MW00783228

THE BOOK OF LEGENDS

Sefer Ha-Aggadah

THE BOOK OF LEGENDS

Sefer Ha-Aggadah

LEGENDS FROM THE TALMUD AND MIDRASH

EDITED BY

HAYIM NAHMAN BIALIK

AND

YEHOSHUA HANA RAVNITZKY

•

TRANSLATED BY WILLIAM G. BRAUDE

•

Introduction by David Stern

SCHOCKEN BOOKS • NEW YORK

To my grandchildren,
Yosef, Yoni, Rachel, and Naomi,
whose lives are my assurance,
I dedicate this book.
—W. G. B.

 Published in the United States by Schocken Books Inc., New York, and simultaneously in Canada by Random House of Canada Limited, Toronto. Distributed by Pantheon Books, a division of Random House, Inc., New York.

Originally published in Hebrew in Odessa, 1908–1911, the *Sefer ha-Aggadah* has gone through eighteen impressions, including an enlarged edition published in Tel Aviv, 1936, by Dvir Publishing. This translation is based on the latest revised edition published by Dvir Publishing, Tel Aviv, in 1952. Published by arrangement with Zmora-Bitan Publishing Ltd., Tel Aviv.

Library of Congress Cataloging-in-Publication Data
Sefer ha-aggadah. English.
The Book of Legends : the first complete translation of Sefer ha-aggadah / [compiled by] Hayim Nahman Bialik and Yehoshua Hana Ravnitzky.
p. cm.
Translation of: Sefer ha-aggadah.
Includes index.
1. Aggada—Translations into English. 2. Midrash—Translations into English. 3. Legends, Jewish. I. Bialik, Hayim Nahman, 1873–1934. II. Ravnitzky, Yehoshua Hana, 1859–1944. III. Title.
BM516.B482E5 1992 296.1'420521—dc20 91-52700
ISBN 0-8052-4113-2

Book Design by Robert Bull Design
Manufactured in the United States of America
9 8

C O N T E N T S

CHAPTER SIX
JUDGES, KINGS, AND PROPHETS

CHAPTER SEVEN
THE DESTRUCTION OF THE FIRST TEMPLE

CHAPTER EIGHT
THE ERA BETWEEN THE FIRST AND SECOND TEMPLES

CHAPTER NINE
THE SECOND TEMPLE— ITS STRUCTURE AND ITS SERVICE

CHAPTER TEN
THE DESTRUCTION OF THE SECOND TEMPLE AND OF THE LAND

PART II

CHAPTER ONE
THE DEEDS OF THE SAGES

PART III

CHAPTER ONE
ISRAEL AND THE NATIONS OF THE WORLD

CHAPTER TWO
THE LAND OF ISRAEL

CHAPTER THREE
LANGUAGE

CHAPTER FOUR
EXILE

CHAPTER FIVE
REDEMPTION AND THE DAYS OF THE MESSIAH

CHAPTER SIX
IN THE TIME-TO-COME

•

CHAPTER SEVEN
TORAH

CHAPTER EIGHT
WISDOM, PROPHECY, AND SONG

CHAPTER NINE
SABBATH, FEASTS, AND FASTS

PART IV

CHAPTER ONE
THE HOLY ONE, BLESSED BE HE, AND RELATIONS BETWEEN HUMAN BEINGS AND HIM WHO IS EVERYWHERE

CHAPTER TWO
GOOD AND EVIL

PART V

CHAPTER ONE
MAN AND HIS NEEDS

CHAPTER TWO
A MAN'S HOUSEHOLD

CHAPTER THREE
BETWEEN MAN AND MAN

CHAPTER FOUR
TRAITS AND ATTITUDES

CHAPTER FIVE
THE COMMUNITY, THE STATE AND THEIR REQUIREMENTS

●

PART VI

CHAPTER ONE
THE WORLD AND ALL THAT IT HOLDS

CHAPTER TWO
MATTERS PERTAINING TO DIVINATION AND HEALING

CHAPTER THREE
PARABLES, PROVERBS, AND SAYINGS

CHAPTER FOUR
A MISCELLANY

PUBLISHER'S NOTE

William G. Braude, the distinguished translator of rabbinic literature and rabbi emeritus of Temple Beth El in Providence, Rhode Island, finished this translation shortly before his death in 1988. We regret that he did not live to see the publication of his labor of love.

This translation of Bialik and Ravnitzky's classic work is complete except for a subsection of one-line proverbial sayings in Part Six of the Hebrew original.

The Book of Legends/Sefer Ha-Aggadah is a compendium of rabbinic lore culled from many sources. The reader should bear in mind that many apparent inconsistencies result from the fact that the selections of *Aggadah* are taken from entirely distinct and separate sources. Thus the reader will encounter such anomalous situations as a paragraph about the death of R. Judah I the Patriarch (Part II, chap. 1, § 328) followed by a paragraph in which he is described as ill.

For some reason, there are occasional variant spellings of the same name (e.g., R. Bannai and R. Benaiah; R. Hoshaia and R. Oshaia; R. Zera and R. Ze'era). Bialik and Ravnitzky retained these variant spellings in deference to their sources, and they are retained in this translation as well.

Another feature that requires explanation is the presence of numerous "parallel passages"—stories that are repeated several times throughout the book. Bialik and Ravnitzky chose to repeat certain stories, parables, anecdotes, and proverbs which are relevant in more than one context in the overall thematic organization of the book. For example, the story of R. Zadok's fasting to save the Temple from destruction (Part I, chap. 10, § 2) also appears in the section entitled "The Deeds of the Sages" (Part II, chap. 11, § 26).

The parable of a vineyard grown wild, which is not razed because of the presence in it of a single rose-colored lily—Israel—included in "Israel and the Nations of the World" (Part III, chap. 1, § 15), replicates an earlier telling of the same parable to illustrate Israel's eagerness to hear God's word at Sinai (Part I, chap. 5, § 28).

These parallel passages are not necessarily rendered identically. Bialik and Ravnitzky frequently provided more than one version in Hebrew of an Aramaic passage. Some inconsistencies may have been accidental, but other variations reveal a clear intention: to show the range of possibilities in interpreting a text.

In this English version, translations of Scripture are generally based on the Jewish Publication Society's translation of the Masoretic text, *The Holy Scriptures* (1917). Other modern translations were consulted as well, and, in some instances, the translator provided his own translation of biblical verses.

The Hebrew term *shene'emar,* which typically heralds a direct quotation from the Bible, is generally translated by the phrase "as is said" or "as Scripture says." On occasion, a colon is substituted for the phrase. The Hebrew epithet for God, literally "the Holy One, blessed be He," is rendered as "the Holy One." R. Judah I the Patriarch is sometimes referred to simply as Rabbi, or our holy Rabbi; the title "Rabbi" is generally abbreviated as "R."

Phrases appearing in brackets throughout the text indicate the translator's interpolations for sense and comprehension. The translator also verified the source citations given by Bialik and Ravnitzky, and when necessary provided his own source citations for many passages.

The Publisher wishes to thank Beverly Colman and Professor Everett Fox for their help in editing and preparing the manuscript for publication.

To Rabbi Braude ז"ל we owe heartfelt gratitude for this living legacy.

ACKNOWLEDGMENTS

Above all I am grateful to my wife, Pen, whose help and unwavering support enabled me to complete this work. My son, Benjamin Braude, dealt with countless matters to ensure its publication. Leon Nemoy, former editor of the Yale Judaica Series, read the entire manuscript, and his comments and suggestions are incorporated in notes throughout this translation. Brother Caedmon Holmes of the Portsmouth Abbey also read the manuscript, made numerous and valuable suggestions, and helped me verify the accuracy of source references. Professor Jakob J. Petuchowski of the Hebrew Union College helped me resolve many textual difficulties. Professor Edward Brookner of Boston University generously responded to numerous questions of style. Cynthia Agronik assisted in many ways the progress of the work. Elizabeth Homans faithfully typed and retyped the manuscript numerous times.

Special thanks go to my many dear friends who, during my stay at the Rhode Island Hospital and later the Verks Rehabilitation Center, read my translation aloud while I reread the Hebrew text to see if any word, line, or passage in the translation had been inadvertently omitted. For this, I am grateful to my sister, Dorothy Fuerst, my sons, Daniel and Joel Braude, and my friends, Abraham Adelman, Louis Astrachan, Rabbi Herman Blumberg, Paul Chernov, Samuel David, Samuel Eisenstadt, Herman Feinstein, Dr. Max Fershtman, Geraldine Foster, Leah Franks, Louis Gilbert, Zelda Gourse, Rabbi Jerome Gurland, Rabbi Jacob Handler, Rabbi Alvin Kaunfer, Seymour Krieger, Rabbi Saul Leeman, Abbot Lieberman, Bernard Margulis, Allan C. Metz, Dr. Samuel Pritzker, Sarah Rosenthal, Professor Albert Salzberg, Rabbi Lawrence Silverman, Pauly Strasmich, Herbert Wagner, and Dorothy Weiner.

Finally, I wish to thank the people of Temple Beth El, especially my colleague and successor, Rabbi Leslie Y. Gutterman, and president Carl Feldman for their support and encouragement.

William G. Braude

After completing the first draft of the translation of *Sefer Ha-Aggadah*, my father suffered a stroke in February of 1983 which left his intellect intact but his speech slurred and his body half paralyzed. He had been working day and night, for he had a foreboding of the affliction. As he was carried into the ambulance, he somehow managed to let us know that we must stuff into his case his worn-out copy of *Sefer Ha-Aggadah* and the sections of the translation he was then reviewing. Installed in the hospital with all the miracles of modern medicine around him, he quickly brought himself back to Bialik and Ravnitzky's world of the ancient rabbis. Within a day he started organizing a troupe of family, friends, visitors, patients, and anyone else who happened into his room, to read aloud his translation so he could check it against the original. Eventually, after months of rehabilitation, he recovered and returned home and, working with the constant support and assistance of my mother, was able to complete his final revisions. Throughout this labor against illness, his determination and dedication never flagged. What kept him going was the conviction that he was part of a tradition, ancient and yet living, of engagement with sacred writ. In each generation the sages had told and retold the stories of Jewish lore. At the beginning of this century, Bialik and Ravnitzky had made them more accessible by recasting them in modern Hebrew. Now my father strove to open this treasure to the English-speaking world. He drew sustenance from the hope that the ongoing tradition of Jewish legend, lore, and study of Scripture would attract and delight yet new generations of readers.

Benjamin Braude

ACKNOWLEDGMENTS

NOTE ON TRANSLITERATION

The transliteration system of Hebrew and Aramaic words and names adopted in this volume is designed for the general reader. It follows fairly closely the pronunciation of modern spoken (Sephardic) Hebrew, with the exception that the letter *het*, which has a rather guttural sound, is not distinguished from *heh*—both are represented by the English *h*. Diacritical marks, such as those distinguishing the silent letters *ayin* from *alef*, have been omitted, except in cases where they are needed for pronunciation (as in *Be'er* instead of *Beer*) or to make a grammatical point.

Biblical names generally follow the usage found in conventional English Bible translations. On the other hand, the names of the rabbis are transcribed in a manner closer to their Hebrew pronunciation, and in general follow the usage found in the *Encyclopaedia Judaica*.

In all transliterated words, the letter *a* is to be pronounced as the *a* in *father*.

INTRODUCTION

BY DAVID STERN

In the first decade of the twentieth century, two leading representatives of the Hebrew renascence in Russia, Hayim Nahman Bialik and Yehoshua Hana Ravnitzky, commenced the creation of this massive compendium of Rabbinic legend and lore. It is telling indeed that Bialik, already recognized as the national poet of the Jewish people, and Ravnitzky, editor, journalist, and co-founder with Bialik of the prestigious Hebrew publishing house of Dvir, chose this project and this material to spearhead the revival of a Hebrew national ethos for their contemporaries. First published in Odessa in 1908–11, *Sefer Ha-Aggadah (The Book of Legends)* was reprinted numerous times in Israel after Bialik and Ravnitzky emigrated to the land of Israel. An instant classic, "an inheritance for all Jews everywhere," as one admirer wrote, *Sefer Ha-Aggadah* was more than just a charming collection of classical Jewish stories and sayings. It was, as many recognized immediately, a masterwork in its own right, a monument to the capacity of modern Jewish culture to assimilate and appropriate its classical heritage.

In the original Hebrew Introduction to the first edition of *Sefer Ha-Aggadah*, Bialik and Ravnitzky articulated the vision behind their work. *Aggadah* (pl. *Aggadot*), the traditional name for all the nonlegal teachings of the early sages of Rabbinic Judaism, from their homilies to their tales, was, Bialik and Ravnitzky wrote, "the principal literary form" of the Jewish people, the "classic expression of their spirit." The product of the creative powers of generations of rabbis, it was like "a beautiful palace" in which "the spirit and soul of the Jews permanently dwelled." Alas, in their own day, that palace had become a ruin; forsaken by all except for a few pedantic scholars and talentless popularizers, it resembled more "an ownerless field, an abandoned grove in which wild vegetation and aftergrowth increase and multiply on their own."

It was this ruined palace, this ownerless and abandoned field of classical Hebrew literature, that Bialik and Ravnitzky sought to restore to its original state of "pristine glory," as they wrote, and thereby to make this literature available to their contemporaries. The task was neither a simple nor an obvious one. Even in Bialik's time, *Aggadah* was among the more inaccessible branches of classical Jewish literature, surely the least structured, and the most inchoate. To make *Aggadah* comprehensible to a contemporary audience, Bialik and Ravnitzky faced numerous challenges, most of which arose from the very nature of the material they wished to present.

For one thing, *Aggadah* presented itself as an almost entirely unsystematized, unorganized body of materials of a truly bewildering variety. As the term was used by the rabbis, and as it continues to be employed by scholars today, *Aggadah* essentially designates all the traditions, statements, and beliefs in early Judaism that fall outside the bounds of the *Halakhah*, the system of Rabbinic law. The literary record of Jewish existence during the first seven centuries in the Common Era in the two main centers of Rabbinic culture—initially, the land of Israel, Roman Palestine; later, Babylonia—*Aggadah* touches upon virtually every conceivable aspect of human life, every subject and matter that drew the sages' attention or shaped their world. Its literary forms similarly range across the entire spectrum: from biblical exegeses and extra-biblical legends—stories elaborating upon biblical characters and episodes in their careers not found in the Bible itself—to fully developed sermons that may once have been delivered in ancient synagogues, to snippets of popular folklore, anecdotes about the sages' own lives and about their contemporary history, and, not least of all, the entire body of Rabbinic thought—every belief held by the sages, from their theological ideas about God to their views on the creation, the reasons for the commandments, and much material that some would call popular religion and others superstition—namely, topics like magic, angelology, demonology, folk medicine, the sciences of amulets, secret charms, astrology, and so on.

To be sure, the richness of *Aggadah*'s contents has always been a major source of its interest; if nothing else, it shows how fully involved the Rabbinic sages were in every imaginable facet of their world. But for a modern reader, the diversity of the material, its sheer heterogeneity, could also be overwhelming, and especially so on account of the way *Aggadah* tends to be preserved and recorded in Rabbinic literature. In its beginnings an oral tradition passed down from generation to generation—the word *Aggadah* itself literally means "that which is told"—its various strands were committed to writing only at a time far removed from their origins. As a result, it is often difficult to date an *Aggadah* or to understand the context in which it was created or its original meaning. The same aggadic story or saying, like many types of oral literature, is frequently preserved in multiple versions that differ from one another significantly, and there is often little indication in the sources as to which one is more authentic.

Moreover, when the various traditions were finally written down, they were not preserved for posterity in collections devoted specifically to *Aggadah*. Instead, they were recorded in seemingly haphazard fashion throughout the breadth of Rabbinic literature, in the numerous anthologies devoted to Midrash, biblical commentary, and in the two massive editions of the Talmud, one compiled in the land of Israel and the other in Babylonia. And even within these classical compilations, *Aggadah* was typically not preserved as generically independent or self-standing material. Rather, most *Aggadot* typically appear within the context of a more complex literary form or in the course of a lengthier, extended discussion. They can be found in a complicated biblical exegesis, a précis of a sermon or lecture, or even as part of a legal debate, as a precedent for one opinion's view, or as an exemplum, a story used to illustrate how a certain commandment was to be performed or the great rewards that observance will bring to the person who piously performs a particular religious deed.

Finally—this was the greatest challenge of all posed to a modern audience—the vast part of *Aggadah*, as preserved in Rabbinic literature, is recorded in a style that is typically fragmentary and elusive and written in a language so condensed and given to allusion that, to the uninitiated reader, it is sometimes barely intelligible and nearly always difficult to appreciate in any profound or sensitive way without some help or guidance from the outside. Futhermore, for many of Bialik's contemporaries, the language of Rabbinic Hebrew itself—different from both biblical Hebrew and the new modern Hebrew that was then in the process of being born—was an obstacle on account of both its unfamiliar expressions and its inclusion of numerous Greek and Latin loanwords that even scholars today have difficulty deciphering. And last of all, a large part of *Aggadah* is composed not in Hebrew but in Aramaic, a closely related but distinct Semitic language that, in one or another of its dialects, was the *lingua franca*, the common language, of Jews living in both Palestine and Babylonia in late antiquity. Even an adept Hebraist would find the Aramaic hard to comprehend unless he was already familiar with Rabbinic literature and its idioms.

In resolving these difficulties, the rabbis themselves were not of much help. In general, they were not interested in either systematizing or conceptualizing their thoughts, or in otherwise facilitating their readers' way through the maze of Rabbinic literature. The rabbis preferred to exemplify the *quality* of an idea through a well-chosen simile or a memorable anecdote rather than theorize about its meaning or explicate it discursively. Consider the term *Aggadah* itself. In not a single place, in all of Rabbinic literature, do the rabbis ever offer a true definition of *Aggadah* or of its significance as a literary genre. Rather, when they discuss *Aggadah*, they tend to do it as follows:

> "Manna . . . was like coriander seed, white" (Exod. 16:31) . . . . Some sages say that, like manna [which drew the heart of a hungry man], *Aggadah* draws a man's heart [to Torah], even as water [draws the heart of a thirsty man].
>
> "The delights of the sons of men" (Eccles. 2:8).
> These are the *Aggadot*, which give delight to
> [the study of] Scripture.
>
> "His lips are as lilies" (Song 5:13). These are the *Aggadot* [whose fragrance is like that of lilies].
>
> —(*The Book of Legends/Sefer Ha-Aggadah*, p. 3)

These passages, all formulated in the guise of biblical interpretations or Midrashim, as though the verses in Scripture were originally meant to refer to *Aggadah*, suggest its *feel*—the taste, the smell, the almost tactile seductiveness of *Aggadah*. But they hardly define the term or its genre. What makes them memorable is the cleverness of their exegeses, their use of startling similes derived from Scripture to convey the delights and attractions of *Aggadah*.

Similarly, when the rabbis wished to describe the importance of the parable, one of their favorite literary forms, they chose to do so by telling a parable *about* parables:

> Do not let the parable appear of little worth to you. Through a parable a man can fathom words of Torah. Consider the king who has lost a gold coin or a precious pearl in his house. May he not find it by the light of a wick worth no more than an *issar* [a Roman penny]? Likewise do not let the parable appear of little worth to you. By its light a man may fathom words of Torah. (SA, p. 3)

For the rabbis, the value of the parable, like that of *Aggadah* in general, lay in its didactic function, its use as a medium for understanding Torah, God's Law. Yet even this characterization of the parable's use, of its ideological function (for what the rabbis meant by Torah was *their* understanding of Torah, that is, the worldview of Rabbinic Judaism), never tells us *what* the parable is or *why* the rabbis so loved to use it. All it tells us is what a parable is *like*: a valuable thing but worth no more than a penny!

To be sure, this last feature, the rabbis' acute sense of paradox, along with their lack of concern with setting out their views or ideas systematically, is also a major source of *Aggadah*'s charm. Indeed, a large part of its rhetorical and literary art lies in its ability effortlessly to communicate a decidedly abstract and difficult idea through a concrete example, a sensuous image or memorable word-picture rather than through a more precise but prosaic formulation. And this art must surely have been fully appreciated by Bialik, the poet. But to the reader unfamiliar with *Aggadah*'s obscure language and intimidated by the massive edifice of Rabbinic discourse, the lyrical quality of *Aggadah* with its frequently associative, rather than logical, structures of thought, could pose a formidable obstacle to its comprehension.

These were some of the challenges that Bialik and Ravnitzky faced in compiling *Sefer Ha-Aggadah*—challenges that arose from the very nature of *Aggadah* itself. To meet and surmount them, Bialik and Ravnitzky spent three years combing through the entirety of Rabbinic literature in order to select what appeared to them "the best" of aggadic tradition—best, that is, in *their* judgment, which, though in general highly reliable, certainly reflected the biases of their age. In making their selection, the two editors followed several guidelines. When there existed multiple versions of the same *Aggadah*, they chose the one that seemed to them most representative (preferring, in general, the versions found in the Babylonian Talmud, which, though probably the latest in date and hence the least original, Bialik and Ravnitzky selected because they were the best known). If the two halves of what seemed to them a single *Aggadah* were found in separate sources, they combined them. When the aggadic passages selected were in Aramaic, or if they contained Aramaic sections, they faithfully translated them into a contemporary Hebrew that managed to blend easily into the Rabbinic Hebrew of the remainder of the texts; from the second edition on, they also vocalized the text with grammatical precision. And, last of all, they wrote brief but extremely helpful glosses to nearly the entire book, which are incorporated into this translation.

Finally the greatest contribution of Bialik and Ravnitzky was the thematic organization of the material they collected. In their own minds, the disorderliness of *Aggadah,* its hapless dispersion throughout Rabbinic literature, was its greatest failing. "Not every person," they wrote in their introduction, "is willing or able to rummage through the piles and piles in [these Rabbinic] works, heaped up through the duration of so many generations as tall as mountains—just in order to find pearls beneath them! . . . Contemporary man . . . [is] accustomed to seek order, method, and the possibility of completeness in his study."

To assist in the attainment of such completeness, Bialik and Ravnitzky divided the *Aggadot* into six main sections and numerous subsections. Parts One and Two are the lengthiest and most historical in nature: they encompass the history of the world from creation through the destruction of the Second Temple in the year 70 C.E., and the lives of the Rabbinic sages themselves. The other four main sections are organized topically: Part Three deals with *Aggadot* relating to the Jewish people, the land of Israel, the Hebrew language, Torah, and the redemption; Part Four with God and Good and Evil; Part Five with traditions pertaining to the human being's place in the world; and Part Six, the final section, is a miscellany of *Aggadot* dealing with the world, folk medicine, popular religion (demons, the evil eye, magic), and selected proverbs and folk sayings.

It is difficult to overestimate the conceptual achievement of this job of organization, or the sheer work that Bialik and Ravnitzky invested in it; indeed, the two men preferred to think of themselves as the *mesadrim,* the "organizers" or "arrangers" of *Aggadah,* rather than as its editors. But for Bialik in particular the project was more than just an intellectual task. The "structured arrangement" of the completed work, *Sefer Ha-Aggadah*—in Bialik's own words, "fragments of stones . . . joined into layers, layers into walls, and walls into a complete fortress, a fortress into which whoever enters finds everything arranged and installed in its proper place"—was a means to a greater end. For this completed fortress, he wrote, would ultimately allow the reader to "grasp finally that worldview and perspective on life in whose spirit the *Aggadah* was originally created, an entity unique to the Jewish people." *Aggadah,* in other words, was the key to Jewish uniqueness, and this anthology a means for revealing that uniqueness once again.

For Bialik, this project of reconstruction, of gathering and rearranging the dispersed fragments of *Aggadah,* of restoring the ruined palace to its original glory, was in fact a trope, a figure in his mind for the reconstruction, the restoration, of the Jewish people themselves. Like the fragments of *Aggadah* in Rabbinic literature, the Jews, too, were scattered, dispersed among the nations; they, too, could recapture their special glory, their singular worldview and perspective on life, only by being reassembled and reconstituted in their homeland, their "palace."

Yet restoration to a geographical homeland alone was not enough. The danger, as Bialik and other cultural Zionists like him saw it, was that, though the Zionist movement might succeed in physically restoring the Jews to their homeland, the spiritual regeneration of the Jewish people, the restoration of the Jewish ethos, would be overlooked and forgotten in the process. Important as the political restoration was, it was only through an equivalent cultural rehabilitation that the Jewish people would truly be reconstituted and their future existence guaranteed. And this rehabilitation was to be achieved partly through the recovery of the national literary past. *Sefer Ha-Aggadah* was, in fact, the foundation of a larger project that Bialik called *kinus,* the "ingathering" of the classical Jewish literary heritage, which, he hoped, would become a kind of national library. For Bialik was certain that the national genius resided in that literary past and that only by recovering it could the future promise of that genius be ensured; indeed, it was the classical literature of the Jews, and the literature of *Aggadah* especially, that most fully expressed the national genius.

This last estimation was, in a sense, axiomatic for Bialik. But there are additional reasons that may explain why the *Aggadah* of the rabbis in particular held such a deep attraction for him. For one thing, he may very well have felt a deep parallel between the historical predicament of his own age and that of the rabbis. And from that perspective, *Aggadah* may have seemed to Bialik an exemplary response, an instance of Jewish creativity at its most intense. Hence the urgency of Bialik's belief not only that his contemporaries needed to familiarize themselves with *Aggadah* as an important chapter in the history of Jewish culture but also that they needed to absorb and assimilate its meaning: this would be key to their own capacity for responding to the challenges of their contemporary historical predicament.

This last point requires some words of explanation. Both *Aggadah* and its parent, Rabbinic Judaism, were born out of a complex of historical factors that include some of the most productive and most catastrophic moments in all of Jewish history. Rabbinic Judaism, the religious system eventually created by the rabbis, originated in the period of the Second Temple, in the last centuries before the Common Era. During this period, partly under the impact of the confrontation of the biblical heritage of Israel with that of the Hellenistic world—in the early fourth century B.C.E. the land of Israel first came under the rule of Alexander the Great's empire—the religion of Israel, whose observance had previously centered on the Temple and its sacrificial cult, began to shift to a new type of worship that was more egalitarian, extending to all Jews the kinds of religious piety and obligation that had formerly been the prerogatives of the priestly class alone, and more intellectual in tenor. The latter shift can be seen in the emergence of the scribe, later the Pharisee, a religious figure who anticipated the Rabbinic sage, and it was accompanied by a new emphasis on study—specifically, study of the Bible, God's revealed Law—as a religious activity in its own right, as a medium for discovering God's will in the present time through the words of Scripture. This latter tendency eventually came to its fullest fruition in Rabbinic Judaism both in midrashic interpretation and in the Talmud's studious explication of *Halakhah.*

These revolutionary changes in Judaism were immanent developments; if nothing else had happened in history during their course, they would have continued from their own impetus and still would have radically altered the face of Judaism as a religion. But these changes were only hastened and exacerbated by contemporary historical events. First, in 70 C.E., the Second Temple was destroyed, a national tragedy that climaxed a three-year-long war waged by the Jews of Palestine against their Roman rulers. Then, some sixty-five years later, there was a second military defeat, that of the Bar Kokhba Rebellion, a last aborted attempt at regaining national independence.

Both the destruction of the Temple and the calamitous Bar Kokhba Rebellion were watersheds in the history of Rabbinic Judaism. The former was the immediate cause of immense religious despair. With the Temple's destruction, the main avenue of worship in Israel, the offering of sacrifices, along with many other religious practices and observances connected to the Temple cult, were all rendered impossible. How could Jews now worship God? This was a question asked by many, and the feelings of desperation and hopelessness that it engendered for the future were only deepened by an implicit and equally pressing question: Was the destruction an unequivocal sign that God had finally decided to reject Israel as His chosen people? The Bar Kokhba Rebellion, its defeat even bloodier and more devastating than that of the earlier war, drove home a second message only hinted at by the destruction: It proved to the Jews, once and for all, that there would be no quick deliverance from their state of political subjection to the Romans, no miraculous resolution to their spiritual dilemma.

The achievement of the rabbis in the aftermath of the two catastrophes was to respond to their crises on the political, social, and religious planes by remaking Judaism. In part, they did this by turning Judaism into a portable possession. They recentered Judaism, shifting its forms of worship from a particular place, a special class of religious functionaries, and a specific type of worship dependent upon both that place and its functionaries (the Temple, the priests, and the Temple cult) to a complex of newly important institutions—the synagogue, Torah-study, communal worship, *Halakhah* in all its details, and so on—that could more readily be transported and adapted to changing geographical locations and historical situations.

Even more crucially, however, the rabbis offered a reinterpretation—a transvaluation, as it were—of the entire temporal and spatial framework in which the success and failure of Jewish existence had previously been gauged. No longer, in their view, was the truth of Judaism to be measured by the rules of conventional history, by the external appearance of the Jewish national condition. Yes, the Jews would again be returned to a politically independent homeland, in the time of the future redemption. And yes, the kingdom of David would be restored then, too; and the Temple rebuilt. But in the meantime, that is to say, for the rest of human history, Jewish existence would take place in a more inner-directed realm. And its success and failure would be counted in the coinage of that realm: mastery of Torah and devotion to *Halakhah.* In this way, the rabbis made the Jews' personal spiritual and communal life take the place, in effect, of a national political existence. And so, too, they transferred the meaning of Jewish existence to a realm whose conditions they could determine, whose fate and destiny they could control.

It is this transformation, this remaking of Judaism, that *Aggadah* records. In addition, though, *Aggadah* also embodies the process of remaking in its own creations—in its anecdotes about the sages and their careers, in its pseudohistorical accounts, and especially in its retellings and elaborations of the biblical past. At the heart of the latter lies Midrash, the name for the Rabbinic mode of Scriptural study. To appreciate Midrash it is crucial to understand that, for the rabbis, the Bible was not only Torah, the divine source for Israel's Law and its history. The words of the Torah, its text, were also the lens, the prism, through which the sages viewed their own world. The Torah gave them the terms of reference in which they experienced their daily lives, the vocabulary through which they articulated their every feeling and thought. When they sought knowledge, any kind of knowledge, they sought it first in Torah. And when they sought the meaning of Torah itself or, as was the case more frequently, the meaning of a particular verse or phrase in the Torah—or even, more precisely, the meaning*fulness* of that verse or phrase—they would search after it, first, in themselves, in their own experiences and in what they knew to be true. If Scripture could not lie, neither could it be false or contradictory to the rabbis' own selves and to their knowledge, their sense of the world and of their place in it.

The collapsing of time and history that is so characteristic of Midrash—as when the rabbis unselfconsciously portray figures from the distant past like the patriarchs in their own image—should not be viewed as a matter of naïve anachronizing on the rabbis' part or as self-serving exploitation of Scripture for their own ends. Rather, its meaning is a symbolic one. By bringing their own experiences to the interpretation of the words of Torah, and taking back from the Torah the language that allowed them to articulate their own experiences, the rabbis created a kind of mythical, timeless realm removed from the travails and injustices of contemporary history. In this realm, the beliefs they valued, the lives they wished to live, their hopes, their dreams, even their moments of anguish, could take shape, unimpeded by hostile forces, and be realized, however complexly so. And from this mythical, legendary realm, they could also learn how to live in this imperfect world. Precisely because the rabbis' beloved ancestors, the patriarchs, had faced the same dilemmas and challenges as the rabbis themselves and overcome them, or so the rabbis' aggadic retelling of the biblical narrative asserted, they could serve as such perfect examples for their descendants.

Through this midrashic model the rabbis found the creativity, the national genius, to remake Judaism and to overcome the crises of their time. And this was the model, too, that Bialik sought by recovering *Aggadah* so as to enable the remaking of Judaism in his own time, in the face of its own crises. Of all these, the greatest crisis, the one Bialik himself had personally suffered through most terribly, was the loss of faith, the collapse of the traditional structures and tenets of Jewish belief, the erosion of the security of existence that those religious structures and tenets had previously ensured. If traditional faith could not be recovered, a surrogate for it nonetheless had to be found, and it was such a surrogate that Bialik, somewhat paradoxically perhaps, looked for in the cultural heritage epitomized by *Aggadah*. In a poem entitled "Before the Bookcase" (*Lifnei Aron Hasefarim*, 1910), as the literary critic Dan Miron has suggested, Bialik expressed his deep ambivalence toward the project of *Sefer Ha-Aggadah* and the years of his life he had devoted to it. Bialik described his loss of faith figuratively, through the image of a necklace of black pearls whose string had suddenly given way. By collecting the scattered pearls of *Aggadah* and restringing them to form the necklacelike compilation of *Sefer Ha-Aggadah*, he was in a deep sense trying to reconstruct, recover, something of his lost faith.

Yet here lay an important difference between the modern poet and the ancient rabbis. For the rabbis, the study of *Aggadah* had been an intrinsically religious pursuit, a path to worshiping God. "If you wish to know Him by whose word the world came into being, study *Aggadah;* you will thereby come to know the Holy One, blessed be He, and hold fast to His ways," a famous Rabbinic statement declares (SA, p. 3). In his introduction to *Sefer Ha-Aggadah*, Bialik paraphrased this saying as follows: "Whoever wishes to know the nation of Israel . . . let him 'go to the *Aggadah*' . . ." In place of the knowledge of God, *Aggadah*, for Bialik, held the knowledge of the nation of Israel, the secret of the Jewish genius, of the national ethos. Or to put the same point somewhat differently: The recovery of a national ethos had become for cultural Zionists like Bialik a kind of religious calling, a sacred vocation. It was not merely that in *Aggadah* lay the secret to recovering the national ethos. Because it was literature—"the principal literary form" of the Jewish people, the "classic expression of their spirit"—*Aggadah was* the national genius.

Bialik's identification of Aggadah as "literature" was a decidedly Romantic idea. While he did not view *Aggadah* as real folklore, as did some of his contemporaries, Bialik did seem to believe that the fragments of *Aggadah* in Rabbinic literature preserved what had once been an epic literature of the Jewish people. Part of the purpose of *Sefer Ha-Aggadah* was to recover that epic. Although he and Ravnitzky claimed in their introduction not to have "reworked" the form of the *Aggadah,* they did admit to having made a few alterations in the name of "modesty." In fact, they made numerous unacknowledged revisions whose purpose was to make *Aggadah* more like their idea of literature.

Thus, in the case of some narrative *Aggadot*, they eliminated homiletical digressions that distracted from the plot. More seriously, they tried to wrest *Aggadot* from their midrashic, exegetical settings, which, to Bialik, seemed particularly cloying, all too reminiscent of the *beit midrash*, the dusty, suffocating house of study, the home of traditional piety, from which he had fled as a youth. And finally, he and Ravnitzky joined and conflated separate *Aggadot* into lengthier, more continuous narratives in order to make their "epic" character more recognizable. In some cases, this was not particularly objectionable, merely a matter of attaching together exegetically discrete units that were, however, all of a piece. In other cases, though, as the Israeli scholar Joseph Heinemann has shown in a particularly brilliant study of *Sefer Ha-Aggadah*, this tendency resulted in the creation of absolutely new narratives, some of which were quite brilliant but were the inventions of Bialik and Ravnitzky, not the rabbis. It was more than slightly ironic that, precisely in order to recover *Aggadah*, Bialik and Ravnitzky found themselves reworking the very tradition they wished to save.

And yet, even with these criticisms, the achievement of *Sefer Ha-Aggadah* is hardly diminished. Bialik and Ravnitzky were not the only ones in their generation to concern themselves with recovering *Aggadah*. Indeed, the project was, in a sense, the project of their generation. The same period that witnessed the publication of *Sefer Ha-Aggadah* saw the appearance of two other important works devoted to *Aggadah*, Louis Ginzberg's *The Legends of the Jews* and Micah Yosef (bin Gorion) Berdichevsky's *Mimekor Yisrael*. The difference between these works and *Sefer Ha-Aggadah* is revealing. Berdichevsky was primarily interested in recovering *Aggadah* as folklore; although he published the separate versions of the same *Aggadah* if they were sufficiently different, he limited himself to what he considered folkloric material; while his anthology extended to include folklore far beyond the Rabbinic period, he did not include much *Aggadah* that is in *Sefer Ha-Aggadah* because he did not consider it folklore. In contrast, Ginzberg's work was limited to Rabbinic elaborations of the biblical narrative. A monument to its author's scholarly erudition, indeed one of the great monuments of Jewish scholarship in this century, *The Legends of the Jews* was not, however, a genuine anthology. Ginzberg did not print the rabbis' own *Aggadot;* he paraphrased and retold them in his own somewhat mannered voice and in a continuous narrative that was incomparably further from the style of aggadic narration than any revision that Bialik and Ravnitzky ventured.

For all their subtle revisions, Bialik and Ravnitzky preserved the rabbis' own voices; even when they altered the details of an *Aggadah*, they treated their material with a tact and sensitivity that are hard to fault. Indeed, it may even be suggested that, in editing the *Aggadot*, Bialik and Ravnitzky were acting in the spirit of *Aggadah* itself. For the rabbis, too, had altered and adapted many *Aggadot* that they received from earlier hands in the course of handing them on to their own audiences. The history of *Aggadah* is in large part the story of such adaptations and transformations. It is the history of tradition: the reshaping of the past precisely in order to make it capable of transmission to a future generation. In this sense, when they turned *Aggadah* into literature in order to make it available to their contemporaries, Bialik and Ravnitzky were acting in the spirit of the very tradition they believed would revitalize the Jewish ethos for their time. And this no doubt is one reason why *Sefer Ha-Aggadah* remains for our time as much as it was for that of Bialik and Ravnitzky the incomparable treasury that it is.

THE BOOK OF LEGENDS

Sefer Ha-Aggadah

PART I

CHAPTER ONE

PROEM

The Meaning of *Aggadah* and of the Parable

1. Those who look for Scripture's inherent meaning say: If you wish to know Him by whose word the world came into being, study [Scripture's homiletical interpretations in the] *Aggadah;* you will thereby come to know the Holy One, blessed be He, and hold fast to His ways.[1]

2. Do not let the parable appear of little worth to you. Through a parable, a man can fathom words of Torah. Consider the king who has lost a gold coin or a precious pearl in his house. May he not find it by the light of a wick worth no more than an *issar?* Likewise, do not let the parable appear of little worth to you. By its light, a man may fathom words of Torah.[2]

3. "A further word: Because Koheleth[3] was a sage, he continued to instruct the people. He listened to and tested the soundness of many parables" (Eccles. 12:9). R. Nahman said: What Solomon did may be understood by the parable of a great palace which had many hallways, so that whoever entered it got lost. What did a clever man do? He took a coil of reedgrass, tied it to an entrance, went in unwinding the coil, and came out rewinding the coil. Then everybody proceeded to go in and come out using such a coil. Likewise, until Solomon appeared, no man could properly grasp words of Torah; but after Solomon appeared, all men could comprehend Torah's words.

Another example: What Solomon did may be understood by the parable of a thicket of reeds so dense that no man dared enter. Whoever entered it got lost. What did a clever man do? He took a sickle, cut down a few reeds, and went in a step, cut down a few more reeds, and went in farther; and so on, until finally he went all the way in by the path he had cut and returned by the same path. Thereafter, everybody proceeded to enter and leave by that path. Such was the way of Solomon.

R. Yose said: What Solomon did may be understood by the parable of a large basket full of fruit. Since the basket had no handles, it could not be moved about until a clever man came and made handles for it, so that it could be carried by the handles. So, too, until Solomon appeared, no man could properly grasp words of Torah; but after Solomon appeared, everyone began to comprehend Torah. R. Shela said: Solomon's role reminds us of a large cruse that was full of boiling water and had no handle which it could be carried about. Then a man came and made a handle for it by which it could be carried. R. Hanina said: Solomon's role reminds us of an exceedingly deep well full of water that was cold, sweet, and wholesome. But no creature could get a drink out of it until a man came and tied rope to rope and cord to cord, drew water from it, and drank; then everyone began to draw and drink. So, too, proceeding from one word to another, from one parable to another, Solomon penetrated to the hidden meaning of Torah.[4]

4. Rich in possessions and rich in popular acclaim—such is the master of *Haggadot.*[5]

5. "A man to whom God giveth riches . . . yet God giveth him not the power to decide what thereof to eat" (Eccles. 6:2)—such a one is the master of *Aggadah,* for he does not have the power to prohibit or to permit, to declare unclean or to declare clean.[6]

6. "Because they regard not the works of the Lord, nor the operation of His hands" (Ps. 28:5). This applies, according to R. Joshua ben Levi, to men who have no regard for *Aggadot.*[7]

7. "Their words to the world's uttermost ends" (Ps. 19:5). This refers to the study of *Aggadot,* which its master tellers hallow the Holy One's great Name to the ends of the world.[8]

8. "Manna . . . was like coriander (*gad*) seed, white (*lavan*)" (Exod. 16:31). Some sages—who derive *gad* from the verb *ngd,* "to draw," and read *libban,* "their heart," for *lavan*—say that, like manna [which drew the heart of a hungry man], *Aggadah* draws a man's heart [to Torah], even as water [draws the heart of a thirsty man].[9]

9. "The delights of the sons of men" (Eccles. 2:8). These are the *Aggadot,* which give delight to [the study of] Scripture.[10]

10. "His lips are as lilies" (Song 5:13). These are the *Aggadot* [whose fragrance is like that of lilies].[11]

11. "And wilt do that which is right in thine eyes" (Exod. 15:26)—heed, that is, the exemplary *Aggadot,* which [unlike *Halakhot*] are readily understood and deemed right by all men.[12]

---

1. Sif Deut., §49.
2. Song R. 1:1, §8.
3. Solomon is said to have been Koheleth, the author of Ecclesiastes.
4. Song R. 1:1, §8; Gen. R. 12:1, 93:4; Eccles. 2:11, §1.
5. He expounds to large and receptive audiences. B. BB 145b.
6. P. Hor 3:5, 48c.
7. MTeh 28:5.
8. TdE, ed. Friedmann p. 11 (JPS, p. 61); Yalkut, Ps., §672.
9. B. Yoma 75b.
10. Eccles. R. 2:8, §1.
11. Yalkut, Song, §991.
12. Mek, *Be-shallah,* Va-yassa, 1.

12. As certain as a formal covenant is the assurance that he who studies *Aggadah* from a book will not soon forget it.[1]

The Meaning of *Aggadah* and *Halakhah*

13. "My teaching shall drop as the rain" (Deut. 32:2). Even as one rain falling on various trees gives to each a special savor in keeping with its species—to the vine the savor of grapes, to the olive tree the savor of olives, to the fig tree the savor of figs—so the words of Torah are one, yet within them are Scripture and Mishnah, *Halakhot* and *Aggadot*.[2]

14. "It is not an empty thing even if it seems so to you" (Deut. 32:47):[3] although matter that you say is empty may seem empty to you, it is, in truth, your life and the light and length of your days. So that you should not say, "I have studied *Halakhot*—that is enough," Scripture asserts, "You shall be mindful of this entire instruction" (Deut. 11:22)—the instruction in its entirety: learn Midrash,[4] as well as *Halakhot* and *Aggadot*. In this connection, Scripture also says, "Man doth not live by bread alone" (Deut. 8:3)—by Midrash—"but by every thing that proceedeth out of the mouth of the Lord doth man live" (ibid.), by both *Halakhot* and *Aggadot*.[5]

15. "As banks (*migdelot*) of sweet herbs" (Song 5:13). R. Tanhuma said: Just as the spicemaker's casket (*migdelot*) is full of all kinds of spices, so should a scholar be full of Scripture, Mishnah and Talmud, *Halakhot* and *Aggadot*.[6]

16. R. Eleazar ben Shammua said: Three types of disciples of the wise are exemplified by a hewn stone [in a wall], a cornerstone, and a polished stone [in a massive pier].

What disciple is like a hewn stone [in a wall]? The one who has studied only Midrash, so that when a colleague comes to him and asks about Midrash, he can reply. He is like a hewn stone [in a wall], which has only one side exposed.

What disciple is like a cornerstone? The one who has studied Midrash and *Halakhot*, so that when a colleague comes to him and asks about Midrash, he can reply; about *Halakhot*, he can reply. He is like a cornerstone, which has two sides exposed.

What disciple is like a polished stone [in a massive pier]? The one who has studied Midrash, *Halakhot*, *Aggadot*, and Toseftot, so that when a colleague comes to him and asks about Midrash, he can reply; about *Halakhot*, he can reply; about Toseftot, he can reply; about *Aggadot*, he can reply. He is like a polished stone [in a massive pier], which has all four sides exposed.[7]

1. P. Ber 5:1, 9a.
2. Sif Deut., §206.
3. JV: "It is not an empty thing for you."
4. Sifra and Sifre. So R. Hillel, as quoted by Meir Friedmann.
5. Sif Deut., § 48.
6. Song R. 5:13, §1.
7. ARN p. 28.

17. "He meteth out the water [of Torah] by measure (Job 28:25). R. Yudan said in the name of R. Samuel: Even words of Torah—Scripture, Mishnah, Talmud, *Halakhot*, and *Aggadah*—that were given in great abundance] from above were meted out in different measures, so that one man may have a capacity only for Scripture, another only for Mishnah, another only for Talmud, and still another only for *Aggadah;* yet, now and then, there is a man who has the capacity for all of Torah.[8]

18. R. Simlai came to R. Jonathan with a request: Teach me *Aggadah*.[9] R. Jonathan answered: I hold to a tradition from my forebears not to teach *Aggadah* to anyone from Babylonia or from southern Israel, because such persons are arrogant and know little of Torah[10]—and you are both a native of Nehardea [in Babylonia] and a resident of the south.[11]

19. "The Lord spoke with you face (*panim*) to face (*panim*)" (Deut. 5:4). The first *panim*, being a plural [literally, "faces"],[12] implies at least two faces, and the second *panim* implies at least two more faces. Thus a total of four faces, referring respectively to Scripture, Mishnah, Talmud, and *Aggadot:* an awestricken face for Scripture, an equanimous face for Mishnah,[13] a friendly face for Talmud, and a joyous face for *Aggadah*.[14]

20. "Sustain me with *ashishot*" (Song 2:5)[15] that is, with *Halakhot*, laws, which are closely reasoned and precisely expressed (*meushashot*). "Refresh me with apples" (ibid.)—with *Haggadot*, whose fragrance and taste are like those of apples.

[In another comment], the words usually read, "I am lovesick" (Song 2:5), are read, "Because I am sickly, I require love." When a man is well, he can eat anything he gets; but when he becomes sick, he wants only delicate foods: "Sustain me with delicacies.[16] Hence R. Isaac said: Formerly, when people were [well], familiar with the main outlines of Torah, they were eager to listen to a matter in Mishnah, in *Halakhah*, or in Talmud. But now that people are [not well], not familiar with the main outlines of Torah, they are willing to listen only to a passage in Scripture or a theme in *Aggadah* [delicacies].[17]

"But I yearn for love" (Song 2:5)[18] R. Levi said:

8. Lev. R. 15:2.
9. Proper interpretation of Scripture.
10. And therefore twist Scripture to suit themselves or simply ridicule it.
11. P. Pes 5:3, 32a.
12. The Hebrew word for "face" is *panim*, a plural that has no singular form.
13. Because the Mishnah is regulatory and does not involve discussion and reasoning.
14. Sof 16; PRKM 12:25.
15. JV: "with dainties."
16. Ibid.
17. Or: In former times, everyone knew God's law [Torah] and therefore was interested in Mishnah and Talmud [which interpret and carry forward Torah]; nowadays, people are ignorant of law [Torah] and want to hear only scriptural lessons and homilies on them. So Leon Nemoy (former editor of the Yale Judaica Series).
18. JV: "For I am lovesick." But *hlh* ("to be sick") can also mean "to yearn."

Formerly, when there was money enough to live on, people were strong enough to study a topic in Mishnah or a topic in Talmud; but now that there is not enough money to live on, and at the same time we are made to suffer from apprehension [by the kingdoms], a man yearns only for words of blessing and comfort.[1]

21. R. Abbahu and R. Hiyya bar Abba happened to come to a certain place where R. Abbahu lectured on *Aggadah* while R. Hiyya bar Abba lectured on *Halakhah*. All the people left R. Hiyya bar Abba and went to hear R. Abbahu, so that R. Hiyya bar Abba was greatly upset. To comfort him, R. Abbahu said: May I tell you a parable to illustrate what each of us represents? Two men came to a certain city, one to sell precious stones and pearls, and the other to sell different kinds of [cheap] notions. To whom will people run? Will they not run to him who sells the different kinds of notions:[2]

22. The verse usually read, "The rich man is wise in his own eyes; but the poor man that hath understanding searcheth him through" (Prov. 28:11), R. Samuel son of R. Yose son of R. Bun read differently, taking it to imply; "The man wise in comprehension of Gemara may in his own eyes appear to be rich; but he who understands *Aggadah* may, through his small change, outdo him."[3] [R. Samuel's reading of the verse can be illustrated by] the parable of two men who come into a city—one with gold bars and the other with small change. The man with gold bars cannot use them to pay for his daily needs [and may starve to death], while the man with small change can easily spend it and keep alive.[4]

23. When R. Ammi and R. Assi sat before R. Isaac Nappaha, one said, "Will the master please lecture on *Halakhah?*" while the other said, "Will the master please discourse on *Aggadah?*" When R. Isaac started on a theme of *Aggadah*, the one did not let him go on; and when he started on a theme of *Halakhah*, the other did not let him go on. So R. Isaac said, I will tell you a parable to illustrate my plight. A man had two wives, one young and the other of advanced years. The younger one used to pluck out his white hair, while the older one used to pluck out his black hair—in the end he became quite bald![5]

24. "Every prop of food" (Isa. 3:1)—these are the masters of Talmud;[6] "and every stay of water" (ibid.)—these are the masters of *Aggadah*, who draw men's hearts with *Aggadah* as easily as one draws water from a well.[7]

25. The words "of the dew of heaven" (Gen. 27:28) apply to Scripture;[8] "and of the fat places of the earth" to Mishnah;[9] "new grain" (ibid.) to Talmud; "and wine" (ibid.) to *Aggadah*.[10]

26. The words "kidney-fat of wheat" (Deut. 32:14) apply to *Halakhot*, which are the essence of Torah; and the words "of the blood of the grape thou drankest foaming wine" (ibid.) apply to *Aggadot*, which, like wine, draw a man's heart.[11]

27. The words "They shall bring to life new grain" (Hos. 14:8) apply to Talmud; and the words "shall blossom as the vine" (ibid.) apply to *Aggadah*.[12]

1. Song R. 2:5, §1; Sof 16.
2. B. Sot 40a and En Yaakov, ad loc.
3. Apparently R. Samuel associates *dal* ("poor") with "reduced to little, handing out small change"; and *hkr* ("search through") with *bsr* ("despise," as in Targum, ad loc.)—hence, "worst," "defeat" "outdo."
4. P. Hor 3:5, 49c.
5. B. BK 60b.
6. Their teachings are as essential as bread.
7. B. Hag 14a.
8. Like the dew, it came from heaven.
9. Apparently a play on *mi-shemane* ("fat places") and Mishnah.
10. Gen. R. 66:3.
11. Sif Deut., §317.
12. Lev. R. 1:2.

CHAPTER TWO

THE WORK OF CREATION AND THE FIRST GENERATIONS

The Creation of the World

1. Quoting the verse "Inquire now concerning the days past" (Deut. 4:32), [1] the sages said: These words might be taken to imply that one is allowed to inquire concerning the entire pre-creation period which is "past." Hence Scripture goes on to allow inquiry only "since the day that God created man upon the earth" (ibid.). But these words might be taken to imply that one is also not allowed to inquire concerning the six days of creation [that preceded the making of man]; therefore Scripture extends the time when inquiry is allowed to "the [six] days past, which were [immediately] before thee" (ibid.). Since Scripture's extending the range of inquiry might be taken to imply that one is also allowed to inquire concerning what is above [the heavens] and what is below [the deep], what is before [the beginning of time] and what is after [its end], therefore, with the phrase "from one end of heaven unto the other" (ibid.), Scripture limits inquiry [to the finite span of time and space that the phrase suggests]. Accordingly, you are allowed to inquire concerning the things that are from one end of heaven to the other, but not concerning what is above [the heavens], what is below [the deep], what is before [the six days of creation], and what is after [the world's existence].[2]

2. Why was the world created with the letter *bet*:[3] Just as *bet* is closed on three sides and open only in front, so you are not permitted to investigate what is above [the heavens] and what is below [the deep], what is before [the six days of creation] and what is [to happen] after [the world's existence]—you are permitted only from the time the world was created and thereafter [the world we live in].[4]

3. "The wise man, his eyes are at the beginning" (Eccles. 2:14)—he is one who inquires from the world's beginning, from the six days of creation and thereafter [the world we live in]. "But the fool walketh in darkness" (ibid.)—he is one who puts aside the time of the world's existence and inquires only concerning the time prior, the time of darkness.[5]

4. "Now the earth was worthless and waste (*toho va vohu*)" (Gen. 1:2). R. Eleazar said in the name of Ben Sira: "Do not pry into things too hard for you or examine what is beyond your reach. Meditate on the commandments you have been given; what the Lord keeps secret is no concern of yours" (Ecclesiasticus 3:21). One reason for such limiting of inquiry is suggested by the parable of a king who built a palace on a site of dunghills, sewers, and waste matter. Should a man come and say, "This palace was built on a site of sewers, dunghills, and waste matter," would one not be likely to value the palace less? So, too, should a man come and say, "This world was created upon that which 'was worthless and waste, *tohu-va-vohu*' " (Gen. 1:2), does he not demean [God's creation? Hence] R. Huna stated in the name of Bar Kappara: Were not the account set down in Scripture, it would be impossible to say such a thing as "In the beginning God created" (Gen. 1:1). Created on what sort of site? On "the earth which was worthless and waste, *tohu va-vohu*" (Gen. 1:2).[6]

5. A pagan philosopher argued with Rabban Gamaliel: "Your God is indeed a great artist, but surely He found on hand suitable materials which were of help to him!"[7] "What are they?" asked Rabban Gamaliel. The philosopher replied, "*Tohu, bohu*, darkness, water, wind, and the depths."[8] Rabban Gamaliel exclaimed, "May the breath of a man such as you be blasted out! Since the term 'creation' is used by Scripture for all of them, [it is clear that God Himself brought them into being]. *Tohu* and *bohu:* 'I make peace [perfection] and create evil [lack of perfection]' (Isa. 45:7);[9] darkness: 'I form the light, and create darkness' (ibid.); water: 'Praise Him, ye heavens of heavens, and ye waters' (Ps. 148:4). Why the water's praise? 'Because He commanded, and they were created' (Ps. 148:5); wind: 'For, lo, He that formeth the mountains and created the wind' (Amos 4:13); the depths: 'When there were no depths, I created them' " (Prov. 8:24).[10]

6. "God created" (Gen. 1:1). It happened that a heretic came to R. Akiva and asked "This world—who created it?" R. Akiva replied: "The Holy One, blessed be He." The heretic said, "Show me clear proof." R. Akiva replied, "Come back to me tomorrow." The next day, when the

---

1. In the parallel B. Hag 11b, the text goes on: "*One* may inquire but *two* may not."
2. B. Hag 11b.
3. The first letter in *Bereshit*, "In the beginning" (Gen. 1:1).
4. Gen. R. 1:10. This may refer either to space or to time, or to both space and time. So Tosafot on B. Hag 11b, s.v. *yakhol*.
5. MhG Gen., pp. 7–8.
6. P. Hag 2:1, 47c; Gen. R. 1:5.
7. The philosopher believed that God had indeed created the world, but in his question implied that He had used primeval matter, which was preexistent.
8. The philosopher construed "In the beginning God created heaven and earth" as a topical sentence that is followed by a detailed account of creation in which are mentioned *tohu, bohu*, darkness, etc., elements he presumed to be preexistent.
9. "By *tohu* and *bohu* the philosopher meant primeval matter without form. Thereupon Rabban Gamaliel quoted: "I made *shalom* (that which is whole, i.e., what contains both matter and form) and evil, i.e., that which is defective, consisting of matter only without form.' Thus that too was created" (I. Husik). Perhaps, too, this is an allusion to the view that matter is a source of evil" (Gen. R. Soncino, p. 8, n. 5).
10. Gen. R. 1:9 (Soncino, p. 8, n. 1: "Since at one time there were no depths, God must have created them"); MhG Gen. 20.

heretic came, R. Akiva asked him, "What are you wearing?" The heretic replied, "A garment." R. Akiva asked, "Who made it?" The heretic: "A weaver." "I don't believe you," said R. Akiva; "show me clear proof." The heretic: "What can I show you? Don't you know that a weaver made it?" R. Akiva then asked; "And you, do you not know that the Holy One made His world?" After the heretic departed, R. Akiva's disciples asked him, "But what is the clear proof?" He replied, "My children, even as a house proclaims its builder, a garment its weaver, or a door its carpenter, so does the world proclaim the Holy One, blessed be He, that he created it."[1]

7. R. Judah ben Pazzi expounded: At the beginning the world was nothing but water, as is said, "And the spirit of God hovered over the face of the waters" (Gen. 1:2). Then He proceeded to make it into snow: "He tosseth down hail like crumbs" (Ps. 147:17). Finally He made it into earth: "He said to the snow: 'Become earth' " (Job 37:6).[2]

8. R. Judah bar Simon said: "He revealed [to the prophets] deep and secret things" (Dan. 2:22) concerning the world's beginning. Thus Genesis merely says, "In the beginning God created the heaven" (Gen. 1:1), but does not explain how heaven was created. Who explains it? Isaiah: "He stretched out the heavens as a curtain, and spread them out as a tent to dwell in" (Isa. 40:22). Genesis says, "Created . . . the earth" (Gen. 1:1), but does not explain how it was created. Who explains it? Job: "He said to the snow: "Become loose earth' " (Job 37:6), and presently "the loose earth stuck together" (Job 38:38). Genesis says, "God said: "let there be light' " (Gen. 1:3), but does not explain how the light came into being. Who explains it? A psalm: "Thou didst cover Thyself with light as with a garment" (Ps. 104:2).[3]

9. Six things preceded the creation of the world. Some were actually created, and others came up only in God's thought as what was to be created. Torah and the throne of glory were created. The creation of the fathers, Israel, the Temple, and the name of the Messiah came up only in God's thought. R. Ahavah son of R. Ze'era said: So, too, repentance. And some say: Also the Garden of Eden and Gehenna.[4]

It is said in the name of R. Samuel son of R. Isaac that the thought of creating Israel preceded all else.[5] Had not the Holy One foreseen that after twenty-six generations Israel would accept the Torah, He would not have written in the Torah: "Command the children of Israel" (Num. 5:2) or "Speak to the children of Israel" (Exod. 25:2).

R. Bannai said: The world and the fullness thereof were created only for the sake of Torah.[6]

1. B. Tem 3.
2. P. Hag 2:1, 77a.
3. Gen. R. 1:6.
4. The idea that all these came before the creation described in Genesis is based on Prov. 8:22, Ps. 93:2, Hos. 9:10, Ps. 74:2, Jer. 17:12, Ps. 72:17, Ps. 90:2–3, Gen. 2:8, and Isa. 30:33. See Gen. R. 1:4; TdE, ed. Friedmann, p. 160.
5. Including Torah.
6. So that its words may be studied and its precepts obeyed. Gen. R. 1:4.

10. R. Hoshaia Rabbah began his discourse with the verse "Then I was by Him as a nursling (*amon*)" (Prov. 8:30). The word *amon* may be read *umman*, meaning "overall design"—I was in the mind of the Holy One, says the Torah, like the overall design in the mind of a craftsman. In the way of the world, when a king of flesh and blood builds a palace, he builds it not according to his own whim, but according to the idea of an architect. Moreover, the architect does not build it out of his own head; he has [a design]—plans and diagrams to know how to lay out the chambers and where to put in wicket doors. Even so the Holy One looked into the Torah as He created the world.[7]

11. R. Zutra bar Tobiah said in the name of Rav: The world was created by means of ten capacities and powers: By wisdom, by understanding,[8] by reason,[9] by strength,[10] by rebuke,[11] by might,[12] by righteousness, by judgment, by loving-kindness, and by compassion.[13]

12. "The Lord God[14] made earth and heaven" (Gen. 2:4). A parable of a king who had cups made of delicate glass. The king said: If I pour hot water into them, they will [expand and] burst; if cold water, they will contract [and break]. What did he do? He mixed hot and cold water, and poured it into them, and so they remained unbroken. Likewise, the Holy One said: If I create the world with the attribute of mercy alone, its sins will be too many; if with justice alone, how could the world be expected to endure? So I will create it with both justice and mercy, and may it endure![15]

Heaven and Earth

13. The sages taught: The school of Shammai says, Heaven was created first and the earth was created afterward, for it is said, "In the beginning God created heaven and earth" (Gen. 1:1). But the school of Hillel says: The earth was created first and heaven afterward, for it is said, "In the day that the Lord God made earth and heaven" (Gen. 2:4). The school of Hillel said to the school of Shammai: According to you, a man should build the upper story of the house first and the lower story afterward, for in the verse "It is He that buildeth His upper chambers

7. Gen. R. 1:1.
8. The ability to understand what one learns.
9. Deductive power.
10. Physical strength.
11. "In Job 26:11 it is implied that at first the pillars of heaven were weak and shaky, till God rebuked them, when, like a person taken aback by astonishment, they stiffened and hardened" (Israel Abrahams in Hag, Soncino, p. 65, n. 6).
12. Moral power.
13. The aforementioned capacities and powers are taken to be intimated in Prov. 3:19–20, Ps. 65:7, Job 26:11, Ps. 89:15, and Ps. 25:6. B. Hag 12a.
14. In rabbinic conception, Adonai ("Lord") represents the attribute of mercy, while Elohim ("God") represents the attribute of justice. Both, according to Gen. 2:4, were brought together at the making of heaven and earth.
15. Gen. R. 12:15; Yalkut, *Bereshit*, §19.

in the heaven, and hath founded His [lower] vault upon the earth" (Amos 9:6), [the upper chambers are identified with heaven]. The school of Shammai replied to the school of Hillel: According to you, a man should first make a footstool and then make the throne,[1] for in the verse "The heaven is My throne and the earth is My footstool" (Isa. 66:1) [the earth is identified as God's footstool]. But the sages say: Both were created at one and the same time, for it is said, "Yea, Mine hand hath laid the foundation of the earth, and My right hand hath spread out the heavens; when I called unto them, they stood up *together*" (Isa. 48:13).[2]

In the name of the sages, R. Yohanan said: In creation, heaven was first; in being brought to completion, earth was first. R. Tanhuma said, I will state the proof for this statement: the verse "God created heaven and earth" (Gen. 1:1) shows that heaven was first in creation; while the verse "In the day the Lord God completed making earth and heaven" (Gen. 2:4) shows that earth was first in being brought to completion.[3]

14. R. Eleazar son of R. Simeon observed: Why does Scripture at times put earth before heaven, and at other times heaven before earth? To teach that the two are of equal value.[4]

15. "From the beginning . . . [the inhabitants of] the earth [were such dissemblers that they] set one to wonder what their true nature (*tohu va-vohu*) was" (Gen. 1:2).[5] And so R. Berekhiah began his discourse with the verse "Though his actions appear to be innocent and proper, even a child may in fact dissemble in his behavior" (Prov. 20:11).[6] Accordingly, R. Berekhiah went on to say: At the very beginning, mankind was like a young fig tree which put forth thorns even before it bore fruit. Hence, in prophetic vision it was to be said, "I looked at [the inhabitants of] the earth, and they set one to wonder what their true nature was" (Jer. 4:23).[7]

Differing, R. Abbahu [construed the verse "The inhabitants of the earth were bewildered and confounded (*tohu va-vohu*)" (Gen. 1:2) and in explanation] told the parable of a king who bought two slaves, both on one bill of sale and at the same price. For one, he decreed that he be fed by the royal treasury; and for the other, that he must toil to eat. The latter sat bewildered and confounded (*toheh u-voheh*), and said: Both of us were acquired through one bill of sale and at the same price. Yet he is fed by the treasury, and I am fed only for my toil! Likewise, the earth sat bewildered and confounded (*tohah u-vohah*), saying: The beings above and the beings below were created at the same time. Yet those above are nourished by the splendor of the Presence, while those below do not eat if they do not toil. I am perplexed!

R. Judah bar Simon told the parable of a king who bought two maidservants, both on one bill of sale and at the same price. For one, he decreed that she need never leave the palace; while for the other, he decreed banishment. The second one sat there bewildered and confounded (*tohah u-vohah*), and said: Both of us were acquired through the same bill of sale and at the same price. Yet she need never leave the palace, while for me the king has decreed banishment. I am perplexed! Likewise, the earth sat bewildered and confounded (*tohah u-vohah*), saying; The beings above and the beings below were created at the same time. Yet the beings above live on, while the beings below die. Hence Scripture: "The earth was bewildered and confounded (*tohu va-vohu*)" (Gen. 1:2).

R. Tanhuma told the parable of a prince who slept in a cradle while his nurse sat by anxious and troubled (*tohah u-vohah*). Why? Because she knew she was to receive her punishment through him. Likewise, the earth foresaw that she was to receive her punishment through Adam, as is said, "Cursed be the earth because of thee" (Gen. 3:17). Hence Scripture: "The earth was bewildered and confounded.[8]

16. "And God made the firmament" (Gen. 1:7). This is a verse whose apparent implication caused Ben Zoma to shake the world [of Jewish learning]. " 'And God made!'—an unbelievable utterance," he said. "Did not the firmament come into being by God's word—"by the word of the Lord were the heavens made, and all the host of them by the breath of His mouth' (Ps. 33:6)?"[9]

17. Concerning the verse "And God said: "Let there be a firmament in the midst of the waters' " (Gen. 1:6), the sages observed: When the Holy One commanded, "Let there be a firmament in the midst of the waters," the middle layer solidified, and thus the separation between the lower heaven and the upper heaven of heavens came into being.[10]

"Let there be a firmament." But was not heaven already made on the first day? Rav explained: On the first day, heaven was in a form that was still fluid, but on the second day, it congealed. Hence, "Let there be a firmament" is to be understood as meaning: Let the firmament congeal, let it be covered by an overlay, let it be stretched out, let it become firm.[11]

R. Hanina said: Fire descended from above and licked the top surface of the firmament. Hence, whenever R. Yohanan came to the verse "By His [fiery] breath heaven was smoothed"[12] (Job 26:13), he would say, "R. Hanina taught me well."[13]

---

1. "The size of the footstool cannot be determined till the throne has been made" (Israel Abrahams in Hag, Soncino, p. 66, n. 6).
2. B. Hag 12a; Gen. R. 1:15.
3. Gen. R. 1:15.
4. Ibid. Accordingly, the difference in order has no bearing on the priority of either in creation.
5. JV: "Now the earth was unformed and void." But *tohu* ("unformed") may be derived from *thh* ("to wonder"); and *bohu* [*vohu*] ("void"), broken into the syllables *bo* [*vo*] ("within") and *hu* ("it"), may be taken to mean "what is in it."
6. NJV: "A child may be dissembling in his behavior even though his actions be innocent and proper."
7. JV: "I beheld the earth, and, lo, it was waste and void."
8. Gen. R. 2:1–2.
9. "Made" would seem to imply almost blasphemously that God had to work at the "making" of the firmament. Gen. R. 4:6; Yalkut, *Bereshit*, §6.
10. Gen. R. 4:2.
11. P. Ber 1:1, 2c; Gen. R. 4:2.
12. JV: "was serene."
13. Gen. R. 4:2.

18. "And God called the firmament heaven (*shamayim*)" (Gen. 1:8). Rav said: *Shamayim* is a composite of *esh* ("fire") and *mayim* ("water"). The Holy One took fire and water, and worked them into each other; and out of the two, heaven was made.

Another comment: *Shamayim* is so called because men wonder (*mishtomemim*) at it, saying: Of what (*shel mah*) is it composed? Of fire? Of water? It is an enigma![1]

19. "All that has been generated in heaven and on earth is now in the form in which it was created[2] on the day the Lord God made earth and heaven" (Gen. 2:4), which implies, R. Nehemiah stated: On the very same day that heaven and earth were created, they brought forth at once the generations that have since issued from them. R. Judah objected: But is it not said, "And there was evening and there was morning, one day . . . a second day . . . a third day . . . a fourth day . . . a fifth day . . . a sixth day"?[3] R. Nehemiah replied: All that has been generated from heaven and earth corresponds to the experience of those who harvest figs [4]—each being [was created at the beginning but] became visible only at the time designated for it.

[In agreement with R. Nehemiah], R. Berekhiah said: The words "And the earth brought forth" (Gen. 1:12) imply that what was brought forth had already been deposited within it.[5]

20. A Caesar said to Rabban Gamaliel [of Yavneh]: He who created the mountains did not create the wind, for it is written, "There is He that formed the mountains and there is He that created the wind" (Amos 4:13).[6] Rabban Gamaliel replied: If so, then in the account of the making of Adam, where Scripture says, "He created" (Gen. 1:27) and "He formed" (Gen. 2:7)—would you, in keeping with your reasoning, also say that He who created one part of Adam did not create any other part of him? Further, there is an area of the human body no more than a handbreadth square, which contains two openings,[7] of which it is written, "He that planteth the ear, shall He not hear? He that formeth the eye, shall He not see?" (Ps. 94:9)[8]—would you maintain here, too, that He who created the one did not create the other? "Yes, even so," answered Caesar. "Yet," Rabban Gamaliel retorted, "Would you say that at a creature's death the creators of the eye and the ear agree to let their creature die?"[9]

The Light

21. "And God said: "Let there be light' " (Gen. 1:3). R. Judah taught: The light was created first, and then [all that is in] the world.[10] A parable of a king who wanted to build a palace, but the site was dark. What did he do? He lit lamps and lanterns to see where to lay the foundations. Hence, light had to be created first. But R. Nehemiah maintained: The world was created first; just as a king would first build a palace and then adorn it with lights and lanterns.[11]

22. R. Simeon ben Jehozadak interrogated R. Samuel bar Nahman, saying: Since I hear that you are a master of *Aggadah*, tell me how light was created. R. Samuel bar Nahman replied: God wrapped Himself in a white garment, and the radiance of His majesty illuminated the world from one end to the other.[12]

23. "And God saw the light, that it was [for the] good, and God set it aside" (Gen. 1:4). R. Eleazar said: By the light that the Holy One created on the first day, one could see from one end of the world to the other. But as soon as the Holy One observed the generation of the flood and the generation of the dispersion of mankind, [13] and saw that their conduct was to be depraved, He proceeded to secrete His light from them. And for whom did He secrete it? For the righteous in the time-to-come, just like a king who has a goodly treasure and sets it aside for his son. And where did He hide the light? In the Garden of Eden.[14]

24. "And God divided the light from the darkness" (Gen. 1:4). R. Berekhiah said: Two men of renown, R. Yohanan and R. Simeon ben Lakish, took the words "And . . . divided" to imply actual division of domains and illustrated this interpretation by a parable: A king had two chiefs of the guards who argued with each other. One said: I am to be in charge during the day. And the other said: No! I am to be in charge during the day. So the king summoned the first, saying to him: So-and-so, daytime is to be your domain; then he summoned the second: So-and-so, nighttime is to be your domain. Likewise, "for the light God summoned the day" (Gen. 1:5), saying, "Daytime is to be your domain"; "and for the darkness He

1. Gen. R. 4:7.
2. JV: "These are the generations of the heaven and of the earth when they were created."
3. Which would indicate that only heaven and earth were created on the first day, whereas what issued from them was created on subsequent days.
4. Figs on the tree assume their shape at about the same time but do not all ripen simultaneously. So, too, all that was to issue from heaven and earth had already been created on the first day: only their appearance was delayed to subsequent days.
5. Gen. R. 12:4.
6. JV: "He that formeth the mountains, and createth the wind." Caesar took these words to refer to two divine beings.
7. The face, which contains the eye and the ear.
8. "Two different expressions are used for the creation of the eye and ear respectively" (Jacob Shachter in Sanh, Soncino, p. 249).
9. B. Sanh 39a. "The one who *planted* and the one who *created*, i.e., assuming that there were two creators of man, he could not completely die unless both agreed; otherwise, the creator of the eye might insist that the eye go on living, whilst the creator of the ear might wish it to die" (Jacob Shachter in Sanh, Soncino, p. 249).
10. According to R. Judah, "In the beginning God created the heaven and the earth" (Gen. 1:1) is a general statement, followed by details which begin with the command "Let there be light" (Gen. 1:3).
11. Gen. R. 3:1; Exod. R. 34:2.
12. Gen. R. 3:4; MTeh 104:4.
13. See Gen. 11:9.
14. B. Hag 12a; Gen. R. 3:6; Exod. R. 35:1.

summoned the night" (ibid.), saying, "Nighttime is to be your domain."[1]

25. "And there was evening and there was morning, one day" (Gen. 1:5). Scripture says here not, "Let there be evening," but, "There was evening." Hence, it follows that the order of time had already existed before creation.[2]

The Water

26. "And God made the firmament, and divided the waters which were under the firmament from the waters which were above the firmament" (Gen. 1:7). R. Yohanan said: The Holy One took all the primeval waters and put half of them in the firmament and half of them in the Great Ocean, as is said, "Each half (*peleg*) of the river (*peleg*) of God is [always] full of water" (Ps. 65:10)[3]—*peleg* in the verse being construed [in a dual sense: "river" and] "half."[4]

R. Berekhiah said: The lower waters did not part from the upper waters without weeping. This is implied in the verse "Because of weeping, He had to bind the streams with poultices" (Job 28:11).[5]

27. A heretic asked R. Meir, "Is it possible that the upper waters are prevented from pouring down by God's mere word?" "Yes," R. Meir answered, and added, "Bring me a water clock."[6] When he brought the water clock, R. Meir placed a plate of gold on top of it. But the water did not stop flowing out. He then placed a plate of silver on top of it. But the water still did not stop flowing out. When R. Meir put his finger on top of it, the water stopped flowing out.

The heretic said, "But you put your finger on top of it!" R. Meir replied, "I am no more than flesh and blood, yet my finger stops the water's flow; how much more and more powerful is the finger—the word—of the Holy One."[7]

28. Why is "It was good" not written about the second day [of creation]? R. Samuel bar Nahman said: Because the disposition of the waters was not yet finished.[8] Consequently, "It was good" is written twice in connection with the third day, once about the disposition of the waters and a second time about the work that was begun and completed on that day.

A Roman noblewoman asked R. Yose, "Why is 'It was good' not written about the second day?" He replied, "But in fact, Scripture subsequently does include all the days in the words 'And God saw *everything* that He had made, and behold, it was very good' " (Gen. 1:31). She said, "Suppose six men came to you, and you gave to each of five one *maneh*, but you did not give one to the sixth, and then you gave a second *maneh* to all of them together. Would not each of the first five now have a *maneh* and one-sixth, while the sixth man would have only one-sixth of a *maneh?* I am still baffled."

At that, R. Yose, retracting his own explanation, explained the matter in the same way as R. Samuel bar Nahman.

R. Simon, in the name of R. Joshua ben Levi, told the parable of a king who had an excessively fierce legion, and he said: Since the legion is so fierce, let it not bear my name. Likewise, the Holy One said: Since the generation of the flood, the generation of Enosh,[9] and the generation of the dispersion of mankind will be punished by water, let not "It was good"[10] be set down concerning water.

But R. Hanina explained: Because separation [that is to say, disunion] was brought into being on the second day, as indicated in "Let [the firmament] separate water from water" (Gen. 1:6), [the statement "It was good" does not occur]. In this regard, R. Tavyomi noted: If there is no mention of "It was good" about an act of separation conducive to the world's improvement and well-being, all the less should such words occur in describing occasions leading to the world's disarray.[11]

29. On the third day, the earth was as flat as a plain, and the waters covered the entire surface of the earth. And when out of the mouth of the Almighty there issued the command "Let the waters be gathered together . . . and let the dry land appear" (Gen. 1:9), mountains and hills rising up in different parts of the earth emerged over its entire surface, so that it became pitted with many valleys. As the core of the earth rose up, the waters rolled down into the valleys [and became seas]. Forthwith, swelling with pride, the waters rose in order to cover the earth as at the beginning. But then the Holy One rebuked them, subdued them, placed them beneath the soles of His feet, and measured out their extent with His own span, so that they should neither enlarge nor diminish. And as a man makes a hedge for his vineyard, so He made the sand into a hedge for the seas, so that when the waters rise and see the sand before them, they turn back and recede.[12]

30. "Let the waters under the heaven be gathered together to one place" (Gen. 1:9). R. Yudan said in the name of R. Levi, and R. Berekhiah in the name of R. Judah son of R. Simeon: The whole earth is filled with waters within waters, and yet you say, "To one place"?

1. Gen. R. 3:6.
2. Gen. R. 3:7.
3. JV: "With the river of God that is full of water."
4. Gen. R. 4:4.
5. JV: "He bindeth the streams that they trickle [literally, "weep"] not." Gen. R. 5:4.
6. "The meaning of the word is doubtful. It would appear to mean a *clepsydra*, a contrivance for measuring time by the flow of water. The bottom was perforated with such small holes that if the upper apertures were completely closed, the water would not flow out from the bottom" (H. Freedman in Gen. R., Soncino, p. 28, n. 6).
7. Gen. R. 4:4.
8. "It was good" may be said only of a work that has been completed.
9. The generation of Enosh suffered partial flood. See PR 48:2 (YJS 2:816).
10. One of God's names is "Good."
11. Gen. R. 4:6.
12. PRE 5; MTeh 93:5 (YJS 2:126); Yalkut, *Bereshit*, §8.

How is such a thing possible? Consider the parable of ten wineskins fully inflated with air, lying in a banqueting hall [and occupying a great deal of space]. When the king needs the space they occupy, what does he do to them? He unties them, lets out the air, and moves them into a corner [of the hall]. So, too, the Holy One trod down upon the primeval waters, causing the air to come out of them, and then moved them into the Great Ocean. It is about this that Scripture says, "He compressed the waters as though they had been in a wineskin, and then put the deeps in vaults" (Ps. 33:7)[1] and "He pressed[2] upon the waters, and they dried up" (Job 12:15) and "He trod upon the waves" (Job 9:8).[3]

31. R. Joshua son of R. Nehemiah said: The waters ascended mountains and descended into depths, until they reached the Great Ocean. Of this, Scripture says, "They ascended the mountains, they descended into valleys, unto the place which Thou hadst founded for them" (Ps. 104:8). Which place hadst Thou founded for them? The great Ocean.[4]

Grasses and Trees

32. In expounding the verse "The glory of the Lord endures for ever; the Lord rightly rejoices in His works" (Ps. 104:31), R. Hanina bar Papa said: The angel of the universe [5] uttered this verse. For when the Holy One enjoined each fruit tree to bear fruit "after its kind" (Gen 1:11), the grasses applied to themselves an *a fortiori* argument, saying: If God enjoined "after its kind"[6] upon trees, which by nature do not grow up in promiscuous miscellany, how much more does it apply to us! Immediately, each grass sprouted forth after its kind, as is said, "The earth sprouted grass, herb yielding seed after its kind" (Gen. 1:12). Then the angel of the universe declared, "The glory of the Lord endures forever; the Lord rightly rejoices in His works!"[7]

33. R. Assi pointed out a [seeming] contradiction between two verses. One verse, referring to the third day, says, "And the earth brought forth grass" (Gen. 1:12), whereas another verse, when speaking of the sixth day, says, "No vegetation of the field was yet in the earth" (Gen. 2:5). However, the two verses, seemingly contradictory, teach us that the plants commenced to grow [on the third day] but stopped just as they were about to break through the soil, until Adam came [on the sixth day] and besought the mercy [of rain] for them; and when rain fell, they sprouted forth.[8]

34. "No one to converse with (*siah*, 'tree') in the field" (Gen. 2:5). All trees converse (*mesihim*)[9], as it were, with one another. Indeed, one may add, all trees converse with mortals; all trees—created, as trees were, to provide fellowship[10] for mortals.[11]

35. R. Simon said: There is not one herb without its own constellation (*mazzal*) in heaven, which slaps it and says, "Grow!"[12]

The Moon

36. R. Simeon ben Pazzi pointed out a [seeming] contradiction between two parts of the same verse. The verse begins by saying, "And God made the two great lights" (Gen. 1:16), and then goes on to speak of "a greater light . . . and a lesser light" (ibid.) [However, this is what happened]: The moon dared say to the Holy One, "Master of the universe, is it possible for two kings to wear the same size crown?" The Holy One answered, "Go, then, and make yourself smaller." But the moon protested, "Master of the universe, must I make myself smaller merely because I suggested to You something that is sensible?" The Holy One conceded, "Very well. Go and rule by day[13] as well as by night."[14]

37. "And the stars" (Gen. 1:16). R. Aha said: [The association of the stars with the moon] will be understood by the parable of a king who had two administrators, one ruling in the city and the other ruling over the [rest of the] province. The king said: Since one was willing to be diminished to rule only in the city, I decree that whenever he goes forth, the city council and the populace shall go forth with him, and whenever he returns, the city council and the populace shall return with him. So, too, did the Holy One: Since the moon was willing to be diminished and to rule by night, I, [said God], decree that when she comes forth, the stars shall go forth with her, and when she returns, the stars shall return with her.[15]

38. When the Holy One rebuked the moon, and it fell, some sparks fell from it into the sky—these are the stars.[16]

The Variety of Creatures

39. R. Akiva used to quote, "What variety Thou hast created, O Lord!" (Ps. 104:24). You have creatures that grow in the sea and You have creatures that grow on dry

---

1. JV: "He gathereth the waters of the sea together as a heap; He layeth up the deeps in storehouses." But *nd* may mean "heap" or "wineskin."
2. JV: "Withholdeth." But the verb *'ter* can mean "withhold" and also "press." Cf. Targum on Judg. 6:38.
3. Gen. R. 5:2; MTeh 93:5 (YJS 2:127).
4. Gen. R. 5:3.
5. Metatron. See Tosafot on B. Hul 60a.
6. This phrase appears in connection with the trees but not in connection with grasses.
7. B. Hul 60a.
8. B. Hul 60b.
9. The usual word for "tree" is *etz*. Hence *siah*, used instead, is construed in a dual sense: "tree" and "converse, provide fellowship."
10. "Fellowship"—Gen. R. TA; BR: "benefit."
11. Gen. R. 13:2.
12. Gen. R. 10:6. On *mazzal*, cf. Sanh, Soncino, p. 629, n. 10. Here it is stated that not only each man but each herb has its own *mazzal*.
13. The moon is at times visible during the day.
14. B. Hul 60b.
15. Gen. R. 6:4.
16. Yalkut Reuveni, quoting Midrash Toledot Yitzhak (BhM, 5; 156).

land. If those of the sea were to come up on dry land, they would immediately die; and if those of the dry land were to go down into the sea, they would immediately die. You have creatures that grow in fire,[1] and You have creatures that grow in the air. If those of the fire were to come up into the air, they would immediately die. [If those of the air were to come down into the fire, they would immediately die.] The place of life for the one is the cause of death for the other; and the place of death for the one is the cause of life for the other. "What variety Thou hast created, O Lord!"[2]

40. "And all the host of them" (Gen. 2:1). Even those creatures that you may look upon as superfluous in the world, such as flies, fleas, or gnats—they too are part of the entirety of creation. The Holy One effects His purpose through all creatures, even through a frog or a flea.[3]

41. R. Judah said in the name of Rav: Of all that the Holy One created in His world, He did not create a single thing that is useless.[4]

42. Elijah told the following: One day, as I was walking through the greatest city of the world,[5] there was a draft roundup and I was peremptorily seized and brought into the king's house. Presently a Parsee priest came and asked me, "Are you a man of books?" I replied, "A bit of one." He said, "If you can answer the particular question I am about to ask, you may go in peace." I replied, "Ask." He then asked, "Why did God create loathsome reptiles and creeping things?"[6] I replied, "God is a judge who is indeed holy and just, but He is also loving because He is perceptive [of man's condition] forever and ever and ever. He knows both beginning and end, and can tell from the beginning what the end of anything is to be, long, long before it has been made; still, He chooses to see the good and chooses not to see the evil [in whatever is made]. In His wisdom and with His understanding He created His world and set it on its foundation. Then He created Adam and brought him into the world. And He created him for no other purpose than to serve Him with a whole heart; He would thus find contentment in him and in his descendants after him until the end of all generations. But then, after Adam complied with the command to be fruitful and multiply, one [descendant] worshiped the sun and the moon, and another worshiped wood and stone, and thus every day Adam's descendants came to be deemed by Him as deserving annihilation. Nevertheless, upon reconsidering all the work of His hands in the world of His creation, God said: These [human beings] have life, and those [other creatures] have life. These have breath and those have breath; these crave food and drink, and those crave food and drink. Human beings ought therefore to be deemed as important as cattle or wild beasts, or, at worst, as important as the variety of loathsome reptiles and creeping things that I created upon the earth. At once He felt some measure of contentment and resolved not to annihilate mankind. And so you see that reptiles and creeping things were created in the world as a means of mankind's preservation.[7]

43. [The Roman general Quintus asked Rabban Yohanan ben Zakkai]: One verse speaks of fowl as having been created out of the waters of the sea: "God said, 'Let the waters bring forth abundantly . . . fowl that may fly above the earth' " (Gen. 1:20). But another verse speaks of them as having been created out of the earth: "Out of the ground the Lord God formed . . . every fowl of the air" (Gen. 2:19). Rabban Yohanan ben Zakkai replied: [Both are true.] Fowl were created out of the alluvial mud.

R. Samuel of Cappadocia commented: Just the same, [fowl are related to fish], for the skin of chickens' feet resembles the scale-covered skin of fish [and so fowl are considered fishlike].[8]

Man

44. "And God said: 'Let *us* make man' " (Gen. 1:26). With whom did He take counsel? R. Ammi said: He took counsel with His own heart. He was like a king who built a palace with the counsel of an architect. When he saw the palace, it did not please him. At whom was he indignant? Was it not at the architect? Hence, "and it grieved Him at His heart" (Gen. 6:6) [with which He had taken counsel at the making of man].

R. Hanina said: He consulted the ministering angels.

R. Berekhiah said: When the Holy One was about to create Adam, he saw both the righteous and the wicked who were to issue from him. So He said: If I create him, wicked men will issue from him; if I do not create him, how are righteous men to be born? What did the Holy One do? He diverted the way of the wicked from before His sight,[9] partnered the quality of mercy[10] with Himself, [saying to it, "Let us make man], and then created him.[11]

45. R. Judah said in the name of Rav: When the Holy One was about to create man, He first created a company of ministering angels and asked them: Is it your desire that "we make man in our image" (Gen. 1:26)? They replied: Master of the universe, what will be his deeds? God said: Such-and-such will be his deeds. Indignantly, they exclaimed: Master of the universe, "what is man that Thou art mindful of him, and the son of man that Thou thinkest of him" (Ps. 8:5)? At once He stretched out His little

1. Salamanders were believed to live in fire.
2. B. Hul 127a; Yalkut, Ps., §862.
3. Gen. R. 10:7; Exod. R. 10:1.
4. B. Shab 77b.
5. Probably Ctesiphon, capital of the Sassanids. See Jacob Mann, "Date and Place of Redaction of Seder Eliahu Rabbah and Zuta," *HUCA* 4,: 302–10, particularly n. 137. (To a Babylonian Jew, Ctesiphon no doubt seemed the largest city in the world—Leon Nemoy.)
6. In Zoroastrian teaching, such creatures are the work of Ahriman, the god of darkness and evil. But for Elijah, as will become evident, such creatures serve an admirable purpose.
7. TdE, Ed. Friedmann, pp. 5–6.
8. B. Hul 27b, and Tosafot and En Yaakov, ad loc.
9. He deliberately disregarded it.
10. Mercy is often hypostatized.
11. Gen. R. 8:3–4; Yalkut, *Bereshit*, §13.

finger among them and consumed them with fire. The same thing happened with a second company. The third company said to Him: Master of the universe, what did it avail the former [angels that they spoke to You] as they did? The whole world is Yours, and whatever You wish to do therein, do it.

When God came to the generation of the flood and to the generation of the dispersion of mankind, whose deeds were so corrupt, the angels said: Lord of the universe, did not the first [company of angels] speak justly? He retorted, "Even to old age . . . and even to hoar hair will I put up [with man]" (Isa. 46:4).[1]

46. R. Simon said: When the Holy One was about to create Adam, the ministering angels formed themselves into groups and companies, some of them saying, "Let him be created," while others urged, "Let him not be created." Thus it is written, "Love and truth fought together, righteousness and peace combated each other" (Ps. 85:11).[2] Love said, "Let him be created, because he will perform acts of love." Truth said, "Let him not be created, because all of him will be falsehood." Righteousness said, "Let him be created, because he will do righteous deeds." Peace said, "Let him not be created, because he will be all strife." What did the Holy One do? He took truth and cast it to the ground, as is said, "Thou didst cast down truth to the ground" (Dan. 8:12). The ministering angels dared say to the Holy One, "Master of the universe, why do You humiliate Your seal?[3] Let truth arise from the earth." Hence it is written, "Let truth spring up from the earth" (Ps. 85:12).[4]

The elder R. Huna of Sepphoris said: While the ministering angels were parleying with one another and disputing with one another, the Holy One created Adam and then said: What are you parleying about? Man is already made.[5]

47. R. Huna said in the name of R. Aibu: God created Adam with due deliberation. He first created the means of man's sustenance and only then did He create him. The ministering angels spoke up to the Holy One: "Master of universes, "what is man that Thou art mindful of him, and the son of man that Thou thinkest of him?' [Ps. 8:5]. This source of trouble—why should he be created?" "If what you hint in your question is to be followed," God replied, " 'sheep and oxen, all of them' [Ps. 8:8]—why should they have been created? Why should 'the fowl of the air and the fish of the sea' [Ps. 8:9] have been created? I am like a king who has a tower full of good things, but no guests. What joy can the tower give the king who filled it?" At that, the ministering angels declared, "Master of universes, 'Lord, our Lord, how glorious is Thy Name in all the earth' [Ps. 8:10]. Do what pleases You."[6]

48. R. Samuel bar Nahman said in the name of R. Jonathan: At the time when Moses was engaged in writing the Torah, he had to set down what happened on each of the six days of creation. When he got to the verse "And God said: "Let *us* make Adam' " (Gen. 1:26), Moses dared ask, "Master of the universe, why do You give heretics their opportunity?"[7] "Write, O son of Amram," God replied: "Whoever wishes to err, let him err." The Holy One then added, "O Moses, this Adam whom I created by Myself—will I not cause both greater and lesser men to issue from him? Accordingly, whenever a great man is inclined to seek approval [for an important act] from one who is less than he and holds back, saying, 'Why should I seek approval from one who is less than I?' he will be told: Learn from your Creator, who created the creatures above and the creatures below [on His own], yet when He was about to create Adam, He took counsel with the ministering angels."[8]

R. Hila[9] differed: No taking counsel is implied here. What happened will be understood by the parable of a king who was strolling at the entrance to his palace when he saw a clump of earth lying about. So he said: What shall we[10] do with it? Some might suggest: [Use it to build] public baths; others might suggest: Private baths. But I will make a statuelike figure out of it! Who is to hinder me?[11]

49. R. Aha said: When the Holy One desired to create the first man, He consulted the ministering angels and said to them, "Shall we make man?"[12] They asked, "What is to be his character?" God replied, "This being whom I desire to create—his wisdom will be greater than yours." How did God prove it? He assembled all domestic animals, all wild beasts, and all fowls, and made them pass before the angels. Then He asked, "What are the names of these creatures?" The angels did not know. Subsequently, when He created the first man, He again assembled all domestic animals, all wild beasts, and all fowl, and made them pass before him. He asked him, "What are the names of these creatures?" Adam replied, "This one—the name 'ox' fits him. This one—'ass.' And this one—'horse.' And this one—'camel.' And this one—'lion.' And this one—'vulture.' " And he named the others as well. Thus it is written, "And the man gave names to all cattle, to the fowl of the air," etc. (Gen. 2:20). God asked him, "And you, what is your name?" He replied, "The name Adam fits me." God asked, "Why?" He replied, "Because I was fashioned out of the earth (*adamah*)." God asked, "And I, what is My Name?" "The name Lord fits You." God asked, "Why?" "Because You are Lord over all Your works."[13]

---

1. B. Sanh 38a.
2. JV: "Mercy and truth are met together; righteousness and peace have kissed each other." But the commentator interprets "met" in the sense of "fought," and derives *nashaku* ("kissed") from *neshek* ("arms"), reading: "have taken arms against each other."
3. Truth is the seal of God.
4. Gen. R. 8:5.
5. Gen. R. 8:5 (Soncino, p. 58). R. Huna thus reads not *na'aseh* ("Let us make") but *ne'esah* ("is already made").
6. Gen. R. 8:6.
7. They will say that there are numerous deities.
8. Gen. R. 8:8.
9. So Gen. R. TA; BR: "R. Levi."
10. The royal plural.
11. Gen. R. 8:8.
12. JV: "Let us make man."
13. PR 14:9 (YJS 1; 272–73): Tanhuma, *Hukkat*, §6; Gen. R. 17:4; Num. R. 19:3.

50. R. Meir used to say: Adam—the dust out of which he was made was gathered from the entire earth.[1]

51. R. Simeon ben Yohai, quoting "The Craftsman,[2] His work is perfect" (Deut. 32:4), said: The Craftsman who wrought the world and man, His work is perfect. In the way of the world, when a king of flesh and blood builds a palace, mortals who enter it say: Had the columns been taller, how much more beautiful the palace would have been! Had the walls been higher, how much more beautiful it would have been! Had the ceiling been loftier, how much more beautiful it would have been! But does any man come and say: If I had three eyes, three arms, three legs, how much better off I would be! If I walked on my head, or if my face were turned backward, how much better off I would be! I wonder. To assure that no one would say such a thing, the King of kings of kings, the Holy One and His court had themselves, in a manner of speaking, polled concerning the placing of every part of your body and set you up in a way that is right for you.[3]

52. R. Levi bar Haita said: Were a king of flesh and blood to build a palace and place a rainspout over its entrance, it would be unseemly. But the King of kings of kings, the Holy One, created man, and placed the spout [his nose] over the entrance [his mouth], and that makes man's beauty, man's comeliness.[4]

53. "And God created man in His own image" (Gen. 1:27). R. Hoshaia said: At the time the Holy One created the first man, the ministering angels mistook him [for God Himself] and were about to say "Holy" before him. What did the Holy One do? He put him into a deep sleep, and all the angels realized that he was no more than man. [God and man together in the world were then] like a king and a governor riding together in a state carriage. The people of the province were about to cry. "Hail, *domine!*" but did not know which one was king. What did the king do? He pushed aside the governor and put him out of the carriage, whereupon all realized that that one was no more than a governor.[5]

54. Man was created alone in order to teach you that if anyone causes a single soul to perish from Israel, Scripture imputes to him the destruction of the entire world; and if anyone saves alive a single soul in Israel,[6] Scripture imputes to him the saving alive of the entire world. Again, [man was created alone] for the sake of peace among men, that one might not say to his fellow, "My father was greater than yours"; and that heretics might not say, "There are many ruling powers in heaven." Another reason: To proclaim the greatness of the Holy One. For if a man strikes many coins from one die, they all resemble one another; in fact, they are all exactly alike. But though the King of kings of kings, the Holy One, blessed be He, fashioned every man from the die of the first man, not a single one of them is exactly like his fellow. Hence, each and every person should say, "The world was created for my sake."[7]

55. The sages taught: Man was created alone. And why so? For the sake of the righteous and for the sake of the wicked. That the righteous might not say, "Ours is a righteous heredity,"[8] and that the wicked might not say, "Ours is an evil heredity."[9]

Another answer: For the sake of [the different] families, that they might not quarrel with one another.[10] Now, if at present, though originally but one man was created, they quarrel anyway, how much more would they have quarreled had two been created?

Another answer: Because of brigands and plunderers. If at present, though originally but one man was created, people rob and plunder, how much more so had two been created?[11]

And why are men's faces not like one another? Lest a man see a beautiful dwelling or a beautiful woman [belonging to someone else] and say, "she is mine."[12]

56. Man was created on the eve of Sabbath, [the last of all created beings]. And why? Lest heretics say, "The Holy One had [Adam as] partner in His work of creation."

Another answer: Should a man's opinion of himself become overweening, he may be reminded that the gnat preceded him in the order of creation.

Another answer: So that immediately [after his creation] he could proceed to fulfill the precept [of hallowing the Sabbath].

Another answer: So that he might at once go to the banquet.[13] Thus, God was like the king of flesh and blood who built a palace, decorated it, and made arrangements for a banquet [so that all would be in readiness when his guests arrived].

57. The words "Man is raised aloft" (Prov. 29:4)[14] refer to the first man, who was the climax of creation—lifted out, as the world's dough offering.[15]

58. When the Holy One created the first man, He took him and led him around all the trees of the Garden of Eden, and said to him: Behold My works, how beautiful, how splendid they are. All that I have created, I created

1. B. Sanh 38b.
2. Instead of *tzur* ("Rock" [=God]), R. Simeon ben Yohai read *tzayyar* ("Craftsman").
3. Sif Deut., §307; Gen. R. 12:1.
4. Gen. R. 12:1.
5. Gen. R. 8:10.
6. Some texts omit "from Israel" and "in Israel."
7. B. Sanh 38a.
8. Therefore we have no need to shun temptation.
9. And therefore we cannot avoid succumbing to temptation.
10. On the superiority of their respective ancestry.
11. I.e., if they had come from different stocks.
12. B. Sanh 38a.
13. All nature was ready for his sustenance.
14. JV: "He that exacteth gifts." But *terumot* ("He that exacteth gifts") may also mean "raised aloft."
15. After a woman pours water on the flour, she separates *hallah*, the dough offering. Similarly, after God watered the ground (Gen. 2:6), He separated *hallah*, which was man, thus making him the sacred part of creation (see P. Shab 2:6, 5b). Gen. R. 14:1.

for your sake. Take care that you do not become corrupt and thus destroy My world. For once you become corrupt, there is no one after you to repair it.[1]

59. "Both last and first You made me" (Ps. 139:5).[2] When a man is worthy, he is told: You preceded the ministering angels.[3] But if he is not, he is told: The fly preceded you, the gnat preceded you, this earthworm preceded you in the work of creation.[4]

60. R. Jeremiah ben Eleazar said: When the Holy One created Adam, He created him hermaphrodite [bisexual],[5] as is said, "Male and female created He them[6] . . . and called their name Adam" (Gen. 5:2).

R. Samuel bar Nahman said: When the Holy One created Adam, He made him with two fronts; then He sawed him in half[7] and thus gave him two backs, a back for one part and a back for the other part. Someone objected: But does not Scripture say, "And He took one of his ribs (*mi-tzalotav*)" (Gen. 2:21)? R. Samuel replied: *Mi-tzalotav* may also mean "his sides," as in the verse "And for the second side (*tzela*) of the Tabernacle" (Exod. 26:20).[8]

61. "And man became an animal being" (Gen. 2:7).[9] R. Judah said: These words teach us that He first provided him with a tail like an animal, but then removed it from him for the sake of human dignity.[10]

62. "And the Lord God created man *afar*"[11] (Gen. 2:7). R. Judah bar Simon said: Read the word *ofer*,[12] "a young man"—Adam was created as a young man, in the fullness of vigor. R. Eleazar son of R. Simeon added: Eve also was created fully developed.

[Even more precise], R. Yohanan said: Adam and Eve were created as at the age of twenty.[13]

63. It is said in the name of R. Eleazar: As the Lord was creating Adam, He had come to the stage when Adam had the form of a *golem*, an unarticulated lump, which lay prone from one end of the world to the other. With regard to this, Scripture says, "Thine eyes did see my *golem*" (Ps. 139:16).[14]

"This is the book of the generations of Adam" (Gen. 5:1). R. Judah bar Simon said: While the first man lay prone as a *golem* before Him who spoke and the world came into being, He caused to pass before him each generation with its expounders of Scripture, each generation with its sages, each generation with its scribes, and each generation with its leaders, as is said, "O [Adam], when thou wast still a *golem*, thine eyes did see all [the worthies whose names were] inscribed in thy book" (Ps. 139:16). O *golem*, all that your eyes have seen had already been written in your book, the book of the first man.[15]

64. While the first man lay prone as a *golem*, the Holy One showed him each and every righteous man that was to issue from him—some hung on Adam's head, some hung on his hair, some on his forehead, some on his eyes, some on his nose, some on his mouth, some on his ears, some on his teeth.[16]

The Upper Worlds and the Lower Worlds

65. "These are the generations of heaven and earth" (Gen. 2:4). R. Simeon ben Halafta said: Great is peace, for when the Holy One created His world, He made peace between the upper and lower worlds. Thus, what He created on the first day, He created out of both upper and lower worlds, as is said, "In the beginning God created heaven and earth" (Gen. 1:1). What He created on the second day, He created out of the upper worlds, as is said, "Let there be a firmament" (Gen. 1:6). What He created on the third day, He created out of the lower worlds, as is said, "Let the earth put forth grass" (Gen. 1:11). What He created on the fourth day, He created out of the upper worlds, as is said, "Let there be lights" (Gen. 1:14). On the fifth, out of the lower worlds, as is said, "Let the waters swarm" (Gen. 1:20). On the sixth, as He was about to create man, He said, If I create him out of the upper worlds, the upper worlds will outnumber the lower worlds by one; if I create him out of the lower worlds, the lower worlds will outnumber the upper worlds by one. As a result, there will be no peace in the world. I will therefore create him out of both upper and lower worlds, as is said, "Then the Lord God formed man of the dust of the ground" (Gen. 2:7)—out of the lower worlds; "and breathed into his nostrils the breath of life" (ibid.)—out of the upper worlds.[17]

---

1. Eccles. R. 7:13, §1.
2. JV: "Thou hast hemmed me in behind and before."
3. Since man's soul, the spirit, came into being at creation's beginning, while the angels were created on the second day or, according to some, on the fifth day. Tanhuma, *Bereshit*, §1.
4. Gen. R. 8:1; B. Sanh 38a.
5. Normally *androgynos* means one who has both male and female genitals; but here it means two bodies, male and female, joined together.
6. Thus Adam was originally male and female.
7. Thus Eve was created out of half of Adam's body and not out of a mere rib (Leon Nemoy).
8. Gen. R. 8:1.
9. The literal meaning of *nefesh hayyah*. JV: "And man became a living soul."
10. Gen. R. 14:10.
11. JV: "out of the dust."
12. The word *afar* ("dust") is superfluous, as Scripture could have stated, "Then the Lord God formed man of the ground." By a play on words, *afar* ("dust") is connected with *ofer* ("a youth," "a strong man").
13. Gen. R. 14:7.
14. R. Eleazar construes these words as saying: So large was the *golem* that wherever You, O God, looked, You saw it.
15. Gen. R. 24:2; PR 23:2 (YJS 1: 472–73).
16. Or: "earlobes." The different members of the body are taken to suggest the particular qualities of heart and mind that single out a righteous man. Exod. R. 40:3.
17. When Scripture speaks of the creation of animals, it does not add that God breathed into their nostrils the breath of life. But with regard to man, Scripture says that God did breathe such breath into his nostrils. Hence the commentator concludes that the breath of life refers to man's creation out of the upper worlds. Gen. R. 12:8; Lev. R. 9:9.

66. "Then the Lord God formed (*va-yitzer*) man" (Gen. 2:7). There were two formations,[1] a formation partaking of the nature of beings below and a formation partaking of the nature of beings above.

R. Tifdai said in the name of R. Aha: The celestial beings were created in the image and likeness [of God], but they do not reproduce, while the terrestrial beings reproduce but were not created in the image and likeness [of God]. Said the Holy One: I will create man in My image and likeness, [and thus he will partake] of the [character of] celestial beings, but he will also reproduce [as is the nature] of terrestrial beings.

R. Tifdai said further in the name of R. Aha: The Holy One also declared: If I create man out of celestial elements, he will live [forever] and not die; if out of terrestrial elements, he will die and not live [in a future life]. Therefore I will create him out of both celestial and terrestrial elements. If he sins, he will die; if not, he will live in a future life.[2]

Things Created at Twilight on Sabbath Eve

67. Ten things were created on the eve of the Sabbath at twilight.[3] They are (1) the mouth of the earth [which engulfed Korah],[4] (2) the mouth of the well [which supplied Israel with water in the wilderness],[5] (3) the mouth of the ass [which spoke to Balaam],[6] (4) the rainbow [given as a sign after the flood],[7] (5) the manna [dropped from heaven], (6) the rod [of Moses],[8] (7) the *shamir* [a mythical creature employed for splitting stones at the building of the Temple],[9] (8) the shape of the written characters [on the Tablets],[10] (9) the writing,[11] and (10) the Tablets.[12] And some say; also the destructive forces [that afflict mankind], the grave of Moses,[13] and the ram of Abraham our father.[14] R. Judah said: Also the original tongs, for, as he put it, [in human conception] tongs can be made only by means of other tongs.[15]

The Order of, and Changes in, the Work of Creation

68. R. Jeremiah ben Eleazar said: With everything that was created during the six days of creation, God made certain stipulations, about which Scripture says, "I, even My hands, have stretched out the heavens, and all their host have I commanded" (Isa. 45:12). I commanded the Red Sea to split apart for Israel; I commanded heaven and earth to be silent before Moses; I commanded the sun and the moon to stand still before Joshua; I commanded the ravens to feed Elijah; I commanded the heavens to open before Ezekiel; I commanded the fish to spew out Jonah; I commanded the fire to do no hurt to Hananiah, Mishael, and Azariah; I commanded the lions not to harm Daniel.[16]

---

1. Scripture spells *va-yitzer* here with two *yods* not with one, as in verse 10, where the formation of animals is spoken of.
2. Gen. R. 14:3 (Soncino, p. 112). Or, as in Gen. R. TA, p. 128: "but when he dies, he will live forever."
3. At the end of the six days of creation prior to the first Sabbath.
4. "And if the Lord shall be found to have created a special creation, and the ground open her mouth, and swallow them up, with all that appertain unto them" (Num. 16:30).
5. Possibly the Well of Miriam, which may be the well referred to in Num. 21:16–18.
6. Num. 22:28–30.
7. Gen. 9:13–17.
8. Exod. 4:1–5.
9. "Iron is created to shorten man's life, whereas the altar was created to prolong man's life" (Mid 3:4 and MTeh 78:12 [YJS 2:30–35]). Hence, no iron was used in the building of the Temple.
10. "The letters having been cut right through, the stones were not only equally readable on both sides, but a letter such as the ancient *ayin*—which was O-shaped—could in such circumstances have been possible only by a miracle (see B. Shab 104a). This belief was based on Exod. 32:15: 'Tablets that were written on both their sides; on the one side and on the other were they written' " (J. Israelstam in Avot, Soncino, pp. 63–64, n. 7).
11. "And the writing was the writing of God" (Exod. 32:16). Others (e.g., Rashi) vocalize here in the Mishnah *makhtev* or *mekhattev*, "writing, or engraving, instrument" (J. Israelstam, in Avot, Soncino, pp. 63–64, n. 8).
12. "And the Tablets were the work of God" (Exod. 32:16).
13. Deut. 34:6.
14. Gen. 22:13. "It was ordained on the eve of the first Sabbath at twilight that a certain ram in Abraham's time should be ownerless (*hefker*), so that when Abraham would require one as a last-minute substitute for Isaac, he might find it ready at hand and could rightfully (i.e., without robbing anyone) appropriate it for a sacrifice" (J. Israelstam in Avot, Soncino, p. 64, n. 3, in which he quotes Israel Lipschütz, ad loc.).
15. "Who then made the tongs which held the first tongs while they were being made?" (Hertz, APB, p. 689). Avot 5:6. "All phenomena that seemed to partake at once of the natural and the supernatural were conceived as having had their origin in the interval between the close of the work of creation and the commencement of the Sabbath [APB, p. 200]. It is generally held that what is meant is that these things were created on the Sabbath eve at twilight, *in posse*, to become available *in esse*, when the right time for their use would arrive" (J. Israelstam in Avot, Soncino, p. 64, n. 5).

   In his commentary on Avot, Menahem Ha-Meiri explains the meaning of the aforementioned miracles as follows: Immediately upon creation, certain principles of faith became obligatory: (1) that the wicked are punished, as intimated by the opening of the mouth of the earth; (2) that the righteous are rewarded, as intimated by the mouth of the well; (3) that God protects Israel, as intimated by Balaam's ass, which spoke; (4) that God also protects mankind, as signified by the rainbow (but for such protection, mankind would have perished during the flood); (5) that God's protection of Israel was to be made evident by the giving of manna and (6) the miracles performed in their behalf by the rod of Moses; (7) that the transcending significance of the Temple is attested by the miraculous character of the *shamir;* (8–9) that the wondrous nature of the Hebrew tongue was to be made evident by the shape of its characters and by the Divine Person who first wrote them; (10) that the Torah whose Tablets God wrought was revealed by Him; that the destructive passions without which no man would wed, beget children, or build a house are providential (MTeh 9:1 [YJS 1:131]). See *Perushe ha-Mishnah le-ha-Meiri* (Jerusalem, 1974). Avot 5:242. Avot 5:9; B. Pes 54a.
16. The incidents hinted at are described in Exod. 14, Deut. 32:1, Josh. 10, 1 Kings 17, Ezek. 1, Jon. 2, and Dan. 3 and 6. Gen. R. 5:5; Yalkut, *Be-shallah*, §238.

69. "I know that whatever God doeth, it shall be forever; nothing can be added to it, nor anything taken from it; yet [at times] God hath acted [exceptionally], that men should fear before Him" (Eccles. 3:14). R. Eleazar said: From the very beginning of His creation of the world, the Holy One issued a decree and commanded: "Let the waters under the heaven be gathered together unto one place [the sea]" (Gen. 1:9). Why then does Scripture elsewhere say twice, "Who summoned the waters of the sea and poured them out upon the face of the earth" (Amos 5:8 and 9:6)—once in the generation of Enosh and again in the generation of the dispersion of mankind?[1] Because in these instances "God acted [exceptionally]," in order "that men should fear before Him" (Eccles. 3:14). A parable of a province that rebelled against its king. So the king dispatched a fierce legion to march throughout the province in order that the people would see it and come to fear him. So, too, why does Scripture say, "He gathereth the waters of the sea as a [towering] heap, and layeth up the deeps in storehouses" (Ps. 33:7)? In order that "all the inhabitants of the world may stand in awe of Him" (Ps. 33:8).

Another comment: The Holy One so created the world that day should be day and night should be night. Along came Jacob and turned day into night, since for his sake the Holy One had the sun set before its proper time;[2] and Joshua came and turned night into day.[3] Thus the righteous both diminish and add to the words of the Holy One, so that mortals may fear Him.

Likewise, the Holy One created the world that the sea should be sea and the dry land should be dry land. Moses came and turned the sea into dry land,[4] and Elisha came and turned the dry land into sea.[5]

So, too, the Holy One created the winter that it should be winter and the summer should be summer. Elijah came and turned the winter into rainless summer,[6] and Samuel came and turned the summer into [the rainy season], winter.[7]

So, too, the Holy One created [the world] that the realms above should be for celestial beings and the realms below for terrestrial beings, for, as Scripture says, "The heavens are the heavens of the Lord, but the earth hath He given to the children of men" (Ps. 115:16). Moses came and converted the realms below into realms above and the realms above into realms below, as Scripture says, "Moses went up unto God" (Exod. 19:3) and "the Lord came down upon Mount Sinai" (Exod. 19:20).[8]

1. During these two generations there was a partial flood (PR 48:2 [YJS 2; 816–17]), which seemingly reversed His decree that the waters should be gathered in one place and stay there.

2. See Gen. R. 68:10.

3. See Josh. 10:12.

4. Exod. 14:21.

5. 2 Kings 3:16ff.

6. 1 Kings 17:1.

7. 1 Sam. 12:17.

8. Gen. R. 5:6; Duet. R. 10:2; and Eccles. R. 3:14, §1.

The Handiwork of the Holy One

70. In the Torah, Moses set down many matters that remained obscure until David arose and clarified them. Thus we find in the account of creation that after He had created heaven and earth, He created the light, for it says, "In the beginning God created the heaven and the earth" (Gen. 1:1), and then, "God said: "Let there be light' " (Gen. 1:3). But David clarified the sequence in creation. After God created the light, He created the heaven, for, as David stated in a psalm: "Thou didst cover Thyself with light as with a garment" (Ps. 104:2), and then, "Thou didst spread out the heaven like a curtain" (ibid.).[9] And so we learn that only after He created light did He create heaven.

Three creations preceded the making of the world: water, wind (spirit), and fire.[10] Water conceived and gave birth to thick darkness,[11] fire conceived and gave birth to light, wind (spirit) conceived and gave birth to wisdom. The world is maintained by means of these six creations: by wind (spirit), wisdom, fire, light, darkness, and water.[12]

"Bless the Lord, O my soul" (Ps. 104:1). When a man sees a beautiful pillar, he exclaims: Blessed be He who created the quarry from which the pillar was hewn. Blessed be He who hewed out the pillar, bringing it into being with a mere word.[13] Blessed art thou, O world, in which the Holy One is King.

"O Lord my God, Thou art very great" (Ps. 104:1). When a king of flesh and blood engraves his image on a wooden tablet, the tablet, it goes without saying, is larger than the image on it. But since He, may His Name be blessed, who wrought worlds is very great, His image [man] must also be very great, [so that by comparison] the world [the tablet on which the image appears] is small, for man, God's image, is greater than the world, [even as God], to whom it is said, "O Lord my God, Thou art very great," [is ever so much greater than man].

"Thou didst cover Thyself with light as with a garment" (Ps. 104:1). After God covered Himself with light, He proceeded to create the world.

"Thou didst spread out the heaven like a curtain" (Ps. 104:2). When a man builds a house, he builds the upper story last. But God did not do so,[14] for after He spread—stretched out—the roof. He built the top story;[15]

9. "This is not a contradiction, but rather shows that, in view of David's statement, Gen. 1:1f. must be translated: In the beginning of God's creating the heaven and the earth, God said: Let there be light (cf. Rashi, ad loc.)" (S. M. Lehrman in Exod. R., Soncino, p. 188, n. 1).

10. The three are not, accordingly, to be regarded as eternal, uncreated matter, which formed God's raw material, as it were.

11. The commentator perhaps finds this intimated in the words "and darkness [appeared] on the face of the deep" (Gen. 1:2)—on the watery deep, that is.

12. All six are mentioned in Ps. 104. So *Yede Moshe*, ad loc.

13. So emended by *Yefeh Toar* on Exod. R. 15:22.

14. He first made the heavens. Such is the view of the school of Shammai. See above in this chapter, §13.

15. Under this roof.

and after He built the top story, He suspended it above the earth's atmosphere, resting on nothing.[1] After that, He formed clouds as His chariot, with its base on a whirlwind.

"Who layest the beams of water for Thine upper chambers" (Ps. 104:3)—beams not of brass or iron, but of jetting columns of water. [Then He built the top stories] not with stone or hewn blocks, but with walls of congealed water.

"Who makest the clouds Thy chariot" (Ps. 104:3). A man makes his chariot sturdy—of brass or iron, of silver or gold—so that it will bear all his weight. But God, may His Name be blessed, makes His chariot of clouds—though clouds have no substance, yet He makes His chariot of clouds.

"Who walkest upon the wings of the wind" (Ps. 104:3). A man confronted by ground so swampy that one sinks into it will walk on stepping stones, which are hard. But not God. He walks upon the wings of the wind; abandoning the cloud that is visible, He chooses to walk upon the wind, which is invisible.

"Who makest winds Thy messengers" (Ps. 104:4). A mortal will enlist men who are strong and sturdy as his soldiers, and will have them wear helmets and mail, and carry weapons. But the Holy One makes winds His messengers—He enlists soldiers who are invisible: "His messengers [are followed by] flaming fire, His ministers" (ibid.). The wind comes first, and then lightning [His weapon].

"Who didst establish the earth upon its foundations. . . . [Then] Thou didst cover it with a vesture" (Ps. 104:5–6). At first He made the deep without a vesture[2] and the earth with a vesture [of water]. As in the parable of a man with two servants who stripped the vesture off one and put it on the other, God said, "Let the waters be gathered . . . so that the part that is to be dry be seen" (Gen. 1:9), thus laying bare the earth and covering the deep.

"The waters stood above the mountains" (Ps. 104:6). A parable of a man who saw his vat full of grapes, while his vineyard was ready for further vintaging. What did he do? He first trod on the grapes in the vat, little by little pressing them down. Then, when he brought in the rest of the grapes from the vineyard, the vat was able to contain them all. Likewise, the world was full of water upon water, and the earth was sunk deep in the water. And so when the Holy One said, "Let the dry land appear" (Gen. 1:9), the waters replied: Behold, we fill the whole world; if we hardly had sufficient room hitherto, where shall we go now? At that, the Holy One tamped down the waters of the Great Ocean and slew its prince, as is said, "With His power He made the sea shrink, and by His understanding He smote through Rahab"[3] (Job 26:12). After He slew him, the waters wept. Indeed, they still weep to this day. Why did God slay Rahab? Because a place that can hold a hundred living can hold a thousand dead.

"At Thy rebuke they fled, at the voice of Thy thunder they hasted away" (Ps. 104:7). At the sound of the Ocean's cry, the waters elsewhere fled but did not know where they were to flee. "They went up mountains, they went down into the valleys—unto the place which Thou hadst founded for them" (Ps. 104:8). They were like a slave to whom his master said, "Wait for me in the marketplace," without specifying the particular spot. The slave pondered: Maybe he wanted me to wait at the forum, or at the bathhouse, or at the theater. When the master came and found the servant, he slapped him on the cheek, saying, "I sent you to the gate of the prefect's palace!"[4] So, too, when the waters heard, "Let the waters under the heaven be gathered together in one place" (Gen. 1:9), God did not let them know whether it was to be in the north or in the south. So they went to and fro—"they went up mountains, they came down into valleys" (Ps. 104:8). The Holy One struck them a blow, saying: I told you to go to the place of Leviathan [the sea], "unto this place which Thou hadst founded for them" (Ps. 104:8).[5]

"Thou didst set a bound which they should not pass over" (Ps. 104:9). Just like a man who brings his cattle into the shed and bolts the lock so that they should not go out and eat the corn in the fields, so, too, did God enclose the sea with sand and make it swear that it would not go beyond the sand.

"Thou causest springs to gush forth in torrents, after they make their way from between the mountains" (Ps. 104:10). Just like a man who has two bales of olive pulp and presses each with the pressing beam so that pure oil spurts down [into the vat], so, too, a mountain on one side and a mountain on the other side compressed the springs, and from between the mountains clear water gushed forth in torrents.[6]

In the World's Praise

71. "And God saw everything that He had made, and, behold, it was very good" (Gen. 1:31). R. Tanhuma began his discourse with the verse "He has made everything beautiful in its time" (Eccles. 3:11), a verse that implies that the world was created in its proper time, and before that it was not deemed right for the world to be created. As R. Abbahu said: From this verse it may be deduced

1. "The conception is of an upper world ('the roof') resting on heaven ('the top story'), which in turn is suspended on nothing above the world, i.e., [above] the earth" (S. M. Lehrman in Exod. R., Soncino, p. 189, n. 2).

2. "The deep was naked before Him, Abaddon had no vesture" (Job 26:6), while the earth was covered with water. But then God covered the deep with the water that hitherto had covered the earth. So A. A. Ha-Levi in his edition of Exod. R., p. 198.

3. The prince of the Ocean is called Rahab [Rahav].

4. "And you should have understood that!"

5. The waters, to be sure, were told to go to "this place which Thou hadst founded for them." But how were they to know where "this place" was? The commentator, however, identifies "this place" as the sea, because later in the same psalm the word "this" in the phrase "This is Leviathan" (Ps. 104:26) clearly refers to the sea; in rabbinic commentary, Leviathan is a synonym for the sea. From the occurrence of "this" in both verses, he infers that in each instance God directed the waters to the sea, a direction they should have understood. The phrase "This is Leviathan" is cited in Exod. R. 15:22 and Tanhuma, *Hayye Sarah*, §3, BR's sources for the passage.

6. Exod. R. 15:22, Tanhuma, *Hayye Sarah*, §3.

that the Holy One kept creating worlds and destroying them, creating worlds and destroying them, until He created these [heaven and earth]. Then He said: Those did not please Me, but these do please Me.[1]

72. "And God saw everything that He had made, and [said], Would that[2] at all times it were very good." R. Hama bar Hanina told the parable of a king who built a palace. When he looked at it, it pleased him, and he said: O palace, palace, may you find favor in my eyes at all times just as you find favor in my eyes at this moment, So, too, the Holy One said to His world: My world, My world, may you find favor in My eyes at all times just as you find favor in My eyes at this moment.[3]

73. "And on the seventh day God finished" (Gen. 2:2). Isn't this statement curious?[4] Geniva explained it by the parable of a king who made a bridal chamber, which he painted and decorated. Now, what did the bridal chamber still lack? The bride to enter it. So, too, what did the world still lack? The Sabbath.[5]

74. "[In Eden] . . . He put the man whom He had formed" (Gen. 2:8). If one dare say such a thing, the Holy One exults in His world, saying: Behold the creature I made, the shape I formed.[6]

"These are the generations of the heaven and of the earth when they were created" (Gen 2:4). Since their Creator praises them, who dare disparage them? Since their Creator lauds them, who dare find fault with them? Indeed, heaven and earth are beautiful and worthy of praise.[7]

Eve

75. "But for Adam there was not found a helpmeet for him" (Gen. 2:20). For God had caused all cattle, beasts, and birds to pass before Adam in pairs [male and female]. Said Adam: Every one has a mate, yet I have none!

And why did God not create a mate for Adam at the beginning? Because the Holy One foresaw that Adam would bring charges against Eve. Therefore He did not create her until Adam expressly asked for her. As soon as he did, at once "God causes a deep sleep to fall upon Adam, and he slept" (Gen. 2:21).[8]

76. "And the Lord God built (*va-yiven*) the rib" (Gen. 2:22). R. Joshua of Sikhnin said in the name of R. Levi: The text says *va-yiven*, which can also mean, "He considered well (*hitbonen*)[9] from what part to create her." God said: I will not create her from Adam's head, lest she be conceited; nor from the eye, lest she be a coquette; nor from the ear, lest she be an eavesdropper; [nor from the neck, lest she be haughty];[10] nor from the mouth, lest she be a gossip; nor from the heart, lest she be prone to jealousy; nor from the hand, lest she be light-fingered; nor from the foot, lest she be a gadabout—so He made her from the rib, a part most modest and chaste. Still, even though, as He was creating each and every member of her body, He kept saying, "Be modest, be chaste," "Ye have [nevertheless] set at naught all My counsel" (Prov. 1:25), for all the aforementioned undesirable qualities are in her.[11]

77. R. Hanina son of R. Idi said: [The letter *samekh* appears here for the first time in the Torah, which implies that] at Eve's creation, Satan was created with her.[12]

78. A Caesar once said to Rabban Gamaliel:[13] "Your God is a thief, for it is written, 'And the Lord God caused a deep sleep to fall upon Adam, and He took one of his ribs' " (Gen. 2:21). Rabban Gamaliel's daughter said, "Leave him to me and I will answer him." [Turning to Caesar], she said, "Send me a police officer." "Why do you need one?" he asked. She replied, "Thieves came to us during the night and took a silver pitcher from us, leaving one of gold in its place." "Would that such a thief came to *us* every day," he exclaimed. "Ah!" said she, "was it not Adam's gain that he was deprived of a rib and given a wife to serve him?"[14]

79. R. Simeon ben Menasya expounded the verse "And with the rib which the Lord God had taken from the man, He plaited the hair (*banah*) of the woman[15] and brought her unto the man" (Gen. 2:22). The word *banah* suggests that the Holy One plaited Eve's hair and brought her [thus adorned] to Adam, for in cities far beyond the sea a woman's plaited hair is called *binyata*.[16]

---

1. R. Abbahu may construe *hinneh* ("behold") as derived from *hnh* ("to please") and so reads Gen. 1:31: "And God saw all that he made, which, being good, pleased Him." Gen. R. 9:2; MTeh 34:1; Exod. R. 30:3.
2. The word *hinneh* ("behold" is taken to be a variant of *hen* ("would that").
3. Gen. R. 9:4.
4. Did not God finish His work of creation in six days? Why then does Scripture say He finished on the seventh day?
5. Geniva construes *va-yekhal* ("finished") as derived from the root *kallah* ("bride") and so he reads the verse: "On the seventh day He invited the bride to enter." Gen. R. 10:9.
6. An implication drawn from the fact that Scripture has already stated in Gen. 2:7 that God had formed man. Why then the repetition?
7. The phrase "These are" is understood to mean that, like a craftsman, God points to the excellence of what He has made. Gen. R. 12:1.
8. Gen. R. 17:4.
9. The commentator regards *va-yiven* as a form of *bin* ("understand").
10. Interpolated by BR.
11. Gen. R. 18:2; Deut. R. 6:11; Tanhuma, *Va-yeshev*, §6.
12. In "And He closed up (*va-yisgor*) the place with flesh" (Gen. 2:21), the verb *sgr* ("close up") begins with the letter *samekh*. R. Hanina takes the letter to hint the presence of Satan, who personifies evil passions. The word "Satan," usually spelled with a *sin*, is for the purpose of the comment spelled with a *samekh*. Gen. R. 17:6.
13. Gamaliel II, who visited Rome twice, once during the reign of Domitian and again during that of Nerva, his successor (end of the first century C.E.).
14. B. Sanh 39a.
15. JV: "And the rib, which the Lord God had taken from the man, made He (*banah*) a woman."
16. B. Ber 61a; B. Er 18a; MTeh 25:11.

80. "And He [Himself] brought her to Adam" (Gen. 2:22). These words intimate that the Holy One acted for Adam as the one who escorted Eve. No, said R. Judah son of R. Simon: Michael and Gabriel were Adam's escorts who brought in Eve.[1]

81. It is taught in the name of R. Simeon ben Yohai: God Himself adorned Eve like a bride and brought her to Adam. In this connection, R. Hama bar Hanina said: What do you suppose—that He brought Eve to Adam [as one might bring something found] under a carob tree or a sycamore tree? The fact is that only after He had decked her out with twenty-four kinds of finery[2] did He bring her to Adam. Thus Scripture: "Thou wast in Eden the garden of God; every precious stone was thy covering" (Ezek. 28:13).[3]

82. "And Adam said: *Zot ha-paam*," etc. (Gen. 2:23).[4] If *paam* here is taken to mean "bell," as in the phrase "a golden bell (*paamon*)" (Exod. 28:34), Adam said of Eve, "This is the one whose impending arrival rang like a bell through me (*mephaamtani*) all night," a woman's capacity to do so being intimated, said Resh Lakish, in the fact that Eve made her first appearance before Adam during a dream [in the night].[5]

The Serpent and Sin

83. "God made Adam upright" (Eccles. 7:29). Adam was upright and straightforward, it being said of him, "Behold, Adam is as one of us" (Gen. 3:22), as one of the ministering angels. However, once Adam and Eve became a pair, "they sought out many inventions" (Eccles. 7:29).[6]

84. R. Judah ben Tema used to say: Adam reclined in the Garden of Eden, while ministering angels, hovering over him, roasted flesh and strained wine for him. When the serpent looked in and saw the honor bestowed on him, he became envious.[7]

85. "Now the serpent was most subtle" (Gen. 3:1). The serpent reasoned to himself: If I go and speak to Adam, I know that he will not listen to me, for it is difficult to lead a man away from his own mind. So I shall go and speak to Eve, for I know that she will listen to me, since women are light-headed and easily led by everybody.

"For God doth know" (Gen. 3:5). R. Judah of Sikhnin said in the name of R. Levi: The serpent spoke slander against his Creator, saying to Eve: Our Creator ate of this tree and then created the world. And because every craftsman hates to have a rival in his craft, He said to you, "You shall not eat of it," so that you might not create other worlds.

[The serpent also said to Eve]: Whatever was created after its companion dominates it. Now, Adam was created after all creatures in order to rule over all of them. So make haste and eat [of the tree] before God creates other worlds which will rule over both of you.

Then the serpent touched the tree with his hands and feet, shaking it until its fruit fell to the ground. The tree then cried out: Villain, do not touch me—"Let not the foot of pride overtake me, and let not the hand of the wicked shake me" (Ps. 36:12). The serpent said to the woman, "Look, I touched the tree, yet I did not die. You, too, if you touch it, will not die." Right away, he pushed her and she touched the tree.

When she saw the angel of death coming toward her, she said, "Woe is me! I am as good as dead, and the Holy One will make another woman and give her to Adam." Immediately, "she took of its fruit and ate; and she also gave some to her husband, and he ate" (Gen. 3:6).

R. Aibu said: She squeezed grapes[8] and gave the juice to Adam.

R. Simlai said: She came at him with her answers all rehearsed, saying to him, "What do you suppose—that I will die and another Eve will be created for you? [There will be no new Eve]—'there is nothing new under the sun' [Eccles. 1:9]. Or that I will die and you will have no obligations? 'He created it not a waste, He formed it to be inhabited' " (Isa. 45:18). But our masters maintained: She raised her voice in howling at him, as is said, "Because thou hast hearkened unto the [loud] voice of thy wife" (Gen. 3:17).

["And she also gave unto her husband" (Gen. 3:6).] The world "also" is a word that suggests she also gave the fruit to others to eat, to cattle, beasts, and birds. All obeyed her, except for a certain bird named *hol* (phoenix), of which it is said, "I shall die with my nest, yet I shall multiply my days as the *hol*"[9] (Job 29:18). The school of R. Yannai maintained: The *hol* lives a thousand years. At the end of a thousand years, a fire issues from its nest and burns it up, yet of the bird a piece the size of an egg is left; it grows new limbs and lives again. But R. Yudan son of R. Simeon said: At the end of a thousand years, its body dries up and its wings drop off, yet of the bird a piece the size of an egg is left; it grows new limbs and lives again.[10]

86. "And the woman said unto the serpent" (Gen. 3:2). Now, where was Adam during this conversation? Abba bar Guria said: He had [engaged in intercourse and] fallen asleep. But the sages said: At that time the Holy One was taking him around the entire world, saying to him: Here is a place fit for planting trees, here is a place fit for sowing cereals.[11]

---

1. Michael represents mercy and love; Gabriel represents stern justice. Hence, the presence of the two angels may perhaps signify the alternatives that Adam and Eve had before them, whereas God's presence symbolizes a yearning father's blessing. Gen. R. 18:3.
2. The ones mentioned in Isa. 3:18–24.
3. Gen. R. 18:1.
4. Gen. 2:23 will apparently be construed: "This one rings through me as though it were a bone of my bones and flesh of my flesh." JV: "This is now bone of my bones and flesh of my flesh." Gen. R. 18:4.
5. Thus Eve was, so to speak, created out of a dream. Gen. R. 18:4.
6. Eccles. R. 7:29, §1.
7. B. Sanh 59b.
8. See below in this chapter, §91.
9. JV: "as the phoenix."
10. Gen. R. 19:4–5; PRE 13; MhG Gen., pp. 95–96; ARNA, p. 2b (YJS, p. 9); ARNB, 2b–3a (trans. Saldarini, pp. 33–34): Yalkut, *Bereshit*, §27.
11. Gen. R. 19:3.

87. R. Simeon ben Yohai said: By what parable may what happened to Eve and Adam [at that time] be illustrated? By the parable of a man who had a wife at home. He went and brought a cask, and put a certain number of figs and a certain number of nuts into it. Then he caught a scorpion and put it at the mouth of the cask, sealed the cask with a tight-fitting lid, and put it in a corner. "My dear," he said to her, "everything I have in this house is in your hands, except this cask, which you may not touch at all because there is a scorpion in it."

When her husband left for the marketplace, an old woman came calling on her, like those who drop in to borrow a little vinegar. The woman asked, "How does your husband treat you?" The wife replied, "My husband treats me wonderfully—he has given me authority over everything he owns, except for this cask." The old woman said, "Very likely all his precious jewels are inside it. And he didn't tell you that, because he intends to marry another woman and give them to her." What did the wife do then? She proceeded to open the cask and put her hand into it. Whereupon the scorpion stung her. She stepped back and collapsed upon her couch.

When her husband returned from the marketplace, he asked, "What is this?" "I put my hand in the cask," she replied, "and a scorpion stung me, and now I am dying." "Did I not tell you in the beginning" he cried out, "everything I own in this house is in your hands except this cask, which you may not touch at all?" He grew angry at her and no longer thought of her as his wife.[1]

88. "[The trees] were heard voicing amazement: 'There walking about is the thief (*gannav*) [at whose formation the epithets] Lord and God [were used]' " (Gen. 3:8).[2] Thus, the trees were saying, "That one walking about turned out to be a thief, a deceiver who even sought to deceive his Creator."

Or, the verse is read, "The ministering angels were heard voicing delight:[3] 'That one walking about will soon be dead and gone.' "[4]

1. ARNA 3b (YJS 12–13); ARNB 4a (trans. Saldarini, pp. 35–36); PRE 13; Gen. R. 19:10.

2. The word *va-yishmeu* ("they heard") is read *va-yashmiu* ("caused to be heard, were heard"). The reference to the Lord God in the verse is understood to allude to the exceptional use of both "Lord" and "God" in the account of the formation of Adam and Eve (Gen. 2:7 and 2:22). Finally, *ba-gan* ("in the garden"), is transposed to read as though it were a contraction of *gannav* ("thief, deceiver"). JV: "And they heard the voice of the Lord God walking in the garden."

3. Some ministering angels, unhappy to begin with at the making of man (see above in this chapter, §46), were naturally delighted about what they believed to be the imminence of his death.

4. The verb *mt'hlk* appears to be used in a dual sense: "walking"; and also, by dividing it into *mt* ("dead") and *hlk* ("gone"), "dead and gone." Gen. R. 19:8. Or: They heard the voice of the trees saying, Here is the one who stole the Lord God's mind, and the voice of the ministering angels saying, Here is the one who walketh to his death. So Leon Nemoy.

89. "Cursed to the ground on account of thee" (Gen. 3:17). Why curse the ground? It is like a man who says, "Cursed be the breast that suckled such a person."[5]

The Tree of Life and the Tree of Knowledge

90. The tree of life—meaning the tree that spreads its branches over all things alive. R. Judah bar Ilai said: The tree of life spread over an area that at an ordinary rate of speed would require five hundred years to traverse, and all the primeval waters branched out in streams from under it. It was not only that its boughs required a five hundred years' journey—even to go around its trunk required a five hundred years' journey.[6]

91. What kind of tree did Adam and Eve eat of? Wheat, according to R. Meir. When a man has no understanding, people say of him: He has never put bread made of wheat [the source of wisdom] into his mouth.[7] (R. Samuel son of R. Isaac put the following question to R. Ze'era: "How can you say it was a grain—wheat?" "Nevertheless, it was so," R. Ze'era replied. R. Samuel argued: "But Scripture speaks of a tree." R. Ze'era replied: "[In the Garden of Eden] stalks of wheat were like trees, for they grew to the height of cedars of Lebanon."

[Adam ate] grapes, according to R. Judah bar Ilai, for Scripture says, "Grapes of gall, they have clusters of bitterness" (Deut. 32:32)—those grape clusters brought bitterness into the world.

According to R. Abba of Acco, it was the etrog,[8] for it is said, "And the woman saw that the tree [its wood] was good for food" (Gen. 3:6). Go forth and see what tree there is whose wood, like its fruit, may be eaten. You will find none but the etrog.

R. Yose said: They were figs, as may be inferred from the context. A parable of a king's son who disgraced himself with one of the maidservants. When the king heard of it, he deprived his son of high rank and expelled him from the palace. The son then went about to the doorways of the other maidservants, and none would take him in. But she who disgraced herself with him opened the door of her house and received him. So, too, when Adam ate of that tree, the Holy One deprived him of lofty status and expelled him from the Garden of Eden. Adam then went about among all the trees, but none would receive him. (What did they say to him? They said, so R. Berekhiah taught, Behold the thief who sought to deceive his Creator. "Let not the foot of pride come unto me" [Ps. 36:12]—the foot that stepped forward in pride toward its Creator; "and let not the hand of the wicked shake me" [ibid.] to take even one leaf from me.) But the fig tree whose fruit Adam had eaten opened its doors [so to speak] and received him, as is said, "They sewed fig leaves together" (Gen. 3:7).

5. Gen. R. 5:9.

6. Gen. R. 15:6, Song R. 6:9, §2–3.

7. Wheat was the first cereal to be domesticated. Hence it is considered both source and symbol of wisdom.

8. A citron used during the Feast of Sukkot (Tabernacles).

The sages taught in the name of R. Joshua ben Levi: Heaven forbid [that we should try to guess the identity of the tree]. The Holy One did not reveal it, nor will He reveal it, for He who is everywhere spares [the honor of a tree,[1] even as He spares] man's honor.[2]

The Primeval Serpent

92. Our masters taught: The primeval serpent set its eyes on that which was not meant for it; what it sought was not given to it, and what it had was taken away from it. The Holy One said: I declared, "Let the serpent be king over all cattle and beasts," but now, "cursed art thou above all cattle and above every beast of the field" (Gen. 3:14). I declared: Let the serpent walk with an erect posture, but now, "upon thy belly shalt thou go" (ibid.). I declared: Let its food be the same as man's, but now, "dust shalt thou eat" (ibid.). The serpent said: I will slay Adam and wed Eve. But now, "I will put enmity between thee and the woman" (Gen. 3:15).[3]

93. R. Simeon ben Menasya said: What a pity that a great servant was lost to the world! Had the serpent not been cursed, everyone in Israel would have had two useful serpents at his beck and call, and would have been able to send one north and the other south to bring him valuable sardonyx, precious stones, pearls of purest ray, and every kind of exquisite thing of great worth in the world. Not only that, but the serpent could have been used instead of a camel or donkey or mule, for a strap could have been fastened under its tail and it would then have brought earth and manure for everyone's garden and wasteland.[4]

Adam after the Sin

94. What was Adam's garment [before his sin]: A fragrant mist of onycha[5] and a divine aura of glory covered him. After he ate the fruit of the tree, the onycha's mist was divested from him, the aura of glory departed from him, and he saw himself naked.[6]

95. R. Judah said in the name of Rav: Adam's body reached from one end of the world to the other. But after he acted offensively, the Holy One laid His hand upon him and diminished him, as is said, "Thou hast hemmed me in behind and before, so that Thou wast able to lay Thy hand upon me" (Ps. 139:5).[7]

1. That it be not said, "Through this tree Adam brought death to the world."
2. Gen. R. 15:7.
3. B. Sot 9b.
4. B. Sanh 59b; ARN 1.
5. An incense used in the Temple.
6. PRE 14.
7. B. Sanh 38b.

96. "[Speed in] heaven and [growth on] the earth were diminished (*va-yekhullu*)" (Gen. 2:1).[8] R. Efes—so said R. Hoshaia—preached in Antioch,[9] saying that the word *va-yekhullu* refers to God's punitive measures, which led to diminution in the speed of growth. To illustrate with a parable: When a king entered a province, the people in the province praised him greatly, and their praise was pleasing to him. So he increased the number of fleet-footed runners and rapidly moving chariots in the local arena. Later on, when the people in the province angered him, he reduced the number of such runners and chariots. Likewise, before Adam sinned, the constellations revolved in short courses and at great speed [bringing springtime sooner and causing greater speed in the growth of vegetation]. But after Adam sinned, God made the constellations revolve in long courses and at a slow pace. Thus, by way of an example which R. Phinehas cited in the name of R. Hanan of Sepphoris, nowadays white figs produce their fruit only once in three years, whereas at their creation[10] they produced fruit that very day. However, in the time-to-come the Holy One will [again speed up the growth of vegetation and thus] heal the injury inflicted; as is said, "He will heal the injury it has suffered" (Isa. 30:26),[11] meaning that He will heal the injury the world has suffered.[12]

97. R. Berekhiah said in the name of R. Samuel bar Nahman: Though all living things [such as white figs] came into being in the fullness of their growth, they shriveled up as soon as Adam sinned and will not return to their perfection until a scion of Perez [the Messiah][13] comes. [To summarize]: After Adam sinned, the Holy One deprived Adam of six things: splendor of visage, lofty stature, life without death, perfection of the earth's fruit, the Garden of Eden, and brilliance of the luminaries in heaven. In the time-to-come, the Holy One will restore them.[14]

98. Our masters taught: When Adam on the day of his creation saw the sun sinking in the sky before him, he said, "Woe is me! Because I acted offensively, the world is darkening for me and is about to return to darkness and desolation—indeed, this is the death that Heaven has decreed for me." So he sat down to fast and to weep throughout the night, while Eve wept beside him. But when the dawn began slowly rising like a column, he said, "Such

8. JV: "The heaven and the earth were finished." But *klh*, the root of *va-yekhullu*, can mean "finish" and "reduce, diminish."
9. The capital of Syria on the Orontes, founded by Seleucus Nicator.
10. Plants were created on the third day, while Adam was made on the sixth day, the very day he sinned. See Gen. 1:11–12 and 1:26–27.
11. The context of the passage is messianic.
12. Gen. R. 10:4.
13. Throughout Scripture the word *tldt* [*toledot*] ("generations") is written defectively, lacking one or even both *vavs*. But in describing the generations of heaven and earth (Gen. 2:4), and in setting down the generations of Perez (Ruth 4:18), the word *tldt* is spelled out—thus; *tvldvt* or *toledot*, with two *vavs*. Hence it is concluded that at the Messiah's coming, all things created will return to their perfection.
14. The restoration of these six is taken to be intimated by inclusion of the *vav* in *toledot*, a letter whose numerical value is six. Gen. R. 12:6; Tanhuma, *Bereshit*, §6.

is the way of nature, and I did not realize it," and then proceeded to offer up a bullock.[1]

99. R. Yose said: There was the thought [in God's mind] that fire be brought into being on Sabbath eve. In the event, it was brought into being at Sabbath's outgoing. At Sabbath's outgoing the Holy One gave Adam knowledge that partook of the knowledge that is above, and he procured two flints which he struck one against the other. From these issued fire, and over it Adam uttered the blessing "[Blessed be Thou] who createst divers lights of fire."[2]

100. Others of our masters taught: When Adam saw the day gradually diminishing, he said, "Woe is me! Perhaps because I acted offensively, the world around me is growing darker and darker, and is about to return to chaos and confusion, and this is the death Heaven has decreed for me." He then sat eight days in fast and prayer. But when the winter solstice arrived, and he saw the days getting gradually longer, he said, "Such is the way of the world," and proceeded to observe eight days of festivity. The following year he observed both the eight days preceding and the eight days following the solstice as days of festivity.[3]

Cain and Abel

101. "Cain said to Abel his brother" (Gen. 4:8). What Cain said to Abel was: Come and let us divide the world between us. Abel replied: Very well. So Cain said: You take chattel, and I will take land.[4] And it was stipulated between them that neither should have any claim against the other about this division.

Nevertheless, when Abel proceeded to graze the flock, Cain said: The land you are standing on is mine. Abel replied: The wool you are wearing is mine. "Strip!" said Abel. "Seat!" said Cain. At that, "Cain rose up against Abel his brother" (Gen. 4:8). [The meaning of "rose up" will be explained in what follows]: Cain proceeded to chase Abel from hill to dale and from dale to hill, until the two grappled. Abel overcame Cain, so that Cain fell underneath Abel. Cain, aware how badly it was going with him, began to plead aloud: Abel my brother, there are only two of us in the world. What are you going to tell our father? . . . Abel, filled with compassion for his brother, let him go. At once Cain rose up against him and slew him. For the verse "Cain rose up against Abel his brother, and slew him" (ibid.) implies that at first Cain had been underneath Abel.

How did he slay him? Cain took a stone and inflicted many contusions and bruises on Abel's arms and legs, for he did not know what part of the body the soul goes out of, until, when he got to his neck, Abel died.

After he slew him, Cain said: I must flee from my father and mother. Since, except for Abel and me, there is no one else in the world, they will demand an accounting from me. Immediately the Holy One revealed Himself to him, saying, "You may flee from your parents, but not from Me. 'Can any hide himself in secret places that I shall not see him?' [Jer. 23:24]. 'Where is Abel thy brother?' " (Gen. 4:9). Cain replied, "I do not know. Why ask me about him? I should be asking You where he is!" "O wicked one," the Holy One replied, "the voice of thy brother's blood crieth unto me" (Gen. 4:10).

God's reply may be illustrated by the parable of a man who entered a garden patch, took some mulberries, and ate them. When the owner ran after him, saying, "What's in your hands?" and the man replied, "Nothing," the owner said, "But your hands are stained!"

Or God's reply may also be illustrated by the parable of a man who entered a pasture, seized a kid, and slung it over his back. When the owner of the pasture ran after him, saying, "What are you holding?" and the man replied, "Nothing," the owner said, "But the kid is bleating behind your back!"

"The voice of thy brother's blood cries out against Me[5] from the ground" (Gen. 4:10). R. Simeon ben Yohai said: This verse is all but intolerable to recite and impossible to explain. For it seems to regard Cain and Abel as two gladiators, wrestling in the king's presence [in an arena, where] if the king desires it, he may separate them; or if he does not desire to separate them, and one gladiator prevails over the other and is about to kill him, the other may cry out, "Who will intercede for me with the king?"[6] [Therefore God said: Since I, the King, did not interfere between Cain and Abel] "The voice of thy brother's blood cries out against Me."

Another comment. Cain said to God, "Am I [expected to be] my brother's keeper?" (Gen. 4:9). You are the keeper of all creatures, yet You call me to account for him. Cain's question may be understood by the parable of a thief who stole some vessels during the night and was not caught. The following morning, the gatekeeper did catch him and asked, "Why did you steal the vessels?" The thief replied, "I, thief that I am, did not slacken at my trade, but you—your trade is to keep watch at the gate. Why did you slacken in your occupation?" Accordingly, Cain's question is in fact a defiant assertion: I slew Abel—it was You who created in me the impulse to evil. But You are the keeper of all things—yet You let me slay him. It is You who slew him. Had You accepted my offering as You did his, I would not have been jealous of him. Immediately the Holy One countered, "What have *you* done? 'The voice of thy brother's blood crieth' " (Gen. 4:10). Then [in self-defense] Cain pleaded: Master of the universe, I never in

1. B. AZ 8a.
2. B. Pes 54a; Gen. R. 11:2.
3. B. AZ 8a.
4. Scripture does not tell what Cain said. So, in view of the fact that Cain brought an offering of the fruit of the earth, while Abel brought of the firstlings of his flock, it is surmised that each offering represented the share in the world that each brother had taken.

5. Since "unto Me" is regarded as unnecessary, the word *elay* ("unto Me") is read *alay* ("Against Me").
6. The spectators in the arena sometimes asked the king to spare the life of the gladiator who was down. See Ignaz Ziegler, *Die Königsgleichnisse des Midrasch* (Breslau, 1908), p. 312.

my life knew or saw anyone slain. How was I to know that if I struck Abel with a stone, he would die? Cain went on, "Is my sin so great that it cannot be borne?" (Gen. 4:13).[1] He said further: Master of the universe, are there, in Your presence, informers who come up to denounce a person before You? My father and mother are on the earth, and yet they do not know that I slew Abel. You are in heaven—how do You know? The Holy One replied: Fool! The whole world, all of it, I bear. Cain then said: The whole world, all of it, You bear, yet my sin You cannot bear! "Is my sin so great that it cannot be borne?"

[Now that Cain spoke of his act as a sin], the Holy One said: Since you vowed repentance, go forth as a wandering exile from this place, "and Cain went out from the presence of the Lord and dwelt in the land as a wanderer" (Gen. 4:16).[2]

As he went forth, wherever he walked, the earth quaked beneath him,[3] and all animals, wild and tame, shaken at the sight of him said, "What sort of a creature is this?" Then, to one another, "Cain has slain his brother Abel; so the Holy One has decreed for Cain, 'A fugitive and a wanderer shalt thou be' [Gen. 4:12]. Let's go at him and devour him," and they surrounded him and came at him to exact reckoning for Abel's blood.

The tears began to flow from Cain's eyes as he said:

Whither shall I go
  From Thy spirit?
Or whither shall I flee
  From Thy Presence?
If I ascend up into heaven,
  Thou art there;
If I make my bed in the nether world,
  Behold, Thou art there.
If I take the wings of the morning,
  Or dwell in the uttermost parts of the sea;
Even there would Thy hand
  Apprehend me,
And Thy right hand would
  Seize me (Ps. 139:7–10).

At that, the Holy One [reassuring him] said, "Whosoever slayeth Cain, sevenfold vengeance shall be taken on him" (Gen. 4:15).[4]

102. After Abel was slain, he was lying in a field, his blood spattered over sticks and stones. The dog who had been guarding Abel's flock now also guarded Abel's corpse from the beasts of the field and the birds of the sky.

Adam and his mate came and sat by the corpse, weeping and mourning for him—but they did not know what to do with Abel's body.

A raven whose companion had just died said: I will teach Adam what to do. The raven took his dead companion, dug up the earth before the eyes of Adam and his mate, and buried him in it. Adam said: We will do as the raven. At once he took Abel's corpse and buried it in the ground.[5]

103. "And the Lord provided Cain with a token for his protection" (Gen. 4:15). He gave him a dog,[6] according to Rav; but according to Abba Yose, He made a horn sprout on his forehead.[7]

104. "Cain went out from the Presence of the Lord" (Gen. 4:16). How can it be said that a man went out from the Presence of the Lord?[8] However, according to R. Yudan, citing R. Aibu, the verse signifies that Cain left [his consciousness of] the Lord's Presence by tossing off the words ["My sin is greater than can be forgiven"], as if by mouthing them he could blunt the Almighty's awareness of his sin.[9]

105. "Cain went out from the Presence of the Lord" (Gen. 4:16). Cain [did not speak deceitfully, but] went forth as one glad in heart. Adam met him and asked, "What was done in punishment of you?" Cain replied, "I vowed repentance and was granted clemency." Upon hearing this, Adam, in self-reproach, began to stroke himself in the face as he said, "Such is the power of repentance, and I knew it not." Then and there Adam exclaimed, "It is a good thing to confess to the Lord" (Ps. 92:2).[10]

106. Lamech, seventh in the generations of mankind, who was Cain's grandson, was blind. One time he went out hunting, with his young son holding him by the hand. The child saw something that looked like a beast's horn and said, "I see something that looks like a beast." Lamech bent the bow, [let go the arrow], and slew Cain. When the child, still at a distance, saw that it was a dead man with a horn on his forehead, he said to Lamech, "My father, this looks like a slain man with a horn on his forehead." Lamech cried out, "Woe is me! It is my grandfather." In contrition, he clapped his two hands together, inadvertently striking the child's head and killing him. It is con-

---

1. JV: "My punishment is greater than I can bear."
2. At first he was told, "A fugitive and a wanderer shalt thou be" (Gen. 4:12); but since he vowed repentance, half the punishment—being a fugitive—was remitted.
3. Apparently, the commentator reads here Gen. 4:16: "He sought to find a place on the earth, [though it was] *nod*, quaking [under him]."
4. Tanhuma, *Bereshit*, §9; Gen. R. 22:9. In Gen. R. 22:12 and in Tanhuma, *Bereshit*, §9, R. Nehemiah interprets Gen. 4:15 as follows: Cain's sentence shall not be like that of other murderers. Cain, slayer though he is, had no way of knowing the enormity of his crime. Henceforth, however, "all who slay shall be slain" (Gen. R. 22:12).
5. PRE 21; Yalkut, *Bereshit*, §38.
6. To ward off the animals that threatened to attack him, Adam had domesticated the dog. *Yefeh Toar* suggests that the commentator read not *le-kayin ot* ("a sign for Cain") but *lo kinot* (= Greek *kuon*, genitive *kunos*): "for him a dog").
7. Gen. R. 22:12. To terrify foes, ancient tribesmen put horns on their foreheads.
8. An impossible feat. Does not the psalmist say, "Whither shall I go from Thy spirit?" (Ps. 139:7).
9. Or: Cain reversed his garment front to back and went out thinking that he had deceived [literally, stolen the mind of] the Holy One. So Leon Nemoy. Gen. R. 22:12; PRKM 24:11 (PRKS, pp. 371–72).
10. Gen. R. 22:12. In the parallel in PRKM (PRKS, p. 372), the word *yotze* ("went out") is taken to indicate the connotation of that word in the verse "He goeth out (*yotze*) to meet thee, he will be glad in his heart" (Exod. 4:14).

cerning this double slaying that Lamech said, "By a wound of mine [my blindness] I slew a man, and by a blow of mine [clapping my hands] a child" (Gen. 4:23).[1]

The Corruption of Succeeding Generations

107. R. Jeremiah ben Eleazar said: In all the years that Adam was under the ban,[2] he begot evil spirits—male demons and female demons, for it is said, "Adam lived a hundred and thirty years, and begot a son in his own likeness, after his own image" (Gen. 5:3), from which it follows that until Adam reached the age of one hundred and thirty, he did not beget after his own image.[3]

Abba Kohen bar Dala was asked: [Why does Scripture list] "Adam . . . Seth, Enosh" (Gen. 4:25–26), and no more?[4] "Down to Enosh," he replied, "They were created in the image and likeness of God. But thereafter, the generations having become corrupt, centaurs came into being."[5]

Four things changed in the days of Enosh son of Seth: Mountainsides turned rocky [unfit for plowing]; corpses putrefied and generated worms; men's faces turned apelike; and [the divine image having departed from human beings], demons became free to work their will upon them.[6]

Noah

108. "And he called his name Noah, saying: 'This same shall comfort us in our work and in the toil of our hands' " (Gen. 5:29). Before Noah's birth, what was reaped was not what had been sewn. Where wheat or barley was sown, thorns and thistles were reaped. But after Noah was born, the earth returned to orderly growth. What was sown was reaped—when wheat was sown, wheat was reaped; when barley was sown, barley was reaped. More! Until Noah's birth men worked the soil with their bare hands, as implied by "the toil of our hands." But after Noah was born, he, to help them, invented the plow, the scythe, the hoe, and other implements for cultivating the ground.[7]

109. R. Yohanan said: When the Holy One created man, He gave him dominion over all things—the heifer was obedient to the plowman; so, too, the furrow responded to the plowman. But after Adam sinned, both rebelled against him—a heifer was no longer obedient to a plowman, nor was a furrow responsive to a plowman. However, after Noah came, they submitted again.

R. Simeon ben Lakish said: Until Noah came, the tides[8] would rise high twice, once in the morning and once in the evening, flushing corpses out of their graves. With the coming of Noah, the tides were stilled.[9]

The Generation of the Flood

110. "The Lord said: 'I will blot out man' " (Gen. 6:7). A parable of a king who built a palace and tenanted it with mutes, who would rise early and—with a gesture or a finger or a kerchief—salute the king. The king said: If these, who are mute, rise early and salute me with gestures, with fingers, or with kerchiefs, how much more and more would they do if they possessed the faculty of speech? So he replaced them with people capable of normal speech. But these at once seized the palace, saying: The palace is not the king's—it is ours. At that, the king said: Let the palace be restored to its former tenants.

Similarly, at the beginning of the world's creation, the praise of the Holy One came only from the waters. Of their praise of Him, it is written, "From the voices of many waters" (Ps. 93:4). What did these voices proclaim? "The Lord on high is mighty" (ibid.). Said the Holy One, "If these, who have neither say nor speech, praise Me, how much more and more will I be praised when I create man?" But when the generation of Enosh rose up and rebelled against Him, and the generation of the flood rose up and rebelled against Him, the Holy One said, "Let these be removed, and let the waters come into their place."[10]

111. R. Joshua ben Levi said: Before bringing the flood, the Holy One grieved seven days over His world, as is said, "And He grieved in His heart" (Gen. 6:6).[11]

112. "And He blotted out every living substance which was upon the face of the ground, both man and cattle" (Gen. 7:23). Man, to be sure, sinned, but in what way did cattle sin? It is taught in the name of R. Joshua ben Korhah: The question may be answered with the parable of a man who set up a bridal canopy for his son and prepared all kinds of food for the festive meal. But within a few days, the son died. So the man dismantled the canopy [and threw out the food], saying: I have prepared all of this for the sake of my son. Now that he is dead, what need have I of [food or] canopy? Likewise, the Holy One said: I have created animals, wild and tame, only for the sake of man; now that man has sinned, what need have I of animals, wild or tame?[12]

1. JV: "I have slain a man for wounding me and a child for bruising me." Tanhuma, *Bereshit*, §11; MhG Gen., pp. 126–27.
2. Because he ate the fruit of the tree of knowledge.
3. Semen discharged not for procreation is said to be utilized by evil spirits to procreate their own kind. B. Er 18b.
4. Instead of continuing the genealogical record of Adam, the narrative is interrupted and starts afresh with, "This is the book of the generations of Adam" (Gen. 5:1).
5. Centaurs were men in the upper portion of their bodies and horses in the lower portion. The implication: succeeding generations gave themselves to copulation in the manner of horses.
6. Gen. R. 23:6.
7. Tanhuma, *Bereshit*, §11.
8. Waters of a partial flood meant to serve as a warning that a great flood was to come.
9. Note the alliteration: Noah and *nahu* ("were stilled"). Gen. R. 25:2.
10. Gen. R. 5:1 and 28:2.
11. Gen. R. 27:4. The proof is drawn from the later statement "And it came to pass after the seven days, that the waters of the flood were upon the earth" (Gen. 7:10), the seven days being understood as God's seven days of anticipatory mourning prior to the flood.
12. B. Sanh 108a.

113. When the generation of the flood arose and gave themselves over to lewd idolatry, the Holy One was grieved. Two angels, Shamhazai and Azzael, rose up and said: Master of the universe, did we not say to You when You created Your world, "What is man that Thou art mindful of him" (Ps. 8:5)? God asked: But [if I destroy mankind], what is to become of the world? They replied: Master of the universe, we will make use of it. He said: It is revealed and known to Me that, if you lived in the world, the impulse to evil would gain mastery over you, and you would be more obdurate than the children of men. They replied: Nevertheless, give us permission to dwell among mortal creatures, and You will see how we hallow Your Name. Then God said: Go down and dwell among them. They immediately misbehaved with the daughters of men, who were so beautiful that the angels could not conquer their impulse.[1]

Thus, when Shamhazai noticed a certain maiden whose name was Istahar, he gazed lustfully upon her and pleaded, "Do my bidding." She replied, "I will not do your bidding until you give me your wings and teach me the Explicit Name, which you go up to heaven upon uttering."

So he gave her his wings and taught her the Name, whereupon she uttered it, went up to heaven, and was spared from corruption.

The Holy One said: Since she shunned transgression, go and set her among the seven stars yonder. Thus, it came about that Istahar was set in the constellation of Draco. When Shamhazai and Azzael saw this, they took wives, and Shamhazai begot sons: Hiva and Hayya.

Metatron[2] sent an emissary to tell Shamhazai: The Holy One will destroy His world by bringing a flood upon it. Shamhazai fell to weeping, grieving over the world and his sons. What would his sons do? What would they eat, should the world be destroyed? For every day each of them ate a thousand camels, a thousand horses, and a thousand oxen.

That night Hiva and Hayya both had dreams. The first saw a stone on the ground, lying flat like a table, its top incised with many lines of script. An angel came down from heaven, in his hand a kind of chisel with which he scraped and erased all the lines, until he left only four letters.[3] The second saw a large and beautiful orchard planted with all kinds of trees. In the orchard were angels, and in their hands axes with which they felled the trees until they left only one tree with three branches.

Upon waking, Hiva and Hayya stood up in consternation and went to their father, who said to them: The Holy One is about to bring a flood [upon the world] and will leave only Noah and his [three] sons. Hearing this, they fell to wailing and weeping. He said to them: Grieve not, your names will never cease among mortals. Every time mortals saw lumber, heave stones, or haul in ships, they will mention your names—Hiva and Hayya.[4] At that, Hiva and Hayya grew calm.

Shamhazai repented and suspended himself, head down and feet up, between heaven and earth, and to this day he continues thus suspended in repentance. Azzael did not repent and still continues in his corruption.[5]

114. "For all flesh had become dissolute" (Gen. 6:12). R. Azariah said in the name of R. Judah bar Simon: In the generation of the flood, all had become dissolute—the dog mated with the wolf, the rooster with the peacock. R. Luliani bar Tibrin said in the name of R. Isaac: Even the earth acted like a harlot—when planted with wheat, it brought forth tares. In fact, tares stem from the generation of the flood.[6]

115. "Lamech took him two wives" (Gen. 4:19). R. Azariah said in the name of R. Judah bar Simon: This is what the men of the generation of the flood used to do—each would take to himself two wives, one for procreation and the other for sexual pleasure. The one for procreation was almost like a widow, though her husband was still alive; while the one for sexual pleasure was made by her husband to swallow a potion[7] so that she would not conceive. She sat in his house painted like a harlot.

You can readily see that it was so, for even Lamech, the best among that generation, took two wives—Adah, "apart from [scorned by] him"; and Zillah [Tzillah],[8] "who dwelt in his shadow [was inseparable from him]."[9]

116. R. Isaac said: [The people of the generation of the flood] needed to plant only once [to raise enough food for] forty years, could walk from world's end to world's end in no time at all, and while walking could [easily] uproot cedars of Lebanon. As for the bite of lions or leopards, it was regarded by the people of that generation as no more dangerous than a flea's prick in the flesh. Besides, they constantly enjoyed the kind of beautiful weather that prevails from Passover to Pentecost.[10]

117. "They send forth their sucklings as though they were sheep in a flock, their newly born are able to skip about" (Job 21:11).[11] When a woman gave birth during the day, she would say to her newborn infant: Go and fetch me a flint, and I will cut your umbilical cord. When she gave birth during the night, she would say to her infant: Go and kindle a lamp for me, and I will cut your cord.

Once a woman who had given birth during the night

---

1. The story of the two angels, an elaboration of Gen. 6:1–2, intends to link the two verses with the account of the flood in Gen. 6:5ff., which follows.
2. The angel of the Presence.
3. *Yod, he, vav, he* (?): God's Name.
4. These names became exclamations of encouragement, like "Heave-ho!" or "way-haul-away!"
5. Midrash Avkir; BhM 4:127–28.
6. The Hebrew word for tares, "*zonin*," is similar to the word for harlotry. Gen. R. 28:8.
7. Literally, "a cup of root-drink."
8. In Aramaic, *adah* means "being apart"; *tzel* in Hebrew means "shade."
9. Gen. R. 23:2.
10. Approximately from April through May. Gen. R. 36:1.
11. JV: "They send forth their little ones like a flock, and their children dance." But Job 21:1ff. is often construed as referring to the generation of the flood. See, e.g., Mek, La 2:13; and PR 42:8 (YJS 2:749).

said to her newborn son: Go, kindle a lamp for me so that I can cut your cord. When he went out, he met the demon Shamdon, prince of all evil spirits. While the two were talking, the cock crowed. So Shamdon said: You may go and boast before your mother that [you managed to survive until] the cock crowed. For had the cock not crowed, I would have killed you with one blow. The newborn retorted: You go and boast before your mother's mother that [you survived] because my mother had not cut my cord—had my mother cut my cord, I would have killed you with but one blow![1]

Noah and the Flood

118. "These are the generations of Noah. Noah was a righteous man, and perfect in his generation" (Gen. 6:9). In his generation, R. Yohanan pointed out, but not in other generations. However, according to Resh Lakish, the verse intimates that even in his generation Noah was a righteous man, all the more so in other generations.

R. Hanina said: R. Yohanan's view may be illustrated by the parable of a jar of wine stored in a cellar filled with jars of vinegar. In such a place, the fragrance of the wine is sensed [because of the vinegar's fumes]; in any other place, its fragrance might not be sensed.[2]

R. Oshaia said: Resh Lakish's view may be illustrated by a vial of [fragrant] spikenard oil lying amid excrement: if its fragrance is sensed even in such surroundings, how much more so amid spices![3]

119. "Noah walked with God" (Gen. 6:9). R. Judah said: The phrasing may be understood from the parable of a king who had two sons, one grown up and the other a child. To the child he said, Walk *with* me; but to the adult, Walk *before* me. Likewise to Abraham, whose [spiritual] strength was great, he said, "Because you are wholehearted, walk *before* me" (Gen. 17:1). But to Noah, whose [spiritual] strength was feeble, Scripture says, "Noah walked *with* God."[4]

120. "Make thee an ark of cedarwood"[5] (Gen. 6:14). R. Huna said in the name of R. Yose: For one hundred and twenty years, the Holy One kept warning the generation of the flood in the hope that they would resolve to repent. When they did not repent, He said to Noah, "Make thee an ark of cedarwood." Noah proceeded to plant cedars. When asked, "Why these cedars?" he would reply, "The Holy One is about to bring a flood upon the world, and He told me to make an ark, that I and my family might escape." They mocked and ridiculed him. In the meantime, he watered the cedars, which kept growing.

When asked again, "What are you doing?" he gave them the same reply, and the generation of the flood continued to ridicule him. Finally he cut the cedars down, and, as he sawed them into planks, he was again asked, "What are you doing?" He replied, "What I said I would do," even as he continued to warn the generation of the flood.

When they did not repent even then, the Holy One brought the flood upon them.

At last, when they realized that they were about to perish, they tried to overturn the ark. What did the Holy One do then? He surrounded the ark with lions.[6]

121. "A light (*tzohar*) shalt thou make for the ark" (Gen. 6:16). R. Levi said: *Tzohar* means a pearl of purest ray. Throughout the twelve months that Noah was in the ark, he had no need of the light of the sun by day, nor of the light of the moon by night. For he had a pearl which he hung up: while it was dim, he knew that it was day, and while it glowed, he knew that it was night.[7]

122. "And of every living thing, of all flesh, two of every sort, thou shalt bring into the ark" (Gen. 6:19). R. Judah said: The *re'em*[8] did not enter the ark; only his whelps did.[9] R. Nehemiah differed: Neither he nor his whelps did, but Noah tied him to the ark, and as he swam, he plowed furrows in the water as long as the distance from Tiberias to Susitha.[10]

123. As the floodwaters swelled, Og, king of Bashan, sat himself on one of the rungs of the ark's ladders and swore to Noah and to his sons that he would be their slave forever. What did Noah do? He punched a hole in the ark, and through it he handed out food to Og every day.

Og's survival is intimated in the verse "Only Og remained of the remnant of the Rephaim" (Deut. 3:11).[11]

124. R. Yohanan said: Each and every raindrop the Holy One caused to come down upon the generation of the flood, He first brought to a boil in Gehenna; then He carried it out and dropped it on them.[12]

125. "Behold, I will destroy them with the earth" (Gen. 6:13). It is said in the name of R. Kahana bar Malkia: Even the three handbreadths of the earth's soil that the plow turns up were washed away. It is as if a prince had a nurse, and whenever he did wrong, his nurse was punished. So the Holy One said, "Behold, I will destroy them with the earth"—I will destroy them, and together with them that part of the earth[13] [that gives them sustenance].[14]

1. Gen. R. 36:1; Lev. R. 5:1.
2. In other generations, Noah would not have been deemed exceptional.
3. How much more righteous would Noah have been had he lived in a generation of righteous men. B. Sanh 108a.
4. Gen. R. 30:10.
5. So Targum Onkelos; JV: "of gopher wood."
6. Tanhuma, *Noah*, §5.
7. Gen. R. 31:11.
8. A fabulous animal of giant proportions.
9. The comment is based on the phrase "of every living thing," which is deemed to be superfluous.
10. Tiberias is on the western side of Lake Kinneret, while Susitha is on its eastern bank. Gen. R. 31:13.
11. The Rephaim are identified as the generation of the flood. PRE 23.
12. Gen. R. 28:8.
13. The three handbreadths that are said to be turned by the plow.
14. Gen. R. 31:7.

126. R. Yohanan said: During the twelve months of the flood, the planets did not perform their function. R. Jonathan differed: They did perform their function, but their effect was imperceptible.[1]

127. "And he sent forth a raven, and it went forth to and fro" (Gen. 8:7). It to-and-fro'ed,[2] argued with him, saying: Of all the cattle, beasts, and fowl you have here, you send none but me! Noah replied: What need has the world of you? You are fit neither for food nor as an offering.

Then, said Resh Lakish, the raven gave Noah an irrefutable retort: Your Lord hates me and you hate me. Your Lord showed His hatred of me by ordering that seven pair of the clean fowl be taken into the ark, but only two pair of the unclean. And you hate me, seeing that you spare the species of which there are seven pair, but from the species of which there are only two pair, you send me. Should the prince of heat or the prince of cold smite me, might not the world lose one entire species of creature?

Nevertheless, "Noah did send out the raven" (Gen. 8:7) to learn what was going on in the world. The raven flew out and, finding a man's corpse flung on a mountaintop, perched itself over this food and did not come back to its sender with word concerning its errand. Then Noah sent out the dove, and she did bring back word.

"And lo, in her mouth an olive leaf freshly plucked" (Gen. 8:11). From where did the dove bring it? R. Bebai said: The gates of the Garden of Eden were opened for her, and she brought it from there. R. Aibu said to him: Had she brought it from the Garden of Eden, would she not have brought something finer, such as a stick of cinnamon or a leaf of balsam? But in truth the dove's olive leaf was a way of hinting to Noah: My master Noah, I would rather have something even more bitter than this from the hand of the Holy One than something sweet from your hand.[3]

128. "And lo, in her mouth an olive leaf freshly plucked" (Gen. 8:11). The dove said to the Holy One: Master of the universe, let my sustenance be bitter as this olive leaf, just so it comes from you, rather than sweet as honey but coming from flesh and blood.[4]

129. "And God spoke to Noah, saying: 'Go forth from the ark' " (Gen. 8:15–16). R. Yudan said: Had I been there, I would have made a breach in the ark and left without ado. But Noah said: Even as I did not go into the ark except with God's permission, so I shall not leave it except with His permission. "Come thou into the ark"—"and Noah went in." "Go forth from the ark"—"and Noah went forth."[5]

130. "After their kinds they went forth from the ark" (Gen. 8:19). Eliezer [Abraham's servant] asked Shem, Noah's oldest son: How did you manage to take care of the many kinds of animals [with habits so divergent]? Shem replied: The truth is, we had much trouble in the ark. The creature whose habit it was to eat by day, we fed by day; the one who ate by night, we fed by night. As for the chameleon, my father did not know what it ate. One day, as my father was sitting and cutting a pomegranate, a worm fell out of it and the chameleon consumed it. After that, he would knead some prickly reeds infested with worms and feed it with them. As for the phoenix, my father found him sleeping in a corner of the ark and asked him: Why did you not request food? He replied: I saw you were busy, and I said to myself that I should not trouble you. Noah responded: Since you were concerned about my trouble, may it be the Lord's will that you never die. Hence it is said, "I shall multiply my days as the phoenix"[6] (Job 29:18).

131. Our masters said: During the twelve months Noah spent in the ark, he did not savor the taste of sleep—neither he nor his sons, neither by day nor by night, occupied as he was with feeding the creatures that were with him. One creature fed in the first hour of the day, another in the second hour, still another in the third hour, and yet another in the fourth hour; one creature fed at the end of the first third of the night, another in the middle of the night, and still another at the time of the cock's crowing. What did Noah feed them? Each and every species got what it was accustomed to eat—straw for camels, vine tendrils for elephants, barley for donkeys, cistus shrubs for gazelles, glass for ostriches.[7]

Once, as he was late in feeding the lion, the beast struck him and he went out limping. That this happened is implied in the words "And only (*akh*)[8] Noah remained" (Gen. 7:23). In these words it is also implied that he was coughing and spitting up blood because of overwork in the tending of animals and beasts.[9]

132. R. Levi taught: When the Holy One said to Noah, "Gather unto thee two living creatures of every kind into the ark," all the creatures came and each of them entered the ark with his mate. Falsehood also came and wished to enter, but Noah said, "You cannot enter unless you wed a proper mate." So Falsehood went looking for a mate and encountered Vexation. Vexation asked, "Where are you coming from?" Falsehood replied, "From Noah. I wanted

1. Neither the sun nor the moon provided the usual illumination. Gen. R. 25:2.
2. In the play on words, *shov* ("return") is associated with *hashev*, ("retort"). Gen. R. 33:5.
3. Gen. R. 33:6; Lev. R. 31:10; Song R. 1:15, §4; Yalkut, *Noah*, §58.
4. B. Er 18b; B. Sanh 108b; PRE 23; Yalkut, *Noah*, §58.
5. Gen. R. 34:4; Yalkut, *Noah*, §59.
6. A legendary bird which is immortal. B. Sanh 108b; Yalkut, *Noah*, §59.
7. The ostrich is said to keep stones in its gizzard, which it digests over a period of time (Aelian *De Natura Animalium* 14:7), and is also capable of digesting iron (Alexander of Aphrodisias *Problems*, preface, 249:15). Professor David Pingree of Brown University provided this information.

   Accordingly, since bringing stones or iron into the ark was impractical, the ostrich had to make do with glass.
8. The commentator regards "only" as superfluous. Hence he construes *akh* as implying *nkh* ("smite"), which accounts for his limping, as well as *khh* ("hacking, spitting up blood"). See Tanhuma, *Noah*, §9.
9. Tanhuma B. *Noah*, §3 and §14; Tanhuma, *Noah*, §9; Gen. R. 31:11; Rashi on Gen. 7:23.

to enter the ark, but he would not allow me to do so unless I had a proper mate with me. Would you be willing to be my mate?" Vexation asked, "What will you give me?" Falsehood replied, "I pledge you that all that I may lay by, you shall take." [Vexation agreed to Falsehood's proposal] and they both entered the ark. After they left the ark, Falsehood went about laying things by, and Vexation took them, one by one. When Falsehood came and inquired, "Where are all the things I laid by?" Vexation replied, "Was it not agreed between us that I would take everything you might lay by?" Falsehood had nothing more to say.

"Yea, Vexation has become heavy with what Falsehood has brought forth" (Ps. 7:15).[1] As the proverb puts it: What falsehood begets, vexation takes over.[2]

133. "And Noah the tiller of the soil became profane" (Gen. 9:20).[3] He profaned himself and became profane. How did he bring this about? Scripture says, "And planted a vineyard" (ibid.). Should he not have planted something of use, say a young fig shoot or an olive shoot? But no—he "planted a vineyard."

But where did he get the grapevines? R. Abba bar Kahana said: He had taken some vine tendrils into the ark with him, as well as fig saplings and olive saplings.

As he set about to plant the vineyard, the demon Shamdon met him and suggested: Take me into partnership. But beware, do not trespass into my part. If you do, I will hurt you.[4]

134. When Noah began planting, Satan came, stationed himself before him, and asked, "What are you planting?" Noah: "A vineyard." Satan: "What is its nature?" Noah: "Its fruit, whether fresh or dried, is sweet, and from it one makes wine, which gladdens a man's heart." Satan: "Will you agree to let both of us plant it together?" Noah: "Very well."

What did Satan do? He brought a ewe lamb and slaughtered it over a vine. After that, he brought a lion, which he likewise slaughtered. Then a monkey, which he also slaughtered over it. Finally a pig, which he again slaughtered over that vine. And with the blood that dripped from them, he watered the vineyard.

The charade was Satan's way of saying that when a man drinks one cup of wine, he acts like a ewe lamb, humble and meek. When he drinks two, he immediately believes himself to be as strong as a lion and proceeds to brag mightily, saying, "Who is like me?" When he drinks three or four cups, he immediately becomes like a monkey, hopping about giggling, and uttering obscenities in public, without realizing what he is doing. Finally, when he becomes blind drunk, he is like a pig, wallowing in mire and coming to rest among refuse.

All the above befell Noah.[5]

---

1. JV: "Yea, he conceiveth mischief, and bringeth forth falsehood."
2. MTeh 7:11; Yalkut, *Noah*, §56.
3. EV: "And Noah the tiller of the soil began . . . " But since the verb in Hebrew is placed at the opening of the verse, suggesting special emphasis, the commentator understands it as stemming not from *hvl* [*hul*] ("begin") but from *hll* ("profane").
4. Gen. R. 36:3 and 31:14.
5. Tanhuma, *Noah*, §13.

Nimrod and the Generation of the Dispersion of Mankind

135. "[The animals' prostrating themselves before Nimrod's garment made all think] he was a mighty lord" (Gen. 10:9).[6] R. Judah said: The garment of glory that the Holy One made for Adam and for his wife was with Noah in the ark. When they left the ark, Noah's son Ham took it, brought it out with him, and bequeathed it to Nimrod. Whenever Nimrod wore it, all cattle, beasts, and fowl, upon seeing the garment on him, would come and prostrate themselves before him. Now, human beings supposed that the greatness of Nimrod's own strength brought about such adoration, and so they made him king over them. Whereupon he said to his people, "Come, let us build us a city and a tower" (Gen. 11:4).[7]

136. "Let us build us a city and a tower with its top in heaven" (Gen. 11:4). They said: Once every one thousand six hundred and fifty-six years, the firmament topples. Come and let us make supports for it [under each of its four sides].

Another interpretation of what they said: It is not for Him to choose for Himself the worlds above and give us those below. Come, let us make us a tower, place an image on its top, and put a sword in its hand, and it will seem that it is waging war against Him.[8]

137. "Come, let us make brick . . . and for them a small brick grow to the size of a foundation stone, and a handful of slime became a heap of mortar" (Gen. 11:3). So greatly did their work prosper, said R. Huna, that a man laying one brick found that two bricks had been laid; another plastering one row found that two rows had been plastered.[9]

138. The tower had seven levels on its east and seven on its west. The builders brought the bricks up on one side and came down on the other. If a man fell down and died, no heed was given to him. But when a brick fell down, they stopped work and wept, saying, "Woe unto us! When will another be brought up in its stead?"

When Abram son of Terah passed by and saw them building the city, he cursed them in the name of his God: "O Lord, confound their speech, confuse it!" (Ps. 55:10).[10]

139. "Come . . . let us confound their language" (Gen. 11:7). When one said to another, "Bring me water," he brought him earth. Whereupon the one cracked the other's skull. When one said to another, "Bring me an ax," he brought him a spade. Whereupon the one cracked open the other's skull.[11]

---

6. JV: "He was a mighty hunter before the Lord."
7. PRE 24; MhG Gen., p. 194.
8. Gen. R. 38:6.
9. Gen. R. 38:8.
10. PRE 24.
11. Gen. R. 38:10.

140. "And they said . . . 'Lest we be dispersed upon the face of the whole earth.' . . . So the Lord dispersed them from thence upon the face of all the earth" (Gen. 11:4 and 11:9). R. Levi said: In its foreboding, the generation that was to be dispersed was like a woman who said to her husband, "In a dream I saw you divorcing me." The husband replied, "Why only in a dream? Here is your bill of divorce—a real one."[1]

141. R. Yohanan said: The tower—one-third [of its height] was burned, one-third was swallowed up, and the lowest third still stands. Whoever ascends the part still standing sees palm trees below him as no bigger than grasshoppers.[2]

142. R. Eliezer said: Who is more reprehensible—he who says to the king, "Either you or I in the palace," or he who says, "I and not you in the palace"? Clearly he who says to the king, "I and not you in the palace," is the more reprehensible. Thus, the generation of the flood said to Him, "What is the Almighty that we should serve Him? And what profit should we have, if we pray unto Him?" (Job 21:15). But the generation of the dispersion of mankind said: It is not for Him to choose for Himself the worlds above and give us those below. Come, let us make us a tower, place an image on its top, and put a sword in its hand, and it will seem that it is waging war against Him.

Consequently, the generation of the flood [which sought to displace God]—of them, no remnant survived; whereas the generation of the dispersion of mankind [which sought to share God's power with Him]—of these, a remnant did survive.

Besides, the generation of the flood was steeped in malfeasance, as is said, "They remove the landmarks, they carry off flocks and pasture them" (Job 24:2). Therefore no remnant of them survived. But the latter generation, because they cherished love for one another, as is said, "And the whole earth was of one language" (Gen. 11:1)—of them, a remnant did survive.[3]

1. Out of fear that they might be dispersed all over the world, the generation that was to be dispersed set out to build a tower with its top in the sky. God said, " 'If this is how they have begun (*hahilam*) to act,' etc. [Gen. 11:6], I will disperse them at once." R. Levi, associating the unusual form *hahilam* with *halom* ("dream"), translates the word "the dream that they dreamed"; their being dispersed has become a reality—they have been dispersed, they did receive their divorce, so to speak, from God. Gen. R. 23:7.

2. B. Sanh 109a; Gen. R. 38:4.

3. Gen. R. 38:6.

C H A P T E R   T H R E E

THE DEEDS OF THE FATHERS

Our Father Abraham

1. There were ten generations from Adam to Noah—to make known God's patience, for all these generations kept provoking Him until finally [in the days of Noah] He brought the waters of the flood upon them.

There were ten generations from Noah to Abraham—to make known God's patience, for all these generations kept provoking Him until our father Abraham came and received the reward [saving] all of them.[1]

2. There were ten generations from Noah to Abraham, and in all of these God spoke to only one of their number, to Abraham. R. Berekhiah taught in the name of R. Nehemiah: [God's sifting through the generations until he found Abraham] may be illustrated by the parable of a king who, while traversing from place to place, lost a pearl from [the crown on] his head. The king halted and had his retinue halt. When passersby asked, "What is going on here with the king and his entire retinue?" they were told, "A pearl has fallen from the king's head." What did the king do? He heaped the soil in a number of piles, brought sieves, and sifted the first pile, but did not find the pearl; he sifted the second, but did not find it; but when he sifted the third pile, he found it. Then the passersby said, "The king has finally found his precious pearl."

Likewise, the Holy One said to Abraham, "Go—for you"[2] (Gen. 12:1), it was for you I was waiting. Otherwise, what need had I to record the [lengthy] genealogy of Shem, Arpachshad, Shelah, Eber, Peleg, Reu, Serug, Nahor, and Terah? Was it not on account of you? Hence it is written, "Thou didst choose Abram . . . because Thou foundest his heart faithful before Thee (Neh. 9:7–8).[3]

3. R. Abba bar Kahana said: In the world's practice, when a man joins a pair of beams so that they come together at an angle, where does he place them? Does he not place them in the middle of the chamber, so that they give support to the beams in front of them and behind them? So, too, why did the Holy One create Abraham in the middle of the generations? In order that he might sustain the generations before and after him.[4]

4. "And told Abram the Hebrew (*ha-ivri*)" (Gen. 14:13). R. Judah used to say: [*Ha-ivri*, "he who is on the other side," signifies] the whole world was on one side, while he was on the other side (*ever*).[5]

5. When our father Abraham was born, a star rose in the east and swallowed four stars in the four corners of heaven. Nimrod's wizards said to him: To Terah, at this hour, a son has been born, out of whom will issue a people destined to inherit this world and the world-to-come. With your permission, let his father be given a house full of silver and gold, on condition that his newly born son be slain.

Nimrod sent word to Terah, saying: Last night a son was born to you. Now give him to me, that we may slay him, and I will fill your house with silver and gold. Terah said: "I reply with a parable that will make you understand my anguish. A horse was told, "Let us cut off your head, and we will give you a barnful of barley." The horse replied, "You fools! If you cut off my head, who will eat the barley?" So, too, if you slay my son, who will make use of the silver and gold? King Nimrod said: From what you say, I gather that a son has indeed been born to you. Terah: A son was born, but he died. Nimrod: My offer was for a live son, not a dead one. What did Terah do then? He hid his son in a cave for three years, and the Holy One provided for the child two apertures—out of one issued oil, out of the other fine flour.

When Abraham was three years old, he went out of the cave and [observing the world] wondered in his heart: Who created heaven and earth and me? All that day he prayed to the sun. In the evening, the sun set in the west and the moon rose in the east. Upon seeing the moon and the stars around it, he said: This one must have created heaven and earth and me—these stars must be the moon's princes and courtiers. So all night long he stood in prayer to the moon. In the morning, the moon sank in the west and the sun rose in the east. Then he said: There is no might in either of these. There must be a higher Lord over them—to Him will I pray, and before Him will I prostrate myself.[6]

6. R. Simeon ben Yohai said: Our father Abraham—his own father did not teach him, nor did he have a master to teach him. From whom, then, did Abraham learn Torah? It was the Holy One who had provided him with reins that were like two pitchers overflowing and filling him with Torah and wisdom all through the night.[7] R. Levi, however, said: Abraham learned Torah all by himself.[8]

---

1. Avot 5:2.
2. JV: "Get thee out."
3. Gen. R. 39:10; Ruth R. 8:1.
4. Gen. R. 14:6; Eccles. R. 3:11, §2.
5. Of all mankind, he alone believed in the true God. Gen. R. 42:8.
6. BhM 2:118–196.
7. Abraham, with the help of God, discovered the Law through his own conscience and reason; the reins, or kidneys, are conceived of in the Bible and the Talmud as the seat of the moral conscience as well as of intellectual deliberation.
8. Gen. R. 61:16 and 95:3; Mteh 1:13.

7. R. Isaac told the parable of a man who was traveling from place to place when he saw a mansion in flames.[1] He wondered: Is it possible that the mansion is without someone to look after it? At that moment the owner of the mansion peered out at him and said: I am the owner of this mansion! So, too, as Abraham was wondering, Is it possible that the world should be without someone to look after it? the Holy One peered down at him and said: I am the world's Owner![2]

8. Abraham's family used to make images and sell them in the market. One day, when it was Abraham's turn to sell, his father Terah gave him several baskets of household gods and set him up in the marketplace. A man came to him and asked: Have you a god to sell? Abraham: What kind of god do you wish to buy? The man: I am a mighty man—give me a god as mighty as I am. So Abraham took an image that was standing on a shelf higher than all the others and said: Pay the money and take this one. The man asked: Is this god as mighty as I am? Abraham replied: You good-for-nothing! Don't you know the way of gods? The one who sits above all others is the mightiest of all. As the man was about to leave, Abraham asked him: How old are you? The man answered: Seventy years. Abraham said: Woe to a man who is seventy, yet prostrates himself before this thing which was made only today. At that, the man flung that god back into Abraham's basket, demanded the return of his money, and went his way.

Next came a widow, who said to Abraham: I am a poor woman—give me a god as poor as I am. At once Abraham took an image that was on a shelf lower than all the others and said: To suit your poverty, take this god who is humble, placed as he is on a shelf below all the others; but he will not budge until you pay me the money. [So she paid the price] and, as she was about to depart, he asked her: How old are you? She replied: Quite old. Abraham then said: May the breath of such a woman be blasted! To think that one so old prostrates herself before a god who is only one day old. She immediately dropped the god into the basket, got back her money from Abraham, and went her way.

Then Abraham took all the gods and brought them back to his father Terah. Terah's other sons said to their father: This Abraham does not know how to sell gods; come, then, and let us make him a priest. Abraham asked: What is a priest's work? They replied: He waits upon the gods, offers sacrifices to them, and serves them food and drink. So they made him priest. Abraham promptly set food and drink before the images and said to them: Come and eat, come and drink, so that you may be able to bestow good upon human beings. But not one of them took anything at all to eat or to drink. Then Abraham began to recite the verse "They have mouths but they speak not; eyes have they, but they see not; they have ears, but they hear not; noses have they, but they smell not; they have hands, but they handle not; feet have they, but they walk not" (Ps. 115:5–7).

A woman came carrying a bowl of fine flour and said: Here, offer it to the gods. At that, Abraham seized a stick, smashed all the images, and placed the stick in the hand of the biggest of them. When his father came, he asked: Who did this to the gods? Abraham answered: Would I hide anything from my father? A woman came with a bowl of fine flour and said: Here, offer it up to them. When I offered it, one god said, "I will eat first," and another said, "No, I will eat first." Then the biggest of them rose up and smashed all the others. His father replied: Are you making sport of me? They cannot do anything! Abraham answered: You say they cannot. Let your ears hear what your mouth is saying!

Terah took hold of Abraham and turned him over to Nimrod.

Nimrod asked Abraham: Are you Abraham son of Terah? Abraham: Yes. Nimrod asked: Do you not know that I am Lord of all [the heavenly] works—sun, moon, stars, and planets—and that all men go forth at my pleasure? Now, you—how dare you destroy what I hold in awe?

In that instant the Holy One gave Abraham the capacity to argue ingeniously, so that he answered Nimrod: May I, with your permission, say something that will redound to your greatness? Nimrod: Say it. Abraham: It is the way of the world that, from the day the world was created until now, the sun goes forth in the east and sets in the west. Tomorrow, bid the sun to go forth in the west and set in the east, and I shall bear witness for you that you are indeed Lord of the world. More: If you are Lord of the world, surely all hidden things are known to you. If so, tell me now what is in my heart and what I intend to do.

The wicked Nimrod stroked his beard in perplexity. Abraham said: Be not perplexed—you are not Lord of the world. You are the son of Cush. If you were Lord of the world, why could you not deliver your own father from death? The truth is, as you did not deliver your father from death, so will you not deliver your own self from death.

Nimrod summoned Terah and asked him: What judgment shall be imposed on your son Abraham, who destroyed my divinities? None other than burning. Then he turned back to Abraham and said: Bow down to fire, and you will be saved. Abraham: Perhaps I should bow down to water, which quenches fire. Nimrod then said: Very well, bow down to water. Abraham: If so, I should bow down to a cloud, which is laden with water. Nimrod: Then bow down to a cloud. Abraham: Perhaps I should bow down to the wind, which scatters the cloud. Nimrod: Then bow down to the wind. Abraham: Let me rather bow down to man, who withstands wind. Nimrod: You are playing word games with me. I bow down to nothing but fire, and I am about to cast you into the midst of it—let the God to whom you bow down come and save you!

They immediately took Abraham out to cast him into an open fire. They bound him hand and foot, and put him on the stony ground. Then they surrounded him on all sides with wood—five cubits wide on every side, and five cubits high—and set the wood on fire.

Just then Terah's neighbors and townsmen came by,

[1] So, too, Abraham saw the world devoured by the flames of evildoing.
[2] Gen. R. 39:1.

tapped him [jeeringly] on the head, and said: What a great and bitter shame! This son of yours, who you have been saying was to inherit both this world and the world-to-come—Nimrod is burning him in fire!

At once the Holy One's mercies crested and He came down and saved Abraham.

Now, Haran, Abraham's brother, was standing there undecided. If Abraham is victorious, he thought, I will say that I share Abraham's belief. Should Nimrod win, I will say that I share Nimrod's belief. So after Abraham went down into the open fire and was saved, and Haran was asked, "Whose side are you on?" he replied, "Abraham's." He was immediately seized and thrown into the fire. His innards were scorched, so that, upon emerging, he died in the presence of his father, as is said, "Haran died in the presence of his father Terah" (Gen. 11:28).[1]

9. When wicked Nimrod cast our father Abraham into the open fire, Gabriel[2] spoke up to the Holy One, "Master of the universe, may I go down and cool the fire, to save the righteous man from burning in it?" The Holy One replied, "I am the Unique One in My world, even as he is the unique one in his. It is fitting that the Unique One deliver the unique one." But since the Holy One does not hold back the reward of any creature, he said to Gabriel, "Yours will be the privilege of saving three of his descendants."[3]

10. "I was with thee when thou didst offer thyself willingly" (Ps. 110:3).[4] The verse is to be understood as the Holy One's saying, "I was with you when for My Name's sake you willingly consented to enter the open fire. 'In the day of thy hosts'[5] [ibid.]—the day you gathered unto Me all those hosts of people [who, following your trial in the open fire, became converted]. 'In beauties, holiness' [ibid.]—out of the beauties of the [eastern part of the] world,[6] I [God] hallowed you; 'from the very creation ["womb"] of the world I sought you out.[7] Let it be the dew of your childhood to you' " (ibid.). Abraham was afraid and said, "Perhaps I bear guilt all those years I [seemingly] worshiped idols." Hence the Holy One went on, " 'Let it be the dew of your childhood to you'—even as dew evaporates, so have your sins evaporated. Even as dew is a sign of blessing for the world, so are you a sign of blessing for the world."[8]

11. When the Holy One said to Abraham, "Get thee out of thy country and from thy kindred" (Gen. 12:1), what did Abraham resemble? A vial of scent with a tight-fitting lid put away in a corner so that its fragrance could not go forth. As soon as it was moved from that place [and opened], its fragrance began to go forth. So the Holy One said to Abraham: Abraham, many good deeds are in you. Travel about from place to place, and the greatness of your name will go forth in My world. "Get thee out . . . and I will have thee acclaimed a great nation."[9]

12. "And I will make thy name great" (Gen. 12:2). That is, coinage with Abraham's name was current in the world. And what symbols did his currency bear? An old man and an old woman on one side, and a young man and a young woman on the other.[10]

13. "Walk [before Me], in My very presence" (Gen. 17:1). To whom may Abraham be likened? To a king's friend, who saw the king walking about in dark alleys[11] and began lighting the way for him through a window. When the king looked up and saw him, he said: Instead of lighting the way for me through a window, come out and light the way for me in my very presence. So, too, the Holy One said to our father Abraham: Instead of lighting the way that leads to Me from Mesopotamia and neighboring territories, come down here and light the way to Me in My very presence—in the Land of Israel.[12]

14. R. Levi said: When Abraham was traveling through Aram-naharaim and Aram-nahor, he saw the inhabitants eating and drinking and reveling. "May my portion not be in this land," he exclaimed. But when he reached the Ladder of Tyre[13] and saw the people there engaged in weeding at weeding time, and in hoeing at hoeing time, he exclaimed, "Would that my portion be in this land." At that, the Holy One said, "Unto thy seed will I give this land" (Gen. 12:7).[14]

15. "The souls that they had made in Haran" (Gen. 12:5). The verse implies: Our father Abraham would bring people into his home, give them food and drink, befriend them, and thus attract them, and then convert them and bring them under the wings of the Presence. Hence you learn that a man who brings a single creature under the wings of the Presence is accounted as if he had created him, shaped him, and articulated his parts.[15]

16. "And Abraham planted an *eshel*"[16] (Gen. 21:33). R. Judah said: *Eshel* means a fruitful orchard, the word implying, "Ask (*she'al*) of it anything you wish—figs, grapes, or pomegranates." R. Nehemiah differed: *Eshel* means a

1. TdE, pp. 27–28; Gen. R. 38:13.
2. Gabriel is the angel who ordinarily executes God's judicial decrees.
3. Hananiah, Mishael, and Azariah. Dan. 3; B. Pes 118a.
4. The commentator assumes that Ps. 110 refers to Abraham and so makes the following change: Since Abraham had no "people," he reads *ammekha* ("thy people") as *immekha* ("[I was] with thee"). JV: "Thy people offer themselves willingly."
5. The word *hel* can mean "warfare, retinue, hosts of people."
6. Babylon.
7. JV: "from the womb of the dawn." But *mishhar* ("dawn") can also be read as a form of *shhr* ("seek out").
8. Gen. R. 39:8; Yalkut, Ps., §869.
9. Gen. R. 39:2; Song R. 1:3, §3.
10. Abraham and Sarah, Isaac and Rebekah. Gen. R. 39:11; B. BK 97b.
11. Where people steeped in idolatry lived.
12. Gen. R. 30:10.
13. Scala Tyriorum, a promontory south of Tyre.
14. Since the Land requires constant care and cultivation, allowing no time for idleness which leads to drinking and reveling, Abraham hoped that his children would settle in it. Gen. R. 39:8.
15. Sif Deut., §32; Gen. R. 39:14; Song R. 1:3, §3; PR 43:6 (YJS 2:764).
16. JV: "tamarisk tree."

[well-stocked] inn, the word suggesting, "Ask (*she'al*) anything you wish—bread, meat, wine, or eggs.[1]

17. "And he called there on the Name of the Lord, the [everlasting] God[2] of the world" (Gen. 21:33). Resh Lakish said: Read not, "And he called," but, "And he caused to call," meaning that our father Abraham caused the Name of the Holy One to be called by the mouth of every passerby. How did it come about? After travelers [whom he made his guests] had eaten and drunk, they stood up to bless him. He said to them: Was it of mine that you ate? You ate of that which belongs to the [everlasting] God of the world. Thank, praise, and bless Him who spoke and the world came into being.[3]

18. Abraham used to receive wayfarers. After they had eaten and drunk, he would suggest, "Say grace." When they asked, "What shall we say?" he would reply, "[Say], 'Blessed be the everlasting God of the world, of whose bounty we have partaken.' " If the wayfarer, having eaten and drunk, accepted the suggestion and said grace, he would be allowed to depart. But if he refused, Abraham would say, "Pay what you owe me." When the wayfarer asked, "How much do I owe you?" Abraham would reply, "A jug of wine—so much; a pound of meat—so much; a loaf of bread—so much. Who do you suppose is giving you wine in the wilderness? meat in the wilderness? bread in the wilderness?"

The wayfarer, now aware that he must either pay or thank God by saying grace, would say, "Blessed be the everlasting God of the world, of whose bounty we have partaken." This is the meaning of the description of Abraham as one who "bestows free bounty and justice" (Gen. 18:19)—first bounty, then justice.[4]

19. Until Abraham made his way into the wider world, the Holy One was, if one dare say such a thing, sovereign only in heaven, for in referring to his earlier years, Abraham said, "The Lord, God of heaven, who took me from my father's house" (Gen. 24:7). But after Abraham made his way into the wider world, he was able to declare Him sovereign over both heaven and earth, as when Abraham said to Eliezer, "I will make thee swear by the Lord, the God of heaven and the God of earth" (Gen. 24:3).[5]

20. "And Abram went down to Egypt" (Gen. 12:10). The Holy One said: Go and tread out a path for your children.[6]

21. "And it came to pass, that when Abram was come into Egypt, the Egyptians beheld . . ." (Gen. 12:14). [Only Abram is mentioned as having come into Egypt]—where was Sarah? Abram put her in a box and locked her in it so that the Egyptians should not see her. When Abram reached the portals of Egypt, the customs people asked, "What are you carrying in this box?" He replied, "Barley." Said they, "You are carrying [something more valuable] wheat." "Very well," he replied, charge me the duty on wheat." "You are carrying pepper." "Charge me the duty on pepper." "You are carrying gold." "Charge me the duty on gold." "You are carrying silks." "Charge me the duty on silks." "You are carrying precious stones." "Charge me the duty on precious stones." They figured: If he did not have something of extraordinary worth in his possession, he would not have agreed to whatever duty was asked of him. So they said to him, "You will not stir from here until you open the box and show us what is inside."

When he opened the box, all of Egypt was illuminated by the radiance of Sarah's beauty.[7]

22. "And Abram went up out of Egypt. . . . And there was a strife between the herdsmen of Abram's cattle and the herdsmen of Lot's cattle" (Gen. 13:1 and 13:7). R. Berekhiah said in the name of R. Judah bar R. Simon: Abraham's cattle used to go out muzzled,[8] but Lot's cattle did not go out muzzled. When Abraham's herdsmen asked, "Since when is robbery permitted?" Lot's herdsmen replied, "You know that the Holy One said to Abraham: 'Unto thy seed have I given this Land' [Gen. 24:7]. But Abraham is a barren mule and cannot beget children. Soon he will die and his nephew Lot will be his heir. So if these cattle eat outside of Lot's fields, it is their own that they eat."

The Holy One then said to Lot's herdsmen: I did, to be sure, tell Abraham, "Unto thy seed have I given this Land." When? After the seven nations are uprooted from it. But now "the Canaanite and the Perizzite still dwell in the Land" (Gen. 13:7). Up to now, the right to the Land has been granted them.[9]

23. In the words "Who hath raised up those from the east?" (Isa. 41:2), Isaiah meant: Who raised—bestirred—the hearts of peoples of the east that they came [to the Land, and there] fell by the hand of Abraham?[10]

In going on to say, "Tzedek (Righteous) called him to His feet" (Isa. 41:2),[11] Isaiah implied that [it was Tzedek, the Righteous One], Life of all worlds, who illumined[12] Abraham's path wherever he went.

But R. Berekhiah said that, according to Isaiah, it was the planet Tzedek (Jupiter) that illumined Abraham's path.[13]

However, R. Reuben said that, according to Isaiah, it was righteousness (tzedek) that cried out and said,

1. Gen. R. 54:6.
2. The Hebrew *el olam* can be translated either "everlasting God" or "God of the world."
3. Sot 10a and En Yaakov, ad loc.
4. Gen. R. 49:4, 43:7 and 54:6.
5. Sif Deut., §313.
6. What is said in Scripture of the patriarchs intimates what is to happen to their descendants, the people of Israel. Gen. R. 40:6, B. BB 100a.
7. Gen. R. 40:5; Tanhuma, *Lekh Lekha*, §5; Tanhuma B, *Lekh Lekha*, §8, pp. 65–66.
8. So as not to graze in other people's fields.
9. Gen. R. 41:5.
10. See Gen. 14.
11. JV: "At whose step victory attendeth."
12. The commentator may associate the word *yikraehu* ("attendeth") with *ykr* ("brightness"): "The moon walking in brightness (*ykr*)" (Job 31:26).
13. Jupiter was Abraham's planet. See B. Shab 156b.

"If there is no Abraham, no one will do my bidding."[1]

"He giveth nations before him, and maketh him rule over kings; his sword maketh them as the dust, his bow as the driven stubble" (Isa. 41:2). R. Judah said: Abraham threw dust at the four kings, which turned into swords; stubble, which turned into arrows.

But R. Nehemiah objected: The text does not say, "He maketh dust [his sword]," but "Maketh them as the dust": the four kings threw swords at Abraham, which turned to dust, and shot arrows, which became stubble.

"He pursueth them and passeth on safely; the way with his feet he toucheth not" (Isa. 41:3). R. Nehemiah said in the name of R. Abbahu: The feet of Abraham and his companions were no more soiled by dust than the feet of one who walks from his house to the synagogue.

"And the king of Sodom went out to meet him" (Gen. 14:17). The king began, as it were, wagging his tail at Abraham, saying: Even as you went down into a fiery furnace and were saved, so did I descend into the bitumen[2] and was saved.

"At the Vale of Shaveh—the same is the King's Vale" (Gen. 14:17). In the name of R. Samuel bar Nahman, the sages said: There all the nations acting in concert (*hushvu*)[3] cut down cedars, made a large dais, seated Abraham on top of it, and extolled him, saying, " 'Hear us, lord; thou art ruler—god' [Gen. 23:6]. You are to be king over us! You are to be ruler over us! You are to be god over us!" Abraham replied, "The world is not without its [true] King—the world is not without its [true] God."[4]

24. "Fear not Abram, I am thy shield, thy reward shall be exceedingly great" (Gen. 15:1). R. Levi said: God spoke to him thus, because Abraham was filled with misgiving, saying to himself: Possibly there was a righteous or a God-fearing man among those hosts I slew. Abraham's misgiving may be illustrated by the parable of a straw merchant who, while passing the king's orchard, saw a pile of thorns. He descended [from his wagon] and picked it up. At that moment the king looked out and caught sight of him, whereupon the straw merchant tried to hide. The king asked, "Why are you trying to hide? How many laborers would I have required to gather those thorns! Now that you have gathered them, come and receive your reward." So, too, the Holy One said to Abraham, "The hosts you slew were thorns, meant to be cut down."[5]

25. "And the Lord appeared unto him in the terebinths of Mamre" (Gen. 18:1). When the Holy One told Abraham to circumcise himself, he went and consulted his three friends, Aner, Eshkol, and Mamre. Aner said to him, "You are now about one hundred years old—are you going to inflict such pain upon yourself?" Eshkol said, "Why should you make yourself readily identifiable in battle among your enemies?" But Mamre said, "Your God, who stood by you in a fiery furnace, in your battle against the four kings, and during famine—will you not heed Him in this matter?"

The Holy One said to Mamre, "You gave Abraham good advice that he circumcise himself. As you live, I will appear to him neither in the palace of Aner nor in the palace of Eshkol—only in your palace." Hence, "the Lord appeared unto him in Mamre's [palace built out of] terebinths" (Gen. 18:1).[6]

26. "And the Lord appeared unto him . . . on a day that was very hot" (Gen. 18:1). Why did God make that day very hot? R. Hama bar Hanina explained: It was the third day after Abraham's circumcision,[7] and the Holy One came to ask how Abraham was; so He drew the sun out of its sheath [to make the day so hot], that the righteous Abraham would not be troubled by attending to wayfarers. [Since no one came because of the heat], Abraham sent out Eliezer [to look around]. He went out but found no wayfarers. So, in accord with the proverb "Never trust a slave," Abraham said, "I do not believe you," and he himself went out. "And he lifted up his eyes, and looked, and lo, three men stood by him" (Gen. 18:2). What kind of people were these three [who were able to stir abroad on such a hot day]? They were the angels Michael, Raphael, and Gabriel. Michael came to announce to Sarah [that she was to bear a child]; Raphael, to heal Abraham; and Gabriel, to overturn Sodom.[8]

27. "And Abraham ran after the calf" (Gen. 18:7).[9] The calf had run away from Abraham and entered the cave of Machpelah. When Abraham entered after it, he saw Adam and his mate lying asleep on couches, lamps burning above them, and their bodies giving forth a goodly odor, sweet in savor. This is how it came about that Abraham was eager to have the cave of Machpelah as a burying place.[10]

Abraham's Prayer and Sodom's Sins

28. "Abraham drew near and said: 'The Judge of all the earth must not exercise justice too strictly' " (Gen. 18:23 and 18:25).[11] According to R. Levi, the verse means that Abraham said: If You seek to have a world, strict justice cannot be exercised; and if You seek strict justice, there will be no world. Do You expect to take hold of the well's

1. Three opinions are stated here concerning the meaning of *tzedek* in Isa. 41:2: (1) An anonymous opinion: God, the Righteous One, brought Abraham near Him, to His feet, so to speak, and thus illumined Abraham's path. (2) R. Berekhiah's: Abraham's natural talent, his affinity with Tzedek, the planet Jupiter, illumined a path for his feet. (3) R. Reuben's: Righteousness (*tzedek*), personified in the verse, required Abraham's presence; so that its feet, so to speak, might be advanced in the world through Abraham's righteous deeds.
2. He fell into a bitumen pit. See Gen. 14:10.
3. *Shaveh*, ("equal") is thus taken to imply unanimity.
4. Gen. R. 42:5.
5. Gen. R. 44:5.
6. Gen. R. 42:8.
7. When he was particularly weak. See Gen. 34:25.
8. B. BM 86b.
9. JV: "And Abraham ran unto the herd."
10. PRE 36.
11. JV: "Shall not the Judge of all the earth do justly?"

rope at both ends? You desire a world and You also desire justice? You can have only one of the two. If You do not relent a little, the world will not endure.[1]

29. "Peradventure the fifty will be lacking—there will be only five" (Gen. 18:28).[2] R. Hiyya bar Abba said: In his plea, Abraham was about to come down at once from fifty to five. But the Holy One said to Abraham, "Go back to the fifty you mentioned first [and reduce gradually the number of the righteous whose presence would save the cities]." The matter may be illustrated by R. Levi's parable of a water clock full of water:[3] only as long as it contains water may the defending counsel plead. However, when the judge wishes the defending counsel to continue his defense, he will say: Add water to the water clock.[4]

30. Our masters taught: The people of Sodom were arrogant because of the bounty the Holy One had bestowed upon them. How is Sodom described in Scripture? "As for [Sodom's] earth, out of it cometh bread [in abundance]. The stones of it are the place of sapphires; and it hath dust of gold. Its paths no bird of prey knoweth, and no falcon's eye hath seen" (Job 28:6–7). There was not a path in Sodom that did not have the foliage of seven trees over it, each shading the one below it: foliage of the vine, fig, pomegranate, walnut and almond, apple, and peach, so that each path was fully sheltered. R. Levi said in the name of R. Yohanan: There is a species of falcon [so keen-sighted] that even when it soars eighteen *mil* in the sky, it can sight its food. Yet when that falcon stood upon Sodom's trees, it could not see the ground below because of the massive foliage of those trees.

More. When a man would go to a gardener and say to him, "Give me an *issar*'s worth of greens," and the gardener would rinse the greens in water, he would shake down gold flakes out of the soil clinging to their roots.

So the [inhabitants of] Sodom said, "We live in peace and plenty—food can be got from our land, gold and silver can be mined from our land, precious stones and pearls can be obtained from our land. What need have we to look after wayfarers, who come to us only to deprive us? Come, let us see to it that the duty of entertaining foot travelers be forgotten in our land, as is said, "They who keep aloof from [wayfaring] men, turning away [in disdain] from them, had come to forget utterly [their duty toward] foot travelers" (Job 28:4).[5]

So the Holy One said: Because of the bounty I bestowed upon you, you would make the very memory of wayfarers' feet forgotten in your midst—therefore I will cause the memory of [anything good in you] to be utterly forgotten in the world.

Rava expounded: What is meant by the verse "How long will ye imagine mischief against men, all of you plan murder by devices such as a leaning wall or a tottering fence" (Ps. 62:4)? The verse intimates that the Sodomites would cast envious eyes upon a wealthy man. So they would seat him in the shadow of a leaning wall, push the wall down on him, and then seize his money.

What is meant by "In the dark they dig into houses, which they had marked for themselves in the daytime" (Job 24:16)? This verse likewise shows that the Sodomites used to cast envious eyes upon men of wealth. In order to mark the exact place where the wealthy men stored their valuables, Sodomites would deposit their precious scented oil (ostensibly for safekeeping) with the wealthy men, who would store this oil with their own valuables. Then later, in the dark of night, these Sodomites would come and, like dogs, sniff out the oil's whereabouts, dig there, and haul away the wealthy men's valuables.

[Their rules were calculated to do injury to the poor.] Thus they said, "He who has an ox is obliged to render one day's herding service; but he who has no ox has to give two day's service." It happened that an orphan, a widow's son, was made to care for the oxen of many owners. To get even, he proceeded to kill all the oxen. Then he said, "He who had one ox may take one hide, but he who had none is to take two hides." When asked, "How does such a rule make sense?" he replied, "The latter rule is no more twisted than the former rule."

When a bricklayer had set out a row of bricks, the inhabitants of Sodom would come and each of them help himself to a brick. When accused, each would say, "But I took only one."

When a greengrocer spread out garlic or onions [to season them], the inhabitants of Sodom would come and each of them steal one; when accused, each would say, "But I took only one."

In Sodom there were four judges: Shakrai ("liar"); Shakrurai ("archdeceiver"); Zayyefai ("forger"); and Matzle-dina ("perverter of justice").

When a man struck his neighbor's wife and caused her to miscarry, the husband would be told, "Give her to this man to impregnate her again."

When a man cut off the ear of another man's donkey, the aggrieved owner would be told, "Give the donkey to this man to keep until its ear grows back."

When a man wounded another, the victim would be told, "Pay the man a fee for having bled you."

When a man crossed a bridge, he would be charged four *zuz*; but if he waded through the water [to avoid the toll] he would be charged eight *zuz*.

It happened that a launderer came to Sodom and was told, "Pay four *zuz*." When he said, "But I waded through the water," he was told, "In that case, pay eight." When he refused, they roughed him up until he bled. Then he appeared before Sodom's judges, who ruled: Pay the men of Sodom a fee for having bled you, besides the eight *zuz* for having waded through the water.

When Eliezer, Abraham's servant, happened to be in Sodom, he was roughed up until he bled. So he appeared before a judge, who ruled: Pay the man a fee for having bled you. At that, Eliezer took a stone, wounded the judge with it, and said: Pay the fee you owe me for bleeding you to this man; as for my own money, it will remain in its place.

Among the people of Sodom, it was agreed that a

---

1. Gen. R. 39:6 and 49:9; PR 29/30a (YJS 2:576).
2. JV: "Peradventure there shall lack five of the fifty righteous."
3. Used in courts of justice for measuring the time allowed for argument.
4. Gen. R. 49:12.
5. So apparently the commentator construes the verse. JV: "They are forgotten of the foot that passeth by; they hang afar from men, they swing to and fro."

man who invited a stranger to a banquet should be punished by being stripped of his cloak. Eliezer happened to come to Sodom when a feast was about to take place, and of course no one invited him to join them. But since he wanted to eat, he sat down at the end of the table. When asked, "Who invited you?" he whispered to the man sitting next to him, "You invited me." The man thought: If they hear that I invited a stranger, I will be stripped of my garment. So he picked up his cloak and ran out. Eliezer did the same thing to each and every one at the table, until they all fled. Then he ate his fill of the meal [in peace].

In Sodom they had a bed on which wayfarers were made to lie. If a wayfarer was too long for the bed, they cut him down to fit it. If he was too short, they stretched his limbs until he filled it. When Eliezer came to Sodom and was told, "Come on up and lie down on this bed," he replied, "Since the day my mother died, I vowed never to lie down on a bed."

When a poor man came to the land of Sodom, each Sodomite would give him a denar with the Sodomite's name inscribed on it, but not one of them would sell him a morsel of bread to eat. Eventually, when the poor man died of hunger, each Sodomite would come to claim his denar. There was a maiden in Sodom who once brought a morsel of bread concealed in her pitcher to a poor man. When three days passed and the poor man did not die, the reason for his staying alive became clear. The Sodomites smeared the maiden with honey and placed her on a rooftop, so that bees came and stung her to death. Of this maiden's anguish, Scripture says, "The cry of Sodom and Gomorrah is great (*rabbah*)" (Gen. 18:20)—the cry was so great because of what befell that maiden (*rivah*).[1]

31. It once happened that two maidens went down to draw water from a well. One asked the other, "Why is your face so sickly?" The other answered, "We have no food left, and we are about to die." What did the first one do? She filled her own pitcher with flour, and the two exchanged pitchers, each taking the other's. When the Sodomites became aware of this, they seized the one who saved the other's life and burned her alive. The Holy One said, "Even if I wished to remain silent, justice for that maiden does not allow Me to do so." Hence: "Whether they have done according to her cry" (Gen. 18:21)—the cry of that maiden.[2]

32. R. Judah said: It was proclaimed in Sodom, "He who sustains a stranger or a poor and needy person with a morsel of bread is to be burned alive."

Lot's daughter Pelotit was married to one of Sodom's notables. Seeing a poor man languishing in the town square, she felt sorry for him. What did she do? Every day when she went down to draw water, she would put into her pitcher some of every kind of food she had in her house, and thus sustained the poor man. The people of Sodom kept wondering: How does this poor man manage to stay alive? Finally they figured out the reason, and they brought Pelotit out to be burned.

She prayed, "God of the universe, exact justice and judgment in my behalf from the Sodomites." Her cry rose up before the throne of glory. The Holy One said, "I will go down and see whether they have done according to her cry" (Gen. 18:21)—if the people of Sodom have indeed done according to the cry of this young woman, I will turn the city's foundations over to the top and the city's top to the bottom.[3]

33. Sodom had five principal judges: Follower of False Principles, Archliar, Archvillain, Perverter of Justice, and Flayer of Human Beings. As chief judge, Lot's status was higher than that of the others. When he said something that pleased the other judges, they would say to him, "Go further" (Gen. 19:9), take an even higher rank; but when he said something that displeased him, they would say, "The fellow settled among us as a stranger, and he would lay down the law for us!" (ibid.).[4]

34. R. Jeremiah ben Eliezer said: The real prosperity of the Sodomites lasted only fifty-two years, during twenty-five of which the Holy One made mountains tremble because of them and caused quakes because of them, so that they might resolve on penitence—but they did not so resolve. Hence Scripture: "He moved mountains, yet they took no cognizance" (Job 9:5), so that in the end "He overturned them in His anger" (ibid.).[5]

35. "But his wife looked back from behind him, and she became a pillar of salt" (Gen. 19:26)—because, R. Isaac said, she sinned through salt. On the night that the angels visited Lot, Lot said to his wife, "Give these guests a bit of salt." But she replied, "[Besides entertaining guests], is it your wish to introduce into Sodom another vile custom [that of seasoning their food]?" What did she do? She went around among all her neighbors, saying to each, "Give me salt—we have guests," intending thereby to have the townspeople become aware of the presence of guests in her home [and penalize Lot for it]. Hence, "she herself became a pillar of salt."[6]

Abraham's Progeny

36. "So shall thy seed be" (Gen. 15:5). R. Levi said in the name of R. Yohanan: How is God's promise to be understood? By the parable of a man who set out on a journey and traveled through the wilderness a day, two days, three days, up to ten days, without finding either town or wayside inn, either tree or water or any living creature. After traveling ten days,[7] he espied a tree in the distance and thought: There may be water under it. When

1. B. Sanh 109b; Num. R. 9:24; Lev. R. 5:2; Gen. R. 42:5; and Rashi, ad loc.
2. Gen. R. 49:6; Yalkut, *Va-yera*, §18.
3. PRE 25.
4. The two parts of the verse appear to be inconsistent; hence the comment. Gen. R. 50:3.
5. Gen. R. 49:6.
6. Gen. R. 51:5 and 50:4.
7. The ten days allude to the ten generations between Noah and Abraham.

he reached the tree, he found that it indeed stood over a spring. He saw how beautiful it was, how delicious its fruit, how graceful its branches, how tempting its shade. So he sat down and cooled himself in the tree's shade, partook of its fruit, drank at the spring, and felt with pleasure that his spirit was refreshed. When he rose to go, he addressed himself to the tree: Tree, O tree, what blessing can I bestow upon you, and what parting word shall I offer you? That your wood may be fine? It is fine. That your shade be pleasant? It is already pleasant. That your branches be graceful? They are graceful. That your fruit be delicious? It is delicious. That a spring issue from beneath your roots? Such a spring already issues from beneath your roots. That you stand in a desirable spot? You already stand in such a spot. How then shall I bless you? Only that all the seedlings arising from you shall be like you.

So it was when the Holy One created the world. Twenty generations came and went, but no good was found in them. Not a single righteous man rose up among them[1] until after twenty generations. It was then that the Holy One espied Abraham hidden away in Chaldea.

The Holy One said: How is one to know whether he will have the power to stand firm? But after he was cast into a fiery furnace, sanctified God's Name, and stood up to the test, at once the Holy One brought him nearer [to Himself, that is], to the Land of Israel. There Abraham set to and built an inn, where he gave food to wayfarers and brought men beneath the wings of the Presence, making known the glory of the Holy One throughout the world.

Then the Holy One said: Abraham, Abraham, what can I say to you or what blessing can I bestow upon you? That in My Presence you be deemed perfectly righteous? That Sarah your wife be deemed righteous in My Presence? Even in My Presence, both you and Sarah are so deemed. That all the members of your household be deemed righteous? Even in My Presence, they are so deemed. How then shall I bless you? Only that all children who spring from you be like you.[2]

37. "Who would have said unto Abraham that Sarah would give children suck?" (Gen. 21:7). How can it be asserted that Sarah suckled more than one child? R. Levi explained: On the day that Abraham weaned his son Isaac, he made a great feast, but the peoples of the world ridiculed him, saying, "Look at this old man and old woman who have picked up a foundling from the street and say, 'He is our own son,' and now they have the gall to make a great feast in an attempt to establish so preposterous a claim." What did our father Abraham do then? He invited all the notables of that generation, even as our mother Sarah invited their wives. Each woman brought her child with her, but not the wetnurse. A miracle was then wrought for our mother Sarah—her nipples poured out milk like two jets of water, so that she was able to suckle all these children. But people continued to scoff. "Even assuming that Sarah could give birth at the age of ninety, is it conceivable that Abraham, at the age of one hundred, could beget children?" At once the lineaments of Isaac's visage changed and became like Abraham's. Then all the people cried out as one, "Abraham did beget Isaac" (Gen. 25:19).[3]

38. Our mother Sarah was exceedingly modest, so that our father Abraham had to say to her, "This is not a time for modesty. To hallow God's Name, uncover your breast, that all may be aware of the miracles the Holy One has begun to perform." Sarah uncovered her breast, and her nipples poured out milk like two jets of water. Noble ladies came forward to have their children suckled by Sarah, saying, "We do not merit having our children suckled on the milk of such a righteous woman."[4]

39. "And Abraham made a great feast" (Gen. 21:8). R. Judah bar R. Simon said: Not "a great feast" but a feast for great personages—Og and all other great ones like him were there. At that time Og was asked, "Did you not use to say, 'Abraham is like a barren mule and cannot beget a child'?" Nevertheless, when Og looked at Isaac, he was able to reply, "So this gift given to Abraham—what's it worth? Is not the creature a puny thing? Were I to put my finger upon him, I could crush him." The Holy One said to Og, "How dare you belittle My gift? As you live, you will see thousands and myriads issue from his children's children." And it was at the hands of Isaac's descendants that this evil man [Og] was to fall.[5]

40. "God hath given me occasion for joy; everyone that heareth will rejoice with me" (Gen. 21:6). R. Samuel bar R. Isaac was quoted as speculating: If one person—let us call him Reuben—rejoices, why should another person—let us call him Simeon—rejoice with him? So also, if Sarah was remembered [and she conceived], why should others rejoice with her? However, when our mother Sarah was remembered, many other barren women were remembered with her, many sick people were healed, many deaf people gained their hearing, many blind people were given sight, many madmen were cured of their madness—an amnesty was granted to the world.

R. Levi said: [At Isaac's birth] the Holy One added brilliance to the luminaries. Accordingly, when Isaac was born, all—heaven and earth, sun and moon, stars and planets—rejoiced.

"And Abraham called the name of his son . . . Isaac (Yitzhak)" (Gen. 21:3). The name Yitzhak signifies that at his birth Torah's Law went forth (*yatza hok*) to the world, went forth as God's bounty to the world.[6]

---

1. The first ten generations, from Cain until Noah, were altogether wicked. The next ten, from Noah until Abraham, had not one among them worthy of preparing mankind to receive the Torah and make the world fit to have the Presence abide in it. Mah.
2. Num. R. 2:12; B. Ta 5b; Tde 25 (JPS, pp. 522–23).
3. B. BM 87a.
4. Gen. R. 53:9; Yalkut, *Va-yera*, §93.
5. Gen. R. 53:10; Deut. R. 1:25.
6. Had Sarah named her child, the name might have signified "laughter" (Gen. 18:12). But since Abraham named him, a serious, not derisive, significance is given to the name. The word *hok* may mean "law," as well as "portion, gift." Gen. R. 53:7; Yalkut, *Va-yera*, §92.

41. "Wherefore she said to Abraham: 'Cast out this bondwoman and her son' " (Gen. 21:10). R. Akiva expounded: The verse implies that Sarah saw Ishmael build altars, catch locusts,[1] and offer them with incense to an idol. So Sarah said, "It may be that my son also will learn such practices and be inclined to such worship, and in the end Heaven's Name will be profaned." But Abraham replied, "After bestowing high status upon a person, are we to demean him? After we declared Hagar mistress and had her enter into a role of such importance, are we now to expel her from our house? What will people say of us? Would not Heaven's Name be profaned by our action?" Sarah replied, "Since you say that the Name would be profaned through Hagar's banishment, let Him who is everywhere decide between you and me."

R. Simeon ben Yohai commented: This passage is one of four that R. Akiva expounded but that I do not expound as he did, and what I say appears to me to be more accurate. I say: God forbid that in the household of that righteous man there were ever such goings-on. Is it conceivable that in the household of the one of whom God had said, "For I know him" (Gen. 18:19)—is it conceivable that in his household idolatry was practiced? Rather, Ishmael's "making sport" (Gen. 21:9) [which incensed Sarah and signifies mockery or ridicule] has to do [not with idolatry but] with inheriting Abraham's estate. For after Isaac was born to our father Abraham, everyone rejoiced, saying, "A son is born to Abraham! A son is born to Abraham! He will inherit [two portions in] the world." Ishmael responded with ridicule, "Don't be foolish, utterly foolish—I am the firstborn, and mine is the right to inherit the double portion."[2]

42. R. Azariah said in the name of R. Levi: Ishmael suggested to Isaac, "Come, let us test our mettle in the field." Then Ishmael took a bow and arrows, and shot them in Isaac's direction, pretending that he was merely making sport. When Sarah saw such "making sport," she told Abraham about it.[3]

43. "And Abraham rose up early in the morning . . . and sent her away" (Gen. 21:14). Abraham took a wheeled water tub and tied it to Hagar's loins so that it would be pulled behind her, in order that whenever Abraham wished to see his son Ishmael, he might readily make out the direction in which Hagar and Ishmael had gone.

Presently Ishmael settled in the wilderness of Paran and took for himself a wife from the plains of Moab—her name was Aissa.

At the end of three years, Abraham went to see his son Ishmael in the wilderness of Paran, after first swearing to Sarah that he would not dismount from his camel at the place where Ishmael was living. Abraham reached there at midday, found Ishmael's wife, and asked her, "Where is Ishmael?" She replied, "He and his mother went to bring some fruits and brooms[4] from the wilderness." Abraham said, "Give me a little water and a little bread, for I am weary from the journey through the wilderness." She replied, "No bread, no water." Abraham said, "When your husband Ishmael returns, tell him, "An old man from the land of Canaan came to see you and said to tell you, 'The household of this house is not in good repair.' " When Ishmael returned, his wife gave him the message—whereupon he divorced her. Then his mother sent for a woman from her father's house in the land of Egypt. Her name was Fatima, and Ishmael took her as his wife.

At the end of another three years, Abraham went again to see his son Ishmael, after once more swearing to Sarah that he would not dismount from the camel at the place where Ishmael lived. He reached there at midday, found Ishmael's wife, and asked her, "Where is Ishmael?" She replied, "He and his mother have gone to graze the camels in the wilderness." He said, "Give me a little bread and a little water, for I am weary from the journey through the wilderness." She brought these out and gave them to him. Then Abraham entreated the Holy One in his son's behalf, and Ishmael's house was filled with all manner of good things. When Ishmael came back, his wife told him what had happened. Then Ishmael realized that his father still loved him.[5]

The Binding of Isaac

44. Had the Holy One asked our father Abraham for even the apple of his eye, Abraham would have given it to Him, indeed would have given Him not only the apple of his eye—would have given Him his very soul.[6]

45. "And it came to pass after these things that God tried Abraham" (Gen. 22:1). After what things? According to R. Yohanan, citing R. Yose ben Zimra, after the things Satan had to say. [Following the feast given] upon the "child's having grown and being weaned" (Gen. 21:8), Satan spoke up to the Holy One, "Master of the universe, out of the entire feast that this old man, upon whom You bestowed fruit of the womb at the age of one hundred—out of the entire feast he prepared, could he not have spared, say, one turtledove, one fledgling, as an offering to You?"

The Holy One replied, "Is it not true that Abraham prepared the feast in honor of his son? Still, if I say to him, 'Sacrifice your son to Me,' he will sacrifice him at once." Satan said, "Try him." At once "God tried Abraham."

"And He said: 'Take, I beg thee (*na*), thy son' " (Gen. 22:2).[7] R. Simeon bar Abba said: The word *na* can imply only entreaty. The matter may be illustrated by the parable of a king of flesh and blood who had to face many wars,

---

1. Being still very young, those were the only living things he could catch.
2. See Deut. 21:17. Tos Sot 5:6; Gen. R. 53:11.
3. Gen. R. 53:11; PRE 30.
4. Reading with David Luria not *temarim* ("dates") but *retamim* ("brooms").
5. PRE 30; MhG Gen. pp. 339–40.
6. Sif Deut., §313.
7. JV: "Take now thy son."

in all of which he had one mighty warrior who invariably achieved victory. In the course of time, he faced a war particularly severe. The king said to the mighty warrior, "I beg you, stand to with me in this war, that mortals should not say, 'The earlier wars were of no substance.' "

Likewise, the Holy One said to Abraham, "I have tried you with many tests, and you have stood up to them all. Now, I beg you, stand to with Me in this test, that it not be said, 'The earlier ones were of no substance.' "

"Take now thy son" (Gen. 22:2). Abraham: "I have two sons [which one do you mean]?" God: "Thine only son" (ibid.). Abraham: "[Both are only sons]—Isaac is the only son I have from his mother, and Ishmael is the only son I have from her who is his mother." God: "The son whom thou lovest" (ibid.). Abraham: "Master of the universe, are there separate compartments in one's inmost self for love? I love both of them." God: "Very well, then—Isaac." Why did God drag out His command to such length? So that Abraham's mind might not be stunned [by such a heartrending demand].

"And offer him up there for a burnt offering upon one of the mountains" (Gen. 22:2). Abraham asked, "Which mountain?" God: "Wherever you see My glory standing and waiting for you."

Abraham meditated in his heart, saying: What am I to do? Shall I tell Sarah? Women tend to think lightly of God's commands. If I do not tell her and simply take off with him—afterward, when she does not see him, she will strangle herself. What did he do? He said to Sarah, "Prepare food and drink for us, and we will rejoice today." She asked, "Why today more than other days? Besides, what is the rejoicing about?" Abraham: "Old people like ourselves, to whom a son was born in our old age—have we not cause to rejoice?" So she went and prepared the food. During the meal, Abraham said to Sarah, "You know, when I was only three years old, I became aware of my Maker, but this lad, growing up, has not yet been taught [about his Creator]. Now, there is a place far away where youngsters are taught [about Him]. Let me take him there." Sarah: "Take him in peace."

"And Abraham rose up early in the morning" (Gen. 22:3). Why early in the morning? Because he said: It may be that Sarah will reconsider what she said yesterday and refuse to let Isaac go. So I'll get up early and go while she is still asleep. Moreover, it is best that no one see us.[1]

"And he [himself] saddled his ass" (Gen. 22:3). Love disregards dignity! How many menservants, how many maidservants did that righteous man have, yet he himself saddled his ass in his eagerness [to do God's will].

"And took two of his young men with him" (Gen. 22:3). These were Ishmael and Eliezer. He said: While I am offering up Isaac, these two will take care of our gear. At once, rivalry set in between Ishmael and Eliezer. Ishmael said, "Now that my father is about to bring his son Isaac as a burnt offering, I, being my father's firstborn, will be heir." Eliezer replied, "But he has exiled you and sent you into the wilderness! Whereas I am the servant who waits on him day and night—I am to be his heir." But the holy spirit replied to both of them, "Neither the one nor the other is to be the heir."

"And rose up, and went" (Gen. 22:3). On the way, Satan ran ahead of Abraham, appeared before him in the guise of an old man, and asked, "Where are you going?" Abraham: "To pray." Satan: "Why should one going to pray have fire and a knife in his hand, and kindling wood on his shoulder?" Abraham: "We may abide there a day or two, and we will have to slaughter an animal, bake bread, and eat." Satan: "Old man, do you think I was not there when the Holy One said to you, 'Take now thy son'? Old man, you are out of your mind. A son who was given you at the age of one hundred—and you are setting out to kill him!" Abraham: "Even so." Satan: "And should He test you even more severely, will you still stand firm?" Abraham: "Yes, even more and more severely." Satan: "But tomorrow He will call you murderer for shedding the blood of your son." Abraham: "Even so."

Seeing that his efforts were in vain, Satan left Abraham and, disguising himself as a young man, stood at Isaac's right and said, "Where are you going?" Isaac: "To study Torah." Satan: "While still alive or after your death?" Isaac: "Is there a man who can study after his death?" Satan: "O hapless son of a hapless mother! How many fasts did your mother fast, how many prayers did she utter until at last you were born! And now this old man has gone mad in his old age and is about to slit your throat." Isaac: "Nevertheless, I shall not deviate from the will of my Maker and from the bidding of my father." Satan: "If so, shall all those fine tunics your mother made [for you] become a legacy for Ishmael, for him who hates your family?[2] Apparently you give no thought [to what would follow upon your death]." As the proverb has it, "If the whole word does not enter [the listener's mind], half of it does." For Isaac turned to his father and said: "Father, listen to what this one is saying to me!" Abraham replied, "Pay no attention to him!"

When Satan saw that neither Abraham nor Isaac heeded what he had to say, he proceeded to turn himself into a wide stream. At once [having to cross the stream], Abraham went down into the water until it reached to his knees and then said to his lads: Follow me. They went down after him. Halfway across the stream, the water came up to his neck. In that instant, Abraham lifted his eyes heavenward and said: Master of the universe, You chose me. You appeared to me, saying: "I am unique and you are unique. Through you shall My Name become known in My world—so bring your son Isaac before Me as a burnt offering." And I did not hold back. As You see, I am occupied with your bidding. But now "I am come into deep waters" (Ps. 69:3). If either I or Isaac were to drown, who will fulfill Your commands, and by whom will the uniqueness of Your Name be proclaimed? The Holy One replied:

1. They may find out what he is about to do and seek to dissuade him.

2. Or, "All the things done by your mother against Ishmael have been for nought, and he who hates your family will be the heir?" See Gen. R. TA, p. 598, which quotes Joseph B. Schönak, *Ha-Mashbir* (Jerusalem, 1858).

As you live! My Name shall be proclaimed in the world through you.

The Holy One rebuked the stream and it dried up, so that they found themselves standing on dry land.

What did Satan do? He said to Abraham, "This is what I heard from behind the [heavenly] curtain: 'A lamb will be the burnt offering—Isaac is not to be the burnt offering.' " But such is the punishment of a liar—even when he tells the truth, no one listens. [Hence Abraham gave Satan no heed.]

"Then on the third day Abraham lifted up his eyes, and saw" (Gen. 22:4). Why on the third day? Why not on the first, or on the second? That the nations of the world might not say: God deranged Abraham so that he cut his son's throat.

"And saw the place from afar" (Gen. 22:4). [But since the place was hollowed out], how could it have been seen from afar?[1] The place was originally hollowed out. But when the Holy One decided to cause His Presence to dwell there and to make it His sanctuary, He said: It is not fitting for a king to dwell in a valley, but only on a high and lofty mountain, resplendent in beauty and visible to all. So He beckoned the valley's environs to come together and provide a suitable place for the Presence.

Then Abraham asked Isaac, "Do you see what I see?" Isaac replied, "I see a mountain, radiant in majesty, with a [mysterious] cloud hovering over it." Abraham asked the two lads, "Do you see anything?" They replied, "We see nothing other than stretches of wilderness." Abraham: "O people the like of asses! As the ass sees but does not comprehend, so it is with you. 'Abide ye here, people like the ass' " (Gen. 22:5).[2]

"Abraham took the wood of the burnt offering and laid it upon Isaac his son" (Gen. 22:6), as upon one [condemned] who is made to carry the cross upon his shoulder.

"And Isaac said . . . 'Behold, the fire and the wood, but where is the lamb for the burnt offering?' " (Gen. 22:7). In that instant, fear and dread terror fell upon Isaac, when he saw in Abraham's hand nothing at all fit for an offering. So, suspecting what was intended, he asked, "Where is the lamb for the burnt offering?" Abraham replied, "The Holy One has chosen you." Isaac said, "If He has so chosen, my life is given to Him, but I grieve for my mother." Nevertheless, "they went both of them together" (Gen. 22:8)—one to bind, the other to be bound; one to slaughter, the other to be slaughtered.

"And they came to the place" (Gen. 22:9)—both carrying stones [for the altar], both carrying the fire, both carrying the wood. For all that, Abraham acted like one making wedding preparations for his son, and Isaac like one making a wedding bower for himself.

Then Isaac said, "Father, hurry, do the will of your Maker, burn me into a fine ash, then take the ash to my mother and leave it with her, and whenever she looks at it she will say, 'This is my son, whom his father has slaughtered.' . . . Father, what will you do in your old age [without me]?" Abraham replied, "My son, we know that we can survive you for but a short time. He who comforted us in the past will comfort us until the day we die."

When Abraham was about to begin the sacrifice, Isaac said, "Father, bind my hands and my feet, for the urge to live is so willful that when I see the knife coming at me, I may flinch involuntarily [causing the knife to cut improperly] and thus disqualify myself as an offering. So I beg you, bind me in such a way that no blemish will befall me." So Abraham "bound his son well" (Gen. 22:9). Then Isaac said to Abraham, "Father, don't tell Mother about this while she is standing over a pit or on a rooftop, for she might throw herself down and be killed."

"And he placed him on the altar" (Gen. 22:9). Abraham's eyes were directed at Isaac's, and Isaac's at the heaven of heavens. Tears were flowing from Abraham's eyes, until his entire body was all but afloat in them. He took the knife in order to cut Isaac's throat deeply enough so that a quarter of a *log* of blood would issue from him.[3] At that instant Satan appeared and shoved Abraham's arm aside, so that the knife fell out of his hand. When he reached out to pick it up, his mouth fell wide open with weeping as a great cry of anguish erupted from him. Then, his eyes blinking frantically, he looked up to the Presence and pleaded in a rising voice, "I lift mine eyes to the mountains; whence will my help come?" (Ps. 121:1). At that, the Holy One appeared above the angels and flung open the firmament. Isaac lifted up his eyes, and, as he beheld the chambers of the chariot, he trembled and shuddered. The ministering angels stood in rows upon rows, crying and weeping, as they said to one another, "Behold, one who is unique is about to slaughter, and one also unique is about to be slaughtered. Master of the universe, the oath 'Thus shall be thy seed' [Gen. 15:5]—what is to become of it?" The Holy One said to the angel Michael, "Why are you standing still? Do not let Abraham go on!" "Then the angel of the Lord called unto him out of heaven, and said: 'Abraham, Abraham,' " (Gen. 22:11), twice, as one who cries out in distress, "What [dreadful] thing are you about to do?"

When Abraham turned his face toward the angel, the angel said again, "What are you about to do? 'Do not lay thy hand upon the lad!' " (Gen. 22:12). Abraham asked, "Who are you?" Michael replied, "I am an angel." Abraham: "When the Holy One told me to offer my son, He Himself spoke to me; so too, if He now wishes something else, He Himself should speak to me."

At once the Holy One flung open the firmament, as well as the thick cloud [covering it], and said, "By Myself I swear" (Gen. 22:16). Abraham replied, "You have sworn, and I too swear that I will not go down from this altar until I say all that I need to say." God: "Say it." Abraham: "Did you not say to me, 'Count the stars . . . so shall thy seed be' (Gen. 15:5)?" The Holy One: "Yes."

---

1. In Gen. 22:2, Moriah is spoken of as "land," presumably not elevated; in 2 Chron. 3:1, it is described as "mount." In the comment that follows, the inconsistency is explained by assuming that Moriah had been lowland, but because God was to appear there, the land (*mora yah*), in reverence of God, elevated itself to the height of a mountain. See Yalkut, *Va-yera*, §100, and *Zayit Raanan*, ad loc.

2. JV: "Abide ye here with the ass." But by a slight change in vowels, the word *im* ("with") may be read *am* ("people").

3. The amount of blood required for ritually valid *shehitah*.

Abraham: "Out of whom?" God: "Out of Isaac." Abraham: "When You commanded me to sacrifice Isaac, I should have replied: Yesterday You told me, 'In Isaac shall thy seed be called' [Gen. 21:12]; now You say to me, 'Offer him there for a burnt offering' [Gen. 22:2]. Nevertheless, I restrained my impulse and did not reply as I should have done. Even so now [I say to You], When Isaac's children shall sin and find themselves in distress, be You mindful on their behalf of the binding of Isaac; let it be reckoned in Your presence as though his ash were in fact heaped upon the altar—be then filled with compassion for his children, forgive them, and redeem them from their distress." The Holy One replied, "You had your say, and now I will have Mine. Isaac's descendants will sin in My very presence, and I will have to judge them on New Year's Day. However, should they implore Me to seek out some merit on their behalf, and to remember on their behalf the binding of Isaac, let them blow in My presence the horn of this creature." Abraham: "The horn of what creature?" God: "Turn around." At once "Abraham lifted up his eyes, and looked, and behold a ram" (Gen. 22:13).

R. Eliezer said: The ram came from the mountains, where he had been grazing. R. Joshua differed: An angel brought him from the Garden of Eden, where he had been grazing beneath the tree of life and drinking out of the waters that passed under it, and the fragrance of that ram went forth throughout the world. When was the ram placed in the Garden? During twilight at the end of the six days of creation.

Throughout that day, Abraham saw the ram become entangled in a tree, break loose, and go free; become entangled in a bush, break loose, and go free; then again become entangled in a thicket, break loose, and go free. The Holy One said, "Abraham, even so will your children be entangled in many kinds of sin and trapped within successive kingdoms—from Babylon to Media, from Media to Greece, from Greece to Edom." Abraham asked, "Master of the universe, will it be forever thus?" God replied, "In the end they will be redeemed at [the sound of] the horns of this ram, as is said, 'The Lord shall blow the horn [shofar] when He goes forth in the whirlwinds at Teman [Edom]' " (Zech. 9:4).[1]

46. R. Zechariah said: The ram that had been created [for this purpose] at the twilight [of the sixth day of creation][2] was running to and fro [in its eagerness] to be offered in place of Isaac, but Samael [Satan] kept blocking him in order to make Abraham's [substitute] offering impossible, with the result that both the ram's horns got entangled in the branches of a tree. What did that ram do then? It stretched out its foreleg to tap Abraham's cloak. Abraham looked behind him, saw the ram, extricated him, and brought him as an offering instead of his son.

[At the time Isaac was bound], Satan went to Sarah, appearing to her in the form of Isaac. When Sarah saw him, she asked, "My son, what did your father do to you?" He replied, "My father took me, led me up hills and down into valleys, until finally he brought me up to the summit of a high and towering mountain, where he built an altar, set out the firewood, bound me upon the altar, and grasped a knife to cut my throat. Had not the Holy One said to him, 'Lay not thy hand upon the lad,' I would have been slaughtered. Even before Satan finished his tale, Sarah's soul left her.[3]

47. Our father Abraham was tested with ten trials, and he stood firm in all of them, showing how great was our father Abraham's love [of God].[4]

48. "There was Abraham buried next to Sarah his wife" (Gen. 25:10). R. Samuel bar Nahman said: [At the time of Sarah's funeral], Shem and Eber, walking before her bier, determined that the place next to where she was to be buried was the one intended for our father Abraham, and then they buried her in [that place in Machpelah] in Abraham's twin chamber.[5]

After the Death of Abraham

49. R. Simeon ben Yohai said: Our father Abraham wore a precious stone hanging from his neck that brought immediate healing to any sick person who looked for it; and when our father Abraham departed this world, the Holy One took it and suspended it from the orb of the sun. Hence, said Abbaye, the proverb "As the day advances, illness eases."[6]

50. R. Hanan bar Rava said in the name of Rav: On the day our father Abraham departed from this world, all the notables of the world's nations stood in a line[7] and said: Alas for the world that has lost its leader! Alas for the ship that has lost its pilot.[8]

Isaac, Rebekah, and Their Progeny

51. "Isaac brought her into the tent [and behold, she was like][9] his mother Sarah" (Gen. 24:67). As long as Sarah lived, a cloud [of glory] hovered over the entrance to her tent. After she died, the cloud disappeared. But when Rebekah came, the cloud returned. As long as Sarah lived, her doors were wide open to wayfarers; at her death, such openness ceased. But when Rebekah came, openness returned. As long as Sarah lived, blessing was dispatched into the dough she baked; at her death, such

1. Tanhuma, *Va-yera*, §22–23; Tanhuma B, *Va-yera*, §46; B. Sanh 89b; PRE 31; P. Ta 2:4, 65d; Yalkut, *Va-yera*, §101; *Va-Yosha* (BhM 1:37–38); PR 40:6 (YJS 2:713–21).
2. See above, chap. 2, §67.
3. Tanhuma, *Va-yera*, §23; Eccles. R. 9:7, §1.
4. Avot 5:3.
5. Gen. R. 62:3.
6. Literally, "As the day rises, the sick man rises." B. BB 16b.
7. The custom followed by those who would offer comfort to mourners.
8. B. BB 91a–b.
9. The meaning, the commentator assumes, cannot be "into his mother Sarah's tent," for the word *ha-ohelah*, which has the definite article, is not in the construct state.

blessing ceased. But when Rebekah came, the blessing returned. As long as Sarah lived, a lamp was alight [in her tent] from one Sabbath eve to the next; at her death, the light ceased. But when Rebekah came, the light returned.[1] When Isaac saw her following his mother's ways, separating her *hallah*[2] in ritual cleanness, and cutting up her dough in ritual cleanness, "Isaac brought her into the tent [and behold, she was like] his mother Sarah."[3]

52. "And Isaac was forty years old when he took Rebekah, the daughter of Bethuel the Aramean, of Paddan-aram, the sister of Laban the Aramean, to be his wife" (Gen. 25:20). R. Isaac taught: If Scripture means to tell us no more than that Rebekah came from Aram-naharaim, why add again and again "Aramean"? "The daughter of Bethuel the Aramean," "the sister of Laban the Aramean"—she has already been described as coming from Paddan-aram. But Scripture means to tell us that her father was a cheat,[4] her brother was a cheat, and the people of her town were cheats. Hence, this righteous woman who sprang from their midst—what is she to be likened to? To a "lily among thorns" (Song 2:2).[5]

53. "And the children seemed to be ever on the run within her"[6] (Gen. 25:22). When Rebekah passed synagogues or houses of study, [the unborn] Jacob was scurrying within her in his eagerness to get out; and when she passed houses of idolatry, [the unborn] Esau was scurrying in his eagerness to get out.[7]

54. "And she went to inquire of the Lord" (Gen. 25:22). But were there synagogues or houses of study in those days? Surely she could have gone only to inquire personally of Shem and Eber! Hence Scripture intimates that visiting a sage is like visiting the Presence.[8]

55. "And when the boys grew up" (Gen. 25:27). R. Levi said: [At first] they were like a myrtle and a wild rose growing side by side. But when they grew up, the former yielded its characteristic fragrance (*reho*) and the latter its thorns (*hoho*). So, for the first thirteen years, both Jacob and Esau went to school and came home from school. But at the end of the thirteen years,[9] one went to houses of study and the other to shrines of idolatry.[10]

56. "Now Isaac loved Esau, because he provided choice viands for his palate".[11] (Gen. 25:28)—choice meat for Isaac's palate and choice wine for Isaac's palate. "But Rebekah loved Jacob more and more" (ibid.):[12] the more she heard his voice [engaged in study of Torah], the more she loved him.[13]

57. "There was [the cunning of] a trap in his mouth" (Gen. 25:28).[14] Esau knew how to entrap and deceive his father with his mouth, by asking such questions as "How should salt be tithed? How should straw be tithed?"[15]

58. "And Esau came in from the field, and he was faint" (Gen. 25:29). One day, when Esau went out to hunt beasts and birds, he saw a gazelle in front of him and ran after it. Nimrod espied Esau and asked him, "Why do you hunt in my forest? I demand that you meet me on the field of battle." Nimrod then fixed the day for the battle. In the interim, Esau had time to go and seek Jacob's counsel. Jacob told Esau, "As long as Nimrod wears Adam's garments,[16] you cannot defeat him. Induce him to remove them, and then fight him." That is what Esau did. When Nimrod took off Adam's garments, Esau cunningly managed to get hold of them and put them on. Then he rose up and slew Nimrod. That is why he felt faint, as is said, "My soul fainteth as [the soul] of murderers" (Jer. 4:31).[17]

59. "And Esau said to Jacob: 'Stuff me with food' " (Gen. 25:30). R. Zera observed: That wicked man opened his mouth wide, as though he were a camel, and said to Jacob, "I'll keep my mouth open, and you pack it in." "And he did eat and drink, then rose up and came back" (Gen. 25:34), bringing with him a company of ruffians who said, "We will eat what is Jacob's and poke fun at him."[18]

60. "And his eyes were dim from seeing" (Gen. 27:1). R. Eleazar ben Azariah taught: From seeing the evil deeds of wicked Esau. For the Holy One said: Shall Isaac go out into the marketplace and hear people say, "This is that scoundrel's father"? I shall therefore dim Isaac's eyes so that he will stay home.[19]

Or, the phrase "from seeing" is to be explained by the tale of a distinguished man who had a beautiful and well-appointed reception room, next to which his neighbors used to burn stubble and straw, sending smoke in through

1. The cloud over the tent is taken to represent modesty; the open doors, hospitality and compassion; blessing in the dough, bliss in the household; and the lamp alight, industry (Moshe Aryeh Mirkin on Gen. R. 60:16, Midrash R. [Tel Aviv, 1956–67], p. 316).
2. The portion of the dough given to priests. See Num. 15:20.
3. Gen. R. 60:16.
4. By a slight transposition, the Hebrew *aram* ("Aramean") may be read *ramai* ("rogue, cheat").
5. Gen. R. 63:4; Lev. R. 23:1.
6. JV: "struggled within her." But the word *va-yitrotzetzu* ("struggled") may also be construed as a form of *rvtz* [*rutz*] ("run, scurry").
7. Gen. R. 63:6; Yalkut, *Toledot*, §110.
8. Gen. R. 63:6.
9. Maturity is reached at thirteen years and one day.
10. Gen. R. 63:10.
11. JV: "He did eat of his venison." But *be-fiv* ("he did eat" [literally, "in his mouth"]) also means "for his palate."
12. In Hebrew the present tense, "she loves," is taken to mean that her love kept growing stronger and stronger. So *Yefeh Toar* on Gen. R. 63:10.
13. Gen. R. 63:10.
14. JV: "He did eat of his venison." The translation suggested by the commentator is likewise possible. The word *tzayid* ("venison") also means "trap"; and *be-fiv* ("he did eat") translated literally is "in his mouth."
15. Although he knew very well that these are not subject to tithing. Rashi on Gen. 25:28.
16. See above, chap. 2, §135.
17. BhM 5:157; PRE 24.
18. Gen. R. 63:12, 14.
19. Gen. R. 65:10; Midrash Avkir.

the window. The man felt constrained to seal the window. Likewise, while Esau's wives worshiped idols, Isaac saw them and was so greatly distressed that at once his eyes grew dim—[his "windows" had to be sealed].

Or: "From seeing"—from the effect of what he saw at his binding. When our father Abraham bound his son upon the altar, the ministering angels wept and tears dropped from their eyes into Isaac's eyes, leaving their mark upon them. And when he grew old, his eyes grew dim.[1]

Isaac's Blessing

61. "And he called his son Esau" (Gen. 27:1). As the nightfall of Passover approached, Isaac called his elder son Esau and said to him, "My son, on this night the entire world, all of it, sings psalms of praise to God; on this night the treasuries of beneficent dews are opened. Make me some savory food and I will bless you while I am still in this world." To this the Holy Spirit retorted, "Eat not the bread of one who is up to no good, and desire not his savory morsels" (Prov. 23:6). Esau went to fetch what Isaac wanted but found himself hindered [by all manner of mishaps; in the interval thus gained] Rebekah said to Jacob, "My son, on this night the treasuries of beneficent dews are opened; on this night angels above utter song. Make some savory food for your father, that he may bless you while he is still in this world." So Jacob went and fetched two kids of the goats.[2]

62. "He called Esau his imposing[3] son" (Gen. 27:1). R. Eleazar son of R. Simeon said: The description of Esau as "imposing" may be understood by the parable of a principality that was recruiting a bodyguard of tall men for its king. A certain woman there had a son, a dwarf, whom she used to call "Tallswift." So she protested, "My son is tall and swift. Why do you not enroll him?" They replied, "In your eyes he may be tall and swift, but in ours he is a dwarf even among dwarfs." Likewise, Esau's father called him "imposing"—"he called Esau his imposing son." His mother called him "imposing"—"Rebekah took the choicest garments of Esau her imposing son" (Gen. 27:15). "Nevertheless," said the Holy One to them both, "if in your eyes he is imposing, in Mine he is small [a dwarf]. 'Behold, among the nations I regard thee [Esau] as small, greatly despised' " (Obad. 1:2).[4]

63. "Make me food that is savory" (Gen. 27:4).[5] Here Isaac is saying, "In the past, I used to relish the pleasures of sight, but now [that I am blind], I can enjoy only the pleasure of taste." Solomon also noted that this is true of blind people: "When food looks appetizing, many can share in the eating of it. What makes it possible for the provider of such food to serve many? Its being seen" (Eccles. 5:10).[6] Hence we learn that the blind [who do not see the food] cannot be fully satisfied [and therefore long for its savor and aroma]. So, too, one who sees a basket empty of food will become even more hungry, unlike one to whom the mere sight of a basket full of food will give some satisfaction.[7]

64. "Upon me thy curse, my son" (Gen. 27:13), [said Rebekah to Jacob]—so R. Abba bar Kahana understood this verse. When a man sins, is it not his mother who is cursed? Even so, Adam was told, "Cursed is the earth[8] on account of thee" (Gen. 3:17). So, too, Rebekah said to Jacob, "Upon me thy curse, my son." But according to R. Isaac, [what Rebekah meant was, "Upon me the responsibility for averting the curse]; it is my duty to go in and tell your father, "Jacob is the righteous one, and Esau is the wicked one." "And Jacob went and fetched [the garments], and brought[9] them to his mother" (Gen. 27:14). Still, [despite his mother's reassurance], he did so reluctantly, bowed down with distress, and weeping.[10]

65. "Because the Lord thy God sent me good speed" (Gen. 27:20). In using God's name, said R. Yohanan, Jacob was like a raven that carries fire into his own nest. For the moment Jacob said, "Because the Lord thy God sent me good speed," Isaac thought to himself: I know that Esau never mentions the Name of the Holy One. Since this one just did, he cannot be Esau, he must be Jacob. Then, when Isaac said to Jacob, "Come near, I pray thee, that I may feel thee, my son" (Gen. 27:21), urine ran down Jacob's thighs, and his heart turned as soft as wax. But the Holy One provided him with two angels, one at his right and one at his left, who supported him by his elbows so that he should not fall.[11]

66. [Why] "Isaac was seized with great terror" (Gen. 27:33) [when Esau returned with the game will be explained in what follows. But to begin with], note that earlier in the passage it is said, "Jacob was yet scarce gone out from the presence of Isaac his father" (Gen. 27:30). How can one go out and the other come in at the same moment [without their seeing each other]? He who is in bright light cannot see one who is in the dark; but he who is in the dark will readily see the one who is in the bright light. Since Esau came in from the outdoors, he could not see Jacob, who was inside the house. Jacob, however, saw

---

1. Gen. R. 65:10; Midrash Avkir.
2. PRE 32.
3. JV: "elder." But *gadol* in the sense of "elder" is deemed unnecessary, since we already know that Esau was the elder son. Hence, "great, imposing."
4. Gen. R. 65:11.
5. The commentator will endeavor to explain why the patriarch Isaac, who was no glutton, would have asked for food that was savory, aromatic.
6. JV: "When goods increase, they are increased that eat them; and what advantage is there to the owner thereof, saving the beholding of them with his eyes?"
7. "Even without eating, for the mere knowledge that one has something to eat often satisfies him" (Soncino). Gen. R. 65:13.
8. The earth out of which Adam was created may be considered his mother.
9. Each of these three verbs begins with *va*[*y*] ("and"), whose sound, suggesting "woe," is taken to intimate that Jacob did his mother's bidding with woeful foreboding.
10. Gen. R. 65:15.
11. Gen. R. 65:19.

Esau from inside the house and hid himself behind the door, and the moment Esau came in, Jacob stepped out. Did Jacob calculate the hours so as to make certain that Esau would not arrive [first] and receive Isaac's blessings? [It was not Jacob but God who did the reckoning.] Because, as soon as Esau went out to hunt, the Holy One dispatched Satan, who prevented Esau from succeeding in his hunt until Jacob had come and received the blessings. How? Esau ran after one gazelle, caught it, tied it up, and left it; then ran after another gazelle, caught it, tied it up, and left it; and so forth, while Satan undid the bonds and shooed the gazelles away, so that each time Esau returned, he did not find any of them. This happened two or three times, thus delaying Esau for hours until after Jacob had come and received the blessings from his father.

When Esau finally entered the house, he called to his father in a rude tone, "Let my father arise and eat of his son's venison" (Gen. 27:31)—"let my father arise," he ordered. Jacob, however, had not spoken in the same tone, but said, "Arise, I pray thee, sit and eat" (Gen. 27:19)—both "I pray thee" and the three verbs implying respectful entreaty, humility, and submissiveness. That wicked Esau, however, said, "Let my father arise and eat," all but saying, "He'd better" [in a curt and peremptory tone].

At that moment, Isaac recognized Esau's voice and, seized with fear, asked Esau, "Who are you?" For when Jacob had come in, the fragrance of the Garden of Eden, a sweet savor, came in with him, and Isaac, feeling refreshed, exclaimed, "See, the smell of my son is as the smell of the field [of Eden] which the Lord hath blessed" (Gen. 27:27), as he proceeded to bless him. But when Esau came in, Gehenna gaped wide before Isaac, so that "Isaac was seized with great terror" (Gen. 27:33). Perturbed in his heart, he said to himself: I see Gehenna with Esau's body kindling the fire therein: "Who is the one to be roasted in it? None other than the hunter [Esau], who has himself become game" (ibid.).[1] [That the verse is to be read thus is suggested by the way Isaac phrased the question "Who is he that hunted the hunt?"[2]—"hunted" would have been sufficient.] However, Isaac's use of the two words suggests that in sheer terror he found himself saying to Esau, "You went out to hunt and will discover that you are the one hunted [you will become game]."[3]

Our Father Jacob When He Left Beersheba

67. "And Jacob went out from Beersheba" (Gen. 28:10).[4] The departure of a righteous man from a city leaves its mark. When a righteous man is in the city, he is its luster, its renown, its glory. Once he leaves, gone is its luster, gone its renown, gone its glory.[5]

"And he got to Haran" (Gen. 28:10).[6] After Jacob reached Haran, he asked himself: Is it possible that I passed by [Moriah], the place where my fathers prayed, and I did not pray? As he was deciding to return, the earth contracted [bringing Moriah to Haran], so that he "encountered the place" (Gen. 28:11) [as it came up to meet him]. After he finished praying, he wanted to return to Haran. But the Holy One said: This righteous man has come to My dwelling place—shall he depart without a night's lodging there? Immediately the sun set.[7]

"Because the sun had set (*ki va*)" (Gen. 28:11)—read rather *kibbah*, "extinguished." God extinguished the sun, that is, God caused the sun to set prematurely, so that he might speak with Jacob in privacy. God's action may be understood by the parable of the king's close friend who visited him occasionally. The king would command, "Extinguish the lamps, extinguish the lanterns, because I wish to speak to my friend in privacy."[8]

"And he took of the stones of the place" (Gen. 28:11). Fearful of wild beasts, Jacob put stones around him in a circle, the way a drainpipe encircles a roof [hoping that the enclosure would provide protection]. Then the stones began quarreling among themselves. One said, "Let the righteous one put his head against me," and the other said, "Let him put it against me," until finally the stones coalesced one with the other and became one stone. Hence Scripture could go on to say of those stones, "He took the stone, which he put at his head" (Gen. 28:18).[9]

"And he dreamed . . . and behold, angels of God ascending and descending" (Gen. 28:12). The Holy One showed Jacob the angelic princes of the four kingdoms[10] ascending and descending. But then, "Behold,[11] the Lord stood beside him" (Gen. 28:13). R. Simeon ben Lakish said: Were it not expressly stated in Scripture, we would not dare suggest that when God [comes to protect Israel],[12] He comes as close to them as a man fanning his son.

R. Abbahu said: God's presence in that dream may

1. JV: "Who is he then that hath taken venison." But the word *efo* ("then") is construed to be a form of *'fh* (*afoh*, "bake")—"a body being baked" or "roasted." The identification of the body as Esau's is derived from "that hath taken venison," which is read, "The hunter, namely, Esau, will himself become game," ending up as he will in Gehenna.

Instead of "I see Gehenna with Esau's body . . . [you will become game]," Leon Nemoy suggests the following translation: "I see Gehenna and Esau kindling the fire therein: 'Who then is the one who has hunted game?' Why the repetition of 'hunted game'? ['Hunted' would have been sufficient.] What Isaac meant was, 'Who then is the hunter who has become game [has been foiled in his hunt by Satan]?' "

2. Such is the literal meaning. JV: "Who is he . . . that hath taken venison?"

3. Tanhuma, *Toledot*, §11.

4. The text should have stated, "Jacob went to Haran." What need to mention that he left Beersheba? Hence the comment that follows.

5. Gen. R. 68:6.

6. JV: "And he went toward Haran." The commentator assumes that *va-yelekh*, being opposite to *va-yetze* ("went out") which precedes it, means not "went toward" but "got to."

7. B. Hul 91b; B. Sanh 95b.

8. Gen. R. 68:10.

9. Gen. R. 68:11.

10. Babylon, Media, Greece, and Rome, the four kingdoms among whom the Jewish people were to be exiled.

11. The word "behold" is construed as intimating the introduction of an element that disrupts the hitherto undisturbed sway of the kingdoms.

12. From the fury of the four kingdoms. Here Jacob is taken to represent the people Israel.

be illustrated by the parable of an infant prince who was sleeping in his cradle while flies were settling upon him. The moment his wetnurse came by and bent over him, they fled. So, too, at first, "Behold, the angels of God ascending and descending on it" (Gen. 28:12). But the moment the Holy One revealed Himself hovering over Jacob, they fled.[1]

68. "The land whereon thou liest, to thee will I give it and to thy seed" (Gen. 28:13). R. Isaac said: The verse implies that the Holy One folded up the entire Land of Israel and put it under our father Jacob, as if to say to him that it will be easily conquered by his children.

R. Simeon said in the name of Bar Kappara: God folded it up like a register tablet and put it under Jacob's head, as the saying goes, "Whatever is under your head is yours."[2]

69. "Then Jacob lifted up[3] his feet" (Gen. 29:1). R. Aha said: "Exhilarating news gives healing to a [weary] heart" (Prov. 14:30).[4] As soon as Jacob received the exhilarating news [of God's promise to his progeny], his heart lifted up his feet, causing them to move [at great speed].

"And he asked the [herdsmen]: 'Is Laban at peace [with his employees]?' " (Gen. 29:6).[5] Is there peace between him and you?

"And they replied: 'There is peace' " (Gen. 29:6); but if you wish to engage in chitchat,[6] "Behold, Rachel his daughter cometh with the sheep" (ibid.). As the saying goes, "Women are chatterboxes."

"And it came to pass, when Jacob saw Rachel . . . that Jacob went near, and rolled the stone from the well's mouth" (Gen. 29:10). [He moved it as easily], said R. Yohanan, as one pulls the stopper out of a vial.

"And Jacob kissed Rachel" (Gen. 29:11). All kisses are frivolous, except three: the kiss of homage, the kiss after long separation, and the kiss at parting. The kiss of homage: "Samuel took the vial of oil and poured it upon Saul's head, and kissed him" (I Sam. 10:1); the kiss after long separation: "[Aaron] went and met [Moses] at the mountain of God, and kissed him" (Exod. 4:27); the kiss at parting: "Orpah kissed her mother-in-law" (Ruth 1:14). Also the kiss of kinship, said R. Tanhuma, as when "Jacob kissed Rachel," she being his kinswoman.

"[Jacob] lifted up his voice and wept" (Gen. 29:11). Why did he weep? Because he said: What is said about Eliezer when he went to fetch Rebekah? "The servant took ten camels [of . . . goodly things]," etc. (Gen. 24:10), whereas I have not even one earring or one bracelet.

Another reason for his weeping: He saw that because he kissed Rachel, the herdsmen were whispering among themselves: What, is this one come to bring unchastity back into our midst? For ever since the world was smitten during the generation of the flood, the nations imposed restraint upon themselves with regard to unchastity, as the saying goes, "People of the east hedge themselves in from unchastity."

"And it came to pass when Laban heard," etc. (Gen. 29:13). He reasoned: Eliezer was an insignificant member of Abraham's household. Yet it is written of him, "The servant took ten camels" (Gen. 24:10). This one, who is the household's favorite—how much more and more is he apt to have [to offer me]. But when Laban did not even see a food sack on him, "He embraced him" (Gen. 29:13), [feeling his waist and] thinking: He must have money, and it is in his belt. When he found not a penny, "he kissed him" (ibid.), thinking that perhaps he had pearls and was keeping them safe in his mouth. Only then did he realize that Jacob brought nothing at all. Jacob said: What do you think—that I came laden with wealth? All I have come laden with is the grievous account of what happened to me.[7] "And he told Laban" (ibid.). "In that case," Laban said, " 'surely for thee a mere bone' " (Gen. 29:14).[8] I had intended to treat you like a king, but since you have nothing, I need do no more than toss you a bone. "Nevertheless," Laban went on, " 'art thou expected to serve me for nought?' " (Gen. 29:15). Jacob replied, "Do you suppose that I have come to haggle about money? I have come only because of the two maidens."

"And Laban had two daughters" (Gen. 29:16), who were, so to speak, like two joists reaching from one end of the world to the other.[9] One produced generals and the other produced generals; one produced kings and the other produced kings;[10] Out of one arose lion slayers and out of the other arose lion slayers.[11] Out of one arose prophets and out of the other arose prophets. Out of one arose judges and out of the other arose judges. Out of one arose conquerors of countries and out of the other arose conquerors of countries.[12] Out of one arose apportioners of allotted parts in lands and out of the other arose apportioners of allotted parts in lands.[13]

---

1. Gen. R. 68:6, 68:10–11, and 69:3; B. Hul 91b; Yalkut, *Va-yetze*, §119.
2. Or: "Possession is nine points of the law." B. Hul 91b; Gen. R. 69:4.
3. One would expect "The feet lifted up Jacob." Saying that "Jacob lifted them" stimulates the comment that follows.
4. JV: "A tranquil heart is the life of the flesh." But *besarim* ("flesh") can mean "tidings, news."
5. JV: "Is it well with him?" But the commentator is puzzled: Why does Jacob not also inquire about the well-being of Laban's family? Hence he assumes that Jacob, fully aware of Laban's reputation as a trickster, inquires not about Laban's well-being but about his relations with his employees.
6. It may be that, busy as they were with their chores, they wanted to cut the conversation short.
7. Upon Jacob's departure from Beersheba, Eliphaz, a son of Esau, ambushed Jacob and took away all his belongings. See Ginzberg, *Legends* 1:346.
8. JV: "Surely thou art my bone."
9. The word *banot* ("daughters") is read *bonot* ("joists" or "beams"), for through Rachel and Leah the House of Israel, the Jewish people, was built.
10. Out of Leah, David's dynasty and some monarchs of the kingdom of Israel; out of Rachel, Saul, Ish-Bosheth, Jeroboam son of Nebat, Nadab, and the dynasty of Jehu.
11. Out of Leah, David (I Sam. 17:36) and Benaiah (2 Sam. 23:20). Out of Rachel, Samson (Judg. 14:5–6) of the tribe of Dan, descended from Bilhah, who was Rachel's maid.
12. Moses and David from Leah; Joshua and Saul from Rachel.
13. Moses, e.g., who apportioned the land east of the Jordan among two and a half tribes, and Joshua, who apportioned the Land of Israel among the nine and a half tribes. Gen. R. 70:8 and 70:11–15.

70. "Leah had weak eyes" (Gen. 29:17). Rav said: That they were weak was no disgrace to her, but cause for praise. For at the crossroads she used to hear people say, "Rebekah has two sons, and Laban has two daughters— the older daughter should wed the older son, and the younger, the younger son." So she sat at the crossroads asking all passersby, "The older one—what kind of person is he?" and was told, " 'A cunning hunter' [Gen. 25:27], a wicked man, given to robbing people." "And the younger—what kind of person is he?" "A quiet man, dwelling in tents" (ibid.). At this, Leah wept so much that her eyelids seemed to disappear.[1]

71. R. Jonathan said: God's intention was that the birthright should have stemmed from Rachel, for it is said, "These are the generations of Jacob, Joseph" (Gen. 37:2).[2] But through [her prayers for] God's mercy [to spare her from marrying Esau], Leah got ahead of Rachel in the birthright. Nevertheless, because of Rachel's effacing herself, the Holy One restored the birthright to Rachel. And what showed Rachel's capacity to efface herself? The following verse, as will be explained: "And Jacob told Rachel that he was her father's brother" (Gen. 29:12). Was Jacob her father's brother? Was he not in fact a son of her father's sister? However, Jacob [described himself as "her father's brother" after he] asked Rachel, "Will you marry me?" and she replied, "Yes, but my father is a trickster, and you cannot beat him in trickery." Jacob asked, "How would he trick me?" She replied, "I have an older sister, and he will not have me marry ahead of her." It was then that Jacob said, "In trickery, I am your father's brother." She asked, "But is it proper for a righteous man to resort to trickery?" He replied, "Yes, for we read: 'With the pure thou dost show thyself pure, and with the crooked thou dost show thyself wily' " (2 Sam. 22:27). So he gave her certain tokens [by which to identify herself]. But when the wedding night came, Rachel said to herself: Now my sister will be humiliated. So she turned the tokens over to Leah. Hence it is said, "And it came to pass in the morning that, behold, it was Leah" (Gen. 29:25). Are these words to be construed as saying that until morning she was not Leah? No, what is meant is that, because of the tokens Rachel had turned over to her, Jacob did not know until morning that it was Leah.[3]

72. "Jacob . . . said: 'I will serve thee seven years for Rachel thy younger daughter' " (Gen. 29:18). Because I know that the people of your town are tricksters, I make my request thoroughly clear: "I will serve thee . . . for Rachel"—for Rachel, not for Leah—"thy . . . daughter." So that you will not bring some other woman from the marketplace who happens to be named Rachel—the "younger"—do not try to have them exchange names. "Nevertheless, when evening came, Laban took his daughter Leah and brought her to him" (Gen. 29:23). [Thus Jacob's explicit stipulations did not avail him, for, as the saying goes], "Even if you clamp a scoundrel in a carpenter's vise, it will not avail you [he will wriggle out of it].

"And Laban gathered together all the men of the place, and made a feast" (Gen. 29:22). He gathered all the men of the place where he lived and said, "You know how short of water we were. But as soon as this righteous man appeared, water became abundant." They asked, "So what do you have in mind?" He replied, "If you go along, I will trick him and give him Leah instead. But since he loves Rachel much more, he is bound to work for you[4] yet another seven years." They replied, "Do as you wish." He said, "Give me pledges that not one of you will disclose my plan to anyone." They brought the pledges, and Laban used them to buy oil, wine, and meat for the wedding. (For this reason he was dubbed Laban the Aramean, that is to say, the cheat, because he cheated even the people of his own place.) All day long, the people gathered at the feast wished Jacob joy. At dusk [as they continued to do so], Jacob asked, "Why so much congratulation?" They replied, "Your merit conferred a great boon upon us. So we, too, wish to confer a boon upon you." Then, while apparently engaged in nothing other than wishing him well, they yodeled, "Ha-liah; Ha-liah!" [seemingly a cry of joy, but in fact a hint, "It is Leah, it is Leah"].[5] In the evening, having led the bride into the nuptial chamber, the ushers put out the lamps. When Jacob asked, "Why are you doing this?" they replied, "What do you think—that we are as shameless as you?"[6]

All that night Jacob kept calling his bride Rachel, and Leah answered to the name. In the morning, "Behold it was Leah" (Gen. 29:25). Said Jacob to Leah, "What is this, O trickstress and daughter of a trickster? Did I not call you Rachel all night long and you answered to the name?" She replied, "Is there a teacher who has no pupils? Did not your father once call you Esau, and you answered to that name?"[7]

73. "And the Lord saw that Leah was held in disdain" (Gen. 29:31). All held her in disdain—sea rats[8] disdained her, vagrants disdained her, even the [loose] grape-treading women behind the beams [of the winepress] disdained her, saying, "This Leah—she's not in private what she is in the open. She looks like a good woman but really isn't. If she were, she would not have tricked her sister."

R. Hanin said in the name of R. Samuel bar R. Isaac: When our father Jacob saw how Leah had deceived him, he made up his mind to divorce her. But after the Holy One visited her with children, he said, "Shall I divorce the mother of these children?"[9]

---

1. She wept at the prospect of being married to Esau. B. BB 123a; Gen. R. 70:16.
2. The implication: that Rachel would give birth to Joseph before Leah gave birth to Reuben.
3. B. Meg 13b; B. BB 123a and Rashi, ad loc.
4. "Shepherds grazed all the livestock together; hence Jacob actually worked for *all* the owners" (Leon Nemoy).
5. A hint Jacob did not understand.
6. It is deemed indecent for a marriage to be consummated in a lighted chamber.
7. Gen. R. 70:17 and 70:19; Yalkut, *Va-yetze*, §117.
8. Pirates?
9. Gen. R. 71:2.

74. R. Hinnena bar Isaac said: Rather the threatening mien of the fathers than the conciliatory manner of their descendants. That the threatening mien of the fathers is endurable, we learn from our father Jacob: "Though Jacob, becoming wroth, took up his grievance with Laban, he said no more to Laban than 'What is my sin, that thou hast hotly pursued after me?' " (Gen. 31:36). You might have supposed that such words were a preamble to blows or bruises, but in fact Jacob went on to conciliate his father-in-law with calming words: "Though thou hast rummaged through all my stuff, what single one of all thy household things hast thou found?" (Gen. 31:37). R. Simon pointed out: Usually, when a son-in-law has been living with his father-in-law, is it not likely at the very least that there will be found in his possession some trifle such as a knife? But here, " 'Thou hast rummaged through all my stuff,' and not even a needle or a pin did you find."

On the other hand, that the conciliatory manner of the descendants of the fathers is not endurable, we may learn from David: "David fled from Naioth in Ramah, and came and said before Jonathan: 'What have I done? What is my guilt? And what is my sin before thy father that he seeketh my life?" (1 Sam. 20:1). Thus, though seeking conciliation, David mentioned Saul's murderous intent. But all Jacob said to Laban was, "Thou hast hotly pursued after me" (Gen. 31:36).[1]

Jacob, Esau, and the Angels

75. "And he called the name of that place Mahanaim" (Gen. 32:3). What is the meaning of "Mahanaim"? Two camps. For when Jacob set out for Aram-naharaim, the guardian angels of the Land of Israel protected him and escorted him until he was out of the Land. Then these angels left, and other angels came to escort him. When he returned from Laban, the angels who had been assigned to him continued to escort him as far as the Land of Israel. Once the guardian angels of the Land of Israel became aware that Jacob was coming, they went out [of the Land] to join the escort, as is said, "The angels[2] of God met him [before he crossed the Jordan]" (Gen. 32:2). Thus it came about that two camps [of angels] were standing at Jacob's side—he sent emissaries from both on the mission in his behalf.[3]

76. "And Jacob sent emissaries ahead to Esau his brother" (Gen. 32:4). R. Jonathan said: When anyone seeks to conciliate a king or a ruler, and does not know his ways and usages, let him set before himself this portion of Scripture, and he will learn from it the proper procedure in attempting conciliation and appeasement.[4]

77. "And Jacob sent messengers [i.e., angels] before him to Esau his brother unto the land of Seir . . . saying: 'Thus saith thy servant Jacob' " (Gen. 32:4–5). The Holy One reproached Jacob: Esau was going in another direction, yet you submissively sent word to him, "Thus saith thy servant Jacob" (Gen. 32:5).[5]

R. Judah bar Simon began his discourse with the verse "A righteous man submitting to the wicked is as a fountain that gets muddied, or a spring that becomes polluted" (Prov. 25:26). Still, a righteous man will not remain in submission before the wicked any more than a fountain will remain muddied or a spring polluted [since their waters soon become clear]. Nevertheless, when a righteous man does submit to the wicked, he [for a while at least] is like a muddied fountain or a polluted spring. Hence the Holy One reproached Jacob: Esau was going his own way, and you submissively sent word to him, "Thus saith thy servant Jacob!"

"And Jacob sent" (Gen. 32:4). R. Huna began his discourse with the verse "He that passeth by, and stirreth [memories of] a quarrel no longer in [the adversary's] mind,[6] is like one that taketh a dog by the ears" (Prov. 26:17). He went on to cite R. Samuel bar Nahman's parable of a robber chieftain who was asleep at a crossroads when a man passed and woke him up, saying, "Wake up! In this place a bad thing happened between us. [Remember?]" The robber chieftain jumped up and began beating the man, who cried out, "Look at him—he woke up as evil as ever!" To which the robber chieftain replied, "I was sound asleep, and you woke me up [for no good reason]!" So, too, the Holy One told Jacob: Esau was going his own way, and you, [stirring up memories], send emissaries to him, who are asked to declare, "Thus saith thy servant Jacob."

R. Judah bar Simon began his discourse with the verse "What wilt thou do when He rebuke thee—it is thou who hast taught them [to be raised] against thee, directed them [so to speak] to be against thy head" (Jer. 13:21).[7] Accordingly, the Holy One reproached Jacob: Esau was going his own way, and you sent emissaries to him who were to declare, "Thus saith thy servant Jacob."[8]

78. When Jacob called Esau "my lord," the Holy One said to him: Eight times have you abased yourself in calling Esau "my lord." As you live, I will raise up eight kings out of his descendants before [there will be one king of] your descendants, as is said, "These are the kings that reigned in the land of Edom, before there reigned any king over the children of Israel" (Gen. 36:31).[9]

79. "Then Jacob was greatly afraid and was distressed" (Gen. 32:8). R. Judah bar R. Ilai asked: Are not fear and distress identical? The meaning, however, is that "he was afraid" lest he should be slain "and was distressed" lest he should slay. For he thought: If Esau proves stronger

1. Gen. R. 74:10; PRKM, p. 240 (PRKS, p. 267).
2. The Hebrew word *mal'akh* means both "angel" and "emissary."
3. Tanhuma, *Va-yishlah*, §3.
4. Lekah Tov, *Va-yishlah*, beginning.

5. When Esau, heading for Seir, realized that Jacob was afraid of him, he decided to detour in order to take him on. So *Yefeh Toar*. Gen. R. 75:1.
6. JV: "He that passeth by, and meddleth with strife not his own."
7. JV: "What wilt thou say when He shall set thy friends over thee as head, whom thou thyself hast trained against thee?" But see *The Holy Bible with the Confraternity Text* (Chicago, 1963), ad loc.
8. Gen. R. 75:1–3.
9. Gen. R. 75:11.

than I, he might slay me, and if I prove stronger than he, I might slay him.[1]

80. "And Jacob sent angels" (Gen. 32:4). Jacob was given two camps of ministering angels. How many angels are in each camp of God? Two thousand myriads, for it is said, "God's mounted angels are twice a thousand myriads (Ps. 68:18).[2] They looked like royal troops—some clad in iron armor, some mounted on horses, some seated in wagons. When Esau met those clad in iron armor, he asked, "To whom do you belong?" They replied, "To Jacob." When he met those mounted on horses, he asked, "To whom do you belong?" They replied, "To Jacob." When he met those seated in wagons, he asked, "To whom do you belong?" They replied, "To Jacob." All these questions and answers are implied in Esau's words "Who has given you the many encampments of troops that I have encountered?" (Gen. 33:8).[3]

81. "Who has given you the many encampments of troops that I have encountered?" (Gen. 33:8). All that night, the ministering angels kept forming themselves into many bands, into many companies. As they attacked Esau's forces, they asked, "To whom do you belong?" When told, "To Esau," they shouted, "Strike, strike! Give it to them!" When told, "We belong to Abraham's grandson," they continued saying, "Give it to them!" When told, "To Isaac's son," they still shouted, "Give it to them!" But when Esau's forces entreated, "We belong to Jacob's brother," the ministering angels called out, "Let them be, they are ours." In the morning, Esau asked Jacob, "Who has given you the many encampments of troops that I have encountered?" Jacob replied by asking, "Did they say anything at all to you?" Esau answered, "[No], but I have been roundly battered by them." [Unaware that angels had been interceding for him], Jacob said, "[But I only sent them to deliver a message], to find favor in the sight of my lord" (Gen. 33:8). "And Esau said: 'I have had enough of battering [messages]! My brother, let that which thou hast remain thine' " (Gen. 33:9).[4]

82. "For to see thy face is like seeing the face of God" (Gen. 33:10). Jacob mentioned God's Name to Esau in order to intimidate him, to frighten him. By what parable may Jacob's mention of God be understood? By the parable of a man who invited his friend to dine with him. When the guest perceived that the host planned to murder him, he said, "This dish tastes like the dish I had in the royal palace." So he knows the king, said the host to himself, and, seized with fear, he did not try to go through with his murderous scheme.

Even so it was with Jacob. As soon as he said to Esau, "For to see thy face is like seeing the face of God," wicked Esau said to himself: Since the Holy One brought him to such honor, I stand no chance against him.[5]

83. "And there wrestled a man with him" (Gen. 32:25). Some say it was the angel Michael, who said to Jacob, "If to me—one of the foremost princes in heaven—if to me you have done what you did, why should you be afraid of Esau?"

R. Tarfon said: Michael had no permission to move from the place where he had been wrestling until Jacob gave him leave—for Michael had to beg, "Let me go, for the day breaketh" (Gen. 32:27). Jacob retorted, "Are you a thief or a gambler, that you fear daybreak?"

Just then, many bands of ministering angels came by and said, "Michael, up with you, for 'the time of singing [God's praise] has come' " (Song 2:12)—meaning: If you do not begin, there will be no [morning] song. Michael began pleading with Jacob, "I beg you, let me go, lest the ministering angels in Aravot [the seventh heaven] incinerate me for delaying the song." Jacob replied, "I will not let thee go, except thou bless me" (Gen. 32:27). Michael then asked, "Who is more beloved—the servitor or the son? I am the servitor and you are the son. Do you require my blessing?" Jacob replied, "Nevertheless." At once Michael said, "Thy name shall be called no more Jacob, but Israel" (Gen. 32:29), and went on, "Blessed are you, born of woman, for you entered the palace above and remained alive."

While Jacob and Michael were wrestling, Michael's band of angels were about to put Jacob's life in jeopardy. At that, the Holy One revealed Himself to them. When Michael saw the Holy One, his strength was depleted, as is said, "When he saw that he was unable to prevail against him, he could do no more than touch the hollow of his thigh" (Gen. 32:26). Then the Holy One said to Michael, "Was it seemly for you to cripple my priest?" Michael answered, "Master of the universe, am *I* not your priest?" God replied, "You are My priest above, while Jacob is My priest on earth." At once Michael summoned Raphael and said, "My comrade, I beg you, stand to with me in my distress, for you are in charge of healing." So Raphael went down and healed Jacob.[6]

84. "Let my lord, I pray thee, pass over before his servant" (Gen. 33:14). Esau suggested to Jacob, "Will you agree that the two of us be partners in your world?"[7] Jacob responded, "[No], 'let my lord, I pray thee, pass through [this world] ahead of his servant.' " Esau asked, "Are you not afraid of my captains, prefects, and commanders?"[8] Jacob replied, " 'I will journey on gently' [ibid.], meekly, very meekly. I will walk as if my face were covered[9] [so that I see nothing]."

"Until I come unto my lord unto Seir" (Gen. 33:14). R. Abbahu said: We went through all of Scripture to and fro, and did not find that Jacob ever went to the mountain

1. Gen. R. 76:2.
2. JV: "The chariots of God are myriads, even thousands upon thousands."
3. JV: "What meanest thou by all this camp which I have met?" Gen. R. 75:11.
4. Gen. R. 75:10; Tanhuma *Va-yishlah*, §3.
5. B. Sot 41b; Gen. R. 45:11.
6. Midrash Avkir.
7. In the rewards of the world-to-come. In return, you will enjoy with me the pleasure of this world.
8. Should you reject your share in this world, you will be at their mercy.
9. Relating *le'itti* ("gently") to *l't* ("cover"), as in 1 Sam. 21:10.

of Seir to see Esau. Is it possible that Jacob, the truthful one, would have deceived Esau? So when is Jacob to come to Esau? In the time-to-come, when "liberators shall come up on Mount Zion to wreak judgment on Mount Esau" (Obad. 1:21).[1]

85. "He established a [token] abode outside the city" (Gen. 33:18).[2] The verse implies that Jacob entered on the eve of the Sabbath as the sun was setting. Then, [leaving the city] while it was yet day, [he established his token abode] and thus fixed the Sabbath boundaries.[3] This proves that Jacob observed the Sabbath before it was ordained [on Sinai].[4]

The Portions of Jacob and Esau

86. When Jacob and Esau were in their mother's womb, Jacob said to Esau, "Esau, my brother, our father has two of us, even as there are two worlds before us—this world and the world-to-come. In this world there is eating, drinking, and the give-and-take of business. But with regard to all such activities, the world-to-come is quite different. If it be your wish, you take this world, and I will take the world-to-come." Thus it came about that Esau took this world as his portion, and Jacob took the world-to-come as his.

Now, when Jacob came back from Laban's house and Esau saw that Jacob had wives, children, menservants and maidservants, livestock, and silver and gold, he said to him, "Jacob, my brother, did you not say to me that you would take the world-to-come as your portion and that I would take this world as mine? How, then, did you come to all this wealth—wives, children, money, menservants, and maidservants? Why do you, like me, make use of this world?" Jacob replied, "What few possessions I have are what the Holy One has given me for my use in this world as the need arises." In that instant, weighing the matter in his mind, Esau said to himself: If the Holy One has given him so much of this world, even though it is not his portion, how much more and more will He give him of the world-to-come, which is his portion![5]

Rebekah's Death and Rachel's Burial

87. When Rebekah died, it was asked: Who will walk before her bier? Abraham is dead. Isaac stays at home because his eyes are dim, and Jacob has gone to Paddanaram. Should wicked Esau walk before her bier, people will say, "A curse on the breast that gave suck to such a one." What did they do? They took her out for burial at night. For this reason, Scripture does not record her death.[6]

"And Rachel died, and was buried on the road to Ephrath" (Gen. 35:19). Why did Jacob see fit to bury Rachel on the road to Ephrath [and not in the cave of Machpelah]? Because our father Jacob foresaw that they who were to be exiled[7] would pass by way of Ephrath. Therefore he buried her there, so that she might beseech mercy for them. Referring to this, Scripture says, "A voice is heard in Ramah,[8] lamentation, and bitter weeping, Rachel weeping for her children" (Jer. 31:15).[9]

The House of Jacob and the House of Esau

88. "And Jacob dwelt" (Gen. 37:1). What precedes this passage? "These are the kings that reigned in the land of Edom. . . . And these are the names of the chiefs that came of Esau" (Gen. 36:31, 40). R. Hunia said: Jacob's decision to dwell in a land near Esau's may be understood by the parable of a man who, while on a journey, saw a pack of dogs and was seized with fear of them. What did he do? He sat down among them.[10] So also, when our father Jacob saw Esau and his chiefs, he too, though afraid of them, settled down among them.

R. Levi said: What Jacob did may be illustrated by the parable of a blacksmith whose forge opened onto the middle of the street, while the workshop of his son, a goldsmith, opened opposite him. Once he saw many, many bundles of thorns being brought into the city. Upset, he exclaimed, "Alas for the town. See what is coming into it!"[11] A clever man who was there called him: "Are you afraid of these? One spark from your forge and one spark from your son's, and all the thorns will go up in flames." So, too, when our father Jacob saw Esau and his chiefs, he was afraid. The Holy One said to him: Are you afraid of these? One spark from you and one spark from your son, and you will consume them, all of them. Thus it is written, "The house of Jacob shall be a fire, and the house of Joseph a flame, with Esau's house like straw to be kindled and consumed" (Obad. 1:18).[12]

---

1. Gen. R. 78:14.
2. JV: "and encamped before the city."
3. Thus he was enabled to go anywhere on the Sabbath within a radius of two thousand cubits from the spot where, prior to the Sabbath, he had made his token abode.
4. Gen. R. 79:6.
5. TdEZ 19 (JPS, p. 494).
6. As, e.g., Sarah's death, which is recorded in Gen. 23:1. Tanhuma, *Ki Tetze*, §4; PR 12:4 (YJS 1:224).
7. By Nebuchadnezzar.
8. Ramah, near where Jacob buried Rachel, lay north of Jerusalem in the path of the exiles driven toward Babylon. Hebron is south of Jerusalem, and the patriarchs and matriarchs buried there in the cave of Machpelah were out of the way of the exiles going northeast to Babylon.
9. Gen. R. 82:10.
10. Had he fled, the dogs, seeing that he was afraid, would have pursued him.
11. "Alas . . . coming into it"—Gen. R. TA, p. 1005. BR: "Where will all these bundles be put?"
12. Gen. R. 84:5; En Yaakov, B. BB 123a; Yalkut, Obad. §549; Tanhuma, *Va-yeshev*, §1.

Joseph and His Brothers

89. "Joseph, though only seventeen years old . . . was already a [sophisticated] youth" (Gen. 37:2).[1] He did the things that such youths do: he made eyes at girls, he walked with a swagger, and he styled his hair.

"Now Israel loved Joseph more than all his children" (Gen. 37:3), because Joseph's radiant features were like his.

"And he made him a coat of *passim*"[2] (Gen. 37:3). The word *passim* means that the coat's sleeves reached Joseph's wrists (*pas*).[3] Or, it was so delicate and light that it could be folded up into the palm (*pas*) of one's hand.

"And Joseph dreamed a dream . . . and he told it to his father, and to his brethren; and his father rebuked him, and said unto him: . . . 'Shall I and thy mother and thy brethren indeed come to bow down to thee?' " (Gen. 37:5 and 37:10). I and your brothers, perhaps. But how can I come with your mother? Your mother is dead. Jacob did not realize that the dream had to do with Bilhah, Rachel's maidservant, who brought up Joseph like a mother.

"But his father kept the saying in mind" (Gen. 37:11). He took a pen and recorded the day, the hour, and the place.[4] Likewise, the Holy Spirit declared: Keep what Joseph reported in mind—it will touch [significantly all of your progeny].

"And Israel said unto Joseph: 'Do not thy brethren graze the flock in Shechem? Go now, and I will send thee unto them.' And he said to him: 'Here am I' " (Gen. 37:13). R. Hama bar Hanina asserted: Whenever our father Jacob recalled this conversation, his innards were slashed by remorse. "You[5] knew that your brothers hated you, and yet you said, 'Here am I!' "[6]

90. "And they saw him from afar" (Gen. 37:18). They said, "Let us sic the dogs on him [so they tear him to pieces]."[7]

"And it came to pass when Joseph was come to his brothers" (Gen. 37:23), he came strutting like a peacock [as was his wont].[8]

"They cast him into the pit—and the pit was empty, there was no water in it" (Gen. 37:24). Empty of water, but full of snakes and scorpions.

"And they sold Joseph to the Ishmaelites" (Gen. 37:28). Is it possible that Joseph, already seventeen years old, saw his brothers selling him, yet remained silent? Indeed not, for he threw himself at the feet of each one of them, imploring them to take pity on him, but not one did. [Later, recollecting Joseph's pleas], the brothers are quoted as saying, "In that we saw the distress of his soul, when he besought us" (Gen. 42:21).[9]

91. R. Tarfon and the elders were sitting in the shade of the dovecote in Yavneh, and the question arose: What is the significance of Scripture's saying, "With their camels bearing spicery and balm and ladanum" (Gen. 37:25)? It is to make known how very much the merit of the righteous helps them. For if this one [Joseph], who was both chosen and beloved, had had to go down with an ordinary caravan of Arabs, would they not have suffocated him with the stench of their camels laden with foul-smelling resin? But for his sake the Holy One arranged that the sacks be full of spices and fragrant balm, so that he should not be suffocated by the stench of the camels and the foul smell of resin.[10]

The Going Down of Judah

92. "Judah went down from his brethren" (Gen. 38:1). It was indeed a going down, for he married a heathen.

"Judah . . . turned in to a man of Adullam" (Gen. 38:1). Judah, the most distinguished in his father's house, took a Canaanite woman! That is why, at Judah's "going down," the Holy Spirit cried out—so said R. Isaac—"[Judah], Israel's glory, had to go down to Adullam!" (Mic. 1:15).[11]

"Judah saw there a daughter of a certain Canaanite" (Gen. 38:2). To illustrate what Judah did, the sages told the parable of a dog who came upon a carcass and smelled it, but did not eat it. Then a lion came upon it and ate it. All the [beasts] then proceeded to berate him: What the dog disdained, the lion ate. So, too, Esau disdained the daughters of Canaan, as is said, "Esau saw the daughters of Canaan were evil" (Gen. 28:8). But Judah, likened to a lion, took one of them, as is said, "He took her" (Gen. 38:2).

Another comment on "Judah went down" (Gen. 38:1). With regard to this verse, Scripture says, "Judah hath dealt treacherously, and an abomination was committed in Israel" (Mal. 2:11). "Judah dealt treacherously" when, [showing Joseph's coat dipped in blood], he said to Jacob, "Know now whether it is thy son's coat" (Gen. 37:32). "An abomination was committed in Israel" when the brothers told Joseph. "Judah hath profaned the holiness of the Lord" (Mal. 2:11)—Judah profaned himself when, going down from among his brothers and his father's house, "he married a woman who worshiped an alien god" (ibid.).

---

1. JV: "Joseph, being seventeen years old . . . being still a lad." But the commentator seems to take *na'ar* as a nominal form of the stem *'r* ("to awake, to become sexually mature"). So Rabbi Julius Kravitz of Tucson, Ariz.
2. JV: "coat of many colors."
3. Long sleeves suggest that Joseph was to do no heavy work.
4. "Though he had rebuked him, that was because he stirred up his brethren's hate, but actually he believed in the dream" (Gen. R., Soncino, p. 778, n. 4).
5. "I"—Gen. R. TA, p. 1014; BR: "You."
6. Gen. R. 84:7–8 and 84:12–13.
7. This comment is based on the second half of the verse: "And before he came near unto them, they conspired against him to slay him."
8. The comment intends to account for the brothers' hardheartedness to Joseph.
9. Gen. R. 84:14, 84:16, and 91:8.
10. Mek, *Be-shallah*, *Va-yehi*, 5; Yalkut, *Be-shallah*, §247.
11. For Judah's "descent" to Adullam began the chain of events leading to the marriage of Judah and Tamar, out of which the Messiah was to spring. See Gen. 38:29 and Ruth 4:18–22.

And how was Judah punished? "To the man that did thus, the Lord cut off Er as well as Oneh" (Mal. 2:12).[1] Er and Onan [his two sons by the Canaanite woman] died.[2]

93. "For My thoughts are not your thoughts" (Isa. 55:8). The Holy One's thoughts are not at all like the thoughts of flesh and blood. How so? The tribe fathers were engaged in selling Joseph, Joseph was engaged in his own work, Jacob engaged with his sackcloth and his fasting, Judah engaged in taking a wife. And the Holy One also was engaged—He was creating the light of Messiah the king. Hence it is written, "Before [Israel] travailed [in servitude], she already had given birth" (Isa. 66:7). Before Pharaoh, the first enslaver, was born, the last redeemer already had his birth.[3]

Joseph in Egypt

94. "Joseph was brought down to Egypt" (Gen. 39:1). Read not, "Was brought down," but, "Brought down,"[4] for he brought down his father and the tribe fathers to Egypt. R. Tanhuma asked: How may what happened be illustrated? By the parable of a heifer upon whose neck her owners tried to place a yoke, but who resisted their efforts. What did the owners do? They took her calf from behind her and dragged it to the place they wanted to have plowed. As the calf was being pulled, it lowed disconsolately. When the heifer heard her offspring lowing, she felt constrained because of her offspring to follow him. Likewise, the Holy One sought to carry out the decree "Know of a surety that thy seed shall . . . serve them" (Gen. 15:13), and so He brought about the cause of all that was to happen, until finally Jacob and his family felt constrained to go down to Egypt, there to discharge the obligation [of living in the servitude] imposed on them.[5]

95. "Potiphar . . . an Egyptian bought him of the hand of the Ishmaelites" (Gen. 39:1). R. Levi observed: A slave buys, the son of a bondmaid sells, and a freeborn son becomes slave to both.[6]

96. "The Lord made all that he did to prosper in his hand" (Gen. 39:3). Whenever Joseph served his master spiced wine, the master would ask, "What have you poured me?" When Joseph replied, "Spiced wine," the master would say, "But I want bitter wine"—and it became bitter wine. When the master said, "I want mulled wine," it became mulled. The same happened with water—indeed, with each and every thing, as is said, "The Lord made all that he did to prosper in his hand." When his master became aware of it, he turned over all the keys to Joseph, so that Joseph was able to say, "My master has no concern about anything that is in the house" (Gen. 39:8). When Joseph found himself so comfortably situated, he began to eat and drink well, to frizz his hair, and to say, "Blessed be He who is everywhere, who helped me forget my father's house." Then the Holy One said to Joseph: Your father is mourning for you in sackcloth and ashes, and you eat and drink well, and frizz your hair—you pampered brat! As you live, I shall sic a she-bear on you. At once, "it came to pass that his master's wife cast her eyes upon Joseph" (Gen. 39:7). A parable of a strong man who stood in the marketplace, made eyes at the women, kept combing his hair, walked with a swagger, and said, "How fit I am, how well endowed I am—how strong! how handsome!" He was told, "If you are so strong and so fit, here is a bear—try to overpower it."[7]

97. Joseph was seventeen, with all the charm of his youth, and each and every day his mistress, Potiphar's wife, endeavored to entice him by various wiles. Each and every day she would wear three different outfits—the garments she wore in the morning she did not wear at noon, and those at noon she did not wear as the sun was setting. Why all this? So that he might gaze at her.

On one occasion a group of Egyptian women gathered [in Potiphar's house], eager to see Joseph's beauty. What did Potiphar's wife do? She took citrons, placed them before the women, and gave each of them a knife. Then she summoned Joseph and had him stand before them. As they peeled the citrons, at the same time gazing at Joseph's beauty, they cut their fingers. Then Potiphar's wife said: You, who saw him only for one instant, are thus overcome; how much more and more am I, who see him all the time.

And though each and every day she sought to entice him with her wiles, he nevertheless stood fast against his impulse.[8]

98. A Roman noblewoman asked R. Yose: Is it possible that Joseph, at seventeen, with all the hot blood of youth, could act with such self-restraint? R. Yose brought out the book of Genesis and began reading to her the story of Reuben and Bilhah, and the story of Judah and Tamar, and said: If Scripture does not cover up for these, who were adult and still under their father's authority, how much less likely is it that Scripture would cover up for one who was a minor and on his own![9]

Joseph before Pharaoh

99. "But there was none that could interpret them unto Pharaoh" (Gen. 41:8). R. Joshua of Sikhnin said in the name of R. Levi: They did interpret them, but Pharaoh

1. JV: "May the Lord cut off to the man that doeth this him that calleth and him that answereth." By not translating the two nouns, the play on words that follows is made possible.
2. See Gen. 38:7 and 38:10. Gen. R. 85:1; Tanhuma B, *Va-yeshev*, §9; MhG Gen., pp. 642–44.
3. Ibid. Perez, child of Judah and Tamar (Gen. 38:29), and ancestor of David (Ruth 4:18–22), thus of the Messiah, had his birth before the birth of the pharaoh who was to subject Israel to slavery.
4. A slight change in vowels makes possible the reading suggested.
5. Tanhuma, *Va-yeshev*, §4; Yalkut, *Va-yeshev*, §145.
6. Potiphar was Pharaoh's slave; the Ishmaelites were descendants of Hagar, a bondmaid. Gen. R. 86:3.
7. Tanhuma, *Va-yeshev*, §8; Gen. R. 86:5.
8. Tanhuma, *Va-yeshev*, §5.
9. Gen. R. 87:6.

did not like what they said. For example, they said: The seven fat cows mean that you will beget seven daughters; the seven lean cows mean that you will bury seven daughters. Or: The seven full ears of corn mean that you will conquer seven principalities; the seven thin ears that seven principalities will rebel against you.

What was the purpose of all of this? So that Joseph would come at the end and be raised to high rank. For the Holy One said: If Joseph were to come right away and interpret the dream, he would not receive the recognition that should be his. The magicians would say to Pharaoh, "Had you asked us, we would at once have interpreted the dream for you in the same sense." Therefore He waited for the magicians to wear themselves out in their attempts and to exhaust Pharaoh's spirit, until Joseph would come and restore it.[1]

100. R. Hiyya bar Abba stated in the name of R. Yohanan: When Pharaoh said to Joseph, "Without thee shall no man lift up his hand or his foot" (Gen. 41:44), his astrologers said to him, "Will you set over us a slave whose master bought him for twenty pieces of silver?" He replied, "I see traits of royalty in him." They said, "If so, he should know the world's seventy languages." "Very well," said Pharaoh, "I'll test him tomorrow."

During the night [the angel] Gabriel came and taught Joseph the seventy languages, so that in the morning, whatever language Pharaoh spoke, Joseph replied in the same language. But then Joseph began talking to Pharaoh in the holy tongue, and Pharaoh did not understand what Joseph was saying. Pharaoh said, "Teach me [this language]." Joseph tried to teach it to him, but Pharaoh could not learn it. Pharaoh said, "Swear to me that you will not reveal this."[2] So Joseph swore to him.

Subsequently, when Joseph said to Pharaoh, "My father made me swear, saying, 'In the land of Canaan, there shalt thou bury me' " (Gen. 50:5), Pharaoh urged him, "Go ask to be released from your oath."[3] Joseph replied, "Very well, but then I will also ask to be released from the oath I swore to you." And so, reluctantly, Pharaoh said to Joseph, "Go up and bury thy father, according as he made thee swear (Gen. 50:6).[4]

101. "And Joseph went out from the presence of Pharaoh, and went throughout all the land of Egypt" (Gen. 41:46). Whenever he went into a marketplace, he used to see the different peoples clustered in many, many groups, in many, many companies, each speaking in their own tongue, and he could understand what each was saying. And when he rode in his chariot and passed through Egypt's entire domain, young Egyptian women used to climb walls and throw golden rings at him, hoping that he might look up and see the beauty of their appearance, as is said, "Joseph was a young man full of grace. . . . Young women used to climb over walls to have him gaze at them" (Gen. 49:22).[5]

102. "Young women used to run on top of walls" (Gen. 49:22). You find that when Joseph went forth to rule over Egypt, royal princesses used to peer at him through lattices and throw bracelets, necklets, earrings, and finger rings, hoping that he might lift up his eyes and look at them. Nevertheless, he did not do so.[6]

Joseph's Brothers in Egypt

103. "And Jacob said to his sons: 'Why should you make yourselves conspicuous?' " (Gen. 42:1).[7] My sons, you are all mighty men and you are all handsome. Do not all enter together by the same gate. Do not stand together in the same place, that the evil eye may have no power over you.[8]

104. "Joseph's brethren went down" (Gen. 42:3). Scripture should have said, "Jacob's sons." Why "Joseph's brethren?" Because in the beginning they did not treat him like a brother, for they sold him into servitude, but in the end they regretted what they had done. Every day they would say, "When shall we be going down into Egypt to bring our brother back to his father?" And when their father told them to go down to Egypt, they were all as one in their resolve to bring him back.

R. Judah bar Simon said: Joseph knew that his brothers had come down to Egypt to buy food. How did he know? He had guards stationed at all the gates and instructed them, "Take note of everyone who enters to buy food—record his name and his father's name, and each evening bring me your records." They did so. When Jacob's sons came, as each one entered by a different gate, his name and the name of his father were recorded. In the evening, when the guards brought the lists to Joseph, one had the entry "Reuben son of Jacob," another, "Simeon son of Jacob," and so on.

Joseph ordered, "Shut all storehouses, but leave one storehouse open." Then he gave the brothers' names to the official in charge of that one storehouse, saying to him, "When these men come to buy food, seize them and dispatch them to me."

Three days passed, but they did not come. So Joseph sent [a company of] mighty men to look for them in the marketplace, supplying the men with personal descriptions of the brothers. Joseph's men set out and found the brothers in the harlot's district, going from one street to another, from one alley to another. What were the brothers doing

---

1. Gen. R. 89:6.
2. That he did not know Hebrew. A king was supposed to know every tongue.
3. In Jewish law, only proper authorities can release a man from his oath. Pharaoh did not want Joseph to leave Egypt to bury his father.
4. B. Sot 36b.
5. JV: "Joseph is a fruitful vine. . . . Its branches run over the wall." But *ben* ("vine") also means "young man"; *porat* ("fruitful") is associated with the Aramaic *apiryon* ("treading gracefully"); *banot* ("branches") can also mean "young women"; *tzaadah* ("run over") also means "climb" and "armlets"; and *shur* ("wall") is construed in a dual sense, "wall" and "gaze." See Rashi on Gen. 49:6. PRE 39.
6. Gen. R. 98:18.
7. JV: "Why do you look one upon another?"
8. Ten such brothers together would expose them to the evil eye. Tanhuma, *Mi-ketz*, §8; Gen. R. 91:6; Yalkut, *Mi-ketz*, §148.

in the harlot's district? They figured: Our brother Joseph, being handsome, may have been set up [as a male harlot] in a harlot's stall. So Joseph's men seized them and brought them before Joseph.

"And when Joseph saw his brethren, he knew them . . . but they knew him not" (Gen. 42:7–8). The sages said: Because they had beards when he left them, "Joseph knew his brethren" (Gen. 42:8). But "they knew him not" (ibid.), because he had yet no sign of a beard when they left him.

"He made himself appear as a non-Jew[1] (*va-yitnakker*) unto them" (Gen. 42:7). He acted like a non-Jew, in that [seemingly resorting to divination][2] he took his goblet, tapped it, and said to them, "I see in the goblet that you are spies." They replied, "We are upright men" (Gen. 42:11). He said, "If you are upright men, why did you not enter through the same gate?" They: "Our father commanded us, 'Do not enter through the same gate.' " He: "Then what business had you being all together in the street of the harlots? Were you not afraid of the evil eye?" They: "We had lost something and were searching for it there." He: "What was it that you lost? [You are lying!] I see in my goblet that two of you have destroyed the great city of Shechem [which I believe is what you intend to do here]." They: "Who were the two?" He again tapped the goblet and said, "Simeon and Levi." Seized with trembling, the brothers blurted out, "We, thy servants, are twelve brethren" (Gen. 42:13). He: "Where are the other two?" They: "One, the youngest, is this day with our father, and the other is we know not where" (ibid.). He: "Bring your youngest brother unto me, so that your words may be verified" (Gen. 42:20). He then seized Simeon, bound him before their eyes, and said, "This one will stay in prison until you bring me the youngest." Why did he bind Simeon? Because it was Simeon who had pushed him into the pit; and also because Joseph wished to separate him from Levi, lest the two devise a plot against him. Simeon then said to his brothers, "What you did to Joseph, are you now about to do to me?" They: "What can we do? Shall the people of our household die of famine?" He: "Do what you will. As for me, let me see who can throw me into prison!"

At that, Joseph sent word to Pharaoh, "Dispatch seventy strongmen from your personal guard, for I have found brigands whom I wish to put in fetters." Pharaoh dispatched them, and Joseph's brothers were watching attentively to see what Joseph would do. He ordered the strongmen, "Throw this man into prison, and be sure to put fetters on his legs." But when some of them came near him, Simeon shouted at them, and as they heard the shout, they fell flat on their faces so hard that their teeth were broken. Now, Manasseh, Joseph's son, was seated in front of his father. So his father said, "Up with you!" Manasseh jumped up, knocked Simeon out with one blow, and threw him into prison, where he put fetters on his legs.

"You may think," Simeon said to his brothers, "that this was an Egyptian kind of blow. It wasn't! It had the kind of knockout punch we are familiar with in Father's house." When Joseph's brothers learned this, a great fear came over them.

They went back to their father and related all that had befallen them. When their father asked, "Where is Simeon?" they replied, "That man, the lord of the land, seized him as a hostage, to force us to bring our youngest brother." Jacob said, "Me have ye bereaved of my children; Joseph is not, and Simeon is not, and ye will take Benjamin away?" (Gen. 42:36). Then "Reuben spoke unto his father, saying: 'Thou shalt slay my two sons, if I bring him not to thee' " (Gen. 42:37). Jacob replied, "You foolish firstborn, are not your sons my sons also?" Judah then counseled his brothers: Let the venerable old man be until the last morsel of bread is gone.

"And it came to pass, when they had eaten up the corn" (Gen. 43:2), Judah spoke up: "Father, should Benjamin go with us, he may be seized; then again, he may not. But if he does not go with us, all of us are sure to die. It is better that you disregard the uncertain and go by the certain." Jacob asked, "Who will stand surety for him?" Judah replied, "I will be surety for him" (Gen. 43:9). So Jacob sent Benjamin with them.[3]

105. "God Shaddai (Almighty) give you mercy" (Gen. 43:14). Why did Jacob see fit to invoke "God Shaddai" when he blessed his sons? He used this name to indicate that more than enough afflictions had come upon him. While he was yet in his mother's womb, Esau strove with him. When he fled from Esau to Laban, he spent twenty years there in many kinds of distress. After he left, Laban pursued him in order to slay him. As soon as he was delivered from Laban, Esau came and sought to slay him, and because of Esau he had to give up a huge tribute [of cattle, camels, and so on]. After he extricated himself from Esau, the distress with Dinah befell him. After he extricated himself from that distress, there was the distress of Rachel['s death]. After such a chain of distress, he wanted a little repose, but then there befell him the distress of Joseph, the distress of Simeon, and the distress of Benjamin. That is why Jacob invoked "God Shaddai[4] (Almighty)," as if to say: May He who said to heaven and earth, "Enough (*dai*)!" say also to my affliction, "Enough (*dai*)!"

The brothers brought Benjamin and presented him to Joseph. "And he lifted up his eyes and saw Benjamin his brother, his mother's son" (Gen. 43:29), and rejoiced at the sight of him, because he saw in him the very likeness of his mother.

Then Joseph asked, "Is this your younger brother of whom you spoke unto me?" (Gen. 43:29). They replied, "Yes." He invited them to dine with him. Now he wanted to have Benjamin seated next to him but did not know how to go about it. So he picked up his goblet and pre-

1. JV: "But made himself strange."
2. Divination is foreign to Jewish belief.

3. Gen. R. 91:6; Yalkut, *Va-yeshev*, §148; Tanhuma, *Mi-ketz*, §8; Tanhuma, *Va-yiggash*, §4.
4. Shaddai is read: *She [amar] dai* ("He who said, 'Enough' ").

tended to divine by tapping and sniffing it. Finally he said, "Judah, who is king, shall sit at the head of the table; Reuben, who is firstborn, next to him"; and so on with the others, until only Benjamin was left. Then he said, "I have no mother, and Benjamin, whose mother died when giving birth to him, has no mother. I had a brother who was separated from me, and he had a brother who was separated from him. Therefore let him come and rest his head next to mine."[1] Hence it is said, "And they sat before him, the firstborn according to his birthright, and the youngest according to his youth" (Gen. 43:33).

"And portions were taken unto them" (Gen. 43:34). Of the portions brought to the meal, Joseph gave each of the brothers his portion and, of course, gave Benjamin his. Then Joseph took his own portion and gave it to Benjamin. Asenath[2] also took her portion and gave it to Benjamin. Then Ephraim and Manasseh likewise took their portions and gave them to Benjamin, so that Benjamin now had five portions. Hence, "Benjamin's portion was five times as much as any of theirs" (Gen. 43:34).[3]

106. "And the goblet was found in Benjamin's sack" (Gen. 44:12). The [indignant] brothers pummeled Benjamin's shoulders, saying, "O thief, son of a she-thief! You have disgraced us. You are a true son of your mother—even so did your mother disgrace our father."[4]

On account of the blows struck on Benjamin's shoulders [for an offense he did not commit], he won the privilege of having the Presence dwell "between his shoulders" [that is, in his territory]—for Benjamin is spoken of as "the beloved of the Lord" (Deut. 33:12). [And Scripture goes on to say that] "God shieldeth him all the day, for He dwelleth [with him because of his humiliation at the pummeling] between his shoulders" (ibid.).[5]

Joseph Makes Himself Known to His Brothers

107. "Then Judah came near unto him" (Gen. 44:18). R. Samuel bar Nahman said in the name of R. Jonathan: While Judah and Joseph were arguing with each other, the ministering angels said to one another: Let us go down and watch a bull and a lion[6] trying to gore each other. Ordinarily, a bull fears the lion, but here bull and lion are at it, trying to hoist each other.

R. Yohanan said: When Joseph seized Benjamin and said to his brothers, "He in whose possession the goblet was found shall be my slave" (Gen. 44:17), Judah became enraged and roared in a voice so loud that it was heard a distance of four hundred parasangs, so that even Hushim son of Dan [who was hard of hearing] heard it. He sprang up out of the land of Canaan and rushed to Judah's side, and, with the two roaring together, the land of Egypt was almost turned upside down.

R. Joshua the Levite said: The other brothers, when they saw that Judah was enraged, were likewise filled with rage and stamped their feet on the earth, making furrows in the ground under them.

When Joseph saw the signs of Judah's rage, he was seized with trembling and said to himself: Woe is me! He may kill me! What were these signs? Blood oozed out of Judah's right eye. Some say that he wore five coats of mail over five sets of clothing. He had a single bristle on his chest, and whenever he became enraged, that bristle turned so hard that it pierced through all he wore. Furthermore, when he wished to stoke his rage, he would fill his belt bag with pea-sized pellets of brass, grab some, put them into his mouth, and grind them down with his teeth as his fury mounted.

In saying, "My lord asked his servants," etc. (Gen. 44:19), Judah argued with Joseph: "From the very beginning, you intended to frame us. From how many countries have people come to Egypt to buy food? Did you ask any of them the kinds of questions you asked us, as though we had come to wed your daughter or you to wed our sister? Nevertheless, we concealed nothing from you." Joseph retorted, "Judah, why do you act as spokesman for your brothers, when I see in the goblet that you have brothers older than you?" Judah replied, "My brothers bear no responsibility for Benjamin, whereas I—my innards are twisted like a rope with anguish." Joseph: "Why?" Judah: "Because I stood surety for him." Joseph: "Why did you not feel it necessary to stand surety for your other brother at the time you sold him to the Ishmaelites for twenty pieces of silver and inflicted pain upon your aged father by telling him that 'without doubt Joseph has been torn in pieces by a beast of prey' [Gen. 37:33]? That brother did no harm to you, while this one sinned, for he stole the goblet. So tell your father, 'The rope has followed the bucket into the well.' " When Judah heard this, he broke out into sobs and cried in a loud voice, "How shall I go up to my father, if the lad be not with me?" (Gen. 44:34).

Then Joseph said, "Come, let us discuss the matter calmly. State what you have in mind and set forth your plea in an orderly fashion."

At that, Judah said to Naphtali [in an aside], "Go and see how many districts there are in Egypt." Naphtali leaped out,[7] bounded back, and reported, "Twelve." Judah then said to his brothers, "I will smash three of them, each of you will take one, and we shall not leave a man alive among them." His brothers replied, "Judah, Egypt is not Shechem. If you destroy Egypt, you destroy the whole world." At this, "Joseph could not refrain himself . . . and he cried, 'Cause every man to go out from

---

1. In antiquity, men reclined on couches at dinner.
2. Joseph's wife. See Gen. 41:50.
3. Tanhuma, *Va-yiggash*, §5; Tanhuma B, *Mi-ketz*, §12; Gen. R. 92:5.
4. See Gen. 31:30–35.
5. Or: "He dwells amid his slopes"; the mountain on which the Temple stood is in the territory assigned to the tribe of Benjamin.
   "R. Yose said: May my portion be with one who is suspected unjustly. You can readily see this in the experience of Benjamin, who was suspected of doing something he had not done. What did he win? The privilege of the Presence in his portion" (see MhG Gen., p. 746; B. Shab 11a–b; B. MK 18b). Tanhuma, *Mi-ketz*, §10.
6. Joseph is described as "a firstling bull" (Deut. 33:17), and Judah is spoken of as "a lion's whelp" (Gen. 49:9).
7. Naphtali is described as a "hind let loose" (Gen. 49:21).

me' " (Gen. 45:1), thus putting himself in great danger, for if his brothers had decided to slay him, no creature in the world would have known who did it. Nevertheless, Joseph said to himself: It is better that I be slain than that I put my brothers to shame in front of the Egyptians.

As soon as the Egyptians left, Judah again confronted Joseph: "You swore by the life of wicked Pharaoh, and I swear by the life of my righteous father—if I draw my sword out of its sheath, I will fill Egypt with corpses." Joseph replied: "If you pull the sword out of its sheath, I will wrap it around your neck." Judah: "If I open my mouth, I will swallow you." Joseph: "If you dare open your mouth, I will plug it with a rock." Judah then asked Joseph, "What are we to tell our father?" Joseph: "I already told you. Tell him, 'The rope has followed the bucket.' " Judah said, "You pass a judgment upon us based on lies." Joseph replied, "Lies to liars—no judgment is as full of lies as the sale of your brother." Judah: "The fire that burned Shechem[1] is rekindled within me." Joseph: "It is rather the fire you unjustly intended for Tamar your daughter-in-law, and I will quench it."

In that instant, Judah's rage flared up, and he kept putting pellets of iron into his mouth and spitting them out as dust, saying, "Now I will go out and dye all the districts of Egypt with blood." Joseph replied, "You have always been dyers, for you dyed the coat of your brother with blood and told your father that 'without doubt Joseph was torn in pieces' " (Gen. 37:33).

Sensing that the brothers were at one in their resolve to destroy Egypt, Joseph said to himself: I had better make myself known to them, to prevent Egypt's destruction. And so Joseph spoke up: "Did you not say that this one's brother is dead? The fact is, I bought him. I will call him, and he will come to you."[2] He proceeded to call, "Joseph son of Jacob, come to me! Joseph son of Jacob, come to me and speak to your brothers who sold you." The brothers turned their eyes to the four corners of the chamber. Joseph asked them, "Why are you looking this way and that? I am Joseph, your brother." Instantly their souls flew out of them, and they could say nothing in reply. But the Holy One performed a miracle in their behalf, and their souls were restored to them. Then Joseph said, " 'Behold, your eyes see, and so can the eyes of my brother Benjamin, that it is Joseph that speaketh unto you' [Gen. 45:12], for I speak the sacred tongue." Still they did not believe him. Why not? Because he left them beardless, and now he stood before them with a beard on his face.

When they did recognize him, they wanted to slay him. But an angel came down and flung them apart to the four corners of the chamber.

In that instant Judah let out a mighty roar, so loud that all walls in Egypt collapsed, all pregnant women miscarried, Joseph fell off his seat, Pharaoh rolled off his throne, and all the strongmen who had been standing in Joseph's presence had their faces twisted around backward, and their teeth fell out.

When Joseph perceived that his brothers felt such deep shame, he said to them, " 'Come near to me, I pray you.' And they came near" (Gen. 45:4), each of them kissing Joseph and weeping over him.[3]

1. Gen. 34.
2. Gen. 38.

Jacob's Going Down to Egypt

108. R. Hiyya bar Abba said in the name of R. Yohanan: By rights, Jacob should have gone down into Egypt in chains of iron.[4] But his merit availed him, as is said, "Because of My love for [Jacob], I drew [Israel] with cords, with bands of love. Thus I was to [Israel] as one that lifteth up the yoke from the jaws of animals, making it easier for [Israel] to sustain [the burden of servitude]" (Hos. 11:4).[5]

109. [Of Jacob's going down to Egypt], R. Berekhiah, citing R. Judah bar Simon, told a parable: An attempt was made to drag a cow to the slaughterhouse, but she refused to move. What was done? Her young one was pulled ahead of her, and she, reluctantly, unwillingly, followed. So, too, Jacob should have gone down to Egypt in shackles, with an iron collar about his neck. But the Holy One said: Shall I have my firstborn son go down in such disgrace? Even if I induce Pharaoh to bring him down personally, I will not have Jacob's going down turned into a public spectacle. Instead, I shall draw Jacob's son in front of him, and then [on his own, albeit] reluctantly, unwillingly, Jacob will quietly follow.

[Another interpretation: "With Joseph, He was brought down to Egypt" (Gen. 39:1)]:[6] Joseph brought down the Presence with him into Egypt.[7]

The Death and Burial of Jacob

110. "And Jacob called unto his sons, and said: 'Gather yourselves together, that I may reveal to you . . .' " (Gen. 49:1). What Jacob was about to reveal to his sons was when the time of redemption was to come. But the Presence departed from him.[8] So he said, "Could it be, God forbid, that my bed has produced an unfit son—as happened to Abraham, my father's father, out of whom sprang Ishmael, or as happened to my father Isaac, out of whom sprang Esau?" His sons assured him of their steadfastness: " 'Hear, O Israel [our father], the Lord is our God, the Lord alone' [Deut. 6:4]. Just as in your heart there is only

3. Tanhuma, *Va-yiggash*, §4; Tanhuma B, *Va-yiggash*, §8; Gen. R. 93:7; Yalkut, *Va-yiggash*, §151.
4. Since it was the beginning of Israel's servitude.
5. JV: "I drew them with cords of a man, with bands of love; and I was to them as they that take off the yoke on their jaws, and I fed them gently." Literally, the last clause may also be read: "I extended [strength] to them, making it possible to sustain the burden." B. Shab 89b.
6. JV: "And Joseph was brought down to Egypt."
7. A conclusion drawn from the assertion "The Lord was with Joseph" (Gen. 39:2). Gen. R. 86:2.
8. The Presence departed because the exact time of redemption is hidden knowledge and not to be revealed to mortals. But Jacob feared that the Presence departed because one of his sons was unfit to be told.

the One, so in our hearts there is only the One." Then our father Jacob pronounced for the first time the benediction "Blessed be the Name whose glorious kingdom is forever and ever."

Hence—it is reported in the name of R. Samuel—every day, morning and evening, Jews say, "In the cave of Machpelah [where you are at rest], 'Hear, O Israel [our father].' What you commanded us we still practice: 'The Lord is our God, the Lord alone.' "[1]

111. "And they came to a threshing floor for brambles" (Gen. 50:10).[2] But is a threshing floor ever used for brambles? R. Abbahu explained: The verse implies that, as a threshing floor is fenced by a hedge of brambles, so was Jacob's coffin encompassed by crowns. For sons of Esau, of Ishmael, and of Keturah also came. They came, so it is taught, to wage war [against the sons of Jacob]. But when they saw Joseph's crown hung upon Jacob's coffin, they all took off their crowns, and they, too, hung them upon Jacob's coffin. It is taught that thirty-six crowns were thus hung upon Jacob's coffin, encompassing it.[3]

When they came to the cave of Machpelah, Esau appeared and sought to prevent Jacob's burial in it, saying, "This cave has room for only four couples.[4] Since Jacob buried Leah in his place, the plot that remains is mine." Jacob's sons replied, "But you sold your portion to our father." Esau retorted, "Even if I did sell my claim as firstborn [to an additional portion in my father's estate], did I sell also the original single portion due me as an heir?" They said, "You sold that also." Esau: "Show me the bill of sale." They: "The bill of sale is in Egypt. Who will go and bring it from there? Let Naphtali go—he is as swift as a hind."

It so happened that Hushim son of Dan, who was hard of hearing, was standing there. When he asked, "What's going on?" he was told, "This one is holding us up until Naphtali returns from Egypt." Hushim asked, "And until Naphtali returns from Egypt, is my father's father to lie shamefully unburied?" So he seized a club and struck Esau on the head so hard that his eyes fell out of their sockets and dropped at Jacob's feet. At that, Jacob opened his eyes and smiled. Hence Scripture's assurance that "the righteous man will rejoice when he seeth revenge; he will bathe his feet in the blood of the wicked" (Ps. 58:11).

At that moment Rebekah's prophecy "Why should I be bereaved of you both in one day?" (Gen. 27:45) was fulfilled.[5]

112. "And when Joseph's brethren saw that their father was dead, they said, 'It may be that Joseph bears a grudge against us' " (Gen. 50:15). What did they see that made them afraid? As they were returning from burying their father, they saw that Joseph turned off the road and went to look at the pit into which his brothers had cast him. Upon seeing this, they said, "He still bears a grudge in his heart. Now that our father is dead, he will make his hatred of us felt." But in fact Joseph's motive was a pious one—he wanted to utter a blessing for the miracle wrought for him in that place.[6]

113. "And he comforted them, and spoke persuasively to them" (Gen. 50:21). R. Eleazar taught: What Joseph had to say was indeed persuasive. He said: If ten lamps could not extinguish one, how is one lamp to extinguish ten?[7]

1. B. Pes 56a; Gen. R. 98:4.
2. JV: "of Atad," a place-name. But since it occurs nowhere else, the commentator explores *atad* in its literal meaning of "brambles."
3. Joseph's crown, twelve crowns of the sons of Ishmael (Gen. 25:13–15), and twenty-three crowns of the chiefs of Esau (Gen. 36:15–18). See Rashi, ad loc.
4. For Adam and Eve, Abraham and Sarah, Isaac and Rebekah. As for the fourth place, the one next to Leah, Esau claimed that it should be reserved for him.

5. B. Sot 13a.
6. Tanhuma, *Va-yehi*, §17; Gen. R. 100:8; Lekah Tov, ad loc.
7. B. Meg 16b.

C H A P T E R   F O U R

ISRAEL IN EGYPT AND THE DEPARTURE FROM EGYPT

The Servitude in Egypt

1. "I found Israel like grapes in the wilderness, I saw your fathers as the first ripe in the fig tree at her first season" (Hos. 9:10). R. Yudan said: At first a fig tree's fruit is picked one by one, then two by two, then three by three, until the figs ripen so abundantly that baskets and shovels have to be used to gather them. So, too, at the beginning, "Abraham was one, and he inherited the Land" (Ezek. 33:24). Then two: Abraham and Isaac. And after that, three: Abraham, Isaac, and Jacob. Until finally, "the children of Israel were fruitful, and increased abundantly, and multiplied, and waxed exceeding mighty" (Exod. 1:7).[1]

2. "Now there arose a new king over Egypt" (Exod. 1:8). Rav and Samuel differed in their explanations of the verse. One said that he was actually a new king; the other, that new decrees were issued by him.[2] But if so, how can the verse go on to say, "Who knew not Joseph" (ibid.)? Because it seemed as though he was not aware that Joseph ever existed.

The sages asked: Why then is he called a new king? Was he not the same pharaoh? What happened was that the Egyptians said to Pharaoh, "Come, let us attack this people." He replied, "You are idiots. To this day we are eating what one might say belongs to them—how can we [even think of] attacking Joseph's people? But for Joseph, we would not have survived." When Pharaoh refused to listen to them, they deposed him from his throne for three months, until he said to them, "I agree to whatever you wish." Then they restored him. Hence, "There arose a new king" [signifies that Pharaoh was forced to issue new decrees].[3]

3. "Who knew not Joseph." When Joseph died, the Israelites, saying, "Let us be like the Egyptians," abolished the covenant of circumcision. After they did this, the Holy One turned the love the Egyptians had for them into hatred, as is said, "He turned their heart to hate His people, to deal craftily with His servants" (Ps. 105:25).[4]

4. "Come, let us deal craftily with him" (Exod. 1:10). The text does not say "with them," but "with him," which implies, so asserts R. Hama son of R. Hanina, that Pharaoh said, "Come, let us deal craftily with Israel's deliverer."

How shall we afflict Israel? [asked the Egyptians]. Shall we afflict them by fire? But Scripture says [that, in retribution], "the Lord will come with fire" (Isa. 66:15) and "by fire will the Lord contend" (Isa. 66:16). Shall we afflict Israel with the sword? But the verse continues, "And by His sword against all flesh" (ibid.). Come then, let us afflict Israel with water, for the Holy One has already sworn that He would not bring another flood upon the world, as is said, "I have sworn that the waters of Noah should no more go over the earth" (Isa. 54:9). What the Egyptians did not know was that He would indeed not cause floodwaters to go over the entire earth, but that He might bring them upon a single people. Or, He might not cause such waters to go over even a single people, but conceivably a people may go and fall into the waters. Thus Scripture: "The Egyptians fled at the sea's approach; but the Lord hurled the Egyptians into the sea" (Exod. 14:27). In connection with what happened to the Egyptians, R. Eleazar construed Scripture as saying, "In the thing that [the Egyptians] cooked up" (Exod. 18:11)[5]—in the very pot where the Egyptians cooked up their mischief against the Israelites, they themselves were cooked.[6]

5. "And they embittered their lives with harsh labor . . . and in all sorts of work in the fields" (Exod. 1:14). What is implied by "in all sorts of work in the fields"? After finishing their work in mortar and bricks, the Israelites would return to their homes to rest. Then an Egyptian would come and say, "Go out and gather greens for me in the garden patch," "Split this log for me," "Fill this cask for me from the river." Hence: "In all sorts of work in the fields."

What does Scripture mean by "With all the tasks that they ruthlessly imposed upon them" (Exod. 1:14)? That the Egyptians imposed men's work upon women and women's work upon men. Thus, a man would be told, "Up, and bake," and a woman would be told, "Fill this cask, split this log. Go to the patch and fetch some greens."[7]

6. R. Samuel bar Nahmani said: Why were the Egyptians compared to *maror*?[8] To teach you that, just as *maror* is soft as it begins to grow and hard at the end, so were the Egyptians soft and mild at the beginning,[9] but tough and hard in the end.[10]

1. Gen. R. 46:1; Yalkut, Hos., §525.
2. After all, Scripture does not say that the old king died.
3. B. Sot 11a; Exod. R. 1:8.
4. Exod. R. 1:8.

5. Literally, "In the thing wherein they dealt proudly (*zaddu*)." But *zaddu* can also mean "cooked up."
6. B. Sot 11a and En Yaakov, ad loc.
7. Tanhuma, *Va-yetze*, §9.
8. Chicory or horseradish.
9. Offering payment for work done.
10. B. Pes 39a.

7. "Therefore they did set over him" (Exod. 1:11)—not "over them," but "over him." In the school of R. Eleazar son of R. Simeon it was taught: The use of "over him" implies that [to con Israelites into believing that Pharaoh himself worked at making bricks] a brick-mold was brought and hung around the neck of Pharaoh, and whenever an Israelite complained that he was too delicate for such work, he was asked, "Are you more delicate than Pharaoh?"[1]

8. "And the Egyptians made the children of Israel serve with *parekh*."[2] R. Eleazar said: The word means "with gentle speech (*peh rakh*)." After Pharaoh said, "Let us act craftily," he gathered all Israel and, affecting gentleness, said, "I beg you, as a special favor, work alongside me today." Then Pharaoh picked up a basket and a shovel, and everyone who saw him pick up the basket and shovel and work at the making of bricks did likewise. Thus it came about that Israelites worked to the fullness of their strength and with great eagerness alongside Pharaoh. But when it grew dark, he stationed taskmasters over the Israelites and said, "Reckon up the number of bricks." After the taskmasters counted them, the Israelites were told, "This is to be the number you are to provide me each and every day."[3]

9. "Every boy that is born ye shall throw into the Nile" (Exod. 1:22). R. Hanan said: What did the chaste and virtuous Israelite women do? They took their infants and hid them in holes [in their houses]. So the wicked Egyptians would take their own young children, bring them into the homes of the Israelites, and pinch their young until they cried. When the Israelite infants in their hiding places heard the Egyptian children cry, they cried with them. Then the Egyptians would seize the Israelite infants and cast them into the Nile.

At that time the Holy One said to the ministering angels: Descend from My Presence and look at the children of My beloved Abraham, Isaac, and Jacob being thrown into the river. The ministering angels rushed headlong down from His Presence and, standing up to their knees in the water, caught the children of Israel in their arms and set them upon rocks. Then out of each rock the Holy One brought forth nipples, which suckled the Israelite children.[4]

10. R. Avira expounded: Israel was redeemed from Egypt on account of the righteous women of that generation. When they went to draw water, the Holy One for their sake caused so many small fish to be scooped up into their pitchers that only half of what they drew up was water and the other half fish. They would then heat two pots, one with hot water and the other with fish, both of which they brought to their husbands in the field. There the women washed their husbands, anointed them, fed them, and gave them to drink. Then, lying secluded between mounds in the fields, they responded to their men. After that, they returned to their homes. When the time for giving birth came, they went into the fields and gave birth under an apple tree,[5] as is said, "Under an apple tree I roused thee; there thy mother was in labor with thee, there was she in labor and brought thee forth" (Song 8:5). Then from the heights of heaven the Holy One sent an angel, who cleansed the infants and massaged their bodies as a midwife does to make a child look beautiful. Then He selected for each of them two breast-shaped stones, one filled with honey and the other with oil, as is said, "And He made him suck honey out of the crag, and oil out of the flinty rock" (Deut. 32:13). When the Egyptians became aware of these infants, they came to slay them. But then another miracle occurred, for the infants were swallowed up by the ground. At that, the Egyptians brought oxen and plowed the area where they had disappeared. But as soon as the Egyptians left, the infants burst forth out of the ground like grass in the field. As the infants grew up, they came running to their homes in flocks.

Later, when God revealed Himself at the Red Sea, these infants, [now grown up], were the first to recognize Him, for they said, "This is my God" (Exod. 15:2).[6]

11. In Egypt, the Israelites gathered to dwell as a group, all of them becoming as one, and they convenanted to act with loving-kindness toward one another; to be loyal to the covenant of Abraham, Isaac, and Jacob; not to forsake the language of the house of their father [Jacob]; and not to adopt the language of Egypt, because it might lead them to idolatry.

And when Israel in Egypt continued to circumcise their sons, the Egyptians would say to them, "Why do you circumcise your sons? Will they not in no time at all be flung into the river?" Israel replied, "We will circumcise them nevertheless. You do with them as you wish—he who is to die will die, he who is to be slain will be slain, and he who is destined to live will live."[7]

12. "And the king of Egypt spoke to the Hebrew midwives" (Exod. 1:15). Who were the midwives? A woman and her daughter, that is, Jochebed and Miriam. So said R. Samuel bar Nahmani. Miriam was then only five years old, but she would accompany her mother and attend zealously to all her needs.[8]

"[Miriam was called] Puah" (Exod. 1:15) because she defied (*hophiah*) Pharaoh, all but thumbing her nose at him, saying, "Woe to this man when God comes to settle with him." Pharaoh, filled with rage, was about to have her put to death. [But Jochebed, who was called] Shiphrah (ibid.) because she used to smooth over (*meshapperet*) her daughter's impudence, conciliated Pharaoh by saying, "Need you pay attention to her? She is only a child and doesn't know a thing."

---

1. B. Sot. 11b; Exod. R. 1:10.
2. JV: "with rigor." But *peh* means "mouth," and *rakh*, "soft."
3. B. Sot 11b; Tanhuma B, *Be-haalotekha*, §23.
4. Song R. 2:15, §2; TdE, ed. Friedmann, p. 43.
5. The commentator assumes that giving birth under an apple tree was made necessary out of fear of the Egyptians.
6. B. Sot 11b; Exod. R. 1:12.
7. TdE, ed. Friedmann, p. 123.
8. She did not act as a midwife, but merely advised her mother.

"But they kept the men-children alive" (Exod. 1:17).[1] The praise of the midwives here goes beyond the praise given them in the first part of the verse. Not only did they not do what Pharaoh told them, they even dared to do deeds of kindness for the children they saved. In behalf of poor mothers, the midwives would go to the houses of rich mothers and collect water and food, which they gave to the poor mothers and thus kept their children alive.[2]

The Birth and Growing Up of Moses

13. "And there went a man from the house of Levi" (Exod. 2:1). Did Amram, the man referred to in the verse, go anywhere? No! Nowhere, so taught R. Judah bar Zevina, but Amram went and acted upon his daughter's advice. He, as is well known, was the most eminent man of his generation. Aware that Pharaoh had decreed, "Every son that is born ye shall cast in the river" (Exod. 1:22), he said, "We labor in vain," and was the first to divorce his wife. At that, all the others divorced their wives. Then his daughter said to him, "Father, your decree is more cruel than Pharaoh's, for Pharaoh has decreed only against the males, while you decree against both males and females. Pharaoh decreed only concerning this world, while you decree concerning both this world and the world-to-come.[3] Now, since Pharaoh is a wicked man, there is doubt whether his decree will or will not be fulfilled; but since you are a righteous man, your decree is sure to be fulfilled." At once he went and took back his wife, and so did all the others.

"And he took" (Exod. 2:1). Scripture does not say, "He restored," but "He took," implying, said R. Judah bar Zevina, that he took her back in a formal wedding ceremony, seating her in a bridal litter, Miriam and Aaron dancing before her, while the ministering angels sang, "The mother of children will [again] rejoice" (Ps. 113:9).[4]

14. As Rabbi Judah [I, the Patriarch] was once expounding Scripture, the congregation became drowsy. Wishing to rouse them, he said: A certain woman in Egypt brought forth sixty myriad infants at one birth. A disciple, named R. Ishmael son of R. Yose, was there, and he asked: Who was that woman? R. Judah replied: It was Jochebed, who gave birth to Moses, deemed equal to sixty myriads of Israel.[5]

15. "She took for him an ark of bulrushes, and daubed it with bitumen and pitch" (Exod. 2:3). It is taught: The bitumen was inside and the pitch outside, in order that the infant who was to grow up so righteous should not be made to smell the bad odor.[6]

16. "And his sister stood afar off" (Exod. 2:4). What is meant by the statement that Miriam stood afar off? Rav explained that Miriam had prophesied, "My mother is destined to give birth to a son who will save Israel from Egypt." And so, when Moses was born and the house, all of it, was flooded with radiant light, Miriam's father stood up and kissed her on the head, saying, "My daughter, your prophecy is fulfilled!" But after Moses was put into the river, her father tapped her on her head and whispered sadly, "My daughter, what is to become of your prophecy?" Hence the verse is to be read, "And his sister pondered over what would be done to him afar off"—pondered over the ultimate outcome of her prophecy in a time far off.[7]

17. "And she sent her handmaid" (Exod. 2:5).[8] When her handmaids saw that Pharaoh's daughter wished to save Moses, they said to her, "Our lady, in the world's practice, when a king issues a decree, even if the whole world does not obey it, his own children and the members of his household do obey it. Yet you would violate your father's decree!" At that, Gabriel came down and smote them to the ground [leaving the princess but one handmaid].[9]

18. "Shall I go and call thee a nurse of the Hebrew women?" (Exod. 2:7). Why of the Hebrew women? The question proves that Moses had already been taken around to ever so many Egyptian women to nurse him, but he rejected them all, for the Holy One said: Shall the mouth that will speak with Me suck anything unclean?[10]

19. "And she brought him unto Pharaoh's daughter," etc. (Exod. 2:10). Pharaoh's daughter used to kiss and hug Moses, loved him as if he were her own son, and would not allow him out of the royal palace. Because he was so handsome, everyone was eager to see him, and whoever saw him could not turn his eyes away from him. Pharaoh also used to kiss and hug him, and Moses used to grab Pharaoh's crown and put it on his own head. The magicians of Egypt sitting there said, "We fear this one who grabs your crown and puts it on his own head may be the one, as we have been saying, who will take your kingdom away from you." Some of the magicians suggested that he be slain, others that he be burned alive. But Jethro, who sat among them, said, "This child has yet no understanding. Why not test him? Place before him a vessel with a gold piece and a burning coal in it. If he reaches for the gold, he has understanding, and you may slay him. But if he reaches for the coal, he has no understanding, and a sentence of death is not called for." The items were brought at once. Then, as Moses put forth his hand to grab the gold, Gabriel came down and shoved it to the side, so that

1. Since it was already stated that the midwife did not do what Pharaoh ordered them to, why add these words? Hence the comment that follows.
2. Exod. R. 1:13 and 1:15.
3. "The drowned babes would live again in the Hereafter; but unborn children are denied such bliss" (Sot, Soncino, p. 60, n. 4).
4. B. Sot 12a; Exod. R. 1:19.
5. Song R. 1:15, §3.
6. B. Sot 12a.
7. B. Sot 12b–13a; Exod. R. 1:22; Mek, *Be-shallah*, *Shirata*, end.
8. The commentator's implied question: Does the verse signify that a royal princess had but one handmaid?
9. B. Sot 12b; Exod. R. 1:23.
10. From the breasts of a woman who worships idols. B. Sot 12b; Exod. R. 1:25.

Moses not only seized the coal but also put the hand with the coal into his mouth and burned his tongue. As a result he became slow of speech and slow of tongue.[1]

Moses Goes Forth to His Brethren

20. "And he went out unto his brethren, and he looked on their burdens" (Exod. 2:11). How did he feel as "he looked on"? As he looked on their burdens he wept, saying, "Woe is me for your servitude! Would that I could die for you!" Since no work is more strenuous than that of handling clay, Moses used to shoulder the burdens and help each worker.

R. Eleazar son of R. Yose the Galilean said: He saw heavy burdens put upon small people, and light ones upon big people; men's burdens upon women, and women's burdens upon men; the burden that an old man could carry on a youth, and that of a youth on an old man. So he would from time to time step away from his retinue and rearrange the burdens, making believe that his intention was to be of help to Pharaoh.[2] The Holy One said: You left your own concerns and went to look with compassion at the distress of Israel, behaving like a brother toward them. So, I, too, will leave those on high and those below, and speak [only] with you.

Another comment on "He looked on their burdens." He saw that they had no rest whatever. So he said to Pharaoh, "When a man has a slave and the slave does not rest at least one day during the week, the slave will die. These are your slaves. If you do not let them rest one day during the week, they will surely die." Pharaoh replied, "Go and do with them as you say." So Moses went and ordained the Sabbath day for them to rest.[3]

21. "And he saw an Egyptian" (Exod. 2:11). Who was this Egyptian? The father of the blasphemer, "whose mother was Israelite and whose father was Egyptian" (Lev. 24:10). The verse in Exodus goes on: "Beating a Hebrew"—the Hebrew was the husband of Shelomith, the daughter of Dibri.[4]

What preceded the Egyptian's beating the Hebrew? [The account that follows will explain]: The taskmasters were Egyptian but the foremen were Israelite, one taskmaster over ten foremen, and one foreman over ten Israelites. The taskmasters used to go around early in the morning to the foremen's homes to get them out to work at cockcrow. Once an Egyptian taskmaster saw an Israelite foreman's wife, Shelomith, the daughter of Dibri, who was beautiful—free of any blemish—and he cast his eye upon her. So the next day at cockcrow, he went to that foreman's home and quietly said to him, "Go, gather your team of ten men." Then he hid himself behind the staircase. The moment the husband left, the Egyptian got into the bedchamber and defiled the woman. It so happened that the husband turned back and saw the Egyptian as he was leaving the house. The husband reentered his house and asked his wife, "Did the Egyptian touch you?" She replied, "Yes, but I thought it was you!"

When the taskmaster became aware that the husband had found him out, he put the husband back to heavy labor and beat him all day, saying, "Work harder, work harder," trying to kill him.

"And he saw what had happened and what was now happening (Exod. 2:12).[5] Through the holy spirit, Moses saw what the Egyptian had done to the Hebrew in his home and what he intended to do to him in the field, and said: It is not enough for this wicked one that he defiled the wife—he is also determined to kill the husband.

"And when he saw that there was no man" (Exod. 2:12)—saw that there was no one who would be zealous for God and slay the Egyptian—"he smote the Egyptian" (ibid.). Taking a shovel used for mixing clay, [he split the Egyptian's skull] so that his brain spilled out.[6]

22. "And . . . he smote the Egyptian, and hid him in the sand" (Exod. 2:12). Moses said to the Israelites present, "You are to be like sand. When sand is taken from here and put over there, it makes no sound; even so, let not a word [about what I did] issue from your mouth.[7]

23. "Thinkest thou to kill me, as thou didst kill the Egyptian? And Moses . . . said: 'Surely the thing is known' " (Exod. 2:14). For Moses had been meditating in his heart: Wherein have Israel sinned, that they should be enslaved more than any other nation? But upon hearing one of the quarreling men say right out what he, Moses, had done, he said to himself: "Now the thing is known"—now I know why Israelites are enslaved—talebearing is rife among them. How can they ever be worthy of deliverance?[8]

24. "Now when Pharaoh heard" (Exod. 2:15). For Dathan and Abiram [the two Israelites who had been quarreling] at once rose up and informed on Moses. Whereupon "he sought to slay Moses" (ibid.). Pharaoh sent for a sword that had no equal and had him struck with it ten times upon his neck,[9] but Moses' neck became like a marble pillar, and the sword did him no harm.

"Then Moses fled from the face of Pharaoh" (Exod. 2:15). Said R. Yannai: Is it possible for a man to escape from a king? Yes, for after Moses was seized, taken to the scaffold, and tied up, had the sword laid upon his neck, and was condemned to be beheaded, an angel disguised in the form of Moses descended from heaven. So they seized the angel, while Moses escaped. R. Joshua ben Levi said: As for all the counselors who sat before Pharaoh

---

1. Exod. R. 1:26.
2. Moses' staff did not realize that he was a Hebrew.
3. Exod. R. 1:27–28; Lev. R. 37:2. "The passage in the Sabbath *Amidah* 'Moses rejoiced in the gift of his portion' is taken as a reference to the joy he felt when God ordained the day he had chosen as the day of rest for all" (Exod. R. 1:28 [Soncino, p. 35, n. 3]).
4. See Lev. 24:11.
5. JV: "He looked (*koh ve-khoh*) this way and that way." But *koh ve-khoh*—literally, "here and there"—may also be construed as the commentator does.
6. Exod. R. 1:28–29; Lev. R. 32:4; Tanhuma, *Shemot*, §9, and *Emor*, §24.
7. Tanhuma, *Shemot*, §9.
8. Exod. R. 1:30.
9. Possibly taking the letter *yod* (10) in *va-yevakkesh* ("he sought") as intimating that the sword struck Moses ten times. *Yefeh Toar*.

at that time—some became mute, some deaf, some blind, some lame. When Pharaoh asked the mute, "Where is Moses?" they could not speak. When he asked the deaf, they did not hear; the blind, they did not see; the lame, they were unable to walk.[1]

Moses in Midian

25. "Now the priest of Midian had seven daughters" (Exod. 2:16). Does not the Holy One hate idolaters? Yet He apparently allowed Moses to find refuge with an idolater. The fact is that Jethro had been a priest for idolatrous worship but then realized that it had no substance, rejected it, and thought of turning to God in penitence even before the arrival of Moses. So he summoned his townsmen and said, "I have been ministering to you until now. But I am grown old. Choose another priest for yourselves." And then and there he brought forth all the paraphernalia used in that worship and turned it over to his townsmen. They excommunicated him immediately, declaring that no man should keep him company or work for him; and when he asked the shepherds to tend his flock, they would not hear of it. That is why his daughters had to go out to tend it: "And the shepherds came and drove them away" (Exod. 2:17).

Jethro's daughters said, "An Egyptian delivered us" (Exod. 2:19). Was Moses an Egyptian? Of course not. He was a Hebrew, but his dress was Egyptian.

A parable provides another explanation for the reference to an Egyptian in the daughters' account of their deliverance: A man was bitten in the foot by a lizard and ran to immerse his feet in water. When he got to the river, he saw a child drowning in it; he stretched out his hand and pulled him out. The child said, "But for you, I would now be dead." The man replied, "It was not I who saved you. It was the lizard who bit me and from whom I was fleeing—it was he who saved you." So, too, when Jethro's daughters said to Moses, "May you grow in strength—you saved us from the shepherds," Moses replied, "It was the Egyptian whom I slew—he saved you." That is why, in speaking to their father, Jethro's daughters mentioned an Egyptian, meaning: "Who caused this man Moses to come to our aid? The Egyptian whom he had slain."[2]

The Groaning of the Children of Israel and the Mission of Moses

26. "The king of Egypt died" (Exod. 2:23). These words really mean that he became leprous, for a leper is regarded as dead. Thus, when Miriam became a leper, Moses prayed, "Let her not be as one dead" (Num. 12:12).[3] [On account of Pharaoh's leprosy], "the Israelites groaned" (Exod. 2:23). Why did they groan? Because the magicians of Egypt said to Pharaoh: There is no cure for you unless we slay a hundred and fifty Israelite children in the evening and a hundred and fifty in the morning, and you bathe twice daily in their blood. When the Israelites heard this decree, they began to groan and lament.

"And God heard their moaning" (Exod. 2:24). R. Akiva said: Pharaoh's executioners used to suffocate Israelites by immuring them in the walls of buildings. These would cry out from the structure, from its walls, and the Holy One heard their moaning.[4]

27. "Now Moses was tending the flock" (Exod. 3:1). The Holy One tested Moses by means of the flock, as our masters explained: When Moses our teacher was tending Jethro's flock in the wilderness, a lamb scampered off, and Moses followed it, until it approached a shelter under a rock. As the lamb reached the shelter, it came upon a pool of water and stopped to drink. When Moses caught up with it, he said, "I did not know that you ran away because you were thirsty. Now you must be tired." So he hoisted the lamb on his shoulder and started walking back with it. The Holy One then said: Because you showed such compassion in tending the flock of a mortal, as you live, you shall become shepherd of Israel, the flock that is Mine.[5]

28. "And God called unto him out of the midst of the bush" (Exod. 3:4). The Holy One said to Moses: Do you not sense that I live in distress whenever Israel find themselves in distress? Just look at the place out of which I speak to you—out of a thornbush. I—if one dare attribute such words to God—fully share in their distress, as implied in the words "In all their affliction, He is afflicted" (Isa. 63:9).[6]

29. "And Moses was tending the flock . . . and the . . . Lord appeared unto him in a flame of fire out of the midst of a bush" (Exod. 3:1–2). R. Simeon ben Yohai said: When the Holy One revealed Himself from the heights of heaven, why did He choose to speak to Moses out of a thornbush? Because of all bushes in the world, the thornbush is the most apt to inflict harm. Whenever a bird flies into it, the bird cannot emerge unscathed, for many parts of its body will be ripped open. So, too, for Him who is everywhere, the task of aiding anyone to emerge free and unscathed out of slavery in Egypt was more delicate by far than out of any other slavery in the world. No manservant or maidservant, other than Hagar, had ever before emerged out of Egypt free and unscathed.[7]

Another comment: "Out of the midst of a thornbush." R. Yose said: Why out of a thornbush? It is characteristic of a thornbush that when a man sticks his hand into it, he is not injured, because the sharp ends of its thorns are

---

1. Exod. R. 1:31; Song R. 7:5, §1; Mek, *Yitro, Amalek*, 1.
2. Exod. R. 1:32; Tanhuma, *Shemot*, §11.
3. Had Pharaoh actually died, Scripture would have said, "The king of Egypt died, a new king arose, and the children of Israel groaned." As the text reads now, it is difficult to understand why the king's death should have caused Israel's groaning, unless, as the comment that follows suggests, the attempts to heal the stricken king brought on the slaughter of young children.
4. Exod. R. 1:34; PRE 48.
5. Exod. R. 2:2.
6. Exod. R. 2:5.
7. To reassure Moses, who feared that being freed from Egypt (the thornbush) was impossible, God appeared in the thornbush in a flame of fire, by way of saying that the fire of freedom for Israel will nevertheless burst forth.

pointed downward; but when he attempts to draw his hand out of the bush, the thorns will fasten on to it. Likewise, when the Israelites first entered Egypt, they were well received, being told, "The land of Egypt is open before thee; in the best of the land make thy father and thy brethren to dwell" (Gen. 47:6). But when they wanted to leave, the Egyptians fastened on to them, as when Pharaoh said, "I will not let Israel go" (Exod. 5:2).[1]

30. A heathen asked R. Joshua ben Korhah: Why did the Holy One see fit to speak to Moses out of a thornbush and not out of another kind of tree? He replied: Had he spoken to Moses out of a carob tree or out of a sycamore tree, you would have asked me the same question; but to dismiss you with no reply is not right. So I will tell you why. To teach you that no place on earth, not even a thornbush, is devoid of the Presence.[2]

31. "The bush burned with fire, and the bush was not consumed" (Exod. 3:2). Why did the Holy One show Moses such a symbol? Because Moses had thought to himself that the Egyptian might consume Israel. Therefore the Holy One showed Moses a fire burning in a thornbush which was nevertheless not consumed, saying to him: As the thornbush, though burning, is not consumed, so the Egyptians will be unable to consume Israel.[3]

32. "Moses Moses" (Exod. 3:4). Here the Hebrew text provides no stop equivalent to a comma between the two occurrences of the name Moses.[4] Why not? This question may be answered by the parable of a man overloaded by an excessively heavy burden, who cries out all in one breath, "Somebody somebody, come quickly, take this load off me!"[5]

33. R. Joshua the Priest bar Nehemiah said: When God revealed Himself to Moses, Moses was but a novice in prophecy. The Holy One said: If I reveal Myself to him in a thunderous voice, I will terrify him; if in a whisper, he will take little note of prophecy. What did God do? He revealed Himself in the voice of Moses' father, whereupon Moses answered, "Here am I. What does my father wish?" God said, "I am not your father. I am the God of your father. In My need to win you over, I addressed you in a familiar voice so that you would not be afraid."[6]

34. "And Moses hid his face" (Exod. 3:6). R. Joshua ben Korhah said: Moses did not act properly in hiding his face, for had he not done so, the Holy One would have revealed to him what is above and what is below, what had been and what is destined to be. Therefore, when subsequently Moses did want to see it all, saying, "Show me, I pray Thee, Thy glory" (Exod. 33:18), the Holy One chided him, saying: When I came to show you [My] face, you hid yours. Now I am telling you that "man shall not see Me and live" (Exod. 33:20). When I wished to have you see Me, you did not wish it—now, when you wish to see Me, I do not wish it.

But R. Hoshaia Rabbah differed: Moses acted properly in hiding his face. The Holy One said to Moses: Since you showed Me respect by hiding your face when I came to show you My face, as you live, you will be seeing Me on the mountain forty days and forty nights. You will neither eat nor drink, but will be feasting upon the splendor of the Presence, as is said, "Moses knew not that the skin of his face sent forth beams [of splendor]" (Exod. 34:29).[7]

35. "And Moses said to God: 'Who am I that I should go to Pharaoh?' " (Exod. 3:11). Moses was saying to the Holy One—so asserted R. Nehorai—You say to me: Go and bring Israel out. How can I manage it with so many people to take care of? Where can I shelter them from the heat in summer and from the cold in winter? Whence can I provide food and drink? How many midwives are there among them? How many pregnant women? How many infants? What food have You prepared for their midwives? What delicacies have You prepared for those who are pregnant? How many parched grains and nuts have You prepared for the little ones? The Holy One replied: You will understand from the parched bread Israel will take with them out of Egypt, bread that will suffice them for thirty days, how I intend to provide for them.[8]

36. "I am forever I am" (Exod. 3:14).[9] The Holy One said to Moses: Go tell Israel, I am He who is with you in this servitude, and I am also He who will be with you during servitude under other kingdoms. Moses replied: Master of the universe, sufficient unto the hour is its own affliction.[10] [Why call to mind affliction yet to come?] The Holy One said: Very well, just tell them, "I-am hath sent me unto you" (Exod. 3:14).[11]

37. "And thou shall take in thy hand this rod" (Exod. 4:17). The rod that was created at twilight [on creation's sixth day] was handed to Adam in the Garden of Eden. Adam handed it to Enoch, Enoch to Shem, Shem to Abraham, Abraham to Isaac, Isaac to Jacob; Jacob took it to Egypt and handed it to his son Joseph. When Joseph died, all his household effects were moved and deposited in Pharaoh's palace. Now, Jethro was one of Pharaoh's magicians. When he saw the rod and the signs on it, he coveted it in his heart and took it, brought it to his place, and planted it in the garden by his house. No man could

1. Mek RSbY, p. 1.
2. Exod. R. 2:5; Song R. 3:10, §2.
3. Exod. R. 2:5.
4. Unlike other instances where a name, such as Abraham or Jacob, occurs twice, separated by a mark equivalent to a comma. See Gen. 22:11 and 46:2; 1 Sam. 3:10.
5. Exod. R. 2:6.
6. Exod. R. 3:1.
7. Ibid.
8. Though parched bread appeared to be the only food available, the entire multitude miraculously subsisted on it until the manna came down. Exod. R. 3:4; Song R. 1:7, §1.
9. The Hebrew for "I am that I am" is very difficult, and many translations have been suggested. This one takes *asher* ("that") in the sense of "confirm, make abide"; hence, "forever."
10. Cf. Matthew 6:34.
11. B. Ber 9b.

come near it until Moses arrived in the land of Midian, entered the garden of Jethro's house, saw the rod, made out the signs on it, stretched forth his hand, and took it. When Jethro saw this, he said: This man is destined to redeem Israel from Egypt. That is why he gave his daughter Zipporah to Moses as his wife.[1]

Moses Returns to Egypt

38. "And Moses went" (Exod. 4:18). Where did he go? To get his wife and children. Jethro asked him, "Where do you propose to take them" Moses: "To Egypt." Jethro: "Those who are in Egypt wish to get out, and you would take your family there?" Moses: "Soon Israel will go out and stand at Sinai to hear from the mouth of the Holy One, 'I am the Lord thy God' [Exod. 20:2]; should not my children, like the others in Israel, hear this?" So Jethro said to Moses, " 'Go in peace' [Exod. 4:18]—go in peace, enter Egypt in peace, and come back in peace."[2]

39. "Go, return to Egypt" (Exod. 4:19). R. Reuben said: When the Holy One told Moses in Midian, "Go, return to Egypt," the command was divided into two distinct voices and assumed two personae. Moses heard one voice saying in Midian, "Go, return to Egypt"; while Aaron [in Egypt] heard the other voice saying, "Go into the wilderness to meet Moses" (Exod. 4:27). Hence, "God thundereth miraculously [in two places] with His voice" (Job 37:5).[3]

40. "And Moses took his wife and his sons" (Exod. 4:20). At that very time [the Holy One] said to Aaron, "Go into the wilderness to meet Moses" (Exod. 4:27). Aaron went to meet him, embraced him, and kissed him, saying, "Moses, where have you been all these years?" Moses: "In Midian." Aaron: "Who are the little ones and the woman with you?" Moses: "My wife and children." "Where are you taking them?" "To Egypt." Aaron: "We are worrying about those already there, and now we shall also have to worry about these." Immediately [Moses] said to Zipporah, "Go back to your father's house." Scripture later refers to this act in saying, "After [Moses] had sent her away" (Exod. 18:2).[4]

Moses before Pharaoh

41. "And afterward Moses and Aaron came" (Exod. 5:1). What happened to the elders of Israel, who are not included [as having come with Moses and Aaron], even though the Holy One had said to Moses, "Thou shalt come, thou and the elders of Israel, unto the king of Egypt" (Exod. 3:18)? The elders started out to go with them—so taught our masters—but they kept themselves at some distance from Moses until, one by one, or even two by two, they managed to slip away, so that when Moses and Aaron reached Pharaoh's palace, not one of the elders was there, as implied in "And afterward Moses and Aaron came." Question: Where were the elders? They had slipped away. The Holy One said to them: Is this what you have done? As you live, I shall requite you. When did the requital take place? When Moses and Aaron went up with the elders to receive the Torah, the Holy One turned the elders back: "Unto the elders He said: 'Tarry ye here' " (Exod. 24:14).

"And they said to Pharaoh: 'Thus saith the Lord, the God of Israel: Let My people go' " (Exod. 5:1). R. Hiyya bar Abba asserted: That day was Pharaoh's reception day for vassals, when all kings from east and west came to honor him, bringing gifts of crowns with which to crown him cosmocrator—monarch of all the world, king over all other kings. After the kings had crowned him, Moses and Aaron were still standing at the door of Pharaoh's palace. His servants came in and reported, "Two old men are standing at the gate." Pharaoh: "Let them come up." Now, in Pharaoh's palace there were four hundred doors, and at each and every door there were lions, bears, and other wild beasts, and until these were fed meat, no mortal could enter any of the doors. But when Moses and Aaron came, all the wild beasts gathered around them, licking their feet, and proceeded to accompany them until they reached Pharaoh's presence. When Moses and Aaron stationed themselves in Pharaoh's presence, all the kings saw that the two seemed like ministering angels, the height of their stature like that of cedars of Lebanon, the orbs of their eyes like the radiant spheres of Venus, their beards like bunches of dates, the splendor of their visage like the splendor of the sun, their hands holding the sapphire rod of God upon which was inscribed the Explicit Name, and the utterance of their mouths like a flame of fire. Seeing that, the fear of the two fell upon all of the kings, every one of them, and a shaking and a trembling, a shudder of awe seized each of them, so that they removed the crowns from their heads and bowed down to Moses and Aaron. All the while Pharaoh sat and looked at Moses and Aaron, expecting that they too wished to crown him and present their paeans of praise.[5] But they did not even salute him.

Pharaoh asked, "Who are you?" They: "The ambassadors of the Holy One." Pharaoh: "What do you seek?" They: "Thus saith the Lord, the God of Israel: 'Let My people go,' " etc. (Exod. 5:1). At this, Pharaoh became angry, saying, " 'Who is the Lord, that I should hearken unto His voice to let Israel go?' [Exod. 5:2]. Has He not sense enough to send me a crown, and you who come to me with mere words [expect me to hearken to Him]? 'I know not the Lord; moreover, I will not let Israel go' " (ibid.).[6] Then he added, "But wait, I shall search my records." And then he went into his archives and brought out a list of divinities, which he proceeded to read: "The god of Moab, the god of Ammon, the god of Zidon" [and so forth]. Finally he decreed, "You see, I looked for the

1. PRE 40; Yalkut, *Shemot*, §170.
2. Exod. R. 4:4.
3. Exod. R. 5:9.
4. Mek, *Be-shallah*, *Amalek*, 3 (La 2:167–68).

5. So David Luria. Others: "credentials," as ambassadors from one more vassal.
6. First he said, "Who is the Lord?" implying doubt, and then, "I know not the Lord," implying certainty. Mah.

name of your God in my archives, and did not find it."

R. Levi said: Pharaoh was like a priest's servant who was an utter fool. When the priest happened to leave the city, the servant went to look for his master in a burial ground, blubbering to the people standing there, "Have you seen my master here?" When asked, "Who is your master?" he replied, "So-and-so, the priest." They retorted, "World's biggest fool that you are! Does one look for a priest in a burial ground?"[1] So, too, Moses and Aaron said to Pharaoh, "Utter fool that you are! Are the living to be sought among the dead? The divinities in your records are dead. But our God is a living God, the King of the universe."

Pharaoh asked, "Is He young or old? How old? How many cities has He subdued? How many provinces has He conquered? How long is it since He ascended the throne?" They replied, "Our God—His strength and might fill the universe. He was before the world was created, and He will be after the world's end. He formed you and gave you the breath of life." Pharaoh: "What are His notable deeds?" Moses and Aaron: "He stretched forth the heavens and laid the foundations of the earth; His voice hews out flames of fire; He splits mountains and shatters rocks. His bow is fire, His arrows flame, His spear a torch, His shield clouds, His sword lightning. He forms mountains and hills; He covers heaven with clouds; brings down rain and dew; makes grasses grow, fruits to be succulent; answers those about to give birth; fashions the embryo in its mother's womb and brings it forth into the air of the world; He removes kings and sets up kings."

Pharaoh replied, "From the very outset you have spoken lies. I am lord of the universe. I created myself as well as the Nile." Then and there he gathered all the sages of Egypt and asked them, "Have you ever heard the name of the God of these two?" They replied, "We did hear that He is a 'son of the wise, son of ancient kings' [Isa. 19:11], [but no more]." At that, Pharaoh told Moses and Aaron, "Your God—I have no idea who He is. 'Who is the Lord, that I should hearken to His voice?' " (Exod. 5:2).[2]

The Brutality of the Enslavement

42. "And the foremen of the Israelites . . . were flogged" (Exod. 5:14). Pharaoh appointed Egyptian taskmasters over the Israelite foremen, and these foremen were appointed over the rest of the people. After Pharaoh had commanded the taskmasters, "Ye shall no more give the people straw" (Exod. 5:7), the taskmasters came and counted the bricks. Whenever the tally was short, the taskmasters flogged the foremen, who surrendered themselves to be flogged for the sake of the people in their charge. Refusing to turn over to the taskmasters the names of those who fell short, they said: We prefer to submit to the lash, rather than have the people in our charge fall into the hands of the taskmasters.

Therefore, when the Holy One said to Moses, "Gather for Me seventy men" (Num. 11:16), Moses replied, "Master of the universe, I do not know who is worthy and who is not." God said, "The foremen who had been set over them thou wilt know as worthy to be elders of the people" (Num. 11:16)[3]—the same foremen who surrendered themselves to be flogged because of the tally of bricks are to come and receive this distinction.[4]

43. "Be off now to your work! No straw shall be issued to you" (Exod. 5:18). After that, the Israelites had to gather stubble in the wilderness and tread clay into the stubble; the coarse stubble pierced their heels, mingling their blood with the clay. Even Rachel, the daughter of Shutelah's son,[5] although about to give birth, had to tread the clay by the side of her husband, with the result that the infant emerged from its mother's womb and fell into and was engulfed by the mix of the brick-mold. At that moment the angel Michael descended, took that brick-mold [with the dead infant], and brought it up before the throne of glory. That very night the decree of punishment against Egypt was issued.[6]

44. "To put a sword in their hand to slay us" (Exod. 5:21). R. Judah the Levite son of R. Shallum taught that the people said to Moses: To what may we be compared? To a lamb that a wolf has come to snatch. Though the shepherd runs after the lamb to save it from the mouth of the wolf, the lamb, pulled this way by the shepherd and that way by the wolf, is torn apart. So, too, Israel said, "Moses, between you and Pharaoh, we are being pulled to death."[7]

45. R. Eliezer son of R. Yose said: Once, during a visit to Alexandria in Egypt, I came upon a learned elder who said to me: Come, let me list for you what my ancestors did to yours—they drowned some in the sea, they slew some by the sword, they crushed some in buildings.[8] It was because of these afflictions that Moses was punished. For Moses had the presumption to say, "Since I came to Pharaoh to speak in Thy Name, it has gone worse with this people; and Thou hast shown no capacity to deliver Thy people" (Exod. 5:23). Then the Holy One told Moses: Alas for those who are gone and are no longer. How many times did I reveal Myself to Abraham, Isaac, and Jacob as "God Almighty," yet they did not question My ways. They did not say, "How do You justify Your attribute 'Almighty' "? I commanded Abraham, "Arise, walk through the land in the length of it and in the breadth of it; for I will give it unto thee" (Gen. 13:17). Yet when he sought a place to bury Sarah and could not find one until he purchased one for four hundred silver shekels, he still did not question My ways. I told Isaac, "Sojourn in this land, and I will be with thee, and will bless thee" (Gen.

1. A priest may not defile himself by contact with the dead. Lev. 21:1.
2. Exod. R. 5:14; Tanhuma, *Va-era*, §5; Yalkut, *Shemot*, §172.
3. JV: "Whom thou knowest to be elders of the people; and officers over them."
4. Tanhuma B, *Be-haalotekha*, §25.
5. Of the tribe of Ephraim. See Num. 26:36.
6. PRE 48.
7. Exod. R. 5:21.
8. By using them as bricks; when an Israelite did not provide his tally of bricks, one of his infants was immured in the wall.

26:3). Yet when his servants sought water to drink and found it only after engaging in a dispute [for, as Scripture says, "The herdsmen of Gerar did dispute with Isaac's herdsmen, saying, 'The water is ours' " (Gen. 26:20)], he too did not question My ways. I assured Jacob, "The Land whereon thou liest, to thee will I give it" (Gen. 28:13). Yet when he sought a place to pitch his tent and could not find one until he bought it for a hundred pieces of money, he also did not question My ways. None of them challenged My attribute "Almighty." But you—at the very beginning you wanted to know by what right [in view of Israel's affliction] did I speak of Myself as "Almighty" and now have dared say to Me, "Thou hast shown no capacity to deliver Thy people." Therefore, "now shalt thou see what I will do to Pharaoh" (Exod. 6:1)—you will see the warfare against Pharaoh, but you will not see the war against the thirty-one kings.[1]

46. "And the king of Egypt said unto them: *Lammah*" (Exod. 5:4).[2] What is meant by *lammah*? "You, Aaron and Moses, are good for nothing (*le-mah*), and what you say amounts to nothing (*le-mah*). 'Get back to the chores assigned to you' " (ibid.). Since the tribe of Levi, as R. Joshua ben Levi taught, was exempt from servile work, Pharaoh said to Moses and Aaron, "Because you are exempt from such work, you [having little to do] say, 'Let us go and sacrifice to our God' [Exod. 5:3]. Get back to the household chores that are yours."[3]

47. "Let heavier work be laid upon the men" (Exod. 5:9). When the entire verse is read, it tells us that the Israelites possessed scrolls that contained assurances that the Holy One would redeem them. The Israelites took delight in reading them from one Sabbath to the next, for at that time they were still allowed to rest on the Sabbath. But now Pharaoh said to the taskmasters, " 'Let heavier work be laid upon the men, and make them keep at it [even on the Sabbath], so that they will not delight (*yish'u*) in lying words' [ibid.]—let them not divert themselves and rest on the Sabbath day."[4]

The Signs and the Plagues

48. "And Aaron cast down his rod before Pharaoh. . . . Then Pharaoh also called[5] for the wise men and the sorcerers" (Exod. 7:10–11). In that instant, Pharaoh began ridiculing Moses and Aaron, all but cackling in triumph like a mother hen as he said to them, "So these are the signs of your God! In the world's practice, people bring merchandise to a place that needs it. But who in his right mind would bring fish brine to Apamea or fish to Acco? Don't you know that every kind of sorcery is available in my domain?" He had children brought from school and had them do the same kind of tricks. He even called his wife and said to her, "Look what these Jews did to make me appear ridiculous," and she also did the same.

"For they cast down every man his rod" (Exod. 7:12). The Egyptian sorcerers Yohani and Mamre[6] asked Moses, "Would you carry straw to Afarayim?"[7] Moses replied, "People do say, To Herbtown carry herbs."[8]

49. "A dullard venteth all his rage" (Prov. 29:11). These words apply to Pharaoh, who scoffed at the Holy One, imagining that what Moses and Aaron had done was the work of witchcraft, and therefore called all the members of his household to do likewise. At that time the Holy One said: "If Aaron's serpent were to swallow up the serpents of the Egyptians, there would be nothing remarkable in that, for a serpent usually swallows another serpent. Therefore, let the rod that turned serpent first resume its original form and only then swallow the serpents of the Egyptians.

"But Aaron's rod swallowed up their rods" (Exod. 7:12). R. Eleazar said: A double miracle occurred. For the verse implies that the rod resumed its original form and swallowed the serpents of the Egyptians. When Pharaoh beheld this, he was amazed and said to himself: What will happen if Aaron should now say to his rod, "Swallow up Pharaoh and his throne"? It would at once swallow me up.

R. Yose son of R. Hanina said: In addition, another great miracle happened to that rod, for although it swallowed up all the rods that had been cast down, enough to make ten heaps, still that rod did not become any thicker, and all who saw it recognized it as Aaron's rod.[9]

50. "And Pharaoh's heart was hardened" (Exod. 7:14). The sages asked: How is the hardening of Pharaoh's heart to be understood? By a story: A lion and all kinds of beasts, including a fox, were about to sail on a ship. The ass was collecting the fare for the journey, saying to each animal, "Pay me the fare." The fox said to the ass, "How brazen-faced you are! You know that the king of beasts is with us, yet you demand the fare." The ass replied, "After I take it from the king, I will put it back in his treasury." [Upon hearing these words], the lion ordered, "Bring the ship to." He then got off, ripped the ass apart, and told the fox, "Lay out the parts of this fool's carcass for me [to feed]." The fox laid them out. But when he saw the ass's heart, he ate it up. When the lion came back and saw all the parts cut up, he asked, "Where is the fool's heart?" The fox replied, "My lord king, he had no heart. If he had had one, he would not have presumed to collect the

1. Moses would not be permitted to enter the Promised Land and witness its conquest. See Josh. 12:24. B. Sanh 111a.
2. JV: "Wherefore." But since Moses and Aaron had already told Pharaoh the reason they wanted to go, why should he ask, "Wherefore?" Hence *lammah* is construed not as a question but as a reproach.
3. Exod. R. 5:16.
4. Exod. R. 5:18.
5. There may be a play on *va-yikra* ("called") and *mekarker* ("cackle").
6. The two chief Egyptian sorcerers (B. Men 85a), also referred to as Jannes and Jambres (*EJ* 9:1277).
7. Josh. 19:19. "Carry coals to Newcastle?"
8. Such a place becomes a specialized market town, and purchasers are likely to be found there. So, said Moses, people come to Egypt from everywhere to watch feats of magic and are likely to be impressed by mine, which are better than yours. Exod. R. 9:6–7; B. Men 85a; Tanhuma B, *Va-era*, §12.
9. Exod. R. 9:7.

fare from the king." So, too, if wicked Pharaoh had a heart,[1] he would not have said to the King who is King of kings, "Pay me my due [paeans of praise]."[2]

51. "Behold God is so great in power—hence, who dare give instructions as He does?" (Job 36:22).[3] The custom of the world is that when a man wishes to bring sudden evil upon his enemy, he will maneuver to catch him unawares. God, however, warned Pharaoh before each and every plague that it was coming, to give him an opportunity to repent.[4]

52. "And the Lord said unto Moses: 'Say unto Aaron' " (Exod. 7:19). R. Tanhum taught: Why were the waters not smitten by Moses himself? Because the Holy One said to Moses: It is not proper that the waters that protected you when you were cast into the river should now be smitten by you. As you live, they shall be smitten by none other than Aaron.[5]

53. Why did God begin by bringing the plague of blood upon the Egyptians? Because Pharaoh and the Egyptians worshiped the Nile. Therefore the Holy One said to Moses, "Go, and in their very presence smite their gods," in accord with the saying "When idols are smashed, their priests are abashed." God will not punish a people until He first punishes its gods.

"Over their rivers" (Exod. 7:19): wherever there was water, it turned into blood. "And over all its bodies of water" (ibid.): even water that was in a kettle turned into blood. Even what an Egyptian spit out of his mouth turned into blood, as is said, "And there shall be blood throughout all of Egypt" (ibid.).

R. Avun the Levite said: The Israelites became rich from the plague of blood. How did that happen? If an Egyptian and an Israelite dwelled in a house where there was a vat full of water, and the Egyptian went to fill a kettle from it, the water turned into blood, but the Israelite would continue to drink water from the same vat. When the Egyptian said to him, "Give me some water with your own hand," and was given water, it still turned into blood. Even if he said, "Let us both drink from one vessel," the Israelite drank water, but the Egyptian drank blood. It was only when the Egyptian bought water from the Israelite for money that he was able to drink water, and this is how the Israelites became rich.[6]

54. R. Berekhiah asked: What is meant by the phrase "The waters . . . turned themselves" in the verse "And because all the waters that were in the river turned themselves, all were turned into blood" (Exod. 7:20)? He explained the phrase with the parable of a slave flogged by his master; after being flogged on the stomach, he turned himself over,[7] [was flogged again, and] thus was flogged over all of his body. So it was with the Nile, which turned its waters upside down in the hope that the plague would not affect it; but it was of no avail, for all of it turned into blood.[8]

55. The Holy One brought the plagues upon Egypt with the tactics of warrior kings. What does a king of flesh and blood do when a city rebels against him? He sends troops to encircle it. Then he shuts off its water conduits. If its people submit, he desists. But if not, he brings loud noises upon them to confuse them. If they submit, he desists. But if not, he shoots arrows at them. If they submit, he desists. But if not, he sets savage units against them. If they submit, he desists. But if not, he deprives them of their source of food.[9] If they submit, he desists. But if not, he flings burning naphtha upon them. If they submit, he desists. But if not, he catapults stones at them. If they submit, he desists. But if not, he arrays multitudes [of scalers of walls] against them. If they submit, he desists. But if not, he puts them in prison. If they submit, he desists. But if not, he slays the notables among them.

So, too, at the beginning, the Holy One shut the Egyptians' water conduits: "He turned their rivers into blood" (Ps. 78:44). Since they did not submit, He brought loud noises to confuse them—frogs, whose croaking was very hard for the Egyptians to endure; for, entering the Egyptians' innards, they kept up their "co-ax, co-ax." Since they did not submit, He shot arrows at them—gnats, which penetrated the bodies of the Egyptians like arrows. Since they did not submit, He brought savage units against them—swarms of wild beasts. Since they did not submit, He deprived them of their source of food—by sending murrain, of which their cattle died. Since they did not submit, He flung burning naphtha at them—skin boils. Since they did not submit, He catapulted stones at them—hail. Since they did not submit, He sicced multitudes [of wall scalers] on them—locusts. Since they did not submit, He put them in prison—darkness. Since they still did not submit, He slew the notables among them: "The Lord smote all the first in rank"[10] (Exod. 12:29).

All that the Egyptians planned against the Israelites, the Holy One brought upon their own persons. The Egyptians intended Israelites to draw water for them. So "He turned their rivers into blood" (Ps. 78:44). The Egyptians intended Israelites to carry wares for them. So He brought frogs, which chewed up those wares. The Egyptians intended Israelites to till the soil for them. So He made the soil swarm with gnats. The Egyptians intended Israelites to carry their young children about in the manner of tutor escorts. So He sent against the Egyptians wild beasts—lions, wolves, leopards, bears, and serpents. For example, an Egyptian with five sons would customarily put them

---

1. The heart was presumed to be the seat of understanding.
2. See above, chap. 4, §41. Yalkut, *Va-era*, §182.
3. JV: "Behold, God doth loftily in His power; who is a teacher like unto Him?"
4. Exod. R. 9:9.
5. Exod. R. 9:10.
6. See "And afterward shall they come out with great substance" (Gen. 15:14). Tanhuma B, *Va-era*, §14; Exod. R. 9:10.
7. To gain relief.
8. Exod. R. 9:11.
9. Literally, "wreaks destruction [upon their source of food]."
10. JV: "all the firstborn." However, in limiting the lethal extent of the plague, the commentator endeavors to diminish the impression that God is unbelievably cruel.

under the care of an Israelite, who would escort the five in the street. A lion would snatch one, a wolf another, a bear another, a leopard another, and a fiery serpent still another, so that the Israelite would come back to the house of the Egyptian alone. The Egyptian would ask, "Where are my children?" and the Israelite would reply, "Sit down, and I will give you an accounting—a lion took one, a wolf another, a bear another, a leopard another, and a fiery serpent still another." The Egyptians intended that Israelites tend their cattle. So He sent murrain upon their cattle. The Egyptians intended that Israelites serve as bath attendants for them. So He brought boils upon them. The Egyptians intended to stone the Israelites. So He brought hail upon them. The Egyptians intended that Israelites be their vintagers. So He brought locusts, which consumed their vines. The Egyptians intended to put them in prison. So He brought darkness upon them. The Egyptians intended to slay them. So "the Lord smote all their first in rank" (Exod. 12:29). The Egyptians intended to drown them in water. So He "hurled Pharaoh and his host into the Red Sea" (Ps. 136:15).[1]

56. "And the frogs[2] came up, and covered the land of Egypt" (Exod. 8:2). R. Akiva said: It was only one frog, but it bred so rapidly that it filled the entire land of Egypt. R. Eleazar ben Azariah said to him: Akiva, what business have you with *Aggadah?* Leave your attempts at homiletical interpretation and turn to Negaim[3] and Ohalot.[4] True, at the beginning there was only one frog, but this one croaked for the others, and they came in swarms.[5]

57. "The Nile shall swarm with frogs, which shall go up and come into thy house . . . and into thine ovens, and into thy kneading troughs" (Exod. 7:28). Whenever an Egyptian woman was kneading dough, or heating her oven with bread inside, frogs would come and settle on the dough and devour it, or hop into the oven, cool it,[6] and get at the bread.

R. Aha said: From the phrase "And upon thee" (Exod. 7:29), the inference may be drawn that when an Egyptian drank water and a drop fell on his chest, the drop would burst apart and become a frog.

R. Yohanan said: Wherever there was a little earth and a drop of water touched it, it would become a frog.[7] Hezekiah Berabbi said to R. Yohanan: But according to your line of interpretation, noblemen's palaces made of marble and massive piers could not have been affected. The fact is, as Scripture tells us, the frog coming up from the deep would say to the marble, "Make room for me, that I may come up [into the palace] and do the will of my Maker." At that, the marble split apart and the frog came up, took hold of the nobleman's private parts, and mutilated them.[8]

58. "But when Pharaoh saw that there was respite," etc. (Exod. 8:11). This is just like the wicked: when they are in trouble, they affect humility; but as soon as they have respite, they return to their perversity.[9]

59. "And the Lord said unto Moses: 'Say unto Aaron: Stretch out thy rod, and smite the dust of the earth' " (Exod. 8:12). [Aaron, not Moses, was told to smite the earth], for, according to R. Tanhum, the Holy One said to Moses: It is not proper that the earth, which protected you when you slew the Egyptian,[10] should now be smitten by you.[11]

60. "There was . . . fire flashing continually amidst the hail" (Exod. 9:24). A miracle within a miracle! R. Judah said that vials made of hail and filled with fire came down, yet the frozen water did not quench the fire nor did the fire consume the frozen water. R. Nehemiah said: Fire and hail, mingling, were made to work together. R. Judah's explanation, said R. Hanan, brings to mind the pomegranate, whose seeds are visible through its pulp; while R. Nehemiah's explanation, R. Hanan went on to say, brings to mind a crystal lamp in which water and oil work together to keep the flame of the wick burning.[12]

The interaction of the water and the oil may be illustrated by the parable of two fierce legions that were bitter rivals. When the time came for the king to wage war, what did he do? He made peace between them, and they both marched out and executed the king's orders together. So, too, fire and hail are bitter rivals, yet when the time came to wage war against Egypt, the Holy One made peace between them, and together they smote the Egyptians. Hence the verse is to be read, "There was fire flashing up within the hail," so that when an Egyptian sat down, he was scorched by hail, and when he stood up, he was scorched by fire.[13]

61. "Behold, tomorrow at this time[14] I will cause it to rain a very grievous hail" (Exod. 9:18). Zavdi ben Levi said: Moses scratched a mark on a wall and said: When the sun reaches this mark tomorrow, the hail will descend.[15]

62. R. Yohanan taught: When the locusts came, the Egyptians, endeavoring to find some joy in their plight,

1. Tanhuma, *Bo*, §4.
2. The word for "frogs" is in the singular in the Hebrew text.
3. A treatise dealing with laws concerning suspected leprosy.
4. A treatise dealing with laws concerning staying under the same roof with a ritually unclean object. The two treatises, which are very difficult, are, according to R. Eleazar, appropriate subjects for R. Akiva's keen mind.
5. B. Sanh 67b.
6. By their natural coldness.
7. He interprets "their land swarmed with frogs" (Ps. 105:30) as suggesting that the land itself—the earth—turned into frogs.
8. Exod. R. 10:2–3.
9. Exod. R. 10:6 and 12:7; Tanhuma B, *Va-era*, §22.
10. The earth "protected" Moses because he hid the Egyptian in it. See Exod. 2:12.
11. Exod. R. 10:7.
12. The oil, being lighter than the water, floats on its surface and feeds the burning wick.
13. Exod. R. 12:4; Num. R. 12:8; Song R. 3:11, §1.
14. The word *ka-et* ("at this time") implies "at exactly the same time." Cf. Gen. R. 33, end.
15. Exod. R. 12:2.

said: Let us gather the locusts, pickle them, and put them up in casks. The Holy One retorted sharply: Scoundrels, do you expect to find any joy in the plague I bring upon you? Immediately "the Lord turned an exceeding strong sea wind" (Exod. 10:19)—the westerly wind—"which took up the locusts," etc. (ibid.). What is signified by the words that follow: "There remained not one locust" (ibid.)? That even those that had been pickled in the Egyptians' pots and casks took wing and fled.[1]

63. "And there was a thick darkness" (Exod. 10:22). R. Avdimi said: The darkness was twice and twice again thicker [than the darkness of any other night, so that] "no one was able to move from his place for three days" (Exod. 10:23). During those three days, he who was seated could not stand up, he who was standing could not sit down, and he who was lying down could not raise himself up.

During the three days of darkness, the cover of thick cloud made it dark for the Egyptians but gave light to the Israelites, so that Israelites were able to enter the houses of the Egyptians and see all that they had. Subsequently, when the Holy One said, "Tell the people that each man shall borrow of his neighbor," etc. (Exod. 11:2), Israelites would enter the houses of Egyptians and say [each man to his neighbor], "Lend me the vessel you have." If the Egyptian replied, "I do not have such a vessel," the Israelite would say, "I know that you have it—it is in such-and-such a place." The Egyptian would then say to himself: If [in saying they merely wish to borrow] the Israelites are lying [and are in fact planning to appropriate the vessels], they could have filched these vessels during the days of darkness, when we would not have been aware of it.[2]

64. "But all the children of Israel had light in their dwellings" (Exod. 10:23). Scripture does not say, "In the land of Goshen," but, "In their[3] dwellings," to show that wherever a Jew entered, light entered with him and illuminated for him what was in casks, chests, and hidden depositories.[4]

65. Why did the Holy One bring darkness upon the Egyptians? Because there were transgressors in Israel who had patrons among the Egyptians, lived in their midst in affluence and honor, and were therefore unwilling to leave Egypt. The Holy One said: If in the sight of all I bring a plague upon them also and they die, the Egyptians will say, "Just as plagues have befallen us, so has a plague befallen them."[5] For this reason, He brought darkness upon the Egyptians for three days, so that the Israelites could bury their [disloyal] dead without their enemies seeing what they were doing.[6]

66. "When Thy judgments are in the earth, the inhabitants of the world learn righteousness" (Isa. 26:9). Our masters taught: The plagues that the Holy One brought upon the Egyptians were the means of establishing peace for them. How so? There had been a dispute between the Ethiopians and the Egyptians, the Egyptians claiming, "Our borders extend to here," and the Ethiopians claiming, "No, our borders extend to here." But when the frogs came, they made peace between them, for the frogs entered only Egyptian territory, and thus the fields that did not belong to the Ethiopians were clearly identified.[7]

67. How may Pharaoh's actions be illustrated? By the parable of a swineherd who found a ewe lamb and put her among his swine. When its owner sent word, "Give me back my ewe lamb," the swineherd replied, "No lamb of yours is with me." Then the owner asked [the other herdsmen], "Tell me, where does the swineherd water his herd?" When he was told, he stopped up the springs [the swineherd used]. Again he sent word to the swineherd, "Return my ewe lamb," and again came the reply, "No lamb of yours is with me." The owner then inquired [of the herdsmen], "Tell me, where does he stall his animals?" When told, he tore down the swineherd's folds and sent word once more, "Return my ewe lamb." Once more came the reply: "No lamb of yours is with me." The owner then inquired, "Tell me, where do his beasts feed?" When told, he burned all the grass that the swineherd had and again sent word, "Return my ewe lamb." The reply again was: "No lamb of yours is with me." The owner then asked, "Let me know which school his son attends." The owner went and took the swineherd's son into his own custody, and once again sent word, "Return my ewe lamb." This time the reply was: "Here is your lamb." The owner took it and then detained the swineherd as he had his son. The swineherd protested, "Now that your lamb is no longer in my possession, why do you detain me? What of yours do I still hold?" The owner replied, "I claim all that she gave birth to, and also the worth of her shearings all the time that she was in your possession." At this, the swineherd began to shout, "Would that I had not given back the lamb at all! People would then have said, 'He stood by his [original] word and did not give up the ewe lamb—evidently her owner was only seeking a pretext to slay him!' "

The owner is the King, King of kings, the Holy One, blessed be He; the ewe lamb is Israel; the swineherd, Pharaoh. When Israel came down to Egypt, Pharaoh subjected them to forced labor. Then the Holy One told Moses, "Say to Pharaoh, 'Let My people go, that they may serve Me.' " When Moses went and said that to Pharaoh, he replied, "Who is the Lord, that I should hearken to His voice?" (Exod. 5:2). Moses reported to the Holy One, "Pharaoh said, 'Who is the Lord?' and refuses to set the people free." God then asked, "Whence do the Egyptians drink?" Moses: "Out of the Nile." God: "Turn it into blood." When the Egyptians sought to drink and found no water, God again sent word, "Let My people go." But Pharaoh refused. Then God asked, "Where do his cattle feed—is it not in the wilderness?" He then sent [fiery] hail upon him, breaking all his trees and burning every-

1. Exod. R. 13:7; Tanhuma, *Va-era*, §14.
2. Exod. R. 14:3; Tanhuma, *Bo*, § 3; Yalkut, *Bo*, §186.
3. The word "their" is taken to refer to the dwellings of Egyptians.
4. Exod. R. 14:3.
5. Proving that the plagues did not come from God, but were natural phenomena.
6. Exod. R. 14:3; Mek, *Be-shallah*, *Va-yehi*, beginning (La 1:175).
7. Exod. R. 10:2 and 13:4.

thing. Next He visited him with locusts, which devoured every green sprout; He also took His rod and broke the neck of all his beasts. God visited all these plagues upon him, but he still refused to set Israel free. Finally He took Pharaoh's son and imprisoned him. Only then did Pharaoh say to the Israelites, "Up, depart!" Then he immediately [changed his mind and] pursued them, but he was seized and detained as his son had been,[1] as it says, "He . . . hurled Pharaoh and his host in the Red Sea" (Ps. 136:15).[2] Pharaoh began to wail, "Would that I had not let them go! For then people would have said, 'See, here is a man who stood by his word; for even though he set them free, the Owner has slain him.' "[3]

Events Preceding the Exodus

68. "Speak *na* in the ears of the people, and let them ask every man of his neighbor . . . objects of silver and objects of gold" (Exod. 11:2). In the school of R. Yannai it is taught: The word *na* implies entreaty. Thus the Holy One said to Moses, I beg you, go and say to Israel: Please, ask the Egyptians for objects of silver and objects of gold, so that the righteous Abraham should not complain, "The one promise—'They shall serve them, and they shall afflict them' [Gen. 15:13]—God did fulfill for my children; but the other promise—'Afterward they shall come out with great substance' [Gen. 15:14]—He did not fulfill for them." The Israelites replied to Moses, "If only we ourselves could get out!" Their reply may be illustrated by the story of a man in prison who was told: Tomorrow you will be released from prison and be given plenty of money. The man replied: Please, just let me go free today, and I will ask for nothing more.[4]

69. "And he called for Moses and Aaron by night" (Exod. 12:31). Pharaoh went around to all the doorways of his servants, rousing each one of them out of his home, then walked with his servants into every street, asking, "Where is Moses? Where does he live?" Now, the Israelite children made fun of him, asking him, "Pharaoh, where are you going?" He replied, "I am looking for Moses." They would say, "He lives here. No, he lives here," thus making sport of him, until finally Pharaoh succeeded in locating Moses and said to him, "Rise up, get you forth from among my people." Moses replied, "Are we thieves, that you expect us to get out during the dark of night? Thus has the Holy One commanded us: 'None of you shall go out of the door of his house until the morning' [Exod. 12:22]—we will not go out except with heads held high, in the sight of all Egypt."[5]

1. Just as his firstborn was killed in Egypt, so was he drowned in the Red Sea.
2. "There is no explicit statement in Exodus that Pharaoh was actually drowned, hence the quotation from Psalms" (Exod. R., Soncino, p. 243, n. 3).
3. Exod. R. 20:1.
4. B. Ber 9a–b.
5. Tanhuma B, *Bo*, §19.

The Spoils of Egypt

70. R. Judah said in the name of Samuel: Joseph gathered and brought to Egypt all the silver and gold in the world, as is said, "Joseph gathered up all the silver that was found in the land of Egypt [and in the land of Canaan]" (Gen. 47:14). Here we are told only concerning the treasures of Egypt [and of Canaan]. But how do we know that he also gathered the treasures of other countries? Because Scripture says, "And all the countries came into Egypt . . . to buy corn" (Gen. 41:57). When the Israelites left Egypt, they brought the silver and gold out with them, as is said, "And they emptied Egypt" (Exod. 12:36), turning it, according to R. Assi, into a fort empty of provisions; according to R. Simeon ben Lakish, into a pond empty of fish.[6] The treasure remained [in the Land of Israel] until the time of Rehoboam, son of Solomon, when Shishak, king of Egypt, came up against Jerusalem and took it from Rehoboam, as is said, "Shishak . . . took away the treasures of the house of the Lord, and the treasures of the king's house" (1 Kings 14:26). Then Zerah, king of Ethiopia, took it from Shishak. Asa came, took it from Zerah, king of Ethiopia, and sent it to Hadadrimmon the son of Tabrimmon. Then came the Ammonites and took it from Hadadrimmon the son of Tabrimmon. Next Jehoshaphat came and took the treasure back from the Ammonites.[7] It remained in the Land until the time of Ahaz, when Sennacherib came and took it from Ahaz. Then came Hezekiah, who took it from Sennacherib, and it remained in the Land until Zedekiah, when the Chaldeans came and took it from Zedekiah. Then came the Persians, who took it from the Chaldeans; the Greeks, who took it from the Persians; the Romans, who took it from the Greeks. And the treasure is still in Rome.[8]

Joseph's Coffin

71. "And Moses took the bones of Joseph with him" (Exod. 13:19). The sages taught: Pause and consider how beloved were commandments to Moses our teacher—while Israel, all of them, were occupied with spoils, he was occupied with performing commandments.

But how did Moses know where Joseph was buried? It is said: Serah daughter of Asher, who was of Joseph's generation, was still living. Moses went to her and asked, "Do you know where Joseph is buried?" She replied, "The Egyptians made a metal coffin for him, which they sank into the Nile, in order that its waters might be blessed thereby. Then, too, the magicians and the sorcerers told Pharaoh, 'Do you wish that this people should never leave

6. Both comments take *va-yenatzelu* to mean "they emptied." But R. Assi, regarding the *lamed* as interchangeable with *dalet*, also takes the verb to be a form of *tzvd*, hence *metzudah* ("fort"), while R. Simeon relates the verb to *metzulah* ("deep," "pond"). In either case, the despoiling amounted to "emptying."
7. See 2 Chron. 20.
8. B. Pes 119a and En Yaakov, ad loc.

Egypt? If they do not find the bones of Joseph, they will never be able to leave.' "

Then Moses went to the bank of the Nile and called out, saying: Joseph, Joseph, the time in which the Holy One swore to redeem Israel has come, as has the time of the oath you had Israel swear.[1] Give honor to the Lord, God of Israel. The Presence is waiting for you. Israel are waiting for you. If you show yourself, well and good. If not, we shall be released from the oath you made our forebears swear. Immediately, Joseph's coffin began bubbling upward, rising out of the depths as though no heavier than a reed, and Moses took it.

R. Nathan said: Joseph was buried in the royal sepulchers. Moses went and stood by these sepulchers, saying: Joseph, the time in which the Holy One swore to redeem Israel has come, as has the time for the oath you had Israel swear. If you show yourself, well and good. If not, we shall be released from the oath you made our forebears swear. At that, Joseph's coffin began to shake. Moses took it and carried it with him.

During all the years that Israel were in the wilderness, the arklike coffin of Joseph and the Ark of the Presence moved side by side. When passersby asked, "What is the significance of these two arks?" they were told, "This one is the coffin of a mortal, and that one is the Ark of the Presence." "But is it proper that a corpse move side by side with the Presence?" Israel replied, "The corpse in this ark fulfilled all that is written in that Ark."[2]

72. "The bones of Joseph" (Exod. 13:19). The significance of taking the bones back to Canaan may be understood by the parable of thieves who entered a wine cellar, took a flask of wine, and drank it. The owner of the cellar looked in on them and said, "I hope you found the wine satisfying—fragrant and sweet. But now that you have drunk the wine, put the flask back in its place!" So did the Holy One say to the tribe fathers, "You sold Joseph—now return his bones to their rightful place."[3]

The Exodus from Egypt

73. The children of Israel were redeemed from Egypt because of four meritorious acts: they did not change their names, they did not change their language, they did not reveal their secrets,[4] and they did not abandon circumcision.[5]

74. "God . . . bringeth out the prisoners *ba-kosharot*"[6] (Ps. 68:7). R. Akiva said: He brought Israel out during a month when it was most suitable to go out—not in Tammuz, because of the heat, nor in Tevet, because of the cold, but in Nisan, when it is most suitable to set out on a journey, the sun being not too oppressive nor the cold too severe. And should you say, Why not Tishri?—that month begins the rainy season.[7]

75. "Egypt was glad when they departed" (Ps. 105:38). R. Berekhiah told the parable of a fat man riding an ass. The ass kept wondering: When will this fellow get off me? And the man kept wondering: When can I get off this ass? When he did get off, the man was glad and the ass was glad. And we do not know which was the more glad [but you might say that the ass was the more glad]. So with Israel in Egypt. As the plagues came down on the Egyptians, the Egyptians kept wondering: When will Israel leave Egypt? and the Israelites too kept wondering when the Holy One was going to redeem them. After they went forth and were redeemed, the former were glad and the latter were glad. But we did not know which was the more glad until David came and said, "Egypt was glad when they departed." [Then we knew that the Egyptians were the more glad.][8]

76. "And it came to pass (*va-yehi*) when Pharaoh had let the people go" (Exod. 13:17). R. Levi told the parable of a man who had a field that contained a sprawling heap of barren rocks; he sold it for a trifle. The purchaser removed the heap and found running water underneath. He planted rows and rows of vines in the field, planted all kinds of spices in it, planted pomegranates in it—for all of these he put up stakes. He also built a tower in it,[9] wherein he placed a keeper. Whoever passed by the field praised it. When the one who sold the field passed by and saw that it was full of all kinds of good things, he said: Woe is me (*oy li*) that I gave up such a field! Woe is me (*oy li*) that I let such a wonderful field out of my hand!

Even so, Israel in Egypt were no more than a heap of barren rocks. But after they left Egypt, they became like a flourishing orchard of pomegranates. At whatever time people saw Israel, they praised them. When Pharaoh perceived them so transformed, he raised his voice in grief: Woe to (*oy lo*) that man—me—who let go of such a people. "And there was (*va-yehi*) woe after Pharaoh had let the people go.[10]

77. It is taught in the school of R. Ishmael: To what may Israel when leaving Egypt be compared? To a dove who fled from a hawk and was about to enter a cleft in a rock when she came upon a serpent nesting there. If she enters the cleft, the serpent will hiss at her threateningly. If she turns back, the hawk stands outside ready to seize her. What did the dove do? She began to cry and beat her wings, so that the owner of the cote would come and deliver

1. Gen. 50:25.
2. B. Sot 13a; Mek, *Be-shallah, Va-yehi,* 1; Deut. R. 11:7; Tanhuma, *Be-shallah,* §2.
3. Gen. R. 85:3.
4. At the beginning Moses told Israel in secrecy that they would leave with many of Egypt's possessions (Exod. 3:21–22). No Israelite betrayed this secret.
5. MTeh 114:4; TdE, p. 123.
6. JV: "into prosperity." But *ba-kosharot* may be taken to be a form of *kosher* ("suitable").
7. Num. R. 3:6.
8. MTeh 105:11.
9. Symbolic of the Temple.
10. Exod. R. 20:5; Mek, *Be-shallah, Va-yehi,* 2 (La 1:197–98). The story is based on the phonetic similarity in Hebrew of "woe is me (to him)" and "and there was."

her. Israel at the Red Sea were in a similar plight. They could not go down into the sea, because the sea had not yet split. Nor could they go back, because Pharaoh had already drawn near. What did they do? "They were sore afraid; and the children of Israel cried out unto the Lord" (Exod. 14:10). At once, "the Lord delivered Israel that day" (Exod. 14:30).[1]

78. "And the heart of Pharaoh and of his servants was turned," etc. (Exod. 14:5). Only a little while before, "Pharaoh's servants said unto him: 'How long shall this man [Moses] be a snare unto us? Let the men go' " (Exod. 10:7). But now, "the heart of Pharaoh and of his servants was turned, and they said: 'What is this we have done?' " (Exod. 14:5). [Distraught by what had happened], they said: If we had been plagued and not let them go, it would have been enough. Or if we had not been plagued and let them go, and they had not taken our treasures, it would have been enough. As it is, we were plagued, we let them go, and our treasures have been taken! By what parable may the Egyptians' distress be illustrated? By that of a man who said to his slave, "Get me a fish from the market." The slave went and brought him a foul-smelling fish. The man said, "I order you to eat the fish, or receive one hundred lashes, or pay me one hundred *maneh.*" The slave replied, "I will eat the fish." He began to eat, but before he could finish it, he said, "I will take the lashes." After receiving sixty lashes, he could take no more and cried out, "I will pay the hundred *maneh.*" The result: He ate [most of] the fish, received [most of] the lashes, and still paid the hundred *maneh*. The same thing happened to the Egyptians: They were plagued, they let Israel go, and their treasures were taken.[2]

79. [R. Nehemian said that Ezekiel reproached those prophets in Israel who "have not gone up into the breaches, nor repaired the walls for the House of Israel, to stand in the battle, in the day of the Lord" (Ezek. 13:5). But be it noted], Moses could say "unto the people: 'Fear ye not' " (Exod. 14:13). For to whom may Moses our teacher be compared? To a faithful shepherd the entire fence of whose sheepfold collapsed as it was growing dark. He got busy and succeeded in repairing three of its sides. But a breach remained on the fourth side; and since there was no more daylight left to complete the repair, he himself stood in the breach. When a lion came, he confronted him. When a wolf came, he confronted him.[3]

80. "The angel of God, who had been going ahead of the Israelite host, now moved and followed behind them" (Exod. 14:19). To understand what the angel of God did, consider the parable of a man walking on the road and making his son walk in front of him. When brigands attempting to capture the son came up in front, the father pulled his son from in front of him and put him behind. When a wolf came up behind, the father pulled his son from behind and put him in front. When brigands came up in front while a wolf came up behind, he took the son into his arms. When the son began to suffer from the heat, the father spread his cloak over him. When he was hungry, he fed him; when he was thirsty, he gave him to drink. So too did the Holy One: When the sea was in front of Israel and the Egyptians behind, He took them into His arms—"taking them upon His arms" (Hos. 11:3). When they began to suffer from the sun, He spread His garment over them, as is said, "He spread a cloud for a screen" (Ps. 105:39). When they were hungry, He fed them: "Behold, I will cause to rain bread from heaven for you" (Exod. 16:4). When they were thirsty, He gave them water to drink: "He brought forth streams from a rock" (Ps. 78:16).[4]

81. "And it came between the camp of Egypt and the camp of Israel; and there was the cloud [of fire] and the darkness" (Exod. 14:20)—the cloud [of fire] upon Israel and the darkness upon the Egyptians. The Egyptians, being placed in the dark, could see the Israelites in the light and shot arrows and catapulted stones at them. But the cloud and the angel shielded the Israelites.

Likewise, Scripture says, "How I bore you on eagles' wings" (Exod. 19:4). How is the eagle different from all other birds? All other birds carry their young between their feet, because they are afraid of birds flying above them. But the eagle is afraid only of man, who might shoot an arrow at him. [Therefore the eagle carries his young upon his wings], saying, "I would rather have the arrow lodge in me than in my young."[5]

The Splitting of the Red Sea and the Plunder at the Sea

82. It is taught that R. Meir said: When the Israelites stood at the Red Sea, the tribes were vying with one another, one saying, "I will be first to go down into the sea," and the other saying, "I will be first to go down into the sea." As they stood there wrangling, the tribe of Benjamin sprang forward and went down first into the sea. At that, the princes of Judah began hurling stones at them. For this reason, righteous Benjamin won the privilege of becoming host for the Almighty [in the Holy of Holies], as is said, "He dwelleth between his shoulders" (Deut. 33:12).[6] R. Judah said to R. Meir: That is not quite the way it happened. In fact, one tribe said, "I will not be the first to go into the sea"; and another tribe also said, "I will not be the first to go into the sea." While they were standing there deliberating, Nahshon the son of Amminadab [of the tribe of Judah] sprang forward and was the first to go down into the sea. Because it was Nahshon who

1. Song R. 2:14, §2; Mek, *Be-shallah, Va-yehi*, 3 (La 1:211).
2. Mek, *Be-shallah, Va-yehi*, 2 (La 1:195).
3. Ruth R., proem 5.
4. Mek, *Be-shallah, Va-yehi*, 5 (La 1:224–25); Tanhuma, *Be-shallah*, §10.
5. Mek, *Be-shallah, Va-yehi*, 5 (La 1:226–27); Mek, *Yitro, Ba-hodesh*, 2 (La 2:202–3); Yalkut, *Yitro*, §276.
6. That is, the Presence, the Holy of Holies, is to be in the territory of Benjamin. The phrase "between his shoulders" may perhaps have been construed: "Because of the blows sustained by his shoulders from the stones thrown at him."

sprang forward, Judah was to obtain [a site that was sacred, as well as] royal dominion in Israel, as is said, "Judah became His sanctuary, Israel his dominion" (Ps. 114:2).[1] For what reason, accordingly, did Judah come to have God's sanctuary [in his territory] and obtain dominion over Israel? Because "the sea saw [him] and fled" (Ps. 114:3).[2]

In the meantime, Moses was standing and praying at greath length. So the Holy One said to him, "My beloved are on the verge of drowning in the sea, and you spin out lengthy prayers before Me." Moses spoke up to God, "But Master of the universe, what else can I do?" God replied, "Speak unto the children of Israel, that they go forward. And lift up thy rod," etc. (Exod. 14:15ff.).

83. "Speak unto the children of Israel, that they go forward" (Exod. 14:15). According to R. Eliezer, the Holy One said to Moses: There is a time to be brief and a time to be lengthy. My children are in great distress, the sea is enclosing them, the enemy is in pursuit, and you stand here praying away! "Speak unto the children of Israel, that they go forward."[3]

84. "Speak unto the children of Israel, that they go forward" (Exod. 14:15). R. Hama bar Hanina said in his father's name: God's command to Moses may be explained by the parable of a shepherd who was leading his sheep across a river when a wolf came up to attack the sheep. What did this experienced shepherd do? He took a large he-goat and threw it to the wolf, saying, "Let him wrestle with this one until we cross the river, and then I will return to recover it."

So, too, when Israel departed from Egypt, the angel Samael arose to accuse them, saying to the Holy One: Master of the universe, until now they have been worshiping idols—would You split the sea for such as these? What did the Holy One do? He turned Job over to him; even though Job was one of Pharaoh's counselors,[4] yet "he was wholehearted and upright" (Job. 1:1). And God said to Samael, "Behold, he is in thy hands" (Job 2:6).[5] The Holy One reckoned: While Samael is busy with Job, Israel will go down into the sea and come up, and then I will save Job. Then, the Holy One said to Moses: Moses, I turned over Job to Satan. Now is the time for you to "speak unto the children of Israel, that they go forward."[6]

1. Except for Benjamin's tiny stretch of land upon which the Holy of Holies stood, the site where the Temple was erected, as well as the rest of the land, belonged to and was ruled by descendants of the tribe of Judah.
2. For the sake of clarity, the words "Because it was Nahshon . . . and fled (Ps. 114:3)" are transposed from below to the end of this paragraph. B. Sot 36b–37a; Mek, *Be-shallah, Va-yehi*, 6 (La 1:233–35).
3. Exod. R. 21:8.
4. That he was Pharaoh's counselor is mentioned as justification for God's action. Otherwise, it would have been unjust to make Job suffer in order to save Israel. *Etz Yosef* ((Exod. R., Soncino, p. 269, n. 1).
5. "Since Job was an upright man, Samael would have a hard task to triumph over him, just as the wolf would have with the he-goat in the parable" (Exod. R., Soncino, p. 269, n. 2).
6. Exod. R. 21:8.

85. "And the children of Israel went into the midst of the sea upon the dry ground" (Exod. 14:22). [How is it possible?] If they went into the sea, why does it say, "Upon the dry ground"? And if they went "upon the dry ground," then why does it say, "Into the midst of the sea"? Hence you learn that the sea was not split for them until they stepped into it, indeed until the waters reached up to their very noses.[7] Only then did the passage become dry land.

In a discourse, R. Nehorai said: When an Israelite woman was walking through the sea, leading her son by the hand, and he began to weep, she had merely to reach out her hand, pluck an apple or a pomegranate from the sea, and give it to him, for "He led them through the depths as [He was to do later] through the wilderness" (Ps. 106:9)—as they were to lack nothing in the wilderness, so also they lacked nothing in the depths.[8]

86. When the Holy One was about to drown the Egyptians in the sea, Uzza, heavenly prince of Egypt,[9] rose up and prostrated himself before the Holy One, saying: Master of the universe, You created the world by the measure of mercy. Why then do You wish to drown my children? The Holy One gathered the entire heavenly household and said to them: You be the judge between Me and Uzza prince of Egypt. At that, the heavenly princes of the other nations began to speak up in behalf of Egypt. When Michael[10] perceived this, he gave the sign to Gabriel, who in one swoop darted down to Egypt, where he pulled out a brick with its clay enclosing a [dead] infant who had been immured alive in the structure. He then came back, stood before the Holy One, and said: Master of the universe, thus did the Egyptians enslave Your children. Whereupon the Holy One sat in judgment over the Egyptians in accord with the measure of justice and drowned them in the sea.

In that instant the ministering angels wished to utter song before the Holy One, but He rebuked them, saying, "The works of My hands are drowning in the sea, and you would utter song in My presence!"[11]

87. The verse "The horse together with his rider hath He thrown into the sea" (Exod. 15:1) implies that the horse was tied to the rider even as the rider was tied to the horse, and that together they were thrown into the air, then down into the deep, and were not separated one from the other.[12]

88. "The horse and his rider hath He thrown (*ramah*) into the sea" (Exod. 15:1). The waves of the sea appeared in the form of mares; the Egyptians rode lusty stallions, which kept running after the apparitions of the mares until they were thrown into the sea to drown. When an Egyptian would say to his stallion, "Yesterday I had to pull you to

7. As a way of testing their faith.
8. Hence, though they "went into the midst of the sea," it was as though they were "upon the dry ground," finding everything there. Exod. R. 21:10.
9. Each nation has its own heavenly prince or guardian angel.
10. Israel's heavenly prince.
11. Midrash Avkir; B. Sanh 39b.
12. Mek, *Be-shallah, Shirata*, 2.

the Nile to water you, and you were reluctant to follow me; but now you are about to sink me in the sea," the lusty stallion replied, "[I can't help myself.] Look what (*re'eh mah*) is in the sea."[1]

89. R. Yose the Galilean expounded: When Israel came out of the sea, they gazed upward to chant their song. But how were all of them—even the infant lying upon his mother's knees and the suckling feeding at his mother's breast—able to do so? When they saw the Presence, the infant raised his neck, the suckling let go of his mother's nipple, and all said, "This is my God, and I will glorify Him" (Exod. 15:2).

It is taught that, according to R. Meir, even fetuses in their mothers' wombs chanted the song. But were they [being in the womb] able to see [the Presence]? Yes, said R. Tanhum, the wombs became as transparent as glass, and so even the fetuses were able to see the Presence.[2]

90. "Then sang Moses and the children of Israel" (Exod. 15:1). R. Avin the Levite said: When Israel stood up to chant the song at the sea, Moses did not let them chant it by themselves, but like a teacher who recites a portion in Scripture with a child when he is young, so did Moses recite it with Israel—"then sang Moses and the children of Israel," they being like a child who repeats after his teacher. But after forty years [in the wilderness], Israel grew up and on their own proceeded to chant the Song of the Well, as is said, "Then sang Israel" (Num. 21:17).[3]

91. R. Huna said: Israel of that generation, having little faith, said: Even as we are coming up on the one side, so the Egyptians are probably coming up on the other side. So the Holy One ordered the prince of the sea, "Spew forth the Egyptians onto dry land." "But," the prince of the sea dared reply, "Master of the universe, is there any other servant whose master first gives him a gift and then takes it back from him?" "I will give you," God replied, "one and a half times their number." Again the prince of the sea spoke up: "Master of the universe, dare any servant claim a debt from his master?"[4] God said, "Let the brook of Kishon be surety for Me." At once the sea spewed forth the Egyptians, casting them onto dry land, and Israel came and saw them, as is said, "Israel saw the Egyptians dead upon the seashore" (Exod. 14:30).

What is alluded to in "One and a half times their number"? [The following]: Of Pharaoh it is written, "He took six hundred chosen chariots" (Exod. 14:7); but of Sisera it is written that he "gathered . . . nine hundred chariots of iron" (Judg. 4:13). When Sisera came to fight Israel, he advanced against them with iron staves. The Holy One brought forth the stars out of their orbits against Sisera's men, and as the stars of heaven descended upon them, the iron staves they held began heating up, and Sisera's men had to go down to cool themselves in the brook of Kishon. Then the Holy One said to the brook of Kishon, "Go and fulfill the pledge given in your name." At once the brook swept them out and cast them into the sea, as is said, "The brook Kishon swept them away, that ancient brook" (Judg. 5:21). What is meant by "That ancient brook"? The brook that was declared surety in ancient times.

In that instant the fish in the sea opened their mouths and exclaimed, "The faithfulness of the Lord endureth forever" (Ps. 117:2).[5]

92. "Israel saw the Egyptians dead" (Exod. 14:30). What did the children of Israel do to them? Each man in Israel took his dog, went down, and, placing his foot upon an Egyptian's neck, said to his dog, "Eat of this hand, which used me as a slave. Eat of these bowels, which had no mercy on me."[6]

93. "And Moses made Israel move on from the Red Sea" (Exod. 15:22). He had them move against their will, for they were not ready to leave the shore. Why not? Because when Israel left Egypt, Pharaoh, together with all those hosts, set out to pursue them. What else did he do? As he set out in pursuit of Israel with his chariots and horsemen, he adorned all the horses with precious stones and pearls. When they reached the sea and the Holy One drowned them, all these precious stones and pearls floated on the surface and were cast on shore, so that every day Israelites would come down and gather them. That is why they did not wish to move from there. Moses, perceiving this, said, "Do you think that the sea will continue to bring up precious stones and pearls for you every day?" So, against their will, Moses had them move on.[7]

1. Exod. R. 23:14; Song R. 1:9, §6.
2. B. Sot 30b–31a; P. Sot 5:6, 20c.
3. Yalkut, *Hukkat*, §263.
4. So what chance have I to get back the bodies I am now forced to give up?
5. B. Pes 118b and En Yaakov, ad loc.
6. Mteh 22:1.
7. Tanhuma B, *Be-shallah*, §16.

CHAPTER FIVE

ISRAEL IN THE WILDERNESS

From Egypt into the Wilderness

1. "As a lily among thorns, so is My love among the maidens" (Song 2:2). R. Eliezer applied the verse to the deliverance from Egypt: Just as a lily placed among thorns is difficult for its owner to pluck, so was the deliverance of Israel difficult for the Holy One, as is said, "Hath God ever assayed to go and take Him a nation from the midst of another nation?" (Deut. 4:34).

[No, Israel was not like a lily among thorns], R. Joshua said in the name of R. Hanan: Scripture does not say here, "A nation from the midst of a people," or, "A people from the midst of a nation," but, "A nation from the midst of a nation," for these were uncircumcised even as the others were uncircumcised, these let their forelocks grow[1] even as the others let their forelocks grow, these wore garments made of fibers of diverse seed even as the others wore garments made of fibers of diverse seed. Accordingly, God's measure of justice alone would not have demanded Israel's deliverance from Egypt.[2]

2. "Thou didst pluck up a vine out of Egypt" (Ps. 80:9). R. Tanhuma bar Abba asked: "Why is Israel compared to a vine? Consider what owners of a vine, seeking to improve it, do. They pluck it from its place and replant it elsewhere, and there it flourishes. So, too, when the Holy One sought to make Israel known throughout the world, what did He do? He plucked them out of Egypt and brought them into the wilderness, and there they began to thrive; there they received the Torah and their name went forth throughout the world.[3]

The Manna

3. "Moses said: 'It is the Lord who will give you flesh to eat in the evening, and bread in the morning to the full' " (Exod. 16:18).[4] R. Aha bar Jacob said: At first Israel were like hens randomly pecking away in a heap of refuse, until Moses came and fixed definite mealtimes for them.[5]

4. The disciples of R. Simeon ben Yohai asked him: Why did the manna not come down for Israel just once a year? He replied: Let me answer you with the parable of a mortal king who had a son. When the king provided him with his sustenance once a year, the son visited his father only once a year. When the father began to provide him with his sustenance daily, the son had to call on his father every day. So it was with Israel. If an Israelite had, say, four or five children, he would worry, saying: Perhaps the manna will not come down tomorrow, and all my children will die of hunger. And so [because the manna was coming down daily] the Israelites were compelled to direct their hearts to their Father in heaven [every day].

Another reason [for daily manna]: They were able to eat it while it was still warm.

Still another reason [for daily manna]: To lighten the burdens that had to be carried during the journey.[6]

5. Manna is described in Scripture as "bread," as "honey," and as "oil." How are the differing descriptions to be reconciled? Young men tasted in it the taste of bread, old people the taste of honey, and infants the taste of oil.[7]

6. It is written, "When the dew fell in the camp in the night, the manna fell upon it" (Num. 11:9); it is also written, "The people shall go out and gather," etc. (Exod. 16:4); and it is also written, "The people went about to and fro to gather it" (Num. 11:8). How are the three statements to be reconciled? For the righteous, it came right down to the doors of their tents; ordinary people had to go out and gather it; but the wicked had to go about to and fro to gather it.

Manna is also described as "bread" (Exod. 16:4) and as "unbaked dough" (Num. 11:8), and Scripture also says, "They ground it" (ibid.). How reconcile the differing descriptions? Well, the righteous received it as [baked] bread, ordinary Israelites as unbaked dough, and the wicked as grain yet to be ground in a hand mill.[8]

7. Our rabbis taught: "Each [Israelite] ate the bread of the mighty" (*abbirim*) (Ps. 78:25), the same kind of bread, so said R. Akiva, as [mighty] ministering angels eat. When these words were reported to R. Ishmael, he said: Go and say to Akiva: Akiva, you are mistaken. Do ministering angels really eat bread? Did not Moses [after being in heaven] say, "I ate no bread" (Deut. 9:18)? How then should one interpret "bread of *abbirim*"? Read rather "bread of *evarim*," bread that was directly absorbed by the two hundred and forty-eight parts (*evarim*) of the body.[9]

---

1. Deemed an act of idolatry.
2. God's mercy had to be joined to His justice. Song R. 2:2, §2.
3. Exod. R. 44:1.
4. Manna in the morning and quails in the evening.
5. B. Yoma 75b.
6. B. Yoma 76a.
7. Since bread was difficult for old people and infants to chew. Exod. R. 25:3.
8. B. Yoma 75a.
9. Hence, there was no waste matter. B. Yoma 75b and En Yaakov, ad loc.

8. "And the taste of it was the taste of a cake (*leshad*) baked with oil" (Num. 11:8) R. Abbahu said: [Read not *leshad*, "cake," but *shad*, "breast"].[1] Hence, just as an infant, whenever he touches the breast, finds many flavors in it, so it was with manna. Whenever Israel ate it, they found many flavors in it.

Some read *leshad* as *le-shed*, "of a demon"—even as the demon changes himself into many shapes, so manna changed into many flavors.[2]

9. "Thou preparest a table before me in the presence of mine enemies" (Ps. 23:5). Issi ben Judah said: "The manna that came down for Israel piled up to such a height that all kings of the east and the west could see it.[3]

10. "And as the sun waxed hot, it melted" (Exod. 16:21). When the sun shone upon the manna, it began to melt and formed rivulets which flowed into the Great Sea. Harts, gazelles, roebuck, and all kinds of other animals would come and drink from the rivulets. The nations of the world would then hunt these animals, eat them, and, tasting in them the taste of the manna that came down for Israel, say, "Blessed is the people who have it so" (Ps. 144:15).[4]

11. It is taught that R. Yose said: Just as a prophet can tell Israel what might be hidden in holes and clefts, so would the manna reveal to Israel what was hidden in holes and clefts. How so? When two men came before Moses with a lawsuit, one saying, "You stole my slave," the other saying, "You sold it to me," Moses would say to both of them: Judgment will be pronounced tomorrow.[5] The next day, if the slave's measure of manna was found in the house of the claimant, it was clear that the respondent had stolen him; if it was found in the house of the respondent, it was clear that the claimant had sold the slave to him.[6]

12. "He subjected thee to the hardship of hunger when He gave thee manna to eat" (Deut. 8:3). R. Hananiah and R. Jonathan asked Menahem the Baker: Can this verse possibly intimate that the manna the Holy One gave to Israel was food that left them hungry? How did Menahem answer them? He set before his questioners two cucumbers, one whole and the other crushed, and asked, "How much is the whole one worth?" "Two silver *zuz*." "And how much the crushed one?" "One silver *zuz*." "But is not the crushed cucumber just as large as the whole one?" asked Menahem, and then, answering his own question, said, "Even as a man derives enjoyment from the taste of food, so he derives enjoyment from the appearance of food.[7]

The Well

13. R. Yohanan said: The well used to water all kinds of garden herbs, all kinds of seeds for planting, and all varieties of trees. You can see for yourself that it was so, for after Miriam died and the well stopped watering plants, the people said, "This is no longer a place of seed, of figs, or of vines" (Num. 20:5).[8]

14. The well that was with Israel in the wilderness had extraordinary properties. It resembled a rock the size of a beehive, from which, as out of a narrow-necked jug,[9] water coming out in a trickle shot high up into the air like a geyser. The well rolled up mountains with Israel and went down into valleys with them. Indeed, wherever Israel encamped, the well rested close by on an elevated spot opposite the entrance to the Tent of Meeting. The princes of Israel would come and walk around the well with their staves as they chanted the song "Spring up, O well, sing ye unto it" (Num. 21:17). At that, the waters welled up, rising high like a lofty pillar; and each of the princes, digging [into the ground] with his staff, channeled water toward his tribe and toward his family, as is said:

> The well, which the princes dug,
> Which the nobles of the people delved,
> With maces, with their own staffs
> (Num. 21:18).

Thus the well flowed in all directions throughout Israel's camp, watering all the surrounding wasteland. It branched out into streams so large that Israelites would seat themselves in small boats and go visiting one another. [There was no need to row], for a man who went upstream on the camp's right side would [as the current reversed itself][10] return downstream on the right side; and so it was with the man who set out on the camp's left side. Even the overflow of drinking water spilled on the ground became a wide river, which coursed toward the Great Sea and, upon its return, brought back from there all the things in the world that were desirable.[11]

Clouds of Glory

15. "And the Lord went before them by day in a pillar of cloud to guide them," etc. (Exod. 13:21). How many clouds of glory encompassed Israel in the wilderness? Seven clouds: one at each of the four sides; one above them; one beneath them; and the one that advanced before

1. Interpolated by Bah.
2. B. Yoma 75a.
3. B. Yoma 76a.
4. Mek, *Be-shallah*, *Va-yassa*, 5 (La 2:117).
5. See Jer. 21:12.
6. B. Yoma 75a.
7. Though the manna had all kinds of flavors, it always looked the same, and so those who ate it did not have the pleasure of seeing the different foods that they tasted in the manna. Eccles. R. 5:10, §1. See also above, chap. 3, §63.
8. Song R. 4:12, §3.
9. The Hebrew *pakh* is a narrow-necked clay vessel, known in Greek as an oinochoe.
10. According to popular belief, through underground tunnels. So Rashi and Targum on Eccles. 1:7.
11. Tos Suk 3:11–13; Num. R. 1:2.

them, raised every lowland, lowered each highland, and thus turned them all into level ground. As that cloud advanced, it also killed snakes and scorpions, and swept and sprinkled the road before them.[1]

Amalek's War

16. "Is the Lord among us, or not? Then came Amalek" (Exod. 17:7–8). R. Levi said: What parable applies here to Israel? The parable of a child who was perched on his father's shoulders [in the marketplace]. Each time the child saw a desirable object, he said to his father, "Buy it for me," and his father bought it for him the first time, the second time, and the third time. While they were walking, the child saw his father's friend and asked him, "Have you seen my daddy?" The father spoke sharply to his son, "Silly boy, you are riding astride my shoulder, whatever you want I buy for you, and yet you ask this man, 'Have you seen my daddy?' " What did the father do then? He dropped him from his shoulder, and a dog came by and bit the son.

So, too, as soon as Israel went out of Egypt, seven clouds of the Holy One's glory encompassed them. They asked for manna, and the Holy One sent it down for them; for quail, and He brought it to them. After He had given them all that they wanted, they began to have doubts, demanding to know, "Is the Lord among us, or not?" (Exod. 17:7). The Holy One said to them: [You doubt My Presence in your midst?]. As you live, I shall make you aware of it. Look, here comes a dog to bite you! And who was the dog? Amalek, for the very next verse says, "Then came Amalek" (Exod. 17:8).[2]

17. R. Levi said in the name of R. Simeon ben Halafta; With what may Amalek be compared? With a fly greedy to get at an open wound. Just so, Amalek, the dog, was panting to get at Israel.[3]

18. "And it came to pass, when Moses held up his hand, that Israel prevailed" (Exod. 17:11). But did the hands of Moses actually wage war or win victories? Not actually; what the text means is that so long as Israel turned their thoughts upward and submitted their hearts to their Father in heaven, they prevailed. Otherwise, they fell.[4]

19. "But Moses' hands were heavy; and they took a stone, and put it under him, and he sat thereon" (Exod. 17:12). Did Moses have no cushion or bolster to sit on? Of course, but Moses said: When Israel are deep in distress, I must be in it with them.[5]

20. "Remember what Amalek did unto thee . . . how he cooled thee"[6] (Deut. 25:17–18)—made you appear lukewarm before other nations. What Amalek did may be understood by the parable of a pool of scalding water into which no living creature dared to descend. Then a worthless fellow came along and jumped right into the pool, so that even though he was scalded, he made it appear lukewarm in the eyes of others. So, too, when Israel went out of Egypt, and the sea was split before them and the Egyptians drowned in it, fear of them fell upon all the nations of the earth, as is said, "Then were the chiefs of Edom affrighted. . . . Terror and dread falleth upon them," etc. (Exod. 15:15–16). But after Amalek came and waged war against Israel, though he got the scalding he deserved from them, still he made Israel appear lukewarm in battle in the eyes of the nations of the earth.[7]

21. "Remember what Amalek did unto thee by the way, as ye came forth out of Egypt" (Deut. 25:17). R. Levi said: Like a highwayman, he came upon you from the wayside. In this connection, the parable is told of a king who had a vineyard, which he enclosed with a fence and in which he put a dog who was a vicious biter. The king said: If anyone comes and breaches the fence, the dog will bite him. Some days later, the king's own son came and breached the fence, and the dog bit him. Afterward, whenever the king wished to remind his son of his sin in breaching the vineyard fence, he would ask him, "Do you remember how the dog bit you?" So, too, whenever the Holy One wished to remind Israel of their sin at Rephidim in demanding to know, "Is the Lord among us, or not?" (Exod. 17:7), He would say to them, "Remember what Amalek did unto thee" (Deut. 25:17).[8]

22. "Amalek dwelleth in a land south [of the Land of Israel]" (Num. 13:29). Why then did the scouts begin their account of the peoples living in the Land with a reference to Amalek [who did not live in it? It was to remind Israel of the punishment that might once more befall them]. What parable illustrates the spies' mention of Amalek? The one of a child who, having misbehaved, was beaten with a strap. Whenever people wanted to intimidate him, they reminded him of the strap with which he was beaten. Even so, [the scouts' mention of] Amalek, Israel's painful strap, [was to serve as a reminder and a warning].[9]

23. "The hand of Amalek is against the t'ron' of the Lor' "[10] (Exod. 17:16). R. Levi said in the name of R. Hama bar Hanina: The Name of God will not be complete and the throne of the Lord will not be whole as long as Amalek's seed remains in the world. Only after

---

1. Mek, *Be-shallah*, *Va-yehi*, §1; Num. R. 1:1, §2.
2. Tanhuma B, *Yitro*, §4; Exod. R. 26:2; PRKM, p. 33 (PRKS, p. 40).
3. Tanhuma B, *Ki Tetze*, §12; PRKM 3:8 (PRKS, p. 51).
4. B. RH 29a.
5. B. Ta 11a.
6. JV: "how he met thee." But *krk* [*korkha*] ("how he met thee") may be associated with the stem *kr* [*kar*] ("cold").
7. Tanhuma, *Ki Tetze*, §9; Tanhuma B, *Ki Tetze*, §13; PRKM 3:10 (PRKS, p. 52).
8. Tanhuma, *Ki Tetze*, §9; Tanhuma B, *Ki Tetze*, §12; PRKM 3:9 (PRKS, p. 51).
9. Tanhuma B, *Shelah*, §18; Num. R. 16:18.
10. The defective spelling of the words "throne" and "Lord" is an attempt to reproduce in English the defective spelling of the Hebrew: the words, which should be written *kisse YHVH*, are written *kes Yah*.

the seed of Amalek is blotted out from the world will the throne of the Lord be whole and the Name of God complete.[1]

24. "Write this for a memorial in the book" (Exod. 17:14). The sages of yore say: Throughout all generations there obtains the rule that the scourge with which Israel is smitten will in the end itself be smitten. All mankind should learn proper conduct from what happened to Amalek, who came to harm Israel, and the Holy One erased him from life in this world as well as from life in the world-to-come, as is said, "I will utterly blot out" (ibid.). Likewise, every nation and every kingdom that set out to harm Israel God always judges according to this rule.[2]

The Giving of Torah

25. R. Isaac said: Israel were worthy of receiving the Torah immediately upon leaving Egypt. But the Holy One said: Because of their servitude in clay and bricks, My children's look of good health has not yet come back, and therefore they cannot receive the Torah at once. God's delay in giving the Torah may be illustrated by the parable of a king's son who had just got up from his sickbed. His tutor said: Let your son go back to school. The king replied: My son's look of good health has not yet come back, yet you say, "Let him go back to school!" Let my son be indulged for two or three months with good food and drink, so that he may fully recover—then he can go back to school. Likewise, the Holy One said: My children's look of good health has not yet come back—they have just been released from slaving with clay and bricks—shall I now give them the Torah? Let My children be indulged for two or three months—with the manna, with the waters of the well, with the quail—then I will give them the Torah.[3]

26. R. Joshua ben Levi said: When Israel left Egypt, there were among them men crippled by heavy labor, for as they worked in clay and bricks, now and then a stone, dropping from the structure, would break a man's arm or sever his leg. Hence the Holy One said: It is not right that I give My Torah to cripples. What did He do? He beckoned to the ministering angels, and they came down and healed them.[4]

27. [As to the consequences of Israel's refusal to accept the Torah], Resh Lakish said: Why is it written, "And there was evening, and there was morning, the sixth day" (Gen. 1:31)? What is the significance of using the definite article?[5] Singling out the "sixth day" by means of the definite article shows that the Holy One stipulated with the preceding works of creation, saying to them: If Israel accept the Torah [on the sixth day of Sivan], you will continue to exist; if not, I will return you to desolation and chaos.[6]

28. "As a lily among thorns" (Song 2:2). R. Azariah, citing R. Judah son of R. Simon, illustrated the verse by the parable of a king who had an orchard planted with a row of fig trees, a row of grapevines, a row of pomegranate trees, and a row of apple trees. The king turned this orchard over to a keeper and went away. After a while the king came back and looked into the orchard to see how it had done, and found it overgrown with thorns and thistles. He summoned woodcutters to raze it, but as he looked again at the thorns, he noticed among them a rose-colored lily. He took hold of it and breathed in its fragrance, and his spirit was calmed. Then the king said: Because of this lily, let the entire orchard be spared.

Likewise, the whole world, all of it, was created only for the sake of the Torah. But after twenty-six generations,[7] when the Holy One looked closely at His world to ascertain what it had done, He found it [muddy] water within [muddy] water[8]—the generation of Enosh, water within water;[9] the generation of the flood, water within water; the generation of the dispersion of mankind, water within water.[10] He summoned destroyers to raze the world, but then he noticed there a rose-colored lily—Israel. He took hold of it and breathed in its fragrance—He gave Israel the Ten Commandments. When he heard their response, "We will do and we will hearken" (Exod. 24:7), His spirit was calmed.

The Holy One then said: Because of a lily, an orchard was spared. Because of Torah and of Israel, let the world be spared.[11]

29. "The Lord came unto Sinai; after having [first] risen at Seir unto the people thereof, then having shined forth at Mount Paran,[12] He came unto the myriads holy, at His right hand a fiery law for them" (Deut. 33:2).[13] When he who is everywhere revealed Himself to give the Torah to Israel, He revealed Himself not only to Israel but to all the other nations as well. At first God went to the children of Esau. He asked them: Will you accept the Torah? They said right to His face: What is written in it? He said: "Thou shalt not murder." They replied: Master of the universe, this goes against our grain. Our father, whose "hands are

1. Tanhuma B, *Ki Tetze*, §18.
2. Mek, *Be-shallah*, *Amalek*, 2.
3. Eccles. R. 3:11; §2; Song R. 2:5, §2.
4. Tanhuma, *Yitro*, §8.
5. The preceding days are referred to as "a second day," "a third day," and so on, with the indefinite article.

6. B. Shab 88a.
7. In the generation when the Torah was given.
8. Wicked people in a wicked environment. For a further explanation of "water within water," see below, part 3, chap. 1, §15, n.o.
9. It was partly wiped out by water. See Gen. R. 23:6 on Gen. 4:26.
10. Also inundated in part. See Gen. R. 38:10.
11. Lev. R. 23:3; Song R. 2:2, §3.
12. Seir is a reference to Edom, and Paran to Ishmael.
13. JV: "The Lord came from Sinai, and rose from Seir unto them. He shined forth from Mount Paran, and He came from the myriads holy, at His right hand was a fiery law unto them." Here the commentor attempts to solve the meaning of God's peregrinations; he is also baffled by the strange statement that God came *from* Sinai, whereas in truth He came *to* Sinai. Accordingly, the commentator takes the proposition *mi* (usually rendered "from") as meaning rather "the place or region in or at which a thing is" (see Gesenius, *Lexicon*, p. 584; cf. Gen. 12:8). The "myriads holy" are the myriads of Israel.

the hands of Esau" (Gen. 27:22), led us to rely only on the sword, because his father told him, "By thy sword shalt thou live" (Gen. 27:40).[1] We cannot accept the Torah.

Then He went to the children of Ammon and Moab, and asked them: Will you accept the Torah? They said right to His face: What is written in it? He said: "Thou shalt not commit adultery." They replied: Master of the universe, our very origin is in adultery, for Scripture says, "Thus were both the daughters of Lot with child by their father" (Gen. 19:36). We cannot accept the Torah.

Then He went to the children of Ishmael. He asked them: Will you accept the Torah? They said right to His face: What is written in it? He said: "Thou shalt not steal." They replied: Master of the universe, it is our very nature to live off only what is stolen and what is got by assault. Of our forebear Ishmael, it is written, "And he shall be a wild ass of a man: his hand shall be against every man, and every man's hand against him" (Gen. 16:12). We cannot accept the Torah.

There was not a single nation among the nations to whom God did not go, speak, and, as it were, knock on its door, asking whether it would be willing to accept the Torah.

At long last He came to Israel. They said, "We will do and hearken" (Exod. 24:7). Of God's successive attempts to give the Torah, it is written, "The Lord came unto Sinai; after having [first] risen at Seir unto the people thereof, then having shined forth at Mount Paran, He finally came unto the myriads holy, at His right hand a fiery law for them" (Deut. 33:2).[2]

30. "Why do you scurry about and contend, ye mountains that are crookbacked?"[3] (Ps. 68:17). R. Yose the Galilean said: When the Holy One came to give the Torah to Israel on Sinai, the mountains scurried about, striving with one another, one saying, "The Torah should be given on me," and another, "It should be given on me." Mount Tabor came from Beth-elim, and Mount Carmel from Apamea, one saying, "I have been summoned," and another saying, "I have been summoned." Finally, the Holy One said, "Why do you scurry about and contend, ye mountains that are crookbacked?" You are, to be sure, lofty mountains, but you are crookbacked, blemished, since idolatry has been practiced at the top of each one of you. But Sinai—idolatry has never been practiced upon it—Sinai is "the mountain which God has desired for His abode" (ibid.).[4]

31. Whence did Sinai come? R. Yose taught: Out of Mount Moriah—the place where our father Isaac had been bound as a sacrifice—Sinai plucked itself as a priest's portion is plucked out of the dough.[5] For the Holy One said: Since their father Isaac was bound upon this mount, it is fitting that his children receive the Torah upon it.[6]

32. "And they stood under the mount" (Exod. 19:17).[7] R. Avdimi bar Hama said: The verse implies that the Holy One overturned the mountain upon them, like an inverted cask, and said to them: If you accept the Torah, it is well; if not, your grave will be right here.[8]

33. R. Simai expounded: When Israel hastened to say, "We will do," before saying, "We will hearken,"[9] sixty myriads of ministering angels came down and fastened two crowns upon each and every one in Israel, one as a reward for saying, "We will do," and the other as a reward for saying, "We will hearken." But when Israel sinned,[10] a hundred and twenty myriads of destroying angels came down and removed the crowns, as is said, "The children of Israel were stripped of their ornaments from Mount Horeb" (Exod. 33:6).[11]

R. Eliezer said: When Israel hastened to say, "We will do," before saying, "We will hearken," a divine voice went forth and exclaimed: Who has disclosed to My children this secret, which only the ministering angels make use of? For they are told, "Bless the Lord, ye angels of His, that do what He saith, [and then] hearken to the voice of His Word" (Ps. 103:20)—first they are described as "doing," and then as "hearkening [obeying]."[12]

34. R. Abbahu said in the name of R. Yohanan: When the Holy One gave the Torah, no bird chirped, no fowl flew, no ox lowed, not one of the *ofannim*[13] stirred a wing, not one of the seraphim said, "Holy, holy, holy!" The sea did not roar, creatures did not speak—the whole world was hushed into breathless silence; it was then that the voice went forth: "I am the Lord thy God" (Exod. 20:2).[14]

35. "I am the Lord thy God." Because the Holy One appeared to them at the Red Sea as a mighty man waging war,[15] at Sinai as a pedagogue teaching Torah, in the days of Solomon as a young man, and in the days of Daniel as an aged man full of mercy, the Holy One said: Because you see Me in many guises, do not imagine that there are many gods—for I am He who was with you at the Red Sea, I am He who was with you at Sinai, I am the same everywhere. "I am the Lord thy God."[16]

36. "His mouth is most sweet" (Song 5:16). It is said in the name of R. Yohanan: The moment Israel at Sinai heard

1. Here not BR but the text in PRF is followed.
2. Sif Deut., §343; PR 21 (PRF, p. 99b; YJS 1:417).
3. JV: "Why look ye askance, ye mountains of peaks." But in the comment that follows, *teratzedun* ("look askance") will be construed as portmanteau for *rvtz* [*rutz*] ("run, scurry") and *dvn* [*dun*] ("contend, strive").
4. Gen. R. 99:1.
5. On *hallah*, the priest's share of the bread, see Num. 15:20.
6. MTeh 68:9; BhM 5:72–73.
7. The translation is literal. JV: "And they stood at the nether part of the mount."
8. B. Shab 88a; AZ 2b.
9. Exod. 24:7.
10. Through the golden calf.
11. That is, what they had received at Mount Horeb.
12. B. Shab 88a.
13. "Wheel-angels." See Ezek. 1:16.
14. Exod. R. 29:9.
15. Exod. 15:3.
16. Yalkut, *Yitro*, §286; Mek, *Be-shallah*, *Shirata*, 4.

the word "I," their souls left them, as is written, "My soul left me when He spoke" (Song 5:6). At once, the Word returned to the Holy One and said: Master of the universe, You are ever alive and enduring, the Torah is ever alive and enduring, yet You are sending me to the dead?—they are all dead! So, for Israel's sake, the Holy One went back and sweetened [made soft] the Word, as is said, "The voice of the Lord is powerful, the voice of the Lord is stately" (Ps. 29:4), which, as R. Hama bar Hanina explained, means that the voice of the Lord was powerful for young men and had measured stateliness for the aged. [In agreement with R. Hama bar Hanina], R. Levi said: Had it been written, "The voice of the Lord is in His strength," the world could not have stood it. Hence Scripture says, "The voice of the Lord is fitted to the strength" (Ps. 29:4),[1] that is to say, to the strength of each and every person—the young, according to their strength; the aged, according to their strength; the little ones, according to their strength; the sucklings, according to their strength; the women, according to their strength.

R. Simeon ben Yohai, however, taught: The Torah that the Holy One gave to Israel was the one who helped restore their souls to them. She pleaded before the Holy One for mercy on their behalf, saying: Is there a king who gives his daughter in marriage and slays the courtier whom she is to wed? The entire world rejoices for my sake, yet Your children [Israel, to whom I am being given], are dying! At that, their souls returned. "The Law of the Lord is perfect, it restores souls" (Ps. 19:8).

Another exposition of "His mouth is most sweet" (Song 5:16): [The Holy One was] like a king who spoke so harshly to his son that the latter fell into a faint. When the king saw that he had fainted, he began to hug him, kiss him, and speak softly to him, saying, "What is it with you? Are you not my only son? Am I not your father?" So, too, as soon as the Holy One said, "I am the Lord thy God," then and there Israel's souls left them. When they died, the angels began to hug them and kiss them, saying to them, "What is it with you? Be not afraid—'ye are children of the Lord your God' " (Deut. 14:1). At the same time, the Holy One repeated the Word softly for their sake as He said, "Are you not My children, even as I am the Lord your God? You are My people. You are beloved unto Me." He kept speaking gently to them until their souls returned.[2]

37. "Thus thou shalt say to the house of Jacob" (Exod. 19:3)—that is, to the women, meaning that God said to Moses: Tell them those essentials that they can understand; "and tell the children of Israel" (ibid.)—that is, the men, meaning: You may tell them also specific details of precepts, which they [unlike women] can understand.

Another explanation: Why did He mention the women first? Because they are prompt in fulfilling commandments.

Still another explanation: In order that they might lead their children to the study of Torah.[3]

38. R. Joshua ben Levi said: With each and every word that issued from the mouth of the Holy One, the entire world, all of it, was filled with the fragrance of spices. But if the first word filled the world, where did the fragrance of the second word go? Out of His treasuries the Holy One brought forth a wind, which carried each fragrance along in orderly succession.

R. Joshua ben Levi said also: At each and every word that issued from the mouth of the Holy One, the souls of Israel departed, as is said, "My soul departed when He spoke" (Song 5:6). But if their souls departed at the first word, how could they receive the next word? He brought down the dew, with which He will in time resurrect the dead, and restored Israel to life.

R. Joshua ben Levi said further: At each and every word that issued from the mouth of the Holy One, the Israelites recoiled a distance of twelve *mil*[4] and the angels moved from back [to Sinai], as is said, "Hosts of angels[5] flee, they flee" (Ps. 68:13). Read not *yiddodun* ("they flee") but *yedaddun* ("they move").[6]

39. Hananiah son of R. Joshua's brother said: Just as in the sea there are ripples and wavelets between each major wave, so between each of the Ten Commandments there were Torah's unwritten minutiae, as well as all of Torah's letters.[7]

40. "For who is there of all flesh, that hath heard the voice of the living God speaking out of the midst of the fire, as we have, and lived?" (Deut. 5:23). Come and see how the voice went forth to all of Israel, to each and every one in keeping with his particular capacity—to the elderly in keeping with their capacity, to young men in keeping with their capacity, to the little ones in keeping with their capacity, and to the women in keeping with their capacity. R. Yose bar Hanina said: If you are astounded at such an assertion, then draw the relevant inference from the manna, which came down for Israel varying in taste, in keeping with each Israelite's particular need—to young men it tasted like bread, to the elderly it tasted like wafers made with honey, to sucklings it tasted like milk from their mother's breast, to the sick it tasted like fine flour mingled with honey, while for the heathen it tasted as bitter as linseed. Now, if the manna, which was all of the same kind, changed into so many kinds to provide for the particular need of each individual, was it not possible for the voice, in which there is such divine strength, to vary according to the capacity of each individual, so that no harm should befall him? Hence Job said, "God thundereth marvelously with His voice" (Job 37:5).[8]

---

1. Literally, "The voice of the Lord is in strength," a deviation from normal syntax, which would require suffixing the appropriate personal pronoun—e.g., "Jacob lifted his feet" (Gen. 29:1), not simply "lifted feet"—whenever a part or an attribute of the body is mentioned. Cf. Tanhuma, *Shemot*, §25.
2. Song R. 5:16, §3; Exod. R. 5:9 and 29:4.
3. Exod. R. 28:2.
4. A *mil* is about 1,620 yards.
5. MT: "Kings of armies."
6. B. Shab 88b.
7. That is, all the details of the Oral Law, as well as the six hundred and thirteen precepts. P. Shek 6:1, 49d.
8. Exod. R. 5:9.

41. At Sinai, when the Holy One gave the Torah to Israel, He manifested marvels upon marvels for Israel with His voice. How so? As the Holy One spoke, the voice reverberated throughout the world. At first Israel heard the voice coming to them from the south,[1] so they ran to the south to meet the voice there. It shifted to the north, so they ran to the north. Then it shifted to the east, so they ran to the east; but from the east it shifted to the west, so they ran to the west. Next it shifted to heaven. But when they raised their eyes toward heaven, it seemed to rise out of the earth. Hence Israel asked one another, "But wisdom, where shall it be found? And where is the place of understanding?" (Job 28:12).

"And all the people perceived the thunderings" (Exod. 20:15). Since there was only one voice, why "thunderings" in the plural? Because God's voice mutated into seven voices, and the seven voices into seventy languages, so that all the nations might hear it.[2]

42. R. Yohanan asked; What is implied in "The Lord gave the word: great was the company of those that published it" (Ps. 68:12)? That each and every word that issued from the mouth of the Almighty divided itself into seventy languages. Accordingly, citing the verse "As a hammer that breaketh the rock in pieces" (Jer. 23:29), the school of R. Ishmael taught: Just as a hammer that strikes a rock causes sparks to fly off in all directions, so each and every word that issued from the mouth of the Holy One divided itself into seventy languages.[3]

43. R. Yohanan said also: Each and every word that issued from the Holy One was transmuted into seventy languages. R. Joshua ben Levi said: As when a man strikes an anvil and causes sparks to fly off in all directions. R. Yose bar Hanina said: As when a man strikes a rock with a hammer and causes chips to fly off in all directions, so, too, did "the great company of those that published it."[4]

44. It is taught: "Remember" and "observe" were spoken in one utterance, something that is beyond the human mouth to articulate or the human ear to absorb.[5]

45. "And God spoke all these words, saying"[6] (Exod. 20:1). God can do all kinds of things at one and the same time—He can put to death and bring to life at one and the same time. He can wound and heal at one and the same time. If there is a woman giving birth; people going down to the sea, traveling through deserts, or being kept in prison—though one is in the east and another in the west, one in the north and another in the south—He can hear them all at one and the same time.[7]

46. "And God spoke all these words, saying" (Exod. 20:1). R. Isaac said: At Mount Sinai the prophets of each and every generation received what they were to prophesy, for Moses told Israel, "But with him that standeth here with us this day before the Lord our God, and also with him that is not here with us this day" (Deut. 29:14). He did not say, "That is not standing here with us this day," but, "That is not here with us this day," a way of referring to souls that are destined to be created. Because as yet these had no substance, Moses did not use the word "standing" for them. Still, even though they did not as yet exist, each one received his share of the Torah. Nor were the future prophets the only ones who received at Sinai the prophecy they were to utter. The sages who were to rise in each and every generation—each and every one of them also received at Sinai the wisdom he was to utter.[8]

47. When the Holy One gave the Torah to Israel, His voice traveled from one end of the world to the other, and in their palaces all kings of the nations were seized with trembling, yet they were constrained to chant a song in praise of God. All of them gathered themselves about the wicked Balaam and asked, "What is this loud tumult we hear? Is another flood coming upon the world?" Balaam replied, "The Holy One has already sworn that He will not bring another flood upon the world." "Perhaps," they asked further, "He will bring not another flood of water but a flood of fire?" Balaam reassured them: "He has already sworn that He would not destroy all flesh." "What, then," they asked, "is this loud tumult we hear?" Balaam replied, "The Holy One has a precious thing in His treasury that had been stored with Him nine hundred and seventy-four generations before the world was created,[9] and now He wishes to give it to His children, as is said, 'The Lord giveth strength to His people' " (Ps. 29:11). The kings of the nations, all as one, immediately exclaimed, "May the Lord bless His people with peace" (ibid.).[10]

48. As soon as Israel accepted the Torah, the Holy One invested them with some of the splendor of His own majesty. What precisely did He invest them with? Crowns, according to R. Yohanan; weapons, according to R. Simeon ben Yohai, upon which God's Explicit Name was engraved—as long as these weapons were in their hands, the angel of death had no power over them.[11]

49. R. Joshua ben Levi taught: When Moses went up on high, the ministering angels dared say to the Holy One:

1. When facing east, the south is on the right side, the side where the Torah was given. Hence the commentator begins with the south.
2. The Torah is intended for all nations—it is not to remain Israel's sole prerogative. Exod. R. 5:9; Tanhuma B, *Shemot*, §22.
3. B. Shab 88b.
4. Ibid., as cited in Yalkut, Ps., §695.
5. In Exod. 20 the fourth commandment begins with the words "Remember the Sabbath day," whereas in Deut. 5 it begins with "Observe." B. RH 27a.
6. "All these words, saying," being regarded as redundant, is construed as implying that at one and the same time God can do even things mutually opposed.
7. Exod. R. 28:4.
8. Exod. R. 28:6.
9. The Torah was to have been given at the end of a thousand generations. But God advanced the time and gave it during the twenty-sixth generation from Adam. See TdE, ed. Friedmann, p. 9.
10. B. Zeb 116a and En Yaakov, ad loc.
11. Exod. R. 51:8.

Master of the universe, what business does one born of woman have in our midst? God replied: He came to receive the Torah. They argued: This precious thing, which has been stored with You for nine hundred and seventy-four generations before the world was created, You are about to give to mere flesh and blood? "O Lord, our Lord, how glorious is Thy Name in all the earth! Let Thy majesty continue to be celebrated above the heavens. . . . What is man that Thou shouldst be mindful of him, and the son of man that Thou shouldst think of him?" (Ps. 8:2 and 8:5). Then the Holy One said to Moses: Let you be the one to reply to the ministering angels. Moses spoke right up: Master of the universe, I fear that they will consume me with the fiery breath of their mouths. God said: Take hold of the throne of My glory and reply to them. Moses spoke up again: The Torah You are about to give me—what is written in it? "I am the Lord thy God, that brought thee out of the land of Egypt" (Exod. 20:2). Then, turning to the angels, he asked: Did *you* go down to Egypt? Were *you* enslaved to Pharaoh? What need have you for the Torah? What else is written in it? "Ye shall have no gods that others worship" (Exod. 20:3)—do *you* live among nations who worship idols? What else is written in it? "Thou shalt not take the Name of the Lord thy God in vain" (Exod. 20:7)—are there business dealings among *you* [that might lead to swearing a false oath]? What else is written in it? "Remember the Sabbath day, to keep it holy" (Exod. 20:8)—do *you* do the kind of work that requires you to rest? What else is written in it? "Honor thy father and thy mother" (Exod. 20:12)—do *you* have father or mother? What else is written in it? "Thou shalt not murder, thou shalt not commit adultery, thou shalt not steal" (Exod. 20:13)—is there rivalry among *you*, is the impulse to evil within *you?*

At that, the angels conceded to the Holy One, for at the psalm's end, they said once more, "O Lord, our Lord, how glorious is Thy Name in all the earth," although they did not add [as before], "Let Thy majesty continue to be celebrated above the heavens."[1]

Then each of the angels came to be favorably disposed toward Moses and gave him a token of his favor, as is implied by what was said to him: "Thou hast ascended on high; thou hast taken the prize [of Torah]; thou hast received gifts [to compensate for the angels' calling thee] a mere man [a groundling]" (Ps. 68:19). Even the angel of death turned over his secret to Moses, for later, after the plague had begun, it is said of Moses that he told Aaron to "put on the incense and make atonement for the people" (Num. 17:12); and Scripture goes on to say, "And he stood between those who were about to die and those who were to remain alive" (Num. 17:13). How would Moses have been able to distinguish between the two, had not the angel of death made him a gift of the secret?[2]

50. R. Simeon ben Lakish said: The Torah given to Moses was written with black fire upon white fire, sealed with fire, and swathed with bands of fire. While writing it, Moses wiped off the reed on his hair—thus he received the radiance that was to emanate from his countenance.[3]

51. R. Joshua ben Levi said: After Moses had come down from the Holy One's Presence, Satan appeared and asked Him bluntly: Master of the universe, where is the Torah? He answered: I gave it to the earth. Satan went to the earth and asked: Where is the Torah? The earth replied, "God understandeth the way thereof, and He knoweth the place thereof" (Job 28:23). He then went to the sea, which replied, "It is not with me" (Job 28:14). Finally he went to the deep under the earth, which replied, "It is not in me" (ibid.). So he returned and said to the Holy One: Master of the universe, I searched for it throughout the world, but did not find it. God said, "Go to the son of Amram." Satan went to Moses and asked, "Where is the Torah the Holy One gave you?" Moses replied, "Who am I that the Holy One should have given the Torah to me?" The Holy One asked: Moses, are you a liar? Moses replied: Master of the universe, You had hidden away a precious thing in which You took delight every day—shall I now claim credit for myself about it? The Holy One said to Moses: Since you make so little of yourself, the Torah shall be called by your name—"remember ye the Torah of Moses My servant" (Mal. 3:22).

R. Joshua ben Levi said also: When Moses went up on high, he found the Holy One busy joining crowns to the letters [of the Torah,[4] and Moses remained respectfully silent]. Finally, God asked, "Moses, where you come from, were you not taught to extend greetings?" Moses replied, "May a servant presume to greet his master?" "Nevertheless," said God, "you should have encouraged Me [by saying something]." Presently [during a later ascent] Moses cried out [without being reminded], "May the power of the Lord increase!" [Then he added], "Is not this what You told me to do?" (Num. 14:17).[5]

52. R. Hanina ben Agil asked R. Hiyya son of R. Abba: Why does it not say in the first version of the Ten Commandments, "That it may go well with thee," while in the second version there is such a promise?[6] He replied: Before asking me why "That it may go well with thee" is not mentioned in the first version, you should ask me whether such a promise does or does not occur in the second version—the fact is, I do not know whether it occurs or not.[7] Go to R. Tanhum bar Hanilai, who visits regularly with R. Joshua ben Levi, an expert in *Aggadah.* When he went to him, R. Tanhum said: From R. Joshua ben Levi, as it happens, I never heard anything on this matter. But Samuel bar Nahum told me, "Because [the Tablets containing the Commandments' first version] were

1. That is, they conceded that the Torah need not remain in heaven.
2. B. Shab 88b–89a.
3. P. Shek 6:1, 49d; Yalkut, *Berakhah,* §951.
4. The crowns (*tagin*) are three small strokes that are added on the top of certain letters. See *JE,* s.v.
5. B. Shab 89a.
6. In Deut. 5:16, it is stated, "That thy days may be prolonged, and that it may go well with thee."
7. No halakhic point was involved in this text. Hence R. Hiyya could not recall its exact wording.

destined to be broken,[1] [the promise of well-being does not occur in them]. But even if they were destined to be broken, how would that eventuality affect the promise of well-being?" R. Ashi explained: Well-being would then, God forbid, have altogether ceased in Israel.[2]

53. In the way of the world, when a king of flesh and blood issues a decree, it may or may not be obeyed; and even if you find that it is obeyed, it may be so only while he is living but not after his death. However, Moses our teacher issued many decrees and introduced many enactments—and these abide forever and ever and ever.[3]

54. Come and see that the way of the Holy One is not like the way of human beings. The way of a human being: when he sells a valuable object to his fellow,[4] the seller grieves, while the buyer rejoices. Not so the Holy One. When He gave up the Torah to Israel, He rejoiced: "I have given you a good purchase;[5] forsake not My teaching" (Prov. 4:2).[6]

55. A certain Galilean expounded in the presence of R. Hisda: Blessed be He who is everywhere, who has given the three-fold Torah[7] to a three-fold people[8] through a third[born][9] on the third day[10] in the third month.[11]

Nadab and Abihu

56. "Unto Moses He said: 'Come up unto the Lord, thou, and Aaron, Nadab, and Abihu' " (Exod. 24:1). The verse intimates that Moses and Aaron walked first, followed by Nadab and Abihu, then by all of Israel. [Treading, so to speak, on the heels of Moses and Aaron], Nadab said to Abihu, "When will these two old men die, so that you and I may lead this generation?" The Holy One said to them, " 'Boast not thyself of tomorrow' [Prov. 27:1]—We shall see who will bury whom." As R. Papa, quoting a common proverb, put it: Many a young ass has died and had its hide turned into saddlecloths for its dam's back.[12]

1. Exod. 32:19.
2. Had the promise of well-being been inserted in the first version of the Ten Commandments, such well-being might have ceased altogether after the Tablets containing that version were broken. B. BK 54b–55a.
3. Moses' own decrees and enactments deal with such matters as the public reading of Scripture and the division of priests into rotas or watches. B. Shab 30a.
4. When forced to do so by poverty.
5. JV: "Good doctrine." But *lekah* ("doctrine") may in postbiblical Hebrew also mean "purchase."
6. By praising it, God showed He was pleased that He made the "sale." B. Ber 5a.
7. Pentateuch, Prophets, and Writings.
8. Israel was made up of priests, Levites, and Israelites.
9. Moses was born after Aaron and Miriam.
10. The third day after separation from their wives. Exod. 19:11.
11. In Sivan. B. Shab 88a.
12. B. Sanh 52a; Lev. R. 20:10.

The Sin of the Golden Calf

57. "And when the people saw that Moses delayed (*boshesh*) to come down from the mount" (Exod. 32:1). "Six hours (*ba'u shesh*) of the day[13] have passed," they said, "and Moses has not yet come down, even though when he went up on high he promised, 'After forty days, at the beginning of the day's sixth hour, I will be back.' "

At the end of forty days, there gathered forty thousand [of the mixed multitude][14] that had come up with Israel, together with two of Egypt's magicians, whose names were Jannes and Jambres[15]—it was they who performed all those acts of witchcraft in Pharaoh's presence, as is said, "They also, the magicians of Egypt, did in like manner with their secret arts" (Exod. 7:11). All of them gathered against Aaron and said, "Moses will not come down again." Aaron and Hur responded, "Any moment he will be coming down from the mount." But the mixed multitude paid no attention to them.

Some say that Satan came and brought confusion to the minds of the people. Satan began by asking, "Where is Moses your teacher?" "He went up on high." "But the sixth hour of the day is here." The people paid no attention to him. "He is dead," [Satan said]. They still paid no attention to him. Finally he showed them a likeness of Moses' bier suspended in the air between heaven and earth. Then the people pointed with their fingers, saying, "This is indeed Moses, a mere man" (Exod. 32:1).

Hur stood up and rebuked them: "You stiff-necked people! Do you not remember how many miracles he performed in your behalf?" But the people rose up and slew him.

Then they gathered against Aaron and said, "If you make a god for us, well and good; but if not, we will do to you what we did to Hur."

When Aaron saw how things stood, he was afraid and attempted to distract them with subterfuges. Thus he said, "Break off the golden rings, which are in the ears of your wives" (Exod. 32:2), a difficult request to execute, since the wives were likely to balk. Indeed, when the men went to their wives [they did balk, but for a different reason]—they defied them, saying, "God forbid that we should make an idol and betray the Holy One, who wrought such miracles and mighty deeds in our behalf." So, since the wives refused, "all the [men among the] people broke off the golden rings which were in their ears (Exod. 32:3)[16]—their own ears.

When the men brought the golden rings—so said R. Jeremiah—Aaron raised his eyes toward heaven and said, " 'Unto Thee I lift up my eyes, O Thou that art enthroned in the heavens' [Ps. 123:1]. You know all thoughts—it is against my will that I am about to do this." But as he threw the gold rings into the fire, the magicians came and

13. Twelve noon—thus, six hours have passed of the fortieth day, the day Moses promised he would be back.
14. See Exod. 12:38.
15. See *JE* 7:71.
16. In this verse, the wives are not mentioned.

worked their secret arts. Some say it was Micah (the one who was nearly crushed to death in a building, where he had been immured in lieu of bricks,[1] and who was saved by Moses)—it was this Micah who took a tablet upon which was written, "Rise up, O bullock," and threw it into the pit among the golden rings. Then a bull-calf emerged, lowing as it leaped about. Whereupon the people said, "This is thy God, O Israel" (Exod. 32:4).

"And when Aaron saw this, he built an altar before it" (Exod. 32:5). The people wanted to build it with him. But he said, "Allow me to build it by myself. It is not in keeping with the respect due to the altar that others build it with me." Aaron's intent: In the time it will take me to build the altar by myself, I hope Moses will come down. But after he finished building it, Moses still had not come down, so he announced, "Tomorrow shall be a feast to the Lord" (Exod. 32:5), saying to himself: Let the "happening" be deferred until tomorrow.

At that moment the ministering angels began to lament, "They forgot God their savior, who had done great things in Egypt" (Ps. 106:21). And the holy spirit moaned, "They soon forgot His works" (Ps. 106:13).[2]

58. "And the Lord spoke unto Moses: 'Go, get thee down' " (Exod. 32:7). By way of rebuke, the Holy One said to Moses, "This is a downgrading for you." Moses asked, "My Master, what is my offense?" God replied, "Thy people have dealt corruptly" (Exod. 32:7). Moses asked, "Are they my people? 'They are Thy people and Thine inheritance that Thou didst bring out by Thy great power' [Deut. 9:29]. But wherein did they sin?" God: "They exchanged their glory for the likeness of an ox" (Ps. 106:20). Moses spoke up: "Master of the universe, this calf would be just right to assist You." The Holy One: "How can he assist Me?" Moses: "You cause the winds to blow, and he might bring down rain; You cause the sun to shine, and he might do the same with the moon; You cause trees to grow, and he might make [smaller] plants sprout." God: "Like them, even you, Moses, seem to be led astray by the calf!" Moses: "so—the thing isn't much. It eats grass, and at any time may be slaughtered [like any other calf]. 'Why, then, should Thy wrath wax hot against Thy people?' " (Exod. 32:11).[3]

59. "Go, get thee down" (Exod. 32:7). According to R. Isaac, when the Holy One said to Moses, "Go, get thee down," Moses' face grew dark. In the greatness of his distress, he became as one blind and so did not know which way to go down. The ministering angels, saying, "This is the time to slay him," were indeed about to slay him.[4] But the Holy One was aware of what they planned. And what did He do? It is said in the name of R. Abba bar Aibu that the Holy One opened a wicket door under His throne of glory and said, "Go, get thee down."

In the name of R. Judah bar Ilai, it is said: When Moses was about to get down, the angels came to slay him. What did he do? He took hold of the throne of the Holy One, and the Holy One spread His mantle over him, so that they should not harm him.[5]

60. "Go, get thee down" (Exod. 32:7). The Holy One said to Moses: Go, Moses, get you down from your greatness.[6] It was only because of Israel that I bestowed such greatness upon you. But now that Israel have sinned, what need have I of you? At that, Moses' strength was so depleted that he did not have strength to utter even a single word. But when God said to him, "Let Me be, that I may destroy them" (Deut. 9:14), Moses reasoned: So the outcome depends on me! At once he rose up and prayed vigorously as he pleaded for mercy. A parable: A king of flesh and blood became angry at his son and beat him severely. Now, the king's friend, seated in the king's presence, was afraid to utter even one word [in demurral]. But when the king said [to his son], "Were it not for my friend who is seated in my presence, I would slay you," the friend said: So the outcome depends on me! At once he rose up and rescued the son.

"And now let Me be" (Exod. 32:10). R. Abbahu said: Were Scripture not so explicit, it would have been impossible to say such a thing. For the verse implies that, like a man who grabs hold of his fellow by his garment, Moses, if one dare say it, grabbed hold of the Holy One and brazenly said to Him: Master of the universe, I will not let You be until You pardon and forgive Israel.[7]

61. "Now therefore let Me alone, that My wrath may wax hot against them, and that I may destroy them" (Exod. 32:10). Does the verse imply that Moses was physically holding the Holy One, so that He had to say, "Let Me alone"? How may the matter be understood? By a parable of a king who became angry at his son and brought him into a chamber for punishment. There, as he began preparing himself to beat him, he kept shouting loudly, "Let me alone, that I may beat him!"—so loudly that he could be heard outside the chamber. The son's tutor, standing in the reception room, said to himself: The king and his son are [alone] inside the chamber. Why does the king keep shouting, "Let me alone," unless he wants me to come in and plead on behalf of his son? That is why he keeps shouting, "Let me alone." Likewise, when the Holy One said to Moses, "Now therefore let Me alone," Moses reasoned: Because the Holy One wishes me to plead on Israel's behalf, that is why He said, "Now therefore let Me alone." At once he began to beseech mercy in their behalf—"Moses besought the Lord his God" (Exod. 32:11). During the time Moses besought God, said R. Hiyya, he left no corner in heaven upon which he did not prostrate himself.

"Moses . . . said: 'Oh, this people have sinned a great sin' " (Exod. 32:31). Moses made it appear, said R. Isaac, as though he were angry at Israel. When the Holy

1. See above, chap. 4, §26, and below, part 1, chap. 6, §33–35.
2. Tanhuma, *Ki Tissa*, §19; Tanhuma B, *Ki Tissa*, §13; B. Shab 89a; Exod. R. 41:7.
3. Tanhuma, *Ki Tissa*, §22; Exod. R. 43:6.
4. Angry as they were at Moses for taking the Torah away from heaven.
5. Exod. R. 42:4.
6. Moses' going down is thus construed not as a physical but as a symbolic descent.
7. B. Ber 32a.

One saw Moses' anger, He said: Moses, shall two faces be boiling with anger? Shall you and I both be angry at Israel? Both faces should not be boiling with such anger! Rather, when I pour hot, you must pour cold; and when you pour hot, I will be pouring cold. Moses responded: Master of the universe, now I know that You love Your children and are only looking for a person who will plead in their behalf.[1]

62. "Why doth Thy wrath wax hot against Thy people that Thou hast brought forth out of the land of Egypt?" (Exod. 32:11). Why did Moses [in the course of his plea] see fit to mention the going out from Egypt? Because Moses was pleading: Master of the universe, whence did You bring them? Was it not out of Egypt, where they worship calves?[2] The aptness of Moses' plea will be understood, said R. Huna in the name of R. Yohanan, by the parable of a sage who opened a perfume shop for his son in the street of harlots. The street plied its trade, the perfume business plied its trade,[3] and the lad, like any young male, plied his natural inclination—he strayed into depraved ways. When the father came and caught him with a harlot, he began to shout, "I'll kill you!" But the sage's friend was there, and he spoke up. "You yourself ruined your son, and now you are yelling at him! You ignored all other occupations and taught him to be a perfumer; you ignored all other streets and deliberately opened a shop for him in the street of harlots." Likewise, Moses said: Master of the universe, You ignored the entire world and deliberately enslaved Your children in Egypt, where the inhabitants worship calves; and so Your children learned from the Egyptians, and now have even made a calf for themselves. Therefore Moses said, "That Thou hast brought forth out of the land of Egypt"—bear in mind from what kind of place You brought them forth.[4]

63. They taught at R. Yannai's school: Moses protested to the Holy One, saying, "It is the silver and gold that You showered upon Israel that led them to make the calf. A lion does not roar over a heap of straw, but he goes wild in his delight over a heap of [freshly killed] flesh." [In illustrating Moses' protest], R. Oshaia told another parable: A man had a heifer that was lean but of large build [so that its appetite was huge]. When he fed it tasty vetches, the heifer, [in sheer delight, inadvertently] kicked him. So the man said: What led you to kick me, if not the tasty vetches that I fed you?[5]

In explaining Moses' protest, R. Hiyya bar Abba told in the name of R. Yohanan still another parable: A man had a son whom he bathed, anointed, gave ample food and drink, and hung a purse about his neck. Then he set him down at the door of a brothel. How could the young man do other than sin?

R. Samuel bar Nahmani taught in the name of R. Jonathan: How do we know that in the end the Holy One, reversing Himself, admitted to Moses that He was wrong? Because God said, "I . . . multiplied unto her silver and gold, which [I should have known] they would use for Baal" (Hos. 2:10).[6]

64. "Remember Abraham, Isaac, and Israel, Thy servants, to whom Thou didst swear by Thine own self" (Exod. 32:13). According to R. Eleazar, Moses spoke right up to the Holy One: Master of the universe, had You sworn to them by heaven and earth, I would have said, Just as heaven and earth shall cease, so Your oath may cease. But You have sworn by Your great Name; even as Your great Name shall live and endure forever and ever and ever, so must Your oath endure forever and ever and ever.

"And all this Land that I have spoken of" (Exod. 32:13). R. Samuel ben Nahmani pointed out that the verse does not read, [as one might have expected], "That You have spoken of." Hence he concluded that Moses actually dared say to the Holy One, "Master of the universe, [the inviolable oath concerning Israel's inheriting the Land], which You commanded me, 'Go tell Israel in My Name,' I went ahead and told in Your Name. Now what am I going to say to them?"

"Because the Lord had no ability (*yekholet*)" (Num. 14:16). Note that here Scripture does not say, "Was not able" (*yakhol*).[7] R. Eleazar explained that Moses said to the Holy One, "Now the nations of the earth will be saying, He has grown feeble like a female, and He has no ability to deliver them [out of the wilderness]." The Holy One asked Moses, "Son of Amram, have they not already seen the miracles and mighty acts you performed in Israel's behalf at the Red Sea?" Moses replied, "Master of the universe, they may still say, 'He could stand up against one king but has no ability to stand up against the thirty-one kings [of Canaan].' "

R. Yohanan said: How do we know that in the end the Holy One, reversing Himself, conceded to Moses that he was right? Because, later, "the Lord said: 'I have pardoned according to thy plea' " (Num. 14:20). The phrase "according to thy plea"—actually "pleas" in the plural,[8] as noted in the school of R. Ishmael—refers to Moses' plea [for God's forbearance (Num. 14:17–18) as well as his earlier plea] that God preserve His reputation (Num. 14:16). God thus admitted that the nations of the world would indeed have mocked Him as having grown feeble.

Happy is the disciple whose Master, when conceding to him, adds in the very next verse, "But in very deed, I live" (Num. 14:21), which, Rava said in the name of R. Isaac, intimates that the Holy One said to Moses: Moses, your words have kept Me alive [helped preserve My reputation].[9]

65. When the Holy One gave Moses the Tablets, they carried themselves [as though weightless]. But when he

1. Exod. R. 42:9; Deut. R. 3:11; Yalkut, *Ki Tissa*, §392.
2. So Israel made for itself a calf.
3. Since harlots use perfume.
4. Exod. R. 43:7.
5. Fodder so good that human beings eat it in emergencies.
6. B. Ber 32a.
7. The ordinary form, which is masculine; *yekholet*, the form used, is feminine.
8. Not *dbrk* [devarkha] ("thy word") but *dbryk* [devarekha] ("thy words"), a spelling that, according to Rudolf Kittel's *Biblia Hebraica* (Leipzig, 1909), occurs in many manuscripts of Scripture.
9. B. Ber 32a.

descended and approached the camp, and saw the calf, the writing on the Tablets flew off, and the Tablets became heavy in the hands of Moses, as is said, "When Moses' anger waxed hot, he had to cast the Tablets out of his hands" (Exod. 32:19).[1]

66. It is taught: When Moses ascended on high, he found the Holy One sitting and writing down His attribute "long-suffering." Said Moses, "Master of the universe, [I presume this means] long-suffering toward the righteous?" He replied, "Even toward the wicked." Moses exclaimed, "The wicked—let them perish [at once]." God replied, "You will find in good time that you need My willingness to suffer the wicked." When Israel sinned [with the golden calf], God said to Moses, "Did you not say, 'Long-suffering toward the righteous [only]'?" Moses spoke up, "Master of the universe, did You not assure me then that it applies to the wicked also?" Hence Moses prayed, "Great be the Lord's power of long-suffering, as Thou hast spoken" (Num. 14:17).[2]

67. "And he would return into the camp," etc. (Exod. 33:11).[3] According to R. Abbahu, the Holy One said to Moses, "Now it will be said, 'Since the Master is angry and the disciple is angry, what will become of Israel?' So, if you restore your tent to its place [in the camp], well and good; but if not, Joshua the son of Nun, your disciple, will serve in your stead."[4]

68. "Nevertheless, on any day that I visit retribution, I will visit upon them this sin of theirs" (Exod. 32:34). R. Isaac said: No retribution comes upon the world without its fraction[5] of retribution for [the sin of] the first calf. The fact is, said R. Yudan in the name of R. Assi, there is no generation that does not receive a particle [of retribution] for the making of the golden calf.[6]

The Tabernacle and Its Vessels

69. "The pattern of the Tabernacle" (Exod. 25:9). R. Levi said: When the Holy One said to Moses, "Make the Tabernacle for Me," Moses might simply have brought four poles and stretched skins over them to form the Tabernacle. Since he did not do so, we may infer from the verse cited below that while Moses was on the mount, the Holy One showed him red fire, green fire, black fire, and white fire, and said to him: Make the Tabernacle for Me. Moses asked the Holy One: Master of the universe, where [on earth] am I to get red fire, green fire, black fire, and white fire? The Holy One replied, "*After the pattern*, which is shown thee in the mount" (Exod. 25:40).[7]

70. "And thou shalt make the boards for the Tabernacle" (Exod. 26:15). Where did the boards come from? Jacob our father had planted them. When he came down to Egypt, he said to his sons: My sons! You are destined to be redeemed from here, and when you are redeemed, the Holy One will tell you that you are to make a Tabernacle for Him. Rise up and plant cedars now, so that when He tells you to make a Tabernacle for Him, these cedars will be on hand. So Jacob's sons set to planting cedars, doing just what he had told them. Hence Scripture speaks of "*the* boards," the boards their father had arranged should be on hand.[8]

71. Even as the stars are above, so the Tabernacle's clasps were here below, a parallel that proves, according to R. Hiyya bar Abba, that the Tabernacle's golden clasps looked like stars fixed in the firmament.[9]

72. "This is how the lampstand was made" (Num. 8:4). When Moses came up on the mount and the Holy One [commanded him] concerning the lampstand, he was baffled how he was to make it. The Holy One said: I will make [a pattern of] it in your presence. What did the Holy One do? He showed him white fire, red fire, black fire, and green fire, and out of these He made the lampstand, its cups, its calyxes, its petals, and the six branches. Then He said to him, "This is how the lampstand is made," implying that, with His finger, the Holy One showed Moses the details of the making of the lampstand.[10]

73. "These seven, which are the eyes of the Lord, that run to and fro through the whole earth" (Zech. 4:10)—the seven lamps of the lampstand correspond to the seven planets, which range over the whole earth.[11]

74. "When thou lightest the lamps" (Num. 8:2). Israel said to the Holy One: Master of the universe, are You asking us to give You light? You are the light of the world, light dwells with You, and You ask us to provide light in "front of the lampstand"? (ibid.). Hence, "it is for Thee to light my lamp" (Ps. 18:29). The Holy One replied: It is not that I need your help. Still, I want you to give Me light, even as I have given you light [during your wanderings]. A parable will explain God's answer. A sighted man and a blind man were walking on the way. The sighted man said to the blind man, "When we enter the house, please kindle this lamp and give me light. The blind man replied, "Out of your kindness, when I was on the road, you supported me, and until we came to the house, you accompanied me, and now you say, 'Kindle the lamp and

---

1. Thus Moses' act was not one of petulant anger. Tanhuma, *Ki Tissa*, §26.
2. B. Sanh 111a–b.
3. Because of his anger at Israel, Moses pitched his tent outside the camp.
4. B. Ber 63b.
5. "Literally, 'a twenty-fourth part of the overweight of a *litra*.' By 'the overweight' is meant the slight addition that is made to tip the scales in the direction of the weights" (Sanh, Soncino, p. 694, n. 1).
6. B. Sanh 102a; Exod. R. 43:2, Eccles. R. 9:11, §1.
7. The Tabernacle was to be made in the colors of these fires, not out of fire itself. PRKM 1:3.
8. Tanhuma, *Terumah*, §9.
9. PRKM 1:3.
10. Tanhuma B, *Shemini*, §11.
11. Tanhuma, *Be-haalotekha*, §5.

give me light!' Will you be good enough to explain why?" The sighted man replied, "The reason I asked you to give me light is to relieve you of any obligation to me for having accompanied you on the road. Hence, I said to you, 'Give me light.' "[1]

75. R. Avina said [that God added]: The orb of the sun is only one of My servants, and when it goes forth into the world, [its direct light is so intense that] no creature can feed its eyes on it—do I then require your light? Lightning is a thing generated from the fire above, and its light dazzles the world from end to end—do I then require your light? As R. Aha stated, "That which the Lord desireth is, for His righteousness' sake, to make Torah great and glorious" (Isa. 42:21). I have come, says God, for no other purpose than to endow you [to whom Torah was given] with the merit [of observing her precepts].

R. Berekhiah said: Consider the eyeball—a man sees not through the white of it, but through the black. So, said the Holy One, if out of darkness I created light for you, do I require your light?

Another comment: A mortal lights a lamp from another lamp that is already kindled. Can he possibly light a lamp out of darkness? Yet of God it is said, "And darkness was on the face of the deep" (Gen. 1:2), followed immediately by, "And God said: 'Let there be light' " (Gen. 1:3). If out of darkness I brought forth light, do I require your light? I only told you to kindle lamps in order to elevate you—"continually to elevate through the lamp"[2] (Exod. 27:20).[3]

76. R. Samuel bar Nahmani said in the name of R. Jonathan: Bezalel [Betzalel] was so called on account of his wisdom. When the Holy One said to Moses: Go and tell Bezalel to make me the Tabernacle, Ark, and vessels,[4] Moses went and reversed the order, saying, "Make an Ark, vessels, and the Tabernacle." Bezalel countered, "Moses our teacher, as a rule a man first builds a house and then brings his vessels into it; but you say, 'Make me an Ark, vessels, and the Tabernacle?' The vessels I make—where am I to put them? Perhaps the Holy One said to you, 'Make the Tabernacle, Ark, and vessels?' " Moses replied, "You may well have been in the shadow of God (*betzel el*), and so you know!"[5]

77. R. Judah said in the name of Rav: Bezalel knew how to combine the letters by which heaven and earth were created.[6]

78. R. Hanina ben Pazzi said: No tribe was greater than the tribe of Judah, and none more lowly than the tribe of Dan. Hence the Holy One commanded: Let Dan come and be associated with Judah, that he be not despised and that the other not become arrogant toward him, for in the eyes of Him who is everywhere, the great and the small are alike. Bezalel came from the tribe of Judah and Oholiab from Dan—hence, the latter was to be associated with the former [in the building of the Tabernacle].[7]

79. "And there was woe (*va-yehi*)[8] on the day that Moses had made an end of setting up the Tabernacle" (Num. 7:1). Woe on the day Moses brought his task to an end? However, the matter may be understood by the parable of a king who had a quarrelsome wife. Once the king said to her, "Make me a purple cloak," and she proceeded to work on it. All the time she was busy with it, she did not grumble. When the work was finished, she brought it to the king. He saw it and liked it, but began to say, "Woe, woe!" His wife asked, "What is this, my lord? I went to great trouble to fulfill your wish, and now you say, 'Woe, woe' "? He replied, "The work is good and suits me well. But as long as you were busy with the work, you did not fly into a temper and did not nag me. Now that you are free, I am afraid that you will begin to rile me again."

Likewise, the Holy One said: As long as My children were busy with the Tabernacle, they did not grumble at Me. Now they will begin to nag Me again. "*Va-yehi* on the day that Moses had made an end"—there was woe on the day the building of the Tabernacle came to an end.[9]

80. "These are the accounts of the Tabernacle" (Exod. 38:21). Moses said: I know that Israel are grumblers. So I will give them an accounting of all the work of the Tabernacle. He then proceeded to give them such an account—"these are the accounts of the Tabernacle"—giving them an accounting for each and every item, whether gold, silver, or brass, that was used in the Tabernacle, in order of their use: "The silver of them that were numbered of the congregation was a hundred talents, and a thousand seven hundred and three score and fifteen shekels. . . . And the hundred talents of silver were for casting" . . . (Exod. 38:25 and 38:27). As he was going on with his accounting, he forgot to mention the one thousand seven hundred and seventy-five shekels that he used to make hooks for the pillars. Since these hooks were not visible [he forgot to mention them]. So he stood there perplexed; he said to himself: Now Israel will think they have found good cause for saying that I took the silver. So he proceeded to go over each and every item in the work. At that, the Holy One enlightened his eyes, so that, as he raised them, he saw that the silver had been made into hooks for the pillars. Then in a loud voice he began a reply to the anticipated reproach: "And of the thousand seven hundred seventy and five shekels he made hooks for the pillars" (Exod. 38:28). Then Israel were pacified. What brought about their change of heart? The fact that Moses sat down and gave an accounting—"these are the accounts of the Tabernacle" (Exod. 38:21).

1. Num. R. 15:5.
2. JV: "Cause a lamp to burn continually."
3. Lev. R. 31:8; Num. R. 15:7.
4. This is the order in Exod. 31:7.
5. B. Ber 55a.
6. Ibid. "The Kabbalah assigns mystic powers to the letters of the Hebrew alphabet" (Ber, Soncino, p. 336, n. 6).
7. Exod. R. 40:4.
8. Play on the syllable *va[y]* in *va-yehi* ("And it came to pass"), which in Aramaic means "woe."
9. Tanhuma, *Naso*, §12.

Now, why did he feel he had to give an accounting? The Holy One trusted him, as is said, "He is trusted in all My house" (Num. 12:7). Why then did he give an accounting? Because he heard the scoffers of the generation talk behind his back, as is said, "And it came to pass, when Moses went out . . . that the people looked after Moses" (Exod. 33:8). And what were they saying? Eyeing him with contempt from behind, one would say to the other: Look at his [beefy] neck! Look at his [fat] thighs! He stuffs himself with what belongs to us and guzzles what is ours. And the other would reply: Stupid! A man appointed over the work of the Tabernacle, over talents of silver and talents of gold whose weight and number are too great to measure—what do you expect? That he would not enrich himself?

When Moses heard this talk, he said: As you live, when the work of the Tabernacle is finished, I will give you an accounting. When it was finished, he said, "These are the accounts of the Tabernacle" (Exod. 38:21).[1]

81. The Roman general Contricos questioned Rabban Yohanan ben Zakkai: "At the collection of the money,[2] you count two hundred and one *kikkar*[3] and eleven *maneh*,[4] for Scripture states, 'A beka for every man, that is, half a shekel after the shekel of the Sanctuary' [Exod. 38:26], whereas when the money was given,[5] you find only one hundred *kikkar*, for it is written, 'And the hundred talents of silver were for casting,' etc. [Exod. 38:27]. Moses your teacher was either a thief, or a swindler, or a bad arithmetician. He spent a half, held back a half, but did not return a complete half."[6] R. Yohanan replied, "Moses our teacher was a trustworthy treasurer and a good arithmetician, only the sacred *maneh* was double the common."[7]

The Roman general questioned Rabban Yohanan further: "In the detailed record of the numbering of the Levites, you find the total is twenty-two thousand, three hundred,[8] whereas in the sum total you find only twenty-two thousand. Where did the remaining three hundred go?" He replied, "The remaining three hundred were [Levite] firstborn, and a firstborn cannot cancel the holiness of another firstborn."[9]

Israel's Journey and Encampment in the Wilderness

82. How did Israel's journeying in the wilderness proceed? A sign would appear in the cloud for Moses when it was about to move. When he saw by this sign that the cloud was about to move, he would say, "Rise up, O Lord, and let Thine enemies be scattered" (Num. 10:35). Then the cloud moved. As the cloud moved, all made preparations for the journey and began loading their utensils. Whoever had an animal would load the utensils on it, and the cloud would take on the rest. After all the utensils were loaded, the trumpets sounded and Judah, led by his standard, set out: first Judah's prince, and then his tribe. The other tribes followed in the same order—"every man to his own standard, according to the emblems" (Num. 2:2). Each prince had his own emblem and his own standard of a color corresponding to the tribe's precious stone on the breast of Aaron. (It was from these that the governments of the world learned to provide themselves with flags of different colors.) Thus, each tribe had its prince and its standard, whose color corresponded to the color of the tribe's stone in the breastplate and the ephod. Reuben's stone being ruby, the color of his standard was red, and embroidered on it as its emblem were mandrakes.[10] Simeon's being chrysolite, his standard was of a green color; the town of Shechem[11] was embroidered on it. Levi's[12] stone being sardonyx, the colors of his standard were equal fields of white, black, and red; embroidered on it were the Urim and Tummim.[13] Judah's stone being turquoise, the color of his standard was something like that of the sky; embroidered on it was a lion.[14] Issachar's stone being sapphire, the color of his standard was [blue-] black, like stribium; and embroidered on it were the sun and the

1. Tanhuma, *Pekudei*, §7.
2. When every Israelite was asked to give half a shekel.
3. "A weight of silver or gold, a talent. Now a *kikkar* contains sixty *maneh*, a *maneh* has twenty-five *sela* or holy shekels, therefore we have one thousand and five hundred shekels in one *kikkar*. Six hundred and three thousand five hundred and fifty half-shekels collected from the people make three hundred and one thousand seven hundred and seventy-five shekels. Divide one thousand and five hundred into this, we have two hundred and one *kikkar* with the remainder of two hundred and seventy-five shekels, i.e., eleven *maneh*" (Bekh, Soncino, p. 24, n. 2).
4. A weight in gold or silver of twenty-five common shekels (Bekh, Soncino, p. 24, n. 3).
5. When Moses rendered the account to the Israelites (Bekh, Soncino, p. 24, n. 5).
6. "For a complete half would have been one hundred and a half *kikkar* and five and a half *maneh*, and he only returned one hundred *kikkar*. And although Scripture says: 'And of the thousand seven hundred seventy and five shekels he made hooks,' and consequently he returned more than a half, the general did not mention this verse, for he wanted to catch him with words" (Bekh, Soncino, p. 24, n. 7).
7. "There were therefore one hundred and twenty *maneh* in a *kikkar*. The hundred *kikkar* were therefore really two hundred, and the remaining *kikkar* and eleven *maneh* were the one thousand seven hundred and seventy-five shekels mentioned, from which hooks were made" (Bekh, Soncino, p. 24, n. 8).
8. "The families of Gershom numbered seven thousand and five hundred, the families of Kohath numbered eight thousand and six hundred, and the families of Merari numbered six thousand and two hundred, making a grand total of the families of the Levites of twenty-two thousand and three hundred" (Bekh, Soncino, p. 23, n. 7).
9. Since the Levite firstborn has to free his own person from the necessity of being ransomed, he cannot very well serve as ransom for an Israelite firstborn. See Num. 3:39. B. Bekh 5a.
10. "And Reuben went in the days of wheat harvest, and found mandrakes in the field" (Gen. 30:14). See Gen. R. 72:5.
11. His courage and strength were fully displayed in his attack on the inhabitants of Shechem. See Gen. 34:25ff.
12. "Perhaps the reference to Levi should, with R. Behayye, be deleted, since he was not included among the twelve tribes [David Luria]" (Num. R., Soncino, p. 29, n. 4).
13. See Deut. 33:8.
14. In his final blessings, Jacob likened Judah to a lion. Gen. 49:9.

moon.[1] Zebulun's stone being an opal, the color of his standard was white,[2] with a ship embroidered on it. Dan's stone being a jacinth, the color of his standard was similar to sapphire, and embroidered on it was a serpent.[3] Gad's stone being an agate, the color of his standard was neither white nor black, but a blend of black and white; on it was embroidered a camp of tents.[4] Naphtali's stone being an amethyst, the color of his standard was like clarified wine of a not very deep red; embroidered on it was a hind.[5] Asher's stone being a beryl, the color of his standard was like the clear color of that precious stone [aquamarine] with which women adorn themselves; embroidered on it was an olive tree.[6] Joseph's stone being an onyx, the color of his standard was jet black; the embroidered design on it, for the two princes of Ephraim and of Manasseh, was [a symbol of] Egypt. On the standard of Ephraim there was also embroidered a bullock.[7] On the standard of Manasseh there was also embroidered a wild ox.[8] Benjamin's stone being a jasper, the color of his standard was a combination of the colors of all twelve stones; embroidered on it was a wolf.[9] Hence the meaning of the phrase "according to the emblems" is that each prince had an emblem that identified his standard.

Thus did Israel proceed—with the clouds over them. Now and then a beam of light would issue from one of the clouds, by which they knew in which direction they were to journey. When [it was God's] wish that they encamp, the cloud that was above the Tabernacle, in the center of Israel's camp, halted. Then the Levites would set up the Tabernacle first, before the camps of the several tribes arrived. When they did arrive, they would halt, and each one would encamp in the place assigned to it, with the clouds of glory hovering above them. Such was the distinction of Moses that the cloud of the Presence did not come down upon the Tabernacle until Moses said, "Come to rest, O Lord, upon the ten thousands of the families of Israel" (Num. 10:36).

When Israel journeyed, the Ark preceded them, and from between its staves sparks of fire would issue, which burned serpents and scorpions, and slew Israel's enemies.

What was the form of Israel's encampment? They were encamped around the Tabernacle in a circle whose perimeter was four thousand cubits. Moses, Aaron and his sons, and their families were to the east of the Tent of Meeting. The well, which was near the tent of Moses at the entrance to the court of the Tabernacle, indicated to the tribes where they were to encamp. How did the well do it? In this way: After the hangings for the court of the Tabernacle were put in place, the twelve princes stationed themselves at the well and uttered the song "Spring up, O well." At that, its waters would spring up and presently form many streams. At first, only one stream encircled the camp of the Presence [i.e., of the Tabernacle]. Out of this one stream, four streams flowed toward the four corners of the court of the Tabernacle, where they joined, thus encompassing the entire camp of the Levites, as well as coursing in between the areas to be occupied by the Levite families. Each of these areas—squares of dry land circling the camp of the Presence—was thus set apart for occupancy.

Then a larger stream encompassed the perimeter of Israel's entire camp. Its waters formed themselves into a number of streams, which flowed between every two tribes, encompassing them inside and out, marking off throughout the area squares of dry land, thus indicating the boundaries of each tribe. The stream made all kinds of good things to grow for Israel. Their cattle grazed just beyond the encampment—the cloud that spread over Israel separated them from their cattle. Because of the cloud's radiance of blue, the streams sparkled with the reflection of dawn, of the moon, and of the sun. Hence the peoples of the world, sighting them from many *mil* away, would extol them, saying, "Who is this shining like the dawn, beautiful as the moon, clear as the sun?" (Song 6:10).[10]

83. R. Judah bar Ilai taught: Two Arks journeyed with Israel in the wilderness—one in which the Torah was placed, and the other in which the Tablets broken by Moses were placed.[11] The one in which the Torah was placed was kept in the Tent of Meeting; the other, containing the broken Tablets, would come and go with them.

But the sages said: There was only one Ark; one time, in the days of Eli, it went forth and was captured.[12]

The Scouts

84. "Send thou men" (Num. 13:2). These words are to be considered in the light of what Scripture says elsewhere: "The stouthearted are bereft of sense . . . and none of the men of might could lift a hand" (Ps. 76:6). The words "bereft of sense" and "none . . . could lift a hand" apply to Moses and Aaron, who sent out the scouts. When these came and spoke slander about the Land, no one knew what to do—even Moses and Aaron could not, so to speak, lift a hand.

"Moses sent them to scout the land of Canaan, and said unto them: 'Get you up here into the southland, and go up into the mountains' " (Num. 13:17). Such is the way

1. The descendants of Issachar were astronomers and experts in calculation.
2. "Like silver, symbolical, according to R. Bechaye, of their great wealth. . . . They were merchants and seafaring traders" (Num. R., Soncino, p. 29, n. 8).
3. "Dan shall be a serpent in the way" (Gen. 49:17).
4. "Gad, a troop shall troop upon him" (Gen. 49:19).
5. "Naphtali is a hind let loose" (Gen. 49:21).
6. "As for Asher, his bread shall be fat" (Gen. 49:20).
7. The words "his firstling bullock" (Deut. 33:17) are applied to Joshua, of the tribe of Ephraim, who was first in rank and power.
8. "His horns are the horns of the wild ox" (ibid.) is applied to Gideon, who came from that tribe.
9. "Benjamin is a wolf that raveneth" (Gen. 49:27).
10. Num. R. 2:7; Tanhuma, *Be-midbar*, §12; Yalkut, *Pekudei*, §426; Yalkut, *Be-midbar*, §686.
11. Another tradition identifies the second ark as containing the bones of Joseph. See above, chap. 4, §71.
12. P. Shek, 1:1, 49c; Yalkut, 1 Sam. §101.

of traders—they show the inferior wares first, and then display the best.[1]

85. "And see . . . what the Land is" (Num. 13:18). "Look carefully," Moses said, "at the Land—one land rears strong men, and another weaklings; there is a land that increases its population, and another that diminishes it."

"And the people that dwelleth therein, whether they are strong or weak" (Num. 13:18). How are you to tell their strength? If they dwell in open camps, they are strong, since they seem to rely on their own strength. But if in fortresses, they are weak, and their spirits timorous.

"Is the soil rich or poor?" (Num. 13:20). Are the fruits of the soil light in weight, or rich, heavy? [To help determine the quality of the fruit], Moses told the scouts, "Examine the stones and pebbles of the soil—if they are granitelike, the fruits are heavy, succulent;[2] but if they are [brittle] like earthenware, the fruits are poor, shriveled.

86. "And they went up into the south, but he came unto Hebron" (Num. 13:22). One would have expected the text to say, "They came." However, according to Rava, "he came" implies that Caleb dissociated himself from the counsel of the scouts and went off [to Hebron] to prostrate himself on the graves of the patriarchs and to plead: My fathers, beseech mercy in my behalf, that I may be delivered from the counsel of the scouts. As for Joshua, Moses had already sought mercy in his behalf, as is said, "On behalf of Joshua the son of Nun, Moses cried out Yehoshua" (Num. 13:16),[3] which means: *Yah yoshia*, "May the Lord save you from the counsel of the scouts." As for the fulfillment of Caleb's prayer, Scripture says, "Caleb . . . had another spirit within him" (Num. 14:24).[4]

87. "And they came unto the valley of Eshkol and cut down," etc. (Num. 13:23). They did not wish to take any of the fruit of the Land of Israel. But Caleb drew his sword and, as he ran ahead of them [into the Land], said, "If you will not take it, then either you will have to kill me or I shall kill you." Otherwise, they would not have taken any of it.

"And they went and came unto Moses and unto Aaron. . . . And they told him, and said: 'We came unto the Land . . . surely it floweth with milk and honey. . . . Howbeit the people are fierce' " (Num. 13:26–28). Such is the way of those who speak slander: they begin by speaking well of one and end by speaking ill.

"And moreover we saw [giants] the children of Anak there" (Num. 13:28). As the scouts went up [into the south], so said R. Berekhiah the Priest Berabbi, they found there the three sons of Anak: Ahiman, Sheshai, and Talmai.

Why was the first called Ahiman? Because he used to boast, "O my brothers (*ahai*), who (*man*) dare come against me?" Sheshai? Because he was strong as marble (*shaish*). Talmai? Because as he walked he made furrows (*telamim*) in the earth. The sons of Anak? Because they were so tall that it seemed as though they wore the sun as a decorative chain about their necks (*maanikim*).

When the scouts saw the three, they were afraid. At once they went and said, "They are stronger than He"[5] (Num. 13:31), thus, as Resh Lakish interpreted it, casting insults at Him above; or, as R. Hanina bar Papa interpreted it, saying that even the Master of the house would be unable to fetch His belongings thence.[6]

88. "A land that eateth up the inhabitants thereof" (Num. 13:32). Rava expounded: The Holy One said: Certain occurrences, which I intended for the scouts' safety, they took to signify the Land's undesirability. What occurrences? When the scouts came into a city, pestilence had consumed its notables, and the people of the city were so occupied with burying them that no one paid any attention to the scouts.[7] Some say: Job had died, and all the people were occupied with his funeral. But the scouts, interpreting these occurrences in a bad sense, described the Land as one "that eateth up the inhabitants thereof." Thus, they gave an evil report even of the miraculous timing of these occurrences that the Holy One had brought about for their benefit.[8]

89. "And we were in our own eyes as grasshoppers, and so were we in their eyes" (Num. 13:33). The Holy One said to the scouts: You don't know what you have just let your mouths utter. I am ready to put up with your saying, "We were in our own eyes as grasshoppers." But I do take offense at your asserting, "And so were we in their eyes." Could you possibly know how I made you appear in their eyes? How do you know but that in their eyes you were like angels?

R. Mesharsheya said: The scouts were liars. As to "We were in our own eyes as grasshoppers"—sure enough [being cowards, they knew it]; but how did they know that "so we were in their eyes"?

Moreover [the scouts were not only liars but also fools]. Because when [a city's inhabitants] provided the funeral meal for the mourners, they served it under [tall] cedar trees. At the sight of such a gathering, the scouts scampered high up in the trees and sat there [hiding]. There they heard the people saying [jokingly]: Up in the trees we espy human beings as tiny as grasshoppers.[9]

90. "And Caleb stilled (*va-yahas*) the people concerning Moses" (Num. 13:30). That is, said Rabbah, Caleb won

1. The rocky and arid Negev, or southland, was the Land of Israel's least desirable part. Num. R. 16:2 and 16:12; Yalkut, *Shelah*, §742.
2. Num. R. 16:12; Tanhuma, *Shelah*, §6. A hard-rock subsurface retains water.
3. JV: "And Moses called Hoshea the son of Nun Joshua [Yehoshua]."
4. B. Sot 34b.
5. JV: "stronger than us." But *mimmennu* ("than us") may also mean "than He."
6. B. Sot 34b–35a; Num. R. 16:14, 16:17, and 16:11.
7. Who thus came and went in safety.
8. B. Sot 35a; Tanhuma, *Shelah*, §7.
9. Ibid.

them over (*hesitam*) with what he had to say. For Caleb had seen Joshua attempt to speak to the people, and they responded by insulting him, saying, "How dare this gelding[1] speak to us?" Hence Caleb decided: If I attempt to speak to them [as Joshua did], they will hurl another insult at me and shut me up. So he said to them, "Is this the only thing that Amram's son has done to us?"[2] Thinking that Caleb was about to speak in disparagement of Moses, they became silent. Then he said to the people, "Did he not bring us out of Egypt? Did he not split the Red Sea for us? Did he not bring down manna for us? So, even if he were to say, 'Make ladders and go up to heaven,' should we not obey him?"[3]

91. "And all the congregation lifted up their voice, and cried" (Num. 14:1). When the scouts returned from reconnoitering the Land, they scattered at once among the several tribes, each scout to his own tribe. There each scout flung himself into every corner of his house, crying and weeping, as one who has just had a death in his family. When his sons and daughters came and asked, "Sir, what ails you?" he made believe, as he stood up, that he was about to collapse, yet managed to say, "Alas, alas, I grieve for you, my sons, my daughters, my daughters-in-law. How the Amorites will abuse you! How they will lord it over you! How can anyone face the Amorites [much less resist them]?" Then all—the sons, daughters, daughters-in-law—began to sob loudly. When the neighbors heard the sobbing, they too began to weep—thus each family made its weeping heard by the next, until throughout the tribe there was nothing but weeping.

At the same time, each of his fellow scouts brought his family to weeping, until the sixty myriads [of Israel] became a single company, all of them sobbing, so that the sound of their weeping reached on high.[4]

92. Rabbah said in the name of R. Yohanan: That night was the night of the ninth of Av, concerning which the Holy One said: Now they give themselves to weeping without cause—so, throughout the generations, I will make [this very night] an occasion for weeping for them![5]

"But all the congregation bade stone them with stones, even as the glory of the Lord appeared" (Num. 14:10). According to R. Hiyya bar Abba, the verse implies that they took stones and threw them also at Him above.

"These men that did bring up an evil report of the Land died by the plague before the Lord" (Num. 14:37). R. Simeon ben Lakish said: They died an unnatural death. According to R. Hanina bar Papa, R. Shela of Kefar Temarta construed the verse to imply that the tongue of each spy grew so long that it reached down to his navel, and worms crawled out of his tongue into his navel and from his navel into his tongue.[6]

The Controversy of Korah and His Company

93. "Now Korah . . . took men . . . and they assembled themselves together against Moses. . . . 'All the congregation are holy, every one of them, and the Lord is among them; wherefore then lift ye up yourselves?' " etc. (Num. 16:1 and 16:3). What is written directly before this passage? "Instruct them to make for themselves . . . fringes . . . and to attach to the fringe at each corner a thread of blue" (Num. 15:38). Korah jumped up and asked Moses, "If a cloak is entirely blue, what is the law? Should it be exempt from the obligation of fringes?" Moses replied, "It is still subject to such obligation." Korah retorted, "The blueness of a cloak entirely blue cannot free it from the obligation, yet four blue threads can do so?" He went on, "If a house is full of Torah scrolls, what is the law? Should it be free from the obligation of having a mezuzah?" Moses replied, "It is still under the obligation of having a mezuzah." Korah snapped back, "The entire Torah cannot exempt a house, but the two sections[7] in a mezuzah exempt it? These things—you have not been commanded concerning them, you are just making them up."

The sages said that Korah was a man of great subtlety and one of the bearers of the Ark. When Moses commanded "that they put with the fringe of each corner a thread of blue" (Num. 15:38), Korah instantly ordered that two hundred and fifty cloaks of blue be made, in which the two hundred and fifty heads of the Sanhedrin who rose against Moses were to wrap themselves. Then Korah made a feast for them, before which they wrapped themselves in their blue cloaks. When Aaron's sons came to receive their dues, the breast and the shoulder,[8] the two hundred and fifty rose against them, saying, "Who told you that you entitled to take these? Was it not Moses? We will give nothing. He who is everywhere said no such thing." When the priests who were thus repulsed went back and told Moses, he tried to pacify the people [assembled at Korah's feast], but they rose against him also.[9]

94. When the Holy One said to Moses, "Take the Levites from among the children of Israel, and cleanse them; and thus thou shalt do unto them, to cleanse them. . . . let them cause a razor to pass over all their flesh" (Num. 8:6–7), Moses had it done at once to Korah. Then Korah's wife

1. Joshua was childless. So, since he had no children to conquer the Land, what right did he have to offer counsel? So Rashi. The difficult *resh ketiah* [BR: *rosh katua*] ("gelding") may also be rendered "head-chopper" (N. Bronznick, *Leshonenu* 41 [1977]: 3). Joshua, being a cruel man, the scouts charged, was not concerned about the frightful loss of lives.
2. He hoped that the ambiguously phrased question would lead the people to suppose that, like them, he was against Moses.
3. B. Sot 35a and En Yaakov, ad loc; Tanhuma, *Shelah*, §10.
4. Yalkut, *Shelah*, §743.
5. Weeping over the destruction of both Temples and over other calamities in the life of Israel.
6. "Measure for measure. They had sinned with their tongues, therefore their tongues grew long. . . . Hence Scripture says that they died by 'the' plague and not by 'a' plague. The words 'before the Lord' mean that they died by that plague which befitted them, in keeping with the norms 'before the Lord,' who metes out measure for measure." Rashi on Num. 14:37. B. Sot 35b.
7. Deut. 5:4–9 and 11:13–21.
8. Of the animals that had been slaughtered for the feast. See Lev. 7:31ff.
9. Num R. 18:3; Tanhuma, *Korah*, §2.

said to him, "Look at what else Moses has been doing. He had himself made king, his brother he made high priest, his nephews deputy high priests. When heave offering is brought, he says, 'That belongs to the priest.' When tithe is brought, and you, as Levites, take it, as is proper, he says to you, 'Give one portion out of ten to a priest.' As if this were not bad enough, he now has your hair cut off—the fact is, he is making sport of you, because he despises you; for some reason, he cast his eyes in envy upon your hair." Korah replied, "But he has done the same to himself." Said his wife, "Since every kind of eminence is his, he is applying the principle of 'Let me die with the Philistines' [Judg. 16:30]; [he is willing to be deprived of his own hair, so long as others are thus deprived]."

Korah, [his hair cut off], went around among the Israelites, and at first they did not recognize him. When he was asked, "Who did this to you?" he replied, "Moses. Moreover, I was seized by my arms and legs, and swung back and forth, and then told, 'Now you are clean.' Presently Aaron, the brother of Moses, was brought in. Moses had *him* decked out like a bride and seated in the Tent of Meeting!"

At that, Moses' enemies began to incite Israel against him, saying, "Moses is king, his brother Aaron high priest, his sons deputy high priests. Heave offering goes to the priest, twenty-four special gifts go to the priest,[1] heave offering of the first tithe goes to the priest." Then, we are told, "they assembled themselves together against Moses" (Num. 16:3).

Korah was a scorner and spoke in scorn against Moses and Aaron. What did he do? He assembled all the congregation and in their presence began to speak words of scorn, saying, "In my neighborhood there was a widow, and with her were her two fatherless daughters. The widow had only one field, and when she was about to plow, Moses said to her, 'Thou shalt not plow with an ox and an ass together' [Deut. 22:10]. When she was about to sow, Moses said to her, 'Thou shalt not sow thy field with two kinds of seed' [Lev. 19:19]. When she was about to reap the harvest and to stack the sheaves, Moses said to her, 'Thou shalt not harvest the gleanings, the overlooked sheaves, and the corners of the field' [cf. Lev. 19:9; Deut. 24:19]. When she was about to bring the harvest into the granary, Moses said to her, 'Give heave offering, first tithe, and second tithe.' She submitted ot the law and gave them to him. What did the poor woman do then? She sold the field and bought two sheep, so that she might clothe herself in the wool shorn from them and profit by the production of lambs. As soon as the sheep brought forth their young, Aaron came and said to the widow, 'Give me the firstling males, for this is what the Holy One said to me: "All the firstling males that are born of thy herd and of thy flock thou shalt sanctify unto the Lord thy God" ' [Deut. 15:19]. Again she submitted to the law and gave the firstling males to Aaron. When the time for shearing arrived, she sheared her two sheep. Then Aaron came again and said to the widow, 'Give me the first portion of the shearing, for the Holy One said, "You shall give him . . . the first shearing of your sheep" [Deut. 18:4]. She said, 'There is no strength in me to withstand this man; behold, I will slaughter the sheep and eat them.' After she slaughtered them, Aaron came once more and said to her, 'Give me the shoulder, the jaws, and the maw.' The widow said, 'Even after I have slaughtered my sheep, I am still not free of his demands; behold, I devote my sheep to the Sanctuary.' But Aaron said to her, 'In that case, they belong entirely to me, for thus said the Holy One, "Everything devoted in Israel shall be thine" ' [Num. 18:14]. Aaron picked up the sheep, went his way, and left her weeping—her and her two daughters. This is what happened to the poor woman. All such [evil] things Moses and Aaron do on their own; but they hang the blame on the Holy One!"

On, the son of Peleth, was saved by his wife, who said, "What will you get out of it? Either Moses remains master and you a follower, or Korah becomes master and you are still no more than a follower." On asked, "But what can I do? I have taken part in the deliberations, and I have sworn loyalty to Korah." "Stay home," she said, "and I will save you." Then she plied him with wine [until he was drunk], put him to bed [within their tent], and seated herself at its entrance. She then loosened her hair, so that whoever of Korah's company came [to summon On] and saw her had to withdraw.[2] In the meantime, Korah and his company were swallowed up.

Thus, "A wise woman buildeth her house" (Prov. 14:1) may be applied to the wife of On, the son of Peleth; and "The foolish woman plucketh it down with her own hands" (ibid.) to the wife of Korah.[3]

95. "Do this: Take ye censers . . . and put fire therein . . . and it shall be that the man whom the Lord doth choose, he shall be holy" (Num. 16:6–7). What did Moses have in mind in speaking thus? He meant: In the religions of idolaters, there are many false divinities, many evil rites, and many would-be priests who need not gather in a single edifice [to worship]. We, on the other hand, have only God, one Torah, one law, one altar, and one high priest. Yet you—all two hundred and fifty of you—are seeking the one high priesthood![4]

96. "And Moses said unto Korah: '. . . Is it not enough for thee that the God of Israel hast set thee apart? . . . Truly, it is against the Lord that thou and all thy company have banded together' " (Num. 16:8–11). Moses tried to win Korah over with this argument and others, yet nowhere will you find that Korah gave an answer. Clever as he was in his wickedness, Korah thought: If I answer Moses, I know that, being resourceful, he will certainly overwhelm me with his arguments, so that I might find myself reconciled with him against my will. It is better

1. In the Temple, ten, such as offerings, part or entire; in Jerusalem, four, such as firstlings and firstfruits; in the provinces, ten, such as the first of the shearing, heave offering, money for redeeming a firstborn, and so on. See Tos Hal 2:7.

2. It is immodest to look upon a married woman with her hair down.

3. B. Sanh 109b–110a; MTeh 1:15; Tanhuma, *Korah*, §3; Num. R. 18:4.

4. Tanhuma B, *Korah*, §11; Num. R. 18:8.

for me not to respond. When Moses saw that he could do nothing with Korah, he parted from him.[1]

97. "So they, and all that appertained to them, went down alive into Sheol" (Num. 16:33)—the opening of the earth adjusted itself to the girth of each person. Beginning at a man's soles, it opened slightly to admit the feet, widened for the legs, the thighs, and the abdomen, and then finally narrowed again for the neck. Korah and his company sank slowly bit by bit, and, as the earth was suffocating them, they kept crying in anguish: Moses is the truth, and his Torah is truth.[2]

98. "So they, and all that appertained to them, went down . . . into Sheol" (Num. 16:33). Our masters said: Even if they had clothes at a washerman's, these came rolling over and over, and were swallowed up with Korah and his company.[3]

99. R. Berekhiah said in the name of R. Helbo: Their very names vanished from the scrolls where they were recorded. R. Yose bar Hanina added: Even a needle borrowed by an Israelite from one of them was swallowed up with them.[4]

The Waters of Meribah

100. "And Moses and Aaron gathered the assembly together before the rock" (Num. 20:10). Moses and Aaron were walking with all Israel behind them, and whenever Israel saw a rock, they would halt and stand around it.

Now, there is no generation without its scoffers. And so the scoffers who happened to be near Moses and Aaron would say, "Don't you know that the son of Amram used to be Jethro's shepherd, and shepherds are expert in locating water? This being so, he wants to drag us to a place where he knows there is water and then say to us, "Look, I brought forth water for you," and thus deceive us. If that is indeed so, let him bring forth water from the rock we are at."

In fact, the Holy One had instructed Moses, "Out of any rock they wish, bring forth water for them." But Moses had his face turned forward, thinking that Israel behind him were following him, whereas actually they were standing in many groups at different rocks. When he said, "Come with me, that I may bring forth water for you," they [each group standing near a different rock] replied, "We want water from this one, [from this one], and if you fail to bring it forth from the rock we are at, we do not want it from any other rock." Moses' face paled with wrath, and he swore that he would indeed bring forth water, but only from the rock of his own choice.[5]

101. "And Moses lifted up his hand, and smote the rock with his rod twice" (Num. 20:11). After he smote it once, water began to trickle from the rock drop by drop. The people said [mockingly], "Son of Amram, is this water only for sucklings or infants just weaned from mother's milk?" At that, Moses lost his temper and smote the rock a second time, and so much water came forth that it swept everything before it.[6]

Litigious [Impertinent, and Suspicious] Persons

102. "How can I myself alone bear your litigiousness?"[7] (Deut. 1:12). So litigious were they that when one of them perceived his opponent in a lawsuit about to prevail, he would say: I have more witnesses to bring and further evidence to cite; tomorrow I shall demand a retrial, with more judges added to the panel. Such is meant by Scripture's "your litigiousness."

"And the burden of your impertinence?" (Deut. 1:12). They were so impertinent that when Moses left his tent early in the morning, they would say, "What made Amram's son leave so early? He is probably not on good terms with his family." On the other hand, when he was late in going out, they would say, "Why is Amram's son late? What do you think he is up to? Probably hatching schemes and designing plots against us!"[8]

103. "These are the words [of rebuke] that Moses spoke beyond the Jordan [for what they had done] in the desert" (Deut. 1:1). He rebuked them, Scripture implies, for what they had done in the desert—they used to grab their young children, toss them into the bosom of Moses, and say: Son of Amram, what rations did you prepare for these little ones? What sustenance did you provide for them?[9]

Aaron

104. "Oh that thou wert as my brother" (Song 8:1). Like what kind of brother? From the beginning of the world's creation until the present, you find brothers who hate each other—Cain hated Abel and slew him, Ishmael hated Isaac and sought to slay him, Esau hated Jacob, and the tribe fathers hated Joseph. Like what kind of brother, then? Like Moses and Aaron—of them it is said, "Behold, how good and how pleasant it is for brethren to dwell together in unity" (Ps. 133:1). Each loved the other, each cherished the other. Thus, when Moses was given the kingship and Aaron the high priesthood, not only was neither brother envious of the other, but each rejoiced in the distinction accorded to the other. You can see for yourself that it was so. For you find that when the Holy One told Moses, "Come now therefore, and I will send thee unto Pharaoh" (Exod. 3:10), Moses replied, "O Lord, make someone else Thy messenger" (Exod. 4:13). Can you suppose Moses held back because he did not wish to go? Not at all. He spoke

1. Num. R. 18:9.
2. Yalkut Reuveni, Num. 16:31.
3. Num. R. 18:13.
4. P. Sanh 10:1, 28a.
5. Yalkut, *Hukkat*, §763.
6. Tanhuma, *Hukkat*, §9; Tanhuma B, *Hukkat*, §30.
7. JV: "your cumbrance."
8. Sif Deut., §12.
9. Sif Deut., §1; Yalkut, *Devarim*, §790.

as he did only out of respect for Aaron. For Moses said to himself: Before I appeared, my brother Aaron prophesied to Israel in Egypt for eighty years. (And the proof that Aaron prophesied to Israel in Egypt? The verse [in which Eli, a descendant of Aaron, is told], "I revealed Myself to the house of thy forebear, when they were in Egypt in bondage to Pharaoh's house; and at the same time I chose him out of all the tribes of Israel to be My priest" [1 Sam. 2:27–28].) So Moses said to God: Aaron has been prophesying to Israel during all those years—am I now to enter my brother's domain, and he be made to grieve?

That is the real reason why Moses did not wish to go. So the Holy One said to him: Aaron will not be disturbed because of what I ask you to do. Not only will he not grieve, he will even rejoice, as you will find out when he goes forth to meet you, as is said, "Behold, he cometh forth to meet thee; and when he seeth thee, he will rejoice in his heart" (Exod. 4:14)—not merely in [the words of] his mouth, but also in his heart; indeed, even more in his heart than in his mouth. When God told him this, Moses consented to go.

R. Simeon ben Yohai said: The heart that rejoiced in the distinction accorded to his brother deserved to wear the Urim and Tummim.

"And he went, and met him at the mountain of God, and kissed him" (Exod. 4:27). These words are to be considered in the light of the verse "Mercy and truth are met together; righteousness and peace have kissed each other" (Ps. 85:11). In this verse, "mercy" alludes to Aaron, who is referred to in the words "And of Levi he said: 'Thy Tummim and thy Urim be with Thy merciful one' " (Deut. 33:8); "truth" alludes to Moses, of whom God said, "He is trusted in all My house" (Num. 12:7); "righteousness" refers to Moses, who "executed the righteousness of the Lord" (Deut. 33:21); and "peace" refers to Aaron, of whom God said, "He walked with Me in peace and uprightness" (Mal. 2:6).

Thus the verse "Mercy and truth are met together; righteousness and peace have kissed each other" (Ps. 85:11) alludes to Moses and Aaron.[1]

105. Moses used to say, "Let the law pierce the mountain."[2] But Aaron loved peace, pursued peace, and made peace between man and man, as is said, "The law of truth was in his mouth, and unrighteousness was not found in his lips; he walked with Me in peace and uprightness, and did turn many away from iniquity" (Mal. 2:6).[3]

106. "It is like the precious oil . . . coming down upon the beard, even Aaron's beard," etc. (Ps. 133:2). Our masters taught: Two drops of oil like pearls hung from Aaron's beard. It is further taught—so said R. Papa—that when Aaron spoke, they [did not fall off, but] rolled up and nestled in the roots of his beard.[4]

1. Tanhuma, *Shemot*, §27–28; Tanhuma, *Shemot*, §24–25.
2. "The law must prevail, even if it involves great loss or difficulty. The Latin equivalent of this principle is 'Fiat justitia ruat coelum' (Let justice prevail, even if the heavens fall)" (Leon Nemoy).
3. B. Sanh 6b.
4. B. Hor 12a.

Aaron's Death

107. "The mount of the mount" (Num. 20:22)[5]—that is, a mount on top of another mount, like a small apple on top of a large apple. For even though the cloud that went before Israel leveled heights and raised valleys, nevertheless the Holy One left this mount on top of a mount as a token to remind Israel of the miracles the Holy One had performed for them. For in order that Israel not become weary from going up and down mountains, the Holy One left no mountain standing in the wilderness. There were, however, important exceptions: even though the cloud turned the wilderness into a plain, it always left one elevated area for the Tabernacle to encamp on. And it also left these three mountains standing: Mount Sinai for the Presence, Mount Nebo as a burial place for Moses, and the mount on the mount as a burial place for Aaron.[6]

108. When Aaron's time came to depart from this world, the Holy One said to Moses, "Go tell Aaron of his impending death." So Moses rose early in the morning and went to Aaron. As soon as he called out, "Aaron, my brother," Aaron came down and asked, "What made you come here so early today?" Moses replied, "During the night I meditated on a matter in Scripture which I found distressing, and so I rose early and came to you." "What was the matter?" Aaron asked. "I do not remember, but I know it was in the book of Genesis. Bring it and we'll read it." They took the book of Genesis, read each and every section in it, and said about each one of them, "The Holy One wrought well, created well." But when they came to the creation of Adam, Moses asked, "What is one to say of Adam, who brought death to the world, so that I, who prevailed over the ministering angels, and you, who held back death[7]—are not even you and I to have a like end? After all, how many more years have we to live?" "Not many," Aaron answered. Moses continued talking, until finally he mentioned to him the precise day when death was to come. At that moment, Aaron's bones felt the imminence of his own demise. So he asked, "Is it because of me that you found the matter in Scripture so distressing?" Moses answered, "Yes."

At once Israel noticed that Aaron's height had diminished, even as Aaron said, "My heart doth writhe within me; and the terrors of death are fallen upon me" (Ps. 55:5). Moses asked, "Is dying acceptable to you?" Aaron: "Yes." Moses: "Then let us go up to the mount on the mount." At that, the three—Moses, Aaron, and Eleazar—went up in the sight of all Israel.

Had Israel known that Aaron was going up to die, they would not have allowed it but would have besought mercy in his behalf. However, they thought that the Divine Word had summoned him.

When the three reached the top of the mount, a cave opened up for them. In it they found a burning lamp and

5. JV: "Mount Hor"; Hebrew: *hor ha-har*.
6. Tanhuma B, *Hukkat*, §37.
7. See above in this chapter, §49, and Num. 17:12–13.

a couch, both wrought by Heaven. Then Aaron proceeded to remove his garments one by one, and Eleazar donned them, until finally a celestial cloud enveloped Aaron's body.

Moses said to Aaron, "Just think, Aaron, my brother, when Miriam died, you and I attended her. Now that you are about to die, I and Eleazar are attending you. But I—when I die, who will attend me?" The Holy One said to Moses, "As you live! I will attend you."

Then Moses said to Aaron, "My brother, go up [and lie] on this couch," and he went up. "Stretch out your arms," and he stretched them out. "Shut your eyes," and he shut them. "Close your mouth," and he closed it. At once the Presence came down, and as it kissed him, his soul departed. Then, as Moses and Eleazar kissed him on his cheeks, the cloud of glory rose up and covered him. The Holy One commanded them, "Go hence." The moment they left, the cave was sealed.

As Moses and Eleazar were coming down, all Israel stood waiting apprehensively to see Aaron, because he loved peace and pursued peace. When they realized that while three had gone up, only two had come down, Satan began circulating among Israel, trying to incite all of them against Moses and Eleazar. Israel split into three groups holding differing views: one said, "Moses slew Aaron because he was envious of him"; another, "Eleazar slew him, wishing to inherit the high priesthood"; and the third, "Aaron died by the will of Heaven."

The people seized Moses and Eleazar, and demanded, "Where is Aaron?" Moses replied, "The Holy One has hidden him away for life in the world-to-come." The people said, "We do not believe you. It may be that he said something that did not suit you, and you imposed the death penalty on him." And they were about to stone Moses and Eleazar. What did the Holy One do? He beckoned to some angels, who opened the cave and brought forth Aaron's bier, which then floated in the air, while other angels intoned praise before it. Thus all Israel saw Aaron, as is said, "All the congregation *saw* that Aaron was dead" (Num. 20:29). And what did the angels intone? "He entereth into peace, as he resteth on his couch" (Isa. 57:2).[1]

109. "They wept for Aaron thirty days, even all the House of Israel" (Num. 20:29); whereas for Moses only men wept, because he rendered judgment strictly according to the truth and used to rebuke people besides. But Aaron never said to a man or to a woman, "You have acted offensively." More! He sought peace, as is said, "He walked with Me in peace and uprightness" (Mal. 2:6). What is meant by the words that follow in the verse: "And did turn many away from iniquity" (ibid.)? These words teach that when Aaron would walk along the road and meet a wicked man, he greeted him warmly. The next day, when that man was about to go and commit a transgression, he would say to himself: Woe is me, how could I ever raise my eyes and face Aaron? I would be too embarrassed by the man who greeted me so warmly. The result: That wicked man would refrain from further transgression.

Likewise, when two men quarreled, Aaron would go, sit with one of them, and say, "My son, look how your friend beats his breast and tears his hair out as he says, 'Woe is me, how can I raise my eyes and face my friend? I would be too embarrassed, for it is I who acted offensively toward him.' "

Aaron would sit with him until he removed all rancor from his heart. Then Aaron would go and say the same thing to the other man. Later, when one met the other, they would hug and kiss each other. Hence it is said, "They wept for Aaron . . . even *all* the House of Israel."[2]

The Miracles in the Valley of Arnon

110. "Spring up, O well, sing ye unto it" (Num. 21:17). What were the miracles in the valley of Arnon [that inspired Israel to sing, "Spring up, O well"]? A man could stand on top of a mountain on one side of the valley and speak to a friend seven miles away on top of a mountain on the other side. Now, the road [to the Promised Land] ran down to the valley [between these two mountains] and then ascended, for Israel's path lay through several valleys on their way [to the Land]. At that spot, endless armies of all the nations assembled, some of them taking up positions within the valley. The mountain on one side of the valley was riddled with caves, while facing these caves in the mountain on the other side of the valley there were numerous rocks projecting breastlike formations.

The armies entered the caves, figuring: When Israel go down into the valley, our men positioned there will confront them, while here, our men high up in the caves will strike them from the rear, and so we shall slay them all.

However, when Israel reached that spot, the Holy One did not make it necessary for them to go down into the valley, for He beckoned to the mountains [and they came together], the "breasts" of one mountain entering into the opposite caves of the other, so that all within the caves were killed. Moreover, the two mountains brought their summits close to each other, forming a road so level that it was impossible to tell one mountain from the other.

This valley formed the boundary between the Land of Israel and the land of Moab. The mountain in the land of Moab, containing the caves, did not move, while the mountain from the Land of Israel, with its pointed rocks resembling breasts, moved and locked with the mountain facing it. Why was it the one to move? Because it belonged to the Land of Israel. The mountain's eagerness to move may be understood by the parable of a maidservant who, on seeing her master's son coming toward her, leaped forward in her eagerness to welcome him.[3]

After the rocks had entered the caves and crushed all the mighty warriors in them, the well came down into the valley,[4] and, as its water swelled, it drowned the armies stationed there, even as the Red Sea had drowned the

1. Yalkut, *Hukkat*, §764.

2. ARN 12; Yalkut, *Hukkat*, §764.

3. The maidservant is the mountain, the master is God, and the son Israel.

4. It had remained intact, although the tops of the mountains had come together.

Egyptians. Israel passed over the top of the mountains without being aware of these miracles. The Holy One said: I will now let the children of Israel know how many hosts I destroyed for their sake. So the well, flowing down into the caves, flushed out skulls, arms, and legs in unending profusion. Subsequently, when Israel returned to look for the well, they saw it in the midst of the valley shining like the moon, still bringing up the limbs of the warriors. Then Israel, standing over the valleys, sang a song about the well: "Spring up, O well, sing ye unto it."[1]

Og, King of Bashan

111. When Moses and the children of Israel came to the border of Edrei, Moses said, "Let us encamp here, and tomorrow at dawn we shall breach Edrei and subdue it." They got up at dawn, when the eye can take in very little, and were about to attempt to breach Edrei. Just then Moses raised his eyes and saw Og sitting on the wall with his feet reaching down to the earth. Moses said, "I know not what I see, unless these people have built another wall in the night." The Holy One said to him, "Moses, what you see is Og." Moses was afraid, but the Holy One said to him, " 'Fear him not' (Num. 21:34)—I will cause him to fall before you." Israel then proceeded to wage war against him.

Og said: How large is the camp of Israel? Three parasangs in circumference. I will pluck up a mountain three parasangs in circumference, hurl it upon them, and kill them. He went and plucked up a mountain three parasangs in circumference and carried it on his head. But the Holy One sent ants, which bored holes in it, so that it slipped down around his neck. He tried to pull it up, but since his teeth began jutting out from both sides of his mouth, he could not pull it past them.

How tall was Moses? Ten cubits.[2] So he took an ax ten cubits long, jumped ten cubits into the air, struck Og on his ankles, and killed him.

It is taught that Abba Saul said: I used to be a gravedigger. Once I chased a deer, which entered the thighbone of a corpse. I pursued the deer for three parasangs, but I neither caught up with the deer nor reached the end of the thighbone. When I returned the way I came, I was told, "The thighbone was part of the corpse of Og, king of Bashan."[3]

Balaam

112. "And Moab said unto the elders of Midian" (Num. 22:4). What brought the elders of Midian to Moab? When the Moabites saw Israel victorious in a way that transcended human experience, they said: Their leader grew up in Midian. Let us find out from the Midianites what his powers are. The elders of Midian reported: His power is only in his mouth.[4] So the Moabites said: We, too, shall come against them with a man whose power is in his mouth.

"And Moab said unto the elders of Midian." But do you not find Midianites generally fighting Moabites, and the hostility between them of long standing? A parable of two dogs who always fought each other will answer the question. When a wolf attacked one of them, the other thought: If I do not come to his aid, the wolf will kill him today, and tomorrow he will have a go at me. Reasoning thus, Moab joined with Midian. As the proverb has it: The weasel and the cat, though natural enemies, make a joint meal on the fat of their luckless prey.

"God said to Balaam: 'Thou shalt not go with them [Balak's messengers]' " (Num. 22:12). So he said, "If so," I shall curse the people of Israel from here.' " When God replied, "Thou shalt not curse the people" (ibid.), Balaam said, "I shall bless them." God replied, "They do not need your blessing, 'for they are blessed' " (ibid.). There is a proverb: To the wasp we say, "Neither your honey nor your sting."

"And God came upon Balaam, who said unto Him: 'I have prepared seven altars,' " etc. (Num. 23:4). The Holy One said to him, "O wicked one, what are you doing?" He replied, "I have prepared seven altars." Balaam was like the moneychanger who gave false weights. The chief of the market, becoming aware of it, asked the moneychanger, "Why are you cheating by giving false weights?" The latter replied, "I have already taken care of you with a gift sent to your home." So, too, Balaam. When the holy spirit spoke sharply to him, saying, "Villain, what are you doing?" he replied, "I have [already] prepared seven altars."

"So the Lord put a thing in the mouth of Balaam" (Num. 23:5). The "thing," said R. Eleazar, was an angel;[5] a hook lock, said R. Jonathan.

R. Yohanan said: From the blessings uttered by that wicked man you learn what he had really intended. He wished to say to them that they are to have neither synagogues nor houses of study, [but he was forced to utter], "How goodly are thy tents,[6] O Jacob" (Num. 24:5). He wished to say that the Presence is not to rest upon them, [but he was forced to utter], "And thy Tabernacles,[7] O Israel" (ibid.). He wished to say that their kingdom is not to endure, [but he was forced to utter], "As valleys are they stretched out" (Num. 24:6). That they are to have neither olive trees nor vineyards, [but he was forced to utter], "As gardens by the riverside" (ibid.). That their fragrance is not to go forth, [but he was forced to utter], "As aloes planted of the Lord" (ibid.). That they are to have no kings of stature, [but he was forced to utter], "As cedars beside the waters" (ibid.). That they are to have no king who is the son of a king,[8] [but he was forced to utter], "He shall pour water out of his buckets"[9] (Num. 24:7). That their kingdom is not to rule over other nations, [but he was forced to utter], "And his seed shall be in

1. Tanhuma B, *Hukkat*, §47; Num. R. 19:25.
2. About fifteen feet.
3. Deut. R. 1:24; Yalkut, *Devarim*, §810; B. Ber 54b; B. Nid 24b.
4. Prayer and intercession.
5. To curb his speech.
6. "Tents" is a metaphor for synagogues.
7. The Tabernacle symbolizes the Divine Presence.
8. That, because of civil war, there are to be no dynasties.
9. That each king shall be the descendant of his predecessor.

many waters" (ibid.). That their kingdom is not to be strong, [but he was forced to utter], "And his king shall be higher than Agag" (ibid.). That their kingdom is not to inspire awe, [but he was forced to utter], "And their kingdom shall be exalted" (ibid.).

R. Abba bar Kahana differed: All the blessings Balaam [was forced to utter] did in fact turn into curses,[1] except for the curse on synagogues and houses of study,[2] as is said, "But the Lord thy God turned the curse into a blessing for thee, because the Lord thy God loved thee" (Deut. 23:6). Note that the verse reads, "The curse," but not, "The curses" [i.e., Balaam's other curses].

"For from the top of the rocks I see him" (Num. 23:9). The verse tells you how great was that wicked man's hatred—from his blessings you may surmise what his real thoughts were. To whom may he be compared? To a man about to cut down a tree. If not an expert woodsman, he will cut down the branches, one by one, and soon grow weary; but an experienced woodsman first of all exposes the roots and then chops down the whole tree in one blow. So, too, that wicked one said: Why curse each tribe separately? I'll go for the roots and thus chop down all the tribes in one blow. But when he attempted to strike at the roots, he found them unyielding, as implied in his admission "From the top of the rocks[3] I see him [Israel, the patriarchs' progeny, as unyielding]." A rock that rests only on the surface is easily pulled up. Not the rocks [who are the patriarchs]—they, as well as their progeny, are held fast by layers of earth which reach all the way to the deep.

"Behold (*hen*),[4] a people that dwells apart" (Num. 23:9)—the word *hen* [spelled *hn*] in Greek means "one" ["unique"]. Israel's uniqueness is intimated by the numerical values of the letters in *hn*—the epithet given to Israel in this verse—which cannot be combined in the manner that such numerical values of letters in epithets given to other nations can.[5] You can see this for yourself. When you examine all the letters in the alphabet, you will find that each of them has a mate [with which the number 10 or 100 may be formed], except the letters *he* and *nun* in *hn*, the epithet for Israel; these two letters have no such mates. Thus the letter *alef* (1) together with *tet* (9) adds up to 10. The letter *bet* (2) together with *het* (8) also adds up to 10. And just as *alef* (1) + *tet* (9) and *bet* (2) + *het* (8) add up to 10, so *gimmel* (3) + *zayin* (7) and *dalet* (4) + *vav* (6) [add up to 10]. But the *he* (5) cannot be mated in this way [since it has no mate except itself to make 10]. Likewise, in another series of combinations, the letters *yod* (10) + *tzade* (90) and *kaf* (20) + *pe* (80) and *lamed* (30) + *ayin* (70) and *mem* (40) + *samekh* (60)—[each adds up to 100]. But the *nun* (50) cannot be mated in this way.[6]

113. "And now behold, I go unto my people; come, and I will counsel thee," etc. (Num. 24:14). Balaam said to Balak, "The God of these people hates fornication, and [as it happens] these people are very fond of linen garments.[7] Listen, I have useful counsel for you. Make tents partitioned by hanging draperies and put harlots inside—old ones in the front part and young ones in the rear, and let them sell linen garments. So, all the way from snow-capped Hermon [in the north] to Beth-ha-yeshimot [in the south], Balak erected such tents and placed harlots inside—old ones in front and young ones in the rear. Whenever an Israelite ate, drank, and became mellow, and went out for a stroll in the marketplace, an old harlot would say to him, "Aren't you interested in linen garments?" She would offer them at the going price, while the young harlot in the rear of the tent offered them for less. After two or three sales, the young harlot would say, "You are now like one of the family. Sit down and select any other garment you desire." Near her, there would be a cooler filled with Ammonite wine, which is strong and stimulates the body to lascivious thoughts. Then she would say, "Will you have a cup of wine?" After he drank, his passion aroused, he would say, "Yield to me." At that, the harlot would take her idol from her bosom and say "[First] worship this." He: "But I am a Jew." She: "What difference does that make? You need do no more than uncover yourself." (He did not know that was the way the idol was worshiped.) "What is more, I will not satisfy you until you reject the Torah of Moses your teacher."[8]

The Daughters of Zelophehad

114. "Then drew near the daughters of Zelophehad," etc. (Num. 27:1). When the daughters of Zelophehad heard that the Land was about to be divided among the tribes—but only for males, not for females—they gathered to take counsel. They decided that the mercies of flesh and blood are not like the mercies of Him who is everywhere. Flesh and blood is apt to be more merciful to males than to females. But He who spoke and the world came into being is different—His mercies are for males as well as females, His mercies being for all: "The Lord is good to all, and His tender mercies are over all His works" (Ps. 145:9).

"Give unto us a possession" (Num. 27:4). R. Nathan said: Women's tenacity is stronger than men's. The men of Israel [being willing to give up the Land], said,[9] "Let us make a captain and let us return to Egypt" (Num. 14:4). But Israel's women insisted, "Give unto us a possession."[10]

---

1. What Balaam had in mind was eventually fulfilled.
2. Unlike other boons, such as kingship, which Balaam did not wish Israel to retain, synagogues and houses of study never disappeared.
3. The phrase "the top of the rocks" is taken to refer to the patriarchs, as, e.g., in the verse "Look unto the rock whence ye were hewn" (Isa. 51:1). In this passage, the patriarchs are spoken of as "Israel's tough roots," the sight of which persuaded Balaam that his proceeding against Israel would prove futile.
4. The form *hen* is a demonstrative adverb less widely used than *hinneh*.
5. Thus, the concluding part of Num. 23:9 is read not, "Shall not be reckoned among the nations," but, "The letters in its name will not be combined in the way letters in the names of other nations may be combined."
6. The *nun* has no mate—only itself—to make 100. Num. R. 20:18–19; B. Sanh 105a–b; Tanhuma B, *Balak*, §19; Tanhuma, *Balak*, §12; Yalkut, *Balak*, §768.
7. Having grown accustomed to them in Egypt. Samuel Edels.
8. B. Sanh 106a; P. Sanh 10:2, 28d.
9. Or, "Women's tenacity is stronger than men's. The men of Israel, [willing to give up freedom], said . . ." So Leon Nemoy.
10. Sif Num., §133.

115. "And they stood before Moses" (Num. 27:2). Each of the five daughters presented one of the five pleas. The first said, "Our father died in the wilderness" (Num. 27:3). The second said, "He was not one of the faction, Korah's, that banded together against the Lord" (ibid.). The third: "But he died in his own sin" (ibid.)—[he gathered wood on the Sabbath day]. The fourth: "He had no sons" (ibid.). The fifth: "Why should our father's name be lost to his family?" (Num. 27:4).[1]

116. It is taught: The daughters of Zelophehad were exceedingly wise, knew well how to expound Scripture, and were perfectly virtuous. They were exceedingly wise, since they chose to speak at the right time; for just then, so stated R. Samuel bar R. Isaac, Moses our teacher was engaged in interpreting the section on levirate marriage. So they said, "If in levirate marriage our status is like that of sons,[2] give us—as to a son—a possession. If not,[3] let our mother be subjected to levirate marriage. At once "Moses brought their cause before the Lord" (Num. 27:5).

The daughters also knew well how to expound Scripture, for they said, "If our father had a son, we would not have spoken;[4] or even if that son had a daughter, we would not have spoken."[5]

They were also perfectly virtuous, since they married only men who were worthy of them.[6]

117. "And the Lord spoke unto Moses, saying: 'The plea of Zelophehad's daughters is just' " (Num. 27:6–7)—this indeed is the law. The Holy One went on, "Did you not say to the people, 'Any cause that is too difficult for you ye shall bring unto me, and I shall hear it' [Deut. 1:17]? Now you find a law you did not know set forth by women!" A parable of a moneychanger who said to his apprentice, "If *sela* are brought to you to be changed into small coins, change them; but if pearls are brought [to be appraised and sold], bring them to me." When a bead of glass was brought to the apprentice, he took it to his master. But his master had to consult someone else about it.

R. Simeon ben Lakish differed: Moses our teacher did know this law, but first the women came before the chiefs of tens, who said, "This, being a case concerning inheritance, is not in our jurisdiction; it belongs to our superiors." Then the women came to the chiefs of fifties, who, seeing that the chiefs of tens had shown them deference, said, "We, too, have those who are superior to us in knowledge." A like reply was given by the chiefs of hundreds, the chiefs of thousands, and the princes. All answered the same way, because they were unwilling to adjudicate the case before their superiors did. So the daughters of Zelophehad went to Eleazar, who told them, "There is Moses our teacher. [Go to him]." They, together with all the aforementioned dignitaries, appeared before Moses. When Moses realized that each dignitary had shown deference to his superior, he said: If I tell them the law, I shall be snatching eminence not properly mine. So he said, "I, too, have a superior." Hence, "Moses brought their cause before the Lord" (Num. 27:5).[7]

The War with Midian

118. "Avenge the children of Israel of the Midianites" (Num. 31:2).[8] These words make known the exellence of Israel's leaders, who refuse to depart from the world until they wreak vengeance for Israel, which is also simultaneously the vengeance of Him who spoke and the world came into being.[9]

119. "And Moses sent them" (Num. 31:6). The Holy One had told Moses, "Avenge," meaning, you yourself are to do it. Yet he sent others! However, since he was highly regarded in the land of Midian, he thought: It is not right for me to cause distress to a people who have been good to me. As the proverb puts it: Do not cast a stone into the cistern from which you drank.[10]

120. "They also put Balaam son of Beor to the sword" (Num. 31:8). What was Balaam doing there? He came to take his reward for the twenty-four thousand Israelites he caused to die.[11] As people say, "When the camel demands horns, he gets his ears lopped off."[12]

R. Jonathan said: At the time Phinehas went to war against Midian, all his troops went with him. The instant wicked Balaam saw Phinehas, he made his two arms as firm as stone tablets and [using them for wings] flew off, rising heavenward. The instant Phinehas saw him, he also few off, rising behind Balaam until he found him standing before the throne of glory about to prostrate himself in supplication. At that, Phinehas showed Balaam the high priest's plate, upon which is written, "Holy unto the Lord," and Balaam instantly fell [down to earth]. Phinehas then seized him and brought him to Moses, where he was tried and condemned to death.[13]

1. Yalkut, *Pinhas*, §773.
2. Like the existence of a son, the existence of a daughter also obviates levirate marriage, since the deceased father was not childless.
3. If, in the matter of inheritance, daughters are not to be treated like sons, as legal issue of the deceased father.
4. "This plea shows that they knew the exposition of Num. 27:8, according to which a daughter has no claim where there is a son. See B. BB 110a" (BB, Soncino, p. 490, n. 16).
5. Knowing that a son's daughter has preference over the daughter of the deceased. See B. BB 115b; BB, Soncino, p. 491, n. 1.
6. They married the sons of their uncles. See Num. 36:11; B. BB 119b; Yalkut, *Pinhas*, §773.
7. Tanhuma, *Pinhas*, §8–9; Num. R. 21:12.
8. In the same verse, Moses is told, "Afterward shalt thou be gathered unto thy people."
9. Sif Num., §157.
10. Num. R. 22:4.
11. These were victims of the plague, caused by Israel's lechery resulting from Balaam's scheme. See Num. 25:9 and above in this chapter, §113.
12. So, too, Balaam demanded a reward and lost his life.
13. B. Sanh 106a; Num. R. 22:5; Yalkut, *Mattot*, §785.

Israel's Provisioning in the Wilderness

121. R. Eliezer asked R. Simeon, saying to him, "When the children of Israel went out of Egypt, did weavers' gear go out with them?" R. Simeon replied, "No." "Then how did they clothe themselves during those forty years?" R. Simeon replied, "With garments that the ministering angels gave them." "But did not their garments wear out?" "Have you not read that Moses said to Israel in the wilderness, 'Thy raiment waxed not old upon thee' (Deut. 8:4)?" "But did not the little ones among the children of Israel grow up?" "Go out and learn from the snail: all the while that he grows, his shell grows with him!" "But did not the garments require washing?" "The cloud of fire cleansed their garments and made them white." "But were not the garments scorched in the process?" "Go out and learn from the amiant,[1] which is cleansed only by fire." "But did not the children of Israel get vermin?" "Since worms and maggots had no power over dead bodies in Israel, how much less did they have over living bodies of Israel!" "But since the children of Israel did not change their garments, did they not reek with sweat?" "The well of living waters brought up varieties of plants and spices for the children of Israel, and they rolled in these, so the fragrant smell of them was carried from world's end to world's end."

When Israel saw how the Holy One led them, made their garments white, and refreshed them in the wilderness, they began to sing in praise as they said, "The Lord is my shepherd; I shall not want. He maketh me to lie down in green pastures" (Ps. 23:1–2).[2]

122. "And I have led you forty years in the wilderness" (Deut. 29:4). The Holy One asked Israel, "Have I been as a wilderness unto Israel?" (Jer. 2:31), have I led you as though you were in a wilderness? In the way of the world, when a king of flesh and blood goes forth into a wilderness, does he do so in order to find quiet or fine food and drink such as he finds in his own palace? No. Yet you were slaves in Egypt, and I brought you forth from there, caused you to be sheltered under clouds of glory, appointed three redeemers for you—Moses, Aaron, and Miriam, ever ready to serve you. The clouds of glory were seven in number: one above you, one below you, four at the four points of the compass; and the seventh in front of you smote serpents and scorpions, leveled hills and valleys, burned thorns and thistles, and caused smoke to go up. Seeing the smoke, all kings of the east and of the west said, "Who is this that cometh up out of the wilderness, like columns of smoke?" (Song 3:6). I caused manna to come down for you, the well to spring up for you, even brought you quails. Have I then been a wilderness unto Israel? Have I guided you as in a wilderness? Or would you say that "it has been for you a land of thick darkness" (Jer. 2:31)? Have I not Myself given light for you in the dark that beset you?

In the way of the world, when a man receives a guest, he will slaughter a calf for him the first day and hens the second day; he will cook pulse the third day; but on the fourth day he will give the guest something less delicious, and even less so on succeeding days. Thus, the first day is not at all like the last day. Do you suppose the Holy One also acted in this way? Hence Scripture says, "These forty years the Lord thy God hath been with thee" (Deut. 2:7)—the last day as much as the first.[3]

The End of the Forty Years in the Wilderness

123. During all the years that Israel was in the wilderness, on the eve of every ninth of Av, Moses sent a herald throughout the camp to proclaim, "Go out and dig graves, go out and dig graves!" and the people went out and dug graves, in which they spent the night. In the morning, the herald went out and announced, "Let those who are alive separate from the dead!" The living then stood up and found themselves some fifteen thousand short.[4] [And so it continued year after year in this way] until Israel was sixty myriads short. In the last of the forty years, they did the same thing and, upon finding that they were all still alive, said: Perhaps we have erred in calculating the new moon.[5] So, to make sure [they had the right date], they did the same thing the night of the tenth, each one spending it in the grave he had dug. In the morning, all of them again stood up alive. Then, to make quite sure, they did the same thing the night of the eleventh, twelfth, thirteenth, fourteenth, and fifteenth of the month. Finally, when they saw that not one of them had died, they said: It appears that the Holy One has removed the harsh decree from over us. They declared that day a festival. Accordingly, the sages taught: Israel had no days more festive than the fifteenth of Av and the Day of Atonement.[6]

124. For forty years the Holy One made Israel go in a roundabout way through the wilderness, saying, "Should I now lead them on a straight route, each one will take possession of a field or a vineyard and regard himself as not obligated to study Torah. I shall therefore lead them by way of the wilderness, where they will eat manna, drink the waters of the well, and so [give themselves to the study of] Torah, which will then be inculcated in them." Moreover, when the Canaanites heard that Israel was about to enter the Land, they burned the newly planted seeds, uprooted trees, cut down saplings, demolished buildings, and stopped up wells. The Holy One said: I promised Abraham to bring his children into a land full of good things. So I shall detain them for forty years in the wil-

1. A variety of asbestos, with flexible filaments.
2. Deut. R. 7:11; MTeh 23:4; PRKM 11:21.
3. Deut. R. 7:9; Yalkut, *Be-midbar*, §683.
4. One-fortieth of the adults died each year.
5. So that the night they spent in the graves was not the night ushering in the ninth of Av.
6. On these days young people used to gather in vineyards for formal courtship (Ta 4:8). P. Ta 4:10, 69c; Lam. R., proem 33; Midrash Sam. 32:5.

derness, until the Canaanites get busy and repair what they have damaged.[1]

125. "When you enter the Land and plant" (Lev. 19:23). When her chicks are tiny, the mother hen gathers them together and places them beneath her wings, warming them and grubbing for them. But once they are grown up, if one of them attempts to get near her, she pecks at its head and says, "Go grub in your own dunghill!" So also, during the forty years that Israel were in the wilderness, manna fell, the well came up for them, quails were at hand for them, clouds of glory encircled them, and the pillar of cloud led the way before them. But once Israel were about to enter the Land, Moses said, "Let everyone pick up his hoe, go out, and plant his own saplings."[2]

126. "These are the stages of the children of Israel" (Num. 33:1). The listing of the stages may be understood by a parable. A king had a son who was sick. He took him to a distant place to have him cured. On their way back, the father began listing the stages of the journey: Here we slept, here we were chilled, here you had a headache. Likewise, the Holy One said to Moses: List for Me all the places where Israel caused Me anxiety. Hence: "These are the stages."[3]

The Prophecy of Moses

127. "There hath not arisen a prophet since in Israel like unto Moses" (Deut. 34:10). It is taught: All the prophets looked into a glass that was dim, as is said, "By the ministry of the prophets I appear dimly" (Hos. 12:11).[4] But Moses our teacher looked through a glass that was translucent, for of him it is said, "The similitude of the Lord doth he behold" (Num. 12:8).[5]

Fifty gates of understanding were created in the world, and at Sinai all but one was opened to Moses, of whom it is said, "Thou hast made him but little lower than God" (Ps. 8:6).[6]

128. "And Moses said unto the Lord" (Exod. 19:23). How may the give-and-take between Moses and the Lord be illustrated? By the parable of a cave situated at the edge of the sea. The sea rises and fills it. Henceforth, the waters of the sea flow freely into the cave, and the waters of the cave into the sea. So, too, [was the give-and-take between Moses and the Lord]: "The Lord said unto Moses," "Moses said unto the Lord," "The Lord said unto Moses."[7]

129. "And I will draw upon the spirit which is on thee, and put it upon them" (Num. 11:17). Since the spirit of the prophecy in the elders was drawn from Moses, do you suppose that his prophecy was at all diminished? In no way! To what may Moses be compared at that moment? To a lamp that is alight—though many lamps are lit from it, still, its own light is not at all diminished. So it was with Moses. Though many prophets drew upon his prophecy, Moses' own prophecy was not at all diminished, as is said, "There hath not arisen a prophet since in Israel like unto Moses" (Deut. 34:10).[8]

130. "Moses, Moses" (Exod. 3:4). He was Moses before God had spoken to him, and [the same] Moses after God had spoken to him.[9]

131. How did Moses come to have rays of splendor [emanate from his countenance]? When Moses wrote the Torah [in fiery letters], so said R. Judah bar Nehemiah, a small tongue of fire was left on the reed, which Moses brushed against his head. From that spark, rays of splendor were wrought for him.[10]

Eldad and Medad

132. "But there remained two men in the camp" (Num. 11:26). Some say: Eldad and Medad remained in the camp [as commoners, not elders], because they drew blanks from the urn. For when the Holy One said to Moses, "Gather unto me seventy of the elders of Israel" (Num. 11:16), Moses asked himself: How shall I do it? If I choose six out of each tribe, there will be [seventy-two], two more than required; if I choose five out of each tribe, there will be [sixty], ten fewer than required. If, on the other hand, I choose six out of ten tribes and five out of two tribes, I shall [have seventy but also] cause jealousy among the tribes. What did he do? He selected six men [out of each tribe] and brought seventy-two slips, on seventy of which he wrote the word "elder," leaving the remaining two blank. Then he shook them up, deposited them in an urn, and said, "Come and draw your slips." To each who drew a slip bearing the word "elder," he said, "Heaven has already consecrated you." But to him who drew a blank, he said, "He who is everywhere does not want you; so what can I do for you?" But R. Simeon said: On their own, Eldad and Medad chose to remain in the camp. For when the Holy One ordered Moses, "Gather unto Me seventy of the elders of Israel" (Num. 11:16), Eldad and Medad said to themselves: We are not worthy of such distinction. The Holy One said, "Because you have humbled yourselves, I will add to your distinction even greater distinction." How did He add to their distinction? All [other prophets] prophesied [for a while] and then ceased, but Eldad and Medad kept on prophesying without cease. What did they prophesy? They announced, "Moses will die, and Joshua will bring Israel into the Land."[11]

---

1. Tanhuma, *Be-shallah*, §1.
2. Lev. R. 25:5.
3. Tanhuma B, *Mas'e*, §3.
4. They imagined they saw the deity, but in fact did not. Rashi.
5. Moses saw a similitude, but he knew that no mortal eye could see God Himself.
6. B. Yev 49b; B. Ned 38a. Ps. 8 is construed as referring to Israel in the wilderness and to Moses.
7. Exod. R. 45:3; Tanhuma B, *Ki Tissa*, §14.
8. Tanhuma B, *Be-haalotekha*, §28; Sif Num., §93.
9. As meek as ever. Num. R. 14:21.
10. Tanhuma B, *Ki Tissa*, §20.
11. The phrase "in the camp" is now construed as meaning "concerning what would happen to the camp of Israel"—that quail would be swept from the sea into the camp and that not Moses but Joshua would lead Israel's camp into the Land. So Samuel Edels. B. Sanh 17a.

133. "Moses said to him: 'Dost thou think I am jealous because of my self-esteem?' " (Num. 11:29).[1] [I am not jealous of Eldad and Medad because they are prophesying.] But I am jealous of you, Joshua. Would that my children were like you. Would that all Israel were like you.[2]

Moses and Joshua

134. "Moses spoke unto the Lord, saying: 'Let the Lord, the God of the spirits of all flesh, set a man over the congregation' " (Num. 27:15–16). The verse proclaims the excellence of the righteous: even when about to depart from the world, they set aside their own needs and occupy themselves with the needs of the community.

"Let the Lord, the God of the spirits of all flesh." When Moses saw that his sons were not worthy to succeed him in the dignity of his office, he wrapped himself in his tallit and, standing up in prayer before the Holy One, said: Master of the universe, let me know who shall come and go [in leadership] before the people. "Let the Lord, the God of the spirits of all flesh, set [the right] man over the congregation." Master of the universe, the disposition of every one of them is revealed to You—the disposition of one is not at all like the disposition of another. After I depart from them, when You will be setting another leader over them, I beg you, set over them a leader who will put up with each and every man according to his particular disposition. So, in saying, "Let the Lord, the God of the spirits of all flesh, set [the right] man over the congregation," Moses asked: Will the man You set over the congregation have within himself the spirits of sixty myriads, so that he will be able to converse with each man according to his particular disposition? The Holy One replied: Moses, you have made a proper request. So I shall show you all the judges and all the prophets whom I will set up over My children from this time until the dead shall be brought back to life. For, as R. Simon said, the verse "He showed him all the earth" (Deut. 34:1) means: He showed him that Joshua would rise up in his stead, and Joshua would turn over his authority to Othniel, as will all subsequent leaders to their successors. Then the Holy One said to Moses: Each of these I showed you has one disposition and one spirit. But as to what you asked for earlier, at the end of time there will be a person within whom, to be sure, there will be but one spirit, yet it will have the capacity to bear the weight of the spirits of all men—that person is the Messiah.

"A man over the congregation, who may go out before them, and who may come in before them" (Num. 27:17)—that he not act like others, who have their legions go forth while they themselves remain in their homes; "who may lead them out, and who may bring them in" (ibid.)—that he not lead them out in myriads and bring them back in thousands, or lead them out in thousands and bring them back in hundreds.

[Moses went on]: "That the congregation of the Lord be not as sheep that have no shepherd" (Num. 27:17). To whom may Moses be compared? To a faithful shepherd. When the owner of the flock said to him, "Remove yourself from my flock," he replied, "I will not remove myself until you tell me whom you will set as shepherd in my place."

"The Lord said to Moses: 'Single out' [Num. 27:18]—one you trust; 'single out' one who has been tested by you: 'Joshua the son of Nun' [ibid.]. You know how long Joshua has served you, how much honor he accorded you, how he came early and stayed late in your meeting place, arranging the benches and spreading the mats. 'A man in whom there is spirit' [ibid.], one who will know how to face up to the spirit of everyone. Let him take on authority, to confirm the verse 'Whoso keepeth the fig tree shall eat the fruit thereof' " (Prov. 27:18).[3]

135. Then Moses said to Joshua: The people I am putting in your cave are not yet goats but only kids, not yet sheep but only lambs. Hence, "go follow the tracks of the lambs, and graze thy kids by the shepherds' tents" (Song 1:8).[4]

136. "And thou shalt put of thy honor upon him" (Num. 27:20)—"of thy honor," but not "all thine honor." Hence the elders of that generation used to say, "The countenance of Moses was like that of the sun, but the countenance of Joshua is merely that of the moon. What a fading of glory! What a comedown."[5]

The Death of Moses

137. "And the Lord said unto Moses: 'Behold, thy days approach that thou must die' " (Deut. 31:14). These words are to be considered in the light of the verse "Though his excellency mount up to the heavens, and his head reach unto the clouds; yet he shall perish. . . . They that have seen him shall say: 'Where is he?' " (Job. 20:6–7). To whom does this verse refer? To none other than [to him who nears] the day of death. Even if a man should make himself wings like a bird and go up to heaven, once his time comes to die, his wings will be broken and he will fall down.

The words "though his excellency mount up to the heavens" apply particularly to Moses, who went up to heaven, whose feet trod on thick clouds, who became like the ministering angels, who spoke with the Holy One face to face, who received the Torah from His own hand—yet when his time came, the Holy One said, "Behold, thy days approach that thou must die!" (Deut. 31:14).

When Moses realized that the decree [of death] had been sealed against him, he drew a small circle around himself, stood in it, and said, "Master of the universe, I

1. JV: "Art thou jealous for my sake?"
2. See Sif Num., §96 (ed. H. S. Horovitz [Frankfurt am Main, 1917], p. 96). Text emended as suggested in a note, ad loc. Gershom and Jonathan, Moses' sons, were less than mediocre, whereas prophets were among the descendants of Joshua.
3. Yalkut, *Pinhas*, §776; Sif Zuta, *Pinhas*, §16; Yelammedenu.
4. ARN 17.
5. B. BB 75a.

will not budge from here until You void that decree." At the same time, he donned sackcloth—indeed, wrapped himself in it—strewed ashes upon himself, and persisted in prayer and supplications before the Holy One, until heaven and earth—indeed, all things made during the six days of creation—were shaken, so that they said, "Perhaps the intention of the Holy One to remake His world is about to be executed. A divine voice came forth and said: As yet, the Holy One's intention to remake His world is not about to be executed. But the words "in whose hand is the soul of every living thing" (Job 12:10) [are in force and apply even to Moses].

What did the Holy One do then? He had it proclaimed at every gate of every firmament that Moses' prayer be not accepted nor brought up to His presence, because the decree concerning him had been sealed.

Still, as the sound of Moses' prayer to Him above grew even stronger, the Holy One summoned the ministering angels and commanded them: Go down in haste, bolt all the gates of every firmament—for Moses' prayer was like a sword, ripping and tearing, and nothing could stop it.

In that instant, Moses said to the Holy One, "Master of the universe, known and revealed to You is the trouble and pain I suffered on account of Israel, until they came to believe in Your Name. How much pain I suffered because of them, until I inculcated among them the Torah and its precepts! I said to myself: As I witnessed their woe, so will I be allowed to witness their weal. Yet now that Israel's weal has come, You tell me, 'You shall not go over this Jordan' [Deut. 3:27]. Thus Your Torah, which asserts, 'In the same day thou shalt give him his hire' [Deut. 24:15], You manifestly turn into fraud. Is such the reward for forty years of labor that I labored until Israel became a holy people loyal to their faith?" The Holy One replied, "Nevertheless, such is the decree that has gone forth from My Presence!" Then Moses said, "Master of the universe, if I am not to enter the Land alive, let me enter dead, as the bones of Joseph are about to enter." The Holy One replied, "Moses, when Joseph came to Egypt, he did not deny his identity.[1] He declared openly, 'I am a Hebrew.' But when you came to Midian, you denied yours."[2]

Then Moses said, "Master of the universe, if You will not let me enter the Land of Israel, allow me to remain [alive] like the beasts of the field, who eat grass, drink water, and thus savor the world—let me be like one of these." At that, God replied, "Enough. Speak no more to Me of this matter" (Deut. 3:26).

But Moses spoke up again, "Master of the universe, if not [like a beast of the field], then let me become like a bird that flies daily in every direction to gather its food and in the evening returns to its nest—let me be like one of these." The Holy One replied again, "Enough."

When Moses saw that his prayer was not heeded, he went to implore heaven and earth, saying: Entreat mercy in my behalf. They replied: Before entreating mercy for you, we should entreat mercy for ourselves, for it is said, "The heavens shall vanish away like smoke, and the earth shall wax old like a garment" (Isa. 51:6). He then went to implore the sun and the moon, and said: Entreat mercy in my behalf. But these replied: Before entreating mercy for you, we should entreat mercy for ourselves, for it is said, "The moon shall be confounded and the sun ashamed" (Isa. 24:23).

Then he went to implore the stars and the planets, and said: Entreat mercy in my behalf. But these replied: Before entreating mercy for you, we should entreat mercy for ourselves, for it is said, "All the host of heaven shall molder away" (Isa. 34:4).

Then he went to implore the mountains and the hills, and said: Entreat mercy in my behalf. But these also replied: Before entreating mercy for you, we should entreat mercy for ourselves, for it is said, "The mountains will depart, and the hills be removed" (Isa. 54:10).

Then he went to implore the sea and cried: Entreat mercy in my behalf. The sea replied: Son of Amram, why is this day different from former days? Are you not the same son of Amram who came to me with your rod, smote me, split me into twelve paths, when I could not withstand you because the Presence was proceeding at your right? What's happened to you now? As the sea reminded Moses of what he was able to do in his younger years, he cried out in anguish, "Oh that I were as in the months of old" (Job 29:2). [O sea], at the time I stood over you, I was a king in the world, but now, though I prostrate myself, no heed is given me.

Then Moses went to the angel of the Presence[3] and implored: Entreat mercy in my behalf, that I not die. The angel replied: Moses my master, of what avail is this effort? For I have heard from behind the curtain above that your prayer in this matter will not be heard.

Moses put his hands on his head and lamented and wept, as he said: To whom am I to go now to entreat mercy in my behalf? In that instant the Holy One was filled with anger at Moses, so that Moses was constrained to remind God that He had described Himself as "the Lord, the Lord, God, who is merciful and compassionate" (Exod. 34:6). Whereupon the holy spirit was assuaged.

Then the Holy One said to Moses: Moses, I have sworn two oaths: one concerning Israel—after they did that deed[4]—that I would destroy them from the world; and the other that you are to die and not enter the Land. The oath I had sworn concerning Israel, I set aside at your plea when you entreated Me, "Pardon, I pray Thee" (Num. 14:19); and now you entreat once again that I set aside My oath to comply with your plea "Let me go over, I pray Thee" (Deut. 3:25). You seize the well's rope at both ends—do you not?[5] If you wish to have "Let me go over, I pray Thee" fulfilled, you must nullify "Pardon, I pray

1. Joseph told the chief butler, "I was stolen away out of the land of the Hebrews" (Gen. 40:15).
2. So that Jethro's daughters, reporting to their father, said that an Egyptian helped them (Exod. 2:19).
3. Metatron.
4. Made the golden calf.
5. The rope for a well has two ends—as one comes up, the other goes down. But when a man holds both ends of the rope, he can neither lower nor raise the bucket.

Thee"; or if you wish to have "Pardon, I pray Thee" fulfilled, then nullify "Let me go over, I pray Thee." When Moses our teacher heard this, he said: Master of the universe, let Moses and a thousand like him perish, but let not a fingernail of one person in Israel be hurt.

Nevertheless, Moses said to God: Master of the universe, shall the feet that went up to the firmament, the face that confronted the Presence, the hands that received the Torah from Your hand—shall these now lick dust?

The Holy One replied: Such was My thought [from the very beginning], and such must be the way of the world: each generation is to have its own interpreters of Scripture, each generation is to have its own providers, each generation is to have its own leaders. Until now it had been your portion to serve Me, but now your disciple Joshua's portion to serve has come.

Moses said to the Holy One: Master of the universe, if I must die [to vacate my post] for Joshua, let me be his disciple [in my remaining hours]. The Holy One replied: If that is what you wish to do, go and do it.

So Moses rose early to be at Joshua's doorway, where Joshua sat and interpreted Scripture. [In order to hide his identity] Moses stooped and put his hand over his heart [thus covering his face with the crook of his arm]. At the same time, Joshua's eyes were veiled [by God], making him unable to see Moses, so that Moses would be humiliated and come to be reconciled to his dying.

In the meantime, when people came to Moses' doorway to study Torah and asked, "Where is our teacher Moses?" they were told, "He rose early and went to Joshua's doorway." They went and found him at Joshua's doorway—Joshua seated and Moses standing. They said to Joshua: What has come over you, that you allow our teacher Moses to stand while you sit? When Joshua's eyes were again clear and he recognized Moses, he rent his garments, cried out, and wept: My master, my master! My father, my father!

Then the people said to Moses, "Moses our teacher, teach us Torah." He replied, "I no longer have the authority." They: "We will not leave you." Then a divine voice came forth and commanded the people, "Be willing to learn from Joshua." With that, the people submitted to the command to sit and learn from Joshua's mouth.

Joshua sat at the head, Moses at his right, and Aaron's sons at his left, while Joshua taught in Moses' presence. At that session, the tradition of wisdom was taken away from Moses and given to Joshua.

When they went out, Moses walked at Joshua's left, and as they entered the Tent of Meeting, the pillar of cloud came down and formed a partition between the two. After the cloud departed, Moses went over to Joshua and asked, "What did the Word say to you?" Joshua replied, "When the Word used to reveal itself to you, did I know what it said to you?"

In that instant, Moses cried out in anguish and said, "Rather a hundred deaths than a single pang of envy. Master of universes, until now I sought life. But now my soul is surrendered to You."

After Moses became reconciled to his dying, the Holy One spoke up, saying: " 'Who will rise up for Me in behalf of evildoers?' [Ps. 94:16]. Who will rise up in Israel's behalf at the time of My anger? Who will stand up for them during My children's warfare [with enemies]? Who will entreat mercy in their behalf when they sin before Me?"

At that time Metratron came and, prostrating himself before the Holy One, sought to comfort Him: Master of the universe, Moses during his life was Yours, and when dead he will still be Yours. The Holy One replied: Let Me tell you a parable. I am like a king who had a son. Day after day the son so provoked his father that the father wished to slay him. But his mother kept saving him from the father's hand. Then, when the mother died, the king wept on and on without cease, so that finally his servants asked, "Our lord king, why are you weeping so disconsolately?" He replied, "I weep not only for my wife; I weep for her and for my son as well. Many times when I became angry at him and wished to slay him, his mother would save him from me."

So it is with Me, the Holy One said to Metratron. I weep not only for Moses; I weep for him and for Israel as well. Many times when they provoked Me and I was angry at them, it was he who stood in the breach before Me to turn back My anger.

In that instant, the Holy One said to Gabriel: Go forth and bring the soul of Moses. Gabriel replied: He who is equal in importance to sixty myriads—how can I bear to watch him dying?

Then the Holy One said to Michael: Go and bring the soul of Moses. Michael replied: I was his teacher, and he my pupil. How can I bear to watch him dying?

Then the Holy One said to Samael: Go and fetch the soul of Moses. Now, the angel Samael, chief of all satanic spirits, had long been awaiting the soul of Moses, as he kept saying, "When will the instant arrive in which Moses is to die, so that I might come down and snatch his soul from him? When will Michael weep, while I fill my mouth with laughter?" He immediately clothed himself with anger, girded on his sword, wrapped himself in ruthlessness, and went forth to encounter Moses. Samael found him seated and writing the Ineffable Name in a scroll. The radiance of his appearance was like the radiance of the sun's visage; indeed, Moses looked like an angel of the Lord of hosts.

Samael was so frightened by the sight of Moses that trembling seized him, so that he found himself unable to open his mouth to say anything, until Moses asked Samael, "Evil one, what are you doing here?" "I have come to take away your soul." "Who sent you?" "He who created all beings." "Go away. I want to praise the Holy One—'I shall not die, but live, and declare the works of the Lord' " (Ps. 118:17). Samael: "Moses, why do you vaunt yourself? The Lord has those who would praise Him—'The heavens declare the works of the Lord' " (Ps. 19:2). Moses: "I shall silence them, and I will voice His praise—'Give ear, O ye heavens, and I will speak; and let the earth hear the words of my mouth' " (Deut. 32:1). Samael: "The souls of all the world's inhabitants are placed under my authority." Moses: "But I have power greater than that of all the world's inhabitants." Samael: "Wherein is your power?" Moses: "I, Amram's son, at the age of three prophesied that out of flames of fire I would receive the Torah; [at that age] I entered the palace of a king and took his crown from his head.[1] At eighty I performed signs and wonders in Egypt, and in the sight of all Egyptians brought forth sixty myriads; split the [Red] Sea into twelve paths; ascended to, and broke a path in, heaven; took hold [of the throne of glory]; and engaged in strife with angels, until I prevailed over heaven's retinue and had them disclose their secrets to the children of men.[2] I spoke with the Holy One face to face, received the fiery Torah from His right hand, and taught it to Israel. I waged war against Sihon and Og, two giants of the peoples of the world, struck them with the rod in hand, and slew them. I made the sun and the moon stand still in the zenith of the world. Who among the world's inhabitants could have done such things? Away, get out of my sight! I won't give you my soul!"

Samael went back and reported to the Almighty. The Holy One commanded once more: Go, bring the soul of Moses.

Samael straightaway drew his sword from its sheath and stood over Moses. At that, Moses became angry at him, took the rod upon which God's Ineffable Name was graven, and struck Samael with all his might, until Samael fled from him. With God's Ineffable Name in his hand, Moses pursued Samael until he [overtook him], plucked a radiant beam from between his own eyes, and blinded the eyes of Samael.

But a divine voice came forth and said, "The time has come for you to depart from the world." Moses pleaded with the Holy One, "Master of the universe, for my sake, remember the day when You revealed Yourself to me at the bush; for my sake, remember the time when I stood on Mount Sinai forty days and forty nights. I beg You, do not hand me over to the angel of death."

Again a divine voice came forth and said, "Fear not, I Myself will attend you and your burial."

Moses pleaded, "Then wait until I bless Israel. On account of the warnings and reprimands I heaped upon them, they never found any ease with me." Then he began to bless each tribe separately, but when he saw that time was running short, he included all the tribes in a single blessing.[3]

Then he said to Israel, "Because of the Torah and its precepts, I troubled you greatly. Now, please forgive me."

They replied, "Our master, our lord, you are forgiven." In their turn they said to him, "Moses our teacher, we troubled you even more, we made your burden so heavy. Please forgive us." Moses replied, "You are forgiven."

Again a divine voice came forth: "The moment has come for you to depart from this world." Moses replied, "Blessed be His Name! May He live and endure forever and ever!" Then he said to Israel, "I implore you, when you enter the Land, remember me and my bones, and say, 'Alas for the son of Amram, who had run before us like a horse, yet his bones fell in the wilderness.' "

Again a divine voice came forth and said, "Within half a moment you are to depart from the world."

Moses lifted both his arms, placed them over his heart, and called out to Israel, "Behold the end of flesh and blood." Moses arose and washed his hands and feet, and thus became as pure as a seraphim.

Then, from the highest heaven of heavens, the Holy One came down to take the soul of Moses, and with Him the three ministering angels, Michael, Gabriel, and Zagzagel. Michael laid out his bier, Gabriel spread a fine linen cloth at his head, while Zagzagel spread it at his feet. Michael stood at one side and Gabriel at the other. Then the Holy One said to Moses, "Moses, close your eyes," and he closed his eyes. "Put your arms over your breast," and he put his arms over his breast. "Bring your legs together," and he brought his legs together. Then the Holy One summoned Moses' soul, saying, "My daughter, I had fixed the time of your sojourn in the body of Moses at a hundred and twenty years. Now your time has to come to depart. Depart. Delay not."

She replied, "Master of the universe, I know that You are God of all spirits and Lord of all souls. You created me and placed me in the body of Moses one hundred and twenty years ago. Is there a body in the world more pure than the body of Moses? I love him, and I do not wish to depart from him."

The Holy One exclaimed, "Depart, and I will take you up to the highest heaven of heavens, and will set you under the throne of glory, next to the cherubim and seraphim."

In that instant, the Holy One kissed Moses, and took his soul with that kiss.

At that, the holy spirit wept and said, "There hath not arisen a prophet since in Israel like unto Moses" (Deut. 34:10).

The heavens wept and said, "The godly man is perished out of the earth" (Mic. 7:2).

The earth wept and said, "The upright among men is no more" (Mic. 7:2).

The ministering angels wept and said, "He executed the righteousness of the Lord" (Deut. 33:21).

Israel wept and said, "And His ordinances are with Israel" (Deut. 33:21).

These as well as those said together, "Let him enter in peace and rest on his couch" (Isa. 57:2).[4]

138. It is taught: "So Moses the servant of the Lord died there" (Deut. 34:5). Is it possible that Moses, while still alive, would have written, "So Moses . . . died"? The truth is, Scripture up to this passage was written by Moses; from this passage on, Scripture was written by Joshua son of Nun. Such is the opinion of R. Judah—some say, of R. Nehemiah. But R. Simeon said to R. Judah: Is it possible that the Torah scroll is short of even a single letter? If it were short, how could Moses have commanded, "Take this book of Torah" (Deut. 31:26)?[5] Rather, the

1. See above, chap. 4, §19.
2. See above in this chapter, §49.
3. See Deut. 33:27–29.

4. Deut. R. 7:10 and 11:10; Tanhuma, *Va-et'hannan*, §6; Yalkut, *Va-et'hannan*, §821.
5. If he had not finished writing the Torah, he would not have referred to it as "the book of Torah."

meaning is that, up to this passage, the Holy One dictated, and Moses repeated the words and wrote them out, but from this passage on, the Holy One dictated, and Moses [without repeating the words][1] wrote them down with tears in his eyes.[2]

139. It is taught that R. Eliezer the Elder said: Over an area of twelve by twelve *mil*, the dimension of the camp of Israel, a divine voice kept reverberating, "Moses is dead—Israel's great scribe!"[3]

140. Moses died on the seventh of Adar, and he was born on the seventh of Adar.[4]

Moses' Burial Place

141. "And he was buried in the valley in the land of Moab over against Beth-peor" (Deut. 34:6). R. Berekhiah commented: Although Scripture thus provides one clue within another about its location, nevertheless [it goes on to say], "No man knoweth of his sepulcher" (ibid.). The wicked kingdom of Rome once dispatched a request to the military garrison at Beth-peor: "Locate the spot where Moses is buried." When the soldiers stood on high ground, the spot seemed to them to be below; when they stood on low ground, it seemed to them to be above, fulfilling the words, "No man knoweth of his sepulcher to this day."[5]

142. R. Hama bar Hanina asked: Why was the sepulcher of Moses hidden from the eyes of mortals? and answered: Because it was revealed and known to the Holy One that the Temple was to be destroyed and Israel banished from their Land; hence [the spot was hidden], lest at that time Israel should come to the sepulcher of Moses and stand there, weeping and beseeching Moses, saying, "Moses our teacher, rise up for prayer in our behalf." Then Moses would rise and nullify the decree [of banishment]. For after their death, the righteous are even more beloved by God than while alive.[6]

1. Because of his grief.
2. B. BB 15a; B. Men 30a.
3. B. Sot 13b and En Yaakov, ad loc.; Sif Deut., §357.
4. B. Meg 13b.
5. B. Sot 13b–14a.
6. B. Sot 13b and En Yaakov, ad loc.

CHAPTER SIX

JUDGES, KINGS, AND PROPHETS

The Chosen Land

1. R. Simeon ben Yohai began his discourse with the verse "He stood, and measured the earth" (Hab. 3:6). That is, the Holy One took the measure of all peoples and found no people other than Israel worthy of receiving the Torah. The Holy One took the measure of all generations and found no generation other than the generation of the wilderness worthy of receiving the Torah. The Holy One took the measure of all mountains and found no mountain other than Sinai worthy of having the Torah given on it. The Holy One took the measure of all cities and found no city other than Jerusalem worthy of having the Temple built within it. The Holy One took the measure of all lands and found no land other than the Land of Israel worthy of being given to Israel.[1]

Joshua

2. R. Judah said in the name of Rav: When Moses our teacher was about to depart for the Garden of Eden, he said to Joshua: Ask me about any matters of law about which you are in doubt. Joshua replied: My master, have I ever left you, even for as little as one hour, and gone elsewhere? Have you not in fact written of me, "His servant Joshua the son of Nun departed not out of the Tabernacle" (Exod. 33:11) [where I studied Torah constantly]? At that, Joshua's mental strength grew so weak[2] that he forgot three hundred laws and found himself in doubt concerning seven hundred other matters of law. The people of Israel [frustrated by Joshua's confusion] were all but ready to slay him. So the Holy One said to him: It is impossible to teach you right now, but go and distract the people with warfare. Hence; "And it came to pass after the death of Moses . . . Joshua commanded: . . . Prepare you victuals, for within three days ye . . . go in to possess the Land" (Josh. 1:1 and 1:10–11).[3]

3. R. Simeon ben Gamaliel said: Before Israel's entry into the Land, Joshua sent three proclamations to the [inhabitants of the] Land of Israel: He who wishes to leave, let him leave; he who wishes to capitulate, let him capitulate; he who wishes to wage war, let him wage war. The Girgashites left and went to Africa; the Gibeonites capitulated;[4] the thirty-one kings waged war and fell in battle.[5]

4. "And Joshua the son of Nun sent out of Shittim two spies *heresh*[6] (Josh. 2:1). Who were they? They were, so taught our rabbis, Phinehas and Caleb, who went and, risking their lives, succeeded in their mission. But what is the meaning of *heresh?* R. Judah said: They carried carpentry (*harash*) tools, pretending to be carpenters. R. Nehemiah, however, said: They pretended to be makers of earthenware (*heres*) and hawked their wares, crying, "Here are pots (*heres*)! Whosoever wishes, let him come and buy!" Why did they do this? In order that the Canaanites might not become aware of their real identity.

But R. Simeon ben Yohai taught: The word *heresh* is to be taken literally as "deaf." For Joshua said to Phinehas and Caleb: Make believe you are deaf, and you will find out their secrets. R. Simeon ben Eleazar said: By pretending to be deaf, you will find out their true character.[7]

5. The verse "The waters . . . stood, and rose up in one heap" (Josh. 3:16) implies that the waters stacked up in heaps upon heaps to a height of more than three hundred *mil*, so that all the kings of the east and of the west beheld them.[8]

6. "Israel hath sinned" (Josh. 7:11). When the Holy One said to Joshua, "Israel hath sinned," Joshua asked, "Who is the one who has sinned?" The Holy One replied, "Do you expect Me to be an informer? Cast lots, and find out." Joshua went and cast lots, and the lot fell on Achan. Achan said to Joshua, "Are you making charges against me on the strength of a lot? Cast the lot between yourself and Eleazar the High Priest, and it will surely fall on one of you."

In that instant, Joshua looked at the twelve precious stones among the stones in the ephod that was on the breast of the high priest and saw that the brilliance in the stone of Judah's tribe had dimmed. (Such was the way of the breastpiece of judgment: whenever a tribe performed a precept, its stone grew in brilliance and it's light was intensified; but whenever a tribe committed a transgression, its stone dimmed.) When Joshua perceived this, he said, "My son, give, I pray thee, glory to the Lord, the God of Israel" (Josh. 7:19). At once Achan answered, "Of a truth, I have sinned" (Josh. 7:20).[9]

7. When Joshua said, "Sun, stand thou still upon Gibeon" (Josh. 10:12), the sun responded, "You say to me, 'Stand still'? How dare a youngster open his mouth and say to his elder, 'Stand still'? I was created on the fourth

---

1. Lev. R. 13:2; Yalkut, Hab. §543.
2. Because he was so certain of himself.
3. B. Tem 16a and En Yaakov, ad loc.
4. Josh. 9:1–18.
5. Josh. 12:7–24; P. Shev 6:1, 36c.
6. JV: "secretly."
7. Num. R. 16:1; Ruth R. 2:1; Yalkut, Josh., §7.
8. B. Sot 34a.
9. All the loot taken at Jericho was proscribed for the Lord. But Achan stole for himself a fine mantle, shekels of silver, and a wedge of gold, thus violating the proscription. Tanhuma, Va-yeshev, §2.

day and you on the sixth, and yet you say to me, 'Stand still'!" Joshua answered the sun, "You upstart slave! Are you not a mere chattel of one of my forebears? Did not my forebear Joseph see you as a slave in the dream in which he reported, 'Behold, the sun and the moon and eleven stars bowed down to me' (Gen. 37:9)?" At once "the sun stood still, and the moon stayed" (Josh. 10:13).[1]

8. The Land of Israel was divided only by lot and by the command of the Urim and Tummim. How could it be done by both?[2] [In the following manner]: Eleazar wore the Urim and Tummim, while Joshua and all Israel stood before him. An urn containing the names of the twelve tribes and another urn containing the outlines of their boundaries were placed before him. At the prompting of the holy spirit [in the Urim and Tummim], Eleazar would declare: The name "Zebulun" is coming up from the first urn, and with his name, the boundary lines of Acco are coming up from the second urn. Then he dipped into the urn containing the names of the tribes, and Zebulun came up in his hand; he dipped into the urn containing the boundaries, and the boundaries of Acco came up in his hand. Again at the prompting of the holy spirit [in the Urim and Tummim], Eleazar would declare: "Naphtali" is coming up, and with his name the boundary lines of Gennesar.[3] Then he dipped into the urn containing the names of the tribes, and "Naphtali" came up in his hand; he dipped into the urn containing the boundaries, and the boundaries of Gennesar came up in his hand. The procedure was the same for each of the other tribes.[4]

9. Joshua was deeply concerned with Israel's well-being, so he provided roads and highways for them.[5]

10. [On his entry into the Land], Joshua laid down ten stipulations:[6] that cattle be permitted to pasture in [private] woods; that wood may be gathered by all in [private] fields; that [fodder] grasses may be gathered anywhere, with the exception of a field where Greek hay is growing;[7] that everyone be permitted to cut off plantings from all trees everywhere except from branches left on the stumps of olive trees; that a spring, though private, may be used by the people of the town, even if it first emerged [after the division of the Land];[8] that it be permitted to fish with an angle in the Sea of Tiberias,[9] provided there be no setting out of reed barriers [to confine the fish] that cause boats to slow down; that it be permitted to ease oneself at the back of a fence even in a field full of saffron;[10] that it be permitted to use paths in private fields until the time when the second rain is expected;[11] that it be permitted to turn off the road [into private fields] to avoid walking on the road's hardened lumps of clay; that he who loses his way in the vineyards may force his way through [the vines] when going up a hillside or when coming down; and that an unidentified corpse, which anyone who finds is obligated to bury,[12] acquires [the right of burial] on the spot [where it is found].[13]

[To return to the stipulation about fishing in the Sea of Tiberias. Our masters taught: On Israel's entry into the Land], it was the tribes of Israel [not Joshua] who stipulated that there be no setting out of reed barriers that cause boats to slow down and that fishing be permitted [not only with an angle but also] with small nets and traps.[14]

11. "And his fame was in all the Land" (Josh. 6:27). Joshua's coinage became current in the world. What was stamped on it? A bullock on one side and a wild ox on the other.[15]

12. "And they buried him in the border of his inheritance . . . on the north of the mountain of Gaash" (Josh. 24:30). It is said in the name of R. Joshua ben Levi: We have gone through all of Scripture and did not find a place called Gaash. What then is meant by "the mountain of Gaash"? That at the time of Joshua's death Israel were so preoccupied (*nitgaashu*) that they failed to pay him the honor due him.[16] The land of Israel had just been divided among the tribes, who were completely taken up both by details of the division and by the use they planned to put the land to. Thus, one was occupied with his field, another with his vineyard, still another with his olive trees, and still another with his household chores, so that they were negligent in paying Joshua the honor due him. The Holy One was about to cause the earth, all of it, to quake under its inhabitants. What, then, R. Judah asked in the name of Rav, is meant by "the mountain fo Gaash"? That the mountain began to quake, and [had it continued], it would have slain them.[17]

In the Days When the Judges Judged

13. "And it came to pass in the days when the judges were judged" (Ruth 1:1).[18] Woe unto the generation that judges its judges, and woe unto the generation whose

1. Tanhuma B, *Ahare*, §14; Yalkut, Josh., §10; Gen. R. 6:9 and 84:11.
2. If by lot, what need for the Urim and Tummim? If by the Urim and Tummim, what need for the lot?
3. Gennesar or Gennesaret, from the Hebrew Kinneret, is a district in Galilee named after the lake of the same name.
4. B. BB 122a.
5. B. Er 22b.
6. Not ten but eleven stipulations will be listed. However, the first two—pasturing cattle and gathering wood—may be deemed to be related.
7. Since Greek hay benefits from the grasses.
8. A provision for the continuing accessibility of water.
9. Even though the whole of it was the possession of Naphtali.
10. Even though feces injure the delicate plant.
11. The seventeenth of Marheshvan. After that day, the seedlings begin to sprout. Walking over them would injure them.
12. Even a high priest who is forbidden under all other circumstances to come into contact with the dead.
13. The owner of the property may not protest.
14. B. BK 80b–81b; Tos BK 8:17.
15. When Joshua's forebear Joseph was blessed, the bullock and the wild ox were mentioned (Deut. 33:17). Gen. R. 39:11.
16. Scripture makes no reference to a period of mourning following Joshua's death.
17. The several comments exploit the meanings implicit in *gaash* ("to quake, rage."). Ruth R. proem 2; B. Shab 105b; Yalkut, Josh., §35; Yalkut, Prov., §959.
18. JV: "And it came to pass in the days when the judges judged."

judges are in need of being judged. When a judge would say, "Remove the toothpick from between your teeth," the man would reply, "Remove the beam from between your eyes."[1]

14. "Slothfulness casteth into a deep sleep, and the soul given to deceiving[2] shall suffer hunger" (Prov. 19:15). At that time, Israel were deceiving the Holy One, many worshiping idols and only a few worshiping the Holy One. Therefore the Holy One starved them of the holy spirit, as is said, "And the word of the Lord was rare in those days" (1 Sam. 3:1).[3]

15. When Israel entered their Land, the members of the Great Sanhedrin, which Moses, Joshua, and Phinehas son of Eleazar had left with Israel, should have bound ropes as strong as iron around their loins, should have rucked up their garments above their knees and gone about to all the towns in Israel, spending one day in Lachish, one day in Hebron, one day in Jerusalem, and so forth in all places in Israel, teaching proper conduct for a year, or two, or even three, until Israel had settled down in their Land, so that the Name of the Holy One would have been hallowed. But they did not do so. Instead, when they entered the Land, each member of the Sanhedrin went to his own vineyard and to his own olive grove, saying, "Ah! It is for the good of my soul!"[4]

16. What parable applies to Israel in the days when the judges ruled? The parable of a mortal king who acquired houses, menservants, and maidservants. He had brought up some of the servants at his table from the time they were six years old, some from the time they were five, some from the time they were four, some from the time they were three, some from the time they were two, some from the time they were one. All of them ate what the king ate; all of them drank what the king drank. After he had brought them up, he built houses for them, planted vines, trees, and shrubs for them, and instructed them: Take care of these shrubs, these vines, these trees. But after they had eaten and drunk, they proceeded to uproot the vines, chop down the trees, hack down the shrubs, and break up the houses. When the king came and found what they had done, he lowered his opinion of them, saying: They are still behaving like schoolchildren. What shall I do with them? He summoned them and flogged them. But they repeated their offense again and again. So also, in the days when the judges ruled, were Israel regarded in the eyes of their Father in heaven: each time they befouled themselves with their deeds, He turned them over to [alien] kingdoms for punishment. When they changed their ways and repented, the Holy One forgave them right away and redeemed them.[5]

17. "Now these are the nations which the Lord left, to try Israel by them" (Judg. 3:1). By what parable may the verse be understood? By the one of a king who planted a vineyard in which there were both cedars and thorns. The king went and cut down the cedars [to make room for vines] but left the thorns. His servants demurred: Our lord king, you left untouched the thorns which catch hold of your garments, but you cut down the cedars! The king replied: Had I cut down the thorns, with what would I have hedged in my vineyard? Likewise, Israel is the Holy One's vineyard, as is said, "The vineyard of the Lord of hosts is the House of Israel" (Isa. 5:7). When He brought them into the Land, He cut down the cedars there, as is said, "I destroyed the Amorite before them, whose height was like the height of cedars" (Amos 2:9). But I left the Amorites' progeny "to try Israel by them," so that Israel would be impelled to keep the Torah.[6]

18. "And the children of Israel again did that which was evil in the sight of the Lord, and served the Baalim, and the Ashtaroth, and the gods of Aram, and the gods of Zidon, and the gods of Moab, and the gods of the children of Ammon, and the gods of the Philistines; and they forsook the Lord, and served Him not" (Judg. 10:6). Since Scripture says, "They forsook the Lord," do I not learn from it that they served Him not? Why then go on to say, "They served Him not"? R. Eleazar explained that the Holy One said: My children responded to Me even less than a lupine, which, when boiled seven times, becomes sweet and is eaten for dessert.[7]

The Prophetess Deborah

19. "Deborah, a prophetess . . . judged Israel" (Judg. 4:4). With regard to this verse, R. Berekhiah had four sayings: Woe unto the living who need help from the dead; woe unto the strong who need help from the weak; woe unto the seeing who need help from the blind; woe unto the generation that has to be led by a woman.[8]

20. "Now Deborah, a prophetess, the wife of Lappidoth, she judged Israel at that time" (Judg. 4:4). What was the special character of Deborah that qualified her to prophesy about Israel and to judge them? Was not Phinehas son of Eleazar still alive at that time? In the school of Elijah it was taught: I call heaven and earth to witness that whether it be a heathen or a Jew, a man or a woman, a manservant or a maidservant, the holy spirit will suffuse any one of them in keeping with the deeds he or she performs.

[What were Deborah's meritorious deeds?] It is said that Deborah's husband was unlettered [in Torah]. So his wife told him; "Come, I will make wicks for you; take them to the Holy Place in Shiloh. Your portion will then

1. Ruth R. 1:1; Yalkut, Ruth, §596. Cf. Matthew 7:5.
2. JV: "the idle." But *remiyyah* ("idle") may also mean "given to deceiving."
3. Ruth R., proem 2; Yalkut, Prov., §959.
4. TdE, ed. Friedmann, p. 56. Or, "Abide in place, O my soul!" In other words: I have discharged my duty—now I am free to attend to my personal affairs. So Leon Nemoy.
5. TdE, ed. Friedmann, p. 55.
6. Yalkut, Judg., §41.
7. After seven boilings, the lupine is sweet; whereas Israel were chastised (boiled) seven times for serving the seven aforementioned deities, and they still remained obdurate. B. Betz 25b.
8. MTeh 22:20; Yalkut, Judg., §42.

be with men of worth in Israel [who will be studying by the light of your wicks], and you will be worthy of life in the world-to-come." She took care to make the wicks thick, so that their light would be ample. He brought these wicks to the Holy Place [in Shiloh]. The Holy One, who examines the hearts and reins of mankind, said to her: Deborah, since you took care to make the light for the study of My Torah ample, I will make the light of your prophecy ample in the presence of Israel's twelve tribes.[1]

21. The point of the words "She sat under the palm tree of Deborah" (Judg. 4:5) is taken to be that, since it is improper for a woman to be alone in a house with a man, Deborah went outside and sat down under a palm tree where she instructed multitudes in Torah.[2]

22. "Barak said unto her: 'If thou will join me, then I will go' " (Judg. 4:8), which, according to R. Nehemiah, means that Barak said to Deborah: If you are willing to join me [in a lesser role] in the song [praising God], I will go with you [as a subordinate] into battle, but if you are unwilling to join me in the song, I will not go with you into battle. "She replied: 'I will certainly go with thee. But desist [from setting conditions]. The glory of the song shall not be thine' " (Judg. 4:9),[3] by which, according to R. Reuben, she meant: "What do you suppose—that [the major role in] the song will be given to you for your glory alone?" As it turned out, "Deborah sang, and [in a lesser role] Barak the son of Abinoam" (Judg. 5:1).[4]

23. Sisera attacked them with forty thousand chiefs of armies, each army numbering one hundred thousand men. He was then thirty years old, and in his might had conquered the entire world—there was no city whose wall he could not cause to collapse with his voice; as for beasts in the field, once he bellowed at them, they were unable to budge from their place.

It is said: Whenever Sisera went down into the brook of Kishon to bathe, he would bring back enough fish entangled in his beard to feel a multitude. His chariot was pulled by nine hundred horses, and the strain in pulling it was so great that not one horse would ever return sound in body.[5]

Jephthah and His Daughter

24. Jephthah was no more lettered than a block of sycamore wood, and because of his ignorance he lost his daughter. When? At the time he fought the children of Ammon, when he vowed, "Whatsoever cometh forth of the doors of my house to meet me . . . I will offer it up for a burnt offering" (Judg. 11:31). The Holy One, provoked by him, said, "Suppose a dog, a pig, or a camel came forth out of his house, would he offer it to Me?" So He had his daughter come forth.

"And it came to pass, when he saw her . . . he moaned: 'Alas, my daughter! . . . I have opened my mouth unto the Lord, and I cannot go back' " (Judg. 11:35). But was not Phinehas there [to absolve him of his vow]?[6] However, Phinehas said: Shall I, high priest son of a high priest, demean myself by calling on an ignoramus? While Jephthah said: Shall I, chief of the tribes of Israel, foremost of its leaders, demean myself by calling on a commoner? Between the two of them, the hapless one perished from the world, and both men were held liable for her blood: Phinehas was deprived of the holy spirit, while Jephthah died by having his limbs drop off one by one. Wherever he went, a limb would drop off from him, and it was buried there on the spot.[7]

As Jephthah was making ready to offer up his daughter, she wept before him and pleaded, "My father, my father, I came out to meet you full of joy, and now you are about to slaughter me. Is it written in the Torah that Israel should offer the lives of their children upon the altar?" Jephthah replied, "My daughter, I made a vow." She answered, "But Jacob our father vowed, 'Of all that Thou shalt give me I will surely give the tenth unto Thee' [Gen. 28:22]. Then, when the Holy One gave him twelve sons, did he perchance offer one of them on an altar to the Holy One? Moreover, Hannah also vowed, 'I will give him unto the Lord all the days of his life' [1 Sam. 1:11]—did she perchance offer her son [on an altar] to the Lord?"

Though she said all these things to him, Jephthah did not heed her, but he went up to the altar and slaughtered her before the Holy One.

At that moment, the Holy Spirit cried out in anguish: Have I ever asked you to offer living souls to Me? "I commanded not, nor spoke it, neither came it into My mind" (Jer. 19:5).[8]

Samson

25. The words "The spirit of the Lord began to ring[9] for him" (Judg. 13:25) imply, so said R. Isaac of the school

1. TdE, ed. Friedmann, p. 48; Yalkut, Judg., §42.
2. TdE, ed. Friedmann, p. 50; Yalkut, Judg., §42.
3. JV: "notwithstanding . . . [it] shall not be for thine honor." But R. Reuben construes *efes* ("notwithstanding") as the Greek *afes* ("let go, desist").
4. Gen. R. 40:4.
5. Yalkut, Judg., §43.
6. A right that was given to priests and sages.
7. With reference to the manner of his death, Scripture says, "Jephthah was dying; he was buried in the cities of Gilead" (Judg. 12:7). Since Scripture does not say, "In a city in Gilead," but, "In the cities of Gilead," the commentator infers that Jephthah's limbs were interred in several cities in Gilead. JV: "was buried in one of the cities of Gilead."
8. Tanhuma, *Be-hukkotai*, §5; Tanhuma B, *Be-hukkotai*, §7; Gen. R. 60:3.
9. JV: "to move." But *p'm* ("to move") may mean "to ring" and also, as in R. Judah's comment below in §27, "to enlarge his stride."

of R. Ammi, that the Presence rang out for him like a bell [so powerful that it overwhelmed him].[1]

26. Or, the meaning may be: "The spirit of the Lord began to ring within him, [giving him such power that he was able to eliminate the distance] between Zorah and Eshtaol" (Judg. 13:25). For, as R. Assi said: Zorah and Eshtaol were two lofty mountains, and Samson plucked them up and ground them one against the other.[2]

27. Likewise, asserting that "The spirit of the Lord began to ring within him between Zorah and Eshtaol" [means that God endowed Samson with great physical strength], R. Samuel bar Nahman said: Like a man who picks up two pebbles and strikes one against the other, so Samson plucked two mountains and slammed them one against the other.

Or, [reading "The spirit of the Lord began to enlarge his stride"], R. Judah maintained that after the Presence rested upon him, Samson could, in a single stride, cover a distance equal to that between Zorah and Eshtaol.[3]

28. "And it came to pass afterward, that he loved a woman in the valley of Sorek, whose name was Delilah" (Judg. 16:4). It is taught that Rabbi [Judah I, the Patriarch] said: Even if her name had not been Delilah, she should have been called Delilah; for she weakened (*dildelah*) his strength, weakened his understanding, and weakened his merits.[4]

29. Samson followed the lust in his eyes; therefore the Philistines gouged out his eyes.[5]

30. It is taught that R. Simeon the Pious said: The width of Samson's shoulders was sixty cubits. For it is said, "Samson lay in bed only till midnight. At midnight he arose, grasped the doors of the gate of the city, and the two posts, and pulled them out, bar and all, and put them upon his shoulders" (Judg. 16:3); and we have a tradition that the width of the two doors in the gate of Gaza was not less than sixty cubits.[6]

31. [Of those that were slain by Samson in Gaza], "there were upon the roof about three thousand" (Judg. 16:27). Such was the number on the edge of the roof, but no one knows how many crowded behind those on the edge, and how many there were crowded behind these.[7]

32. "And Samson called unto the Lord, and said: 'O Lord God, remember me, I pray Thee, and strengthen me, I pray Thee, only this once' " (Judg. 16:28). Samson pleaded with the Holy One: Master of the universe, remember on my behalf the twenty-two years I judged Israel and never presumed to say to anyone, "Carry my staff from here to there."[8]

Micah's Idol

33. "Why hast Thou done evil to this people?" (Exod. 5:22). In speaking thus to God, Moses charged Him: It is You who have done evil to this people, for now, whenever there are not enough bricks, the Egyptians immure Israelite children into the structure [in place of bricks]. The Holy One replied: The Egyptians are merely weeding out thorns, for it is revealed to Me that had such children remained alive, they would have grown up utterly wicked. If you wish to test what I say, take out one of these children. Moses took out Micah. In fact, the name Micah, "the crushed one," was given him precisely because he was crushed (*nitmaknek*) when he was immured into the structure.[9]

34. "Now there was a man of the hill-country of Ephraim, whose name was Micah. . . . And the man Micah had a house of god, and he made an ephod, and teraphim" (Judg. 17:1 and 17:5). Micah's idol was in the days of Cushan-rishathaim,[10] as was the incident with the concubine in Gibeah.[11]

35. The verse "And he passed over the sea with what was to be such a source of distress that it stirred up waves in the sea" (Zech. 10:11)[12] alludes, so said R. Yohanan, to Micah, who stirred up the Red Sea with his idol.[13]

36. It is taught that R. Nathan said: It is three *mil* from Gareb[14] to Shiloh, close enough for the smoke from [God's] altar in Shiloh and the smoke from Micah's idol [in Gareb] to mingle with each other. When the ministering angels wished to do away with Micah, the Holy One said, "Let

---

1. B. Sot 9b. The problem that R. Isaac deals with in §25, and R. Assi, R. Samuel bar Nahman, and R. Judah in §26 and §27, is the role "the spirit of the Lord" played in the life of Samson. For Samson, it could not have been what it had been for the prophets of Israel, since after it had "moved him," instead of saying something significant, he took unto himself a Philistine girl; or, as later on, displayed great prowess. Hence, R. Isaac suggests that Samson's taking a Philistine girl, quite a departure from the pattern of a Nazirite, came about as a result of God's overwhelming Samson. R. Assi (in §26), R. Samuel bar Nahman, and R. Judah (in §27) understand "the spirit of the Lord" in Samson as endowing him with extraordinary physical strength.
2. B. Sot 9b.
3. Two kilometers. Lev. R. 8:2.
4. B. Sot 9b.
5. Ibid.
6. B. Sot 10a.
7. Gen. R. 98:17–18.
8. B. Sot 10a.
9. Rashi on B. Sanh 101b, using an aggadic source.
10. First of the kings of the area who oppressed Israel. See Judg. 3:8–11.
11. The commentator places Micah at the beginning of Israel's occupation of the Land, even though both the account concerning him and the account concerning the concubine in Gibeah occur at the end of Judg. 18 and 19. SOR 12; Yalkut, Judg., §41.
12. JV: "And over the sea affliction shall pass, and the waves shall be smitten in the sea."
13. Thus Micah had already made an idol for himself in Egypt. B. Sanh 103b.
14. The town where Micah's idol was set up.

him be, since his bread is available to wayfarers." On the other hand, because of Micah's idol in Gareb, [which his neighbors permitted], the [death] penalty was visited upon many men of Israel who fought the tribe of Benjamin to avenge the concubine in Gibeah.[1] The Holy One said to the men of Israel, "For My honor, [tarnished by Micah's idol], you put up no fight, but for a woman's honor, you did."[2]

37. "The children of Dan set up for themselves the graven image; and Jonathan, the son of Gershom, the son of Manasseh, he and his sons were priests to the tribe of the Danites" (Judg. 18:30). But was Gershom the son of Manasseh? Was he not, in fact, a son of Moses, as is said, "The sons of Moses: Gershom, and Eliezer. The sons of Gershom: Shebuel" (1 Chron. 23:15–16), the latter [alias Jonathan] being further identified elsewhere as "Shebuel the son of Gershom, the son of Moses" (1 Chron. 26:24)? However, because he acted [wickedly] like [King] Manasseh,[3] Scripture assigned his ancestry to Manasseh. Still, the letter *nun* in Manasseh is suspended above the line, indicating that, if deserving, he will be spoken of as a descendant of Moses; if undeserving, as a descendant of Manasseh.[4]

R. Eleazar said: One should always take care to intermarry with virtuous people, for out of Moses, who married Jethro's[5] daughter, there issued Jonathan.[6]

38. The sages asked R. Samuel bar Nahman: How is it that Jonathan, although a priest for idolatry, had such a long life? He replied: Because Jonathan made a mockery out of his idol. Thus, when a man came to offer a bullock, a lamb, or a goat to his idol, saying, "Draw its favor upon me," Jonathan would reply, "How can this thing help you? It cannot see, hear, or speak; it can do neither good nor harm." The man asked, "As you live, what am I to do?" Jonathan replied, "Go and bring me a bowl of fine flour, add ten eggs, and set the repast before it. It will eat all that is brought, and I will draw its favor upon you." After the man [did so, and] left, Jonathan himself ate up every bit of the offering.

Once an impudent fellow came, and when Jonathan said the same thing to him, he asked, "If the idol gives no help at all, what are you doing here?" Jonathan answered, "Making my living."

[When the Danites reached the house of Micah, they recognized Jonathan as a Levite, so "they asked him]: 'Who brought thee hither? and what doest thou in this place? and what hast thou here?' " (Judg. 18:3). By these inquiries, the Danites meant: Are you not a descendant of Moses? Yet now you act as a priest to an idol? He replied, "I have a tradition from my grandfather's house that a man should hire himself out to officiate at idol-worship rather than be dependent on fellow mortals." (He supposed that in the tradition referred to, *avodah zarah* meant idol-worship. But in fact, such was not the tradition's meaning—it meant work that was strange, uncongenial.)[7]

In later years, when David perceived that Moses' grandson had an exceptional appreciation for money, he appointed him over the treasuries, as is said, "Shebuel, the son of Gershom, the son of Moses, was chief officer in charge of the treasuries" (1 Chron. 26:24). But was his name Shebuel? Was it not Jonathan? However, as R. Yohanan explained, the name Shebuel [Hebrew: Shevuel] means that he returned to God (*shav la-el*) with all his heart.[8]

The Scroll of Ruth

39. "And it came to pass (*va-yehi*) in the days when the judges judged" (Ruth 1:1). In the name of R. Hiyya and R. Eleazar, it is reported: We brought the following rule in exegesis from the Babylonian exile: Wherever the word *va-yehi* occurs, there is woe.[9]

In the verse "And it came to pass (*va-yehi*) in the days when the judges judged," what woe is implied? "There was (*va-yehi*) a famine in the Land" (Ruth 1:1). But why does the word *va-yehi* occur twice in this verse? Once to intimate the famine for bread, and again to intimate the famine for Torah. [The word is repeated] to teach that when a generation is not possessed of Torah, it will find itself possessed of famine.[10]

40. "And a certain man of Bethlehem in Judah went . . . and the name of the man was Elimelech" [Hebrew: Elimelekh] (Ruth 1:1–2). He used to say, "To me (*eli*) shall kingship (*melekh;* read *malkhut*) come." "And the name of his wife was Naomi" (ibid.), her actions being comely and sweet (*neimim*); "and the name of the two sons Mahlon and Chilion" (ibid.), Mahlon, because he was blotted out (*nimmah*) from the world; and Chilion, because he perished (*kalah*) from the world.[11]

41. "And a certain man of Bethlehem in Judah went . . . and the name of the man was Elimelech" (Ruth 1:1–2). Why was Elimelech punished? Because he caused the hearts of Israel to fall [into despair]. Elimelech may be compared to a magnate who lived in a certain province. The people of that province, depending on him, used to say, "Should years of drought come, he could supply the entire province with food for ten years." However, when a year of drought did come, his maidservant went walking

---

1. In the initial battles, the men of Israel lost forty thousand of their number. See Judg. 20:21 and 20:25.
2. B. Sanh 103b.
3. Hezekiah's son, one of Judah's most wicked kings.
4. In Hebrew, Menasheh with the letter *nun;* without it, Mosheh.
5. The rabbis are divided in their judgment of Jethro. Some, as R. Eleazar, regard him as an idolatrous priest of Midian; others as a true proselyte.
6. An idolatrous priest for the tribe of Dan. B. BB 109b; P. Ber 9:3, 13d.
7. *Avodah zarah* may mean either "strange worship" or "strange, uncongenial work."
8. P. Ber 9:3, 13d; B. BB 110a; Yalkut, Judg., §73.
9. Play on the syllable *va[y]* in *va-yehi; vay* in Aramaic means "woe."
10. Ruth R., proem 7; Yalkut, Ruth, §596.
11. Ruth R. 2:5; Yalkut, Ruth, §600.

about the marketplace with her [empty] basket in her hand. The people of the province said, "He on whom we depended in the event of a drought to feed the entire province for ten years—look! There in the marketplace stands his maidservant, basket in hand—empty! So with Elimelech. He was one of the notables of the realm, one of the sustainers of the generation. Still, when the years of famine came, he said to himself: Now all of Israel will come knocking at my door [begging for food], one with a large basket, and another with a small basket. So he got up and ran away from them.[1]

42. "They came into the fields of Moab, and chose to remain there" (Ruth 1:2). At first they came to country towns, where they found a scarcity of water; then they went to large cities, but found the inhabitants utterly dissolute. So they returned to the country towns: "They came into the fields of Moab, and chose to remain there."[2]

43. "And they took them wives of the daughters of Moab; the name of the one was Orpah, and the name of the other Ruth" (Ruth 1:4). Orpah, because she turned her back (*oref*) on her mother-in-law;[3] and Ruth, because she understood (*raatah*) her mother-in-law's true wish.

Ruth and Orpah, so said R. Bebai in the name of R. Reuben, were the daughters of Eglon [king of Moab],[4] to whom the Holy One said: Rising from your throne in deference to me (Judg. 3:20), you accorded Me honor. As you live, I shall cause to rise out of you a son whom I will seat on My throne.[5]

44. "And Elimelech . . . died . . . and Mahlon and Chilion died both of them" (Ruth 1:3 and 1:5). It is taught: The Master of Mercy [in His exercise of justice] puts off taking human life. Thus, their horses died first, then their asses, then their camels; after that, "Elimelech died," and after that, "Mahlon and Chilion died, both of them."

"And the woman was left" (Ruth 1:5), left, said R. Hanina, as the leavings of a meal offering.[6]

45. "And she went forth out of the place" (Ruth 1:7). Was she the only one who went forth from the place? Did not many cameleers go forth? Did not many ass drivers go forth? However, as R. Azariah explained in the name of R. Judah bar Simon, the notable of a city is its radiance, its splendor, its adornment, its renown. When he departs, its radiance departs, its splendor departs, its adornment departs, and its renown departs.[7]

46. "And she went forth out of the place . . . and her two daughters-in-law with her, and they walked on the way" (Ruth 1:7)—walking was agonizing for them: being unshod, their bare feet were lacerated by the hard ground.[8]

47. "And Naomi said: 'Turn back, my daughters.' . . . And Ruth said: 'Entreat me not to leave thee, and return from following after thee' " (Ruth 1:11 and 1:16), for in any event, I intend to be converted, but I prefer that it come about through you and not through another. When Naomi heard this, she began to set forth the rules for conversion, saying also, "My child, it is not the practice for daughters of Israel to go to the theaters and circuses of the heathen."[9] Ruth replied, "Whither thou goest, I will go" (Ruth 1:16). Naomi continued, "It is not the practice for daughters of Israel to dwell in a house that has no mezuzah." Ruth replied, "Where thou lodgest, I will lodge; thy people shall be my people, and thy God my God" (ibid.).[10]

48. "So they two went. . . . And it came to pass, when they were come to Bethlehem" (Ruth 1:19). That day Boaz's wife died, and all Israel assembled to give her a loving farewell. Just then Ruth came with Naomi—as Boaz's wife was taken out, Naomi came in, and "all the city was astir concerning them, and the women said: 'Is this Naomi?' [ibid.]—the one whose appearance used to be so comely, so attractive. At one time she used to be carried about in a palanquin, and now she walks barefoot. At one time she wore garments of fine wool, and now she is covered with rags. At one time her face was ruddy from food and drink, and now her face is a sickly green from hunger." Naomi replied, "Call me not Naomi,[11] call me Marah"[12] (Ruth 1:20).

49. "Then said Boaz . . . :'Whose damsel is this?' " (Ruth 2:5). Did he not recognize her? Yes, but noticing how sweet she was and how demure her conduct, he was moved to inquire about her. All the other women bent down to gather ears of corn, while she sat down to gather them; all the other women hitched up their skirts, while she kept hers down; all the other women bantered with the reapers, while she was reserved—"she sat apart from the reapers" (Ruth 2:14), not in their midst. All the other women gathered from between the sheaves, while she gathered only what was already abandoned—two sheaves, not three.[13]

50. "Then she said: 'Let me find favor in thy sight, my lord . . . though I be not as one of thy handmaidens' " (Ruth 2:13). Boaz replied, "God forbid! You are not as one of the handmaidens (*amahot*) but as one of the matriarchs (*immahot*)."[14]

---

1. Ruth R. 1:4; Yalkut, Ruth, §598.
2. Ruth R. 2:6; Yalkut, Ruth, §600.
3. She left Naomi, after Naomi's plea that she do so.
4. Judg. 3:12.
5. Ruth R. 2:4; Yalkut, Judg., §42.
6. These are of no value whatever, even as Naomi came to feel about herself following her husband's and sons' deaths. Ruth R. 2:10
7. Ruth R. 2:12.
8. Ibid; Yalkut, Ruth, §601.
9. These had a reputation for lewdness.
10. Ruth R. 2:22; Yalkut, Ruth, §601.
11. Pleasant.
12. Bitter. Ruth R. 3:6; Yalkut, Ruth, §601.
13. Two sheaves are deemed "forgotten," that is, belong to the poor (see Pe 6:5). Ruth R. 4:6 (in printed eds., as opposed to medieval manuscripts, 4:9); Yalkut, Ruth, §601.
14. Ruth R. 5:5; Yalkut, Ruth, §603.

51. R. Yohanan said: Why was she called Ruth [the one who fills to overflowing]? Because such was her merit that from her was to issue David, who filled to overflowing (*rvh*) the Holy One with songs and hymns.[1]

52. R. Ze'era said: The Scroll of Ruth tells us nothing of the laws of cleanness or uncleanness, of what is prohibited or what is permitted. Why then was it written? To teach you how great is the reward of those who do deeds of kindness.[2]

Elkanah and Hannah

53. Elkanah used to make a pilgrimage to Shiloh four times a year—three times as required by Scripture and one time in fulfillment of what he required of himself on his own. Elkanah went up together with his wife, his sons, his daughters, his brothers, his sisters, and his kin.

When Elkanah and his retinue were on the way, they would lodge in the broad place of a city. As a result, the city was astir as people kept asking, "Where are you bound?" Elkanah and his kin would reply, "To the house of God in Shiloh, whence Torah and commandments come. Why don't you come with us? We'll all go together." At that, tears came to the eyes of the questioners, and they said, "Indeed we will go with you." So [one year] five families went up; the year after, ten; and the year after that, the entire city was astir, set on going up to Shiloh.

Moreover, the way Elkanah would go one year he would not go the following year, but he would go another way instead. Thus, Elkanah kept bringing up more and more Israelites with him, until all of them began to go up. As a result, the Holy One said to him: Elkanah, you tipped the balance on the scales in Israel's favor and trained them in the observance of the commandments, so that many people earned merit because of you. Therefore I will have a son issue from you who will likewise tip the balance on the scales in Israel's favor and train them in the observance of commandments, so that many will grow in merit through him.[3]

54. "And her rival vexed her sore" (1 Sam. 1:6). Peninnah would vex Hannah [who was childless] with one annoying taunt after another. What would Peninnah say to her? "Did you get a scarf for your older son and an undergarment for your second son?" Then, too, Peninnah would get up early—so said R. Nahman bar Abba—and say to Hannah, "Why don't you rouse yourself and wash your children's faces, so that they will be fit to go to school?" At twelve o'clock,[4] she would say, "Hannah, why don't you rouse yourself and welcome your children who are about to return from school?"

R. Tanhuma bar Abba said: When they sat down to eat, Elkanah would give each of his children his proper portion. Intending to vex Hannah, Peninnah would say to Elkanah, "Give this son of mine his portion and that son of mine his portion. You have given no portion to this [unborn] one."[5] Why did Peninnah speak this way? "To make her fret (*hrmh*)" (1 Sam. 1:6) against God [for making her barren].

In another comment, the word *hrmh* is interpreted not "to make her fret" but "to make her thunder" against God in prayer on her own behalf. The Holy One said to Peninnah, "You make her 'thunder' against Me. As you live, there are no thunders that are not followed by rain. I shall remember her at once."[6]

55. "O Lord of Tzevaot ['hosts'], if Thou wilt but look on the affliction of Thy handmaid!" (1 Sam. 1:11). R. Eleazar said: From the day the Holy One created His world, there was no one who called the Holy One [Lord of] Tzevaot ("hosts") until Hannah came and called Him [Lord of] Tzevaot—for she spoke up to the Holy One: Master of the universe, out of all the hosts of hosts that You created in Your world, is it so difficult for You to give me just one son? By what parable may Hannah's petition be illustrated? By the one of a king of flesh and blood who made a feast for his servants. A poor man came and, standing by the doorway, begged them, "Give me a morsel of bread," but no one heeded him. So he forced his way into the presence of the king and said, "My lord king, out of the entire feast you have made, it is so difficult in your sight to give me one morsel of bread?"

Another comment: Hannah used to go up to the Sanctuary on festal pilgrimages, and when she observed all Israel gathered there, she would say to the Holy One: Master of the universe, You have all these hosts, but among them not even one is mine.[7]

56. "Now Hannah, she spoke about[8] her heart" (1 Sam. 1:13), about matters, so said R. Eleazar in the name of R. Yose ben Zimra, that were in her heart.[9] She spoke right up to the Holy One: Master of the universe, of all that You created in woman, there is not one part without its purpose—eyes to see, ears to hear, a nose to smell, a mouth to speak, hands to work with, legs to walk with, breasts to give suck. The breasts You placed over my heart—what are they for? Are they not to give suck? Give me a son, that I may give him suck with them.[10]

57. "For *this* child I prayed" (1 Sam. 1:27). [The significance of "this" will be explained in what follows: The child] Samuel presumed to give a decision in the presence of his teacher, as implied in "When a bullock was about to be slaughtered, the child was brought to Eli" (1 Sam. 1:25). Just because a bullock was about to be slaughtered, they brought the child to Eli? [No. Rather] the bullock

---

1. B. Ber 7b; Yalkut, Prov., §964, end.
2. Ruth R. 2:14.
3. TdE (8) 9 (ed. Friedmann, pp. 47–48; JPS, pp. 149–50); Yalkut, 1 Sam., §377.
4. Literally, "the sixth hour."
5. Pointing to Hannah's barren belly.
6. PR 43:8 (YJS 2:768); Midrash Sam. 5; Yalkut, 1 Sam., §77.
7. B. Ber 31b; PR 43:3 (YJS 2:757).
8. JV: "in." The use of *al* in the sense of "on, of, about" is exceptional.
9. In Hebrew, the word for "heart" also means "chest," thus allowing for Hannah's disquisition that follows.
10. B. Ber 31b.

was brought to be offered up. Eli said, "Call a priest, and have him come and slaughter it properly."[1] When the child Samuel saw the people look for a priest to do the slaughtering, he said, "Why do you go about looking for a priest? A commoner's slaughtering is just as valid."

At that, [the child] Samuel was brought before Eli, who asked, "Where did you get such a decision?" Samuel replied, "Does Scripture say, 'The priest shall slaughter'? All that it says is, 'The priests shall present [the blood]' [Lev. 1:5], that is, the priest's obligation begins with receiving the blood. Hence, proper slaughtering may be performed by a commoner." Eli said, "You have reasoned well. But you presumed to give a decision in the presence of your teacher, and one who presumes to give a decision in the presence of his teacher is liable to the death penalty." Hannah immediately appeared and cried out in anguish, "I am the woman that stood by thee here" (1 Sam. 1:26). Eli replied, "Let me be, that I may condemn him to death. Afterward, I will invoke God's mercy in your behalf, and He will give you a son better than this one." But she said to him, "For *this* child I prayed."[2]

The Sons of Eli

58. "Now the sons of Eli were base men; they knew not the Lord. . . . Yea, before the fat was made to smoke, the priest's servant came with a three-pronged fork . . . and whatever the fork brought up, the priest would take away for himself" (1 Sam. 2:12–15). R. Simeon ben Yohai taught that the Holy One said to the sons of Eli: Why do you devour the remnants of the meal offering and leave to the flies the handful [that should be burned on the altar]? Why do you devour the flesh of offerings and leave its pieces of fat lying about in the sun?

What did Israel keep saying to the priest? "Let the priest sprinkle the blood, make the pieces of fat go up in smoke on the altar, and only then consume the flesh of the offering." What did the priest, [the son of Eli] say in reply? "The blood I will not sprinkle, the fat I will not make go up in smoke. [Why make such a fuss!] 'Give the priest flesh to roast . . . or else I will take it by force' " (1 Sam. 2:15–16).

Hence, in summing up the story, Scripture says, "The sons of Eli were men without a yoke[3] (*beli-yaal*)" (1 Sam. 2:12), that is, men who cast off from themselves the yoke (*ol*) of Heaven. "They knew not the Lord" (ibid.)—they said, "There is no [divine] kingship in heaven."[4]

Samuel

59. "Before the lamp of God had gone out, Samuel was laid down to sleep" (1 Sam. 3:3). R. Hiyya bar Abba said in the name of R. Yohanan: No righteous man ever departs from the world before a righteous man like him is brought into being: "A sun ariseth, even as another sun goeth down" (Eccles. 1:5). Thus, even before the sun of Eli set, the sun of Samuel the Ramathite began to shine.[5]

60. "Samuel was laid down"—like a lamb[6]—said R. Yohanan, without a blemish.[7]

61. We find that Moses and Samuel are regarded as equal in worth, as implied in the verse "Moses and Aaron among His priests; Samuel among them that call upon His Name" (Ps. 99:6). Pause to consider the difference between Moses and Samuel: Moses had to enter the Tabernacle and thereby come to the Holy One in order to hear the Divine Word; whereas the Holy One would come to Samuel, as is said, "The Lord came and stood" (1 Sam. 3:10). Why the difference? Because, the Holy One says, "I deal with every man in keeping with justice and equity." Moses used to sit in his place, and whoever had a case in law would come to him and have it judged, as is said, "And Moses sat to judge the people" (Exod. 18:13). But Samuel wearied himself going around from place to place to act as judge, so that people would not be put to the trouble of coming to him, as is said, "And he made the rounds from year to year" (1 Sam. 7:16).

Hence the Holy One said: Let Moses, who sits in one place to judge Israel, come to Me to the Tent of Meeting, to hear the Divine Word. But Samuel, who goes about to Israel in their many settlements to act as judge on their behalf—to him I will go and speak, in keeping with the verse "A just balance and scales is the Lord's" (Prov. 16:11).[8]

62. Samuel was regarded as equal to Moses and Aaron together, as is said, "Moses and Aaron among His priests; Samuel among them that call upon His Name" (Ps. 99:6).[9]

62a. [10] "And they answered them, and said, He is; behold, He is before thee" (1 Sam. 9:12). According to R. Yudan, who cited R. Mari bar Jacob, [when Saul and his servant asked some young women where Samuel could be found, and the young women in their reply finished by saying, "He is before thee," they meant that Samuel could be found where God in the cloud was conversing with him]. "Do you not see," they asked, "the cloud that always hovers about Samuel's courtyard?"[11]

The Destruction of Shiloh

63. "And the Philistines fought, and Israel was smitten. . . . And the Ark of God was taken. . . . And there

1. Perform *shehitah* (ritual slaughter).
2. B. Ber 31b; Yalkut, 1 Sam., §80.
3. JV: "base men."
4. Yalkut, 1 Sam., §86; Midrash Sam. 6:11.
5. B. Yoma 38b.
6. Here there may be a play on the words *shkv* ("laid down,") and, by metathesis, *kvs* ("lamb").
7. Yalkut, 1 Sam., §97.
8. Exod. R. 16:4
9. Num. R. 18:8.
10. Transposed by the translator from §72 below in this chapter.
11. Yalkut, 1 Sam., §108.

ran a man of Benjamin out of the army, and came to Shiloh the same day" (1 Sam. 4:10–12). The man of Benjamin was Saul, who, according to R. Levi, ran sixty *mil* that day. He was in the front lines, but when he heard that the Tablets had been captured, he went, snatched them from Goliath, and came [to Eli].[1]

64. "And it came to pass when the Benjamite made mention of the Ark of God, [Eli] fell . . . backward . . . and his neck broke" (1 Sam. 4:18). R. Joshua bar Nehemiah said: Neither five [iron] claws nor five [iron] styli[2] killed Eli, but at the news that the Ark was captured, his neck broke asunder.[3]

65. "Now the Philistines had taken the Ark of God . . . and brought it into the house of Dagon, and set it by Dagon" (1 Sam. 5:1–2). The Philistines, so stated R. Yohanan, honored the Ark, saying, "This one is a god, and the other [Dagon] is a god. Let this god come and abide with the other god." Resh Lakish argued, "If that were so, would the Philistines' reward have been so humiliating? In fact, what they actually said was, 'This one is the vanquished, while the other [Dagon] is the victor. Let the vanquished one come and serve the victorious one.' But the Holy One said, '[just for this], you will be scalded not by tepid water but by furiously boiling water.'[4] Hence, 'when they arose early the next morning, behold, Dagon was fallen upon his face. . . . And the head of Dagon and both the palms of his hands lay cut off upon the threshold' " (1 Sam. 5:4).[5]

66. "But the hand of the Lord was heavy upon them of Ashdod, and He destroyed them, and smote them with mice" (1 Sam. 5:6). [Deluding themselves], the wicked men of Ashdod said, " 'So this is the God who smote the Egyptians!' [1 Sam. 4:8] He had ten plagues, but they have been used up." The Holy One replied, "Do you suppose I have no other plague left? I will bring a plague upon you, the like of which has not been in the world—mice that will pull out your innards [when you sit down to ease yourselves]." Even when the men of Ashdod, in an attempt to protect themselves, made copper vessels on which to sit, a mouse would say to the vessel, "We are the emissaries of Him who spoke and the world came into being, and you are one of His creatures. Give honor to Him who created you." Then the vessel would split open of itself, and the mouse would leap up out of the deep and pull out the man's innards.

This is one of the instances when God endowed the frail with mastery over the strong.[6]

67. It is said in the name of R. Abba: Why were the people of Beth-shemesh smitten?[7] Because they behaved disrespectfully toward the Ark, so that the Holy One was constrained to say: If a hen belonging to one of the people of Beth-shemesh had been lost, would not its owner have gone around to many doorways to recover it? Yet My Ark has been seven months in the country of the Philistines, and not one of you gave it any heed. Since you are not giving it any heed, it is for Me to give heed to it. [God's bestirring Himself for the Ark is set forth in the verse] "His right hand and His holy arm hath wrought deliverance for Him" (Ps. 98:1).[8]

68. "And the heifers took the straight way (*va-yisharnah*) by the way to Beth-shemesh" (1 Sam. 6:12). What is the dual significance of *va-yisharnah?* Rav said: The heifers directed (*yashar*) their visages toward the Ark and uttered a song (*shirah*). What song did they utter? R. Isaac Nappaha said:

> Sing, sing, O [Ark of] acacia!
> Exult in all your radiance,
> You who are overlaid with woven gold,
> Extolled in God's holiest place,
> Made resplendent with delicate traceries,
> Sheltered between the wings of cherubim.

R. Samuel bar Nahman said: How much toil did [Moses] the son of Amram expend until he had taught song to the Levites! Yet you, on your own, utter song. All strength (*yeyasher*) to you.[9]

The Sons of Samuel

69. "And it came to pass when Samuel was old . . . his sons walked not in his ways, but turned aside for lucre" (1 Sam. 8:1 and 8:3)—they did not follow the pattern set by their father. The righteous Samuel used to travel throughout Israel's habitations, dispensing justice for them in the cities they dwelled in: "And he made the rounds from year to year of Bethel, and Gilgal, and Mizpah; and judged Israel in all those places" (1 Sam. 7:16). His sons, however, did not do so—they remained in their towns, in order to provide lucrative income for their beadles and scribes.[10]

70. The words "they turned aside for lucre" mean, according to R. Meir, that the sons of Samuel asked outright for the portions due them [as Levites];[11] or, according to R. Judah, that they forced people to sell the excess produce for them; or, according to R. Akiva, that they extorted an extra basket of tithe beyond what they were entitled to;

1. Midrash Sam. 11; Yalkut, 1 Sam., §102.
2. Clawing and penetrating attachments to weapons of war.
3. Midrash Sam. 11.
4. I thought you would understand a slight hint, but apparently you require a more unambiguous assertion.
5. Midrash Sam. 10.
6. MTeh 78:11 (YJS 2:30); Yalkut, 1 Kings, §222.
7. See 1 Sam. 6:19.
8. The only instance in Scripture where it is said that God came to His own aid. Gen. R. 54:4.
9. B. AZ 24b; Gen. R. 54:4; Yalkut, 1 Sam., §103.
10. The beadles were sent to summon litigants, and the scribes recorded the proceedings. B. Shab 56a.
11. Because of their importance, they received what they demanded, thus depriving Levites of humbler status, indeed reducing them to near starvation. But they were not guilty of perversion of justice.

or, according to R. Yose, that they extorted additional sacred gifts.[1]

King Saul

71. Why did Saul merit kingship? Because of his humility. He said on one occasion: "Lest my father cease caring for the asses, and become anxious concerning *us*" (1 Sam. 9:5), thus making the servant to whom he was speaking equal to himself in his father's affection. And again, when Saul sought to evade kingship, what did God say of him? "Behold, he hath hid himself among the baggage" (1 Sam. 10:22).[2]

72. [This section is transposed to §62a, above in this chapter.]

73. "As soon as ye are come into the city, ye shall straightway find him, before he go up to the high place to eat; for the people will not eat until he come, because he doth bless the sacrifice; and afterward they eat that are bidden. Now therefore get you up; for at this time ye shall find him" (1 Sam. 9:13). Why did the maidens talk at such great length? Because women are fond of talking, said Rav. Because, said Samuel, they wanted to gaze at the beauty of Saul, of whom it is written, "From his shoulders and upward he was higher than any of the people" (1 Sam. 9:2). But R. Yohanan said: The maidens had to talk at such length [to detain Saul], because one reign may not overlap another even by as little as a hairbreadth.[3]

74. "Then Saul drew near . . . and said: 'Tell me, I pray thee, where the seer's house is.' And Samuel answered . . . : 'I am the seer' " (1 Sam. 9:18–19). The Holy One then said to Samuel, "So you are the seer, are you? As you live, I will make you see that you are not much of a seer." When did He make Samuel see it? When He said to him, "Fill thy horn with oil. . . . And it came to pass, when [the sons of Jesse] were come, that he beheld Eliab, and said: 'Surely the Lord's anointed is before Him.' But the Lord said unto Samuel: 'Look not on his countenance . . . for it is not as man seeth' " (1 Sam. 16:1 and 16:6–7).[4]

75. When the Holy One said to Saul, "Now go and smite Amalek" (1 Sam 15:3), Saul said to himself: If at the death of a single person, the Torah ordains, "Bring a heifer whose neck is to be broken,"[5] how many more and more such heifers would have to be brought for the death of so many! In any event, even if a human being has sinned, what sin has the animal committed? And if grownups have sinned, what sin did the little ones commit? A divine voice came forth and said, "Be not righteous overmuch" (Eccles. 7:16). Subsequently, after Saul had said to Doeg, "Turn thou and fall upon the priests" (1 Sam. 22:18), another divine voice came forth and said to him, "Be not overmuch wicked" (Eccles. 7:17).

Because brazenness dwelled in King Saul, he was slain and his royal line was extirpated. Thus, when Samuel asked him, "Wherefore then didst thou not hearken to the voice of the Lord?" (1 Sam. 15:19), Saul answered brazenly, "Yea, I have hearkened to the voice of the Lord" (1 Sam. 15:20). Saul was all the more at fault! For thereafter, because of David, he nursed hostility and vengefulness in his heart against Israel wherever they dwelled.[6]

76. "Seek me a woman that divineth by a ghost, that I may go to her, and inquire of her" (1 Sam. 28:7). In speaking thus, to whom may Saul be likened? To a king, said Resh Lakish, who entered a province and issued a decree that all the cocks in it should be slaughtered. The next night he decided to depart early in the morning, so he inquired; "Is there a cock here that will crow at dawn?" At that, he was asked "Are you not the one who issued a decree that all cocks in this province be slaughtered?" So, too, Saul first removed from the Land all who divined by ghosts or familiar spirits, then he turned around and said, "Seek me a woman that divineth by a ghost."

"And Saul disguised himself, and put on other raiment" (1 Sam. 28:8), a commoner's raiment. "And went, and two men with him" (ibid.)—Abner and Amasa. "And they came to the woman by night" (ibid). But was it night?[7] No, but "at night" intimates that the hour was as gloomy for them as night.

"And Saul swore to her by the Lord" (1 Sam. 28:10). To whom may Saul at that time be compared? To a woman, said Resh Lakish, who while in the company of her lover, swears by the life of her husband. So, too, Saul, while inquiring of a diviner by a ghost and a familiar spirit, said, "As the Lord liveth, there shall no punishment happen to thee for this thing" (ibid.).[8]

77. "Then said the woman: 'Whom shall I bring up unto thee?' And he said: 'Bring me up Samuel' " (1 Sam. 28:11). The woman did what she had to, and said what she had to, and brought up Samuel. "And Samuel said to Saul: 'Why hast thou disquieted me?' And Saul answered: 'I am sore distressed . . . and God is departed from me, and answereth me no more, neither by prophets, nor by dreams' " (1 Sam. 28:15). But why did Saul not also say, "Nor by the Urim and Tummim"?[9] "The heart knoweth its own bitterness" (Prov. 14:10), said R. Isaac son of R.

---

1. Either the priestly dues—the shoulder, cheeks, and maw of animals—though the sons of Samuel were not priests; or the Levitical dues—the first tithes. The sin of the sons of Samuel was that they used force. Tithes were to be given voluntarily, not collected.
2. Tos Ber 4:18.
3. B. Ber 48b.
4. Sif Deut., §17; Midrash Sam. 14.
5. See Deut. 21.
6. Yalkut, 1 Sam., §120; TdE, ed. Friedmann, p. 159. He charged that even the Benjamites—his own tribe—were all conspiring against him (1 Sam. 22:7–8). For a different view of Saul, see MTeh 7:2 (YJS 1:101–3).
7. Saul's disguise would have been unnecessary at night. *Mattenot Kehunnah*, ad loc.
8. Lev. R. 26:4; Tanhuma, *Emor*, §2.
9. Since Saul did inquire of them and received no answer. See 1 Sam. 28:6.

Hiyya: Had Saul mentioned the Urim and Tummim,[1] Samuel might have said to him: Are you not the one who brought it upon yourself? Are you not the one who smote Nob, the city of priests [including Ahimelech, the high priest]?[2]

"Then Saul fell straightway his full length upon the earth, and was sore afraid, because of the words of Samuel" (1 Sam. 28:20). When Abner and Amasa asked, "What did Samuel say to you?" he replied [untruthfully], "He said, 'Tomorrow when you go down to battle you will be victorious. More! Your sons will be appointed to high office.' "

Then Saul took his three sons, and they went forth to war. At that very moment, said Resh Lakish, the Holy One summoned the ministering angels and said to them: Come and behold the extraordinary being I created in My world! Ordinarily, even a man going to a feast will not take his sons with him, because of the evil eye. But this man is going forth to war and, though he knows that he will be slain, takes his sons with him, facing cheerfully the measure of justice that is sure to strike him.[3]

The Death of Saul

78. R. Joshua of Sikhnin said in the name of R. Levi: The Holy One showed Moses every generation and its judges, every generation and its kings, every generation and its sages, every generation and its leaders, every generation and its teachers of Mishnah, every generation and its officers, every generation and its communal heads, every generation and its extortionists, every generation and its brigands, every generation and its prophets. When He showed him Saul and his sons falling by the sword, Moses spoke up: Shall the first king raised over Your children be pierced by the sword? The Holy One answered: Why are you speaking of this matter to Me? Speak to the priests whom he ordered slain. They are now acting as accusers against him. "And the Lord said unto Moses: 'Speak unto the priests' " (Lev. 21:1).[4]

79. R. Judah said in the name of Rav: Why was Saul punished? Because he waived the honor due him, as when "certain base fellows said: 'How shall this one save us?' And they despised him. . . . But he held his peace" (1 Sam. 10:27).[5]

But in the name of Samuel, R. Judah said: Why did the dynasty of Saul not continue? Because Saul was above reproach.[6]

80. "And there was a famine in the days of David. . . . And the Lord said: 'It is because of Saul' " (2 Sam. 21:1), because he was not mourned in the manner required by law. The Holy One asked David: David, is he not the Saul who was anointed with the oil of anointing? Is he not the Saul in whose day no idolatry was practiced in Israel?[7] Is he not the Saul whose portion in heaven is with Samuel the Prophet?[8] Yet you are in the Land and he is outside it.[9]

At once David got busy and gathered all the elders and notables of Israel. They crossed the Jordan, came to Jabesh-gilead, and found the bones of Saul and of his son Jonathan—bones over which worms had exercised no power. They took the bones, put them in a coffin, and went back across the Jordan. Then David commanded that Saul's coffin be borne through the territory of each and every tribe. Upon the coffin's arrival in a tribe's territory, the entire tribe—the men, their sons and daughters, as well as their wives—came out and paid affectionate tribute to Saul and to his sons, thus discharging the obligation of loving-kindness to the dead. When the Holy One saw that Israel had shown such loving-kindness, He, immediately filled with compassion, sent down rain.[10]

David the Shepherd

81. "The Lord testeth the righteous" (Ps. 11:5). He tested David by means of the sheep and found him a good shepherd, as is said, "He took him because of [his] separations[11] of the sheep" (Ps. 78:70). What is meant by "[his] separations"? It means that David kept some sheep separate from the others. He would first lead out the young lambs and let them feed on the upper part of the herbage, which is tender; then he would lead out the rams and let them feed on the middle part of the herbage, which is neither tender nor tough; and finally he would lead out the old ewes and let them feed on the stubble of the herbage, which is tough. So the Holy One said: He who knows how to look after sheep, each according to its capacity, is to look after My sheep—Israel. Hence, "from following the ewes that give suck He brought him, to be shepherd over Jacob His people" (Ps. 78:71).[12]

82. While David was tending sheep, he came upon the *re'em*[13] asleep in the wilderness and, thinking it was a mountain, climbed upon it and continued to tend his sheep. The *re'em* woke up and arose, and David, astride its horns, was lifted up as high as the heavens. [At that moment David prayed before the Holy One to bring him down from the horns of the *re'em*.] What did the Holy One do? He caused a lion to come toward the *re'em*, and when the *re'em* saw the lion, he was afraid of it and cringed before it, for the lion is king of all animals and beasts. When David saw the lion, he also was afraid of it. Then

1. Which are in the hands of the high priest.
2. See 1 Sam. 22:11–19.
3. Lev. R. 26:8.
4. Lev. R. 26:7.
5. A king should be resolute and firm.
6. He had no family skeletons, which might have softened his arrogance. B. Yoma 22b.
7. "Saul had put away those that divined by a ghost or a familiar spirit out of the Land" (1 Sam. 28:3).
8. See Lev. R. 26:7.
9. Buried in Jabesh-gilead. See 1 Sam. 31:13.
10. Num. R. 8:4; PRE 17; Yalkut, 2 Sam., §154.
11. JV: "from the sheepfolds."
12. MTeh 78:21; Exod. R. 2:2; Yalkut, Ps., §823.
13. A fabulous animal of giant proportions.

the Holy One caused a gazelle to come along, and as the lion sprang after it, David descended and went his way. Hence David said, "Save me from the lion's mouth: for Thou hast answered me from the horns of the *remim*" (Ps. 22:22).[1]

David and the Works of the Lord

83. "A psalm of David when he feigned madness" (Ps. 34:1). [Why David had to feign madness will be explained in what follows]: David said to the Holy One, " 'How manifold are Thy works, O Lord! All those that Thou hast made in wisdom' [Ps.104:24]. All that You have made in Your world, You have made beautiful, yet the most beautiful of all Your works is wisdom. But madness, which You also made—what profit is there for the world in madness? When a man goes about the marketplace and rends his garment, and children run after him and mock him, is this beautiful in Your eyes?" The Holy One answered, "David, are you raising a cry against madness? By your life, you shall have need of it and you shall find yourself praying for madness before I give you a touch of it."

Not long after David spoke thus to God, he set out to go to Achish, king of the Philistines. The Holy One asked, "David, are you going to Achish?! Yesterday you slew Goliath—his blood is not yet dry—and Goliath's brothers serve as the king's bodyguard, and yet you are going to Achish with Goliath's sword in your hand?"

When David did come to Achish, Goliath's brothers said to Achish, "Let us slay him who slew our brother!" Achish replied, "Was it not in fair battle that David slew your brother? Is it not true that your brother stipulated with him, 'If he be able to fight with me and kill me, then we will become your slaves' (1 Sam. 17:9)?" The brothers said to Achish, "If so, get up off your throne, surrender your kingship to David, and let us become his slaves, for this is what Goliath stipulated." Thus they hammered at him with their words.

In that instant David grew afraid and began to pray to God, saying, "Master of the universe, answer me!" The Holy One asked, "David, what do you require?" David said, "Give me a touch of that thing [that madness You have created]." The Holy One replied, "Did I not say to you, "Whoso despiseth a thing shall be taken by it' (Prov. 13:13)?"

Then David made himself out to be a madman and started writing on the doors, "Achish, king of Gath, owes me one hundred myriads, and his wife fifty myriads." Now, the daughter of Achish and her mother were both mad, and the two were screaming and carrying on in madness within, while David was screaming and feigning madness without. So Achish said to his servants, "Do I lack madmen, that you have brought this fellow to rave for me?" (1 Sam. 21:16).

In that instant David rejoiced greatly [that madness had come to his aid] and said to the Holy One, "Master of the universe, how very good is madness! 'I will bless the Lord at all times' [Ps. 34:2]—both in time of reason and in time of madness."[2]

84. Once, while seated on the roof of his house, David, king of Israel, saw a wasp eating a spider. David spoke up to the Holy One: Master of the universe, what benefit is there from these two You created in Your world? The wasp merely despoils the nectar of flowers—no benefit from it. Throughout the year, the spider spins but makes no garments. The Holy One replied: David, you belittle My creatures! The time will come when you shall have need of both of them.

Later, when fleeing from King Saul, David had taken refuge in a cave. The Holy One sent a spider, which spun a web across the cave's entrance, sealing it. When Saul came and saw the cave's entrance with the web across it, he said: Surely no man has come in here, for had he come, he would have torn the web into shreds. So Saul went away without going into the cave.

And when David went out of the cave and saw the spider, he all but kissed him, saying: Blessed is your Creator, and blessed are you.

Subsequently, David found Saul asleep within a barricade [in the royal tent] and Abner lying prone across the tent's entrances, his head in one entrance and his feet in the opposite entrance. But Abner's knees were raised up, and so David was able to come in under them and pick up the cruse of water.[3] As he was about to leave the way he came, Abner stretched out his legs, which in size were like two gigantic columns, pinning David down. Beseeching the Holy One's compassion, David prayed, "My God, My God, why hast Thou forsaken me?" (Ps. 22:2). Then the Holy One performed a miracle for him—He sent him a big wasp, which stung Abner's legs so that he again bent his knees, and thus David was free to leave.

In that instant David said, in praise of the Holy One: Master of the universe, who can imitate Your works, Your mighty acts—all Your works are beautiful![4]

David's Harp

85. "At midnight I will rise to give thanks unto Thee" (Ps. 119:62). A harp was hung above David's couch, across his window. When midnight arrived, the north wind blew upon the harp and made it swing to and fro, so that it played of itself. David would immediately rise and occupy himself with Torah until the break of dawn. And after dawn's break, the sages of Israel would come in to see him and say, "Our lord king, your people Israel require sustenance." He would reply, "Let them go out and make a living one from the other."[5] They would answer, "A handful cannot satisfy a lion, nor can a cistern be filled by rain falling into its surround."[6] So he said, "Go forth in troops and help yourselves [to the enemy's posses-

1. MTeh 22:28; Yalkut, 1 Sam., §131.
2. MTeh 34:1; Yalkut, 1 Sam., §131.
3. See 1 Sam. 26:12.
4. Alphabet of Ben Sira, in Eisenstein.
5. Let the poor be supported by the prosperous.
6. To fill a cistern, water must be channeled in.

sions]."[1] The sages took counsel with Ahithophel, sought advice from the Sanhedrin, and inquired of the Urim and Tummim. [After that, they would go forth to wage war.]

And the proof that David was awakened in such a way and at such an hour? The verse, so said R. Isaac bar Adda, "Wake up my royal glory, let the psaltery and the harp wake it, and I then wake the dawn" (Ps. 57:9).[2]

86. "A prayer of David. . . . Preserve my life, for I am pious" (Ps. 86:1–2). David dared to say to the Holy One: Master of the universe, am I not a truly pious man? All the kings of the east and of the west sleep into the third hour of the day,[3] while "I at midnight rise to praise Thee" (Ps. 119:62). All the kings of the east and of the west sit in pomp in the midst of retinues, while I, in order to declare a woman clean for her husband, have my hands soiled with the blood [of menstruation] or with an aborted fetus and its placenta.[4] What is more, in all that I do, I consult my master Mephibosheth, for I ask him: My master Mephibosheth, is my decision right—have I properly convicted, properly acquitted, properly declared clean, properly declared unclean? I [the king] am not ashamed [to ask an underling]. Hence, unlike other kings [who spend their time feasting], "I speak of Your decrees, and am not ashamed [to ask concerning them]" (Ps. 119:46).[5]

87. [David said]: "Let me dwell in Thy tent forever" (Ps. 61:5). Could David have actually believed that he would live forever? No. What David asked the Holy One was: May it be the will of Your Presence that my songs and paeans of praise be uttered in synagogues and houses of study forever.[6]

88. It is reported of King David that when he finished the book of Psalms, he became complacent, saying to the Holy One: Master of the universe, is there a creature You created in Your world who utters songs and paeans of praise more than I? In that instant a frog confronted him and said: David, do not be so complacent—I utter more songs and more paeans of praise than you.[7]

David's Sin and Repentance

89. For twenty-two years the holy spirit was taken away from David, king of Israel,[8] and in his grief he shed a cupful of tears every day and ate his bread sprinkled with ashes.[9]

90. R. Judah said in the name of Rav: When David said to Mephibosheth: "Thou and Ziba divide the Land" (2 Sam. 19:30), a divine voice came forth and said: Rehoboam and Jeroboam will divide the kingdom.[10]

91. No generation is without its scorners. What did such impudent ones do in David's generation? They would go to David's windows and say: David, David, when will the Temple be built? When will we be able to go to the house of the Lord? And David would say to himself: Although they intend to provoke me, may such-and-such befall me if I did not rejoice should what they ask be fulfilled. That David spoke thus is implied in the words "I rejoiced when they said unto me: 'Would that we were able to go to the house of the Lord' " (Ps. 122:1).[11]

David's Humility

92. "And David danced (*mekarkher*) before the Lord with all his might" (2 Sam. 6:14). Just what did he do? He was dressed, say our masters, in glistening garments embroidered with fringes shining like fine gold (*paz*), and he struck his hands one against the other, clapping them. As he danced, crying, "[Hail], exalted Lord (*kiri ram*)!"[12] the glistening gold fringes that he wore made a tinkling sound (*pozez*). More! He pulled up his skirts [thus baring his legs] and cavorted as Israel cheered loudly, sounding horns and trumpets and all kinds of musical instruments. When he reached Jerusalem [cavorting thus], all the women looked at David from roofs and windows, and he did not mind. But Michal did not let him come into the house. Instead, she ran out into the street and pummeled him with reproaches, saying, "Didn't the king of Israel do himself honor today—exposing himself in the sight of the slave-girls of his subjects, as one of the riffraff might expose himself!" (2 Sam. 6:20). She went on, "Today the nobility of my father's house was made evident. Look at the difference between you and my father's house. Everyone in my father's house was modest and godly. [Of the house of

---

1. Saying, in effect: If you are so inept that you cannot manage the people's economy, there is only one alternative for you—despoil the neighboring nations by brute force. So Leon Nemoy.
2. B. Ber 3b–4a and En Yaakov, ad loc.; P. Ber 1:1, 2c.
3. 9:00 A.M.
4. "The restrictions of Lev. 12:2ff. do not apply to all cases of abortion, nor is all discharge treated as menstrual, and David is represented as occupying himself with deciding such questions instead of feasting. [The Munich] ms. omits 'with the blood [of menstruation] or' " (Maurice Simon in Ber, Soncino, p. 11, n.5).
5. B. Ber 4a.
6. P. Ber 2:1, 4a.
7. Perek Shirah.
8. In the seventeenth year of his reign, during his campaign against Ammon, he took Bathsheba. And the next twenty-two years until the day of his death he spent in penitence. See 2 Sam. 11:2–17 and 12:15–23; 1 Chron. 3:5; and *EB* 2:634 and 2:641–42, s.v. "David."
9. TdE, ed. Friedmann, p. 7; Yalkut, 2 Sam., §165.
10. B. Shab 56b.
11. David had been told that he would not build the Temple. Hence, the request of "the impudent ones" to go to the house of the Lord was in effect a wish that he die. P. Ber 2:1, 4b; P. Shek 2:7, 47a; Yalkut, Ps. §879.
12. Play on *mekharker: kiri* (Greek *kyrios:* "lord, master"); *ram* (Hebrew: "exalted, high").

Saul, it is said that in all their lives no one had ever seen the naked heel or toe of any of them] While you—you stand and uncover yourself like one of the riffraff." David replied, Am I acting up before a king of flesh and blood? Am I not acting up for the King who is King of kings? They of your father's house sought honor for themselves and put aside the honor of Heaven. I do not do so—I seek the honor of Heaven and put aside my own honor. Moreover, "I will gladly be honored among the slavegirls you speak of" (2 Sam. 6:22). Those daughters of Israel whom you call slavegirls (*amahot*) are not slavegirls, but matriarchs (*immahot*). Would that my share were with them in the time-to-come.

"Lord, my heart was not haughty" (Ps. 131:1) when Samuel anointed me king: "nor mine eyes lofty" (ibid.) when I slew Goliath; "nor did I strut in high office" (ibid.) when God restored me to kingship; "or in tending to marvels beyond my scope" (ibid.) when I brought up the Ark. "Surely I disposed my person like a weaned child with his mother" (Ps. 131:2)—even as an infant is not ashamed to be uncovered before his mother, so I disposed my person before You; I felt no shame in abasing myself for the sake of Your glory.[1]

David and Abner

93. Why was Abner punished? The sages said: Because he did not let Saul be reconciled with David when David said to Saul, "Please, sir, take a close look at the corner of thy cloak in my hand; for when I cut off the corner of thy cloak, I did not kill thee" (1 Sam. 24:12).[2] At that, Abner said to Saul, "Why pay attention to the corner of the cloak displayed by this [boastful liar]? It was probably torn away by a thornbush." And afterward [when David took away the spear and the cruse of water from near Saul's head][3] in the barricade where Saul lay, David cried to Abner, "Abner, aren't you going to answer?" (1 Sam. 26:14), as if to say, "Are you not he who declared, '[The corner of Saul's cloak] was probably torn away by a thornbush'? The spear and the cruse—were they also torn away by a thornbush?"

Some say that Abner was punished [because, as one of Saul's guards], he had an opportunity to protest [the slayings] at Nob, the city of priests, but did not protest.[4]

R. Simeon ben Lakish said: It was because Abner made of young men's blood something to play with, as is written, "Abner said to Joab: 'Let the young men, I pray thee, arise and play before us' " (2 Sam. 2:14) [that is, engage in a sword-fighting duel to the death].[5]

David and Israel's Enemies

94. "David . . . also defeated the Moabites. He made them lie down on the ground and he measured them off with a cord; he measured out two lengths of a cord for those who were to be put to death, and one length for those to be spared" (2 Sam. 8:2). As is known, when David was fleeing from Saul, he took his father and his mother to the king of Moab, whom, as a descendant of Ruth the Moabite, he trusted. Thus it is written, "David went thence to Mizpeh of Moab; and he said unto the king of Moab: 'Let my father and my mother, I pray thee, come and stay with you,' " etc. (1 Sam. 22:3). But the king of Moab slew them and not one of them escaped, except a brother of David's who fled to Nahash, king of the Ammonites. The king of Moab sent for him, but the king of Ammon would not give him up. (That was the kindness Nahash showed to David.) Because of what the king of Moab had done to his family, David waged war against the Moabites.[6]

95. When David sent Joab against Aram-naharaim and Aram-zobah, he at first was about to attack the Edomites [to protect his rear], intending to neutralize them.[7] But they showed him a document that bore God's injunction,[8] "Be very careful not to start a fight with [the descendants of Esau]" (Deut. 2:4–5). Then, when he was about to attack the Moabites [also in his rear], wishing to neutralize them, they likwise produced a document bearing God's injunction "Do not harass the Moabites, or engage them in war" (Deut. 2:9). So Joab desisted, but sent emissaries to David, saying: I was about to attack the Edomites, but they showed me a document bearing the injunction "Be very careful not to start a fight with [the descendants of Esau]." Then I was about to attack the Moabites, and they too showed me a document bearing the injunction "Do not harass the Moabites."

Then David, disregarding royal dignity, arose, doffed his purple and his crown, wrapped himself in his cloak, and went to the Sanhedrin, to whom he said: My masters, ordinarily I come here to learn, but this time, with your permission, I would instruct. I sent Joab to Aram-naharaim and to Aram-zobah, and when he was about to attack the Edomites [in his rear], they showed him a document with the injunction "Be very careful not to start a fight with [the descendants of Esau]." But were they not the first to breach the border? For "[Eglon] brought the Ammonites and the Amalekites[9] together . . . and went and defeated Israel" (Judg. 3:13) Then Joab was about to attack the Moabites, wishing to neutralize them, but they also brought forth a document with the injunction "Do not harass the Moabites." But were they not the first to breach the "border"? For "Balak . . . king of Moab . . . sent messengers to Balaam . . .: 'Come, put a curse upon this people for me' " (Num. 22:4–6).

The aforegoing is implied in the psalm's caption,

1. Num. R. 4:20.
2. That is, David could have killed Saul in the cave in En Gedi, but instead he cut off the corner of Saul's cloak; and later, having followed Saul out of the cave, he showed Saul the cloak as proof that he had refrained from killing him.
3. 1 Sam. 26:5 and 26:12.
4. See 1 Sam. 22:17 and Rashi.
5. Yalkut, 1 Sam., §133; Num. R. 23:13; Tanhuma, *Hukkat*, §4.
6. Num. R. 14:1.
7. Literally, "to crop their tails."
8. Instead of quoting, "Ye have compassed this mountain long enough" (Deut. 2:3), the translator quotes the words that follow directly.
9. Descendants of Esau.

"Mikhtam for David to instruct" (Ps. 60:1): [Though cloaked (*mikh*)] in genuine humility (*mikhut*), [yet compelled (*tam*) by his] integrity (*tammut*), David presumed to instruct [the Sanhedrin].[1]

95a.[2] R. Judah said in the name of Rav: [In his army] David had four hundred young squires, all of them sons of women taken captive in battle. All trimmed their hair in front and grew long locks [in heathen fashion]; all went about in golden chariots. They formed the army's vanguard, David's strike force—wherever they went, they terrified the enemies of Israel.[3]

David and His Son Absalom

96. When a man refrains from chastising his son for disobedience, the son will in the end fall into evil ways and come to hate his father. . . . Because David neither rebuked nor chastised his son Absalom, Absalom fell into evil ways, sought to slay his father, forced him to walk [out of Jerusalem] barefoot and weeping—in consequence of which many thousands, many myriads fell in Israel—and brought upon his father many, many other cruel afflictions without end.[4]

97. R. Yohanan said in the name of R. Simeon ben Yohai: An evil brood in a man's house is worse than the war of Gog and Magog.[5] For the words "A psalm of David when he fled from his son Absalom" (Ps. 3:1) are followed at once by David's saying, "O Lord, my foes are so many! Many are those who attack me" (Ps. 3:2); while concerning the war of Gog and Magog, the words "Why do the nations assemble, and the peoples plot vain things?" (Ps. 2:1) are not followed by David's saying, "O Lord, my foes are so many."[6]

98. "A psalm of David when he fled from his son Absalom" (Ps. 3:1). "A psalm of David"? Scripture should have said, "A lamentation of David." R. Simeon ben Avishalom explained David's use of "psalm" by the parable of a man against whom a writ of debt is issued. Before he pays it, he is troubled; but after he has paid it, he is glad. So it was with David. When the Holy One said to him, "Behold, I will raise up evil against thee out of thine own house" (2 Sam. 12:11), he was troubled, saying to himself: Perhaps it will be a slave or a bastard who will have no pity on me. But when he saw that it was Absalom, he was relieved, saying; A son is likely to have pity on his father.[7]

99. "I pray thee, let me go and pay my vow" (2 Sam. 15:7). Absalom said to David, "I ask you one favor—that you give me two elders to accompany me, so that whatever I do will be done by their authority." So David gave him a writ directing that two elders whom Absalom might pick from each and every city accompany him. Absalom then took the writ and went from city to city, where he called upon its most distinguished elders and, showing them the writ issued by his father, said, "Read what my father wrote in my behalf. Only because I favor you [over others] did I seek you out." Absalom did this in every city, until he got himself two hundred elders, as is said, "Out of Jerusalem there accompanied Absalom two hundred men who were invited and went in good faith, suspecting nothing" (2 Sam. 15:11)—they had no idea for what purpose they were accompanying Absalom.

Then Absalom prepared a feast for all the elders, where he had them recline in twos—between each two, one who had joined him in the conspiracy would keep saying, "Look how comely Absalom is. Kingship becomes him. Let us abandon David and go with Absalom."

How did the elders respond? Though they seemed to go along with Absalom, yet they prayed in behalf of David, saying, "May it be God's will that we fall into David's hands and not David into our hands. For if we fall into David's hands, he will have pity on us; but if David falls into our hands, we will [be compelled to] show no pity to him."[8]

David and Ishbi-benob

100. "Ishbi-benob tried to kill David—he was a descendant of the [giant] Raphah; his bronze spear weighed three hundred shekels" (2 Sam. 21:16). What is the meaning of the name Ishbi-benob? R. Judah, citing Rav, defined it as "the man who was dispatched (*ish she-ba*) [by God against David] because of the set-to at Nob." The Holy One asked David, "How long shall the misdeed at Nob go unatoned for by you? Because of your doing, Nob, a city of priests, was put to the sword. Because of your doing, Doeg the Edomite was banished from life in the world-to-come. Because of your doing, Saul and his three sons were slain.[9] Therefore, take your choice: either [the royal power of] your descendants will be abrogated or you will be delivered into the hands of your enemy." David replied, "Master of the universe, it is better that I be delivered into the hands of my enemy than that [the royal power of] my descendants be abrogated."

[Some time later] David went out to hunt, and Satan appeared to him in the guise of a gazelle. David shot an arrow at him but did not hit him; then he found himself drawn on and on by Satan, until he reached the land of the Philistines. When Ishbi-benob saw David, he said, "This man is he who slew my brother Goliath.'" He swung his shield [to crush] David, but David leaped back eighteen

1. Gen. R. 74:15.
2. Section 95a, in BR §104, is transposed and renumbered.
3. Literally, "the world." B. Kid 76b.
4. Exod. R. 1:1.
5. Prior to the Messiah's coming, Gog and Magog will, according to Ezek. 38–39, wage a terrible war against Israel.
6. B. Ber 7b.
7. Ibid.
8. Yalkut, 2 Sam., §149; Num. R. 9:24.
9. By his lack of precaution, he caused Saul's suspicion against the priests of Nob. Doeg reported what had taken place (1 Sam. 22:22) and so lost his life in the future world. The subsequent defeat and death of Saul were, in part, punishment for what he had done to the priests. David was thus ultimately responsible for all that grief.

cubits. Each was then afraid of the other. Ishbi-benob was afraid of David, thinking; If he can leap back that far, how far forward might he leap? And David, too was afraid of Ishbi-benob, thinking; If he can swing his shield[1] so easily, how can I stand up to him?

In that instant, David whispered: O that one of my sister's sons would come to help me.

Meanwhile, Ishbi-benob seized David, tied him up, and weighted him down by putting him under the beam of an olive press. Ishbi-benob stretched out on that beam, saying; I will have a bite to eat, something to drink, and then amuse myself with him at my pleasure. But a miracle was wrought for David—the earth receded under him [so that he was not crushed].

That day was the eve of the Sabbath, and Abishai the son of Zeruiah,[2] who was washing his head in four *seah* of water, saw bloodstains in the water. Some say that David's mule came to him whinnying plaintively. And some say that a dove came and stood fluttering its wings before him. Abishai said, "The congregation of Israel is likened to a dove in the saying 'Ye are as the wings of a dove covered with silver' " (Ps. 68:14). [Since Israel is not now in distress], it must be that David, Israel's king, is in torment. He went to David's house and did not find him. He sent to inquire at the house of study and did not find him. When he asked there, "Where is David?" he was told, "He went out in the morning and did not come back."

Then he said to himself: We were taught that "one may neither ride a king's horse nor sit on his throne nor use his scepter."[3] But what may be done in an emergency? He made inquiry in the house of study and was told that these things are permitted in an emergency. He then mounted David's mule and rode off. Instantly, the earth contracted under Abishai [so that he arrived quickly]. On the way, Abishai saw Orpah, Ishbi-benob's mother, spinning silk. When she saw him, she took her spindle and threw it at him, intending to slay him, [but she missed]. Then she said, "Young man, fetch me my spindle." Abishai [picked up the spindle], threw it at the top of Orpah's head, and slew her.

When Ishbi-benob saw Abishai, he said, "Now that they are two, they will surely slay me." So he tossed David into the air and, at the same time, drove his spear into the ground, thinking; David is sure to fall upon it and be slain. But Abishai uttered God's Ineffable Name and so kept David suspended between heaven and earth.

Abishai then asked David, "How do you happen to be here?" David replied, "God gave me a choice, and I chose to be delivered into the hands of an enemy." Abishai said, "Reverse your prayer. Spare yourself sorrow, even if your son's son shall have to sell wax." David said, "If so, succor me with *your* prayer." Of Abishai's prayer in David's behalf, it is said, "Abishai the son of Zeruiah succored him" (2 Sam. 21:17). Then Abishai again uttered the Ineffable Name and brought David down. Ishbi said, "Two against one?" They replied, "After we slay you, go up to the city and boast that ten men slew you." Since Ishbi-benob seemed determined to attack them, they said to him, "Go [first] and find your mother in her grave."[4] At their mentioning of his mother's name, his strength failed, and Abishai and David were able to kill him.

Following this incident, "the men of David swore unto him, saying: 'Thou shalt go no more out with us to battle, that thou quench not the lamp of Israel' " (2 Sam. 21:17).[5]

[1] Since the weight of Ishbi-benob's spear was three hundred shekels, his shield must have been very heavy.

[2] David's sister's son, brother of Joab, and one of the captains of David's army.

[3] Sanh 2:5.

David's Death

101. "Lord, make me to know mine end and the measure of my days, what it is; let me know the day I will cease to be" (Ps. 39:5). When David pleaded with the Holy One, "Master of the universe, let me know when mine end is to come," God replied, "This decree has gone forth from Me: the end of a mortal is not to be made known to him." "And the measure of my days, what it is?" "This decree has gone forth from Me: a man's span of life is not to be made known to him." "Let me know the day I will cease to be." God replied, "You will die on the Sabbath." "Let me die on the first day of the week."[6] "By then the time for the reign of Solomon your son will have come, and one reign may not overlap another even by a hairsbreadth." "Then let me die on the sixth day of the week." God replied, "[Remember your saying], 'Better is a day in Thy courts than a thousand . . .' [Ps. 84:11]? So, too, for Me, the one extra day you sit in the courts [of study] where you occupy yourself with Torah is better than the thousand burnt offerings your son Solomon will bring to Me on the altar."[7]

Hence, every Sabbath David would sit and study Torah all day.[8] On the day that his time to die came, the angel of death stationed himself before David, but could not prevail, because learning did not cease from his mouth. The angel of death said to himself: What am I to do with him? Now, behind David's house there was a garden. So the angel of death entered it, then flew up and soughed in the trees. David went out to see [what caused the sound]. As he climbed a ladder, it broke under him [and, silenced for an instant, learning ceased]. At that, his soul left him, and he died.[9]

102. Since King David's body was lying in the hot sun, Solomon beckoned to eagles, who spread their wings over the body so that the sun would not beat down upon it.[10]

[4] They said that she was dead.

[5] B. Sanh 95a; Gen. R. 59:11; Yalkut, *Hayye Sarah*, §107; Yalkut, 2 Sam., §154–55.

[6] So that my body could at once be made ready for burial. On the Sabbath, such activity is prohibited.

[7] "Thus your life is too precious for a single day to be renounced. Study itself is regarded in Judaism as an act of worship, indeed, the greatest, though only when it leads to piety; cf. Pe 1:1" (Shab, Soncino, p. 134, n. 5).

[8] "The angel of death cannot approach one who is studying the Torah. Sot 21a" (ibid.).

[9] B. Shab 30a–b; Eccles. R. 5:10, §2.

[10] Ordinarily, a body may not be moved on the Sabbath. Ruth R. 3:2.

103. In the verse "And the fame of David went out into all lands" (1 Chron. 14:17), the word "fame" means that coins bearing his name were current throughout the world. What was stamped on them? On one side a shepherd's staff and pouch, and on the other a royal tower.[1]

104. [This section is transposed and renumbered 95a.]

The Wisdom and Greatness of King Solomon

105. "God said: 'Ask what I shall give thee.' And Solomon replied: . . . 'Give thy servant an understanding heart' " (1 Kings 3:5–6 and 3:9). R. Simon said in the name of R. Simeon ben Halafta that Solomon resembled a counselor who was raised [from childhood] in the king's court. When the king said to him, "Ask me for anything you want," the counselor said to himself: If I ask for silver and gold, that is all I shall have; for precious stones and pearls, that is all I shall have. So he said [to himself]: I will ask for the king's daughter, and that will include everything. Even so, "in Gibeon the Lord appeared to Solomon in a dream by night, and God said, 'Ask what I shall give thee' " (1 Kings 3:5). Solomon said to himself: If I ask for silver and gold, for precious stones and pearls, that is all I shall ever have. So I shall ask for wisdom, which encompasses everything. God then said: Solomon, you have asked for wisdom, not for wealth and possessions or the life of your enemies. As you live, wisdom and understanding are hereby given you, and by means of these I will also give you wealth and possessions.[2]

106. "Solomon . . . was wiser than all men" (1 Kings 5:11). All kings feared him. Nations speaking divers languages obeyed him and brought tribute to him. Fishes of the sea and birds of heaven, together with cattle and beasts of the field, would come as one to the slaughterhouse to be slaughtered for Solomon's banquet. He was rich and powerful, acquiring property, silver, and gold in great abundance. He interpreted parables, told what is hidden, and made known mysteries without end. His enemies and his foes alike turned into his friends. All kings deferred to him. All of them stood together to behold his countenance and were eager to hear his words of wisdom, for his fame had spread among kings, and the vigor of his understanding among sages. He was an upright man who shunned evil. He was so wise that he even knew the mysteries of heaven. Princes of all realms would offer their sons and daughters to be his menservants and maidservants. To him was given the great key whereby all gates of wisdom and understanding are opened. He knew and understood the speech of birds, cattle, and beasts of the field. Deer and gazelles were his forerunners, lions and tigers his armor bearers.[3]

107. One day Ashmedai, king of demons, came to King Solomon and asked, "Are you the one of whom it is written, 'He was wiser than all men' (1 Kings 5:11)?" Solomon replied, "Yes, that is what the Holy One promised me." Ashmedai said, "If you allow me, I will show you something you have never seen before." Solomon: "Very well." Ashmedai reached down into the subterranean region called Tevel and out of it brought up a man with two heads and four eyes. Solomon, shaken and terrified, said, "Bring him into a private chamber."

Then Solomon sent for Benaiah the son of Jehoiada, whom he asked, "Would you say that human beings exist beneath us?" Benaiah replied, "As you live, my lord king, I do not know. But I heard from Ahithophel that human beings do exist beneath us." Solomon: "What will you say if I show you one of them?" Benaiah: "How can you show me something that is below the depth of the earth—below our earth, which extends downward a distance that at an ordinary pace would require five hundred years to traverse; and below the distance between our earth and the next earth[4] a distance that at an ordinary pace would likewise require five hundred years to traverse?" So Solomon had the [subterranean] man brought into his presence. When Benaiah the son of Jehoiada saw him, he fell on his face [in fright], saying, "Blessed are You who has granted me life and substance, and permitted me to reach such a day."

Solomon then asked the man, "Whose son are you?" The man: "I am Adam's descendant, of the progeny of Cain." "Where do you live?" "In the earth known as Tevel." "Do you have a sun or a moon there?" "Yes." "Whence does the sun rise and where does it set?" "It rises in the west and sets in the east." "What is your occupation?" "We plow and reap and graze flocks and herds." "Do you pray?" "Yes." "What is your prayer?" "How manifold are Thy works, O Lord! In wisdom hast Thou made them all" (Ps. 104:24).

Solomon told the man, "If you wish, we shall return you to your place." The man replied, "Out of your goodness, do so—please return me to my place."

The king immediately summoned Ashmedai and said, "Go, return the man to his place." Ashmedai replied, "I can never restore him to his own place."

When the man saw how things were, he took a wife and begot seven sons by her—six in the likeness of the mother, and one in the likeness of the father: he had two heads and four eyes.

The man plowed and reaped, and presently became very rich, as rich a man as there was in the world.

In due time, the man died and left an inheritance to his sons, who proceeded to quarrel, the six saying, "There are seven of us to divide our father's estate." But the man with the two heads contended, "We are eight, and I am entitled to take two portions of the inheritance."

So they all went to Solomon and said, "Our lord king, we are seven, but our two-headed brother says that we are eight and wishes to divide our father's estate into eight parts and take two parts himself."

Solomon called together the Sanhedrin, whom he asked, "What is your opinion in this matter?" They kept

---

1. Gen. R. 39:11.
2. Song R. 1:1, §9.
3. Targum Sheni on Esther, beginning.

4. Just as there are seven firmaments, so there are said to be seven earths, the lowest of which is Tevel. See PRKM 23:10.

silent. Solomon said, "Tomorrow morning there will be justice" (Jer. 21:12).

At midnight Solomon entered the Temple and, standing in prayer before Him who is everywhere, said, "Master of the universe, in Gibeon, when you revealed Yourself to me, You said, 'Ask what I shall give thee' [1 Kings 3:5]. I asked for neither silver nor gold, only wisdom, in order to be able to judge men with equity. Now lend light to my eyes, that I may issue a verdict that is just." The Holy One replied, "In the morning I shall give you the wisdom you require."

In the morning Solomon sent for and gathered the entire Sanhedrin, to whom he said, "Bring the two-headed man into my presence." After he was brought, Solomon said, "Observe—if one head is aware of and feels what I am going to do to the other head, the man is one person. If not, he is two."

Then Solomon said, "Bring hot water." Hot water was brought and sprayed over one head. The other head cried out, "My lord king, we are dying, we are dying!"

When Israel saw the way Solomon arrived at the verdict, they were amazed and shaken, and all were awed by him.[1]

108. Once a man was walking in a field with a jug of milk in his hand. A snake, moaning with thirst, met him. "Why are you moaning?" asked the man. "Because I am thirsty," replied the snake; "what is this that you have in your hand?" The man: "Milk." The snake: "Give me the milk to drink, and I will show you so much money that you will be rich." The man gave the milk to the snake, and it drank.

After the snake had drunk, the man said, "Show me the money you spoke of." The snake: "Follow me." He followed it until they came to a big stone. "The money [is hidden]," said the snake, "under the stone." The man lifted the stone, dug down, and found the money, which he took and was about to carry to his house.

But what did the snake do? It leaped up and wrapped itself around the man's neck. "Why are you doing this?" the man asked. The snake: "I am going to kill you because you took all my money." The man: "Come with me to Solomon and his court."

They went and appeared before Solomon—the snake still around the man's neck, and the man sobbing in the king's presence.

"What are you after?" the king asked the snake. It answered, "In accord with Scripture's 'Thou shalt attack him in the heel' [Gen. 3:15], I want to kill him." "Get off his neck," said the king; "since both of you are in court, it is not right that you, and not I, should hold him!" So the snake slithered off the man's neck to the ground. The king: "Now you can have your say." The snake: "I wish to slay the man, in keeping with what the Holy One said to me: 'Thou shalt attack him in the heel.' " The king to the man, "And of you the Holy One said, 'He shall attack [the snake] in the head' " (ibid.). At once the man sprang forward and stamped on its head.

Hence the proverb "Smash the head of even the best of snakes."[2]

109. "And Solomon's wisdom excelled . . . all the wisdom of Egypt" (1 Kings 5:10). What sort of wisdom was there in Egypt? You find that when Solomon wished to build the Temple, he sent word to Pharaoh-necoh, saying: Send me craftsmen to work for a wage, for I wish to build the Temple. What did Pharaoh do? He gathered all his astrologers and said to them, "Gaze into the future and see which of our craftsmen are destined to die during the coming year, and I will send these to Solomon." When they came to Solomon, he perceived through the holy spirit that they were destined to die during that year. So he gave them their shrouds and sent them back, together with a written message: Didn't you have enough shrouds to bury your dead? Here are the ones about to die, together with their shrouds.[3]

110. "And Solomon became allied to Pharaoh king of Egypt by marriage, and took Pharaoh's daughter" (1 Kings 3:1). It is said: When Solomon married Pharaoh's daughter, Gabriel came down and stuck a reed into the sea. That reed gathered around itself a sandbank, on which the great city of Rome was eventually built.[4]

Solomon as Builder

111. Our masters taught: Solomon built the Temple with the help of the *shamir*. For the verse "When the house was built, only unbruised stones from the quarry were used" (1 Kings 6:7) implies that [because of the *shamir*] the stones emerged in a hewn state. Such was the opinion of R. Judah. But R. Nehemiah argued: How can you say so? Does not Scripture declare, "All these buildings were of choice stones, according to the measures of hewn stone, sawed with saws" (1 Kings 7:9)? [R. Judah replied: But if the stones were sawed with saws], why does it say, "No iron tool was heard in the house while it was being built?" (1 Kings 6:7)? [R. Nehemiah replied]: Scripture means that the stones were made ready outside and then were brought in.

Rabbi [Judah I, the Patriarch] observed: R. Judah's opinion is reasonable in connection with the stones for the Sanctuary, while R. Nehemiah's opinion is likely in connection with the stones for Solomon's own house. How, then, according to R. Nehemiah, was the *shamir* used? In readying the stones for the shoulder pieces on the ephod [and the stones for the breastplate]. For concerning these we are taught: The precious stones for the ephod and the breastplate could not have the names of the twelve tribes inscribed on them in ink, inasmuch as Scripture requires "engravings of a signet" (Exod. 28:11); nor could a chisel be used to make an incision in the stones, inasmuch as Scripture requires that the stones remain "in their

1. BhM 4:151–52.

2. Tanhuma B, introduction, p. 157.

3. Num. R. 19:3; PR 14:9 (YJS 1:272).

4. Thus, Solomon's straying led ultimately to the destruction of the Jewish state. B. Shab 56b; B. Sanh 21b.

fullnesses"[1] (Exod. 28:20). Hence the stones had first to be marked lightly with ink; then, with the markings on their outer surfaces, they were held up and passed in front of the *Shamir*. At that, the stones, of their own accord, split at the markings, like a fig that opens up during the summer and nothing thereof is lost; or, like a valley that opens up during the rainy season [2] and nothing thereof is lost.

The *shamir* is a creature about the size of a grain of barley and was created during the six days of creation.[3] Nothing is hard enough to withstand it. How then was it kept? It was wrapped in tufts of wool and placed in a leaden tube full of barley bran.

And who brought the *shamir* to Solomon? The eagle fetched it from the Garden of Eden. For "Solomon [who] spoke also to beasts and to birds" (1 Kings 5:13) asked the birds, "Where is the *shamir* hidden away?" and the eagle went and fetched it.[4]

112. Iron was created to shorten man's days, while the altar was created to lengthen his days. What shortens life should not be listed as a tool to build what lengthens life.[5]

113. "And for the house he made windows, broad and narrow" (1 Kings 6:4). R. Avin the Levite explained: You find that when a man makes openings for windows, he makes them broad on the inside and narrow on the outside. Why? So that they draw in the greatest amount of light. But the windows in the Temple were broad on the outside and narrow on the inside. Why? So that the light would flow out from the Temple and illumine the world.[6]

114. "Thus all the work was finished *va-tishlam* (1 Kings 7:51). [Read not *va-tishlam* but] *va-tehi shalom*, "the work was accomplished in peace": of all the craftsmen who were building the Temple, not one died, not one took sick; no trowel or ax was broken; not a tool used in the work of building was even dented.[7]

115. After Solomon built the Temple, he attempted to bring the Ark into the Holy of Holies, but the gates held fast one to the other, and although Solomon cried out twenty-four times, he was given no response.[8] Then, when he opened his mouth and said, "O gates, lift up your heads! Up high, ye everlasting doors, that the King of glory may come in" (Ps. 24:7), the gates rushed at him to swallow him up. "Who [did you say, they asked], is the King of glory?" (Ps. 24:8).[9] Solomon replied, "The Lord strong and mighty" (ibid.). Then he repeated the plea: "O gates, lift up your heads! Up high, ye everlasting doors, that the King of glory may come in" (Ps. 24:9). The gates asked again, "Who is the King of glory?" (Ps. 24:10), and Solomon answered, "The Lord of hosts, He is the King of glory forever" (ibid.), and still he was given no response. But when he said, "O Lord God, turn not away the face of Thine anointed, remember the good deeds of David Thy servant" (2 Chron. 6:42), he was given a response immediately. Then the faces of David's enemies turned as black as the bottom of a pot, for all the people—all Israel—knew that God had forgiven him that sin [with Bathsheba].[10]

116. "He built the house of the forest of Lebanon"[11] (1 Kings 7:2). R. Oshaia said: When Solomon built the Temple, he planted in the Temple area all sorts of golden fruit-bearing trees, which brought forth their fruit in season. When the wind blew through them, the fruit would fall to the ground [in great abundance], as indicated by the verse "Let his fruit thrive like the forest of Lebanon" (Ps. 72:16)—[in such abundance] that the priests had their full maintenance from that fruit. But after heathens entered the Holy Place, the fruit withered, as is said, "The blossom of Lebanon withered" (Nah. 1:4). But the Holy One will restore the abundance of Lebanon's trees, as Scripture says, "It shall blossom abundantly, it shall also exult and shout. It shall [again] receive the glory of Lebanon" (Isa. 35:2).[12]

117. R. Ishmael said: On the night Solomon completed the work of the Temple, he married Bithiah, the daughter of Pharaoh. There was shouting in celebration of the Temple, and there was shouting in celebration of Pharaoh's daughter. But the shouting for Pharaoh's daughter was more joyous than the shouting for the Temple. At that time the thought of destroying Jerusalem came to the Holy One. Hence R. Hillel bar Helene said of the verse "This city hath been a provocation to My nose[13] and to My fury" (Jer. 32:31): God felt like a man who, passing a filthy place, turns his nose away.

R. Hunia said: Pharaoh's daughter danced eighty kinds of dances that night. The sages add: She brought Solomon a thousand kinds of musical instruments and

1. Use of a chisel would, it goes without saying, chip off particles of the stones, so that they would not remain "in their fullnesses." JV: "in their settings."
2. The dried-up stream bisecting the valley is now in flood stage and sweeps away the accumulation of sand and debris that blocked the entrances to the valley. So Leon Nemoy.
3. See above, chap. 2, §67.
4. B. Sot 48b and En Yaakov, ad loc.; Yalkut, 1 Kings, §182, which cites MTeh 78:11.
5. Mid 3:4.
6. Tanhuma, *Be-haalotekha*, §2; Yalkut, 1 Kings, §182.
7. PR 6:7 (YJS 1:126).
8. The expressions "cry," "prayer," and "supplication" are repeated twenty-four times in the account of the dedication of the Temple. See 2 Chron. 6.
9. They thought he was describing himself.
10. B. Shab 30a.
11. *Lebanon*, "that which whitens (*malbin*) the sins of Israel," is taken to refer to the Temple, which Solomon built with cedars of Lebanon. In the present verse, R. Oshaia resolves the inconsistency between "house" and "forest" by saying that fruit grew in the Temple area. That the fruit was golden is derived from the assertion that Solomon garnished the House with "gold of Parvaim" (2 Chron. 3:6); and by associating "Parvaim" with the verb *prh* ("to bear fruit"), he concludes that the fruit was golden. See Samuel Edels on B. Yoma 39b.
12. B. Yoma 39b and 21b.
13. JV: "Mine anger." But *af* means "nose" as well as "anger."

ordered that each of them be played to him that night. As each instrument was played, she would say to Solomon: Thus it is played before such-and-such an idol, and thus it is played before such-and-such another idol. What else did Pharaoh's daughter do? Over his bed she spread a kind of canopy, in which she set all kinds of precious stones and pearls that shimmered like stars and planets, so that whenever Solomon was about to get up, he saw those stars and planets, and kept going back to sleep until the fourth hour in the day.[1]

R. Levi said, That day the morning offering was brought not at dawn[2] but during the fourth hour. And Israel grieved, for although it was the day of the Temple's dedication, they could not bring the offering on time because Solomon was asleep with the keys of the Temple under his head, and, in their awe of royalty, they hesitated to wake him. So they went and told Bathsheba, his mother, who came in, woke him up, and chastised him. With regard to this, it is said, "The utterance of his mother, followed by her chastising him"[3] (Prov. 31:1). She took off her slipper and slapped him on one cheek, then on the other, as she said, "What, my son? and what, O son of my womb?" (Prov. 31:2).

Or, the verse is read: "The utterance of his mother, followed by her intention to chastise him." R. Yohanan said in the name of R. Simeon ben Yohai: The verse implies that Bathsheba tied Solomon to a post [intending to chastise him], as she said, "What, my son? and what, O son of my womb? And what, O son of my vows?" (Prov. 31:2). In saying, "What, my son," she meant: All know that your father feared God, [but now it will be said: His mother made him what he is, and you will be spoken of not as your father's son, but as my son]. In saying, "And what, O son of my vows," she meant: Each woman in your father's household made vows as she prayed, "May I have a son fit for the throne," while I made vows as I prayed, "May I have a son eager and keen to study Torah, and fit for prophecy." Continuing her reprimand of Solomon, Bathsheba said, "Not with kings [who say], 'Lemuel' " (Prov. 31:4). Why do you imitate kings who say, "*Lamah lanu el*," "What need have we of God?" "Not with kings who drink wine" (ibid)—why do you act like those kings who imbibe wine, get drunk, then indulge in all kinds of lewdness? "Not for the master of secrets (*rozenim*) [to keep asking], 'Where is strong drink?' " (ibid.)—not for him to whom all mysteries of the world (*raze olam*) are revealed to imbibe and get drunk. Some read the verse, "Not for [one sought out by] the world's princes (*rozenim*) [to keep asking], 'Where is strong drink?' "—shall he whose door to the world's princes seek out early in the morning give himself to drinking wine?

How do we know, said R. Isaac, that Solomon repented and admitted to his mother that she was right? From the verse "Surely I am more brutish than that man, and have not the understanding of Adam" (Prov. 30:2). In saying, "I am more brutish than that man," Solomon referred to Noah, of whom it is said, "Noah, the man engaged in farming, profaned himself [by getting drunk]" (Gen. 9:20–21).[4] In saying, "And have not the understanding of Adam," he referred to the first man['s eating of the grape].[5]

Solomon's Throne

118. "Moreover the king made a great throne of ivory" (1 Kings 10:18). The throne was overlaid with the fine gold of Ophir, studded with lapis lazuli, jacinth and emerald, turquoise and chalcedony, as well as pearls and other precious stones—white, green, and ruby red. No other like it was made for any other king—indeed, no kingdom had the means to construct a throne like it. The details of its structure were as follows: at its two sides stood [six groups of] twelve golden lions, and opposite them [six groups of] twelve golden eagles, each lion opposite an eagle even as each eagle was opposite a lion. The pairs were thus standing face to face, so that the right paw of each golden lion was opposite the left wing of each golden eagle even as the right wing of each eagle was opposite the left paw of each lion. Thus there were seventy-two lions and seventy-two eagles. At the apex of the throne was a circular area that served as the royal seat.

The throne had six steps [leading up to the seat]. On the first step crouched a golden lion, and opposite him a golden ox; on the second step crouched a golden wolf, and opposite him a golden lamb; on the third a golden tiger, and opposite him a golden kid; on the fourth a golden bear, and opposite him a golden gazelle; on the fifth a golden eagle, and opposite him a golden dove; on the sixth a golden hawk, and opposite him a golden sparrow. At the very top of the throne rested a golden dove, her claw holding a golden blossom. Over the seat hung a golden lampstand, set up with all its parts—its lamps, its calyxes, its tongs and its fire pans, its cups and its petals. From one side of the lampstand there extended seven golden branches, upon which were wrought the likenesses of the seven patriarchs of the world: Adam, Noah, his eldest [son] Shem, Abraham, Isaac, and Jacob, together with Job. From the other side of the lampstand there also extended seven golden branches, upon which were wrought the likenesses of the seven pious men of the world: Levi['s son] Kohath, Amram, Moses and Aaron, Eldad and Medad, with Hur between them. Attached to the top of the lampstand was a golden bowl filled with the purest olive oil, the kind that is used for illumination in the Temple; and below, a golden basin filled with pure olive oil for the lamps of the lampstand. The likeness of Eli was wrought upon the basin. From this large basin there extended two golden faucets, upon which were wrought the

1. 10:00 A.M.
2. As prescribed.
3. JV: "the burden wherewith his mother corrected him." But the root *ysr* ("to correct") may also mean "to chastise, give the lash."
4. See above, chap. 2, §133.
5. According to the opinion that the fruit of the forbidden tree was the grape, which Adam ate but did not get intoxicated by (see above, chap. 2, §91). B. Sanh 70b; Lev. R. 12:5; Num R. 10:4; Midrash Prov., ad loc.

likenesses of Eli's two sons, Hophni and Phinehas. From the golden faucets protruded two golden spouts, upon which were wrought the likenesses of Aaron's two sons, Nadab and Abihu.

At the two sides of the throne there were two high-backed chairs of gold, one for the high priest and one for the deputy high priest. Surrounding the throne there were seventy high-backed chairs of gold, upon which sat the seventy elders, members of Israel's Sanhedrin, who administered justice in Solomon's presence. Close by the king's ears there hovered two sirens [who sang sweetly], so that he would not be agitated. Twenty-four golden vines rising at both sides of the throne provided shade for the king. Around the throne there were also palms canopied with white linen and all kinds of dyed cloth hanging from cords of fine linen and purple wool, so loosely woven that fresh air come come in. The vines and the palms covered an area of a hundred cubits around the throne. The vines and palms with their multicolored covering had the appearance of lightning, the appearance of dazzling flashes of fire, and the appearance of a rainbow. Golden bells were tied to the edges of the multicolored covering, and whenever the wind blew through them, the bells started ringing. On the treetops were ivory peacocks, which faced the wings of [ivory] eagles. Above the throne, in an upper chamber of Solomon's, stood two golden lions, hollowed out and filled with all kinds of perfumes exuding fragrance.

When Solomon, about to ascend to his seat, put his foot on the first step, the wheels in the mechanism of the throne began to whirl, so that at the king's right the lion reached out his paw, and at the king's left the ox reached out his foreleg. The king leaned upon these as he went up. Thus, aided by the different animals at succeeding steps, he kept going up until he reached the top. There the eagles came down, took hold of him, and helped him to his seat. When the king sat down, a great eagle circling above picked up the royal crown and placed it on the king's head.

There was also a silver serpent in the elaborate mechanism of the throne. [The moment Solomon sat down], that great serpent sprang forward [and, pressing] against the machinery, forced the lions and the eagles upward until they formed themselves into a protective cover above the king's head.

Then a golden dove came down from the reader's stand, opened the Ark, took out a scroll of Torah, and placed it in the king's hand, to fulfill the precept "It shall be with him, and he shall read therein all the days of his life" (Deut. 17:19).

When the high priest and the elders arrived, they would pay homage to the king, then sit at his right and at his left, and, together with him, administer justice. Whenever witnesses inclined to give false testimony appeared before Solomon, the machinery of the throne came into motion: the wheels turned, the oxen bellowed, the lions roared, the wolves howled, the lambs baa'ed, the leopards snarled, the goats bleated, the bears growled, the hinds cried, the hawks screamed, the sparrows chirped, the eagles flew above, and the peacocks scurried about. Why? In order to grip and terrify the hearts of the witnesses and prevent them from giving false testimony. The witnesses would say to themselves: We'd better give true testimony. If we do not, the world will be destroyed on account of us.

When Pharaoh-necoh, king of Egypt, carried the throne from Jerusalem into captivity in Egypt, and tried to ascend and sit on it, the lion stretched forth his right foreleg and struck him on his hip, so that he limped to the day of his death. He was thenceforth called Pharaoh-necoh, "Pharaoh the Lame."

When wicked Nebuchadnezzar destroyed Jerusalem and came to conquer Egypt, he found the throne there, seized it, and brought it to Babylon so that he might sit on it in Babylon. But as he put his foot upon the first step, the lion struck him, and he fell to the ground.

When Darius became king and destroyed Babylon, he took the throne and brought it to Media, but no one dared sit on it. When Alexander of Macedon became king, he captured the throne and brought it back to Egypt.

When Antiochus Epiphanes came and devastated Egypt, he captured the throne and put it on a ship. A golden chain within the throne's leg was pulled out of place. He brought all the craftsmen and artificers in the world to fix the leg of the throne, but they have been unable to fix it to this day.[1]

Solomon and the Queen of Sheba

119. When Solomon was in a cheerful mood from wine, he sent word summoning all the kings of the east and of the west who were near the Land of Israel, and had them quartered in the royal palace. After a while he commanded that there be brought psalteries and cymbals, tabors and harps that his father used to play upon, and he had these played before him. Then he commanded that the birds of heaven, the beasts of the field, the creatures that creep on the ground, demons, spirits, and night harpies dance before him, in order to demonstrate his greatness to all the kings seated in his presence. The king's scribes summoned the animals and the spirits by name, and all gathered and came to the royal palace of their own accord, neither fettered nor bound, with no human hand to lead them.

Among the birds who came, the hoopoe was looked for but could not be found. Greatly provoked, the king commanded that the bird be fetched, intending to punish him. When the hoopoe appeared, he said: My lord, king of the world, listen to me—let what I say enter your ears. For three months, while endeavoring to grasp [the extent of your kingdom], I reflected so intensely that I ate no bread and drank no water. Then I said: Let me roam throughout the world and see whether there is any principality or government that has not submitted to my lord king. I kept looking about until I found one such principality, the city of Kitor in the east. Dust there is more valuable than gold, and silver is as common as manure in

---

1. Midrash Abba Gorion, ed. Buber, pp. 4–8; Midrash Panim Aherim, ed. Buber (Vilna, 1886), pp. 57–58; Targum Sheni on Esther 1; BhM 5:34–37.

its streets. Its trees, planted since the beginning of creation, drink water from the Garden of Eden. In it are many warriors whose heads are crowned with laurels, but these warriors do not know how to wage war—they are unable even to bend a bow. Indeed, I saw a woman ruling all of them—she is called the queen of Sheba. Now if it please my lord king, I will gird my loins as if I were a man, go to the city of Kitor in the principality of Sheba, fetter its princes with chains and its governors with iron bands, and bring them to my lord king.

What the hoopoe had to say pleased the king. The king's scribes were summoned, and they wrote a letter which they bound to the hoopoe's wings. Then the hoopoe rose up and ascended to the heights of heaven, uttering a cry of joy. In triumph he flew among the other birds, who immediately followed him to the city of Kitor in the principality of Sheba.

In the morning, when the queen went out to prostrate herself to the sun, behold, a cloud of birds darkened the sun's light. In bewilderment and desolation, she took hold of her garments and rent them. Then, as the hoopoe alighted near her, she saw a letter bound to his wing. She untied the letter and read what was written in it: "From me, King Solomon. Peace be upon you and upon your princes! Did you not know that the Holy One made me king over the beasts of the field and the birds of heaven, over demons, over spirits, and over night harpies? All kings, east and west, north and south, come to pay me homage. Now then, if you will come and pay me homage, I will accord you honor greater than that accorded to any of the kings who attend me. But if you refuse to come and pay me such homage, I will dispatch potentates with their legions and riders against you. Do you ask, Who are King Solomon's potentates, legions, and riders? The beasts of the field are the potentates; the birds of heaven are the riders; the spirits, the demons, and the night harpies are the legions who will strangle you in the beds within your houses. The beasts of the field will slay you in the fields, and the birds of heaven will devour the flesh from off your bones!"

After the queen of Sheba fully perceived what the letter demanded of her, she again put her hands to her garments and rent them anew. Then she sent for the counselors and princes, whom she asked, "Will you not assent to the request King Solomon dispatched to me?" They replied, "We know nothing of King Solomon, and we owe no homage to his royal power." However, she felt no confidence in them and paid no heed to what they said. So she summoned all her sea captains and had them load their vessels with cypress wood, pearls, and precious stones. She also sent to Solomon six thousand youths and maidens, all born in the same year, in the same month, on the same day, in the same hour, all of equal stature and size, all clothed in purple garments. She wrote the following letter to King Solomon, which she sent with them: "From the city of Kitor to the Land of Israel is normally a journey of seven years. Nevertheless, I plead and petition: Let me come to you at the end of three years."

At the end of the three years, the queen of Sheba came to King Solomon. When King Solomon heard that the queen of Sheba had arrived, he had Benaiah the son of Jehoiada go out to meet her. Benaiah looked like the hind at dawn leaping into the sunlight, like the evening star always aglow among other stars, like a lily swaying by brooks of water. When the queen of Sheba saw Benaiah the son of Jehoiada, she descended from her chariot. Benaiah the son of Jehoiada spoke up and asked, "What made you descend from your chariot?" "Are you not King Solomon?" she queried. Benaiah replied, "I am not King Solomon—I am but one of the servants who attend him." The queen turned around, and, quoting the proverb "You have not yet seen the lion, come and behold his den," said to her princes, "You have not yet seen King Solomon; come and behold the beauty of him who attends him."

Then Benaiah the son of Jehoiada conducted her to the king, who, upon hearing that she was about to arrive, went to a glass house to receive her. When the queen of Sheba beheld the king seated in the glass house, the thought came to her that the king was seated in water. So [to pass through what she believed to be water, she lifted her skirts], exposing her thighs, and the hair on her legs became visible. The king was moved to say, "Your beauty is a woman's, but the hair [on your legs] is that of a man—hair, an ornament in a man, is disfiguring in a woman."

Then the queen of Sheba spoke up and said, "My lord king, allow me to put three riddles to you. If you can solve them, I will know that you are a wise man. If not, you are like other men." Then she went on: "A wooden well with an iron bucket, which draws up grains of sand and pours out water—what is it?" The king replied, "A kohl tube."[1]

"It issues as dust from the earth, its food is dust of the earth, it is poured out like water, and it gives light to the house—what is it?" The king replied, "Naphtha."[2]

"When the wind rushes over the tops of all these, each makes a loud, anguished noise; each bends its top like a reed; each enhances the distinction of nobles and reflects the lowliness of the poor;[3] each is the glory of some who are dead and the disgrace for some who are alive;[4] each is the delight of birds and the cause of mourning for fish[5]—what is it?" The king replied, "Flax."

Then the queen brought before the king a number of males and females of the same appearance—the same height, and wearing the same garb—and said to him, "Sort out the males from the females for me." At once he beckoned to his eunuchs, who brought him nuts and roasted ears of corn, which he proceeded to distribute among the males and the females. The males, not bashful, put the nuts and corn into their robes [whose lower edges they lifted up to form a pocket]; but the females, who were

1. The kohl (mascara) applicator is "the iron bucket" that draws up the kohl powder, "grains of sand," from its container, the "wooden well." When mascara inadvertently gets into the eye, it causes tears, "the pouring out of water."
2. Naphtha was used for lighting lamps.
3. Both fine linen and coarse sackcloth may be made out of flax.
4. Shrouds, as well as cords for binding prisoners or for hanging men condemned to die, are made out of flax.
5. Birds eat the seed of flax, and nets to catch fish are made out of flax.

modest, put them into their head kerchiefs.[1] The king said, pointing, "These are males, and those are females."

To test him once more, the queen set another exhibit before him. She had a number of men, some circumcised, some uncircumcised, stand in his presence and said, "Sort out for me the circumcised from the uncircumcised." The king beckoned to the high priest to open the Ark of the Covenant, whereupon those who were circumcised bowed their bodies to half their height—more, their countenances seemed to be filled with the radiance of the Presence. But the uncircumcised ones fell on their faces.[2] Solomon spoke up and said, "These are circumcised, and those are not."

The queen said, "I did not believe the reports until I came and saw with my own eyes that not even the half had been told me; your wisdom and wealth surpass the reports I have heard. How fortunate are your men, and how fortunate are these your servants" (1 Kings 10:7–8). Then Solomon brought the queen into an inner hall of the royal palace, where she presented him with fine gold and silver, and he gave her everything she wanted.[3]

120. R. Yose said: [In the days of Solomon], the population was divided into four groups [each wearing garments of a different color]. Thus the king and his courtiers, the sages and their disciples, the priests and the Levites wore blue; all Israelites who lived in Jerusalem wore white; those who came from the provincial cities, the villages, and from other places wore red; and the nations of the world who would come from afar to bring presents to the king wore green. R. Yose's disciples asked: Why garments of these particular colors? He replied: The colors correspond to the [colors associated with the] four cycles in the year. During the cycle from Tishri to Tevet, the [sparkling] days are like the color blue; during the cycle from Tevet to Nisan, snow comes down, so white garments were worn; from Nisan to Tammuz, the green sea is fit to sail upon, so the garments worn were green; and from Tammuz to Tishri, fruits are shapely and red-cheeked, so the garments worn were red.[4]

121. [Who has been able to move as rapidly[5] as I?" (Eccles. 2:25). Who has done, Solomon asked, what I have done? Thus,] in the words "And he built Tadmor in the wilderness" (2 Chron. 8:4), there is the implication, according to R. Jeremiah, who cited R. Samuel bar R. Isaac, that Solomon had a large eagle upon whose back he used to ride to and from Tadmor in the wilderness[6] in one day.[7]

1. The kerchiefs were wound as turbans and served as pockets without being removed from their heads.
2. "Those who are not sons of the covenant of Abraham cannot bear the Divine Presence" (Ginzberg, *Legends* 6:290).
3. Targum Sheni on Esther; Yalkut ha-Makhiri, ed L. Grünhut (Jerusalem, 1902), Prov. 20.
4. BhM 5:39.
5. JV: "Who will enjoy?" But *hush* ("to enjoy,") also means "to move fast, rapidly."
6. Palmyra, an oasis in the Syrian desert.
7. Eccles. R. 2:25, §1.

Solomon—King and Commoner

122. "I got me male and female demons" (Eccles. 2:8).[8] [Male and female demons?] For what purpose did Solomon get them? Because it is said, "The house, when it is in building, is to be built of stone made ready before it is brought thither: so that neither hammer nor ax nor any tool of iron shall be heard in the house, while it is in building" (1 Kings 6:7). Solomon asked the sages, "Then how can it be built?" They said to him, "You could build it if you had the *shamir*, which Moses brought to cut the stones in the ephod." Solomon asked, "Where is the *shamir* to be found?" They replied, "Get a male and a female demon, and press them hard one against the other. Perhaps they know and will tell you." So Solomon went and got a male and a female demon, and pressed them one against the other. But the demons said to him, "We do not know. Perhaps Ashmedai, king of the demons, knows." Solomon asked them, "Where is he?" They answered, "He is in such-and-such a mountain, where he has dug himself a pit, filled it with water, covered it with stone, and sealed it with his signet. Every day Ashmedai goes up to heaven and studies in the academy on high. Then he comes down to the earth and studies in an academy below. After that, he examines his seal, opens the pit, and drinks from it; then he covers it again, seals it, and goes on his way."

At once Solomon sent for Benaiah the son of Jehoiada and gave him a chain and a signet ring with the Ineffable Name engraved on each. He also gave him wool fleece and jugs of wine.

Benaiah went and dug a ditch from below to Ashmedai's pit and drained the water into it. Then he stopped up the ditch with the wool fleece. Above the pit he dug another ditch, through which he poured the wine into Ashmedai's pit. He covered both ditches with earth, climbed to the top of a tree, and seated himself there.

When Ashmedai came, he examined the seal, opened the pit, and found wine. He said, "It is written, 'Wine is a mocker, strong drink is riotous; and whosoever is deceived thereby is not wise' " (Prov. 20:1). And so he did not drink. But when he grew very thirsty, he could no longer restrain himself; he drank, became drunk, and fell asleep. Then Benaiah came down and threw over him the chain [on which the Ineffable Name was engraved] and bound him. When Ashmedai woke up and began to struggle madly, Benaiah said, "The Name of your Master is upon the chain," and grasped him firmly, so that Ashmedai had to go with him. Yet, when Ashmedai came to a palm tree, he rubbed himself against it and threw it down, and when he came to a house, he overturned it. When he reached the hut of a widow, she came out and begged mercy of him. So he jerked his bulk away from the hut so abruptly that he broke a bone, at which he said, "This

8. JV: "I got me men singers and women singers." But the words *shiddah* and *shiddot*, which in JV are translated "men singers and women singers," are obscure. The meaning "demon" (*shed*) is as admissible as any proposed.

bears out the verse 'A soft tongue breaketh the bone' " (Prov. 25:15). When he saw a blind man wandering off the path, he brought him back. When he saw a drunken man staggering off the path, he brought him back. When he saw a wedding procession on its merry way, he wept. When he heard a man say to a shoemaker, "Make me a pair of shoes that will last seven years," he laughed. When he saw a diviner practicing divination upon a loaf of bread, he laughed again.

After they arrived in Jerusalem, Ashmedai was not taken before Solomon for three days. On the first day, he asked, "Why am I not summoned before the king?" and when he was told, "Drink has overcome the king," he picked up a brick and placed it upon another. When this was reported to Solomon, he said, "By this Ashmedai meant that you are to give me more wine to drink." The next day Ashmedai again asked, "Why am I not summoned before the king?" and when he was told, "Too much food constrains the king," Ashmedai took the brick and set it back on the ground. When they came and reported this to Solomon, he said, "Ashmedai meant that you are to deny me food."

At the end of the third day, when Ashmedai was brought before Solomon, he measured off four cubits on a reed and, throwing it before Solomon, said, "When you are dead, you will own nothing in this world but four cubits [of earth]. Yet now, having subdued the whole world, you were not satisfied until you also subdued me." Solomon replied, "I want nothing at all that is yours. But because I desire to build the Temple, I need the *shamir*." Ashmedai said to him, "The *shamir* was not placed in my charge but given to the prince of the sea, and he gave sole charge of it to the wild cock,[1] who is entrusted with it on his oath. Do you know what he does with it? He takes it to an uninhabited mountain and sets it down upon the peak, and the mountain splits asunder. Then the wild cock gathers seeds of trees and scatters them in the split, which consequently attracts settlers." (Hence the Aramaic Targum calls the wild cock the "splitter of mountains.")

They sought out the nest of the wild cock and found fledglings in it, so they covered it with a white glass. The wild cock came and tried to get into the nest, but could not. He went and fetched the *shamir*, and was about to set it down upon the glass that covered the nest. But at that moment they threw a pebble at the wild cock, causing him to drop the *shamir*, and thus they were able to take it away. When the wild cock realized that he had failed to keep his oath, he went and strangled himself.

[After the *shamir* was brought in], Benaiah asked Ashmedai, "When you saw the blind man wander off the path, why did you bring him back?" Ashmedai replied, "Because in heaven it was proclaimed of the blind man that he was a completely righteous man, and that whoever did him a kindness would merit life in the world-to-come."

"And when you saw the drunken man stagger off the path, why did you bring him back?" [Ashmedai replied], "Because in heaven it was proclaimed that he was a completely wicked man, and so I help him enjoy life in this world."

"And when you saw the wedding procession, why did you weep?" [Ashmedai replied], "Because the husband was to die within thirty days, and the wife would have to wait thirteen years before the husband's [infant] brother would be of an age to marry her."

"And when you saw the man say to the shoemaker, 'Make me shoes that will last seven years,' why did you laugh?" [Ashmedai replied], "The man did not have seven days to live, and he wanted shoes for seven years!"

"And when you saw the diviner divining, why did you laugh?" [Ashmedai replied], "He was sitting over a king's treasure and should have divined and found out what was underneath him!"

Solomon detained Ashmedai while the Temple was being built. One day when the two were standing alone, Solomon said to him, "In what way is your power superior to ours?" Ashmedai answered, "Remove the chain from my back and give me your ring, and I will show you how great is my power." Solomon removed the chain from his back and gave him the ring. Ashmedai swallowed it, and, setting one of his wings down on the earth and the other in the sky, he hurled Solomon a distance of four hundred parasangs [and then went and sat himself down on the throne in the guise of the king]. Of that time, Solomon said, "What profit hath a man of all his labor, wherein he laboreth under the sun" (Eccles. 1:3), and, "This is my portion from all my labor" (Eccles. 2:10)—all I have is my walking stick. At the beginning, "I, Koheleth, was king over Israel" (Eccles. 1:12), and now I am king only over my walking stick.

Solomon had to go begging at doorways, and wherever he went he would declare, " 'I, Koheleth, was king over Israel in Jerusalem'." And people said, "King Solomon is seated on his throne in Jerusalem; you are out of your mind." And they tapped him with a length of reed [as is done to quiet a lunatic] and set before him a dish of boiled grits. It was then that Solomon said to himself: This is my portion after all my labor. When he reached the Sanhedrin, the sages said, "A madman does not hold fast to the same illusion. What kind of man is this person?" So they went to Benaiah and asked him, "Does the king summon you?" and he said, "No!" They sent to the queens: "Does the king come to you?" They replied, "Yes." They sent word again: "Examine his feet." The queens replied, "He comes to us with socks on his feet."[2]

They brought Solomon back and gave him the ring and the chain on which the Name was engraved. As soon as Solomon came in, Ashmedai saw him and fled.[3]

123. When Solomon had been removed from his throne and went from door to door begging for food, a man met him and, prostrating himself before him, said, "My lord king, if you please, deign to visit me today." At once Solomon went with the man, who took him to an upper chamber in his home, where he slaughtered an ox for him

1. In §119 above in this chapter, *tarnegol ha-bar* is translated not as "wild cock" but as "hoopoe."

2. The socks concealed Ashmedai's cloven hoofs.

3. B. Git 68a–b; MTeh 78:12; Tanhuma B, *Ahare*, §2.

and served him many viands. Then the man began to remind Solomon of matters that had taken place when he was king: "Do you remember your doing such-and-such when you were king?" The moment the man reminded Solomon of the time he was king, Solomon broke down and wept. He wept thus throughout the meal and continued to weep even after he stood up to leave.

The next day, another man met Solomon. He, too, prostrated himself before him and said, "My lord king, if you please, deign to visit me today." Solomon replied, "What will you do for me?" Will you perhaps do to me what your friend did yesterday?" The man said, "My lord, I am only a poor man. But if you will visit me, I have a few greens, which I will set before you. So if you are willing, come with me to my house." Solomon went with him. When Solomon reached his house, the man washed Solomon's face, hands, and feet, and served him the few greens he had. Then he began to comfort him, saying, "My lord, the Holy One swore an oath to your father that royalty would not cease in his seed. However, such is the way of the Holy One—He reprimands, but then comes back and conciliates. Be assured that the Holy One will restore you to your throne."

After Solomon did return to the throne, in his wisdom he spoke of this experience with the force of prophecy, " 'Better is the dinner of greens' [Prov. 15:17] that I ate at the poor man's home 'than the fattened ox' [ibid.] that the rich man fed me only to remind me of my distress."[1]

124. "It came to pass, when Solomon was old, that his wives turned away his heart after other gods" (1 Kings 11:4). R. Hiyya bar Abba said: It would have been better for Solomon to have cleaned sewers than to have such a verse written of him.[2]

Jeroboam

125. R. Judah said in the name of Rav: When David said to Mephibosheth, "Thou and Ziba divide the land" (2 Sam. 19:30), a divine voice came forth and said: Rehoboam and Jeroboam will divide the kingdom. In this connection, R. Judah said further in the name of Rav: Had David been unwilling to accept Ziba's slanderous talk [about Mephibosheth], not only would David's kingdom not have been divided, but Israel would not have given themselves to idolatry,[3] nor would we have been exiled from our Land.[4]

126. "Rehoboam went to Shechem; for all Israel were come to Shechem to make him king" (1 Kings 12:1)—to a place, so it is taught in the name of R. Yose, predestined for calamity. Dinah was ravished in Shechem, Joseph's brothers sold Joseph in Shechem, even as the kingdom of the house of David was to be divided in Shechem.[5]

127. Our masters taught: The name Jeroboam [Yerov'am] implies that he fomented strife (*merivah*) among the people (*am*). Another interpretation: It implies that he caused strife between Israel and their Father in heaven.

R. Yohanan said: Why did Jeroboam merit kingship? Because he reproved Solomon. Why then was he punished? Because he reproved him in public, as is said, "And this was the cause that [Jeroboam] lifted up his hand against the king: Solomon built Millo, and repaired the breach of the city of David his father" (1 Kings 11:27). What Jeroboam said to Solomon was: Your father David made breaches in the wall, so that Israel could readily come up to Jerusalem in pilgrimage for the festivals; but you closed them to make a tollgate for the benefit of Pharaoh's daughter.[6]

R. Nahman said: The arrogance that possessed Jeroboam drove him out of the world,[7] for "Jeroboam said in his heart: 'Now will the kingdom return to the house of David. If this people go up to offer sacrifices in the house of the Lord at Jerusalem, then will the heart of this people turn back unto their lord, even unto Rehoboam king of Judah; and they will kill me' " (1 Kings 12:26–27). He reasoned thus: It is a tradition that sitting in the court of the Temple is prohibited except to kings of the house of David. Now, when the people see Rehoboam seated and me standing, they will say of him, "Here is the king," and of me, "There is the servant." Were I to sit down, I would be deemed a rebel against royal authority. I would be put to death, and the people would follow Rehoboam. "Wherefore the king took counsel, and made two calves of gold" (1 Kings 12:28). How did he go about procuring the counsel he sought? [In the council chamber], so said R. Judah, he seated a wicked man right next to a righteous one and asked both, "Will you sign your consent to all I may do?" They replied, "Yes." He then said, "I wish to be made king." They said, "Yes, good." "Will you obey all that I bid you do?" "Yes." "Even to worship idols?" "God forbid," the righteous man replied. The wicked one asked the righteous one, "Can the thought enter your mind that a man such as Jeroboam would worship idols? He merely wishes to test all of you, to see whether you are willing to accept what he has to say." In the end, even Ahijah of Shiloh erred and signed his consent.[8]

128. On the very day that Jeroboam introduced two golden calves, one into Bethel and the other into Dan, far away there was built a hut [to which more and more and more huts were added, until] the area became known as Magna Graecia.[9]

---

1. Yalkut, Prov., §953.
2. Tanhuma, *Va-era*, §5; Exod. R. 6:1.
3. To maintain the independence of his kingdom, Jeroboam set up the golden calves at Dan and Bethel.
4. As punishment for such idolatry. B. Shab 56b.
5. B. Sanh 102a.
6. Since few openings were left in Jerusalem's walls, visitors could be checked closely and made to pay for the privilege of coming to Jerusalem.
7. Led to his destruction.
8. B. Sanh 101b.
9. Greek Italy, that is, Rome. B. Shab 56b.

129. R. Oshaiah said: Until Jeroboam, Israel used to suck its proneness to idolatry from only one calf; but thenceforth from two—indeed, from three—calves.[1]

130. "After this occurrence Jeroboam returned not from his evil way" (1 Kings 13:33). After what occurrence? R. Abba said: After the Holy One had seized Jeroboam by his garment and said, "Repent; then I, you, and the son of Jesse will walk together in the Garden of Eden." "But who," Jeroboam asked, "shall be at the head?" [God]: "The son of Jesse shall be at the head." [Jeroboam]: "If so, I will not have it."[2]

Omri and Ahab

131. R. Yohanan taught: Why did Omri merit kingship? Because he added a large city to the Land of Israel, as is said, "He bought the hill Samaria from Shemer . . . and called the name of the city which he built . . . Samaria" (1 Kings 16:24).[3]

132. In the school of Elijah it is taught: One day I was seated in the presence of sages in the great academy of Jerusalem, and I asked them: My masters, why was Omri, captain of the hosts of Israel, treated differently [from those who had occupied the throne of Israel previously]? Before him, no king had his grandson accede to the throne, whereas after Omri, three of his descendants [a son and two grandsons] came successively to the throne.[4] They replied: We have not heard [any explanation of this.] I said: My masters, Omri was treated differently because he added a large city[5] to the number of cities in Israel: his purpose was to make Samaria for the kings of Israel the same as Jerusalem was for the kings of Judah.[6]

133. Our masters taught: Though the men of Ahab's generation—all of them—worshiped idols, they were victorious when they went into battle because there were no informers among them. Therefore, when Elijah called out to the people on Mount Carmel, "I, even I only, am left a prophet of the Lord" (1 Kings 18:22), though all the people knew otherwise, none made it known to the king [that there were a hundred prophets whom Obadiah had hidden].[7]

134. The verse "Their altars are as heaps in the furrows of the fields" (Hos. 12:12) implies that there was not one furrow in the Land of Israel upon which Ahab did not set up an idol and prostrate himself before it.[8]

135. Every day Ahab used to adorn himself; then, standing in front of Hiel, who was in charge of his treasuries, he would ask, "How handsome am I today?" Hiel would reply, "Each day, more and more." Then Ahab would turn over the equivalent of his worth in money to shrines of idolatry. With regard to this, Ahab was told, "[I will bring disaster upon you, because] to do evil in the sight of the Lord, [you kept selling your person]" (1 Kings 21:20).

"But there was none like unto Ahab, who gave himself to do what was evil in the sight of the Lord" (1 Kings 21:25). For six months R. Levi expounded this verse, to Ahab's discredit. Then Ahab appeared to him [in a dream] during the night and asked, "In what way have I sinned or transgressed against you? For you expand upon the verse's beginning, but ignore its conclusion—'Jezebel his wife stirred him up' " (ibid.). Thereafter, for the next six months, R. Levi expounded the entire verse: "There was none like unto Ahab . . . whom Jezebel his wife stirred up."[9]

136. Ahab was equally balanced between good and evil, as implied by the words "The Lord said: Who shall entice Ahab so that he will . . . fall? One [of the host of heaven] said: 'On the one hand [he deserves to fall]'; but another said: 'On the other hand [he does not deserve to fall]' " (1 Kings 22:20).[10] R. Joseph objected [to such a characterization of Ahab]: He of whom it is said, "There was none like unto Ahab, who kept giving himself to do that which was evil in the sight of the Lord, whom Jezebel his wife stirred up" (1 Kings 21:25), and of whose wife it is taught that every day she used to weigh out gold shekels for shrines of idolatry—you say of such a man that he was equally balanced between good and evil! He was not! But Ahab was generous with his money—with his means he used to benefit disciples of the wise. Hence, half his sins were forgiven him.[11]

137. The name Ahab [Ah'av] means that he was a wavering brother (*ah*) to Heaven, but a loving father (*av*) to idolatry.[12]

138. Naboth had a good voice, and whenever he came up to Jerusalem, all Israel would gather to hear his voice [in song]. The one time he failed to make the pilgrimage, witnesses [suborned by Jezebel], vile rogues, testified against him [so that he was condemned to be stoned] and thus perished out of the world.[13]

139. "And there came forth a spirit, and stood before the Lord, and said: 'I will entice him' " (1 Kings 22:21).[14]

---

1. The one they made at Sinai and the two Jeroboam made at Bethel and Dan. B. Sanh 102a.
2. Ibid.
3. B. Sanh 102b.
4. Omri's son Ahab, and Ahab's two sons, Ahaziah and Joram (1 Kings 16:29 and 22:40; 2 Kings 3:1). Of Omri's predecessors, Jeroboam's and Baasa's sons, but not their grandsons, came to the throne. See 1 Kings 15:25–27 and 16:8–9.
5. Before Samaria, the capital Tirzah was presumably a city of lesser importance. See 1 Kings 14:17, 15:33, 16:6, 16:8–9, and *passim.*
6. TdE, ed. Friedmann, p. 49.
7. See 1 Kings 18:3–14. Yalkut, 1 Kings, §213; Tanhuma, *Hukkat*, §4.
8. B. Sanh 102b.
9. P. Sanh 10:2, 28b.
10. The verse is interpreted thus by Samuel Edels, ad loc. JV: "And one said: On this manner; and another said: On that manner."
11. B. Sanh 102b.
12. Ibid.
13. Yalkut, 1 Kings, §221; PR 25:2 (YJS 2:517).
14. Entice Ahab to march against Ramoth-gilead, where he would fall.

Whose spirit was it? "The spirit," said R. Yohanan, "of Naboth the Jezreelite."[1]

Elijah and the Worshipers of Baal

140. "Let them therefore give us two bullocks" (1 Kings 18:23). Elijah said to the prophets of Baal: Select two bullocks equal in all respects, from the same dam, reared at the same trough. Then cast lots for them, one for the Lord and the other for Baal. So the prophets of Baal chose for themselves one of the bullocks. Elijah's bullock followed him immediately. As for the bullock intended for Baal, though all the prophets of Baal and all the prophets of the Asherah gathered around to make it lift its feet from the ground, they could not get it to do so until Elijah began to speak to it, urging, "Go along with them." The bullock replied by saying to Elijah in the presence of all the people, "My brother and I have come from the same belly, from the same sire: have grown up on the same pasture and fed from the same trough. Yet he has fallen to the lot of Him who is everywhere, and the Name of the Holy One will be sanctified in him, while I have fallen to the lot of Baal to provoke my Creator." Elijah said to it, "Bullock, bullock, feat not! Go with them, so that they will find no excuse for failure. Indeed, even as the Name of the Holy One will be sanctified through the bullock that is with me, so will it be sanctified through you." The animal replied, "Is such the advice you give me? Then I swear I shall not budge from here until you yourself turn me over into their hands." At that, "they took the bullock which he gave them" (1 Kings 18:26). Who gave it to them? Elijah.[2]

141. "And it danced in halting wise about the altar which he made" (1 Kings 18:26). Hiel made the altar hollow, and he was placed inside it and told, "As soon as you hear the sound of dancing feet, stir up the embers you have and make a fire under the altar." At that, the Holy One had a serpent come—it bit Hiel and he died.[3]

Jonah

142. "But Jonah rose up to flee unto Tarshish from the Presence of the Lord" (Jon. 1:3). Why did Jonah flee? Because the first time, when the Holy One sent him to announce the restoration of Israel's borders, his words were fulfilled, for Jeroboam did "restore the borders of Israel from the entrance of Hamath unto the Sea of Arabah" (2 Kings 14:25). Then the Holy One sent him a second time to Jerusalem to announce that He would destroy it. But when Israel resolved to repent, the Holy One, in the abundance of His mercy, regretted the evil decree and did not destroy Jerusalem. Hence Israel called Jonah "a lying prophet."[4] The third time, the Holy One sent him against Nineveh. Jonah reasoned with himself: I know that this people are [more] prone to repentance [than Israel], and so they are likely to repent. Then the Holy One will direct His anger at Israel [who are slow to repent]. It is not enough that Israel call me "a lying prophet"? Shall the nations of the world do likewise? I have no choice but to flee.

Jonah went down to Joppa, but found no ship in which he could embark. So the Holy One sent a windstorm against a ship two days' journey away and blew it back to Joppa. When Jonah saw it, he rejoiced, saying, "Now I know that my conduct is deemed right by the Holy One." So he asked the ship's crew, "May I embark with you?" They replied, "We are going to the islands of the sea, to Tarshish." Jonah: "I would like to go with you to Tarshish."

After they had traveled one day's journey on the sea, a windstorm rose up against them at their right as well as at their left. While all other ships in the sea passed to and fro in safety, the ship on which Jonah had embarked was in great peril. "And the mariners were afraid, and cried every man unto his god" (Jon. 1:5). R. Hananiah said: On the ship there were men speaking the world's seventy languages, and each man, with his god in his hand, said: Let each of us cry out to his god, and the god who answers and delivers us from this peril shall be proclaimed the true god. But though each man cried out to his god, it availed not at all.

"Jonah was gone down into the innermost parts of the ship" (Jon. 1:5) and, despite the anguish in his soul, dozed off and fell asleep. The captain came to Jonah and said, "We are hovering between life and death, and you are off sleeping! Who are your people?" "I am a Hebrew" (Jon. 1:9). The captain: "Have we not heard that the God of the Hebrews is great? 'Rise, call upon thy God, that He bestir Himself in our behalf' [Jon. 1:6] and perform miracles for us even as He did for you at the Red Sea." Jonah: "I dare not hide from you that the trouble that has befallen you is because of me. Take me up and cast me forth into the sea; that the sea may be calm unto you" (Jon. 1:12). However, the crew would not cast him into the sea. "But they cast lots, and the lot fell upon Jonah" (Jon. 1:7). Nevertheless, it was all kinds of the ship's utensils that they took and cast into the sea to lighten its weight, but that did not avail them. They tried to row hard to dry land, but they could not. What did they finally do? They took Jonah, and, stationing themselves at the side of the ship, they said, "God of the universe, Lord! Do not lay upon us innocent blood, that we may not be doomed because of the life of this man, whose character and deeds we do not know but who keeps saying loud and clear, 'This trouble is yours because of me.' " Then they took him and lowered him into the water up to his knees, and the sea's wrath abated. When they hoisted him to their own level into the ship, the sea resumed its raging at them. Then they lowered him to his neck, and the sea's wrath abated once more. But when they lifted him up again to their own level into the ship, the sea again resumed its raging at them. Finally, after they put all of him in, the sea's wrath ceased.

"The Lord had designated a great fish to swallow up Jonah" (Jon. 2:1). That fish, said R. Tarfon, had been designated since the six days of creation to swallow up Jonah. Jonah entered its mouth just as a man might enter a big house, and he was able to remain standing there.

---

1. B. Sanh 102b.
2. Tanhuma, *mas'e*, §8; Num. R. 23:9; Yalkut, 1 Kings, §214.
3. Yalkut, 1 Kings, §214.
4. The prophet in 2 Kings 9:4–12 is identified by Rashi and Kimhi as Jonah.

The two eyes of the fish were like two windows giving light to Jonah. But, according to R. Meir, a pearl was suspended from the innards of the fish, and, like the sun, which gives light at noon, it gave light to Jonah and made it possible for him to see all around him in the sea and in the depths.

The fish asked Jonah, "Are you not aware that my day has come to enter the mouth of Leviathan [and be devoured]?" Jonah: "[Take me] to him, and I will save you and myself." The fish immediately took Jonah to Leviathan's place, and Jonah said, "Leviathan, you should know that it is on account of you that I came down to see the place where you abide. For [in the time-to-come] I am destined to put a rope around your tongue, bring you up, and slaughter you for the great feast of the righteous." At that, Leviathan precipitously swam away from Jonah a distance of two days' journey.

Then Jonah said to the fish: Now that I have saved you from the mouth of Leviathan, show me everything that is in the sea and in the depths below. The fish showed him the great river whence the waters of the Ocean issue; showed him the paths in the Red Sea through which Israel had passed; showed him the place whence the breakers of the sea and its waves originate; showed him the pillars of the earth and its foundations; showed him Gehenna and nethermost Sheol; showed him the Temple of the Lord in heaven and the earth's foundation stone fixed in the deep directly under the Temple of the Lord—on this stone, the sons of Korah continue to stand and pray.[1]

The fish said to Jonah: Look, you now stand near the Temple of the Lord. Pray, and you will be answered. Jonah said to the fish: [Yes, indeed!] Remain still where you are, because I do wish to pray.

The fish remained in its place, and Jonah began to pray to the Holy One, saying: Master of the universe, You are called "the One who casts down and the One who brings up"—behold, I have been cast down; now bring me up. You are called "the One who kills and the One who restores life"—behold, my soul has all but reached death; now restore me to life. But Jonah was not answered until he said, "That which I have vowed, I will perform" (Jon. 2:10). What I vowed—to bring up Leviathan and slaughter him in Your presence for the great feast of the righteous—I will perform on the day of Israel's deliverance. The Holy One immediately beckoned to the fish, and it cast forth Jonah onto dry land.[2]

The Banishment of the Ten Tribes

143. In the twentieth year of Pekah, king of Israel, "came Tiglath-pileser, king of Assyria," etc. (2 Kings 15:29). He took the golden calves, smashed them, and went away. In the twelfth year of Ahaz, "the God of Israel stirred up the spirit of Pul, king of Assyria . . . and he carried them away, even the Reubenites and the Gadites" (1 Chron. 5:26), and also took the golden calf at Bethel, and went away. When [King] Hoshea son of Elah perceived that both golden calves had been carried away, he removed the border posts that Jeroboam son of Nebat had set up to prevent Israel [in the north] from coming up to Jerusalem as pilgrims. Note that Scripture says of every other king of Israel, "And he went in the way of Jeroboam," but of Hoshea son of Elah it says, "He did that which was evil in the sight of the Lord, yet not as the kings of Israel that were before him" (2 Kings 17:2).

"Against [Hoshea] came up Shalmaneser" (2 Kings 17:3). Why had the decree for the banishment of Israel not been sealed prior to his time? Because until Hoshea, Israel could hang responsibility for their corruption on their kings. [But upon Hoshea's coming to the throne], Scripture could say, "I, even I, know Ephraim, and Israel is not hid from Me; for now, O Ephraim, thou [on thine own] hast gone awhoring [with idols]. Hence, Israel defiled itself" (Hos. 5:3).[3]

144. In what way was Hoshea son of Elah different, so that the ten tribes were exiled during his reign? He was different because, until he came to the throne, the transgression of idolatry was identified with a single individual [each successive king], and it was difficult for the Holy One to exile the congregation [of Israel] because of the iniquity of an individual. But when Hoshea son of Elah came along and abolished all the border posts, every one of them, he announced, "Whoever wishes to go up to Jerusalem may go up"—he did not say, "Everyone *must* go up to Jerusalem." Hence, "because of him, came up Shalmaneser king of Assyria" (2 Kings 17:3). For what Hoshea did was to remove the iron collar from his own neck and hang it on the neck of the many [by allowing them to choose not to go up]. Hence the sages said: He who begins performing a precept but does not carry it through makes himself liable to the death penalty.[4]

145. "As the shepherd rescueth out of the mouth of the lion two legs or a piece of an ear" (Amos 3:12). The verse refers to those of the ten tribes who relied on Hezekiah and found safe refuge with him. Whereas, of the Israelites who lived in Samaria, only one in eight remained.[5]

146. Where did Sennacherib deport the ten tribes? To Africa,[6] according to Mar Zutra; to the mountains of Salug,[7] according to R. Hanina.[8]

147. R. Judah bar Simon said: The tribes of Judah and Benjamin were not banished to the place where the ten tribes had been banished. The ten tribes were banished beyond the river Sambatyon, while the tribes of Judah and Benjamin are dispersed in all lands.[9]

---

1. The three sons of Korah survived the death of Korah and his followers. See Num. 26:10.
2. PRE 10; Midrash Jon. in Eisenstein, pp. 218–19.
3. SOR 22.
4. TdE, ed. Friedmann, p. 188.
5. SOR 22.
6. Abrik, 150 kilometers northwest of Diarbekir (Obermeyer, pp. 11ff.).
7. The mountains of Salak in the district of Adiabene. Ibid.
8. B. Sanh 94a.
9. Gen. R. 73:6.

148. In the name of R. Samuel bar Nahman, it is said: Israel were exiled in three successive banishments: the first, beyond the river Sambatyon; the second, to Daphne of Antioch; and the third—a cloud came down upon them and concealed them.[1]

149. The ten tribes will not return [to the Land of Israel], for it is said: "The Lord . . . will cast them into another land, like this day" (Deut. 29:27). Just as this day goes and does not return, so the ten tribes who have gone will not return. Such is the opinion of R. Akiva. But R. Eliezer said: Scripture's saying "like this day" implies that just as the day grows dark and then grows light again, so, too, after darkness has fallen upon the ten tribes, light shall shine for them hereafter.[2]

The Cutheans [Samaritans]

150. The Cutheans are not to be regarded as one of the seventy nations in the world. For they were the remnant of the five nations of Babylon, Cuthah, Avva, Hamath, and Sepharvaim, which the king of Assyria had captured. R. Yose added other peoples as having been included among the Cutheans, namely, the Dinites, the Apharesattechites, the Tarpelites, the Apharesites, the Archevites, the Babylites, the Shushanchites, the Dehites, the Elamites (Ezra 4:9).

After the Israelites were banished from Samaria, Sennacherib stationed officers in Samaria to raise tribute for his kingdom. So the Holy One dispatched lions against the officers, which kept killing them. The survivors wrote to the king: Our lord king, the Land to which you sent us will not accept us—out of many, only a few of us are left. So the king sent word to the elders of Israel, saying: All the years you were in the Land, beasts of the field did not devour you, but now the Land will not accept my officers. The elders responded with advice that they hoped might lead the king to restore the banished Israelites to their own Land. They said: Our lord king, the Land will not accept aliens who are uncircumcised and who do not study Torah. The king replied: Let me have two of your number, who will go and circumcise the newcomers and teach them Torah. Since the king's command may not be denied, the elders sent R. Dostai ben Yannai and R. Zechariah, who wept as they taught the Cutheans Torah in the Notarikon script.[3] Thereafter, the nations [settled in Samaria] followed the statutes of the Torah as well as the statutes of their own gods, until Ezra, together with Zerubbabel son of Shealtiel and Joshua son of Jehozadak, came up from Babylon and began building the Temple. At that time the Samaritans came with a hundred and eighty thousand men to fight against them. (But were they Samaritans? Were they not in fact Cutheans? Yes, but they were called Samaritans after the city of Samaria in which they lived.) They also sought to kill Nehemiah through trickery and for two years caused the work on the Temple of the Lord to cease. What did Ezra, Zerubbabel, and Joshua do? They gathered the entire congregation in the Temple and brought three hundred priests with rams' horns in their hands and three hundred children with Torah scrolls in their arms. [The priests] blew the rams' horns, the Levites hymned songs and praises, and, using the secret Explicit Name, whose letters were incised on the Tablets, they excommunicated the Cutheans by a ban of the court of justice here below and a ban of the court of justice above, [and decreed] that no Jew may eat a Cuthean's bread (hence it is said: He who eats a Cuthean's bread is deemed as though he had eaten the flesh of swine), that no Jew may convert a Cuthean, and that the Cutheans shall have no portion in the resurrection of the dead and neither portion nor inheritance nor memorial in Israel.

The elders sent the writ of the ban to the Jews in Babylonia, who added an additional ban, which King Darius ordained to be a perpetual ban upon them: "May the God that hath caused His Name to dwell there overthrow all kings and peoples that shall put forth their hand to alter the same" (Ezra 6:12).[4]

Hezekiah and the Fall of Sennacherib

151. The name Hezekiah means "he whom God (Yah) has strengthened (*hizzeko*)." Or, "He who fastened (*hizzek*) Israel to their Father in heaven."[5]

152. The verse "The yoke shall be destroyed because of the oil" (Isa. 10:27) means, said R. Isaac Nappaha, that Sennacherib's yoke was destroyed because of Hezekiah's providing oil that burned in synagogues and in houses of study. What did Hezekiah do? He thrust a sword into the ground at the entrance to a house of study and said: He who will not occupy himself with Torah will be transfixed with this sword. After that, search was made from Dan to Beersheba, and no ignoramus was found; from Gabbath to Antipatris, and no boy or girl, no man or woman was found not thoroughly versed even in the laws of cleanness and uncleanness.[6] Of that time, Scripture says, "It shall come to pass on that day that a man will be content to nourish only one young cow and two sheep"[7] (Isa. 7:21), and also, "On that day it shall come to pass that every place where there had been a thousand vines at a thousand silver shekels shall become a wilderness of briers and thorns" (Isa. 7:23): though a thousand vines were worth a thousand silver shekels, yet that vineyard will be abandoned to briers and thorns.[8]

153. The words "The curse of the Lord is in the house of the wicked" (Prov. 3:33) apply to Pekah son of Remaliah, who used to eat forty *seah* of young birds as a

---

1. P. Sanh 10:6, 29c.
2. B. Sanh 110b; Yalkut, *Nitzavim*, §940.
3. The ancient Hebrew script, used before the introduction of the present-day "square" script.
4. PRE 38; Tanhuma, *Va-yeshev*, §2; Yalkut, 2 Kings, §234.
5. B. Sanh 94a.
6. Which are exceedingly difficult to understand.
7. Leaving ample time for study.
8. People will neglect the vines for study of Torah. B. Sanh 94b.

mere dessert;[1] and the words "But He blesseth the habitations of the righteous" (ibid.) apply to Hezekiah, king of Judah, who ate but a *litra* of vegetables as his entire meal.[2]

154. "These also are the proverbs of Solomon, which the men of Hezekiah copied out (*he'etiku*)" (Prov. 25:1). [They were copied out and circulated] after having been suppressed. Or, *he'etiku*, construed as "removed," means that the men of Hezekiah moved them out of circulation [as part of the canon].[3]

155. Our masters taught: King Hezekiah did six things, three of which the sages approved and three others that they did not. The three they approved: He hid away the Book of Cures,[4] and they approved; he smashed the brazen serpent,[5] and they approved; he dragged the bones of his father [to the grave] on a bed of ropes,[6] and they approved.[7] The three they did not approve: He stopped up the waters of Gihon,[8] and they did not approve; he stripped [the gold] from the doors of the Temple and sent it to the king of Assyria, and they did not approve;[9] and he intercalated the month of Nisan during the month of Nisan,[10] and they did not approve.[11]

156. R. Joshua ben Levi said: Sennacherib dared say, "Am I now come up without the Lord against this place to destroy it? The Lord said to me: 'Go up against this Land to destroy it' " (2 Kings 18:25), because he had heard the prophet declare, "Forasmuch as this people refuseth the waters of Shiloah that go gently" (Isa. 8:6)—refused, that is, the kings of the house of David, who led the people gently even as the waters of Shiloah flow gently. Hence Sennacherib applied to himself the words "Now therefore, behold, the Lord will bring up upon them the waters of the river, strong and many, even the king of Assyria" (Isa. 8:7). Why then was Sennacherib punished? Because the prophet prophesied only of the ten tribes, whereas Sennacherib set his face against the whole of Jerusalem. In fact, when the prophet declared, "He who wearies himself will not be for the oppressor" (Isa. 8:23), he meant, so said R. Eleazar bar Berekhiah, that the people that makes itself weary through intensive study of Torah will not be made victim of an oppressor. "Aforetime, the land of Zebulun and the land of Naphtali took [its burden] lightly; but the latter generations who held the burden [of Torah] in high regard—for them, it will be like the way through the sea, like the passing over the Jordan" (ibid.).[12] Unlike [the experience of] former generations,[13] who took the yoke of Torah lightly, the latter generations [Judah and Benjamin] who persisted in making the yoke of Torah ever heavier for themselves will have miracles performed for them—miracles like those that were performed for the Israelites who crossed the Red Sea and who passed over the Jordan.

[Nevertheless, even they of Jerusalem were to be punished for the massacre of the priests at Nob.[14] However, God set a time limit for imposing such punishment.] "Only one day yet remained to stand [against Jerusalem] on account of Nob" (Isa. 10:32).[15] R. Huna said: Only that one day was left for punishing the crime committed at Nob. So Sennacherib's astrologers said to him: If you set out now to attack, you will conquer Jerusalem; if not, you will not conquer it.[16] Therefore, the journey that should have taken ten days,[17] he completed in only one day. When the Assyrians reached Jerusalem, Sennacherib's soldiers piled up a great many mattresses for him, so that, by mounting the pile, he was able to sit on a level higher than the city wall and see all of Jerusalem. As he gazed on it, it appeared so small in his eyes that he was moved to ask his troops, "Is this the city on whose account I scared up all my soldiers, summoned the entire might of my realm? Why, it is smaller and weaker than any one of the cities of the nations I subdued with [but a portion of] my armed strength." Then he stood up and, shaking his head in disbelief [at the number of troops brought], contemptuously waved his hand back and forth from the direction of fair Zion's mount to the Temple Court in Jerusalem. In the meantime, the astrologers kept urging, "Let us attack today—at once." But Sennacherib said to his soldiers, "You are weary today, having just come from a distant land. So rest up for the night. Tomorrow [you will conquer Jerusalem so easily that] each of you will bring me a stone from its demolished wall."

As Sennacherib was speaking, his court official, Rabshakeh, looking at the wall, heard Israel chanting the Passover *Hallel*.[18] So he said to Sennacherib, "Go back. On this night miracles are wrought for Israel." But Sennacherib made little of the warning, as again he contemptuously "waved his hand toward fair Zion's mount" (Isa. 10:32). Whereupon "it came to pass that night that the angel of the Lord went forth and smote in the camp

1. Even then his hunger was not satisfied. The metaphor may refer to the fact that Pekah, a mere captain, conspired against the legitimate king and slew him.
2. And was nevertheless satisfied. B. Sanh 94b.
3. See Eliezer (Louis) Finkelstein, *Mavo le-Massekhtot Avot ve-Avot de-R. Natan* (New York, 1951), pp. 126–27. Yalkut, Prov., §961; Midrash Prov. 25 (ed. Buber, p. 97).
4. So the sick would direct their hearts to Heaven.
5. 2 Kings 18:4.
6. Instead of giving him a royal burial.
7. Because his father Ahaz was a wicked man.
8. To deprive the Assyrian invaders of water. 2 Chron. 32:30.
9. 2 Kings 18:16.
10. A second Nisan must not be intercalated. Or: He intercalated a second Adar so late in the month of Adar that it seemed as though he were intercalating the second Adar when Nisan had already set in.
11. B. Ber 10b.
12. JV: "Now the former hath lightly afflicted the land of Zebulun and the land of Naphtali, but the latter hath dealt a more grievous blow by the way of the sea, beyond the Jordan."
13. The ten tribes, who were exiled in 722 B.C.E.
14. 1 Sam. 22:17–19.
15. Literally, "And yet shall he halt at Nob that day."
16. Sennacherib was king of Assyria in 705–681 B.C.E. He invaded Judah in the fourteenth year of Hezekiah's reign.
17. The ten days' journey is deduced from the listing of the ten marches in Isa. 10:28–31.
18. Psalms in praise of God—Pss. 113–118.

of the Assyrians. . . . And the following morning, they were all dead corpses" (2 Kings 19:35; Isa. 37:36).

Concerning the above, R. Papa cited the proverb "Sentence delayed overnight is sentence repealed."[1]

157. R. Judah said in the name of Rav: [In the days of Hezekiah], wicked Sennacherib advanced against Israel with forty-five thousand princes, each seated in a golden chariot, each accompanied by his consorts and concubines; with eighty thousand warriors in coats of mail; with sixty thousand swordsmen at a run in front of him, and the rest on horseback.

It is taught: The length of Sennacherib's camp was four hundred parasangs; the horses standing neck to neck formed a line forty parasangs in width; and the total of his army numbered two million six hundred thousand less one. The troops were so numerous that, although the vanguard had to swim across rivers, the midmost were able to wade across them, while the feet of the rearguard kicked up the sand [from riverbeds][2] where no water was found to drink until brought from elsewhere—only then were they able to satisfy their thirst.

(But it is not written, "And it came to pass that night that the angel of the Lord went forth and smote in the camp of the Assyrians a hundred fourscore and five thousand; and the following morning, they were all dead corpses" [2 Kings 19:35]?[3] R. Abbahu replied: These were just the army captains.)

The Holy One asked Gabriel: Is your sickle sharpened [to cut down the Assyrians]? He replied: Master of the universe, it has been sharpened and made ready ever since the six days of creation. It was the time of year, so said R. Simeon ben Yohai, for fruits to ripen. Hence the Holy One told Gabriel: On your way to ripen fruits,[4] as you pass [the Assyrians], attack them, in keeping with the advice "As he passeth, he should take you on" (Isa. 28:19).

R. Papa said: The saying, "When you pass, make your enemy aware of you" applies here.[5]

"While the king sat at his table" (Song 1:12). R. Yudan said: While Hezekiah and his company were still eating their paschal lambs in Jerusalem, God had already wrought their deliverance that very night: "It came to pass that night that the angel of the Lord went forth and smote in the camp of the Assyrians" (2 Kings 19:35).[6]

158. Some say: Gabriel huffed out of his nose at the Assyrians and they died, as is said, "He huffed upon them, and they withered" (Isa. 40:24). R. Jeremiah bar Abba said: Gabriel struck his hands together at them and they died, as is said, "I will strike hand against hand, and will satisfy my fury upon you" (Ezek. 21:22). R. Isaac Nappaha said: He unsealed their ears for them, so that they were able to hear the song of the celestial creatures in the chariot,[7] and they died, as is said, "At the [sound of] exaltation of Thee the heathen were shattered" (Isa. 33:3).

How many [Assyrians] were left? Ten, said Rav, for it is written, "The remnant of the trees of his forest shall be so few that a child may write them down" (Isa. 10:19). What number can even a child write? Ten.[8] Six, said R. Eliezer, the length of a scratch that a young lad can make in a wall.[9]

159. Pharaoh king of Egypt and Tirhakah king of Ethiopia, who had come to help Hezekiah,[10] benefited from that miracle. [Before they reached Hezekiah], Sennacherib became aware that they were coming. What did the wicked Sennacherib do to them? [He managed to capture them and] in the evening put them in fetters. At midnight the angel went forth and smote the hosts of Sennacherib. When Hezekiah rose in the morning and found the two kings in fetters, he said, "It appears that the two had come to help me." So of course he released them, and both of them went forth to tell the miracles and mighty acts of the Holy One.[11]

160. When Sennacherib came and laid siege to Jerusalem, Shebna wrote a note declaring, "Shebna and his followers are willing to make peace; Hezekiah and his followers are not willing," [and inserted the note] in an arrow, which he shot [into the enemy's camp. When he heard about the note], Hezekiah was afraid, saying, "Perhaps the mind of the Holy One will, Heaven forbid, incline toward the majority [who wish to surrender]." The prophet came and said, "Do not dignify it with the name 'confederacy' merely because most of this people say it is a confederacy [Isa. 8:12]: it is a confederacy of the wicked, and a confederacy of the wicked cannot be counted [in arriving at a decision]."

[Parenthetically, prior to Shebna's organizing his conspiracy, he aspired to the throne of David.] He even went to hew out a sepulcher for himself among the sepulchers of the house of David. It was then that the prophet Isaiah came and said to him, " 'What hast thou here, and whom hast thou here, that thou wouldst hew thee out a sepulcher here? . . . Take note, the Lord will continue to drive you

1. B. Sanh 95a; Targum Jonathan on Isa. 10:32; Yalkut, Isa., §415.
2. "The draining of the rivers may be another way of indicating the size of Sennacherib's army, which began its approach at the end of the rainy season, when the rivers were swollen, and reached its goal only at the end of summer, when the rivers ran dry." (Pearl F. Braude, Providence, R.I.).
3. Proving that the total of Sennacherib's army was much less than two million.
4. One of Gabriel's tasks.
5. B. Sanh 95b.
6. Song R. 1:12, §3.
7. Possibly metaphors for, respectively, a khamsin, an earthquake, and thunder and lightning. So Ze'ev Wolf Rabinovitz, *Shaare Torat Bavel* (Jerusalem, 1961), p. 167.
8. Represented in Hebrew by the letter *yod*, which "being formed by the mere stroke of a pen, is the easiest letter for a child to write" (Isidore Epstein in Sanh, Soncino, p. 645, n.11).
9. The length of the letter *vav* in the Assyrian script used today—not in the ancient Hebrew script current in Hezekiah's time (BR's note). B. Sanh 95b; Lam.R. 4:12, §15.
10. See Isa. 36:6 and 37:9.
11. Song R. 4:8, §3.

from place to place like a cock'[1] [Isa. 22:16–17]. You drifter and son of a drifter,[2] [what gives you the right to aspire to royalty]? What wall have you ever built here? What pillar have you ever set up here? Indeed, what nail have you ever driven in here?"

[To come back to the conspiracy: When Shebna went out of Jerusalem to surrender to Sennacherib], Gabriel came and shut the city gate in the face of his troops, [cutting him off from them]. On being asked, "Where are your followers?" Shebna answered, "They deserted me." So, saying, "You made us appear ridiculous," the Assyrians bored holes through Shebna's heels, and through these holes tied him to the tails of their horses and dragged him over thorns and thistles.[3]

161. R. Yohanan said: [Why did Sennacherib], that evil man, merit being referred to as "the great and noble Asenappar" (Ezra 4:10)? Because he did not speak disparagingly of the Land of Israel, for his aide Rab-shakeh quoted him as saying, "Until I come and take you away to a land like your own Land" (2 Kings 18:32). Rav and Samuel [differ as to what Sennacherib's saying "a land like your own Land" reveals about his mental capacity]. One maintained he was a wise king, for had he said, "A land that is better than your own," they would have replied, "You lie." The other maintained that he was a foolish king, because if the land to which they were to be taken was no better than their own, what inducement was offered them [to leave it]?[4]

162. Maintaining that Sennacherib was a foolish king who did not know how to win people, R. Simeon ben Yohai told the parable of a man who, wishing to marry a certain woman, said to her: Your father is a king, and I, too, am a king. Your father is rich and I am rich. Your father gives you meat and fish to eat and aged wine to drink, and I, too, will give you meat and fish to eat and aged wine to drink. Such talk is not likely to win the lady's heart. What would have been an effective way of winning her? His saying: Your father is a commoner, but I am a king; your father is poor, but I am rich; your father gives you vegetables and pulse to eat and water to drink, but I will give you meat and fish to eat and aged wine to drink; your father takes you to the baths on foot, but I will take you in a palanquin.[5]

163. R. Berekhiah said in the name of R. Eleazar: By rights Hezekiah should have hymned a song of praise over the fall of Sennacherib, but Scripture records that "Hezekiah rendered not according to the benefit done unto him" (2 Chron. 32:25). Why did he not do so? Because "his heart was puffed up" (ibid.). Think about it! Though a king, Hezekiah was nevertheless a righteous man, yet Scripture says of him, "His heart was puffed up." It can only mean that he felt himself to be above chanting a hymn of praise. So when Isaiah came to Hezekiah and his retinue, and said to them, "Sing unto the Lord" (Isa. 12:5), they replied, "Why?" Isaiah said, "Because He hath done gloriously" (ibid.). They said, "But this is already known in all the earth" (ibid.). And, according to R. Abba bar Kahana, Hezekiah went on to say, "The Torah in which I am engaged makes up for the lack of song"; and, according to R. Levi, Hezekiah continued in the same vein: "What need have we to proclaim the miracles and mighty deeds of the Holy One? They are already known from world's end to world's end. Did not the orb of the sun stand still in the midst of the firmament long ago, so that the miracles and mighty deeds of the Holy One were seen to the ends of the world?"[6]

164. There were four kings, David, Asa, Jehoshaphat, and Hezekiah—not one asked of God what each of the others was to ask. David asked, "Let me pursue mine enemies and overtake them, and not turn back till they are consumed" (Ps. 18:38; 2 Sam. 22:38). The Holy One replied, "I will help you do so." Then "David smote them from dawn until evening into the morrow of the next day" (1 Sam. 30:17)—[thus on two nights the Holy One gave him light by shooting stars and lightning flashes]. Hence David said, "Thou dost light my lamp; the Lord my God doth lighten my darkness" (Ps. 18:29; 2 Sam. 22:29).

Then Asa rose up and asked, "I—in me there is no strength to slay them. All that I can do is pursue them. You slay them." The Holy One replied, "I will do so." Hence it is said, "Asa and the people that were with him pursued them. . . . None remained alive: for they were shattered before the Lord" (2 Chron. 14:12)—not "before Asa," but "before the Lord."

Then Jehoshaphat rose up and asked, "I—I have not the strength either to slay or to pursue, but I will utter a song, and You do [the pursuing and the slaying]." The Holy One replied, "I will do so." Then, "when they began to sing and to praise, the Lord set an ambush against the Ammonites . . . and they were smitten" (2 Chron. 20:22).

Finally, Hezekiah rose up and asked, "I—I have not the strength to slay, to pursue, or to utter song, but I will sleep in my bed, and You do what is required." The Holy One replied, "I will do so." Then "it came to pass that night that the angel of the Lord went forth and smote in the camp of the Assyrians" (2 Kings 19:35).[7]

165. "Of the increase (*le-marbeh*) of [Hezekiah's] government and of peace there shall be no end" (Isa. 9:6). R. Tanhum related that Bar Kappara expounded this verse in Sepphoris as follows: Why is every *mem* in the middle

1. JV: "Behold, the Lord will hurl thee up and down with a man's throw." But *gever* ("man") also means "cock."
2. In Isa. 22:15, Shebna is called *sokhen*, usually translated "steward." But here the commentator takes the word to mean "the man from Sikhnin," a town in northern Galilee, who came to Jerusalem as a kind of carpetbagger.
3. B. Sanh 26a–b; Lev. R. 5:5.
4. B. Sanh 94a.
5. Sif Deut. §37; Yalkut, 2 Kings, §238.
6. Song R. 4:8, §3.
7. At a time when, it is assumed, Hezekiah was in bed. Lam R., proem 30; Yalkut, 2 Sam., §163.

of a word open while the one in this verse is closed?[1] Because the Holy One was about to designate Hezekiah as the Messiah, and Sennacherib as Gog and Magog.[2] But the attribute of justice[3] spoke up to the Holy One: Master of the universe, David, king of Israel, who uttered so many hymns and praises before You, You did not make the Messiah, yet Hezekiah, for whom You performed all manner of miracles and who uttered no hymn in praise of You—him You are about to make the Messiah? Following the argument by the attribute of justice, the letter *mem* was closed.[4] Immediately, the earth exclaimed: Master of the universe, as proxy for this righteous man, I will utter song before You—designate him the Messiah. And the earth broke into song before Him, as is written, "From the uttermost ends of the earth have we heard song: 'Glory to the Righteous' " (Isa. 24:16). Then the prince of the world spoke up before the Holy One: Master of the universe, as proxy for this righteous man, the earth has just now fulfilled Your desire [for a song of praise].[5] But a divine voice cried out and said, "[The delay in the Messiah's coming] 'is My secret, My secret' " (Isa. 24:16). To which the prophet replied, " 'Woe is me' [ibid.], woe is me, how long [must we wait]?" In response, a divine voice cried out, "Until 'the faithless who acted faithlessly will themselves have been betrayed.' " (ibid.).[6]

It was taught in the name of R. Pappias: It is a reproach to Hezekiah and his retinue that they uttered no song [to God] until the earth had first broken out into singing.[7]

Hezekiah and Isaiah

166. [King Hezekiah and the prophet Isaiah refused to go to each other's home], Hezekiah saying, "Let Isaiah come to me, for we find that Elijah went to Ahab," and Isaiah saying, "Let Hezekiah come to me, for we find that Joram son of Ahab went to Elisha." What did the Holy One do? He brought illness upon Hezekiah and then said to Isaiah: "Go, visit the sick."[8]

"And Isaiah . . . came to him and said: . . . Thou shalt die and not live" (Isa. 38:1)—"thou shalt die" in this world; "and not live" in the world-to-come. Hezekiah asked, "Why punishment so severe?" Isaiah: "Because you did not wed." Hezekiah: "I did not wed because through the holy spirit I saw that unworthy children would issue from me." Isaiah: "What business have you with the mysterious ways of the Holy One? What you are commanded, you must do, and the Holy One will do what pleases Him." Hezekiah: "Then give me your daughter [as wife]—perhaps, because of my merits and your merits, worthy children will issue from me." Isaiah: "The decree against you has already been sealed." Hezekiah: "Son of Amoz, be done with your prophesying and get out! From the house of my father's father[9] there has been handed down to me the tradition: 'Even if a sharp sword rests on a man's neck, he should not despair of mercy.' " In the end, Isaiah gave Hezekiah his daughter, and Manasseh and Rab-shakeh issued from him. Once, when Hezekiah put both of them on his shoulders and was carrying them to the house of study, one said, "Father's head could be used to fry fish on"; and the other: "Father's head could be used as an altar for idolatrous sacrifice." In anger, Hezekiah flung them to the ground—Manasseh remained alive, while Rab-shakeh died.[10]

167. "And Hezekiah slept with his fathers, and they buried him in the best[11] of sepulchers of the house of David" (2 Chron. 32:33). R. Eleazar said: By "the best" is meant: near the best of the family. And who were they? David and Solomon. "And they did honor to him at his death" (ibid.) means that thirty-six thousand[12] [warriors] marched before his bier with shoulders bared.[13] Such is the opinion of R. Judah. But R. Nehemiah said to him: Was not the same done for Ahab [who was an evildoer]? What the verse means is that a Torah scroll was placed on Hezekiah's bier, and the people declared: This one fulfilled all that is written in that scroll.[14]

168. Since when was the merit of the fathers exhausted? Ever since the days of Hezekiah.[15] So taught R. Yohanan.[16]

The Reward for the Three Steps Merodach-baladan Took

169. Merodach-baladan, who worshiped the sun, used to eat at midday,[17] then go to sleep till three in the afternoon. In the days of Hezekiah, when the orb of the sun

1. "There are two forms of *mem:* medial, which is open ( ), and final, which is closed ( ). In this sentence, however, the final form occurs in the middle of a word" (Sanh, Soncino, p. 630, no 6).
2. It is believed that Gog and Magog will lead all the nations in a powerful attack on Israel. Their defeat will usher in the days of the Messiah.
3. "The attributes of justice and mercy are often hypostatized and represented as interceding with the Almighty" (Isidore Epstein in Sanh, Soncino, p. 630, n. 8).
4. Therefore the word *le-marbeh* appears in the text with the closed *mem* to indicate that the matter of Hezekiah's designation as Messiah (a word that begins with the letter *mem*) was closed.
5. So Samuel Edels. BR take it to mean: "Fulfill the desire of this righteous man," i.e., "Make him the Messiah." The two comments are based on different readings of the phrase *tzevi la-tzaddik* ("Glory to the righteous").
6. So NJV. That is, until Israel's enemies and the enemies of their enemies have been destroyed.
7. B. Sanh 94a and En Yaakov, ad loc.
8. Part of the Jewish code of charitable conduct.
9. David. See 1 Chron. 21:15–17.
10. B. Ber 10a and En Yaakov, ad loc.
11. JV: "in the ascent of." But *be-maaleh* ("ascent") can also mean "best."
12. "The figure was arrived at by the numerical value *lv* [*lo*] (30 + 6), 'to him,' occurring here in the text" (BK Soncino, p. 75, n. 4).
13. "As a sign of mourning for a righteous man and a scholar" (Isidore Epstein in BK, Soncino, p. 75).
14. B. BK 16b–17a.
15. Since his time it is said, "The zeal of the Lord of hosts [not the merit of the fathers] shall bring this to pass" (Isa. 9:6).
16. B. Shab 55a.
17. "Midday" or, literally, "the sixth hour," instead of BR's "nine in the morning" or, literally, "the third hour."

went back [ten degrees],[1] Merodach had gone to sleep [in the afternoon] as usual, but when he rose and found it was morning, he was about to slay all his servants, saying accusingly to them: You let me sleep all day and all night. They replied: It is the orb of the day that went backward [while you slept]. He asked: Which god made it go backward? They: Hezekiah's God. He: Can there be a god greater than mine? They: Hezekiah's God is greater than all gods in the world.

At that, "Merodach-baladan the son of Baladan, king of Babylon, sent letters and a present to Hezekiah" (Isa. 39:1; 2 Kings 20:12). The letters he wrote began, "Peace to King Hezekiah, peace to Jerusalem, and peace to the great God." No sooner were the letters dispatched than he bethought himself, saying, I have not done right. I have put my salutation to Hezekiah and to his city before my salutation to his great God.

At once he rose from his throne, took three steps to have the letters brought back, and composed other letters in their stead. In these, he first wrote, "Peace to the great God," and then, "Peace to Jerusalem, and peace to Hezekiah."

The Holy One said to Merodach: You rose from your throne and took three steps in My honor. I will raise up from you three kings, Nebuchadnezzar, Evil-merodach, and Belshazzar, each of whom will rule from one end of the world to the other.[2]

Manasseh

170. It is taught that Simeon ben Azzai said: In Jerusalem I found a genealogical scroll in which was written, "Manasseh slew Isaiah." For as soon as Manasseh brought the idol into the Temple, Isaiah began prophesying to Israel, saying to them in the name of the Lord, "Wherefore do you exalt yourselves? Is it because of this house that you built for Me?[3] The upper and the lower worlds cannot contain My glory. Do I then require this house that you built? 'Where is the house that ye may build unto Me?' [Isa. 66:1].[4] Behold, Nebuchadnezzar will come and destroy it, and exile you." At once Manasseh was enraged at Isaiah and said [to his servants], "Seize him." They ran after him to seize him. But he fled into a forest where, on his pronouncing the Name, a cedar opened up and took him in. Still, the fringes of his garment remained visible outside the tree. So the servants returned and reported it to Manasseh, who brought carpenters and had them saw into the cedar until Isaiah's blood flowed forth. Finally, when [the saw] reached Isaiah's mouth, his soul left him, because it was with his mouth that he sinned when he said, "I dwell in the midst of a people of unclean lips" (Isa. 6:5).[5]

171. Manasseh appeared in a dream to R. Ashi, who asked him: Why did you worship idols? Manasseh replied: Had you been living in my time, you would have seized the skirt of my garment and run to join me.[6]

172. "These are also the proverbs of Solomon, which the men of Hezekiah king of Judah copied out" (Prov. 25:1). Now, would Hezekiah king of Judah have taught Torah to everyone in the entire world but not to his own son Manasseh? Of course not, but all the pains Hezekiah spent on him and all the labor he lavished upon him did not bring Manasseh back to the right path. Only Manasseh's suffering did.[7]

173. "They placed him in a device made of copper" (2 Chron. 33:11).[8] A copper caldron with many holes in it was devised for [the torture of] Manasseh. After he was put into the caldron, a slow fire was started under it. When Manasseh saw that his peril was indeed great, there was not an idol anywhere in the world that he failed to call upon by name: O idol So-and-so, and O idol Such-and-such, come and deliver me. When he perceived that his appeal availed him nothing at all, he said: I remember that my father had me read a particular verse: "In thy distress, when all these things come upon thee . . . return to the Lord thy God" (Deut. 4:30). All right, then, I will call upon my father's God; if He answers me, well and good, but if not, then all dieties are alike—equally worthless. At this point, the ministering angels began shutting heaven's windows so that Manasseh's prayer would not come up before Him who is everywhere. They put the question before Him: Master of universes, a man who set up an idol in the Temple—can You possibly accept the repentance of such a man? The Holy One replied: If I do not receive him in his repentance, I shall be barring the door to all those who would repent. What did the Holy One [proceed to do for Manasseh]? He contrived an opening (*htyrh*) under His very throne of glory [where the angels could not interfere with] His listening to Manasseh's supplication. Hence it is written, "And he prayed unto Him; and He was entreated (*vy'tr*) of him," etc. (2 Chron. 33:13). The word *vy'tr* may be regarded as another form of *vyhtr* [meaning that God Himself made the opening for Manasseh—let Himself be dug into, so to speak].[9]

King Zedekiah

174. "For these things I weep" (Lam. 1:16)—for Zedekiah's lack of sense and for the departure of the Presence, said R. Judah. How could Zedekiah, aware that [his children would be put to death and that then] the sadists[10]

1. See Isa. 38:8.
2. Tanhuma, *Ki Tissa*, §8; Esther R. 3:1; PRKM 3:5 (PRKS, pp. 28–29).
3. Literally, "Wherefore do ye boast of this house ye have built for Me?"
4. Cf. Acts 7:49.
5. B. Yev 49b; PR 4:3 (YJS, pp. 88–89); P. Sanh 10:2, 28c.

6. B. Sanh 102b.
7. B. Sanh 101b.
8. JV: "They bound him with fetters." But *nehushtayim*, ("double fetters") literally means "something double made of copper."
9. P. Sanh 10:2, 28c; PRKM 24:11 (PRKS, pp. 375–76); Ruth R. 5:6.
10. Literally, "others," which the translator takes to mean "other than normal," hence, "sadists."

would pierce his eyes, not have had the sense to dash his head against the wall until life left him?[1]

Nebuchadnezzar

175. R. Yohanan said: As long as that wicked man lived, the sound of mirth was never heard in the mouth of any living creature, for [in the song of scorn at Nebuchadnezzar's death] the words "The whole earth is at rest and untroubled; they break forth into singing" (Isa. 14:7) imply that until [his death] there had been no singing.[2]

176. "Excellent greatness was added to me" (Dan. 4:33).[3] The verse implies, so said R. Judah in the name of R. Jeremiah bar Abba, that Nebuchadnezzar rode on a male lion, to whose head he tied a snake [for reins], in fulfillment of "And the beasts of the field also have I given him to serve him" (Jer. 27:6).[4]

Jehoiakim and Jeconiah

177. It is said: At the time Nebuchadnezzar went up to destroy Jerusalem, he first came to Daphne of Antioch, where he took up his abode. When the Great Sanhedrin went down to pay their respects to him, they asked, "Has the time come for this house to be destroyed?" He replied, "No, it is only that Jehoiakim has rebelled against me; deliver him to me, and I shall go away." They went and told Jehioakim, "Nebuchadnezzar demands your person." He replied, "Is this the way to act—sacrifice one life for another? Sacrifice my life, so that you may save yours? Does not Scripture say, 'Thou shalt not deliver a bondman unto his master' (Deut. 23:16)?" They said, "Has not a female forebear of yours[5] done this very thing to Sheba son of Bichri, saying, 'Behold, his head shall be thrown to thee over the wall' (2 Sam. 20:21)?" When they saw that Jehoiakim would not heed them, they seized him, put him in chains, and lowered him down [the city wall] to Nebuchadnezzar.

What did Nebuchadnezzar do to him? According to R. Judah, Nebuchadnezzar took him, carried him around through all the cities of Israel, and put him to death by tearing open an ass and sewing Jehoiakim into it, in fulfillment of "He shall have his burial in an ass" (Jer. 22:19). But according to R. Nehemiah, Nebuchadnezzar took Jehoiakim, carried him around through all the cities of Israel, and put him to death, then cut his body into olive-sized pieces, which he threw before dogs, in fulfillment of "He shall be buried with the burial of an ass." Where is the burial of an ass? Is it not in the innards of a dog?

After Jehoiakim was put to death, Nebuchadnezzar made Jehoiakim's son Jeconiah king in his father's place and went down to Babylon. As all the people of Babylon came out to salute and praise him, they asked: What have you accomplished? He replied: Jehoiakim, king of Judah, rebelled against me, so I had him put to death, and I made his son Jeconiah king in his place. They: There is a proverb "Don't expect to tame any puppy sired by a vicious dog," all the less so a vicious puppy sired by a vicious dog.

He took heed of what they said and again took up his abode in the arena of Antioch. Again the Great Sanhedrin came down to pay their respects to him, and again they asked, "Has the time come for the house of the Lord to be destroyed?" He replied, "No. But the one I have just made king—deliver him to me and I shall go my way." They went and told Jeconiah, "Nebuchadnezzar demands your person." What did Jeconiah do then? He gathered all the keys of the Temple, went up to its roof, and said, "Master of the universe, since we are deemed by You unworthy custodians, here are the keys to Your house."[6] At that, what appeared to be a fiery hand came down and took them from Jeconiah's hand.

Then what did Nebuchadnezzar do? He seized Jeconiah and put him in prison; and in Nebuchadnezzar's time, a man put in prison never left it.[7]

178. R.Hiyya bar Avuyah said: On Jehoiakim's skull are inscribed the words: "This and yet another" [which R. Hiyya explained with the following story]: At the gates of Jerusalem, R. Perida's grandfather found a skull with the words "This and yet another" inscribed on it. He buried it, but it burst up out of the ground. He buried it again; it burst up again. Then he said to himself: This must be the skull of Jehoiakim, about whom it is said, "He shall have the burial of an ass, dragged out and left lying outside the gates of Jerusalem" (Jer. 22:19). Still, he reflected, Jehoiakim was a king, and it is not right to subject him to such disgrace. So R. Perida's grandfather took the skull, wrapped it in silk, and put it in a casket. When his wife came home and saw what was in the casket, she went out and spoke of it to her women neighbors, who said: It is no doubt the skull of his first wife, whom he cannot forget. So she lit the oven and burned the skull.

When R. Hiyya bar Avuyah heard of the incident, he said: No doubt it is the skull that is inscribed with the words "This and yet another."[8]

---

1. Apparently R. Judah is willing to condone suicide in the face of great anguish. Lam. R. 1:16, §51.
2. B. Shab 149b.
3. After Nebuchadnezzar lived seven years as a wild beast and had regained his sanity.
4. B. Shab 150a.
5. She was "the wise woman" (2 Sam. 20:16) of Abel of Beth-maacah who persuaded the people of her town to cut off the head of Sheba son of Bichri, in order to save them from Joab's sword (2 Sam. 20:21). One commentator suggests that "the wise woman" was of the tribe of Asher, whose daughters were deemed fit to wed royalty, and that a descendant of "the wise woman" did so, thus making her a forebear of Jehoiakim's. See Lev. R., ed. Mordecai Margulies (Jerusalem, 1953–60), 1:432, n. 6.
6. The words "Up to now we have been faithful householders before You" in BR and in printed editions of Lev. R. are omitted, as in Lev. R., ed. Margulies, ad loc.
7. Lev. R. 19:6 (ed. Margulies, p. 436); P. Shek 6:3, 50a; Yalkut, 2 Kings, §249–50.
8. A dual disgrace: lying about in the streets and being burned. B. Sanh 82a.

C H A P T E R   S E V E N

THE DESTRUCTION OF THE FIRST TEMPLE

The Destruction of the Temple

1. The Holy One said to Jeremiah: Go and prophesy against Israel. But Jeremiah kept responding to the Holy One, "I am but a child, I know not how to speak" (Jer. 1:6) the dire prophecy You would have me utter against Israel. Until finally the Holy One told him, "Before I formed thee in the belly I knew thee, and before thou camest forth out of the womb I sanctified thee; I have appointed thee a prophet unto the nations" (Jer. 1:5). At once he accepted the burden of prophecy, thinking that he was to prophesy only against the nations. No sooner did Jeremiah accept the burden of prophecy than God said to him, "Take this cup of the wine of fury" (Jer. 25:15). Jeremiah took it, as is said, "I took the cup from the Lord's hand" (Jer. 25:17), still thinking that he was to cause only the nations to drink it. But then the Holy One said to Jeremiah: Go forth and learn [a lesson in] proper conduct. Is not drink served [first] to him who reclines in the most prominent position at a banquet? See who reclines in the most prominent position among the world's capitals and serve that one first—Jerusalem: she is the one most prominent among the world's capitals.

What parable applies here? That of a woman to whom infidelity was imputed, who entered the Temple Court to drink the water such a woman is asked to drink.[1] When the priest came to have her drink it, he looked at her, and behold, she was his mother. Deeply embarrassed, he drew back and began to moan and weep for his mother. So it was with Jeremiah. When the Holy One said to him, "Make Jerusalem drink," Jeremiah replied, "Master of the universe, did You not say to me, 'I have appointed thee a prophet unto the nations'? Yet now the beginning of my prophecy is to be directed against my own people! 'O Lord, Thou hast enticed me, and I let myself be enticed' " (Jer. 20:7). The Holy One said, "You have already accepted the burden of prophecy and cannot go back on your word."

And so it came about that Jerusalem took [the cup] from Jeremiah's hand and drank it, all of it, even sucked its shards dry, as is said, "Thou shalt drink it and drain it, and gnaw its shards" (Ezek. 23:34).

When Jeremiah realized that the decree of doom for Jerusalem was sealed, he began to raise his voice and wail bitterly, "How doth the city sit solitary" (Lam. 1:1).[2]

2. When wicked Nebuchadnezzar, together with the other kings, came to Jerusalem, they supposed that they would capture it within a short time. But the Holy One strengthened the men of Jerusalem up to the third year of the siege, in the hope that they would return in penitence. Unending was the number of heroes in Jerusalem who fought the Chaldeans and felled many of them. One such hero was Avuka son of Gavtri. Whenever the Chaldean warriors shot big stones [from catapults] in order to demolish the wall, Avuka would catch the stones in his hand and hurl them back at the warriors, killing many of them. After a while, [when his arm grew weary] he began catching them with his foot and hurled them back at the [Chaldean] army. But Israel's sin brought it about that a wind came up and blew him off the wall—his body split open and he died.

What did Hanamel, Jeremiah's uncle, do then? He called up certain ministering angels by their names and made them come down to the walls, armed with all kinds of weapons. When the Chaldeans saw the angels, they fled in fear of them, until the Holy One changed the angels' names and brought them back to the firmament. Hanamel tried to bring them down again, but could not.[3] What did Hanamel do then? He called up the prince of the world, who raised Jerusalem and kept it suspended in the air, until from heaven the Holy One kicked it, and it fell back to earth. At that, Jerusalem's walls split apart, so that the Chaldeans were able to enter the city. When they came into the Temple Hall and were about to set it on fire, the Holy One summoned Gabriel and Michael, and asked, "Who is most beloved by you?" They replied, "Israel." "And after Israel, who is most beloved by you?" They replied, "The Temple." God then said, "By My great Name I swear that you yourselves shall set fire to it."[4] At once Gabriel and Michael took two flaming torches and set fire to the Temple of the Lord, so that, in lamentation for itself, the Temple cried out, "From above, He sent a fire down into my bones" (Lam. 1:13).[5]

3. R. Joshua of Sikhnin said in the name of R. Levi: For six years the coals were kept dimly glowing in the hands of Gabriel, who thought that Israel would yet resolve on repentance. When they failed to repent, he, in his wrath, wanted to fling the coals at the people. But the Holy One called out to him: Gabriel, Gabriel, go easy, go easy, there are people among them who practice charity toward one another.[6]

4. For eighteen years a divine voice kept reverberating in Nebuchadnezzar's palace, saying, "Wicked servant, go up and destroy the house of your Master, whose children do not listen to Him." But Nebuchadnezzar was afraid and did not go up. He said to himself: He only wishes to entrap

1. See Num. 5
2. Yalkut, Lam., §909.
3. Because, not knowing their new names, he could no longer command them.
4. According to tradition, no human hand was capable of destroying the Temple; only God or His angels could do so.
5. Yalkut, Lam., §909.
6. Lam. R. 1:13, §41.

me and do to me what He did to my grandfather.[1] What did Nebuchadnezzar do? He went and set up residence in Daphne of Antioch, but sent Nebuzaradan, the captain of the guard, to destroy Jerusalem. Nebuzaradan spent three and a half years there, maintaining the siege of Jerusalem day after day, but was unable to subdue it. Then, when he decided to retreat, the Holy One put a new idea in his head. He began to measure the height of the wall, which at once began sinking two and a half handbreadths every day, until all of it sank into the ground. After it was wholly sunk, the foes entered Jerusalem. Concerning that time: "The kings of the earth believed not, neither all the inhabitants of the world, that the adversary and the enemy would enter into the gates of Jerusalem" (Lam. 4:12).[2]

5. Rava said: Nebuchadnezzar sent Nebuzaradan three hundred mules laden with iron axes [so sharp] that they could crack iron, and all of them vanished when a single gate of Jerusalem opened up and sucked them in, as is said, "And now a single [gate] opened upon the axes and pikes they battled with" (Ps. 74:6). Nebuzaradan wanted to retreat, saying to himself: I fear that what happened to Sennacherib will happen to me.[3] But a divine voice went forth: "O leaper, and son of a leaper, Nebuzaradan, leap! The time for the Temple to be destoyed, and for the Sanctuary to be consumed by fire has come." He had only one ax left. Leaping up, he struck that gate with the ax's wooden shaft, and the gate opened wide, as is said, "A man became famous for lifting the part of an ax that is wrought from the sturdy portion of a tree" (Ps. 74:5). Nebuzaradan leaped in and kept hewing down [Jews], until he reached the Sanctuary. When he tried to set it on fire, the Sanctuary lifted itself up. But from heaven it was trod upon so hard [that it was forced down]: "As in a winepress the Lord trod upon the most sacred[4] part of fair Judah" (Lam. 1:15). Nebuzaradan was elated. But a divine voice came forth and proclaimed, "A people already slain you slew, a Sanctuary already consumed by fire you set on fire, flour already ground you ground.[5]

6. "Even now our eyes pine away in vain for deliverance" (Lam. 4:17). What did the ten tribes do? They carried oil to Egypt, and from there brought produce, which they sent on to Assyria, saying, "If our foes advance against us, these peoples will be a help for us." As Scripture says, "Now they make a covenant with Assyria, now oil is carried to Egypt" (Hos. 12:2), and also, "We hold out a hand to Egypt, to Assyria, for its fill of bread" (Lam. 5:6). When the foes did come upon the ten tribes, they immediately sent to Pharaoh-necoh [for help], saying, "Send up soldiers from your army." And he did send the soldiers. But as they sailed upon the sea, the Holy One beckoned to the sea, and it floated before their eyes distended leather skins, which looked like corpses with human innards trailing in the water. They asked one another, "What are these corpses?" They were told, "These are the remains of your forebears who enslaved the forebears of the Jews [you are sailing to help]. As soon as the forebears of these Jews were redeemed from your forebears, they rose up and drowned them in the sea." At that, the Egyptian soldiers said, "Jews acted thus to our forebears, and we are going to assist them?" They returned at once, as is said, "The army of Pharaoh, which set out to help you, shall return to Egypt, into its own land" (Jer. 37:7).[6]

The Ninth of Av

7. It is taught: Good things come to pass on an auspicious day, and bad things on an ill-starred day.

It is said: The first time the Temple was destroyed was on the ninth of Av, on a Saturday evening, at the end of a sabbatical year, when a watch of the family of Jehoiarib was on duty, and the Levites standing at their posts were singing a psalm. What psalm did they sing? "He shall bring upon them their own iniquity, and shall cut them off in their own wickedness" (Ps. 94:23). But before they had time to sing the end of the psalm, "Yea, the Lord our God shall cut them off entirely" (ibid.), the heathens entered and silenced them.[7]

Upon the Ruins of Jerusalem

8. "The famine was sore in the city" (2 Kings 25:3). The well-born daughters of Zion used to congregate in the streets of the city, staring at each other, until at last one would say to her friend, "Why have you come out into the street? You never came out into the street before." And in anguish the other would reply, "What have I to hide from you? The 'boon of'[8] famine is hard to accept. I cannot bear it." Then, supporting one another, the daughters of Zion walked around looking for food in the city, for something to put into their mouths.[9] And not finding anything to eat, they would clutch at the house pillars and, wherever the street turned, fall dead at the base of the pillars. Their infants who still needed to suck their mother's milk came crawling after them on their hands and knees. Each child, recognizing his own mother, came up, took the breast he knew, and put it against his mouth, expecting to draw milk. But he drew none, and so, driven into a frenzy, he died in his mother's bosom.

At that time the Lord said to Jeremiah, "Rise, go to Anathoth and buy the field from thine uncle Hanamel."[10]

As soon as Jeremiah left Jerusalem, the angel of the Lord came down from heaven, set his feet against the walls of Jerusalem, and breached them. Then the angel cried

1. Sennacherib.
2. Lam. R., proem 30; Lam. R. 4:12, §15.
3. After his abortive siege of Jerusalem, he was assassinated.
4. Literally, "virgin."
5. B. Sanh 96b.
6. Lam. R. 4:17, §20 (ed. Buber [Vilna, 1899], p. 152); Rashi on Lam. 4:17.
7. B. Ta 29a.
8. "Boon of"—so YJS.
9. "For food" and "for something to put into their mouths" added, as in YJS.
10. See Jer. 32:6–44.

out, saying, "Let the enemies come and enter the house, for the Master of the house is no longer within. Let them despoil and destroy it. Let them go into the vineyard and cut down its vines, for the Watchman has gone away and left it." [And to the enemies he said], "Do not boast that you have vanquished the city. Nay, a conquered city you have conquered, a dead people you have put to death. A Temple consumed by fire you set on fire."

The enemies came and set up a platform for themselves on the Temple Mount, in a place that happened to be the very same spot where Solomon used to sit when he took counsel with the elders about how to decorate the Temple. There the enemies sat and took counsel about how to burn the Temple. As they were deliberating, they lifted their eyes and saw four angels descending, in their hands four flaming torches which they put at the four corners of the Holy Place, setting it on fire.

When the high priest saw that the Temple was on fire, he, together with many companies of young priests, went up to the roof of the Temple Hall, holding the keys of the Temple Hall, and cried out, "Master of the universe! Since we have been unworthy custodians of it, here are the keys of Your house," and then cast them heavenward. Something that looked like the palm of a hand came forth and received them. As the high priest started to go down, the enemies seized him and slaughtered him at the altar, in the very place where he used to offer the daily sacrifice. His daughter ran out wildly, crying, "Woe is me! My dear father, the delight of my eyes!" They seized her and slaughtered her also, and mingled her blood with the blood of her father.

When the priests and the Levites saw that the Temple was on fire, they took their harps and trumpets, let themselves fall with them into the flames, and were consumed. When the virgins who wove the curtain for the Sanctuary saw that the Temple was on fire, they too let themselves fall into the flames [so that the enemies should not violate them] and were consumed.

When Zedekiah saw all that was happening, he sought to flee through an underground passage—used as a water main—that led to the plains of Jericho. But the Holy One provided a gazelle that walked on top of the underground passage. The Chaldeans chased after the gazelle, and just as they got to the egress of the passage onto the plains of Jericho, Zedekiah and his sons were emerging. The Chaldeans saw them and seized them. Nebuzaradan sent all of them to Nebuchadnezzar, who asked, "Tell me, Zedekiah, what made you rebel against me? By what law shall I judge you? If by the law of your God, you deserve the death penalty, for you swore in His Name falsely; if by the laws of the state, you likewise deserve the death penalty, for he who violates his oath to the king deserves the death penalty."

Zedekiah replied, "I beg you, slay me first, so that I may not see the blood of my sons." And his sons pleaded, saying, "Slay us first, so that we may not see the blood of our father shed upon the earth."

So Nebuchadnezzar did what they asked: he slaughtered them before their father. Then he gouged out Zedekiah's eyes, put them in an oven [to burn], and took him to Babylon. And Zedekiah kept crying out, "Come and see, all you children of men, that Jeremiah prophesied truly about me when he said to me, 'You will go to Babylon and in Babylon you will die, but your eyes will not have seen Babylon.' I would not listen to his words. And here I am in Babylon, and my eyes do not see it."

In the meantime, the prophet Jeremiah left Anathoth to come back to Jerusalem. He lifted his eyes and saw the smoke of the Temple rising up. So he said in his heart: Perhaps Israel has returned in penitence to bring offerings, and now the smoke of incense is rising up. But when he climbed closer and stood upon the wall, he saw the Temple turned into heap upon heap of stones and the wall of Jerusalem broken down.[1] He cried to God, saying, "Thou hast enticed me, O Lord, and I was enticed; Thou hast overcome me, and hast prevailed," etc. (Jer. 20:7). As he continued on his way, he kept moaning and saying, "What road have the sinners taken? What road have those taken who are about to perish? I will go and perish with them." As he went on, he saw the path covered with blood and the ground on both sides soaked with the blood of the slain. He brought his face close to the ground and made out the footprints of sucklings and children who were walking into captivity. He threw himself on the ground and kissed the footprints. When he caught up with the host going into captivity, he embraced them and kissed them. When Jeremiah saw a band of young men tied by neck chains one to the other, he put his head into a neck chain with them, but Nebuzaradan came along and released him. Then later, when he saw a band of old men bound together by chains, he put the chains on his own neck, but once more Nebuzaradan came by and released him. Even as Jeremiah wept with them and they wept with him, he spoke up and said, "My brethren and my people, all that has befallen you is the consequence of your not hearkening to the words of the prophecy that God uttered through me."

When Jeremiah reached the Euphrates River, Nebuzaradan spoke, saying to him, "If it seem good unto thee to come with me into Babylon, come" (Jer. 40:4). So Jeremiah thought in his heart: If I go with the exiles to Babylon, there will be no comforter for the captivity left in Jerusalem. With that, he started to go forth from among them. When the exiles lifted their eyes and saw that Jeremiah was taking leave of them, all of them broke out weeping and wailing as they implored, "Our father Jeremiah, you are in truth abandoning us!" There they sat down and wept, for thus it is written: "By the rivers of Babylon, there we sat down, yea, we wept" (Ps. 137:1). Jeremiah answered and said, "I call heaven and earth to witness that if you had wept even once while you dwelled in Zion, you would not have been driven out."

As Jeremiah went, he wept and said, "Alas for you, most precious of cities." [After he was released by Nebuzaradan] and was on his way back [to Jerusalem], Jeremiah saw fingers and toes [of captive Israelites] that had been cut off and flung on mountain paths. He picked them up, held them close, kissed them, put them in his cloak, and wept over them, saying, "O my children, did I not keep

---

1. YJS: *mfvgrt* [mefuggeret] ("destroyed") and not *msvgrt* [mesuggeret] ("closed up" or "shut in").

warning you, 'Give glory to the Lord your God, before it grow dark, and before your feet stumble on the mountains in shadow' (Jer. 13:16)?" Of that time, Scripture says, "On the mountains I take up weeping and wailing, on the pastures in the wilderness a dirge" (Jer. 9:9)—on those mountains, once majestic in splendor, I now am weeping and wailing; and for Jacob's pastures, so desolate [that the sight of them] evokes a dirge.

Jeremiah said: [After I left the exiles and] was going back up to Jerusalem, I lifted my eyes and saw at the top of a mountain a seated woman, clothed in black, her hair disheveled, crying and pleading for someone to comfort her, just as I was crying and pleading, "Who will comfort me?" I came near her and spoke to her, and said, "If you are a woman, speak to me, but if you are a spirit, depart from me." She answered, "Do you not recognize me? I am the woman who had seven sons. Their father went away to a city far across the sea. As I was going up to lament him, messengers came and said, 'Your house has collapsed over your seven sons and slain them.' And in my distraction I know not for whom I am to cry or for whom I am to disarray my hair." I replied, "You are not more deserving of comfort than Mother Zion, who has been made into a pasture for the beasts of the field." She replied, saying, "I am your Mother Zion, the mother of seven." Jeremiah said, "Your chastisement is like Job's chastisement. Job's sons and daughters were taken from him, and your sons and daughters have been taken from you. Job's gold and silver were taken from him, and your gold and your silver have been taken from you. Job was cast upon a dungheap, and you have been turned into a heap of dung. But even as the Holy One turned back and comforted Job, so will He turn back and comfort you."[1]

9. There was a man with four sons, who asked his wife, "Do we have any food in the house?" She replied, "One jarful." He: "Cook it, and we shall eat it." So she cooked it in a pot, and [after it was served] a drop was left. When the eldest son came to scrape it out, the man pushed him aside and said, "Do not rob your brothers." Before the eldest had a chance to eat it, the Chaldeans came,[2] took the children away, and slew all of them. The father went and found each in the place where he fell. He then took the index finger of his eldest son, thrust it into his own eye, and said, "Because I did not let you scrape out a drop of food, let a finger of yours take out the eye of him who denied it."

It is told: A woman had three grown-up sons who were about to join a sortie against the besiegers. She took the infant she was giving suck to and cooked it in a pot. As the grown-up brothers ate from it, they recognized their infant brother's hands. So they went up to the roof, flung themselves down, and died. Concerning them, Jeremiah lamented, "Better off are the slain of the sword than those slain by famine" (Lam. 4:9). And the mother cried in anguish, "Woe is me! Would that I had the leavings of a harvest, the gleanings of a vintage. I have not even one cluster to enjoy" (Mic. 7:1).[3] She meant: a harvester leaves aftergrowths, a vintager leaves gleanings. But I—for me nothing remained. I have been turned over to Nebuchadnezzar's hand like a ewe to the claws of a lion, like a lamb to the hands of a slaughterer.[4]

The Departure of the Presence

10. "The glory of the Lord went forth from off the threshold of the house" (Ezek. 10:18). R. Aha said: God was like a king who was leaving his palace in anger. Nevertheless, as he was leaving, he turned back, embraced and kissed the walls of the palace, and the pillars of the palace, wept, and said: Farewell, my palace! Farewell, my royal residence! Farewell, my cherished home! Farewell! Farewell henceforth! So, too, as the Presence was departing from the Temple, it turned back, embraced and kissed the walls of the Temple and the columns of the Temple, wept, and said: Farewell, My Sanctuary! Farewell, My royal residence! Farewell, My cherished home! Farewell! Farewell henceforth![5]

The Holy One Weeping

11. "And in that day did the Lord, the God of hosts, call to weeping, and to lamentation" (Isa. 22:12). When the Holy One was about to destroy the Temple, He said: So long as I am within it, the peoples of the world will be unable to touch it. However, I will shut My eyes from it and swear that I will have nothing to do with it again till the messianic end of time. Meanwhile, let the enemies come and devastate it. Then He swore by His right hand and put it behind Him, as is said, "He put back His right hand from before His enemy" (Lam. 2:3). At once the enemies entered into the Temple Hall and burned it. After it was burned, the Holy One said: Once again I have no dwelling place in the Land. So I shall remove My Presence from it and go up to My former residence. The Holy One wept and said: Woe is Me! What have I done? For Israel's sake I caused My Presence to dwell below. But now that Israel sinned and I am returning to My former place, I have, Heaven forbid, become the laughingstock of the nations and an object of derision for mortals. In that instant Metatron[6] came, fell upon his face, and spoke before the Holy One: Master of the universe, let me weep, but You must not weep. God replied: If you do not let Me weep, I will go into a place where you have no authority to enter and weep there. That such was God's response is intimated in the verse "If you cannot bear to hear it, My spirit will weep in the secret place" (Jer. 13:17).[7]

Then the Holy One said to the ministering angels:

---

1. PR 26:6 (YJS 2;533–38); Lam. R., proem 32; Rashi on Jer. 39:4.
2. The words "led them to the battlefield" are omitted.
3. JV: "Woe is me! For I am as the last of the summer fruits, as the grape gleanings of the vintage: There is no cluster to eat."
4. Yalkut, Lam., §1015–16.
5. Lam. R,. proem 25.
6. The angel of the Presence.
7. JV: "But if ye will not hear it, my soul shall weep in secret."

Come and let us go, you and I, to My house, and see what the enemies have done to it. At once the Holy One and the ministering angels went forth, Jeremiah leading the way. When the Holy One saw the Temple, He said: Beyond doubt, this was My house, this was My resting place, into which enemies came and did as they pleased. Then and there the Holy One wept and cried out in anguish: Woe is Me for My house! My children, where are you? My priests, My Levites, where are you? What else might I have done with you, seeing that I kept warning you again and again, but you would not return in penitence?

Then the Holy One said to Jeremiah: I am today like a man who had an only son for whom he prepared a marriage bower, but, while in it, the son suddenly died. Will you show no anguish for Me or for My children? Go, summon Abraham, Isaac, Jacob, and Moses from their graves. They know how to weep. Jeremiah replied: Master of the universe, I do not know where Moses is buried. The Holy One said: Go, stand on a bank of the Jordan, lift up your voice, and cry out: Son of Amram, son of Amram, arise and gaze at your flock, which enemies have ripped apart.

But first Jeremiah went to the cave of Machpelah and said to the fathers of the world: Arise, the time has come when your presence is required by the Holy One. They asked: Why is our presence required by the Holy One on this day more than on any preceding day? Jeremiah replied: I do not know—he was afraid[1] lest they say in reproach, "This has befallen our children in your days."

Jeremiah left the fathers of the world and, standing on a bank of the Jordan, called out: Son of Amram, son of Amram, arise! The time has come when your presence is required by the Holy One. Moses replied: Why is my presence required by the Holy One on this day more than on any preceding day? Again Jeremiah replied: I do not know.

Moses left Jeremiah and went to the ministering angels, whom he had come to know at the time of the giving of Torah. He asked them: Ministers on high, do you know why my presence is required by the Holy One? They replied: Son of Amram, do you not know that the Temple is destroyed and Israel is exiled? Moses immediately rent the garments of glory with which the Holy One had clothed him, put his hands on his head, and walked weeping and moaning until he reached the fathers of the world. When the fathers of the world asked him: Moses, shepherd of Israel, wherein is this day different from any preceding day? he replied: Fathers of my fathers, do you not know that the Temple is destroyed and Israel exiled among the peoples of the world? They also rent their garments, put their hands on their heads, and walked weeping and moaning until they reached the gates of the Temple. When the Holy One saw them, at once "the Lord the God of hosts called on that day to weeping and to lamentation, to shaving the head and to girding on sackcloth" (Isa. 22:12). (Were such words not explicitly set down in Scripture, it would be impossible to utter them.) As the fathers walked from gate to gate, they wept like a man in whose presence the corpse of a dear one is lying; while the Holy One lamented as He said: Woe to the king who prospered in his youth but did not prosper in his old age.[2]

[1] To tell them of the catastrophe that had befallen Israel.

Mourning by the Fathers

12. When the Temple was destroyed, Abraham came weeping before the Holy One, plucking his beard, pulling out the hair of his head, striking his face, rending his garments. With ashes on his head, he kept walking about the site of the Temple, lamenting and crying, until finally he spoke up to the Holy One: "Why am I dealt with differently than [the forebear of] any other nation or tongue, in that I am brought to such shame and humiliation?" When the ministering angels saw him, they arranged themselves in row upon row, like mourners, and composed a dirge: "The highways are desolate, wayfarers have ceased" (Isa. 33:8). The highways You provided for Jerusalem, on which wayfarers were not to cease—how desolate they have become! The roads on which Israel came and went during festivals—how deserted they are!

The Holy One frowned upon the ministering angels and asked: Why did you arrange yourselves in row upon row, like mourners, composing a dirge [about the just punishment of Israel]? They replied: Master of the universe, for the sake of Abraham, Your friend who loves You. He came to Your house, lamenting and weeping—why did You not respond to him? He replied: Ever since My friend departed from My Presence to his eternal abode, he came not to My house, but now, "why should My beloved be in My house?" (Jer. 11:15). Then Abraham spoke up again to the Holy One: Master of the universe, why did You exile my children and turn them over to heathen nations, who put them to death in all kinds of unnatural ways and destroyed the Temple on whose site I once brought my son Isaac as a burnt offering before You? The Holy One replied: Your children sinned and transgressed against the entire Torah and against the twenty-two letters[3] in which it is written. Abraham spoke further to the Holy One: Master of the universe, who will testify against them, against Israel, that they have indeed transgressed Your Torah?[4] God: Let the Torah herself come and testify against them, against Israel.

At once the Torah came to testify against Israel. But Abraham said to her: My daughter, have you come to testify against Israel, that they transgressed your commandments? Have you no shame in my presence? Remember the day when the Holy One went around with you to every nation and tongue, and not one of them would have you until my children came to Mount Sinai and accepted you and honored you. Yet now you come to testify against them in the day of their misfortune. Upon hearing this, the Torah stood aside and gave no testimony against them.

Then the Holy One said to Abraham: Let the twenty-two letters of the alphabet come and testify against them,

[2] Lam. R., proem 24; Yalkut, Lam., §996.

[3] The Hebrew alphabet has twenty-two letters.

[4] The accused cannot be judged guilty unless there are witnesses attesting his guilt.

against Israel. At once the twenty-two letters came. As the *alef* came forward to testify against Israel, that they transgressed the Torah, Abraham said to her: *Alef*, you who are the first among the letters would testify against Israel in the day of their misfortune? Remember the day the Holy One appeared on Mount Sinai and began [the Ten Commandments] with you: *Anokhi*,[1] "I am the Lord your God" (Exod. 20:2)? No nation or tongue would have you, save only my children, yet you are here to testify against my children. At once the *alef* stepped back and gave no testimony against them.

Then the *bet* came to testify against them, against Israel. Abraham said to her: My daughter, you come to testify against my children who are diligent in the study of the Five Books, at whose beginning you stand?[2] At once the *bet*, too, stepped back and gave no testimony whatever.

When all the other letters saw that Abraham had silenced those who appeared, they were embarrassed, stepped aside, and did not testify against Israel.

Then Abraham began to speak to the Holy One and said: Master of the universe, when I was already a hundred years old, You gave me a son, and when he reached the age of understanding, a mature man of thirty-seven,[3] You said to me, "Bring him as a burnt offering before Me." I steeled my heart against him with cruelty and showed no compassion for him; on the contrary, I myself bound him. Will You not remember this on my behalf, and will You not have mercy on my children?

Then Isaac began to speak and said: Master of the universe, when my father said to me, "God will provide Himself the lamb for a burnt offering, my son" (Gen. 22:8),[4] I did not balk at what You had to say. I willingly let myself be bound upon the altar and stretched out my neck under the knife. Will You not remember this on my behalf, and will You not have mercy on my children?

Next, Jacob began and said: Master of the universe, did I not stay in Laban's house for twenty years? When I left his house and wicked Esau met me and wished to slay my children, I risked my life for them.[5] And now they have been delivered into the hands of their enemies like sheep for slaughter—my children whom I had reared as tenderly as hens' chicks, and for whose sake I suffered the pain of parenting. Will You not remember this on my behalf, and will You not have mercy on my children?

Moses began and said: Master of the universe, was I not a faithful shepherd of Israel for forty years, trotting before them like a horse in the wilderness? Yet when the time came for them to enter the Land, You decreed for me that my bones were to fall in that wilderness. And now that they are exiled, You send for me to lament and weep over them. It is as the proverb puts it: "I have no share in my master's good fortune, but a full share of his misfortune."

Without waiting for a reply, Moses said to Jeremiah: You go before me, so that I may lead them [back to the Land of Israel] and see who dares to lay a hand upon them. Jeremiah replied: It is impossible to walk along the road because of the slain. Moses said: Nevertheless, let us go.

Forthwith, Moses went, Jeremiah walking before him, until they reached the rivers of Babylon. When the exiles saw Moses, one said to the other, "The son of Amram has come up from his grave to deliver us from the hand of our adversaries." But then a divine voice came forth and said, "It is a decree from My Presence." At that, Moses said to them, "It is impossible to bring you back now, since the decree has already been issued, but He who is everywhere will bring you back soon," and then he left them. Then the exiles lifted their voices in loud weeping, so that the sound of their weeping reached the heights above. Thus it is written, "By the rivers of Babylon, there we sat down, yea, we wept" (Ps. 137:1).

When Moses returned to the fathers of the world, they asked him: What have the enemies done to our children? He replied: Some they slew with the sword; they bound the hands of others behind their backs; some were fettered with iron chains; others were stripped naked; some died by the way, their corpses serving as food for the birds of heaven and the beasts of the earth; and others were exposed to the burning sun, hungry and thirsty.

At once all the fathers began to weep and utter lamentations: Woe for what has befallen our children! How you have become like orphans without a father! How you had to sleep at noon during summer without garments or cover! How you were forced to walk over mountains and rocks without shoes, without sandals! How you were made to bear heavy loads of sand! How your hands were bound behind your backs! How you were [so parched by thirst] that there was no saliva left in your mouths to swallow!

Then Moses began to say: Cursed be you, O sun! Why did you not plunge into darkness when the enemy entered the Temple? The sun replied: By your life, O Moses, faithful shepherd, how could I have turned into darkness? I was not allowed to, for I was not left alone, but was beaten unceasingly with sixty whips of fire and told: Go forth, pour out your light.

Moses continued: Alas for your splendor, O Temple! How tarnished! Alas that the time has come for the Temple to be destroyed! The Temple Hall is burned, schoolchildren are massacred, and their parents are going into captivity and exile.

Moses again lifted up his voice and said: O captors, as you live, if you kill, do not kill with a cruel death; do not bring on them total extermination; do not kill a son in the presence of his father, or a daughter in the presence of her mother. For the time will come when the Holy One will requite you. But the wicked Chaldeans did even worse things: they put a child in its mother's bosom and said to the father, "Up, and kill it." As the mother wept, her tears fell on the child, while the father raised the child's head [to cut his throat].

Moses went on defying the Holy One: Master of the

1. The word *anokhi* begins with the *alef*.
2. Genesis begins with the letter *bet* in *Bereshit* ("In the beginning").
3. Isaac was born when Sarah was 90 (Gen. 17:17). She died at 127. She died, it is said, when she learned that Abraham had taken him to be sacrificed.
4. In rabbinic interpretation, the verse is construed as hinting that Isaac was to be the lamb for the burnt offering.
5. Jacob's passing in front of them (Gen. 33:2ff.) is construed as an attempt to defend them.

universe, in Your Torah You wrote, "Whether it be a cow or ewe, ye shall not kill it and its young both in one day" (Lev. 22:28). But have not mothers and sons been killed again and again? Yet You remain silent!

At that moment our mother Rachel broke forth into speech before the Holy One and said: Master of the universe, it is revealed and known to You that Your servant Jacob cherished a great love for me; indeed, because of me he worked for my father seven years. When the time for the marriage to my husband arrived, my father conspired to substitute my sister for me. Yet I was not jealous of my sister and did not expose her to shame. Now if I, who am flesh and blood, dust and ashes, was not jealous of my rival, then why should You—the King, living, enduring, merciful—be jealous of idols, which have no substance, and banish my children because of them?

At once the mercy of the Holy One crested, and he said: For your sake, O Rachel, I will restore Israel to their place. Of this it is said:

> Thus saith the Lord:
> A cry was heard in Ramah,
> Wailing, and bitter weeping,
> Rachel weeping for her children.
> She refuseth to be comforted for her children
> Who are gone
> (Jer. 31:15).

These words are followed by:

> Restrain thy voice from weeping,
> Thine eyes from shedding tears;
> For there is a reward for thy labor . . .
> There is hope for thy future,
> Thy children shall return to their country
> (Jer. 31:16).[1]

The Blood of Zechariah

13. R. Joshua ben Korhah said: An old man of the inhabitants of Jerusalem told me that Nebuzaradan, the captain of the guard, killed two hundred and eleven myriads in this valley, and in Jerusalem he killed ninety-four myriads on one stone, so that, as their blood flowed, it touched the blood of Zechariah. Nebuzaradan noticed that the blood of Zechariah kept seething and bubbling up. He asked, "What's the matter with this blood?" and was told, "It is the blood of sacrifices, which was spilled." So he said: Bring some blood of sacrifices, and I will check [the accuracy of what you say]. The blood was brought, and the two kinds were found not to be the same. Then Nebuzaradan said, "If you tell me the truth, well and good, but if not, I will scrape your flesh with iron combs." They replied, "What can we say to you? There was a priest among us who was also a prophet. He used to reprove us for the transgressions we committed, and so we rose up against him and killed him. It is now many years that his blood has not been still." Nebuzaradan said, "I will quiet it." At that, he brought the [members of the] Great Sanhedrin and the Small Sanhedrin[2] and slew them over the blood, but the blood did not become still. He then slaughtered young priests, but the blood did not become still; youths and maidens, but the blood did not become still; schoolchildren, but it did not become still—until he slew ninety-four myriads all together. Then Nebuzaradan drew near the blood and said, "Zechariah, Zechariah, I have slain the best of them. Will it please you to have me slay all of them?" The blood promptly became still.

In that instant, thoughts of remorse came to Nebuzaradan's mind as he said to himself: If such is the penalty for them who slew but one person, how much greater will be the punishment imposed on me, who have slain all these multitudes? He fled away, sent a last will and testament to his family, and became a convert.[3]

The Sufferings of the Exiles

14. "And [Jerusalem's] tears are on her cheeks" (Lam. 1:2)—on the cheeks of Jerusalem's young men. You find that when the foes entered Jerusalem, they seized young men and bound their hands behind their backs. They wept, and the tears ran down their cheeks. They were unable to wipe them, so the tears remained on their cheeks, smarting like the burn of a [skin] boil.[4]

15. "I called upon those who were supposed to love me, but they deceived me" (Lam. 1:19). R. Joshua ben Levi said: When the wicked Nebuchadnezzar abducted the children of Israel to Babylon—their hands tied behind their backs, chained together with iron chains, and going naked like beasts—the children of Israel, as they passed by Ishmael's land, said to Nebuchadnezzar's officers in charge, "Show us compassion and pity, and take us by way of our kinsmen, the children of our uncle Ishmael." And the officers did so. The children of Ishmael came out to meet them with salted bread and brine [to dip it in]. They also brought empty leather bottles made to appear as though filled with water and hung these at the entrances of their own tents. When the Israelites saw such seeming concern, their anxieties subsided, for they assumed that the leather bottles were filled with water. The Ishmaelites said, "First eat some bread, and then we will bring you water." After the Israelites had eaten the bread, the Ishmaelites came and said, "We could not find any water." So the Israelites tore with their teeth at those bottles, and, because the hot air in them rushed into their innards, they died.[5]

16. R. Yohanan said: Eighty thousand novice priests, bearing eighty thousand golden shields, broke through the ranks of Nebuchadnezzar's army and escaped to the Ish-

1. Lam. R., proem 24.

2. The first had seventy-one members; the second had twenty-three.
3. B. Git 57b; B. Sanh 96b.
4. Or: "fell upon the cheeks like the burn of a boil." Lam. R. 1:2, §25.
5. Tanhuma, *Yitro*, §5.

maelites, to whom they said, "You are our cousins. Give us water to drink." The Ishmaelites replied, "Eat first, and then you will drink water." What did the Ishmaelites do? They set before them salted foods. After the Israelites had eaten, the Ishmaelites brought forth empty leather bottles distended with air. As each Israelite untied a bottle's neck and put it into his mouth, the air in it penetrated the Israelite's innards, so that he was thrown into convulsions and died.[1]

By the Rivers of Babylon

17. "By the rivers of Babylon, there we sat down, yea, we wept" (Ps. 137:1). What made Israel sit down and weep by the rivers of Babylon? R. Yohanan explained: It was the Euphrates, which slew more of the children of Israel than the wicked Nebuchadnezzar had slain. While the children of Israel were living in the Land of Israel, they drank only rainwater, running water, or spring water. But when they were exiled to Babylon, they had to drink the water of the Euphrates, and many of them died. And so the exiles wept—wept for the dead whom their enemies had slain, wept for the dead who had perished in the way and whom the Babylonians had not permitted to be buried, and wept for the dead whom the Euphrates had slain. They had even more cause to weep! For the wicked Nebuchadnezzar was seated in a ship—he and all his nobles and all his officers—and they had with them all kinds of instruments to sing with, as is said, "The Chaldeans, in the ships of their singing" (Isa. 43:14). At the same time, all the members of the royal house of Judah, who had been put into iron chains, were walking naked along the edge of the river. The wicked Nebuchadnezzar looked up and saw them. He said to his servants, "Why are such as these walking with their heads held high and without burdens? Have you no burdens to load upon their necks?" Instantly the servants brought Torah scrolls, shaped them into sacks, filled them with sand, and loaded them on the shoulders of the members of the royal house of Judah until their heads were bent low. At that, the members of the royal house of Judah said of themselves, "To our very necks we are pursued" (Lam. 5:5). And in that hour all Israel moaned loudly, until their cry came up to heaven.

R. Aha bar Abba taught: It was at this moment that the Holy One wished to return the world to chaos and emptiness, saying, "I will strike hand against hand, and will satisfy My fury" (Ezek. 21:22). By these words the Holy One meant" All that I created in the world, I created with My two hands—"My left hand hath laid the foundation of the earth, My right hand hath spread out the heavens" (Isa. 48:13)—I created only for the sake of Israel, and now I return it to chaos and desolation.

R. Tahalifa bar Keruya taught: It was at this moment that all the ministering angels came and stood before the Presence of the Holy One and said to Him: Master of the universe! The entire universe, and all that is in it, is Yours. Is it not enough for You that You have already destroyed Your dwelling place on earth? Must You also destroy Your dwelling place in heaven? God replied: Am I flesh and blood, that I require your comforting? I foresee the beginning, and I foresee the end: "Even to your old age I am He" (Isa. 46:4). "Therefore say I, 'Look away from Me, I will weep bitterly; labor not to comfort Me' " (Isa. 22:4). [The verse does not say, as in usual discourse, "Comfort Me no more," but says, "Labor not," employing an unusual verb, which signifies that] God said to the ministering angels, "These words of comfort with which you would console Me are as blasphemies[2] to Me. Go down out of My presence and lift the burden from My children." Instantly the ministering angels went down and lifted the burden from them. And not only the ministering angels, but the Holy One Himself, if one dare say such a thing, reached out to help in lifting the burden, as is said, "For your sake I have reached out to Babylon" (Isa. 43:14).

When Nebuchadnezzar came and burned the Temple and exiled Israel, taking them into captivity, he allowed [them] no halts for rest while traversing all the Land of Israel, for the Babylonians pressed hard upon the Israelites. Why did they press so hard upon them? Because the Babylonians feared for their own lives, saying, "The God of this nation is waiting for them to repent. It may be that they will repent while they are still in their own Land, and He will then deal with us as He dealt with Sennacherib." Therefore the Babylonians allowed no halts for rest in the entire Land of Israel. It was only when the children of Israel came to the rivers of Babylon, where the Babylonians felt that the Israelites were completely in their power on Babylonian land, that Nebuchadnezzar allowed a halt. At that, some Israelites turned to food and drink; and some turned to weeping and mourning.

Nebuchadnezzar asked, "Why do you sit weeping?" And he called to the tribe of Levi and said to them, "Get ready! While we eat and drink, I want you to stand and strike your harps before me, as you struck them in your Temple before your God." The Levites looked at one another and said, "Is it not enough [of a torment] for us that we destroyed His Temple by our sins? Must we now strike our harps for this dwarf?"[3] They all stood up with one accord, hung their harps upon the willows there by the river, and then, with extraordinary self-command, put their thumbs into their mouths and either mangled them or bit them off.

That this happened is implied in what David, quoting the Levites, says: "How shall we sing the Lord's song?" (Ps. 137:3–4). They did not say, "We shall not sing," but said, "How shall we sing?" The Levites showed the Babylonians their [mangled] fingers and said, "Are you not aware that our hands were so tightly manacled by the irons that our fingers were mangled? Look! How can we now sing?"[4]

18. "Mine eye shall weep sore, and run down with tears, because the Lord's flock is carried away captive" (Jer.

---

1. Lam. R. 2:2, §4; Yalkut, Isa., §421.

2. Rendering *ta'itzu* ("labor") as if it read *tin'atzu* ("blaspheme"): "Do not blaspheme in order to comfort Me."
3. See "the lowest of men" (Dan. 4:14).
4. PR 31:4 (YJS 2:606–7); Yalkut, Ps., §883.

13:17). You find that before Israel were exiled, they were made up of several flocks—flocks of priests unto themselves, flocks of Levites unto themselves, and flocks of lay Israelites unto themselves. But after they were exiled, they became one flock—"the Lord's flock is carried away captive."

R. Yohanan ben Zakkai used to say: Why should Israel have been exiled to Babylon more than to any of the other lands? Because Abraham's family came from there. By what parable may the matter be explained? By the one of a woman who was unfaithful to her husband. Where is he likely to send her? Back to the house of her father.[1]

Yearnings

19. "These things I remember and pour out my soul within me" (Ps. 42:5). Whom did the sons of Korah have in mind when they uttered this verse? None other than the congregation of Israel, for the congregation of Israel said to the Holy One: Master of the universe, I recall the trust and serenity in which I used to abide. Now these are far removed from me. I weep and sigh as I say: Who will restore me as in former days, when the Temple was standing, and You used to come down into it from the highest heaven and have Your Presence abide over me, and the peoples of the world spoke in praise of me; and when I sought compassion for an iniquity of mine, You answered me? But now I am covered with shame and humiliation.

The congregation of Israel said also: Master of the universe, my soul is desolate within me, for when I pass Your house, which is destroyed, and am plunged in utter silence, I ask myself: The place where the seed of Abraham used to bring offerings to You, where priests used to minister on the dais, where Levites used to intone praise with harps—is it right for foxes to be romping about in it?

"How I passed on with the throng (*sakh*), and led them (*eddaddem*) to the house of God" (Ps. 42:5). Here the congregation of Israel is saying to the Holy One: In the past, I used to go up with the throng (*sakh*) to Jerusalem along well-kept roads, but now [I have to make my way] through thorny hedges (*sakh*)—"I will hedge up (*sakh*) her roads with thorns" (Hos. 2:8). In the past, when I used to go up, trees furnished shade (*mesakekhim*) over my head, but now I am fully exposed to the sun.[2] In the past, I used to go up in the shade of the Holy One, but now I am in the shadow of [oppressive] kingdoms.

According to R. Berekhiah, the congregation of Israel also said to the Holy One: In the past, I used to go up carrying baskets of firstfruits on my head, but now [I go] "in silence" (*eddaddem*)[3]—I go up in silence (*demumah*) and come down in silence (*demumah*). In the past, I used to go up with songs and psalms of praise before the Holy One. But now I go up with weeping and come down with weeping. In the past, I used to go up in "a festive throng" (Ps. 42:5), throngs and throngs caught up in festivity—(Indeed, as R. Levi said, the congregation of Israel was then like a cataract whose flow stops neither day nor night)—but now I sneak up like a thief, and like a thief sneak down.[4]

Comforting

20. The words "Comfort ye, comfort ye My people" (Isa. 40:1) are, according to R. Berekhiah the Priest, to be read, "Comfort Me, comfort Me, O My people." In the world's use, if a man owns a vineyard and robbers come and cut it down, who is to be comforted, the vineyard or the owner of the vineyard? And so, too, if a man owns a house and robbers come and burn it down, who is to be comforted, the house or the owner of the house? You are My vineyard. But Nebuchadnezzar came and, having destroyed it, exiled you and burned My Temple; it is I that need to be comforted. Hence, "Comfort *Me*, comfort *Me*, O My people."[5]

21. "A Psalm of Asaph. O God, the heathen are come into Thine inheritance" (Ps. 79:1). Should not Scripture have used a phrase such as "weeping of Asaph," "lament of Asaph," "dirge of Asaph"? Why does it say "A Psalm [song] of Asaph"? Well, the use of the word "psalm" may be accounted for by the parable of a king who made a bridal bower for his son, which he plastered, paneled, and painted. But his son entered upon an evil course of living. So the king came up into the bower and tore the curtains and broke the rods. Then the son's tutor took a reed pipe and played on it. He was asked, "The king has just now overthrown his son's bower, and you sit here playing a tune?" The tutor replied, "I play a tune because the king overthrew his son's bower but did not pour out his wrath[6] upon his son." So, too, when it was said to Asaph, "The Holy One has just destroyed both Temple Hall and Sanctuary, and you sit here singing a psalm?" he replied, "I sing because the Holy One poured out His wrath upon sticks and stones, but did not pour out His wrath upon Israel."[7]

1. Lam. R., proem 25; Tos BK 7:3.
2. Reading not *teluyah* ("hung") but *geluyah* ("exposed"). So David Luria and Midrash Ekhah, ed. Buber (Vilma, 1899), p. 80.
3. JV: "led them."
4. Lam. R. 1:17, §52. The source of the first two paragraphs in this section is unknown to the translator.
5. PR 29/30:9 (YJS 2:586).
6. Play on words: *huppato* ("his bower") and *hamato* ("his wrath").
7. Lam. R. 4:11, §14.

CHAPTER EIGHT

THE ERA BETWEEN THE FIRST AND SECOND TEMPLES

Daniel and the Dragon in Babylon

1. "I will punish Bel in Babylon, and I will bring forth out of his mouth that which he hath swallowed up" (Jer. 51:44). Nebuchadnezzar had a great dragon, which swallowed up everything thrown to it. [Nebuchadnezzar said to Daniel, "How great is its might, that it swallows up everything thrown to it!"] "Give me permission," Daniel replied, "and I will deplete his strength." Nebuchadnezzar gave him permission. What did Daniel do? He took straw, hid nails in it, and threw the straw to the dragon, and the nails lacerated his innards.[1]

The Dead whom Ezekiel Brought Back to Life

2. Our masters taught: When Nebuchadnezzar threw Hananiah, Mishael, and Azariah into the fiery furnace, the Holy One said to Ezekiel, "Go and bring the dead in the Valley of Dura back to life." As Ezekiel was quickening them, the [utensils made from] bones of the dead, [which Nebuchadnezzar had been using, also came to life and] began slapping Nebuchadnezzar in the face. When he asked, "What in the world are these? his courtiers replied, "Ezekiel, the companion of the three you threw into the fiery furnance, has brought the dead in the Valley of Dura back to life."

At that, Nebuchadnezzar broke into song:

How great are His signs!
And how mighty are His wonders!
His kingdom is an everlasting kingdom,
And His dominion is from generation to generation!
(Dan. 3:33).

R. Isaac said: May molten gold be poured into the mouth of that wicked one! If an angel had not come and struck him upon his mouth, he would have sought to excel all the songs and praises that David had uttered in the book of Psalms.[2]

3. It is taught that R. Eliezer said: The dead whom Ezekiel brought back to life stood up on their feet, uttered song, and [immediately] died. What song did they utter? "The Lord slayeth in justice, and in mercy bringeth back to life." R. Joshua said that their song was: "The Lord killeth and maketh alive; He bringeth down to the grave, and bringeth up" (1 Sam. 2:6). R. Judah said: The account in Ezekiel[3] was the truth, and it was also a parable. R. Nehemiah asked him: If truth, how a parable? And if a parable, how truth? [R. Judah]: It was a true event that served as a parable.[4]

R. Eliezer son of R. Yose the Galilean said: The dead whom Ezekiel brought back to life went up to the Land of Israel, married, and begot sons and daughters. At this, R. Judah ben Betera jumped up on his feet and said: I am one of their descendants, and here are the tefillin that my grandfather left me [as an heirloom] from them.[5]

Hananiah, Mishael, and Azariah

4. "My son, fear thou the Lord and the king" (Prov. 24:21). When Nebuchadnezzar ordered Hananiah, Mishael, and Azariah to worship idols, and they refused to obey him, he said to them, "Did not the Holy One command you to obey the government in whatever it tells you to do, [as is said], 'I [counsel thee], keep the king's command' (Eccles. 8:2)?" They replied, "You are king over us in the matter of taxes and imposts. But to worship idols? O Nebuchadnezzar, in this respect you and a dog are alike."[6]

5. R. Simeon the Shilonite expounded: When the wicked Nebuchadnezzar cast Hananiah, Mishael, and Azariah into the fiery furnace, Yurkami, the [heavenly] prince of hail, appeared before the Holy One and said, "Master of the universe, let me go down, cool the furnace, and thus save those righteous men from the fiery furnace." Gabriel spoke up, "The might of the Holy One will not be made evident this way, for you are the prince of hail, and everyone knows that water quenches fire. But I am the prince of fire. Let me go down, and I shall cool it within and heat it without,[7] and thus perform a miracle within a miracle." At that, the Holy One said to Gabriel, "Go down." It was then that Gabriel burst forth: "True is the Lord forever" (Ps. 117:2).[8]

6. "O Lord, goodness is Thine, but shame falls to us" (Dan. 9:7). R. Eleazar asked: Who uttered this verse? and he himself replied: Hananiah, Mishael, and Azariah uttered it. When they came out of the fiery furnace, all the peoples of the world gathered and, slapping Israel on their faces, said jeeringly, "You have such a God, yet you were willing to worship the image [of Nebuchadnezzar]." They

---

1. Gen. R. 68:13.
2. B. Sanh 92b. Rabbinic tradition has a grudging admiration for Nebuchadnezzar as an outstanding personality.
3. Ezek. 32.
4. It foreshadowed the rebirth and revival of the Jewish people.
5. B. Sanh 92b.
6. Num. R. 15:14.
7. To burn those who put them into it.
8. At the time of Abraham's deliverance from the fire, God promised Gabriel that he would deliver Abraham's descendants, and God kept His word. B. Pes 118b.

spit in the faces of Israel until their entire bodies seemed to be covered with spittle. Then Hananiah and his companions lifted their eyes to heaven above and, justifying the [humiliating] punishment meted out to Israel, said, "O Lord, goodness is Thine, but shame falls to us."

After Hananiah, Mishael, and Azariah came out of the furnace, where did they go?[1] They, so said R. Joshua, drowned in the spittle.[2]

7. R. Yohanan said: It is written, "The sun was darkened in his going forth" (Isa. 13:10). Would that it had been dark on that day and the sun had not risen at all! For Cyrus went out to walk through his capital and saw that the capital was deserted. He asked: What has gone wrong with this city, that it is so deserted? Where are the goldsmiths? Where are the silversmiths? He was answered: Are you not the one who decreed, "The Jews may leave and build the Temple"? Some of those Jews were goldsmiths and others were silversmiths, and they went up to rebuild the Temple. So Cyrus decreed, "He who has already crossed the Euphrates may remain across; but he who has not yet crossed may no longer cross." At that very moment Daniel and his followers had already [completed the crossing and] gone up to the Land, saying: [Instead of eating the abundant food of Babylon], it is better to eat the meager food of the Land of Israel and say grace in the Land of Israel. But Ezra and his followers did not go up at that time.

Why did Ezra not go up at that time? Because he had to clarify his grasp of Torah, which he learned from Baruch son of Neriah.[3] But should not Baruch son of Neriah himself have gone up? Yes, the sages said, but Baruch was so old[4] and so enfeebled that he could not travel even in a litter.

Resh Lakish suggested: Ezra did not go up at that time, in order that the Temple might retain its sanctity. Had Ezra gone up at that time, Satan would have been given an opportunity to make mischief by saying: It is better that Ezra should take over the high priest's office than that Joshua son of Jehozadak serve as high priest. But Joshua son of Jehozadak was high priest by right of descent, whereas Ezra, a righteous man to be sure, had no such hereditary claim to serve in that office. The Holy One, R. Simon said, is reluctant to disrupt claims of succession based on descent.[5]

8. It is taught that R. Eliezer ben Jacob said: Three prophets[6] went up with the Jews from exile in Babylon: one informed them about [the dimensions of] the altar and the site of the altar; another informed them that they could bring offerings, even though there was as yet no Temple; and the third informed them that the Torah should be written in Assyrian characters.[7]

Ezra

9. We learn that R. Yose said: Had Moses not preceded him, Ezra would have been worthy of having the Torah given to Israel through him. And even though the Torah was not given through him, its script was changed through him.[8]

10. "If she be a wall, we will build upon her a turret of silver; and if she be a door, we will enclose her with boards of cedar" (Song 8:9). If, in the days of Ezra, you had made yourselves solid like a wall and all of you had come up together in solid unity, you would have been likened to silver, which no rot can affect. But since you came up like doors, you are like cedarwood, which succumbs to rot.[9]

Men of the Great Assembly

11. R. Joshua ben Levi asked: Why were they called "Men of the Great Assembly?" Because, he answered, they restored the manner[10] [of praising God's greatness] to its ancient form. Moses said, "The great God, the mighty, the awesome" (Deut. 10:17). Then Jeremiah came and said: Heathens are battering at His Holy Place—where are the feelings of awe that He is said to inspire? Hence he did not say that God was awesome. Then Daniel came and said: Heathens are enslaving His children—where are His mighty acts? So he did not say that God was mighty.[11] Then came the Men of the Great Assembly, who said: On the contrary, the greatness of His might is in that He suppresses His wrath and is forbearing toward the wicked. His awesome deeds are in that but for the awe of the Holy One, how could a single people remain alive among the heathens?[12]

In the Days of Mordecai and Esther

12. In the verse "For the Leader; upon the hind of the dawn" (Ps. 22:1), Scripture speaks of the generation of Mordecai and Esther, [a time that was more dark than] the night. For though it is night, one has the light of the moon, the stars, and the planets. Then when is it really dark? Just before dawn! After the moon sets and the stars set and the planets vanish, there is no darkness deeper than the hour before dawn, and in that hour the Holy One answers the world and all that is in it: out of the darkness, He brings forth the dawn and gives light to the world.

---

1. The question is asked because they are not mentioned again.
2. A figurative way of saying that they died of broken hearts, humiliated as they were at Israel's acquiescence in idolatry. So Meir Ha-Levi, as quoted by Adin Steinsaltz in his edition of Sanh (Jerusalem, 1974). B. Sanh 93a; Tanhuma, *Ki Tissa*, §14.
3. Jeremiah's disciple. See Jer. 45.
4. The *Ot Emet* suggests that "stout" in the text be changed to "old."
5. Song R. 5:5, §1.
6. Haggai, Zechariah, and Malachi.
7. The square form of Hebrew now in use. B. Zev 62a.
8. See preceding note. B. Sanh 21b.
9. B. Yoma 9b.
10. Literally, the crown [of God's greatness].
11. See Jer. 32:18 and Dan. 9:4.
12. B. Yoma 69b and En Yaakov, ad loc.

Then, too, why is Esther likened to the hind of the dawn? What is true of the light of dawn? Its light rays out as it rises; at the beginning, light comes little by little; then it spreads wider and wider, grows and increases; and at last it bursts into shining glory. So, too, Israel's redemption through Esther came about little by little. At the beginning "Mordecai sat in the king's gate" (Esther 2:21); then "the king saw Esther the queen" (Esther 5:2); then "on that night the king could not sleep" (Esther 6:1); then "Haman took the apparel and the horse" (Esther 6:11); then "they hanged Haman" (Esther 7:10); then Ahasuerus said to Esther and Mordecai, "Write concerning the Jews as you see fit" (Esther 8:8); then "Mordecai went forth from the presence of the king in royal apparel" (Esther 8:15); and at last "the Jews had light and gladness" (Esther 8:16).

The sages said: When a hind is thirsty, she digs a hole, fixes her horns in it, and in her distress cries softly to the Holy One. The Holy One causes the deep to come up, and the deep causes water to spring up for her. So, too, Esther: when wicked Haman decreed cruel decrees against Israel, she, in her distress, began to cry softly in prayer to the Holy One, and the Holy One answered her.

R. Assi said: As the dawn ends the night, so all miracles [recorded in Scripture] ended with Esther.[1]

Deborah and Esther

13. R. Judah bar Simon taught: You find that when a house in which a snake nests is fumigated with a hind's horn or a woman's hair, the snake immediately flees. So, too, Deborah and Esther were as effective as a hind's horn, for Deborah did not budge until she destroyed Sisera and his hosts; and Esther did not budge until she had Haman and his ten sons hanged.[2]

The Feast of Ahasuerus

14. His disciples asked R. Simeon ben Yohai: Why was Israel[3] of that generation deemed to deserve extermination? He said to them: You tell me. They replied: Because Israel relished the feast of that wicked one. He said: If so, the Jews in Susa should have been condemned to die, but not those in the rest of the world. They: You tell us then. He: Because they bowed down to the graven image.[4] They: Was there a show of favor toward them [on God's part] in this matter? He: No. Since they only pretended to worship the graven image, God only pretended that He was about to exterminate them.[5]

15. "The couches were of gold and silver" (Esther 1:6). It is taught that R. Judah said: He who was rated worthy of silver was invited to recline on a couch of silver, and he who was rated worthy of gold was asked to recline on a couch of gold. R. Nehemiah argued: Such show of favor would have stirred up resentment at the feast. Rather, what the verse really means is that all the couches were made of silver, and only their legs were of gold. These couches were placed "upon a pavement of . . . shell (*dar*) and onyx marble (*tzoharet*)" (Esther 1:6). Samuel said: In cities far across the sea, there is a precious pearl shell called *darah*, which Ahasuerus placed in the center of the pavement, and it provided the guests with light as bright as midday (*tzahara*).[6]

16. "And the drinking was according to the manner [of each country]; none did compel" (Esther 1:8). The first part of the verse implies that each guest was given the wine native to his own province. Of the verse's second part, R. Levi said: Such was the practice of the people of Persia: they had a large cup holding five-eighths of a *kav*,[7] which each guest was made to drink—even if he were to die or go out of his mind as a result, he was not allowed to return it until he had drunk all of it. The wine steward used to get rich from those guests who winked at him and gave him ever so many gold denars so that they would not be compelled to drink from it. But Ahasuerus did not have this cup brought to his banquet. Rather, he said: Whoever wishes to drink may drink as much as he chooses.[8]

17. "According to every man's wish" (Esther 1:8). The Holy One said: O wicked one, if two men wish to marry the same woman, can she possibly wed both? If two ships are sailing on the Great [Mediterranean] Sea, one seeking a southerly wind and the other a northerly wind, can the same wind drive both of them? Tomorrow two men, Mordecai and Haman, will come to you. Do you think you can possibly satisfy both as you might if there were only one? You will have no choice but to exalt one and hang the other.

No one except the Holy One can satisfy the wish of every human being. Of Him it is said, "Thou satisfiest the wish of every living thing" (Ps. 145:16).[9]

Bigthan and Teresh

18. "In those days, while Mordecai sat in the king's gate, two of the king's chamberlains, Bigthan and Teresh . . . had a grievance" (Esther 2:21). What brought on their grievance? R. Levi said: Bigthan and Teresh were Tarseans,[10] and both sat in the gate of the king. But the king removed them and put Mordecai in their place. So they felt they had a grievance. What did they do? They said: Let us put poison in the [king's] bowl, so that the king will die and everyone will say, "When Bigthan and Teresh guarded the king, all was well; but now that a Jew was put in their place, the king is murdered." They were stand-

1. MTeh 22:13; B. Yoma 29a.
2. Aggadat Esther on 7:11 (ed. Buber [Cracow, 1897], p. 68).
3. Literally (and euphemistically), "the enemies of Israel."
4. Set up by Nebuchadnezzar.
5. B. Meg 12a.
6. Ibid.
7. The equivalent of the contents of fifteen eggs.
8. Midrash Abba Gorion on Esther 1:8; Yalkut, Esther, §1048.
9. Midrash Abba Gorion on Esther 1:8; Esther R. 2:14.
10. There was a Tarsus in Cilicia and another in Cappadocia.

ing and talking of their scheme in the Tarsean language, not knowing that Mordecai was one of those who had sat in the Chamber of Hewn Stone[1] and therefore knew the seventy languages [of the world].[2]

19. "So they were both hanged on a tree" (Esther 2:23). "After these things did King Ahasuerus promote Haman" (Esther 3:1). [In explaining the sequence of these two verses], R. Phinehas used to tell a fable: A lion gave a feast for animals, tame and wild. He provided a tent covering for them made from skins of lions, wolves, and other ferocious animals. After they had finished eating and drinking, they said, "Who is going to sing for us?" and looked to the fox. He said, "Will you repeat the song after me?" They answered, "Yes." He lifted his eyes to the skins above their heads and said, "May He who has shown us what has become of those above[3] show us also what is to become of those below."[4] So, too, He who has shown us the hanging of Bigthan and Teresh will show us also the downfall of Haman.[5]

The Promotion of Haman

20. "After these things did King Ahasuerus promote Haman" (Esther 3:1). R. Levi said: Haman was promoted only for his downfall. Why then bother to promote him? The answer will be provided by the parable of a common soldier who cursed the king's son. The king said: If I put the scoundrel to death, everyone will say, "The king has executed a common soldier." I will first promote him, and then execute him. So he made him a tribune, then a general, and after that he cut off his head. Likewise, the Holy One said: Should Haman be put to death when he sank so low as to advise Ahasuerus to stop the building of the Temple, no one will know who he is. Let him therefore be promoted and then be hanged. So "he first set his seat above all the princes" (Esther 3:1), and after that "they hanged Haman" (Esther 7:10). This shows how the enemies of the Holy One become great only as prelude to their downfall. And so Scripture says, "Though the wicked bloom, they are like grass; though all evildoers blossom" (Ps. 92:8). What follows at the end of the verse? "It is only that they may be destroyed forever" (ibid.). Similarly it is said, "He exalts the nations, then destroys them" (Job 12:23).[6]

21. "King Ahasuerus promoted Haman . . . and set his seat above all the princes" (Esther 3:1). A parable of a man who had a filly, a she-ass, and a sow. He measured out fodder to the she-ass and to the filly, but let the sow eat as much as she wanted. The filly complained to the she-ass, "What is the idiot doing? To us, who do the work of the master, they ration food, but to the sow, who does nothing, they give as much as she wants." The she-ass replied, "The time will come when you will see that she is stuffed with fodder not out of deference to her but to her own harm." When the Roman Calends[7] came, they took the sow and stuck her. So, too, first "King Ahasuerus promoted," and in the end "they hanged Haman" (Esther 7:10).[8]

Haman's Intention

22. "Wherefore Haman sought to destroy all the Jews" (Esther 3:6). To what may the wicked Haman be compared? To a bird that made its nest at the edge of the sea, only to have it swept away when the tide was high. What did the bird do? It proceeded to take water into its beak and pour it out on the dry land, then take sand from the dry land and drop it into the sea. Its companion came, stood by, and asked: What are you doing, wearing yourself out so? The bird answered: I will not budge from here until I turn the sea into dry land and the dry land into sea. Its companion said: Biggest fool in the world! After all this effort, what do you think you can accomplish? So, too, the Holy One said to wicked Haman: You are the biggest fool in the world! I said I would destroy Israel, and found—if one dare ascribe such words to God—I could not. As Scripture says, "[God] intended to destroy them, but then Moses His chosen stood before Him in the breach, that . . . He should not destroy them" (Ps. 106:23). Yet you expect "to destroy, to slay, and to cause to perish." By your life, your head will be removed and not theirs! They are for deliverance, and you are for hanging.[9]

Haman's Slander and Ahasuerus's Decree

23. "Haman said: 'There is (*yeshno*) one people' " (Esther 3:8). Rava commented: There never was a slanderer as skillful as Haman. Haman said to Ahasuerus, "Come, let us engage them in battle." Ahasuerus answered, "I am afraid. Their God punishes anyone who engages them in battle." Haman: "But they are negligent (*yashenu*)[10] of God's precepts." Ahasuerus: "Nevertheless, there are righteous men in Israel who will seek mercy for the transgressors." Haman: "But they are 'one people' [ibid.].[11] Should you argue [that by obliterating them] I will make a barren area in your kingdom, [please remember] that they are 'scattered' [ibid.]—scattered among many peoples. Should you say, 'But surely there is some benefit to be derived from them,' remember that they are *meforad*[12] [ibid.]—they are like a *firdah*, a mule that bears no progeny. Should you argue, 'But they are outside my domain,' and so you cannot act against them, they are 'in all the provinces of thy kingdom' [ibid.].

1. As a member of the Sanhedrin.
2. Midrash Panim Aherim on Esther 2:29; B. Meg 13b.
3. The skins of the dead beasts hung above their heads.
4. The host—the lion—himself.
5. Esther R. 7:3; Yalkut, Esther, §1054.
6. Midrash Abba Gorion on Esther 3:1; Esther R. 7:2.
7. The first day of the Roman month, usually observed as a feast.
8. Midrash Abba Gorion on Esther 3:1; Esther R. 7:1.
9. Midrash Abba Gorion on Esther 3:1; Esther R. 7:10.
10. Literally, "They are as negligent as if they were asleep."
11. All of them are transgressors; or, all of them bear responsibility for one another.
12. JV: "dispersed." The word *meforad* is construed as an adjectival form of *firdah* ("mule").

"Beside, 'their laws are diverse from those of every people' [Esther 3:8]—they do not eat with us, drink with us, or intermarry with us. 'Neither keep they the king's laws' [ibid.]—they spend the entire year dawdling and lolling about.[1] They say, 'It is the Sabbath, it is a festival,' and thus get out of doing the king's work." Haman then proceeded to reckon the Jewish festivals: the Feast of Unleavened Bread, Feast of Weeks, Feast of Tabernacles, New Year's Day, and the Fast of Atonement. At that, the Holy One said to Haman, "Villain, you would cast an evil eye on their festivals? I will cause you to fall down before them, and to celebrate your downfall they will add still another festival."

Haman went on, " 'It profiteth not the king to suffer them' [Esther 3:8], for they eat and drink, and hold the king in contempt. If a fly falls into the cup of one of them, he flings it out and drinks the wine. But if my lord king touches the cup of one of them, he dashes it to the ground and will not drink from it. Therefore, 'if it please the king, let it be written that they be destroyed; and I will pay ten thousand talents of silver,' " etc. (Esther 3:9).

"And the king said unto Haman: 'The silver is given thee, the people also, to do with them as it seemeth good to thee' " (Esther. 3:11). R. Abba said: By what may the give-and-take between Ahasuerus and Haman be illustrated? By the parable of two men, one of whom had a mound in the middle of his field, while the other had a ditch in the middle of his. The owner of the mound said: Who will sell me that ditch? The owner of the ditch said: Who will sell me that mound? One day the two met, and the owner of the ditch said to the owner of the mound: Sell me your mound. The other replied: I wish that such a request had been made long ago! Take it for nothing.[2]

24. "Then were the king's scribes called . . . and there was written . . . and letters were sent" (Esther 3:12–13). What was written in those letters? [The following]: To all peoples of diverse races and languages: May your well-being increase! Be it known unto you that there came to us a man, who is not of our city or of our land, an Amalekite, the son of distinguished forebears, and his name is Haman. He put a small—one may say, trifling—request to us, saying: In our midst there dwells a nation more despicable than any other nation. Arrogant in spirit, they are ever ready for treachery and corruption. They hold us in contempt and rejoice in our misfortune. Evening, morning, and noon the cursing of the king is habitual in their mouths. They keep saying, "The Lord is king forever and ever. May the nations vanish from His earth" (Ps. 10:16) when "He wreaks vengeance upon the nations, punishment upon the peoples" (Ps. 149:7).

The scions of this despicable and arrogant people are notorious ingrates. Look what they did to poor Pharaoh. When their forebears came down to Egypt, he welcomed them with extraordinary kindness—he even allowed them to settle in the very best part of his land. During years of famine he did not merely feed them, he gave them choice viands. Then, when he asked that they build him just one palace, they came with a trumped-up tale, saying, "Let us go, we pray thee, three days' journey into the wilderness and sacrifice unto the Lord our God" (Exod. 5:3); after that we will come back. In the meantime—they said—please lend us silver vessels, gold vessels, and garments. So the Egyptians lent them their silver, their gold, and their finest clothing. Then each one of these ingrates loaded ever so many asses, until they emptied Egypt. After that, they made their getaway. Naturally, Pharaoh—he and his entire camp—had no choice but to pursue them to retrieve their stolen treasure. What did these ingrates do? They had among them a certain person whose name was Moses son of Amram. By means of his witchcraft he took a staff, uttered incantations over it, and with it smote the sea, until it became dry. Then all of them went into the midst of the sea on dry land, and all of them got across. I do not know by what means they were able to cross the sea or by what means its waters were dried up. When Pharaoh saw this, he went in after them—I do not know how they managed to push him into the sea—but he and his entire host drowned in it. The ingrates, you see, chose not to remember the good things Pharaoh had done for them.

Then do you know what they did to Amalek, Haman's ancestor? After they had come up out of the sea, Amalek went to Balaam to seek advice from him, saying: Look what this people has done to Egypt. Now, if they have done this to Egypt, which bestowed so many boons upon them, how much more are they likely to do to other peoples! What do you advise? Balaam replied: Go and wage war against them. If you cannot prevail against them, no mortal will ever prevail against them, because they depend on the merit of Abraham, and so do you.

At that, Amalek went to war against them. What did their leader Moses do then? He had an understudy named Joshua son of Nun, cruel—utterly without mercy. Moses said to him, "Choose us men, and go out, fight with Amalek" (Exod. 17:9). I do not know the kind of men he chose—whether they were wizards or just mighty warriors. But Moses took a stick in his hand—I do not know precisely what he did with it—and also took a stone and sat on it—again I do not know what incantations he whispered over it. All I know is that Amalek's strength grew weak; and, powerless, they fell, slain by them.

Then they attacked Sihon and Og, the mightiest warriors in the world. No mortal could stand up to these two. I still do not know how they managed to slay them.

After that, what did Joshua, that person's understudy, do? He led Israel into the land of the Canaanites, not only taking their land, but slaying thirty-one of their kings. He then divided the land of the Canaanites among the Israelites. Even the Gibeonites, who made peace with them, they forced to become menservants and maidservants. Then Sisera and his multitude attacked Israel. What they did to him, I do not know, but the brook of Kishon swept away Sisera and his multitude, carried them off, and cast them into the Great [Mediterranean] Sea.

As their first king, they had a man named Saul. He went to the land of Haman's ancestor Amalek, where in

1. Hebrew: *shihi pihi*, which may be an acronym for *Shabbat ha-yom, Pesah ha-yom*, "Today is Sabbath, today is Passover."

2. B. Meg 13b–14a; Midrash Panim Aherim 3 (ed. Buber, p. 68).

one day Saul slew a hundred thousand horsemen—he had no pity on man or woman, child or suckling. How he managed to slay them, I do not know. Then what did they do to Haman's grandfather, Agag, whom they first had spared? After a while one of them, named Samuel, came forth, cut him in pieces, and served his flesh as food to the birds of heaven. I do not know why Samuel felt he had to inflict such a horrible death upon Agag.

After that, they had another king, David son of Jesse by name, who destroyed and exterminated ever so many realms, and showed no pity to their inhabitants.

After David, his son Solomon rose up and built for Israel an edifice he called "the sacred house." What they had in it, I do not know. But whenever enemies came to fight them, they entered that edifice and performed their witchcraft in it, and when they emerged from it, they killed [enough] to destroy the entire world. There was not a virtue they did not boast of having, and because of their extraordinary prosperity, no other people or tongue was deemed by them to amount to anything.

But when that God of theirs grew old, Nebuchadnezzar attacked them and burned that edifice of theirs, and their wizardry no longer availed them. Some he slew; others, after fettering in irons, he exiled from their Land and brought into our midst. But they still did not change their ugly ways. Even though they are in exile in our midst, they mock us and mock what we hold in awe. In their eyes, we are an abomination. So now all of us have agreed to cast lots to determine the best time to exterminate them from the world. The lot against them fell on the month of Adar, the thirteenth day in it. Accordingly, when these presents reach you, get ready for that day. He who draws a bow, let him draw it. He who wields a sword, let him wield it. Be ready to kill, to exterminate in one day all the Jews in your midst—young and old, little ones and women; do not allow even one of them to escape or get away.[1]

The following is the text of the letter Haman the Agagite wrote and sent to all the kingdoms of the world and to all the notables of the peoples of the world: I, chief officer of the king, second only to him, first of all prefects and most distinguished among the nobles in the realm, I, in full agreement with the king's eparchs and officers, satraps and governors, speaking as one, in the same language, using the same words, which King Ahasuerus has authorized, do herewith indite this writing, which is sealed with his signet and is therefore irreversible. The writing concerns the great vulture [Israel] whose wings had been spread over the whole world. No fowl, no beast, tame or wild, could withstand him. But then came the great lion [Nebuchadnezzar], who dealt the vulture a mortal blow. His wings were broken, his feathers plucked out, his feet hacked off. From the day the vulture was forced out of his eyrie until this day, the entire world, all of it, has had bestowed upon it calm, quiet, and serenity. But now we see the vulture determined to grow feathers and wings once again, determined to overshadow us and the entire world, all of it, as he once overshadowed and plundered our earliest forebears. Therefore we, all the foremost regents of Media and Persia, under the authority of King Ahasuerus, with common consent, are writing to you as follows: "Set snares for this vulture and trap him before he renews his strength and returns to his eyrie. We advise you to pluck his feathers and break his wings, to feed his flesh to the fowl of heaven, to crack his eggs, to crush his fledglings, and to root out his memory from the world. Let not our counsel be like Pharaoh's, who decreed only against males but let the females be; nor like Amalek's, who smote the stragglers and left the strong unscathed; nor like Sennacherib's, who exiled them to a land like their own; nor like Nebuchadnezzar's, who only exiled them but let them live, even seating some of them near his throne. Clearly aware [of the threat], we are resolved to slay, to exterminate all Jews, young and old, so that there be left of them no memorial, no name, no posterity in the world. Thus, they will be unable to do to us what they did to our forefathers and fathers. For whoever did them a favor, they paid back only with evil."

After the letters were sealed and given to Haman, he, together with his entire band of associates, left the royal palace, overjoyed.

When Mordecai met them [and learned of the fate in store for the Jews], he happened to see three Jewish children coming from school and hastened to catch up with them. Haman and his band, seeing Mordecai hasten after the children, followed him to find out what he might say to them.

When Mordecai caught up with the children, he asked one of them: Recite for me the verse in Scripture you studied today. He replied, "Be not afraid of sudden terror, neither of the destruction of the wicked, when it cometh" (Prov. 3:25). The second child followed him, saying: Today in school I studied the verse "Take counsel together, and it shall be brought to naught; speak the word, and it shall not stand; for God is with us" (Isa. 8:10). The third added, "Even to old age I am the same, and even to hoar hairs will I carry you; I have made and I will bear; yea, I will carry, and will deliver" (Isa. 46:4). When Mordecai heard these verses, he not only cheered up, he became jubilant. Haman asked him: What did the children say to you that made you so joyful? Mordecai replied: They gave me the good tidings that I need not fear the evil counsel you have devised against us. Enraged, wicked Haman said: I will make these children the first to feel the blow of my hand.

Then Haman said to Ahasuerus: The God of these people hates lewdness. So make a feast for them and seat women next to each one of them. Order that all of them come, eat and drink, and do whatever they desire. The king gave the order. At once Mordecai rose up and issued a proclamation: My children, go not to the place of Ahasuerus's feasting, so that Satan will not be given cause to make accusations against you. But they disregarded the words of Mordecai, and all of them went to the place of feasting.

---

1. "All this is a masterpiece of satirical parody of a people's history. I know only one other work in this genre—Count Alexis (no relation to Leo) Tolstoy's parody (in verse) of Russian history, as murderous in its characterization of the Russian czars as this is of the Jewish leaders. Perhaps there is an English counterpart—I cannot recollect a German or a French one (Voltaire? Heine?—I can't remember). There is certainly no Arabic one" (Leon Nemoy).

R. Ishmael said: Eighteen thousand five hundred men went to the place of feasting, where they ate, drank, became drunk, and committed acts of depravity, giving no thought whatever to the destruction of their Temple.

At once Satan rose up and, in the presence of the Holy One, brought charges against the Jews, saying bluntly to the Holy One: Master of the universe, how long will You cleave to this people, who keep provoking You? If You please, cause this people to perish from the world. The Holy One asked: But what will happen to the Torah? Satan replied: Master of the universe, You will have to make do with [the allegiance to it of] those on high. Indeed, the Holy One Himself, becoming reconciled with Satan's counsel, said: What need have I of this people, because of whom I have had so many reasons for anger? "I will make their memory cease from among men" (Deut. 32:26). At once the Holy One said to Satan: Bring Me a scroll and I will write in it: "Extermination." Satan went and brought God a scroll, which He inscribed and sealed.

At once the Torah went forth in a widow's garb and lifted her voice in weeping before the Holy One. At the sound of her weeping, the ministering angels too cried out to the Holy One and said: Master of the universe! If Israel were not in the world, of what use are we? When the sun and the moon heard this, they withdrew their brightness, and heaven and earth and all the works of creation went into mourning.

At that moment, Elijah, ever remembered on good occasions, ran in all haste to the fathers of the world and to the first prophets, and said to them: Fathers of the world, heaven and earth and all the host on high are weeping bitterly. The entire world is seized with pangs, like a woman in labor, and you lie here unruffled? They asked: What is happening? Elijah replied: A decree of extermination has been issued against Israel.[1] Abraham, Isaac, and Jacob said: If the decree against them has been sealed, what can we do? Elijah turned around and went to Moses, to whom he said: Alas, O faithful shepherd, how many times did you stand in the breach in Israel's behalf and cause a decree against them to be nullified, so that they were not destroyed. How will you respond to this present peril? Moses asked: Is there one virtuous man in this generation? Elijah: Yes, his name is Mordecai. Moses: Go and tell him about it, so that he might stand in prayer there, as we will here. Elijah responded quickly: But, O faithful shepherd, the decree against Israel is already indited, already sealed. Moses: If it is sealed with clay, our prayer will be heard; but if with blood, what must be, must be. Elijah: It is sealed with clay. Moses: Go and tell Mordecai.

At once Elijah went and told Mordecai.

"And in every province whithersoever the king's commandment and his decree came, there was intense mourning among the Jews" (Esther 4:3). Why is it spoken of as "intense mourning"? Because it is the way of mourning to be intense the first day, but, as it continues, it grows less intense. This mourning, however, kept growing more intense as it went on, for each man would say to himself: Tomorrow I am to be slain.

[1] Literally (and euphemistically), "the enemies of Israel."

"And the thing pleased Haman, and he caused the gallows to be made" (Esther 5:14). What did he do? He went and cut down a cedar in the palace garden, and with chants and songs had it taken out and set up at the entrance to his house. Then he said: Tomorrow morning I will hang Mordecai upon it. After he had it set up, he measured himself against it; at that a divine voice spoke up, saying: These gallows fit you fine. Indeed, these gallows have been ready for you ever since the six days of creation.[2]

After Haman made the gallows, he went to Mordecai and found him seated in a house of study, with young children before him, their heads sprinkled with ashes, sackcloth about their loins, engaged in the study of Torah, even though they were crying aloud and weeping. Haman counted them and found that there were twenty-two thousand of them. He put iron collars about their necks, and fetters of iron on their legs, set guards over them, and said: Tomorrow I will slaughter these first, and then hang Mordecai.

The mothers of the children came to bring them bread and water, and said to them: Children, eat and drink before you die tomorrow—do not die hungry. The children put their hands on their scrolls and swore: By the life of our teacher Mordecai, we will neither eat nor drink, but will die worn out from fasting. Then each child rolled up his scroll, returned it to his teacher, and said: We thought that through the merit of Torah we would live long. But now that we have no such merit, take the scrolls from our hands. Then all moaned loudly as they wept, the mothers lowing like heifers outside the house of study, and the children bawling like calves within it, until their cry reached the height above. The Holy One heard the sound of their weeping at the end of the third hour in the night. In that instant the Holy One rose from the throne of justice, seated Himself on the throne of mercy, and asked: What is this loud noise I hear, like that of kids and lambs? Moses our teacher stood up before God and said: Master of the universe! These are neither kids nor lambs. They are the little ones of Your people, who have been fasting now for three days and three nights, and tomorrow, like kids and lambs, they will be made to stand up for slaughtering.

With that, the compassion of the Holy One crested, and He broke the seals, tore up the letters [of doom] and that night cast dismay on Ahasuerus.[3]

The Fall of Haman and the Exaltation of Mordecai

25. "On that night could not the king sleep" (Esther 6:1). R. Hama bar Gorion said: All those who wished to sleep had no sleep that night. Esther was busy with the feast for Haman; Mordecai was busy with his sackcloth and fasting; Haman was busy with his gallows. At that time

[2] The assertion is the result of what appears to be an outrageous play on words: the phrase *hmn h-'tz* [*ha-min ha-etz*] "of the tree" (Gen. 3:11), is read, "For Haman the tree [*Haman ha-etz*]," hence, "the gallows."

[3] Aggadat Esther, ed. Buber, pp. 38–40 and 45–46; Esther R. 7:13 and 9:4; Midrash Abba Gorion 4–5; Yalkut, Esther, §1055.

the Holy One said to the angel in charge of sleep: My children are in peril, yet this wicked king is sleeping in his bed. Go and cause his sleep to desert him. At once the angel came down, stood over Ahasuerus, and disturbed his spirit, saying to him: Ingrate, go and repay with favor him who deserves it. Ahasuerus began to muse: Who has served me well and has not been repaid? So "he commanded to bring the book of the records of the chronicles" (ibid.)

R. Levi said: Haman's son, who was the king's scribe, read the writ before the king. When he came to the parallel of Scripture's "It was found written, that Mordecai had told of Bigthana and Teresh" (Esther 6:2), he started rolling the scroll. But the words "Mordecai had told of Bigthana and Teresh" kept leaping into his sight, and, [agitated, he] continued rolling the scroll. The king asked, "How long must you keep rolling that scroll? Read what is before you." Haman's son said, "I cannot make myself read these words." At that, the words beginning "Mordecai had told" started reading themselves aloud. The instant Mordecai's name was recalled to Ahasuerus, sleep came over him. Near morning, as the king was sleeping, he saw in a dream Haman standing over him with an unsheathed sword in his hand, divesting him of the royal purple, removing the crown from his head, and aiming to slay him. In that instant Haman came and knocked on the door. Startled out of his sleep, the king called out, "Who is in the court?" and was told, "Behold, Haman standeth in the court" (Esther 6:4–5). So the king said to himself: That was no dream—it was the truth. "At once the king commanded: 'Let him come in' " (Esther 6:5).

When Haman came in, the king asked, "What shall be done unto the man whom the king delighteth to honor?" (Esther 6:6). Haman, puffed up by the pride in his heart, said to himself: Who is greater than I? Who deserves honor more than I? So whatever I ask, I ask for myself. Accordingly, he said, "My lord king, 'for the man whom the king delighteth to honor, let royal apparel be brought . . . and the horse . . . [and] a royal crown' " (Esther 6:7–8). The moment Haman asked for the crown, the king's countenance changed and he said to himself: That's it! That is what I saw in my dream—he wishes to slay me. So he told Haman, "Make haste, and take the apparel, etcetera, and do even so to Mordecai" (Esther 6:10). Haman said, "My lord king, there are many Mordecais in the world." The king: "Mordecai the Jew" (ibid.). Haman: "Among the Jews also there are many Mordecais." The king: "That sitteth at the king's gate" (ibid.). Haman: "If he is the one, the gift of a village or a river would be enough for him." The king roared at him like a lion and said, "Let nothing fail of all that thou hast spoken" (ibid.). The king summoned Hathach and Harbonah to accompany Haman, and ordered them: See to it that he omits nothing of all that he has mentioned. So the two went with Haman.

By the time Haman entered the king's storehouse, his body was bent low, his head covered like a mourner's; a hangdog look about his ears, his eyes lackluster, his mouth twisted, his spirit benumbed, and his knees knocking against each other. He took the king's apparel and the insignia of royalty from the storehouse, hurried out from there, and entered the royal stable, where out of its foremost stall he took the horse with a gold chain hanging from its neck. He seized the horse's halter and placed on its shoulders all the insignia of royalty. Then he went on to Mordecai.

When Mordecai saw Haman coming toward him leading a horse, he said to himself: I have a feeling that this wicked man is coming with his horse to trample me to death. Mordecai's disciples were then seated before him, studying. So he said to them, "Up, run off, lest you be scorched by the coal meant for me." They replied, "We will not part from you. Whether we live or die, we are with you." Then Mordecai wrapped himself in his prayer shawl and stood up to pray. In the meantime, Haman came in, sat down in the midst of the disciples, and asked, "What are you so busy with?" They replied, "With the precept of the *omer*,[1] which Israel used to offer in the days when the Temple was standing." He asked, "And what was that *omer* made of—silver or gold?" They replied, "Barley." He asked, "And what was its value?" They replied, "At the most, ten *meah*."[2] He said to them, "Your ten *meah* have prevailed over my ten thousand talents of silver."

Then, as soon as Mordecai finished praying, Haman said to him, "Rise up, righteous Mordecai, descendant of Abraham, Isaac, and Jacob. Your sackcloth and ashes count for more than my ten thousand talents of silver. Rise up from your sackcloth and ashes, put on royal apparel, and ride the king's horse." Mordecai replied to Haman, "Wicked one, son of the seed of Amalek, wait a bit while I eat the bread of bitterness and drink the water of gall. Then take me out and hang me on the gallows." Haman said, "Rise up, righteous Mordecai, from of yore great miracles have been performed for your people. The gallows I prepared, I prepared for my own undoing. And now rise up, put on this purple robe, place this crown on your head, and ride this horse, for the king wishes to honor you." Then Mordecai understood that the Holy One had performed a miracle in his behalf. So he raised his voice and said to Haman, "You are the biggest fool in the world! Here I am seated in ashes, my body is filthy, and I am to wear royal apparel! It is not the seemly thing to do. I shall not put these on until I bathe and have my hair shorn." So Haman went looking for a bath attendant and a barber, but could find neither. Then he himself took Mordecai into a bathroom, girded his loins and rolled up his sleeves, and served as bath attendant for Mordecai. He brought all kinds of perfumes and fragrant oils, applied them carefully to Mordecai, and washed and anointed him. Afterward, he fetched a pair of shears from his house and served as Mordecai's barber. As he was cutting his hair, Haman began to sigh. Mordecai asked, "Why are you sighing?" He answered, "Alas for a man like me, who had been the greatest among the nobles, whose seat was above their seats, and now has become bath attendant and barber." Mordecai then said, "Wicked one, did I not know your father, who for twenty-two years was bath attendant and barber at the village of Kiryanos? In fact, these are his own instruments."

---

1. The sheaf of barley, also called the "sheaf of waving," brought on the sixteenth of Nisan. See Lev. 23:9–14 and below, part 1, chap. 9, §72–73.

2. Small silver coins.

After Haman groomed and clothed him, he said to Mordecai, "Rise up, mount this horse." Mordecai replied, "I am an old man, and because of the fast my strength is depleted." Haman bent down and lowered his neck. Mordecai stepped on Haman's back, mounted the horse, and sat on it. As Mordecai mounted the horse, he kicked Haman, at which Haman said, "Mordecai, 'Rejoice not when thine enemy falleth' " (Prov. 24:17). Mordecai replied, "Wicked one, my people were told, 'You shall tread on their backs' " (Deut. 33:29).

Now, as Mordecai rode on, Haman walked ahead of him, proclaiming, "Thus shall it be done to the man whom the king delighteth to honor" (Esther 6:11). From the royal palace twenty-seven thousand young men with golden cups in their right hand and silver goblets in their left also walked, proclaiming, "Thus shall it be done to the man whom the king delighteth to honor." As all these were singing his praise, others were carrying flaming torches ahead of him.

Haman's daughter looked out of a window, and when she saw her father in such degradation, she collapsed and died.

When Israel saw the honor bestowed on Mordecai, they too walked at his right and at his left, proclaiming, "Thus shall it be done to the man whom the King in heaven delighteth to honor."

Mordecai on his part chanted God's praise, saying, "I will extol Thee, O Lord; for Thou hast raised me up, and hast not suffered mine enemies to rejoice over me" (Ps. 30:2).

His disciples were saying, "Sing praise unto the Lord, O ye His godly ones, and give thanks to His holy Name. For His anger is but for a moment. His favor is for a lifetime" (Ps. 30:5–6).

Esther was saying, "Unto Thee, O Lord, did I call, and unto the Lord I made supplication: 'What is to be gained from my death?' " (Ps. 30:9–10).

And Israel cited, "Thou didst turn for me my mourning into dancing" (Ps. 30:12).

"But Haman hastened to his house" (Esther 6:12) with four skills in hand—bath attendant, barber, foot soldier, and herald.[1]

26. "For Mordecai was great in the king's house, and his fame went forth throughout all the provinces" (Esther 9:4). Coins bearing the name Mordecai circulated throughout [Persia's] provinces. What were the effigies on his coins? Sackcloth and ashes on one side, and a golden crown on the other.[2]

The Hanging of Haman

27. "The king said: 'Hang him' " (Esther 7:9). Haman spoke up and said to Mordecai: Before I am taken to the gallows, I beg you, O righteous Mordecai, that I not be hanged the way commoners are hanged. The mightiest men in the world were not considered very much in my presence, and potentates of the realm submitted to me like bondmen. With the words of my mouth I frightened regents, and with the breath of my lips I terrified provinces. I, Haman, was known as second only to the king. I, Haman, used to be called "the king's father–counselor." I now fear that you will do to me what I intended to do to you. Take pity on my honor, and do not slay me in the manner that my grandfather Agag was slain. Act in keeping with the kindness that is natural to you. After all, there are no deliberate murderers among you. Do not hold Agag's hatred and Amalek's jealousy against me. Do not bear a grudge as did my forebear Esau, who bore a grudge and took vengeance. My eyes, grown dim, can barely see your face, and I find it difficult to plead with you, because of the advice against you that I accepted from my friends and from my wife Zeresh. Still, I beg you! Have pity on my person, my lord, O righteous Mordecai, do not hang my gray head on a gallows. Have me put to death any other way, but not by hanging. Have my head severed with the king's sword, the way officers of the realm are usually executed.

Even though Haman cried out in anguish and wept, Mordecai did not incline his ear to him. When Haman saw that no heed was given to his pleas, he raised his voice in the palace garden in weeping and lamentation, exclaiming; O trees and saplings planted in the earth since the six days of creation, hearken unto me: The son of Hammedatha is about to be hanged from a tree.

All the trees gathered together to take counsel and concluded that the tree that was fifty cubits high should have Haman hanged from its top. The grapevine said: I am too short, and besides, I, from whom wine is taken for libations, will not have Haman hang from me. The fig tree said: I, from whom firstfruits are taken and from whom Adam and Eve made themselves loincloths, will not have Haman hang from my top. The olive tree said: I, from whom oil is taken for the [holy] lampstand, will not have Haman hang from me. The palm spoke up to the Holy One: Everyone knows that wicked Haman is a descendant of Agag, who is a descendant of Amalek—shall he be hanged from my top? The Holy One replied: May your strength continue to be firm. He will not be hanged from your top, for you are one of a pair[3] with the congregation of Zion who was favored by Me. The etrog said: I will not have Haman hang from me, to whom all nations come to take my fruit to praise Thee with it! The myrtle spoke up and said: I, being partnered with the etrog, over whom the words "joy and gladness" are spoken [in the benediction during Sukkot], will not have Haman hanging from my top. The oak cried out and said: I, under whom Deborah, Rebekah's nurse, is buried, will not have Haman hang from me. The terebinth cried out and said: I, in whose lower branches Absalom the son of David was caught and hanged, will not have Haman hanging from my upper branches. The pomegranate said: I, to whom the righteous are likened, will not have Haman hanging from me.

"Listen to me," said the cedar, "hang Haman on me, on the tree that he in fact prepared for himself."[4]

---

1. B. Meg 16a; Esther R. 10:4; Midrash Panim Aherim, ed. Buber, 6; Eccles R. 5:2, §1; PR 18:6 (YJS 1:389–91).
2. See Esther 4:1 and 8:15. Gen R. 39:11.
3. Perhaps an allusion to "Thy stature is like a palm tree" (Song 7:8).
4. Targum Sheni on Esther 9:7.

CHAPTER NINE

THE SECOND TEMPLE—ITS STRUCTURE AND ITS SERVICE

The Temple in Its Glory

1. Our masters taught: He who never saw Jerusalem in its glory has never seen an exquisite city. He who never saw the Temple in its final construction has never seen a magnificent building.[1]

2. The Land of Israel is the navel of the world, being situated at its center; Jerusalem is at the center of the Land of Israel; the Temple, at the center of Jerusalem: The Temple Hall, at the center of the Temple; the Ark, at the center of the Temple Hall. And in front of the Temple Hall is the foundation stone upon which the world was founded.[2]

3. The house in which God chose to dwell was built in the territory of Benjamin on a triangle[3] wedging out of his territory into Judah's, as implied in the words "And He dwelleth between [Judah's] shoulders" (Deut. 33:12).[4] Why did Benjamin merit having the Presence dwell in his territory? The answer is provided by the parable of a king who from time to time visited his sons, each of whom would say in turn, "The king is to dwell with me," except the youngest son, who [gloomily] said to himself: Is it conceivable that my father would disregard my older brothers and choose to dwell with me? So, his visage sad and his spirit low, he stood up and was about to leave. The king said [to the other sons], "Did you notice, when my youngest son stood up, that his visage was sad and his spirit low? Henceforth, my food and my drink are to come from you, my elder sons, but my dwelling is to be with him." Likewise, the Holy One said, "The house I chose to dwell in is to be in Benjamin's territory, but the offerings in it are to come from all the tribes."

Another explanation: Why did Benjamin merit having the Presence dwell in his territory? Because all the tribe fathers were in on the sale of Joseph, while Benjamin had nothing to do with it. So the Holy One said: Am I to tell these to build the house I choose to dwell in, so that they may pray to Me in it and I may be filled with compassion for them? No. They were not compassionate to their brother, so I shall not have My compassionate Presence dwell in their territory.

Another explanation: Why did Benjamin merit having the Presence dwell in his territory? The reason will be made clear by the parable of a king who had many sons. After they grew up, each went off and claimed the place that was his. But the father dearly loved the youngest of them all, so he ate and drank with him, leaned on him when he came into the house, and leaned on him when he went out. So it was with the righteous Benjamin, the youngest of the tribe fathers: Jacob ate and drank with him, leaned on him when he went out of the house, and leaned on him when he came in. Hence the Holy One said: The place where that righteous man laid his hands to receive support, there I shall have My Presence dwell. Hence, "He dwelleth between his shoulders."[5]

4. The shape of the Temple, like that of a lion, was narrow at the rear[6] and wide in front.[7]

5. All gates in the Temple had been changed to gold, except the Nicanor gate, because of the miracles wrought for its doors. But some say: Because the bronze of its doors had a golden hue, for, according to R. Eliezer ben Jacob, the bronze was Corinthian,[8] which shines like gold.

What miracles happened to the bronze doors of the Nicanor gate? It is reported: On Nicanor's way back from Alexandria in Egypt, where he went to fetch those doors,[9] a fierce gale arose and was about to sink the ship. [To lighten the load] the mariners picked up one of the doors and cast it into the sea, yet the sea would not cease its raging. As they were about to cast the companion door into the sea, Nicanor jumped up, clung to it, and said, "Cast me in with it." At that, the sea stopped raging. But Nicanor continued to grieve about the other door. When the ship arrived at the harbor of Acco, the other door, bursting through the water, emerged from under the sides of the ship.

Some say: A sea creature had swallowed it and disgorged it onto dry land.[10]

6. At the entrance to the Temple Hall stood a trellised vine laden with gold, for whoever presented a leaf, a berry, or a cluster of golden grapes would bring it and hang it there. [So abundant was the gold on the vine], said R. Eliezer son of R. Zadok, that on one occasion three hundred priests were delegated to clear it.

R. Simeon ben Gamaliel said in the name of R. Simeon, deputy [high priest]: The curtain[11] was a handbreadth thick and was woven on seventy-two strands, each

---

1. B. Suk 51a.
2. Tanhuma B, *Kedoshim*, §10.
3. Literally, "ox head."
4. Cf. above, chap. 3, §106, and chap. 4, §82.
5. Yalkut, *Berakhah*, §957.
6. The western side, whose width was seventy cubits.
7. The eastern side, whose width was one hundred cubits. Mid 4:7.
8. "Corinthian bronze was refined, hence the light weight, hence the golden hue, as against the duller tone of the heavier bronze" (Yoma, Soncino, p. 175, n. 2).
9. The doors for the great eastern gate of the Temple Court.
10. B. Yoma 38a and En Yaakov, ad loc.
11. Between the Holy of Holies and the Temple Hall, where the golden altar stood.

strand consisting of twenty-four threads. Its length was forty cubits and its breadth twenty cubits, made up in its entirety of eighty myriads [of threads]. They used to make two curtains every year, and three hundred priests were required to immerse them.[1]

R. Isaac bar Nahmani said in the name of Samuel: With regard to the curtain as well as the vine, the sages used hyperbole.[2]

7. Our masters taught: In the Sanctuary, from the days of Moses, there was a flute, which was smooth and thin, and made of reed. The king commanded that it be overlaid with gold, whereupon its sound was not as pleasant as it had been. When the overlay was removed, its sound was again pleasant as before.

In the Sanctuary, from the days of Moses, there was a cymbal made of bronze, and its sound was pleasant. Then it was damaged. The sages sent for craftsmen from Alexandria in Egypt who patched it, whereupon its sound was not as pleasant as it had been. When the patch was removed, its sound was again pleasant as before.

In the Sanctuary, from the days of Moses, there was a mortar made of bronze; the incense was pounded in it. Then the mortar was damaged. The sages sent for craftsmen from Alexandria in Egypt who patched it, but it no longer was possible to pound in it as well as before. When the patch was removed, the mortar became again what it had been before.

The latter two vessels were left over from the First Temple, but after they were damaged there was no way of repairing them.[3]

8. Samuel said: In the Sanctuary there was a [musical instrument called a] *magrefah*; it had ten holes, each of which produced ten different kinds of pitches—thus it produced altogether one hundred different kinds of pitches.

[In a differing tradition] the sages taught: The instrument was one cubit long and one cubit high; from it projected a handle that had ten holes, each producing one hundred different kinds of pitches. Thus it produced altogether one thousand different kinds of pitches.

R. Nahman bar Isaac said: With regard to this instrument also, the sages used hyperbole.[4]

9. There were two chambers in the Temple complex, one the Chamber of Secrets, and the other the Chamber of Utensils. The devout used to deposit their gifts secretly in the Chamber of Secrets, and the poor whose families had seen better days were able to receive support from there in secret. The Chamber of Utensils: whoever made a gift of any utensil used to toss it into that chamber, which the treasurers opened every thirty days. Any article that they found useful for the maintenance of the Temple, they left there; but the others were sold, and the money received went to the fund for the maintenance of the Temple.[5]

10. R. Phinehas said in the name of R. Huna of Sepphoris: The spring that issued from the Holy of Holies resembled at its source the [tiny] antennae of locusts; when it reached the entrance to the Temple Hall,[6] it became as wide as a thread of warp; when it reached the entrance to the Porch,[7] it grew as wide as a thread of weft; when it reached the entrance to the Temple Court, it became as wide as the mouth of a small narrow-necked jug. From there onward, it grew wider and wider as it rose, until it reached the entrance to the house of David.[8] After it reached the entrance to the house of David, it became a swiftly flowing brook in which those [who were ritually unclean] immersed themselves [in order to become clean].[9]

The Hiding of the Ark

11. There were five matters in which the First Temple differed from the Second: (1) the Ark, its cover, and the cherubim; (2) the fire;[10] (3) the Presence; (4) the Holy Spirit; and (5) the Urim and Tummim.

When the Ark was hidden, there were hidden with it the jar containing the manna,[11] the flask of anointing oil,[12] the staff of Aaron with its petals and almond blossoms, and the chest that the Philistines had sent as a gift to the God of Israel. Who hid the Ark? Josiah, king of Judah, hid it. What was his reason for hiding it? When he came upon the verse "The Lord will bring thee, and thy king whom thou shalt set over thee, unto a nation that thou hast not known" (Deut. 28:36), he rose up and hid it. Concerning his decision to hide it, Scripture says, "And he said unto the Levites . . . : 'Put the holy Ark in the house which Solomon . . . did build; it need be no longer carried upon your shoulders' " (2 Chron. 35:3). Josiah went on to say to the Levites: If the Ark should be exiled with you to Babylon, then [when you return] you will not be permitted to restore it to its place in the Holy of Holies.[13] And so, henceforth [without the Ark], "serve the Lord your God, and His people Israel" (ibid.).[14]

12. Members of the household of Rabban Gamaliel and of the household of R. Hananiah, deputy high priest, used to prostrate themselves in front of the Temple's woodshed, for among them was a tradition going back to their forebears that the Ark lay hidden there.[15]

13. Once, while working [in the woodshed], a priest became aware that a block of pavement sounded different from the others. He went to tell his friends, but before he

1. Like all holy things, it was immersed in water before being used.
2. B. Hul 90b; B. Tam 29b.
3. B. Ar 10b; Tos Ar 2:3–5.
4. B. Ar 10b–11a.
5. Shek 5:6.
6. The hall where the golden altar stood.
7. The vestibule leading into the interior of the Temple Hall.
8. Mount Zion, outside Jerusalem.
9. B. Yoma 77b–78a and En Yaakov, ad loc.
10. In the First Temple it came from heaven.
11. See Exod. 16:33.
12. See Exod. 30:25.
13. The Ark's removal from the Land of Israel would have profaned it.
14. B. Yoma 21b and 52b; P. Shek 6:1, 49.
15. Shek 6:2.

had time to reveal the exact place, his soul left him. Thus they knew for certain that the Ark was hidden in the Temple's woodshed. What had the priest been doing? R. Helbo said: While chopping wood, he happened to strike the pavement with his ax.[1]

The school of R. Ishmael taught: Two priests, both physically blemished, were separating worm-eaten sticks from the other sticks of wood[2] when the ax of one of them slipped out of his hand and fell up on that [secret] place. At that, flame burst forth and consumed him.[3]

The Crown of Priesthood

14. In the Chamber of Hewn Stone, the Great Sanhedrin of Israel used to sit and [among other matters] investigate the [lineage of] priests. A priest in whom a disqualification [in lineage][4] was found would put on black garments, veil himself in black, and go away. He in whom no such disqualification was found would put on white garments, veil himself in white, go into the Temple area, and minister alongside his brother priests. They used to declare a day on which no disqualification was found in [the lineage of] any of the seed of Aaron the high priest a festal day and say: Blessed be He who is everywhere, blessed be He, that no disqualification has been found in the seed of Aaron. Blessed be He who has chosen Aaron and his sons to stand and serve before the Lord in the house most holy.[5]

15. "And the priest that is greatest among his brethren" (Lev. 21:10). Why was he called "greatest"? Because he was greatest in five matters—in comeliness, in strength, in wealth, in wisdom, and in personality.

It happened that Phinehas the Stonecutter was appointed high priest. When his brother priests went out and saw him still cutting stones, they did not allow him to go on and filled the quarry before him with gold denars.

How do we know that, if he has no means, his brother priests must make his means great? Because Scripture says, "The priest who has been made great by his brothers" (Lev. 21:10), which implies: Make his means great from the possession of his brother priests.[6]

Simeon the Righteous

16. Our masters taught: During the forty years that Simeon the Righteous ministered as high priest, the lot designating the goat for the Lord[7] would always come up in his right hand; after Simeon, it would sometimes come up in the right hand, sometimes in the left. [During those forty years] the crimson-colored strand[8] would turn white. After Simeon, it would at times turn white, at others not. Also during those forty years, the westernmost light[9] did not cease burning; after Simeon, it would at times burn and at other times go out. Also, the wood fire on the altar was burning so intensely [throughout the day][10] that the priests did not have to bring any wood other than the two logs[11] in order to fulfill the command of providing wood for the pile on the altar; after Simeon, however, the fire would at times remain intense, at other times not, so that throughout the day the priests had no choice but bring more wood for the pile [on the altar]. Also, [during those forty years], blessing was bestowed on the *omer*,[12] the two loaves of bread,[13] and the shewbread. Of the priests who ate a piece of the shewbread the size of an olive—some felt sated after eating it, some felt so sated that they even left a bit of it. After Simeon, however, a curse struck the *omer*, the two loaves of bread, and the shewbread, so that every priest received a portion as small as a cowpea. Those priests who were unassuming withdrew their hands from it, while the voracious ones took it [greedily] and devoured it. It happened that one such priest grabbed not only his portion but that of his fellow as well, and until his dying day he was called Ben Hamtzan, "the Grabber."[14]

17. It is taught: The twenty-fifth day of Tevet is the day of Mount Gerizim [when public mourning is permitted]. On that day the Cutheans sought permission from Alexander of Macedon to destroy the house of our God, and he granted it to them. So people came and informed Simeon the Righteous. What did he do? He put on priestly undergarments,[15] as well as his priestly outergarments;[16] then, with the nobility of Jerusalem carrying flaming torches in their hands alongside him, he and they set out to walk all night. It so happened that as the Jews were marching on one side of the road, Alexander's men marched on the other [each not seeing the other in the darkness], and did not come into contact until the break of dawn. At dawn, Alexander asked the Cutheans with him, "Who are these?" The Cutheans replied, "They are the Jews who rebelled against you."

---

1. And became aware of a hollow area underneath.
2. Being physically blemished, these priests were excluded from participation in the cult and were assigned to outside chores such as this.
3. Shek 6:2; B. Yoma 54a.
4. E.g., that his mother was a divorced woman.
5. Mid 5:4.
6. P. Yoma 1:2, 39a; Tanhuma B, *Emor*, §6.
7. The goat that was offered as a sin offering on the Day of Atonement; the other goat was designated by lot for Azazel (Lev. 16:6–10).
8. Tied between the horns of the he-goat sent off to the wilderness. Or possibly the one tied at the entrance to the Porch. The strand's turning white was taken to signify God's forgiveness. See Isa. 1:18.
9. The westernmost light in the lampstand, into which as much oil was put as into the others. Even though it was kindled first, the others were first to go out. The continuing light that it gave was a sign that the Presence rested in the midst of Israel.
10. The fire was kindled in the morning.
11. Two logs had to be presented daily in fulfillment of the command to bring wood to the altar. B. Yoma 26b.
12. Literally, "sheaf." The sheaf of barley offered on the sixteenth of Nisan; before that offering, the new cereals of that year were forbidden for use (Lev. 23:10).
13. Lev. 23:17ff.
14. B. Yoma 39a–b and En Yaakov, ad loc.
15. Breeches and sash.
16. Breastpiece, ephod, robe, fringed tunic, headdress, and gold frontlet. See Exod. 28:4 and 28:36.

By the time Alexander reached Antipatris,[1] the sun had risen and the two columns were face to face. When Alexander saw Simeon the Righteous, he descended from his chariot and bowed down before him. He was asked: Should a great king like you prostrate himself before this Jew? He answered: In my military campaigns, a vision of this man's likeness has always led me to victory.

Then Alexander turned to the Jews: "What brought you here?" They replied, "Is it possible that heathens should have wrongly induced you to destroy the house in which prayers are offered constantly that neither you nor your kingdom be destroyed? He asked the Jews, "Which heathens?" The Jews replied, "These [treacherous] Cutheans—the very ones standing in your presence." Alexander: "They are herewith put in your hands."

At once they pierced the heels of the Cutheans, tied them [through the holes] to the tails of their horses, and dragged them over thorns and thistles, until they reached Mount Gerizim, which they then plowed and planted with wild vetches, even as the Cutheans had intended to do to the house of our God.

That day was declared a festal day.[2]

The Temple of Onias

18. It is taught: The year in which Simeon the Righteous was to die, he foretold that he would die during that year. When asked, "How do you know?" he replied, "On every Day of Atonement an old man, dressed in white and veiled in white, would join me, enter [the Holy of Holies] with me, and leave with me; but this year the old man, dressed in black and veiled in black, joined me, entered [the Holy of Holies] with me, but did not leave with me." After the Festival [of Sukkot], Simeon was ill for seven days, and died. [That year] his brother priests refrained from mentioning the Explicit Name in the [priestly] blessing.[3] In the hour of his departure, he said to the priests, "My son Onias is to assume the high priesthood after me."

Being two and a half years older then he, Onias's brother Shimei was jealous of him and [pretending to be helpful] said to him, "Come, let me teach you the order of the Temple service." So he attired him in a woman's lounging gown,[4] tied a woman's sash around his waist, and had him stand near the altar. Then Shimei called out to his brother priests, "See what this one promised his ladylove and has now fulfilled. He vowed, 'The day I begin to serve in the high priesthood, I will put on your gown and tie your sash around my waist.' " His brother priests were about to kill Onias, but he ran away. Though they ran in pursuit of him, he outran them and managed to reach Alexandria in Egypt, where he built an altar and brought offerings to an idol upon it. When the sages heard of the incident, they said, "If this one [Onias], who had not yet been officially installed as high priest, has turned out to be such a turncoat [by apostatizing into idol-worship], what might have happened had he actually been installed as high priest?"[5] Such is the account of the events according to R. Meir. But R. Judah said to him: This is not what happened. Onias in fact refused to accept the office because Shimei was two and a half years older than he. Even so, Onias was jealous of his brother Shimei, to whom he said, "Come, let me teach you the order of the Temple service." So Onias attired Shimei in a woman's lounging gown, tied a woman's sash around his waist, placed him near the altar, and then called out to his brother priests, "See what this one promised his ladylove and has now fulfilled. He vowed, 'The day I begin to serve in the high priesthood, I will put on your gown and tie your sash around my waist.' " The priests were about to kill Shimei, but he explained to them all that had occurred. Then the priests sought to kill Onias, who ran away from them, and they ran in pursuit of him. Though he ran into the king's palace,[6] they continued to pursue him. Everyone who saw him said, "This is he, this is he!" Finally he managed to reach Alexandria in Egypt, built an altar there, and brought offerings upon it in honor of God, in fulfillment of the verse "In that day shall there be an altar to the Lord in the midst of the land of Egypt" (Isa. 19:19). When the sages heard of the incident, they said: If this is what happened [through the jealousy] of one [such as Onias] who had at first shunned the honor, what would happen [through the jealousy] of one who seeks the honor?[7]

Alexandria's Synagogue with the Double Colonnade

19. We are taught that R. Judah said: He who has never seen Alexandria in Egypt's synagogue with the double colonnade has never seen the glory of Israel. It is said that it was like a huge basilica, one colonnade within another, and it sometimes held twice the number of people that had gone out of Egypt. In it, corresponding to the seventy-one elders of the Sanhedrin, there were seventy-one golden cathedras, each of them weighing not less than twenty-one[8] talents of gold. In the middle of the synagogue was a wooden *bimah*, upon which the sexton of the synagogue stood with scarves in his hand. When the time came to answer, "Amen,"[9] he waved the scarves and the congregation responded with "Amen." Moreover, they

---

1. On the way from Jerusalem to Caesarea. It was built by King Herod and called Antipatris after his father, Antipater.
2. On it, public mourning was prohibited. B. Yoma 69a and En Yaakov, ad loc.
3. The Explicit Name could be pronounced only if the Presence rested in the Sanctuary. The priests took Simeon's death to indicate the departure of the Presence, and so that year they did not dare utter the Name. Tosafot on Sot 38a.
4. An egregious insult to the cult.
5. "Moral: let no high priest, even one as righteous as Simeon, appoint his successor. He may suggest one, but the candidate must be scrutinized and examined by the sages to ascertain his moral fitness for the office" (Leon Nemoy).
6. " 'The king's mount,' the region stretching from the Valley of Jezreel to the south of Judah, including the mountains of Samaria" (Git, Soncino, p. 254, n. 4).
7. B. Men 109b; B. Yoma 39b.
8. "Myriads of" omitted, as in mss.
9. As when the reader concluded a benediction.

were not seated haphazardly. Goldsmiths sat separately, silversmiths sat separately, blacksmiths separately, master weavers separately, and apprentice weavers separately, so that when a stranger or a poor man entered the synagogue, he was able to identify the members of his craft. He would then join them, and through them earn a livelihood for himself and the members of his family.[1]

Priestly Families

20. Our masters taught: The Garmu family were expert in preparing the shewbread but would not teach others [how to do it]. The sages sent for specialists from Alexandria in Egypt, who knew how to bake as well as they. However, they did not know how to take [the loaves] down [from the oven] as well as the Garmus, who heated the oven from the outside and baked the bread outside,[2] while the Alexandrians heated the oven from the inside and baked the bread inside—with the result that the bread of the Alexandrians would become moldy, while the bread of the Garmus did not turn moldy. When the sages heard that, they said: Everything the Holy One created, He created for His own glory [so that we need not insist upon having our way]. Let the Garmu family return to their task. The sages sent for them, but they would not come. Then they doubled their pay, and they came. Until that day they used to get twelve *maneh;*[3] after that day, twenty-four *maneh.* R. Judah said: Until that day, twenty-four *maneh;* after that day, forty-eight *maneh.*

The sages asked them: What reason do you have for not teaching [your art] to others? They replied: Our father's family knew that the Temple would be destroyed, and conceivably an unworthy man might learn the art and proceed to use it in serving an idol.

However, the memory of the Garmu family [who may appear to have been greedy] was held in high esteem for the following reason: fine bread was never found in their children's homes, lest people say: These feed from the preparation of the shewbread. Thus they endeavored to fulfill the command "Ye shall be clear before the Lord, and before Israel" (Num. 32:22).[4]

21. Our masters taught: The Avtinas family were skilled in preparing the incense but would not teach [their art]. The sages sent for experts from Alexandria in Egypt, who knew how to compound incense as well as they but did not know how to make the smoke rise as well as they. The smoke of the former ascended [as straight] as a stick, while the smoke of the latter was dispersed in every direction.

When the sages heard that, they said: The Holy One created everything for His own glory [so that we need not insist upon having our way]. Let the Avtinas family return to their task. The sages sent for them, but they would not come. Then they doubled their pay, and they came. Until that day they used to get twelve *maneh;* after that day, twenty-four *maneh.* R. Judah said: Until that day, twenty-four *maneh;* after that day, forty-eight.

The sages asked them: What reason do you have for not teaching [your art] to others? They replied: Our father's family knew that the Temple would be destroyed, and conceivably an unworthy man might learn the art and proceed to use it in serving an idol.

Nevertheless, the memory of the Avtinas family was held in high esteem for the following reason: never did a bride of their family go forth perfumed, and when they married a woman from elsewhere, they stipulated that she was not to go forth perfumed, lest people say: They perfume themselves from the preparation of the Temple incense. Thus they endeavored to fulfill the command "Ye shall be clear before the Lord, and before Israel" (Num. 32:22).

R. Ishmael said: Once I was walking on the way, and I met one of their descendants, to whom I said: [By refusing to teach their art], your forebears sought to enhance their own glory and to reduce the glory of their Creator. Nevertheless, the glory of Him who is everywhere remains, but their glory He reduced.[5]

R. Akiva said: R. Ishmael ben Logah told me the following: One day I and one of their descendants went to the field to gather herbs, and I saw him cry, then laugh. I asked, "Why did you cry?" He answered, "Because I recalled the glory of my ancestors." "And why did you laugh?" "Because the Holy One will restore it to us." "And what caused you to recall the glory that had been yours?" "A 'smoke raiser'[6] in front of me." "Show it to me." "We are under oath not to show it to any person."

R. Yohanan ben Nuri said: Once I met an old man who had a scroll [containing recipes] for the making of fragrant spices. I asked him, "From whom are you descended?" He replied, "I come from the family of Avtinas." I: "What have you in your hand?" He: "A scroll for the making of fragrant spices." I: "Show it to me." He: "As long as my father's house had the authority, they would not turn it over to anyone. Now you may have it. Take care [that no one else sees it]." [R. Yohanan ben Nuri concluded]: When I came and told my experience to R. Akiva, he said to me: From now on, I say, it is forbidden to speak disparagingly of these people.[7]

22. Our masters taught: Ben Kamtzar would not teach [his art] of writing. It is said of him that he would hold four pens between his five fingers, and if there was a word of four letters, he could write it in one movement.[8] He was asked, "What reason have you for refusing to teach [your art]?" The others mentioned earlier provided an explanation for their refusal, but Ben Kamtzar provided none. To the former apply the words "The memory of the righteous shall be for a blessing" (Prov. 10:7). While to

1. B. Suk 51b and En Yaakov, ad loc.
2. By slapping the flat cakes of dough to the heated outside of the oven wall.
3. One *maneh* equaled one hundred common shekels.
4. B. Yoma 38a and En Yaakov, ad loc.
5. Though the Temple was destroyed, God continues to be honored—but the art of the Avtinas family is no longer in demand.
6. The name of a plant used in the making of incense. Both its identity and the way it was used were known only to the Avtinas family.
7. B. Yoma 38a and En Yaakov, ad loc.
8. Perhaps a form of rapid lettering that the sages wished to become more widely known.

Ben Kamtzar and his like apply the words "But the name of the wicked shall rot" (ibid.)[1]

23. Hygros ben Levi excelled in the art of singing but would not teach others. It is told of him that when he was about to make a high trill, he would put his thumb into his mouth, place his index finger between the two parts of his mustache, and produce all kinds of sounds at such high intensity that, to a man, his brother priests would be thrown backward.[2]

24. Our masters taught: Four times did the Temple Court cry out. The first time: "Depart hence, ye sons of Eli, for you defiled the Holy Place of the Lord!" The Temple Court cried out another time: "Depart hence, Issachar of Kefar Barkai, who takes such care of himself that he profanes the sacred offerings to Heaven!"—he used to wrap his hands with silk while performing the service in the Temple.[3] The Temple Court cried out a third time: "Lift up your heads, O ye gates, and let Ishmael ben Phiabi, a disciple of Phinehas,[4] enter and serve in the high priesthood." And still another time the Court cried out: "Lift up your heads, O ye gates, and let Yohanan ben Narbai, a disciple of Pinkai,[5] enter and fill his stomach with the divine offerings." It is said of Yohanan ben Narbai that at his meal he would eat three hundred calves, drink three hundred bottles of wine, and consume forty *seah* of young pigeons for dessert.[6]

It is said: As long as Yohanan ben Narbai lived, *notar*[7] was never found in the Temple.

After R. Ishmael ben Phiabi died, the splendor of the high priesthood ceased.

What punishment befell Issachar of Kefar Barkai? It is related: As the king and queen[8] were dining, the king said; "Goat's flesh is best." The queen: "Lamb is best." Both said, "Who knows for certain? The high priest, who brings offerings every day." When Issachar came, he dismissed the question with a [contemptuous] flick of his right hand: "If the goat were best, it would be brought as the daily offering."[9] The king said, "Since he seems to have no respect for royalty, let his right hand be cut off." But Issachar bribed the executioners, and his left hand was cut off instead. When the king heard of it, he had them cut off his right hand also as well.

R. Joseph commented: Blessed be He who is everywhere, for having ordained that Issachar of Kefar Barkai receive his punishment in this world.[10]

25. We are taught that Abba Saul said: There were trunks of sycamore trees in Jericho, which strong-arm men used to grab for themselves, until the owners finally consecrated them to Heaven. Of such violent men and the likes of them, Abba Saul ben Botnit, quoting Abba Joseph ben Hanin, used to say:

Woe is me because of the family of Boethus! Woe is me because of their forked staves![11]

Woe is me because of the family of Hanin! Woe is me because of their whisperings![12]

Woe is me because of the family of Katros![13] Woe is me because of their pens!

Woe is me because of the family of Ishmael ben Phiabi! Woe is me because of their fists! They were high priests, their sons Temple treasurers, their sons-in-law trustees—and their servants beat people with sticks.[14]

26. It is told of R. Ishmael ben Phiabi that his mother made him a tunic worth one hundred *maneh,* which he put on to officiate at a "private" service and then handed over to the community.[15]

It is told of R. Eleazar ben Harsom[16] that his mother made him a tunic worth twenty thousand *maneh,* but his brother priests did not allow him to put it on, because it was so transparent that he appeared to be naked.[17]

27. A story concerning the sons of Martha daughter of Boethus. With but two fingers, each of the sons could grasp two legs of an ox bought for a thousand denars and walk heel touching toe as prescribed, until he placed the two legs of the ox on the altar.[18]

28. R. Yohanan said: What is implied by the verse "The fear of the Lord prolongeth days, but the years of the wicked shall be shortened" (Prov. 10:27)? "The fear of the Lord prolongeth days" applies to the First Temple, which remained standing for four hundred and ten years, and in which there served only eighteen high priests. "But

---

1. B. Yoma 38b.
2. Ibid.; Song R. 3:6, §6.
3. More than a desire to protect his hands may have been involved here. It is possible that Issachar imitated the pagan practice of veiling one's hands while performing rites in a temple. On the *velum humerale,* see Pearl F. Braude, " 'Cokkel in oure Clene Corn': Some Implications of Cain's Sacrifice," *Gesta* 7 (1968): 27, n. 29. Reprinted in Joseph Gutmann, ed., *No Graven Images: Studies in Art and the Hebrew Bible* (New York, 1971), p. 596, n. 29.
4. It is suggested that Agrippa appointed him. Though he sprang from a lower-class family of priests, his zeal and devotion won him praise. So Adin Steinsaltz in his translation of Pes. (Jerusalem, 1972–73), p. 239.
5. Pinkai may be a play on *pinka,* a meat dish, and thus suggest that he liked to eat well.
6. A hyperbolical way of paying tribute to his hospitality to poor people and to wayfarers.
7. Portions of sacrifices left over after the prescribed time during which they had to be eaten.
8. Hasmonean monarchs.
9. Which is contrary to law.
10. B. Pes 57b; B. Sot 49a.
11. With which they beat people.
12. During secret gatherings to devise oppressive measures.
13. Said to be identical with Cantheras (Josephus *Antiquities* 19.6.1 [Loeb ed., p. 355]), given to writing evil decrees.
14. The high priesthood meant considerable political power, which a high priest retained even after he was deposed. Even after being deposed, he may have retained his title. Hence, there were often several priests who held the title of high priest simultaneously. B. Pes 57a.
15. The removal of the spoon and coal pan may be done even when the community is absent. Hence, such activity is called a private service.
16. High priest in the days of Agrippa II.
17. B. Yoma 35b.
18. Tos Yoma 1:14.

the years of the wicked shall be shortened" applies to the Second Temple, which remained standing for four hundred and twenty years, and in which there served more than three hundred high priests. Deduct from those years the forty years Simeon the Righteous served as high priest, and the eighty years the high priest Yohanan [Hyrcanus] served, and the ten Ishmael ben Piabi served; some say also the eleven that R. Eleazar ben Harsom[1] served. Deducting the sum of the years during which the aforementioned served, you will find that not one of the others completed a year in office.

R. Yohanan ben Torta said: And why did the others not complete even one year in office? Because they bought the high priesthood for money. Thus R. Assi reported that Martha daughter of Boethus brought two *kav* of denars to King Yannai to get him to nominate Joshua ben Gamla as high priest.[2]

Alexander of Macedon

29. Our masters taught: When the Africans[3] came before Alexander of Macedon to sue the Jews, they said: The land claimed by Israel belongs to us, since it is described as "the land of Canaan with its various boundaries" (Num. 34:2), and our forebear was Canaan. At that, Gebiha ben Pesisa [a doorkeeper in the Temple] said to the sages: Give me permission, and I will go and contend with them before Alexander of Macedon. If they defeat me, say to them, "You defeated a mere commoner among us." If I defeat them, say, "The Torah of Moses defeated you."

The sages gave him permission, and he went and argued against the Africans, saying, "Whence do you bring proof?" They replied, "From the Torah." He said, "I, too, will bring proof only from the Torah, where it says, 'Cursed be Canaan, the lowest of slaves shall he be to his brothers' (Gen. 9:25). Now, if a slave acquires property, since he is a slave, to whom does the property belong?[4] Besides, you have not served us for ever so many years."[5] Alexander said to the Africans, "Answer him." "Give us three days' time," they requested. So he gave them the respite, during which they sought, but found no answer. At that, they fled, leaving behind their fields, which had been sown, and their vineyards, which had been planted.

That year was a sabbatical year.[6]

30. On another occasion, the Egyptians came to sue Israel before Alexander of Macedon. They pleaded, "Behold, the Torah says, 'The Lord gave the people favor in the sight of the Egyptians, and they lent them gold and precious stones' (Exod. 12:36). Return to us immediately the gold and silver that you took from us." Gebiha ben Pesisa said to the sages: Give me permission to go and contend with them before Alexander. If they defeat me, say to them, "You defeated a mere commoner among us." If I defeat them, say, "The Torah of Moses our teacher defeated you." The sages gave him permission, and he went and argued against the Egyptians, saying, "Whence do you bring proof?" They replied, "From the Torah." "Then I, too," he said, "will bring you proof only from the Torah, where it is said, 'The sojourning of the children of Israel, who dwelt in Egypt, was four hundred and thirty years' (Exod. 12:40). Pay us wages for the toil of sixty myriads whom you enslaved in Egypt for four hundred and thirty years." Alexander of Macedon said to the Egyptians, "Answer him." "Give us three days' time," they requested. So he gave them the respite, during which they sought, but found no answer. At that, they left their fields, which had been sown, their vineyards, which had been planted, and fled.

That year was a sabbatical year.[7]

31. On another occasion, the Ishmaelites and the Ketureans brought suit against the Jews before Alexander of Macedon. They pleaded: The land of Canaan is ours as well as yours, for it is written, "Now these are the generations of Ishmael, Abraham's son" (Gen. 25:12); and it is written, "And these are the generations of Isaac, Abraham's son" (Gen. 25:19); and it is further written, "But he shall acknowledge the firstborn, the son of the hated, by giving him a double portion of all that he hath" (Deut. 21:17)—accordingly, Ishmael should by right take a double portion.

Gebiha ben Pesisa said to the sages: Give me permission, and I will go and argue against them before Alexander. Should they defeat me, say, "You defeated a mere commoner among us." Should I defeat them, say, "The Torah of Moses our teacher defeated you." The sages gave him permission, and he went and argued against them, saying, "Whence do you bring proof?" They replied, "From the Torah." He said, "I, too, will bring proof only from the Torah, where it is written, 'And Abraham gave all that he had unto Isaac. But unto the sons of the concubines, that Abraham had, Abraham gave gifts' [Gen. 25:5–6]. If a father, while still living, bequeaths his property to one of his sons and then sends the son who has been given only gifts away from the son who has received the bequest, can either have a claim upon the other?" Shamefaced, they departed.[8]

32. Alexander of Macedon wanted to go up to Jerusalem. But the Cutheans went and told him: Take heed—they will not let you enter their Holy of Holies. When Gebiah ben Kosem learned of this, he went and had a pair of felt shoes specially made, which he set with two precious

1. He is described elsewhere as a rich man who gave up his money to devote himself to Torah. See B. Yoma 35b.
2. B. Yoma 9a and En Yaakov, ad loc.
3. In Jewish tradition, they are taken to be Girgashites, one of the seven peoples of Canaan; they left Canaan and settled in Carthage, North Africa.
4. "Obviously to the owners. Therefore, even if the land was given to the Canaanites, it belongs to their masters, the Jews, descendants of Shem" (Sanh, Soncino, p.609, n. 3).
5. "So you owe us your toil too for all that time" (ibid.).
6. So that Jews, who had no crops of their own, appropriated the crops of the Africans. B. Sanh 91a; Megillat Ta 3.
7. B. Sanh 91a.
8. Ibid.; Gen. R. 61:7.

stones worth twenty thousand silver [*zuz*]. When Alexander reached the Temple Mount, Gebiah said to him, "My lord king, so that you should not slip, remove your shoes and put on these felt shoes—the pavement is slippery."[1] When they came to the area of the Holy of Holies, he said, "Thus far we may enter. From here on, even we may not enter."[2] Alexander replied, "When we come out, I will straighten your hump."[3] Gebiah: "If you can do that, you will be famed as a great surgeon and receive large fees."[4]

33. Alexander of Macedon put ten questions to the elders of the Negev, the south country. He asked: Which is farther—from heaven to earth or from east to west? They replied: From east to west. The proof is that when the sun is in the east, [it is so far away that] all can look at it, but when the sun is in the middle of the sky, [it is so close that] no one can look at it.

He asked: Was heaven created first, or the earth? They replied: Heaven was created first, as Scripture says, "In the beginning God created the heaven and then the earth" (Gen. 1:1).

He asked: Was light created first, or darkness? They replied: This question cannot be solved. (Why did they not reply that darkness was created first, since it is written, "Now the earth was unformed and void, and darkness" [Gen. 1:2], and after that, "God said, 'Let there be light,' and there was light" [Gen. 1:3]? They thought to themselves: Perhaps he will go on to ask what is above and what is below, what is before and what is after.)[5]

He asked: Who is called wise? They replied: He who discerns what is about to come to pass.

He asked: Who is called a mighty man? They replied: He who subdues his impulse to evil.

He asked: Who is called a rich man? They replied: He who rejoices in his lot.

He asked: What shall a man do to live? They replied: Let him mortify himself.

What should a man do to kill himself? They replied: Let him live it up.

He asked: What should a man do to make himself popular? They replied: Let him hate sovereignty and authority. He commented: I have a better answer than yours. Let him love sovereignty and authority, and confer favors on mankind.

He asked: Is it better to dwell on the sea or on dry land? They replied: It is better to dwell on dry land, because those who set out to sea are never free from anxiety till they reach dry land again.

He asked: Which among you is the wisest? They replied: All of us are equal, since we all concur in giving the same answers to your questions.

He asked: Why do you resist me [and refuse to submit to my authority]? They replied: [Authority is yours only because] Satan prevails.

He said to them: [For saying such a thing] I may have you put to death by royal command. They replied: Power is in the hands of the king, but it is not seemly for a king to be false [to his assurances of immunity]. At that, he clothed them in garments of purple and placed gold chains upon their necks.[6]

34. One time Alexander told his sages: I want to go to the province of Africa. They replied: You cannot go there, because the Mountains of Darkness are in the way. He said to them: The idea of not going is unacceptable. I only ask you how I am to go about it. They replied: Take Libyan asses, which can travel in the dark, and bring coils of rope and lay them down at the side [of the road], so that when you return you may hold on to them and thus get back to the place you came from. After providing himself with what his sages suggested, he set out. Presently he came to Carthage, a realm inhabited only by women. He was about to make war against them. But they said to him: If you slay us, people will say that he killed women; and if we slay you, they will speak of you as the king whom women killed. So he said: Bring me bread. They brought him bread of gold and apples and pomegranates of gold placed upon a golden table. He asked them: Do people in your realm eat bread of gold? They replied: If you wanted bread, did you have no bread in your own country, that you had to bestir yourself and come here?

When he left, he wrote on the gate of the city: "I, Alexander of Macedon, was a fool until I came to Carthage and learned good counsel from women."[7]

35. From there Alexander of Macedon paid a visit to a king at the end of the world,[8] who showed him much silver and gold. Alexander said, "I have not come to see your silver and gold—it is your legal customs I have come to observe."

As Alexander and the king were engaged in discourse, two men came before the king for judgment. One said: My lord king, I bought a ruin from this man, and while digging in it, I found a treasure; so I said to him, "Take your treasure. I bought a ruin—I did not buy a treasure." The other replied: Just as you are afraid of the punishment for robbery, so am I afraid of it. The fact is, I sold you the ruin and everything in it—from the depths of the earth to the heights of heaven.

The king addressed one of them and asked him, "Have you a son?" He replied, "Yes." The king asked the other, "Have you a daughter?" He replied, "Yes." "Go then," said the king, "wed the one to the other, and let the two make use of the treasure." Alexander showed his amazement. The king asked, "Why are you amazed? Have I not judged well?" Alexander: "Yes, well." The king asked, "If such a case had come up before you in your country, how would you have handled it?" Alexander replied, "I would have chopped off the head of the one and

---

1. The real reason was that one was not permitted to enter the Temple Mount wearing leather shoes.
2. The hint to Alexander was unmistakable.
3. Gebiah means "humpbacked."
4. Gen. R. 61:7; Yalkut, *Hayye Sarah*, §110.
5. Questions man was not to ask. See above, chap. 2, §1.
6. B. Tam 31b–32a.
7. B. Tam 32b; Lev. R. 27:1; Tanhuma B, *Emor*, §9.
8. Believed to have been Africa, where, according to authors of antiquity, men led ideal lives. The Aramaic *Katzia* is taken to mean "End-of-the-World Land." See Saul Lieberman's note in PRKM, p. 274.

the head of the other, and the treasure would have gone to the king's house." The king: "Does the sun shine where you dwell?" Alexander: "Yes." "Does rain come down upon you?" Alexander: "Yes." The king: "There are small cattle in your country, are there not?" Alexander: "Yes." The king: "May the breath of life in such a man as you be blasted out! It is only for the sake of the small cattle that the sun still shines for you, that the rain still comes down upon you."[1]

On his return, Alexander sat by a certain spring eating bread. When he washed some salted fish he had, they gave off a sweet odor. So, saying, "This spring seems to be coming from the Garden of Eden," he scooped up some of the water and washed his face with it. Then he followed the course of the spring until he came to the entrance to the Garden of Eden. He cried out, "Open the gate for me." They replied, "This is the gate of the Lord; only the righteous shall enter into it" (Ps. 118:20). He replied, "I, too, am a lord; I, too, am of some account. Give me a token [to show that I was here]." They gave him an eyeball.

When he returned to this place, he put all the silver and gold he had on a scale over against the eyeball, and the silver and gold did not tip the scale. He asked the sages, "How do you account for this?" They replied, "It is the eyeball of a human being, which is never satisfied." He asked, "How can you prove that this is so?" They replied, "Take a little dust and cover it." He did so, and at once the silver and gold tipped the scale.[2]

The Servitude under Greece and the Jews Who Betrayed the Covenant

36. The words "A leopard watcheth over their cities" (Jer. 5:6) allude to Greece, which fired at Israel a variety of decrees culminating with the demand: "Write on the horns of an ox that you have no share in the God of Israel."[3]

37. In the days of the wicked kingdom of Greece, it was decreed against Israel that he who had a bolt on a door of his house should inscribe on it, "I have neither portion nor heritage in the God of Israel." All Jews promptly went and removed all bolts from their houses.

It was also decreed that he who had an ox should write on its horns, "I have neither portion nor heritage in the God of Israel." All Jews promptly went and sold their oxen.[4]

38. "And when he took in the smell even of those false to Him,[5] he blessed him" (Gen. 27:27)—"those false to Him," such as Joseph Meshita and Yakum of Tzerorot.

Joseph Meshita: When the [Greek] enemies wished to enter the sacred area of the Temple Mount, they said, "Let one of their own go in first," and told Joseph, "Go in, and anything you bring out is yours." So he went in and brought out the golden lampstand. They said to him, "It is not fitting for a commoner to make use of such a thing. Go in a second time, and whatever you bring out will be yours." But he refused. Though they offered him remission of taxes for three years, so said R. Phinehas, he still refused, saying, "Is it not enough that I angered my God once? Am I to anger Him a second time?"

What did the enemies do to him? They tied him to a carpenter's sawhorse and sawed him apart, while he kept crying, "Woe, alas, alack! That I should have angered my Creator!"

Yakum of Tzerorot, the son of the sister of Yose ben Joezer of Tzeredah, became an apostate. Presently, when the decree was issued that Yose ben Joezer be hanged, the beam for the hanging was carried before him. Just then—it was the Sabbath—Yakum rode by on a horse; Yakum said to his uncle, "Look at the horse my master has given me to ride, and look at the horse your Master gives you to ride." R. Yose replied, "If so much is given to those who provoke Him, how much more shall be given to those who obey His will!" Yakum asked, "Is there anyone who obeys His will more than you?" R. Yose replied, "If such [affliction] is meted out to those who obey His will, how much more to those who anger Him!" The answer got to Yakum like the venom of a snake. He went away and imposed upon himself the four judicial death penalties of stoning, burning, beheading, and strangling. How did he do it? He brought a beam, drove it into the ground, and tied a rope to the beam. He placed sticks of wood in a row and built a wall of stones over them. Then he piled up the fuel in front of the beam and put a sword, pointing upward, in the midst of the fuel. After lighting a fire under the sticks of wood beneath the stones, he hanged himself from the beam and thus strangled himself. The rope broke, and he fell into the fire, the sword met him, and the wall of stones tumbled upon him. The soul of Yakum departed, and because of his repentance he was received. Yose ben Joezer, in the drowse of death, spied Yakum's bier flying through space and said, "See ye, this man by a brief hour precedes me into the Garden of Eden.[6]

39. A story: Miriam the daughter of Bilgah became an apostate and married a military officer of the royal house of Greece.[7] When the Greeks entered the Temple Hall, she struck the top of the altar with her sandal, crying out, "*Lykos! Lykos!*[8] How long will you consume Israel's money and not stand by them in a time of distress?" When the

1. PRKM 9:1 (PRKS, pp. 171–72).
2. B. Tam 32b.
3. Lev. R. 13:5. The translator was unable to locate the source where Jer. 5:6 is used as the verse in the comment.
4. Midrash le-Hanukkah, BhM 6:1.
5. The commentator reads *begaday*, ("his clothes") as *bogeday*, ("those false to Him"). Isaac's blessing of Jacob, despite his awareness of the apostates that would spring out of Israel, is taken to point to the extraordinary qualities that even apostates were to have.
6. Gen. R. 65:22; MTeh 11:7, Yalkut, *Toledot*, §115.
7. Greece in Syria.
8. Greek for "Wolf! Wolf!" "For this expression applied to the altar with an allusion to its construction and situation rather than to its voraciousness, see Gen. R. 99 and [Nehemiah] Brüll" (Isidore Epstein in Suk, Soncino, p. 276, n. 6).

sages heard of the incident, they made the ring of her family immovable and blocked up its alcove.[1]

The Mother of Children

40. "Nay, but for Thy sake are we killed all the day; we are accounted as sheep for the slaughter" (Ps. 44:23). R. Judah said: This verse applies to a certain woman and her seven children, specifically Miriam daughter of Tanhum, who, together with her seven sons, was taken captive. The seven sons were taken and placed within the innermost of the seven enclosures of a temple for idol-worship.

The eldest was brought before the emperor and told, "Bow down to the idol." He replied, "It is written in the Torah, 'I am the Lord thy God' " (Exod. 20:2). At once he was taken out and put to death. Then the second son was brought to the emperor and told, "Bow down to the idol." He replied, "It is written in the Torah, 'Thou shalt have no other gods before Me' " (Exod. 20:3). He was taken out and put to death. Then the third son was brought and told, "Bow down to the idol." He replied, "It is written in the Torah, 'Thou shalt bow down to no other god' " (Exod. 34:14). He was taken out and put to death. Then the fourth was brought and told, "Bow down to the idol." He replied, "It is written in the Torah, 'He that sacrificeth unto the gods shall be utterly destroyed' " (Exod. 22:19). He was taken out and put to death. Then the fifth son was brought and told, "Bow down to the idol." He replied, "It is written in the Torah, 'Hear, O Israel, the Lord our God, the Lord is one' " (Deut. 6:4). He was taken out and put to death. The sixth son was brought and told, "Bow down to the idol." He replied, "It is written in the Torah, 'Know therefore this day, and lay it to thy heart, that the Lord, He is God in heaven above and upon the earth beneath; there is none else' " (Deut. 4:39). He was taken out and put to death. The seventh son, the youngest, was brought, and the emperor said to him, "My son, bow down to the idol." He replied, "God forbid." The emperor asked, "Why not?" The lad replied, "Because it is written in our Torah, 'Thou hast avowed the Lord this day to be thy God . . . and the Lord hath avowed thee this day' [Deut. 26:17–18]. We have long ago sworn to the Holy One that we will not exchange Him for any other God, and He also has sworn to us that He will not exchange us for any other people." The emperor said, "Your brothers have had [in part] their fill of years, fill of life, and savored that which is sweet; you are but a child, you have not had your fill of years, your fill of life, and as yet not savored that which is sweet in the world. [Listen to me, and] bow down before the idol." He replied, "It is written in our Torah, 'The Lord shall reign forever and ever' [Exod. 15:18], and also, 'The Lord is King forever; the nations will perish out of His Land' [Ps. 10:16]. You will cease. Your kingdom will cease. But the Holy One lives and endures forever." The emperor said, "Look at your brothers lying dead before you. I will throw my ring to the ground in front of the idol—[bend over] just enough to pick up the ring, so that it will be said, 'He obeyed the emperor's command.' " The lad replied, "Alas for you, O emperor! Alas for you, O emperor! If your honor is so important, how much more and more the honor of the Holy One." As he was taken out and put to death, his mother pleaded, "Give me my son, that I may kiss him." They gave him to her. Then she said, "By the life of your head, O emperor, put me to death first, and then put him to death." The emperor replied, "I cannot agree to that, because in your Torah it is written, 'Ye shall not kill it and its young both in one day' " (Lev. 22:28). She said, "Wicked one, have you already fulfilled all the other commandments, and this one alone remains for you to fulfill?" At once the emperor ordered that the child be put to death. The mother threw herself upon the child, embraced and kissed him, and said, "My son, go to your father Abraham and tell him, 'This is what my mother said: "Do not be proud. You built one altar, but I built seven altars. Yours was only a test, but mine a reality." ' " Even as she was embracing and kissing her child, they put him to death in her arms.

Then she went up to the roof and jumped to her death. A divine voice proclaimed, "The mother of such children causeth rejoicing" (Ps. 113:9).[2]

The House of the Hasmoneans

41. At whose hand will the kingdom of Greece fall? At the hands of the Hasmoneans, who are of the tribe of Levi.

Levi (*Lvy*) is rightly matched with Greece (*Yvn*), the former being the third tribe, the latter the third kingdom.[3] The name of the former consists of three letters, and the name of the latter of three letters. The former blow horns, the latter trumpets.[4] The former wear turbans, the latter wear helmets. The former wear breeches, and the latter femorals.[5] Now the former are few, while the latter are many; yet the many came and fell by the hands of the few.[6]

42. On the twenty-third of Iyyar, the [heathen] occupants of Akra[7] withdrew from Jerusalem. They used to harass the Jewish inhabitants, who because of them could neither come nor go during the day—only in the night [did they dare go out]. When [the might of] the Hasmonean house grew strong, the heathens were banished. The day the Hasmoneans expelled them was declared a festal day.

1. Each of the twenty-four courses, or watches, of priests had its own ring and its own alcove in the area where the animals to be offered were slaughtered. The head of the animal to be slaughtered was placed in the ring; and the knives were kept in the alcove. The course (*mishmar;* "watch") of Bilgah was punished in that henceforth it had to make use of the rings and alcoves that belonged to other priestly courses. This was done, so it is explained, in keeping with the adage "Woe to the wicked and woe to his neighbor." B. Suk 56b, P. Suk 5:8, 55d.

2. B. Git 57b; Lam. R. 1:16, §50; Yalkut, Lam., §1029.
3. Egypt, Babylon, then Greece.
4. So Gen. R. TA, p. 1274.
5. Knee breeches for military use.
6. Gen. R. 99:2.
7. It lay just north of the Temple. In later years it was known as Antonia. See 1 Macc. 13:50–51.

On the twenty-seventh of Iyyar, the garlands were removed from Judea and from Jerusalem. In the days of the kingdom of Greece, garlands of roses used to be brought and hung at the doorways of their temples for idolatry, as well as at doorways of shops and at entrances to courtyards. Songs to idols were sung. The foreheads of oxen and the foreheads of asses bore the inscribed declaration that their owners had no portion in the God of Israel. When the might of the Hasmonean house grew strong, the garlands were abolished, and the day they were abolished was declared a festal day.

On the seventeenth of Sivan, the fortress of Tyre, later called Caesarea daughter of Edom,[1] situated in a sandy area, was conquered. In the days of the Greeks, it had been a painful thorn in Israel's side. When the might of the Hasmonean house grew strong, the Greeks were conquered and expelled, and the Jews were settled in its midst. The day the Hasmoneans conquered it was declared a festal day.

On the fifteenth and the sixteenth of Sivan, the [heathen] inhabitants of Beth Shean and of the Valley [of Jezreel] were expelled. In the days of the Greeks, they too had been a menacing threat whenever Israel sought to resist Arab [invaders]. In the early days these heathens were not adjudged as deserving expulsion. Therefore neither Joshua son of Nun nor David king of Israel expelled them. Then later, when they were adjudged to deserve expulsion, the might of the Hasmonean house grew strong, and they were expelled. Those two days were declared festal.[2]

43. When the Greeks entered the Temple Hall, they defiled all the oils that were in it. Hence, when the royal house of the Hasmoneans grew strong and defeated the Greeks, they searched [in the Temple Hall] and found only one cruse of oil that had the seal of the high priest intact upon it.[3] There was enough oil in it for only one day's lighting. But a miracle was wrought, and with that oil [a lamp] was lit for eight days. The following year, these eight days were fixed in the calendar as festal days to be celebrated with *Hallel*[4] and thanksgiving.[5]

44. It is taught: Nicanor was a Greek general. Every day he used to raise his hand in threat against Judea's Jerusalem and say, "When will it fall into my hands so that I may trample it to dust?" When the royal house of the Hasmoneans grew strong, and they conquered the Greeks, Nicanor's thumbs and great toes were cut off and hung at the gates of Jerusalem, as if to say: The mouth that spoke in arrogance and the hands that moved threateningly against Judea's Jerusalem—vengeance is wrought upon them![6]

1. As an outpost of the Roman Empire, it was called "Daughter of Edom," i.e., of Rome.
2. The conquests referred to probably took place during the reigns of Simon (142–135 B.C.E.) and Yohanan Hyrcanus (135–104 B.C.E.). Megillat Ta 2–3; B. Meg 6a.
3. Hence not tampered with, undefiled.
4. P. 113–18.
5. The lighting took place in 165 B.C.E. (see 1 Macc. 4:50 and 2 Macc. 10:3). B. Shab 21b.
6. B. Ta 18b.

45. Why are lamps kindled during Hanukkah? Because when the sons of the Hasmoneans triumphed and entered the Temple, they found there eight spits of iron. They grooved these out and kindled wicks in the oil they poured into the grooves.[7]

46. On the third of Tishri, the mention [of God's Name] in legal bonds was abolished. For at one time the wicked government of Greece had issued a decree against Israel that at no time should the Name of Heaven be mentioned by them. When the royal house of the Hasmoneans grew strong, and they triumphed, they ordained that the Name of Heaven might be mentioned even in legal bonds. Thus they used to write: "In the year such-and-such of Yohanan [Hyrcanus], high priest, priest to God Most High." When the sages heard of it, they said: The day after someone pays his debt, the [canceled] bond might be thrown on a dung hill. So they stopped the mention of the Name of Heaven on such bonds. That day was declared a festal day.[8]

47. It is taught: There is the [memorable] story of King Yannai,[9] who went to Kohalith in the wilderness and conquered sixty towns there. On his return, he celebrated with great rejoicing and, after a while, summoned all the sages of Israel, to whom he said, "Our forefathers ate mallows while they were engaged with the building of the [Second] Temple; let us likewise eat mallows[10] in memory of our forefathers." So mallows were served on golden tables, and they ate. Now, there was a man there, frivolous, evil-hearted, and worthless, named Eleazar ben Poirah, who said to King Yannai, "O King Yannai, the hearts of the Pharisees are against you."

The king: "Then what shall I do?"

Eleazar: "By wearing the high priest's frontlet between your eyes, force them to stand up in deference."[11]

So he tested them by putting the high priest's frontlet between his eyes. An elder who was present, named Judah ben Gedidiah, said to King Yannai, "O King Yannai! Let the royal crown suffice you, and leave the high priestly crown to the seed of Aaron." [Judah spoke thus], voicing the rumor that Yannai's mother had been taken captive [by Greeks] in Modiim [and raped by them]. The rumor was investigated, but proved untrue. Small wonder that the sages of Israel had to depart in royal disfavor.[12] Upon their departure, Eleazar ben Poirah [dissatisfied with the mildness of the punishment] said to King Yannai, "O King

7. PR 2:1 (YJS 1:5).
8. Megillat Ta 7; B. BH 18b.
9. Alexander Yannai (103–76 B.C.E.).
10. After the king had feasted sumptuously, he invited the sages to "feast" on a poor man's salad.
11. You will then see how they react to your being high priest.
12. "There is probably a lacuna in the narrative, which may be supplied from Josephus *Antiquities* B.10.6. That rabbis sentenced [Judah ben Gedidiah] to flagellation, in accordance with the law of slander; but Eleazar urged that this was altogether inadequate, in view of Yannai's exalted position, and proved that [the sages] secretly [agreed] with the slanderer (Lazarus Goldschmidt)—in fact, the status of a person is taken into account when bodily injury is sustained (BK 83b), but not for slander" (Kid, Soncino, p. 333, n. 10).

Yannai! That is the law for the most humble man in Israel, but you, King and high priest—shall such a law be applied in your case also?"

The king: "Then what shall I do?"

Eleazar: "If you will take my advice, trample them to death."

The king: "But what will become of the Torah?"

Eleazar: "Look, it is rolled up and lying in a corner. Whoever wishes to study, let him come and study!"

Right away, evil sprouted through Eleazar ben Poirah. All the sages of Israel were massacred, and the world was desolate until Simeon ben Shetah came and restored the Torah to its pristine [glory].[1]

48. It is told: When King Yannai took sick, he had seventy elders of the elders of Israel seized, confined them in prison, and told the warden: If I die, put these elders to death, so that while the Jews rejoice at my death, they will at the same time be forced to grieve for their teachers. It is further told that King Yannai had a good wife whose name was Shalmonin.[2] The instant her husband died, she removed a ring from his hand and sent it to the warden with the message: As a result of a dream, your master has ordered the elders released. He released them, and they went back to their homes. It was only then that she announced: King Yannai is dead.

The day King Yannai died was declared a festal day.[3]

49. On the twenty-eighth of Tevet, a [qualified] Sanhedrin was seated again to dispense justice. For when the Sadducees sat in the Sanhedrin, which they controlled, King Yannai was with them, with his wife Queen Shalmonin seated next to him; and, except for Simeon ben Shetah, no one [who was not of their party] sat with them. Hence, when responsa concerning legal questions were solicited, no one knew how to adduce the required proof from the Torah.

Then Simeon ben Shetah said: Whoever knows how to adduce such proof from the Torah deserves to be seated in the Sanhedrin. Nevertheless, [nothing was done about it until] a certain occasion, when there arose a practical issue concerning which again no one knew how to adduce proof from the Torah—no one, except an old man who babbled in opposition to R. Simeon. Finally, the old man said, "Give me time; by tomorrow, I will have the answer." Simeon gave him the time asked, and the old man meditated in private on the issue. When he realized the next day that he still had no proof from the Torah, he was too embarrassed to come and sit in the Great Sanhedrin. At that, Simeon ben Shetah summoned one of his disciples and seated him in the old man's place, explaining: The Sanhedrin may not have fewer than seventy-one men. He kept doing this day after day, until all the Sadducees were removed, and a Sanhedrin of like mind to his was seated in authority.

When the Sanhedrin of the Sadducees was finally removed and a Sanhedrin of Jews [who were Pharisees] was seated, that day was declared a festal day.[4]

50. Our masters taught: When the princes of the Hasmonean house were contending with one another, Hyrcanus was outside [the wall of Jerusalem], and Aristobulus inside [the wall]. Every day those inside the wall would let down a sum of denars in a basket to those outside the wall, and, in exchange, lambs for the daily sacrifice were sent up. There happened to be [among the besiegers] an old man who had some knowledge of Greek wisdom. So, citing this wisdom to them in the original Greek, he said: As long as they carry on the daily services, they will never surrender to you.

The following day, when the sum of denars was let down in the basket, a swine was sent up. When it reached halfway up the wall, it thrust its nails into the wall, and an area in the Land of Israel four hundred by four hundred parasangs was shaken.

At that time it was declared: Cursed be the man who breeds swine, and cursed be the man who teaches his son Greek wisdom.[5]

Herod's Temple

51. Herod, a slave of the Hasmonean house, set his eyes on a certain maiden of that house. One day he heard a divine voice proclaim, "Every slave who rebels now will succeed." So he rose up and slew everyone in his master's household, leaving alive only that maiden. When she saw that he wanted to marry her, she went up on a roof and cried out, "Anyone who appears and says that he is of the Hasmonean house is really a slave, since I am the only one left of it." Then the maiden threw herself from the roof, fell to the ground, and died.

Herod preserved her body in honey for seven years, so that it could be said, "Herod wed a king's daughter."

"Who are they," he said, "who expound the verse 'From the midst of thy brethren thou shalt set up a king over thee' [Deut. 17:15]? The sages." Then he rose up and slew all the sages, leaving alive only Bava ben Buta, so that he might take counsel of him. He placed a garland of leeches around his head and put out his eyes.

One time Herod came, sat down before Bava, and [disguising his voice] said to him, "Did you see what this wicked slave [Herod] has been doing?"

Bava asked, "What do you expect me to do to him?"

"Curse him."

"It is said, 'Curse not the king, not even in thy thoughts' " (Eccles. 10:20).

"But he is not a [rightful] king."

"Even if he is no more than a rich man, for it is said, 'Curse not the rich in thy bedchamber' " (Eccles. 10:20).

"But in saying, 'A prince of thy people thou shalt not curse' [Exod. 22:27], Scripture has in mind a prince who conducts himself as your people are expected to, and not one who does not so conduct himself."

1. B. Kid 66a and En Yaakov, ad loc.
2. She was the sister of Simeon ben Shetah (*fl.* 1st century B.C.E.). See below, part 2, chap. 11, §2.
3. Megillat Ta 11.
4. Megillat Ta 10.
5. B. Sot 49b; B.BK 82b.

"Still, I fear that someone will hear and go and tell him."

"But, except for you and me, there is no one here who might go and tell him."

"A bird of the air shall carry the voice" (Eccles. 10:20).

Then Herod said, "I am he. Had I known that the sages were so circumspect, I would not have slain them. Now tell me what amends one such as I can make."

Bava ben Buta replied, "He who has extinguished the light of the world [the sages], who in their persons give reality to the words 'The commandment is a lamp, and the Torah is light' [Prov. 6:23), should go and occupy himself with the light of the world [the building of the Temple], of which it is written, 'All the nations shall have light through it' " (Isa. 2:2). Some say that Bava replied, "He who has blinded the eye of the world should occupy himself with the eye of the world [the Temple]."

Herod said, "But I fear the government of Rome." Bava replied, "Send an envoy to Rome, let him take a year on the way, stay in Rome a year, and take a year in coming back. In the meantime, you can pull down the old Temple and rebuild it." Herod did so, and received word from Rome: "If you have not pulled it down, do not do so. If you have pulled it down, do not rebuild it. If you have pulled it down and already rebuilt it, you are one of those who, after doing something wrong,[1] ask permission. Though you strut with your sword, the record of your birth is here for all to see: 'Neither king nor son of a king—before he made himself a freedman, he was Herod the slave.' "

In the days of Herod, while the people were occupied with building the Temple, rain fell during the night, but in the morning the wind blew, the clouds dispersed, and the sun shone, so that the people were able to go out to their work. Thus, they knew that what they were doing was work for the sake of Heaven.

It is said: He who has not seen the Temple of Herod has never seen a beautiful building. Of what did he build it? Rabbah said: Of yellow and white marble. Some say: Of blue, yellow, and white marble. The building rose in tiers,[2] in order to provide a hold for the plaster. Herod originally intended to cover it with gold, but the sages said to him: Leave it alone, for it is more beautiful as it is, since it has the appearance of the waves of the sea.[3]

The Service in the Temple

52. Until the Temple was built, the world rested on a [shaky] throne with only two legs; after the Temple was built, the world stood firm, its well-being assured.[4]

53. "If any man of the House of Israel slaughtereth an ox or sheep or goat in the camp . . . [he is to] offer them as . . . peace offerings" (Lev. 17:3 and 17:5). R. Phinehas said in the name of R. Levi: The precept may be understood by the parable of a king's son who thought he could do what he liked, and so fell into eating animals improperly slaughtered or torn by wild beasts. The king said: "I shall have him always at my table, and, thus learning to restrain himself, [he will be weaned from improper conduct]. So, too, because Israel in Egypt came to lust for idolatry and used to bring offerings to satyrs, they were told, "They shall no more sacrifice their sacrifices unto the satyrs" (Lev. 17:7). The word "satyrs" here can refer only to demons, as indicated by the assertion "Satyrs shall dance there" (Isa. 13:21).[5] Then, too, Israel used to bring their offerings in private high places, which were forbidden, and on account of which punishments came upon them. So the Holy One said, "Let them bring their offerings to Me at all times in the Tent of Meeting, and thus be weaned from idolatry and saved from punishments."[6]

54. It is taught that R. Simeon ben Azzai said: Pause and consider what is stated in the chapter on sacrifices. Neither the term *El* nor the term *Elohim* is found there—only "Lord," so as not to give a would-be disputant the opportunity to differ [with regard to God's unity].[7] Furthermore, of the ox, which is large, it is said, "An offering made by fire, of a sweet savor" (Lev. 1:9); of a bird, which is small, "an offering made by fire, of a sweet savor" (Lev. 1:17); and of a meal offering, "an offering made by fire, of a sweet savor" (Lev. 2:2)—to teach you that it is the same whether a man offers much or little, so long as he directs his heart to Heaven.

Lest you say, He needs the offering for food, Scripture states, "If I were hungry, I would not speak to thee of it" (Ps. 50:12). I did not bid you offer sacrifices, that you might be able to say, "I will do His will, so that He will do my will." You sacrifice not for My sake, but for your own sake, as is said, "You shall sacrifice it for your sake" (Lev. 19:5).[8]

55. Rava said: R. Joseph used to test us with the following question: If a priest snatches the priestly dues,[9] is he considered zealous in performing the precept or disdainful of the precept? We replied: Scripture says, "They shall give" (Deut. 18:3), not, "He shall take on his own."

Abbaye said: At first I used to snatch the priestly portions, saying to myself, "I thus show my zeal for the precept"; but when I heard the Baraita "In asserting, 'They shall give' [Deut. 18:3], Scripture implies that the priest is not to take them on his own," I no longer snatched them, but would merely say, "Give them to me." And when I heard another Baraita that taught, "The verse 'They turned aside after lucre' [1 Sam. 8:3] means, according to R.

1. In BR, the Aramaic "one of those who, after doing something wrong" is mistranslated "one of those bad servants."
2. Literally, "It sent forth an edge, and drew in an edge."
3. Because of the differing hues of marble, B. BB 3b–4a; B. Ta 23a; B. Suk 51b.
4. Tanhuma, *Terumah*, §9.
5. Dance in the ruins to which Isaiah refers earlier. Demons were said to inhabit empty places. Instead of Isa. 13:21, BR cite "They sacrificed unto demons" (Deut. 32:17).
6. Lev. R. 22:8.
7. The absence of other names for God is intended to make it clear that there is only one God and that names such as *el* and *elohim* are no more than other designations for Him.
8. B. Men 110a.
9. From children on their way to give it to another priest.

Meir, that Samuel's sons used to ask right out for the portions due them,"[1] I decided not to ask for them, but would accept them only when given to me. But when I heard a third Baraita that declared, "The [priests who were] modest withdrew their hands from them, but the greedy took them," I decided not to accept them at all, save on the day before Yom Kippur, so as to establish myself as one of the priests.[2]

56. The priests on duty, the Levites on their dais and the Israelites at their lay posts[3]—they did not turn their backs completely as they were leaving but, half turning, kept their faces looking sideways as they left.[4]

57. The watch of priests leaving the Temple used to say to the watch coming in, "May He who has made His Name dwell in this house make love and brotherliness, peace and friendship dwell in your midst."[5]

58. R. Eleazar said: To what do the seventy bullocks [that were offered during the seven days of Sukkot] correspond? To the seventy nations [of the earth]. To what does the single bullock [offered on the Eighth Day Festival—Shemini Atzeret] correspond? To the unique nation [Israel]. A parable of a king of flesh and blood who [for seven days] said to his servants, "Prepare a great feast for me." Then on the eighth day he said to the special friend who loved him, "Prepare a simple meal for me, that I may have the pleasure of your company."

R. Yohanan observed: Woe to the nations of the world who sustained a loss[6] and are not even aware of what loss they sustained. When the Temple stood, the altar made atonement for them. But now who makes atonement for them?[7]

59. According to R. Judah bar Simon, the Holy One said to Israel: My children, I have made available as food for you ten clean beasts—three of these subject to your control, and seven not subject to your control. Three subject to your control: the ox, the lamb, and the goat. Not subject to your control: the deer, the gazelle, the roebuck, the wild goat, the ibex, the antelope, and the mountain sheep. I have not burdened you—I have not told you to climb up mountains or to tramp through forests in order to fetch Me an offering out of those that are not subject to your control. I told you to fetch only such as are subject to your control—those reared at your trough.

R. Judah bar Simon said in the name of R. Yose bar Nehorai: A bullock is pursued by the lion, a lamb by the wolf, a goat by the leopard. But the Holy One said: Bring no offering to Me from those who pursue, only from those who are pursued.[8]

60. R. Isaac taught: Why is the meal offering distinguished in that the word "soul" is used in connection with it (Lev. 2:1)?[9] Because the Holy One said: Who is it that usually brings a meal offering? It is the poor man. I account it for him as though he had offered his very soul to Me.

R. Isaac said further: Why is the meal offering distinguished in that five kinds of oil dishes[10] are listed in connection with it? A parable provides the answer: A king of flesh and blood had a friend who was about to prepare a feast for him. Since the king knew that his friend was poor, he said: Prepare for me [whatever you have] as five kinds of flour[11] dishes, so that I may enjoy your company longer.[12]

61. King Agrippa[13] once desired to bring a thousand burnt offerings in one day and sent word to the high priest: "Let no man except me bring an offering on that day." And so, when a poor man with two doves in his hand came and said to the high priest, "Offer up these doves for me," the high priest answered, "The king charged me, saying, "No man other than I is to bring an offering this day." But the poor man said, "My lord high priest, each day I capture four doves; two I offer up, and two I eat. If you do not offer these up for me, you cut off my livelihood." So the high priest took the doves and offered them up.

It was disclosed to Agrippa in a dream: "A poor man's offering has preceded yours!" So he sent word to the high priest: "Did I not command you: Let no man except me bring an offering on that day?" The high priest replied, "My lord king, a poor man came with two doves in his hand and said to me, 'Offer these up for me.' I said to him, 'The king has charged me, saying, 'Let no man except me bring an offering this day,' and he said to me, 'Each day I capture four doves; two I offer up, and two I eat. If you will not offer these up for me, you cut off my livelihood.' Should I not have offered them up?" Agrippa replied to the high priest, "You have done well."

It happened that a woman brought one handful of fine flour for a meal offering, and the priest ridiculed her, saying, "See what such people offer up! What is there in this to eat? Indeed, what is there in this to offer up?" Later on, it was disclosed to the priest in a dream: "Do not despise her. I reckon it for her as if she had offered up her very soul."[14]

---

1. See above, chap. 6, §70.
2. So that it should not be forgotten that he was a priest. B. Hul 133a.
3. Delegations from the people out in the country. Some of the lay post accompanied the daily offerings in the Temple by gathering for services in Jerusalem, while others assembled for such services in the provinces.
4. B. Yoma 53.
5. B. Ber 12a.
6. The Temple.
7. B. Suk 55b.
8. Tanhuma B, *Emor*, 13; Tanhuma, *Pinhas*, §12; Lev. R. 27:6.
9. JV: "And when anyone bringeth a meal offering" is literally in the Hebrew "And when a *soul* bringeth a meal offering."
10. Each of the five kinds of meal offerings is prepared with oil. See Lev. 2.
11. Prepared with coarse flour fried in olive oil, which even the poorest person could afford.
12. B. Men 104b.
13. Probably Agrippa I (ca. 10 B.C.E.–44 C.E.), who treated religious law with respect. See *JE*, s.v.
14. Lev. R. 3:5: MTeh 22:31.

62. [The details concerning] the lay posts are as follows. It is said, "Command the children of Israel and say unto them: My food which is presented unto Me" (Num. 28:2). Now, how can a man's offering be brought on the altar and he not be present? The earlier prophets[1] therefore instituted twenty-four watches.[2] During each watch, there was present in Jerusalem a post of priests, of Levites, and of lay Israelites. When the time came for a particular watch to go up to Jerusalem, the priests and Levites [as well as the lay Israelites of that watch] went up to Jerusalem, while the bulk of Israelites belonging to that watch assembled in their cities and read the story of creation (Gen. 1). On Sunday they read "In the beginning" and "Let there be a firmament"; on Monday, "Let there be a firmament" and "Let the waters be gathered together"; on Tuesday, "Let the waters be gathered together" and "Let there be lights"; on Wednesday, "Let there be lights" and "Let the waters swarm"; on Thursday, "Let the waters swarm" and "Let the earth bring forth"; on Friday, "Let the earth bring forth" and "The heavens and the earth were finished."

Between them, two persons read a long section[3] and one person read a short section. This procedure was followed only at the morning and at the *Musaf* services, but at the afternoon service everybody entered and recited the entire text for himself by heart, in the same way one recites for himself the Shema. On Fridays, the gathering in synagogues for the afternoon service did not take place, because the time was needed for preparations in honor of the Sabbath.

Our masters—as already said—taught: There were twenty-four priestly watches in the Land of Israel. When the turn of a particular watch arrived, half of the watch would go up from everywhere in the Land to Jerusalem, and the other half would go to Jericho, in order to provide [from there] water and food for their brethren in Jerusalem.

Only four priestly families returned from the [Babylonian] exile. They were: Jedaiah, Harim, Pashhur, and Immer.[4] The prophets of that generation divided these four families into twenty-four watches in the following manner: [twenty-four] lots [numbered from one to twenty-four, six for each of the four families] were mixed and placed in an urn. A member of the family of Jedaiah was the first to draw a lot. He was followed by five other members of his family, thus determining the sequence of the watches for the six families of Jedaiah. The same procedure was carried out by Harim, then Pashhur, and finally Immer.[5] The prophets who were among those who returned from Babylon stipulated that even if the house of Jehoiarib, which at the time of the First Temple was the foremost of all the watches, were to decide to go up to Jerusalem, Jedaiah should not be removed from his newly acquired place—he should remain foremost, and Jehoiarib subsidiary to him.[6]

The men of the lay post used to fast on four days of the week, from Monday through Thursday. On Friday they did not fast, out of respect for the Sabbath; nor did they fast on Sunday, so that they not go suddenly from rest and delight into fasting, and, as a result, die. Another reason: Because of the Christians, who should be given no reason to say, "Because we rejoice on Sunday, they fast on it." But of this reason the sages said: At the time the lay posts existed, there could have been no fear of Christian hostility.[7]

Our masters also taught: The men of the [lay post attached to the] watch of priests on duty prayed over the sacrifices of their brethren, that they might be favorably accepted, while the bulk of the men of the lay post assembled in their synagogues [throughout the Land] and also observed four fasts, on Monday, Tuesday, Wednesday, and Thursday during that week. On Monday [they fasted] for the safety of those who were on the high sea; on Tuesday, for those who were traveling in the deserts; on Wednesday, that croup would not attack children; on Thursday, for pregnant women and nursing mothers—that the pregnant women would not miscarry and that the nursing mothers would safely nurse their children.[8]

The Miracles in the Temple

63. Ten miracles were wrought for our fathers in the Temple: No woman miscarried from the odor of the sacrificial meat; the sacrificial meat never became putrid; no fly was seen in the Temple slaughterhouse; no nocturnal emission of semen ever happened to a high priest on the eve of Yom Kippur; the rain never quenched the fire of the woodpile [on the altar, which was under the open sky]; no wind ever prevailed against the column of smoke [from the altar fire, so that the smoke was not blown downward]; no disqualifying defect was ever found in the *omer* [of new barley, offered on the second day of Passover] or in the two loaves [baked of the first grain of the wheat harvest and offered up on the Feast of Weeks] or in the shewbread [which was changed on the Sabbath];[9] though the people

1. Samuel and David.
2. Twenty-four watches of lay people, as well as of priests and Levites.
3. Containing at least six verses.
4. Ezra 2:36–39.
5. At bimonthly intervals during the year, the six families of each watch were to serve in the Temple in the order in which the lots bearing their numbers were drawn.

6. Among the priestly families that returned with Ezra (Ezra 2:36–39), Jehoiarib, which headed the watches in the First Temple, is not mentioned. Hence it is presumed that the family refused to return.
7. Since it was much later that Christianity became the official religion of the Roman Empire.
8. B. Ta 26–27 and En Yaakov, ad loc.; Sof 17.
9. "*Lehem ha-panim*, 'bread of the Presence,' the unleavened bread that the priest placed before the Lord in the Sanctuary (Exod. 25:30). This consists of twelve loaves, representing the twelve tribes of Israel, and was expressive of man's constant indebtedness to God, who is the source of every material blessing. It had to be baked before the Sabbath; if there had been anything wrong with it, they could not have changed the bread for another week. Similarly, if the *omer* had been found defective, it would have been impossible to provide another supply in time for the offering. The baking of the two loaves of the new grain of wheat had to be done before the commencement of *Shavuot*, the Feast of Weeks; had they been defective, others could not have been prepared. The permission to bake on holy days is restricted to food required for those days" (Philip Birnbaum, *The Daily Prayer Book* [New York, 1949], pp. 513–14). Avot 5:5.

stood in closely pressed rows, they found ample space to prostrate themselves; never did a serpent or a scorpion injure anyone in Jerusalem; and no man ever said to his fellow, "There is no room for me to lodge overnight in Jerusalem."

64. Though the people stood in close rows, they found ample space to prostrate themselves. R. Aha said: Each person had four cubits, a cubit on each side, so that no one should hear his neighbor's prayer.[1]

65. It is taught: Five things were reported about the fire of the woodpile on the altar: It lay like a lion,[2] it was clear as the sun, its flame was of solid substance, it consumed freshly cut wood as though it were dry wood, and it caused no smoke to rise from it. It lay like a lion? But has it not been taught that R. Hanina, deputy high priest, had said: I myself saw it, and it lay low like a dog? [The answer is]: The first description refers to the First Temple, the second to the Second Temple.[3]

66. Rabbah bar Bar Hana said: It is a distance of ten parasangs[4] from Jerusalem to Jericho. The turning of the door hinges in the Temple Hall was heard eight Sabbath limits away,[5] while [the fragrance of the incense in the Temple Hall traveled all the way to Jericho], so that the goats in Jericho used to sneeze because of the fragrance of the incense, and the women of Jericho had no need to perfume themselves because of that fragrance. Neither did a bride in Jerusalem.[6]

Diligent Priests

67. With torches before him, the officer of the Temple Mount used to make the rounds during every watch, and if any priest in the watch failed to rise and say, "Officer of the Temple Mount, peace be unto you," it was clear that he was asleep, and the officer would strike him with his staff; the officer was also permitted to burn his clothes. The other priests would ask, "What noise is that in the Temple Court?" [They were told], "It is the cry of a son of Levi who is being beaten, and whose garments are being burned, because he was asleep at his post." R. Eliezer ben Jacob said: Once they found my mother's brother asleep, and they burned his clothes.[7]

68. Originally, whatever priest [of the family on duty] desired to remove the ashes from the altar did so. If such priests were many, they would run up the ramp of the altar,[8] and he who came first within four cubits [of its top] won that privilege. It once happened that as two priests were running neck-and-neck up the ramp, one pushed the other, who fell and broke his leg. When the High Court saw that the rivalry exposed priests to physical danger, it ordained that the ashes from the altar be removed only by lot.

Our masters taught: [Before the lot was instituted] it once happened that two priests were running neck-and-neck up the ramp. When one of them came first within four cubits of the top of the altar, the other took a knife and thrust it into his rival's heart. At this, R. Zadok, standing on the steps of the Porch, cried out in anguish, "Our brethren of the House of Israel, hear ye! Behold, Scripture says, 'If one be found slain in the Land . . . then thy elders and judges shall come forth' [Deut. 21:1]. Who is to assume the guilt and provide the heifer whose neck is to be broken—the city of Jerusalem or the priests in the Temple Courts?" All the people burst out weeping. The father of the young priest who was knifed came and, finding his son still in his death throes, said, "Look, he is atonement for you! See, my son is still moving [not yet dead]; the knife has not become unclean."[9]

The cleanness of their utensils, it would seem, was of greater concern to them than the shedding of blood.[10]

The Paschal Lamb

69. The paschal lamb was slaughtered by the people in three groups.[11] After the first group entered and the Temple Court was filled, they closed the doors of the Temple Court; then they sounded *tekiah*, *teruah*, and *tekiah*.[12] The priests stationed themselves in two rows, facing each other; in their hands were basins of silver and basins of gold.[13] The row of priests who held the silver basins, held only silver basins; and the row of priests who held the gold basins, held only gold basins. The vessels were not intermixed—[silver vessels were in one row and gold vessels in the other]. The basins had no flat bottoms, lest the priests put them down and the blood become congealed.

As an Israelite slaughtered [his own lamb], the priest caught [the blood] in the basin; he handed it to the colleague next to him, and that colleague to his colleague, each receiving the basin full and returning it empty.[14] The priest nearest the altar dashed the blood in one movement against the base [of the altar].[15]

As the first group of Israelites went out, the second entered; as the second went out, the third entered. Like the procedure with the first [group] was the procedure with the second and with the third. [In the meantime] the Levites chanted the *Hallel*;[16] if they finished it before a group

1. Gen. R. 5:7
2. So powerful was the flame.
3. B. Yoma 21b.
4. Approximately thirty miles.
5. Approximately five miles.
6. B. Yoma 39b.
7. B. Tam 27b–28a.
8. At the south of the altar; it was thirty-two cubits long.
9. Since only a dead body can render a weapon unclean.
10. B. Yoma 22a and 23a.
11. Irrespective of the number sacrificing.
12. *Tekiah* is a long, straight blast on the shofar (ram's horn); *teruah* is a series of three consecutive short blasts.
13. To receive the blood.
14. After the blood in it had been dashed against the altar.
15. On the north and west sides of the altar, where its base projects. See Mid 3:1.
16. Ps. 113–18. Literally, "praise."

was done slaughtering, they repeated it; and if, after repeating it, that group was still not done, they would have to chant it a third time, though in fact it never was necessary to chant it a third time. R. Judah said: Never during the turn of the third group did the Levites reach the words "I love that the Lord should hear", etc. (Ps. 116:1), because the people in that group were so few.

How did they hang up the carcasses and flay them? There were iron hooks fixed in the walls and in the pillars, on which the carcasses were suspended and flayed. If anyone found no place to suspend and flay his animal, there were thin, smooth staves that a man could rest on his own shoulder and on the shoulder of his neighbor, and so hang and flay it.

After the Israelite slit the animal and took out its sacrificial portions,[1] he placed them on a tray, and [a priest] burned them on the altar.

[When Passover eve fell on a Sabbath], the first group went out [from the Temple Court] but remained on the Temple Mount.[2] The second remained in the rampart,[3] while the third group remained where they were [in the Temple Court]. After it grew dark, they all went home and roasted their paschal lambs.[4]

70. Our masters taught: No man was ever crushed in the Temple Court,[5] except during one Passover in the days of Hillel, when an old man was crushed, and they called it "the Passover of the Crushed."

King Agrippa once wished to number the hosts of Israel.[6] After he told the high priest, "Number the paschal lambs," the high priest took a kidney from each paschal lamb, and six hundred thousand pairs of kidneys were found to have been there, twice as many as the number of people who departed from Egypt. The total [it goes without saying] does not include those Jews who were unclean and those who were on a distant journey and therefore [could not bring paschal lambs]. One must also realize that there was not a single paschal lamb for which more than ten people had not registered. That Passover came to be known as "the Passover of Dense Throngs."[7]

1. See Lev. 3:3–4.
2. Since on the Sabbath they could not carry the paschal lambs home, they had to wait for the evening.
3. A place within the fortification of the Temple (Jastrow). See Mid 2:3.
4. B. Pes 64a–b.
5. In spite of the enormous crowds that thronged it.
6. Literally, "to cast his eyes on the hosts of Israel." Such "casting of eyes" is regarded in Jewish tradition as casting an evil eye, as Satan did when he "moved David to number Israel" (1 Chron. 21:1). "In addition, a census was looked upon with suspicion as being the possible precursor of fresh levies and taxation, and the decision of Quirinius, the governor of Syria, to take a census in Judea (ca. 6–7 C.E.) nearly precipitated a revolt; see [Heinrich] Graetz. According to Graetz, the present census was undertaken by Agrippa II in the year 66 C.E. as a hint to the Roman powers not to underrate the strength of the Jewish people, and therefore avoid driving them too far by the cruelty and greed of the Procurator, at that time Gessius Florus" (Pes, Soncino, p. 326, n. 2).
7. B. Pes 64a–b and En Yaakov, ad loc. The actual census figure of Israel was thus considerably more than twice six hundred thousand.

71. A story is told of a certain idolater who used to go up and partake of the meat of paschal lambs in Jerusalem. Once he came to R. Judah ben Betera and boastfully said, "It is written, 'No foreigner shall eat of it' [Exod. 12:43], and, 'No uncircumcised person shall eat of it' [Exod. 12:48], yet I manage to eat its very best portions!" R. Judah ben Betera asked him, "Did they give you a big chunk of the fat-tail?" "No," he replied. "Then," said R. Judah, "when you journey up there again, say to them, 'Give me a big helping of the fat-tail.' " When he went up, he said, "Give me a big chunk of the fat-tail." They replied, "How can you make such a demand? The fat-tail belongs to the Most High!" Then they asked, "Who told you to ask for it?" He answered, "R. Judah ben Betera." They wondered: What in the world is going on here? Upon investigating his background, they discovered that he was a foreigner, and they immediately put him to death. Then they sent word to R. Judah ben Betera: "Peace be with you, R. Judah ben Betera, for though you may be in Nisibis, your net is spread out all the way to Jerusalem."[8]

The Sheaf of the *Omer* (Lev. 23:9–11)

72. What was the procedure for preparing the *omer*? Messengers of the High Court used to go out on the day before Passover and tie the unreaped stand of barley grain in bunches to make it easier to reap. [On the night following the first day of Passover] all the inhabitants of the nearby towns assembled at a particular field so that the sheaf of the *omer* might be reaped in the midst of great commotion.[9] As soon as it became dark, the one assigned to reap the barley called out, "Has the sun set?" And they shouted, "Yes!" "Has the sun set?" And they shouted, "Yes!" "[Shall I reap] with this sickle?" And they shouted, "Yes!" "[Shall I reap] with this sickle?" And they shouted, "Yes!" "Into this basket?" And they shouted, "Yes!" "Into this basket?" And they shouted, "Yes!" If it was the Sabbath, he called out further, "On this Sabbath?" And they shouted, "Yes!" "On this Sabbath?" And they shouted, "Yes!" "Shall I reap on the Sabbath?" And they shouted, "Reap!" Three times he inquired concerning each act, and three times they answered, "Yes!" "Yes!" "Yes!" And why was it necessary to inquire three times? By way of demonstrating against the Boethusians,[10] who maintained that the reaping of the *omer* was not to take place at the conclusion of the [first day of the] Passover festival.

After they reaped the *omer*, they put it into baskets

8. B. Pes. 3b.
9. To impress the Boethusians. See the following note.
10. "A sect in opposition to the Pharisees and often regarded as synonymous with the Sadducees. They held that the expression (Lev. 23:11) 'the morrow after the Sabbath' must be taken in its literal sense, the day following the first Saturday in Passover. The Pharisees, however, argued that the Sabbath meant here 'the day of cessation from work', i.e., the Festival of Passover. Accordingly the *omer* was to be offered on the second day of the Festival, and the reaping of [the sheaf of barley] on the night preceding, at the conclusion of the first day of the Festival" (Men, Soncino, p. 384, n. 4).

and brought it to the Temple Court. They singed it over fire by putting it in a [copper] pipe, which was perforated so that the fire might get at all of the grains. Then they spread it out in the Temple Court, so that the wind blew over it.[1] Next they put it into a grist mill,[2] and out of it they took a tenth [of an *ephah* of flour], which was then sifted through thirteen sieves [and was finally offered up].

As soon as the *omer* [of the new harvest] had been offered, they would go out and find the markets of Jerusalem already filled with both flour and parched grain.[3]

73. The precept for the *omer* requires that it be brought [from barley] that grows near Jerusalem. If the crop near Jerusalem was not yet ripe, it could be brought from any place.

Once, when the time arrived, they did not know where to find newly grown barley.[4] So they had a herald announce the difficulty. A deaf-mute came forward and pointed with one hand to a [flat] roof, and with the other to a cone-shaped hut. Mordecai[5] inquired, "Is there a place anywhere named Gaggot Tzerifin[6] or Tzerifin Gaggot?" They searched and found the place [and the newly grown barley].

Another time, when they had to bring the two loaves [baked of the new wheat harvest and offered on the Feast of Weeks], they did not know where to find newly grown wheat. So they had a herald announce the difficulty. A deaf-mute came forward and put one hand over his eye and the other hand over a bolt. Mordecai inquired, "Is there a place anywhere named En Sokher[7] or Sokher En?" They searched and found the place [and the newly grown wheat].[8]

The Bringing of the Firstfruits

74. How are the firstfruits set aside? When a man goes down to his field and sees a ripe fig[9] or a ripe cluster of grapes or a ripe pomegranate, he ties reed grass around it and says, "Let these be firstfruits."[10] R. Simeon differs: Even so, he should again designate them as firstfruits after they are plucked from the soil where they grew.

How are the firstfruits taken up [to Jerusalem]? All [the inhabitants of] the towns that make up a lay post assemble in the city of the [head of that] post, but spend the night in its open place without entering any of the houses.[11] Early in the morning, the head of the post says, "Let us arise and go up to Zion, unto the house of the Lord our God" (Jer. 31:6).[12]

Those who live near [Jerusalem] bring fresh figs and grapes, but those from a distance bring dried figs and raisins.[13] Before them walks an ox, its horns overlaid with gold, a crown of olive leaves on its head.[14] A flute strikes the tempo for their procession until they approach Jerusalem. When they arrive close to Jerusalem, they send messengers to announce their coming. Meanwhile, they arrange their firstfruits in an ornamental display.[15] Governors of priests, chiefs of the Levites, and treasurers [of the Temple] go out to meet them. The number of those going out varies in keeping with the number of the entrants. All the skilled artisans of Jerusalem are required to rise up before them and greet them:[16] "Brethren, men of such-and-such a place, peace be upon you in your coming."

The flute continues to strike the tempo before them until they reach the Temple Mount. When they reach the Temple Mount, even King Agrippa places a basket on his shoulder and walks as far as the Temple Court. As they approach the Court, the Levites sing, "I will extol Thee, O Lord, for Thou hast raised me up, and hast not suffered mine enemies to rejoice over me" (Ps. 30:2).

The turtledoves [tied to] each basket[17] are [offered up as] burnt offerings, but the baskets of firstfruits that the people hold in their hands they present to the priests.

While the basket is yet on his shoulder, each man recites the passage beginning: "I profess this day unto the Lord thy God" (Deut. 26:3), until he reaches the end of the passage (Deut. 26:10). R. Judah said: Until he reaches "A wandering Aramean sought to slay my father" (Deut. 26:5). When he reaches these words, he takes the basket off his shoulder and holds it by its rim, and the priest places his hand under it and waves it. Then the Israelite begins to recite "An Aramean sought to slay my father," until he completes the entire passage. He then deposits the basket by the side of the altar,[18] prostrates himself, and departs.

Originally, all who knew how to recite the prescribed words [in Hebrew] would recite them, while those unable to do so repeated them after the priest. But when people began to refrain from bringing firstfruits in shame [of their ignorance], it was decided that both those who could as

1. To cool and dry the grains.
2. Which grinds very coarsely, so that only the husk is separated from the grain.
3. See Lev. 23:9–14. To have it ready on the same day, the shopkeepers must have prepared it in advance, thus handling the new crop while it was yet prohibited. B. Men 65a and 66a; Pes 10b.
4. Because of the devastation around Jerusalem wreaked by Roman forces.
5. A high Temple official, who on account of his sagacity bore the name of Mordecai. See Shek 5:1.
6. A place-name whose literal meaning is "[flat] roofs, cone-shaped huts."
7. The literal meaning is "eye of a bolt."
8. B. Men 64b.
9. Though the vine is listed first in Deut. 8:8, the fig is the first to ripen. Cf. Song 2:13.
10. He is now exempted from further designation at the time of harvesting.
11. Lest impurity be contracted through contact with the dead.
12. On their way to the Temple Mount, they recite various psalms (Bertinoro). According to Israel Lipschütz, *Tiferet Yisrael* (Vilna, 1935), the fifteen Songs of Ascents (Ps. 120–134) are recited.
13. Fresh fruit would rot on the way.
14. The ox is to serve as the peace offering.
15. "Fresh figs would be placed as the top layer of a basket containing dried ones, and raisins would be covered by fresh grapes; while the choicest of the fruit would be placed on top of a basket containing only fresh fruits" (Bik, Soncino, p. 400, n. 7).
16. Men working at their craft were not required to rise for a scholar, but they were to rise before the procession of firstfruits.
17. They were suspended from the sides of the basket so as not to soil the fruit.
18. At its southwest corner.

well as those who could not recite them [in Hebrew] should repeat the words after the priest.

The rich bring their firstfruits in baskets overlaid with silver and gold, while the poor bring them in wicker baskets made of peeled willow branches and give both baskets and firstfruits to the priests.[1]

The Service of Yom Kippur [the Day of Atonement]

75. Seven days before the Day of Atonement, the high priest is removed from his house to the counselors'[2] chamber, and another priest is held ready to take his place should anything befall him to render him unfit.[3] From the elders of the High Court, they appoint for him a few elders, who [throughout the seven days] read to him [Lev. 16, which sets forth] the rites for the day. Then they say to him, "Most esteemed high priest, now you yourself, with your own mouth, read these words, in case you may have forgotten them or may never have learned them."

The morning of the eve of Yom Kippur, they have him stand at the eastern gate and have oxen, rams, and sheep pass before him, so that he may scrutinize them and rehearse in his mind what he must do during the service.

Throughout the seven days, they do not withhold food or drink from him. But on the eve of Yom Kippur toward nightfall, they do not let him eat much, because food induces sleep.

The elders of the High Court hand him over to elders of the priesthood, and they escort him to an upper chamber in the house of Avtinas.[4] They adjure him, then take their leave, saying to him, "Most esteemed high priest, we are messengers of the High Court, and you are our messenger as well as the messenger of the High Court. By Him that made His Name dwell in this house, we adjure you not to change anything of what we have said to you."[5] He turns aside and weeps, and they turn aside and weep.[6]

If he is a sage, he expounds [Scripture]; if not, disciples of the wise expound it before him. If he is familiar with reading [Scripture], he reads it; if not, they read it to him. From what books do they read to him? From Job, Ezra, and Chronicles.[7] Zechariah ben Kevutal said: Often have I read to the high priest from Daniel.

If he tries to doze off, novices in the priesthood snap their middle finger before him and say, "Most esteemed high priest, rise up and drive sleep away by taking a turn on the [cool] pavement." The novices also engage him in conversation to divert him until the time for slaughtering [the daily burnt offering] has come.

(Some of the nobility of Jerusalem do not go to sleep all night, in order to make the high priest hear the reverberating noise [made by many people] and so prevent him from being suddenly overcome by sleep.)

The officer on duty says to the priests, "Go forth and see whether the time for slaughtering [the burnt offering] has come." If it has come, he who perceives it says, "It is daylight!" Matia ben Samuel used to ask, "Has the dawn lighted up the entire east, even as far as Hebron?" And the lookout would answer, "Yes."

(And why is it necessary to make the inquiries so precise? Because once the light of the moon rose so bright that they thought the east was alight with sunrise,[8] and they slaughtered the daily burnt offering, which then had to be taken away at once to the place where unfit offerings are burned.)

[When it is announced, "The whole east is alight,"] the high priest is led down to the place of immersion. The high priest undergoes five immersions and ten washings of hands and feet that day.

A sheet of byssus [linen] is hung between him and the people. Then he strips off [his ordinary clothes], goes down and immerses himself, and comes up and dries himself. They bring him his golden vestments;[9] he puts them on, and washes his hands and feet. They bring him the lamb for the daily burnt offering. He makes the initial incision,[10] and someone else finishes it for him. He receives the blood and sprinkles it. He goes inside [the Temple Hall] to burn the morning incense[11] and to trim the lamps.[12]

If the high priest is either old or in delicate health, they prepare boiling water for him, which they pour into the cold water [of the pool] to temper its chill.

They escort him to the Parvah[13] Chamber—which is on holy ground[14]—where a sheet of byssus linen is hung

1. Bik 3.
2. The name "counselors" is used to designate high priests, who changed so frequently that they had become in effect like officers of the crown who come and go. See B. Yoma 8b.
3. By becoming ritually unclean or suffering certain bodily defects. See above in this chapter, §63.
4. "There the famly of Avtinas prepared the incense, there the high priest was taught the skillful manipulation that would enable him to take up the incense without spilling one grain" (Yoma, Soncino, p. 80, n. 7).
5. That he would not follow the practices of the Sadducees, but hold fast to those of the Pharisees.
6. The elders, because they had such suspicions; and he, because they found it necessary to voice them.
7. These books, less known, might arouse his interest and keep him awake. Sleep was to be prevented because of the risk of a seminal emission during the night, making him unclean.
8. "When the sky is clouded, the light coming from the moon may be confused with that of the sun. But it never reaches as far as the latter, hence the question of the officer whether the horizon is alight even unto Hebron" (Yoma, Soncino, p. 131, n. 6).
9. For the daily service they were: tunic, breeches, headdress, sash, breastpiece, ephod, rode, and frontlet. See Exod. 28:2ff.
10. "To enable the high priest to put the knife aside and to take hold of the holy bowl in which he receives the blood. On other days one priest would slaughter, and another receive the blood. Both functions were to be performed by the high priest on the Day of Atonement" (Yoma, Soncino, p. 145, n. 8).
11. See Exod. 30:7.
12. I.e., clean them and provide them with wick and oil; according to Maimonides, also light them.
13. Parvah is the name of a Persian magus who, according to Menahem Ha-Meiri, became a proselyte (as quoted in Yoma, ed. Adin Steinsaltz [Jerusalem, 1977], p. 146).
14. "The first immersion, on top of the water gate, took place on profane ground; this one, however, had to be performed on holy ground, as part of the service of the Day of Atonement" (Yoma, Soncino, p. 161, n. 1).

between him and the people. He washes his hands and feet, and strips. Then he goes down, immerses himself in the pool, and comes up and dries himself. Afterward, they bring him white garments.[1] He puts them on and again washes his hands and feet. The white garments that he puts on at dawn are made of Pelusium linen worth twelve *maneh*, and at twilight, of Indian linen worth only eight hundred *zuz*.[2] These garments are paid for by the community, but if he wants to spend more on them from his own money, he may do so.

The high priest comes to his bullock,[3] which is already standing between the Outer Hall leading into the Temple's interior and the altar,[4] its body north to south and its face turned to the west. The high priest, his back to the east,[5] his face to the west, stands [by the bullock]. He presses both hands [between its horns] and makes confession, saying: I beseech Thee, O Lord![6] I have committed iniquity, I have transgressed, I have sinned before Thee, I and my house. I beseech Thee, O Lord! cleanse the iniquities, the transgressions, the sins that I have committed, transgressed, and sinned before Thee, I and my house, for in the Torah of Moses Thy servant it is written, "On this day shall atonement be made for you, to cleanse you; from all your sins shall ye be clean before the Lord" (Lev. 16:30). [And the priests and the people in the Temple Court, prostrating themselves],[7] respond after him: Blessed be the Name of His glorious kingdom forever and ever!

He then goes back to the eastern side of the Temple Court, to the north of the altar, the deputy high priest at his right and the head of the priestly family ministering that week at his left. Two he-goats are there (Lev. 16:5 and 16:7), and an urn containing two lots. (At one time they were made of boxwood. Ben Gamla made them of gold, and he was praised.)

The high priest shakes the urn and brings up the two lots. On one is inscribed, "For the Lord," and on the other, "For Azazel." The deputy high priest is at his right hand, the head of the ministering family at his left. If the lot with the inscription "For the Lord" comes up in his right hand, the deputy high priest says to him: Most esteemed high priest, raise your right hand! If the lot with the inscription "For the Lord" comes up in his left hand, the head of the ministering family says: Most esteemed high priest, raise your left hand! Then the high priest places his hands on both he-goats and says: To the Lord! And the two priests respond: Blessed be the name of His glorious kingdom forever and ever.

He ties a strand of crimson wool on the head of the he-goat that is to be sent away,[8] and he places it at the gate through which it will be sent away; and [he ties another strand around the neck of] the he-goat that is to be slaughtered. Then he returns to his bullock, presses his two hands on it, and makes confession, saying: I beseech Thee, O Lord! I have committed iniquity, I have transgressed, I have sinned before Thee, I and my house, and the children of Aaron, Thy holy company. I beseech Thee, O Lord, cleanse the iniquities, the transgressions, and the sins that I have committed, transgressed, and sinned before Thee, I and my house, and the children of Aaron, Thy holy company, for in the Torah of Moses Thy servant it is written, "On this day shall atonement be made for you, to cleanse you," etc. And the two priests respond: Blessed be the name of His glorious kingdom forever and ever.

Then the high priest slaughters the bullock and receives its blood in a bowl. He gives it to the priest standing in the Temple Court on the fourth block of pavement [the one closest to the Outer Hall's entrance], who keeps stirring the blood so that it will not congeal. He then takes the coal pan and goes up to the top of the altar, where he clears away the cinders to both sides and scrapes out a panful of glowing coals from below. Then he comes down and places the coal pan in the Temple Court on the fourth block of pavement [away from the altar].

On other days in the year, he scrapes out the glowing coals with a silver coal pan and empties it into one of gold. But this day he scrapes them out with the same golden coal pan in which he is to bring the glowing coals into the Holy of Holies. On other days the coal pan is of yellowish gold. On this day it is of red gold.

They bring the empty ladle and the incense pan to him. From the pan he fills both hands with incense, which he puts into the ladle—more incense if he is a man of large build, and less if of small build. The amount of incense required is determined by the high priest's size. Then he takes the pan with the glowing coals in his right hand and the ladle with the incense in his left hand. He goes through the Temple Hall until he comes to the area between the two curtains that separate the Temple Hall from the Holy of Holies; between these is [a cubit's space]. The outer curtain is looped up on the south side, and the inner curtain on the north side.[9] He walks along between them until he reaches the north side. When he reaches the north, he turns to the south and walks along with the curtain at his left, until he reaches the Ark. When he reaches the Ark, he puts the pan with the glowing coals between the two bars of acacia wood.[10] He heaps the incense upon the glowing coals, and the whole house comes

1. The four garments prescribed for the special service of the Day of Atonement: the tunic, the breeches, the sash, and the headdress. See Lev. 16:4.

2. Equal to eight *maneh*.

3. "Two bullocks were offered up on that day, one from community funds at the additional sacrifice (Num. 29:8), the other from the high priest's own means: the latter, here dealt with, is therefore called 'his bullock.' " (Yoma, Soncino, p. 164, n. 7).

4. The outer altar in the Temple Court.

5. The altar was at his back, and he faced the Temple Hall.

6. Literally, "O, the Name."

7. On hearing him pronounce the Ineffable Name of God, they prostrated themselves.

8. "Destined for Azazel, in the wilderness, where it was hurled to its death from a rock. The word Azazel has been variously interpreted, but it seems to be the name of a place (a rough rock) rather than that of a demon" (Yoma, Soncino, p. 196, n. 7).

9. "The two curtains formed a corridor one cubit wide. Access from the Sanctuary, or Holy Place, to the corridor was on the left side, and from the corridor to the Holy of Holies on the right (north) side" (Yoma, trans. Herbert Danby [Oxford, 1933; repr. 1974], p. 167, n. 7.)

10. See Exod. 25:13 ff.

to be filled with the fragrance of burning incense. He comes out by the same way he went in, and in the outer area [the Temple Hall] he utters a short prayer. He does not make the prayer long, so as not to frighten Israel.[1]

(After the Ark had been taken away, a stone remained there from the days of the early prophets,[2] called the Foundation Stone.[3] It was higher than the ground by three fingerbreadths. On this stone he puts the coal pan.)

He then takes the bowl from the priest who has been stirring it, enters again into the place where he had entered previously, and stands where he had stood previously [between the two bars of the Ark]; he sprinkles the blood from the bowl by moving his hand[4] palm up one time and palm down seven times, each time lowering his hand closer to the ground in the manner of one giving the lash (*ke-matzlif*), who begins at the upper part of the body and proceeds downward. At each movement of his hand, he counts: one, one and one, one and two, one and three, one and four, one and five, one and six, one and seven. Then he goes out and puts the bowl with its remaining blood on a golden stand in the Temple Hall.

The he-goat marked "For the Lord" is brought to him. He slaughters it and receives its blood in a bowl. He enters again into the place where he had entered previously and stands in the place where he had stood previously, and he sprinkles the blood from the bowl by moving his hand palm up one time and palm down seven times . . . in the manner of one giving the lash (*ke-matzlif*). . . . Then he goes out and puts the bowl with its remaining blood on the second golden stand in the Temple Hall.

He then comes to the he-goat to be sent away, lays his two hands on it, and makes confession, in which he says: I beseech Thee, O Lord, Thy people the House of Israel have committed iniquity, transgressed, and sinned before Thee. I beseech Thee, O Lord, cleanse the iniquities, the transgressions, and sins that Thy people the House of Israel have committed, transgressed, and sinned before Thee, for in the Torah of Moses Thy servant it is written, "On this day shall atonement be made for you, to cleanse you," etc.

And when the priests and the people standing in the Temple Court hear the Explicit Name come forth from the mouth of the high priest, they bend their knees and, prostrating themselves, fall on their faces as they call out: Blessed be the name of His glorious kingdom forever and ever.

He hands over the he-goat that is to be sent away to him who is to lead it on a ramp provided to protect the goat from the Jews of Babylonia, who were apt to pull at its hair, shouting to it, "Take our sins, and be off with you! Take our sins, and be off with you!"

Some of the nobility of Jerusalem go up to the first booth with the man who leads the he-goat. There were ten booths from Jerusalem to the *tzok*,[5] a distance of ninety *ris*.[6] At every booth, those within it say to the man, "Here is food and here is water." Then they accompany him from each booth to the next, but not from the last booth. The one in the last booth does not go up with the man to the *tzok*, but stands at a distance and watches what he is doing.[7]

What does he do? He cuts the strand of crimson wool in half, tying one half to the rock and the other half between the horns of the goat. Then he pushes the goat from behind, and it goes rolling down over and over. Before it reaches halfway down the hill, it is dashed to pieces. Then the man comes back and sits down inside the last booth until it grows dark.

Meanwhile, the high priest comes to the bullock and the goat that are to be burned . . . and burns them.

Presently the high priest is told: The he-goat has reached the wilderness. How do they know that the he-goat has reached the wilderness? They set up sentinel posts. From these posts scarves are waved, and thus they learn that the he-goat has reached the wilderness.

The high priest then comes to [the Women's Court] to read two passages in Scripture. If he wishes to read them while wearing byssus linen, he may do so; otherwise, he reads them while wearing his own white robe. The synagogue sexton takes a Torah scroll and gives it to the head of the synagogue, the head of the synagogue gives it to the deputy high priest, the deputy high priest gives it to the high priest, and the high priest stands up to receive it and reads the passage beginning "After the death . . ." (Lev. 16) and the passage beginning "Howbeit on the tenth . . ." (Lev. 23:27–32). Then he rolls up the Torah scroll and, holding it at his bosom, says, "Much more is written here than what I have read before you."

The golden vestments are brought to him. He puts them on, washes his hands and feet, goes out, and brings his own ram and the ram of the people as burnt offerings.[8]

He then washes his hands and feet, and immerses himself.

The white vestments are brought back to him; he puts them on and washes his hands and feet. Then he goes in [to the Holy of Holies] to bring out the ladle and the coal pan. He again washes his hands and feet, and immerses himself. The golden garments are brought back to him. He puts them on, washes his hands and feet, and goes into the Temple Hall to burn the twilight incense on the altar and to trim the lamps. He again washes his hands and feet, and takes off the golden garments. After that, they bring him his own garments, which he puts on. Finally they accompany him to his house, where, together with his friends, he celebrates his having come forth from the Holy of Holies unscathed.[9]

1. If the prayer were long, they might fear that something untoward had happened to him in the Holy of Holies.
2. This term includes Samuel, David, and Solomon (B. Sot 48b).
3. See above, chap 6, §142, and chap. 9, §2.
4. In the direction of the Ark cover but not on it.
5. Literally, "the peak," the mountain from which the scapegoat was cast down.
6. The equivalent of twelve *mil*.
7. Possibly to signal to the sentinel posts the completion of the act.
8. See Lev. 16:24.
9. Yoma, selections from chaps. 1–7.

76. R. Simeon said in the name of R. Joshua: Why does the high priest not enter the Holy of Holies clad in garments of gold?[1] Because whatever invites accusation should not be in sight when defense is required. [Hence no garments of gold], in order that Satan not be given the opportunity to say in accusation: Only yesterday these people made themselves a god of gold [the calf], and today they have the temerity to serve God in garments of gold.

But R. Joshua of Sikhnin said in the name of R. Levi: It is because the Holy One is greatly concerned not to have Israel's possessions go to waste.[2]

77. Our masters taught: At one time, a strand of crimson wool would be tied on the outside of the entrance to the Porch.[3] If it turned white, they rejoiced; if it did not turn white, they were sad and shamefaced. Then it was arranged to have it tied on the inside of the entrance to the Porch. But people still managed to have a look at it, and if it became white, they rejoiced, but if it did not become white, they were sad and shamefaced. Then it was ordained to have one half of the strand tied to the rock and the other half tied between the horns of the he-goat that is sent away.

R. Nahum bar Papa said in the name of R. Eleazar ha-Kappar: At one time the strand of crimson wool would be tied on the inside of the entrance to the Porch. As soon as the goat reached the wilderness, the strand turned white; then people knew that the precept concerning the he-goat that is sent away had been performed, in keeping with the promise "If your sins be as scarlet, they shall be as white wool" (Isa. 1:18).[4]

78. Our masters taught: It once happened that [after leaving the Holy of Holies] a high priest was so long at his prayer that his brother priests voted to go into [the Temple Hall] to find out what happened to him. As they were about to enter, he walked out. They asked, "Why were you so long at your prayer?" He replied, "Do you object to my having prayed at greater length for you and for the Temple, that it not be destroyed?" They said, "Please make no habit of this, for we have been taught: 'The high priest does not make the prayer long, so as not to frighten Israel.' "[5]

79. Our masters taught: There was a Sadducee [high priest] who prepared the incense outside and brought it inside [the Holy of Holies]. As he was leaving, greatly exuberant, his father met him and said: My son, even though we are Sadducees, yet [we are not to prepare the incense outside] for fear of the Pharisees. The son replied: All my days I have been troubled by the verse "I appear in the cloud upon the Ark cover" (Lev. 16:2), saying to myself: When shall the opportunity come my way, and I will be able to fulfill the precept?[6] Now that it came my way, should I not have fulfilled it?

It is reported: In but a few days he died, his body was thrown on a dungheap, and worms came crawling out of his nose. Some say: He was smitten as he came out [of the Holy of Holies]. For R. Hiyya taught: Some sort of noise was heard in the Temple Court because an angel came and struck him, so that he fell face down. When his brother priests came in, they found the imprint of something like a calf's foot on his shoulder.[7] For of angels it is written, "Their feet were straight feet; and the sole of their feet was like the sole of a calf's foot" (Ezek. 1:7).[8]

80. It is told of [the high priest] R. Ishmael ben Kimhit that one day, while he was talking with an Arab king,[9] a spray of saliva spurted from the king's mouth on R. Ishmael's garments, making him ritually unclean.[10] So his brother Yeshevav entered and ministered in his stead. Thus, their mother saw both her sons high priests on the same day. According to our masters, Kimhit had seven sons, and all of them served in the office of high priest. The sages asked her: What good deeds are there to your credit [that you should be so honored in your sons]? She replied: The ceiling beams of my house have never seen the hair of my head or the skirt of my petticoat.[11] They responded: Others were equally careful, but it did not avail them.

It used to be said: Flour (*kemahim*) is flour, but Kimhit is the very flower of flowers.[12]

81. Our masters taught: Once a high priest was going out of the Temple, followed by a great multitude. Upon seeing Shemaiah and Avtalion, however, they left him and followed Shemaiah and Avtalion instead.[13] After a while, when Shemaiah and Avtalion called upon the high priest

---

1. See Exod. 28:6ff.
2. The garments the high priest wore on the Day of Atonement had to be stored away and were never to be worn again. Lev. R. 21:10.
3. The vestibule leading into the Temple Hall.
4. B. Yoma 67a and En Yaakov, ad loc.
5. Because they feared either that he did not obtain forgiveness or that something untoward had happened to him. B. Yoma 53b.
6. "The Sadducees interpreted the passage 'For I appear in the cloud' as if it said: For I am to be seen only with the cloud (of incense) upon the Ark cover. The whole verse, according to them, is to mean: 'Let him not come into the Holy Place except with the cloud' (of incense), for only thus, with the cloud, 'am I to be seen on the Ark cover.' Hence the Sadducees' effort to enter the Holy of Holies with the fire pan asmoke, prepared and lit outside" (Yoma, Soncino, p. 84, n. 5).
7. "The high priest, in coming out of the Holy of Holies, walked backward so as not to turn his back on the Holy of Holies. When he reached the threshold and his back first emerged behind the curtain, the angel who was outside the curtain struck him on his back between the shoulders and threw him down, making him fall forward into the Holy of Holies with his face to the ground. There he lay till his brother priests came and threw him out. Cf. B. Yoma, 1, 5. J. Z. Lauterbach" (Yoma, Soncino, p. 84, n. 6).
8. B. Yoma 19b and En Yaakov, ad loc.
9. Who may have come to observe the rites of the Day of Atonement.
10. The spittle defiled him, and he was unable to minister further.
11. Uncovering the hair was an act of immodesty, particularly for a married woman.
12. An attempt to reproduce the pun of *kemahim* and Kimhit. Literally: "All flours (*kemahim*) are coarse flours, but the flour of Kimhit is fine flour," that is, "Smiths are Smiths, but this one is a Smythe." B. Yoma 47a; PRKM 26:10; Lev. R. 20:11.
13. The teachers of Hillel and Shammai. According to one tradition, they were descendants of Sennacherib, a heathen.

to ask permission to leave, he said to them: May the descendants of heathens go in peace.[1] They replied: May the descendants of heathens who do the work of Aaron go in peace, but descendants of Aaron who do not do the work of Aaron are not to go in peace.[2]

The Lulav Cluster

82. In time past, how was [the rite of] the lulav fulfilled [on the Sabbath]? If the first day of the [Sukkot] Festival[3] fell on a Sabbath, the people brought their lulavim to the Temple Mount [on Friday], and the sextons received them and arranged them in rows on the benches that surrounded the Temple Mount,[4] while the elders laid theirs in a special chamber.[5] And the people were instructed to say, "Should anyone get my lulav in his hand, let it be his as a gift."[6] The next day, the people arrived early [at the Temple Mount], and the sextons threw the lulavim before them. They snatched at them and in doing so often came to blows. When the High Court saw that bringing the lulavim to the Temple Mount on a Friday had consequences that endangered human life, they ordained that [when the Festival fell on a Sabbath] each man should say the blessing over the lulav in his own home.

How was [the rite of] the willow branch carried out? There was a place below Jerusalem called Moza.[7] [Every day of the Festival] the people went down there and cut themselves young willow branches. Then they came and set these up at the sides of the altar, so that their tops were bent over the altar. After that, they sounded on the shofar a *tekiah* [a long blast], a *teruah* [tremulous blast], and again a *tekiah*. Every day [of the first six days of the Festival] they went around the altar once, saying, "We beseech Thee, O Lord, save now! We beseech Thee, O Lord, make us now to prosper!" (Ps. 118:25). But on the seventh day [Hoshana Rabbah], they went around the altar seven times. Before they departed, what did they say? "Yours, O altar, is the beauty! Yours, O altar, is the beauty!"[8]

As the rite was carried out on a weekday, so was it carried out on the Sabbath, except that the willow branches were cut on the eve of the Sabbath and placed in golden basins [filled with water], so that they might not wither. R. Yohanan ben Beroka said: On the seventh day, not willow branches but branches of palms were brought and beaten on the ground at the sides of the altar. That day was called "the Day of Beating the Palm Fronds."

Upon the conclusion of the rite, youngsters would pull the lulav clusters apart and eat the etrogim.[9]

1. An expression of his malice.
2. B. Yoma 71b and En Yaakov, ad loc.
3. Also referred to in this work as Feast of Tabernacles or Booths.
4. Above them there was a cover that provided shelter from rain.
5. To avoid the crush on the following day.
6. Since the blessing recited over it would be invalid if it belonged to someone else.
7. Cf. Josh. 18:26.
8. Since upon you are placed offerings that cleanse us of sin.
9. Suk 4:4–7.

The Water Libation

83. How was the water libation [performed]? A golden flagon with the capacity of three *log* was filled with water from the Siloam.[10] When they arrived at the water gate,[11] they sounded on the shofar a *tekiah*, a *teruah*, and again a *tekiah*. The priest [whose turn of duty it was] then went up the ramp [on the south side] of the altar and turned to his left, where there were two silver bowls. (R. Judah said: They were of plaster [but they looked like silver] because their surfaces were darkened from the wine.) Each bowl was pierced by a small snout; the snout of one bowl was wide and the snout of the other was narrow, so that both bowls could be emptied simultaneously [into the pits of the altar].[12] The bowl farther to the west was for water [and the libation was to be poured into it]; the bowl east of it was for wine. To [the priest] who performed the libation, they used to say, "Raise your hand high";[13] for one time a certain priest[14] poured out the water [not into the bowl, but] on his feet, and all the people pelted him with their etrogim.

As the rite was performed on weekdays, so was it performed on the Sabbath, except that on the eve of the Sabbath an unhallowed golden jar[15] was filled with water from the Siloam and put in a special chamber. If the water in that jar was spilled or uncovered, the jar had to be refilled from the laver,[16] for, upon being uncovered, both wine and water are unfit for the altar.[17]

84. Our masters taught: It once happened that a Sadducee [priest] poured the water libation on his feet, and all the people pelted him with their etrogim. On that day a horn of the altar was damaged.[18] A handful of salt was brought and the hole was stopped up; not that the altar was thereby rendered fit for use in the service, but merely in order that it not be seen in a damaged state. For, it should be noted, an altar that does not have its ramp, its horn,[19] its base,[20] and its square shape[21] is unfit for the service.[22]

10. A pool near Jerusalem.
11. One of the gates of the Temple Court.
12. The water was poured through the narrow snout, and the wine, being thick, through the wide snout. See B. Suk 48b.
13. So all may see that the water is poured into the bowl.
14. "A Sadducee. Josephus *Antiquities* 13.13.5 ascribes the incident to Alexander Yannai, king and high priest 107–76 B.C.E. The Sadducees denied the validity of this precept, and in this way he showed his contempt of the Pharisees" (Suk, Soncino, p. 226, n. 15).
15. That is, a jar in ordinary or household use. Water remaining in it overnight is fit for the rite. If, however, the water is in a hallowed jar—a vessel used in the Temple—water remaining in it overnight becomes unfit for use in the rite. See Men 7:4.
16. The laver (see Exod. 30:18) was, of course, a hallowed vessel. But on the eve of a festival it was lowered into a well, giving the water in it the status of well water and therefore fit for Temple use, even though it had remained in the laver overnight. See B. Yoma 37a.
17. Suk 4:9–10.
18. Because some of the etrogim struck it.
19. A projection of one cubic cubit at each of the four corners.
20. "A ledge of one cubit in width and one cubit in height from the ground round the altar" (Suk, Soncino, p. 229, n. 8).
21. See Exod. 27:1.
22. B. Suk 48b–49a.

The Rejoicing at the Place of the Water-drawing

85. He who has not seen the rejoicing at the place of the water-drawing has never in his life seen true rejoicing. At the conclusion of the first day of Sukkot, the priests and the Levites went down to the Women's Court,[1] where they put up an elaborate structure [to separate men from women].[2] In the Women's Court were also installed golden lampstands, each with four golden bowls at its top. Each lampstand had four ladders by which four novices of the priesthood, holding jars of oil, each jar containing one hundred and twenty *log*, were able to ascend to its top[3] and pour oil into each of its bowls. The wicks used by the novices to kindle the lamps were made out of priests' worn-out undergarments and sashes, which they tore into strips. [So abundant was the light that] there was no courtyard in Jerusalem that was not illumined by the light coming from the place of the water-drawing.

With burning torches in their hands,[4] men of piety and good deeds[5] used to dance in front of the people, singing songs and praises.[6] And Levites without number, with harps, lyres, cymbals, trumpets, and other musical instruments were there on the fifteen steps leading down from the Court of the Israelites to the Court of the Women. (The steps corresponded to the fifteen Songs of Ascents in the Psalms.)[7] It was on these steps[8] that the Levites stood with their musical instruments and played their music. Two priests stood by the upper gate, which leads down from the Court of the Israelites to the Court of the Women, each with a trumpet in his hand. When the cock crowed, they sounded a *tekiah*, a *teruah*, and again a *tekiah*.[9] When they reached the tenth step, they sounded a *tekiah*, a *teruah*, and a *tekiah*. When they reached the floor of the Women's Court, they sounded a *tekiah*, a *teruah*, and a *tekiah*. They proceeded, sounding their trumpets, until they reached the gate that leads out to the east. When they reached that gate, they turned their faces from east to west [toward the Temple] and proclaimed "[In the days of the First Temple] our forebears who were in this place [stood] with their backs toward the Temple of the Lord, their faces to the east, and they bowed low to the sun in the east.[10] But we—our eyes are turned to the Lord!" R. Judah stated: They used to repeat the last words and then say, "We are the Lord's, and our eyes are turned to the Lord."

When they separated one from the other, what did they say to one another? "The Lord bless thee out of Zion; and see thou the good of Jerusalem all the days of thy life; and see thy children's children. Peace be upon Israel!" (Ps. 128:5–6).[11]

86. It is taught of Hillel the Elder: When he celebrated during the rejoicing at the place of the water-drawing, he used to recite, "When I am here, everyone is here; but when I am not here, who is here? To the place that I love, there my feet lead me." The Holy One's response: If you come into My house, I will come into your house; if you come not into My house, I will not come into your house: "In every place where I cause My Name to be mentioned, I will come to thee and bless thee" (Exod. 20:21).[12]

87. Our masters taught: Some used to say, "Happy our youth, which has not disgraced our old age." These were the men of piety and good deeds. Others used to say, "Happy our old age, which has atoned for our youth." These were the penitents. Both the former and the latter used to say, "Happy is he who has not sinned; but let him who has sinned return, and the Lord will pardon him."[13]

88. It is reported of R. Simeon ben Gamaliel: When he celebrated during the rejoicing at the place of the water-drawing, he used to take eight burning torches in one hand and throw them into the air; as he threw one, he caught another, and not one torch touched the other. When he prostrated himself, he used to fix his thumbs firmly on the ground [and, while leaning on them], lower himself, kiss the ground, and draw himself up again, a feat that no other man could perform, and this is what is meant by the genuflexion called *kiddah*.[14]

89. R. Joshua ben Hananiah said: When we used to celebrate at the place of the water-drawing, we never had a wink of sleep. Why not? Because the first hour [was occupied with] the daily morning sacrifice; then we proceeded to prayers; then to the additional sacrifice; then to the prayers at the additional sacrifice; then to the house of study; then to eating and drinking; then to the afternoon prayer; then to the daily twilight sacrifice; after that to the [all night] celebration at the place of rejoicing.[15]

The King's Passage in Scripture

90. At the end of the first day of Sukkot in the eighth year following a seven-year cycle, a wooden dais upon which the king is seated is erected in the Temple Court. The synagogue sexton takes a Torah scroll and gives it to the head of the synagogue, the head of the synagogue gives it to the deputy high priest, the deputy high priest gives

1. See Mid 2:5.
2. Above the Court, balconies were erected for the women.
3. Each lampstand was fifty cubits high.
4. They threw up and caught again four or eight torches. So Rashi, ad loc.
5. Or, "miracle workers." See below in this chapter, §87, and part 2, chap. 11, §68.
6. See below in this chapter, §87.
7. Ps. 120–134.
8. And not at the side of the altar, where they served when sacrifices were offered.
9. The signal to set out for the Siloam to draw the water of libation.
10. Cf. Ezek. 8:16.
11. Suk 5:1–5; Tos Suk 4:9.
12. B. Suk 53a and En Yaakov, ad loc.
13. Ibid.
14. B. Suk 53a.
15. Ibid.; P. Suk 5:2, 55b.

it to the high priest, and the high priest gives it to the king. The king stands up to receive it and then sits down and reads.

King Agrippa[1] stood up as he received it, and read standing, for which the sages praised him. When he reached "Thou mayest not put a foreigner over thee who is not thy brother" (Deut. 17:15), tears flowed from his eyes.[2] They said to him: Fear not, Agrippa, you are our brother, you are our brother.

It is taught in the name of R. Nathan: In that instant, Israel[3] made themselves liable to extermination, because they flattered Agrippa.[4]

The Eighth Day Festival [Shemini Atzeret] and the Night Following the Seventh Day of Sukkot

91. "On the eighth day ye shall have a festival for yourselves" (Num. 29:35). This verse is to be considered in the light of what Scripture says elsewhere: "In return for my love, for prayer offered by me, they nevertheless are my adversaries" (Ps. 109:4). During the seven days of Sukkot, Israel offer seventy bullocks for the seventy nations. One might therefore have expected them to love us. But not only do they not love us—they hate us. Therefore the Holy One said to Israel: During the seven days of Sukkot, you have been bringing offerings to Me in behalf of the seventy nations. Now bring offerings in your own behalf only. "On the eighth day ye shall have a festival for yourselves."

"Ye shall present a burnt offering . . . one bullock, one ram" (Num. 29:36). A parable: A king arranged a feast to last seven days and invited all the people of the province to the seven days of feasting. After the seven days of feasting were over, he said to his friend: Now that we have discharged our obligation to the people of the province, you and I will make do with whatever you find—a bit of meat, a fish, some greens. So, too, the Holy One said to Israel: All the offerings you brought during the seven days of Sukkot you brought in behalf of the nations of the world. But now—"on the eighth day—ye shall have a festival for yourselves." Make do with what you find—one bullock, one ram.[5]

92. R. Isaac bar Avdimi said: On the night following the seventh day of Sukkot, all gazed upon the smoke rising from the pile of wood [on the altar]. If the smoke inclined toward the north, poor people rejoiced and the prosperous ones were dejected, because the rains of the coming year were going to be excessive, and fruits would have to be left to rot.[6] If the smoke inclined toward the south, poor people were dejected and the prosperous ones rejoiced, because the rains of the coming year were going to be scanty, and the fruit would be preserved. If the smoke turned toward the east, everyone rejoiced;[7] if toward the west, all were dejected.[8]

Festival Pilgrimage to Jerusalem

93. Rava said: What is meant by "How beautiful are thy feet in sandals" (Song 7:2)? How beautiful are the feet of Israel when they go up in pilgrimage.[9]

94. "No man shall covet they land when thou goest up [to appear before the Lord thy God]" (Exod. 34:24). The verse implies that your heifer will graze in the pasture and no wild beast will hurt it; your hen will go grubbing in the dungheap and no weasel will harm it.

Once, a man forgot to lock the doors of his house when he went up on a pilgrimage. When he returned, he found a serpent entwined in the ring handles of his door.

On another occasion, a man forgot to bring his chickens into the house when he went up on a pilgrimage. When he returned, he found some cats torn to pieces in front of them.

On still another occasion, a man forgot to bring a stack of wheat into the house when he went up on a pilgrimage. When he returned, he found lions standing guard around it.

There is a story of two wealthy brothers in Ashkelon who had two invidious gentile neighbors. The neighbors said: When these Jews go up to pray in Jerusalem, we will go into their houses, ransack them, and take everything they have. The time came when the two brothers went up on their pilgrimage, whereupon God appointed two angels in their likeness to go in and out of their houses. When the brothers returned from Jerusalem, they sent their neighbors gifts out of all they brought back with them from Jerusalem. The neighbors asked, "Where have you been?" The brothers, "In Jerusalem." "When did you go up?" "On such-and-such a day." "When did you come back?" "On such-and-such a day." "Whom did you leave in your house?" "We left no one." The neighbors: "Blessed be the God of the Jews, who did not leave them and does not ever leave them."[10]

95. R. Isaac said: Why are there no fruits like those of Gennesaret[11] in Jerusalem? So that the pilgrims should not say, "Had we gone up to Jerusalem only to eat the fruits of Gennesaret, it would have been enough," with the result that the pilgrimage would not have been undertaken for its own sake.

Similarly, R. Dostai son of R. Yannai said: Why are hot springs like those of Tiberias not found in Jerusalem? So that the pilgrims should not say, "Had we gone up only in order to bathe in the hot springs of Tiberias, it would

---

1. Agrippa I, probably in 41 C.E.
2. On his father's side, he was not of Jewish descent.
3. Literally (and euphemistically), "the enemies of Israel."
4. B. Sot 41a–b and En Yaakov, ad loc.
5. Tanhuma B, *Pinhas*, §14–15.
6. So the poor would be able to buy them cheaply.
7. Since it indicated normal rainfall and normal prices.
8. Because the east wind dries up the seeds and causes famine. B. BB 147a; B. Yoma 21b.
9. They must wear sandals for such a journey. B. Hag 3a.
10. B. Pes 8b; P. Pe 3:7, 17d; Song R. 7:2, §1.
11. A lake so named from the fertile plain lying on its western side. The biblical and modern name is Yam Kinneret.

have been enough," with the result that the pilgrimage would not have been undertaken for its own sake.[1]

Pilgrimage to Jerusalem during the Time of an Adverse Decree

96. It is reported that the ruling power once decreed that Israel not bring their firstfruits to Jerusalem and, to prevent Israel from going up on pilgrimages for the festivals, placed guardposts on the roads, as Jeroboam son of Nebat had done. What did the pious and sin-fearing men of that generation do? They took the baskets of firstfruits, covered them with dried figs, and put them, as well as a pestle, on their shoulders. When they reached the guardposts and were asked, "Where are you going?" they replied, "We are going to make two cakes of pressed figs in the mortar yonder with the pestle on our shoulders." As soon as they passed the guards, they rearranged their baskets in ornamental display and brought them to Jerusalem.[2] These pious men are known as the family of pestle smugglers and fig pressers.[3]

Another time, the ruling power decreed that Israel should not bring wood for the altar and, to prevent Israel from going up on pilgrimage for festivals, placed guardposts on the roads, as Jeroboam son of Nebat had done. What did the pious and God-fearing men of that generation do? They took cuts of wood and made them into ladders (*sullamot*), which they put on their shoulders and proceeded thus. When they reached the guardposts and were asked, "Where are you going?" they replied, "We are going with these ladders on our shoulders to fetch young pigeons from the dovecote yonder." As soon as they passed the guards, they took the ladders apart and brought the wood to Jerusalem. They are known as "the family of Sulmai ha-Netotzati [the family that took ladders apart]."[4]

It is of them and of men like them that Scripture says, "The memory of the righteous shall be for a blessing" (Prov. 10:7); and of Jeroboam and his companions, the verse adds, "But the name of the wicked shall rot.[5]

97. On the twenty-second of Shevat the decree requiring worship of idols, which the enemy intended to bring into the Temple Hall, was nullified. On that day, there is to be no public mourning.

The news that on a certain day Caligula had sent idols to be set up in the Temple Hall[6] reached Jerusalem on the eve of the first day of Tabernacles. Simeon the Mild[7] said: Observe the days of your Festival with joy, for not one of the things you heard will come to pass. For He who has made His Name dwell in this house will perform miracles for us at this time, even as He performed miracles for our fathers in each and every generation. At that, a voice was heard out of the Holy of Holies, saying, "The worship of idols in the Temple is nullified—Caligula has been slain, and his decrees are nullified." The precise hour these words were spoken was set down in writing.

When it became evident that [Caligula] Caesar's soldiers were slowly coming closer to Jerusalem, one of the Jewish leaders said, "Go and meet them [and attempt to stop them].[8] As soon as the leader's word became known, all the Jewish notables assembled, went out to Caligula's legate, and said, "All of us are ready to die rather than have this decree imposed upon us." As they kept crying aloud and beseeching the legate, he responded, "Instead of crying aloud and beseeching a mere emissary, why don't you plead and cry aloud to your God in heaven to help you?"

As the legate approached one city after another, he saw people coming toward him from each city. At the sight of them he was overwhelmed, saying, "How numerous they are!" The informers told him, "These are Jews going out from each of the cities to confront you." However, when the legate came into each city, he saw men lying in sackcloth and ashes in its marketplaces.

No sooner did he reach Antipatris than a letter came apprising him that Caligula had been assassinated and his decrees nullified. At that, the Jews seized the idols and dragged them through the streets.

That day was declared a festal day.[9]

The Cleverness of the People of Jerusalem

98. "She that was numerous among the nations" (Lam. 1:1). But has it not just been said, "She whose people was numerous"? What, then, is implied by saying again, "She that was numerous (*rabbati*) among the nations"? Here *rabbati* means not "numerous" but "superior in intellect." R. Huna said in the name of R. Yose: Whenever a Jerusalemite went into the provinces, they provided him with a high-backed chair to sit on, in order to listen to his wisdom.

Once, when a Jerusalemite went to a certain province, he became aware that the time of his death was near. So he summoned the owner of the house where he was lodging and entrusted him with his money, saying, "If my son comes from Jerusalem and performs three clever acts in your presence, give him the money; otherwise, do not give it to him." Presently the man died and departed to his eternal rest. After a while, his son arrived. (Now, it was the practice among the inhabitants of this city that not one of them would point out the house of a neighbor to any stranger who inquired for it.) When the son reached the gate of that city and saw a man carrying a load of twigs, he asked, "Will you sell me that load?" The man answered, "Yes." "Then take the money for it and carry it to So-and-so." The man took the money and set out to carry the

1. P. Pes 8b.
2. See above in this chapter, §74.
3. Ta 4:5.
4. See Ezra 2:46 and 1 Chron. 2:54.
5. B. Ta 28a and En Yaakov, ad loc.
6. In 41 C.E.
7. A high priest under Agrippa I. See Josephus *Antiquities* 19.7.4 and Ben-Zion Luria, ed. Megillat Ta (Jerusalem, 1964), p. 186.
8. Unlike Simeon, who believed in miracles, he relied on political action (Luria, ed. Megillat Ta, p. 187).
9. Megillat Ta 11.

twigs to the courtyard named. As he walked, the son followed him, until they arrived at that courtyard. Then the man called to the owner of the house, "Ho, there, come and receive this load of twigs!" The owner of the house replied, "Did I ask you to bring me a load of twigs?" The man said, "True, you did not tell me to do so; but the person behind me did—the load belongs to him." Immediately the owner of the house opened his home to the son, and they greeted each other.

This was the first clever act.

Then the owner of the house asked him, "Who are you?" He replied, "I am the son of the man who died in your house." The householder took him in and prepared a meal for him. Now, this householder had two sons and two daughters. When the meal was ready, the householder set before the Jerusalemite's son five young chickens as the main course, and as they were about to begin the meal, the host said to his guest, "You divide the portions and serve." The guest answered, "It is not mine [that I should be serving]." The householder said, "Please, it is my wish that you divide and serve." At that, the guest divided one chicken between the man and his wife, a second between the two sons, a third between the two daughters, and set two before himself. They ate without making any comment.

That was the second clever act.

In the evening the host brought in a fat hen for supper and again asked the guest to serve it. Again he replied, "It is not mine." The host again said, "It is my wish that you divide the hen and serve it." At that, the guest served the head to the host, the entrails to the wife, the two legs to the two sons, and the two wings to the two daughters, and set the rest of the hen's body before himself.

That was the third clever act.

The host inquired, "Is this how people portion out food where you come from? The first time you served, I said nothing to you. So now you do it again the same way." The Jerusalemite's son replied, "Did I not say to you that the food was not mine? Nevertheless, what I was asked to serve, I apportioned properly. The first time, five chickens were served for the meal. You, your wife, and one chicken add up to three; your two sons and one chicken add up to three; your two daughters and one chicken add up to three; and I and two chickens add up to three. So can you say that I have taken any part of your portion? This time, a hen was served for supper. I took the head and gave it to you, because you are the head of the household. I took the entrails and set them before your wife, because children issue from the womb. I took the two legs and gave them to your two sons, because they are the pillars of the house. I took the two wings and gave them to your two daughters, because in the future they will fly away from your house and go to their husbands. I took the [rest of the hen's body, which is shaped like a] boat, because I came in a boat and will leave in a boat. Now come and give me my money, which my father entrusted to you, and I will leave right away." The host turned over his money to him, and he departed in peace.[1]

99. Our masters taught: It once happened that two Jerusalemites were taken captive on Mount Carmel, and their captor was walking behind them. One of them said to the other, "The camel walking in front of us is blind in one eye and is laden with two skins, one containing wine and the other oil. And of the two men who lead it, one is a Jew and the other a heathen." Their captor, sharply, "You arrogant fellows, how do you know this?" They replied, "Because, from the grasses in front of him, this camel eats only on the side he can see, and not on the side he cannot see. He is laden with two skins, one containing wine and the other, oil—wine drips and is absorbed [into the ground], while oil drips and remains on the surface. As for the two men leading it, one is a Jew, the other, a heathen—a heathen eases himself on the roadway, while a Jew turns aside."

The captor hastened after the two men leading the camel and found that it was as his captives had said. At that, he kissed the captives on their heads, brought them to his house, and prepared a great feast at which he danced in attendance before them as he exclaimed, "Blessed be He who chose the seed of Abraham and imparted to them some of His wisdom, so that, wherever they go, they tower over their masters!"

Then he freed them, and they returned to their homes in peace.[2]

100. A story of a heathen who in the Land of Israel took two children captive and made them run before his horse. When the heathen reached the gateway of Rome, one child said to his companion, "I smell Judean leek-heads cooking in a pot made in Kefar Hananiah." This angered their master, who said, "Your God could not put up with you, so how will I be able to?" As he was cursing them, a royal emissary approached and the heathen asked him, "Where did you come from?" The emissary: "I have just come from Judea in one day." The heathen: "How could you come in one day from Judea, a distance of four hundred parasangs?" The emissary: "A wind favored the ship, and I arrived in one day. If you don't believe me, here are some Judean leek-heads being cooked in a pot. I have not yet tasted them."

When the children's captor came into his home, his mother got busy and killed a lamb, preparing all kinds of dishes for her son, and opened a cask of wine. As he was reclining for the meal, with the two children standing over him, one said to his companion, "Look, the smell of this meat is like the smell of a dog, and the smell of the wine is like the stench of a corpse." [When the heathen heard these words], he asked his mother, "What kind of meat is this?" She replied, "I had a ewe that was giving birth to a lamb, and it died while giving birth. So our bitch suckled the lamb until it grew up. Now I killed it, and you are dining on it." Then he asked, "What kind of wine is this?" She replied, "This wine is from the vineyard that extends over your father's grave. Of all the vineyards your father left you, no other yields wine as good. So I filled one cask for you from that vineyard. I plugged the cask,

1. Lam. R. 1:1, §4.

2. B. Sanh 104a–b.

sealed it, and said: I will not open it until my son comes back. Now, when I saw you, I rejoiced greatly and opened the cask."

The heathen ate and drank, greatly pleased with the two children he had brought back with him.

After he got through eating and drinking, he stood up and danced around. One of the children said to his companion, "Look, the feet of our master are like the feet of a circus clown—his mother must have fornicated with a song-and-dance man to give birth to this one."

When the heathen heard this, he grabbed a sword, went to his mother, and asked her, "Whose son am I?" She: "My son, you are your father's son." He: "If you won't tell me the truth, I will kill you." She: "Don't kill me. I'll tell you the truth. Your father was unable to beget, and I was afraid that the kinsmen might take away my estate.[1] One day your father brought this song-and-dance man, whose singing was sweet. So I conceived from him and gave birth to you. Did I not do well by bringing you to inherit all this wealth?" Upon hearing what she told him, he said, "I brought with me a pair who may reveal my shame to the neighbors."

He went out to the children and said, "Go in peace. I am not worthy of being waited on by such as you." He gave them all kinds of food and provisions for the journey, escorted them, and then returned to his home. After that, his mind was at peace.[2]

101. A Jerusalemite went to see a certain merchant in Athens. On his arrival, he put up at a shop[3] where he found several persons sitting and drinking wine. After he had eaten and drunk, he wished to go to bed. They said to him, "We have agreed among ourselves not to allow a guest to stay until he has made three long-distance jumps." He replied, "How do I know what you consider a long-distance jump. Let one of you get up, do it before me, and I will do likewise." One of them stood up and jumped, and found himself in the middle of the shop; he jumped again, and found himself at the shop's entrance; he jumped a third time, and found himself outside. The Jerusalemite got up, bolted the door in his face, and said to the others, "By your lives, what you intended to do to me, I have done to you.[4]

102. An Athenian came to Jerusalem, where he met a child to whom he gave a few coppers, saying, "Go and bring me something of which I can eat my fill and have enough left over to take on my journey." The child went and brought him salt. The man asked the child, "Did I tell you to bring me salt?" The child replied, "But did you not tell me to go and bring you something of which you can eat your fill but have enough left over to take on your journey? By your life, there is enough for you here to eat your fill and leave an ample supply to take on your journey!"[5]

103. An Athenian came to Jerusalem, where he found a broken mortar which had been thrown away. He picked it up and took it to a tailor, saying, "Sew this broken mortar for me." The tailor scooped up a handful of sand and said, "Twist this into threads for me, and I will sew it."[6]

104. An Athenian came to Jerusalem, where he met a child, to whom he gave a few coppers, saying, "Bring me eggs and cheese." On the child's return, the man said to him, "Show me which cheese is from a white goat and which from a black goat." The child replied, "You are a man well on in years, so show me which egg is from a white hen and which from a black hen!"[7]

105. An Athenian came to Jerusalem and went into a school, where he found the children sitting without their teacher. He put some questions to them, which they answered. Then they said to him, "Come, let us agree among ourselves that if one of us asks a question that the other is unable to answer, he will win the other's garments." He said, "Very well." They said, "You ask first, since you are older than we." He replied, "You ask first, since you belong here." So they said to him, "Identify the following: nine go out but only eight come in, two pour but only one drinks, while twenty-four are ready to serve." He was unable to respond, and so the children took his garments from him. He then went to the home of R. Yohanan, their teacher, and complained to him, "Hey, master, what dreadful mischief there is among you! When a stranger comes into your midst, you apparently rob him of his garments!" R. Yohanan answered, "Did the children put a question to you that you were unable to answer, and they took your garments from you?" "Yes." "What was the question they asked you?" He related it to him, and the teacher explained, "My son, the nine that go in are the nine months of gestation, and the eight that come out are the eight days of circumcision; the two that pour are the two breasts, and the one who drinks is the child that is born; and the twenty-four that are ready to serve are the twenty-four months of nursing." At that, the Athenian went back to the school, gave the answer, and regained his garments. The children, taunting him, quoted, "If ye had not plowed with my heifer, ye had not found out my riddle" (Judg. 14:18).[8]

106. An Athenian went to Jerusalem and upon his return ridiculed its inhabitants. When the Jerusalemites heard this, they said, "Who will go and bring him back to us?" One volunteered: "I will go and bring him back with his head shaved." The Jerusalemite went to Athens and was

---

1. That is, her widow's right to her husband's estate.
2. Yalkut, Lam., §1004.
3. A food and wine shop with rooms for overnight guests.
4. Lam. R. 1:1, §5.
5. Lam. R. 1:1, §7.
6. Lam. R. 1:1, §8.
7. Lam. R. 1:1, §9.
8. Lam. R. 1:1, §11.

given hospitality by that man. In the morning, the two went out to walk in the marketplace. When one of the Jerusalemite's sandals broke, he said to a workman, "Take this *tremis*[1] and repair the sandal." The Athenian asked, "Are sandals so costly where you live?" "Yes." "How many denars do they cost?" "Nine or ten. Even when cheap, seven or eight denars." The Athenian asked, "If I were to come to your city with a stock of sandals, would they sell?" "Certainly," he answered, "only do not enter the city without first informing me."

So the Athenian went and bought a stock of sandals, set forth for Jerusalem, and sat down at the gate of the city. He sent for the Jerusalemite, who came to him. When he arrived, the Jerusalemite said, "We have agreed among ourselves that nobody may enter to sell his wares unless his head is shaved and his face blackened." The Athenian replied, "What do I care if my head is shaved, so long as I sell my goods!" After shaving his head, the Jerusalemite took him and seated him in the middle of the marketplace. When a customer came to buy sandals of him and asked him, "How much is this pair of sandals?" he would answer, "Ten denars—well, nine denars; but I will not take less than eight." On hearing this, each would-be purchaser struck him on his head with a sandal and went away without buying. The Athenian said to the Jerusalemite, "Did I treat you so badly when you were in my place?"[2] The Jeusalemite replied, "Henceforth, do not ridicule the men of Jerusalem."[3]

107. It happened that Israel had need of a Red Heifer and could not find one; at long last they found one at a heathen's. They went to him and said, "Sell us the heifer you have." He replied, "Give me my price for her and take her." "And what is your price for her?" "Four gold coins at the most." They replied, "We shall pay it." While they went to fetch the money, the heathen guessed for what purpose they needed the heifer. And so when they came back and brought the money, he said to them, "I will not sell her to you." They asked, "Perhaps you wish to increase the price? If so, we will pay you all you require."

When the scoundrel realized that they were pressing for the heifer, he kept raising the price. When they said, "Take five gold coins," he did not want to. "Take ten, take twenty, thirty, fifty, a hundred," he still refused to sell, until they reached a thousand. He consented to sell them the heifer for a thousand gold coins. Having finally come to an agreement, they once again went to fetch the gold coins for him.

What did the wicked man do then? He said to another heathen, a boon companion of his, "Come and see how I shall fool these Jews. The only reason they are trying to get the heifer from me and are willing to pay me all that money is because a yoke has never been put on her neck. I will take the yoke, put it on her neck, have some fun at their expense, and get their money just the same." Here is what he did: he took the yoke and put it on the heifer for the entire night. Now, this is the sign that shows that a heifer has never borne a yoke: on her neck, in the place where the yoke is set, are two particular hairs which stand upright as long as she has never borne a yoke. But as soon as a yoke is set upon her neck, the two hairs are at once bent down. And there is still another sign of her never having borne a yoke. As long as no yoke has been on her, both eyes look straight ahead. After a yoke has been upon her, her eyes have an anxious look as she turns her head and rolls her eyes, straining to see the yoke.[4]

When they came back with all the gold in their hands to take the heifer from the heathen, he went in and, first removing the yoke from the heifer, led her out to them. As soon as he led her out, they proceeded to examine her and saw that the two particular hairs that should have been straight were bent down and that her eyes were rolling back because the yoke had been on her.

They said to him, "Take your heifer. We cannot use her now. We will not accept her even if you give her to us for nothing."

When the wicked heathen saw that they were returning his heifer to him and that he had come out with hands empty of all those gold coins, the very mouth that had said, "I will have my fun at their expense," proceeded to say, "Blessed be He who has chosen this nation." Then he went into his house, strung up a rope, and hanged himself.[5]

108. R. Joshua was once walking along a highway and met a child holding a covered dish. He asked, "What have you in that covered dish?" The child replied, "If my mother had wanted you to know, she would not have said to me, 'Cover it.' "

When R. Joshua entered the city, he met a little girl standing and filling her pitcher from a well. He said to her, "Give me some water to drink." She: "For you as well as for your ass."

After he had drunk and was turning to go on his way, he said, "My daughter, you acted like Rebekah." She: "I acted like Rebekah, but you did not act like Eliezer."[6]

---

1. A Roman coin, a third of an *aureus*, which was a gold piece. He paid him an absurdly high price.
2. He understood now that a trick had been played on him.
3. Lam. R. 1:1, §13.
4. See H. Yalon, "PLL and PLPL in Hebrew and Aramaic" [Hebrew], *Tarbitz* 6 (1935): 225–26.
5. PR 14:1 (YJS 1: 280–81); Tanhuma B, *Hukkat*, §3.
6. Isaac's servant who rewarded Rebekah's kindness with the gift of a gold nose ring and gold bands for her arms; see Gen. 24. Lam R. 1:1, §19.

CHAPTER TEN

THE DESTRUCTION OF THE SECOND TEMPLE AND OF THE LAND

The Years before the Destruction

1. Our masters taught: During the forty years preceding the destruction of the Temple, the lot "For the Lord"[1] did not come up in the high priest's right hand, nor did the crimson strand turn white, nor did the westernmost lamp burn continually. And [ominously] the doors of the Temple Hall would open by themselves, until Rabban Yohanan ben Zakkai reprimanded them, saying, "Temple Hall, Temple Hall, why do you yourself keep sounding the alarm? I already know about you, that you are to be destroyed, for long ago Zechariah, a descendant of Iddo, prophesied to you, 'Open thy doors, O Lebanon[2] [whitener of sins], that the fire may devour thy cedars' " (Zech. 11:1).[3]

Why the Land Was Destroyed

2. R. Yohanan said: What demonstrates the truth of the verse "Happy is the man that feareth always, but he that hardeneth his heart shall fall into mischief" (Prov. 28:14)? The fact that the destruction of Jerusalem came about through a Kamtza and a Bar Kamtza, that the destruction of King's Mountain[4] came about through a cock and a hen, that the destruction of Bethar came about through the shaft of a royal litter.

The destruction of Jerusalem came about through a Kamtza and a Bar Kamtza in this way. A certain man, who had a friend named Kamtza and an enemy named Bar Kamtza, once arranged a banquet and said to his servant, "Go and bring Kamtza." But the servant [mistakenly] went and brought Bar Kamtza. When the host found his enemy Bar Kamtza seated in his home, he said, "You hate me, so what are you doing here? Pick yourself up and get out!" Bar Kamtza: "Now that I am here, let me stay, and I will pay you for whatever I eat and drink." The host: "No!" Bar Kamtza: "Then let me give you half the cost of your banquet." "No, sir!" "I will pay the full cost for your entire banquet." "Under no circumstances!" Then the host grabbed Bar Kamtza by his arm, pulled him up from his seat, and threw him out.

The ousted Bar Kamtza said to himself: Since the sages sitting there did not stop him, it would seem that what happened met with their approval. So I will go to the king and inform against them. He went and said to Caesar, "The Jews are about to rebel against you." Caesar: "How can one prove such an accusation?" Bar Kamtza: "Send them an offering [for their Temple] and see whether they will be willing to offer it." So Caesar sent a fine calf with Bar Kamtza. While on the way, Bar Kamtza inflicted a blemish on its upper lip, or, some say, injured its eye, in a place where we [Jews] count it a blemish but heathens do not. The sages were inclined to offer it in order to maintain peace with the government. But R. Zechariah ben Avkulas protested, "People will say that blemished animals may be offered on the altar." Then it was proposed to have Bar Kamtza assassinated, so that he would not continue to inform against them. Again R. Zechariah ben Avkulas demurred: "Is one who makes a blemish on consecrated animals to be put to death?" (R. Yohanan was to remark: The scrupulousness of R. Zechariah ben Avkulas, as well as his forebearance, destroyed our [holy] house, burned our Temple Hall, and caused us to be exiled from our Land.)

Presently Nero Caesar advanced against the Jews. When he got close [to Jerusalem], he shot an arrow toward the east, and it turned back and fell in Jerusalem. He then shot another arrow toward the west, and it too turned and fell in Jerusalem. And the same thing happened when he shot toward the other points of the compass. Then he said to a [Jewish] boy, "Recite [the last] verse of Scripture you learned." The boy: "And I will lay My vengeance upon Edom by the hand of My people Israel" (Ezek. 25:14). Hearing that, Nero said to himself: The Holy One desires to lay waste His house and wipe His hands clean on me. So he ran away and became a proselyte. R. Meir was descended from him.

Then Vespasian [who was eventually to become] Caesar advanced against them. He laid siege to Jerusalem for three years. Three men of great wealth, Nakdimon ben Gorion, Ben Kalba Savua, and Ben Tzitzit ha-Keset, lived in Jerusalem. Nakdimon ben Gorion was so called because the sun continued shining (*nakedah*) for his sake.[5] Ben Kalba Savua was so called because one would go into his house hungry as a dog (*kelev*) and come out full (*savea*). Ben Tzitzit ha-Keset was so called because his fringes (*tzitzit*) used to trail on cushions (*keset*).[6] One of the three said, "I will keep the people of Jerusalem in wheat and

---

[1] See above, chap. 9, §75.

[2] Lebanon is another name for the Temple Hall, because the word *Levanon* means "whitener [of sins]."

[3] B. Yoma 39b.

[4] "The whole mountainous region stretching from the Valley of Jezrael to the south of Judah, including the mountains of Samaria (Israel Horowitz, as cited by Isidore Epstein in Git, Soncino, pp. 254–55, n. 4).

[5] An official of the Roman government offered Nakdimon water from cisterns for the use of pilgrims, with the stipulation that on a certain day that water was to be replenished by Nakdimon. If unable to do so, Nakdimon was to pay gold in lieu of the water. When the due day came, Nakdimon had no water. But as the day was drawing to a close, rain began to fall, and for Nakdimon's sake the sun broke through the clouds, thus lengthening the day, until the cisterns were filled again—on the day promised.

[6] Which were put on the pavement before him as he walked.

barley." A second said, "I will keep them in wine, oil, and salt." The third said, "I will keep them in firewood." (The sages considered the offer of wood the most generous. They pointed out that R. Hisda [used to hand all his keys to his servant, except the one to the woodbin, for, he] would say, "To bake one load of wheat requires sixty loads of wood.")

When the three men inspected their storehouses, they figured they could maintain the city for twenty-one years.

At that time the Zealots dominated the city. When the sages said to them, "Let us go out and make peace with the Romans," they did not allow them to, saying, "No, we will go out and fight them." The sages countered, "Such an attempt will accomplish nothing at all for us." But the Zealots rose up and burned the stores of wheat and barley, so that presently a famine ensued [in the city].

Martha daughter of Boethus, who was one of the richest women in Jerusalem, sent out her manservant, saying, "Go and bring me some fine flour." By the time he went, the fine flour was sold out. He came back and told her, "There is no fine flour, but there is plain white bread." She said to him, "Go and bring me some." By the time he went, he found the white bread also sold out. He came back again and told her, "There is no white bread, but there is coarse black bread." She said to him, "Go and bring me some." By the time he went, that, too, was sold out. He returned and said to her, "There is no coarse black bread, but there is barley flour." She said, "Go and bring me some." By the time he went, this also was sold out. Even though [she was partly undressed], having taken off her shoes, she said, "I will go out and see if I can find anything at all to eat." [So out she rushed.] Then, when some dung stuck to her foot, [her revulsion was such] that she died. To the way she died, Rabban Yohanan ben Zakkai applied the verse "She who is most tender and delicate among you, so tender and delicate that she never ventured to set a bare foot on the ground" (Deut. 28:56). Some report that she found a bone-dry fig discarded by R. Zadok, tried to eat it, choked, and died. As Martha was dying, she brought out all her gold and silver, and threw it into the street, saying, "What good is this to me?" To her applies the verse "They shall cast their silver in the streets" (Ezek. 7:19).

What was special about a dried fig discarded by R. Zadok? R. Zadok observed [continual] fasts for forty years, in order that Jerusalem might not be destroyed. He became so emaciated that when he ate anything at all, the food could be seen going down his gullet. When he wanted to restore himself, they would bring him dried figs, and he could only suck the juice and throw the figs away.

When Rabban Yohanan ben Zakkai went out to walk in the marketplace and saw men of Jerusalem stewing straw and drinking its water, he said to himself: Can men who are reduced to cooking straw and drinking its water withstand Vespasian's troops? Matters cannot be remedied unless I go out of the city [and attempt to make peace with the Romans].

Abba Sicara[1] ben Battiah, head of the Zealots in Jerusalem, was the son of Rabban Yohanan ben Zakkai's sister. Rabban Yohanan sent word to him: "Come to visit me in secret." When Abba Sicara came, Rabban Yohanan asked him, "How long will you men continue what you are doing? You are killing all the people by famine." Abba Sicara replied, "What choice have I? If I dare object to them, they will kill me." Rabban Yohanan: "Devise a scheme for me to leave the city. Perhaps the saving of a few lives may still be possible." Abba Sicara: "We have agreed among ourselves that no man may leave the city except as a corpse." Rabban Yohanan: "Then have me taken out as a corpse." Abba Sicara ben Battiah: "Pretend to be ill, and let everyone come to visit you. Have something foul-smelling brought and put at your side, so that they will say, 'Rabban Yohanan is dead!' Then let your disciples come and carry the casket [with you in it]. Make sure that others are not allowed to carry it, so that your body's light weight will not be noticed. It is well known that a living body weighs less than a corpse."

Rabban Yohanan acted on Abba Sicara's advice. He sent for his disciples R. Eliezer and R. Joshua, and said to them, "Bestir yourselves, my children, and have me taken out of Jerusalem. Make a coffin for me, and I will lie down in it." Presently R. Eliezer took hold of the upper part of the coffin and R. Joshua of its lower part, and they carried it slowly along until the setting of the sun, when they reached the gates of Jerusalem. Some of the Sicarii guards asked, "Who is this?" The disciples: "A dead body. Don't you know that dead bodies may not be kept overnight in Jerusalem?"[2] Some of the Sicarii wanted to drive a dagger through the body, but Abba Sicara restrained them: "It will be said of you, 'They pierced their master.' " Then they wanted to push the body about, but again he restrained them: "It will be said of you, 'They pushed their master about.' " So they opened the gate for the coffin, and it left the city.

The disciples continued to carry the coffin until they got to Vespasian. When they opened the coffin, R. Yohanan stood up before him and said, "Peace to you, O king! Peace to you, O king!" Vespasian replied, "Your life is forfeit on two counts. To begin with, you call me king, and I am not a king. Moreover, if I am a king, why did you not come to me until now?" R. Yohanan replied, "As for your saying that you are not a king, you are in fact a king. If you were not a king, Jerusalem would not be delivered into your hand, for it is written, 'And Lebanon[3] shall fall by a mighty one' [Isa. 10:34], and the epithet 'mighty one' is applied only to a king. As for your question, 'If I am a king, why did you not come to me till now?'—the Zealots among us did not let me." Vespasian asked, "If there is a jar of honey around which a draco[4] is coiled, would not the jar be broken to get rid of the draco?" Rabban Yohanan did not respond. (R. Joseph—some say R. Akiva—applied to him the verse "[God] turneth wise men backward, and maketh their knowledge

1. Abba Sicara means "the chief of the Sicarii, (daggermen)," the epithet given to the Zealots.

2. See below, part 3, chap. 2, §116.

3. The Temple, "that which makes Israel's sins white (*malbin*)."

4. A brilliantly colored flying lizard. The idea is a metaphor for the Zealots.

foolish" [Isa. 44:25]. He should have responded, "We take a pair of tongs, grip the draco, and kill it, leaving the jar intact.")

Some say there were four generals at that confrontation: the general of the Arabs, whose name was Pangar; the general of Africa; the general of Alexandria; and the general of Palestine. These began setting forth parables before Rabban Yohanan ben Zakkai: "If a snake nests in an amphora, how is the snake[1] to be dealt with?" He replied, "A charmer should be brought to charm the snake and leave the amphora intact." To which Pangar retorted, "The snake should be killed, even if that means breaking the amphora." Then the generals asked, "If a snake nests in a tower, how is the snake to be dealt with?" Rabban Yohanan replied, "A charmer should be brought to charm the snake, and leave the tower intact." Again Pangar retorted, "The snake should be killed, even if the tower has to be set on fire." Rabban Yohanan then said to Pangar, "All neighbors who do harm [to others] find that they have done it to themselves.[2] Not only do you not speak in our defense, you even argue for the prosecution against us." Pangar replied, "I seek only your good, for so long as the Temple stands, the heathen kingdoms will strive against you. Once it is destroyed, they will no longer do so." Rabban Yohanan said to him, "Only your heart knows whether you are on the level or in league with the devil."[3]

At this point a messenger came from Rome to Vespasian and said, "Arise! Caesar is dead, and the notables of Rome have decided to make you head of the state." Vespasian had just finished putting on one boot, but when he tried to put on the other, his foot could not get into it; then, when he tried to take off the first boot, he could not pull his foot out of it. Vespasian said, "What is the meaning of this?" Rabban Yohanan replied, "Be not distressed. The good news has done it, as Scripture says, 'Good tidings make the bones fat' [Prov. 15:30]. How may your condition be remedied? Let someone you dislike come and pass before you, for Scripture also says, 'A broken spirit drieth up the bones' " (Prov. 17:22). Vespasian did so and was able to get his foot into the second boot. Then he asked Rabban Yohanan, "Seeing that you are so wise, why did you not come to me till now?" Rabban Yohanan said, "Have I not already told you?" Vespasian: "I, too, told you."

Then Vespasian said to Rabban Yohanan, "I am now going away from here and will send someone else to take my place. You may, however, make a request of me, and I will grant it." Rabban Yohanan: "Give me Yavneh and its sages,[4] the dynasty of Rabban Gamaliel,[5] and physicians to heal R. Zadok." (R. Joseph—some say R. Akiva—applied to him the verse "[God] turneth wise men backward, and maketh their knowledge foolish" [Isa. 44:25]. He should have said, "Let Jerusalem off this time." But Rabban Yohanan thought that Vespasian would deny such a request, and so there would not even be the saving of a few.)

[Some say that Rabban Yohanan ben Zakkai answered Vespasian as follows]: "I beg you to let this city be." Vespasian: "Did the Romans proclaim me king so that I should let this city be? Make another request of me, and I will grant it." Rabban Yohanan: Let the western gate, which leads to Lydda,[6] remain open, and let everyone who departs up to the fourth hour in the day be spared."

When Vespasian was laying siege to Jerusalem, he asked Rabban Yohanan, "Have you any friend or relative in the city? Send for him and bring him out before my troops enter." Rabban Yohanan sent R. Eliezer and R. Joshua to bring out R. Zadok. They went and found him at the city gate. When R. Zadok arrived, Rabban Yohanan stood up before him. Vespasian asked, "You stand up in deference before this emaciated old man?" Rabban Yohanan: "By your life, if there had been one more like him in Jerusalem, you would not have been able to conquer it, even if your army were twice its size." Vespasian: "What is his power?" Rabban Yohanan: "He eats one ripened fig, and with the strength he derives from it, he teaches one hundred sessions at the academy." "But why is he so emaciated?" "Because of his numerous abstinences and fasts." Vespasian sent for physicians, who came and fed R. Zadok small portions of food and small doses of liquid until his normal weight was restored. R. Zadok's son, Eleazer, said to him, "Father, give them their reward in this world, so that they will have no merit on your account in the world-to-come."[7] So R. Zadok taught the Romans how to calculate by using one's fingers and how to weigh by means of a balance beam.[8]

When Vespasian had subdued the city, he assigned the destruction of its four ramparts to the four generals, the western gate being allotted to Pangar. Now, it had been decreed by Heaven that this gate should never be destroyed. Why not? Because the Presence abode in the west. The other three demolished the parts assigned to them, but Pangar did not demolish his. Vespasian sent for him and asked, "Why did you not destroy the part assigned to you?" He replied, "By your life, I acted as I did for the honor of Rome. If I had demolished it, mortals would never have known what fortified installations you destroyed.[9] But now when people look [at the western wall], they will exclaim, 'Behold Vespasian's might! What a strong fortification he demolished!' " Vespasian: "You have done well. But since you disobeyed my command, you are to ascend the roof and throw yourself down. If you live, you live; and if you die, you die." Pangar ascended,

1. The snake is Israel in rebellion against Rome, the amphora is Jerusalem, and, in the next question, the tower is the Temple. R. Yohanan's answer was a plea for leniency in behalf of the Jews.

2. After he was done with the Jews, Vespasian would presently turn on the Arabs, who were their neighbors.

3. Literally, "Only the heart knows whether you are *akel* ('weaving') or *akalkalot* ('twisting')."

4. I.e., permission to found a seminary at Yavneh (Jamnia).

5. Rabban Yohanan was particularly solicitous for Rabban Gamaliel and his family, as they were said to be of the house of David.

6. A town to the southeast of Jaffa.

7. It was Eleazar's reaction to the way the Romans had dealt with Jerusalem.

8. The crossbar of a balance from which scales are suspended.

9. There would have been no relic to show how strong the walls had been.

threw himself down, and died.[1] Thus the curse of Rabban Yohanan ben Zakkai struck him down.

Vespasian went away and sent the wicked Titus in his place. When Titus arrived, he stood up and said, "Where is their God, the Rock in whom they trusted?" (Deut. 32:37). What did Titus do? He took hold of a harlot, entered the Holy of Holies, spread out a Torah scroll, and fornicated with her on it. He then took a sword and slashed the curtain [in front of the Holy of Holies]. At this, a miracle happened: blood began to spurt from the curtain, so that Titus thought he had slain God Himself.

Then he began to revile and curse Him above, saying: One who wages war against a king in the wilderness and is victorious is not as mighty as one who wages war against a king in his own palace and is victorious.

(Abba Hanan said, "Who is a mighty one like unto Thee, O Lord?" [Ps. 89:9]. Who is like You, mighty in self-restraint? Though You heard the insults and revilings of that scoundrel, yet You kept silent! In the school of R. Ishmael, it was taught: "Who is like Thee among the gods [*elim*]?" [Exod. 15:11]. Who is like You among the silent ones [*illemim*]!)

Then Titus took the curtain, folded it to serve as a sack, fetched all the vessels of the Temple, packed them in it, and put them on board ship to accompany him at the triumphal procession in his city.

A giant wave rose up, threatening to sink his ship. So Titus said: Apparently the power of the God of these people is only over water: when Pharaoh came, He drowned him in water; when Sisera came, He drowned him in water. I, too—when I was in His house and in His domain, He could not stand up to me. But now here He has overtaken me and rises up against me, trying to drown me in water. If He is really mighty, let Him come up on dry land and fight with me. A voice went forth from heaven, saying, "O wicked man, son of a wicked man, descendant of the wicked Esau! I have a tiny creature in My world called a gnat. Go up on dry land and wage war against it." Presently Titus succeeded in reaching dry land. When he got to Rome, all the people of Rome went out and hailed him as conqueror of the barbarians. Then they heated a bath for him. He went in and washed himself, and when he came out, they mixed a cup of wine for him. At that moment a gnat appeared, entered through his nose, and proceeded to burrow into his brain for the next seven years.

One day, as Titus was passing by a blacksmith's shop, the gnat heard the noise of a hammer and stopped its burrowing. Titus said: I see there is a remedy! So every day they brought a blacksmith, who hammered away before him. If the blacksmith was a pagan, he was paid four *zuz* a day; if he was a Jew, he was told, "It is enough payment that you see your enemy in such distress." This went on for thirty days, but then the creature got used to the hammering[2] [and went back to its burrowing].

(It is taught: R. Phineas ben Aruva said: I was in company with the notables of Rome and was told that when Titus died, his skull was split open, and inside it there was found a creature resembling a sparrow, two *sela* in weight. Abbaye said: We have a tradition that its beak was of brass and its claws of iron.)

When Titus lay dying, he said: Cremate me and scatter my ashes over the seven seas, so that the God of the Jews should not find me and bring me to trial.

Onkelos son of Kalonikos was the son of Titus's sister. He was thinking about becoming a proselyte. So he went and, with the aid of a necromancer, raised Titus from the dead and asked him, "Who is held in greatest repute in the other world?" Titus: "Israel." "What then," Onkelos asked, "would you say about my joining them?" Titus: "Their observances are so numerous that it is impossible to endure them. Instead, go and attack the Jews in your world, and you will become master over them, for it is written, 'Her adversaries are now masters' [Lam. 1:5]; whoever harasses Israel becomes a master of men." Onkelos asked Titus, "What is your punishment [in the other world]?" Titus: "What I decreed for myself. Every day my ashes are collected and sentence is passed upon me; I am cremated and my ashes are scattered again over the seven seas."

Then Onkelos went and, with the aid of a necromancer, raised Balaam from the dead. He also asked him, "Who is held in greatest repute in the other world?" Balaam: "Israel." "What then," Onkelos asked, "do you say about my joining them?" Balaam: "Thou shalt not seek their peace nor their prosperity all thy days forever" (Deut. 23:7).

Then Onkelos went and, with the aid of a necromancer, raised Jesus [a sinner in Israel] from the dead. He asked him, "Who is held in greatest repute in the other world?" Jesus: "Israel." "What do you say about my joining them?" Jesus: "Seek their welfare, seek not their harm. Whoever touches them touches the apple of God's eye." Observe the difference in behavior between the sinners in Israel and the prophets among the nations of the world.

It is taught that R. Eleazar said: [From the aforementioned tale about the humiliation of Bar Kamtza] you can see what a serious offense it is to put a man to shame. For take note—the Holy One espoused the cause of Bar Kamtza and, as an aftermath, destroyed His house and burned His Temple.[3]

3. Another story [that accounts for Jerusalem's destruction]: A certain man—a carpenter's apprentice—conceived a desire for the wife of his master. There came a time when his master needed to borrow some money. The apprentice said, "Send your wife to me, and I will lend the money to her." The master sent his wife to the apprentice, and she stayed three days with him. Finally, the master went to the apprentice's home and asked, "My wife, whom I sent to you, where is she?" The apprentice replied, "I sent her away at once, but I heard that on her way back some young men had their will with her." "What shall I do?" the master asked. "If you listen to my advice," the apprentice replied, "divorce her." "But," the master said,

1. His fate proved that his intentions against Israel were hostile.
2. Literally, "once it begins threshing, it keeps threshing."

3. B. Git 55b–57a; Gen. R. 10:7; Lam. R. 1:5, §32; ARN 4 and 6; Lev R. 22:3; Eccles. R. 5:8, §4; Yalkut, *Haazinu*, §546.

"she has a large marriage settlement [payable to her upon divorce]." The apprentice: "I will lend you money to pay her settlement." So the master divorced his wife, and the apprentice immediately married her. When the loan fell due and the master was unable to repay it, the apprentice said, "Come and work off your debt with me." Then the apprentice and his wife would sit eating and drinking, while the master waited on them, tears flowing from his eyes and dropping into their cups. From that hour, the doom [of Jerusalem] was sealed.[1]

4. Why was the First Temple destroyed? Because of three evils in it: idolatry, immorality, and bloodshed. But why was the Second Temple destroyed, seeing that during the time it stood people occupied themselves with Torah, with observance of precepts, and with the practice of charity? Because during the time it stood, hatred without rightful cause prevailed. This is to teach you that hatred without rightful cause is deemed as grave as all the three sins of idolatry, immorality, and bloodshed, together.[2]

5. Because of a cock and a hen, King's Mountain was destroyed. How did it happen? It was the custom that when a bride and a bridegroom were being escorted [to the nuptial chamber], a cock and a hen were carried before them, as if to say: Be fruitful and multiply like these fowl. One day, when a band of Roman soldiers passed by, they snatched the cock and the hen from the bridal procession. The Jews fell on the soldiers and beat them up. The soldiers came to Caesar and reported, "The Jews are rebelling against you." So Caesar marched against them.

There was at that time among the Jews a certain Bar Deromi who would leap a *mil*'s distance and was thus able to kill many Romans. So Caesar took off his crown, placed it on the ground, and said, "Master of the universe, may it please You not to deliver me and my kingdom into the hands of one man." Presently Bar Deromi was tripped up by his own mouth, for he bragged, "Mayest thou not just as well, O God, cast us off, since there is no need for Thee, O God, to go forth with our hosts?" (Ps. 60:12).[3] Then, when Bar Deromi went into a privy, a draco came and pulled out his lower bowel, and he died. At that, Caesar remarked, "Since a miracle has been wrought for me, I will let them off this time." So he left them and went away. They leaped for joy; they ate and drank and lit so many lamps that the design on a seal a *mil* away could be made out by their light. [Informed of their rejoicing] Caesar said, "These Jews are making merry at my expense and ridiculing me!" And he returned to attack them. According to R. Assi, three hundred thousand men with drawn swords invaded King's Mountain, and for three days and three nights kept up the slaughter on one side of the city, while on the other side dancing and feasting were still going on. So big was the area that the people on one side were unaware of what was happening on the other side.

"The Lord hath swallowed up all the habitations of Jacob and hath not pitied" (Lam. 2:2). R. Yohanan said: The verse refers to the sixty myriads of towns that King Yannai had on King's Mountain. Each of them had as many inhabitants as had come out of Egypt. Ulla said: I saw that area—it cannot hold even sixty myriads of reeds. As a matter of fact, a certain heretic taunted R. Hanina: You tell a heap of lies. R Hanina replied: Palestine is called "land of the deer" (Jer. 3:19).[4] Just as the skin of a deer shrinks after the animal is killed, so that it cannot hold its flesh, so the Land of Israel has ample room when it is inhabited; but when not inhabited, it seems to shrink.[5]

6. It is told that when Trajan[6] was about to execute Lilianus and his brother Pappus in Laodicea [Lydia], he said to them, "If you are of the people of Hananiah, Mishael, and Azariah, let your God come and deliver you from my hand, as He delivered Hananiah, Mishael, and Azariah from the hand of Nebuchadnezzar." They replied, "Hananiah, Mishael, and Azariah were utterly righteous men, and they merited having a miracle wrought for their sake. Besides, Nebuchadnezzar was a worthy king, deserving to have a miracle wrought through him. But as for you, you are a wicked and mindless man—you do not deserve to have a miracle wrought through you. As for us, no doubt we have been condemned by Him who is everywhere to be put to death. So even if you do not execute us, He who is everywhere has many other executioners—many bears, many lions, many leopards—who can attack and kill us. The only reason the Holy One handed us over to you is that He intends to exact vengeance from you for our blood." Because they dared speak thus, he killed them at once. It is reported that hardly had Trajan's entourage moved from there than two officials arrived from Rome and split Trajan's skull with clubs.[7]

7. Another tale: The wife of Trajan—may his bones be ground to dust—gave birth to a child on the night of the ninth of Av, while the Jews [of Rome] were mourning [the destruction of the Temple]. The child died on Hanukkah.[8] The Jews wondered: What shall we do? Shall we kindle the lights or not? They decided: Let us kindle them, come upon us what may. And they kindled them. Certain persons maligned the Jews to Trajan's wife, saying, "Those Jews! When your child was born, they mourned; and when it died, they kindled lights!" She sent a letter to her husband: "Instead of subduing the barbarians, come back and subdue these Jews who have revolted against you." He boarded a ship, figuring to make the voyage in ten days, but the wind favored him and brought him home in five. On his arrival, he entered an academy where he found

1. B. Git 58a.
2. B. Yoma 9b.
3. JV: "Hast not Thou, O God, cast us off, and Thou goest not forth, O God, with our hosts?"
4. JV: "land, the goodliest." But *tzevi* ("the goodliest") also means "deer."
5. B. Git 57a.
6. It is suggested by Paul Cassell that Trajan is a misreading for Seron, a commander of the army of Syria in the days of Judah Maccabee (Ben-Zion Luria, Megillat Ta, p. 191).
7. B. Ta 18b.
8. The Feast of Dedication, which marks the victory of Judah Maccabee over Antiochus Epiphanes. It is observed by kindling lights for eight days.

Jews occupied with the verse "The Lord will bring a nation against thee from far . . . as the vulture swoopeth down" (Deut. 28:49). So Trajan said to them, "I am that vulture. I figured to come in ten days, but the wind brought me in five." He surrounded them with his legions and slaughtered them. Then he said to the women, "Yield to my legions, or I will do to you what I did to your men." They replied, "Do to the women what you did to the men!" He promptly surrounded them with his legions and slaughtered them, so that their blood mingled with that of the men and kept streaming as far as the river Kypris.[1] And the holy spirit kept crying out, "For these things I weep" (Lam. 1:16).[2]

8. "Bethar[3] was destroyed through the shaft of a royal litter."

When a boy was born, it was the custom to plant a cedar tree; and when a girl was born, an acacia. When they wed, the tree [planted at birth] was cut down and the wedding canopy made from its branches. One day, as Caesar's daughter was passing [through Bethar], the shaft of her litter broke. Her servants cut down a cedar tree and repaired the litter with it. Immediately, the Jews fell upon the servants and beat them up. The Romans went and told Caesar, "The Jews are rebelling against you." And so he marched against them.

According to R. Yohanan, eighty thousand trumpeters besieged Bethar. Ben Koziva was located in the city, and he had with him two hundred thousand men, each with an amputated finger.[4] The sages sent him the message: "How long will you continue to maim the men of Israel?" He said, "How else are they to be tested?" They answered, "Let anyone who cannot uproot a cedar from Lebanon while riding a horse be denied enrollment in your army."

Thus, Ben Koziva came to have an army composed of two hundred thousand men with amputated fingers and another two hundred thousand who had uprooted cedars of Lebanon. No matter how many troops Hadrian sent against them, these men would go forth and slay them. So the Romans decided: There is no way of remedying the situation unless we bring a crown for Hadrian, place it on his head, and hail him as emperor.

One day, as Ben Koziva's men went out to battle, an old man met them and said, "May your God be your help." Their mouths tripped them up, and they said in reply, "May He neither help nor hinder—'Mayest Thou not, O God, just as well cast us off, since there is no need for Thee, O God, to go forth with our hosts?' " (Ps. 60:12).

How great was the strength of Ben Koziva? He would intercept the stones shot by Roman catapults with one of his knees, heave them back, and thus slay ever so many Roman soldiers. When R. Akiva beheld Ben Koziva, he exclaimed, " 'A star (*kokhav*) has risen out of Jacob' [Num. 24:17]—Koziva[5] has risen out of Jacob! He is the king Messiah." R. Yohanan ben Torta responded, "Akiva, grass will be growing out of your cheeks and David's son the Messiah will still not have come."[6]

Hadrian Caesar laid siege to Bethar for three and a half years.[7] In the city was R. Eleazar of Modiim,[8] who day after day wore sackcloth and fasted.[9] Day after day, he prayed, "Master of the universe, sit not in judgment this day!" After a time, Hadrian seriously considered returning home.[10] But just then a Cuthean came and said to Hadrian, "My lord, so long as that old rooster wallows in ashes, you will not conquer the city. Give me time, and I will do something that will enable you to subdue it today." He entered Bethar through the gate of the city, where he found R. Eleazar standing and praying. He [walked over to him and] pretended to whisper in his ear. People went and informed Ben Koziva, "Your uncle, R. Eleazar, wishes to surrender the city to Hadrian." Ben Koziva had the Cuthean brought before him and asked him, "What did you say to R. Eleazar, and what did he say to you?" The Cuthean replied, "If I tell you, the king will kill me; and if I do not tell you, you will kill me. It is better that I kill myself, so that the secrets of the government will not be divulged." Ben Koziva was thus convinced that R. Eleazar wanted to surrender the city. So he sent for R. Eleazar, had him brought into his presence, and asked him, "What did that Cuthean tell you?" He answered, "I do not know what he whispered in my ear. I was standing in prayer, so that I did not hear a thing." "And what did you say to him?" "Not a word." Ben Koziva flew into a rage and kicked him once with his foot so fiercely that he killed him. At this, a divine voice came forth and proclaimed, "Woe to the worthless shepherd who abandons his flock! The sword shall descend upon his arm, and upon his right eye" (Zech. 11:17). It intimated to Ben Koziva: "You smashed the arm of Israel and blinded their right eye; therefore shall your arm wither and your right eye be utterly darkened!" (ibid.). The sins [of the people] caused Bethar to be captured, and Ben Koziva was slain.

When his head was brought to Hadrian, he asked, "Who killed him?" A Cuthean said, "I killed him." "Bring his body to me," he ordered. The Cuthean went off to get it and found a snake curled around its neck. When Hadrian heard about the snake, he exclaimed, "If his God had not slain him, who else could have?"

The eighty thousand trumpeters entered Bethar and went about slaying men, women, and little children, so that their blood flowed in streams out of doorways, even out of grates and pivots. Horses waded in blood up to their nostrils, and the blood flow was so swift that it rolled stones weighing forty *seah* over and over, until it finally flowed into the sea, coloring the sea a distance of four *mil*. You

1. Perhaps a misreading of Tybris (Tiber). So Leon Nemoy.
2. Lam. R. 1:16, §45; Lam. R., ed. Buber, p. 83; P. Suk 5:1, 55b.
3. In southern Palestine, the center of the revolt of Bar Kokhba (Bar Kozeva).
4. As a test of fortitude, he ordered each recruit to cut off a finger.
5. Hence, not *Koziva* ("false hope") but *kokhba* ("star").
6. You will be dead in your grave a long time.
7. "This is not historically correct and is a reminiscence of Vespasian's siege of Jerusalem. The siege lasted about a year and the whole campaign three and a half years. It is probable, however, that the Midrash includes in this period the battles preceding the actual siege" (Lam. R., Soncino, p. 158, n. 4).
8. A small town near Jerusalem, famous as the home of the Maccabees.
9. In order to avert the fate that was threatening the people of Bethar.
10. So great was the power of R. Eleazar's piety.

might suppose that Bethar was close to the sea. Not at all—it was a whole *mil* distant from it.

Now, Hadrian owned a large vineyard eighteen *mil* square, covering an area equal to the area from Tiberias to Sepphoris. They surrounded it with a kind of fence made up of the corpses of Bethar's slain, their bodies placed upright with arms spread out. By Hadrian's decree, those corpses remained unburied, until finally another king came to power and ordered their burial.

It is taught that R. Eliezer the Elder said: [From that blood] two streams formed in the valley of Yadaim, one flowing in one direction and the other in the opposite direction. The sages estimated that the streams were two parts water and one part blood.

We are taught: For seven years the nations of the world harvested their vineyards without manuring them, because they were so well fertilized by Jewish blood.

It is reported in the name of Rabban Simeon ben Gamaliel: There were five hundred schools in the city of Bethar. In the smallest there were no fewer than five hundred children, who used to say: Should the enemies come at us, we will go forth with our styluses and gouge out their eyes. When Israel's sins brought it about that the enemies did prevail and were able to capture the children, they wrapped them in the scrolls they had been studying and set them on fire.

R. Yohanan said: Three hundred brains of children were found on a single stone.

R. Assi said: Four *kav* of brains were found on a single stone.[1]

The Wickedness of Hadrian

9. A Jew passed in front of Hadrian and greeted him. The king asked, "Who are you?" He answered, "I am a Jew." Hadrian exclaimed, "How dare a Jew pass in front of Hadrian and greet him?" and ordered, "Off with his head!" Another Jew passed and, seeing what happened to the first man, did not greet him. Hadrian asked, "Who are you?" He answered, "A Jew." He exclaimed, "How dare a Jew pass in front of Hadrian without giving a greeting?" and again ordered, "Off with his head!" His senators said, "We cannot understand your actions. He who greeted you was put to death, and he who did not greet you was put to death!" Hadrian replied, "Do you dare advise me how I am to execute those I hate?" And the holy spirit kept crying out, "O Lord, Thou hast seen my wrong. . . . Thou hast seen all their vengeance and all their devices against me" (Lam. 3:59–60).[2]

10. Hadrian—may his bones be ground to dust—set up three garrisons, one in Emmaus, another in Kefar Lekatia, and the third in Bethlehem of Judea,[3] saying, "He who succeeds in evading the one will be captured by the other, and he who succeeds in evading the other will be captured by the third." He also sent out heralds to proclaim, "Wherever there is a Jew in hiding, let him come forth—the king is pleased to give him assurance [of safety]." Those who understood [the ruse] did not come out [from their hiding places]; but those who did not understand—the sort described in Scripture as "Ephraim has acted like a silly dove, without understanding" (Hos. 7:11)—came out and found themselves trapped. All of these were presently gathered in the valley of Beth Rimmon.[4] Hadrian said to the captain in command, "By the time I consume this slice of white bread and the leg of this fowl, I expect to find not even one of them still standing on his two feet." At once his legions surrounded the Jews and slaughtered them, so that their blood streamed [to the coast and colored the sea] as far as Cyprus.[5]

Those who remained hidden [in caves] used to go out at night, follow the scent of the corpses of their dead, and bring back some, which they ate. Every day one of their number would go out and forage for a corpse. Once one of them, a young man, went out and found the corpse of his slain father. He picked it up, hid it, and put a marker over it. Then he came back to the cave and reported, "I found nothing." So they said, "Let another person go." The other scout went out and, led by the scent of that same corpse, found it and brought it back. After they had eaten, he was asked, "Where did you bring this corpse from?" He replied, "From such-and-such a corner." The young man who went out first asked him, "What kind of marker was over it?" "Such-and-such a marker." The young man moaned, "Woe to him who has consumed the flesh of his own father."[6]

Zion's Precious Children

11. The story of Doeg son of Joseph, whose father died, leaving him a small child with his mother. Every day his mother would measure his height by handbreadths, estimating the weight he had gained, and give its equivalent in gold to the Sanctuary. Yet when the enemy prevailed, she slaughtered him and ate him. Concerning her, Jeremiah lamented, "Alas, women eat their fruit, the children that are dandled in their arms!" (Lam. 2:20). The holy spirit replied, "Shall the priest and the prophet be slain in the Sanctuary of the Lord?" (ibid.).[7]

12. A story of four hundred boys and girls who were carried off for immoral purposes. They sensed what they were wanted for and said among themselves, "If we drown in the sea, we shall attain life in the world-to-come." The eldest among them cited the verse "The Lord said: 'I will bring back from Bashan, I will bring them back [to life]

---

1. Lam. R. 2:2, §4; P. Ta 4:5, 68d; B. Git 57 and 58; Lam. R., ed. Buber, pp. 101–4.
2. Lam. R. 3:60, §9. Cf. Romans 8:26–27, where the holy spirit, as it were, personifying Israel, prays to God on Israel's behalf. Brother Caedmon Holmes (Abbey of St. Gregory the Great, Portsmouth, R.I.).
3. Strategic points in preventing the escape of Jews from the country.
4. See 2 Kings 5:18. The valley where the temple to the idol Rimmon was located.
5. The text has "the river of Cyprus." See above, p. 194, n. 1.
6. Lam. R. 1:16, §45; Lam. R., ed. Buber, p. 82.
7. The reference is to the prophet Zechariah son of Jehoiada the Priest. See above, chap. 7, §13. B. Yoma 38b and En Yaakov, ad loc.

from the depths of the sea' " (Ps. 68:23) and interpreted it as promising: "I will bring back from Bashan," from between the lion's teeth (*ba-shen* [*ben shinne*]); "I will bring them back from the depths of the sea"—those who drown in the sea. When the girls heard this, all of them jumped up and leaped into the sea. The boys then drew an inference for themselves, saying: If they—for whom being mounted for the sexual act is natural—prefer death to submission, we—for whom being mounted is unnatural—should all the more prefer death to submission. At that, they also leaped into the sea. Of them, Scripture says, "It is for Thy sake that we are slain all day long, that we are regarded as sheep to be slaughtered" (Ps. 44:23).[1]

13. It is related that the son and daughter of R. Ishmael ben Elisha were carried off [and bought] by two masters, who happened to meet after a while. One said, "I have a manservant—in the entire world, no man is his equal in appearance." The other said, "I have a maidservant—in the entire world, all of it, no woman is her equal in beauty." So they decided: Let us wed them to each other and share the children. [That night] they put them in a darkened chamber, where the boy sat down in one corner and the girl sat down in the opposite corner. The boy said to himself: Am I, a priest, descended from high priests, to wed a slavegirl? The girl said to herself: Am I, a priestess, descended from high priests, to be wed to a slave? And so all night they wept. When day dawned, they recognized each other, fell on each other's neck, and continued to weep bitterly until their souls left them. For them, Jeremiah lamented, "For these I weep; mine eye, mine eye runneth down with water" (Lam. 1:16).[2]

14. A story of a certain woman named Zaphenath daughter of Peniel (she was called Zaphenath because all gazed [*tzophin*] at her beauty, and "daughter of Peniel" because she was the daughter of a high priest privileged to minister in the inner shrine [*lifne ve-lifnim*]). It is told that after she was taken captive, her captor abused her the entire night. In the morning he put seven wraps around her and took her out to sell her. A certain man, who was exceptionally ugly, came by and said, "Show me her beauty." The captor replied, "You good-for-nothing, if you want to buy, buy her. I can assure you that in the entire world, all of it, no woman equals her in beauty." "Nevertheless," the would-be buyer said, "I want to have a look." The captor took six wraps off her, and she herself tore off the seventh, sprinkled ashes upon herself, and cried out, "Lord of the universe, even if You have no pity on us, why have You no pity on the sanctity of Your mighty Name?"[3] With her in mind, Jeremiah quoted God as saying, "O daughter of My people, gird thee with sackcloth and sprinkle ashes upon thyself . . . for the spoiler shall suddenly come upon us" (Jer. 6:26). Jeremiah ended by saying not "upon thee" but "upon us"—meaning: the spoiler is come, if one dare say such a thing, upon Me and upon thee.[4]

15. A story of a young girl taken captive together with her ten maidservants. A Gentile bought her, and she was brought up as part of his household. One day, when he gave her her pitcher and said, "Go out and bring me some water," one of the girl's maidservants jumped up and took it from her. "What is the meaning of this?" he demanded. "By the life of your head, master!" the maidservant replied. "I was one of five hundred maidservants of this girl's mother!" When he heard these words, he set the girl free, along with her ten maidservants.

Another story: A young girl was taken captive. A Gentile bought her, and she was brought up as part of his household. The angel in charge of dreams appeared to him and told him, "Send this girl from your house." But the Gentile's wife said, "Do not send her away." Then the angel in charge of dreams appeared to him again and said, "If you do not send her away, I will kill you."

So he sent her away but followed after her. I will go, he said to himself, and see what happens to this girl.

As she was walking along the road, she grew thirsty and stepped down to drink water from a fountain. But when she put her hand on the fountain's wall, a serpent leaped at her and bit her, and she died, her body left floating on the surface of the water. The Gentile came down, took hold of the body, lifted it, and buried it. Then he came home and said to his wife, "This people whom you have just seen something of—none other than their Father in heaven Himself is angry with them."[5]

16. It is taught: It was said of Nakdimon ben Gorion that when he walked from his home to the academy, woolen cloths were spread beneath his feet, and the poor, following behind, rolled them up [and kept them for themselves].

It is told of the daughter of Nakdimon ben Gorion that, to provide perfumes for her toilet, the sages granted her four hundred gold denars a day [out of her deceased husband's estate]. Nevertheless, dissatisfied, she said, "May you grant such skimpy allowances to your own daughters!" They replied, "Amen."

Another story. When the sages granted to the daughter-in-law of Nakdimon an allowance from Sabbath eve to Sabbath eve of two *seah* of wine for her puddings, she, dissatisfied, said to them, "May you grant such skimpy allowances to your own daughters!" This time they did not say, "Amen," because she was then a woman awaiting [the decision whether or not] her brother-in-law [would marry her].[6]

R. Eleazar son of R. Zadok said: May I [not] behold the consolation [of Zion] if I have not seen the daughter of Nakdimon ben Gorion picking up barley grains in Acco from among horses' hoofs. I then applied to her the verse "If thou know not, O thou fairest of women, go follow the

1. B. Git 57b.
2. B. Git 58a.
3. Such desecration of a woman's honor is deemed desecration of God's Name.
4. B. Git 58a.
5. ARN 17.
6. They did not wish their own daughters to be widows and await the decision of a brother-in-law to marry them or free them by the rite of *halitzah*.

tracks of the sheep and graze thy kids" (Song 1:8). Read not, "Thy kids" (*gediyyotayikh*), but, "Thine own person" (*geviyyotayikh*).

Another story. When Rabban Yohanan ben Zakkai left Jerusalem riding on an ass, with his disciples following him, he saw a girl picking barley grains out of the dung of some Arabs' cattle. The moment she saw him, [not wishing to be recognized] she wrapped her hair about her face and stood up before him: "Master, feed me." "My daughter," he asked her, "who are you?" She remained silent. When he asked her again, "Who are you?" she replied, "I am the daughter of Nakdimon ben Gorion." "My daughter, where did the wealth of your father's house go?" "Master, is there not a proverb current in Jerusalem: 'Money has no (*hsr*) salt to preserve it'?" (Others read: Only *hsd*,—"charity"—can preserve money.)[1] "And where is the wealth of your father-in-law's house?" "Master, the one came and caused the other to disappear.[2] Do you remember, Master, when you signed my *ketubbah?*" "I remember," he said to his disciples, "that when I signed the *ketubbah* of this woman, I read therein, 'A thousand thousand gold denars from her father's house besides [the amount] from her father-in-law's house.' "[3] Then Rabban Yohanan ben Zakkai wept and said, "How fortunate are Israel! When they do the will of Him who is everywhere, no nation or tongue can prevail over them. But when they do not do the will of Him who is everywhere, He delivers them into the power of an ignoble people; indeed, not only into the power of an ignoble people, but into the power of beasts belonging to an ignoble people.[4]

The Holy One Mourns

17. It is reported in the name of R. Joshua ben Levi: The Holy One summoned the ministering angels and asked them, "When a king of flesh and blood loses a dear one and he wishes to mourn, what is customary for him to do?" They replied, "He hangs sackcloth over his door." God said, "I will do likewise." Hence it is written, "I clothe the heavens with blackness, and I make sackcloth their covering" (Isa. 50:3).

"What else does a king of flesh and blood do [when mourning]?" They replied, "He extinguishes the lanterns." God said, "I will do likewise." Hence it is written, "The sun and the moon are become black, and the stars withdraw their shining" (Joel 4:15).

"What else does a king of flesh and blood do?" They replied, "He walks barefoot." God said, "I will do likewise." Hence it is stated, "The Lord, in the whirlwind and in the storm is His way, and the clouds are the dust beneath His [bare] feet" (Nah. 1:3).

"What else does a king of flesh and blood do?" They replied, "He rends his purple robe." God said to them, "I will do likewise." Hence it is written, "After the Lord did what He purposed, He rent His purple robe (*bitza imrato*)"[5] (Lam. 2:17).

"What else does a king of flesh and blood do?" They replied, "He sits in silence." God said, "I will do likewise." Hence it is stated, "He sitteth alone and keepeth silence, because he was taken away" (Lam. 3:28).[6]

18. "My soul shall weep in a secret place for pride" (Jer. 13:17). What is meant by "a secret place"? R. Samuel bar Unia said in the name of Rav: The Holy One has a place where He weeps—it is called the "secret place." And what is meant by "for [your] pride"? R. Samuel bar Isaac said: For Israel's pride, which was taken from them and given to the heathen. R. Samuel bar Nahmani said: For the pride of the kingdom of Heaven, which was taken away.

"Mine eye shall drop tears after tears, and run down with tears, because the Lord's flock is carried away captive" (Jer. 13:17). R. Eleazar asked: Why are tears mentioned here three times? Once for the First Temple, once again for the Second Temple, and once more for Israel exiled from their home.[7]

19. R. Aha said: The Presence will never move from the Temple's western wall, for it is said, "Behold, He standeth behind our wall" (Song 2:9).[8]

Menahem the Comforter

20. The day the Temple was destroyed, the redeemer was born.

It happened that while a certain man was plowing, his heifer lowed. An Arab passed by, heard the lowing, and asked, "Who are you?" He answered, "I am a Jew." The Arab said, "Jew, O Jew, unharness your heifer and unhitch your plow [and go into mourning]." "Why?" "Because the Temple of the Jews is destroyed." "How do you know this?" "I know it from the lowing of your heifer." While they were conversing, the heifer lowed again. The Arab said, "Jew, O Jew, harness your heifer and hitch up your plow, because the Messiah, deliverer of Israel, has been born." "What is his name?" "His name is Menahem, 'Comforter.' " "What is his father's name?" "Hezekiah." "Where does he live?" "In Birat Arba, in Bethlehem of Judah."[9]

The man immediately sold his heifer, sold his plow, and became a merchant for children's felt garments. He journeyed from one region to another and from one city to another until he reached that place. Women came from all the villages in the area to buy felt garments from him,

---

1. Because the members of her family were not charitable, they lost their money.
2. The two were mixed together, so that when one estate was lost, the other disappeared with it.
3. The addition made to her *ketubbah* by the bridegroom.
4. B. Ket 65–67; ARN 17.
5. JV: "He performed His word." But *bitza*, ("performed") may also mean "rent," and *imrato* ("His word") may be read "His robe." This is an allusion to the curtain before the Holy of Holies, which He allowed Titus to rend.
6. Lam. R. 1:1, §1.
7. B. Hag. 5b.
8. Tanhuma B, *Shemot*, §10.
9. In P. Ber. 5a, the reading is: "in the royal capital of Bethlehem."

except for one woman—the mother of Menahem the Comforter—who bought nothing. Then he heard the voices of the other women urging her, "Mother of Menahem, mother of Menahem, come and buy felt garments for your son." The mother: "I would rather have Israel's enemies strangled." They asked, "Why [do you say such things]?" She: "Because the day he was born, the Temple was destroyed." The man said to her, "I am confident that even as at your son's arrival it was destroyed, so because of his arrival it will be rebuilt." The mother: "But I have no money." The man: "That is of no concern to me. Come and take for your son whatever he needs. After a while, I will come to your house, and you will pay me." Some time later, he came back to the city and said to himself: I will go and see that child to find out what has been happening to him. When he came to the woman and asked, "Your child—what has been happening to him?" she replied, "Right after you saw me, winds and storms came, snatched him out of my hand, and carried him off and away."

Of the foregoing, Scripture says, "Menahem the Comforter is far from me, even he who should revive my spirit" (Lam. 1:16).[1]

The Mourners for Zion

21. Our masters taught: When the Temple was destroyed the second time,[2] large numbers in Israel became ascetics, binding themselves neither to eat meat nor to drink wine. R. Joshua got into conversation with them and said, "My sons, why do you eat no meat and drink no wine?" They replied, "Shall we eat meat, which formerly was brought as an offering on the altar, now that the altar has ceased to be? Shall we drink wine, which formerly was poured as a libation on the altar, now that it is poured no longer?" He said to them, "If so, we should eat no bread, because the meal offerings have ceased." They: "Perhaps we will manage with fruit."

"We should not eat fruit either, because firstfruits are offered no more."

"Perhaps we will manage with other fruits.[3]

He: "Well, then, we should not drink water, because the rite of pouring water[4] is no longer observed. [Since they had no answer] they kept silent. So he said to them, "My sons, come and let me advise you. Not to mourn at all is impossible, because the decree that the Temple be destroyed has been executed [and requires mourning]. But to mourn too much is also impossible, because we may not impose a hardship on the community unless the majority can endure it. Therefore the sages have ordained the following: A man may plaster his house, but he should leave a small space uncovered. A man who is preparing all that is needed for a feast should leave out some small ingredient. And if a woman is putting on all her ornaments, she must omit one of them. For it is said, 'If I forget thee, O Jerusalem . . . let my tongue cleave to the roof of my mouth' [Ps. 137:5–6]. He who mourns for Jerusalem will merit seeing the renewal of her joy, as is said, 'Rejoice ye with Jerusalem . . . join in her jubilation, all ye that have mourned for her' " (Isa. 66:10).

It is taught that R. Ishmael ben Elisha said: Since the day of the destruction of the Temple, we should by rights bind ourselves to eat no meat and drink no wine. However, we may impose no hardship on the community unless the majority can endure it. And from the day that a foreign government has come into power, which issues cruel decrees against us and forbids us to observe the Torah and its precepts, and does not allow us to enter into the "week of the son"[5]—some say, "the deliverance of the son"[6]—we ought by rights to bind ourselves not to marry nor to beget children. But the result would be that the seed of our father Abraham would of itself come to an end. Rather, let Israel go their way—it is better that they should err in ignorance than in presumptuousness.[7]

22. R. Akiva said: He who works on the ninth of Av will never see a sign of blessing. But the sages differed: Only he who works on the ninth of Av and does not mourn for Jerusalem will not see the renewal of her joy, as is said, "Rejoice ye with Jerusalem . . . join in her jubilation, all ye that have mourned for her" (Isa. 66:10). Hence it is said: He who mourns for Jerusalem will merit seeing the renewal of her joy; and he who does not mourn for Jerusalem will not see the renewal of her joy.[8]

23. "Weeping she maketh weep (Lam. 1:2).[9] She weeps and makes the Holy One weep with her. She weeps and makes the ministering angels weep with her. She weeps and makes heaven and earth weep with her. She weeps and makes mountains and hills weep with her.[10]

24. "She weepeth, yea, she weepeth in the night" (Lam. 1:2).[11] Why this double weeping? Rabbah said in the name of R. Yohanan: Once for the First Temple and once for the Second. "In *the* night"—because of the goings-on during a particular night, the night of which it is written, "All the congregation lifted up their voice, and cried, and the people wept that night" (Num. 14:1).[12] The Holy One said to Israel, "You wept without cause; and so I will make for you an occasion for weeping that will continue throughout the generations." Another interpretation: "In the night"—when a man weeps at night, his voice is heard better.[13] And another interpretation: When a man weeps at night, the stars and planets weep with him. Still another interpretation: When a man weeps at night, whoever hears him weeps [in sympathy.]

1. P. Ber 2:4, 4a; Lam. R. 1:16, §51.
2. In 70 C.E.
3. Fruit ripening later than the firstfruits.
4. On Sukkot. See above, chap. 9, §83.
5. The male infant is circumcised on the eighth day after his birth.
6. *Yeshuat-pidyon ha-ben*, the redemption of the firstborn son on the thirty-first day after his birth. See Exod. 13:13 and Num. 18:16.
7. B. BB 60b and En Yaakov, ad loc.
8. B. Ta 30b.
9. JV: "She weepeth sore in the night."
10. Lam. R. 1:2, §23.
11. Literal meaning of Lam. 1:2.
12. After the discouraging report of the spies.
13. Because of the stillness of the night.

A story of a woman who was a neighbor of Rabban Gamaliel: When her child died, she wept for him during the night. On hearing her, Rabban Gamaliel was reminded of the destruction of the Temple and wept in sympathy with her, so much that his eyelids seemed to disappear. The next day, when his disciples noticed how swollen his eyes were, they removed the woman from his neighborhood.[1]

25. Rabbi [Judah I, the Patriarch] was once holding the book of Lamentations and reading in it. When he came to the verse "He hath cast down from heaven unto the earth the beauty of Israel" (Lam. 2:1), the book slipped from his hand as he said, "From a vault so high to a pit so deep."[2]

26. Rav said: A sigh breaks down half of the human body [as witness this story]: A Jew and an idolater were once walking together on the same road, and the idolater could not keep pace with the Jew. When the idolater reminded him of the destruction of the Temple, the Jew [grew faint] and sighed, but still the idolater was unable to keep pace with him. "Do you Jews not say," the idolater asked, "that a sigh breaks down half of a person's body?" "This applies only," the Jew replied, "to a fresh calamity, not to one with which we are already familiar. As people say: A woman accustomed to miscarriages is not alarmed when another occurs."[3]

27. "All conversation (*siah*) is of the field" (Gen. 2:5).[4] All conversation of mortals concerns the growth of crops in the fields: "Have the fields yielded produce? Have the fields not yielded produce?" The prayers of mortals, too, concern the growth of crops in the fields: "My Lord, may the fields yield produce! My Lord, may the yield of the fields prosper." But Israel's prayer is concerned solely with the "field" that is the Temple: "Master of the universe, may the Temple be rebuilt. Master of the universe, when will the Temple be rebuilt?"[5]

28. R. Hisda quoted the verse "Thus saith the Lord God: 'When the miter is removed, the crown is taken off' " (Ezek. 21:31) and asked: What has the miter to do with the crown? It is to teach you that when the miter is worn by the high priest, there is a crown on the head of every man; but when the miter has been removed from the head of the high priest, the crown is removed from the head of every man.[6]

Since the Temple Was Destroyed

29. Since the day the Temple was destroyed, there is no laughter for the Holy One, nor does the firmament appear in its full clarity.

R. Eleazar said: Since the day the Temple was destroyed, a wall of iron has been interposed between Israel and their Father in heaven.

R. Phinehas ben Yair said: Since the Temple was destroyed, sages and freemen are put to shame and walk with covered heads, and men of good deeds have grown feeble, while men of violence and men given to slander prevail. Nobody inquires [about Israel's plight]; nobody prays [in Israel's behalf]; and nobody asks [about the welfare of his neighbor]. Upon whom then are we to rely? Upon our Father in heaven.

The elder R. Eliezer said: Since the day the Temple, our beloved house, was destroyed, the sages began to be like schoolteachers, schoolteachers like synagogue sextons, synagogue sextons like disciples, and disciples like common people; and common people are becoming more and more debased. And there is none to inquire [about Israel's plight] and none to pray [in Israel's behalf]. Upon whom then are we to rely? Upon our Father in heaven.

Rabban Simeon ben Gamaliel said in the name of R. Joshua: Ever since the Temple was destroyed, there is no day without a curse.

Rava said: And the curse of each day is greater than that of the preceding day.[7]

30. R. Jeremiah ben Eleazar said: Ever since the Temple was destroyed,[8] it is enough for the world to use only two letters[9] [of the tetragrammaton], *yod* and *he*, as is said, "Let everything that hath breath praise by saying *Yah*"[10] (Ps. 150:6).[11]

Consolations

31. "If fire break out . . . he that kindled the fire shall surely make restitution" (Exod. 22:5). Hence the Holy One said: It is for Me to make restitution for the fire that I kindled. It was I who kindled the fire in Zion, as is said, "He hath kindled a fire in Zion, which hath devoured the foundations thereof" (Lam. 4:11); and it is I who one day will build it anew by fire, as is said, "For I, saith the Lord, will be unto her a wall of fire round about, and I will be the glory in the midst of her" (Zech. 2:9).[12]

---

1. B. Sanh 104b; Lam. R. 1:2, §24.
2. How great Israel's downfall—from heaven to earth. B. Hag 5b.
3. B. Ket 62a.
4. JV: "No shrub of the field." But *siah* ("shrub") may mean "conversation" and also, as later in the comment, "prayer"; while "field" will be taken to refer to the Temple. See Gen. R. 22:7 and above, chap. 2, §34.
5. Gen. R. 13:2.
6. B. Git 7a.
7. B. AZ 3b and B. Ber 59a (conflated); B. Ber 32b; B. Sot 49a and 48a.
8. And the priests stopped using the tetragrammaton YHVH. See B. Hag 16a.
9. In extolling God, or in ordinary greeting.
10. Spelled YH. To this day, Jews do not pronounce God's full name, YHVH, substituting for it Adonai or Adoshem. Such names as Jehovah or Yahveh, which attempt vocalizing YHVH, are not accepted by the Jews because they do not know how the Ineffable Name was pronounced in the days of the Temple.
11. B. Er 18b.
12. B. BK 60b.

32. As Rabban Gamaliel, R. Eleazar ben Azariah, R. Joshua, and R. Akiva were walking on the road at Puteoli,[1] they could hear the noise of the crowds in Rome, one hundred and twenty *mil* away. Three of the sages burst into weeping, but R. Akiva continued to be cheerful. They asked him: Why are you so cheerful? He replied: Why are you weeping? They: These heathen, who bow down to images and burn incense to idols, live in safety and tranquility, whereas we—whose Temple, the "footstool" of our God,[2] is burned down by fire—are we not to weep? He replied: For that very reason, I am cheerful. If they who offend Him fare thus, how much better by far will fare those who please Him!

Another time, the same sages were coming up to Jerusalem together, and when they reached Mount Scopus they rent their garments. When they got to the Temple Mount and saw a jackal emerging from the Holy of Holies, they began to weep, but R. Akiva laughed. Why, they asked him, are you laughing? He replied: Why are you weeping? They: The place of which Scripture says, "The common man that draweth nigh shall be put to death" (Num. 1:51), is now become the haunt of jackals. Should we not weep? He said to them: For that very reason, I am laughing. For it is written, "And I call reliable witnesses, Uriah the Priest and Zechariah the son of Jeberechiah" (Isa. 8:2).[3] Now what connection is there between Uriah and Zechariah? Did not Uriah live during First Temple, while Zechariah [lived and prophesied] during the Second Temple? Still, Scripture links the [later] prophecy of Zechariah with the [earlier] prophecy of Uriah. In the [earlier] prophecy, [in the days] of Uriah, it is written, "Because of you, Zion shall be plowed as a field, Jerusalem shall become heaps of ruins, and the Temple Mount a shrine in the woods" (Mic. 3:12),[4] and in Zechariah, it is written, "Thus saith the Lord of hosts: There shall yet old men and old women sit in the broad places of Jerusalem" (Zech. 8:4). So long as Uriah's [dire] prophecy had not yet had its fulfillment, I feared that Zechariah's prophecy would not be fulfilled; now that Uriah's prophecy has been fulfilled, it is quite certain that Zechariah's prophecy also is to be fulfilled. They said to him: Akiva, you have comforted us! Akiva, you have comforted us![5]

---

1. A great seaport in Italy. The incident took place during their journey to Rome in the year 95 C.E.
2. Ps. 99:5 and 132:7; Lam. 2:1.
3. Cf. Zech. 1:1.
4. See Jer. 26:18–20.
5. B. Mak 24a–b and En Yaakov, ad loc.; Sif Deut., §43.

PART II

CHAPTER ONE

THE DEEDS OF THE SAGES

R. Simeon ben Shetah (fl. 1st century B.C.E.)

1. After King Yannai[1] massacred the sages, the world was desolate, until Simeon ben Shetah set to and restored the Torah to its pristine glory.[2]

2. Three hundred Nazirites came up [to Jerusalem] in the days of Simeon ben Shetah and sought to bring nine hundred offerings.[3] For one hundred and fifty of the Nazirites, he found grounds for absolution;[4] but for the other one hundred and fifty, he found no such grounds. Then he went to King Yannai and said to him: Three hundred Nazirites have come up, and they look for nine hundred[5] offerings, which they cannot afford. May I suggest that you provide half out of your means, and I shall provide the other half out of mine, so that they will be able to bring the required offerings. King Yannai provided the half out of his means, and the offerings were brought. But then some people came to King Yannai and informed on R. Simeon ben Shetah, saying: You should know that whatever was offered was offered out of your means only, for Simeon ben Shetah provided nothing at all out of his own means. At that, King Yannai became very angry. When R. Simeon ben Shetah heard that the king was angry at him, he fled in fear.

Soon after, some notables from the kingdom of Persia, who were dining at King Yannai's table, said to him, "Our lord king, we remember that there used to be a venerable man here who regaled us with wise sayings. [We miss him.]" Yannai said to his wife, R. Simeon's sister, "Send for him to come back." She replied, "Swear to me that you will not cause him distress, and send him your signet ring, so that he may feel it is safe to come." He swore to her and sent his ring to R. Simeon, who came back at once.

The king asked, "Why did you flee?" R. Simeon replied, "I heard that my lord king was angry with me and I was afraid you were going to put me to death, and so I took the advice in the verse 'Hide thyself but a little moment, until the indignation be overpast' " (Isa. 26:20).

The king asked, "Why did you make a fool of me?" R. Simeon replied, "God forbid! I had no intention of making you appear foolish. You contributed your share out of your wealth and I out of my Torah [my wisdom]. Thus it is said, 'For wisdom extendeth its shade [freely to those who seek relief from the burning sun], just as wealth extendeth its shade' " (Eccles. 7:12).

"But why didn't you tell me?"

"Had I told you, you would not have contributed."

Yannai seated R. Simeon between himself and the queen, and said, "See what honor I pay you." R. Simeon replied, "It is not you who honor me—it is the Torah that honors me, as Ben Sira put it: 'Exalt her and she shall raise thee high, and make thee sit among great men' " (Prov. 4:8 and Ecclesiasticus 11:1). Yannai said to his queen, "You see, he still does not accept [my] authority." Presently he gave R. Simeon a cup [of wine] with which to say grace.[6] R. Simeon said, "How shall I word the grace? Shall I say, 'Blessed be He of whose sustenance Yannai and his companions have eaten'?" Yannai said, "You persist in your contrariness. Never before have I heard Yannai's name included in the grace." R. Simeon: "What do you expect me to say? [The customary] 'Let us say grace for what we have eaten'? [How can I], since I have not eaten?" So food was brought to him, which he ate, and then he uttered the [customary] blessing, "For what we have eaten."[7]

3. One of King Yannai's slaves killed a man. Simeon ben Shetah said to the sages, "Set your eyes [boldly] on him and let us sit in judgment upon him." So they sent word to the king, "Your slave has killed a man." The king sent him to them [to be tried]. But they again sent word to the king, "You, too, must come here, for the Torah says, 'If warning has been given to its owner' [Exod. 21:29], meaning that if an ox has done damage, the owner must come and stand by his ox."[8] The king came, was given a seat next to Simeon ben Shetah, and sat down.

Then Simeon ben Shetah said, "Stand up on your feet, King Yannai, and let the witnesses testify against you." The king replied, "[I shall do it] not when you say so, but when your colleagues say so." Simeon turned to the right, and they looked down to the ground; he turned to the left, and they too looked down to the ground. Simeon ben Shetah said to them, "You appear to be sunk in deep thought. Let the Master of men's thoughts come and requite you." Gabriel immediately came down and smote them to the ground, so that their souls left them. The king was visibly shaken.

1. A Hasmonean king (103–76 B.C.E.).
2. He was responsible for setting up schools for children from the age of five or six (P. Ket, 8, end). B. Kid 66a.
3. At the conclusion of his Naziriteship, a Nazirite was expected to bring a male lamb for a burnt offering, a ewe lamb for a sin offering, and a ram for a peace offering. See Num. 6:14.
4. From the Nazirite vow. Since such absolution was retroactive, it was as though these had never been Nazirites and so were under no obligation to bring offerings.
5. Because one hundred and fifty were absolved from their vows, Simeon in fact needed only one-half the amount he asked the king to pay for. By asking him to contribute one-half of nine hundred, Simeon was actually asking the king to underwrite the entire project.
6. Even though he had not partaken of the meal.
7. Gen. R. 91:3; B. Ber 48a; P. Ber 7:2, 11b.
8. The owner is responsible for his slave, since the latter's legal status is that of a chattel.

Simeon ben Shetah said to him once more, "Stand up on your feet and let the witnesses testify against you. It is not before us that you stand, but before Him who spoke and the world came into being, as is said, 'Both the men, between whom the controversy is, shall stand before the Lord" (Deut. 19:17). At that, King Yannai stood up.[1]

4. It is told of R. Simeon ben Shetah that he once purchased an ass from an Ishmaelite. When his disciples came, they found a jewel suspended from its neck and said to him, "Master, 'The blessing of the Lord, it maketh rich' " (Prov. 10:22). Simeon ben Shetah replied, "I purchased an ass—I did not purchase a precious stone." He went and returned the jewel to the Ishmaelite, who thereafter used to say, "Blessed be the Lord God of Simeon ben Shetah."[2]

5. After R. Simeon ben Shetah was designated head of the Sanhedrin, some people came and told him, "There are eighty witches in a cave in Ashkelon, bent on destroying the world." On that day there was a heavy rainstorm. Still R. Simeon ben Shetah arose at once, gathered eighty young men of tall stature, and took them with him. He gave each one a new jug with a cloak folded up in it, and they placed the jugs upside down on their heads. Then R. Simeon said to them, "When I chirp the first time,[3] put on your cloaks. When I chirp a second time, all of you enter the cave together. After you enter, each of you is to take one of the witches into his arms and lift her off the ground." For such is the way of a witch—once you lift her off the ground, she can do nothing at all.

Then R. Simeon went and stationed himself at the entrance to the cave and called to the witches, "*Oyim, oyim,*[4] open for me, for I am one of you." They asked, "How did you manage to come here bone-dry at such a rainy hour?" He replied, "I walked between the raindrops." They: "What did you come to do here?" He: "To study and to teach, and to have each of you do what she knows." So one intoned whatever [incantation] she intoned and produced a loaf of bread; another intoned something else and produced a cut of meat; a third produced a cooked dish; and a fourth produced wine. Then they asked him, "And you, what can you do?" He said, "I can chirp twice and produce for you eighty young men wearing dry cloaks. They will find joy in you and give joy to you." He chirped once, and the young men put on their cloaks. He chirped a second time, and all of them entered the cave together. R. Simeon said, "Let each select his mate." They picked them up, went out, and hanged them.

The kinsmen of the eighty women were thereby provoked to anger. Two of them came and bore witness to a charge against R. Simeon ben Shetah's son, which made him liable to the death penalty, and he was sentenced to be put to death. On his way to be stoned, he said, "If I am guilty of this iniquity, let not my death be my expiation; but if I am not guilty, may my death be expiation for all my iniquitous deeds and may the collar [of perjury] encircle the necks of the witnesses."

When the witnesses heard what he had said, they retracted and confessed, "We are false witnesses." The father wished to bring his son back [from the place where he was to be stoned]. But the son said, "If you really wish to bring deliverance during your regime,[5] regard me as though I were not your son[6] [and let the Sanhedrin decide my fate].[7]

Honi the Circle Maker and His Progeny (fl. 2d half of 1st century B.C.E.)

6. Our masters taught: Once it happened that most of [the month of] Adar passed by, and rain did not come down. So the people sent word to Honi the Circle Maker: "Pray for rain to fall." He replied, "Go out and bring in the ovens [in which you roast] the paschal lambs, so that they do not disintegrate."[8] He then prayed, but no rain fell. What did he do? He drew a circle, stationed himself within it, as the prophet Habakkuk had done—Habbakkuk, who is quoted as having said, "I will stand upon my watch, and station me within a circle" (Hab. 2:1). Then Honi exclaimed before the Holy One, "Master of the universe, Your children have turned to me because they regard me as a member of Your household. By Your great Name I swear that I will not move from here until You have mercy on Your children." At once rain began to fall drop by drop. His disciples said, "Master, only because of your merit have we been allowed to see you [cause such a miracle] without being struck dead. But it seems to us that the rain is coming down merely to release you from your vow." In reply, he exclaimed, "Not for this [gentle] rain did I pray, but for pouring rain that would fill cisterns, ditches, and caves." The rain immediately came down so furiously that each drop was the size of the mouth of a cask, and the sages estimated that no drop was less than a *log*[9] in bulk. Again the disciples said, "Master, only because of your merit have we been allowed to see you without being struck dead. But it seems to us that the pouring rain is coming down to destroy the world."

Again Honi exclaimed before God, "It is not for this that I prayed, but for rains of benevolence, benediction, and grace." At once the rain moderated to a normal volume but continued so steadily that all the people had to go up to the Temple Mount [to escape the rising waters]. Then they said to Honi, "Master, just as you have prayed for rain to come down, pray now for it to cease." He replied, "I have it by tradition that one may not pray for the cessation of superabundant good. Nevertheless, bring me a bullock for a thank offering." They brought him the bullock. He laid both his hands upon it and said to the Holy One, "Master of the universe, Your people Israel, whom

1. The king was thus made to submit to the jurisdiction of the Sanhedrin. B. Sanh 19b; Tanhuma B, *Shofetim*, §6.
2. Deut. R. 3:3.
3. From the cave, which he was to enter alone.
4. A cry used by sorcerers to summon thier creations.
5. In his days, lawlessness prevailed.
6. Literally, "as ownerless as a threshold."
7. P. Hag 2:2, 77d; Rashi on B. Sanh 44b.
8. These portable ovens were usually made of clay.
9. The equivalent in volume of six eggs; one pint.

You brought out of Egypt, cannot endure either superabundant good or superabundant punishment. When You are angry with them, they cannot endure it; and when You shower superabundant good upon them, they cannot endure it. May it be Your will that the rain cease and there be relief for the world." Immediately a wind blew, the clouds dispersed, and the sun shone. The people went out into the fields and began to gather mushrooms and truffles.

Simeon ben Shetah sent word to Honi: "Were you not Honi, I would place you under a ban.[1] But what can I do to you, seeing that you ingratiate yourself with Him who is everywhere, who then grants you your wish, just like a son who ingratiates himself with his father, who then grants him his wish. Thus the son may say, 'Father, take me to where I may bathe in warm water,' and he takes him there; 'to where I may shower in cold water,' and he takes him there; 'Give me walnuts, almonds, peaches, and pomegranates,' and he gives them to him. Of you [Honi], Scripture says, 'Thy Father-and-thy-Mother[2] is glad, therefore she [the congregation of Israel] that bore thee must likewise rejoice' " (Prov. 23:25).

Our masters taught: They who sat in the Chamber of Hewn Stone [the Sanhedrin] sent the following missive to Honi the Circle Maker: "Thou decreest a thing, and because of thee it is established" (Job 22:28ff.)—[on the earth] below you decree, and [in heaven] above the Holy One fulfills your word. "And light shines upon thy ways" (ibid.)—with your prayer you give light to a generation in darkness. "When they were cast down, thou saidst, 'There is lifting up' " (ibid.)—with your prayer you lifted the spirit of a generation that was cast down. "The lowly person thou savest" (ibid.)—with your prayer you saved a generation whom [sin] brought low. "Thou didst deliver him that is not innocent" (ibid.)—with your prayer you delivered a generation that is not innocent. "Yea, it was delivered through the cleanness of thy hands" (ibid.)—you, through the deeds of your clean hands, have delivered it.[3]

7. R. Yohanan said: Through all the days of that righteous man, he was troubled about the meaning of the verse "A Song of Ascents. When the Lord brought back those that returned to Zion, we were like unto them that dream" (Ps. 126:1). Is it possible for a man to doze off and dream continuously for seventy years?[4] [But the following incident clarified the verse's meaning for him.] One day, as he was walking on the road, he saw a man planting a carob tree. He asked him, "How long will it take this tree to bear fruit?" The man replied, "Seventy years." He asked, "Are you quite sure you will live another seventy years to eat its fruit?" The man replied, "I myself found fully grown carob trees in the world; as my forebears planted for me, so am I planting for my children."

Once, when Honi sat down for a meal, sleep overcame him, and he dozed off. During his sleep, a grotto formed itself about him and hid him from sight, so that he continued sleeping for seventy years. When he awoke, he saw a man gathering the fruit of that same carob tree. He asked, "Are you the man who planted this tree?" The man replied, "That was my grandfather." Next, when Honi saw the herds and herds descended from his own she-ass, he exclaimed, "No doubt I slept for seventy years." He went to his home and inquired, "Where is the son of Honi the Circle Maker?" He was told, "Honi's son is no longer in this world, but his grandson is." At that, he announced, "I am Honi the Circle Maker," but no one believed him. Next he went to the house of study, where he overheard the sages say, "This tradition is as clear to us now as it was in the days of Honi the Circle Maker," for whenever he came to the academy, he would settle any difficulty the sages had. Hearing these words, he cried out, "But I am Honi!" Since the sages neither believed him nor accorded him the honor due him, he was so mortified that he besought God's mercy—and he died.

Rava observed: For this reason mortals say, "The fellowship of men or the fellowship of death."[5]

8. Abba Hilkiah was Honi the Circle Maker's grandson. Whenever the world was in need of rain, the sages sent word to him, and he besought God's mercy and rain fell. Once, when there was urgent need for rain, the sages sent a pair of scholars to ask him to beseech God's mercy. When they came to his home and did not find him, they went on to his field, where they found him hoeing. They greeted him, but he took no notice of them. Toward evening, he gathered sticks of wood, and, after loading the sticks of wood and the hoe on one shoulder, and his cloak on the other shoulder, he started for home. On the way, he did not wear his shoes, but when he got to a body of water, he put them on; when he came to thorns and thistles, he lifted up his garments. When he reached the city limit, his wife, bedecked in her finery, came out to meet him. When he arrived at the entrance to his house, his wife entered first, then he, and then the sages. He sat down to eat but did not say to the sages, "Please join me." When he distributed the bread[6] among his children, he gave one portion to the elder son and two to the younger.

Then Abba Hilkiah whispered to his wife: I know that the sages have come to me on account of rain. So [without making them aware of it] let us go up to the roof and beseech God's mercy. Perhaps the Holy One will be reconciled and rain will fall, and in that event you and I will not be credited for it. When they went up to the roof, he stood in one corner and she in another, both beseeching God's mercy, and a cloud appeared first over the corner where his wife stood. When he came down, he said to the sages, "Blessed be He who is everywhere, who has not made you depend on Abba Hilkiah." They replied, "We know that the rain has come because of your merit—be that as it may. But, sir, we would like to have explained

1. God must have imposed the drought in punishment for Israel's transgressions, and pressing Him to cancel His judgment would have been sinful.
2. In speaking of God as "Father-and-Mother," Simeon ben Shetah resorts to a very bold epithet for God the Creator.
3. B. Ta 19a and 23a; En Yaakov, ad loc.
4. The number of years the exile in Babylon lasted.
5. B. Ta 23a and En Yaakov, ad loc.
6. Literally, "doubled the bread" [after placing salt and herbs upon it].

those actions that so baffled us: Why did you take no notice of us when we greeted you?"

He answered, "I was working as a hired man for the day, and felt I had no right to take any time out."

"Why did you load the sticks of wood on one shoulder and the cloak on the other?"

"The cloak was borrowed—borrowed to be worn, not to serve as padding for some sticks of wood."

"Why did you not wear your shoes the entire way, but when you came to a body of water, you put them on?"

"Everything on the road I could see; I could not see what was in the water."

"Why did you lift up your garments when you came to thorns and thistles?"

"A scratch on the body heals itself, but a rent in clothing does not."

"When you reached the city limit, why did your wife come out to meet you wearing all her finery?"

"So that I would not set my eyes on any other woman."

"Why did she enter [the house] first, you after her, and then we?"

"You are not known to me."[1]

"When you sat down to eat, why did you not say, 'Please join us?"

"The food was not abundant, and I preferred not to have the sages thank me for something they could not have had."

"Why did you give one portion to the elder son and two portions to the younger?"

"The elder one stays at home, but the younger is usually away at school."[2]

"Why did the cloud appear first in the corner where your wife stood and then in the corner where you stood?"

"My wife, staying at home, gives bread to the poor, which benefits them right away, while I give them money, which does not benefit them right away."[3]

9. Honi the Circle Maker's daughter had a son called Hanan ha-Nehba. When the world was in need of rain, the sages would send schoolchildren to him; they would take hold of the hem of his garment and say to him, "Father, father, give us rain." Then he would plead with the Holy One, "Master of the universe, do it for the sake of these who do not know the difference between a Father who can give rain and a father who cannot." And why was he called Hanan ha-Nehba? Because he used to hide (*mahbi*) himself.[4]

Hillel the Elder (fl. end of 1st century B.C.E.)

10. R. Levi said: In Jerusalem there was found a genealogical scroll in which was written, "Hillel is of David's stock."[5]

1. And so I preferred not to leave her unchaperoned.
2. Where he gets little food.
3. Immediate relief is best. B. Ta 23a–b.
4. Out of modesty and humility.
5. P. Ta 4:2, 68a.

11. Hillel and Shebna were brothers. Hillel engaged in the study of Torah [in dire poverty], while Shebna engaged in trade [and prospered]. Eventually [after Hillel became famous], Shebna said to Hillel, "Come, let us be partners and share [the profits]."[6] A divine voice went forth and proclaimed, "If this man were to give all the substance of his house for the love [of Torah, which he now professes], he would be utterly contemned" (Song 8:7).[7]

12. It is reported about Hillel the Elder that every day he used to work and earn one *tropaic*,[8] half of which he would give to the watchman at the house of study; the other half he used on food for himself and the members of his household. One day he was unable to earn anything, so the watchman at the house of study did not let him in. He then climbed [to the roof] and hung on, sitting over the opening of the skylight, so that he could hear the words of the living God from the mouths of Shemaiah and Avtalion. It is said that the day was a Sabbath eve in the winter solstice, and snow came down on him from heaven. When the dawn rose, Shemaiah said to Avtalion, "Brother Avtalion, every day this house is bright with light, but today it is dark. Is the day cloudy?" When they looked up, they saw the figure of a man in the skylight. They climbed to the roof and found Hillel, covered with three cubits of snow. They removed the snow from him, bathed and anointed him, and, as they seated him in front of an open fire, they said, "This man deserves to have the Sabbath profaned on his behalf."[9]

13. Our masters taught: On one occasion, the fourteenth of Nisan fell on a Sabbath, and the Bene Betera[10] forgot the law, so that they did not know whether offering the paschal lamb does or does not override the Sabbath. They asked, "Is there anyone at all who knows whether or not the paschal lamb overrides the Sabbath?" They were told, "There is a certain man who has come up from Babylonia—he is known as Hillel the Babylonian. Since he ministered to the two notables of the generation, Shemaiah and Avtalion, he must know whether or not offering the paschal lamb overrides the Sabbath." So they sent for him and asked, "Do you know whether or not the paschal lamb overrides the Sabbath?" He replied, "Have we only one lamb—the lamb offered on Passover—that might override the Sabbath? Have we not in fact more than two hundred so-called paschal lambs during the year that override the Sabbath?"[11] The Bene Betera, taken aback, asked, "How can you make such a statement?" He replied, "In con-

6. The reward for Torah in the world-to-come and the profits of business in this world.
7. So *Iyyun Yaakov*, ad loc. B. Sot 21a.
8. Half a denar.
9. The Sabbath may be profaned to save a human life. B. Yoma 35b and En Yaakov, ad loc.
10. Sages of Judea who were at the helm after the death of Shemaiah and Avtalion until the appointment of Hillel as patriarch (1st century B.C.E.)
11. The lamb offered in the morning and evening of fifty Sabbaths during the year plus the two additional daily offerings on a Sabbath add up to more than two hundred during a year.

nection with the paschal lamb, Scripture prescribes that it be offered 'in its appointed time' [Num. 9:2], and in connection with [its analogue] the daily lamb, Scripture likewise prescribes that it be offered 'in its appointed time' [Num. 28:2]—just as 'its appointed time' said in connection with the daily lamb involves overriding the Sabbath, so 'its appointed time' said in connection with the paschal lamb involves overriding the Sabbath. Besides, there is an argument *a fortiori:* if the daily lamb, whose omission is not punished by excision, overrides the Sabbath, then should not the paschal lamb, whose neglect is punished by excision, without question override the Sabbath? Immediately Hillel was placed foremost in the house of study and appointed patriarch over them, and the rest of the entire day he sat and lectured concerning the laws of Passover. In the course of his remarks, he was moved to chide the people of Jerusalem, saying, "Who brought it about that I have come from Babylonia and have been made patriarch over you? It was your own indolence—you did not minister to the two notables of the generation, Shemaiah and Avtalion, who dwelled in your very midst." No sooner did he rebuke them than the answer to a question in *Halakhah* was hidden from him, so that when they asked him, "Master, what is the rule if a man forgot to bring in a knife on the eve of the Sabbath?" he had to reply, "I have heard the answer to this question but forgotten it. But depend on the people of Israel: if they themselves are not prophets, they are the children of prophets!" Indeed, the next day, one whose Passover offering was a lamb stuck the knife in its wool; one whose Passover offering was a goat tied the knife between its horns.[1] When Hillel saw what was being done, he recollected the *Halakhah* and said, "What these men are doing is in line with the tradition I received from the mouths of Shemaiah and Avtalion."[2]

14. Our masters taught: It once happened that two men made a wager with each other, agreeing that he who was able to arouse the anger of Hillel would win four hundred *zuz*. So one of them said, "I will go [first] and arouse his anger." Since it was before the onset of Sabbath, Hillel was washing his head. The man went, passed by the door of Hillel's house, and called out, "Is there a Hillel[3] here? Is there a fellow named Hillel around this place?" Hillel pulled his robe on and went out to him, saying, "My son, what do you wish?" "I have a question to ask." "Ask, my son, ask."

"Why are the heads of the Babylonians round?"[4]

"My son, you have asked quite a question. The answer is that their midwives are unskilled."

The man left, stayed away for a while, then came back, calling out, "Is there a Hillel here? Is there a fellow named Hillel here?" Again Hillel pulled on his robe and went out to him, saying, "My son, what do you wish?" "I have a question to ask." "Ask, my son, ask."

"Why are the eyes of the Palmyrians bleary?"

"My son, you have asked quite a question. The answer is that they live in a [windswept] sandy country."

The man left, stayed away for a while, and again came back, calling out, "Is there a Hillel here? Is there a fellow named Hillel around this place?" Once again Hillel pulled on his robe and went out to him, saying, "My son, what do you wish?" "I have a question to ask." "Ask, my son, ask."

"Why are the feet of the Ethiopians so wide?"

"My son, you have asked quite a question. The answer is that they live in watery marshes."[5]

"I have many questions to ask," said the man, "but I am afraid that you may become angry [at me]." At that, Hillel wrapped his robe around himself, sat down before the man, and said, "All the questions you have to ask, go ahead and ask." The man: "Are you the Hillel who is called patriarch of Israel?" Hillel: "Yes." The man: "If you are the one, may there not be many like you in Israel." Hillel: "Why, my son?" The man: "Because on account of you I just lost four hundred *zuz*." Hillel: "Calm your spirit. Losing four hundred *zuz*, and even an additional four hundred *zuz*, was well worth it, [for you have learned that, whatever the provocation], Hillel will not lose his temper."[6]

15. Our masters taught: A certain heathen once came before Shammai and asked him, "How many Torahs have you?" "Two," he replied, "the Written Torah and the Oral Torah." "I will believe you about the Written Torah, but not about the Oral Torah. Take me as a proselyte, on condition that you teach me only the Written Torah." In response, Shammai scolded him and angrily ordered him to get out. When he went before Hillel, the latter accepted him as a proselyte. On the first day he taught him the letters of the alphabet in order: *Alef, bet, gimmel, dalet* [and so on to *tav*]. The following day he reversed the order of the letters. "But yesterday you did not teach them to me in this order," the heathen protested. "Is it not upon me," Hillel asked, "that you have to rely to know the correct order of letters in the alphabet? Then you must also rely upon me for the validity of the Oral Torah."

On another occasion, it happened that a certain heathen came before Shammai and said to him, "Take me as a proselyte, but on condition that you teach me the entire Torah, all of it, while I stand on one foot." Shammai instantly drove him away with a builder's measuring rod he happened to have in his hand. When the heathen came before Hillel, Hillel said to him, "What is hateful to you, do not do to your fellow man. This is the entire Torah, all of it; the rest is commentary. Go and study it."

On another occasion, it happened that a certain heathen passing behind a synagogue heard the voice of a teacher reciting, "And these are the garments which they shall make: a breastpiece, and an ephod" (Exod. 28:4).

1. And thus avoided having to carry the knife on the Sabbath.
2. B. Pes 66a and En Yaakov, ad loc.: P. Pes 6:1, 33a.
3. Insolently, without the courtesy of a prefixed title, besides being contemptuous, as if Hillel were an unknown nobody and not the premier scholar of his age.
4. Intended as a dig at Hillel, who was a Babylonian.
5. Just as ducks' feet are webbed, so the feet of Ethiopians must be wide to enable them to get about.
6. B. Shab 30b–31a.

He asked: "For whom are these intended?" He was told, "For the high priest." The heathen said to himself: I will go and become a proselyte so that I may be appointed high priest. He went before Shammai and said to him, "Take me as a proselyte, on condition that you appoint me high priest." Shammai promptly drove him away with a builder's measuring rod he happened to have in his hand. When the heathen went before Hillel, Hillel made him a proselyte, but then asked, "Is a king appointed unless he knows the details of governance? Go now and study details of [the Temple's] governance!" The new proselyte went and read Scripture. When he came to the verse "The layman that cometh nigh shall be put to death" (Num. 1:51), he asked Hillel, "To whom does this verse apply?" "Even to David, king of Israel." At that, that proselyte applied to himself an argument *a fortiori:* Israel are called sons of Him who is everywhere—indeed, He speaks of them as "Israel, My firstborn son" (Exod. 4:22) out of the love He has for them. Yet of them it is written, "The layman that cometh nigh shall be put to death." Surely how much more and more do these words apply to a lowly proselyte, who comes with his staff and his shoulder bag! Then he went before Shammai and said to him, "Could I ever have been eligible to become high priest?[1] Is it not written in the Torah, 'The layman that cometh nigh shall be put to death'?" Next, he went before Hillel and said to him, "O gentle Hillel, may blessings rest on your head for bringing me under the wings of the Presence!"

Some time later, when the three aforementioned proselytes happened to meet in one place, they said, "Shammai's severity nearly drove us from the world [-to-come], but Hillel's gentleness brought us under the wings of the Presence." [Hence, say the sages]: A man should always be as flexible as Hillel, not as inflexible as Shammai.[2]

16. "He who does good to his own person is a man of piety" (Prov. 11:17),[3] as may be inferred from what Hillel the Elder once said. After concluding a session of study with his disciples, he kept walking along with them. His disciples asked him, "Master, where are you going?" He answered, "To perform a precept." "What precept?" He replied, "To wash up in the bathhouse." "But is this a precept?" "It is indeed. Kings' statues set up in theaters and circuses have to be scoured and washed down by a man specially appointed to look after them, who receives maintenance for the work. More—he is esteemed as being among the notables of the kingdom. How much more and more am I required to scour and wash myself, I who have been created in God's image and likeness—I, of whom it is written, 'In the image of God made He man'!" (Gen. 9:6).

Another exposition: "He who does good to his own person is a man of piety," as may be inferred from what Hillel the Elder once said. After concluding a session of study with his disciples, he walked along with them. His disciples asked him, "Master, where are you going?" He replied, "To do a good turn to a guest in my house." They said, "You seem to have a guest every day." He replied, "Is not my poor soul a guest in my body—here today, and tomorrow here no longer?"[4]

17. It is related of Hillel the Elder that, for a certain poor man who was of good family, he hired[5] a horse to ride on and a slave to run before him. Once, when he could not find a slave to run before the man, he himself ran before him a distance of three *mil.*[6]

18. On one occasion Hillel the Elder had a meal prepared for a certain man. [Before they were called to sit down] a poor man came by, stood at Hillel's doorway, and said, "I am scheduled to marry today and have no provisions whatever." Hearing that, Hillel's wife took the entire meal and gave it to the poor man [without telling her husband]. Then she kneaded fresh dough, cooked another pot of stew, and, when it was ready, placed it before Hillel and his guest. Hillel asked, "My dear, why did you not bring it sooner?" She told him what happened. He said, "My dear, in asking about the delay, I meant to judge you not on the scale of guilt but on the scale of merit, because I was certain that everything you did, you did for the sake of Heaven."[7]

19. Our masters taught: It once happened that Hillel the Elder, while returning from a journey, heard a cry of anguish in the city and said to himself: I am confident that this cry does not come from my house. To him apply the words "He shall not be afraid of evil tidings; his heart is steadfast, trusting in the Lord" (Ps. 112:7).[8]

20. When the Torah was forgotten in Israel, Ezra came up from Babylon and reestablished it. [Some of] the Torah was again forgotten, and Hillel the Babylonian came up and he, too, reestablished it.

Hillel came up from Babylonia at the age of forty, ministered to the sages for forty years, and guided Israel for forty years.

It is said of Hillel that there were no sages' words that he put aside and did not study. Then, too, [he studied] all languages, even those of mountains, hills, and valleys; of trees and herbs; of beasts, wild and tame; and of demons; as well as the parables of fullers and [fables of] foxes.[9]

21. Our masters taught: Hillel the Elder had eighty disciples. Thirty of them were worthy of having the Presence rest upon them, as it did upon Moses our teacher. Thirty were worthy of having the sun stand still for them, as it did for Joshua son of Nun; and the remaining twenty were more moderately competent. The oldest was Jonathan ben Uzziel;[10] the youngest was Rabban Yohanan ben Zakkai.[11]

---

1. Meaning: "I apologize to you for demanding something you could not possibly grant me."
2. B. Shab 31a.
3. JV: "The merciful man doeth good to his own soul."
4. Lev. R. 34:3.
5. "He hired"—Alfasi; BR: "bought."
6. B. Ket 67b.
7. DER 6.
8. B. Ber 60a.
9. B. Suk 20a; Sif Deut., §357; Sof 16.
10. It is said he wrote a Targum to the Prophets. B. Meg 3a.
11. B. Suk 28a and En Yaakov, ad loc.

22. Once, when Hillel took sick, all his disciples came to visit him, but Rabban Yohanan ben Zakkai remained in the courtyard. Hillel asked, "Where is the youngest of you, the one who is father of wisdom, father of the generations, and, needless to say, the most distinguished among you?" They replied, "He is in the courtyard." Hillel: "Let him come in." When he came in, Hillel said to his disciples, "To this one apply the words 'I [Torah] cause those that love me to inherit substance, and I fill their treasuries' " (Prov. 8:21).[1]

23. Our masters taught: After the death of the last prophets, Haggai, Zechariah, and Malachi, the holy spirit departed from Israel; yet they were still served by the divine voice. Once, when the rabbis were gathered in the upper chamber of Guria's house in Jericho, a divine voice sounded above them from heaven, saying, "There is one among you who is worthy of having the Presence rest upon him as it did upon Moses our teacher, but his generation does not merit it." The sages set their eyes on Hillel the Elder. When he died, they lamented and said, "Alas for the pious man, alas for the humble man, the disciple of Ezra [is no more]!"[2]

Akavia ben Mahalalel (fl. middle of 1st century C.E.)

24. Akavia ben Mahalalel testified to the validity of four legal opinions. He was told: Akavia, retract what you said about these four legal matters, and we will make you president of Israel's High Court. He replied: Better for me to be called a fool all my days than to be wicked in the sight of God even for one hour, so people would say of me, "He retracted for the sake of advancement in office." At that, they put him under a ban, and when he died while still under the ban, the court put a stone on his coffin.[3] R. Judah said: God forbid saying that Akavia was put under a ban, for [on a Passover eve] when the Temple Court [was so filled with people that it] had to be closed, there was not a man in the multitude who was equal to Akavia ben Mahalalel in wisdom and in the fear of sin.

In the hour of Akavia's death, he said to his son, "Retract the four opinions I used to maintain." His son asked, "Why did you yourself not retract them?" He replied, "I heard them from the mouths of a majority of my teachers, and my opponents heard [the contrary] from the mouths of a majority [of their teachers].[4] I stood fast by the tradition I had heard, and my opponents stood fast by the tradition they had heard. But you have heard [my tradition] from the mouth of only one individual [myself], and [my opponents' tradition] from the mouths of a majority. It is better to leave the opinion of an individual and take hold of the opinion of the majority." The son then said, "Father, commend me to your colleagues." Akavia replied, "I will not commend you." The son: "Have you found some wrong in me?" "No," said Akavia, "but your own deeds may bring you near to them, and your own deeds may remove you far from them."[5]

Rabban Gamaliel the Elder (fl. 20–50 C.E.)

25. We have been taught: One may not register simultaneously for two paschal lambs.[6] Yet it once happened that the king and queen instructed their servants, "Go out and slaughter a paschal offering on our behalf." However, the servants [on their own] slaughtered two offerings [a lamb and a goat]. When they went to ask the king [which one he desired], he answered, "Go ask the queen." When they went to ask the queen, she said, "Go ask Rabban Gamaliel." They went and asked Rabban Gamaliel, who said, "The king and queen, who [having much food] are not greatly concerned [and therefore cannot be said to have committed themselves], may eat the first animal slaughtered; but [in a similar case] we may eat neither the first nor the second."

On another occasion, a lizard was found in the slaughterhouse of the palace, and they were ready to declare the entire repast about to be served unclean.[7] They went and asked the king, who answered, "Go ask the queen." When they went and asked the queen, she said, "Go ask Rabban Gamaliel." So they went and asked Rabban Gamaliel, who said, "Was the lizard lying in hot water or in cold water?" "In hot water." "Then pour a glass of cold water over it." They poured a glass of cold water over it, and it began to stir.[8] At that, Rabban Gamaliel declared the entire repast clean.

Thus, the king was dependent on the queen, and the queen was dependent on Rabban Gamaliel. Hence the entire repast [for king and queen], all of it, was dependent on Rabban Gamaliel.[9]

R. Zadok and His Son R. Eleazar (fl. 2d half of 1st century C.E.)

26. R. Zadok observed fasts for forty years in order that Jerusalem not be destroyed [and he became so emaciated that] when he ate anything, the food could be seen [as it passed through his gullet]. When he wanted to restore himself, they used to bring him figs, and he would suck their juice and throw the rest away.

When Vespasian was laying siege to Jerusalem, Rabban Yohanan ben Zakkai came before him. Vespasian said, "If you have any friend or relative in the city, send for him and bring him out before my troops enter." Rabban Yohanan sent R. Eliezer and R. Joshua to bring out R. Zadok. They went and found him at the city gate. When

---

1. P. Ned 5:7, 39b.
2. B. Sanh 11a.
3. As a symbolic gesture of stoning.
4. The controversy between Akavia and the sages was over what had been the opinion of the majority of the sages before them.
5. Ed 5:6–7.
6. To subsequently eat whichever one chooses, since choosing one or the other later is not deemed to have retroactive power.
7. A dead lizard (*haltaah*) defiles anything in contact with it.
8. They now saw that it was alive.
9. The king and queen in the two stories may have been Agrippa I and his wife. B. Pes 88b.

R. Zadok arrived, Rabban Yohanan ben Zakkai stood up before him. Vespasian asked, "You stand up in deference to this emaciated old man?" Rabban Yohanan: "By your life, if there had been one more like him in Jerusalem, you would have been unable to conquer it, even if your army were twice its size." Vespasian: "What is his power?" Rabban Yohanan: "He eats one ripened fig and, with the strength he derives from it, he teaches one hundred sessions at the academy." "But why is he so emaciated?" "Because of his numerous abstinences and fasts." Vespasian sent for physicians, who fed R. Zadok small portions of food and small doses of liquid until his normal weight was restored.[1]

27. R. Zadok was the greatest man of the generation. When he was taken captive, a certain Roman noblewoman acquired him and assigned him a beautiful maidservant. The moment he saw her, he turned his eyes to the wall, so as not to look at her. And he sat studying all night. In the morning she went and complained to her mistress, saying, "I would rather die than be given to this man." The mistress sent for him and asked, "Why did you not do with that woman as men are accustomed to do?" He replied, "How else could I have acted—I who come from a line of high priests, from a family of great distinction?" When she heard what he said, she ordered that he be freed with great honor.[2]

28. R. Eleazar bar Zadok said: When I was studying Torah with R. Yohanan the Horonite,[3] I noticed that during a year of drought he used to eat dry bread with salt. I went home and told it to my father, who said, "Bring him some olives." When I brought them and he noticed that they were moist,[4] he said to me, "I do not eat olives."[5] I came back and told my father, who said to me, "Go tell him that the jar was broached,[6] only the lees had blocked up the breach."[7]

29. R. Eleazar bar Zadok said: When my father was dying, he gave me the following instructions: "My son, bury me first in a fosse. In due time, gather my bones and put them in an ossuary; but be sure not to gather them with your own hands."

And thus did I do for him: Yohanan entered the fosse, gathered the bones, and spread a sheet over them. Then I entered, rent my garments [in mourning] over the bones [as though they were the original corpse of my deceased father], and sprinkled dried herbs over them.

As my father had done for his father, so I did for him.[8]

30. It is said of R. Eleazar bar Zadok and of Abba Saul ben Batnit, who throughout their lives were shopkeepers in Jerusalem, that on the eve of a festival they would fill their measures [with oil][9] and give it to their customers on the day of the festival. In order to avoid neglect of the house of study—so said R. Hananiah ben Akavia—the same thing used to be done [on the eves of] the intermediate days of the festival.[10] On weekdays also—said the sages—the same thing was done by tipping the vessel beforehand, so that it emptied completely into the buyer's vessel. In fact, Abba Saul ben Batnit had collected three hundred jars of oil from what clung to the vessel after it was measured, and his companion, Eleazar bar Zadok, had collected three hundred jars of wine from the foam left over in the measures they used; they brought these to the treasurers dispensing charity. The treasurers said, "You are not required to do so."[11] They replied, "But we do not wish to keep them." The treasurers: "Since you are determined to be stringent with yourselves, the liquids will be turned over to the community, to be used for communal purposes.[12]

The School of Shammai and the School of Hillel (middle of 1st century C.E.)

31. When the disciples of Shammai and Hillel who had not studied sufficiently grew numerous, disputes multiplied in Israel, and the Torah became two Torahs.[13]

32. R. Abba said in the name of Samuel: For three years there was a dispute between the school of Shammai and the school of Hillel, the ones asserting, "The law is according to our views," and the others asserting, "The law is according to our views." Then a divine voice went forth and said, "The utterances of the one and those of the other are both the words of the living God, but the law is according to the school of Hillel."

Since both are the words of the living God, what entitled the school of Hillel to have the law fixed according to their rulings? Because they were kindly and humble; they taught their own rulings as well as those of the school of Shammai.[14] And even more, they taught the rulings of the school of Shammai before their own.

1. B. Git 56a; Lam. R. 1:5, §31.
2. ARN 16.
3. Perhaps from Hauran, mentioned in Ezek. 47:18, between Damascus and Gilead.
4. Moisture renders fruit susceptible to ritual uncleanness.
5. He hesitated to eat them because of the possibility that the earthen jar in which they were kept had been touched by an *am ha-aretz* (an ignorant man who gave little heed to the laws of ritual purity); thus, according to rabbinical enactment, the jar would have become unclean. Upon being moistened, the olives receive uncleanness from the jar.
6. "Keeping olives in a broached container is clear evidence that the owner had no desire to retain the sap that exudes from the olives, and only liquids which are desired by the owner render the fruit susceptible to Levitical uncleanness" (Yev, Soncino, p. 83 n. 1).
7. "And thus the undesired moisture remained in the olives. . . . Such may safely be eaten even by the scrupulous" (Yev, Soncino, p. 83, n. 2). B. Yev 15b.
8. Sem 12 (YJS 17:82).
9. Measuring out oil during the festival was prohibited.
10. Measures would be filled in the evening.
11. Those who purchased the wine and the oil were assumed to have resigned what was left in the measures.
12. Tos Betz 3:8; P. Betz 3:8, 62b.
13. There was controversy concerning many matters. B. Sanh 88b.
14. E.g., in saying the Shema, R. Tarfon, a member of the school of Hillel, followed a Shammaitic ruling at the risk of his life. B. Ber 10b.

This should teach you that he who humbles himself is exalted by the Holy One, and he who exalts himself is humbled by the Holy One.[1]

33. Although the school of Shammai and the school of Hillel were in disagreement—what the one forbade, the other permitted—nevertheless the school of Shammai did not refrain from marrying women of the families of the school of Hillel, nor did the school of Hillel refrain from marrying those of the school of Shammai. This should teach you that they showed love and friendship toward one another, thus putting into practice the injunction "Love ye truth, but also peace" (Zech. 8:19).[2]

Jonathan ben Uzziel (fl. middle of 1st century C.E.)

34. It is said of Jonathan ben Uzziel that when he sat and occupied himself with Torah, every bird that flew over him was instantly incinerated.[3]

35. The Targum of the Five Books of Moses—Onkelos the Proselyte composed it under the guidance of R. Eliezer and R. Joshua. The Targum of the Prophets—Jonathan ben Uzziel composed it under the guidance of Haggai, Zechariah, and Malachi.[4] At the time [of its completion], the Land of Israel quaked over an area four hundred parasangs by four hundred parasangs, and a divine voice went forth and exclaimed, "Who is this that has revealed My secrets to mankind?"[5] Jonathan ben Uzziel stood up and said, "It is I who have revealed Your secrets to mankind. It is revealed and known to You that I did so not for my own honor nor for the honor of my father's house, but I have done it for Your honor alone, so that dissension may not increase in Israel."[6]

He further sought to reveal by a Targum [the inner meaning of] the Writings. But a divine voice went forth and said, "Enough!" What was the reason? Because in that part of Scripture, the exact time of the Messiah's coming is foretold.[7]

36. Our masters taught: A tale is told of a certain person whose sons did not conduct themselves properly. He got busy and assigned his estate in writing to Jonathan ben Uzziel. What did Jonathan ben Uzziel do? One third he sold;[8] one third he consecrated;[9] and the remaining third he returned to the man's sons. Shammai came at him with staff and bag.[10] Jonathan replied, "Shammai, if you think you have the right to take back what I sold and what I consecrated, then you also have the right to take back what I returned to the sons. But if not, you cannot take back what I returned."[11]

Shammai exclaimed, "The son of Uzziel has insulted me![12] The son of Uzziel has insulted me!"

R. Yose son of R. Bun said: What actually happened was the following: Jonathan ben Uzziel's father vowed that his son was to derive no benefit from his estate and proceeded to assign it in writing to Shammai. What did Shammai do? A part he sold, a part he consecrated, and the remainder he gave to Jonathan as a gift. Then he said, "Let whoever finds fault with this gift first take back what the purchasers and the Temple got, and then take back what Jonathan got.[13]

Samuel the Little (fl. 1st century C.E.)

37. It is told that Rabban Gamaliel [II] once said, "Early in the morning, seven scholars are to meet me in the upper chamber[14] [to intercalate a month in the year]." But when he came in early that morning, he found eight. So he said, "Whoever has come without permission should leave." Samuel the Little stood up and said, "It is I who came without permission. I came up not to participate in the intercalation of the year, but because I felt the need to learn the practical application of the law." Rabban Gamaliel answered, "Sit down, my son, sit down. You are worthy of intercalating all the years that require it. However, the rabbis have declared, 'Years may be intercalated only by those specially invited for the purpose.' "

In reality, it was not Samuel the Little [who was the uninvited one] but another man; Samuel merely wished to save the intruder from humiliation.[15]

38. Once Samuel the Little ordained a fast [for the following day], but rain fell before sunrise [before the people had begun to fast and to pray]. The people thought that it was due to the merit of the congregation.[16] But Samuel said to them: To have you understand what happened, I will tell you the parable of a servant who asked his master for a gratuity, and the master said to his other servants, "Give it to him, just so I do not have to listen to his whining."

Another time, Samuel the Little ordained a fast [for the following day], and rain fell the next day after sunset

---

1. B. Er 13b and En Yaakov, ad loc.
2. B. Yev 14b.
3. Burned by the fire of the ministering angels, who gathered to listen to his teaching. So Rashi, ad loc. B. Suk 28a and En Yaakov, ad loc.
4. He may have used traditions ascribed to them. Samuel Edels.
5. "Jonathan ben Uzziel's Targum is very paraphrastic and applies many of the prophetic verses to the Messianic Age" (Meg, Soncino, p. 9, n. 8).
6. "Through different interpretations being placed on the prophetic allusions" (Meg, Soncino, p. 9, n. 9).
7. In the book of Daniel. B. Meg 3a and En Yaakov, ad loc.
8. And kept the money.
9. For Temple use.
10. In vehement objection. Shammai maintained that Jonathan had no right to return any part of the money to the sons, for in doing so he flouted the father's last wish.
11. "If the sale and the transaction are valid, it follows that the estate has passed into the absolute ownership of Jonathan. Consequently he is entitled to dispose of it in any way he pleases. Hence his gift to the sons of the deceased is also legally valid" (BB, Soncino, p. 562, n. 7).
12. Literally, "covered me with plaster."
13. B. BB 133b–134a and En Yaakov, ad loc.; P. Ned 5:7, 39b.
14. The meeting place of the rabbis.
15. B. Sanh 11a.
16. Inasmuch as rain came even before their prayers of entreaty.

[after the people had fasted and entreated God]. The people thought that it was due to the merit of the congregation. But Samuel said to them: To have you understand what happened, I will tell you the parable of a servant who asked his master for a gratuity, and the master said to his other servants, "Keep him waiting until he is made submissive by hunger and is wracked by pain. Then give it to him."

Then, according to Samuel the Little, how is one ever to determine whether a congregation's own merit is responsible for the coming of rain? Only when a congregation recites the prayer "He causeth the wind to blow" and the wind blows at once; and when it recites "He causeth the rain to fall," and rain falls at once.[1]

39. Our masters taught: In Yavneh, at the request of Rabban Gamaliel, Simeon ha-Pakuli[2] fixed the order of the Eighteen Benedictions.

Later Rabban Gamaliel asked the sages: Is there anyone here who can compose [a nineteenth] benediction—[the imprecation] against heretics? Samuel the Little arose and composed it. The next year [while reciting the benedictions in the synagogue service], he forgot this nineteenth benediction. He tried for two or three hours to recall it. Still, he was not removed [from his post as reader].[3]

40. Once the sages were reclining at a meal in an upper chamber in Yavneh, and a divine voice from heaven came over them: One man here is worthy of having the Presence rest upon him, but his generation does not merit the privilege. The sages set their eyes on Samuel the Little. And when he died, they said: Alas for the pious man, alas for the humble man, the disciple of Hillel [is no more]!

Why was he called "the Little"? Because he made little of himself. Some say: Because he was just a little less than the other Samuel, the one of Ramah.[4]

41. When Samuel the Little died and left no heir, his key and ledger were suspended from his coffin.[5] Rabban Gamaliel the Elder and R. Eliezer eulogized him, saying:

Over him it is well to weep.
Over him it is well to mourn.
When kings die,
They leave their crowns to their children.
When the rich die,
They leave their wealth to their children.
Samuel the Little
Took all the world's treasures and went off [with them].

(The words "They will be thine alone; others have no part with thee" [Prov. 5:17] apply to his death.)

In the hour of his death, Samuel the Little spoke thus: "Simeon and Ishmael,[6] for the sword; their companions, for execution; the rest of the nation, for plunder. And afterward, great disasters will come to the world." He said this in Aramaic.[7]

Rabban Yohanan ben Zakkai (1st century C.E.)

42. All the years of Rabban Yohanan ben Zakkai were one hundred and twenty: forty years he engaged in business; forty years he studied; and forty years he taught.[8]

43. It is said of Rabban Yohanan ben Zakkai that during his entire life he never used profane speech, nor walked four cubits without studying Torah or without wearing tefillin; nor did any man arrive earlier than he at the house of study, nor did he sleep or even doze while there; nor, when he went out, did he leave anyone in the house of study; nor when he happened to be in a filthy alleyway did he meditate [on sacred subjects]; nor did anyone ever find him sitting silent—he was always engaged in study; no one but himself opened the door to his disciples; never in his life did he say anything that he had not heard from his teacher;[9] and, except on the eve of Passover,[10] or the eve of Yom Kippur,[11] he never said, "It is time to leave the house of study." After him, his disciple R. Eliezer conducted himself likewise.[12]

44. It is said of Rabban Yohanan ben Zakkai that no man ever greeted him first, not even a heathen in the marketplace.[13]

45. It is said of Rabban Yohanan ben Zakkai that he did not leave unstudied Scripture, Mishnah, Gemara,[14] *Halakhah*,[15] *Aggadah*,[16] details of the Torah,[17] details of the scribes,[18] inferences from the minor to the major, analogies,[19] calendrical computations,[20] gematrias,[21] the speech

1. B. Ta 25b.
2. The word may mean "cotton seller."
3. Because his piety was unquestioned. Another person would have been suspected of heresy and removed immediately. B. Ber 28b–29a.
4. B. Sanh 11a; P. Sot 9:13–14, 24b.
5. The key and the ledger symbolized the fact that Samuel the Little was taking all his property with him. So Gedaliah Alon, quoted in Sem, YJS 17:15.
6. Rabban Simeon ben Gamaliel and R. Ishmael the High Priest. See below in this chapter, §180.
7. So that those around him would not understand his prophecy. B. Sanh 11a; Sem 8:7 (YJS 17:59).
8. B. RH 31b.
9. That is, at public gatherings he offered no decision on law unless he had heard it from his teacher. So Adin Steinsaltz in his edition of Suk (Jerusalem, 1979), ad loc.
10. When it was necessary to hurry home, so that the seder could start early and the children stay awake through it.
11. When the last meal had to be eaten early.
12. B. Suk 28a and En Yaakov, ad loc.
13. B. Ber 17a.
14. Explanations of the Mishnah.
15. Decisions of law.
16. The nonhalakhic parts of the Talmud, including homilies, ethics, folklore, legends, etc.
17. Minute details and subtle points in exposition of Scripture.
18. Subtle implications of rabbinic enactments.
19. The second of the thirteen hermeneutical principles of R. Ishmael.
20. The calculations of the solstice, etc.
21. Inferences derived from the numerical equivalents and other computations of letters.

of ministering angels, the speech of demons, the speech of palm trees,[1] fullers' parables and fables of foxes, great matters or small matters. ["Great matters" means the Work of the Chariot[2] and "small matters" means the discussions of Abbaye and Rava],[3] in order to fulfill "That I [Torah] may cause those that love me to inherit substance, and that I may fill their treasuries" (Prov. 8:21).

It was also related of him that he said: If all the heavens were sheets [of parchment], all trees pens, and all the seas ink, they would not suffice to record the wisdom that I acquired from my masters; and yet I drew of their wisdom no more than a fly, dipping in the Great Sea, diminishes it by the tiniest drop.[4]

46. Our masters taught: Once, when on a journey, Rabban Yohanan ben Zakkai was riding an ass and his disciple R. Eleazar ben Arakh was driving the ass from behind. R. Eleazar said: Master, teach me a chapter in the Work of the Chariot. He answered: My son, have I not instructed you that the Work of [the Chariot] is not to be taught even to one person, unless he is a sage and able to draw inferences on his own? R. Eleazar entreated: Master, then permit me to say something before you that you already taught me. He answered: Say it.

Rabban Yohanan ben Zakkai immediately dismounted from the ass, wrapped his cloak around himself, and sat down on a stone beneath an olive tree. R. Eleazar said to him: Master, why did you dismount from the ass? Rabban Yohanan ben Zakkai: While you are expounding the Work of the Chariot, the Divine Presence might be with us, and the ministering angels might accompany us—is it proper that I should continue riding an ass? As soon as R. Eleazar ben Arakh began his exposition of the Work of the Chariot, fire came down from heaven and lapped at all the trees in the field, which then burst into song. What was the song they sang? "Praise the Lord from the earth, ye sea monsters, and all deeps . . . fruitful trees and all cedars. . . . Hallelujah" (Ps. 148:7, 148:9, and 148:14). And an angel was heard from the fire, saying: "Surely this is the very Work of the Chariot!"

Then Rabban Yohanan ben Zakkai arose, kissed him on his head, and said: Blessed be the Lord, the God of Israel, that has given to Abraham our father a son who knows how to speculate upon, to examine, and to expound the Work of the Chariot. There are some who expound well but do not carry out precepts well; some who carry them out well but do not expound well. But you expound well and carry out precepts well. Happy are you, O Abraham our father, that R. Eleazar ben Arakh has come forth from your loins![5]

[1] On a windless day, if a man stands between two palms and observes how they incline, signs that afford information may be discerned. So Hai Gaon.

[2] Esoteric lore concerning the divine chariot described in Ezek. 1.

[3] They lived long after Rabban Yohanan ben Zakkai. "Rashi suggests that they were forgotten, and Abbaye and Rava retaught them" (Suk, Soncino, p. 124, n. 3).

[4] B. Suk 28a; Sof 16:8.

[5] B. Hag 14b and En Yaakov, ad loc.

47. Rabban Yohanan ben Zakkai had five [distinguished] disciples: R. Eliezer ben Hyrcanus, R. Joshua ben Hananiah, R. Yose the Priest, R. Simeon ben Nathaniel, and R. Eleazar ben Arakh.

He used to sum up their merits: Eliezer ben Hyrcanus—[his memory is so retentive that he is like] a cemented cistern that does not lose a drop; Joshua ben Hananiah—happy is she that bore him;[6] Jose the Priest—the embodiment of piety; Simeon ben Nathaniel—the embodiment of sin-fearing; Eleazer ben Arakh—[his originality is so great that he is like] a spring with ever-welling strength.

Rabban Yohanan ben Zakkai said to them: Go into the world and observe the right course a man should steadfastly follow. R. Eliezer came back and said: Be generous with your means.[7] R. Joshua said: Be a good friend; R. Yose said: Be a good neighbor. R. Simeon said: Consider the consequences of your actions. R. Eleazar said: Cultivate an unselfish heart. Rabban Yohanan said to them: I prefer what Eleazar ben Arakh said to what you have said, because his definition includes all of yours.[8]

48. When his disciples asked Rabban Yohanan ben Zakkai a question, he replied, "Thus-and-thus." They reminded him, "But this is not what you taught us before." He said, "Even if I taught you something that is constructed by hand and seen by the eyes—even such an unforgettable experience I could have forgotten. How much more easily could I have forgotten something that had imprinted itself only on my sense of hearing [the least retentive of man's five senses]!"

Not that he didn't know. But he sought to spur his disciples [to be wary in the issuance of rulings].[9]

49. Simeon of Sikhnin, and [more precisely] of Itzah, used to dig wells, trenches, and caves in Jerusalem. Once he said to Rabban Yohanan ben Zakkai, "I am as great a man as you." Rabban Yohanan: "How is that?" Simeon: "Because, like you, I am occupied with the public weal." Then Simeon explained, "When a man comes to you for a decision or with an inquiry, you tell him to drink from a certain well [which I dug], because its waters are pure and cold. Or when a woman asks you concerning her ritual uncleanness, you say to her: Immerse yourself in a certain well [which I dug], because its waters cleanse."

At that, Rabban Yohanan applied to Simeon the verse "Be ready to hearken; it is better than the 'offering' of fools [like Simeon], who are not even aware that they say things that are wrong" (Eccles. 4:17).[10]

[6] "Great credit for his scholarship was due to his mother, who is said to have taken him as an infant to the academy of learning so that his ears might become attuned to the sound of Torah. Rabbi Joshua ben Hananiah successfully debated with Greek philosophers and was famous as the representative of Jewish wit and wisdom" (Birnbaum, *The Daily Prayer Book*, p. 488).

[7] Literally, "a good eye."

[8] Avot 2:10–11 and 2:13.

[9] Tos Oh 16:8.

[10] Eccles. R. 4:17, §4.

50. R. Ulla said: Rabban Yohanan ben Zakkai spent eighteen years in Arav,[1] and only two inquiries on matters of law came before him. So he said: Galilee, O Galilee, you have no use for the Torah. In the end you will have to cope with malfeasants.[2]

51. Once, when Rabban Yohanan ben Zakkai was going up to Maon in Judea, he saw a girl picking barleycorn out of a horse's excrement. Rabban Yohanan ben Zakkai said to his disciples: Look at this poor child. Who is she? They replied: She is a Jewish girl. And to whom does the horse belong? To an Arab horseman. Then Rabban Yohanan ben Zakkai said to his disciples: All my life I have been troubled by this verse: "If thou understandest not, O thou fairest among women, thou wilt be forced to follow the tracks of the sheep" (Song 1:8). I read it over and over but failed to grasp its meaning [until now. The verse says]: You were unwilling to subject yourselves to Heaven; behold, now you are subjected to the heathen. You were unwilling to pay the head tax to heaven, "a mere beka[3] a head" (Exod. 38:26); now you are paying a head tax of fifteen shekels under a government of your enemies. You were unwilling to repair the roads and highways for pilgrims going up to the Temple; now you have to keep in repair [Roman] road posts and way stations for travelers to the royal plantations. And thus it says, "Because thou didst not serve the Lord thy God" (Deut. 28:47) with love, "therefore shalt thou serve thine enemy" (ibid.) with hatred; "because thou didst not serve the Lord thy God" in time of plenty, "therefore shalt thou serve thine enemy . . . in hunger and in thirst, in nakedness, and in want of all things" (ibid.).[4]

When Rabban Yohanan ben Zakkai's son died, his disciples came in to comfort him. R. Eliezer entered, sat down before him, and said, "Master, by your leave, may I say something to you?"

"Speak," he replied.

R. Eliezer said, "Adam had a son who died, yet he was comforted for the loss of him. How do we know that he was comforted for him? Because it is said, 'And Adam knew his wife again' [Gen. 4:25], and [after she bore a son, Adam said], 'God has provided me with another offspring in place of Abel' [ibid.]. You, too, must be comforted."

Rabban Yohanan said to him, "Is it not enough that I grieve over my own? Do you have to remind me of Adam's grief?"

R. Joshua entered and said, "Master, by your leave, may I say something to you?"

"Speak," he replied.

R. Joshua said, "Job had sons and daughters, all of whom died in one day, and he was comforted for the loss of them. You, too, must be comforted. How do we know that Job was comforted? Because Job said, 'The Lord gave, and the Lord hath taken away; blessed be the Name of the Lord' " (Job 1:21).

1. Near Sepphoris in Upper Galilee.

2. P. Shab 16:7, 15d.

3. Half a shekel.

4. Mek, *Yitro, Ba-hodesh*, 1 (La 2:193–95).

Rabban Yohanan said to him, "Is it not enough that I grieve over my own? Do you have to remind me of Job's grief?"

R. Yose entered, sat down before him, and said, "Master, by your leave, may I say something to you?"

"Speak," he replied.

R. Yose said, "Aaron had two grown sons, both of whom died in one day, yet he was comforted for the loss of them, as it is said, 'And Aaron was silent' [Lev. 10:3]—his silence implies a willingness to be comforted. You, too, must be comforted."

Rabban Yohanan said to him, "Is it not enough that I grieve over my own? Do you have to remind me of Aaron's grief?"

R. Simeon entered and said, "Master, by your leave, may I say something to you?"

"Speak," he replied.

R. Simeon said, "King David had a son who died, yet he allowed himself to be comforted for the loss of him. How do we know that David was comforted? Because it is said, 'And David comforted Bathsheba his wife, and went in unto her, and lay with her; and she bore a son, and he called his name Solomon [Peace, Consolation]' [2 Sam. 12:24]. You, too, Master, must be comforted."

Rabban Yohanan said to him, "Is it not enough that I grieve over my own? Do you have to remind me of King David's grief?"

R. Eleazar ben Arakh entered. As soon as Rabban Yohanan saw him, he said to his servant, "Take my clothing and follow me to the bathhouse,[5] for he is a great man, and I shall be unable to resist him."

Having entered, R. Eleazar sat down before him and said, "May I tell you a parable? To whom may you be likened? To a man with whom the king deposited an object. Each and every day the man would weep and cry out, saying, 'Woe is me! When shall I be safely relieved of this trust?' You too, master, had a son: he studied the Torah, the Prophets, the Writings; he studied Mishnah, *Halakhah*, and *Aggadot*, and departed from this world without sin. You should be comforted because you have returned unimpaired what was given you in trust."

Rabban Yohanan said to him, "Eleazar, my son, you have comforted me the way men should give comfort!"[6]

52. When Rabban Yohanan ben Zakkai fell ill, his disciples went in to visit him. The moment he saw them, he began to weep. His disciples asked: O our master, lamp of Israel, pillar at the right side,[7] mighty hammer! Why are you weeping? He replied: If I were being taken before a king of flesh and blood, who is here today and in the

5. "R. Yohanan realized that R. Eleazar would succeed in consoling him and therefore he prepared to go to the bathhouse, a luxury normally forbidden to a mourner. The phrase 'Take my clothing,' etc., was suggested (according to Professor Louis Ginzberg) by the reference to 2 Sam. 12:20, where it is said that David terminated the mourning for his son by bathing and putting on his clothes" (ARN, YJS, p. 192).

6. ARN 14.

7. The reference is to Jachin, one of the two pillars in the Temple. See 1 Kings 7:21.

grave tomorrow, whose anger if he is angry with me does not last forever, who if he imprisons me does not imprison me forever, who if he puts me to death does not put me to everlasting death, and whom I can persuade with words or bribe with money—even so I would weep. Now that I am being taken before the supreme King of kings, the Holy One, blessed be He, who lives and endures forever and ever and ever, whose anger if He is angry with me is an everlasting anger, who if He imprisons me imprisons me forever, who if He puts me to death puts me to death forever, and whom I cannot persuade with words or bribe with money—even more, now that there are two ways before me, one leading to the Garden of Eden and the other to Gehenna, and I do not know by which I shall be taken—should I not weep?

They said to him: Our master, bless us. He said to them: May it be God's will that the fear of Heaven shall be as much upon you as the fear of flesh and blood. His disciples asked: Is that all?[1] He replied: Would that you attained no less than such fear! You can see for yourselves the truth of what I say: when a man is about to commit a transgression, he says, "I hope no man will see me."

At the moment of his departure, he said to them: Remove the vessels [from this chamber] so that they will not become unclean [by contact with my dead body], and prepare a seat for Hezekiah king of Judah, who is coming [to attend my funeral].[2]

53. After Rabban Yohanan ben Zakkai died, the radiance of wisdom ceased.[3]

54. As long as Raban Yohanan ben Zakkai made his home [in Berur Hayyil],[4] his five disciples remained in his presence. After he passed away, four went to Yavneh.[5] However, Eleazar ben Arakh joined his wife at Emmaus,[6] a place of good water and beautiful situation, where he waited for the others to come to him, but they did not. When they failed to come, he wanted to go to them, but his wife would not let him, saying, "Who needs whom?" He answered, "They need me." She said, "When there is a leather vessel [containing food] and there are mice, who goes to whom—the mice to the vessel, or the vessel to the mice?" He listened to her and remained there until he forgot his learning.

After a while the other disciples came to him and asked him about a matter in Torah, but he was unable to answer.[7]

R. Dosa ben Horkinas (fl. 1st century C.E.)

55. In the days of R. Dosa ben Horkinas [word came to the academy, presumably in his name, of] a ruling that if a man dies leaving two widows—one of them his brother's daughter—then his brother is permitted to marry the other widow.[8] The ruling was very disturbing to the sages[9] because R. Dosa was a great sage [who had previously supported the rule that forbade such marriages]. But now, because of his advanced years and his failing eyesight, he was unable to come to the academy. Hence they deliberated about who should go and tell him [that his recent ruling would be disregarded]. R. Joshua said, "I will go." "And who will go along to back him up?" "R. Eleazar ben Azariah." "And who will back up R. Eleazar?" "R. Akiva." The three of them went and sat down at the entrance of R. Dosa's house. His maidservant entered the house and told R. Dosa, "Master, the sages of Israel are come to you." He said, "Bid them enter." When they came in, he took hold of R. Joshua and had him sit on a gilded couch. The latter said to R. Dosa, "My master, will you ask another disciple of yours to sit?" R. Dosa asked, "Who is he?" R. Joshua replied, "R. Eleazar ben Azariah." R. Dosa asked, "Does our colleague Azariah have a son?" [He was told, "Yes."] At that, R. Dosa quoted, "I have been young and now am old, and [knowing that Azariah is blessed with a son, I can affirm] I have not seen the righteous forsaken" (Ps. 37:25). R. Dosa took hold of R. Eleazar and had him sit on a gilded couch. Then R. Eleazar said, "Will you ask one more disciple of yours to sit?" R. Dosa asked, "Who is he?" R. Eleazar replied, "Akiva son of Joseph." R. Dosa said, "Are you really Akiva son of Joseph, whose name has gone forth from one end of the world to the other? Sit down, my son, sit down. May there be many like you in Israel!" And he applied to him the verse "A good name is better than precious oil" (Eccles. 7:1).

Then the sages began to encircle R. Dosa with all sorts of legal questions until they came around[10] to the subject of the special case mentioned above. When they reached it, they asked him, "What is the ruling that applies

---

1. Should not the fear of God exceed fear of a mortal?
2. Perhaps Rabban Yohanan's way of saying that even Hezekiah, who did not submit to Assyria, approves of Rabban Yohanan's submission to Rome (see above, part 1, chap. 10, §2). So Rabbi Isaac Herzog, as quoted by Adin Steinsaltz in his translation of Ber (Jerusalem, 1967). B. Ber 28b and En Yaakov, ad loc.
3. He is said to have embraced all the sciences known in his day (see above in this chapter, §48). B. Sot 49a.
4. A small town near Yavneh.
5. Where Rabban Yohanan had established an academy after the destruction of the Temple.
6. A town on the road between Jerusalem and Jaffa.
7. Eccles. R. 7:7, §2; ARN 14.
8. The other widow—co-wife of a relative whom one is forbidden to marry—is herself deemed such a relative and is therefore, according to law, exempt from both *halitzah* and levirate marriage (Yev 1:1–2; Maimonides, Code IV, iii, vi, 14–15 [YJS 19:307–8]). Still, because of neglect of the study of Torah, the prohibition against such marriages—imposed, as will be presently stated, in the days of Haggai (4th century B.C.E.)—came to be lifted, purportedly in the name of Dosa ben Horkinas, the highest legal authority in the land.
   In rabbinic law, an uncle may marry his niece (but an aunt may not marry her nephew).
9. They were reluctant to act against his decision without having consulted him first.
10. "This is a shining example of the sages' mastery of style and of pregnant brevity—*multum in parvo*.
   "Being polite, the disciples did not attack Dosa frontally with the query "What about the co-wife of a daughter?" Rather, they began with utterly irrelevant points of law, going in concentric circles until they reached forbidden marriages, then levirate marriage, and finally, perhaps a whole hour later, co-wife of a daughter. This is, of course,

when a man with two wives dies and his brother—who is the father of one of the widows—wishes to marry the other widow?" "This," he answered, "is a question in dispute between the school of Shammai and the school of Hillel." "And what is the final ruling?" "The ruling is in keeping with the opinion of the school of Hillel [that such a marriage is forbidden]."[1] "But it has been said in your name that [such a marriage is permitted], in accordance with the ruling of the school of Shammai." Dosa asked, "Did you hear the name given as 'Dosa' or 'the son of Horkinas'?" "By the life of our master," they replied, "we heard no first name given." "I have a younger brother," Dosa said, "who is a 'limb of Satan'[2] [first in stubborn debate], and his name is Jonathan, one of the disciples of the school of Shammai. Beware lest he overwhelm you on questions of established practice, because he has three hundred answers to prove that the sort of marriage we are discussing is permitted. But I call heaven and earth to witness that the prophet Haggai[3] sat on this very seat and declared that marriage between one widow of a man and his brother, who is the father of the man's other widow, is forbidden.

It is taught: When the sages came, they had all entered through one door, but when they left, they left through three different doors [to avoid Jonathan].[4] But Jonathan accosted R. Akiva and put a difficult question to him, which R. Akiva answered. [Dissatisfied with the reply], Jonathan said, "Are you the Akiva whose name has gone forth from one end of the world to the other? You are lucky that you have achieved such fame [for, judging by your answer], you are not even the equal of one of the cattle herdsmen." R. Akiva replied [with the sort of soft answer that turns away wrath], "I beg your pardon, not even the equal of one of the [more lowly] shepherds."[5]

R. Hanina ben Dosa (fl. 1st century C.E.)

56. Every day a divine voice goes forth and declares: The whole world is supplied with food only on account of My son Hanina, while My son Hanina is satisifed with just one *kav*[6] of carobs from Sabbath eve to Sabbath eve.[7]

57. Every Friday the wife of R. Hanina ben Dosa would heat the oven by burning smoke-producing fuel in it, because she was ashamed [to have it known that she had nothing to bake for the Sabbath]. But she had a malicious neighbor, who said, "I know that these people have nothing; let me go and see what causes that smoke." She went and knocked on the door. Embarrassed by the unexpected visit, the wife of R. Hanina withdrew to an inner room. A miracle was wrought [for her], so that the neighbor found the oven full of bread and the kneading trough full of rising dough. Seeing that, she called out, "Madam, madam, bring your shovel, your bread is about to get charred." R. Hanina's wife called back, "Yes, I just went to the other room to fetch one."

Once Hanina's wife said to him, "How long are we to go on suffering so much?" He replied, "What shall we do?" She said, "Pray that some of what is stored up for the righteous in the world-to-come may be given you here and now." He prayed, and [from above] there emerged the semblance of a hand, which gave him the leg of a golden table. That night in a dream he saw each of the other righteous men [in the world-to-come] dining at a table with three legs, but he and his wife were dining at a table with only two legs. So he said to his wife, "Are you content to have all the righteous dine at three-legged tables, while you and I will be dining at a table with one of its legs missing?" She: "What shall we do? You have no choice but to pray that the leg be taken from you." He prayed, and it was taken back.

The sages taught: The latter miracle was greater than the former. For we have a tradition that Heaven gives but never takes back.[8]

58. Once, on a Friday eve at dusk, when R. Hanina noticed that his daughter looked sad, he asked her, "My daughter, why are you so distressed?" She replied, "I mistook a vessel containing vinegar for a vessel containing oil, and used the vinegar to light the Sabbath lamp." He replied, "My daughter, why should you be concerned? He who ordained that oil should burn will ordain that even vinegar should burn." The sages taught: Indeed, the lamp continued burning, so that [on Saturday evening] they were able to use its light for the *Havdalah*.

59. R. Hanina ben Dosa had some goats and was told, "Your goats are damaging people's property." He replied, "If they really cause damage, may bears devour them; but if not, in the evening may each of them bring a bear impaled on its horns." That evening each of the goats did bring home a bear on its horns.

How did R. Hanina ben Dosa [who was poor] come to have goats? R. Phinehas said: Once it happened that a man passed by his house and [inadvertently] left behind some hens there, and R. Hanina ben Dosa's wife found them. However, he said to her, "Do not eat their eggs." The eggs and the hens increased so much that they distressed R. Hanina and his wife. So he sold them and bought the goats with the proceeds. One day, the man who had lost the hens passed by [the house] again and

typical Near Eastern good manners, especially toward an esteemed and venerated elder.

"What took me a whole paragraph, the sages expressed in *one word*—'encircled' and 'came around' are feeble shadows of the Hebrew word *mesovevim*, but at least they try to reproduce the pregnant meaning of *svv* in such a context" (Leon Nemoy).

1. According to this school, one widow may not marry her deceased husband's brother if he is the father of the other widow.
2. Literally, "the firstborn of Satan." R. Dosa seems to be playing upon the rhyme *ah katan, bekhor satan*, and *Yonatan* ("younger brother," "firstborn of Satan," "Jonathan").
3. "This means that he had an incontrovertible tradition on the matter" (Menahem ha-Meiri, as quoted in B. Yev 16a, Soncino).
4. Or, conversely, in the hope that at least one of them might meet him.
5. B. Yev 16a and En Yaakov, ad loc.
6. Four pints.
7. B.Ta 24b.
8. B. Ta 24b–25a.
9. B. Ta 25a.

said to a companion, "It was here I left my hens." R. Hanina overheard him and asked him, "Have you any mark [by which to identify them]?" The man said, "Yes." He told him what the mark was and took the goats away.

These are the same goats that brought home bears on their horns.[1]

60. R. Hanina ben Dosa had a neighbor, a woman who was building a house and found that the beams were not long enough to reach from wall to wall. She came to him and said, "I am building a house, but the beams do not reach far enough." He asked, "What is your name?" She replied, "My name is Eikhu." He said, "Eikhu,[2] may your beams reach [farther]." Immediately, they reached [the walls].

Pelimo said: I saw that house, and its beams projected a cubit on each side; and I was told: This is the house that, through his prayer, R. Hanina ben Dosa framed with beams.[3]

61. Once R. Hanina, seeing the men of his town taking vowed offerings and free-will offerings up to Jerusalem, exclaimed, "All of them take vowed offerings and free-will offerings up to Jerusalem, and I [being poor] can take up nothing! What did he do?" He went out to the grazing area near his town and found a stone, which he proceeded to chisel, polish, and scour, and then said, "I vow to take this up to Jerusalem." He wanted to engage some carriers. Five men happened to come along. He asked them, "Will you take this stone up to Jerusalem for me?" They said, "Pay us fifty *sela* and we will take it up to Jerusalem." He would have been willing to pay them, but he had no such sum, so the five men left him and went away. Immediately the Holy One placed in his path five angels in the guise of men. He asked them, "Will you take up this stone for me?" They replied, "Give us five *sela* and we will take your stone up to Jerusalem, but you must give us a hand." He no sooner put his hand to the stone than they all found themselves standing in Jerusalem. Then he wanted to pay them their hire, but he could not find them. He entered the Chamber of Hewn Stone,[4] asked about them, and was told, "It would appear that ministering angels brought your stone up to Jerusalem." To him was applied the verse "Seest thou a man diligent in his work, he shall stand before kings (*melakhim*)" (Prov. 22:29)—stand before *mal'akhim*, angels.[5]

62. R. Hanina ben Dosa was walking along the road with a basket of salt on his head, when it began to rain. He exclaimed, "Master of the universe, the whole world is at ease, but Hanina is in distress!" The rain stopped. When he reached his home, he said, "Master of the universe, the whole world is in distress, but Hanina is at ease." The rain fell again.[6]

63. Our masters taught: In a certain place there was once a lizard[7] who used to injure human beings. People came and told R. Hanina ben Dosa about it. He said: Show me its hole. They showed it to him, and he put his heel over the hole. The lizard came out, bit him, and died. He put the dead lizard on his shoulder, brought it to the house of study, and said: See, my children, the lizard does not kill; it is sin that kills!

On that occasion they said: Woe to the man who meets up with a lizard, and woe to the lizard that meets up with R. Hanina ben Dosa![8]

64. Once R. Hanina ben Dosa saw a lion and said to him, "O you weakling of a king, have I not adjured you not to be seen in the Land of Israel?" At once the lion fled. R. Hanina ran after him and said, "Forgive my having called you weakling, while He who created you called you mighty when He spoke of you as 'the lion, which is mightiest among beasts' " (Prov. 30:30).[9]

65. It is said of R. Hanina ben Dosa that when he prayed in behalf of the sick, he would say, "this one will live," "That one will die." When he was asked, "How do you know?" he would reply, "If my prayer comes fluently to my mouth, I know that the patient is accepted [for recovery]; if not, I know he is rejected."

A story is told that when the son of Rabban Gamaliel fell ill, the father sent two scholars to R. Hanina ben Dosa to ask him to beseech mercy for his son. As soon as R. Hanina saw them, he went up to his upper chamber and besought mercy for him. When he came down, he said, "Go, the fever has left him." The scholars asked, "Can it be that you are a prophet?" He replied, "I am neither a prophet nor the son of a prophet, but I learned this from experience: if my prayer comes fluently to my mouth, I know that the patient is accepted [for recovery]; but if not, I know that he is rejected." They sat down and made a note of the exact moment [when, according to R. Hanina, the fever left]. When they came to Rabban Gamaliel, he said to them, "By the Temple service! The time you put down is not an instant before or after what happened—at that very moment the fever left my son and he asked us for a drink of water."

On another occasion it happened that R. Hanina ben Dosa went to study Torah with Rabban Yohanan ben Zakkai. When the son of Rabban Yohanan ben Zakkai fell ill, the father said to R. Hanina, "Hanina my son, beseech mercy for me, that he may recover." R. Hanina lowered his head between his knees and besought mercy for him, and the son recovered. Rabban Yohanan ben Zakkai said, "If I, Ben Zakkai, had kept knocking my head between my knees the entire day, no one would have heeded me." His wife asked, "Is Hanina greater than you?" He replied,

1. Ibid.
2. The name Eikhu suggested to him the Greek *eike*, ("would that"). So Henry Malter in his translation of Ta (Philadelphia, 1928), p. 188, n. 351.
3. B. Ta 25a and En Yaakov, ad loc.
4. The room in the Temple where the Sanhedrin sat.
5. Eccles. R. 1:1, §1; Song R. 1:1, §4.
6. B. Ta 24b.
7. Perhaps a crossbreed of a snake and a lizard.
8. B. Ber 33a and En Yaakov, ad loc.
9. Tanhuma, *Va-yiggash*, §3.

"No, but he, like a servant attending the king [can go in and out before the royal presence], while I, like a nobleman attending the king [may appear only at fixed times]."[1]

66. Our masters taught: There is a story about the daughter of Nehonia, the digger of cisterns.[2] When she fell into a large pit [that he had dug], people came and reported the accident to R. Hanina ben Dosa. During the first hour, he said to them, "She is all right." During the second hour, he again said, "She is all right." In the third, he said, "She has got out safely." Her father asked her, "My daughter, who saved you?" "A ram,[3] with an aged man[4] leading it, came to my help." "Are you a prophet?" the people asked R. Hanina ben Dosa. He replied, "I am neither a prophet nor the son of a prophet; but I said to myself: It is inconceivable that his own seed should come to grief through the very same beneficent work in which a righteous man is engaged!"

(R. Abba stated: [To be sure, Nehonia's daughter was saved, but] Nehonia's son died of thirst, for the Holy One deals strictly with those round about Him, even [if they stray] by a hairsbreadth, as is said, "Round about Him, it is by a hairsbreadth"[5] [Ps. 50:3]).[6]

67. A story: The ass of R. Hanina ben Dosa was stolen by brigands, who tied it up in a yard and put straw, barley, and water before it. But the ass would neither eat nor drink. So, asking themselves, "Why would we let it die and stink up our yard?" they opened the gate before it and chased it out.

The ass walked along braying until it reached the house of R. Hanina ben Dosa. As soon as it reached the house, his son heard its voice. "Father," he said, "that sounds like our beast." R. Hanina said to him: "My son, open the gate for it—it is almost dead of hunger." He rose up, opened the gate, and put before it straw, barley, and water, and it ate and drank.

Therefore people say: Even as the righteous of old were saintly, so their beasts, like their masters, were saintly.[7]

68. When R. Hanina ben Dosa died, men of deed[8] ceased to be.[9]

1. B. Ber 34b and En Yaakov, ad loc.
2. Because of the large influx of pilgrims during the festivals, the water in the year-round wells did not suffice. Nehonia devoted himself as a volunteer to provide additional sources of water.
3. The ram of Isaac, according to Rashi.
4. Abraham, according to Rashi.
5. JV: "feared by all them that are round about Him." But *s'r* ("fear") also means "hairsbreadth."
6. B. Yev 121b.
7. ARN 8.
8. "Men capable of performing miracles; or men who devoted their lives to deeds of lovingkindness" (Adolf Büchler, as quoted in Sot, Soncino, p. 265, n. 13).
9. B. Sot 49a.

Rabban Gamaliel II (fl. 90–115 C.E.)

69. A vignette about Rabban Gamaliel: When he got married, he recited the Shema on his wedding night. His disciples said to him: Our master, did you not teach us that a bridegroom is exempt from the recital of the Shema? He replied: I will not listen to the suggestion that I should cast off the kingship of Heaven from myself even for a moment.

[Years later] Rabban Gamaliel bathed on the first night after his wife's death. His disciples said to him: Our master, did you not teach us that a mourner is forbidden to bathe? He replied: I, being very delicate, am not like other people.[10]

70. Rabban Gamaliel[11] was once a passenger on board ship with R. Joshua [who was traveling to earn his living]. Rabban Gamaliel had taken only bread with him, while R. Joshua had taken bread and flour. When Rabban Gamaliel's bread gave out and he had to depend on R. Joshua's flour, he asked him, "Did you know that we could be so much delayed that you decided to bring flour?" R. Joshua answered, "There is a certain star that rises once in seventy years and leads mariners[12] astray, and I said to myself: Perhaps it will rise this time and lead us astray." Rabban Gamaliel: "You possess so much knowledge and yet must travel on board ship to earn your livelihood!" R. Joshua: "Before you marvel about me, marvel first at two disciples you have on land, R. Yohanan ben Gudgada[13] and R. Eleazar Hisma, who can calculate how many drops there are in the sea and yet have no bread to eat nor clothes to wear."

Rabban Gamaliel decided to appoint them to high official posts [where they could earn a living]. When he landed, he sent for them, but they could not come.[14] He sent for them again, and they came. He said to them, "Do you imagine that I offer you mastery? It is servitude [the true status of a person in authority] that I offer you, as indicated by the elders' saying to Rehoboam, 'If thou wilt be a servant unto this people this day' " (1 Kings 12:7).[15]

71. Rabban Gamaliel used to have a diagram of the phases of the moon on a tablet [hung] on the wall of his upper chamber, and he used to show it to the unlearned[16] and say, "Did the new moon look like this or like that?"[17]

72. Our masters taught: Once the heavens were overcast with clouds, and the likeness of the new moon was visible on the twenty-ninth of the month. The public wanted to

10. His bathing was thus medicinal. B. Ber 16a–b.
11. On his journey to Rome in the year 95 C.E.
12. Who steer their course by the stars.
13. "R. Yohanan ben Gudgada belonged to a much earlier generation, and the reference must be to R. Yohanan ben Nuri; see Wilhelm Bacher (Isidore Epstein in Hor, Soncino, p. 71, n. 3.
14. They were too modest to accept a position of authority.
15. B. Hor 10a–b and En Yaakov, ad loc.
16. Who came to testify that they had seen the new moon.
17. B. RH 24a.

declare the day New Moon, and the court was about to sanctify the new month, but Rabban Gamaliel said: I have it on the authority of my father's house that the renewal of the moon takes place not before twenty-nine and a half days, two-thirds of an hour, and seventy-three *halakin*[1] of the old month have elapsed.

On that day, the mother of Ben Zaza died, and Rabban Gamaliel delivered a lengthy funeral oration for her—not because she merited it, but so that the public would know that the court had not yet sanctified the new month.[2]

73. On one occasion, two witnesses came and said, "We saw the new moon in the morning in the east and in the evening in the west."[3] R. Yohanan ben Nuri said curtly, "They are false witnesses."[4] However, when they came to Yavneh, Rabban Gamaliel accepted their testimony.

On another occasion, two witnesses came and said, "We saw the new moon at its proper time,"[5] but on the night that should have been New Moon,[6] it was not visible. However, by that time Rabban Gamaliel had already accepted their testimony [and declared the thirtieth day as New Moon]. R. Dosa ben Horkinas said, "They are false witnesses. How can it be testified that a woman has given birth if on the next day her belly is still swollen?"[7] R. Joshua said to him, "I agree with what you say."

Then Rabban Gamaliel sent word to R. Joshua: "I order you to come to me with your staff and your money on the day that according to your reckoning should be Yom Kippur.[8] When R. Akiva went [to R. Joshua] and found him distraught,[9] he asked, "Master, why are you so distraught?" R. Joshua replied, "Akiva, that man [Gamaliel] deserves to be laid up in a sickbed for twelve months without the opportunity to issue such an order." R. Akiva: "I can bring proof [from Scripture] that whatever Rabban Gamaliel has done is valid, because it says, 'These are the appointed seasons of the Lord, holy convocations which ye shall proclaim in their appointed seasons' [Lev. 23:4], meaning that God says: Whether they are proclaimed at their proper time or not at their proper time, I have no appointed seasons other than these." R. Joshua then went to R. Dosa ben Horkinas, who said to him, "If we call in question the decisions of the court of Rabban Gamaliel, we may very well question the decisions of each and every court that has arisen since the days of Moses up to now. For Scripture says, 'Then went up Moses and Aaron, Nadab and Abihu, and seventy of the elders of Israel' [Exod. 24:9]. Why are the names of the elders not expressly mentioned if not to teach that every three judges who have risen up as a court over Israel are to be deemed like the court of Moses."[10]

Hearing that, R. Joshua took his staff and his money, and went to Yavneh to Rabban Gamaliel on the day on which, according to his own reckoning, Yom Kippur fell. As soon as Rabban Gamaliel saw him, he rose up from his chair, kissed R. Joshua on his head, and said to him, "Come in peace, my master and my disciple—my master in wisdom and my disciple because you adopted my decision. Blessed is the generation in which men of great distinction obey those of little distinction."[11]

74. R. Zadok [a priest] owned a firstling for whom he set down barley in a wicker basket made of peeled willow twigs. While it was eating, it split its lips. R. Zadok came before R. Joshua to inquire whether he, as a fellow (*haver*), would not be suspected of having deliberately caused a blemish in the firstling he owned, so that, since it was blemished, he would be allowed to eat it.[12] By way of arguing for R. Joshua's approval, he asked, "Have we not said that there was a difference between [a priest who is] a fellow (a *haver*) and [a priest who is] 'unlearned' (an *am ha-aretz*)?" R. Joshua replied, "Yes."[13] Then R. Zadok came before Rabban Gamaliel, whom he also asked, "Have we not said that there was a difference between [a priest who is] a fellow (a *haver*) and [a priest who is] 'unlearned' (an *am ha-aretz*)?" Rabban Gamaliel replied, "No." R. Zadok said to him, "But R. Joshua told me yes!" Rabban Gamaliel: "Wait until the expert debaters[14] enter the house of study." When they entered the house of study, R. Zadok arose and asked, "Have we not said that there was a difference between [a priest who is] a fellow (a *haver*) and one who is 'unlearned' (an *am ha-aretz*)?" R. Joshua replied, "No."[15] At that, Rabban Gamaliel asked, "Was not the answer yes reported to me in your name? Joshua, stand on your feet and let the facts as reported testify against you." R. Joshua stood up and said [to himself]: What am I to do? If I were alive and he dead, the living might conceivably contradict the dead; but since he is alive and I am alive, how can the living successfully con-

1. "Lit., 'parts' (sc. of one hour), i.e., $^{73}/_{1080} \times 60$ m = 4 m 3⅓ sec. The new moon, therefore, could not be seen in the twenty-ninth day" (RH, Soncino, p. 110, n. 7).
2. A funeral oration may not be delivered on the New Moon, regarded as a holy day. B. RH 25a.
3. "We should naturally suppose this to mean that they saw the old moon in the morning and the new moon in the evening" (RH, Soncino, p. 108, n. 1).
4. "Presumably because according to what has been stated above the old moon is never visible for twenty-four hours before the new appears" (RH, Soncino, p. 108, n. 2).
5. "Apparently this must have been on the thirtieth day shortly before nightfall" (RH, Soncino, p. 108, n. 3).
6. "Lit., 'the night of its carryover,' i.e., after the nightfall with which the thirty-first day begins, when it should have been clearly visible" (RH, Soncino, p. 108, n. 4).
7. "Lit., 'between her teeth.' Similarly the old moon would still be 'between the teeth' of the new" (RH, Soncino, p. 108, n. 6).
8. "The New Moon in question was that of Tishri, and consequently the Day of Atonement according to R. Joshua would fall a day later than according to R. Gamaliel" (RH, Soncino, p. 108, n. 7).
9. Because he was ordered to profane the Day of Atonement.
10. Seeing that most of the members of the Moses' court also bore no names of distinction.
11. B. RH 24b–25a and En Yaakov, ad loc.
12. An unblemished firstling must be brought as an offering. See Deut. 15:19 and Joseph Reider's comment in Deut. (Philadelphia, 1937), p. 156.
13. There is a difference, and therefore you, being a *haver*, are not suspected of deliberately blemishing your firstling.
14. Literally, "shield bearers."
15. Not wishing to give a contrary decision in the presence of Rabban Gamaliel.

tradict the living?[1] In the meantime, while R. Joshua remained on his feet, Rabban Gamaliel, seated, continued his discourse until all the people began to grumble and finally told Hutzpit, Rabban Gamaliel's interpreter,[2] "Stop interpreting Rabban Gamaliel's words," and he stopped.[3]

75. Our masters taught: A certain disciple came before R. Joshua and asked him, "Master, is the evening *Tefillah* optional or obligatory?" He replied, "It is optional." Then the disciple presented himself before Rabban Gamaliel and asked him, "Is the evening *Tefillah* optional or obligatory?" He replied, "It is obligatory." "But," said the disciple, "what if R. Joshua told me that it is optional?" Rabban Gamaliel: "Wait until the expert debaters enter the house of study." When they came in, the disciple arose and inquired, "Is the evening *Tefillah* optional or obligatory?" Rabban Gamaliel replied, "It is obligatory," and then asked the sages, "Is there anyone who disputes me in this matter?" R. Joshua: "No." Rabban Gamaliel: "Was not the answer Optional reported to me in your name?" He then went on: "Joshua, stand on your feet and let the facts as reported testify against you!" R. Joshua stood up and said [to himself]: Were I alive and he dead, the living might conceivably contradict the dead; but since he is alive and I am alive, how can the living successfully contradict the living? In the meantime, while R. Joshua remained standing on his feet, Rabban Gamaliel, seated, continued his discourse, until all the people there began to grumble and finally said to Hutzpit, Rabban Gamaliel's interpreter, "Stop interpreting his words," and he stopped. Then the people said to R. Zinon, the precentor: "Read [verses that are appropriate]." After he began reading, the people stood up and said, "Read 'Upon whom hath not thy wickedness passed continually?' " (Nah. 3:19). Then they said, "How long is Rabban Gamaliel to go on insulting R. Joshua? On New Year's Day last year, he insulted him; in the matter of the firstborn in the affair of R. Zadok, he insulted him; now he insults him again! Come, let us depose him! Whom shall we appoint in his place? Shall we appoint R. Joshua? [No], because he is one of the parties involved. Shall we appoint R. Akiva? [No], because since he has no ancestral merit, Rabban Gamaliel may bring a curse on him. Let us then appoint R. Eleazar ben Azariah, who is wise and rich and tenth in descent from Ezra." [He is wise, so that if anyone puts a question to him, he will be able to answer it. He is rich, so that if occasion rises for paying court to Caesar, he will be able to do so. He is tenth in descent from Ezra, so that he has ancestral merit, and Rabban Gamaliel will be unable to bring a curse on him.] They went and said to him, "Will it please the master to become head of the academy?" He replied, "Let me go and consult the members of my family." He went and consulted his wife. She said to him, "Perhaps they will depose you too." He replied to her, "[There is a proverb]: Let a man use a crystal cup for one day, even if it be broken the next." She said to him, "You have no hoary hair." He was only eighteen years old that day, but a miracle was wrought for him, and he was adorned with eighteen streaks of gray hair. (That is why R. Eleazar ben Azariah said: Behold, I am like a seventy-year-old—he did not say: I am seventy years old.)

R. Akiva, seated there, was distressed and said, "R. Azariah is not my superior in learning, but he is my superior in lineage.[4] Happy is the man whose forebears convey such merit on him. Happy is the man who has an ancestral peg to hang on to."

A Tanna taught: On that day the doorkeeper was removed and the disciples were allowed unrestricted entry—previously Rabban Gamaliel had issued a proclamation: "No disciple whose inner self does not live up to his acceptable exterior[5] may enter the house of study." On that day several benches were added.

Before that, Rabban Gamaliel had become alarmed and said, "I may, God forbid, be depriving Israel of Torah!"[6] But in a dream he was shown white casks[7] filled with ashes.[8]

We have been taught: Eduyyot[9] was formulated on that day—wherever the expression "on that day" is used, it refers to that day—and there was no *Halakhah* about which any doubt existed in the house of study that was not fully elucidated. Rabban Gamaliel also did not absent himself from the house of study a single hour, as we have been taught: On that day, Judah, an Ammonite proselyte, came before them in the house of study and asked, "Am I permitted to [marry a Jewess, and thus] enter the assembly [of the Lord]?" Rabban Gamaliel said, "You are forbidden to enter the Lord's assembly." R. Joshua, however, said to him, "You are permitted to enter the Lord's assembly." "But," said Rabban Gamaliel to R. Joshua, "has it not been laid down long ago, 'An Ammonite or a Moabite shall not enter into the assembly of the Lord' " (Deut. 23:4)? R. Joshua replied, "But now, do Ammon and Moab still reside in their original homes? Long ago, did not Sennacherib king of Assyria come up and mingle all the nations, as it says, 'I have removed the bounds of the peoples, and have robbed their treasures, and have brought down as one mighty their inhabitants'?" (Isa. 10:13). Rabban Gamaliel replied to him, "But has it not already been said, 'Afterward I will bring back the captivity of the children of Ammon' [Jer. 49:6]? So, then, they have returned." To this R. Joshua replied, "But it has also been said, 'And I will turn the captivity of My people Israel' [Amos 9:14], and as yet they have not returned. Rather, Scripture means that in time Israel will return; even as in time Ammon will return." They per-

1. "I did say it and now withdraw" (Rashi). Tosafot: "I had in mind concealing what I said but am unable to do so now."
2. The man who expounded the ideas of the teacher to the public. In later usage he is called *amora*.
3. B. Bekh 36a and En Yaakov, ad loc.
4. R. Akiva's father, Joseph, was a proselyte. So Maimonides, in the introduction to his Code.
5. Literally, "whose inside is not as his outside."
6. By keeping out so many disciples.
7. Or, "stone jars."
8. Those kept out did not deserve to be admitted.
9. Literally, "testimonies," not necessarily the tractate Eduyyot we now have.

mitted the Ammonite [to marry a Jewess, and thus] to enter the Lord's assembly.

Rabban Gamaliel then said, "Since the decision sides with R. Joshua, I will go and apologize to him." When he reached R. Joshua's house, he saw that its walls were coal-black. He said to him, "From the walls of your house, it is apparent that you are a charcoal burner."[1] R. Joshua replied, "Woe to the generation whose leader you are, and woe to the ship whose pilot you are! For you know nothing of the troubles of the scholars, how they make their living, and how they sustain themselves!"

Rabban Gamaliel: "In all humility, I ask you to forgive me."

But R. Joshua was unmoved.

"Do it, then," Rabban Gamaliel said, "out of respect for my father."

At this, R. Joshua made his peace with Rabban Gamaliel.

They asked, "Who will go and tell the sages?" A certain fuller said to them, "I will go." R. Joshua sent word [through him] to the house of study, saying, "Let him who is accustomed to wear the robe wear it again; for is it conceivable that he who is not accustomed to wear the robe should keep saying to him who is accustomed to wear it, 'Take off your robe, and I will put it on'?" At this, R. Akiva said to the sages, "Lock the doors, so that the servants of Rabban Gamaliel may not enter and [in support of their master's reinstatement] resort to violence against the sages."

R. Joshua said, "I had better get up and go to them myself." He came, knocked at the door, and called out to them, "Let the sprinkler, son of a sprinkler, sprinkle.[2] Shall he who is neither a sprinkler nor the son of a sprinkler dare say to a sprinkler son of a sprinkler, 'Your water is cave water[3] and your ashes are oven ashes'?"[4] R. Akiva said to him, "R. Joshua, you are now reconciled with Rabban Gamaliel, and since we have done nothing except out of regard for your honor, [we, too, are reconciled with Rabban Gamaliel's reinstatement]. Early tomorrow morning, you and I will wait on R. Eleazar ben Azariah [to inform him]."

Nevertheless, they did not remove R. Eleazar ben Azariah entirely from his office. For after that, Rabban Gamaliel lectured on two Sabbaths, and then R. Eleazar ben Azariah lectured on one Sabbath. It is in reference to this that a master inquired, "Whose Sabbath was it?" and was told, "It was the Sabbath of R. Eleazar ben Azariah."[5]

76. Such was Rabban Gamaliel's conduct: When he walked into [the academy] and said, "Ask,"[6] it had been made known to him [in advance] that there would be no remonstrance. But when he entered and did not say, "Ask," it had been made known to him that remonstrance was to be expected.[7]

77. It once happened that while traveling from Acco to Chezib, Rabban Gamaliel was riding on an ass and R. Ilai was following behind him on foot. Noticing a loaf of white bread on the road, Rabban Gamaliel said, "Ilai, pick up the loaf from the road." Later, he met a certain heathen. "Mavgai,"[8] he said, "take that loaf from Ilai." R. Ilai then approached the heathen and asked, "Where are you from?" The other replied, "From one of the settlements in the vicinity of the road station for travelers." "What is your name?" "My name is Mavgai." "Did R. Gamaliel ever meet you before?" "No," the other replied.

From this incident we learned that R. Gamaliel divined [the heathen's name] by the holy spirit. At the same time, we learned three other things. We learned that edibles lying on the ground may not be passed by [but must be picked up];[9] that one must assume that the loaf belongs to one of the majority of those traveling on that road, namely, to a heathen;[10] and that it is permitted to derive benefit from a heathen's leavened bread after the Passover.[11]

When Rabban Gamaliel arrived at Chezib, a man approached him and asked to be absolved from a vow he had made. At that, Rabban Gamaliel asked R. Ilai, who accompanied him, "Have we perchance [during our journey] drunk a quarter of a *log* of Italian wine?" "Yes," the other replied. "In that case," he said, "let this man walk behind us until the effect of the wine we drank has been dissipated." The man walked behind them for three *mil*, until Rabban Gamaliel reached the Ladder of Tyre.[12] Having arrived at the Ladder of Tyre, R. Gamaliel dismounted the ass, wrapped his cloak around himself, sat down, and absolved the man from his vow.

From that incident we learned many things. We learned that a quarter of a *log* of Italian wine causes intoxication; that an intoxicated man may not render decisions in legal matters; that a journey causes the effects of wine to dissipate; and that absolution from vows may not be granted while riding, walking, or standing, but must be done sitting.[13]

78. We have been taught: Rabban Gamaliel had a tube through which he could see at a distance of two thousand cubits across land, and likewise two thousand cubits across the sea.[14]

79. It once happened that at a banquet in the home of Rabban Gamaliel's son, R. Eliezer, R. Joshua, and R.

---

1. Or, "blacksmith."
2. That is, a priest, son of a priest, should sprinkle the water of purification—Rabban Gamaliel, who has a hereditary claim to the patriarchate, should be reinstated.
3. And not "living water" from a stream, as required. See Num. 19:17.
4. And not from the Red Heifer.
5. See B. Hag 3a. B. Ber 27b–28a; P. Ber 4:1, 7c–d; En Yaakov.
6. Questions may be asked.
7. Sif Deut., §16.
8. A Samaritan proper name. Cf. B. Mak 11a.
9. Since R. Ilai was requested to pick up the loaf.
10. And therefore was forbidden to an Israelite.
11. The loaf was nevertheless presented to a heathen. But he would naturally be grateful for the gift and likely to reply to it by some act of kindness.
12. Scala Tyriorum, a promontory south of Tyre.
13. B. Er 64b and En Yaakov, ad loc.
14. B. Er 43b and En Yaakov, ad loc.

Zadok were reclining on couches, while Rabban Gamaliel was standing over them and serving drinks. He offered a cup to R. Eliezer, but he would not take it; then he offered it to R. Joshua, who did take it. R. Eliezer said to him, "How can we allow this, Joshua? We are seated, while Gamaliel Berabbi[1] is standing over us and serving us drinks!" R. Joshua replied, "In Scripture we find one even greater than he acting as servitor. Abraham was the greatest man of his generation, yet of him it is written, 'And he stood over them'[2] [Gen. 18:8]. Do you suppose that his guests appeared to him openly as ministering angels? They appeared to him disguised as mere Arabs.[3] Then should not Rabban Gamaliel Berabbi stand over us and serve us drinks?"

Now R. Zadok spoke up: "How long will you disregard the honor due Him who is everywhere and concern yourselves with the honor due to His creatures? The Holy One causes winds to blow, clouds to rise, rain to fall, and the earth to sprout, and before each and every one of us He sets a table, and we—should not Rabban Gamaliel, even though a Berabbi, stand and serve us drinks?"[4]

80. Rabban Gamaliel gave his daughter in marriage. "Father," she requested, "pray for me." He replied, "May [it be God's will that] you not come back here." When she gave birth to a son, she asked, "Father, pray for me." He replied, "May [it be God's will that] 'Woe' never leave your mouth." She cried out, "Two joys befell me, and you curse me!" "Both were prayers for you," he replied. "[My prayer was] that peace reign for you in your home, so that you will not return here; and that your son may survive, so that 'Woe' will not leave your mouth, [so that you will not have to wail] 'Woe, my son has not eaten! Woe, my son has not drunk! Woe, my son has not gone to the synagogue!' "[5]

81. It happened that by accident Rabban Gamaliel put out an eye of his slave Tabi.[6] He rejoiced over it greatly [eager as he was to have his meritorious slave set free]; and when he met R. Joshua, he said, "Do you know that my slave Tabi is getting his freedom?" "How did it happen?" R. Joshua asked. "Because I [accidentally] put out his eye."[7] R. Joshua: "Your admission is not legally effective, since there are no witnesses testifying for the slave.[8]

82. Male and female slaves are not customarily addressed as "Father So-and-so" or "Mother So-and-so." However, those of Rabban Gamaliel were addressed as "Father So-and-so" and "Mother So-and-so."

When his slave Tabi died, he accepted condolences for him. His disciples asked, "But did you not teach us, our master, that condolences are not to be accepted for a slave?" He replied, "My slave Tabi was not like other slaves. He was a worthy man."[9]

83. Proclos son of Philosophos put a question to Rabban Gamaliel while he was bathing in Acco in the bath of Aphrodite.[10] Proclos asked, "It is written in your Torah, 'And there shall cleave nought of the devoted thing to thy hand' [Deut. 13:18]; why, then, are you bathing in the bath devoted to Aphrodite?" Rabban Gamaliel replied, "Questions relating to Torah may not be answered in a bath."[11] When he came out, he said to Proclos, "I did not come into her domain—she has come into mine.[12] People do not say, 'The bath was made as an adornment for Aphrodite,' but rather, 'Aphrodite was made as an adornment for the bath.' "[13]

84. When the wicked tyrant Rufus plowed the site of the Temple Hall, Rabban Gamaliel was condemned to death. A certain general then appeared, stood up in the house of study, and said, "The man with the nose,[14] the man with the nose is wanted." When Rabban Gamaliel heard this, he hid himself [from the Romans]. But the general called on him secretly and said, "If I save you, will you bring me into the world-to-come?" Rabban Gamaliel: "Yes." "Swear it to me." And Rabban Gamaliel so swore. At that, the general went up to the roof, threw himself down, and died. [The decree against Rabban Gamaliel was then annulled], in keeping with the practice among the Romans that when a decree is issued and one of their own leaders dies, that decree is annulled.[15] Then a divine voice went forth and declared, "This general is destined for life in the world-to-come.[16]

85. Our masters taught: From the days of Moses down to Rabban Gamaliel, the Torah was studied only while standing. When Rabban Gamaliel died, feebleness descended on the world, and they studied the Torah sitting. Such is the implication of what we learned: "From the time that Rabban Gamaliel died, [full] honor ceased to be paid to the Torah.[17]

---

1. A title of distinction.
2. Over the three angels who appeared to him in the guise of human beings.
3. When Abraham bade them wash their feet, it was because he suspected them of being Arabs, who worship the sand on their feet.
4. B. Kid 32b and En Yaakov, ad loc.
5. Gen. R. 26:5.
6. Giving Tabi freedom would have violated the injunction "These shall become your property: you are to keep them as a possession for your children after you" (Lev. 25:45–46).
7. He would thereby, in accordance with Exod. 21:26, receive his freedom.
8. Under such circumstances, the slave does not go free, the penalty for the master being no more than a fine. B. BK 74b.
9. B. Ber 16b.
10. Baths were frequently adorned with the statues of deities.
11. Where people are naked.
12. The bath existed before the image of Aphrodite was set up in it, and it was constructed for general use.
13. B. AZ 44b.
14. The Roman officer may have confused the Hebrew title Nasi with the Latin word *nasus*, ("nose"). Hence he called out, "Baal *ha-hotem*"—in Latin, "*Vir nasi*" ("the man with the nose"). So Goldschmidt, ad loc.
15. They regard the death as punishment for the evil decree.
16. B. Ta 29a and En Yaakov, ad loc.
17. B. Meg 21a.

86. After the death of Rabban Gamaliel, R. Joshua entered [the house of study] to abrogate a certain ruling of his.[1] But R. Yohanan ben Nuri stood up and exclaimed, "The body, I declare, must follow the head [the earlier authority]. Throughout Rabban Gamaliel's lifetime, we set the law in agreement with Rabban Gamaliel's ruling, and now you seek to abrogate it? Since the law has already been set in agreement with Rabban Gamaliel, we shall not listen to you, Joshua."

And there was not a single person who raised any objection whatever to this statement.[2]

R. Eliezer [the Elder] ben Hyrcanus (fl. 2d century C.E.)

87. R. Aha taught in the name of R. Hanina: When Moses went up to heaven, he heard the voice of the Holy One, who sat engaged in the study of Torah, quoting a law in the name of its author and saying, "R. Eliezer says . . ." Moses spoke up, "Master of universes, may it please You that this scholar issue from my loins." God replied, "By your life, he will indeed be from your loins." Hence it is written, "And the name *of the one* Eliezer" (Exod. 18:4)[3] as much as to say, "the name of that uniquely gifted one."[4]

88. What were the beginnings of R. Eliezer ben Hyrcanus? At the age of twenty-two, he had not yet studied Torah. His father was very rich and had many plowmen working for him. One day R. Eliezer's brothers were plowing arable ground [in a valley] while he was plowing a stony plot [on a hill]. Presently he sat down and wept. His father asked, "Why are you weeping? Are you distressed because you have to plow a stony plot? From now on, you will plow arable land." But he sat down on the arable land and wept again. The father asked, "Why are you weeping? Are you distressed because you are plowing arable land [in the heat of the valley]?" R. Eliezer: "No." The father: "Then why are you weeping?" R. Eliezer: "Because I wish to study Torah." The father: "But you are already twenty-two, and you wish to study Torah? Take a wife. She will bear children for you, and you will take them to school."

Nevertheless, R. Eliezer resolved: I will go and study Torah in the presence of Rabban Yohanan ben Zakkai. His father retorted, "You will not get a taste of food until you have plowed the entire furrow."

R. Eliezer got up early and plowed a full furrow. But then his heifer fell and broke its leg. Saying, "My heifer's leg broke for my sake," he quickly took off and went to Rabban Yohanan ben Zakkai in Jerusalem.

It is said: That day was the eve of the Sabbath, and he had tasted nothing from six hours before Sabbath eve until six hours after the Sabbath's departure. As he was walking along the road, he saw a pebble in a cultivated field, picked it up, and put it in his mouth.

When he came before Rabban Yohanan ben Zakkai, he sat down and wept. "Why are you weeping?" R. Eliezer: "Because I wish to study Torah." "Have you never studied it?" "No." So Rabban Yohanan began to teach him the Shema, the *Tefillah*, the grace after meals, and two rules of law every day. On the Sabbath, R. Eliezer repeated the prayers and the rules till he memorized them. Eight days he kept at it, without eating a thing, until the foul odor from his mouth attracted the attention of Rabban Yohanan ben Zakkai, who asked, "Eliezer, my son, did you eat anything at all today?" Silence. Rabban Yohanan ben Zakkai repeated the question. Again silence. "By your life, today you will eat with me." R. Eliezer: "But I already ate at the place where I stay." Rabban Yohanan said to his disciples, "As you live, look into the matter."

So his disciples went around all the streets of Jerusalem, inquiring at the inns, "Do you have a guest who is a scholar? Do you have a guest who is a scholar?" The reply was no until they came to a woman who said yes. They asked, "Does he have anything here?" She: "He has a sack into which he puts his head and appears to suck from it as from a leather wine bottle." They: "Show it to us." She brought the sack. When they opened it, they found it full of earth. Then they asked her, "Has Eliezer eaten anything in your place today?" She replied, "No. We thought he was eating at his master's house." Thus they realized that he had not eaten for eight days.

They went and reported to Rabban Yohanan ben Zakkai, who then turned to R. Eliezer and said, "Alas for you, Eliezer, so greatly neglected in our midst. But I say to you: Even as foul breath rose out of your mouth before me, so shall the fragrance of Torah issuing out of your mouth [travel] from one end of the world to the other."

Then Rabban Yohanan set up regular meals for R. Eliezer, and he was healed. For three years he occupied himself with study in the presence of Rabban Yohanan ben Zakkai.

The other sons of Hyrcanus said to their father, "See what our son Eliezer did to you—he left you in your old age and went off to Jerusalem. Go there and disinherit him." So Hyrcanus went up to Jerusalem to disinherit Eliezer.

It is said: That day was a festal day for Rabban Yohanan ben Zakkai. All the notables of the city were dining with him, including Ben Tzitzit ha-Keset, Nakdimon ben Gorion, and Ben Kalba Savua. When Rabban Yohanan ben Zakkai heard that Hyrcanus had come, he said, "Make room for him." Thus finding himself [unexpectedly] placed among the notables of the city, he sat trembling in their midst.

Rabban Yohanan ben Zakkai set his gaze upon R. Eliezer and said, "Begin your discourse." R. Eliezer pleaded, "I cannot begin, for I am like a well, which cannot bring forth more water than it draws [from the earth]—so, too, I cannot utter more words of Torah than those I have received from you." Rabban Yohanan said, "My son, you

---

1. That a fast which has begun on a Friday may continue even into the onset of the Sabbath, which begins before the sun sets.
2. B. Er 41a.
3. Since Eliezer was the second son of Moses, one would expect the verse to read, "And the name of the second son was Eliezer." But the text reads instead, "And the name of the one Eliezer." Hence R. Hanina assumes that in this context the word hints at R. Eliezer, who lived in the first–second centuries C.E.
4. Num. R. 19:7.

are rather like a spring, which wells up and brings forth water of itself. You are like such a spring." Rabban Yohanan pressed him, and the disciples pressed him. So he arose and delivered a discourse on things that no ear had ever heard before. R. Eliezer's face was as radiant as the light of the sun; rays came forth from him like the rays that came forth from Moses, so that no one could tell whether it was day or night.

Then Rabban Yohanan ben Zakkai stood up, kissed him on his head, and said, "Abraham, Isaac, Jacob, happy are you that such a son has issued from your loins." Hyrcanus asked, "To whom is he saying this?" When told, "To your son, Eliezer," he said, "Rabban Yohanan should not have spoken thus. He should have told me to say, 'How happy am I that such a one has issued from my loins.' "

Then Hyrcanus climbed up on a bench and declared in the presence of the people of Jerusalem, "Masters, I came here for no other purpose than to disinherit my son Eliezer. But now all my possessions will be given to my son Eliezer, while his brothers are to have no portion whatever in them."

Eliezer said to Hyrcanus, "Had I sought landed properties, the Holy One would have given them to me, for 'the earth is the Lord's and the fullness thereof' [Ps. 24:1]. Had I sought silver or gold, He would have given them to me, for 'Mine is the silver, and Mine the gold, saith the Lord of hosts' [Hag. 2:8]. I sought from the Holy One nothing other than Torah."[1]

89. R. Eliezer—he is like a plastered cistern, which does not lose a drop; like a flask coated with pitch which retains its wine.[2]

90. R. Eliezer said: If all seas were ink, and all reeds pens, and heaven and earth scrolls, and all mankind scribes, they would not suffice to write the Torah that I have learned, even though I abstracted from it no more than a man would take by dipping the tip of his painting stick into the sea.[3]

91. [To accommodate his many disciples], R. Eliezer's house of study was almost as large as an arena, and in it there was a stone that was reserved for him to sit on. Once R. Joshua came in and began kissing the stone and saying: This stone is like Mount Sinai, and he who sits on it is like the Ark of the Covenant.[4]

92. Our masters taught: It happened that R. Eliezer passed the Sabbath in Upper Galilee, and they asked him for thirty decisions in the laws of Sukkah. Of twelve of these, he said, "I heard them [from my teachers]"; of eighteen, he said, "I have not heard." According to R. Yose son of R. Judah, R. Eliezer said the reverse: of eighteen, he said, "I have heard them"; of twelve, he said, "I have not heard them." When he was asked, "Master, is all you say nothing other than what you have heard?" he replied, "You finally force me to say something I have not heard from my teachers. [I may tell you that] during all my life no man arrived earlier than myself at the house of study; I never slept or dozed there; I never quit the house of study leaving another person inside it; nor did I ever engage in chitchat; nor have I ever in my life said a thing that I did not hear from my teacher.[5]

93. Our masters taught: It happened that R. Eliezer passed the Sabbath [of Sukkot] in Upper Galilee in the sukkah of R. Yohanan ben R. Ilai at Caesarea, and when the sun reached the sukkah, R. Yohanan asked R. Eliezer, "May I spread a cloth over it [for more shade]?"[6] R. Eliezer answered, "There was not a tribe in Israel that did not produce a judge."[7] When the sun reached the middle of the sukkah, R. Yohanan again asked, "May I spread a cloth over it?" R. Eliezer answered, "There was not a tribe in Israel from which there did not come prophets, and the tribes of Judah and Benjamin appointed their kings at the behest of the prophets."[8] When the sun reached the feet of R. Eliezer,[9] R. Yohanan took a cloth and spread it over the sukkah. At that, R. Eliezer folded up his cloak, threw it over his back, and went out.[10] It was not in order to distract him [to another subject that he answered irrelevantly], but because R. Eliezer never said anything he had not heard from his master.[11]

94. Our masters taught: It happened that R. Eliezer was once sitting and lecturing the whole day [of a festival] on the laws of that festival. When the first group left [the lecture hall], he said: These are people who have casks;[12] when the second group left, he said: These are people who have amphorae; when the third group left, he said: These are people who have pitchers;[13] when the fourth group left, he said: These are people who have flasks; when the fifth group left, he said: These are people who have only goblets.[14] When the sixth group began to go out, he said: These are the people who will receive a curse.[15] Then he fixed his eyes on his disciples and their faces began to change

1. PRE 1; ARN 6; Gen. R. 42:1; Tanhuma B, *Lekh Lekha*, § 10.
2. Avot 2:8; ARN 14.
3. Song R. 1:3, §1.
4. Suggesting that R. Eliezer's rulings were as authoritative as the words on the Tablets placed in the Ark. Song R. 1:3, §1.
5. Nor will I give today any decision I have not heard from my teachers. B. Suk. 28a.
6. The point of his question: Is spreading a cloth regarded as extending a temporary tent, an act that is forbidden on the Sabbath.
7. He changed the subject, since he never gave a decision that had not been handed down. R. Eliezer's outstanding characteristic was his rigid conservatism.
8. Saul and David, for instance, were appointed by Samuel.
9. As the sun climbed the sky, its rays penetrated farther and farther into the sukkah.
10. To avoid responsibility for R. Yohanan's action.
11. B. Suk 27b and En Yaakov, ad loc.
12. "I.e., very rich, counting their wine by casks. They have left thus early because of the large quantities of food and drink waiting for them. These are gluttons" (Betz, Soncino p. 78, n. 7).
13. "I.e., less rich than the second but wealthier than the next group" (Betz, Soncino, p. 78, n. 8).
14. "Less keen on their pleasures" (Betz, Soncino, p. 78, n. 9).
15. "The emptiness of the lecture hall roused his ire" (Betz, Soncino, p. 78, n. 10).

color.[1] At that, he said to them: My children, not of you did I speak thus, but of those who have gone out, putting aside life eternal and occupying themselves with the life temporal. At the end of the lecture, when the disciples [who had remained behind] were about to take their leave, he said to them: "Go your way, eat the fat and drink the sweet, and send portions unto him for whom nothing is prepared; for this day is holy unto the Lord; neither be ye grieved, for the joy of the Lord is your strength" (Neh. 8:10).[2]

95. A story is told of a certain disciple who gave a decision in law in the presence of his master, R. Eliezer. Later, R. Eliezer said to his wife, Imma Shalom, "Alas for the wife of this man! He will not live out the week!" The week was hardly over when that disciple died. As the sages came in [to offer their condolences], his other disciples asked him, "Are you a prophet?" He replied, " 'I am neither a prophet nor the son of a prophet' [Amos 7:14], but I have the following tradition: a disciple who gives a decision in law in the presence of his master is liable to the death penalty."[3]

96. A Roman noblewoman asked R. Eliezer: How is it that, though only one sin had been committed in the making of the golden calf, yet the Israelites died by three kinds of death?[4] He replied: Women have no wisdom except for wielding the distaff, for, as Scripture says, "All the women that were wise-hearted did spin with their hands" (Exod. 35:5).[5] R. Eliezer's son, Hyrcanus, said to his father: Because you would not give her an answer drawn from the teachings of Torah, you caused us the loss of three hundred *kor* of tithe that she used to give us every year. R. Eliezer replied: Let the three hundred *kor* be burned, rather than have the words of Torah entrusted to women.[6]

97. When the bondwoman of R. Eliezer died, his disciples came in to condole with him. At the sight of them, he went to an upper chamber, and they went up after him. Then he went into the bath chamber, and they followed him there. Next he went into the great dining hall,[7] and they followed him there. Finally, he said to them: I thought that lukewarm water would be enough to scald you, but apparently even boiling water cannot do so.[8] Have I not taught you that a row of comforters is not provided at the death of male or female slaves, that the mourner's blessing [after the first meal] is not recited, nor are condolences offered for them? What then is said over them? Even as for the loss of an ax or an ass, a man is told, "May the Almighty replenish your loss," so, at the death of a male or female slave, he is told, "May the Almighty replenish your loss."[9]

98. We have been taught: Say a man made an oven out of separate coils [of clay, placing one upon another], then put sand between each of the coils[10]—such an oven, R. Eliezer declared, is not susceptible to defilement, while the sages declared it susceptible. The oven discussed was the oven of Akhnai—"snake" [so called because it precipitated arguments as numerous as the coils of a snake].

It is taught: On that day R. Eliezer brought forward every imaginable argument, but the sages did not accept any of them. Finally he said to them, "If the *Halakhah* agrees with me, let this carob tree prove it!" Sure enough, the carob tree was uprooted [and replanted] a hundred cubits away from its place. "No proof can be brought from a carob tree," they retorted.

Again he said to them, "If the *Halakhah* agrees with mme, let the channel of water prove it!" Sure enough, the channel of water flowed backward. "No proof can be brought from a channel of water," they rejoined.

Again he urged, "If the *Halakhah* agrees with me, let the walls of the house of study prove it!" Sure enough, the walls tilted as if to fall. But R. Joshua rebuked the walls, saying, "When disciples of the wise are engaged in a halakhic dispute, what right have you to interfere?" Hence, in deference to R. Joshua they did not fall, and in deference to R. Eliezer they did not resume their upright position; they are still standing aslant.

Again R. Eliezer said to the sages, "If the *Halakhah* agrees with me, let it be proved from heaven!" Sure enough, a divine voice cried out, "Why do you dispute R. Eliezer, with whom the *Halakhah* always agrees?" But R. Joshua stood up and protested, "It [the Torah] is not in heaven" (Deut. 30:12). We pay no attention to a divine voice, because long ago, at Mount Sinai, You wrote in the Torah, "After the majority must one incline" (Exod. 23:2).

R. Nathan met [the prophet] Elijah[11] and asked him, "What did the Holy One do in that moment?" Elijah: "He laughed [with joy], saying, 'My sons have defeated Me, My sons have defeated Me.' "

It is said: On that day all objects [that had been placed within that oven—objects] R. Eliezer had declared clean—[were pronounced unclean. Presently they] were brought and burned in fire. [After R. Eliezer's departure] the sages took a vote, excommunicated R. Eliezer, and

1. "I.e., to turn pale, because they thought he was angry with them for not leaving earlier—apparently they thought that he considered himself bound to go on as long as he had hearers" (Betz, Soncino, p. 79, n. 2).
2. B. Betz, 15b.
3. P. Git 1:2, 43c; Lev. R. 20:6.
4. By the sword, by the plague, and by dropsy.
5. He regarded her question as too trivial to deserve a reasoned reply. R. Eliezer's attitude to women is exceptional. We find, for example, R. Eleazar saying, in the name of R. Yose ben Zimra, "Woman was endowed with more understanding than man" (Gen. R. 18:1).
6. P. Sot 3:4, 19a; B. Yoma 66b; Num. R. 9:48.
7. A mourner usually spent the period of mourning in a room downstairs. R. Eliezer's demonstrative going to the upper chamber, the bathing quarters, and the festive dining area was meant to say that he did not observe mourning for the bondwoman.
8. As much as to say: I thought you would take the first hint, and you do not even take the last!
9. B. Ber 16b.
10. Since each portion in itself is not a utensil, and the sand between the portions prevents the oven's being regarded as a single utensil, therefore, according to R. Eliezer, the oven is not liable to uncleanness. The sages, however, hold that the oven's outer coating of mortar or cement unifies the coils so that the oven is liable to uncleanness.
11. It was believed that Elijah, who had never died, often appeared to the sages.

asked, "Who will go and tell him?" "I will go," R. Akiva volunteered, "lest an unsuitable person go and tell him, and thus destroy the whole world."[1] What did R. Akiva do? He donned black garments and wrapped himself in black,[2] and sat at a distance of four cubits from him. "Akiva," said R. Eliezer to him, "why the different garb today?" "Master," R. Akiva replied, "it seems to me that your companions are parting from you." At that, R. Eliezer rent his garments, removed his shoes, slipped off his seat, and sat on the ground, tears streaming from his eyes. The world was then smitten: a third of the olive crop, a third of the wheat crop, and a third of the barley crop [were ruined]. Some say that even the dough in women's hands fermented [and was spoiled]. The sages taught: Great was the wrath that befell [the world] that day, for anything R. Eliezer cast his eyes on was incinerated.

Indeed, on that day Rabban Gamaliel was traveling on shipboard when a huge wave arose, threatening to drown him. It appears to me, he reflected, that it is on account of R. Eliezer ben Hyrcanus. Then he stood up and called out, "Master of the universe! It is known and revealed to You that I have not acted for my honor, nor for the honor of my father's house, but for Your honor—that dissension might not multiply in Israel!" At that, the sea's rage subsided.

Imma Shalom was R. Eliezer's wife and Rabban Gamaliel's sister. From the time of this incident on she did not permit R. Eliezer to prostrate himself upon his face [in prayer].[3] One time a poor man came and stood at the door, so she took out some bread for him. [On her return] she found R. Eliezer prostrated upon his face. "Get up!" she cried out to him. "You have just slain my brother!" Even as she was speaking, a horn's blast coming from the house of Rabban Gamaliel announced that he had died. R. Eliezer asked her, "How did you know [that my prayer would bring about his death.]?" She replied, "I have a tradition from my grandfather's house: all gates may be locked, except the gates for wounded feelings."

99. Our masters taught: When R. Eliezer, suspected of [Judeo-Christian] heresy, was arrested, he was brought up on a torturer's scaffold to be examined. The Roman governor said to him, "How can a venerable sage like you occupy himself with such drivel?"[4] R. Eliezer replied, "I acknowledge the Judge as right." The governor, thinking that R. Eliezer referred to him—in fact he referred to his Father in heaven—said, "Because you have acknowledged me as the right judge, I dismiss you. You are acquitted." When R. Eliezer came home, his disciples called on him to console him,[5] but he would accept no consolation. Said R. Akiva to him, "Master, will you permit me to say something you taught me?" He replied, "Say it." "Master, is it possible that some heretical teaching was reported to you and pleased you, and for that reason you were arrested?" He exclaimed, "Akiva, you have reminded me. I was once walking in the upper market of Sepphoris, when I came across one of the disciples of Jesus the Nazarene, Jacob of Kefar Sekhania[6] by name, who said to me: It is written in your Torah, 'Thou shalt not bring the hire of a harlot . . . into the house of the Lord thy God' [Deut. 23:19]. May such money be applied to the building of a privy for the high priest? To this I made no reply. He said to me: I was taught [by Jesus the Nazarene]: 'For of the hire of a harlot hath she gathered them and unto the hire of a harlot shall they return' [Mic. 1:7]—since it came from a place of filth, it should go to a place of filth [such as the high priest's privy]. This interpretation pleased me very much, and that is why I was arrested for apostasy, for in reacting thus, I transgressed Scripture: 'Remove thy way far from her,' meaning heresy, 'so that you will not have to come nigh to the door of her house' [Prov. 5:8]—to the house of the ruling power."[7]

100. Rabban bar Bar Hanah taught: R. Eliezer fell sick, and when his disciples came to visit him, he said to them, "There is fierce wrath in the world."[8] They broke into tears, but R. Akiva laughed. "Why do you laugh?" they inquired of him. "Why do you weep?" he replied. They answered, "Shall [R. Eliezer], a [veritable] scroll of Torah, be lying in pain and we not weep?" R. Akiva then said, "For that very reason I laugh. As long as I see that my master's wine is not souring, nor is his flax smitten, nor is his oil gone rancid, nor does his honey ferment,[9] I thought, God forbid, that my master might have received all his reward in this world [leaving nothing for the next]; but now that I see him lying in pain, I rejoice [knowing that punishment for his sins is exacted in this world, while the reward for his righteousness is treasured up for him in the next]."

R. Eliezer said, "Akiva, have I neglected anything in the entire Torah?"[10] R. Akiva replied, "You, our master, taught us, 'No man on earth is so righteous that he does only good and never sins' " (Eccles. 7:20).[11]

101. Our masters taught: When R. Eliezer fell sick, four elders—R. Tarfon, R. Joshua, R. Eleazar ben Azariah,

1. I.e., commit a great wrong by informing him tactlessly.
2. As a sign of mourning, which a person under the ban had to observe.
3. After the Eighteen Benedictions, there follows a short interval for private prayer, during which each person offers up his own individual supplications to God as he prostrates himself upon his face. She feared that her husband might pour out his sense of injury and that God would punish Rabban Gamaliel, her brother.
4. B. BM 59a–b and En Yaakov, ad loc.
5. R. Eliezer was greatly troubled: what sin had he committed that God should have made him the victim of such a charge?

6. Possibly James son of Alphaeus (Mark 3:18) or James the Younger (Mark 15:40). So Isidore Epstein in AZ, Soncino, p. 85, n. 3.
7. B. AZ 16b–17a and En Yaakov, ad loc.
8. "He referred to himself—God must be very angry with him so to have afflicted him. So Rashi. [Heinrich] Graetz conjectures that his death took place shortly before Trajan's attack upon the Jews of many countries (ca. 116–17 C.E.), to which he was alluding in this remark, as the storm was already brewing" (Sanh, Soncino, p. 686, n. 2).
9. He was prosperous in everything.
10. R. Eliezer means: "I am being punished; hence I must have neglected some biblical ordinances. Now, I can't recollect any such lapses on my part. Do you recollect any? If you do, please tell me, so that I may atone for them" (Leon Nemoy).
11. B. Sianh 101a.

and R. Akiva—came to visit him. R. Tarfon spoke up and said, "You are more valuable to Israel than drops of rain; for drops of rain sustain us in this world, while you, my master, [sustain us] in this world and in the world-to-come."[1]

R. Joshua spoke up and said, "You are more valuable to Israel than the orb of the sun: the orb of the sun is but for this world, while you, my master, are for this world and for the world-to-come."

R. Eleazar ben Azariah spoke up and said, "You are better for Israel than a father and a mother: a father and a mother are only for this world, whereas you, my master, are for this world and for the world-to-come."

But R. Akiva spoke up and said, "Suffering is precious."[2]

Then R. Eliezer said to his disciples, "Prop me up, so that I may hear better the words of Akiva, my disciple, who said, 'Suffering is precious.' What proof have you, Akiva, for saying it?" R. Akiva replied, "I draw such inference from the verse 'Manasseh was twelve years old when he began to reign, and he reigned fifty and five years in Jerusalem . . . and he did that which was evil in the sight of the Lord' [2 Kings 21:1–2]. I consider this verse in the light of another: 'These are also the proverbs of Solomon, which the men of Hezekiah king of Judah copied out [for widespread instruction]' [Prov. 25:1]. Now, would Hezekiah king of Judah have taught Torah to the whole world, to all of it, and not taught Torah to his own son Manasseh? However, all the pains that Hezekiah took with him and all the labors he expended for him did not bring him to the right path. Only Manasseh's suffering did so, as is written, 'And the Lord spoke to Manasseh, and to his people; but they gave no heed. Wherefore the Lord brought upon them the captains and the host of the king of Assyria. . . . And when [Manasseh] was in distress, he besought the Lord his God, and humbled himself greatly before the God of his fathers, and He answered his entreaty' [2 Chron. 33:10–13]. Thus you may learn how precious is suffering."[3]

102. We have been taught: When R. Eliezer fell sick, R. Akiva and his companions came to visit him. He was seated in a canopied four-poster, while they sat in the reception room. That day was Sabbath eve, and R. Eliezer's son Hyrcanus came in to his father's room to remove the tefillin his father had on.[4] But his father rebuked him, and he retreated, crestfallen. "It seems to me," Hyrcanus said to them, "that my father's mind is deranged."[5] But R. Akiva said to them, "[R. Eliezer's mind is clear], but Hyrcanus's mind and that of his mother are deranged. How is it that both have neglected acts [kindling the Sabbath lights and putting away the Sabbath meal to keep it hot] that are punishable on scriptural authority by stoning if performed on the Sabbath, while they concern themselves with tefillin, the wearing of which on the Sabbath is forbidden not on scriptural but only on rabbinic authority?"[6]

The sages, persuaded that his mind was clear, entered R. Eliezer's room and sat down at a distance of four cubits from him.[7] "Why have you come?" he asked. "We have come to study Torah,"[8] they replied. "And why did you not come before now?" he asked. "We had no time," they replied. Then he said to them, "I wonder if such as you will die a natural death." When R. Akiva asked, "And what kind of death will be mine?" he answered, "Yours will be more cruel than theirs."

Then R. Eliezer placed his arms over his heart and bewailed them, saying, "Alas for you, arms of mine, that are like two Torah scrolls about to be rolled up [and put away]. Much Torah have I learned, and much have I taught. Much Torah have I learned, yet I have not taken from my teachers even as much as the water a dog laps up from the sea. Much Torah have I taught, yet my disciples have taken from me no more than the paint a paint stick picks up from its tube. Moreover, I have studied three hundred laws on the subject of a bright discoloration on the skin,[9] yet no man has ever asked me about them. Even more, I have studied three hundred rules about planting cucumbers [by magic], and no man other than Akiva ben Joseph ever asked me about them. Once, while he and I were walking on a road, he said to me, 'My master, teach me the planting of cucumbers [by magic].' I uttered a single word, and the whole field about us was filled with cucumbers. Then he said, 'Master, you just taught me how to plant them. Now teach me how to pluck them.' I uttered another word, and all the cucumbers gathered into one place."

Then his disciples kept asking him about the laws of cleanness and the laws of uncleanness: concerning that which was unclean, he kept saying, "Unclean," and concerning that which was clean, he kept saying, "Clean," until his soul departed as he uttered the word "clean." Then R. Joshua stood up and exclaimed, "The ban is lifted, the ban is lifted!"

At the end of the Sabbath, on the way between Caesarea and Lydda, R. Akiva met R. Eliezer's bier. In his grief, R. Akiva lacerated his flesh until the blood dripped on the ground, and, sobbing and moaning, he lamented, "Woe is me for the loss of you, woe is me for the loss of you, my master, for you have left an entire generation fatherless." In the mourners' row he began his eulogy with

1. "R. Tarfon compares R. Eliezer's teaching to rain (a very valuable phenomenon in the Near East): after all, rain is a boon only on earth, whereas R. Eliezer's teaching will continue benefiting successive generations of scholars long after his death—the rain of his teaching will, as it were, continue falling out of heaven even after it has ceased falling out of the clouds of his physical terrestrial mouth" (Leon Nemoy).

2. It makes atonement for the sufferer.

3. B. Sanh 101a–b.

4. The Sabbath, when tefillin may not be worn, was drawing near.

5. Since he would not let me remove his phylacteries.

6. Wearing tefillin indoors on the Sabbath is forbidden by the rabbis for fear that the wearer may forget himself and go out in the street with them—carry them from home to a public domain—an act forbidden by Scripture. See Shab 1:1.

7. Because R. Eliezer had been placed under the ban. See above in this chapter, §98.

8. They preferred not to say that they came because he was gravely ill.

9. A form of leprosy. Lev. 13:2.

[Elisha's words at the departure of Elijah]: " 'My father, my father, the chariots of Israel and the horsemen thereof' [2 Kings 2:12]. I have many coins, but no moneychanger to sort them out."[1]

103. When R. Eliezer died, the Torah scroll was hidden away, the book of wisdom was hidden away.[2]

R. Joshua ben Ḥananiah (fl. ca. 90–130 C.E.)

104. R. Joshua—happy is she who gave birth to him!

When R. Dosa ben Horkinas saw R. Joshua, he applied to him the verse "To whom is one to give instruction? . . . Even to those newly weaned from the milk" (Isa. 28:9). I remember R. Joshua's mother taking his cradle to the house of study so that his ears would become attuned to words of Torah.[3]

105. R. Joshua said: If all seas were ink, and all reeds pens, heaven and earth scrolls, and all mankind scribes, they would not suffice to write down the Torah I learned, even though I abstracted [from my masters' teaching] no more than a man would take when dipping the point of a painting stick in the paint tube.[4]

106. Once the daughter of a Caesar[5] said to R. Joshua ben Hananiah, "What a pity! Such glorious wisdom in so ugly a vessel!" He replied, "My daughter, in what kind of vessel does your father keep his wine?" She: "In an earthenware vessel." R. Joshua: "But ordinary people keep wine in earthenware vessels; do you, too, keep your wine in such vessels?" She: "What else should we keep it in?" R. Joshua: "You, who are such important persons, should keep it in vessels of silver or even gold." So she went off and spoke to her father, who immediately had the wine put into vessels of silver and gold, where it soon turned sour. Then Caesar asked his daughter, "Who gave you such advice?" She: "R. Joshua ben Hananiah." Caesar had him summoned and asked him, "Why did you give my daughter such advice?" R. Joshua: "The same question she asked me, I [turned around and] asked her."

Caesar: "But are there not learned people who are handsome?"

R. Joshua: "If these handsome people were ugly, they would be even more learned."[6]

107. Once, when R. Joshua ben Hananiah and R. Yose the Priest were walking along a highway, they said: Let us expound the Work of the Chariot. So R. Joshua began his exposition. Now, that day was the day of the summer solstice;[7] nevertheless, the heavens became overcast with clouds, a kind of rainbow[8] appeared in the cloud, and the ministering angels assembled and came to listen, just like people who assemble and come to watch the entertainment for a bridegroom and bride. Later on, R. Yose the Priest went and related what happened to Rabban Yohanan ben Zakkai, who said: Happy are you, and happy is she that bore you! Happy are my eyes that behold you who have seen such a sight! Moreover, in a dream I beheld you and me reclining on Mount Sinai when a divine voice was sent to us from heaven [saying], "Ascend hither, ascend hither! Here are great banqueting chambers and beautiful couches spread out for you. You and your disciples and your disciples' disciples are designated for the third company of the upright."[9]

108. R. Joshua ben Hananiah said: I can take cucumbers and melons, and turn them into hinds and gazelles, who will even give birth to hinds and gazelles.[10]

109. In the days of R. Joshua ben Hananiah, the wicked Roman government issued a decree that the Temple was to be rebuilt. Pappus and Lulianus set up tables all the way from Acco to Antioch, to provide gold and silver and sundry needs to those who were to come up from the exile [in Babylonia]. At that, the notorious Cutheans went and warned the king, "Let Caesar know that the Jews are about to rebel against you." "But what can I do," he asked, "seeing that I have already issued the decree?" "Send word to them that they must either change its site, or add five cubits to it, or diminish it by five cubits, and then of their own accord they will withdraw from rebuilding their Temple."[11]

Now, all the people were assembled in the valley of Beth Rimmon. When the new royal writ arrived, they wept in frustration and wanted to revolt against Caesar. [Alarmed], the sages decided: Let a wise man go to pacify the assembly. Who is the one to go? R. Joshua ben Hananiah should be the one, since he is a master of Torah. R. Joshua ben Hananiah stepped before the assembly and sought to pacify them by means of a fable: As a lion was devouring his prey, a bone stuck in his throat. He wailed, "[I have a bone in my throat and] I shall give a [great] reward to anyone who removes it!" An Egyptian heron, which has a long beak, came forward, plunged his beak into the lion's throat, pulled out the bone, and demanded, "Give me my reward." The lion roared, "Move off! Go boast, prattling, 'I entered a lion's mouth in peace and came out in peace.' You can have no greater reward than that." So, too, it should be enough for us that we entered

1. His many questions on Torah would now go unanswered. B. Sanh 68a and En Yaakov, ad loc.; ARN 25.
2. Thorough understanding of Torah and wisdom was no longer available to disciples. B. Sot 49b; P. Sot 9:16, 24c.
3. Avot 2:8; P. Yev 1:6, 3a.
4. Song R. 1:3, §1.
5. Perhaps Hadrian. See *JE* 7:291.
6. B. Ta 7a–b; B. Ned 50b.
7. Literally, "the cycle of Tammuz" (the fourth month). On such a day the sky in the Land of Israel should be cloudless.
8. Cf. Ezek. 1:28.
9. See MTeh 11:6 (YJS 1:164–65). B. Hag 14b.
10. P. Sanh 7:13, 25d.
11. Th Cutheans' wily counsel led to the Roman government's subsequent withdrawal of permission to rebuild the Temple, an act that may have precipitated Bar Kozeva's rebellion during Hadrian's reign. See Ben-Zion Luria, "When Locks Were Let Loose in Israel" [Hebrew], *Sinai* 93, nos. 3–4 (1983): 100.

into dealings with this Roman people in peace and have emerged in peace.[1]

110. R. Joshua ben Hananiah was standing in the presence of Caesar when a certain heretic spelled out in pantomime: "Here is a people whose Lord has turned His face away from them." R. Joshua responded in pantomime: "But His hand is still stretched protectively over us."

Caesar asked R. Joshua, "What did he show you?" " 'A people whose Lord has turned His face away from them.' And I responded by saying, 'His hand is still stretched protectively over us.' " Then Caesar asked the heretic, "What did you show him?" "A people whose Lord has turned His face away from them." "And what did he show you?" "I do not know." Then Caesar said, "A man who does not understand the figures he is shown dares to draw figures in pantomime before Caesar!" They led him forth and put him to death.[2]

111. Hadrian said to R. Joshua ben Hananiah, "How difficult it is for a flock to be grazing among seventy wolves." R. Joshua replied, "How strong the Keeper who is able to save it from all of them.[3]

112. Our masters taught: Once, when R. Joshua ben Hananiah happened to go to a great city in the Roman Empire, he was told that there in a prison was a child with beautiful eyes and face, and curly locks. He went, stood at the doorway of the prison, and said, "Who gave Jacob for a spoil, and Israel to the robbers?" (Isa. 42:24). The child answered, "Is it not the Lord, against whom they sinned, in whose ways they would not walk, and whose teaching they would not obey?" (ibid.). Upon hearing the child speak so aptly, R. Joshua applied to him the verse "The precious sons of Zion, comparable to fine gold" (Lam. 4:2). R. Joshua's eyes were flowing with tears and he said: I feel sure that this one will be a teacher in Israel. By the Temple service, I swear that I will not budge from here until I ransom him, whatever price may be demanded.

It is reported that R. Joshua did not leave the spot until he had ransomed him for a substantial sum; nor did many days pass before the child became a teacher in Israel. Who was the child? R. Ishmael ben Elisha.[4]

113. It happened once that bones were found in Jerusalem in the chamber where wood for the altar was stored. [Out of fear that bones might be buried throughout the city], the sages were about to impose a decree of ritual uncleanness on all of Jerusalem. R. Joshua ben Hananiah rose up and said: Would it not be a shame and a humiliation for us to impose a decree of uncleanness on the city of our ancestors? Where are [the bones of] those who died during the flood? Where are [the bones of] those who were slain by Nebuchadnezzar? Where are the bones of those who were slain during the war against Rome and until now? [Surely they must all be here.] However [he concluded], the sages said: Only that which is certain may be declared unclean; but that which is uncertain remains clean.[5]

114. R. Joshua ben Hananiah remarked: No one has ever had the better of me except a woman, a little boy, and a little girl.

What was the incident with the woman? I was once staying at an inn where the proprietress prepared [a meal of] beans for me. The first day I ate all of it, leaving nothing. The second day I again ate all of it, leaving nothing. The third day she overseasoned the beans with salt, and, upon tasting them, I drew my hand away from the plate [and stopped eating]. "My master," she asked, "why do you not eat?" I replied, "I have already eaten earlier in the day." She said, "You should then have drawn your hand away from the bread [I served and eaten less of that]." She continued, "My master, may it be that you left beans on the plate today to make up for what you failed to do on the two preceding days, for have not the sages taught, 'No food need be left in the pot [for the servant], but something must be left for him on the plate'?"

What was the incident with the little girl? I was once on a journey, and, observing a path across a field, I made my way through it. A little girl called out to me, "Master! Is not this part of the field?" "No," I replied, "this is a trodden path." "Poachers like you," she retorted, "have trodden it down."

What was the incident with the little boy? I was once on a journey when I noticed a little boy sitting at a crossroads. I asked him, "My son, by what road do we go to the town?" "This one," he replied, "is short but long, and that one is long but short." I proceeded along the "short but long" road. When I approached the town, I discovered that [the road became a dead end] because gardens and orchards blocked access to the town. I turned back and said to him, "My son, did you not tell me that this road was short?" He replied, "Did I not also tell you, 'But long'?" I kissed him on his head and said to him, "Happy are you, O Israel, for all of you, from the oldest to the youngest among you, are wise."[6]

A story of R. Joshua: When a certain person called on him early in the morning, he gave him food and drink, [entertained him, and in the evening] took him up to the roof to sleep, and then removed the ladder leading down from the roof. What did that man do? In the middle of the night he arose, collected the articles [kept on the roof], and wrapped them in his cloak. But when he tried to come down, he [unaware that there was no ladder] fell from the roof and broke his neck. The following morning, R. Joshua rose early and found the man where he had fallen. R. Joshua said to him, "You good-for-nothing, do all persons like you act as you have?" The thief replied, "Master, I did not know that you had removed the ladder from under me." R. Joshua replied, "You good-for-nothing, did you

1. Gen. R. 64:10; Yalkut, *Toledot*, §111.
2. B. Hag 5b.
3. Israel is the flock; the seventy gentile nations are the wolves. Esther R. 10:11; Tanhuma, *Toledot*, §5.
4. B. Git 58b; Lam. R. 4:2, §4.
5. Tos Ed 3:3; B. Zev 113a.
6. B. Er 53b and En Yaakov, ad loc.

not realize that from the moment you arrived yesterday we were wary of you?"

Hence, R. Joshua said: Always consider all men as brigands, but honor them as you would honor Rabban Gamaliel.[1]

116. Hadrian Caesar asked R. Joshua ben Hananiah, "Does the world have a master?" R. Joshua: "Can you possibly suppose that the world is ownerless?" Hadrian: "And who created heaven and earth?" R. Joshua: "The Holy One, as stated: 'In the beginning God created heaven and earth' " (Gen. 1:1). Hadrian: "Then why does He not reveal Himself twice a year, so that mortals may see Him and the awe of Him be upon them?" R. Joshua: "Because the world cannot endure His radiance, as is said, 'No man shall see Me and live' " (Exod. 33:20). Hadrian: "If you do not show Him to me, I will not believe you." At midday R. Joshua had Hadrian stand facing the sun and said, "Look directly at the sun and you will see Him." Hadrian: "Who can possibly look directly at the sun?" R. Joshua: "Do your ears not hear what your mouth is saying? If no creature can look at the sun, which is but one of the thousand thousands and myriad myriads of servitors who minister before Him, all the less can a creature look at Him, at the Holy One, whose radiance fills the world." Hadrian: "Then when will He reveal His glory?" R. Joshua: "When idols shall have perished from the world."[2]

117. The same Caesar said to R. Joshua ben Hananiah, "I wish to prepare a banquet for your God." R. Joshua: "You cannot do so." "Why not?" "Because His attendants are too numerous." Caesar: "Nevertheless, I wish to do it." "Then go and prepare it on the banks of the river Revita,[3] where there is ample room." Accordingly, Caesar spent the six months of summer in making preparations, but then a tempest arose and swept everything into the sea. So he spent the six months of winter in making new preparations, but then the rains came and again everything was washed into the sea. "What is the meaning of this?" demanded Caesar. R. Joshua replied, "These are but the sweepers and sprinklers that march ahead of Him!" "In that case," Caesar concluded, "I admit I cannot do it."[4]

118. The same Caesar once said to R. Joshua ben Hananiah, "Your God is likened to a lion, for it is written, 'The lion hath roared, who will not fear?' [Amos 3:8]. Wherein, then, lies His greatness? Surely a horseman can easily kill a lion!" R. Joshua: "He has been likened not to an ordinary lion, but to the lion of [the forest] on high!" "I desire," said Caesar, "that you show it to me." R. Joshua: "You will be unable to look at it." Caesar: "Nevertheless, I insist." So R. Joshua ben Hananiah entreated God's mercy, and the lion set out from its place. When it was four hundred parasangs distant, it roared once, and all the pregnant women miscarried and the walls of Rome collapsed. When it was three hundred parasangs distant, it roared again, and the teeth of men fell out—Caesar himself fell from his throne to the ground. "I beg of you," he implored, "entreat God's mercy that this lion may return to its place." R. Joshua entreated God's mercy, and it was returned to its place.[5]

119. Hadrian—may his bones be ground to dust—said to R. Joshua ben Hananiah, "I am better than your teacher Moses." "What makes you say so?" "Because I am alive and he is dead, and it is written, 'A living dog is better than a dead lion' " (Eccles. 9:4). R. Joshua said to him, "Can you order that no one should kindle a fire in Rome for three days?" "Certainly I can," and at once Hadrian issued a decree that no fire be kindled in Rome [for three days]. But on that very day, toward evening, when Hadrian went up to the roof of his palace, together with R. Joshua ben Hananiah, the two lifted their eyes and saw smoke rising from a distant corner. R. Joshua asked, "What is the meaning of that smoke?" Hadrian replied, "A captain is ill. A physician went in to examine him and said that unless the patient is given hot drinks he will not recover." R. Joshua lifted his eyes again and saw smoke rising from another corner and again asked, "What is the meaning of that smoke?" Hadrian replied, "You will find that a prefect is ill. A physician went in to examine him and said that unless he is kept warm by a hot vessel he will not recover." R. Joshua then said, "May the breath of a man like you be blasted out. While you are still alive, your decree has not endured even for one day, whereas since the day our teacher Moses decreed for us, 'Ye shall kindle no fire throughout your habitations upon the Sabbath day' [Exod. 35:3], have you ever seen any Jew kindle a fire on the Sabbath? And yet you say, 'I am better than Moses!' "[6]

120. The same Caesar said to R. Joshua ben Hananiah, "If you are wiser than the sages of Athens, go and defeat them in argument, and bring them to me." R. Joshua asked, "How many Athenian sages are there?" "Sixty men." R. Joshua said, "Make me a ship containing sixty cabins, and in each cabin place sixty chairs." He did this for him.

When R. Joshua reached Athens, he went up to a slaughterhouse, where he found a man skinning a carcass. When he asked him, "Is your head for sale?" the man replied, "Yes." "For how much?" "For a half a *zuz*." R. Joshua gave him half a *zuz* and said, "Give me your head." The man gave him the animal's head. R. Joshua exclaimed, "Did I say the head of an animal? I said, 'Your head.' " Finally R. Joshua said to the man, "If you want me to let you be, go and point out to me the entrance to the School of Athens." The man replied, "I am afraid, for whoever points out its door is put to death." R. Joshua then said, "Take a bundle of reeds, and when you reach the spot, [as a signal to me] set it down as if to rest."

Having reached the school, R. Joshua found guards stationed inside and outside the building. For when the elders saw the footprints of someone about to enter [without

1. DER 5.
2. Yalkut, *Ki Tissa*, §394; B. Hul 59b–60a.
3. Or, "the shore of the Great Sea." The river is near Yavneh, in the Land of Israel.
4. B. Hul 60a.
5. B. Hul 59b.
6. Eccles. R. 9:4, §1; Yalkut, Eccles., §989.

permission], they would kill the outside guards; and when they saw the footprints of someone about to leave [without permission], they would kill the inside guards.[1] So R. Joshua reversed his sandals, and they killed the inside guards. He then turned the sandals back to their normal position, and they killed the outside guards.[2]

Thus free to enter, he found the young men sitting high up [in the upper chamber] and the elders below. So he said to himself: If I give greetings to the elders first, the young men will kill me, for they will say, "We are more important than the elders, for we sit high up, while they sit below." And if I give greetings to the young men first, the elders will kill me, for they will say, "We are older than they and they are mere youngsters." So R. Joshua said no more than: "Peace upon [all of] you." When he was asked, "What are you doing here?" he replied, "I am one of the sages of the Jews, and I have come to learn wisdom from you." They said, "If so, we will ask you a question." He replied, "Very well. If you defeat me, you will do with me as you please; if I defeat you, you will break bread with me on my ship."

They said to him, "Tell us some tall tales." He said, "After a she-mule gave birth to a colt, they hung around the colt's neck a document in which was written, 'The colt has filed a claim against his sire's house for one hundred[3] thousand *zuz.*' " They retorted, "But can a she-mule give birth?" He replied, "This is one of the tall tales you asked for."

"When salt becomes stale, with what is it salted?" He replied, "With the afterbirth of a mule." "But can a mule have an afterbirth?" "And can salt become stale?"

"Build us a house in the sky." R. Joshua: "[First] bring clay and bricks up there for me."

"Where is the center of the world?" He pointed a finger [to a spot in the ground] and said, "Here." They replied, "Who says so?" He said, "[If you do not believe me], bring ropes and measure."

They said, "We have a wellspring in the field. Bring it into the town." He replied, "Twist ropes of bran flour for me, and I will bring it in."

"We have a broken millstone. Sew it up." "Pull the original sewing threads out of the pieces for me, and I shall mend the millstone."

"A bed of knives—with what should one reap it?" "With the horns of an ass." [They asked, "But has an ass horns?" "And is there a bed of knives?" he replied.]

They brought him two eggs. "Which is from a white hen and which is from a black?" He brought them two cheeses and asked them, "Which is from a white goat and which from a black?"

"A chick that died in its shell—where has its spirit gone?" "From where it came, there it went."

"Show us an article whose value is not worth the loss it may cause." He brought a mat of reeds and spread it out. It could not get through the door [being too long and too wide]. So he said to them, "Bring a pickax and demolish the wall. Here you have an article whose value is not worth the loss it may cause."

In the end, he brought each of them to the ship. When each saw the sixty chairs in his chamber, he supposed that all his companions would soon come there. In the meantime, R. Joshua ordered the captain to set sail. But before starting the journey, R. Joshua had taken some earth from the Athenians' native soil. When they reached the straits,[4] he drew a jug of water from its waters.[5]

When Joshua returned to his own place, he presented the sages to Caesar, who, seeing that they appeared subdued, said, "These cannot possibly be the sages of Athens." Then R. Joshua took a clod of the earth [he had brought] from their native land and tossed it at them. Smelling it, they became haughty[6] toward Caesar, who then said to R. Joshua, "Do with them as you wish." So R. Joshua fetched the water he had taken from the straits and poured it into a jug. Then he said to them, "Fill this jug, and you can go your way." They tried to fill it, but every bit of water they poured into the jug kept being absorbed. They kept trying to fill the jug, until their shoulders were wrenched out of place, and thus one by one they perished.[7]

121. Twelve questions did the people of Alexandria put to R. Joshua ben Hananiah: three of these concerned matters of *Aggadah;* three were mere nonsense; and three concerned matters of proper conduct.

Three matters of *Aggadah:* One verse says, "For I desire not the death of him that dieth" (Ezek. 18:32), but another verse says, "Because the Lord desireth to slay them?" (1 Sam. 2:25).

R. Joshua replied: The first verse refers to those who are penitent, while the second refers to those who are not penitent.

One verse says, "Who lifteth not His countenance nor taketh bribe" (Deut. 10:17), but another verse says, "The Lord lift up His countenance to thee" (Num. 6:26).

R. Joshua: The first verse refers to the time before sentence is passed, while the second refers to the time after sentence has been passed.

One verse says, "For the Lord hath chosen Zion" (Ps. 132:13), but another verse says, "For this city [Zion] hath been to Me a provocation of Mine anger and of My fury from the day that they built it even unto this day" (Jer. 32:31).

R. Joshua: The first verse applies to the time before Solomon married the daughter of Pharaoh, while the second verse applies to the time after Solomon married the daughter of Pharaoh.

Three were mere nonsense: Does the wife of Lot[8] convey uncleanness? He replied: A corpse conveys uncleanness, but no pillar of salt conveys uncleanness.

---

1. Bran flour or dust was scattered over the threshold so that the footprints of those entering or departing were made visible.
2. The two footprints seen on the threshold, pointing in different directions, suggested to the Athenians that there had been two persons, one leaving and the other entering.
3. Goldschmidt reads: "one thousand."
4. Probably Scylla and Charybdis. So Jastrow.
5. Its waters are said to be capable of absorbing all other waters.
6. After smelling their native earth, they imagined that they were back again in their own country.
7. B. Bekh 8b–9a and En Yaakov, ad loc.
8. Who was turned to a pillar of salt; see Gen. 19:26.

Does the son of the Shunammite[1] convey uncleanness? R. Joshua replied: A corpse conveys uncleanness, but no live person conveys uncleanness.

Will the dead in the time-to-come require to be sprinkled upon[2] on the third and the seventh day,[3] or will they not require it? R. Joshua replied: When they come back to life, we shall go into the matter.

Three were concerned with matters of proper conduct: What must a man do to become wise? R. Joshua replied: Let him engage much in study and very little in business. They objected: Many did just that, and it did not avail them. R. Joshua: In such cases, let them beseech mercy from Him to whom wisdom belongs, for it is said, "The Lord giveth wisdom, out of His mouth cometh knowledge and discernment" (Prov. 2:6).

What must a man do to become rich? R. Joshua replied: Let him engage much in business, and give and take in honesty. They objected: Many did just that, but it did not avail them. R. Joshua: In such cases, let them beseech mercy from Him to whom riches belong, for it is said, "Mine is the silver, and Mine the gold" (Hag. 2:8).

What must a man do to have male children? R. Joshua replied: He should marry a wife who is worthy of him and dispose his mind toward saintliness at the time of marital intercourse. They objected: Many did just that, but it did not avail them. R. Joshua: In such cases, let them beseech mercy from Him to whom children belong, for it is said, "Lo, children are a heritage of the Lord; the fruit of the womb is a reward" (Ps. 127:3).[4]

122. The daughter of a Caesar once said to R. Joshua ben Hananiah, "Since your God is a carpenter—for it is written, 'Who layeth the beams of His upper chambers in the waters' [Ps. 104:3]—ask Him to make me a spool." He replied, "Very well." He prayed for mercy in her behalf, and she was smitten with leprosy, whereupon she was made to sit in the open square of Rome and given a spool. (Such was the custom in Rome: whoever was smitten with leprosy was given a spool, made to sit in the open square, and provided with skeins to undo [and wind on the spool], so that people seeing him would pray for his recovery.) One day, as R. Joshua was passing through the Forum of Rome, he saw Caesar's daughter seated, undoing skeins and winding their wool on a spool. He said, "Is the spool that my God has given you good enough for you?" She replied, "Tell your God to take back what He has given me." R. Joshua: "Our God gives, but never takes back."[5]

123. A Caesar asked R. Joshua ben Hananiah, "Why did you not attend Be Avidan?"[6] He replied, "The mountain is covered with snow; it is surrounded by ice; its dogs no longer bark; and its stones no longer grind."[7]

124. When R. Joshua ben Hananiah was about to die, the sages asked him: Who will now stand up in our behalf against heretics? He replied: "Counsel is perished from children, their wisdom vanishes" (Jer. 49:7)—counsel is perished from the children of Israel, the wisdom of the heathen vanishes.[8]

125. When R. Joshua died, [men of] counsel and thought ceased.[9]

Nahum the Man of Gamzo (fl. ca. 90–130 C.E.)

126. It is related of Nahum of Gamzo[10] that he was blind in both eyes, stumped in both hands, and crippled in both legs; his entire body was covered with boils. The legs of his bed stood in four basins of water to prevent ants from crawling all over him. Once, when his bed was in a house about to collapse, his disciples proposed first removing the bed and then clearing the furniture out of the house, but he said to them, "My children, remove the furniture first and then remove my bed, for you may be sure that so long as I am in the house it will not collapse." So they cleared out the furniture, then they removed his bed, and in the next instant the house collapsed. His disciples asked, "Master, since you are so perfectly righteous, why has all this [affliction] come upon you?" He replied, "My children, I invoked it on myself. Once I was journeying to the house of my father-in-law and had with me three heavily laden asses, one with food, another with drink, and the third with all kinds of delicacies. A poor man appeared and stopped in front of me on the road, saying, 'Master, give me something to sustain me.' I replied, 'Wait until I unload the ass.' I had barely managed to unload the ass when the man died [of hunger]. I then threw myself over him and said, 'Let these eyes of mine which had no pity upon your eyes be blinded, let these hands of mine which had no pity upon your hands be stumped, let these legs of mine which had no pity upon your legs be crippled!' Nor could my soul rest thereafter, until I added, 'Let my whole body be covered with boils.' " At this, his pupils exclaimed, "Woe unto us that we see you in such a state!" Nahum replied, "Woe indeed, but even greater woe unto me if you did not see me in such a state."[11]

127. Why was he called Nahum of Gamzo? Because whenever something untoward befell him, he would declare, "This too is for good. [*Gam zo le-tovah*]." It happened once that the Jews, wishing to send a gift to Caesar, deliberated who was to go and decided that Nahum of Gamzo should go, because he was one to whom miracles always happened. They sent him with a chest full of precious stones and pearls. On the way, he spent the night at a certain inn. During the night the innkeepers opened the chest, took all that was in it, and filled it with earth.

---

1. Whom Elisha restored to life; see 2 Kings 4:35.
2. As is required of one in contact with a corpse.
3. The days that are to be counted after one has contracted uncleanness.
4. B. Nid 69b and 70b–71a.
5. B. Hul 60a.
6. Meanings suggested: (1) house of the Ebionites; (2) *Avadan* (Persian), "forum"; Be Mevedhan (Persian), "house of the chief magus."
7. My hair and beard are white, my voice is barely audible, and my teeth are worn to the gums. B. Shab 152a.
8. B. Hag 5b.
9. B. Sot 49b.
10. Gamzo is mentioned in 2 Chron. 28:18 as the name of a place. The name here is not of a place but a surname or epithet—the combination of *gam* ("also") and *zo* ("this"). See below in this chapter, §127.
11. B. Ta 21a.

When he got to Caesar and the chest was opened, they found it full of earth. "The Jews are making a laughingstock of me," said Caesar, and was about to put Nahum to death. Nevertheless, Nahum again said, "This too is for good." Just then Elijah appeared to Caesar, disguised as one of his courtiers, and remarked, "Perhaps this earth is the same kind of earth their father Abraham used—for when Abraham threw earth [against an enemy], it turned into swords, and when [he threw] stubble, it changed into arrows, as is written, 'He turns what appears to be earth into his sword, and driven stubble into his bow' " (Isa. 41:2).[1]

Now, there was one province that hitherto Caesar had not been able to conquer. They tried some of this earth against it and succeeded in conquering it. Then they brought Nahum to the royal treasury, filled his chest with precious stones and pearls, and sent him back with great honor. On his return journey, he again spent the night at the same inn. The innkeepers asked him, "What did you bring with you, that they showed you such great honor?" He replied, "What I had taken from here, the same I brought there." Hearing that, the innkeepers tore down their inn, took some of its earth to Caesar, and said, "The earth that was given to you [by Nahum] was brought from our land." When the earth [they brought] was tested, and nothing [of the aforementioned qualities] was found to be in it, the innkeepers were put to death.[2]

R. Tarfon (fl. ca. 110–35 C.E.)

128. R. Tarfon—father of all Israel, master of all Israel.[3]

129. R. Tarfon—a pile of walnuts: when a person removes one of them, all come clattering down as they fall over one another. So was R. Tarfon! Whenever a disciple of the wise came to him and said, "Teach me," he would cite for him Scripture and Mishnah, Midrash of *Halakhot* and of *Aggadot*. When the disciple left, he went away laden with blessing and [intellectual] wealth.[4]

130. When a man made a sound observation before R. Tarfon, he would say, "A knop and a flower—[well ordered]" (Exod. 25:33). And when a man uttered drivel before him, he would say, "My son shall not go down with you" (Gen. 42:38).[5]

131. It is related of R. Tarfon that once, while he was eating some dried figs in his own garden [leased to a tenant], the tenant came by and found him there but did not recognize him. "So you're the one," the tenant shouted, "who has been stealing my grapes all year!" He then proceeded to thrash him with a stick, dumped him into a sack, and carried him to the river to drown him. When R. Tarfon perceived himself to be in mortal danger, he said, "As you live, go to the house of Tarfon and say, 'Prepare shrouds for him.' " Upon hearing this, the tenant [released R. Tarfon], prostrated himself before him, tore his hair, and wept as he cried, "My master, forgive me!" R. Tarfon replied, "May such-and-such come upon me if at each and every blow of the stick that descended upon me I did not forgive you for every preceding blow."

It is said in the name of R. Hananiah ben Gamaliel: Throughout all the days of that righteous man he continued to be distressed about the incident, saying, "Woe is me! I made [selfish] use of the crown of the Torah."[6]

132. It is related of R. Tarfon that, although he was very wealthy, he did not give many gifts to the poor. Once R. Akiva met him and said to him, "Master, would you like me to purchase one or two villages for you?" He replied, "Yes," and handed R. Akiva four thousand gold denars. R. Akiva took the money and distributed it among poor disciples of the wise. Later on, R. Tarfon met him and asked, "Where are the villages that you purchased for me?" R. Akiva took him by the hand and led him to the house of study; he brought over a child who had the book of Psalms in his hand and made him read until he came to the verse "He hath scattered abroad, he hath given to the needy; his righteousness endureth forever" (Ps. 112:9). Then R. Akiva said, "This is the village I bought for you." At that, R. Tarfon stood up, kissed him, and said, "You are my teacher and my friend—my teacher in wisdom, my friend in proper conduct," and gave him additional money to distribute.[7]

133. It happened that R. Tarfon's mother went off on the Sabbath for a walk in her courtyard. Her slipper split [and since she could not repair it then and there, because it was the Sabbath], R. Tarfon held his hands under the soles of her feet, and she walked on his hands until she reached her couch.

Later, when R. Tarfon took sick and the sages came in to visit him, she said to them, "Pray for my son Tarfon, for he treats me with too much honor." They asked her, "In what way?" So she told them the story. They said, "Even if he did what you say—did so a thousand thousand times—he still has not come halfway to showing the full honor that the Torah says a son owes a parent."[8]

134. One day, as R. Tarfon sat teaching his disciples, an [indigent] bride passed by before him. He ordered that she be invited to his house and said to his mother and his wife, "Bathe her, anoint her, adorn her, and dance before her, until she goes to her husband's house."[9]

135. It once happened that R. Tarfon had not been present at the house of study the previous evening. The next

1. JV: "His sword maketh them as dust, his bow as the driven stubble."
2. B. Ta 21a; B. Sanh 108b–109a.
3. P. Yoma 1:1, 38d; P. Hor 3:2, 37d.
4. ARN 18.
5. That is, "I would not permit my son to associate with an ignorant idiot like you." In Genesis, Jacob says, "My son shall not go down with you," in response to Reuben's foolish proposal.
6. By disclosing his identity and rank; by rights, he should not have trespassed on the tenant's garden, particularly when eating what seemed to be stolen produce. P. Shev 4:2, 35b; Ka 2; B. Ned 62a.
7. Ka 2.
8. P. Pe 1:1, 15c.
9. ARN 41.

morning Rabban Gamaliel met him and asked, "Why were you not at the house of study last night?" R. Tarfon [who was a priest] replied, "I performed an act required in a priest's service." Rabban Gamaliel: "Your words are beyond comprehension. How could you at this time [when there is no Temple] perform an act required in a priest's service?" R. Tarfon: "It is said, 'I regard [priestly] gifts you make use of as a service of priesthood' [Num. 18:7][1]—my act of eating a heave offering [*terumah*] in the provinces is equal to performing an act of priestly service in the Temple."[2]

136. It is told of R. Tarfon that, while he was walking on a road, an old man accosted him and asked him, "Why do people find fault with you? Are not all your ways faithful and upright? It must be because you accept heave offering from all sorts of people throughout the year."[3] R. Tarfon: "May I bury my children if I do not have in hand a *Halakhah* from Rabban Yohanan ben Zakkai, who said to me, 'Throughout the year you are allowed to receive heave offering from all sorts of people.' Still, because [you say that] mortals find fault with me, I decree for myself not to receive heave offering from all sorts of people throughout the year, save only if there be in it a fourth of a *log* [of wine or oil] sacred for use in the Sanctuary."[4]

137. "The sons of Aaron, the priests, shall blow with the trumpets" (Num. 10:8)—the priests must be whole, without physical blemish. Such is the opinion of R. Akiva. R. Tarfon said to him: May I bury my sons if I did not see my mother's brother, one of whose legs was lame, standing in the Temple Court, a trumpet in his hand, blowing it. R. Akiva replied: My master, perhaps what you witnessed took place at the time of *Hak'hel*, the time of the great assembly.[5] I, however, have in mind the time when offerings are presented. R. Tarfon: May I bury my children—in proposing your opinion, you veered not a whit to the right or to the left. It is I who saw what happened but forgot the exact circumstances. I should not have interpreted the rule as I did, whereas you expound in precise agreement with the true tradition. So anyone who sets himself apart from you sets himself apart from his own life.[6]

138. At one time the Ineffable Name was uttered [by the high priest] in a loud voice. But after skeptics grew in number, it came to be uttered in a low voice. R. Tarfon said: Once, while standing in a row with my brother priests [on the Day of Atonement], I inclined my ears toward the high priest [to catch his pronunciation], but he muffled it in the priests' chanting. One time, however—continued Rabban—I did hear it and fell upon my face [in awe].[7]

R. Akiva (fl. 95–135 C.E.)

139. Resh Lakish said: What is meant by "This is the book of the generations of Adam" (Gen. 5:1)? It intimates that the Holy One showed him each generation and its expounders of Scripture, each generation and its sages. When He reached the generation of R. Akiva, Adam rejoiced in R. Akiva's Torah but grieved over his death and protested, "How precious to me Thy friends [each sage, each expounder of Scripture], O God" (Ps. 139:17).[8]

140. R. Judah said in the name of Rav: When Moses ascended on high, he found the Holy One affixing crowns to letters.[9] Moses asked, "Lord of the universe, [why use crowns to intimate what You wish]? Who hinders Your hand [from writing out in full all of Torah's precepts]? God replied, "At the end of many generations there will arise a man, Akiva ben Joseph by name, who will infer heaps and heaps of laws from each tittle on these crowns." "Lord of the universe," said Moses, "permit me to see him." God replied, "Turn around." Moses went and sat down behind eight rows [of R. Akiva's disciples and listened to their discourses on law]. Not being able to follow what they were saying, he was so distressed that he grew faint. But when they came to a certain subject and the disciples asked R. Akiva, "Master, where did you learn this?" and R. Akiva replied, "It is a law given to Moses at Sinai," Moses was reassured. He returned to the Holy One and said, "Lord of the Universe, You have such a man, yet You give the Torah [not by his hand] but by mine?" God replied, "Be silent—thus has it come to My mind." Then Moses said, "Lord of the universe, You have shown me his Torah—now show me his reward." "Turn around," said God. Moses turned around and saw R. Akiva's flesh being weighed out in a meat market.[10] "Lord of the universe," Moses cried out in protest, "such Torah, and such its reward?" God replied, "Be silent—thus has it come to My mind."[11]

141. R. Akiva was a shepherd forty years; he studied Torah forty years; and guided Israel forty years.[12]

142. Who are the fathers of the world? R. Ishmael and R. Akiva.[13]

1. JV: "I give you the priesthood as a service of gift."
2. B. Pes 72b–73a.
3. Even though their reputation for scrupulous observance of the laws of cleanness is not the best.
4. Even the ignorant person (*am ha-aretz*), who is not trusted with regard to proper care of the heave offering, is trusted concerning an item that is used in the Sanctuary. The incident may have occurred in the days of Bar Kozeva, when people resumed bringing gifts for the cultus. See Saul Lieberman, ed., Tos Hag (New York, 1962), 7:1333. Tos Hag 3:33.
5. Once every seven years, the entire people assembled during the Feast of Tabernacles to listen to the reading of the Torah. See Deut. 31:12.
6. P. Yoma 1:1, 38d.
7. P. Yoma 3:7, 40d; Eccles. R. 3:11, §3.
8. The psalm is understood to deal with Adam. B. Sanh 38b. JV: "How weighty . . . Thy thoughts to me, O God." However, *re'ekha* ("Thy thoughts") can also mean "Thy friends"; and *yakeru* ("weighty") can also mean "precious."
9. See above, part one, chap. 5, §51.
10. R. Akiva died a martyr's death at the hands of the Romans during the Hadrianic persecution. See below in this chapter, §180.
11. B. Men 29b.
12. Sif Deut., §357.
13. P. RH 1:1, 56d.

143. Had Shaphan not arisen in his time, and Ezra in his time, and R. Akiva in his time, would not the Torah have been forgotten in Israel?[1]

144. After the death of Yose ben Joezer of Tzeredah and Joseph ben Yohanan of Jerusalem, men of comprehensive learning (*eshkolot*)[2] ceased, so that one could say, "There is no bunch of grapes (*eshkol*) to eat, no choice morsel of a fig" (Mic. 7:1). Not until R. Akiva did a man of comprehensive learning (*eshkol*) arise.[3]

145. R. Akiva worked as a shepherd for Kalba Savua.[4] When Rachel, Kalba Savua's daughter, saw that even though Akiva was unassuming, there was something extraordinary about him, she said, "If I am willing to be betrothed to you, will you attend a house of study?" R. Akiva answered, "Yes." So she betrothed herself to him in secret. When Kalba Savua learned what she had done, he drove her out of his house and vowed that she was not to benefit from any of his property. At that, she went off and [openly] married Akiva. When winter came, [they were so poor that] they had to sleep in a straw bin. As R. Akiva picked the straw from her hair, he would say, "If I had the means, I would give you a 'Jerusalem of gold.' "[5]

Presently [the prophet] Elijah, disguised as a mortal, came and cried out at the door, "Please give me a bit of straw—my wife is about to give birth, and I have nothing for her to lie on." R. Akiva said to his wife, "Look at this man—he does not even have the straw [that we have]!"

Soon after, she insisted, "Go now, and learn Torah in a house of study." He went away, and for twelve years he sat in a house of study in the presence of R. Eliezer and R. Joshua.

At the end of twelve years, he arose and returned to his home, bringing with him twelve thousand disciples. Everyone went out to meet him. When his wife heard [of his arrival], she too went out to meet him. Her neighbors said to her, "Borrow some clothes, put them on, and make yourself presentable." But she replied, "A righteous man will recognize his loyal creature" (Prov. 12:10). When she came near him, she fell upon her face and was about to kiss his feet. But his disciples sought to push her aside. R. Akiva shouted at them, "Let her be—mine and yours are rightly hers."

Her father, on hearing that a great man had come to town, said, "I shall go to him, perhaps the great man will release me of my vow." When the father came to him, R. Akiva asked, "Would you have made your vow if you had known that her husband was to become a great man?" The father replied, "[Had her husband known] even one chapter, even one *Halakhah* [I would not have made such a vow]." R. Akiva then said, "I am your daughter's husband." The father fell upon his face and kissed R. Akiva's feet. Presently, he gave him half of his wealth.[6]

146. What were Akiva's beginnings?

It is said: Up to the age of forty, he had not yet studied a thing. One time, while standing by the mouth of a well in Lydda, he inquired, "Who hollowed out this stone?" and was told, "Akiva, haven't you read [in Scripture] that 'water wears away stone' [Job 14:19]?—it was water [from the well] falling upon it constantly, day after day."

At that, R. Akiva asked himself: Is my mind harder than this stone? I will go and study at least one section of Torah. He went directly to a schoolhouse, and he and his son began reading from a child's tablet. R. Akiva took hold of one end of the tablet, and his son of the other end. The teacher wrote down *alef* and *bet* for him, and he learned them; *alef* to *tav*, and he learned them; the book of Leviticus, and he learned it. He went on studying until he learned the whole Torah.

Then he went and sat before R. Eliezer and R. Joshua. "My masters," he said to them, "reveal the sense of Mishnah to me."

When they told him one *Halakhah*, he went off to reason with himself. This *alef*, he wondered, what was it written for? That *bet*—what was it written for? This teaching—what was it uttered for? He kept coming back, kept inquiring of R. Eliezer and R. Joshua, until he reduced his teachers to silence.

All the twelve years that R. Akiva was with R. Eliezer, R. Eliezer paid little attention to him, so that when R. Akiva offered his first clinching argument to him, R. Joshua quoted the verse "There is the army you paid no attention to; now go out and fight it" (Judg. 9:38).

R. Simeon ben Eleazar said: I shall tell you a parable to illustrate what R. Akiva did. He was like a stonecutter hacking away at mountains. One time he took his pickax in his hand, went and sat on top of the mountain, and began to chip small stones from it. Some men came by and asked him, "What are you doing?"

"I mean to uproot the mountain and cast it into the Jordan."

"Can you possibly do such a thing?"

"Yes." He continued hacking away until he came to a big boulder. He placed an iron claw under it, pried it loose, uprooted it, and cast it into the Jordan. Then he espied another, even bigger boulder, placed an iron claw under it, and cast it into the Jordan, saying, "Your place is not here, but there."[7]

R. Akiva had to perform such uprooting of "big boulders" with [the instruction of] R. Eliezer and R. Joshua, in keeping with the verse "He falls to work upon the flinty rocks, he turns mountains up by the roots, he carves out channels through rock, and his eye beholds every precious thing" (Job 28:9–10).

Each day R. Akiva would gather a bundle of twigs—half of it he would sell to provide food for himself, and

---

1. Sif Deut., §48.
2. The word *eshkolot* is construed as portmanteau: *ish* ("a man") *she-ha-kol bo* ("in whom there is everything").
3. P. Sot 9:10, 24a.
4. At the time of Vespasian's siege, one of Jerusalem's three richest men. See above, part 1, chap. 10, §2.
5. A gold tiara with "Jerusalem" engraved on it.
6. B. Ket 62b–63a; B. Ned 50a.
7. By perseverance and skill, he achieved what appeared to be impossible.

the other half he would use for his personal needs. His neighbors rose up in protest, saying, "Akiva, you are all but choking us with smoke! Sell us the twigs, buy oil with the money, and study by the light of a lamp." He replied, "I find many uses for the twigs. To begin with, I study by the light they give; then I keep warm by their heat; finally, I sleep on some of them."

It is said: Before R. Akiva departed from the world, he owned tables made of silver and of gold—he even ascended his couch by a stepladder made of gold. His wife used to go out shod with golden sandals and wearing a golden tiara.

"Master," his disciples said to him, "you put us to shame [before our wives] by what you are doing for her."

He replied, "Much suffering did she endure with me for the sake of Torah."[1]

147. A story is told of R. Akiva, who had a "Jerusalem of gold" made for his wife. When the wife of Rabban Gamaliel saw it, she was envious of her, went to her husband, and said so. He replied, "Would you have done for me what she did for her husband? She used to sell the braided locks of her hair and give him the money, so that he could occupy himself with Torah."[2]

148. It is taught that R. Akiva said: When I was untutored (*am ha-aretz*), I used to say, "Would that I had a scholar before me! I would bite him as does an ass." His disciples said, "Master, you mean, as does a dog." He replied, "No, when an ass bites, he breaks bones; when a dog bites, he breaks no bones."[3]

149. R. Yohanan ben Nuri said: I call heaven and earth to witness that many times R. Akiva was punished on account of me, because I used to bring charges against him before Rabban Gamaliel in Yavneh, but I know that nevertheless R. Akiva's love for me grew, in keeping with the verse "Reprove a man of sense, and he will love thee" (Prov. 9:8).[4]

150. One day R. Akiva was delayed in getting to the house of study, so that when he did come, he sat down outside. A question arose: "Is such-and-such the *Halakhah*?" They said, "The *Halakhah* is outside." Again a question arose. They said, "Akiva is outside." So a space was found for him, and he came in and sat down [in an unassuming way] at the feet of R. Eliezer.[5]

151. R. Akiva—"a treasury with compartments." To whom may R. Akiva be likened? To a laborer who took his basket and went forth to the field. When he found wheat, he put some into it; when he found barley, in it went; emmer, likewise; beans, the same; lentils—they too went into the basket. Upon returning home, he sorted out the wheat by itself, the barley by itself, the emmer by itself, the beans by themselves, the lentils by themselves. This is how R. Akiva acted: all the Torah [he amassed], he sorted into its various compartments.[6]

152. To R. Akiva, who provided scriptural grounding for *Halakhot* and *Haggadot*, R. Jonah applied the verse "I will give him [fame] among many as his portion, because he divided spoil with those who sought hard [to understand]" (Isa. 53:12).[7] Some say, the Men of the Great Assembly[8] provided such grounding. What, then, did R. Akiva provide? General principles and detailed regulations.[9]

153. Once, as R. Akiva sat teaching his disciples and recalling what he had done in his youth, he exclaimed:

I give thanks unto You,
O Lord my God,
that You have set my portion
among those who sit in the house of study
and have not set my portion
among those who loiter at street corners in the
marketplace.[10]

154. R. Tarfon said to him, "Akiva, when a man separates himself from you, he separates himself from life."

R. Tarfon also said to him, "Akiva, of you Scripture says, 'The thing that is hid, bringeth he forth to light' [Job 28:11]—things concealed from men, [you] R. Akiva brought forth to light.[11]

155. Ben Azzai said: Compared to me, all sages in Israel are as thin as the husk of garlic—except for this baldhead [R. Akiva].[12]

156. Some time ago, a legal decision [about the ash of the Red Heifer] was put to thirty-eight elders in a vineyard in Yavneh, who declared its flesh ritually clean. The issue was one of the matters R. Yose the Galilean debated with R. Akiva. R. Akiva disposed of R. Yose, who subsequently found a rejoinder and asked R. Akiva, "May I go back to the subject?" R. Akiva: "No other man but you may, because you are Yose the Galilean." Then R. Yose set forth the rejoinder he had thought of.

Recalling this incident, R. Tarfon quoted, "I saw the ram pushing westward, and northward, and southward; and none of all the beasts could stand before him, neither was there any that could deliver out of his hand; but he did according to his will, and grew great" (Dan. 8:4). The ram is R. Akiva.

1. ARN 6; ARNB 12.
2. P. Shab 6:1, 4d.
3. B. Pes 49b.
4. B. Ar 16b and En Yaakov, ad loc; Sif Deut., §1.
5. Song R. 1:3, §1.
6. Literally, "rings [upon] rings"—like a chain whose links are connected. R. Akiva not only systematized the body of tradition he acquired, but formulated it in abstract general rules. ARN 18.
7. JV: "Therefore will I give him a portion among the great, and he shall divide the spoil with the mighty."
8. A legislaive body of one hundred and twenty men, said to have functioned about five centuries before the Common Era.
9. P. Shek 5:1, 48c.
10. ARN 21.
11. B. Kid 66b; ARN 6.
12. B. Bekh 58a.

"And as I was considering, behold, a he-goat came from the west over the face of the whole earth, and touched not the ground; and the he-goat had a conspicuous horn between his eyes. And he came to the ram that had the two horns . . . and ran at him in the fury of his power. . . . And he was moved with choler against him, and smote the ram, and broke his two horns; and there was no power in the ram to stand before him; but he cast him down to the ground, and trampled upon him, and there was none that could deliver the ram out of his hand" (Dan. 8:5–7). The he-goat is R. Yose the Galilean.[1]

157. It is related of R. Akiva that he never said, "It is time to quit [the house of study] except on the eve of Passover and the eve of Yom Kippur. On the eve of Passover, for the sake of children, so that they would not fall asleep [during the seder]. On the eve of Yom Kippur, so that the disciples could feed their children.[2]

158. When R. Simeon, the son of R. Akiva, fell ill, the father did not neglect his house of study, but arranged for his messengers to stand by [the sickbed].

The first messenger came and said, "He is very ill."
"Carry on!" said R. Akiva to his disciples.
The second came and said, "He is getting worse."
He had them resume their study of Torah.
The third came and said, "He is dying."
"Carry on!"
The fourth came and said, "He is gone."

Hearing this, R. Akiva rose, removed his tefillin, rent his clothes, and said to his disciples: "Up to now we were obliged to study Torah. From this moment on, you and I are obligated to honor the dead."

A large gathering assembled for the burial of R. Akiva's son and showed great grief over his demise. As they were about to leave, R. Akiva stood up on a large stool and said: O House of Israel, our brethren, hear me! Even if my son had been a bridegroom, I would still be comforted, because of the honor you accorded him.

It is not because I am wise:
There are those here who are wiser than I.
And it is not because I am rich:
There are those here who are richer than I.
The people of the south know R. Akiva,
But how do the people of Galilee know him?
The men know R. Akiva,
But how do the women and children know him?
If you came for the sake of someone named Akiva,
how many men named Akiva are there in the
marketplace?

I know that you troubled yourselves to come for the sake of the commandment [of comforting the bereaved], as well as for the honor of Torah, saying, "The law of his God is in his heart" (Ps. 37:31). It is therefore certain that your reward will be twofold. I am comforted. Go to your homes in peace.[3]

159. R. Akiva sat weeping on the Sabbath. His disciples said: Our master, you taught us, "Call the Sabbath a delight" (Isa. 58:13). R. Akiva: This is my delight.[4]

160. It happened that the synagogue sexton publicly asked R. Akiva to step over to the [lectern] to read the Torah lesson, but R. Akiva did not rise. After they left the synagogue, he began to apologize to the disciples, saying: May such-and-such befall me if it was out of arrogance that I did not rise to read in the Torah. So they asked: Then why did not the master rise? He replied: Because I had not prepared myself.

The disciples fell to wondering about what R. Akiva had said.[5]

161. We have been taught that, according to R. Judah, such was the practice of R. Akiva: when he prayed with a congregation, he used to make his prayer brief and conclude the service, in order not to inconvenience the congregation; but when he prayed by himself, a man would leave him praying in one corner and find him later [still praying] in another corner, because of his many genuflexions and prostrations.[6]

162. Our masters taught: Four men entered the "Garden,"[7] namely, Ben Azzai, Ben Zoma, Aher,[8] and R. Akiva. R. Akiva said to them: When you arrive at the slabs of pure transparent marble, do not say: Water, Water! For it is said, "He that speaketh falsehood shall not be established before Mine eyes" (Ps. 101:7) Ben Azzai cast a look and died: of him Scripture says, "Precious in the sight of the Lord is the death of His saints" (Ps. 116:15). Ben Zoma looked and became demented; of him Scripture says, "Hast thou found honey? Eat so much as is sufficient for thee, lest thou be filled therewith, and vomit it" (Prov. 25:16). Aher mutilated the shoots. R. Akiva departed unhurt.[9]

---

1. Sif Num., §124; Yalkut, *Hukkat*, §761.
2. B. Pes 109a.
3. Sem 8:13 (YJS 17:63); B. MK 21b and En Yaakov, ad loc.
4. *Shibbolei ha-Leket*, which cites a Midrash. "As he thought of the Temple in Jerusalem, it was a relief for R. Akiva to shed tears, even on a Sabbath" (private communication to the translator from Dr. Louis Finkelstein, chancellor emeritus of the Jewish Theological Seminary of America, New York). Another possibility: R. Akiva belonged to those who believed that the Sabbath should be observed by fasting and weeping (see Yitzhak D. Gilat, "On Fasting on the Sabbath" [Hebrew], *Tarbitz* 52, no. 1 [1982]: 1–15).
5. The disciples marveled that even R. Akiva, who was so well versed, felt he needed special preparation to read and expound a lesson in Scripture. Tanhuma, *Yitro*, §15.
6. B. Ber 31a.
7. "A figurative expression for the mystical realm of theosophy." So Jastrow and Goldschmidt.
8. Elisha ben Avuyah, R. Meir's teacher. See below in this chapter, §191.
9. Ben Azzai and Ben Zoma penetrated into the forbidden regions of the divine mystery and were smitten accordingly. Aher, misinterpreting the mystery, fell into heresy. Only Akiva survived the experience. B. Hag 14b.

163. R. Akiva came up unhurt and went down unhurt. Of him, Scripture says, "Draw me, we will run after Thee" (Song 1:4). The ministering angels sought to thrust R. Akiva away; but the Holy One said: Let this venerable elder be. He is worthy of making use of My glory.[1]

164. It is said that R. Akiva had twelve thousand pairs of disciples between Gabbath[2] and Antipatris.[3] All died during his lifetime, at the same time, between Passover and Pentecost [Shavuot], because they did not treat one another with respect. The world was desolate[4] until R. Akiva came to our masters in the south and taught them Torah—he thus taught R. Meir, R. Judah, R. Yose, R. Simeon, R. Eleazar ben Shammua. He said to them, "The previous disciples died only because they begrudged one another the knowledge of Torah. See to it that you do not act like them." They rose and filled all the Land of Israel with Torah.[5]

165. Rabban Gamaliel said: Once, while traveling on shipboard, I saw another ship wrecked and grieved greatly for a disciple of the wise who was on it. (Who was he? R. Akiva.) After I landed, there was R. Akiva, who sat down before me and held forth upon decisions in *Halakhah*. I asked him: Who brought you here? He replied: A ship's plank came my way, and as each wave came toward me, I dipped my head under it.[6]

166. Once, while on a journey, R. Akiva came to a certain place where he looked for lodging but was not given any. He said, "Whatever the Holy One does is for the best." So he went off and spent the night in the open field. He had with him an ass, a cock, and a lamp. A lion came and ate the ass, a weasel came and ate the cock, and a gust of wind came and blew out the lamp. Again he said, "Whatever the Holy One does is for the best." That same night, troops came and took the people of that city into captivity. Said R. Akiva to his disciples, "Did I not tell you, 'Whatever the Holy One does is for the best'?"[7]

167. Our masters taught that R. Akiva gave seven charges to his son Joshua: My son, do not live and study in the business district of the city;[8] do not dwell in a town whose leaders are scholars;[9] do not enter your own house unexpectedly, much less your neighbor's house; do not withhold shoes from your feet.[10] Rise early and eat—in summer, on account of the sun's heat, and in winter, on account of the cold.[11] Treat your Sabbath like a weekday rather than be dependent on [the charity of] mortals. Strive to be on good terms with a man upon whom the hour smiles.[12]

168. One of R. Akiva's disciples fell ill, and the sages did not come to visit him. So R. Akiva went to visit the disciple, and because he saw to it that the ground was swept and sprinkled for him, he recovered and said, "My master, you have brought me back to life."

R. Akiva went out and expounded, "He who does not visit the sick is as though he had shed blood."[13]

169. R. Akiva said: This is how my attendance upon sages began. Once, while walking on a road, I found a slain man. I carried him a distance of four *mil* until I brought him to a burial place, where I interred him. When I came to R. Eliezer and R. Joshua, I told them what had happened. They said to me, "Every step you took is accounted for you as though you had shed blood."[14] Then I said to myself: If I incurred sin when I thought to do good, how much more sin would I have incurred had I not thought to do good!

Henceforth, I did not budge from attending upon sages.

R. Akiva used to say: He who does not attend upon sages deserves death.[15]

170. R. Akiva became rich from six sources:

(1) From Kalba Savua.[16]

(2) From a ship's ram—for every ship is provided with the figurehead of a ram. Once one was forgotten on the seashore, and R. Akiva found it.[17]

(3) From a ship's coffer. Once he gave four *zuz* to mariners, saying, "Bring me such-and-such a thing [that I need]." But they found only a coffer on the seashore, which they brought to him and said, "Our master will have to make do with this." The coffer was found to be filled with denars. For it so happened that a pirate ship had sunk, and all their wealth was in that coffer found just then.

(4) And from a Roman noblewoman. One time the sages needed a lot of money for the house of study. So they sent R. Akiva to a certain Roman noblewoman, from whom he borrowed a large sum, and he fixed with her the time of repayment. When she asked, "Who will guarantee me in this matter that you will repay on time?" he replied, "Whoever you wish." So she said, "Let it be the Holy One and the sea"—for her house was on the seashore. R. Akiva replied, "Very well."

When the time for repayment came, R. Akiva took sick and could not bring the money. So the noblewoman

---

1. B. Hag 15b and En Yaakov ad loc.
2. Gibbethon, in the territory of Dan.
3. Northwest of Jerusalem.
4. Without Torah.
5. B. Yev 62b; Gen. R. 61:3; Eccles. R. 11:6, §1.
6. B. Yev 121a.
7. B. Ber 60b.
8. Where the movement of people disturbs study.
9. They are too busy with their studies to pay attention to its affairs.
10. "One should sell even the beams of his house and buy shoes for his feet" (B. Shab 129a).
11. So that your breakfast will be well digested by the time you have to face the summer's heat or the winter's cold.
12. B. Pes 112a.
13. B. Ned 40a and En Yaakov, ad loc.
14. "His own blood, and the blood of others against whom Rome might take reprisals" (Sem: Dov Zlotnick, ed., *The Tractate "Mourning"* [New Haven, Conn., 1966; YJS 17] 22). R. Akiva should have buried the corpse on the spot at once.
15. P. Naz 7:1, 56a; Sem 4.
16. See above in this chapter, §145.
17. It was full of gold coins.

went out to the seashore and said, "Master of the universe, to You it is known and revealed that R. Akiva is sick and is unable to pay the debt owed me. Be advised that You and the sea are guarantors in the matter."

At once the Holy One sent a spirit of folly into the heart of Caesar's daughter, who entered the royal treasury, took a basket filled with precious stones and gold denars, and threw it into the sea. The sea discharged it at the doorway of the noblewoman, who picked it up. After a while, R. Akiva recovered and came to the noblewoman with the money in his hand. She said, "Let all you brought remain with you, for I went to the Guarantor and He paid the entire debt, and here is the extra He gave." In addition to this, she bestowed on him substantial gifts and sent him away in peace.

(5) And from the wife of the tyrant Rufus.[1] The tyrant Rufus would voice silly arguments against R. Akiva and, in the presence of Caesar, R. Akiva would overwhelm these arguments with verses—even dared rebuke him. Once, when the tyrant Rufus came home greatly put out, his wife asked, "Why are you so put out?" He: "Because of R. Akiva, who manages every day to rebuke me." The wife: "Give me permission, and I will make him stumble." (It should be said that she was very beautiful.) He gave her permission. She adorned herself and went to R. Akiva's house. When R. Akiva saw her, he spat, wept, and yet seemed elated. She: "What is the meaning of these three reactions?" He: "I will explain two, but not the third. I spat because you originated from a fetid drop [of sperm]; I wept because of such great beauty, which is to decay into dust." But he did not explain why he was elated—he was elated because he foresaw through the holy spirit that she would be converted and be wed to him.

She: "Is repentance possible?" He: "Yes."

At once she went away, became a convert, was wed to him, and brought him much wealth.

(6) And finally from Ketia bar Shalom. He became a convert, was sentenced to death, and said, "All my possessions are to go to R. Akiva and his companions."[2]

171. It happened that the tyrant Rufus asked R. Akiva, "Why does the Holy One so hate us that He wrote, 'But Esau I hate' (Mal. 1:3)?" R. Akiva: "Tomorrow I will give you an answer." In the morning Rufus asked, "R. Akiva, what did you dream last night, and what did you see [in your dream]?" R. Akiva: "In my dream I saw two dogs, one named Rufus and the other named Rufina." Angered, Rufus said, "You call your dogs by names no other than mine and my wife's! You deserve death [for an offense] against the government." R. Akiva: "But how do you differ from dogs? You eat and drink, and they eat and drink. You procreate, and they procreate. You die, and they die. You are angry because I called them by your name. Now consider: It is the Holy One who has stretched out the heavens and established the earth. It is He who consigns to death and restores to life. Yet you take a block of wood [which does nothing] and call it god by His Name. Does it not stand to reason that He should be angry with you? Hence, 'But Esau I hate.' "[3]

172. When R. Akiva went to a foreign land, its ruler sent him two beautiful women who had been bathed, anointed, and adorned like brides. All night they kept thrusting themselves at him, one saying, "Turn to me," and the other saying, "Turn to me." But he sat there spitting in disgust and turned to neither. [In the morning] they went away and complained to the ruler, saying, "We would rather die than be given to this man."

The ruler sent for him and asked, "Why did you not do with these women as men usually do? Are they not beautiful? Are they not human beings like you? Did not He who created you also create them?"

R. Akiva answered, "What could I do? Their breath came at me like the odor of the carrion, torn beasts, and creeping things [they eat].[4]

173. R. Akiva used to scoff at sexual transgressors. Once Satan, disguised as an [alluring] woman, appeared to him on top of a palm tree. Akiva took hold of the tree and started to climb it. But when he reached halfway, his [impulse to evil] let go of him. Satan said to him: Had it not been proclaimed of you in the firmament "Take heed of R. Akiva and his learning," I would have valued your life at no more than two *meah*.[5]

174. Our masters related the following story: When R. Akiva was confined in prison and R. Joshua the Grits Maker served him, only a limited amount of water was brought in to him every day. One day R. Joshua was stopped by the keeper of the prison, who asked him, "Why is your water today above the set limit? Do you perhaps require that much to breach the prison walls?" At this, the keeper poured out half of the water and left the other half. When R. Joshua, [delayed by the encounter, finally] came in to R. Akiva, R. Akiva said, "Joshua, do you not know that I am an old man and that my life depends on yours? [Why are you so late?]" After R. Joshua told him all that had happened, R. Akiva said, "Give me some water to wash my hands." R. Joshua replied, "The water I brought will not suffice for drinking—how can it also suffice for washing your hands [for the meal]?" R. Akiva: "But what else am I to do? I would rather starve myself to death than disregard the opinion of my colleagues."[6]

It is related that he tasted nothing until R. Joshua managed to bring him more water with which to wash his hands. When the sages heard of the incident, they remarked, "If he is so scrupulous in his old age, how much more so must he have been in his youth; and if he behaves thus in prison, how much more scrupulous must his behavior be in his own home."[7]

---

1. Governor of Judea, 1st century C.E.
2. B. AZ 10b and 20a; R. Nissim and Rashi on B. Ned 50a–b.
3. Tanhuma, *Terumah*, §3.
4. ARN 16.
5. A small coin. That is, your life would not have been worth two cents. B. Kid 81a.
6. Who ruled that before a meal one's hands must be washed.
7. B. Er 21b and En Yaakov, ad loc.

175. R. Yohanan the Cobbler, pretending to be a peddler, passed by R. Akiva's prison cell, calling out, "Who needs needles? Who needs hooks? What if a widow performed *halitzah*[1] without witnesses?" R. Akiva looked out from the prison window and said, "Do you have spindles? Do you have . . . The act is valid."[2]

176. When R. Akiva was on trial before the tyrant Rufus, and R. Joshua the Grits Maker was standing in prayer with him, a cloud came down and covered them. At this, R. Joshua said, "It seems to me that the cloud came down and covered us only so that the prayer of my master would not be heard." With regard to this, Scripture says, "Thou hast covered Thyself with a cloud, so that no prayer can pass through" (Lam. 3:44).[3]

177. Our masters taught: Once the wicked Roman government issued a decree forbidding the Jews to study and practice the Torah. Pappus ben Judah came by and, upon finding R. Akiva publicly holding sessions in which he occupied himself with Torah, Pappus asked him: Akiva, are you not afraid of the government? R. Akiva replied: You, Pappus, who are said to be wise, are in fact a fool. I can explain what I am doing by means of a parable: A fox was walking on a river bank and, seeing fishes hastening here and there, asked them, "From whom are you fleeing?" They replied, "From the nets and traps set for us by men." So the fox said to them, "How would you like to come up on dry land, so that you and I may live together the way my ancestors lived with yours?" They replied, "You—the one they call the cleverest of animals—are in fact a fool. If we are fearful in the place where we can stay alive, how much more fearful should we be in a place where we are sure to die!" So it is with us. If we are fearful when we sit and study the Torah, of which it is written, "For that is thy life and the length of thy days" (Deut. 30:20), how much more fearful ought we to be should we cease the study of words of Torah!

It is related that soon afterward R. Akiva was arrested and thrown into prison, and Pappus ben Judah was also arrested and put in prison next to him. R. Akiva asked: Pappus, who brought you here? He replied: Happy are you, R. Akiva, that you have been seized for occupying yourself with the Torah! Alas for Pappus, who has been seized for occupying himself with vain things!

When R. Akiva was taken out to be executed, it was the hour for the recital of the Shema, and the executioners were combing his flesh with iron combs, while he was lovingly making ready to accept upon himself the yoke of the kingship of Heaven. His disciples asked: Our teacher, even to such a degree? He replied: All my days I have been troubled by this verse "With all thy soul" (Deut. 6:5), which I have interpreted as meaning "Even if He takes your soul." But I said: When shall I have an occasion to fulfill the precept? Now that I have the occasion, shall I not fulfill it? He prolonged the Shema's concluding word, *ehad* ("one"), until he expired as he finished pronouncing it. A divine voice went forth and proclaimed: Happy are you, Akiva, that your soul has departed with the word *ehad!* The ministering angels spoke out bluntly to the Holy One: Such Torah, and such its reward? He should have been "of those that die by Thy hand, O Lord" (Ps. 17:14). God replied: "Their portion is in life" (ibid.). Just then, another divine voice went forth and proclaimed: Happy are you, R. Akiva, destined as you are for life in the world-to-come.[4]

178. While R. Akiva was confined in prison, the eve of Yom Kippur came, and his disciple and servant R. Joshua the Grits Maker went home.

Then the prophet Elijah, ever remembered for good, appeared and, standing at the doorway of R. Joshua's house, said: Peace upon you, my master. Joshua: Peace upon you, my master and teacher. Elijah: Do you need anything? R. Joshua: Who are you? Elijah: I am a priest and I came to tell you that R. Akiva has died in prison. At once they both went to the prison and found the door of the prison open, the chief officer of the prison asleep, and all the prisoners asleep as well. They laid out R. Akiva's corpse on a bier and were about to leave when Elijah, ever remembered for good, bestirred himself and hoisted the bier on his shoulders. Seeing this, R. Joshua said: My master, did you not just tell me that you are a priest, and is not a priest forbidden to defile himself by contact with the dead? Elijah: Enough, R. Joshua, my son. God forbid that disciples of the wise or even their disciples should convey uncleanness.

So all that night the two carried R. Akiva's bier, until they reached Antipatris of Caesarea. When they arrived there, they went up three steps, then went down three steps, and a cave opened up before them. In it they saw a seat, a footstool, a table, and a lamp. They laid down R. Akiva's bier and left. The moment they left, the cave closed, and the light in the lamp was lit. When Elijah saw this, he burst out in blessing: Blessed are you, O righteous! Blessed are you who labor in Torah! Blessed are you who fear God! In the time-to-come, a place in the Garden of Eden is reserved, saved, and lovingly kept for you. Blessed are you, R. Akiva, that at the time of your death a transient lodging was made available for you.[5]

179. When R. Akiva died, the glory of Torah ceased, the arms of Torah lost their strength, and the fountains of wisdom were stopped up.[6]

The Ten Martyrs

180. When the wicked Roman government decreed that the sages of Israel be put to death, his companions said to R. Ishmael the High Priest, "Go up to heaven and inquire whether the decree has been inspired by the Holy One." R. Ishmael stood up, purified himself, wrapped

1. The ceremony of removing the shoe of the brother of a husband who died childless. Deut. 25:5–9.
2. P. Yev 12:5, 12d.
3. Lam. R. 3:44, §9.
4. B. Ber 61b and En Yaakov, ad loc.
5. Midrash Prov. 9 (ed. Buber, pp. 61–62); Yalkut, Prov., §944.
6. B. Sot 49a–b.

himself in tallit and tefillin, and pronounced the Explicit Name. A wind lifted him at once and brought him up to heaven. When the angel Gabriel encountered him, he asked him, "Are you Ishmael whose Maker boasts every day that He has a servant on earth who resembles His own visage?" R. Ishmael: "I am he." Gabriel: "Why did you come up here?" Ishmael: "I came up to ascertain if the decree had been sealed by the Holy One." Gabriel: "Ishmael, my son, as you live, thus have I heard from behind the curtain [in heaven]: ten sages of Israel will be turned over to be slain at the hand of the wicked government. R. Ishmael: "Why?" Gabriel: "Because of the sale of Joseph. Every day the measure of justice has been speaking in accusation before the throne of glory, saying, 'Did You write in vain a single letter in the Torah?' You said, 'He that stealeth a man, and selleth him . . . shall surely be put to death' [Exod. 21:16]. Yet the ten tribe fathers sold Joseph, and until now You did not requite them or their progeny. Therefore a decree was issued against ten sages of Israel." R. Ishmael: "Has the Holy One been unable to find anyone but us to requite until now?" Gabriel: "As you live, Ishmael, my son, since the day the tribe fathers sold Joseph, the Holy One has not found in any generation men as righteous and pious as the tribe fathers, save only you. Hence He will requite through you."

When the wicked angel Samael saw that the Holy One was about to seal the decree, he rejoiced greatly as he boasted, saying, "I have prevailed over Prince Michael!" At that, the wrath of the Holy One was kindled at Samael, and, summoning the angel Metatron, He said to him, "Write and seal—brimstone and fire upon wicked Rome, upon humans and cattle, upon silver, upon gold, upon everything that is theirs."

When R. Ishmael heard this, his indignation immediately abated. As he walked back and forth in heaven, he saw an altar near the throne of glory. So he asked Gabriel, "What is this?" Gabriel: "An altar." R. Ishmael: "What do you offer on it every day?" Gabriel: "We offer on it the souls of the righteous." R. Ishmael: "Who offers them?" Gabriel: "The great prince Michael."

At once R. Ishmael went down to the earth and informed his colleagues that the decree had been sealed. Those seated on the right complained that a harsh decree had been issued against them; and those seated on the left rejoiced that the Holy One held them to be equal to the tribe fathers.

R. Simeon ben Gamaliel and R. Ishmael the High Priest were seized to be executed. R. Simeon burst into tears. R. Ishmael said to him, "Avrekh,[1] you are but two steps away from being put in the bosom of the righteous, yet you weep!" R. Simeon: "My heart fails me, because I do not know why I am to be killed." R. Ishmael: "In your lifetime, did a man ever come to you for judgment or with a question, and you kept him waiting while you drank your cup or tied your sandal or donned your cloak, even though the Torah says, 'If thou delayest at all' [Exod. 22:22][2]—whether the delay be long or short?" At that, R. Ishmael said, "You have comforted me, my master."

Both pleaded with the executioner. R. Ishmael said, "I am a high priest son of a high priest, of the seed of Aaron, the High Priest. Slay me first, so that I shall not have to witness the death of my colleague." And R. Simeon said, "I am a prince son of a prince, of the seed of David, king of Israel. Slay me first, so that I shall not have to witness the death of my colleague."

The executioner said, "Cast lots." The lot fell on R. Simeon ben Gamaliel. At once the executioner seized the sword and cut off his head. Then R. Ishmael took R. Simeon's severed head and clasped it to his bosom as he wept and cried out, "Holy mouth, faithful mouth! Holy mouth, faithful mouth, the mouth that uttered beautiful gems, precious stones, and pearls—who consented to have you put in the dust? Who allowed your tongue to be filled with dust and ashes? Woe unto the Torah! And woe to its 'reward'!"

As he was weeping, Caesar's daughter looked down from a window and saw the beauty of R. Ishmael, for he was one of the seven most handsome men in the world, his face resembling the face of an angel of the Lord of hosts. She was filled with compassion for him and sent word to her father: "Grant me but one petition." He replied, "My daughter, I will do whatever you say, except concerning R. Ishmael and his colleagues." The daughter: "I beg of you, let him live." The father: "I have already sworn." The daughter: "If so, I beg of you, command that his scalp be removed, so that I may look at it instead of a mirror." Caesar then issued an order to remove R. Ishmael's scalp.

When the executioner reached the place on the forehead where the tefillin are worn, R. Ishmael uttered a great and bitter cry, so that heaven and earth were shaken. When he cried out a second time, even the throne of glory quivered.

Then the ministering angels spoke bluntly to the Holy One, "A man so righteous that you showed him all the treasures of the worlds above and the mysteries of the worlds below—should he be put to death in such a horrible way? Such Torah, and such a reward?"[3]

The Holy One: "But what can I do for my son? It is a decree, and no one may nullify it." Then a divine voice came forth and said, "If I hear one more such cry, I will turn the world to void and desolation." When R. Ishmael heard this, he fell silent.

Caesar said to him, "Do you still trust your God?" R. Ishmael: "Yea, though He slay me, yet will I trust in Him" (Job 13:15). At that, the soul of R. Ishmael left him.

When word reached R. Akiva that R. Simeon and R. Ishmael were slain, he rose, rent his garments, girded himself with sackcloth, and said to his disciples, "Prepare yourselves for calamity. Had good been destined to come to us in our generation, then surely none but R. Simeon and R. Ishmael would have received it. But now, since it

1. *Av*, "father in wisdom," and *rakh*, "tender in years."

2. The punishment, stated in the next verse, is being put to the sword. See Avot 5:11. JV: "If thou afflict in any wise."

3. Cf. B. Men 29b. Professor Jakob J. Petuchowski of Hebrew Union College in Cincinnati suggested the interpretation and provided the parallel to the translator.

is revealed and known to Him who spoke and the world came into being that great calamity is destined to come to the world, therefore the two were removed from our midst in keeping with the verse 'The righteous perisheth. . . . The righteous is taken away because of the evil to come' " (Isa. 57:1).

After R. Simeon and R. Ishmael were slain, they brought out for execution R. Akiva ben Joseph, who was capable of expounding the meaning of the crowns on letters and thereby disclosing facets of Torah like those shown to Moses at Sinai.[1] As he was being taken out to be slain, a missive came to Caesar that the king of Arabia was threatening to expand into Caesar's territory. Feeling pressed to go forth at once, he ordered R. Akiva back to prison until his return from the war. As soon as he came back from the war, he ordered that R. Akiva be brought out and his flesh be combed with combs of iron. Each time a comb tore into his flesh, he would say, "The Rock, His work is perfect; for all His ways are justice; a God of faithfulness and without iniquity, true and upright is He" (Deut. 32:4). A divine voice came forth and said, "Blessed are you, R. Akiva—you yourself were true and upright, and your soul left you with the words 'true and upright.' "

When the news that R. Akiva had been put to death reached R. Hanina ben Teradion and R. Judah ben Bava, they rose up, rent their garments, girded themselves with sackcloth, and said, "Our brothers, hear us. R. Akiva was put to death only as a sign [of evil to come]."

After R. Akiva was slain, they brought out R. Hanina ben Teradion for execution.

It is said of him—of R. Hanina ben Teradion—that he was pleasing to the Holy One as well as to men. Never did a word condemning his fellow cross his lips. When the Caesar of Rome decreed that Torah was not to be taught, he openly arranged public assemblies and occupied himself in expounding Torah [before him].

When R. Yose ben Kisma took sick, and R. Hanina ben Teradion went to visit him, R. Yose said, "Hanina, my brother, do you not know that this [Roman] nation was given reign by Heaven? For though it has laid waste His house, burned His Temple Hall, slain His pious ones, and caused His favorites to perish, it endures nevertheless. Yet I hear of you that you continue to occupy yourself with Torah, openly arrange public assemblies, and carry a Torah scroll in your bosom." R. Hanina: "Heaven will show mercy." R. Yose: "I speak sense to you, and you reply, 'Heaven will show mercy'! I shall not be surprised if both you and your Torah scroll are burned in fire."

R. Hanina: "Master, what is my chance with regard to the world-to-come?" R. Yose: "Is there any particular act of yours that troubles you?" R. Hanina: "Money that I had for the feast of Purim I took to be money intended for charity."[2] R. Yose: "If so, I wish that your portion were my portion, and your lot my lot."

It is said that within a few days R. Yose ben Kisma died and all the notables of Rome joined in arranging an elaborate funeral for him. Upon their return, they saw R. Hanina ben Teradion sitting and occupying himself with Torah, openly arranging public assemblies, and holding a Torah scroll in his bosom. He was brought and asked, "Why do you occupy yourself with Torah?" He replied, "Even as the Lord my God commanded me" (Deut. 4:5). It was immediately decreed that he be burned, his wife slain by the sword, and his daughter placed in a brothel.

They brought him out, wrapped him in the Torah scroll, placed bundles of vine shoots around him, and set them on fire. Then they brought tufts of wool, soaked them in water, and placed them over his heart, so that he should not expire quickly. His daughter exclaimed, "Oh, Papa, that I should see you in such a state!" He replied, "If I alone were being burned, it would have been hard for me to bear; but now that I am burning together with a Torah scroll—He who will have regard for the humiliation of the Torah will also have regard for my humiliation." His disciples called out, "Rabbi, what do you see?" He answered, "Sheets of parchment being burned, but the letters [on them] soaring on high." The disciples: "Open your mouth, so that the fire will enter into you quickly."[3] R. Hanina: "Let Him who gave me my soul take it away—no one has the right to put an end to his own life." The executioner then said to him, "Master, if I raise the flame and take away the tufts of wool from over your heart, will you bring me into the life of the world-to-come?" "Yes." "Swear to me." R. Hanina swore to him. Hearing that, the executioner raised the flame and removed the tufts of wool from over his heart, and R. Hanina's soul departed quickly. The executioner then jumped up and threw himself into the fire. A divine voice exclaimed, "Both R. Hanina ben Teradion and his executioner have been assigned to life in the world-to-come."

When Rabbi [Judah I, the Patriarch] heard it, he wept and said, "One may acquire eternal life in a single hour, another only after so many years!"

Our masters taught: When R. Hanina ben Teradion and R. Eleazar ben Perata were arrested, R. Eleazar ben Perata said to R. Hanina ben Teradion, "Happy are you, R. Hanina, that you have been arrested on only one charge! Woe is me, for I am arrested on five charges." R. Hanina replied, "Happy are you who have been arrested on five charges but will be saved! Woe is me, who, though arrested on only one charge, will not be saved. For you have occupied yourself with the study of Torah as well as with acts of benevolence, while I occupy myself only with the Torah."

When they brought up R. Eleazar ben Perata for his trial, he was asked, "Why have you been studying the Torah and why have you been stealing?" He answered, "If a man is a thief, he is not a scholar; if he is a scholar, he is not a thief.[4] And as I am not the one, neither am I the other." "Why then are you called 'master'?"[5] "I am a

[1] See above in this chapter, §140.

[2] R. Hanina was collector of alms and mistakenly distributed to the poor money meant to provide meals for them on the Festival of Purim, thus violating the rule that such monies must be spent only for the particular purpose for which they were collected, and not diverted to other purposes, even if equally charitable.

[3] And put an end to your agony.

[4] Literally, "If [one's tool is a] sword, [he will] not [wield] a book; if [one's tool is] a book, [he will] not [wield a] sword.

[5] The third charge.

master of weavers." Then they brought him two coils of yarn and asked, "Which is for the warp and which for the weft?" A miracle was wrought for him, and a male bee came and sat on the weft, and a female bee came and sat on the warp. "This coil," said R. Eleazar, "is for the warp and that one for the weft." Then they asked him, "Why did you not attend Be Avidan?"[1] to which he replied, "I am old and fear lest I be trampled under your feet." "How many old people have been trampled till now?" he was asked. A miracle was again wrought and on that very day an old man was trampled. "And why did you let your slave go free?"[2] He replied, "No such thing ever happened." One of the Romans was about to give evidence against R. Eleazar, but just then Elijah, disguised as one of the dignitaries of the government, appeared and said to that man, "Let him be. As miracles were wrought for him in all the other matters, so will a miracle be wrought in this one, and you will be regarded merely as an evildoer." But the man ignored Elijah and was about to stand up to bear witness when a written communication from the dignitaries of Rome had to be sent to Caesar, and they sent it by that man. [On the road] Elijah came and hurled him a distance of four hundred parasangs. So that man went off [in haste][3] and did not return. Thus R. Eleazar ben Perata was saved.

After R. Joshua ben Teradion was slain, R. Judah ben Bava was put to death.

It is said of R. Judah ben Bava that, from the age of eighteen to the age of eighty, he savored no more sleep than a horse.

The wicked Roman government[4] issued a decree that he who ordained an elder should be put to death, he who was ordained should also be put to death, the town in which such ordination took place should be laid waste, and the area surrounding the town[5] in which the ordination took place should be uprooted. What did R. Judah ben Bava do? He went and sat down between two mountains, between two large towns, and between two Sabbath areas[6]—namely, between Usha and Shefaram[7]—and there he ordained five elders: R. Meir, R. Judah [bar Ilai], R. Simeon, R. Yose, and R. Eleazar ben Shammua. Seeing that the foes had become aware of their presence, he said to the newly ordained elders, "Flee, my children!" But they replied, "And you, O master, what about you?" "I," he said, "will lie still before them, as a stone that is not turned."

It is said that the Romans did not move from there until they drove three hundred iron spears into his body, making his corpse look like a sieve!

After R. Judah ben Bava was slain, they brought out R. Judah ben Dama for execution. The day was the eve of Shavuot.

R. Judah said to Caesar, "By your life, wait for me a while, that I may fulfill the command of Shavuot by saying the Kiddush praising the Holy One for giving us the Torah." Caesar: "Do you still put your trust in the Torah and the God who gave it?" R. Judah: "Yes." Caesar: "What reward is there for your Torah?" R. Judah: "David, peace be upon him, said of it, 'Oh, how abundant is Thy goodness, which Thou hast laid up for them that fear Thee' " (Ps. 31:20). Caesar: "No fools in the world are like you, who suppose that there is another world." R. Judah: "No fools in the world are like you, who deny the living God. Woe to you, and woe to the shameful thing you call god; you will see us in the light of life, while you go down to the nethermost Sheol."

At once Caesar's wrath was kindled, and he ordered that R. Judah be tied by the hair of his head to the tail of a horse and dragged through every street in Rome. He commanded that the corpse be dismembered afterward.

The prophet Elijah, ever remembered for good, came up and gathered the members of R. Judah's body, and buried them in a cave near the river that flows down through Rome. For thirty days the Romans heard the sound of lamentation and weeping in that cave. When they came and told Caesar about it, he said, "Even if the whole world turn to void and desolation, I will not rest until I have my will with these elders."

After R. Judah ben Dama was slain, they brought out R. Hutzpit the Interpreter for execution.

It is said of R. Hutzpit the Interpreter that he was one hundred and thirty years old when he was taken out to be slain—he was handsome in countenance, beautiful in appearance, resembling an angel of the Lord of hosts.

They came and told Caesar of his beauty and of his venerable years, saying, "Sire, by your life, have mercy on this old man." Caesar asked R. Hutzpit, "How old are you?" R. Hutzpit: "One hundred thirty less one day, and I beg of you that you wait until this my last day reaches its end." Caesar: "What does it matter whether you die today or tomorrow?" R. Hutzpit: "So that I may fulfill two more precepts." Caesar: "What precepts do you wish to perform?" R. Hutzpit: "Reciting the Shema of the evening and of the morning, whereby I assert over me the kingship of the unique, great, and awesome Name." Caesar: "O impudent ones! O arrogant ones! How long will you persist in trusting your God? He is now old and has no strength to save you from my hand. If He still had such strength, He would have taken vengeance for Himself, vengeance for His people, and vengeance for His house, as he did to Pharaoh, to Sisera, and to all the kings of Canaan."

When R. Hutzpit heard this, he broke down in unrestrained weeping and rent his garments at the blasphemy against the Lord and the reviling of Him. Then he said to Caesar, "Woe unto you, Caesar! What will you do on the last day, when the Lord will visit punishment on Rome and on your gods?"

Caesar: "How long am I to argue with this one?" He commanded that R. Hutzpit be put to death. They stoned him and then hanged him.

1. The fourth charge brought against him; see above in this chapter, §123.
2. In accordance with the biblical injunction to free all Jewish slaves after six years, or at the advent of the jubilee year. Manumitting slaves, the fifth offense with which he was charged, had been forbidden by the Roman government.
3. Without giving the intended evidence.
4. During the Hadrianic persecutions in 135 C.E..
5. Literally, *tehum* ("a Sabbath limit"), an area of 2,000 cubits (about 1,000 yards) around an inhabited place, within which it is permitted to walk on the Sabbath.
6. In an area adjacent (in the meaning of the decree) to neither of the two towns.
7. Towns in Galilee, near Tiberias.

After R. Hutzpit was slain, they brought out R. Hanina ben Hakinai for execution.

Of R. Hanina ben Hakinai it is said that throughout his days, from the age of twelve to ninety-five, he kept observing fasts. The day they took him out to be slain was the eve of Sabbath. His disciples asked, "Master, do you wish to eat something before you are put to death?" He replied, "I fasted until now. I know not what road I am about to take, and you tell me to eat and drink!"

He began the Kiddush for the day with "And were finished" and reached "He made holy," but they did not let him conclude it before they slew him. A divine voice came forth and said, "Blessed are you, R. Hanina ben Hakinai—you were holy, and your soul left you at the word 'holy.' "

After R. Hanina ben Hakinai was slain, they brought out R. Yeshevav the Scribe for execution.

As he was being brought out, his disciples came to him and said, "Our master, what is to become of Torah?" R. Yeshevav: "My children, Torah is destined to be forgotten in Israel. For this wicked [Roman] nation in its insolence is brazenly plotting to have us lose our precious pearls [the sages]. Oh, if only I could be the expiation for the people of this generation! But I foresee that not a street in Rome will be without one slain by the sword, for this wicked nation will persist in shedding innocent blood in Israel." The disciples: "Our master, what will become of us?" R. Yeshevav: "Strengthen one another. Love peace and justice. There may be hope."

Caesar asked R. Yeshevav, "Old man, how old are you?" R. Yeshevav: "Ninety years old this day. But even before I left my mother's womb, a decree came forth from the Holy One to turn me and my colleagues over to your power. But the Holy One will demand our blood from you." Caesar: "Hasten and put to death this one also, and let me see the power and strength of his God." Caesar gave the command, and they burned him.

And after R. Yeshevav was slain, they brought out R. Eleazar ben Shammua for execution.

Of R. Eleazar ben Shammua it is said that he was one hundred and five years old, and that, from his childhood to the end of his days, no man heard a frivolous word issue from his mouth; he did not allow himself to become annoyed with his colleagues, either by what they said or by what they did; he was humble and meek, and for eighty years observed more fasts than the number prescribed. The day he was put to death was Yom Kippur. His disciples came to him and asked, "Our master, what do you see?" R. Eleazar: "I see R. Judah ben Bava's bier being carried side by side with the bier of R. Akiva ben Joseph, and they are arguing with each other over a question in *Halakhah*." The disciples: "And who endeavors to bring harmony between them?" R. Eleazar: "R. Ishmael the High Priest." They: "Who prevails?" R. Eleazar: "R. Akiva, because he labored with all his might in Torah." R. Eleazar went on, "My children, I see more—the soul of each and every righteous man purifies itself in the waters of Siloam to enter in purity this day into the academy on high and listen to R. Akiva's exposition of the passage for the day. And each and every angel brings a golden chair for each and every righteous man to sit upon in purity."

Caesar commanded that he be put to death. A divine voice came forth and said, "Blessed are you, R. Eleazar ben Shammua. You were pure, and your soul left you with the word 'purity.' "

R. Yohanan said: Woe unto the nations of the world, for there is no mending for them. Scripture says, "For brass [of the nations] I will bring gold, and for iron I will bring silver, and for wood, brass," etc. (Isa. 60:17). But for R. Akiva and his colleagues, what more precious commodity could be brought? Concerning those nations, Scripture asserts, "Though I cleanse them [of other transgressions], from the blood they shed I shall not cleanse them" (Joel 4:21).[1]

R. Meir, Elisha ben Avuyah (Aher), Beruriah (fl. ca. 130–60 C.E.)

181. R. Akiva said: Once, while sailing on shipboard, I saw another ship about to capsize in the sea and was distressed about a certain disciple of the wise who was on it. (Who was he? R. Meir.) But when I went up to the province of Cappadocia, he came to me, sat down, and held forth before me on *Halakhah*. When I asked him, "My son, who rescued you from the sea?" he replied, "One wave tossed me over to the wave that followed, and that one to the next wave, until I was cast up on dry land."[2]

182. R. Meir was an accomplished—indeed, superb—scribe. By working hard, he earned three *sela* a week. One *sela* he spent on food and drink, another on clothing, and with the third he used to provide sustenance to disciples of the wise. His disciples said to him: Our master, what is to become of your children? He replied: If they are righteous, they will fare as David has declared: "I have not seen the righteous forsaken, nor his seed begging bread" (Ps. 37:25). But if not, why should I leave what is mine to enemies of Him who is everywhere?[3]

183. R. Meir said: When I came to study Torah with R. Ishmael, he asked me, "My son, what trade do you ply?" I replied, "I am a scribe." He said, "Be careful in your work, for your work is the work of Heaven. Should you omit a single letter[4] or add an extra letter,[5] you may find yourself destroying the entire world, all of it."[6]

184. It is told of R. Meir that he went to Asya to intercalate the [thirteenth] month in the year.[7] Since there was no Scroll [of Esther] there, he wrote it out from memory[8] and read it aloud.[9]

---

1. Midrash Eleh Ezkerah, BhM 2:64–72; B. Sanh 14a; B. AZ 8b and 17b–18a; Mek, *Mishpatim, Nezikin*, 18 (La 3:141–42); ARN 38; Sem 8; B. RH 23a and En Yaakov, ad loc.
2. B. Yev 121a.
3. Eccles R. 2:18, §1.
4. Should one leave out the *alef* in "[the Lord God is] *emet* ['truth']" the result would be "is *met*" ("dead").
5. Should one mistakenly add a *vav* to [*va-yedabber*] *Adonai*—"the Lord [spoke]"—the result would be "the lords [spoke]."
6. B. Er 13a; B. Sot 20a.
7. By adding a second Adar.
8. He did not copy it from another scroll.
9. B. Meg 18b.

185. In [the margin of] R. Meir's Torah scroll, instead of "And behold, it was very (*meod*) good" (Gen. 1:31), they found the deliberate change to "And behold, death (*mot*) was very good." They found there: "The Lord God made for Adam and his wife garments of light (*or*)"[1] (Gen. 3:21), as well as "And the son[2] of Dan: Hushim" (Gen. 46:23).[3]

186. In the margin of R. Meir's codex they found, instead of "The burden of Dumah" (Isa. 21:11), "The burden of Rome."[4]

187. R. Meir was both sage and scribe.[5]

188. When one observed R. Meir in the house of study, he appeared to be uprooting mountains and grinding them one against the other.[6]

189. R. Aha bar Hanina said: It is known and revealed to Him who spoke and the world came into being that in R. Meir's generation there was none like him. Why, then, was the law not fixed in keeping with his opinion? Because his colleagues were unable to follow his reasoning to its ultimate end. For he would declare that which was unclean clean and provide credible evidence; and he would contrariwise declare that which was clean unclean and provide equally credible evidence.

It is taught: His real name was not R. Meir but R. Nehorai. Then why was he called R. Meir? Because he illumined (*meir*) the eyes of sages in *Halakhah*.[7]

190. R. Yose ben R. Halafta used to praise R. Meir to the people of Sepphoris as a great man, a holy man, and an unassuming man.

One time, on a Sabbath, R. Meir noticed some mourners and greeted them.[8] Witnessing that, R. Yose's disciples asked him: Our master, is R. Meir the one whose praise you speak? He replied: What did R. Meir do [that makes you ask about him]? They told him: He noticed some mourners on the Sabbath and greeted them. R. Yose: Would you like to know the extent of his mastery [of Torah]?[9] He meant to teach us that there may be no mourning on the Sabbath. For "The blessing of the Lord, it maketh rich" (Prov. 10:22)[10] refers to the special blessing on the Sabbath, and the following "He is to add no sorrow with it" (ibid.) refers to mourning [which is to be set aside for the duration of it].[11]

1. Instead of *or* ("skin").
2. Instead of "sons."
3. Gen. R. 9:5, 20:12, and 94:9.
4. The *dalet* in "Dumah" is easily mistaken for the *resh* in "Rome." P. Ta 1:1, 64a.
5. B Git 67a.
6. So great was his acumen. B. Sanh 24a.
7. B. Er 13b.
8. Exchange of greetings with mourners is prohibited.
9. No one before R. Meir had the acumen to apply Prov. 10:22 to mourners' conduct on the Sabbath.
10. Cf. also Ps. 37:4: "So shalt thou delight thyself in the Lord; and He shall give thee the petitions of thy heart," which could also be understood to mean: "[On the Sabbath] when you take delight in the Lord, He allows exchange of greetings [even when in mourning]."
11. P. MK 3:5, 82d.

191. R. Meir was seated in the house of study in Tiberias on the Sabbath, expounding, while his teacher Elisha was passing through the marketplace astride his horse. People came by and told R. Meir: Look, your teacher Elisha is here riding through the marketplace. R. Meir interrupted his expounding and went out to him. Elisha asked: What verse have you been expounding today? R. Meir: "So the Lord blessed the latter end of Job more than his beginning" (Job 42:12). Elisha: What did you say about it? R. Meir: "The Lord gave Job twice as much as he had before" (Job. 42:10)—He doubled his possessions. Elisha: Alas for those who are gone and are no more—your teacher Akiva would not have spoken thus. He would have construed these words "The Lord blessed the latter end of Job because of the beginning"—because of the observance of precepts and good deeds that had been Job's at the beginning.

Elisha: What other verse did you expound? R. Meir: "Better is the end of a thing than the beginning thereof" (Eccles. 7:8). Elisha: What did you say about it? R. Meir: You have a man who acquired merchandise in his youth and sustained a loss, but in his old age makes a profit from it. Or, you have a man who learned Torah in his youth and forgot it, but it comes back to him in his old age. Elisha: Alas for those who are gone and are no more—your teacher Akiva would not have spoken thus. He would have construed it "Good is the end of a thing from the beginning"—when it is good from its beginning. So it happened with me. Avuyah, my father, was one of the notables of Jerusalem. When he was arranging for my circumcision, he invited all the notables of Jerusalem, among them, R. Eliezer and R. Joshua. After they had eaten and drunk, they began to clap their hands and dance. Some of the notables sang songs, and others composed alphabetical acrostics. R. Eliezer said to R. Joshua, "These are occupied with what interests them; shall we not occupy ourselves with what interests us?" They began with subjects connected with the Five Books of Moses, then with the Prophets, and after that with the Writings. Fire came down from heaven and surrounded them, at which Avuyah said to them, "My masters, have you come to set my house afire over me?" They replied, "God forbid! We were merely sitting and stringing words of Torah, then from the Torah we went on to the Prophets, and from the Prophets to the Writings. The words were as joyful as when they were given at Sinai. For, when originally given at Sinai, they were given in the midst of fire, as is said, 'The mountain burned with fire unto the heart of heaven' " (Deut. 4:11). Elated, my father Avuyah remarked, "My masters, since the power of Torah is so great, if this child stays alive for me, I will dedicate him to the Torah." But because the intent of my father's resolve was not for the sake of Heaven, my study of the Torah did not endure with me.

Elisha: What other verse did you expound? R. Meir: "God hath made the one corresponding to the other" (Eccles. 7:14). Elisha: What did you say about it? R. Meir: Whatever the Holy One created in His world, He created its analogue: He created mountains, then created hills; He created seas, then created rivers. Elisha: Your teacher Akiva would not have spoken thus. He would have said: God created the righteous, then created the wicked. He created the Garden of Eden, then created Gehenna. Thus each man has two portions assigned to him—a portion in the Garden of Eden and a portion in Gehenna. When a man is declared righteous, he takes his own portion and the portion of another who [by his action] forfeited his in the Garden of Eden. When a man is declared wicked, he takes his own portion and the unclaimed portion of a righteous man in Gehenna.

Elisha: What other verse did you expound? R. Meir: "Gold and glass cannot equal it; neither shall the exchange thereof be vessels of fine gold" (Job 28:17). Elisha: What did you say about it? R. Meir: These are the words of Torah—they are as difficult to acquire as vessels of gold or of fine gold and are as readily destroyed as vessels of glass. Elisha: By God, even as readily as earthenware vessels. But your teacher Akiva would not have spoken thus. He would have said: As vessels of gold and even vessels of glass can be repaired if broken, so can a disciple of the wise recover his learning if it has disintegrated.

R. Meir: So you, too, must come back. Elisha: I cannot. R. Meir: Why not? Elisha: I was riding a horse behind the house of study on a Day of Atonement that fell on the Sabbath, and I heard a divine voice reverberating: "Return, O backsliding children" (Jer. 3:14), "return unto Me, and I will return unto you" (Mal. 3:7), except for Aher, who knew My strength and yet rebelled against Me.

When R. Meir and Elisha reached the Sabbath limit,[1] Aher (Elisha) said to him: Meir, turn back, for I have just measured by the paces of my horse that the Sabbath limit extends only thus far. He replied: You, too, go back! Aher answered: Have I not just told you that I have already heard from behind the curtain [in heaven], "Return ye backsliding children—except Aher"? Nevertheless, R. Meir prevailed upon him and took him into a schoolhouse, where Aher said to a child: Recite for me your verse. The child answered, "There is no peace, saith the Lord, unto the wicked" (Isa. 48:22). R. Meir then took him to another schoolhouse, where Aher said to a child: Recite for me your verse. The child answered, "For though thou wash thee with niter, and take thee much soap, yet thine iniquity is marked before Me, saith the Lord God" (Jer. 2:22). R. Meir took him to yet another schoolhouse, where again Aher said to a child: Recite for me your verse. The child answered, "And thou that art spoiled, what doest thou, that thou clothest thyself with scarlet, that thou deckest thee with ornaments of gold, that thou enlargest thine eyes with paint? In vain dost thou make thyself fair. . . . They seek thy life," etc. (Jer. 4:30). And thus R. Meir took Aher to thirteen schools, one after the other, where in like vein all the children quoted verses boding evil. When Aher said to the last child: Recite for me your verse, he answered, "But unto the wicked God saith: 'What hast thou to do to declare My statutes?' " etc. (Ps. 50:16). That child had a speech defect, so it sounded as though he answered, "But to Elisha[2] God saith."

[1] Two thousand cubits in all directions from the place where a man makes his abode for the Sabbath.

[2] The child pronounced *ve-la-rasha* ("and unto the wicked") like *ve-le-Elisha* ("and unto Elisha"). The child could not distinguish between *resh* and *lamed*, so that his *r* sounded like an *l*.

At that, Elisha said: Had I a knife in my hand, I would have cut him to pieces.

It is said of him, of Aher, that when he entered a meeting place for scholars and saw youngsters with scrolls in front of them, he would say: Why do these sit here and occupy themselves thus? This one's craft should be that of a builder. This one's, that of a carpenter. That one's, that of a painter. And that other one's, that of a tailor. When the youngsters heard such talk, they left their scrolls and went away.

It is also said of him, of Aher, that Greek song did not cease from his mouth and that whenever he rose to leave the house of study, many heretical books would fall out of his lap.

What did Aher see that made him go wrong? It is said that once, while sitting and studying in the valley of Gennesar, he saw a man climb to the top of a palm tree on the Sabbath, take the mother bird with the young, and descend in safety. At the end of the Sabbath, he saw another man climb to the top of the same palm tree and take the young, but let the mother go free; as he descended, a snake bit him and he died. Elisha exclaimed: It is written, "Let the mother go and take only the young, that you may fare well and have a long life" (Deut. 22:7). Where is the well-being of this man, and where is the prolonging of his life? (He was unaware how R. Akiva had explained it, namely, "that you may fare well," in the world [-to-come], which is wholly good; "and have a long life" in the world whose length is without end.)

Some say that [Elisha became a heretic] when he saw a pig dragging along in its mouth R. Hutzpit the Interpreter's tongue. He said then: The tongue from which pearls of purest ray used to come forth is to lick the dust? Immediately, he resolved to commit sin. He went out and, espying a harlot, beckoned to her. She asked: Are you not Elisha ben Avuyah? It was the Sabbath, and he pulled a radish out of a furrow and gave it to her. So she said: He is clearly *aher*, "another."

(There are some who say: [Elisha became a heretic because] when his mother was pregnant with him, she passed by temples for idolatry and smelled the aroma [of their offerings, whose meat she craved]. They gave her some, and she ate it. The meat permeated her innards like the venom of a snake [and affected Elisha].)

Some time later Elisha ben Avuyah fell ill, and R. Meir was told, "Your master is ill." He went to visit him and said: Repent! Elisha asked: Having gone so far, will I be accepted? R. Meir replied: Is it not written, "Thou allowest man to turn, up to his being crushed" (Ps. 90:3), up to the time that life is being crushed out of him? In that instant Elisha ben Avuyah began to weep, and then he died. R. Meir rejoiced, saying: My master, it would appear, departed in a state of repentance. However, after he was buried, fire came forth from heaven to burn his grave. They went and told R. Meir: The grave of your master is on fire! R. Meir went out, spread his cloak over the grave, and said to him, "Tarry this night" (Ruth 3:13)—in this world which is wholly night—"and it shall be in the morning" (ibid.)—the world-to-come, all of which is morning—"if He who is good will redeem thee" (ibid.)—that is, the Holy One, who is good, of whom it is said, "The Lord is good to all" (Ps. 145:9). But if He is not willing to redeem thee, then, as the Lord liveth, I [Meir] will redeem thee. "Lie down until morning" (Ruth 3:13). The fire was then extinguished.

R. Meir's disciples asked him: In the world-to-come, should you be asked, "Whom do you wish to be placed next to—your father or your teacher?" what will you say? He replied: My dear father, and then my teacher. They asked: And will they listen to you? He answered them: Have we not learned in a Mishnah that [in the event of fire on the Sabbath], the case in which a scroll is kept should be saved, together with the scroll?"[1] So, too, because of the merit of his Torah, Elisha should be saved [from the fire of Gehenna].

According to some, when Aher died, it was said: Let him not be judged, nor let him enter the world-to-come. Let him not be judged, because he engaged in the study of the Torah; nor let him enter the world-to-come, because he sinned. R. Meir said: It is better that he should be judged and afterward enter the world-to-come. When I die I shall cause smoke to rise from his grave.[2] When R. Meir died, smoke rose up from Aher's grave.

R. Yohanan said: What a mighty deed [of R. Meir's] to burn his master with fire! Only one such sinner was in our midst, and we could not save him! If Elisha had been in my care, who would have dared snatch him from me? So he said: When I die, I shall extinguish the smoke from Elisha's grave.[3] When R. Yohanan died, the smoke ceased from Aher's grave. Then the public mourner began [his oration] concerning R. Yohanan thus: Even Gehenna's gatekeeper could not stand up to you, O master![4]

192. Aher's daughter once came before Rabbi [Judah I, the Patriarch] and said to him, "O master, provide for me!" He asked her, "Whose daughter are you?" She replied, "I am Aher's daughter." Said he, "Are any of his [male] children still left in the world? Is it not written, 'He shall have neither son nor son's son among his people, nor any remaining in his dwellings!' (Job 18:19)?" She answered, "My master, remember his Torah; do not remember his deeds." A fire came down and lapped R. Judah's bench. Then R. Judah burst into tears and cried, "If such is done in behalf of those who have dishonored Torah, how much more is certain to be done in behalf of those who have honored her!"[5]

193. Rabbah bar R. Shila once met the prophet Elijah and asked him, "What is the Holy One doing?" Elijah answered, "He is reciting traditions concerning law in the name of all the sages, but He is not reciting them in the name of R. Meir." Rabbah: "Why not?" "Because he learned Torah from the mouth of Aher." Rabbah: "What does that matter? R. Meir found a pomegranate, ate the pulp within it, and threw away the rind!" Elijah: "Henceforth God will begin to say, 'My son Meir says.' "[6]

194. R. Yohanan said: When R. Meir used to deliver one of his public lectures, during one third of it he would expound *Halakhah;* during another third, *Aggadah;* and during the final third, parables.

R. Yohanan added: R. Meir had three hundred parables of foxes, of which we have only one left:

"The fathers have eaten sour grapes, and the children's teeth are set on edge" (Ezek. 18:2). It happened that the fox said to the wolf, "Go into a Jewish courtyard on a Sabbath eve, and help them prepare whatever is needed for the meal, and you will eat with them on the Sabbath." But when the wolf was about to enter, the courtyard's residents banded together against him with clubs.

Then the wolf was set on killing the fox, but the fox said, "They beat you only because of your father, who on one occasion helped them prepare a meal and then devoured every luscious morsel." The wolf: "Should I be beaten up because of my father?" The fox: "Yes—'fathers eat sour grapes, and their children's teeth are blunted.' But come with me, and I will show you a place where you can eat your fill." The fox led the wolf to a well. Across the well's mouth was a beam, with a rope wound over it. At each end of the rope was tied an empty bucket. The fox climbed into the upper bucket, and his weight caused it to plunge downward, while the lower bucket flew upward. The wolf called to him, "Why did you go down there?" The fox: "Because here there is meat and cheese enough to eat one's fill," and he pointed to the reflection of the moon in the water. It looked like a round cheese. The wolf: "How am I to go down?" The fox: "Climb into the upper bucket." The wolf did so, and his weight caused it to plunge down, while the bucket with the fox flew up. The wolf: "How am I to get up again?" The fox: " 'The righteous is delivered out of his trouble, and the wicked cometh in his stead' [Prov. 11:8]. Is it not written, 'Just balances, just weights' (Lev. 19:36)?"[7]

195. Some say the parable was told like this: It once happened that a fox, about to be devoured by a lion, pleaded, "What [meat] is there on me to fill you? Come along, and I will show you a fat man whom you can raven and be filled with." At that spot there was a covered pit, beyond which a man sat praying. When the lion saw him, he said to the fox, "I fear this man's prayer. [I hope] you are not entrapping me." The fox: "You need not fear, nor need your posterity fear. It is the posterity of your posterity upon whom punishment will fall. Now satisfy your hunger. There is lots of time before your posterity's posterity. The lion was persuaded and leaped over the pit, but [miscalculated and] fell into it. The fox came over, stood at the edge of the pit, and stared gleefully at the lion. The lion: "Did you not say, 'No punishment will befall you [nor your posterity], but the posterity of your posterity will be seized for it'?" The fox: "But there is a charge of iniquity against

1. Shab 16:1.
2. As a sign that Elisha was judged and punished for his sins.
3. As a sign that he was forgiven.
4. B. Hag 15a; P. Hag 2:1, 77a–b; Eccles. R. 7:8, §1; Ruth R. 6:4; B. Kid 39b.
5. B. Hag 15b and En Yaakov, ad loc.
6. Ibid.
7. B. Sanh 38b–39a and En Yaakov, ad loc; Rashi, ad loc.

the sire of your sire. On account of that charge, you are now seized." The lion: "The fathers eat sour grapes, but it is the children's teeth that are blunted!" The fox: "Why did you not think of this before?"[1]

196. R. Meir had a favorite saying: Resolve with all your heart and all your soul to know My ways, and try hard to master those parts of Torah [that are within your capacity].[2] Keep My Torah in your heart, and the awe of Me will be before your eyes. Keep your mouth from all sin, and purify and sanctify yourself by avoiding all trespass and iniquity. Then will I be with you everywhere.[3]

197. Once the Roman government sent word to our masters: Send us one of your torches. Our masters reasoned: Rome has so many torches, so many precious stones and pearls of purest ray, and yet they want a torch from us. Apparently they want nothing other than one who will illuminate (*meir*) facets of meaning in *Halakhah.* So they sent R. Meir. The Romans asked him questions, and he answered them. They asked him more questions, and he answered them as well.[4]

198. R. Zechariah the son-in-law of R. Levi would tell this story: R. Meir used to give regular discourses in the synagogue of Hamath every Sabbath eve. A certain woman of that town made it a habit to listen to his weekly discourses. On one occasion when he extended it to a late hour, she waited [and did not leave] until he finished. But when she came to her home, she found that the lamp was out. Her husband asked her, "Where have you been until now?" She told him, "I have been listening to a lecturer's discourse." Now, the husband was a scoffer. So he said to her, "I swear by such-and-such that you are not to enter my house again until you spit in the lecturer's face." She left the house and stayed away one week, a second, and a third. Finally the neighbors asked her, "Are you still angry with each other? Let us go with you to the lecturer." When R. Meir saw them, he perceived the reason [for their coming] by means of the holy spirit. And so, pretending to be suffering from pain in the eyes, he asked, "Is there among you a woman skilled in whispering a charm for eye pain?" Her neighbors said to her, "Go, whisper in his ear and spit lightly in his eyes, and you will be able to live with your husband again." So she came forward. However, when she sat down before R. Meir, she was so overawed by his presence that she confessed, "My master, I do not know how to whisper a charm for eye pain." But he said to her, "Nevertheless, spit in my face seven times, and I will be healed." She did so, whereupon he said, "Go and tell your husband, 'You bade me do it only once. I spat seven times!' "[5]

His disciples said to him, "Master! Is the Torah to be treated with such contempt? If you had only mentioned it to us, would we not have brought that man and flogged him at the post until he consented to be reconciled with his wife?" R. Meir replied, "The dignity of Meir ought not to be greater than that of his Maker. If Scripture enjoins that God's holy Name, which is inscribed in sanctity, may be obliterated in water in order to bring about peace between a man and his wife, all the more so may Meir's dignity be disregarded.[6]

199. There were two men who were incited by Satan, so that every Sabbath eve, as the sun was about to set, they fell to quarreling. R. Meir happened to visit them and for three Sabbaths stopped them from their quarreling, until peace was made between them. Then R. Meir heard Satan cry out, "Woe! R. Meir has put me out of my home."[7]

200. There was a certain guardian in the quarter where R. Meir lived, who was selling the land of the orphans in his charge and buying slaves with the proceeds. R. Meir forbade the guardian to do so.[8] A voice [Satan's] said to him in a dream, "I mean to destroy, and will you presume to build?" Nevertheless, R. Meir gave no heed, saying, "Dreams are of no significance one way or the other.[9]

201. There was once a certain innkeeper in the south who used to arise in the night, put on his clothes, and say to his guests, "Wake up and go forth [to your destination]—I will provide you with an escort." When they went out, robbers lying in wait for them would rob them, then come to the inn and share the spoils with the innkeeper. On one occasion, R. Meir happened to lodge there overnight. The innkeeper arose, put on his clothes, and said to R. Meir, "Wake up and go forth—I will provide you with an escort." R. Meir replied, "I have a brother; I must remain here and wait for him." The innkeeper: "Where is he?" "In the synagogue." "Tell me his name, and I will go and call him." R. Meir: "*Ki tov.*"

The innkeeper went off and all that night kept calling at the gate of the synagogue, "*Ki tov, Ki tov,*" but no one answered to the name. In the morning, R. Meir arose and untied his ass. As he was about to take off, the innkeeper said, "Where is the brother of whom you spoke?" R. Meir: "Behold, he has just come—'And God saw the [morning] light (*ki tov*)—that it was good' " (Gen. 1:4).[10]

202. [On the eve of a Sabbath] R. Meir, R. Judah, and R. Yose were journeying on a road. (R. Meir used to pay attention to people's names, whereas R. Judah and R. Yose did not.) When they got to a certain inn, they asked the innkeeper, "What is your name?" He replied, "*Ki dor.*" R. Meir said to his companions, "Very likely a wicked man, for it is written, 'They are a treacherous breed (*ki dor*)' " (Deut. 32:20). Nevertheless, R. Judah and R. Yose

---

1. *Teshuvot ha-Geonim,* ed. Abraham Elijah Harkavy (Berlin, 1887; Repr. 1965), §362.
2. So *Etz Yosef* on En Yaakov, ad loc. Literally, "doors of my Torah."
3. B. Ber 17a.
4. Eccles. R. 19, §1.
5. God's name in the passage written on a scroll is washed out by the "water of bitterness," which a woman suspected of infidelity is made to drink. Num. 5:23–24.
6. P. Sot 1:4, 16d; Num. R. 9:20; Deut. R. 5:15; Lev. R. 9:9.
7. B. Git 52a.
8. Because slaves are perishable property, whereas land is not.
9. B. Git 52a.
10. Gen. R. 92:6.

deposited their purses with the innkeeper [over the Sabbath], while R. Meir did not. Instead, R. Meir went off and placed his purse in a jug, which he buried at the head of the grave of the innkeeper's father. That night the innkeeper's father came to his son in a dream, saying, "Come and take the purse lying at my head." In the morning the innkeeper told the sages, "Such-and-such was shown me in a dream." They said to him, "There is no substance in dreams on Sabbath eves."[1] Nevertheless, R. Meir went [to the grave], guarded the purse all day, and brought it back in the evening. The next morning, when R. Judah and R. Yose said to the innkeeper, "Give us our purses," he replied. "[What purses?] There never were any!" R. Meir then said to them, "Why didn't you pay attention to people's names?" They replied, "Why did you not tell us right out [that this innkeeper was a thief]?" R. Meir: "[Because of his name] I merely suggested that one should be suspicious, but could I have said anything definite? [In order to find a way to recover their purses], R. Judah and R. Yose took the innkeeper into a shop. As they plied him with wine, they noticed lentils on his mustache.[2] They quickly went to his wife and, as a countersign, told her that she and her husband had eaten lentils the evening before. Thus they obtained their purses from her. From then on, they too paid close attention to names.[3]

203. R. Meir used to ridicule [sexual] transgressors.[4] One day Satan appeared to him in the guise of a woman standing on the opposite bank of a river [beckoning him toward her]. As there was no bridge across the river, R. Meir grabbed a rope [which stretched from bank to bank] and proceeded to cross. When he reached halfway along the rope, Satan [resuming his usual form] let him go,[5] saying: Had they not proclaimed in heaven, "Beware of R. Meir and his Torah," I would have valued your life at no more than two *meah*.[6]

204. One may not beat together wine and oil for an invalid on the Sabbath. However, R. Simeon ben Eleazar said in R. Meir's name: Without hesitation, one may beat together wine and oil.

R. Simeon ben Eleazar later related: Once [on a Sabbath] R. Meir was suffering pain in his stomach, and we wished to beat some wine and oil for him, but he would not permit us. We pleaded with him, "Are your words to be disregarded during your own lifetime?" He replied, "Though, to be sure, I rule that it is permitted, yet my colleagues rule that it is not. In all my days I never presumed to go counter to the opinion of my colleagues."[7]

205. It happened that while R. Meir was expounding in the house of study on a Sabbath afternoon, his two sons died. What did their mother do? She put them both on a couch and spread a sheet over them.

At the end of the Sabbath, R. Meir returned home from the house of study and asked, "Where are my two sons?" She replied, "They went to the house of study." R. Meir: "I looked for them there but did not see them."

Then she gave him the cup for *Havdalah*,[8] and he pronounced the blessing. Again he asked, "Where are my two sons?" She replied, "They went to such-and-such a place and will be back soon." Then she brought food for him. After he had eaten, she said, "My teacher, I have a question." R. Meir: "Ask your question." She: "My teacher, a while ago a man came and deposited something in my keeping. Now he has come back to claim what he left. Shall I return it to him or not?" R. Meir: "My daughter, is not one who holds a deposit required to return it to its owner?" She: "Still, without your opinion, I would not have returned it."

Then what did she do? She took R. Meir by his hand, led him up to the chamber, and brought him near the couch. Then she pulled off the sheet that covered them, and he saw that both children lying on the couch were dead. He began to weep and say, "My sons, my sons, my teachers, my teachers. My sons in the way of the world, but my teachers because they illumined my eyes with their understanding of Torah."

Then she came out with: "My teacher, did you not say to me that we are required to restore to the owner what is left with us in trust? 'The Lord gave, the Lord took. May the Name of the Lord be blessed' " (Job 1:21).[9]

206. In R. Meir's neighborhood there lived some ruffians, who annoyed him so much that he prayed for them to die. His wife Beruriah said to him: What are you thinking of? Are you relying on the verse "Let sinners be consumed" (Ps. 104:35)? But, in fact, is the word "sinners"? It is rather "sins."[10] Moreover, look at the end of the verse [and you will see]: "And let the wicked be no more," which implies that when sins come to an end, the wicked will be no more. You should seek mercy for them, that they turn in penitence, so that they will be wicked no more. Accordingly, he besought mercy for them, and they did turn in penitence.[11]

207. A Judeo-Christian said to Beruriah, "It is written, 'Sing, O barren, thou that didst not bear' [Isa. 54:1]. Because she did not bear, is she to sing?" Beruriah: "Fool, look at the end of the verse: 'For more are the children of

---

1. The Sabbath rest gives rise to idle thoughts, which are then reflected in dreams.
2. Leon Nimoy informed the translator that the story is set forth more clearly in a parallel: Before the innkeeper went off to work in the morning, he said to his wife, "Don't surrender the two purses to anyone, unless he tells you as a countersign that we had lentils for supper the evening before." When the two rabbis saw the lentils on the innkeeper's mustache, they deduced that this was the remainder of his last meal, etc. See *Elegant Composition*, pp. 1108–10.
3. B. Yoma 83b; Yalkut, *Haazinu*, §945.
4. He believed that they could easily subdue their sexual desires.
5. And thus freed R. Meir from temptation.
6. B. Kid 81b.
7. B. Shab 134a.
8. The blessing by which the Sabbath or any other holy day is ushered out.
9. Midrash Prov. 31:10 (ed. Buber, pp. 108–9); Yalkut, Prov., §964.
10. The word *hataim* may mean "sins" or "sinners."
11. B. Ber 10a.

the desolate than the children of the married.' " "But what is the meaning of 'O barren, that thou didst not bear'?" "It means: Sing, O congregation of Israel—which is likened to a barren woman—which, unlike you people, did not bear children who are destined for Gehenna."[1]

208. R. Yose the Galilean was once walking on a road when he met Beruriah, whom he asked, "Which road should I take to go to the city of Lydda?" She replied, "Foolish Galilean, did not the sages say, 'Do not multiply talk with women'?[2] You should have said, "Which way to Lydda?' "[3]

209. Beruriah once came upon a student who was studying his lesson by whispering it. She spoke sharply to him: "Does not Scripture say, 'Set up everywhere, and secured (2 Sam. 23:5)?[4] If the Torah is set up [everywhere—that is], in the two hundred and forty-eight parts of your body—it is secure; but if not,[5] it is not secured."[6]

210. Beruriah, the wife of R. Meir, was a daughter of R. Hanina ben Teradion. She said [to her husband], "It is humiliating to me that my sister is [forced] to serve in a brothel." So he took a container holding three *kav* of denars and set out for that place. He thought: If she has not yet been subjected to anything sinful, a miracle will be wrought for her; but if she has already committed a sin, no miracle will be wrought. He disguised himself as a stable attendant, came to her, and said, "Give in to my desire." She replied, "The monthly uncleanness of women is upon me." "I am prepared to wait," he said. She: "But there are many here prettier than I." So he said to himself: It is clear that she has not committed any sin. No doubt she says this to everyone who comes to her. He then went to her keeper and said, "Hand her over to me." He replied, "I am afraid of the government." "Take the three *kav* of denars—use half as a bribe [to be paid out when inquiry is made], and the other half shall be yours." "But what will I do when the denars are spent [and further inquiry is made]?" "Then," R. Meir replied, "say, 'O God of Meir, answer me!' and you will be saved." "Still, who says that it will be so?" R. Meir: "You will have a chance to see right now." There were some man-eating dogs nearby. R. Meir took a pebble and threw it at them, and, as they sprang at him to devour him, he exclaimed, "O God of Meir, answer me!" and they let him be. The keeper then handed over Beruriah's sister to R. Meir.

Presently the matter became known to the Roman emperor, and when the keeper was brought and taken to the scaffold to be hanged, he exclaimed, "O God of Meir, answer me!" They took him down at once and asked him, "What does this mean?" He answered, "This is what happened," [and told them of his encounter with R. Meir]. They then engraved R. Meir's likeness on the gate of Rome and proclaimed that anyone seeing a person resembling it should seize him.

One day [some Romans] saw him and pursued him, so he ran away from them and entered a brothel.[7] (Some say: He saw a dish cooked by Gentiles. So he dipped one finger into it but licked another.) "God forbid," they said. "If it were R. Meir, he would not have done such a thing," [and they stopped their pursuit of him]. At that, he rose up and fled until he reached Babylonia.[8]

211. When Rabbi [Judah I, the Patriarch] married off his son R. Simeon, the people were clapping the backs of their hands on the Sabbath.[9] R. Meir passed by and, upon hearing the sound, he asked, "My masters, has the Sabbath been suspended?" R. Judah heard him and answered, "Who has come to chastise us in our own home?" When R. Meir heard R. Judah's voice, he fled. Runner after runner went after him. Then a wind caused the part of the scarf that covered the back of R. Meir's head to fly up. Looking through a window, R. Judah saw the exposed back of R. Meir's head.

Subsequently, R. Judah used to say: I am keener [in Torah] than my colleagues only because I saw R. Meir from the back. Had I seen his face, I would have been even keener, since it is said, "Thine eyes are to see thy teacher" (Isa. 30:20).[10]

212. R. Simeon ben Eleazar said: During the two times that he was a refugee, I was R. Meir's servant, and R. Meir's staff was in my hand. From it, I acquired understanding.[11]

213. R. Meir's time to die came when he was in Asya. He said, "Tell the people of the Land of Israel: [Burying in the Land] your anointed teacher is ultimately your obligation." But in the meantime, to those with him, he said, "Place my bier by the seashore, for 'He hath founded [the Land] upon the sea, set it upon the nether streams' " (Ps. 24:2).[12]

214. When R. Meir died, makers of parables ceased.[13]

215. Our masters taught: After the death of R. Meir, R. Judah said to his disciples, "Do not allow the disciples of R. Meir to enter here, for, being contentious, they come not to learn Torah but only to put me down with citations of *Halakhah*." Yet Symmachus pushed his way through, entered [and proceeded to put R. Judah down with such citations]. Greatly provoked, R. Judah said to his disciples, "Did I not tell you that R. Meir's disciples were not to enter here because they are contentious?"

---

1. Ibid.
2. Avot 1:5.
3. B. Er 53b.
4. JV: "Ordered in all things, and sure."
5. If the organs of speech are not used.
6. B. Er 53b–54a.
7. So as not to be identified with R. Meir, who naturally would not enter such a place.
8. B. AZ 18b and En Yaakov, ad loc.
9. By changing the manner of clapping, they thought that they were not violating the Sabbath.
10. P. Betz 5:2, 63a; B. Er 13b.
11. P. MK 3:1, 82a.
12. Thus it would be possible for his bier to float to the Land of Israel. P. Kil 9:4, 32c.
13. B. Sot 49a.

Then R. Yose remarked, "People will say: R. Meir is dead, R. Judah is provoked, R. Yose is silent, and Torah—what is now to become of her?"[1]

216. Again and again R. Judah recited to his son R. Simeon the words "Others say," etc., until finally the son asked: Who are they whose waters we drink but whose names we do not mention? R. Judah replied: They are the men who sought to root out your glory and the glory of your father's house. R. Simeon: "Their loves, their hates, their jealousies have long since vanished" (Eccles. 9:6). R. Judah: "The enemy has, to be sure, perished, but the swords[2] are forever" (Ps. 9:7). R. Simeon: What you say applies to instances where the "swords" of contention prevailed, but these sages [whose names you omit] did not prevail. After that, R. Judah changed and began to recite, "It is said in the name of R. Meir."

Rava observed: Even R. Judah, who was [so] self-effacing, resorted to "It is said in the name of R. Meir"; he still would not say, "R. Meir said."[3]

R. Simeon ben Yohai (fl. ca. 130–60 C.E.) and His Son R. Eleazar (fl. end of 2d century C.E.)

217. R. Abba said: Formerly, each master used to ordain his own pupils: thus Rabban Yohanan ben Zakkai ordained R. Eliezer and R. Joshua; R. Joshua ordained R. Akiva; R. Akiva ordained R. Meir and R. Simeon. But when R. Akiva added, "Let R. Meir sit in the first place," R. Simeon's face turned pale. At this, R. Akiva said to R. Simeon, "Let it suffice you that I and your Creator recognize your [intellectual] strength."[4]

218. It is reported that R. Simeon ben Yohai used to say: I see those who will behold the Presence in the hereafter, and they are few. If there be a thousand, I and my son are among them. If a hundred, I and my son are among them. If only two, I and my son are the ones.

It is further reported that R. Simeon ben Yohai used to say: [The suffering and privation that have been mine] would make it possible for me to exempt from judgment the entire world from the day I was born until now. Were my son Eleazar with me, [we would exempt it] from the day the world was created until now. Were Jotham son of Uzziah[5] with me, [we could] exempt it from the day the world was created until its end.[6]

219. R. Simeon ben Yohai said: Had I stood at Mount Sinai at the time when the Torah was given to Israel, I would have asked the Holy One that He create two mouths in a man, one to be occupied with Torah, the other to serve all his other needs. Then, retracting his words, R. Simeon said: If, when man has only one mouth, the world can barely endure all the informing it does, how much less if he had two.[7]

220. Isi ben Judah used to say: R. Simeon grinds much [grain] and wastes very little, which means, so it is taught, he forgets little, and even what he forgets is only bran.

Once R. Simeon came upon Isi ben Judah and asked him: Why do you spout idle chatter before the sages? Isi replied: Why should it bother you? I never said anything derogatory about you other than that you study much, forget little, and what you forget is no more than the bran of your learning.

R. Simeon used to say to his disciples: Learn my rules, for my rules surpass the very best of R. Akiva's rules.[8]

221. On one occasion, while R. Judah, R. Yose, and R. Simeon were sitting together, Judah the son of proselytes happened to sit with them. R. Judah began the discussion by observing, "How noble are the works of this [Roman] nation! They laid out streets, they built bridges, they erected baths." R. Yose remained silent, but R. Simeon ben Yohai spoke up and said, "All that they made, they made to serve themselves: they laid out streets to settle harlots in them; baths, to pamper themselves; bridges, to levy tolls. Now, Judah the son of proselytes went off and kept retelling the sages' words, until they were heard by the [Roman] government, which decreed: Judah, who acclaimed, shall be acclaimed [as spokesman for the Jews]; Yose, who remained silent, shall be exiled to Sepphoris; Simeon, who vilified, shall be put to death.

As a result, R. Simeon and his son hid out in the house of study, where every day R. Simeon's wife would bring them bread and a jug of water, with which they sustained themselves. But when insistence on carrying out the decree became intense, R. Simeon said to his son, "Women's resolution is frail—your mother, put to the torture, may reveal the place where we are hiding."

So they went and hid in a cave. A miracle occurred—a carob tree and a well were created for them. They would remove their garments and sit up to their necks in sand, and study the entire day. When it was time for prayer, they put on their garments, wrapped themselves in their prayer shawls, and prayed. Afterward, they again removed their garments, so that they would not wear out.

They dwelled twelve years in the cave. Then the prophet Elijah came and, standing at the entrance to the cave, announced, "Who will inform the son of Yohai that Caesar is dead and his decree annulled?" So they went out, and, seeing people plowing and sowing, R. Simeon exclaimed, "These men forsake life eternal and engage in life temporal!" Whatever they cast their eyes upon was immediately incinerated. At that, a divine voice went forth and said, "Have you come out to destroy My world? Return to your cave!"

So they returned and remained there twelve months

1. B. Naz 49b–50a; B. Kid 52b.
2. JV: "waste places"; but *horavot* also means "swords."
3. B. Hor 13b–14a.
4. P. Sanh 1:2, 19a.
5. During the many years his father was leprous, Jotham forbore to take over the kingship. He is regarded as a most pious king.
6. B. Suk 45b and En Yaakov, ad loc.
7. B. Ber 1:5, 3b.
8. B. Git 67a; ARN 18 (YJS 10:92–93).

longer. Finally they said, "Even the punishment of the wicked in Gehenna is no more than twelve months." A divine voice then came forth and said, "Leave your cave!" They went out and sat down at the entrance to the cave, where they saw a trapper attempting to catch birds by spreading his net. When R. Simeon heard a divine voice say, "Mercy, mercy," the bird escaped; and when he heard the voice say, "Death," the bird was trapped and stayed caught. At this, R. Simeon declared, "Without the will of Heaven, even a bird may not be trapped, all the less so a human being," and they left the cave for good. Wherever R. Eleazar bruised anyone's feelings, R. Simeon would heal them, saying, "My son, it is enough for the world if only you and I [occupy ourselves with Torah]."

On the Sabbath eve, as it was getting dark, they saw an old man running in the twilight with two bunches of myrtles in his hands. When they asked him, "What are these for?" he replied, "They are in honor of the Sabbath."

"But one bundle should be enough!"

"One is for 'Remember' [Exod. 20:8] and the other for 'Observe' " (Deut. 5:12).

Said R. Simeon to his son, "See how precious commandments are to Israel!" Then their minds were put at ease.

When R. Phinehas ben Yair, R. Simeon's son-in-law, heard that R. Simeon had left the cave, he went out to meet him and immediately took him to the baths in Tiberias, where he began to massage him. Seeing the abrasions in his skin caused by the sand, R. Phinehas burst into weeping, his tears falling on R. Simeon's body so that R. Simeon cried out in pain. R. Phinehas lamented, "Woe is me that I see you in such a state!" R. Simeon replied, "Happy are you that you see me thus. Had you not seen me thus, you would not have found as much learning in me."

R. Simeon said to himself: Since a miracle has been wrought for me, I will go and rectify that which requires rectification. So he asked R. Phinehas, "Is there anything that requires rectifying?" R. Phinehas: "There is a place here suspected of being unclean,[1] so that priests, who have to make a detour around it, are distressed." R. Simeon: "Does anyone here know whether at any time in the past this place was believed to be clean?" A certain old man replied, "Here Rabban Yohanan ben Zakkai [who was a priest] cut down lupines for the heave offering [*terumah*]." So R. Simeon, too, declared it clean. Where the ground was hard [and showed no trace of having been dug into to make a grave], he declared it clean; and where it was loose, he marked it [as a grave site]. Later the old man remarked derisively, "The son of Yohai has declared a whole cemetery clean!" R. Simeon responded, "If you had not been with us at the time, or even if you had been with us but did not vote with us, you might properly have made such a remark. But since you were with us and actually voted with us, [you should not subsequently criticize my decision], for people ought to be able to say, 'If whores are willing to paint one another, certainly disciples of the wise should do the same, and more." Then R. Simeon thrust such a look at the old man that the man died.

An ignorant Cuthean saw what R. Simeon was doing, and he said: Shall I not go and make sport of this elder of the Jews? So he got hold of a corpse and buried it in a thoroughfare that R. Simeon ben Yohai had purified that morning. The Cuthean then went to him and said, "Did you not cleanse such-and-such a throughfare?" He replied, "Yes." The Cuthean said, "Suppose I produce a corpse for you from that very place?" R. Simeon: "Produce it." The Cuthean did so, and R. Simeon, having perceived by the power of the holy spirit that the Cuthean had placed it there, declared, "I decree that he who is aboveground [shall die and] be put underground, and that he who was underground shall be [revived and] raised aboveground." And so it came to pass.[2]

When R. Simeon went out into the street and saw Judah the son of proselytes, he exclaimed, "That man is still in the world!" He cast his eyes upon him, and he was turned into a heap of bones.[3]

222. The [Roman] government once issued a decree that Jews should not keep the Sabbath nor circumcise their children. R. Reuben ben Istroboli trimmed the front of his hair [in Roman fashion], went up and sat among the Romans, and asked them, "If a man has an enemy, what should he wish him to be, poor or rich?" They replied, "Poor." He said to them, "If so, let the Jews do no work on the Sabbath, so that they may grow poor." They: "Right you are!" Then he went back and asked them again, "If one has an enemy, what should he wish him to be, weak or healthy?" They: "Weak." He said to them, "Then let their children be circumcised when they are only eight days old, and they will be weak." They again declared, "Right you are!" and immediately annulled the decree. Later, however, when they realized that he was a Jew, the decree was reinstituted.

The Jews then said among themselves, "Who shall go [to Rome] to work for the annulment of the decree? Let R. Simeon ben Yohai, for whom miracles are frequently wrought, go. And who should accompany him? R. Eleazar son of R. Yose." At this, R. Eleazar's father, R. Yose, said to them, "If my father Halafta were still alive, would you have said to him, 'Surrender your son [Yose] to be slain'?"[4] R. Simeon retorted sharply, "If Yohai my father were still alive, would you have said to him, 'Surrender your son [Simeon] to be slain'?" So R. Yose said to them, "Then I myself will go, for I fear that during the journey R. Simeon may inflict punishment on my son." So R. Simeon undertook to inflict no punishment on him. Nevertheless, in the event, he did inflict it, for during their journey the following question was put to them: How do we know that a reptile's blood [like its flesh] is also unclean? [Without waiting for R. Simeon to reply] R. Eleazar

1. A grave or human bones were believed to have been lost there.

2. The Cuthean died and was buried, while the corpse was restored to life.

3. B. Shab 33b–34a; P. Shev 9:1, 38d; Gen. R. 79:6.

4. R. Yose was afraid to expose his son to R. Simeon's vile temper. But R. Simeon understood him to fear the Romans. So he answered that he too was risking his life.

son of R. Yose said [in an undertone] out of the side of his mouth, "[The blood's uncleanness is derived from] 'And these are the items in reptiles that are unclean unto you' " (Lev. 11:29). R. Simeon said to him [with biting irony], "From your way of speaking out of the side of your mouth, one can see that you are indeed some scholar! May such a son never return to his father!"[1]

Then [the demon] Ben Temalion came to meet him, inquiring, "Do you wish me to accompany you?" At these words, R. Simeon burst into tears and said, "[Hagar], handmaid of my ancestor's house, was found worthy of meeting an angel three times,[2] while I had no such privilege, not even once. However, let a miracle be wrought [whether through an angel or through a demon]." So Ben Temalion went ahead [to the palace] and entered the body of Caesar's daughter [who kept calling for R. Simeon]. When R. Simeon arrived at the palace [and was asked to help her], he ordered, "Ben Temalion, leave her! Ben Temalion, leave her!" And as his name was called, Ben Temalion left her and went away. At that, Caesar said to R. Simeon, "Ask for whatever you wish, then go into the treasure house and take whatever you desire." They went in, found the document of the decree, took it, and tore it to pieces.[3]

223. The story is told of a disciple of R. Simeon ben Yohai who left to go outside of the land and came back wealthy. When the other disciples saw him, they envied him and wished that they too might go abroad. Having learned of this, R. Simeon brought all his disciples to a certain valley near the village of Meron, where he began to pray, "Valley, O valley, fill up with gold denars!" Immediately, before his very eyes, the valley began to give forth a stream of gold denars. He then said to the disciples, "If it is gold you want, here is your gold, take it. But you should know that he who takes it now is taking his share of the world-to-come, since the reward for studying Torah is not in this world, but in the world-to-come."[4]

224. The story is told of a woman in Sidon who lived ten years with her husband without bearing him a child. Deciding to part from each other, the two came to R. Simeon ben Yohai, who said to them, "By your lives, even as you were wed with food and drink, so should you be separated with food and drink." They followed his advice and, declaring the day a festal day for themselves, prepared a great feast, during which the wife gave her husband too much to drink. Being thus put in a good humor, he said to her, "My dear, pick any fine article you want in my home and take it with you when you return to your father's house." What did she do? After he fell asleep, she beckoned to her manservants and maidservants, and said to them, "Pick him up with the couch, take him along, and carry him to my father's house." At midnight, he woke up from his sleep. The effects of the wine had left him, and he asked, "My dear, where am I?" She replied, "You are in my father's house." He: "But what am I doing in your father's house?" She: "Did you not say to me last night, 'Pick any fine article you like from my house and take it with you when you return to your father's house'? There is no fine article in the world I care for more than for you." They again went to R. Simeon ben Yohai, and he arose and prayed for them, and they were remembered [by God and granted children].[5]

225. R. Jonathan ben Akhmai and R. Judah the son of proselytes studied the passage on vows at the school of R. Simeon ben Yohai. They had taken leave of him in the evening, but in the morning they came back and took leave of him again. When he asked, "But did you not take leave of me last night?" they replied, "Our master, you taught us that a disciple who took leave of his master and then remained to lodge overnight in the city is required to take leave of him once again." At this, R. Simeon said to his son, "These men are men of consequence. Go along with them, that they may bless you." So the son went to them. When they asked him, "What do you wish?" he replied, "My father told me, 'Go along with them, that they may bless you.' " They said to him, "May it be Heaven's will that you sow but reap not; that you bring in but not bring out; that you bring out but not bring in; that your home remain desolate but your lodging place lived in; that your table be in turmoil and you not behold a new year." When he came home to his father, he said to him, "Not only did they not bless me—they greatly upset me." His father asked, "What did they say to you?" "They said thus and so." The father: "Those are all blessings. 'That you sow but reap not' means that you beget children and they do not die. 'That you bring in but not bring out' means that you bring home daughters-in-law and your sons do not die, so that the wives would be obliged to go back to their father's homes. 'That you bring out but not bring in' means that you give your daughters in marriage and their husbands do not die, so that your daughters are not obliged to come back to you. 'That your home be desolate but your lodging place lived in'—this world is the lodging place and the grave your home. 'That your table be in turmoil' because of many sons and daughters; and 'that you not behold a new year' [with a new wife]—that your wife does not die and you are not obliged to wed a new wife."[6]

226. A man once said to his wife, "I vow that you are not to derive any benefit from me until you make R. Judah and R. Simeon taste your cooking. R. Judah consented to taste it, as he reasoned *a fortiori:* if, in order to make peace between husband and wife, Torah quotes God as saying, "My Name which is written in sanctity is to be dissolved in 'the waters that curse' " (Num. 5:23)—even when it is doubtful whether or not the wife is guilty of adultery—how much less should I stand on my honor [and refuse to taste the woman's cooking]?

But R. Simeon refused to taste the food, exclaiming,

1. May he die for his rashness in replying without his teacher's permission.
2. See Gen. 16.
3. B. Me 17a–b.
4. Exod. R. 52:3; Yalkut, Prov., §964.
5. Song R. 1:4, §2.
6. B. MK 9a–b.

"Even though the woman be widowed and her children die, Simeon will not be budged from his position, in order that people should not fall into the habit of vowing."[1]

227. Whenever R. Simeon ben Yohai saw his mother engage in long chitchat on the Sabbath, he would say, "Mother, it is the Sabbath!"[2]

228. R. Simeon used to carry a basket on his shoulder, saying, "Great is labor, for it gives honor to the worker."[3]

229. A story about R. Eleazar son of R. Simeon: Some donkey drivers, wishing to buy grain, came to his father's house, where they saw R. Eleazar seated near the oven, from which his mother kept taking out loaves of [freshly baked] bread. As she took them out, he kept eating them, until he had consumed all the troughs of bread. They said, "What a shame! A pernicious snake must be lodged in this young man's belly. He may well bring a famine on the world!" R. Eleazar heard what they said, so, when they went out to fetch their load, he took hold of their donkeys and hoisted them up onto the roof. When they returned, they looked for the donkeys but could not find them, until they raised their eyes and saw them on the roof. [Chagrined], they went to his father and told him what had happened. He asked, "Perhaps you said something to offend him?" They replied, "No, sir, but this and this is what happened." R. Simeon: "Why did you say something that might make him a victim of the evil eye? Was it perhaps your food he ate? Do you have to pay for his food? Did not He who created him also create food for him? Nevertheless, go and tell him in my name to fetch the donkeys down, and he will do so."

[They went and said to R. Eleazar what his father had told them to say.] The second feat was more striking than the first. In taking up the donkeys, Eleazar had hoisted them up one by one; in bringing them down, he carried them down two by two.

However, once he began to study Torah, he could not carry even his own cloak.[4]

230. R. Yose ben Halafta saw Eleazar the son of R. Simeon ben Yohai and said: You come from the stock of righteous men, yet you are not a student of Torah. Eleazar: What am I to do? R. Yose: Do you wish to study? Eleazar: Yes. So R. Yose began by teaching him one chapter of Scripture, then a second, and then a third; finally, he brought him down to the place where scholars assemble. When Rabbi [Judah I] saw him, he asked R. Yose: Did you have to bring such a one with you? R. Yose: He comes from the stock of R. Simeon ben Yohai. Later, R. Yose brought Eleazar up to Sepphoris, where he taught him Mishnah. The following year, he brought him down again to the place where scholars assemble, and Eleazar proceeded to respond to questions with proper answers. At that, our holy rabbi [Judah I] applied to Eleazar the verse "The fruit of the righteous is a tree of life" (Prov. 11:30).

Who caused Eleazar to become a student of Torah? Was it not R. Yose ben Halafta?[5]

231. R. Eleazar ben Simeon became a porter. One time Elijah the Prophet came to him, disguised as an old man, and said to him, "Get a beast of burden ready for me." Eleazar asked, "And what do you have to load on the animal?" Elijah replied, "This baggage, my cloak, and myself as rider." Eleazar said [to the bystanders], "Look at this old man—I could load him [on my back] and carry him to the end of the world, yet he says to me, 'Get a beast of burden ready for me!' " So he asked Elijah, "Do you insist on riding?" Elijah: "Yes." Then he put Elijah astride his own back and took him up mountainsides, down into valleys, and across fields of thorns. But Elijah began to bear down with his weight upon Eleazar. Finally Eleazar said, "Old man, old man, ride more lightly. If not, I shall throw you off." Then he asked Elijah, "Would you like to rest a bit?" Elijah replied, "Yes." What did Eleazar do next? He took Elijah to a field, set him down under a tree, and gave him something to eat and drink. After Elijah ate and drank, he asked Eleazar, "What will all this heavy labor get you? Would it not be better for you to take up the vocation of your forebears?" Eleazar asked, "Will you teach me their vocation?" Elijah replied, "Yes." Then, according to some, Elijah taught Eleazar Torah for thirteen years, until he was able to recite the Sifra.[6] [So much of his strength went into learning, that] once he was able to recite the Sifra, he could not even carry his own cloak.[7]

232. While R. Simeon ben Gamaliel and R. Joshua ben Korhah sat on benches, R. Eleazar son of R. Simeon and Rabbi [Judah I] sat in front of them on the ground,[8] raising questions and answering them. Finally, the other sages, also seated on benches, said, "We drink the water [the learning] of these two, yet they sit on the ground." Then seats were provided, and they were seated on them. But R. Simeon ben Gamaliel protested, "I have an only son among you, and you wish to make me lose him!"[9] S. R. Judah was asked to get down from the bench. At that, R. Joshua ben Korhah said, "Shall he who has a father live, while he who has no father[10] die?"[11] So R. Eleazar son of R. Simeon was also asked to get down from his bench. [Not knowing why this was done], R. Eleazar felt hurt, saying, "Do you regard R. Judah as my equal?" Now, until that day, whenever R. Judah made a statement, R. Eleazar son of R. Simeon would support him. But from then on, as soon as R. Judah said, "I have an objection," R. Eleazar son of R. Simeon would retort, "You should object thus

1. B. Ned 66b.
2. P. Shab 15:3, 15b.
3. B. Ned 49b.
4. Song R. 5:14, §3; PRKM 11:18.
5. Tanhuma B, *Va-yera*, §38.
6. The tannaitic Midrash on Leviticus, a particularly difficult treatise.
7. PRKM 11:22.
8. The usual way of study: the master on a seat, the disciples on the ground.
9. He, R. Judah's father, feared that his son's promotion would excite the evil eye and cause him to die.
10. R. Simeon ben Yohai, R. Eleazar's father, was dead.
11. R. Eleazar might likewise become victim of an evil eye.

and so—this should be your objection. Instead, you encompass us with bundles of objections that have no substance." R. Judah felt humiliated and went off to complain to his father, who told him, "My son, do not take it to heart, for Eleazar is a lion the son of a lion, whereas you are a lion the son of a mere fox."[1]

233. R. Eleazar son of R. Simeon once met a detective who was assigned to catch thieves. R. Eleazar asked, "How can you recognize them? Are they not like wild beasts that prowl at night and hide during the day? Perhaps you sometimes arrest the innocent and leave the guilty free?" The detective answered, "What shall I do? It is the king's command." R. Eleazar: "Come, I will teach you what to do. At nine o'clock in the morning,[2] go into a tavern. Should you see a man dozing with a cup of wine in his hand, inquire about him. If he is a disciple of the wise, [you may assume that] he has risen very early in the morning to pursue his studies [and that is why he is now dozing]; if he is a laborer, he too must have been up early to do his work. But if he is neither, he is a thief—arrest him." The report [of this conversation] was brought to the king's attention, and the decision was [as the proverb puts it]: "Let the reader of the message become the messenger."[3] R. Eleazar son of R. Simeon was accordingly sent for and was appointed to arrest thieves. R. Joshua ben Korhah sent word to him, "O Vinegar son of wine! How long will you deliver up the people of our God for slaughter!" R. Eleazar sent back: "I weed out thorns from the vineyard." R. Joshua replied, "Let the Owner of the vineyard come and Himself weed out its thorns."

One day a mere fuller met him and called him "Vinegar son of wine." R. Eleazar said to himself: Since he is so insolent, he must surely be a felon. So he gave the order to his attendant, "Arrest him!" and they arrested him. When R. Eleazar's anger cooled, he went back in order to secure the fuller's release, but could not do so. Then he applied to himself the verse "Whoso keepeth his mouth and his tongue, keepeth his soul from troubles" (Prov. 21:23). When they subsequently hanged the fuller, R. Eleazar stood under the gallows and wept. His disciples said to him, "Master, do not grieve, for this fuller and his son together raped a betrothed maiden on Yom Kippur."[4] At this, R. Eleazar laid his hand on his belly and exclaimed, "Rejoice, my innards, rejoice! If matters you were in doubt about fall out thus, how much more so matters about which you are certain! I am well assured that neither worms nor decay will have power over you."

Nevertheless, his conscience [troubled by the thought that he might have caused an innocent man's death] had no rest. So he was given a sleeping draught and taken into a marble chamber, where his abdomen was opened. Out of it baskets and baskets of fat were removed and placed in the sun during [the summer months of] Tammuz[5] and Av, yet the fat did not putrefy. Consequently, he applied to himself the verse "My flesh, too, shall dwell in safety" (Ps. 16:9).

Yet even so,[6] R. Eleazar son of R. Simeon's conscience continued to trouble him. He therefore invoked painful afflictions upon himself, so that although sixty sheets were spread under him in the evening, sixty basins of blood and pus were removed from under him in the morning. Every morning his wife prepared a mixture of sixty kinds of fig pap for him, and when he ate it, he recovered. But his wife did not permit him to go to the house of study, lest the sages [who disapproved of his work as a thief catcher] should cause him distress. In the evening R. Eleazar would invite his afflictions back, saying, "Come back, my brethren and friends!" and in the morning he would say to them, "Depart, lest you disturb my studies!"

One day his wife, overhearing him, cried out, "So it is of your own volition that you bring these afflictions upon yourself, and to pay for their treatment, you squander the money of my father's house!" With that taunt, she went off to her father's house, in defiance of her husband. Just then, sixty mariners were sailing on the sea. When a huge wave crested over them and was about to sink their vessel, they rose up in prayer, saying, "O God of Eleazar, answer us!" and the sea's wrath abated. When the mariners reached dry land, they brought R. Eleazar a gift of sixty slaves bearing sixty purses. The slaves prepared a mixture of sixty kinds of fig pap for him, and he ate it.

One day, R. Eleazar's wife said to her daughter, "Go and find out how your father is faring, how he is now." She went to him and [on her arrival] her father said to her, "Go tell your mother that our [wealth] is still greater than that of her father's house." He then applied to himself the verse "[Torah] is like the merchant ships, fetching foodstuffs from afar" (Prov. 31:14).

He ate, drank, and recovered, then went to the house of study. Sixty specimens of blood were brought before him [with the question whether they were or were not menstrual blood], and he declared all the specimens clean [not blood of menstruation]. But the sages criticized him, saying, "Is it possible that there was not even one specimen about which there might have been some doubt?" He responded, "If it is as I have said, let all the future children borne by these women be males; if not, let there be one female among them." All the children born were males and were named Eleazar after him.

[In his last illness], R. Eleazar's arm once happened to be exposed, and his wife both laughed and wept. She laughed because she said to herself: How happy I am—how happy my lot, that I have been able to cleave to the body of so righteous a man! She wept because she said: Alas that the body of so righteous a man is destined for the dust.

As he was dying, he said to his wife, "I know that the sages are angry with me and will not properly attend

---

1. That is to say, Eleazar's father, R. Simeon ben Yohai, was more learned than I. B. BM 84b.
2. Literally, the fourth hour of the day.
3. You made the motion—now you can become chairman of the committee.
4. A triple sin.
5. A sign that he had acted rightly and would be proof against decay.
6. Even though his fat did not putrefy.

to my burial. Let my body repose in the upper chamber, and do not be afraid of my presence there.

R. Samuel bar Nahmani said: R. Jonathan's mother told me that the wife of R. Eleazar son of R. Simeon had told her, "He lay in his upper chamber not less than eighteen nor more than twenty-two years. Whenever I ascended there, I would examine his hair, and if even a single hair happened to fall out, blood would spurt forth. One day, when I saw a worm issue from his ear, I [fearful that his body had begun to decompose] was much grieved. But then he appeared to me in a dream and told me to think nothing of it. 'This has happened,' he said, 'because I once heard a disciple of the wise being belittled and did not protest as I should have done.' "

Whenever two people in a lawsuit came before him, they stood at the door, and each stated his case. Then a voice would issue from the upper chamber, saying, "So-and-so, you are liable; So-and-so, you are in the clear."

One day R. Eleazar's wife was quarreling with a neighbor woman who cursed her, "May you be like your husband, who had no proper burial!" Consequently the sages said, "Now that R. Eleazar's being unburied has come to be known, it is not right to have it continue thus." Others say: R. Simeon ben Yohai appeared to the sages in a dream and said to them, "I have a dear child among you, whom you refuse to bring to me." Then the sages decided to attend to his burial. But the townspeople of Akhbera[1] would not let them, because during all the years that R. Eleazar son of R. Simeon lay asleep in his upper chamber, no wild beast had come to their town. However, one day—it was the eve of Yom Kippur—while the people of Akhbera were preoccupied, the sages sent [word] to the townspeople of Biri,[2] and they took his bier down and carried it to the cave where his father was buried. When they found a snake coiled at its entrance, they said to it, "Snake, O snake, open your mouth [and let go of your tail], so that a son may join his father." At that, the snake opened its mouth and they were able to enter.[3]

When R. Eleazar son of R. Simeon died, his generation applied to him the verse, "Who is this that cometh up out of the wilderness like pillars of smoke perfumed with myrrh and frankincense, with all the powders of the merchant?" (Song 3:6). What did they mean by "with all the powders of the merchant"? That he had rare powers—that he was master of Scripture and Mishnah, that he was a composer of hymns, and that he was a gifted preacher.[4]

R. Yose ben Halafta (fl. 2d half of 2d century C.E.) and His Son R. Ishmael (fl. 1st half of 3d century C.E.)

234. R. Levi said: In Jerusalem there was found a genealogical scroll in which was written, "R. Yose son of Halafta is of the descendants of Jonadab son of Rechab."[5]

235. When R. Yose ben Halafta was a boy, he used to play with other boys. A man saw him and called out, "Your father should be told that [instead of studying, you waste your time] playing with the boys." R. Yose answered, "What is that to you? If you tell my father, he will only spank me, whereas you will accustom your tongue to speaking slander."[6]

236. R. Yose said: Once, while traveling on the road, I entered one of the ruins of Jerusalem in order to pray. Elijah the prophet, ever remembered for good, appeared and waited for me at the door until I finished my prayer. After I had prayed, he said to me, "Peace be unto you, my master!" I replied, "Peace be unto you, my master and my teacher!" He asked, "My son, why did you enter this ruin?" I replied, "To pray." He said to me, "You could have prayed on the road." I replied, "I feared lest passersby might interrupt me." Elijah: "My son, what sound did you hear in this ruin?" I replied, "I heard a divine voice cooing like a dove and saying:

Woe is me that I have destroyed My house,
burned My Temple Hall,
and exiled My children among the nations!"

Elijah went on, "By my life and by your head, my son! Not in this moment alone does the voice so lament—it laments three times every day! And more than that! Each time Jews go into houses of prayer and houses of study and respond, 'Amen! May His great Name be blessed,' the Holy One, if one dare speak thus, shakes His head and says:

Happy is the King who is thus acclaimed in His own house!
What has caused the Father to banish His children?
And woe to the children who had to be banished from the table of their Father!"[7]

237. During a lecture in Sepphoris, R. Yose said: Father Elijah [the prophet] was a hot-tempered man.[8] So Elijah, who used to visit him regularly, stayed away for three days and did not come. When he did come again, R. Yose asked him, "Why have you stayed away, sir?" Elijah replied, "Because you called me hot-tempered." R. Yose responded, "But, sir, even in this you have shown your temper."[9]

238. R. Yose's wife used to quarrel with her maidservant. Once, in front of the maidservant, he said that his wife was wrong. When she asked, "Why do you declare me wrong in front of my maidservant?" he replied, "Did not Job say, 'Have I ever despised the case of my servants, man or maid, even they made a complaint against me?' " (Job 31:13).[10]

---

1. A town north of Tiberias.
2. A neighboring town, a bit farther north.
3. B. BM 83b–84a and En Yaakov, ad loc.; Eccles R. 11:2, §1.
4. Lev. R. 30:1; Song R. 3:6, §7.
5. See Jer. 35. Since the Rechabites were descendants of Jethro, R. Yose was thus of proselyte stock. P. Ta 4:2, 68a.
6. MTeh 50:3 (YJS 1:470).
7. B. Ber 3a and En Yaakov, ad loc.
8. In that he dealt with Ahab severely. See 1 Kings 17:1.
9. B. Sanh 113a–b.
10. Gen. R. 48:3.

239. R. Yose said: Never have I called my wife "my wife" or my ox "my ox"; rather, I called my wife "my house" and my ox "my field."

R. Yose also said: Never have the beams of my house seen the seams of my shirt.[1]

And R. Yose said: Never have I contradicted the words of my colleagues. Though I know full well that I am not a priest, yet, should my colleagues say to me, "Go up to the dais,"[2] I would go up.

R. Yose also said: Never have I said a thing and then had to take back what I said.

And R. Yose said: May my portion be with those who eat three meals on the Sabbath.[3]

R. Yose also said: May my portion be with those who recite the entire *Hallel* every day.[4]

And R. Yose said: May my portion be with those who pray at the red glow of the sun.[5]

R. Yose also said: May my portion be with those who die of illness of the bowels, for a master once said: Most of the righteous die of a disease of the bowels.[6]

And R. Yose said: May my portion be with those who die as they are about to perform a precept.

R. Yose also said: May my portion be with those who welcome the Sabbath as if they were in Tiberias and usher it out as if they were in Sepphoris.[7]

And R. Yose said: May my portion be with those who inspire pupils to enter and sit in the house of study, and not with those who inspire them to rise up and leave the house of study.

R. Yose also said: May my lot be with those who collect charity, and not with those who distribute charity.[8]

R. Yose also said: May my portion be with those who are suspected for no cause.[9]

240. R. Yose said: All my life I have been perplexed by the verse "And thou shalt grope at noonday as the blind gropeth in darkness" (Deut. 28:29). What difference [I asked], does it make to a blind man whether it be dark or light? [Nor did I find the answer] until the following incident occurred. I was once walking at the darkest time of the night when I saw a blind man walking on the road with a torch in his hand. I said to him, "My son, what need have you for this torch?" He replied, "As long as I have this torch in my hand, people see me and save me from holes, thorns, and briers."[10]

1. When he undressed he did not turn the shirt inside out, but pulled it over his head while in bed; out of modesty, he remained covered as much as possible.
2. To recite the priests' benediction. Num. 6:22–27.
3. He held himself in such low esteem that he hoped he would be deemed the equal of men who regularly observed a precept that was not too difficult to carry out.
4. See *APB*, pp. 84–96. The practice was apparently new, and he approved of it.
5. Both at dawn and at sunset.
6. The pain they suffer purges them of sin.
7. That is, prolong the Sabbath's observance. In Tiberias, situated in a valley, the Sabbath began earlier; in Sepphoris, which was on a mountain, it ended later.
8. It is difficult to be fair and impartial in performing the latter task.
9. B. Shab 118b and En Yaakov, ad loc.
10. B. Meg 24b.

241. R. Yose always had a profound reason for his views.[11]

242. When R. Yose bar Halafta died, the roof gutters of Sepphoris ran with blood.[12]

243. When R. Yose died, understanding ceased.[13]

244. Whenever Rabbi [Judah I, the Patriarch] was about to offer a refutation of one of R. Yose's teachings, he would say: We who are lowly dare attempt to refute a teaching of R. Yose's! For as things utterly common are to things utterly holy, so is our generation to the generation of R. Yose.

R. Ishmael son of R. Yose said: As dust is to gold, so is our generation to the generation of my father.[14]

245. R. Ishmael son of R. Yose asked Rabbi [Judah I, the Patriarch]: Who are those who are said to "dwell before the Lord" in the verse "Her grain shall be for them that dwell before the Lord" (Isa. 23:18)? R. Judah replied: Such as you and your colleagues and those two [sages][15] wearing plain cloaks as you choose to do, who hold yourselves in no special esteem.[16]

246. R. Ishmael son of R. Yose, while walking on a road, met a man carrying a bundle of sticks. The man put it down, rested, and then said, "Help me pick it up." "What is it worth?" R. Ishmael inquired. "Half a *zuz*." So R. Simeon gave the man the half-*zuz* and declared the fagot ownerless. But then the man resumed possession of the bundle. R. Ishmael gave him another half-*zuz* and again declared the fagot ownerless. Seeing that the man was again about to resume possession of the bundle, R. Ishmael said to him, "I have declared it ownerless for everyone else, but not for you."[17]

247. The tenant of R. Ishmael son of R. Yose used to bring him a basket of fruit [as rent] every Friday afternoon. On one occasion, he brought it on Thursday. When R. Ishmael asked, "Why the change in day?" the tenant replied, "I have a lawsuit [to be adjudicated by you], and I thought that on my way to attend it I would bring the rent to the master." R. Ishmael did not accept it from him and said, "I am disqualified from adjudicating your suit." He then appointed two disciples of the wise to try the tenant's case. While arranging matters, R. Ishmael found himself thinking: If the tenant wished, he might plead this way; then again, he might plead otherwise. Then R. Ishmael

11. Or, "carried his learning with him." B. Git 67a; ARN 18.
12. By way of mourning. B. MK 25b; P. AZ 3:1, 42c.
13. P. Sot 9:15, 24c.
14. P. Git 6:7, 48b.
15. Two highly regarded sages who were exceedingly humble.
16. Eccles. R. 1:7, §9.
17. R. Ishmael was ready to help the man but preferred not to strain himself physically. So he bought the bundle and declared it ownerless, i.e., public property. The man accepted the money twice and, since the bundle became ownerless, each time declared himself the owner, until R. Ishmael felt forced to restrict that man's right to take possession of the bundle. B. BM 30b.

said: "May the breath of those who take bribes be blasted! If I—who have not taken the fruit; and even if I had taken it, I would have taken what is mine—[find myself providing pleas for my tenant], how much more and more do they who do accept bribes."[1]

248. It once happened that a man said to his wife: I vow that you are to derive no benefit from me until you manage to show to R. Ishmael son of R. Yose that at least one of your features is beautiful. So R. Ishmael said to those who reported the incident to him, "Perhaps her head is beautiful?" "It is round," they replied. "Perhaps her hair is beautiful?" "It is like limp stalks of flax." "Perhaps her eyes are beautiful?" "They are bleary." "Perhaps her ears are beautiful?" "They are deformed." "Perhaps her nose is beautiful?" "It is bloated." "Perhaps her lips are beautiful?" "They are thick." "Perhaps her neck is beautiful?" "It is squat." "Perhaps her belly is beautiful?" "It protrudes." "Perhaps her feet are beautiful?" "They are as broad as those of a duck." "Perhaps her name is beautiful?" "It is Likhlukhit ['marred']." He said to them, "She is beautifully called *likhlukhit*, marred as she is by her many defects." And he absolved her husband of his vow.[2]

249. R. Ishmael son of R. Yose was going up to Jerusalem to pray. As he passed Neapolis, a Cuthean saw him and asked him, "Where are you going?" R. Ishmael: "I am going up to pray in Jerusalem." The Cuthean: "Would it not be better to pray on this mountain,[3] singled out for blessing, rather than on that dungheap?" R. Ishmael: "May I tell you to what you may be compared? To a dog whose tongue is out for carrion. Because you know that there are idols hidden beneath Gerizim, as is said, 'And Jacob hid them' [Gen. 35:4], your tongue is out for them."[4] The Cutheans said, "This man wants to take the idols away," and took counsel on how to put him to death. Hearing that, R. Ishmael arose and fled during the night.[5]

250. Once a certain disciple, following R. Ishmael son of R. Yose in a marketplace in Zion, noticed that R. Ishmael seemed afraid of something. So he said: You must be a sinner, because it is written, "The sinners in Zion are afraid" (Isa. 33:14). R. Ishmael replied: But it is also written, "Happy is the man that feareth alway" (Prov. 28:14). The disciple: That verse refers to words of Torah.[6]

251. R. Ishmael son of R. Yose used to say: I could write down all of Scripture from memory.[7]

252. The same thing that happened to R. Eleazar ben Simeon happened to R. Ishmael son of R. Yose.[8] The prophet Elijah met him and reproved him, "How long will you deliver the people of our God to be executed?" "But what can I do?" R. Ishmael replied. "It is the king's decree." Elijah: "Your father fled to Asya.[9] You—flee to Laodicea."[10]

253. R. Ishmael son of R. Yose happened to visit R. Simeon son of R. Yose ben Lakonia and was given a goblet, which he emptied in one swallow. R. Simeon then asked R. Ishmael: Did not the master declare that a man who drinks his goblet in one swallow is a tippler? R. Ishmael replied: The master did not speak of your goblet, which is small, of your wine, which is sweet, and of my stomach, which is big.[11]

254. When R. Eleazar son of R. Simeon and R. Ishmael son of R. Yose met, a yoke of oxen could pass under their bellies without touching them.[12]

R. Judah bar Ilai (2d half of 2d century C.E.)

255. On all occasions, R. Judah was first to speak.[13]

256. "Beauty is deceitful. . . . It is the fear of the Lord whereby one is adorned" (Prov. 31:30). The verse applies to the generation of R. Judah son of R. Ilai, of which it is said: [Though their poverty was so great that] six of R. Judah's disciples had to make do with one cloak for all of them, yet they occupied themselves with Torah.[14]

257. R. Judah's wife got busy, bought some wool ends, and made a wrap of mixed colors. When she went out to market, she would cover herself with it, and when R. Judah went out to pray, he, too, would cover himself with it and pray. As he was about to cover himself, he would utter the blessing, "Blessed be He who has provided me with a robe."[15]

258. Once Rabban Simeon ben Gamaliel declared a fast, but R. Judah did not appear at the special service for the fast. When Rabban Simeon was told that R. Judah had nothing to wear, he sent him a robe, but R. Judah refused to accept it; lifting up the mat [upon which he sat, he] said to Rabban Simeon's emissary, "See what [treasures][16] I have here [under the mat], but I do not find it right to benefit from this world."[17]

259. A Roman noblewoman saw R. Judah son of R. Ilai, his face aglow. So she said: Old man, old man, one of

1. B. Ket 105b.
2. B. Ned 66b.
3. Mount Gerizim. See Deut. 27:12.
4. You only pretend to worship the true God. In fact, it is the idols hidden beneath the mount that you worship.
5. Gen. R. 81:3; P. AZ 5:4, 44d.
6. A man should always fear the possibility of forgetting them. B. Ber 60a.
7. P. Meg 4:1, 74d.
8. He also was asked to be a Roman officer in charge of arresting thieves. See above in this chapter, §233.
9. R. Yose ben Halafta fled after he was ordained by R. Judah ben Bava. See B. Sanh 14a.
10. B. BM 83b–84a.
11. B. Pes 86b.
12. Their bellies were so large. B. BM 84a.
13. See above in this chapter, §221. B. Shab 33b.
14. B. Sanh 20a.
15. B. Ned 49b.
16. Their appearance came about through a miracle.
17. B. Ned 49b–50a.

three things must be true of you: either you have drunk too much wine, or you lend money upon interest, or you raise swine.[1] R. Judah replied: By the faith that is mine, none of these things is true of me. I do not lend money upon interest, since it is said, "Thou shalt not lend upon interest to thy brother" (Deut. 23:20). I do not raise swine, since it is forbidden for a Jew to raise swine. Nor am I drunk with wine. I drink wine only for the Kiddish and *Havdalah* rites; and the four cups [required at the Passover seder] make me feel as though I had a tight cord around my temples from Passover to Shavuot. The noblewoman: Then why does your face shine? R. Judah: It is teaching Torah that makes my face shine, as is said, "A man's wisdom makes his face to shine" (Eccles. 8:1).[2]

260. When R. Judah went to the house of study, he used to carry on his shoulder a large pitcher to sit on, saying: Great is work, for it gives honor to the worker.[3]

261. When R. Judah was seated in the presence of R. Tarfon, R. Tarfon said to him: Your face shines today. R. Judah: Last night your servants went out to the field and brought beets for us, which we ate without salt. Had we eaten them with salt, our faces would have shone with even greater joy.[4]

262. R. Yose and R. Judah ate porridge out of the same bowl. One ate with his fingers, and the other used a palm leaf [for a spoon]. He who was eating with the palm leaf asked the one who ate with his fingers, "How long will you make me eat the filth on your fingers?" The one who ate with his fingers replied to the one who ate with a palm leaf, "How long will you make me eat your spittle?"[5]

263. Lesbian figs[6] were set before R. Judah and R. Simeon. R. Judah ate them, but R. Simeon did not. R. Judah asked: Why is the master not eating? R. Simeon replied: These do not pass out of the stomach. R. Judah: All the more reason [to eat them], since one may depend on them for sustenance tomorrow.[7]

264. R. Judah said in the name of Rav: Such was the practice of R. Judah bar Ilai: on the eve of the Sabbath, a tub filled with warm water would be brought to him. In it, he washed his face, his hands, and his feet. Then, as he sat wrapped in his fringed linen robes, he seemed like an angel of the Lord of hosts.[8]

265. R. Judah said in the name of Rav: Such was the practice of R. Judah son of R. Ilai: on the eve of the ninth of Av, dry bread seasoned with salt would be brought to him. He would sit between the oven and the stove, and eat it, washing it down with a pitcher of water and behaving as though his deceased loved one were lying before him.[9]

266. R. Judah said: Once I was walking behind R. Akiva and R. Eleazar ben Azariah. When the time for reading the Shema came, I supposed that they refrained from reading it [before sunrise].[10] But then I realized that they were busy with communal matters. So I kept repeating the Shema [until its conclusion coincided with the instant of sunrise]. Then they began reciting it, when the sun was already seen over the summits of the mountains.[11]

267. It is said of R. Judah bar Ilai that he used to interrupt his study of Torah only to participate in a funeral procession or to lead a bride [to the bridal bower].

It is also said of R. Judah bar Ilai that he used to seize the twig of a myrtle and dance before the bride, chanting, "O bride, beautiful and charming."[12]

R. Eleazar ben Shammua (fl. 2d half of 2d century C.E.) and His Son R. Simeon (1st third of 3d century C.E.)

268. R. Yohanan said: The intellectual powers of former generations were as wide as the entrance[13] into the Outer Hall [leading to the Temple's interior], and those of recent generations narrower, like the entrance[14] into the Temple Hall; but ours is like the eye of a small needle. R. Akiva is reckoned as one of the former generations; R. Eleazar ben Shammua as one of the recent generations.

Some say R. Eleazar ben Shammua is reckoned as one of the former generations, and R. Oshaia Berabbi as one of the recent generations.[15]

269. Rav used to speak of R. Eleazar ben Shammua as the strongest among the sages.[16]

270. Rabbi [Judah I, the Patriarch] said: When I went to R. Eleazar ben Shammua to have my learning examined (others say, to sound the learning of R. Eleazar ben Shammua), I found Joseph the Babylonian, who was very dear

1. Both immensely profitable occupations.
2. P. Shab 8:1, 11a; B. Ned 49b; Eccles. R. 8:1, §4.
3. B. Ned. 49b.
4. Ibid.
5. Because the leaf was not wiped after being put in the mouth; ibid.
6. Figs from Lesbos were said to be difficult to digest.
7. B. Ned 49b.
8. B. Shab 25b.
9. B. Ta 30a–b.
10. To indicate disagreement with R. Eliezer, who maintained that the Shema must be read before sunrise.
11. After sunrise. Tos Ber 1:4 (ed. Saul Liberman [New York, 1955], 1:2). See his comments in Lieberman, TKF 2:2–3. Leon Nemoy responds: "What troubles me is 'refrained from' for *nityaashu*. Refraining is a deliberate action, whereas *hityaesh* is a lack of any action. Moreover, as I read the story, it is a simple account of events. The two sages were busy with public affairs and could not interrupt their deliberations to recite the Shema. R. Judah was doing nothing, so he recited the Shema at the appointed time. When the two sages completed their business, a little after sunrise, they too recited the Shema. Ergo, important public business is a valid reason to delay the Shema, at least according to these two sages."
12. B. Ket 17a.
13. Twenty cubits.
14. Ten cubits.
15. B. Er 53a.
16. B. Ket 40a.

to him, seated before him. Joseph asked, "Master, what is the law if one has slaughtered an offering, intending to leave some of the blood for the morrow?" "The offering is valid," R. Eleazar replied. In the evening [when asked the question again], he again replied, "It is valid." The next morning he again replied, "It is valid." At midday he again replied, "It is valid." In the afternoon he again replied, "It is valid, but R. Eliezer declares it to be invalid." At that, the face of Joseph the Babylonian brightened. R. Eleazar: "Joseph, it seems to me that we did not get our traditions straight until now." "Quite so, master," he replied, "quite so. For R. Judah taught me that such blood was invalid; but when I went around among all his disciples to find the same opinion, I could not find any.[1] Now that you teach me that according to R. Eliezer, too, such blood is invalid, [you provide me with another opinion in agreement with R. Judah's] and thus restore to me words of Torah I thought I had lost." R. Eleazar ben Shammua's eyes filled with tears of joy and he exclaimed, "Happy are you, O disciples of the wise, to whom the words of Torah are so dear!" He then said that Joseph could justly declare, "O how I love Thy Torah! It is my meditation all the day" (Ps. 119:97). "But you should know that it is only because R. Judah was the son of R. Ilai, and R. Ilai was the disciple of R. Eliezer, that R. Judah taught you R. Eliezer's opinion."[2]

271. Rabbi [Judah I, the Patriarch] used to say: When we studied Torah at the home of R. Eleazar ben Shammua, six of us used to sit in the space of one cubit.[3]

272. Rabbi [Judah I, the Patriarch] also said: When I went to study Torah in the school of R. Eleazar ben Shammua, his disciples banded together against me like the cocks of Beth Bukya[4] and did not let me learn more than one ruling in this Mishnah we are now studying.[5]

273. A story of R. Eleazar ben Shammua and R. Yohanan the Cobbler, who were traveling to Nisibis [in Babylonia] to study Torah in the school of R. Judah ben Beterah. When they reached Zidon and remembered the Land of Israel, they lifted their tear-filled eyes, rent their garments, and recited the verse "Ye shall possess it. By dwelling therein, ye will be able to do all the statutes" (Deut. 11:31–32). At that, they turned back and went home, saying: Dwelling in the Land of Israel is the equivalent to performing all precepts in the Torah.[6]

274. R. Eleazar ben Shammua, while walking on the shore of the Great Sea, saw a ship being tossed about in the water and, in the twinkling of an eye, sink with all its passengers. Then he espied a man holding on to a ship's plank and being carried from wave to wave until he got to dry land. Being naked, he hid himself [among the rocks] on the shore. The incident happened while Jews were going up to Jerusalem for a festival. So the man called out to them, "I am of the descendants of Esau, your brother. Give me any kind of garment to cover my nether parts, because the sea has tossed me about, leaving me with nothing." They replied, "So may all your people be likewise tossed about!" As he looked around, he noticed R. Eleazar walking among these Jews. So he said to him, "I see that you are a venerable man and respected by your people; you recognize the dignity of all creatures. Help me, and give me a garment to cover my nether parts, because the sea has tossed me about." R. Eleazar ben Shammua, who was wearing seven robes, took off one of them and gave it to the man. Then R. Eleazar brought him to his house, provided him with food and drink, and gave him two hundred denars. After that, R. Eleazar had him ride [his own donkey] for fourteen Persian *mil*, conveying him with great honor until he brought him to his home.

Some time later, the wicked Caesar died and the man [who had been shipwrecked] was elected to rule in his stead. He decreed concerning that province: "All its men are to be put to death, and all its women to be taken as spoil." The Jews of the province said to R. Eleazar ben Shammua, "Go and intercede for us." He replied, "Are you not aware that this government does nothing without being paid?" They said to him, "Here are four thousand denars. Take them—go and intercede for us." He took them, went, and, when he reached the gate of the royal palace, said to [the guards], "Go tell the emperor that a Jew is standing at the gate and wishes to greet the emperor." The emperor said, "Bring him in." When the emperor saw R. Eleazar, he leaped up from his throne and prostrated himself before him. Then he asked him, "My lord, what is your quest here, and why have you taken the trouble to come here?" R. Eleazar replied, "In behalf of that province, I came to ask that you annul the decree you just issued." The emperor asked, "Is anything false written in the Torah?" R. Eleazar: "No." The emperor: "Is it not written in your Torah, 'An Ammonite or a Moabite shall not enter into the assembly of the Lord' [Deut. 23:4]? For what reason? 'Because they met you not with bread and with water in the way' [Deut. 23:5]. But it is also written, 'Thou shalt not abhor an Edomite, for he is thy brother' [Deut. 23:8]; and am I not a descendant of Esau, your brother? Nevertheless, the Jews of this province did not treat me with the kindness enjoined! And whoever transgresses the Torah incurs the penalty of death." R. Eleazar ben Shammua replied, "Although they are guilty toward you, forgive them and have mercy on them." The emperor: "Do you know that this government does nothing without being paid?" R. Eleazar: "I have with me four thousand denars. Take them and have mercy upon the people." The emperor: "The four thousand denars are presented to you in exchange for the two hundred you gave me; and on your account, in return for the food and drink in which you provided me, the whole province will be spared. Now enter

1. And I therefore thought that I must have been mistaken in what I believed R. Judah had said, since his other disciples had not heard it.
2. B. Men 18a and En Yaakov, ad loc.
3. Because we were so anxious to learn, we crowded into a small space. B. Er 53a.
4. According to Rashi, a place in Upper Galilee where the cocks allow no strange cock to enter.
5. B. Yev 84a.
6. Sif Deut., §80.

my treasury and take seventy robes, in return for the robe you gave me. Go in peace to your people."

They applied to R. Eleazar the text "Cast thy bread upon the waters" (Eccles. 11:1).[1]

275. Once R. Simeon son of R. Eleazar, coming from Migdal Eder, from the house of his teacher, was riding leisurely on his donkey along the lakeshore, feeling greatly elated and thoroughly satisfied with himself because he had studied much Torah. [While in this mood] he chanced upon an exceedingly ugly man, who greeted him, "Peace be upon you, my master." R. Simeon did not return the greeting but instead said to him, "You worthless creature! How ugly you are! Are all the people of your city as ugly as you?"

The man replied, "I do not know, but go and say to the Craftsman who made me, 'How ugly is the vessel You have made!' "

No sooner did R. Simeon realize that he had done wrong than he got down from the donkey and, prostrating himself before the man, said to him, "I apologize to you; forgive me!"

The man replied, "I will not forgive you until you go to the Craftsman who made me and say to Him, 'How ugly is the vessel You have made!' "

R. Simeon followed him until he reached the man's city. When the people of the city came out to meet R. Simeon, greeting him with the words "Peace be upon you, master, O our master, teacher, O our teacher," the man asked them, "Whom are you addressing as 'master, O our master'?"

They replied, "The man who is walking behind you." Then the man said, "If he is a master, may there be no more like him in Israel!" When the people asked him, "Why?" he replied, "He behaved to me thus and so."

They said to him, "Nevertheless, forgive him, for he is a man greatly learned in the Torah."

The man replied, "For your sakes, I forgive him, but only on condition that he does not make a habit of such misbehavior."

Right after this, R. Simeon son of R. Eleazar entered the house of study and preached, "At all times a man should be pliant as a reed and not hard as a cedar."[2]

Rabban Simeon ben Gamaliel II (2d half of 2d century C.E.)

276. According to R. Judah, Samuel said in the name of Rabban Simeon ben Gamaliel:[3] "I should bring my eyes to tears because of what was done to the families of the city, as shown in my own experience" (Lam. 3:51).[4] In my dear father's house, there were a thousand young men—five hundred of them studied Torah, and the other five hundred studied Greek wisdom—and out of all of them only I here and the son of my father's brother in Asia[5] remain alive.

277. Rabban Simeon ben Gamaliel was patriarch, R. Meir counselor sage, and R. Nathan president of the court. Whenever Rabban Simeon ben Gamaliel entered, all stood up for him; when R. Meir and R. Nathan entered, all stood up for them as well. So Rabban Simeon ben Gamaliel said: Should there be no distinction between my [office] and theirs?[6] So he instituted the following procedure: when the patriarch enters, all the people rise and do not sit down until he says, "Be seated." When the president of the court enters, a row on one side of him and another row on the other side of him rise [to provide a passageway, and remain standing] until he sits down in his place. When the counselor sage enters, each person he passes rises to make room for him and sits down after he passes, while the last person he passes sits down only after he sits down in his place.

R. Meir and R. Nathan were not present in the house of study on the day Rabban Simeon instituted the new procedure. When they came the next day and saw that the people did not rise for them as had been their wont, they inquired, "What's going on here?" When they were told that Rabban Simeon ben Gamaliel had instituted the new procedure, R. Meir said to R. Nathan, "I am counselor sage and you are president of the court. Let us institute something against him." "What do you suggest we do?" "Suppose we say to him, 'Lecture to us upon the tractate Uktzin, a tractate with which he is unfamiliar,' and since he will be unable to lecture upon it, we shall say to him, 'Who may tell the mighty acts of the Lord? He who can proclaim all His praises' [Ps. 106:2]: for whom is it fitting to 'tell the mighty acts of the Lord'? Only for one who can proclaim *all* His praises. We shall then depose him; you will become patriarch and I president of the court."

R. Jacob ben Korshai happened to overhear the conversation and said to himself: This plot may, God forbid, lead to [Rabban Simeon's] humiliation. So he went and sat down behind Rabban Simeon ben Gamaliel's upper chamber, where he kept studying and reciting, studying and reciting the tractate Uktzin, until finally R. Simeon ben Gamaliel asked himself: What can this mean? Could there be, God forbid, a plot against me in the house of study? So he paid close attention [to R. Jacob's recitation] and familiarized himself with the tractate.

The following day, when R. Meir and R. Nathan said to him, "Will our master lecture on Uktzin?" he started lecturing upon it. After he finished, he said to R. Meir and R. Nathan, "Had I not familiarized myself with it, you would have disgraced me publicly!" Then he issued an order, and the two men were removed from the house of study.

After that, R. Meir and R. Nathan would write down

---

1. Eccles. R. 11:1, §1.
2. B. Ta 20a; ARN 41.
3. A survivor of the massacre at Bethar.
4. JV: "Mine eye affected my soul because of all the daughters of my city."
5. The Roman province of Asia, originally the territory of Pergamum in western Asia Minor, B. BK 83a; Sot 49b.
6. "R. Simeon had made this agreement, not from personal motives, but in order to increase the authority of the college over which the *nasi* [patriarch] presided, and to promote the due respect for learning" (J. Z. Lauterbach in *JE* 7:347).

scholastic problems on tablets, which they threw into the house of study. When the problems were dealt with satisfactorily, that was the end of it; but when they were not solved, R. Meir and R. Nathan would write down the solutions, which they again threw into the house of study. R. Yose said to the sages, "Torah is outside but we are inside!" At this, Rabban Simeon ben Gamaliel conceded, "[Very well], we will readmit them, but let us impose on them the penalty that no ruling in *Halakhah* is to be reported in their names." Thereafter, a ruling by R. Meir was quoted anonymously as "Others say," and a ruling by R. Nathan as "Some say."

[Presently], in their dreams, R. Meir and R. Nathan were told, "Go and make peace with Rabban Simeon ben Gamaliel." R. Nathan went, but R. Meir did not, saying, "Dreams are of no consequence."

When R. Nathan came, Rabban Simeon ben Gamaliel remarked to him, "If the exilarch's girdle worn by your father has helped you to become president of the court, who will avail you to become patriarch?"[1]

278. Rabbi [Judah I, the Patriarch] said: Three were humble—my father,[2] the Bene Betera,[3] and Jonathan son of Saul.[4]

279. Isi ben Judah used to call Rabban Simeon ben Gamaliel "a shop stocked with superb purple."[5]

280. When Rabban Simeon ben Gamaliel died, locusts came up,[6] and troubles abounded.[7]

R. Phinehas ben Yair (1st third of 3d century C.E.)

281. It is said of R. Phinehas ben Yair that never in his life did he say grace over a piece of bread that was not his own;[8] and that, from the day he reached the years of discretion, he did not avail himself even of his own father's table.[9]

282. It is related of R. Phinehas ben Yair that when he was living in a city in the south, two poor men came there to seek a livelihood. They had with them two *seah* of barley, which they deposited with him, but then forgot about them and went away. Year after year R. Phinehas ben Yair sowed the barley, reaped it, gathered it, and stored it in a granary. After a lapse of seven years, the two men returned and asked for their barley. R. Phinehas ben Yair recognized them and said, "Fetch camels and asses, and come to take your stores [of grain].[10]

283. While R. Phinehas ben Yair was on his way to ransom captives, he came to the river Ginnai. "O Ginnai," said he, "split your waters for me, that I may pass through you." The river: "You are traveling to do the will of your Maker; I, too, am flowing to do the will of my Maker. You may or may not accomplish your task. I am certain to accomplish mine." R. Phinehas: "If you will not split, I shall decree against you that no water ever pass through you again." The river split. A certain man who was carrying wheat for Passover happened to be there. So R. Phinehas told the river, "Split for this man also, since he is occupied with performing a precept." The river split again. Now, an Arab who had joined them earlier during the journey was there too, and R. Phinehas once again told the river, "Split for this one as well, so that he should not say, 'Is this how a fellow traveler is treated?' " The river split a third time.

His disciples asked, "Can we cross it too?" R. Phinehas replied, "He who feels certain that never in his life has he put a Jew to shame can cross and suffer no harm."

R. Joseph exclaimed: How great is this man [R. Phinehas]—as great as Moses and the sixty myriads [of Israelites together].[11]

Continuing on his journey, R. Phinehas came to a certain inn, where some barley was placed before his donkey, but she would not eat. The barley was sifted, but the donkey would not eat. It was carefully picked; still the donkey would not eat. "Perhaps," suggested R. Phinehas, "the barley has not been tithed?" The barley was tithed, and then the donkey ate it. R. Phinehas said, "This poor creature is on a journey to do the will of her Creator, and you try to feed her untithed grain!"

His disciples asked him, "Our master, did you not teach us that he who purchases [grain from an unlearned person] for an animal is exempt from the obligations about grain that may not have been tithed?" R. Phinehas replied, "But what can I do with this poor creature if she chooses to be strict with herself?"

When Rabbi [Judah] heard of the arrival of R. Phinehas, he went out to meet him and asked him, "Will you please dine with me?" "Certainly," R. Phinehas answered. Rabbi [Judah]'s face at once brightened with joy. So R. Phinehas said, "Did you suppose that I had vowed not to derive any benefit from an Israelite? Oh, no. The people of Israel are holy. But there are some who desire [to benefit others] and have not the means; while others have the means but not the desire, and it is written, 'Never dine with a niggardly man, never fancy his dainties,' etc. [Prov. 23:6]. But you have the desire and also the means. However, right now I am in a hurry, for I am engaged in performing a mitzvah. But on my return, I will come and visit you."

When R. Phinehas returned, he happened to enter

1. B. Hor 13b and En Yaakov, ad loc.
2. Rabban Simeon ben Gamaliel.
3. They were heads of the Sanhedrin in the days of Herod. When they found themselves unable to answer a question concerning Passover, they resigned their post in favor of Hillel, who provided the answer.
4. He told David, "You are going to be king over Israel, and I shall be second to you" (1 Sam. 23:17). B. BM 84b–85a.
5. ARN 18.
6. Possibly tax gatherers who robbed the people.
7. B. Sot 49b.
8. He accepted no invitations.
9. B. Hul 7b.
10. Deut. R. 3:3; P. Dem 1:3, 22a.
11. The river split for him as the sea did for Moses.

[Rabbi (Judah)'s courtyard] by a gate near which some white mules were standing. He exclaimed, "The angel of death is in this house,[1] and I am to dine here!" As soon as Rabbi [Judah] heard what R. Phinehas had said, he went out to him and announced, "I shall sell the mules." R. Phinehas replied, " 'Thou shalt not put a stumbling block before the blind' " (Lev. 19:14). "I shall abandon them." "You would be causing damage [as they run wild]." "I shall hamstring them." "There is a prohibition against inflicting pain on living creatures." "I shall kill them." "That would be counter to the ruling prohibiting wanton waste." As Rabbi [Judah] kept pressing R. Phinehas, a mountain rose up between them.[2]

Then Rabbi burst into tears and said, "If such is [the power of the righteous] while they are alive, how much greater must it be after their death!"[3]

284. A story is told of a pious man who used to dig cisterns, pits, and holes [to contain water] for those who come and go. Once, his daughter, on her way to be wed, was crossing a river and was swept away [by the current]. All the people came to the pious man seeking to comfort him, but he refused the comforting. Even when R. Phinehas ben Yair came to comfort him, he refused his comforting as well. So R. Phinehas asked, "Is this the man you regard as pious?" The people replied, "Our master, the man has been doing such good deeds, and yet such a [cruel] thing befell him." R. Phinehas: "Is it possible that God would chastise with water a man who honored his Creator with water?" Just then a rumor reverberated in the city: The daughter of So-and-so is back. Some say that [as she fell into the water] she was held up by a branch of a thorny tree. Others say that an angel in the likeness of R. Phinehas ben Yair came down and saved her.[4]

285. A story is told of the king of Saracenia, who happened to drop a pearl. A mouse [scampered by and] swallowed it. So the king came to R. Phinehas ben Yair, who asked him, "Am I a worker of magic?" The king: "I came because of your good name." Then R. Phinehas commanded all mice to gather around him. When he saw one of them come in waddling, he said, "Here, the pearl is in this one." Then he commanded the mouse to disgorge, and it spewed out the pearl.[5]

R. Judah I, the Patriarch (Rabbi, Our Holy Rabbi); R. Hiyya the Elder and His Sons (fl. last quarter of 2d century to beginning of 3d century C.E.)

286. As soon as R. Akiva died, Rabbi was born.[6]

287. At one time the [Roman] government issued a decree prohibiting Israel from circumcising their children. During that period, our holy Rabbi was born. His father, Rabban Simeon ben Gamaliel, asked: How dare we set aside the decree of the Holy One and comply with the decree of these wicked ones? Immediately he rose up and circumcised his son.

When the magistrate in charge of the city heard of this, he had Rabban Simeon ben Gamaliel summoned and asked him: Why did you violate the emperor's decree? Rabban Simeon: We are only doing what the Holy One commanded us. The magistrate: I have great respect for you, since you are the head of your people. But it is the emperor's decree, and I cannot allow you to violate it. Rabban Simeon: What do you intend to do? The magistrate: We will send your family to the emperor, and he will do what he wishes. So he dispatched our holy Rabbi and his mother to the emperor. After journeying all day, toward evening, they arrived at the inn kept by the grandfather of Antoninus.[7] And as it happened, Antoninus was born at the very time our holy Rabbi was born. Our holy Rabbi's mother, held in affection by Antoninus's mother, went to her at once. [Upon seeing her distress], Antoninus's mother asked: What troubles you? The mother of our Rabbi: Such-and-such—that we do not circumcise—was decreed against us, and since I did circumcise my son, he and I are being taken to the emperor. When the mother of Antoninus heard this, she said: If you wish, take my child, who is not circumcised, and give me your child. She did what was suggested, and the mother of our holy Rabbi continued her journey.

Upon her arrival, the magistrate in charge of her city brought her into the presence of the emperor. The emperor commanded that the child be examined, and they found him to be uncircumcised.

At that, the emperor, furious at the magistrate, roared: My decree concerned circumcised children, and you brought me an uncircumcised child! The emperor commanded that the magistrate be put to death, while our holy Rabbi and his mother were sent away in peace.

When the two returned to the house of Antoninus, his mother said: Since the Holy One has wrought a miracle for you through me and for your son through my son, let them always be friends.[8]

288. From the days of Moses to Rabbi, we find no other person in whom Torah and wealth were combined.[9]

289. R. Simeon ben Menasya said in the name of R. Simeon ben Yohai: Beauty and strength, wealth and honor, wisdom and hoary age, and children are an ornament to the righteous and an ornament to the world.

The aforementioned seven qualities, which the sages specified as becoming to the righteous, were all realized in Rabbi and his sons.[10]

---

1. White mules are prone to kick and kill.
2. So that dining at Rabbi's home became impossible.
3. B. Hul 7a–b; P. Dem 1:3, 22a.
4. P. Dem 1:3, 22a; Deut. R. 3:3.
5. P. Dem 1:3, 22a.
6. B. Kid 72a.
7. Marcus Aurelius, surnamed Antoninus, was to become emperor of Rome (161–80 C.E.).
8. BhM 6:130–31; Tosafot on B. AZ 10b.
9. B. Git 59a.
10. B. Avot 6:8; P. Sanh 11:4, 38a.

290. After R. Eleazar son of R. Simeon died, Rabbi sent messengers to propose marriage to his widow. She responded with the question "Shall a untensil used for holy food be used for profane food?" Rabbi sent messengers again: "Granted that he may have outstripped me in learning, but was he at all my superior in good deeds?" She replied, "As for learning, I do not know whether or not he was greater than you. But [that he was greater than you] in good deeds, I know full well, since he invoked suffering upon himself."[1]

So, declaring, "Suffering is precious," Rabbi invoked suffering upon himself for thirteen years, six through stones in the kidneys, and seven through scurvy.

Rabbi's steward was wealthier than King Shapur. [So numerous were his cattle that] when he set out fodder for them, their lowing could be heard for three *mil*; and he deliberately set out their fodder just when Rabbi was entering the privy [in order that Rabbi's cries of pain would not be heard]. Yet even so, Rabbi's voice [lifted in pain] was louder than that of the cattle and could be heard even by distant seafarers.

Nevertheless, the sufferings of R. Eleazar son of R. Simeon were superior [in virtue] to those of Rabbi. For whereas those of R. Eleazar son of R. Simeon came to him directly in consequence of his love [of God] and departed in such love, those of Rabbi came to him as the result of an incident [in which he acted improperly] and departed as a result of another incident in which he acted properly.

They came to him because of an incident [in which he acted improperly]: A calf was being taken to be slaughtered. Just then Rabbi was seated in front of the Babylonians' house of study in Sepphoria. The calf broke away, hid its head under Rabbi's skirts, and lowed pitifully, as though pleading, "Save me." "Go," said Rabbi. "For this you were created."

Then it was said [in heaven], "Since he has no pity, let the suffering [he invoked sometime ago] come upon him now."

And they departed because of another incident [in which he acted properly]: One day Rabbi's maidservant was sweeping the house. [Seeing] some young weasels lying there, she was about to sweep them away. "Let them be," he said to her, "for it is written, 'And His tender mercies are over all His works' " (Ps. 145:9).

Then it was said [in heaven], "Since he is compassionate, let Us be compassionate to him."[2]

291. R. Yose bar Avin said: During the entire thirteen years that Rabbi suffered from pain in his teeth [brought on by scurvy], there were no miscarriages in the Land of Israel and no women suffered pain in childbirth.

Our Rabbi was very modest and used to say, "I am prepared to do whatever any person tells me, except what the Bene Betera did for my ancestor [Hillel]—they actually relinquished their high office and promoted him to it. Still, if R. Huna the Exilarch were to come up to the Land, I would [relinquish my office and] seat him above me, for he is descended from Judah, while I am descended from Benjamin; he is descended from Judah on the male side, while I am descended [from Judah] only on the female side." But when R. Hiyya the Elder said to him, "Look, R. Huna is outside!" Rabbi's face went pale. When R. Hiyya saw that Rabbi's face had gone pale, he said, "It is R. Huna's coffin that has come." Rabbi said to R. Hiyya, "Go and see who wants you outside." When he went out and found no one, he knew that he was placed under a ban—and a ban is no fewer than thirty days.

R. Yose bar Avin remarked: During those thirty days that R. Hiyya the Elder was under Rabbi's ban, he taught Rav, his sister's son, all the [exegetical] principles of the Torah—the source for the halakhic rulings of the Babylonians.

At the end of the thirty days, the prophet Elijah, ever remembered for good, came before Rabbi disguised as R. Hiyya the Elder and laid his hand upon his teeth, which were promptly cured. The next day, when R. Hiyya visited Rabbi and asked him, "How are your teeth?" Rabbi replied, "Since you laid your hand upon them, they have been cured." "I know nothing about it," R. Hiyya said, and then went on to say, "Alas for you, O women in the Land of Israel who are about to give birth. Alas for you, O unborn infants."[3]

When R. Hiyya told Rabbi, "I know nothing about it," Rabbi realized that it was Elijah, ever remembered on good occasions, who had healed him. Thereafter Rabbi began to defer to R. Hiyya—so much so that he told his disciples to seat R. Hiyya on an inner bench [near his own person]. R. Ishmael son of R. Yose protested, "Even in front of me?" Rabbi: "Heaven forbid! Such a thing shall not be done in Israel. R. Hiyya is to be seated on an inner bench, but R. Ishmael son of R. Yose is to be seated on an innermost bench."[4]

292. Our masters taught: Once Rabbi, suffering from a pain in his stomach, asked, "Does anyone know whether a heathen's apple cider is prohibited or permitted?" R. Ishmael son of R. Yose replied, "My father once had the same complaint, and they brought him a heathen's apple cider which was seventy years old; he drank it and recovered." Rabbi: "All this time you knew the law as well as the cider's effectiveness, and you let me suffer!" Upon inquiry, they found a heathen who possessed three hundred kegs of apple cider seventy years old. Rabbi drank some of it and recovered. At that, he exclaimed, "Blessed be He who is everywhere, who has delivered His universe into the keeping of those who guard its well-being."[5]

293. Once, when R. Hiyya and R. Simeon bar Rabbi sat together, one of them began the following discussion: A man at prayer should direct his eyes downward [toward the place here on earth where the Temple once stood], in keeping with the verse "And Mine eyes and Mine heart

1. See above in this chapter, §233.
2. B. BM 84b–85a; Gen. R. 33:3.
3. Now that Rabbi, freed of his pain, no longer shields you.
4. Gen. R. 33:3 and 96:5; P. Kil 9:3, 32b.
5. He thanked God that the beverage that could cure him had been preserved for the seventy years needed to make it effective. B. AZ 40b.

shall be there perpetually" (1 Kings 9:3). But the other said: He should direct his eyes upward [toward the heavens], for it is said, "Let us lift up our heart with our hands, unto God in the heavens" (Lam. 3:41). Meanwhile R. Yose bar Avin son of R. Yose had joined them, and he asked, "What subject are you discussing?" "One's posture at prayer." R. Ishmael: "My father ruled thus: 'A man at prayer should direct his eyes downward and direct his heart upward so that both verses may be complied with."

While this discussion was going on, Rabbi entered the house of study.[1] R. Hiyya and R. Simeon, being nimble, got to their places quickly and sat down. But R. Ishmael son of R. Yose, who moved slowly because of his corpulence, sought to take a shortcut to his place by laboriously striding [over the heads of the disciples seated on the ground].[2] Avdan[3] cried out to him, "Who is this person who dares stride over the heads of a holy people?" R. Ishmael: "It is I, Ishmael son of R. Yose, who have come to learn Torah from Rabbi." Avdan: "Are you qualified to learn Torah from Rabbi?" R. Ishmael: "Was Moses qualified to learn Torah from the lips of the Almighty?" "Are you Moses?" "Is your Rabbi God?"

While this was going on, the widow of a man who had died without issue came before Rabbi [to ask for release through the rite of *halitzah*]. Rabbi said to Avdan, "Go out, and arrange to ascertain [whether she has reached puberty].[4] After Avdan had gone out, R. Ishmael said to Rabbi, "Thus said my father: 'In the relevant portion in Scripture [Deut. 25:7], the future husband of the widow is designated as "[adult] man,"[5] whereas the age of the widow, whether adult or minor, is not specified. [Hence her release through *halitzah* is effective in any case.]' " "Come back," Rabbi cried after Avdan. "You need not [arrange for any examination]; the venerable sage has already taught us the decision [on the subject]." Avdan, in a hurry to get back, proceeded to stride [over the heads of disciples seated on the ground]. So R. Ishmael son of R. Yose said to him, "A man [like me], whom the holy people need, may stride over the heads of a holy people. But how dare a man [like you], whom the holy people do not need, dare stride over the heads of a holy people?" At that, Rabbi said to Avdan,"Stay where you are."[6]

294. Rabbi sat [in the teacher's chair] and said, "[On the Sabbath] it is forbidden to store cold [water in sand to keep the water cold]." R. Ishmael son of R. Yose timidly spoke up: "My father permitted it." Rabbi: "[So be it.] The venerable sage has already taught us the proper ruling."

Regarding Rabbi's response, R. Papa said: Pause and consider how much the two sages cherished each other. Were R. Yose alive, he would have sat deferentially before Rabbi, since we know that R. Ishmael son of R. Yose, fully as learned as his forebears, sat deferentially before Rabbi. Yet Rabbi said of R. Yose, "The venerable sage has already taught us the proper ruling."[7]

295. Rabbi kept extolling R. Hiyya the Elder in the presence of R. Ishmael son of R. Yose, saying, "A great man, a holy man!" One day, R. Ishmael saw him in the bathhouse, and R. Hiyya did not stand up for him. So R. Ishmael said to Rabbi, "I saw this disciple of yours, whom you praised so highly, in the bathhouse, and he did not stand up for me." Later, Rabbi asked R. Hiyya, "Why did you not stand up for R. Ishmael?" R. Hiyya replied, "I was absorbed in the *Aggadah* on Psalms." When Rabbi heard this, he assigned two disciples to accompany R. Hiyya, so that he should not expose himself to danger [by falling into a pit or stumbling over a stone].[8]

296. While Rabbi was expounding Scripture, he became aware of the odor of garlic. So he said, "Let him who has eaten garlic leave." R. Hiyya got up and left. Then all the other disciples got up and left [to share the blame]. The next morning R. Simeon, Rabbi's son, met R. Hiyya and said to him, "So it is you who upset my father yesterday!" R. Hiyya: "God forbid that I should be guilty of such a thing in Israel."[9]

297. The prophet Elijah used to frequent Rabbi's house of study. One day—it was the new moon—Elijah was late. [When he did come] Rabbi asked him, "Why was the master delayed today?" Elijah replied, "[I had to wait] until I woke Abraham, washed his hands, let him say his prayers, and put him back to bed. And the same for Isaac and for Jacob."

"But why did not the master wake the three of them at the same time?"

"I feared that the three, praying forcefully together, might bring the Messiah before his time."

Rabbi: "And are their likes to be found in this world?" Elijah: "There are—R. Hiyya and his sons." So Rabbi proclaimed a fast, and R. Hiyya and his sons were requested to descend [to the reading desk].[10] When the three read, "He causeth the wind to blow," a wind blew; when they read, "He causeth the rain to descend," rain descended. When they were about to read, "He quickeneth the dead," the universe trembled. At that, it was asked in heaven, "Who has revealed this secret to the world?"[11] The reply: "Elijah." So Elijah was summoned and flogged with sixty lashes of fire. Then Elijah, disguised as a fiery bear, came into the midst of the three at prayer and dispersed them.[12]

1. When everyone present was expected to take his usual place.
2. During a master's discourses, the disciples were seated in Eastern fashion on the ground.
3. One of Rabbi's disciples. Avdan is a contraction of Abba Yudan, the name by which he is known in the Palestinian Talmud.
4. And is consequently eligible to perform *halitzah*.
5. Which excludes a minor.
6. B. Yev 105b and En Yaakov, ad loc.
7. B. Sanh 24a.
8. Gen. R. 33:3; P. Kil 9:3, 32b.
9. He assumed the blame for the offensive odor, in order to avoid a lengthy interruption devoted to finding out who the real offender was. B. Sanh 11a and En Yaakov, ad loc.
10. In talmudic times the reading desk in a synagogue was on a level lower than the rest of the building. On fast days, three men instead of one led the congregation in prayer.
11. That R. Hiyya's prayers are so efficacious.
12. B. BM 85b.

298. On one occasion, Rabbi decreed that disciples should not be taught in the marketplace. Nevertheless, R. Hiyya went out into the marketplace and taught Rav and Rabbah bar Bar Hana, sons of his two brothers. When Rabbi heard of this, he took offense. So the next time R. Hiyya appeared before him, Rabbi said to him, "Iyya,[1] go see who is calling you outside."[2] Realizing that Rabbi had taken his disobedience to heart, he submitted on his own for thirty days to the ban following a reproof. On the thirtieth day, Rabbi sent word to him: "Come." When he came, Rabbi asked him, "Why did you disregard my decree?" "Because," R. Hiyya replied, "it is written, 'Wisdom crieth aloud in the streets' " (Prov. 1:20). Rabbi said to him, "You may have read Scripture once but not twice, or if twice not thrice, or if thrice, then it was not explained to you properly. What the text means is that when one studies Torah indoors, the Torah proclaims his merit outside [in the streets]."[3]

299. Rabbi and R. Hiyya were on a journey, and when they came to a certain town, they said, "If there is a disciple of the wise here, we shall go and pay our respects to him." They were told, "There is one disciple of the wise here, but he is blind." R. Hiyya said to Rabbi, "Stay [here]. You must not lower your patriarchal dignity. I shall go and pay my respects for both of us." But Rabbi took hold of R. Hiyya and went with him. As they were about to leave that disciple of the wise, he said to them, "You have paid your respects to one who can be seen but cannot see; may you be granted the privilege of paying your respects to Him who sees but cannot be seen." Hearing that, Rabbi said to R. Hiyya, "And you would have deprived me of such a blessing!"[4]

300. After Rabbi had learned thirteen variant interpretations in *Halakhah*, he taught R. Hiyya only seven of them. Eventually Rabbi fell sick [and forgot his learning]. Then R. Hiyya restored to him the seven interpretations that Rabbi had taught him, but the other six were lost. Now, there was a certain fuller who had overheard Rabbi when he was studying them by himself, and he had come to know all of them. So R. Hiyya went to the fuller's house and learned them from his mouth, and then he was able to restore them to Rabbi. When Rabbi met the fuller, he said to him, "You taught[5] both R. Hiyya and me." Others say that Rabbi said to the fuller, "You taught R. Hiyya, and he taught me."[6]

301. On the eve of the fast of the ninth of Av, which fell on a Sabbath, from the time of the afternoon prayer onward, Rabbi, R. Hiyya the Elder, and R. Ishmael son of R. Yose were engaged in setting forth the literal meaning of the Scroll of Lamentations. [Because it was already growing dark], they left out one of the acrostic chapters, saying, "We shall complete the scroll tomorrow." When Rabbi was about to leave for home, he caught his small toe [and fell down, hurting himself]. So he applied to his own person the words "Many are the sufferings of the wicked" (Ps. 32:10). R. Hiyya said to him, "This befell you because of our wrongdoing, as it is written, 'The breath of our nostrils, the anointed of the Lord, was caught through our fault' " (Lam. 4:20). R. Ishmael son of R. Yose said to him, "Even if this were not from the passage we failed to deal with, we might have quoted it to Rabbi; all the more so when it is precisely the passage we failed to deal with."[7]

302. Judah and Hezekiah, the [twin][8] sons of R. Hiyya, once sat at table with Rabbi without uttering a word. Finally Rabbi said: Give the lads plenty of wine, to induce them to say something. When they were feeling the wine's effect, they began by saying: [Messiah] the son of David will not appear before the two ruling houses in Israel—the exilarchate in Babylonia and the patriarchate in the Land of Israel—come to an end, for it is written, "And [the son of David] shall be for a Sanctuary, for a stone of stumbling, and for a rock of offense to both houses of Israel" (Isa. 8:14). Rabbi exclaimed: sons, you are thrusting thorns into my eyes![9] At this, R. Hiyya remarked: Master, do not be angry, for the numerical value of the letters in *yayin*[10] is seventy, and likewise the letters in *sod.*[11] When *yayin* ("wine") goes in, *sod* ("secret") comes out.[12]

303. The people of Simonia[13] came to Rabbi and said: Please give us a man who can act as expounder of Scripture, judge, children's preceptor, scribe, and teacher of the Oral Law, thus providing all the services we need. He gave them Levi ben Sisi. They erected a large dais, had him sit in a seat high above it, and proceeded to ask him a question in *Halakhah*, which he could not answer. So they said: He may not be a master of *Halakhah*. Then they asked him a question in *Aggadah*, and again he could not answer. So they went to Rabbi and said: Is this the kind of person we asked you go give us? He replied: As you live, I have given you a man as good as I. Rabbi and Levi sent for and asked him about the same *Halakhah*, and he gave the relevant answer; about the same *Aggadah*, and again he gave the relevant answer. Then Rabbi asked Levi: Why were you unable to answer the people of Simonia? Levi replied: They erected a huge dais for me and had me sit in a seat high above it, and my opinion of myself grew so exalted that words of Torah escaped me. Rabbi applied to him the verse "If thou hast been humiliated, it is because of exaltation so great that thou didst have to clap thy hand

1. He imitated R. Hiyya's inability to distinguish between the several gutturals.
2. A polite way of commanding him to leave the academy.
3. M. MK 16b and En Yaakov, ad loc.
4. B. Hag 5b.
5. Literally, "made."
6. B. Ned 41a.
7. P. Shab 16:1, 15c; Lev. R. 15:4.
8. See B. Yev 65b.
9. Foretelling as they did the abolition of the patriarch's office, which he occupied.
10. *Yod* (10) + *yod* (10) + *nun* (50) = 70.
11. *Samekh* (60) + *vav* (6) + *dalet* (4) = 70.
12. B. Sanh 38a.
13. A town in Lower Galilee.

over thy mouth" (Prov. 30:32).[1] What caused you to be humiliated in matters of Torah [you knew so well]? Your having allowed yourself to be exalted on account of them.[2]

304. There were two mutes in Rabbi's neighborhood, and whenever Rabbi entered the house of study, they, too, entered. Sitting down before him, they nodded their heads and moved their lips. Rabbi besought mercy in their behalf, and they were healed. Then it was discovered that they were versed in *Halakhah*—in the Sifra [on Leviticus], in the Sifre [on Numbers and Deuteronomy], in the Tosefta; indeed, in the entire Talmud.[3]

305. R. Hone said: The sages did not know what the words *serugin, haloglogot,* and *matate* meant; nor who is to be more deferred to—one greater in wisdom or one greater in years. They decided: Let us go and inquire at the house of Rabbi. When they got there, one said to the other, "Let So-and-so go in first." "No, let So-and-so go in first." A maidservant of Rabbi's came out and said, "Enter according to your seniority in years." They began entering at intervals. So she asked them, "Why are you entering *serugin, serugin* ('in a broken line')?" Among them was a young man carrying purslane, which fell from his hand. So the maidservant said, "Young man, your *haloglogot* ('purslane') has fallen all over the place. I will bring a matate," and she brought a broom [and swept it up].[4]

306. Once when Rabbi happened to visit the place where R. Eleazar son of R. Simeon lived, he inquired of the inhabitants, "Did that righteous man leave a son?" "Yes," he was told, "and [he is so handsome that] every harlot whose hire is two *zuz* hires him for four." So Rabbi had him brought into his presence [and was so impressed by him that] he ordained him and entrusted him to R. Simeon ben Issi ben Lakonia, his mother's brother [to be taught]. Every day R. Eleazar's son would say, "I want to go back to my village," to which R. Simeon would reply, "They have made you a sage [at the ceremony of ordination] and spread over you a cloak trimmed with gold; they address you as 'Rabbi.' And yet you say, I want to go back to my village!" Finally R. Eleazar's son said, "I swear not to speak of it again [and henceforth will devote myself to study]." When he became a great scholar, he went and sat in Rabbi's academy. On hearing his voice, Rabbi observed, "This voice is like the voice of R. Eleazar son of R. Simeon." He was told, "He is his son." So Rabbi applied to him the verse "The fruit of the righteous is a tree of life; and he that winneth souls is the true sage" (Prov. 11:30). [Thus] "the fruit of the righteous is a tree of life" applies to R. Yose son of R. Eleazar son of R. Simeon; "and he that winneth souls is the true sage" applies to R. Simeon ben Issi ben Lakonia.

When R. Yose died, he was carried to the cave in which his father was buried. The cave's entry was girdled by a snake. "Snake, O snake," they adjured it, "open your mouth [to release your tail] and let the son come to be with his father"; but it would not open its mouth for them. Now, the people thought that it was because the father was greater in learning than the son. But a divine voice came forth and proclaimed, "It is not because the father is greater in learning than the son, but because the father underwent suffering in the cave, and the son did not.[5]

307. Rabbi once happened to visit R. Tarfon's town, where he asked the inhabitants, "Has that righteous man, who used to swear by the life of his children, left a son?" They replied, "He left no son, but a daughter's son remains, and [he is so handsome that] every harlot who is hired for two *zuz* hires him for four." So Rabbi had him brought into his presence [and was so impressed by him that he] said to him, "Should you repent, I will give you my daughter in marriage." He did repent. Some say, he married Rabbi's daughter but later divorced her; others that in fact he did not marry her, lest it be said that his repentance was on her account.[6]

308. During years of scarcity, Rabbi opened his storehouse of victuals, proclaiming: Let those who are masters of Scripture, masters of Mishnah, masters of Gemara, masters of *Halakhah*, or masters of *Aggada* enter, but those who are unlearned may not. R. Jonathan ben Amram pushed his way in and said to Rabbi, "Master, give me food." Rabbi asked him, "My son, have you studied Scripture?" He replied, "No." "Have you studied Mishnah?" "No." "If so, how can I give you food?" R. Jonathan: "Give me food, for even a dog and a raven are given food."[7] So he gave him some food. After he went away, Rabbi's conscience troubled him, and he said: Woe is me that I have given my bread to a man without learning! R. Simeon bar Rabbi ventured to say to him, "Perhaps it is your disciple Jonathan ben Amram, who all his life has refused to derive any perquisite from honor paid to the Torah." Upon inquiry, it was found to be so. As a result, Rabbi said, "All may enter."[8]

309. All a disciple of Rabbi's had was two hundred *zuz* less one.[9] Every three years,[10] Rabbi was in the habit of bestowing on him the tithe for the poor. Once it happened that some of Rabbi's disciples cast a jaundiced eye upon this disciple and [gave him one *zuz*], bringing the amount he owned to two hundred *zuz*. When Rabbi came, as had been his custom, to give him the tithe, the disciple said, "Master, now I own the minimum that makes it impossible for me to accept the poor man's tithe." Rabbi replied,

1. JV: "If thou hast done foolishly in lifting up thyself, or if thou hast planned devices, lay thy hand upon thy mouth." But *zammota* ("thou hast planned devices") may also mean "thou art muzzled," hence, "clap thy hand over thy mouth."
2. P. Yev 12:6, 13a; Gen. R. 81:2.
3. B. Hag 3a and En Yaakov, ad loc.
4. P. Meg 2:2, 73a.
5. See above §221 in this chapter, and §233. B. BM 85a.
6. B. BM 85a.
7. The verse "He giveth to the beast his food, to the young ravens which cry" (Ps. 147:9), R. Jonathan takes to mean, "As God feeds these, so you, feed me."
8. B. BB 8a.
9. Which gave him the status of poverty.
10. The third and sixth years in the seven-year cycle.

"The kind of stratagem hypocrites use has struck this poor man." So he hinted to the other disciples that they take this one into a food shop where, through a small purchase, he would be made poorer by one coin the size of a carob seed. Then, as had been his custom, Rabbi was again able to bestow the tithe on the poor disciple.[1]

310. Our Rabbi used to declare pounded beans ownerless [public property] so that R. Simeon ben Halafta might acquire them.[2]

311. Rabbi made a feast for his disciples, serving them tongues that were tender as well as tongues that were tough. They proceeded to select the tender tongues and passed up the tough ones. So he said to them: Take heed of what you are doing. Even as you select the tender and pass up the tough, so let your tongues be tender, gentle toward one another.[3]

312. Rabbi said: Trouble comes to the world only because of the unlearned.

The incident of the royal crown for whose payment the inhabitants of Tiberias were taxed confirms what Rabbi said. For at that time, when the inhabitants of Tiberias came to Rabbi and said, "Let the sages give their share with us," he refused. "Then we will run away," they said. "Run," he replied. So half the unlearned ran away. At that, the [Roman] emperor remitted half the sum demanded. The other half of the inhabitants then came to Rabbi and said, "Let the sages give their share with us." He again refused. "We will run away," they said. "Run," he replied. So they, too, ran away, leaving only a certain fuller. The money was then demanded of him, and he also ran away. Consequently, the demand for money for the crown was dropped.

At this, Rabbi said, "You see, trouble comes to the world only because of the unlearned."[4]

313. R. Judah said in the name of Samuel: For each festal day of the Romans, the household of Rabbi had to present them with a fatted ox. A sum of forty thousand coins had to be paid for the concession to present the ox not on the festal day itself but on the following day. Another forty thousand coins had to be paid for permission to present the ox not alive but slaughtered. Finally, forty thousand coins more had to be paid for exemption from the obligation of presenting the ox at all.[5]

314. The story is told of thirteen brothers—twelve of them died childless—whose widows came before Rabbi, asking to marry the surviving brother. Rabbi said to him: Go and take them in levirate marriage. The brother: I do not have the means to maintain all of them. The widows: Each of us will maintain the household for one month during the year. The brother: But who will maintain it during the thirteenth month that is intercalated?[6] Rabbi: I will maintain the household during that month. He prayed in their behalf, and they went away. After three years, they came carrying thirty-six babies—came and stood in front of Rabbi's house. Rabbi was told: A village of babies are here to greet you. Rabbi looked out of a window and saw them. He asked: What brings you here? The women: We are here to ask that you maintain us during this thirteenth month. So that month, maintain them he did![7]

315. Rabbi came out of the bathhouse, wrapped himself in his garments, and sat down to attend to the people's needs. Though Rabbi's servant mixed a cup of water and wine for him, Rabbi was so busy attending to people's needs that he could not spare a moment to take it from his servant, who [kept holding it until he] dozed off. Then Rabbi turned and gazed at him, and said, Solomon put it well: "Sweet is the sleep of the laboring man, whether he eat little or much; but the satiety of the rich will not suffer him to sleep" (Eccles. 5:11)—those [rich in Torah] like ourselves are so busy attending to the people's needs that we are not even allowed to sleep.[8]

316. Rabbi showed respect to rich men.

Thus, when Bonyos ben Bonyos once visited Rabbi, Rabbi called out, "Make room for the owner of one hundred *maneh.*" When another person entered, he called out, "Make [more] room for the owner of two hundred *maneh.*" "Master," R. Ishmael son of R. Yose said, "Bonyos's father has a thousand ships at sea and an equal number of hamlets on land [yet to the one who came later you gave more room]." So Rabbi said, "When you meet Bonyos's father, tell him, 'Do not send your son to me wearing garments so drab.' "[9]

317. Rabbi once asked R. Joshua ben Korhal, "How have you managed to reach such long life?" R. Joshua: "Do you begrudge me the length of my life?" Rabbi: "My inquiry is concerned with Torah, [whose precepts for long life] it is necessary for me to learn." R. Joshua: "In my life I never gazed at the countenance of a wicked man."[10]

As R. Joshua was about to die, Rabbi said to him, "Bless me." R. Joshua: "May it be [Heaven's] will that you reach half my days." Rabbi: "Not their entire number?" R. Joshua: "[While you go on living], will you have the generation after you do nothing but graze cattle?"[11]

318. It was said of Antoninus and Rabbi that during summer or winter, neither radishes nor lettuce nor cucumbers ever ceased being served at their tables.[12]

1. P. Sot 3:4, 19a.
2. Ruth R. 5:17, §7.
3. Lev. R. 33:1; Yalkut, Ps., §767.
4. It was only because of them that money for the crown was demanded in the first place. B. BB 8a.
5. B. AZ 16a.
6. In a leap year.
7. P. Yev 4:12, 6b.
8. Eccles. R. 5:11, §1.
9. B. Er 85b–86a.
10. Thus Elisha said to wicked King Jehoram, "Were it not that I respect King Jehoshaphat of Judah, I would not look at you or notice you" (2 Kings 3:14).
11. Since they are going to be scholars, they will have no positions of dignity if you continue to live. B. Meg 28a.
12. Vegetables conducive to good health and good appetite. B. AZ 11a.

319. Our Rabbi instructed R. Aphes: Write a letter in my behalf to our lord, the emperor Antoninus. So he wrote, "From Judah the Patriarch to our lord emperor Antoninus." Rabbi took it, read it, and tore it up. Then he said, "Write, 'From your servant Judah to our lord emperor Antoninus.' " R. Aphes asked, "Master, why do you make so little of your dignity?" Rabbi replied, "Am I better than my ancstor Jacob? Did not Jacob say, 'Thus saith thy servant Jacob' (Gen. 32:5)?"[1]

320. Whenever our Rabbi had to travel to the government [in Rome], he would look at this text[2] and then not take any Roman with him. One time he neglected to look at this text and took some Romans with him. Before he reached Acco, he had to sell even his traveling cloak.[3]

321. It happened once that when Antoninus came to Caesarea, he sent for our holy Rabbi, who arrived accompanied by his son R. Simeon and by R. Hiyya the Elder. When R. Simeon saw there a legion whose soldiers were comely, strong, and so tall that their heads seemed to reach the capitals of columns, he said to R. Hiyya, "See how fattened Esau's calves are." R. Hiyya then took R. Simeon and led him to the marketplace, where he saw a basket of grapes and figs with flies [buzzing] over them. R. Hiyya said, "These flies and that legion are alike." Later, when R. Simeon came up to his father's home, he said, "This is what I said to R. Hiyya, and that is how he replied to me." Rabbi commented, "R. Hiyya the Babylonian ascribed too much substance to them by likening them to flies. These legions are regarded [by God] as nothing at all. But flies—through them, God executes His commissions."[4]

322. Antoninus asked Rabbi, "Why does the sun rise in the east and set in the west?" Rabbi: "Were it the other way around, you would have asked the same question." Antoninus: "My question still stands—why should the sun set in the west? [Why does it not return to the east, where it has risen, or to any other point in the sky?]" Rabbi: "The sun sets in the west to make obeisance to its Maker,[5] as is said, 'The host of the heavens makes obeisance to Thee' " (Neh. 9:6). Antoninus: "Then let the sun go midway in heaven, make obeisance,[6] and set at once." Rabbi: "For the sake of workers and wayfarers [the sun sinks gradually]."[7]

323. Antoninus asked our holy Rabbi, "Is one allowed to pray every hour?" "It is forbidden." Antoninus: "Why?" Rabbi: "So that one should not become irreverent toward the Almighty." Antoninus refused to accept this explanation. What did our holy Rabbi do? Early in the morning he went to the palace of Antoninus and called out, "Hail, O lord."[8] An hour later, he came again: "[Hail], Emperor." After another hour: "Peace upon you, O King." At this, Antoninus asked, "Why do you treat royalty with such contempt?" Rabbi replied, "Let your ears hear what your mouth utters. If you, who are no more than flesh and blood, characterize him who salutes you every hour as one who holds you in contempt, surely a man should not burden every hour [with his prayers] the King who is King of kings."[9]

324. Antoninus came to Rabbi and said, "Pray for me." Rabbi: "May it be [Heaven's] will that you be delivered from cold." Antoninus: "This prayer makes no sense. Add a garment, and the cold goes away." So Rabbi said, "May it be [Heaven's will] that you be delivered from dry heat." Antoninus: "Now this prayer makes sense. O that your prayer could be accepted, for Scripture says, 'Nothing can escape the sun's heat' " (Ps. 19:7).[10]

325. When our Rabbi entertained Antoninus on the Sabbath, he served him cold dishes, which Antoninus ate and liked. On another occasion, our Rabbi entertained him on a weekday, when he served him hot dishes. Antoninus said, "I found the cold dishes more tasty than the hot." Our Rabbi: "The hot dishes lack one seasoning." Antoninus: "Can there be anything at all lacking in the emperor's pantry?" Our Rabbi: "The hot dishes lack Sabbath. Does your pantry have Sabbath?"[11]

326. Antoninus once said to Rabbi, "It is my desire that my son Severus should reign in my stead and that Tiberias should be declared a [Roman] colony [free of taxes]. Were I to make just one request of the senators, they would comply. But if there were two requests, they would not." At that, Rabbi brought a man, had him climb atop his companion, handed the one on top a dove, and then had the one below tell the one on top to let the dove in his hand go free. So Antoninus said to himself: It seems that Rabbi intimates: Ask the Senate to confirm my son Severus to reign in my stead, and tell Severus that Tiberias is to be made a colony.

[On another occasion] Antoninus said to Rabbi, "Certain prominent Romans distress me." At that, Rabbi proceeded to bring him into a garden, where on each of several days, in Antoninus's presence, he pulled out a single radish from the radish patch. Antoninus said to himself: It seems that Rabbi intimates: Do away with them singly, one at a time, but do not attack all of them at once.

Antoninus had a daughter named Gira, who had gone astray. So he sent Rabbi a *gargira* [a garden rocket (an herb also known as arugula), intimating that Gira had *gar*, "gone astray"]. Rabbi in return sent him *kusbarta* [cor-

1. The point: Jacob, R. Judah's ancestor, was submissive to Esau, Rome's ancestor. Gen. R. 75:5.
2. In which Jacob rejected Esau's offer "Let me now leave with thee some of the folk" (Gen. 33:15).
3. Because they robbed him. Gen. R. 78:15; Yalkut, *Va-yishlah*, §133.
4. Tanhuma, *Va-yeshev*, §3.
5. The Presence dwells in the west.
6. At some distance from its Maker, as is done in royal courts.
7. If the sun sank suddenly, they would have no way of planning when to stop work or halt in their journey. B. Sanh 91b.
8. *Kiri keri*; Greek: *Kyrie chaire*.
9. Tanhuma, *Mi-ketz*, §9.
10. P. Sanh 10:5, 29c.
11. B. Shab 119a; Gen. R. 11:4.

iander, intimating, *kus*, "slay," *barta*, "the daughter"]. Antoninus then sent *karata* [leeks, intimating, "If so, my line will be *karata*—cut off"]. So in response, Rabbi sent him *hassa* [lettuce, intimating *hus*, "spare her"].

Each and every day, Antoninus would send Rabbi a leather bag filled with granules of gold, topped with a layer of wheat, saying to his messenger, "Carry this wheat to Rabbi." After a while, Rabbi said, "I do not need your gold; I have enough gold of my own." But Antoninus answered, "Then leave it to those who will come after you, for they will be forced to give it [as bribes] to those who will come after me."

Antoninus had an underground passage whereby he went from his palace to Rabbi's house. Every time [he visited Rabbi], he had two slaves with him—one he put to death at the door of Rabbi's house, and the other [who had been left behind] he put to death [on his return] at the door of his own home. Antoninus also said to Rabbi, "When I call, make sure that no one else is with you." One day, when he found R. Hanina ben Hama sitting there, he said to Rabbi, "Did I not tell you that no man should be with you when I call?" Rabbi replied, "He is not an [ordinary] man." "Then," said Antoninus, "let him go and summon the servant who is asleep outside the door." R. Hanina ben Hama went out and found that he was dead. He reasoned: What shall I do? Shall I go and tell Antoninus that his servant is dead? It may cost me my life to bring bad news to the emperor. Shall I leave him and run away? I would then be guilty of acting disrespectfully toward royalty. So he besought mercy for the servant, brought him back to life, and sent him in. Said Antoninus, "I now see that even the least among you can bring the dead back to life. Nevertheless, when I visit, let no one else be with you."

Every time [Antoninus visited], he used to attend Rabbi, waiting on him with food and drink. When Rabbi wanted to get up to his bed, Antoninus would crouch in front of it, saying, "Get up to your bed by stepping on me." Rabbi, however, would demur, "It is not proper to treat royalty so disrespectfully." Antoninus would say, "O that I might be placed as a mattress under you in the world-to-come!" Once he asked him, "Will I enter the world-to-come?" "Yes!" said Rabbi. "But," said Antoninus, "is it not written, 'There will be no remnant to the house of Esau' (Obad. 1:18)?" "That," Rabbi replied, "applies only to those [descendants of Esau] whose evil deeds are like those of Esau."

When Antoninus died, Rabbi said, "The bond [of our love] is snapped."[1]

327. A certain Judeo-Christian once said to Rabbi, "He who formed the mountains did not create the wind, and He who created the wind did not form the mountains, for it is written, 'For, lo, He that formeth the mountains and createth the wind' " (Amos 4:13). Rabbi replied, "You fool, go on to the end of the verse: 'The Lord, [the disciple] of hosts, is His Name" (ibid.). The Judeo-Christian said, "Give me three days' time, and I will come back with a reply." Rabbi spent those three days fasting. Then, just as he was about to partake of food, he was told, "A Judeo-Christian is waiting at the door." Rabbi exclaimed, "Yea, they put poison into my food" (Ps. 69:22).[2] But the waiting Judeo-Christian said, "My master, I bring tidings that prove you right. Your adversary could find no answer, and so he threw himself off the roof and died." Rabbi: "Will you dine with me?" The Judeo-Christian. "Yes." After they ate and drank, Rabbi [suspicious of his guest's Jewish loyalty] said to him, "Do you wish to drink the cup of wine over which the blessing following grace [after meals] is said, or in lieu of it accept forty gold coins?"[3] The Judeo-Christian replied, "I would rather drink the cup for the blessing." Subsequently Rabbi's willingness to pay forty gold coins for the cup of wine for the blessing that follows grace was widely quoted.[4]

R. Isaac[5] said: [In the event, Rabbi's suspicion proved right. For the Judeo-Christian left Israel and went to Rome, and] this family, still to be found among [the Christian] notables of Rome, is known as the family of Bar Livianus.[6]

328. Our masters taught: As Rabbi lay dying, he said, "I need to see my sons." When his sons entered, he instructed them: "Be sure to accord honor to your mother. My lamp is to burn in its usual place, my table is to be set in its usual place, and my bed is to be spread in its usual place. Joseph of Haifa and Simeon of Efrath, who attended me in my lifetime, are to attend me at my death."

He went on, "I need to see the sages of Israel." When the sages of Israel entered, he said to them, "Do not have me eulogized in the small towns [when my funeral procession passes through],[7] and reassemble the academy after thirty days. My son Simeon is to be counselor sage, my son Gamaliel patriarch, and Hanina ben Hama head of the academy.

"I need to see my younger son." When R. Simeon entered, he passed on to him the principles of [esoteric] wisdom.

"I need to see my elder son." When R. Gamaliel entered, he passed on to him the regulations of the patriarchate. "My son," he said, "surround your patriarchate

1. B. AZ 10a–b.

2. Rabbi thought that it was the same heretic who had argued with him three days earlier.

3. A guest's leading the grace after meals was a way of thanking the host for hospitality. What began as politeness became in time the guest's prerogative, all but his property. For yielding the right to lead in the grace, Rabbi offered his guest forty gold coins—ten coins for each amen voiced by the guest following each of the four blessings in the grace spoken by the host.

4. Here *bat kol*, generally translated "a divine voice," is taken in its literal meaning of "echo, reverberation," hence, "widely quoted." See Tosafot, s.v. "*bat kol*" on B. Sanh 11a. Rabbi Mordecai Savitsky of Boston, Mass., provided the reference to the translator.

5. He lived in the fourth century C.E. in Palestine, when Christianity became the state religion.

6. For the interpretation of R. Isaac's remark, the translator is indebted to his friend Rabbi Gershon B. Chertoff of Elizabeth, New Jersey. B. Hul 87a and En Yaakov, ad loc.

7. On the way from Sepphoris, where he died, to Beth Shearim, where he was to be buried. So Rashi on B. Sanh 47a.

with people of distinction, and discipline students with severity."

On the day Rabbi appeared to be on the verge of death, the sages decreed a public fast to beseech God's mercy [for the continuance of Rabbi's life]. They also threatened, "He who says that Rabbi is dead will be stabbed with a sword."

Rabbi's handmaiden went up to the roof and prayed, "They on high desire Rabbi [to join me], and those below desire Rabbi [to remain with them]. May it be [God's] will that those below prevail over those above." But when she saw that he was in great pain, she prayed, "May it be [God's] will that those above prevail over those below." However, since the sages did not cease praying for [God's] mercy [to extend Rabbi's life], she picked up a jar and threw it from the roof to the ground. Startled at the noise made by the smashed jar, the sages ceased their prayers [for an instant], and the soul of Rabbi departed.

[But not knowing that Rabbi had died], the sages said to Bar Kappara, "Go and find out." He went, and, upon finding that Rabbi was dead, he, with head covered and garments rent, walked over to the window [of the room where Rabbi lay], looked out, and began the announcement, saying:

> Our brethren of the family of Jedaiah,[1] hear me, hear me!
> Angels and the just who are earth's foundations gripped the holy ark.
> The angels prevailed over the just who are earth's foundations—
> The holy Ark is taken captive.

The sages asked, "Is Rabbi dead?" Bar Kappara: "You have said it. I did not say it." They rent their garments, and the sound of their rending reached as far as Gofefata, a distance of three *mil* [from Sepphoris].

As he lay dying, Rabbi stretched his ten fingers toward heaven and said, "Lord of the universe, to You it is revealed and known that with all my ten fingers I labored hard to perform Torah's precepts and that I did not derive any worldly benefit, not even as little as may be enjoyed by the smallest finger. May it be Your will that there be peace in my [last] resting place."

A divine voice came forth and said, "He shall enter into peace; he shall have rest on his couch" (Isa. 57:2).

The day Rabbi died, a divine voice came forth and said, "Whoever was present at Rabbi's death is destined for life in the world-to-come."

There was a fuller who used to visit Rabbi every day but did not visit him on that day. When he heard the voice, he went up to a roof, threw himself to the ground, and died. Again a divine voice came forth and said, "The fuller also is destined to life in the world-to-come."[2]

1. Jedediah was the priestly family whose home was Sepphoris, where Rabbi died.
2. B. Ket 103a–104a; P. Kil 9:4, 32a–b; Eccles. R. 7:12, §1 and 9:10, §9.

329. When Rabbi fell ill, R. Hiyya visited him and found him weeping. "Master," he asked, "why are you weeping? Have we not learned: 'When a man dies smiling, it is a good omen for him; when he dies weeping, it is a bad omen for him'?" Rabbi replied, "I weep because [I am about to part from] Torah and her precepts."[3]

330. When Rabbi Judah [I] the Patriarch died, R. Yannai proclaimed: The restrictions on priests do not hold today.[4]

331. After Rabbi died, humility and fear of sin ceased.[5]

332. R. Hiyya said: The day Rabbi died, holiness ceased.[6]

333. R. Hiyya also said: Whenever I see Rabbi's grave, I shed tears over it.[7]

334. Whenever R. Hanina and R. Hiyya were in a dispute, R. Hanina would say to R. Hiyya, "Do you presume to dispute with me? If—God forbid!—the Torah were forgotten in Israel, I could restore it by my dialectical power." R. Hiyya would reply, "But I see to it that the Torah is not forgotten in Israel. What do I do? I go and sow flax, make nets [from the flax cords], and trap deer, whose flesh I give to orphans and out of whose skins I prepare scrolls, upon which I write the Five Books [of Moses]. Then I go to a town that has no teachers for the young and teach the Five Books to five children and the six divisions [of Mishnah] to six young people. And I say to them, 'Until I return, read Scripture to one another and recite Mishnah to one another.' Thus I see to it that the Torah is not forgotten in Israel."

It is to such preoccupations of R. Hiyya that Rabbi referred when he said, "How great are the words of Hiyya!" When R. Simeon son of Rabbi asked his father, "Greater than yours?" he replied, "Yes." When R. Ishmael son of R. Yose asked Rabbi, "Even greater than my father's?" he replied, "God forbid. Such a thing should not be said in Israel!"[8]

335. As for R. Hiyya, the angel of death could not come near him. So one day he took on the guise of a poor man and came knocking on the door, saying, "Bring out some bread to me." It was brought out to him. Then the angel of death called to R. Hiyya [who remained indoors], "Won't you be kind to a poor man? Why don't you show sympathy to a poor man [by coming out of the house and saying a few kind words to him]?" R. Hiyya opened the door. The angel of death showed him a rod of fire, and he yielded his soul.[9]

3. B. Ket 103b.
4. They are allowed by way of exception to participate in Rabbi's funeral rites. P. Ber 3:1, 6a.
5. B. Sot 49b.
6. B. Ket 103b.
7. Ibid.
8. B. Ket 103b; B. BM 85b.
9. B. MK 28a.

336. R. Haviva said: R. Haviva ben Surmaki told me: I saw a certain disciple of the wise whom the prophet Elijah used to visit. That morning the disciple's eyes were clear, but in the evening they looked as though they had been burned by fire. When I inquired, "What happened?" he replied, "I asked Elijah, 'Show me the [departed] sages as they ascend to the academy in heaven.' He replied, 'You may look upon all of them, except the throne of R. Hiyya—upon it you may not look.' 'How am I to distinguish the various thrones?' 'All, when they ascend and descend, are accompanied by angels, except R. Hiyya's throne, which ascends and descends of its own accord.' But I could not control my curiosity. So I gazed upon it, whereat two sparks of fire came forth, smote me, and blinded my eyes. The following day, I went and prostrated myself upon R. Hiyya's grave, crying out, 'Master, it is your Baraita that I study!'[1] and I was healed."[2]

337. R. Yose observed a fast for eighty days in order to see R. Hiyya the Elder. Finally, when R. Yose did see him, his hands began to tremble and his eyesight was dimmed. You might suppose [from this incident] that R. Yose was a man of little consequence. Far from it. For a weaver once came to R. Yohanan and said to him, "In my dream I saw the firmament about to fall, and one of your disciples propped it up." R. Yohanan asked, "Do you think you could identify him?" The weaver: "If I see him, I will recognize him." Then R. Yohanan had all his disciples come before the weaver, and he identified R. Yose.

R. Simeon ben Lakish—some say R. Joshua ben Levi—observed three hundred fasts to be able to see R. Hiyya the Elder, but did not succeed. In the end, he felt aggrieved, saying, "Did he perchance labor more in Torah than I?" and was told, "R. Hiyya spread Torah in Israel more than you. What's more, he was willing to wander from place to place [in doing so]." R. Simeon: "Was I not willing to wander from place to place?" He was told, "You wandered to study. He wandered to teach."[3]

338. Resh Lakish was marking the caves where sages were buried.[4] But when he approached the cave of R. Hiyya, it eluded him. Dejected, he said, "Master of the universe, did I not discuss the subtleties of Torah as much as he did?" A divine voice came forth and told him, "You discussed Torah's subtleties as much as he did. But you did not spread Torah as much as he.[5]

339. Resh Lakish said: May my life be an expiatory sacrifice for R. Hiyya and his sons. For in ancient times, when Torah was forgotten in Israel, Ezra came up from Babylon and reestablished it. When it was again forgotten in Israel, Hillel the Babylonian came up and reestablished it. When it was once again forgotten in Israel, R. Hiyya and his sons came up and reestablished it.[6]

1. There were several sets of Baraitas—laws not included by Rabbi in his compilation of the Mishnah—the most important of which was the one put together by R. Hiyya and R. Oshaia.
2. Yet the redness of the burning was still perceptible. B. BM 85b.
3. P. Kil 9:3, 32b.
4. To alert priests not to go there and be defiled.
5. B. BM 85b.

Bar Kappara (1st half of 3d century C.E.)

340. When Rabbi made a wedding banquet for his son, he invited all the sages but forgot to invite Bar Kappara. So Bar Kappara went and wrote on the door [of the banqueting hall], "The end of all rejoicing is death; so what is gained by your rejoicing?"

Rabbi went out, looked at the writing on the door, and asked, "Who did this to us?" He was told, "It was Bar Kappara, whom you forgot to invite." Next morning Rabbi arranged another banquet to which he invited all the sages, including Bar Kappara. They sat down to dine, and at each and every course during the meal, Bar Kappara related three hundred fox fables. The guests enjoyed them so much that the food became cold, and they touched none of it. Rabbi asked his servants, "Why do our courses go in and come back without being touched by the guests?" The servants answered, "Because of an old man who sits there and, as each course is brought in, relates three hundred fables." Rabbi went over to him and said, "Why do you do this? Allow the guests to eat!" He replied, "So that you should not say that I came here for your dinner; I came here to be with my colleagues." Presently, each apologized to the other, and they made peace.[7]

341. Rabbi made a wedding feast for his son R. Simeon but did not invite Bar Kappara. So Bar Kappara wrote on the pavilion in which the nuptial canopy was set up, "Twenty-four thousand myriads of denars were spent for this pavilion, yet the father of the groom did not invite Bar Kappara." He went on to say of Rabbi, "If they who do not do His will are so well off, how much better off will be those who do His will." At that, Rabbi invited Bar Kappara, who then modified his dictum: "If they who do His will are so well off in this world, how much better off by far will they be in the world-to-come.[8]

342. Rabbi used to honor Ben Elasah.[9] So Bar Kappara said to him, "Everyone inquires of Rabbi [in matters of *Halakhah*], but you do not make such inquiry." Ben Elasah: "Tell me what I should inquire about." Bar Kappara: Inquire about the meaning of

> He who is lowest of the low[10] manages to look down
> from heaven,
> In whose innermost parts he has been making quite
> a stir,
> Terrifying scholars whose minds take wing.
> Young men see him and hide,
> Old men stand up [in deference].

6. B. Suk 20a.
7. Lev. R. 28:2; Eccles. R. 1:3, §1.
8. B. Ned 50b.
9. Rabbi's son-in-law, who was very rich but no scholar.
10. Bar Kappara dubs Ben Elasah "Sheol"—the netherworld—hence, "lowest of the low."

He who gets away says [behind his back], "Ho, ho."
But he who is trapped [into honoring such a one] is
trapped by his own inquiry.

[After Ben Elasah made his inquiry of Rabbi], Rabbi turned his face around and saw Bar Kappara smiling. Rabbi said to Bar Kappara, "Elder, I don't think I know who you are." Bar Kappara then was certain that he was not going to be ordained.[1]

343. R. Simeon son of Rabbi and Bar Kappara were once sitting and studying together. When they came to a tradition they could not understand, R. Simeon said to Bar Kappara, "This matter needs Rabbi." Bar Kappara said to R. Simeon, "What, pray, can Rabbi possibly say about this?" When R. Simeon went and told his father what Bar Kappara had said, Rabbi took great exception to the remark. The next time Bar Kappara visited Rabbi, Rabbi said, "Bar Kappara, I don't believe I know you at all." Bar Kappara realized that Rabbi had taken the matter to heart, and so for thirty days imposed upon himself the disability of a reprimand.[2]

344. On the day Rabbi laughed, punishment came to the world.[3] So he said to Bar Kappara [who was given to practical jokes], "Do not make me laugh, and I will give you forty measures of wheat." Bar Kappara replied, "But let the master see to it that I take the measures of wheat in whatever way I choose." Presently he took a large basket, covered it with pitch,[4] placed it on his head, and came and said to Rabbi, "Let the master measure out for me the forty measures I claim." [At the sight of Bar Kappara's getup] Rabbi burst out laughing and said, "Did I not warn you not to make me laugh?" Bar Kappara said, "I have come merely to take the wheat to which I have a claim."[5]

345. Bar Kappara said to Rabbi: I dreamed that my nose (*af*) fell off. Rabbi replied: God's wrath (*af*) will fall away from you.

Bar Kappara: I dreamed that my hands were cut off. Rabbi: You will not require the labor of your hands.

Bar Kappara: I dreamed that my legs were lopped off. Rabbi: You will ride horseback.[6]

346. Bar Kappara was walking up and down the seashore of Caesarea when he saw a ship sinking in the Great [Mediterranean] Sea and the proconsul [of Caesarea] emerging from it all but naked. On seeing him, Bar Kappara went over to him, greeted him, and gave him food and drink, and handed him three more *sela*, saying, "For a distinguished man like you, it is right to expend three more *sela*." Some time later, Jews were arrested during a roundup following a riot. When it was asked, "Who will go and intercede for us?" one said to another, "Bar Kappara [is the man to go], because he is highly esteemed by the government." When he told them, "You know that this government does nothing without being paid," they said to him, "Here are five hundred denars. Take them and go to intercede for us." He took the five hundred denars and went to the government. When the proconsul saw him, he stood up, greeted him, and asked, "Why has the master troubled to come here?" Bar Kappara answered, "I beg of you to have mercy upon these [arrested] Jews." The proconsul: "You know that this government does nothing without being paid." Bar Kappara: "I have with me five hundred denars. Take them and intercede for us." He replied, "These denars are to be kept by you in return for the five *sela* you gave me; your people are spared in return for the food and drink you provided for me in your house; and as for you, go in peace and great honor."

To Bar Kappara they applied the text "Cast thy bread upon the waters" (Eccles. 11:1).[7]

347. Once, while two disciples were seated before Bar Kappara, cabbage, prunes, and young chickens were set before him. Bar Kappara gave permission to one of the disciples to pronounce the appropriate blessing. When that disciple in his haste said the blessing over chickens,[8] his colleague sniggered at him. Bar Kappara became angry and said, "I am not angry with the one who pronounced the blessing but with the one who sniggered. If it appears that your colleague acted like one who has never tasted meat before, what right have you to snigger at him?"[9] But then Bar Kappara changed his mind and said, "I am not angry at the one who sniggered, but I am angry at the one who pronounced the blessing," adding, "Even if there be no wisdom in me, there is my seniority."[10]

R. Simeon ben Halafta (1st half of 3d century C.E.)

348. Once, on the eve of Passover (some say on the eve of Yom Kippur), while R. Hiyya the Elder and R. Simeon ben Halafta were seated studying Torah in the great house of study in Tiberias, they heard the sound of people running about in excitement. When R. Simeon asked R. Hiyya, "What are these people doing?" R. Hiyya answered, "He who has money is purchasing [what he needs for the festival], and he who has no money is running to his employer, who gives it to him." R. Simeon said, "If so, I too will run to my Master and He will give it to me." He went out and prayed in a cave in Tiberias, and beheld

1. P. MK 3:1, 81c.
2. B. MK 16b.
3. During the thirteen years R. Judah the Patriarch suffered pain, no drought came to the world. See B. BM 85a.
4. So that it would retain the wheat.
5. B. Ned 50b–51a.
6. Rabbi interpreted Bar Kappara's dreams in keeping with the practice of giving bad dreams a good meaning. B. Ber 56b.
7. Eccles R. 11:1, §1.
8. The proper order would have been a blessing over the prunes, "fruit of the tree"; then over the cabbage, "fruit of the ground"; and last, over the chickens, "by whose will everything was created."
9. In such a case the sequence of blessings would be reordered, since the preferred food is given priority.
10. Hence he should have asked me before hastily pronouncing the blessing. B. Ber 39a.

a hand holding out a pearl to him. So R. Simeon took it to our Rabbi, who asked him, "Where did you get this? It is priceless. Take these three denars—go and prepare food in honor of the day, and after the festival we shall advertise it, and you will take whatever money it brings in." R. Simeon took the three denars, went to make his purchases, and then came home. His wife said to him, "Simeon, have you turned thief? All your possessions amount to no more than a hundred *meah*. How were you able to make all these purchases?" He replied, "They were made out of what the Holy One provided." At that, she said, "If you won't tell me where you got the money, I will taste nothing at all." He told her, "This is what I prayed to Heaven for and what was given me from Heaven." She said, "Do you wish that your canopy in heaven should have one pearl less than that of your colleagues?" When he asked, "What shall I do?" she replied, "Go and return your purchases to their owners, the denars to their owner, and the pearl to its Owner."[1]

When our Rabbi heard that R. Simeon was grieved, he sent for his wife and said to her, "You have caused much anguish to this righteous man!" She replied sharply, "What do you want—that his canopy should have one pearl less than yours in the world-to-come?" He said to her, "And even if it should, will not one among us make it up to you?" She answered him, "Rabbi, how do we know that we will be privileged to see your face in the world-to-come? Will not each and every righteous man have his own chamber?" Rabbi admitted that she was right.

As soon as R. Simeon heard what Rabbi had said, he went and returned the pearl. The instant he stretched out his hand to return it, an angel came down and took it.

When R. Simeon received the pearl, the palm of his hand was below [the hand from heaven]. But when he reached out to return it, the palm of his hand was above [the hand from heaven], as when a man lends to his fellow.

Our masters taught: The second miracle was greater than the first, for it is the way of those on high to give, but not to take back.

349. R. Simeon ben Halafta received from R. Hiyya a field in tenancy. R. Simeon asked: How much does it bring in? R. Hiyya: A hundred *kor* [of produce]. R. Simeon sowed and harvested it, but it brought in less than a hundred *kor*. So he asked: Did not you, my teacher, say that the field brings in a hundred *kor?* R. Hiyya: Yes. R. Simeon: But I sowed it, gathered in the crop, and found that it produced less than a hundred *kor*. R. Hiyya: Where did you set up the threshing floor? R. Simeon: At the highest point of the city. R. Hiyya: But is it not written, "Get thee down to the threshing floor" (Ruth 3:3)? Nevertheless, go and sift the chaff again, and you will find that what was left over will make up the hundred *kor*.[2]

[1] Ruth R. 3:4; Exod. R. 52:3.

[2] Ruth R. 5:12

350. R. Simeon ben Halafta said: It happened that a cabbage stalk in our field grew so tall that I could go up and down it as one goes up and down a ladder.[3]

351. R. Simeon ben Halafta said: I had a stalk of mustard in my field, and I used to climb it as one climbs to the top of a fig tree.[4]

352. R. Simeon ben Halafta was a fat man. One day the heat all but overpowered him. So he climbed to the top of a boulder, where he sat down, and said to his daughter, "Daughter, fan me with your fan, and I will give you talents' worth of spikenard." Just then a breeze began to blow. So he exclaimed, "How many talents' worth of spikenard do we owe the Proprietor of this breeze?"[5]

353. It is said of R. Simeon ben Halafta that he was given to experimenting. What kind of experimenting? R. Mesharsheya said: It is written, "Go to the ant, thou sluggard; consider her ways and be wise; which having no chief, overseer, or ruler, provideth her bread in the summer" (Prov. 6:6–8). R. Simeon ben Halafta said, "I shall go and find out whether it is true that ants have no king." At the summer solstice, he went and spread his cloak over an ant hill. When one of the ants came out, he marked it. It immediately went back into the hill and informed the other ants that the shady time of the day had already come.[6] At that, all the ants went outside. Just then he raised his cloak so that the sun beat down upon the ants. So, they set upon this ant and killed it.[7] He then said, "It is clear that they have no king. Otherwise, they would have had to obtain royal sanction!"[8]

354. R. Simeon had a tree trunk in his garden, and [one day] he saw a hoopoe building a nest for itself in that trunk. So, saying to himself: What does that unclean bird want in my orchard? R. Simeon went and demolished the nest. But the hoopoe put it together again. What did R. Simeon ben Halafta do then? He brought a board and placed it over the face of the nest and drove a nail into it. What did the hoopoe do? It went and brought a certain herb, wound the herb around the nail, and pulled it out. Seeing that, R. Simeon ben Halafta said: It is advisable that I hide this herb, so that thieves may not learn to use it [in burglaries] and ruin mankind.[9]

355. R. Simeon ben Halafta had a hen that lost its plumage. So he wrapped the hen in the [leather] apron used by coppersmiths and put it into an oven, and then its feathers grew back thicker than before.[10]

[3] Sif Deut., §317.

[4] P. Pe 7:4, 20b.

[5] B. BM 86a.

[6] Ants avoid the fierce heat of the sun and only venture forth in the shade.

[7] For having deceived them.

[8] To execute the ant whose information proved wrong. B. Hul 57b.

[9] Lev. R. 22:4.

[10] B. Hul 57b.

356. R. Simeon ben Halafta had a hen whose femur was dislocated. So he had a tube of reed made for it [as support], and it recovered.[1]

357. Once, when R. Simeon ben Halafta was walking on a road, some roaring lions closed in on him. As soon as he quoted, "The young lions roar after their prey" (Ps. 104:21), two joints of meat came down [from heaven]. The lions ate one joint and left the other. R. Simeon ben Halafta brought the remaining joint to the house of study and asked, "Is this a clean or an unclean thing?" He was told, "No unclean thing can come down from heaven."[2]

358. One of the notables of Sepphoris had occasion to celebrate the circumcision of his son, and the inhabitants of En Te'enah came up to honor him [with their presence], R. Simeon ben Halafta among them. Upon arriving at the city gate, they noticed youngsters standing around and playing in front of a courtyard. When they saw R. Simeon ben Halafta, who was both distinguished and handsome, they heckled him: "You will not get away from here until you do a little dance for us." He said to them, "You cannot expect this of me—I am an old man." Though he rebuked them, they were neither frightened nor cowed. He lifted up his face and saw [the wall of] the courtyard about to collapse [on the youngsters because of their impertinence]; so he said to them, "Will you say loudly what I am about to tell you? Say to the owner of this courtyard that if he is asleep, he had better wake up, because while the beginning of sin is sweet, its end is bitter."

At the sound of their conversation, the owner of the courtyard woke up. He came out and fell at R. Simeon ben Halafta's feet, saying, "My master, I beg you to pay no attention to the words of these youngsters, who are both young and foolish." R. Simeon: "But what can I do for you, seeing that the decree [for the wall's collapse] has already been issued? I will, however, postpone it for you until you remove everything you own from this courtyard." As soon as the owner removed all that he had in the courtyard, [the wall of] the courtyard trembled and collapsed.

R. Simeon and his companions then went on to share in the observance of the circumcision [to which they had been invited]. There the child's father gave them seven-year-old wine to drink, saying, "Drink some of this wine; I trust that at the child's wedding feast the God of heaven will again allow me to offer you more of this wine, which I am aging." They responded, "As you brought this child into the covenant [of Abraham], so may you bring him to Torah and to the nuptial canopy." They feasted until midnight.

Then, at midnight, R. Simeon ben Halafta, who relied on his [spiritual] strength, set out to walk to his town. The angel of death met him on the road and asked, "Is it because you rely on your good deeds that you venture out at an hour that is not the [safe] time [to be abroad]?" R. Simeon: "And you, who are you?" The angel of death [smiling]: "I am God's emissary." R. Simeon: "What are you smiling at?" The angel: "At the talk of mortals who say, 'Thus-and-thus shall we do,' though not one of them knows when he may be summoned to die. The same man in whose home you have just feasted, who said to you, 'I am aging more of this wine to serve at my son's wedding feast'—look, his son's nametag is with me. After thirty days, I am to take him."

R. Simeon ben Halafta then asked the angel of death, "As you live, show me my tag." The angel: "As you live, I have no power over you or the likes of you." R. Simeon: "Why not?" The angel: "Because day after day, as you labor in Torah and mitzvot, and perform deeds of mercy, the Holy One keeps adding years to your years." R. Simeon: "May it be the Holy One's will that even as you have no power over our nametags, so may you have no power over the prayers we utter." He besought mercy, and the infant remained alive.[3]

359. Rabbi asked R. Simeon ben Halafta, "Why did we not have the pleasure of receiving you during the recent festival, as my forebears had the pleasure of receiving your forebears?" R. Simeon replied, "Rocks have become higher, near ones have become distant, distant ones have become near, and that which makes peace in the home has ceased to be."[4]

R. Hanina bar Hama (fl. 1st half of 3d century C.E.)

360. As he was about to die, Rabbi enjoined his son to appoint R. Hanina bar Hama as head of the academy. Why did he himself not appoint him? R. Derosai said: Because the people of Sepphoris [where R. Hanina was born] protested his appointment. But just because the people of Sepphoris protested, should their wishes have been deferred to? [Besides], even now these people protest and protest. So if we deferred to them with regard to R. Hanina [in Rabbi's time], we should have deferred to them with regard to R. Hanina in Rabbi's son's time as well.

R. Eleazar son of R. Yose said: The reason R. Hanina bar Hama was not appointed is because on one occasion he publicly refuted Rabbi. Rabbi was sitting and reciting [from memory] the verse "But they that shall at all escape of them, shall be on the mountains like doves of the valleys, all of them moaning" (Ezek. 7:16). Rabbi read the word for "moaning" as *homiyyot*, and R. Hanina corrected him: "The word is *homot*." Rabbi asked him, "With whom did you study Scripture?" R. Hanina: "With R. Hamnuna, the scribe in Babylonia." Rabbi: "When you go down there, tell *him* to appoint you elder." R. Hanina then understood that Rabbi would never appoint him.

When Rabbi died, his son wished to appoint R. Hanina [head of the academy]. But he would not accept the

1. Ibid.
2. B. Sanh 59b.
3. Eccles. R. 3:2, §3; Deut. R. 9:1; Yalkut, Prov. 10, §947.
4. "I have become old. My eyes, which could see far in the distance, barely see at close range. My ears do not hear, even when something is repeated many times. My sexual capacity is no more." B. Shab 152a; Lev. R. 18:1.

appointment, saying, "I will not accept the appointment until you first appoint R. Aphes of Daroma."

A certain elder was there who said, "Whether R. Hanina or R. Aphes is appointed first, I should be second." R. Hanina agreed to be appointed third and merited living a great many years. R. Hanina used to say, "I do not know how I earned the merit of living a great many years—whether because of my willingness to have my appointment deferred, or whether because, when going up from Tiberias to Sepphoris, I took a detour to pay my respects to R. Simeon ben Halafta in En Te'enah."[1]

361. R. Hanina lived in Sepphoris, where many times questions in *Halakhah* were put to him, which he decided by himself. Even though R. Yohanan and Resh Lakish lived there, he did not associate them with him in his deliberations. The two said, "This elder is fully aware that his knife is sharp [his mind is keen]."

On one occasion, he did associate them with him. They asked, "Master, why did you take note of us this time?" He replied, "[Yes, I have resolved many questions by myself.] But may such-and-such befall me if—with each and every question that I resolved on my own—I had not heard Rabbi dealing in theoretical discourse as many times as there are hairs on my head, and in actual cases at least three times. However, this particular question was considered by Rabbi only twice. That is why I associated you with me this time."[2]

362. There was an epidemic in Sepphoris, which did not affect the street where R. Hanina lived. So the people of Sepphoris said: How is it that this old man—he and his quarter—live among us in peace, while the rest of the city is in distress? R. Hanina came to them and said: Though there was only one Zimri[3] in his generation, twenty-four thousand perished in Israel; and how many Zimris have we in our generation! Yet [believing yourselves wronged], you are indignant!

Once a fast was decreed [in Sepphoris], yet no rain came down; while R. Joshua [ben] Levi decreed a fast in the south, and it did rain. So the people of Sepphoris said: R. Joshua ben Levi brings down rain for the people in the south, while R. Hanina withholds rain from the people of Sepphoris. They concluded that it was necessary to decree a second fast.

R. Hanina sent for R. Joshua ben Levi and said to him: Look here, master, join us for the service of the fast. So both of them went out to the special service, but rain still did not come down.

Then R. Hanina appeared before the people of Sepphoris and said: R. Joshua ben Levi does not bring down rain for the people in the south, nor does R. Hanina withhold rain from the people of Sepphoris. But the people of the south have receptive hearts—when they hear words of Torah, they submit themselves to those words; while the people of Sepphoris have unreceptive hearts—when they hear words of Torah, they refuse to submit.

When R. Hanina returned to his home, he looked up and saw that the air was still clear. So he said: That's enough of that [henceforth rain must come]! At once, rain came down. He then vowed never again to utter such an impertinent command, saying: What right have I to tell the Creditor not to collect the debt owed Him?[4]

363. R. Hanina, who dealt in bees' honey, happened to have some date honey[5] which he [inadvertently] sold as bees' honey. After a while, when those who purchased it came by, he said to them, "I must not mislead you—I want you to know that the honey I sold you was date honey." They replied, "That was the kind we wanted; it was just right for the use we put it to." Nevertheless, R. Hanina set aside the money he received for that honey and [used it when he] built a house of study in Sepphoris.[6]

364. A story is told of a certain butcher in Sepphoris who sold to Jews [forbidden] flesh of animals that died of themselves or were torn by beasts. One Sabbath eve he drank [too much] wine, went up to the roof, fell down, and died. When dogs were licking up his blood, people came and asked R. Hanina: May his body be moved [on the Sabbath] away from the dogs? R. Hanina replied: It is said, "Ye shall not eat any flesh that is torn by beasts in the field; ye shall cast it to the dogs" (Exod. 22:30). This one robbed dogs [of their natural food], which he then fed to Jews. Let the dogs be—they are eating what is theirs.[7]

365. On Sabbath eve at twilight, R. Hanina used to wrap himself in a [special] robe, stand up, and say, "Come, let us go forth to welcome Queen Sabbath.[8]

366. Simeon bar Abba came to R. Hanina and said: Write me a letter of recommendation, so that I may go abroad for my livelihood. R. Hanina replied: Before long, when I join your forebears, they will say to me: We had a precious sapling in the Land of Israel, and you allowed it to go abroad!

A certain priest came to R. Hanina and asked: May I go to Tyre to perform a commandment—to undergo *halitzah*[9] by, or to marry, the childless widow of my deceased brother? R. Hanina replied: Your brother left the bosom of his motherland and embraced the bosom of an alien land—may He who is everywhere be blessed for having smitten him—and you would do what your brother did![10]

367. A woman once attempted to take some earth from under R. Hanina's feet, [in order to work magic against

1. P. Ta 4:2, 68a; Eccles. R. 7:7, §2.
2. P. Nid 2:7, 50b.
3. A prince from the tribe of Simeon who, by flagrantly cohabiting with a Midianitish woman, caused a plague that struck down twenty-four thousand Israelites. See Num. 25.
4. P. Ta 3:4, 66c.
5. Date honey was regarded as inferior.
6. P. Pe 7:3, 20b.
7. P. Ter 8:4, 45c.
8. B. Shab 119a.
9. The ceremony whereby one is freed from the obligation of marrying the childless widow of one's deceased brother.
10. You should stay in the land and let the widow come here. P. MK 3:1, 81a.

him]. R. Hanina said to her: If you think you can succeed, go ahead. [I am not afraid], because Scripture says, "There is none else beside Him" (Deut. 4:35).[1]

368. When R. Hanina's daughter died and he did not weep for her, his wife asked: Was it a mere hen that you carried out of your house? He replied: Do you want me to suffer two evils—not only bereavement but also blindness [from incessant weeping]?[2]

369. R. Hanina said: My son Shivhat died [before his time] only because he cut down a fig tree before its time.[3]

370. While R. Hanina and R. Jonathan were walking on a road, they came to two paths, one leading to the door of a place for idolatry and the other to the door of a brothel. One sage said to the other: Let us [take the path leading] to the place of idolatry, since the inclination for it has been killed [it is easily resisted]. The other said: Let us [take the path] to the brothel, overcome our inclination, and receive our reward.

As they approached the brothel, they realized that the harlots made themselves scarce.[4] So one sage asked the other: What made you so certain that you could overcome your inclination? In reply, the other quoted: "[Torah] shall watch over thee against lewdness, discernment shall guard thee" (Prov. 2:11).[5]

371. It is told of R. Hanina that when he was eighty he could remove his shoe or put it on while standing on one foot.

Concerning his continuing suppleness, R. Hanina said: Warm baths and oil with which my mother anointed me in my youth stood me in good stead in my old age.[6]

372. At the time R. Hanina was ordained by R. Hiyya bar Abba in Sepphoris, he saw a great many people running by. When he asked, "Where are all these people running?" he was told, "To R. Benaiah's house of study. There, R. Yohanan is sitting in the teacher's chair and explaining Scripture, and all the people are hastening to hear him." So R. Hanina said, "Blessed be He who is everywhere for having shown me the fruit [of my labor] while I am still alive: except for Proverbs and Ecclesiastes, I explained the *Aggadot* [on all other books of Scripture] to R. Yohanan."[7]

373. R. Hanina fell ill in Sepphoris. When R. Yohanan heard of it, he set out to go up from Tiberias to Sepphoris, intending to visit him. On the way, he saw a man coming down from there, and he asked, "What news of the city?" The man: "A certain master has just died, and all the people are hastening to tend to his burial." R. Yohanan understood that it was R. Hanina. So he got off the donkey, took out his Sabbath garments—thirteen robes of fine wool—and rent them, saying, "The man in whose presence I stood in awe is gone.[8]

R. Oshaia the Elder ben R. Hama (fl. 1st half of 3d century C.E.)

374. R. Hama bar Bisa went away [from home and] spent twelve years at a house of study. When he returned, he said, "I will not act as did Ben Hakinai."[9] So he entered the local house of study and stayed there, sending word to his home [that he was back]. Just then, his son R. Oshaia happened to walk into the house of study, sit down before him, and inquire concerning rulings in *Halakhah*. Seeing how sharp he was in the relevant traditions, R. Hama became quite depressed as he said to himself: Had I remained home, I, too, might have had such a son.[10] Later, after R. Hama entered his home, his son came in. R. Hama, believing that the young man wished to inquire about other rulings in *Halakhah*, stood up before him. At that, R. Hama's wife asked, "What father stands up before his own son?" Rami bar Hama then applied to R. Hama the verse "A threefold cord is not quickly broken" (Eccles. 4:12), the threefold cord being the line of R. Oshaia the son of R. Hama bar Bisa.[11]

375. R. Yohanan said: In his generation, R. Oshaia Berabbi was as great as R. Meir in his generation. Even as in R. Meir's generation, his colleagues could not fathom the depth of his knowledge, so R. Oshaia's colleagues could not fathom the depth of his knowledge.

R. Yohanan said: The understanding of former generations was as wide as the door of the Outer Hall leading into the Temple's interior; the understanding of the latter generations no wider than the door into the Temple Hall.[12] But ours is as narrow as the eye of a needle. By "former generations" was meant such as R. Akiva. By "latter generations," such as R. Eleazar ben Shammua. But there are some who say that "former generations" means such as R. Eleazar ben Shammua, and "latter generations" means such as R. Oshaia Berabbi.[13]

376. R. Oshaia was the first interpreter of the Mishnah.[14]

---

1. He will protect me from you. B. Sanh 67b.
2. B. Shab 151b.
3. B. BK 91b.
4. Literally, "hid themselves from them," in apparent certainty that the two would not solicit them.
5. JV: "Discretion shall watch over thee, discernment shall guard thee." But *mezimmah* ("discretion") also means "lewdness." B. AZ 17a–b.
6. B. Hul 24b.
7. P. Hor 3:4, 48b.
8. P. MK 3:8, 83d; P. BM 2:12, 8d; B. MK 24a.
9. Who entered his house unexpectedly and nearly caused the death of his wife as a result. See B. Ket 62b.
10. He did not recognize him after twelve years and thought he was another man's son.
11. B. Ket 62b.
12. The door into the Outer Hall leading into the Temple's interior was twenty cubits wide; the one into the Temple Hall, ten cubits.
13. B. Er 53a.
14. P. BK 4:6, 4c.

377. "I made me gardens and parks" (Eccles. 2:5). These words refer to such voluminous collections of Mishnah as the collection of R. Hiyya the Elder, the collection of R. Oshaia the Elder, and the collection of Bar Kappara.[1]

378. [On Purim] R. Yudan the Patriarch[2] sent a joint of meat and a jug of wine to R. Oshaia the Elder, who replied: You fulfilled for us the injunction of "gifts to the poor" (Esther 9:22). At that, R. Yudan sent a whole calf and a huge jar of wine to R. Oshaia, who replied: Now you have fulfilled for us the injunction "of sending portions, each man to his colleague" (ibid).[3]

379. R. Oshaia the Elder was the teacher of his own blind son, who used to dine with him daily. One day, when guests came to R. Oshaia, he did not invite his son to dine with them. In the evening R. Oshaia came to his son's room and said: Young master, do not be angry at me. Because I had guests, I did not wish to embarrass the young master. For that reason I preferred not to dine with you today. The son replied: You have reassured one who is seen but cannot see. May He who sees and cannot be seen ever accept your reassurances.[4]

380. R. Oshaia the Elder went to a certain place where, on the Sabbath, he saw mourners and greeted them, saying: I do not know the custom of your place, but I greet you in keeping with the custom of our place.[5]

381. While R. Hama bar Hanina and R. Oshaia were walking among the synagogues of Lydda, R. Hama bar Hanina said to R. Oshaia: How much money my forebears sank here! R. Oshaia replied: How many souls your forebears sank here! Would it not have been better if your forebears had made it possible for people to labor in Torah?[6]

382. A certain Christian said to R. Hanina: We are more compassionate than you. Of you it is written, "Joab and all Israel remained there six months, until he had cut off every male in Edom" (1 Kings 11:16). But we—just consider how many years you have been living in our midst, yet we do you no harm whatsoever. R. Hanina replied: Will you allow a disciple of mine to join you [in debating the matter? Accordingly,] R. Oshaia joined them and said to the Christian: It is because you do not know how to go about it. You would like to exterminate all of us. But all of us are not living among you. Should you exterminate only those of us who are in your midst, you will be called a suicidal kingdom. The Christian said: By the Roman eagle! It's a tough nut to crack—whatever we do involves as much loss as profit.[7]

383. A pagan philosopher asked R. Hoshaia [Oshaia]: If circumcision is so beloved [of God], why was the mark of circumcision not given to Adam at his creation? R. Hoshaia replied: According to your reasoning, why should a man like you shave the hair of his head [with which he was born], but at the same time leave the adult hair of his beard intact?[8] The pagan sage replied: Because the hair of his head grew with him in the days of his foolish childhood. Rabbi Hoshaia then argued: If so, he should blind his eyes, lop off his hands, and break his legs, which also grew along with him since the days of his foolish childhood. The philospher exclaimed: Have we come down to such drivel? R. Hoshaia replied: I cannot let you go without a proper answer. So observe that everything that was created during the six days of creation needs finishing: mustard needs sweetening, vetches need sweetening, wheat needs grinding, and even man needs finishing.[9]

384. People came and told R. Oshaia, "The judges whom you appointed drink wine in the marketplace,"[10] but he did not believe them. One time, he came out and in fact did find his judges drinking wine in the marketplace; then he applied to himself the verse "So I came to hate life" (Eccles. 2:17) and died peacefully.[11]

R. Joshua ben Levi (fl. 1st half 3d century C.E.)

385. R. Hanina and R. Joshua ben Levi appeared before the proconsul of Caesarea, who stood up at the sight of them. When asked, "Are you standing up for these Jews?" he replied, "I beheld the visages of angels."[12]

386. R. Joshua ben Levi went up to Rome, and when [on his way back] he arrived in Acco, R. Hanina went out to meet him. Noticing that R. Joshua was limping on his hip, R. Hanina quipped: You are like your grandfather—he, too, "limped on his hip" (Gen. 32:32).[13]

387. R. Hiyya the Elder [bar Abba] went to Darom, where he stayed as the guest of R. Joshua ben Levi. [At dinner] when twenty-four courses were set before him, R.

---

1. Only some of the Mishnayyot in these collections were included in R. Judah's less bulky collection, which came to be known as "the Mishnah." Eccles. R. 2:8, §1.
2. Grandson of R. Judah I, the Patriarch.
3. P. Meg 1:4, 70d.
4. P. Pe 8:8, 21b; P. Shek 5:4, 49b. See above in this chapter, §190.
5. Where we do greet mourners on the Sabbath. P. MK 3:5, 82d.
6. The money spent to erect buildings would have been better spent to support promising scholars. P. Pe 8:7, 21b.
7. The literal translation may be: "With this concern we lie down, and with it we get up." But *yoredim* may also mean "weigh" or "consider loss," and *olim* may mean "weigh" or "consider profit. So Leon Nemoy. B. Pes 87b.
8. "Pagan philosophers in Roman times often cut the hair of their head very short but let their beard grow long" (Brother Caedmon Holmes).
9. Gen. R. 11:6.
10. Thus violating the injunction "It is not for rulers to drink wine" (Prov. 31:4).
11. Eccles. R. 2:17, §1.
12. P. Ber 5:1, 9a.
13. Even as Jacob limped after encountering Esau's guardian angel, so you limp after encountering Rome, identified with Esau. Gen. R. 78:5.

Hiyya asked: What on earth do you do on the Sabbath?[1] R. Joshua replied: We double the number of courses. Later R. Joshua ben Levi went to Tiberias, where he was the guest of R. Hiyya the Elder. R. Hiyya gave the disciples of Joshua ben Levi some drachmas and said: Go and provide your master with everything he is accustomed to eating.[2]

388. On Friday afternoons, R. Joshua ben Levi used to listen regularly to a portion of Scripture recited by his grandson. Once he forgot to do so, and, as he was going to the baths of Tiberias, leaning upon the shoulder of R. Hiyya bar Abba, he remembered that he had not listened to his grandson's portion. So he turned around and left the baths. (How was he dressed then? Still in his usual clothes, according to R. Derosai; already undressed, according to R. Eliezer son of R. Yose.) R. Hiyya bar Abba asked R. Joshua: But, my master, did you not teach me that once started at the bath, one may not interrupt it? R. Joshua: Hiyya, my son, what I am about to do may appear trivial to you. You should understand that listening to one's grandson recite a portion in Scripture is like listening to it at Mount Sinai, for it is said, "When you make the words [of Torah] known to your children and children's children, [it is like] the day that thou stoodest before the Lord thy God in Horeb" (Deut. 4:9–10).[3]

389. R. Joseph, the son of R. Joshua ben Levi, became ill and his spirit left him.[4] After his spirit returned to him, his father asked him, "What did you see?" He replied, "I saw a world turned upside down. The people high up here were low there, and people low here were high there." R. Joshua: "You saw a world in which right is made clear. But what of you and me—where were we placed?" "Just as we are here, so were we there. I also heard them say, 'Happy is he who comes here with his learning in hand.' I also heard them say, 'They who were martyred by Rome—no man is allowed to stand within their compartments.' " Who are they? The martyrs of Laodicea.[5]

390. The grandson of R. Joshua ben Levi had an obstruction in his throat. To remove it, R. Joshua went and brought one of the followers of [Jesus] bar Pandera,[6] who whispered an incantation over him and the grandson breathed freely. As he was about to leave, R. Joshua ben Levi asked him, What did you whisper over my grandson? He replied: Such-and-such a verse from Scripture[7] [as interpreted by Jesus bar Pandera]. R. Joshua exclaimed: It were better if he were dead and not have to hear a verse [so misused]. And thus it befell the grandson, [who died] as a result of "the inadvertent remark that came from the mouth of a ruler [in matters of Torah]" (Eccles. 10:5).[8]

391. In the neighborhood of R. Joshua ben Levi there lived a Judeo-Christian who annoyed him with his interpretation of verses in Scripture. One day R. Joshua took a cock, placed it between the legs of his bed, and looked at it steadily, saying, "When the right moment [of the day or night, when a cure takes effect], arrives, I will curse him." But when that moment did arrive, R. Joshua had dozed off. On waking, he said, "This shows that it is not proper to attempt such a thing, for 'His tender mercies are over all His works' " (Ps. 145:9). Hence "it is not good for the righteous to attempt to punish" (Prov. 17:26).[9]

392. Ulla the Conspirator[10] was summoned [on a charge] by the Roman government. He fled and reached the house of R. Joshua ben Levi in Lydda. The Romans came, surrounded the city, and said to the inhabitants, "If you do not turn him over to us, we will destroy the city." R. Joshua ben Levi undertook to persuade Ulla [to give himself up], saying, "It is better that only you be put to death and that the community not be put to death on account of you." Ulla let himself be persuaded, and R. Joshua turned him over to the Romans.

Now, the prophet Elijah, ever remembered on good occasions, used to appear to R. Joshua. After R. Joshua had done this, Elijah no longer appeared to him. So R. Joshua fasted for thirty days, and Elijah again appeared to him. R. Joshua asked, "Sir, why did you cease to come?" Elijah answered, "Am I to be a companion of informers?" R. Joshua: "Did I not act in keeping with the Baraita [which reads: If a company of people are told by Gentiles, 'Give us one of you, and we will slay him.' all are to submit to death and not turn over a Jewish person. But if the Gentiles name the person wanted, the company are to give him up rather than that all die]?"[11] "But is that a teaching for the pious?" Elijah asked. "Such an act should be committed by others and not by you."[12]

393. When R. Joshua ben Levi was standing with the prophet Elijah, ever remembered on good occasions, he asked him, "Will you not show me where the stones of chalcedony[13] are?" Elijah said, "Yes," and showed them to him by means of the following miracle.

It so happened that at that time a ship was sailing in the Great Sea. The ship was filled with heathens, but there was also a Jewish lad on it. When a mighty wave seized the ship, so that it was tossed about in the sea, Elijah appeared to the lad and said, "If you will go on an errand for me, I will save this ship for your sake." The lad: "I

---

1. When the fare should be more elaborate.
2. Lam. R. 3:17, §6.
3. P. Shab 1:2, 3a.
4. He lost consciousness.
5. Lulianus and Pappus, the two brothers who took upon themselves the guilt for the death of a princess so as to save the Jewish people. So Rashi on B. Pes 50a.
6. A pejorative implying that a soldier named Pandera seduced Jesus' mother.
7. It is forbidden to use scriptural verses for incantations and similar illicit practices.
8. P. Shab 14:4, 14d; P. AZ 2:2, 14d; Eccles. R. 10:5, §1.
9. B. Ber 7a.
10. "The Conspirator" (*kosher*)—Gen. R. TA, p. 1184; BR: "son of Koshav."
11. Tos Ter 7:20.
12. P. Ter 8:4, 46b; Gen. R. 94:9.
13. The stones that were to be used for the construction of the Temple.

will." Elijah: "Go [to the bottom of the sea, gather some stones of chalcedony, and] show them to R. Joshua ben Levi." The lad: "R. Joshua ben Levi, who is the most distinguished man of this generation, may give no credence to my tale." Elijah replied, "He will give you credence, for he is a humble man. However, when you show the stones to him, do not show them to him in the presence of any other person. Take him to a cave three *mil* distant from Lydda and show them to him there." The lad agreed to do what Elijah asked him to do, and a miracle was wrought [the ship was saved] and the lad got away safely. When he went to R. Joshua ben Levi, he found him in the teacher's chair in the great academy of Lydda and said, "Sir, I have a secret matter to confide to you. Follow me." At once R. Joshua ben Levi rose and followed him.

(Pause and consider the humility of R. Joshua ben Levi, who, though he had to follow the lad for three *mil*, did not first inquire of him, "What is it that you wish to tell me?")

When they reached the cave, the lad said, "Sir, these are stones of chalcedony [which I brought from the bottom of the sea for the construction of the Temple]." As he showed them to R. Joshua, their brightness shone forth so strongly that all of Lydda was lit up. Startled, he let them fall to the ground, and they disappeared.[1]

394. When R. Joshua ben Levi found the prophet Elijah standing by the entrance of the cave where R. Simeon ben Yohai was buried, he asked him, "Will I attain the world-to-come?" Elijah: "If the Lord here desires it."[2] R. Joshua ben Levi said, "I saw two, but heard the voice of a third."[3] He then asked him, "When will the Messiah come?" "Go and ask him yourself," was his reply. "Where is he sitting?" "At the entrance to the city of Rome." "And by what sign may I recognize him?" "He is sitting among the poor [lepers] burdened with sicknesses. All of them first untie all the bandages over their sores and then retie them, whereas he unties and reties each bandage separately, saying to himself: Should I be wanted, I must not be delayed."

So R. Joshua went to the Messiah and greeted him, saying, "Peace be upon you, my master and my teacher." "Peace upon you, O son of Levi," the Messiah replied. "When will you come, O master?" R. Joshua asked. "Today," was the Messiah's answer.

When R. Joshua came back to Elijah, Elijah asked, "What did he say to you?" R. Joshua: "Peace be unto you, O son of Levi." Elijah observed, "Thereby he assured you and your father of [a portion in] the world-to-come." R. Joshua: "[How can I believe him, since] he spoke falsely to me, for he told me that he would come today, yet he did not come." Elijah: "What he said to you was the beginning of the verse, "Today—if you would but hearken to His voice" (Ps. 95:7)."[4]

1. PRKM 18:5; Yalkut, Isa., §477; PR 32:3/4 (YJS 2:624).
2. He referred to the Presence, which was with them (Rashi). Samuel Edels renders: "When you are worthy thereof."
3. I.e., he saw only himself and Elijah there, but heard a third voice—that of the Presence.
4. B. Sanh 98a.

395. R. Joshua ben Levi attached himself to sufferers of *raatan*[5] and thus studied Torah; for, quoting, "A lovely hind and a graceful doe" (Prov. 5:19), he said, "If the Torah bestows grace upon those who study it, would it not also protect them [from infection]?"

When R. Joshua was about to die, the angel of death was instructed, "Go and do whatever he wishes." The angel came and showed himself to him, and R. Joshua said, "Show me my place [in Eden]." The angel: "Very well." R. Joshua: "But give me your knife, since otherwise you may terrify me with it on the way." The angel gave it to him. When they arrived, the angel lifted up R. Joshua and showed him [his place in Eden]. At that, R. Joshua jumped over and dropped on the other side [of the wall]. When the angel seized hold of him by the hem of his cloak, R. Joshua exclaimed, "I swear that I will not leave." The Holy One said, "If R. Joshua ever had an oath of his annulled, he must return; but if not, he need not return." [Thus, without experiencing death, R. Joshua remained in Eden.] The angel said, "Give me back my knife," but R. Joshua would not return it to him. A divine voice went forth and said to R. Joshua, "Give it to him, since it is needed for mortals."

Elijah heralded R. Joshua's arrival, "Make room for the son of Levi, make room for the son of Levi." As he proceeded on his way, he found R. Simeon ben Yohai sitting on thirteen golden mats. R. Simeon: "Are you the son of Levi?" R. Joshua: "Yes."

R. Simeon: "Has a rainbow ever appeared in your lifetime?"[6] R. Joshua: "Yes."

"If that is so [the other said], you are not the son of Levi."

(In fact, the rainbow did not appear [in his lifetime], but he thought: I must take no credit to myself.)[7]

396. R. Hanina ben Papa was R. Joshua ben Levi's friend, and when R. Hanina was about to die, the angel of death was commanded, "Go and do whatever he wishes." When he went to R. Hanina's house and revealed himself to him, R. Hanina said, "Allow me thirty days in which to go over my studies, for it is said, 'Happy is he who comes here in full possession of his learning.'" The angel of death left him and after thirty days appeared to him again. R. Hanina said, "Show me my place [in Eden]." "Very well," the angel replied. R. Hanina: "But give me your knife, since otherwise you may terrify me with it on the way." The angel: "Are you about to treat me as your friend has done?" R. Hanina: "Bring a Torah scroll and see if there is anything written in it that I have not fulfilled." The angel: "Have you attached

5. A skin disease causing nervous trembling and extreme weakness (Jastrow).
6. The rainbow in the sky, the token of God's pledge never again to bring a flood, does not, according to R. Simeon ben Yohai, appear in the sky during the lifetime of one like himself, who in his own person is a kind of rainbow and whose presence therefore shields his generation from extinction by floodwaters.
7. B. Ket 77b.

yourself to sufferers of *raatan* and engaged thus in study of Torah?"[1]

Nevertheless, when his soul passed to its eternal rest, a pillar of fire came between him and the world;[2] and we have a tradition that such a pillar of fire comes to set apart only one person in a generation, or at most two persons in a generation.

Approaching as close as he could to R. Hanina's bier, R. Alexandri said, "Remove the pillar out of deference to the sages," but R. Hanina disregarded him. "Remove it out of deference to your father." But again R. Hanina disregarded him. "Remove it," [R. Alexandri finally pleaded], "out of deference to your own person,"[3] and the pillar of fire departed.

Abbaye remarked, [The purpose of the pillar of fire was] to keep away anyone who failed to observe [even a single letter of] the Torah.

At that, R. Adda bar Matena retorted: This would also exclude you, sir, since you have no parapet on your roof. (However, R. Adda's reproach was not fair, for Abbaye did have such a parapet, which, as it happened, the wind had just then blown down.)[4]

397. At the time of their departure from this world, Zavdi ben Levi, R. Yose ben Petros, and R. Joshua ben Levi each quoted one of the following three verses. One quoted, "For this let every one that is godly pray unto Thee" (Ps. 32:6); another quoted, "So shall all those that take refuge in Thee rejoice" (Ps. 5:12); and the third quoted, "Oh how abundant is Thy goodness, which Thou hast laid up for them that fear Thee" (Ps. 31:20).[5]

Zavdi ben Levi yearned to behold the face of R. Joshua ben Levi, who appeared to him in a dream and showed him men whose faces looked straight ahead and others whose faces were lowered. Zavdi asked: What is the meaning of this? R. Joshua answered; Those whose faces look straight ahead are men who have their learning well in hand, while those whose faces are lowered do not.[6]

R. Yohanan ben ha-Nappah (died ca. 279 C.E.) and R. Simeon ben Lakish [Resh Lakish] (2d half of 2d century C.E.)

398. There was a woman [with child] who inhaled the smell of food on the Day of Atonement [and was seized with a craving to eat]. People came before Rabbi to question him whether food might be served to her. He replied: Go and whisper in her ear that it is the Day of Atonement. They whispered it to her, and she instantly overcame her craving. Rabbi applied to [the unborn child] the verse "Before I formed thee in the belly I knew thee" (Jer. 1:5).[7] From that woman issued R. Yohanan.[8]

399. R. Yohanan—when his mother conceived him, his father died; when his mother gave birth to him, she died.[9]

400. R. Yohanan said: Once, as I rode on my grandfather's shoulder, I heard R. Simeon ben Eleazar reciting the lore of Torah as he sat in his teacher's chair.[10]

401. R. Yohanan said: R. Oshaia Berabbi had twelve disciples. During the eighteen days I spent among them, I came to know the intellectual capacity and wisdom of every one of them.

R. Yohanan also said: When we were studying Torah in R. Oshaia's home, four of us used to sit in the space of one cubit.[11]

402. R. Yohanan said: I am the only one remaining of Jerusalem's men of outstanding beauty.

Let him who wishes to perceive R. Yohanan's beauty take a silver goblet as it emerges from the silversmith's, fill it with the seeds of red pomegranates, encircle its brim with a garland of red roses, and set it between the sun and the shade. Its lustrous glow will be an approximation of R. Yohanan's beauty.[12]

403. When R. Yohanan [a corpulent man] was ascending a staircase, with R. Ammi and R. Assi supporting him, the step [he stood on] began to sag under the weight. So he climbed the remainder of the staircase rapidly by himself, pulling up his two aides with him. The sages asked him, "Since your strength is so great, why do you require support?" R. Yohanan replied, "Otherwise, what strength will I have left [for Torah] in my old age?"[13]

404. R. Yohanan fell ill. When R. Hanina came to visit him, he asked, "Are your sufferings cherished by you?" R. Yohanan replied, "Neither they nor the reward for them." R. Hanina: "Give me your hand." R. Yohanan gave him his hand, and R. Hanina raised him up from the sickbed.

R. Eleazar ben Pedat fell ill, and R. Yohanan came to visit him. When R. Yohanan saw that R. Eleazar was lying in a dark room,[14] he bared his arm and light radiated from it. Then he noticed that R. Eleazar was weeping. So he asked, "Why are you weeping? Is it because you did not study enough Torah? Surely we have learned: 'The one

1. You were not as pious and staunch in your faith as R. Joshua ben Levi, who trusted in Torah's power to protect him from all evil. If R. Joshua, despite his extreme piety, did not hesitate to outwit me, the angel of death, how much more likely are you to do so!
2. To show that the rest of mankind are not worthy of being near him.
3. So that you may be eulogized.
4. B. Ket 77b.
5. P. AZ 3:1, 42c; Gen. R. 62:2; MTeh 5:11.
6. Eccles. R. 9:9, §1.
7. It is suggested here that when the woman with child inhaled the smell of food and craved it, it was in fact not she but the embryo that had the craving. The mother's ready acceptance of the whispered suggestion was thus due to the piety of the unborn child. (This note is derived from Yoma, Soncino, p. 405.)
8. B. Yoma 82b.
9. B. Kid 31b.
10. P. Maas 1:2, 48d.
11. B. Er 53a.
12. B. BM 84a.
13. B. Ket 62a.
14. R. Eleazar was a poor man and lived in a room without windows.

who does much and the one who does little have the same merit, provided that their hearts are directed to Heaven.' Is it perhaps because of your meager livelihood? Not everybody has the privilege of enjoying two tables—Torah and wealth. Is it perhaps because of [your lack of] children? Here is the bone of my tenth son!"[1]

R. Eleazar replied, "I am weeping on account of this beauty of yours, which will in the end waste away in the earth." R. Yohanan: "On that account, you surely have good reason to weep." And they both wept.

Presently, R. Yohanan asked him, "Are your sufferings cherished by you?" R. Eleazar replied, "Neither they nor the reward for them." R. Yohanan: "Give me your hand." R. Eleazar gave him his hand, and R. Yohanan raised him up [out of bed].[2]

405. Ilfa and R. Yohanan studied Torah together, but when they found themselves greatly distressed by poverty, one said to the other, "Let us go into business and make true the words 'Howbeit there shall be no needy among you' [Deut. 15:4] in our own lives." Then they went and sat down to eat at the foot of a deteriorating wall. While they were eating, two ministering angels came, and R. Yohanan overheard one angel saying to the other, "Let us bring down the wall upon them and kill them, for they are about to neglect life eternal and occupy themselves with life temporal." The other angel, however, replied, "Let them be: the time is not up yet for one of them." R. Yohanan asked Ilfa, "Did you hear anything?" Ilfa replied, "No." R. Yohanan then said to himself: Since I did hear and Ilfa did not, I must be the one whose time is not yet up. He said to Ilfa, "I will go back [to my studies] and make true in my own life the words 'The poor shall never cease out of the land' " (Deut. 15:11). So R. Yohanan returned to his studies, while Ilfa did not. By the time Ilfa came back to the city, R. Yohanan was made head of the academy, and the people of the town said to Ilfa, "Had you remained and devoted yourself to study, might you not have become the academy's head?"[3] Hearing that, Ilfa suspended himself from the top of a mast and said, "If anyone will put to me a question regarding a Baraita handed down by R. Hiyya and R. Oshaia, and find me unable to answer it by quoting a corroborating parallel from our Mishnah, I will throw myself from the mast into the water and drown."[4]

406. A story is told of when R. Yohanan was taking a walk up from Tiberias to Sepphoris, leaning on the shoulder of his disciple R. Hiyya bar Abba. When they came to a certain farm, R. Yohanan said: You see this farm—it had been mine and I sold it, because I wanted to devote myself entirely to the study of Torah. When they came to an olive orchard, R. Yohanan said: You see this olive orchard—it had been mine and I sold it, because I wanted to devote myself entirely to the study of Torah. When they came to a vineyard, R. Yohanan said: You see this vineyard—it had been mine and I sold it, because I wanted to devote myself entirely to the study of Torah. Then R. Hiyya began to weep. R. Yohanan asked: Why are you weeping? His companion replied: I weep because you did not put anything aside for your old age. R. Yohanan said: Hiyya, my son, is what I did really as foolish as you seem to think? I gave up something that took no more than six days to be created and acquired something that took forty days and forty nights to be revealed. For it took God no more than six days to create the entire world, as is written, "In six days the Lord made heaven and earth" (Exod. 31:17). But to reveal the Torah took him forty days and forty nights, as is written, "And Moses was there with the Lord forty days and forty nights" (Exod. 34:28).[5]

407. Whatever R. Yohanan had to eat, he would give the same to his [heathen] slave, about whom he would quote the verse "Did not He that made me in the womb make him? And did not the One fashion us both in the womb?" (Job 31:15).[6]

408. When R. Yohanan came to the verse "Behold, He putteth no trust in His holy ones" (Job 15:15), he wept [as he asked]: If He does not put His trust in His holy ones, in whom will He put His trust? One day, as he was walking on a road, he saw a man who was gathering figs leave those that were ripe and take those that were unripe. So he asked the man: Are not those that are ripe better? The man answered: I need these for the road. The unripe ones will keep, but the ripe ones will spoil.

Then R. Yohanan said to himself: I now understand the verse "Behold, He putteth no trust in His holy ones."[7]

409. R. Hana the Moneychanger said: Once Bar Nappaha stood over me and asked me for a Gordian denar with which to measure the size of a defect.[8] When I was about to stand up for him, he restrained me, saying, "Sit, my son, sit. Craftsmen when engaged in their work are not allowed to stand up for disciples of the wise."[9]

410. R. Yohanan was seated in the teacher's chair reading Scripture to the people of the Babylonian synagogue in Sepphoris. When the archon of the city passed by, R. Yohanan did not stand up. At that, the archon's servants were ready to whip him, but the archon said: Let him be; he is engaged in doing what his Creator commands."[10]

411. Whenever R. Eleazar was about to part from R. Yohanan [he would do the following]: If R. Yohanan had to leave first, R. Eleazar would remain standing, bowed over, until R. Yohanan disappeared from sight. But if R.

1. R. Yohanan, who lost ten sons, kept a bone of the tenth as a kind of grisly reminder.
2. B. Ber 5b.
3. Because Ilfa was older, he might well have been elected in place of R. Yohanan.
4. B. Ta 21a.
5. Exod. R. 47:5; Lev. R. 30:1; PRKM 27:1.
6. P. Ket 5:5, 30a.
7. God fears that the righteous, like the ripe figs, may later lose their savor of righteousness. Hence they are taken away when young. B. Hag 5a.
8. In, say, an animal's lung, to determine whether the animal is kosher.
9. B. Hul 54b.
10. P. Ber 5:1, 9a.

Eleazar had to leave first, he would keep walking backward until R. Yohanan could no longer be seen.[1]

412. R. Yohanan went for a walk, leaning on R. Jacob bar Idi. When R. Eleazar saw him, he sought to hide out of sight. R. Yohanan took offense, saying: This Babylonian has done two things to me—to begin with, he did not greet me; and secondly, he does not say, when citing a tradition, that it came from me. R. Jacob bar Idi replied: [R. Eleazar did not greet you] because it is the custom in Babylonia that the inferior person does not greet his superior.[2] For in Babylonia they comply literally with Job's remark "Young men saw me and hid themselves" (Job 29:8).

[Continuing his explanation of R. Eleazar's conduct] R. Jacob bar Idi asked: Should one give way to a procession of idols? R. Yohanan: Why should one accord them any kind of honor? The thing to do is to pass in front of them as if you do not see them. Then R. Jacob bar Idi said: If so, R. Eleazar did well in not passing in front of you.[3]

But why, R. Yohanan asked, did he not cite the tradition [he taught] as having come from me? As he was asking the question, R. Ammi and R. Assi came by, and, finding him very angry, cautioned him: A like outburst of anger occurred in the synagogue in Tiberias when R. Eliezer and R. Yose differed concerning a certain matter, until in the end, because of their anger, a scroll of Torah was ripped apart. A certain elder, R. Yose ben Kisma by name, who happened to be there, said, "I shall be surprised if this synagogue is not converted into a shrine for idolatry." Indeed, this is what happened.[4] R. Yohanan was even more deeply offended and asked R. Ammi and R. Asssi: But is R. Eleazar my colleague?[5]

As they were walking and saw a house of study, R. Jacob bar Idi said to R. Yohanan: Here R. Meir used to sit in the teacher's chair and cite rulings on law in the name of R. Ishmael, but he did not cite rulings on law in the name of R. Akiva. R. Yohanan replied: But everyone knows that R. Meir was R. Akiva's disciple.[6] R. Jacob bar Idi responded: So, too, does everyone know that R. Eleazar is R. Yohanan's disciple.

R. Jacob bar Idi went on: It is said, "As the Lord commanded Moses His servant, so did Moses command Joshua; and so did Joshua" (Josh. 11:15). But are we to suppose that at each and every command Joshua uttered, he would say, "This is what Moses told me"? The fact is that Joshua used to expound in the teacher's chair without indicating the source. But of course everyone knew that his teaching was that of Moses. So, too, when your disciple R. Eleazar sits in the teacher's chair and expounds without indicating the source, everyone naturally knows that his teaching is yours.

R. Yohanan then chided R. Ammi and R. Assi: Why do you not know how to conciliate as skillfully as our friend R. Jacob bar Idi?[7]

413. In the winter, when R. Yohanan's head did not ache, he wore the head tefillin as well as the arm tefillin; but in the summer, when his head ached, he would wear only the arm tefillin.[8]

414. R. Yohanan said: In my case, God's Name is profaned when I walk four cubits without uttering Torah or wearing teffilin.[9]

415. R. Yohanan said: [Once] on the Day of Atonement I was seized with ravenous hunger, and I went to the eastern side of a fig tree[10] and made true by my example the verse "Wisdom preserveth the life of him who hath it" (Eccles. 7:12).[11]

416. Zeira kept evading R. Yohanan, who was pressing him: "Marry my daughter." One day, as they were walking on a road, they came to a pool of water. Zeira hoisted R. Yohanan on his shoulder and carried him across. R. Yohanan said to Zeira: My teaching seems to be right [for you], but my daughters are not![12]

417. Hezekiah son of R. Hiyya used to say of R. Yohanan, "This one is not a son of man."[13] According to others, he used to say, "This one is indeed a son of man."[14]

418. Throughout Rav's days, R. Yohanan used to address him in writing, "Greetings to our master in Babylonia." After Rav's departure from this world, he wrote to Samuel, "Greetings to our colleague in Babylonia." Samuel said to himself: Is there nothing in which I am R. Yohanan's master? So he sat down and sent him calculations for intercalating months sixty years in advance. But R. Yohanan said: Now, he knows only calculations. Samuel then sent R. Yohanan thirteen parchment scrolls[15] of questions concerning doubtful cases of meat of animals torn by beasts in the field. Then R. Yohanan said: It is clear that I have a master in Babylonia. I must go to see him.

He asked a child, "Recite for me the last verse you

---

1. B. Yoma 53a.
2. In order to spare the superior the trouble of responding. Cf. above, part 1, chap. 5, §51.
3. Since he felt he had no right to greet you, he would have had to seem to ignore you and thus appear to be disrespectful.
4. The point: One is not to take offense at the acts or words of fellow scholars.
5. Since he is only my disciple, my anger is warranted.
6. So there was no need for R. Meir to cite R. Akiva by name.
7. P. Ber 2:1, 4b; P. Shek 2:7, 47a; B. Yev 96b; Midrash Sam. 19.
8. P. Ber 2:3, 4c.
9. Unaware that I stopped studying Torah only because of weariness, people might, seeing my example, take even greater liberties. B. Yoma 86a.
10. Figs on a tree do not ripen at the same time. Those that are on the tree's eastern side, exposed to the sun, ripen first. Their aroma relieved R. Yohanan's hunger.
11. B. Yoma 83b.
12. "What R. Yohanan is saying to Zeira is: My teaching seems to fit you—you know enough of it to act helpfully toward me, as a disciple should act toward his teacher—but my teaching failed to teach you the desirability of marrying a wife bred in a scholar's family. In other words, 'When will you come to your senses and marry my daughter?' " (Leon Nemoy). B. Kid 71b.
13. He is superhuman.
14. Fully a man. B. Shab 112b.
15. *Gevillim* ("parchment scrolls")—R. Hananel. BR: *Gemallim* ("camel loads").

learned." The child replied, "Now Samuel is dead" (1 Sam. 28:3). R. Yohanan said to himself: This means that [my master] Samuel is gone.

But it was not so. In fact Samuel was not dead then, but the verse came to be cited so that R. Yohanan would not be put to the trouble [of going to Babylonia to visit Samuel].[1]

419. When Resh Lakish sold himself [for a good sum] to the Lydians,[2] he took along a waterskin with a stone in it, "Because," he said, "I have heard that on the last day [before combat in the arena] they grant any request the gladiator may make, in order that his blood may be sweet [i.e., that he may face combat with his mind at ease]." On the last day, when they asked him, "What would you like?" he replied, "I want you to let me tie your arms, set you down, and give each of you a blow and a half with this waterskin." He then bound them and seated them. As each of them received a blow and was stunned, each [grimaced and] gnashed his teeth. Resh Lakish said, "Are you laughing at me? Remember, you still have half a blow coming." Then he killed them all.

Thus he procured his freedom. Later, as he sat [on the ground] eating and drinking, his daughter asked, "Don't you want something to recline on?" He replied, "Daughter, my belly is my cushion."

[Having been fond of spiced food], he left, at the time of his death, a *kav* of saffron, thus applying to himself the verse "And they shall leave to others their substance" (Ps. 49:11).[3]

420. One day R. Yohanan was bathing in the Jordan when Resh Lakish saw him and jumped into the Jordan after him. R. Yohanan said to him, "Your strength should be devoted to Torah." Resh Lakish replied, "Your beauty should be devoted to women." R. Yohanan: "If you repent, I will let you wed my sister, who is more beautiful than I." He undertook to repent, but when he tried to jump back and collect his gear, he could not do so.[4]

Subsequently R. Yohanan had him read Scripture and study Mishnah, and he became a great man.[5]

421. R. Yohanan and Resh Lakish both said: We won the privilege of studying Torah only because we saw Rabbi's toes showing out of the Roman shoes he wore, which leave the wearer's toes uncovered.[6]

422. When R. Kahana went up to the Land of Israel, Rav said, "Be sure not to point out any difficulty to R. Yohanan for the next seven years." When he arrived, he found Resh Lakish sitting and [for the benefit of younger scholars] going over the lecture R. Yohanan had given that day. Since he had never met Resh Lakish, he quietly asked them, "Where is Resh Lakish?" They asked him, "Why do you wish to know?" R. Kahana replied, "This point [in the lecture] is difficult and that point is difficult, but this could be given as an answer to the one and that could be given as an answer to the other." When they mentioned this to Resh Lakish, he went over to R. Yohanan and said, "A lion has come up from Babylonia; the master should therefore prepare tomorrow's lecture carefully." The next day R. Kahana was seated in the first row of disciples, right in front of R. Yohanan. But, as R. Yohanan gave one ruling in law and R. Kahana raised no difficulty, and he gave another ruling and R. Kahana still raised no difficulty, R. Kahana was moved back seven rows and seated in the very last row. Then R. Yohanan said to Resh Lakish, "The lion you mentioned turns out to be no more than a fox." At this, R. Kahana whispered the prayer "May it be the will [of Heaven] that these seven rows be regarded as the equivalent of the seven years Rav spoke of." At that, R. Kahana rose to his feet and said to R. Yohanan, "Will the master start the lecture from its beginning?" As R. Yohanan proceeded to give the first ruling in law, R. Kahana pointed out a difficulty; when R. Yohanan gave the second ruling, R. Kahana again pointed out a difficulty, until finally R. Kahana was put back in the first row. R. Yohanan had been sitting on seven cushions, and each time R. Kahana pointed out a difficulty, R. Yohanan pulled out one of the cushions from under himself, until finally all the cushions were pulled out from under him and he remained seated on the bare ground.[7]

R. Yohanan was then a very old man, and his eyebrows overshadowed his eyes. So he said to his disciples, "Raise up my eyebrows. I want to see him." They raised up his eyebrows with a silver Kohl stick, and when R. Yohanan saw that R. Kahana's lips were cleft,[8] he thought that R. Kahana was laughing at him. He was greatly humiliated. Seeing R. Yohanan in such a state, R. Kahana's soul left him. The next day, when R. Yohanan said to the sages, "Have you noticed how this Babylonian carried on?" they told him, "But such is his natural appearance." Hearing that, R. Yohanan went to the cave [where R. Kahana's body was placed] and, seeing a snake coiled at its entrance, said, "Snake, O snake, open your mouth [and let your tail go][9] to allow the master to visit his disciple." But the snake did not open its mouth. He then said, "To allow a colleague to visit his associate!" But it still did not open [its mouth, until he said], "To allow a disciple to visit his master." At that, the snake opened its mouth. Then R. Yohanan besought God's mercy and brought R. Kahana back to life, and said to him, "Had I known that such was the master's appearance, I would not have felt humiliated. Now will the master please go with us [to the academy]." R. Kahana replied, "If you are able to beseech God's mercy that I would not die [should you again be humiliated], I will go, but if not, I will not go. For, having experienced the ordeal of death once [because of your

1. B. Hul 95b.
2. In his early years, Simeon ben Lakish was a gladiator.
3. B. Git 47a.
4. The mere decision to study Torah so depleted his strength that he was unable to haul his heavy equipment. Cf. above in this chapter, §229.
5. B. BM 84a.
6. P. Betz 5:2, 63a.
7. A way of showing that he no longer considered himself worthy of occupying the elevated place of master.
8. Because of a physical defect following an accident.
9. The snake held its tail in its mouth. The Munich ms. reads: "open the door."

sensitivity], I do not wish to experience it again." Then R. Yohanan shook him, stood him up, and proceeded to consult him on all doubtful points, which R. Kahana cleared up for him.

[In subsequent years] R. Yohanan used to say [to his Palestinian disciples], "Do you think it is your [Palestinian] learning that I utter? It is theirs [the Babylonians']." [1]

423. Anyone with whom Resh Lakish talked in the marketplace could get a loan without witnesses.[2]

424. One who saw Resh Lakish in the house of study would think that he was uprooting mountains and grinding them one against the other.[3]

425. Because Resh Lakish meditated much in Torah, he would [sometimes] walk beyond the Sabbath limit[4] and, in keeping with the verse "Because of thy love for it, thou errest always" (Prov. 5:19), was not aware of having done so.[5]

426. Resh Lakish made it his practice to set in order what he had learned forty times—to correspond to the forty days needed for the Torah to be given—before he presumed to come into the presence of R. Yohanan.

Resh Lakish used to say: When you see a disciple to whom studying is as hard as iron, it is because what he attempts to learn is not set in order in his mind.[6]

427. Resh Lakish[7] said: There are those who know how to string [scriptural passages one to another by showing linkages in meaning] but do not know how to penetrate [into the sense of each passage]; there are others who know how to penetrate but do not know how to string. But I am one who knows both how to string and how to penetrate.[8]

428. R. Simeon ben Lakish used to study Torah with great intensity in a cave outside Tiberias, where every day a water carrier would have a pitcher of water ready for him, so that when he entered feeling very tired, he would take the pitcher and drink its water. Once, when the water carrier came by and sat down next to him to rest a bit, he said, "Master, do you remember that you and I used to go to school together? But you were deemed worthy [of higher study of Torah], while I was not deemed worthy of it. Pray for me that in the world-to-come my portion may be next to yours." Resh Lakish replied, "What can I pray for in your behalf [other than] that your portion may be with your fellow craftsmen, since each and every man will be made to dwell only with the fellows in his craft?"[9]

1. B. BK 117a–b.
2. Since one could trust the honesty of such a man. B. Yoma 9b.
3. B. Sanh 24a.
4. Two thousand cubits.
5. P. Ber 5:1, 9a.
6. B. Ta 8a.
7. The editions attribute the utterance to R. Levi, not to Resh Lakish.
8. Song R. 1:10, §2.
9. Eccles. R. 3:9, §1.

429. R. Simeon ben Lakish was sitting and studying Torah in a cave outside Tiberias. When two women came out of that cave, one said to the other, "Blessed be He who made it possible for me to leave Tiberias's bad climate." R. Simeon called out to them, "Where do you come from?" The women: "From Mazga." R. Simeon: "I know Mazga—[its climate is so bad that] it has only two columns [left standing, all other structures having deteriorated]. Blessed be He who endows each place with charm for its inhabitants."[10]

430. During a sabbatical year, R. Hiyya bar Zarniki and R. Simeon ben Jehozadak went to Asya[11] to intercalate a month in the year. Resh Lakish happened to meet them and attached himself to them, saying, "I will come and watch how they go about it." When he saw a man plowing, he said, "That man a priest, and plowing [during the sabbatical year]!" They replied, "The man might say, 'I am a servant on an imperial estate [and must obey my Roman master].' " Farther on, he saw a man pruning his vineyard. So Resh Lakish said, "That man a priest, and pruning his vineyard!" They replied, "The man might say, 'I need the twigs to weave a bale (*akal*)[12] for my olive press [to supply olive oil].' " Resh Lakish commented, "Only the man's heart knows whether he is *akel*, 'weaving,' or *akalkallot*,[13] 'twisting [the law].' "

They decided that Resh Lakish was a troublemaker. So, upon reaching their destination, they went to the upper chamber and pulled up the ladder from under it, so that Resh Lakish could not follow them.

Presently Resh Lakish went to R. Yohanan and asked, "Are people who appear to be easygoing about the observances of the sabbatical year[14] fit to intercalate the year?" But then Resh Lakish reconsidered, saying, "R. Hiyya and R. Simeon present no difficulty, for they are like the sages who once accepted the testimony of three herdsmen concerning intercalation; then they did the calculating on their own." Subsequently, however, considering the matter further, he said, "The two instances are not alike. In the case of the herdsmen, the sages went back, voted, and intercalated the year on their own. Here [in the matter of tolerating flagrant violation of the sabbatical year] we have what amounts to a confederacy of wicked men, and men who are in such a confederacy with the wicked may not be part [of an intercalary board]." R. Yohanan observed, "It is indeed a painful problem."

When R. Hiyya bar Zarniki and R. Simeon ben Je-

10. Gen. R. 34:15.
11. "[Isaac] Halevy . . . suggests that Assia [Essa, east of the Sea of Tiberias] was especially chosen for the intercalation as it was considered a safe place owing to its hot springs, which attracted many visitors from far and wide, and the arrival of the rabbis would not rouse the suspicion of the Romans" (Isidore Epstein in Sanh, Soncino, p. 151, n. 2).
12. "A bale of loose texture containing the olive pulp to be pressed" (Jastrow).
13. A play on the sound of the two Hebrew words can be approximated by opposing "honest weaving" to "deceiving"; or "being on the level" to "in league with the devil."
14. They were so ready to excuse people who were violating it.

hozadak came before R. Yohanan, they complained, "Resh Lakish described us as herdsmen, and you did not object." R. Yohanan replied, "Even if he had called you shepherds,[1] what could I have said in your defense?"[2]

431. At one time Resh Lakish was a watchman in an orchard. When a man came and helped himself to some figs, he threw a stone at him. But the man paid him no heed. So Resh Lakish said, "Let the man be put under a ban." "On the contrary," the man replied, "let the one who invoked the ban be put under it. I agree I am liable to pay money for trespassing, but does my liability extend to being put under a ban?"

When Resh Lakish went to the house of study [and reported the incident], he was told, "The man's ban against you is valid; your ban against him is not valid." "What remedy is there for me?" Resh Lakish asked. "Go to the man and ask him to absolve you." "But I do not know who or where he is." "Then go to the patriarch, and he will absolve you."[3]

432. Once, when Resh Lakish was walking on a road and reached a pond, a man came along, hoisted him on his shoulders, and started taking him across. Resh Lakish asked the man, "Have you read Scripture?" The man: "Yes, I have read it." "Have you recited Mishnah?" "Yes, I have recited four divisions of Mishnah." "Then you have hewn for yourself four mountains of Torah, yet you carry Resh Lakish on your shoulder! Throw Resh Lakish into the water."[4]

433. When R. Abbahu and Resh Lakish were about to enter that notorious city of Caesarea, R. Abbahu said to Resh Lakish, "Why should we enter a city of blasphemers and revilers?" Resh Lakish got off his donkey, gathered some sand, and stuffed it into R. Abbahu's mouth. When R. Abbahu asked, "Why do you do this to me?" Resh Lakish replied, "The Holy One is not pleased with one who speaks ill of Israel."[5]

434. When R. Imi was kidnapped in Sifsufa, R. Jonathan said, "The corpse may as well be wrapped in its shroud." Resh Lakish replied, "Before I say that R. Imi is already slain, I myself am willing to run the risk of being slain. I will go and do what I can to rescue him." So he went and persuaded the kidnappers to return R. Imi alive. Then Resh Lakish said to them, "Come with me to a certain elder who will pray in your behalf." They went with him to R. Yohanan, who said to them, "May what you intended to do to R. Imi be done to you; indeed, may it befall all people like you."

Sure enough, even before the kidnappers got to Apiphserus, all of them were slain.[6]

[1] Shepherds, who are disqualified as witnesses, are more lowly in status than herdsmen.

[2] B. Sanh 26a.

[3] B. MK 17a.

[4] You should not act as my servant. B. Meg 28b.

[5] Song R. 1:6, §1.

[6] P. Ter 8:10, 46b.

435. R. Yohanan was robbed in Ale-kaniah. When he came up to the sages' meeting place, Resh Lakish kept asking him questions, which he did not answer. Finally Resh Lakish asked, "What is wrong with you?" R. Yohanan: "All parts of the body depend on the heart, and the heart depends on the purse." Resh Lakish: "Why such an adage?" R. Yohanan: "I was robbed in Ale-kaniah." Resh Lakish: "Show me the spot." R. Yohanan went out and showed it to him. When Resh Lakish espied the men of Ale-kaniah in the distance, he began ringing a bell. [Alarmed] they said, "If the one robbed is R. Yohanan, he may take back one-half [of what was robbed]." But R. Yohanan said, "By your lives, I will take back everything!" And he took it all back.[7]

436. One day the sages in the house of study were divided on the following question: At what stage [in their manufacture] are a sword, a knife, a dagger, a spear, a handsaw, and a scythe deemed to be [finished] utensils and susceptible to uncleanness? The answer first suggested was: when their manufacture is finished. But when is their manufacture finished? R. Yohanan stated, "After they have been tempered in a furnace." Resh Lakish maintained, "Only after they have been quenched in water." R. Yohanan: "A robber is an expert in his trade."[8] Resh Lakish [resentful]: "What special benefit have you bestowed upon me? There [as a robber] I was called master, and here I am called master." R. Yohanan: "I bestowed upon you the benefit of bringing you under the wings of the Presence." Nevertheless, R. Yohanan was mortified [by the sharpness of the exchange], while Resh Lakish [was so overcome by remorse that he] fell ill. Thereupon his wife came and wept before R. Yohanan, pleading: "Forgive him for the sake of my sons." He replied: "Scripture says, 'Leave thy fatherless children with Me. I will rear them' " (Jer. 49:11). "For the sake of my widowhood then!" He replied: "Scripture says, 'And let thy widows rely on Me' " (ibid.). [Soon afer that], Resh Lakish died.

R. Yohanan grieved so much for Resh Lakish that he no longer came down to the scholars' assembly. And so the sages deliberated: "Who is to go and ease his mind? Let R. Eleazar ben Pedat go, since his knowledge of *Halakhot* is acute." R. Eleazar went and sat down before him; and whatever R. Yohanan said, R. Eleazar observed, "There is a Baraita that supports you." R. Yohanan finally exclaimed, "Do you think you are at all like Ben Lakish? When I would state a matter, Ben Lakish used to raise twenty-four objections, which I responded to with twenty-four rebuttals, forming a debate that led to a fuller comprehension of the tradition. But all you say is, 'There is

[7] Ibid.

[8] "This was quoted only proverbially, though in later times it was taken literally, and Resh Lakish was held to have been a robber. Actually, he had been a circus attendant, to which his necessitous circumstances had reduced him, and these weapons were used in the course of that calling. (Heinrich Graetz: [Isaac Hirsch] Weiss . . . understands the phrase literally, but translates *listaah* as 'thief catcher.' If that be correct, Resh Lakish at one time helped the Roman government, just as R. Eleazar ben R. Simeon and R. Ishmael ben Jose [Yose] had done" (BM, Soncino, p. 481, n. 4).

a Baraita that supports you,' as though I do not know on my own that what I said was right." Then R. Yohanan stood up, rent his garments, and, bursting into tears, cried out, "Where are you, Ben Lakish? Where are you, Ben Lakish?" He kept crying in anguish until he went out of his mind. Then the sages besought mercy in his behalf, and he died.[1]

437. Once [after Resh Lakish died], when R. Yohanan met the young son of Resh Lakish and said to him, "Recite for me the verse [you learned today]," the son replied, "Tithe that you may be able to tithe again" (Deut. 14:22), and went on to ask, "What do these words imply?" R. Yohanan answered, "Tithe that you may become rich[2] [and be able to tithe again]." The son then asked, "What proof have you for what you say?" R. Yohanan replied, "Go test it [for yourself]." The son asked, "Is it permissible to test the Holy One? Is it not written, 'Ye shall not test the Lord' (Deut. 6:16)?" R. Yohanan replied, "Thus taught R. Oshaia: 'Testing God is forbidden except in this instance, for it is said, "Bring ye the whole tithe and test Me now herewith, saith the Lord of hosts, if I will not open you the windows of heaven, and pour you out a blessing, that there shall be more than sufficiency" [Mal. 3:10]. (What is the meaning [of the words] 'that there shall be more than sufficiency'? R. Rami bar Hama said in the name of Rav: Until your lips shall grow weary from saying, 'It is sufficient')". The son then exclaimed, "Had I already come to this verse in my studies, I would have had no need of you or R. Oshaia, your teacher."

On another occasion, R. Yohanan met the young son of Resh Lakish sitting and reciting the verse "The foolishness of man perverteth his way; and his heart fretteth against the Lord" (Prov. 19:3). R. Yohanan sat down, and, after pondering the verse's implication for a while, he said, "Is it possible that in the Writings there is something not alluded to in the Torah?" The son replied, "Is not this verse in fact alluded to in the Torah? Is it not written, 'And their heart failed them, and they turned trembling one to another, saying [indignantly]: "What is this that God hath done unto us?" (Gen. 42:28)?"[3] R. Yohanan lifted his eyes and gazed at him [in astonishment]. At that, his mother rushed in and took him away, saying to her son, "Get away from him, lest he do to you what he did to your father."[4]

438. When R. Yohanan died, all images were bowed down—a way of saying that no image was as beautiful as he.[5]

439. When R. Yohanan died, his generation applied to him the verse "When a man giveth all the substance of his house for love" (Song 8:7); for such love as R. Yohanan had for the Torah, "he will be given rich spoil [in the world-to-come]" (ibid.).[6]

440. When R. Yohanan died, R. Isaac ben Eleazar began his eulogy: Grievous is this day for Israel as a day when the sun sets at noon.

When R. Yohanan died, R. Ammi [no immediate kin] observed the seven [days of mourning] as well as the thirty.[7]

R. Judah [II] the Patriarch (R. Yudan the Patriarch) (fl. 225–53 C.E.)

441. R. Yohanan once visited R. Yudan the Patriarch, who came out to greet him wearing a plain flaxen garment. R. Yohanan said, "Go back and put on your woolen garment, because we are told, 'Thine eyes shall see the king in his beauty' " (Isa. 33:17). As R. Yohanan was about to leave, R. Yudan said, "Bring him a choice snack." R. Yohanan said, "Be sure to send for Menahem, the [renowned] pastry cook, in keeping with the verse 'The law of kindness is on her tongue' " (Prov. 31:26).[8]

When R. Yohanan left, he saw R. Hanina bar Sisi, [R. Yudan's coadjutor] splitting wood. He said, "Master, this does not suit your dignity." R. Hanina: "But what am I to do? I have no one to help me." R. Yohanan: "If you could not afford help, you should not have accepted the office to which you were appointed."[9]

442. In a synagogue in Tiberias, Yose of Maon[10] interpreted in Aramaic the verse "Hear this, O ye priests" (Hos. 5:1)—why do you not labor in study of Torah? Did I not allow you twenty-four gifts as a prerogative?"[11] The priests' reply: But Israel give us nothing now.[12]

He went on: "Attend, ye House of Israel" (Hos. 5:1)—why do you not give to the priests the twenty-four gifts that I commanded you at Sinai? They replied: The [Roman] king takes everything.

He continued, "Give ear, O house of the king,[13] for unto you will come judgment" (Hos. 5:1). It is to you that I said, "This then shall be the priests' [prerogative]" (Deut. 18:3). Therefore shall I sit in judgment over the king's house to bring their rule to an end and have them perish from the world.

When R. Yudan heard what Yose had said, he was enraged and Yose, frightened, fled. Both R. Yohanan and

1. B. BM 84a, P. Meg 1:11, 72b.
2. A play on words: *isser* ("to tithe") and *hit'asher* ("to become rich").
3. First they sold their brother Joseph, and then they complained at the punishment meted out to them by God.
4. B. Ta 9a.
5. P. AZ 3:1, 42c.
6. So Targum, ad loc. JV: "he would be utterly contemned." But the stem *bz* can mean both "contemn" and "spoil, booty." Lev. R. 30:1.
7. An immediate kin's first seven days of obligatory mourning, which is intense, are followed by twenty-three days during which the mourning is of lesser intensity.
8. So that the snack will be pleasing to the palate.
9. P. Sanh 2:6, 20c–d.
10. A town near Tiberias.
11. Most of them are listed in Num. 18. Receipt of them, it was anticipated, would have given priests time to study Torah.
12. Now that the Temple is no longer in existence and the priests no longer serve.
13. The phrase "house of the king" is code for the patriarchate.

Resh Lakish went in to pacify R. Yudan. They said, "Master, we should be grateful to the nations of the world who bring mimes into their theaters and circuses to entertain them. They are thus induced to converse amicably among themselves without lapsing into foolish quarrels. It was [in order to wean people from vain pursuits] that Yose of Maon expounded words of Torah, yet you are enraged at him! He is an eminent scholar." R. Yudan: "But does he know anything at all of Torah?" They: "Yes." R. Yudan: "Was he an apprentice to sages?" They: "Yes." R. Yudan: "If so, let him come to see me." When R. Yose came, R. Yudan asked him, "What is meant by 'Their mother hath played the harlot' [Hos. 2:7]? Was our mother Sarah a harlot?!" Yose: "As the daughter, so the mother—'Like mother, like daughter' [Ezek. 16:44]—as the generation, so its patriarch; as the patriarch, so the generation; as the altar, so its priests." Some quote him as having said, "As the garden, so the gardener."

R. Yudan then reproached Yose: "It is not enough that you insulted me once behind my back, now you insult me to my face three times over."[1]

443. Once, while R. Yannai was out for a walk, leaning on the shoulder[2] of Simlai, his attendant, R. Yudan the Patriarch came toward them. The attendant said to R. Yannai, "The man coming toward us looks elegant, even as his cloak looks elegant." When R. Yudan came close, R. Yannai felt the cloak and said, "This has the same legal minimum to incur ritual uncleanness as does a sack. [In short, the material of this cloak is like sackcloth."][3]

Then R. Yannai set forth before R. Yudan a matter of *Halakah*, and R. Yudan responded in a superficial way. At that, R. Yannai said to his attendant, "Move along! This man does not wish to learn."[4]

444. Resh Lakish expounded: When the patriarch commits a sin, he may be sentenced to flogging by a court of three. When R. Yudan the Patriarch heard of this, he was so enraged that he sent a detachment of Goths to seize him. They kept after him until Resh Lakish fled [for safety] to a tower near Tiberias. (Some say he fled to Kefar Hittim.) The next day R. Yohanan went up to the scholars' assembly, as did R. Yudan the Patriarch, who asked R. Yohanan, "Why does our master not discuss with us a matter of Torah?" R. Yohanan began to make believe that he was clapping by using only one hand. R. Yudan: "Can one clap with one hand?" R. Yohanan: "No, but when Resh Lakish is not here, I have only one hand." R. Yudan: "Where is he? I will let him go free." R. Yohanan: "In the tower." R. Yudan: "Tomorrow you and I will go to see him." R. Yohanan sent word to Resh Lakish: "Prepare a theme in Torah, because the patriarch is coming to see you." Resh Lakish went out to greet the patriarch and said, "The example you set is like that of your Creator. When the Holy One came to redeem Israel, He sent no emissary, no angel—He [came] Himself as it is said, 'I will go through the land of Egypt' [Exod. 12:12], He and His staff of angels."[5] R. Yudan then asked him, "Why did you make that statement about flogging the patriarch?" Resh Lakish: "What do you suppose—that out of fear of you I should withhold words of God's Torah? As R. Samuel bar Isaac put it, 'Nay, my sons; for it is no good report which I hear—the Lord's people should remove' [1 Sam. 2:24]—should remove such a person from his high office."[6]

445. When the patriarch's family appointed a judge who was unlearned in Torah, the sages said to Judah bar Nahmani, Resh Lakish's interpreter,[7] "Go and stand at his side as interpreter." Judah stationed himself by the judge and bent down [to hear what he wished to say], but he said nothing. So Judah began to expound, "Ah, you who say, 'Wake up' to wood, 'Awaken' to inert stone! Can this person teach? Why, he is encased in gold and silver, but there is no spirit in him" (Hab. 2:19). The Holy One will requite those who appoint such a person, for the verse goes on to say, "The Lord is in His holy Temple; let all the earth keep silence before Him" (ibid.).[8]

446. Resh Lakish went to pay his respects to our Rabbi [Judah I, the Patriarch]. "Pray for me," R. Judah begged him, "for this Roman government is very evil."[9] Take nothing from anyone," Resh Lakish told him, "and then you will not have to give anything." While Resh Lakish was sitting with R. Judah, a woman came in, bringing R. Judah a dish with a knife in it. He took the knife and returned the dish to the woman. At that moment an imperial courier came in and saw the knife, took a fancy to it, and carried it off. Toward evening Resh Lakish again went to pay his respects to our Rabbi and saw him laughing. "Why are you laughing?" Resh Lakish asked. R. Judah: "That knife you saw—an imperial courier came in, saw it, coveted it, and took it away." Resh Lakish: "Did I tell you that if you take nothing from anyone, you will not have to give anything to anyone?"[10]

447. At one time, Diocletian[11] was a swineherd near Tiberias. Whenever he approached the house of study of R. Yudan the Patriarch, the children used to go out and rough him up. Presently, when he became emperor, he took up residence in Panias[12] and sent a letter to Tiberias: I command the notables of the Jews to come and appear

1. P. Sanh 2:6, 20d; Gen. R. 80:1.
2. When R. Yannai became old, his sight was defective.
3. Unlike a garment whose minimum to incur uncleanness is three by three handbreadths, a sack, being of lesser importance, has a minimum of four by four handbreadths (Kel 27:2; Ned 7:3). In other words. R. Yudan's elegance is not real, since the cloak is of cheap material.
4. B. BB 111a.
5. R. Yohanan.
6. P. Sanh 2:1, 19d–20a; R. Hor 3:1, 47a.
7. He expounds aloud and in detail to the gathering what the judge has uttered concisely and in a low voice.
8. B. Sanh 7b.
9. Its demands are exorbitant.
10. Gen. R. 78:12.
11. Diocletian was emperor of Rome from 285 to 305 C.E.; his father was a slave.
12. Caesarea Philippi, a city in the north of Palestine.

before me immediately after the conclusion of the Sabbath. He also commanded his emissary: "Be sure to give the letter to the Jews on Sabbath eve as it begins getting dark."[1]

When R. Samuel bar Nahman went down to bathe, he saw R. Yudan the Patriarch standing in front of the great house of study, his face quite pale. R. Samuel asked, "Why is your face so pale?" R. Yudan replied, "Such-and-such an order has been sent to me by the Roman government." R. Samuel: "Come down and bathe, for your Creator will perform miracles for you." When the two entered the bathhouse, a bath sprite came jesting and dancing toward them. R. Yudan the Patriarch wished to scold him, but R. Samuel bar Nahman said, "Master, leave him alone, for sometimes he shows himself before miracles." Then to the sprite: "Your master is in distress, yet you stand here jesting and dancing." The sprite: "Eat and drink and keep the Sabbath with good cheer, for your God will perform miracles for you and I will set you before the emperor immediately after the conclusion of the Sabbath."

At the outgoing of the Sabbath, immediately after the service, the sprite took them and set them in front of the gate [for Panias]. When the emperor was informed, "Lo, they are standing before the gate," he ordered, "Shut the gate." At that, the sprite took them and set them in the center of the town. When the emperor was informed, he exclaimed, "I command that the bathhouse be heated for seven days and seven nights. Then have them enter and bathe, and after that appear before me." Accordingly, the bathhouse was heated for seven days and seven nights, but the sprite entered it and tempered the heat for them, so that when they entered it they could bathe, and afterward appear before the emperor, who said to them, "Because you know that your God performs miracles for you, you insult the emperor!" They replied, "We did insult Diocletian the swineherd, but to Diocletian the emperor we willingly submit." "Even so," the emperor replied, "you should not insult the humblest Roman citizen or the lowest-ranking Roman soldier."[2]

448. Hiyya bar Abba came to Eleazar and said to him: Please ask R. Yudan the Patriarch to write a letter of commendation on my behalf so that I may go abroad for my livelihood. Eleazar asked for the letter, and R. Yudan wrote: We are sending you a distinguished man. Since he is sent by us, he is to be treated as our own emissary, indeed as we would be treated, provided he intends to return to us in the Land. (According to some, R. Yudan wrote: We are sending you a distinguished man. Wherein his distinction? He is not ashamed to say, "[Regarding this matter] I have not heard any tradition.").[3]

449. Resh Lakish said in the name of R. Judah the Patriarch: The world endures only for the sake of the breath of schoolchildren. Not even for the building of the Temple are children to be deprived of their study of Torah.

Resh Lakish said to R. Judah the Patriarch: I have a tradition from my forebears (others say: from your forebears) that if there are no schoolchildren in a town, it is bound to be destroyed.

R. Judah the Patriarch sent R. Hiyya, R. Ammi, and R. Assi to go through the small cities of the Land of Israel to set up teachers of Scripture and teachers of Mishnah in them. When they came to a place where they found neither teachers of Scripture nor teachers of Mishnah, they said, "Bring us the guardians of the city." When the city's bailiffs were brought, the sages said, "Are these the guardians of a city? They may well turn out to be its destroyers." They were asked, "Who, then, are the true guardians of a city?" They replied, "The teachers of Scripture and teachers of Mishnah. As Scripture says, 'Except the Lord guard the city, the watchman waketh but in vain' " (Ps. 127:1).[4]

450. When R. Yudan the Patriarch, grandson of R. Judah [I] the Patriarch, died. R. Hiyya bar Abba pushed R. Zera [a priest] into the synagogue of Gufta near Sepphoris[5] and caused him to be ritually unclean.[6]

R. Eleazar ben Pedat (fl. 1st half of 4th century C.E.)

451. R. Yohanan said to Resh Lakish: I have observed that when Ben Pedat is seated in the teacher's chair and expounding Torah, he is like Moses expounding from the mouth of the Almighty.[7]

452. "Because of thy love for her, thou forgettest always" (Prov. 5:19), as did R. Eleazar ben Pedat. It is said of R. Eleazar ben Pedat that he used to sit occupied with Torah in the lower marketplace in Sepphoris, while his [forgotten] cloak lay in the upper marketplace.

R. Isaac ben Eliezer said: A man once came to pick it up and found a venomous serpent in it.[8]

453. R. Yohanan said to R. Eleazar, "Come, and I will teach you the Work of the Chariot."[9] He replied, "I am not old enough." When he did become old enough,[10] R. Yohanan died. Then R. Assi said to him, "Come, and I will teach you the Work of the Chariot." R. Eleazar replied, "Had I had the merit, I would have learned it from your teacher R. Yohanan."[11]

454. R. Eleazar said: I saw R. Yohanan in a dream. So I am sure I will now say something worthwhile.[12]

1. Making it impossible to carry out his command.
2. P. Ter 8:8, 46b–c; Gen. R. 63:8.
3. P. Hag 1:8, 76d.
4. B. Shab 119b; P. Hag 1:7, 76c.
5. Where the funeral was held.
6. Since all, even priests, are obligated to participate in the funeral of a patriarch (Maimonides, Code, XIV, iv, iii, 10 [YJS 3:172]). P. Ber 3:1, 6a.
7. B. Yev 72b.
8. Guarding it. B. Er 54a.
9. The mysteries of God's providence as discerned in the exposition of Ezek. 1.
10. Reached the age of fifty.
11. B. Hag 13a.
12. B. Men 84b.

455. R. Judah and R. Eleazar used to study together. R. Judah wed a wife, so that R. Eleazar got ahead of him because of the wedding's seven days of feasting; and though R. Judah endeavored for many years to catch up with him, he did not succeed.[1]

456. When R. Eleazar went up to the land of Israel, he said: I have now escaped the first [of the maledictions]. When he was ordained, he said: I have now escaped the second [of the maledictions]. When he was seated in the council of those charged to intercalate the year, he said: I have now escaped the third [of the maledictions]. The three are referred to in the verse "My hand shall be against the prophets that see vanity. . . . They shall not be in the council of My people" (Ezek. 13:9)—not be in the council of those in charge of intercalating the year; "neither shall they be written in the register of the House of Israel" (ibid.)—not in the register of those who are ordained; "neither shall they enter into the Land of Israel" (ibid.), in its literal meaning.[2]

457. R. Helbo, R. Avira,[3] and R. Yose bar Hanina once visited a certain place in the Land of Israel where a peach as large as a stew pot of Kefar Hino[4] was brought to them. (And how big is a stew pot made in Kefar Hino? Five *seah.*) A third they ate; a third they declared free for all; and a third they fed to their mounts.

R. Eleazar visited the place again a year later and was served peaches so small that he could hold them all in one hand. So he recited the verse "A fruitful land into a salt waste, because of the wickedness of them that dwell therein." (Ps. 107:34).[5]

458. When presents were sent to R. Eleazar from the house of the patriarch, he would not accept them; and when he was invited there for a meal, he would not go, but would say, "You evidently are not pleased to see me alive, for he that hateth gifts shall live" (Prov. 15:27).[6]

459. R. Eleazar dropped a denar. Simeon bar Abba [picked it up and] handed it to him. R. Eleazar: "I have already resigned possession of it."

The sages said: R. Eleazar had no other purpose than to convey possession of the denar to R. Simeon bar Abba, who was a poor man.[7]

460. R. Eleazar was a custodian of charity. Once he came home and asked the members of his household, "What deed of charity have you done [today]?" They answered, "A company of people came here. We gave them food and drink, and they offered prayers in your behalf." R. Eleazar: "That is not a proper response."[8] Again he came to his house and asked, "What deed of charity have you done [today]?" They replied, "Another company came here. We gave them food and drink, and they reviled you." "That," he said, "is a proper response."[9]

461. "And God blessed the Sabbath day" (Gen. 2:3). R. Eleazar said: He blessed it by [increasing the capacity of] the Sabbath lamp, as I myself have experienced. I once lit a lamp for Sabbath eve, and at the conclusion of the Sabbath I found it still burning and the oil not at all diminished.[10]

462. R. Eleazar entered a privy, and a Roman came in after him and demanded that he get out. R. Eleazar got up and left. Then a serpent came and ripped out the Roman's gut. At that, R. Eleazar applied to him the verse, "I give a man (*adam*) in exchange for you" (Isa. 43:4). Read not *adam*, "a man," but Edom [a Roman].[11]

463. R. Eleazar ben Pedat was so greatly distressed by poverty that once, after being bled, he had nothing to eat except some green garlic he found and put into his mouth. But then he grew so faint that he dozed off. Those who came to see him noticed that he was both crying and laughing, and that a ray of light issued from his forehead. [When he spoke], they asked him: Why did you cry and laugh, and why did a ray of light issue from your forehead? He replied: Because I saw the Holy One sitting by my side, and I asked Him, "Master of the universe, how long will I suffer such distress in this world?" And He replied, "Eleazar, my son, would you rather had Me turn the world back to its very beginnings? Perhaps you might then be born at a time when you would have adequate sustenance." I replied, "All this, for only a 'perhaps'?"[12] I then asked, "Is the time I have already lived greater, or is the time I have yet to live greater?" He replied, "The time that you have already lived [is greater]." Then I said, "If so, I do not ask to be reborn." He replied, "As a reward for not asking to be reborn, I will grant you in the world-to-come thirteen rivers of balsam oil as clear as the Euphrates and the Tigris, in which you will find pleasure." When I asked, "Is that all? Nothing more?" He replied, "If you take everything, what shall I give your colleagues?" Then I said, "Am I making my request of flesh and blood, which has not the wherewithal?" At this, He snapped at my forehead and said, "Eleazar, my son, I have no choice but to dispatch My arrows at you."[13]

464. R. Eleazar was eating *terumah* [the heave offering given to a priest] when the angel of death appeared to him. So R. Eleazar said: Am I not performing the mitzvah of eating *terumah*, and is not such food designated "holy

1. Eccles. R. 1:15, §2.
2. B. Ket 112a.
3. Munich ms.: "R. Azariah."
4. Kefar Hananiah in Galilee.
5. B. Ket 112a.
6. B. Meg 28a.
7. P. BM 2:3, 8c.
8. Custodians of charity should not expect or receive a reward for their service.
9. P. Pe 8:6, 21a.
10. This was said to encourage people not to stint in outlay for the Sabbath. Gen. R. 11:2.
11. B. Ber 62b.
12. He would not give God such trouble for a mere possibility.
13. These accounted for the ray of light issuing from R. Eleazar's forehead. B. Ta 25a.

food"?[1] As a result, the moment for the angel of death to act passed by.[2]

R. Abbahu (fl. 1st half of 4th century C.E.)

465. R. Abbahu's beauty had something of the quality of our father Jacob's beauty.[3]

466. "A man to whom favor is shown" (Isa. 3:3) is one for whose sake his generation is shown favor in the world above—one such as R. Hanina ben Dosa;[4] or one for whose sake his contemporaries are shown favor here below—one such as R. Abbahu in Caesar's court.[5]

467. When R. Abbahu used to go from the academy to Caesar's palace, the Roman noblewomen in Caesar's palace would go out to greet him and begin by saying:

> Great one of your people,
> Spokesman for your nation,
> Lantern of light,
> May your coming be in peace.[6]

468. R. Abbahu said: I used to think that I was a humble man. But when I saw R. Abba of Acco offer one reason for a particular decision, and his interpreter[7] offer an entirely different reason, and R. Abba was not annoyed, I said, "I am not such a humble man after all."

In what way did R. Abbahu's humility show itself? The wife of R. Abbahu's interpreter once said to R. Abbahu's wife, "My husband really does not require [what] your husband [whispers to him, My husband knows the material], and when he bends down, seemingly to listen to R. Abbahu, and then straightens up, it is only out of deference to R. Abbahu's prestige." When R. Abbahu's wife went and reported this to him, he said, "Why be concerned? Whether it is out of my mouth or his mouth, what matters is that the Name of Heaven is magnified."

Another instance of R. Abbahu's humility: The sages voted to designate R. Abbahu as head [of the academy]. But when he became aware that R. Abba of Acco had numerous creditors [pressing for payment], he said to the sages, "You have a scholar greater than I."

According to some, R. Abbahu replied, "I will not take office until I extricate R. Abba [from his creditors]." And until he extricated him, he did not take office.[8]

469. When R. Abbahu went south, he ruled [about disputed practices] as did R. Hanina, and when he went to Tiberias, he ruled as did R. Yohanan, not wishing to differ with the local authority in his place of residence.[9]

470. As R. Abbahu sat and expounded Scripture, fire flashed around him. So he said, "Perhaps I do not know how to string [one scriptural passage to another properly, by showing linkages in meaning]."[10] For Resh Lakish said: "There are those who know how to string, but do not know how to penetrate [into the sense of each passage]; there are others who know how to penetrate, but do not know how to string [the meaning of one passage to another]. But I am one who knows both how to string and how to penetrate [into the sense of each passage]."[11]

471. R. Abbahu and R. Hiyya bar Abba happened to be in a place at the same time, where R. Abbahu lectured on *Aggadah* while R. Hiyya bar Abba lectured on *Halakhah.* All the people left R. Hiyya bar Abba and went to hear R. Abbahu, so that R. Hiyya bar Abba was greatly upset. To comfort him, R. Abbahu said: May I tell you a parable to illustrate what each of us represents? Two men came to a certain city, one to sell precious stones and pearls, and the other to sell different kinds of cheap notions. To whom will people run? Will they not run to him who sells the different kinds of cheap notions?

Every day, in deference to the imperial court's esteem of R. Abbahu, R. Hiyya bar Abba used to accompany him to his lodging place. But that day R. Abbahu accompanied R. Hiyya bar Abba to his lodging place; nevertheless, R. Hiyya's mind was still not set at rest.[12]

472. R. Abbahu went to Caesarea and returned from there to Tiberias, his face shining. When R. Yohanan's disciples saw him, they came and told R. Yohanan, "R. Abbahu must have found a treasure." R. Yohanan asked, "How do you know?" They replied, "Because his face is shining." He asked, "Could it be that he heard a new interpretation of Torah?" When R. Abbahu came in to see him, R. Yohanan asked him, "What new interpretation of Torah have you heard?" R. Abbahu replied, "Something in an ancient Tosefta."

R. Yohanan applied to him the verse "A man's wisdom maketh his face to shine." (Eccles. 8:1).[13]

473. On Sabbath eves, while fanning the fire, R. Abbahu used to sit on a stool made of ivory.[14]

A three-year-old calf used to be prepared for R. Abbahu's meal at the end of the Sabbath. Of it, he would eat only a kidney. When his son Avimi grew up, he asked, "Why waste so much meat? Let us save one kidney from

1. Were he to die at that moment, the *terumah* would be defiled, something the angel of death would surely not wish to have happen. Besides, "a good deed is a shield against tribulation" (Avot 4:1)—in this instance, R. Eleazar's death.
2. B. MK 28a.
3. B. BM 84a.
4. See above in this chapter, §56.
5. B. Hag 14a.
6. B. Ket 17a; B. Sanh 14a.
7. The one who repeated and read aloud to the assembly and occasionally expounded the master's brief utterances, which were spoken in a low voice.
8. B. Sot 40a.
9. P. Ber 8:1, 12a.
10. He feared that the flashes of fire threatened punishment.
11. Cf. above in this chapter, §427. Song R. 1:10, §2.
12. B. Sot 40a.
13. P. Shab 8:1, 11a; Eccles. R. 8:1, §4.
14. He was so wealthy.

last night's Sabbath meal." So they saved it, but a lion came and devoured the calf that was left unslaughtered.[1]

474. When R. Abbahu went down to bathe in the baths of Tiberias, he would lean on two slaves. [Because he was so heavy], they used to give way under his weight and then raise themselves, give way and then raise themselves. When he was asked, "Why do you put them to such trouble," he would reply, "Because I want to husband my strength for [Torah in] my old age."[2]

475. R. Judah said: He who eats three shekels' weight of asafetida[3] on an empty stomach will lose his skin. R. Abbahu said: I had such an experience when I ate only a shekel's weight of asafetida. Had I not quickly sat down in water [to cool the fever], I would have lost my skin. I then applied to myself the verse "Wisdom preserveth the life of him that hath it" (Eccles. 7:12).[4]

476. R. Abbahu said in the name of R. Yohanan: A man is allowed to teach his daughter Greek, because knowledge of the language is deemed an accomplishment. When Simeon bar Abba heard this, he said: Just because R. Abbahu wishes to teach his daughters Greek he attributes the saying to R. Yohanan. When R. Abbahu learned what Simeon had said, he protested; May such-and-such befall me if I have not heard this rule from R. Yohanan.[5]

477. When R. Abbahu, who lived in Caesarea, sent his son R. Hanina to study Torah in Tiberias, people came and told him, "Your son busies himself in tending to burial of the dead." So R. Abbahu sent a letter to his son: "Is it because there are no graves in Caesarea that I sent you to Tiberias? Long ago it was decided in the upper chamber of the house of Bet Arim in Lydda that the obligation to study takes precedence over the obligation to do good deeds."[6]

478. A misfortune happened to R. Abbahu—a child of his died. R. Jonah and R. Yose visited his home to comfort him. Because of their awe of him, they did not utter Torah [on the theme of consolation]. He said, "Let my masters honor me with a theme of Torah." They replied, "Let our master honor us." So he said, "Under the jurisdiction here below, where there is lying, falsehood, deception, favoritism, and bribery, where a judge is here today and gone tomorrow—still, here below the kinsmen of one condemned to death come and salute the judges and the witnesses, as if to say, "We have naught against you in our hearts, for you gave a true judgment.'[7] Then surely under the jurisdiction above, where there is no lying, no falsehood, no deception, no favoritism, no bribery, where the Judge lives and endures forever and ever and ever—all the more are we required to submit ourselves willingly to the measure of justice, so 'that the Lord may show thee mercy, and have compassion upon thee, and multiply thee, as He hath sworn unto thy fathers' " (Deut. 13:18).[8]

479. In a dream, R. Abbahu saw Pentakaka[9] pray for rain, and rain came down. So R. Abbahu sent for him and asked him, "What is your occupation?" He replied, "Every day I commit five sins: I send out harlots for hire; I decorate a theater; I carry harlots' bags to the bath; there I clap hands and dance before them; I even beat a drum before them." R. Abbahu: "But what good deed have you done?" Pentakaka: "Once, while I was decorating a theater, a woman came, stood behind a pillar [seeming to offer herself to me], and wept. I asked her, 'What is the matter with you?' She replied, 'The husband of a certain woman is in prison [and I need money to free him]. I wanted to see what I could do to [help her] release him. So I sold my bed and my mattress, gave her the money they brought, and said to her, 'Here, take it, release your husband, and don't resort to the sin [of adultery].' "

Then I [R. Abbahu] said to him, "You are worthy of praying and having your prayer answered."[10]

480. R. Abbahu, R. Yose ben Hanina, and R. Simeon ben Lakish passed an orchard in Doron. The tenant farmer brought them a peach so large that they and their donkeys ate of it and left some. They estimated its size as that of a stewing pot made in Kefar Hananiah, which can hold a *seah* of lentils. After a while, they again passed that place, and the tenant farmer brought them two or three peaches so small that he could hold them in one hand. They said, "We would rather have fruit of that other tree." He replied, "They are of that other tree." So they recited the verse "A fruitful land into a salt waste, for the wickedness of them that dwell therein" (Ps. 107:34).[11]

481. R. Hiyya, R. Yose, and R. Ammi convicted a certain woman named Tamar [according to Jewish law].[12] So she went and denounced them to the proconsul in Caesarea. The three sent a letter to R. Abbahu, who wrote back to them: We have already won over three advocates, Good Boy (*Eutokos*), Good Pupil (*Eumousos*), and Sea Boy (*Thalassios*). But *Tamar-tamrurim* (Bitterness) persists in her bitterness. Though we sought to sweeten her, "in vain doth the founder refine" (Jer. 6:29).[13]

482. When R. Abbahu made use of enigmatic speech, he would say, "Make the coal appear to be citrous,[14] then

1. B. Shab 119a–b.
2. P. Betz 1:6, 60c. Cf. above in this chapter, §403.
3. A fetid gum resin of Persian plants formerly used in medicine as an antispasmodic.
4. B. Hul 59a.
5. P. Shab 6:1, 7d.
6. P. Pes 3:7, 30a; P. Hag 1:7, 76c.
7. Sanh 6:6.
8. P. Sanh 6:10, 23d–24a.
9. Greek for a man guilty of five kinds of wrongdoing.
10. P. Ta 1:4, 64b.
11. P. Pe 7:3, 20a.
12. Not in keeping with Roman law.
13. P. Meg 3:2, 74a.
14. Yellow, like the color of the fruit.

turn the golden coal sky-blue,[1] and prepare for me two of those who in the dark announce dawn's coming.[2]

The sages said to R. Abbahu: Unconceal to us where R. Ilai is concealed. He replied: He rejoices with his most recent wife (*aḥaronit*), an Aaronite maiden (*aharonit*), a wakeful one (*eronit*) who keeps him awake (*hinirattu*). Some say that it was in fact a woman.[3] Others, that it was a tractate in the Talmud.[4]

The sages said to R. Ilai: Unconceal to us where R. Abbahu is concealed. He replied: He has been consulting with the Patriarch who bestows the crown [of ordination] upon sages; and now is off to the south to call on noted scholars dubbed Mephibosheths.[5]

483. A certain heretic said to R. Abbahu: Your God is a practical joker, for He said to Ezekiel, "Lie down on thy left side," etc. (Ezek. 4:4), and then, "Lie on thy right side," etc. (Ezek. 4:6). Just then a disciple happened to come and ask, "What is the reason for the sabbatical year?" R. Abbahu replied, "Now I will tell you something that will be applicable to both your questions. The Holy One said to Israel: Sow seed six years, but omit the seventh, so that you may know that the earth is Mine.[6] They did not do so, but sinned and were banished. As you know, it is the way of the world that a king of flesh and blood, against whom the people of a province rebel, will slay all of them if he is cruel, will slay half of them if he is merciful, and, if he is exceedingly merciful, will impose chastisement only on the province's notables. Likewise, the Holy One afflicted Ezekiel, [one of their notables, three hundred ninety days[7] to correspond to the number of years during which Israel failed to keep the sabbatical year] and through him purged Israel of their iniquities [so that, instead of being slain, they were banished]."

484. A certain heretic said to R. Abbahu: Clearly your God is a priest, for He said, "That they take for Me a heave offering" (Exod. 25:2).[8] Now, when He had buried Moses,[9] in what did He immerse Himself [after contact with the corpse]? Should you reply, "In water," is it not written, "Who hath measured the waters in the hollow of His hand" (Isa. 40:12)? R. Abbahu replied: He immersed Himself in fire, for it is written, "Behold, the Lord will come in fire" (Isa. 66:15). The heretic: But does immersion in fire count? R. Abbahu: Fire is indeed the most effective means of purification, for it is said, "Everything that may abide the fire, ye shall make go through the fire, and it shall be clean . . . and all that abideth not the fire ye shall make to go through the water" (Num. 31:23).[10]

485. An infidel whose name was Sason said to R. Abbahu: In the world-to-come, you will be drawing water for me, since it is said, "Ye shall draw water for joy (*sason*)" (Isa. 12:3).[11] R. Abbahu replied: Had the text read "for joy" (*le-sason*), you would have been right. But in fact it reads "in joy" (*be-sason*), which implies that your skin will be made into a bottle with which we shall draw water.[12]

486. Heretics challenged R. Abbahu, saying: We find no mention [in Scripture] of death experienced by Enoch. R. Abbahu: What makes you say so? The heretics: With regard to Enoch it is said, "God took him" (Gen. 5:24); and with regard to Elijah [who did not die] it is said, "Knowest thou that the Lord will take away thy master from thy head today?" (2 Kings 2:3). R. Abbahu: If you insist on interpreting "taking" literally, I will grant you that it may be so in regard to Enoch. But "taking" is used by Scripture also with regard to Ezekiel's wife: "I take away from thee the desire of thine eyes" (Ezek. 24:16)—[do you insist that she too did not die?].[13]

487. A heretic asked R. Abbahu, "When will the Messiah come?" R. Abbahu: "When darkness covers people like you." "You curse me [but do not answer my question]," the heretic exclaimed. R. Abbahu: "I do no more than quote Scripture, 'for, behold, the darkness shall cover the earth, and gross darkness the peoples; but upon thee the Lord shall shine, and His glory shall be seen upon thee' " (Isa. 60:2).[14]

488. R. Abbahu lauded R. Safra to the *Minim* [Judeo-Christian authorities] as an exceedingly learned man, and he was thus exempted by them from paying taxes for thirteen years. One day, on coming across R. Safra, they said to him, "It is written: 'You only have I affectionately known from all the families of the earth; therefore I will visit upon you all your iniquities' [Amos 3:2]—is it right for one in a bad humor to let it out on a friend?" R. Safra remained silent and gave them no answer. So they wound a scarf around his neck and tormented him by tightening it. When R. Abbahu came and found them at it, he asked, "Why do you torment him?" They replied, "Did you not tell us that he was an exceedingly learned man? Yet he cannot explain to us the meaning of a verse!" R. Abbahu: "I told you [that he was learned] in Mishnah. Did I tell you [that he was equally learned] in Scripture?" They: "How come you know both?" R. Abbahu: "We who are frequently in

1. Fan the coal so as to have a blue flame.
2. Cocks.
3. So that now during the day he is asleep, and therefore not in the academy.
4. Dealing with the laws of priests. Its subtlety kept him awake during the night.
5. Saul's grandson, Mephibosheth, was reputed to be a great sage. B. Er 53b.
6. See Lev. 25:3 and 25:23.
7. See Ezek. 4:5. Abarbanel, quoted by Malbim, reckons the period of Samaria's guilt symbolized by Ezekiel's lying on his left side from the time when the schism took place under Rehoboam (ca. 952 B.C.E.) until the fall of Jerusalem (S. Fisch in Ezek., Soncino, pp. 20–21). B. Sanh 39a.
8. Such offerings are for priests.
9. Deut. 34:6.
10. B. Sanh 39a.
11. JV: "Therefore with joy shall ye draw water."
12. The story of Sason may have been directed at heresiarchs who by various means "found" allusions to themselves in Scripture. R. Abbahu was known for his skill in debating such heretics. B. Suk 48b.
13. Gen. R. 25:1.
14. B. Sanh 99a.

contact with you set ourselves the task of studying Scripture thoroughly, but others[1] do not do so." They: "Then you tell us the verse's meaning." R. Abbahu: "I will explain it by a parable. To whom may God in this verse be compared? To a man who is the creditor of two persons, one his friend and the other his enemy. From his friend he is willing to accept payment little by little, but from his enemy he will exact payment in one lump sum!"[2]

489. The heretic Jacob applied [what he claimed to be] a medicine to R. Abbahu's leg, and but for R. Ammi and R. Assi who [hastened] to suck the poison out of the leg, R. Abbahu would have had to have it amputated.

[So distraught were the heretics by R. Abbahu's influence with the government that they] were willing to face what Samson did when he said, "Let me die with the Philistines" (Judg. 16:30).[3]

490. Simeon bar Abba was expert even in precious stones, and yet he had not a loaf of bread to eat. So, applying to him the verse "Nor is bread won by the wise" (Eccles. 9:11), R. Yohanan said, "Not even by such as Simeon bar Abba [whose father was given to deeds of mercy to such an extent that] one who did not know the good deeds of our father Abraham could come to know them through the deeds of Simeon bar Abba's father."[4]

[Ultimately, because he could not make a living, Simeon bar Abba had to leave the Land. Years later], when Simeon bar Abba was in Damascus, R. Abbahu sent him a letter in which, enclosing some of his gray hair, he wrote, "In deference to these gray hairs of mine, rise up and come back to the Land of Israel."

Abbahu speculated to himself: Who, O R. Yohanan, will remove the dust from your eyes, [so that you might explain why] Abbahu, who resembles a scrawny ear of corn, was appointed to an important post, while Simeon bar Abba, who resembles a full ear of corn, received no appointment whatever.[5]

491. When R. Abbahu died, even the pillars of Caesarea wept. Still the Cuthean [heretics] said: On the contrary, the pillars rejoice. Jews asked: How can they who are so far removed [living as they do on Mount Gerizim] know whether the pillars that are near us are rejoicing [or weeping]?

At the time of R. Abbahu's death, thirteen rivers of balsam passed in front of him. When he asked, "For whom are these?" and was told, "For you," he said, "All these for Abbahu? 'Yet to me, all my labor seemed useless, my strength worn out in vain. But my case rested with the Lord' " (Isa. 49:4). For in this world the Holy One shows the righteous their reward, so that their soul is satisfied, and they go to sleep peacefully. It is like a king who made a feast and imaged on the tablecloth the many varieties of food prepared for it. When the guests entered, they saw the images, their souls were satisfied, and they dozed peacefully [waiting to be served the meal].[6]

R. Zera (Ze'era) (fl. 1st half 4th century C.E.)

492. R. Zera used to hide himself to avoid ordination, because R. Eleazar had said, "Stay obscure and remain alive." But later he heard yet another saying of R. Eleazar's: "No man attains high office until his sins are forgiven him [so that his life is prolonged]." [Thus reassured], he allowed himself to be found.

When they ordained R. Zera, they began the ordination with a wedding song: "No kohl, no rouge, no hair dye—yet full of grace."[7]

493. "Most men cite [traditions] from those whom they personally favor" (Prov. 20:6)[8]—true enough of most men." But who can find a trustworthy man[9] [capable of citing traditions from reliable sources without partiality]?" (ibid.)—such a man was R. Ze'era. Hence R. Ze'era used to say, "We are not required to give heed to the traditions of R. Sheshet, since he is blind."[10]

When R. Ze'era asked R. Yose, "Does my master personally know Ben Pedaiah, in whose name you quote traditions?" R. Yose replied, "R. Yohanan used to quote him."

When R. Ze'era asked R. Abba bar Zavdi, "Does my master know personally Rav, in whose name you quote traditions?" R. Yose replied, "R. Adda bar Ahavah used to quote him."[11]

494. When R. Ze'era was told, "The traditions you cite are set forth sharply," he would reply, "They are the result of daytime study."[12]

495. R. Zera said: Formerly, when I saw sages running to attend a lecture on the Sabbath, I thought they were desecrating the Sabbath.[13] But I too took to running after I heard the saying of R. Tanhum in the name of R. Joshua ben Levi: "One should run to listen to a matter of *Halakhah*, even on the Sabbath, as is said, 'For He shall roar, and His children shall come hurrying after Him' " (Hos. 11:10).[14]

---

1. I.e., those of Babylonia.
2. So does God punish Israel only by intermittent visitations. B. AZ 4a.
3. B. AZ 28a.
4. Among other things, Simeon bar Abba's father was unbelievably scrupulous in guarding orphans' money entrusted to his care. See below in the chapter, §552.
5. On this passage, see Ze'ev Wolf Rabinovitz, *Shaare Torat Eretz Yisrael* (Jerusalem, 1940), p. 144. P. Bik 3:3, 65d.
6. P. AZ 3:1, 42c.
7. B. Sanh 14a.
8. JV: "Most men will proclaim every one his own goodness (*hasdo*)." But the commentator takes *hasdo* to mean "that which is favored," hence, "[traditions from men] favored."
9. JV: "But a faithful man who can find?"
10. Since R. Shashet was unable to look at the man who conveyed a particular tradition to him and observe his face, eyes, etc., he was not altogether reliable.
11. P. Shab 1:2, 3a.
12. Not during the night, when one's mind is not clear. Others thought that nighttime study is more productive than daytime study. B. Er 65a.
13. It is forbidden on the Sabbath to take long steps. See B. Shab 113b.
14. B. Er 6b.

496. While R. Ze'era, R. Abba bar Kahana, and R. Levi were sitting together, R. Ze'era belittled those who expound *Aggadah*, calling such works no better than books of augury. R. Abba bar Kahana asked, "Why do you find fault with them? Put a question to them, and they will answer you to the point." So R. Ze'era asked, "What is meant by 'Surely the wrath of man shall praise Thee; the residue of wrath shalt Thou gird upon Thee' (Ps. 76:11)?" They responded, " 'Surely the wrath of man shall praise Thee' in this world; 'the residue of wrath shalt Thou gird upon Thee' in the world-to-come." R. Ze'era replied, "But we can just as well construe the verse the other way around: 'Surely the wrath of man shall praise Thee' in the world-to-come; 'the residue of wrath shalt Thou gird upon Thee' in this world." R. Levi retorted, "The verse means: 'When You rouse Your wrath against the wicked, the righteous, seeing what You do to them, praise Your Name.' " Then R. Ze'era cut it short with the remark: "Whichever way you turn it, *Aggadah* teaches us nothing. So, Jeremiah my son, hold fast to *Halakhah*, for it is better than all else."[1]

497. Once R. Jeremiah said to R. Zera, "Let the master come teach Mishnah." R. Zera: "My strength is depleted, and I cannot." R. Jeremiah: "Then let the master teach something in *Aggadah*."[2]

498. When R. Zera was tired from studying, he used to go to the door [of the academy] of R. Judah bar Ammi, saying: As the sages go out and come in, I will rise for them and receive the reward for honoring them.[3]

499. When R. Zera was tired from studying, he used to go and sit at the door of the academy headed by R. Nathan bar Tobi, saying: As the sages pass by, I will rise for them and receive a reward. Out came R. Nathan bar Tobi, and R. Zera asked him, "Who set forth *Halakhah* in the academy?" R. Nathan: "R. Yohanan stated that such-and-such was the decision in a particuliar *Halakhah*." R. Zera: "You are quite sure that R. Yohanan himself stated it?" R. Nathan: "Yes." Then R. Zera repeated it after him forty times. R. Nathan: "Are you repeating it so many times because it is the only decision in *Halakhah* you learned from R. Yohanan, or because the decision is new to you?" R. Zera: "I repeated it because it is new to me. Until now I had an uncertain feeling that the decision might have been R. Joshua ben Levi's."[4]

500. R. Zera was avoiding R. Judah, because he wanted to go up to the Land of Israel, despite R. Judah's having said: "When a man goes up from Babylonia to the Land of Israel, he violates the positive commandment: 'They shall be brought to Babylon, and there they shall remain, until the day I remember them' " (Jer. 27:22).

1. P. Mass 3:10, 51a.
2. B. Ta 7a.
3. B. Er 28b.
4. B. Ber 28a.

Finally R. Zera decided: I will go hear something from R. Judah's own mouth, leave, and then go up to the Land. He went and found R. Judah standing in the bathhouse and saying to his attendants, "Bring me natron, bring me a comb, open your mouths to absorb the vapor [of steam and let out the vapor of perspiration], then drink the waters heated in the bathhouse." Thereupon R. Zera said: Had I come to hear only this, it would have been sufficient.[5]

501. When a man sees barley in a dream, it is a sign that his iniquities are removed, for it is said, "Thine iniquity is removed, and thy sin is expiated" (Isa. 6:7).[6] R. Zera said: I did not decide to go up from Babylonia to the Land of Israel until I saw barley in a dream.[7]

502. On his way to the Land of Israel, when R. Zera found no ferry to take him across [the Jordan], he held on to a rope bridge and crossed over. Watching him, a certain heretic said, "O you impulsive people, who opened your mouths before you opened your ears![8] You still persist in your impulsiveness [exposing yourselves to the danger of drowning]." R. Zera: "A Land that neither Moses nor Aaron was deemed worthy of entering—who could possibly assure me that I would be deemed worthy of entering?"[9]

503. R. Zera crossed the Jordan wearing all his clothes [and they did not get wet].[10]

504. When R. Zera came up to the Land of Israel, he kept a hundred fasts to forget the Babylonians' [subtle] method of study,[11] so that it should not disturb him; and another hundred fasts that R. Eleazar should not die during his lifetime, so that he would have to shoulder the burden of taking care of public needs; and yet another hundred fasts that the fire of Gehenna should have no power over him. Every thirty days he used to test himself [to see whether his body could resist fire]. He would heat an oven and sit on it, and the fire had no power over him. One day, however, the sages cast [envious] eyes upon him, and his thighs were scorched. Thereafter he was called, "Scorch-thighed Shorty."[12]

505. When R. Ze'era came to the Land of Israel, he had himself bled, and immediately went to buy a *litra* of meat from a butcher,[13] whom he asked, "How much is a *litra?*"

5. Since these instructions were given in Hebrew, R. Zera realized that secular matters may be set forth in the sacred tongue even in a bathhouse. B. Shab 41a.
6. A play on *seorim* ("barley") and *sar avon* ("iniquity is removed").
7. Going up to the Land of Israel was a way of having one's sins expiated. B. Ber 57a.
8. At Sinai you said, "We will do," before saying, "We will hear" (Exod. 24:7).
9. The ferry might have foundered, and I might have perished just the same. B. Ket 112a.
10. He was so agile and quick on the rope bridge that his clothes did not touch the water. P. Shev 4:9, 35c.
11. The method of study in the Land of Israel was less complicated.
12. B. BM 85a.
13. As an antidote.

The butcher: "Fifty small coins and a stroke of the lash." R. Ze'era: "[Instead of the lash], take sixty." The butcher refused. "Take seventy." He still refused. "Take eighty, take ninety," until he reached one hundred. But the butcher continued to refuse. "Very well, then," said R. Ze'era, "follow your custom."

In the evening R. Ze'era went to the assembly of scholars and complained, "What a wicked custom you have here! A man cannot eat a *litra* of meat without being given one stroke of the lash." When asked, "Who told you that?" he said, "So-and-so, the butcher." The scholars sent for him to bring him in, and [the messenger] found his coffin being taken out. So the scholars asked R. Ze'era, "Master, did you have to impose such [dreadful] punishment?" He replied, "May such-and-such befall me if I became at all angry! [On the contrary], I supposed that was the custom here."[1]

506. R. Ze'era used to grieve much, saying, "If my dear father and my dear mother were living, I would then have earned a portion in the Garden of Eden by honoring them."[2] But after hearing the sages' tales concerning the way R. Tarfon honored his mother and the way R. Ishmael honored his mother, he said, "Blessed be He who is everywhere that I have neither father nor mother, for I could not have acted like R. Tarfon and could not have shouldered the unpleasant burden that R. Ishmael shouldered."[3]

507. In R. Zera's neighborhood there lived brigands whom R. Zera befriended in the hope that they might repent. But the sages were annoyed [by his conduct]. When R. Zera died, the brigands said, "Until now we had Scorch-thighed Shorty to beseech mercy for us. Who will do so now?" They were thus led to thinking [about the kind of life they led] until they resolved to repent.[4]

508. After R. Zera had an altercation with a man, he would pass to and fro before him, making himself accessible, in the hope that the man would accost him, pour the grievance out of his heart, [and thus bring about a reconciliation].[5]

509. R. Haggai was supporting R. Ze'era, when a man bearing a bundle of woodchips passed by. R. Ze'era said to R. Haggai, "Fetch me a chip to pick my teeth," but then retracted, saying, "Do not bring it. Should everyone come and help himself to a chip, the man's bundle would be entirely used up. Not that I, R. Ze'era, am so pious. But one should be precise in observing our Creator's commandments."[6]

1. I did not cause his death. P. Ber 2:8, 5c.
2. Evidently they died before R. Ze'era was old enough to be able to honor them.
3. See below, part 5, chap. 2, §277. P. Pe 1:1, 15c.
4. B. Sanh 37a.
5. B. Yoma 87a.
6. Even taking a woodchip without the owner's consent is theft. P. Dem 3:2, 23b.

510. R. Judah ben Eliakim testified in the name of the holy community of Jerusalem:[7] He who brings together the *Geullah* and the *Tefillah* [at the very instant the sun rises] will suffer no harm throughout that day.[8] R. Ze'era said, "That is not so. I did join the two, and yet suffered harm, for I was seized for forced labor and made to carry a myrtle branch to the king's palace." They replied, "That was a preferment. There are people who pay to have the palace pointed out to them, so that they may behold the king's visage."[9]

511. When R. Ze'era fell down in a burial ground, and people came over to pick him up, they found that he had fainted. They asked him, "What caused the faint?" He replied, "[The thought that] all of us are heading for this place—'for that is the end of all men' " (Eccles. 7:2).[10]

512. When gifts were sent to R. Zera from the patriarch's house, he would refuse to accept them. But when he was invited to a meal, he would go, saying, "They derive honor from my presence."[11]

513. R. Zera's disciples asked him: How did you manage to live such a long life? He replied: In all my years I never lost my temper in the midst of my family. I have never walked even one step ahead of one greater than I. When I found myself in an alley soiled with excrement, I endeavored not to meditate on Torah. I have never walked four cubits without studying Torah and without wearing tefillin. I have never slept in the house of study—neither a long slumber nor a short nap. I have never rejoiced at my fellow scholar's discomfiture, nor have I ever called him by his nickname.[12]

514. When R. Zera fell ill, R. Abbahu went to visit him and made a vow: "If Scorch-thighed Shorty recovers, I will make a feast for the sages." R. Zera recovered, and R. Abbahu made a feast for all the sages.[13]

515. When R. Zera died, a certain eulogizer began his lament:

> The land of Shinar conceived and bore him,
> The Land of Beauty[14] made eminent him who was her delight.

7. Even though Rome prohibited Jews from residing in Jerusalem after Bar Kozeva's rebellion (135 C.E.), the Jewish community—"the holy community"—in Jerusalem continued its existence.
8. The practice here referred to is the recital of the morning Shema in such a way that the *Geullah* benediction ("Blessed art Thou, O Lord, who hast redeemed Israel"), which concludes the Shema, is said the instant the sun starts to rise over the horizon, and at that very moment the *Tefillah* (the *Shemoneh Esreh*, or Eighteen Benedictions) is begun.
9. P. Ber 1:1, 2d; B. Ber 9b.
10. P. Ber 3:1, 6b.
11. B. Meg 28a.
12. Ibid.
13. B. Ber 46a.
14. R. Zera migrated from Shinar (Babylonia), to the Land of Israel (the Land of Beauty).

Now Rakkath[1] laments. Woe to her,
She has lost her most precious ornament.[2]

Rav (R. Abba bar Aibu) (fl. 219–47 C.E.)

516. Rav was the tallest man in his generation, and R. Judah reached up to his shoulder.[3]

517. Rav's beauty had something of the beauty of R. Abbahu, and R. Abbahu's beauty had something of the beauty of our father Jacob.[4]

518. When Issi bar Hini came up to the Land of Israel, R. Yohanan met him and asked, "Who is the head of the academy in Babylonia?" Issi: "Tall Abba [Abba Arika]." R. Yohanan: "You refer to him as mere Tall Abba! I remember when I was sitting before Rabbi [Judah I, the Patriarch] seventeen rows behind Rav, and sparks of fire issued from the mouth of Rav into the mouth of Rabbi and from the mouth of Rabbi into the mouth of Rav, and I could not understand what they were saying. And you refer to him as mere Tall Abba![5]

519. When R. Hiyya bar Joseph came up [to the Land of Israel], he found both R. Yohanan and Resh Lakish stating that an animal known to have been attacked by a beast of prey need only have its intestines examined to determine whether it died as a result of the attack. He said, "By God! Rav has ruled: '[All its internal organs], from the brainpan to the hips, must be examined.' " Resh Lakish retorted, "Who is this Rav? Who is he anyway? I don't know him!" R. Yohanan said to him, "Don't you remember the disciple who attended the lectures of Rabbi and of R. Hiyya the Elder? By God! During all those years that disciple was allowed to sit in the presence of his teachers,[6] while I had to remain standing! And who [do you think] excelled? He excelled in everything [in Torah and in piety]!" At this, Resh Lakish exclaimed, "Truly, the man who repeated the ruling of Rav's is to be remembered for good!"[7]

520. Once, while Rav was expounding a portion of Scripture before Rabbi, and R. Hiyya entered, Rav started from the beginning. When Bar Kappara entered, Rav started from the beginning again. When R. Simeon Berabbi entered, Rav started from the beginning a third time. But when R. Hanina bar Hama came, Rav said, "Do I have to keep going back again and again?" And when he did not go back, R. Hanina took offense. Rav went to [pacify] him on thirteen eves of Yom Kippur, but R. Hanina refused to be pacified.[8]

1. An ancient name for Sepphoris or Tiberias, where R. Zera lived.
2. B. MK 25b.
3. B. Nid 24b.
4. B. BM 84a.
5. B. Hul 137b.
6. As an advanced student.
7. B. Hul 54a.
8. B. Yoma 87b.

521. Rav was the son of R. Hiyya's brother and the son of R. Hiyya's sister.[9] When Rav came up to the Land of Israel, R. Hiyya asked him, "Is your father still alive?" Rav replied, "You might ask, 'Is Mother still alive." "Well, *is* your mother alive?" R. Hiyya asked. Rav replied, "Is Father still alive?" At that, R. Hiyya said to his attendant, "Take off my shoes [but carry my bathing gear after me to the bathhouse].[10]

522. When Rabbah bar Hana was about to go down to Babylonia, R. Hiyya said to Rabbi, "My brother's son is going down to Babylonia. May he decide on matters of ritual law?" "He may." "May he decide in disputes about money?" "He may." "May he declare firstborn animals permissible for slaughter?"[11] "He may." When Rav was about to go down to Babylonia, R. Hiyya asked Rabbi, "My sister's son is going down to Babylonia. May he decide on matters of ritual law?" "He may." "May he decide in disputes about money?" "He may." "May he declare firstborn animals permissible for slaughter?" "He may not."

"He may not? Why not?" "Because he is not expert in examining blemishes."

"But did not Rav say, 'I spent eighteen months with shepherds to learn which blemish was permanent and which was temporary'?"

Nevertheless, Rabbi withheld the authorization from Rav out of deference to Rabbah bar Hana.[12]

523. Rabbi authorized Rav to absolve vows and examine bloodstains.[13] After Rabbi died, Rav asked Rabbi's son for authorization to examine the blemishes of firstborn animals. Rabbi's son said: I will not add to what my father gave you.[14]

524. While Samuel and Karna were sitting by the bank of the Royal Canal,[15] they saw its water rising and becoming turbid, a phenomenon that prompted Samuel to say to Karna, "A great man is arriving from the west, who suffers from a disorder of the bowels, and the water is rising to welcome him.[16] [Since you appear to be skeptical about the extent of his learning], go and test for yourself the 'wine in his vessel.' " So Karna went and met Rav, whom he asked, "How do we know that tefillin are to be engrossed

9. Aibu, Rav's father, was R. Hiyya's paternal half-brother, while Rav's mother was R. Hiyya's half-sister on his mother's side.
10. He meant to show that one may mourn only for an hour if one hears of a death that occurred more than thirty days before. After such a brief period of mourning, R. Hiyya told his attendant to follow him to the bathhouse—he is no longer a mourner, and bathing is now permitted. B. Pes 4a.
11. After the destruction of the Temple, firstborn animals could be slaughtered for food only if they had permanent blemishes.
12. Who had to be propped up, so to speak. Rav required no propping up. B. Sanh 5a.
13. In inquiries concerning menstruation.
14. P. Hag 1:8, 76c.
15. The canal connecting the Euphrates and the Tigris at Nehardea and Mahoza (Obermeyer, pp. 144ff.).
16. Water welcomes the great and those of patriarchal lineage. It is said that the water in the well rose up to enter Rebekah's jar. Thus Eliezer knew that the woman was Rebekah (Gen. R. 60:5).

only on the skin of a clean animal [which may be eaten]?" Rav replied, "Because it is written, 'That the law of the Lord may be in thy mouth' [Num. 13:9], meaning that which is permitted to your mouth." Karna: "How do we know that blood must be red [to be considered menstrual]?" Rav: "Because it is said, 'The Moabites saw the water over against them as red as blood' " (2 Kings 3:22).

Rav asked, "What is your name?" "Karna." "May it be [Heaven's] will that a horn (*keren*) sprout from between your eyes."[1]

After that, Samuel took Rav into his house, fed him barley bread and a stew of small fish, and had him drink strong beer, so that his bowels might be loosened, but he did not show him the privy.[2]

Rav [who did not know what Samuel had in mind] uttered a curse, saying, "May he who caused me such distress have no sons rise from him," and so it was.[3]

525. After Rav returned to Babylonia, he, Samuel, and R. Assi met at the circumcision of a boy (or, as some say, at the redemption of a firstborn). Rav would not enter ahead of Samuel, nor Samuel ahead of R. Assi,[4] and R. Assi would not go in ahead of Rav. They kept arguing who should go in last, and it was decided that Samuel would go in last.[5] But why should not Rav and [his disciple] R. Assi have gone in last? Because Rav regularly deferred to Samuel to make up for the time a curse unwittingly escaped his lips.[6]

526. When Rav came down [to Babylonia], he used to say: I am the Ben Azzai[7] of these parts.[8]

527. R. Eleazar said: The words "I shall be to them as a little sanctuary" (Ezek. 11:16) apply to the school in Babylonia of our master, Rav.[9]

528. When the main body of students departed for home from the school of Rav, one thousand two hundred still remained.[10]

529. Rav came to R. Shela's school when there happened to be no interpreter[11] to stand next to R. Shela. So Rav stood next to him and interpreted *keriat ha-gever*[12] as "a man's calling the priests." R. Shela: "Sir, would you mind transalting this phrase as 'cockcrow'? Rav: "A flute's sound is music to nobles' ears, but ignorant weavers will have none of it.[13] When I used to stand next to R. Hiyya and interpreted *keriat ha-gever* as 'a man's calling the priests,' he did not object. Yet you insist, 'Say, cockcrow.' " R. Shela: "Sir, are *you* the teacher here? [I thought *I* was the teacher, and *you* were the meturgeman (the interpreter). Now please be good enough to translate literally what I am telling you; or, if this does not suit you, go back to your seat and] take a load off your feet." Rav: "People say, 'If you hire yourself out to someone, be ready for any task, however menial—even to carding wool for him.' "[14] According to some, Rav said, "In matters pertaining to things holy, go up, not down."[15]

530. It happened that when a man drowned in the marsh of Simki, R. Shela permitted the man's wife to marry again. Hearing that, Rav sent word to Samuel: "Come, let us put him under a ban."[16] Samuel: "Let us first inquire of R. Shela [what led him to do it]." So they sent the inquiry: "If a man has fallen into water that has no [visible] limit, is his wife forbidden or permitted to marry again?" R. Shela replied, "His wife is forbidden." Rav and Samuel again inquired, "Is the marsh of Simki regarded as water that has [a visible] limit or as water that has [no visible] limit?" R. Shela: "It is water that has no visible limit." Rav and Samuel: "Why then did the master act as he did?" R. Shela: "I made a mistake. At first I thought that since the water in the marsh was enclosed on all sides and stands still, it is to be regarded as water that has [a visible] limit."

At that, Samuel applied to Rav the words "There shall no mischief befall the righteous" (Prov. 12:21),[17] and Rav applied to Samuel the words "But in the multitude of counselors there is safety" (Prov. 24:6).[18]

531. A young deer whose hind legs were broken was brought before the exilarch. Rav examined it at the bunch of sinews converging in the thigh. [Upon finding them uninjured], he declared that the young deer could be eaten. In fact, he was getting ready to eat a portion of it rare. But just then Samuel said to him, "Abba, have you no fear that it might have been bitten by a snake [and is full of poison]?" "Then what is the remedy?" Rav asked. Samuel: "Let it be put into an oven, and it will test itself [as to whether poison is in it or not]." It was put into an oven and it fell to pieces.

At that, Samuel applied to Rav the words "There shall be no mischief befall the righteous" (Prov. 12:21), and Rav applied to Samuel the words "No secret troubleth thee" (Dan. 4:6).[19]

1. Rav probably deemed Karna's questioning as effrontery.
2. So that he had to restrain himself from moving his bowels. It was part of the cure that Samuel, who was a physician, prescribed.
3. Samuel had no sons who lived. B. Shab 108a.
4. R. Assi was older.
5. Samuel being the youngest. The words "that Rav and R. Assi should go in," which follow, are deleted as in various manuscripts and *Arukh*. See BK, ed. E. Z. Melamed (Jerusalem, 1968), p. 128.
6. B. BK 80b.
7. Distinguished by keenness of mind and authoritative teaching.
8. P. Pe 6:3, 19c.
9. B. Meg 29a.
10. The students went home for a festival, which was preceded by a *kallah*, a period of intense study under Rav's guidance. B. Ket 106a.
11. The rabbi was seated and spoke Hebrew in a low voice to the interpreter, who translated the rabbi's words into Aramaic, more and more the language of the people.
12. "The call of the *gever*" ("man" or "cock"). Hence it may mean that the work in the Temple began either at cockcrow or when the man in charge called the priests to their respective duties.
13. An insult to R. Shela.
14. I will not stand on my dignity.
15. Another interpreter is not likely to have my learning. B. Yoma 20b.
16. For permitting the remarriage of a married woman.
17. For challenging R. Shela's action and preventing it from becoming a precedent.
18. Samuel's counsel saved Rav from acting precipitately. B. Yev 121a.
19. B. Hul 59a.

532. Isaac bar Samuel bar Martha came down to Nisibis, where he found R. Simlai of Darom seated in a teacher's chair and expounding: Rabbi [Judah I, the Patriarch] and his court allowed the use of oil [owned by Gentiles]. Samuel ate the oil, but Rav was unwilling to eat it. When Samuel said to Rav, "Eat, or I will have you set down as a contumacious elder,"[1] Rav replied, "While I was still over there [in the Land of Israel], I knew the one who demurred with regard to using oil of Gentiles—it was Simlai of Darom." Samuel: "Did he do so on his own authority? Did he not in fact do so in the name of R. Yudan the Patriarch?"

So Samuel insisted, and Rav began to eat such oil.[2]

533. Samuel and the people of the school of Shela used to pay their respects to the exilarch every day. Those of the school of Shela used to enter first and be seated first. Then, in deference to Samuel, they had him seated first. When Rav returned to Babylonia, Samuel, in deference to him, had him seated first. Annoyed, those of the school of Shela said, "We insist on being second." So Samuel was willing to be seated third.[3]

534. In Nehardea there was a dilapidated wall which Rav and Samuel did not walk by, even though it had been standing in such condition for thirteen years and had not collapsed. Once, when R. Adda bar Ahavah happened to visit, Samuel said to Rav, "Master, let us make a detour around it." Rav replied, "No need for that now. Since we have with us R. Adda bar Ahavah, whose merit is so great, I am not afraid."[4]

535. The exilarch appointed Rav market commissioner, and he dispensed floggings for dishonest measures but not for inflated prices. [Because he thus limited his duties], the exilarch had him put in prison, where Rav-karna visited him. Rav said, "According to the sages, a market commissioner is expected to deal with measures but not with prices, yet you changed the commissioner's duties to deal with both measures and prices. So go out and tell them at the exilarchate that a market commissioner is expected to deal only with measures and not with prices." Rav-karna went out and said, "A man who [in disobedience to the exiliarch] presumes to say even such a thing as that a cake of pressed unripe dates is something other than what it is deserves to be put in prison [let alone one who on his own changes the duties of the market commissioner]."[5]

536. A man whose adversary in a lawsuit was rich wanted to have his suit tried before Rav. Rav sent for the rich man, who said, "If all the camels of Arabia were to come, they could not carry even the keys of my storehouses. So how do you expect me to appear in a lawsuit with such a one?" When Rav heard this, he said, "Where does he get off boasting about what is not really his?" At that, a Roman decree was issued that the rich man [be pressed into forced labor] and his possessions confiscated by the imperial treasury. [Humbled], he went at once to Rav and pleaded, "Pray in my behalf that my freedom and my possessions be restored." Rav prayed, and restored they were.[6]

537. Once a man [the offspring of a Jewish woman and an idolater], appeared before Rav and asked him, "What [is the legal status of the child] begotten of an idolater or a slave who had intercourse with the daughter of an Israelite?" Rav replied, "The child is legitimate." The man: "If so, then give me your daughter." Rav: "I will not give her to you." Subsequently Shimi bar Hiyya said to Rav, People say that, in Media,[7] a camel can dance on a *kav*.[8] Here we have a *kav*, we have a camel, we have Media, but there is no dancing!"[9] Rav: "Even if he were the equal of Joshua son of Nun, I would not have given him my daughter." Shimi: "If he were the equal of Joshua son of Nun, others would have given him their daughters, if the master had not given him his; but with this man, if the master will not give him, others also will not give him."[10] As Shimi refused to go away, Rav fixed his eye upon him, and he died.[11]

538. Rav once had an altercation with a certain butcher, and when the butcher did not come to him on the eve of Yom Kippur [to seek reconciliation], he said: I will go to him to seek to be reconciled. When R. Huna met Rav and asked him, "Sir, where are you going?" Rav replied, "To seek to be reconciled with So-and-so." To himself, R. Huna said: Abba[12] is about to cause someone's death.[13] Rav went on until he stood before the butcher, who was sitting and splitting up an animal's head When the butcher raised his eyes and saw Rav, he said, "You are Abba—go away, I will have nothing to do with you." Just then, as he was splitting up the animal's head, a bone glanced off, struck his windpipe, and killed him.[14]

539. Rav was constantly tormented by his wife. When he said to her, "Prepare lentils for me," she would prepare beans; "beans," she would prepare lentils. After Rav's son, Hiyya, grew up, he took to reversing his father's requests, until finally Rav said to his son, "Your mother has grown kind [to me]." R. Hiyya said, "It was I who reversed your requests." So Rav said, "What you have done bears out the saying, 'Your offspring in season may teach you reason.' Nevertheless, do not continue to do so, lest you become like those of whom Scripture says, 'They have trained their tongues to speak falsely' " (Jer. 9:4).[15]

1. Who refuses to heed the decision of the Sanhedrin. B. Sanh 86b.
2. P. AZ 2:8, 41d.
3. P. Ta 4:2, 68a.
4. B. Ta 20b.
5. P. BB 5:5, 15b.
6. P. Ned 9:4, 41c.
7. A way of referring to foreign lands where wonders occur (Goldschmidt).
8. A small measure of capacity equal to a pint.
9. In his ruling, Rav displayed courage, but he stopped short of carrying it into practice.
10. They would regard the master's refusal as an indication that the man was really illegitimate.
11. B. Yev 45a.
12. Rav's real name was Abba.
13. As he knew that the butcher was a hard man and would not take up Rav's offer of reconciliation.
14. B. Yoma 87a.
15. B. Yev 63a and En Yaakov, ad loc.

540. Rav said to his son Aibu: I have labored to teach you *Halakhah*, but without success, so come and I will teach you worldly wisdom. Sell your wares while the sand is still on your feet.[1] Everything you sell, you may regret,[2] except wine, which you may sell without regret.[3] Untie your purse and then open your sack.[4] Better a *kav* from the ground than a *kor* from the roof.[5] Once the dates are in your bag, run to the brewery.[6]

Rav said to his son Hiyya: Do not take drugs;[7] do not try to jump over a brook;[8] do not have a tooth extracted; do not provoke serpents; and do not provoke a heathen.

Rav said to R. Assi: Do not dwell in a town in which no horse neighs and no dog barks.[9] Do not dwell in a town where the leader of the community is a physician.[10]

Rav said to R. Kahana: Better turn a carcass around than turn your words around. Flay a carcass in the marketplace and earn a wage, and do not say, "I am a priest, I am a great man, and such a task is odious to me." Even if you merely ascend the roof, [take] victuals with you. Even if a hundred pumpkins sell for one *zuz* in town, let them be under your skirts.[11]

541. On concluding his *Tefillah*, Rav would add the following: May it be Your will, O Lord our God, to grant us a long life, a life of peace, a life of well-being, a life of blessing, a life of sustenance, a life of bodily vigor, a life in which there is fear of sin, a life free from shame and disgrace, a life of wealth and honor, a life in which we may be filled with the love of Torah and the fear of Heaven, a life in which You will fulfill all our heart's desires for what will truly benefit us.[12]

542. Ardavan sent a pearl of purest ray to our master [Rav] and requested: Send me something equally precious in return. Rav sent him a mezuzah. Ardavan sent back word: I sent you something beyond price, and you sent me something that sells for a debased coin of no value. Rav: Neither my possessions nor yours can match it. Besides, you sent me something that I have to guard, whereas I sent you something that guards you while you lie asleep, as is said, "When thou walkest, it shall lead thee, when thou liest down, it shall guard thee" (Prov. 6:22).[13]

543. Ardavan ministered to Rav. When Ardavan died, Rav exclaimed: The bond [of friendship] is snapped![14]

544. When Rav died, his disciples followed his bier. On their way back,[15] they said: Let us go and have a meal by the river Danak. After they had eaten, they sat and discussed a question concerning the invitation to the saying of grace and the proper response. When they were unable to find an answer, R. Adda bar Ahavah rose, reversed his garment, which was rent in front,[16] and then made another rent in its back, saying: Rav has departed![17]

545. When Samuel was told, "Rav has departed," he made rents in twelve of his garments, saying, "Gone is the man before whom I stood in awe."[18]

546. When Rav died, R. Isaac bar Bisna decreed that myrtles and palm branches with the accompaniment of small bells not be brought to a wedding.[19]

547. It was the practice of people to take some earth from Rav's grave, and apply it [as a remedy] on the first day of an attack of fever.[20]

548. Shila bar Avina gave a practical decision in agreement with the view of Rav. At the time Rav was about to depart from this world, he said to R. Assi, "Go and tell Shila to reverse his decision [as I did], and if he does not listen to you, bend him with strong words."[21] R. Assi thought that he was told, "[If he does not listen to you], ban him with strong words."[22] After Rav died, R. Assi came to Shila and said to him, "Retract, for Rav has also retracted." Shila: "If Rav had retracted, he would have said so to me."[23] Since Shila would not listen, R. Assi put him under the ban. Shila: "Is not the master afraid of being burned by the glow of my fire?" R. Assi: "I am Issi ben Judah,[24] who is Issi ben Gur-aryeh,[25] who is Issi ben Gamaliel, who is Issi ben Mahalalel, a brazen mortar (*assita*) over which rust has no power." Shila: "And I am Shila ben Avina, an iron pestle that can break even an iron mortar." Soon after that, R. Assi fell ill, alternately burning up with fever and shivering with chills, until finally he died. Shila then went to his wife and said to her, "Prepare my shroud for me—R. Assi is likely to go to Rav and denounce me." She prepared his shroud for him, and at once Shila died. When people saw a myrtle

1. After buying, sell quickly.
2. Since the price may go up.
3. Had you waited, it might have turned to vinegar.
4. Be sure to get the money for the merchandise before delivering it to the purchaser.
5. Rather earn little near home, than much far away.
6. To brew beer from them—otherwise, you may eat them or they may deteriorate.
7. Even as medicine, as they are habit forming.
8. The strain affects the eyesight.
9. These guard the town: the dogs raise the alarm, and the marauders are pursued on horseback.
10. A doctor might be too busy to give proper attention to communal matter.
11. Keep them in stock and do not wait until you actually need them. B. Pes 113a.
12. This prayer is now said on the Sabbath on which the New Moon is announced. B. Ber 16b.
13. P. Pe 1:1, 15d; Gen. R. 35:16.

14. B. AZ 10a–11b.
15. Rav was not buried in the town where his academy was.
16. Which he had done when he heard of Rav's death.
17. B. Ber 42b–43a.
18. B. MK 24a.
19. B. Shab 110a.
20. B. Sanh 47b.
21. *Garyeh*, literally, "incite him."
22. *Gadyeh*, literally, "cut him off."
23. He was a disciple of Rav.
24. He probably meant that his name Assi resembled that of Issi ben Judah, who bore a variety of names. See Pes, Soncino, p. 585., n. 6.
25. Literally, "a lion's whelp" (see Gen. 49:9).

branch[1] flying from Shila's bier to R. Assi's, they said, "Evidently the two sages have made peace with each other."[2]

549. Once an epidemic broke out in Sura, but it did not appear in the neighborhood where Rav lived. People thought that this was due to Rav's extraordinary merit. However, it was made clear in a dream that the miracle was too slight to be attributed to Rav's great merit and it came about on account of the merit of a certain man who made it a practice to lend hoe and shovel for the digging of graves.[3]

Samuel (fl. 219–54 C.E.)

550. Abba, Samuel's father, dealt in silks. Once he came to R. Judah ben Betera in Nisibis [to sell him some silk] and reached an understanding with him about price. After a while, Abba asked him, "Does my master want that item?"[4] R. Judah replied, "But were there not only words between us?" Abba: "Do I not trust your word more than money?" R. Judah: "You trusted my word. May you be privileged to raise up a son like the prophet Samuel, of whom it is said, 'All Israel . . . knew that Samuel was trustworthy as a prophet' " (1 Sam. 3:20).[5]

551. Once Samuel's father found Samuel crying and asked him, "Why are you crying?"

"Because my teacher beat me."

"Why?"

"Because he said, 'You fed my son and did not wash your hands before doing it.' "

"But why did you not wash your hands?"

"It was he who ate, so why should I wash?"

"Is it not enough that your teacher is ignorant; must he also beat you?"[6]

552. Samuel's father was entrusted with money belonging to orphans. When he died, Samuel was not with his father, and the orphans dubbed Samuel "Son of the Orphans' Money Eater. So he went after his father to the cemetery and said to those buried there, "I am looking for Abba." They replied, "There are many Abbas here." "I want Abba ben Abba." They replied, "There are several Abbas ben Abba here." He then said to them, "I want Abba ben Abba, Samuel's father. Where is he?" They replied, "He has gone up to the academy on high." [When he got there] and saw Levi sitting outside, he asked him, "Why are you sitting outside? Why have you not gone up into the academy?" Levi replied: "Because they said to me, 'As many years as you would not go up to the academy of R. Aphes and so kept hurting his feelings, we will not let you go up into the academy on high.' " In the meantime, Samuel's father came by, and Samuel noticed that he was both weeping and smiling. Samuel asked him, "Why are you weeping?" He replied, "Because you will be coming here soon." "And why are you smiling?" "Because you are highly esteemed in this world." So Samuel said, "If I am esteemed, let Levi be allowed up." And Levi was allowed up.

Then Samuel asked his father, "Where is the orphans' money?" He replied, "You will find it in the rack of millstones. The money on the upper and lower millstones is ours; that on the middle one is the orphans'." Samuel: "Why did you put the orphans' money on the middle millstone?" He replied, "So that if thieves got at it [from the top], ours would be stolen; and if the earth eroded it [from below] ours would be eroded."[7]

553. Samuel Yarhinaah[8] was Rabbi's physician. When Rabbi was afflicted with a disease in one eye, Samuel said, "I will put a medicine in it." Rabbi: "I cannot bear such a thing." "Then let me apply it as a poultice." "That, too, I cannot bear." So Samuel placed a vial containing the medicine under Rabbi's pillow, and he was cured.[9]

Rabbi all but ached to ordain Samuel, but somehow it did not come about. So Samuel said to Rabbi, "Let it not grieve you. I have seen it written in the stars:[10] Samuel Yarhinaah will be called 'sage' but not 'rabbi,' and Rabbi's healing shall come through him."[11]

554. Samuel said: Except for the comet, whose nature I do not understand, I know the lanes of heaven as well as I know the lanes of Nehardea.[12]

555. "It is not in heaven" (Deut. 30:12). Samuel said, "Torah is not to be found among astrologers." People said to Samuel, "But you yourself are an astrologer and also a great man in Torah." Samuel: "I engage in astrology only when I am free from studying Torah." "When is that?" "When I go into a privy."[13]

556. Samuel said: I was able to make out the facial features of the midwife who assisted at my birth.[14]

---

1. According to Rashi, it was customary to lay a myrtle branch on a bier.
2. B. Nid 36b–37a.
3. B. Ta 21b.
4. Meanwhile the price of silk had risen, but Abba would not raise it to R. Judah.
5. Midrash Sam. 10:3; Yalkut, 1 Sam., §100.
6. He who eats must wash his hands—lift them, so to speak, in holiness (Ps. 134:2)—before blessing the Lord for the food he takes. Even a person who is fed must wash his hands, since his hands may inadvertently touch the food he is eating. On the other hand, he who feeds another is under no such obligation. B. Hul 107b.
7. B. Ber 18b.
8. The expert on the moon, or astronomer.
9. By the vapor.
10. "Written in the stars"—Solomon Funk, as quoted in BM, Soncino, p. 493, n. 4; BR: "Book of Adam."
11. B. BM 85b–86a.
12. B. Ber 58b.
13. Deut. R. 8:4.
14. P. Ket 5:6, 30a.

557. It happened that a fetus was brought to Samuel, and he said, "This is forty-one days old"; and what he said was found to be accurate.[1]

558. Samuel's tenant farmer brought him some dates. When he ate them, he tasted wine in them. He asked, "How did that come about?" The tenant: "The date palms were placed between vines." Samuel: "So date palms deplete the soil[2] that much! [Uproot them] and bring me their roots tomorrow."[3]

559. King Shapur [I] once said to Samuel, "You Jews profess to be very clever. Tell me what I shall see in my dream." Samuel replied, "You will see the Romans come, take you captive, and make you grind date stones in a golden mill." He thought about it all day, and in the night saw it in his dream.[4]

560. Samuel used to juggle eight cups of wine in the presence of King Shapur.[5]

561. Once, while Samuel and Avlat[6] were sitting together and happened to see some people going to a meadow, Avlat [pointing to one of them] said to Samuel, "That man is going but will not return, for a snake will bite him and he will die." Samuel replied, "If he is a Jew, he will go and return."[7] While they were still sitting, that man who went, returned. Avlat arose, removed the man's pack, and in it found a snake cut in two. Samuel asked the man, "What good deed did you do?"[8] He replied, "Every day we pool our bread and eat it. But today one among us had no bread, and he was embarrassed. So I said: I shall undertake to [collect the bread and] put it in the basket. When I got to him, in order to relieve him of his embarrassment, I pretended to take bread from his hand." Samuel said to the man, "You have done a wonderful deed." Then Samuel went forth and expounded the words "Charity delivereth from death" (Prov. 10:2)—not merely from unnatural death, but from death in any form.[9]

562. Even though "during the war of Vespasian[10] the use of crowns for bridegrooms was prohibited,"[11] R. Jeremiah plaited a crown of olive branches and put it on [in honor of a couple]. When Samuel heard of this, he said, "He should not have done such a thing. He deserves to have his head chopped off." And "due to this hasty remark which proceeded from a ruler [in Torah]" (Eccles. 10:5), that is exactly what happened to R. Jeremiah.[12]

1. B. Nid 25b.
2. "Soil"—BK, ed. E. Z. Melamed (Jerusalem, 1953), p. 151, BR: "wine."
3. B. BK 92a.
4. B. Ber 56a.
5. B. Suk 53a.
6. A Persian sage and friend of Samuel.
7. Prayer can set aside what is determined by the stars. So Rashi.
8. To escape your fate.
9. B. Shab 156b.
10. Roman emperor, 67–79 C.E.
11. Sot 9:14.
12. P. Sot 9:15, 24b.

563. When Samuel and Mar Ukba[13] were sitting together going over a theme in *Halakhah*, Mar Ukba sat deferentially before him at a distance of four cubits. But at a judicial session [when Samuel and Mar Ukba were sitting together, the arrangement was reversed, and] Samuel sat deferentially before Mar Ukba at a distance of four cubits. Nevertheless, in order that [his seat might not be on a level higher than Samuel's and also that] Samuel's words might be well heard, a place was hollowed out in the ground and a mat spread there for Mar Ukba the Exilarch to sit on.[14]

Every day Mar Ukba [walked ahead of Samuel] and escorted him to his lodging place. But one day Mar Ukba continued to be so preoccupied by a lawsuit [over which he had presided] that Samuel found himself walking on and on behind him, beyond his lodging place. Finally, when Mar Ukba reached his home [having forgotten that Samuel was still behind him], Samuel spoke up: "Has not the day already ended? Please, master, release me from the bind I am in and allow me to go to my own home."[15] Realizing that Samuel was miffed, Mar Ukba imposed upon himself for one day the isolation prescribed for a man under formal reproof.[16]

564. Phinehas, Samuel's brother, suffered a bereavement, and Samuel came to comfort him. When he saw that Phinehas's nails were long, he asked, "Why did you not trim them?"[17] Phinehas replied, "Had you been bereaved, would you have made so little of it [as to trim your nails]?" His words were [as ill omened] "as an ill-considered word that proceedeth from a ruler" (Eccles. 10:5),[18] and before long Samuel, too, suffered a bereavement. When his brother Phinehas called on him to console him, Samuel took his nail trimmings, tossed them to his brother, and said, "Are you not aware that, as a covenant's clauses follow each other, so does calamity follow ill-considered words?"[19]

565. Once certain women captives were brought to Nehardea. When Samuel's father placed watchmen with them,[20] Samuel asked him, "And who watched them till now?" The father replied, "If they had been your own daughters, would you also have made so little of it?" His words were [as ill omened] "as an ill-considered word that

13. " 'Mar' is a Babylonian title of rank and is sometimes also borne by Samuel, but mostly by the members of the exilarch's family. Samuel was the principal of the academy at Nehardea . . . while Mar Ukba was both a disciple of Samuel and exilarch, the supreme head [and judge] of the Jewish community invested with authority by the Persian king. . . . See Wilhelm Bacher" (MK, Soncino, p. 102, n. 2).
14. Isidore Epstein in MK, Soncino, p. 102, n. 4.
15. The translation follows the exposition and readings in the commentary of an anonymous disciple of Rabbenu Yehiel of Paris (*Kitve Makhon Harry Fischel* [Jerusalem, 1937], p. 34).
16. B. MK 16b.
17. In keeping with Samuel's belief that a person may trim his nails during the period of mourning.
18. One of the ruler's servants is apt to act on it at once—hence, inauspicious.
19. B. MK 18a.
20. To guard them until they were redeemed.

proceedeth from a ruler." Before long, Samuel's daughters were taken captive and brought to the Land of Israel. They persuaded their captors to remain outside while they walked into the school of R. Hanina. One said, "I was taken captive, but I am unsullied." The other said, "I was taken captive, but I, too, am unsullied." So [accepting their testimony] the sages gave them permission [to marry even priests]. As they left, and the captors entered,[1] R. Hanina said, "It is clear that the young women are children of a sage."[2] Then it became known that they were the daughters of Samuel. So R. Hanina said to Simeon bar Abba [Samuel's brother] "Go take care of your relatives." He married one, and she soon died; then he married the other, and she also died.[3]

566. R. Papa said: A man who was following the bier of Samuel made derogatory remarks about him, and a beam fell from the roof and crushed his skull.[4]

R. Judah (bar Ezekiel) (fl. 254–99 C.E.)

567. As Rabbi was about to die, he said: Today R. Judah will be born in Babylonia.[5]

568. Samuel said of R. Judah: This man cannot have been born of woman.[6]

569. Rav was the tallest man in his generation, and R. Judah reached only to his shoulder. R. Judah was the tallest man in his generation, and his attendant Adda reached only to his shoulder.[7]

570. Samuel [who was R. Judah's teacher] used to say to him, "Sharp wit, stand up in deference to your father!"[8]

R. Ezekiel was a man of such good deeds that even Mar Samuel used to stand up in deference to him.[9]

571. R. Judah used to pray only once every thirty days. So he had to go over his *Tefillah* [and prepare it] before saying it.[10]

572. A certain man from Nehardea entered a butcher's shop in Pumbedita and peremptorily demanded, "Give me meat!"

He was told, "Wait until R. Judah bar Ezekiel's attendant takes his order, and then we will serve you."

"Who is Judah bar Sheviskel,"[11] he exclaimed, "to take precedence over me and be served before me?"

They went and told R. Judah. Enraged, he brought out a ram's horn, [sounded it], and imposed a ban on that man.

They also told R. Judah, "That man is in the habit of calling people slaves." R. Judah then had him proclaimed a slave. So the man went off and summoned R. Judah to a lawsuit before R. Nahman. When the summons was served on R. Judah, he went to R. Huna and asked him, "Shall I go or not?"[12] "As a matter of fact," R. Huna replied, "you are not obligated to go, since you are a distinguished man; yet in deference to the exilarch's house,[13] arise and go."

On his arrival there, he found R. Nahman making a parapet for the roof of his house.[14] He said to him, "Does not the master accept Samuel's dictum 'Once a man is appointed head of a community, he may not do manual labor in the presence of three people'?"[15]

"I am [merely] making a little bit of a *gundrita*,"[16] R. Nahman replied.

R. Judah: "Is not *maakeh*,[17] as written in the Torah, or *mehitzah*,[18] as used by the sages, good enough? Why such highfalutin language?"

R. Nahman: "Sit down on a *keraphita* [seat]."

R. Judah: "Is not *safsal*, as used by the rabbis, or *itztaba*, as commonly used, good enough?"

R. Nahman: "Will you partake of *etronga* [citron]?" R. Judah: "Thus did [my teacher] Samuel say: 'He who says *etronga* has in him a huge measure of arrogance': either *etrog*, as it is called by the sages, or *etroga*, as popularly called."

R. Nahman: "Will you drink an *anbaga* [a small cup of wine]?"

R. Judah: "Are you then dissatisfied with the *ispharagus*, as it is called by the sages, or *anpak*, as it is popularly called?"

R. Nahman: "Let [my daughter] Donag come and serve drinks."

R. Judah: "Thus said [my teacher] Samuel: 'One may not make use of a woman.' "

"But she is only a child!"

"[My teacher] Samuel distinctly said, 'One may make no use of a woman at all, whether grownup or child.' "

"Will the master send greeting to [my wife] Yalta?"

"Thus said [my teacher] Samuel: '[To listen to] a

1. To demand ransom money for them.
2. Since they saw to it that their captors remained outside, so that they could act as their own witnesses, in which case the principle of "the mouth that forbids may also be the mouth that permits" applies.
3. Their dying indicated that their testimony was untruthful. B. Ket 23a; P. Ket 2:6, 26c.
4. B. Ber 19a.
5. B. Kid 72b.
6. He was so extraordinary. B. Nid 13a.
7. B. Nid 24b.
8. Even though you are superior to him in scholarship.
9. B. Kid 33b.
10. B. RH 35a.
11. A willful and contemptuous mispronunciation of Ezekiel, meaning: "meat eater," "glutton." The Arabic word *shiwā'* means "roast hunk of meat."
12. His eminent position entitled him to refuse to recognize R. Nahman's jurisdiction over himself.
13. R. Nahman was a son-in-law of the exiliarch, the official head of Babylonian Jewry.
14. See Deut. 22:8.
15. R. Nahman would be seen by at least that many people walking in the street below.
16. Balustrade.
17. The Hebrew name for it.
18. Literally, "barrier," the rabinnical term.

woman's voice'—[for your wife will respond to my greeting]—'is indecent.' "

"Then perhaps through a messenger?"

"Thus said [my teacher] Samuel: 'One may not inquire after a woman's welfare.' "

"Then through her husband?"

"Thus said [my teacher] Samuel: 'One may not inquire after a woman's welfare in any way whatsoever.' "

[When] R. Nahman's wife [heard of the interchange, she] sent word to her husband; "Adjudicate this case and get rid of him, lest he make you out to be a common ignoramus!"

R. Nahman to R. Judah: "Why did the master take the trouble to come here?"

R. Judah: "You, master, had a summons served on me."

R. Nahman: "Seeing that I barely know the master's manner of speaking, would I presume to send the master a summons?"

R. Judah drew out the summons from his bosom and showed it to him. "Here is the man and here the summons!"

R. Nahman: "Since the master did trouble himself to come here, let him set forth his plea, so that it will not be said, 'Disciples of the wise show favor to one another.' " After listening to R. Judah's account, R. Nahman asked him, "Why did the master put the man under a ban?"

"Because he abused a sage's messenger."

"Then the master should have had him lashed, for you know, of course, that Rav used to have the lash given to one who abused a messenger of the sages."

"I chose to deal with him more severely."

"Why did the master have it proclaimed, 'He is a slave'?"

R. Judah: "Because he is in the habit of calling people slaves, and we have been taught that he who declares [others unfit is] himself unfit. Since such a one never speaks well of anyone, he, in [my teacher] Samuel's words, 'stigmatizes others with his own blemish.' "

"But when Samuel said this, he meant that such a man is to be suspected of being a slave. Who said that he is actually to be proclaimed a slave?"

At this stage, his Nehardean opponent appeared on the scene and said to R. Judah, "You call me a slave—I who am descended from the royal house of the Hasmoneans!" R. Judah: "Thus taught [my teacher] Samuel: 'Whoever says, "I am descended from the Hasmonean house," is a slave.' "[1] R. Nahman: "Do you not agree with what was stated by R. Abbahu in the name of R. Huna in Rav's name: When a disciple of the wise [involved in a lawsuit] cites a ruling in the name of his master, he is heeded only if he cites it before the pleas are set forth; if after they are set forth, he is not heeded?" R. Judah: "But R. Mattenah [not involved in this lawsuit], who is ready to affirm what I have just cited, is here in the court."

Now, R. Mattenah had not seen Nehardea for thirteen years and only arrived there that day. So R. Judah asked him, "Does the master remember what Samuel said while he was standing with one foot on the riverbank and the other foot on the bridge?" R. Mattenah replied, "Thus indeed taught Samuel: 'Whoever says, "I am descended from the Hasmonean house," is a slave, because there remained of them only one maiden, who ascended a roof and cried out, "Whoever says, 'I am descended from the Hasmonean house' is a slave." Then she leaped from the roof and died.' "

After hearing R. Mattenah's reply, R. Nahman proclaimed the man a slave. [As a result, in Nehardea, the marriages of many women who sprang from that family were declared invalid] and their marriage contracts were torn up.[2] So, as R. Judah was leaving the city, its inhabitants came out after him to stone him. But he threatened them, "If you will desist, do so. If not, I will make known about you what [the master] Samuel said: There are in Nehardea two families, one called the House of the Dove, and the other the House of the Raven, and the mnemonic for them is 'The clean is clean, and the unclean is unclean.' "[3] They promptly dropped the stones they held in their hands, and the stones were so numerous that they clogged up the Royal Canal.[4]

573. R. Zera found R. Judah standing by the door of his father-in-law's house and noticed that he was in such a cheerful mood that if he were to ask him about all the secret processes of the universe, he would tell them to him. So he asked him: Why do the goats walk at the head of a flock, while the sheep follow after them? R. Judah: It is in keeping with the order of creation—darkness first, and light afterward.[5]

Why is the rear end of sheep covered with a fat-tail, while goats are uncovered? Those whose wool we cover ourselves with are themselves covered, while those whose hair we do not cover ourselves with are uncovered.

Why is a camel's tail short? Because it feeds on thorns.[6]

Why is an ox's tail long? Because it grazes in meadows and needs [a long tail] to beat off the gnats.

Why is the proboscis of a locust flexible? Because it dwells among young shoots. If the proboscis were hard, it would be dislocated, and the locust would go blind. For, as Samuel said, if one wishes to blind a locust, let him extract its proboscis.

Why is a fowl's [lower] eyelid bent upward?[7] Because it dwells among the rafters, and if smoke entered [its eyes], it would go blind.

---

1. Because the dynasty was wiped out by Herod, who, in spite of his having become king, was always regarded by the Jews as an Idumean slave. To ennoble his children, he called them Hasmoneans. See above, part 1, chap. 9, §51.

2. Since the women who belonged to that family were consequently reduced to the status of slaves, their marriages to freemen became null and void.

3. The dove, being a clean bird, is fit for food; the raven, being unclean, is unfit. Descendants of the two families were probably numerous in Nehardea, and their origin was forgotten.

4. B. Kid 70a–b and En Yaakov, ad loc.

5. In that part of the world, goats are dark, while sheep are light.

6. In which a long tail would be entangled.

7. When its eyes are closed, the lower eyelid turns upward and lies upon the upper. So Rashi. The reference is to a thin membrane beneath the lower lid of the eye capable of extending across the eyeball.

The word *dasha*, "entrance," is an acronym for *derekh sham*, "there is the way."[1] *Darga*, "stairs, ladder," is an acronym for *derekh gag*, "the way to the roof." *Metukhilta*, "a relish," is portmanteau for *Matai tikleh da*, "When will this end?"[2] *Beta*, "a house," is an acronym for *Bo ve-etiv bah*, "Come and settle it." *Biketa*, "a small house," is an acronym for *Be akta*, "confined place." *Kufta*, "a low seat," is an acronym for *Kof ve-tiv*, "Invert it, and sit down." *Livne*, "bricks," implies *li-vene vanim*, "to last for one's children's children." *Hutza*, "prickly shrubs," is a variant of *hatzitzah*, "barrier." *Hatzba*, "pitcher," is so called because it is used to draw (*hotzev*) water from the river. *Kuzah*, "a small jug," is a variant of *ka-zeh*, "like this."[3] *Shotita*, "a myrtle branch," is a variant of *shetuta*, "folly."[4] *Meshikhla*, "a washbasin," is an acronym for *mashe khullah*, "a vessel capable of washing everybody." *Mashkilta*, "another kind of washbasin," is an acronym for *mashiya khalata*, "a vessel in which brides are washed." *Assita*, "mortar," suggests *hasirta*, "hollow interior." *Bukhna*, "a pestle," is an acronym for *Bo ve-akkennu*, "Come, and I will pound it." *Levusha*, "upper garment," is an acronym for *los vusha*, "no shame." *Gelima*, "a cloak," is so called because in it one looks like a shapeless mass (a *golem*).[5] *Gulta*, "a long woolen cloak," is acronym for *Geli ve-etiv*, "Remove it and then sit down." *Puria*, "bed," is so called because in it human beings procreate, *parin ve-rabbin*. *Bur zinka*, "a well that springs up only occasionally," is an acronym for *Bor zeh naki*, "This well is empty." *Sudra*, "turban,"[6] is an acronym for *Sod adonai li-re'av*, "The secret of the Lord is revealed to those that fear Him." *Apadna*, "royal palace," is an acronym for *Apit'ha din*, "the door to which all come for judgment."[7]

574. When Ulla happened to visit Pumbedita, R. Judah said to his son R. Isaac, "Go offer him a basket of fruit, and observe how he recites *Havdalah*.[8] R. Isaac did not go, but sent Abbaye instead. When Abbaye returned, R. Isaac asked him, "How did he recite it?" " 'Blessed be He who distinguishes between sacred and profane,' " he replied, "and no additional blessing." When R. Isaac came to his father, his father asked him, "How did he say it?" R. Isaac replied, "I did not go. I sent Abbaye, and he told me that Ulla recited, 'Who distinguishes between sacred and profane.' " His father said, "Sir, your pride and arrogance are responsible for the fact that Ulla's practice will not be reported in your name."[9]

575. When Ulla visited R. Judah's home in Pumbedita, he realized that R. Isaac, R. Judah's son, was already grown up but remained unmarried. So he asked R. Judah, "Why does the master not find his son a wife?" R. Judah replied, "Do I know from whose stock[10] to take one?" Ulla replied, "Do we know the stock we ourselves come from? Perhaps from those of whom it is said, 'They ravished the women in Zion, the maidens in the cities of Judah' " (Lam. 5:11).[11]

576. R. Judah was reading with his son R. Isaac the verse "I find more bitter than death the woman" (Eccles. 7:26). R. Isaac: "What woman, for instance?" R. Judah: "For instance, your mother."

But did not R. Judah [on another occasion] teach his son R. Isaac: A man finds joy only with his first wife, for it is said, "Let thy fountain be blessed and have joy with the wife of thy youth" (Prov. 5:18)? When R. Isaac asked, "What wife, for instance?" R. Judah replied, "For instance, your mother." The truth is that R. Judah's wife was easily provoked and just as easily pacified.[12]

577. R. Judah permitted eye painting on the Sabbath [for medicinal purposes]. R. Samuel bar Judah commented sharply, "He who listens to R. Judah [in this matter] profanes the Sabbath." After a while, when R. Samuel himself had a sore eye, he sent an inquiry to R. Judah: "Is painting it permitted or prohibited?" R. Judah sent a reply: "For everyone else it is permitted, but for you it is prohibited." [R. Samuel bar Judah protested]: "Was it on my own that I had the temerity to differ with you? I merely cited what I learned from Mar Samuel."[13]

578. Once R. Judah, seeing two men using bread wastefully, exclaimed, "It seems that there is a superfluity of food in the world." He cast an angry look at the two wastrels, and suddenly there was a great scarcity of food. So the sages said to R. Kahana son of R. Nehunia, a disciple ministering as R. Judah's attendant, You, sir, who are constantly with him, persuade him to go out by the door next to the marketplace.[14] He prevailed upon him, and R. Judah went out into the marketplace. Seeing a large crowd there, he asked, "What is the matter?" He was told, "They stand around the offal of crushed dates, which is for sale." At this, he exclaimed, "There is evidently famine in the land," and said to his attendant, "Take off my shoes." As soon as R. Kahana had taken off one shoe, rain began to fall. As R. Kahana was about to take off the other shoe, the prophet Elijah appeared and said to him, "The Holy One says: If you take off the other shoe, I will lay waste the world [with flood]."[15]

R. Mari, the son of Samuel's daughter, related: On that day I was standing on the bank of the river Papa[16] and saw angels disguised as mariners bringing sand and

1. The following words, similarly treated, may be regarded as examples of popular etymology or as jeux d'esprit, not to be taken seriously.
2. Since relishes are used sparingly and last a long time.
3. "Give me a glass of this size to drink."
4. People danced with them at weddings and looked like fools as they did so!
5. Since there are no openings for the arms.
6. The distinctive turban worn by rabbinical scholars.
7. B. Shab 77b.
8. The benediction of separation recited at the close of a Sabbath or festival.
9. But in Abbaye's name. B. Pes 104b.

10. What stock is pure.
11. B. Kid 71b.
12. B. Yev 63b.
13. Who was his teacher. B. AZ 28b.
14. That he might see for himself how people were suffering because of the famine he had brought about.
15. R. Judah should not importune God with too much self-humiliation, as rain was about to come.
16. The canal passing through Pumbedita (Obermayer, p. 237).

loading ships with it, and the sand turned into fine flour. When everybody came to purchase it, I called out to them, "Do not buy this flour, because it was produced by a miracle." Next day, boatloads of rice [long overdue] came in.[1]

579. R. Judah was sitting before Samuel when a certain woman came and cried out in his presence [about a wrong inflicted on her]. But Samuel ignored her. So R. Judah said to him, "Does the master not agree that 'Whoso stoppeth his ears at the cry of the helpless, he also will cry but not be heard'?" (Prov. 21:13). Samuel replied, "O sharp wit, I, your superior, may have cold water poured on me [as punishment for ignoring a cry for justice]. But your superior's superior [Mar Ukba] will have hot water poured on him [as punishment for failure to judge rightly]. For Mar Ukba is head of the court, which is told, 'O house of David, thus saith the Lord: Execute justice in the morning, and deliver the spoiled out of the hand of the opppressor, lest My fury go forth like fire, and burn that none can quench it, because of the evil of your doings' " (Jer. 21:12).[2]

580. Zutra bar Tobiah was once expounding a lesson in Scripture in the presence of R. Judah. When he came to the verse "And these are the last words of David" (2 Sam. 23:1), he asked R. Judah, " 'Last words' would imply, would it not, that there were first words—what were they?" R. Judah was silent, saying not a word. So Zutra repeated the question: " 'Last words' would imply, would it not, that there were first words—what were they?" R. Judah then replied, "What do you think—because one [like myself] has no explanation for this verse, I am not a man of distinction?" Zutra, realizing that R. Judah was offended, took upon himself the disability [of a reproof] for one day.[3]

581. A certain man died in R. Judah's neighborhood. Since there were no kin to be comforted, R. Judah assembled ten men every day who sat [in mourning] in the home of the deceased. After seven days, the deceased appeared to R. Judah in a dream and said, "May your mind be at rest, for you set my mind at rest."[4]

582. A certain woman of Nehardea came before R. Judah[5] in a lawsuit and was declared guilty. When she asked, "Would your teacher Samuel[6] have judged this way?" he asked her, "Did you know him?" She replied, "Yes. He was short, big-bellied, and soot-black, and he had large teeth." R. Judah: "So you came to insult him! Let this woman be put under the ban." Then and there her body swelled up and she died.[7]

583. There was once a certain disciple of the wise whose reputation was not very good. So R. Judah said, "What are we to do? If we put him under a ban, the sages will miss him [because he is an able teacher]. If we do not put him under the ban, the Name of Heaven will be profaned." Then R. Judah asked Rabbah bar Bar Hana, "Have you heard anything concerning such a problem?" Rabbah replied, "Thus said R. Yohanan: What is meant by 'The priest's lips should keep knowledge and they should seek the law from his mouth; for he is the messenger of the Lord of hosts' [Mal. 2:7]? It can only mean that if a master is like the messenger of the Lord of hosts, people should seek the law from his mouth; but if he is not, they should not seek it from him." At that, R. Judah pronounced the ban on that disciple. In the end, R. Judah fell ill and the sages came to visit him, and that disciple came with them. When R. Judah beheld the disciple, he began to laugh with joy. The disciple said to him, "As though it were not enough that you put me under the ban—now you even laugh at me!" R. Judah replied, "I am not laughing at you. But as I am about to go to the world-to-come, my spirit rejoices at the thought that, even in dealing with such a learned person as you, I allowed myself no partiality."

After R. Judah died, the same disciple came to the house of study and said to the sages, "Release me from the ban." The sages replied, "There is no man here of R. Judah's standing who could release you. Go to R. Judah the Exilarch[8]—he will release you." When the disciple came to him, R. Judah the Exilarch said to R. Ammi, "Examine his case. If releasing him is required, release him." R. Ammi examined his case and was inclined to release him from the ban. Then R. Samuel bar Nahmani got up on his feet and said, "Why, even a ban of 'separation' imposed by a maidservant in Rabbi's house was not treated lightly by the sages for three years. How much more so a ban imposed by our colleague R. Judah!" R. Zera asked, "What is signified by the appearance of the venerable [R. Samuel bar Nahmani], who for many years has not come to the house of study, but did come today? It signifies that we are not required to release the man from the ban he is under." So R. Judah the Exilarch did not release him. The disciple went out weeping as he walked away. Then a hornet came at him and stung him, and he died. When he was brought to a cave of the pious, they refused to receive him.[9] Then he was brought to a cave of public lecturers, where they did receive him.[10]

584. In Sura, people did not eat the udder of an animal. In Pumbedita, they did.

Rami bar Tamri, also known as Rami bar Dikuli, of Pumbedita once happened to be in Sura on the eve of Yom

1. B. Ta 24b.
2. B. Shab 55a.
3. B. MK 16b.
4. B. Shab 152a–b.
5. He lived in Pumbedita, where he had his school.
6. After the death of Rav and R. Assi, R. Judah was Samuel's pupil for a short time.
7. B. Ned 50b.
8. R. Judah II, grandson of Rabbi Judah I and son of Rabban Gamaliel III. *Nesiah*, the Aramaic form of *nasi* ("prince" or "exilarch"), is conveniently used to indicate the second Judah (and sometimes the third).
9. A serpent was coiled at the cave's entrance. See above in this chapter, §233 and §306.
10. Since he was a lecturer who had repented. B. MK 17a and En Yaakov, ad loc.

Kippur. When the townspeople took all the udders and threw them away, he immediately went to collect them and ate them. Then he was brought before R. Hisda, who asked him, "Why did you do it?" He replied, "I come from the place of R. Judah, where eating the udder is permitted." R. Hisda asked him, "But do you not accept the rule: [When a person arrives in a town], to him is applied the more stringent usage of the town he left, as well as the more stringent usage of the town he has come to?"[1] Rami replied, "I ate them outside the city's boundary." R. Hisda: "And with what did you roast them?" Rami: "With grape kernels." R. Hisda: "Perhaps they were kernels of grapes from which men had made wine used as libation for idols?" Rami: "They had been lying there more than twelve months."[2] R. Hisda: "Perhaps they were stolen?" Rami: "Since shoots were growing among them, the owners must have given up all hope of recovering them." Then R. Hisda noticed that Rami was not wearing tefillin and asked him, "Why do you not wear tefillin?" Rami replied, "I suffer from loose bowels, and R. Judah has said, 'One who suffers from loose bowels is exempt from wearing his tefillin.' " R. Hisda further noticed that Rami was not wearing fringes [on his coat] and asked him, "Why are you not wearing fringes?" Rami replied, "The coat [I am wearing] is borrowed, and R. Judah has said, 'A borrowed coat is exempt from fringes for thirty days.' " While this was going on, a man was brought in [to the court] charged with failure to honor his father and mother. They bound him [for flogging], but Rami said to them, "Let him go, for it has been taught, 'Any commandment whose reward is stated right after it is not to be enforced by a court below.' "[3] R. Hisda said to him, "I see that you are very sharp." He replied, "If you would but come to R. Judah's school, I could really show you how sharp I am!"[4]

R. Jeremiah (fl. middle of 4th century C.E.)

585. Abbaye said: One of those [who dwell in the Land of Israel] surpasses any two of us [Babylonians]. Rava responded: But when one of ours goes up there [to the Land of Israel], he is as good as two of theirs, for while R. Jeremiah was here, he was not able to grasp what the sages were saying. But when he went up there, he began to speak of us as "the stupid Babylonians."[5]

586. We have been taught: A young pigeon that is found on the ground within fifty cubits from a cote, belongs to the owner of the cote. If found beyond fifty cubits from the cote, it belongs to the finder. [Upon hearing these words], R. Jeremiah raised the question: "If one foot of the pigeon is within fifty cubits and the other is beyond them, how do we decide?" It is because of this question that they turned P. Jeremiah out of the house of study.[6]

587. On another occasion, the associate scholars in the Land of Israel sent a query on a matter of *Halakhah* to R. Jeremiah. He sent back his reply: "I am unworthy to rule on the query you sent me, but this is the view to which I, your disciple, incline." And he set forth the right *Halakhah* in the matter. For this [act of becoming modesty], they readmitted R. Jeremiah to the house of study.[7]

588. R. Isaac bar Redifa had a practical question in law. So he went and put the question to R. Jeremiah, who said: You have lions to consult, and you put the question to foxes?[8]

589. In the days of R. Jeremiah, a distressing tax was imposed on the people of Tiberias. So R. Jeremiah sent a request to R. Jacob son of R. Bun for a silver lampstand. R. Jacob replied with the words "Jeremiah has still not turned back from his evildoing"[9] and wanted to place R. Jeremiah under a ban. At this, R. Hiyya son of R. Isaac Atushaia, who was seated there, protested, "I understand that an elder is not put under the ban unless he has acted like Jeroboam the son of Nebat and his companions." R. Jacob replied, "Akavia ben Mahalalel was put under a ban because he said, 'Only in show did they make her drink.'[10] Was there anything in such a charge that could match what Jeroboam the son of Nebat and his companions did?"[11]

So each put the other under a ban; each minded the other's ban; and finally each had to release the other from it.[12]

590. R. Jeremiah was seated before R. Zera, and both were engaged in *Halakhah*. Evening drew near, the time for prayer arrived, and R. Jeremiah insisted on reciting it. R. Zera then applied to him the verse "He that turneth away his ear from hearing Torah, even his prayer is an abomination" (Prov. 28:9).[13]

591. Once, when R. Abba had a grievance against R. Jeremiah, R. Jeremiah went and sat down at R. Abba's door [waiting for him to come out so that he might ask to be forgiven]. Just then a maidservant of R. Abba's came

1. Pes 4:1.
2. Even if they were kernels of wine that had been used in idolatry, after twelve months they are permitted. See B. AZ 34a.
3. The reward for honoring parents is stated right after the commandment. See Exod. 20:12.
4. B. Hul 110a–b.
5. B. Ket 75a.
6. B. BB 23b.
7. B. BB 165b.
8. P. Shev 9:4, 39a.
9. Scholars were not called upon to pay such taxes.
10. There was a dispute as to whether a female proselyte or a freed bondwoman suspected of infidelity may be made to drink the water of bitterness (Num. 5). Akavia said No. The sages said Yes. When the sages recalled that Shemaiah and Avtalion had Karkemith, a freed bondwoman, drink such water, Akavia replied, "Only in show did they make her drink." For imputing the integrity of Shemaiah and Avtalion, Akavia was put under a ban.
11. Accordingly, an elder may be put under a ban for an offense of lesser gravity.
12. P. MK 3:1, 81d.
13. B. Shab 10a.

out to empty some dirty water into the dungheap, and as she was pouring it, jets of that water fell on R. Jeremiah's head. He remarked: They have used me for a dungheap, and in his own behalf he prayed, "May He raise up the needy one out of the dungheap" (1 Sam. 2:8). As soon as R. Abba heard what happened, he hastened out to R. Jeremiah, who in the meantime had turned around and was about to ask R. Abba's forgiveness. Interrupting him, R. Abba said: No need for you to beg to be forgiven. Now it is for me to remove from your heart [the memory of your humiliation], as Scripture says, "Go, grovel [if need be], in order to restore your neighbor's dignity" (Prov. 6:3).[1]

592. As he lay dying, R. Jeremiah left word: Wrap me in white shrouds that are hemmed; put socks on me, sandals on my feet, and a staff in my hand; and lay me down at the side of the road, so that I shall be ready when the Messiah comes.[2]

R. Huna (fl. 257–97 C.E.)

593. R. Huna once came before Rav with reed grass tied around his waist. Rav: "What is the meaning of this attire?" R. Huna: "I had no wine for Kiddush. So I pledged my girdle, and with the money got wine for Kiddush." Rav: "May it be Heaven's will that one day you be covered with silks."

Soon after, on the day when Rabbah, R. Huna's son, was getting married, R. Huna, who was a small man, happened to be lying asleep on a bed. [Unaware of R. Huna's presence], his daughters and daughters-in-law came in to change and threw their discarded garments over him, so that he was [temporarily] covered with silks.

When Rav heard of the incident [and realized how short-lived his well-meant blessing turned out to be], he was annoyed. "Why," he asked, "when I blessed you, did you not respond with 'The same to you, sir'? [Had you done so, you would have continued to be covered with silks.]"[3]

594. R. Huna was once carrying a hoe on his shoulder. When R. Hana bar Hanilai came over and wished to relieve him of it, R. Huna said: If you are accustomed to carry such gear in your own town, carry it. But if not, I refuse to be deferred to through abasement of your person.[4]

595. Once a certain man came to R. Huna for a lawsuit. [In reply to his request], R. Huna said, "Bring me a man who will take my place at work on my palm plantation."

R. Huna, who used to graze oxen, once knew of some evidence in behalf of a certain person. That person said to R. Huna, "Come and bear witness in my behalf." R. Huna replied, "Reimburse me for the wages [I will lose]."[5]

596. When a lawsuit was brought before R. Huna, he used to say to the litigants, "Provide me with a man who will draw the water [to irrigate my field], and I will adjudicate your case."[6]

597. R. Huna frequently passed the door of R. Avin the Carpenter. Seeing that R. Avin was scrupulous in kindling [Sabbath] lights, he said, "Two great men will issue from this household." And indeed, R. Idda bar Avin and R. Hiyya bar Avin did issue from there.[7]

598. When R. Huna was delivering a discourse, he required thirteen interpreters.[8] After such a discourse, when the disciples rose up and shook out their garments, the dust rose so high that it obscured the light of day. Indeed, even in the west,[9] they would say, "The disciples in the academy of R. Huna the Babylonian have just now stood up."[10]

599. When R. Huna went forth to hold court, he took ten scholars with him from the house of study, in order, he said, that only one chip of the beam might fall on him.[11]

600. R. Hisda asked R. Huna, "What do you think of a disciple whom his master needs?"[12] "Hisda, Hisda," R. Huna exclaimed, "I do not need you, but you will have need of me till the age of forty." After that, they were so angry at each other that they did not even visit each other. [But subsequently] R. Hisda kept forty fasts because R. Huna had felt humiliated; while R. Huna kept forty fasts because he had suspected R. Hisda [unjustly].[13]

601. Rava said to Rafram bar Papa: Tell us some of the good deeds R. Huna did. He replied: Of his earlier years, I remember nothing; but of his later years, I remember that on stormy days he used to be taken out in a gilded carriage to inspect every part of the city, and wherever a wall appeared to be wobbly, he would order its demolition. If the owner was in a position to rebuild it, he had to do so; if not, R. Huna would have it rebuilt at his own expense. Every Friday, at the approach of evening, R. Huna would send his emmisary to the market to buy up all the

1. JV: "Go, humble thyself, and urge thy neighbor." But *rehav* ("urge") can also mean "dignity," "pride." En Yaakov version of B. Yoma 87a.
2. For the resurrection and for meeting the Messiah. P. Kil 9:2, 32b; Gen. R. 100:2.
3. To have a blessing flow fully, the one blessed must respond by voicing his thanks. Otherwise, the blessing may be, so to speak, short-circuited. B. Meg 27b. Rabbi Mordecai Savitsky provided the interpretation to the translator.
4. B. Meg 28a.
5. P. Sanh 1:1, 18b.
6. B. Ket 105a.
7. B. Shab 23b.
8. Each of whom spoke to a small portion of the large gathering.
9. The column of dust rose so high that it was visible even in the Land of Israel.
10. B. Ket 106a.
11. That, in the event of a wrong decision, responsibility for it would be shared by the others. B. Hor 3b.
12. Because the disciple may have traditions of which his teacher is unaware. R. Hisda was R. Huna's disciple, so R. Huna regarded the question as an affront.
13. B. BM 33a.

gardeners' leftover vegetables and have them thrown into the river.

Should he not rather have distributed these among the poor?

[He was afraid] that at times they would rely on these gifts and would fail to come and buy [for the Sabbath].

Why then did he not feed the vegetables to domestic animals?

He was of the opinion that food fit for human beings should not be fed to animals.

Then why did he purchase them at all?

Because if he had not done so, the gardeners might have been tempted [not to grow enough vegetables for the community] in the future.[1]

When he had a meal, he used to open the doors and declare, "Whoever is in need, let him come and eat."

Rava said: All these things I, too, could do, except the last one, because there are so many soldiers in Mahoza.[2]

602. Once four hundred jars of wine belonging to R. Huna turned sour. The sages came to visit him and said to him: The master ought to examine his [past] actions. He asked them: Am I suspect in your eyes? They replied: Is the Holy One suspect of executing judgment without justice? He said to them: If anyone has heard something against me, let him speak up. They replied: We have heard that you do not give your tenant his [lawful share of] vine shoots.[3] R. Huna replied: Does he leave me any of them? He steals them all! They said to him: That is exactly what the proverb says: "Even if you steal [what is your own] from a thief, you also are a bit of a thief!" He said to them: [From now on] I pledge myself to give them to him.

Then vinegar went up so high that it sold at the same price as wine.[4]

603. R. Huna had wine stored in a dilapidated building. When he wanted to remove it, he took R. Adda bar Ahavah into that building and kept him occupied in a learned discussion until he removed the wine. Then, as soon as R. Adda bar Ahavah left the building, it collapsed. When R. Adda ben Ahavah realized that he was used for such a purpose, he was annoyed and quoted R. Yannai, who once said, "A man should never stay in a place of danger in the hope that 'surely a miracle will be wrought for me,' for it might be that no miracle will be wrought for him. But even if it is wrought for him, it will be charged against his merits [in the world-to-come]."[5]

604. R. Hisda praised R. Hamnuna before R. Huna as a great man. So R. Huna said, "When he visits you, bring him to me." R. Hamnuna came, and R. Huna noticed that he was not wearing the distinctive turban[6] of scholars. "Why," R. Huna asked, "are you not wearing your turban?" R. Hamnuna: "Because I am not married." R. Huna turned his face away from him and said, "See to it that you do not appear before me again until you are."[7]

605. R. Huna died suddenly, and the sages were greatly concerned [for, according to a Baraita, "If one dies suddenly, it is deemed that he was 'snatched' "]. However, Zoga from Adiabene recited another Baraita: "Sudden death is called 'snatching' only when it occurs before one attains [eighty], the age of strength; after a man has attained this age, sudden death is called 'death by a kiss.' "[8]

606. When R. Huna died, the sages were about to place a Torah scroll on his bier. But R. Hisda said to them: Should one do something for him that he disapproved of while he was alive? Remember that R. Tahalifa told us, "I once saw R. Huna about to sit down on a couch on which there lay a Torah scroll. He inverted a jar on the ground and laid the Torah scroll upon it." Clearly he thought that sitting on a couch that had a Torah scroll lying on it was forbidden.

When R. Huna's bier could not be got through the doorway, they thought of letting it down from the roof. But R. Hisda said: This is what I learned from R. Huna: "Deference to a deceased sage requires that his bier should pass through the door." They thought of moving the corpse from one bier to another, but R. Hisda again said to them: I have also learned from him: "Deference to a deceased sage requires that he be taken out on the original bier upon which he was placed." So they broke the door and carried him out.

R. Abba began his eulogy: "Our master was worthy of having the Presence rest upon him, but his being in Babylonia prevented it."[9]

But then a son of R. Hisda challenged R. Abba's statement by quoting, "The word of the Lord came unto Ezekiel the Priest, the son of Buzi, in the land of the Chaldeans [Babylonia] by the river Chebar" (Ezek. 1:3). His father gently tapped him with his sandal and said: Haven't I told you not to worry your head too much with such matters? In saying "came," Scripture means that "the word of the Lord" came in the past [but no more].

When the bier was brought to the Land of Israel, R. Ammi and R. Assi[10] were told, "R. Huna has arrived." They said, "While we were in Babylonia, we could not raise our heads because of him;[11] now that we have come here, he is still after us." When they were told that it was his bier that had arrived, R. Ammi and R. Assi went out to meet it. They asked themselves: Where shall we lay him to rest? and decided: Let us bring him into R. Hiyya's grotto, for R. Huna disseminated Torah in Israel, just as

---

1. Causing a rise in prices, as a result of which the poor would suffer.
2. B. Ta 20b.
3. The tenant is entitled to as great a share in the shoots cut during the vintage as in the grapes. BM 9:1.
4. B. Ber 5b.
5. B. Ta 20b.
6. The *sudarium*.
7. B. Kid 29b.
8. B. MK 28a.
9. See below, part 3, chap. 2, §45.
10. Two Babylonians who had become leading scholars in the Land of Israel. Cf. B. Ket 17a.
11. Being aware of his superiority and seniority. See B. Meg. 22a.

R. Hiyya disseminated Torah in Israel. But who was to bring him into the grotto? R. Hagga spoke up, "I shall bring him in; because I corroborated R. Huna's teaching, he made me his attendant, and I know of his pious deeds. One day, when a thong of his tefillin was [accidentally] reversed, he fasted forty days to atone for the accident." So R. Hagga brought R. Huna's bier to the grotto, where Judah was reposing at the right of R. Hiyya, his father, and [his twin] Hezekiah at R. Hiyya's left. Judah spoke up to Hezekiah, "Rise from your place; it is not good manners to have R. Huna remain outside." As Hezekiah rose, a column of fire rose with him. When R. Hagga saw it, he was overcome with fear. So he stood the bier up [as a shield between himself and the column of fire] and left.[1]

R. Hisda (died 300 C.E.)

607. R. Hisda [who was a priest] used to hold up high two priestly gifts given him as his due[2] from the flesh of an ox and say: Whoever comes to me with a new utterance of Rav's, I will give him these.[3]

608. R. Hisda said: The reason I am superior to my colleagues is that I was married at sixteen.[4] Had I married at fourteen, I would have said to Satan, "An arrow in your eye!"[5]

609. R. Hisda was in the habit of frequently passing the door of R. Shizbi's father's house, where he regularly saw many lights [in honor of the Sabbath]. He said: A great man will issue from there.[6] Indeed, R. Shizbi issued from that household.[7]

610. R. Huna and R. Hisda were once sitting together when Geniva happened to pass by. One said to the other: Let us stand up for him—he is a man of Torah learning. The other replied: Are we to stand up for a quarrelsome man?[8]

611. R. Hisda said to his disciples: There is something I would like to say to you, but if I say it, I am afraid you may leave me and go elsewhere. [I will nevertheless say it]: "Whoever learns Torah from only one master will never see a sign of blessing in his studies." Hearing these words, they left him and went to sit before Rabbah, who explained to them that the dictum applied only to logical analysis and that oral traditions are better learned from only one master, for then the disciple will not be confused by a variety of terms.[9]

1. B. MK 25a and En Yaakov, ad loc.
2. The shoulder, the jaws, and the maw were the priest's due.
3. B. Shab 10b.
4. So that my mind was entirely free for study.
5. "I defy you." B. Kid 29b–30a.
6. In keeping with "Where the command of the Sabbath lamp is heeded, there will be the light of Torah" (Prov. 6:23).
7. B. Shab 23b.
8. B. Git 31b.
9. B. AZ 19a.

612. The exilarch [Mar Ukba II] asked R. Huna, "By what authority are nuptial crowns for grooms prohibited?" R. Huna replied, "By the sages on their own authority." After R. Huna got up to leave the room, R. Hisda[10] said to the exilarch, "There is scriptural authority for the prohibition: 'Thus saith the Lord God: The miter shall be removed, and the crown taken off; this shall be no more the same: that which is low shall be exalted, and that which is high abased' [Ezek. 21:31]. It may be asked," he continued, "what the miter has to do with the crown. It is to indicate that when the miter is worn by the high priest,[11] ordinary persons can wear the crown; once the miter has been removed from the head of the high priest, the crown must be removed from the head of all ordinary persons." At this point R. Huna returned, and, finding them still discussing the matter, he said, "I swear to you that the prohibition was made by the sages on their own authority, but as your name is Hisda, 'favor,' so do your words find favor."[12]

613. R. Huna asked his son Rabbah, "Why are you not to be found in the presence of R. Hisda, whose traditions are so keen?" Rabbah replied, "Why should I go to him? When I go to him, he treats me to secular discourses![13] Thus he tells me, 'When one enters a privy, one should not sit down abruptly nor strain overmuch, for the rectum is supported by three teethlike glands, and should these teethlike glands become dislocated, one's health would be endangered.' " R. Huna: "R. Hisda treats of matters that concern the life of mankind, and you call them secular discourses! All the more reason for you to go to him!"[14]

614. Whenever R. Hisda had to walk among thorns and thistles, he lifted up his clothes, saying, "The body heals itself, but clothes do not."[15]

615. R. Hisda noticed date-palm shoots sprouting in his vineyard, so he said to his tenant farmer, "Uproot them—grapevines [produce enough income to] buy date palms, but date palms do not [produce enough income to] buy grapevines."[16]

616. R. Hisda used to hand all his keys to his servant except the key to the woodbin, for R. Hisda would say: A storehouse of wheat requires sixty stores of wood for fuel.[17]

617. R. Hisda said: Neither when poor nor when rich did I ever eat vegetables. When I was poor, because they whet the appetite; when rich, because I said: Where veg-

10. He was R. Huna's disciple and therefore did not like to speak up in his presence.
11. I.e., while the Temple is standing.
12. B. Git 7a.
13. I.e., not Torah.
14. B. Shab 82a.
15. Cf. above in this chapter, §8. B. BK 91b.
16. B. BK 92a.
17. To bake the bread. B. Git 56a.

etables are to enter, fish and meat [which are more nourishing] may as well enter.

R. Hisda also said: If a scholar has but little bread, he should take care not to break it up in small pieces, but eat it all at once [and feel sated at least for a while].

R. Hisda also said: If a scholar has but little bread, he should not break it into smaller portions. Why not? Because [the portions being skimpy], he is not likely to recite the blessing for bread with a willing heart.

R. Hisda also said: Formerly [when I was poor] I did not break bread for the blessing until I put my hands into the basket to make sure I found in it all that I required.[1]

R. Hisda advised his daughters: Act modestly before your husbands. When someone calls at the door, do not say, "Who is he who wishes to enter?" but, "Who is she who wishes to enter?"[2] R. Hisda used to take a jewel in one hand and a berry in the other. He showed them the jewel, but he did not show them the berry until they were distressed by their eagerness to know what was in the other hand. Only then did he show it to them.[3]

618. R. Hisda's daughter was sitting on her father's lap, and before him sat Rava and Rami bar Hama. Her father asked her, "Which of them would you like to marry?" She replied, "Both." Rava asked, "May I be the second?" And thus it came to pass.[4]

619. Rava said: [Length of] life, children, and sustenance depend not on merit but on *mazzal*.[5] Take Rabbah and R. Hisda, both of whom were sages, both saintly. When one prayed for rain, it came, even as it came when the other prayed for rain. Yet R. Hisda lived to the age of ninety-two,[6] while Rabbah died at the age of forty.[7] In R. Hisda's house, sixty[8] wedding feasts were celebrated; in Rabbah's house, sixty bereavements. In R. Hisda's house, dogs were fed bread of fine flour, which was never missed; in Rabbah's, barley bread was for human beings, and even that was hardly to be had.[9]

620. Once, when Ulla and R. Hisda were walking along the road, they came to the door of the house of R. Hana bar Hanilai. R. Hisda broke down and began to sigh. Ulla said to him: Why are you sighing? Remember what Rav said: A sigh breaks half a man's body, as evident from, "Sigh therefore, thou son of man, with the breaking of thy loins," etc. (Ezek. 21:11). And R. Yohanan said: Indeed, it breaks all of a man's body as evident from "And it shall be, when they say unto thee, wherefore sighest thou? . . . every heart shall sink and all hands hang nerveless" (Ezek. 21:12). R. Hisda replied: How shall I refrain from sighing? Here is a house in which there were once sixty bakers by day and sixty bakers by night, who baked for everyone who was in need. Nor did R. Hana ever take his hand away from his purse, thinking that perhaps a poor man of good family might come and be put to shame as R. Hana was reaching for his purse. Moreover, the house had four doors, opening to the four cardinal points, and whoever came in hungry went out full. In years of scarcity, wheat and barley were piled outside, so that anyone who was ashamed to take some by day might come and take some by night. Now that this house has fallen into ruins, shall I not sigh? Ulla replied: Thus said R. Yohanan: Since the day the Temple was destroyed, a decree was issued against the houses of the righteous, that they should become desolate, as is said, "In mine ears said the Lord of hosts: Of a truth many houses shall be desolate, even great and fair, without inhabitants" (Isa. 5:9). R. Yohanan said further: The Holy One will someday restore them to their inhabited state, as is said, "A Song of Ascents. They that trust in the Lord are as Mount Zion, which cannot be moved, but abideth forever" (Ps. 125:1). Just as the Holy One will restore Mount Zion to its inhabited state, so will He restore the houses of the righteous to their inhabited state. Observing that R. Hisda was still not reassured, Ulla said to him: Enough for the servant that he should be like his Master.[10]

621. R. Hisda's daughter asked him: Wouldn't you like to take a short nap? He replied: Soon enough there will come days that are both long and short, when we will have plenty of sleep.[11]

622. R. Hisda was sitting in the school [of Rav] studying, so that the angel of death was unable to come near him, for his mouth did not cease reciting the words of the lore he was at. But when he proceeded to sit down on a cedar bench in the school, [the angel of death saw to it that] it split under him, so that R. Hisda was silent for a moment. In that very moment the angel of death prevailed over him.[12]

623. When R. Hisda died, it was suggested that a Torah scroll be placed on his bier. But R. Isaac bar Ammi said: Shall we do for him what he disapproved of doing for his master? Then it was suggested that the [mourning] rent in their garments not be sewn. But R. Isaac bar Ammi said: With regard to a deceased sage, as soon as the faces of those who follow the bier are turned away, the rent may be sewn together again.[13]

624. R. Hisda used to find quail among the logs in his woodshed, while Rava's gamekeeper used to bring Rava

---

1. And thus could say the blessing with a whole heart.
2. To indicate that you do not associate with strange men.
3. He thus proved the folly of being curious and lacking in reserve. B. Shab 140b.
4. Ten years after the death of her husband Rami bar Hama, Rava married her (B. Yev 34b). B. BB 12b.
5. Destiny.
6. He died in 390 C.E.
7. He died in 330 C.E.
8. A proverbial number.
9. B. MK 28a.
10. That R. Hana's house should be like the house of God. B. Ber 58b and En Yaakov, ad loc.
11. "The days in the grave are long in quantity but short in quality. In the grave one cannot continue his studies or perform any of the other good deeds" (Er, Soncino, p. 453, n. 15). B. Er 65a.
12. B. Mak 10a.
13. B. MK 25a.

quail daily from the meadow. But one day the gamekeeper failed to bring them, and Rava wondered why. He went up to the roof, where he heard a child reciting the verse "When I heard, my inward parts trembled" (Hab. 3:16). At that, Rava said: The child's verse intimates that R. Hisda is dead and that [I] the disciple was able to eat quail only by the grace of the master.[1]

R. Sheshet (fl. 1st half of 4th century C.E.)

625. R. Hama applied to R. Sheshet the verse "Wisdom is good with an inheritance" (Eccles. 7:11).[2]

626. Every thirty days R. Sheshet used to go over his studies, and then, leaning on the door bolt of his house, he would say, "Rejoice, O my soul; rejoice, O my soul. For you have I read Scripture. For you have I recited Mishnah."[3]

627. [During the reading of Scripture], R. Sheshet used to turn his back to the reader and, reviewing [interpretations of the text], would say: We are busy with ours [advanced study], while they are busy with theirs [cursory perusal].[4]

628. Rabbah said: A hard man who is as hard as iron[5] raised a question. And who was it? R. Sheshet.[6]

629. Whenever R. Hisda and R. Sheshet met each other, R. Hisda's lips trembled because of R. Sheshet's great command of Mishnah,[7] and R. Sheshet trembled all over his body because of R. Hisda's capacity for keen analysis.[8]

630. R. Isaac bar Judah used to attend Rami bar Hama's lectures, but then left him and began to attend R. Sheshet's lectures. One day Rami bar Hama met R. Isaac and said, "Just because a high dignitary took us by the hand, do we think that his [sweet] scent remains on [our] hand? Just because you have gone to R. Sheshet, do you think you will be [esteemed] like R. Sheshet?" "That was not the reason," R. Isaac replied. "When I ask you a question, you give me an answer based on logic; then I find a mishnaic passage[9] that refutes your answer. But when I put a question to R. Sheshet, his answer is based on a mishnaic passage, so that if I come upon another mishnaic passage that refutes him, it is merely a case of one passage against the other."[10]

1. B. Yoma 75b.
2. B. Bekh 52b.
3. B. Pes 68b.
4. B. Ber 8a.
5. "A scholar who is not as hard as iron is no scholar" (B. Ta 4a).
6. B. Men 95b.
7. Since many Mishnayyot appeared to contradict one another, R. Sheshet would embarrass R. Hisda by challenging him to reconcile them.
8. So keen that R. Sheshet was embarrassed. B. Er 57a.
9. Or a Baraita.
10. A controversy: I have my choice of which to follow. B. Zev 96b.

631. When R. Sheshet and R. Ahadboi bar Ammi [were discussing a question in *Halakhah*], R. Ahadboi finally voiced his dissent from R. Sheshet in a derisive fashion, so that R. Sheshet felt deeply humiliated. Soon after that, R. Ahadboi lost his speech and forgot his learning. R. Ahadboi's mother came weeping before R. Sheshet, but, in spite of her [pitiful] cries, he gave her no heed. Finally she said to him: Look at these breasts from which you sucked.[11] At this, R. Sheshet prayed in R. Ahadboi's behalf, and he was healed.[12]

632. R. Sheshet was blind. Still, on one occasion, when all the people went out to welcome the king, R. Sheshet arose and went with them. A certain heretic came across him and said to him, "Sound pitchers are taken to the river, but why should cracked ones go there?"[13] R. Sheshet replied, "I will show you that I know more than you."

When the first legion passed by and a shout arose, the heretic said, "The king is coming," but R. Sheshet retorted, "He has not yet come." When a second legion passed by, and again a shout arose, the heretic said again, "The king is coming now," but R. Sheshet once more retorted, "Not yet." When a third legion passed by in perfect silence, R. Sheshet said to the heretic, "Now it is certain that the king is coming." The heretic asked, "How do you know this?" R. Sheshet replied, "Because royalty on earth is like royalty in heaven, about which it is written, 'The Lord was not in the earthquake; and after the earthquake a still small voice' " (1 Kings 19:12).

When the king came, R. Sheshet pronounced the appropriate blessing over him. The heretic asked, "You pronounce a blessing over one you cannot see?" R. Sheshet fixed his eyes upon him, and sparks of fire came forth and quenched the sight of the heretic's eyes.[14]

633. The exilarch once asked R. Sheshet, "Why, sir, will you not dine with us?" R. Sheshet: "Because your servants are not decent people, for they are suspected of serving limbs cut from live animals." "Who says so?" asked the exilarch. R. Sheshet: "I will show you," and he [quietly] said to his attendant, "Steal an animal's leg and bring it to me." After the attendant brought it to R. Sheshet, the latter said to the exilarch's servants, "Set out all the pieces of the animal before me." They brought three of its legs and placed them before him. R. Sheshet asked, "Was this a three-legged animal?" When the exilarch's servants produced another leg from outside [the exilarch's house], R. Sheshet said to his attendant, "Now produce yours." R. Sheshet's attendant did so. R. Sheshet asked the exilarch's servants, "Was this then a five-legged animal?"

The exilarch said to R. Sheshet, "Let the food be prepared in the presence of your own attendant and then eat." "Very good," replied R. Sheshet. So they brought a

11. She had nursed R. Sheshet.
12. B. BB 9b.
13. Why should a blind man be going to see the king?
14. B. Ber 58a.

table to him, upon which was placed meat, and in front of him was set a portion containing a tiny bone.[1] He felt it, picked it up, and wrapped it in his turban. [The servants noticed that he had wrapped something in his turban.] So after he finished eating, they said, "A silver cup has been stolen from us."[2] They searched him and found the piece of meat wrapped in his turban. They said to the exilarch, "Sir, you can see that he does not want to eat—he only wants to vex us." R. Sheshet: "I started to eat, but found it tasting of a leprous animal." They replied, "We slaughtered no leprous animal today." He said to them, "Examine the skin in the place where my portion came from."

They examined it and found that it was as he said.

When R. Sheshet was about to leave, the exilarch's servants dug a pit, threw a mat over it, and said to him, "Come, sir, and recline here." R. Hisda uttered a snort of warning behind him. So R. Sheshet said to a boy, "Tell me the last verse you studied." The boy: "Turn thee aside to thy right hand or to thy left" (2 Sam. 2:21). Then he asked his attendant, "What do you see?" The attendant: "A mat placed in front of us." R. Sheshet: "Turn away from it." After he got away safely, R. Hisda asked him, "How did the master come to know?" He replied, "For one thing, because you, sir, warned me by your snort; then, too, from the verse the boy quoted; and finally, because the exilarch's servants are not decent people."[3]

634. The angel of death showed itself to R. Sheshet in the marketplace. R. Sheshet said to him: Will you seize me in the marketplace like cattle? Come to my house.[4]

R. Nahman [bar Jacob] (died 329 C.E.)

635. After Rabbi died, humility and fear of sin ceased. But R. Nahman said to the teacher [who taught this]: Do not include "fear of sin," because I am still here.[5]

636. R. Nahman himself used to carry [whatever was needed for the Sabbath] on his shoulder in and out on the eve of the Sabbath, saying: Were R. Ammi and R. Assi to visit me, would I not be carrying in and out [whatever they needed]?[6]

637. R. Nahman used to send men from his personal guard[7] [to give a hand to the aged, but he would not do so himself], saying, "But for Torah, how many Nahman bar Abbas would there be in the marketplace?"[8]

638. R. Nahman and R. Isaac once were dining together, and R. Nahman said to R. Isaac, "Let the master expound something," R. Isaac replied, "R. Yohanan said the following: One should not converse while eating, lest the windpipe open before the gullet and thus endanger life." After they had dined, R. Isaac said, "Thus declared R. Yohanan: Jacob our patriarch is not dead." R. Nahman objected: "Was it then for nought that mourners mourned, embalmers embalmed, and gravediggers dug a grave?" R. Isaac replied, "I derive this teaching from Scripture, where it is said, 'Therefore fear thou not, O Jacob, My servant . . . for, lo, I will save thee from afar, and thy seed from the land of their captivity' [Jer. 30:10]. Here the verse likens Jacob to his seed [Israel]—as his seed is alive, so, too, he is alive."

When R. Nahman was about to take leave of R. Isaac, he said, "Please, master, bless me." R. Isaac replied, "Let me tell you a parable by which I would respond to your request—the parable of a man who was journeying in the desert. He was hungry, weary, and thirsty, and he lighted upon a tree whose fruits were delicious and its shade pleasant, and a stream of water was flowing beneath it. He ate of its fruits, drank water from the stream, and rested under the tree's shade. When he was about to continue his journey, he said: Tree, O tree, what blessing shall I bestow upon you? If I say to you, 'May your fruits be delicious,' behold, they are delicious. If I say, 'May your shade be pleasant,' behold, it is pleasant. If I say, 'May a stream of water flow beneath you,' behold, a stream of water does flow beneath you. Therefore I say, 'May it be [God's] will that all the seedlings taken from you be like you.' You, too, [dear Nahman]—what blessing shall I bestow upon you? Knowledge of Torah? Behold, you already possess such knowledge. Eminence? You are already eminent. Honor? You are already honored. Riches? You are already rich. Children? You already have children. Hence I say, 'May it be [God's] will that your offspring be like you.' "[9]

639. Ulla happenend to visit the house of R. Nahman. They had a meal, after which Ulla said grace and then handed the cup of blessing[10] to R. Nahman to recite the blessing over it. R. Nahman said to him, "Please send the cup to [my wife] Yalta, that she may recite it.[11] Ulla replied, "Thus taught R. Yohanan: The fruit of a woman's body is blessed only from the fruit of a man's body, since Scripture says, 'He will also bless the fruit of thy body' [Deut. 7:13]—it does not say, 'The fruit of *her* body,' but, 'The fruit of *thy* [that is, a man's] body.' [So if you recite the blessing over the cup, there is no need for her to recite it.]" Yalta heard[12] [that Ulla had refused to send her the cup], and she flew into a rage, stormed into the wine pantry, and smashed four hundred jugs of wine. R. Nahman again said to Ulla, "Would the master please send her the cup." Ulla [again refused and] sent her a message: "The huge quantity of wine you splattered should provide the cup of blessing you demand." She shot back the reply:

---

1. Literally, "the portion intended to choke a mother-in-law." It is a part containing a tiny bone and is taken from flesh just above the animal's hind leg. So Rashi.
2. A pretext in order to search him.
3. B. Git 67b–68a.
4. B. MK 28a.
5. B. Sot 49b.
6. How much more so to welcome the Sabbath. B. Shab 119a.
7. As the exilarch's son-in-law, he had them at his disposal.
8. I must therefore husband my time for teaching Torah. B. Kid 33a.
9. B. Ta 5b–6a and En Yaakov, ad loc.
10. The blessing over a full cup of wine following the grace after a meal in which at least three men have partaken.
11. Apparently, Yalta, with R. Nahman's consent, expected that women be given the right to utter such a blessing.
12. Yalta sat in an adjoining room during the meal, as was the custom for women.

"Insulting words from itinerant peddlers[1] are as inevitable as vermin from rags."

640. While seated at the bedside of R. Nahman, Rava saw him falling into the sleep [of death], yet R. Nahman managed to say to Rava, "Master, tell the angel of death not to torment me." Rava replied, "But, master, are you not important enough [to say so to him yourself]?" R. Nahman: "Who is sufficiently important, esteemed, or well enough put together [to make such a request]?" Then Rava asked R. Nahman, "Master, show yourself to me in a dream." When [after his death] he did show himself, Rava asked him, "Master, did you suffer any pain?" And he replied, "As little as in pulling a hair out of milk. Still, if the Holy One were to say to me, 'Go back to that world and become again what you were,' I would not wish it, the fear of the angel of death being so great."[2]

Rabbah [bar Nahmani] (died 339 C.E.)

641. Rabbah's brothers sent him an urgent message:[3] Since [the patriarch] Jacob knew that he was a completely righteous man [and knew that] the dead [buried] outside the Land were to come back to life, why did he impose on his sons [the task of carrying his corpse to Canaan]? Because he could not reconcile himself to the distress he would experience in going back to the Land through underground passages.[4]

Ilfa added to Rabbah's brothers' words the following: There was once a man who ached to marry a certain woman living outside the Land and was about to move there. But when he heard of the journey [made by the dead] through underground passages, he resigned himself to the distress of giving up the woman he loved [and remained in the Land] until the day of his death.

[In their plea, Rabbah's brothers went on]: Even though you are a great scholar, you must admit that a man who learns by himself is not the equal of a man who learns from a master. And if you suppose that there is no master fit for you [in the Land of Israel], there is one. Who? R. Yohanan.[5]

642. R. Joseph was "Sinai,"[6] and Rabbah was "an uprooter of mountains."[7] When the time came for one of them to be needed [to head the academy of Pumbedita], their colleagues sent an inquiry to the Land of Israel: As between "Sinai" and "the uprooter of mountains," which should have the preference? Word came back: Sinai, because everybody needs the master of the wheat.[8] Nevertheless, R. Joseph would not accept the post, because the astrologers had told him, "You would be head for only two years." So Rabbah served as head for twenty-two years, and after him R. Joseph for two years and a half.[9]

During all the time that Rabbah was head, he did not so much as summon a cupper[10] to come to his house.[11]

643. When the main body of sages left the schools of Rabbah and R. Joseph, and only four hundred remained, they described themselves as orphans.[12]

644. Before Rabbah began his discourse to the sages, he told them a humorous story to put them in a cheerful mood. Then, in a solemn manner, he sat down and began the discourse on *Halakhah*.[13]

645. Rav said: During the day, [when a man ought to be studying Torah], his sleep should last no longer than the sleep of a horse. And how long is that? Sixty respirations.

Abbaye said: The sleep of the master [Rabbah bar Nahmani] is as short as that of Rav.[14]

646. [On the eve of a Sabbath], Rabbah and R. Joseph used to split wood.[15]

647. Abba bar Martha (sometimes called Abba bar Manyumi),[16] who owed Rabbah money he had lent him, brought it to Rabbah's house in the seventh year of a septenary.[17] Rabbah said: I cancel the debt. So Abba bar Martha took his money and went away. Subsequently, Abbaye, seeing that Rabbah looked sad, asked him, "Sir, why are you sad?" Rabbah told him what had happened. So Abbaye went to Abba bar Martha and asked him, "Did you offer money to Rabbah?" R. Abba replied, "Yes." Abbaye: "And what did he say to you?" R. Abba: "I cancel the debt." Abbaye: "And did you say to him, 'Nevertheless, take it'?" R. Abba: "No." Abbaye said to him, "If you had said to him, 'Nevertheless, take it,' he would have taken it. At any rate, go now, offer it to him, and say, 'Nevertheless, take it.' " R. Abba went and offered it to Rabbah, saying, "Nevertheless, take it." Rabbah took it from him and said, "Until now, this disciple of the wise did not have the sense to know what to do!"[18]

648. At first the sages said: If an associate scholar[19] becomes a tax collector, he is expelled from the fellow-

1. She was referring to Ulla's journeying from Babylonia to the Land of Israel and back again. B. Ber 51b.
2. B. MK 28a.
3. Pleading with him to move to the Land of Israel. He lived in Pumbedita, Babylonia.
4. And only then come back to life.
5. B. Ket 111a and En Yaakov, ad loc.
6. His knowledge of the traditions was encyclopedic.
7. He was exceptionally skillful in dialectics.
8. One who is master of the authentic traditions.
9. Rabbah was head in 309–30 C.E. R. Joseph, who succeeded him, died in 333 C.E.
10. One who draws blood from the body by means of a cupping glass as a form of medical treatment.
11. But instead went to him, like any other individual. B. Ber 64a.
12. See above in this chapter, §528. B. Ket 106a.
13. B. Shab 30b.
14. B. Suk 26b.
15. B. Shab 119a.
16. Martha was the name of his mother, by whose name he was designated because it was she who once cured him from the bite of a mad dog. See B. Yoma 84a.
17. When loans are canceled.
18. B. Git 37b.
19. One scrupulous in observance of the law, particularly with regard to ritual cleanness and separating priestly and Levitical dues.

ship.[1] If he gives up the office, he is not again accepted as a fellow. Subsequently, however, they declared: If he resigns, he is treated like any other person.

It so happened that the sages required the presence of R. Huna bar Hiyya.[2] So Rabbah and R. Joseph set out to go to him, together with four hundred pairs of sages. When he learned that they were coming, he arranged four hundred mats to seat them. [On their way], when they heard that he had become a tax collector, they [decided not to go to him, but] sent a [contemptuous] message: "Go on to your important post, go on to your eminent office!" He sent back word to them: "I regret what I have done." R. Joseph did not go to visit him, but Rabbah did. R. Joseph reasoned: We have been taught: If he gives up the office, he is not again accepted as a fellow. However, Rabbah reasoned: We have been taught: Subsequently they declared that if he resigns, he is treated like any other person.[3]

649. Abbaye asked Rabbah: For the likes of you, sir, whom all of Pumbedita hates [because of your outspokenness], who will offer a eulogy? Rabbah replied: You and Rava bar R. Hanan are enough for me.[4]

650. R. Kahana said: R. Hama, the son of the daughter of Hassa, related to me [that] Rabbah bar Nahmani died as a result of religious persecution, having been denounced to the king by informers, who said: Among the Jews there is one man who for one month in summer and one in winter prevents twelve thousand Jews from paying their royal poll tax.[5] At that, a royal emissary was sent to bring him in, but he could not find him, for Rabbah kept fleeing from Pumbedita to Akra, from Akra to Agam, from Agam to Shahin, from Shahin to Tzarif, from Tzarif to En Damim,[6] and from there back to Pumbedita. Finally the emissary chanced to visit the inn in Pumbedita where Rabbah was staying. A small table was placed before the emissary, he was served two goblets [of liquor], and then the table was removed, whereupon his face was turned backward [by demons].[7] "What shall we do with him?" the inn attendants asked Rabbah. "He is, after all, a royal emissary." Rabbah: "Put the table before him again, and make him drink another goblet; then remove the table, and he will recover." They did so, and he recovered. The emissary then said, "I know that the man I am seeking is here." He looked for Rabbah, and when he caught sight of him, he said, "I will go away from here. Even if I am sentenced to die, I will not reveal his whereabouts. Still, if I am tortured, I am likely to reveal it." So he had Rabbah brought into his presence, had him taken into a chamber, and locked the door [to keep him there as a prisoner]. But Rabbah invoked God's mercy, and the wall of the chamber fell down. Then he fled to Agam, where he sat on the stump of a fallen palm and studied Torah.

Meanwhile, in the academy on high they were debating an instance in the laws concerning leprosy, where the Holy One ruled, "Clean," while the entire academy on high maintained, "Unclean." Finally, they asked, "Who is to decide the matter?" and answered "Rabbah bar Nahmani, the one who said, 'I am unique in understanding the laws of leprosy and the laws of tents in which there is a corpse.' " A messenger was sent for him, but the angel of death could not touch him, because his mouth did not stop studying even for one instant. In the meantime, a wind blew up and soughed in the reeds. Imagining it to be a legion of horsemen, he said, "Let me die at the hands of the angel of death, rather than be delivered into the hands of the government." As he was dying, he exclaimed, "Clean, clean!"[8] A divine voice cried out, "Happy are you, O Rabbah bar Nahmani, whose body is pure and whose soul has departed with [the word] 'clean.'

In Pumbedita a tablet fell from heaven upon which was written, "Rabbah bar Nahmani has been summoned to the academy on high." So Abbaye and Rava left [their homes] to attend to his burial,[9] but they did not know where his body lay. They went to Agam, where they saw birds shading something with their wings. They said, "He must be over there." When they found him, they eulogized him for three days and three nights. Then another tablet fell: "He who [will now] cease eulogizing should consider himself under a ban." So they eulogized him for [another four days, making it] seven in all. Finally a third tablet fell: "Return to your homes in peace."

On the day Rabbah died, a mighty storm lifted an Arab riding his camel from one bank of the river Papa and flung him across to the other bank. He asked, "What does this signify?" and was told, "Rabbah bar Nahmani is dead." At that, he cried out to the Holy One, "Lord of the Universe! The whole world is Yours, and Rabbah bar Nahmani also is Yours. You are [the friend] of Rabbah, and Rabbah is Your [friend]. Why then would You destroy the world?" With that, the storm subsided.[10]

651. When Rabbah and R. Joseph died, it seemed as though the cliffs on both sides of the Euphrates had kissed each other.[11]

R. Joseph (died 333 C.E.)

652. When Rabbi died, humility and fear of sin ceased. R. Joseph said to the one who taught this: Do not mention humility, for I am still here.[12]

1. "Publicans or customs collectors had the taxes farmed out to them by the crown and as a rule recouped themselves by imposing iniquitous burdens on the people: consequently they were considered robbers in Jewish law" (Bekh, Soncino, p. 196, n. 5).
2. To consult him on a question in Jewish law. Literally, "the time needed him."
3. B. Bekh 31a.
4. B. Shab 153a.
5. They used to come to the academy in Nisan and Tishri, months during which popular lectures were given; in consequence, the tax collectors could not collect their taxes during those months. So Rashi.
6. All these places appear to be in the neighborhood of Pumbedita.
7. To drink an even number of glasses was believed to excite the ill will of certain demons.
8. As though the subject of the heavenly controversy had already been communicated to him.
9. See above in this chapter, §649.
10. B. BM 86a.
11. The mourners were so numerous that they seemed to have crowded out the water. B. MK 25b.
12. B. Sot 49b.

653. A woman [whose husband had vanished] came to Abbaye to inquire about her status. He deferred answering her for the time span of three festivals.[1] So R. Adda bar Abba said to her: Go to R. Joseph, whose mind is as keen as the blade of a knife.[2]

654. Rava said: Rabbah and R. Joseph found a certain matter difficult for twenty-two years, with no answer forthcoming, until R. Joseph became head of the academy and solved it.[3]

655. R. Joseph applied to himself the verse "Good crops come from the work done by the ox" (Prov. 14:4).[4]

656. On the Feast of Weeks [Shavuot], R. Joseph would say, "Prepare for me a calf thirdborn of its dam.[5] But for this day,[6] how many Josephs would there be in the marketplace!"[7]

657. R. Joseph [who was blind] said: Formerly, I thought that if anyone were to tell me, "The *Halakhah* agrees with R. Judah that a blind person is exempt from the [observance of the] precepts," I would have made a festive meal for the sages, since even though I am not obliged to observe the precepts, I do observe them. But now, having heard what R. Hanina said—"He who is commanded to observe the precepts and does observe them is greater than he who observes them though not commanded to do so"—the contrary has become true. Were anyone to tell me, "The *Halakhah* does not agree with R. Judah," I would make a festive meal for the sages.[8]

658. When R. Joseph took sick and forgot his learning, Abbaye restored it to him. Hence the exchange that occurred frequently: R. Joseph saying, "I have not heard this tradition," and Abbaye responding, "You yourself taught it to us—deduced it in fact from this particular Baraita."[9]

659. R. Joseph was studying the Work of the Chariot,[10] while the elders of Pumbedita were studying the Work of Creation.[11] They said to R. Joseph, "Will our master teach us the Work of the Chariot?" He replied, "Teach me the Work of Creation." After they had taught him, they said to him, "Now teach us the Work of the Chariot." He replied, "Concerning it, we have been taught, 'Honey and milk are under thy tongue' [Song 4:11][12]—the things that are as sweet as honey should remain under your tongue."

R. Abbahu said, "The restriction of teaching the Work of the Chariot is inferred from the verse 'The lambs [*kevasim*] will be for thy clothing' [Prov. 27:26]. Read not *kevasim*, 'lambs,' but *kevushim*, 'things mysterious'—the things that are the mystery [*kivshon*] of the world should remain under your clothing [in your bosom]." But the elders of Pumbedita said to him, "We have already studied these mysteries up to the verse 'And he said unto me: Son of man' " (Ezek. 2:1). R. Abbahu replied, "This verse is the very essence of the Work of the Chariot."[13]

660. R. Joseph observed a fast for forty days and [in a dream] had read to him, "They shall not depart out of thy mouth" (Isa. 59:21). He observed forty more fasts and [in a dream] had read to him, "They shall not depart out of thy mouth, nor out of the mouth of thy seed" (ibid.). He observed still another forty fasts and [in a dream] had read to him, "They shall not depart out of thy mouth, nor out of the mouth of thy seed, nor out of the mouth of thy seed's seed" (ibid.). "From now on," he said, "I have no need to fast. The Torah will keep coming back to the place where it has been made to feel at home."[14]

661. When from a distance Abbaye saw only the ear of Joseph's donkey as it was approaching, he would rise up.[15]

662. When Rava took leave of R. Joseph, he would walk backward, so that his feet were bruised and the threshold of R. Joseph's house was stained with blood. People told R. Joseph what Rava did.[16] R. Joseph said to him, "May it be [Heaven's] will that your person be raised above the entire city."[17]

663. In the days of R. Joseph, when there came the affliction of famine,[18] the sages said to R. Joseph: Let the master entreat for mercy. He replied: [During a like famine], after the main body of Elisha's disciples left, there remained two thousand two hundred sages[19] [for whom he had to provide]. Yet he did not entreat God's mercy. Should I, then, left with a mere four hundred to provide for,[20] entreat God for mercy?[21]

---

1. When scholars who assembled to listen to discourses were asked to consider difficult problems in law that had come up during the preceding months.
2. B. Yev 121b–122a.
3. B. Kat 42b.
4. Since his name was Joseph, he spoke of himself as an ox, in keeping with what was said of the tribe father Joseph: "Like a firstling ox in his majesty" (Deut. 33:17). B. Sanh 42a.
5. Choice; and, being thirdborn, it corresponds to the third month in the year, Sivan, during which the Feast of Weeks occurs.
6. When the Torah is said to have been given to Israel.
7. But for my knowledge of Torah, I would be but another Joseph. B. Pes 68b.
8. B. Kid 31a.
9. B. Ned 41a.
10. Intimated at the beginning of Ezekiel.
11. Intimated in Genesis.
12. Song of Songs is construed as a mystical dialogue between God the groom and Israel the bride.
13. B. Hag 13a.
14. B. BM 85a.
15. B. Kid 33a.
16. R. Joseph, being blind, did not see it.
17. The blessing was fulfilled. Rava became head of the academies of Sura and Pumbedita. B. Yoma 33b.
18. Perhaps during the time he was head of the academy.
19. The number is arrived at by close examination of 2 Kings 2:42–44. See Rashi.
20. See above in this chapter, §643.
21. B. Ket 106a.

664. R. Joseph owned small date palms under which cuppers [with his permission] used to sit and draw blood. When ravens, coming to drink up the spilled blood, would land on the palm trees and damage the dates, R. Joseph said to the cuppers: Get your croakers away from here![1]

665. R. Joseph had a garden plot which he hoed repeatedly, and it produced wine that, when mixed, could take twice the usual amount of water.[2]

666. Rava bar R. Hanan had small palm trees growing next to R. Joseph's vineyard, and birds roosting in the palms would fly down into the vineyard and damage the grapes in it. R. Joseph said to Rava, "Go, cut down your palms." Rava: "I will not cut them down, for Rav has said, 'It is forbidden to cut down a palm that bears a *kav* of dates'; and R. Hanina has said, 'My son Shibhat died because he cut down a fig tree before its time.'[3] However, if it pleases the master, let him cut down the palms himself."[4]

667. The sages taught: There are three kinds of men whose life is no life: those who are overly compassionate, those who are too prone to anger, and those who are too fastidious. R. Joseph said: The three qualities are in me.[5]

668. R. Joseph said: I once entered the baths after Mar Ukba. When I was about to leave, he made me drink a cup of [*aluntit*] wine,[6] and I then experienced a cooling sensation from the hair of my head right down to the nails of my toes. Had he made me drink a second cup, I fear that my merits in the world-to-come would have been diminished.[7]

Abbaye bar Kaylil (280–338/39 C.E.)

669. When Abbaye's mother conceived him, his father died. When she gave birth to him, she died. But did not Abbaye used to say, "Mother told me"? He meant his foster mother.[8]

670. Abbaye's foster mother trained a lamb to go with him into the privy.[9]

671. A boy who knows to whom a benediction is addressed may be invited by the partakers to say grace with them after a meal.

[When they were still very young], Abbaye and Rava sat in the presence of Rabbah, who asked them, "Whom do we address when we pronounce a benediction?" The two: "God."

"And where does God dwell?"

Rava pointed to the ceiling, while Abbaye went outside and pointed to the sky. Rabbah said to them: Both of you will grow up to be sages.

Hence the popular saying: Each young pumpkin can be told by its stalk.[10]

672. Abbaye, Rava, R. Zera, and Rabbah bar Mattenah once sat studying together at a time when the need had arisen to appoint a head [for the school of Pumbedita].[11] Rabbah suggested: He who makes a statement that cannot be refuted by others shall be appointed head. The statements of three of them were refuted, but not Abbaye's. When Rabbah realized that Abbaye was destined to become head, he said: Nahmani[12] begin to expound.[13]

673. Abbaye said: In the streets of Tiberias I am like Ben Azzai.[14]

674. When the main body of disciples departed from the school of Abbaye, there still remained two hundred. Nevertheless, [because they believed they were too few], they described themselves as most orphaned among orphans.[15]

675. Abbaye said: May it be counted as merit for me that whenever I saw a disciple of the wise finish a tractate, I made a festive day for the sages.[16]

676. Rabbah and Abbaye sprang from the house of Eli[17] [doomed to be short-lived]. Still, because Rabbah occupied himself with Torah, he lived forty years; and because Abbaye occupied himself with Torah and deeds of loving-kindness, he lived sixty years.[18]

677. Abba, who was a cupper, used to receive greetings daily from the academy on high, while Abbaye received such greetings only on Sabbath eve, and Rava only on Yom Kippur eve. When Abbaye was depressed because of the signal honor shown to Abba the Cupper, people said to him: You cannot do what Abba the Cupper does.

What was the special merit of Abba the Cupper? When he let blood, he had a separate place for men and

---

1. Go away and find another spot to do your work. R. Joseph presumed to ask the cuppers to remove themselves, even though the damage they caused was indirect. B. BB 23a.
2. "Usually wine was adulterated with water in the proportion of three parts of water to one of wine (cf. Shab 77a); this wine could stand an admixture of water in the proportion of six parts of water to one of wine" (Men, Soncino, p. 526, n. 6). B. Men 87a.
3. Before it withered.
4. B. BB 26a.
5. B. Pes 113b.
6. A mixture of old wine, clear water, and balsam.
7. B. Shab 140a.
8. B. Kid 31b.
9. So that he should not be afraid. B. Ber 62a.
10. B. Ber 48a.
11. "After the death of R. Joseph" (Isidore Epstein in Hor, Soncino, p. 105, n. 10).
12. Nahmani, a nickname for Abbaye, may mean "one who brings comfort."
13. B. Hor 142.
14. "Said humorously—'I am ready to face all comers.' Ben Azzai was the keen scholar able to answer all questions. Cf. Bekh 28a" (Kid, Soncino, p. 92, n. 6). B. Kid 20a.
15. B. Ket 106a.
16. B. Shab 118b–119a.
17. See 1 Sam. 1:3 and 2:22ff.
18. B. RH 18a.

a separate place for women. Then, too, he had a garment to which the cup for receiving the blood was attached; the garment was slit at the shoulder blades, and whenever a woman patient came to him, he would have her wear this garment in order not to see the exposed parts of her body [and would stand behind her as he worked]. Outside his office, he had a discreet place where small coins were to be deposited [as his fee]. Whoever had money put it there; whoever had none could come to him without feeling embarrassed. Whenever a disciple of the wise happened to consult him, he would accept no fee from him. When he saw a man who [he felt sure] had no means, as that man was leaving, he would hand him some small coins, saying, Go and [use the money to] regain your strength.

One day Abbaye sent two disciples of the wise to Abba the Cupper in order to test him. Abba received them, gave them food and drink, and in the evening spread mattresses for them [to sleep on]. In the morning the two disciples of the wise rolled up the mattresses and took them to the marketplace. [Then Abbaye[1] saw to it that Abba the Cupper came to the marketplace, where the two, making believe they were hawking the mattresses], said to Abba, "Sir, appraise them—how much are they worth?" He replied, "So much." The two: "Perhaps they are worth more?" Abba: "This is what I paid for some like them." Then they said to him, "They are yours—we took them from you."

They asked him, "Please, tell us: what did you suspect we were up to?" He replied, "I said to myself: Perhaps the sages needed money to redeem captives and were too embarrassed to say so to me." The two: "Now, sir, take back what is yours." Abba: "From the moment I missed them, I diverted my mind from them by considering them assigned to charity."

When Rava felt depressed because of the special honor shown to Abbaye, the latter appeared to him in a dream and said to him: Be content that your merit protects the entire city.[2]

678. During the rejoicing at the place of the water-drawing,[3] Abbaye used to juggle eight eggs before Rabbah, tossing one into the air and catching another without having them touch each other.[4]

679. Abbaye was seated before Rabbah, who noticed that he seemed quite joyous. Rabbah cautioned him, "It is written, 'Rejoice with trembling' " (Ps. 2:11). Abbaye replied, "But I have my tefillin on."[5]

680. When Abbaye was riding a donkey along the bank of the Sagya Canal, R. Mesharsheya and other sages seated on the opposite bank did not rise for him. He protested, "Am I not your distinguished teacher?" They replied, "We were otherwise occupied [and did not see you]."[6]

1. See Ta, trans. Henry Malter, p. 158.
2. B. Ta 21b–22a.
3. For a description of the rejoicing, see above, part 1, chap. 9, §85.
4. B. Suk 53a.
5. Therefore I may be joyful. B. Ber 30b.
6. B. Kid 33a.

681. When Ravin and Abbaye were traveling on a [narrow] road, Ravin's donkey got in front of Abbaye's donkey, yet Ravin did not stop and say to Abbaye, "Let the master get ahead of me." So Abbaye muttered sharply, "Since this one has come up from the west [the Land of Israel], he has grown arrogant." But when they reached the entrance of a synagogue, Ravin said, "Let the master enter first." Abbaye: "And until now I have not been master?" Ravin then quoted R. Yohanan: One gives precedence to a master only as one enters a structure with doorposts.[7]

682. When Abbaye lost a donkey in a place inhabited by Cutheans, he sent word to them: Have it brought back to me. The Cutheans: Let us have a mark of identification. Abbaye: Its belly is white. The Cutheans: Were you not Nahmani, we would not have sent it back to you. Do not all donkeys have white bellies?[8]

683. R. Shimi bar Ashi appeared before Abbaye and asked him: Will the master give me private instruction?[9] Abbaye: I have to use my private time for my own studies. R. Shimi: Will the master instruct me at night? Abbaye: At that time I must irrigate [my field]. R. Shimi: I will irrigate the master's field in daytime; let the master instruct me during the night. Abbaye: Very well. Then R. Shimi went to the people above Abbaye's field and said to them: The people below have the right to draw water first. After that, he went to those below Abbaye's field and said to them: The people above have the right to draw water first. Meanwhile, he dammed the watercourse and irrigated Abbaye's field. When he presented himself before Abbaye, Abbaye was greatly distressed and would not taste anything of that year's produce.[10]

684. Abbaye used to inspect his properties daily. One day he came upon his tenant farmer carrying a bundle of vine shoots. When Abbaye asked him, "Where are you taking them?" the tenant farmer replied, "To the master's house." Abbaye said, "The sages anticipated you long ago."[11]

685. Abbaye said: One who is required to present a specimen of his signature at a court of law should not write it at the foot of a blank scroll, lest someone find it and write above it that the signer owes him money.

A customs collector once came before Abbaye and said to him: Will the master let me have his signature, so that when the sages come by and show it to me with your authorization, I will allow them to pass without payment.[12]

7. If such deference were shown on a narrow road, others hurrying to work, etc., would be held back. So Menahem ha-Meiri, quoted by Adin Steinsaltz, Ber, 205. B. Ber 47a.
8. B. Git 45.
9. Literally, "Let me sit by the master during study."
10. B. Git 60b.
11. In advising daily inspection of property to stop pilfering. B. Hul 105a.
12. "His possession of Abbaye's signature, he contended, would enable him to verify Abbaye's signature on any authorization that might be presented to him" (BB, Soncino, p. 726, n. 16).

Abbaye wrote it down for him at the head of a scroll. As the customs collector had tried to pull the scroll up [so that a blank space would be left above Abbaye's signature], Abbaye said to him: The sages anticipated you long ago.[1]

686. There was a certain magus who used to rummage among graves.[2] When he came to the burial cave of R. Tobi ben Mattenah, R. Tobi grabbed hold of him by his beard. Abbaye[3] came and said to him, "Pray, let go of him." A year later the magus came back, and the dead man again seized hold of his beard; Abbaye came again [to rescue him], but this time the dead man would not let go, so that they had to bring scissors and cut off the magus's beard.[4]

687. Abbaye used to offer his hand to old Arameans to lean on.[5]

688. When Rabbah was about to send Abbaye to Mari bar Mar with a basketful of dates and a cupful of flour made from roasted ears of corn, Abbaye said to Rabbah: Mari is now apt to say, "Even when a villager becomes a king, he still does not take the basket off his neck."[6] Later, when in return Mari was about to send [Abbaye] to Rabbah with a basketful of ginger and a cupful of long-stalked pepper, Abbaye said to Mari: Rabbah is now apt to say, "I sent him sweet things, and he sends me things sharp."

Subsequently Abbaye reminisced: When I left my master's house, I was pretty full, but when I reached Mari's place, sixty dishes containing different entrees were set before me, and I partook of sixty portions from them. The last entree, which was called potroast, [I liked so much that] I wanted to lick the dish that contained it.

This, Abbaye went on, bears out the proverb: The poor man is hungry, but does not know it.[7] Or the other proverb: There is always room for a savory dish.[8]

689. Abbaye said: At first I used to snatch the priestly portions, saying to myself, "I shall show my zeal for the precept." But when I heard the tradition "In saying, 'They shall give' [Deut. 18:3], Scripture implies that the priest is not to take them on his own," I no longer snatched them, but would merely say, "Give them to me." And when I heard the Baraita that taught, " 'They turned aside after lucre' [1 Sam. 8:3] means, according to R. Meir, that Samuel's sons used to ask right out for the portions due them."[9] I decided not to ask for them, but would accept them only when they were given to me. And when I heard the Baraita that taught, "The [priests who were] modest withdrew their hands from them, but the greedy took their share," I decided not to accept them at all, save on the day before Yom Kippur, so as to establish my status as a priest.[10]

690. Abbaye suffered from dropsy. Rava said: I know about this, about Nahmani—he practices hunger [being always engaged in fasting].[11]

691. Abbaye heard a certain man say to a woman, "Let us get up early and be on our way." He said to himself: I will follow them to keep them from doing what is prohibited. He followed them through meadows a distance of three parasangs. Then, as they were about to separate, he heard them say, "The company is pleasant, but the way is long." Abbaye had to admit: If I were in their place, I could not have restrained myself. And in deep anguish he leaned against the bolt in a doorway. An elder came and recited the tradition: "The greater the man, the greater his impulse to evil."[12]

Rava bar Joseph bar Hama (fl. 299–352 C.E.)

692. When R. Judah died, Rava was born.[13]

693. When Rava and Rami bar Hama were studying before R. Hisda, they first went over the Gemara [the traditional statements on the *Halakhah* in hand], and then they investigated the logical underpinning.[14]

694. Rava said: In the streets of Tiberias, I am deemed [as keen witted] as Ben Azzai.[15]

695. R. Nahman bar Isaac observed: A legal decision must be as clear as a day when the north wind blows.

Abbaye said: If my foster mother had said to me, "Bring me the *kuttah*,"[16] I would not have been able to study.[17]

Rava remarked: If a louse bit me, I could not study.[18]

696. Rava said: Three things I asked for from Heaven; two were granted me, and one was not. I asked for the scholarship of R. Huna and the wealth of R. Hisda, which

1. B. BB 167a.
2. Persian fire-worshipers considered it sinful to defile the earth by the burial of dead bodies in it. Accordingly, they would exhume bodies and expose them to the birds.
3. Who was apparently a friend of the magus.
4. B. BB 58a.
5. B. Kid 33a.
6. Although you, Rabbah, have become head of the academy in Pumbedita, you keep sending ordinary gifts. See above in this chapter, §642.
7. He is so inured to hunger that he is not aware of its pangs until he sits down to eat.
8. B. Meg 7b.
9. See above, Part 1, chap. 6, §70.
10. When his abstention from the many gifts brought at that time to priests would make it seem that he was not one of them. B. Hul 133a.
11. B. Shab 33a.
12. B. Suk 52a.
13. B. Kid 72b.
14. B. Suk 29a.
15. See above in this chapter, §673. B. Er 29a.
16. A dish of bread crusts, sour milk, and salt.
17. Even so slight a chore would have distracted his mind.
18. B. Er 65a.

were granted me; but the humility of Rabbah bar R. Huna[1]—that was not granted me.[2]

697. A certain heretic saw Rava utterly absorbed in his studies, with his hands under his feet, which pressed down so hard that his fingers spurted blood. The heretic exclaimed: O you precipitous people, who put your mouth before your ears![3] You continue to be precipitate! You should have listened first to determine whether you could accept the Commandments, and if not, not accept them. Rava replied: To us, who walk in integrity, the words "The integrity of the upright shall guide them" (Prov. 11:3) apply. But to others, who walk in perversity, apply the words "The perverseness of the treacherous shall destroy them" (ibid.).[4]

698. When Rava saw R. Hamnuna overlong at his prayers, he said, "There are people who give up [study, which is] eternal life, and occupy themselves [with praying] for transient needs.[5]

699. [As a mark of humility], Rava used to remove his [costly] upper cloak, clasp his hands, and pray, explaining what he did: [I pray] like a slave in the presence of his master.[6]

700. Whenever Rava went to [preside at] court, he used to say: Out of his own will, he [the judge] goes toward death; he does not supply the needs of his household, for he returns empty[7] to his home. May his coming back be like his going forth. And when Rava saw a crowd escorting him, he would say, "Though his excellency mount up to heaven, and his head reach into the clouds, yet shall he perish forever like his own dung; they that have seen him shall say: 'Where is he?' " (Job 20:6–7).[8]

701. R. Joseph bar Hama used to seize slaves belonging to people who owed him money and make them work [for him]. His son Rava said to him: Sir, why do you allow this to be done?[9] R. Joseph: Because R. Nahman stated that a slave is not worth the bread he puts into his stomach. Rava: But of whom did R. Nahman say such a thing? Only of one like Daru, his own slave, who spent his time dancing in taverns. Did R. Nahman speak thus of other slaves who do in fact work?" R. Joseph: I hold with R. Daniel bar R. Ketina, who stated in Rava's name that he who seizes another man's slave and makes him work [for him] is exempt from any payment, a statement that proves that preventing a slave from being idle is beneficial to his owner. Rava: Such a statement is valid only when the owner of the slave does not owe money to the man who seizes him. As for you, sir, since the slave's owner owes you money, seizing that slave to work for you is clearly a form of interest. R. Joseph: I retract what I said.[10]

702. R. Abba, to whom R. Joseph bar Hama owed money, said to R. Safra, "When you go there, bring me back the money owed me." Upon R. Safra's arrival, Rava, R. Joseph's son, asked R. Safra, "Has the creditor given you a written statement that he will deem your receiving the money as though he himself had received it?" When R. Safra said, "No," Rava went on, "Then you must first go back and have him execute such a written statement." But in the end Rava said, "Even if he were to prepare such a statement, it would still avail nothing, since before your return, R. Abba [being an old man] might die. Then his right to the money my father owes him would devolve to the heirs, and the written statement executed by him would be of no avail."[11] "What, then," R. Safra asked, "is the remedy?" Rava: "Go back and let him transfer to you the ownership of the money he claims by giving you title to some land[12] he owns. Then come back and execute for us your written statement that you received the money."[13]

703. [Before his death], the son of Mar Samuel ordered that thirteen thousand *zuz* out of the income from his produce be given to Rava. Rava sent R. Joseph a request to define "produce," but then did not accept the definition R. Joseph sent him.[14] So R. Joseph was annoyed, saying, "Since he does not need us, why did he send the inquiry to us?" Rava heard [that R. Joseph was annoyed], and as the eve of Yom Kippur came around, he said to himself: I will go and appease him. He went off and found R. Joseph's attendant mixing him a cup of wine. He said to him, "Give it to me, and I will mix it for him." The attendant gave it to Rava, and he mixed the wine for R. Joseph, who, upon tasting it, said, "This mixture is like that of Rava son of R. Joseph bar Hama." Then Rava spoke up, "I am he."[15]

704. Once Rava came to Hagronia[16] and ordained a fast. The people entreated [Heaven] for mercy, but no rain fell. So he said to them: Continue fasting overnight. Next morning he said: If there is anyone among you who had a dream, let him tell it. R. Eleazar from Hagronia spoke up: In my dream, the following was said to me: Greetings of well-being to the good teacher from the good Lord who dispenses from His bounty good things to His people. At that, Rava

1. Died 309 C.E.
2. B. MK 28a.
3. Referring to the Israelites' reply to Moses: "All that the Lord hath spoken will we do and hear" (Exod. 24:7).
4. B. Shab 88a–b.
5. B. Shab 10a.
6. Ibid.
7. Judges were not paid for their services.
8. B. Yoma 86b–87a.
9. Is not the benefit you derive from such work a form of interest?
10. B. BK 97a; B. BM 64b–65a.
11. The death of the principal renders a contract of agency null and void.
12. In accordance with the principle that property such as money, for which there is no security, can be transferred in conjunction with property such as land, for which there is security. Kid 1:4.
13. Since you will then be the legal owner of the sum claimed. B. BK 104b.
14. Does "produce" mean only the produce of fields, or is income from other sources also to be included?
15. B. Er 54a; B. Ned 55a.
16. A city near Nehardea.

said: This is a favorable time to pray. So they prayed, and rain fell.[1]

705. Once, when Rava came to Tigris,[2] he said to Bar Avin, "Get up and utter a prayer for God's mercy."[3] He rose and said:

More than a third of the land is already submerged in water;
Remember Your covenant[4] and have mercy upon us.
We have strayed from You like a wife who strayed from her husband.[5]
O do not abandon us,
But save us as [You saved our fathers] at Marah.[6]

706. Thieves broke in and stole a few rams owned by Rava. Presently the thieves returned the rams, but he refused to accept them, saying, "Rav has ruled: If a thief breaks into a house, steals some items, and gets away, he is exempt from punishment. Why? Because he acquired them with his blood."[7]

707. When R. Dimi of Nehardea brought a ship's load of figs, the exilarch said to Rava, "Go and see if he is a disciple of the wise. If he is, reserve a place in the market for him."[8] So Rava said to R. Adda bar Ahavah, "Go and smell the wine [of his learning]." R. Adda went out and put to R. Dimi the following question: "If an elephant swallows a basket made of palm fronds and passes it in his excrement, is it still subject to uncleanness?"[9] R. Dimi could not give an answer and asked R. Adda, "Sir, are you Rava?" R. Adda tapped him with his sandal and said, "There is a great difference between me and Rava, but evidently I can be your teacher, so that Rava is the teacher of your teacher." In the event, a place in the market was not reserved for R. Dimi, and his figs were a dead loss. He appealed to R. Joseph: "See what R. Adda did to me." R. Joseph responded: "He who did not delay avenging the wrong done to the king of Edom will not delay avenging the wrong done to you."[10] Shortly afterward, R. Adda bar Ahavah died.

R. Joseph said: It is through me that he was punished [by his untimely death], because I invoked God's vengeance upon him.

R. Dimi of Nehardea said: It is through me that he was punished, because he made me lose my figs.

Abbaye said: It is through me that he was punished, because he said to the disciples, "Instead of gnawing at bones in the school of Abbaye, come eat fat meat in the school of Rava."[11]

Rava said: It is through me that he was punished, because, when he went to the meat market to buy meat, he used to say to the butchers, "Serve me before Rava's servant, because I am superior to him."

R. Nahman bar Isaac said: It is through me that he was punished. R. Nahman bar Isaac was the principal lecturer during a *kallah.*[12] Every day, before delivering his lecture, he used to go over it with R. Adda bar Ahavah, and only then would he enter the *kallah.* One day R. Papa and R. Huna ben R. Joshua detained R. Adda bar Ahavah. Dusk set in, and R. Nahman bar Isaac was still waiting for him. The sages came and said to R. Nahman, "Stand up to lecture. It is already dusk. Why does the master remain seated?" R. Nahman replied, "I remain seated because I am waiting for the bier of R. Adda bar Ahavah." Even as he said this, the report came that R. Adda bar Ahavah had died.[13]

708. Rava and R. Nahman bar Isaac were sitting together when R. Nahman bar Jacob went by in a gilded litter with a shabby green cloak spread over him. Rava went out to meet him, but R. Nahman bar Isaac did not stir, saying: He is probably a member of the exilarch's court. Rava needs them, but I do not.[14]

709. Rava said: May the merit of what I used to do stand by me. Whenever a disciple of the wise came before me in a lawsuit, I did not lay my head on the pillow [to sleep] before I considered what might be said in his favor.[15]

710. A poor man once applied to Rava [for maintenance]. Rava asked him, "What do your meals ordinarily consist of?" He replied, "Of fat chicken and aged wine." Rava: "Do you not consider the burden you impose on the community?" The poor man: "Do I eat what is theirs? I eat [the food] of the Holy One. For we are taught: In the verse 'The eyes of all wait for Thee, and Thou givest them their food in his season' [Ps. 145:15], it is not said, 'In *their* season,' but, 'In his season,' implying that the Holy One provides food for every individual in keeping with his 'season,' his particular habits." Just then Rava's sister, who had not seen him for thirteen years, arrived and

1. B. Ta 24b.
2. "Tagrit or Tekrit lies higher up on the Tigris between Mosul and Baghdad and is often mentioned in Syriac literature" (MK, Soncino, p. 161, n. 3).
3. When the Tigris overflowed in April and May.
4. With Noah, that a flood not come again. See Gen. 9:15–16.
5. Such a wife was tried by the ordeal of water, which caused her death (Num. 5:22). So, too, when the water of the Tigris rose, it was unfit to drink, and many who drank it died.
6. Where You sweetened the bitter water. See Exod. 15:23–25. B. MK 25b.
7. The owner might have taken his life (Exod. 22:1). B. Sanh 72a.
8. So that no one else should sell until he has disposed of his stock.
9. Is it regarded as a basket and subject to uncleanness, or as excrement, which is not subject to it?
10. A reference to "Thus saith the Lord, for three transgressions of Moab, yea, for four, I will not turn away the punishment thereof; because he burned the bones of the king of Edom into lime" (Amos 2:1).
11. Where the instruction is greatly superior.
12. The *kallah* was the semiannual gathering of Babylonian scholars during the months of Adar and Elul under the leadership of the heads of the academies.
13. B. BB 22a.
14. See Aaron Mordecai Hyman, *Toledot Tannaim ve-Amoraim* (London, 1911; repr. 1964) 3:930. B. Git 31b.
15. So high was his opinion of scholars that he felt they would not be involved in a lawsuit unless they were certain of being in the right. So Samuel Edels. B. Shab 119a.

brought him a fat chicken and aged wine. "What a remarkable coincidence!" Rava exclaimed, and he said to the poor man, "I defer to your request—come and eat."[1]

711. Rava said: At first I thought that all the people of Mahoza[2] loved me. When I was appointed judge, I thought that some hated me and some loved me. After I became aware that he who is held wrong today is held right tomorrow, I decided that if I am loved, all love me, and if I am hated, all hate me.[3]

712. A certain man who had intercourse with a gentile woman was sentenced by Rava's court to be flogged. After Rava had him flogged, the man died. When news of the incident reached King Shapur,[4] he wanted to punish Rava, but Ifra Hormiz, the king's mother, said to him, "Do not meddle with the Jews, because anything they ask of their Lord, He grants them." The king asked her, "What, for instance?" She replied, "They ask for mercy, and rain falls." The king retorted, "That is simply because it is the season for rain. Let them ask for such mercy now, in the Tammuz solstice, and make rain come down." So they sent word to Rava, "Concentrate your mind and ask for mercy that rain come down now." Rava did so, but no rain came. Then he pleaded, "Lord of the universe, 'We have heard with our ears, our fathers have told us, what work Thou didst in their days, in the days of old' [Ps. 44:2]. But we have not seen it with our eyes." Immediately rain came down so heavy that the gutters of Mahoza carried the water into the Tigris. Rava's father then appeared to Rava in a dream and said to him, "Is there another man who puts Heaven to such trouble? Change your [sleeping] place, change your [sleeping] place."[5] He did so, and the next morning he found that his regular bed was lacerated with knife cuts.[6]

713. Ifra Hurmiz, King Shapur's mother, sent four hundred denars to R. Ammi [in Tiberias], but he would not accept them. Then she sent them to Rava, who, to maintain cordial relations with the government, accepted them and distributed them to poor Gentiles.[7]

714. On a heathen feast day, Rava once sent a present to Bar Sheshak, saying, "I know that he does not worship idols." But when he called on him, he found him sitting up to his neck in a bath of rose water, with naked harlots standing before him. When Bar Sheshak asked, "Will you [Jews] have anything like this in the world-to-come?" Rava replied, "We will have something much finer than this." Bar Sheshak asked, "Is there anything finer than this?" Rava answered, "Upon you is the fear of the ruling power,[8] but for us there will be no such fear." Bar Sheshak asked, "What fear have I of the ruling power?" But even as the two were sitting together, a king's courier arrived with the message: "Arise, the king requires your presence." As Bar Sheshak was about to depart, he said to Rava, "May the eye of him who wishes you ill burst!" Rava responded, "Amen," and Bar Sheshak's eye burst [out of its socket].

R. Papi said: Rava should have answered him by quoting the verse "Kings' daughters are for thine honor;[9] at thy right hand doth stand the queen in gold of Ophir" (Ps. 45:10). R. Nahman bar Isaac said: Rava should have answered him by quoting the verse "No eye hath seen [the rewards awaiting us], O God, but Thou who acts for those who trust in Thee" (Isa. 64:3).[10]

715. Bar Hadaya was an interpreter of dreams. He would give a favorable interpretation to one who paid him [a fee] and an unfavorable interpretation to one who did not. Abbaye and Rava each had [the same] dream. Abbaye gave him a *zuz*, and Rava gave him nothing. The two said to him: In our dream, we had read to us the verse "Thine ox shall be slain before thine eyes, and thou shalt not eat of it" (Deut. 28:31). To Rava, Bar Hadaya said: Your merchandise will depreciate, and because of the distress in your heart, you will be unable to eat. To Abbaye, he said: Your merchandise will appreciate so much that you will be unable to eat because of the joy in your heart.

Another time, the two reported: We had read to us the verse "Thou shalt beget sons and daughters, but they shall not be thine, for they will go into captivity" (Deut. 28:41). To Rava, he interpreted the verse in its [literal] unfavorable sense. To Abbaye, he said: You will have many sons and daughters, and your daughters will wed abroad, and it will seem to you as if they had gone into captivity.

Another time, the two reported: We had read to us the verse "Thy sons and thy daughters shall be given unto another people" (Deut. 28:32). To Abbaye, he said: You will have numerous sons and daughters; you will want your daughters to marry your kin, and your wife will want them to marry her kin, and she will force you to marry them off to her kin, which will seem to you like giving them to an alien people. To Rava, he said: Your wife will die, and her sons and daughters will come under the sway of another wife.

The two further reported: We had read to us the same verse "Go thy way, eat thy bread with joy" (Eccles. 9:7). To Abbaye, he said: Your merchandise will appreciate, and you will eat and drink and read this verse with joy in your heart. To Rava, he said: Your merchandise will depreciate, you will eat and drink, and you will read this verse to counteract your distress.

---

1. B. Ket 67b.
2. A Jewish trading center in the vicinity of Babylon.
3. B. Ket 105b.
4. Shapur II, king of Persia (310–79 C.E.).
5. "It was a general belief that by changing one's place (here the bed in which Rava was to sleep), one might escape the evil that was to befall him" (Ta, trans. Henry Malter, p. 185, n. 348).
6. B. Ta 24b.
7. B. BB 10b and En Yaakov, ad loc.

8. Your fate is in the hands of your king, who can at will deprive you of all you possess.
9. That is, Jews will be attended by noble ladies in the world-to-come, and not by harlots, as this heathen was. JV: "among thy honorable women."
10. That is, the good things in the world-to-come cannot be conceived by the mind of man. B. AZ 65a.

The two reported: We had read to us the verse "Thou shalt carry much seed out into the field, and shalt gather little in" (Deut. 28:38). To Abbaye, he interpreted only from the first half of the verse; to Rava, only from the second half.

The two reported: We had read to us the verse "Thou shalt have olive trees throughout all thy borders, but thou shalt not anoint thyself with the oil" (Deut. 28:40). To Abbaye, he interpreted only from the first half of the verse; to Rava, only from the second half.

The two reported: We had read to us the verse "And all the peoples of the earth shall see that the Name of the Lord is called upon thee; and they shall be afraid of thee" (Deut. 28:10). To Abbaye, Bar Hadaya said: Your fame will go forth, you will become head of the academy, and people will be afraid of you. To Rava, he said: You will be arrested in the company of thieves, and because of what will be done to you, all will be the more afraid for themselves.[1] The next day, the royal treasury was broken into by thieves, and the authorities arrested Rava.

The two told Bar Hadaya: We saw a head of lettuce lying over the mouth of a cask. To Abbaye, Bar Hadaya said: Your merchandise—deemed as flavorful as lettuce—will be snapped up. To Rava, he said: Your merchandise—deemed as bitter as lettuce—will be rejected.

The two reported: We saw some meat lying over the mouth of a jar. To Abbaye, Bar Hadaya said: Your wine will be sweet, and everyone will come to buy meat and wine from you. To Rava, he said: Your wine will turn to vinegar, and everyone will come to buy meat to dip in it.

The two reported: We saw a jar hanging from a date palm. To Abbaye, Bar Hadaya said: Your merchandise will rise in price as high as a date palm. To Rava, he said: Your goods [will depreciate so much that to the purchaser they] will be as sweet as dates.

The two reported: We saw a pomegranate sprouting from the mouth of a jar. To Abbaye, Bar Hadaya said: Your goods will be as high priced as a pomegranate. To Rava, he said: Your goods will be as tough as a [dry] pomegranate.

The two reported: We saw a jar falling into a pit. To Abbaye, Bar Hadaya said: Your goods will be in demand.[2] To Rava, he said: Your goods will be spoiled and be thrown into a pit.

They reported: We saw a young ass (*hamor*) standing upon a block and braying. To Abbaye, Bar Hadaya said: You will be head of the academy, and [an interpreter] will stand by you [and "bray"]. To Rava, he said: The words "the firstborn of an ass" (Exod. 13:13) are erased in your tefillin.[3] Rava said to him: I have just looked at them, and those words are there. Bar Hadaya replied: Certainly the letter *vav* in the word *hamor* has been erased in your tefillin.[4]

1. Saying: If Rava, who is rich and powerful, is suspect, how much more so are we.
2. Like something valuable that has accidentally fallen into a pit and is eagerly retrieved.
3. This passage is one of the four contained in the tefillin.
4. The scribe erroneously wrote in the letter *vav*, which he then erased, since in that verse *hamor* is spelled without it.

Later, Rava went alone to Bar Hadaya and reported: In my dream I saw that the outer door [of my house] fell out. Bar Hadaya: Your wife will die.

Then Rava reported: I dreamed that my back and front teeth fell out. Bar Hadaya: Your sons and daughters will die.

Rava reported: I saw two doves flying away. Bar Hadaya: You will divorce two wives. Rava said to him: I saw two turnip tops.[5] He replied: You will receive two blows with a cudgel. Rava went and sat all that day in the house of study, where he came upon two blind men quarreling with each other and went to separate them, and they gave him two blows with their cudgels. They raised their cudgels to give Rava a third blow, but he said, "Enough! [In my dream] I saw only two."

Finally, Rava went over, paid Bar Hadaya a fee, and reported: I saw a wall fall down. To which Bar Hadaya replied: You will acquire wealth without limit.

He reported: I saw Abbaye's mansion fall, and its dust covered me. Bar Hadaya replied: Abbaye will die, and [his presidency of] the academy will pass to you.

Rava reported: I saw my own mansion collapse, and everyone came and took it away brick by brick. Bar Hadaya replied: Your teachings will spread throughout the world.

Rava reported: I dreamed that my head was split open and my brains spilled out. Bar Hadaya replied: The feathers stuffed in your pillows will burst forth bit by bit. He reported: In my dream I had the *Hallel* of Egypt[6] read to me. Bar Hadaya replied: Miracles will happen to you.

Once, when Bar Hadaya was traveling with Rava by ship, he said to himself: Why should I accompany a man to whom a miracle will happen?[7] As Bar Hadaya was disembarking, he accidentally dropped a book, which Rava found: He saw written in it: All dreams follow the [interpreter's] mouth. At that, he exclaimed, "Wretch! It all depended on you, and you caused me such great distress! Still, I forgive you everything, except [what you said about] the daughter of R. Hisda.[8]

716. Rava said to R. Hisda's daughter, "The sages are criticising you [for remaining unmarried]." She replied, "All these years I had my mind set on you."[9]

717. [After Abbaye died], Homah, Abbaye's wife, came to Rava and asked him, "Grant me an allowance for food [from my husband's estate]. He granted it to her. "Grant me an allowance for wine." "I know," Rava said to her, "that Nahmani[10] did not drink wine." "By your life, master, [I swear]," she replied, "that he gave me drink from beakers as long as this arm." As she was exhibiting her arm,

5. Which look like cudgels.
6. Pss. 113–18, recited on Passover eve to celebrate the going forth from Egypt.
7. He will be saved, but I will not.
8. Rava's wife, whose death Bar Hadaya had foretold. B. Ber 56a–b.
9. She married Rava ten years after her husband Rami ben Hama died. She even had children with Rava which rarely happens after such a prolonged widowhood. B. Yev 34b.
10. Literally, "my comforter," a name by which Abbaye was often referred to. See above in this chapter, §672.

it was uncovered and [its beauty] lit up the court chamber. At once Rava rose and went home.[1] His wife, R. Hisda's daughter, noticing that his appearance was greatly changed, asked, "Who was at court today?" Rava replied, "[Homa], the wife of Abbaye." Rava's wife immediately went after her, whipping her with litter straps, until she chased her clean out of Mahoza. "You have already killed three men,"[2] she kept saying to her, "and now you come [flirting] to kill another!"[3]

718. Rava said to his sons: When you cut meat, do not cut it while holding it in your hand (some say because of danger, and some say because of spoiling the meat); do not sit on the bed of an Aramean woman; and do not walk around the rear of a synagogue when the congregation is at prayer.

Do not sit upon the couch of an Aramean woman. Some explain: Do not go to sleep without first reciting the Shema. Others: Do not marry a proselyte woman.[4] And still others: Literally, "the couch of an Aramean woman," on account of the kind of thing that happened to R. Papa. R. Papa went to an Aramean woman. She pulled out a couch for him and said, "Sit down." He said to her, "I will not sit down until you lift the bedding." When she lifted the bedding, they found a dead infant there.[5]

719. R. Seorim, Rava's brother, while sitting at Rava's bedside, saw him about to fall into the sleep of death. Still, Rava managed to say, "Tell the angel of death not to torment me." R. Seorim asked, "Are you not [as a teacher of Torah] the angel's intimate friend?"[6] Rava: "Since my *mazzal*[7] has already been delivered to him, the angel of death has no regard for me."

Then R. Seorim said to his brother, "Please, master, show yourself to me in a dream." When Rava did appear to him [after his death], he asked, "Master, did you suffer pain?" Rava: "No more than from the prick of the cupping lancet."[8]

720. When Abbaye and Rava died, it seemed as though the cliffs on both sides of the Tigris had kissed each other.[9]

R. Papa (died 375 C.E.)

721. R. Papa and R. Huna son of R. Joshua once came before Rava, who asked them, "Have you mastered such-and-such a tractate and such-and-such a tractate?" They: "Yes." Rava: "Are you a little better off now?" They: "Yes, we bought a parcel of land." He explained: Happy are those righteous men who receive in this world what the wicked receive in this world [for the few good deeds they perform].[10]

722. R. Papa said: Had I not brewed beer, I would not have become wealthy.

He also said: Had I not married a priest's daughter, I would not have become wealthy.[11]

723. R. Papa said: Whoever can drink beer but drinks wine violates "Thou shalt not waste" (Deut. 29:19).[12]

724. R. Yose said: May my portion be with those who, though innocent, are under suspicion. R. Papa said: I was suspected of something I was innocent of.[13]

725. R. Papa was asked, "What is your name?" He replied, "Rav Papa." He was told, "But is it not said, 'Let others praise thee [with titles], but not thine own mouth' (Prov. 27:2)?" He replied, "But if there are no others, then it must be one's own mouth.[14]

726. R. Papa and R. Huna son of R. Joshua were once walking along the road, when they met R. Hanina son of R. Ika. They said to him: The instant we saw you we recited two blessings, "Blessed be He who has imparted of His wisdom to them that fear Him" and "That has kept us alive." He replied: And the instant I saw you, I, deeming you to be equal to the sixty myriads of the House of Israel, recited three blessings, the two you mentioned and "Blessed is He that discerns secrets.[15]

727. R. Papa and R. Huna son of R. Joshua bought sesame seed on the bank of the Royal Canal and hired some boatmen who guaranteed to bring it across[16] regardless of any mishap that might occur. When, as it turned

1. It was deemed indecent for a woman to expose her arm, even when washing clothes.
2. Homah had already married three times, and each of her husbands had died. See B. Yev 64b.
3. B. Ket 65a.
4. Rava's aversion to female proselytes is exceptional. Generally, they are welcomed and reckoned as desirable spouses.
5. B. Ber 8b. She herself had smothered the infant and planned to accuse R. Papa of having killed it when he sat down on it. See below in this chapter, §733.
6. The teacher of Torah is a messenger of the Lord of hosts (Mal. 2:6–7), hence a bosom friend of another messenger, the messenger of death.
7. My guardian angel.
8. B. MK 28a.
9. The mourners were so numerous that they seemed to have crowded out the water. Cf. above in this chapter, §651. B. MK 25b.
10. "As a rule, the righteous suffer in this world, so as to atone for their earthly sins and be worthy of full reward in the world-to-come. The wicked on the other hand, prosper in this world, so as to receive condign punishment for their wickedness in the world-to-come. Hence, if they do occasionally perform a righteous deed, they are immediately rewarded for it in this world, so as to retain their record of wickedness in the world-to-come. Rava expressed his pleasure at seeing the two rewarded for their devotion to Torah in this world by a bit of material prosperity (Leon Nemoy). B. Hor 10b.
11. "R. Joshua said, 'He who desires to become wealthy, let him cleave to the seed of Aaron.' " B. Pes 113a and 49a.
12. B. Shab 140b.
13. See above in this chapter, §718. B. Shab 118b.
14. *Teshuvot ha-Rashba*, in *Rishonot* 84.
15. The blessing spoken at the sight of the hosts of Israel. B. Ber 58b.
16. To Naresh, the home of R. Papa. The boats had to sail up the Euphrates and from there pass into the Naresh Canal.

out, passage through the Royal Canal was blocked, the sages said to the boatmen: Hire ass drivers and deliver the stuff to us, since you have guaranteed us against any mishap. The boatmen appealed to Rava, who said to the sages: You wizened geezers, you would strip men of the very clothes they wear. This mishap is of a kind that could not possibly have been anticipated.[1]

728. R. Papa once visited Tuakh[2] and said: If there is a disciple of the wise in this town, I would like to go and pay him my respects. An old woman said to him: There is a disciple of the wise here—his name is R. Samuel, and he is able to recite tannaitic traditions. May it be [Heaven's] will that you become his equal. R. Papa said to himself: Since she blesses me by praying that I become his equal, he must be a God-fearing man. So R. Papa went to R. Samuel, who in his honor slaughtered an ox and then all but "slaughtered" his guest with legal queries. R. Papa sought to answer them, but R. Samuel refused to accept his answers. Finally R. Papa exclaimed: May it be [Heaven's] will that the rest of the ox be eaten in peace [without further wrangling]. Then he left R. Samuel and went to R. Shimi bar Ashi.[3]

729. R. Shimi bar Ashi would frequently attend [the discourses] of R. Papa and annoy him greatly with his questions. One day he observed that R. Papa fell on his face [in prayer] and heard him say, "May God preserve me from the insolence of Shimi." After that, he vowed silence and annoyed him no more with such questions.[4]

730. While making arrangements for his son to be married into the house of Abba of Sura,[5] R. Papa went there to have the marriage contract written for the bride. Judah bar Meremar heard [that R. Papa was on his way] and went out to welcome him. However, when, upon reaching the door of Abba Sura's house, R. Papa said to him, "Will the master come in with me?" Judah asked permission to take his leave. Realizing that Judah was reluctant [to come in], R. Papa asked him, "What is your reason? [Are you reluctant to come in] because Samuel said to R. Judah [bar Ezekiel], 'Keen wit, do not be present at a transfer of inheritance,[6] even if it be from a bad son to a good son, because one never knows what issue may come forth from the bad son; all the more so [when such transfer is] from a son to a daughter?[7] But surely you are aware that a father's duty to provide a dowry for his daughter is confirmed by an enactment of the sages."[8] Judah replied, "The enactment applies only to a father who does so voluntarily. Does it also imply that the father should be compelled to do so?" R. Papa: "Did I tell you to come in and compel him? What I meant was: Come in, but exercise no pressure upon him." "My coming in," Judah replied, "would amount to pressure."[9] Nevertheless, R. Papa kept urging Judah until he came in and sat down, but remained silent.[10] Abba thought that Judah was vexed [by the paltriness of the dowry he was offering] and consequently assigned [to his daughter as dowry] all that he possessed. Finally, Abba asked Judah, "Will you remain silent even now? By your life, I left nothing for myself!" "If the matter depended on me," Judah replied, "any amount [however small] you might have assigned would have been unacceptable." "If so," Abba said, "I will renege." Judah: "I did not suggest that you turn into a reneger."[11]

731. A certain beggar who used to go from door to door came to R. Papa [for alms], but he did not respond to him. R. Samma son of R. Yeva said to R. Papa: If you do not respond, he will die. R. Papa: But we have been taught: If he is a beggar who goes from door to door, we need not respond. R. Samma: We need not respond with a large donation to be sure, but with a small donation, we must.[12]

732. As R. Papa was climbing a ladder, his foot slipped, and he almost fell down. So he said: It is evident that I—may my enemy incur such liability—am guilty of a trespass as grave as that of a Sabbath breaker or an idolater.[13] R. Hiyya bar Rav from Difti[14] said to him: Perhaps a poor man came to you and you did not feed him, for we have been taught that R. Joshua ben Korhah said: He who shuts his eye to an appeal for alms is deemed to be the same as a worshiper of idols. For in one place it is written, "Beware that there be not a base thought in your heart[15] . . . so that you are mean to your needy kinsman and give him nothing" (Deut. 15:9), and elsewhere, "Certain base[16] fellows are gone out from the midst of thee and have subverted the inhabitants of their town, saying, 'Come, let us worship other gods' " (Deut. 13:14). Even as the sin in the second instance is idolatry, so the sin in the first instance is idolatry.[17]

733. An Aramean woman owed money to R. Papa, and he used to go to her home to collect it. One day she strangled her child and placed him under [the bedding of] her couch. When R. Papa came, she pointed to the couch and said to him: Sit there until I fetch your money. He

1. B. Git 73a.
2. Near Naresh, not far from Sura (Obermeyer, p. 208).
3. B. Nid 33b.
4. B. Ta 9b.
5. R. Papa's father-in-law. R. Papa's son married the sister of R. Papa's wife.
6. From persons legally entitled to be heirs.
7. By giving his daughter a dowry, the father deprives his sons of a portion of their inheritance.
8. Allowing one's daughter a dowry.
9. The father of the bride would be ashamed to offer a small dowry in the presence of a distinguished legal scholar.
10. While R. Papa was discussing the amount of the dowry with the bride's father.
11. B. Ket 52b–53a.
12. B. BB 9a.
13. They were executed by stoning, before which the condemned was thrown down from a high place. See B. Sanh 45a.
14. A town near Apamea on the Tigris. See Obermeyer, p. 197.
15. The "base thought" is not to lend to the poor before the onset of the sabbatical year.
16. In both instances, the Hebrew for "base" is *beli-yaal*, a word sharply condemnatory.
17. B. BB 10a.

replied: I will not sit down unless you lift up the bedding. She lifted the bedding, and the dead child was exposed.

Hence, said the sages: It is prohibited to sit on the couch of an Aramean woman.[1]

734. R. Papa ordained a fast. Feeling very weak, he ate a morsel, then prayed for God's mercy, but no rain came. So, in his ravenous hunger, he gulped down a plateful of grits and prayed again, but still no rain came. R. Nahman bar Ish Prati ("Man of the Euphrates")[2] said tauntingly, "If the master had gulped down a second plateful of grits, rain would surely have come." R. Papa felt humiliated. And then the rain came.[3]

R. Ashi (352–427 C.E.)

735. When Rava died, R. Ashi was born.[4]

736. In the book of Adam[5] it is written, "R. Ashi and Ravina will conclude authentic teaching."[6] A hint of their activity is to be found in the verse "Until I went to the Sanctuary (*mikdeshe* [*she* = Ashi]) of God, where I understood (*avinah* = Ravina) that the task of concluding was to be theirs" (Ps. 73:17).[7]

737. R. Adda bar Ahavah said: From the days of Rabbi to R. Ashi we did not find Torah and high office in the same person. You say, "We did not? But was there not Huna bar Nathan?"[8] Huna bar Nathan was subordinate to R. Ashi in matters of instruction.[9]

738. When R. Ashi noticed cracks in the synagogue of Mata Mehasia,[10] he had the area of the crack pulled down. Then he put his couch there and did not remove it until the very gutters [of the repaired area] had been completed.[11]

739. R. Ashi said: The people of Mata Mehasia are "stubborn of heart" (Isa. 46:12), for twice a year[12] they see the glory of the Torah and yet never has even one of them become converted.[13]

740. When an animal afflicted with an organic disease [and therefore possibly unfit for consumption] was brought to R. Ashi, he would have all the butchers of Mata Mehasia gather, in order, as he put it, that each of them should carry one chip of the beam.[14]

741. R. Ashi made a wedding feast for his son. When he saw the sages very merry, he fetched a white crystal goblet and smashed it in their presence. Then they grew pensive.[15]

742. R. Ashi had a grove in Shelania, and on a weekday during a festival, he went to cut down some trees in it. R. Shela of Shelania protested: "What justification have you for doing this? Is it because R. Hananel, citing Rav, said: During the weekdays of a festival a man may lop off branches from a date palm, even if he requires no more than its sawdust? But did not Abbaye vehemently denounce such a practice?" R. Ashi responded, "I have not heard it"—a way of saying, "I do not concur." Then his hatchet slipped and just missed slicing his thigh. So he abandoned the task and came back on another day [not during the festival].[16]

743. R. Ashi had a grove that he sold to a Parsee temple. Ravina said to him: But there is the injunction "Thou shalt not put a stumbling block before the blind" (Lev. 19:24)![17] R. Ashi replied, "Most wood is used for ordinary heating."[18]

744. Amemar, Mar Zutra, and R. Ashi were sitting at King Yezdegerd's gate. When the king's butcher passed by them [carrying a tray of meat], R. Ashi saw that Mar Zutra's face had turned pale [from hunger]. So R. Ashi picked up some food with his finger and put it in Mar Zutra's mouth. The butcher said, "[By putting your finger in the food], you spoiled the king's meal." When the king's officers asked him, "Why did you do this?" R. Ashi replied, "Because a commoner who touches the king's food renders it unfit." They: "Then why did you render it unfit?" R Ashi: "Because I saw an unwholesome piece of meat in it." They examined the dish but did not find such meat. He placed his finger on the unwholesome piece and asked them, "Did you examine here?" They examined it and found it unwholesome. The sages asked R. Ashi, "Why did you depend on a miracle?" He replied, "I sensed the vapor of leprosy hovering over it."[19]

745. Once [during prayer] Ravina was standing behind R. Ashi. When Ravina felt an urge to spit, he spat out behind him. R. Ashi asked him, "Does not the master agree with R. Judah's dictum that sputum may be stanched with one's turban?" Ravina replied, "But I am squeamish."[20]

---

1. B. Ber 8b; Rashi on B. Pes 112b. See above in this chapter, §718.
2. Or, "Man of Sparta" (Leon Nemoy).
3. B. Ta 24b.
4. B. Kid 72b.
5. The book containing the genealogy of the whole human race, which God showed to Adam.
6. They compiled and arranged in order in the Gemara the mass of accumulated Amoraic discussion of the laws set down in the Mishnah.
7. JV: "Until I entered the Sanctuary of God." B. BM 86a.
8. "According to Sherira's *Epistle*, he was exilarch in the time of R. Ashi" (Isidore Epstein's note in Sanh, Soncino, p. 227).
9. B. Sanh 36a.
10. A suburb of Sura, which attained fame as a center of learning in the days of R. Ashi (Obermeyer, p. 289).
11. B. BB 3b.
12. During the semiannual *kallah* assemblies in which the Torah was expounded.
13. B. Ber 17b.
14. Share in responsibility for the decision. B. Sanh 7b.
15. B. Ber 31a.
16. Throughout the week of a festival, wood may be chopped for the preparation of food, but not for any other purpose. B. MK 12b.
17. That is, nothing may be done to aid idolatry.
18. Not for idolatrous service. B. Ned 62b.
19. B. Ket 61b.
20. And the awareness of spittle under my turban would distract me from my prayer. B. Ber 24b.

746. The angel of death appeared to R. Ashi in the marketplace. He said: Give me thirty days' respite, so that I may go over my studies, inasmuch as it is said [in heaven], "Happy is he who comes here with his learning in hand."

When the angel of death came back on the thirtieth day, R. Ashi asked him: What is the urgency? [The angel of death replied]: R. Huna bar Nathan is close on your heels,[1] and remember, "No sovereignty may encroach upon another even by as little as a hairsbreadth."[2]

747. R. Ashi said to Bar Kipok: [On the day of my repose], what will you say about me? Bar Kipok responded:

If a flame felled lofty cedars,
What chance for lowly hyssop on the wall?
If a hook hauled up Leviathan,
What chance for fishes in shallow streams?
If drought stilled cascading torrents,
What chance for water in tranquil pools?

Bar Avin said to Bar Kipok: God forbid that I would use words such as "hook" or "flame" with regard to the death of the righteous. Then what would you say? Bar Kipok asked. Bar Avin: I would say:[3]

Weep for the mourners,
Not for the soul that is gone—
It to its repose,
We to grief.

Patriarch and Exilarch

748. "Thou hast manifested princely power over an angel, and wilt do so over men" (Gen. 32:29).[4] The angel thus intimated to Jacob that two lines of princes would issue from him: the exilarch in Babylon and the patriarch in the Land of Israel.[5]

749. We have been taught: The words "The scepter shall not depart from Judah" (Gen. 49:10) refer to the exilarchs of Babylonia, who rule over Israel with the authority of a scepter;[6] and the words "Nor a lawgiver from between his feet" (ibid.) refer to the descendants of Hillel, who teach Torah's laws to multitudes.[7]

750. R. Judah son of R. Nahmani, the interpreter of R. Simeon ben Lakish, expounded in a discourse: When a man looks at any one of three things, his eyes become dim: at the rainbow, at the patriarch, and at the priests [standing on their dais and blessing Israel with the Ineffable Name]. At the rainbow, because it is written, "As the appearance of the bow that is in the cloud in the day of rain . . . so was the appearance of the likeness of the glory of the Lord" (Ezek. 1:28). At the patriarch, because Moses was told concerning Joshua his successor, "Thou shalt put thine honor upon him" (Num. 27:20).[8]

751. Rabban Gamaliel said: [On a festival] my father's household never baked bread in twisted loaves[9] but only in thin wafers. The sages said to him: How can we counsel others to follow the example of your father's household, who were stringent toward themselves and lenient toward all Israel, permitting them to bake bread in twisted loaves and in thick cakes?[10]

752. Our masters taught: When the patriarch enters, all the people rise and do not sit down until he says, "Be seated." When the president of the court enters, a row on one side of him and another row on the other side of him rise [to provide a passageway and remain standing] until he sits down. When the sage counselor enters, each person rises as he passes and sits down after he passed, while the last person he passes sits down only after he has sat down.[11]

753. Our masters taught: When the sage counselor dies, his house of study is closed [the day of his death]. When the president of the court dies, all the houses of study [in his city] close [on the day of his death]; and when the people of his town enter their synagogues, they change their usual places: those who usually sit in the north sit in the south, and those who usually sit in the south sit in the north. When the patriarch dies, all houses of study [in the area] close [the day of his death], and the people of all synagogues gather in his synagogue, where seven persons read [the weekly lesson in the Torah],[12] and then all leave the synagogue. R. Joshua ben Korhah added that, afterward, people are not to talk about idly in the street, but are to sit at home in [mournful] silence.[13]

754. There [in Babylonia], upon the death of an exilarch, the Torah scroll was taken to his home [where the weekly lesson was read]. Because the [exilarchs, who are] descendants of David, are settled in Babylonia, things that

---

1. Waiting to succeed you.
2. B. MK 28a.
3. B. MK 25b and En Yaakov, ad loc.
4. JV: "Thou hast striven with God and with men." But *sarita* ("thou hast striven") may also, by association with *sar* ("prince"), be understood as "showing princely power."
5. B. Hul 92a.
6. Backed in their office by the government.
7. But are not backed by the government. B. Sanh 5a. Leon Nemoy differs sharply with the translator: "I don't believe your interpretation of *ba-shevet* will wash—the reference is not to the *scepter* of the Persian Empire, but to the *rod* of tyrannical power. There was no love lost between the exilarch and the sages, nor between him and the rank and file of the people, who groaned under his taxation and the arrogance of his bureaucracy (one of the causes of the rise of Karaism, by the way)."
8. Moses could not be looked at. B. Hag 16a.
9. Because they were burdensome, handling them would not be in keeping with the observance of the festival. It would constitute a violation of *shevut*, an act forbidden not in Scripture but by the rabbis.
10. Betz 2:6.
11. B. Hor 13b and En Yaakov, ad loc.
12. But they pray individually, not as a congregation. So Rashi.
13. B. MK 22b–23a and commentary by a disciple of R. Yehiel of Paris (*Kitve Makhon Harry Fishel* [Jerusalem, 1937], section 3: *Rishonim* 1:97–98); Tosafot of R. Asher, pp. 69–70.

were done for their ancestors [the Davidic kings] are also done for them.[1]

755. R. Aha son of Rava said: From the days of Rabbi [Judah I, the Patriarch] to the days of R. Ashi, Torah and high office were not found in the same person. Not found? But were they not found in Huna bar Nathan? It was not the same thing with Huna bar Nathan, for he submitted to R. Ashi [in decisions on law].[2]

756. R. Ashi said: Huna bar Nathan told me: Once while I was standing before King Yezdegerd, my girdle was tied too high up. He pulled it down while saying to me: It is written of you, "Ye shall be unto Me a kingdom of priests and a holy nation" (Exod. 19:6).[3] When I came before Amemar, he said to me: The promise "Kings shall be thy foster fathers" (Isa. 49:23) has come to be fulfilled in you.[4]

757. Rav said: When one wishes to decide monetary suits by himself and be free from liability [to reimburse the injured party] in the event of an erroneous decision, he should obtain permission [in advance] from the exilarch.[5]

758. R. Zera said to R. Simon: The master should rebuke the exilarch's household. R. Simon: They do not heed me. R. Zera: Even if they do not heed you, master, you should still rebuke them.[6]

759. [Before he became], the exilarch Mar Ukba,[7] who used to go to bed and rise to the accompaniment of music, sent a writ to his predecessor in office, saying, "No rejoicing, Israel, no cries of gladness now! Wouldst thou be like the heathen?" (Hos. 9:1).[8]

760. [After becoming exilarch], Mar Ukba sent a query to R. Eleazar: "Certain men are against me, but I am able to get them into trouble with the government. Shall I do so?" R. Eleazar scribbled his answer on the same paper: "I said, 'I will take heed to my ways, that I sin not with my tongue; I will keep a curb upon my mouth, while the wicked is before me' [Ps. 39:2], meaning, even though the wicked is before me, I will still keep a curb on my mouth." Mar Ukba sent another message to R. Eleazar: "They are troubling me very much, and I no longer can put up with them." Eleazar replied, " 'Resign thyself unto the Lord, and wait patiently [*hit'holel*] for him' [Ps. 37:7]; [that is to say], he added, "Wait for the Lord, and He will [utterly prostrate them (*halalim*)] before you. [Pay them no heed], go to the house of study morning and evening, and they, by their own doing, will soon come to an end."

R. Eleazar had hardly written these words when Geniva[9] was placed in chains [for execution].[10]

761. The exilarch once came to Hagronia to the house of R. Nathan. Rafram and all the sages attended the lecture. R. Huna did not. The next day Rafram wished to remove the hurt caused by R. Huna from the exilarch's heart. So [in the exilarch's presence] he asked R. Huna: Why did the master not come to the lecture? R. Huna: Because my foot hurt.[11]

762. Samuel said to R. Hinena bar Shila: No sage associated with the exilarch should go out [on the Sabbath] wearing a cloak fastened by a brooch with the exilarch's insignia[12] on it, except you, at whom the exilarch's household take no offense.[13]

763. A certain old woman[14] came before R. Nahman[15] and said to him: The exilarch and all the sages of the exilarch's household are sitting in a stolen sukkah. She complained loudly, but R. Nahman paid no attention to her. She persisted: A woman whose ancestor[16] had three hundred and eighteen slaves is crying out to you, and you pay her no heed. R. Nahman said to the sages: She is a noisy woman, but all she can claim is the value of the wood.[17]

764. A certain person cut down a date palm belonging to his neighbor, and then came to the exilarch [to inquire what he should pay]. The exilarch said: I myself saw the place. Three date palms stood there close together, and the three were worth one hundred *zuz*. Go therefore and pay your neighbor thirty-three and one-third *zuz*. At this, the man exclaimed: What have I to do with an exilarch who judges according to Persian law? And he went to R. Nahman [who ruled in keeping with the laws of Israel].[18]

The Merit of the Sages

765. Rabban Yohanan ben Zakkai had five distinguished disciples. He used to sum up their merits: R. Eliezer ben

1. P. Yoma 7:1, 44a. Ordinarily, the Torah scroll may not be taken out of the synagogue to be read elsewhere, except to honor a Davidic king.
2. B. Git 59a.
3. Hence, like priests, you must not wear your girdle too high up.
4. B. Zev 19a.
5. B. Sanh 5a.
6. B. Shab 55a.
7. See above in this chapter, §563.
8. P. Meg 3:2, 74a.
9. He was one of Mar Ukba's chief antagonists.
10. B. Git 7a.
11. B. Yoma 78a.
12. If the insignia should fall off, the sage, fearful of being seen without it, might remove the cloak, fold it, put it over his shoulder, and thus find himself carrying it, an act forbidden on the Sabbath.
13. B. Shab 58a.
14. Who felt that the exilarch's household had helped themselves to her wood to build their sukkah.
15. The exilarch's son-in-law.
16. Abraham. See Gen. 14:14.
17. No need to demolish the sukkah to return to her the wood she claims. B. Suk 31a.
18. The amount of damages to be paid by the person who chopped down the palm tree is equivalent to the amount of depreciation in value that a stand of sixty palm trees would suffer if one of the palm trees were to be chopped down. Thus the amount of damages to be paid in Jewish law would be less than in Persian law. B. BK 58b.

Hyrcanus—[his memory is so retentive that he is like] a cemented cistern, which does not lose a drop; R. Joshua ben Hananiah—she who gave birth to him is happy; R. Yose the Priest—the embodiment of piety; R. Simeon ben Nathanel—the embodiment of sin-fearing; R. Eleazar ben Arakh—[his originality is so great that he is like] a spring with ever-welling strength.

He also used to say: If all the sages of Israel were in one pan of a scale and R. Eliezer ben Hyrcanus in the other, he would outweigh them all. Abba Saul, however, quoted him otherwise: If all the sages of Israel, including R. Eliezer ben Hyrcanus, were in one pan of a scale, and R. Eleazar ben Arakh in the other, he would outweigh them all.[1]

766. In like manner[2] Rabbi Judah [I] the Patriarch used to list the merit of the sages Rabbi Tarfon, Rabbi Akiva, Rabbi Eleazar ben Azariah, Rabbi Yohanan ben Nuri, and Rabbi Yose the Galilean:

R. Tarfon he called "a pile of stones"—some say, "a pile of walnuts." When a person removes one of them, all come clattering down as they fall over one another. Such was R. Tarfon. Whenever a disciple of the wise came to him and said, "Teach me," he would bring forth for him Scripture and Mishnah, Midrash of *Halakhot* and of *Aggadot*. When the disciple left R. Tarfon's presence, he went away laden with blessing and [intellectual] wealth.

R. Akiva he called "a treasury with compartments." To whom may R. Akiva be likened? To a laborer who took his basket and went forth to the field. When he found wheat, he put some into it; when he found barley, in it went; emmer, likewise; beans, the same; lentils, too, went into the basket. Upon returning home, he sorted out the wheat by itself, the barley by itself, the emmer by itself, the beans by themselves, the lentils by themselves. This is how R. Akiva acted: all the Torah [he amassed], he sorted into its various compartments.

R. Eleazar ben Azariah he called "spice peddler's basket." For to whom may R. Eleazar be likened? To a spice peddler who takes up his basket and comes into a city; when the people of the city come up and ask him, "Have you good oil with you? Have you spikenard ointment with you? Have you balsam with you?" they find that he has everything with him. Such was Rabbi Eleazar ben Azariah. When a disciple of the wise came to him and asked him about Scripture, he answered him; about Midrash, he answered him; about *Halakhah* he answerred him; about *Aggadah*, he answered him. So when the disciple left R. Eleazar's presence, he went away filled with [intellectual] wealth and blessing.

R. Yohanan ben Nuri he called "a basket filled with *Halakhot*."

R. Yose the Galilean he called "a man who gathers [traditions] with discrimination." Utterly without arrogance, he held fast to meek lowliness, a requirement that the sages inferred from [the fact that] Mount Sinai [was a lowly mountain], and in such a spirit of lowliness he taught all the sages of Israel.[3]

1. Avot 2:8.
2. Even as Rabban Yohanan ben Zakkai described the distinction of his disciples, so R. Judah described those of his masters.

767. Issi ben Judah used to count the distinctive merits of various sages. R. Meir—sage and scribe; R. Judah—a sage whenever he chose to speak;[4] R. Tarfon—a pile of walnuts; R. Ishmael—a well-stocked shop; R. Akiva—a treasury with compartments; R. Yohanan ben Nuri—a basket of fancy goods; R. Eleazar ben Azariah—a basket of spices. The Mishnah of [the elder] R. Eliezer ben Jacob was small in quantity but good.[5] R. Yose always had his reasons [for his decisions]. R. Simeon used to grind much but discard little, and what little he did discard was only bran. R. Simeon used to say to his disciples: My sons, learn my rules, for my rules are the cream of the cream of R. Akiva's.[6]

768. R. Joshua said: Happy are you, O our father Abraham, that R. Eleazar ben Azariah issued from your loins! The generation in whose midst R. Eleazar ben Azariah lives is not one that is orphaned.[7]

769. Ben Azzai used to say: Except for this baldhead [R. Akiva], all of Israel's sages are as thin as a garlic's husk compared to me.[8]

770. He who has disciples and disciples of disciples is called Rabbi. When his disciples are forgotten, he is called Rabban. When both his disciples and the disciples of his disciples are forgotten, he is called by his name alone [without titles].[9]

771. Rabbi [Judah I, the Patriarch] and R. Nathan concluded the Mishnah. R. Ashi and Ravina concluded [authentic] teaching [by redacting the Talmud].[10]

The Former and the Latter Generations

772. R. Haggai said in the name of R. Samuel bar Nahman: The former generations plowed and sowed, weeded and trimmed, hoed and reaped, piled up sheaves, threshed, winnowed, and sifted, ground the grain and sifted the flour, kneaded the dough, tore it in pieces, and baked. Yet we do not know how to make use of what was prepared for us.[11]

3. ARN 18.
4. See above in this chapter, §261.
5. His rulings were always accepted.
6. B. Git 67a.
7. P. Hag 14b and 3b.
8. B. Bekh 58a.
9. Hillel, for example. Such a master is so outstanding that his teachings are cited directly in his name only, omitting the names of the disciples who transmitted them. Tos Ed 3:4.
10. They arranged Amoraic discussions in systematic order, even as R. Judah I, the Patriarch, arranged tannaitic utterances in such order. B. BM 86a.
11. Literally, "Yet we have no mouths to eat it with." P. Shek 5:1, 48c.

773. R. Zera said in the name of Rava bar Zemina: If the former generations were like sons of angels, we are like sons of men; and if the latter generations were like sons of men, we are like asses—and not even like the asses of R. Hanina ben Dosa and R. Phinehas ben Yair,[1] but like ordinary asses.[2]

774. R. Yohanan said: The intellectual powers of former generations were as wide as the door of the Outer Hall leading into the Temple's interior; the powers of latter generations were narrower like the door of the Temple Hall;[3] but ours is as narrow as the eye of a fine needle.

R. Akiva is classed with the former generations. R. Eleazar ben Shammua with the latter generations. Others say: R. Eleazar ben Shammua is classed with the former generations, and R. Oshaia Berabbi with the latter generations.

"But ours is as narrow as the eye of a fine needle." Abbaye said: With regard to Gemara, we find mastering it as difficult as forcing a peg into a wall [with bare hands]. Rava said: With regard to logical reasoning, we are like a finger trying to press into hardened wax.[4] R. Ashi said: As to forgetfulness, we are like a finger inserted into a bowl of seeds[5] [and taken out].[6]

775. R. Yohanan said: The fingernail of former generations has more substance than the entire body of the latter generations. Resh Lakish replied: On the contrary, the latter generations have more substance, for they occupy themselves with Torah despite oppression by the kingdoms. R. Yohanan retorted: The Temple proves what I say. It was restored for former generations but was not restored for the latter generations.

R. Eleazar was asked: Were the former generations superior, or were the latter generations superior? He replied: Set your eyes upon the Sanctuary! Some say, he said: Your evidence[7] is the Sanctuary.[8]

776. R. Judah [I] the Patriarch said of R. Yose ben Halafta: Like the difference between the holiest of the holy and the most common of the common is the difference between our generation and the generation of R. Yose.[9]

777. R. Papa asked Abbaye: Why were miracles performed for former generations, and no miracles are performed for us? Is it on account of learning? In the days of R. Judah, the sum of their learning was Nezikin,[10] wherreas we range over the entire six orders [of the Mishnah]. And when R. Judah happenend to reach the tractate Uktzin,[11] he would say in despair, "I find myself helpless in confronting the intricate theses of Rav and Samuel"; whereas, in matters of Uktzin, we on our own are able to advance thirteen ways of interpreting it. Nevertheless, R. Judah had only to draw off one of his shoes[12] and rain came, while we fast and cry out, but no one [on High] seems to need us.

Abbaye replied: Former generations gave up their lives for the hallowing of the Name; but we do not give up our lives for the hallowing of the Name.[13]

778. Abba Saul was the tallest man in his generation, and R. Tarfon reached only to his shoulder. R. Tarfon was the tallest man in his generation, and R. Meir reached only to his shoulder. R. Meir was the tallest man in his generation, and Rabbi reached only to his shoulder. Rabbi was the tallest man in his generation, and R. Hiyya reached only to his shoulder. R. Hiyya was the tallest in his generation, and Rav reached only to his shoulder. Rav was the tallest man in his generation, and R. Judah reached only to his shoulder. R. Judah was the tallest man in his generation, and his waiter Adda of Pumbedita reached only to his shoulder. Parshtabina of Pumbedita reached to half the height of the waiter Adda, while everybody else reached only to the loins of Parshtabina of Pumbedita.[14]

779. R. Zera said: Last night [in a dream], R. Yose son of R. Hanina appeared to me, and I asked him, "Near whom are you seated [in the academy on high]?" "Near R. Yohanan." "And R. Yohanan, near whom?" "Near R. Yannai." "And R. Yannai?" "Near R. Hanina." "And R. Hanina?" "Near R. Hiyya." I then asked, "Is not R. Yohanan [worthy of a seat] near R. Hiyya?" He replied, "In the region of sparks of fire and tongues of fire, who needs to bring in a smith's son?"[15]

The Sages of the Land of Israel and the Sages of Babylonia

780. R. Oshaia said: What is the meaning of the verse "And I took unto me the two staves; the one I called *Noam*, "graciousness," and the other I called *Hovelim*, "binders" (Zech. 11:7)? *Noam* refers to the disciples of the wise in the Land of Israel, who, when engaged in halakhic debates, treat each other graciously [*manimim*]; *Hovelim* refers to the disciples of the wise in Babylonia, who, when discus-

1. See above in this chapter, §67 and §283.
2. B. Shab 112b.
3. The door of the Outer Hall was twenty cubits wide, while the door of the Temple Hall was only ten cubits wide.
4. We can no more penetrate the reasoning than we can press a finger into hard wax—we merely depress the surface.
5. Instead of *bira* ("pit"), according to Tosafot, ad loc., R. Hananel reads *bizra* ("seeds").
6. Once the finger is taken out, no trace of its having been there is left. B. Er 53a.
7. The words *eneykhem* ("your eyes") and *edeykhem* ("your evidence") differ but slightly.
8. B. Yoma 9b.
9. P. Git 6:7, 48b.
10. The old name for Bava Kamma, Bava Metzia, and Bava Batra, which made up one tome (the law of torts).
11. A tractate dealing with the definition of a fruit—are its leaves, its stem end, or its bottom end deemed to be part of the fruit or extraneous?
12. To prepare for a fast, during which people sat on the ground without wearing shoes.
13. B. Ber 20a.
14. B. Nid 24b–25a.
15. To work the bellows and fan the fire. (R. Yohanan was known as Bar Nappaha, "the smith's son.") B. BM 85b.

sing *Halakhah*, injure each other's feelings [*mehabbelim*].[1]

It is written, "And two olive trees by it. These are the two *yitzhar*, anointed ones" (Zech. 4:3 and 4:14). R. Isaac said: *Yitzhar* designates the disciples of the wise in the Land, who, when engaged in halakhic debates, are soothing to one another like olive oil; while "And two olive trees stand by it" symbolizes the disciples of the wise in Babylonia, who in halakhic discussions make each other as bitter as [unripe] olives.[2]

781. Why are disciples of the wise in Babylonia so particular about their attire? Because they are not too well learned.[3] R. Yohanan said: Because they are not in their [original country].[4] As people say, "In my own town, my name is what matters; away from home, my attire."[5]

782. "In days to come . . . Israel shall blossom and bud" (Isa. 27:6). R. Joseph taught: The verse refers to disciples of the wise in Babylonia, who by their discourses wreathe Torah with blossoms and buds.[6]

783. Ulla happened to visit Pumbedita, where he was offered a basketful of dates. He asked, "How much are these worth?" He was told, "One *zuz*."[7] Ulla said, "So in Babylonia one may have a basketful of date honey for only one *zuz*, and yet the Babylonians do not occupy themselves with Torah!" During the night, the dates he had eaten upset his digestion. He remarked, "A basketful of [poison that cuts like] knives for one *zuz*. And yet the Babylonians occupy themselves with Torah!"[8]

784. What does the name Babel [Babylonia] suggest? R. Yohanan said that, in Babylonia, study is a proper blend (*belulah*) of Scripture, Mishnah, and Talmud. But R. Jeremiah applied the verse "He hath made me dwell in dark places like those that have been long dead" (Lam. 3:6) to the study of the Talmud in Babylonia.[9]

785. R. Jeremiah said: Those foolish Babylonians! Because they dwell in a dark country,[10] they voice murky utterances.[11]

786. The verse "Indeed, it shall be said of Zion: 'This man and that man also was born there' " (Ps. 87:5), R. Meyasha grandson of R. Joshua ben Levi explained, means that [it will be said, "He is of Zion"] of a man born in Zion as well as of a man yearning to see Zion.

Abbaye said: Yet one of them [of Zion] is better than any two of us. Rava added: Still, when one of ours goes up to Zion, he is as good as any two of theirs. Thus, when R. Jeremiah was with us, he actually did not understand what the sages were saying. But when he went up there, he used to call us "foolish Babylonians."[12]

787. When R. Zera went up to the Land of Israel, he kept a hundred fasts, to help him forget the Babylonian method of study, so that it should not confuse him.[13]

Sages at Their Going In and Their Coming Out of the House of Study

788. When he went into the house of study and also when he came out, R. Nehunia ben ha-Kaneh used to say a short prayer. He was asked: Why is such prayer necessary? He replied: When I go in, I pray that no offense should occur through me,[14] and when I come out, I voice thanks for my lot.

Our masters taught: On going in, what should a man say? "May it be Your will, O Lord my God, that no offense may occur through me, that I may not stumble in a matter of *Halakhah* and allow my colleagues to rejoice at my discomfiture,[15] that I may not declare the unclean clean or the clean unclean, or that my colleagues may not stumble in a matter of *Halakhah* and allow me to rejoice at their discomfiture." On his coming out, what should he say? "I give thanks to You, O Lord my God, that You have set my portion among those who sit in the house of study and not set my portion with those who loiter at street corners.[16] For I rise early and they rise early—I rise early for words of Torah and they rise early for idle talk. I labor and they labor—I labor and receive a reward, while they labor and receive no reward. I run and they run, but I run to life in the world-to-come, while they run to the pit of destruction."[17]

789. When the main body of disciples departed from the school of Rav, one thousand two hundred disciples were left; [when they departed] from the school of R. Huna, eight hundred were left; when they departed from the schools of Rabbah and R. Joseph, four hundred were left, yet they spoke of themselves as orphans. When they departed from the school of Abbaye (some say, from the school of R. Papa, others, from the school of R. Ashi), two hundred were left, and they spoke of themselves as most orphaned among orphans.[18]

---

1. In the Babylonian academies, discussions were carried on far more energetically than in the Palestinian ones; consequently, there is considerably more controversy in the Babylonian than in the Jerusalem Talmud.
2. B. Sanh 24a.
3. So they have nothing but attire to distinguish them.
4. They are immigrants from the Land of Israel.
5. B. Shab 145b.
6. Ibid.
7. So Munich ms., as quoted by Isidore Epstein, Pes, Soncino, p. 465, n. 4. BR read: " 'How many baskets for a *zuz*?' 'Three.' "
8. B. Pes 88a; Ta 9b.
9. B. Sanh 24a.
10. Perhaps an allusion to the Parsees' prohibition of kindling lights during Parsee festivals. Leon Nemoy writes, "Darkness is a common synonym of ignorance. Palestinian scholars were contemptuous of Babylonian scholars."
11. B. Men 52a.
12. B. Ket 75a.
13. The Babylonian dialectics were complicated and at times obscure. Palestinian analysis was clear and simple. B. BM 85a.
14. By giving a wrong decision.
15. And so bring sin upon themselves.
16. Or, shopkeepers. So Rashi.
17. B. Ber 28b.
18. B. Ket 106a.

790. When the disciples left the school of R. Ammi, they used to say to him:

During your life, may you see your worldly needs provided,
But may your ultimate reward be in the world-to-come,
And may hope for it endure through the generations that spring from you.
May your heart meditate understanding,
Your mouth speak wisdom,
And your tongue be moved to song.
May your gaze scan what lies ahead,
Your eyes shine with light of Torah,
Your face be radiant as the brightness of the firmament.
May your lips utter knowledge,
Your reins rejoice in uprightness,
And your steps hurry to hear the words of the Ancient of Days.[1]

791. When the disciples left the school of R. Hisda, they used to say to him:

"Our learned ones[2] are well laden" (Ps. 144:14)—our men learned in Torah and obedient to percepts are well laden with suffering.

"May there be no breach" (Ps. 144:14)—may our fellowship not be like the fellowship of Saul, from whose midst issued Doeg the Edomite [who caused so great a breach].[3]

"And no going forth" (Ps. 144:14)—may our fellowship not be like the fellowship of David, from whose midst Ahithophel went forth.[4]

"That there be no complaining" (Ps. 144:14)—may our fellowship not be like the fellowship of Elisha, from which issued Gehazi.[5]

"In our streets" (Ps. 144:14)—may we have no son or disciple who disgraces himself in public.[6]

The Death of Sages and Their Eulogies

792. Our masters taught: When the elder Rabban Gamaliel died, the glory of Torah ceased and Levitical purity and abstinence died out. When Rabban Yohanan ben Zakkai died, the radiance of wisdom ceased. When R. Eliezer died, the Torah scroll was hidden. When R. Joshua died, counsel, speculation, and [the blessing of] plenty ceased in the world. When R. Ishmael ben Phiabi died, the radiance of priesthood ceased. When Rabban Gamaliel died, locusts came[7] and tribulations increased. When R. Akiva died, the strong arms of Torah ceased, and the wells of wisdom were stopped up. When R. Eleazar ben Azariah died, the crowns of wisdom ceased, for the crown of sages is their wealth. When R. Hanina ben Dosa died, workers of miracles ceased. When R. Yose Ketanta died, men of piety died out. (And why was he called Ketanta? Because he was the youngest [*katan*] of the pious men.) When Ben Azzai died, the assiduous students of Torah ceased. When Ben Zoma died, the expounders of Scripture ceased. When R. Meir died, the tellers of parables ceased. When Rabbi died, humility and fear of sin ceased.[8]

793. When R. Akiva died, Rabbi was born. When Rabbi died, R. Judah was born. When R. Judah died, Rava was born. When Rava died, R. Ashi was born. This teaches that a righteous man does not depart from the world until another righteous man like himself is brought into being, as is said, "The sun riseth, as the sun goeth down" (Eccles. 1:5). Before Eli's sun was extinguished, the sun of Samuel the Ramathite rose, as is said, "Even before the lamp of God was extinguished [in Eli], Samuel was . . . already in the Temple of the Lord" (1 Sam. 3:3).[9]

794. When R. Abbahu died, the columns of Caesarea ran with tears.[10] At the death of R. Yose, the gutters on the roofs of Sepphoris ran with blood. (It is said that he was willing to lay down his life for performing circumcision.) When R. Jacob died, stars were visible during the day. When R. Samuel bar R. Isaac died, all cedars in the Land of Israel were uprooted. At the death of R. Hiyya [bar Abba], fiery stones came down from the sky; at that of R. Nahum bar Simai, the Man of the Holy of Holies, all images were covered with mattings. (Why was he called Nahum the Man of the Holy of Holies? Because during his entire life he never gazed at the image engraved on a coin. And so, people said: Even as he did not gaze at images during his life, so he should not have to gaze at them after his death.) When Rabbah and R. Joseph died, it seemed as though the cliffs on both banks of the Euphrates were kissing one another.[11] When Abbaye and Rava died, it seemed as though the cliffs on both banks of the Tigris were kissing one another. When R. Mesharsheya died, the date trees were laden with thorns.[12]

795. When Rabbah bar R. Huna and R. Hamnuna died, their coffins were carried up [to the Land of Israel]. When the cortege reached a bridge, the camels halted. An Arab asked: What's happening? The sages [accompanying the cortege] replied: The deceased scholars are deferring to each other, one saying, "Master, you go first," and the

---

1. B. Ber 17a.
2. JV: "oxen." But *aluf* ("ox") may be associated with the stem *alef* ("to learn, to study").
3. See 1 Sam. 22:9–23.
4. See 2 Sam. 16:21–23.
5. See 2 Kings 5:20–27.
6. By heretical teaching, as did—so munich Ms. of the Talmud—the Nazarene. B. Ber. 17a.
7. Some take it to refer to the plague of locusts in 164 C.E., when Rabban Gamaliel died; others, to the proliferation of tax collectors.
8. B. Sot 49a and En Yaakov, ad loc.; P. Sot 9:16, 24c; P. BK 3:7, 3c.
9. B. Kid 72b.
10. Munich ms.; BR: "Water."
11. So numerous were the mourners that they seemed to have crowded out the water.
12. B. MK 25b; P. AZ 3:1, 42c.

other saying, "You, master, go first." The Arab interjected: By rights, a lion son of a lion should go first. Accordingly, the camel carrying Rabbah bar H. Huna went first.

The eulogizer at Rabbah bar R. Huna's funeral began:

A scion of noble lineage is brought up from Babylon,
And with him a book of Torah's battles.
Double the number of jackdaws and owls[1]
To mourn the crushing loss brought from Shinar.[2]
God, angered at His world,
Snatches souls from it
But rejoices in them, as at the coming of a new bride.
He who rides the skies rejoices, jubilates
When a soul pure and just comes to Him.[3]

When Ravina died, the eulogizer at the funeral began:

Palm trees sway their heads,
Mourning the palmlike righteous man.
He turned nights into days [meditating in Torah].
So must we
Turn night into days
Lamenting him.

R. Ashi asked Bar Kipok: [On the day of my repose], what will you say about me? Bar Kipok responded: I shall say:

If a flame felled lofty cedars,
What chance for lowly hyssop on the wall?
If a hook hauled up Leviathan,
What chance for fishes in shallow streams?
If drought stilled cascading torrents,
What chance for water in tranquil pools?"

Bar Avin said to Bar Kipok: God forbid that I would use words such as "hook" or "flame" at the death of righteous men. Then what would you say? Bar Kipok asked. I would say:

Weep for the mourners,
Not for the soul that is gone—
It to its repose,
We to grief.

R. Hanin, the patriarch's son-in-law, had no children. He besought God's mercy, and a son was born to him. The day his son was born, R. Hanin died. The eulogizer at the funeral began:

Joy is turned to sorrow,
Gladness and grief, commingle.
In the father's moment of joy, he sighed [his last breath].
At the very instant the child was being caressed (*haninato*),
He who was caressing him (*hanino*) died.

The child was named Hanin after his father.

When R. Yohanan died, R. Isaac ben Eleazar began the funeral oration:

Grievous is this day for Israel,
As a day when the sun sets at noon.

When R. Zera died, the eulogizer at the funeral began:

The land of Shinar conceived and bore him,
The Land of Beauty[4] made eminent him who was her delight.
Now Rakkath[5] laments. Woe to her,
She has lost her most precious ornament.[6]

1. Birds whose presence signifies mourning.
2. Babylon. See Gen. 14:1.
3. See MTeh 116:7 (YJS 2:226–27).
4. R. Zera migrated to the Land of Israel.
5. An ancient name for either Sepphoris or Tiberias, where R. Zera lived. See B. Meg 6a.
6. B. MK 25b and En Yaakov, ad loc.

PART III

CHAPTER ONE

ISRAEL AND THE NATIONS OF THE WORLD

God's Love for Israel

1. R. Akiva used to say: Israel are beloved, called as they are "children of God." As a special token of His love, it was made known to them that they are called "children of God," for He said to them, "You are children of the Lord your God" (Deut. 14:1). Israel are beloved, the precious instrument [Torah] having been given to them. As a special token of His love, it was made known to them that the precious instrument through which the world was created was given to them, for He said, "I give you good doctrine; forsake not My Torah" (Prov. 4:12).[1]

2. "Thou hast affirmed the Lord this day . . . and the Lord hath affirmed thee" (Deut. 26:17–18). The Holy One said to Israel: You have declared Me a unique entity, and I shall declare you a unique entity. You made Me a unique entity in the world by saying, "Hear, O Israel, the Lord our God is the only Lord" (Deut. 6:4); and I shall declare you a unique entity by having it said, "Who is like Thy people Israel, a nation one in the earth" (1 Chron. 17:21).[2]

3. R. Simeon ben Lakish said in the name of R. Yannai: The Holy One partnered His great Name with Israel. What He did may be illustrated by the parable of a king who had a small key to a treasure chest. He said to himself: If I leave the key without identification, it may be lost. So I will attach a chain to it, and if it should be lost, the chain will identify it. So, too, the Holy One said: If I leave Israel without identification, they may be lost among the nations. So I shall join My great Name to them and they will remain alive [as a distinct entity]. Hence [when there was danger that Israel's name might be wiped out] Joshua asked, "What wilt Thou do for Thy great Name?" (Josh. 7:9), by which he implied that the Name is partnered with us.[3]

4. "I sleep; nevertheless, my heart waketh" (Song 5:2). R. Hiyya bar Abba asked: Where do we find that the Holy One is actually identified as the heart of Israel? In the verse "God is the rock, my heart, and my portion forever" (Ps. 73:26).[4]

5. Israel are more beloved by the Holy One than the ministering angels . . . for the ministering angels do not utter song above until Israel first utter it below.[5]

6. "He will give His angels charge over thee, to guard thee" (Ps. 91:11). R. Meir said: Who is greater, the guardian or the guarded? Since it is written, "He will give His angels charge over thee, to guard thee," it follows that the guarded is greater than the guardian.

"They shall bear thee upon their hands" (Ps. 91:12). R. Judah said: Which is the greater, he who is borne up by another or he who bears another up? Since Scripture says, "They shall bear thee upon their hands," you must conclude that he who is borne up is greater than he who bears another up.[6]

7. R. Nehemiah said: See how great is the love of the Holy One for Israel, for He has designated the ministering angels, the "mighty creatures who do His bidding" (Ps. 103:20), to be watchmen over Israel. Who are those angels? Michael and Gabriel, of whom it is said, "I have set watchmen upon thy walls, O Jerusalem" (Isa. 62:6).[7]

"And saviors shall come up on Mount Zion to judge the Mount of Esau" (Obad. 1:21), the saviors being Michael and Gabriel. However, our holy Rabbi [Judah I, the Patriarch] maintained that the verse refers to Michael alone, for Scripture says, "At that time shall Michael stand up, the great prince who standeth for the children of thy people" (Dan. 12:1), because he it is who presents Israel's needs and pleads for them, as Scripture says, "Then the angel of the Lord spoke and said: 'O Lord of hosts, how long wilt Thou not have compassion on Jerusalem?' " (Zech. 1:12), and also, "And there is none that holdeth with me against these, except Michael your prince" (Dan. 10:21).

R. Yose said: To whom may Michael and Samael[8] be compared? To an advocate and a prosecutor before a tribunal. The one speaks and then the other speaks. And when the one finishes what he has to say, and the other finishes what he has to say, if the advocate knows that he has prevailed, he begins to praise the judge in the hope that he will give his verdict [in the defendant's favor]. Then, if the prosecutor wishes to say more, the advocate tells him, "You be quiet and let us hear the judge." So also do Michael and Samael stand before the Presence, with Satan making accusations and Michael pointing to Israel's merits. When Satan wishes to say more, Michael silences him, as indicated in the verse "Let me hear what God, the Lord, will speak: for He will speak of well-being to His people" (Ps. 85:9).[9]

---

1. Avot 3:15.
2. B. Ber 6a.
3. The name Israel includes *El* ("God"); and the name Yehudah includes YHVH ("Lord"). P. Ta 2:6, 65d; Yalkut, Josh., §17.
4. Yalkut, Song, §988.
5. B. Hul 91b.
6. Gen. R. 78:1; MTeh 104:3.
7. The verse continues: "They shall never hold their peace day nor night." Such capacity can be attributed only to angels.
8. Satan.
9. The whole psalm pleads for God's mercy on Zion and is understood to have been uttered by Michael. Exod. R. 18:5.

8. Beloved are Israel, for when God calls them by a pet name, He calls them "priests," as is said, "Ye shall be called the priests of the Lord" (Isa. 61:6).[1]

9. R. Ashi said: R. Huna bar Nathan told me: Once I was standing before King Yezdegerd and my girdle was tied too high. He pulled it down, saying to me: You are described as "a kingdom of priests, and a holy nation" (Exod. 19:6).[2] When I came before Amemar, he said to me: The promise "Kings shall be thy foster fathers" (Isa. 49:23) has come to be fulfilled in you.[3]

10. R. Simeon said: All Israel are royal princes.[4]

11. R. Simeon said: Great is God's love for Israel. The Holy One revealed Himself in a place of idolatry, in a place of sexual pollution, in a place of ritual uncleanness in order to redeem them, as is said, "I am come down to deliver them out of the hand of the Egyptians" (Exod. 3:8).[5]

12. R. Simeon ben Yohai asked R. Eleazar bar R. Yose:[6] Have you perhaps heard from your father an interpretation of the verse "The crown wherewith his mother hath crowned him" (Song 3:11)? R. Eleazar replied: Yes. R. Simeon: How does it go? R. Eleazar: The verse may be understood by the parable of a king who had an only daughter whom he loved exceedingly. He called her "my daughter," but as time went on and his love kept increasing, he came to call her "my sister" and finally "my mother." So at first, in His endearment of Israel, the Holy One called her "My daughter"—"Hearken, O daughter, and consider" (Ps. 45:11). As His love increased, he called her "My sister"—"My sister, My bride" (Song 5:1). And finally, as His love grew more intense, he called her "My mother," as is indicated by the verse "Attend unto Me, O My people, and give ear unto Me, O My nation" (Isa. 51:4), where *u-leummi*, "O My nation," is spelled defectively and may also be read *u-le-immi*, "O My mother."

[Upon hearing this interpretation] R. Simeon ben Yohai rose, kissed R. Eleazar on the brow, and said: Had I come into the world only to hear this interpretation from you, it would have been enough for me.[7]

13. Elijah said: Once while I was traveling from place to place, a certain man came to me and asked me about matters pertaining to Torah, saying, "My master, there are two things in my heart I love with a very great love—Torah and Israel. But I do not know which of them comes first." I replied, "Generally people say that Torah is to be put first before all else. But I used to say: Israel, being holy, comes first."[8]

14. The verse "But now thus saith the Lord: Jacob created thee, Israel formed thee" (Isa. 43:1)[9] means, so said R. Phinehas in the name of R. Reuben, that the Holy One said to His world: My world, My world, who created you? Who formed you? Jacob created you. Israel formed you.

R. Berekhiah [hastened to explain]: Heaven and earth were created only for the sake of Israel, for it is said, "On account of the beginning God created" (Gen. 1:1). Here, by "the beginning" is meant Israel, of which Scripture says, "Israel is the Lord's hallowed portion, the beginning of His harvest" (Jer. 2:3).[10]

15. "As a lily among thorns" (Song 2:2). R. Azariah, citing R. Judah son of R. Simon, illustrated the verse by the parable of a king who had an orchard planted with a row of fig trees, a row of grapevines, a row of pomegranate trees, and a row of apple trees. The king turned the orchard over to a keeper and went away. After a while, the king came back and inspected the orchard to see how it had done, and found it overgrown with thorns and thistles. So he summoned woodcutters to raze the orchard. But when he saw there a rose-colored lily, he picked it up and breathed in its fragrance, and his spirit was calmed. The king said, "Because of this lily, let the orchard be spared."

Likewise, the world was created only for the sake of Israel. After twenty-six generations, [in the time of Moses], the Holy One inspected His world to see how it had done, and He found it had reverted, as it were, to water in water:[11] the generation of Enosh—water in water; the generation of the flood—water in water; the generation of the dispersion—water in water. Finally, He brought destroyers to raze the world, but then He saw there a rose-colored lily—Israel. He picked it up and breathed in its fragrance at the time Israel received the Ten Commandments, and His spirit was calmed. When Israel said, "We will do and obey" (Exod. 24:7), the Holy One said: On account of a lily, an orchard was spared; on account of the Torah and Israel [who study it], let the world be spared.[12]

16. "There is none like unto God of Jeshurun" (Deut. 33:26). Israel says, "There is none like unto God." And

1. Sif Num., §119.
2. Like a priest, he was not to wear his girdle too high.
3. B. Zev 19a.
4. B. Shab 128a.
5. Exod. R. 15:5.
6. R. Simeon ben Yohai turned to R. Eleazar because R. Eleazar's father, the historian R. Yose ben Halafta, was the best judge of the range of meaning in any verse of the Song of Songs. R. Simeon's turning to R. Eleazar would indicate that the Song's interpretation had long been linked with the crossing of the Red Sea, the revelation at Sinai, and the building of the Tabernacle. The Song was systematically interpreted as symbolizing each of these events, and it was for this reason that R. Simeon asked R. Eleazar how Song 3:11 was to be construed in reference to the building of the Tabernacle (see Saul Lieberman's appendix D in Gershom G. Scholem, *Jewish Gnosticism, Merkabah Mysticism, and Talmudic Tradition* [New York, 1960], pp. 118–26).
7. Song R. 3:11, §2; Exod. R. 52:5; Num. R. 12:8.
8. TdE, ed. Friedmann, p. 71.
9. JV: "But now thus saith the Lord, that created thee, O Jacob, and He that formed thee, O Israel."
10. Lev. R. 36:4; Yalkut, Isa., §452.
11. "The creation can be thought of as the act of separating the waters from the waters, i.e., making order out of chaos by setting limits; so sin, the disruption of the order decreed by Heaven, can be thought of as mixing once again the waters with the waters from which they were separated by Heaven's decree" (Brother Caedmon Holmes).
12. Lev. R. 23:3; Song R. 2:2, §3.

the holy spirit replies, "Like unto God is Jeshurun—[unique].

Israel says, "Who is like unto Thee, O Lord, among the mighty?" (Exod. 15:11). And the holy spirit replies, "Happy art thou, O Israel, who is like unto thee?" (Deut. 33:29).

Israel says, "Hear, O Israel, the Lord our God, the Lord is one" (Deut. 6:4). And the holy spirit replies, "Who is like unto Thy people Israel, a nation one on the earth?" (1 Chron. 17:21).

Israel says, "As an apple tree among the trees in the wood, so is my Beloved among the sons" (Song 2:3). And the holy spirit replies, "As a rose among thorns, so is My love among the daughters" (Song 2:2).

Israel says, "This is my God, and I will glorify Him" (Exod. 15:2). And the holy spirit replies, "The people which I formed for Myself" (Isa. 43:21).

Israel says, "Thou art the glory of their strength" (Ps. 89:18). And the holy spirit replies, "Israel, in whom I will be glorified" (Isa. 49:3).[1]

Between Israel and the Nations

17. It is taught in the name of R. Meir: Why was the Torah given to Israel? Because they are of a fiery temper. For in the school of R. Ishmael it is taught: "At His right hand was a fiery law unto them" (Deut. 33:2) means that the Holy One said, "It is right that they be given a fiery law [to restrain them]." Some say, Israel's laws had to be of fire, for if the Torah had not been given them, no people or tongue could withstand them. In this connection, R. Simeon ben Lakish said: There are three creatures of a fiery temper: among nations, Israel; among beasts, the dog; and among fowls, the cock.

R. Isaac bar Redifa said in the name of R. Ammi: You may think that such a description of Jews [as fiery tempered] is disparaging. In fact, it is complimentary. Their attitude is: Let me be a Jew or be crucified! Indeed, as R. Avin said, to this day Jews outside the Land are called "stiff-necked people."[2]

18. R. Yohanan said in the name of R. Eleazar son of R. Simeon: Wherever you find the words of R. Yose the Galilean in *Aggadah*, make your ear like a funnel.[3] [Thus R. Yose said: The verse] "It was not because you were greater than any people that the Lord set His love upon you and chose you, but because you were the humblest of all peoples" (Deut. 7:7) means that the Holy One said to Israel: I love you because even when I shower greatness upon you, you humble yourselves before Me. I bestowed greatness upon Abraham, yet he said to Me, "I am but dust and ashes" (Gen. 18:27); upon Moses and Aaron, yet they said, "And we are nothing" (Exod. 16:8); upon David, yet he said, "But I am a worm and no man" (Ps. 22:7). But the nations of the world do not act thus. When I bestowed greatness upon Nimrod, he said, "Come, let us build us a city," etc. (Gen. 11:4); upon Pharaoh, he said, "Who is the Lord?" (Exod. 5:2); upon Sennacherib, he said, "Who are they among all the gods of the countries?" etc. (2 Kings 18:35); upon Nebuchadnezzar, he said, "I will ascend above the heights of the clouds" (Isa. 14:14); upon Hiram king of Tyre, he said, "I sit in the seat of God, in the heart of the seas" (Ezek. 28:2).[4]

19. "God seeketh that which is pursued" (Eccles. 3:15). R. Judah son of R. Simon said in the name of R. Yose son of R. Nehorai: The Holy One always demands satisfaction from pursuers for the blood of the pursued. You can see that this is so, for Abel was pursued by Cain, and the Holy One chose Abel, as may be inferred from "The Lord had respect unto Abel and to his offering" (Gen. 4:4). Noah was pursued by his generation, and the Holy One chose none but Noah, as He Himself said, "For thee have I seen righteous before Me in this generation" (Gen. 7:1). Abraham was pursued by Nimrod, and the Holy One chose Abraham, as Scripture says, "Thou art the Lord, the God who didst choose Abram" (Neh. 9:7). Isaac was pursued by the Philistines, and the Holy One chose Isaac, as inferred from the Philistines' saying, "We saw plainly that the Lord was with thee" (Gen. 26:28). Jacob was pursued by Esau, and the Holy One chose Jacob, as Scripture says, "For the Lord hath chosen Jacob unto Himself" (Ps. 135:4). Joseph was pursued by his brothers, and the Holy One chose Joseph, as inferred from "He appointed it in Joseph[5] for a testimony" (Ps. 81:6). Moses was pursued by Pharaoh, and the Holy One chose Moses, as the verse indicates: "Had not Moses His chosen stood before Him" (Ps. 106:23). Saul was pursued by the Philistines, and the Holy One chose Saul, as is said, "See ye him whom the Lord hath chosen?" (1 Sam. 10:24). David was pursued by Saul, and the Holy One chose David, as the verse indicates: "He chose David also His servant" (Ps. 78:70). Israel are pursued by the nations, and the Lord has chosen Israel, as Scripture says, "And the Lord hath chosen thee to be His own treasure" (Deut. 14:2).[6]

20. "And they gave him the name Esav [Esau]" (Gen. 25:25)—["fully developed,"[7] the firstborn. But] God said of him: Look here at "a mere nothing," *he shav*, that I created in My world! Moreover, added R. Isaac, God says: You people have given a name to your sow[-like issue Edom–Rome]. I too am giving a name to My firstborn son. [Not "Esow" is to be My firstborn, but Jacob (Gen. 25:26) to whom I give the name Israel]. "Thus saith the Lord: 'My firstborn son is Israel' " (Exod. 4:22).[8]

1. Sif Deut., §355.
2. B. Betz 25b; Exod. R. 42:9.
3. To receive his teaching, even as a funnel or hopper at the top of the mill receives the grain.
4. B. Hul 89a.
5. In the Hebrew, the exceptional spelling "Yehoseph" is taken to mean that God inserted the letter *he*, one of the letters of His Name, to show that He had chosen Joseph [Yosef].
6. Lev. R. 27:5.
7. Taking Esav to be derived from *asoh* ("fully developed"); hence, the firstborn.
8. Not Yaakov, ("holding on to Esau's heel [*akev*]," but Israel ("capable of confronting both God and men"). Gen. R. 63:8.

21. "Are ye not as the children of the Cushites unto Me?" (Amos 9:7). But were they named children of Cushites? Was not their name "children of Israel"? However, what is meant by calling the children of Israel Cushites is that even as a Cushite is different in the color of his skin, so in their deeds Israel are different from every nation and tongue.[1]

22. R. Levi said: All Israel's activities are different from the corresponding activities of the peoples of the earth—in their plowing, in their sowing, in their harvesting, in their gathering the sheaves, in their threshing, [in furnishing liberally from] their threshing floors and their winepresses, in the cutting of their hair, in their counting and reckoning of time. In their plowing: "Thou shalt not plow with an ox and an ass together" (Deut. 22:10). In their sowing: "Thou shalt not sow thy vineyard with two kinds of seed" (Deut. 22:9). In their harvesting: "Neither shalt thou gather the gleaning of thy harvest" (Lev. 19:9). In their gathering the sheaves: "When thou reapest . . . in thy field, and hast forgot a sheaf in the field, thou shalt not go back to fetch it" (Deut. 24:19). In their threshing: "Thou shalt not muzzle the ox when he treadeth out the corn" (Deut. 25:4). In [furnishing liberally from] their threshing floors and their winepresses: "Thou shalt furnish [the Hebrew servant] liberally . . . out of thy threshing floor, and out of thy winepress" (Deut. 15:14). In the cutting of their hair, as is said, "Ye shall not round off the side growth on your head, nor destroy the side growth of your beard" (Lev. 19:27). And finally in their counting and reckoning of time, for the nations of the earth count years by the sun, but Israel count by the moon, as is said, "This, [the determination of time by the] moon, is to be yours" (Exod. 12:2).[2]

23. R. Levi said in the name of R. Yose son of R. Ilai: It is but natural that the large should count by the large, and the small by the small. Esau (Rome), who is large, counts by the sun, which is large; Jacob, who is small, counts by the moon, which is small. And indeed, as R. Nahman said, "This difference is a happy augury: Esau counts by the sun—just as the sun rules by day but does not rule by night, so [wicked] Esau has a portion in this world but no portion in the world-to-come; Jacob counts by the moon—just as the moon rules by day[3] and by night, so Jacob has a portion in both this world and in the world-to-come.

R. Nahman made another observation: As long as the light of the larger luminary shines in the world, the light of the lesser one is not noticed; but when the light of the larger one declines, the light of the lesser one becomes conspicuous. Even so, as long as the light of Esau shines brightly in the world, the light of Jacob is not noticed; but when the light of Esau declines, the light of Jacob becomes conspicuous.[4]

24. R. Meir said: R. Dostai of Kokaba asked me: What is meant by "The belly of the wicked shall want" (Prov. 13:25)? I replied: In our city there was a heathen who prepared a banquet for all the elders of the city, and he invited me along with them. He had [his servants] set before him all that the Holy One created in His world during the six days of creation, and indeed his table lacked nothing at all except soft-shelled nuts. [When the heathen saw that they were wanting], what did he do? He took away the tabletop—worth something like six talents of silver—from before us and smashed it. I asked him, "Why did you do this?" He replied, "You say this world is ours and the world-to-come is yours. So if we cannot eat every kind of food we want now, when shall we eat it?" To him I applied the verse "The belly of the wicked shall want."[5]

25. [When] Israel eat and drink, they begin with discussions on Torah and with words in praise of God. When the peoples of the world eat and drink, all they begin with is words of frivolity.[6]

26. Rava made the following exposition: What [are the allusions] in the verse "Come, my Beloved, let us go forth into the field," etc. (Song 7:12)? "Come, my Beloved," said the congregation of Israel to the Holy One: O Master of the universe, do not judge me as You judge inhabitants of [heathen] cities who are guilty of robbery, unchastity, and taking vain and false oaths. Rather, "let us go forth into the field" (ibid.)—Come, and I will show You disciples of the wise who [live in rural areas and] study Torah in poverty. "Let us lodge in the villages" (ibid.)—read not *ba-kefarim*, "in the villages," but *ba-koferim*, "among the unbelievers"—come, and I will show You the descendants of Esau, upon whom You have showered much bounty, yet they refuse to believe in You. "Let us get up early to the vineyards" (Song 7:13), meaning to synagogues and houses of study. "Let us see whether the vine hath budded" (ibid.), budded with students of Scripture; "whether the vine blossoms be opened" (ibid.), opened to students of Mishnah; "and the pomegranates be in flower" (ibid.), flowered with students of Gemara; "there will I give Thee my love"—I will show You the honor and greatness that are mine, the glory of my sons and my daughters.[7]

27. Isaac left two legacies to his two sons: to Jacob he left the voice—"The voice is the voice of Jacob" (Gen. 27:22); while to Esau he left the hands—"But the hands are the hands of Esau" (ibid.). Esau took pride in his legacy, as Scripture says, "Edom said unto him: 'Thou shalt not pass through me, lest I come out with the sword against thee' " (Num. 20:18). Jacob also took pride in his legacy, for Scripture says, "And we cried unto the Lord, the God of our fathers, and the Lord heard our voice" (Deut. 26:7). In the time-to-come, both will receive their

---

1. B. MK 16b and En Yaakov, ad loc.
2. PR 15:5 (YJS 1:312); Num. R. 10:1.
3. During part of its cycle, the moon is visible by day.
4. Gen. R. 6:3; PR 15:2 (YJS 1:334–35); Yalkut, *Bereshit*, §8.
5. PR 16:6 (YJS 1:351); Num. R. 21:20; Midrash Prov., ed. Buber, p. 74.
6. B. Meg 12b.
7. B. Er 21b and En Yaakov, ad loc.

rewards. Esau will receive his, as Scripture says, "For My sword hath drunk its fill in heaven; behold, it shall come down upon Edom" (Isa. 34:5). Jacob will receive his reward, for Scripture says, "Yet again shall be heard in this place . . . the voice of mirth and the voice of gladness" (Jer. 33:10–11).[1]

28. "The voice is the voice of Jacob" (Gen. 27:22)—no prayer avails unless the seed of Jacob shares in voicing it. "The hands are the hands of Esau" (ibid.)—no war is won unless the seed of Esau has a part in it.[2]

29. "Behold, *hen*,[3] a people that dwells apart" (Num. 23:9). What is implied by the word *hen?* Israel's uniqueness, which is intimated by the numerical values of the letters in *hn*—the epithet given to Israel in this verse. When you examine all the letters in the alphabet, you will find that each of them has a mate [with which the number 10 or 100 may be formed; the exceptions are the letters *he* and *nun* in *hn*, the epithet for Israel—these two letters have no such mates]. Thus the letter *alef* (1) together with *tet* (9) adds up to 10. The letter *bet* (2) together with *het* (8) also adds up to 10. And just as *alef* (1) + *tet* (9) and *bet* (2) + *het* (8) add up to 10, so *gimmel* (3) + *zayin* (7) and *dalet* (4) + *vav* (6) add up to 10. But the *he* (5) cannot be mated in this way [since it has no mate except itself to make 10]. Nor has the *nun* (50) a mate [except itself to make 100]. Likewise, in another series of combinations, the letters *yod* (10) + *tzade* (90) and *kaf* (20) + *pe* (80) and *lamed* (30) + *ayin* (70) and *mem* (40) + *samekh* (60)—each adds up to 100. But the *nun* (50) cannot be mated in this way.[4]

The Holy One said: Even as the letters *he* and *nun* cannot be mated with other letters except themselves to form either ten or one hundred, so Israel cannot be joined with other peoples, but must stand apart. Even if a king decrees that they violate the Sabbath, abolish circumcision, or worship idols, they let themselves be put to death rather than commingle with the nations.[5]

30. A Gentile asked R. Avina: Your Scripture says, "Who is like Thy people, like Israel, a nation unique in the earth?" (2 Sam. 7:23). But wherein lies your greatness? You, too, are reckoned as one of us in the verse "All the nations are nothing before Him" (Isa. 40:17). R. Avina replied: [Balaam], one of your own, has already testified about us: "Israel is not to be reckoned among the nations" (Num. 23:9).[6]

31. "The notable ones whose names derive from the first of the nations" (Amos 6:1)[7]—Israel, who derive their name [Semites] from Shem and [Hebrews] from Eber.[8]

[Or the verse may be read: "Like the nations who name their notables as gods], Israel, coming into their midst, [do likewise]." When the nations dwell in peace, they eat and drink, get drunk and engage in idle chatter. What do they say [by way of glorifying themselves? They say], "Who is as wise as Balaam, as mighty as Goliath, as rich as Haman?" And in imitation of them, Israel come and say to the nations, "Was not Ahithophel wise? Was not Solomon wise? Was not Samson mighty? Was not David mighty? Was not Korah rich? Was not Solomon rich?"[9]

32. R. Isaac said: It happened once that a provincial lady had an Ethiopian maidservant who went down with her friend to draw water from the spring. The maidservant said to her, "My friend, soon my master is going to divorce his wife and marry me." When the friend asked, "Why?" the Ethiopian maidservant replied, "Because he saw her hands covered with soot." The friend: "You are the most foolish woman in the world! Let your ears hear what your mouth is saying: a wife greatly loved by your master—you say he is about to divorce her because just once he saw her hands covered with soot. Then all the less will he want you, whose entire body is covered with soot, and who have been black all your days from your mother's womb!" [As the maidservant was mistaken], so, too, are the nations of the world who taunt Israel, saying, "[God will give up] this nation, which has bartered its glory [for a golden calf, and He will take us]." Israel reply, "If we, who have done such a thing only once, are punished this way, how much more and more will you be punished!"[10]

33. Straw, stubble, and chaff were contending with each other. One claimed, "It was for my sake that the field was sown," while another claimed, "No, for my sake." But the wheat said, "Wait till threshing time comes—then we shall know for whose sake the field was sown." When threshing time came and the owner went out to winnow the crop, the chaff was scattered in the wind; he threw the straw on the ground; he burned the stubble. But he took the wheat and stacked it in a heap—and whoever passed by kissed it. So it is with the peoples of the world. Some of them say, "We are essential; it was for our sake that the world was created." Others say, "No, for our sake." But Israel said, "Wait till God's day comes—then we shall know for whose sake the world was created." Thus it is written, "Behold, the day cometh, it burneth as a furnace" (Mal. 3:19), the day when "Thou shalt winnow them and the wind shall carry them off; the whirlwind shall scatter them" (Isa. 41:16). But Israel is told, "Thou shalt rejoice in the Lord, thou shalt glory in the Holy One of Israel" (ibid.).[11]

34. R. Hanina bar Papa—some say R. Simlai—commented: In the time-to-come, the Holy One will bring out a Torah scroll, hold it to His bosom, and say, "Whosoever

---

1. Exod. R. 21:1.
2. B. Git 57b.
3. The form *hen* is a demonstrative adverb less widely used than *hinneh*.
4. Thus the concluding part of Num. 23:9 is read not, "Shall not be reckoned among the nations," but, "The letters in its name will not be combined in the way letters in the names of other nations may be combined."
5. Exod. R. 15:7.
6. B. Sanh 39a.
7. JV: "The notable men of the first of the nations."
8. See Gen. 10:21.
9. Lev. R. 5:3; Num. R. 10:3.
10. Song R. 1:6, §3.
11. Gen. R. 83:5; Song R. 7:3, §3.

has occupied himself with a scroll such as this—let him come and get his reward." Immediately all the peoples of the world will gather together in an indiscriminate crowd, as is said, "All the nations gathered together indiscriminately," etc. (Isa. 43:9). Then the Holy One will say, "Come not before Me indiscriminately, but let each and every people come by itself with its own scribes." The empire of Rome will come before Him first. The Holy One will ask, "How have you occupied yourselves?" They will reply, "We set up many forums, built many baths, accumulated much silver and gold—and all this we did only for the sake of Israel, so that they might have the leisure to occupy themselves with Torah." The Holy One will reply, "More than anyone else in the world, you are given to deluding yourselves. In fact, whatever you did, you did only to serve your own needs. You set up forums to station harlots in, baths to pamper yourselves in. As for the silver and gold, it is Mine—'Mine is the silver, and Mine is the gold, saith the Lord of hosts' [Hag. 2:8]. Is there anyone among you who has been voicing 'This'? 'Who among them has ever voiced *This?*' [Isa. 43:9]. '*This*' means nothing other than Torah, as indicated in the verse '*This* is the Torah which Moses set before the children of Israel' " (Deut. 4:44).

Immediately those of Rome will leave, utterly thwarted.

After the empire of Rome leaves, the kingdom of Persia will step forward. The Holy One will ask, "How have you occupied yourselves?" They will reply, "Master of the universe, we built many bridges, conquered many capital cities, waged many wars, all of which we did only for the sake of Israel, so that they might have the leisure to occupy themselves with Torah." The Holy One will reply, "Whatever you did, you did only to serve your own needs. You built bridges to collect tolls on them; you took cities to impose forced labor upon them. As for wars, it is I who wage them—'The Lord is Master of war' [Exod. 15:3]. But is there anyone among you who voiced 'This'?"

Immediately they will leave, utterly thwarted. And the same will happen to each and every nation.

Then the peoples will speak up before Him, "Master of the universe, did you ever suspend a mountain over us like the vault You had to suspend over Israel,[1] and we then refused to accept 'This'?" The Holy One will answer them, " 'Let the first [Noachide] commandments tell us' [Isa. 43:9]: the seven commandments[2] you did accept—in what way did you bestir yourselves to keep them?" The peoples of the world will reply, "Master of the universe, in what way did Israel, who did accept the whole Torah, bestir themselves to keep it?" The Holy One will then say, "I bear witness concerning Israel, that they kept the Torah, all of it." The peoples will respond, "Master of the universe, may a father—You being the one who said, 'Israel is My son, My firstborn' [Exod. 4:22]—bear witness concerning his own son?" The Holy One: "Let heaven and earth testify concerning them, that they kept the Torah, all of it." The peoples: "Master of the universe, heaven and earth as witnesses have a selfish stake in Israel's continuance, for it is said, 'If not for My covenant, [Torah, which is to be studied day and night], I would not sustain the fixed ways of heaven and earth' " (Jer. 33:25). Then the Holy One will say, "Let individuals out of your midst come forward and testify in behalf of Israel that they kept the Torah, all of it. Let Nimrod come and testify in behalf of Abraham, that he refused to worship an idol. Let Laban come and testify in behalf of Jacob, that he could not be suspected of theft [Gen. 31:37]. Let Potiphar's wife come and testify in behalf of Joseph, that he could not be charged with unchastity. Let Nebuchadnezzar come and testify in behalf of Hananiah, Mishael, and Azariah, that they refused to prostrate themselves before an image. Let Darius come and testify in behalf of Daniel, that he did not neglect the daily prayers.[3] Let Bildad the Shuhite, Zophar the Naamathite, Eliphaz the Temanite, and Elihu the son of Barachel the Buzite come and testify in behalf of Israel, that they kept the Torah, all of it,[4] as is said, 'Let the peoples bring their own witnesses, that Israel may be justified' " (Isa. 43:9).

The peoples will then say, "Master of the universe, offer us the Torah anew, and we shall practice it." The Holy One will reply, "You are the biggest fools in the world! He who took the trouble to prepare on the eve of the Sabbath can eat on the Sabbath; but he who has not troubled himself on the eve of the Sabbath—where will he get food to eat on the Sabbath? Nevertheless, I have an easy commandment called [the commandment of the] sukkah—go and carry it out."

Each one of them will pick himself up and go to build his sukkah on his rooftop. But then the Holy One will cause the sun to blaze down on them as at the summer solstice,[5] and each one of them will kick his sukkah down and leave it, saying, "Let us break their bonds asunder, and cast away their cords from us" (Ps. 2:3).

Then the Holy One will sit and laugh at them, as is said, "He that sitteth in heaven laugheth" (Ps. 2:4).[6]

The Character of Israel

35. This people are said to be like dust[7] and said to be like stars.[8] When they go down, they go down to the very dust. When they reach up, they reach up to the stars.[9]

1. See above, part 1, chap. 4, §32.
2. To refrain from (1) idolatry, (2) blasphemy, (3) shedding blood, (4) unchastity, (5) seizing what belongs to another, (6) eating flesh cut from a living animal; and (7) to institute civil courts. In rabbinic thought, these are regarded as binding upon all mankind.
3. "His windows were open in his upper chamber toward Jerusalem and he kneeled upon his knees three times a day and prayed" (Dan. 6:11).
4. These four heard Job, a pious Gentile, blaspheme, thus proving that he was not equal to the test, as Jews are.
5. Literally, "the cycle of Tammuz," which lasts from June 21 to September 22.
6. B. AZ 2a–3b and En Yaakov, ad loc.; Yalkut, Isa., §43.
7. "Thy seed shall be as the dust of the earth" (Gen. 28:14).
8. "I will multiply thy seed as the stars of the heaven" (Gen. 22:17).
9. B. Meg 16a.

36. When Israel reach the lowest degradation, they are certain to go up again, as is intimated in the words "He will go up from the earth" (Exod. 1:10).[1]

37. Israel are said to be like sand. You dig a pit in sand in the evening, and in the morning you find that the pit has filled itself up. Likewise, the loss of all those hosts in the days of David was made up in the days of Solomon, as is said, "Judah and Israel increased as the sand which is by the sea in multitude" (1 Kings 4:20).

Another comment: Israel are said to be like sand and the peoples of the world like lime, as is said, "The peoples shall be as the burnings of lime" (Isa. 33:12). If sand is not put into lime, it lacks staying power. So too without Israel, the peoples would be unable to stand up. Thus, but for Joseph, Egypt would have perished during the famine; but for Daniel, the wise men of Babylon would have perished.[2]

38. Why did the Holy One choose to speak to Moses out of a thornbush? Because, so said R. Yohanan, just as one makes a fence for a garden out of thornbushes, so is Israel[3] a fence for the world.

Another answer: Just as thornbushes grow both in a garden patch and by a river, so Israel share both in this world and in the world-to-come. Another answer: Just as a thornbush grows thorns and roses, so in Israel there are both righteous and wicked.

R. Phinehas the Priest bar Hama said: Just as when a man puts his hand into a thornbush, he feels no pain at first, but when he pulls it out, his hand is lacerated,[4] so no one noticed Israel when they came into Egypt, but when they left, they left with signs, with wonders, and with warfare.[5]

39. "The righteous shall flourish like the palm tree" (Ps. 92:13). As no part of the palm tree is without worth—the dates for food, the branches to wave during *Hallel*,[6] the fronds to cover the sukkah, the bast to make rope, the leaves for sweeping, the planed boards for ceilings of houses, so there are none in Israel without worth. Some are versed in Scripture, others in Mishnah, some in Talmud, others in *Aggadah*, some in deeds of piety, still others in deeds of charity.

What is true of the palm and the cedar? Whoever climbs to their top and does not take care will fall down and die. So, too, whoever comes to attack Israel will take his comeuppance at their hands.[7]

40. "As an apple tree among the trees of the wood," etc. (Song 2:3). Why are Israel said to be like an apple tree? Because just as in an apple tree the fruit [buds] appear before the leaves, so Israel voiced, "We will do" before, "We will hear" (Exod. 24:7).[8]

41. "I went down into the garden of nuts" (Song 6:11).[9] The nut, if it falls into muck, may be picked up, wiped, rinsed, and washed. It is thus restored to its original condition and is fit to eat. So, too, with Israel: however much they may be soiled with iniquities during all the days of the year, when the Day of Atonement comes, it washes them clean.

Another comment. A nut tree may have Perekh[10] nuts, whose shells are soft; nuts whose shells are moderately hard; and nuts whose shells are very hard. The nut with a soft shell bursts open (*niphrakh*) of itself; the nut with a moderately hard shell will crack open when you strike it; and the nut with a hard shell is too hard to be cracked, so that you must strike it with a stone to shatter it, and even then you do not get much good out of it. So, too, Israel: there are some among them who do good of their own accord; there are others who, when you ask them for charity, will give at once; and there are those who will not give, even when pressed hard.

Another comment. Nuts cannot escape customs, because they make themselves heard and are thus recognized. So it is with Israel: wherever one of them goes, he cannot say that he is not a Jew, for he is recognized as such: "All that see them shall recognize them, that they are the seed which the Lord hath blessed" (Isa. 61:9).

Another comment. With nuts, if you take one out of a pile, all the others tumble down, rolling over one another. So it is with Israel: when one man is punished, all of them feel it.

Another comment. With all other fruits—whether dates, mulberries, or figs—it is possible to take some of a particular kind out of a sack, and the other fruit will not be disturbed. But with nuts, as soon as you reach in and take a few of them, all the others are in commotion. So it is with Israel: when one of them sins, all the others are disturbed. "When one man sins, You are wrathful with the whole community" (Num. 16:23).[11]

42. "To the garden of nut trees" (Song 6:11). R. Joshua ben Levi said: Israel is likened to a nut tree. Why? Because when a nut tree is pruned, it renews itself; and since it renews itself, the pruning is for its own good. [The nut tree is thus] like hair, which grows quickly after being shorn, or like nails, which grow again after being pared. So, too, whenever Israel allow themselves to be shorn of the fruit of their labor in this world in order to give freely to those who labor at Torah, they are being shorn for their own good.

R. Joshua of Sikhnin taught in the name of R. Levi:

1. Exod. R. 1:9.
2. See Dan. 3. PRKM 2:9; Num. R. 2:17.
3. Their Torah and their deeds.
4. Since the thorns bend downward, they grip the hand only when it is taken out.
5. Exod. R. 2:5.
6. Pss. 113–18, recited during the waving of the lulav cluster on Sukkot, the Feast of Tabernacles.
7. Gen. R. 41:1; Num. R. 3:1.
8. P. Shab 88a.
9. In Jewish commentary, the Song of Songs is interpreted as a dialogue between God and Israel. The nut, according to Philo, "signifies perfect virtue" (*The Life of Moses* 2.181 [ed. Colson 6:539]).
10. Nuts from Perekh, the modern Ferka near Samaria, were noted for their soft shells. See Or 3:7.
11. Song R. 6:11, §1; PR 11:2 (YJS 1:200–1).

All other kinds of saplings thrive if, when planted, their roots are covered with earth; but with roots uncovered, they do not thrive. The sapling of a nut tree, however, will not thrive if its roots are covered with earth at the time it is planted. The same is true of Israel: "He that covereth his transgressions shall not prosper" (Prov. 28:13).[1]

43. "Thy name is as oil poured forth" (Song 1:3). Just as oil is bitter at its beginning and sweet in the end, so, "though thy beginning was distressing, yet thy end shall greatly increase [in sweetness]" (Job 8:7).[2] Just as oil is improved only by crushing [the olives thoroughly], so are Israel brought to repent by being crushed in affliction. Just as oil will not mix with other liquids, so Israel will not mix with other nations of the world. Just as oil brings light to the world, so are Israel light to the world, for Scripture says, "Nations shall walk at thy light" (Isa. 60:3). Just as oil rises above all other liquids, so Israel rises above all other peoples, as Scripture says, "The Lord thy God will set thee on high above all the nations of the earth" (Deut. 28:1). Just as oil makes no noise when poured, so in this world Israel makes no noise.[3]

44. "As a lily among thorns" (Song 2:2). R. Avun said: The lily, when the sun's heat beats upon it, withers, but it blooms again when dew falls upon it. So Israel. As long as the shadow of Esau endures, Israel in this world appear—if one dare say such a thing—withered. But in the time-to-come, when the shadow of Esau will have disappeared, Israel will become moist and bloom again. Just as the lily will not cease to exist until its fragrance does, so will Israel not cease to exist unless their observance of precepts and doing of good deeds come to an end. Just as the lily is readily recognized among plants, so are Israel recognized among the peoples of the world, as is said, "All that see them shall recognize them" (Isa. 61:9).

R. Hanina son of R. Abba applied the verse to [oppression by] the kingdoms. Just as a lily among thorns, bending toward the south when the north wind blows, is pricked by thorns, and bending toward the north when the south wind blows, is pricked by thorns, yet its heart remains steadfastly turned upward; so, too, Israel: though produce tax is collected from them and forced labor imposed on them, their heart remains steadfastly directed toward their Father in heaven.

R. Aibu interpreted the verse as alluding to the redemption soon to come. When the lily is among thorns, it is difficult for its owner to pluck it. What does he do? He brings fire, burns everything around the lily, and then plucks it. So "the Lord hath commanded concerning Jacob, that they that are round about him should be his adversaries" (Lam. 1:17). Accordingly, when the time of redemption nears, what will the Holy One do? He will bring fire and burn all around Israel, as is said, "The peoples shall be as the burnings of lime" (Isa. 33:12). What is said about Israel? "The Lord shall lead him alone" (Deut. 32:12). Even as the lily is held ready for Sabbath and festivals, so are Israel held ready for the redemption soon to come.[4]

45. "Thou didst pluck up the vine [Israel] out of Egypt" (Ps. 80:9). The vine is not planted in stony ground, but first the ground is gone over and the stones removed; and only then is it planted. So, too, Israel: "Thou didst remove the nations and didst plant it" (ibid.). The more you clear away from under the vine, the better it becomes. So, too, Israel: "Thou didst clear it" (Ps. 80:10) of the thirty-one kings of Canaan, and after that, Israel "took deep root, and filled the Land" (ibid.). The vine is not planted haphazardly but is arranged in ordered rows. So, too, Israel are arranged under separate standards—"every man with his own standard, according to their emblems" (Num. 2:2). The vine is lower than all other trees, yet it is deferred to more than any other tree. So, too, Israel: they appear to be lowest in this world, but in the time-to-come they are destined to inherit from one end of the world to the other. A single bough may come forth the vine and spread its tendrils over many trees. So, too, Israel: one righteous man may come forth from them, and his influence will be felt from one end of the world to the other. The vine's leaves give shelter to clusters of grapes. So, too, Israel: the unlearned among them give shelter to students of Torah. Upon the vine are clusters large and small, the larger one appearing to be lower than its mate. So, too, Israel: he who surpasses his fellow in Torah holds himself to be lower than his fellow. Upon the vine are grapes as well as raisins. So, too, Israel: among them are masters of Scripture, masters of Mishnah, masters of Talmud, masters of *Aggadah*. The vine yields wine as well as vinegar, the one requiring a benediction and the other requiring a benediction. So, too, Israel are required to utter a benediction for good as well as for evil. The vine's fruit is first trodden underfoot but in the end ascends to the table of kings. So, too, Israel: they appear to be contemned in this world, as is said, "I am become a laughingstock to all peoples, the butt of their jibes all day long" (Lam. 3:14); yet in the time-to-come "the Lord thy God will set thee on high" (Deut. 28:1) and "kings shall be thy foster fathers" (Isa. 49:23). When a man drinks wine from the vine, his countenance brightens. [So, too, "a man's wisdom maketh his face to shine" (Eccles. 8:1) when he is asked a question and is able to answer.] When a man attacks the vine's unripe fruit, his teeth are set on edge. So, too, Israel: he who attacks them in battle will receive his due at their hands. Because the vine is propped up by dried sticks of [dead] wood, it remains moist and alive. So, too, Israel: only because [they are propped up] by the merit of their [dead] fathers do they remain alive. The vine's keeper stands above it and watches over it. So, too, Israel: their Keeper stands above them and watches over them, as is said, "Behold, He that keepeth Israel doth neither slumber nor sleep" (Ps. 121:4).[5]

---

1. Song R. 6:11, §7.
2. The study of Torah, difficult at the beginning, becomes pleasant in the end. JV: "Though thy beginning was small, yet thy end shall greatly increase." But *mitz'ar* ("small") may be associated with *tz'r* ("to distress").
3. Song R. 1:3, §2.
4. Song R. 2:2, §5–6; Lev. R. 23:6.
5. Lev. R. 36:2; Exod. R. 44:1; Yalkut, Ps., §829; Midrash Sam. 16.

46. R. Simeon ben Lakish said: This people is like a vine: its branches are the householders; its clusters, the sages; its leaves, the unlearned; its twigs, those in Israel devoid of learning as well as of good deeds. The importance of their being together was implied in the message sent [to Babylonia] from the Land of Israel: Let the clusters pray for the leaves—if not for the leaves, the clusters could not exist.[1]

47. [With the nations of the world in mind], R. Eliezer the Elder said: Since the House of Israel is the Holy One's vineyard, do not peek into it. But if you should peek into it, do not enter it. If you should enter it, do not breathe in its fragrance. If you should breathe in its fragrance, do not eat of its fruit. Now, if you do peek into it, enter it, breathe in its fragrance, and eat of its fruit, the end of such as you is that you will be rooted out of the world.[2]

48. "Thine eyes are doves" (Song 1:15). As a dove is artless, so were Israel artless with the Holy One at Sinai, for they did not say, "Ten commandments are enough, or twenty, or thirty," but, "All that the Lord hath spoken, we will do and obey" (Exod. 24:7). As a dove is distinguished [by its cooing], so are Israel distinguished by their deeds. As a dove is chaste, so are Israel chaste. As a dove is graceful when it moves, so are Israel when they move as pilgrims for the festivals. The dove will not leave its cote even when a man takes its young from it; so Israel continue to go up to Jerusalem even though the Temple is destroyed. As the dove goes away but comes back, so Israel: "They shall come trembling as a bird out of Egypt, and as a dove out of the land of Assyria" (Hos. 11:11). As a dove brings others with her, so proselytes are brought along with Israel. As a dove stretches out her neck for slaughter and does not struggle as other birds do, so Israel offer up their lives for the Holy One. As a dove does not desert its mate, so Israel do not desert the Holy One. As a dove brought as an offering atones for iniquities, so Israel atone for the nations.[3]

49. "Oh My dove, that art in the clefts of the rock" (Song 2:14). Scripture does not say, "O dove," but, "O My dove," implying that the Holy One said: To Me they are as innocent as a dove, although to the nations they may seem as wily as serpents.[4]

50. "He made thee and wound thee" (Deut. 32:6).[5] R. Meir used to say: Israel is a roll in which all kinds of people are wound—its priests are within it, its prophets within it, its scribes within it, as intimated in the verse "Within it are cornerstones, within it are tent pegs" (Zech. 10:4).[6]

1. B. Hul 92a and En Yaakov, ad loc.
2. TdE, ed. Friedmann, p. 43 (JPS, p. 141).
3. Song R. 1:15, §2; Yalkut, Song, §985.
4. BhM 5.
5. JV: "Hath He not made thee and established thee?" But *knn* ("to establish") may also mean "to wind."
6. Sif Deut., §309.

51. Let Israel be; [they will know what to do]. For if they are not prophets, they are sons of prophets.[7]

Israel's Afflictions

52. "Behold, Thou art fair, my Beloved, pleasing even in wrath" (Song 1:16).[8] [The congregation of Israel] said: Master of the universe, the wrath You bring upon me is pleasing. Why? Because You thus restore me to Yourself, bringing me back to the right way.[9]

53. R. Yohanan said: Why is Israel said to be like the olive? Because as the olive will not yield its oil unless it is crushed, so Israel do not return to the right way unless they are crushed by affliction.[10]

54. "A leafy olive tree, fair with goodly fruit" (Jer. 11:16). Olives, while still on the tree, are marked for shriveling, after which they are knocked down and brought up to a roof, where they are left to dry;[11] then they are placed in a grinding mill, where they are ground; their pulp is then tied up in a hempen bale, upon which heavy stones are placed. Only after all of that do olives yield their oil. So, too, Israel. The nations of the earth knock them down, drive them from place to place, imprison them, put chains around their necks, and post soldiers all around them. Only then do Israel resolve on repentance, and the Holy One responds to them.[12]

55. R. Abba bar Kahana said: Ahasuerus's removal of his signet ring [and his giving it to Haman] was more effective than the forty-eight prophets and seven prophetesses who prophesied to Israel. All of these were unable to bring Israel back to the right way. But Ahasuerus's removal of his signet ring brought them back right away.[13]

56. R. Eleazar said: Calamity comes to the world only because of Israel, for it is said, "I wiped out nations; their corner towers are desolate. . . . And I thought that she would fear Me, would learn a lesson" (Zeph. 3:6).[14]

57. [The prophet] Elijah said to Ben He He (some say to R. Eleazar): The verse "Behold, I refine you, but not as silver; I test you in the furnace of poverty" (Isa. 48:10) implies that, among all the good states of being that the Holy One scrutinized to give to Israel, He found none better than poverty.[15]

7. B. Pes 66b and En Yaakov, ad loc.
8. JV: "Behold, thou art fair, my beloved, yea, pleasant." But *af* ("yea") also means "anger, wrath."
9. Song R. 1:16, §1.
10. B. Men 53b and En Yaakov, ad loc.
11. The passage "Olives while the tree . . . left to dry" represents the text as emended by A. A. Ha-Levi on the basis of the Oxford manuscript and the first edition of Exod R. See his edition of Shemot R. (Tel Aviv, 1959), p. 475.
12. Exod. R. 36:1.
13. The dread of Haman made them turn to God. B. Meg 14a.
14. B. Yev 63a.
15. B. Hag 9b.

58. R. Akiva said: Poverty is as becoming to the daughter of Jacob as a red ribbon on the neck of a white horse.[1]

59. R. Aha said: Carobs [are poor men's fare, and poor fare] is what Israel require to put them on the road to repentance.[2]

60. "Thy desolation is comely" (Song 4:3).[3] According to R. Levi, the Holy One said: In its state of desolation, Israel raised up righteous men for Me, but when it was in its state of prosperity, it raised up wicked men for Me. In its state of desolation, it raised up righteous men for Me—Daniel and his associates, Mordecai and his associates, Ezra and his associates. But in its state of prosperity, it raised up wicked men for Me—men such as Ahaz and his associates, Manasseh and his associates, Amon and his band. Beside R. Levi's comment, R. Avin bar Kahana, citing R. Yohanan, used to quote the verse "Far more are the children of the desolate than the children of the married wife" (Isa. 54:1).[4]

61. "Surely he that toucheth you toucheth the apple of His eye" (Zech. 2:12). R. Simeon ben Eleazar said: No part of the body is more precious than the eye: when a man is struck on the head, he closes only his eyes. Thus you can see that no part of the body is more precious than the eye, and it is to God's eye that Scripture likens Israel.[5]

62. "He hath burned in Jacob like a flaming fire, which then devoured round about" (Lam. 2:3). R. Simeon ben Lakish said: When calamity comes to the world, the first to feel it is Jacob. And the proof? "He hath burned in Jacob . . . a fire." And when boons come to the world, the first to feel them is Jacob, as is said, "Let Jacob rejoice, let Israel be glad" (Ps. 14:7).[6]

63. R. Simeon ben Lakish said: The Holy One does not smite Israel unless He creates healing for them beforehand, as is said, "When I would heal Israel" (Hos. 7:1), and only after that "does the punishment of Ephraim reveal itself" (ibid.). Not so with other nations. First He smites them, and then He creates a healing for them, as is said, "The Lord will smite Egypt, smiting and healing" (Isa. 19:22)—first "smiting" and then "healing."[7]

The Characteristics of Israel

64. R. Ishmael said: The children of Israel—may I be an atonement for them—are like boxwood, neither black nor white but of an intermediate shade.[8]

65. This people is distinguished by three characteristics: they are merciful, modest, and benevolent. He who has these three characteristics is fit to join this people. He who does not have these three characteristics is not fit to join them.[9]

66. R. Abba bar Aha said: It is difficult to fathom the character of this people: when asked to contribute to making the [golden] calf, they respond; when asked to contribute to building the Tabernacle, they respond![10]

Transgressors in Israel

67. We have been taught: "Ye are sons of the Lord your God" (Deut. 14:1). When you conduct yourselves like sons, you are called sons. When you do not conduct yourselves like sons, you will not be called sons. Such is the opinion of R. Judah. But R. Meir said: The verse means that in either event you are called sons, for elsewhere it is said, "They are sottish sons" (Jer. 4:22), and, "They are sons in whom is no faith" (Deut. 32:20), and, "A seed of evildoers, sons that deal corruptly" (Isa. 1:4).[11]

68. "Their baseness has played Him false—still, despite their blemishes, His sons" (Deut. 32:5).[12] Though full of blemishes, said R. Meir, they are still His sons. For R. Meir used to say: If they are still called sons when full of blemishes, how much and more so when they have no blemishes. The same inference may be drawn from "A seed of evildoers, sons that deal corruptly" (Isa. 1:4): if they are called "sons" when they deal corruptly, how much and more so when they do not deal corruptly.[13]

69. "Thy temples (*rakkatekh*) are like a pomegranate" (Song 6:7). R. Simeon ben Lakish said: Read not *rakkatekh*, but *rekatekh*, "thine empty ones," signifying that even those among you who are "empty" are nevertheless as full of good deeds as [there are seeds] in a pomegranate.[14]

70. "Israel hath sinned" (Josh. 7:11). R. Abba bar Zavda said: Even though they sinned, they are still called Israel. R. Abba commented: Hence people say: Though a myrtle stands among thorns, its name is still myrtle, and people call it myrtle.[15]

71. A certain heretic said to R. Hanina: You are surely unclean, for Scripture says, "Her filthiness was in her skirts" (Lam. 1:9). R. Hanina replied: Look what else it says of them: "That dwelleth with them in the midst of their uncleanness" (Lev. 16:16), that is, the Presence dwells among them even at the time they are unclean.[16]

---

1. Lev. R. 35:5; Yalkut, Isa., §389.
2. PRKM 14:3 (PRKS, p. 268).
3. *Midbar* may mean "mouth, speech" or "wilderness, ruin."
4. Song R. 4:4, §9.
5. Sif Num., §84.
6. The repetition of the terms for "joy" is taken to imply that Israel will be first to feel it. Lam. R. 2:3, §7.
7. B. Meg 13b and En Yaakov, ad loc.
8. Neg 2:1.
9. B. Yev 79a and En Yaakov, ad loc.
10. Shek 2b and En Yaakov, ad loc.
11. B. Kid 36a.
12. JV: "Is corruption His? No, His children's is the blemish."
13. Sif Deut., §308.
14. B. Er 19a.
15. B. Sanh 44a.
16. B. Yoma 56b–57a.

72. "We are the people of His pasture, and the sheep of His hand" (Ps. 95:7). When are we His people? When we are the sheep of His pasture, as is said, "When ye are My sheep, ye are the sheep of My pasture" (Ezek. 34:31). But when we are lions, God hates us, as is said, "My heritage is unto Me as a lion in the forest. . . . Therefore have I hated her" (Jer. 12:8).[1]

73. When Israel repose trustfully in the shadow of their Creator, they bestow blessing—since they are kind and loving, there is benefit for the world from them. But when they turn away from their Creator, they bestow curses—since they are malevolent and bitter, there is no benefit for the world from them.[2]

74. When the congregation of Israel will stand for judgment before Him who is everywhere and say: Master of the universe, I know not who sinned against whom and who changed toward the other—whether Israel did in fact sin against Him who is everywhere or whether He who is everywhere changed toward them—toward Israel. But since Scripture says, "The heavens declare His righteousness" (Ps. 50:6), one must assume that Israel had sinned against the Holy One and that the Holy One had not changed toward Israel, as is said, "For I the Lord change not" (Mal. 3:6).[3]

75. "Give ear, ye heavens, and I will speak; and let the earth hear the words of my mouth" (Deut. 32:1). Moses asked two witnesses [heaven and earth] who endure forever and ever to be ready to testify against Israel, saying to them, "I am flesh and blood—soon I will die. Should Israel wish to say, 'We did not receive the Torah,' who will come forward to contradict them?" Therefore he called two witnesses who endure forever and ever to be ready to testify against them. And the Holy One called the song to be ready to testify against them, saying, "That this song may be a witness for Me against the children of Israel" (Deut. 31:19). God said: The song will bear witness against them on earth below, and I in heaven above.[4]

76. "A foolish people, and not wise" (Deut. 32:6)—a people foolish with regard to past [boons], and unwise in [not mending its ways] for the future.[5]

77. "They are Thy people, and Thine inheritance" (Deut. 9:29). In the name of R. Levi, R. Berekhiah told the parable of a king who had a vineyard that he turned over to a tenant. When the vineyard produced good wine, the king used to say, "How good is the wine of my vineyard!" When it produced bad wine, he used to say, "How bad is my tenant's wine!" So the tenant said to him, "My lord king, when the vineyard produces good wine, you say it is yours, but when it produces bad wine, you say it is mine. Yet good or bad, the wine is still yours." Likewise, the Holy One first said to Moses, "Come now . . . that thou mayest bring forth My people" (Exod. 3:10). But after Israel did that deed of theirs [the golden calf], what did He say? "Go, get thee down, for thy people . . . have dealt corruptly" (Exod. 32:7). Then Moses replied to the Holy One, "When they sin You say they are mine, and only when they are free from sin do You say they are Yours. Yet sinful or sinless, they are still Yours—'They are Thy people, and Thine inheritance' " (Deut. 9:29).[6]

78. R. Eleazar said: Moses spoke reproachfully to Him above, for it is said, "Moses prayed unto the Lord" (Num. 11:2). Read not *el*, "unto the Lord," but *al*, "against the Lord."

The school of R. Yannai drew the same inference from "And Di-zahav" (Deut. 1:11): What can the place-name Di-zahav suggest but that Moses spoke reproachfully to the Holy One: Master of the universe, it is the silver and gold (*zahav*) You lavished upon Israel until they had to say "Enough (*dai*)!" that is what led to their making the golden calf. For, so the school of Yannai continued, a lion does not get excited over a heap of straw but goes wild in his delight over a heap of flesh.

[To illustrate Moses' reproach], R. Oshaia told a parable: A man had a heifer who was lean but of large build [so that its appetite was huge]. When he fed it tasty vetches, the heifer [in its delight inadvertently] kicked him. So the man said: What led you to kick me, unless it was the tasty vetches I myself fed you?[7]

[To illustrate Moses' reproach], R. Hiyya bar Abba, citing R. Yohanan, told another parable: A man had a son, whom he bathed and anointed. He gave him food and drink, but then hung a purse around his neck and seated him at the entrance to a brothel. What was that son to do but sin? As R. Aha the son of Ravina said in the name of R. Sheshet, the above bears out the proverb "A full belly leads to rebellious deeds." Thus Scripture: "When they were fed, they became full, they were filled, and their heart was exalted; therefore have they forgotten Me" (Hos. 13:6). Or, according to R. Nahman: "Then thy heart be lifted up and thou forget the Lord" (Deut. 8:14). Or, according to the sages: "They shall have eaten their fill, and waxen fat, and turned unto other gods" (Deut. 31:20). Or, if you prefer, derive the proverb from "But Jeshurun waxed fat and kicked" (Deut. 32:15).

R. Samuel bar Nahmani taught: How do we know that in the end the Holy One, reversing himself, admitted to Moses that He was wrong? Because God said, "I . . . multiplied unto her silver and gold, which [I should have known] they would use for Baal" (Hos. 2:10).[8]

79. When the Holy One said to Hosea, "Your children sinned," Hosea should have replied, "They are Your children, children of those You greatly loved, children of Abraham, Isaac, and Jacob. Let the measure of Your mercy roll gently over them." Not only did Hosea not speak

---

1. MTeh 95:2.
2. PRE 9.
3. Sif Deut., §306; Yalkut, Mal., §589.
4. Sif Deut., §306.
5. Ibid.
6. Yalkut, *Ki Tissa*, §391, based on PRKM 16:9.
7. Vetches are so tasty that human beings ate them in emergencies.
8. B. Ber 32a; Yalkut, *Devarim*, §792.

in this way, but he actually dared say to God, "Master of the universe, all the world is Yours [to do with as You like]. Put another people in their place."

The Holy One said: What shall I do with this so-called sage? I will tell him, "Take yourself a whoring wife, who will bear you children of whoredom." Later I will tell him, "Send her away from you." If he is able to do so, I, too, will send Israel away [from Me]. So Hosea went and took Gomer the daughter of Diblaim [a woman of ill repute]. After two sons and a daughter were born to him, the Holy One said to Hosea, "Should you not follow the example of your teacher Moses, who separated from his wife as soon as I began speaking to him? You too should live apart from yours." Hosea replied, "Master of the universe, I have children by her—I cannot send her away or divorce her." The Holy One: "You—whose wife is a whore and whose children are children of whoredom, so that you do not know whether your children were fathered by you or by others—still reply in this way. Yet you dare say of Israel who are My children, children of those tested by Me, children of Abraham, Isaac, and Jacob, Israel who are one of the four masterpieces—Torah, heaven and earth, the Temple, and Israel—I wrought in My world, yet you dare say of them, 'Put another people in their place!' " Thus made aware that he had sinned, Hosea started to beseech mercy for himself. But the Holy One rebuked him: "Before beseeching mercy for yourself, beseech mercy for Israel."[1]

80. R. Hana bar Bizna said in the name of R. Simeon the Pious: A fast in which transgressors of Israel do not participate is no fast. For consider: though the odor of galbanum is vile, yet it is included among the ingredients for the incense.[2]

81. R. Joshua ben Levi contrasted two verses, one saying, "Ye have not followed the norms of the nations that were round about you" (Ezek. 5:7),[3] while the other asserts, "Ye have followed the norms of the nations that were round about you" (Ezek. 11:2). The right norms that were theirs you did not adopt, while the wrong ones you did.[4]

82. "Then flew unto me one of the seraphim, with a glowing stone (*rtzph*) in his hand" (Isa. 6:6). The usual word for "glowing coal," *ghlt*, is not used here; the word *rtzph*, "glowing stone," is used instead. What is intimated by the word *rtzph?* R. Samuel bar Nahman explained *rtzph* as signifying "Silence (*rtz*)[5] the mouth (*ph*) of him who denounces My children."[6]

83. R. Abbahu and R. Simeon ben Lakish were about to enter the notorious city of Caesarea when R. Abbahu said to R. Simeon ben Lakish, "What business do we have entering a city filled with blasphemers and revilers?" R. Simeon ben Lakish got off his donkey, scraped up some sand, and stuffed it into R. Abbahu's mouth. R. Abbahu: "What is the meaning of this?" R. Simeon: "God is displeased with him who denounces Israel. For Israel pleads, 'Regard me not as one swarthy' [Song 1:6], and Scripture enjoins, 'Slander not a servant unto his Master' " (Prov. 30:10).[7]

84. "In the womb he attacked his brother at the heel" (Hos. 12:4). The verse will be understood by the parable of a widow who was about to bring charges against her son before a judge. But when she saw the judge sitting in judgment and sentencing people to be punished with fire, with pitch, and with whips, she said: If I denounce the misconduct of my son to the judge, he may even sentence him to death. So she waited until the judge finished trying the cases before him. After he had done so, he asked her: This son of yours—how did he offend against you? She replied: My lord, he kicked me when he was in my womb. He asked her: Has he done anything to you since? She replied: No. He said to her: Go your way. There is no offense in what he did.[8]

Israel—One Cluster

85. Of the four plants that make up the lulav cluster, two bear fruit and two do not. The ones that bear fruit must be combined with those that do not bear fruit; and the ones that do not bear fruit must be combined with those that bear fruit. And a man does not fulfill his obligation until the four plants are bound together in one cluster. And so it is with Israel's endeavor to conciliate God, which is successful only when all of Israel are together in one cluster, as is said, "He buildeth his upper chambers in the heaven and establisheth [Israel] on the earth when it is together in one cluster" (Amos. 9:6).[9]

86. "The fruit of goodly trees" (Lev. 23:40), the etrog symbolizes [a type of man in] Israel: even as the etrog tree has edible fruit and fragrance, so Israel have men in their midst who have knowledge of Torah and the fragrance of good deeds. "Branches of palm trees" (ibid.) also symbolize [a type of man in] Israel: as the palm tree has edible fruit but no fragrance, so Israel have men in their midst who have knowledge of Torah but not the fragrance of good deeds. "And branches of a tree screened by its network of foliage" (ibid.) also symbolize [a type of man in] Israel: as the myrtle tree has fragrance but does not bear edible fruit, so Israel have men in their midst who have the fragrance of good deeds but do not have Torah. "And willows of the brook" (ibid.) also symbolize [a type of man in] Israel: even as the willow has neither edible fruit nor fragrance, so Israel have men in their midst who have

1. B. Pes 87b and En Yaakov, ad loc.; Yalkut, Hos., §515.
2. See Exod. 30:34. B. Ker 6b.
3. What, for example, Eglon king of Moab did. Upon being told, "I have a message from God unto thee" (Judg. 3:20), he at once rose up in respect.
4. In sacrificing human beings, as was the usage of another king of Moab (2 Kings 3:27). B. Sanh 39b.
5. Literally, "break" or "smash." Cf. Rashi on Isa. 6:6.
6. PR 33:3; Song R. 1:6, §1.
7. Song R. 1:6, §1; Yalkut, 1 Kings, §218.
8. Lev. R. 27:6.
9. JV: "He buildeth . . . And hath founded His vault upon the earth." The word *aguddah* can mean "vault" or "cluster." B. Men 27a.

neither knowledge of Torah nor the fragrance of good deeds. What does the Holy One do with the last? To destroy them is out of the question. So the Holy One says: Let all of them be joined together in one cluster, and the ones will atone for the others. If you are willing to act in this way, I will be exalted. With reference to such a cluster, Scripture says, "He buildeth His upper chambers in the heaven" (Amos 9:6). When is He thus exalted? When Israel are joined together in one cluster, as the verse goes on to say: "When [Israel] on earth is established as His cluster" (ibid.).[1]

87. "Ye are standing this day erect all of you" (Deut. 29:9). When are you described as "standing erect"? As on this day when "all of you" are joined together in one cluster.

"When His cluster [is one], He will establish it upon the Land" (Amos 9:6).[2] In the nature of things, when a man picks up a cluster of reeds, can he possibly break them at one time? But if picked up one by one, then even a child can break them. Thus you find that Israel cannot be redeemed until they are one cluster, as is said, "In those days the house of Judah shall walk with the House of Israel, and together [in one cluster] they shall come out of the land of the north" (Jer. 3:18).[3]

88. "And He was acclaimed Sovereign over Jeshurun" (Deut. 33:5). When Israel are unanimous in counsel below, His great Name is acclaimed above. For the words "And He was acclaimed Sovereign over Israel" imply that it is so when, as the verse goes on to say, "the heads of the people are gathered, all the tribes of Israel together" (ibid.)—when they are together in one [large] cluster, not when they are made up of many [small] clusters.[4]

89. As long as Israel are joined together in one cluster on the earth below, the kingdom of Heaven—if one dare speak thus—is in its place.[5]

90. "He buildeth firmly His upper chambers in the heaven, after He hath set up His cluster on earth" (Amos 9:6). The verse may be explained by the parable of a palace built on pontoons. As long as the pontoons are joined together, the palace on them stands firm. Likewise—if one dare speak thus—His throne stands firm above when Israel are joined in one cluster [below].[6]

91. "Mine eye shall weep sore, and run down with tears, because the Lord's flock is carried away captive" (Jer. 13:17). You find that before Israel were exiled, they were divided into several flocks—flocks of priests apart, flocks of Levites apart, flocks of Israelites apart. But when they were exiled, they became one flock: "The Lord's flock is carried away captive." Scripture does not say, "The Lord's flocks are carried away captive," but, "The Lord's flock is carried away captive."[7]

92. "They shall stumble one because of another" (Lev. 26:37)—one because of the iniquity of another. The verse teaches that all Israel are responsible for one another.[8]

93. All Israel are responsible for one another. With what may this responsibility be compared? With a ship in which one compartment has split apart. Of something like this, it is not said, "A compartment in the ship has split apart." What people say is, "The entire ship—the whole thing—split apart."[9]

94. Hezekiah taught: "Israel are scattered sheep" (Jer. 50:17). What is true of a sheep? When it is smitten in one of its limbs, all the other limbs feel it.[10] So it is with Israel: when one of them sins, all the others feel it.

"When one man sins, Thou art wroth with all the congregation" (Num. 16:22).[11] R. Simeon ben Yohai taught: The verse may be illustrated by the parable of men on a ship, one of whom took a drill and began to drill [a hole] under his own seat. When his companions asked him, "Why are you doing this?" he replied, "Why should it bother you? Am I not drilling only under my own seat?" His companions: "But the water will rise up and flood the ship for all of us."[12]

The Enemies and Friends of Israel

95. R. Samuel bar Nahmani said in the name of R. Jonathan: What is signified by the verse "Faithful are the wounds of a friend; but the kisses of an enemy are importunate" (Prov. 27:6)? Better was the curse that Ahijah the Shilonite uttered against Israel than the blessing the wicked Balaam bestowed upon them. Ahijah the Shilonite cursed them by likening them to a reed. He said to Israel, "The Lord will strike Israel until it sways like a reed in water" (1 Kings 14:15). What is true of a reed? Because a reed grows in a well-watered area, its stock keeps driving up new shoots; and because its roots are many, even if all the winds of the world come and blow at it, they cannot move it from its place, for it sways to and fro with them. When the winds have subsided, the reed resumes its erect stance. But the wicked Balaam blessed them by comparing them to a cedar, saying of Israel, "As cedars" (Num. 24:6). What is true of a cedar? Because it does not grow in a well-watered area, its stock does not drive up new shoots and its roots are few. Still, even if all the winds of the world come and blow at it, they cannot move it from its

1. Lev. R. 30:12; Yalkut, *Emor*, §651.
2. JV: "And hath founded His vault upon the earth." But *aguddato* ("His vault") also means "His cluster"; and *eretz* ("earth") also means "the Land of Israel."
3. Tanhuma B, *Nitzavim* §4; Yalkut, *Nitzavim*, §440.
4. Sif Deut., §346.
5. Midrash Sam. 5.
6. Num. R. 15:18.
7. Lam. R., proem 25.
8. B. Shevu 39a.
9. TdE, ed. Friedmann, p. 56.
10. True of all animals, but more so of a sheep because of its small size.
11. In JV, the sentence is interrogative.
12. Lev. R. 4:6; Yalkut, Jer., §334.

place. If, however, the south wind blows at the cedar, it uproots it at once and lays it flat on its face.

What's more, [because it yields so readily], the reed has the privilege of being used for pens with which to write the books of Torah, Prophets, and Writings.[1]

96. "These are the rebukes" (Deut. 1:1). R. Aha son of R. Hanina said: The rebukes should have been uttered by Balaam and the blessings by Moses. But had Balaam uttered the rebukes, Israel would have said, "An enemy rebukes us. [So what?]" Had Moses blessed them, the nations of the world would have said, "A friend blesses them. [So what?]" Therefore the Holy One declared: Let Moses, who loves them, rebuke them, and let Balaam, who hates them, bless them, so that the genuineness of the blessings and of the rebukes bestowed upon Israel will be made clear.[2]

97. When a heathen met R. Ishmael and greeted him with a blessing, R. Ishmael replied: The response to you has already been spoken. When another heathen met him and cursed him, he again replied: The response to you has already been spoken. His disciples wondered: Master, you replied to the second as you did to the first! R. Ishmael: But it has been spoken! "Cursed by everyone that curseth thee, and blessed by everyone that blesseth thee" (Gen. 27:29).[3]

98. "Ah, the uproar of many peoples, that roar like the roaring of the seas" (Isa. 17:12). Israel is said to be like sand (Hos. 2:1) and the nations like the sea. They take counsel against Israel, but the Holy One depletes their strength.

Isaiah said, "The wicked are like the troubled sea" (Isa. 57:20), in which the first wave says, "I now rise up and will flood the entire world." But when it reaches the sand, it bows before it and is shattered. Should not the second wave have learned from the first? To illustrate: Pharaoh came and vaunted himself over Israel. So the Holy One hurled him down, as is said, "He . . . hurled Pharaoh and his host down into the sea" (Ps. 136:15). Should not Amalek have learned from Pharaoh? Yet "then came Amalek" (Exod. 17:8), but "Joshua discomfited Amalek" (Exod. 17:13). Should not Sihon and Og have learned from Amalek? Still "Sihon . . . went out against Israel" (Num. 21:23), and "Og . . . went out against them" (Num. 21:33). Balak, likewise. Should he not have learned from Sihon and Og? Yet Balak was determined to wage war against Israel, and so he sent for Balaam to come and curse Israel.[4]

99. "The sons of Japheth . . . Dodanim" (Gen. 10:2, 4). This verse calls them Dodanim, but another verse elsewhere calls them Rodanim (1 Chron. 1:7). R. Simon and R. Hanin differ in their explanations. R. Simon: They are called Dodanim because they are Israel's kinsmen (*dodim*) and called Rodanim because they keep coming to persecute (*rodim*) them. R. Hanina: When Israel are on the rise, they say; We are your kinsmen; but when Israel are in decline, they come and persecute them.[5]

100. "Jacob arrived in peace" (Gen. 33:18). "A Song of Ascents. 'Much have they attacked me from my youth up,' Israel kept saying" (Ps. 129:1). The Holy One asked Israel (Jacob), "But have they prevailed against you?" And he answered, "Indeed, they have not prevailed against me" (Ps. 129:2)—[I, Jacob, have arrived in peace].[6]

Constellations Have No Power over Israel

101. Our masters taught: When the sun is in eclipse, it is a bad sign for the entire world, all of it. By what parable may the matter be illustrated? By the one of a king of flesh and blood who made a feast for his servants and placed a lamp before them. But then he became angry at them, so he told one of his servants, "Take away the lamp from them and let them sit in the dark." But we are told, R. Meir said: When the luminaries are in eclipse, it is a bad sign for Israel—may such fate befall its enemies—accustomed as Israel are to being scourged. Thus, when a teacher comes with a strap in his hand, who is the one who worries? He who is accustomed to be whipped day after day is the one who worries.

On the contrary, when Israel obey the will of Him who is everywhere, they do not fear any such signs, as is said, "Learn not the way of the nations, and you will not be dismayed at the signs of heaven; for only the nations are dismayed at them" (Jer. 10:2). The nations are dismayed, but Israel will not be dismayed."[7]

102. "And He had him go forth beyond" (Gen. 15:5). When Abraham spoke up to God, "Master of the universe, I looked in the sign of the zodiac that guides my destiny and [found] I am not destined to have a son," the Holy One replied, "Go forth beyond what you see in the stars—no sign of the zodiac has power over Israel."[8]

103. No sign of the zodiac has power over Israel.

In the days of Jeremiah, Israel were willing to subject themselves to the power of the zodiac, but the Holy One did not let them, for He said, "Learn not the ways of the nations, and be not dismayed at the signs of heaven, for only the nations are dismayed at them" (Jer. 10:2). Long ago, your father Abraham was willing to subject himself to such power, but I did not let him. Abraham said, "Behold, to me Thou wilt give no seed" (Gen. 15:3), since my zodiac sign discourages me, saying, "Abram, you are not to beget." At once God "had him come forth beyond" (Gen. 15:5), which means that the Holy One showed him

1. B. Ta 20a.
2. Deut. R. 1:4.
3. P. Ber 8:9, 12c.
4. Tanhuma, *Va-yikra*, §12; Yalkut, *Balak*, §765.
5. Gen. R. 37:1.
6. Gen. R. 79:2.
7. B. Suk 29a and En Yaakov, ad loc.
8. B. Ned 32a.

the paths of heaven [beyond the stars] and said, "Go beyond stargazing. You are a prophet, not an astrologer."

In the name of R. Yohanan, it was said: The Holy One had Abraham go up above the vault of the firmament. Such is the implication of "Look now toward heaven" (Gen. 15:5)—the word "look" (*habbet*) means looking down from above to below. The Holy One went on, "He who is placed below the stars is afraid of them. But you who are placed beyond them—hold your head high at the sight of them."[1]

104. A story: R. Yannai and R. Yohanan were seated at the gate of Tiberias where there were two astrologers. When they saw two Jews go forth to their work, the two stargazers said: These two men will go forth but not come back, for a serpent will sting them. R. Yannai and R. Yohanan overheard these words. What did they do? They remained at the entrance to the city to find out whether the two men who went forth to their work would come back. They did in fact come back, and when R. Yannai and R. Yohanan saw them, they said to the astrologers: Did you not say that these two men would go forth and not come back, because a snake would sting them? The astrologers: Yes. The sages: But they went forth in peace and came back in peace. The astrologers kept looking at the two men and finally asked: What in particular did you do today? The two men: We did nothing other than what we are accustomed to do—we read the Shema and prayed. The astrologers: Oh, you are Jews? Astrologers' predictions are not fulfilled in people such as you, who are Jews. For "to you the Lord your God has not assigned the like" (Deut. 18:14).[2]

Israel Endure Forever

105. R. Simeon ben Yohai said: It is written, "As the days of a tree shall be the days of My people" (Isa. 65:22), and here "tree" can only mean Torah, of which it is said, "She is a tree of life to them that lay hold upon her" (Prov. 3:18). Who was created for the sake of whom? Torah for the sake of Israel, or Israel for the sake of Torah? Was it not Torah that was created for the sake of Israel? Now, if Torah, which was created for the sake of Israel, will endure forever and ever, all the more so Israel, who were created for their own sake.[3]

106. R. Joshua ben Levi said: Scripture says, "I have spread you abroad as the four winds of heaven, saith the Lord" (Zech. 2:10). As the world cannot endure without winds, so the world cannot endure without Israel.[4]

107. R. Berekhiah said: The congregation of Israel requested something not suitable for her, but the Holy One responded by giving her something suitable. She asked, "Let us know, eagerly strive to know the Lord . . . and He shall come unto us as the rain" (Hos. 6:3). The Holy One responded: My daughter, you ask for something [rain] that is desired at times and not desired at other times. But I will be something for you that is desired at all times: "I will be as the dew unto Israel" (Hos. 14:6).

On another occasion the congregation of Israel asked for something not suitable for her, when she said to Him: Master of the universe, "set me as a seal upon Thy heart, as a seal upon Thine arm" (Song 8:6). The Holy One replied: My daughter, you ask for something that is seen at times and not seen at other times.[5] But I will do something for you that is seen at all times: "Behold, I have graven thee upon the palms of My hands" (Isa. 49:16).[6]

108. "But Zion said: 'The Lord hath forsaken me, the Lord hath forgotten me' " (Isa. 49:14). Is not forsaken the same as forgotten? Resh Lakish explained: The congregation of Israel said to the Holy One: Master of the universe, when a man weds a second wife, forsaking the first, he still remembers the deeds of the first. But You have both forsaken me and forgotten me. The Holy One replied: My daughter, in the firmament I created twelve constellations. For each constellation I created thirty hosts; for each host I created thirty legions; for each legion I created thirty cohorts; for each cohort I created thirty maniples; for each maniple I created thirty camps. And to each camp I attached three hundred and sixty-five thousands of myriads of stars corresponding to the days of the solar year. And all of them I created only for your sake. Yet you say, "Thou hast forsaken me, Thou hast forgotten me"! "Can a woman forget her sucking child (ullah)?" (Isa. 49:15). By which the Holy One meant: Can I possibly forget the burnt offerings (*olah*) of rams you brought Me in the wilderness? Israel replied: Master of the universe, since there is no forgetfulness before the throne of Your glory, You will probably not forget my making the golden calf. The Holy One replied, " 'These' shall be forgotten" (Isa. 49:15).[7] Your saying to the images of the golden calf, "These are thy gods, O Israel" (Exod. 32:4), shall be forgotten. The congregation of Israel spoke up: Master of the universe, since there is forgetfulness before the throne of glory, will You perhaps forget my instant obedience at Mount Sinai? God replied: Your response to the "I" in "I am the Lord thy God" (Exod. 20:2), I shall not forget.[8]

109. R. Hanina bar Papa said: What is meant by "I the Lord repeat not" (Mal. 3:6)?[9] I have never smitten a people and had to repeat the smiting. "But ye, O sons of Jacob, have not been consumed" (ibid.). These words are clarified by the verse "I will consume My arrows upon them" (Deut. 33:23)—Mine arrows will be consumed, but they will not be consumed. Israel was therefore able to say, "He hath bent His bow, and set me as a mark for His arrow" (Lam. 3:12). How may what Israel said be illustrated? By the parable of a warrior who sets up a post at which he shoots

1. Gen. R. 44:12; Tanhuma, *Hayye Sarah*, §6.
2. Tanhuma, *Shofetim*, §10.
3. Eccles. R. 1:4, §4.
4. B. Ta 3b.
5. Being covered by clothing.
6. B. Ta 4a.
7. JV: "Yea, these shall be forgotten."
8. B. Ber 32b.
9. JV: "I the Lord change not." But *shaniti* ("change") also means "repeat."

his arrows. The arrows are consumed, but the post remains standing. So, too, Israel. Despite the fact that at all times affliction comes at them, the affliction is consumed, but Israel remain as they are.[1]

110. "But fear not, O Jacob My servant" (Isa. 44:2). In the name of R. Meir, it is said: The verse teaches that [in the dream of the ladder (Gen. 8:12)] the Holy One showed Jacob the prince of Babylon going up and coming down, the prince of Media going up and coming down, the prince of Greece going up and coming down, the prince of Edom [Rome] going up and coming down. Then the Holy One said to Jacob: You, too, go up. In that instant our father Jacob grew fearful and said: Perhaps, God forbid, as there is a coming down for these, there will be a coming down for me as well. The Holy One replied, "But thou, fear not, O Jacob My servant" (Jer. 30:10). Though you go up, you will never experience a coming down.[2]

111. "Their bodies were as of sapphire" (Lam. 4:7). Do you think the sapphire is fragile? R. Phinehas told the story of a man who went up to Rome to sell a sapphire. The buyer made the purchase of the sapphire contingent upon his testing it. He laid it on an anvil and proceeded to strike it with a hammer. The anvil split, the hammer was shattered, but the sapphire remained undamaged.[3]

112. "The Lord called thy name a leafy olive tree" (Jer. 11:16). R. Joshua ben Levi taught: Why is Israel said to be like the olive tree? To tell you that even as the leaves of an olive tree fall neither during the summer season nor during the rainy season, so Israel will never cease to be, neither in this world nor in the world-to-come.[4]

113. "I will make thy seed as the dust of the earth" (Gen. 13:16). As the dust of the earth is from one end of the world to the other, so your children will be dispersed from one end of the world to the other. As dust is trodden by all, so will your children by trod upon by the peoples of the world. As dust outlives all vessels of metal while it endures forever, so all the peoples of the world will cease to be, while Israel endures forever.[5]

114. "One generation passeth away, and another generation cometh; but the earth abideth forever" (Eccles. 1:4). Solomon meant: Even though "one generation passeth away, and another generation cometh," one kingdom passes away and another kingdom comes, one decree passes away and another decree comes, "the earth abideth forever": Israel abide forever—they have not been forsaken, nor will they be forsaken. As Scripture says, "I the Lord change not; and ye, O sons of Jacob, are not consumed" (Mal. 3:6). Even as I have not changed and will not change, so you, O house of Jacob, have not been consumed and will not be consumed. "But ye that did cleave unto the Lord your God are alive every one of you this day" (Deut. 4:4).[6]

The Purity of Families in Israel

115. R. Hama bar Hanina said: When the Holy One causes His Presence to dwell, He causes it to dwell only upon families in Israel whose lineage is unsullied, as is said, "At that time, saith the Lord, will I be the God of all the families of Israel" (Jer. 31:1). Scripture does not say, "Of all Israel," but, "Of all the families of Israel [whose lineage is unsullied]."[7]

116. R. Eleazar said: Ezra did not go up from Babylon until he made [the Jewish families in] it as pure as the purest sifted flour.[8] Only then did he go up.[9]

117. R. Judah said in the name of Rav: When you see two men continually at strife, there is some blemish in the lineage of one of them, and therefore the two men should be discouraged from becoming related to each other [by ties of marriage].

R. Joshua ben Levi said: If you see two families continually at strife, there is some blemish in the lineage of one of them, and therefore the two families should be discouraged from becoming related to each other [by ties of marriage].[10]

118. "And he . . . shall purge them as gold and silver, there will also be those that will be permitted to offer unto the Lord offerings because of His charity" (Mal. 3:3). The Holy One, said R. Isaac, shows charity to Israel, for even a blemished family, once assimilated [in Israel beyond tracing back], should be deemed to be fully assimilated.

There was the family named Bet ha-Tzerifah beyond the Jordan, which Ben Zion declared unfit [to marry Jews of unblemished lineage], and another family he declared fit. There was yet another family whose identity the sages declined to reveal, but once every seven-year period they confided its name to their children and their children's children.[11]

119. Mari bar R. Judah said: Ever since the day when the Book of Genealogies was hidden,[12] the strength of the sages has been depleted and the light in their eyes dimmed.[13]

---

1. B. Sot 9a; Tanhuma, *Nitzavim*, §1.
2. Lev. R. 29:2.
3. The sapphire is second in hardness only to the diamond. Nevertheless, if subjected to the test mentioned above, it would shatter, even as a diamond would. The translator thanks his friend Albert M. Schaler of Providence, R.I., for this information. Lam. R. 4:7, §10.
4. B. Men 53b.
5. Gen. R. 41:9; Gen. R. 69:5; Yalkut, *Lekh Lekha*, §70.
6. Per Sha.
7. B. Kid 70b.
8. That is, established purity of lineage by careful investigation.
9. B. Kid 69b and 71b.
10. B. Kid 71b and En Yaakov, ad loc.
11. B. Kid 71a.
12. Suppressed or forgotten. It contained reasons for certain laws in Scripture. So Rashi.
13. B. Pes 62b.

120. R. Yose said: Earlier generations, who knew their lineage, named their children after an event,[1] whereas we, who do not know our lineage, name our children after our immediate forebears. But R. Simeon ben Gamaliel said: Earlier generations, who were able to make use of the holy spirit, named their children for events that were to occur; whereas we, who are unable to make use of the holy spirit, name our children after our immediate forebears.[2]

Proselytes in Israel

121. "And they shall be My people" (Ezek. 37:27). Rabbah bar R. Huna said: Compared to proselytes, Israel are given somewhat higher status, for of Israel it is written, "I will be their God, and they shall be My people" (ibid.), whereas Scripture says of proselytes "Whosoever hath pledged his heart to approach unto Me, saith the Lord, ye shall then be My people, and I will be your God" (Jer. 30:21–22).[3]

R. Helbo said: Proselytes are as troublesome to Israel as the itch (*sappahat*),[4] for it is said, "The proselyte who joins himself with them shall be like the itch for the house of Jacob" (Isa. 14:1).[5]

122. R. Eliezer ben Jacob said: An assembly of proselytes is not called an assembly [of the Lord].[6]

123. There are three kinds of proselytes: a proselyte who is still in every respect a heathen; a proselyte who is like [Shechem son of] Hamor;[7] and a proselyte who is like our father Abraham. How so? A proselyte of the first kind, who had in his house flesh of carrion, of diseased animals, and of abominable and creeping creatures [all forbidden to Jews], said, "Isn't it time that I go and become a proselyte, and live among Jews, whose food is wholesome, who eat delicate food on their festivals and Sabbaths, so that I shall no longer have vile food in my house?" So, forcing himself, he went and became a proselyte. Of him, the Holy One said to Israel: My children, even as he has come to love you, so are you to love him, as is said, "Love ye therefore the proselyte" (Deut. 10:19).

Another kind of proselyte is like [Shechem son of] Hamor. How so? He sought to wed a Jewish maiden, and was told [by her kinsmen], "We will not give her to you as a wife until you consent to become a proselyte." So, forcing himself, he went and became a proselyte. Of such a one, the Holy One said to Israel: My children, as this one sought the security [of your congregation from you], so you must give security to him, as is said, "A proselyte shalt thou not wrong, neither shalt thou oppress him" (Exod. 22:20).

Finally, the third kind of proselyte is like our father Abraham. How so? He went about making inquiries among all the nations, and, having heard all of them speak of the excellence of Israel, he said, "I will go and become a proselyte, and enter under the wings of the Presence." Of such a man, it is said, "Neither let the alien, that hath joined himself to the Lord, speak, saying: 'The Lord will keep me apart from His people.' . . . For thus saith the Lord: I will give them in My house and within My walls a monument and a name" (Isa. 56:3–5).[8]

124. "Happy is everyone that feareth the Lord, that walketh in His ways" (Ps. 128:1). The psalm does not say, "Happy is Israel," "Happy are the priests," "Happy are the Levites," but says, "Happy is everyone that feareth the Lord." It refers to proselytes who, because they fear the Lord, are included in the apostrophe "happy." Even as Israel is told, "Happy art thou, O Israel" (Deut. 33:29), so it is said of proselytes, "Happy is everyone that feareth the Lord." Of what sort of proselyte is "happy" said? Of one who is a true proselyte, not one like these Cutheans, of whom it is said, "They feared the Lord, and served their own gods" (2 Kings 17:33), but like the proselyte who fears the Holy One and walks in the ways of the Holy One, of whom it is said, "That walketh in His ways" (Ps. 128:1).

The words "When thou eatest the labor of thy hands" (Ps. 128:2) are spoken to a proselyte who has no merit of the fathers. In order that he should not say, "Woe is me who has no merit of the fathers, so that, for all the good deeds I may accumulate, I shall have reward only in this world," the psalm announces good tidings to him: because of his own merit, he will "eat" in this world as well as in the world-to-come. Hence, "when thou eatest the labor of thine own hands"—the good deeds he has labored to perform in this world—what is to be his reward? "Happy shalt thou be, and it shall be well with thee" (ibid.). "Happy shalt thou be" in this world, and "it shall be well with thee" in the world-to-come.

"Thy wife shall be as a fruitful vine" (Ps. 128:3). Even though his wife became a proselyte with him and is not of the daughters of Israel, she shall be like the daughters of Israel, "as a fruitful vine" that is heavy with fruit. Not as a barren vine—she will be privileged to have children. "In the innermost parts of thy house" (ibid.)—if she conducts herself according to the Jewish religion and is modest, she will be privileged to produce children who are masters of Scripture, masters of Mishnah, masters of good deeds.

---

1. Since their forebears lived long lives, the descendants knew their identity and did not need to name children after them to keep their memory alive.
2. Gen. R. 37:7.
3. Proselytes must first come to God.
4. A skin disease that produces itchy sores.
5. JV: "shall cleave (*nispehu*) to the house of Jacob." "R. Helbo's words did not embody a religious objection. They merely expressed a political fact. It was dangerous for Jews who lived at the time of the Council of Nicaea (325 C.E.) to receive proselytes, and R. Helbo said so" (William G. Braude, *Jewish Proselyting in the First Five Centuries of the Common Era* [Providence, R.I., 1940], p. 48). B. Kid 70b.
6. Unlike born Jews, proselytes may marry bastards or other stock that is deemed blemished. B. Yev 57a.
7. Hamor, the father of Shechem who seduced Dinah, the daughter of Jacob and Leah. See Gen. 34.
8. TdE, ed. Friedmann, p. 146; Yalkut, *Shelah*, §745.

"Thy children like olive plants" (Ps. 128:3). The olive plant has olives for eating, olives to be dried, olives for oil; its oil burns better than all other oils, and its leaves fall neither during the summer season nor during the rainy season. So, too, do the children of proselytes turn out: some as masters of Scripture, some as masters of Mishnah, some as masters of the give-and-take of business, some as sages, some as men of common sense, some as knowing the right time to do something. And besides, they will have progeny who will endure forever. "Round about thy table" (ibid.). Your merit will stand your children in good stead. Because [of the generosity] of your table, your children will be endowed with noble virtues.

"Behold, surely thus shall the man be blessed that feareth the Lord" (Ps. 128:4). Even as we find that Abraham and Sarah became proselytes and were blessed, so shall all proselytes who pattern themselves after their conduct be blessed.

"The Lord bless thee out of Zion" (Ps. 128:5). The Holy One will bless them out of the same place whence He blesses Israel, for blessings come out of Zion. "And see . . . the good of Jerusalem" (ibid.)—they will see the good of Jerusalem in the time-to-come.

"And see thy children's children. Peace be upon Israel" (Ps. 128:6). But how does it follow that, just because the proselyte will see the children of his children, peace will come to Israel? What the verse means is that the proselyte will be privileged to wed his daughter to a priest, and from her children, who are his children's children, will arise priests, who will bless Israel, saying, "May the Lord bless thee . . . and give thee peace" (Num. 6:24 and 6:26).[1]

125. At the time the Gibeonites said to Joshua, "Come up to us quickly, and save us and help us" (Josh. 10:6)—at that time Joshua asked himself: Shall we burden the community for the sake of these proselytes? The Holy One said to him: Joshua, if you keep away those who have been far off, you will end up keeping away those who are near. Besides, consider your own origin—is it not from proselytes?[2]

126. "The hand upon the throne of the Lord: the Lord will have war with Amalek from generation to generation" (Exod. 17:16). The Holy One swore a solemn oath: "By My right hand and again by My right hand, by My throne and again by My throne, I swear that if would-be proselytes come from any of the nations of the earth, I will receive them, but if from the seed of Amalek, I will not receive them.[3]

127. Our masters taught: If, at the present time, a man comes seeking to be a proselyte, he should be asked: What makes you wish to be received as a proselyte? Are you not aware that at this time Israel is broken down, pushed about, swept from place to place, driven here and there, and overcome by afflictions? If he says, "I am fully aware. But I am scarcely worthy of [the privilege of becoming a Jew]," he is to be received at once and instructed in a few minor and a few major precepts. He should be told of the sin of not giving gleanings,[4] forgotten sheaves,[5] corner crop,[6] and poor man's tithe.[7] He is also to be told of the punishments for disobedience to divine commands. He should be told further: You are to be aware that before coming to this state, had you eaten forbidden fat, your life would not have been shortened; had you profaned the Sabbath, you would not have been subject to stoning. But henceforth, should you eat forbidden fat, your life will be shortened; should you profane the Sabbath, you will be subject to stoning. Even as he is told the punishment for disobeying divine commands, so should he be told the reward for obeying them. He should be told further: You are to be aware that the world-to-come is prepared only for the righteous and that at this time [in this world] Israel are unable to receive very much reward or very much punishment.[8]

One should take care not to impose on him too many commandments nor go into fine details about them.[9]

128. A proselyte has the legal status of a newborn child.[10]

129. "A proselyte shalt thou not vex" (Exod. 22:20). You are not to vex him with words. You are not to say to him, "Only yesterday you worshiped idols and up until just now swine's flesh was between your teeth."

Because the proselyte's origin may be tainted, Scripture warns about him in a great many passages.[11]

130. "And the Levite . . . and the proselyte shall come" (Deut. 14:29). Moses spoke up to the Holy One: Is a proselyte as important to You as a Levite? God replied: He is more important to Me, since he became a proselyte for My sake. A parable of a stag who grew up in the wilderness and on his own joined the flock. The shepherd not only gave him food and drink, but loved him more than any of the other animals in his flock. He was asked: How is it that you love the stag more than any other in the flock? He replied: I had to perform many kinds of labor for my flock until they grew up: I took them out in the morning and brought them back in the evening. But this one, who grew up in the wilderness and forests, came into my flock on his own. Should I not love him very much? Likewise the Holy One said: Much did I have to labor for Israel: I brought them out of Egypt, lit the way for them, sent down manna for them, swept in quail for them, made the well gush up for them, and encompassed them with clouds of glory before they were willing to accept My Torah.

---

1. Num. R. 8:9.
2. Through Ephraim, Joshua descended from Asenath, an Egyptian. Num. R. 8:4.
3. PRKM 3:16.
4. Lev. 19:9 and 23:22.
5. Deut. 24:19.
6. Lev. 19:9 and 23:22.
7. Given to the poor in the third and sixth years of a seven-year cycle.
8. Since they are incapable of coping with the impulse to evil.
9. B. Yev 47a–b.
10. B. Yev 22a.
11. If provoked, he may lapse into idolatry. Ger 4.

But this one came on his own. He is therefore deemed by Me the equal of an Israelite, even of a Levite.[1]

131. Proselytes are beloved, for in each and every passage Scripture likens them to Israel.[2]

132. Why are proselytes at this time oppressed and visited with afflictions? Abba Hanan said in the name of R. Eleazar: Because they perform divine commands not out of love but out of fear of punishment.[3]

133. "And Rizpah the daughter of Aiah took sackcloth . . . and she suffered not the birds of the air to nest on them . . . by night" (2 Sam. 21:10). But it is written, "If a man have committed a sin worthy of death . . . and thou hang him on a tree, his body shall not remain all night upon the tree" (Deut. 21:22–23). [Why then were the bodies of the sons of Saul, who were executed, allowed to remain unburied all night?] R. Yohanan said in the name of R. Simeon ben Jehozadak: It is well to have one word [the word "not" in the phrase "not remain all night"] rooted out of the Torah, so that the Name of Heaven is openly hallowed thereby. For passersby, seeing the bodies thus exposed, would ask, "What sort of men were these?" "They were princes." "But what did they do?" "They laid violent hands on proselytes who came in from improper motives." Hearing that, the passersby would say: "There is no people so worth attaching oneself to as Israel. If princes were punished thus, how much more and more would commoners be punished. If this was done for the sake of proselytes who came in from improper motives, how much more and more would be done for Israelites!"

Immediately one hundred and fifty thousand [proselytes] were added to Israel.[4]

134. "And he looked on the Kenite, and took up his parable, and said: Firm be thy dwelling place" (Num. 24:21). A parable of a bird hunter who caught one bird and was about to catch another, but he stopped in indecision because the bird had flown off and perched on a statue of the king. So he spoke of the bird in this way: If I throw a stone at her, I may forfeit my life; if I poke at her with a stick, I fear it might strike the king's image. I do not know what to say to you, except that you fled to a perfect place and made good your escape. So, too, Balaam, aware that Jethro and Amalek had been present in Pharaoh's deliberation [about the fate of Moses],[5] confronted Amalek and pronounced doom upon his name.[6] But then, when he looked at Jethro and realized that he had repented [indeed, had become a proselyte], Balaam said: You have fled to a perfect place; "firm be thy dwelling place."[7]

135. "And the souls they made in Haran" (Gen. 12:5)—these are the proselytes they welcomed, which shows that he who brings a stranger near and causes him to become a proselyte is deemed as though he had created him.[8]

136. A story of Monobazos and Zotos, King Ptolemy's sons, who sat reading the book of Genesis. When they reached the verse "And ye shall be circumcised in the flesh of your foreskin" (Gen. 17:11), each turned his face to the wall and began to weep. Then each of them went and had himself circumcised. After a while, when they again sat and read the book of Genesis, and reached the verse "And ye shall be circumcised," one said to the other, "Alas, my brother." The other replied, "Alas for you, my brother, but not for me." Then each disclosed to the other what he had done. When their mother became aware of it, she went and told their father, "Your sons had a growth on their member, and the physician ordered that they be circumcised." He said to her, "Then let them be circumcised."[9]

137. "He declareth His word unto Jacob" (Ps. 147:19). Akilas[10] once said to Hadrian Caesar: I wish to convert and become a Jew. Hadrian: You would join this people, which I have humiliated so greatly, so many of whom I have slain? You would get mixed up with the very lowest of nations? What do you see in them that makes you wish to become a proselyte? He replied: The least among them knows how the Holy One created the world, what was created on the first day and what was created on the second day, how long it is since the world was created, and on what the world is founded. Besides, their Torah is truth. Hadrian: Go ahead, then, and study their Torah, but do not be circumcised. Akilas: Unless he be circumcised, even the wisest man in your kingdom, even a venerable man who is a hundred years old, cannot study their Torah, concerning which it is said, "He declareth His word unto Jacob, His statutes and His ordinances unto Israel. He doth not accord these to any other nation" (Ps. 147:19–20). To what nation alone? To Israel.[11]

138. Akilas, who was Hadrian's nephew, wished to become a proselyte but was afraid of his uncle Hadrian. So he said to him: I want to go into business. Hadrian: Does that mean you are in need of silver or gold? My treasures are open before you. Akilas: I still want to go into business, to get outside, to learn what people think. And I seek your counsel on how to go about it. Hadrian: Any merchandise whose price is depressed, all but sunk in the ground—go and deal in it, for in the end its price will rise and you will realize a profit. So Akilas went to the Land of Israel and studied Torah. After a while R. Eliezer and R. Joshua came upon him, and, noticing a change in his countenance, they said to each other: Akilas is apparently studying Torah. When he came into their presence, he

1. Num. R. 8:2; MTeh 146:8.
2. Num. R. 8:2.
3. B. Yev 48b.
4. B. Yev 79a.
5. See above, part 1, chap. 4, §19; Exod. R. 27:6.
6. He said: "His end shall come to destruction" (Num. 24:20).
7. Exod. R. 27:6.
8. Gen. R. 39:14.
9. Gen. R. 46:10; Yalkut, *Lekh Lekha*, §82.
10. After his conversion, he became a disciple of R. Akiva and translated the Bible into Greek. See *JE*, s.v. "Aquila."
11. Exod. R. 30:12.

proceeded to put many questions to them, which they answered. Then he went up to his uncle Hadrian, who asked him: Why is your countenance changed? I suspect that either your merchandise sold at a loss, or can it be that someone has distressed you? Akilas: No. You are my kinsman—would any man dare distress me? Hadrian: Then why is your countenance changed? Akilas: Because I have studied Torah. What is more, I have had myself circumcised. Hadrian: Who told you to do so? Akilas: It was you I consulted. Hadrian: When? Akilas: When I told you that I wanted to go into business, and you said to me, "Any merchandise whose price is depressed, all but sunk in the ground—go and deal in it, for in the end it will rise in value." I then went around among all nations and found none held in lower esteem and deemed to be more deeply sunk in the ground than Israel. But in the end they will be exalted, as Isaiah said, "Thus saith the Lord, the Redeemer of Israel, his Holy One, to him who is despised of men, to him who is abhorred of nations, to a servant of rulers: Kings shall see him and rise, princes, they shall prostrate themselves (Isa. 49:7).[1]

139. Akilas the Proselyte once came to R. Eliezer and asked: Is all the love the Holy One bestowed upon a proselyte shown only in giving him bread and raiment—"He . . . giveth him bread and raiment" (Deut. 10:18)? Why, I have so many peacocks, so many pheasants, that even my servants pay no attention to them. R. Eliezer reprimanded him: Is such a gift so trivial in your eyes? It is one for which the venerable [Jacob] prostrated himself, saying, "If God . . . will give me . . . bread to eat, and raiment to put on" (Gen. 28:20). And now a person like yourself comes, and it is offered to you [daintily] at the tip of a reed.

Akilas then came to R. Joshua's home, who began to console him, saying: "Bread" means Torah, which says, "Come, eat of my bread" (Prov. 9:5). "Raiment" means a sage's cloak. When a man acquires Torah, he acquires such a cloak. More: proselytes may marry off their daughters into the priesthood, and children of their children may become high priests.

It is said: But for R. Joshua's patient treatment of Akilas, Akilas might have reverted to his evil past. To R. Joshua was applied the verse "He that is slow to anger is better than the mighty" (Prov. 16:32).[2]

140. One day a certain Caesar, an enemy of the Jews, asked the princes of his realm: If one has a sore on his foot, should he cut off the sore and enjoy life, or leave it and suffer distress? They replied: He should cut it off and enjoy life. But Ketia[3] bar Shalom said: To begin with, you cannot get rid of all of those of whom God said, "I have spread you abroad as the four winds of the heaven" (Zech. 2:10). Besides, yours will be called "a realm part of which has been cut away." Caesar: You have spoken well. But he who defeats Caesar in an argument is thrown into the potter's kiln.

[1] Tanhuma, *Mishpatim*, §5.
[2] Gen. R. 70; Num. R. 8:9; Eccles. R. 7:8, §1.
[3] Ketia means "he who is to undergo the cut [of circumcision]."

When Ketia was seized, a Roman noblewoman said to him: Alas for the ship that sets out to sail without paying the toll![4] At this, he picked up a knife to cut off his foreskin. Others say that he bit off the foreskin with his teeth and announced: I have paid the toll and will pass into Paradise. As he was thrown into the kiln, he cried out: I bequeath all my possessions to R. Akiva and his companions.

A divine voice came forth, proclaiming: Ketia bar Shalom is destined for life in the world-to-come.

[On hearing what happened], Rabbi [Judah I, the Patriarch] wept and said: One may acquire eternal life in a single hour, another only after so many years![5]

141. Once, when our masters R. Eliezer, R. Joshua, and Rabban Gamaliel were in Rome, the imperial Senate issued a decree that after thirty days no Jew should remain in the entire [Roman] world. One senator, who feared Heaven, came to Rabban Gamaliel and disclosed the decree to him. Our masters were greatly distressed, but the man who feared Heaven said to them: Be not distressed. Within the next thirty days the God of the Jews will stand by them. After twenty-five days, he disclosed the decree to his wife, who said: But twenty-five days are already gone. He: Five days are still left. His wife, even more righteous than he, said: Have you no ring? Suck the poison concealed in it and die. Then the sessions of the Senate will be suspended for thirty days in mourning for you, and the decree will not take effect.[6] He heeded what she had to say, sucked the ring, and died.

When our masters heard of this, they came to his wife to express their sympathy. While there, they said: Alas for the ship that set out to sail without paying the toll. She replied: I understand what you mean. As you live, the ship did not sail until she paid the toll due. Then she went into the bedchamber and brought them a box in which lay the foreskin, wrapped in blood-stained rags. At that, our masters applied to that senator the verse "They among the peoples who volunteer are gathered together, the people of the God of Abraham; for unto God belong the shields of the earth; He is highly exalted" (Ps. 47:10). What is signified by "the shields of the earth?" God said: To Abraham I became a shield of strength. And the proof? Because it is said, "I am thy shield" (Gen. 15:1). But to this senator I will become many shields. To Abraham I said, "I will make of thee a great nation, and I will bless thee, and make thy name great" (Gen. 12:2), and only after that did he have himself circumcised. But to this senator I made no such promise. What then is signified by "He is highly exalted"? That this one is exalted high above Abraham.[7]

142. When Onkelos son of Kalonymos became a proselyte, Caesar sent a troop of Romans to arrest him. But

[4] Entry into Paradise might be denied him, since circumcision is the "toll" for admission.
[5] B. AZ 10b and En Yaakov, ad loc.
[6] "The Romans had a rule that if the Senate made a decree, and before it was carried into effect one of the senators died, the decree was annulled" (Deut. R. Soncino, p. 52, n. 3).
[7] Deut. R. 2:24; Yalkut, Ps., §754.

he won them over by citing verses from Scripture, and they too became proselytes. Caesar then sent another troop of Romans and instructed them: Say nothing at all to Onkelos. After they seized him and went off [with him], he said to them: May I speak to you about a matter that is not Scripture? A torchbearer carries a torch before a litter carrier, a litter carrier before a commander, a commander before a general, a general before the emperor. But does an emperor bear a torch before other people? They replied: No. Then he said: But the Holy One carries a torch before Israel, as is said, "And the Lord went before them by day in a pillar of cloud . . . by night in a pillar of fire, to give them light" (Exod. 13:21). At that, all of them too became proselytes. Then Ceasar sent still another troop and enjoined them: Do not engage in any conversation whatsoever with Onkelos. As they seized him and went off with him, they saw a mezuzah affixed to the doorway, and when he put his hand on it and smiled, they asked him: Why are you smiling? He replied: It is the way of the world that a king is seated inside while his servants stand guard outside. But the Holy One—His servants are inside, while He stands guard outside, as is said, "The Lord shall guard thy going out and thy coming in," etc. (Ps. 121:8). At this, they too became proselytes. Caesar did not send soldiers for him again.[1]

Those Who Became Proselytes Because of Lions

143. R. Nehemiah used to say: They who become proselytes because of lions,[2] because of dreams, or because of fear of Mordecai and Esther are not deemed proselytes unless they are ready to be converted again at a time such as ours.[3]

144. The ways of the Samaritans (Cutheans) are at times like those of Gentiles and at other times like those of Jews, but most of their ways are like those of Jews.

Why are Samaritans forbidden to marry Jews? Because they intermarried with the priests of heathen high places.

When are they to be received as proselytes? When they deny the sanctity of Mount Gerizim and acknowledge Jerusalem's preeminence and the resurrection of the dead.[4]

145. Whenever the Samaritans adhere to a precept, they adhere to it more firmly than the Jews.[5]

146. R. Meir sent R. Simeon ben Eleazar to fetch wine from a Samaritan home. A certain venerable man met him and quoted, "If thou art a man of conscience, put a knife to thy throat" (Prov. 23:2).[6] When R. Simeon ben Eleazar went and reported to R. Meir what he was told, R. Meir prohibited the use of Samaritan wine. What was his reason? Because, said R. Nahman bar Isaac, on the summit of Mount Gerizim the sages discovered the likeness of a dove, which the Samaritans worshiped.[7]

147. R. Meir met a certain Samaritan and asked him, "From whom are you descended?" The Samaritan: "From Joseph." R. Meir: "No." The Samaritan: "From whom then?" R. Meir: "From Issachar." The Samaritan: "What is your proof?" R. Meir: "Because in the verse 'The sons of Issachar: Tola . . . and Shimron' [Gen. 46:13] the latter name refers to the Samaritans." The Samaritan then went to their patriarch and reported, "The elder of the Jews told me something astonishing." The patriarch: "What was it?" The Samaritan: "He asked me from whom I was descended. When I told him, 'From Joseph,' he said to me, 'No, from Issachar, because in the verse "The sons of Issachar: Tola . . . and Shimron" the latter name refers to the Samaritans.' " The patriarch: "As you live, he excluded you from the lineage of Joseph but did not bring you into the lineage of Issachar."[8]

148. On his way to pray in Jerusalem, R. Ishmael son of R. Yose was passing that notorious Mount [Gerizim] when a Samaritan saw him and asked: Master, where are you going? R. Ishmael: I am going up to pray in Jerusalem. The Samaritan: Would it not be better for you to pray at this mountain, upon which a blessing was pronounced,[9] than at that dunghill? R. Ishmael: I will tell you whom you resemble: a dog eager for carrion. You know that idols are hidden under this mountain, of which it is said, "Jacob hid them under the terebinth which was by Shechem" (Gen. 35:4). That is why you are eager about Mount Gerizim. Then the Samaritans suspected R. Ishmael of wishing to remove those idols. When he heard them say: We will rise early in the morning and destroy the thorns, he knew that they planned to slay him. So he rose up and fled during the night.[10]

149. R. Jonathan was going up to pray in Jerusalem. When he reached Mount Gerizim, a Samaritan met him and asked: Where are you going? R. Jonathan: To pray in Jerusalem. The Samaritan: Would it not be better for you to pray at this mountain, upon which blessing was bestowed, than at that dunghill? R. Jonathan: In what way is this mountain blessed? The Samaritan: It was not covered by water during the flood. The appropriate response escaped R. Jonathan for the moment, so he was unable to reply. But his ass driver said to him: Master, permit me,

---

1. B. AZ 11a.
2. Like the Samaritans (2 Kings 17:25), who became proselytes after a visitation of lions, because they regarded their coming as a manifestation of divine wrath.
3. In 135 C.E., after the Hadrianic wars, when only love of God and Torah could move people to become Jews. B. Yev 24b.
4. Kut 1–2; B. Kid 74b.
5. B. Ber 47b.
6. Meaning: You may as well kill yourself if you, an observant Jew, do not abstain from using their wine.
7. B. Hul 6a.
8. The Samaritans came to their name because they settled in Samaria, a place so named because the site was purchased from Shemer (1 Kings 16:25). Hence, they could not be descendants of Shimron son of Issachar, a far more ancient person. Gen. R. 94:7.
9. See Deut. 27:12–13.
10. Gen. R. 81:3; P. AZ 5:4, 44d.

and I will answer him. He asked that Samaritan: What do you consider Mount Gerizim to be? One of the high mountains? But Scripture says that during the flood "all the high mountains . . . were covered" (Gen. 7:19). One of the low mountains? Scripture gave it no heed and mentioned it not at all. The Samaritan remained silent, for he found no answer.

At that, R. Jonathan dismounted the ass, and had his driver ride it for three *mil.* With regard to him, R. Jonathan quoted three verses: (1) "Thou shalt be blessed above all peoples; there shall not be male or female barren [of wisdom] among you, or among your cattle (*behemtekha*)" (Deut. 7:14)—for "cattle," he said, read "cattle drivers (*behamim*)"; (2) "No weapon that is formed against thee shall succeed; and every tongue that shall rise against thee in debate thou shalt defeat" (Isa. 54:17); and (3) "Thine empty ones (*rakkatekh*)[1] are like a pomegranate split open" (Song 6:7)—in Israel, even an ass driver seemingly empty of knowledge (*rekan*) is as full of pertinent replies as a pomegranate is full of seeds.[2]

The Nations of the World

150. [The prophet] Elijah said: One day, as I was walking along a road, a man accosted me. He came toward me like one coming at another aggressively and charged: "You Jews say that seven prophets[3] have arisen to admonish the heathen nations of the world that they must [change their ways, or else] they will go down to Gehenna." I said, "My son, that is so." The man said, "But after the seven generations [contemporary with the seven prophets] have passed away, the nations of the world may argue: Torah was not given to us [as a guide], and no prophets have subsequently come to admonish us. Why then should we be doomed to go down to Gehenna?"

I replied, "My son, the sages have taught thus: If a heathen seeks to become a proselyte, a hand of welcome should be held out to bring him under the wings of the Presence. Thereafter, the proselytes in each succeeding generation are there to admonish their heathen brethren."[4]

151. The Holy One declares no creature unfit, but receives all. The gates [of mercy] are open at all times, and he who wishes to enter may enter.

R. Meir said: What is the proof that even a Gentile who occupies himself with Torah is like a high priest? Scripture says, "With which if a man occupy himself, he shall live by them" (Lev. 18:5). It does not say, "A priest, a Levite, an Israelite," but, "A man." Hence you may infer that even a non-Jew who occupies himself with Torah is like a high priest.

R. Jeremiah used to say: What is the proof that even a Gentile who keeps the Torah is like a high priest? The verse "Which if a man do, he shall live by them." Scripture also says, "This is the Torah of man,[5] O Lord God" (2 Sam. 7:19)—not "of priests, Levites, or Isralites," but "of man." Scripture also says, "Open ye the gates, that the righteous Gentile . . . may come in" (Isa. 26:2)—not that "priests, Levites, or Israelites may come in," but that "the righteous Gentile who keeps the faith may come in." Scripture also says, "This is the gate of the Lord; the righteous shall enter it" (Ps. 118:20)—not "priests, Levites, or Israelites shall enter it," but "the righteous shall enter it." Scripture also says, "Rejoice in the Lord, O ye righteous" (Ps. 33:1)—not "Rejoice, O ye priests, Levites, and Israelites," but "Rejoice . . . O ye righteous." Scripture also says, "Do good, O Lord, unto the good" (Ps. 125:4)—not "to priests, Levites, and Israelites," but, "Do good, O Lord, unto the good."

Thus, even a Gentile who keeps the Torah is like a high priest.[6]

152. [The prophet] Elijah said: I call heaven and earth to witness that whether it be Jew or Gentile, man or woman, manservant or maidservant, the holy spirit will suffuse each in proportion to the deeds he or she performs.[7]

153. "Thy priests are clothed with righteousness" (Ps. 132:9). These are the righteous of the nations of the world, such as [Emperor] Antoninus and his companions, who in this world are as priests for the Holy One.[8]

154. Should a person tell you that there is wisdom among the nations, believe it, for of their wisdom it is written, "I will make the wise vanish from Edom" (Obad. 1:8). That there is Torah among the nations—do not believe it, for it is said, "Her king and her princes are among the nations, where Torah is not" (Lam. 2:9).[9]

155. "May God endow Japheth[10] with beauty (*yapht*), and may it dwell in the tents of Shem" (Gen. 9:27)—may the beauty of Japheth [forebear of Yavan: Greece] dwell in the tents of Shem.[11]

156. Canaan enjoined five things upon his sons: Love one another, love robbery, love lewdness, hate your masters, and do not tell the truth.[12]

157. R. Meir said: Among cities, you have none as wicked as Sodom. When a man is wicked, he is called a Sodomite. Among peoples, you have none as cruel as the Amorites. When a man is cruel, he is called an Amorite.[13]

---

1. *Rakkatekh* can mean "thy Temples" or "thine empty ones."
2. Gen. R. 32:10; Song R. 4:1, §5; Deut. R. 3:6.
3. Shem, Eliphaz, Zophar, Bildad, Elihu, Job, and Balaam.
4. TdE, ed. Friedmann, p. 35; Lev. R. 2:9.
5. JV: "This too after the manner (*torah*) of great men." But *torah* may mean not only "manner," but also "instruction" or "Torah."
6. B. BK 38a; Exod. R. 19:4; Sif Lev. 86b.
7. TdE, ed. Friedmann, p. 48.
8. Yalkut, Isa., §429. The citation from the Yalkut is incorporated in the editions of TdEZ preceding Meir Friedmann's.
9. Lam. R. 2:9, §13.
10. JV: "God enlarge Japheth." But *yapht* may be derived from *pth* ("to enlarge") or *yph* ("to make beautiful").
11. B. Meg 9b.
12. B. Pes 113b.
13. Gen. R. 41:7.

158. Hypocrisy and arrogance descended to Babylon.[1]

159. Ten *kav* of wealth descended to the world: the Romans took nine, and all the rest of the world one.

Ten *kav* of poverty descended to the world: Babylon took nine, and all the rest of the world one.

Ten *kav* of presumptuousness descended to the world: Elam[2] took nine, and all the rest of the world one.

Ten *kav* of might descended to the world: the Persians took nine, and all the rest of the world one.

Ten *kav* of vermin descended to the world: Media took nine, and all the rest of the world one.

Ten *kav* of witchcraft descended to the world: Egypt took nine, and all the rest of the world one.

Ten *kav* of harlotry descended to the world: Arabia took nine, and all the rest of the world one.

Ten *kav* of impudence descended to the world: Mesene[3] took nine, and all the rest of the world one.

Ten *kav* of drunkenness descended to the world: the Ethiopians took nine, and all the rest of the world one.[4]

160. There are ten portions of stupidity in the world—nine among the Ishmaelites, and one in the rest of the world.

There are ten portions of outlawry in the world—nine among the Ishmaelites, and one in the rest of the world.

There are ten portions of physical beauty in the world—nine in Media, and one in the rest of the world.

There are ten portions of ugliness in the world—nine in the east, and one in the rest of the world.

There are ten portions of physical strength in the world—nine among the Chaldeans, and one in the rest of the world.[5]

161. "I looked up again and saw two women come soaring with the wind in their wings—they had wings like those of a stork—and carry off the tub between earth and sky. 'Where are they taking the tub?' I asked the angel who talked with me. And he answered: 'To build a shrine for it in the land of Shinar' " (Zech. 5:9–11). R. Yohanan said in the name of R. Simeon ben Yohai: The two women symbolize hypocrisy and arrogance, which made their home in Babylon.

But did arrogance really make its home in Babylon? Did not the master say: Ten *kav* of presumptuousness descended to the world—Elam took nine, and all the rest of the world one? Yes, it first descended to Babylon, but then it spread out into Elam.[6]

162. R. Hiyya bar Abba and R. Assi sat before R. Yohanan, and R. Yohanan was dozing off. So R. Hiyya bar Abba asked R. Assi: Why are the fowl of Babylon fat? He replied: Go to the wilderness of Gaza, and I will show you fatter ones.

Why are festivals in Babylon so joyous?

Because its people are poor.[7]

Why are disciples of the wise in Babylon so elegant in their attire?

Because they are not true sons of Torah.[8]

Why do heathens exude a fetid odor?

Because they eat forbidden animals and reptiles.

Just then R. Yohanan woke up with a start and said: You amateurs! Did I not teach you: "Say unto wisdom: 'Thou art my sister' " (Prov. 7:4)? If a matter is as clear to you as that your sister is forbidden to you [in marriage], say it. Otherwise, do not say it. So they asked him: Will the master answer the several queries for us, beginning with "Why are the fowl of Babylon fat?"

Because they were never banished,[9] as is said, "Moab hath been at ease from his youth. . . . Neither hath he gone into captivity; therefore his taste remaineth in him" (Jer. 48:11).

Why are festivals in Babylon so joyous?

Because they were not included under that curse which declared, "I will also cause all her mirth to cease, her feasts, her New Moons, and her Sabbaths" (Hos. 2:13), and, "Your New Moons and your appointed seasons My soul hateth; they are a burden unto Me" (Isa. 1:14).

Why are disciples of the wise in Babylon so elegant in their attire?

Because they are not of local origin.[10] As people say, "In my own town, my name's my fame; elsewhere, it's what I wear."

Why do heathens exude a fetid odor?

Because Israel stood at Mount Sinai, their stench ceased.[11] But the stench of the heathens, who did not stand at Mount Sinai, did not cease.

R. Aha son of Rava asked R. Ashi: What about proselytes? R. Ashi replied: Even though they were not present, their constellations were, as is said: "I make this covenant . . . with him that standeth here with us this day . . . and also with him that is not here" (Deut. 29:14).[12]

163. "And behold, another beast, a second, like to a bear" (Dan. 7:5). R. Joseph taught: The verse refers to the Persians, who eat and drink like a bear, are fleshy like a bear, are as hairy as a bear, and as restless as a bear.

Whenever R. Ammi saw a Persian riding by, he would say, "There goes a wandering bear."

When Rabbi [Judah I, the Patriarch] said to Levi: Tell me what Persians are like, he replied: They are as mighty as the hosts of David.

What are the Habbars[13] like?

---

1. B. Kid 49b.
2. The country named after the oldest son of Shem (Gen. 10:22). Babylon was west of it.
3. An island formed by the confluence of the Euphrates, the Tigris, and the Royal Canal.
4. B. Kid 49b.
5. Esther R. 1:17.
6. B. Sanh 24a.
7. Since their lives are so drab, they are eager to live it up.
8. They display their raiment in lieu of Torah, which they do not possess.
9. Unlike the fowl of the Land of Israel, which were banished and then returned.
10. So many of them emigrated from Palestine.
11. The moral stench injected by the serpent in Eden was curbed by Torah.
12. B. Shab 145b–146a and En Yaakov, ad loc.
13. Parsee priests who were fanatical Zoroastrians. They were put in power by Ardavan (in 226 C.E.), who established the Sassanid dynasty. The Sassanids' original home was Haber near Shiraz. Hence the name Habbar. See Git, Soncino, p. 63, n. 2.

They are like destroying angels.
What are Ishmaelites like?
Like demons of the privy.
What are disciples of the wise in Babylon like?
Like ministering angels.[1]

164. "I will provoke them with a vile nation" (Deut. 32:21). These are the people of Tunisia and Britannia,[2] who go naked in the streets. For nothing is more abominable and detestable to Him who is everywhere than one who walks naked in the street. But. R. Yohanan said: These are the Parsees.

When. R. Yohanan was told: The Parsees have come to Babylon, he reeled and fell. When told they would accept bribes, he recovered and sat up again.

The Parsees issued three decrees: that ritually slaughtered meat not be eaten, that bathhouses not be used, that graves be dug up.[3]

165. When Rabbah bar Bar Hanah fell ill, R. Judah and Rabbah came to visit him and inquired about a certain matter of law. Meanwhile, a Habbar came in and removed the lamp.[4] Said Rabbah bar Bar Hanah: Master of the universe, either in Your shadow or in the shadow of the scion of Esau![5]

Are we actually to say that the Romans are better than the Parsees? Did not R. Hiyya interpret "God understandeth the way thereof, and He knoweth the place thereof" (Job 28:23) as meaning that since the Holy One knew that Israel could not endure the decrees of the Romans, He banished them to Babylon? There is no contradiction: one dictum refers to the time before the Parsees arrived in Babylon; the other, to the time after the Parsees came to Babylon.[6]

166. R. Hiyya bar Abba said: The kings of Media were blameless. The Holy One had nothing against them other than the idolatry their forebears had transmitted to them.[7]

167. R. Akiva said: I like the Medes for three things: when they cut meat, they cut it only on the table; when they kiss, they kiss only the back of the hand; when they hold counsel, they hold counsel only in the field.[8]

Rabban Gamaliel said: I like the Persians for three things: they are temperate in their eating, modest in the privy, and restrained in sexual matters.[9]

168. The exilarch said to R. Sheshet: Even though you are venerable sages, yet the Persians are better versed in arrangements for a meal. When two couches are set up, the senior guest takes his place first and the junior one above him.[10] When three couches are set up, the senior occupies the middle couch; the next to him in rank takes the place above him; and the third, one below him.[11] R. Sheshet said: So when the senior wants to talk to the one above him, he has to sit up? The exilarch: This does not bother the Persians, who [do not speak during a meal, but] communicate in sign language.

R. Sheshet further asked: With whom do they begin the washing of the hands before a meal? The exilarch: With the senior guest.

Is the senior guest forced to wait, making sure his hands remain clean until all the others have washed?

The exilarch: No. A table with food upon it is brought to him immediately.

With whom does the washing after the meal begin?

The exilarch: With the most junior guest present.

And does the senior guest sit with greasy hands until all have washed?

The exilarch: Until the water is brought to him, his table is not removed.[12]

169. R. Huna said: The kingdom of Greece excels the wicked kingdom [of Rome] in three matters: in laws, in keeping records,[13] and in oratorical style.[14]

170. R. Joseph taught: Edom is told, "Thou art greatly despised" (Obad. 1:2)—for the Romans have neither literary form nor oratorical style of their own.[15]

171. "The boar out of the wood doth ravage it" (Ps. 80:14). Why is the kingdom of Rome said to be like a boar? Because like the boar, which extends its cloven hooves when lying down, as if to say, "See how kosher I am,"[16] so this wicked kingdom of Edom [Rome] robs and despoils, yet makes it appear that the legal tricks it resorts to are fair practice.

It happened that a Roman ruler who kept executing men guilty of theft, adultery, and sorcery confided to his counselors: In a single night I committed all three of these acts.[17]

172. "And behold, it is very good" (Gen. 1:31). R. Simeon ben Lakish said: The words "Behold, it is very good" refer to the kingdom of Heaven; the words "And behold, it is very good" refer to the kingdom of the Romans.[18] Why

---

1. B. Kid 72a.
2. The text reads, "Barbaria and Mauretania." But see Jastrow, p. 190.
3. The Parsees, sometimes called Habbars, believed that corpses buried in the earth polluted it. Hence corpses were burned or thrown to beasts and birds of prey. B. Yev 63b.
4. Because it was a Habbar festival, on which lighting of fire in homes was forbidden.
5. Edom, the Roman Empire; rather than live in the shadow of Zoroastrian Persia.
6. B. Git 16b–17a.
7. Esther R. 1:18.
8. Because walls have ears.
9. B. Ber 8b.
10. Head to head.
11. With his head to the senior's feet.
12. In the meantime, he can go on eating. B. Ber 46b.
13. Another reading: "in the building of ships and palaces."
14. Gen. R. 16:4.
15. B. AZ 10a. They borrowed both from the Greeks.
16. Clean (kosher) animals have cloven hooves and chew the cud; the pig has cloven hooves but does not chew the cud, hence is not clean.
17. Gen. R. 65:1; Lev. R. 13:5; Yalkut, *Shemini*, §536.
18. "The word 'and' seems superfluous; hence it is assumed that it adds something to the meaning of the statement. Therefore, since 'Behold, it is very good' refers to the kingdom of Heaven, the added 'and' must refer to another kingdom, that of Edom/Rome" (Leon Nemoy).

is the kingdom of the Romans called "very good"? Because it endeavors to protect the wronged, as implied in "I, even I, have made the earth, and created Edom[1] upon it. . . . [I summoned him to execute righteousness]" (Isa. 45:12–13).[2]

173. On one occasion, while R. Judah, R. Yose, and R. Simeon ben Yohai were sitting together, Judah the son of proselytes happened to join them. R. Judah began the discussion by observing, "How noble are the works of this [Roman] nation! They laid out streets, they built bridges, they erected bathhouses." R. Yose remained silent, but R. Simeon ben Yohai spoke up and said, "All that they made, they made to serve themselves: they laid out streets to settle harlots in, baths to pamper themselves in, bridges to levy tolls on." Judah the son of proselytes went off and retold the sage's words, until they were heard by the Roman government, which decreed: Judah, who acclaimed [Rome], shall be acclaimed [as spokesman for the Jews]; Yose, who remained silent, shall be exiled to Sepphoris; Simeon, who vilified, shall be put to death.[3]

174. You find no nation smitten unless its gods are smitten with it, as is said, "And also against all the gods of Egypt I will execute judgments" (Exod. 12:12).[4]

175. "And, behold, *Mitzrayim*[5] was marching after them" (Exod. 14:10). The name of their prince in heaven was Mitzrayim. The Holy One does not fell a nation before he first fells its prince in heaven.

"While the word was in the king's mouth, Kal[6] fell in heaven" (Dan. 4:28). R. Joshua bar Avin said: Nebuchadnezzar's prince in heaven was Kal, and the Holy One felled him first. So, too, Pharaoh's prince in heaven was Mitzrayim, and he, too, was flying in pursuit of the children of Israel. Accordingly, when the Holy One sank the Egyptians in the sea, He first sank their prince, as is said, "And the Lord hurled down Mitzrayim" (Exod. 14:27), meaning the prince of Egypt; and only then "Pharaoh's chariots and his hosts hath He hurled down into the sea" (Ps. 136:15).[7]

176. Every distress in which Israel and the nations are partnered is distress indeed; but a distress that is Israel's alone is no distress.[8]

177. "Grant not, O Lord, the desires of the wicked; draw not out his muzzle"[9] (Ps. 140:9). Jacob prayed to the Holy One: Master of the universe, grant not to wicked Esau his heart's desire. What then is implied by "Draw not out his muzzle?" Jacob prayed: Master of the universe, make a muzzle for the wicked Esau, that his serenity not be complete. And what muzzle did the Holy One make for Esau? The Barbarians and the Germans,[10] said R. Hama bar Hanina, of whom the Romans are afraid. But for them, the Romans would have proceeded to destroy the entire world.

R. Hama bar Hanina also said: In Germania, a province of Rome, there are three hundred crowned heads, and in Babylonia there are three hundred and sixty-five generals. Every day the ones go out against the others, and one of the crowned heads or generals is slain, and so they are too busy to appoint a supreme king under whose command they would conquer the world.[11]

178. "Deliver me, I pray Thee, from the hand of my brother, from the hand of Esau" (Gen. 32:12): In the time-to-come, deliver my children from Esau's children's children, who will come at them with the power of Esau. Of Jacob's prayer, it is written, "I considered the horns, and behold, there came up among them another horn, a little one" (Dan. 7:8)—the son of Natzar[12]—"before which three of the first horns were plucked up by the roots" (ibid.)—Macrinus, Carinus, and Kyriades.[13] "And behold, in this horn were eyes like the eyes of a man, and a mouth speaking great things" (ibid.): the wicked empire [of Rome], which drafts soldiers from all the nations in the world.

Quoting "As for the ten horns, out of this kingdom shall ten kings arise" (Dan. 7:24), R. Yohanan said: Scripture speaks of all these as descendants of Esau, but "I considered the horns, and behold, there came up among them another horn, a little one" (Dan. 7:8)—this one is the wicked empire [of Rome]; "before which three of the first horns were plucked up by the roots" (ibid.)—these are the three preceding empires;[14] "and behold, in this horn were eyes like the eyes of a man" (ibid.)—this [describes] the wicked empire [of Rome], which casts an envious eye upon a man's possessions, saying, "So-and-so is rich—we will make him a magistrate;[15] so-and-so is rich—we will make him a counselor."[16]

179. At the time Israel crossed the sea, the ministering angels were about to chant their daily song before the Holy One. But the Holy One said to them: The works of My hands are drowning in the sea, and you would chant song before Me?[17]

---

1. JV: *adam* ("man"). Scripture seemingly equates the creation of Edom to the creation of the earth.
2. Gen. R. 9:13.
3. B. Shab 33b.
4. B. Suk 9a.
5. JV: "the Egyptians." The Hebrew text says, "Egypt was marching after them," not, as one would expect, "the Egyptians."
6. JV: "a voice (*kol*)."
7. Exod. R. 21:5.
8. Because God quickly responds to Israel's urgent pleas for help (Mah). Deut. R. 2:22.
9. JV: "further not his evil device." But *zemam* may mean "evil desire" as well as "a muzzle."
10. The Goths and the Huns.
11. B. Meg 6a–b; Gen. R. 75:9.
12. According to Heinrich Graetz, he was Odenathus of Palmyra, a robber chief who became the founder of a dynasty (Gen. R., Soncino, p. 705, n. 8).
13. Three Roman generals who fell before Odenathus. Possibly Quietus should be read, instead of Kyriades. So Gen. R. TA.
14. Babylon, Persia, and Greece.
15. An office that ruins its holder.
16. A post equally ruinous. Gen. R. 76:6.
17. B. Meg 10b; B. Sanh 39b; Exod. R. 23:7.

180. Our masters taught: If a Jew on the road happens to come upon a heathen [walking in the same direction], he should keep him walking at his right. R. Ishmael son of R. Yohanan ben Beroka said: If the heathen has a sword, one should keep him walking at one's right; if he has a stick, at one's left.[1] If the Jew and the heathen are going up or down [a hill], the Jew should make sure that he is not below and the heathen above. The Jew should also make sure not to bend down before him, lest the heathen smash his skull. If the heathen asks him where he is going, he should mention a place beyond his destination. This is what our father Jacob did with the wicked Esau, when he said, "Until I come to my lord in Seir" (Gen. 33:14), while, in fact, "Jacob journeyed to Sukkoth"[2] (Gen. 33:17).

It once happened that some disciples of R. Akiva, who were journeying to Chezib, were overtaken by robbers. The robbers asked them where they were going. They replied, "To Acco."[3] But when they reached Chezib, they turned in to their destination. The robbers asked them, "Whose disciples are you?" "R. Akiva's." The robbers: "Happy are R. Akiva and his disciples, whom no evil man is likely to do mischief to."[4]

181. When Rabbi [Judah I, the Patriarch] and R. Yose son of R. Judah, who were walking along a road, saw a heathen coming toward them, they said: He will ask us three things: Who are you? What is your occupation? Where are you going? When asked "Who are you?" we will say, "Jews." "What is your occupation?"—we will say, "Merchants." "Where are you going?"—we will say, "To buy wheat from the granaries of Yavneh."

Rabbi [Judah] stood facing the heathen to see what he would ask, but R. Yose son of R. Judah waited [in the background], thinking: If the heathen continues to question, I will [step forward and] give another answer. Later, Rabbi Judah asked R. Yose: Where did you learn [the need for] such [precaution]? R. Yose: From our father Jacob, who instructed the foremost to say, "He also is behind us. And he instructed also the second" (Gen. 32:19–20).[5]

182. R. Eleazar said: A Jew should never stick his finger into the mouth of a heathen unless the heathen first sticks his finger into the mouth of a Jew.[6]

183. R. Yohanan said: I remember that it used to be said in the academy: He who concedes to heathens falls into their hands; and he who trusts them—what belongs to him will become theirs.[7]

1. A sword is worn on the left side; a stick is carried on the right side. The Jew will thus be instantly alerted in the event of an attack.
2. Much nearer than Seir.
3. Beyond Chezib.
4. B. AZ 25b.
5. Gen. R. 76:8.
6. The Jew is not the one to initiate strife. Or: With his finger in the Jew's mouth, the heathen is not likely to bite the Jew's finger for fear of getting his own finger bitten off. Gen. R. 80:7.
7. B. BB 91b.

C H A P T E R   T W O

THE LAND OF ISRAEL

The Land and Israel

1. The Holy One said to Moses: The Land is precious to Me, and Israel are precious to Me. I shall bring Israel who are precious to Me into the Land that is precious to Me.[1]

2. There is a man who is comely, but his clothes fit badly; there is another who is ungainly, but his clothes fit him well. Israel becomes the Land, and the Land becomes Israel: "Yea, the heritage becomes me well" (Ps. 16:6).[2]

3. Beginning his discourse with the verse "He stood and measured the earth" (Hab. 3:6), R. Simeon ben Yohai said: The Holy One took the measure of all lands and found no land but the Land of Israel worthy of being given to Israel.[3]

4. R. Isaac said: The Torah should have started with no other verse than "This month shall be unto you" (Exod. 12:2), which is the first precept enjoined upon Israel. Why then does it begin with "In the beginning" (Gen. 1:1)? Because "He wished to declare to His people the power of His works, to be able to give them the heritage of the nations [without causing protest]" (Ps. 111:6). For, should the peoples of the world say to Israel: You are a people of robbers, for you conquered the lands of seven nations, Israel will be able to reply: The entire earth and the fullness thereof belong to the Holy One. He created it and gave it to whoever seemed right to Him. So when He chose, He gave it to you, and when He chose, He took it from you and gave it to us.[4]

5. There are three sites concerning which the peoples of the world cannot taunt Israel and say, "They are yours by acts of robbery." The three are: the cave of Machpelah, the grave of Joseph, and the area for the Temple.[5]

6. It is taught that R. Simeon ben Yohai said: The Holy One gave Israel three precious gifts, each of them through suffering: Torah, the Land of Israel, and the world-to-come. The proof for Torah? "Happy is the man whom Thou chastenest, O Lord, for thus Thou teachest him Thy Torah" (Ps. 94:12). The Land of Israel? "As a man chasteneth his son, so the Lord thy God chasteneth thee" (Deut. 8:5), followed by: "The Lord thy God bringeth thee into the good Land" (Deut. 8:7). And the world-to-come? "The commandment is a lamp, and the teaching is light, and reproofs of suffering are the way to life[-to-come]" (Prov. 6:23).[6]

7. Three things—the Land of Israel, the Temple, and the dynasty of David—were given conditionally. Proof for the Land of Israel? "Take heed to yourselves, lest your heart be deceived . . . and the anger of the Lord be kindled against you . . . and ye perish quickly from off the good Land" (Duet. 11:16–17). Proof for the Temple? "As for this house which thou art building, if thou wilt walk in My statutes," etc. (1 Kings 6:12); but if not, "this house which is so high [shall become desolate]" (1 Kings 9:8).[7] Proof for the dynasty of David? "If thy children keep My covenant . . . their children also forever shall sit on thy throne" (Ps. 132:12); if not, "I will visit their transgression with the rod" (Ps. 89:33).[8]

The Land and Its Settlement

8. Our masters taught: A man should ever strive to live in the Land of Israel, even in a city whose inhabitants are mostly heathens, and should avoid living outside the Land, even in a city whose inhabitants are mostly Jews. For he who lives in the Land of Israel is like one who has a God, whereas he who lives outside the Land is like one who has no God.[9] Therefore it is said, "To give you the land of Canaan, to be your God" (Lev. 25:38). But is it conceivable that he who lives outside the Land has no God? No, but what Scripture means is that he who lives outside the Land is regarded as though he worshiped idols. Thus David is quoted as saying, "They have driven me out this day, that I should not cleave unto the inheritance of the Lord, saying: Go, serve other gods" (1 Sam. 26:19). Could it be supposed that anyone would actually say to David, "Go, worship other gods"? Rather, the verse implies that he who lives outside the Land is regarded as though he worshiped idols.[10]

9. It is taught that R. Ishmael said: Jews outside the Land worship idols without meaning to. How? When a heathen prepares a feast for his son and invites all the Jews in his city, even though they eat their own [kosher food] and drink their own [kosher wine], and their own attendant waits on them, Scripture regards them as though

---

1. Num. R. 23:7.
2. Num. R. 23:6.
3. Lev. R. 13:2.
4. Gen. R. 1:2; Yalkut, *Bo*, §187; Rashi on Gen. 1:1 and Ps. 111:6.
5. Each of these sites was purchased. See Gen. 23:9, Josh. 24:32, and 1 Chron. 21:25–26. Gen. R. 79:7; Yalkut, *Va-yishlah*, §133.
6. B. Ber 5a and En Yaakov, ad loc.
7. So Mek, La 2:188. BR quote Mic. 7:13, which is less to the point.
8. Mek, *Yitro*, *Amalek*, 4.
9. "They mingled themselves with the nations, and learned their works" (Ps. 106:35).
10. B. Ket 110b and En Yaakov, ad loc.

they had eaten sacrifices to inert idols, as is said, "When he invites thee, thou eatest of his sacrifice" (Exod. 34:15).[1]

10. "And I will give unto thee, and to thy seed after thee, the land of thy sojournings, all the land of Canaan . . . and I will be their God" (Gen. 17:8). R. Yudan said: If your children enter the Land, they agree to accept My Godhead; otherwise, they do not.[2]

11. "My soul hath them still in remembrance, and is bowed down within me" (Lam. 3:20). R. Hiyya taught: The verse will be understood from the parable of a king who used to go to the hot baths of Gedor[3] and take his sons with him. On one occasion his sons provoked him, and he swore that he would not take them again. After that, when the king went forth by himself without his sons, he would remember them and say tearfully: Would that my sons were with me, even if they did provoke me. The king in the parable is the Holy One. The sons are Israel. After Israel were no longer in the Land, He kept saying: Would that Israel were with Me, even if they did provoke Me. In expressing this wish, God said, "Oh that I were again in the wilderness with the complaints[4] of wayfaring men" (Jer. 9:1), by which the Holy One meant: Oh that My sons were with Me now, as they were in the wilderness, where they kept complaining against Me. Likewise, "let the House of Israel dwell in their land, even if they defile it" (Ezek. 36:17),[5] by which the Holy One meant: Oh that My children were still with Me in the Land of Israel, even if they were to keep defiling it.[6]

12. R. Eleazar said: He who makes his home in the Land of Israel lives untainted by iniquity, as is said, "The people that dwelleth therein has its iniquity lifted" (Isa. 33:24).[7]

13. "And the spirit to them that walk therein" (Isa. 42:5) teaches, so said R. Jeremiah bar Abba in the name of R. Yohanan, that anyone who walks even as little as four cubits in the Land of Israel is assured that he is destined for the world-to-come.[8]

14. "Oh that I had wings like a dove" (Ps. 55:7). Why like a dove? Because, said R. Azariah in the name of R. Yudan, all other birds rest on a rock or on a tree when tired; but when a dove is tired, she draws in one of her wings and continues flying. "Since I will have to keep moving farther and farther away" (Ps. 55:8)—moving and moving on again, exile and on to another exile—"I would lodge in the wilderness" (ibid.)—I would rather dwell in the wilderness of the Land of Israel than in palaces outside the Land.[9]

15. "Ye shall dwell in your Land safely" (Lev. 26:5). Inside your Land, you dwell safely; but outside it, you do not.[10]

16. R. Simlai expounded: Why did Moses our teacher long to enter the Land of Israel? Are we to suppose that what he needed was to eat its fruit or be sated with its bounty? Rather, what Moses had in mind was that many precepts given to Israel could not be fulfilled except in the Land of Israel.[11]

17. A story of R. Judah ben Betera, R. Matia ben Heresh, R. Hanina the nephew of R. Joshua, and R. Jonathan, who were going to settle abroad. When they came to Platus and remembered the Land of Israel, they lifted their tear-filled eyes, rent their garments, and recited the verse "Ye shall possess it, and dwell therein, for in it ye can observe all the laws" (Deut. 11:31–32). Then they turned around and went back, saying: Living in the Land of Israel is equivalent to performing all the commands in the Torah.

Another story of R. Eleazar ben Shammua and R. Yohanan the Sandal Maker, who were traveling to Nisibis [in Babylonia] to study Torah in the school of R. Judah ben Betera. When they reached Zidon and remembered the Land of Israel, they lifted their tear-filled eyes, rent their garments, and recited the verse "Ye shall possess it, and dwell therein, for in it ye can observe all the laws" (Deut. 11:31–32). Then they turned around and went back, saying: Living in the Land of Israel is equivalent to performing all the commands in the Torah.[12]

18. "Dwell in the cities that ye have taken" (Jer. 40:10). Hezekiah said: How did you take them? By dwelling in them. The school of R. Ishmael taught: "Ye shall possess it, and dwell therein" (Deut. 11:31). How do you come to possess it? By dwelling in it.[13]

19. R. Yohanan taught: Why did Omri merit kingship? Because he added a large city to the Land of Israel, as is said, "He bought the hill Samaria from Shemer . . . and called the name of the city which he built . . . Samaria" (1 Kings 16:24).[14]

20. "Then will I remember My covenant with Jacob . . . and I will remember the Land" (Lev. 26:42). From this verse you may infer that the Land is equivalent to [the covenant of] circumcision. Accordingly, even as the Sabbath is set aside for circumcision, so the Sabbath is set aside for the conquest of the Land.[15]

---

1. B. AZ 8a.
2. Gen. R. 46:9.
3. On the Yarmuk River.
4. JV: "lodging place." But *malon* ("lodging place") could also be derived from the root *lvn* ("to complain").
5. JV: "When the House of Israel dwelt in their own land, they defiled it."
6. Lam. R. 3:20, §7; Yalkut, Lam., §638.
7. B. Ket 111a.
8. Ibid. For the holy spirit's role in the resurrection, see Sot. 9:15ff.
9. Gen. R. 39:8; Yalkut, Ps., §771.
10. Sif Lev. 111a.
11. B. Sot 14a.
12. Sif Deut., §80; Yalkut, Deut. §877.
13. B. Kid 26a.
14. B. Sanh 102b.
15. Yalkut, Deut., §861.

21. When a man purchases a house in the Land of Israel, the bill of sale for it may be written even on the Sabbath.[1]

22. From the very beginning of creation, the Holy One was occupied first with the planting of trees, as is shown by the verse "The Lord God first planted a garden in Eden" (Gen. 2:8). You, too, when you enter the Land, must occupy yourselves first with nothing else but planting trees, as is said, "When you come into the Land, ye shall plant . . . trees" (Lev. 19:23).[2]

23. R. Levi said: When Abraham was traveling through Aram-naharaim and Aram-nahor, he saw the inhabitants eating and drinking and reveling. "May my portion not be in this land," he exclaimed. But when he reached the promontory of Tyre and saw the people there engaged in weeding at weeding time and in hoeing at hoeing time, he exclaimed, "Would that my portion be in this land." At that, the Holy One said, "Unto thy seed will I give this land" (Gen. 12:7).[3]

24. R. Yohanan ben Zakkai used to say: If you have a sapling in your hand and are told, "Look, the Messiah is here," you should first plant the sapling and then go out to welcome the Messiah.[4]

25. "Walk [before Me] in My very presence" (Gen. 12:1). To whom may Abraham be likened? To a king's friend, who, seeing the king walking about in dark alleys,[5] began lighting the way for him through a window. When the king looked up and saw him, he said: Instead of [indirectly] lighting the way for me through a window, come and light the way [directly] for me in my very presence. So, too, the Holy One said to our father Abraham: Instead of [indirectly] lighting the way to Me from Mesopotamia and neighboring territories, come down here and light the way to Me [directly] in My very presence—in the Land of Israel.[6]

26. After Jacob had brought his sons and his flocks to the Land of Israel, he got busy and sold all the flocks he had brought with him from outside the Land. He set up the proceeds in piles of gold. Then he said to Esau, "You own an equal share with me in the area of Machpelah. Which do you prefer—to take these piles of gold or share Machpelah with me?" Esau said to himself: What do I have to do with this cave? I would rather have the gold.

Do you suppose that Jacob lost anything by that? Not at all. For the Holy One made up his loss and at once restored everything to him.[7]

27. "Better is a handful quietly come by," etc. (Eccles. 4:6). R. Isaac interpreted this verse as applicable to the tribes of Reuben and Gad,[8] who, upon coming into the Land of Israel, saw how many areas suitable for sowing grain were there, how many areas suitable for planting trees were there.[9] And so they said, "Better is a handful quietly come by" in the Land of Israel "than two fistfuls after much struggle" (Eccles. 4:6) on the east bank of the Jordan. After reflecting, they asked themselves: Are we not the ones who chose [the east bank in preference to the Land]?[10]

28. "Better is a dry morsel and quietness therewith, than a house full of feasting with strife" (Prov. 17:1). R. Yohanan said, "Better is a dry morsel"—the Land of Israel, where even if day after day a man eats no more than a morsel with salt, yet because he lives in the Land he gains the world-to-come; "than a house full of feasting with strife"—than living outside the Land, where acts of violence and robbery are rife.[11]

29. Our masters taught: One may not leave the Land to go outside the Land unless two *seah* of wheat cost four denars. R. Simeon [ben Yohai] objected: When may one leave the Land? Only if there is no wheat to be purchased; but if one does find wheat for purchase, then even if one *seah* costs as much as four denars, one may not leave.

Indeed, R. Simeon ben Yohai taught: Elimelech, Mahlon, and Chilion were the notables who led their generation. Why then were they punished [by untimely death]? Because they left the Land to go outside it, for it is written, "All the city was astir concerning them, and the women said: 'Is this Naomi?' " (Ruth 1:19). What did they mean by "Is this Naomi?" They meant, said R. Isaac, "Look at Naomi, who left the Land to go outside the Land—look what happened to her."[12]

30. Simeon bar Abba came to R. Hanina and said: Write me a letter of recommendation, so that I may go abroad for my livelihood. R. Hanina replied: Before long, when I join your forebears, each of them will say to me: I had a precious sapling in the Land of Israel and you allowed it to go abroad!

A certain priest came to R. Hanina and asked: May I go to Tyre to perform a commandment—to undergo *halitzah* by or to marry the childless widow of my deceased brother? R. Hanina replied: Your brother left the bosom of his motherland and embraced the bosom of an alien land. May He who is everywhere be blessed for having smitten him—and you would do what your brother did![13]

31. "And the Lord said unto Jacob: Return unto the Land of thy fathers, and unto her who begat thee; and I will be with thee" (Gen. 31:3). In saying, "Return unto the Land of thy fathers," etc., the Holy One said, "Your father is

---

1. B. BK 80b.
2. Lev. R. 25:3.
3. Since the land required constant care and cultivation, allowing no time for idling, which leads to drinking and reveling, Abraham hoped that his children would settle in it. Gen. R. 39:8.
4. ARNB 31.
5. Where people steeped in idolatry lived.
6. Gen. R. 30:10.
7. Tanhuma B, *Va-yishlah*, §11.
8. The two tribes chose to settle on the east bank of the Jordan.
9. Unlike the grazing land on the east bank.
10. Lev. R. 3:1; Eccles. R. 4:6, §1.
11. Yalkut, Prov., §556.
12. B. BB 91a; Gen. R. 25:3.
13. You should stay in the Land and let the widow come here. P. MK 3:1, 81a.

waiting for you, your mother is waiting for you, and I Myself am waiting for you," meaning, so taught R. Assi in the name of Resh Lakish, that there is no enduring blessing in wealth acquired outside the Land, but once you return to the Land of your fathers, I Myself will be with you.[1]

32. Even when a man has the merit of his fathers, it does not stand by him once he leaves the Land and goes outside it.[2]

Love for the Land

33. "I will give thee a desirable Land" (Jer. 3:19)—a Land all the notables of the world deemed desirable.[3]

34. "I had rather stand on the threshold (*histopheph*) of the house of my God" (Ps. 84:11). What is meant by *histopheph?* R. Tanhum son of R. Hanilai and Rav differed. According to one, David said to the Holy One: Master of the universe, even if I had an antechamber and a chamber outside the Land, and only a threshold (*saph*) in the Land, "I had rather stand on the threshold." According to the other: Even if in the Land of Israel I had nothing to eat other than the leavings (*sippuph*) of carobs, "I would settle for the leavings."[4]

35. On his way to the Land of Israel, when R. Zera found no ferry to take him across [the Jordan], he held on to a rope bridge and crossed over. Watching him, a certain heretic sneered: "O you impulsive people, who opened your mouths before you opened your ears![5] You still persist in your impulsiveness [exposing yourselves to the danger of drowning]." R. Zera replied, "A Land that neither Moses nor Aaron was deemed worthy of entering—who could possibly assure me that I would be deemed worthy of entering?[6]

36. R. Abba used to kiss the cliffs of Acco. R. Hanina used to repair broken sections of the roads in the Land. R. Hiyya ben Gamda used to roll himself in its dust, in keeping with "Thy servants take pleasure in her stones, and love her dust" (Ps. 102:15).[7]

37. Ulla came down [from the Land of Israel to Babylonia], where he died. [As he was dying] he began to weep. When asked, "Why are you weeping? We will carry your coffin up to the Land of Israel," he replied, "What good will it do me? I am about to lose the precious pearl given me in a land that is unclean. He who discharges this pearl into the bosom of his motherland is not like him who discharges it into the bosom of an alien land."

When R. Eleazar was told of Ulla's death, he exclaimed, "O that you, Ulla, 'had to die in a land that is unclean' " (Amos 7:17). When informed, "But his coffin has just arrived [in the Land]," he said, "He whom the Land receives while still alive is not at all like one whom it has to receive after his death."[8]

38. A story. As R. Berokia and R. Eleazar ben Pedat were strolling through the city gate to the outskirts of Tiberias, they saw some coffins arriving from abroad. R. Berokia asked R. Eleazar, "What good will it do them? While alive, they left the Land, and now, dead, they have had themselves brought back to her? To such I apply the verse 'You regarded My heritage as an abomination' [Jer. 2:7] while you were alive, and 'when ye entered as corpses ye defiled My Land' [ibid.]." R. Eleazar replied, "What you imply is not right. For as soon as they are buried in the Land of Israel, and a clod of the Land's earth is thrown over them, it will make expiation for them, as is said, "And His Land shall make expiation for His people" (Deut. 32:43).[9]

39. R. Levi said: Moses pleaded with the Holy One: Master of the universe, Joseph's bones are being allowed to enter the Land—should I not be allowed to enter? The Holy One replied: He who acknowledged it as his Land is rightfully buried in the Land.[10] But he who did not acknowledge it as his Land[11] cannot claim the right to burial in it.[12]

40. R. Eleazar said: The dead [buried] outside the Land of Israel will not come back to life, for it is said, "I will set glory in the Land of the living" (Ezek. 26:20): in the Land, where My glory is set, the dead will come back to life; but not so the dead in a land where My glory is not.[13]

41. "Bury me not, I pray thee, in Egypt" (Gen. 47:29). Why did all the patriarchs demand and yearn for burial in the Land of Israel? R. Eleazar said: There is a reason for it. R. Joshua ben Levi explained that in saying, "There is a reason for it," R. Eleazar alluded to the verse "O that I might walk before the Lord in the lands of the living" (Ps. 116:9), a verse our masters, in the name of R. Huldah, explained as follows: Why did the patriarchs yearn for burial in the Land of Israel? Because the dead buried in the Land of Israel will be the first to come to life in the days of the Messiah and will enjoy the age of the Messiah. But he who dies outside the Land and is buried there has, said R. Hananiah, two agonies to contend with [the agony of dying and the agony of burial outside the Land].

Does this mean, asked R. Simon, that the righteous buried outside the Land will lose out? No. What will the Holy One do for them? For their sake, He will provide

1. Gen. R. 74:1.
2. B. BB 91a.
3. Tanhuma, *Mishpatim*, §23.
4. Tanhuma, *Re'eh*, §8.
5. At Sinai you said, "We will do," before saying, "We will hear." See Exod. 24:7.
6. B. Ket 112a.
7. Ibid.
8. P. Kil 9:4, 32c; B. Ket 111a.
9. PR 1:6 (YJS 1:44–45); P. Kil 9:5, 32d; Gen. R. 96:5.
10. Joseph said: "I was stolen out of the Land of the Hebrews" (Gen. 40:15).
11. Moses allowed the daughters of Jethro to say of him, "An Egyptian delivered us out of the hand of the shepherds" (Exod. 2:19).
12. Deut. R. 2:8.
13. B. Ket 111a.

underground passages, which go on and on like subterranean caves, and the righteous will roll through them until they reach the Land of Israel, where the Holy One will restore the spirit of life to them and they will stand up. And the proof? The verse "I will open your graves, and cause you to come up out of your graves, O My people, when I bring you into the Land of Israel" (Ezek. 37:12), followed by "I will put My spirit in you and ye shall live" (Ezek. 37:14).[1]

42. "Of Zion it shall be said: 'This man and that man was born in her' " (Ps. 87:5). R. Meyasha grandson of R. Joshua ben Levi explained: The phrase "This man and that man" refers to the man actually born in Zion and to the man yearning to see her.[2]

The Holiness of the Land

43. The Land of Israel is the holiest of all lands.[3]

44. Why did the holy spirit dwell in the territory of Benjamin? Because all the other tribe fathers were born outside the Land, while Benjamin was born in the land of Israel.[4]

45. "And the Lord spoke unto Moses and Aaron in the land of Egypt, saying" (Exod. 12:1). "In the land of Egypt" implies that it was outside the city. But perhaps it means inside the city? However, since Scripture says, "Moses said unto him: 'As soon as I am gone out of the city, I will spread forth my hands unto the Lord' " (Exod. 9:29), may not the matter be argued *a fortiori?* If, in order to pray—an ordinary event—Moses would insist on going outside the city, how much more so would he go outside the city to receive a communication from God—an extraordinary event? And why would God speak to him only outside the city? Because the city was full of abominations and idols.

Before the Land of Israel had been chosen, all lands were suitable for God to speak in. After the Land of Israel was chosen, all other lands were excluded.

Before the eternal Temple had been chosen, all of Jerusalem was fit for the Divine Presence. After the eternal Temple was chosen, the rest of Jerusalem was eliminated, as is said, "The Lord hath chosen Zion" (Ps. 132:13), and goes on to quote God as declaring, "This is to be My resting place forever" (Ps. 132:14).

Should you say, "But I can mention prophets to whom God spoke outside the Land": even though to be sure, He did speak to some prophets outside the Land, He spoke to them only because of the merit of the fathers. And, it might be added, even though He did speak to them outside the Land because of the merit of the fathers, He spoke to them only in a place that was clean, near water. As Daniel said, "I was by the stream Ulai" (Dan. 8:2) and "I was by the great river, which is Tigris" (Dan. 10:4): and as is said, "The word of the Lord came expressly unto Ezekiel . . . by the river Chebar" (Ezek. 1:3).

R. Eleazar ben Zadok pointed out that Scripture also says to Ezekiel: "Arise, go forth into the plain" (Dan. 3:2), which shows that a plain was a suitable place for divine utterance.

You can see for yourself that the Presence does not reveal itself outside the Land, for Scripture says, "Jonah rose up to flee unto Tarshish from the Presence of the Lord" (Jon. 1:3). Could he have thought that it was possible to flee from the Lord? Had not David said, "Whither shall I go from Thy spirit? Or whither shall I flee from Thy Presence" (Ps. 139:7)? Rather, what Jonah had in mind was: Gentiles are more inclined [than Israel] to repent. So, in order not to put Israel in a bad light, I will go outside the Land, to a place where the Presence neither dwells nor reveals itself.[5] The matter may be illustrated by the parable of a priest's heathen slave who said: I will flee to the cemetery, where my master cannot follow me.[6] But his master said to him: You are not the only heathen slave I have. So, too, Jonah said: Since Gentiles are more inclined to repent, in order not to put Israel in a bad light, I will go outside the Land, where the Presence does not reveal itself. But the Holy One said to him: [I do not depend on you.] You are not the only emissary I have, as is said, "The Lord hurled a great wind into the sea" (Jon. 1:4).[7]

46. We have been taught: Before Israel entered the Land, miracles in whatever land they occurred were commemorated with hymns of praise [*Hallel*]. After Israel entered the Land, miracles occurring in other lands were no longer commemorated in this way.[8]

Torah of the Land

47. The Holy One said: A small company in the Land of Israel is more precious to Me than the Great Sanhedrin outside the Land.[9]

48. Even when there are saintly men and sages outside the Land, and in the Land none but shepherds and cowherds, the year is intercalated only on the testimony of the shepherds and cowherds who are within the Land of Israel. More! Even if there are prophets outside the Land, and in the Land none but unlearned men, the year is intercalated only on the testimony of the unlearned men within the Land.[10]

49. R. Safra said that R. Abbahu used to tell the following: When Hananiah the son of R. Joshua's brother

---

1. Gen. R. 96:5.
2. B. Ket 75a.
3. Kel 1:6.
4. Mek, *Yitro, Ba-hodesh*, 4.
5. Lest it become evident that Israel were not as ready to heed the prophets as were the people of Nineveh.
6. A priest may not enter a cemetery.
7. Mek, *Bo, Pis'ha* 1; Yalkut, *Bo*, §187.
8. B. Meg 14a.
9. P. Ned 6:8, 40a.
10. PRE 8.

went down to the Diaspora, he used to intercalate years[1] and fix New Moons[2] outside the Land. So [the High Court] dispatched two disciples of the wise, R. Yose ben Kippar and the grandson of Zechariah ben Kevutal. When Hananiah saw them, he asked: Why did you come? They replied: We came to learn Torah [from you]. At that, he had it announced: These men are notables of the generation and their forebears ministered in the Temple, for we are taught, "Zechariah ben Kevutal said: 'Many times I read the Book of Daniel to the high priest.' "[3] Before long, R. Hananiah proceeded to declare unclean what was declared clean by the two disciples of the wise from the Land and to prohibit what they permitted. This time he had it announced: These are men of falsehood and chaos. They replied: You already built us up and cannot tear us down. You have already built a fence [of good repute about us] and cannot break it down. So he asked them: Why do you declare clean what I declare unclean? Why do you permit what I prohibit? They replied: Because you intercalate years and fix New Moons outside the Land. He said: But did not Akiva ben Joseph himself use to intercalate years and fix New Moons outside the Land? They replied: Let R. Akiva be—he did not leave his equal in the Land of Israel. Hananiah retorted: I, too, did not leave my equal in the Land of Israel. They replied: The kids you left have become goats with horns, and it is they who sent us to you, saying, "Go speak to him in our name. If he listens, well and good. If not, he will be placed under a ban. Also tell our brethren in the Diaspora [not to obey him]. If they listen to you, well and good. If not, they may as well go up a mountain top [and make themselves a high place], where Ahiah[4] will build the altar, Hananiah[5] will play the harp, and all of them will become renegades who declare that they have no portion in the God of Israel."

Hearing this, all of the people burst into weeping as they said: God forbid! We do have a portion in the God of Israel.

Why all this to-do? Because Scripture says, "Out of Zion shall go forth the Law, and the word of the Lord from Jerusalem" (Isa. 2:3).[6]

50. We have been taught that R. Eleazar ha-Kappar said: Synagogues and houses of study outside the Land are destined to be implanted in the Land of Israel, for it is said, "As Tabor among the mountains and Carmel by the sea did come" (Jer. 46:18).[7] The matter may be argued *a fortiori:* If Tabor and Carmel, which came only for a while to learn Torah, are implanted in the Land of Israel, all the more so synagogues and houses of study, where Torah is constantly read and expounded.[8]

1. That is, add a month to certain years.
2. Fix the day when the new month begins.
3. Yoma 1:6.
4. He was head of the community.
5. He was a Levite.
6. B. Ber 63b and En Yaakov, ad loc.
7. There is a tradition that the two mountains originally stood outside the Land of Israel, but because they offered themselves as mountains on which the Torah could be given—that is, the mountains wanted to study Torah—they were permitted to enter the Land of Israel. See Gen. R. 99:1 and Strashun's note; MTeh 68:9.
8. B. Meg 29a.

51. R. Yose bar Halafta said to his son R. Ishmael: If you would see the face of the Presence in this world, then occupy yourself with Torah in the Land of Israel.[9]

52. The air of Israel's Land makes one wise.[10]

53. "Among the nations there is no Torah" (Lam. 2:9) implies that Torah is in the Land of Israel, [the Land] "where there is gold" (Gen. 2:11)—where there are words of Torah more to be desired than gold, than much fine gold.

"And the gold of that Land is good" (Gen. 2:12). These words assert that there is no Torah like the Torah of Israel's Land and no wisdom like the wisdom of Israel's Land.

"There is bdellium and the onyx stone" (Gen. 2:12)—Scripture, Mishnah, Talmud, Tosefta, and *Aggadah.*[11]

54. R. Simeon ben Eleazar said: A sage who dwells in the Land of Israel but then goes to live abroad diminishes himself, so that one who continues to dwell in the Land is superior to him. Even though he has diminished himself, he is still superior to all the superior ones in foreign lands. By what analogy may the matter be illustrated? By analogy with Indian iron, which comes from a land far across the sea. Even when deteriorated through use, it is still better than the best in all other lands.[12]

55. "A well of living waters" (Song 4:15)—such is the Torah in Israel's Land.[13]

56. R. Ze'era said: Even the everyday talk of people in the Land of Israel is Torah.[14]

57. Ten *kav* of wisdom came down to the world—the Land of Israel took nine, and all the rest of the world one.[15]

The Dimensions of the Land

58. R. Abba bar Hanina said: Had Israel not sinned, they would have been given only the five books of Torah and the book of Joshua, the latter containing the dimensions of Israel's Land.[16]

59. "Then shalt thou arise, and get thee up unto the place which the Lord thy God shall choose" (Deut. 17:8). These words teach that the Temple is on higher ground than the entire Land of Israel and that the Land of Israel is on higher ground than all other lands.[17]

60. Ever since the early prophets, there was a stone [in the Temple] called the foundation stone, because, so it is taught, upon it the world was founded.

9. MTeh 105:1.
10. B. BB 158b.
11. Sif Deut., §37; Gen. R. 16:4.
12. ARN 28.
13. Yalkut, Song, §537.
14. Lev. R. 34:7.
15. B. Kid 49b.
16. B. Ned 22b.
17. B. Zev 54b.

We have been taught: R. Eliezer the Elder said: "These are the generations of the heaven and of the earth, when they were created in the day that the Lord God made earth and heaven" (Gen. 2:4)—that is, the progeny of heaven[1] was generated from heaven, and the progeny of earth was generated from earth. However, the sages said: Both were generated from Zion, for Scripture says, "God, God, the Lord, hath spoken and called the earth, from the rising of the sun unto the going down thereof" (Ps. 50:1), and goes on to say, "Out of Zion, the perfection (*mikhlal*) of beauty" (Ps. 50:2), which implies that out of Zion was the world's beauty perfected (*mukhlal*).[2]

61. "I made me gardens and parks, and I planted trees in them of all kinds of fruit" (Eccles. 2:5). Even as the navel is in a man's middle, so the Land of Israel, it is said, "dwells in the middle of the earth" (Ezek. 38:12). It is situated in the world's middle, and from there the foundation of the world extends. Now, Jerusalem is in the middle of the Land of Israel, and the Temple area in the middle of Jerusalem, the Holy of Holies[3] in the middle of the Temple, the Ark in the middle of the Holy of Holies, and the foundation stone out of which the world was founded in the front of the Ark. Since Solomon was wise, he came to know the "roots" issuing from it to the entire world. If an artery went to Ethiopia, he planted pepper upon it, and on other arteries he planted all kinds of trees that brought forth all kinds of other fruit.[4]

62. When R. Dimi came [to the Land], R. Yohanan said: The verse "He hath founded it upon the seas, and established it upon the floods" (Ps. 24:2) refers to the seven seas and four rivers that surround the Land of Israel. The seven seas: the Sea of Tiberias, the [Salt] Sea of Sodom, the Sea [Gulf] of Elath, the Sea of Shalith, the Sea of Samachonitis,[5] the Sea of Apamea, and the Great [Mediterranean] Sea. The four rivers: the Jordan, the Yarmuk, the Keramiyon, and the Pigah.

But is there not also the Sea of Emessa? No, because Diocletian brought the waters of several rivers together to form that sea.[6]

63. We have been taught that the Jordan issues from the cave of Panias, passes through the Sea of Samachonitis and the Sea of Tiberias, and rolls down into the Great Sea, where it rolls on until it rushes into the mouth of Leviathan, who is described as "confident, because the Jordan rushes forth to his mouth" (Job 40:23).[7]

64. We have been taught that R. Simeon ben Gamaliel said: The pool of Siloam used to bring forth a steady flow of water through a narrow mouth the size of an *issar*.[8] At the king's order, the pool's mouth was widened so that its flow would increase. Instead, it diminished. Then they went back and narrowed its mouth as before, and the pool again brought forth its steady flow.[9]

A Land Flowing with Milk and Honey

65. "*Tevel* is supreme among terrains" (Prov. 8:26).[10] The word *tevel*, said R. Simeon ben Yohai, refers to the Land of Israel, for of the Torah it is said, "Playing in *tevel* which is His own Land" (Prov. 8:31). Why is it called *tevel?* Because it is seasoned (*metubbelet*) with everything, for, among all other terrains, each has something the others lack. But the Land of Israel lacks nothing, as is said, "Thou shalt not lack anything in it" (Deut. 8:9).[11]

66. "And of Joseph he said: Blessed of the Lord be his land" (Deut. 33:13). The verse teaches that Joseph's land was the most blessed of all lands. Dew is always available for it; it is irrigated by springs, open to the sun, open to the moon, abundant, and not lacking any blessing.[12]

67. "A land of hills and valleys" (Deut. 11:11). In mentioning hills,[13] does the verse speak in disparagement of the Land of Israel? Not at all, for the verse also mentions valleys—as valleys are mentioned in praise of the Land, so are hills mentioned in praise of it. Besides, there is a reason for hills and a reason for valleys. Fruits growing on a hill ripen early; fruits growing in a valley are more succulent.

R. Simeon ben Yohai said: When an area is a valley, it produces a *kor*[14] of grain. When it is a hill, it produces a *kor* on its eastern side, a *kor* on its western side, a *kor* on its southern side, a *kor* on its northern side, and a *kor* on its summit—a fivefold crop.

"Thus saith the Lord God: This is Jerusalem! I have set her in the midst of nations, and lands are round about her" (Ezek. 5:5). It is a land that has many kinds of soil—areas of soil for tillage, areas of sand [from which glass may be made], and areas of soil completely free of rocks or stones.

Another comment: "A land of hills and valleys." The verse indicates that the taste of fruit growing on a mountain is not like the taste of fruit growing in a valley, and the taste of fruit growing in a valley is not like the taste of fruit growing on a mountain. And the proof that the taste of fruit growing on each and every hill and fruit growing in each and every valley is distinct? The verse "A land of hills and valleys"—many, many hills, and many, many valleys.

R. Simeon ben Yohai said: There are twelve different

1. Sun, moon, and stars.
2. B. Yoma 54b.
3. Literally, "the Temple Hall," which in this instance includes chambers west of the Holy of Holies, as well as the Holy of Holies itself.
4. Tanhuma, *Kedoshim*, §10.
5. North of the Sea of Tiberias.
6. B. BB 74b; P. Kil 9:4, §32c; P. Ket 12:3, §35b; MTeh 24:6.
7. B. BB 74b.
8. A small Roman coin.
9. B. Ar 10b.
10. JV: "The beginning of the dust of the world."
11. Sif Deut., §37.
12. Sif Deut., §353.
13. Where plowing is difficult.
14. Thirty *seah*.

kinds of lands corresponding to the twelve tribes, and the fruits growing in one tribe were not like the fruits growing in another tribe.

R. Yose ben Meshullam said: Where is the proof that even as there are different savors in that which grows on land, so there are different savors in that which grows in the sea? The verse "And the gathering together of the waters called He seas" (Gen. 1:10), a verse that indicates that the taste of a fish caught in Acco is not like the taste of a fish caught in Tyre, nor is the taste of a fish caught in Tyre like the taste of a fish caught in Apamca.

Or, since the soil on a mountain is poor and the soil in a valley rich, you might suppose that the rainwater will wash the poor soil of the mountain down into the valley [and this poor soil will cause the water to sink below the ground], thus depriving plants of water.[1] Scripture therefore speaks of "hills and valleys," meaning that a hill will remain what it is and a valley will remain what it is.

Or, since rocks in the Land of Israel are fractured, producing hills, one might suppose that only the bare summits of the hills will be watered, while the sheltered sides of the hills will not be watered.[2] Therefore Scripture says, "It drinketh water from the precipitation[3] of heaven" (Deut. 11:11), meaning that both the bare summits and the sheltered sides of the hills will be watered. Scripture also says, "Yea, He ladeth the thick cloud with moisture, He spreadeth abroad the cloud of His lightning" (Job 37:11), which implies that the clouds encompassed every part of the Land, irrigating every side of it.

Or, because the Land drinks rainwater, it might perhaps not drink water from brooks? Hence Scripture: "A land of brooks of water" (Deut. 8:7). Or, because it drinks water from brooks, it might perhaps not drink water of snows? Hence Scripture: "It drinks water from [every kind of] precipitation from heaven"—since water is mentioned, it must also include melted snow, as indeed is clearly stated in "The rain cometh down, and the snow from heaven" (Isa. 55:10).

Or, since it drinks water of snows, it might perhaps not drink water of dews? Hence Scripture: "It drinketh water from the precipitation of heaven," implying that the Land drinks water of dews as well.[4]

68. "The Land . . . is not as the land of Egypt" (Deut. 11:10). The land of Egypt drinks the water of its own streams; the Land of Israel drinks rainwater. The land of Egypt—a low-lying area drinks; an elevated area cannot drink. The Land of Israel—both low-lying and elevated areas can drink. The land of Egypt—bare hilltops drink; sheltered sides do not. The Land of Israel—both bare hilltops and sheltered sides drink. The land of Egypt first drinks and then is sown;[5] the Land of Israel drinks, is sown, may be sown again, and then drinks again. The land of Egypt does not drink every day; the Land of Israel drinks every day. The land of Egypt—if one does not toil over it, [channeling its water] with mattock and ax, depriving oneself of sleep, one gets nothing from it. Not so the Land of Israel—people sleep in their beds while He who is everywhere brings down rain for them.

A parable of a king who during a journey met a man of good family and gave him one of his own slaves to serve him. Later, the king saw another person also of good family, delicately reared, working hard at a task. Since the king knew that person and his forebears as well, he said to him: I decree that you are to stop working with your hands—I myself will maintain you. So, too, all other lands were given servants to minister to them: Egypt drinks from the Nile, Babylon from the Euphrates. Not so the Land of Israel: people sleep in their beds while the Holy One brings down rain for them. To teach you incidentally that the ways of mortals are not like the ways of Him who is everywhere: a mortal acquires for himself servants in order that they may feed and sustain him, but He who spoke and the world came into being acquires for Himself servants in order that He may feed and sustain them.[6]

69. The sages taught: In her blessed years, an area in Israel's Land sown with a *seah* of grain would produce five myriad *kor* of grain; whereas even in the days of her prosperity, the same area in Zoan yielded no more than seventy *kor*. Now, among all the countries none is more fertile than the land of Egypt, of which it is said, "Like the garden of the Lord, like the land of Egypt" (Gen. 13:10); and in the entire land of Egypt there is no area more fertile than Zoan, where Egypt's kings used to be reared, as is said, "Its princes are in Zoan" (Isa. 30:4). Further: In all the Land of Israel, no ground is more rocky than Hebron, where the dead are buried.[7] Nevertheless, Hebron was seven times more fertile than Zoan, as may be inferred from the verse "Hebron was built (*mevunneh*) seven years before Zoan in Egypt" (Num. 13:22). What can the meaning of *mevunneh* be here? If it be suggested that it means "built," is it likely that [Ham] would build a house for his younger son [Canaan] before he built one for his elder son [Egypt]? The order of the birth of the two sons is given in the verse "The sons of Ham, Cush and Mizraim [Egypt], and Put and Canaan" (Gen. 10:6). The meaning of *mevunneh*[8] must be that Hebron [in Canaan] was seven times more fertile than Zoan.[9] This refers to stony ground; but in ground where there are no stones, an area in which a *seah* of grain is sown would yield at least five hundred *kor*.[10] This applies to times when the area was not blessed; but of a time when it was blessed, Scripture says, "Isaac sowed in that Land and reaped in the same year a hundredfold" (Gen. 26:12).[11]

1. Not only rain, but snow and dew as well.
2. In the valleys, encompassed by the sheltered hillsides, the air mass is thicker and warmer, so there is less precipitation. Professor Bruno Giletti of Brown University provided the meteorological information.
3. Interpretation follows Elijah of Vilna and David Hoffmann. See Sif Deut., ed. Eliezer (Louis) Finkelstein (New York, 1983), p. 79.
4. Sif. Deut., §39; Yalkut, *Ekev*, §858.
5. If it is sown before the inundation by the Nile, its water will wash away the sown seed.
6. Sif Deut., §38.
7. See Gen. 49:31.
8. The root *bnh* may mean "to build" or "to produce."
9. Seven times seventy *kor* is four hundred ninety *kor*.
10. Only ten more *kor* than rocky ground.
11. A hundred times five hundred equals fifty thousand or five myriads. B. Ket 112a.

70. When Sennacherib came to persuade Israel to make peace, what did he say to them? "I come and will take you away to a land like your own land" (2 Kings 18:32). He did not say, "To a land better than your own land," but, "To a land like your own land." The matter may be argued *a fortiori:* when one who comes to speak in praise of his own land is unable to find any fault with Israel's Land, all the less so when one wishes to speak in praise of Israel's Land.

R. Simeon ben Yohai said: Sennacherib was a fool who did not know how to persuade effectively, as may be illustrated by the parable of a man who, intending to wed a wife, said to her, "Your father is a king, and I am a king. Your father is rich, and I am rich. Your father gives you meat and fish to eat and aged wine to drink, and I will give you meat and fish to eat and aged wine to drink." This is not effective wooing. What kind of wooing is effective? If he were to say to her, "Your father is a commoner and I am a king; your father is poor and I am rich; your father feeds you nothing but varieties of greens and pulse, while I will feed you meat and fish; your father takes you to the baths on foot, while I will take you in a sedan chair." Now, if one who came to speak in praise of his own land was unable to find any fault with Israel's Land, all the less so he who comes to speak in praise of Israel's Land.[1]

71. "That thou mayest gather in thy corn, and thy wine, and thine oil" (Deut. 11:14)—that the Land of Israel may be full of new grain, wine, and oil, and that all lands will send their overflow of silver and gold [to buy its produce].[2]

72. "I shall give thee a land of desire, a heritage of beauty desired by the nations (*tziv'ot goyim*)" (Jer. 3:19). What does *tziv'ot goyim* mean? It means that the Land of Israel is desired (*tzovin*) and coveted by all the nations (*goyim*).[3]

73. "I shall give thee a land of desire, a heritage of beauty desired by the nations"—a land of desire, a land set up with many castles for kings and rulers. For any king or ruler who had not acquired a site in the Land of Israel would say, "I have accomplished nothing." In this connection, R. Judah said: The thirty-one kings whom Joshua subdued—could all of them have been in Israel's Land? Of course not. The situation then was like the one nowadays in Rome, where any king or ruler who has not acquired an estate and a castle in Rome says, "I have accomplished nothing." So, too, a king or a ruler who had not acquired an estate and a castle in the Land of Israel would say, "I have accomplished nothing."[4]

74. "They invite their kin to the mountain" (Deut. 33:19). From this verse one may infer that peoples and kings setting out in companies come looking for the wares of the Land of Israel. Then they will say: Since we took such trouble to come here, let us go and see the nature of the Jews' own wares. So they go up to Jerusalem [the mountain of the Lord's house], where they see Jews worshiping one God and following one kind of diet. Since among the nations the god of one is not the god of another, nor is the diet of one the diet of another, they say, "There is no better nation to cleave to than this nation."

And the proof that they will not budge from there until they become proselytes and bestir themselves to bring sacrifices and burnt offerings? The end of the verse: "There shall they offer the sacrifices of righteousness" (Deut. 33:19).[5]

75. "They shall draw upon the riches streaming into the sea" (Deut. 33:19), that is, into the sea of Haifa,[6] which is being kept for the righteous in the time-to-come. Whence the proof that in the case of all ships lost in the Great Sea with treasures of silver and gold, precious stones and pearls, and other valuables—all these the Great Sea spews up into the Sea of Haifa, which is being kept for the righteous in the time-to-come? The verse "They shall draw upon the riches streaming into the sea."[7]

R. Yose said: Once, while I was on a journey from Chezib to Tyre, I came upon an old man whom I greeted and asked, "How do you make your living?" "From the purple snail."[8] I asked, "But where is it found?" He replied, "By Heaven, there is an area in the sea where the creature lies between mountains. Spiders bite it, and it dies and dissolves in its place." I said, "By Heaven, they do say that it is kept for the righteous in the world-to-come."[9]

76. "The hidden treasures of the sand" (Deut. 33:19). The word "hidden" refers to the purple snail, "treasures" refers to the *torit,*[10] and "sand" to glass. The tribe of Zebulun protested to Him who is everywhere, saying: Master of the universe, to my brothers You gave lands, while to me You gave seas. To my brothers You gave fields and vineyards, while to me You gave the purple snail. God replied: In the end I will make them dependent on you for this purple snail. Zebulun: Master of the universe, what means will I have of making certain that the purple snail will be utilized only by me? God: Take this as a sign: anyone who steals it will see no blessing in his trade.[11]

77. "Nebuzaradan . . . left the poorest of the land to be *koremim* and *yogevim*"[12] (Jer. 52:16). The *koremim,* R. Joseph taught, were the balsam gatherers from En Gedi

1. Sif Deut., §37.
2. Sif Deut., §42.
3. MTeh 5:1.
4. Sif Deut., §33 and §353; Yalkut, *Berakhah,* §959.
5. Sif Deut., §354; Yalkut, *Berakhah,* §961.
6. "Haifa," as emended by Samuel Klein (see Sif Deut., ed. Finkelstein, p. 416). Some editions read "Jaffa."
7. Sif Deut., §354; Yalkut, *Berakhah,* §961.
8. A snail yielding a special kind of blue dye (*tekhelet*).
9. Sif Deut., §354; Yalkut, *Berakhah,* §961.
10. Salted or pickled fish; all three items in this sentence were valuable articles in commerce.
11. Sif Deut., §354. "Making dye from the purple snail was a highly profitable and highly skilled trade, and its secrets were jealously kept. Hence, an outsider who stole a basketful of snails could get no profit from it" (Leon Nemoy).
12. JV: "Vinedressers and husbandmen."

to Ramah, while the *yogevim* were those who catch the purple snail from the Ladder of Tyre as far as Haifa.[1]

78. Hammath (Josh. 19:35) is Tiberias. Why was it called Hammath? Because of the hot baths (*hamme*) of Tiberias.

Rakkath (Josh. 19:35) is Sepphoris. Why was it called Rakkath? Because it is situated high up, like the steep bank (*rakkat*) of a river.

"And Kinneret" (Josh. 19:35). Kinneret is Gennesaret. Why was it called Kinneret? Because its fruit is as sweet as the music of harps (*kinnorot*).

Rava said: Hammath is the hot baths of Geder.[2] Rakkath is [not Sepphoris but] Tiberias.

R. Jeremiah said: Its real name is Rakkath. Why then is it called Tiberias [Teveria]? Because it is situated in the center (*tabbur*) of the Land of Israel. Rather, said Rabbah, because its scenery is superb (*tovah re'iyat*).

Zeira said: Kitron (Judg. 1:30) is Sepphoris. Why is it called Sepphoris? Because it is perched on top of a mountain like a bird (*tzippor*).

Resh Lakish said: I myself have seen the trail of milk and honey[3] around Sepphoris, and it was sixteen by sixteen *mil*.

"Ekron shall be rooted up" (Zeph. 2:4)—that is, Caesarea daughter of Edom,[4] situated in a sandy area. In the days of the Greeks it had been a painful peg in Israel['s side]. When the might of the Hasmonean house grew strong and the Greeks [there] were overpowered, the event came to be spoken of as the Capture of the Tower of Tyre.[5]

79. R. Isaac said: Leshem (Josh. 19:47) is Pamias.[6] "And Ekron shall be rooted up" (Zeph. 2:4)—that is, Caesarea daughter of Edom, which was a metropolis of kings. Some say this means that kings were brought up there, while others say that kings were appointed from there.[7]

80. Michmas and Zanoha rank first in the quality of their fine flour. Second to them is Afarayim in the valley.[8]

81. Our masters taught: "I will give you rains in their season" (Lev. 26:4). The verse means that the soil will be neither saturated nor parched, but moderately rained upon. For when rain is excessive, it makes the soil muddy, so that it yields no fruit.

Another comment: The words "in their season" mean that rain would fall only on the nights ushering in Wednesday[9] and the Sabbath. Thus we find that in the days of R. Simeon ben Shetah, rain fell only on the eve of Wednesdays and Sabbaths, so that grains of wheat grew to the size of kidney beans, and grains of barley to the size of olive pits, and lentils to the size of gold denars. Specimens of these were stored for the generations.[10]

82. "The early rain" (*yoreh*) (Deut. 11:14)—so called because it indicates (*moreh*) to people that they are to bring in their fruits, to caulk their roofs, and to attend to all their other needs [for the coming of winter].

Another explanation: Being concerned with the earth's well-being, the early rain does not come down (*yored*) with vehemence.

Or: It saturates (*marveh*) the ground, watering it right down to the abyss.

The text goes on to call the late rain *malkosh*, because it puts an abundance (*memalle*) of produce into the stalks (*kash*).

Or: *Malkosh* because it comes down on ripe ears (*melilot*), as well as on the stalks (*kash*).[11]

83. Rafram bar Papa said in the name of R. Hisda: Ever since the day the Temple was destroyed, rain does not come down from the good treasure. In saying, "The Lord will open unto thee His good treasure," etc. (Deut. 28:12), Scripture implies that when Israel[12] dwell in their Land, rain comes down from the good treasure; but when Israel do not dwell in their Land, rain does not come down from the good treasure.[13]

84. "I give thee a pleasant land, the heritage of the deer"[14] (Jer. 3:19). Why is the Land of Israel compared to a deer? To tell you that even as the hide of a deer, upon being flayed, [shrinks and] cannot contain its flesh, so the Land of Israel[15] cannot contain its produce.

Or: As the deer is the swiftest of all animals, so is the Land of Israel swiftest of all lands in the ripening of its fruits. Now, one might suppose that, just as the deer is swift but its flesh is not succulent, so the Land of Israel is swift to ripen but its fruits not succulent. Therefore Scripture says, "Flowing with milk and honey" (Exod. 3:17), implying that its fruit is as rich as milk and as sweet as honey.[16]

85. The fruits of the Land of Israel are easier to digest than the fruits of all other lands.[17]

---

1. B. Shab 26a.
2. Or, Gerar.
3. "Left by the goats eating dates" (Meg, Soncino, p. 28, n. 7).
4. As an outpost of the Roman Empire, it was called "daughter of Edom," i.e., of Rome.
5. "The reference is probably to the conquest of Caesarea by Alexander Jannaeus [Yannai]. . . . The old name of Caesarea was Strato's Tower, after the Phoenician king Strato, its founder" (Isidore Epstein in Meg, Soncino, p. 28, n. 5). B. Meg 6a.
6. "More correctly Panias, Caesarea Philippi, the modern Banias, a place near the source of the Jordan" (Meg, Soncino, p. 29, n. 5).
7. B. Meg 6a.
8. The three sites are mentioned in Scripture: the first in Ezra 2:27; the second in Josh. 15:34 and 15:56; the third in Josh. 19:19 and 2 Chron. 13:19. Men 9:1.
9. People did not venture out during the night ushering in Wednesday, since it was believed that demons were abroad then. Cf. B. Pes 112b.
10. B. Ta 22b–23a.
11. Sif Deut., §42; B. Ta 6a.
12. The words "obey the will of Him who is everywhere" are deleted. So Bah.
13. B. BB 25b.
14. JV: "a goodly heritage." But *tzevi* can mean "deer" as well as "goodly."
15. Its storehouses or granaries.
16. B. Ket 112a; Sif Deut., §37.
17. Sif Deut., §37.

86. R. Meir used to say: From Scripture's saying "Ye shall count the fruit thereof as forbidden" (Lev. 19:23), would I not understand that trees for food are being spoken of here? Then why does it say in the same context, "Of trees for food" (ibid.)? In order to include a tree whose wood has the same taste as its fruit. What is that tree? The pepper tree. This teaches you that the Land of Israel lacks nothing, as Scripture says, "A land wherein thou shalt eat bread without scarceness; thou shalt not lack anything in it" (Deut. 8:9).[1]

87. Rami bar Ezekiel once visited Bene Berak, where he saw some goats grazing under fig trees. Honey oozed down from the figs, and milk dripped from the goats, and they mingled with each other. So he quoted, "A land flowing with milk and honey" (Exod. 3:17).[2]

88. It happened that R. Jonathan ben Eleazar was sitting under a fig tree, which was full of succulent figs. When dew came down, the figs oozed honey, which the wind kneaded into the soil. Then a she-goat came along and dripped milk into the honey. So he called out to his pupils, saying to them: Come and see a paradigm of the world-to-come, of which it is said, "It shall come to pass in that day that the mountains shall drop down new wine, and the hills shall flow with milk" (Joel 4:18).[3]

89. R. Jacob ben Dostai said: From Lod to Ono is about three *mil*. Once I got up early in the morning twilight and walked in fig honey all the way up to my ankles.[4]

90. "And He made him suck honey out of the crag" (Deut. 32:13) applies to Sikhnin and cities nearby.

Once R. Yudan said to his son in Sikhnin: Go up [to the roof] and bring us dried figs from the jar. So he went up, put his hand into the jar, and found it full of fig honey. When he said to his father, "Papa, but this is a jar of honey," the father said, "Put your hand deeper into the jar, son, and you will bring up dried figs."

"[And He made him suck] oil out of the flinty rock" (Deut. 32:13). These are olives from Gush Halav.[5]

Once R. Yose said to his son in Sepphoris: Go and bring us olives from the upper chamber. He went up and found the upper chamber flooded with olive oil.[6]

91. "And of Asher he said: . . . Let him dip his foot in oil" (Deut. 33:24). The land of Asher gushed oil like a spring. It is told that when the people of Laodicea were in need of oil, they appointed an agent and instructed him, "Go and purchase for us a hundred myriad [*maneh*] worth of oil." He first went to Jerusalem and said, "I need a hundred myraids' worth of oil"; he was told, "Go to Tyre." He went to Tyre and said, "I need a hundred myriads' worth of oil"; there he was told, "Go to Gush Halav." He went to Gush Halav and said, "I need a hundred myriads' worth of oil"; he was told, "Go to So-and-so." Going to So-and-so's house, he did not find him, but he was told, "He is in the field." He went to the field and found him there, breaking up the earth under his olive trees. When the agent told him, "I need a hundred myriads' worth of oil," the man in the field replied, "Wait until I finish with the olive trees." After the man had finished with his olive trees, he slung his tools over his back and proceeded on his way, kicking stones from his path as he went. The agent asked himself: Is it likely that such a man would have a hundred myriads' worth of oil? It would seem that the Jews have had a good laugh at my expense. When the man got home, his maidservant brought him a kettle of hot water, and he washed his hands and feet in it. Then she brought him a golden bowl full of oil, and he dipped his hands and feet in it (in fulfillment of "Let him dip his foot in oil"). After they ate and drank, the man got up and measured out to the agent a hundred myriads' worth of oil. Then he asked, "Do you need more?" The agent: "Yes, but I have no more money with me." The man: "If you wish to buy more, take it, and I will go back with you for the money." The man then measured out to him an additional eighteen myriads' worth of oil. It is said that there was not a horse, a mule, a camel, or an ass in the Land of Israel the agent did not hire [to transport the oil]. When he got back to his city, the citizens came out to give him a hero's welcome. He said, "No one deserves your applause but this man; all of this oil is his, and I still owe him for eighteen myriads' worth."

The story illustrates the verse "There is that pretendeth himself rich, yet hath nothing; there is that pretendeth himself poor, yet hath great wealth" (Prov. 13:7).[7]

92. R. Hanina said: When I came up from exile, I undid my own girdle, my son's, and my animal's, [and I tied them together in order] to encircle the trunk of a carob tree, but it was so thick I was unable to do it.

R. Hanina also said: When I first came up from exile, I cracked a carob pod I happened to find, and out of it gushed enough honey to fill my hand.[8]

93. R. Yohanan said: I remember that when a child would crack a carob pod, a thread of honey would run down both his arms.

And R. Eleazar said: I remember that when a raven would pick up a piece of meat, a thread of fat would run down from the top of the wall to the ground.[9]

94. When R. Dimi came [to Babylonia], he said: The verse "Binding its colt unto the vine" (Gen. 49:11) implies that there is not a vine in the Land of Israel that does not require a colt to carry off the harvest from it. And "Two

1. B. Ber 36b.,
2. B. Ket 111b.
3. Tanhuma B, *Tetzavveh*, §10; Tanhuma B, *Ve-hizhir*, p. 100b.
4. B. Ket 111b.
5. In Upper Galilee, where olive trees grew in the midst of rocks. The place-name means "lump of milk."
6. P. Pe 7:3, 20a; Sif Deut., §316.
7. Sif Deut., §355; B. Men 85b; Yalkut, *Berakhah*, §962.
8. P. Pe 7:3, 20a.
9. B. BB 91b.

asses to a wild tree" (ibid.)[1] means that not even a wild tree in the Land of Israel fails to produce a load[2] for two she-asses. Lest you suppose that such grapes make no wine, Scripture says, "He washes his garments in wine" (ibid.). Lest you suppose that such wine is not red, Scripture says, "In the blood of grapes" (ibid.). Lest you suppose that such wine does not intoxicate, Scripture says, "Its intoxicating power" (ibid.).[3] Lest you suppose that such wine has no flavor, Scripture says, "*Hakhlili* after tasting what looks like wine" (Gen. 49:12),[4] which means: Any palate (*hekh*) that tastes it says, "More of it for me, more of it for me (*li, li*)." Lest you suppose it may be suitable for young people but not suitable for aged people, Scripture says, "And *le-ven shinayim* with milk" (ibid.). Read not *le-ven shinayim*, "his teeth white," but *le-ven shanim*, "[suitable] for aged people."[5]

95. R. Hiyya bar Adda, who was the teacher of Resh Lakish's young children, took time off for three days and did not come [to teach]. When he did come, Resh Lakish asked him: Why did you absent yourself? He replied: My dear father left me a trellis laden with vines. On the first day I gathered three hundred clusters, each cluster yielding one keg [of wine]. On the second day I gathered three hundred clusters, each two clusters yielding one keg [of wine]. On the third day I gathered three hundred clusters, each three clusters yielding a keg [of wine]. And even then, I had to declare ownerless (*hefker*) more than half of the grapes on the trellis. Resh Lakish said: Had you not taken time off from teaching Torah, the trellis would have yielded even more.[6]

96. A certain heretic said to R. Hanina: You may well boast of your Land. My father left me a parcel of land fifty by fifty cubits, and from it I get oil, wine, and grain, and my ox also feeds on it.[7]

---

1. JV: "and his ass's colt unto the choice vine." But *beni* (singular) is read as the plural *bene*, and *serekah* ("choice vine") is read *serakah* ("wild tree").
2. "A wild tree . . . is one that bears no fruit and is generally used either for shade or for firewood. Hence it seems that the two she-asses were laden with something other than fruit fit for human consumption. What was it? Acorns fit for animal feed? Or dead twigs fit for fuel?" (Leon Nemoy).
3. JV: "its vesture." But *svt* ("vesture") may be associated with the verb *svt:* "to agitate, to incite, to intoxicate."
4. JV: "His eyes shall be red (*hakhlili*) with wine." But *enayim* ("eyes") is taken to mean "to look like," as in Num. 11:7. Leon Nemoy differs: "I find several stumbling blocks here: *enayim* is a noun, not a verb—it can't mean 'to look like'; *enayim* does not describe yayin—it is affected by *yayin;* hence *yayin* is not something that looks like wine—it is wine.

   "Hence JV's 'His eyes shall be red with wine' seems to me to be perfectly suitable for this context with a slight modification: 'His eyes, affected by the wine [made out of the aforementioned abundant harvests of grapes], [cry out], "The palate [says]; More for me, More for me!" ' "
5. B. Ket 111b and En Yaakov, ad loc.
6. The successive reduction in the clusters' yield was intended as a hint to R. Hiyya that, by interrupting his teaching activity, he was not acting properly. Ibid.
7. B. Ket 112a.

97. We have been taught that R. Yose said: A parcel of land in Judah fifty by fifty cubits sown with a *seah* of seed used to yield five *seah:* a *seah* of ordinary flour, a *seah* of fine flour, a *seah* of ordinary bran, a *seah* of coarse bran, and a *seah* of short bran.[8]

98. We have been taught that R. Yose said: It once happened in Shihin that a man was left by his father a mustard stalk with three twigs, one of which split and was found to contain nine *kav* of mustard seed. A potter's hut was roofed with its timber.

R. Simeon ben Tahalifa said: Father left us a cabbage stalk, and we used to climb up and down on it, as on a ladder.[9]

99. A story of a scribe who used to go up to Jerusalem year after year, and people in Jerusalem became aware that he was greatly learned in Torah. So they said to him: Take fifty gold coins a year and stay with us. He replied: I have one vine that is more productive for me than all the other vines. It yields three crops a year and produces six hundred jars of wine every year—three hundred jars from the first crop, two hundred from the second, and a hundred from the third. I sell all of them for a very considerable sum.[10]

100. When R. Dimi came [to Babylonia], he said that King Yannai had a city in King's Mountain, to which from Sabbath eve to Sabbath eve they used to bring [11] sixty myriad bowls of salted fish for the men trimming fig trees.

When Ravin came [to Babylonia], he said that King Yannai had a tree in King's Mountain from which forty *seah* of pigeon chicks from three broods used to be taken down every month.[12]

101. R. Joshua ben Levi once visited Cabla,[13] where he saw [vines laden with] grape clusters as big as calves. "Calves among the vines!" he exclaimed, and was told, "They are clusters of ripe grapes." At that, he again exclaimed, "Land, O Land, withhold your fruit. For whom are you producing your fruit? For these Arabs, who on account of our sins have risen up against us?" The following year, R. Hiyya happened to visit there. When he saw clusters of grapes as big as goats, he exclaimed, "Goats among grapes!" So they said to him, "Go away. Do not do to us what your companion did."[14]

102. Rabbi [Judah I, the Patriarch] said to R. Perida, "Will you not show me that famous cluster in your vineyard?" R. Perida replied, "Very well," and went out [with Rabbi], intending to show it to him. At some distance, R. Judah saw something that looked like an ox and asked,

---

8. B. Ket 112a.
9. B. Ret 111b; Sif Deut., §317.
10. Tanhuma B, *Tetzavveh*, §10.
11. Literally, "King's Mountain, for whose sake . . . there used to be produced."
12. B. Ber 44a.
13. Southeast of the Dead Sea.
14. He cursed the crop. B. Ket 112a.

"Does this ox not injure the vineyard?" R. Perida: "What you take to be an ox is that grape cluster." Then Rabbi Judah cited the verse "While the King sat at His table, my spikenard sent forth its fragrance" (Song 1:12). But now the Temple is destroyed, yet you, O vineyard, stubbornly continue to produce such grapes.

From then on, when people looked for those grapes, they could not be found.

Between New Year's Day and the Day of Atonement—it happened to be at the end of a sabbatical year—two radishes as heavy as the weight of a camel's load were brought to R. Judah, who asked, "Are they not prohibited? Are they not the aftergrowths of a sabbatical year?" He was told, "They were planted at the end of the sabbatical year.[1]

It was on that occasion that R. Judah permitted the purchase of greens soon after the end of a sabbatical year.[2]

103. An Amorite once asked an Israelite who entered the Land of Israel [with Joshua], "How many dates do you gather from that date palm standing on the bank of the Jordan?" The Israelite: "Sixty *kor*." The Amorite: "You have just come into the Land, and you have already ruined it. We used to gather one hundred and twenty *kor* from it." The Israelite: "[So do we]—the amount I mentioned to you is from only one side of the date palm."[3]

104. R. Huna said in the name of R. Avun: Cinnamon, which Israel produced, [was so abundant] that it was used as feed for goats.[4]

105. R. Yohanan said: There used to be sixty myriads of townships between Gabbath and Antipatris.[5] The smallest was Beth-shemesh, whose population you may estimate from the fact that Scripture says, "And He smote of the men of Beth-shemesh . . . seventy men, and fifty thousand men" (1 Sam. 6:19). And these were from just one side of Beth-shemesh. But now, if you were to plant in Beth-shemesh as many reeds as the men smitten, its area could not contain them. Israel has, as R. Hanina said, shrunk greatly.[6]

106. At one time, it used to be said: Grain is in Judea, straw in Galilee, and chaff on the other side of the Jordan. But [after the Land was laid waste] the saying was: In Judea there is no grain [only straw], in Galilee there is no straw—only chaff, and on the other side of the Jordan there is neither the one nor the other.[7]

107. R. Ze'era said: Pause and consider how irrepressible is the Land of Israel, for it continues to bear fruit. Why does it? Two Amoraim differ in their answers. One said: Because it is well manured. The other: Because the soil is [carefully] turned over.[8]

108. R. Helbo, R. Avira, and R. Yose bar Hanina once visited a certain place in the Land of Israel where a peach as large as a stewpot of Kefar Hino[9] was brought to them. (And how big is a stewpot of Kefar Hino? Five *seah*.) A third they ate: a third they declared free for all; and a third they fed to their mounts.

R. Eleazar visited the place again a year later and was served peaches so small that he could hold them all in one hand. So he recited the verse "A fruitful land into a salt waste, because of the wickedness of them that dwell therein" (Ps. 107:34).[10]

109. "And I will bring the Land into desolation" (Lev. 26:32). There is some consolation in this curse, in that Israel need not say, "Now that we are exiled from our Land, the enemies will come in and find satisfaction in it." For the verse goes on to say, "Your enemies that settle therein shall be astonished at it" (ibid.), meaning that the enemies who come in afterward will find no satisfaction there.[11]

Jerusalem

110. R. Hanina bar Papa said: The Holy One wished to confine Jerusalem within definite measurements, for it is said, "Then said I: Whither goest thou? And he said unto me: To measure Jerusalem, to see what is the breadth thereof, and what is the length thereof?" (Zech. 2:6). But the ministering angels spoke up before the Holy One: Master of the universe, You have created in Your world many cities for the nations of the earth, and You did not fix the measure of their length or the measure of their breadth. Yet now for Jerusalem, in whose midst is Your Name, in whose midst is Your Sanctuary, in whose midst are the righteous—for it You fix a measure? "Thereupon [one angel speaking to another] said unto him: 'Run, speak to this young man, saying: Jerusalem shall be inhabited without walls, for the multitude of men and cattle therein' " (Zech. 2:8).[12]

111. "I went down to the bottoms of mountains . . . into Thy holy Temple" (Jon. 2:7–8).[13] Jerusalem is situated on seven hills.[14]

---

1. But grew so rapidly.
2. P. Pe 7:3, 20b.
3. B. Ket 112a.
4. P. Pe 7:3, 28a.
5. Gabbath was in the territory of Dan, and Antipatris was northwest of Jerusalem.
6. P. Ta 4:5 and 4:8, 69b; Meg 1:1, 70a.
7. ARN 27.

---

8. P. Ta 4:5, 69b; Lam. R., proem 34.
9. "Identified by Klein . . . as Kefar Hananiah in Upper Galilee" (Isidore Epstein in Ket, Soncino, p. 724, n. 9).
10. B. Ket 112a.
11. Sif Lev. 112a.
12. B. BB 75b.
13. The words "From this verse we learn that" are omitted, as suggested by Elijah of Vilna. See David Luria's commentary, ad loc.
14. PRE 10. Leon Nemoy writes: "Rome, too, was built on seven hills. Is the implied conclusion here to say to the Romans, 'Quit bragging about your seven-hilled imperial capital—Jerusalem has seven hills, too, in addition to lots of precious things that Rome never had and never will have.'?"

112. Ten *kav* of beauty came down to the world—Jerusalem took nine, and all the rest of the world one.

You will find no beauty like the beauty of Jerusalem.[1]

113. Ten portions of suffering are in the world—nine in Jerusalem, and one in the rest of the world.

Ten portions of physical strength are in the world—nine in Judea, and one in the rest of the world.

Ten portions of wisdom are in the world—nine in Jerusalem, and one in the rest of the world.

Ten portions of hypocrisy are in the world—nine in Jerusalem, and one in the rest of the world.

Ten portions of Torah are in the world—nine in Jerusalem, and one in the rest of the world.[2]

114. R. Joshua ben Levi said: "Jerusalem that art builded as a city that is compact together" (Ps. 122:3)—a city that makes all Israel feel the fellowship that binds them together.[3]

115. "The valley of vision" (Isa. 22:1)—the valley concerning which all seers have prophesied, the valley out of which all seers rise. For, as R. Yohanan said, any prophet whose city is not named is a Jerusalemite.[4]

116. Ten things are said about Jerusalem: It is not impossible to buy back one's house there;[5] no heifer is brought to have its neck broken [when someone slain is found lying in the open in the vicinity of Jerusalem and the identity of the slayer is unknown];[6] it may not be declared a condemned city;[7] it is not subject to uncleanness from house plagues;[8] attachments to windows or balconies may not protrude over its thoroughfares;[9] dungheaps may not be located within it; artisans' kilns may not be built there; other than rose gardens that existed from the days of the early prophets, gardens and orchards may not be cultivated in it;[10] chickens are not to be raised within it;[11] and a corpse may not be kept overnight there.[12]

117. Our masters taught: In Jerusalem there was a Stone of Losses. He who lost an article went there [and so did he who found one]. The finder stood up and announced what he found, and its owner stood up and called out the identifying marks and had the lost article restored to him.[13]

118. R. Yohanan said: Outside of Jerusalem there was an arcade called the Arch of Accounts, and when people had accounts to settle, they used to go and settle them under the arch. Thus, it could not happen that a man, while reckoning his account, would be brought to grief—a thing that must not be allowed to occur, because Jerusalem is called "the joy of the whole earth" (Ps. 48:3). True, as soon as Jerusalem was destroyed (*harevah*), that joy was darkened (*arevah*) and the gladness of the whole earth was exiled. But when the Holy One rebuilds Jerusalem, He will restore to it all the joy, as is said, "The Lord hath comforted Zion. . . . Joy and gladness shall be found therein, thanksgiving and the voice of melody" (Isa. 51:3).[14]

119. Rabban Simeon ben Gamaliel said: The Siloam used to issue through a narrow mouth the size of an *issar*. So it was suggested: Let us widen the mouth, and its water will increase. They did widen it, but its water diminished. So they narrowed its mouth again, and the flow returned to what it had been before.[15]

120. R. Judah said: Jerusalem's [fuel] logs were of cinnamon, and when they were burning, their fragrance pervaded the entire Land of Israel. After Jerusalem was destroyed, they were hidden, only as much as the size of a barley grain being left, and it is found in Queen Zimzemai's collection of rarities.[16]

121. Caesarea and Jerusalem [are rivals]. If someone says to you that both are destroyed, do not believe him; if he says both are flourishing, do not believe him; if he says Caesarea is waste and Jerusalem is flourishing, believe him. Or that Jerusalem is waste and Caesarea is flourishing—you may believe him. For Scripture says, "I shall be filled, she is laid waste" (Ezek. 26:2)—if this one is filled, the other is laid waste; and if the other is filled, this one is laid waste.[17]

122. R. Joshua ben Levi taught that the Holy One said to Israel: You people caused My house to be destroyed and My children to be banished. Now go on inquiring about Jerusalem's peace, and I will give you peace.[18]

123. R. Samuel bar Nahmani said: According to an *Aggadah* transmitted through the generations, Jerusalem will not be rebuilt until all the exiles have been gathered. If someone says to you: All the exiles have been gathered, but Jerusalem is still not rebuilt, do not believe him, for Scripture says, "The Lord will rebuild Jerusalem" (Ps. 147:2) and then "He will gather together the dispersed of Israel" (ibid.).[19]

124. R. Yohanan said: Jerusalem is destined to become the metropolis of all lands.[20]

---

1. B. Kid 49b; ARN 28.
2. ARNB 48.
3. P. Hag 3:6, 79d.
4. Lam. R., proem 24.
5. Unlike other walled cities. See Lev. 25:29–34.
6. See Deut. 21.
7. See Deut. 13:13–28.
8. See Lev. 14:35–53.
9. Lest pilgrims be hurt.
10. Lest they spread the stench of manure.
11. By going into dung to pick for grains, they proliferate uncleanness.
12. B. BK 82b.
13. B. BM 28b.
14. Exod. R. 52:5.
15. P. Suk 5:6, 55d.
16. B. Shab 63a.
17. B. Meg 6a.
18. Per Sha.
19. Tanhuma B, *Noah*, §17.
20. Exod. R. 23:10.

125. Jerusalem is destined to be widened and to rise upward, until it reaches the throne of glory and says, "The place is too narrow for me" (Isa. 49:20).[1]

126. R. Nahman asked R. Isaac: What is meant by the verse "The Holy One in the midst of thee, and I will not come into the city"[2] (Hos. 11:9)? Surely it cannot mean that the prophet said, "Because the Holy One is in the midst of thee, I will not enter the city"! R. Isaac replied that R. Yohanan explained it in this way: "The holy one" refers not to God but to the holy city, and God the Holy One is saying, "I will not come into the city of Jerusalem that is above until I first come into the city of Jerusalem that is below."

But can it be that there is a Jerusalem above?

Yes. Scripture says, "Jerusalem that art builded like the city with which it is companioned" (Ps. 122:3).[3]

---

1. Song R. 7:5, §3.
2. JV: "in fury." But *ir* ("fury") can also mean "city."
3. JV: "Jerusalem, that art builded as a city that is compact together (*hubberah lah*)." B. Ta 5a.

CHAPTER THREE

LANGUAGE

The Sacred Tongue

1. It is taught in the name of R. Meir: Everyone who dwells permanently in the Land of Israel, recites the Shema morning and evening, and speaks the sacred tongue is assured that he will dwell in the world-to-come.[1]

2. "And ye shall teach them to your children, to speak of them" (Deut. 11:19). From this verse it is inferred: When a child begins to speak, his father should speak to him in the sacred tongue and teach him Torah; if he does not speak to him in the sacred tongue and does not teach him Torah, it is as though he were burying him, for Scripture says, "Ye shall teach them to your children, to speak of them . . . that your days may be multiplied, and the days of your children" (Deut. 11:19 and 11:21). If you teach them to your children, your days and the days of your children will be multiplied; if you do not, your days and the days of your children will be made fewer.

For the rule is that a negative commandment implies the corresponding positive commandment, and a positive commandment the corresponding negative commandment.[2]

3. Israel were redeemed from Egypt because they did not change their names. They went down there as Reuben and Simeon, and came back up as Reuben and Simeon. Reuben was not called Rufus, nor Judah Julianus, nor Joseph Justus, nor Benjamin Alexander. Also, because they did not change their language—they continued to speak the sacred tongue, for Scripture says, "When the house of Jacob [went forth] from a people of strange language" (Ps. 114:1), and Joseph also said, "It is my mouth that speaketh unto you" (Gen. 45:12)—speaks to you in the sacred tongue.[3]

4. "She shall be called woman (*ishah*) because she was taken out of man (*ish*)" (Gen. 2:23). It is said in the name of R. Simon: Just as the Torah was given in the sacred tongue, so was the world created with the sacred tongue. Have you even heard anyone say *gune, gunya; anthrope, anthropia; gavra, gavarta?*[4] But *ish* and *ishah* are used. Why? Because [in Hebrew] the masculine form and the feminine form correspond to each other.[5]

5. It is written, "And the whole earth was of one language, even though they used *ahadim* words" (Gen. 11:1). R. Eleazar and R. Yohanan differed on the meaning of *ahadim.* According to one, it means "several," that is, the seventy languages of the world. According to the other, it means the language of the One that is unique in the world—the sacred tongue.[6]

6. R. Assi asked R. Yohanan: What is the law governing wine mixed (*mesakho*) with water[7] by a heathen? R. Yohanan replied: The correct verb is *mezago.* R. Assi: I used the verb that occurs in Scripture, "She hath killed her beasts, she hath mingled (*masekhah*) her wine" (Prov. 9:2). R. Yohanan: For mixing wine with water, *mesakho* is still not the right word. Torah has its language, and the sages have theirs.[8]

When Assi bar Hini came up [to the Land of Israel], R. Yohanan found that, while teaching R. Yohanan's son Mishnah, Assi used the masculine plural *rehelim* for "ewes." R. Yohanan said: The correct plural is feminine: *rehelot.* Assi: But it is written, "Two hundred *rehelim*" (Gen. 32:15). R. Yohanan: Torah has its language, and the sages have theirs.[9]

7. R. Hiyya the Elder and R. Simeon bar Halafta forgot the meaning of several words in the Aramaic version of Scripture and went to a marketplace of Arabs [who spoke Nabatean] to learn from them. They heard a man who meant to say to his companion, "Place this burden on me," say instead, "Place this *yehav* on me," from which they concluded that *yehav* means "burden," as in the verse "Cast *yehavekha* (thy burden) upon the Lord, and He will sustain thee" (Ps. 55:23). Then again, they heard a man who wished to say to his companion, "Why do you tread (*mevasseh*) on me?" say instead, "Why do you *measseh* on me?" They accordingly interpreted the verse "*Ve-assotem* (Ye shall tread down) the wicked" (Mal. 3:21). They then heard a woman say to her companion, "Come and bathe," and receive the reply, "I am *galmudah,*" meaning "menstruating." They accordingly interpreted the verse "Seeing I have been bereaved and *galmudah*"[10] (Isa. 49:21). They then heard another woman who meant to say to her companion, "Come, raise your lament," say, "Come, raise your *livyah.*" They accordingly interpreted the verse "Who are ready to raise their *livyah*" (Job 3:8). For "Lend me

1. Sif Deut., §333; P. Shab 1:3, 3c.
2. Sif Deut., §46.
3. Lev. R. 32.6; Song R. 4:12, §1; MTeh 114:4.
4. "In Greek, *gune* means 'woman'; but to reflect nature, there should be a *gune–gunya* word pair for 'man'–'woman.' Instead, *anthrope* in Greek means 'man,' with no corresponding *anthropia* to mean 'woman.' Likewise, Aramaic *gavra* ('man') has no corresponding *gavarta* for 'woman' " (Brother Caedmon Holmes).
5. Gen. R. 18:4.
6. The word *ahadim* may be taken as the plural of "one"—hence, seventy; or as a plural of majesty—hence, the One who is unique. P. Meg 1:9, 71b.
7. Wine was usually diluted with water before drinking.
8. In rabbinic Hebrew, *masakh* means not to mix wine with water but to mix strong wine with weaker wine.
9. B. AZ 58b; B. Hul 137b.
10. "Shunned" (as one unclean).

your broom," a woman said, "Lend me your *matate.*" They accordingly interpeted the verse, "I will sweep it with the *matate* of destruction" (Isa. 14:23). For "Lend me your pearls," they heard a woman say, "Lend me your *cesitha.*"[1] For "Take this ewe out to pasture," they heard, "Take this *kesitah* out to pasture." Hence: "A hundred *kesitah*" (Gen. 33:19).[2]

8. R. Honi said: The sages did not know what the words *serugin, haloglogot,* and *matate* meant; nor which is to be deferred to—one greater in wisdom or one greater in years. They decided: Let us go and inquire at the house of Rabbi [Judah I, the Patriarch]. When they got there, one said to the other, "Let So-and-so go in first." "No, let So-and-so go in first." A maidservant of Rabbi [Judah's] household came out and said, "Enter according to your seniority in years." They began entering at intervals. So she asked them, "Why are you entering *serugin, serugin,* 'in a broken line'?" Among them was a young man carrying purslane, which fell from his hand. The maidservant said to him, "Young man, your *haloglogot,* 'purslane,' has scattered all over. I will bring a *matate.*" And she brought a broom [and swept it up].[3]

9. At the baths, secular matters may be discussed in the sacred tongue.[4]

The Sacred Tongue and Other Languages

10. "And he said: 'The Lord came from Sinai' " (Deut. 33:2). When the Holy One revealed Himself to give Torah to Israel, He revealed Himself not in one language, but in four. "And he said: 'The Lord came from Sinai' " in Hebrew; 'and rose from Seir unto them' (ibid.) in the language of Rome; 'and shined forth from Mount Paran' (ibid.) in the Arab language; 'and He came from Meribath-Kadesh' "[5] (ibid.) in the Aramaic language.[6]

11. Ben Damah, R. Ishmael's nephew, asked R. Ishmael: May one such as I, who have studied the entire Torah, also study Greek wisdom?[7] R. Ishmael recited to him the verse "The book of Torah shall not depart out of thy mouth, but thou shalt meditate therein day and night" (Josh. 1:8)—go and find a time that is neither day nor night, and in it you may study Greek wisdom.[8]

12. R. Joshua was asked: May a man teach his son Greek? He replied: He may teach him at a time that is neither day nor night, for Scripture says, "Thou shalt meditate therein day and night" (Josh. 1:8). [The inquirer objected], "But according to you, one should be forbidden to teach his son a craft, because Scripture says, 'Thou shalt meditate therein day and night.' Yet R. Ishmael taught: The words 'Thou shalt choose life' (Deut. 30:19) refer to learning a craft."

R. Abba son of R. Hiyya bar Abba, citing R. Yohanan, said: [Greek should not be taught] because of informers [who might use their proficiency in Greek to curry favor with the gentile authorities by denouncing innocent persons].

R. Abbahu said in the name of R. Yohanan: A man may teach his daughter Greek, because it is an ornament for her. When Simeon bar Abba heard this, he said: Just because R. Abbahu wishes to teach Greek to his daughter, he attributes to R. Yohanan permission to do so. When R. Abbahu heard this, he said: May such-and-such befall me if I have not actually heard this permission from R. Yohanan himself.[9]

13. We have been taught that Rabbi [Judah I, the Patriarch] asked: Why should anyone speak Syriac—Aramaic—in the Land of Israel? Either the sacred tongue or the Greek tongue!

R. Yose said: Why speak Aramaic in Babylonia? Either the sacred tongue or the Persian tongue.[10]

14. R. Samuel bar Nahman said in the name of Yohanan: Do not think lightly of the Syriac language, for we find that the Holy One pays honor to it in the Torah, in the Prophets, and in the Writings. In the Torah: "Jegar-sahadutha" (Gen. 31:47);[11] in the Prophets: "Thus shall ye say unto them: 'The gods that have not made the heavens and the earth, these shall perish from the earth' " (Jer. 10:11);[12] in the Writings: "Then spoke the Chaldeans to the king in Aramaic: 'O king, live forever!' " (Dan. 2:4).[13]

15. R. Hanina said: It was to Babylonia that the Holy One exiled Israel because their language is close to the language of Torah.[14]

16. R. Judah said in the name of Rav: Adam spoke Aramaic.[15]

17. R. Judah said: A man should never pray for his needs in Aramaic.

R. Yohanan said: When a man prays for his needs

1. The spelling variation may, Leon Nemoy suggests, be a scribe's error; the two words would have been pronounced the same.
2. So Jacob may have bought the land either for a hundred precious pearls or for a hundred sheep. JV: "a hundred pieces of money." Gen. R. 79:7.
3. P. Meg 2:2, 73a.
4. B. Shab 41a.
5. So Meir Friedmann, Sif Deut. (Vienna, 1864). JV: "from the myriads holy." The verse itself is of course entirely in Hebrew. But the three places mentioned in addition to Sinai—Seir = Edom = Rome, Paran = Arabian desert, and Kadesh = Syria—suggests that God also revealed Himself in the languages of these countries. So Leon Nemoy.
6. Sif Deut., §342.
7. Perhaps Greek philosophy.
8. B. Men 99b.
9. P. Sot 19:15, 24c; P. Shab 6:1, 7d.
10. B. BK 82b–83a.
11. "The heap of witness."
12. The text is in Aramaic (Syriac).
13. Gen. R. 74:14; P. Sot 7:2, 21c.
14. B. Pes 87b.
15. "This may have been said in justification of the abandonment by the Babylonian Jews of the Hebrew language in favor of Aramaic" (Isidore Epstein in Sanh, Soncino, p. 243, n. 6). B. Sanh 38b.

in Aramaic, the ministering angels, who do not understand Aramaic, will not respond to him.[1]

18. R. Jonathan of Beth Gubrin said: There are four beautiful languages, which all the world should use: Greek for song, Roman—Latin—for battle, Syriac—Aramaic—for lamentation, and Hebrew for conversation. Some add: Assyrian for writing.

Assyrian has a script but is no longer a spoken language. Hebrew is a spoken tongue but has no script of its own. The Hebrews chose for themselves the Assyrian script and the Hebrew tongue. Why is the Hebrew script called Assyrian? Since it is clear, easy reading of it is assured. R. Levi said: Because it came to them from Assyria.[2]

19. "I will . . . saith the Lord . . . cut off from Babylon name and remnant" (Isa. 14:22). "Name" refers to the script [whereby a nation's name spreads abroad and comes to be known], and "remnant" refers to the spoken tongue [whereby a nation survives as such, and so has a remnant in the world].[3]

20. "Thou art greatly despised" (Obad. 1:2), for Rome possesses neither script nor tongue.[4]

21. "And Balaam said: . . . Because thou hast mocked (*hit'alalt*) me" (Num. 22:29). Even when he speaks in the sacred tongue, a heathen's language is foul.[5]

22. "Come, let us go down, and there confound their language" (Gen. 11:7). He confounded their language, so that one did not understand the language of the other. The first language they had been speaking was the sacred tongue, by which the world had been created.

So the Holy One said: In this world, because of the impulse to evil, My creatures have been separated and have become divided into seventy languages. But in the time-to-come, all of them will come as one to call upon My Name and worship Me, as is said, "Then I will make the peoples pure of speech, so that they will all invoke the Lord by name, and serve Him with one accord" (Zeph. 3:9).[6]

Exactness in the Use of Language

23. R. Judah said in the name of Rav: The Judeans, who were particular about their language, retained their learning in Torah, but the Galileans, who were not particular about their language, did not retain their learning.

The Judeans were particular about their use of language. For example, a Judean once announced that he had a cloak to sell. He was asked, "What is the color of your cloak?" He replied, "Like that of beets on the ground."

The Galileans were not particular about their use of language. For example: A certain Galilean went around asking, "Who has *amar*?"[7] "Which do you mean, O foolish Galilean?" he was asked. "An ass for riding, wine to drink, wool for clothing, or a lamb for slaughtering?"[8]

---

1. "Angels were held to mediate between God and man, carrying the prayers of the latter to the former" (Shab, Soncino, p. 48, n. 3). B. Shab 12b.
2. P. Meg 1:9, 71b; Esther R. 4:12.
3. B. Meg 10b.
4. "Greek remained the spoken and written language throughout the East even after the establishment of the eastern Roman Empire, to which allusion is here made" (Isidore Epstein in AZ, Soncino, p. 50, n. 2). B. AZ 10a.
5. The expression *hit'olel* is used in connection with acts of obscenity (see Judg. 19:25). Num. R. 20:14.
6. Tanhuma, *Noah*, §22.
7. Since he did not pronounce some sounds distinctly, it was not clear whether he meant *hamar* ("an ass"), *hamar* ("wine"), *amar* ("wool"), or *immar* ("a lamb").
8. B. Er 53a.

CHAPTER FOUR

EXILE

The Hardship of Exile and the Enslavement by Kingdoms

1. Heavy is the burden of exile: it outweighs all other divine afflictions.[1]

2. In the academy of Rav, it was said: There are four things the Holy One regrets having created, and one of them is exile.[2]

3. "And you I will scatter among the nations" (Lev. 26:33). This is a particularly severe measure against Israel. For if the people of a province, all of them, are banished to one place, they at least see one another and so are comforted. But here Scripture says, "And I will scatter you among the nations"—I will disperse you among the nations so that not one of you will be near another, in keeping with "I will scatter thee among the nations, and disperse thee through the countries" (Ezek. 22:15). Scripture says again, "I will scatter them as with a winnowing fork through the settlements of the earth" (Jer. 15:7), the way a man does who scatters barley with a winnowing fork, so that one grain will not stick to another.[3]

4. "Judah is gone into exile" (Lam. 1:3). Do not the peoples of the world also go into exile? They do, but inasmuch as they eat of each other's bread and drink of each other's wine, their exile is not true exile. Whereas for Israel, who do not eat other nations' bread and do not drink other nations' wine, exile is true exile.[4]

5. "Sell me the birthright, and a day as well" (Gen. 25:31).[5] Jacob said to Esau: Sell me just one day of your many days. In this regard, R. Aha said: He who can reckon up the days in exile will find that in fact Jacob did spend one day [a short period] in peace under the shadow of Esau.[6]

6. "If they are driven hard a single day, all the flocks will die" (Gen. 33:13). R. Huna said in the name of R. Aha: But for the mercies of the Holy One, when they were driven hard one day, all the flocks [that is to say, all Israel] would have died in Hadrian's day.[7]

7. "Put a space betwixt drove and drove" (Gen. 32:17). Jacob said to the Holy One: Master of the universe, if troubles are to befall my children, let these not come one right after the other, but let them have a breathing space between their troubles.[8]

8. "I was transpierced by the yoke of my transgressions" (Lam. 1:14). The congregation of Israel meant: I was transpierced by the kingdoms. I had supposed that He would impose them on me one by one. I had not realized that He would bring them on me in pairs: Babylon and the Chaldea, Media and Persia, Greece and Macedon, Edom and Seir.[9]

"They come in broken succession" (Lam. 1:14). The pairs of kingdoms He brought on me alternated in their treatment of me: Babylon was severe, but Media was mild; Greece severe, but Edom mild; Chaldea severe, but Persia mild; Macedon severe, but Seir mild.[10] With regard to such alternation, Scripture says, "Some of the kingdoms will be fierce, and some mild" (Dan. 2:42).[11]

9. "Behold a smoking furnace and a torch of fire" (Gen. 15:17). Simeon bar Abba said in the name of R. Yohanan: The Holy One showed four things to our father Abraham: Gehenna, [the yoke of] the kingdoms, the giving of Torah, and the Temple. And He said to him: As long as your children occupy themselves with the latter two, they will be saved from the former two. If they neglect the latter two, they will be punished by the former two. The Holy One also asked Abraham: How do you wish your children to be chastised—by Gehenna or by the kingdoms? According to R. Hanina bar Papa, Abraham chose the yoke of the kingdoms, as implied in "Their rock had given them over" (Deut. 32:30), "their rock" being Abraham, and "The Lord had delivered them up" (ibid.), meaning that the Holy One ratified Abraham's choice.

However, R. Yudan, R. Idi, and R. Hama bar Hanina maintained that Abraham chose Gehenna, but the Holy One changed his choice to the yoke of the kingdoms. This is implied in the verse "Thou hadst caused man to ride over our heads, which is as though we went through fire and water [through Gehenna]" (Ps. 66:12).

---

1. Enumerated in Deut. 27–28. Sif Deut., §43 (ed. Finkelstein, p. 100).
2. B. Suk 52b.
3. Sif Lev., *Be-hukkotai* 6:6 (ed. Isaac Hirsch Weiss [Vienna, 1862], p. 112a); Yalkut, *Be-hukkotai*, §675.
4. Lam. R. 1:3, §28.
5. AV: "Sell me this day (*ka-yom*) the birthright." Since *ka-yom* is deemed superfluous, R. Aha construes it as a request for something in addition to the birthright.
6. R. Aha may be referring to the period of the Maccabees, 160 B.C.E.; to the coming of Pompey, 66 B.C.E.; or to the time of Agrippa I, ca. 41–44 C.E. So A. A. Ha-Levi in Bereshit R. (Tel Aviv, 1956), p. 489. Gen. R. 63:13.
7. Gen. R. 78:13.
8. Gen. R. 75:13.
9. Possibly Rome and Byzantium.
10. To correct the chronological order, David Luria emends as follows: "Chaldea was severe, but Babylon mild; Persia severe, but Media mild; Greece severe, but Macedon mild; Edom severe, but Ishmael mild."
11. Lam. R. 14, §42.

According to R. Huna, citing R. Aha, all that day our father Abraham sat wondering and asking himself: Which shall I choose, since Gehenna is cruel and the yoke of the kingdoms is cruel? The Holy One said: Abraham, how long will you sit and search your heart? Cut short the deliberation and choose the yoke of the kingdoms. "In that day the Lord cut short Abram" (Gen. 15:18).[1]

10. "And lo, a dread, a darkness, a great one, fell upon him" (Gen. 15:12). "Dread" refers to Babylon; "darkness," to Media, which darkened the eyes of Israel with fasting and self-affliction; "a great one," to Greece; and "fell upon him" refers to Edom.

"[Who led thee through a . . . wilderness] wherein were serpents, fiery serpents, and scorpions" (Deut. 8:15). By "serpents" is meant Babylon; by "fiery serpents," Media; by "scorpions," Greece.[2]

11. R. Yohanan said: "Wherefore a lion out of the forest doth slay them" (Jer. 5:6)—that is Babylon;[3] "a wolf of the deserts doth spoil them" (ibid.)—that is Media; "a leopard watcheth over their cities" (ibid.)—that is Greece; "everyone that goeth out thence is torn in pieces" (ibid.)—that is Edom.[4]

12. "And again I lifted up mine eyes, and behold, there came four chariots" (Zech. 6:1)—these are the four chariots of the four kingdoms. "In the first chariot were red horses" (Zech. 6:2)—this is the kingdom of Babylon, which spilled so much of Israel's blood. "And in the second chariot black horses" (ibid.)—this is the kingdom of Persia and Media, under which the faces of Israel were made black [with grief] by the decree of Haman. "And in the third chariot white horses" (ibid.)—this is the kingdom of Greece, which through blasphemies and revilings whitened the faces of Israel with humiliation. "And in the fourth chariot grizzled bay horses" (ibid.)—this is the fourth kingdom [Rome], which issued decrees of so many varieties, each different from the others.[5]

13. "I was not at ease, neither was I quiet, neither had I rest; but trouble came" (Job 3:26). "I was not at ease" because of Babylon; "neither was I quiet" because of Media; "neither had I rest" because of Greece; "but trouble came" because of Edom.[6]

14. "There are four things which are little upon the earth" (Prov. 30:24)—these are the four kingdoms. "The ants are a people not strong" (Prov. 30:25)—this is Babylon, of which it is said, "Behold, the land of the Chaldees—this is the people that was not" (Isa. 23:13). "The rock badgers are but a feeble folk" (Prov. 30:26)—this is Media. "Yet they would erect [Israel's] house upon the crags" (ibid.)—this is Cyrus, who wished to build the Temple. "The locusts have no king" (Prov. 30:27)—this is Greece and refers to Alexander of Macedon, who roved about the entire world like locusts, which rise high and fly about in the air. "The spider thou canst take with the hands" (Prov. 30:28)—this is Edom, for even as, among creeping things, none is as hated as a spider, so, too, is it said, "But Esau I hate" (Mal. 1:3). "Yet she is in the king's palaces" (Prov. 30:28), for Edom destroyed the Temple of the King who is King of kings.[7]

15. "Who is she that looketh forth as the dawn, fair as the moon, clear as the sun, terrible as an army with banners" (Song 6:10). Here are four articles of praise for Israel, as against the four kingdoms, since under these four kingdoms that subjugated Israel, Israel did not deny the Holy One. The proof concerning the kingdom of Babylon referred to in "Who is she that looketh forth as the dawn?": Nebuchadnezzar worshiped the sun, for to him Scripture says, "Thou who worshipest (*heilel*) the rising (young) daybreak (sun) (Isa. 14:12).[8] Daniel, too, used to rise at dawn and pray evening, morning, and noon[9] to Him who is everywhere, for Scripture says, "Now his windows were open in his upper chamber toward Jerusalem, and he kneeled upon his knees three times a day" (Dan. 6:11). For what did he rise at dawn to pray? That the Holy One have mercy upon Israel. With regard to him, Solomon prophesied, "He who diligently rises at dawn to pray [will find] favor" (Prov. 11:27). Indeed, God let Himself be found by them at the time of their trouble, as is said, "I love them that love Me, and those that seek Me at dawn shall find Me" (Prov. 8:17). And so we find that when Daniel was cast into the lions' den, he was not harmed; when Hananiah, Mishael, and Azariah were cast into the fiery furnace, they, too, were not harmed. Instead, they gave light to the world, just as the dawn gives light to the world. Moreover, they prevailed upon heathen nations to recognize the Holy One and to acclaim Him.

When the kingdom of Media was the enemy, Israel was said to be "fair as the moon." You find that when the moon is not visible in the sky at night, the darkness in the world is such that a man cannot [see to] walk about even in the city. But once the moon appears in the sky, all rejoice and are able to walk about. So, too, in the days of Ahasuerus, when it was decreed that Israel should be destroyed, slain, and exterminated. But then Esther appeared and gave light to Israel, as is said, "The Jews had light and gladness, and joy and honor" (Esther 8:16).

When Greece was the enemy, Scripture uses the phrase "clear as the sun." The reference is to Alexander son of the sun[10] and to Greece, identified with the sun. The sun is called a mighty man, as in the verse "He rejoiceth as a mighty man to run his course" (Ps. 19:6).

1. "In that day the Lord made a covenant with Abram." Gen. R. 44:21; PR 15:2 (YJS 1:305–7); Tanhuma, *Pekudei*, §9.
2. Gen. R. 44:17.
3. The kingdom of which Jeremiah said, "A lion is gone up from his thicket" (Jer. 4:7).
4. Exod. R. 51:7; Lev. R. 13:5.
5. Yalkut, Zech., §574.
6. Exod. R. 26:1.
7. Midrash Prov. 30 (ed. Buber, pp. 106–7); Yalkut, Prov., §964.
8. The interpretation of Isa. 14:12 was suggested by Leon Nemoy.
9. "The word *shahar* is played on here: it can mean 'rise at dawn,' and it can mean 'be diligent,' 'seek it diligently' " (Brother Caedmon Holmes).
10. His name is given in Greek: Alexandros uios Hēliou.

Who can stand up to the sun during the summer solstice? All flee from it, as is said, "There is nothing hid from the heat thereof" (Ps. 19:7). Likewise, during the ascendancy of Greece, all fled from it. But Mattathias the Priest and his sons stood up in their faith in the Holy One. The armies of Antiochus fled before them and were all slain. For to Mattathias and his sons, the Holy One had said, "Beat your plowshares into swords, and your pruning hooks into spears; let the weak say: 'I am mighty' " (Joel 4:10). In the end it could be said, "So perish all Thine enemies, O Lord; but they that love Him be as the sun when he goeth forth in his might" (Judg. 5:31).

When Israel was said to be "terrible as an army with banners," Edom was the enemy. Why should Israel then have been called terrible? Because it stood up to a kingdom that inspired terror, the kingdom referred to in the words "And behold a fourth beast, dreadful and terrible, and strong exceedingly" (Dan. 7:7). What then is implied by saying that Israel is "terrible as an army with banners"? You find that there are twelve constellations in the sky. Even as the heavens cannot endure without the twelve constellations, so the world cannot endure without the twelve tribes, as is said, "If these ordinances [concerning the constellations] depart from before Me, saith the Lord, then the seed of Israel shall also cease from being a nation before Me forever" (Jer. 31:36).

"Terrible as an army with banners." The use of the term "banners" implies hosts, as indicated in the verse "The banner of the camp . . . and its host, and those that were numbered of them" (Num. 2:3–4). Just as the banners of heaven are the angels, so are Israel the banners of the earth—the Lord of both is the Holy One. And just as all fear the Holy One and the angels, so will the heathen peoples fear Israel, as is said, "All the peoples of the earth shall see that the Name of the Lord is called upon thee; and they shall fear thee" (Deut. 28:10).[1]

16. "At nights on my bed" (Song 3:1). The congregation of Israel said to the Holy One: Master of the universe, in the past You were wont to give me light between one night and another—between the night of Egypt and the night of Babylon, between the night of Babylon and the night of Media, between the night of Media and the night of Greece, and between the night of Greece and the night of Edom. But now one night follows immediately upon another.[2]

17. When Israel were driven into exile, the peoples of the world said: The Holy One no longer desires this people, as is said, "Silver melted down[3] shall men call them" (Jer. 6:30). Just as silver is refined and made into a utensil, then is refined again and made into a new utensil, and so many times over, until what is left of it finally breaks in one's hand and is no longer fit for any useful purpose; so Israel were saying that they had no hope of being restored [as with silver refined beyond use], that the Holy One had rejected them. When Jeremiah heard this, he came to the Holy One and said: Master of the universe, is it true that You have rejected Your children? "Hast Thou utterly rejected Judah? Hath Thy soul loathed Zion? Why hast Thou smitten us, and there is no healing for us?" (Jer. 14:19). If You desire to drive us out [of this world], then smite us until we die.[4]

18. R. Simeon ben Gamaliel said: Our forebears had only a whiff of the distress inflicted by the kingdoms, yet they lost their courage. All the more so we, who have been swallowed up in the kingdoms' very innards for so many days, so many years, so many periods, so many epochs![5]

19. "Or hath God assayed to go and take Him a nation from the midst of another nation?" (Deut. 4:34). R. Avin taught in the name of R. Simon: What is meant by "from the midst of another nation"? That the children of Israel were swallowed up in the very innards of Egypt, as is said, "They had swallowed us up alive" (Ps. 124:3).[6]

20. "As a lily among thorns" (Song 2:2). R. Eliezer interpreted the verse as referring to the redemption from Egypt. Just as a lily, when growing between thorns, is difficult for its owner to pluck, so the redemption of Israel was difficult for the Holy One, as is said, "Or hath God assayed to go and take a nation from the midst of another nation?"

Note, said R. Joshua citing R. Hanan, that the text does not say, "A nation from the midst of a people" or "A people from the midst of a nation," but, "A nation from the midst of a nation," for Israel were uncircumcised even as the Egyptians were uncircumcised; Israel grew locks even as the Egyptians grew locks; Israel put on garments made of mixed fibers even as the Egyptians put on garments of mixed fibers. So the measure of justice [alone] would not have allowed that Israel ever be redeemed.[7]

21. Our masters taught: Who wrote the Scroll of Fasts?[8] The answer: Hananiah ben Hezekiah and his company, because they cherished [the memory of] past tribulations [from which they had been rescued]. R. Simeon ben Gamaliel said: We, too, cherish our tribulations. But what are we to do? Were we to attempt writing them down, we would not have enough time [our tribulations being so many]. Or [perhaps] a fool is not aware of being oppressed. Or the flesh of a corpse does not feel the scalpel.[9]

22. "That they have said to thy soul: 'Bow down, that we may go over' " (Isa. 51:23). What did they do to them? They made them lie down in the streets and had paving rollers go over them.[10]

---

1. Exod. R. 15:6.
2. Song R. 3:1, §1.
3. JV: "Rejected (*nim'as*) silver shall men call them." But here *nim'as* is apparently equated with *nimas* ("melted down").
4. Exod. R. 31:10.
5. Song R. 3:4, §2; Lam. R. 5:9, §1.
6. MTeh 114:6.
7. Song R. 2:2, §2.
8. In it, the days commemorating Jewish victories were set down as festal days, on which fasting was prohibited.
9. B. Shab 13b.
10. Gen. R. 69:5.

23. Once the wicked empire [of Rome] issued a decree that Israel should not occupy themselves with Torah nor circumcise their sons, and should profane the Sabbath. What did Judah ben Shammua and his companions do? They went and consulted a Roman noblewoman whose home all the notables of Rome used to visit. She advised: Go and make proclamation [of your sorrows] at night.[1] They went and proclaimed them at night, saying, "In Heaven's name, are we not your brothers? Are we not sons of one father, are we not sons of one mother? How are we different from any other nation and tongue, that you issue such hard decrees against us?" The decrees were subsequently annulled.[2]

24. "Her adversaries are the chief" (Lam. 1:5). Rabbah said, citing R. Yohanan: Everyone who oppresses Israel becomes a chief.[3]

25. R. Hiyya taught: What is meant by "God understandeth the way thereof, and He knoweth the place thereof" (Job 28:23)? The Holy One knows that Israel would be unable to endure the cruel decrees of Esau or of Ishmael, so He exiled them to Babylonia.

R. Hanina said: The Holy One exiled them to Babylonia because the language is akin to the language of the Torah. R. Yohanan said: Because He thus sent Israel back to their mother's house. As when a man grows angry at his wife, where does he send her? Back to her mother's house. Ulla said: [God sent them to Babylonia] so that they might eat dates and occupy themselves with Torah.[4]

26. R. Avin opened his discourse with the verse "He changeth the times and the seasons" (Dan. 2:21), meaning that Jeremiah said to Israel: Had you been worthy, you would be dwelling in Jerusalem and drinking the waters of Siloam, whose waters are pure and sweet. But now that you are unworthy, you are being exiled to Babylon, where you will be drinking the waters of the Euphrates, whose waters are impure and ill smelling, as Scripture says, "And now, what is the good of your going to Egypt to drink the waters of the Nile? And what is the good of your going to Assyria to drink the waters of the Euphrates?" (Jer. 2:18).[5]

27. Rabbah bar Bar Hanah took sick, and R. Judah and Rabbah came to visit him. At this point a Habbar[6] came in and took away their lamp.[7] So Rabbah bar Bar Hanah said: Master of the universe, either in Your shadow or in the shadow of the son of Esau.[8]

28. We have been taught that R. Yose said: Throughout my days I was baffled by the verse "And thou shalt grope at noonday as the blind gropeth in darkness" (Deut. 28:29). What difference, I kept asking myself, does it make to a blind man whether it is dark or light? Then the following incident occurred: once I was walking on a pitch-black night when I saw a blind man walking on the road with a torch in his hand. So I said to him, "My son, this torch—why do you need it?" He replied, "As long as a torch is in my hand, people see me and keep me away from holes in the ground, from thorns and briers."[9]

29. R. Judah said: Exile atones for three decrees [which otherwise would have been imposed], for Scripture says, "Thus saith the Lord: . . . He that abideth in this city shall die by the sword, and by the famine, and by the pestilence; but he that goeth out and falleth away to the Chaldeans that besiege you, he shall live" (Jer. 21:9).[10]

R. Yohanan said: Exile atones for everything. Thus it is written, "Thus saith the Lord: Write ye this man childless" (Jer. 22:30). But after this man was exiled, it is said, "The sons of Jeconiah—the same is Assir-Shealtiel his son," etc. (1 Chron. 3:17).[11]

30. R. Sheshet said in the name of R. Eleazar ben Azariah: I can justify the exemption of the entire [Jewish] world from condign judgment from the destruction of the Temple until the present time, for Scripture says, "Therefore hear now this, thou afflicted, and drunken, but not with wine" (Isa. 51:21).[12]

31. "Jacob said to his sons: 'Why should you show yourselves?' " (Gen. 42:1).[13] What Jacob meant was: "Do not show yourselves when you are full, either to Esau or to Ishmael, lest they envy you [and rob you].[14]

32. "Thy sons have fainted, they lie at the head of all the streets, as an antelope in a net" (Isa. 51:20). Even as an antelope, when fallen into a net, is shown no pity, so Israel's possessions are shown no pity when fallen into the hands of heathens.[15]

33. "The sound of a driven leaf shall chase them" (Lev. 26:36). R. Joshua ben Korhah said: Once, while we were seated in the midst of trees, the wind began to blow and the leaves rustled. So we jumped up and ran, crying: Woe unto us, the horsemen may catch up with us. After a while we turned around and saw not a creature there. So we sat down where we were and wept as we said: Woe unto us, for unto us has been fulfilled the verse "The sound of a driven leaf shall chase them."[16]

---

1. The Jews' lament would keep the citizenry awake, and the public would demand that the Jews be pacified so that Romans could sleep. Suggested hesitantly by Leon Nemoy.
2. B. RH 19a and En Yaakov, ad loc.
3. B. Sanh 104b.
4. B. Pes 87b–88a; Git 17a.
5. Lam. R. proem 19.
6. A fire worshiper.
7. It was a Habbar festival, when kindling a fire was forbidden.
8. B. Git 16b–17a.
9. B. Meg 24b and En Yaakov, ad loc.
10. Wandering in exile and the hardships that attend it are taken to be a lesser evil than the three evils in the city.
11. B. Sanh 37b.
12. Since Israel is described as "drunken" [with troubles], it cannot be held responsible for its actions. B. Er 64b–65a and En Yaakov, ad loc.
13. JV: "Why do you look upon one another?"
14. B. Ta 10b.
15. B. BK 117a.
16. Sif Lev. 112b; Yalkut, *Be-hukkotai*, §675.

34. Our masters taught: It once happened that evil edicts were brought to the notables of Sepphoris. They went and asked R. Eleazar ben Perata, saying to him, "Master, evil edicts came to us from the [Roman] government. What do you advise? Shall we flee?" Fearful of saying to them, "Flee," he replied in veiled language, "Are you asking me? Go ask Jacob, Moses, and David."

What is written of Jacob? "And Jacob fled" (Hos. 12:13). So also of Moses: "But Moses fled from before Pharaoh" (Exod. 2:15). And so it was with David: "Now David fled, and escaped" (1 Sam. 19:18). It is in this spirit that Scripture says, "Come, My people, enter thou into thy chambers. . . . Hide thyself for a little moment, until the indignation be overpast" (Isa. 26:20).[1]

35. "Come, My people, enter thou into thy chambers." When you see that a particular time is brazen, do not attempt to stand up against it, but be willing to make room for it. Look at Me—if one dare say such a thing—when I saw that, because of your sins, the time was brazen, I made room for it, as is said, "He hath drawn back His right hand" (Lam. 2:3).[2]

Israel: An Object of Derision among the Nations

36. "I am become a derision to all my people" (Lam. 3:14). R. Abbahu began his discourse with the verse "They that sit in the gate talk of me" (Ps. 69:13), "they" being the nations of the world who are seated in theaters and circuses. "And I am the song of the drunkards" (ibid.)—after they eat and drink and get drunk, they start talking of me and ridiculing me, saying, "We do not live on carobs as the Jews have to." Then they ask one another, "How many years do you wish to live?" and reply, "As long as a Jew's shirt lasts, which he wears only on the Sabbath." Then they bring a camel into their theaters, with his [black] covers upon him, and ask one another, "Why is this one in mourning?" and they answer, "These Jews are observing the sabbatical year, and since they have no greens, they eat up the thorns used by this camel, and he mourns the loss of them." Then they bring a clown into their theaters, his head shaven, and ask one another, "Why is the head of this one shaven?" and they reply, "These Jews keep the Sabbath, and whatever they toil for during the week, they consume on the Sabbath. Since they have no wood to cook with, they break up their [wooden] beds and use them for fuel. Then they have to sleep on the ground, get covered with dust, and need to anoint their hair with oil, [which Jews use in such quantities] that the price of oil has become prohibitive."[3]

37. R. Judah said in the name of Samuel: They have yet another festival in Rome: once every seventy years they bring a healthy man and have him ride on a lame man. They dress him in Adam's choice garments,[4] place on his head R. Ishmael's scalp,[5] hang on his neck [a chain] of fine gold in the weight of four *zuz*, stud his thighs with emeralds, and proclaim before him in Greek: *Sak kyriou plastēr*, meaning: The reckoning of the ruler is wrong. The brother of our Lord is an impostor. Let him who sees this see it. For he who does not see it will not live to see it again.[6] Of what avail is fraud to a cheat or deceit to a deceiver?

And they conclude: Woe unto the one when the other arises![7]

38. R. Phinehas said: It happened that two harlots in Ashkelon were quarreling. In the course of their quarrel, one said to the other: Why don't you leave town? You look like a Jewess! After a while, they became reconciled, and the one said to the other: Everything is forgiven you, except your remark "You look like a Jewess"—that I cannot forgive. Hence it is said, "See, O Lord, and behold, how abject I am become" (Lam. 1:11).[8]

39. "Make me not the reproach of the base" (Ps. 9:9). R. Hama bar Hanina said: The nations of the earth should have no sickly or broken-down people among them.[9] Why then are there sickly and broken-down people among them? So that they should not taunt Israel and say, "Are you not a people made up of those who are sickly and broken down?" Thus Israel's prayer "Make me not the reproach of the base" is fulfilled.

R. Samuel bar Nahman said: None among the nations of the earth should have persons with running sores. Why then are there among them some who have running sores? So that they should not taunt Israel, saying, "Are you not a people of lepers?" Israel's prayer "Make me not the reproach of the base" is thus fulfilled.[10]

The Holy One Is Partner in Israel's Travail

40. Whenever the Holy One calls to mind His children deep in travail among the nations of the world, He—if one dare say this—lets fall two tears into the Great [Mediterranean] Sea. Their splash is heard from world's end to world's end, and that is the cause of earthquakes.

The sages say: He treads heavily upon the sky. Others say: He roars with His voice, and makes worlds shake, as

1. Tanhuma B, *Mas'e*, §1; Num. R. 23:1.
2. Tanhuma B, *Va-yetze*, §5; Yalkut, *Shemot*, §168.
3. And since the clown cannot afford the high cost of oil, he shaves his head. Lam. R., proem 17; Lam. R. 3:14, §5.
4. Which God made for Adam and Eve. See above, part 1, chap. 2, §135, and chap. 3, §98.
5. See above, part 1, chap. 11, §180.
6. Since the spectacle is to be seen only once in seventy years.
7. The healthy man in the charade is Esau; the lame one, Jacob (see Gen. 32:32). "The reckoning of the ruler" refers to Jacob's calculation of the time of Israel's redemption. The "fraud" and "deceit" allude to Jacob's deception of his brother Esau. And the conclusion is a warning to Israel to beware of the power of Rome. So Rashi. B. AZ 11b and En Yaakov, ad loc.
8. Lam. R. 1:11, §39.
9. Since this world is to be theirs.
10. Gen. R. 88:1; Yalkut, *Va-yeshev*, §146.

is said, "The Lord doth roar from on high. . . . He doth mightily roar because of His fold" (Jer. 25:30).[1]

41. Baltza asked R. Akiva: What causes earthquakes? R. Akiva: When the Holy One observes heathen temples and their worshipers enjoying peace and prosperity in this world, and sees His own Temple destroyed and in the hands of idolaters, He—if one dare ascribe such feeling to Him—becomes jealous and roars. As a result, heaven and earth shake, as is said, "The Lord roars from Zion, and utters His voice from Jerusalem, and the heavens and the earth shake" (Joel 4:16).[2]

42. We have been taught that R. Yose said: Once, while on a journey, I entered into one of the ruins in Jerusalem to pray. [The prophet] Elijah, ever remembered on good occasions, appeared and waited for me at the door until I finished my prayer. After I finished my prayer, he said to me, "Peace be with you, my master." I replied, "Peace be with you, my master and teacher." He asked, "My son, why did you go into this ruin?" I: "To pray." He: "You should have prayed on the road." I: "I was afraid that passersby might interrupt me." He: "What sound did you hear in the ruin?" I: "I heard a divine voice cooing like a dove and saying:

> 'Alas that I destroyed My house,
> burned my Temple Hall,
> and exiled My children among the peoples.' "

Elijah said to me, "By your life and by the life of your head, not only at this time alone does it so exclaim. But every day, three times a day, it exclaims thus. More; when Israel enter synagogues and houses of study, and respond, 'Amen, may the great Name be blessed,' the Holy One—if one dare speak thus—nods His head and says:

> 'Happy the King who is thus praised in His own house!
> What is one to say of a Father who banished His children?
> Alas for children banished from their Father's table.' "[3]

43. "My dove, My twin"[4] (Song 5:2). R. Yannai said: As with twins, when the head of one aches, the other also feels it, so, too—if one dare utter such a thing—the Holy One said, "I am with him in trouble" (Ps. 91:15). And again, "In all their affliction, He too was afflicted" (Isa. 63:9). The Holy One said to Moses: Are you not aware that I am wracked with pain even as Israel is wracked with pain? Take note of the place whence I speak to you—from the midst of a thornbush. I am—if one may ascribe such a statement to God—a partner in their pain.[5]

44. Pause and consider how plentiful always are the mercies of the Holy One for the people of Israel. For in any generation that you find righteous, faithful, and worthy men [grieving in exile], the Holy One claps both hands together, then He clasps them over His heart, then He folds His arms as He weeps secretly for the righteous. Why does He weep for them secretly? Because it is unseemly for a lion to weep before a fox, unseemly for a sage to weep before his disciple, unseemly for a king to weep before the least of his servants, as is said, "So that you will not hear it, My soul shall weep in secret" (Jer. 13:17).[6]

45. We have been taught that R. Simeon ben Yohai said: Pause and consider how beloved are Israel in the sight of God. Wherever they were exiled, the Presence was with them. When they were exiled to Egypt, the Presence was with them, for Eli was told, "Did I not reveal Myself to thy forebear [Aaron's] house when they were in Egypt?" (1 Sam. 2:27). When they were exiled to Babylon, the Presence was with them, as is said, "For your sake I had Myself sent to Babylon" (Isa. 43:14). When they were exiled to Elam, the Presence was with them, as is said, "I will set My throne in Elam" (Jer. 49:38). When they were exiled to Edom, the Presence was with them, as is said, "Who is this that cometh from Edom, with crimsoned garments from Bosrah?" (Isa. 63:1). And when they are redeemed, the Presence will be with them, as is said, "The Lord thy God will return with thy captivity" (Deut. 30:3). Scripture does not say, "Cause to return thy captivity"; rather, it says, "Return," proving that the Holy One will return with them out of the several exiles. Thus also it is said, "Come with Me from Lebanon, My bride, with Me from Lebanon; look from the top of Amana, from the top of Senir and Hermon, from the lions' dens, from the mountains of the leopards" (Song 4:8).

Rabbi [Judah I, the Patriarch] said: How may the matter be illustrated? By the parable of a king who said to his servant: If ever you seek me, you will find me with my son. Whenever you seek me, you will find me with my son. Thus Scripture: "That dwelleth with them in the midst of their uncleanness" (Lev. 16:16).[7]

46. "My soul shall weep in secret for the glory"[8] (Jer. 13:17). R. Samuel bar Unia said in the name of Rav: The Holy One has a place, and its name is Secret. What is meant by "for the glory"? R. Samuel bar Isaac said: For the glory of Israel, which was taken from them and given to the peoples of the world.[9]

47. Zavdi ben Levi began his discourse with the verse "God seated the unique ones together in a house, after He brought forth the prisoners into prosperity. But then, as rebellious ones, they were made to dwell in a parched

---

1. B. Ber. 59a and En Yaakov, ad loc.
2. Exod. R. 29:9.
3. B. Ber 3a and En Yaakov, ad loc.
4. The word *tammati* ("My undefiled") is read as though spelled *te'omati* ("My twin").
5. Exod. R. 2:5.
6. TdE, ed. Friedmann, p. 154.
7. B. Meg 29a; Sif Num., §161.
8. JV: "for the pride."
9. B. Hag 5b.

land" (Ps. 68:7).[1] You find that before Israel were redeemed from Egypt, they dwelled by themselves, and the Presence dwelled by itself. But after they were redeemed, Israel and the Presence became one entity. Then, after they were exiled, the Presence resumed existence apart, and Israel resumed existence apart.[2] Hence Scripture: "How doth she sit solitary" (Lam. 1:1).[3]

48. "Open to Me, My sister, My love, My dove, My undefiled; for My head is filled with dew" (Song 5:2). In the time-to-come, when the Holy One comes to redeem Israel, they will say: Master of the universe, You exiled us among the nations and thrust us out of Your house. And now You come to redeem us? The Holy One will reply: I will tell you the parable of a king who divorced his wife and the next day came to bring her back. She said: My lord king, yesterday you drove me out of your house, and today you come to take me back? He said: You should know that since you left my house, I, too, have not gone into my house. If you do not believe me, look at the dew on my head. Likewise, the Holy One will say to Israel: Ever since the day you left My house, I, too, have not gone into My house. If you do not believe Me, put your hands upon My head, and you will see that "My head is filled with dew, My locks with the drops of the night" (ibid.).[4]

The Guardian of Israel

49. R. Joshua ben Levi said: Why are they called "the Men of the Great Assembly"?[5] Because they restored the manner of praising God to its ancient form.

Moses instituted the order of prayer for Israel when he said, "The great God, the mighty, the awesome" (Deut. 10:17). Then came Jeremiah and said: Heathen nations are battering at His Temple Hall—where are His awesome deeds? So He decided not to say, "The awesome God." Then came Daniel and said: Heathen nations are enslaving His children—where are His mighty acts? So [in his order of prayer] Daniel decided not to say, "The mighty God."

Then came the Men of the Great Assembly and said: On the contrary! The greatness of His might lies precisely in His restraining His wrath and extending patience to the wicked. And these are His awesome deeds: but for the awe of the Holy One, blessed be He, how could one nation exist among seventy hostile nations?

But how dared flesh and blood[6] assert that God has limitations?

Because, so said R. Isaac ben Eleazar, the prophets knew that their God demanded truth, and they did not attempt to flatter Him.[7]

1. JV: "God maketh the solitary to dwell in a house; He bringeth out the prisoners into prosperity; the rebellious dwell but in a parched land."
2. "In a parched land," where the Presence is not.
3. Lam. R., proem 29.
4. Midrash based on Yalkut Eliezer 68.
5. A supreme authority established under Ezra and Nehemiah.
6. Jeremiah and Daniel.
7. B. Yoma 69b and En Yaakov, ad loc.; P. Ber 7:3, 11c.

50. Hadrian said to R. Joshua: The lamb that stays alive among seventy wolves must be great. R. Joshua: Even greater is the shepherd who delivers it, protects it, and destroys the wolves around it. Hence, "no weapon that is formed against thee shall prosper" (Isa. 54:17).[8]

51. A philosopher asked R. Eleazar: Did not a prophet attribute to God the words "They shall build, but I will throw down" (Mal. 1:4)? Yet all buildings [of the nations of the world] remain standing! R. Eleazar replied: Scripture speaks not about physical buildings, but about plans [behind them]. All that you plot to build up against us in order to destroy us—the plan you come to, He demolishes. The philosopher then said: By your life, this is so. Every year we meet to figure out how to destroy you, but a certain elder comes and nullifies [what we intend].[9]

52. R. Abbahu extolled R. Safra to the *Minim*[10] as a learned man, and he was thus exempted by them from paying taxes for thirteen years.[11] One day, on coming across R. Safra, they said, "It is written, 'You only have I loved of all the families of the earth; therefore will I visit upon you all your iniquities' [Amos 3:2]. Is it just that an irate person should let out his ire on his friend?" R. Safra remained silent and gave no answer. So they wound a scarf around his neck and tormented him. When R. Abbahu came and found them at it, he asked, "Why do you torment him?" They replied, "Did you not tell us that he was a great man? Yet he cannot explain the meaning of this verse in Amos." R. Abbahu: "I told you [that he was learned] in Mishnah. Did I tell you that [he was equally learned] in Scripture?" They: "How come you know it?" R. Abbahu: "We, who are now under your rule, set ourselves the task of studying Scripture thoroughly, but others[12] do not study it as carefully." They: "Then you tell us the verse's meaning." R. Abbahu replied, "I will explain it by a parable. To whom may God in this verse be compared? To a man who is the creditor of two persons, one a friend and the other an enemy. From his friend he is willing to accept payment little by little; but from his enemy he will exact immediate payment in one lump sum."[13]

53. "O Lord, rebuke me not in Thine anger" (Ps. 6:2). R. Eleazar said: With whom may God in His punishment [of Israel] be compared? With a king who became angry at his son and at that moment, holding in his hand an unsheathed Indian sword, swore that he would whip it across his son's head. But then the king softened and said: If I whip it across my son's head, his life will be gone, and who will inherit my kingdom? And yet it is impossible for me to revoke my royal word. What did the king do? He put the sword back into its sheath and then whipped it across his son's head, and so his son was spared while his royal word was kept.

8. Tanhuma, *Toledot*, §5.
9. Yalkut, Mal., §587.
10. The Judeo-Christian authorities.
11. Such exemption was granted to scholars.
12. Those of Babylonia.
13. B. AZ 4a.

R. Hanina taught: God may be compared with a king who became angry at his son and, seeing at that moment a large stone before him, swore that he would heave it at his son. But then the king said: If I throw it at my son, his life will be gone. What did the king do? He ordered that the stone be broken up into small pebbles and that these be thrown, one by one, at his son. And thus the king spared his son and yet kept his royal oath.[1]

54. R. Oshaia said: What is meant by "The merciful act of His dispersing Israel" (Judg. 5:11)?[2] The Holy One showed mercy to Israel in dispersing them among the nations.

In this regard, a certain Christian said to R. Hanina: We are more compassionate than you. Of you it is written, "Joab and all Israel remained there six months until he had cut off every male in Edom" (1 Kings 11:16). But we—just consider how many years you have been living in our midst, yet we do you no harm whatsoever. R. Hanina replied: Will you allow a disciple to join you [in debating the matter? Accordingly,], R. Oshaia joined them and said to the Christian: It is because you do not know how to go about it. You would like to exterminate all of us. But all of us are not living among you. Should you exterminate only those of us who are in your midst, you will be called a suicidal kingdom. The Christian said: By the Roman eagle! It's a tough nut to crack—whatever we do involves as much loss as profit for us.[3]

55. "Then Judah went down from his brethren" (Gen. 38:1). The brothers said: Come, let us disperse. As long as we are together, the writ of debt [for the sale of Joseph] may be called.[4]

56. R. Judah son of R. Simon said: The tribes of Judah and Benjamin were not exiled to the same place that the other tribes were. The ten tribes were exiled beyond the river Sambatyon, while the tribes of Judah and Benjamin were dispersed in all lands.[5]

57. "And he said: 'If Esau come to the one camp, and smite it' " (Gen. 32:9). This alludes to our brethren in the south. "Then the camp which is left, shall escape" (ibid.) alludes to our brethren in Galilee. Even though they escaped, said R. Oshaia, we nevertheless fast in their behalf on Mondays and Thursdays.[6]

58. R. Eleazar said: The Holy One exiled Israel among the peoples only in order that proselytes might be multiplied, as is said, "I will sow her unto Me in the Land" (Hos. 2:25). Does not a man sow a *seah* [seed] in the ground only so that it may bring in many *kor* [of harvest]?[7]

Watchman, What of the Night?

59. "One calleth unto me out of Seir: 'Watchman, what of the night?' " (Isa. 21:11). Israel said to Isaiah: Our master Isaiah, what will come for us out of this night? He replied: Wait until I ask. After he had asked, he came back to them, and they asked again: "Watchman, what did He say?" (ibid.)[8]—what did the Watchman of both worlds [this world and the next] say? Isaiah replied: "The Watchman said: 'The morning cometh and also the night' " (Isa. 21:12). They asked: [After the morning], is night to come again? Isaiah replied: It is not as you suppose. There will be morning for the righteous and night for the nations of the world. They asked: When? Isaiah replied: When you wish it, He will wish it—"If you desire it, He will desire it" (ibid.).[9] They asked: What hinders it? Isaiah: [Your lack of] repentance—"Return, come" (ibid.).[10]

60. "Arise, shine, for thy light is come" (Isa. 60:1). R. Yohanan said: A parable of a man walking on a road after sunset. Someone came and kindled a lamp for him, but it went out. Another person came and kindled a lamp for him, but it, too, went out. The man then said: From now on, I will wait for nothing but the light of morning. So, too, Israel said to the Holy One: We made a candelabrum for You in the days of Moses, and it went out. We made another in the days of Solomon, and it, too, went out. From now on, we will wait for nothing but Your light, as is said, "For with Thee is the fountain of life; in Thy light do we see light" (Ps. 36:10).[11]

61. "I adjure you, O daughters of Jerusalem, by the gazelles and by the hinds of the field, that ye awaken not, nor stir up love, until it please" (Song 2:7). R. Yose son of R. Hanina said: What is the purpose of these three adjurations?[12] One: that Israel [repent and thus earn their redemption, and] not attempt to return to the Land en masse [until they are cleansed of sin]. Another: the Holy One adjured Israel that they should not rebel against the nations of the world. Third: the Holy One adjured the nations of the world that they should not enslave Israel too harshly.

"By the gazelles and by the hinds of the field." R. Eleazar said: The Holy One told Israel: If you abide by the adjuration, well and good; but if not, I will have your flesh be lawful prey, like the flesh of gazelles and hinds of the field.[13]

1. MTeh 6:3; Yalkut, Ps., §633.
2. JV: "The righteous acts of His rulers (*pirzono*) in Israel." But by metathesis, *pirzono* is read *pizrono* ("His dispersing").
3. The literal translation may be: "With this concern we lie down, and with it we get up." But *yoredim* may also mean "weigh" or "consider loss," and *olim* may mean "weigh" or "consider profit." So Leon Nemoy. B. Pes 87b.
4. Gen. R. 85:2.
5. Gen. R. 73:6.
6. Gen. R. 76:3; Yalkut, *Va-yishlah*, §131.
7. A *kor* is thirty *seah*. B. Pes 87b.
8. JV: "Watchman, what of the night (*millel*)." But the word can also mean "he said."
9. Reading *be'iyo* for *be'ayu* ("do ye desire it").
10. P. Ta 1:1, 64a.
11. Yalkut, Isa., §499.
12. The other two are in Song 3:5 and 5:8.
13. B. Ket 111a.

62. "I adjure you . . . that ye awaken not, nor stir up love, until it please" (Song 2:7). R. Onia said: The Holy One addressed four adjurations to Israel, corresponding to the four generations who tried to hasten the time destined for redemption and came to grief: once in the days of Amram; once in the days of Dinai[1] (some say, in the generation of [Hadrian's] persecution); once in the days of Ben Kozeva; and once in the days of Shuthelach son of Ephraim, as is said, "The children of Ephraim were as archers handling the bow" (Ps. 78:9).[2]

63. "But the dove found no rest" (Gen. 8:9). R. Judah said in the name of R. Simeon ben Lakish: Had the dove found a place of rest, it would not have returned. So, too, "she dwelleth among the nations, she findeth no rest" (Lam. 1:3). Had she found rest, she would not have returned [in contrition to God]. So, too, "among the nations shalt thou have no repose, and there shall be no rest for the sole of thy foot" (Deut. 28:65). Had they found it, they would not have returned [in contrition to God].[3]

64. Moses said, "Ye shall perish among the nations" (Lev. 26:38). Then came Isaiah and said, "It shall come to pass in that day, that a great horn shall be blown, and they shall come that were lost in the land of Assyria" (Isa. 27:13).

Rav said: I am fearful about that verse which asserts, "Ye shall perish among the nations."

[But R. Papa demurred at Rav's apprehension]: May not "being lost" be taken in the sense of something lost and then eagerly sought, as in the verse "I have gone astray like a lost sheep; seek Thy servant" (Ps. 119:176)?

It was, however, the latter part of the verse—"and the land of your enemies shall eat you up" (Lev. 26:38)—that frightened Rav.

[Mar Zutra]: May not the eating be like the eating of cucumbers and pumpkins [whose seeds are left to sprout anew]?[4]

65. "She is become as a widow" (Lam. 1:1). R. Judah said in the name of Rav that the verse has an aspect of blessing: "As a widow," but not an actual widow—more like a woman whose husband has gone to a city far across the sea, with the firm intention of returning to her.[5]

66. "And be thou like to a gazelle" (Song 8:14). Even as a gazelle may wander to the end of the world and yet invariably returns to its place, so are Israel: even though they are dispersed throughout the world, they are destined to return.[6]

67. We have been taught: "And yet, for all that, when they are in the land of their enemies, I have not rejected them" (Lev. 26:44)—in the days of the Chaldeans, when I raised up for them Daniel, Hananiah, Mishael, and Azariah. "Neither have I abhorred them" (ibid.)—in the days of Haman, when I raised up for them Mordecai and Esther. "To destroy them utterly" (ibid.)—in the days of the Greeks, when I raised up for them Simeon the Righteous and the high priest Mattathias son of Yohanan Hasmonai and his sons. "To break My covenant with them" (ibid.)—in the days of the Romans, when I raised up for them the sages of the house of Rabbi [Judah I, the Patriarch] and the sages of successive generations. "For I am the Lord their God" (ibid.)—also in the time-to-come, when no people or tongue will be able to prevail over them.[7]

68. "Know, yea, know, that thy seed shall be a stranger" (Gen. 15:13): "Know" that I shall disperse them, but "know" also that I will gather them together; "know" that I shall give them in pledge,[8] but "know" also that I will redeem them; "know" that I will allow them to be enslaved, but "know" also that I will deliver them.[9]

69. "The Lord answer thee in the day of trouble" (Ps. 20:2). A parable of a father and son who were journeying on a road. The son, growing weary, asked his father, "Father, where is the city?" The father replied, "My son, take this as a sign: when you see a burial ground before you, then surely the city is near you." Likewise, the Holy One said to the children of Israel: When you see troubles hard by you, surely in that very hour you will be redeemed, for it is said, "The Lord will answer thee in the day of trouble."[10]

70. The children of Israel said to the Holy One, "Master of the universe, when will You redeem us?" He answered, "When you have gone down to the very bottom of the pit. In that very hour I shall redeem you, as is said, 'The children of Judah and the children of Israel shall be gathered together—and shall rise up from the earth' " (Hos. 2:2). So, too, the sons of the Korah said, "We are at the very bottom of the pit, as is said, 'For our soul is sunk deep in the dust' " (Ps. 44:26). [And what did they go on to say?] "Arise for our help" (Ps. 44:27).[11]

71. "The voice is the voice of Jacob, but the hands are the hands of Esau" (Gen. 27:22). R. Judah bar Ilai said that Rabbi [Judah I, the Patriarch] used to expound the verse: The voice of Jacob cries out because of what the hands—the hands of Esau—have done to him.[12]

72. What is meant by the words "And Thou, O Lord, how long" (Ps. 6:4)? In answer, R. Kahana told the parable of a sick man who was under a physician's care. The sick man was eagerly waiting for the physician: when will he come—at the fourth hour, the fifth hour, the sixth, or the

1. Probably during the Second Temple.
2. See 1 Chron. 7:21. Song R. 2:7, §1.
3. Gen. R. 33:6; Lam. R. 1:3, §29.
4. B. Mak 24a.
5. B. Ta 20a; B. Sanh 104a; Lam. R. 1:1, §3.
6. Yalkut, Song, §964.
7. B. Meg 11a and En Yaakov, ad loc.
8. Being in exile is intended as a pledge that Israel will expiate their sins.
9. Gen. R. 44:18.
10. MTeh 20:4; Yalkut, Ps., §680.
11. MTeh 45:3; Yalkut, Hos., §533.
12. Gen. R. 65:21.

seventh? But the physician did not come. The eighth, ninth, and tenth hours passed by. Still he did not come, and only as the sun was setting was the physician seen approaching, feeling his way in the dark. The sick man said, "Had you delayed your coming a little longer, my soul would have left me!" So, too, David cried out. When he saw the kingdoms continuing to enslave the people of Israel, he exclaimed, " 'And Thou, O Lord, how long?' You, who are my healer, are delayed in Your coming to me."[1]

73. The verse "Therefore fear thou not, O Jacob My servant, saith the Lord; neither be dismayed, O Israel" (Jer. 30:10) applies to an episode in Jacob's life, when "he dreamed, and behold a ladder . . . and . . . angels of God ascending and descending on it" (Gen. 28:12). These angels were the princes of the nations of the earth. Further, this verse indicates that the Holy One showed to our father Jacob the prince of Babylon climbing up seventy rungs of the ladder, then climbing down; the prince of Media climbing up fifty-two rungs; the prince of Greece, one hundred and eighty rungs; and the prince of Edom [Rome] climbing and climbing, no one can tell how many rungs. At the sight of Edom's climbing, our father Jacob grew afraid and said: Is one to suppose that this prince will have no comedown? The Holy One replied, "Fear thou not, O Jacob My servant" (Jer. 30:10). Even if—as though such a thing were possible!—you were to see Edom come up and sit next to Me, I will have him eventually brought down from there. Indeed, Edom is told in Scripture, "Though thou make thy nest as high as the eagle, and though thou set it among the stars, I will bring thee down from thence, saith the Lord" (Obad. 1:4).[2]

74. "Surely blood of your lives will I require; at the hand of every beast will I require it" (Gen. 9:5). This refers to the four kingdoms.[3] "Even at the hand of a man's brother" (ibid.)—of Esau, about whom Jacob prayed, "Deliver me, I pray thee, from the hand of my brother, from the hand of Esau" (Gen. 32:12).[4]

75. "For He hath clothed me with garments of salvation" (Isa. 61:10), with the seven garments that, according to Scripture, the Holy One will have put on successively from the day the world was created until the day He requites wicked Edom. When He created the world, He put on glory and majesty. When He appeared to us at the Red Sea, He put on pride. When He gave the Torah to His people, He put on strength. When He requited the Chaldeans, He put on vengeance. When He will have forgiven the iniquities of Israel, He will put on a white garment. And when the Messiah appears, God will be clothed in righteousness. Finally, when He comes to requite Edom, He will put on red apparel, as is said "Wherefore is Thine apparel red?" (Isa. 63:2)—that is, red with vengeance against Edom. At that time the ministering angels will say to the Holy One: Master of the universe, the comely apparel You wear now becomes You more than all the apparel You put on before.[5]

76. It is taught in the name of R. Eliezer: Vengeance on Israel comes through the agency of the poor, as is said, "And he cry unto the Lord against thee, and it be sin against thee" (Deut. 15:9). So, too, will vengeance on Edom come through the agency of [poor, oppressed] Israel, as is said, "I will lay My vengeance upon Edom by the hand of My people Israel" (Ezek. 25:14).[6]

77. R. Judah said in the name of Rav: [Messiah] son of David will not come until the kingdom of Edom [Rome] will have spread its power over the whole world for nine months, as is said, "Therefore will He give them up, until the time that she who is with child hath brought forth; then the residue of his brethren shall return with the children of Israel" (Mic. 5:2).[7]

78. "Some of this red, red pottage" (Gen. 25:30). He was red, his food red, his land red, his warriors red, his garments red. He who requites him will likewise be red and clad in red garments. He was red: "And the first came forth ruddy" (Gen. 25:25). His food was red: "Let me swallow, I pray thee, some of this red, red pottage" (Gen. 25:30). His land was red: "To Esau his brother unto the land of Seir, the field of red"[8] (Gen. 32:4). His warriors are red: "The shield of his warriors is painted red" (Nah. 2:4). Their garments are red: "The valiant men are in scarlet" (ibid.). He who requites him will be red: "My Beloved is white and ruddy" (Song 5:10), clad in red: "Wherefore is Thine apparel red?" (Isa. 63:2).[9]

79. R. Jonathan said: Three things were given as a gift to the world: Torah, the luminaries, and rain. R. Azariah said in the name of R. Simeon ben Lakish: Also peace. R. Joshua ben Nehemiah: Also deliverance. R. Tanhuma: Also the Land of Israel. R. Isaac ben Maryon: Also the crossing of the Great [Mediterranean] Sea. But for this gift, a man would perish as soon as he went down into the sea. The sages say: Also compassion. And some say: Also vengeance on Edom.[10]

1. MTeh 6:5.
2. PRKM 23:2; Tanhuma, *Va-yetze*, §3; Yalkut, Jer., §312.
3. Babylon, Persia, Greece, and Rome, the four beasts in Daniel's vision (Dan. 7:3 and 7:17).
4. Gen. R. 34:13.
5. PR 37:2.
6. Lev. R. 34:9.
7. B. Yoma 10a.
8. Literally: "Edom."
9. Gen. R. 63:12.
10. Gen. R. 6:5; Lev. R. 35:8.

C H A P T E R   F I V E

REDEMPTION AND THE DAYS OF THE MESSIAH

Archives of Travails and Archives of Deliverance

1. R. Ishmael said: [When I went up to the firmament], the angel of the Presence said to me: My beloved, sit in my lap, and I will tell you what is to befall Israel, the holy people. I sat in his lap, and he looked at me and wept; his tears, flowing from his eyes, dripped down and fell on me. I said to him, "Splendor of my radiance, why are you weeping?" He replied, "Beloved, come, and I will bring you into the innermost chambers and innermost archives."

He then took hold of me and brought me within, and showed me documents on which were indited travails, each more monstrous than the one preceding. I asked, "For whom are these intended?" He replied, "For Israel." I asked, "Can Israel withstand these?" He said, "Come tomorrow, and I will show you travails even more cruel than these." The next day he led me into the innermost chamber and showed me travails even more cruel than the previous ones: "Such as are for the sword, to the sword; and such as are for the famine, to the famine" (Jer. 15:2); "such as are for the plunder, to the plunder"; "and such as are for captivity, to captivity" (ibid.). I said to him, "Splendor of my radiance, did only Israel sin?" He replied, "Every day new travails as cruel as these are intended for them. But when they enter synagogues and houses of study, and say, 'Amen! May His great Name be blessed,' we do not let these travails go forth from the innermost chambers."

When I came down from before him, I heard a voice speaking Aramaic proclaim:

The holy Sanctuary will turn into a ruin;
Its Temple Hall will burn in fire.
The King's dwelling will stand guard over desolation.
Young maidens and young men will be plunder,
Royal princes will be slain,
The pure altar will be defiled,
Jerusalem—to mounds of rubble,
And the Land of Israel—to quaking.

In that instant I was so shaken that I fell down on my back. The angelic prince Hadarmiel came and stood me on my feet and said to me, "Come, I will bring you into the archives of deliverances and consolations."

He brought me in and showed me companies and companies of ministering angels sitting and weaving garments of deliverance, making crowns of life set with precious gems and pearls, pounding all kinds of spices and aromatics of the world, and sweetening wines for the righteous in the time-to-come. I asked, "Splendor of my radiance, for whom are these intended?" He replied, "For Israel."

Then I saw one crown different from all the other crowns—the sun, the moon, and the twelve constellations were set in it. I asked, "For whom is this exquisite crown intended?" He replied, "For David, king of Israel." I said, "Splendor of my radiance, show me the glory of David." He replied, "My beloved, wait three hours. David will come, and you will see him in his greatness."

He took hold of me, seated me in his lap, and asked me, "What do you see?" I replied, "I see seven lightnings flashing together as one." He said, "Shut your eyes, my son, lest you be frightened. These lightnings are going forth to meet David, king of Israel." At that, all the *ofannim*,[1] seraphim, sacred creatures, wheels of the chariot,[2] clouds of glory, storehouses of snow, storehouses of hail, stars and constellations, ministering angels, and other fiery beings of the fourth heaven[3] were stirred to say, "For the Leader. A Psalm of David. The heavens declare the glory of God" (Ps. 19:1). Then I heard the sound of a great commotion coming from Eden, reverberating the words "The Lord will reign forever and ever" (Exod. 15:18).

And behold, David, king of Israel, coming out first, and all the kings of the house of David following him, each one with his crown on his head. But David's crown was brighter and more beautiful than all the others, so that its radiance reached to the end of the world. Then David went up to the heavenly Temple, where a fiery throne was prepared for him. He sat on it with all the kings of the house of David seated facing him and all the kings of Israel standing behind him. Then David rose up and uttered songs and praise no ear had ever heard. After David had begun with the songs and praises, Metatron and the entire heavenly household began to proclaim, "Holy, holy, holy is the Lord of hosts" (Isa. 6:3).

And the sacred creatures uttered praise, saying, "Blessed is the glory of the Lord wherever His place be" (Ezek. 3:12).

And the firmaments declared, "The Lord will reign forever and ever" (Exod. 15:18).

And the earth followed with: "The Lord reigns, the Lord did reign, the Lord will reign forever and ever."

And all the kings of the house of David responded, "The Lord shall be King over all the earth; in that day shall the Lord be One, and His Name One" (Zech. 14:9).[4]

2. "This I recall to my mind, therefore have I hope" (Lam. 3:21). R. Abba bar Kahana, citing R. Yohanan, said: By what parable may the verse be understood? By the one of a king who wed a noblewoman. He wrote out a substantial marriage settlement for her and told her, "I am to provide

1. Wheel-angels.
2. See Ezek. 1.
3. The site of the heavenly counterpart of Jerusalem.
4. BhM 5:167–68.

so-and-so many state apartments for you. I am to give you so-and-so many purple garments. I am to give you so-and-so many seagoing ships. I am to give you so-and-so many towns on the mainland." Then the king left her, went away to a country far across the sea, and tarried there. Meanwhile, her neighbors visited her and sought to provoke her, saying, "The king has left you, gone away to a country far across the sea, and he will never come back to you." She wept and sighed. But then she would go into her bridal pavilion, open [the chest in which her marriage settlement was deposited], take it out, and read it. On seeing, "I am to provide so-and-so many state apartments for you. I am to give you so-and-so many purple garments. I am to give you so-and-so many seagoing ships. I am to give you so-and-so many towns on the mainland," she was at once comforted.

After a long time, the king came back and said to his wife, "My little one, I marvel how you were able to wait for me all these years!" She replied, "My lord king, but for the substantial marriage settlement you wrote out and gave me, my neighbors would long since have caused me to feel that you were lost to me."

[As her companions mocked the king's wife], so the nations of the earth mock Israel, saying to them, "Your God has hidden His face from you and removed His Presence from you. How long will you die for your God, letting yourselves be slain for His sake, giving up your lives for His sake? He will never come back to you." And Israel weep and sigh. But then they go into synagogues and houses of study, open the Torah scroll, read in it, and find written in it, "I will have respect unto you, and make you fruitful, and I will set My tabernacle among you . . . and I will walk among you" (Lev. 26:9 and 26:11–12). Then they are comforted.

In the future, when the time of redemption comes, the Holy One will say to Israel, "My children, I marvel how you were able to wait for Me all these years." And Israel will reply, "Master of the universe, but for Your Torah You gave us, the nations of the earth would long since have caused us to feel that You were lost to us."

David said likewise, "But for Thy Torah, my delight, then in my affliction I would have felt that You were lost to me" (Ps. 119:92).[1]

The Merit of the Fathers

3. "These two anointed ones, that stood by the Lord of the whole earth [provide the merit for Israel's redemption]" (Zech. 4:14). R. Levi said: The verse implies that the Holy One went about seeking some justification for redeeming Israel and could not find it until He came upon the merit of Moses and Aaron. It was the merit of these two that stood by Israel. How may the matter be illustrated? By the parable of a king who wanted to wed a woman but was told that she was poor, possessing only two nose rings. [He replied: The two nose rings are sufficient for me to wed her.] So, too, God said: The merit of Moses and Aaron provides sufficient reason for Israel to be redeemed.

"Hark! my Beloved! Behold, He cometh" (Song 2:8). When Moses went and told Israel: Thus did the Holy One speak to me: "This day go ye forth, in the month of Aviv" (Exod. 13:4), they asked: Where is He? Moses replied: Behold, He is about to stand before you—"Hark! my Beloved, He cometh" (Song 2:8). But what, asked R. Judah, is the meaning of "Leaping upon the mountains" (ibid.)? The Holy One said: If I look closely at the deeds of Israel, they will never be redeemed. Upon whom then should I look closely? Upon their holy forefathers. I will redeem them because of the merit of their forefathers. Hence: "Leaping upon the mountains"—"mountains" here meaning the fathers.

R. Nehemiah gave another interpretation: What, he asked, is meant by "Leaping upon the mountains"? The Holy One said: Israel have no good deeds that would justify their redemption, other than the merit of their elders. "Go, gather the elders of Israel together" (Exod. 3:16). Hence "mountains" means "the elders."[2]

4. "Then will I remember my covenant with Jacob . . . and I will remember the Land" (Lev. 26:42). Why, in mentioning the merit of the fathers, does Scripture mention with them the merit of the Land? Resh Lakish told the parable of a king who had three sons, all of them brought up by one of his maidservants. So whenever the king inquired about the well-being of his sons, he would add: Inquire also about the well-being of her who brought them up. So, too, whenever the Holy One mentions the fathers, He mentions the Land with them.[3]

5. R. Perida began his discourse with the verse "I said unto the Lord, 'Thou art my Lord.' [God]: 'My gratitude is not with thee' " (Ps. 16:2). The congregation of Israel said to the Holy One, "Master of the universe, show me gratitude for having made You known in the world." God replied, "My gratitude is not with you. I am grateful to none other than Abraham, Isaac, and Jacob, who were first to make Me known to the world—'with the holy ones that were on the earth; they are the mighty ones in whom is all My delight' " (Ps. 16:3).[4]

6. How long will the merit of the fathers endure? R. Aha said: The merit of the fathers endures forever.

R. Yudan bar Hanan taught in the name of R. Berekhiah that the Holy One said to Israel: My children, when you see the merit of the fathers declining and the merit of the mothers shaken, go and hang on to God's kindness, as is said, "The mountains may decline" (Isa. 54:10)—the merit of the fathers; "and the hills be shaken" (ibid.)—the merit of the mothers. Thenceforth you may be certain that "My kindness shall not move from thee, neither shall the power of my covenant of peace decline, saith the Lord that hath compassion on thee" (ibid.).[5]

---

[1] JV: "I should then have perished in mine affliction." Lam. R. 3:21, §7; PR 21:15.

[2] Exod. R. 15:3–4.

[3] Lev. R. 36:5.

[4] B. Men 53a.

[5] P. Sanh 10:1, 27d; Lev. R. 36:6.

7. R. Isaac said: At the time the Temple was being destroyed, the Holy One found Abraham standing in the Temple and asked him, "What hath My beloved to do in My house?" (Jer. 11:15). Abraham: I have come because of what is happening to my children. God: Your children sinned and are to go into exile. Abraham: May it be that they sinned unwittingly? God: "She wrought with premeditation" (ibid.).[1] Abraham: Perhaps only a few of them sinned? God: "With many" (ibid.). Abraham: You should have remembered in their behalf the covenant of circumcision. God: "The hallowed flesh they pass from thee" (ibid.).[2] Abraham: Perhaps had You waited for them, they would have repented? God: "When thou doest evil, then thou rejoicest" (ibid.). Then Abraham put his hands on his head [in a gesture of grief], wept bitterly, and cried: Can it be, God forbid, that there is no mending for them? A divine voice came forth and said to him, "The Lord called thy name a leafy olive tree, fair with goodly fruit" (Jer. 11:16). As the olive tree produces its best only at the very end,[3] so Israel will flourish at the end of time.[4]

8. R. Samuel ben Nahmani said in the name of R. Jonathan: What is meant by "Thou art our Father; for Abraham knoweth us not; and Israel doth not acknowledge us; Thou, O Lord, art our Father, our Redeemer" (Isa. 63:16)? In the time-to-come, the Holy One will say to Abraham: Your sons have sinned against Me. He will answer: Master of the universe, let them be wiped out, that Your Name may be hallowed. God will then say: I will speak to Jacob, who had great distress in bringing up his children—perhaps he will entreat mercy on their behalf. So He will say to Jacob: Your children have sinned against Me. He, too, will reply: Master of the universe, let them be wiped out for the hallowing of Your Name. Then, deciding that there is no reason in men advanced in age [such as Abraham], nor counsel in those young in years [such as Jacob], God will say to Isaac [who is in his middle years]: Your children have sinned against Me. But Isaac will reply: Master of the universe, are they now my children—not Your children? When they said to You, "We will do," before saying, "We will hear," You called them "Israel, My son, My firstborn" (Exod. 4:22). But now they are *my* sons, not *Your* sons! Moreover, how much have they sinned? How many are a man's years? Seventy. Deducting the first twenty, during which You do not inflict punishment,[5] fifty remain. Subtract the twenty-five that comprise the nights, and so twenty-five are left. Subtract twelve and a half spent in prayer, eating, and answering calls of nature. Twelve and a half are left. If You are willing to bear all of these years, well and good; if not, let half be upon me and half upon You. Should You say that they must all be upon me, remember, I once offered myself as a sacrifice before You. At this, Israel will begin to say to him, "You are our father" (Isa. 63:16). But Isaac will say: Before you acclaim me, acclaim the Holy One. And Isaac will show them the Holy One, for them to see with their own eyes. At once they will lift their eyes on high and say, "Thou, O Lord, art our Father, our Redeemer from everlasting is Thy Name" (ibid.).[6]

The Time of Redemption

9. "Gather yourselves together, that I may tell you that which shall befall you in the end of days. . . . Reuben, thou art my firstborn" (Gen. 49:1–3). The verse teaches that when Jacob was about to reveal to them the time of redemption, it was hidden from him. A parable of a man who bore the title of the king's friend[7] and who knew the king's secrets. In the course of time, the king's friend was about to die. He started to say to his sons gathered around his couch, "Come, and I shall reveal to you the secrets of the king." But just then he lifted his eyes and saw the king. Instead, he said to them: "My sons, heed the honor of the king." So, too, our father Jacob lifted his eyes and saw the Presence standing over him, whereupon he said, "My sons, heed the honor of the Holy One."[8]

10. "The day of vengeance is in My heart, and the year of My redemption is come" (Isa. 63:4). What is meant by "The day of vengeance is in My heart"? According to R. Yohanan, God said: I have revealed it to My heart but not to My limbs. According to R. Simeon ben Lakish, God said: I revealed it to My heart, but not to the ministering angels.[9]

11. R. Samuel bar Nahmani said in the name of R. Jonathan: Blasted be the bones of those who presume to calculate the time of redemption. For they are apt to say, "Since redemption has not come at the time expected, it will never come." Rather, one must wait for it, as is said, "Though it tarry, wait for it" (Hab. 2:3). Lest you say, "We are looking forward to its coming, but He does not seem to," Scripture asserts, "Truly the Lord is waiting to show you grace, truly He will arise to pardon you" (Isa. 30:18). But since we look forward to it and He also looks forward to it, what then delays its coming? The measure of justice delays it. But since the measure of justice delays it, what point is there in our waiting for it? To receive reward [for hoping], as is said, "Blessed are all they that wait for it" (ibid.).[10]

12. Rav said: All times set for redemption have passed, and the matter now depends only on repentance and good deeds. But Samuel said: To endure the experience of mourning is sufficient punishment for the mourner [for the people of Israel].[11]

1. JV: "She hath wrought lewdness (*mezimmatah*)," a word that can also mean "premeditation."
2. They sought to disguise their circumcision by blistering the skin.
3. It bears fruit only after years of growth.
4. B. Men 53b and En Yaakov, ad loc.
5. Even as the people under twenty were not punished for having accepted the slanderous report of the spies (see Num. 14:29). So Rashi, ad loc.
6. B. Shab 89b and En Yaakov, ad loc.
7. A court title, as was "companion of the king." Cf. Polybius 31.3.7.
8. Gen. R. 98:2; PR 21:13.
9. Who serve God as limbs serve man. B. Sanh 99a.
10. B. Sanh 97b.
11. Regardless of repentance, Israel's suffering warrants redemption.

How redemption is to come about is also disputed among the Tannaim. For R. Eliezer said: If Israel repent, they will be redeemed; but if not, they will not. R. Joshua retorted: You say they will not be redeemed if they do not repent. On the contrary, they will be redeemed, for the Holy One will raise up against them a king whose decrees will be as cruel as Haman's, so that Israel will be driven to repentance, and thus He will bring them back to the right path.[1]

13. In the school of Elijah it is taught: The world, as we know it, was intended to exist for six thousand years—two thousand years in desolation [without Torah], two thousand years with Torah, and two thousand years of the Messiah's reign. Because of our many, many iniquities, the years [God had intended to be the Messiah's] were [temporarily] withheld.[2]

14. R. Hanan bar Tahalifa sent word to R. Joseph: I once met a man who possessed a Hebrew scroll written in Assyrian characters.[3] I asked him: Where did you get this? He replied: I had hired out as a mercenary in the Persian army and found it in the Persian archives. In it is written that four thousand two hundred and ninety-one years after creation, the world will be orphaned.[4] [As to the years that follow], some will be spent in the war of the great sea monsters;[5] some in the war of Gog and Magog; and the remaining period will be the years of the Messiah's reign. The Holy One will renew His world only after seven thousand years. After five thousand years, said R. Aha son of Rava.

We have been taught that R. Nathan said: There is a verse that pierces to the very abyss [in the mystery of its implication]: "For the vision is yet for an appointed time, but at the end it shall speak and not lie. Though it tarry, wait for it; because it will surely come, it will not delay" (Hab. 2:3).[6]

15. "I sleep; nevertheless, my heart waketh" (Song 5:2). The congregation of Israel said to the Holy One: Master of the universe, "I sleep" in ignorance of the time set for redemption; "nevertheless, my heart waketh" for the time of redemption.[7]

16. R. Joshua ben Levi pointed out a [seeming] contradiction within a verse, which asserts, "In its time [redemption will come]" (Isa. 60:22), and then goes on to say, "I will hasten it" (ibid.). However, he said, the meaning is: If they are worthy, "I will hasten it"; if not, "in its time."[8]

17. [R. Joshua ben Levi sid]: Israel's redemption is compared to four things: to harvesting, to vintaging, to gathering of spices, and to a woman with child.

It is compared to harvesting, because when a field is harvested prematurely, even the straw is unusable; if the field is harvested in its proper time, even the straw is fully usable. Hence Scripture: "Put ye in the sickle, for the harvest is ripe" (Joel 4:13).

It is compared to vintaging, because when a vineyard is vintaged before its time, even the vinegar made from it is not good; but if gathered in its time, even its vinegar is good. Thus: "Sing ye of her: A vineyard of foaming wine" (Isa. 27:2)—only when the grapes in the vineyard are full of juice are you to gather them.

It is compared to spices, because if spices are gathered when they are still moist and soft, they do not give off fragrance; but if gathered when they are dry, they give off fragrance, as is said, "That the spices thereof may flow out" (Song 4:16).

It is compared to a woman with child, because if the woman gives birth before the time, the child will not live; but if at the right time, the child lives. So it is written, "Therefore He will give them up until the time that she who travaileth hath brought forth" (Mic. 5:2).[9]

18. When R. Joshua ben Levi found the prophet Elijah standing by the entrance to the cave in which R. Simeon ben Yohai was buried, he asked him, "Will I be allowed to enter the world-to-come?" Elijah answered, "If this master here desires it." R. Joshua later said, "I saw two [Elijah and myself] but I heard the voice of a third."[10] He then asked Elijah, "When will the Messiah come?" "Go and ask him yourself," was his reply. "Where is he sitting?" "At the entrance to the city [of Rome]." "And by what sign may I recognize him?" "He is sitting among the poor who are stricken with illnesses; all of whom untie and retie all the bandages over their sores at the same time, whereas he unties and reties each bandage separately, saying to himself; Should I be wanted, I must not be delayed."

So R. Joshua went to the Messiah and greeted him: "Peace be upon you, my master and teacher." "Peace be upon you, son of Levi," the Messiah replied. R. Joshua: "When will you come, O master?" "Today," was the Messiah's answer.

When R. Joshua came back to Elijah, the latter asked him, "What did he say to you?" R. Joshua: "Peace be upon you, son of Levi." Elijah observed, "By that he assured you and your father of a portion in the world-to-come." R. Joshua: "[How can I believe him, seeing that] he spoke falsely to me, for he told me that he would come today, yet he has not come." Elijah: "When he told you, 'Today,' he was quoting the first word of a verse that goes on to say, 'If you will hear His voice' " (Ps. 95:6).[11]

19. When R. Yose ben Kisma's disciples asked him, "When will [Messiah] son of David come?" he replied, "I fear you will ask me for a sign that my answer is right." They: "We will ask for no sign." R. Yose: "After this

1. B. Sanh 97b.
2. B. Sanh 97a–b.
3. The square characters.
4. Will be in great distress.
5. The great nations.
6. B. Sanh 97b.
7. Song R. 5:2, §1.
8. B. Sanh 98a.
9. Song R. 8:14, §1; Yalkut, Ps., §639.
10. The Presence.
11. B. Sanh 98a.

gate[1] falls down and is rebuilt, falls down again and is again rebuilt, falls down a third time—then, before there will be time to rebuild it, [Messiah] son of David will come." They said, "Our master, give us a sign." R. Yose: "Did you not promise me that you would not ask me for a sign?" They replied, "Just the same, please." R. Yose: "If so, let the waters of the grotto of Paneas turn to blood." And turn to blood they did.

When R. Yose was dying, he said, "Place my coffin deep in the ground, for there is not a palm tree in Babylonia to which a Persian horse will not be tied and not a coffin in the Land of Israel out of which a Median horse will not eat straw.[2]

20. Israel have been assured that Elijah will not come on the eve of a Sabbath or the eve of a festival, when people are preoccupied with preparations.[3]

21. Abbaye said: The Messiah will come only on the ninth of Av, which is set apart as our time for mourning but which the Holy One will turn into a festive day, as is said, "I will turn their mourning into joy," etc. (Jer. 31:12).[4]

22. R. Hanina ben Dosa said: The ram that was created at twilight on the sixth day of creation—not a part of it was without purpose. The ram's ash was the foundation for the altar within the Temple Hall; its sinews provided the ten strings for the harp David played on; its hide became the leather girdle on the loins of Elijah, ever remembered on good occasions; its two horns were made into shofars—the left horn is the one the Holy One blew on Mount Sinai; and the right horn, larger than the left one, the Holy One will blow in the time-to-come, as is said, "And it shall come to pass on that day, that a large horn shall be blown" (Isa. 27:13).[5]

The Footprints of the Messiah

23. R. Yohanan said: When you see a generation ever dwindling, expect the Messiah then, for Scripture says, "The afflicted people Thou wilt save" (2 Sam. 22:28).

R. Yohanan also said: When you see a generation that is overwhelmed by many troubles, as by a river in flood, expect the Messiah then, for Scripture says, "When the enemy shall come in like a river, the spirit of the Lord shall lift up a standard against him" (Isa. 59:19), and then Scripture goes on to say, "The redeemer shall come to Zion" (Isa. 59:20).

R. Yohanan said further: [Messiah] son of David will come only in a generation that is altogether righteous or altogether wicked. In a generation altogether righteous, for it is said, "Thy people shall be all righteous, they shall inherit the Land forever" (Isa. 60:21). Or altogether wicked, for it is written, "And He saw that there was no man, and was astonished that there was no intercessor," etc. (Isa. 59:16), and elsewhere it is written, "Then for Mine own sake, for Mine own sake will I do it" (Isa. 48:11).[6]

24. R. Isaac said: [Messiah] son of David will not come until every kingdom is converted to the belief of the sectarians. And the proof? Rava quoted, "It is all turned white: he is clean" (Lev. 13:13).[7]

25. R. Eleazar bar Avina said: When you see the [great] kingdoms fight one another, look for the footprints of the Messiah.[8]

26. R. Simlai said in the name of R. Eleazar son of R. Simeon: [Messiah] son of David will not come until all judges and officers[9] are gone from Israel.

R. Zeiri said in the name of R. Hanina: [Messiah] son of David will not come until arrogant men cease to be in Israel.[10]

27. R. Assi said: [Messiah] son of David will not come until all souls in the treasury of souls[11] have been used up, as is said, "The spirit that is before Me will enwrap [mankind] when all souls I made [have been used up]" (Isa. 57:16).[12]

28. The sages said: King Messiah will not come until all souls that have been considered for creation have been created; and these are the souls referred to in the Book of Adam.[13]

29. Rav said: The Torah is destined to be forgotten in Israel, because it is said, "Then the Lord will make thy plagues wonderful" (Deut. 28:59). Now, I do not know what "wonderful" in such a context signifies. However, it is said, "Therefore, behold, I will proceed to do a wonderful work among this people, even a wonderful work and a wonder, and the wisdom of their wise men . . . shall perish" (Isa. 29:14). Hence one may conclude that "the wonder" refers to Torah['s being forgotten].

Our masters taught: When our masters entered the vineyard[14] in Yavneh, they said: The Torah is destined to

1. "The gate of Caesarea Philippi, the home of R. Yose. Its fall would be a signal of the destruction of the Roman power by the Parthians" (Isidore Epstein in Sanh, Soncino, p. 665, n. 1).
2. The Persian invaders will be so numerous that coffins will be used as cribs for their horses. B. Sanh 98a–b.
3. B. Er 43b.
4. PR 28:3.
5. PRE 31.
6. B. Sanh 98a.
7. In leprosy, a white swelling is a symptom of uncleanness; however, when the skin on the entire body turns white, the whiteness is declared a mark of cleanness. So, too, when the entire world turns sectarian, the Messiah, the purifier, is sure to come. B. Sanh 97a.
8. Gen. R. 42:4.
9. Who are apt to abuse their power or pervert justice.
10. B. Sanh 98a.
11. Literally *guf* ("body") where the souls of the unborn are kept.
12. That is, assigned to bodies of living men.
13. A book containing the entire history, past and future, of mankind. Gen. R. 24:4; Lev. R. 15:1.
14. Vineyard is a metaphor for an academy where scholars sat in rows resembling rows of vines.

be forgotten in Israel, for it is said, "Behold the days come, saith the Lord, that I will send a famine in the Land, not a hunger for bread, nor a thirst for water, but a hunger for hearing the words of the Lord" (Amos 8:11); and it also says, "And they shall wander from sea to sea, and from the north even to the east; they shall run to and fro to seek the word of the Lord, and shall not find it" (Amos 8:12). It is said: A woman is destined to take a loaf of *terumah*[1] and go around to synagogues and academies in order to find out whether it is clean or unclean, and no one will even understand the question.

We have been taught that R. Simeon ben Yohai said: God forbid that the Torah be forgotten in Israel, for it is said, "It shall not be forgotten out of the mouths of their seed" (Deut. 31:21). What then is implied in the words "They shall run to and fro to seek the word of the Lord, and shall not find it"? That they will not find a clear and intelligible *Halakhah* or a clear and intelligible Mishnah in any of the places [where they will seek it].[2]

30. R. Yohanan said: In the generation in which [Messiah] son of David comes, disciples of the wise will grow fewer and fewer. And as for those who remain, their eyes will be consumed with sorrow and sighing. And many agonies [will afflict the entire people]—harsh decrees added one to anoother, so that while one is still in force, another is quickly promulgated.

Our masters taught as follows of the particular seven-year period at whose end [Messiah] son of David will appear. The first year there will be fulfilled the verse "And I will cause it to rain upon one city, and cause it not to rain upon another city" (Amos 4:7). The second year, arrows of famine will be launched. The third year, there will be a universal famine; men, women, little children, and men of piety and good deeds will die, and [because of hunger] the Torah will be forgotten by those who study it. The fourth year, there will be a scarcity of one thing and a surplus of another. The fifth year, there will be a great plenty; people will eat and drink and rejoice, and the Torah will return to those who study it. During the sixth year, there will be rumors [of war]; and during the seventh, wars. And with the departure of the seventh, [Messiah] son of David will appear.[3]

31. At the approaching of the Messiah, insolence will increase and honor will be held in contempt. The vine will yield abundant fruit, but wine will be costly and there will be none to reprove.[4] The chamber where scholars meet for study will be used for harlotry. Galilee will be laid waste; the Gavlan region[5] will be made desolate. The men of the border region will go about from town to town and find no pity. The wisdom of scribes will be deemed a stench, those who fear sin will be despised, and truth will be lacking. The face of the generation will be [brazen] like the face of a dog. The young will cause the faces of their elders to go pale [with humiliation], and the great will wait upon those of little worth. A son will revile his father. A daughter will rise up against her mother, a daughter-in-law against her mother-in-law. A man's enemies will be the inmates of his own house (Mic. 7:6). A son will feel no shame before his father.

Upon whom then can we rely? Upon our Father in heaven.[6]

32. Our Masters taught: "For the Lord shall vindicate His people . . . when He seeth that their power is gone, and there is no one being ruled and no one being helped"[7] (Deut. 32:36): [Messiah] son of David will not come until informers are so numerous [that Israel appears helpless]. Another interpretation [of "Their power is gone"]: Until disciples [of the wise] dwindle to a few. Others say: Until the last copper is gone from the purse. Another interpretation: Until hope of redemption is given up, as is said, "There is no one being ruled and no one being helped"—until, if one dare say such a thing, there is neither Supporter nor Helper for Israel.

Whenever R. Zera found sages engaged [in calculating the time of the Messiah's coming], he would say to them: I beg of you, do not put it further off, for we have been taught that three come without warning: Messiah, something found, and a scorpion.[8]

33. Ulla said: Let the Messiah come, but let me not see him. Rabbah said likewise: Let him come, but let me not see him.

R. Joseph, on the other hand, said: Let him come, and may I be worthy of sitting in the shadow of the saddle of his ass.

Abbaye asked Rabbah: What is your reason for not wishing to see him? Should you say, "Because of the birth pangs preceding the Messiah's coming," have we not been taught: R. Eliezer's disciples asked him, "What should one do to be spared the pangs of the Messiah?" [He answered], "Let him engage in study of Torah and in good deeds." And you, master—in you are Torah and good deeds. Rabbah replied: Still, sin may bring on [suffering].[9]

34. R. Hillel[10] said: There will be no Messiah for Israel, because they have already used him up in the days of Hezekiah.[11]

R. Joseph said: May R. Hillel's heavenly Master forgive him for saying so. When did Hezekiah live? In the days of the First Temple. Yet Zechariah, prophesying in the days of the Second Temple, proclaimed, "Rejoice

1. Of grain given as a heave offering to priests.
2. B. Shab 138b–139a.
3. B. Sanh 97a.
4. There will be so much drinking that no one will be able to reproach another.
5. "East of the Sea of Galilee and of the upper Jordan" (Sanh, Soncino, p. 655, n. 4).
6. B. Sot 49b; B. Sanh 97a and En Yaakov, ad loc.
7. A euphemism for "There is no one ruling and no one helping." AV: "and then is none shut up, or helped."
8. B. Sanh 97a and En Yaakov, ad loc.
9. B. Sanh 98b.
10. "A brother of R. Judah II" (Sanh, Soncino, p. 669, n. 4).
11. Who was saved from total defeat at the hands of the invading Assyrian army. Instead, God Himself will redeem Israel. So Rashi.

greatly, O daughter of Zion; shout, O daughter of Jerusalem; behold, thy king cometh unto thee, he is just and brings salvation," etc. (Zech. 9:9).[1]

35. R. Joshua ben Levi cited two verses that seemed mutually contradictory. One verse says, "And behold, one like the son of man came with the clouds of heaven" (Dan. 7:13); while the other says, "[Behold, thy king cometh unto thee] . . . lowly, and riding upon an ass" (Zech. 9:9). However, the two verses declare: If Israel are meritorious, Messiah will come "with the clouds of heaven"; if not, he will be "lowly, and riding upon an ass."

King Shapur [I] said to Samuel: You say that the Messiah will come riding upon an ass. I would like to send him a brightly colored steed of mine. Samuel replied: Do you have a thousand-hued steed?[2]

Redemption and the Ingathering of Exiles

36. "So that I come back to my father's house in peace, [and it shall come to pass (*ve-hayah*) that He be a God unto me]" (Gen. 28:21). R. Joshua of Sikhnin said in the name of R. Levi: The Holy One took the words used by the patriarchs and made them a key for the redemption of their descendants. Thus the Holy One said to Jacob: You said, "And it shall come to pass (*ve-hayah*) that He be a God unto me." By your life, all boons, blessings, and consolations I will give to your children, I will bestow with this very expression, as is said, "And it shall come to pass (*ve-hayah*) in that day, that living waters shall go out from Jerusalem" (Zech. 14:8); "And it shall come to pass (*ve-hayah*) in that day, that the Lord will set His hand again the second time to recover the remnant of His people" (Isa. 11:11); "And it shall come to pass (*ve-hayah*) in that day, that the mountains shall drop down sweet wine" (Joel 4:18); "And it shall come to pass (*ve-hayah*) in that day, that a great horn shall be blown," etc. (Isa. 27:13).[3]

37. "Gather yourselves together . . . assemble yourselves" (Gen. 49:1). Jacob warned them against dissension, bidding them, "Be you all joined in a unified gathering." Thus it says, "And thou, son of man, take thou one stick, and write upon it: For Judah, and for the children of Israel his companions; then, take another stick, and write upon it . . . that they may all come to be joined in thy hand" (Ezek. 37:16–17). Once Israel are joined in a single cluster, you may prepare yourselves for redemption. For what follows directly? "I will make them one nation in the Land, upon the mountains of Israel" (Ezek. 37:22).[4]

38. R. Abba said: There is no sign of the coming of redemption more evident than what is set forth in the verse "But ye, O mountains of Israel, ye shall shoot forth your branches, and yield your fruit to My people Israel. Then will My day of redemption be at hand" (Ezek. 36:8).[5]

39. R. Hiyya the Elder and R. Simeon ben Halafta were walking in the valley of Arbel and saw the light of daybreak. R. Hiyya the Elder said to R. Simeon: Eminent master, Israel's redemption will be like this—little by little at the beginning; but as it advances, it will grow larger and larger.[6]

40. In the book of Samuel it is said, "God . . . is the mighty tower (*migdol*) of deliverance for His king" (2 Sam. 22:51), while the parallel verse in Psalms, taken literally, reads: "Mightily He enlargeth (*magdil*) deliverance for His king" (Ps. 18:51). "This means," R. Yudan said, "that deliverance will come to this people not all at once, but little by little." Can "mightily He enlargeth" be understood in any way except that deliverance for Israel will gradually grow larger and larger (*mitgaddelah*)? The children of Israel now live in the midst of great troubles, and if deliverance were to come all at once, they would be unable to bear such great deliverance. . . . Hence, it will come little by little and will be enlarged gradually for Israel. Therefore is deliverance likened to the dawn, as is said, "Then shall thy light break forth as the dawn" (Isa. 58:8). Why is deliverance likened to the dawn? Because you know no darkness greater than that in the hour nearest to dawn; were the whole sphere of the sun to wheel up at that hour, when creatures are still sleeping, they would all be stunned. Therefore, the first streak of dawn appears and gives light to the world; after that, the whole sphere of the sun wheels up and gives its light, and so creatures are not stunned, as is said, "The path of the righteous is as the dawning light, that shineth more and more unto the perfect day" (Prov. 4:18).[7]

41. R. Aha said, Israel is likened to an olive tree: "A leafy olive tree fair with goodly fruit" (Jer. 11:16). And the Holy One is likened to a lamp: "The lamp of the Lord is the spirit of man" (Prov. 20:27). What use is made of olive oil? It is put into a lamp, and then the two together give light as though they were one. Hence the Holy One will say to Israel: My children, since My light is your light and your light is My light, let us go together—you and I—and give light to Zion: "Arise, give light, for thy light has come" (Isa. 60:1).

R. Hoshaia said: Jerusalem is destined to become a torch for the nations of the world, who will walk by its light, as is said, "Nations shall walk at thy light" (Isa. 60:3).[8]

42. "Said [the angel of Esau (Edom, Rome)] to Jacob: 'Let me go, for dawn is breaking' " (Gen. 32:27). Regarding the verse "Renewed in the mornings, [we know that] great is Thy faithfulness" (Lam. 3:23), R. Alexandri

1. B. Sanh 99a.
2. B. Sanh 98a.
3. Gen. R. 70:6.
4. Gen. R. 98:2.
5. So Targum Jonathan, ad loc. JV: "for they are at hand to come." B. Sanh 39a.
6. P. Ber 1:1, 2c.
7. MTeh 18:36.
8. PRKM 21:4; Yalkut, Isa., §499.

said: From the fact that You have renewed us in the morning [after the night of the ascendancy] of each of the three kingdoms, we know that great is Your faithfulness to redeem us [from Edom, the fourth kingdom].[1]

43. "The Lord will create over the whole habitation of Zion, and over her invited guests"[2] (Isa. 4:5). Rabbah said in the name of R. Yohanan: Jerusalem of the world-to-come will not be like Jerusalem of this world. For anyone who wishes to go up to Jerusalem of this world goes up. But only those invited will be able to go up to Jerusalem of the world-to-come.[3]

44. R. Yohanan said: The day of the gathering of exiles will be as momentous as the day heaven and earth were created.[4]

45. "In those days the house of Judah shall walk unto the House of Israel" (Jer. 3:18), the House of Israel being the ten tribes, who were exiled beyond the river Sambatyon. The exiles of Judah and Benjamin will go to them to bring them over, so that, together with themselves, these may merit the days of the Messiah and life in the world-to-come.[5]

46. The ten tribes are not destined to come back, for it is said, "The Lord . . . cast them into another land, as [it is] this day" (Deut. 29:27). As the day goes and does not return, so they went and will not return. Such is the opinion of R. Akiva. But R. Eliezer takes "as this day" to mean: As the day begins with darkness and then lights up, so their darkness is destined to light up for them.[6]

47. "Therefore, behold, the days come, saith the Lord, that they shall no more say: 'As the Lord liveth, that brought up the children of Israel out of the land of Egypt'; but 'As the Lord liveth, that brought up and that led the seed of the House of Israel out of the north country, and from all the countries whither I had driven them' " (Jer. 23:7–8). This does not mean that recounting the exodus from Egypt shall be abolished; rather that [the deliverance from] subjection to the kingdoms will become the principal theme, and the exodus from Egypt secondary.

Thus also Scripture says, "Remember ye not the former things." This refers to subjection to the kingdoms. "Neither consider the things of old" (Isa. 43:18). This refers to the exodus from Egypt.

"Behold, I will do a new thing; now shall it spring forth" (Isa. 43:19). R. Joseph taught: This verse speaks of the war of Gog and Magog. By what parable may the matter be illustrated? By the one of a man who, while traveling on the road, was attacked by a wolf but was saved. Afterward, he kept telling about his experience with the wolf. Later a lion attacked him, and he was saved from it. So he started telling about his experience with the lion. Finally a snake attacked him, and when he was saved from it also, he forgot his experience with the wolf and the lion, and proceeded to tell about his experience with the snake. So, too, Israel—the later troubles make them forget the earlier ones.[7]

48. Samuel said: The only difference between this world and the days of the Messiah is the subjection to the kingdoms, for it is said, "The poor shall never cease out of the Land" (Deut. 15:11).[8]

49. "O Israel, that art saved by the Lord with an everlasting salvation; ye shall not be ashamed nor confounded" (Isa. 45:17). For the children of Israel say to the Holy One, "Did You not long ago redeem us by the hands of Moses, and by the hands of Joshua, and by the hands of judges and kings? Yet now we are again enslaved and despised, as though we had never been redeemed." And the Holy One replies, "Because your redemption was through creatures of flesh and blood, and because your leaders were mortal men, here one day and in the grave the next, your redemption was but a temporary one. But in the time-to-come, I Myself shall redeem you; I, who live and endure forever, shall redeem you with a redemption that will last forever, as is said, 'O Israel, that art saved by the Lord with an everlasting salvation' [Isa. 45:17]. Therefore, 'ye shall not be ashamed nor confounded, world without end' " (ibid.).

Then the Holy One will say further, "In days gone by, you could live in shame, in subjection to contempt, because you were young. But now that you are grown old, there is no strength in you to bear the shame of exile. Hence it is said, 'Fear not, for thou shalt not remain ashamed. . . . Indeed, thou shalt forget the shame of thy youth' " (Isa. 54:4).[9]

The Day of Darkness and Light

50. R. Simlai expounded: What is meant by the verse "Woe unto you that desire the day of the Lord! Wherefore would ye have the day of the Lord? It is darkness, and not light" (Amos 5:18)? Its meaning will be understood by the parable of a cock and a bat who were waiting for the light of day. Said the cock to the bat: I wait for daylight because daylight is mine [to announce]. But what is daylight to you?

Similarly, a heretic asked R. Abbahu: When will the Messiah come? R. Abbahu replied: When darkness covers certain persons. The heretic: You are cursing me. R. Abbahu: The verse is explicit: "For behold, the darkness shall cover the earth, and gross darkness the peoples; but

1. Gen. R. 78:1.
2. JV: "her assemblies." But *mikra'eha*, ("her assemblies") may also mean "her invited guests."
3. B. BB 75b.
4. B. Pes 88a.
5. Yalkut, Song §985.
6. B. Sanh 110b; Yalkut, Deut., §960.
7. B. Ber 12b–13a; Tos Ber 1:10–11.
8. Never—not even in the days of the Messiah. B. Ber 34b.
9. MTeh 31:2.

upon thee the Lord will arise, and His glory shall be seen upon thee" (Isa. 60:2).[1]

51. A Roman general asked Rabban Gamaliel: Who will seize royal power after us? [In reply], Rabban Gamaliel brought a piece of blank paper, took a quill, and wrote, "After that came forth his brother [Jacob], and his hand had hold of [Esau's] heel" (Gen. 25:26).

With regard to Rabban Gamaliel's reply, the comment was made: See how ancient words become new in the mouth of a sage.[2]

52. R. Yose bar Simon said: The nations of the earth will bring gifts to the king Messiah. When they come to the king Messiah, he will ask: Are there Israelites among you? Bring them as gifts to me, as is said, "O ye peoples, bring families unto the Lord" (Ps. 96:7), that is, "O ye nations, bring the families of Israel unto Me."

R. Aha said: This verse also implies [that the Messiah will say to the nations of the earth, "When you bring the families of Israel to me], bring them not in contempt but in honor," for the words that follow, namely, "Bring unto the Lord honor and strength, bring unto the Lord the honor of His Name" (Ps. 96:7), mean: "Bring unto the Lord those who have honored God's Name in the world."[3]

53. R. Kahana said: When R. Ishmael son of R. Yose fell ill, Rabbi [Judah I, the Patriarch] sent word to him: Tell us two or three things of the kind you are wont to tell in your father's name. R. Ishmael sent back: Thus did my dear father say: Egypt is destined to send a gift to the Messiah, who will be inclined not to accept it. But the Holy One will say to him: Accept it from them, since they offered hospitality to My children in Egypt. And so "nobles shall come out of Egypt [bringing gifts]" (Ps. 68:21). Then Ethiopia will draw an inference for itself: if these who had enslaved them have their gifts accepted, how much more are our gifts likely to be accepted, seeing that we have not enslaved them. The Holy One will say to the Messiah: Accept gifts from these. At once, "Ethiopia shall hasten to stretch out her hands unto God" (ibid.). Then will the [wicked] kingdom of Edom draw an inference for itself: if these two, who are not Israel's kin, have their gifts accepted, all the more so by far should gifts be accepted from us, who are Israel's kin. But the Holy One will say to Gabriel, "Rebuke the wild beast of the reeds" (Ps. 68:31)—rebuke the wild animal that dwells among the reeds,[4] of which it is written, "The boar out of the wood doth ravage it, that which moveth in the field feedeth on it" (Ps. 80:14).

R. Hiyya bar Abba, citing R. Yohanan, interpreted this verse in the sense that God said to the Messiah: Rebuke the wild beast, all of whose actions [which intend evil for Israel] may be recorded with the same stroke of the reed pen. "The multitude of the valiant ones[5] as calves of peoples" (Ps. 68:31)—they slaughtered [Israel's] valiant ones as if they were ownerless calves. "Everyone opening his hand with the desire for money"[6] (ibid.)—they put forth their hands to receive money but then do not carry out the wishes of those who give them the money. "He hath scattered the people that delight in approaches"[7] (ibid.). What caused Israel to be scattered among the nations? The approaches to those whom Israel eagerly sought.[8]

54. An unlearned man said to R. Hoshaia, "If I tell you a good thing, will you repeat it in public in my name?" R. Hoshaia: "What is it?" "All those gifts," he replied, "that our father Jacob gave to Esau, the nations of the world are going to give back to the king Messiah in the time-to-come." "What proof have you?" "The verse 'The kings of Tarshish and of the isles shall return tribute' [Ps. 72:10]. Scripture does not say, 'Shall bring,' but, 'Shall return.' " "By your life," R. Hoshaia exclaimed, "you said a good thing, and I will teach it in your name."[9]

55. R. Samuel bar Nahmani said: We have a traditional *Aggadah* that Esau will fall only at the hands of the descendants of Rachel. Why so? Because if the other tribes should come to judgment with Esau and ask him, "Why did you persecute your brother?" he could respond with, "Why did you persecute Joseph, your own brother? You are no better than I." But should Esau turn for help to Joseph,[10] Joseph, too, would ask him, "Why did you persecute your brother? Should you say, 'Because he did evil unto me,' my brothers also requited me with evil, yet I requited them with good." Then Esau will have to remain silent.[11]

The Messiah

56. "In Thy light do we see light" (Ps. 36:10). What light is it that the congregation of Israel looks for as from a watchtower? It is the light of the Messiah, of which it is said, "And God saw the light, that it was good" (Gen. 1:4). This verse proves that the Holy One foresaw the generation of the Messiah and his works before the world was created, and then stored it away under His throne of glory for the Messiah until the time of the generation in which he is to appear.

Satan asked the Holy One: Master of the universe, for whom is the light that is stored away under Your throne of glory?

God replied: For him who will turn you back and put you to utter shame.

---

1. B. Sanh 98b–99a.
2. Gen. R. 63:9; Yalkut, *Toledot*, §110.
3. MTeh 87:6.
4. See above, part 1, chap. 6, §110.
5. The word *abbirim* may mean "bulls," as in JV, or "valiant ones."
6. *Mitrappes*, ("submitting himself") is read *mattir pas* ("opening his hand"); and *ratze* ("pieces") is read as a form of *rtzh* ("to desire").
7. Or, as in JV, "wars." Had they submitted to Nebuchadnezzar and to Titus, and not made war, they would not have been exiled. So Samuel Edels.
8. B. Pes 118b and En Yaakov, ad loc.
9. Gen. R. 78:12.
10. Esau would naturally think that Joseph would side with him, since Joseph's brothers had sold Joseph into slavery.
11. Tanhuma B, *Va-yetze*, §15; Yalkut, Judg., §51.

Satan said: Master of the universe, show him to me.

God replied: Come and see him. Now, the moment he saw him, Satan was shaken. He fell down upon his face and said: Surely this is the Messiah, who will cast into Gehenna both me and all the heavenly counterparts of the princes of the earth's nations.

In that hour all [the princely counterparts of] the nations, greatly agitated, will say to Him: Master of the universe, who is this whose power we are to fall into? What is his name? What kind of being is he? The Holy One will reply: His name is Ephraim, My true Messiah, who will elevate his own stature and the stature of his generation, and who will light up the eyes of Israel and deliver his people; and no nation or tongue will be able to withstand him. And all his enemies and adversaries shall be overawed and flee from him. And even rivers will [yield to the power] of his right hand and stop flowing.

[At the time of the king Messiah's creation], the Holy One will tell him in detail what will befall him: These souls that have been put away with you—their sins will put you in a yoke of iron and make you like a calf whose eyes grow dim [with suffering]. They will strangle your breath with the yoke, and because of the sins of these souls, your tongue will cleave to the roof of your mouth. Are you willing to endure such trials?

The Messiah will ask the Holy One: Master of the universe, will my suffering last many years?

The Holy One will reply: Upon your life and the life of My head, I have decreed for you a period of seven years. But if your soul is saddened by the prospect of your suffering, I shall at this moment banish these sinful souls.

The Messiah will say: Master of universes, I take this suffering upon myself with joy in my soul and gladness in my heart, so that not one person in Israel may perish; that not only those who are alive may be saved in my days, but also those who are buried in the earth; not only those who died in my days, but also those who died ever since the days of Adam up to the time of redemption; and that not only these may be saved in my days, but also those who died as abortions; and that not only abortions, but all those the thought of whose creation came to Your mind but who were not created. Such are the things I desire, and for these I am ready to take upon myself [whatever You decree].

The sages said: During the seven-year period preceding the coming of [Messiah] son of David, iron beams will be brought and loaded upon the Messiah [son of Joseph's] neck, until his body is bent low. Then he will cry and weep, his voice will rise up to heaven, and he will say to God: Master of the universe, how much can my strength endure? How much can my spirit endure? How much my breath before it ceases? How much can my limbs suffer? Am I not flesh and blood?

At that time the Holy One will say to him: Ephraim, My true Messiah, long ago, ever since the six days of creation, you took this ordeal upon yourself. At this moment, let your pain be My pain. Ever since the day the wicked Nebuchadnezzar came up and destroyed My house, burned My Temple Hall, and banished My children among the nations of the world—and this I swear by your life and the life of My own head—I have not been able to ascend My throne. And if you do not believe Me, see the night dew that has fallen on My head.

At these words, the Messiah will reply: Master of the universe, now I am reconciled. The servant is content to be like his Master.

R. Isaac taught: In the year when the king Messiah reveals himself, all the kings of the nations of the earth will be at strife with one another. All the nations of the world will be agitated and frightened; they will fall upon their faces and be seized with pangs like the pangs of a woman in labor. And Israel, agitated and frightened, will say: Where shall we go, where shall we take ourselves? God will reply: My children, be not afraid. All that I have done, I have done only for your sake. Why are you afraid? Fear not. The time of your redemption is come. And this latter redemption will not be like your previous redemption, for following your previous redemption you again suffered anguish and enslavement by the kingdoms; but following this one, you will have no such anguish or enslavement.

At the time the Holy One redeems Israel, three days before the Messiah comes, [the prophet] Elijah will come and stand upon the mountains of Israel, and weep and lament over them, and then will say: O mountains of Israel, how long will you continue to be wasteland, dry and desolate? Elijah's voice will be heard from world's end to world's end. But then he will say to the mountains of Israel: Peace has come to the world.

On the second day, Elijah will come and stand upon the mountains of Israel, and say: Good has come to the world. On the third day, he will come and say: Salvation has come to the world.

In that hour, the Holy One will show His glory and His kingship to all the inhabitants of the world: He will redeem Israel, and He will appear at the head of them.

Our masters taught: When the king Messiah appears, he will come and stand on the roof of the Temple and make a proclamation to Israel, saying: Meek ones, the time of your redemption is come. And if you do not believe me, behold my light, which shines upon you: "Arise, shine, for thy light is come, and the glory of the Lord is risen upon thee" (Isa. 60:1). And it has risen only upon you and not upon the nations of the earth: "For behold, darkness shall cover the earth, and gross darkness the peoples; but upon thee the Lord will arise, and His glory shall be seen upon thee" (Isa. 60:2).

Then the Holy One will brighten the light of the king Messiah and of Israel, and all the nations shall walk by the light of the Messiah and of Israel: "And the nations shall walk at thy light, and kings at the brightness of thy rising" (Isa. 60:3). And they shall all come and lick the dust touched by the feet of the king Messiah. And all of them shall fall down upon their faces before the Messiah and before Israel, and say: Let us be slaves unto you and unto Israel.

"As a bridegroom putteth on a priestly diadem" (Isa. 61:10). This verse declares that the Holy One will clothe Ephraim, our true Messiah, with a garment whose splendor will radiate from world's end to world's end. And Israel will make use of his light and say:

Blessed is the hour in which he was created!
Blessed is the womb whence he came!
Blessed is the generation whose eyes behold him!
Blessed is the eye that waited for him,
Whose lips open with blessing and peace,
Whose speech is pure delight,
Whose heart meditates in trust and tranquility.
Blessed is the eye that merits seeing him,
Whose tongue's utterance is pardon and forgiveness
for Israel,
Whose prayer is a sweet savor,
Whose supplication is purity and holiness.
Fortunate are Israel in what is stored up for them!

Our masters taught: In the month of Nisan the patriarchs will arise and say to the Messiah: Ephraim, our true Messiah, even though we are your forebears, you are greater than we, because you suffered for the iniquities of our children, and harsh and grievous ordeals befell you, ordeals such as did not befall earlier generations or later ones. For the sake of Israel you became a laughingstock and a derision among the nations of the earth, and you sat in darkness, in thick darkness, your eyes seeing no light, your skin cleaving to your bones, your body dry as a stick of wood, your teeth falling out from fasting, and your strength dried up like a potsherd—all these afflictions on account of the iniquities of our children. If it please you, let our children benefit by that goodness which the Holy One will bestow in abundance upon Israel. Or is it that, because of the anguish you suffered on their account and because they caused you to be imprisoned, you are displeased with them?

He will reply: O patriarchs, all that I have done, I have done only for your sake and for the sake of your children, so that they may benefit from the goodness that the Holy One will bestow in abundance upon Israel.

The patriarchs will say to him: Ephraim, our true Messiah, be content with what you have done, for you have made content the mind of your Maker and our minds as well.

Then—so taught R. Simeon ben Pazzi—the Holy One will lift the Messiah up to the heaven of heavens and cloak him in some of the splendor of His own glory as protection against the wicked nations of the earth. He will say to him: Ephraim, My true Messiah, you be the judge of these and do with them what your soul desires, for the nations would long since have destroyed you in an instant had not My mercies been exceedingly mighty in your behalf.

And then the Holy One will make seven canopies of precious stones, including pearls and emeralds, for him. Out of each canopy will flow forth four rivers—one of wine, one of honey, one of milk, and one of pure balsam. And the Holy One will embrace the Messiah in the sight of the righteous and bring him within the canopy, where all the righteous will gaze upon him. The Holy One will then say to the righteous: O righteous of the world, Ephraim, My true Messiah, has not yet been repaid for even half his anguish. I have one more measure of reward that I will give him, one that no eye in the world has ever seen. Then the Holy One will summon the north wind and the south wind, and say to them: Come, sweep and sprinkle all kinds of spices from the Garden of Eden before Ephraim, My true Messiah, as is said, "Awake, O north wind; and come, thou south wind; blow upon My garden, that the spices thereof may flow out" (Song 4:16).

At that moment, the Holy One will bring Elijah and the Messiah, a flask of oil in their hands and their staves in their hands, with all Israel gathered before them—the Presence will be at the head of Israel, the prophets at their rear, the Torah at their right, the ministering angels at their left—and they will lead Israel to the valley of Jehoshaphat, where all the nations will be gathered [for judgment].

At that time the Holy One will bring the worshipers of idols and say: Let them walk across the bridge over Gehenna. So they will start walking across it, but as they reach the middle, the bridge will seem to have shrunk to the thinness of a thread, and they will fall into Gehenna.

At this, Israel, seized with fear, will ask: Master of the universe, will You do with us as You have done with these? The Holy One will ask: Who are you? Israel will reply: We are Israel, Your people and Your inheritance. The Holy One will ask: Who will bear witness for you? Israel will reply: Abraham. The Holy One will summon Abraham and ask him: Will you bear witness that they are My people and I their God? Abraham will reply: Master of the universe, did You not say to me, "Also that nation whom they shall serve, I shall judge" (Gen. 15:14)? He will ask them further: Who else will bear witness? Israel will reply: Isaac. The Holy One will summon Isaac and ask him: Will you bear witness that they are My people and I their God? Isaac will reply: Master of the universe, did You not say to me, "Unto thee, and unto thy seed, I will give all these lands" (Gen. 26:3)? The Holy One will ask: Who else will bear witness? Israel will reply: Jacob. The Holy One will summon Jacob and ask him: Will you bear witness that they are My people and that I am their God? Jacob will reply: Master of the universe, did You not say to the children of Israel, "Thou shalt have no other gods before Me" (Exod. 20:3), and did they not say, "Hear, O Israel, the Lord is our God, the Lord alone" (Deut. 6:4)?

Then the Holy One will bring the Torah, put it in His bosom, and make the radiance of Israel shine from world's end to world's end.

And Gabriel will say to the Holy One: Master of the universe, let all the worshipers of idols come and see Israel's well-being.

Forthwith Gehenna will open its mouth, and all the worshipers of idols will come out and, seeing Israel's well-being, fall down on their faces and say: How comely is this Lord! How comely is this people whom He loves exceedingly, as is said, "Blessed is the people that is in such a case" (Ps. 144:15).[1]

57. "We will rejoice and be glad in Thee" (Song 1:4). A parable of a noblewoman whose royal husband, sons, and sons-in-law went to a country far across the sea. Pres-

---

[1] PR, *Piskas* 35–37; Yalkut, Isa., §499.

ently she was told, "Your sons have come back!" She replied, "What does that matter to me? Let my daughters-in-law be glad." When her sons-in-law came back, she was told, "Your sons-in-law have arrived." She replied, "What does that matter to me? Let my daughters rejoice." But when she was told, "The king, your husband, is back!" she replied, "O perfect joy, O joy of joys!" Likewise, when in the time-to-come the prophets say to Jerusalem, "Thy sons have come from afar" (Isa. 60:4), Jerusalem will reply, "What does that matter to me?" Told, "Thy daughters are carried [to thee] on uplifted arms" (ibid.), Jerusalem will reply, "What does that concern me?" But when the prophets say to her, "Behold, thy King cometh unto thee" (Zech. 9:9), she will reply, "O perfect joy! 'I will greatly rejoice in the Lord, my soul shall be joyful in my God' " (Isa. 61:10).[1]

1. Song R. 1:4, §2.

CHAPTER SIX

IN THE TIME-TO-COME

The Good That Is to Be

1. R. Hiyya bar Abba said in the name of R. Yohanan: All the prophets prophesied only about the days of the Messiah, but as for the world-to-come, "Eye hath not seen beside Thee, O God, who worketh for him that waiteth for Him" (Isa. 64:3).

What does "Eye hath not seen" refer to? Resh Lakish said: Eden, upon which the eye of no mortal has rested.[1]

2. Rabban Gamaliel, sitting in the teacher's chair, expounded: [In the time-to-come] a woman will bear a child every day. But a certain disciple ridiculed him by quoting, "There is no new thing under the sun" (Eccles. 1:9). Come, said Rabban Gamaliel, and I will show you its like in this world. He went out and showed him a chicken.

On another occasion, Rabban Gamaliel, sitting in the teacher's chair, expounded: Trees will yield fruit every day. The same disciple, ridiculing him, asked, But does not Scripture say, "There is nothing new under the sun"? Rabban Gamaliel replied: Come, and I will show you their like in this world. He went out and showed him the caper bush.[2]

On still another occasion, Rabban Gamaliel, sitting in the teacher's chair, expounded: The earth of Israel's land will bring forth loaves of bread and choice wool robes. The same disciple ridiculed him by quoting, "There is nothing new under the sun." Rabban Gamaliel replied: Come, and I will show you their like in this world. He went out and showed him morels and truffles;[3] and for the like of choice woolen robes, he showed him the bark of a young palm shoot.[4]

3. R. Yohanan, sitting in the teacher's chair, expounded: The Holy One will bring gems and pearls measuring thirty by thirty cubits, and, after hollowing out in them openings ten cubits wide and twenty cubits high, will set them up as the gates of Jerusalem, for Scripture says, "And I will make thy pinnacles of rubies, and thy gates of gems hollowed out"[5] (Isa. 54:12). The same disciple ridiculed him, saying: Why, you can't find a gem or pearl even as large as a pigeon's egg—how can such giant gems be found?

Sometime afterward the disciple sailed far out to sea, where he beheld ministering angels sawing gems and pearls that measured thirty by thirty cubits and hollowing out in them openings ten cubits wide and twenty cubits high. He asked: What are these for? The angels replied: These are the gems and pearls the Holy One is to set up as the gates of Jerusalem.

When the disciple returned and found R. Yohanan sitting in his teacher's chair and expounding the same passage in Isaiah, he said: Expound, my teacher, It is right for you to expound. What you spoke of, I actually saw. R. Yohanan replied: You good-for-nothing! If you had not seen, you would not have believed? You are given to ridiculing the words of the sages. R. Yohanan set his eyes on him, and in that instant he turned into a heap of bones.[6]

4. Our masters taught: The verse "A handful of wheat in the Land will reach up to the top of the mountains" (Ps. 72:16)[7] means that a stalk of wheat will rise as high as a palm tree, reaching up to the top of mountains. But you may say, "Then it will be difficult to reap it." Therefore Scripture says, "Its fruit shall rustle like Lebanon" (ibid.)—out of His treasury the Holy One will bring a wind, which will blow upon the wheat and cause its fine flour to drop. Then a man will go out into the field and bring in a mere handful of the flour, out of which there will be enough for his own and his household's maintenance.

"With the fat of kidneys of wheat" (Deut. 32:14). It is inferred from these words that a grain of wheat will be as large as the two kidneys of a big bull. And do not be astounded at this! For a fox once made his lair in a turnip, and when [the remainder of] the vegetable was weighed, it was found to weigh sixty *litra* by the standard of the *litra* of Sepphoris.

"And of the blood of the grape thou drankest foaming wine" (Deut. 32:14). It is inferred from these words that this world is not at all like the world-to-come. In this world, the harvesting and treading of grapes is wearisome. But in the world-to-come, a man will bring a single grape by wagon or ship, put it in a corner of his house, and use its contents as if it were a large cask; and he will use its stalk to kindle fire under a stewpot. There will not be a grape, mind you, that will contain less than thirty kegs of wine.[8]

5. R. Jeremiah sat before R. Zera and declared: The Holy One will bring forth from the Holy of Holies a stream along whose sides will grow all kinds of precious fruits. At this,

---

1. B. Ber 34b; B. Sanh 99a.
2. Whose various products are eaten successively. So Jastrow.
3. Which resemble slabs of bread.
4. On the inside it has a downy, silklike substance. B. Shab 30b and En Yaakov, ad loc.
5. Apparently, R. Yohanan interprets *kdh* in the sense of "to bore, hollow out" and not in the sense of "kindle" (hence "carbuncles" in JV). See Rashi on B. Sanh 100a. "For pearls as gates, cf. Apocalypse 21:21" (Brother Caedmon Holmes).
6. B. BB 75a; B. Sanh 100a and En Yaakov, ad loc.
7. JV: "May he be as a rich (*pissat*) cornfield in the land upon the top of the mountains." But *pissat* ("rich, spreading") can also mean "handful."
8. A *gerev* (keg) is the equivalent of a *seah*. B. Ket 111b.

a certain old man[1] said to him, "Well spoken!" And R. Yohanan taught likewise.[2]

6. R. Hiyya bar Ashi said in the name of Rav: All the wild trees in the Land of Israel will bear [edible] fruit.[3]

7. In the time-to-come, the Holy One will renew ten things: The first: He will illumine the whole world, for Scripture says, "The sun shall be no more thy light by day . . . but the Lord shall be unto thee an everlasting light" (Isa. 60:19). But is there a man able to look at God? Rather, what will God do to the sun? He will make it give forty-nine times as much light, for Scriptures says, "And the light of the moon shall be as the light of the sun, and the light of the sun shall be sevenfold"[4] (Isa. 30:26). Even when a man is sick, God will order the sun to heal him, as it says, "But unto you that fear My Name shall the sun of righteousness arise with healing in its wings" (Mal. 3:20). The second thing: He will bring out living water from Jerusalem to heal all those who have a disease, as it says, "Every living creature wherewith it swarmeth, whithersoever the rivers shall come, shall live . . . that all things be healed and may live whithersoever the river cometh" (Ezek. 47:9). The third thing: He will make trees yield their fruit each month, and when a man eats of them, he will be healed, for Scripture says, "And by the river upon the bank thereof, on this side and on that side, shall grow every tree for food. . . . It shall bring forth new fruit every month . . . and the leaf thereof for healing" (Ezek. 47:12). The fourth thing: All the waste cities will be rebuilt, so that there shall not be one waste place left in the world; even Sodom and Gomorrah will be rebuilt in the time-to-come, as Scripture says, "And thy sisters, Sodom and her daughters, shall return to their former estate" (Ezek. 16:55). The fifth thing: He will rebuild Jerusalem with sapphire stones, as it says, "Behold, I will set thy stones in fair colors, and lay thy foundations with sapphires" (Isa. 54:11), and, "I will make thy pinnacles[5] of rubies" (Isa. 54:12). These precious stones will shine like the sun, and the nations of the world will come and see the glory of Israel, as is said, "And nations shall walk at thy light" (Isa. 60:3). The sixth: "The cow and the bear shall feed together" (Isa. 11:7). The seventh: He will bring all the wild beasts, birds, and creeping things, and make a covenant with them and with all Israel, for Scripture says, "And in that day I will make a covenant for them with the beasts of the field, and with the fowls of heaven, and with the creeping things of the earth" (Hos. 2:20). The eighth: There will be no more weeping or wailing in the world, for it says, "And the voice of weeping shall be no more heard in her, nor the voice of crying" (Isa. 65:19). The ninth: There will be no more death in the world, for it says, "He will swallow up death forever," etc. (Isa. 25:8). The tenth is that there will no longer be any sighing, wailing, or anguish, but all will be rejoicing, for Scripture says, "And the ransomed of the Lord shall return, and come with singing unto Zion [and sorrow and sighing shall flee away]" (Isa. 35:10).[6]

8. "It shall come to pass in that day, that though there shall be no light, yet precious things will come to be perspicuous" (Zech. 14:6)[7]—that is, the explanation of things concealed from you in this world will be as clear to you as crystal in the time-to-come.[8]

9. R. Simeon ben Lakish said: In the time-to-come, there will be no Gehenna, but the Holy One will take the sun out of its sheath: the righteous will be healed and the wicked condemned by it. The righteous will be healed by it, for it is written: "But unto you that fear My Name shall the sun of righteousness arise with healing in its wings" (Mal. 3:20). More—the righteous will be kept young by it, as is said, "Ye shall go forth and grow up as calves of the stall" (ibid.). But the wicked shall be condemned by it, as is written, "Behold, the day cometh, it burneth as a furnace; and all the proud, and all that work wickedness shall be stubble; and the day that cometh shall set them ablaze" (Mal. 3:19).[9]

10. In the time-to-come, the impulse to evil will have no power.[10]

11. "And God created the great sea monsters" (Gen. 1:21)—Leviathan the bolt-straight serpent and Leviathan the coiled serpent, so said R. Yohanan.

R. Judah said in the name of Rav: All that the Holy One created in His world, He created male and female. So, too, Leviathan the bolt-straight serpent and Leviathan the coiled serpent He created male and female, and if they had mated with each other, [their numerous progeny] would have destroyed the entire world, all of it. What did the Holy One do? He castrated the male and killed the female, preserving her in salt for the righteous in the world-to-come. Also the Behemoth,[11] which [daily] eats up the grass of a thousand hills, He created male and female. And if they had mated with each other, [their numerous progeny] would have destroyed the entire world, all of it. What did the Holy One do? He castrated the male and froze the female, preserving her for the righteous in the world-to-come.[12]

12. R. Dimi said in the name of R. Jonathan: Gabriel will stage a hunt of Leviathan, and but for the Holy One's helping him, he would be unable to prevail against it.

R. Dimi said in the name of R. Yohanan: When Leviathan is hungry, it emits a fiery breath from its mouth and brings all the waters of the deep to a boil, and but

1. Elijah?
2. B. Sanh 100a.
3. B. Ket 112b.
4. Interpreting "sevenfold" as seven times seven.
5. The word *shimshotayikh* can mean both "thy pinnacles" and "thy suns."
6. Exod. R. 15:2.
7. JV: ". . . not be light; but heavy clouds and thick."
8. Num. R. 19:6.
9. B. Ned 8b; B. AZ 3b.
10. Gen. R. 48:11.
11. See Ps. 50:10.
12. B. BB 74b.

for Leviathan's sticking its head into the Garden of Eden, no creature could endure the stench of its breath. When Leviathan is thirsty, it makes many furrows in the sea.

Rabbah said in the name of R. Yohanan: The Holy One will make a feast for the righteous out of the flesh of Leviathan, and what is left will be portioned out and made available as merchandise in the marketplaces of Jerusalem.

Rabbah also said in the name of R. Yohanan: The Holy One will make a sukkah for the righteous out of Leviathan's skin. The Holy One will spread the rest of the skin over the walls of Jerusalem, and its radiance will shine bright from one end of the world to the other, as is said, "Nations shall walk by thy light, and kings by thy shining radiance" (Isa. 60:3).[1]

13. Our masters taught: It happened that R. Eliezer and R. Joshua were traveling on a ship. R. Eliezer was sleeping and R. Joshua was awake. But then R. Joshua shuddered, and R. Eliezer, waking up with a start, asked: What happened, Joshua? What caused you to shudder? R. Joshua: I saw a great light in the sea. R. Eliezer: You may have seen the eyes of Leviathan, for it is written, "His eyelids are like the eyelids of the morning" (Job 41:10).[2]

14. "Every beast of the forest is Mine, and Behemoth upon a thousand mountains" (Ps. 50:10). I have a certain kind of cattle, which I created as food for you in the time-to-come—it is Behemoth, couched upon a thousand mountains, and the thousand mountains produce all kinds of grasses and all kinds of food for it to eat.

How does the Behemoth drink? Some say that its head is opposite the mouth of the Jordan and its mouth open against the Jordan's mouth, so that the river flows directly into Behemoth's mouth, and in this way it drinks the river's water. Others say that all the water the Jordan gathers up in six months, Behemoth swallows in a single draft, which is only enough to moisten its mouth.[3]

15. "Eye hath not seen" (Isa. 64:3). What hath eye not seen? The wine, so said R. Joshua ben Levi, that is preserved within its grapes since the six days of creation.[4]

16. R. Avira lectured: What is meant by the verse "When the child has grown, He will manifest His bountiful dealings" (Gen. 21:8)?[5] That the Holy One will make a great feast for the righteous on the day He manifests His bountiful dealings (*yigmol*) with the progeny of Isaac. After they eat and drink, the cup over which grace is to be said will be given to our father Abraham to say grace. But he will reply, "I cannot say it, for out of me came Ishmael." Then the cup will be given to Isaac, who will be bidden, "Take the cup and say grace." But he will reply, "I cannot say grace, for out of me came Esau." Then the cup will be given to Jacob, and he will be bidden, "Take the cup and say grace." But he will reply, "I cannot say grace, for I married two sisters[6] while both were alive, even though the Torah was to forbid such marriages." Then Moses will be bidden, "Take the cup and say grace." But he will reply, "I cannot say grace, since neither in life nor in death did I merit entering the Land of Israel." Then Joshua will be bidden, "Take the cup and say grace." But he will reply, "I cannot say grace, since I was not privileged to have a son."[7] When David will be bidden, "Take the cup and say grace," he will reply, "I shall say grace. It is proper for me to say it, since, because of His bountiful dealings with me, 'I will lift up the cup of salvation, and call upon the Name of the Lord' " (Ps. 116:13).[8]

17. R. Eleazar said: The Holy One will form a circle of righteous men in the Garden of Eden with Himself in the center, so that each of them will be able to point with his finger and say, "Lo, this is our God, for whom we waited, that He might save us; this is the Lord, for whom we waited, we will be glad and rejoice in His salvation" (Isa. 25:9).[9]

Resurrection of the Dead

18. "They are new every morning; great is Thy faithfulness" (Lam. 3:23). R. Alexandri said: Because you renew our spirits each and every morning [as we awaken], we are certain that in Your great faithfulness You will restore our spirits to us at the resurrection.[10]

19. A Caesar asked Rabban Gamaliel: You maintain that the dead will come back to life. But they turn to dust—can dust come to life? Caesar's daughter said to Rabban Gamaliel: Let me answer him. In our town are two potters. One fashions his wares from liquid [sperm], and the other from clay. Which deserves greater praise? Caesar replied: He who fashions them from liquid. His daughter then said: If He can fashion His wares [men] from liquid, He can surely fashion them from clay.

In the school of R. Ishmael it is taught: The inference may be drawn from glassware. If glassware—which is made by the breath of human beings—may be mended when broken, how much the more so flesh and blood made by the breath of the Holy One, blessed be He.[11]

20. A Sadducee said to R. Ammi: You maintain that the dead will revive, but they turn to dust—can dust come to life? R. Ammi replied: I will respond with a parable. What is to happen may be illustrated by the parable of a king

1. B. BB 74b–75a and En Yaakov, ad loc.
2. B. BB 74b.
3. PR 16:4 and 48:3 (YJS 1:347 and 2:824); Lev. R. 22:10.
4. B. Ber 34b.
5. "And the child grew, and was weaned (*va-yiggamel*)." But R. Avira reads the word in its active form, *va-yigmol*, hence, "will manifest His bountiful dealings."
6. Leah and Rachel.
7. "Nun his son, Joshua his son" (1 Chron. 7:27), but the text does not indicate that Joshua himself had sons.
8. B. Pes 119b and En Yaakov, ad loc.
9. B. Ta 31a and En Yaakov, ad loc.
10. Gen. R. 78:1.
11. B. Sanh 90b–91a.

of flesh and blood who commanded his servants, "Go and build me a great palace in a place where there is neither water nor earth." So they went and built it. But after some time it collapsed. He said to them, "Go back and rebuild the palace in the place where there is now both water and earth." They replied, "Impossible!" He became angry with them and said, "You could build in a place where there was neither water nor earth; surely you can do so where there are both!"[1] Yet, [continued R. Ammi], if you do not believe [this], go out into the field and observe a mouse, which today is half flesh and half dust,[2] and yet by tomorrow it will develop and become entirely flesh. And should you object, "But that takes a long time,"[3] go up to a mountain and see: where today there may be but one snail, tomorrow, after rain has come down, the mountain will be filled with snails.[4]

21. A Sadducee said to Gebiha ben Pesisa: Woe to you, O you scoundrels who maintain that the dead will come back to life! The living die—how can the dead live? Gebiha replied: Woe to you, O you scoundrels who maintain that the dead will not come back to life! If those who had never lived before now live, surely those who have lived before will live again. The Sadducee: You called me scoundrel. If I get up and kick you, I could remove the hump from your back. Gebiha: If you do that, you will be called a great physician and command large fees.[5]

22. Queen Cleopatra asked R. Meir: I know that the dead will come back to life. But when they rise up, will they arise nude or clad in their garments? R. Meir replied: You may come to the answer by inference from a grain of wheat. If a grain of wheat, which is buried naked, sprouts forth clad in many robes, how much more and more so the righteous, who are buried in their raiment.[6]

23. "Behold, I will open your graves, and cause you to come up . . . and I will bring you into the Land of Israel'" (Ezek. 37:12). R. Eleazar, who cited R. Simon, said: The Holy One will make underground passages for the righteous, who will roll through them until they reach the Land of Israel, and when they get to the Land of Israel, He will restore the breath of life to them, and they will stand up. For Scripture says, "I will bring you into the Land of Israel," and after that, "I will put My breath in you, and you shall live" (Ezek. 37:14).

But R. Simeon ben Lakish differed: Scripture is explicit in asserting that the instant they get to the Land of Israel, the Holy One will restore their souls to them, as is said, "He that giveth souls unto the people upon it, and spirits to them that walk therein" (Isa. 42:5).[7]

24. Hadrian—may his bones be ground—asked R. Joshua ben Hananiah: In the time-to-come, from what part of the body will the Holy One cause man to blossom forth? R. Joshua: From the nut in the spinal column. Hadrian: How do you know that? Then and there R. Joshua had such a nut brought and put it into fire, but it was not burned. He put it into water, but it did not dissolve. He tried to grind it between millstones, but it was not to be ground. He put it on an anvil and struck it with a hammer—the anvil was split apart, the hammer broke, but the nut of the spinal cord remained intact.[8]

25. As he was dying, R. Jeremiah ordered: Dress me in white raiment with borders, put socks on my legs, sandals on my feet, and a staff in my hand. Lay me on my side near the road, so that when the Messiah comes, I will be ready.[9]

26. "That which is hath been long ago, and that which is to be hath already been" (Eccles. 3:15). If a man says to you, "The Holy One will quicken the dead for us," say in reply, "This has already been done by the hand of Elijah, by the hand of Elisha, and by the hand of Ezekiel." For, as R. Aha said in the name of R. Eliezer ben Halafta, all that the Holy One intends to do or to renew in the time-to-come, He has already done in part by the hands of His righteous prophets in this world.[10]

27. In the school of Elijah it was taught: The righteous whom the Holy One will quicken will not return to the dust. You may ask, "In the thousand years during which the Holy One will renew His world,[11] what will they do?" [The answer is that] the Holy One will provide them with wings like eagles, and they will fly above the water.[12]

1. If God can make life without these, surely He is able to resuscitate those who have turned to dust.
2. It was believed that a species of mice sprang from the earth.
3. Whereas resurrection must happen in a moment.
4. Thus proving that God can create life with great speed. B. Sanh 91a.
5. Ibid.
6. B. Sanh 90b.
7. PR 1:6 (YJS 1:45); Tanhuma B, *Va-yehi*, §6.
8. Gen. R. 28:3; Lev. R. 18:1.
9. P. Kil 9:3, 32b; Gen. R. 100:2.
10. Lev. R. 27:4.
11. Years of desolation, between their resurrection during the Messiah's reign and the inauguration of the world-to-come.
12. B. Sanh 92a–b.

CHAPTER SEVEN

TORAH

On the Value and Study of Torah

1. The world endures because of three activities: study of Torah, divine worship, and deeds of loving-kindness.[1]

2. But for Torah, heaven and earth could not endure, as Scripture says, "But for My covenant with [those who took upon themselves to study] day and night, I would not have continued the ordinances for heaven and earth" (Jer. 33:25).[2]

3. Great is Torah, which in this world as well as in the world-to-come gives life to those who obey it, as is said, "[Words of Torah] are life to those who find them" (Prov. 4:22).[3]

4. "Light" (Esther 8:16)—this is Torah.[4]

5. The splendor of human beings is Torah.[5]

6. "Nevertheless, I will not reject them, neither will I abhor them" (Lev. 26:44). But was there anything left to Israel, so that it could still be said that they would not be rejected nor abhorred? Were not all good gifts that had been bestowed upon them taken away from them? What, then, did remain with them? The Torah scroll. Had it not been left with Israel, they would have been in no way different from the nations of the world.[6]

7. These are the activities whose income a man can enjoy in this world but whose principal remains undiminished for him in the world-to-come: honoring father and mother, deeds of loving-kindness, making peace between a man and his fellow. The study of Torah, however, equals all of these put together.[7]

8. Ben Bag Bag said: Turn to it, and turn to it again, for everything is in it. Pore over it, grow old and gray over it. Do not budge from it. You can have no better guide for living than it.[8]

9. The study of Torah ranks above the building of the Temple;
The study of Torah ranks above honoring father and mother;
The study of Torah ranks above the saving of lives;
Torah ranks above priesthood and royalty.[9]

10. R. Hananiah, deputy high priest, said: He who takes words of Torah to heart will be relieved of anxieties about war, anxieties about famine, anxieties about foolish preoccupations, anxieties about unchastity, anxieties about the impulse to evil, anxieties about craving another man's wife, anxieties about trifles, and anxieties about the yoke of flesh and blood. For in the book of Psalms, it is written by David, king of Israel, "The precepts of the Lord are right, a joy to the heart," etc. (Ps. 19:9). But he who does not take words of Torah to heart will be burdened by anxieties about war, anxieties about famine, anxieties about foolish preoccupations, anxieties about unchastity, anxieties about the impulse to evil, anxieties about craving another man's wife, anxieties about trifles, and anxieties about the yoke of flesh and blood. For it is written in Deuteronomy by our teacher Moses, "They shall serve as signs and proofs against you and your offspring for all time. Because you would not serve the Lord your God in joy and gladness over the abundance of everything, you shall serve—in hunger and thirst, naked and lacking everything—the enemies whom the Lord will let loose against you" (Deut. 28:46–48).[10]

11. Rava said: He who occupies himself with study of Torah needs neither burnt offering, nor meal offering, nor sin offering, nor guilt offering. R. Isaac asked: What is the proof for such a statement? and replied: Scripture's saying "This Torah for a sin offering" (Lev. 6:18) and "This Torah for a guilt offering" (Lev. 7:1). The two verses imply that he who occupies himself with the part of the Torah that details the sin offering—it is as though he brought a sin offering; and he who occupies himself with the part of the Torah that details the guilt offering—it is as though he brought a guilt offering.[11]

12. R. Meir used to say: Where do we find the proof that even a Gentile who pursues the study of Torah is like a high priest? From the assertion about Torah's ordinances that "by pursuing their study man shall live" (Lev. 18:5), where Scripture speaks not of priest, Levite, or Israelite, but of "man." So you learn that even a Gentile who pursues the study of Torah is like a high priest.[12]

13. R. Hisda said: What is meant by the verse "The Lord loveth the gates of Zion (Tziyyon) more than all other tabernacles of Jacob" (Ps. 87:2)? That the Lord loves gates

---

1. Avot 1:2.
2. B. Pes 68b.
3. Avot 6:6.
4. B. Meg 16b.
5. DEZ 5.
6. Sif Lev. 26:4 (ed. Weiss, p. 112c).
7. Pe 1:1.
8. Avot 5:25.
9. B. Meg 16b; B. Er 63b; Avot 6:6.
10. ARN 20; Zohar, Idra Zuta 15.
11. B. Men 110a.
12. B. Sanh 59a.

distinguished (*metzuyyanim*) by study of *Halakhah* more than [elaborate] synagogues and houses of study. This assertion supports what R. Hiyya bar Ammi said in the name of Ulla: Since the day the Temple was destroyed, the Holy One limits Himself in His world to an area no larger than the four square cubits of [him who studies] *Halakhah*.

Abbaye said: Formerly, I used to study in my home and pray in a synagogue. But after I heard the saying of R. Hiyya bar Ammi in the name of Ulla, I pray only where I study.

Though R. Ammi and R. Assi had [their choice of] thirteen synagogues in Tiberias, they would pray only between the pillars [of the academy] where they studied.[1]

14. R. Jeremiah was seated before R. Zera while the two were engaged in the study of *Halakhah*. As the sun was setting and the time for evening prayer arrived, R. Jeremiah was pressing [to adjourn study and pray]. R. Zera applied to him the verse "He that turneth away from hearing Torah, even his prayer is an abomination" (Prov. 28:9).

When Rava saw R. Hamnuna prolonging his prayers, he remarked: Some people forsake eternal life and concern themselves with temporal life.[2]

15. Our masters taught: "Therefore shall ye lay up (*vesamtem*) these My words" (Deut. 11:18). The word *samtem* is to be understood as a compound of *sam*, "remedy," and *tam*, "perfect," the Torah being compared to a lifesaving remedy. A parable of a man who gave his son a severe blow and then put a plaster on the sore spot, saying: My son, as long as this plaster is on your sore, you may eat what you like, drink what you like, bathe in hot or cold water, and need not be afraid. But if you remove it, the sore will open up [and fester]. So, too, the Holy One said to Israel: My children, I created the impulse to evil, and I created the Torah as its antidote. If you occupy yourselves with Torah, you will not be delivered into the power of the impulse to evil, for Scripture says, "If thou occupiest thyself with that which is good, thou wilt be exalted" (Gen. 4:7). If you do not occupy yourself with Torah, you will be delivered into the power of the impulse to evil, "thou wilt couch at the door of sin" (Gen. 4:7).[3] More: all concerns of the impulse will be to make you sin, as is said, "Unto thee will be its desire" (ibid.). But if you choose, you can master it, as is said, "Thou wilt be master over it" (ibid.).[4]

16. R. Judah son of R. Hiyya said: Pause and consider how the effect of human action is not at all like the effect of the Holy One's action. In human action, when a man gives a drug to his fellow, it may be beneficial to one part of the body but injurious to another. Not so the Holy One: He gave Israel the Torah—a lifesaving drug for the entire body, as is said, "Healing to all his flesh" (Prov. 4:22).[5]

17. R. Joshua ben Levi said: When a man is on a journey and has no company, let him occupy himself with study of Torah, for Scripture says, "They[6] are to be companions of grace" (Prov. 1:9). When a man feels pain in his head, let him occupy himself with Torah, since the verse goes on to prescribe "for thy head" (ibid.). When a man feels pain in his throat, let him occupy himself with Torah, for the verse likens Torah's words to "a necklace about thy throat." When he feels pain in his innards, let him occupy himself with Torah, for another verse says of Torah that "it shall be healing to thy navel" (Prov. 3:8). When he feels pain in his bones, let him occupy himself with Torah, since the verse goes on to describe Torah as "marrow for thy bones" (ibid.). When he feels pain in his entire body, let him occupy himself with Torah, since another verse speaks of it as "healing for his whole body" (Prov. 4:22).[7]

18. R. Joshua ben Levi said: What is the meaning of the verse "This is the Torah which Moses set (*sam*) before the children of Israel" (Deut. 4:44)? If a man merits it, it becomes a potion (*sam*) of life for him; if not, a potion of death. That is what Rava meant in saying, "If used the right way, it is a potion of life; if not used the right way, a potion of death."[8]

19. "These are the words" (*devarim*) (Deut. 1:1). Just as bees (*devorim*) reserve their honey for their owner and their sting for others, so are words of Torah an elixir of life for Israel but deadly poison for the nations of the earth.[9]

20. R. Judah said in the name of Samuel: What is meant by "Thou makest men as the flesh of the sea" (Hab. 1:14)? In what way can men be spoken of as being like fish of the sea? In this way: as the fish of the sea, once they go up on dry land, promptly die, so human beings, as soon as they give up Torah and its precepts, promptly perish.[10]

21. We have been taught: "They went three days in the wilderness, and found no water" (Exod. 15:22). Those who expound the inner meaning of Scripture say that here "water" can mean only Torah, of which it is said, "Ho, everyone that thirsteth, come ye for water" (Isa. 55:1). Since the Israelites went for three days without Torah, they grew weary. So prophets and elders among them bestirred themselves and ordained that Torah be read on the Sabbath and not read on Sunday; read on Monday and not read on Tuesday and Wednesday; read on Thursday and not read on Friday. Thus Israelites will never go on for three consecutive days without hearing Torah.[11]

22. Words of Torah are likened to waters: "Ho, everyone that thirsteth, come ye to the waters" (Isa. 55:1). As waters reach from one end of the world to the other, so Torah

1. B. Ber 8a.
2. B. Shab 10a.
3. JV: "If thou doest well, shall it not be lifted up? and if thou doest not well, sin coucheth at the door."
4. B. Kid 30b.
5. B. Er 54a and En Yaakov, ad loc.
6. The Written and the Oral Torah.
7. B. Er 54a and En Yaakov, ad loc.
8. B. Yoma 72b.
9. Deut. R. 1:6.
10. B. AZ 3a.
11. B. BK 82a; Mek, *Be-shallah, Va-yassa*, §1.

reaches from one end of the world to the other. As waters give life to the world, so Torah gives life to the world. As waters are given without cost to the world, so is Torah given without cost to the world. As waters are given from heaven, so is Torah given from heaven. As waters are given to the accompaniment of powerful thunderings, so was Torah given to the accompaniment of powerful thunderings. As waters restore a man's spirit, so Torah restores a man's spirit. As waters cleanse a man from uncleanness, so Torah cleanses an unclean person from his uncleanness. As waters come down in myriads of drops and become a multitude of brooks, so are words of Torah; today a man learns two *Halakhot*, tomorrow two more, [and so on], until he becomes like a bubbling brook. As waters leave a high place and flow to a low place, so Torah leaves him whose opinion of himself is high and cleaves to him whose spirit is lowly. As water is not kept in vessels of silver or gold, but only in the cheapest of vessels, so Torah abides only in him who regards himself as lowly as an earthenware vessel. As when thirsty, a grown man is not ashamed to say to a child, "Let me have a drink of water," so in studying Torah an [unlearned] grown man should not be ashamed to say to a child, "Teach me a chapter," "Teach me a verse," "Teach me a word," even "Teach me a single letter." As with water, if one does not know how to swim in it, he will end by drowning, so with words of Torah: if one does not know how to swim in them and teach them, he will drown in the end.[1]

23. "At His right hand was a fiery law unto them" (Deut. 33:2). The verse asserts that words of Torah are likened to fire. As fire was given from heaven, so were words of Torah given from heaven. (Israel were told, "Ye yourselves have seen that I talked with you from heaven" [Exod. 20:22].) Even as fire is life for the world, so words of Torah are life for the world. Fire: close up to it, one is scorched; away from it, one is chilled; near but not too near, one enjoys it. So are words of Torah: as long as a man labors in them, they are life for him; but when he separates himself from them, they slay him. Even as fire is made use of in this world and in the world-to-come, so words of Torah are made use of in this world and in the world-to-come. Even as fire when used leaves a mark on a man's body, so words of Torah when used leave a mark on the body. Fire: they who work with it are readily distinguishable from other mortals. So, too—by their walk, by their speech, by their garments in the marketplace—disciples of the wise are just as readily distinguishable.[2]

24. "My doctrine shall drop as the rain" (Deut. 32:2). Even as rain gives life to the world, so words of Torah give life to the world. But while some people in the world rejoice in rain, others are grieved by it. Thus he whose pit or vat is full of wine, or his threshing floor full of grain, is distressed by rain. Is the same true of words of Torah? [No indeed], for Scripture goes on to say, "My speech shall distill as the dew" (Deut. 32:2). As all people in the world—all—rejoice in dew, so all people in the world, in all of it, rejoice in words of Torah.

"As showers upon the tender grass" (Deut. 32:2)—as showers coming down upon blades of grass raise them up and make them grow, so words of Torah raise up those who study them and make them grow. "And droplets upon the herb" (ibid.)—as the droplets that come down upon herbs refresh them and make them beautiful, so words of Torah refresh those who study them and make them beautiful.[3]

25. "Whoso keepeth the fig tree shall eat [all] the fruit thereof" (Prov. 27:18). Why is Torah likened to a fig tree? Because all other fruits contain useless [inedible] matter. Dates have pits, grapes have seeds, pomegranates have rinds. But the fig, all of it, is edible. So words of Torah have no worthless matter in them, as is said, "For it is not a thing [any part of which is] without use for you" (Deut. 32:47).[4]

26. R. Joshua ben Levi said: Each and every day a divine voice goes forth from Mount Horeb[5] to proclaim these words: "Woe unto [you], mankind, because of the humiliation Torah suffers from your neglect." For he who does not occupy himself with Torah is said to be under divine censure.[6]

27. Upon him who has the means to study Torah but does not study it, the Holy One brings unsightly afflictions, which affect him to the depths of his being, as is said, "When I keep silent, away from the good, my afflictions become unsightly" (Ps. 39:3).[7]

28. Rava said: All bodies are sheaths. Blessed is he who is privileged to be a sheath for Torah.[8]

29. R. Jeremiah ben Eleazar said: A house in which words of Torah are heard at night will never be destroyed, for it is said, "No one who giveth forth songs [of Torah] in the night saith: 'Where is God my Maker?' " (Job 35:10).[9]

30. R. Hananiah ben Teradion said: When two sit together and no words of Torah are spoken between them, theirs is a session of scorners. But when the two sit together and words of Torah are spoken between them, the Presence abides with them.[10]

31. R. Simeon said: If three eat at a table without speaking words of Torah, it is as though they were eating sacrifices offered to lifeless [idols]. But if the three eat at a table while speaking words of Torah, it is as though they were eating at the table of Him who is everywhere.[11]

---

1. Song R. 1:2, §3; MTeh 1:18; Sif Deut., §48.
2. Sif Deut., §343; Yalkut, *Berakhah*, §951.
3. Sif Deut., §306; Yalkut, *Haazinu*, §942.
4. Yalkut, Josh., §2, citing Yelammedenu.
5. That is, Mount Sinai, the place of the revelation of the Torah.
6. Avot 6:2.
7. B. Ber 5a.
8. B. Sanh 99b.
9. B. Er 18b.
10. Avot 3:2.
11. Avot 3:3.

32. R. Halafta ben Dosa of Kefar Hananiah said: When ten men sit together and occupy themselves with Torah, the Presence abides among them, as is said, "God abideth in the congregation of God"[1] (Ps. 82:1). How do we know that this is true even when there are only five? Because it is said, "When a band[2] is His, He establisheth [His Presence] upon the earth" (Amos 9:6). And from what do we infer that the same is true even when there are only three? From the verse "In the midst of the judges,[3] He judgeth" (Ps. 82:1). How do we know that the same is true when there are only two? From the verse "When they that fear the Lord spoke each to the other, the Lord hearkened, and heard" (Mal. 3:16). And how do we know that the same is true even of one? From the verse "In every place where I hear My Name mentioned, I will come to thee and bless thee" (Exod. 20:24).[4]

33. When one person sits and meditates on Torah, his reward is approved on high, for Scripture says, "When a man sits alone and meditates, [he will be rewarded], because he took it upon himself" (Lam. 3:28). How may the matter be illustrated? By the parable of a young son who, being left behind when his father went to the marketplace, up and took a Torah scroll, sat down, placed it between his knees, and began to make out its words. When his father came back from the marketplace, he said: Look what he did! My little boy, whom I left when I went out to the marketplace—on his own, he up and took the scroll, placed it between his knees, and now sits and studies it![5]

34. R. Simeon ben Eleazar reported a tradition in the name of R. Joshua ben Hananiah: He who recites a verse at the time appropriate for it brings good to the world, as is said, "How good is a word rightly timed" (Prov. 15:23).

Our masters taught: He who recites a verse from Song of Songs and treats it as a secular air [disregarding the traditional cantillation] or he who during a meal recites a verse out of the context where it belongs[6] [for no purpose other than to entertain] brings evil upon the world. Because the Torah girds itself in sackcloth, stands before the Holy One, and says, "Master of the universe, Your children have turned me into a harp to be played by frivolous people." When God replies, "My daughter, while they are eating and drinking, what else shall they occupy themselves with?" the Torah says, Master of the universe, if they are skilled in Scripture, let them occupy themselves with the Five Books, the Prophets, and the Writings; if they are skilled in Mishnah, let them occupy themselves with Mishnah—with *Halakhot* and *Aggadot*; if they are skilled in Talmud, let them occupy themselves with the laws of Passover on Passover, with the laws of the Feast of Weeks on the Feast of Weeks, and with the laws of Tabernacles on Tabernacles.[7]

35. "Thine oils have a goodly fragrance" (Song 1:3). Just as when you hold a cup full of oil and a drop of water falls into it, a drop of oil of equal volume will be forced out, so, too, when a word of Torah enters the heart, a scoffing word equal in volume will be forced out. And contrariwise, when a scoffing word enters the heart, a word of Torah equal in volume will be forced out.[8]

36. R. Levi said: A man who breaks off the study of Torah to engage in idle talk will be made to eat cinders of the broom tree.[9]

37. R. Simeon said: He who while walking on a road is repeating aloud what he learned, but then interrupts himself to say, "How beautiful is this tree," "How beautiful is this newly plowed field"—Scripture regards him as if he had incurred a guilt expiable only by his life.[10]

38. R. Hanina ben Hakinai said: He who while lying awake during the night, or walking alone on a road, makes room in his heart for thoughts that are trifling incurs a guilt expiable only by his life.[11]

39. Shammai said: Make your study of Torah a regular practice.[12]

40. It was taught in the school of R. Ishmael: Let not words of Torah be a [burdensome] duty to you, [to be avoided as far as possible], for you are never at liberty to desist from them.[13]

41. R. Tarfon used to say: It is not your duty to finish the task, but neither are you free to desist from it. If you study much Torah, a high wage will be paid you, and your Employer may be depended on to pay you in full the wages for your labor.[14]

42. Hillel said: Do not say, "I shall study when I have leisure." Perhaps you will never have leisure.[15]

43. "He that committeth adultery with a woman lacketh understanding" (Prov. 6:32). Resh Lakish said: This verse applies to one who studies Torah at [irregular] intervals.[16]

---

1. Ten men constitute a congregation. When such a congregation is described as "of God," it is one where words honoring Him are spoken.
2. "R. Halafta takes *aguddah*, 'band,' to mean a number of things held together by the five fingers of the hand, as well as the hand itself, consisting as it does of five separate fingers knit together" (Avot, Soncino, p. 30, n. 5, which cites Maimonides). JV: "His vault."
3. The smallest Jewish court consisted of three judges.
4. Avot 3:6.
5. ARN 8.
6. Such as verses recited in the saying of Kiddush or grace.
7. B. Sanh 101a.
8. Song R. 1:3, §2.
9. The broom tree's hot cinders, it is said, never die out. B. Hag 12b.
10. Avot 3:7.
11. Avot 3:4.
12. Avot 1:15.
13. B. Men 99b.
14. Avot 2:16.
15. Avot 2:4.
16. In the manner of an adulterer. B. Sanh 99b.

44. R. Jonathan said: One should never keep himself away from the house of study or from words of Torah, even when he is about to die, as is said, "This Torah, when a man dieth—[he is still to be] in [its] tent" (Num. 19:14): even at the time of death, a man should still occupy himself with Torah.[1]

45. Ben Damah, the son of R. Ishmael's sister, asked R. Ishmael: May one like myself, who has studied the entire Torah, study Greek wisdom? R. Ishmael cited to him the verse "This book of Torah shall not depart out of thy mouth, but thou shalt meditate therein day and night" (Josh. 1:8). Go and find an hour that is neither day nor night, and study Greek wisdom then.

But R. Samuel bar Nahmani said in the name of R. Jonathan: This verse sets forth neither a duty nor a precept, but a blessing. For the Holy One saw that words of Torah were most precious to Joshua, as is said, "His minister Joshua, the son of Nun, even when young, departed not out of the tent [for the study of Torah]" (Exod. 33:11). So the Holy One said to him: Joshua, since words of Torah are so precious to you, "This book of Torah will not depart out of thy mouth."[2]

46. We have been taught that R. Judah ben Betera used to say: Words of Torah are not susceptible to uncleanness. Once a disciple, who was seated above R. Judah ben Betera, was mumbling indistinctly[3] as he read from the Torah. So R. Judah said to him: My son, open your mouth and let your words shine, for words of Torah are not susceptible to uncleanness, since Scripture says, "Is not My word like as fire?" (Jer. 23:29). As fire is not susceptible to uncleanness, so words of Torah are not susceptible to uncleanness.[4]

47. Our masters taught: Every day the Holy One weeps over three: over him who can occupy himself with Torah but does not, over him who cannot occupy himself with Torah but does so nevertheless [and misunderstands it], and over a communal leader who lords it over the community.[5]

48. Our masters taught: When a poor man, a rich man, and a sensual man come before the [heavenly] court for judgment, the poor man is asked, "Why have you not occupied yourself with Torah?" If he answers, "I was poor and preoccupied with making a living," he is asked, "Do you mean to say that you were poorer than Hillel?"

The rich man is asked, "Why have you not occupied yourself with Torah?" If he answers, "I was rich and preoccupied with tending to my possessions," he is asked, "Do you mean to say that you were richer than R. Eleazar ben Harsom?"

It is reported about R. Eleazar ben Harsom that his father left him a thousand hamlets on land and, matching them, a thousand ships at sea. Still, every day he would put on his shoulder a sack of flour [as food for himself] and travel from city to city and from province to province to study Torah. One day his servants came upon him and [not recognizing him] seized him for public service. When he said to them, "I beg of you, let me go to study Torah," they replied, "By the life of R. Eleazar ben Harsom, we shall not let you go." So he gave them much money to let him go. [Neither he nor they knew one another] because he had never seen his servants, sitting as he did all day and all night, occupied with Torah.

The sensual person is asked, "Why have you not occupied yourself with Torah?" If he answers, "I was handsome and obsessed by my sensual passion," he is asked, "Do you mean to say that you were more handsome and more obsessed by passion than the virtuous Joseph?" It is told of the virtuous Joseph that every day Potiphar's wife endeavored to win him with [flattering] words. Besides, she did not wear for him in the evening the garments she put on to [entice] him in the morning, and she did not wear for him in the morning those she put on for him in the evening. She kept saying to him, "Yield to me!" and he kept saying, "No!" Finally she said, "I shall have you imprisoned." He replied, "The Lord sets prisoners free" (Ps. 146:7). She said, "I shall bend down your proud stature." He replied, "The Lord makes those who are bent down stand straight" (Ps. 146:8). She said, "I shall blind you." He replied, "The Lord restores sight to the blind" (ibid.). Even when she offered him a thousand talents of silver, he still would not listen to her.

Thus Hillel shows up the poor, R. Eleazar ben Harsom shows up the rich, and the virtuous Joseph shows up the sensual.[6]

49. It was said of R. Judah ben Ilai's generation: [Their poverty was so great that] six disciples had to cover their bodies with but one cloak. Nevertheless, they occupied themselves with Torah.[7]

50. R. Yohanan said: When we studied Torah at the home of R. Oshaia, four of us used to sit [crowded] in the space of one cubit.[8]

Rabbi [Judah I, the Patriarch] said: When we studied Torah at the home of R. Eleazar ben Shammua, six of us used to sit [crowded] within the space of one cubit.[9]

51. [The prophet] Elijah, ever mentioned on good occasions, said: Once, as I was walking on the road, a man who met me mocked and reviled me. I asked him, "My son, since you have refused to learn Torah, what will you say on the Day of Judgment?" He replied, "I have an answer: Understanding, knowledge, and spirit were not given me from Heaven [so how could I study Torah]?" I said, "My son, what is your work?" He replied, "I am a

---

1. B. Shab 83b.
2. B. Men 99b.
3. Having had a seminal emission during the night, he was reluctant to utter the Scriptural words distinctly.
4. B. Ber 22a and En Yaakov, ad loc.
5. B. Hag 5b and En Yaakov, ad loc.
6. B. Yoma 35b and En Yaakov, ad loc.
7. B. Sanh 20a.
8. So anxious were we to study with R. Oshaia.
9. B. Er 53a.

trapper of fowls and fish." I asked, "Who gave you knowledge and spirit to take flax, spin it into cords, weave the cords into nets, use the nets to trap fish and fowls, and sell them?" He replied, "Understanding and knowledge [to do my work] were given me from Heaven." I said, "To take flax, spin it into cords, weave cords into nets, and use nets to trap fish and fowls, understanding and knowledge were given to you from Heaven. But do you suppose that, for words of Torah, about which it is written, 'The word is very nigh unto thee' [Deut. 30:14], understanding and knowledge were not given to you?"[1]

52. R. Nehunia ben Ha-Kanah said: He who takes upon himself the yoke of Torah will be relieved of the yoke of government and the yoke of worldly concerns. But he who breaks off the yoke of Torah from himself will have the yoke of government and the yoke of worldly concerns imposed upon him.[2]

53. "The writing was the writing of God, graven (*harut*) upon the Tablets" (Exod. 32:16). Read not *harut*, "graven," but *herut*, "freedom," for no man is truly free unless he occupies himself with study of Torah.[3]

54. R. Eleazar ben Azariah said: Where there is no Torah, there are no good manners. Where there are no good manners, there is no Torah. . . . Where there is no bread, there is no Torah; where there is no Torah, there is no bread.[4]

55. It is said in the name of R. Judah bar Ilai: Pause and consider how recent generations are not like the former generations. The former generations made the study of Torah their regular concern and their daily work their occasional concern, and they succeeded in the one and in the other.[5] The recent generations have made their daily work their regular concern and their study of Torah their occasional concern, and they have succeeded neither in the one nor in the other.[6]

56. R. Judah ben Ilai said: Anyone who makes words of Torah his primary concern and worldly matters secondary will be made primary in the world-to-come. But anyone who makes worldly matters primary and words of Torah secondary will be made secondary in the world-to-come.[7] [But R. Judah ben Ilai also said: Anyone who does not teach his son a trade is as though he taught him to be a brigand;[8] and also: Work is primary in importance, honoring him who engages in it.[9] In fact, R. Judah counsels a middle course.] How is what he counsels to be illustrated? By the parable[10] of a highway that runs between two paths, one of fire and the other of snow. If a man walks too close to the fire, he will be scorched by the flames; if too close to the snow, he will be bitten by the cold. What is he to do? He is to walk in the middle, taking care not to be scorched by the heat nor bitten by the cold.[11]

57. It has been taught in the name of R. Meir: As great as the superiority of light over darkness is the superiority of Torah's words over the vaporous words [of worldly wisdom].[12]

58. R. Nehorai said: I prefer to put aside all worldly skills and teach my son nothing but Torah, whose interest a man enjoys in this world, while the principal endures for him in the world-to-come. It is not so with other occupations. For when a man falls ill or reaches old age or is beset by afflictions and thus is unable to engage in his work, he will die of hunger. Not so the Torah: it stands by a man, guards him in his youth from all evil, and gives him a future and a hope in his old age. Of the time of his youth, what does Scripture say? "They that wait upon the Lord shall renew their strength; they shall mount up with wings as eagles" (Isa. 40:31). Of his old age, what does Scripture say? "They shall bring forth fruit in old age; they shall be full of sap and richness" (Ps. 92:15).[13]

59. "For I give you a good acquisition" (Prov. 4:2). In the way of the world, if two merchants stand side by side, one with silk yarn and the other with silk cloth, should the one say to the other, "Come, let us trade," and one takes all the silk yarn and the other all the silk cloth, then what the one now has the other has no longer; and what the other now has the one has no longer. Not so the Torah. If the one studies the Order of Seeds and another the Order of Festivals, and the one teaches the other, then the one is now master of two Orders and the other is master of two Orders. Can there be a better acquisition than this? Hence, "I give you a good acquisition."

Then, too, he who acquires merchandise and goes out on the highway is afraid of robbers. But with the Torah, it is not so. Can robbers possibly seize Torah out of a man's heart? Hence, "I give you a good acquisition."

A story of an associate scholar who was traveling with many merchants on a ship. When asked, "Where is your merchandise?" he replied, "My merchandise is more substantial than yours." They searched throughout the ship but found nothing that belonged to him. So they fell to making sport of him. Presently pirates attacked them and took everything they found in the ship. Consequently, when the travelers reached dry land and entered a city, they had neither bread to eat nor a garment to wear. But what did the associate scholar do? He went into a house

1. Tanhuma, *Va-yelekh*, §2; TdEZ 14; Yalkut, *Nitzavim*, §960.
2. Avot 3:5.
3. Avot 6.2.
4. Avot 3:17.
5. See "Man doth not live by bread alone, but by everything that proceedeth out of the mouth of the Lord" (Deut. 8:3).
6. B. Ber 35b.
7. So emended in ARN, p. 86; BR: "in this world."
8. B. Kid 29a.
9. B. Ned 49b.
10. This parable sets forth the mysteries of the chariot and of creation. P. Hag 2:1, 77a. See B. Z. Bacher, *Aggadot ha-Tannaim* (Berlin, 1922) 3:137. n. 3.
11. ARN 28.
12. Eccles. R. 2:13, §1.
13. B. Kid 82b; Sof 16.

of study, sat down, and expounded Scripture. When the people of the city realized that he was profoundly learned in Torah, they accorded him much respect and proceeded to maintain him. When the merchants saw this, they came to him, apologized, and asked him, "We beg of you, since you know us, speak favorably of us to the people of the city, so that we will not die of hunger." He replied, "Did I not tell you that my merchandise is more substantial than yours? Yours is perishable, while mine endures." Hence Scripture: "I have given you a good acquisition."[1]

60. R. Yose ben Kisma said: Once, as I was traveling on a road, a man met me and greeted me, and I returned his greeting. He asked, "Master, what place are you from?" I replied, "From a great city of sages and scribes." He said, "Master, if you consent to live with us in our place, I will give you a thousand thousand gold denars, besides precious stones and pearls." I replied, "If you were to give me all the silver and gold and precious stones and pearls in the world, I still would live nowhere except in a place of Torah. For thus it is written in the book of Psalms by David, king of Israel: 'The Torah of Thy mouth is worth more to me than thousands of gold and silver' " (Ps. 119:72). More: in the hour of a man's departure from the world, neither silver nor gold, neither precious stones nor pearls accompany him, but Torah and good deeds—only they, as is said, "When thou walkest, it shall lead thee; when thou liest down, it shall watch over thee; and when thou wakest, it shall talk with thee" (Prov. 6:22). "When thou walkest, it shall lead thee"—in this world; "when thou liest down, it shall watch over thee"—in the grave; "and when thou wakest, it shall talk with thee"—in the world-to-come.[2]

61. R. Yohanan said: Whoever has wearied himself with Torah in this world is not allowed to sleep in the world-to-come. He is taken to the house of study of Shem and Eber, of Abraham, Isaac, and Jacob, and of Moses and Aaron. For how long? "Until I make thee a great name, like unto the name of the great ones that were in the earth" (2 Sam. 7:9; 1 Chron. 17:8).[3]

How Torah Is Acquired and in Whom It Maintains Itself

62. Torah demands forty-eight attributes [from its students]: study [aloud]; attentive listening; distinct pronunciation; alertness of mind; intuitive insight; awe [of one's master]; reverence [for God]; humility; cheerfulness; cleanness; attendance on sages; intense examination of a matter in the company of colleagues; subtle discussion with disciples; unhurried reflection; persistence in study of Scripture and Mishnah; strict moderation in business, in sleep, in chitchat, in pleasure, in hilarity, and in worldly interests; patience; a good heart; faith in the sages; resignation to afflictions; knowing one's place; contentment with one's lot; restraint in one's words; refraining from claiming merit for oneself; being loved; loving Him who is present everywhere; loving fellow creatures; loving reproof and rectitude; shunning honor; avoiding pride in one's learning; taking no delight in laying down the law; bearing the yoke with one's fellow; judging him charitably; guiding him to the true [*Halakhah*]; urging him to reconciliation [in a dispute]; being systematic in study; asking and answering; listening and being ready to answer [when asked]; learning in order to teach; studying in order to practice [precepts]; making his teacher wiser [by pointed questions]; noting with precision what he is hearing; and giving credit for a comment to the one who made it.[4]

63. Seek not greatness for yourself. Covet not honor. Your study should lead to practice. Crave not the [luxurious] table of kings, for your table [of learning] is greater than their table [of food], and your crown is greater than their crown. And faithful is your Employer to pay you the recompense for your work.[5]

64. "The small is great there, and the servant is free from his master" (Job 3:19). He who makes himself small—humbles himself—in this world for the sake of words of Torah is deemed to be great in the world-to-come; and he who in this world is willing to be a servant [so that he may learn words of Torah] will be a free man in the world-to-come.[6]

65. R. Hanina bar Idi said: Why are words of Torah likened to water, as in the verse "Ho, everyone that thirsteth, come ye for water" (Isa. 55:1)? To teach you that, just as water flows from a higher level to a lower level, so words of Torah abide only with one who is meek in spirit.

R. Oshaia said: Why are words of Torah likened to the three beverages water, wine, and milk, as in "Ho, everyone that thirsteth, come ye for water" and in "Come ye, buy and eat . . . wine and milk without money, and without price" (Isa. 55:1)? To teach you that, just as these three beverages are preserved only in the most humble of [earthenware] vessels, so words of Torah abide only with one who is humble in spirit.[7]

66. R. Eleazar said: What is meant by "And chains about thy neck" (Prov. 1:9)? If a man trains himself to be like a chain, which hangs loosely around the neck, at times visible and at other times not visible, his learning will remain with him. But if not, his learning will not remain.

R. Eleazar also said: What is meant by "His cheeks are as a furrow of spices" (Song 5:13)? If a man allows himself to be treated as a furrow, upon which everybody treads, and as spices, with which everybody perfumes himself, his learning will endure. But if not, his learning will not endure.[8]

---

1. Tanhuma, *Terumah*, §2; Tanhuma B, *Terumah*, §1.
2. Avot 6:9.
3. By "the great ones" are meant the patriarchs. Eccles. R. 5:11, §5.
4. Avot 6:6.
5. Avot 6.4.
6. B. BM 85b.
7. B. Ta 7a and En Yaakov, ad loc.
8. B. Er 54a.

67. R. Akiva said: He who exalts himself because of [his knowledge of] words of Torah—to what may he be likened? To a carcass cast upon the road. Every passerby, putting his hand on his nose [and mouth], tries to get far away from it, as is said, "When you exalt yourself, you turn yourself into a carcass; when you think so loftily of yourself, everyone's hand is on his mouth" (Prov. 30:32).[1]

Ben Azzai said: If one is willing to be degraded for the sake of Torah's words, willing to eat carobs and lupines and wear filthy clothes in order to sit assiduously at the doors of sages, though every passerby says, "That one is an idiot," he will in the end become a scribe, and you will find the entire Torah to be with him.[2]

68. R. Yose bar Hanina said: Words of Torah dwell only with one who is willing to remain naked [destitute] in their behalf, as is said, "I, wisdom, make my dwelling with nakedness"[3] (Prov. 8:12).

R. Yohanan said: Words of Torah endure only with one who is willing to make himself as nothing, for it is said, "Wisdom shall be found in nothing (Job 28:12).[4]

69. "Wisdom crieth aloud in the streets" (Prov. 1:20). Rava said: When one studies Torah in his home, Torah proclaims his merit in the streets.[5]

70. R. Yohanan of En Te'enah said: As firm as a formal covenant is the assurance that he who labors at his studies without ostentation will not soon forget them. And the proof? "Wisdom is with the unostentatious" (Prov. 11:2).[6]

71. Torah's sandal is humility; Torah's crown is fear [of God].[7]

72. R. Yohanan ben Zakkai used to say: Do not give yourself airs if you have learned much Torah, because for this purpose you were created.[8]

73. R. Yose said: Make yourself fit to study Torah, for it is not [something that will come automatically] to you as an inheritance.[9]

74. This is the way of life [usual for] study of Torah: You will eat bread with [nothing more than] salt, drink water by measure, sleep on the [bare] ground, live a life of privation, yet still keep laboring in Torah. If you act thus, "thou wilt be happy, and it shall be well with thee" (Ps. 128:2)—"happy" in this world and "well with thee" in the world-to-come.[10]

75. R. Jonathan said: If a man persists in the study of Torah in poverty, he will eventually find himself persisting in such study in the midst of wealth; if he puts aside the study of Torah in the midst of wealth, he will put aside study of Torah in [abject] poverty.

R. Meir said: Give little time to business, and occupy yourself assiduously with Torah. Be lowly in spirit before all men. If you have once been remiss in study of Torah, soon you will find many other occasions to be remiss in studying. But if you have toiled [assiduously] at the study of Torah, God has abundant reward to give you.[11]

76. The Torah said to the Holy One: Let my portion be in the tribe [of Levi],[12] which is marked by [its] poverty. For when rich people are at all occupied with me, they swell up with pride. But people who are poor, even when occupied entirely with me, continue to be mindful that they are hungry and lowly.[13]

77. The Torah was given to be expounded only by those who [are so poor that they] have [nothing but] manna to eat and only secondarily by those who eat [fat] *terumah* [heave offering].[14]

78. R. Yohanan said: The words "It is not in heaven" (Deut. 30:12) imply that Torah will not be found among those who are arrogant. "Neither is it beyond the sea" (ibid.)—it will not be found among merchant princes or petty traders.[15]

79. "It is not in heaven" (Deut. 30:12). Samuel said, "Torah is not to be found among astrologers, who spend [most of] their time gazing at the heavens." Samuel was disputed: "But you yourself are an astrologer and also great in Torah?" He replied, "I engage in astrology only when I am free from studying Torah." "When is that?" "When I enter the privy."[16]

80. "Surely business[17] turneth a wise man into a fool" (Eccles. 7:7). When a sage busies himself (*mitasek*) with many [worldly] matters, his wisdom gets addled. "And destroyeth the gift in the heart" (ibid.)[18]—the many matters destroy the Torah, which was given as a gift to man's heart.

1. JV: "If thou hast done foolishly in lifting up thyself, or if thou hast planned devices, lay thy hand upon thy mouth."
2. ARN 11; Yalkut, Prov., §964.
3. JV: "prudence." But *ormah* ("prudence") may, with a slight change in vocalization, also mean "nakedness."
4. B. Sot 21b.
5. B. MK 16b.
6. P. Ber 5:1, 9a.
7. Tanhuma, *Bereshit*, §1.
8. Avot 2:8.
9. Avot 2:12.
10. Avot 6:4.
11. Avot 4:9–10.
12. The tribe that received no allotment of land.
13. Yalkut, Ruth, §597.
14. "This is a bitterly sarcastic dictum: since manna fell only once in history, a person said to have only manna to eat is totally destitute and starving. The priesthood, eating of fat sacrifices, was often criticized for its selfishness" (Leon Nemoy). Mek, *Be-shallah*, *Va-yassa*, 3.
15. B. Er 55a.
16. Deut. R. 8:6.
17. Reading not *oshek* ("oppression") but *esek* ("business").
18. JV: "And a gift destroyeth the heart."

Another interpretation: "Surely business turneth a wise man into a fool." He who busies himself with the needs of the community causes his knowledge of Torah to be forgotten.

R. Joshua ben Levi said: R. Judah ben Pedaiah taught me sixty laws concerning a grave that has been plowed over. I have forgotten all of them because I have been busy with the needs of the community.[1]

81. We have been taught that R. Simeon ben Yohai said: The Holy One gave Israel three precious gifts—Torah, the Land of Israel, and the world-to-come—each given only by means of chastisements. And the proof for Torah? The verse "Blessed is the man whom Thou chastenest, O Lord, and teachest him out of Thy Torah" (Ps. 94:12).[2]

82. What are the chastisements of love? Those that do not cause the study of Torah to cease.[3]

83. R. Bisna said: There is no man in the world who does not experience suffering. A man with pain in his teeth cannot sleep or with pain in his eyes cannot sleep; one who labors in Torah likewise does not sleep. The first two are kept awake, and the last one is kept awake. "Blessed is the man whom Thou chastenest, O Lord, by teaching him out of Thy Torah" (Ps. 94:12).[4]

84. Resh Lakish said: What is the proof that words of Torah abide only with a man who all but kills himself for their sake? The verse "This is the Torah, [to be studied] even if a man die in [his] tent [while at it]" (Num. 19:14).[5]

85. "When I was in a frenzy, my wisdom stayed within me" (Eccles. 2:9).[6] R. Hanina bar Papa said: Torah, which I studied in a [kind of] frenzy, stayed with me.[7]

86. "The doctrine I acquired is as shattering as the rain" (Deut. 32:2). The sages said that Moses asked Israel: Are you aware of the pain I suffered for Torah's sake, the toil I put into it, the backbreaking labor I devoted to it, as is said, "And he was there with the Lord forty days and forty nights" (Exod. 34:28)? Moreover, I had to go into the midst of angels, had to go into the midst of the celestial creatures, had to go into the midst of seraphim, any one of which could incinerate the entire world, all of it. I all but gave my life for its sake. As I have learned it in pain, so will you learn it in pain. But now, as you have learned it in pain, will you also teach it by inflicting pain [on your pupils]? Therefore Scripture says, "My speech shall be as low in cost as dew" (Deut. 32:2)[8]—you will dispense it at low cost [painlessly].[9]

87. It was taught in the school of Elijah: For words of Torah, a man should be ever ready to submit himself like an ox to the yoke or like an ass to the burden.[10]

88. Sages in the school of R. Yannai taught: Concerning the verse "As milk under pressure produces butter" (Prov. 30:33): in whom do you find the "butter" [the richness] of Torah? In him [who puts himself under such pressure for its sake that he] all but regurgitates the milk he sucked at his mother's breast.[11]

89. R. Judah son of R. Simon expounded: He who is willing for the sake of Torah is to have his face blackened [by deprivation] in this world, the Holy One will make his countenance shine in the world-to-come.[12]

90. "In early hours, as in the evening" (Song 5:11).[13] In whom will you find words of Torah? In him who comes early and stays on into the evening at the house of study for their sake.

Rabbah, reading the verse "Black as a raven," took it to refer to one who for the sake of words of Torah is willing to have his face made as black [by deprivation] as a raven. Rava said: The verse refers to one who can bring himself to be as cruel to his children and to the members of his household as is the raven.[14] Such was the case with R. Adda bar Mattena, who was leaving [home] to study Torah. When his wife asked him, "How will I provide food for your children?" he answered, "Is watercress no longer in the marsh?"[15]

91. R. Isaac said: If a man claims, "I labored but did not find," do not believe him; "I did not labor but found nevertheless," do not believe him; "I labored and found," believe him.[16]

92. R. Eleazar said: Never in my life has anyone preceded me into the house of study, nor have I departed from it leaving anyone there. Once I rose early and found the carriers of manure and straw already abroad. So I recited the verse "If thou seek her as silver, and search for her as for hidden treasure, then shalt thou understand the fear of the Lord" (Prov. 2:4). Should we not carry our "manure and straw" at least [as industriously] as professional carriers of manure and straw?

---

1. Exod. R. 6:2.
2. B. Ber 5a.
3. Ibid.
4. Tanhuma B, *Mi-ketz*, §16; *Yalkut*, Ps., §850.
5. B. Ber 63b.
6. JV: "Also (*af*) my wisdom stood me in stead." But *af* can also mean "frenzy, ferment."
7. Yalkut, Eccles., §968.
8. JV: "My speech shall distill (*tizzal*) as the dew." But *tizzal* can also be construed as a form of the noun *zol* ("low in price").
9. Sif Deut., §307.
10. B. AZ 5b.
11. B. Ber 63b.
12. B. Sanh 100a.
13. JV: "Black (*shehorot*) as a raven (*orev*)." But here the commentator boldly associates *shehorot* with *shaharit* ("early morning") and *orev* with *arevit* ("evening").
14. On the raven's neglect of its young, see B. Ket 49b and B. BB 8a.
15. Implying that water plants could be cooked for food. B. Er 21b–22a and En Yaakov, ad loc.
16. B. Meg 6a.

R. Phinehas ben Yair inferred from the verse just cited: Zeal [in the study and practice of Torah] leads to fastidiousness; fastidiousness leads to cleanness; cleanness leads to holiness; holiness leads to humility; humility leads to fear of sin; fear of sin leads to pious conduct; pious conduct leads to the holy spirit; the holy spirit leads to the resurrection of the dead; the resurrection of the dead leads to Elijah the Prophet, ever mentioned on good occasions.[1]

93. R. Eleazar says: Be diligent in studying Torah . . . and know in whose Presence you toil.[2]

94. R. Eliezer said: If all seas were ink, all reeds quills, heaven and earth scrolls, and all men scribes, they would not suffice to write down the amount of Torah I have learned, even though I abstracted no more from it than a man might take by dipping a painting stick in the sea.

So, too, R. Joshua said: If all seas were ink, all reeds quills, heaven and earth sheets of parchment, and all men scribes, they would not suffice to write down the amount of Torah I have learned, even though I abstracted from it no more than a man might take by dipping a painting stick in the sea.

R. Akiva said: As for me, I am in no position to say what my teachers[3] said. For, in fact, my teachers did abstract something, while I have abstracted no more than one who smells [the fragrance of] an etrog—he who smells it benefits, while the etrog itself is not diminished—or than one who fills his pitcher from a canal or kindles one lamp from another.[4]

95. Once, as Ben Azzai sat expounding Scripture, fire was flashing around him. They went and told R. Akiva, "Master, Ben Azzai sits and expounds, while fire flashes around him." R. Akiva went to Ben Azzai and said, "I hear that while you have been expounding, fire was flashing around you." Ben Azzai: "Yes." R. Akiva: "Were you perhaps discussing the innermost secrets of the divine chariot?" Ben Azzai: "No. But I was sitting and stringing words of Torah with one another, and words of Torah with words of the Prophets, and words of the Prophets with words of the Writings, and the words were as full of joy as when they were given at Sinai, as sweet as at the time of their first utterance. And were they not at their first utterance uttered in fire?"[5]

96. R. Hanina ben Hakinai and R. Simeon ben Yohai went to study Torah with R. Akiva in Bene Berak and remained there thirteen years. R. Simeon ben Yohai used to send home for news and so knew what was happening in his home. But R. Hanina ben Hakinai [did not send home for news], so he did not know [anything about his home]. Finally, his wife sent word to him: "Your daughter has come of age. Come back and get her married." So he got leave from R. Akiva and went home. Upon his return, he found that the lanes of his city had changed so much that he did not know how to get to his house. What did he do? He sat down on the bank of the river, where he heard the voices of young girls calling to one of them, "Daughter of Hakinai, fill your pitcher and let's go." He said: It is clear that this young girl is of my family. He followed her and entered his house unannounced. His wife was sitting and sifting flour. When she raised her eyes and became aware of him, her soul left her. At that, he said to the Holy One, "Master of the universe, this poor woman—is such to be her recompense?" He entreated mercy for her, and her soul returned to her body.[6]

97. R. Hama bar Bisa went away [from his home] and spent twelve years at a house of study. When he returned, he said: I will not do what Ben Hakinai did. So he entered the [local] house of study and stayed there, while he sent word to his home [that he was back]. Just then his son R. Oshaia happened to walk into the house of study and sit down before him. R. Hama proceeded to ask him about some rulings in *Halakhah*. Seeing how sharp he was in the relevant traditions, R. Hama[7] became quite depressed as he said to himself: Had I remained home, I also might have had such a son. When R. Hama finally entered his home, his son also happened to walk in. R. Hama, believing that the young man wished to inquire about some other rulings in *Halakhah*, stood up in deference to him. At this, R. Hama's wife asked, "What father stands up for his own son?"

Rami bar Hama then recited the verse "A threefold cord is not quickly broken" (Eccles. 4:12), the threefold cord being [young] R. Oshaia, his father R. Hama, and his grandfather Bisa.[8]

98. R. Joseph son of Rava was sent by his father to the house of study to study with R. Joseph [the Elder], and it was arranged that he stay there six years. After three years passed, and the eve of the Day of Atonement came, the son said: I will go and see the members of my household. When the father heard of his son's coming, he picked up a stick and went out to meet him. "Are you here because you thought of [your wife, whom you call] your [little] pigeon?" They fell to quarreling, and neither was able to eat the final meal before the fast.[9]

99. There was a certain heretic who saw Rava utterly engrossed in his studies, with his hand under his leg, which pressed down so hard that his finger spurted blood. The heretic exclaimed: You precipitous people, who put your mouth before your ears.[10] You continue to be precipitous. You should have listened first to determine

1. Elijah is the herald of the Messiah and the Day of Judgment. Song R. 1:1, §9; P. Shab 1:3, 3c.
2. Avot 2:14.
3. R. Eliezer and R. Joshua.
4. Song R. 1:3, §1.
5. Song R. 1:10, §2.
6. B. Ket 62b; Lev. R. 21:8.
7. Who did not recognize him after twelve years and thought that he was some other man's son.
8. B. Ket 62b.
9. B. Ket 63a.
10. The heretic refers to Israel's having said "We will do," before saying, "We will listen." See Exod. 24:7.

whether you could accept the commandments. And if not, not accept them. Rava replied: Of us who walk in integrity, Scripture says, "The integrity of the upright shall guide them" (Prov. 11:3). But of those [like you] who walk in perversity, Scripture says, "The perverseness of the treacherous shall destroy them" (ibid.).[1]

100. "Attend and hear, O Israel: this day thou art become a people unto the Lord thy God" (Deut. 27:9). Was it on this day that the Torah was given to Israel? Was not this day in fact forty years after the Torah was given? However, the verse intends to teach you that, to those who study Torah, it is as beloved every day as the day when it was given from Mount Sinai.[2]

101. Hour after hour, words of Torah are loved as much by those who study them as when they first made their acquaintance with them.[3]

102. "Her breasts will satisfy thee at all times" (Prov. 5:19). Why are words of Torah likened to a breast? As with a breast, however often the infant feels it, he finds milk in it, so, too, with words of Torah—whenever a man meditates on them, he finds savor in them.

"With love for her wilt thou be ravished always" (Prov. 5:19),[4] as happened to R. Eleazar ben Pedat. It is said of R. Eleazar ben Pedat that he would sit in the lower marketplace of Sepphoris, while his linen cloak lay abandoned in Sepphoris's upper marketplace.

R. Isaac ben Eleazar related: Once a man was about to take it, but he found a venomous serpent lying [as guard] upon it.[5]

103. "And let them be like fish" (Gen. 48:16). Fish, though they grow in water, nevertheless, when a drop [of rain] falls from above, leap for it thirstily as if they had never tasted water in their lives. So, too, Israel: though brought up in the waters of Torah, nevertheless, when they hear a new exposition of it, they receive it thirstily, as though they had never before heard a word of Torah in their lives.[6]

104. We have been taught that Rabbi [Judah I, the Patriarch] said: When I went to R. Eleazar ben Shammua to have my learning examined (others say: to sound the learning of R. Eleazar ben Shammua), I found Joseph the Babylonian, whom R. Eleazar cherished exceedingly, seated before him. Joseph asked, "Master, what is the law if one has slaughtered an offering intending to leave the blood's sprinkling for the morrow?" "The blood is valid," R. Eleazar replied. The next morning he again replied, "It is valid." At midday he again replied, "It is valid." In the afternoon he replied, "It is valid." In the evening, however, he replied, "It is valid, but R. Eliezer declares it invalid." At that, the face of Joseph the Babylonian brightened. R. Eleazar: "Joseph, it seems to me that we did not get our traditions straight until now." "Quite so, master," he replied, "quite so. For R. Judah taught me that such blood is invalid; but when I went around among all his disciples to find the same opinion, I could not find any.[7] Now that you teach me that according to R. Eliezer, too, such blood is invalid [you provide me with another opinion in agreement with R. Judah's] and thus restore to me words of Torah I thought I had lost." R. Eleazar ben Shammua's eyes filled with tears of joy and he exclaimed, "Happy are you, O disciples of the wise, to whom the words of Torah are so dear!" He then said that Joseph might justly declare, "O how I love Thy Torah! It is my meditation all the day" (Ps. 119:97).[8]

105. R. Abbahu went to Caesarea and from there returned to Tiberias, his face shining. When R. Yohanan's disciples saw him, they came and told R. Yohanan, "R. Abbahu has found a treasure!" R. Yohanan asked, "How do you know?" They replied, "Because his face is shining." He said, "Perhaps he has heard a new interpretation of Torah." When R. Abbahu came in to see him, R. Yohanan asked him, "What new interpretation of Torah have you heard?" R. Abbahu replied, "Something in an ancient Tosefta."

R. Yohanan applied to him the verse "A man's wisdom maketh his face to shine" (Eccles. 8:1).[9]

106. A heretic who saw R. Judah bar Ilai with his face aglow said, "One of three things must be true of that man: either he is drunk with wine, or he lends money upon interest, or he raises swine."[10] R. Judah bar Ilai, overhearing the heretic's remark, said to him, "May the breath of life in that man be blown out of him, for not one of these things is true of me. I do not lend money upon interest. I do not raise swine. Both activities are prohibited to Jews. Nor am I drunk with wine. Even the four cups of wine I drink on the eve of Passover make my head ache from Passover to the Feast of Weeks." The heretic asked, "Why then is your face aglow?" He replied, "It is Torah that makes my face shine, as is written, 'A man's wisdom maketh his face to shine' " (Eccles. 8:1).[11]

107. Abbaye said: May good come to me, because whenever I see a disciple of the wise complete a tractate, I declare it a festal day [for all the sages].[12]

108. How do we know that a blessing is to be spoken over the reading of the Torah? R. Ishmael said: By infer-

1. B. Shab 88a–b.
2. B. Ber 63b.
3. B. Er 54b.
4. Or: " 'Because of love for her, thou makest a fool of thyself,' leaving both cloak and wares unattended." So Rashi, ad loc.
5. B. Er 54a–b and En Yaakov, ad loc.
6. Gen. R. 97:3.
7. And I therefore thought that I must have been mistaken in what I believed R. Judah had said, since his other disciples had not heard it.
8. B. Men 18a and En Yaakov, ad loc.
9. P. Shab 8:1, 11a; Eccles. R. 8:1, §4; PR 14:10.
10. Both immensely profitable occupations.
11. P. Shab 8:1, 11a; Eccles. R. 8:1, §4; PR 14:10.
12. Abbaye was head of the academy of Pumbedita. B. Shab 118b–119a.

ence. If a blessing must be pronounced over an occasion that brings temporal life, all the more so by far over the reading of the Torah, which brings life eternal.[1]

Torah for Its Own Sake

109. R. Eleazar said: What is signified in the verse "She openeth her mouth with wisdom, and the Torah of loving-kindness is on her tongue" (Prov. 31:26)? Is there a Torah of loving-kindness and another Torah not of loving-kindness? What the verse means is that Torah studied for its own sake is a "Torah of loving-kindness," while Torah studied not for its own sake [for an ulterior motive] is a Torah not of loving-kindness.[2]

110. We have been taught: The verse "That thou . . . mayest love the Lord thy God, to hearken to His voice, to cleave unto Him" (Deut. 30:20) means that one should not say, "I will read Scripture so that I may be called 'sage,' I will recite Mishnah so that I may be called 'master,' I will study so that I may be designated an elder and have a seat in the academy." Rather, study out of love, and honor will come in the end.

R. Eleazar ben R. Zadok said: Do good deeds for the doing's sake, and speak of words of Torah for their own sake. Do not use them as a crown to magnify yourself with, or as a spade to hoe with. The foregoing may be confirmed by inference: if Belshazzar, who made use of the sacred vessels only after they had been profaned, was rooted out of the world, how much more so by far he who turns to his own use the crown of Torah, the crown whose holiness abides and endures forever.[3]

111. R. Zadok said: Make them not a crown to magnify yourself with, nor a spade to dig with. Even so Hillel was wont to say, "He who makes [unworthy] use of the crown of Torah shall perish." Hence, you are to conclude: anyone who derives benefit from words of Torah removes his life from the world.[4]

112. R. Meir said: He who occupies himself with Torah for its own sake acquires many boons. More: the entire world is under obligation to him. He is called [God's] companion, [God's] beloved, one who loves Him who is everywhere, one who loves his fellow men, one who gladdens Him who is everywhere, one who gladdens his fellow men. The Torah clothes him with humility and fear of God, and fits him to be virtuous and devout, upright and faithful. It keeps him far from sin and draws him near to the doing of good deeds. Men are aided by his counsel, sagacity, understanding, and strength. It gives him a regal appearance, a manner that commands respect, and the capacity to be searching in judgment. Secret meanings of the Torah are revealed to him, and he becomes a fountain that never ceases and a stream that gathers strength. With it, he is modest, long suffering, and forgiving of personal slight. The Torah makes him great and exalts him above all of God's works.[5]

113. R. Alexandri said: He who studies Torah for its own sake makes peace in the household above and in the household below. Rav said: It is as though he built the Temple above and the Temple below. R. Yohanan said: He shields the whole world, all of it, [from the consequences of sin]. Levi said: He also brings redemption nearer.[6]

114. R. Jeremiah said in the name of R. Eleazar: When two disciples of the wise sharpen each other['s wit] through discussion of *Halakhah*, the Holy One gives them success, for Scripture says, "In thy majesty [*va-hadarekha*] be successful" (Ps. 45:5). Read not *va-hadarekha*, but *va-hadadekha*, "thy sharpening."

Moreover, they rise to greatness, as is said, they "ride on prosperously" (Ps. 45:5). One might have supposed that this is so even when the discussion in *Halakhah* is not for its own sake. Therefore the verse goes on to say, "In behalf of truth" (ibid.). One might have supposed that this is so even if the disciple of the wise becomes arrogant. Therefore the verse goes on to speak of "meekness and righteousness" (ibid.).[7]

115. We have been taught that R. Banaah used to say: He who occupies himself with Torah for its own sake—the Torah he masters becomes an elixir of life for him. But he who occupies himself with Torah not for its own sake—the Torah becomes for him a deadly poison.[8]

116. R. Judah said in the name of Rav: A man should in any case occupy himself with Torah and its precepts, even if it be not for their own sake, for as he occupies himself with them not for their own sake, he will end up occupying himself with them for their own sake.[9]

They Who Teach Torah and the Ways of Study

117. R. Ishmael said: He who studies in order to teach is afforded adequate means both to study and to teach.[10]

118. R. Yohanan said: He who studies Torah but does not teach it is like a myrtle in the wilderness [from which no one benefits]. Some report the saying as follows: He who studies Torah and teaches it in a place where there are no disciples of the wise[11] is like a myrtle in the wilderness, which is particularly precious, because whoever wishes to take instruction from him can do so.[12]

---

1. B. Ber 48b.
2. B. Suk 49b.
3. B. Ned 62a and En Yaakov, ad loc.
4. Avot 4:5.
5. Avot 6:1.
6. B. Sanh 99b.
7. B. Shab 63a.
8. B. Ta 7a.
9. B. Naz 23b.
10. Avot 4:5.
11. That is, no mature students, but students eager to learn.
12. B. RH 23a.

119. In expounding the verse "Thine ointments have a goodly fragrance" (Song 1:3), R. Nahman son of R. Hisda said: To what may a disciple of the wise be compared? To a flask containing spikenard ointment. When it is opened, its fragrance goes forth; but when it is covered up, its fragrance does not go forth.[1]

120. R. Judah said in the name of Rav: Whoever withholds a *Halakhah* from a disciple is as though he had robbed him of his ancestral heritage, as is said, "Moses commanded us the Torah, which is the inheritance of the congregation of Jacob" (Deut. 33:4). Ever since the six days of creation, it has been the heritage of all Israel.

P. Hana bar Bizna said in the name of R. Simeon the Pious: When a man withholds a *Halakhah* from a disciple, even fetuses in their mothers' wombs curse him.

And when a man does teach a disciple, what is his reward? He will merit blessings like Joseph's, said R. Sheshet, for it is written, "Blessings shall be upon the head of a *mashbir* [of him that purveyeth]" (Prov. 11:26). The word *mashbir* can refer only to Joseph, of whom it is said, "Joseph was *ha-mashbir* [he that purveyed food] to all the people of the land" (Gen. 42:6).[2]

121. Citing the verse "In the morning sow thy seed, and in the evening withhold not thy hand" (Eccles. 11:6), R. Akiva said: If you raised up many disciples when you were young, do not sit back and raise no others when you are grown old. Indeed, this happened to R. Akiva, who when young had three hundred disciples, all of whom died. Had he not raised seven more disciples when he grew old, he would not have left even one disciple spoken of as his.[3]

122. We have been taught that R. Meir used to say: He who studies Torah but does not teach it is one who "despiseth the word of the Lord" (Num. 15:31).[4]

123. "Though wealth and riches [Torah] are in his house, his generosity endureth forever" (Ps. 112:3). R. Huna and R. Hisda differed in their interpretation of this verse. One said: It applies to a man who studies Torah and teaches it to others. The other said: It applies to a man who writes out the Five Books, the Prophets, and the Writings, and lends these scrolls to others.[5]

124. "Such as have none to take their place[6] fear not God" (Ps. 55:20). R. Yohanan and R. Joshua ben Levi differed concerning the implication of this verse. One said: It refers to a man who has no son. The other said: It refers to a man who leaves no disciple.[7]

125. "And thou shalt teach them diligently to thy sons"[8] (Deut. 6:7)—to your disciples. And so you find in ever so many instances that disciples are called "sons," as in "Ye are the sons of the Lord your God" (Deut. 14:1) and in "The sons of the prophets . . . come forth" (2 Kings 2:3). Were these really sons of the prophets? Were they not in fact disciples? Hence it follows that disciples are called "sons." Thus you also find that Hezekiah king of Judah, who taught the entire Torah to Israel, called them "sons," as in "My sons, be not now negligent" (2 Chron. 29:11). And even as disciples are called "sons," so is the teacher called "father," as in "Elisha saw it, and he cried: 'My father, my father' " (2 Kings 2:12) and in "Now Elisha was fallen sick . . . and Joash the king of Israel came down unto him, and wept over him, and said 'My father, my father' " (2 Kings 13:14).[9]

126. R. Samuel bar Nahmani said in the name of R. Jonathan: When a man teaches Torah to his neighbor's son, Scripture speaks of him as though he had begotten him. Thus it says, "These are the generations of Aaron and Moses" (Num. 3:1), and right after that, "These are the names of the sons of Aaron" (Num. 3:3). This tells you that although Aaron begot them, nevertheless, because Moses taught them, they are [also] called after the name of Moses.[10]

127. Where is the proof that he who teaches Torah to his fellow man is deemed as though he had formed him, articulated his limbs, and brought him into the world? The verse "If thou bringest forth the noble out of that which is worthless, thou shalt be as My mouth" (Jer. 15:19).

Whoever brings even one person under the wings of the Presence is deemed as though he had formed him, articulated his limbs, and brought him into the world.[11]

128. R. Joseph bar Honi said: A man envies everyone except his son and his disciple. One's son, as shown by the example of Solomon;[12] and one's disciple, as shown by Elisha's saying to Elijah, "I pray thee, let a double portion of thy spirit be upon me" (2 Kings 2:9); or, if you prefer, Moses' giving of his spirit to Joshua: "He laid his hands upon him, and commissioned him" (Num. 27:23).[13]

129. He who teaches his neighbor's son Torah will earn the merit of sitting in the academy on high, for Jeremiah is told, "If thou wilt cause [Israel] to repent, then will I bring thee again, and thou shalt stand before Me" (Jer. 15:19). And he who teaches Torah to the son of an unlearned man [*am ha-aretz*]—even if the Holy One has issued an evil decree [against him], He will annul it because of what he is doing, as is said, "If thou bringest forth the noble out of that which is worthless, thou shalt be as My mouth" (ibid.).[14]

---

1. B. AZ 35b.
2. B. Sanh 91b–92a.
3. Tanhuma, *Hayye Sarah*, §6; Tanhuma B, *Hayye Sarah*, §8.
4. B. Sanh 99a.
5. B. Ket 50a.
6. JV: "Such as have no changes."
7. B. BB 116a.
8. There is no duty to teach Torah to daughters.
9. Sif Deut., §34.
10. B. Sanh 19b.
11. Tos Hor 2:7.
12. David's servants came to David and said, "God make the name of Solomon better than thy name!" (1 Kings 1:47), and they were not fearful that David might resent it.
13. B. Sanh 105b.
14. B. BM 85a.

130. Be heedful of the children of the unlearned, for out of them Torah proceeds.[1]

131. Once Rav came to a certain place where, though he had decreed a fast, no rain fell. Presently a reader [in the synagogue] stepped down in front of Rav before the Ark and recited, "He causeth the wind to blow," and the wind blew; then, "He causeth the rain to fall," and rain fell. Rav asked him: What is your occupation? He replied: I am a teacher of young children, teaching Scripture to children of the poor as well as to children of the rich. From him who cannot afford it, I take no payment. Besides, I have a fishpond, and I bribe with fish any boy who refuses [to study] until he comes in to study Scripture.[2]

132. Be heedful of the children of the poor, for out of them Torah proceeds.[3]

133. "Behold, I have taught you statutes and ordinances" (Deut. 4:5). Even as I have taught for free, so you are to teach for free. One might think this applies also to Scripture and its Aramaic translation. But Moses speaks of "statutes and ordinances"—you are to teach statutes and ordinances for free, but you are not expected to teach Scripture and its Aramaic translation for free.[4]

134. "Behold, I have taught you statutes and ordinances, even as the Lord my God commanded me" (Deut. 4:5). Even as I teach for free, said R. Judah, citing Rav, so you should teach for free. And the proof that if you do not find someone who will teach for free, you must be ready to pay for being taught? The verse "Buy the truth" (Prov. 23:23). And the proof that one may not say, "Even as I learned the Torah by paying, so shall I teach it for payment"? [The complete verse] "Buy the truth, but do not sell it" (ibid.).[5]

135. Raise up many pupils.

The school of Shammai says: A man is to teach only one who is wise, humble, of good stock, and rich.

But the school of Hillel says: Every man is to be taught. For there were many transgressors in Israel who were attracted to the study of Torah, and out of them sprang righteous, pious, and worthy men. What parable may illustrate the matter? The one of a woman who sets a hen to brood on eggs—out of many eggs, she may hatch only a few chicks; but out of a few eggs, possibly not even one.[6]

136. R. Hanina bar Papa pointed to a [seeming] contradiction between two verses, one saying, "Unto him that is thirsty, bring ye water" (Isa. 21:14), and the other saying, "Ho, everyone that thirsteth, come ye for water" (Isa. 55:1). The solution is: If the disciple is worthy, "Unto him that is thirsty, bring ye water"; but if he is not, then, "Ho, everyone that thirsteth, come ye for water."

R. Hanina bar Hama pointed to another [seeming] contradiction between two verses, one saying, "Let thy springs be dispersed abroad" (Prov. 5:16), and the other, "Let them be only thine own" (Prov. 5:17). The solution is: If the disciple is worthy, "Let thy springs be dispersed abroad"; but if he is not, "Let them be thine own."[7]

137. R. Zera said in the name of Rabbi [Judah I, the Patriarch]: When a man teaches a disciple who is unworthy, he is as much of an idolater as one who tosses a pebble on a statue of Mercury, as is said, "As a pebble upon a statue of stones,[8] so is he that giveth honor to a fool" (Prov. 26:8), "honor" here meaning Torah, as in the verse "The wise shall inherit honor" (Prov. 3:35).[9]

138. Our masters taught: Always, while your left hand repulses, make your right hand draw near. Not like Elisha, who repulsed Gehazi with both hands, and not like Joshua ben Perahiah, who repulsed Jesus with both hands.[10]

139. Hillel the Elder said: When scholars keep [the Torah] to themselves, you must disseminate [it]; and when they disseminate [it], you may keep [it] to yourself.[11] When you see that the Torah is beloved by Israel and all rejoice in it, spread it abroad, as is said, "There is that scattereth, and yet increaseth" (Prov. 11:24). But when you see that the Torah is forgotten in Israel and that the generality give it no heed, keep it to yourself, as is said, "It is time to work only for the Lord, when they make void Thy Torah" (Ps. 119:126).[12]

140. R. Simeon ben Yohai taught: If you see whole villages of people that have been plucked up from their place in the Land of Israel, know that it is because they failed to provide fees for teachers of Scripture and teachers of Mishnah. And the proof? The words "Wherefore is the Land perished?" (Jer. 9:11), which are followed directly by "Because they have forsaken My Torah" (Jer. 9:12).[13]

141. R. Judah said in the name of Rav: The name of that man, Joshua ben Gamla, should always be mentioned on good occasions. But for him, the Torah would have been forgotten in Israel. Formerly, if a child had a father [living], his father taught him Torah; if he had no father, he did not learn Torah. By what verse did they guide themselves? By the verse "Ye shall teach them to your children" (Deut. 11:19), which they read, "Ye shall teach, even ye,[14] [to your children]. Then it was ordained that

1. B. Sanh 96a.
2. B. Ta 24a and En Yaakov, ad loc.
3. B. Ned 81a.
4. A father is expected to teach the basics to his own son. P. Ned 4:3, 38a.
5. B. Bekh 29a.
6. Avot 1:1; ARN 2; ARNB 4.
7. B. Ta 7a.
8. The word *margemah*, found only here, has been variously rendered. The Vulgate follows the rabbinic interpretation, namely, that a shrine of Mercury is referred to.
9. B. Hul 133a and En Yaakov, ad loc.
10. B. Sot 47a and En Yaakov, ad loc.
11. Do not endeavor to compete.
12. Tos Ber 7:24; B. Ber 63a.
13. P. Hag 1:7, 76c.
14. The word *otam* ("them") is read *attem* ("even ye," "you yourselves").

teachers of young children should be set up in Jerusalem. By what verse did they guide themselves? By the verse "The Torah shall go forth out of Zion" (Isa. 2:3). Even so, if a child had a father, the father would take him up to Jerusalem and have him taught; if he had no father, the child would not go up and study. Then it was ordained that teachers of youths be set up in each district and that youths enter school at the age of sixteen or seventeen. But when a teacher was annoyed with one of them, that one would rebel against the teacher and leave school. So Joshua ben Gamla came along and ordained that teachers of little children be set up in each district and in each town, and that children enter school at the age of six or seven.[1]

142. "And they that turn the many to righteousness shall be as the stars" (Dan. 12:3). These are teachers of young children. Such as who, for example? Such, Rav said, as R. Samuel bar Shilat.

Rav once found R. Samuel bar Shilat standing in his garden patch. Rav asked him, "Have you given up the task entrusted to you?" R. Samuel replied, "I have not looked at this patch for thirteen years, and even at this moment my thoughts are with the children."[2]

143. Rav advised R. Samuel ben Shilat: Do not accept a child before the age of six. After that age, accept him, and stuff Torah into him as though he were an ox [to be fattened].

Rav also advised R. Samuel ben Shilat: When you spank a child, use only the thongs of a sandal. He also advised: The bright child who is quick to learn will learn to read quickly [by himself]; and the one who is not quick—seat him next to one who is.[3]

144. Rava said: The maximum number of pupils to be assigned to each teacher of little children is twenty-five. If there are fifty children, two teachers are to be appointed. If there are forty, the teacher should be given an assistant to be paid by the city.

Rava also said: If there is a teacher of children who studies just enough to keep up with them, and there is another who studies more than enough, do not remove the first, lest the second become indolent. Rather, said R. Dimi of Nehardea, if the first were allowed to continue, the second would be likely to exert himself even more, for "the jealousy of scribes increases wisdom."

Rava further said: If there are two teachers, one of whom covers much ground but is not exact, and the other is exact but does not cover much ground, the one who covers ground but is not exact is to be appointed. And the reason? In time, mistakes correct themselves. However, R. Dimi of Nehardea maintained that the one who is exact and does not cover much ground is to be appointed. The reason? A mistake once implanted [in a mind] stays. That this is so can be shown from the following verse: "Joab and all Israel remained until he had cut off every male in Edom" (1 Kings 11:16). When Joab came before David, David asked him: Why have you acted thus [killed only the males]? Joab replied: Because it is written, "Thou shalt cut out the males [*zekhar*] of Amalek" (Deut. 25:19). David: But we read, "The remembrance [*zekher*] of Amalek." Joab: I was taught to read *zekhar* ["male"]. He then went to his teacher and asked: How did you teach me to read it? The teacher: *Zekhar* ["male"]. At that, Joab seized a sword to kill him. The teacher: Why? Joab: Because it says, "Cursed be he that doeth the work of the Lord negligently" (Jer. 48:10). The teacher: Let me be. It is enough that I am to be cursed. Joab: But the verse goes on to say, "Cursed be he that keepeth back his sword from blood" (ibid.). Some say Joab did kill him. Others say that he did not.[4]

145. When you teach your son, teach him from a corrected scroll.[5]

146. Hillel said: An impatient man is not fit to be a teacher.[6]

147. A Persian came to Rav and said, "Teach me the Torah." Rav consented and said to the Persian, "Say *alef*." The Persian: "Who says this is *alef*? Perhaps this is not an *alef*." Rav: "Say *bet*." The Persian: "Who says this is *bet*?" At that, Rav scolded him and drove him out in anger. He then went to Samuel and said, "Teach me the Torah." Samuel: "Say *alef*." The Persian: "Who says this is *alef*?" Samuel: "Say *bet*." The Persian: "Who says this is *bet*?" Samuel then grabbed the Persian's ear. The Persian: "My ear, my ear!" Samuel: "Who says this is your ear?" The Persian: "Everybody knows this is my ear." Samuel: "The same way everybody knows this is *alef* and that is *bet*." At that, the Persian kept quiet and accepted the instruction.

Hence, "the patient in spirit is better than the proud in spirit" (Eccles. 7:8).[7]

148. Rava said: If you see a student whose studies come as hard to him as iron, it is because his teacher does not encourage him.[8]

149. R. Perida had a pupil to whom he had to repeat his lesson four hundred times before he was able to learn it. One day R. Perida was invited to a religious celebration; that day also R. Perida kept repeating the lesson, but the student did not learn it. R. Perida: "Why are you different today?" The student: "The moment the master was told, 'There is a religious celebration,' my attention wandered, for I kept saying to myself: The master is about to get up and leave, the master is about to get up and leave." R. Perida: "Pay attention now, and I will teach you [once more]." He repeated the lesson another four hundred times, and the student learned it.

---

1. B. BB 21a and En Yaakov, ad loc.
2. B. BB 8b.
3. B. BB 21a and En Yaakov, ad loc.
4. B. BB 21a–b.
5. B. Pes 112a.
6. Avot 2:5.
7. Eccles. R. 7:8, §1.
8. B. Ta 7b–8a.

Then a divine voice came forth and said, "Do you prefer that four hundred years be added to your life, or that you and your generation merit life in the world-to-come?" R. Perida: "I prefer that I and my generation merit life in the world-to-come." The Holy One said, "Give him the one and the other as well."[1]

150. "And the Lord spoke to Moses of facet after facet" (Exod. 33:11).[2] According to R. Isaac, the Holy One said to Moses: Moses, both of us—I [to you] and you [to Israel]—are to make clear *Halakhah*'s varying facets. But according to others [who read the verse "face to face"], the Holy One said to Moses: Moses, even as I showed you a cheerful face [to encourage you to study Torah], so you are to show a cheerful face to Israel [to encourage them to study Torah].[3]

151. R. Hanina bar Papa said: The Holy One appeared to Israel with an awe-inspiring face, with an equanimous face, a friendly face, a joyous face. With an awe-inspiring face for Scripture—when a man teaches his son Scripture, he should teach it in the spirit of awe; an equanimous face for Mishnah; a friendly face for Talmud; a joyous face for *Aggadah.*[4]

152. We have been taught: "Make them known unto thy children and thy children's children" (Deut. 4:9). Directly after that it is said, "The day that thou stoodest before the Lord thy God in Horeb" (Deut. 4:10). Even as at Sinai it was with awe and fear, with trembling and trepidation, so in teaching, it should be with awe and fear, with trembling and trepidation.[5]

153. Before beginning his discourse to the sages, Rabbah used to say something humorous in order to amuse them. After that, he sat down and with awe began to discourse on *Halakhah.*[6]

154. Once, while R. Akiva was in the teacher's chair expounding Scripture, the assembly became drowsy. Wishing to stir them awake, he said: Why did Esther think she deserved to rule one hundred and twenty-seven provinces? Because, [R. Akiva suggested], Esther, being a descendant of Sarah, who lived one hundred and twenty-seven years, [thought that she] should come and rule one hundred and twenty-seven provinces.[7]

155. As Rabbi [Judah I, the Patriarch] was in the teacher's chair expounding Scripture, the assembly became drowsy. Wishing to stir them awake, he said, "A woman brought forth six hundred thousand in a single birth." There was a certain disciple there, named R. Ishmael son of R. Yose, who asked, "Who can that have been?" Rabbi [Judah] replied, "That was Jochebed, who bore Moses, deemed equal to six hundred thousand of Israel."[8]

156. Our masters taught: What procedure was followed at instruction in the Oral Torah? Moses learned from the mouth of the Almighty. Then Aaron entered, and Moses taught him his lesson. Aaron then moved aside and sat down at Moses' left. Then Aaron's sons entered, and Moses taught them their lesson. The sons then moved aside, Eleazar taking his seat at Moses' right and Ithamar at Aaron's left. Then the elders came in, and Moses taught them their lesson. After the elders moved aside, all the people came in, and Moses taught them their lesson. It follows that Aaron heard the lesson four times, his sons three times, the elders twice, and the people once. At this time Moses left, and Aaron taught them his lesson. Then Aaron left, and his sons taught them their lesson. Then the sons left, and the elders taught them their lesson. It thus follows that everybody heard the lesson four times. From the aforementioned procedure, R. Eliezer inferred: It is a man's duty to repeat a lesson to his pupil four times, a practice that may be deduced by an argument *a fortiori:* if Aaron, who learned from Moses, and Moses, who learned [directly] from the Almighty, had to have their lesson repeated four times, all the more so by far an ordinary pupil who learns from an ordinary teacher.

But R. Akiva said: How do we know that a man must keep repeating a lesson to his pupil until he has taught it to him? From the verse "And *teach* thou it to the children of Israel" (Deut. 31:19). And the proof that the lesson must be so put to them that they get a systematic grasp of it? The verse "Put it in their mouths" (ibid.). And the proof that the various facets of meaning must be set forth? The verse "These are the ordinances which thou shalt set forth in the facets of their meaning"[9] (Exod. 21:1). "Thou shalt set before them" (Exod. 21:1)—set these ordinances before them as a table is set, just as Scripture says, "Unto thee it was shown, that thou mightest know" (Deut. 4:35).[10]

157. What purpose was served by the empty spaces that occur from time to time in the written text of Scripture?[11] To give Moses time to reflect between one passage and the next, between one subject and the next. This is a matter that may be inferred *a fortiori:* if he who hears words from the mouth of the Holy One and himself speaks with the holy spirit requires reflection between one passage and the next, between one subject and the next, how much more by far is reflection required by one who is a mere commoner taught by another commoner.[12]

1. B. Er 54b.
2. JV: "face to face." But the implication that God has a face being inadmissible stimulates the two comments that follow.
3. B. Ber 63b.
4. See above, part 1, proem, §19. Tanhuma B, *Yitro,* §17; Yalkut, Exod., §286.
5. B. Ber 22a.
6. B. Pes 117a.
7. Gen. R. 58:3.
8. Song R. 1:15, §3.
9. JV: "set forth before them [*lifnehem*]." But *lifnehem* may also mean facets, or meaning and reasons for the commandments.
10. B. Er 54b and En Yaakov, ad loc; Mek, *Mishpatim, Nezikin,* 1.
11. Passages that begin at the beginning of a line are called *petuhot* (open); those beginning in the middle of a line are called *setumot* (closed). Each such passage is preceded by empty space, which contains only the letter *pe* for *petuhah* or the letter *samekh* for *setumah.*
12. Sif Lev. 1:1 (ed. Weiss, p. 3c).

158. It is said in the name of R. Meir: A teacher should always teach in as few words as possible. Thus we have been taught that Rabbi [Judah I, the Patriarch] said: It is known and manifest to Him who spoke and the world came into being that unclean animals outnumber those that are clean; therefore Scripture enumerates only the clean. On the other hand, it is known and manifest to Him who spoke and the world came into being that clean birds outnumber those that are unclean; therefore Scripture enumerates only the unclean.[1]

159. Our masters taught: "*Ve-shinnantam* ['Make them sharp']" (Deut. 6:7)[2]—see to it that words of Torah are sharply and readily articulated in your mouth, so that if a man inquires of you about a certain matter, you will not have to hem and haw before answering him, but you will be able to answer him at once. As is said, "Say unto wisdom: 'Thou art my sister,' and call understanding thine intimate friend" (Prov. 7:4); and, "Happy is the man that hath his quiver full of them; they shall not be put to shame, when they speak with their enemies in the gate" (Ps. 127:5).[3]

160. R. Yohanan ben Torta once came before R. Akiva, who said to him, "Stand up and read the portion of the week." R. Yohanan replied, "But I have not yet gone over it." The sages said that he was right to refuse.[4]

161. "And God spoke all these words, saying" (Exod. 20:1). The Torah teaches you: if you are a man of learning, do not be so arrogant as to say something in front of an assembly before you have made the matter clear to yourself by going over it two or three times.

It happened to R. Akiva that the sexton of the synagogue publicly invited him to read the Torah before the congregation, but he refused to go up. His disciples asked him: Our master, did you not teach us: "That is thy life, and the length of thy days" (Deut. 30:20)? Why then did you refuse to go up [to the dais]? R. Akiva replied: By the [Temple] worship, it was not that I refused to read the Torah portion. I did not go up because [I was not prepared for it]. I had not gone over the portion carefully two or three times. For a man is not allowed to read a portion of Scripture in public unless he has made its words thoroughly clear to himself by going over them two or three times. We find this to be so even in the Holy One, who has given the capacity of speech to all mortals and to whom the Torah is as clear as a star [in heaven]. Yet of Him, when He was about to give the Torah to Israel, Scripture says, "Then He did see it, and declare it; He prepared it thoroughly, and searched it out" (Job 28:27). And only after that, Scripture says, "Unto man He said" (Job 28:28). So, too, it is written, "And the Lord spoke all these words" (Exod. 20:1)—spoke them first to Himself; and only after that, "saying" (ibid.) to Israel.[5]

162. R. Abbahu said: What is the proof that a master should not sit on a couch teaching a disciple who sits crouched on the ground? From the verse "But as for thee, do thou stand here by Me" (Deut. 5:28).

Our masters taught: From the days of Moses until Rabban Gamaliel, Torah was studied only while standing. But after Rabban Gamaliel died, feebleness came down upon the world, and they began to study Torah while seated. Indeed, this is what we conclude from the saying "Ever since Rabban Gamaliel died, adequate honor ceased to be given to the Torah."[6]

163. Avtalion said: O sages, be careful with your words, lest you be condemned to exile[7] and be exiled to a place of evil waters,[8] and the disciples who follow you [into exile] drink of them and die [spiritually], with the result that the Name of Heaven will be profaned.[9]

They Who Study Torah and the Ways of Study

164. Resh Lakish said in the name of R. Judah [II] the Patriarch: The world endures only because of the breath of schoolchildren. R. Papa asked Abbaye: what about my breath and yours [the breath of men who have given themselves to Torah]? Abbaye answered: The breath of one who now has sin is not like the breath of one who is still without sin.

Resh Lakish said in the name of R. Judah [II] the Patriarch: One may not neglect schoolchildren even in order to erect the Temple.

Resh Lakish also said to R. Judah [II] the Patriarch: I have a tradition from my forebears (according to some, [Resh Lakish said]: from your forebears) that a city that has no children at school will be destroyed.[10]

165. R. Meir said: When Israel stood before Mount Sinai to receive the Torah, the Holy One said to them: By the [Temple] worship, I am about to give you the Torah. But you must [first] give Me good sureties that you will keep it, and then I will give it to you. They replied: Master of the universe, our patriarchs will be sureties for us, our prophets will be sureties for us. The Holy One: These also require sureties for their own persons. You yourselves must bring Me better sureties, and I will give it to you. Israel: Behold, our children will be surety for us. The Holy One: Certainly these are excellent sureties. On account of them will I give you the Torah.[11]

166. R. Hamnuna said: Jerusalem was destroyed only because teaching children at school had ceased, as is said, "Pour it [God's wrath] out upon the children in the street"

1. See Lev. 11 and Deut. 14. B. Hul 63b.
2. JV: "Thou shalt teach them diligently."
3. B. Kid 30a–b.
4. Exod. R. 40:1.
5. Tanhuma, *Yitro*, §15.
6. B. Meg 21a.
7. By the Sadducees in power.
8. Of heretical teachings—a place such as Alexandria.
9. Avot 1:11.
10. B. Shab 119b.
11. Song R. 1:4, §1.

(Jer. 6:11). Why "Pour it out"? Because "children [are] in the street" and not at school.[1]

167. "And it came to pass [*va-yehi*][2] in the days of Ahaz the son of Jotham" (Isa. 7:1). What occasion for woe was there in this instance? The answer may be provided by the parable of a king who turned over his son to a tutor, who hated the son. So he said: If I slay him right away, I will forfeit my head to the king. Instead, I will withdraw his wetnurse,[3] and he will presently die naturally. Ahaz said the same thing: If there are no kids, there will be no he-goats. If there are no he-goats, there will be no flocks. If there are no flocks, there will be no shepherd. If there is no shepherd, there will be no world [for people will have no food]. So Ahaz said to himself: If there are no little ones, there will be no disciples. If there are no disciples, there will be no sages. If there are no sages, there will be no elders. If there are no elders, there will be no prophets. If there are no prophets, there will be no holy spirit. If there is no holy spirit, the Holy One will not cause His Presence to rest upon Israel. What did Ahaz do? He sealed up all synagogues and houses of study. This is implied in the words "Bind up the testimony, seal up instruction among My disciples" (Isa. 8:16). When everyone saw that Ahaz had seized [*ahaz*] synagogues and houses of study, they began crying, "Woe, woe!"[4]

168. R. Abba bar Kahana said: Among the nations of the world there have risen no philosophers like Balaam son of Beor and Oenomaus of Gadara.[5] When all the nations came to them and asked, "Can we take on this nation of Israel in battle?" they replied, "Go out and make the rounds of their synagogues and houses of study. If you come upon children within them, chirping away in their childish voices, you will be unable to take on this nation in battle. For what [Isaac] their father promised to his descendants was this: 'Either the voice of Jacob; or else the hands—the hands of Esau' (Gen. 27:22).[6] As long as the voice of Jacob is heard in synagogues and houses of study, the hands will not be the hands of Esau. But if not, 'the hands will be the hands of Esau,' that is, you will be able to take them on in battle."[7]

169. Every day an angel goes out from the presence of the Holy One to destroy the world and to turn it back to what it used to be. But once the Holy One observes young children in their schools and disciples of the wise in their houses of study, His anger immediately turns into mercy.[8]

1. B. Shab 119b.
2. The word *va-yehi* is taken to suggest an occasion for woe (*vay*).
3. In the East, children are nursed years longer than in the West.
4. P. Sanh 10:2, 28b; Gen. R. 42:3; Lev. R. 11:7.
5. A cynic philosopher of Gadara in the Land of Israel who lived during the reign of the emperor Hadrian (117–38 C.E.).
6. JV: "The voice is the voice of Jacob, but the hands are the hands of Esau."
7. Gen. R. 65:20; Lam. R., proem 2.
8. Ka R. 2.

170. R. Judah said in the name of Rav: What is meant by "Touch not Mine anointed ones, and do My prophets no harm" (Ps. 105:15)? "Touch not Mine anointed ones"—children in school; "and do My prophets"—disciples of the wise—"no harm."[9]

171. R. Judah son of R. Simon said: Come and see how beloved children are before the Holy One. When the ten tribes were banished, the Presence did not go into exile with them. When Judah and Benjamin were banished, the Presence did not go into exile with them. When the Sanhedrin was banished, the Presence did not go into exile with it. When the priestly watches on duty were banished, the Presence did not go into exile with them. But when schoolchildren were banished, the Presence did go into exile with them. Scripture refers to this in the verse "Her young children are gone into captivity before the adversary" (Lam. 1:5), which is followed at once by "Gone is from fair Zion all her splendor" (Lam. 1:6).[10]

172. "I went down into the garden of nuts" (Song 6:11)—this is the world; "to look at the green plants of the valley" (ibid.)—these are Israel; "to see whether the vine had blossomed" (ibid.)—this is synagogues and houses of study; "and the pomegranates were in flower" (ibid.)—these are young children who sit occupied with Torah and are arrayed in row upon row, like the seeds of a pomegranate.[11]

173. The sages said to R. Joshua ben Levi: Today some young children came to the house of study and told us things[12] the likes of which had not been said even in the days of Joshua son of Nun:

Alef bet means "Learn wisdom (*alef binah*)."

Gimmel dalet means "Be kind to the poor (*gemol dallim*)." Why is the foot of the *gimmel* stretched toward the base of the *dalet?* Because it is the way of the benevolent to run after the poor [to help them out].

And why is the foot of the *dalet* stretched toward the *gimmel?* Because the poor must make himself available to the benevolent.

And why is the face of the *dalet* averted from the *gimmel?* Because help must be given in secrecy, so that the poor will not be humiliated by the presence of the giver.

He and *vav* are two letters that form [part of] the [Ineffable] Name of the Holy One, blessed be He.

Zayin, het, tet, yod, kaf, lamed: If you act thus [as commanded], the Holy One will sustain (*zan*) you, be gracious (*han*) to you, show goodness (*metiv*) to you, give you a heritage (*yerushah*), and bind a crown (*keter*) about your head in the world-to-come (*le-olam ha-ba*).

The open *mem* and the closed [final] *mem* signify that one utterance [in Scripture] may be open and another may be closed [esoteric].[13]

9. B. Shab 119b.
10. Lam. R. 1:5, §32.
11. Song R. 6:11, §1.
12. About the Hebrew alphabet, which they had just learned.
13. And inquiry into it may be forbidden. See above, part 1, chap. 2, §1–3.

The bent *nun* and the upright [final] *nun* mean that he who is faithful (*ne'eman*) when bent with suffering [in this world] will be made upright [in the world-to-come].

Samekh and *ayin* stand for "Uphold the poor (*semokh aniyyim*)." (Others say: The two letters stand for "Devise [*aseh*] mnemonics [*simmanim*] in Scripture and thus commit it to memory.")

The bent *pe* and the [final] open *pe* signify that there are times when the mouth (*peh*) should be open and times when it should stay closed.

The bent *tzade* and the erect [final] *tzade* signify that while in this world the righteous man (*tzaddik*) is bent down, in the world-to-come he will be enabled to stand erect.

Kof signifies "holy (*kadosh*)." *Resh* signifies "wicked (*rasha*)."

Why is the face of the *kof* averted from the *resh*? Because the Holy One says, "I cannot bear looking at the wicked."

And why is the upper tip on the crown over the *kof* turned toward the *resh*? Because the Holy One says: If the wicked (*rasha*) repents, I will bind a crown over his head like the crown over the *kof*.

And why is the leg of the *kof* detached from its upper part? To show that when the wicked man (*rasha*) repents, he can enter through the opening between the two parts of the *kof*.

Shin stands for "falsehood (*sheker*)," and *tav* for "truth" (*emet*). Why do the letters of *sheker* in the alphabet closely follow one another, while the letters of *emet* are far apart?[1] Because falsehoods follow close upon one another, while truth is encountered only at intervals far apart.

And why does *sheker* (falsehood) stand on one leg,[2] while *emet*, (truth) is made up of the letters *alef*, *mem*, and *tav*, which have [solid] bricklike bases?[3] Because truth stands firmly; falsehood does not.[4]

174. R. Assi said: Why are young children started with [Leviticus], the Torah of priests, and not with Genesis? Because the Holy One said: Young children are pure and offerings are pure—let them who are pure engage themselves with matters of purity.[5]

175. Elisha ben Avuyah used to say: When a man learns Torah while young, the words of Torah are absorbed into his very blood and issue from his mouth in explicit form. But when a man learns Torah in his old age, the words of Torah are not absorbed into his blood and do not issue from his mouth in explicit form. Hence the proverb: If you did not long for them in your youth, how do you expect to attain them in your old age?

He also used to say: When a man learns Torah in his youth, what may he be compared to? To ink written on a clean sheet. When a man learns in his old age? To ink written on a sheet from which the original writing has been erased.[6]

176. R. Nehorai used to say: When a man learns Torah in his youth, he may be compared to dough that has been kneaded with warm water.[7] When a man learns Torah during his advanced years, he may be compared to dough that has been kneaded with cold water.[8]

177. Rabban Simeon ben Gamaliel said: When a man learns Torah while young, he is like a young man who has married a virgin—she is right for him and he is right for her; she feels passion for him and he feels passion for her. But when a man of advanced years studies Torah, whom may he be compared to? To a man of advanced years who has married a virgin—she may be right for him, but he is not right for her; she may feel passion for him, but he shies away from her.[9]

178. At the age of three, a child is ready for the letters of the alphabet.[10]

179. Judah ben Tema used to say: At the age of five, [a child is ready] for Scripture. At ten, for Mishnah. . . . At fifteen, for Talmud.[11]

180. A pupil who shows no discernible advance in his studies after five years is not likely ever to show it. R. Yose asserted: After three years, for it is said, "To be taught the learning and the language of the Chaldeans . . . they are to be trained three years" (Dan. 1:4–5).[12]

181. "His delight is in the Torah of the Lord" (Ps. 1:2). Rabbi [Judah I, the Patriarch] said: A man learns well only that part of the Torah which delights him, for the verse implies, "[The part of] the Torah of the Lord a man delights in [becomes his]."

Levi and R. Simeon Berabbi were seated before Rabbi [Judah I, the Patriarch] and were expounding verses of Scripture. When the book they were at was finished, Levi said: Let the book of Proverbs be brought. R. Simeon Berabbi said: Let the book of Psalms be brought. Levi was overruled, and the book of Psalms was brought. When they got to the verse "His delight is in the Torah of the Lord," Rabbi, expounding it, said: A man learns well only that part of the Torah which delights him. At that, Levi said: Master, you have just now given me permission to get up and leave.[13]

---

1. The *alef* at the beginning, the *mem* in the middle, and the *tav* at the end.
2. The long stroke of *kof*, the second letter of the *sheker*, extends below the line, so the word looks as if it is standing on one leg.
3. Both the *alef* and the *tav* rest on two legs, while the *mem* has a horizontal bar as its base.
4. B. Shab 104a.
5. Lev. R. 7:3; Yalkut, *Tzav*, §479.
6. ARN 24; Avot 4:20.
7. And stays together.
8. It does not stay together. ARN 23.
9. Ibid.
10. Midrash cited by *Darkhe Moshe* on Tur Yoreh Deah, §245. See also Tanhuma, *Kedoshim*, §14.
11. Avot 5:21.
12. B. Hul 24a.
13. B. AZ 19a.

182. Resh Lakish said: If you see a disciple whose studies are as hard as iron for him, it is because he has not arranged his study in systematic fashion. What is his remedy? To attend the sessions of the sages more regularly.[1]

183. R. Ammi said: What is signified by the verse "It is a pleasant thing if thou keepest them in thy belly; then they will be established altogether upon thy lips" (Prov. 22:18)? When are words of Torah "pleasant"? "When you guard them within your inmost being [in your belly, so to speak]." And when may you be said to keep them within your inmost being? When they are "established altogether upon thy lips."[2]

184. Beruriah [wife of R. Meir] once came upon a disciple who merely whispered the words while studying. She reprimanded him sharply. Is it not said, "If ordered in all parts, then sure" (2 Sam. 23:5)? If what you study is "ordered" [reverberates] in the two hundred and forty-eight parts of your body, "it is sure." If not, it is not sure.

R. Eliezer ben Jacob had a disciple who merely whispered the words while studying. After three years, he forgot his learning.[3]

185. Samuel said to R. Judah: You may be a keen scholar. Nevertheless, when you read Scripture, speak out When you repeat Mishnah, speak out, so that you may retain what you study, for Scripture says, "They are life to those that find them" (Prov. 4:22). Read not, "To those that find them (*motz'ehem*)," but, "To those that enunciate them clearly with their mouths (*motzi'ehem*)."[4]

186. R. Yohanan said: As certain as a formal covenant is the assurance that he who studies *Aggadah* from a book will not soon forget it, for Scripture says, "Thou wilt not forget the things which thine eyes saw" (Deut. 4:9).[5]

187. R. Shefatiah said in the name of R. Yohanan: When a man reads Scripture without its cantillation or recites Mishnah without its tune, [his not singing Scripture or Mishnah with love all but implies, says God, that] "I gave them statutes that they do not find pleasing, and ordinances they will not live by" (Ezek: 20:25).[6]

188. When words of Torah come out from the mouths of those who utter them in the way they should, the words are sweet to those who hear them. But when they come out indistinctly, they are bitter to those who hear them.[7]

189. R. Simeon ben Lakish said: He who utters words of Torah so that they are not sweet to those who hear them would do better not to utter them at all.[8]

1. B. Ta 7b–8a.
2. By your clear and systematic utterance of them. B. Er 54a.
3. B. Er 53b–54a.
4. B. Er 54a.
5. P. Ber 5:1, 9a.
6. B. Meg 32a.
7. P. Sanh 10:1, 28a.
8. Exod. R. 41:5.

190. Rava said: One should always study Torah first, then meditate upon it. For Scripture says, "His delight is in the Torah of the Lord" (Ps. 1:2), and only after that, "And in His law doth he meditate" (ibid.).

Rava also said: A man should keep studying, even though he forgets, even though he does not quite understand what he is studying, for it is said, "My soul breaketh up for the longing that it hath unto Thy ordinances at all times" (Ps. 119:20). The psalm says, "Breaketh up," and not, "Grindeth thoroughly."[9]

191. The systematic arranger of traditions is more highly regarded than the dialectician.[10]

192. R. Judah said: A man should always gather words of Torah in the form of general principles and bring them forth as specific details. For if he gathers them as specific details, they will so weary him that he will find himself helpless. A parable of a man who, when about to go to Caesarea, needed one or two hundred *zuz* for expenses. If he took them in the form of one-*zuz* coins, they would so wear him out that he would be helpless. But if he changes the *zuz* into [large coins]—*sela* or gold denars—and then, as needed, changes them back into *zuz*, he can spend them whenever he wishes.[11]

193. R. Hisda said: The Torah can be acquired only by mnemonic signs, for it is said, "Put it (*simah*) in their mouths" (Deut. 31:19). Read not *simah*, "put it," but *simanah*, "its mnemonic signs."[12]

194. "See, and remember" (Num. 15:39). Seeing assures remembering.[13]

195. All words of Torah need one another, for what one word closes, another opens.[14]

196. The sages taught in the name of R. Nehemiah: "She is like the merchant ships; she bringeth her food from afar" (Prov. 31:14). Words of Torah that are meagerly expressed in one passage [are illumined by] a related passage in which their meaning is richly set forth.[15]

9. In the verse as construed, the intellect (soul) is compared to a mill and is seen as satisfied by merely breaking up the kernels of grain without turning them into fine flour. B. AZ 19a.
10. P. Hor 3:5, 48c.
11. Sif Deut., §306 (ed. Finkelstein, p. 336).
12. B. Er 54b and En Yaakov, ad loc.
13. B. Men 43b.
14. Tanhuma B, *Hukkat*, §52.
15. The verse "And the Lord spoke unto Moses and unto Aaron, and gave them a charge unto the children of Israel" (Exod. 7:13) is "meager," because the nature of the charge is not indicated. But this verse, it should be noted, follows another in which Moses is commanded to tell Pharaoh to let the children of Israel go out of servitude. The rich meaning of the "meagerly expressed" passage becomes clear when it is read together with the account of the Judeans who, despite a solemn covenant, brought back into servitude the slaves they had freed (Jer. 34:8–12). This "covenant" is taken to refer to the "charge unto the children of Israel" given by Moses. Thus a "meager" passage is illumined by a related passage "rich" in import. P. RH 3:5, 58d.

197. "As the small rain upon the tender grass" (Deut. 32:2). As the light rain coming down upon tender blades of grass stirs them up so that they do not become wormy, so must you keep stirring the memory of words of Torah, in order not to forget them. Thus R. Jacob son of R. Hanina said to Rabbi [Judah I, the Patriarch]: Come, let us stir up *Halakhot,* lest our memory of them become rusty.[1]

198. R. Hiyya bar Abba, expounding Scripture in the name of R. Yohanan, said: "Whoso keepeth the fig tree shall eat the fruit thereof" (Prov. 27:18). Why are words of Torah likened to the fig tree? As with the fig tree, the more one tends it, the more figs one finds on it, so with words of Torah: the more one studies them, the more relish one finds in them.[2]

199. He who repeats his chapter one hundred times does not compare to him who repeats it a hundred and one times.[3]

200. R. Joshua ben Korhah said: He who studies Torah and does not go over what he has studied is like a man who sows but does not reap.

R. Joshua also said: He who studies Torah and forgets it is like a woman who bears a child and buries it.

R. Akiva said: Chant it every day, chant it every day![4]

201. R. Dostai bar Yannai said in the name of R. Meir: When a man forgets a single word of what he has studied, Scripture deems it as though he had forfeited his life, for it is said, "Only take heed to thyself and keep thy soul diligently, that thou forget not the things thine eyes saw" (Deut. 4:9). One might have inferred that this is so even when study proves too difficult for him. Hence Scripture goes on to say, "That they be not removed from thy heart all the days of thy life" (ibid.)—a man forfeits his life only if he deliberately removes words of Torah from his heart.[5]

202. Elisha ben Avuyah used to say: A man may study Torah for twenty years and forget it in two. How? If he sits idly for six months without reviewing [what he has learned], he will find himself declaring that which is unclean clean and that which is clean unclean. If he is idle for twelve months without reviewing, he will find himself mixing up the names of the sages. If he is idle for eighteen months without reviewing, he will forget the substance of whole tractates he had studied. If he is idle for twenty-four months without reviewing, he will forget the substance even of individual chapters. Now, since he has declared what was unclean clean and what was clean unclean, mixed up the name of one sage with another, and forgot the substance of whole tractates he studied and the substance of individual chapters he studied, in the end he will be compelled to sit in silence. Of him, Solomon said, "I went by the field of the slothful, and by the vineyard of the man void of understanding; and lo, it was all grown over with thistles, the face thereof was covered with nettles, and the stone wall thereof was broken down" (Prov. 24:30–31). Once the wall collapses, the entire vineyard, all of it, goes to rack and ruin.[6]

203. R. Simeon ben Lakish said: In the Scroll of the Pious[7] the following was found: "If you leave me [Torah] for one day, I will leave you for two." These words may be illustrated by the parable of two men who set out, one from Tiberias and the other from Sepphoris, and met at an inn. Then, not long after they separated, one had walked a *mil* [one way] and the other had walked a *mil* [the other way], so that they found themselves two *mil* apart from each other. Or by the parable of a woman who was waiting for a man. As long as he intended to wed her, she sat waiting for him. But once his interest in her waned, she went and wed another.[8]

204. "Gold and glass cannot equal it; neither shall the exchange thereof be vessels of fine gold" (Job 28:17). This refers to words of Torah, which are as expensive to acquire as vessels of gold or vessels of fine gold and are as fragile as vessels of glass.[9]

205. Words of Torah are like garments of Milesian wool.[10] Even as garments of Milesian wool are not readily acquired and are easily torn, so words of Torah are not readily acquired and are easily forgotten. Words of folly, on the other hand, are like a garment made of sackcloth: even as a garment of sackcloth is readily acquired but not easily torn, so words of folly are readily acquired but difficult to forget.[11]

206. Why are words of Torah likened to water, wine, and milk? Because just as these three liquids may become unfit for consumption only through inattention,[12] so words of Torah are forgotten only through inattention.[13]

207. It is harder to retain in memory something old than to commit to memory something new; the former is like trying to make [new] cement out of [old] cement.[14]

208. It is said in the name of R. Huna: What is meant by the verse "Wealth gotten in bundles (*ḥevel*)[15] shall be diminished, but he that gathereth little by little shall in-

1. Sif Deut., §307.
2. B. Er 54a–b.
3. B. Hag 9b.
4. B. Sanh 99a–b.
5. Avot 3:8.
6. ARN 24.
7. Apparently a work no longer extant.
8. P. Ber 9:8, 14d.
9. B. Hag 15a.
10. The city of Miletus used to be a center of trade in wool.
11. ARNB 31.
12. By not covering them.
13. B. Ta 7a–b.
14. It is hard to dissolve it and use it again. B. Yoma 29a.
15. JV: "Wealth gotten by vanity (*hevel*)." But the word *hevel* ("vanity") is read as though spelled *ḥevel*, ("bundle"). "The idea, I suppose, is of studying several biblical books or mishnaic tractates at the same time, instead of taking up one book or tractate at a time, digesting it thoroughly, and only then proceeding to the next" (Leon Nemoy).

crease" (Prov. 13:11)? When a man acquires his Torah bundle by bundle [much at a time], his learning diminishes; but if little by little, it increases. Rava said: The sages are fully aware of this counsel, yet they disregard it. R. Nahman bar Isaac said: I acted in keeping with this counsel, and what I learned stayed with me.

R. Dimi said: He who studies by the right method may be compared to a fowler. If he breaks the wings of each bird as he captures it, his catch is secure. Otherwise, it is not.[1]

209. "For it is no vain thing for you; because it is your life, and through this thing ye shall prolong your days upon the Land" (Deut. 32:47). What you suppose to be a vain thing is in fact your very life. R. Simeon ben Yohai said: There is a parable of two brothers who saved money out of what their father had given them. One, after accumulating small coins adding up to a denar, spent them and found himself with nothing. The other, after accumulating small coins adding up to a denar, set them aside and after a while found himself a rich man. So it is with a disciple of the wise. He studies two or three matters a day, two or three chapters a week, two or three weekly portions a month. After a while he finds himself a "rich" man. To him apply the words "He that gathereth little by little shall become rich" (Prov. 13:11). But he who says, "Am I to study today? I prefer studying tomorrow. Am I to recite Mishnah today? I prefer to do so tomorrow"—such a man finds that he has nothing. To him applies the verse "He who sleepeth during the harvest is an incompetent" (Prov. 10:5).[2]

210. "Whoso keepeth the fig tree shall eat the fruit thereof" (Prov. 27:18). Why is the Torah likened to a fig tree? Because the fruit of most trees, such as the olive tree, the vine, and the date palm, is gathered all at once, while the fig tree's fruit is gathered little by little. So it is with the Torah. One studies a little each day and eventually learns much, because the Torah is not to be learned in one or even two years.[3]

211. "It is to be cleared away as heaps" (Song 5:11).[4] R. Hanin of Sepphoris applied the verse to what is done with a mound of earth. What does one who is slow witted say? "Who," he says, "can ever clear away such a mound?" But what does he who is intelligent say? "I will clear away two basketfuls today and two basketfuls tomorrow, until I have cleared it away entirely." So also he who is slow witted says, "How can I learn the entire Torah—Nezikin with its thirty chapters,[5] Kelim with its thirty chapters?"[6] But what does he who is intelligent say? "I will study two *Halakhot* today and two *Halakhot* tomorrow, until I have learned the entire Torah, all of it."

R. Yannai cited: "Wisdom seems unattainable to the fool; hence he is unable to open his mouth in the gate" (Prov. 24:7). A parable of a loaf of bread hanging high up in a house. He who is dull witted will say, "Who can possibly bring down this loaf?" But an intelligent man says, "Did not somebody hang it up? So I will get a ladder or a long stick and bring it down." So, too, a dull-witted man says, "Who can possibly learn the Torah that is in the heart of a sage?" But an intelligent man says, "Did not the sage also learn it from another person? So I will study two *Halakhot* today and two tomorrow, until I learn the entire Torah, all of it.

R. Levi said: There is a parable of a feed bag with a hole in it, and its owner hires workmen to fill it with water. The dull-witted worker will say, "Of what avail is my labor? If I put water in at this end, it will flow out of the other." But the intelligent worker says, "Do I not get paid for each and every jug of water I pick up?" So, too, the dull-witted man will say, "Of what avail is my labor? If I do study Torah, I will only forget it." But the intelligent man says, "Does not the Holy One give me a reward for each and every effort I make?"

The sages said: The foolish man enters a synagogue, and when he sees people there engaged in Torah, he asks, "How does a man begin to learn Torah?" They tell him: First a man reads from a [beginners'] scroll, then he reads from one of the Five Books, then from the Prophets, then from the Writings. After he finishes Scripture, he studies Talmud, then *Halakhot*, then *Aggadot*. Upon hearing such a list, the dull-witted man says, "When can I learn all of this?" and departs from the gate of the synagogue. Such is the thrust of "He openeth not his mouth in the gate" (Prov. 24:7).[7]

212. "Better is a handful of quietness, than both the hands full of labor and striving after wind" (Eccles. 4:6). R. Isaac said: Better is he who studies two divisions of Mishnah and is familiar with them than he who studies *Halakhot* and is not familiar with them.[8]

Better is he who leases one field, manures it, and hoes it than he who leases many fields and leaves them untilled.[9]

213. R. Sheshet used to go over his studies every thirty days. Then he would stand up, lean upon the bar of the doorway, and say, "Rejoice, O my soul, rejoice, O my soul! For your sake I have read Scripture, for your sake I have studied Mishnah.[10]

1. B. Er 54b and En Yaakov, ad loc.
2. Sif Deut., §48.
3. Num. R. 21:15.
4. JV: "His locks are curled." The word *kevutzotav* ("his locks") is construed as a nominal form of *ktzh* ("to clear away") and *taltalim* ("curls") as another form of *telulit*, ("heap" or "mound").
5. At one time the three tractates Bava Kamma, Bava Metzia, and Bava Batra which are now separate tractates, comprised one tractate known as Nezikin.
6. The first tractate in the division of Toharot, the sixth division of the Mishnah.
7. Lev. R. 19:2; Deut. R. 8:3; Song R. 5:11, §2.
8. Perhaps the laws in the six divisions of the Mishnah, So Etz Yosef.
9. Lev. R. 3:1; Yalkut, Eccles., §971.
10. Being blind, R. Sheshet was under no obligation to perform any commandments. Hence his study of Torah qualified him for no reward. Accordingly, he said: Not to seek reward, but for Torah's own sake—for the sake of his soul—did he persist in his studies. So Hayyim Zundel Makkaby as quoted in Hyman, *Toledot Tannaim ve-Amoraim* 3:1232. B. Pes 68b.

214. R. Tanhum said: He who thinks through what he studies will not quickly forget it. And the proof? The verse "Thou wilt not forget the things which thine eyes saw" (Deut. 4:9).[1]

215. Pause and consider that the way of the Holy One is not at all like the way of flesh and blood. The way of flesh and blood: something may be put into an empty vessel, but nothing can be put into a full vessel. But with the Holy One it is not so. More may be put into a full vessel, but nothing may be put into an empty vessel. For it is said, "If hearkening, thou wilt hearken" (Exod. 15:26). If you hearken [to learning], you will continue to hearken. But if not, you will be unable to hearken.

Another explanation: If you hearken to the old,[2] you will continue to be able to hearken to what is new. But if your heart turns away, you will not be able to hearken again.[3]

216. R. Nahman bar Isaac said: Study of *Halakhot* requires clarity of mind as [perfect as the clarity of light on] a day when the north wind blows.

Abbaye said: Even if my [foster] mother had said to me no more than "Bring me the *kuttah* (porridge)," I would have been rendered unable to study.[4]

Rava said: If a louse bit me, I would have been rendered unable to study.

Seven garments, one for each of the seven days of the week, were made for Mar[5] son of Ravina by his mother.[6]

217. A disciple was seated before R. Yose, who was explaining a matter that the disciple could not comprehend. Finally R. Yose asked him, "Why can't you grasp the matter?" The disciple: "Because I am away from my home." R. Yose: "Where do you come from?" "From Gobat-Shammai." "What is its climate?" "When a child is born, we crush juicy grapes and smear them on his head so that mosquitoes will not eat him up." R. Yose: "Blessed be He who inspires the inhabitants of a place with love for it."[7]

218. R. Hiyya bar Adda was seated before Rav, who was explaining a matter to him, but he could not comprehend it. Finally, Rav asked him, "Why can't you grasp the matter?" The disciple replied, "Because my she-ass is about to foal, and I am afraid that she may catch cold and die."[8]

1. P. Ber 5:1. 9a.
2. If you keep on going over it.
3. B. Ber 40a.
4. He found the least distraction disturbing.
5. Mar was usually used as a title of honor: "Sir, master"; it is not clear whether it was used also as a proper name (cf. Jastrow, p. 834).
6. So that he would feel completely clean and thus be induced to study. B. Er 65a.
7. Gen. R. 34:15.
8. Gen. R. 20:6.

219. Hillel said: A bashful person is not apt to learn.[9]

220. R. Giddol said in the name of Rav: When a disciple of the wise sits before his master, and his lips do not tremble in anxiety and awe[10]—those lips deserve to be scorched.[11]

221. Is a lesson in Gemara to be recited merely as a singsong?[12]

222. When Rabbi [Judah I, the Patriarch] is engaged with one tractate, you are not to question him about another.[13]

223. Happy is the disciple whose master concedes that he is right.[14]

224. R. Judah said, "The night was created only for sleep." "Still," R. Simeon ben Lakish rejoined, "moonlight was created only for study."

When R. Zera was told, "The traditions you report are stated immaculately," he would reply, "They are the result of daytime study."

When R. Hisda's daughter asked her father, "Don't you wish to take a short nap?" he would reply, "Soon days that are both long and short[15] will come, and I shall have ample time to sleep."

R. Nahman bar Isaac said: We are meant to be daytime workers.

When R. Aha bar Jacob had to borrow [time ordinarily devoted to study during the day], he repaid [it during the night].[16]

225. Resh Lakish said: When a man occupies himself with Torah in the night, the Holy One extends to him a thread of grace during the day, as is said, "By day the Lord will command His loving-kindness, and in the night His song shall be with me" (Ps. 42:9). Why will "the Lord command His loving-kindness by day"? Because "His song is with me in the night."[17]

226. R. Zera said: If a man dozes off in the house of study, his knowledge will become raggedy,[18] for it is said, "Drowsiness shall clothe a man with rags" (Prov. 23:21).[19]

227. There are four types of disciples: quick to learn and quick to forget—his gain is dissipated in his loss; slow to comprehend and slow to forget—his loss is offset by his gain; quick to comprehend and slow to forget—that

9. One must have the determination to ask questions. Avot 2:5.
10. Literally, "drop bitterness."
11. B. Shab 30b; B. Pes 117a.
12. Whether or not correct. B. Betz 24a.
13. B. Shab 3b.
14. B. Ber 32a.
15. Long in quantity, but short in quality, since one cannot study in the grave.
16. B. Er 65a.
17. B. AZ 3b.
18. He will forget much of it.
19. B. Sanh 21a.

is a good portion; slow to comprehend and quick to forget—that is a bad portion.[1]

228. There are four types of those who sit before the sages: a sponge, a funnel, a strainer, and a sieve. The sponge absorbs everything. The funnel lets in at one end and lets out at the other. The strainer lets out the wine and retains the lees. The sieve lets out the powdery stuff and retains the good flour.[2]

229. Be like a deep pit, which holds its water; like a cylinder lined with pitch, which preserves the wine in it; and like a sponge, which absorbs everything.[3]

230. R. Judah said: Be careful in study, for an inadvertent error in study amounts to deliberate wrong.[4]

231. "This stumbling block is under thy hand" (Isa. 3:6). A man does not fully understand words of Torah until he has stumbled over them.[5]

232. "But the Lord hath not given you a heart to know . . . until this day" (Deut. 29:3). Rabbah said: From this verse it follows that it may take forty years before one truly knows the mind of one's master.[6]

233. "My doctrine shall drop as the rain" (Deut. 32:2). Even as the same rain falling upon various trees gives to each a special savor in keeping with its species—to the vine the savor of grapes, to the olive tree the savor of olives, to the fig tree the savor of figs—so the words of Torah are the same, yet within them are Scripture, Mishnah, and Midrash of *Halakhot* and *Aggadot*.

"Like droplets of rain upon the tender grass" (Deut. 32:2). Even as droplets of rain come down upon tender blades of grass and cause them to rise up—some green, some red, some black, and some white—so do words of Torah affect human beings. Some become savants, some men of worth, some sages, some righteous men, and some saintly men.[7]

234. Lest you say, "I will read a difficult portion and set the easy one aside," Scripture declares, "It is no vain thing for you" (Deut. 32:47). Lest you say, "I studied *Halakhot* and that is enough for me," Scripture declares, "Ye shall be mindful of this entire commandment" (Deut. 11:22). You are to study Midrash of both *Halakhot* and *Aggadot*.[8]

235. Our masters taught: Those who occupy themselves with Scripture earn merit in one respect and none in another;[9] with Mishnah, earn merit and receive reward for it; with Talmud—no merit is greater. Nevertheless, run to Mishnah more than to Talmud.[10]

236. "With bundles[11] thou shalt make thy war" (Prov. 24:6). R. Assi said in the name of R. Yohanan: In whom will you find [skill to prevail in] the "war" of Torah? In him who has many bundles of Mishnah.[12]

237. "Neither is there any peace for him that goes out or comes in" (Zech. 8:10). Rav said: When a man goes out of the realm of *Halakhah* into the realm of Scripture, he no longer has peace. Samuel said: The verse refers to one who leaves Talmud for Mishnah.[13] R. Yohanan said: It applies even to one who leaves one Talmud for the other.[14]

238. R. Banaah said: A man should always immerse himself in the study of all of Mishnah, for when he knocks, it will open [the door] to Talmud for him, if he wishes to study Talmud; or to *Haggadah*, if he wishes to study *Haggadah*. But, as R. Eleazar said in the name of R. Joshua ben Levi, the massive pier of iron [upon which all else rests] is Mishnah.[15]

239. "It is good that thou shouldst take hold of the one" (Eccles. 7:18)—that is, Scripture. "Yea, also from the other withdraw not thy hand" (ibid.)—that is, Mishnah.[16]

240. "Prepare thy work without" (Prov. 24:27)—that is, Scripture. "And make it ready for thee in the field" (ibid.)—that is, Mishnah. "And afterward build thine house" (ibid.)—that is, Talmud.[17]

241. R. Safra said in the name of R. Joshua ben Hananiah: A man should divide his daily study into three parts—a third for Scripture, a third for Mishnah, and a third for Talmud.[18]

242. R. Isaac ben Phinehas said: He who has command of Midrash [*Aggadah*] but not of *Halakhot* has not savored the taste of wisdom. He who has command of *Halakhot* but not of Midrash [*Aggadah*] has not savored the taste of revulsion from sin.

He also used to say: He who has command of Midrash but not of *Halakhot* is strong [in fear of Heaven], but without weapons [in meeting controversy]. He who has command of *Halakhot* but not of Midrash is weak [in fear of Heaven], but has the weapons [to meet controversy].

1. Avot 5:12.
2. Avot 5:15.
3. DEZ 1.
4. Avot 4:13.
5. B. Git 43a.
6. Moses was with Israel in the wilderness forty years. B. AZ 5b.
7. Sif Deut., §307; Yalkut, *Haazinu*, §942.
8. Sif Deut., §48 (ed. Finkelstein, p. 113).
9. Because Scripture cannot be understood without exposition.
10. For when a man has no command of the details set forth in Mishnah, he is incapable of participating in talmudic discussion. B. BM 33a and En Yaakov, ad loc.
11. JV: "With wise advice (*tahbulot*)." But the word may be associated with *havilah* ("bundle").
12. B. Sanh 42a.
13. The study of Talmud, which explains obscure or contradictory Mishnayyot, is also required for the proper understanding of Scripture.
14. The Palestinian for the Babylonian, or vice versa. B. Hag 10a.
15. Lev. R. 21:5.
16. Eccles. R. 7:18, §1.
17. B. Sot 44a.
18. B. Kid 30a.

He who has command of both the one and the other is strong and is also provided with proper weapons.[1]

243. Our masters taught: Rich in possessions and rich in popular acclaim—such is the master of *Haggadot*. Rich in money and rich in oil[2]—such is the master of dialectics.[3] Rich in products and rich in stores—such is the master traditions. All, however, are dependent on the master of wheat, that is, of Talmud.

R. Zera said in the name of Rav: The verse "All the days of the poor are evil" (Prov. 15:15) applies to the master of Gemara.[4] "But he that is of a merry heart hath a continual feast" (ibid.) applies to the master of Mishnah.[5]

Rava reversed the applications of the verse, as R. Mesharsheya, quoting another verse, stated in Rava's name: "Whoso quarrieth stones shall be hurt therewith" (Eccles. 10:9) applies to masters of Mishnah. "And he that cleaveth wood is warmed thereby" (ibid.) applies to masters of Gemara.[6]

244. R. Isaac bar Judah used to attend Rami bar Hama's sessions, but then left him to attend R. Sheshet's sessions. One day Rami bar Hama met R. Isaac and said, "When the noble has taken you by the hand, do you suppose that the scent has been transferred into your hand? Because you went to R. Sheshet's sessions, do you think you will come to have a reputation like that of R. Sheshet?" R. Isaac replied, "That was not the reason. When I used to ask you a question, you would give me an answer based on logic. Then, when I found a Mishnah[7] [that taught contrariwise], your answer was refuted. But when I ask a question of R. Sheshet, he answers it with a [tannaitic] teaching, so that even if I find another passage in Mishnah that contradicts it, it is one [tannaitic] teaching against another.[8]

245. We have been taught that R. Ishmael said: He who wishes to be wise should occupy himself with the laws that concern disputes about money—no branch of Torah surpasses them, since they are like an ever-flowing fountain of instruction.[9]

1. ARN 29.
2. Literally, "rich in *sela* and rich in [that which comes from] Tekoa."
3. "Who by his creative powers is continually able to establish new points and evolve new principles, thus making his knowledge as continually productive as the possession of money and choicest oils" (Isidore Epstein in BB, Soncino, p. 627, n. 6).
4. "Who is often in difficulty in finding his way through the maze of the involved and difficult argumentation" (Isidore Epstein in BB, Soncino, p. 672, n. 12).
5. Where teachings are clear and precise.
6. "The study of the Gemara affords a sensible appreciation of the principles of the teaching of the Mishnah, and thus enables the students to make practical applications of the Mishnah" (Isidore Epstein in BB, Soncino, p. 627, n. 18). B. BB 145b.
7. Or a Baraita.
8. A controversy, and I may choose to follow the first tannaitic teaching. B. Zev 96b.
9. B. Ber 63b; B. BB 175b.

246. "He meteth out the waters [of Torah] by measure" (Job 28:25). R. Yudan said in the name of R. Samuel: Even words of Torah—Scripture, Mishnah, Talmud, *Halakhot* and *Aggadah*—although given from above, were meted out only by measure. Thus, one man may have a capacity only for Scripture, another only for Mishnah, another only for Talmud, and still another only for *Aggadah*. Yet now and then there is one man who has the capacity for all of Torah.[10]

247. "One man among a thousand have I found" (Eccles. 7:28). In the way of the world, when a thousand men take up the study of Scripture, a hundred of them go on to Mishnah, ten of the hundred to Talmud, and one of the ten to decisions on questions of law. With regard to this, Scripture says, "One man among a thousand have I found."[11]

Teacher and Companion: Attending Upon [Sages in] Torah[12]

248. Rabban Gamaliel used to say: Provide yourself with a teacher, and thus remove yourself from doubt.[13]

249. A man who studies on his own is no match for one who studies with a teacher.[14]

250. R. Yohanan said: The verse "The lips of a priest keep knowledge—Torah should be sought from his mouth, if he is an angel of the Lord of hosts" (Mal. 2:7) means that if the teacher is like an angel of the Lord of hosts [if he dreads sin], Torah should be sought from his mouth; but if not, Torah should not be sought from his mouth.[15]

251. R. Yose bar Judah of Kefar ha-Bavli said: To whom is he who learns from the young to be compared? To one who eats unripe grapes or drinks new wine fresh from his vat. And to whom is he who learns from the old to be compared? To one who eats ripe grapes or drinks aged wine.

Rabbi [Judah I, the Patriarch][16] differed: Look not at the container, but at what is in it. A new container may be full of aged wine, while an old container may be empty even of new wine.[17]

252. "And he shall be like a tree transplanted by streams of water" (Ps. 1:3). Sages said in the name of the school of R. Yannai: The psalm speaks of "a tree transplanted,"

10. Lev. R. 15:2.
11. Eccles. R. 7:28, §1.
12. "Personal attendance on scholars, constituting apprenticeship to them" (Avot, Soncino, p. 84, n. 11).
13. A scholar should seek out a greater authority, whom he is to consult in the event of doubt. Avot 1:16.
14. B. Ket 111a.
15. B. MK 17a.
16. "R. Meir" in BR is an error. It should read Rabbi [Judah I, the Patriarch].
17. Avot 4:27.

not of a tree planted in only one place, implying that he who learns from only one teacher will never see a sign of blessing.[1]

R. Hisda said to his [young] students, "I am about to tell you something, even though I fear that as a result you may leave me and go elsewhere: he who studies under only one teacher will never see a sign of blessing." His students did leave him and went to sit before Rabbah, who, however, explained to them that the saying applies only to matters requiring analysis. But as to matters that are to be committed to memory, it is better to learn them from only one teacher, lest the student be confused by differing versions taught by his several teachers.[2]

253. R. Meir used to say: To whom may he who learns Torah from only one teacher be compared? To a man who had a field, part of which he sowed with wheat, another part with barley; a third part he planted with olive trees, and a fourth part with trees bearing no edible fruit. That man will have an overflow of well-being and plenty. But when a man learns from two or three teachers, he may be compared to a man who has several fields, one sowed with wheat, another sowed with barley, a third planted with olive trees, and a fourth planted with trees bearing no edible fruit. This man, spread out in several areas, will have neither well-being nor plenty.[3]

254. R. Eliezer said: He who utters something he has not heard from his teacher causes the Presence to depart from Israel.[4]

255. A man must cite the exact language of his teacher.[5]

256. When a man cites a tradition in the name of the person who uttered it, he must speak as if that person were standing right before him.[6]

257. Joshua ben Perahiah said: Provide yourself with a teacher and get yourself a companion [to study with].

"Provide yourself with a teacher." For what reason? The saying implies that a man should provide himself with a single[7] teacher and study Scripture, Mishnah, and Midrash, *Halakhot* and *Aggadot*, with him. Then the interpretation the teacher neglected to tell him while studying Scripture, he will presently tell him while studying Mishnah; the interpretation he neglected to tell him while studying Mishnah, he will presently tell him while studying Midrash; the interpretation he neglected to tell him while studying Midrash, he will presently tell him while studying *Halakhot;* the interpretation he neglected to tell him while studying *Halakhot,* he will presently tell him while studying *Aggadah.*

"Get yourself a companion [to study with]." For what reason? This saying implies that a man is to get himself a companion who will eat with him, drink with him, read Scripture with him, study Mishnah with him, sleep next to him, and disclose all his secrets to him—secrets of Torah and secrets of worldly matters. Thus, when the two sit and occupy themselves with Torah, if one errs in *Halakhah* or in the substance of a chapter, or says of what is unclean that it is clean or of what is clean that it is unclean, of what is prohibited that it is permitted and of what is permitted that it is prohibited, his companion will bring him back [to right thinking], as is said, "Two are better than one, in that they have greater benefit from their labor" (Eccles. 4:9).[8]

258. R. Nehorai said: Go as a [voluntary] exile to a place of Torah, and do not suppose that the Torah will seek you out, for it is only your companions in study who can make it your permanent possession. And as for your own understanding, don't depend on it.[9]

259. "Attend (*hasket*), and you will understand" (Deut. 27:9). The word *hasket* is to be read as a composite of *asu kittot kittot,* "Form yourselves into many groups" and occupy yourselves with Torah, since its knowledge can be acquired only in companionship with others. Indeed, this is what R. Yose ben R. Hanina said: What is meant by "A sword is upon the boasters (*baddim*), and they shall become fools" (Jer. 50:36)? A sword—may such things happen to the enemies of the disciples of the wise—is upon those disciples of the wise who sit separately (*bad be-vad*) while studying Torah. What is more, they become dull witted, as is said, "And they shall become fools."[10]

260. R. Hama son of R. Hanina said: What is implied in the verse "Iron sharpeneth iron" (Prov. 27:17)? It tells you that just as one piece of iron sharpens another, so two scholars sharpen each other's mind by discussion of *Halakhah.*

Rabbah bar Bar Hanah said: Why are words of Torah likened to fire, as in the verse "Is not My word like as fire? saith the Lord" (Jer. 23:29)? To teach you that just as fire does not ignite of itself, so words of Torah do not abide in him who studies by himself.[11]

261. R. Nahman bar Isaac said: Why are words of Torah likened to a tree, as in the verse "She is a tree of life to them that lay hold upon her" (Prov. 3:18)? To teach you that just as a small tree may set a big tree on fire, so lesser scholars sharpen the minds of greater scholars. This agrees with what R. Hanina said: I have learned much from my teachers, and from my companions more than from my teachers, but from my disciples even more than from all the others.[12]

1. Will not achieve outstanding success.
2. B. AZ 19a–b.
3. Because he cannot provide proper care for each of his fields. ARN 8.
4. B. Ber 27b.
5. Ed 1:3.
6. B. Shek 7b.
7. Literally, "fixed, permanent."
8. Avot 1:6; ARN 8.
9. Avot 4:15.
10. B. Ber 63b.
11. B. Ta 7a.
12. Ibid.

262. A knife can be sharpened only on the side of another knife.[1]

263. Jealousy among scribes increases wisdom.[2]

264. "They shall not be ashamed when they speak with their enemies in the gate" (Ps. 127:5). What is meant by "With their enemies in the gate"? R. Hiyya bar Abba said: Even father and son or teacher and disciple occupied with Torah in the same gate [of the house of study] become "enemies" [as they dispute] with each other, yet they do not stir from there until they come to love each other.[3]

265. R. Samuel bar Nahmani asked R. Jonathan son of R. Eleazar, who was standing in a marketplace, "Teach me one chapter." R. Jonathan: "Go to the house of study and I will teach you there." R. Samuel: "But our master, did you not teach us, 'Wisdom crieth aloud in the street, she uttereth her voice in the broad places' (Prov. 1:20)?" R. Jonathan: "You may have read this verse, but you didn't understand it. What do you think is meant by 'Wisdom crieth aloud in the street'? It means, in the street of Torah. After all, where is a precious pearl sold? Is it not sold in its own street [of jewelers]? So it is with Torah, for Torah is to be taught in a street of its very own. What do you think 'She uttereth her voice in the broad places' means? It means in a place where room is made for her. And where is such room made for her? In synagogues and houses of study."[4]

266. We have been taught: If a disciple has to go into banishment,[5] his teacher should be banished with him, as is said, "That fleeing into one of those cities he might live" (Deut. 4:42). This means: Provide him with whatever he needs to live [including needs of the spirit]. R. Ze'era remarked: For this very reason it is said that a man should not teach a disciple who is unworthy.

R. Yohanan went even further: If a teacher is banished, his entire house of study should be banished with him.[6]

267. "The sluggard saith: 'There is a lion in the way' " (Prov. 26:13). When a sluggard is told, "Your teacher is in the city nearby; go and learn Torah from him," he replies, "But I fear the lion in the way—'There is a lion in the way.' " When he is told, "Your teacher is within your township; bestir yourself and go to him," he replies, "I fear that the lion may be in the streets—'Yea, a lion is in the streets' " (ibid.). When he is told, "Behold, your teacher is in his house," he replies, "If I go to his house, I am certain to find the door bolted." Then he is told, "But it is open; 'the door is turning upon its hinges' " (Prov. 26:14). At that point, when he is at a loss to reply, he says, "Whether the door is open or bolted, I want to sleep just a little longer." Hence: " 'How long wilt thou sleep, O sluggard?' . . . Still the sluggard replies: 'Yet a little sleep' " (Prov. 6:9–10).[7]

268. R. Yohanan said in the name of R. Simeon ben Yohai: A disciple's attending upon a sage in Torah is more valuable than the sage's direct teaching. For Scripture says, "Here is Elisha, the son of Shaphat, who poured water on the hands of Elijah" (2 Kings 3:11). The text does not say, "Who studied," but, "Who poured water." It thus implies that a disciple's attending upon a sage is more valuable than the sage's direct teaching.[8]

269. Yose ben Joezer of Tzeredah used to say: Make your house a meeting place for sages, be willing to be covered by the dust of their feet,[9] and drink in their words thirstily.[10]

270. Warm yourself before the fire of sages. But beware of their glowing coals, that you may not be singed. For their bite is the bite of a fox, their sting is the sting of a scorpion, their hiss is the hiss of a serpent, and all their words are like coals of fire.[11]

271. The Torah is all fire. It was given out of fire and it is like fire. What is the way of fire? When a man comes too close to it, he is scorched; when too far from it, he is chilled. So, too, a man should make certain that he is no more than warmed by the fire of the sages.[12]

272. If a man reads Scripture but does not study Oral Law, he is still standing outside [Torah's inner mysteries]; if he studies Oral Law but does not read Scripture, he is still standing outside; if he reads Scripture and studies Oral Law but does not attend upon the sages, he is like one from whom the inner mysteries of Torah remain hidden.[13]

Honoring Torah and Those Who Study It

273. R. Yose said: Whoever honors the Torah is himself held in honor by men, and whoever dishonors the Torah is himself held in dishonor by men.[14]

274. He who learns from his companion a single chapter, a single *Halakhah*, a single verse, a single expression, or even a single letter[15] should treat him with respect. For we find that although David, king of Israel, learned only two things from Ahithophel, yet he called him master—guide and teacher: "Thee, my guide and my teacher,

1. Gen. R. 69:2.
2. B. BB 21a.
3. B. Kid 30b.
4. Tanhuma, *Be-hukkotai*, §3; Tanhuma B, *Be-hukkotai*, §3.
5. For manslaughter.
6. B. Mak 10a.
7. Deut. R. 8:6; Yalkut, Prov., §961.
8. B. Ber 7b.
9. Either (1) follow them closely or (2) sit on the ground while they teach.
10. Avot 1:4.
11. Avot 2:10.
12. Tanhuma, *Yitro*, §12.
13. Lev. R. 3:7.
14. Avot 4:6.
15. Whether a word is to be spelled with an *alef* or *ayin*. See Ka 7.

though a commoner, I call my equal" (Ps. 55:14).[1] And is there not in this matter an inference *a fortiori?* if David, king of Israel, who had learned only two things from Ahithophel, called him master, guide, and teacher, how much more should one pay honor to one's companion from whom one has learned a single chapter, a single *Halakhah*, a single verse, a single expression, even a single letter.[2]

275. If one finds a lost article belonging to his father and a lost article belonging to his teacher, the teacher's article must be returned first, because his father brought him into this world, whereas his teacher, who instructed him in wisdom, is bringing him to life in the world-to-come. But if his father is a sage, his father's article takes precedence. If his father and his teacher are [each] carrying a burden, he must [first] assist his teacher to lay the burden down and then assist his father. If his father and his teacher are in captivity, he must redeem his teacher [first] and then his father. But if his father is a sage, he must [first] redeem his father and then his teacher.

Our masters taught: The teacher referred to above is the one who has instructed him in the wisdom [of Gemara], not the one who has taught him Scripture and Mishnah. Such is R. Meir's view. But R. Judah said: The teacher is the one from whom he derived the greater part of his knowledge [in any area of learning]. Whereas R. Yose said: Even if the teacher has illuminated the meaning[3] of but one Mishnah, he is his teacher.[4]

276. Our masters taught: A sage takes precedence over a king of Israel,[5] for when a sage dies, there is none to replace him, but when a king of Israel dies, all Israel are fit for kingship. A king takes precedence over a high priest, a high priest over a prophet, a prophet over the high priest anointed for service in war only, a high priest anointed for service in war only over a deputy high priest, a deputy high priest over a priest who has charge of the keys and vessels of the Temple, a priest who has such charge over a Temple treasurer, a Temple treasurer over the chief of the weekly watch of priests, a chief of the weekly watch of priests over the chief of the men of the daily watch, a chief of the men of the daily watch over a common priest, a priest over a Levite, a Levite over a lay Israelite, a lay Israelite over a bastard, a bastard over a *Nathin*,[6] a *Nathin* over a proselyte, a proselyte over an emancipated slave. When is this order of precedence to be followed? When all of them are equal. If, however, a bastard is a disciple of the wise and the high priest is an unlearned man, the learned bastard takes precedence over the unlearned high priest.[7]

277. R. Eleazar ben Shammua said: Let the honor of your disciple be as dear to you as your own, the honor of your companion as great as the awe you feel for your teacher, and the awe for your teacher as great as your fear of Heaven.[8]

278. We have been taught that Simeon Imsoni[9] (others say: Nehemiah Imsoni) used to expound every *et*[10] in the Torah as implying some extension of meaning. But when he came to "Thou shalt fear (*et*) the Lord thy God" (Deut. 6:13 and 10:20), he desisted.[11] His disciples said to him: Master, what will now happen to all the *ets* you have interpreted [to indicate extension]? He replied: Just as I received reward for interpreting them, so will I now receive reward for desisting. Subsequently, R. Akiva came and expounded: The word *et* in "Thou shalt fear (*et*) the Lord thy God" extends the obligation to fearing the disciples of the wise.[12]

279. It is said in the name of R. Hisda: If a father renounces the honor due him, it is renounced; but if a teacher renounces the honor due him, it is not renounced. R. Joseph said: Even if a teacher renounces the honor due him, it is renounced, for Scripture says, "The Lord went before them by day" (Exod. 13:21).[13]

280. R. Hisda said: When a man contends against [the ruling of] his teacher, it is as though he contended against the Presence, for [of Korah and his followers, who strove only against Moses], Scripture says, "When they strove against the Lord" (Num. 26:9). R. Hama bar Hanina said: When a man quarrels with his teacher, it is as if he quarreled with the Presence, as is said, "This is the water of Meribah; because the children of Israel strove with the Lord[14] (Num. 20:13).

R. Hanina bar Papa said: When a man expresses resentment against his teacher, it is as though he expressed it against the Presence, as is said, "Your murmurings are not against us, but against the Lord" (Exod. 16:8). R. Abbahu said: When a man speaks evil of his teacher, it is as though he spoke evil of the Presence, as is said, "And the people spoke against God when [they spoke] against Moses" (Num. 21:5).[15]

---

1. JV: "It was thou, a man mine equal, my companion, and my familiar friend." But *enosh* ("man") often means "ordinary man," hence, "commoner"; *aluf* ("companion") is here derived from the verb *'lf* ("to train, to direct"), hence, "my guide"; and by a slight change in vocalization, *meyudda'i* ("my familiar friend") is read *meyadde'i* ("one who conveys knowledge to me"), hence, "my teacher."
2. Avot 6:3.
3. Literally, "enlightened his eyes."
4. B. BM 33a.
5. With regard to saving of life, restoration of lost property, or redemption from captivity.
6. A descendant of the Gibeonites who deceived Joshua. See Josh. 9:3ff.
7. B. Hor 13a; Num. R. 6:1.
8. Avot 4:12.
9. Possibly from Amasia in Pontus. So Jastrow.
10. The Hebrew particle that precedes the direct object of a verb. The sages often interpreted it as evidence of additional objects which are not specified.
11. He could not accept the idea that such supreme fear should extend to anyone other than God. And so he concluded that even as the *et* in this verse cannot signify extension, it may not signify extension elsewhere.
12. B. Pes 22b.
13. Thus God, renouncing the honor due Him, condescended to act as a guide for Israel. B. Kid 32a.
14. But in the narrative they are said to strive only with Moses.
15. B. Sanh 110a.

281. R. Joshua ben Levi said: In twenty-four instances we find that the High Court imposed the ban for an insult to a teacher, and they are all recorded in our Mishnah. R. Eleazar asked him: Where? He replied: See if you can find them. R. Eleazar went to search [in the Mishnah] and found only three instances: one of a person who belittled the requirement of washing the hands, another of a person who made disparaging remarks over the biers of disciples of the wise, and a third of a person who acted arrogantly toward the One above.[1]

282. R. Judah stated: Jerusalem was destroyed only because disciples of the wise were despised there, as is said, "They mocked the messengers of God, and despised His words, and scoffed at His prophets, until the wrath of the Lord arose against His people, till there was no remedy" (2 Chron. 36:16). What does "Till there was no remedy" suggest? That for the illness of him who despises disciples of the wise, so said R. Judah in the name of Rav, there is no remedy.[2]

283. R. Joshua ben Levi said to his children: Take care to respect an old man who through unavoidable circumstances has forgotten what he knew, for Scripture says that both the whole Tablets and the shattered Tablets were placed in the Ark.[3]

284. We have been taught: If three men walk together on a road, the teacher should be in the middle, the elder of the other two on his right, and the younger on his left.[4]

285. A disciple taking leave of his teacher should not turn around and walk away, but must turn sideways to depart. We find that R. Eleazar walked this way when he took leave of [his teacher] R. Yohanan. If R. Yohanan was about to leave first, R. Eleazar, head bowed down, would remain standing in his place until R. Yohanan disappeared from sight. If R. Eleazar wanted to leave first, he would walk backward until R. Yohanan disappeared from sight.

When Rava took leave of R. Joseph [his teacher], he walked backward until his heels struck the threshold so sharply that it was stained with his blood. When R. Joseph was told[5] that Rava acted thus, he said: May it be [God's] will that your head be raised above the entire city.[6]

286. When R. Zera grew too weak to study, he used to go and sit by the door of R. Nathan ben Tobi's house, saying to himself: When the sages pass by, I will stand up and receive a reward [for it in the world-to-come].[7]

287. Rava said: How stupid are those people who stand up for a Torah scroll but do not stand up for a distinguished personage. They should realize that even though in the Torah scroll it is said, "Forty stripes he may give him" (Deut. 25:3), the sages came and [through interpretation] reduced the number of stripes by one.[8]

288. R. Eleazar said: A disciple of the wise who does not rise before his teacher is called wicked. He will not live long and will forget his studies, for Scripture says, "It shall not go well with the wicked, neither shall he prolong his days, which are as a shadow, because he feareth not before God" (Eccles. 8:13). But I do not know what is meant here by "fear." Since it says, "Thou shalt rise up before the hoary head . . . and fear thy God" (Lev. 19:32), I conclude that here "fear" is shown by rising up.

R. Aibu said in the name of R. Yannai: A disciple of the wise is allowed to rise before his teacher only [twice], morning and evening, so that the deference shown to him may not exceed the deference shown to Heaven.[9]

289. R. Abba the Priest bar Papa said: When I used to see a group of people [sitting together], I would turn off to another road so as not to inconvenience them, for were they to notice me, they would feel impelled to rise before me. When I told R. Yose bar Zevida what I did, he said: You should pass before them, so that they may see you and rise for you, and you will thus lead them to fear of Heaven, as Scripture says, "Thou shalt rise up before the hoary head . . . and then thou shalt fear thy God" (Lev. 19:32).[10]

290. We have been taught that R. Eliezer said: One who places himself behind his teacher while praying,[11] one who gives a perfunctory greeting to his teacher or responds with lack of deference to his teacher's greeting,[12] one who disputes a decision arrived at in the academy of his teacher, and one who says something in the name of his teacher that he has not actually heard from his teacher—all such cause the Presence to depart from Israel.[13]

291. Resh Lakish said: One who coughs up phlegm and spits in the presence of his teacher deserves an untimely death, as is said, "All that hate Me love death" (Prov. 8:36). Read not, "That hate Me," but, "That cause Me to be hated."[14]

292. R. Hiyya bar Ammi said in the name of Ulla: A man should always live in the same town as his teacher. For as long as Shimei son of Gera was alive, Solomon did not dare marry Pharaoh's daughter. When does this rule

1. B. Ber 19a.
2. B. Shab 119b.
3. See above, part 1, chap. 5, §83. B. Ber 8b.
4. B. Er 54b.
5. R. Joseph was blind.
6. The prayer was fulfilled. Rava became head of the academies of Sura and Pumbedita. B. Yoma 53a.
7. B. Ber 28a.
8. B. Mak 22b.
9. One rises before God in prayer only twice a day, morning and evening. B. Kid 33b.
10. Tanhuma B, *Be-haalotekha*, §20.
11. It would seem as though he were directing his prayer to his teacher (Tosafot on B. Ber 27b).
12. He says, "Shalom," without adding, "My master."
13. B. Ber 27b.
14. The disciples' manners bring Torah into disrepute. B. Er 99a, and En Yaakov, ad loc.

apply? When a person is submissive to his teacher; but if he is not submissive, he should not dwell there.[1]

293. When the words of the teacher and the words of a pupil clash, whose words are to be followed?[2]

294. Our masters taught: When our masters entered the vineyard[3] at Yavneh, among them were R. Judah, R. Yose, R. Nehemiah, and R. Eliezer the son of R. Yose the Galilean. In appreciation of the hospitality shown them, they began their discourses by expounding [relevant] texts. R. Judah, who was the one delegated to speak first on all occasions,[4] began his discourse on the honor due to Torah by expounding the text "Now Moses used to take the Tent [of Meeting] and pitch it without the camp" (Exod. 33:7). Have we not here, he said, an argument *a fortiori?* The Ark of the Lord was never more than twelve *mil* distant [from the Israelite encampment], yet the Torah speaks of those who went out as "everyone that sought the Lord went out unto the Tent of Meeting" (ibid.). How much more [is the title "they who seek the Lord" applicable to] disciples of the wise, who go from city to city and from province to province to learn Torah!

R. Judah, speaking further on the honor due to Torah, expounded another text: "Attend and hear, O Israel: this day thou art become a people unto the Lord thy God" (Deut. 27:9). Now, was it on this day that the Torah was given to Israel? Was not this day in fact forty years after Sinai? However, use of "this day" in the verse is meant to teach you that the Torah is as beloved every day by those who study it as on the day when it was given from Mount Sinai.

R. Nehemiah began his discourse, in appreciation of the hospitality shown them, by expounding the text "And Saul said unto the Kenites, Go, depart, get you down from among the Amalekites, lest I destroy you with them; for ye showed kindness to all the children of Israel when they came up out of Egypt" (1 Sam. 15:6). Have we not here an argument *a fortiori?* If such was the reward of Jethro [the father of the Kenites], who befriended Moses only for his own benefit, how much greater by far will it be for one who entertains a disciple of the wise in his house, gives him food and drink, and supports him with his possessions!

R. Yose began his discourse, in appreciation of the hospitality shown them, by expounding the text "[Thou shalt not abhor an Edomite, for he is thy brother]; thou shalt not abhor an Egyptian, because thou wast a stranger in his land" (Deut. 23:8). Have we not here an argument *a fortiori?* If such was the reward of the Egyptians, who befriended the Israelites only for their own purposes, as Pharaoh had declared: "And if thou knowest any able men among them, then make them rulers over my cattle" (Gen. 47:6), how much greater by far will be the reward of one who entertains a disciple of the wise in his house, gives him food and drink, and supports him with his possessions!

R. Eliezer the son of R. Yose the Galilean began his discourse, in appreciation of the hospitality shown them, by expounding the text "And the Lord blessed Obed-edom and all his house . . . because of the Ark of God" (2 Sam. 6:12). Have we not here an argument *a fortiori?* If such was the reward for attending to the Ark, which required neither food nor drink, but before which Obed-edom merely swept and laid the dust, how much greater by far will it be for one who entertains a disciple of the wise in his house, gives him food and drink, and supports him with his possessions![5]

295. At the end of Hadrian's persecution,[6] when our masters—R. Judah, R. Nehemiah, R. Meir, R. Yose, R. Simeon ben Yohai, R. Eliezer the son of R. Yose the Galilean, and R. Eliezer ben Jacob—gathered at Usha, they sent word to the elders of Galilee, saying, "Whoever has studied, let him come and teach; and whoever has not studied, let him come and learn." After they came together and studied, they decreed sundry measures that were necessary.[7] When the time came for them to depart, they said, "We cannot leave a place where we have been received so well without a word of blessing." They gave R. Judah the honor of speaking first, not because he was the most learned among them, but because his home was in Usha, and the place in which a man lives gives him certain privileges. So R. Judah came forward and took as his text "Now Moses used to take the tent and pitch it without the camp, afar off (*harhek*) from the camp" (Exod. 33:7). The word "afar off" (*harhek*) is used here, and in another place Scripture says, "Yet there shall be a space (*rahok*) between you and it, about two thousand cubits by measure" (Josh. 3:4). Just as the word *rahok* in Joshua means two thousand cubits, so *harhek* in Exodus must mean two thousand cubits. The verse in Exodus continues, "And it came to pass, that everyone that sought,"—not everyone that sought Moses, but "everyone that sought the Lord."[8] From this we learn that welcoming companions in Torah is like welcoming the Presence. As for you, our brethren, our masters, who are distinguished in knowledge of Torah, since some of you have taken the trouble to come ten *mil*, some twenty *mil*, and some thirty mil, and some even forty *mil* to hear words of Torah, you may all the more rest assured that the Holy One will not withhold your reward in this world and in the next!

R. Nehemiah then came forward and expounded the text "An Ammonite or a Moabite shall not enter the assembly of the Lord" (Deut. 23:4). He began by saying: We have been taught: Two great nations were excluded from marrying into the assembly of the Lord. Why? "Because they met you not with bread and with water" (Deut. 23:5). Now, at that time did Israel require bread and water? During all the forty years that Israel were in the wilderness, did not the manna descend for them and the well come

1. So as to avoid confrontations with his teacher outside of study hours. B. Ber 8a.
2. Clearly those of the teacher. B. Kid 42b.
3. That is, sat in formal session, in rows, like rows of vines in a vineyard.
4. See above, part 2, chap. 1, §225.
5. B. Ber 63b.
6. After the war of Bar Kozeva, 135 C.E.
7. "The havoc caused by the wars had rendered a number of new enactments urgently necessary; these were now decided upon and promulgated" (Song R., Soncino, p. 106, n. 3).
8. Though in actual fact the man would visit Moses.

up for them; were not quails provided for them; did not clouds of glory surround them and the pillar of cloud journey before them? And yet you say [as the reason for excluding Ammonites and Moabites], "Because they did not meet them with bread and water"? However, as R. Eleazar explained, courtesy requires that one who comes from a journey is to be welcomed with food and drink. Come and see how God punished these two nations [for their discourtesy toward Israel]—of them it is written in Scripture, "An Ammonite or a Moabite shall not enter the assembly of the Lord." But as for you, men of Usha, who have welcomed our masters with your food, your drink, and your couches to recline on, the Holy One will surely requite you with a good reward.

R. Meir then came forward and took as his text "Now there dwelt an old prophet in Bethel" (1 Kings 13:11). Who was that prophet? Amaziah the Priest of Bethel.[1] R. Yose interrupted: Meir, you are confusing matters.[2] Who [you just asked] was that prophet? He was Jonathan the son of Gershom the son of Moses. As a matter of fact, in the verse "Jonathan, the son of Gershom, the son of Manasseh" (Judg. 18:30), the letter *nun* in the name Manasseh is suspended, to intimate that if virtuous, Jonathan would be accounted a descendant of Moses; and if not, a descendant of Manasseh.[3]

[Be that as it may, whether the old prophet was Amaziah or Jonathan, R. Meir went on to quote]: "And the old prophet said unto [the man of God]: 'I also am a prophet as thou art' . . . [but in fact] he lied (*kihesh*) unto him" (1 Kings 13:18). But how can you say that he lied unto him? [He was a prophet, was he not? Yes], but have *kihesh* means: He deceived him. How did he deceive him? He deceived the man of God into believing that he was allowed to eat the food proffered to him.[4] Nevertheless, in the same passage it is written, "And it came to pass, as they sat at the table, that the word of the Lord came unto the old prophet that brought him back [by deceit]" (1 Kings 13:20). Does it not then stand to reason: If the old prophet, who deceived the man of God into believing he was allowed to eat the food proffered, was yet privileged to have the holy spirit rest upon him, you, our brethren, men of Usha, who welcomed our masters with food that is not deceitful, with drink, and with couches to recline on—the Holy One will surely requite you with a good reward!

R. Yose then came forward and took as his text "And the Ark of the Lord remained in the house of Obed-edom the Gittite. . . . And it was told King David, saying: 'The Lord hath blessed the house of Obed-edom and all that pertaineth unto him' " (2 Sam. 6:11–12). For what merit? "Because of [service to] the Ark of God" (ibid.). Now, it stands to reason: the Ark of God neither eats nor drinks nor speaks, but merely contains two Tablets of stone, and yet, merely because Obed-edom kindled one lamp in front of it, he was blessed for honoring it. How much more and more will you, our brethren, men of Usha, be blessed!

R. Simeon ben Yohai then came forward and took as his text "And it fell on a day, that Elisha passed to Shunem, where a wealthy woman lived, and she constrained him to eat bread" (2 Kings 4:8). This Shunammite woman, because she gave Elisha a cordial welcome and ministered to him, merited having her son brought back to life. How much more and more will you, our brethren, men of Usha, who treated us with such kindness, be blessed!

R. Eliezer the son of R. Yose the Galilean then came forward and took as his text "And Saul said unto the Kenites: 'Go, depart, get you down from among the Amalekites, lest I destroy you with them; for ye showed kindness to all the children of Israel, when they came up out of Egypt' " (1 Sam. 15:6). Now, did Jethro show kindness to all Israel? Surely it was only to Moses that he showed kindness! This text, however, teaches you that if anyone shows kindness to one of Israel's great men, it is accounted to him as if he had shown it to all Israel. How much more and more, then, does this apply to you, our brethren, men of Usha!

Finally R. Eliezer ben Jacob came forward and took as his text "Moses and the Levitical priests spoke unto all Israel, saying: 'Be silent, and hear, O Israel: this day thou art become a people' " (Deut. 27:9). Was it on this day that they received the Torah? Had they not already received the Torah forty years before this day? Yet you say, "On this day"? However, the text teaches that since Moses repeated to them the Torah and they received it gladly, it was accounted to them as if they had received it that very day on Mount Sinai. Therefore it is said, "On this day thou art become a people unto the Lord thy God." To you, then, our brethren, men of Usha, who have received us so gladly, how much more and more does this apply.[5]

296. R. Yose son of R. Hanina said in the name of R. Eliezer ben Jacob: When a man entertains a disciple of the wise in his home and supports him with what he possesses, Scripture accounts it to him as if he were bringing the daily offerings.[6]

297. "There came a man from Baal-shalishah, and brought the man of God bread of the firstfruits," etc. (2 Kings 4:42). But was Elisha [who was not a priest] entitled to eat firstfruits? The verse, however, tells you that he who brings a gift to a disciple of the wise [is doing as good a deed] as if he were offering firstfruits.[7]

298. R. Eleazar said: Whoever does not support disciples of the wise out of his possessions will never see a sign of blessing.[8]

299. Rava said: He who loves sages will have sons who are sages. He who honors sages will have sons-in-law who are sages. He who stands in awe of sages will himself

1. Mentioned in Amos 7:10.
2. You are mixing up two different people. Literally, "there are broken eggs here."
3. The infamous king of Judah who spread idolatry. See above, part 1, chap. 6, §170–73.
4. Which in fact he was not, having been instructed by God "to eat no bread nor drink water there" (1 Kings 13:9).
5. Song R. 2:5, §3; Lev. R. 34:8.
6. B. Ber 10b.
7. B. Ket 105b.
8. B. Sanh 92a.

become a disciple of the wise. But if he is not fit for such study, his words will be heeded as though he were a disciple of the wise.[1]

300. Rava said: Merit, I pray, will be mine, for whenever a disciple appears before me in a lawsuit, I do not place my head on the pillow before I consider arguments in his favor.[2]

Mar bar R. Ashi said: I am not fit to judge in a sage's lawsuit. Why not? Because he is as dear to me as my own person, and a man is not likely to find fault with himself.[3]

301. R. Hiyya bar Abba said in the name of R. Yohanan: Many specific boons were promised by all the prophets only to him who weds his daughter to a disciple of the wise, who conducts business on behalf of a disciple of the wise, or who provides for a disciple of the wise out of his possessions. But as for the disciples of the wise themselves, "Eye hath not seen, O God, beside Thee, what Thou wilt do," etc. (Isa. 64:3).[4]

The Disciple of the Wise and the Unlearned Person

302. R. Yohanan said: The builders—these are disciples of the wise who throughout their days are occupied with building up the world.[5]

303. R. Eleazar said in the name of R. Hanina: Disciples of the wise increase peace in the world, as is said, "Because of all thy children who are taught by the Lord, great shall be the peace of thy children" (Isa. 54:13).[6]

304. "Gone is from fair Zion all her splendor" (Lam. 1:6). These are disciples of the wise, with regard to whom it is said, "Thou shalt regard the person of a sage as splendid" (Lev. 19:32).[7]

305. "The commandment is a lamp, and the teaching is light" (Prov. 6:23). A parable of one who stands in a dark place. No sooner does he start walking than he stumbles over a stone or comes to a gutter and falls into it, striking the ground with his face. Why does this happen? Because he has no lamp in his hand. So, too, is the unlearned man who possesses no Torah. When he comes upon a transgression, he stumbles into it and dies. But they who study Torah give light wherever they are. A parable of one who stands in the dark with a lamp in his hand. When he comes upon a stone, he does not stumble [over it]; when he comes upon a gutter, he does not fall into it. Why not? Because he has a lamp in his hand, as Scripture says, "Thy word is a lamp unto my feet, and a light unto my path" (Ps. 119:105).[8]

306. We have been taught: "Thou shalt love the Lord thy God" (Deut. 6:4), so that the Name of Heaven may come to be loved because of you.[9] When a man reads Scripture, studies Mishnah, ministers to the needs of disciples of the wise, is honest in his business dealings, speaks gently to people—what do people say of him? Happy is So-and-so who has studied Torah! Happy is his father who had him taught Torah! Happy is his teacher who taught him Torah! Alas for people who have not studied Torah. So-and-so who has studied Torah—mark how pleasant are his ways, how perfect his deeds! To him apply the words "Thou art My servant Israel, in whom I will be glorified" (Isa. 49:3). On the other hand, he who reads Scripture, studies Mishnah, and ministers to the needs of disciples of the wise, but is not honest in his business dealings and not gentle in his speech with people—what do people say of him? Alas for So-and-so who has studied Torah! Alas for his father who had him taught Torah! Alas for his teacher who taught him Torah! So-and-so who has studied Torah—mark how vile his deeds, how ugly his ways! To him apply the words "They profaned My holy Name, in that men said of them: These are the people of the Lord, and are gone forth out of His land" (Ezek. 36:20).[10]

307. Fifteen characteristics are mentioned of a disciple of the wise. He is pleasant when he comes in and pleasant when he departs. He is unassuming in his academy, resourceful in bringing about fear of God, prudent in awareness, wise in his ways. He collects [words of Torah] and remembers them well, takes pains to reply properly, makes his questions relevant and his replies to the point, listens carefully before replying, adds something novel of his own to each and every chapter, goes to a sage [to minister to him], and studies in order to teach and to practice.[11]

308. He who is a disciple of the wise does not eat standing up, does not lick his fingers, does not belch in the presence of his companion; he is not given to much talk, much laughter, much sleep, much indulgence, and much saying [carelessly], "Yes, yes," or, "No, no."[12]

309. A disciple of the wise should be modest at eating, at drinking, at bathing, at anointing himself, at putting on his sandals; in his walking, in dress, in the sound of his voice, in the disposal of his spittle, even in his good deeds. A bride, while still in her father's house, acts so modestly that when she leaves it her very presence proclaims:

---

1. B. Shab 23b.
2. Because of his great respect for scholars, Rava was certain that the scholar in the lawsuit sought what was right. So Samuel Edels.
3. B. Shab 119a.
4. To reward the disciples of the wise themselves. B. Ber 34b.
5. B. Shab 114a.
6. B. Ber 64a.
7. JV: "Thou shalt . . . honor (*hadarta*) the face of the old man (*zaken*)." But *hadarta* literally means "regard as splendid," and *zaken* is frequently understood as an acronym for *zeh she-kanah hokhmah* ("he who has acquired wisdom"). Lam R. 1:6, §33.
8. Exod. R. 36:3.
9. *Ve-ahavta* ("thou shalt love") is read *ve-ehavta* ("thou shalt cause to be loved").
10. B. Yoma 86a and En Yaakov, ad loc.
11. DEZ 3.
12. He makes few promises. DEZ 5.

"Whoever knows of anything to be testified against me, let him come and testify." Likewise, a disciple of the wise should be so modest in his actions that his ways proclaim what he is.[1]

310. The way of a disciple of the wise: humble, meek, eager, full of goodwill, submissive to discourtesy, loved by all people, undemanding even with the people in his own house, fearful of sin, appraising each person according to his deeds, ever saying, "All that is in this world I have no desire for, because this world is not mine." He keeps studying and is ever ready to throw his robe on the ground and sit on it at the feet of other disciples of the wise. And no man ever espies in him anything evil.[2]

311. There are seven characteristics in a boor and seven in a sage. A sage will not speak in the presence of one greater than he in wisdom,[3] does not interrupt his companion, does not hasten to answer, asks questions that are relevant, and replies to the point; he speaks first of the first point raised and last of the last point raised; concerning that which he has not heard, he says, "I have not heard this"; and he acknowledges the truth.[4] The opposites of these characteristics are true of a person who is a boor.[5]

312. Disciples of the wise may be recognized by four characteristics: their out-of-purse spending, tippling, temper, and attire. Some say, also by their speech.[6]

313. From the way a man phrases his benedictions, it may be recognized whether or not he is a disciple of the wise.[7]

314. From the way you curve your lips when you speak, one can tell that you [pronounce the words correctly and therefore] are a disciple of the wise.[8]

315. It was said in the name of Rav: Whence do we learn that even the everyday conversation of disciples of the wise requires study? From the verse "Even his leaf doth not wither" (Ps. 1:3).[9]

316. He who undertakes to be an associate scholar (*haver*)[10] will not sell to "the unlearned" (*am ha-aretz*) produce that is moist or dry[11] and will not buy from him produce that is moist.[12] He will not be a guest in the home of an unlearned person, nor will he have him in his home as a guest as long as he continues to wear his own [unclean] garment.[13] R. Judah said: Nor should he raise small cattle[14] or be lavish in making vows or in jesting. R. Judah was told: What you mention are not [among the obligations of an associate scholar], not being within the scope of precautions against uncleanness.[15]

317. R. Hanina of Hoza[16] said: One may presume that an associate scholar (*haver*) will not sell[17] produce that is untithed.[18]

318. Rava said: A young disciple of the wise is like a seed under a hard clod of earth: once he sprouts, he grows fast.[19]

319. "Within and without thou shalt overlay it [with gold]" (Exod. 25:11). Rava said: Any disciple of the wise who is not on the inside what he appears to be on the outside is no true disciple of the wise.[20]

320. R. Akiva: When a disciple of the wise exalts himself because of his mastery of words of Torah, to what may he be likened? To a carcass thrown on the road. Every passerby clamps his hand over his nose and walks speedily away from it, as is said, "When exalting thyself, thou becomest like a carcass" (Prov. 30:32).[21]

321. If a disciple of the wise lacks common sense, a carcass is better than he.[22]

322. R. Abba said in the name of R. Simeon ben Lakish: Even if a disciple of the wise is vengeful and malicious like a serpent, gird him about your loins.[23] But if a man is unlearned, even if he should be pious, do not dwell in his neighborhood.[24]

323. R. Yohanan said in the name of R. Simeon ben Jehozadak: Any disciple of the wise who is not vengeful and malicious like a serpent [toward violators of Torah] is no genuine disciple of the wise.[25]

---

1. DEZ 7.
2. DEZ 1.
3. "Or in years" is omitted, as in many editions.
4. He accepts defeat gracefully.
5. Avot 5:7.
6. DEZ 5.
7. B. Ber 50a.
8. B. Me 17b.
9. B. Suk 21b; B. AZ 19b.
10. To be scrupulous in the observance of regulations concerning ritual purity.
11. Since through his lax observance of the regulations of cleanness, the unlearned may make unclean not only the moist produce but also the dry.
12. Since the "unlearned" is always ritually unclean, he inevitably conveys uncleanness to moist produce, which is susceptible to uncleanness. On the other hand, dry produce is not susceptible to uncleanness, and the "unlearned" may be trusted if he says that it has not become unclean.
13. The garments "the unlearned" wear cause ritual defilement.
14. Being given to grazing in other people's fields, such small cattle make one guilty of misappropriation.
15. Dem 2:3.
16. A province of southwestern Iran, now known as Khuzistan.
17. Literally, "will not let out of his hand."
18. B. Er 32a; B. Pes 9a.
19. B. Ta 4a.
20. B. Yoma 72b.
21. JV: "If thou hast done foolishly (*navalta*) in lifting up thyself." R. Akiva associates *navalta* with *nevelah* ("carcass"). ARN 11.
22. Lev. R. 1:15.
23. You will benefit from his learning.
24. His piety is sure to be tainted by his ignorance. B. Shab 63a.
25. B. Yoma 23a.

324. Rava said: If a disciple of the wise is boiling with rage, it is the Torah that brings him to such a boil, as is said, "Is not My word like as fire? saith the Lord" (Jer. 23:29).

R. Ashi said: A disciple of the wise who is not as hard as iron is no genuine disciple of the wise, for it is said, "Is not My word . . . like a hammer that breaketh the rock in pieces?" (Jer. 23:29). Nevertheless, said Ravina, a man should train himself to be gentle, for it is said, "Remove anger from thy heart" (Eccles. 11:10).[1]

325. R. Hiyya bar Ashi said in the name of Rav: A disciple of the wise should have an eighth of an eighth of pride; which, said R. Huna the son of R. Joshua, crowns him as the awn crowns a stalk of wheat. Rava said: [A disciple of the wise who possesses such pride] deserves being placed under a ban, and one who does not, also deserves being placed under a ban. R. Nahman bar Isaac said: He should not possess it at all, not even a smidgin of it. Is what has been written about pride a trifling matter? Namely, "Everyone that is proud in heart is an abomination to the Lord" (Prov. 16:5).[2]

326. R. Hiyya bar Abba said in the name of R. Yohanan: Any disciple of the wise on whose garment a grease spot is found deserves death, for it is said, "All they that despise Me (*mesane'ai*) love [merit] death" (Prov. 8:36). Read not *mesane'ai*, "that despise Me," but *masni'ai*, "that cause Me to be despised."[3]

327. Issi ben Judah said: Why do [some] disciples of the wise die before their time? Because they despise themselves.[4]

328. Our masters taught: Six things are unbecoming for a disciple of the wise. He should not go out into the marketplace scented; he should not go out in patched sandals; he should not go out alone at night; he should not chat with a woman in the marketplace; he should not be the last to enter the house of study; he should not recline for a meal in a company of the unlearned. Some say: He should not take long strides or walk with a stiff posture.[5]

329. R. Yohanan asked R. Banaah: How long should the undergarment of a disciple of the wise be? So long that no part of his flesh is visible below it. How long should the upper garment of a disciple of the wise be? So long that no more than a handbreadth of his undergarment is visible below it. How long should the table of a disciple of the wise be? Two-thirds should be covered with a cloth and the other third be left bare for dishes and greens to be put on. The ring [by which the tabletop is hung when not in use] should be on the outside edge of the tabletop.[6] The table of the unlearned is like a hearth with pots all around.[7] What is special about the bed of a disciple of the wise? That under it nothing is kept except for sandals during summer and shoes during winter. But that of an unlearned person is like a crowded storeroom.[8]

330. R. Yohanan said: What disciple of the wise has a lost garment returned to him on his mere say-so?[9] The one who takes care to turn even his undershirt inside out [to see whether there is any spot on it].[10]

331. Disciples of the wise are pleasant when they are together in a company. The unlearned are not pleasant when they are in a company.[11]

332. R. Avin the Levite said: If one shares in a meal at which a disciple of the wise is present, it is as though he feasted amid the splendor of the Presence, for Scripture says, "Aaron came and all the elders of Israel to eat bread with Moses' father-in-law before God" (Exod. 18:12). Was it before God that they ate? Did they not eat before Moses? However, the verse informs you that if one shares a meal at which a disciple of the wise is present, it is as if he feasted amid the splendor of the Presence.[12]

333. We have been taught that R. Simeon said: A disciple of the wise is not allowed to share in a feast that is not associated with a religious act.[13]

334. Our masters taught: Every disciple of the wise who feasts much everywhere ends up by destroying his home, widowing his wife, and orphaning his young. Eventually, his learning will be forgotten; he will be involved in many disputes; nobody will listen to what he says; he will profane the Name of Heaven, the name of his father, and the name of his teacher; and he will bring an evil name upon himself, his children, and his children's children, to the end of time.

How will his son come to be known? He will be called "Son of him who warms himself at every oven," said Abbaye. "Son of the tavern dancer," said Rava. "Son of the plate licker," said R. Papa. "Son of the folder-of-garments-to-sleep-on-anywhere," said R. Shemaiah.[14]

335. "As the tents of Kedar, as the curtains of Solomon" (Song 1:5). Like tents of Kedar, which from the outside look unsightly, sooty, and tattered, but inside contain precious stones and pearls, so are disciples of the wise: they appear to be ungainly and sooty, but within them is Torah—Scripture, Mishnah, Midrashim, *Halakhot*, Talmud, Toseftas, and *Aggadot*.[15]

---

1. B. Ta 4a.
2. B. Sot 5a.
3. B. Shab 114a.
4. By neglecting their appearance. ARN 29.
5. B. Ber 43b and En Yaakov, ad loc.
6. If it were in its middle, it would interfere with the diners.
7. Because the bread and the cloth are in the middle, and the dishes are all around.
8. B. BB 57b–58a.
9. He is not required to identify it. See above, part 3, chap. 2, §117.
10. If he is so meticulous, it may be presumed that he will recognize his shirt by a mere glance. B. Shab 114a.
11. DEZ 4.
12. B. Ber 64a.
13. B. Pes 49a.
14. Ibid.
15. Song R. 1:5, §1.

336. R. Judah son of R. Ilai expounded: What is meant by "Declare unto My people their transgression, and to the house of Jacob their sins" (Isa. 58:1)? "Declare unto My people their transgressions"—to the disciples of the wise, whose unwitting errors are held against them as presumptuous transgressions; "and to the house of Jacob their sins"—to the unlearned, whose presumptuous transgressions are accounted against them as mere unwitting sins.[1]

337. Resh Lakish said: A disciple of the wise who has sinned is not to be put to shame in public, for Scripture says, "Therefore when thou stumblest in the day, and the prophet also stumbleth with thee, then as the night" (Hos. 4:5). That is, cover the prophet's stumbling as with the darkness of night.[2]

338. "Gold and glass cannot equal it" (Job 28:17). R. Akiva said: Just as vessels of gold and vessels of silver, though they are broken, may be mended, so a disciple of the wise, though he has sinned, may be mended.[3]

339. Sages in the school of R. Ishmael taught: If you see a disciple of the wise commit a sin during the night, do not think ill of him the next day, for perhaps he has already turned penitent.

You say, "Perhaps"?

No, he has certainly turned penitent!

This applies only to carnal offenses. But if [he has misappropriated money, you may continue to criticize him] until you know that he has returned the money to its owner.[4]

340. Rava expounded: What is meant by "I went down into the garden of nuts, to look at the green plants of the valley" (Song 6:11)? Why are disciples of the wise likened to the nut? To tell you: As with a nut, even though dirtied in mud and offal, what is within it is not rejected, so it is with a disciple of the wise—even though he has sinned, the Torah within him is not to be rejected.[5]

341. "That which is crooked, cannot be made straight" (Eccles. 1:15). R. Simeon ben Yohai said: Only he can be called "crooked" who was straight at first and then became crooked. Thus we are told not, "Inspect a camel, inspect a pig," but, "Inspect a lamb [to determine whether it is fit as an offering]." Who, accordingly, is referred to as "crooked"? A disciple of the wise who forsakes the Torah. R. Judah ben Lakish said: Any disciple of the wise who forsakes the Torah, Scripture says of him, "As a bird that wandereth from her nest, so is a man that wandereth from his place" (Prov. 27:8).[6]

342. R. Jeremiah bar Abba said in the name of Resh Lakish: A disciple of the wise may not afflict himself by fasting, because thereby he diminishes his capacity for the work of Heaven.

R. Sheshet said: The disciple who would afflict himself by fasting—may a dog devour the meal [that is to break his fast]![7]

343. "Unto you, O men[8] of might, I call" (Prov. 8:4). R. Berekhiah said: These are disciples of the wise, whose strength appears to be like that of women but who do mighty deeds like men.[9]

344. "Wonderful is His counsel, and great is His *tushiyyah*"[10] (Isa. 28:29). Why is Torah called *tushiyyah*, "depleter"? asked R. Hanan. Because it depletes (*mat-teshet*) a man's strength.[11]

345. Rabban Gamaliel had in his household a man who could pick up a basket containing forty *seah* [of flour] and carry it to the baker. Rabban Gamaliel said to him, "Your strength is so great, yet you do not occupy yourself with Torah?" Once the man began to occupy himself with Torah, he found himself able to pick up a basket only of thirty, then of twenty, then of twelve, and then of only eight *seah*. After he finished studying Sifra [the commentary on Leviticus], he could not carry a basket containing even one *seah*. Some say he could not even stand the weight of the head cover that fell over his shoulders. In fact, others had to remove it from his head, since he was unable to do so.[12]

346. "And he carried away all Jerusalem . . . all the mighty men of valor . . . all of them strong and apt for war" (2 Kings 24:14–16). Now, what mighty acts are men capable of performing if they are carried off into exile? And what war are men apt for if they are bound by fetters and weighted down with chains? These can have been no other than the acts of men mighty in the warfare of Torah.[13]

347. R. Yohanan said: What sort of disciple of the wise is appointed leader of a community? One who is asked a *Halakhah* in any area of study and can state it.[14]

348. R. Yohanan also said: What sort of disciple of the wise is he whose townspeople are required to perform his work for him? The one who sets aside his own interests and engages in the interests of Heaven.[15]

349. R. Judah said in the name of Rav: Anyone who flaunts himself in the cloak of a disciple of the wise but

1. B. BM 33b.
2. B. Men 99b.
3. B. Hag 15a.
4. B. Ber 19a.
5. B. Hag 15b.
6. B. Hag 9a and En Yaakov, ad loc.
7. B. Ta 11b.
8. "*Ishim*, used instead of *anashim*, the usual plural for men, is taken as a plural common both to *ish* ('man') and to *ishah* ('woman')" (Brother Caedmon Holmes).
9. B. Yoma 71a.
10. JV: "wisdom."
11. B. Sanh 26b.
12. Song R. 5:14, §3.
13. Sif Deut., §321 (ed. Finkelstein, p. 370); Tanhuma, *Noah*, §3.
14. B. Shab 114a and En Yaakov, ad loc.
15. Ibid.

is not truly a disciple of the wise will not be admitted within the precinct of the Holy One.[1]

350. R. Berekhiah said: He who sees that Torah is running thin in his family should wed the daughter of a disciple of the wise, for Scripture says, "Though the root thereof wax old in the earth, and the stock thereof die in the ground; yet through the scent of water it will bud" (Job 14:8–9).[2]

351. R. Parnakh said in the name of R. Yohanan: When a man is himself a disciple of the wise, and his son is a disciple of the wise, and his son's son is a disciple of the wise, Torah will never run thin in his seed, as is said, "As for Me, this is My covenant with them . . . : When My words . . . do not depart out of thy mouth, nor out of the mouth of thy seed, nor out of the mouth of thy seed's seed, saith the Lord, from henceforth and forever" (Isa. 59:21). What is implied by "saith the Lord"? That the Holy One said, "I am surety to you in this matter." And what is meant by "henceforth and forever"? That from then on, said R. Jeremiah, the Torah will keep returning to the lodging it has become accustomed to.[3]

352. Why is it not common for sages to sire sages? R. Joseph suggested: That it not be said: Torah is a legacy for them. R. Shisha son of R. Idi said: That they should not lord it over the community. Mar Zutra said: [On the contrary], because they do lord it over the community. R. Ashi said: [Indeed], because they call ordinary people "asses."[4]

353. R. Hama said: What is meant by "In the heart of him that hath understanding wisdom resteth quietly, but among fools it seeketh to be known" (Prov. 14:33)? "In the heart of him that hath understanding wisdom resteth quietly" refers to a disciple of the wise who is the son of a disciple of the wise. And "among fools it seeketh to be known" refers to a disciple of the wise who is the son of an unlearned father. As Ulla, quoting a popular adage, put it: "A single coin in a bottle goes clink-clink."[5]

354. The unlearned who are getting on in years—the older they get, the more addled their minds become, as is said, "He taketh away the sense of the aged" (Job 12:20). But with disciples of the wise who are on in years, it is not so. The older they get, the more composed their minds become, as is said, "With learned men there is greater wisdom and more understanding in length of days" (Job 12:12).[6]

355. There are four things commonly used in the world, for each of which, when lost, a substitute is available: "There is a mine for *silver*, and a place for *gold* which they refine. *Iron* is taken out of the dust, and *brass* is molten out of the stone" (Job 28:1–2). Each of these metals, when lost, has a substitute. But when a disciple of the wise dies, who can provide us with a substitute for him? Who can provide us with an alternate for him? "Whence shall wisdom come, and where is the place of understanding? Seeing it is hid from the eyes of all living" (Job 28:21).[7]

356. R. Hiyya bar Ashi said in the name of Rav: Disciples of the wise have no rest either in this world or in the world-to-come, for it is said, "They go from strength to strength, every one of them that appeareth before God in Zion" (Ps. 84:8).[8]

357. R. Judah quoted in the name of Rav: "Let me dwell in Thy tent forever" (Ps. 61:5). Could the thought have come into David's mind that he might live forever? Rather, it means that David prayed to the Holy One: Master of the universe, may words heard from my mouth be uttered forever in this world. For, as R. Yohanan said in the name of R. Simeon ben Jehozadak: When a word heard from the mouth of a disciple of the wise is uttered in this world in his name, the lips of that disciple move and give utterance in the grave. R. Isaac ben Ze'era said: Where do we learn such a thing? From "The speech of thy mouth is like the best wine . . . moving the lips of those that are asleep" (Song 7:10). Just as a mass of heated grapes gives forth its juice as soon as a man puts his finger on it, so, too, the lips of disciples of the wise, as soon as a word once heard from their mouth is uttered in this world in their name, give utterance in the grave.[9]

358. R. Judah said: Every day a man should say the blessing, "Blessed be He who has not made me a boor," for an unlearned man does not fear sin. By what parable may the matter be illustrated? By the one of a king of flesh and blood who asks his servant to cook him a dish. Since that servant has never before in his life cooked a dish, he is sure to burn it and incense his master.[10]

359. A boor [who does not know what sin is] is incapable of fearing sin; and an unlearned person is incapable of being truly pious.[11]

360. We have been taught: Who is an *am ha-aretz*, an "unlearned person"? He who does not eat profane [nonsacred] food in ritual cleanness. So said R. Meir. But the sages say: Anyone who does not tithe his produce in the proper way.

Our masters taught: Who is an *am ha-aretz*? He who does not read the Shema morning and evening—such is the opinion of R. Eliezer. R. Joshua said: Anyone who

1. B. BB 98a.
2. Water means Torah (see above in this chapter, §220). B. Yoma 71a.
3. B. BM 85a.
4. B. Ned 81a and En Yaakov, ad loc.
5. B. BM 85b.
6. Kin 3:6; B. Shab 152a.
7. P. Ber 2:8, 5c.
8. Eager as they are to advance their understanding of Torah. B. Ber 64a.
9. B. Yev 96b–97a; B. Sanh 90b.
10. Tos Ber 7:18.
11. He is incapable of looking beyond the letter of the law into its spirit. Avot 2:5.

does not put on tefillin. Ben Azzai said: Anyone who has no tzitzit attached to his garments. R. Nathan said: Anyone who has no mezuzah at his doorway. R. Nathan ben Joseph said: Anyone who has sons but does not bring them up to the study of Torah. Others say: Even if he has read Scripture and studied Mishnah but has not attended upon disciples of the wise [mixing with them and thereby learning the explication of Scripture and Mishnah], he is an *am ha-aretz.*[1]

361. Anyone who is versed in Scripture and Mishnah and has a gainful occupation will not readily sin, for Scripture says, "A threefold cord is not readily broken" (Eccles. 4:12). But anyone who has no Scripture, no Mishnah, and no gainful occupation does not belong to orderly society.

Bar Kappara expounded: If anyone has neither Scripture nor Mishnah nor gainful occupation, make a vow not to benefit from him, as is said, "Nor sitteth in the seat of scoffers" (Ps. 1:1). When such a one [who has nothing else to do] is in his seat, it is a seat of scoffers.[2]

362. R. Eleazar said: How is a disciple of the wise regarded by an *am ha-aretz*? At first, as a golden ladle. After the disciple of the wise has chatted with him, as a silver ladle. After the disciple of the wise has benefited from him, as a clay ladle, which once broken cannot be mended.[3]

363. Our masters taught: Six things were enjoined concerning the *am ha-aretz:* we may not ask him to act as a witness; we may not accept testimony from him; we may not reveal a secret to him; we may not appoint him as a guardian for orphans; we may not appoint him supervisor of charity funds; and we may not attach ourselves to him on the road.[4]

364. It is told that a certain company of rogues in Kefar Hittim used to eat and drink at the synagogue every Friday before sunset. As they were eating, they would take up the bones and throw them at the teacher's assistant. When one of them was about to die and he was asked, "To whose charge will you commit the guardianship of your son?" he replied, "To the teacher's assistant." He had so many friends, yet he said, "To the teacher's assistant." The reason was that he knew the ways of his companions as well as the ways of the teacher's assistant and knew well who was good [for his son].[5]

365. Our masters taught: One should always sell all that he has in order to marry the daughter of a disciple of the wise, for should he die or be exiled, he will be assured that his sons will turn out to be disciples of the wise. He should not marry the daughter of an *am ha-aretz,* for should he die or be exiled, his sons will turn out to be unlearned.

One should always sell all that he has in order to marry the daughter of a disciple of the wise. For this is like mingling grapes of one vine with grapes of another, a proper and acceptable procedure. And let him not marry the daughter of an *am ha-aretz.* For this is like mingling grapes of a vine with berries of a thornbush, an improper and unacceptable procedure.

One should accordingly be ever willing to sell all he has in order to marry the daughter of a disciple of the wise. If he cannot find the daughter of a disciple of the wise, let him marry the daughter of one of the notables of the generation. If he cannot find the daughter of one of the notables of the generation, let him marry the daughter of the head of a synagogue. If he cannot find the daughter of the head of a synagogue, let him marry the daughter of a collector of charity funds. If he cannot find the daughter of a collector of charity funds, let him marry the daughter of a teacher of young children—just so he does not marry the daughter of an *am ha-aretz,* because such men are detestable, their wives are vermin, and of their daughters it is said, "Cursed be he that lieth with any manner of beast" (Deut. 27:21).[6]

We have been taught that R. Meir used to say: He who weds his daughter to an *am ha-aretz* is as though he had bound her and laid her down before a lion: just as a lion first rips apart and then devours, and feels no shame, so an *am ha-aretz* first beats his wife [into submission] and then copulates with her, and feels no shame.[7]

366. Greater is the hatred the *amme ha-aretz*[8] feel for a disciple of the wise than the hatred heathens feel for Israel. Their women hate even more fiercely than the man. It is further taught: He who has studied Torah and then given up his study hates disciples of the wise even more fiercely than all the aforegoing.

We have been taught that R. Akiva declared, "When I was an *am ha-aretz,* I used to say: Would that I had a disciple of the wise before me, so I could bite him as an ass bites." His disciples said to him, "Master, you mean as a dog bites." "No," he replied. "When the ass bites, he breaks bones; when the dog bites, he does not break bones."

We have been taught that R. Eliezer said: But for our being needed by them for the give-and-take of trade, they would kill us.

R. Eleazar said: A man should not attach himself to an *am ha-aretz* on the road, because it is said, "[The Torah] is thy life, and the length of thy days" (Deut. 30:20). If [by abandoning the study of Torah] the *am ha-aretz* shows that he has no concern for his own life, how much less so for the life of his fellow man.

R. Samuel bar Nahmani said in the name of R. Yohanan: One may rip an *am ha-aretz* apart [down his front] as one does a fish. And down his back as well,[9] R. Samuel bar Isaac added.

R. Eleazar said: It is permitted to stab an *am haaretz* on a Day of Atonement that falls on the Sabbath. His

1. B. Ber 47b.
2. B. Kid 40b–41a.
3. B. Sanh 52b and En Yaakov, ad loc.
4. B. Pes 49b and En Yaakov, ad loc.
5. Gen. R. 65:16.
6. Lacking as they do a moral sense and intellectual perception.
7. B. Pes 49a–b.
8. The plural of *am ha-aretz.*
9. Which is more painful.

disciples said to him: You mean to slaughter him? No, he replied, slaughtering requires a blessing; stabbing does not.[1]

367. R. Eleazar said: The *amme ha-aretz* will not be brought back to life. R. Yohanan argued: It is not acceptable to their Master that you should speak of them thus. R. Eleazar rejoined: I do no more than expound the verse that asserts, "When thy dew is as the dew of light, the earth shall bring to life the dead" (Isa. 26:19). When a man makes use of Torah's light, Torah's light will bring him back to life; but he who does not make use of Torah's light, Torah's light will not bring him back to life. Still, when R. Eleazar noticed that R. Yohanan was deeply troubled, he added: My master, I have found a remedy for them in the Torah: "Ye that did cleave unto the Lord your God are alive, every one of you this day" (Deut. 4:4). But is it possible to cleave to the Presence, of which it is said, "The Lord thy God is a devouring fire" (Deut. 4:24)? Rather, what the verse means is that when a man weds his daughter to a disciple of the wise, or carries on trade in behalf of disciples of the wise, or supports disciples of the wise out of what he possesses, Scripture accounts it to him as though he were cleaving to the Presence.[2]

368. A favorite saying of the sages of Yavneh: I am God's creature, and my fellow man is God's creature. I—my work is in the city; he—his work is in the field. I rise early for my work, even as he rises early for his work. Just as he does not encroach on my work, so I do not encroach on his work. Lest you say, "I do much [in study of Torah], while he does little," we have been taught: One may may do much and another may do little. What is important is that he direct his heart to Heaven.[3]

369. R. Judah son of Ilai expounded the verse "Your brethren [that, is the *amme ha-aretz*] who spurn you" (Isa. 66:5). Lest you suppose their expectation [for future life] is gone, their hope for it has ceased, the verse goes on: "We will see your joy" (ibid.).[4]

370. A man should not adopt the rule: Love the sages, . . . love disciples of the wise, and hate the *amme ha-aretz*. You should love all of them.[5]

371. R. Ammi said: We learn from the words of R. Yose[6] that even if a man studies but one chapter in the morning and one chapter in the evening, he fulfills the precept "This book of Torah shall not depart out of thy mouth" (Josh. 1:8). R. Yohanan said in the name of R. Simeon ben Jehozadak: Even if a man merely recites the Shema in the morning and in the evening, he fulfills the precept "This book of Torah shall not depart," etc. It is forbidden, however, to say such a thing in the presence of *amme ha-aretz*.[7] But Rava said: On the contrary, it is a mitzvah [a religious duty] to say this in the presence of *amme ha-aretz*.[8]

372. R. Eleazar said in the name of R. Hanina: Let not the blessing of a common man seem trivial in your eyes.

R. Eleazar also said in the name of R. Hanina: Let not the curse of a common man seem trivial in your eyes.[9]

The Oral Torah

373. Moses received the Torah at Sinai and handed it on to Joshua, Joshua to the elders, the elders to the prophets, and the prophets to the Men of the Great Assembly.[10]

374. R. Eleazar said: The greater portion of the Torah is found in the written text,[11] and only the smaller portion in the Oral Torah, for Scripture says, "I wrote for him the major portion of [the precepts of] My Torah" (Hos. 8:12). But R. Yohanan maintained: The greater part was given orally, and only the smaller part is in the written text, for Scripture says, "By the mouth of these words" (Exod. 34:27).

R. Judah bar Nahmani, the interpreter of R. Simeon ben Lakish, said: Scripture asserts, "Write thou these words" (Exod. 34:27), and also asserts, "According to the mouth whereby these words [were uttered]" (ibid.). How are both assertions to be maintained? You are not allowed to say orally [but only to read from a scroll] the words that are written; and you are not allowed to set down in writing the words that were uttered by word of mouth.

Sages in the school of R. Ishmael taught: Scripture says, "These"—"these" you may write down, but you are not to write down *Halakhot* [which were given orally].

R. Yohanan said: God made a covenant with Israel only for the sake of matters that were given by word of mouth, for Scripture says, "By the mouth of these words I have made a covenant with thee and with Israel" (Exod. 34:27).[12]

375. The Holy One foresaw that the nations of the world would get to translate the Torah and, reading it in Greek, would declare, "We are Israel." And to this day the scales appear to be evenly balanced between both claims. But then the Holy One will say to the nations of the world, "You claim you are My children? I have no way of knowing other than that My children are those who possess My

1. B. Pes 49a–b.
2. B. Ket 111b.
3. B. Ber 17a.
4. All of us will be together in the joy to come. B. BM 33b.
5. ARN 16.
6. Who ruled that if the old shewbread remains on the table for a while in the morning and the new for some time in the evening, the prescription "continually" is deemed to be observed.
7. Lest they conceive the erroneous idea that neither they nor their children need study Torah.
8. They may conclude that if, merely for recitation of the Shema, Scripture promises, "Then thou shalt make thy way prosperous, and then thou shalt have good success," how much greater by far is the reward of those who devote themselves to Torah. B. Men 99b.
9. B. Meg 15a.
10. Avot 1:1.
11. Explicitly or implicitly.
12. B. Git 60b.

secret lore." What secret lore? Mishnah, which was given by word of mouth.

"And the Lord said to Moses: 'Write thou these words' " (Exod. 34:27). When the Holy One came to give the Torah to Israel, he uttered it to Moses in its order, Scripture and Mishnah, Talmud and *Aggadah*, as is said, "The Lord spoke all these words" (Exod. 20:1). Even what a faithful student was someday to ask his teacher, the Holy One uttered to Moses at that time. After Moses had learned the Torah, the Holy One said: Go and teach it to My children. Moses replied: Master of the universe, write it down for Your children. The Holy One then said: What do you wish? That the Mishnah also be in written form? Then what would be the difference between Israel and the nations of the world? With regard to this response, Scripture quotes God as saying, "Had I written the full abundance[1] of My law for him" (Hos. 8:12)—had I indeed done such a thing, "the children of Israel would by now have been accounted as strangers [the same as the nations of the world]" (ibid.). Therefore give them Scripture in writing and Mishnah by word of mouth. "Write thou these words"—Scripture. Then: "By these words uttered with the mouth I have made a covenant with thee" (ibid.)—these words being Mishnah and Talmud, which make it possible to tell Israel and the nations of the world apart.[2]

376. The sages taught: Some time ago Rome's wicked government sent two military officers to the sages of Israel with the request: Teach us your Torah. They read it through once, a second time, and a third time. When they were about to take their leave, they said: We scrutinized your entire Torah, and it is true, except for one thing. You say, "An ox belonging to an Israelite that gores an ox belonging to a Gentile is exempt from paying damages; but if a Gentile's ox gores an Israelite's ox, whether for the first time or the third time, the Gentile owner must pay full damages."[3] There are only two alternatives here: if the term "another's" (Exod. 21:35) excludes anyone who is not a Jew, then a Gentile's ox that gores an Israelite's ox should also be free of paying damages; if on the other hand the term "another's" is not exclusive, then the Israelite's ox that gores the Gentile's ox should also be liable. But we will not divulge this inconsistency to the government.[4]

377. Elijah said: Once, as I was walking along a road, a man accosted me. He came at me aggressively with the sort of argument that leads to heresy. It turned out that the man had Scripture but no Mishnah. He asserted: Scripture was given us from Mount Sinai, but not Mishnah. I replied: My son, were not both Scripture and Mishnah given by the Almighty? Does the fact that they are different from each other mean that both cannot have been given by Him? By what parable may the question be elucidated? By the one of a mortal king who had two servants, whom he loved with perfect love. To one he gave a measure of wheat, and to the other he gave a measure of wheat; to one a bundle of flax, and to the other a bundle of flax. What did the clever one of the two do? He took the flax and wove it into a napkin. He took the wheat and made it into fine flour by sifting the grain and grinding it. Then he kneaded the dough and baked it, set the loaf of bread on the table, spread the napkin over the bread, and left it to await the coming of the king.

But the foolish one of the two did not do anything at all.

After a while the king came into his house and said to the two servants: My sons, bring me what I gave you. One brought out the table with the loaf of bread baked of fine flour on it, and with the napkin spread over the bread. The other brought out his wheat in a basket with a bundle of flax over the wheat grains.

What a shame! What a disgrace!

So, too, when the Holy One gave the Torah to Israel, He gave it as wheat to be turned into fine flour and as flax to be turned into cloth for garments.[5]

378. Our masters taught: A story of R. Yohanan ben Beroka and R. Eleazar ben Hisma who went to Pekiin[6] to pay their respects to R. Joshua in his old age. He asked them, "What new teaching was there in the academy this time?" They replied, "Master, we are your disciples and drink only of your water." R. Joshua: "Even so, it is impossible for a session in the academy to take place without at least one interpretation that is new. Whose Sabbath was it?"[7] "It was the Sabbath of R. Eleazar ben Azariah." "And what did the haggadic exposition deal with that day?" "With the portion 'Assemble' (Deut. 31:12)." "How did he expound it?" " 'Assemble the people, the men and the women and the little ones'—the men, to be sure, came to learn, and the women to listen. But why did the little ones have to come? In order to bestow reward upon those who brought them." R. Joshua: "[There you are!] You had a precious jewel in your hands and were about to deprive me of it!"

R. Yohanan and R. Eleazar went on to say, "R. Eleazar ben Azariah also expounded the verse 'The words of the wise are as goads, as nails planted by masters of assemblies; they are given from one Shepherd' [Eccles. 12:11]. Why are words of Torah likened to goads? To tell you that even as a goad directs the heifer along her furrows to bring life to the world, so words of Torah direct the hearts of those who study them from ways of death to ways of life. The words are spoken of as 'planted': even as a planted tree bears fruit and multiplies, so words of Torah bear fruit and multiply. 'Masters of assemblies'—these are disciples of the wise who sit in many assemblies and occupy themselves with Torah. Some declare 'unclean' and others declare 'clean.' Some prohibit and others permit. Some declare 'unfit' and others declare 'fit.' Lest a man say, "How, then, can I possibly learn Torah?" Scripture

1. Mishnah as well as Scripture.
2. Tanhuma B, *Ki Tissa*, §17; Tanhuma, *Ki Tissa*, §60; Exod. R. 47:1.
3. An ox belonging to a Jew that does injury for the first time incurs payment for only half the damage.
4. B. BK 38a.
5. TdEZ 2 (JPS, pp. 407–8).
6. A southern town in the Land of Israel between Lydda and Yavneh.
7. Rabban Gamaliel used to lecture on two Sabbaths and R. Eleazar on the third Sabbath. See above, part 2, chap. 1, §75.

asserts, 'They are given from one Shepherd.' One God gave and one leader uttered all of them at the command of the Lord of all works, blessed be He, as is said, 'And God spoke all these words, saying' [Exod. 20:1]. It is up to you to make your ear like a hopper and get yourself a perceptive heart to understand the intent of those who declare 'clean' and those who declare 'unclean,' of those who prohibit and those who permit, of those who declare 'unfit' and those who declare 'fit.' "

When he heard this interpretation, R. Joshua said, "It is no orphaned generation in whose midst R. Eleazar ben Azariah lives."[1]

379. "They are given from one shepherd" (Eccles. 12:11). The Holy One said: If you hear a word of Torah that pleases you from a lowly one in Israel, regard it not as something you heard from such a lowly one, but as though you had heard it from a man of note—indeed, not merely from a man of note, but as though you had heard it from a sage; indeed, not merely from a sage, but as though you heard it from a prophet; indeed, not merely from a prophet, but as though you had heard it from *the* shepherd, the shepherd being none other than Moses.[2]

380. R. Yannai said: Had the Torah been given in the form of clear-cut decisions, Israel would have had no leg to stand on. And the proof? After "the Lord spoke to Moses," Moses asked: Master of the universe, let me have the clear-cut rule. God replied: The majority is to be followed.[3] When a majority acquits, acquit. When a majority condemns, condemn. Therefore [to allow the possibility of differering opinions], the Torah may be expounded with forty-nine arguments by which something may be declared unclean and forty-nine other arguments by which the same thing may be declared clean.[4]

381. Once, while Rabban Gamaliel and the elders were reclining in an upper chamber in Jericho, dates[5] were brought in. They ate them, and Rabban Gamaliel gave permission to R. Akiva to say grace. R. Akiva quickly said the one blessing that is a summary of three. Rabban Gamaliel said to him: Akiva, how long will you stick your head into a quarrel [not of your making and decide against my opinion]? R. Akiva replied: Our master, you, to be sure, say one thing, and your colleagues say another. Nevertheless, you yourself taught us that when an individual differs from the majority, the *Halakhah* is decided with the majority.[6]

382. "The words of the wise are *ka-dorbonot*" (Eccles. 12:11)—as a ball (*kaddur*) of children (*banot*). Just as a ball children play with is tossed from hand to hand but never falls on the ground, so Moses received the Torah at Sinai and handed it on to Joshua, Joshua to the elders, the elders to the prophets, and the prophets to the Men of the Great Assembly, etc.[7]

383. "Thy cheeks are comely with circlets (*torim*)" (Song 1:10)—with two Torahs, the one in writing and the one by word of mouth.[8]

384. The Torah in writing is made up of general rules; the Torah by word of mouth is made up of specific details.[9]

385. [The rules concerning] release from vows, which have no basis in Scripture, hover in the air. The laws concerning the Sabbath, festal offerings, and acts of trespass[10] are as mountains hanging by a hair, for they have scant proof from Scripture but many *Halakhot.* The laws concerning civil cases, the offering of sacrifices, ritual cleanness and uncleanness, and forbidden sexual relations (Lev. 18:6ff.) have their basis in Scripture. Nevertheless, both kinds of laws are essentials of the Torah.[11]

386. "*Kevutzotav taltallim*" (Song 5:11).[12] R. Hisda said in the name of Mar Ukba: The verse shows that on every single stroke (*kotz ve-kotz*) [over the letters of Torah], there are mounds upon mounds (*tille tillim*) of *Halakhot.*[13]

387. Hananiah son of R. Joshua's brother said: Between each commandment and the next [on the Tablets] were written the related portions of Torah and the minutiae derived from them.

When R. Yohanan, while studying Scripture, came to the verse "In the hands [of God] was something resembling waves (*gelile*) as radiant as gold, [the troughs between them] filled with Tarshish" (Song 5:14),[14] he would say: The son of R. Joshua's brother has instructed me well. Just as in the sea there are small waves (*gallim*) between one large wave and another, so the related portions of Torah and the minutiae derived from them were written between one commandment and the next on the Tablets, for in going on to say, "[The troughs between them] filled with Tarshish," Scripture means that these were filled with Talmud, which is like the Great Sea.[15]

---

1. B. Hag 3a and En Yaakov, ad loc.; ARN 18.
2. P. Sanh 10:1, 28a; Sif Deut., §41.
3. Exod. 23:2.
4. P. Sanh 4:2, 22a.
5. One of the seven species listed in Deut. 8:8 as "honey." For these, Rabban Gamaliel maintained, the full-length—not a summary—grace should be said.
6. B. Ber 37a.
7. Eccles R. 12:11, §1.
8. Song R. 1:10, §1.
9. E.g., the general prohibition in Scripture of work on the Sabbath and the specification in rabbinic tradition of the thirty-nine kinds of prohibited work. Tanhuma, *Noah,* §3.
10. Misappropriation of holy things to secular use. See Lev. 5:14–16.
11. B. Hag 10a.
12. "His locks are curled."
13. B. Er 21b.
14. JV: "His hands are rods of gold set with beryl." But *gelile* ("rods") can also mean "waves"; *memullaim* ("set" or "studded") can also mean "filled"; and the meaning of "Tarshish," variously rendered "beryl," "jacinth," or "topaz," is uncertain. In saying that "Jonah rose up to flee to Tarshish" (Jon. 1:3), it is suggested as Targum Jonathan makes clear, that Jonah sought to flee to the Great Sea from the Presence of the Lord.
15. Song R. 5:14, §2; P. Shek 6:1, 49d.

388. R. Meir had a disciple whose name was Symmachus. If anything was ritually unclean, he could supply forty-eight reasons to prove its uncleanness, and if anything was ritually clean, he could supply forty-eight reasons to prove its cleanness.[1]

389. "His legs are as pillars of marble set upon sockets of fine gold" (Song 5:15). A pillar that does not have a capital above and a pedestal beneath does not strike one as handsome. Thus, there is no section in Torah that does not have a capital before it and a pedestal after it.[2]

390. The sages in the school of R. Ishmael taught: "As a hammer may be shattered by a rock" (Jer. 23:29). Just as a hammer that strikes a rock may itself be shattered into many fragments, so may a verse [encountering the scrutiny of a keen mind] yield many meanings.[3]

391. "And the smell of thine ointment because of all manner of spices" (Song 4:10). R. Samuel bar Nahman said: Of itself, oil is without scent, but when you perfume it with spices, it gives forth all kinds of fragrance. So, too, as you expound a verse, you find in it all kinds of rich meaning.[4]

392. R. Kahana said: By the time I was eighteen I had studied all six divisions of the Mishnah, yet until today I did not know that a verse cannot depart from its plain meaning.[5]

393. The sages of former generations were called *soferim* ["scribes"], because they counted (*soferim*) all the letters in the Torah.

Or: *Soferim*, because they arranged the laws in the Torah by numbers.[6]

394. "Black as a raven" (Song 5:11). R. Alexandrai bar Haggai said in the name of R. Alexandrai the Hymn Writer: If all the inhabitants of the world were to gather and try to turn one wing of a raven white, they would be unable to do so. So, too, if all the inhabitants of the world were to gather and try to remove a *yod*, the smallest letter in the Torah, they would be unable to do so.[7]

395. The words "Because he hath despised the word of the Lord" (Num. 15:31) refer to an *epikoros* [Epicurean], "one irreverent toward religion."

Or, the words refer to one who maintains that the Torah is not from Heaven. Even if he says that the entire Torah is from Heaven, except for one verse that [he contends] was not said by the Holy One but was said by Moses on his own, he is included in "He that despised the word of the Lord." Even if he says, "The entire Torah, all of it, is from Heaven, except for this fine point, except for this *a fortiori* argument, except for this inference from analogy, he is included in "He that despised the word of the Lord." A parable of a heap of stones: when only one of them is disturbed, all of them are disturbed.[8]

396. What kind of person is meant by *epikoros*? R. Joseph said: The kind who jeers: "What use have the sages been to us? They read Scripture for their own benefit and study Mishnah for their own benefit."

Rava said: People like the family of Benjamin the Physician, who say: "What use have the sages been to us? They could never allow us [to eat] the raven or forbid us to eat the dove."[9] R. Papa said: Like one who says, "Oh, those sages!"[10]

397. He who ridicules the words of the sages will be punished with boiling excrement.[11]

398. R. Yudan said: At one time Mordecai went around among all the nursing women, but just then he could not find one for [the infant] Esther. So he himself gave her suck, for, as R. Berekhiah and R. Abbahu declared in the name of R. Eliezer, milk came to him and he was able to give her suck. When R. Abbahu cited this tradition before an assembly, the assembly laughed derisively at what he had to say. But he asked: Does not a Mishnah affirm this? "R. Simeon ben Eleazar says: Milk of a male is ritually clean" (Makh 6:7).[12]

399. Polemon asked Rabbi [Judah I, the Patriarch], "He who has two heads—which head should he put tefillin on?" R. Judah replied, "Either leave [the house of study] or consider yourself under the ban." Just then a man came in and said, "A child with two heads has been born to me. How much am I to give the priest for his redemption?"[13]

400. The ordinances of Torah need no additional strengthening; but the ordinances of the scribes do need such strengthening.[14]

401. Resh Lakish said: There are times when the nullifying of the Torah may lead to the establishing of it. Thus it is said, "Which (*asher*) thou didst break" (Exod. 34:1; Deut. 10:2), by which the Holy One meant: You did well (*yishar*) to break the Tablets.[15]

---

1. B. Er 13b and En Yaakov, ad loc.
2. What precedes and what follows each lesson help to explain its meaning. Tanhuma B, *Be-har*, §2.
3. B. Sanh 34a.
4. Song R. 4:10, §1.
5. "In the narrative and poetical passages" [Shab, Soncino, p. 296, n. 5]. B. Shab 63a.
6. Such as four kinds of injury (BK 1:1) and thirty-nine kinds of work prohibited on the Sabbath (Shab 7:1). B. Kid 30a; P. Shek 5:1.
7. Lev. R. 19:2; Song R. 5:11, §3.
8. B. Sanh 99a; P. Sanh 10:1, 27b.
9. Bound as they are by what is written in the Torah.
10. B. Sanh 99b–100a.
11. B. Er 21b.
12. Gen. R. 30:8.
13. The fixed sum for one firstborn was five shekels (see Num. 18:16). B. Men 37a.
14. B. Ta 17b.
15. B. Men 99a–b.

402. R. Yohanan and Resh Lakish used to look into a book of *Aggadah*[1] on Sabbaths and, citing the verse "When work is to be done for the Lord, [one ordinance of] Thy Torah may be violated" (Ps. 119:126), expounded it thus: It is better that a single letter in the Torah be uprooted, so that the [entire] Torah may not be forgotten in Israel.[2]

Holy Writings and Other Books

403. R. Yohanan said in the name of R. Banaah: The Torah was given in separate scrolls, for David declared, "Then I said, I, who am alluded to in a scroll in the book of Torah, am come" (Ps. 40:8).[3] But R. Simeon ben Lakish said: The Torah was given as [one] sealed [book], for it is said, "[When Moses had finished writing the words of this Torah in a book, to the very end, Moses commanded the Levites], 'Take this book of Torah' " (Deut. 31:26).[4]

404. "Write thou" (Exod. 34:27). The ministering angels began to say to the Holy One: Are You giving permission to Moses to write down anything he wishes? He may well say to Israel, "I gave you the Torah—it is I who wrote and gave it to you." The Holy One replied: No, Moses would never do such a thing! But no matter what he does, he is trusted, as is said, "Not so with my servant Moses; he is trusted in all My house" (Num. 12:7).[5]

405. R. Simeon ben Lakish said: In the Temple Court were found three Torah scrolls: The scroll of *maon*, the scroll of *zaatute*, and the scroll of *hu*. In one scroll they found written, "The eternal God is a dwelling place (*maon*)" (Deut. 33:27), but in two other scrolls the word for dwelling place was given as *meonah*. So the sages discarded the one and kept the two. In one scroll it was written, "And he sent the young men (*zaatute*) of the children of Israel" (Exod. 24:5), but in two other scrolls the word for "young men" was *naare*. So they discarded the one and kept the two. In one scroll they found the word for "she" represented eleven times by the masculine form *hu*, "he," but in two others they found the word for "she" represented eleven times by the word *hi*, "she." So they discarded the one scroll and kept the two.[6]

406. "The secret things belong unto the Lord our God; but the things that are revealed belong to us and to our children forever" (Deut. 29:28). Each of the letters that spell out the words "to us and to our children" and the first letter in the word "forever" have a dot over them. Why? Because Ezra said: If the prophet Elijah comes and asks me, "Why did you write it thus?" I will reply, "But I did put dots over the letters [to indicate my uncertainty about the text]." If, however, he says to me, "You wrote out the text accurately," I will remove the dots.[7]

407. Our masters taught: "And it came to pass when the Ark set forward that Moses said," etc. (Num. 10:35). For this section the Holy One provided signs to precede it and signs to follow it,[8] in order to indicate that the section is not in its proper place.[9] But Rabbi [Judah I, the Patriarch] said: This is not the real reason. The signs indicate that the section is to be regarded as a separate book in itself.

Rabban Simeon ben Gamaliel said: The section is destined to be moved from its present place and put where it belongs. Why then was it put here to begin with? In order to provide a break between the account of one calamity and the account of another calamity that immediately followed.[10]

408. Many sections in Scripture are placed next to each other even though they are as distant from each other as the east is from the west.[11]

409. "The enemy said: 'I will pursue,' " etc. (Exod. 15:19). This was really the beginning of the section. Why then was it written here [in the middle of the section]? Because no strict order of "earlier" and "later" is observed in Scripture.

A similar instance: "And it came to pass on the eighth day, that Moses called Aaron and his sons," etc. (Lev. 9:1). This was really the beginning of the section. Why then was it written here [in the middle of the section]? Because no strict order of "earlier" and "later" is observed in Scripture.

A similar instance: "In the year that King Uzziah died," etc. (Isa. 6:1). This was really the beginning of the book. Why then was it written here? Becuse no strict order of "earlier" and "later" is observed in Scripture.

A similar instance: "Son of man, stand upon thy feet, and I will speak with thee" (Ezek. 2:1)—some say it is: "Son of man, put forth a riddle" (Ezek. 17:2)—was really the beginning of the book. Why then was it written here? Because no strict order of "earlier" and "later" is observed in Scripture.

A similar instance: "Go, and cry in the ears of Jerusalem" (Jer. 2:2). This was really the beginning of the book. Why then was it written here? Because no strict order of "earlier" and "later" is observed in Scripture.

1. Even though the writing down of *Aggadah* was prohibited.
2. B. Tem 14b.
3. JV: "Lo, I am come with the roll of a book which is prescribed for me." The allusion to David is said to be found in Gen. 19:15, where the clause "The two daughters that are found" is read "The two daughters who are finds"; and the word "finds" is construed as an adumbration of God's saying in later years, "I regard David as a 'find' " (Ps. 89:21).
4. B. Git 60a.
5. Exod. R. 47:9.
6. Sof 6; Sif Deut., §356.
7. ARN 34.
8. The letter *nun* upside down precedes and follows the section.
9. It properly belongs to Num. 2, where Israel's disposition according to the banners of the tribes is set forth.
10. The three days' journey from the mount of the Lord (Num. 10:33), which is construed as a departure from God, and the account of the murmurers who spoke evil (Num. 11:1). B. Shab 115b–116a and En Yaakov, ad loc.
11. Sif Num., §131.

A similar instance: "Israel was a luxuriant vine" (Hos. 10:1). This was really the beginning of the book. Why then was it written here? Because no strict order of "earlier" and "later" is observed in Scripture.

A similar instance: "I, Koheleth, have been king over Israel in Jerusalem" (Eccles. 1:12). This was really the beginning of the book. Why then was it written here? Because no strict order of "earlier" and "later" is observed in Scripture.[1]

410. "Man knoweth not the order thereof" (Job 28:13). R. Eleazar taught: The sections in Scripture are not given in sequential order.[2]

411. "And Jacob vowed a vow" (Gen. 28:20). R. Abbahu and R. Jonathan differed. One maintained that the narrative is in scrambled order, but the other said that it follows the order in which the events took place. He who says that the account is in scrambled order [bases himself on the argument that since] God had already promised, "And behold, I am with thee" (Gen. 28:15), why should Jacob now be saying, "If God will be with me" (Gen. 28:20)? But how does he who maintains that the narrative is in order explain Jacob's saying, "If God will be with me"? Because Jacob declared: If the conditions [namely, my refraining from sin] are fulfilled, so that God will [find it possible to] be with me and to protect me, then I will fulfill my vow.[3]

412. Our masters taught: The order of the Prophets is: Joshua and Judges, Samuel and Kings, Jeremiah and Ezekiel, Isaiah and the Twelve [Minor Prophets].

The order of the Writings is: Ruth and the book of Psalms and Job and Proverbs; Ecclesiastes, Song of Songs, and Lamentations; Daniel and the Scroll of Esther; Ezra[4] and Chronicles.

Moses wrote his own book, as well as the oracles of Balaam (Num. 23–24), and Job. Joshua wrote the book that bears his name and the last eight verses of the Five Books. Samuel wrote the book that bears his name, as well as Judges and Ruth. David wrote the book of Psalms, including in it the work of ten elders. Jeremiah wrote the book that bears his name, the book of Kings, and Lamentations. Hezekiah and his colleagues published Isaiah, Proverbs, Song of Songs, and Ecclesiastes. The Men of the Great Assembly published Ezekiel and the Twelve [Minor Prophets], Daniel and the Scroll of Esther. Ezra wrote the book that bears his own name and the genealogies in the book of Chronicles up to his own time.

David wrote the book of Psalms, including in it the work of ten elders: Adam, Melchizedek, Abraham, Moses, Heman, Jeduthun, Asaph, and the three sons of Korah.[5]

413. R. Huna said in the name of R. Assi: Though certain psalms bear the name of one of the ten authors, the book as a whole bears the name of David, king of Israel. As a parable tells us, there was a company of musicians who sought to sing a hymn to the king. The king said to them: To be sure, all of you are skilled musicians, all of you are devout, all of you are worthy of taking part in the singing of a hymn before me, yet let the hymn be sung by So-and-so only, on behalf of all of you. Why? Because his voice is sweetest.

Similarly, when ten righteous men sought to sing the book of Psalms, the Holy One said to them: To be sure, all of you are skilled musicians, devout, and worthy of taking part in the singing of hymns to Me, yet let the hymn be sung by David in behalf of all of you. Why? Because his voice is the sweetest, as is said, "The saying of David the son of Jesse . . . the sweet singer of the psalms of Israel" (2 Sam. 23:1). Who, therefore, makes the psalms of Israel sweet? David son of Jesse.[6]

414. R. Simon said: Be'eri[7] uttered only two verses in prophecy, and since these were not sufficient to make up a separate book, they were attached to the book of Isaiah. The two verses were "And when they shall say," etc. (Isa. 8:19) and the verse that follows it.[8]

415. A certain sage who was sitting before R. Samuel bar Nahmani said: Job never was and never existed—he is no more than a paradigm. R. Samuel replied: To confound such as you, Scripture says, "There was a man in the land of Uz, Job was his name" (Job 1:1).

The sage retorted: If it is as you say, what of the verse "The poor man had nothing, save one little ewe lamb, which he had bought and reared," etc. (2 Sam. 12:3)? Did such a thing really happen? Was not the tale a paradigm? So, too, Job was a paradigm.

R. Samuel: But if so, why are his name and the name of his land mentioned?[9]

416. Resh Lakish said: Job [as described in Scripture] never was and never existed. What did Resh Lakish mean by saying Job never was and never existed? He meant only that the unbelievable sufferings Job underwent according to Scripture [never took place]. Why then were they set down about him? Because if they had come upon him, he would have been able to withstand them.

R. Hanina said: Job was a Gentile. For, R. Hiyya taught, the Holy One said: One righteous Gentile rose up for Me among the nations. so I gave him [his extraordinary] reward [in this world] and let him go. Who was He? Job.[10]

417. We have been taught that R. Eliezer said: The dead whom Ezekiel had brought back to life stood up on their feet, uttered song, and died again at once. What song did

1. Mek, *Be-shallah, Shirata*, 7; Yalkut, *Be-shallah*, §249.
2. MTeh 3:2.
3. Gen. R. 70:4; Yalkut, *Va-yetze*, §122.
4. Ezra and Nehemiah were originally one book.
5. The verses beginning "Thine eyes did see mine unformed substance" (Ps. 139:16 and Ps. 92) are ascribed to Adam; Ps. 110 to Melchizedek; Ps. 90 to Moses; Ps. 89 to Ethan the Ezrahite, who is identified as Abraham. B. BB 14b–15a.
6. Song R. 4:1, §1; Eccles. R. 7:19, §4.
7. The father of Hosea. See Hos. 1:1.
8. Lev. R. 6:6.
9. B. BB 15a.
10. See Job 42:10–17. Unlike Jews, whose reward is in the world-to-come, Job was given a greater reward in this world. Gen. R. 57:4.

they utter? The Lord slayeth in righteousness and bringeth back to life in mercy. R. Joshua said, The song they sang was: "The Lord killeth and maketh alive; He bringeth down to the grave, and bringeth up" (1 Sam. 2:6). R. Judah said: It was truth—it was parable. R. Nehemiah asked him: If it was truth, how can you speak of it as a parable? And if it was a parable, how can you say it was truth? Say, then: In truth it was parable.

R. Eliezer son of R. Yose the Galilean said: The dead whom Ezekiel had brought back to life went up to the Land of Israel, wed wives, and begot sons and daughters. R. Judah ben Betera stood up on his feet and said: I am one of their descendants, and these are the tefillin my dear father's father left me [as a keepsake] from them.[1]

418. R. Simon said in the name of R. Joshua ben Levi, and R. Hama the father of R. Hoshaiah in the name of Rabbi [Judah I, the Patriarch]: The book of Chronicles was given for no other purpose than that the meaning underlying it be expounded.[2]

419. R. Simeon ben Pazzi said: When my dear father Pazzi began a discourse on the book of Chronicles, he would speak to the book and say: All that is set down in you is baffling. Still, we know how to bring forth the inner meaning that is yours.[3]

420. R. Simlai came before R. Yohanan and said, "Let my master teach me the Book of Genealogies."[4] R. Yohanan: "Where are you from?" "From Lydda."[5] "And where do you live?" "In Nehardea." R. Yohanan: "We do not teach it to people of Lydda or of Nehardea, much less to a native of Lydda who lives in Nehardea." But R. Simlai kept urging R. Yohanan until he consented. Next R. Simlai asked, "Will you teach it to me in three months?" R. Yohanan picked up a pebble and tossed it at R. Simlai as he said, "Beruriah, wife of R. Meir, daughter of R. Hanina ben Teradion, who could master three hundred *Halakhot* a day, was nevertheless unable to discharge in three years what she had taken upon herself to do in the study of this book. Yet you speak of doing it in three months!"[6]

421. Rami bar R. Yuda said in the name of Rav: Ever since the Book of Genealogies was suppressed, the strength of the sages has been depleted and the light of their eyes dimmed.[7]

Mar Zutra said: The words between "Azel" and "Azel" were laden with so many exegetical interpretations that, if set down, they would have required four hundred camels to carry them.[8]

1. B. Sanh 92a.
2. Lev. R. 1:3; Ruth R. 2:1.
3. B. Meg 13a and En Yaakov, ad loc.; Yalkut, 1 Chron., §674.
4. A commentary on Chronicles.
5. Southern Palestine.
6. B. Pes 62b.
7. It contained reasons for the commandments. So Rashi, ad loc.
8. So enormous was the number of interpretations in the passage beginning "And Azel had six sons" (1 Chron. 8:38) and ending with "And Azel had six sons" (1 Chron. 9:44). B. Pes 62b.

422. R. Simeon ben Lakish said: Were a man to tell me that in Babylonia there is a Midrash on Chronicles, I would go and bring it. But as things stand, even if all our masters were to gather, they would not have the strength to bring it from there.[9]

423. R. Judah said in the name of Rav: Truly, there is a man whose name should be remembered for blessing. He is Hananiah ben Hezekiah. But for him, the book of Ezekiel would have been suppressed,[10] for its words contradicted the Torah.[11] What did he do? He had three hundred kegs of oil taken up to him and sat in an upper chamber until he so expounded them [that the contradictions were reconciled].

R. Judah son of R. Samuel bar Shilat said in the name of Rav: The sages wished to suppress the book of Ecclesiastes, because its words contradicted one another.[12] Why did they not suppress it? Because its beginning is religious teaching, and its end religious teaching.[13]

They also wished to suppress the book of Proverbs, because its statements contradicted one another.[14] And why did they not suppress it? Because they said: Did we not examine the book of Ecclesiastes and discover reasons for not suppressing it? Let us also examine the book of Proverbs more diligently.[15]

424. Formerly they used to say, "Proverbs, Song of Songs, and Ecclesiastes should be suppressed," because these books spoke in parables that could not be understood and should therefore not be included in the Writings. Indeed, these books were suppressed. But then the Men of the Great Assembly came along and interpreted them.[16]

425. R. Isaac ben Levi said: The sages were about to suppress the Book of Ecclesiastes, having found in it ideas that savored of heresy. They said: Should Solomon have given utterance to advice such as "Rejoice, O young man, in thy childhood; and let thy heart cheer thee in the days of thy youth" (Eccles. 11:9)? Even though Moses had said, "Go not about after your own heart and your own eyes" (Num. 15:39), Solomon said, "Walk in the ways of thy heart, and in the sight of thine eyes" (Eccles. 11:9), as though all restraint were removed and there were neither [ultimate] justice nor [Supreme] Judge. But since Solomon went on to say, "But know thou that for all these things God will bring thee into judgment" (ibid.), [the sages decided that] Solomon had spoken well after all.[17]

9. P. Sanh 10:1, 28a.
10. Excluded from the biblical canon.
11. E.g., Ezek. 44:31, where dietary regulations differ; and 45:20, where an unheard-of festival is described.
12. "I said . . . of mirth: 'What doth it accomplish?' " (Eccles. 2:2) and "I commended mirth" (Eccles. 8:15).
13. "For what profit hath he that worketh in that he laboreth (Eccles. 3:9) and "Fear God, and keep His commandments" (Eccles. 12:13).
14. Such as: "Answer not a fool according to his folly" (Prov. 26:4), and "Answer a fool according to his folly" (Prov. 26:5).
15. B. Shab 13b and 30b.
16. ARN 1.
17. Lev. R. 28:1.

426. All the holy writings make the hands unclean.[1] Song of Songs and Ecclesiastes make the hands unclean. R. Judah said: Song of Songs does make the hands unclean, but there is a difference of opinion concerning Ecclesiastes. R. Yose said: Ecclesiastes does not make the hands unclean,[2] but there is a difference of opinion concerning Song of Songs.

R. Simeon said: [The ruling about] Ecclesiastes is one of the [few] leniencies of the school of Shammai and one of the [few] stringencies of the school of Hillel.[3]

R. Simeon ben Azzai said: I have a tradition from the seventy-two elders[4] that on the day R. Eleazar ben Azariah was appointed to be head of the academy,[5] a decision was made that Song of Songs and Ecclesiastes were declared to make the hands unclean.

R. Akiva said: God forbid! No man in Israel differed concerning Song of Songs and maintained that it does not make the hands unclean, for the whole world is not as worthy as the day on which Song of Songs was given to Israel. For while all songs in Scripture are holy, Song of Songs is the holiest of the holy. Accordingly, if there was a difference of opinion, it concerned only Ecclesiastes.[6]

427. The Aramaic parts of Ezra and Daniel make the hands unclean. If an Aramaic section is translated into Hebrew, or a Hebrew section is translated into Aramaic or is written in the ancient Hebrew script, it does not make the hands unlcean. A part of Scripture never makes the hands unclean until it is written in Assyrian script, on hide, and in ink.[7]

428. "Add thou not unto His words" (Prov. 30:6). We have been taught that R. Eliezer said: Esther was composed by inspiration of the holy spirit, for Scripture states, "And Haman said in his heart" (Esther 6:6).[8] R. Akiva said: Esther was composed by inspiration of the holy spirit, for Scripture states, "And Esther obtained favor in the eyes of all that looked upon her" (Esther 2:15). R. Meir said: Esther was composed by inspiration of the holy spirit, for Scripture states, "And the thing became known unto Mordecai" (Esther 2:22).[9] R. Yose ben Durmaskit said: Esther was composed by inspiration of the holy spirit, for Scripture states, "But on the spoil they laid not their hands" (Esther 9:10).[10]

Samuel said: If I had been there [among the Tannaim], I would have provided proof superior to all the verses they cited. In saying, "They confirmed what they took upon them" (Esther 9:27), Scripture implies that they confirmed in heaven above what the Jews took upon themselves on the earth below. R. Joseph said: [The matter can be proved] from here—from the verse "These days of Purim shall not fail from among the Jews" (Esther 9:28). R. Nahman bar Isaac said: It can be proved from here—from the latter part of that verse: "Nor the memorial of them perish from their seed" (ibid.).[11]

429. [Queen] Esther sent word to the sages: Set my book down in writing for the generations [to come, as one of the books of Scripture]. They replied, "Have I not written for thee three parts?" (Prov. 22:20)[12]—three parts [the Five Books, the Prophets, and the Writings], not four. They finally found support for what she requested in the verse "Write this [the war against Amalek] a memorial in a scroll" (Exod. 17:14).

R. Judah said in the name of Samuel: The Scroll of Esther does not make the hands unclean. But did not Samuel say that Esther was composed by inspiration of the holy spirit? Composed to be read as Holy Writ; but its written text is not regarded as Holy Writ.[13]

430. R. Ze'era said: This Scroll [of Ruth] contains no rules concerning ritual uncleanness and cleanness or what is prohibited and what is permitted. Why then was it written? To teach you how adamant is the reward for those who practice loving-kindness.[14]

431. "And it came to pass at that time that Judah went down," etc. (Gen. 38:1). Surely Scripture should [not have interrupted the narrative about Joseph, but] should have continued with, "Joseph was brought down to Egypt" (Gen. 39:1). So, too, in the passage "They were not ashamed. Now the serpent was more subtle" (Gen. 2:25 and 3:1), Scripture [should not have brought in the serpent, but] should have continued with "The Lord God made for Adam and for his wife garments of skins" (Gen. 3:21). So, too, the passage in which Nebuchadnezzar says, "Those that walk in pride He is able to abase" (Dan. 4:34), is followed by reference to "Belshazzar the king" (Dan. 5:1) and to "Darius the Mede" (Dan. 6:1). But where is Evil-merodach [who followed Nebuchadnezzar and preceded Belshazzar]? So, too, the passage "In that night Belshazzar the Chaldean

1. Jews deemed the holy writings so sacred that they stored them with heave-offering (*terumah*) produce, which was also holy. However, mice seeking out such produce often chewed up the parchment of the writings. As a result, the sages declared that picking up these writings made the hands unclean. The hope was that this decree would cause Jews to think twice before storing them alongside *terumah*, which would contract uncleanness from contact with such hands. Thus the writings would be saved from destruction.
2. Being excluded from the canon.
3. According to the former, Ecclesiastes did not convey uncleanness to the hands; according to the latter, it did.
4. The usual number in the Great Sanhedrin is seventy-one. J. Z. Lauterbach says that since on that day both Rabban Gamaliel and R. Eleazar ben Azariah were included, the total reached seventy-two. See *JE*, s.v. "Sanhedrin."
5. See above, part 2, chap. 1, §75.
6. Yad 3:5.
7. Yad 4:5.
8. How could the author have known this except through the holy spirit?
9. How, except through the holy spirit, could Mordecai have come to know what the king's chamberlains were plotting?
10. Again, how, except through the holy spirit, would the author have known that all the Jews were so scrupulous?
11. B. Meg 7a.
12. JV: "Have I not written unto thee excellent things (*shalishim*)." But *shalishim* also means "threefold," hence three parts.
13. B. Meg 7a.
14. Yalkut, Ruth, §601.

king was slain. And Darius the Mede received the kingdom" (Dan. 5:30–6:1). But where is the passage "In the third year of King Belshazzar" (Dan. 8:1) [which should certainly have preceded the account of his death]? However, R. Huna said: [This apparent disarray in Daniel exists] so that it should not be said, "These are merely fiction," and to make it known that the text was composed by inspiration of the holy spirit. The sages said: Daniel's vision, which occurred in the third year of Belshazzar's reign, is mentioned after the account of his death in order to combine the entire book of Daniel as a work framed by inspiration of the holy spirit.[1]

432. "And he gave straw and provender for the camels" (Gen. 24:32). R. Aha said: The ordinary conversation of servants in the households of the patriarchs is deemed more important than the Torah given to their descendants. Thus the section dealing with Eliezer covers two or three columns, and what he has to say is not only recorded but repeated. On the other hand, the uncleanness of a creeping creature is one of the essentials of Torah, yet we learn the rule that its blood as well as its flesh defiles[2] only from a particle in Scripture whose meaning has been extended by interpretation.

"And water to wash his feet" (Gen. 24:32). R. Aha said: The washing of the feet of the servants in the households of the patriarchs is more important than the Torah given to their descendants, so that even the washing of their feet must be recorded.[3]

433. R. Adda son of R. Hanina said: Had Israel not sinned, only the Five Books and the book of Joshua, which contains the boundaries of the Land of Israel, would have been given them. And the proof? The verse "Much wisdom, much provocation" (Eccles. 1:18).[4]

434. "And of more than these (*me-hemmah*), my son, beware: of making many books there is no end" (Eccles. 12:12). The word *me-hemmah* is to be read *mehummah*, meaning that confusion (*mehummah*) would overcome you. For he who brings into his house any books other than the twenty-four books of Scripture—books such as Ben Sira [meaning Ecclesiasticus] or the Book of Ben Tagla—brings confusion (*mehummah*) into his house.[5]

435. R. Akiva said: He who reads apocryphal books, such as the books of Ben Sira and the books of Ben Laanah, has no portion in the world-to-come.[6] As for the books of Homer and all other books that have been written since—he who reads them is like one who reads a letter. As is said, "And of more than these, my son, beware: of making many books there is no end, and much study is a weariness of the flesh" (Eccles. 12:12). The other books are intended for light reading—not for wearying oneself with them.[7]

436. Keep your children from light reading.[8]

437. R. Meir said: When I came to R. Ishmael [to study Torah], he asked me, "My son, what is your occupation?" I replied, "I am a scribe." He said, "My son, be careful in your work, for your work is sacred. Should you omit or add a single letter, you will find yourself destroying the entire world, all of it."[9]

438. In the Torah scroll of R. Meir there was found written not "And behold, it was very (*meod*) good" (Gen. 1:31), but "And behold, death (*mot*) was good"; not "And He made for Adam and for his wife garments of skin (*'or*)" (Gen. 3:21), but "Garments of light (*or*)"; not "The sons of Dan: Hushim" (Gen. 46:23), but "The son of Dan: Hushim."[10]

439. In the scroll of R. Meir they found written, instead of "The burden of Dumah" (Isa. 21:11), "The burden of Roma [Rome]."[11]

440. A scroll of a book of Scripture that has not been corrected, R. Ammi said, may be kept for thirty days. From then on, it is forbidden to keep it, for Scripture says, "Let not wrong dwell in thy tents" (Job 11:14).[12]

441. R. Joshua ben Levi said: The Men of the Great Assembly observed twenty-four fasts in behalf of those who write scrolls, tefillin, and mezuzot, praying that they should not grow rich, for were they to become rich, they would cease to write them.[13]

442. "Wealth and riches [of Torah] may be in a man's house, but his merit can endure forever" (Ps. 112:3) if he copies out the Five Books, the Prophets, and the Writings, and then lends them to others.[14]

443. Books may not be thrown about from one place to another, nor may they be treated disrespectfully.

A man is required to have a scroll of Torah written with good ink, a good quill, by competent scribes, on good sheets of parchment made out of the hides of deer. He is then to wrap it in beautiful silks, in keeping with "This my God, and I will glorify Him" (Exod. 15:2).[15]

444. All sacred writings make the hands unclean.

The Sadducees declared: We protest against you, O Pharisees, because you say that sacred writings make the hands unclean, while the writings of Homer do not make

---

1. Gen. R. 85:2.
2. If either is equal in bulk to a lentil.
3. Gen. R. 60:8.
4. B. Ned 22b.
5. Eccles. R. 12:12, §7.
6. Because heretical matter had crept into them.
7. P. Sanh 10:1, 28a.
8. B. Ber 28b.
9. The omission of the letter *alef* in *emet* ("truth") one of God's names, would change the word to *met* ("dead"); the addition of a final *vav* to *va-yedabber* ("God spoke") would change the word to *va-yedabberu* ("the gods spoke"). Such changes would be blasphemy. B. Er 13a.
10. Gen. R. 9:5, 20:2, and 94:9.
11. P. Ta 1:1, 64a.
12. B. Ket 19b.
13. B. Pes 50b.
14. B. Ket 50a.
15. Sof 3.

them unclean. R. Yohanan ben Zakkai replied: Is this all we have against the Pharisees? Look, they say that the bones of an ass are clean, while the bones of Yohanan the High Priest[1] are unclean. The Sadducees replied: Their susceptibility to uncleanness is in keeping with the love cherished for them, lest anyone make [ornamental] spoons out of the bones of his father and mother. R. Yohanan: So, too, the sacred writings—their susceptibility to uncleanness is in keeping with the love cherished for them. But the books of Homer, which are not cherished, are not unclean.[2]

445. All sacred writings, whether used for public reading [on the Sabbath] or not, must be saved from a fire [even on the Sabbath].[3]

Sacred writings, even if written in another language, must be put away properly [when they become unfit for use]. Why are translations of sacred writings not used for public reading [on the Sabbath]? Because such reading would lead to disuse of rabbinic exposition in the houses of study. Whether translated into Coptic, Median, Trans[-Euphratean][4] Aramaic, Elamitic, or Greek, such sacred writings, even though not used for public reading, must be saved from a fire [even on the Sabbath].

Whether translated into Aramaic or into any other language, sacred writings must, as just stated, be saved [even on the Sabbath] from a fire. However, R. Yose said: They need not be saved from a fire. And R. Yose went on: It once happened that my dear father Halafta, while visiting Rabban Gamaliel Berabbi [II] in Tiberias, found him seated at the table of Yohanan ben ha-Nazuf with an Aramaic translation of the book of Job in his hand, which he was reading. My father said to him: I remember that your grandfather Rabban Gamaliel the Elder was sitting on a rise of the Temple Mount[5] when an Aramaic translation of the book of Job was brought to him, and he said to the builder, "Bury it under a course of bricks." On hearing this story, Rabban Gamaliel Berabbi [II] ordered that the same be done to his copy. So it was put away in a genizah.[6]

The Language of Torah and [the Aramaic] Targum

446. When the Holy One came to give the Torah to Israel, He spoke to them in a language they knew and understood.

"I (*anokhi*) am the Lord thy God" (Exod. 20:2). R. Nehemiah said: What kind of word is *anokhi*?[7] It is an Egyptian word. In Egypt, when a man wishes to say to a friend "I (*ani*)," he says *anokh*. How may God's need to use an Egyptian word for "I" be explained? By the story of a mortal king whose son had been captured. The son spent a long time among his captors and learned their language. Finally the king wreaked vengeance on his enemies and brought his son back. But when he tried to talk with his son in his own language, the son did not understand. What did the king do? He began to speak with him in the language of the captors. The Holy One had to do the same thing with Israel. During all the years Israel spent in Egypt, they learned the Egyptian speech. Finally, when the Holy One redeemed them and came to give them the Torah, they could not understand it. So the Holy One said: I will speak to them in the Egyptian tongue. Thus the Holy One inaugurated the giving of Torah by using the word *anokhi*, which is a form of the Egyptian *anokh*.[8]

447. "The Lord came from Sinai," etc. (Deut. 33:2). When the Holy One revealed Himself to give the Torah to Israel, He revealed Himself not in only one language but in four languages: "The Lord came from Sinai"—Hebrew; "and rose from Seir [Edom] unto them" (ibid.)—Latin; "He shined forth from Mount Paran" (ibid.)—Arabic; "and He came[9] from Meribat in Kadesh" (ibid.)—Aramaic.[10]

448. "Thus shalt thou say" (Exod. 19:3). You shall speak to My children in the tongue in which I speak to you—the holy tongue.[11]

449. Mar Zutra (or, as some say, Mar Ukba) said: Originally the Torah was given to Israel in Hebrew characters and in the holy tongue. Then it was given to them again in the time of Ezra in the [square] Ashur script and in the Aramaic tongue. Finally Israel chose for themselves the Ashur script and the holy tongue, leaving the Hebrew characters and the Aramaic tongue to vulgarians.

Who are the vulgarians? The Cutheans, said R. Hisda.[12]

450. What is meant by Hebrew characters? R. Hisda said: The Libbunaah script [the script of the inhabitants of the Lebanon region, that is, the Phoenicians].

We have been taught that R. Yose said: Ezra would have been worthy of having the Torah given to Israel by his hand, had not Moses preceded him. Of Moses it is written, "And the Lord commanded me at that time to teach you statutes and judgments" (Deut. 4:14); and of Ezra it is asserted, "For Ezra had prepared his heart to expound the Torah of the Lord, and to practice it, and to

1. He seems to be referring to the Yohanan who after eighty years of service became a Sadducee. See above, part 1, chap. 9, §28, and B. Ber 29a.
2. Yad 4:6.
3. Even if it means moving them from one domain to another, which is otherwise forbidden.
4. Ancient Persian (Leon Nemoy).
5. To supervise repairs of the Temple, which was a duty of the patriarch. See Lieberman, TKF 5:204.
6. Because, during the second century C.E., written translations of books of Scripture other than those of the Pentateuch were not to be used. B. Shab 115a; Tos Shab 14:2.
7. The word *anokhi* for "I" is found only in the older parts of Scripture. In rabbinic times, *anokhi* was not used at all. Hence R. Nehemiah's attempt to discern the word's special significance in this verse.
8. Tanhuma B, *Yitro*, §16; PR 21:12 (YJS 1:435); Yalkut, *Yitro*, §286.
9. See Deut. 32:51. The proof may be derived from the use of *atah*, an Aramaic word for the usual Hebrew word *ba* ("came").
10. Sif Deut., §343.
11. Mek, *Yitro*, *Ba-hodesh*, 9.
12. B. Sanh 21b.

teach Israel statutes and judgments" (Ezra 7:10). Still, even though the Torah was not given through him, its script was changed through him.

Why is this script called Ashurit? Because it came with them from Ashur.[1]

We have been taught that Rabbi [Judah I, the Patriarch] said: Originally the Torah was given to Israel in the [Assyrian] script. But when they sinned, it was turned for them into *roetz* ["broken, rugged script"].[2] After they repented [in the days of Ezra], the Ashurit characters were restored to them. Why is it called Ashurit? Because its script is *meushar*, "square, upright." But R. Simeon ben Eleazar said in the name of R. Eleazar ben Perata, who said it in the name of R. Eleazar of Modim: The script of the Torah was never essentially changed, for Scripture records, "The *vavs* [hooks] of the pillars" (Exod. 27:10), which implies that their [letter] *vav* was [even then] upright like a pillar. And Scriptures says, "Unto the Jews, according to their writing and language" (Esther 8:9); even as their language had not changed, so their writing had not changed.[3]

451. Our masters taught: How did the Israelites inscribe the Torah? According to R. Judah, they inscribed it on stones, as is said, "Then thou shalt write upon stones all the words of this Torah," etc. (Deut. 27:8) [which they had been told to then "coat . . . with plaster" (Deut. 27:2)]. That is, after writing out the words, they coated them with plaster. R. Simeon asked: But according to your account, how could the nations of that time have learned the Torah? R. Judah replied: The Holy One endowed them with exceptional intelligence, and they sent their scribes to peel off the plaster and carry away [a copy of the words inscribed on the stones]. It is for this reason that the decree against those nations to go down into the pit of destruction was sealed, for they could have learned, but did not. R. Simeon said: The Israelites inscribed the words of Torah over the plaster, and on the bottom line they wrote "[You must proscribe . . . the Canaanites] lest they mislead you into doing all the abhorrent things they have done" (Deut. 20:18). From this you may infer that if the Canaanites and the others had turned in penitence, they would have been received.[4]

452. It is related that five elders wrote the Torah in Greek for King Ptolemy. And that day was as intolerable for Israel as the day the golden calf was made, for the Torah cannot be translated adequately.[5]

453. We have been taught: It is related that King Ptolemy gathered seventy-two elders, put them in seventy-two houses, and did not tell them why he had gathered them. He then visited each of the elders and said to him: "Write for me the Torah of Moses your teacher." The Holy One put in the heart of each and every one of the elders good counsel, so that with one accord they wrote the following: "God created in the beginning" (Gen. 11:1);[6] "I shall make man in image and likeness" (Gen. 1:26);[7] "And He finished on the sixth day,[8] and rested on the seventh day" (Gen. 2:2); "Male and female created He him"[9] (Gen. 1:27); "Come, let me [not "us"] go down, and there confound their language" (Gen. 11:7); "And Sarah laughed among her kinswomen" (Gen. 18:12);[10] "In their anger they slew an ox,[11] and in their self-will they digged up a stall" (Gen. 49:6); "And Moses took his wife and his sons and had them ride a carrier of men"[12] (Exod. 4:20); "Now the time that the children of Israel dwelt in Egypt and in other lands was four hundred and thirty years"[13] (Exod. 12:40); "And he sent young men[14] of the children of Israel" (Exod. 24:5), and "Against the young men[15] of the children of Israel He sent not forth His hand" (Exod. 24:11); "I have not taken one valuable[16] of theirs" (Num. 16:15); "Which the Lord thy God hath allotted to give light to all the peoples"[17] (Deut. 4:19); "And he went and served other gods . . . which I have commanded should not be served"[18] (Deut. 17:3). They also wrote for King Ptolemy: "The creature with small legs" (Lev. 11:6). They did not write, "The hare," Ptolemy's wife's name being "Hare,"[19] lest Ptolemy say, "By putting my wife's name in the Torah [the way they did], they meant to jibe at me."[20]

454. There is no difference between scrolls of Torah, on the one hand, and tefillin and mezuzot, on the other, except

---

1. "Assyria stands here for Babylon. Cf. Jer. 2:18, Ezra 6:22" (Sanh, Soncino, p. 120, n. 4).
2. The writing of the Samaritans. So Jastrow, s.v.
3. B. Sanh 21a–b; Tos Sanh 4:5.
4. And the command "Thou shalt proscribe them" would not have been carried out. B. Sot 35b.
5. Sof 1.
6. Instead of "In the beginning God created" (literally, "In the beginning created God"), which might be misunderstood as "[A god named] In-the-Beginning created God," suggesting dual divinity.
7. Instead of "Let us make man in our image, after our likeness."
8. Instead of "And He finished on the seventh day," which might lead to the notion that God worked on the Sabbath.
9. Instead of "them," which might indicate that He created them separately from the first.
10. Instead of "And Sarah laughed within herself." Since she laughed openly, God took umbrage at her, but not at Abraham who laughed within himself.
11. "Ox" instead of "man," to save the reputations of Jacob's sons.
12. Instead of "ass," which might be taken to imply that Moses owned neither horse nor camel.
13. Adding "and in other lands" because, in Egypt alone, Israel lived two hundred ten years at the utmost.
14. Possibly, Nadab and Abihu. It should be noted that the translation of Exod. 24:5 and 24:11 quoted here is omitted in parallels.
15. JV's "nobles" might seem puzzling, because no nobles have been mentioned previously.
16. As though the text read *hemed*, instead of *hamor* ("ass"), to avoid giving the impression that, while Moses abstained from taking an ass, he did not hesitate to take valuables.
17. They added the words "to give light to all the peoples" to avoid giving the impression that the peoples of the world were meant to worship the heavenly bodies.
18. They added "should not be served." Had the translation read simply, "Which I have commanded not [to come into being]," it would seem that the heavenly bodies brought themselves into being and were thus deities on their own.
19. "In fact, it was Ptolemy's father who was named 'Hare' (Lagos)" (Meg, Soncino, p. 50, n. 9).
20. B. Meg 9a–b and En Yaakov, ad loc.

that scrolls of Torah may be written in any language [and script], whereas tefillin and mezuzot may be written only [in Hebrew and] in the square Ashurit script. R. Simeon ben Gamaliel said that scrolls of Torah also may be written in no foreign language [or script] other than Greek.

R. Yohanan said: What is R. Simeon ben Gamaliel's proof? The verse "God enlarge Japheth, and he shall dwell in the tents of Shem" (Gen. 9:27), that is, the words of Japheth may reside in the tents of Shem, which Bar Kappara took to imply that the words of Shem may be translated into the language of Japheth.[1] R. Yuda said: From this verse it follows that in the Torah itself translation into Aramaic is permitted. With regard to such permission, Scripture says, "And they read in the book, in the Torah of God, what was made explicit" (Neh. 8:8)—"in the Torah of God" in the Hebrew original; "what was made explicit" by translation into Aramaic.

R. Judah said: Even when our masters allowed the use of Greek, they allowed it only for the scroll of Torah, and that came about because of the action taken by King Ptolemy.[2]

455. Akila translated the Torah [into Greek] in the presence of R. Eliezer and R. Joshua, and they applauded him, saying, "Through Grecian grace you are making its beauty known among men" (Ps. 45:3).[3]

456. The Aramaic Targum of the Five Books was composed by Onkelos the Proselyte under the guidance of R. Eliezer and R. Joshua. The Aramaic Targum of the Prophets was composed by Jonathan ben Uzziel under the guidance of Haggai, Zechariah, and Malachi.[4] When he finished it, the Land of Israel was shaken over an area of four hundred parasangs by four hundred parasangs. A divine voice went forth and asked, "Who is he that revealed My secrets to mortals?"[5] Jonathan stood up and said, "I am he who revealed Your secrets to mortals. It is known and manifest to You that I did it not for my own honor nor for the honor of my father's house, but for Your honor, so that controversies [about the meaning of passages] should not abound in the Land."

He was about to reveal through an [Aramaic] Targum the inner meaning of the Writings. But a divine voice went forth and said, "What you have done is enough."

What was the reason? Because in the Writings the exact time of the Messiah's coming is foretold.[6]

1. Shem is the ancestor of Israel, and Japheth [Yephet] the ancestor of the Greeks (Yavan). See Gen. 10:2 and 21.
2. B. Meg 8b–9a; Gen. R. 36:8; Deut. R. 1:1.
3. The Hebrew *yaphyaphita* ("Thou art fairer") is read as two words: *yaphita* ("you made beauty known") and *yaphet* (Japheth), the son of Noah and forebear of Yavan, the Hebrew name for Greece (Gen. 10:2). JV: "Thou art fairer than the children of men." P. Meg 1:9, 71c.
4. Since Jonathan ben Uzziel was actually a contemporary of Hillel's, Samuel Edels suggests that he made use of traditions handed down from these three prophets.
5. The Targum is paraphrastic and applies many verses to the days of the Messiah.
6. B. Meg 3a and En Yaakov, ad loc.

457. Scripture stimulates the need for translation, and translation stimulates the need for Mishnah.[7]

458. R. Simeon ben Pazzi said: What is the proof that he who translates Scripture [in public] is not permitted to raise his voice above that of the reader? From the words "Moses spoke, and God answered him by a voice" (Exod. 19:19). What does Scripture imply in [the apparently unnecessary] "by a voice"? That God answered by a voice [no louder than that] of Moses. Thus we are taught in a Baraita: He who translates Scripture [in public] is not permitted to raise his voice above that of the reader. If, however, he who does the translating is unable to read as loudly as the reader, the reader should lower his voice as he reads.[8]

459. We have been taught that R. Judah said: He who translates a verse literally is a liar, and he who adds [his own words] to it is a blasphemer and reviler.[9]

460. The Torah uses the ordinary language of men.[10]

461. The Torah makes use of hyperbole.[11]

462. The language of Torah is distinctly its own, even as the language of the sages is distinctly their own.[12]

Study and Practice

463. We have been taught that R. Menahem son of R. Yose expounded the verse "The commandment is a lamp and Torah is light" (Prov. 6:23) as follows: Scripture associates a commandment with a lamp, and the Torah with light. A commandment with a lamp, in order to tell you that even as a lamp gives light only for a while, so performance of a commandment shields only for a while. The Torah with light, in order to tell you that even as light always lights up the world, so study of Torah always shields the world. For Scripture says, "When thou walkest, it shall lead thee," etc. (Prov. 6:22). "When thou walkest, it shall lead thee" in this world; "when thou liest down, it shall watch over thee" (ibid.) in death; "and when thou awakest, it shall talk with thee" (ibid.) in the time-to-come. A parable of a man who, walking at dead of night, during its darkest part, is fearful of thorns, thistles, and pits, of wild beasts and robbers, and besides does not know what road to take. Were he to come upon a lighted torch, he would be able to keep clear of thorns, thistles, and pits, but he would remain fearful of wild beasts and robbers, and would still not know what road to take. When dawn breaks, he is saved from wild beasts and robbers, but he still does not know what road to take. When he

7. Sif Deut., §161.
8. B. Ber 45a.
9. He should reproduce the total sense of the verse. B. Kid 49a.
10. B. Ber 31b.
11. Such as "The cities are great and fortified up to heaven" (Deut. 1:28). B. Tam 29a.
12. B. Hul 137b.

finally reaches a crossroads, he is saved from all these fears.[1]

Another explanation: A transgression snuffs out [the merit of] a commandment, but no transgression can snuff out [the merit of] Torah, for it is said, "The mightiest of waters cannot snuff out love" (Song 8:1).[2]

464. R. Tarfon and some elders were reclining in an upper chamber in the house of Nitzah in Lydda[3] when this question was raised before them: Which is greater—study or practice? R. Tarfon spoke up and said: Practice is greater. R. Akiva spoke up and said: Study is greater. [In agreement with him], all spoke up and said: Study is greater, for it leads to practice."[4]

465. R. Abbahu sent his son R. Hanina to study Torah in Tiberias. People came back and reported to R. Abbahu that his son was busy attending the dead. So he wrote to his son, "Did I send you to Tiberias because there are no graves in Caesarea? In an upper chamber in the house of [Nitzah], a tenant farmer[5] in Lydda, the sages voted and decided that study takes precedence over practice." Our masters in Caesarea added: This was said only about a time when there is someone else to engage in the practice required. But if there is no one else to do so, then practice takes precedence.[6]

466. "If ye study in My statutes . . . and practice them" (Lev. 26:3). R. Hiyya taught: This verse speaks of one who studies in order to practice, not of one who studies without intending to practice. As for him who studies without intending to practice, it were better if he had not been created.

R. Yohanan said: He who studies without intending to practice—it were better for him if the caul in which he lay [as a fetus] had been turned over his face and he had not come out into the air of the world.[7]

467. R. Hanina ben Dosa used to say: When a man's good deeds exceed his learning, his learning will endure; but when his learning exceeds his good deeds, his learning will not endure.

R. Eleazar ben Azariah used to say: To what may he whose learning exceeds his good deeds be compared? To a tree whose branches are many and roots few, so that when a wind comes, it uproots the tree and turns it flat on its face. On the other hand, to what may he whose good deeds exceed his learning be compared? To a tree whose branches are few and whose roots are many, so that even if all the winds in the world come and blow at it, they will not move it from its place.[8]

468. Elisha ben Avuyah used to say: To whom may a man who has good deeds and has studied much Torah be compared? To a man who in building [lays] stones first [for a foundation] and then lays bricks [over them], so that however much water may collect at the side of the building, it will not wash it away. Contrariwise, he who has no good deeds even though he has studied much Torah—to whom may he be compared? To a man who in building lays bricks first and then heaps stones over them, so that even if a little water collects, it at once undermines the structure.

He used to say: A man who has good deeds and has studied much Torah—to what may he be compared? To plaster coated over a structure of stones, so that however many rains fall upon it, they will not budge it from its place. On the other hand, a man who has no good deeds even though he has studied much Torah—to what may he be compared? To plaster coated over a structure of bricks, so that, however little rain falls upon it, it immediately softens and crumbles away.[9]

469. R. Simeon ben Eleazar said: He whose good deeds exceed his learning—to whom may he be compared? To the rider of a horse that is bridled; he can turn the horse whichever way he wishes. Contrariwise, he whose learning exceeds his good deeds—to whom may he be compared? To the rider of a horse that is not bridled, for when he rides it, he is likely to fall and break his neck.[10]

470. "To observe to do all His commandments" (Deut. 28:1). R. Simeon ben Halafta said: When a man learns the precepts of Torah but does not fulfill them, his punishment is more severe than that of him who has not studied at all. To what may his situation be compared? To one where a king had an orchard into which he brought two tenants, one of whom planted trees and cut them down, while the other neither planted any nor cut down any. With whom is the king likely to be angry? Surely with the one who planted trees and cut them down. So, too, when a man learns precepts of Torah but does not fulfill them, his punishment is more severe than that of him who has not studied at all.[11]

471. There are four types of attendance at a house of study. One attends but does not practice—at least the reward for attending is his. Another practices but does not attend—at least the reward of practice is his. Another attends and practices, and is a pious man. Another neither attends nor practices, and is a wicked man.[12]

472. There is a man who expounds well and acts well. There is another who acts well but does not expound well.

1. The commandment is a torch, Torah the dawn, and death the crossroads.
2. B. Sot 21a, and En Yaakov, ad loc.
3. The gathering may have taken place during the Hadrianic persecutions.
4. Since both study and observance were prohibited, the question was for which of the two life should be risked. B. Kid 40b.
5. The Hebrew "*arim*" is probably a corruption of *aris* ("tenant farmer") (Leon Nemoy). The rabbis were in such a humble abode so as not to arouse the suspicion of the Roman authorities.
6. P. Pes 3:7, 30b.
7. P. Ber 1:5, 3b; Lev. R. 35:7.
8. Avot 3:9, 17.
9. ARN 24.
10. ARNB 34.
11. Deut. R. 7:4.
12. Avot 5:14.

There is still another who expounds well but does not act well.[1]

473. R. Eliezer son of R. Yose the Galilean said: "Prepare thy work without" (Prov. 24:27)—Scripture, Mishnah, and Talmud; "and make it ready for thee in the field" (ibid.)—good deeds; "and afterward build thy house" (ibid.)—seek the inner meaning of Torah and receive reward.[2]

474. R. Ishmael son of R. Yohanan ben Beroka said: He who learns in order to teach will be afforded means to learn and to teach. He who learns in order to practice will be afforded means to learn and to teach as well as to observe and to practice.[3]

475. R. Huna said: He who occupies himself only with studying Torah acts as if he had no God.[4]

476. He who says that he is interested only in the study of Torah has no reward even for the study of Torah. And the proof? The verse, said R. Papa, "That ye may learn them . . . to do them" (Deut. 5:1): He who is engaged in "doing" the commandments is regarded as engaged in learning them; but he who is not engaged in "doing" them is not regarded as engaged in learning them.[5]

477. R. Samuel bar Nahmani said in the name of R. Jonathan: The verse "Of what avail are the fool's means to acquire learning, when there is no [reverent] heart" (Prov. 17:16) says: Woe to those disciples of the wise who occupy themselves with Torah but have no fear of Heaven.[6]

478. Rabbah bar R. Huna said: He who has Torah but no fear of Heaven is like a treasurer who is entrusted with the inner keys but not with the outer keys. How is he to enter?

R. Yannai cried out: Alas for him who has no courtyard, yet makes a gate for it![7]

479. R. Hoshaia said: Anyone who has knowledge but has no fear of sin really has nothing, just as a carpenter without his tools is no carpenter. Why [is such a one's knowledge worthless]? Because the diadems of Torah are acquired through fear of sin, as Scripture says, "The fear of the Lord is His treasure" (Isa. 33:6).[8]

480. R. Alexandri was once calling out, "Who wants life?" All kinds of people gathered around him, saying, "Give us life." At that, he cited, "Who is the man that desireth life? . . . Keep thy tongue from evil" (Ps. 34:13–14). So that a man should not say, "Since I kept my mouth from evil and my lips from speaking deceit, I will freely indulge in idle living," the psalm goes on to say, "Depart from evil and do good" (Ps. 34:15). By "good" here is meant Torah, of which it is said, "I have given you a doctrine that is good—forsake ye not My Torah" (Prov. 4:2).[9]

481. Rava had a favorite saying: The purpose of learning is repentance and good deeds. A man should not read Scripture and study Mishnah, and then rebel against his father, his mother, his teacher, and anyone else who surpasses him in learning and in years, as is said, "The fear of the Lord is the beginning of learning; a good understanding have they that act accordingly" (Ps. 111:10). Not "who study accordingly," but "who act accordingly"—act out of fear of God, not out of no such fear.[10]

482. Not study, but action, is the essence of the matter.[11]

The Precepts of Torah

483. R. Hananiah ben Akashia said: The Holy One, desiring to bestow upon Israel abundant merit, made Torah and precepts abundant for them, as is said, "The Lord desireth Israel's merit—hence He made Torah [and its precepts] abundant and numerous" (Isa. 42:21).[12]

484. "Thine ointments have a goodly fragrance" (Song 1:3). To the first forefathers You gave the fragrance of a few precepts—one precept to Adam, six precepts to Noah and his sons. But we—when we came to Sinai, "Thy Name is as ointment poured forth" (Song 1:3). Like a man who pours out of an amphora, so did You pour out upon us all the precepts—two hundred and forty-eight positive precepts and three hundred and sixty-five negative precepts.[13]

485. The sons of Noah were enjoined concerning seven matters: idolatry, unchastity, bloodshed, blasphemy, maintenance of civil courts, robbery, and taking flesh cut from a living animal. R. Hanina ben Gamaliel said: Also concerning blood from a living animal. R. Eliezer said: Also concerning planting diverse seeds. R. Simeon ben Yohai: Also concerning witchcraft. R. Yohanan ben Beroka: Also concerning castration. R. Assi added: The sons of Noah were enjoined concerning all the abominations specified in the passage that begins, "There shall not be found among you anyone that maketh his son or daughter to pass through the fire" (Deut. 18:10), and ends, "Because of these abominations the Lord thy God is driving them out from before thee" (Deut. 18:12).[14]

1. B. Yev 63b.
2. B. Sot 44a.
3. B. Avot 4:5.
4. B. AZ 17b.
5. B. Yev 109b.
6. B. Yoma 72b and En Yaakov, ad loc.
7. Through learning one enters the court of piety. B. Shab 31b.
8. Exod. R. 40:1.
9. B. AZ 19b and En Yaakov, ad loc.
10. B. Ber 17a.
11. Avot 1:17.
12. JV: "The Lord was pleased for His righteousness' sake to make the teaching great and glorious." B. Mak 23b.
13. Tanhuma, *Yitro*, §3; Song R. 1:3, §1.
14. Gen. R. 34:8.

486. R. Judah son of R. Simon stated: Adam deserved to have the Torah given through him, for the Holy One said: Shall I not give it to the one I formed with My own hands? But then the Holy One retracted, saying: If now, when I have given him six precepts, he showed himself unable to cope with them, how can I give him six hundred and thirteen precepts—two hundred and forty-eight positive precepts and three hundred and sixty-five negative precepts? So I shall not give the Torah to Adam but to his children: "This book is for the generations of Adam" (Gen. 5:1).[1]

487. R. Yose bar Aibu said in the name of R. Yohanan: Adam, who was not permitted the eating of flesh, was not enjoined concerning flesh cut from a living animal. But the sons of Noah, to whom the eating of flesh was permitted, were enjoined concerning flesh cut from a living animal.[2]

488. "He declareth His word unto Jacob" (Ps. 147:19). R. Abbahu said in the name of R. Yose son of R. Hanina: The verse will be understood by the parable of a king who had an orchard in which he planted all kinds of trees, which he alone entered, because he was its keeper. When his children came of age, he said to them, "My children, hitherto I have guarded this orchard, not allowing anyone to enter it. Now I want you to look after it as I have." So, too, God said to Israel, "Before I created this world, I prepared the Torah, which I did not give to any one of the nations, only to Israel." As soon as Israel rose up and said, "All that the Lord hath spoken will we do, and obey" (Exod. 24:7), they were given the Torah. Hence, "He declareth His word unto Jacob, His statutes and His ordinances unto Israel. He hath not dealt so with any nation" (Ps. 147:19–20). Except with which? Except with [the nation of] Jacob, whom He chose from all other nations. To those others He gave only some [of the commandments]. Thus to Adam [father of all nations] He gave six commandments, to Noah [father of all nations] one more, to Abraham [father of many nations] an eighth, and to Jacob [during his lifetime] a ninth. But to Israel He gave *all*.

R. Simon said in the name of R. Hanina: What God did may be illustrated by the parable of a king who had before him a table set out with all kinds of dishes. When his first servant entered, he gave him a slice [of meat]; to the second he gave an egg, to the third some vegetables, and likewise to each of the others. But when his son came in, he gave him all that was on the table before him, saying to him, "To the others I gave only single portions; to you I put all that is here at your disposal." So also the Holy One gave to the nations only some commandments, but when Israel arose, He said to them, "Behold, the whole Torah is yours," as Scripture affirms: "He hath not dealt so with any nation" (Ps. 147:20).

"He kisseth me with the kisses of His mouth" (Song 1:2). God gave the nations of the world precepts in a raw state, so that they might work out the relevant details on their own. Nor did he elaborate for them the precise distinctions between ritual uncleanness and cleanness. But when Israel came, He made the details of the precepts explicit, for each the punishment [for its violation] and the reward [for its observance]. Hence, "His statutes and His ordinances for Israel."[3]

489. Israel are surety for one another to the Holy One. How did they come to be surety? When God sought to give the Torah, no nation other than Israel would accept it. What happened may be illustrated by the parable of a king who had a field that he wished to turn over to tenants. When the king called the first of them and asked, "Will you accept care of this field?" he replied, "I have no strength. Such work is too hard for me." And so, too, the second, the third, the fourth—not one would accept the care of the field. The king then called the fifth and asked him, "Will you accept the care of this field?" The man replied, "Yes." "With the understanding that you will till it?" "Yes." But when that tenant entered the field, he let it lie fallow. With whom is the king angry? With those who declared, "We cannot accept the care of it," or with the one who accepted its care but, upon coming to the field, let it lie fallow? Is it not with the one who accepted the responsibility? Similarly, when God revealed Himself on Sinai, there was not a nation at whose doors He had not knocked, but not one would accept it. But when He came to Israel, they exclaimed, "All that the Lord hath spoken will we do, and obey" (Exod. 24:7). Therefore it is proper that you all should obey. And if not, you will all be punished as surety for one another.[4]

490. "Now these are the ordinances" (Exod. 21:1). The nations of the world have judges, and Israel have judges, and you do not know the difference between them. The answer is suggested in the parable of a sick man whose physician came to visit him and then said to his family, "Give him to eat whatever he asks for." But when the physician came to another sick man, he said to the family, "Take care not to let him each such-and-such a food." The physician was asked, "About the first, you said that he might eat whatever he wished; but about the second, you said that he must not eat certain food." He replied, "The first had no chance to remain alive, and so I allowed him to eat whatever he likes; but the second will live, and therefore I ordered strict care in his diet." Similarly of the nations of the world who are separated from the Torah [from the hope of life] Scripture says, "I gave them statutes that were not good, and ordinances by which they could not live" (Ezek. 20:25). But with regard to the commandments [given to Israel], Scripture says, "Which if a man do, he shall live by them" (Lev. 18:5).[5]

491. R. Abba said: In the Torah there are two hundred and forty-eight positive commands, as many as the parts of the human body. Each and every one of these parts

1. Gen. R. 24:5.
2. See Gen. 1:29 and 9:3. Gen. R. 34:13; B. Sanh 59b.
3. Exod. R. 30:9.
4. Exod. R. 27:9.
5. Exod. R. 30:22.

cries out to the man, saying: Perform through me the command that applies to me, so that by its merit you will stay alive and your days will be long. And three hundred and sixty-five negative precepts, as many as the days in the solar year. Every day that the sun shines, and until it sets, the sun cries out, saying to the man: I decree upon you in the name of Him who has brought your days to this day, do not commit a transgression during my span of hours, lest you tilt the scale for yourself and the entire world, all of it, toward the side of guilt.

Thus you come to a total of six hundred and thirteen commandments.[1]

492. "Take heed of the heavens" (Deut. 32:1). The Holy One said to Moses: Say to them, to Israel: Gaze at the heavens, which I created to serve you. Have they perhaps changed their ways? Does the orb of the sun perchance not rise out of the east and light up the entire world, all of it? The fact is: the sun rejoices in its commission to do My will, for Scripture says, "The sun . . . is as a bridegroom coming out of his chamber, and rejoiceth as a strong man to run his course" (Ps. 19:6).

"And let the earth be heard" (Deut. 32:1). Gaze at the earth, which I created to serve you. Has it perhaps changed its ways? Have you perchance sown seed and it has not sprouted? Or have you sown wheat and it brought forth barley? Or did the heifer perhaps say, "I will not plow," "I will not thresh"? Or did the ass say, "I will bear no burden," "I will not move"?

Likewise, the sea. "I . . . have placed the sand for the bound of the sea" (Jer. 5:22). Has it perhaps changed its ways and, rising, flooded the world? Is this not a matter to be argued *a fortiori?* The heavens, the earth, and the sea were created to receive neither reward nor penalty. If they earn merit, they receive no reward; if they go astray, they are subjected to no penalty. They need not be concerned about their sons and daughters. Yet they have not changed their ways. You—who receive reward when you earn merit and receive punishment when you sin, who are concerned about your sons and daughters—how much more and more by far should you not change your ways.[2]

493. "That ye may look upon it, and remember" (Num. 15:38). Looking leads to remembering, and remembering leads to doing, as is said, "That ye may remember and do" (Num. 15:40).[3]

494. We have been taught that R. Meir used to say: Why is blue different from all other colors? Because blue is similar to the color of the sea; the color of the sea is similar to the color of the firmament; the color of the firmament is similar to the color of sapphire; and the color of sapphire is similar to the color of the throne of glory, as is said, "There was under His feet the like of paved work of sapphire stone, and the like of the very heaven for clearness" (Exod. 24:10); and also, "The semblance of a throne in appearance like sapphire" (Ezek. 1:26).[4]

495. "Thy glory upon their children" (Ps. 90:16). R. Hezekiah taught: When the children of Israel are wrapped in their prayer shawls, let them not think that they are clothed merely in [ordinary] blue.[5] Rather let the children of Israel look upon the prayer shawls as though the glory of the Presence were covering them.[6]

496. "All the peoples of the earth shall see that the Name of the Lord can be read upon thee" (Deut. 28:10). We have been taught that R. Eliezer the Elder said: These words refer to tefillin worn on the head.[7]

497. Our masters taught: Beloved are Israel, whom the Holy One encompassed with commandments [that are testimonies of the fear of God]: tefillin on their heads, tefillin on their arms, four knotted fringes on their garments, mezuzots on their doorposts. Of these David said, "Seven times a day do I praise Thee by heeding Thy righteous ordinances" (Ps. 119:164). When David went into a bathhouse and saw himself standing naked, he exclaimed, "Woe is me, that I stand naked without a commandment [that is a testimony of the fear of God]." But when he noticed the circumcision in his flesh, his mind was set at rest. And when he came out, he composed a psalm concerning it: "For the Leader; concerning the Sheminith (the eighth), a Psalm of David" (Ps. 12:1)—concerning circumcision, ordained for the eighth day [of the newborn male child's life].[8]

498. R. Ishmael said: Great is the precept of circumcision, for "covenant" is mentioned in connection with it thirteen times.[9] R. Yose said: Great is circumcision, for it even sets aside the rigor of the Sabbath.[10] R. Meir said: Great is circumcision, for notwithstanding all the precepts that our father Abraham had performed, he was not called "perfect" until he circumcised himself, as is said, "Walk before Me as hitherto, and in addition be thou perfect" (Gen. 17:1).

Rabbi [Judah I, the Patriarch] said: Great is circumcision, for it is equal in importance to all precepts in the Torah.[11]

499. "Walk before Me, and be thou perfect (Gen. 17:1). R. Levi said: The verse will be understood by the parable of a Roman noblewoman to whom the emperor said, "Walk before me." As she walked before him, her face turned pale, for she thought: Who knows but that the emperor

---

1. Tanhuma B, *Ki Tetze*, §2; Tanhuma, *Ki Tetze*, §2.
2. Sif Deut., §307; Yalkut, Isa., §387.
3. Tanhuma B, *Shelah*, §30.
4. B. Sot 17a; P. Ber 1:5, 3a.
5. The threads fastened to the four corners of the tallit, or prayer shawl, originally had a cord of blue entwined in them. The blue cord was dyed with the blood of the *hilazon* snail, which was said to appear only once in seventy years and was scarce even in mishnaic times. The authorities therefore agreed that the blue cord might be dispensed with and white threads alone be used. See Men 4:1 and *JE*, s.v. "Fringes."
6. MTeh 90:18.
7. B. Sot 17a.
8. B. Men 43b and En Yaakov, ad loc.; Sif Deut, §36.
9. In Gen. 17.
10. If the eighth day of the infant boy's life falls on a Sabbath, circumcision may be performed on that day, even though it involves what is considered "work of labor."
11. B. Ned 31b–32a and En Yaakov, ad loc.

has found some defect in me? But the emperor said, "You have no defect other than that the nail of your little finger is a bit too long. Pare it, and the defect will be gone." So, too, the Holy One said to our father Abraham, "You have no defect other than this foreskin. Remove it, and you will be free of imperfection. 'Walk before me, and be thou perfect, as soon as I set [the mark of] My covenant between thee and Me' " (Gen. 17:2).[1]

500. A Caesar said to R. Tanhum, "Come, let us all be one people." "Very well," he answered, "but we who are circumcised cannot possibly [go back and] become like you. So you go and circumcise yourselves, and become like us." Caesar: "Well spoken. But he who prevails over the emperor is thrown into the wild animal pen [at the arena]." Accordingly, R. Tanhum was thrown into the pen, but the animals did not eat him. A certain heretic said, "The only reason the animals did not eat him is because they were not hungry." At that, he himself was thrown in, and the animals devoured him.[2]

501. A pagan philosopher asked R. Hoshaia: If circumcision is so beloved [of God], why was it not prescribed for Adam at his creation? R. Hosaia replied: According to your reasoning, why should a man like you shave the hair of his head [with which he was born] but at the same time leave the hair of his adult beard intact?[3] The pagan philosopher replied: Because the hair on my head has grown with me since the days of my foolish childhood. R. Hoshaia retorted: If so, [to be consistent] you should blind your eyes, lop off your hands, and break your legs, which have also grown along with you since the days of your foolish childhood. The pagan philosopher exclaimed: Have we come down to such drivel? R. Hoshaia replied: I cannot let you go without a proper answer. And so observe that everything that was created during the six days of creation needs finishing: mustard needs sweetening, vetch needs sweetening, wheat needs grinding, and even man needs finishing.[4]

502. "The mighty in strength that fulfill His word" (Ps. 103:20). To whom does Scripture refer? R. Isaac said: To those who are willing to observe the Year of Release.[5] In the way of the world, a man may be willing to observe a commandment for a day, a week, a month,[6] but is he likely to continue to do so through the remaining days of the year? But [throughout that year] this [mighty] man sees his field declared ownerless, his trees declared ownerless, his fences broken down, and his produce consumed by others, yet he continues to give up his produce without saying a word. Can you conceive a person mightier than such as he?[7]

1. Gen. R. 46:4; Yalkut, *Lekh Lekha*, §81.
2. B. Sanh 39a.
3. "Pagan philosophers in Roman times often cut the hair of their head very short but let their beard grow long" (Brother Caedmon Holmes).
4. Gen. R. 11:6; PR 23:4.
5. See Exod. 23:10–11 and Lev. 25:2ff.
6. Sabbath for a day, sukkah and lulav for a week, and mourning for a month.
7. Lev. R. 1:1; Tanhuma, *Va-yikra*, §1.

503. R. Judah ben Pedaiah expounded: O that someone would remove the dust from your eyes, Adam! You could not observe a command [not to eat of the tree of knowledge] even for one hour, yet your children wait three years for *orlah*, "uncircumcision."[8] When Bar Kappara heard of R. Judah's exposition, he said: Nephew, you spoke well.[9]

504. Rabbi [Judah I, the Patriarch] said: Be as careful with a light precept as with a weighty one, for you do not know the exact reward for the various precepts. Reckon the loss sustained through the performance of a precept against the reward earned by its observance; and the profit of a transgression against the loss it will entail.[10]

505. R. Aha said in the name of R. Isaac: It is written, "In all that is to be observed, guard thy heart, for in each such observance are the wellsprings of life" (Prov. 4:23).[11] Be observant with regard to all that is prescribed for you in Torah, for you do not know out of which precept life issues for you.

In this regard, R. Abba bar Kahana said: Scripture puts the easiest of commandments on the same level as the most difficult of observances. The easiest of commandments—letting a mother bird go;[12] and the most difficult of commandments—honoring father and mother. And with regard to each, it is written, "That your days may be long."[13]

506. Let an easy precept be as dear to you as a difficult precept.[14]

507. Once a man violates a minor precept, he will end up by violating a major one.[15]

508. Ben Azzai said: Run to perform even a minor precept,[16] and flee from transgression, for one good deed leads to another, and one transgression leads to another. The recompense for doing a good deed is another good deed [to be done], and the recompense for a transgression is another transgression.[17]

509. The "dry bones" (Ezek. 37:4) are men in whom there is no marrow of good deeds.[18]

510. "That ye may remember and do all My commandments" (Num. 15:40). This verse may be illustrated by

8. The law that the fruit of trees within three years after planting is considered *orlah* ("uncircumcised") and entirely forbidden. Lev. 19:23 and 19:25.
9. Gen. R. 21:7.
10. Avot 2:1.
11. JV: "Above all that thou guardest, keep thy heart; for out of it are the issues of life."
12. Deut. 22:6–7.
13. P. Pe 1:1, 14d.
14. Sif Deut., §79, 115.
15. Sif Deut., §186–7.
16. The words "as a major one" in BR are omitted.
17. Avot 4:2.
18. B. Sanh 92b.

the parable of a person thrown into the water, to whom the pilot throws a rope, saying, "Hold on to this rope and do not let go of it. If you let go, you will lose your life." So, too, the Holy One said to Israel, "As long as you hold on to the precepts, the words 'But you who held to the Lord your God are alive all of you this day' [Deut. 4:4] apply to you."[1]

511. "The spirit of man is the lamp of the Lord" (Prov. 20:27). The Holy One said: Let My Lamp be in your hand, and your lamp will be in My hand. What is the Holy One's lamp? The Torah, of which it is said, "The commandment is a lamp, and Torah is light" (Prov. 6:23). What is implied by "The commandment is a lamp?" That he who performs a commandment is accounted as if he had kindled a lamp before the Holy One, and thereby he quickens his own spirit, which is called a "lamp," as in the verse "The spirit of man is the lamp of the Lord."[2]

512. Bar Kappara said: Both the spirit of man and the Torah are said to be like a lamp. The spirit—"The spirit of man is the lamp of the Lord" (Prov. 20:27); and Torah—"The commandment is a lamp, and Torah is light" (Prov. 6:23). The Holy One said to man: My lamp is in your hand, and your lamp is in My hand. My lamp—the Torah—is in your hand; and your lamp—the spirit of life—is in My hand. If you keep My lamp lit, I will keep your lamp lit. But if you extinguish My lamp, I will extinguish your lamp.[3]

513. R. Yohanan and R. Eleazar both said: The Torah was given in forty days, and the soul is formed in forty days.[4] He who keeps the Torah—his soul is kept. He who does not keep the Torah—his soul is not kept.

Sages in the school of R. Ishmael taught: The matter may be illustrated by the parable of a man who entrusted a swallow to his servant and said to him: Do you think that if you allow her to perish, I will take from you no more than an *issar*[5] as her value? I will take your very soul from you.[6]

514. A proverb says: The door that will not open for a good deed will have to open wide for the doctor.[7]

515. R. Simeon ben Yohai said: A loaf of bread and a rod came down from heaven wrapped together. The Holy One said to Israel: If you obey the Torah, here is a loaf to eat; but if not, here is a rod to smite you with.[8]

516. R. Eliezer said: The book and the sword came down from heaven wrapped together. The Holy One said to Israel: If you obey what is written in the book, you will be saved from the sword. But if not, you will be smitten by it.

R. Meir said: When a man performs one precept, he is given one angel; two precepts, he is given two angels; many precepts, he is given many angels, as is said, "For He will give His angels charge over thee" (Ps. 91:11). Why? To protect the man from demons, as is said, "A thousand shall fall [in] at thy side" (Ps. 91:7).[9]

517. R. Eleazar said: They who are sent to perform a precept come to no harm, either in their going or in their returning.[10]

518. Rav was asked: Young scholars who live in the valley outside the town—what about their walking morning and evening to your house?[11] He replied: Let them come. [I take the responsibility] upon myself and upon my neck.[12]

519. R. Judah said: It happened that a certain inspector was examining the validity of mezuzot in the upper market of Sepphoris when a quaestor found him and extorted one thousand *zuz* from him.[13] But did not R. Eleazar say, "They who are sent to perform a precept come to no harm"? Yes, but where danger is certain, the rule is different, for it is written, "And Samuel said: 'How can I go? If Saul hear it, he will kill me' " (1 Sam. 16:2).[14]

520. The precepts were given to Israel for no reason other than for Israel to stay alive, for it is said of the precepts, "Which if a man do, he shall live by them" (Lev. 18:5)—live by them and not die by them. Therefore, when there is danger to life, no precept is to be insisted on except those prohibiting idolatry, unchastity, and murder. When does the rule apply? Not in a time of religious persecution. But during a time of religious persecution, a man must be willing to give up his life even for the least demanding of precepts, as is said, "You shall not profane My Holy Name—I am to be hallowed among the children of Israel" (Lev. 22:32).[15]

521. To affect healing, one may violate any precept except those prohibiting idolatry, unchastity, and murder.

What is the proof that one may not violate the prohibition against murder? If a man were told, "Go slay this person and you will be healed," he may not follow such advice, for it is written, "Whoso sheddeth man's blood, by man shall his blood be shed" (Gen. 9:6). Now, since a man who sheds blood must have his own blood shed, how can one who is sick be healed by the shedding of blood?

What is the proof that one may not resort to an act of unchastity? If a man is told, "Engage in an act of

1. Num. R. 17:6; Tanhuma, *Shelah*, §15.
2. Exod. R. 36:3.
3. Deut. R. 4:4.
4. The soul is planted in the embryo forty days after conception.
5. A small coin.
6. B. Men 99b and En Yaakov, ad loc.
7. Even a miser will become generous when he falls ill. So Meir Friedmann, ad loc. PR 11:2 (YJS 1:201); Song R. 6:11, §1.
8. Sif Deut., §40.

9. Tanhuma, *Va-yetze*, §3; En Yaakov on B. Shab 119b.
10. B. Pes 8b.
11. Even though they run the risk of being attacked by robbers.
12. B. Pes 8b.
13. For violating the interdiction against observance of Torah.
14. B. Yoma 11a.
15. Tos Shab 16:17.

unchastity and you will be healed," he may not do so, for everyone is forbidden to engage himself in unchastity. In the Torah, you will find two sections right next to each other: the section on the Nazirite and the section on the woman suspected of infidelity.[1] When the Nazirite vows not to drink wine, the Holy One says to him, "You have just vowed not to drink wine. So do not say, 'I will continue to eat grapes, and no sin will befall me.' " Hence Scripture: "He shall abstain from wine and ale, neither shall he eat anything in which grapes have been steeped, nor eat grapes fresh or dried" (Num. 6:3–4). Thus, once the Nazirite has vowed not to drink wine, he may not eat grapes, fresh or dried, nor drink anything in which grapes have been steeped or anything that is obtained from the grapevine. Now a woman, too, is called "vine," for Scripture says, "Thy wife shall be as a fruitful vine" (Ps. 128:3). So, with regard to a woman who is not your wife, do not say, "To be sure, I may have no sexual intercourse with her, but I may take hold of her and it will be no sin, or embrace her and it will be no sin, or kiss her and it will be no sin." The fact is that one is forbidden to have any contact at all with such a woman. For whoever touches a woman other than his own wife brings death upon himself, for Scripture says, "She hath cast down many wounded; yea, many a man she has slain" (Prov. 7:26). Now, since such a woman has all these characteristics, how can she give new life to one who is sick?

What is the proof that one may not resort to idolatry? If an ailing Jew is advised, "Approach such-and-such an idol and you will be healed," he is forbidden to approach it, for we are told, "He that sacrificeth to a god other than the Lord shall be proscribed" (Exod. 22:19). Since he who worships other gods is proscribed, it is better for him to die of his illness in this world than bring such proscription upon himself. Not only is idolatry itself forbidden to be used in healing the sick, but so are all things connected with idolatry. For instance, if a man is told, "Take some of the incense offered up to the idol or a piece of wood from the idol's grove and make a charm of it, and thereby be healed," he may not take either of these, for Scripture says, "Let nothing that has been doomed stick to thy hand" (Deut. 13:18). Why not? Because there is no substance in them, and they are of no avail whatsoever, as Scripture says, "Be not afraid of them, for they cannot do evil, neither is it in them to do good" (Jer. 10:5).

The Holy One said: Since an idol is like a mute stone and has no substance, and it must be guarded by others to prevent it from being stolen, how can it possibly give new life to one who is sick?[2]

522. We have been taught that R. Simeon ben Eleazar said: Every precept, such as abstention from idolatry and observance of circumcision, for which Israel were willing to die during Hadrian's persecution is still held on to firmly. On the other hand, every precept, such as use of tefillin, for which Israel were not willing to die during Hadrian's persecution continues to be weakly observed.

When the Roman government decreed that any man who wore tefillin would have a nail hammered into his skull, Elisha continued to wear his tefillin as he went out into the marketplace. A quaestor spotted him, and he ran off, with the quaestor running after him. Just as the quaestor caught up with Elisha, he removed the tefillin from his head and held them in his hand. "What's that in your hand?" the quaestor asked. "The wings of a dove." Elisha opened his hand, and the wings of a dove were in it. After that, he was dubbed "Elisha, the man of wings."

Why did Elisha say to the quaestor, "The wings of a dove," and not the wings of some other bird? Because the congregation of Israel is likened to a dove, as is said, "The wings of the dove are covered with silver, and her pinions with the shimmer of gold" (Ps. 68:14). Just as a dove is protected by her wings, so Israel are protected by precepts.[3]

523. R. Abba bar Zemina did tailoring in the home of a heathen in Rome. [At mealtime] meat of a forbidden animal was served to him, and the heathen said, "Eat." R. Abba answered, "I cannot eat." The heathen: "Eat, for if you do not, I will slay you." R. Abba: "If you wish to slay me, do so, but I cannot eat forbidden meat." The heathen: "How did you know that if you had eaten it, I would have slain you? For a Jew should act like a Jew, even as a heathen should act like a heathen."

R. Mana said: Had R. Abba bar Zemina heeded the words of the sages, he would have eaten.[4]

524. R. Hiyya bar Abba said: If someone told me, "Give up your life for the hallowing of the Name of the Holy One," I would give it up, provided I were put to death at once. But I could not endure the tortures of the generation of [Hadrian's] persecution.

What was done [to people] during that generation? Iron balls would be brought, heated white in fire, then wedged into their armpits until they gave up their souls. Or sharpened reeds were brought and driven in under their fingernails until they gave up their souls. Of such torture, David said, "Unto Thee, O Lord, do I lift up (*essa*) my soul" (Ps. 25:1). It is actually written *assi*, "I give up," indicating that they gave up their souls for the hallowing of the Holy One's Name.[5]

525. During Hadrian's persecution, two of R. Joshua's disciples gave up wearing garments [that identified them as Jews]. A certain [Roman] officer, an apostate, met them and said to them: If you are Torah's children, be willing to give up your lives for her sake; and if you are not Torah's children, why be willing to be slain for her sake?[6] They replied: We are her children and are willing to be slain for her sake, but it is not human nature to commit suicide.[7]

1. Num. 5:11–12, which deals with such a woman, is followed by 6:1ff., which sets forth the proper conduct for the Nazirite.
2. Exod. R. 16:2.
3. B. Shab 130a; Yalkut, Ps., §795.
4. P. Shev 4:2, 35a–b.
5. Song R. 2:7, §1.
6. Give up your faith.
7. Gen. R. 82:8; Yalkut, *Va-yishlah*, §35; Yalkut, Isa., §396.

526. Once, while Rabbah bar Bar Hanah was traveling with a caravan, he had a meal and forgot to say grace. He said to himself: What shall I do? If I say to my fellow companions, "I forgot to say grace," they will say, "Say it here,[1] for wherever you utter a blessing, you are saying it to the Holy One." I had better tell them I forgot a golden dove. So, saying, "Wait for me, I forgot a golden dove," he went back, said grace, and actually found a golden dove.

Why a dove? Because the congregation of Israel is said to be like a dove.[2]

527. R. Nathan said: The words "Of them that love Me and keep My precepts" (Exod. 20:6) apply to Jews who dwell in the Land of Israel and are willing to give up their lives for the sake of the precepts. Why are you led out to be decapitated?" "Because I circumcised my son." "Why are you led out to be burned?" "Because I read Scripture." "Why are you led out to be crucified?" "Because I ate unleavened bread." "Why are you lashed with the whip?" "Because I took up the lulav cluster." " 'Because I was wounded in the house of Him that causes me to be loved' [Zech. 13:6]—these wounds cause me to be loved by my Father in heaven."[3]

528. We have been taught that R. Simeon ben Gamaliel said: Every precept Israel accepted with joy—such as circumcision, of which it is said, "I rejoice at Thy [first] utterance [of the precept][4] as one that findeth great spoil" (Ps. 119:162)—they still continue to observe with joy. On the other hand, every precept Israel accepted in the midst of disaffection—such as the commandments concerning forbidden unions, of which it is said, "Moses heard the people weeping with regard to family relations" (Num. 11:10), that is, weeping on account of the sexual constraints put upon them in family relations—they continue to observe in disaffection. Thus, there is no marriage contract that does not involve [disagreement and] disaffection.[5]

529. "As for God, His word is purifying" (Ps. 18:31). Rav said: Precepts were given only so that mortals might be purified by them. For of what concern can it be to the Holy One whether, in [preparing his meat], a man slaughters an animal at the windpipe or at the gullet? Or of what concern is it to Him whether a man eats animals that are unclean or animals that are clean? Hence, precepts were given only so that mortals might be purified by them.[6]

530. "Thou hast established harmony" (Ps. 99:4). R. Alexandri said: Two ass drivers who hated each other were walking on a road when the ass of one lay down under its burden. His companion saw it, and at first he passed on. But then he reflected: Is it not written in the Torah, "If thou see the ass of him that hateth thee lying prostrate under its burden . . . thou shalt surely release it with him" (Exod. 23:5)? So he returned, lent a hand, and helped his enemy in loading and unloading. He began talking to his enemy: "Release a bit here, pull up over there, unload over here." Thus peace came about between them, so that the driver of the overloaded ass said, "Did I not suppose that he hated me? But look how compassionate he was with me." By and by, the two entered an inn, ate and drank together, and became fast friends. What caused them to make peace and to become fast friends? Because one of them kept what is written in the Torah. Hence: "Thou hast established harmony."[7]

531. If one's friend requires unloading, and one's enemy loading, one's first obligation is toward the enemy, in order to subdue the impulse to evil.[8]

532. Our masters taught: "Mine ordinances[9] ye shall do" (Lev. 18:4), matters that, had they not been set down in Scripture, should have been set down—matters such as the prohibition of idolatry, of unchastity, of shedding blood, of robbery, and of blasphemy. "And My statutes shall ye keep" (ibid.)—matters that Satan and the nations of the world challenge [as having no rational justification], such as not eating swine's flesh, not wearing cloth made of wool and linen (Deut. 22:11), the rite of *halitzah* performed by a widowed sister-in-law (Deut. 25:5ff.), the purification of a leper, the he-goat to be sent away, and the Red Heifer. Lest you think these are vain things, Scripture says, "I am the Lord" (Lev. 18:4): I, the Lord, set them down as statutes, and you have no right to question them.[10]

533. A heathen said to Rabban Yohanan ben Zakkai: "The things you Jews do appear to be a kind of sorcery. A heifer is brought, is burned up, and is pounded [into ashes] and its ashes are gathered up. Then, when one of you gets defiled by contact with a corpse, two or three drops of water mixed with these ashes are sprinkled upon him, and he is told, 'You are now cleansed!' "

Rabban Yohanan asked the heathen, "Has the spirit of madness ever possessed you?" He replied, "No." "Have you ever seen anyone possessed by the spirit of madness? The heathen replied, "Yes." "And have you seen what you people do to the man?" "Roots are brought, they are made to smoke under him, and water is splashed on him, until the spirit flees."

Rabban Yohanan then said, "Do not your ears hear what your mouth is saying? A man defiled is like a man possessed by a spirit. This spirit is a spirit of uncleanness. When water of lustration is splashed on it, it flees."

After the heathen left, Rabban Yohanan's disciples said, "Our master, you thrust off that heathen with a mere reed of an answer, but what reply will you give us?"

---

1. But grace should be said at the place where one eats.
2. B. Ber 53b and En Yaakov, ad loc.
3. Mek, *Yitro, Ba-hodesh,* 6; Lev. R. 32:1.
4. Circumcision was the first precept given to Abraham.
5. B. Shab 130a.
6. Gen. R. 44:1; Tanhuma, *Shemini,* §8.
7. Tanhuma, *Mishpatim,* §1; Tanhuma B, *Mishpatim,* §1; MTeh 99:3.
8. B. BM 32b.
9. The Hebrew for "ordinance," *mishpat,* means a law or a norm whose rightness stands to reason.
10. B. Yoma 67b and En Yaakov, ad loc; Yalkut, *Ahare Mot,* §587.

Rabban Yohanan answered, "As you live, the corpse does not defile, nor does the [mixture of ashes and] water cleanse. The truth is that the rite of the Red Heifer is a decree of the King who is King of kings. The Holy One said: I have set down a statute, I have issued a decree. You are not permitted to transgress My decree. 'This is a statute of the Torah' " (Num. 19:2).

Why are male animals specified for all [communal] sacrifices, whereas a female is specified for the rite of the Red Heifer? R. Aibu said: Consider this parable: There was a maidservant's child who polluted the king's palace. The king said, "Let his mother come and wipe up the excrement." In the same way the Holy One said, "Let the mother of a calf come and atone for the misdeed of the [golden] calf."[1]

534. R. Isaac said: Why were the reasons for [some of] the commandments in the Torah not revealed? Because in two verses reasons were revealed, and yet the greatest man in the world [Solomon] stumbled over them. One verse stated, "A king . . . shall not multiply wives to himself, that his heart turn not away" (Deut. 17:17). Now, Solomon said: I will multiply wives and not turn away. But then we read, "When Solomon was old, his wives turned away his heart" (1 Kings 11:4). Another verse stated, "A king shall not multiply horses to himself, nor cause the people to return to Egypt" (Deut. 17:16). Now, Solomon said: I will multiply horses and not cause [Israel] to return [to Egypt]. But then we read, "A chariot imported from Egypt [cost six hundred shekels of silver]" (1 Kings 10:29).[2]

535. Elijah said: Once, while I was traveling from one place to another, a man learned in Scripture but not in Mishnah came and sat down opposite me. He said to me, "Master, according to the Torah, the eating of human blood is not prohibited." I asked him, "My son, what makes you think so?" He replied, "My master, Scripture says, 'Ye shall eat no manner of blood, whether it be of fowl or of beast' (Lev. 7:26)—no mention of human blood here." I said, "My son, may not the matter be resolved by inference? If eating [the blood of] cattle, beast, and fowl—all customarily regarded as edible—is forbidden to us, surely the blood of man, who is customarily not regarded as edible—should be forbidden to us. Besides, Scripture says, 'Only be steadfast in not eating the blood; for the blood is the life' " (Deut. 12:23).[3]

536. Yalta once said to [her husband] R. Nahman: For everything that the Torah has forbidden us, it has permitted us its equivalent. Thus, it has forbidden us blood, so it has permitted us liver;[4] it has forbidden us certain fat of cattle, so it has permitted us the fat of wild beasts; it has forbidden us swine's flesh, so it has permitted us the brain of the *shibbuta;*[5] it has forbidden us the *gorit,*[6] so it has permitted us tongue of fish;[7] it has forbidden us the married woman, so it has permitted us the divorcee even if her former husband is still living; it has forbidden us the brother's wife, so it has permitted us levirate marriage (Deut. 25:5ff.). Now, I wish to eat flesh seethed in milk. [What is its counterpart?] R. Nahman said to the butchers: Roast some udders for her.[8]

537. A favorite saying of Rava's: It were better not to have been born than to perform [a precept] for a purpose that is reprehensible.[9]

538. Rabbah bar Bar Hanah said in the name of R. Yohanan: The verse "The ways of the Lord are right, and the just do walk in them, but transgressors do stumble therein" (Hos. 14:10) may be illustrated by the parable of two men who roast their paschal lambs: one eats it with the intention of fulfilling the precept, while the other eats it merely to stuff himself. To the one who eats it to fulfill the precept apply the words "The just do walk in them"; and to the one who eats it merely to stuff himself apply the words "But transgressors do stumble therein."[10]

539. R. Nahman bar Isaac said: A transgression performed with a good motive is better than a precept performed for an ulterior motive.

R. Judah said in the name of Rav: A man should always occupy himself with Torah and its precepts, even if it be for an ulterior motive, for out of occupying himself with them for an ulterior motive, he will come to occupy himself with them for the right motive.[11]

540. Precepts do not need to be performed with deliberate intention.[12]

541. The one who performs numerous precepts and the one who performs only a few have equal merit, provided the heart is directed toward Heaven.[13]

542. The Holy One requires the heart, for Scripture says, "The Lord looketh at what is in the heart" (1 Sam. 16:7).[14]

---

1. Tanhuma B, *Hakkut,* §26; PR 14:14; Num. R. 19:8.
2. Implying that merchants went to and from Egypt. B. Sanh 21b; Yalkut, *Shofetim,* §913.
3. "There is no interdict of cannibalism in Jewish law. Neither is there any law prohibiting sexual contact with one's own child. I suppose the answer is that even this far back in the history of Jewish civilization, such acts were regarded as impossible even on the part of otherwise utterly degraded individuals, and no laws to interdict them were thought necessary" (Leon Nemoy). TdE, p. 73 (JPS, p. 204).
4. Because liver is brownish red, Leon Nemoy suggests, it may have a vague similarity to dried blood.
5. According to some, it is the mullet; according to others, the sturgeon.
6. Said to be the moorhen.
7. Said to have the taste of the *gorit.*
8. B. Hul 109b.
9. B. Ber 17a.
10. B. Naz 23a.
11. B. Naz 23b.
12. B. RH 28b.
13. B. Ber 5b.
14. B. Sanh 106b.

543. A story is told of a certain pious man who forgot a sheaf of grain in his field.[1] So he said to his son, "Go and offer [in thanksgiving] on my behalf a bullock as a burnt offering and another bullock as a peace offering." The son asked, "Father, what makes you rejoice at the performance of this precept more than at any of the other precepts in the Torah?" The pious man replied, "He who is everywhere has given us all other precepts in the Torah to be performed consciously, but this one cannot be performed consciously. For if we had knowingly acted on it before Him who is everywhere, the performance of this precept would have been beyond our power. Note that Scripture says, 'When thou reapest thy harvest in thy field, and hast forgot a sheaf in the field' " (Deut. 24:19).[2]

544. "Verily, the word is very nigh unto thee, when it is in thy mouth and in thy heart to do it" (Deut. 30:14). R. Isaac said: When is it very nigh unto you? When readiness to do it is in your mouth as well as in your heart.[3]

545. R. Isaac said: The Torah teaches you a rule of good conduct, namely, that when a man performs a precept, he should do so with a cheerful heart. Had Reuben, for example, known that the Holy One would cause it to be written of him, "Reuben heard it, and delivered him out of their hand" (Gen. 37:21), he would have put Joseph on his shoulder and carried him to his father. And had Boaz known that the Holy One would cause it to be written of him that "he handed her roasted grain" (Ruth 2:14), he would have given Ruth fatted calves to eat.[4]

546. "I went down into the garden of nuts" (Song 6:11). R. Levi said: There are three kinds of nuts: Perekh[5] nuts, whose shell is soft; those whose shell is moderately hard; and those whose shell is very hard. The nut with a soft shell bursts open of itself; the nut with a moderately hard shell will crack open when you strike it; the nut with a hard shell [is too hard to be cracked, so that] when you strike it with a stone, you shatter it, and then you do not get the good of it. So, too, the Israelites: there are some among them who do good of their own accord; there are some among them who, when you ask them to give charity, will give at once; and there are those among them from whom, no matter how hard you press them, nothing good ever comes.[6]

547. We have been taught that R. Simeon ben Eleazar said: Greater is he who acts from love than he who acts from fear.[7]

548. Precious is a precept performed at the time it should be performed.[8]

549. "Ye shall observe [the feast of] unleavened bread (*ha-matzot*)" (Exod. 12:17). R. Josiah said: Do not read it so; read rather, "Ye shall observe the precepts (*ha-mitzvot*)."[9] Just as one should not be slow in making the matzah, lest it leaven, so should one not be slow to perform a mitzvah. When a mitzvah comes your way, do it at once.[10]

550. R. Joshua ben Korhah said: A man should always be as alert as possible to perform a mitzvah.[11]

551. The zealous are prompt in performance of precepts.[12]

552. Judah ben Tema said: Be bold as a leopard, light as an eagle, swift as a hart, and strong as a lion to do the will of your Father in heaven.[13]

553. R. Hama bar Hanina said: When someone begins to perform a precept without finishing it, and someone else comes along and finishes it, Scripture imputes it to the one who finishes it, as though he had performed it from beginning to end.

R. Huna said in the name of R. Eliezer son of R. Yose the Galilean: When a man begins a good deed but does not finish it, and another person comes and finishes it, it is credit wholly to the other. Thus it is written, "The bones of Joseph which the children of Israel brought up out of Egypt" (Josh. 24:32). But did not Moses bring them up, as is said, "And Moses took the bones of Joseph with him" (Exod. 13:19)? However, since it was decreed that Moses was not to enter the Land, so that others had to take charge of the bones, the others were given credit for the deed.[14]

554. He who begins doing a good deed should be told, "Finish it."[15]

555. R. Yose the Galilean used to say: He who is occupied with the performance of a precept is [at that time] exempt from the performance of any other precept.[16]

556. We have been taught: "This is my God, and I will beautify Him" (Exod. 15:2). Beautify yourself before Him

1. Thus enabling a poor man to pick it up. It is one of the ways by which a farmer benefits the poor.
2. Deliberate leaving of a sheaf in the field would not have been proper fulfillment of the precept, which requires that forgotten sheaves be made available to the poor. It would have been merely an act of charity. Forgetting is not a conscious act. Tos Pe 3:8.
3. B. Er 54a.
4. Lev. R. 34:8.
5. Nuts from Perekh, the modern Ferka, near Samaria, were noted for their soft shells. See Or 3:7.
6. PR 11:2 (YJS 1:200–201); Yalkut, Song, §992; Song R. 6:11, §1.
7. B. Sot 31a.
8. B. Pes 68b.
9. The word is spelled the same and may be vocalized either way.
10. Mek, *Bo, Pis'ha*, 9.
11. B. Naz 23b.
12. B. Pes 4a.
13. Avot 5:20.
14. B. Sot 13b; Gen. R. 85:3.
15. P. RH 1:10, 57c.
16. B. Suk 26a.

with the performance of precepts. In His honor make a beautiful sukkah, a beautiful lulav cluster, a beautiful shofar, beautiful fringes, a beautiful scroll of Torah and have it written in His name by a skilled scribe with beautiful ink and a beautiful reed pen, and wrap it in beautiful silks.[1]

557. R. Simeon ben Lakish said: Not for the world's need was gold created. Why was gold created? For the sake of the Tabernacle and for the sake of the Temple.

R. Hanina said: Not for the world's need were cedars created. Why were cedars created? For the sake of the Tabernacle and for the sake of the Temple.[2]

558. R. Zera said: To make the performance of a precept more beautiful, a man should spend up to one-third [beyond the cost ordinarily incurred].[3]

559. It once happened that Rabban Gamaliel, R. Joshua, R. Eleazar ben Azariah, and R. Akiva were traveling on a ship [during Sukkot]. Rabban Gamaliel alone had a lulav, which he bought for one thousand *zuz*. Rabban Gamaliel used it to fulfill his obligation and then gave it as a gift [to R. Joshua, who took it, fulfilled his own obligation with it, and in turn gave it as a gift] to R. Eleazar ben Azariah. R. Eleazar ben Azariah took it, discharged his obligation, and gave it as a gift to R. Akiva. R. Akiva took it, discharged his obligation, and returned it to Rabban Gamaliel.

Why was it necessary to mention that Rabban Gamaliel had bought it for one thousand *zuz?*

In order to let you know how precious to them was an opportunity to perform the precepts.[4]

560. The adornment of a precept is modesty.[5]

561. R. Eleazar ben Azariah declared: A man should not say, "I do not like swine's meat, I do not like wearing linsey-woolsey." He should say, "I like both. But what can I do? My Father in heaven decreed for me not to."[6]

562. R. Hanina said: He who is commanded and fulfills [the precept] is greater than he who fulfills it though not commanded.[7]

563. Hezekiah said: He who is exempt from the obligation to perform a precept and performs it nevertheless is called ignorant.[8]

1. B. Shab 133b.
2. Exod. R. 35:1; MTeh 104:13.
3. B. BK 9b.
4. B. Suk 41b.
5. A man should not boast of his piety. DEZ 5.
6. Sif Lev. 93d.
7. "The idea underlying this principle is the contrast between the Autonomy of the Will and the Law of God as the Authority to Man. The moral act finds its sure basis only when it is conceived as prompted by the command of God. When man acts in obedience thereto, the merit is greater" (Isidore Epstein, who quotes M. Lazarus, in AZ Soncino, p. 6, n. 1). B. Kid 31a.
8. Since in a way he ignores God's command, however laudable his intention. P. Ber 2:9, 5d; P. Shab 1:1, 3a.

564. He who, wishing to be stringent with himself, follows the stringencies of the school of Shammai as well as the stringencies of the school of Hillel—the words "The fool walketh in darkness" (Eccles. 2:14) apply to him. On the other hand, he who takes advantage of the leniencies of the school of Shammai as well as the leniencies of the school of Hillel is a wicked man. Rather, one must live either in full accordance with the opinions of the school of Shammai, with both its leniencies and its stringencies; or in full accordance with the opinions of the school of Hillel, with both its leniencies and its stringencies.[9]

565. R. Yohanan said: What is meant by "Among the dead [I am] free" (Ps. 88:6)? That once a man is dead, he is exempt from the Torah and its precepts.[10]

566. R. Joseph said: In the time-to-come, the precepts will be abolished.[11]

567. R. Simlai expounded: Six hundred and thirteen commandments were revealed to Moses: three hundred and sixty-five negative commandments, corresponding to the days in the solar year, and two hundred and forty-eight positive commandments, corresponding to the parts of the body.

When David came, he summed up the six hundred and thirteen commandments in eleven principles, for he said, "Lord, who shall abide in Thy Tabernacle? Who shall dwell in Thy holy hill? [1] He that walketh uprightly, and [2] worketh righteousness, and [3] speaketh the truth from his heart; [4] he that hath used no deceit in his tongue, [5] nor done evil to his neighbor, and [6] hath not endured a reproach against his kinsman; [7] in whose eyes a vile person is despised; [8] but he honoreth them that fear the Lord; [9] he that sweareth to his own hurt, and changeth not; [10] he that hath not given out his money upon usury, [11] nor taken reward against the innocent. He that doeth these things shall never be moved" (Ps. 15). Now, "He that walketh uprightly" applies to Abraham, who was told, "Walk before Me, and be thou upright" (Gen. 17:1). "Worketh righteousness" applies to such as Abba Hilkiah.[12] Speaketh the truth from his heart" applies to such as R. Safra.[13] "He that hath used no deceit in his tongue" applies to Jacob, who said, "My father peradventure will feel me" (Gen. 27:12).[14] "Nor done evil to his neighbor" applies to a man who does not set himself in trade to compete with

9. Tos Yev 1:13.
10. B. Shab 30a.
11. B. Nid 61b.
12. See above, part 2, chap. 1, §8.
13. An eminent scholar who lived in Caesarea, where he carried on an extensive trade. One day, while R. Safra was reading the Shema, someone offered him a sum of money for an article in his possession. Though willing to sell, R. Safra would not speak during the reading of the Shema. The would-be purchaser, interpreting R. Safra's silence as refusal, kept increasing the offer. After R. Safra finished the Shema, he explained the reason for his silence and indicated his willingness to sell the article at the price originally suggested (see Samuel ben Meir [Rashbam] on B. BB 88a; also B. Hul 94b).
14. Jacob was a reluctant partner in the deception perpetrated upon Isaac. Had Isaac put the question directly to Jacob's real identity, Jacob would have undeceived him immediately.

his neighbor. Hath not endured a reproach against his kinsman" applies to one who has befriended his kinsmen. "In whose eyes a vile person is despised" refers to Hezekiah, king of Judah, who ordered his own father's bones to be dragged along on a pallet of ropes.[1] "But he honoreth them that fear the Lord" refers to Jehoshaphat, king of Judah, who, whenever he saw a disciple of the wise, would rise from his throne, embrace him, kiss him, and call him "My father, my father! My teacher, my teacher! My master, my master!"[2] "He that sweareth to his own hurt, and changeth not" applies to such as R. Yohanan, who used to say, "I shall continue fasting until I have read the allotted portion in Mishnah and the weekly portion of Scripture."[3] "He that hath not given out his money upon usury" applies to a man who does not lend out his money usuriously even to a heathen.[4] "Nor taken a reward against the innocent" applies to such as R. Ishmael ben R. Yose.[5] Hence Scripture says, "He that doeth these things shall never be moved."

Whenever Rabban Gamaliel reached this verse, he would burst into tears and ask: Does this mean that only he who does all these things shall not be moved, but that he who does only one of them shall be moved?

R. Akiva replied: According to your reasoning, the words "Defile not yourselves in all these things" (Lev. 18:24) would mean that for a man to be defiled, he would have to touch all these creeping things, whereas if he touched only one of them, he would not be defiled. Yet the truth is that "in all these things" means that if a man touches a single creeping thing, it is as though he touched all creeping things. Here, too, in the psalm, "He that doeth these things" means that if he does any one of them [it is as though he had done them all].

When Isaiah came, he summed up the six hundred and thirteen commandments in six principles, for Isaiah said, "[1] He that walketh in righteousness and [2] speaketh peaceably; [3] he that despiseth profit from fraudulent dealings, [4] that waveth away a bribe instead of grasping it, [5] that stoppeth his ears from hearing of infamy, and [6] shutteth his eyes from looking upon evil. Such a one shall dwell in lofty security" (Isa. 33:15–16). "He that walketh in righteousness" refers to Abraham, of whom God said, "I have singled him out to instruct . . . by doing what is just and right" (Gen. 18:19). "Speaketh peaceably" refers to a man who does not provoke his fellow [with his words] in public. "He that despiseth profit from fraudulent dealings" refers to such as R. Ishmael ben Elisha.[6] "That waveth away a bribe instead of grasping it" refers to such as R. Ishmael ben R. Yose.[7] "That stoppeth his ears from hearing of infamy" refers to such as R. Eleazar son of R. Simeon,[8] who would not hear defamation of a disciple of the wise and remain silent. "Shutteth his eyes from looking upon evil" is to be construed as R. Hiyya bar Abba construed it. For R. Hiyya bar Abba said: These words refer to a man who will not gaze at women when they are doing the wash.[9]

Of each of the aforementioned, Isaiah said, "Such a one shall dwell in lofty security, with inaccessible cliffs for his stronghold, with his food supplied and his drink assured" (Isa. 35:16).

When Micah came, he summed up the six hundred and thirteen commandments in three principles, for he said, "It hath been told thee, O man, what is good, and what the Lord doth require of thee: [1] only to do justly, and [2] to love mercy, and [3] to walk modestly with thy God" (Mic. 6:8). "To do justly" refers to the maintaining of justice; "to love mercy" refers to the doing of deeds of mercy; and "to walk modestly with thy God" applies even to dowering a bride or providing shrouds for the dead. Now, if in commandments that are customarily not done in private [and thus do not require modesty], the Torah commands, "Walk modestly with thy God," how much more strongly does this precept apply to commandments that have to be done in private.

Upon further consideration, Isaiah summed up the six hundred and thirteen commandments in two principles when he said, "Thus saith the Lord: [1] keep justice and [2] do righteousness" (Isa. 56:1).

When Habakkuk came, he summed up the six hundred and thirteen commandments in one principle, for he said, "The righteous shall live by his faith" (Hab. 2:4).[10]

---

1. He thus deprived his father, the vile Ahaz, of royal burial. Cf. 2 Chron. 28:27.
2. See 2 Chron. 19:4ff. and B. Ket 103b.
3. "Until I have read the allotted portion in Mishnah and in Scripture": parallel in P. Ned 8:1, 40d; BR: "until I come home."
4. According to Scripture, usury from a heathen is not prohibited. See Deut. 23:21 and B. BM 70b–71a.
5. R. Ishmael ben R. Yose was a judge. Upon learning that his tenant gardener was to appear before him in a lawsuit, he refused to accept the regular basket of fruit the tenant brought a day earlier than was his custom. R. Ishmael also disqualified himself from the lawsuit. As he went about getting another judge to act as his substitute, he caught himself unwittingly arguing in behalf of his tenant and thus became more aware than ever of a bribe's insidious effect upon a judge. Cf. B. Ket 105b (Ket, Soncino, p. 677). Also see above, part 2, chap. 1, §233.
6. R. Ishmael ben Elisha was both priest and judge. One day a man brought him the first of the fleece as a priest's gift (see Deut. 18:4). R. Ishmael asked whether there was no priest in the man's own neighborhood to whom he might have given the first of the fleece; the man replied that there was indeed a priest in his neighborhood, but since he—the man—was on the way to attend a lawsuit, he thought that he might as well dispose of the fleece on his way. Upon hearing this, R. Ishmael refused to accept the proffered fleece. He also disqualified himself from the lawsuit. As he went about getting another judge to act as his substitute, he caught himself arguing unwittingly in behalf of the man who had offered him the fleece. See B. Ket 105b and above, part 2, chap. 1, §112.
7. Who similarly refused the bribe of his tenant.
8. After his death, his body was kept for years in an upper chamber and was not infested with worms. However, one day, when his wife saw a worm issue from his ear, she was greatly grieved. But then he appeared to her in a dream and said, "This happened because I once heard a disciple of the wise defamed and did not protest as I should have done." Clearly he offended in this regard only once. See above, part 2, chap. 1, §229–33.
9. Presumably because, as the women lean over toward the water, they expose parts of their bodies.
10. B. Mak 23b–24a; B. Sanh 81a.

A Fence around the Torah

568. "Assure the safety of My charge (Lev. 18:30)[1]—provide a safeguard for My charge."[2]

569. The Men of the Great Assembly used to say: Make a fence for the Torah.[3]

570. "Enter not into the path of the wicked. . . . Avoid it, pass not by it; turn from it, and pass on" (Prov. 4:14–15). R. Ashi said: The verse may be illustrated by the parable of a man who guards an orchard. If he guards it from without, the entire orchard is protected; but if he guards it from within, only the part in front of him is protected, while the part behind him is not protected.[4]

571. Once the wall of a vineyard collapses, the vineyard is as good as destroyed.[5]

572. We have been taught: The sages made a fence for their words, so that a man returning home from a field in the evening should not say, "I will go home, eat a little, drink a little, sleep a little. Then I will recite the Shema and the *Tefillah*."[6] For sleep is likely to overpower him, and he will sleep through the entire night. Rather, a man coming home from the field in the evening should first go into the synagogue. If he is accustomed to read Scripture, he should read Scripture; if he is accustomed to recite Mishnah, he should recite Mishnah. Then he should recite the Shema and the *Tefillah*, eat his meal, and say grace.[7]

573. R. Avira expounded: The ministering angels said to the Holy One: Master of the universe, it is written in your Torah, "Who regardeth not persons" (Deut. 10:17). But You—do You not regard the people of Israel, as Scripture says, "The Lord regardeth thee" (Num. 6:26)? He replied: And shall I not regard Israel, seeing that I wrote for them in the Torah, "And thou shalt eat and be satisfied, and bless the Lord" (Deut. 8:10), and they make sure to say the blessing of grace, even when the quantity [they consume] is only the bulk of an olive or the bulk of an egg?[8]

574. One may not read on the Sabbath by the light of a lamp, lest he tilt it. R. Ishmael ben Elisha said: I will read and not tilt. But once, while reading, he caught himself about to tilt it and he exclaimed: How great are the words of the sages, who used to say, "One may not read by the light of a lamp." According to R. Nathan, R. Ishmael actually did tilt the lamp while reading, and he wrote in his notebook, "I, Ishmael ben Elisha, did tilt a lamp while reading on the Sabbath. When the Temple is rebuilt, I will bring a plump sin offering."[9]

575. R. Eliezer ben Jacob said: I have heard that [when necessary] a court may—even without scriptural authority—impose flogging or even the death penalty, not, however, intending to contravene the Torah, but rather [to safeguard it by] making a fence around it. It once happened in the days of the Greeks that a man rode a horse on the Sabbath. When brought before the court, he was sentenced to be stoned, not because he incurred such a penalty [according to Scripture],[10] but because the exigencies of the time made it necessary.[11]

576. Rava expounded: What is implied in the verse "And furthermore, my son, take care . . . of making many books there is no end" (Eccles. 12:12)? Take greater care [to observe] the ordinances of the scribes than the ordinances of Torah, for in the ordinances of Torah there are [varying penalties for transgressing] positive and negative commandments. But as to the ordinances of the scribes, whoever transgresses any of them incurs the penalty of death. Lest you say, "If there is such substance in them, why were they not written down?" Because "of making many books there is no end."[12]

577. To a Nazirite we say: Go round and round, but not near a vineyard.[13]

578. Rava said: Sanctify yourself even in that which is permitted you.[14]

579. "Sanctify yourselves therefore, and be ye holy" (Lev. 20:7). R. Avin said: The verse may be understood by the parable of a king who had a cellar full of wine. The king set watchmen over it, some of them Nazirites and some tipplers. In the evening, when he came to give them their pay, he gave the tipplers a double wage and the Nazirites only a single wage. The Nazirites asked, "Our lord king, have we not all watched alike? Why give a double wage to these, and only a single wage to us?" He replied, "These are tipplers and are in the habit of guzzling wine. [As a reward for having abstained] I gave them a double wage. But to you [who have no such weakness], I give a single wage." So it is with the beings above. Since the impulse to evil is not present in them, one command to be holy is sufficient. But the beings below—the impulse to evil overcomes them. O that they would resist it after being twice bidden to be holy! Such is the implication in "Sanctify yourselves therefore, and be ye holy."[15]

---

1. JV: "Therefore shall ye keep My charge."
2. B. MK 5a.
3. Avot 1:1.
4. B. Yev 21a.
5. ARN 24.
6. The Eighteen Benedictions, at one time said twice, now three times, daily.
7. B. Ber 4b.
8. B. Ber 20b.
9. B. Shab 12b.
10. Riding a horse on the Sabbath is forbidden only by a rabbinic prohibition.
11. B. Yev 90b; B. Sanh 46a.
12. B. Er 21b.
13. A Nazirite may eat no grapes and drink no wine. B. Shab 13a.
14. B. Yev 20a.
15. Lev. R. 24:8.

580. R. Judah said in the name of Rav: Whenever the sages forbid anything for appearance' sake, it is forbidden even in one's innermost chambers.[1]

581. We have been taught: On the Sabbath one may beat up wine and oil for a sick person. However, R. Simeon ben Eleazar said in the name of R. Meir: One may beat up wine and oil for a sick person on the Sabbath. Nevertheless, R. Simeon ben Eleazar went on to tell: Once [on a Sabbath] R. Meir had pain in his stomach, and as we were about to beat up wine and oil for him, he would not permit us. We asked him, "Shall your ruling be made null and void in your own lifetime?" He replied, "I, to be sure, rule one way, but my colleagues rule another way, and I have never presumed to disregard the rulings of my colleagues."[2]

582. "Ye shall not eat of it, neither shall ye touch it" (Gen. 3:3). In connection with Eve's adding "neither shall ye touch it" to God's words, Scripture warns, "Never add to His words, lest He prove you to be falsifying" (Prov. 30:6). R. Hiyya commented: Do not make the fence taller than what is fenced in, lest it fall down and crush the saplings. Thus, too, after the Holy One said, "In the day that thou eatest thereof, thou shalt surely die" (Gen. 2:17), Eve did not quote Him accurately, saying instead, "God hath said, 'Ye shall not eat of it, neither shall ye touch it, lest ye die.' " Later, when the serpent saw her pass in front of the tree, he took hold of her, pushed her against the tree, and said, "You see, you did not die. Even as you did not die by touching it, so you will not die by eating its fruit."[3]

583. There were certain rulings that all the sages agreed upon in the upper chamber of Hananiah ben Hezekiah ben Gorion.[4] However, one day, when going up to visit him, they took a vote on a matter. Finding that the school of Shammai outnumbered the school of Hillel, they issued eighteen rulings [not universally agreed upon]. That day was as calamitous for Israel[5] as the day the golden calf was made.

[In approval of what had been done], R. Eliezer said: On that day [in issuing rulings that were necessary] they made the measure full to the brim. Differing, R. Joshua said: On that day they in fact made the measure deficient, for when a measure is full to the brim, whatever extra a man puts into it will inevitably cause what is in it to spill out.

The sages taught: By what parable may R. Eliezer's view be illustrated? By the parable of a basket full of cucumbers and gourds. When a man pours mustard seeds into it, it holds the contents more firmly. By what parable may R. Joshua's view be illustrated? By the parable of a tub full of honey. When a man puts pomegranates and walnuts into it, the tub overflows.[6]

584. Hezekiah said: How do we know that he who adds to the word of God subtracts from it? From the verse "God hath said: Ye shall not eat of it, neither shall ye touch it" (Gen. 3:3). But R. Mesharsheya maintained: We derive it from a single word in the verse "*Ammatayim* [two cubits] and a half shall be the length thereof" (Exod. 25:10);[7] while R. Ashi said: We drive it from two words in the verse "*Ashte esreh* [eleven] curtains" (Exod. 26:7).[8]

585. R. Yose said: Better [a fence of] ten handbreadths that stands firm than one of a hundred handbreadths that is sure to fall down.[9]

586. A fence that [though rickety] still stands should be repaired, but one that is clearly deteriorating should be demolished.[10]

587. A restriction should not be imposed on a community unless the majority is able to stand it.[11]

588. A restriction issued by a court but not accepted by the majority of the community is not a valid restriction.[12]

589. R. Tarfon said: One may not light [the Sabbath lamp] with any oil [other than] olive oil. Hearing this, R. Yohanan ben Nuri rose to his feet and exclaimed. What shall the Babylonians do, who have only sesame oil? What shall the Medians do, who have only walnut oil? And what shall the people of Alexandria do, who have only radish oil? And what shall the people of Cappadocia do, who have neither the one nor the other, but only naphtha? Accordingly, you must conclude that oils other than those listed by the sages as not to be used for lamps [are not to be added to the prohibited list].[13]

590. If the interpretation of a law is varying in the courts, and you do not know which interpretation is to be preferred, note how the local people apply this law and act accordingly.[14]

591. Our masters taught: On one occasion, the fourteenth of Nisan fell on a Sabbath, and the Bene Betera forgot the law, so that they did not know whether offering the paschal lamb does or does not override the Sabbath. They asked, "Is there anyone at all who knows whether or not the paschal lamb overrides the Sabbath?" They were told, "There is a certain man who has come up from Babylonia—he is known as Hillel the Babylonian. Since he ministered

---

1. B. Shab 64b.
2. B. Shab 134a.
3. Gen. R. 19:3.
4. Concerning him, see above in this chapter, §423.
5. Because not reasoning but the sheer plurality of numbers prevailed.
6. B. Shab 153b; Tos Shab 1:16.
7. Had the word read *ma'tayim* ("two hundred") and the scribe wrongly added an *alef* in front, making it read *ammatayim* ("two cubits"), God's word would have been diminished.
8. Had the words read *shete esreh*, ("twelve") and the scribe wrongly added an *ayin*, making it read *ashte esreh* ("eleven"), God's word would have been diminished. B. Sanh 29a.
9. ARN 1.
10. Tanhuma B, *Va'yeshev*, §14.
11. B. BK 79b.
12. P. Shab 1:4, 3d.
13. B. Shab 26a.
14. P. M Sh 5:2, 56b.

to the two notables of the generation, Shemaiah and Avtalion, he must know whether or not offering the paschal lamb overrides the Sabbath." So they sent for him and asked, "Do you know whether or not the paschal lamb overrides the Sabbath?" He replied, "Have we only one lamb—the lamb offered on Passover—that might override the Sabbath? Have we not in fact more than two hundred so-called paschal lambs during the year that override the Sabbath?"[1] The Bene Betera, taken aback, asked, "How can you make such a statement?' He replied, "In connection with the paschal lamb, Scripture prescribes that it be offered 'in its appointed time' [Num. 9:2], and in connection with [its analogue] the daily lamb, Scripture likewise prescribes that it be offered 'in its appointed time' [Num. 28:2]. Just as 'its appointed time' said in connection with the daily lamb involves overriding the Sabbath, so 'its appointed time' said in connection with the paschal lamb involves overriding the Sabbath. Besides, there is an argument *a fortiori:* if the daily lamb, whose omission is not punished by excision, overrides the Sabbath, then should not the paschal lamb, whose neglect is punished by excision, without question override the Sabbath?" Immediately Hillel was placed foremost in the house of study and appointed patriarch over them, and the rest of the entire day he sat and lectured concerning the laws of Passover. In the course of his remarks, he was moved to chide the people of Jerusalem, saying, "Who brought it about that I have come from Babylonia and have been made patriarch over you? It was your own indolence—you did not minister to the two notables of the generation, Shemaiah and Avtalion, who dwelled in your very midst." No sooner did he rebuke them than the answer to a question in *Halakhah* was hidden from him, so that when they asked him, "Master, what is the rule if a man forgot to bring in a knife on the eve of the Sabbath?" he had to reply, "I have heard the answer to this question but forgotten it. But depend on the people of Israel: if they themselves are not prophets, they are the children of prophets!" Indeed, the next day, one whose Passover offering was a lamb stuck the knife in its wool; one whose Passover offering was a goat tied the knife between its horns.[2] When Hillel saw what was being done, he recollected the *Halakhah* and said, "What these men are doing is in line with the tradition I received from the mouths of Shemaiah and Avtalion."[3]

592. Custom set aside a rabbinic ruling.[4]

593. All practices must follow the custom of the city.[5]

594. Where the custom is to work on the eve of Passover until midday, one may work. Where the custom is not to work,[6] one may not work. When a man goes from a place where work is done to a place where work is not done, or from a place where work is not done to a place where work is done, both the restrictions of the place he left and the restrictions of the place he went to are imposed on him. [However, if he goes from a place where work is not done to a place where it is done], he need not change his ways out of fear of stirring up controversy.[7]

595. R. Hinena said: All kinds of practices depend on custom. Thus in Migdal Tzabbayim there were acacia trees, and R. Hanina, the associate of scholars, was asked, "May these now be used for secular purposes?"[8] He replied, "Since your fathers regarded such use as prohibited, do not change the practice of your fathers, may they rest in peace."

R. Eleazar said in the name of R. Avun: When a man is not sure whether a certain practice is permitted and he errs in regarding it as prohibited, he may come to the scholars for absolution and they may release him from the prohibition he imposed on himself. But if he knows that a practice is permitted and he nevertheless chooses to regard it as prohibited, then if he seeks absolution from the scholars, they may choose not to give it to him.

One may sit on the [merchandise] bench of a heathen on the Sabbath.[9] It happened that Rabban Gamaliel sat on the [merchandise] bench of a heathen in Acco on the Sabbath. He was told, "Our custom is not to sit on the [merchandise] bench of a heathen on the Sabbath." But since he did not wish to tell them that it was permitted, he [obediently] rose and went his way.

A story is told of Judah and Hillel, the sons of Rabban Gamaliel, who went to bathe in a bathhouse in Cabul. They were told, "It is not our custom to have two brothers bathe together."[10] But since they did not wish to say that such a practice was permitted, they [obediently] went in one after the other. More: When the two brothers came out for a walk on the Sabbath wearing golden shoes, they were told, "It is not our custom to wear golden shoes on the Sabbath."[11] But since they did not wish to say that it was permitted, they [obediently] sent the shoes back home with their servants.

The people of Mesha had taken it upon themselves not to set sail in the Great [Mediterranean] Sea [three days before the Sabbath]. They came and said to Rabbi [Judah I, the Patriarch], "Our fathers followed the custom not to set sail in the Great Sea—we, what should we do?" He replied, "Since your fathers regarded such a practice as prohibited, do not change the custom of your fathers, may they rest in peace."[12]

596. Our masters taught: In R. Eliezer's locality they used to cut timber to make charcoal for forging iron on

1. The lamb offered in the morning and evening of fifty Sabbaths during the year, plus the two additional daily offerings on a Sabbath, add up to two hundred during a year.
2. And thus avoided having to carry it on the Sabbath.
3. B. Pes 66a and En Yaakov, ad loc.; P. Pes 6:1, 33a.
4. P. Yev 12:1, 12c.
5. B. Suk 38a.
6. So that people may have ample time to prepare for Passover.
7. Because those who see him not working will assume that he has no work or is not well enough to work. Pes 4:1.
8. Even though when the Temple stood they were used in its structure.
9. And not worry that he may be suspected of engaging in business on the Sabbath.
10. Because of fear of homosexual intercourse.
11. Out of fear that they may be removed to be shown and the prohibition of carrying on the Sabbath thus be violated.
12. P. Pes 4:1, 30d.

the Sabbath.[1] In the locality of R. Yose the Galilean, they used to eat the flesh of fowl with milk.

Levi visited the home of Joseph the Fowler and was offered the head of a peacock in milk, which he did not eat. When he came to Rabbi [Judah I, the Patriarch], Rabbi asked him, "Why did you not place Joseph under a ban?" Levi replied, "It was in the locality of R. Judah ben Betera, and so I thought: perhaps Joseph the Fowler understood the law in accordance with the interpretation of R. Yose the Galilean."[2]

597. Every river has its own course.[3]

Torah's Mysteries

598. The chapter on creation (Gen. 1) may not be expounded in the presence of two persons, nor the chapters on the chariot (Ezek. 1 and 10; Isa. 6) in the presence of even one person, unless he is a sage who is capable of understanding on his own.

When a man speculates upon four things—what is above [the celestial creatures] and what is beneath them, what preceded creation and what will happen thereafter—it were better for him if he had not come into the world. And anyone who is not delicate about the honor of his Creator—it were better for him if he had not come into the world.[4]

599. The Torah may be likened to two paths, one of fire and one of snow. If one turns too close to the first, he will die in the fire; too close to the second, he will die in the snow. What should he do? He should walk in the middle.[5]

600. Four men entered the "Garden,"[6] namely, Ben Azzai, Ben Zoma, Aher,[7] and R. Akiva. R. Akiva said to them: When you arrive at the slabs of pure marble, do not say, "Water, water!" for Scripture says, "He that speaketh falsehood shall not be established before Mine eyes" (Ps. 101:7). Ben Azzai cast one look [at the Garden] and died; of him, Scripture says, "Precious in the sight of the Lord is the death of His saints" (Ps. 116:15). Ben Zoma looked and became demented; of him, Scripture says; "Hast thou found honey? Eat so much as is sufficient for thee, lest thou be filled therewith, and vomit it" (Prov. 25:16). Aher fell into heresy.[8] R. Akiva came down unharmed. Of him, Scripture says, "Draw Me, I will run after thee" (Song 1:4). The ministering angels sought to thrust even R. Akiva away, but the Holy One said: Let this venerable elder be. He deserves to make use of My glory.[9]

601. Once, R. Joshua ben Hananiah was standing on a step on the Temple Mount when Ben Zoma walked toward him but, after coming close to him, did not salute him.[10] R. Joshua asked, "Whence and whither, Ben Zoma?" Ben Zoma: "I have been meditating on the work of creation, and found that between the upper and the lower waters there is no more than the space of three fingerbreadths, as is said, 'The spirit of God hovered upon the face of the water' [Gen. 1:2], like a dove hovering over its young, touching them and not touching them." At that, R. Joshua said to his disciples, "Ben Zoma is already outside."[11] Not many days passed, and Ben Zoma departed this life.[12]

602. Our masters taught: There was once a child who was reading in the book of Ezekiel at his teacher's house, and he kept speculating about the meaning of *hashmal* [electrum] (Ezek. 1:4). When a fire went forth from the *hashmal* and consumed him, the sages sought to suppress the book of Ezekiel. Hananiah ben Hezekiah objected: "This child, to be sure, was a sage. But do you suppose it likely that all other children will be sages like him [and similarly endangered]?"[13]

603. R. Simeon ben Jehozadak inquired of R. Samuel bar Nahman: "Since I hear that you are a master of *Aggadah*, tell me how light was created?" R. Samuel bar Nahman replied, "The Holy One covered Himself with a white garment, and the radiance of His majesty illuminated the world from one end to the other." But since R. Samuel bar Nahman gave his reply in a whisper, R. Simeon ben Jehozadak pressed him further: "Is this not stated explicitly in the verse 'Who coverest Thyself with light as with a garment' [Ps. 104:2]? Why do you tell it in a whisper?" R. Samuel bar Nahman said to him, "As I received this tradition in a whisper, so I answered you in a whisper."[14]

604. "This is My Name" (Exod. 3:15). But it is also written, "And this is My appellation" (ibid.), by which the Holy One implied: I am not to be called by My Name as written: My Name is written *yod he*, but my appellation is to be *alef dalet*.[15]

Rabbah bar Bar Hanah said in the name of R. Yohanan: The sages confide the exact pronunciation of the Tetragrammaton to their disciples only once in a seven-year cycle. Some say: Twice in a seven-year cycle.

---

1. To make a knife for circumcision.
2. B. Shab 130a.
3. B. Hul 18b.
4. B. Hag 11b.
5. P. Hag 2:1, 77a.
6. A figurative expression for the mystical realm of theosophy. So Jastrow and Goldschmidt.
7. Elisha ben Avuyah, R. Meir's teacher. See above, part 2, chap. 1, §191.
8. Literally, "mutilated the shoots [of true faith]."
9. B. Hag 14b and 15b, and En Yaakov, ad loc.
10. He was lost in thought and failed to show a disciple's respect to his master.
11. Engaged in gnostic speculations, which were heretical.
12. B. Hag 15a; Tos Hag 2:6.
13. B. Hag 13a.
14. Gen. R. 3:4; MTeh 104:4.
15. The Tetragrammaton, *Yod He Vav He*, is read *adonai* (*alef dalet nun yod*). But even this name was apparently pronounced *Ad* (*alef dalet*). See J. Z. Lauterbach, "Substitutes for the Tetragrammaton," *Proceedings of the American Academy for Jewish Research* 2 (1930–31): 43.

Our masters taught: At first the twelve-letter Name used to be entrusted to all people. After the indiscreet became numerous, it was entrusted only to the discreet ones in the priesthood. During the chanting [of the Tetragrammaton] by their brother priests, they pronounced it indistinctly.

We have been taught that R. Tarfon said: One time I ascended the [priests'] dais after my mother's brother, and I inclined my ear to the high priest, who pronounced that [twelve-letter] Name indistinctly during the chanting [of the Tetragrammaton] by his brother priests.

R. Judah said in the name of Rav: The forty-two-letter Name is entrusted only to one who is discreet and meek, in his middle years, free from bad temper, not given to drink, and not insistent on his rights. And he who knows it and is careful about it, taking care to utter it only when he is ritually clean, is beloved above and cherished below, is held in awe by his fellows, and inherits two worlds—this world and the world-to-come.[1]

605. Our masters taught: Once, when on a journey, Rabban Yohanan ben Zakkai was riding an ass, with R. Eleazar ben Arakh driving the ass from behind. R. Eleazar said, "Master, teach me a chapter of the Work of the Chariot." He answered, "My son, have I not instructed you that the Work [of the Chariot] is not to be taught in the presence of even one person, unless he is a sage and able to draw inferences on his own?" R. Eleazar then said, "Master, permit me to say something before you."[2] He answered, "Say it!"

Rabban Yohanan ben Zakkai dismounted from the ass, wrapped himself in his robe, and sat down on a stone beneath an olive tree. R. Eleazar said to him, "Master, why did you dismount from the ass?" Rabban Yohanan answered, "Since you are about to expound the Work of the Chariot, the Divine Presence will be with us, and the ministering angels may be accompanying us—is it proper that I should continue riding the ass?" As R. Eleazar ben Arakh began his exposition of the Work of the Chariot, fire came down from heaven and lapped all the trees of the field, and they all began to utter song. What was the song they uttered? "Praise the Lord from the earth, ye sea monsters, and all deeps . . . fruitful trees and all cedars. . . . Hallelujah" (Ps. 148:7, 148:9, and 148:14).

An angel also was heard from the fire saying, "Of a certainty, this is the very Work of the Chariot."

Then Rabban Yohanan ben Zakkai rose, kissed R. Eleazar on his head, and said, "Blessed be the Lord, the God of Israel, that has given to Abraham our father a son who knows how to speculate upon, to examine, and to expound the Work of the Chariot. There are some who expound well but do not practice well, and some who practice well but do not expound well; but you both expound well and practice well. Happy are you, O Abraham our father, that Eleazar ben Arakh has come forth from your loins."

When these things were told to R. Joshua, while he and R. Yose the Priest were on a journey, the two sages said: Let us also engage in speculations about the Work of the Chariot. After R. Joshua had begun his discourse, even though that day was the summer solstice, the heavens nevertheless became overcast with clouds, a kind of rainbow appeared in the cloud (Ezek. 1:28), and the ministering angels assembled as they came to listen, like people who assemble and come to watch the entertainment for a groom and a bride.

R. Yose the Priest went and told Rabban Yohanan ben Zakkai what had happened. Rabban Yohanan said: "Blessed are you, and blessed are the mothers who bore you. Blessed are my eyes, which saw that it was so. Moreover, in my dream the two of you and I were reclining on Mount Sinai, and a divine voice from heaven was vouchsafed to us: 'Ascend hither! Ascent hither! Here large banqueting chambers are prepared for you, and beautiful dining couches are laid out for you. You, your disciples, and the disciples of your disciples are designated to the third company of the upright.' "[3]

1. B. Kid 71a.
2. The words "that you taught me" are omitted, as in parallels in the Palestinian Talmud.
3. Seven such companies are admitted after death into God's presence (see MTeh 11:6). B. Hag 14b and En Yaakov, ad loc.

CHAPTER EIGHT

WISDOM, PROPHECY, AND SONG

Wisdom

1. The spirit conceived and gave birth to wisdom.[1]

2. R. Ammi said: So great is knowledge [of Torah] that the prayer for it was placed at the beginning of the weekday blessings.[2]

R. Ammi also said: So great is knowledge [of Torah] that it was placed between two of God's Names: "For a God of knowledge is the Lord" (1 Sam. 2:3).

R. Eleazar said: When a man has [Torah] knowledge, it is as though the Sanctuary were built in his days. For just as knowledge was placed between two of God's Names, so the Sanctuary was placed between two of God's Names: "Thou hast made, O LORD, the Sanctuary, O LORD" (Exod. 15:17).

R. Eleazar also said: A man who has [Torah] knowledge will eventually become wealthy, for it is said, "By knowledge are all chambers filled with precious and pleasant riches" (Prov. 24:4).

R. Eleazar also said: When a man lacks [Torah] knowledge, one may have no mercy on him, for it is said, "It is a people that have no understanding [of Torah], therefore He that made them will not have mercy upon them" (Isa. 27:11).

R. Eleazar also said: He who gives his bread to one who has no [Torah] knowledge will be assailed by suffering, for it is said, "They in whom there is no understanding that eat thy bread lay a wound[3] under thee" (Obad. 1:7).

R. Eleazar also said: A man who has no [Torah] knowledge will eventually be exiled, as is said, "Therefore My people are gone into exile, for want of knowledge" (Isa. 5:13).[4]

3. If a disciple of the wise lacks a sense [of propriety], an animal is better than he is.

If a disciple of the wise lacks a sense [of propriety], a carcass is better than he is.[5]

4. The adornment of knowledge is wisdom, the adornment of wisdom is humility.[6]

5. The Torah was not given to fools.[7]

6. "In want of all things" (Deut. 28:48). R. Nahman said: This means: without knowledge.

Abbaye said: We have a tradition that "poor" means poor in [Torah] knowledge. In the west [the Land of Israel], there is a proverb: He who has this has everything; he who lacks this—what has he?[8]

7. R. Tanhuma began his discourse with the verse "There is gold, and a multitude of rubies; but the lips of knowledge are a precious jewel" (Prov. 20:15). It is the way of the world that if a man has gold and silver, priceless gems and pearls, and all kinds of precious vessels in the world, but lacks knowledge, of what worth is what he owns? The proverb says, "If it's knowledge you've got, what do you lack? If it's knowledge you lack, what have you got?"[9]

8. "Ask what I shall give thee" (1 Kings 3:5, 2 Chron. 1:7). R. Simon said in the name of R. Simeon ben Halafta: Solomon at that time was like a counselor who was held in great esteem at the king's court. When the king said to him, "Ask for what I shall give you," the counselor thought: If I ask for silver and gold, that is all I shall be given. If I ask for precious stones and pearls, that is all I shall be given. So he decided: I will ask for the king's daughter, and that will include everything else. So, too, Solomon said: If I ask for silver and gold, precious stones and pearls, that is all I shall be given. What I will ask for is wisdom, and that will include everything else.[10]

9. R. Isaac said: He who desires to become wise, let him turn to the south [when praying]; and he who desires to become rich, let him turn to the north [when praying]. The mnemonic [by which this may be remembered] is that the table [in the Tabernacle] was to the north of the altar and the lampstand to the south (Exod. 26:35).[11]

R. Joshua ben Levi, however, said: One should always turn south, because by obtaining wisdom, he will obtain wealth, as it says, "Length of days are in [wisdom's] right hand; in her left hand are riches and honor" (Prov. 3:16).[12]

10. R. Yohanan said: The Holy One grants wisdom only to one who already has wisdom, for Scripture says, "He giveth wisdom to the wise, and intelligence to the intelligent" (Deut. 2:21). When R. Tahalifa of the West heard it and repeated it to R. Abbahu. R. Abbahu said to him: You infer it from that verse, while we infer it from this one: "In the heart of all that are wise-hearted I have put wisdom" (Exod. 31:6).[13]

---

1. Exod. R. 15:22.
2. See Hertz *APB*, p. 137.
3. JV: "snare."
4. B. Ber 33a; B. Sanh 92a and En Yakov, ad loc.
5. TdE, ed. Friedmann, p. 33; Lev. R. 1:15.
6. DEZ 5.
7. Lekah Tov on Gen. 49:4 (ed. Buber, p. 232).
8. B. Ned 41a.
9. Lev. R. 1:6; Yalkut, *Va-yikra*, §428.
10. Song R. 1:1, §9.
11. The table symbolizing plenty, and the lampstand wisdom—"the commandment is a lamp" (Prov. 6:23).
12. B. BB 25b.
13. B. Ber 55a.

11. "And beyond wisdom, I have filled him with the spirit of God" (Exod. 31:3). Take the shopkeeper as an example. When a man comes to buy wine from him, or honey, or oil, or fish brine, the shopkeeper, if he is knowledgeable, first smells the buyer's vessel. If it had been used for wine, he puts wine into it; so, too, if the vessel had been used for oil, for honey, or for fish brine. Likewise the Holy One, when He sees that there is the aroma of wisdom in a man fills him with more. Hence, "I have filled him with the spirit," implying that the spirit of wisdom had already been in him.[1]

12. A [Roman] noblewoman challenged R. Yose ben Halafta, saying to him, "What sense is conveyed by 'He giveth wisdom to the wise' [Dan. 2:21]? Should the verse not have read, 'He giveth wisdom to fools'?" R. Yose replied, "Have you any jewelry?" She said, "Yes." R. Yose: "If two persons, one rich and the other poor, should come to you to borrow your jewelry, to which would you lend it?" The noblewoman: "To the one who is rich." "Why?" "Because the one who is rich has the means to repay should he lose it; but the one who is poor—how is he to repay?" R. Yose: "Let your ears hear what your mouth is saying. You would lend your jewelry only to a person who is rich. Shall the Holy One, then, give wisdom to fools?"[2]

13. "But wisdom, where shall it be found?" (Job 28:12). The verse implies that Solomon was endeavoring to determine where in man's body wisdom is to be found. R. Eliezer said: [Solomon concluded that it was] in the head. But R. Joshua said: In the heart, for Scripture says, "Thou hast put gladness in my heart" (Ps. 4:8), and with regard to gladness, Scripture says elsewhere, "My son, be wise, and make my heart glad" (Prov. 27:11).[3]

14. "All the streams run into the sea" (Eccles. 1:7). All of man's wisdom is nowhere other than in the heart. "Yet the sea is not full" (ibid.)—the heart is never filled to capacity. You might suppose that when a man lets his wisdom go forth from his heart,[4] it will never flow back to him. Hence Scripture says, "Yet the streams flow back again" (ibid.).[5]

15. The Alexandrians asked R. Joshua ben Hananiah: What should a man do to become wise? He replied: Let him sit long in the academy and engage very little in business. They objected: But many did so, and it did not avail them. [So he suggested]: Let him beseech mercy of Him to whom wisdom belongs, as is said, "For the Lord giveth wisdom, out of His mouth cometh knowledge and discernment" (Prov. 2:6).

R. Hiyya taught: What God does may be understood by the parable of a king who prepared a public feast, but he sent [choice tidbits] to his favorites from what was set before his own person.

R. Isaac taught: The verse may be understood by the parable of a king who was sucking a lozenge. When his son came in, he took the lozenge out of his own mouth and gave it to his son. Thus "the Lord giveth wisdom" to all; but "out of His mouth cometh knowledge and discernment" for Israel.[6]

16. A [Roman] noblewoman said to R. Judah: A teacher and a drunkard?[7] He replied: By my faith! I taste no wine but that of Kiddush, *Havdalah*,[8] and the four obligatory cups on Passover. The latter make me feel as though I had a tight cord around my head from Passover to Pentecost. No; rather, "a man's wisdom maketh his face to shine" (Eccles. 8:1).[9]

17. If there is [no Torah] knowledge, whence the capacity to make distinctions?[10]

18. Who is wise? He who foresees what is about to happen.[11]

19. "A wise man has his eyes in his head" (Eccles. 2:14). Are then a fool's eyes in his feet? No; what the verse means is that when the wise man is at the "head" of a thing, he already foresees what the end will be.

R. Meir used to call the end of a matter its "head."[12]

20. Ben Zoma said: Who is wise? He who learns from everyone, as is said, "Because everyone has been my teacher, I have gained understanding" (Ps. 119:99).[13]

21. "Undertanding in matters" (1 Sam. 16:18)—understanding how to infer one matter from another.[14]

22. R. Eleazar ben Azariah said: If there is no wisdom, there is no fear [of God]; if there is no fear [of God], there is no wisdom. If there is no knowledge, there is no understanding; if there is no understanding, there is no knowledge.[15]

23. What is the difference between a man whose understanding is deep and a man who is merely clever? The man who is merely clever is like a small-time money-changer—when a [gold] denar is brought to him to be examined [for genuineness], he examines it; when no denar is brought to him, he sits in idleness. The man whose understanding is deep is like a prosperous money-changer—when a [gold] denar is brought to him to be examined [for genuineness], he examines it; when no denar is brought to him, he takes out one of his own and examines it, [thus continuing] to refine his knowledge.[16]

1. Tanhuma, *Va-yak'hel*, §2.
2. Tanhuma B, *Mi-ketz*, §9; Yalkut, Job, §919.
3. Midrash Prov., ed. Buber, p. 41.
4. When he teaches.
5. Eccles. R. 1:7, §4.
6. B. Nid 70b; Yalkut, Prov., §932; Yalkut, Song, §981; Exod. R. 41:3.
7. Since his face was always shining, he gave that impression.
8. For the blessing at the outgoing of Sabbath.
9. B. Ned 49b.
10. P. Ber 5:2, 9b.
11. B. Tam 32a.
12. P. Sot 8:10, 23a; Eccles. R. 2:14, §1.
13. Avot 4:1.
14. B. Sanh 93b.
15. Avot 3:17.
16. Sif Deut., §13; Yalkut, *Devarim*, §802.

24. "Get wisdom, get understanding" (Prov. 4:5). He who has wisdom but no understanding is like a man with bread in his hand but nothing to eat with it. And he who has understanding but no wisdom is like a man with a savory dish in his hand but no bread to eat with it. But he who has both wisdom and understanding is like a man who has in his hand bread and a savory dish—he eats both and is fed full.[1]

25. Silence is a [protective] fence for wisdom.[2]

26. R. Hanina ben Dosa said: He whose fear of sin takes precedence over his wisdom—his wisdom will endure. But he whose wisdom takes precedence over his fear of sin—his wisdom will not endure.

He used to say: He whose [good] works exceed his wisdom—his wisdom will endure; but he whose wisdom exceeds his [good] works—his wisdom will not endure.[3]

27. "To understand wisdom and self-restraint" (Prov. 1:2). If wisdom, why self-restraint? And if self-restraint, why wisdom? If a man has wisdom, he will learn self-restraint. But if he has no wisdom, he is incapable of learning self-restraint.[4]

28. Ben Azzai said: If one's mind is serene because of his learning, it is a good sign for him. But if his mind is not serene because of his learning, it is a bad sign for him.[5]

29. He used to say: It is a good sign for a man when his body suffers because of [his concern for] his knowledge [of Torah]. It is a bad sign for a man when his knowledge of Torah suffers because of [his concern for] his body.

He also used to say: It is a good sign for a man when his mind is upset out of concern for his knowledge of Torah. But it is a bad sign for a man when his knowledge of Torah is upset out of concern for his mind.[6]

30. Hillel used to say: The more schooling, the more wisdom; the more counsel, the more understanding.[7]

31. R. Ishmael said: He who would become wise should engage in the study of civil laws, for there is no branch of the Torah more extensive than civil laws; they are like a welling fountain.[8]

32. Rabban Gamaliel, the son R. Judah the Patriarch, used to say: Not everyone who is engaged overmuch in commerce gains wisdom.[9]

---

1. MTeh 119:24.
2. Avot 3:13.
3. Avot 3:9.
4. Midrash Prov., ed. Buber, p. 42.
5. ARN 25.
6. Tos Ber 3:4.
7. Avot 2:7.
8. B. BB 175b.
9. Avot 2:5.

33. "Surely business[10] turneth a wise man into a fool" (Eccles. 7:7). When a wise man busies himself with many matters, his wisdom becomes confused.[11]

34. R. Joshua ben Levi said in the name of Bar Kappara: When a man knows how to calculate the cycles and planetary courses but does not calculate them, Scripture says of those like him, "They regard not the work of the Lord, nor take note of His designs" (Isa. 5:12).

R. Samuel bar Nahmani said in the name of R. Jonathan: What is the proof that to calculate the cycles and the courses of the planets is a religious duty? The verse "This is your wisdom and understanding in the sight of the peoples" (Deut. 4:6). What wisdom and understanding are plainly in the sight of the peoples? It is the calculating of cycles and the courses of the planets.[12]

35. Our masters taught: He who sees sages of Israel should say: Blessed be He who has imparted His wisdom to those who fear Him. He who sees sages of the peoples of the world should say: Blessed be He who has imparted of His wisdom to His creatures.[13]

36. Should someone tell you, "There is wisdom among the nations," believe him. Should he say to you, "There is Torah among the nations," do not believe him."[14]

37. "And he sent and called for all the magicians of Egypt and all the sages thereof" (Gen. 41:8). The verse informs you that every nation that exists in the world appoints five[15] wise counselors to serve it. More: the Holy One endows each nation with wisdom, understanding, and strength. And when the Holy One punishes the world, He takes each of these capacities away from each nation, as is said, "In that day I will destroy the sages of Edom and understanding out of Mount Esau; thy mighty men, O Teman, shall be dismayed" (Obad. 1:8–9).[16]

38. A sage has precedence over a king of Israel. For when a sage dies, we have none like him; but when a king of Israel dies—all Jews are worthy of kingship.[17]

---

10. Reading not *oshek* ("oppression") but *osek* ("business").
11. Exod R. 6:2.
12. The reckoning of cycles and planetary courses, which show order and regularity in the universe, would, it was hoped, undermine belief in astrology (Samuel Edels).

    Or, the scientific expertise shown in connection with the Jewish calendar would impress the people of the world with the logic of Jewish thought and belief (Josiah Pinto, as quoted by Adin Steinstaltz in his edition of Shab [Jerusalem, 1968], 1:314). B. Shab 75a; Yalkut, Isa., §402.
13. B. Ber 58a.
14. Lam. R. 2:13.
15. The number five may be derived in the following manner: the plural "sages" is taken to denote two; the repetition of the word "all," two more; and the repetition of the particle *et* before "magicians" and "sages," one more.
16. Gen. R. 89:6.
17. B. Hor 13a.

39. "I, wisdom, have made subtlety my dwelling" (Prov. 8:12). When wisdom enters a man, subtlety enters with it.[1]

40. The rivalry of scribes increases wisdom.[2]

41. No man loves a rival in his craft, but a sage loves a rival.[3]

42. "Even during a walk, the fool shows lack of sense, for he calls everyone else a fool (Eccles. 10:3)[4]—the fool thinks that all men are fools.[5]

43. For a wise man, a gentle hint; for a fool, a fist.[6]

44. One must not take leave of a friend in the midst of chitchat, in the midst of joking, in the midst of trivial talk, or in midst of irreverent discussion, but only while in the midst of words of *Halakhah*.[7]

45. When a sage dies, all are his kin [and should mourn for him].[8]

46. "Wisdom is good with an inheritance" (Eccles. 7:11). Wisdom is good when it is joined with an inheritance.

Another version: Wisdom is good when the merit of ancestors accompanies it. Happy is the man whose fathers' merit continually lights the way for him.[9]

47. R. Ammi said: At a study session, give precedence to wisdom; at a feast, give precedence to age.[10]

48. R. Avdimi of Haifa said: Though prophecy has been taken from the prophets since the day the Temple was destroyed, it has not been taken from the sages.

Amemar said: A sage is superior to a prophet, for Scripture says, "And a prophet[11] hath a heart of wisdom" (Ps. 90:12). Who is generally compared with whom? Is it not the smaller with the greater?[12]

49. "And Bezalel the son of Uri, the son of Hur, of the tribe of Judah, made all that the Lord commanded Moses" (Exod. 38:22). Here Scripture says not, "What the Lord commanded Moses," but, "All that the Lord commanded Moses," implying that even in matters he had not heard from his master, his mind coincided with what had been told to Moses on Sinai.[13]

50. R. Huna said in the name of Rav: "The law of truth was in his mouth" (Mal. 2:6) refers to matters he heard from his master. "And nothing untoward was found on his lips" (ibid.) refers to matters [he did not utter] because he had not heard them from his master.

The sages said: "The Lord will be with thy folly"[14] (Prov. 3:26). Even in matters wherein you are foolish, God "will keep thy foot from being caught" (ibid.).[15]

51. "According to the law which they shall teach thee" (Deut. 17:11). A prophet and a sage—by what parable may their functions be illustrated? By the parable of a king who sent two of his emissaries to a province. About one, he wrote [to its inhabitants]: "If he does not show you my ring and seal, do not believe him." About the second, he wrote: "Even if he does not show you my ring, believe him without ring and without seal." So, too, of the prophet, Scripture says, "And he give thee a sign or a wonder" (Deut. 13:2). But concerning the sage, Scripture says, "According to the law which they shall teach thee."[16]

Prophecy and the Holy Spirit

52. R. Phinehas ben Yair used to say: Torah leads to strictness, strictness to zeal [in avoiding sin], zeal [in avoiding sin] to cleanliness, cleanliness to purity, purity to abstinence, abstinence to holiness, holiness to humility, humility to fear of sin, fear of sin to saintliness, saintliness to [possession of] the holy spirit, and the holy spirit to ability to revive the dead.[17]

53. The Presence rests only on one who is wise, strong, wealthy, tall in stature, yet unassuming.[18]

54. R. Yohanan said: All the prophets were wealthy. And the proof? From Moses and Samuel, from Amos and Jonah [as will be shown in what follows].

Moses, because he is quoted as saying, "I have not taken one ass from them" (Num. 16:15)—even as a fee.[19] But perhaps it was because of his poverty?[20] On the contrary, that Moses was wealthy is inferred from the verse "Hew for thyself" (Exod. 34:1)—the chips of the broken Tablets are to be yours [and will make you rich].

Samuel, because he is quoted as saying, "Here I am; witness against me before the Lord, and before His anointed; whose ox have I taken, or whose ass have I

---

1. B. Sot 21b and En Yaakov, ad loc.
2. B. BB 21a.
3. Gen. R. 32:2.
4. JV: "Yea, also, when a fool walketh by the way, his understanding faileth him, and he saith to everyone that he is a fool."
5. Eccles R. 10:3, §1.
6. Midrash Prov. 22 (ed. Buber, p. 91).
7. B. Ber 31a.
8. B. Shab 105b.
9. Eccles R. 7:11, §1.
10. B. BB 120a.
11. The word *navi* ("that we may get us") is taken in the sense of "prophet."
12. B. BB 12a. "When A is compared with B, A is usually smaller than B. Since, in the verse just cited, *prophet* is first (A) and *wisdom* is second (B), the former must be smaller than the latter" (Leon Nemoy).
13. P. Pe 1:1, 15b.
14. The word *kislekha* ("thy confidence") is here taken to mean "thy folly."
15. P. Pe 1:1, 15b; Yalkut, Mal, §588.
16. P. Ber 1:7, 3b; Song R. 1:2, §2.
17. JV: "I will put My spirit in you, and ye shall live" (Ezek. 37:14). Sot 9:9; B. AZ 20b. See Adolf Büchler, *Types of Jewish Palestinian Piety* (London, 1922), pp. 42–67.
18. B. Shab 92a; B. Ned 38a.
19. He had so many asses that he had no need to hire one.
20. He had so few possessions that he had no need for an ass.

taken?" (1 Sam. 12:2)—even as a fee. But perhaps it was because of his poverty? On the contrary, that Samuel was wealthy is inferred from the verse "And his return was to Ramah [even though, wherever he went there was his home"] (1 Sam. 7:17), which Rava interpreted as meaning that he had his household with him wherever he went.

Amos, because he is quoted as saying, "I am no prophet, neither am I a prophet's son, but I am the owner of herds, and a tender of sycamore figs" (Amos 7:14).

Jonah, because it is written, "[He found a ship going to Tarshish], and he paid the hire thereof" (Jon. 1:3)—the hire of the whole ship, said R. Yohanan, which, according to R. Romanus, came to four thousand gold denars.[1]

55. Wherever "To David, a Psalm"[2] occurs, it denotes that the Presence first rested on him, and then he uttered that psalm. Wherever "A Psalm of David"[3] occurs, it denotes that he first uttered that psalm, and then the Presence rested on him. This is to teach you that the Presence does not come to rest on a man in the midst of idleness or despair or laughter or frivolity or chitchat or idle talk, but only in the midst of joyous obedience to [divine] commands. [Thus, after Elisha became angry at the king of Israel (2 Kings 3:13–14), his power of prophecy left him. But when he overcame anger, he found joy] "in the playing of the instrument. It was only then that the hand of the Lord [the power of prophecy] came back to him" (2 Kings 3:15).[4]

56. Elijah [the Prophet] said: I call heaven and earth to witness that whether it be a Jew or a heathen, whether it be a man or a woman, a manservant or a maidservant, the holy spirit will suffuse each of them in keeping with the deeds he [or she] performs.[5]

57. R. Hanina bar Isi said: At times the world and its fullness cannot contain the glory of His Godhead, and at other times He speaks to a man out of [a space as tiny as] that between the hairs of his head.[6]

58. R. Yudan said: Very wise in the power of language are the prophets, who [in order to make the children of Israel aware of God's Presence] speak of the form of the Almighty as though it were like the form of a man.[7]

59. R. Isaac ben Eleazar said: The prophets, knowing that their God was truthful, did not wish to flatter Him.[8]

60. R. Yose ben Zimra said: Just as a woman is not ashamed to demand the requirements of her household from her husband, so prophets are not ashamed to demand bluntly the requirements of Israel from the Holy One.[9]

61. There were three types of prophets. One insisted on the honor due the Father as well as the honor due the son;[10] one insisted upon the honor due the Father without insisting upon the honor due the son; and one insisted upon the honor due the son without insisting upon the honor due the Father. Jeremiah insisted upon both the honor due the Father and the honor due the son, for he said, "We have transgressed and rebelled; and Thou hast not pardoned [as Thou shouldst have done]" (Lam. 3:42). Therefore his prophecy was doubled, as is said, "And there were added besides unto them many like words" (Jer. 36:32). Elijah insisted upon the honor due the Father but did not insist upon the honor due the son, as is said, "I have been very jealous for the Lord, the God of hosts" (1 Kings 19:10). Consequently, what was he told? "Go, return on thy way to the wilderness of Damascus . . . and Elisha the son of Shaphat . . . shalt thou anoint to succeed thee as prophet" (1 Kings 19:15–16)—because I am displeased with your prophecy. Jonah insisted upon the honor due the son but did not insist upon the honor due the Father, as is said, "But Jonah rose up to flee into Tarshish from the presence of the Lord" (Jon. 1:3). What is written about him? "The word of the Lord came to Jonah a second time" (Jon. 3:1)—He spoke to him a second time, but not a third.[11]

R. Jonathan said: Jonah embarked upon his voyage only in order to drown himself in the sea, for Scripture says, "And he said unto them: 'Take me up and cast me forth into the sea' " (Jon. 1:12).

And so you find that the patriarchs as well as the prophets offered their lives in behalf of Israel. As to Moses, what is he quoted as saying? "And yet, if Thou wouldst only forgive their sin! If not, blot me, I pray Thee, out of the book which Thou hast written" (Exod. 32:32) And David,[12] what did he say? "Lo, I have sinned, and I have done iniquitously; but these sheep, what have they done? Let Thy hand, I pray Thee, be against me, and against my father's house" (2 Sam. 24:17). Thus you see that everywhere patriarchs as well as prophets offered their lives for Israel.[13]

62. "And he said, I have been very jealous for the Lord, the God of hosts; for the children of Israel have forsaken Thy covenant" (1 Kings 19:14). The Holy one replied to Elijah: "This is My covenant. Is it yours?" Elijah: "Thrown down Thine altars." The Holy One: "These are My altars. Are they yours?" (ibid.). Elijah: "And slain Thy prophets with the sword" (ibid.). The Holy One: "They are My prophets. What concern is it of yours?" Elijah: "And I, even I only am left, and they seek my life, to take it away" (ibid.). See what is written in that context: "And he looked, and behold, there was at his head a cake baked on the hot stones (*retzaphim*)" (1 Kings, 19:6). What is meant by *retzaphim?* R. Samuel bar Nahman said: *Retz peh,*

1. B. Ned 38a.
2. E.g., Ps. 24:1, in the Hebrew.
3. E.g., Ps. 23:1.
4. See Kimhi, ad loc. B. Pes 117a; B. Shab 30b.
5. TdE, ed. Friedmann, p. 48.
6. Gen. R. 4:4.
7. Gen. R. 27:1.
8. P. Ber 7:4, 11c.
9. PRKM 12:1.

10. God is the Father and Israel the son.
11. Since Scripture does not say "again," the phrase "a second time" is taken to exclude a third time.
12. In MTeh 18:8, David is likened to Abraham, a patriarch.
13. Mek, *Bo, Pis'ha,* 1.

"silence[1] the mouth"—silence the mouth of him who spoke calumny of My children.

"Look not upon me that I am swarthy" (Song 1:6). R. Simon began his discourse with the verse "Slander not a servant unto his Master" (Prov. 30:10). Israel are called servants, as Scripture says, "For unto Me the children of Israel are servants" (Lev. 25:55). The prophets are also called servants, as Scripture says, "But He revealeth His counsel unto His servants the prophets" (Amos 3:7). Hence Israel responded to the prophets: Do not look [contemptuously] upon me because of my swarthiness. There was no one who cherished us more than Moses, yet because he said, "Hear now, ye rebels" (Num. 20:10), it was decreed against him that he should not enter the Promised Land.

Another version of Israel's response to the prophets: No one rejoiced in us more than Isaiah, yet because he said, "And I dwell in the midst of a people of unclean lips" (Isa. 6:5), the Holy One said to him, "Isaiah, of your own self you may say, 'Because I am a man of unclean lips' [ibid.]. That I will abide. But will you dare say, 'I dwell in the midst of a people of unclean lips'?" Come see what is written in that passage: "Then flew unto me one of the seraphim, with a glowing stone (*ritzpah*) in his hand" (Isa. 6:6). R. Samuel said: The word *ritzpah* means *rotz peh*, silence the mouth" of him who spoke calumny of My children.[2]

63. "A voice! my Beloved knocketh" (Song 5:2)—by means of the prophets.[3]

64. "I will bring them into the land of their enemies" (Lev. 26:41). This is a good dispensation for Israel, so that they would not say, "Inasmuch as we are exiled among the peoples of the world, we may as well act like them." I will see to it that they do not act that way; I will raise prophets over them who will lead them back to the right place under My wings. And the proof? The verse "And that which cometh into your mind shall not be at all; in that ye say: We will be as the nations, as the families of the countries, to serve wood and stone" (Ezek. 20:32). But "as I live, saith the Lord God, surely with a mighty hand, and with an outstretched arm, and with fury poured out, will I be King over you" (Ezek. 20:33). Against your will, like it or not, I will impose My kingship over you.[4]

65. "And the Lord spoke unto Moses . . . that he say" (Exod. 12:1). R. Akiva taught: "That he say" means: "[Moses], go say to them that it was only because of their merit that He spoke with me." For during all the thirty-eight years in which He was angry with Israel, He did not speak with Moses, as is said, "So it came to pass, when all the men of war were consumed and dead from among the people, that the Lord spoke unto me, to say" (Deut. 2:16–17). R. Simeon ben Azzai stated: I am not arguing against the words of my teacher, but would merely add to what he taught: It was not with Moses alone that God spoke solely because of Israel's merit, but also with the other prophets—all of them—He spoke solely because of Israel's merit, as is said, "And I remained there appalled[5] among them seven days" (Ezek. 3:15). And after that it is written, "And it came to pass at the end of seven days, that the word of the Lord came unto me, to say" (Ezek. 3:16).[6] And similarly, "And it came to pass after ten days, that the word of the Lord came again unto Jeremiah" (Jer. 42:7).[7] In the account of Baruch the son of Neriah, you will also find that he was complaining to Him who is everywhere, so that God had to tell Baruch, "Thou didst say: Woe is me now! for the Lord hath added sorrow to my pain" (Jer. 45:3). [You said], "Why was I treated differently from other disciples of the prophets? Joshua ministered to Moses, and the holy spirit rested upon him. Elisha ministered to Elijah, and the holy spirit rested upon him. Why then was I treated differently from other disciples of the prophets? 'I am weary with my groaning and I find no rest' " (ibid.). The word "rest" here must mean "prophecy," as in the verse "And the spirit rested upon them . . . and they prophesied in the camp" (Num. 11:26) and in the verse "And the spirit of the Lord shall rest upon him" (Isa. 11:2). Note how He who is everywhere told Jeremiah to answer Baruch: "Thus shalt thou say unto him: 'Thus saith the Lord: Behold, that which I have built I am about to break down. . . . And seekest thou great things for thyself?' " (Jer. 45:4–5). "Great things" here must mean "prophecy," as in the verse "Tell me, I pray thee, all the great things that Elisha hath done" (2 Kings 8:4) and in the verse "Call unto Me, and I will answer thee, and will tell thee great things, and hidden, which thou knowest not" (Jer. 33:3). God went on, "Baruch son of Neriah! If there is no vineyard, what need for a fence? If there is no flock, what need for a shepherd?"[8] Why should there be? "Hence, when I bring evil upon all flesh, saith the Lord, in all places whither thou goest, thy life will be granted thee [but not prophecy]" (Jer. 45:5).

Thus, in each of the foregoing instances you see that the prophets prophesy only because of Israel's merit.[9]

66. Ulla said: Wherever a man's name is given along with that of his father as the author of a prophecy, we know that he was a prophet as well as the son of a prophet. Where his own name is given alone, without that of his father, we know that he was a prophet but not the son of a prophet. Where his name and the name of his hometown are stated, we know that he came from that town. Where

1. Literally, "break" or "smash." See Rashi on Isa. 6:6.
2. Song R. 1:6, §1.
3. Yalkut, Song, §988.
4. Sif Lev., ed. Weiss, p. 112b.

5. "Desolate" or "appalled" is taken to mean being without divine communication (see Zeh Yenahemenu and Malbim).
6. "The passage is interpreted to mean that Ezekiel had been without communication from God. But after he dwelled among the people for seven days, the word of God came to him for the sake of the people" (Mek, *Bo Pis'ha* 1 [La's note, ad loc.]).
7. The passage is understood to mean that the word of God came to Jeremiah only because the people, led by Yohanan and Jezaniah, asked for a divine message (Jer. 42:1–3) (Mek, *Bo Pis'ha* 1 [La's note, ad loc.]).
8. Synonym for prophet.
9. Mek, *Bo*, *Pis'ha* 1 (La 1:13–15).

his name is given but not the name of his town, we know that he was from Jerusalem.[1]

67. If a prophet's father's name is stated, we know that the father also was a prophet. But if a prophet's father's name is not stated, he was definitely not a prophet, except for Amos, whose father was a prophet, even though his name is not stated. For Scripture says, "Amos answered Amaziah: 'I am not a prophet, and I am not a prophet's son' " (Amos 7:14). Even as Amos was a prophet, though he said, "I am not a prophet," so Amos's father was a prophet, though he said, "I am not a prophet's son."

If a prophet's home city is stated, we know he came from that city. If a prophet's city is not stated, we know he came from Jerusalem, for the majority of both prophets and sages came from Jerusalem, which Scripture describes as [a city] "full of justice, righteousness lodgeth in her" (Isa. 1:21), implying that they who lodge in her are "sovereigns [prophets, sages] of righteousness.[2]

68. Prophets were called by ten names: envoy, man of faith, servant, messenger, visionary, sentinel, seer, angel, prophet, man of God.[3]

The holy spirit is known by ten names: parable, metaphor, riddle, speech, saying, call, command, pronouncement, prophecy, vision.[4]

69. Prophecy is known by ten names, six gentle and four stern: prophecy, seeing, watching, parable, metaphor, and holy spirit[5] are gentle; vision, pronouncement, preaching,[6] and riddle are stern.

God spoke with the patriarchs through seeing, prophecy, and vision. With Moses our teacher, through prophecy, seeing, and the holy spirit. With the other prophets, He communicated through most or some of these means.

Note: Instruction, speech, command, and saying are no more than explanatory terms for prophecy. In only one instance—"A deep sleep fell upon Abram" (Gen. 15:12)—does deep sleep mean prophecy.

Prophetic speech is to be understood as relevant to the immediate need as well as beyond the immediate need, as in the verse "Walk before Me, and be thou perfect' (Gen. 17:1) and in "Let it not be grievous in thy sight because of the lad . . . [for in Isaac shall seed be called unto thee]" (Gen. 21:12). On the other hand, speech that is not prophetic is to be understood as bearing only on the immediate need, as in the verse "Behold, thou shalt die, because of the woman" (Gen. 20:3) and in "Take heed to thyself that thou speak not to Jacob either good or bad" (Gen. 31:29).

A dream that is not prophetic—he who had it has to ask for its interpretation, as with Pharaoh's dream, Nebuchadnezzar's dream, and the Midianite's dream.[7] But a dream that is prophetic, even if its matter is enigmatic—he who had it need not ask for its interpretation, as with Daniel and his companions.[8]

As for the patriarchs, when the Holy One appeared to them to speak with them, He did not reveal Himself through the celestial creatures, through the chariot, or through other aspects of [God's] glory. For the Presence rested directly upon the patriarchs.

R. Simeon said: The patriarchs themselves are the chariot, for it is said of Jacob, "And God [Himself] went up from him" (Gen. 35:13). But as for the other prophets, God revealed Himself to each of them through aspects of His glory, in keeping with each one's capacity.

When the Holy One spoke to the patriarchs, He revealed Himself to them neither through lightning nor through thunder, neither through terrifying sounds nor through quakes, because they knew full well His strength, His might, His greatness, and His majesty. As for the other prophets—He had to reveal Himself to them in terrifying sounds, in thunderclaps, and in flashes of fire, in keeping with the needs of the people of their generation. Why? Because without such terrifying sounds and lightnings, the people of their generation would not have become aware of the overwhelming might of the Holy One, and even then the other prophets hoped against hope that the people of their generation would submit.

When the Holy One revealed Himself to the patriarchs to give them commands, He did not make stipulations with them, such as "if you walk in My statutes" or "if you spurn My statutes." Why not? Because they knew the reward of the righteous and the punishment of the wicked, and therefore there was no need to make stipulations with them. But with the other prophets, He had no choice but to make the reward of the righteous and the punishment of the wicked explicit for them time after time, in the hope that the people of their generation would submit.

When the Holy One spoke to the patriarchs, His voice did not shake the world, but [He spoke] in a whisper, because there was no need to make the people of their generations hear. As for the other prophets, when the Holy One spoke to them, He shook the world, as is said, "The voice of the Lord breaketh cedars" (Ps. 29:5). When was it so? Until the Tabernacle was set up. But after the Tabernacle was set up, there was a place set aside for God's speech, and He no longer shook the world.

When the Holy One told the patriarchs to move from land to land, He gave no assurances about what He would do for them. Why not? Because they were men of faith. As for the other prophets, how many assurances he had to give in the hope that the people of their generation would believe them! How much did He promise our forebears in Egypt—"unto a land flowing with milk and honey" (Exod. 33:3)! And likewise in the wilderness. Neverthe-

---

1. B. Meg 15a.
2. Mishnat R. Eliezer 6 (ed. Hyman Enelow [New York, 1933], pp. 118–19).
3. The sources in Scripture: Obad. 1:1, Num. 12:7, Isa. 49:5, Isa. 6:8, Amos 7:12, Ezek. 3:17, 1 Sam. 9:9, Hag. 1:13, Jer. 1:5, Ps. 90:1.
4. The sources: Mic. 2:4; Hab. 2:6; Ezek. 17:2; Jer. 5:13, Gen. R. 5:1; Sif Lev., ed. Weiss, p. 3a; Gen. R. 20:2; Isa. 17:1; 2 Chron. 15:8; Joel 3:1. See ARN 34; Gen. R. 44:6.
5. Ps. 51:13.
6. Amos 7:16.
7. Gen. 41, Dan. 2, and Judg. 7:13.
8. Dan. 7.

less, they remained in doubt. How much did He promise us also! "Sing, O barren, thou that didst not bear" (Isa. 54:1); "Arise, shine, for thy light is come" (Isa. 60:1); "Comfort ye, comfort ye My people" (Isa. 40:1); "Rejoice greatly, O daughter of Zion" (Zech. 9:9); "Behold, the day of the Lord cometh" (Zech. 14:1); and "Behold, I send My messenger" (Mal. 3:1). Nevertheless, we are dissolved in doubt.

There was no need to make the Name explicit for the patriarchs. As for the other prophets, God's Name had to be made explicit for them, for the people of their generation required it. Proof for this assertion is that Moses our teacher said, "When they shall say to me: What is His Name? What shall I say unto them? And God said unto Moses: 'I am that I am' " (Exod. 3:13–14). [As for His not having previously made the Name explicit], the Holy One said to Moses, "I appeared unto Abraham . . . but by My Name YHVH I did not need to make Myself known to them" (Exod. 6:3) as I had to make Myself known to you.

For five hundred and two years the Holy One communicated with the patriarchs, and in all those years He voiced to the three of them no more than fifteen utterances, since for them there was no need to keep setting down matters at all times. But as for the other prophets, how very many utterances at all times—because of the people of their generation! And Moses our teacher had the greatest number of such communications. You can see for yourself that it was so. In a single day the Holy One spoke to him fifteen times. What day was it? The day the Tabernacle was set up.[1]

70. "He maketh [specific] weight for the spirit" (Job 28:25). R. Aha said: Even the holy spirit, which rests on the prophets, does so by specific weight—one prophet uttering one book of prophecy; and another, two.

R. Simon said: Beeri uttered two verses as a prophet, and because there was not enough to make a book, they were included in the book of Isaiah. The two verses are "And when they shall say unto you: 'Seek unto the ghosts and the familiar spirits' " (Isa. 8:19) and its companion verse.

"He maketh [specific] weight for the spirit." Each and every prophet had the holy spirit set within him, each according to his capacity.[2]

71. R. Isaac said: Several prophets treated the same theme, yet no two prophets prophesied on that theme [in identical language].[3]

72. "When I spoke unto the prophets, I multiplied visions" (Hos. 12:11). The Holy One said: It is true that "I spoke unto the prophets," but "I multiplied visions," for among all of them, the experience in prophecy of one is not like the experience in prophecy of another. Amos saw Me standing.[4] Micaiah saw Me seated.[5] Moses saw Me as a mighty man.[6] Daniel saw Me as an ancient of days. Therefore it is written, "By the ministry of the prophets have I used similitudes" (ibid.).[7]

73. Some, such as Ezekiel, prophesied through seeing; "I saw visions of God" (Ezek. 1:1); Habakkuk, through hearing: "I have heard that which Thou hast made heard" (Hab. 3:2); Jeremiah, through the mouth: "The Lord touched my mouth. . . . 'Behold, I have put My words in thy mouth' " (Jer. 1:9). Some, through the nose; "And spirit entered into me" (Ezek. 2:2). Some, through the hand: "By the hand of the prophets have I used similitudes" (Hos. 12:11). Some prophesied in enigmas, and some in enigmas within enigmas.[8]

74. "Behold, this I have found, saith (*amerah*) Koheleth" (Eccles. 7:27); the verb *amerah* is feminine. Elsewhere it is written, "Saith (*amar*) Koheleth" (Eccles. 1:2); the verb *amar* is masculine. R. Jeremiah explained: The two forms of the verb allude to the holy spirit, which sometimes speaks using a masculine form and at other times a feminine form. Thus one verse reads, "Thou art my help [*ezri*, masculine] and my deliverer" (Ps. 70:6), while another verse reads, "Thou art my help [ezrati, feminine] and my deliverer" (Ps. 40:18). One verse reads, "How beautiful upon the mountains are the feet of the messenger of good tidings [mevasser, masculine]" (Isa. 52:7), while another verse reads, "O thou that tellest good tidings [*mevasseret*, feminine] to Zion, get thee up into the high mountain" (Isa. 40:9).[9]

75. R. Eleazar taught in the name of R. Yose ben Zimra: As they uttered their prophecies, none of the prophets knew what they were prophesying, except Moses and Joshua, who did know. R. Joshua bar Nehemiah maintained that Elijah also prophesied and knew what he was prophesying.

R. Eleazar further taught in the name of R. Yose ben Zimra: Samuel, the master of prophets, did not know what he was prophesying while uttering his prophecy, as is said, "And the Lord sent Jerubbaal, and Bedan, and Jephthah, and Samuel" (1 Sam. 12:11). Samuel did not say, "The Lord sent . . . me," but, "The Lord sent . . . Samuel," for he did not know what he was prophesying.[10]

76. "And there hath not arisen a prophet in Israel since like unto Moses" (Deut. 34:10). What is the difference between Moses and all the other prophets? R. Judah son of R. Ilai and the sages differed in their explanations. R. Judah said: The prophets beheld prophetic visions through nine lenses. This is intimated in the verse "And the appearance of the vision which I saw was like the vision that I saw when I came to destroy the city; and the visions were like the vision that I saw by the river Chebar; and I

1. Mishnat R. Eliezer 6.
2. Lev. R. 15:2; Yalkut, Job, §916.
3. B. Sanh 89a.
4. Amos 9:1.
5. 2 Chron. 18:18.
6. Exod. 15:3.
7. Dan. 7:9 Aggadat Bereshit 14 (ed. Buber [Cracow, 1902], p. 30).
8. Yalkut Hadash (Warsaw, 1879), *Noah*.
9. Eccles. R. 7:27, §1; Yalkut, Eccles., §977.
10. MTeh 90:4; Yalkut, Ps., §841.

fell upon my face" (Ezek. 43:3)[1]–thus nine visions. Likewise, it is said of Daniel, "And he gave heed to the word, and had understanding of the vision. . . . I lifted up mine eyes and saw . . . his face as the appearance of lightning. . . . And I, Daniel, alone saw the vision; for the men that were with me saw not the vision. . . . So I was left alone, and saw this great vision" (Dan. 10:1 and 10:5–8)—thus again nine visions. But Moses our teacher saw through only one lens, as is said, "With him do I speak in one vision, not in riddles" (Num. 12:8).

However, the sages said: All other prophets saw [prophetic visions] through a blurred lens, as is said, "I have multiplied visions; and by the ministry of the prophets have I used similitudes" (Hos. 12:11). But Moses saw [prophetic visions] through a polished lens, as is said, "The similitude of the Lord doth he behold" (Num. 12:8). All the other prophets heard the voice only in keeping with their capacity, as is said, "The voice of the Lord, according to a man's capacity" (Ps. 29:4). But Moses our teacher heard it in full, as is said, "And he heard the voice" (Num. 7:89)—the voice as it is.[2]

77. R. Jonah said in the name of R. Samuel bar Nahman: Every prophet who arose repeated the prophecy of his predecessor. Why did he repeat the prophecy of his predecessor? To make the predecessor's prophecy quite clear.

But R. Joshua ben Levi said: Every prophet was fully engaged with his own prophecy, except for Moses, who uttered all the prophecies of the other prophets as well as his own, with the result that whoever prophesied later drew from the prophecy of Moses.[3]

78. Rav and Samuel both said: Fifty gates of understanding were created in the world, and all of them but one were opened for Moses at Sinai, as is said, "Thou hast made him [Moses] but little lower than God" (Ps. 8:6).[4]

79. R. Yose bar Hanina said: Our teacher Moses pronounced four adverse decrees against Israel, but four [subsequent] prophets came and nullified them. Moses said, "Israel dwelleth in safety, alone,[5] in Jacob's abode" (Deut. 33:28). But Amos came and nullified it when he prayed to God, "Refrain! How will Jacob survive [alone]? He is so small" (Amos 7:5). We are told in the next verse, "The Lord relented concerning this" (Amos 7:6). Moses said, "Among those nations you shall find no peace" (Deut. 28:65). But Jeremiah came and said, "The people that were left of the sword . . . Israel . . . I go to give him peace" (Jer. 31:1). Moses said, "Visiting the iniquity of the fathers upon the children" (Exod. 34:7). But Ezekiel came and nullified it: "The soul that sinneth, it shall die" (Ezek. 18:20). Moses said, "Ye shall be lost [perish] among the nations" (Lev. 26:38). But Isaiah came and said, "It shall come to pass on that day, that a great horn shall be blown, and they shall come that were lost," etc. (Isa. 27:13).[6]

80. R. Simon said: The face of Phinehas, when the holy spirit rested on him, glowed like torches.[7]

81. "The spirit of the Lord began to ring within him" (Judg. 13:25). R. Nahman said: Samson—when the spirit of the Lord rested upon him, the hairs on his head stood up and clanged against one another as in a bell.[8]

82. "He wakeneth me morning by morning, He wakeneth mine ear to hear what a disciple should hear" (Isa. 50:4). Isaiah said: As I walked about in my house of study, "I heard the voice of the Lord, saying: 'Whom shall I send, and who will go for us?' etc. [Isa. 6:8]. When I sent Micaiah,[9] they smote him on the cheek.[10] When I sent Amos,[11] they mockingly called him 'tongue-heavy.' Now 'whom shall I send, and who will go for us?' "

[Isaiah replied], "Here am I; send me" (Isa. 6:8). The Holy One warned him: "Isaiah, My children are obstinate, troublesome. If you are willing to suffer insults and be smitten by them, you may go on My mission, but if not, you may not go." Isaiah replied, "Even if such be my portion, 'I am ready to give my body to the smiters, and my cheek to them that pluck off the hair' [Isa. 50:6]. But I am unworthy of going to Your children on a mission of Yours." The Holy One answered, "Isaiah, 'thou hast loved righteousness' [Ps. 45:8], you have loved to make out My children to be righteous; 'and hated wickedness' [ibid.], hated to make them out wicked. 'Therefore [I], God, thy God, have Myself anointed thee with the oil of gladness above thy fellows' " (ibid.). What is meant by "above thy fellows"? In using these words, the Holy One meant: As you live, each of the prophets [who prophesied before you] received his prophetic mission from another prophet. As Scripture relates, [the spirit of Moses rested on the seventy elders]: "The Lord . . . took of the spirit that was on him, and put it upon the seventy elders" (Num. 11:25); "The spirit of Elijah rested on Elisha" (2 Kings 2:15). But you alone will prophesy directly from the mouth of the Divine Power, so that you can say, "The spirit of the Lord God is upon me; because the Lord hath anointed me" (Isa. 61:1). More: By your life, all the other prophets who prophesied used single terms in their prophecies. But you will prophesy in double terms [revealing that you prophesy with a double portion of the Divine Power]: "Awake, awake" (Isa. 51:9); "Rouse thee, rouse thee" (Isa. 51:17); "Rejoicing, I will rejoice" (Isa. 61:10); "I, even I, am He that comforteth you" (Isa. 51:12); "Comfort ye, comfort ye my people" (Isa. 40:1).[12]

---

1. "Eight derivations [i.e., forms] of the verb *ra'ah* (to see) occur in this verse, one of these, 'visions,' being plural, so that it stands for at least two; hence altogether nine *specularia*" (Lev. R., Soncino, p. 17, n. 2).
2. Lev. R. 1:14; Mishnat R. Eliezer 6.
3. Exod. R. 42:8.
4. B. Ned 38a.
5. In isolation, not among the nations.
6. B. Mak 24a.
7. Lev. R. 1:1.
8. Lev. R. 8:2.
9. See 1 Kings 22:24.
10. Apparently the commentator construes Micaiah as Muccaiah [*mukkeh*] ("one who is smitten on the cheek").
11. "Amos" [*amus*] can mean "tongue-heavy."
12. Lev. R. 10:2.

83. Rava said: All that Ezekiel saw, Isaiah saw.[1] Whom does Ezekiel resemble? A villager who saw the king.[2] Whom does Isaiah resemble? A city dweller who saw the king.[3]

84. "Before I formed thee in the belly, I knew thee" (Jer. 1:5). That is, even before I formed you in the belly of your mother, I designated you to prophesy to My people. In answer, Jeremiah spoke right up to the Holy One: Master of the universe, I cannot prophesy to them. What prophet ever came before them whom they did not seek to slay? When You set up Moses and Aaron over them to act in their behalf, did they not wish to stone them? When You set up the curly-haired Elijah over them to act in their behalf, they mocked and ridiculed him, saying, "Look how he frizzes his locks, this fancy-haired fellow." And when You set up Elisha over them to act in their behalf, they said derisively to him, "Go away, baldhead! go away, baldhead!" (2 Kings 2:23). Besides, I cannot venture forth in Israel's behalf, because "I don't know how to speak, for I am still a child" (Jer. 1:6). The divine spirit replied, "Is it not because you are a child that I love you?" For Jeremiah had not as yet tasted the savor of sin.[4]

85. "Take this cup of wine—of wrath—from My hand" (Jer. 25:15). Take this cup of wrath and make the nations drink. Jeremiah took the cup and asked, "Whom shall I make drink first?" God replied, "Jerusalem, and the cities of Judah" (Jer. 25:18), for they are the chief of all [earthly] kingdoms." When Jeremiah heard this command, he opened his mouth and cursed the day he was born.

Jeremiah then said, "With whom may I be compared? With a priest who was chosen by lot to give [a woman suspected of adultery] 'the water of bitterness' to drink." They brought the woman to the priest. He bared her head, disarrayed her hair, held out the cup for her to drink—and as he looked closely at her, he saw that she was his mother! Then he began to cry out, saying, 'Woe is me! Mother, I sought ever to honor you, but now behold me abasing you!" Even so, Jeremiah said, "Woe unto me because of you, Mother Zion! I thought I was to prophesy good things and consolations for you, and lo, I prophesy for you inflictions of punishment!"[5]

86. "Who would not fear Thee, O King of the nations?" (Jer. 10:7). The Holy One asked Jeremiah: [You call Me King of the nations], but I am not King of Israel? Jeremiah replied: Because You said to me, "I have appointed thee a prophet to the nations" (Jer. 1:5), therefore I call You also King of the nations.[6]

87. "Who would not fear Thee, O King of the nations?" (Jer. 10:7). The other prophets asked Jeremiah: Why do you see fit to call Him King of the nations? All the other prophets call Him King of Israel, yet you call Him King of the nations. Jeremiah replied: I heard Him say to me, "I have appointed thee a prophet to the nations" (Jer. 1:5), and therefore I say, King of the nations.[7]

88. Jeremiah was one of three prophets who prophesied in that generation—Jeremiah, Zephaniah, and the prophetess Huldah. Jeremiah prophesied in the city squares, Zephaniah [in the Temple and] in synagogues, and Huldah among the women.[8]

89. But if Jeremiah was there, how could Huldah prophesy? In the school of Rav, sages said in Rav's name: Huldah was a kinswoman of Jeremiah, and so he did not object.[9]

90. Although all the prophets begin their books with recitals of Israel's guilt, they end them with words of comfort.[10]

91. "And this is the blessing" (Deut. 33:1). Because at the beginning Moses spoke harsh words to Israel, he then changed and spoke words of comfort to them. And the other prophets learned from him, for at the beginning they spoke harsh words to Israel, but then they changed and spoke words of comfort to them.[11]

92. "And there hath not arisen a prophet since in Israel" (Deut. 34:10). There had not arisen one like him in Israel; but among the nations of the world, one like him did arise. This was done in order that the nations of the world might have no excuse to say, "If we had had a prophet like Moses, we would have worshiped the Holy One." Who was the prophet like Moses they had? Balaam son of Beor. However, there was a difference between the prophecy of Moses and the prophecy of Balaam, in that Moses had three qualities Balaam did not have: when God spoke with Moses, Moses was able to stand on his feet, whereas when God spoke with Balaam, he fell prone on the ground; He spoke with Moses mouth to mouth, whereas He did not speak mouth to mouth with Balaam; He spoke with Moses in plain terms, whereas He spoke with Balaam only in parables. On the other hand, there were three qualities Balaam had that Moses did not have: Moses did not know who was speaking to him, whereas Balaam knew who was speaking to him; Moses did not know when the Holy One would speak to him, whereas Balaam knew when the Holy One would speak to him (Balaam's knowledge in these two respects may be explained by the parable of a king's cook, who knew what fare the king would have on his table and how much money would be spent by the king for this

1. Even though Isaiah, unlike Ezekiel, gave no elaborate description of what he had seen.
2. To convince his audience that he has actually beheld such marvels, he is constrained to give a detailed description of them. So Tosafot, ad loc.
3. To him, the king is a familiar sight. So Rashi. B. Hag 13b.
4. PR 26:1/2 (YJS 2:526–27).
5. Ibid.
6. MTeh 93:1.
7. Exod. R. 29:9.
8. PR 26:1/2 (YJS 2:528).
9. B. Meg 14b.
10. MTeh 4:12; P. Ber 5:1, 8d.
11. Sif Deut., §342.

purpose); Moses could not speak with God whenever he wished, whereas Balaam spoke with Him whenever he pleased, as Scripture says, "Fallen down—his eyes are opened" (Num. 24:4), which implies that whenever he prostrated himself on his face, at once his eyes were opened [to anything that he inquired about].[1]

93. "Balaam also the son of Beor, the soothsayer" (Josh. 13:22). A soothsayer? But he was a prophet! At first, said R. Yohanan, he was a prophet, but subsequently [he became] a mere soothsayer.[2]

94. The Holy One raised up Moses for Israel and raised up Balaam for the nations of the world. Observe the difference between the prophets of Israel and the prophets of the nations of the world! The prophets of Israel warn Israel against transgressions. Thus Ezekiel: "I have appointed thee a watchman unto the House of Israel . . . and thou shalt give them warning" (Ezek. 3:17). But the one prophet who rose up among the nations made a breach in the moral order through his desire to cause human beings to perish from the world.[3] More! All the prophets had a measure of compassion for Israel as well as for the nations of the world. Thus Isaiah said, "Wherefore my heart moaneth for Moab like a harp" (Isa. 16:11). Likewise, Ezekiel said, "Take up a lamentation for Tyre" (Ezek. 27:2). But this one, a cruel man, rose up to root out an entire people for no fault whatsoever.[4]

95. R. Isaac said: Until the Tabernacle was set up, prophecy was also found among the nations of the world; after the Tabernacle was set up, it departed from among them, as Israel said, "I held it [the holy spirit] and will not let it go" (Song 3:4). The sages retorted to R. Isaac: But Balaam did prophesy [after the Tabernacle was set up]! He replied: Yes, but he prophesied for the good of Israel, e.g., 'Who hath counted the dust of Jacob?" (Num. 23:10); "None hath beheld iniquity in Jacob" (Num. 23:21); "There is no augury in Jacob" (Num. 23:23); "How goodly are thy tents, O Jacob" (Num. 24:5); "There shall step forth a star out of Jacob" (Num. 24:17); and "Out of Jacob shall one have dominion" (Num. 24:19).[5]

96. Seven prophets prophesied to the peoples of the world: Balaam and his father, and Job, Eliphaz the Temanite, Bildad the Shuhite, Zophar the Naamathite, and Elihu the son of Barachel the Buzite.[6]

97. What is the difference between the prophets of Israel and the prophets of the nations of the world? R. Hama the son of R. Hanina said: To the prophets of the nations of the world, the Holy One appears with half-speech only; but to the prophets of Israel, with complete speech, clear speech, affectionate speech, in the language of purity, in the language of holiness, in the same language in which the ministering angels chant praise to Him.

R. Yose said: The Holy One appears to the prophets of the nations of the world only [at night] when human beings generally take leave from one another, as Eliphaz said: "A word was secretly brought to me . . . at the time of leave-taking,[7] from the visions of the night, when deep sleep falleth on men" (Job 4:12–13).

R. Hanina bar Papa said: The matter may be illustrated by the parable of a king placed with his friend in a chamber where a curtain was between them. Whenever the king wished to speak to his friend, he would raise the curtain by folding it upward until he saw his friend face to face and then speak to him. But for the nations of the world, God does not fold up the curtain—He speaks to them from behind the curtain.

R. Simon said: The matter may be illustrated by the parable of a king who has a wife and a concubine. To his wife he goes openly, but to his concubine he goes secretly. So, too, the Holy One reveals Himself to the nations of the world only at night, but to the prophets of Israel by day.[8]

98. The prophets of Israel do not know when the Holy One will speak to them, but the prophets of the nations of the world do know when the Holy One will speak to them. Thus it is said of Balaam, "The saying of him who [knows when he is about to] hear the words of God" (Num. 24:4). The prophets of Israel do not know how many utterances He will articulate for them. But the prophets of the nations of the world do know how many utterances He will articulate for them. Thus it is said of Balaam, "Who knoweth the knowledge of the Most High" (Num. 24:16).

Are the prophets of the nations of the world then greater than the prophets of Israel? Not at all. In fact, the prophets of Israel are greater than the prophets of the nations of the world. A parable will explain what the matter resembles. The king's cooks know in advance exactly what expenditures they have to make, what ingredients they have to prepare, because their charge has definite limits. But the king's governors do not know in advance what expenditures they have to make and what items they have to prepare, because their charge has no definite limit.

R. Issachar said: With the prophets of the nations of the world, God speaks only in half-speech. Thus Scripture says, "The Lord called [*va-yikkar*, without the letter *alef* at the end] unto Balaam" (Num. 23:4). But with the prophets of Israel, [He speaks] in full speech, as for example, "The Lord called [*va-yikra*, with the letter *alef* at the end] unto Moses" (Exod. 19:20), a mode of locution the ministering angels use to praise Him, as is said, "And one called (*kara*) unto another, and said" (Isa. 6:6).[9]

99. R. Levi said: The prophecy of the nations of the world is ambiguous, so that they do not know whether they

1. Num. R. 14:20; Yalkut, *Berakhah*, §966; Sif Deut., §357.
2. B. Sanh 106a.
3. Israel's giving themselves to fornication, set forth in Num. 25, is attributed to Balaam's devising.
4. Tanhuma B, *Balak*, §1; Num. R. 20:1.
5. Lev. R. 1:12.
6. B. BB 15b.
7. "Lit. 'at the divisions'—when people separate from each other. This derives *se'ippim* from *se'if*, a branch—when people branch away. EV: 'in thoughts' " (Gen. R., Soncino, p. 454, n. 3).
8. Gen. R. 52:5 and 74:7; Lev. R. 1:13; Yalkut, Job, §897.
9. Mishnat R. Eliezer 6.

are told to slay or told to be slain. A parable of one who, while on a journey, grew tired toward evening. So he said: O that I had just one ass! A Roman, whose she-ass had just then foaled, passed by and said to him: Take this [newborn] foal and carry it on your back. So he said: I see that my prayer has been answered, but I did not put it properly—whether to ride or be ridden upon.

Another parable, of a man who set sail on the Great [Mediterranean] Sea. When a violent storm blew up and was about to sink his vessel, he said: If this crushing wind will moderate, I will bring a calf. When the wind did moderate, he said: I promised nothing.[1]

Such is the prophetic utterance of the nations of the world: "That they should be ready against that day" (Esther 3:14), whether to slay or to be slain. As for Israel, their prophetic utterance is clear: "Should be ready against that day to avenge themselves on their enemies" (Esther 8:13).[2]

100. R. Yohanan said: "The poor useth entreaties" (Prov. 18:23)—the prophets of Israel [when pleading to God]. "But the rich speak out impudently" (ibid.)—the prophets of the nations of the world [when they address God].[3]

101. The Holy One said to the prophets: What do you suppose—if you refuse to go on a mission of Mine, I have no other emissary? "With the superfluities of the earth, with all" (Eccles. 5:8)—I can have My mission carried out with all, even by means of a serpent, even by means of a scorpion, even by means of a frog.[4]

102. Before the Land of Israel had been chosen, all lands were suitable for divine revelations; after the Land of Israel had been chosen, all other lands were eliminated. Before the Temple had been singled out, all of Jerusalem was suitable for the abiding of the Presence; after the Temple had been singled out, the rest of Jerusalem was eliminated.

You might say, "I can cite instances of prophets with whom God spoke outside the Land." True, He did speak to them outside the Land, but only because of the merit of the fathers did He speak with them. And even though, because of the merit of the fathers, He did speak with them outside the Land, He spoke with them only at a spot that was pure, being near water, as Daniel said, "I was by the stream Ulai" (Dan. 8:2); and again, "I was by the side of the great river, which is Tigris" (Dan. 10:4); and elsewhere, Scripture says, "The word of the Lord came expressly unto Ezekiel the Priest the son of Buzi . . . by the river Chebar" (Ezek. 1:3).

R. Eleazar ben Zadok added: Note that Scripture says, "Arise, go forth into the plain" (Ezek. 3:22), asserting that a plain was suitable for divine revelation.[5]

You can see for yourself that the Presence does not reveal itself outside the Land. Scripture says, "But Jonah rose up to flee unto Tarshish from the Presence of the Lord" (Jon. 1:3). Could he really have thought that it was possible to flee from the Lord? Had it not been already said, "Whither shall I go from Thy spirit? Or whither shall I flee from Thy Presence?" (Ps. 139:7)? But Jonah thought: In order not to incriminate the Jews, for Gentiles are more prone to repent, I will go outside the Land, where the Presence does not reveal itself. A parable will illustrate his folly. A priest's servant who fled from his master said: I will go to the cemetery, a place where my master cannot follow me.[6] His master told him, "I have other flunkeys just like you." So, too, when Jonah said, "I will go outside the Land to a place where the Presence does not reveal itself," the Holy One replied, "I have other emissaries like you, as is said, 'The Lord hurled a great wind into the sea' " (Jon. 1:4).[7]

103. When R. Huna died, R. Abba began the eulogy by saying: Our master was worthy of having the Presence rest on him, but his residing in Babylonia prevented it.[8]

104. Many prophets rose up for Israel, twice as many as the number of Israelites who went out of Egypt. But only prophecy required by subsequent generations was set down in writing, while prophecy not required by subsequent generations was not set down.[9]

105. R. Derosa said in the name of R. Samuel bar Isaac: Sixty myriads of prophets rose up for Israel in the days of Elijah. Why was their prophecy not made public? Because it was not required for subsequent generations. Hence you may conclude that any prophecy that had meaning for the time and was also required for subsequent generations was made public, while any prophecy that had meaning for the time but was not required for subsequent generations was not made public. In the time-to-come, however, the Holy One will bring these prophets back and make public their prophecies, as is said, "The Lord my God shall come, and all the holy ones with thee" (Zech. 14:5).

R. Berekhiah said in the name of R. Helbo: Even as sixty myriads of prophets rose up for Israel, so sixty myriads of prophetesses rose up for them, and Solomon came along and made the fact public when he said, "Thy lips also, O My bride, drop honey" (Song 4:11).[10]

106. Our masters taught: After the early prophets died, the Urim and Tummim[11] ceased.[12]

107. After the last prophets—Haggai, Zechariah, and Malachi—died, the holy spirit departed from Israel, who

1. Since I did not specify whether I would bring a calf as an offering or to my table.
2. Midrash Panim Aherim A, pp. 50–51.
3. Deut. R. 2:4.
4. Exod. R. 10:1; Lev. R. 22:3.
5. Since a plain is uninhabited and therefore undefiled by human or animal uncleanness.
6. A priest is not allowed to enter a cemetery.
7. Mek, *Bo, Pis'ha* 1 (La 1:4–8); Yalkut, Ezek., §336.
8. B. MK 25a.
9. B. Meg 14a and En Yaakov, ad loc.
10. The verb *tittofnah* ("drop") is taken to mean "preach in prophecy" (cf. Mic. 2:6). Song R. 4:11, §1; Ruth R., proem 2.
11. See Exod. 28:30.
12. Ceased to have power to indicate God's will. Sot 9:12.

nevertheless were able to avail themselves of the divine voice.[1]

108. R. Avdimi of Haifa said: Ever since the Temple was destroyed, prophecy was taken from the prophets and given to the sages.

R. Yohanan said: Ever since the Temple was destroyed, prophecy was taken from the prophets and given to fools and children.[2]

109. The dream is an unripe form of prophecy.[3]

110. R. Yohanan said: When a man rises early and a verse comes to his mouth,[4] it is a kind of minor prophecy.[5]

111. R. Judah said in the name of Rav: Whoever is boastful—if he is a sage, his wisdom departs from him; if he is a prophet, his prophecy departs from him.

Resh Lakish said: Whoever is prone to anger—if he is a sage, his wisdom departs from him; if he is a prophet, his prophecy departs from him.[6]

112. "These are the commandments" (Lev. 27:34) implies that henceforth no prophet may introduce innovations.[7]

113. Our masters taught: Forty-eight prophets and seven prophetesses prophesied to Israel, but they neither diminished from nor added to anything that is written in the Torah, other than the reading of the Megillah.[8]

How did they [who introduced the reading of the Megillah] infer it [from the Torah]? R. Hiyya bar Avin said in the name of R. Joshua ben Korhah: If we hymn praise for being delivered from slavery into freedom, should we not do so all the more for being delivered from death to life?[9]

114. The false prophet who prophesies what he has not heard or what he has not been told—his death shall be at the hands of man. But he who suppresses his prophecy[10] or disregards the words of another prophet[11] or the prophet who transgresses his own words[12]—his death shall be at the hands of Heaven.

He who prophesies in the name of an alien god and says, "Thus saith the alien god," is liable to death by strangling, even if he follows the *Halakhah* in declaring unclean what is unclean and clean what is clean.[13]

115. R. Abbahu said in the name of R. Yohanan: In every matter, if a prophet tells you, "Transgress the commands of Torah,"[14] listen to him, except in the matter of idolatry: then, even if the prophet should cause the sun to stand still in midheaven [as proof of divine inspiration], do not listen to him.

We have been taught that R. Yose the Galilean said: Because the Torah understood thoroughly the power of idolatry, it gave as an example:[15] If he [who would lure you to idolatry] should have the sun stand still in midheaven,[16] even then you must not listen to him.

R. Akiva said: Far be it from the Holy One to have the sun stand still at the behest of those who transgress His will! But [the Torah refers here to such] as Hananiah son of Azur, who at first was a true prophet and only subsequently became a false prophet.[17]

116. He who shouts loudly during the *Tefillah* is among the false prophets.[18]

Song

117. Rav said: The world was created only for the sake of David.[19] Samuel said: For the sake of Moses. And R. Yohanan said: For the sake of the Messiah.[20]

118. The Holy One said: I will open the tongue of all flesh and blood, that they may hymn praise before Me every day and proclaim Me King in the four corners of the world, because I would not have created my world but for the song and music that they intone for Me daily. And the proof that the Holy One created the world only for the sake of song and music? The verse "Glory and majesty are before Him; strength and beauty are in His Sanctuary" (Ps. 96:6). "Glory and majesty before Him" in heaven, and "strength and beauty in His Sanctuary" on earth. The precise meaning of these words is spelled out in "His glory covereth the heavens, even as the earth is full of his praise" (Hab. 3:3). And the proof that the Holy One created heaven to have it engage in song? The verse "The heavens declare the glory of God, and the firmament showeth His handiwork" (Ps. 19:1). And the proof that ever since the Holy One created the earth, it hymns song to Him? The verse "From the uttermost parts of the earth have we heard songs: 'Glory to the Righteous' " (Isa. 24:16), the Righteous here being the Holy One, of whom it is said, "The Lord is righteous in all His ways" (Ps. 145:17). And the proof

1. B. Sanh 11a.
2. B. BB 12a–b.
3. Gen. R. 17:5.
4. Either he utters it spontaneously or hears a child recite it.
5. B. Ber 55b.
6. B. Pes 66b.
7. B. Shab 104a.
8. The Scroll of Esther on Purim.
9. B. Meg 14a.
10. Jon. 1:3.
11. 1 Kings 20:35.
12. 1 Kings 13:26.
13. Sanh 11:6.
14. As did Elijah, who ordered that sacrifices be brought on Mount Carmel (see 1 Kings 18).
15. Reading *mashelah* ("example") instead of *memshalah* ("power"). So Goldschmidt.
16. "Since Scripture says, 'And giveth thee a sign and a wonder' [Deut. 13:2–3], it follows that the false prophet must have been endowed with such powers" (Sanh, Soncino, p. 599, n. 4).
17. "The 'sign' being given during his first phase, and he supported himself thereon in his second" (Sanh, Soncino, p. 599, n. 5). B. Sanh 90a.
18. Who, it is said, "shouted louder" (1 Kings 18:28). B. Ber 24b.
19. That he might sing the praises of God.
20. That he might bring redemption. B. Sanh 98b.

that seas and rivers also intone song? The verse "Above the voices of many waters" (Ps. 93:4). And the proof that mountains and hills also intone song? The verse "Mountains and all hills . . . let them praise the Name of the Lord, for His Name alone is exalted" (Ps. 148:9, 13). And the proof that all orders of creation intone song? The verse "From the rising of the sun unto the going down thereof, the Lord's Name is to be praised" (Ps. 113:3). And the proof that Adam also opened his mouth with song? The verse "A Psalm. A Song. For the Sabbath day. It is a good thing to give thanks unto the Lord, and to sing praises unto Thy Name, O Most High" (Ps. 92:1–2. "It is a good thing to give thanks unto the Lord" on the earth, in the midst of mankind, "and to sing praises to Thy Name, O Most High" in the heights of heaven, among the ministering angels.[1]

119. "Thine is the day, Thine also the night" (Ps. 74:16). The day praises You and the night praises You. It is right to sing praise to You during the day and right to sing praise to You during the night.[2]

120. At the beginning of the world's creation, the praise of the Holy One ascended only from the water, as is said, "From the voices of many waters" (Ps. 93:4). And what did they proclaim? "The Lord on high is mighty" (ibid.). The Holy One said: If these, which have neither mouth nor the capacity of utterance or speech, praise Me, how much more and more when Adam will be created![3]

121. "From the rising of the sun unto the going down thereof, the Lord's Name is praised" (Ps. 113:3). From the time the sun begins to rise until it sets, the praise of the Holy One does not cease from its mouth. Thus you find that when Joshua rose up in Gibeon and sought to silence the sun, he did not say, "Sun in Gibeon, stop," but "Sun in Gibeon, be still" (Josh. 10:12). For as long as the sun moves, it praises the Holy One, and as long as it praises Him thus, it has the strength to move. Once it grows silent, it stops. Therefore Joshua said to the sun, "Be still."

The sun replied, "Do you presume to tell me to be still?" Joshua: "Yes." The sun: "But if I grow still, who will hymn the praise of the Holy One?" Joshua: "Be still, and I will hymn song, as is said, 'Then spoke Joshua to the Lord' " (Josh. 10:12). Here the word "then," as in "Then sang Moses" (Exod. 15:1), suggests song.[4]

122. R. Judah said in the name of Samuel: How do we know that the indispensability of song is to be inferred from the Torah? From the verse "Then shall he minister with the Name of the Lord his God" (Deut. 18:7). Now, which ministry is performed with the Lord's Name? You must admit that it is in the ministry of song.

R. Mattenah said: It is inferred from the verse "Because thou didst not serve the Lord thy God with joyfulness, and with gladness of heart" (Deut. 28:47). Now, which service is "with joyfulness and with gladness of heart"? You must admit that it is song.[5]

123. We have been taught: Until the Israelites entered the Land of Israel, all lands were deemed fit places to chant a hymn of praise [for miracles done in them]. After they had entered the Land, other lands were not deemed fit places to chant a hymn of praise [for miracles done in them]. After Israel went into exile, other lands were again deemed fit as at first.[6]

124. R. Simon said: Not everyone who wishes to hymn a song may hymn it. But he for whom a miracle has been performed and who does hymn a song—it is well known that all his iniquities are forgiven him and he becomes a new creature.[7]

125. R. Samuel bar Nahmani said in the name of R. Yohanan: How do we know that a song of praise is sung only over wine? Because Scripture says, "And the vine said unto them: Should I leave my wine, which cheereth God and man?" (Judg. 9:13). If wine cheers man, how does it cheer God? [By the song that accompanies it.] From this we learn that a song of praise is sung only over wine.[8]

126. Ten songs are mentioned in Scripture. The first, which was sung in Egypt; "Ye shall have a song, as in the night [of the first Passover] when a feast was hallowed" (Isa. 30:29). The second, which was sung at the Red Sea: "Then sang Moses" (Exod. 15:1). The third, which was chanted at the well: "Then sang Israel" (Num. 21:17). The fourth, which Moses uttered: "So Moses wrote this song" (Deut. 31:22). The fifth, which Joshua recited: "Then spoke Joshua to the Lord" (Josh. 10:12). The sixth, which Deborah and Barak uttered: "Then sang Deborah and Barak the son of Abinoam" (Judg. 5:1). The seventh, which David recited: "And David spoke unto the Lord the words of this song" (2 Sam. 22:1). The eighth, which Solomon recited: "Then spoke Solomon" (2 Chron. 6:1). The ninth, which Jehoshaphat uttered: "And when he had taken counsel with the people, he appointed them that should sing unto the Lord, and praise to the beauty of holiness," etc. (2 Chron. 20:21). The tenth song will be recited in the time-to-come: "Sing unto the Lord a new song, and His praise from the end of the earth" (Isa. 42:10).[9]

127. "Thine ointments have a goodly fragrance" (Song 1:3). R. Yannai ben R. Simeon son of R. Yannai said: The former generations uttered only the fragrance of song before You, but when we came to the Red Sea we did not leave out one song of praise with which to praise Your Name. ["Thy Name is as ointment poured forth" (ibid.).][10]

---

1. Alphabet of R. Akiva (BhM 3: 12–13).
2. Gen. R. 6:2.
3. Gen. R. 5:1.
4. Tanhuma, *Ahare Mot*, §9; Yalkut, Josh., §22.
5. B. Ar 11a and En Yaakov, ad loc.
6. B. Meg 14a.
7. See Rashi on Judg. 6:1. Yalkut, *Be-shallah*, §254.
8. B. Ber 35a.
9. Mek, *Be-shallah*, *Shirata*, 1; Yalkut, *Be-shallah*, §242.
10. Tanhuma, *Yitro*, §3.

128. "Then sang Moses and the children of Israel" (Exod. 15:1). When uttering this song, Moses was equal to all of Israel, and Israel equal to Moses.[1]

Another interpretation: "Moses and the children of Israel." This declares that Moses led the song before Israel [which responded in antiphony].[2]

129. R. Akiva expounded: When Israel came up from the Red Sea, the holy spirit rested on them, and they sought to utter song. How did they utter their song? In the manner of an adult who leads in reciting the *Hallel* in the synagogue, while the congregation responds by repeating each verse of each psalm. Thus Moses said, "I will sing unto the Lord." (Exod. 15:1), and Israel responded, "I will sing unto the Lord." Moses said, "The Lord is my strength and song" (Exod. 15:2), and Israel responded, "I will sing unto the Lord."

R. Eliezer son of R. Yose the Galilean said: They uttered their song in the manner of a child who chants the *Hallel* in his school. Moses said, "I will sing unto the Lord," and they repeated, "I will sing unto the Lord." Moses said, "The Lord is my strength and song," and they repeated, "The Lord is my strength and song."

R. Nehemiah said: They uttered their song in the manner of people who recite the Shema in the synagogue. Moses opened with a verse of praise, and Israel completed it in response. Moses said, "Then sang Israel" (Exod. 5:1), and Israel responded, "I will sing unto the Lord, for He is highly exalted" (ibid.). Moses said, "The Lord is my strength and song" (Exod. 15:2), and Israel responded, "This is my God, and I will glorify Him" (ibid.).[3]

130. R. Avin the Levite said: When Israel stood up to utter the song of the Red Sea, Moses did not allow them to say it by themselves, but even as when a disciple is young, his teacher recites his lesson with him, so also Moses recited it with them: "Then sang Moses *and* the children of Israel," just like a disciple responding after his teacher. Forty years later, when Israel had mastered their lesson, they proceeded to sing the Song of the Well by themselves, as is said, "Then sang Israel" (Num. 21:17). For they said: Master of the universe, it is up to You to perform miracles in our behalf, and it is up to us to utter song, as is said, "It is for the Lord to deliver us, and for us to sing songs with stringed instruments" (Isa. 38:20).[4]

131. "And one approached not the other all night" (Exod. 14:20).[5] In that instant, when the ministering angels sought to utter song before the Holy One, He rebuked them, saying, "The works of My hands are drowning in the sea, and you would utter song in My presence!"[6]

132. "Barak said unto her: 'If thou wilt join me, then I will go' " (Judg. 4:8). According to R. Nehemiah, this means that Barak said to Deborah: If you are willing to join me [in a lesser role] in song [praising God], I will go with you [as a subordinate] into battle, but if you are unwilling to join me [in a lesser role] in song, I will not go with you into battle. "She replied, 'I will certainly go with thee, but desist [from setting conditions]. The glory [of the song] shall not be thine' " (Judg. 4:9),[7] by which, according to R. Reuben, she meant: "What do you suppose—that [the major role in] the song will be given to you for your glory alone?" [As it turned out], "Deborah sang, and [in a lesser role], Barak the son of Abinoam" (Judg. 5:1).[8]

133. King David dwelled in five worlds and composed a song for each one of them. When he abode in his mother's womb, he uttered the song "Bless the Lord, O my soul, and all within which I am, bless His holy Name" (Ps. 103:1). When he came out into the air of the world and beheld the stars and planets, he uttered a song, "Bless the Lord, ye His angels. . . . Bless the Lord, all ye His hosts" (Ps. 103:20–21). When, as he sucked milk from his mother's breasts and beheld her nipples, he uttered a song, "Bless the Lord, O my soul, and forget not all those weaned [from their mother's milk]"[9] (Ps. 103:2). When he saw the downfall of the wicked, he uttered a song, "The sinners are consumed out of the earth, and the wicked are no more. Bless the Lord, O my soul. Hallelujah" (Ps. 104:35). When he reflected on the day of death, he uttered a song, "Bless the Lord, O my soul; O Lord my God, Thou art very great; Thou art clothed with glory and majesty. . . . Thou hidest Thy face, they vanish; Thou withdrawest their breath, they perish" (Ps. 104:1 and 104:29).[10]

134. "At midnight I will rise to give praise unto Thee" (Ps. 119:62). R. Aha bar Bizna said in the name of R. Simeon Hasida: A harp used to hang above David's bed. When midnight arrived, a wind would come up from the north and blow across the strings of the harp, so that it played of itself. He would immediately arise and occupy himself with Torah.

R. Ashi said: Up to midnight he used to occupy himself with Torah. From then on, with songs and praises.[11]

135. It is reported of King David that when he finished the book of Psalms, he became boastful, saying to the

---

1. Otherwise, why should Moses have been singled out?
2. Hence the name of Moses was put first. Mek, *Be-shallah*, *Shirata*, 1.
3. Tos Sot 6:1; Yalkut, *Be-shallah*, §241.
4. Yalkut, *Hukkat*, §764.
5. These words are usually taken to mean that neither army could approach the other during that night. However, the Hebrew *zeh el zeh* ("one to the other") need not necessarily refer to armies. Moreover, the only other instance where this phrase occurs is Isa. 6:3, where we are told that "one seraphim called unto another and said: Holy, holy, holy is the Lord of hosts." Hence, in the comment that follows, *krb* ("approach") is understood as "to sing, to hymn" and the phrase "one to the other" is taken to mean "one angel to another."
6. B. Sanh 39b.
7. JV: "notwithstanding, [it] shall not be for thine honor." But R. Reuben construes *efes* ("notwithstanding") as the Greek *afes* ("let go, desist").
8. Gen. R. 40:4.
9. JV: "His benefits." But another meaning of *gml* ("benefit") is "wean."
10. B. Ber 10a.
11. B. Ber 3b.

Holy One: Master of the universe, is there any [other] creature You created in Your world that utters more songs and paeans of praise than I? In that instant a frog happened to meet him and said: David, don't be so boastful. I utter more songs and paeans of praise than you.[1]

136. "Behold, thou art fair, My love, behold, thou art fair" (Song 4:1). R. Akiva said: The entire world, all of it, is not equal in worth to the day on which the Song of Songs was given to Israel. Why? Because all other books in the Writings are holy, whereas the Song of Songs is holy of holies.

In illustration, R. Eleazar ben Azariah told the parable of a man who took a *seah* of wheat and gave it to a baker, to whom he said: Try to get out of it so much [coarse] flour, so much bran, so much coarse bran, and so much fine flour. And sift out of the fine flour enough for me to bake a cake, elegant, dainty, and savory. So, too, from all of Solomon's wisdom there was sifted out for Israel only the Song of Songs, the most beautiful of songs, the most sublime of songs. See how the Holy One praises Israel in it: "Behold, thou art fair, My love, behold, thou art fair."[2]

137. He who sings selections from the Song of Songs with a tremulous voice in a tavern, turning it into a kind of drinking song, has no portion in the world-to-come.[3]

138. "And the kine took the straight way (*va-yisharnah*)" (1 Sam. 6:12). Their visages looked straight toward the Ark, and they sang a beautiful song.[4] What song did they sing? Elijah taught:

Sing, sing, O Ark of acacia!
Exalted in all your radiance,
You who are overlaid with woven gold,
Extolled in God's holiest place,
Made resplendent with delicate traceries,
Sheltered between the two cherubim.

R. Samuel bar Nahman said: How much toil did [Moses] the son of Amram expend until he succeeded in teaching song to the Levites, and you [kine carrying the Ark] on your own utter song! All strength (*yeyasher*) to you.[5]

139. "Of the increase (*le-marbeh*) of [Hezekiah's] government and of peace there shall be no end" (Isa. 9:6). R. Tanhum related that Bar Kappara expounded this verse in Sepphoris as follows: Why is every *mem* in the middle of a word open, while the one in this verse is closed?[6] Because the Holy One was about to designate Hezekiah as the Messiah and Sennacherib as Gog and Magog.[7] But the attribute of justice[8] spoke up to the Holy One, "Master of the universe, David, king of Israel, who uttered so many hymns and praises before You—You did not make him Messiah. Yet Hezekiah, for whom You performed all manner of miracles and who uttered no hymn in praise of You—him you are about to make the Messiah?" Following the argument by the attribute of justice, the letter *mem* was closed.[9] Immediately the earth exclaimed, "Master of the universe, as proxy for this righteous man, I will utter song before You. Designate him the Messiah." And so the earth broke into song before Him, as is written, "From the uttermost ends of the earth have we heard song: 'Glory to the Righteous' " (Isa. 24:16). Then the [angelic] prince of the world spoke up before the Holy One, "Master of the universe, as proxy for this righteous man, the earth has just now fulfilled Your desire [for a song of praise]."[10] But a divine voice cried out and said, "[The delay in the Messiah's coming] 'is My secret, My secret' " (Isa. 24:16). To which the prophet replied, " 'Woe is me' [ibid.], woe is me, how long [must we wait]?" In response, a divine voice cried out, "Until 'the faithless who acted faithlessly will themselves have been betrayed' " (ibid.).[11]

The sages taught in the name of R. Pappias: It is a reproach to Hezekiah and his retinue that they uttered no song [to God] until the earth broke into song.[12]

140. R. Berekhiah said in the name of R. Eleazar: By rights, Hezekiah should have sung a song of thanks over the fall of Sennacherib. "But Hezekiah rendered not according to the benefit done unto him" (2 Chron. 32:25). Why not? "For his heart was lifted up" (ibid.). But consider the matter. Hezekiah, though a king, was righteous. Yet you say, "For his heart was lifted up." What it means, however, is that he was too puffed up with pride to chant a song.

When Isaiah came to Hezekiah and his retinue, and said to them, "Sing unto the Lord" (Isa. 12:5), they asked, "Why should we?" Isaiah replied, "For He hath done gloriously" (ibid.). They said, "This is already made known in all the earth" (ibid.).

Finally, so said Abba bar Kahana, Hezekiah declared, "The Torah with which I am occupied atones for the absence of song."[13]

---

1. Yalkut, Ps., §889, citing Perek Shirah.
2. Tanhuma, *Tetzavveh*, §5; Song R. 1:11; Rashi on Song 1:1.
3. Tos Sanh 12:10.
4. The word *va-yisharnah* may mean "looked straight" as well as "sang a song."
5. B. AZ 24b; Gen. R. 54:4.
6. "There are two forms of *mem:* medial, which is open ( ), and final, which is closed ( ). In this sentence, however, the final form occurs in the middle of a word" (Sanh, Soncino, p. 630, n. 6).
7. It is believed that Gog and Magog will lead all the nations in a powerful attack on Israel. Their defeat will usher in the days of the Messiah.
8. "The attributes of justice and mercy are often hypostatized and represented as interceding with the Almighty" (Isidore Epstein in Sanh, Soncino, p. 630, n. 8).
9. Therefore the word *le-marbeh* appears in the text with the closed *mem* to indicate that the matter of Hezekiah's designation as Messiah (a word that begins with the letter *mem*) was closed.
10. So Samuel Edels. BR take it to mean: "Fulfill the desire of this righteous man," i.e., "Make him the Messiah." The two comments are based on different readings of the phrase *tzevi la-tzaddik* ("glory to the righteous").
11. So NJV. That is, until Israel's enemies and the enemies of their enemies have been destroyed.
12. B. Sanh 94a and En Yaakov, ad loc; Yalkut, Isa., §415.
13. Song R. 4:8, §3.

141. There were four kings—David, Asa, Jehoshaphat, and Hezekiah—and not one asked of God what each of the others was to ask. David requested, "Let me pursue mine enemies and overtake them, and not turn back till they are consumed" (Ps. 18:38; 2 Sam. 22:38). The Holy One replied, "I will [help you] do so." So "David smote them from dawn until evening and into the morrow of the next day" (1 Sam. 30:17)—on two nights the Holy One gave him light by shooting stars and lightning flashes. Hence David said, "Thou dost light my lamp; the Lord my God doth lighten my darkness' (Ps. 18:29; 2 Sam. 22:29).

Then Asa rose up and requested, "There is no strength in me to slay them. All that I can do is pursue them. You slay them." The Holy One replied, "I will do so." Hence it is said, "Asa and the people that were with him pursued them. . . . None remained alive: for they were shattered before the Lord" (2 Chron. 14:12)—not "before Asa," but "before the Lord."

Then Jehoshaphat rose up and requested, "I have not the strength either to slay or to pursue, but I will utter a song, and You do [the pursuing and the slaying]." The Holy One replied, "I will do so." Accordingly, "when they began to sing and to praise, the Lord set an ambush against the Ammonites . . . and they were smitten" (2 Chron. 20:22).

Finally, Hezekiah rose up and requested, "I have not the strength to slay, to pursue, or to utter song, but I will sleep in my bed, and You do what is required." The Holy One replied, "I will do so." Hence, "it came to pass that night, that the angel of the Lord went forth, and smote in the camp of the Assyrians" (2 Kings 19:35).[1]

142. R. Hananel said in the name of Rav: The ministering angels do not utter song above until Israel utter it below, for it is said, "When [they who are like] the morning stars sing together" (Job 38:7), and after that, "All divine beings shout for joy" (Job 38:7).[2]

143. "As well the singers as the players on instruments shall be there: all my springs are in Thee" (Ps. 87:7). R. Yuda said in the name of R. Meir: Like the spring from which fresh water pours out at every moment, so will the children of Israel sing a new song at every moment.

But the sages expounded: Even as the men will sing songs, so also will the women, as is said, "All my springs are in Thee." Here the word "springs" implies women, as in the verse "A garden shut up is my sister, my bride, a fountain sealed, a spring shut up" (Song 4:12).[3]

144. R. Joshua ben Levi said: He who utters song [in praise of God] in this world will merit uttering it in the world-to-come, as is said, "Happy are they that dwell in Thy house now; they will be praising Thee forever. Selah" (Ps. 84:5).

R. Hiyya bar Abba said in the name of R. Yohanan: All the prophets are destined to utter song with one voice, as is said, "Hark, Thy watchmen raise their voices; as one they shout for joy" (Isa. 52:8)[4]

145. "I am the rose of Sharon" (Song 2:1). I am she, I am the beloved, I am the one who has been both covered and trampled down while in the shadow of the [heathen] kingdoms, but tomorrow, when the Holy One delivers me from the shadow of those kingdoms, I shall freshen like a rose and sing a new song unto Him, as is said, "O sing unto the Lord a new song; for He hath done marvelous things; His right hand, and His holy arm, hath wrought salvation for Him" (Ps. 98:1).

R. Abba bar Kahana taught that the congregation of Israel said to the Holy One: I am she, I am the beloved, deep in the depths of trouble, but when the Holy One lifts me up out of my troubles, I shall freshen like a rose with good deeds and shall sing a song [to Him], as is said, "A Song of Ascents. Out of the depths have I called Thee, O Lord" (Ps. 130:1).[5]

146. "Look (*tashuri*) from the top of Amana" (Song 4:8). R. Yusta said: There is a mountain called Amana which marks the extreme boundary of the Land of Israel. From there and beyond is outside the Land.

R. Eleazar son of R. Yose said: ["Look (*tashuri*)" means that] as soon as the returning exiles reach it, they will utter song (*shirah*). Hence Scripture: "Sing (*tashuri*) from the top of Amana."[6]

147. "Then sang Moses and the children of Israel this song (*shirah*)"[7] (Exod. 15:1). All the songs recited throughout the past by Israel are designated "*song*" in its feminine form, as if to say: [Just as a woman conceives and gives birth again and again, so troubles keep coming]. Observe that the deliverances of the past were followed by servitude, for Babylon, Media, Greece, and Rome were to rise against Israel. But the deliverance destined to come will not be followed by another servitude, as is said, "O Israel, that art saved by the Lord with an everlasting deliverance" (Isa. 45:17). At that time they will sing a song in its masculine form, as is said, "Sing unto the Lord a new song (*shir*)" (Ps. 98:1).[8]

---

1. At a time when, it is assumed, Hezekiah was in bed. Lam R., proem 30; Yalkut, 2 Sam., §163.
2. B. Hul 91b.
3. MTeh 87:7.
4. B. Sanh 91b.
5. Song R. 2:1, §1 and §3.
6. Exod. R. 23:5.
7. A feminine form of *shir* ("song").
8. Exod. R. 23:11; Yalkut, *Be-shallah*, §242.

CHAPTER NINE

SABBATH, FEASTS, AND FASTS

Sabbath

1. "That ye may know that I the Lord sanctify you" (Exod. 31:13). The Holy One said to Moses: Moses, in My treasury I have a precious gift—it is called the Sabbath, and I wish to give it to Israel. Go and make it known to them.[1]

2. "See, for that the Lord hath given you the Sabbath" (Exod. 16:29). What is implied by the word "see"? R. Yose answered that God meant: See the pearl I am giving you.[2]

3. R. Yohanan said in the name of R. Simeon ben Yohai: All commandments the Holy One gave to Israel, He gave publicly, except for the Sabbath, which He gave privately, as is said, "It is a sign between Me and the children of Israel forever" (Exod. 31:17).[3]

4. R. Simeon ben Yohai taught: The Sabbath spoke right up to the Holy One: Master of the universe, each one of the days has a mate,[4] but I have no mate. The Holy One replied: The congregation of Israel will be your mate. And when Israel stood before Mount Sinai, the Holy One said to them: Remember the special thing I told the Sabbath, that "the congregation of Israel is to be your mate." It is this that is implied in the verse "Remember the Sabbath day to hallow it" (Exod. 20:8) [by uniting with it in holy wedlock].[5]

5. "Because for you it is a means of hallowing" (Exod. 31:14).[6] The verse tells us that the Sabbath enhances Israel's holiness: Why is the shop of So-and-so closed? Because he is keeping the Sabbath. Why does So-and-so abstain from work? Because he is keeping the Sabbath.[7]

6. In the Five Books, the Prophets, and the Writings, we find it stated that the Sabbath is the equivalent of all the commandments in the Torah. In the Five Books, Israel are reproached: "How long refuse ye to keep My commandments and My laws?" (Exod. 16:28),[8] and this is followed directly by "See that the Lord hath given you the Sabbath" (Exod. 16:29). In the Prophets: "But the House of Israel rebelled against Me in the wilderness; they walked not in My statutes" (Ezek. 20:13), and this is followed directly by "And My Sabbaths they greatly profaned" (ibid.). In the Writings: "Thou camest down also upon Mount Sinai . . . and gavest them . . . statutes and commandments" (Neh. 9:13), and this is followed directly by "And madest known unto them Thy holy Sabbath" (Neh. 9:14).

The Holy One said to Israel: If you succeed in keeping the Sabbath, I will account it to you as though you had kept all the commandments in the Torah. But if you violate it, I will account it to you as though you had profaned all the commandments. Thus Scripture: "He that keepeth the Sabbath from profaning it is as one who keepeth his hand from doing any evil deed" (Isa. 56:2).[9]

7. When a man keeps the Sabbath, it is as though he had fulfilled the entire Torah, all of it.[10]

8. "He that keepeth the Sabbath keepeth his hand from doing any evil" (Isa. 56:2). Thus we learn that he who keeps the Sabbath is kept far from sin.[11]

9. "It is a sign forever" (Exod. 31:17). The verse tells that the Sabbath will never cease in Israel. You find that any observance for which Israel were willing to give up their lives has been preserved among them. But any observance for which Israel were not willing to give up their lives has not been preserved among them. Thus the Sabbath, circumcision, and study of Torah, for which Israel were willing to give up their lives, have been retained by them. But such institutions as the Temple and the sabbatical and jubilee years, for which Israel were not willing to give up their lives, have not been retained by them.[12]

10. R. Hiyya bar Abba said in the name of R. Yohanan: Even if a man worships idols, as did the generation of Enosh, but keeps the Sabbath as it should be kept, he is forgiven, for Scripture says, "Blessed is Enosh . . . that keepeth the Sabbath from profaning it (*me-hallelo*)" (Isa. 56:2). Read not *me-hallelo*, "from profaning it," but *mahul lo*, "he shall be forgiven."

R. Hiyya bar Abba said: "Better is a handful of quietness" (Eccles. 4:6)—the Sabbath—"than both the hands full of labor and striving after wind" (ibid.)—the six days of work. For R. Hiyya bar Abba used to say: Only through the merit of the Sabbath will Israel be redeemed, as is said, "In sitting still and rest shall ye be saved" (Isa.

---

1. B. Shab 10b; B. Betz 16a.
2. MTeh 92:1; Yalkut, *Be-shallah*, §241; Yalkut, Ps., §843.
3. B. Betz 16a.
4. The six weekdays make three couples.
5. Gen. R. 11:8; Yalkut, *Bereshit*, §17.
6. JV: "For it is holy unto you."
7. Mek, *Ki Tissa, Shabbata*, 1.
8. Even though there was violation of but one commandment, that of the Sabbath.
9. P. Ned 3:9, 38b; Exod. R. 25:12.
10. Pesikta. The translator could not locate the source.
11. Mek, *Be-shallah*, *Va-yassa*, 6.
12. Mek, *Ki-Tissa, Shabbata*, 1; Yalkut, *Ki Tissa*, §391.

30:15). That is, your salvation shall come about through the Sabbath and its rest.[1]

11. R. Judah said in the name of Rav: Had Israel kept the first Sabbath, no nation or tongue would have gained dominion over them, for Scripture says, "And it came to pass on the seventh day, that there went out some of the people to gather" (Exod. 16:27), and this is followed at once by "Then came Amalek" (Exod. 17:1).

R. Yohanan said in the name of R. Simeon ben Yohai: If Israel were to keep but two Sabbaths as they should be kept, they would be redeemed immediately, as is said, "Thus saith the Lord concerning the eunuchs that keep my sabbaths"[2] (Isa. 56:4), and this is followed by "Them will I bring to My holy mountain" (Isa. 56:7).[3]

12. "As for Me, behold, if My covenant is with thee . . . I will give unto thee and to thy seed after thee, the Land of thy sojournings" (Gen. 17:4 and 17:8). R. Yudan took the verse to say: If your children accept the covenant of Sabbath, they will enter the Land; but if not, they will not enter it.[4]

13. Abbaye said: Jerusalem was destroyed only because its inhabitants profaned the Sabbath there, as is said, "They have hid their eyes from the Sabbaths, therefore am I profaned among them" (Ezek. 22:26).[5]

14. Why was Mount Simeon[6] laid waste? Because its inhabitants played ball on the Sabbath.[7]

15. "Thou shalt not bear false witness" (Exod. 20:16). On one Tablet it is written, "Remember the Sabbath to keep it holy"; and facing it, on the opposite Tablet is written, "Thou shalt not bear false witness." Thus Scripture tells us: Whoever profanes the Sabbath—it is as though he were bearing witness in the presence of Him who spoke and the world came into being that He did not create His world in six days and did not rest on the seventh. But whoever keeps the Sabbath bears witness in the presence of Him who spoke and the world came into being that He did create His world in six days and did rest on the seventh, as is said, "Ye are to be My witnesses, saith the Lord" (Isa. 43:10).[8]

16. There are three who bear witness about one another: Israel, the Sabbath, and the Holy One. Israel and the Holy One bear witness about the Sabbath, that it is a day of rest. Israel and the Sabbath bear witness about the Holy One, that He is unique in His world. The Holy One and the Sabbath bear witness about Israel [that they are unique among the nations].[9]

17. "Remember the Sabbath day, to keep it holy" (Exod. 20:8). Here in Exodus it is written, "Remember," but in Deuteronomy it is written, "Take care of" (Deut. 5:12). R. Yudan and R. Aibu said in the name of R. Simeon ben Lakish: Consider the parable of a king who handed his son a coin and a flask, and sent him to the storekeeper. On the way, the son broke the flask and lost the coin. So the king twisted his son's ear and pulled at his hair, and as he gave him a coin and a flask a second time, he said to him, "Take care that you do not lose these as you lost the others." In the same way, because Israel lost in the wilderness[10] the command that began with "Remember," God gave them the command again, this time beginning with the words "Take care of the Sabbath."[11]

18. R. Berekhiah taught in the name of R. Hiyya bar Abba: The Sabbath was given solely for enjoyment. R. Haggai said in the name of R. Samuel bar Nahman: The Sabbath was given solely for the study of Torah. But the two do not really differ. What R. Berekhiah said in the name of R. Hiyya bar Abba about the Sabbath's being given for enjoyment applies to disciples of the wise, who weary themselves in study of Torah throughout the week but on the Sabbath come out and enjoy themselves. What R. Haggai said in the name of R. Samuel bar Nahman about the Sabbath's being given for study of Torah applies to workingmen, who are monopolized by their work throughout the week, but on the Sabbath come in and busy themselves with the Torah.[12]

19. "And Moses assembled" (Exod. 35:1). Our masters who are expert in *Aggadah* say: From the beginning of Torah to its end, there is no section where "Moses assembled" is mentioned except here. For the Holy One said to Moses: Gather large assemblies and publicly expound for them the laws of Sabbath, so that coming generations may learn from you to bring together assemblies in synagogues on each and every Sabbath for the purpose of teaching and instructing Israel in words of Torah—what is prohibited and what is permitted—that thereby My great Name will be honored among My children.[13]

---

1. B. Shab 118b; Eccles. R. 4:6, §1.
2. In rabbinic commentary, an unspecified plural denotes two.
3. B. Shab 118b.
4. Gen. R. 46:9.
5. When Jerusalem is in ruins, God's Name is profaned. B. Shab 119b.
6. The place has not been identified. Its name suggests that it was a stronghold in Judea.
7. P. Ta 4:6, 69a; Lam. R. 2:2, §4.
8. Mek, *Yitro, Ba-hodesh*, 8.
9. Concerning the Sabbath, God and Israel bear witness that "when days were fashioned, one of them was His" (Ps. 139:16). Concerning the Holy One, Israel and the Sabbath bear witness that he is one, as is said, "The Sabbath is a sign between Me and you . . . that ye may know that I am the Lord." Concerning Israel, the Holy One and the Sabbath bear witness that Israel are a unique people, as is said, "What one nation . . . is like . . . Israel, whom God went to redeem to be His own people?" (1 Chron. 8:21). Joseph Davis of Washington University, St. Louis, Mo., provided the reference to *Perushe ha-Torah le-Baale ha-Tosafot*, ed. Gellis (Jerusalem, 1981), vol. 1. Midrash cited in Tosafot on B. Hag 3b.
10. By going out on the Sabbath to gather manna (Exod. 16:27), and by the worship of the golden calf, which led to the breaking of the first Tablets.
11. PR 23:1 (YJS 1:474).
12. PR 23:9 (YJS 1:490–91).
13. Yalkut, *Va-yak'hel*, §407.

20. "Moses . . . saw their burdens" (Exod. 2:11). He saw that they had no rest whatever [from hard labor]. So he went off and told Pharaoh: "When a man has a slave and the slave gets no rest at least one day during the week, the slave will die. Now, these are your slaves. If you do not let them rest during the week, they will surely die." Pharaoh replied, "Go and do with them as you say." So Moses went and ordained the Sabbath day for them to rest.[1]

21. "Let heavier work be laid upon the men" (Exod. 5:9). When the entire verse is read, it tells us that the Israelites possessed scrolls containing assurances that the Holy One would redeem them. The Israelites took delight in reading them from one Sabbath to the next, for at that time they were still allowed to rest on the Sabbath. But now Pharaoh informed Moses [of a new order]: "Let heavier work be laid upon the men, and make them keep at it [even on the Sabbath], so that they will not delight in lying words" (ibid.)—let them not divert themselves and rest on the Sabbath day.[2]

22. The Torah said: Master of the universe, when Israel enter the Land, what will happen to me? Every man in Israel will proceed to sow and plant his field—and I, what will happen to me? God replied: I have a mate which I will provide for you—the Sabbath, when Israel abstain from work, enter the synagogues and houses of study, and occupy themselves with Torah.[3]

23. "Thou that [when at leisure] dwellest in the gardens, the companions hearken for thy voice: 'Cause Me to hear it' " (Song 8:13). R. Nathan said in the name of R. Aha: [God here is compared] to a king who grew angry with some of his servants and threw them into a dungeon. He then took all his soldiers and servants, and went to listen to what they were chanting. When he heard them recite, "Our lord king, he is our praise, he is our life; we will never fail our lord king," he said to them, "My children, raise your voices, so that the companions who are above you may hear." Likewise, although Israel are occupied with their work during the six days of the week, on the Sabbath they rise early and go to the synagogue and recite the Shema; they go over to the lectern, where they read the Torah and conclude the reading with a related passage from the Prophets. Then the Holy One says, "My children, raise your voices, so that the companions standing above you may hear"—the word "companions" here denoting the ministering angels. "Take heed that ye do not hate one another, nor be jealous of one another, nor contend with one another, nor humiliate one another, lest the ministering angels say before me, 'Lord of the Universe, Israel do not concern themselves with the Torah You have given to them, for, as you see, there is enmity, jealousy, hatred, and strife among Israel.' Whereas in fact you are fulfilling the Torah in its entirety."[4]

1. Exod. R. 1:28.
2. Exod. R. 5:16.
3. Midrash, cited in "Some say."
4. Song R. 8:13, §1.

24. In the school of Elijah it was taught: "Among the days that were to be fashioned, one was to be wholly His" (Ps. 139:16). This is Israel's Sabbath day. In what sense is it to be wholly His? Say, a man who labors for six days rests on the Sabbath and so finds it possible to come closer to his children and the other members of his household. Likewise, a man may labor all six days in the midst of people who are hostile to him, but then, as he rests on the Sabbath, he forgets all the vexation he has previously suffered. Such is the nature of man: a good day makes him forget an evil day, and conversely, an evil day makes him forget a good day.[5]

25. "Remember the Sabbath day" (Exod. 20:8). R. Eleazar ben Hananiah said: Remember it continually from the first day of the week. If a good portion happens to come your way, prepare it for use on the Sabbath.[6]

26. We have been taught: It is told of Shammai the Elder that throughout his life he saved the [best] food for honoring the Sabbath. If he came upon a fine animal, he would say; Let this one be for the Sabbath. If subsequently he came upon a finer animal, he put the second aside for the Sabbath and ate the first. But Hillel the Elder had a different trait. Daily throughout the week, all his doings were in utter reliance upon Heaven, in keeping with "The Lord is to be relied on day by day" (Ps. 68:20).[7] Hence we were taught: The school of Shammai says, "From the first day in the week, look to the Sabbath"; whereas the school of Hillel says, "The Lord is to be relied on day by day."[8]

27. "Remember" and "observe"—remember it before it comes, and observe it after it leaves. The sages said: We should always increase what is holy by adding to it [at both ends] out of the time that is not holy, the Sabbath being like a wolf that preys upon [victims] both in front of him and behind him.[9]

28. He who works on the eves of Sabbaths or on the eves of festivals from midday onward, or [too soon] at the outgoing of Sabbath, at the outgoing of a festival, or the outgoing of the Day of Atonement—or at any time when there is the least possibility of transgression—will never see a sign of blessing.

Our masters taught: Some are industrious and profit from it, while others are industrious and suffer loss; some are indolent and profit from it, while others are indolent and suffer loss. An industrious man who profits: he who works the entire week but does not work [after midday] on the eve of Sabbath. An industrious man who suffers loss: he who works the entire week and also works [after midday] on the eve of Sabbath. An indolent man who profits: he who works neither during the entire week nor [after midday] on the eve of Sabbath. An indolent man who suffers

5. TdE, ed. Friedmann, p. 4 (JPS, p. 45).
6. Mek, *Yitro, Ba-hodesh*, 7.
7. He trusted God to provide for the Sabbath.
8. B. Betz 16a and En Yaakov, ad loc.
9. Mek, *Yitro, Ba-hodesh*, 7.

loss: he who does not work the entire week but works [after midday] on the eve of Sabbath.

Rava said: Those women of Mahoza,[1] who only out of self-indulgence do no work [after midday] on the eve of Sabbath—those women, even though they do no work on any other day of the week either—nevertheless may be spoken of as "an indolent person who profits."[2]

29. R. Hisda said: One should market early for the Sabbath, as is said, "It shall come to pass on the sixth day, that they shall prepare that which they bring in" (Exod. 16:5)—the manna, which they gather early in the morning.[3]

30. Seated on an ivory stool,[4] R. Abbahu would fan the fire [in preparing food for the Sabbath]. R. Anan used to wear a smock [over his clean clothes], for he agreed with what was taught in the school of R. Ishmael: the workaday clothes worn when a man cooks a dish for his master, he should not wear when pouring a cup for him. R. Safra would singe the head [of an animal] himself. Rava salted mullet himself. R. Huna kindled a lamp. R. Papa plaited wicks. R. Hisda cut up beetroots. Rabbah and R. Joseph chopped wood. R. Zera used to kindle a woodchip fire himself. R. Nahman bar Isaac carried in and out what was needed for the Sabbath on his shoulder, saying: Were R. Ammi and R. Assi to visit, would I not act as a porter for them?[5]

31. R. Judah said in the name of Rav: Such was the practice of R. Judah bar Ilai: on the eve of Sabbath, a basin filled with warm water would be brought to him. He would wash his face, his hands, and his feet and then wrap himself in his fringed linen robes. He looked like an angel of the Lord of hosts.[6]

32. One Sabbath eve, before sunset, R. Simeon ben Yohai and his son R. Eleazar saw an old man holding two bunches of myrtle and running in the twilight. "What are these for?" they asked him. "To honor the Sabbath," he replied.

"But one should be enough."

"One is for 'Remember,' and one for 'Observe.' "[7]

R. Simeon said to his son, "See how beloved are the commandments to Israel."[8]

33. "As a lily among the thorns, so is My love among the daughters" (Song 2:2). Even as [the fragrance of] the lily is designated for Sabbaths and festivals, so are Israel designated for redemption as early as the very next day.[9]

1. A Jewish town on the Tigris, where Rava's academy was situated.
2. B. Pes 50b.
3. B. Shab 117b.
4. He was a wealthy man.
5. B. Shab 119a.
6. B. Shab 25b.
7. Exod. 20:8: "Remember the Sabbath day," and Deut. 5:12: "Observe the Sabbath day."
8. B. Shab 33b.
9. Lev. R. 23:6.

34. On Sabbath eve, at twilight, R. Hanina would wrap himself in his robe, stand up, and say, "Come, let us go forth to welcome Queen Sabbath!"

On Sabbath eve, R. Yannai would put on his festive garments and say, "Come, O bride! Come, O bride!"[10]

35. "And God blessed the seventh day, and hallowed it" (Gen. 2:3)—blessed the Sabbath with radiance in a man's face; hallowed it with radiance in a man's face. The radiance in a man's face on weekdays is not like that on the Sabbath.[11]

36. "I am black, but comely" (Song 1:5). I am black during the days of the week, but comely on the Sabbath.[12]

37. R. Hisda said in the name of Mar Ukba: When a man praying on the eve of the Sabbath says, "The heaven and the earth were finished" (Gen. 2:1), the two ministering angels who accompany every man place their hands on his head and say to him, "Thine iniquity is taken away, and thy sin purged" (Isa. 6:7).

We have been taught that R. Yose son of R. Judah said: On the eve of Sabbath, two ministering angels accompany every man from the synagogue to his home, a good angel and an evil one. When the man arrives home and finds the lamp lit, the table set, and his couch spread, the good angel says, "May it be God's will that it be thus another Sabbath!" and unwillingly the evil angel responds, "Amen!" But if not [if the room is dark, the table and the couch bare], the evil angel says, "May it be God's will that it be thus another Sabbath!" and unwillingly the good angel responds, "Amen!"[13]

38. "And call the Sabbath a delight" (Isa. 58:13). The word "delight" refers to kindling the lamp on the Sabbath.

"My life was bereft of peace" (Lam. 3:17) refers, according to R. Abbahu, to the lack of a Sabbath lamp. "I had forgotten what happiness was" (ibid.) refers to the lack of a bathhouse. According to R. Yohanan, to the lack of washing hands and feet in warm water. According to R. Isaac Nappaha, to the lack of a beautiful couch and beautiful appointments for it.[14]

39. R. Huna said: He who regularly lights the Sabbath lamp will have sons who are disciples of the wise.

R. Huna used to walk back and forth past the doorway of R. Avin the Carpenter, and he observed that R. Avin regularly lit many Sabbath lamps. So he said: Two distinguished men will issue from this house. Indeed, R. Idi bar Avin and R. Hiyya bar Avin did issue from it.[15]

40. R. Eleazar, quoting "God blessed the seventh day" (Gen. 2:3), said: He blessed the day by the continuous

10. B. Shab 119a.
11. Gen. R. 11:2; Yalkut, *Bereshit*, §17.
12. Song R. 1:5, §2.
13. B. Shab 119b.
14. Tanhuma, *Noah*, §1; B. Shab 25b; Yalkut, Lam., §3.
15. B. Shab 23b.

burning of the lamp lit for it, as I was to learn from my own experience. I once lit a lamp on Sabbath eve, and when I came back I found it still burning at the Sabbath's end.[1]

41. The Sabbath—the lamps thereof are the honor due to it. If you are meticulous about the Sabbath lamps, I will show you the lamps of Zion [lit again], as is said, "And it shall come to pass at that time, that I will free Jerusalem because of the lamps" (Zeph. 1:12).[2]

42. In the school of Elijah it is taught: "Remember the Sabbath day, to hallow it" (Exod. 20:8). With what are you to hallow it? With reading of Scripture, with reciting of Mishnah, with [appropriate] food and drink, with clean garments, and with rest [of body and spirit].[3]

43. "To hallow it" (Exod. 20:8)—with a blessing. On the basis of this verse, the sages said: At the incoming of the Sabbath we hallow it by reciting the hallowing (Kiddush) of the day over wine.[4]

44. R. Zakkai's disciples asked him: How have you managed to reach such an advanced age? He replied: I never gave a derogatory nickname to a colleague, nor have I omitted to say the Kiddush for the [Sabbath] day. I had a grandmother who once, when I had no wine for Kiddush, sold her headdress and brought me the wine for the Kiddush of the day.

The sages taught that when she died, she left him three hundred kegs of wine, and when he died, he left his sons three thousand kegs of wine.[5]

45. R. Eliezer said: A man should always set a full table for Sabbath eve, even if he himself needs no more than an olive's bulk of food.[6]

46. R. Yose said: May my portion be with those who eat three meals on a Sabbath.[7]

47. "Thou shalt call the Sabbath a delight" (Isa. 58:13). With what is one to show his delight in the Sabbath? R. Judah son of R. Samuel bar Shilat said in the name of Rav: With a dish of beets, large fish, and heads of garlic. R. Hiyya bar Ashi said in the name of Rav: So long as it is prepared in honor of the Sabbath, even a humble dish is "a delight." What humble dish, for example? R. Papa said: Fish-hash pie.[8]

48. "And it shall come to pass on the sixth day that they shall prepare . . . and it shall be twice as much (*mishneh)*" (Exod. 16:5). Read *meshunneh*, "different." How? Every day there will be one measure of manna, but for the Sabbath two measures; every day its fragrance will go forth, but more so on the Sabbath; every day it will shine brightly like gold, but more so on the Sabbath.[9]

49. Our masters taught: How many meals is a man duty bound to eat on the Sabbath? Three. R. Hidka said: Four.[10]

50. "And shalt honor it" (Isa. 58:13)—so that your garment for the Sabbath is not like your garment for weekdays.

R. Huna said: If one has a change of garments, he should change them; but if he has nothing to change into, he should let them down.[11]

51. R. Hanina said: A man should have two cloaks, one for weekdays and one for the Sabbath. When R. Simlai preached this to an assembly, the disciples burst into tears in front of him, saying, "Master, our garment on the Sabbath is necessarily the same as our garment on weekdays." He replied, "Nevertheless, you must make some change in it for the Sabbath."[12]

52. "And thou shalt honor it, not doing thy wonted round" (Isa. 58:13): your [leisurely] way of walking on the Sabbath is not to be like your [hurried] way of walking on weekdays. "Not pursuing your affairs" (ibid.): your affairs are forbidden, but the affairs of Heaven may be pursued. "And not [ordinary] talk" (ibid.): your talk on the Sabbath is not to be like your talk on weekdays.[13]

53. Whenever R. Simeon ben Yohai's mother indulged in too much talk on the Sabbath, he would say to her, "It is the Sabbath," and she would grow silent.[14]

54. R. Akiva sat weeping on the Sabbath. His disciples said: Master, you taught us, "Call the Sabbath a delight" (Isa. 58:13). R. Akiva: Such is my delight.[15]

55. Both R. Hisda and R. Hamnuna said: Accounts that have to do with performing a precept may be reckoned on the Sabbath. And R. Eleazar said: One may allocate grants to the poor on the Sabbath. And R. Jacob bar Idi said in the name of R. Yohanan: One may oversee matters of life and death and of communal urgency on the Sabbath, and one may go to synagogues to attend to communal affairs on the Sabbath. R. Samuel bar Nahmani said to R. Jonathan: One may even go to theaters, circuses, and basilicas to attend to communal affairs on the Sabbath.

In the school of R. Manasseh it was taught: One may make arrangements on the Sabbath for the betrothal of a young woman and for teaching reading or a craft to a child,

1. Gen. R. 11:2; Yalkut, *Bereshit*, §17.
2. JV: "that I will search Jerusalem with lamps." But by a slight change, *hps* ("search") may be read *hpsh* ("free"). Yalkut, *Be-haalotekha*, §719.
3. Mek RSbY, p. 149; TdE 26 (ed. Friedmann, p. 133).
4. Mek, *Yitro, Ba-hodesh*, 7.
5. B. Meg 27b and En Yaakov, ad loc.
6. B. Shab 119b.
7. On weekdays, only two meals were eaten. B. Shab 118b.
8. B. Shab 118b.
9. Mek RSbY, p. 107.
10. B. Shab 117b.
11. And not tuck them up, as he does when he is working. B. Shab 113a; Yalkut, *Bereshit*, §17.
12. P. Pe 8:7 21b.
13. B. Shab 113a–b.
14. Lev. R. 34:16.
15. See above, part 2, chap. 1, §159. *Shibbolei ha-Leket*, which cites a Midrash.

for Scripture says, "Not pursuing your affairs," meaning: Your own affairs may not be pursued, but the affairs of Heaven may be pursued.[1]

56. R. Tanhum said in the name of R. Joshua ben Levi: A man is always to run to perform a precept, even on the Sabbath.[2]

57. R. Yohanan said in the name of R. Yose: He who delights in the Sabbath is given a heritage unlimited by boundaries, for Scripture says, "If thou delightest thyself in the Lord . . . I will let thee enjoy the heritage of Jacob thy father" (Isa. 58:14)—not like the heritage of Abraham, who was told, "Arise, walk through the Land in the length of it and in the breadth of it" (Gen. 13:17); nor like the heritage of Isaac, who was told, "Unto thee, and unto thy seed, I will give all these lands" (Gen. 26:3); but like the heritage of Jacob, who was told, "Thou shalt spread abroad to the west, and to the east, and to the north, and to the south" (Gen. 28:14). R. Nahman bar Isaac added: He is saved from servitude under the kingdoms: here, in connection with the Sabbath, it is said, "I will set you astride the heights of the earth" (Isa. 58:14), and elsewhere, in connection with triumph over the kingdoms, it is said, "As you march across their heights" (Deut. 33:29).

R. Judah said in the name of Rav: He who delights in the Sabbath is given his heart's desires, for it is said, "Delight thyself in the Lord; and He shall give thee the desires of thy heart" (Ps. 37:4). Now, I do not know what delight the psalm refers to. But since we read in Isaiah, "Thou shalt call the Sabbath a delight" (Isa. 58:13), one may conclude that by "delight" is meant the Sabbath.[3]

58. In the school of Elijah it is taught: Even though R. Akiva said, "Treat your Sabbath like a weekday rather than be dependent on mortals," one must prepare something, however slight, at home.[4]

59. R. Tahalifa, the brother of Rabinai of [Be] Hozae,[5] taught: A man's entire sustenance [for the year] is fixed for him between New Year's Day and the Day of Atonement, except expenses for Sabbaths, expenses for festivals, and expenses for instructing his children in Torah. If he spends less, he is given less; and if he spends more, he is given more.[6]

60. R. Yohanan said in the name of R. Eleazar son of R. Simeon: The Holy One said to Israel: My children, borrow on My account to mark the holiness of the day, and put your trust in Me, and I will do the repaying.[7]

1. Arranging for a child's instruction is a precept, hence an affair of Heaven. B. Shab 150a.
2. When running is prohibited. B. Ber 6b and En Yaakov, ad loc.
3. B. Shab 118a–b.
4. B. Pes 112a and En Yaakov, ad loc.
5. The province of Khuzistan.
6. B. Betz 15b–16a.
7. B. Betz 15b.

61. Joseph-who-honors-the-Sabbath had in his neighborhood a certain Gentile who owned very much property. Soothsayers told him: All the property you have, Joseph-who-honors-the-Sabbath will eventually enjoy. So the Gentile went and sold his property, and with the proceeds he bought a pearl, which he secured in his headdress. As he was crossing a bridge, the wind blew off the headdress and carried it out to sea, and a fish swallowed it. The fish was caught and brought to the marketplace on the eve of a Sabbath at twilight. They asked, "Who will buy a fish at this late hour?" They were told, "Go, take it to Joseph-who-honors-the-Sabbath. He is always eager to buy [fine food in the Sabbath's honor]. So the fish was brought to him, and he bought it. When he cut it open, he found the pearl in it, which he sold for enough gold denars to fill thirteen upper chambers.

A certain venerable elder[8] met him and said: He who lends to the Sabbath, the Sabbath will repay him.[9]

62. R. Hiyya bar Abba told the following story: Once a man of Laodicea[10] invited me to his house, and a golden table was brought before him. Sixteen men carried it by means of sixteen silver chains attached to it. On the table were set plates, goblets, pitchers, and flasks. All kinds of food, all kinds of precious fruits and spices created during the six days of creation were on it [to be eaten]. In the middle of the table there sat a child, and when the table was set down, the child proclaimed loudly, "The earth is the Lord's, and the fullness thereof; the world and they that dwell therein" (Ps. 24:1). And when the table was removed, the child said, "The heavens are the heavens of the Lord; but the earth hath He given to the children of men" (Ps. 115:16). I asked my host, "My son, how did you merit all this wealth?" He replied, "Master, I was a simple butcher, and I would say of every fat-fleshed animal, 'This one shall be for the Sabbath.' "[11] I told him, "Happy are you that such is your merit, and blessed be He who is everywhere for having allowed you to enjoy all this."[12]

63. R. Eleazar said in the name of R. Yose: "God blessed the seventh day" (Gen. 2:3) in that, on account of people with delicate digestions, he blessed its food with special flavor.[13]

64. A Caesar asked R. Joshua ben Hananiah: Why do Sabbath dishes have such a fragrant aroma? R. Joshua: We have a certain seasoning called Sabbath which we put into the dish, and that gives it its fragrant aroma. Caesar: Give us some. R. Joshua: For him who keeps the Sabbath, it avails; but for him who does not keep the Sabbath, it will not avail.[14]

8. The prophet Elijah?
9. B. Shab 119a.
10. A town in Syria.
11. The butcher took a chance, since the meat might not get sold and would spoil.
12. B. Shab 119a; Gen. R. 11:4.
13. They will thus enjoy the food and have no difficulty in digesting it. Gen. R. 11:4.
14. B. Shab 119a.

65. When our Rabbi [Judah I, the Patriarch] entertained Antoninus on a Sabbath, he served him cold dishes, which Antoninus ate and liked. On another occasion, our Rabbi entertained Antoninus on a weekday, when he served him hot dishes. Antoninus said: I found the cold dishes more tasty than the hot. Rabbi [Judah] replied: The hot dishes lack one seasoning. Antoninus: Can there be anything at all lacking in the emperor's pantry? Rabbi [Judah]: The hot dishes lack Sabbath. Does your pantry have Sabbath?[1]

66. The tyrant Rufus asked R. Akiva: How does the Sabbath day differ from other days? The latter replied: How does one man differ from other men? Rufus: In that the emperor chooses to honor me [and not other men]. R. Akiva: So, too, the King of kings chooses to honor it. Rufus: What I meant was: Who decides that this day is the Sabbath? R. Akiva: It is proved by the fact that the river Sambatyon, which [flows so swiftly] on weekdays [that] it pulls up the stones [from its bed, does not pull them up on] the Sabbath, when it rests. Rufus: For your proof, you go as far afield as the wind? R. Akiva: A necromancer will be my proof, for he can raise a ghost on any weekday, but not on the Sabbath. Or your father's grave will be my proof, for it emits no smoke on the Sabbath.

Rufus: [By speaking of such proof], you shame, disgrace, and revile my father!

At that, Rufus went off and made the test with his own father. Every day he raised him, but on the Sabbath he could not raise him. After the Sabbath he again raised him and asked him: Have you become a Jew since you died? The father replied: He who does not observe the Sabbath when he is in your world can do so by his own choice, but here he is compelled to observe it. Rufus: And what labor do you all perform on weekdays? The father: On weekdays we are punished, but on the Sabbath we are allowed to rest.[2]

Rufus came back to R. Akiva and asked him: If God wishes to honor the Sabbath, as you say, let Him not cause winds to blow on that day, let Him not cause rain to come down on that day, let Him not cause grass to grow on that day. R. Akiva: May the breath of such a man be blasted out! I will tell you a parable to explain the matter: When only one man lives in a courtyard, he is allowed on the Sabbath to carry things anywhere in the courtyard. So, too, since the entire world, all of it, belongs to Him, and no one else shares this domain with Him, He is free to carry things on the Sabbath throughout the world, through every part of it.[3]

67. A story is told of a pious man who took a walk in his vineyard on the Sabbath. When he noticed a breach in it, he resolved to repair it upon the departure of the Sabbath. But then he said: Since the thought of repairing it came to me on the Sabbath, I will leave it unrepaired forever. How did the Holy One reward him? A big caper bush grew up in the vineyard and filled the breach in the fence, and with the fruit of that bush he sustained himself for the rest of his life.[4]

68. Our masters taught: It once happened that a fire broke out in the courtyard of Joseph ben Simai in Shihin, and because he was a steward of the king,[5] the men of the garrison in Sepphoris came to extinguish it. But out of deference to the Sabbath, he would not permit them to do so, saying, "Let the [divine] Collector collect what is due Him." Right away, a miracle happened in his behalf—rain came down and extinguished the fire. In the evening,[6] he sent a *sela* to each of them, and fifty to their captain. But when the sages heard it, they said: He had no obligation to restrain them, for we are taught in a Mishnah: if a Gentile comes to extinguish a fire, we do not say to him either, "Extinguish" or, "Do not extinguish."[7]

69. A story is told of a certain pious man who owned a plowing heifer. In time, the pious man's wealth slipped out of his hands, and he had to sell his heifer to a heathen, who plowed with her for six days of the [first] week. But on the Sabbath, when he brought her out to play, she lay down under the yoke and would do no work. Though he kept beating her, she would not budge from her place. Seeing this, he went to the pious man and said to him, "Come, take back your heifer. For six days I worked her, but when I took her out on the Sabbath, she lay down under the yoke and would do no work whatever. And though I beat her again and again, she would not budge from her place."

When the heathen spoke thus, the pious man understood that the reason she would do no work was because she had become accustomed to rest on the Sabbath. He said, "Come along. I will get her up and make her plow." When he came to her, he whispered in her ear, "Alas, heifer, heifer, when you were in my possession, you rested on the Sabbath. But now that my sins have forced me to sell you to this heathen, I beg you, stand up and do the will of your [new] master!"

At once she stood up and was ready to work. The heathen said to the pious man, "I won't let you go until you tell me what you did to her and what you whispered into her ear. Did you perhaps practice some sorcery upon her?" The pious man replied, "I said such-and-such to her."

When the heathen heard this, he was both amazed and shaken, as he drew an inference *a fortiori* for himself: If this creature—which has no speech, no cognition, no intelligence—affirms her Creator, shall not I, whom the Holy One created in His own image and likeness, and into whom He put cognition and intelligence—shall I not affirm my Creator?

At once he went and became a proselyte. He was

1. Ibid.; Gen. R. 11:4.
2. The rest of the week he is in purgatory. But even the wicked are given a respite on the Sabbath.
3. B. Sanh 65b; Gen. R. 11:5; Tanhuma, *Ki Tissa*, §33; PR 23:8.
4. B. Shab 150b; P. Shab 15:3, 15a–b; PR 23:3.
5. Agrippa II (?).
6. One may not handle money on the Sabbath.
7. B. Shab 121a; P. Shab 16:7, 15d.

privileged to study Torah and came to be called R. Yohanan ben Tortah ("son of a heifer").[1]

70. Comes Sabbath, comes rest.[2]

71. The Sabbath is one-sixtieth of the world-to-come.[3]

72. Sabbath is to the world-to-come as an unripe date to a ripened one.[4]

73. The word "Sabbath" (*shbt*) is an acrostic of "sleep (*shenah*) on Sabbath (*be-shabbat*) is a delight (*taanug*)."[5]

74. R. Isaac said: Sunshine on the Sabbath is an act of kindness toward the poor, as is said, "But unto you that fear My Name shall the sun shine—a kindness" (Mal. 3:20).[6]

75. R. Simeon ben Lakish said: The Holy One gives man an additional soul on Sabbath eve, and at the Sabbath's departure it is taken from him, as is said, "The Sabbath ceased;[7] *va-yinnafash*" (Exod. 31:17). Once the Sabbath ceases, *vay, en nefesh*; "woe, the [additional] soul is no more."[7]

76. R. Hanina said: One should always set a full table at the Sabbath's departure, even if one requires for himself no more food than the bulk of one olive.[8]

Hot water at the Sabbath's departure is soothing. Fresh warm bread also is soothing at the Sabbath's departure.[9]

77. What is the proof that danger to human life suspends the laws of Sabbath? R. Jonathan ben Joseph cited, "For it is holy unto you" (Exod. 31:14). The Sabbath is committed to your keeping, not you to its keeping. R. Simeon ben Menasya cited, "The children of Israel shall keep the Sabbath" (Exod. 31:16). The Torah says: Profane one Sabbath for a man's sake, so that he may keep many Sabbaths.[10]

78. R. Simon said in the name of R. Simeon the Pious: In this world, if a man goes about gathering figs on a Sabbath, the fig tree says nothing at all to him. But in the time-to-come, [if a man should go to pick fruit from a fig tree on a Sabbath], the tree will call aloud to him and say, "It is the Sabbath!"[11]

79. [This number is missing in BR.]

1. PR 14:2; Midrash Aseret ha-Dibberot (BhM 1:74–75).
2. Rashi on B. Meg 9a, citing a Midrash.
3. B. Ber 57b.
4. Gen. R. 17:5. So interpreted by Leon Nemoy.
5. The three letters Sh, B, and T, which make up the word Shabbat ("Sabbath"), are used to suggest that sleep is a delight on the Sabbath. Yalkut Reuveni, *Va-et'hannan*.
6. B. Ta 8b. The sun's warmth is the only pleasure they can afford.
7. JV: "He ceased from work and rested." But *nfsh* may mean "soul" as well as "rest."
8. B. Betz. 16a.
9. B. Shab 119b.
10. B. Yoma 85b.
11. MTeh 73:4; Yalkut, Jer., §315.

Hallowing the New Moon and Intercalating the Year

80. "This reckoning of the month shall be unto you" (Exod. 12:2). R. Joshua ben Levi said: How may the matter be illustrated? By the parable of a king who had a clock. When his son reached puberty, he said to him: My son, until now the clock has been in my keeping. From now on, I turn it over to you. So, too, the Holy One used to hallow new moons and intercalate years. But when Israel arose, He said to them: Until now the reckoning of new moons and of New Year's Day has been in My keeping. From now on, they are turned over to you.[12]

81. There was a large courtyard in Jerusalem called Beth Yaazek, where all the witnesses[13] used to gather, and there the court examined them. As an inducement for them to come, lavish fare was provided for them.

How did they examine the witnesses? The pair that came first was examined first. The senior of the pair was brought in and asked, "Tell us, in exactly what position did you see the moon? Turned toward the sun? Away from it? To the north? To the south? How high in the sky was it? Toward what point of the compass did it incline? How thick was the crescent?"

After that, the second witness [of the pair] was brought in and examined. If their accounts tallied, their evidence was held valid. Then the other pairs were questioned only briefly, not because their evidence was really needed, but in order that they did not go away disappointed and were induced to continue to come.

The head of the court would then declare, "Hallowed," and all the people would repeat after him, "Hallowed, hallowed."

Rabban Gamaliel used to have a diagram of the phases of the moon on a tablet [hung] on the wall of his upper chamber, and as he showed them to the unlearned, he would ask, "Did it look like this, or like this?"[14]

82. At first, testimony concerning [the appearance of] the new moon was received from anyone. However, following the nefarious schemes of the Boethusians, it was enacted that testimony should be received only from persons who were known.

What nefarious schemes did the Boethusians contrive? Because the Boethusians believe that the Feast of Weeks must fall only on a Sunday, they conspired on one occasion to mislead the sages [concerning the day on which the month of Nisan had begun].[15] For four hundred *zuz*,

12. Tanhuma B, *Bo*, §12.
13. Witnesses who had seen the new moon's crescent. The court hallowed the new moon on the basis of their testimony.
14. RH 2:5–8.
15. By making them believe that the new moon of Nisan had been seen on the thirtieth of Adar, which was a Sabbath, when in fact it had not, so that the second day of Passover might fall on a Sunday and the counting of the *omer* might commence literally "on the morrow of the Sabbath" (Lev. 23:15), according to their interpretation of the words in Leviticus (Rashi).

they hired two men, one belonging to our party and one to theirs. The one of their party gave his evidence and departed. Then they asked our man: Tell us how you saw the moon. He replied: As I was going up the Ascent of Adummim,[1] I saw the new moon's crescent couched between two rocks, its head like that of a calf, its ears like those of a kid, its horns like those of a hind, and its tail lying between its legs. when I caught sight of its [strange configuration], I was so startled that I fell backward. [The fact is, I was bribed to make you believe that I had seen the new moon, and I promised that I would. Since you obviously do not believe me, I have not succeeded in doing what I promised to do. Being an honest man, I cannot keep the bribe I have not earned.] Since you do not believe me, here are the two hundred *zuz*. I cannot keep them.[2]

The sages then asked him: Who induced you to do this? He replied: I heard that the Boethusians were conspiring to mislead the sages, so I said [to myself]: I will go and tell the truth to the sages, lest scoundrels come and mislead them. The sages said: The two hundred *zuz* are yours as a gift, and the man who hired you shall be stretched out on the post [to receive a flogging].

There and then it was ordained that testimony should be received only from persons who were known to the sages.[3]

83. Formerly, beacons would be lit. But after the Cutheans spoiled their effectiveness,[4] it was enacted that messengers should go forth.

How were the beacons lit? They used to take long poles of cedarwood, reeds, olive wood, and short fibers of flax; a man would bind them together with a rope and go to the top of a hill, where he would set them on fire and then wave the pole back and forth and up and down, until he saw his fellow do the same on top of the next hill; and so, too, on top of the third hill, [and so on], until he finally saw the entire Diaspora as though it were one big bonfire spread out before him.

But how could the individual torches appear like one big bonfire? Because each and every person took a torch in his hand and went up to his roof.[5]

84. "This new moon is for you" (Exod. 12:2). It is under your authority, and you are not under its authority. [That the moon is under Israel's authority may be seen from] a story told of R. Hiyya the Elder. Once, on the night ushering in [a Wednesday preceding the day when] New Year's Day [had to be set], the [old] moon was so bright that cattle drivers were able to walk three *mil* by its light.[6] When R. Hiyya saw the moon, he threw pebbles and clods of earth at it, saying, "It is tomorrow that we wish to declare you the new moon, yet you have arisen now![7] Go, cover yourself." The moon vanished then and there.[8]

85. Our masters taught: The year may be intercalated [by the court] only in Judea. Still, if [for some reason] the decision was arrived at by the court in Galilee, the year is deemed to have been intercalated. However, Hananiah of Ono testified: If the decision was arrived at in Galilee, the year is not deemed to have been intercalated. Nor may the year be intercalated outside the Land. If it had been intercalated there, it is not to be regarded as intercalated, provided that it is possible to intercalate it in the Land of Israel.

R. Judah son of R. Simeon ben Pazzi said: What is R. Hananiah of Ono's proof? The verse "In His habitation shall ye seek, and thither thou shalt come" (Deut. 12:5). Whatever search you have to make in a religious matter is to be made only in the habitation of Him who is everywhere.[9]

86. R. Hananiah the son of R. Joshua's brother intercalated the year outside the Land. Rabbi[10] sent him three successive missives by the hand of R. Isaac and R. Nathan. In the first, he addressed him [respectfully] as "the saintly Hananiah." In the second, he reminded him: "The kids you left have become goats."[11] In the third, he reproved him: "If you do not yield, you may as well go forth into a wilderness of brambles, [erect a private high place], slaughter an animal, and let Nehunion[12] dash [the blood of the offering]."

After Hananiah read the first missive, he was deferential to the two emissaries. After he read the second, he continued to be deferential. But after he read the third, he started to insult them. They said to him, "How can you treat us so rudely after you had shown deference to us?"

Then R. Isaac stood up and exclaimed [ironically], "In the Torah it is said, 'These are the appointed seasons of Hananiah the son of R. Joshua's brother." They replied, "You mean, 'The appointed seasons of the Lord' " (Lev. 23:4). R. Isaac: "Only when so designated among us [in the Land of Israel]."

R. Nathan stood up and concluded [the interchange] with "For out of Babylonia shall go forth the Torah, and the word of the Lord from Nehar Pekod."[13] They said,

1. See Josh. 15:7.
2. Interpretation suggested by Leon Nemoy.
3. B. RH 22b; Tos RH 1:15.
4. By lighting their own beacons at the wrong time.
5. R. RH 22b–23a.
6. A sign that the new moon would not appear for at least twenty-four hours. See B. RH 20b.
7. Were the old moon visible during the night ushering in Wednesday, Thursday would have to be the thirtieth day in the month of Elul, and not New Year's Day. New Year's Day would then fall on Friday, and ten days later, the Day of Atonement on a Sunday, bringing about an impossible situation in households.

   Rabbi Saul Leeman of Providence, R.I., who explained the passage to the translator, suggests another possibility: R. Hiyya saw not the old moon, but, prematurely, the new moon, which would make Wednesday New Year's Day; the Day of Atonement would fall on a Friday, likewise intolerable in households.
8. B. RH 25a; Tanhuma B, *Bo*, §8.
9. In the Land of Israel. B. Sanh 11b; P. Ned 6:8, 40a.
10. An unnamed patriarch.
11. The young disciples have now become mature scholars, and their decisions should be obeyed.
12. The exilarch who approved of R. Hananiah's action.
13. Hananiah's place of residence in Babylonia.

"You mean—do you not?—'Out of Zion shall go forth the Torah, and the word of the Lord from Jerusalem' " (Isa. 2:3). R. Nathan: "Only when decisions have been reached among us [in the Land of Israel]."

R. Hananiah went and complained about Rabbi to R. Judah ben Beterah in Nisibis. R. Judah responded, "Follow them, follow them."

R. Hananiah: "Am I not aware of the kind of scholars I left there [in the Land of Israel]? Who will persuade me that they know how to reckon the calendar as well as I?"

Just because he says, "They do not know how to reckon the calendar as well as I," must they [in the Land of Israel] heed him? [On the contrary], precisely because they [in the Land of Israel] say, "We know how to reckon," he [R. Hananiah] must heed them [because they are many, and he is only one].

R. Judah ben Beterah rose up, mounted a horse [and rode off to have his opinion made known everywhere]. The places he got to, he got to; in the places where he did not get to, the people guided themselves by the inaccurate calendar [as reckoned by R. Hananiah].[1]

87. The hallowing of the new moon may be performed by three elders, but the intercalation of the year requires ten.

Whenever our masters went in to intercalate a year, ten learned elders entered the house of study, and with them the president of the court. They shut the windows and discussed the matter in detail throughout the night. At midnight they said to the president of the court: We wish to intercalate this year, so that it will have thirteen months. Will you join us in so decreeing? He responded: Whatever your decision, I am with you.

At this moment, a light shone forth from the house of study and illuminated them. Then they knew that God was satisfied with their decision.[2]

88. Our masters taught: The year is to be intercalated only by those who are invited in advance to the proceedings.

It once happened that Rabban Gamaliel [II] said, "Send me up seven scholars[3] early in the morning to the upper chamber[4] [to intercalate an additional month in the year]." But when he arrived in the morning, he found eight. So he said, "Whoever has come up without permission, let him go down." Samuel the Little stood up and said, "It is I who came up without permission. My purpose was not to participate in the intercalation of the year, but I felt the need to learn the practical application of the law." Rabban Gamaliel answered, "Sit down, my son, sit down. You are worthy of intercalating all the years that require it. However, the rabbis have declared, 'It should be done only by those specially invited to the proceedings.' "

In reality, it was not Samuel the Little [who was the uninvited one], but another man [present there]; Samuel only wished to save the intruder from humiliation.[5]

89. Our masters taught: A year cannot be intercalated unless the patriarch approves the decision. It once happened that Rabban Gamaliel was away seeking permission[6] from the governor of Syria, and as his return was delayed, the year was intercalated subject to Rabban Gamaliel's later approval. When Rabban Gamaliel returned, he gave his approval, with the result that the intercalation held good.[7]

90. Our masters taught: A year may be intercalated only when [an additional month] is required to [give time to repair] roads and bridges, [time to dry] ovens[8] [required for roasting] the paschal lambs, or time for pilgrims from distant Diasporas who have already left their homes but are as yet unable to reach [Jerusalem for Passover]. However, a year may not be intercalated because of heavy snows or cold weather,[9] or for the sake of pilgrims from distant Diasporas [who at the time of the court's deliberations] have not yet set out [from their homes].

Our masters taught further: A year may not be intercalated because kids or lambs [set aside for the paschal offering] or doves are still too young.[10] But such circumstances are considered an auxiliary reason[11] for intercalating a year. How so? R. Yannai gave such an instance by quoting [from a letter to the communities in the Diaspora] that Rabban Simeon ben Gamaliel had written: "We beg to inform you that the doves are still tender, the lambs are still too young, and the grain has not yet ripened. After considering the matter, I have deemed it advisable to add thirty days to the year."

We are taught that once Rabban Gamaliel [II][12] was sitting on a step on the Temple Mount, and standing before him was the well-known scribe Yohanan, who had three neatly trimmed sheets of parchment lying before him. "Take one sheet," Rabban Gamaliel said, "and write the following: 'To our brethren in Upper Galilee and to our brethren in Lower Galilee, may your peace grow great! We beg to inform you that the time has come for removing the accumulated tithes from the olive vats.'[13] Take another

1. P. Ned 6:8, 40a.
2. Exod. R. 15:20.
3. The seven, together with Rabban Gamaliel and his two aides, would make ten.
4. The meeting place of the rabbis.
5. B. Sanh 10b–11a.
6. "In order to secure confirmation of his appointment as patriarch . . . or to obtain permission for intercalating the year." (Isidore Epstein in Sanh, Soncino. p. 47, n. 2).
7. B. Sanh 11a.
8. Since these ovens were erected in the open and exposed to the winter rains, they became unfit for use.
9. These need not prevent pilgrims from proceeding to Jerusalem.
10. Doves were prescribed as offerings by women after childbirth and by persons cured from flux. As a rule, these people postponed bringing their offerings until Passover. Since they could bring young pigeons as their offerings in lieu of doves (Lev. 12:8), the year was not intercalated to meet their special needs.
11. Two reasons were required to justify intercalation.
12. He was noted for firmness in enforcing his authority.
13. "Tithes were of four classes: (a) the Levitical or first tithe; (b) the priestly tithe given by the Levites from their own tithe; (c) the second tithe, and (d) the triennial or poor tithe. The second tithe was to be eaten in Jerusalem every year of the septennial cycle, except the

sheet and write the following: 'To our brethren in the south, may your peace grow great! We beg to inform you that the time has come for removing the accumulated tithes from the corn sheaves.'[1] Take the third sheet and write the following: 'To our brethren the exiles in Babylonia and our brethren in Media, and to all the other exiled people of Israel, may your peace grow great forever! We beg to inform you that the doves are still tender, the lambs are still too young, and the crops are not yet ripe. After I, along with my colleagues,[2] have considered the matter, I have deemed it advisable to add thirty days to this year.' "[3]

91. Three cowherds were standing together [and talking], and the sages happened to overhear what they were saying. One said: If the early and the late sowing[4] sprout together [because the air is warm], the month is Adar; if not, it is not Adar, [but still Shevat]. The second cowherd said: If in the morning the frost is severe enough to [almost] kill an ox, and if at midday the ox lies in the shade of a fig tree and rubs its hide [against a tree to get relief from the heat], then it is already Adar; if not, it is not Adar. The third said: When a strong east wind is blowing and your breath can prevail against it, the month is Adar; if not, it is not Adar [but still Shevat]. That year the sages intercalated a month relying on what the cowherds had to say.[5]

92. Once, the following message [from the land of Israel] was sent to Rava: From Rakkath[6] there arrived a pair of scholars who, because they were in possession of certain articles[7] manufactured in Luz, had been apprehended by the eagle.[8] However, through divine mercy and their own merits, they escaped safely. Further, Nahshon's offspring[9] wished to set up a *netziv*,[10] but the Edomite[11] would not permit it.[12] Nevertheless, the members of the council[13] did meet, and they set up a *netziv* in the month in which Aaron the [High] Priest died.[14]

New Year's Day and the Day of Atonement

93. R. Phinehas and R. Hilkiah taught in the name of R. Simon: When all the ministering angels gather before the Holy One and say, "Master of the universe, what day is New Year's Day?" He replies, "Are you asking Me? Let us, you and Me, ask the court on earth."

R. Hoshaiah taught: When an earthly court decrees, "Today is New Year's Day," the Holy One tells the ministering angels, "Set up the judicial dais. Summon the advocates to defend and to prosecute. For My children have decreed that today is New Year's Day." If, however, the court has decided to intercalate the year [and thus to advance New Year's Day to] the next day, the Holy One tells the ministering angels, "Remove the judicial dais, dismiss all the advocates, since My children have decreed, 'Tomorrow is New Year's Day.' " And the proof?

"A decree for Israel is an ordinance for the God of Jacob" (Ps. 81:5). But when it is not a decree for Israel, it is not—if one dare speak thus—an ordinance for the God of Jacob.[15]

94. R. Kruspedai said in the name of R. Yohanan: On New Year's Day, three books are opened—one with the names of the completely righteous, one with the names of the completely wicked, and one with the names of those who are neither completely righteous nor completely wicked. The completely righteous: their verdict —life—is written down and sealed at once. The completely wicked: their verdict—death—is written down and sealed at once. Those neither completely righteous nor completely wicked: their verdict is suspended between New Year's Day and the Day of Atonement. If they are deemed to deserve it [by resolving to repent], they are inscribed for life; if [they fail to repent] and are therefore deemed not to deserve life, they are inscribed for death.[16]

95. R. Isaac said: Why on New Year's Day do we sound a *tekiah* and a *teruah* while seated, and then again a

third and sixth, when it was replaced by the poor tithe. The whole series of tithes reached its completion close upon Passover in the fourth and seventh year, and all the tithes which ought to have been paid in the course of the three years, but which, whether through negligence or other circumstances, were not given, had to be removed on the eve of Passover, and a prayer of confession offered, in accordance with Deut. 26:13." (Isidore Epstein in Sanh, Soncino, p. 48, n. 4).

1. "The chief product of Galilee was olives, and that of the south, wheat" (Isidore Epstein in Sanh, Soncino, p. 48, n. 5).
2. He thus associated his colleagues with the epistle, whereas his son, though noted for his modesty, did not refer to his colleagues.
3. B. Sanh 11a.
4. The wheat sown earlier, and the barley sown later (Rashi).
5. B. Sanh 18b.
6. Tiberias (see B. Meg 6a).
7. Fringes dyed purple and used for garments that had four corners. See Num. 15:38.
8. The eagle was the principal standard of the Roman legions—hence, the Roman government.
9. The patriarch, who descended from Nahshon, the first of the princes of Judah. See Exod. 6:23.
10. *Netziv* ("military post") is a cipher for "month"; that is, they wished to intercalate a month in the year.
11. "Primarily name given to Esau (cf. Gen. 25:30; 36:1). Edom is used by the Talmudists for the Roman Empire, as they applied to Rome every passage of the Bible referring to Edom or Esau. In the Middle Ages it came to be used symbolically of Christianity, and that accounts for the substitution of 'Aramean' in censored editions" (Sanh, Soncino, p. 52, n. 8).
12. "The above messages were sent in this obscure form to prevent them from being stopped by the Government under the reign of Constantius II (337–361 C.E.), when the persecutions of the Jews reached such a height that, as in the days of Hadrian, all religious exercises, including the computation of the calendar, were forbidden under pain of severe punishment. Cf. [Heinrich] Graetz" (Sanh, Soncino. p. 52, n. 9).
13. The Sanhedrin.
14. The month of Av. B. Sanh 12a.
15. P. RH 1:3, 57b; MTeh 81:6.
16. B. RH 16b and En Yaakov, ad loc.

tekiah and a *teruah* while standing? To confuse Satan.[1]

R. Abbahu said: Why do we sound a ram's horn? Because the Holy One said: Sound before Me a ram's horn so that I may remember on your behalf the binding of Isaac son of Abraham and deem it for you as if you had bound yourselves on the altar before Me.[2]

96. R. Abbahu taught: The ministering angels spoke up to the Holy One: Master of the universe, why do Israel not chant praise before You on New Year's Day and on the Day of Atonement? He replied: Is it possible that while the King is seated on the throne of judgment, with books of death open before Him, Israel should be chanting praise?[3]

97. R. Tanhuma said: It once happened on the eve of the Day of Atonement that a certain tailor in Rome went to the market to buy fish and found only one fish.

So he and the governor's servant [who was also there] vied for the purchase [of the fish], this one bidding up the price and that one bidding up the price, until it reached twelve denars. In the end, it was the tailor who bought the fish. At mealtime, the governor asked his servant: Why did you not serve fish? The servant replied: My lord, why conceal from you what happened? I went to the market, where there was only one fish left, and I and a Jew found ourselves vying for it until he bid up the price to twelve denars. I wonder, now, what you would have had me do? Bring you a fish that cost twelve denars? The governor: Who is the Jew? The servant: So-and-so. The governor: Go and summon him, for apparently the Jew owns a treasure that properly belongs to the king. The servant went forth and summoned the Jew. The governor asked him: What is your work? The Jew replied: I am a tailor. The governor asked: How is it that you, a mere Jewish tailor, presume to eat a fish that cost twelve denars? The Jew replied: My lord, we Jews have one day that atones for all the sins we have committed throughout the year. When this day comes, should we not honor it? The governor said: Since you bring such a reason for what you have done, you are free to go.

How did the Holy One requite the tailor? When the tailor cut open the fish, God had him find a pearl of purest ray in it, and on the money he got for the pearl he sustained himself all the rest of his days.[4]

98. He who says again and again, "I will sin and then repent"—he will be given no opportunity to repent. He who says, "I will sin, and the Day of Atonement will procure forgiveness for me"—the Day of Atonement will not procure forgiveness for him. Furthermore, the Day of Atonement procures forgiveness only for man's transgressions against Him who is everywhere, but it does not procure forgiveness for man's transgressions against his neighbor until the man has conciliated his neighbor. R. Eleazar ben Azariah expounded this principle by quoting, "From all your sins before the Lord shall ye be clean" (Lev. 16:30). That is, only for man's transgressions against Him who is everywhere does the Day of Atonement procure forgiveness, but for man's transgressions against his neighbor, the Day of Atonement does not procure forgiveness until he has conciliated his neighbor.

R. Akiva said: Happy are you, Israel! Who is He before whom you are cleansed? And who is He that makes you clean? Your Father who is in heaven, for He said, "I will sprinkle clean water upon you, and ye shall be clean" (Ezek. 36:25). And Scripture further says, "Thou pool[5] of Israel, the Lord!" (Jer. 17:13). Just as the pool cleanses those who are unclean, so the Holy One cleanses Israel.[6]

99. You will find that the numerical value of the letters in *hstn* [Satan], "the Adversary," is three hundred and sixty-four,[7] which is one short of the number of days in the year. Thus the Adversary is given the authority to make accusations against the children of Israel on all the days of the year except the Day of Atonement, for the Holy One said to him, "You have no authority to touch them. Nevertheless, go and see what they are occupied with." Then, when the Adversary goes forth and finds all of them at fasting and prayer, dressed in white [penitential] garments and cloaked like the ministering angels, he immediately returns in shame and confusion. The Holy One asks him, "What have you found out about My children?" He answers, "They are like the ministering angels, and I am unable to touch them." At once, the Holy One shackles the Adversary and announces to the children of Israel, "I have forgiven you."[8]

100. "I am black, but comely" (Song 1:5). "I am black" throughout the days of the year; "but comely" on the Day of Atonement.[9]

101. Rabban Simeon ben Gamaliel said: There never were greater days of joy in Israel than the fifteenth of Av and the Day of Atonement. On these days the daughters of Jerusalem used to walk out in white garments, which they borrowed in order not to put to shame anyone who owned none. The daughters of Jerusalem would go out and dance in the vineyards. What did they chant? "Young man,

---

1. "The devotion of the Jews to the precepts nullifies Satan's accusation against them (Rashi). The shofar on New Year is blown twice: once at the close of the morning prayer and of the reading of the Law while the congregation is seated, and again during the *Musaf* prayers, when the people stand. The shofar was originally blown only at the morning service, whence it was transferred to a later hour in the *Musaf* because their enemies on one occasion took the shofar blasts early in the morning as a call to arms, whereupon they attacked the Jews. The custom of blowing the shofar at *Musaf* service was retained even after the rite had been restored to the morning service" (RH, Soncino, p. 61, n. 5).
2. B. RH 16a–b.
3. B. RH 32b.
4. Gen. R. 11:4; PR 23:6.
5. The Hebrew *mikveh* means "pool for immersion" as well as "hope," the usual translation here.
6. B. Yoma 85b.
7. h = 5, s [*sin*] = 300, t [*tet*] = 9, n = 50.
8. MTeh 27:4.
9. Song R. 1:5, §2.

lift up your eyes and see what you choose for yourself. Do not set your eyes on beauty, but set your eyes on good family. 'Grace is deceitful, and beauty is vain; but a woman that feareth the Lord, she shall be praised' " (Prov. 31:30).

Our masters taught: What did the beautiful women among the daughters of Jerusalem chant? "Set your eyes on beauty—what is woman for, if not for beauty?" What did those among them who came of noble families chant? "Look for good lineage—woman has been created to bring children into the world [and our lineage is good]." What did those among them who were rich chant? "Set your eyes on moneyed ones." What did those among them in modest circumstances, the poor, and the homely chant? "Carry off your 'purchase' in the name of Heaven, but on condition that you crown us with gold coins; [then we, too, will appear to be rich and beautiful]."[1]

Pilgrimage Festivals

102. "On the eighth day, ye shall have a solemn assembly" (Num. 29:35). The Holy One said to Israel: Rejoicing becomes you, appointed seasons become you, festal days become you.

"Thou hast increased for the nation" (Isa. 26:15). When You multiply festal days for the nations of the world, they eat, drink, and carouse, attend their theaters and circuses, and provoke You with their [foul] utterances and [vile] deeds. But Israel are not like that. When You increase festal days for them, they eat, drink, and rejoice, but then attend synagogues and houses of study, and augment the number of their prayers.[2]

103. In Sepphoris, a heathen posed a question to R. Akiva: Why do you go on observing the appointed seasons? Did not the Holy One say to you, "Your New Moons and your appointed seasons My soul hateth" (Isa. 1:14)? R. Akiva replied: Had the Holy One said, "*My* New Moons and *My* appointed seasons My soul hateth," I might have agreed with you. But what He said was: "*Your* New Moons and *your* appointed seasons," meaning the appointed seasons that Jeroboam son of Nebat instituted, of which Scripture says, "Jeroboam ordained a feast in the eighth month . . . even in the month which he had devised of his own heart" (1 Kings 12:32–33). But the appointed seasons you refer to will never cease, nor will the New Moons. Why not? Because they belong to the Holy One, as is said, "These are the appointed seasons of the Lord" (Lev. 23:4).[3]

104. R. Sheshet said in the name of R. Eleazar ben Azariah: He who despises the festivals[4] is as though he worshiped idols, as implied by the fact that "Thou shalt make thee no molten god" (Exod. 34:17) is followed directly by "The [seven-day] feast of unleavened bread thou shalt keep" (Exod. 34:18).[5]

1. B. Ta 26b and 31a, and En Yaakov, ad loc.
2. Yalkut, *Pinhas*, §782.
3. Tanhuma B, *Pinhas*, §17; Yalkut, Isa., §255.
4. Does work during the intermediate days. So Rashbam, ad loc.
5. The juxtaposition implies their being equated. B. Pes 118a.

105. Our masters taught: A man is obligated to cause his wife, his children, and the members of his household to rejoice, as is said, "Thou shalt rejoice in thy feast, thou, and thy son, and thy daughter," etc. (Deut. 16:14). With what is one to cause them to rejoice? With wine. But R. Judah said: Men, with what is suitable for them, and women, with what is suitable for them. Men, with what is suitable for them—with wine. And women, with what? R. Joseph taught: In Babylonia, with colored garments. In the Land of Israel, with shiny linen garments.[6]

106. We have been taught that R. Eliezer said: On a festival, a man is either to eat and drink or to sit and study. But R. Joshua said: Divide the day—half for eating and drinking, and half for spending in the house of study. R. Yohanan noted: Both deduce it from the same verses. One verse says, "A solemn assembly to the Lord thy God" (Deut. 16:8), while another says, "Ye shall have a solemn assembly" (Num. 29:35). How so? R. Eliezer took the two verses to mean: "Either entirely to God or entirely to yourselves," while R. Joshua took them to mean: "Divide the day—half to God and half to yourselves."[7]

107. The appointed seasons were given to Israel for no other purpose than for them to enjoy themselves. The Holy One said: If you enjoy yourselves [this year], you will do so again the following year, as is said, "When thou keepest this ordinance in its season, then from year to year" (Exod. 13:10)—you will be given the opportunity to do so from year to year.[8]

108. "On a festal day be joyful" (Eccles. 7:14). R. Levi interpreted the verse to mean: On the festal days which I have given you, be joyful and cause the Holy One to rejoice. Even when a year of drought[9] comes, go out to your vineyard, look around, and be joyful; look around your olive yard and be joyful.[10]

109. R. Isaac said: A man should purify himself for a festival.[11]

110. R. Isaac said: Where is the proof that during a festival a man should go calling on his master? The verse, "Wherefore wilt thou go to [the man of God] today? It is neither New Moon nor festival"[12] (2 Kings 4:23).

Our masters taught: It once happened that R. Ilai went calling on his master R. Eliezer in Lydda just before a festival. R. Eliezer said, "Ilai, you do not seem to be among those who rest on a festival." For R. Eliezer used to say, "I praise the indolent who do not go out of their houses during a festival, in keeping with 'Thou shalt re-

6. B. Pes 109a and En Yaakov, ad loc.
7. B. Pes 68b; Betz 15b.
8. Tanhuma, *Bereshit*, §4.
9. "Without drought" in BR is a euphemism.
10. Confident that God will bestow rain. Eccles. R. 7:14, §3.
11. B. RH 16b.
12. JV: "neither New Moon nor Sabbath." But "Sabbath" can also mean "festival," as in Lev. 23:11.

joice in thy feast, thou, together with thy son, together with thy daughter,' etc." (Deut. 16:14).[1]

111. You find three verses that command you to rejoice in the Feast of Tabernacles: "And thou shalt rejoice in thy feast" (Deut. 16:14); "And thou shalt be altogether joyful" (Deut. 16:15); "And ye shall rejoice before the Lord your God seven days" (Lev. 23:40). For Passover, however, you will not find even one command to rejoice. Why not? Because in the season of Passover, judgment is being passed on field crops,[2] and no man knows whether the year will bring forth crops or not. So, too, you find that for the Feast of Weeks there is but one command to rejoice: "And thou shalt keep the Feast of Weeks unto the Lord thy God . . . and thou shalt rejoice . . . thou, and thy son," etc. (Deut. 16:10–11). Why that one? Because the field crop has already been brought into the house. Then why not two commands to rejoice? Because judgment is then being passed on fruits of trees. For Tabernacles, however, when both field crops and fruits of the tree have been brought into the house, three commands to rejoice are set down.

Another answer to the question of why Scripture gives no command to rejoice even once during Passover: because the Egyptians died during the Passover. Therefore you find that, though we read the entire *Hallel* on each of the seven days of Tabernacles [an entirely joyful feast], on Passover we read the entire *Hallel* only on the first day and the night preceding it. Why not on the other days of the festival? Because of "Rejoice not when thine enemy falleth, and let not thy heart be glad when he stumbleth" (Prov. 24:17).[3]

112. We have been taught that R. Judah said in the name of R. Akiva: Why did the Torah say, "Offer an *omer* of barley on Passover"? Because Passover is the season of produce. Therefore the Holy One said, "Bring before Me an *omer* on Passover, so that the produce in the fields may be blessed for you." Why did the Torah say, "Bring two loaves of wheat bread on the Feast of Weeks"? Because the Feast of Weeks is the time when fruits ripen on the trees. So the Holy One said, "Bring into My presence two loaves of wheat bread on the Feast of Weeks, in order that the fruits of trees may be blessed for you."[4] And why did the Torah say, "Pour libations of water before Me on Tabernacles"? Because Tabernacles is the time when the year's rains begin. So the Holy One said, "Pour out before Me waters of libation during Tabernacles, so that the year's rains be blessed for you." The Holy One also said, "On New Year's Day, recite before Me texts that mention kingships, remembrances, and shofars—kingships, so that you may proclaim Me King over you; remembrances, so that remembrance of you may rise up before Me for favor. And how will remembrance of you be made to rise up before Me? By the shofar."[5]

113. The Boethusians insisted that the Feast of Weeks must always fall on a day after Sabbath [on a Sunday]. R. Yohanan ben Zakkai joined them in a discussion and finally said, "Fools that you are. What proof have you?" Not one of them could answer him, except an old man, who babbled away, saying, "Moses our teacher loved Israel, and since he knew that the Feast of Weeks lasted only one day, he fixed it on the day after the Sabbath, so that Israel might enjoy themselves for two successive days." R. Yohanan quoted to him the following verse: "It is eleven days' journey from Horeb to Kadesh-barnea by way of Mount Seir" (Deut. 1:2), and went on: "If Moses loved Israel so much, why did he detain them in the wilderness forty years?" "Master," the old man said, "is it with such an argument that you would dismiss me?" "Fool," R. Yohanan answered, "should not our perfect Torah be as convincing as your idle talk? Now, one verse says, 'Ye shall number fifty days' [Lev. 23:16], while another says, 'Seven weeks shall there be complete' [Lev. 23:15]. How can the two verses be reconciled?[6] Only by assuming that the second verse refers to the time when the [first day of the] festival [of Passover] falls on a Sabbath,[7] while the first verse refers to the time when the [first day of the] festival falls on a weekday."[8]

114. Our masters taught: In the words "Ye shall sit in booths" (Lev. 23:42), "sit" means "reside." Hence, they went on to say: During the seven days [of Tabernacles], a man is to make his sukkah the permanent abode, and his home the occasional one. How? If he has beautiful vessels, he should bring them up to the sukkah.[9] If he has beautiful divans, he should bring them up to the sukkah. He should eat and drink, pass his leisure, and study in the sukkah.[10]

115. R. Eliezer said: One is obligated to eat fourteen meals in the sukkah, one each day and one each night.

King Agrippa's administrator asked R. Eliezer: May a man such as I, who eats only one meal a day, eat only one meal in the sukkah and be free of further obligation? R. Eliezer replied: Every day you prolong your meal with all kinds of delicacies to enhance your own honor; for this occasion, will you not prolong the meal with but one more delicacy in honor of your Maker?[11]

116. We have been taught that R. Eleazar bar Zadok said: Such was the custom of distinguished men of Jerusalem: a man would leave his house with the lulav cluster in his hand. He would walk to the synagogue with the lulav cluster in his hand. He would read the Shema and recite the *Tefillah* with the lulav cluster in his hand. But

---

1. B. Suk 27b.
2. RH 1:1.
3. Yalkut, *Emor*, §654.
4. The firstfruits of trees were not brought as offerings until the Feast of Weeks.
5. B. RH 16a and En Yaakov, ad loc.
6. The first verse seems to speak of fifty days regardless of the completeness of the weeks; the second verse, which speaks of "seven weeks . . . complete," seems to imply *full* weeks, each commencing on a Sunday.
7. In which case there are seven complete weeks.
8. Accordingly, the Feast of Weeks may fall on any day of the week. B. Men 65b.
9. The sukkah was built on the roof.
10. B. Suk 28b.
11. B. Suk 27a.

before he read in the Torah or lifted his hands [for the priests' benediction], he laid the lulav cluster on the ground. When he went to visit the sick or comfort the mourners, it was with the lulav cluster in his hand. But when he entered the house of study, he would have his son, his slave, or his messenger take his lulav cluster home.[1] You are thus made aware how zealous those men were in the performance of precepts.[2]

117. "And ye shall take for you" (Lev. 23:40). "For you" here means "what is yours." The sages inferred from this verse that no one may fulfill his obligation on the first day of Tabernacles with a lulav cluster that belongs to his fellow, unless he later has given it to him as a gift.

It once happened that Rabban Gamaliel, R. Joshua, R. Eleazar ben Azariah, and R. Akiva were traveling on a ship, and only Rabban Gamaliel had a lulav, which he had purchased for a thousand *zuz*. Rabban Gamaliel took it up, fulfilled his obligation with it, and gave it to R. Joshua as a gift. R. Joshua took it up, fulfilled his obligation with it, and gave it to R. Eleazar ben Azariah as a gift. Finally, R. Akiva took it up, fulfilled his obligation with it, and gave it back to Rabban Gamaliel as a gift.[3]

118. "On the eighth day ye shall have [an additional] solemn assembly" (Num. 29:35). The need for an additional day may be illustrated by the parable of a king who invited his children to a feast for such-and-such a number of days. When their time came to depart, he said: My children, I beg of you, stay on for an additional day—the prospect of separation from you is hard for me.[4]

119. R. Levi said: God desired to give to the children of Israel a festival for each and every month during the summer, so He gave them Passover in Nisan, the minor Passover[5] in Iyyar, and the Feast of Weeks in Sivan. But as He was about to give them a notable feast in Tammuz, they made themselves the golden calf,[6] and as a result He took away the festivals He had intended for the months of Tammuz, Av, and Elul. He made up, however, for Israel's being deprived of the festivals He had intended them to celebrate during the three previous months by assigning them all to the following month, Tishri, and having the three festivals—New Year's Day, the Day of Atonement, and Tabernacles—celebrated within Tishri's span. Then the Holy One said to them: Since Tishri has been used to make up for the other months and has not been given a festival that is its own, let it be given its own day. Hence, "On the eighth day ye shall have [an additional] solemn assembly" (Num. 29:35).

About this matter, Scripture says, "Give a portion [of honor] to seven, and also to [the day that brings the number up to] eight" (Eccles. 11:2): "Give a portion [of honor]" to Tabernacles' seven days: "and also to [the day that brings the number up to] eight." Here the Holy One charged Israel concerning the eighth day's holiness.[7]

120. "Solemn confining[8] by you" (Num. 29:35). Of the confining enjoined at Passover, Scripture says in Deuteronomy, "Solemn confining by the Lord thy God" (Deut. 16:8), while here in Numbers, Scripture says of the Eighth Day Festival, "Solemn confining by you" (Num. 29:35). R. Hanina bar Adda explained: For your sake, says God, on Passover I confine the winds and the rains in order that you may occupy yourselves with harvesting your fields. But during the present season, during Tabernacles, when for My sake you [make pilgrimages to Jerusalem and there—absent from your fields—] confine yourselves [in sukkahs], I open for the sake of your crops the treasuries wherein are winds, wherein are rains.[9]

121. When you consider the matter, you would say that as the concluding Festival of Weeks follows Passover after an interval of fifty days, so the festival at Tabernacles' conclusion should follow Tabernacles after an interval of fifty days. Why, then, does the festival come right after Tabernacles? In answer, R. Joshua ben Levi asked: What parable is apt here? He replied: The one of a king who had many sons, some married to wives in a place far away and some married to wives in a place nearby. Whenever they wished to, those married to wives in the place nearby would come visit him, and when they wished to leave, he was not distressed. Why not? Because, since the journey was short, whenever they wished to come and return home, they could easily come and go [in one day]. But when those who were married to wives in a distant place came to him and then wished to leave, he would press them to remain with him for yet one more day. Likewise, at Passover the days of summer are to begin soon enough, so that after a fifty days' interim Israel may conveniently come up to Jerusalem for Passover's concluding festival, the Feast of Weeks. But the season after Tabernacles is the rainy season, when the roads are troublesome. Therefore the Holy One said: As long as the children of Israel are here, let them also observe the concluding festival. Hence, "on the eighth day, for your own sake, ye shall have a festival" (Num. 29:35).[10]

Hanukkah and Purim

122. In the days of the wicked kingdom of Greece, it was decreed upon Israel that whoever had a bolt on his door should engrave upon it the words "I have neither portion nor heritage in the God of Israel." At once, Israel went and pulled out the bolts from their doors. It was also

1. His absorption in study might cause him to drop it or forget its very existence.
2. B. Suk 41b.
3. B. Suk 41b.
4. B. Suk 55b; Rashi on Lev. 23:36.
5. See Num. 9:10ff.
6. On the seventeenth of Tammuz, after which Israel remained in disgrace until the tenth of Tishri, the day God pardoned Israel's sin. See PR 26:6; B. Ta 28b; and Rashi.
7. Yalkut, *Pinhas*, §782.
8. JV: "solemn assembly." However, *atzeret* may also mean "solemn confining."
9. Yalkut, *Pinhas*, §782.
10. Ibid.

decreed that whoever had an ox should write on its horn, "I have neither portion nor heritage in the God of Israel." At once, Israel went and sold their oxen.[1]

123. Why are lamps kindled during Hanukkah? At the time that the sons of the Hasmonean triumphed and entered the Temple, they found there eight spits of iron that they set up firmly and then kindled wicks [with oil they poured into the depressions at the top].[2]

124. With the beginning of Adar we may increase indulgence in amusements.[3]

125. R. Samuel bar judah said: Esther sent word to the sages, saying: [By a book or a festival], fix the memory of me for generations to come. They sent word to her: Such an act would cause ill will against us among the nations of the world. She replied to them: But I am already recorded in the Chronicles of the Kings of Media and Persia.[4]

126. Rava said: On Purim it is a man's duty to mellow himself with wine until he cannot tell the difference between "Cursed be Haman" and "Blessed be Mordecai."

Rabbah and R. Zera joined together in a Purim feast. Rabbah became mellow and plied R. Zera with so much drink that he passed out. The next morning, Rabbah besought mercy and revived him.[5] But the following year, when Rabbah said to R. Zera, "Let the master come and we will celebrate Purim together," R. Zera replied, "[Sorry], but one cannot expect a miracle on every occasion."[6]

The Scroll of Fasts

127. Our masters taught: Who wrote the Scroll of Fasts?[7] The sages replied: Hananiah ben Hezekiah and his companions, for, cherishing the troubles [from which they had been redeemed, they wished to record them].

Rabban Simeon ben Gamaliel said: We, too, cherish [the memory of] such troubles. But what are we to do? If we were to attempt to record them, we would be unequal to the task [since there are so many of them]. Another reason: a fool does not realize he is being oppressed. Still another reason: the flesh of a corpse does not feel the scalpel.[8]

128. Rav and R. Hanina hold that the Scroll of Fasts has been annulled, for only while there is stability[9] are those days to be days of joy and gladness. But when there is no longer such stability, public fasts may be proclaimed on those days. R. Yohanan and R. Joshua ben Levi said: The Scroll of Fasts has not been annulled. Only the four fasts[10] that the Holy One linked with the Temple structure[11] are to become occasions for joy, but the others remain what they were [days on which no public fasts are to be proclaimed].[12]

Fasts

129. [In Jewish history] five punishments befell our forebears on the seventeenth day of Tammuz and another five on the ninth of Av. On the seventeenth day of Tammuz, the Tablets were broken [at the foot of Mount Sinai], the daily offering in the Temple ceased, the city of Jerusalem was breached, Apostomos burned a Torah scroll and set up an idol in the Temple.[13] On the ninth of Av, it was decreed upon our forebears [in the wilderness] that they were not to enter the Land, the Temple was destroyed the first time and the second time, Bethar was captured, and the city [of Jerusalem] was plowed over.[14]

130. R. Simeon said: I do not agree with four expositions R. Akiva used to set forth. [One of them]: R. Akiva used to say that "the fast of the fourth month" (Zech. 8:19) is the ninth of Tammuz, when the city was breached. "The fast of the fifth month" (ibid.) is the ninth of Av, on which the house of our God was burned. "The fast of the seventh month" (ibid.) is the third of Tishri, on which Gedaliah son of Ahikam was slain, assassinated by Ishmael son of Nethaniah.[15] [The fact of a fast's being instituted on that day] shows that the death of the righteous is put on a level with the burning of the house of God. "The fast of the tenth month" (ibid.) is the tenth of Tevet, on which the king of Babylon invested Jerusalem. [It might be asked]: Should this not have been mentioned first?[16] Why then was it mentioned in this place [last]? So as to list the months in their proper order. I, however [continued R. Simeon], do not explain the matter in this way. My view is that "the fast of the tenth month" [does not refer to the tenth of Tevet, which was the first of the calamities, but to] the fifth of Tevet, on which news came to the Diaspora that the city had been smitten, and they put the day of the report on the same footing as the day of [the Temple's] burning. My view is more probable than his, because I follow the chronological order. He does not; true, he does follow the order of months, but I [follow also] the order in which the calamities occurred.[17]

1. Midrash le-Hanukkah (BhM 1:133).
2. PR 2:1.
3. B. Ta 29a.
4. B. Meg 7a.
5. So interpreted by Samuel Edels, ad loc.
6. B. Meg 7a.
7. An ancient scroll in which the days on which deliverances had taken place were recorded. On those days, no public fasts were to be observed.
8. B. Shab 13b.
9. While the Temple stands.
10. See below in this chapter, §130.
11. Its burning.
12. B. RH 18b.
13. See Ta 4:6. Gedaliah Alon identified Apostomos as an officer during the revolt against Trajan in 116–17 C.E. See his *Toledot ha-Yehudim be-Eretz Yisrael* . . . 2 vols. (Tel Aviv, 1953–56), 1:259.
14. B. Ta 26b.
15. See Jer. 41:1–2.
16. The event commemorated being chronologically the first of those mentioned.
17. B. RH 18b; Tos Sot 6:10; Yalkut, Zech., §574.

131. With the beginning of Av we must decrease indulgence in amusements.[1]

132. R. Judah said in the name of Rav: Such was the practice of R. Judah son of R. Ilai: on the eve of the ninth of Av, dry bread with salt would be brought to him, and he would sit between the oven and the stove.[2] He would eat the bread with the salt and wash it down with a ladle of water. And he looked as though his dear relative were lying dead before him.[3]

133. Our masters taught: All the laws that apply to mourning apply also to the ninth of Av. On that day eating, drinking, bathing, anointing, wearing shoes, and sexual intercourse are forbidden. It is also forbidden to read in the Five Books, the Prophets, and the Writings, or to study the Mishnah in any of its six divisions, Midrash, *Halakhot* and *Aggadot*.[4] However, according to R. Meir, one may read those parts of the Torah that he has not been in the habit of reading and study those parts of the Mishnah that he has not been in the habit of studying.[5] One may also read the book of Lamentations, Job, and the ominous portions in Jeremiah. The children are not free from school. On the other hand, R. Judah said: One is not allowed to read even parts of the Torah that he has not been in the habit of reading or study parts of the Mishnah that he has not been in the habit of studying, but he may read the book of Lamentations, Job, and the ominous portions of Jeremiah. And children are free from school. The reason for the prohibition [of study] is set down in the verse "The precepts of the Lord are right, rejoicing the heart" (Ps. 19:9).[6]

134. Some [congregations] read the book of Lamentations in the evening, while others postpone it to the [following] morning, after the reading of the Torah. At that time the reader stands up, his head sprinkled with ashes, his clothes covered with them, weeping and lamenting, reads the book of Lamentations. If he is able to translate it, he may do so; but if not, he gives the book to one who knows how to translate, and [that person] translates it, so that the rest of the men, women, and children may understand it. The reader precedes the reading by saying, "Blessed be the true Judge." Some [congregations] place the Torah scroll, wrapped in a black covering, on the ground and say, "The crown is fallen from our head" (Lam. 5:16). Garments are rent and words of mourning are spoken, like that of a man whose dead lies before him. Some change their [customary] places [in the synagogue]; some come down from their benches [and sit on the floor]. All of them, covered with ashes, refrain from greeting one another all night and all day, until the people have finished reading their book of Lamentations.[7]

135. R. Hana bar Bizna said in the name of R. Simeon the Pious: What is the meaning of the verse "Thus saith the Lord of hosts: The fast of the fourth month, and the fast of the fifth, and the fast of the seventh, and the fast of the tenth shall be to the house of Judah joy and gladness" (Zech. 8:19)? How can the prophet call the four days "fasts" and at the same time call them "joy and gladness"? He intimates by this that when there is stability,[8] they will be for "joy and gladness." But as long as there is no stability, they will remain fasts.[9]

136. "And he said: 'If Esau come to the one camp, and smite it' " (Gen. 32:9); this alludes to our brethren in the south. "Then the camp which is left shall escape" (ibid.) alludes to our brethren in the Diaspora.[10]

Nevertheless, said R. Hoshaia, though they escaped, we fast Mondays and Thursdays on their behalf.[11]

1. B. Ta 26b.
2. As an act of humility.
3. B. Ta 30a–b.
4. Because such studies give pleasure.
5. Because they require exertion.
6. B. Ta 30a.
7. Sof 18.
8. The Temple rebuilt.
9. B. RH 18b.
10. To Babylonia. While the Jews in Judea ["our brethren in the south"] were decimated by the Romans, the ones in Babylonia were unscathed.
11. Gen. R. 76:3; Yalkut, *Va-yishlah*, §131.

PART IV

CHAPTER ONE

THE HOLY ONE, BLESSED BE HE, AND RELATIONS BETWEEN HUMAN BEINGS AND HIM WHO IS EVERYWHERE

The Holy One, Blessed Be He

1. Resh Lakish said: In the verse "I will sing unto the Lord, for He is greatly exalted" (Exod. 15:1), the song is to Him who is exalted above all who are exalted. For a master said: The king of beasts is the lion. The king of cattle, the ox. The king of fowl, the eagle. And man is exalted over all of them. But the Holy One, blessed be He, is exalted above them all and above the world, all of it.[1]

2. Every entity regards itself as exalted over another entity. Darkness regards itself as exalted over the deep, because it is above it. Air, as exalted over water, because it is above it. Fire, as exalted over air, because it is above it. The heavens, as exalted over fire, because they are above it. But the Holy One, blessed be He, is truly exalted over them all.[2]

3. "Hear, O Israel, the Lord our God, the Lord is one" (Deut. 6:4). The Holy One, blessed be He, said to Israel: My children, note that all I created, I created in pairs. Heaven and earth are a pair; the sun and the moon are a pair; Adam and Eve are a pair; this world and the world-to-come are a pair. But My glory is one, and unique in the world.[3]

4. R. Hanina said: The seal of the Holy One, blessed be He, is *emet* [spelled '*mt*], "truth." In explaining the significance of the letters in this word, Resh Lakish said: The first letter, *alef*, is the first letter of the alphabet; the second letter, *mem*, is in the middle, and the third letter, *tav*, is the last letter, thus signifying, "I am the first, and I am the last, and beside Me there is no God" (Isa. 44:6). "I am the first"—I did not receive My kingdom from anyone else. "And beside Me there is no God—I have no partner. "And with the last am the same" (Isa. 41:4)—I am not destined to turn over My kingdom to anyone else.[4]

5. R. Isaac taught: A verse in Deuteronomy speaks of "the skies, the dwelling place of the eternal God" (Deut. 33:27). But we would not have known whether the Holy One, blessed be He, is the dwelling place of the world or whether the world is the dwelling place of the Holy One, blessed be He, unless Moses had come and given us the answer by saying, "Lord, Thou hast been our dwelling place . . . from everlasting" (Ps. 90:1).

R. Yose bar Halafta said: We would not have known whether the Holy One, blessed be He, is secondary to His world or whether His world is secondary to Him[5] unless the Holy One Himself, blessed be He, had made the answer plain by saying, "Behold, there is a place by Me" (Exod. 33:21), meaning: "The place is by Me—secondary to Me—and not I to My place."

R. Abba bar Yudan said: He is like a warrior riding upon a horse, with the caparison hanging down on one side and the other; the horse does the bidding of the rider, but the rider does not do the bidding of the horse.

R. Huna said in the name of R. Ammi: Why is the epithet "Place" used for the Name of the Holy One, blessed be He? Because He is the place of the world, and the world is not His place.[6]

6. No spot on earth is devoid of the Presence.[7]

7. R. Hoshaia said: What is meant by "Thou art the Lord, Thou alone . . . and the host of heaven worshipeth Thee" (Neh. 9:6)? Your emissaries are not like the emissaries of flesh and blood. The emissaries of flesh and blood have to report the performance of their task back to the place from which they were sent. But Your emissaries can report the performance of their task at the very place to which they were sent, as is said, "Canst thou send forth lightnings, that they may go, and say unto thee: 'Here we are'?" (Job 38:35). Scripture does not aver "that they may come back and say," but "that they may go and say," which proves that the Presence, being in every place, [is there to receive the lightnings' report].[8]

8. "Bless the Lord, O my soul" (Ps. 103:1). The soul—no man knows where its place is. So, too, the Holy One, blessed be He—no creature knows where His place is. Not even the celestial creatures that carry the throne of glory know where His place is, nor in what place He abides. Therefore they say: Whatever place His glory is, "Blessed be the glory of the Lord wherever His place may be" (Ezek. 3:12).[9]

9. It happened that a certain man asked Rabban Gamaliel, "In what place does the Holy One, blessed be He, abide?" Rabban Gamaliel replied, "I do not know." The man said, "Is this your wisdom—the wisdom of the people who pray to God every day yet do not know where His place is?" Rabban Gamaliel replied, "See here, you ask

---

1. B. Hag 13b.
2. Exod. R. 23:13.
3. Deut. R. 2:31; Yalkut, *Va-et'hannan*, §833.
4. B. Shab 55a; P. Sanh 1:1, 18a; Song R. 1:9, §1.
5. Rather, "appertains to His world or whether His world appertains to Him" (Leon Nemoy).
6. That is to say, without God there would have been no world. Gen. R. 68:9; Exod. R. 45:6; Mteh 90:10.
7. Num. R. 12:4, end.
8. B. BB 25a and En Yaakov, ad loc.
9. MTeh 103:5; PRE 4.

me about something that is thirty-five hundred years away from me.[1] Now I shall ask you about something that abides with you day and night, and you tell me where its place is." The man asked, "And what is that?" Rabban Gamaliel replied, "It is the soul, which abides within you. Tell me precisely, where does it abide?" The man said, "I do not know." Rabban Gamaliel replied, "May the breath of one such as you be blasted out! You do not know the place of something that abides within you day and night, yet you ask me about something that is thirty-five hundred years away from me!"

The man went on to say to Rabban Gamaliel, "We do well to bow down to the work of our own hands, since we can always see it." Rabban Gamaliel answered, "You see the work of your own hands, but it cannot see you. Whereas the Holy One, blessed be He, sees the work of His hands, but the work of His hands cannot see Him, as is said, 'Man shall not see Me, not even a celestial creature' " (Exod. 33:20).[2]

10. R. Tanhuma said: There is a story of a heathen's ship sailing on the Great Sea, and in the ship was a young lad, a Jew. When a fierce storm rose against them in the sea, everyone in the ship proceeded to take the object of his worship into his hand and call [for mercy], but it availed not at all. Upon seeing that the objects of their worship availed not at all, they said to the Jew: Son, rise up and call upon your God, for we have heard that He is mighty and that, when you people cry out to Him, He answers you. At once, the lad stood up and cried out with all his heart, and the Holy One, blessed be He, accepted his prayer, so that the sea was stilled.

When they came to dry land, and each of them went down to buy what he needed, they asked the lad, "Don't you wish to buy anything at all?" He replied, "What a question to ask a hapless stranger like me!" They replied, "You a hapless stranger? The others are hapless strangers—some are here while their idols are in Babylonia; some are here while their idols are in Rome; and some are here and their idols are with them but avail them not at all. You, however—wherever you go, your God is with you."

With regard to God's ubiquity, Scripture says, "The Lord our God is wheresoever we call upon Him" (Deut. 4:7).[3]

11. A Caesar said to Rabban Gamaliel, "You people say, 'At every gathering where there are ten men, the Presence abides.' Well then, how many Presences must there be?" In answer, Rabban Gamaliel summoned Caesar's servant and boxed his ears. When Caesar asked, "Why did you do this?" Rabban Gamaliel replied, "On account of the sun, which your servant allowed to enter Caesar's palace."

Caesar retorted, "But the sun abides over the entire world."

Rabban Gamaliel: "If the sun, which is merely one of the thousand thousands of myriads serving the Holy One, blessed be He, abides over the entire world, how much more true is this of the Presence of the Holy One Himself, blessed be He!"[4]

12. A Roman noblewoman said to R. Yose: My god is greater than your God. He asked her: Why do you say so? She replied: When your God revealed Himself to Moses in the thornbush, Moses hid his face. But when he saw the serpent, who is my god, at once "Moses fled from before it" (Exod. 4:3). R. Yose: May the breath of a woman such as you be blasted out! When our God appeared in the thornbush, Moses had no place to flee to. Where could he have fled? To heaven, to the sea, or to dry land? What is said of our God? "Do not I fill heaven and earth? saith the Lord" (Jer. 23:24). But as for the serpent, who is your god—as soon as a man gets two or three steps away from it, he can escape it.[5]

13. R. Hanina bar Isi said: There are times when the world and the fullness thereof cannot contain the glory of His Godhead, and there are times when He speaks to a man from between the hairs of his head.[6]

14. A certain heretic quizzed R. Meir, saying to him, "Is it possible that He of whom it is written, 'Do not I fill heaven and earth?' (Jer. 23:24), spoke to Moses from between the two staves of the Ark?" R. Meir replied, "Bring me magnifying mirrors." Upon their being brought, R. Meir said to the heretic, "Look at your reflection in them," and the heretic saw how big it was. Then he said, "Bring me reducing mirrors." These were brought, and R. Meir said, "Look at your reflection in them," and the heretic saw how small it was. R. Meir said, "If you, who are flesh and blood, may change your size whenever you wish, how much more by far is this true of Him who spoke and the world came into being, blessed be He. Hence, when He wishes, 'Do not I fill heaven and earth?'; and when He wished, He used to speak to Moses from between the two staves of the Ark."[7]

15. [A proverb]: "When our love[8] was strong, we could lie on the edge of a sword. Now that it has grown weak, a bed sixty cubits wide is not wide enough for us." R. Huna said: We may also infer this truth from verses in Scripture. In the beginning God said, "There I will meet with thee, and I will speak with thee from above the Ark cover" (Exod. 25:22), and we have been taught, "The Ark's height was nine handbreadths, and the Ark cover's thickness one handbreadth, thus ten handbreadths in all." Later on, it was said, "The house which King Solomon built for the Lord, the length thereof was threescore cubits, and the breadth thereof twenty cubits, and the height thereof thirty cubits" (1 Kings 6:2). But in the end it was said,

---

1. The thirty-five hundred years since the creation of the world.
2. Usually rendered; "Man shall not see Me and live," but here the commentator takes the form *hai* ("live") in the substantive sense of a living creature. MTeh 103:5; Yalkut, Ps., §857.
3. P. Ber 9:1, 13b.
4. B. Sanh 39a.
5. Exod. R. 3:12.
6. Gen. R. 4:4.
7. Gen. R. 4:4.
8. A husband's love for his wife.

"Thus saith the Lord: The heaven is My throne, and the earth is My footstool. Where is the house that ye may build unto Me? And where is the place that may be My resting place?" (Isa. 66:1).[1]

16. The norm of flesh and blood: when in his palace, he cannot at the same time be present in the city outside, and vice versa. But with the Holy One, blessed be He, it is not so. He is always present both in the worlds above and in the worlds below, as is said, "The Lord is in His holy abode [above]; let all the earth [here below] keep silent in His presence" (Hab. 2:20).[2]

17. We have been taught that R. Yose said: The Presence never came down below, and Moses and Elijah never ascended on high, for Scripture says, "The heavens are the heavens for the Lord; and it is the earth that He hath given to the children of men" (Ps. 115:16).[3]

18. R. Hiyya bar Abba said in the name of R. Yohanan: Had there been a chink no bigger than the eye of a fine needle in the cave in which Moses and Elijah stood,[4] neither of them would have been able to endure the light of the Presence, for Scripture says, "Man shall not see Me and live" (Exod. 33:20).[5]

19. A Caesar said to R. Joshua ben Hananiah, "I want to see your God." R. Joshua: "You cannot see Him." Caesar: "Nevertheless, I want to see Him." So R. Joshua had Caesar stand facing the sun during the summer solstice of Tammuz and said to him, "Look directly at the sun." Caesar: "I cannot." R. Joshua: "If you say of the sun, which is only one of the servitors standing before the Holy One, blessed be He, 'I cannot look directly at it,' how much less could you look at the Presence itself!"[6]

20. The same Caesar said to R. Joshua ben Hananiah, "I wish to prepare a banquet for your God." R. Joshua: "You cannot do so." "Why not?" "Because His attendants are too numerous." Caesar: "Nevertheless, I wish to do it." "Then go and prepare it on the banks of [the river] Revita,[7] where there is ample room." So Caesar spent the six months of summer toiling over the preparations, but then a tempest arose and swept everything into the sea. He then spent the six months of winter toiling over new preparations, but the rains came and washed everything into the sea. "What is the meaning of this?" demanded Caesar. "These are but the sweepers and sprinklers which march ahead of Him." "In that case," Caesar concluded, "I admit I cannot do it."[8]

21. Elijah [the Prophet] told the following: One day as I was walking through the greatest city of the world, there was a roundup and I was roughly seized and brought into the king's house. Presently a Parsee priest came to me and asked me, "Are you a scholar?" I replied, "A bit of a one." He said, "If you can answer the particular question I am about to ask, you may go in peace." I replied, "Ask."

So the Parsee priest said, "You people assert that fire is not god. Then why is it written in your Torah, 'Fire burning eternally' [Lev. 6:6]?" I replied, "My son, when our forebears stood at Mount Sinai to receive the Torah for themselves, they saw no form resembling a human being, nor one resembling the form of any creature, nor one resembling the form of anything that has breath which the Holy One, blessed be He, created in His world, as is said, 'Take ye therefore good heed unto yourselves—for ye saw no manner of form on the day that the Lord spoke unto you in Horeb' [Deut. 4:15]. For He, the God of gods, the Lord of lords, is the one and only God, whose kingdom endures in heaven and on earth as well as in the highest heaven of heavens. And yet you people say that fire is god! Fire is no more than a rod to be used upon men on earth. Its use may be understood by the parable of a king who took a lash and hung it up in his house, and then said to his servants, to his children, and to the members of his household, 'With this lash I may strike you, may even kill you'—threatening them, so that in penitence they would turn away from sin. If they do not turn back, then God says, 'I will have to strike them with the lash, will even have to kill them.' Hence, 'Fire burning eternally' is to be read in the light of the verse 'For by fire will the Lord threaten judgment' [Isa. 66:16]. You might suppose that this verse is to be read [literally], 'For by fire will the Lord be judged.' Therefore, elsewhere Scripture declares, 'The Lord thy God is a devouring fire' " (Deut. 4:24).[9]

22. "When they say to me: What is His Name? What shall I tell them?" (Exod. 3:13). At that time Moses was asking that the Holy One, blessed be He, make known to him His great Name.

"And God said unto Moses: 'I am what [from time to time] I may be' " (Exod. 3:14). According to R. Abba bar Mammal, the Holy One, blessed be He, said to Moses: You wish to know My Name. I am variously called, in keeping with My divers deeds, El Shaddai, Tzevaot, Elohim, Adonai. When I judge created beings, I am called Elohim, "God." When I wage war against the wicked, I am called Tzevaot, "Hosts." When [while waiting for a man to repent] I suspend [judgment] of a man's sins, I am called El Shaddai.[10] And when I have mercy on My world, I am called Adonai.[11] Hence, "I am what [from time to

1. I.e., there is no place large enough to contain God. B. Sanh 7a.
2. Mishnat R. Eliezer 11:44.
3. B. Suk 5a.
4. "According to tradition, the cave in which Elijah stood when the Lord passed before him was the same as that in which Moses had stood on a similar occasion" (Meg, Soncino, p. 119, n. 3).
5. B. Meg 19b.
6. B. Hul 60a.
7. Near Yavneh in Palestine. Or, on the shore of the Great Sea.
8. B. Hul 60a.
9. "The Parsee cites Isa. 66:16 in its literal sense, as proof that God is judged by fire—hence fire is not only a deity but even one superior to God. 'Not so fast,' says Elijah, 'it is just to prevent such literal exegesis that Scripture declares elsewhere, "God is fire." Fire is one of His manifestations or tools, like wind, thunder, etc.' " (Leon Nemoy). TdE, JPS, pp. 48–50. For explanatory notes, see above, part 1, chap. 2, §42.
10. "The God who says, *She-dai*, 'Enough [affliction for the man].' "
11. "Adonai . . . merciful and gracious" (Exod. 34:6).

time] I may be—I am called in keeping with My divers deeds."[1]

23. Whenever "Adonai" is mentioned, it implies the measure of mercy ("Adonai, Adonai, God, merciful and gracious" [Exod. 34:6]). Whenever "God" is mentioned, it implies the measure of justice ("The cause of both parties shall come before God [the Judge, as represented by a human judge]" [Exod. 22:8]).[2]

24. "This is My Name forever" (Exod. 3:15). *Le-olam,* "forever" [spelled here] without the letter *vav,* may be read *le-alom,* "to be concealed," and thus implies that the letters of God's [Ineffable] Name should not be uttered. "Such is to be My appellation for all eternity" (ibid.) My Name is to be uttered by substituting another word.[3]

25. "Show me, I pray Thee, Thy glory" (Exod. 33:18). Moses said to the Holy One, blessed be He: Show me the rule whereby You guide the world. God replied: You cannot fathom My rules.[4]

26. "What is man that he could fathom the King?" (Eccles. 2:12).[5] If a man tells you, "I can fathom the world's foundation," answer him, "You cannot fathom a king of flesh and blood. How, then, I wonder, do you expect to fathom [the words of] the King who is King of kings, the Holy One, blessed be He?"[6]

27. "The heavens declare the glory of God" (Ps. 19:1). R. Jacob ben Zavdi told the parable of a mighty man who came to a certain city where the inhabitants did not know his strength. A knowing man said, "You can tell his strength from the size of the stone he manages to roll." Even so, we can tell the strength of the Holy One, blessed be He, from [the size of] the heavens.[7]

28. "His splendor is in the skies" (Deut. 33:26). All Israel gathered at Moses' place and said to him: Our master Moses, what is the measure of the Glory that is above? He replied: From the beings below you can tell the measure of the Glory that is above. To illustrate, there is the parable of one who said, "I want to see the king's countenance." He was told, "Go into the capital, and you will see him." As he was about to go into the capital, he saw spread across its entrance a curtain in which precious stones and pearls were set. [At the sight of it], he was so amazed that he fell to the ground in obeisance. He was told, "Your eyes could not bear the sight [of the curtain], and so you fell down. How much more and more, had you entered the capital itself and seen the king's face." Hence, "His splendor is in the skies."[8]

1. Exod. R. 3:6.
2. Gen. R. 33:3.
3. Not YHVH, but Adonai. Exod. R. 3:7.
4. MTeh 25:6.
5. JV: "What can the man do that cometh after the king?"
6. Gen. R. 12:1; Exod. R. 6:1; Eccles. R. 2:12, §9.
7. MTeh 19:6.
8. Sif Deut., §355.

29. It is characteristic of flesh and blood to mention first a man's name and then his accomplishments. "So-and-so the sage, So-and-so the mighty man, So-and-so the rich man." But the Holy One, blessed be He, mentions His accomplishments first and then His Name, "In the beginning created God" (Gen. 1:1).[9]

It is characteristic of a king of flesh and blood to demand that people of his province praise him even before he has built bridges or laid out roads for them. But the Holy One, blessed be He, has not acted thus. First He set everything in order, and after that He demanded worship of Himself, for He created man only as the very last of His creatures.

It is characteristic of a king of flesh and blood that when he is praised, the notables of the realm are praised with him, because they share in carrying his burden. But the Holy One, blessed be He—He alone is praised in His world, He alone is glorified in His world, because no one shares with Him in carrying His burden, as is said, "For Thou art great, and doest wondrous things, Thou art God alone" (Ps. 86:10).

It is characteristic of flesh and blood that when carrying a burden, he is below and the burden he carries is above. But the Holy One, blessed be He, is above, yet He carries both the creatures above and the creatures below, as is said, "Behold, God doeth loftily in His power" (Job 36:22).

It is characteristic of flesh and blood that when he brings his works to a halt, there is no more potential in them for growth. But it is not so with the Holy One, blessed be He—after He brought His works to a halt, there was such potential in them, as is said, "He brought all His work that He had wrought to a half, and bestowed potential for further growth on the seventh day" (Gen. 2:2–3).[10]

30. Pause and consider that the behavior of the Holy One, blessed be He, is not like the behavior of flesh and blood. The behavior of flesh and blood is for the exalted to take notice of the exalted, but not of the lowly. The Holy One, blessed be He, does not act thus. He is lofty, yet He takes notice of the lowly, as is said, "Lofty though the Lord is, He regards the lowly" (Ps. 138:6).[11]

31. It is characteristic of flesh and blood to be more particular about his own honor than about the honor of his emissary. But the Holy One, blessed be He, is more particular about the honor of His emissary than about His own honor. Thus we find that when Jeroboam stood burning incense before an idol, his hand did not dry up. But as soon as he put forth his hand against a righteous man, his hand immediately dried up, as is said, "And it came to pass, when the king heard the saying of the man of God . . . that Jeroboam put forth his hand . . . , saying: 'Lay hold on him.' And his hand dried up" (1 Kings 13:4).

9. This is the order of the words in the Hebrew text.
10. JV: "He rested . . . from all His work which He had made. And God blessed the seventh day." Mishnat R. Eliezer 11:2–3 and 11:10–12, based on Gen. R. 10:9.
11. B. Sot 5a.

It is characteristic of flesh and blood that when a man has a patron, and a time of trouble befalls the man, he cannot go in unannounced to his patron. Instead, he comes and has to stand at the patron's door, and call a servant or a member of the household, who then tells the patron, "So-and-so is standing at the door of your courtyard." The patron may allow him to enter; then again, he may have him remain outside. But the Holy One, blessed be He, does not act thus. When trouble befalls a man, he need cry out neither to Michael nor to Gabriel, but to the Holy One, blessed be He, alone, as is said, "Call unto Me, and I will answer thee" (Jer. 33:3).

It is characteristic of flesh and blood that when a man examines promissory notes in his possession and finds that money is owed him, he will bring them forth and demand payment; if he finds that he owes money to another, he will suppress them. But the Holy One, blessed be He, does not act thus. When He finds a debt [of guilt] charged to us, He suppresses it, as is said, "He will suppress our guilts" (Mic. 7:19), but when He finds the merit [of good deeds] in our favor, He brings it forth [for payment], as is said, "The Lord brought forth our meritorious acts" (Jer. 51:10).[1]

[**31.** R. Simeon ben Lakish said: With flesh and blood, if a man has a rich kinsman, the man acknowledges him; but if the kinsman is poor, the man is apt to deny the kinship. But with the Holy One, blessed be He, it is not so. Even when Israel are most degraded, He continues to call them "My brethren and My companions" (Ps. 122:8).[2]]

32. R. Yohanan said in the name of R. Simeon ben Yohai: The significance of the verse "I the Lord love justice. I hate defrauding even a burnt offering"[3] (Isa. 61:8) may be understood by the parable of a king of flesh and blood who, about to go through a customs house, said to his servants, "Pay the customs to the collectors." They replied, "Our lord king, does not all money collected from customs belong to you?" The king: "Let all travelers learn from me not to defraud customs." So, too, the Holy One, blessed be He, said, "[Though all offerings belong to me, yet] I the Lord hate defrauding, even [if the defrauder's purpose is to present] a burnt offering. Let My children learn from Me to keep themselves from any kind of defrauding" (ibid).[4]

33. R. Yohanan said: Wherever you find the power of the Holy One, blessed be He, mentioned in Scripture, you also find His condescension mentioned, a fact that is stated in the Five Books, repeated in the Prophets, and reasserted in the Writings. In the Five Books it is written, "For the Lord your God, He is God of gods," etc. (Deut. 10:17), and directly after that, "He doth execute justice for the fatherless and the widow" (Deut. 10:18). It is repeated in the Prophets: "For thus saith the high and lofty one: . . . I dwell in the high and lofty place" (Isa. 57:15), and directly after that, "With him also that is of a contrite and humble spirit" (Isa. 57:15). And reasserted in the Writings: "Extol Him that rideth upon the skies, whose name is the Lord" (Ps. 68:5), and directly after that, "A father of the fatherless, and a judge [protector] of the widows" (Ps. 68:6).[5]

34. R. Kahana said in the name of R. Ishmael son of R. Yose: The verse "A psalm for Him who causes others to be victorious" (Ps. 13:1)[6] means: "A psalm for Him who rejoices when others are victorious over Him." Pause and consider that the behavior of the Holy One, blessed be He, is not like the behavior of flesh and blood. The behavior of flesh and blood: when others are victorious over him, he grieves. But when others are victorious over the Holy One, blessed be He, He rejoices, as is said, "Therefore He said that He would destroy them, had not Moses His chosen[7] stood before Him in the breach" (Ps. 106:23).[8]

35. We have been taught that R. Yose said: Pause and consider that the behavior of flesh and blood is not at all like the behavior of the Holy One, blessed be He. The behavior of flesh and blood: when one gives offense to another, the other will attempt to deprive the one of his livelihood. But the Holy One, blessed be He, does not act thus. He cursed the serpent, yet when it goes up to a roof, its sustenance is on hand; and when it comes down, its sustenance is on hand. At Noah's request, He cursed Canaan [to be a slave].[9] Yet a slave eats what his master eats and drinks what his master drinks. He cursed the woman,[10] yet all run after her. He cursed the earth,[11] yet all draw their sustenance from it.[12]

36. R. Eleazar said: Even at the time of the anger of the Holy One, blessed be He, He still remembers compassion.[13]

37. Hezekiah said: Pause and consider that the behavior of the Holy One, blessed be He, is not like the behavior of flesh and blood. A man is apt to allure another from the ways of life unto the ways of death. But the Holy One, blessed be He, allures man from the ways of death unto the ways of life, as is said, "Yea, He hath allured thee out of the mouth of straits" (Job 36:16)—out of Gehenna, whose mouth is strait.[14]

38. "There is none holy as the Lord; for there is none besides Thee (*biltekha*)" (1 Sam. 2:2). R. Judah bar Men-

---

1. P. Ber 9:1, 13a; Exod. R. 25:6; Yalkut, Joel, §535; Mishnat R. Eliezer 11.
2. P. Ber 9:1, 13b.
3. JV: "iniquity." But the Hebrew word also means "burnt offering."
4. B. Suk 30a and En Yaakov, ad loc.
5. B. Meg 31a.
6. JV: "For the Leader (*menatzeah*). A Psalm." But the word can also be construed as in the comment above.
7. Though Moses was victorious over God, God continued to regard Moses as "His chosen."
8. B. Pes 119a and En Yaakov, ad loc.
9. See Gen. 9:6.
10. See Gen. 3:16. The rabbis understand the punishment He imposed on her to be a curse.
11. Gen. 3:47.
12. B. Yoma 75a and En Yaakov, ad loc.
13. B. Pes 87b.
14. B. Men 99b.

asya said: Read not *biltekha*, but *ballotekh*, "There is none can outlive Thee." For the behavior of the Holy One, blessed be He, is not like the behavior of flesh and blood. Flesh and blood: the works of his hands outlive him. But the Holy One, blessed be He: He outlives His works.

"Neither is there any rock (*tzur*) like our God" (1 Sam. 2:2). No artist (*tzayyar*) is like our God. When a man makes a figure on a wall, he cannot put spirit, breath, entrails, and bowels into it. But the Holy One, blessed be He, makes a figure [an embryo] within another figure and then puts spirit, and breath, and entrails, and bowels into it.[1]

39. If a man strikes many coins from the same die, they all resemble one another. But though the King of kings of kings, the Holy One, blessed be He, fashioned every man in the stamp of the first man [Adam], not a single one of them is exactly like his fellow.[2]

40. "Who is like unto Thee (*ne'dar*) in holiness" (Exod. 15:11). [*Ne'dar* is a composite of] "*naeh*, You are gracious [to human beings], even though You are *addir*, mighty in holiness." The nature of the Holy One, blessed be He, is not like the nature of flesh and blood. For it is in the nature of flesh and blood that he cannot say two words at the same time, but the Holy One, blessed be He, spoke the Ten Commandments all at the same time, as is said, "And God spoke all these words, saying [them at one time]" (Exod. 20:1). It is in the nature of a human being that he cannot listen to two people crying out at the same time. The Holy One, blessed be He, is not so—even when all the inhabitants of the world come and cry out at one time before Him, he hears the cries of each of them, as is said, "O Thou that hearest prayer, unto Thee doth all flesh come" (Ps. 65:3).

"Fearful in praises" (Exod. 15:11). It is in the nature of flesh and blood to be more revered by those far from him than by those near to him. Not so the Holy One, blessed be He. He is revered by those near to Him even more than by those who are far from Him, as is said, "By them that are nigh unto Me am I sanctified" (Lev. 10:3), "Round about Him it stormeth mightily" (Ps. 50:3), and, "Held in awe by all around Him" (Ps. 89:8).

It is in the nature of flesh and blood that when he is about to form a figure, he must begin either with its head or with one of the other parts of its body and then complete it. But the Holy One, blessed be He, forms the entire figure all at once, as is said, "For He is the former of the whole" (Jer. 10:16), and also, "Neither is there any rock (*tzur*) like our God" (1 Sam. 2:2)—neither is there any former (*tzayyar*) like our God. It is the norm of flesh and blood that when he goes to a sculptor and says, "Make me an image of my father," the sculptor will reply, Let your father come and pose before me, or bring me likenesses of him, and I will make you his image." Not so the Holy One, blessed be He: out of a drop of fluid he gives a man a son who is the image of his father.[3]

41. It is the norm of flesh and blood that a man who makes a figure can make it only in the light. But the Holy One, blessed be He, makes all who are alive in darkness, in innermost chambers, as is said, "The Lord . . . made the spirit of man within him" (Zech. 12:1).

It is the norm of flesh and blood that when he makes a figure, his figure cannot generate another figure. But the Holy One, blessed be He, makes a figure, and the figure He made in turn generates other figures, as is said, "Be fruitful and multiply" (Gen. 9:1).

It is the norm of flesh and blood that when he puts different ingredients in a boiler, intending to dye with them, they all come out one color. But the Holy One, blessed be He, forms all who are alive out of the same matter, yet each of them emerges in its distinctive species.[4]

42. R. Hanina said: Pause and consider that the norm of the Holy One, blessed be He, is not like the norm of flesh and blood. The norm of flesh and blood is for a king to sit inside while his servants guard him on the outside. But such is not the norm of the Holy One, blessed be He. His servants sit inside while He guards them from the outside, as is said, "The Lord is thy keeper, the Lord is thy shade upon thy right hand" (Ps. 121:5).[5]

43. "He that would break me with a whirlwind, and multiply my wounds without cause" (Job 9:17). Rabbah said: Job blasphemed by speaking of a whirlwind, and he was answered through a whirlwind. He blasphemed by speaking of a whirlwind when he said to God: Master of the universe, [perhaps] a whirlwind passed before You, so that I, Iyyov [Job], was confused with *oyev* ["enemy"]. He was answered in a whirlwind, as is said, "There the Lord answered Job out of the whirlwind [*searah*] and said: . . . Gird up now thy loins like a man, for I will demand of thee" (Job 38:1 and 38:3). [Whirling like a wind over Job's each and every hair (*searah*)], God said to Job: You are the biggest fool in the world! I created many hairs in a man's head, and for each and every hair I created a [root] cavity for itself, so that two hairs should not draw sustenance from the same cavity; for if two hairs had to draw sustenance from the same cavity, the light in a man's eyes would grow dark. If I do not confuse one such cavity with another, am I apt to confuse Iyyov and *oyev*?

"Who hath cleft the waterflood into innumerable molds?" (Job 38:25).[6] I created many drops in the clouds, and for each and every drop a separate mold, so that two drops should not issue from the same mold; for if two drops were to issue from the same mold, they would wash away the soil and it would yield no fruit. If I make sure not to confuse one drop with another, am I apt to confuse Iyyov and *oyev*?

"Or a way for the lightning of the thunder?" (Job 38:25). I created many thunderclaps in the clouds, and

---

1. B. Meg 14a and En Yaakov, ad loc.
2. B. Sanh 37a.
3. Mek, *Be-shallah*, *Shirata*, 8; Mek RSbY, pp. 93–94.
4. Mishnat R. Eliezer 11:24–25 and 11:31.
5. That is to say, outside your body. B. Men 33b.
6. JV: "Who hath cleft a channel for the waterflood?" But *tealah* ("channel") is here taken to mean "mold."

for each and every thunderclap I created a path, so that no two thunderclaps should travel by the same path; for if two thunderclaps did travel by the same path, they would destroy the world. If I make sure not to confuse one thunderclap with another, am I apt to confuse Iyyov with *oyev*?

"Knowest thou the time when the wild goats of the rocks bring forth?" (Job 39:1). The wild goat is cruel toward her young, and when about to crouch to give birth, she goes up to the top of a mountain, so that the young should drop down from her and be killed. Therefore I ready a vulture to catch the young in its wings and set it down before the mother goat. Not even by an instant does the vulture come too soon or too late, for if the vulture were an instant too soon or too late, the youngling would die. If I do not confuse one instant with the next, am I apt to confuse Iyyov and *oyev*?[1]

44. "Woe unto them that seek deep to hide their counsel from the Lord, and their works are in the dark" (Isa. 29:15). A parable of an architect who built a city, making [underground] chambers, passages, and caves in it. Later, he was made collector for the royal treasury. When the people of the province sought to hide from him in the [underground] chambers and caves, he said to them: I am he who built the [underground] caves. To what avail is your hiding in them? Hence, "Woe unto them that seek deep to hide . . . from the Lord."[2]

45. "For Thou art my lamp, O Lord" (2 Sam. 22:29). R. Yohanan said: The eye is white, with a black part in its middle. Out of what part would one be expected to see? Out of the white part surely. But no, one sees out of the black part. Since you cannot fathom the light in your eyes, how can you attempt to fathom the way of the Holy One, blessed be He?

You find that he who is in the dark can see what is in the light, whereas he who is in the light cannot see what is in the dark. But the Holy One, blessed be He, does see what is in the dark.[3]

46. R. Berekhiah said: Consider the eyeball. It is not through the white of it that one sees, but through the black. The Holy One, blessed be He, says: If I create light for you out of the darkness, what need have I of your light?[4]

47. "The Lord . . . understandeth all the shapings of the thoughts" (1 Chron. 28:9). Even before a man shapes a thought in his heart, the Holy One, blessed be He, understands it.[5]

48. Haggai, citing R. Isaac, said that the verse "The Lord searcheth all hearts and understandeth every thought before its birthing" (1 Chron. 28:9) means: Even before a thought is shaped in a man's heart, it is already manifest to Him. In the name of R. Isaac, R. Yudan said: Even before a creature is brought into being, his thought is already revealed to Him. On his own, R. Yudan, citing "For there is not a word on my tongue but lo, O Lord, Thou knowest it altogether" (Ps. 139:4), said: Even before a man's tongue articulates a word, "lo, O Lord, Thou knowest it altogether."[6]

49. "Declareth unto man what is his small talk" (Amos 4:13). Even matters that have no substance—even the small talk a man voices to his wife—is written down in a man's ledger [in heaven] and is read to him at the time of his death.[7]

50. A Caesar said to Rabban Gamaliel: I know what occupies your God. At this, Rabban Gamaliel sighed. Caesar: What's troubling you? Rabban Gamaliel: I have a son in one of the cities far across the sea, and I yearn for him. Please let me see him. Caesar: But do I know where he is? Rabban Gamaliel: You do not know what is on earth. Yet you pretend to know what goes on in heaven.[8]

51. Another time a Caesar said to Rabban Gamaliel: In your Scripture it is written, "He counteth the number of the stars" (Ps. 174:4). What is so great about that? I too can count the stars. So Rabban Gamaliel brought some quince seeds, put them in a basket sieve, and began to whirl them. He said to Caesar: Count them. Caesar: [First] stop whirling them. Rabban Gamaliel: Thus also does the firmament whirl.

Some tell the story differently: Caesar said to Rabban Gamaliel: I know how many stars there are. Rabban Gamaliel: Tell me how many teeth you have. Caesar put his hand into his mouth and began counting them. Rabban Gamaliel: You do not know what is in your mouth, yet you think you know what is in heaven.[9]

52. After Hadrian, emperor of Rome, conquered the world, all of it, he returned to Rome and said to the people in his palace: I desire that you declare me God, for, as you see, I have conquered the entire world. They replied: But you still have no dominion over His city or His house. So Hadrian went and destroyed the Temple, exiled Israel, and then returned to Rome, and said to them: Now that I have destroyed His city, burned His Holy Place, and exiled His people, make me God.

Now, according to R. Berekhiah, Hadrian had three philosophers. The first of them said: No man may rebel against the king within the king's own palace, only outside it. Accordingly, you must first leave His palace and then you will be declared God. Heaven and earth, He created them. Go beyond their bounds and you will be declared God. The second philosopher said: You cannot become God, for through His prophets He said, "The gods that have not made the heaven and the earth, these shall perish from the earth" (Jer. 10:11). The third philosopher said:

1. B. BB 16b and En Yaakov, ad loc.; Yalkut, Job, §904.
2. Gen. R. 24:1; Yalkut, Isa, §436.
3. Tanhuma B. *Tetzavveh*, §4 and 6; Yalkut, 1 Kings, §182.
4. Lev. R. 31:8.
5. MTeh 45:4.
6. Gen. R. 9:3; Yalkut, 1 Chron., §1080.
7. Lev. R. 26:7.
8. B. Sanh 39a.
9. Ibid.

I beg of you, stand by me in this urgent matter. Hadrian: What matter? The philosopher: I have a ship more than three *mil* offshore, and it is being tossed about in the sea. All my merchandise is in that ship. Hadrian: I will send my legions and my ships there, and they will rescue it. The philosopher: Sire, why need you trouble your legions and ships to go there? Dispatch a bit of a wind there, and thus you will rescue it. Caesar: Where am I to get a wind to send there? The philosopher: You cannot create a wind? How then can you make yourself God, in whose name it is said, "Thus saith the Lord, He that created the heavens, and stretched them forth, He that spread forth the earth and that which cometh out of it, He that giveth breath unto the people upon it, and spirit to them that walk therein" (Isa. 42:5)?

Hadrian then went to his home greatly troubled. [When his wife asked him: Why are you troubled? he told her what had happened.] So she said: The three philosophers misled you. You can, in fact, become God, for you are a great and mighty king, and everything is in your power. I suggest one thing: give Him back His deposit, and you will become God. Hadrian: What is His deposit? The wife: The soul. Hadrian: But if the soul leaves [me], what will I be capable of doing? The wife: If you exercise no authority over the soul within you—Scripture says of it, "No man has authority over the lifebreath to hold back the lifebreath; there is no authority over the day of death" (Eccles. 8:8)—how can you become God? In truth, you are a man, not God.[1]

53. "And the Lord saw that the wickedness of man was great . . . and it grieved Him at His heart" (Gen. 6:5–6). A heretic asked R. Joshua ben Korhah: "Do you people not maintain that the Holy One, blessed be He, foresees the future?" R. Joshua: "Yes." The heretic: "But does Scripture not say, 'And it grieved Him at His heart'?"[2] R. Joshua: "Was a son ever born to you?" The heretic: "Yes." R. Joshua: "What did you do?" The heretic: "I celebrated and had all others celebrate." R. Joshua: "Didn't you know that in the end he would die?" The heretic: "Joy at the time of joy, and mourning at the time of mourning." R. Joshua: "Even such was the experience of the Holy One, blessed be He."[3]

54. R. Papa said: There is no grief in the presence of Him who is everywhere, for Scripture says, "Strength and joy are in His place" (1 Chron. 16:27).

But elsewhere Scripture says, "In that day did the Lord, the God of hosts, call to weeping," etc. (Isa. 22:12)!

[This refers to] the destruction of the Temple, which is different, for even the angels wept over it, as is said, "The celestial beings cry. '[The Temple's destruction] is an outrage';[4] the angels of peace cry bitterly" (Isa. 33:7).[5]

[1] Tanhuma, *Bereshit*, §7.

[2] Why then did He first say of everything that he had made, "Behold, it was very good"?

[3] Gen. R. 27:4.

[4] JV: "The valiant ones cry without." But see PR 40:6 (YJS 18:718).

[5] B. Hag 5a.

55. R. Judah said in the name of Rav: The day consists of twelve hours: the first three, the Holy One, blessed be He, sits and occupies Himself with Torah; the next three, He sits and issues judgments for the entire world, all of it—when He sees that the world is so guilty as to deserve extermination, He rises from the throne of judgment and sits down on the throne of compassion; the next three hours, He sits and feeds the entire world, from the horned wild ox to lice; the final three hours, He sits and disports with the Leviathan,[6] as is said, "There is Leviathan, whom Thou hast formed to sport therewith" (Ps. 104:26).[7]

56. A Roman noblewoman, interrogating R. Yose ben Halafta, asked: In how many days did the Holy One, blessed be He, create His world? R. Yose replied: In six days. She asked: And what has He been doing since? R. Yose replied: The Holy One, blessed be He, has been busy making matches—the daughter of Such-and-such to So-and-so. The noblewoman: Is that all He does? I can do the same thing. How many menservants, how many maidservants do I have? In no time at all, I can match them up. R. Yose: Matchmaking may be a trivial thing in your eyes; but for the Holy One, blessed be He, it is as awesome an act as splitting the Red Sea.

R. Yose ben Halafta left the noblewoman and went his way. What did she do? She took a thousand menservants and a thousand maidservants, lined them up, row upon row facing one another, and said, "So-and-so shall marry Such-and-such, and Such-and-such shall be married to So-and-so," and thus matched them all up in a single night. In the morning, the ones thus matched came to the noblewoman, one with his head bashed in, another with his eye knocked out, a third with his arm fractured, a fourth with his leg broken. When she asked them, "What happened to you?" one replied, "I don't want that woman," and another replied, "I don't want that man."

At that, the noblewoman sent for and had R. Yose ben Halafta brought to her. She said to him: Master, your Torah is unerring, completely right, and worthy of praise, and all that you have claimed for it is true.

R. Berekhiah [in differing with the above version of R. Yose ben Halafta's reply to the noblewoman's question about what God has been doing ever since His creation of the world] said that R. Yose's reply was as follows: The Holy One, blessed be He, has been busy making ladders, having this one ascend and that one descend, lifting this one up and putting that one down. [In short, He has been judging mankind.][8]

57. King Ptolemy asked the elders in Rome, "In how many days did the Holy One, blessed be He, create the world?" They replied: "In six days." Ptolemy: "And what has been happening since then?" They: "Gehenna has

[6] "A huge sea monster, real according to some, but according to others imaginary. We have here a magnification of God's power in sporting with the mightiest, as men do with their animal pets" (Isidore Epstein in AZ, Soncino, p. 9, n. 6).

[7] B. AZ 3b.

[8] PRKM 2:4; Gen. R. 68:4; Lev. R. 8:1.

been heated up for the wicked. Woe to the world because of His judgment."[1]

58. R. Judah said in the name of Samuel: Each and every day a divine voice goes forth and proclaims: The daughter of So-and-so to So-and-so! The field of So-and-so to So-and-so![2]

59. "The steps of a man are made firm by the Lord" (Ps. 37:23). R. Hanina said: No man bruises a finger here below unless it was proclaimed for him above.[3]

60. The Holy One, blessed be He, carries out a mission of His through anything, even through a snake, even through a gnat, even through a frog.

There is the story of a scorpion proceeding to the other side of the Jordan to carry out a mission given him. The Holy One, blessed be He, provided him with a frog upon whose back he crossed the river. Then, moving on, he stung a man to death. After the scorpion carried out his mission, the frog brought him back to his place.

R. Yannai was sitting and lecturing at the gate of his town when he saw a snake slithering rapidly toward the town. When it was chased away from one side of the road, it continued its journey on the other side of the road; when chased away from that side, it came back again to the side where it had been first. R. Yannai said: This creature is on the way to carry out its mission. Soon after that, a report spread in the town: So-and-so son of So-and-so was bitten by a snake and is dead.[4]

61. As R. Isaac bar Eleazar was strolling on the cliffs of the Sea of Caesarea, he saw a thighbone rolling on the ground. He hid it,[5] but [it bobbed up out of the ground] and started rolling again. He did it once more, [but it would not stay under] and kept rolling. He said: This thighbone is intent on carrying out the mission assigned it. And indeed, as a courier passed by, it rolled between his feet, so that he stumbled over it and fell to his death. When his body was examined, it was found that he had been carrying documents containing evil decrees against the Jews of Caesarea.[6]

62. R. Joseph expounded: How is the verse "I give thanks to Thee, O Lord! Although Thou wast wroth with me, Thy wrath hath turned back, and Thou comfortest me" (Isa. 12:1) to be understood? Here Scripture alludes to two competitors who were about to set out on a trading venture when a thorn got into the foot of one of them. He began to curse and blaspheme [at this mishap, which delayed him]. After a time, however, when he heard that his competitor's ship had sunk in the sea, he began to thank God and glorify Him [for sparing his life through the thorn]. Hence, "Thy wrath hath turned back, and Thou comfortest me." In this connection, R. Eleazar said: What is implied in the verse "Who doeth wondrous things alone. . . . Blessed be His glorious Name forever" (Ps. 72:18–19)? That even he for whom the miracle is wrought is not aware of the miracle wrought for him.[7]

63. How little does he whom the Lord supports need to grieve or be troubled![8]

64. How many miracles does the Holy One, blessed be He, perform for a man that he is not aware of![9]

65. R. Yohanan said in the name of R. Yose: When a word [of blessing] issues from the mouth of the Holy One, blessed be He, even if it is based on a condition, He never retracts it.[10]

The Household Above

66. Resh Lakish said: There are seven firmaments; curtain, expanse, grinders, habitation, dwelling, depository, and heavy clouds. Curtain: It serves no purpose whatever except that it enters its sheath in the morning and comes out of its sheath in the evening, thus renewing daily the work of creation. Expanse: where the sun, moon, stars, and planets are fixed. Grinder: where millstones stand and grind manna for the righteous. Habitation: where [the heavenly] Jerusalem, the Temple, and the altar are built; where Michael, the great prince, stands and every day brings an offering. Dwelling: where innumerable companies of ministering angels utter song by night and are silent by day for the sake of Israel's glory.[11] Depository: where there are stores of snow and stores of hail; it is the loft of noxious dews, and the loft of raindrops, and the chamber of the storm and the whirlwind, and the cave of vapor—the doors of all the aforementioned are of fire. Heavy clouds: where are stored right, and justice, and mercy; the treasures of life, the treasures of peace, and the treasures of blessing; the souls of the righteous, and the spirits and souls of those destined to be born, and the dew with which the Holy One will revive the dead. There too are the *ofannim*,[12] the seraphim, the celestial creatures, the ministering angels, and the throne of glory; the King, the living and enduring God, high and exalted, dwells above them, and darkness, cloud masses, and thick clouds encompass Him. R. Aha bar Jacob said: There is still another heaven above the celestial creatures.

Thus far you have permission to speak. Beyond that, you have no such permission, for in the book of Ben Sira it is clearly stated:

Do not pry into things too hard for you
Or examine what is concealed from you.

---

1. Gen. R. 10:9.
2. B. MK 18b.
3. B. Hul 7b.
4. Gen. R. 10:7; Tanhuma B, *Hukkat*, §1.
5. To give it burial.
6. Gen. R. 10:7; Lev. R. 22:4.
7. B. Nid 31a.
8. B. Yoma 22b.
9. Exod. R. 24:1.
10. B. Ber 7a.
11. Israel utter God's praise by day.
12. Wheel-angels.

Meditate on the commandments you have been given;
What the Lord keeps secret is no concern of yours.
(Ecclesiasticus 3:21).[1]

67. We have been taught that Rabban Yohanan ben Zakkai said: What answer did the divine voice give to the wicked Nebuchadnezzar when he said, "I will ascend above the heights of the clouds; I will be like the Most High" (Isa. 14:14)? The divine voice went forth and said, "O wicked man, son of a wicked man, grandson of the wicked Nimrod, who during his reign induced the whole world, all of it, to rebel against Me! How many are the years of man? 'Threescore and ten, and even by reason of strength fourscore' [Ps. 90:10]. And is not the following true? It is five hundred years' journey from earth to heaven, and five hundred years' journey across the thickness of heaven, and a like distance between each heaven and the one above it. Above the heavens are the celestial creatures. The journey across each of the feet of the celestial creatures takes as much time as all the previous journeys together; the journey across each of the ankles of the celestial creatures takes as much time as all the previous journeys together; the journey across each of the legs of the celestial creatures takes as much time as all the previous journeys together; the journey across the knees of each of the celestial creatures takes as much time as all the previous journeys together; the journey across the thighs of each of the celestial creatures takes as much time as all the previous journeys together; the journey across each of the bodies of the celestial creatures takes as much time as all the previous journeys together; the journey across the neck of each of the celestial creatures takes as much time as all the previous journeys together; the journey across the head of each of the celestial creatures takes as much time as all the previous journeys together; the journey across each of the horns of the celestial creatures takes as much time as all the previous journeys together. And above them is the throne of glory. The journey across each of the legs of the throne of glory takes as much time as all the previous journeys together; the journey across the throne of glory takes as much time as all the previous journeys together. And upon this throne of glory and above all the celestial creatures dwells God, living and enduring, high and exalted. Yet you dared say, 'I will ascend above the heights of the clouds. I will be like the Most High!' In the event, 'thou shalt be brought down to the nether world, to the uttermost parts of the pit' " (Isa. 14:15).[2]

68. "Till thrones were placed, and one that was ancient of days did sit" (Dan. 7:9). Why thrones? We have been taught; One for Himself and one for David. Such was the opinion of R. Akiva. R. Yose protested: Akiva, how long will you profane the Presence? One throne is for justice and the other for mercy. So R. Akiva accepted R. Yose's interpretation, and on another occasion he expounded the verse as R. Yose did. But this time R. Eleazar ben Azariah retorted to R. Akiva: Akiva, what business have you with *Aggadah*? Stick to the tractates of Negaim and Ohalot.[3] One of the two in the verse serves as the throne, the other a taboret—the throne for Him to sit upon, the taboret as a stool for His feet.[4]

69. Four companies of ministering angels utter praise before the Holy One, blessed be He: the first camp, that of Michael, at His right; the second camp, that of Gabriel, at His left; the third camp, that of Uriel, in front of Him; and the fourth camp, that of Raphael, behind Him.[5] The Presence of the Holy One, blessed be He, is thus in the center. He is seated on a throne high and exalted—high up and suspended above in space. The reflections of His glory have the gleam of amber. Upon His head a crown, the diadem of the Explicit Name on his forehead; His eyes range over the whole earth. Half [of His glory] is fire; the other half, hail. At His right is life; at His left, death. He holds a scepter of fire in His hand, and a veil is spread before Him. Within the veil, which is called the curtain, seven angels minister before Him. His footstool is like [a composite of] fire and hail. Under His throne of glory there is something like a sapphire. Fire is flashing continually around His throne—mercy and justice form the foundation of His throne. Seven clouds of glory surround it, and a whirling wheel-angel, a cherub, and a celestial creature utter praise before Him.[6]

70. "Now as I beheld the living creatures, behold one wheel[-angel] upon the earth by the living creatures" (Ezek. 1:15). R. Eleazar said: The verse refers to a certain angel who stands on the earth with his head reaching up close to the celestial creatures. His name, so we are taught in the Mishnah, is Sandalphon.

It is said of Sandalphon that he is taller than his fellows by a height that would take five hundred years to journey across, that he stands behind the chariot, and that he wreathes crowns for his Maker[7] and adjures each crown [he has wreathed] so that it rises of its own accord and reposes on the head of his Lord. And when a crown goes forth [from Sandalphon], all the hosts on high are fevered with excitement and shaken with awe, and the celestial creatures, silent until now, roar like lions. In that instant they cry out and say, "Holy, holy, holy is the Lord of hosts; the whole earth is full of His glory" (Isa. 6:3). When the crown reaches God's throne, the wheels of the throne revolve and the supports of the footstool tremble, and all the firmaments are seized with a shudder of terror. As the crown goes up above His throne, all the hosts above and His crown, too, open their mouths, saying, "Praised be the glory of the Lord wherever His place be" (Ezek. 3:12).

Come and behold the greatness and the excellence

1. B. Hag 12b–13a and En Yaakov, ad loc.
2. B. Hag 13a; B. Pes 94a–b, and En Yaakov, ad loc.

3. Two difficult treatises, the first dealing with signs of leprosy, the second with "tents" or "overshadowings," under which uncleanness—e.g., that of a corpse—will, even without touching them, convey uncleanness to food or utensils.
4. B. Sanh 38b.
5. Concerning these four angels, see *JE*, svv.
6. PRE 4.
7. He wreathes them out of the prayers of the righteous. See Tosafot, s.v. "Binds crowns," on B. Hag 13b.

of the Holy One, blessed be He! When the crown reaches His head, He brings Himself to accept the crown from His servants. Then all the celestial creatures, the seraphim, the wheels of the chariot, the throne of glory, the mighty ones above and below them—raised in dignity, power, and exaltation—ascribe with one voice glory and royal majesty [to Him], saying, "The Lord will reign forever and ever" (Exod. 15:18).[1]

71. R. Ishmael said: Metatron, the prince of the Presence, related to me: When the Holy One, blessed be He, took me to minister under the throne of glory and under the wheel of the chariot and to all other appurtenances of the Presence, my flesh turned into a flame of fire, my sinews into glowing fire, my bones into coals of broom. My eyelids became like the brightness of the firmament, the orbs of my eyes like torches of fire, the hairs of my head a scorching blaze. All the parts of my body [turned] into pinions of incandescent fire, my entire person into blistering fire; at my right piercing tongues of fire, at my left torches alight, and all about me scurries of a whirlwind's burgeoning.[2]

72. R. Akiva said: Every day in the morning, an angel opens his mouth and says, "The Lord reigns, the Lord did reign, the Lord will reign forever and ever," until he reaches "Bless ye."[3] When he reaches "Bless ye," there stands up in the firmament a creature of the chariot whose name is Israel and upon whose brow "Israel" is inscribed. It stands in the middle of the firmament and says, "Bless ye the Lord who should be blessed." And all the troops [of angels] above respond, saying, "Blessed is the Lord who should be blessed forever and ever."

In the firmament there is one celestial creature on whose brow is the symbol "Truth" when it is day, and thus the angels know that it is day; and "Faithfulness" on its brow in the evening, and thus the angels know that it is night. Each time it says, "Bless ye the Lord who should be blessed," all the troops [of angels] above respond, "Blessed is the Lord who should be blessed forever and ever."[4]

73. Samuel said to Hiyya bar Rav: O son of a lion of a man, come, and I will tell you some of the beautiful things your father used to say: Each and every day ministering angels are created from the fire river, utter song, and then cease to be, as is said, "Because they are new every morning, [the praise of] Thy faithfulness is great" (Lam. 3:23).[5]

74. Hadrian—may his bones be ground to dust—asked R. Joshua ben Hananiah: Do you people maintain that there is no [permanent] company [of angels] above, who praise God and repeat the praise of Him, but that every day the Holy One, blessed be He, has to create a [new] company of angels, who utter song before Him and then go away? R. Joshua: Yes. Hadrian: Where do they go? R. Joshua: To the place where they were created. Hadrian: Where were they created? R. Joshua: In the fire river. Hadrian: What is the nature of the fire river? R. Joshua: It is like the Jordan, which does not cease its flow either by day or by night. Hadrian: Where is its source? R. Joshua: In the [fiery] perspiration of the celestial creatures—they perspire from carrying the throne of the Holy One, blessed be He.[6]

75. When were the angels created?[7] On the second day of creation, said R. Yohanan. On the fifth day, said R. Hanina.

R. Luliani bar Tabrin said in the name of R. Isaac: All agree that the angels were not created on the first day, so that it should not be said, "While Michael was stretching out the firmament in the south, and Gabriel was stretching it out in the north, the Holy One, blessed be He, was stretching out the middle portion." The fact is, God said, "I am the Lord that maketh all things; that stretched the heavens alone; that spread abroad the earth by Myself (*me-itti*)" (Isa. 44:24). *Me-itti*, "by Myself," when read as *mi itti*, "who with Me,"[8] means: "In the work of the world's creation, who was partner with Me?"[9]

76. "The Lord God of differing manifestations of will" (Hos. 12:6)—the will[10] He exercises upon His angels. When He so wills it, He has them come into being seated; at times He has them come into being standing; at other times He makes them in the likeness of women, or of men; at times as winds, and at still other times as fire. When by His command they act as messengers, they are made winds; when they minister before Him, they are made of fire, as is said, "Who makest winds Thy messengers, the flaming fire Thy ministers" (Ps. 104:4).[11]

77. "He maketh peace in His high places" (Job 25:2). Michael is the prince of snow and Gabriel the prince of fire. Yet Michael does not quench Gabriel, nor does Gabriel incinerate Michael. Even when half of an angel is fire and the other half snow, the Holy One, blessed be He, makes peace between the two parts.[12]

78. The angels are kept alive only by the splendor of the Presence, as is said, "Thou keepest them all alive, and

---

1. B. Hag 13b; Hekhalot.
2. Hekhalot.
3. These two utterances form part of the daily liturgy.
4. Hekhalot.
5. B. Hag 14a.
6. Gen. R. 78:1.
7. Gen. 1 does not mention the creation of angels.
8. The commentator's point here is that since the verse has already said that God alone had stretched the heavens, "by Myself" (*me-itti*) at the end of the verse might appear redundant; but the reading *mi itti* ("who with Me?") makes the sense of the verse emphatic and avoids the seeming redundancy.
9. There were indeed sectarians who asserted that God created nothing but a demiurge, a single angel, and that this angel did all the rest of the work of creation. This concept ascribes all the anthropomorphic passages in the Bible to this angel and thus avoids the charge that the Bible represents God in human form. Gen. R. 1:3.
10. *Tzevaot* ("hosts") is here derived not from *tzb* ("host") but from *tzby* ("will").
11. Exod. R. 25:2; PRE 4.
12. Song R. 3:11, §1; Tanhuma, *Va-yiggash*, §6.

the host of heaven prostrate themselves before Thee" (Neh. 9:6).[1]

79. It is taught: Michael arrives with one flap of the wings, Gabriel with two, Elijah with four. The angel of death arrives with eight, but during a pestilence, he, too, arrives with but one flap of the wings.[2]

80. We have been taught: One angel does not perform two [simultaneous] missions, nor do two angels together perform a single mission.[3]

81. The impulse to evil has no power over angels.[4]

82. We have a tradition: In the world above, there is no sitting down and no rivalry. [Angels have] no backs[5] and [experience] no weariness.[6]

83. R. Simeon ben Lakish said: The Jews brought up the names of angels with them from Babylon. Of yore [before they went to Babylon], Scripture has: "Above Him stood the seraphim" (Isa. 6:2) and "Then flew unto me one of the seraphim" (Isa. 6:7). But after they had been in Babylon, Scripture has: "the man Gabriel" (Dan. 9:21) and "Michael your prince" (Isa. 10:21).[7]

84. One verse says, "Each of them had six wings" (Isa. 6:2), while another says, "And every one had four faces, and every one of them had four wings" (Ezek. 1:6). There is no contradiction. The first verse speaks of the time when the Temple was still standing; the second verse of the time the Temple was no longer standing, when, if one dare say such a thing, the wings of the celestial creatures were diminished. Which wings were taken away? Those with which they used to utter song, said R. Hananel in the name of Rav.

One verse says, "Thousand thousands ministered unto Him, and ten thousand times ten thousand stood before Him" (Dan. 7:10), while another verse says, "Is there a number of His armies?" (Job 25:3). There is no contradiction. The first verse refers to the time when the Temple was still standing, while the second verse refers to the time when the Temple was no longer standing, when, if one dare say such a thing, the household above was diminished.[8]

Idolatry

85. Idolatry is so heinous [a sin] that he who rejects it is as though he affirms the entire Torah, all of it.[9]

1. Exod. R. 32:4.
2. B. Ber 4b.
3. Gen. R. 50:2.
4. Gen. R. 48:11.
5. Angels have eyes all around them so that they may constantly see God. See Ezek. 1:6.
6. B. Hag 15a.
7. P. RH 1:2, 56d.
8. B. Hag 13b.
9. B. Kid 40a.

86. R. Abbahu said in the name of R. Yohanan: In every matter, when a prophet tells you to transgress commands of Torah, obey him,[10] except for idolatry. Even if he should have the sun stand still in the middle of the firmament, do not obey him.[11]

87. R. Nahman said: All sneering is forbidden, except the sneering at idolatry, which is permitted, as is said, "Bel boweth down, Nebo stoopeth. . . . They stoop, they bow down together, they could not deliver the burden" (Isa. 46:1–2).[12]

88. "Should a people seek their god, one who is dead, on behalf of the living?" (Isa. 8:19). The verse may be understood, said R. Levi, by the parable of a man whose son disappeared and who went looking for him in a cemetery. A clever man who saw him asked, "Was your son who disappeared alive or dead?" "Alive." "You are the biggest fool in the world. It makes sense that those who are dead be sought among the living—but the living among the dead? Everywhere the living attend to the needs of the dead, but do the dead attend the needs of the living?" So, too, our God lives and endures forever. But the gods of those who worship idols are dead, as is said, "They have mouths, but they speak not" (Ps. 115:5). Are we to leave Him who lives forever and prostrate ourselves before the dead?[13]

89. General Agrippa asked Rabban Gamaliel: "It is written in your Torah, 'For the Lord thy God is a devouring fire, a jealous God' [Deut. 4:24]. But is a wise man jealous of any but another wise man, a warrior of any but another warrior, a rich man of any but another rich man?" Rabban Gamaliel: "I will tell you a parable by which the verse may be understood. When a man marries a second wife, if the second wife is superior, the first will not be jealous of her; but if she is inferior, the first wife will be jealous of her."[14]

90. A philosopher asked Rabban Gamaliel: "It is written in your Torah, 'For the Lord thy God is a devouring fire, a jealous God' [Deut. 4:24]. But why is He jealous of those who worship an idol rather than of the idol itself?" Rabban Gamaliel: "I will tell you a parable by which the verse may be understood. A king of flesh and blood had a son, and this son reared a dog to which he dared give his father's name, so that whenever he took an oath he exclaimed, 'By the life of the dog my father!' When the king heard of it, with whom was he angry—with his son or with the dog? Surely with his son!" [The philosopher]: "In calling the idol a dog, do you not imply that the idol has substance?"[15] Rabban Gamaliel: "What evidence of it have you seen?"

10. As when Elijah ordered sacrifices brought on Mount Carmel. See 1 Kings 18.
11. B. Sanh 90a.
12. B. Sanh 63b.
13. Lev. R. 6:6.
14. B. AZ 55a.
15. A dog, after all, is a living being.

The philosopher: "Once a fire broke out in our city, and the whole town was burned, but the shrine of the idol was not burned." Rabban Gamaliel: "I will tell you a parable to account for what happened. One of the provinces of a king of flesh and blood has rebelled against him. When he wages war against it, will he wage it against the living or against the dead? Surely against the living!" [The philosopher]: "You call the idol a dog, and now you call it a dead thing. If it is no more than either, let Him extirpate it from the world!" Rabban Gamaliel: "If what was worshiped were something the world had no need of, He would have had it cease to exist; but people worship the sun and the moon, the stars and the planets, brooks and valleys. Should He extirpate His world on account of fools?"

Our masters taught: Some philosophers asked [Jewish] elders in Rome, "If your God has no desire for idolatry, why does He not have it cease to exist?" The elders replied, "If what was worshiped were something the world had no need of, He would have made it cease to exist. But people worship the sun and the moon, the stars and the planets. Should He, on account of fools, make the world cease to exist? So the world must go on as is its wont. As for fools, who act wrongly—they will have to render an account." Another example: "Say a man stole a measure of wheat, and went and sowed it in the ground—by right it should not grow, but the world must go on as is its wont. As for fools, who act wrongly—they will have to render an account."[1]

91. [A Jew named] Zonin said to R. Akiva: My heart and yours know that there is no substance in an idol. Still, we see men enter [its shrine] crippled and come out cured. [Why should that be so?] R. Akiva: I will tell you a parable to explain what happens. There was a trustworthy man in a city, with whom all townsmen used to deposit [their money] without witnesses, except for one man who insisted on depositing [his money] in the presence of witnesses. However, on one occasion he forgot and made his deposit with the trustworthy man without witnesses. The wife [of the trustworthy man] said to [her husband], "Come, let us deny that he made a deposit." He answered, "Just because this fool has been acting improperly, shall we abandon our trustworthiness?" So it is with afflictions. When they are dispatched against a man, they are adjured, "You are to proceed against him only on such-and-such a day; and you are to leave him only on such-and-such a day, at such-and-such an hour, under the care of So-and-so, and by means of such-and-such a potion." Precisely when the time arrives for the afflictions to depart, this particular man happens to go to an idol's shrine. At first the afflictions plead, "By right we should not leave this man." But then, reconsidering, they say, "Just because this fool acts improperly, shall we break our oath?"[2]

92. R. Azariah said in the name of R. Hanina: Only the orb of the sun was created to give light. Why, then, was the moon created? Because the Holy One, blessed be He, foresaw that idolaters would declare them [the sun and moon] to be divinities. So the Holy One, blessed be He, said: If when they are two, now and then outshining each other, idolaters declare them to be divinities, how much more and more would they be likely to do so if only one luminary had been created.[3]

93. A heathen asked R. Joshua ben Korhah: "In your Torah it is written, 'One is to follow the many' [Exod. 23:2]. We are more numerous than you. Why, then, do you not agree with us about idolatry?" R. Joshua: "Have you sons?" The heathen: "You remind me of my aggravation." R. Joshua: "Why do you say that?" The heathen: "I have many children. When they sit at my table, one recites a blessing to this god, and another recites a blessing to that god, and they do not rise from the table until they all but crack each other's skulls." R. Joshua: "Do you ever get them to agree with one another?" The heathen: "No." R. Joshua: "Before making us agree with you, go and bring about agreement among your own children." Thus rebuffed, the heathen went away.

After he had gone, R. Joshua's disciples said to him, "Master, you thrust him off with a broken reed; but what answer will you give us?" R. Joshua: "You numskulls, by rights I should not answer you. However . . . In connection with Esau, only six souls are mentioned in Scripture, and they are spoken of in the plural as 'souls' [Gen. 36:6], while in connection with Jacob, Scripture mentions seventy souls, and they are spoken of in the singular as one soul. The reason for Scripture's inconsistency: with regard to Esau, whose descendants worshiped many gods, the phrase 'many souls' is used.[4] But with regard to Jacob, whose entire household worshiped the one God, the phrase 'one soul' is used: 'They who came out of the loins of Jacob were one soul' " (Exod. 1:5).[5]

94. What is [the heathen idol] teraphim? A man, a firstborn, is slaughtered. His head is plucked off and pickled in salt and spices. Then the name of the spirit of uncleanness, written on a plate of gold, is placed under his tongue. The head is affixed to a wall, lamps are lit in front of it, and people prostrate themselves before it.[6]

95. What is [the heathen idol] Molech like? Our masters taught: Even though all other shrines for idolatry were in Jerusalem, Molech's was outside Jerusalem, some distance away. It was a hollowed image, its visage that of a calf, its hands spread out like those of a man who opens his hands to receive something from his fellow, and in one hand it held a copper plate. The image was placed within seven enclosures, which a man entered in keeping with the offering he brought. He who offered a fowl entered the first enclosure and offered it. A goat, the second. A lamb, the third. A calf, the fourth. A bullock, the fifth. An ox, the sixth. He who offered his son would be told by the

1. B. AZ 54b and En Yaakov, ad loc.
2. B. AZ 55a.
3. Gen. R. 6:1.
4. Hence, even though Esau's descendants are numerous, they do not constitute a majority, since they are divided among themselves.
5. Lev. R. 4:6; Yalkut, *Va-yishlah*, §137.
6. Tanhuma, *Va-yetze*, §12; PRE 36.

priests that no one was higher than he, and he was allowed to enter the seventh enclosure, where he would kiss the Molech. With regard to such kissing, Scripture says, "They that sacrifice men kiss calves" (Hos. 13:2). The Molech was heated from within until its hands became as hot as fire. Then the child was taken and placed between the idol's hands on the copper plate. Timbrels were brought and struck to make a loud noise, so that the father should not hear the cry of his son and his heart yearn for him. They who stood there intoned songs, while the priests commended the father as they said to him, "May it please you! May it benefit you! May it agree with you!"[1]

96. R. Isaac said: What is meant by the verse "And now they sin more and more, and they made them molten images of their silver, according to their own understanding, even idols" (Hos. 13:2)? The verse suggests that each of them made a small image of the object of his awe, put it in his purse,[2] and whenever he thought of it, took it from his bosom, fondled it, and kissed it.

"Men sacrifice themselves in homage to calves" (Hos. 13:2).[3] R. Isaac of the school of R. Ammi said: When priests cast covetous eyes upon men of means, they would starve the calves [that were worshiped]. Then they made images in the likenesses of these men of means, which they set at the calves' cribs. After a while, they let loose the calves, which, upon seeing the men [whose images they had learned to associate with food], started running after them, eager to lick them. Then the priests would say to each of these men, "The idol yearns for you. Come and sacrifice yourself to him."[4]

97. "Moreover thou hast taken thy sons . . . whom thou hast borne unto Me, and . . . hast sacrificed them [to the images] of those idols" (Ezek. 16:20). A priest would come to a man and say to him, "Such-and-such an idol has sent me to you, because he has heard you have many sons. Why don't you bring one of them as an offering?" The man would reply, "They are no longer under my authority—one is engaged with silver, another with gold; one with flocks, another with herds." The priest: "But if you come before the idol empty-handed, will he not be angry with you?" The man: "I have a young son at school. Wait until he comes home, and I will give him to you. Then you may go and bring him as an offering." At that, the Holy One, blessed be He, would say to the man, "Thou hast taken thy sons . . . whom thou hast borne unto Me, and . . . hast sacrificed them [to the images] of these idols." Of all the sons you have, you would sacrifice none but the one who [being at school] is consecrated to Me![5]

98. "And I will cast your carcasses upon the carcasses of your idols" (Lev. 26:30). The sages said: Elijah the Righteous, while searching in Jerusalem for those swollen by hunger, found a child swollen and lying [helpless] on a dung-heap. He asked, "From what family are you?" The child: "From such-and-such a family." Elijah: "Does anyone of that family remain alive?" The child: "No one except me." Elijah: "If I teach you something by which you can stay alive, will you learn it?" The child: "Yes." Elijah: "Every day, say, 'Hear, O Israel, the Lord our God, the Lord is one' " (Deut. 6:4). The child: "Be silent, for one must not make mention of the Name of the Lord" (Amos 6:10). He spoke thus because his father and his mother had not taught him [to worship God]. Then the child took the idolatrous object of his awe out of his bosom, fondled it, and kissed it until his belly burst. The object of his awe fell to the ground and he fell upon it, to fulfill the verse "I will cast your carcasses upon the carcasses of your idols."[6]

99. Manasseh appeared in a dream to R. Ashi, who asked him: Why did you people worship idols? Manasseh replied: Had you been living in our time, you would have hiked up the skirt of your garment and come running to join us.[7]

100. "And they cried with a loud voice unto the Lord their God" (Neh. 9:4). What was the cry about? [They cried], "Woe, woe, it is [the impulse to idolatry] that destroyed the Sanctuary, burned the Temple Hall, slew all the righteous, exiled Israel from their Land, and still dances around in our midst! You have given him to us for no purpose other than that we may receive a reward through him, but we want neither him nor the reward through him!" Then a tablet fell down from heaven, upon which was written, "True." They observed a fast for three days and three nights, and the impulse was handed over to them, emerging from the Holy of Holies like a fiery lion. A prophet of Israel said, "This is the wickedness" (Zech. 5:8), namely, the impulse to idolatry. When they seized him [the impulse] and a single hair was pulled from the hair of his head, his cry of pain was heard four hundred parasangs away. The sages asked, "What shall we do? They may, God forbid, take pity on him in heaven." The prophet advised, "Throw him into a leaden pot and cover its mouth with lead, because lead absorbs sound."[8]

101. R. Judah said in the name of Rav: Once, when a gentile woman fell very sick, she vowed, "If this sick woman recovers from her sickness, she will go and worship every idol in the world." She did recover and proceeded to pay homage to every idol in the world, until she reached Peor, where she asked her servants, "How does one worship this one?" "People eat beets, drink beer, and then defecate against it." The gentile woman said, "I would rather fall sick again than worship an idol in such a way."[9]

102. There is the story of Savta of the town of Alas,[10] who hired out his ass to a gentile woman. When she got

1. Tanhuma B, *Va-et'hannan*, supplement, §2; Lam. R. 1:9, §36; Yalkut, Jer., §277.
2. The word *mi-kaspam* ("of their silver") is construed as portmanteau; *mi-kis* ("out of the purse") and *peh* ("[kiss with] the mouth").
3. JV: "They that sacrifice men kiss calves."
4. B. Sanh 63b.
5. Lam. R. 1:9, §36.
6. B. Sanh 63b–64a and En Yaakov, ad loc.
7. B. Sanh 102b.
8. B. Yoma 69b.
9. B. Sanh 64a.
10. In Cilicia.

to Peor, she said to Savta, "Wait until I go in and come out again." After she came out, he said to her, "You, too, wait until I go in and come out." She asked him, "Are you not a Jew?" He replied, "How does that concern you?" He went in, defecated in the idol's presence, and wiped himself on its nose. At that, the idol's retinue applauded him, saying: No one has ever served Peor so well.[1]

103. A Parsee priest said to Amemar: From your middle upward, you belong to Ormazd; and from your middle downward, you belong to Ahriman. Amemar asked: Why then does Ahriman allow Ormazd to send water through his territory?[2]

104. Everywhere you find that the Holy One, blessed be He, requites the kingdoms only after He first requites their idols and their princes. Thus Scripture first says, "It shall come to pass in that day, that the Lord will punish the host of the high heaven on high" (Isa. 24:21), and after that, "And the kings of the earth upon the earth" (ibid.).[3]

105. The proverb says: Idols maimed—their priests are shamed.[4]

106. Our masters taught: If one sees a statue of Mercurius, he is to say, "Blessed be He who shows forbearance toward those who transgress His will." If he sees a place from which idolatry has been uprooted, he is to say, "Blessed be He who has uprooted idolatry from our Land; and as it has been uprooted from this place, so may it be uprooted from all places belonging to Israel, and may the hearts of [Israelites] who serve such idols be turned to serve Thee." It is not necessary to say the latter words outside the Land, where most of the people are Gentiles. However, R. Simeon ben Eleazar said: One should say these words outside the Land as well, because the people there will eventually become proselytes, as is said, "For then I will make the peoples pure of speech, so that they all invoke the Lord by name" (Zeph. 3:9).[5]

107. "Ashamed will be all they that serve graven images, that boast themselves of things of nought; bow down to Him, all ye gods" (Ps. 97:7). R. Nahman said in the name of R. Mana: The idol is destined to come spit in the face of those who worship it and put them to shame, then bow down before the Holy One, blessed be He—and cease to exist.[6]

Heretics

108. R. Yohanan said: Not until twenty-four sects of heretics had come into being were Israel exiled. And the proof? The verse "Son of man, I send thee to the children of Israel, to the rebellious nations that have rebelled against Me" (Ezek. 2:3). God did not say, "To the rebellious nation," but, "To the rebellious nations that have rebelled against Me; they and their fathers have transgressed against Me, even unto this very day" (ibid.).[7]

109. "Remove thy way far from her" (Prov. 5:8)—from heresy. A man is told, "Don't go into the midst of heretics, don't even look in on them, lest you stumble because of them." Should the man say, "I am sure of myself, so that even if I go there, I will not stumble," he is told, "Even though you are sure, don't go, lest you say, 'I think there is something in what they assert, and I will go back to them [to learn more].' Scripture says clearly, 'All who go there will not return and thus not attain the paths of life' " (Prov. 2:19).[8]

110. Scripture says, "She hath prepared her meat; she hath mingled her wine; she hath also furnished her table" (Prov. 9:2). In this verse [the wiles of] heretics are meant. Because, when a man comes into their midst, they feed him, clothe him, shelter him, and give him much money. But as soon as he becomes one of them, each identifies what he gave him and takes it back. Hence Scripture: "Till an arrow strike through his liver; as a bird hasteneth to the snare—and knoweth not that it is at the cost of his life" (Prov. 7:23).[9]

111. One should not engage in give-and-take with heretics, nor should one receive medical treatment from them even to prolong life by ever so little.

It once happened to Ben Dama, the son of R. Ishmael's sister, that he was bitten by a snake. Jacob of Kefar Sekhania[10] came to heal him, but R. Ishmael did not allow him to. Ben Dama pleaded, "Ishmael, my uncle, allow me to be healed by him—I will cite for you proof from the Torah that he is permitted to." He did not finish speaking when his soul departed, just as he was uttering the word "permitted," and he died. R. Ishmael exclaimed, "Happy are you, Ben Dama, that your body is pure, that your soul has left you while you were in a state of purity, and that you have not disregarded the words of your colleagues, who quote 'He who breaketh through a fence, a serpent shall bite him' " (Eccles. 10:8).[11]

112. The Evangels and the books of the heretics are not to be saved from a fire [on a Sabbath].[12] R. Yose the Galilean said: When I find books of heretics, I cut out the divine Names written in them, hide those, and burn the rest. R. Tarfon said: May I bury my sons if, when

1. B. Sanh 64a.
2. Water taken in at the mouth and emptied through urination. B. Sanh 39a.
3. Yalkut, Isa., §418; Yalkut, Jer., §331, based on Mek, *Be-shallah*, *Shirata*, 2, and Tanhuma, *Bo*, §4.
4. Literally, "Strike the idols, and their priests will be confounded." Tanhuma, *Va-era*, §13.
5. B. Ber 57b and En Yaakov, ad loc.
6. P. AZ 4:7, 44a.
7. The nation of Israel is made up of twelve tribes. The plural "nations" is taken to imply double that number—hence twenty-four sects of rebels. So *Kikkar la-Aden*, ad loc. P. Sanh 10:5, 29c.
8. ARN 2; ARNB 2.
9. ARN 2.
10. Possibly James son of Alphaeus (Mark 3:18) or James the Younger (Mark 15:40). So Isidore Epstein in AZ, Soncino, p. 85, n. 3.
11. B. AZ 27b and En Yaakov, ad loc.
12. Which involves labor prohibited on the Sabbath.

books of heretics come into my hands, I do not bury them together with the divine Names in them! For even if a man pursued me to slay me and a serpent were after me to bite me, I would seek refuge in a heathen temple rather than in the houses of heretics, since idolaters do not know the Holy One, blessed be He, and so deny Him, whereas these [the heretics] know Him and still deny Him.

R. Ishmael said: If in order to make peace between a man and his wife, He who is everywhere has said, "My Name, written in sanctity, is to be blotted out in water,"[1] how much more does it follow that the books of heretics, which cause hatred, anger, and strife between Israel and their Father in heaven, are to be burned, together with the divine Names written in them. Of such books Scripture says, "Do I not hate them, O Lord, that hate Thee? And do I not strive with those that rise up against Thee? I hate them with utmost hatred; I count them as my enemies" (Ps. 139:21–22). And just as we are not to save them from a fire, so we are not to save them from under a collapsed house, from water, or from anything else that may destroy them.[2]

113. Our masters taught: When R. Eliezer was arrested on suspicion of [Judeo-Christian] heresy, he was brought up on the [torturer's] scaffold to be examined. The governor said to him, "How can a venerable sage like you occupy himself with such drivel?" R. Eliezer replied, "I acknowledge the Judge as right." The governor, thinking that R. Eliezer referred to him—in fact he referred to his Father in heaven—said, "Because you have acknowledged me as being right, I grant you pardon. You are acquitted." Nevertheless, R. Eliezer felt uneasy about the accusation of heresy. When he came home, his disciples called on him to console him,[3] but he would accept no consolation. R. Akiva said to him, "Master, will you permit me to cite something you taught me?" He replied, "Cite it." "Master, is it possible that some heretical teaching had been reported to you and you found it pleasing, and for that reason you were arrested?" He exclaimed, "Akiva, you have reminded me. I was once walking in the upper market of Sepphoris when I came across one of the disciples of Jesus the Nazarene, named Jacob of Kefar Sekhania. He said to me, 'It is written in your Torah, "Thou shalt not bring the hire of a harlot . . . into the house of the Lord thy God" [Deut. 23:19]. May such money be applied to the erection of a privy for the high priest?' To this I made no reply. He went on, 'Thus was I taught [by Jesus the Nazarene]: "For of the hire of a harlot hath she gathered them, and unto the hire of a harlot shall they return" [Mic. 1:7]—since it came from a place of filth, it should go back to a place of filth [such as the high priest's privy].' Those words pleased me very much, and that is why I was arrested for heresy, for in reacting thus, I transgressed Scripture: 'Remove thy way far from her' [Prov. 5:8], meaning heresy, 'so that you will not have to come nigh to the door of her house' [Prov. 5:8]—to the house of the ruling power."[4]

114. When Hananiah the son of R. Joshua's brother went to Capernaum, the heretics worked a spell on him and brought him into the town riding his ass on the Sabbath. His uncle Joshua visited him and gave him an ointment, and the spell was removed. He said to him: Since the ass of that wicked person[5] is now roused against you, you should not continue living in the Land of Israel. So he went down to Babylonia, where he died in peace.[6]

115. R. Judah ben Nakosah had dealings with the heretics. They kept asking him questions, which he kept answering. They continued goading him with questions, which he answered. Finally he said to them: We argue to no purpose. Come, let us agree between ourselves that he who prevails may hit the opponent's head with a mallet. He kept prevailing and kept hitting them until their heads were covered with bruises.

When he returned, his disciples said to him: Master, you were helped by Heaven, and you prevailed. He replied: To no purpose. Go and pray for me, and also for this bag [passing as my head], which was once filled with precious stones and pearls, and now is filled with [burned-out] coals.[7]

116. Our masters taught: The left hand may always repulse, but the right hand should bring near. Not like R. Joshua ben Perahiah, who repulsed Jesus with both hands.

What was the incident with R. Joshua ben Perahiah? When King Yannai rose up against the sages to put them to death, Simeon ben Shetah was hidden by his sister, and R. Joshua ben Perahiah [and Jesus] fled to Alexandria of Egypt. When peace came,[8] Simeon ben Shetah wrote to R. Joshua, "From me, Jerusalem the holy city, to you, my sister Alexandria of Egypt: My husband dwells in your midst, and I abide desolate." R. Joshua replied, "I understand. Peace upon you." So he rose up, together with his disciple [Jesus], and came to Jerusalem. He happened to put up at a certain inn [run by a woman], where great honor was accorded him. He remarked, "What a beautiful inn." His disciple replied, "Yes, master, but her[9] eyes are bleary." R. Joshua: "You wicked person! So it is with such matters that you occupy yourself!" At that, he brought forth four hundred rams' horns and [had them sound as he] excommunicated him. Though Jesus came day after day before R. Joshua, pleading, "Take me back," R. Joshua paid no attention to him. But one day, as R. Joshua was reciting the Shema, [Jesus] came and stood before him. [Relenting], R. Joshua decided to take him back and motioned to him with his hand. But Jesus interpreted the gesture as a final repulse. So he went off, set up a brick, and worshiped it.

---

1. See Num. 5:23ff.
2. B. Shab 116a; P. Shab 16:1, 15c; Tos Shab 14:5; Tanhuma B, *Korah*, supplement, §1.
3. R. Eliezer was greatly troubled: what sin had he committed that God should have made him the victim of such a charge?
4. B. AZ 16b–17a and En Yaakov, ad loc; Eccles. R. 1:8, §3; Yalkut, Mic., §551.
5. Jesus.
6. Eccles. R. 1:8, §4.
7. Some of the heretics' arguments contaminated his mind. Ibid.
8. At Yannai's death. See above, part 2, chap. 1, §48.
9. *Aksania* (Greek *xenia*) means both "inn" and "hostess of the inn."

R. Joshua implored, "Repent." But Jesus replied, "I have a tradition from you: he who sins and causes others to sin should not be given the opportunity to repent."

A master taught: Jesus practiced magic and incited Israel to heresy, leading them astray.[1]

117. Ben Stada brought out [secrets] of sorcery from Egypt by incising them in his flesh.[2]

118. He who incites to idolatry should be brought to the [High] Court, where he is to be condemned to death by stoning. This was done in Lod to Ben Stada, whose body was hanged [after being stoned].[3]

119. We have been taught: Jesus was executed on the eve of Passover. Forty days prior to the execution, a herald went forth and proclaimed, "He is going forth to be stoned because he practiced sorcery, incited to idolatry, and led Israel astray. Anyone who knows anything in his defense, let him come forward and plead in his behalf." Since no one pleaded, he was hanged on the eve of Passover.

Ulla challenged the account: Do you suppose that he was one for whom such a plea could possibly have been made? He was one who incited to idolatry, of whom the Torah says, "Neither shalt thou spare, neither shalt thou conceal him" (Deut. 13:9).

Jesus had to be treated differently[4] because he was close to the [Roman] government.

The sages taught: Jesus had five disciples: Mattai, Nakkai, Netzer, Bunni, and Todah. When Mattai was brought before the court, he asked [the judges], "Shall Mattai be put to death? Is it not writtten, '*Matai*[5] shall come and appear before God' (Ps. 42:3)?" They replied, "Yes, Mattai is to be put to death, for it is written, '*Matai* shall die, and his name perish' " (Ps. 41:6). When Nakkai was brought before the court, he asked [the judges], "Shall Nakkai be put to death? Is it not written, '*Naki*[6] and the righteous slay thou not' (Exod. 23:7)?" The judges replied, "Yes, Nakkai is to be put to death, since it is written, 'In secret places does *naki* slay' " (Ps. 10:8). When Netzer was brought in, he asked [the judges], "Shall Netzer be put to death? Is it not written, 'And *Netzer* [7] shall grow forth out of his roots' (Isa. 11:1)?" They replied, "Yes, Netzer shall be put to death, for it is written, 'But thou art cast forth away from thy grave like *Netzer*'"[8] (Isa. 14:19). When Bunni was brought, he asked, "Shall Bunni be put to death? Is it not written, '*Beni*,[9] My firstborn' (Exod. 4:22)?" They replied, "Yes, Bunni shall be put to death, for it is written, 'Behold, I will slay *binekha*,[10] thy firstborn' " (Exod. 4:23). When Todah was brought in, he asked, "Shall Todah be put to death? Is it not written, 'A Psalm for *todah*'[11] (Ps. 100:1)?" They replied, "Yes, Todah is to be put to death, for it is written, 'Whoso slaughtereth todah[12] honoreth Me' " (Ps. 50:23).[13]

120. "No man is God" (Num. 23:19)[14] [was uttered] because Balaam foresaw that a certain man would lead mortals astray by claiming to be God.[15]

121. R. Avin said in the name of R. Hilkiah: The minds of those liars who say that the Holy One, blessed be He, has a son are truly dense. Consider what happened to Abraham's son. When God saw that Abraham was about to slaughter him, He could not bear to see him in pain, but immediately cried out, "Do not put forth your hand" (Gen. 22:12). Now, if God had a son, would He have allowed him to be crucified? Would He not have turned the world upside down, reducing it to chaos and desolation? Solomon said, "There is One that is alone, and He hath not a second; yea, He hath neither son nor brother" (Eccles. 4:8).[16]

122. "There is One . . . and He hath not a second." "There is One": the Holy One, blessed be He, of whom it is said, "The Lord our God, the Lord is one" (Deut. 6:4). "And He hath not a second": He has no partner in His world. "He hath neither son nor brother": since He has no brother, how is He to have a son?[17]

123. "I am the Lord thy God" (Exod. 20:2). R. Abbahu said: Consider by way of contrast the parable of a king of flesh and blood who reigns and who has a father or a brother. On the other hand, the Holy One, blessed be He, said: I am not like that. "I am the first" (Isa. 44:6), for I have no father; "and I am the last" (ibid.), for I have no son; "and beside Me there is no God" (ibid.), for I have no brother.[18]

124. R. Yohanan said: In all the passages that heretics cite [as proof for their heretical teaching], the refutation is found near at hand. Thus: "Let *us* make man in *our* image" (Gen. 1:26) is refuted by "And God created [a verb in the singular] man in His own image" (Gen. 1:27). "Come, let us go down and there confound their language" (Gen. 11:7) is refuted by "And the Lord came down [a verb in the singular] to see the city and the tower" (Gen. 9:5). "Because there were revealed to him *Gods*" (Gen. 35:7) is refuted by "Unto God who answereth [a verb in the singular] me in the day of my distress" (Gen. 35:3). "For what great nation is there that hath God so nigh [an

---

1. B. Sot 47a; B. Sanh 107b.
2. B. Shab 104b.
3. B. Sanh 47a, as in Munich and Oxford mss.
4. He was hanged, not stoned.
5. JV: "when."
6. JV: "The innocent."
7. JV: "a twig."
8. JV: "an abhorred offshoot."
9. JV: "My son."
10. JV: "thy son."
11. JV: "of thanksgiving."
12. JV: "[sacrifice of] thanksgiving."
13. All the foregoing are a kind of word game. B. Sanh 43a.
14. JV: "God is not a man."
15. Tanhuma, *Balak*, according to *Etz ha-Daat Tov*, by Hayyim Vital (Zolkiev; 1870).
16. Aggadat Bereshit 31 (ed. Buber, p. 64).
17. Since He has none like Him, whose daughter could he marry to bear Him a son? Eccles. R. 4:8, §1.
18. Exod. R. 29:5.

adverb in the plural] unto it, as the Lord our God is [unto us]" (Deut. 4:7) is refuted by the same verse's conclusion, "Whensoever we call upon Him" [pronoun in singular form] (ibid.). "And what one nation in the earth is like Thy people, Israel, whom God went" [a verb in the plural] (2 Sam. 7:23) is refuted by the verse's conclusion, "To redeem for a people unto Himself" [a pronoun in the singular] (ibid.). "Till thrones were placed" (Dan. 7:9) is refuted by the verse's conclusion, "And *one* that was ancient did sit" (ibid.).

Still, why should the foregoing verbs and nouns have plural forms? Because the Holy One, blessed be He, does nothing without first consulting His household above, as is said, "The matter is by the decree of the watchers, and the sentence by the word of the holy ones" (Dan. 4:14). Now, what was just said explains adequately the use of the plural in all the verses, except "Till thrones were placed." How is this phrase to be explained? One throne was for justice, the other for mercy.[1]

125. "I am the Lord thy God" (Exod. 20:2). The heretics challenged R. Simlai, saying: There are many divinities in the world. R. Simlai asked them: Why do you say so? They replied: Because Scripture says, "Did ever a people hear the voice of *elohim* (gods)?" (Deut. 4:33). R. Simlai: But does Scripture go on to say, "They speak" (*medabberim*, plural)? No; it says, "He speaks" (*medabber*, singular).

At this, R. Simlai's disciples said to him: Master, you put these off with a broken reed of an answer. But how will you reply to us? [R. Simlai]: It was R. Levi who considered this verse and explained it, saying: How is the verse "Did ever a people hear the voices of *elohim* (gods)?" to be understood? [In the light of "The voice of the Lord is fitted to the strength" (Ps. 29:4).] Had it read, "The voice of the Lord is in His strength," the world could not have endured it. Hence Scripture says, "The voice of the Lord is fitted to the strength," that is to say, to the strength of each and every person—the young according to their strength, the aged according to their strength, the little ones according to their strength. By this, the Holy One, blessed be He, intended to say: Because you hear so many voices, do not imagine that there are many gods in heaven. Rather, you are to know that I alone am the Lord your God, as is said, "I am the Lord your God" (Exod. 20:2).[2]

126. We have been taught that R. Simeon ben Azzai said: Pause and consider that in connection with all the offerings in the Torah there is no mention of El or Elohim, no mention of Shaddai, or Tzevaot—only "Lord," in order not to give heretics the opportunity to rebel.[3]

127. A heretic asked R. Ishmael son of R. Yose: Scripture says, "Then the Lord caused to rain upon Sodom and upon Gomorrah brimstone and fire from the Lord" (Gen. 19:24). Should it not have said, "From Him"? A certain fuller interjected, "Leave him to me. I will answer him." [He then proceeded]: "It is written, 'And Lamech said to his wives: Ada and Zillah, hear my voice, ye wives of Lamech' [Gen. 4:23]. He should have said, 'My wives.' But such is the idiom of Scripture. Here, too, such is the idiom of Scripture."[4]

128. "It is not in heaven" (Deut. 30:12). Moses said to them, "Do not say, 'Another Moses will arise and bring us another Torah from heaven,' for I say to you, 'It is not in heaven'—no part of it has remained in heaven."[5]

129. R. Meir calls the heretics' writ *aven-gilion*,[6] "the gospel of falsehood"; R. Yohanan calls it *avon-gilion*, "the gospel of iniquity."

In the vicinity of Imma Shalom, R. Eliezer's wife, who was Rabban Gamaliel's sister, there lived a heretical judge who had a reputation for not accepting bribes. In an attempt to expose him, Imma Shalom brought him a golden lamp. She then appeared before him [in court], where she said, "I desire that a share be given me in my [deceased] father's estate." He ordered, "Divide [the estate]!" But Rabban Gamaliel spoke up, "In our Scripture, it is written, 'Where there is a son, a daughter does not inherit.' " The heretical judge: "Ever since the day you were exiled from your Land, the Torah of Moses has been suspended and another Torah given.[7] In that Torah it is written, 'A son and a daughter inherit equally.' " The next day, after Rabban Gamaliel had brought him a Lybian ass, the judge said to them, "I have read further to the end of the book, where it is written, 'I came not to destroy the Torah of Moses,[8] but only to add to the Torah of Moses,' and as you said, in that Torah it is written, 'A daughter does not inherit where there is a son.' " At this, Imma Shalom said to the judge, "May your light shine forth like a lamp!" Rabban Gamaliel added, "An ass has come and knocked down the lamp!"[9]

130. Heretics challenged R. Abbahu: We do not find death mentioned in connection with Enoch. R. Abbahu: What makes you say so? The heretics: It is said of Enoch, "God took him" (Gen. 5:24), and it is said of Elijah [who did not die], "Knowest thou that the Lord will take away thy master from thy head today?" (2 Kings 2:3). R. Abbahu: If you base your conclusion on the term "taking," consider that, just as it is used of Enoch, so is it used with regard to the death of Ezekiel's wife, of whom it is said, "I take away from thee the desire of thine eyes with a stroke" (Ezek. 24:16) ["with a stroke" clearly implying death]. R. Tanhuma observed: R. Abbahu answered them beautifully.[10]

---

1. B. Sanh 38b.
2. Hence, the voices of what appear to be several gods are in reality varying manifestations of the one and only God. Exod. R. 29:1.
3. By saying that there are many deities. B. Men 110a; Sif Num., §143.
4. B. Sanh 38b.
5. Deut. R. 8:6.
6. A play on the Greek word *evangelion* ("gospel").
7. Or, as in the Oxford Codex: "and the law of the Evangelium has been given."
8. See Matthew 5:17ff.
9. B. Shab 116a–b.
10. Gen. R. 25:1.

131. There were once two heretics; one was called Sason, "joy," and the other Simhah, "gladness." Sason said to Simhah, "I am better than you, since it is said, 'They shall obtain Sason and Simhah' " (Isa. 35:10).[1] "No," said Simhah, "I am better than you, since it is written, 'The Jews had Simhah and Sason' " (Esther 8:17).[2] "One day," said Sason to Simhah, "they will take you out and make you a mere runner, since it is said, 'For with Simhah shall they go forth' " (Isa. 55:12). "One day," Simhah said to Sason, "they will take you out and draw water with you, for it is said, 'Therefore with Sason shall ye draw water' " (Isa. 4:3).

A Sadducee whose name was Sason said to R. Abbahu, "In the world-to-come, you will be drawing water for me, since it is said, 'Ye shall draw water for joy (*be-sason*)' " (Isa. 12:3).[3] R. Abbahu replied, "Had the text actually read 'for joy (*le-sason*),' you would have been right. But since it reads 'in joy (*be-sason*),' it implies that your skin will be made into a bottle for us to draw water."[4]

132. Know how to answer the unbeliever.[5]

Between Man and Him Who Is Everywhere

133. Bar Kappara expounded: What is the brief passage upon which all principles of Torah depend? "In all thy ways be aware of Him" (Prov. 3:6).[6]

134. "It is He that buildeth His upper chamber in the heaven, [which is firm only] as long as it stays tied together; [otherwise it collapses] upon the earth on which He founded it" (Amos 9:6).[7] R. Simeon ben Yohai said: The verse may be understood by the parable of a man who brought two ships and fastened them together with anchors and clamps, then placed them on their keels [on dry land] and built a [chambered] palace over them. As long as the ships stay fastened together, the [chambered] palace stands. Once the ships are separated, the [chambered] palace will not stand. So are Israel: when they obey the will of Him who is everywhere, His upper chamber in heaven stands. But when they do not obey the will of Him who is everywhere, "that which [was] tied together [collapses] upon the earth on which He founded it." Similarly, you say, "This is my God, and I will glorify Him" (Exod. 15:2). When I acknowledge Him, He—if one dare say such a thing—is glorified, but when I do not acknowledge Him, He is glorified merely in name. Similarly, you say, "Ye are My witnesses, saith the Lord, and I am God" (Isa. 43:12). When you are My witnesses, I am God, but when you are not My witnesses, I am not God. Similarly, you say, "Unto Thee I lift up mine eyes, O Thou that art my enthroned one[8] in the heavens" (Ps. 123:1). But for me, You would not be sitting in the heavens.[9]

135. "The God before whom my fathers did walk" (Gen. 48:15). R. Yohanan and Resh Lakish differed in their interpretations of this verse. R. Yohanan said: God is compared to a shepherd who stands and watches his flock. Resh Lakish said: He is like a prince before whom the elders walk. According to R. Yohanan's opinion, we are in need [of the majesty] of His glory.[10] According to Resh Lakish, He is in need [of our eagerness] to glorify Him.[11]

136. "And thou shalt love the Lord thy God," etc. (Deut. 6:5). R. Eliezer the Elder commented: If Scripture says, "With all thy soul," why also say "With all thy might"? On the other hand, if it says, "With all thy might," why say also, "With all thy soul"? The answer is: Should there be a man whose body is more precious to him than his money, Scripture says to him, "With all thy soul"; and should there be a man whose monetary might is more precious to him than his life, Scripture says to him, "With all thy might." But R. Akiva maintained that "With all thy soul" means: Love Him even during the affliction you suffer at His taking the soul from your body. Simeon ben Azzai said: "With all thy soul"—love Him until your soul departs from you.

"Thou shalt love the Lord thy God with thy entire heart" (Deut. 6:5)—with both your impulses, the impulse to good and the impulse to evil.[12]

137. R. Yose said: Let all your deeds be for the sake of Heaven.[13]

138. "The fear of the Lord is His treasure" (Isa. 33:6). Rava said: When a man is led in for judgment [in the world-to-come], he is asked, "In your dealings, did you give and take with integrity? Did you fix definite times for study of Torah? Did you fulfill the duty of being fruitful and multiplying? Did you wait for [God's] deliverance? Did you analyze the wisdom you acquired? Did you draw proper inferences from each utterance?" No matter what the answer to these questions, if "the fear of the Lord is his treasure,"[14] it will go well with him; if not, it will not go well. The latter may be compared to a situation where a man told his agent, "Bring a *kor* of wheat up for me into my upper chamber." After the agent went and brought it

1. "Joy" before "gladness."
2. "Gladness" before "joy."
3. JV: "Therefore with joy shall ye draw water."
4. The stories of Sason and Simhah may have been directed at heresiarchs, who by various means "found" allusions to themselves in Scripture. R. Abbahu was known for his skill in debating such heretics. B. Suk 48b.
5. Avot 2:19. See parallel in 1 Peter 3:15.
6. B. Ber 63a.
7. JV: "It is He that buildeth His upper chambers in the heaven, and hath founded His vault upon the earth." But *aguddato* ("His vault") can also mean "that which He fastened together."
8. "The poetic form *yoshvi* (enthroned one) would in ordinary prose mean 'my enthroned one' " (Brother Caedmon Holmes).
9. Sif Deut., §346.
10. To scare off all kinds of predators.
11. Since we are the ones who speak of His greatness. Gen. R. 30:10.
12. B. Ber 61b; Sif Deut., §32.
13. Avot 2:17.
14. Even if he answers all these questions affirmatively, he is asked the final and most important question: Did he fear the Lord?

up, the man asked him, "Did you mix in with it a *kav* of sandy soil containing salt?"[1] When the agent said no, he replied, "Then it would have been better if you had not carried up the wheat at all."[2]

139. R. Hanina said: Everything is in the hand of Heaven except the fear of Heaven, as is said, "And now Israel, what is the one thing that the Lord thy God requireth of thee, but to fear Him?" (Deut. 10:12). Yet, is the fear of Heaven such a small thing? Did not R. Hanina, citing R. Simeon ben Yohai, say: In His treasuries the Holy One, blessed be He, has naught but the treasure of fear of Heaven, as is said, "His one treasure is fear of the Lord" (Isa. 33:6)? Yes, for Moses it was a small thing, as R. Hanina explained by the parable of a man who is asked for a big utensil he happens to have—it seems a small thing to him. But if he is asked for a small utensil he does not have, it seems a big thing to him.[3]

140. R. Helbo said in the name of R. Huna: He who is filled with the fear of Heaven—his words are listened to, as is said, "The end of the matter, [when] all is heard, Fear God, and keep His commandments, that being all of man" (Eccles. 12:13). What is meant by "That being all of man"? According to R. Eleazar, the Holy One said: The entire world, all of it, was brought into being for such a man. According to R. Abba bar Kahana, such a man is equal in worth to the entire world, all of it. According to R. Simeon ben Azzai, the entire world, all of it, was brought into being only to provide companionship for such a man.[4]

141. R. Hama bar Papa said: When a man is endowed with grace, it is clear that he is one who fears Heaven, as is said, "The grace of the Lord is from everlasting to everlasting upon them that fear Him" (Ps. 103:17).[5]

142. When R. Yohanan ben Zakkai fell ill, his disciples came in to visit him . . . and said to him: Our master, bless us. He replied: May it be God's will that the fear of Heaven shall be [as great] upon you as the fear of flesh and blood. His disciples asked: Is that all?[6] He replied: Would that you might attain even this much fear! You can see for yourselves the truth of what I say: When a man is about to commit a transgression, he says, "I hope no man will see me."[7]

143. R. Simeon ben Eleazar said: Greater is he who acts from love than he who acts from fear. For the latter, the merit remains in effect for only a thousand generations, while for the former, it remains in effect for two thousand generations. With regard to love of God, Scripture says, "He keepeth mercy for two thousand [generations] for them that love Me and keep His commandments [out of love]" (Exod. 20:6); while with regard to fear, Scripture says elsewhere, "For a thousand [generations] for them that keep His commandments [out of fear]" (Deut. 7:9).[8]

144. Judah ben Tema said: Be fierce as a leopard, light as an eagle, swift as a gazelle, and strong as a lion to do the will of your Father in heaven.[9]

145. Rabbi Judah [I] the Patriarch said: If you have done His will as though it were your own will, you have not yet done His will as He wills it. But if you have done His will as though it were not your own will, then you have done His will as He wills it. Is it your wish not to die? Die, so that you will not die [in the world-to-come]. Is it your wish to live? Do not live, so that you may live [in the world-to-come]. It is better for you to die in this world, where you are going to die whether you wish it or not, than to die in the time-to-come, where, if you wish, you need not die.[10]

146. Rabban Gamaliel son of R. Judah [I] the Patriarch used to say: Do His will as though it were your will, so that He may do your will as though it were His will. Set aside your own will in favor of His will, so that He may set aside the will of others in favor of your will.[11]

147. When a man enhances the glory of Heaven and belittles his own glory, the glory of Heaven is magnified and his own glory is likewise magnified. However, if a man belittles the glory of Heaven and enhances his own glory, the glory of Heaven remains undiminished, but his own glory is diminished.[12]

148. "Honor the Lord with whatever excellence He hath bestowed upon thee"[13] (Prov. 3:9)—with whatever He has bestowed upon you. If you are a man with good looks, honor Him with the good looks He has given you. If your voice is pleasing and you are seated in a synagogue, rise up and honor the Lord with your voice.

Hiyya the son of R. Eliezer ha-Kappar's sister had a pleasing voice, so R. Eliezer ha-Kappar would say to him: Hiyya, my son, rise up and honor the Lord with what He has bestowed upon you.[14]

149. R. Yohanan ben Berokah said: He who profanes the Name of Heaven in secret—whether the profanation was done unwittingly or wantonly—shall be requited openly.[15]

---

1. To protect the wheat from vermin.
2. B. Shab 31a.
3. B. Ber 33b.
4. B. Ber 6b.
5. B. Suk 49b.
6. Should not the fear of God exceed fear of mortals?
7. He does not say, "I hope God will not see me." B. Ber 28b and En Yaakov, ad loc.
8. B. Sot 31a.
9. Avot 5:23.
10. ARNB 32.
11. Avot 2:4.
12. TdE 14 (JPS, p. 188): Num. R. 4:20.
13. A play on *hnnk* ("bestowed upon you") and *hvnk* ("the substance given you").
14. PR 25:2 (YJS 18:516–17).
15. Avot 4:4.

150. "There is no wisdom nor understanding nor counsel against the Lord" (Prov. 21:30). Wherever there is profanation of the Lord's Name, no respect is given to a teacher.[1]

151. R. Yohanan said in the name of R. Simeon ben Jehozadak: It is well to have a letter rooted out of the Torah if the Name of Heaven will thereby be openly hallowed.[2]

152. One should expose hypocrites to prevent the profanation of the Name, as is said, "If a righteous man abandoneth his righteousness and doeth wrong [in secret], I shall put a stumbling block before him [to expose him]" (Ezek. 3:20).[3]

153. There should be no delay in punishment for profanation of the Name, whether unwitting or wanton.[4]

154. To what extent is one guilty of profanation of the Name? In my case, said Rav, if I buy meat from the butcher and do not pay him at once.[5]

When Abbaye bought meat from two partners, he paid each of them separately. Afterward, he brought them together and made the reckoning with them [so that each should know that he had paid the other].

In the school of R. Yannai, it was taught: If a disciple's colleagues are ashamed of his [bad] reputation [but nevertheless are willing to put up with it], they are guilty of profanation of the Name. By way of example, R. Nahman bar Isaac cited the case of a disciple about whom people said, "May his Lord forgive him."[6]

155. For him who is guilty of profanation of the Name, penitence has no power to suspend judgment; the Day of Atonement has no power to expiate, nor suffering to purge. All of them together, however, suspend judgment, and death scours it, as is said, "The Lord of hosts revealed Himself in my ears: This iniquity [of profanation] shall not be expiated by you till you die" (Isa. 22:14).[7]

156. Six hundred and thirteen commandments were spoken to Moses. When Habakkuk came, he summed them up in one principle, saying, "The righteous shall live by his faith" (Hab. 2:4).[8]

Prayer

157. We have been taught: "To love the Lord your God and to serve Him with all your heart" (Deut. 11:13). What service is that with the heart? You must say, It is prayer.[9]

158. R. Eliezer ben Jacob said: "The Lord is the hope (*mikveh*) of Israel" (Jer. 17:13) means that as the ritual bath of purification (*mikveh*)[10] cleanses those who are unclean, so the Holy One, blessed be He, cleanses Israel.

Hence, the Holy One, blessed be He, declared to Israel: When you pray, pray in the synagogue in your city; if you cannot pray in the synagogue in your city, pray in your open field; if you cannot pray in your open field, pray in your house; if you cannot pray in your house, pray on your bed; if you cannot pray aloud in your bed, commune with your heart.[11] Hence it is written, "Commune with your own heart upon your bed, and be still. Selah" (Ps. 4:5).[12]

159. R. Yose son of R. Hanina said: The [daily] *Tefillah*s were instituted by the [three] patriarchs. But R. Joshua ben Levi said: They were instituted to replace the [two] daily offerings [in the Temple].[13]

160. Abraham instituted the morning *Tefillah*; Isaac instituted the afternoon *Tefillah*; and Jacob instituted the evening *Tefillah*.[14]

161. "I sleep, yet my heart waketh" (Song 5:2). The congregation of Israel said to the Holy One, blessed be He: Master of the universe, "I sleep" for lack of offerings [since there is no Temple now]; "yet my heart waketh" at the reading of the Shema and the *Tefillah*.[15]

162. R. Eleazar said: Prayer is more efficacious than offerings.

R. Eleazar also said: Ever since the day the Temple was destroyed, the gates of prayer have been closed, for Scripture says, "Yea, when I cry and call for help, He shutteth out my prayer" (Lam. 3:8). But though the gates of prayer are closed, the gates of tears are not closed, for it says, "Hear my prayer, O Lord . . . [but if Thou wilt not hear], keep not silence at my tears" (Ps. 39:13).[16]

163. R. Joshua ben Levi said: Even an iron partition cannot interpose between Israel and their Father in heaven.[17]

164. Blessed be you unto the Lord, ye heavens and ye who go down in the chariot, if you tell and declare to My children what I do when they pronounce the sanctification, saying, "Holy, holy, holy." Be sure to teach them to lift

1. B. Ber 19b; B. Er 63a.
2. B. Yev 79a.
3. B. Yoma 86b.
4. B. Kid 40a.
5. For then people might think that Rav does not pay at all, as a reward for his leniency when the butcher inquires about *kashrut* (the fitness of a slaughtered animal). So *Mikhtam*, cited by Steinsaltz in his edition of Yoma, ad loc.
6. B. Yoma 86a.
7. Ibid.
8. B. Mak 23b–24a.
9. B. Ta 2a.
10. A play on these two homonyms.
11. "That is, if you cannot go to your synagogue because you are busily at work in your field, pray there; if you cannot manage to pray in the field, wait until you reach your home and pray there; if you are traveling and cannot pray in your home, pray on your bed while you rest; if you are on the move and cannot pray on your bed, commune with your heart" (Leon Nemoy).
12. MTeh 4:9.
13. B. Ber 26b.
14. Ibid.
15. Song R. 5:2, §1.
16. B. Ber 32b; B. BM 59a.
17. B. Pes 85b.

their eyes to their [heavenly] house of prayer and thus lift themselves to the region above. For I have no joy in the world like the joy in that hour when their eyes are lifted to Me on high and My eyes meet their eyes. In that hour I take hold of the throne of My glory, which is in the likeness of Jacob, hug them in My arms, kiss them, am mindful of their exile, and hasten their redemption.[1]

165. "Fear not, thou worm Jacob, and ye men of Israel" (Isa. 41:14). Just as the worm has only its mouth with which to smite the cedar, so Israel has only prayer. Likewise, Scripture says, "They were sore afraid, the children of Israel cried unto the Lord" (Exod. 14:10)—they seized upon the occupation of their fathers, the occupation of Abraham, Isaac, and Jacob. Thus, too, Jacob said to Joseph, "Moreover, I have given to thee one portion more than to thy brethren, which I took from the Amorites with my sword and with my bow" (Gen. 48:22). Did Jacob really take it with his sword and his bow? Rather, by "my sword" he meant prayer, and by "my bow" supplication. Likewise, David said to Goliath, "Thou comest to me with a sword, and with a spear, and with a javelin; but I come to thee in the name of the Lord of hosts" (1 Sam. 17:45). And it is also written, "Some trust in chariots, and some in horses; but we will make mention of the Name of the Lord our God. They are bowed down and fallen; but we are risen and stand upright. Save, Lord; let the King answer us in the day that we call" (Ps. 20:8–10). Likewise, Scripture says, "And Asa cried unto the Lord his God, and said: 'Lord, there is none beside Thee to help, between the mighty and him that hath no strength; help us, O Lord our God; for we rely on Thee, and in Thy name are we come against this multitude,' " etc. (2 Chron. 14:10).[2]

166. R. Simeon taught: What skilled craftsmen are Israel, who know just how to conciliate their Creator!

R. Yudan said: Those Cutheans really know how to beg alms. One of them goes to a woman and says to her, "Do you have an onion? Please give it to me." After she gives it to him, he says to her, "But can one eat an onion without bread?" After she gives him bread, he says, "Can one eat without drinking?" Thus he obtains both food and drink.

R. Aha said: There is a woman who is clever at borrowing, and there is a woman who is not clever at borrowing. There is a woman who is clever at borrowing: she goes to her neighbor, and, though the door is open, she knocks on it and says, "Peace unto you, my neighbor. How are you doing? How is your husband doing? How are your children doing?" Should the neighbor reply, "They are well," she will ask, "May I come in?" The neighbor will then say, "Come in. What do you require?" The visitor: "Have you such-and-such a utensil? Would you let me have it?" The neighbor is likely to answer, "Yes." On the other hand, the woman who is not clever at borrowing will go to the neighbor, and, though the door is closed, she will open it and say to her, "Have you such-and-such a utensil?" The neighbor is likely to answer, "No."

R. Hanina said: There is a tenant who is clever at borrowing, and there is another tenant who is not clever at borrowing. The one clever at borrowing: when he sees that he is likely to fall behind in what he will produce during his tenancy, he summons up his courage, combs his hair, cleans his garments, puts on a cheerful face, takes his stick in his hand, places his [seal] ring on his finger, and goes to his landlord. When the latter says to him, "Come in peace, my good tenant. How are you making out?" he responds, "I am doing well." "How is the land doing?" "May you enjoy its produce in plenty." "How are the oxen doing?" "May you enjoy their fat in plenty." "How are the goats doing?" "May you enjoy their kids in plenty." "What do you require?" "If you have ten denars, would you let me have them?" The landlord: "If you need them, take even twenty." As for the tenant who is not clever at borrowing: he will go to his landlord with his hair unkempt, his clothes soiled, and his face gloomy. When the landlord asks him, "How is the land doing?" he replies, "I hope that you will get out of it what you put into it." "How are the oxen doing?" "They are feeble." "What do you need?" "If you have ten denars, give them to me." "Be off, and give me back what you [already] have of mine."[3]

167. "May He regard the prayer of the destitute" (Ps. 102:18). R. Isaac interpreted the verse as referring to the generations in exile, which have neither king nor prophet, neither priest nor Urim and Tummim, and have nothing left to them except prayer. David said to the Holy One, blessed be He: Master of the universe, do not despise their prayer.[4]

168. R. Hama bar Hanina said: If a man sees that he prays and is not answered, he should pray again, for Scripture says, "Wait thou for the Lord, be strong and let thy heart take courage; yea, wait thou for the Lord" (Ps. 27:14).[5]

169. Both R. Yohanan and R. Eleazar said: Even if a sharp sword is actually resting on a man's neck, he should not hold himself back from praying for [God's] mercy.[6]

170. R. Ze'era said: A man may have a favorite who so importunes him with his needs and his wants that the man comes to dislike him and tries to avoid him. But with the Holy One, blessed be He, it is not so. The more a man importunes God with his needs and his wants, the more God loves him, as is said, "Call unto Me, and I will answer thee" (Jer. 33:3).

R. Ze'era said further: A man may have a client [a dependent]. The first time the client comes to visit, he seats him on a couch; the second time the client comes to visit, he seats him on a chair; the third time, he seats him on a bench; but the fourth time, he says of him, "How this fellow forces himself upon me, and how he burdens

1. Hekhalot.
2. Mek, *Be-shallah*, *Va-yehi*, 3; Yalkut, Isa., §450.
3. Lev. R. 5:8.
4. Lev. R. 30:3.
5. B. Ber 32b.
6. B. Ber 10a.

me!" But with the Holy One, blessed be He, it is not so: the more often the children of Israel throng toward His place of prayer, the greater is His joy. Hence it is said, "Who is as the Lord our God whensoever we call upon Him?" (Deut. 4:7).[1]

171. R. Yudan said, Flesh and blood may have a patron, but when a time of trouble befalls him, he cannot go in unannounced to his patron. Instead, he comes and has to stand at the patron's door and call a servant or a member of the household, who will tell the patron, "So-and-so is standing at the door." He then may admit him or may leave him standing at the door. But not such a patron is the Holy One, blessed be He, who says, "Whenever trouble befalls a man, he need call neither Michael nor Gabriel. Let him call Me directly, and I shall answer him at once." As Scripture says, "It shall come to pass, that whosoever shall call on the Name of the Lord shall be delivered" (Joel 3:5).[2]

172. The Holy One, blessed be He, yearns for the prayers of the righteous.[3]

173. "And Isaac was as effective as a shovel" (Gen. 25:21).[4] R. Isaac said: Why is the prayer of the righteous likened to a shovel? Even as a shovel turns the grain from one place to another in the granary, so the prayer of the righteous turns the dispensations of the Holy One, blessed be He, from the measure of anger to the measure of mercy.[5]

174. "For the Leader. Upon the hind of the dawn" (Ps. 22:1). R. Benjamin bar Japheth said in the name of R. Eleazar: Why is the prayer of the righteous compared to a hind? To tell you that as with the hind, whose antlers keep forming more and more branches every year as long as it grows, so with the righteous—the more they pray, the more will their prayer be heard.[6]

175. A man upon whom a calamity has befallen should make it known to the public, so that many people may entreat [God's] mercy for him.[7]

176. Rabbah bar Hinena the Elder said in the name of Rav: He who is able to entreat [God's] mercy for his fellow and does not is called a sinner, for Scripture says, "Moreover, as for me, far be it from me that I should sin against the Lord in ceasing to pray for you" (1 Sam. 12:23). Rava said: If his fellow who is in straits is a disciple of the wise, he must pray for him to the point of making himself sick.[8]

177. He who entreats [God's] mercy for his fellow while he himself is in need of the same thing will be answered first, for it is said, "The Lord changed the fortune of Job when he prayed for his friend" (Job 42:10).[9]

178. When you pray, make your prayer not a routine but a plea for mercy and a supplication before the Holy One, blessed be He.

R. Eliezer said: When a man makes his prayer a routine, it is not supplication.

What is meant by [one whose prayer is a] routine? R. Jacob bar Idi said in the name of R. Hoshaia: Anyone whose prayer is to him nothing but a heavy burden. The sages said: He who does not say it as one supplicating. Rabbah and R. Joseph both said: He who is unable to bring something fresh into it. Abba bar Avin and R. Hanina bar Avin both said: He who does not make an effort to pray [in the morning and in the evening at the proper time, namely] when the sun appears to stand still.[10]

179. [Mornings], R. Yose bar Hanina used to pray at the time the sun appeared to stand still, so that the fear of Heaven might be upon him all day.[11]

180. "And it came to pass, when Moses held up his hand, that Israel prevailed," etc. (Exod. 17:11). But did the hands of Moses actually wage war or win victories? Of course not. What the text signifies is that so long as Israel turned their thoughts upward and submitted their hearts to their Father in heaven, they prevailed; but otherwise, they fell.

In the same way, you read, "Make thee a fiery serpent . . . and it shall come to pass that everyone that is bitten, when he seeth it, shall live" (Num. 21:8). But was it the serpent that killed, or was it the serpent that kept alive? Not so: what the text indicates is that so long as Israel turned their thoughts upward and submitted their hearts to their Father in heaven, they were healed; otherwise, they rotted away.[12]

181. Our masters taught: He who prays should direct his heart toward Heaven. The verse "Thou directest their heart, then Thou causest Thine ear to attend" (Ps. 10:17), said Abba Saul, is a reminder of this requirement.[13]

182. R. Hiyya and R. Simeon bar Rabbi were once sitting together when one of them began [the following discussion]: A man at prayer should direct his eyes toward the place here on earth [where the Temple once stood], in keeping with the verse "And Mine eyes and Mine heart shall be there perpetually" (1 Kings 9:3). But the other said: He should direct his eyes toward [the heavens] above, for Scripture says, "Let us lift up our heart with our hands unto God in the heavens" (Lam. 3:41). In the meanwhile, R. Ishmael son of R. Yose joined them and asked, "What subject are you discussing?" "One's posture at prayer." R. Ishmael: "My father ruled thus: 'A man at prayer should

1. MTeh 4:3.
2. P. Ber 9:1, 13a.
3. B. Yev 64a.
4. JV: "And Isaac entreated." But *'tr* ("to entreat") also means "shovel."
5. B. Yev 64a; B. Suk 14a.
6. B. Yoma 29a.
7. B. Hul 78a.
8. B. Ber 12b.
9. B. BK 92a.
10. Avot 2:13; B. Ber 29b.
11. P. Ber 2:1, 7b.
12. B. RH 29a.
13. B. Ber 31a.

direct his eyes toward the place here on earth [where the Temple once stood] and direct his heart toward [the heavens] above, so as to comply with both verses.' "[1]

183. R. Ammi said: A man's prayer is not heard until he places his very life into his uplifted hands, as is said, "Let us lift up our hearts with our hands unto God in the heavens" (Lam. 3:41).[2]

184. Hezekiah said: A man's prayer is not heard until he makes his heart [soft] like flesh, as is said, "And it shall come to pass that from one new moon to another . . . shall all flesh come to worship before Me" (Isa. 66:23).[3]

185. R. Eleazar would first give a copper to a poor man, and then pray, explaining: It is said, "Through charity I shall behold Thy face" (Ps. 17:15).[4]

186. When a man does not distribute his tithes in generous fistfuls, his prayer will not ascend [to heaven].[5]

187. R. Judah said: Repentance effects half [of the atonement], while prayer effects all [of it]. But R. Joshua ben Levi said the opposite: Repentance effects all [of the atonement], while prayer effects only half.[6]

188. "There shall not be male nor female barren among you" (Deut. 7:14). R. Hanin ben Levi said: This means that your prayer will never prove barren—it will always rise and bear fruit.[7]

189. R. Hanina bar Papa put the following question to R. Samuel bar Nahman: Since I have heard that you are a master of *Aggadah*, [tell me] what is signified by the verse "Thou hast covered Thyself with a cloud, so that no prayer can pass through" (Lam. 3:44). He replied: Prayer is likened to an immersion pool, while repentance is likened to the sea. Even as an immersion pool is at times open and at times barred, so the gates of prayer are at times barred and at times open. On the other hand, the sea is always open, so that whoever wishes to bathe in it bathes in it whenever he wishes. So, too, the gates of repentance are always open. R. Berekhiah and R. Helbo said in the name of R. Anan son of R. Joseph: In truth, the gates of prayer too are never barred.[8]

190. Quoting "As for me, let my prayer be unto Thee, O Lord, in an acceptable time" (Ps. 69:14), R. Yose bar Halafta said: This means that there are acceptable times for prayer and that David prayed to the Holy One, blessed be He: Whenever I pray before You, may it be an acceptable time.[9]

191. "As for me, let my prayer be unto Thee, O Lord, in an acceptable time." For everything the Holy One, blessed be He, set a time and a season, as is said, "There is a time for every experience, including the doom" (Eccles. 8:6)—except for prayer. Whenever a man prays, he is answered. Why is no time set for prayer? Were a man to know the time when, if he prays, he will be answered, he would leave off other times and pray only then. Accordingly, the Holy One, blessed be He, said: For this reason I do not let you know when you will be answered, so that you will be willing to pray at all times, as is said, "Put your trust in Him at all times" (Ps. 62:9).[10]

192. Our masters taught: One should not stand up to say the *Tefillah* when depressed, when indolent, when laughing, when gossiping, when frivolous, or when engaged in idle matters, but only when still rejoicing after the performance of a religious act.[11]

193. One should not stand up to say the *Tefillah* except in a reverent frame of mind. The pious men of yore used to spend an hour [in meditation] and pray only after that, in order to make sure that their hearts would be directed to their Father in heaven.

And the proof from Scripture? From the verse "Worship the Lord in the beauty (*hadrat*) of holiness" (Ps. 29:2), concerning which R. Joshua ben Levi said, Read not *hadrat* but *herdat*, "awe." But R. Nahman bar Isaac said, From another verse: "Serve the Lord with fear and rejoice with trembling" (Ps. 2:11), which, according to Rav, means; Where there is rejoicing, there is also to be trembling.[12]

194. Our masters taught: The pious men of yore used to spend an hour [in meditation], then pray for an hour, and then meditate again for an hour. But seeing that they thus had to spend nine hours a day at prayer,[13] how was their knowledge of Torah preserved, and how did their work get done? Well, because they were pious, their knowledge of Torah was preserved and their work was blessed with success.[14]

195. When you pray, know before whom you stand.[15]

196. R. Hanah bar Bizna said in the name of R. Simeon the Pious: When a man prays, he should regard himself as though the Presence were before him, in keeping with "I regard the Lord as always before me" (Ps. 16:8).[16]

1. B. Yev 105b.
2. B. Ta 8a.
3. B. Sot 5a.
4. B. BB 10a.
5. Num. R. 12:11.
6. Lev. R. 10:5.
7. Deut. R. 3:6.
8. Lam. R. 3:44, §9; MTeh 65:4.
9. P. Mak 2:6, 31d.
10. Aggadat Bereshit 77.
11. B. Ber 31a.
12. B. Ber 30b.
13. Three hours for each of the three daily services.
14. B. Ber 32b and En Yaakov, ad loc.
15. B. Ber 28b.
16. B. Sanh 22a.

197. R. Ashi said: During a period of distress in the world, I saw R. Kahana remove his cloak, clasp his hands, and pray, saying, "I pray like a slave before his master." But during a period of peace, he would put on his cloak, covering and wrapping himself with it, and pray, saying, "Prepare to meet thy God, O Israel" (Amos 4:12).[1]

198. Even if a man is greeted by the king while praying, he may not return the greeting. And even if a snake is wound around his heel, he may not interrupt his prayer.

Our masters taught: It is related that once, when a certain pious man was praying by the roadside, a general came by and greeted him, but he did not return his greeting. So the general waited for him to finish his prayer. When he finished it, the officer said to him: Numskull! Is it not written in your Torah, "Take utmost care, and watch yourself scrupulously" (Deut. 4:9), and also, "Be most careful about yourselves" (Deut. 4:15)? Why, then, when I greeted you, did you not return my greeting? Had I chosen to cut off your head with my sword, who would have demanded your blood from me? The pious man: Wait a moment, and I will try to explain. If you had been standing before a king of flesh and blood, and a friend of yours came by and greeted you, would you have returned his greeting? The general: No. The pious man: And if you did return his greeting, what would have been done to you? The general: My head would have been cut off with the sword. The pious man: Have we not here an instance of *a fortiori*? If such is the penalty for the return of a greeting when standing before a king of flesh and blood, who is here today and tomorrow in the grave, how much greater by far the penalty for the return of a greeting when I stand before the King of kings of kings, the Holy One, blessed be He, who lives and endures forever and ever and ever! The general was instantly mollified, and the pious man returned to his home in peace.[2]

199. Rav said in the name of R. Meir: When addressing the Holy One, blessed be He, a man's words should be few, for Scripture says, "Be not rash with thy mouth . . . to utter a word before God. . . . Therefore let thy words be few" (Eccles. 5:1).[3]

200. The story of a reader who went down[4] [before the Ark] in the presence of R. Hanina and said, "O God, great, mighty, awesome, majestic, powerful, feared, strong, overwhelming, reliable, and honored." R. Hanina waited until the reader finished. Then, when he finished, he asked him, "Have you concluded all epithets of praise to be accorded to your Master? Why did you have to voice so many? We would not have been allowed to utter even the three[5] we do utter, had not Moses our teacher mentioned them in the Torah and had not the Men of the Great Synagogue come and included them in the *Tefillah*; yet you not only uttered the three, but went on and on. It is as if a king of flesh and blood had a thousand thousand gold denars and was praised for possessing silver ones. Would that not be an insult to him?"[6]

201. Our masters taught: Once a certain disciple went down before the Ark in the presence of R. Eliezer and spun out his prayers to great length. R. Eliezer's disciples said to him: Master, what a long-winded fellow this one is! R. Eliezer: Did he spin out his prayer to greater length than did our teacher Moses, who mentioned "the forty days and the forty nights [that I fell down in prayer]" (Deut. 9:25)?

Another time it happened that a certain disciple went down before the Ark in the presence of R. Eliezer and made his prayers very short. R. Eliezer's disciples said to him: What a terse fellow this one is! R. Eliezer: Was he any more terse than our teacher Moses, who prayed, "Heal her, O God, I beseech Thee" (Num. 12:13)?[7]

202. Rava saw R. Hamnuna prolonging his prayers. He said: Some people forsake eternal life [i.e., study of Torah] and occupy themselves with temporal life.[8] But R. Hamnuna held: The time for prayer is reckoned by itself, and the time for study is reckoned by itself.[9]

203. How many *Tefillahs* is one required to utter every day? Our masters taught: One is to utter no more than the three *Tefillahs* which the Fathers of the world ordained. David came and specified the times: "Evening, morn, and noon" (Ps. 55:18). Hence, one is not permitted to utter more than three *Tefillahs* a day. However, R. Yohanan said: Oh that one could continue to pray the entire day![10]

204. Antoninus asked our holy Rabbi [Judah I, the Patriarch]: "Is one allowed to pray every hour?" Rabbi: "It is forbidden." Antoninus: "Why?" Rabbi: "So that one should not become irreverent toward the Almighty." Antoninus refused to accept this explanation. What did our holy Rabbi do? Early in the morning, he went to the palace of Antoninus and called out, "Hail, O Lord."[11] An hour later, he came again: "Hail, Emperor." After another hour: "Peace upon you, O king." At this, Antoninus asked, "Why do you treat royalty with such contempt?" Rabbi replied, "Let your ears hear what your mouth utters. If you, who are no more than flesh and blood, think that he who salutes you every hour holds you in contempt, surely one should not bother [with his prayers] the King who is King of kings every hour."[12]

205. R. Eleazar said: When in doubt whether one has recited the *Tefillah* or not, he need not go back and recite

---

1. B. Shab 10a.
2. B. Ber 30b and 32b–33a, and En Yaakov, ad loc.
3. B. Ber 61a.
4. The reading desk was at a lower level than the floor of the synagogue; hence the expression "went down."
5. "Great, mighty, and awesome" (Hertz, *APB*, p. 131).
6. B. Ber 33b.
7. B. Ber 34a.
8. Prayers for health and sustenance.
9. One should not be shortened for the sake of the other. B. Shab 10a.
10. Tanhuma, *Mi-ketz*, §9; B. Ber 31a.
11. *Kiri keri*; Greek: *Kyrie chaire.*
12. Tanhuma, *Mi-ketz*, §9.

it. But R. Yohanan said: O that one could keep reciting the *Tefillah* all day long![1]

206. "Let every breath praise the Lord" (Ps. 150:6). At each and every breath a man takes, he should praise his Creator.[2]

207. R. Yose son of R. Hanina, citing R. Eliezer ben Jacob, said: The verse that reads "Ye shall not eat before the blood" (Lev. 19:26)[3] means you are not to eat before you say the *Tefillah* for [the gift of] your blood.

When a man eats and drinks, and then says the *Tefillah*, Scripture declares of him, "Thou . . . hast cast Me behind thy back" (1 Kings 14:9). Read not *gavvekha*, "behind thy back," but *ge'akha*, "behind thy arrogance." For the Holy One, blessed be He, says, "Only after this person stoked his arrogance did he deign to accept the kingship of Heaven."[4]

208. A man should not stand on a chair, a footstool, or any place that is elevated when he says the *Tefillah*, but should stand in a place that is low lying and say it there, in keeping with the verse "Out of the depths I call Thee, O Lord" (Ps. 130:1).[5]

209. R. Hiyya bar Abba said in the name of R. Yohanan: One should always pray in a house that has windows, for it is said of Daniel at prayer, "His windows were open in his upper chamber toward Jerusalem" (Dan. 6:11).[6]

210. Our masters taught: A blind man or anyone who cannot direct his gaze toward a particular point of the compass should direct his heart toward his Father in heaven. If he is standing outside the Land, he should direct his heart toward the Land of Israel, as is said, "And pray unto Thee toward their Land" (1 Kings 8:48). If he stands in the Land of Israel, he should direct his heart toward Jerusalem, as is said, "And they pray unto the Lord toward the city which Thou hast chosen" (1 Kings 8:44). If he is standing in Jerusalem, he should direct his heart toward the Temple, as is said, "They pray toward this house" (2 Chron. 6:32). If he is standing in the Temple, he should direct his heart toward the Holy of Holies, as is said, "They pray toward this place" (1 Kings 8:35). If he is in the east, he should turn his face to the west; if in the west, he should turn his face to the east; if in the south, he should turn his face to the north; if in the north, he should turn his face to the south. In this way, all Israel will be turning their hearts toward the same place. The verse that confirms the need for turning toward the same place is "Thy neck is like the tower of David builded with *talpiyyot*"[7] (Song 4:4), *talpiyyot* being understood as a composite word, "the hill (*tel*)[8] toward which all (*piyyot*) mouths are to turn."[9]

211. R. Hamnuna said: How many important rulings may be derived from the verses about Hannah at prayer (1 Sam. 1:10ff.). "Now Hannah, she spoke with her heart"—hence, he who says the *Tefillah* must direct his full heart to the prayer; "only her lips moved"—hence, he who says the *Tefillah* is to do it clearly with his lips; "but her voice could not be heard"—hence, it is forbidden to raise one's voice in the *Tefillah*; "and Eli thought she was drunk"—hence, one who is drunk is forbidden to say the *Tefillah*.[10]

212. The story is told of a man who always regretted not having read Scripture nor recited Mishnah. Once, as he was standing in the synagogue and the reader before the Ark reached the Sanctification of the Divine Name,[11] the man raised his voice, responding loudly to the reader, "Holy, holy, holy is the Lord of hosts" (Isa. 6:3). People asked him, "What impelled you to raise your voice?" He replied, "I have not had the privilege of reading Scripture or reciting Mishnah. Now when I get the opportunity [to respond], should I not raise my voice, so that my [troubled] spirit may be calmed?"[12] Not one year passed by nor a second, nor a third but that [good fortune came to this man]. He went up from Babylonia to the Land of Israel, was made an officer of the Roman emperor's army, and was appointed supervisor of all the fortresses in the Land of Israel. Then they assigned him an area where he built himself a town, in which he settled. And he, his children, and his grandchildren until the end of all the generations came to be recognized as *coloni* [citizens of Rome].[13]

213. R. Yohanan said in the name of R. Simeon ben Yohai: Why was it instituted that the *Tefillah* be spoken in a whisper? In order not to embarrass transgressors.[14] For, note: Scripture does not provide one place on the altar for a burnt offering and another place for a sin offering.[15]

214. He who makes his voice heard during his *Tefillah* is of those whose faith is small.[16]

He who raises his voice during his *Tefillah* is at one with false prophets.[17]

1. B. Ber 21a; B. Pes 54b.
2. Gen. R. 14:9; Deut. R. 2:37.
3. JV: "Ye shall not eat with the blood."
4. B. Ber 10b.
5. Ibid.
6. B. Ber 34b.
7. JV: "turrets."
8. Understood as the hill on which the Temple stands.
9. B. Ber 30a.
10. B. Ber 31a.
11. The *Kedushah*. See Hertz, *APB*, p. 134.
12. "The man is depressed because he never had the chance (too busy, too poor, or no competent teachers nearby) to study Scripture and Mishnah. He is worried and unhappy. At last he sees a ray of hope—he can at least earn merit by loudly responding to the *Sanctus*. Now he feels at least slightly relieved, slightly easier, slightly less guilty. . . . This leads me to conclude that what is meant is *shvh*, ('to go down, to sink,'), from which it is only one step to 'to settle, to calm down, to rest' " (Leon Nemoy).
13. A play on words: Latin *colonus* ("settler," "citizen of Rome") and *koloni* ("one who raised his voice [in prayer])." Num. R. 4:20.
14. Who confess their sins.
15. So that the onlooker is unable to tell which kind of offering is brought. B. Sot 32b.
16. Since it suggests that unless he spoke audibly, God would not hear.
17. See 1 Kings 18:28.

He who belches or yawns during his *Tefillah* is of the arrogant. Some say, It shows that he is vulgar.

It is a bad omen for a man if he sneezes during his *Tefillah*.

When a man spits during his *Tefillah*, it is as if he spat in the face of the king.[1]

215. Our masters taught: One should not respond with a hasty amen,[2] a truncated amen,[3] or an orphaned amen.[4] Nor should one hurl, so to speak, a benediction from his mouth.[5]

216. R. Hiyya bar Ashi said in the name of Rav: He whose mind is not at ease may not say the *Tefillah*, since it is said, "He who is in distress shall not utter that which requires deliberation."

R. Hanina would not say the *Tefillah* on a day when he had succumbed to anger.

Samuel would not say the *Tefillah* in a house where there was alcoholic drink.

R. Papa would not say it in a house where there was a fish hash.[6]

Samuel's father would not say the *Tefillah* for three days after returning from a journey.[7]

217. To entreat concerning what has already happened is to utter a vain prayer. For example: if a man's wife is pregnant and he says, "May it be [God's] will that my wife give birth to a male child," he utters a vain prayer. If, upon returning from a journey, he hears a cry of distress in the town and says, "May it be [God's] will that there is nothing untoward in my home," he utters a vain prayer.[8]

218. There are certain pleas that are prayers uttered in vain. For example: a man gathers a hundred *kor* [of grain] and prays, "May it be [God's] will that they become two hundred." Or he brings in a hundred jars [of wine] and prays, "May it be [God's] will that they become two hundred." Each is a prayer uttered in vain. But he may pray that blessing come into what he has gathered and that no curse come into it.[9]

219. Our masters taught: He who is asked to go down before the Ark [to lead the service] must show reluctance.[10] If he shows no reluctance, he is like an unsalted dish [hurriedly served]. If he shows too much reluctance, he is like an oversalted dish. What should he do? The first time, he should show reluctance; the second time, he should hesitate like a wick just touched by the flame; the third time, he should stretch his legs and go down.[11]

220. If a man makes a mistake in his *Tefillah*, it is a bad omen for him; and if he is a reader for the congregation, it is a bad omen for those who have commissioned him, because a man's agent is like himself. It is told of R. Hanina ben Dosa that he used to pray for the sick and say, "This one will live, this one will die." When asked, "How do you know?" he would reply, "If my prayer comes fluently to my mouth, I know that the sick man is accepted [for recovery]; if not, then I know that he is rejected."[12]

221. R. Helbo said in the name of R. Huna: He who sets a fixed place for his *Tefillah* has the God of Abraham as his helper. And when he dies, people say of him, "Alas for the humble man, alas for the pious man, who was of the disciples of Abraham our father." And what is the proof that our father Abraham set a fixed place for his *Tefillah*? The verse "Abraham got up early in the morning to the place where he had stood before the Lord" (Gen. 19:27).[13]

222. Abba Benjamin said: A man's prayer is heard by God only in a house of prayer, for Scripture says, "[God is willing] to hearken to the song and to the prayer" (1 Kings 8:28). In the place where there is song,[14] there is to be prayer.

223. Ravin bar R. Adda said in the name of R. Isaac: What is the proof that the Holy One, blessed be He, is found in a house of prayer? The verse "God standeth in the congregation of God" (Ps. 82:1). And what is the proof that when ten people pray together, the Presence is with them? The verse "God standeth in the congregation of God."[15]

224. "I will be unto them as a little sanctuary in the countries where they have come" (Ezek. 11:16). The verse, said R. Isaac, refers to the houses of prayer and houses of study in Babylonia.

Rava expounded: The verse "O Lord, Thou hast been our refuge" (Ps. 90:1) refers to houses of prayer and houses of study.[16]

225. "I sleep, nevertheless my heart waketh" (Song 5:2). The congregation of Israel said to the Holy One, blessed be He: Master of the universe, I am [numb as though] asleep, for lack of the Temple; "nevertheless my heart waketh" in houses of prayer and houses of study.[17]

226. He hath delivered My soul by acts of peace, so that none dare wage war with Me—for many strive to come

---

1. B. Ber 24b.
2. "Men" instead of "amen."
3. "Ame" instead of "amen."
4. Spoken without having first heard the benediction.
5. Perfunctorily, as if it were a burden. A benediction should be uttered slowly and solemnly. B. Ber 47a.
6. He could not stand its pungent odor.
7. B. Er 65a.
8. B. Ber 54a.
9. Tos Ber 7:7.
10. By way of saying that he is unworthy of such a responsibility.
11. B. Ber 34a.
12. B. Ber 34b.
13. B. Ber 6b.
14. The song of the congregation and of the precentor. B. Ber 6a.
15. A congregation consists of not less than ten adult males (see B. Sanh 2a). B. Ber 6b.
16. B. Meg 29a.
17. Song R. 5:2, §1.

near Me" (Ps. 55:19).[1] The Holy One, blessed be He, said: When a man occupies himself with Torah and with deeds of charity [which lead to peace], and strives alongside many others to come near Me through prayer, it is as though he has redeemed Me—Me and My children—from the nations of the world.[2]

227. "But as for me, my prayer is unto Thee, O Lord, in an acceptable time" (Ps. 69:14). When is "an acceptable time"? The time when the congregation prays.[3]

228. "O Thou that hearest prayer, unto Thee (*adekha*) doth all flesh come" (Ps. 65:3). R. Phinehas in the name of R. Meir and R. Jeremiah in the name of R. Hiyya bar Abba said: When Israel pray, you do not find them all praying at the same time, but each and every assembly prays separately, first one assembly and then another. When all assemblies have finished all their prayers, the angel appointed over prayers collects all the prayers that have been uttered in all the assemblies, weaves them into garlands, and places them upon the head of the Holy One, blessed be He, for Scripture says, "With a garland for Thee (*adekha*) doth all flesh come." The world *adekha* here means "garland," as in the verse "Thou shalt surely clothe thee with them all as with a garland (*adi*)" (Isa. 49:18). Thus, too, God says, "Israel, in whom I will be glorified" (Isa. 49:3), [implying that] the Holy One, blessed be He, is crowned with the prayers of Israel, for Scripture says, "And a glorious garland upon Thy head" (Ezek. 16:12).

Another comment: "O Thou that hearest prayer, unto Thee doth all flesh come." You are aware that flesh and blood cannot hear the conversation of two persons speaking at the same time. It is not so with the Holy One, blessed be He. All pray before Him, and He hears and receives the prayers of each one.

Another comment: "O Thou that hearest prayer, unto Thee doth all flesh come." Flesh and blood: when a poor man says something to him, he barely listens; but when a [rich] man comes to say something, he is all attention and deference. But the Holy One, blessed be He, does not act thus. Before Him, all are equal—women, slaves, poor, and rich. You can see this for yourself: to designate prayer, Scripture uses the same word for Moses, master of all prophets, and for a poor man. With regard to Moses, Scripture says, "A prayer of Moses, the man of God" (Ps. 90:1), and of a poor man, it says, "A prayer of the poor man, when he fainteth, and poureth out his complaint before the Lord" (Ps. 102:1). "Prayer" in the first instance and "prayer" in the second, so that you should know that at prayer all are equal before Him who is everywhere.[4]

229. Resh Lakish said: He who has a house of prayer in his city and does not enter it to pray is called an evil neighbor, as is said, "Thus saith the Lord: As for all Mine evil neighbors, who barely touch the inheritance which I have caused My people Israel to inherit" (Jer. 12:14). More! Such a person brings exile upon himself and upon his children, as the verse goes on to say, "Behold, I will pluck them up from off their land" (ibid.).[5]

230. Ravin bar R. Adda said in the name of R. Isaac: He who regularly attends a house of prayer, but fails to come one day—the Holy One, blessed be He, inquires about him, saying, "Who is among you that feareth the Lord, that obeyeth the voice of His servant? Yet now walketh off in darkness and hath no light?" (Isa. 50:10). If [he walked off in darkness away from the house of prayer] for a religious purpose, he will continue to have light; if for a secular purpose, he will have no light.

R. Yohanan said: When the Holy One, blessed be He, comes into a house of prayer and does not find ten persons there,[6] He immediately grows angry, saying, "Wherefore, when I came, was there no man? When I called, was there none to answer?" (Isa. 50:2).[7]

231. When R. Yohanan was told, "In Babylonia, there are men who are old," he was surprised. He quoted, " 'That your days may be multiplied, and the days of your children, in the Land' [Deut. 11:21]—but not outside the Land!" But when told further, "These men go to a house of prayer morning and evening," he said, "It is this that made them worthy. For thus did R. Joshua ben Levi say to his sons: Go morning and evening to the house of prayer, that your life may be prolonged."[8]

232. R. Joshua ben Levi said: A man should always come early to the house of prayer, so that he may merit being counted among the first ten. Even if a hundred more come after him, he will receive a reward equal to that of all of them.[9]

233. R. Isaac asked R. Nahman: Why does the master not come to the synagogue to pray? R. Nahman: I have not the strength. R. Isaac: Then let ten men gather at the master's home and pray with him. R. Nahman: There is too much trouble for me in such an arrangement. R. Isaac: Then let the master ask the reader to come and tell the master that the congregation is about to pray [so that he may pray at the same time]. R. Nahman: Why go to such trouble? R. Isaac: Because of what R. Yohanan said in the name of R. Simeon ben Yohai: With regard to the verse "But as for me, my prayer is unto Thee, O Lord, in an acceptable time" (Ps. 69:14). When is the time acceptable? The time when the entire congregation is praying.[10]

---

1. JV: "He hath redeemed my soul in peace so that none came nigh me; for they were many that strove with me." The word *mi-kerav* can mean "wage war" as well as "come near."
2. B. Ber 8a.
3. Ibid.
4. Exod. R. 21:5.
5. B. Ber 8a.
6. The minimum number for a public service. If there are fewer than ten, several important parts of the service cannot be said.
7. B. Ber 6b and En Yaakov, ad loc.; Yalkut, Isa., §473.
8. B. Ber 8a.
9. B. Ber 47b.
10. B. Ber 7b–8a.

234. It happened that R. Eliezer entered a synagogue and did not find ten persons present. He emancipated his slave in order to complete the ten.[1]

235. "Happy is the man that hearkeneth to Me, determined to enter [within] My doors" (Prov. 8:34). What is meant by "determined to enter [within] My doors"? The Holy One, blessed be He, said, When you go to pray within the synagogue, do not remain standing at the outer door, to pray there.[2] But make sure that you go through the door beyond the outer one. Scripture does not say, "Determined to enter within My door," but, "Within My doors"—[at least] two doors. Why? Because God counts your steps and gives you a reward [for each step you take]. The Holy One, blessed be He, said: If you do so, know that you will face the Presence. What follows directly? "Whoso findeth Me findeth life" (Prov. 8:35), intimating that the Holy One, blessed be He, asked: Who ever came to a synagogue and did not find My glory there? Moreover, said R. Aibu, when you sit in a synagogue, the Holy One stands over you [to wait on you], as is said, "God standeth in the congregation of God" (Ps. 82:1). The Holy One, blessed be He, went on to say: Not only do you face the Presence in the synagogue, but you go out of there laden with blessings, as is said, "Whoso findeth Me findeth life, and obtaineth favor of the Lord" (Prov. 8:35).[3]

236. R. Helbo said in the name of R. Huna: When a man leaves the synagogue, he should not take big steps. Abbaye added: Only when one comes from the synagogue; but when he goes to it, it is his duty to run, as is said, "Let us hurry to know the Lord" (Hos. 6:3).[4]

237. We have been taught that Abba Benjamin said: If two men enter to pray, and one finishes his prayer earlier and, not waiting for the other, leaves,[5] his prayer is torn up in his face, as is said, "He teareth his soul['s outpouring] in his own face.[6] Shall the earth be forsaken because of thee?" (Job 18:4). Moreover, such a man causes the Presence to depart from Israel, as the verse goes on to say, "And shall the Rock be removed from His place?" (ibid.).[7]

238. Our masters taught: One is not to behave in a free and easy manner in synagogues. Thus, one should not eat or drink in them, make use of them for one's own pleasure, stroll about in them, or go into them during hot days merely to escape the heat and during rains to escape the rain. Nor is one to deliver in them a eulogy for a person mourned by few. But one may read Scripture in them, study Mishnah in them, and deliver in them a eulogy for a person mourned by many. Synagogue floors are to be swept and sprinkled, lest grass sprout on them. R. Judah said: When should that be done? When they are in use. But when they have been demolished, grass may be allowed to grow in them. When grass does grow in them, one should not pull it out—[its continued presence] will stir up grief [and the synagogues will be rebuilt].

Moreover, R. Judah said: If a synagogue has fallen into ruins, one still may not deliver a eulogy in it [for an ordinary individual], nor may one twist ropes or stretch out nets in it, nor may produce be spread on its roof to dry, nor may it be used as a shortcut, for Scripture says, "I will make your holy places desolate" (Lev. 26:31). Their holiness remains even when they are desolate.

R. Joshua ben Levi said: He who spits in a synagogue is as though he spat in God's eye.[8]

239. R. Assi said: Synagogues in Babylonia are built with the stipulation [that they may be used for ordinary purposes]. Nevertheless, one should not treat them irreverently. In what way, for example? By reckoning personal accounts there. R. Assi went on: A synagogue that is used for reckoning personal accounts may as well be used to keep a corpse overnight.[9]

240. Rav said: Any city whose roofs are higher than its synagogue will ultimately be destroyed, as is said, "To raise high the house of our God and so prevent the city's destruction" (Ezra 9:9).[10] The restriction applies only to houses; there is no objection to fortresses and towers [being higher than synagogues].[11]

241. R. Hisda said: One may not demolish a synagogue before another is built.[12]

242. While R. Hama bar Hanina and R. Hoshaia the Elder were walking among the synagogues of Lydda, R. Hama bar Hanina said to R. Hoshaia the Elder: "How much money my forebears sank here!" R. Hoshaian replied, "How many souls your forebears sank here! Would it not have been better if your forebears had instead made it possible for people to labor in Torah?"

R. Avin had a gate built for the great house of study. When R. Mani came to visit R. Avin, he said: Look at what I have accomplished. R. Mani applied to R. Avin the verse "Israel hath forgotten his Maker and builded palaces" (Hos. 8:14). Would it not have been better if you had instead made it possible for people to labor in Torah?[13]

243. When R. Eleazar concluded his *Tefillah*, he would add: May it be Your will, O Lord our God, that in our lot there dwell love and brotherhood, peace and friendship. May You make our territories abundant in disciples. To the very end of our lives, may You endow us with hope

---

1. B. Ber 47b.
2. Making it seem that you are eager to get away.
3. Deut R. 7:2; B. Ber 8a.
4. B. Ber 6b.
5. Exposing him to the danger of walking by himself from the synagogue, which was at some distance from the town.
6. JV: "He teareth himself in his anger." But *nafsho* ("himself") may also mean "his prayer"; and *af* ("anger") also means "face."
7. B. Ber 5b.
8. B. Meg 28a–b; P. Ber 3:5, 6d.
9. B. Meg 28b.
10. JV: "To set up the house of our God, and to repair the ruins thereof."
11. B. Shab 11a.
12. B. BB 3b.
13. P. Shek 5:4, 49a.

and expectation. May You set our portion in Paradise. May You sustain us in Your world with a good friend and a good impulse. When we rise in the morning, may we find our hearts yearning to fear Your Name, and may You be pleased to regard our contentment with favor.

When R. Yohanan concluded his *Tefillah*, he would add: May it be Your will, O Lord our God, when seeing our shame and glimpsing our evil plight, to clothe Yourself in Your mercies, cover Yourself with Your strength, wrap Yourself in Your loving-kindness, gird Yourself with Your graciousness, and have the attribute of Your kindness and gentleness come into Your presence.

When R. Zera concluded his *Tefillah*, he would add: May it be Your will, O Lord our God, that we sin not, so that we need feel no shame or disgrace in the presence of our forebears!

When R. Hiyya concluded his *Tefillah*, he would add: May it be Your will, O Lord our God, that Your Torah be our occupation, and that [as we study it] our hearts not ache nor our eyes grow dim.[1]

When Rav concluded his *Tefillah*, he would add: May it be Your will, O Lord our God, to grant us a long life, a life of peace, a life of goodness, a life of blessing, a life of sustenance, a life of bodily vigor, a life in which there is fear of sin, a life free from shame and disgrace, a life of sufficiency and honor, a life marked by love of Torah and fear of Heaven, a life in which You will fulfill all the wishes in our hearts that are good for us.

When Rabbi [Judah I, the Patriarch] concluded his *Tefillah*, he would add: May it be Your will, O Lord our God and God of our fathers, to deliver us from the impudent and from impudence, from an evil man, from evil fortune, from the impulse to evil, from an evil companion, from an evil neighbor, from the destructive Accuser, and from a difficult lawsuit and a difficult adversary in the suit, whether he be a son of the covenant or not the son of the covenant!

When R. Safra concluded his *Tefilllah*, he would add: May it be Your will, O Lord our God, to establish peace in the household above and in the household below, as well as among the disciples who occupy themselves with Your Torah, whether they do so for its own sake or not for its own sake; and may it be Your will that all who study Torah not for its own sake come to study it for its own sake!

When R. Alexandri concluded his *Tefillah*, he would add: May it be Your will, O Lord our God, to put us in a corner where there is light and not in a corner where there is darkness, and let not our hearts ache nor our eyes grow dim! According to some, this was the prayer of R. Hamnuna, but when R. Alexandri concluded his *Tefillah*, he would add: Lord of the universe, it is known and manifest to You that our intention is to do Your will. But what is it that hinders us? The leaven in the dough[2] and the servitude to the foreign kingdoms. May it be Your will that in front of us and behind us You subdue them both, so that we may return to do the statutes of Your will with entire heart!

When Rava concluded his *Tefillah*, he would add: My God, before I was formed, I was of no worth, and now that I have been formed, it is as though I had not been formed. Dust am I while alive, all the more so when I am dead. [Aware of my frailty], I stand before You a vessel filled with shame and confusion. May it be Your will, O Lord my God, that I sin no more; and the sins I have committed before You, wipe away in Your abundant mercy, though not by means of suffering and painful diseases.

When Mar son of Ravina concluded his *Tefillah*, he would add: My God, keep my tongue from evil and my lips from speaking falsehood. Let me remain silent before those who slander me. Let me be as humble as dust before all. Open my heart to Your Torah, and may my soul pursue Your commandments. Deliver me from evil fortune, from the evil impulse, from an evil woman, and from all evils that come storming into the world. As for all who plot evil against me—speedily frustrate their designs, make nothing of their schemes! May the words of my mouth and the meditation of my heart be acceptable before You, O Lord, my Rock and my Redeemer![3]

244. R. Ishmael ben Elisha said: Once when I entered into the innermost part [of the Sanctuary] to offer incense, I saw Akhtariel Yah,[4] the Lord of hosts, seated upon a high and exalted throne. He said to me, "Ishmael, My son, bless Me!" I replied, "May it be Your will that Your mercy subdue Your wrath and Your mercy prevail over Your other attributes, so that You deal with Your children according to the attribute of mercy; and may You, on their behalf, stop short of the limit of strict justice!" And He nodded His head toward me.

Here we learn [incidentally] that the blessing of an ordinary man is not to be regarded lightly in our eyes.[5]

245. [In the time-to-come] all prayers will cease, but the prayer of thanksgiving will not cease.[6]

246. When you go forth on a journey, seek the counsel of your Maker. What is meant by "Seek the counsel of your Maker"? It refers to the prayer before setting out on a journey. What is the prayer? May it be Your will, O Lord my God, that You lead me forth in peace, and direct my steps in peace, and uphold me in peace, and deliver me from every foe and ambush on the way, and send blessing in the works of my hands, and cause me to find grace, kindness, and mercy in Your eyes and in the eyes of all who see me. Blessed are You who hears prayer.[7]

247. R. Joshua said: One who is traveling in a dangerous place may entreat God in a shorter prayer, saying, "De-

1. From intense use.
2. The impulse to evil.

3. B. Ber 16b–17a and En Yaakov, ad loc.
4. Literally, "crown of God."
5. A conclusion drawn from God's apparent gratitude to a mortal for the blessing he bestowed upon Him. B. Ber 7a, and En Yaakov, ad loc.
6. Lev. R. 9:7.
7. B. Ber 29b.

liver, O Lord, Your people, the remnant of Israel. On every crossroads, may their needs be before You. Blessed are You, O Lord, who hears prayer."

Our masters taught: One who passes through a place infested with bands of soldiers or robbers may say a shorter prayer. What is the shorter prayer? According to R. Eliezer: "Do Your will in heaven above and grant relief to those who fear You below; nevertheless, do that which is good in Your eyes. Blessed are You, O Lord, who hears prayer." According to R. Joshua: "Hear the entreaty of Your people Israel and speedily fulfill their request. Blessed are You, O Lord, who hears prayer." According to others: "The needs of Your people Israel are many, but their capacity [to concentrate on prayer] is small. May it be Your will, O Lord our God, to give to each and every one enough for his sustenance, and to each and every body enough for what it needs. Blessed are You, O Lord, who hears prayer."[1]

248. He who goes through a capital city [in the course of a journey] should say two prayers, one on entering and one on leaving. Ben Azzai said: Four prayers—two on entering and two on leaving, giving thanks for past mercies and supplicating for the future.

Our masters taught: What should he say on entering? "May it be Your will, O Lord my God, to bring me into this city in peace." After he enters it, he should say, "I give thanks to You, O Lord, my God, that You have brought me into this city in peace." When about to leave, he should say, "May it be Your will, O Lord my God and God of my fathers, to bring me out of this city in peace." When he is outside, he should say, "I give thanks to You, O Lord my God, that You have brought me out of this city in peace, and as You brought me out in peace, so may You guide me in peace, support me in peace, make me proceed in peace, and deliver me from the hand of every enemy and of anyone who lies in ambush on the road."[2]

249. Our masters taught: On entering a bathhouse, one should say, "May it be Your will, O Lord my God, to deliver me from the immoralities practiced here and from the likes of them, and let no perversity or iniquity befall me; and should I succumb to such perversity or iniquity, may my death serve as atonement for all my iniquities."

On leaving the bathhouse, what does he say? According to R. Aha: "I give thanks to You, O Lord my God, that You have delivered me from hellfire."

On going to be cupped,[3] one should say, "May it be Your will, O Lord my God, that this operation be a healing for me, and may You be the one to heal me, for You are a healing God who is faithful and Your healing is sure." When he gets up [after cupping], what should he say? According to R. Aha: "Blessed be He who heals without payment."

On entering a privy, one should say, "Be honored, O honored and holy ones[4] who minister to the Most High. Pay honor to the God of Israel. Wait for me while I enter and attend to my needs, and I will return to you." But Abbaye said: A man should not speak thus, lest the angels leave him and go away. What he should say is: "Watch over me, watch over me, help me, help me, support me, support me, wait for me, wait for me, till I have entered and come forth, for such is the way of human beings."[5]

Benedictions

250. A man should taste nothing before he utters a blessing. Since "the earth is the Lord's, and all that it holds" (Ps. 24:1), a man embezzles from God when he makes use of this world without uttering a blessing.[6]

251. [Of a man condemned to die, it is said], "He who is dead shall be put to death" (Deut. 17:6), for a wicked man is called dead even while alive, because when he sees the sun shining, he is not stirred to utter in blessing, "Who creates light." When he sees it set, he is not stirred to say in blessing, "Who brings on evenings." When he eats and drinks, he is not stirred to speak a blessing. But the righteous are stirred to bless God for each and every thing they eat or drink, or see, or hear.[7]

252. R. Judah said: He who goes abroad in the days of Nisan [springtime] and sees the trees in blossom should say, "Blessed be He who has not deprived His world of aught and has created in it goodly creatures and goodly trees for the enjoyment of mankind." Mar Zutra bar Tobiah said in the name of Rav: What is the proof that a blessing should be said over fragrant odors? The verse "Let every breath praise the Lord" (Ps. 150:6). What is it that gives enjoyment to the breath and not to the body? You must say that it is a fragrant odor.[8]

253. R. Meir said: Even if one merely sees a loaf of bread and says, "Blessed be He who created this bread; how beautiful is this bread!"—that is the same as a blessing over it. Even if he sees figs and says, "Blessed be He who created these figs; how beautiful they are!"—that is the same as a blessing over them.

But R. Yose said: He who changes the formulae the sages have fixed for blessings has not discharged his duty.[9]

254. When a man sees beautiful trees or beautiful people, he should say, "Blessed be He who has created such beautiful creatures in His world."

---

1. B. Ber 28b and 29b.
2. B. Ber 54a and 60a.
3. To be bled for medical purposes by having cups applied to the body.
4. These words are addressed to the angels who are supposed to accompany a man to privies, which were regarded as the haunt of evil spirits.
5. B. Ber 60a.
6. Tos Ber 4:1.
7. Tanhuma, *Berakhah*, §7.
8. B. Ber 43b.
9. Tos Ber 4:4–5.

It happened once that when Rabban Gamaliel saw a beautiful gentile woman, he uttered a blessing at the sight of her.

But was it not said in the name of R. Yohanan that the words "You shall show them no grace" (Deut. 7:2) mean "You shall ascribe no grace to them"?

But what had Rabban Gamaliel said? He did not say, "*Abáskanta*,[1] [May God keep you from harm]." All he said was: "Who has created such beautiful creatures in His world." For even if he had seen a beautiful camel, a beautiful horse, a beautiful donkey, he would have said, "Blessed be He who has created beautiful creatures in His world!"

Was it Rabban Gamaliel's habit to gaze at women? No, but the road was tortuous, and he looked at her without intending to.[2]

255. If one sees a crowd of Israelites, he is to say, "Blessed be He who discerns things that are secret," for the mind of each is different from that of every other, just as the face of each is different from that of every other. Ben Zoma once saw such a crowd on the ascent to the Temple Mount. He said, "Blessed be He who discerns things that are secret," and, "Blessed be He who has created all these people to serve me." For he used to say: What effort Adam had to make before he obtained bread to eat! He plowed, he sowed, he reaped, he bound [the sheaves]; he threshed, winnowed, and sorted the grain; he ground it and sifted [the flour]; he kneaded and baked. And only then, at long last, was he able to eat. Whereas I rise in the morning and find all these things done for me. What effort Adam had to make before he obtained a garment to wear! He had to shear the wool, wash [it], comb it, spin it, and weave it. And only then, at long last, did he obtain a garment to wear. Whereas I rise in the morning and find all these things done for me. All kinds of craftsmen come early to the door of my house, and I rise in the morning and find all these [necessities] before me.

He used to say: What does a good guest say? "How much trouble my host has gone to for me! How much meat he placed before me! How much wine he brought before me! How many loaves of white bread he set before me! And all the trouble he went to was only for my sake!" But what does a bad guest say? "How much, in truth, has my host put himself out? I ate only one loaf of bread, I ate only one slice of meat, I drank only one cup of wine! All the trouble my host went to was in fact only for the sake of his wife and his children!"

How, according to Scripture, does a good guest speak? "As notables are sung to, so shall men laud their conduct" (Job 36:24). But with regard to a bad guest, Scripture says, "Men do therefore shy away from him" (Job 37:24).

Our masters taught: On seeing the sages of Israel, one should say, "Blessed be He who has imparted of His wisdom to them that fear Him." On seeing the sages of other nations, one should say, "Blessed be He who has imparted of His wisdom to His creatures." On seeing kings of Israel, one should say, "Blessed be He who has imparted of His glory to them that fear Him." On seeing kings of the nations, one should say, "Blessed be He who has imparted of His glory to His creatures."[3]

256. On seeing the houses of Israel, when inhabited, one should say, "Blessed be He who sets up anew the boundaries of the widow [Israel]"; if uninhabited, "Blessed be the true Judge."

Once, when Ulla and R. Hisda were walking along the road, they came to the door of the house of R. Hana bar Hanilai. R. Hisda broke down and sighed. Ulla said to him, "Why are you sighing?" R. Hisda replied, "How shall I refrain from sighing on seeing a house in which there used to be sixty cooks by day and sixty cooks by night, who cooked for everyone who was in need. Nor did R. Hana ever take his hand away from his purse, saying to himself: Perhaps a poor man of good family might come and be put to shame while I reach for my purse. Moreover, the house had four doors opening to the four cardinal points, and whoever came in hungry went out full. In years of scarcity, wheat and barley were placed outside, so that anyone who was ashamed to take some by day could come and take it by night. Now that the house is a mound of ruins, shall I not sigh?"[4]

257. When one sees a place where miracles were wrought for Israel, one should say, "Blessed be He who wrought miracles for our ancestors in this place." When one sees a place from which idolatry has been extirpated, one should say, "Blessed be He who has extirpated idolatry from our Land." [In the presence of] shooting stars, earthquakes, thunderclaps, windstorms, and lightning, one should say, "Blessed be He whose power and might fill the world." On seeing mountains, hills, seas, rivers, and deserts, one should say, "Blessed be He who wrought the work of creation." R. Judah said: If one sees the Great [Mediterranean] Sea, one should say, "Blessed be He who has made the Great Sea," provided, that is, one sees it at [considerable] intervals. For rain and for good tidings, one should say, "Blessed be He who is good and bestows good." For evil tidings, one should say, "Blessed be the true Judge." One who has built a new house or bought new vessels should say, "Blessed be He who has kept us alive, preserved us, and brought us to this season."

One should say, "Blessed be the true Judge" on the occasion of evil, even if out of it there emerges some good; and one should say, "Blessed be He who has kept us alive" on the occasion of good, even if out of it there emerges some evil.

A man is obligated to bless [God] for evil in the same way as for good, for Scripture says, "And thou shalt love the Lord thy God with all thy heart, with all thy soul, and with all thy might" (Deut. 6:5). "With all thy heart" means with both your impulses, the impulse to good as well as the impulse to evil. "With all thy soul" means even if He

1. Greek.
2. P. Ber 9:2, 13b–c.
3. B. Ber 58a.
4. B. Ber 58b.

takes away your soul. "With all thy might" means with all your monetary might.

In another interpretation, "With all thy might [*me'odekha*] is read, "With all the measure [*me'oddekha*] given thee." For whatever measure (*middah*) He metes out to you, you are still to thank Him.[1]

258. Is a blessing to be said only for a miracle wrought for many people, but not for one wrought for only one person?

The answer: for a miracle wrought for many people, it is the duty of everyone to say a blessing; for a miracle wrought for one person, he alone is required to say a blessing.

If one sees the place where Israel crossed the Red Sea, or the place where Israel crossed the Jordan, or the place where Israel crossed the valleys of Arnon;[2] or if one sees hailstones at the descent from Beth-horon,[3] or the stone that Og king of Bashan wanted to throw at Israel,[4] or the stone on which Moses sat while Joshua fought with Amalek,[5] or [the pillar of salt into which] Lot's wife [turned],[6] or the wall of Jericho that was swallowed up into the ground upon which it stood[7]—in each of these instances, one should utter thanksgiving and praise to Him who is everywhere.[8]

259. R. Joshua ben Levi said: He who sees his friend after a lapse of thirty days should say, "Blessed be He who has kept us alive, preserved us, and brought us to this season." If after a lapse of twelve months, he should say, "Blessed be He who revives the dead."

He who sees an Ethiopian, a red-spotted or white-spotted person, a hunchback, a dwarf, or a person afflicted with dropsy should say, "Blessed be He who makes strange creatures." He who sees a person with a limb cut off, or blind, or flat-headed, or lame, or smitten with boils, or pockmarked should say, "Blessed be the true Judge!"

On seeing an elephant, a tailless ape, or a long-tailed ape, one should say, "Blessed be He who makes strange creatures." On seeing beautiful creatures or beautiful trees, one should say, "Blessed be He who has such in His world."[9]

260. R. Joshua ben Levi said: On seeing the rainbow in the clouds, one should fling himself down upon his face, in keeping with "At the appearance of the bow that is in the cloud . . . the instant I saw it, I flung myself down upon my face" (Ezek. 1:28). In the west [the Land of Israel], they cursed anyone who did this, because it seemed as though he were bowing down to [worship] the rainbow; but one may certainly say a blessing [over it].

What blessing should one say? "Blessed be He who remembers the covenant,[10] is faithful to His covenant, and fulfills His promise."

R. Joshua ben Levi also said: He who sees the sky in all its purity says, "Blessed be He who wrought the work of creation."[11]

261. The sages taught: He who sees the sun starting on its new cycle,[12] the moon in its power,[13] the planets in their orbits, and the signs of the zodiac in their orderly progress should say, "Blessed be He who wrought the work of creation."[14]

262. When do we begin to say the blessing for rain? When the bridegroom goes out to meet his bride.[15] What blessing should one say? R. Judah taught: "We give thanks unto You for every drop You caused to fall on us."

R. Johanan used to conclude the blessing thus:

Were our mouths filled with
song as the sea [is with water],
And our tongue with ringing
praise as the roaring waves.
Were our lips full of adoration
as the wide expanse of heaven,
And our eyes sparkling
like the sun or the moon.
Were our hands spread out in prayer as eagles' wings
in the sky,
And our feet as swift as the deer,
We should still be unable to thank You enough, O
Lord our God.
Blessed be You, O God, to whom thanksgivings are
due.[16]

263. Our masters taught: He who sees a statue of Mercury should say, "Blessed be He who shows long-suffering to those who transgress His will." He who sees a place from which idolatry has been uprooted should say, "Blessed be He who has uprooted idolatry from our Land; and as it has been uprooted from this place, so may it be uprooted from all places where Israel dwell and may You turn the hearts of those that serve them to serve You."

R. Hamnuna said in a discourse: If one gazes upon wicked Babylon, one should say five benedictions. On seeing [the ruins of] Babylon, one should say, "Blessed be He who has destroyed wicked Babylon." On seeing the [ruins of the] palace of Nebuchadnezzar, one should say, "Blessed be He who destroyed the palace of wicked Nebuchadnezzar." On seeing the fiery furnace or the lions' den,[17] one should say, "Blessed be He who wrought mir-

1. Ber 9:1.
2. See above, part 1, chap. 5, §110.
3. See Josh. 10:11.
4. See above, part 1, chap. 5, §111.
5. See Exod. 17:12.
6. See Gen. 19:26.
7. See Josh. 6:20.
8. B. Ber 54a.
9. B. Ber 58b.
10. Not to cause another flood.
11. B. Ber 59a.
12. Of twenty-two years.
13. In the spring equinox, when it causes extraordinarily powerful tides. So W. M. Feldman in Ber, Soncino, p. 370, n. 1.
14. B. Ber 59b.
15. When the drops of rain first strike the earth.
16. B. Ber 59b.
17. Mentioned in the book of Daniel.

acles for our ancestors in this place." On seeing the statue of Mercury, one should say, "Blessed be He who shows long-suffering to those that transgress His will." On seeing a ruin from which earth is carried away [to be used in building], one should say, "Blessed be He who says and does, who decrees and carries out." When Rava would see asses carrying earth, he used to slap them on their back and say, "Run, O righteous ones, to perform the will of your Creator." When Mar son of Ravina came to [the site of] Babylon, he used to pick up some earth in his kerchief and fling it to the wind, to fulfill the text "I will sweep it with the broom of destruction" (Isa. 14:23).[1]

264. On seeing the graves of Jews, one should say;

Blessed be He who fashioned you in justice,
Who maintained you in justice,
Fed you in justice,
And in justice gathered you in,
And in justice will raise you up again.

Mar son of Ravina, citing R. Nahman, used to conclude the blessing thus:

And He knows the number of all of you,
And He will bring you back to life and preserve you.
Blessed be He who brings the dead back to life.[2]

[1] B. Ber 57b, P. Ber 9:1, 12d.

[2] B. Ber 58b.

CHAPTER TWO

GOOD AND EVIL

The Impulse to Good and the Impulse to Evil

1. R. Nahman son of R. Hisda expounded: Why is the word *Va-yitzer* ["He formed man"] (Gen. 2:17) spelled with two *yods*? Because the Holy One created two *yetzers* ("impulses") in man—the impulse to good and the impulse to evil.[1]

2. Our masters taught: There are two kidneys in man. One counsels to do good, the other to do evil.

It stands to reason that the good kidney is on man's right side and the evil one on his left side, as is written, "A wise man's understanding is at his right hand, but a fool's understanding is at his left" (Eccles. 10:2).[2]

3. Our masters taught: The impulse to evil is hard to bear, since even its Creator called it evil, for He said, "From his youth the impulse in man's heart is evil" (Gen. 8:21).[3]

4. R. Hiyya the Elder said: How wretched the dough that the baker himself admits is bad! [Thus man's Creator declares], "The impulse in a man's heart is evil from his youth" (Gen. 8:21). R. Yose the Potter[4] said: How miserable the leaven that he who kneaded it admits is bad, as is said, "For He knoweth our impulse, He remembereth that we are dust" (Ps. 103:14). The sages said: How inferior the plant that he who planted it admits is bad, as is said, "The Lord of hosts, that planted thee, hath spoken evil of thee" (Jer. 11:17).[5]

5. "There shall no strange god be in thee" (Ps. 81:10). What is the strange god within a man's body? It is none other than the impulse to evil.[6]

6. Rava said: The impulse to evil is first called "wayfarer," then "guest," and finally "master." Thus it is said, "And there came a wayfarer unto the rich man" (2 Sam. 12:4); then, "And he spared to take of his own flock and of his own herd to dress for the guest" (ibid.); and finally, "And dressed it for the master who had come to be with him" (ibid.).[7]

7. R. Assi said: At first the impulse to evil is as thin as a spider's gossamer, but in the end it is as thick as a cart rope, as is said, "Woe unto them that begin to draw iniquity with gossamer strands, and in the end sin as it were with a cart rope" (Isa. 5:18).[8]

8. Such is the art of the impulse to evil: One day it bids a man, "Do this"; the next day, "Do that"; until finally it says to him, "Go worship idols." And he goes and worships them.[9]

9. The impulse to evil is sweet in the beginning and bitter in the end.[10]

10. Rav said: The impulse to evil is like a fly sitting at the entrance to both ventricles of the heart,[11] as is said, "Flies of death make the ointment of the Perfumer fetid and putrid" (Eccles. 10:1).[12]

11. R. Ammi said: The impulse to evil walks not along the sides [of the road] but in its middle, and as soon as it sees a man making eyes at girls, frizzing his hair, and walking with a swagger, it says, "This one is mine."

R. Avin said: If a man indulges his impulse to evil in his youth, it will in the end, in his old age, be his master, as is said, "He that indulgeth his servant in youth shall have him become a master at the last" (Prov. 29:21).[13]

12. Rava said: We have a tradition that the impulse to evil dominates only what its eyes see.[14]

13. "My son, give Me thy heart . . . and let thine eyes observe My ways" (Prov. 23:26). Why did the Holy One deem it necessary to ask Israel to direct their hearts and eyes toward Him? Because transgression is dependent on them. Hence it is written, "That you do not follow your heart and your eyes" (Num. 15:39), the eye and the heart being the two agents of sin.[15]

14. The impulse to evil yearns only for that which is forbidden to a man.[16]

15. R. Simeon ben Lakish said: Satan, impulse to evil, and angel of death—all three are the same thing.[17]

---

1. B. Ber 61a.
2. Ibid.
3. B. Kid 30b.
4. "The Potter"—Gen. R TA; BR: "ha-Torati"—from Torata in Babylonia (see Jaskow, pp. 1658–59).
5. Gen. R. 34:10.
6. B. Shab 105b.
7. B. Suk 52b.
8. B. Suk 52a; Gen. R. 22:6.
9. B. Shab 105b: B. Nid 13b.
10. P. Shab 14:3, 45c.
11. The impulse to evil is said to be at the left ventricle, while the impulse to good is at the right ventricle. Yet the impulse to evil manages to get into the right ventricle by pretending that its counsel is good.
12. B. Ber 61a.
13. Gen. R. 22:6.
14. B. Sot 8a.
15. Num. R. 10:2.
16. P. Yoma 6:4, 43d.
17. B. BB 16a.

16. R. Samuel bar Nahmani said in the name of R. Jonathan: The impulse to evil first incites a man [to sin] in this world and then testifies against him in the world-to-come.[1]

17. Antoninus asked Rabbi [Judah I, the Patriarch], "At what time does the impulse to evil gain mastery over man—at the time of his conception or at the time he is born?" Rabbi: "At the time of his conception." Antoninus: "If so, he would have kicked his way out of his mother's womb. Accordingly, the impulse to evil must gain mastery at the time of birth."

Subsequently, Rabbi used to say: This is one thing that Antoninus taught me, and Scripture supports him, for it is said, "At the door [through which the newborn child issues], sin croucheth" (Gen. 4:7).[2]

18. Come and observe: a kid or a lamb, when it sees a pit, turns back, since in an animal there is no impulse to evil [to lead it to harm]. But an infant—the impulse to evil drives him headlong [to destruction], so that the infant places his hand on a serpent or a scorpion and is stung by it, or he places his hand on glowing coals and is burned.[3]

19. "When a man's ways please the Lord, He maketh even those hostile to him be at peace with him" (Prov. 16:7). R. Joshua ben Levi said: The words "those hostile to him" refer to the impulse to evil. In the way of the world, when a man grows up in a city with another for two or three years, he is bound to the other in affection. But this one [the impulse to evil], though it grows up with a man from youth to old age, [its hostile nature is such that] if it is with him for even seventy years, it will bring him down; and even if it is with him for eighty years, it will still bring him down. In David's question "Who is like unto Thee, who deliverest the wretched . . . and the needy from his despoiler?" (Ps. 35:10), R. Aha identified "his despoiler" by asking, "Is there a despoiler greater than the impulse to evil?"

[In contrast to David, and suggesting that man himself should cope with the impulse], Solomon said, "If he who is hostile to thee be hungry, give him bread to eat, and if he be thirsty, give him water to drink" (Prov. 25:21)—[silence his mouth with] the bread of Torah and the water of Torah.[4]

20. "The impulse of man's heart was evil from the time he was expelled from his mother's womb" (Gen. 8:21).[5] If you argue: "Is it not the Holy One Himself who created the impulse to evil, of which it is written, 'The impulse of man's heart was evil from the time he was expelled from his mother's womb'? Who then can possibly make it good?" the Holy One replies, "You are the one who makes the impulse to evil stay evil. How? When you were a child, you did not sin. Only when you grew up, you began to sin." If you argue: "But no man can guard himself against it!" the Holy One replies, "How many things in the world are even less bearable and more bitter than the impulse to evil, yet you manage to sweeten them. Nothing is more bitter than the lupine, and yet, in order to sweeten it, you carefully boil it in water seven times, until it becomes sweet. Now, if you sweeten for your need bitter things that I alone created, all the greater is your responsibility for the impulse to evil, which was placed under your control."[6]

21. R. Isaac said: A man's impulse to evil renews itself [in allure] every day, as is said, "Every impulse wrought by his mind was sheer evil every day" (Gen. 6:5).

R. Simeon ben Lakish said: A man's impulse to evil grows in strength from day to day and seeks to slay him, as is said, "The wicked watcheth the righteous, and seeketh to slay him" (Ps. 37:32). And but for the Holy One who is his help, he could not withstand it, as is said, "The Lord will not leave him in his hand" (Ps. 37:33).[7]

22. R. Isaac cited: "Even when a living man is in mourning, he is overcome by his proneness to sin [sexually]" (Lam. 3:39).[8] Even during the time of a man's mourning, his impulse is apt to overcome him.[9]

23. The sages said: The impulse to evil is [at least] thirteen years older than the impulse to good. It begins growing with a child in the mother's womb and comes out with him. If the child is about to profane the Sabbath, it does not deter him; if the child is about to take a life, it does not deter him; if the child is about to commit an act of unchastity, it does not deter him. Only at the age of thirteen is the impulse to good born in a child. If then he is about to profane the Sabbath, it warns him: "You fool! Scripture states, 'Everyone that profaneth it shall surely be put to death' " (Exod. 31:14). If he is about to take a life, it warns him: "You fool! Scripture says, 'Whoso sheddeth man's blood, by man shall his blood be shed' " (Gen. 9:6). If he is about to commit an act of unchastity, it warns him: "You fool! Scripture states, 'Both the adulterer and the adulteress shall surely be put to death' " (Lev. 20:10).

When a man stirs up his passion and is about to commit an act of lewdness, all parts of his body are ready to obey him. On the other hand, when a man is about to perform an act of piety, all his parts become laggard, because the impulse to evil in his innards is ruler of the two hundred and forty-eight parts of his body, whereas the impulse to good is like a man confined in a prison.[10]

---

1. B. Suk 52b.
2. B. Sanh 91b.
3. ARN 16.
4. Gen. R. 54:1.
5. JV: "For the impulse of man's heart is evil from his youth." But here the word *mi-ne'urav* ("from his youth") is taken to be a nominal form of *nin'ar* ("expelled [from his mother's womb]").
6. Tanhuma, *Bereshit*, §7; ARN 16.
7. B. Suk 52b; B. Kid 30b.
8. JV: "Wherefore doth a living man complain, a strong man because of his sins?" But *yit'onen* ("complain") also means "be in mourning."
9. B. Kid 80b.
10. ARN 16.

24. R. Ammi bar Abba said: What is meant by "There is a little city, and few men within it," etc. (Eccles. 9:14)? "A little city" refers to a man's body; "and few men within it" to its parts. "And there came the great king against it, and besieged it" (ibid.). "The great king" is the impulse to evil. "And built great bulwarks against it" (ibid.)—the devisings of sin. "Now there was found in it a man poor and wise" (Eccles. 9:15)—the impulse to good. "And he by his wisdom delivered the city" (ibid.)—by means of repentance and good deeds.[1]

25. R. Levi bar Hama said in the name of R. Simeon ben Lakish: A man should always make the impulse to good [within him] rage against the impulse to evil. If he prevails against it, well and good; if not, he should occupy himself with Torah. If he then prevails against it, well and good; if not, he should recite the Shema. If he now prevails against it, well and good; if not, he should remind himself of the day of death.[2]

26. A sage in the school of R. Ishmael taught: My son, if this filthy wretch [the impulse to evil] meets you, drag him to the house of study, where, if he is made of stone, he will dissolve; if made of iron, he will be shattered into pieces.[3]

27. R. Yohanan said in the name of R. BaNaah: Israel are to be congratulated—when they occupy themselves with Torah and with deeds of loving-kindness, their impulse to evil is mastered by them, and not they by their impulse.[4]

28. "Didst Thou will that I not be wicked?[5] Yet there is none that can deliver out of Thy hand" (Job 10:7). Rava said, Job sought to exculpate the entire world from judgment as he said: Master of the universe, You created the ox whose hoofs are cloven, You created the ass whose hoofs are whole, You created the Garden of Eden, You created Gehenna, You created the righteous, you created the wicked—who can restrain You?

What did Job's friends say to him in reply? "Yea, thou doest away with fear, and impairest devotion before God" (Job 15:4). To be sure, the Holy One created the impulse to evil; but He also created Torah as an antidote.[6]

29. R. Simeon ben Eleazar said: The impulse to evil resembles a piece of iron cast into the flame. As long as it is in the flame, one can make of it any vessel desired. So it is with the impulse to evil: there is no way of ameliorating it except by words of Torah, which are like fire.[7]

30. R. Levi told the parable of an isolated settlement thrown into confusion by ravaging troops. What did the king do? He set a guard within it to protect it. The Holy One [acted in a similar way when He] said: The Torah is called a stone, as in the verse "The tables of stone, and the law and the commandment" (Exod. 24:12); the impulse to evil is likewise called a stone, as in the verse "I will take away the heart of stone out of your flesh" (Ezek. 36:26). Thus, since Torah is a stone, and the impulse to evil a stone, let one stone guard against the other stone.[8]

31. R. Ilai the Elder said: When a man sees that his impulse [to evil] is about to gain mastery over him, let him go to a place where he is not known, put on black garments—indeed, wrap himself entirely in black garments[9]—and [if that does not restrain him] do what his heart desires, but let him not openly profane the Name of Heaven.[10]

32. R. Simeon ben Yohai said: "Israel will never see the face of Gehenna," a statement that may be explained by the parable of a king of flesh and blood who had a field of most inferior quality. Some men came and rented it at ten *kor* of wheat a year. They manured it, hoed it, watered it, and weeded it, and still could get it to yield no more than one *kor* of wheat during the year.

The king asked them, "How do you account for such a poor yield?" They replied, "Our lord king! You know that the field you turned over to us had originally yielded nothing for you; now, even after we manured it, weeded it, and watered it, we could get it to yield no more than one *kor* of wheat." In like manner will Israel plead with the Holy One: "Master of the universe, [what do you expect of us]? You know that the impulse to evil has been inciting us, as Scripture states, 'For He knoweth our impulse' " (Ps. 103:14).[11]

33. R. Simeon ben Pazzi said: Woe is me because of Him who formed me (*yotzeri*), and woe is me because of the impulse formed within me (*yitzri*).[12]

34. "And these words which I command thee this day shall be [an oath] upon thy heart" (Deut. 6:6). From here it follows, R. Josiah used to say, that one should adjure his impulse [to evil], even as you find all righteous men adjuring their impulse. Thus, Abraham is quoted in Scripture as saying, "I have lifted up my hand unto the Lord, God Most High, Maker of heaven and earth, that I will not take a thread nor a shoe-latchet nor aught that is thine" (Gen. 14:22–23). Boaz is quoted as saying, "I will do the part of a kinsman unto thee, as the Lord liveth; lie down until morning" (Ruth 3:13). Of David, Scripture records, "David said: 'As the Lord liveth, nay, but the Lord shall smite him, or his day shall come to die, or he shall go down into battle and be swept away' " (1 Sam. 26:10).

1. B. Ned 32b.
2. B. Ber 5a.
3. B. Suk 52b.
4. B. AZ 5b and En Yaakov, ad loc.
5. RV: "Although Thou knowest that I am not wicked."
6. B. BB 16a.
7. ARN 16.
8. Lev. R. 35:5.
9. The color of mourning. Hopefully, these would cool his passion.
10. B. Hag 16a.
11. ARN 16.
12. God will punish me if I obey my evil impulse, yet I cannot resist its incitement. B. Ber 61a.

Elisha is quoted as saying, "As the Lord liveth . . . I will receive none" (2 Kings 5:16).[1]

35. Who is mighty? He who subdues his impulse [to evil].[2]

36. "Happy is the man" (Ps. 1:1). Happy is he who is man enough to subdue his impulse to evil.[3]

37. "Ye mighty in strength, who nevertheless do His bidding, hearkening unto the voice of His word" (Ps. 103:20)—men such as R. Zadok and [R. Akiva, one of] his companions, [who, though possessed of potency for the sexual act, nevertheless did His bidding].

Thus, when a [Roman] noblewoman propositioned R. Zadok, he said to her, "My heart is faint, and I have not the strength to perform. Is there something to eat?" She replied, "There is unclean food." R. Zadok: "So what? A man ready to do what I am about to do will eat such food." She fired the oven, and as she was placing the food in it, he ascended and seated himself in it. She asked him, "What does this mean?" He replied, "He who is about to do the one thing will end up [being roasted] like this." The noblewoman: "Had I known [the act was so heinous to you], I would not have brought you to such distress."[4]

38. When R. Akiva went to Rome, he was slanderously described to a certain general [as one enjoying the company of loose women]. As a result, the general sent him two beautiful women who had been bathed, anointed, and adorned like brides for their grooms. All night, they kept thrusting themselves at R. Akiva, one saying, "Turn to me," and the other saying, "Turn to me." He just sat there, spitting at both and turning to neither.

In the morning the two women went off and complained to the general, saying to him, "We would rather die than be given to such a man." The general sent for R. Akiva and asked him, "Why did you not do with these women what men usually do? Are they not beautiful? Are they not human beings like yourself? Did not He who created you create them?" R. Akiva replied, "What could I do? The odor of the forbidden meat and the creeping things they had eaten revolted me."[5]

39. R. Akiva used to ridicule transgressors [for succumbing to the evil impulse]. One day Satan, in the guise of a woman, appeared to him standing at the top of a date palm. R. Akiva took hold of the date palm and began climbing it. When he reached halfway up the palm, Satan [resuming his usual form] let him go, saying: Had they not proclaimed in heaven, "Beware of R. Akiva and his Torah," I would have valued your life at no more than two *meah*.

R. Meir used to ridicule transgressors [for the same reason]. One day Satan, in the guise of a woman, appeared to him on the opposite bank of a river. As there was no bridge, R. Meir seized a rope [stretching from bank to bank] and proceeded to cross, hand over hand. When he reached halfway along the rope, Satan [resuming his usual form] let him go, saying: Had they not proclaimed in heaven, "Beware of R. Meir and his Torah," I would have valued your life at no more than two *meah*.[6]

40. A story of Matia ben Heresh: He was rich and feared Heaven and, like R. Meir, his teacher, sat all his days in the house of study occupying himself with Torah. Now, the splendor of his countenance shone like the radiance of the sun, and the beauty of his features resembled that of the ministering angels. It was said of him that never in his life had he raised his eyes upon a woman. Once, Satan passed by and, seeing him, was overcome with envy as he said: Is it possible that there is a righteous man entirely without sin in the world? At once he went up to the height above, stood before the Holy One, and said, "Master of the universe, Matia ben Heresh—what sort of man is he in Your sight?" God: "He is utterly righteous." Satan: "Give me permission, and I will test him." God: "You will not prevail over him." Satan: "Nevertheless!" So God gave him permission.

Satan went and found R. Matia seated and occupied with Torah. So he appeared to him in the guise of a beautiful woman, the like of which there had not been in the world since the days of Naamah, Tubal-Cain's sister, on account of whom ministering angels went astray. Satan stood in front of R. Matia, who, upon seeing him, turned his back to him. Satan went around and again stood in front of R. Matia. When R. Matia turned his face to still another direction, Satan was once more in front of him. When R. Matia saw that Satan [in the woman's guise] turned up on all sides, he said to himself: I fear that the impulse to evil will gain mastery over me and cause me to sin. What did that righteous man do then? He summoned one of his disciples, who acted as his attendant, and said to him: My son, go and bring me fire and nails. After he brought them, R. Matia passed the nails through the fire, then plunged them into his own eyes. When Satan saw this, he was shaken, all but knocked out, and left R. Matia.

In that instant, the Holy One summoned Raphael, prince of healings, and said to him, "Go and heal the eyes of Matia ben Heresh." When Raphael came and stood before him, Matia asked, "Who are you?" Raphael answered, "I am the angel Raphael, whom the Holy One had sent to heal your eyes." Matia: "Let me be. What happened has happened."

Raphael returned to the Holy One and reported to Him, "Master of the universe, thus-and-thus did Matia ben Heresh answer me." The Holy One said, "Go and tell him: From this day and henceforth, fear not. I guarantee you in this matter that, throughout your days, the impulse to evil will have no sway over you."

When Matia ben Heresh heard God's guarantee from

1. Sif Deut., §33.
2. Avot 4:1.
3. B. AZ 19a.
4. B. Kid 40a.
5. ARN 16.
6. B. Kid 81b.

the angel, he was willing to accept the angel's healing and was healed.[1]

41. The story of a man who was very scrupulous about the command to wear fringes on his garments. Nevertheless, when he heard of a certain courtesan in one of the cities across the sea who charged four hundred gold denars as her fee, he sent her four hundred gold denars, and she fixed an appointment for him. When his time arrived, he came and sat down at the entrance to her house. Her maidservant went in and told her, "The man [from across the sea] who sent you four hundred gold denars has come and is sitting at the entrance to the house." The courtesan replied, "Let him come in." After he came in, she prepared seven beds for him [one above the other], six with silver [bedclothes] and one with gold. Between one bed and the next there was a silver ladder, but the last ladder was of gold. She then [disrobed and] climbed up to the uppermost bed, and sat down, nude, upon it. He, too, [disrobed and] went up after her to sit across from her. But just then the four fringes [of the one garment he still wore] struck him across his face, whereupon he let himself slide off until he sat on the ground. She also slid off until she sat on the ground, and she said, "By the Roman eagle, I will not let you be until you tell me what blemish you saw in me." "By the Temple," he replied, "never have I seen a woman as beautiful as you. But there is one precept the Lord our God has commanded us called tzitzit, 'fringes.' With regard to it, 'I am the Lord your God' is written twice in Scripture, signifying, 'I am He who will exact punishment, and I am He who will give reward.' And just now the four fringes of the tzitzit seemed to me like four witnesses [ready to testify against me]." She said, "I will not let you be until you tell me your name, the name of your town, the name of your teacher, and the name of your school in which you study Torah." He wrote all this down and gave the script to her. At that, she arose and divided her possessions into three parts—a third for the government, a third for the poor, and a third she took with her in her hand; the aforementioned bedclothes, however, she retained. She then came to the study house of R. Hiyya and said to him, "Master, direct your disciples to make me a proselyte." "My daughter," he replied, "perhaps you have set your eyes on one of the disciples?" She took out the script and gave it to R. Hiyya. "Go," he said, "you deserve the husband you are about to acquire."

Before long, those same bedclothes she had laid out for him for an unlawful purpose she was able to lay out for him for a lawful purpose.[2]

42. While R. Hanina and R. Jonathan were walking on a road, they came to two paths, one leading to the door of a place for idolatry and the other to the door of a brothel. One sage said to the other: Let us [take the path leading] to the place of idolatry, since the inclination for it has been killed [it is easily resisted].[3] The other said: Let us [take the path] to the brothel, overcome our inclination, and receive a reward.

As they approached the brothel, they realized that the harlots made themselves scarce.[4] One sage asked the other: What made you so certain that you could overcome your inclination? In reply, the other quoted, "[Torah] shall watch over thee against lewdness, discernment shall guard thee" (Prov. 2:11).[5]

43. While R. Kahana was selling women's workbaskets, a [Roman] noblewoman propositioned him. Saying to her, "I will go and adorn myself," he went to an upper chamber and hurled himself to the ground. But [the prophet] Elijah came and caught him [before he reached bottom], and then said to him, "You have troubled me to come a distance of four hundred parasangs!" R. Kahana replied, "What brought me [to this mishap]? Poverty."[6]

At that, Elijah gave him a measure full of denars.[7]

44. Several captive women [who had been redeemed] were brought to Nehardea and taken to an upper chamber in the house of R. Amram the Pious. Then the ladder to it was removed from under them. As one of them passed by in the upper chamber, the light [of her beauty] shone through the skylight. At that, R. Amram grabbed the ladder, which ten men could not lift, set it up unaided, and proceeded to climb it. After he had gone halfway up, he forced himself to stand still as he cried out, "A fire in R. Amram's house!" When his disciples came [and found him halfway up to the women's chamber], they reproved him: "You put us to shame!" R. Amram replied, "It is better that you be put to shame in this world because of Amram than that you be put to shame because of him in the next." He then adjured his impulse to depart from him, and it issued from him in the shape of a column of fire. He said to it, "See, you are fire and I am flesh, yet I am stronger than you."[8]

45. Abbaye, hearing a certain man say to a woman, "Let us get up early and go on our way," said to himself: I will follow them to keep them from doing what is prohibited. He followed them through meadows a distance of three parasangs. As they were about to separate, he heard them say, "The company is pleasant, but the way is long." Abbaye said: If I were in their place, I could not have restrained myself. And in deep anguish he leaned against the bolt in a doorway. An elder[9] came and recited the tradition: "The greater the man, the greater his impulse to evil."[10]

---

1. Tanhuma B, *Hukkat*, supplement, §1 (p. 131); Midrash Avkir; Yalkut, *Va-yehi*, §161.
2. B. Men 44a and En Yaakov, ad loc.; Sif Num., §115.
3. After the Temple's destruction. See above, part 4, chap 1, §99–100.
4. Literally, "hid themselves from them," in apparent certainty that the two would not solicit them.
5. JV: "Discretion shall watch over thee, discernment shall guard thee." But *mezimmah* ("discretion") also means "[against] lewdness." B. AZ 17a–b.
6. Poverty forced me to sell women's baskets, thus exposing me to temptation from my customers.
7. B. Kid 40a.
8. B. Kid 81a.
9. The prophet Elijah?
10. B. Suk 52a.

46. Pelimo used to say every day, "An arrow in your eyes, Satan!"[1] One day—it was the eve of the Day of Atonement—Satan disguised himself as a poor man, went to Pelimo's door, and begged for alms. Bread was taken out to him. "On such a day," pleaded Satan, "when everyone is inside, shall I be outside?" At that, he was taken in, and bread was served to him. "On a day like this," he again pleaded, "when everyone eats at the table, am I to eat alone?" So he was taken over and seated at the table. As he sat down, he caused his body to be covered with suppurating sores and proceeded to act in a revolting manner. "Sit properly," he was told. He said, "Give me a cup," and one was given him. Then he became overheated and began spitting his mucus and phlegm into it. Even as they were scolding him, he passed out and died. The rumor went forth: "Pelimo killed a man, Pelimo killed a man!" So Pelimo fled from the city and hid himself. But Satan followed him, and [at the sight of Satan] Pelimo [frightened of being discovered] fell down before him. Seeing how Pelimo was suffering, Satan disclosed his identity, then asked Pelimo, "Why are you in the habit of saying, 'An arrow in your eyes, Satan!'?"

Pelimo: "What else am I to say?"

"Say: 'May the Lord rebuke you, Satan!' "[2]

47. Every time R. Hiyya bar Ashi fell down upon his face,[3] he used to say, "May He who is everywhere save me from the impulse to evil." One day, when his wife heard him pray thus, she said to herself: It is now many years that he has held aloof from me; what need has he to pray in this manner? And so one day, while he was studying in his garden, she disguised herself with [enticing] adornments and kept walking past him, and finally sat down before him. "Who are you?" he asked. "I am Haruta,[4] and today I returned from a journey," she replied. He asked her [to lie with him]. She said to him, "Bring me that pomegranate from the uppermost branch." He jumped up and brought it to her.

When he came back to his house, his wife was firing the oven. He went up and sat in it. "What does this mean?" she asked. He replied, "Such-and-such a thing has just happened." "It was I," she assured him. But he paid no heed to her until she produced the pomegranate. "Nevertheless," he said, "my intention was to commit a forbidden act."

All the rest of his days that righteous man fasted, until he died from his fasts.[5]

48. R. Judah said in the name of Rav: It happened that a certain man set his eyes on a certain woman [and became so enamored of her] that his heart was consumed by his ardent desire [and his life was endangered]. When inquiry was made of physicians, they said, "There is no remedy other than that she submit to him." The sages said, "Let him die rather than that she submit."

"Then let her stand naked before him."

"Let him die rather than that she stand naked before him."

"Then let her [at least] talk to him from behind a screen."

"Let him die rather than that she talk to him from behind a screen."[6]

49. R. Nahman bar Hanin said: He who is consumed by sexual desire will eventually be fed his own flesh [he will commit incest].[7]

50. Even the most pious among the pious should not be designated guardian where there is a possibility of unchastity.[8]

51. Thoughts about illicit copulation are more exciting than the act itself—the analogy being the aroma of meat [which is more pleasing than the meat itself].[9]

52. The beginning of the sin of lewdness is the thought in the heart.[10]

53. R. Simeon ben Eleazar said: When confronting the impulse to evil [in a child or in a woman], the left hand should thrust aside while the right hand should bring near.[11]

54. After people slew the impulse to the evil of idolatry, they said: Since this is a time of grace, let us beseech [God's] mercy against the impulse to the evil of lewdness. They besought God's mercy and the impulse was turned over to them. A prophet warned them: Consider carefully—if you slay it, the world will be destroyed. So [instead of slaying it] they imprisoned it for three days. But then, when a day-old egg was sought throughout the Land of Israel for a sick man, it could not be found. So they said: What shall we do now? If we slay the impulse, the entire world will be destroyed.[12] So they painted its eyes [blinding it] and then let it go. What they did helped weaken its strength.[13]

55. The Holy One created two impulses in His world—the impulse to idolatry and the impulse to lewdness. The impulse to idolatry is already rooted out, but the impulse to lewdness still abides. So the Holy One said: When a

---

1. To restrain him from enticing human beings.
2. B. Kid 81a–b.
3. After reciting the Eighteen Benedictions, each person may pray silently for whatever he desires. Such prayers are called "supplications" (*tahanunim*). When saying them, one would fall down on his face. See Ismar Elbogen, *Der jüdische Gottesdienst* (Frankfurt am Main, 1924), pp. 73ff.
4. A well-known courtesan.
5. B. Kid 81b.
6. Such conduct would disgrace her family. B. Sanh 75a.
7. Gen. R. 41:7.
8. P. Ket 1:8, 25d.
9. B. Yoma 29a.
10. DEZ 6.
11. Otherwise, the child might run away and the woman might take to evil ways. B. Sot 47a.
12. The elimination of the sexual instinct prevents the propagation of all living creatures.
13. B. Yoma 69b and En Yaakov, ad loc.

man succeeds in resisting the temptation to commit an act of lewdness, I will deem it for him as though he had resisted both impulses.[1]

56. R. Samuel bar Nahman said: The words "Behold, it was good"[2] refer to the impulse to good, and the words "Behold, it was very good" (Gen. 1:31) refer to the impulse to evil. But how can the impulse to evil be termed "very good"? Because Scripture teaches that were it not for the impulse to evil, a man would not build a house, take a wife, beget children, or engage in commerce. All such activities come, as Solomon noted, "from a man's rivalry with his neighbor" (Eccles. 4:4).[3]

57. R. Judah said, The world endures because of three things: rivalry, lust, and mercy.[4]

58. Resh Lakish said, Pause and consider how grateful we should be to our forebears—had they not been prone to sin, we would not have come into the world.[5]

59. Israel said to the Holy One: Master of the universe, You know the power of the impulse to evil, how enduring it is. The Holy One replied: Clear out a bit of it in this world, and I will remove it altogether from you in the world-to-come, as is said, "Build up, build up the highway, clear away the rocks" (Isa. 62:10), and also, "Build up, build up a highway! Clear a road! Remove all obstacles from the road of My people" (Isa. 57:14). But in the world-to-come, I will pull it out of you by its roots, as is said, "I will take away the stony heart out of your flesh" (Ezek. 36:26).[6]

60. The impulse to evil will have no sway in the world-to-come.[7]

61. R. Judah bar Ilai expounded: In the time-to-come, the Holy One will bring the impulse to evil and slaughter it in the presence of both the righteous and the wicked. To the righteous, it will have the appearance of a towering mountain; and to the wicked, it will have the appearance of a strand of hair. These will weep, and the others will weep. The righteous will weep, saying, "How were we able to cope with such a towering mountain?" The wicked will weep, saying, "How is it that we were unable to cope with a mere strand of hair?" And the Holy One will also marvel together with them, as is said, "Thus saith the Lord of hosts: If it be marvelous in the eyes of the remnant of this people . . . it will also be marvelous in Mine eyes" (Zech. 8:6).[8]

62. "The end for darkness is set" (Job 28:3). A definite time was set for the world to spend in darkness. As long as the impulse to evil is in the world, darkness and thick darkness are in the world. After the impulse to evil is pulled out by its roots from the world, the end for darkness will have been set.[9]

Precept and Transgression

63. Akavia ben Mahalalel said: Reflect upon three things, and you will not fall into the grip of sin. Know where you came from, where you are going, and before whom you are destined to give an account and reckoning. "Where you came from"—from a putrid drop. "Where you are going"—to a place of dust, worm, and maggot. "And before whom you are destined to give an account and reckoning"—before the King of kings of kings, the Holy One, blessed be He!

R. Abba son of R. Papi and R. Joshua of Sikhnin said in the name of R. Levi: R. Akavia drew the three inferences from one verse, "Remember thy Creator (*bor'ekha*)" (Eccles. 12:1)—your well (*be'erekha*), your pit (*borekha*), your Creator. "Your well": the place where you came from. "Your pit": the place where you are going. "Your Creator": before whom you are destined to give an account and reckoning.[10]

64. Rabbah bar R. Huna, citing R. Huna—some say, R. Huna, citing R. Eleazar—said: From the Five Books, the Prophets, and the Writings, it may be inferred that one is allowed to follow the road he wishes to take. From the Five Books: Balaam was first told, "Thou shalt not go with them" (Num. 22:12), and subsequently was told, "Rise up and go with them" (Num. 22:20). From the Prophets: "I am the Lord thy God, who teacheth thee for thy profit, who leadeth thee by the way thou wouldest go" (Isa. 48:17). From the Writings: "If he is of the scorners, he will [be allowed to] speak scorn; and [if] of the meek, he will be shown grace" (Prov. 3:34).[11]

65. Our masters taught: "Neither shall ye defile yourselves, for ye will become even more defiled thereby" (Lev. 11:43). When a man defiles himself by ever so little, he will be judged greatly defiled. If he defiles himself here below, he will be judged defiled up above. If he becomes defiled in this world, he will be judged defiled in the world-to-come.

"Make yourselves holy therefore, and be ye holy" (Lev. 11:44). When a man reaches out by ever so little for holiness, he will be judged most holy. If he reaches out for holiness here below, he will be judged holy up above. If he reaches out for holiness in this world, he will be judged holy in the world-to-come.[12]

66. Our masters taught: A man should always regard himself as though he were half-guilty and half-meritorious. If he performs even one precept, happy is he, for he has

1. Song R. 7:8, §1.
2. Since there is no such phrase in Gen. 1, it may be a variant reading.
3. Gen. R. 9:7; Eccles. R. 3:11, §3.
4. ARNB 4.
5. B. AZ 5a.
6. Num. R. 15:16.
7. Gen. R. 48:11.
8. B. Suk 52a.
9. Gen. R. 89:1.
10. Avot 3:1; P. Sot 2:2, 18a.
11. B. Mak 10b.
12. B. Yoma 39a.

tilted the scale for himself toward the side of merit; if he commits one transgression, woe to him, for he has tilted the scale for himself toward the side of guilt, as is said, "But one sinner destroyeth much good" (Eccles. 9:18). On account of the single sin he commits, he destroys for himself much good.

R. Eleazar son of R. Simeon said: The world is judged by the majority [of its deeds], and an individual is likewise judged by the majority [of his deeds, good or bad]. A man should therefore always regard himself and the world as half-meritorious and half-guilty. If he performs one good deed, happy is he, for he has tilted the scale both for himself and for the entire world, all of it, toward the side of merit; if he commits even one transgression, woe to him, for he has tilted the scale both for himself and for the entire world, all of it, toward the scale of guilt, as is said, "But one sinner destroyeth much good." On account of a single sin this man has committed, he has destroyed for himself and for the entire world much good.[1]

67. Merit has both stock [for the world-to-come] and fruit [in this world], for it is said, "Hail the righteous man, for he shall fare well; he shall eat the fruit of his works" (Isa. 3:10). Transgression has stock but no fruit, for it is said, "Woe to the wicked man, for he shall fare ill: as his hands have dealt, so shall it be done to him" (Isa. 3:11). Then how do I interpret "The wicked eat the fruit of their own ways, and have their fill of their own counsels" (Prov. 1:31)? Transgression that bears fruit[2] has fruit; that which does not bear fruit[3] has no fruit.

The Holy One adds up a good intention to a [good] deed, as though the intention had been carried out, for it is said, "Then they that feared the Lord spoke one with another; and the Lord hearkened, and heard, and a book of remembrance was written before Him, for them that feared the Lord, and that thought upon His Name" (Mal. 3:16). Now, what is the meaning of "that thought upon His Name"? R. Assi said: Even if one no more than thinks of performing a good deed but is forcibly prevented from doing so, Scripture ascribes it to him as though he had performed it. But the Holy One does not add up an evil intention to a [wicked] deed, as though the intention had been carried out, for it is said, "When I regarded iniquity in my heart, the Lord would not hear" (Ps. 66:18). Well then, how do I interpret "Behold, I will bring evil upon this people, even the fruit of their thoughts" (Jer. 6:19)? The Holy One adds up an intention that bears fruit to a deed, as though the intention had been carried out; an intention that does not bear fruit, the Holy One does not add up to a deed, as though the intention had not been carried out.[4]

68. R. Judah said: Good works are not barren, but bear fruit. Sin, however, is barren.[5]

69. R. Eliezer ben Jacob said: He who performs one precept acquires for himself one advocate, and he who commits one transgression acquires for himself one accuser. Repentance and good works are as a shield against retribution.[6]

70. R. Hinena bar Idi said: He who fulfills a precept as commanded will be spared evil tidings, as is said, "Whoso keepeth the commandment shall know no evil thing" (Eccles. 8:5).

R. Assi—according to others, R. Hanina—said: Even when the Holy One issues a decree, the righteous man can annul it, for the question "Because the King's word hath power, and who may say unto Him, 'What doest Thou?' " (Eccles. 8:4) is answered at once, "Whoso keepeth the commandment shall know no evil thing."[7]

71. R. Hanina ben Dosa said: He whose fear of sin takes precedence over his learning[8]—his learning will endure. But he whose learning takes precedence over his fear of sin—his learning will not endure. For it is said, "The fear of the Lord is the beginning of learning" (Ps. 111:10).

He used to say: He whose [good] works exceed his learning—his learning will endure. But he whose learning exceeds his [good] works—his learning will not endure. For it is said, "We will do [what is right], then we will understand" (Exod. 24:7).

Rabban Yohanan ben Zakkai was asked, "How would you describe a man who is both learned and fearful of sin?" He replied, "He is a craftsman who has the tools of his craft in his hand." "And the man who is learned but does not fear sin?" He replied, "He is a craftsman who has no tools of his craft in his hand." "And the man who fears sin but is not learned?" He replied, "He is no craftsman, but the tools of his craft are in his hand."[9]

72. R. Simon and R. Eleazar were seated when R. Jacob bar Aha passed by. One said to the other, "Let us stand up for him, because he is a sin-fearing man." The other replied, "Let us stand up for him, because he is a man of learning." Said the one, "I will tell you that he is a sin-fearing man, and you tell me that he is merely a man of learning!"[10]

73. "The fear of the Lord is clean, enduring forever" (Ps. 19:10). You find that even when a man studies Midrash of *Halakhot* and *Aggadot*, but has no fear of sin, he really possesses nothing, as may be illustrated by the parable of a man who said to his friend, "I have a thousand measures of grain, a thousand measures of oil, and a thousand measures of wine." His friend asked, "Do you have storehouses in which to keep them? If you have them, all will remain yours; if not, you will possess nothing." So it is with a man who studies everything; he is told, "If you have fear

1. B. Kid 40b; Tos Kid 1:14.
2. When the sinner is imitated by others.
3. When he sins quietly, with none to imitate him.
4. B. Kid 40a and En Yaakov, ad loc.
5. MTeh 62:4.
6. Avot 4:11.
7. B. Shab 63a.
8. His ethical conduct concerns him more than his learning.
9. Avot 3:9; ARN 22.
10. B. Shab 31b.

of sin, you have everything," as is said, "Even if faithfulness to your times of study brings a hoard of salvation, both wisdom and knowledge, still it is the fear of the Lord which is a man's treasury" (Isa. 33:6).[1]

74. R. Abbahu said: When a man causes his companion to perform a precept, Scripture imputes it to him as though he had performed it himself.[2]

75. R. Samuel bar Nahmani said in the name of R. Jonathan: When a man performs a precept in this world, it precedes him—goes ahead of him—in the world-to-come. And when a man commits a transgression in this world, it clings to him and goes before him on the Day of Judgment. R. Eleazar said: It attaches itself to him like a dog.[3]

76. We have been taught that R. Yose son of R. Judah said: When a man commits a transgression, he should be forgiven the first time, forgiven the second time, forgiven the third time, but not forgiven the fourth time, as is said, "Thus saith the Lord: For three transgressions of Israel, [yes]; but for four I will not reverse it" (Amos 2:6), and, "Lo, all these things does God work twice, yea thrice, with a man" (Job 33:29).[4]

77. R. Judah son of R. Nahmani, Resh Lakish's interpreter, expounded: The verse "Trust ye not in evil,[5] put ye not confidence in such an intimate" (Mic. 7:5) means that if the impulse to evil says to you, "Sin, and the Holy One will pardon you," do not believe it. You may say: But who will testify against me? The stones of your house, the beams of your house, even the furnishings of your house will testify against you, for Scripture says, "The stone shall cry out of the wall, and the beam out of the timber shall answer it" (Hab. 2:11). However, the sages assert: The man's own soul will testify against him, for Scripture says, "Keep the doors of thy mouth from her that lieth in thy bosom" (Mic. 7:5). What is it that lies in a man's bosom? You must admit, it is the soul.

R. Zerika said: The two ministering angels that accompany him will testify against him, for it is said, "He will give His angels charge over thee, to watch thee in all thy ways" (Ps. 91:11). But other sages assert: A man's own limbs will testify against him, for they have been told, "Therefore ye are My witnesses, saith the Lord, and I am God" (Isa. 43:12).[6]

78. R. Isaac bar Parnakh said: All of a man's iniquities are engraved upon his bones.[7]

79. R. Hiyya bar Abba said in the name of R. Yohanan: If most of a man's years have passed without sin, he will not sin anymore, as is said, "He will guard the steps of His saintly one" (1 Sam. 2:9).

Sages in the school of R. Shila taught: If a man had the opportunity to sin and then had a similar opportunity once again, and sinned neither time, he will not sin in the future, as is said, "He will guard the steps of His saintly one."[8]

80. R. Huna said: When a man has committed a sin once and a second time, it appears to him as if it were permitted.[9]

81. R. Ulla expounded: What is meant by "Be not much wicked" (Eccles. 7:17)? Is it that a man may not be wicked much, but he may be wicked a little bit? No indeed. Rather, if a man has eaten a bit of garlic and his breath smells, is he to eat more garlic so that his breath will smell even more?[10]

82. Ben Azzai said: Run to perform an easy precept as you would to perform a difficult one,[11] and flee from transgression, since one precept draws another in its train, and one transgression draws another in its train. For the recompense for performing a precept is the opportunity to perform another precept, and the recompense for committing a transgression is the temptation to commit another transgression.[12]

83. He used to say: Recoil from a slight sin so that you will recoil from a grave sin. Anticipate what is commanded, so that retribution does not anticipate you. If you have lapsed into transgression, worry not so much about that transgression as about the one that will come after it. And if observance of a precept has come to your hand, rejoice not so much about the observance of that precept as about the precept that will come after it.[13]

84. "But if any man hate his brother, and lie in ambush for him" (Deut. 19:11). From this verse the sages inferred: When a man violates an easy precept, he will in the end violate a grave precept. If a man violates the precept "Thou shalt love thy neighbor as thyself" (Lev. 19:18), he will in the end violate successively "Thou shalt not hate thy brother" (Lev. 19:17), "Thou shalt not take vengeance, nor bear any grudge" (Lev. 19:18), and "That thy brother may live with thee" (Lev. 36:22), until finally he comes to shed blood, as is said, "If any man hate his neighbor, he will come to lie in ambush for him, and rise up against him, and smite him mortally" (Deut. 19:11).[14]

---

1. Exod. R. 30:14.
2. B. Sanh 99b.
3. B. Sot 3b.
4. B. Yoma 86b.
5. The word *re'a* ("friend") is read as though vocalized *ra'* ("evil").
6. B. Hag 16a and En Yaakov, ad loc.
7. Ka R. 3:1.
8. B. Yoma 38b and En Yaakov, ad loc.
9. B. Yoma 86b.
10. If a man has sinned a little, he should not continue sinning. B. Shab 31b.
11. The words "as you would perform a difficult one" are not found in many versions.
12. Avor 4:2.
13. ARNB 33.
14. Sif Deut., §186–87.

85. "Happy is he who is raised above transgression"[1] (Ps. 32:1). Happy is the man who rises above proneness to transgression, and whose proneness to transgression does not rise above him.[2]

86. Resh Lakish said: No man commits a transgression unless the spirit of madness enters into him.[3]

87. [The prophet] Elijah said to R. Judah brother of R. Salla the Pious: Refrain from anger, and you will not sin; drink not to excess, and you will not sin.[4]

88. A sage of the school of R. Ishmael taught: Sin dulls the heart of man, as is said, "Neither shall ye make yourselves unclean with them, that ye should be defiled thereby" (Lev. 11:43). Read not *ve-nitmetem* "that ye should be defiled," but *ve-nittamtem*, "that ye should become dulled."[5]

89. R. Isaac said: When a man commits a transgression in secret, it is as though he were pushing the feet of the Holy One [off His footstool], as is said, "Thus saith the Lord: The heaven is My throne and the earth is My footstool" (Isa. 66:1).[6]

90. We have been taught that R. Meir used to say: A man may commit a transgression in secret, but the Holy One proclaims it about him in the open.[7]

91. R. Kahana said: I consider a man brazen who sets forth his sin in detail, for it is said, "Happy is the man whose transgression is forgiven, whose sin is covered" (Ps. 32:1).[8]

92. R. Nahman bar Isaac said: A transgression performed with good intention is better than a precept performed with evil intention.[9]

93. One may presume that a man will not commit a sin unless he stands to profit by it.[10]

94. There can be no agent for a sinful act.[11]

95. No man ascribes guilt to himself.[12]

96. A sinner may not be allowed to profit.[13]

1. JV: "whose transgression is forgiven."
2. Gen. R. 22:6.
3. B. Sot 3a.
4. B. Ber 29b.
5. B. Yoma 39a.
6. B. Hag 16a.
7. B. Sot 3a.
8. B. Ber 34b.
9. B. Naz 23b.
10. B. BM 5b.
11. Hence, the agent cannot exculpate himself by pleading that he was no more than an agent. B. BK 51a.
12. B. Shab 119a.
13. Shev 9:9.

97. Woe unto him who cannot distinguish between good and evil.[14]

98. Sin's beginning is sweet, but its end is bitter.[15]

99. Rava expounded: The verse that says, "The mandrakes give forth fragrance" (Song 7:14), alludes to young men in Israel who have never savored the taste of sin.[16]

100. R. Zutra bar Tobiah said in the name of Rav: Young men in Israel who have not savored the taste of sin are destined to give forth sweet fragrance like that of Lebanon, as is said, "His young men[17] shall spread out far, and his beauty shall be as the olive tree, and his fragrance as Lebanon" (Hos. 14:7).[18]

101. "If your sins be in keeping with your years"[19] (Isa. 1:18). When a man's iniquities are in keeping with his years,[20] "they shall be as white as snow" (ibid.).[21]

102. We have been taught that R. Simeon ben Eleazar said: Do works [of righteousness and charity] while you can find [people to do such works for], while you have the opportunity, and while it is still in your power. Indeed, in his wisdom, Solomon said, "Remember then thy Creator in the days of thy youth, before the evil days come"—the days of old age—"and the years draw nigh, when thou shalt say: 'I have no pleasure in them' " (Eccles. 12:1)—the days of the Messiah, when there will be neither merit nor guilt.[22]

103. Quoting "Among the dead I am free" (Ps. 88:6), R. Yohanan said: Once a man is dead, he is free from religious obligations.[23]

The Righteous and the Wicked

104. "Say ye of the righteous, when they are good, that they shall eat the fruit of their doings" (Isa. 3:10). But is it conceivable for there to be one righteous man who is good and another righteous man who is not good? The answer is: he who is good to Heaven and good to man is a righteous man who is truly good; good to Heaven but not good to man is a righteous man who is not truly good. Similarly, you read, "Woe unto the wicked man that is evil; for the reward of his hands shall be given unto him" (Isa. 3:11). But is it conceivable for there to be one wicked man who is evil and another wicked man who is not evil? The answer is: he who is evil to Heaven and evil to man

14. B. Sanh 103a.
15. Lev. R. 16:8.
16. B. Er 21b.
17. JV: "boughs."
18. B. Ber 43b and En Yaakov, ad loc.
19. JV: "like scarlet." But *shanim* ("scarlet") also means "years."
20. So that when old, he does not take to youthful follies.
21. P. Yoma 6:5, 43d.
22. B. Shab 151b.
23. Ibid.

is a wicked man who is truly evil; he who is evil to Heaven but not evil to man is a wicked man who is not truly evil.[1]

105. "They who practice Thy righteousness are like the mighty mountains" (Ps. 36:7). As the mountains are sown and yield fruit, so the deeds of the righteous yield fruit which benefits them and others. By what parable may the matter be illustrated? By that of a golden ball whose clapper is a pearl. "They upon whom Thy judgments are imposed are like the great deep" (ibid.)—these are the wicked. As the deep cannot be sown to yield fruit, so the deeds of the wicked cannot yield fruit, for if they yielded fruit, they would destroy the world.[2]

106. R. Phinehas the Priest bar Hama said: In the heaven called Aravot,[3] the Holy One sows the doings of the righteous and they bear fruit, as is said, "They shall eat the fruit of their doings" (Isa. 3:10).[4]

107. "Now the earth was unformed and void" (Gen. 1:2); this alludes to deeds of the wicked. "And God said: 'Let there be light' " (ibid.); this alludes to deeds of the righteous.[5]

108. Righteous men say little but perform much. Thus, Abraham said, "I will fetch a morsel of bread and stay ye your heart" (Gen. 18:5), but in the event "Abraham ran unto the herd" (Gen. 18:7). On the other hand, the wicked say much but do not perform even a little. Thus we find Ephron saying to Abraham, "The field give I to thee . . . a piece of land worth four hundred shekels of silver—what is that betwixt me and thee?" (Gen. 23:11, 23:15). But in the event, "Abraham weighed to Ephron . . . four hundred shekels of silver, current money with the merchant" (Gen. 23:16). Ephron refused to accept anything but centenaria.[6]

109. R. Yose the Galilean said: The righteous—their impulse to good judges them, as Scripture says, "My heart pierces [my soul] within me" (Ps. 109:22). The wicked—the impulse to evil judges them, as Scripture says, "Transgression speaketh [accusingly] to a wicked man within his heart" (Ps. 36:2). Middling people are judged by one impulse as well as by the other, for Scripture says, "Because He standeth at the right hand of the needy, to save him from those[7] who would judge his soul" (Ps. 109:31). Rabbah said, "People such as ourselves are middling." Abbaye said to him, "[If the master is no more than average], he gives no one else a chance to survive!"[8]

Rabbah further said: "Everyone should himself know whether he is completely righteous or not."[9]

Rava said: The world was created only for the completely wicked and the completely righteous. He went on: Thus, the world was created only for Ahab son of Omri and for R. Hanina ben Dosa—this world for Ahab son of Omri; and for R. Hanina ben Dosa, the world-to-come.[10]

110. If there is no righteous person, there is no wicked either. Hence, the wicked said to the righteous: You should endeavor to show gratitude to me, for were I not wicked, how would you be recognized? Were all men righteous, you would have no superiority.[11]

111. The wicked—they are under control of their hearts. But the righteous—they have their hearts under their control.[12]

112. R. Hanina bar Papa expounded: The name of the angel in charge of conception is Night; he takes each drop [of semen] and places it before the Holy One, saying to Him, "Master of the universe, what is this drop to become, a strong man or a weak man, a wise man or a fool, a rich man or a poor man?" But he does not say, "A righteous man or a wicked man?" R. Hanina added: Everything is in the hands of Heaven except the fear of Heaven, as is said, "And now, O Israel, what is the thing that the Lord thy God requireth of thee? It is to fear [Heaven]" (Deut. 10:12).[13]

113. Our masters taught: When a wicked man enters the world, wrath enters the world. When a wicked man perishes from the world, good comes to the world. When a righteous man departs from the world, evil comes to the world. When a righteous man comes into the world, good comes to the world.[14]

114. The death of the wicked is a benefit to them and a benefit to the world; the death of the righteous is an injury to them and an injury to the world. Wine and sleep of the wicked are a benefit to them and a benefit to the world; wine and sleep of the righteous are an injury to them and an injury to the world. Dispersion of the wicked is a benefit to them and a benefit to the world; dispersion of the righteous is an injury to them and an injury to the world. Gathering of the wicked is an injury to them and an injury to the world; gathering of the righteous is a benefit to them and a benefit to the world.[15] Tranquility of the wicked is an injury to them and an injury to the world; tranquility of the righteous is a benefit to them and a benefit to the world.[16]

---

1. B. Kid 40a.
2. Tanhuma, *Emor*, §5.
3. Here associated with *aravah* ("an arid tract").
4. MTeh 114:2.
5. Gen. R. 2:5.
6. Twenty-five times the worth of the field. The centenarium is a weight equal to 100,000 Roman sesterces, the same as the biblical talent (*kikkar*). B. BM 87a; Tanhuma, *Be-har*, §1.
7. Plural pronoun; hence, two impulses.
8. For if so, the overwhelming majority of mankind is wicked and faces damnation.
9. And if not completely righteous, he should know that he is destined to suffer.
10. B. Ber 61b and En Yaakov, ad loc.
11. Midrash Tem 2 (BhM 1:108).
12. Gen. R. 34:1.
13. B. Nid 16b.
14. B. Sanh 113b.
15. The source for "Gathering of the wicked is an injury . . . to the world . . ." is unknown to the translator.
16. B. Sanh 72a.

115. R. Yohanan said: As long as the wicked live, they evoke the anger of the Holy One, as is said, "Ye have wearied the Lord with your words" (Mal. 2:17). But when they die, they cease to anger the Holy One, as is said, "There the wicked cease from raging" (Job 3:17), which means that there the wicked cease from enraging the Holy One. As long as the righteous live, they must combat their impulse to evil, but when they die, they enjoy rest, in keeping with "And there the weary are at rest" (ibid.), [as the righteous say], "We have labored enough."[1]

116. "It is not good to respect the person of the wicked" (Prov. 18:5); it is not good for the wicked to be favored [by the Holy One] in this world.[2] "[But it is good] to subvert the righteous in judgment" (ibid.); it is good for the righteous that no favor be shown them [for their faults by the Holy One] in this world.[3]

Happy are the righteous! Not only do they acquire merit, but they bestow merit upon their children and children's children to the end of all generations. Aaron had several sons who deserved to be burned like Nadab and Abihu, as is said, "His sons that were left" (Lev. 10:12),[4] but the merit of their father stood up for them. Woe unto the wicked! They render not only themselves guilty, they bestow guilt upon their children and children's children unto the end of all generations. Canaan had many sons who were worthy to be ordained like Tabi, the slave of R. Gamaliel, but the guilt of their ancestor caused them [to be held unworthy].[5]

117. "Visiting the iniquity of the fathers upon the children—upon the third, and upon the fourth generation" (Num. 14:18). Consider the implications of this verse by analogy with a four-level storehouse, one level above the other; on one there is wine; on another, oil; on still another, honey; and on still another, water. If a fire starts on any one of the levels, what is above it will extinguish the fire. But if all four levels should have oil on them, all four will burn down. Likewise, if children persist, generation after generation, in the wicked ways of their forefathers, punishment will be visited upon them. But if the generations alternate, one generation righteous and the next wicked, and so on, then "the fathers shall not be put to death for the children, neither shall the children be put to death for the fathers" (Deut. 24:16). Hearing this, Moses rejoiced, saying, "In Israel, no one is a malicious destroyer of grapevines just because his father was a malicious destroyer of grapevines."[6]

118. Believe not in yourself until the day of your death. The high priest Yohanan ministered in the high priesthood for eighty years, and in the end became a Sadducee [heretic].[7]

119. R. Simeon ben Yohai said: Even if a man is perfectly righteous all his life, but rebels in the end, he annuls the [good] deeds he had previously performed, as is said, "The righteousness of the righteous shall not deliver him in the day of his transgression" (Ezek. 33:12). And conversely, even if a man was completely wicked, but then resolved on penitence, his wickedness is never mentioned to him again, as is said, "Nor shall the wickedness of the wicked cause him to stumble when he turns back from his wickedness" (ibid.).[8]

120. R. Eliezer son of R. Yose the Galilean said: If you are aware of a righteous man about to set out on a journey, and you intend to go in the same direction, start out as many as three days earlier or as many as three days later, so that you set out on the journey together with him, because angels of peace accompany him, he being told, "For He will give His angels charge over thee, to keep thee in all thy ways" (Ps. 91:11). On the other hand, if you are aware of a wicked man about to set out on a journey, and you intend to go in the same direction, start out as many as three days earlier or as many as three days later because of him, so that you will not have to set out with him on the journey, for the angels of Satan will accompany him, as is said, "Set thou a wicked man near him, and Satan will stand at his right hand" (Ps. 109:6).[9]

121. Abbaye said: Woe to the wicked, woe to his neighbor. It is well with the righteous, and well with his neighbor.[10]

122. "God remembered Abraham and removed Lot" (Gen. 19:29). We have been taught: A case in which there is a book of Scripture should be saved [by being carried out of a burning house on the Sabbath], together with the book itself; a case containing tefillin should be saved together with the tefillin themselves. Hence you learn that it is well with the righteous and well with those who cleave to them. And so, too, Scripture says, "God remembered Noah, and every living thing with him" (Gen. 8:1) [remembered them on account of Noah]. But woe to the wicked, and woe to those who cleave to them, for Scripture says earlier, "And He blotted out every living substance which was upon the face of the earth" (Gen. 7:23).[11]

123. A sage in the school of R. Ishmael taught: The verse "When he that is falling falls thence [from the roof that has no parapet]" (Deut. 22:8) implies that he was destined to fall ever since the six days of creation, for even though he had not yet fallen, Scripture speaks of him as "he that is falling," because reward is bestowed through

1. Gen. R. 9:5.
2. So that punishment may be visited upon them in the world-to-come.
3. Because thereby they come to eternal life purged of sin.
4. The suggestion being: "They were left to survive," even though they also deserved the punishment suffered by their two brethren.
5. B. Yoma 87a.
6. Yalkut, *Shelah*, §744.
7. Avot 2:4; B. Ber 29a.
8. B. Kid 40b.
9. Tos AZ 1:17.
10. B. Suk 56b.
11. Tanhuma, *Va-yera*, §9.

a person deserving of reward, and punishment through a person deserving punishment.[1]

124. He who causes the many to be righteous—no sin will occur through him. But he who causes the many to sin will not be provided means to resolve on penitence. Moses was righteous and caused the many to be righteous, therefore the righteousness of the many is deemed to be dependent on him, as is said, "He executed the righteousness of the Lord, and his ordinances[2] with Israel" (Deut. 33:21). But Jeroboam son of Nebat sinned and caused the many to sin. Therefore the sin of the many is deemed to be dependent on him, as is said, "For the sins of Jeroboam which he sinned, and wherewith he made Israel to sin" (1 Kings 15:30).[3]

125. R. Abba bar Kahana said: The root of the Presence had been with those below, for it is said, "And they heard the voice of the Lord God walking through the garden" (Gen. 3:8). When Adam sinned, the Presence withdrew to the first heaven. When Cain sinned, it withdrew to the second heaven; the generation of Enosh—to the third; the generation of the flood—to the fourth, the generation of the dispersion of the races of man—to the fifth; the people of Sodom—to the sixth; the Egyptians in the days of Abraham—to the seventh. Over against these wicked men there rose seven righteous men who brought it about that the Presence came down to the earth. Abraham had the privilege of bringing it down from the seventh to the sixth. Isaac rose up and brought it down to the fifth; Jacob—to the fourth; Levi—to the third; Kohath—to the second; Amram—to the first. Then Moses rose up and brought it down from the world above to the world below.[4]

126. R. Phinehas said in the name of R. Hoshaia: Although you read, "Because on it He rested from all His work" (Gen. 2:3), He rested, to be sure, from the work of [creating] His world, but not from the work of the wicked and the work of the righteous, for He works with the former and also with the latter. He shows the ones [the consequences of] their essential character and the others [the consequences of] their essential character. How do we know that the punishment of the wicked is called work? Because it is said, "The Lord hath opened His armory, and hath brought forth the weapons of His indignation, for it is a work that the Lord God hath to do" (Jer. 50:25). And how do we know that the bestowing of reward upon the righteous is called work? Because it is said, "Oh how abundant is Thy goodness, which Thou hast laid up for them that fear Thee, which Thou hast worked for them that take refuge in Thee" (Ps. 31:20).[5]

127. R. Yohanan said: The righteous are greater than the ministering angels.[6]

128. Rabbah bar Bar Hanah said: The soul of one righteous man equals in weight the entire world, all of it.[7]

129. R. Hiyya bar Abba said in the name of R. Yohanan: When the Holy One saw that the righteous were but few, He planted them in each and every generation, as is said, "The pillars of the earth [the righteous], which are of the Lord, upon them He placed the world" (1 Sam. 2:8).[8]

130. "And the angel of the Lord called unto him out of heaven, and said: 'Abraham, Abraham' " (Gen. 22:11). R. Eliezer ben Jacob stated: [The repetition of the name implies that God spoke] to him as well as to subsequent generations. There is no generation that does not have someone like Abraham, no generation that does not have someone like Jacob, no generation that does not have someone like Moses, and no generation that does not have someone like Samuel.[9]

131. The world rests on twelve pillars, as is said, "He set the borders of the peoples according to the number [of the tribes] of the children of Israel" (Deut. 32:8). Some maintain: On seven pillars, as is said, "She hath hewn out her seven pillars" (Prov. 9:1). R. Eleazar ben Shammua maintained: On one pillar, and its name is Righteous, for it is said, "Righteous is the foundation of the world" (Prov. 10:25).[10]

132. R. Eleazar said: Even for the sake of just one righteous man would the world have been created.

R. Hiyya bar Abba said in the name of R. Yohanan: Even for the sake of just one righteous man would the world endure, as is said, "The righteous is the foundation of the world."[11]

133. Rava said: If the righteous desired [to be utterly free of iniquity], they could create a world, for Scripture says, "It is only your iniquities that have distinguished between you and your God" (Isa. 59:2).

Rava created a man and sent him to R. Zera. R. Zera spoke to him but received no answer. So he said: You are a creature of the associate scholars [*haverim* of the academy]. Go back to your dust![12]

134. You will find that, through the agency of the righteous, the Holy One anticipated in this world everything that He will do in the world-to-come. The Holy One quickens the dead, and [the prophet] Elijah quickened the dead. The Holy One holds back rain, and Elijah held back rain. The Holy One blesses the [ones who have] little, and Elijah

---

1. The man who built a roof without a parapet deserves punishment, and a man who deserves to fall because of guilt is the instrument for punishing the man who built the roof improperly. B. Shab 32a.
2. Not God but Moses is credited with the ordinances.
3. Avot 5:18.
4. Gen. R. 19:7; Num. R. 13:2; Song R. 5:1, §1.
5. Gen. R. 11:10; Yalkut, Jer., §335.
6. B. Sanh 92b–93a.
7. B. Sanh 103b.
8. B. Yoma 38b.
9. See Gen. 46:2, Exod. 3:4, and 1 Sam. 3:10. Gen. R. 56:7.
10. B. Hag 12b.
11. B. Yoma 38b.
12. B. Sanh 65b.

blessed the [ones who have] little.[1] The Holy One quickens the dead,[2] and [the prophet] Elisha quickened the dead. The Holy One remembers barren women, and Elisha remembered barren women.[3] The Holy One blesses the [ones who have] little, and Elisha blessed the [ones who have] little.[4] The Holy One makes the bitter sweet, and Elisha made the bitter sweet.[5] The Holy One sweetens the bitter through the agency of the bitter,[6] and Elisha sweetened the bitter through the agency of the bitter.[7]

135. R. Abbahu interpreted the verse "The God of Israel said, The Rock of Israel spoke to me, the ruler over men—the righteous" (2 Sam. 23:3) as meaning; "The God of Israel said to me: The Rock of Israel spoke to me: I am the ruler over men. Who rules Me? The righteous man. For I issue a decree, and he nullifies it."[8]

136. "And to rule over the day and over the night" (Gen. 1:18). These are the righteous, who rule over what was created to give light during the day and over what was created to give light during the night. Of this power, Scripture says, "And the sun stood still and the moon stayed" (Josh. 10:13).[9]

137. "Thy righteousness is like the mighty mountains, Thy judgments are like the great deep" (Ps. 36:7). R. Josiah the Elder said: Transpose the parts of the verse and read it thus: "Like the mighty mountains over the great deep is Your righteousness over Your judgments," that is: As the mountains hold down the deep so that it does not come up and flood the earth, so the righteous hold down retribution so that it should not come to the world.[10]

138. R. Samuel bar Nahmani said: Woe to the wicked, who turn the measure of mercy into the measure of judgment. Blessed are the righteous, who turn the measure of judgment into the measure of mercy.[11]

139. A heretic once said to R. Joshua ben Hananiah: You are no more than a brier, since it is said of you, "The best of them is as a brier" (Mic. 7:4). R. Joshua replied: You fool, go to the end of the verse, where it is said, "The upright man is better [protection] than a tabernacle" (ibid.).[12] What, then, is meant by "The best of them is as a brier"? Even as briers shield a gap in a fence, so do the best among us provide a shield for the rest of us.[13]

140. R. Isaac observed: When a man says to his friend, "Why do you do this or that?" his friend gets angry. Yet the righteous say to the Holy One, "Why?"[14] and He does not get angry, and the righteous are not punished. Why are the righteous not punished? Because they seek no boon for themselves, but only for the children of Israel.[15]

141. Abbaye said: In the world there are no fewer than thirty-six righteous men, who in each generation are allowed sight of the Holy One's countenance, for it is said, "Blessed are all they who wait on Him (*lo*) [*lv*]" (Isa. 30:18). The numerical value of the letters *lamed* and *vav* in the word *lo* is thirty-six.[16]

142. "It is a brilliant light, which gives off rays on every side—and there His glory is enveloped" (Hab. 3:4). To what, then, may the righteous in the vicinity of the Presence be likened? To a lamp in the presence of a torch.[17]

143. "I am a rose of Sharon, a lily of the valleys" (Song 2:1). R. Eliezer said: The righteous are likened to the most exquisite plant and its most exquisite variety. The most exquisite plant: the lily; its most exquisite variety: the lily of the valley. Not the lily of the mountain, which soon withers, but the lily of the valley, which remains full of sap. But as for the wicked, they are likened to the vilest thing and to its vilest representative—to chaff before the wind. Do not suppose that the wicked are likened to the chaff of the valley, which retains some moisture. No! "They shall be chased as the [utterly dried] chaff of the mountains before the wind" (Isa. 17:13).[18]

144. "The righteous shall flourish like the palm tree; he shall grow like a cedar in Lebanon" (Ps. 92:13). [With this verse] R. Tanhuma bar Abba began his discourse: Why are the righteous likened to a palm tree and a cedar, but not to any other tree? You find that with all other trees a man cannot tell from afar that it is such-and-such a tree. Why not? Because they are low. Whereas the palm tree and the cedar, being tall in stature, can be seen from afar, and all may stand under them and raise their eyes to the trees' stature. Therefore are the righteous likened to a palm tree and to a cedar, since the Holy One elevates the righteous in the world, so that they may be seen from afar.[19]

145. Does a man plant a vineyard to eat grapes from it and drink wine from it or to have it overgrown with weeds? If it becomes overgrown with weeds and thorns, he sets them on fire and burns them. If a few vines survive, he manures it, hoes it, prunes it, and irrigates it to propagate the vines in it. So it is with the righteous in the world—they are like the pillars of a house, and the entire world

1. See Gen. 30:30 and 1 Kings 17:14.
2. 2 Kings 4:32–34.
3. 2 Kings 4:16.
4. 2 Kings 4:43–44.
5. See Exod. 15:25 and 2 Kings 2:21–22.
6. The wood that Moses was told to cast into the water is said to have been olive wood, which is very bitter.
7. Salt. See 2 Kings 2:19–20. Gen. R. 77:1.
8. B. MK 16b and En Yaakov, ad loc.
9. Gen. R. 6:9.
10. Gen. R. 33:1; Lev. R. 27:1; MTeh 36:5.
11. Gen. R. 33:1.
12. JV: "The most upright is worse than a thorn hedge." But R. Eliezer takes *mesukhah* ("thorn hedge") to be a form of *sukkah* ("tabernacle").
13. B. Er 101a.
14. Questions such as "Why do You countenance treachery?" (Hab. 1:13).
15. MTeh 2:2; Yalkut, Ps., §620.
16. B. Sanh 97b.
17. Even as the light of an oil lamp seems dim in the presence of a torch, so does the light of the righteous in God's presence. B. Pes 8a.
18. Song R. 2:1, §3.
19. Adapted from Tanhuma, *Lekh lekha*, §5.

is sustained by them. Such is the meaning of "The pillars of the earth are the Lord's, and He hath set the world upon them" (1 Sam. 2:8).[1]

146. "Hearken unto Me, ye stout-hearted [ye righteous], who are far from having to depend on charity" (Isa. 46:12). The entire world, all of it, is sustained by [God's] charity, while they are sustained by their arm [their own merit]. Some say that the entire world, all of it, is sustained by the merit of the righteous, while they themselves are not sustained even by their own merit.[2] Thus, R. Judah said in the name of Rav: Each and every day a divine voice goes forth from Mount Horeb and proclaims: The entire world, all of it, is sustained on account of My son Hanina. But as for My son Hanina—he has to sustain himself on a *kav* of carobs from Sabbath even to Sabbath eve.[3]

147. "And Jacob would dwell" (Gen. 37:1). R. Aha said: When the righteous dwell in peace and would continue to dwell in peace in this world, Satan comes along and charges, saying: It is not enough for these that the world-to-come is prepared for them—they seek to live in peace in this world as well.[4]

148. "The Lord loveth the righteous" (Ps. 146:8). Why does the Holy One love the righteous? Because their worth stems neither from inheritance nor from family. You find that priests constitute an ancestral house and Levites constitute an ancestral house, as is said, "O house of Aaron, bless ye the Lord; O house of Levi, bless ye the Lord" (Ps. 135:19–20). Accordingly, should a man wish to become a priest, he cannot; to become a Levite, he cannot. Why not? Because his father was not a priest or not a Levite. But should a man—even a Gentile—wish to be righteous, he can, because being righteous does not depend on an ancestral house. Therefore the psalm says, "Ye that fear the Lord, bless ye the Lord" (Ps. 135:20)—not, "Ye house of them that fear the Lord," because they who fear the Lord do not constitute an ancestral house. But they themselves come forth on their own and love the Holy One. Therefore does the Holy One love them.[5]

149. R. Eleazar pointed to an apparent contradiction between two verses. One says, "The Lord is good to all" (Ps. 145:9), while another says, "The Lord is good unto them that wait for Him" (Lam. 3:25). He reconciled the two verses by the parable of a man who has an orchard. When he irrigates it, he irrigates the entire orchard, but when he hoes, he hoes only the best trees.[6]

150. R. Simeon ben Judah said in the name of R. Simeon ben Yohai: Beauty, strength, riches, honor, wisdom, old age and gray hair, and children are comely for the righteous and comely for the world.[7]

151. The Holy One has more consideration for the honor of the righteous than for His own honor.[8]

152. One righteous man may surpass another in seven respects: his wife may be more beautiful than his friend's, his sons more handsome than his friend's; when two righteous men eat from the same dish, one will enjoy the food in keeping with his merits and the other in keeping with his; when two righteous men dye cloth in the same vat, the color comes up brilliant for one and dull for the other. [Further, one may surpass the other] in wisdom, knowledge, and stature, as is said, "One righteous man may surpass another" (Prov. 12:26).[9]

153. R. Hiyya bar Abba said in the name of R. Yohahan: No righteous man ever departs from the world until a righteous man like him is brought into being, as is said, "A sun ariseth, even as another sun goeth down" (Eccles. 1:5). Thus, even before the sun of Eli set, the sun of Samuel the Ramathite began to shine.[10]

154. R. Hama bar Hanina said: The righteous are more powerful after their death than during their life.[11]

155. "For the living know that they died" (Eccles. 9:5)—these are the righteous, who even after their death are called living. "But the dead know not anything" (ibid.)—these are the wicked, who even during their life are called dead.[12]

156. R. Eleazar said in the name of R. Hanina: When a righteous man dies, he dies only to his own generation.[13] A parable of a man who lost a pearl: Wherever the pearl is, it is still a pearl—it is lost only to its owner.[14]

157. "The righteous shall flourish like the palm tree; he shall grow like a cedar in Lebanon" (Ps. 92:13). Why are the righteous likened to a palm and to a cedar? Because you find it true of the majority of trees that, even after they are cut down, a sprout may be taken from them and planted in another place, and they begin to grow again. But when the palm and the cedar are cut down, who can make others grow up in their stead except after many years and much labor? So, too, when a righteous man perishes from the world, who can make another stand up in his stead except after many years?[15]

---

1. TdEZ 5 (JPS, p. 428).
2. The latter part of the verse is now read, "Who are far from receiving [God's] charity."
3. B. Ber 17b.
4. Gen. R. 84:2.
5. Num. R. 8:2.
6. Only the good are fully cared for. B. Sanh 39b.
7. Avot 6:8.
8. PRKM, *Ki Tissa*, 6 (2:25).
9. JV: "The righteous is guided by his friend." ARN 37.
10. B. Yoma 38b.
11. B. Hul 7b.
12. B. Ber 18a–b.
13. Both his reputation and his soul survive.
14. B. Meg 15a.
15. Tanhuma B, *Lekh lekha*, §9.

158. Our masters taught: "The spirit returneth unto God who gave it" (Eccles. 12:7). As He gave it to you in purity, so you [give it back] in purity. The matter may be illustrated by the parable of a king of flesh and blood who distributed royal vestments among his servants. The wise among the servants folded the vestments and placed them carefully in a chest, while the fools among them proceeded to do their ordinary work wearing them. After a time, the king asked for his vestments. The wise among his servants returned them immaculate, while the fools had to return them soiled. The king was pleased with the wise but angry with the fools. Of the wise, he said, "Let my vestments be placed in my treasury, and they may return to their homes in peace"; of the fools, he said, "Let my vestments be given to a fuller, and they who wore them are to be confined in prison." So, too, the Holy One quotes concerning the bodies of the righteous, "Let them enter in peace, let them rest on their couches" (Isa. 57:2); concerning their souls, He quotes, "The soul of my lord shall be treasured in the treasury of life" (1 Sam. 25:29). But concerning the bodies of the wicked, He quotes, "There is no peace, saith the Lord, unto the wicked" (Isa. 48:22); concerning their souls, He quotes, "He will fling away the souls of thine enemies as from the hollow of a sling" (1 Sam. 25:29).[1]

159. R. Hiyya bar Gamda said in the name of R. Yose ben Saul: When a righteous man departs from the world, the ministering angels say to the Holy One, "Master of the universe, such-and-such a righteous man is coming." God responds, "Let the righteous come [from their nesting places] and go forth to meet him, and say to him, 'Let him enter in peace [and then they may go back] and rest on their couches.' " (Isa. 57:2).

R. Eleazar said: When a righteous man departs from the world, three companies of ministering angels go forth to meet him. One says, "Let him come in peace"; another, "Let him rest on his couch"; and still another, "Each may walk in his uprightness" (Isa. 57:2). When a wicked man perishes from the world, three companies of destroying angels come to meet him. One proclaims, "There is no peace, saith the Lord, unto the wicked" (Isa. 48:22); another tells him, "Ye shall lie down in sorrow" (Isa. 50:11); and still another says to him, "Go down, and be thou laid with the uncircumcised" (Ezek. 32:19).[2]

160. The death of the righteous is as grievous as the burning of the house of our God.[3]

161. The sages said in the name of Bar Kappara: When one sheds tears for a virtuous man, the Holy One counts them and lays them up in His treasury, as is said, "Thou countest my grievings. Put Thou my tears into Thy bottle. Are they not in Thy record?" (Ps. 56:9).[4]

1. Shab 152b.
2. B. Ket 104a; MTeh 30:3.
3. B. RH 18b.
4. B. Shab 105b.

162. When R. Hiyya bar Adda, the son of Bar Kappara's sister, died, Resh Lakish, who was his teacher, wept for him, because a disciple is as dear to his teacher as a son. Then he went in and spoke the eulogy for him: "My Beloved is gone down to His garden, to the beds of spices, to feed in the gardens, and to gather lilies" (Song 6:2). "My Beloved" is the Holy One; "went down to His garden"—to the world; "to the beds of spices"—to Israel; "to feed in the gardens"—these are the nations of the world; "and gather lilies"—these are the righteous among the nations, whom He removes from the midst of the nations to plant in Israel. By what parable may the matter be illustrated? By the one of a king who had a son whom he loved exceedingly. What did the king do? He planted an orchard for him. Whenever the son carried out his father's wish, the king would go around the entire world, all of it, and when he saw a beautiful sapling in the world, he would [bring it and] plant it in his orchard. But whenever the son provoked him, he would cut down all his saplings. So, too, whenever Israel carry out the will of Him who is everywhere, He goes around the entire world, all of it, and when He sees a righteous man among the nations of the world, such as Jethro and Rahab, He brings him and has him cleave to Israel. But whenever Israel provoke Him, He removes the righteous who are in their midst.[5]

163. When R. Yose of Milhaia[6] died, R. Yohanan and Resh Lakish went up to attend his funeral, and R. Isaac Passaka went with them. A certain old man who happened to be there wished to deliver the eulogy for R. Yose. R. Isaac Passaka said to him, "Do you dare open your mouth in the presence of these two lions?" But R. Yohanan said, "Let him be—he is an old man and wishes to be accorded honor in the place where he lives." So the old man went in and delivered the eulogy for R. Yose, saying, "The departure of the righteous is more grievous for the Holy One than the hundred less two curses mentioned in Deuteronomy and than the destruction of the Temple. In connection with the curses, it is written, 'Then the Lord will make the plagues wonderful' [Deut. 28:59], and of the destruction of Jerusalem, it is written, 'Therefore is she come down wonderfully' [Lam. 1:9]. But of the departure of the righteous, Scripture says, 'Therefore, behold, I will multiply wonderful work among this people, yea, wonder upon wonder' [Isa. 29:14]. And why such multiplying of God's wonders? Because, as the verse goes on to say, 'The wisdom of their wise men shall perish' " (ibid.). At that, R. Isaac Passaka exclaimed, "May the mouth of this man be blessed,"[7] and R. Yohanan said, "If we had not allowed him to speak, where would we have heard such a pearl [of a eulogy]?"[8]

164. R. Abbahu taught in the name of R. Eleazar: The Holy One records upon His purple robe the name of every righteous man whom the nations put to death. And the

5. P. Ber 2:8, 5b–c.
6. A town in Upper Galilee.
7. The word *gavra* ("man") is in BR mistakenly translated *koah* ("power").
8. Lam. R. 1:9, §37; Yalkut, Isa., §436.

Holy One will demand of the nations of the earth, "Why did you put to death My righteous ones?" When the nations of the earth claim ignorance and reply, "We did not put them to death," what will the Holy One do? He will fetch His royal robe, judge them, and decree their doom.[1]

165. No monuments need be put up for the righteous—their words are their monuments.[2]

166. "The name of the righteous is to be invoked in a blessing" (Prov. 10:7). R. Isaac said: When one mentions a righteous man by name without blessing him, one violates a positive command. What is the proof? "The name of the righteous is to be invoked in a blessing." While he who mentions by name a wicked man without cursing him also violates a positive command. What is the proof? "But the fame of the wicked rots" (ibid.).

R. Samuel bar Nahman said: The names of the wicked are like weaving implements—as long as you use them, they stay taut; but when you lay them aside, they slacken. Thus, have you ever heard a man call his son Pharaoh, Sisera, or Sennacherib? No—he calls him Abraham, Isaac, Jacob, Reuben, or Simeon.[3]

167. Akavia ben Mahalalel said: Better I be called a fool all my days than become wicked for even one hour before Him who is everywhere.[4]

168. Our masters taught: There are four kinds of men who are called wicked. They are, to begin with, he who raises a hand against his fellow to strike him. Even if he does not actually strike him, he is called wicked. Note the language of Scripture: "And he said to the wicked, 'Wherefore wouldst thou strike thy fellow?" (Exod. 2:13). The verse does not say, "Wherefore didst thou strike?" but "Wherefore wouldst thou strike" [implying that the man had not yet struck him]. There is also the kind who borrows but does not repay, of whom Scripture says, "The wicked borroweth and payeth not" (Ps. 37:21). Then there is the kind who is so brazen that he feels no shame in the presence of one superior to him, of whom it is said, "The wicked man is brazen in his presence" (Prov. 21:29). Finally, there is the kind who causes strife. With regard to a band of such, Scripture says, "Depart, I pray you, from the tents of these wicked men" (Num. 16:26).[5]

169. What are the wicked like? Like a man who walks on a road in the dead of night [without a lantern in his hand], so that when he trips over a stone, he falls down; when he bumps into a tree, it bruises his face; when he comes to a pit, he stumbles into it; when he comes to a river, he falls into it—he just does not know where he is going. Of such a one, Scripture says, "The way of the wicked is as darkness; they do not know what will make them stumble" (Prov. 4:19). But the righteous are like a man who carries a torch in his hand while walking in the darkness, so that when he comes to a stone, he steps aside; when he sees a tree, he removes himself from it; when he reaches a pit, he takes care; when he reaches a river, he takes care. Such a man can say, "Thy word is a lamp unto my feet" (Ps. 119:105).[6]

170. "Thou hast broken the teeth of the wicked" (Ps. 3:8). A parable of two men, one righteous and the other wicked, who were walking along a highway. When they came upon an inn, they said to each other, "Let us go in and eat." As they entered the inn, the wicked man saw a great abundance of [food]—fish, bullock, ox, lamb and ram, fowl, and other good victuals. So he said to the righteous man, "We will pay nothing, and eat all we want." The righteous man answered, "Has this inn just opened today? Only if it has just opened today could we try out its food without paying."[7] The two men sat down, each by himself. The wicked man said to the innkeeper, "Fetch me pheasants, fetch me spiced wine, fetch me something of all the victuals in the inn." The righteous man said to the innkeeper, "Bring me a bowl of lentils, a small round bread, and two slices of meat." As the two men sat, each by himself, the wicked man was making sport of the righteous man, saying, "Look at that fool, son of a windbag! All these abundant victuals are before him, and he's eating lentils!" And the righteous man was making sport of the wicked man, saying, "He's been devouring all those delicacies, but he'll soon have his teeth broken."

When the righteous man finally said to the innkeeper, "Let me have two cups of wine," the innkeeper served them to him. The righteous man said grace and stood up. Then the innkeeper said, "Pay me for what you ate—one small round bread, a bowl of lentils, two slices of meat, and two cups of wine." The righteous man asked, "How much am I to pay you?" The innkeeper: "Give me two *issar*." The righteous man: "Here you are." The innkeeper took the money and said to the righteous man, "Go in peace."

When the wicked man stood up to go, the innkeeper said, "Settle your account with me!" The wicked man answered, "What have I eaten? One small round bread." The innkeeper said, "No, you have eaten two!" The wicked man, "Well, I ate two eggs!" The innkeeper insisted, "You have eaten five eggs!" The wicked man: "No, I have not eaten that many." At that, the innkeeper and his servants set upon him and broke his teeth. Hence it is said, "Thou hast broken the teeth of the wicked."

So, too, the wicked think: "How can God know?" (Ps. 73:11). But the righteous say, "There is not a word in my tongue, but what Thou, O Lord, knowest it altogether" (Ps. 139:4).[8]

171. "The wicked are like the troubled sea" (Isa. 57:20). The waves in the sea exalt themselves as they rise, even

---

1. MTeh 9:13; Yalkut, Ps., §643.
2. P. Shek 2:5, 47a.
3. Gen. R. 49:1.
4. Ed 5:6.
5. Tanhuma, *Korah*, §8.
6. MTeh 119:44; PR 8:5.
7. In newly opened inns in Roman times, there was a custom of offering free food on opening day.
8. MTeh 4:13.

though each of them is shattered when it reaches and must go back to the sea. And even though each successive wave sees the preceding shattered, it too exalts itself as it rises and will not return to the sea. So it is with the wicked. Though they see what happened to the others, still they exalt themselves. None of the generations—the generation of Enosh, the generation of the flood, the generation of the dispersion of the races of men—none learned from the other, but kept exalting themselves. Therefore they are likened to the sea: "The wicked are like the troubled sea."[1]

172. "Why do the heathen rage?" (Ps. 2:1). R. Aibu said: All the raging of the wicked, all their wearying of themselves, is in vain, as is said, "The people labor for the fire, and the nations weary themselves for vanity" (Hab. 2:13).

Whom do the wicked resemble? Grasshoppers trapped in an urn, flinging themselves upward, only to fall down. So, too, the wicked, with regard to whom Scripture says, "It is He that sitteth above the circle of the earth, and the inhabitants thereof are as grasshoppers" (Isa. 40:22).[2]

173. R. Simeon ben Lakish said: Even at the entrance to Gehenna, the wicked do not turn in penitence, for it is said, "All flesh . . . shall go forth, and look upon the carcasses of the men that rebel[3] against Me" (Isa. 66:24). Scripture does not say, "That have rebelled against Me," but, "That rebel against Me," implying that they go in rebellion forever.[4]

174. Nittai the Arbelite said: Keep your distance from a bad neighbor and do not associate with a wicked man.[5]

175. "On account of Abel—for it was Cain that [Lamech] slew" (Gen. 4:25).[6] Because of the sin against Abel, Cain was slain. What Eve said may be illustrated by the parable of two trees growing close to each other. A wind knocked down one of them, which fell on the other and knocked it down. So, too, Eve said, "On account of Abel—for it was Cain that [Lamech] slew": because of the sin against Abel, Cain had to be slain.[7]

176. R. Yohanan said: A man is forbidden to gaze at the countenance of a wicked man, for [Elisha said to a wicked king of Israel], "Were it not that I regard the presence of Jehoshaphat the king of Judah, I would not look toward thee, nor gaze upon thee" (2 Kings 3:14).

Rabbi [Judah I, the Patriarch] asked R. Joshua ben Korhah, "How did you manage to reach such long life?" R. Joshua: "Do you begrudge me the length of my life?" Rabbi: "My inquiry is concerned with Torah, [whose precepts for long life] it is necessary for me to learn." R. Joshua: "In my life I have never gazed at the countenance of a wicked man."[8]

177. R. Dostai son of R. Mattan said: It is permitted to contend with the wicked in this world, as is said, "They that forsake the Torah praise the wicked; but such as keep the Torah contend with them" (Prov. 28:4). Should someone whisper to you, "Contend not with evildoers, neither be thou envious of them that work unrighteousness" (Ps. 37:1), say to him, "One who is afraid [of the secular authorities] speaks in such a way. As for the verse in the psalm, it is to be read, 'Strive not with evildoers' by trying to be like evildoers, and 'neither be thou envious of them that work unrighteousness' by trying to be like those who work unrighteousness."

But R. Issac said: If you see a wicked man upon whom the hour smiles, do not contend with him.[9]

178. R. Samuel bar Nahman said: Accursed be the wicked, who never perform an act of unmixed kindness.[10]

179. Accursed be the wicked, for even when they do a kindness, their intention is evil.[11]

180. All the favors of the wicked turn out to be bad for the righteous.[12]

181. The wicked's ease ends in calamity.[13]

182. "And Balak saw" (Num. 22:2). It would have been better for the wicked if they were blind, for their eyes bring a curse to the world. Of the generation of the flood, it is written, "The sons of God saw" (Gen. 6:2).[14] It is also written, "And Ham the father of Canaan, saw" (Gen. 9:22); "The princess of Pharaoh saw her" (Gen. 12:15); and, "Shechem the son of Hamor . . . saw her" (Gen. 34:2). And so, too, "And Balak saw."[15]

183. Rava said: Every man has most concern for his own self, hence no man will declare himself wicked.[16]

184. "As they went out before the vanguard, they said: 'Give thanks unto the Lord, for His mercy endureth forever' " (2 Chron. 20:21). R. Jonathan said: Why are the words "for He is good" omitted from this thanksgiving?

---

1. Tanhuma B, *Va-yikra*, §17.
2. MTeh 2:2.
3. JV: "that have rebelled." But the Hebrew *poshe'im* is in the present tense.
4. B. Er 19a.
5. Avot 1:7.
6. JV: "instead of Abel; for Cain slew him." But the commentator regards the statement that Cain had slain Abel is unnecessary. Hence, from this verse he infers that the man Lamech said he slew (Gen. 4:23) was Cain. See above, part 1, chap 2, §106.
7. Gen. R. 23:5.
8. B. Meg 28a.
9. B. Ber 7b.
10. Gen. R. 89:7.
11. Tanhuma, *Mi-ketz*, §5.
12. B. Yev 103a–b.
13. B. Yoma 86b.
14. After which, they sinned.
15. Num. R. 20:2; Tanhuma, *Balak*, §2.
16. Hence, he may not testify for or against himself. B. Sanh 9b.

Because the Holy One does not rejoice at the downfall of the wicked.

R. Samuel bar Nahmani said in the name of R. Jonathan: What is implied in the verse "And one [angel] approached not another all night" (Exod. 14:20)? In that instant the ministering angels wished to utter song before the Holy One, but He rebuked them, saying, "The works of My hands are drowning in the sea, and you would utter song in My presence!"[1]

185. One is forbidden to pray that the wicked be removed from the world.[2] For had the Holy One removed Terah from the world when he worshiped idols, Abraham would not have come into being.

186. Do not raise a vicious dog's pup, even if it is docile. But if it is vicious, all the less so.[3]

187. Misdeed is [usually] ascribed to a [known] misdoer.[4]

188. R. Simeon said: The Egyptians would have drowned Israel in the sea, and the Edomites would have confronted Israel with the sword, yet Scripture prohibited intermarriage with them for only three generations. But for the Moabites, who took counsel to cause Israel to sin, Scripture prohibited intermarriage with them forever. Hence you learn that he who causes a person to sin is more cruel to him than he who slays him, for he who slays him takes him out of only this world, while he who causes him to sin takes him out of both this world and the world-to-come.[5]

189. "Ye shall burn their groves with fire" (Deut. 12:3). If the Torah decrees with regard to trees, which neither eat, nor drink, nor smell: "Destroy, burn, exterminate," because men stumbled on their account, how much more and more are you to destroy him who leads his fellow astray from the paths of life to the paths of death.

"And ye shall break down their altars" (Deut. 12:13). In what way did wood and stones sin? However, because men stumbled on their account, Scripture says, "Break them down." The matter may be argued *a fortiori*: if the Torah says of wood and stone, which have neither guilt nor merit, neither good nor evil, yet, because man has stumbled on their account: "Break them down," how much more and more does this apply to a man who causes his fellow to sin and turns him from the path of life to the path of death.[6]

190. "Their inward thought is, that within their houses they shall continue forever, and their dwelling places to all generations; they call their lands after their own names" (Ps. 49:12). R. Yudan said: Why do the wicked think that "within their houses they shall continue forever"? Because "they call their lands after their own names," that is, Tiberias after Tiberius's name, Alexandria after Alexander's name, and Antioch after Antiochus's name.

R. Phinehas construed the verse "*Kirbam* ('within') are their houses forever" to mean that tomorrow their houses will become their graves (*kivram*).[7]

191. R. Joshua used to say: A foolish pietist, a cunning rogue, a hypocritical woman, and the wounds of the Pharisees—these wreck the world.

What is a foolish pietist? One who sees a child struggling in the river and says, "As soon as I remove my tefillin, I will save him," and while he is removing his tefillin, the child gives up the ghost. Or he sees a woman drowning in the river and says, "It is not proper for me to look at her as I save her." Or he sees the first ripe fig and says, "I will give it to the first person I meet."[8]

Who is a cunning rogue? R. Yohanan said: He who ingratiatingly tells[9] his case to the judge before the other party to the suit has arrived. R. Abbahu said: He who gives a poor man a denar to bring the poor man's possessions to the total of two hundred *zuz*.[10] For we have been taught: The poor man who has two hundred *zuz* may not take the gleanings, the forgotten sheaves, the produce from the corner of the field, and the poor man's tithe. R. Joseph bar Hama said in the name of R. Sheshet: He who [by the practice of deception] induces others to follow in his ways. R. Zerika said in the name of R. Huna: He who is lenient with himself and strict with others.

What is a hypocritical woman? Our masters taught: A maiden given to prayer and a gadabout widow—these wreck the world. Other masters added: A maiden given to fasting.

"The wounds of the Pharisees." Our masters taught: There are seven kinds of Pharisees: The *shikhmi*[11] Pharisee, the *nikpi*[12] Pharisee, the *kizzai*[13] Pharisee, the *medokhi*[14] Pharisee, the "May-I-know-my-guilt-and-I-will-make-it-up" Pharisee, the Pharisee vaunting his love of God, and the Pharisee vaunting his fear of God.

King Yannai said to his wife: Fear not the Pharisees, nor those who are not Pharisees, but only the hypocrites who make themselves resemble Pharisees, for though their works are like those of Zimri, they demand a reward as though they were Phinehas.[15]

1. B. Sanh 39b.
2. MhG, *Va-yera*. The translator could not locate this rule in MhG. It is found in Zohar, Gen. 105a.
3. Lev. R. 19:6.
4. B. BB 109b.
5. Sif Deut., §252.
6. B. Sanh 55a; Sem 8:16.
7. Gen. R. 23:1.
8. Abstaining from the joy of eating it himself.
9. Literally, "feeds his words."
10. The rogue prevents the poor man from taking any part of the rogue's crop, thus keeping it all for himself. A *zuz* is another name for a denar.
11. *Shikhmi*, the adjectival form of *shekhem* ("shoulder"), may mean the Pharisee who ostentatiously carries on his shoulder the good works he performs.
12. May mean: "Excuse me [while I perform a precept]."
13. He calculates his good deeds to counterbalance his evil ones.
14. From *medokhah* ("mortar")—he is given to bowing and scraping.
15. On Zimri and Phinehas, see Num. 25:1–15, and on the entire passage, see the excellent presentation in ARNB, trans. Saldarini, 45. B. Sot 20a–22b; P. Sot 3:4, 19a and 5:7, 20c.

192. R. Isaac said: What is meant by the verse "But to the wicked God saith: 'What hast thou to do to declare My statutes?' " (Ps. 50:16)? The Holy One said to the wicked Doeg: How dare you declare My statutes? When you come to the section dealing with murderers or the section dealing with slanderers, what can you say in expounding them? "That shouldst take My covenant in thy mouth?" (ibid.). R. Ammi said: Doeg's learning in Torah was [external]—from the lips outward.[1]

193. One should expose hypocrites in order to prevent profanation of the Name.[2]

Repentance

194. R. Abbahu bar Ze'era said: Great is repentance, for it preceded the creation of the world, as is said, "Before the mountains were brought forth . . . Thou turnest men to contrition" (Ps. 90:2–3).[3]

195. "Good and upright is the Lord, because He doth show sinners the way" (Ps. 25:8). He shows [them] the way of repentance.

When Wisdom is asked, "The sinner—what is to be his punishment?" Wisdom answers, "Evil shall pursue sinners" (Prov. 13:21). When Prophecy is asked, "The sinner—what is to be his punishment?" Prophecy replies, "The soul that sinneth, it shall die" (Ezek. 18:4). When Torah is asked, "The sinner—what is to be his punishment?" Torah replies, "Let him bring a guilt offering and his sin will be expiated for him." When the Holy One is asked, "The sinner—what is to be his punishment?" the Holy One replies, "Let him vow penitence, and his sin will be expiated for him."

With regard to this, the psalm says, "Because He doth show sinners the way." He shows sinners the way to resolve on penitence.[4]

196. In the neighborhood of R. Meir there lived hooligans, who annoyed him so much that he prayed for them to die. His wife Beruriah said to him: Why do you suppose [your prayer should be heard]? Is it because of the verse "Let the sinners be consumed" (Ps. 104:35)? But in fact, not "sinners" is written, but "sins." Moreover, look at the end of the verse: "And let the wicked be no more," which implies that once sins cease, the wicked will be no more. Rather, beseech mercy for them, that they may turn in penitence, so they will be wicked no more. He besought mercy for them, and they turned in penitence.[5]

197. In the neighborhood of R. Zera there lived brigands, whom he befriended in the hope that they might repent. But the sages were annoyed. When R. Zera died, the brigands said: Until now we had that Scorch-thighed Shorty[6] beseech mercy for us. Who will do it for us now? Thus were they led to thinking about the kind of people they were, until they resolved to repent.[7]

198. When R. Eliezer said, "Repent, even if only one day before your death," his disciples asked him, "Does any man know what day he will die?" R. Eliezer: "Then all the more reason that he repent today. For should he die tomorrow, his entire life will have been spent in repentance. In his wisdom, Solomon also intimated [the need to repent] when he said, "Let thy garments be always white; and let not thy head lack ointment" (Eccles. 9:8).

Regarding this, Rabban Yohanan ben Zakkai said: The matter may be illustrated by the parable of a king who invited his servants to a banquet without designating the precise time. The wise ones among them adorned themselves and sat at the entrance to the palace, for they said, "Is anything lacking in a royal palace?" The foolish went to their work, saying, "Can there be a banquet without preliminary preparation?" Suddenly the king called for his servants: the wise entered his presence adorned, while the foolish entered his presence wearing their soiled [working clothes]. The king rejoiced in welcoming the wise but was angry with the foolish. "Let those who adorned themselves for the banquet," he ordered, "sit, eat, and drink. But let those who did not adorn themselves for the banquet remain standing and watch."

R. Meir's son-in-law said in R. Meir's name: The foolish might have said, "If only it had been done that way, for then we would have appeared to be attendants." In fact, however, both the wise and the foolish were seated, but the wise ate while the foolish stayed hungry; the wise drank while the foolish stayed thirsty. For it is said, "Therefore thus saith the Lord God: Behold, My servants shall eat, but ye shall be hungry; behold, My servants shall drink, but ye shall be thirsty; behold, My servants shall rejoice, but ye shall be ashamed; behold, My servants shall sing for joy of heart, but ye shall cry for sorrow of heart" (Isa. 65:13–14).[8]

199. R. Jacob said: This world is like a vestibule before the world-to-come. Fix yourself up in the vestibule, so that you may enter the banqueting hall.

He used to say: Better one hour spent in repentance and good deeds in this world than the whole life in the world-to-come; and better one hour of bliss in the world-to-come than the whole life in this world.[9]

200. "A twisted thing cannot be made straight, a lack cannot be made good" (Eccles. 1:15). In this world, he who is twisted can be made straight, and he who lacks something can have it made good. But in the time-to-come, he who is twisted cannot be made straight, and he who

1. B. Sanh 106b; Yalkut, Ps., §761.
2. B. Yoma 86b.
3. MTeh 90:12; Gen. R. 1:4.
4. P. Mak 2:6, 31d; Yalkut, Ps., §702.
5. B. Ber 10a.
6. See above, part 2, chap. 1, §504.
7. B. Sanh 37a and En Yaakov, ad loc.
8. B. Shab 153a and En Yaakov, ad loc.
9. Avot 4:16.

lacks something cannot have it made good. There were two wicked men who were friendly with each other in this world. One of the two was beforehand, in that he repented just before he died, but the other did not repent. Eventually the one finds himself standing in a company of righteous men, while the other stands in a company of wicked men. At the sight of his friend, the latter will exclaim, "Woe is me! Is there perhaps some partiality in divine judgment? He and I stole together, he and I robbed together, and together we did all sorts of evil things in the world. Yet here he stands in the company of the righteous, while I am with the company of the wicked!" He will be told bluntly, "You are the biggest fool in the world! Don't you know that your friend vowed penitence?" At that, he cries out, "Allow me, and I too will go and vow penitence." But he is told, "Alas for you, world's fool that you are! Don't you know that this world is like the Sabbath, and the world from which you came is like a Sabbath eve? If a man does not make preparations on Sabbath eve, what will he eat on the Sabbath? This world is like the sea, and the world from which you came is like dry land. If a man does not make preparations for himself while he is on dry land, what will he eat when at sea? This world is like a wilderness, and the world from which you came is like inhabited land. If a man does not make preparations for himself from what is on inhabited land, what will he eat in the wilderness? This world is like the rainy season, and the world from which you came is like the dry season. If a man does not plow and sow, harvest and vintage during the dry season, what will he eat during the rainy season? At that, he gnashes his teeth and is ready to eat himself alive.[1]

201. "A dog [a scoundrel] may thrive, so that he will be better off than a lion [a noble man] who [because he has been brought low] may, so to speak, die." (Eccles. 9:4).[2] In this world, he who is a dog may become a lion, and a lion may become a dog. But in the time-to-come, he who is a dog cannot become a lion, and he who is a lion cannot become a dog.[3]

202. "When a wicked man dieth, his hope shall perish" (Prov. 11:7). As long as a man lives, the Holy One expects him to repent. But once he is dead, the hope that he will repent is gone. The matter may be illustrated by the parable of a band of robbers confined in a prison. What did they do? They dug an opening and escaped. One alone remained behind—he did not escape. When the warden came, he began beating the prisoner with a stick, saying to him, "Ill-starred and hapless wretch! There was an opening before you, and you did not escape!" So, too, in the time-to-come, the Holy One will say to the wicked, "Repentance was before you, and you did not repent!"[4]

1. Eccles. R. 1:15, §1; Ruth R. 3:3; Midrash Prov. 6 (ed. Buber, p. 55). Yalkut, Eccles., §967.
2. A bold paraphrase suggested by Leon Nemoy. JV: "a living dog is better than a dead lion."
3. Yalkut, Eccles., §989.
4. Eccles. R. 7:15, §1; Yalkut, Job, §906.

203. Two things appear to be near you and yet are far from you, appear to be far from you and yet are near you. Repentance appears to be near you but is far from you,[5] appears to be far from you but is near you.[6] Death is near you but it can be far from you,[7] appears to be far from you but is near you.[8]

204. Hillel used to say: If I am not for myself, who will be for me? But if I care only for myself, what am I? If not now, when?[9]

205. According to R. Isaac, the Holy One told Jeremiah: Go, say to Israel, "Vow repentance." When Jeremiah went and exhorted them, they replied, "Our master, how shall we vow repentance? With what countenance may we come into the presence of Him who is everywhere? Have we not provoked Him? Have we not vexed Him? Those mountains and hills where we sacrificed to idols—are they not still standing?" When Jeremiah came into the Holy One's presence and reported Israel's reply, God said to him, "Go tell them this: If you come to Me [in repentance], will you not be coming to your Father in heaven?"[10]

206. "Open to Me, My sister" (Song 5:2). According to R. Yose, the Holy One said to Israel: My children, open to Me in penitence an opening as small as the eye of a needle, and I shall make an opening in Me for you so wide that through it wagons and coaches could enter.[11]

207. R. Phinehas the Priest bar Hama said: The Holy One does not wish to condemn any creature: "For it is not My desire that anyone shall die, saith the Lord God. Repent, therefore, and live" (Ezek. 18:32); "Thou art not a God who desires to declare guilt" (Ps. 5:5); and, "As I live—saith the Lord God—it is not My desire that the wicked shall die" (Ezek. 33:11). What does He desire? To vindicate His creatures: "The Lord desires His [servant's] vindication" (Isa. 42:21). You can see this for yourself. When creatures sin and provoke Him, and He is provoked at them, what does the Holy One do? He goes around and seeks an advocate who will plead for them, and He Himself provides for the advocate a line [of argument]. Thus, in the days of Jeremiah, you find that He said, "Run ye to and fro through the streets of Jerusalem, and see now, and know, and seek in the broad places thereof, if ye can find a man, if there be any that doeth justly, that seeketh truth, and I will pardon her" (Jer. 5:1). So, too, when the Sodomites sinned, He revealed the matter to Abraham so that he would plead for them, as intimated in the verse "Shall I hide from Abraham," etc. (Gen. 18:17). Indeed, Abraham at once began to plead in their behalf: "And Abraham drew near, and said: 'Wilt

5. Because it is so difficult.
6. Because it is possible to repent.
7. Good deeds may avert it.
8. Wicked deeds may bring it near. Eccles. R. 8:16, §1.
9. Avot 1:14.
10. PRK 24:16.
11. Song R. 5:2, §2; Yalkut, Song, §988.

Thou sweep away the innocent with the guilty?' " (Gen. 18:23).[1]

208. R. Simeon ben Lakish said: What is meant by "If a man wishes to join scorners, he is allowed to; but if a man wishes to join the humble, he will be given grace in their eyes" (Prov. 3:34)?[2] If a man comes to defile himself, doors should be opened for him; but if he comes to purify himself, he should be helped. A sage in the school of R. Ishmael explained the matter by the parable of a man who was selling naphtha and balsam. If [a purchaser] comes to measure out naphtha, [the shopkeeper] says, "Measure it out for yourself." But to one who would measure out balsam, he says, "Wait for me to measure it out together with you, so that both of us may become perfumed by it."[3]

209. "Cain went out from the presence of the Lord" (Gen. 4:16). R. Huna, citing R. Hanina bar Isaac, said: Cain went forth glad at heart. As he went out, Adam met him and asked, "What sentence was given you?" Cain replied, "I vowed repentance and was granted clemency." Hearing this, Adam proceeded to strike himself in the face in self-reproach, saying: "So, repentance has all this power, and I knew it not!" Then and there Adam composed "a psalm, a song for the Sabbath day" (Ps. 92:1).[4]

210. "This shall be written for the generation to come" (Ps. 102:19). From the verse's end, it follows that the Holy One receives the penitent. For, in going on to say, "A people that shall be created shall praise the Lord," it clearly speaks of the penitent to whom God gives a new life—creates anew.[5]

211. "The stranger need not lodge outside" (Job 31:32). The Holy One declares no creature unfit—He receives all. The gates [of repentance] are always open, and he who wishes to enter may enter.[6]

212. R. Helbo asked R. Samuel bar Nahman: Since I have heard of you as a master of *Aggadah*, [tell me] what is meant by the verse "Thou hast covered thyself with a cloud so that no prayer can pass through" (Lam. 3:44). R. Samuel answered: Prayer is likened to an immersion pool, but repentance is likened to the sea. Just as an immersion pool is at times open and at other times locked, so the gates of prayer are at times open and at other times locked. But the sea is always open, even as the gates of repentance are always open.[7]

1. Tanhuma, *Va-yera*, §8.
2. JV: "If it concerneth the scorners, He scorneth them, but unto the humble He giveth grace."
3. B. Yoma 38b–39a.
4. The second verse reads: "It is a good thing to confess to the Lord." Lev. R. 10:5.
5. Lev. R. 30:3.
6. Exod. R. 19:4.
7. Lam. R. 3:43, §9.

213. "Have mercy upon me, O God, according to Thy loving-kindness" (Ps. 51:3). With whom may David be compared? With a man who had a wound on his hand and came to a physician. The physician said, "You cannot be treated. The wound is large, but the money you have is little." The man said, "I beg of you, take all the money that I have here, and as for the rest, let it come from you. Have mercy upon me, have compassion upon me." So, too, David said to the Holy One, "Have mercy upon me, O God, according to Thy loving-kindness." You are compassionate, so "according to the multitude of Thy compassions blot out my transgressions" (ibid.): You have already shown me much mercy. David also said, "Make passing great Thy mercies, O Thou that savest . . . them that take refuge in Thee" (Ps. 17:7): healing comes from You. Because the wound is large, lay on a large poultice for me, as is said, "Wash me thoroughly from mine iniquity" (Ps. 51:4).[8]

214. R. Levi said: The power of repentance is so great that it soars up all the way to the throne of glory, as is said, "Return, O Israel, all the way to the Lord thy God" (Hos. 14:2).[9]

215. "Return, O Israel, all the way to the Lord thy God." Our holy rabbi [Judah I, the Patriarch] expounded the verse: So great is the power of a return in penitence that, as soon as a man meditates in his heart to vow penitence, it soars up at once [straight to God]. It soars up to a height not of ten *mil*, nor of twenty, nor of a hundred, but to a height that would require a journey of five hundred years to accomplish—soaring not merely to the first heaven but all the way to the seventh heaven, soaring ever upward beyond the seventh heaven until it stands before the throne of glory itself. Such was Hosea's thought when he said, "Return, O Israel, all the way to the Lord thy God."[10]

216. R. Simeon ben Lakish said in the name of R. Judah [II] the Patriarch: What is meant by the verse "And they had the hands (*yede*) of a man under their wings" (Ezek. 1:8)? Actually *yado*, "His hand," is written, meaning the hand of the Holy One, which is spread out under the wings of the celestial creatures in order to receive penitents [and shield them] from the measure of justice.[11]

217. R. Yohanan said: He who declares that Manasseh has no share in the world-to-come weakens the hand of penitent sinners.

R. Yohanan went on to say in the name of R. Simeon ben Yohai: What is meant by "Manasseh . . . prayed unto Him, and He was entreated (*'tr*) of him" (2 Chron. 33:13)? That God let Himself be dug into (*htr*).[12] The verse implies that, to prevent inteference by the measure of justice, the

8. MTeh 51:1; Yalkut Ps., §764.
9. B. Yoma 86a.
10. PR 44:9.
11. B. Pes 119a.
12. Some Hebrew dialects, under the influence of Aramaic, made no distinction between the gutturals *het* and *ayin*.

Holy One contrived a kind of opening [*mahteret*] in the firmament to accept Manasseh in his penitence.[1]

218. R. Hama son of R. Hanina said: Great is penitence, for it brings healing to the world, as is said, "I will heal their affliction, generously will I take them back in love" (Hos. 14:5).[2]

219. R. Yohanan said: Great is penitence, for it tears up the decree issued against a man.[3]

220. The repentance of confirmed sinners delays punishment, even if the decree of punishment for them had already been sealed.[4]

221. R. Jonathan said: Great is penitence, for it brings redemption, as is said: "A redeemer will come to Zion, and unto them that turn from transgression in Jacob" (Isa. 59:20).[5]

222. R. Judah said: If Israel do not vow penitence, they will not be redeemed. Yet Israel vow penitence only out of distress and out of wandering hither and yon, and because they have no livelihood. However, they will not vow spontaneous penitence until Elijah, ever remembered on good occasions, comes, as is said, "Behold, I will send you Elijah the Prophet . . . and he shall turn the hearts of the fathers to the children, and the hearts of the children to their fathers" (Mal. 3:23–24).[6]

223. Resh Lakish said: Great is penitence, because it reduces one's deliberate sins to mere errors.

But did not Resh Lakish say at another time: Great is penitence, because it transforms one's deliberate sins into merits?

The latter statement refers to penitence out of love; the former, to penitence out of fear.

R. Samuel bar Nahmani said in the name of R. Jonathan: Great is penitence, because it prolongs one's days and years, as is said, "And when the wicked turneth from his wickedness . . . he shall live thereby" (Ezek. 33:19).

R. Isaac said: In the west [the Land of Israel], the sages said in the name of Rabbah bar Mari: Come and see that the conduct of flesh and blood is not at all like the conduct of the Holy One. The conduct of flesh and blood: when a man angers his friend with words, it is questionable whether or not the friend will agree to be pacified by him. And even if you suppose the friend is willing to be pacified, it is questionable whether he will be pacified by mere words or will have to be pacified by compensation. But with the Holy One, there is no question. When a man commits a sin in secret, He is pacified with mere words, as is said, "Take with you words, and return unto the Lord" (Hos. 14:3). More: He even accounts it to him as a good deed, as is said, "And accept that which is good" (Hos. 14:3). Still more: Scripture accounts it for him as though he had offered up bullocks, as is said, "So will we render bullocks with offerings of our lips" (ibid.). Lest you suppose that Scripture refers here to obligatory bullocks, it is said, "I will love the voluntary offerings [of bullocks]" (Hos. 14:5).[7]

We have been taught that R. Meir used to say: Great is penitence, for on account of one individual who vows penitence, pardon is given to him as well as to the entire world, to all of it, as is said, "I will heal their backsliding, I will love them freely, when mine anger is turned away from him" (Hos. 14:5). Hosea says not, "From them," but, "From him."

How is one to tell whether a penitent is genuine? R. Judah said: When the penitent has the opportunity to commit the same sin once and once again, and he refrains from committing it.[8]

224. We have been taught that R. Eliezer said: It would seem to be impossible to say, "He will clear the guilty" (Exod. 34:7), when Scripture is about to say, "He will not clear the guilty" (ibid.). Nor would it seem to be possible to say, "He will not clear the guilty," having just said, "He will clear the guilty." How is the inconsistency explained? That He clears the guilty who repent, but does not clear the guilty who do not repent.

R. Matia ben Heresh asked R. Eleazar ben Azariah in Rome: Have you heard about the four categories of those who atone for sin that R. Ishmael has set forth? R. Eleazar answered: They are actually three,[9] and in each category penitence is required. When a man transgresses a positive commandment and vows penitence, forgiveness is granted him even before he stirs from the place where he is, as is said, "Return, ye backsliding children, I will heal your backslidings" (Jer. 3:22). If he has transgressed a negative commandment and vowed penitence, his penitence suspends punishment and the Day of Atonement procures atonement, as is said, "For on this day shall atonement be made for you . . . from all your sins" (Lev. 16:30). If he has committed [a sin punishable by] excision[10] or by any of the deaths decreed by the High Court and has vowed penitence, his penitence and the Day of Atonement suspend punishment, and his suffering completes the atonement, as is said, "Then I will punish their transgression with the rod, their iniquity with plagues" (Ps. 89:33). But if the man was guilty of profanation of the Name, penitence has no power to suspend punishment, nor can the Day of Atonement procure atonement, nor will suffering complete it; but all of them together suspend the punishment, and only death completes atonement, as is said, "And the Lord of hosts revealed Himself in my ears:

1. B. Sanh 103a.
2. B. Yoma 86a.
3. B. RH 17b.
4. B. Yoma 86b.
5. Ibid. and En Yaakov, ad loc.
6. PRE 43.
7. JV: "I will love them freely."
8. B. Yoma 86b and En Yaakov, ad loc.; Yalkut, Hos., §530.
9. Since, as will be stated, no atonement for the profanation of God's Name is possible while the offender is alive. So Moses ibn Haviv, as cited by Adin Steinsaltz in his edition of Yoma, ad loc.
10. Shortening the years of his life.

surely this iniquity shall not be expiated by you till ye die" (Isa. 22:14).[1]

225. R. Hiyya bar Abba said in the name of R. Yohanan: All the prophets prophesied only concerning penitences, but as for the reward of the wholly righteous, "Eye hath not seen, O God, beside Thee" (Isa. 64:3).

But R. Abbahu differed. In the place where the penitents stand, even the wholly righteous are not permitted to stand, for Scripture promises, "Peace, peace to him that was far and to him that is near" (Isa. 57:19)—first to him who had been far, and then to him who has been near all along.[2]

226. It is told of R. Eliezer ben Dordia that there was not one courtesan in the world whom he had not patronized. Once, on hearing that there was a certain courtesan in one of the cities across the sea who demanded a purse of denars as her fee, he took such a purse and journeyed forth, crossing seven rivers for her sake. During the foreplay of the sexual act, she broke wind. She said, "As this wind will not return to its place, so Eliezer ben Dordia will never be received in penitence." So he went and dwelled among mountains and hills, imploring them: O you mountains and hills, beseech [God's] mercy for me! They replied: Before beseeching mercy for you, we have to beseech it for ourselves, since it is said, "The mountains shall depart, and the hills be removed!" (Isa. 54:10). He went on to implore: Heaven and earth, beseech mercy for me! They, too, replied: Before beseeching mercy for you, we have to beseech it for ourselves, since it is said, "For the heavens shall vanish away like smoke, and the earth shall wax old like a garment" (Isa. 51:6). He then went on: Sun and moon, beseech mercy for me! But they also replied: Before beseeching mercy for you, we have to beseech it for ourselves, since it is said, "Then the moon shall be confounded, and the sun ashamed" (Isa. 24:23). He went on: Stars and planets, beseech mercy for me. They replied: Before beseeching mercy for you, we have to beseech it for ourselves, since it is said, "And all the hosts of heaven shall moulder away" (Isa. 34:4). So he concluded: The issue of the matter must depend on me alone! He lowered his head between his knees and wept aloud until his soul departed. A divine voice went forth to announce: "Rabbi Eliezer ben Dordia is destined for life in the world-to-come!"

[On hearing this], Rabbi [Judah I, the Patriarch] wept and said: One person may acquire eternal life only after many years, while another in one hour. He went on to say: Not only are penitents accorded acceptance, but they are even granted the title Rabbi.[3]

227. Resh Lakish said: A single self-reproach in a man's heart is better than a hundred lashes, as is said, "A rebuke in a man of understanding goes deeper than a hundred lashes on a fool" (Prov. 17:10).[4]

1. B. Yoma 86a.
2. B. Ber 34b and En Yaakov, ad loc.
3. B. AZ 17a and En Yaakov, ad loc.
4. B. Ber 7a.

228. Bar Hinena the Elder said in the name of Rav: When a man commits a transgression and then is ashamed of it, all his iniquities are forgiven him.[5]

229. R. Adda bar Ahavah said: A man who confesses after committing a transgression but does not change his ways is like one who persists in holding a dead reptile in his hand—even if he immerses himself in all the waters of the world, his immersion will not cleanse him. But once he throws the reptile away and then immerses himself in no more than forty *seah* of water, the immersion is effective in cleansing him, as is said, "Whoso confesseth and forsaketh them shall obtain mercy" (Prov. 28:13), and, "Let us lift up our heart *with* our hands unto God in the heavens" (Lam. 3:41).[6]

230. He who says, "I will sin and then repent, I will sin and then repent," will be given no opportunity to vow penitence.[7]

231. "He openeth their ear for instruction. . . . But they that are godless . . . cry not for help when He bindeth them" (Job 36:10 and 36:13). R. Phinehas the Priest son of R. Hama said: After the Holy One has waited in vain for the godless to vow penitence, then even if in the end they wish to repent, He distracts their hearts so that they cannot vow penitence.[8]

232. Our masters taught: If a man misappropriates a beam and builds it into a palace, he must demolish the palace and return the beam to its rightful owner. So says the school of Shammai. But the school of Hillel says: Because we wish to encourage penitents, the owner may claim no more than the value of the beam.[9]

233. The story of a man who wished to restore an object he had misappropriated. His wife said to him, "You numbskull, if you begin restoring things, even the girdle you are wearing is not yours." So he refrained and did not return a thing.

It was then that the sages declared: If robbers or usurers offer to return the things they misappropriated, these items are not to be accepted; and he who does accept them will not have the approval of the sages.[10]

234. Our masters taught: The left hand may always repulse, but the right hand should bring near. Not like Elisha, who pushed away Gehazi with both hands, or like R. Joshua ben Perahiah, who with both hands[11] repulsed his disciple [Jesus].

5. B. Ber 12b.
6. B. Ta 16a.
7. His so-called repentance not being genuine. B. Yoma 85b.
8. Exod. R. 11:1.
9. B. Git 55a.
10. According to the law, a robber must return, with interest, the very object he stole, even if in the meantime he made such use of it that its return would cause him great loss. Hence the sages' ordinance. B. BK 94b; Tanhuma, *Noah*, §4.
11. 2 Kings 5:20ff.

What was the incident with R. Joshua ben Perahiah? When King Yannai rose up against the sages to put them to death, Simeon ben Shetah was hidden by his sister, and R. Joshua ben Perahiah [and Jesus] fled to Alexandria of Egypt. When peace came,[1] Simeon ben Shetah wrote to R. Joshua: "From me, Jerusalem the holy city, to you, my sister Alexandria of Egypt: My husband dwells in your midst, and I abide desolate." R. Joshua concluded: It is clear from this message that peace has been made. Upon his return [together with his disciple Jesus], he happened to put up at a certain inn, where great honor was accorded him. So he sat down and spoke in praise of the woman who kept the inn. But when he said, "What a gracious hostess,"[2] his disciple observed, "Master, her eyes are bleary." R. Joshua: "You wicked man! So it is with such matters that you occupy yourself!" At that, he had four hundred rams' horns brought and [had them sounded to] put him under the ban. Though Jesus came every day before R. Joshua [pleading to be readmitted], R. Joshua paid no attention to him. One day, while R. Joshua ben Perahiah was reciting the Shema, Jesus appeared before him. R. Joshua, intending to readmit him, gestured with his hand, but Jesus took the gesture to be a final repulse. So he went out and led a depraved life.

When R. Joshua implored him, "Repent," Jesus replied, "I have a tradition from you: he who sins and causes others to sin is not given the opportunity to repent."[3]

235. When a man causes many to earn merit, no sin will come through him; when a man causes many to sin, the opportunity to repent will not be given him. "When a man causes many to earn merit, no sin will come through him"—so that he will not have to be in Gehenna while his disciples are in the Garden of Eden. "When a man causes many to sin, the opportunity to repent will not be given him"—so that he will not manage to get to the Garden of Eden while his disciples are in Gehenna.[4]

Reward and Punishment

236. Antigonus of Sokho[5] received [the Oral Torah] from Simeon the Righteous. He used to say: Be not like servants who serve their master in the hope of receiving a gratuity. Be like servants who serve their master with no expectation of receiving a gratuity.

Antigonus of Sokho had two disciples, who repeated his teaching to their disciples, and so did the disciples to their disciples. But then [two of the latter] disciples rose up and speculated on the implications of what they had been taught, asking, "Why did our masters say such a thing? Is it right for a laborer to toil all day and not [expect to] receive his reward in the evening? Had our forebears been certain that there is another world and that there is to be the resurrection of the dead, they would surely not have taught such a thing!" So they rose up and turned away from the Torah. From these two disciples sprang two sects, the Sadducees and the Boethusians. The Sadducees were named after Zadok and the Boethusians after Boethus. All their lives, both sects used vessels of silver and gold—not because they were personally arrogant but because, as they explained, "it is a [silly] tradition of the Pharisees to subject themselves to austerity in this world,[6] for in the world-to-come they will possess nothing at all."[7]

237. R. Akiva said: Everything is foreseen [by God], but the right [to choose] is given [to man]. The world is judged by [divine] goodness, yet all is in accord with the number of a man's [good] deeds.[8]

He [also] used to say: Everything is given against a pledge, and a net is spread out over all the living.[9] The store is open, the [divine] Storekeeper extends credit, the account book lies open, a[n angel's] hand writes [therein], and whoever wishes to borrow may come and borrow. But the collectors go around regularly every day and exact payment from every man, whether he is aware or not that he is being punished. And the collectors have good authority to rely on, since the judgment is a true judgment, and all is prepared for the banquet.[10]

238. R. Eleazar ha-Kappar used to say: They who are born [are destined] to die, and they that are dead to be brought to life, and the living to be brought to judgment. Therefore men who should know, make known, and be fully aware that He is God, He is the Fashioner, He is the Creator, He is the Discerner, He is the Judge, He is the Witness, He is the Plaintiff, and He, blessed be He, will pass judgment. In His presence there is no guile, no forgetting, no respect of persons, no taking of bribes. For everything is His. And know that all is according to reckoning. Do not let your impulse to evil assure you that Sheol is a place of refuge for you: despite yourself you are formed; despite yourself you are born; despite yourself you live; despite yourself you will die; and despite yourself you are destined to give an account and reckoning before the King of kings of kings, the Holy One, blessed be He.[11]

239. R. Eleazar said: Know before whom you toil, who is your Employer, and who will pay you the wages of your labor.

R. Tarfon said: The day is short, the task is great, the workmen are indolent; but the wages are high and the Master of the house is insistent.

He used to say: It is not your duty to complete the work [of Torah study], yet you are not at liberty to desist

1. At Yannai's death. See above, part 2, chap. 1, §48.
2. *Aksania* (Greek *xenia*) means both "inn" and "hostess of the inn."
3. B. Sot 47a; B. Sanh 107b.
4. B. Yoma 87a.
5. First half of third century B.C.E.
6. Cf. Josephus *Antiquities* 18.1.3: "The Pharisees live simply, and despise delicacies."
7. The two sects reputedly did not believe in the resurrection of the dead. Avot 1:3; ARN, 5.
8. Thus a man who gives a denar each to a thousand poor men is deemed more worthy than one who gives a thousand denars to one poor man.
9. No one can escape judgment.
10. The reward of the righteous is assured. Avot 3:15–16.
11. Avot 4:22.

from it. If you have studied much Torah, high wages will be paid you—your Employer may be trusted to pay you full wages for your labor. But you are to know that the giving of reward to the righteous will be in the time-to-come.[1]

240. Akavia ben Mahalalel said: Reflect upon three things, and you will not fall into the grip of sin. Know where you came from, where you are going, and before whom you shall have to give an account and reckoning. "Where you came from"—from a putrid drop [of semen]. "Where you are going"—to a place of dust, worm, and maggot. "And before whom you shall have to give an account and reckoning"—before the King of kings of kings, the Holy One, blessed be He![2]

241. Rabbi [Judah I, the Patriarch] said: Consider three things, and you will not fall into sin. Know what is above you: a seeing eye, a hearing ear, and all your deeds recorded in a book.[3]

242. With ten [divine] utterances[4] was the world created. What does Scripture teach by this? Could not the world have been created with but one utterance? Yes, but Scripture intimates that God will impose [severe] penalties upon the wicked, who would destroy the world which was created with [no fewer than] ten utterances, and will bestow rich reward upon the righteous, who maintain the world which was created with ten utterances.[5]

243. Ben Azzai said: The reward for performing a precept is [an opportunity to perform] another precept, and the reward for committing a transgression is [a temptation to commit] another transgression.[6]

244. Rabbi [Judah I, the Patriarch] said: Be as careful with an easy precept as with a difficult one, for you cannot know the degree of reward for each precept. Reckon the loss [that may be incurred through observance] of a precept against the reward for it, and the gain that may be had through committing a transgression against the punishment sure to follow.[7]

245. R. Samuel bar Nahmani said in the name of R. Jonathan: What is meant by the verse "Wherefore do *ha-moshelim* ('they that speak in parables') say: Come ye to Heshbon" (Num. 21:27)? The word *ha-moshelim* means here: "they who rule[8] their impulse to evil." "Come ye to Heshbon" means: "Come and consider the account (*heshbon*) of the world—the loss incurred by the fulfillment of a precept against the reward secured by its observance, and the gain made by succumbing to sin against the punishment for it."[9]

246. R. Hiyya told the parable of a king who had an orchard, into which he brought workmen without revealing to them the wages for planting each of the several kinds of trees in the orchard. Had he revealed to them the reward for planting each kind of tree in the orchard, the workmen would have picked out the kind of tree for whose planting there was the greatest wage and would have planted it exclusively; as a result, the work of planting the orchard would have been neglected in one part and maintained in another part. Just so, [concluded R. Hiyya], the Holy One did not reveal to Israel the reward for heeding the individual precepts of Torah. Had He revealed it to them [Israel might have picked out the most rewarding precept and heeded only that one]. Then some of the precepts of Torah would have been maintained, while the others would have been neglected.[10]

247. R. Simeon ben Yohai taught: The Holy One has revealed the reward for heeding two precepts in the Torah: one of these precepts is the least onerous, and the other is the most onerous. The least onerous concerns letting the mother go when chancing on a bird's nest—with regard to it, Scripture promises "that thou mayest prolong thy days" (Deut. 22:7). The most onerous concerns honoring one's father and mother—with regard to it also, Scripture promises "that thy days may be long" (Deut. 5:16).

So the two precepts are alike in the reward received in this world for their observance.[11]

248. Ben He He said: According to the suffering is the reward.[12]

249. One man acquires his [place in the] world[-to-come] only after many years, while another does so in an instant.[13]

250. R. Joshua ben Levi said: What is implied in the verse "Which I command you this day to do them" (Deut. 7:11)? *This day* you are to do them—you may not postpone doing them to a morrow [when in the world-to-come it will be impossible to do them]. You are to do them *this day* and receive reward for them only on a morrow.[14]

251. In this world, there is no reward for any precept.

We have been taught that R. Jacob said: There is not a single precept in the Torah whose reward is specified immediately, where it is not intimated that that reward is

1. Avot 2:14–16.
2. Avot 3:1.
3. Avot 2:2.
4. In Gen. 1:3–29 and 2:18, the words "And God said" occur ten times.
5. Avot 5:1.
6. Avot 4:2.
7. Avot 2:1.
8. The homonym *moshelim* means both "speaking parables" and "ruling."
9. B. BB 78b.
10. Tanhuma, *Ekev*, §2.
11. Ibid.
12. Or, "According to the labor is the reward." Some commentators take Ben He He to have been a proselyte. They understand the word "He" to be made up of the letter *he*, the last letter in *Sarah*, and the letter *alef*, the first letter in *Abraham*—hence a spiritual son of Abraham and Sarah. Avot 5:23.
13. B. AZ 10b.
14. B. Er 22a; B. AZ 3a.

linked with resurrection of the dead. Thus, in connection with honoring one's parents, it is written, "That thy days may be prolonged, and that it may go well with thee" (Deut. 5:16). Again, in connection with letting the mother bird go from a nest one chances upon, it is written, "That it may be well with thee, and that thou mayest prolong thy days" (Deut. 22:7). Suppose a father said to his son, "Go up to the top of the tower and bring me down some young birds," and the son went up to the top of the tower, let the mother bird go, and took the young ones, but on his descent he fell down and was killed. Where is the son's length of days, and where is the son's doing well? Hence, "That thy days may be prolonged" must refer to the world that is wholly long, and "That it may go well with thee" must refer to the world that is wholly good.

But perhaps such a thing could not happen? R. Jacob saw such a thing happen.

R. Joseph said: Had Aher[1] interpreted this verse as R. Jacob, his daughter's son, did, he would not have sinned. What did he actually see? Some say: He saw just such a thing happen. Others say: He saw the tongue of Hutzpit the Interpreter lying on a dunghill and he exclaimed, "Shall the mouth that uttered pearls lick dust!" Then he went off and sinned—he did not realize that the words "That it may go well with thee" refer to the world that is wholly good, and the words "That thy days may be prolonged" refer to the world that is wholly long.[2]

252. "The blessing, if ye shall hearken . . . and the curse, if ye shall not hearken" (Deut. 11:27–28). A parable of an old man seated on a highway from which there branched two roads, [one full of thorns at the beginning but level at the end], and the other level at the beginning but full of thorns at the end. So he sat at the fork of the road and cautioned passersby, saying, "Even though the beginning of this road is full of thorns, follow it, for it will turn level in the end." Whoever sensibly heeded the old man and followed that road did get a bit weary at first, to be sure, but went on in peace and arrived in peace. Those who did not heed the old man set out on the other road and stumbled in the end. So it was with Moses, who explicitly said to Israel, "Behold the way of life and the way of death, the blessing and the curse. 'Therefore choose life, that thou mayest live, thou and thy seed' " (Deut. 30:19).[3]

253. He who took the trouble to prepare on the eve of Sabbath can eat on the Sabbath; but he who has not troubled himself to prepare on the eve of Sabbath—where is he to get food to eat on the Sabbath?[4]

254. R. Aibu said: There are three kinds of men. The first kind says, "Had I been created to do no more than behold the stars and the heavenly bodies, it would have been enough for me," as is said, "When I behold . . . the moon and the stars which Thou hast ordained" (Ps. 8:4). The second kind says, "All that Thou hast to give me, give it to me in the time-to-come." The third kind, made up of slothful laborers, says, "Give us now what is ours and also what was our fathers'."[5]

255. "Get thee up into the high mountain; . . . lift up thy voice with strength. . . . His reward is with him, and his recompense before him" (Isa. 40:9–10). R. Jeremiah son of R. Eleazar said: A divine voice will reverberate on the mountaintops, saying, "Whosoever has wrought with God, let him come and receive the reward due him." And the divine spirit will say, "Who hath given Me anything beforehand that I should repay him?" (Job 41:3). Who could sing out in praise of Me before I put breath in him? Who could perform circumcision in My name before I gave him a male child? Who could build a parapet at My request[6] before I gave him a roof? Who could make a mezuzah at My request before I gave him a house? Who could build a sukkah at My request before I gave him a space? Who could make a lulav cluster at My request before I gave him money? Who could make fringes at My request before I gave him a garment? Who could set aside the corners of the crop at My request before I gave him a field? Who could set aside heave offering for priests at My request before I gave him a threshing floor? Who could set aside the priests' share of the dough[7] at My request before I gave him dough? Who could set aside an offering at My request before I gave him an animal?[8]

256. Antoninus[9] said to Rabbi [Judah I, the Patriarch], "The body and the soul can both free themselves from judgment. Thus, the body can plead, 'The soul has sinned—ever since the day it left me, look, I lie in the grave like a mute stone'; while the soul can plead, 'The body has sinned—ever since the day I departed from it, look, I fly about in the air like a bird.' " Rabbi Judah replied, "I will show you by a parable [that neither the body nor the soul can thus free itself]. A king of flesh and blood who owned a beautiful orchard, which yielded luscious first figs, appointed two watchmen—one lame and the other blind—over it. [One day] the lame watchman said to the blind one, 'I see some early figs in the orchard. Come and take me upon your shoulder, so that we can pick the figs and eat them.' The lame man got up on the blind man, and together they picked figs and ate them. After a while, the owner of the orchard came and inquired, 'Where are those early figs?' The blind man replied, 'Have I eyes to see with?' The lame man replied, 'Have I legs to walk with?' What did the king do? He had the lame man mount upon the shoulders of the blind one and judged them together, as though they were one. So will the Holy One bring the soul, toss it inside the body, and judge the two together, as is written, 'He shall call to the heavens

1. Aher ("the Other") is the name by which Elisha ben Avuyah, an apostate, is often referred to.
2. B. Kid 39a; Hul 142a.
3. Tanhuma, *Re'eh*, §3.
4. B. AZ 3a.
5. MTeh 8:6.
6. See Deut. 22:8.
7. *Hallah*. See Num. 15:20.
8. Lev. R. 27:2.
9. Antoninus has been identified as Marcus Aurelius.

from above, and to the earth, that he may judge his people' [Ps. 50:4). 'He shall call to the heavens from above'—call for the soul; 'and to the earth, that He may judge His people'—call for the body."[1]

257. "God shall bring every work into the judgment concerning every hidden thing" (Eccles. 12:14). R. Levi cited the parable of a bird kept in a cage. Another bird came by, alighted over the caged one, and said, "How happy you must be that the food you require is provided for you!" The bird in the cage responded, "All you see is the feed. You don't see the bars of the cage."[2]

258. "Rejoice, O young man, in thy youth. . . . But know thou that for all these things God will bring thee into judgment" (Eccles. 11:9). R. Hiyya the Elder told the parable of a robber who, as he was fleeing from the examining magistrate, was told, "Don't run too far, so that you will not be exhausted [and will be able to stand on your feet] when you are dragged back here [for sentencing]."[3]

259. "The Rock, His work is perfect. . . . Just and right is He" (Deut. 32:4). The sages said: At the time of a man's departure to his eternal home, all his deeds are set out before him as he is told, "Such-and-such a thing you have done in such-and-such a place on such-and-such a day." And he responds, "Yes." He is then told, "Sign," and he signs, as is said, "It is signed by every man's hand" (Job 37:7). Furthermore, he accepts the verdict as just, saying, "You have judged me fairly."[4]

260. R. Abba Cohen bar Dala said: Woe unto us on the Day of Judgment. Woe unto us on the day of rebuke. Balaam, the wisest of the heathens, could not withstand his donkey's rebuke: "Was I ever wont to do so unto thee?" And he said, "Nay" (Num. 22:30). Joseph was the youngest of the tribe fathers, and yet his brothers could not withstand his rebuke, as is said, "And his brethren could not answer him; for they were affrighted at his presence" (Gen. 45:3). How much more by far will this be true when the Holy One comes to rebuke each man according to his deserts, when, according to Scripture God will say, "I will rebuke thee, and set the cause before thine eyes" (Ps. 50:21).[5]

261. When Hillel saw a skull floating on the water, he said to it: Because you drowned others, you were drowned, and in the end they who drowned you will also be drowned.[6]

262. We have been taught that R. Meir used to say: What is the proof that with the same measure a man measures out it will be measured out to him? The verse "In full measure (*sa'sseah*) . . . Thou dost contend with her" (Isa. 27:8). *Sa'sseah* is taken as a reduplicating form and read: *seah* for *seah* [that is, "measure for measure"]. How do we know that, [just as] small coins add up to a large sum, [so small sins add up to a large guilt]? From Scripture, which says, "Adding one to one, to find out the sum" (Eccles. 7:27).[7]

263. Samson followed [the lust in] his eyes: therefore the Philistines gouged his eyes. Absalom took pride in his hair; therefore he was left hanging by his hair.[8]

264. Our masters taught: The woman suspected of infidelity set her eyes on one who was not proper for her. What she had sought was not given her, and what she had possessed was taken away from her. Because he who sets his eyes on what is not his is not given what he seeks, and what he possesses is taken away from him.

We find this to be true also of the primeval serpent [in the Garden of Eden], which set its eyes on what was not proper for it: what it had sought was not given to it, and what it possessed was taken away from it. For the Holy One said: *I* declared; Let it be king over all cattle and beasts; but now "cursed art thou above all cattle and above every beast of the field" (Gen 3:14). *I* declared: Let it walk with an erect posture; but now "upon thy belly thou shalt go" (ibid.). *I* declared; Let its food be the same as that of man; but now "dust shalt thou eat" (Gen. 3:14). The serpent said: I will kill Adam and marry Eve; but now "I will put enmity between thee and the woman, and between thy seed and her seed" (Gen. 3:15).

We find this to be true also of Cain, Korah, Balaam, Doeg, Ahithophel, Gehazi, Absalom, Adonijah, Uzziah, and Haman, who set their eyes upon what was not proper for them; what they sought was not given to them, and what they possessed was taken away from them.[9]

265. R. Simeon ben Lakish began his discourse with the verse "And if a man lie not in wait, but God cause it to come to hand" (Exod. 21:13). [He went on]: This verse is to be considered in the light of what Scripture says elsewhere. "As saith the proverb of the ancients: Out of the wicked cometh forth wickedness" (1 Sam. 24:14). Of whom does the verse in Exodus speak? Of two men who had each committed murder, one unwittingly and the other deliberately, with no witnesses against the one or against the other. The Holy One has the two meet at an inn, where He has the one who had slain deliberately sit under a stepladder and the one who had slain unwittingly come down the stepladder and fall, killing the other. The murderer who had slain deliberately is thus put to death, and the murderer who had slain unwittingly goes into banishment [to a city of refuge].[10]

266. Ever since the Temple was destroyed, even though the Sanhedrin ceased, the four forms of capital punishment

1. B. Sanh 91a–b and En Yaakov, ad loc.
2. PRKM 24:14; Yalkut, Eccles., §989.
3. PRKM 24:14.
4. B. Ta 11a.
5. Gen. R. 93:6.
6. Avot 2:7.
7. B. Sot 8b.
8. B. Sot 9b.
9. B. Sot 9a–b.
10. B. Mak 10b.

have not ceased. He who would have been sentenced to death by stoning either falls from a roof or is attacked and killed by a wild beast. He who would have been sentenced to death by burning either falls into a conflagration or is stung by a snake. He who would have been sentenced to death by decapitation is either delivered to the government or attacked by brigands. And he who would have been sentenced to death by strangulation either drowns in a river or is suffocated by croup.[1]

267. The arrow maker is slain by his own arrow—paid back by the devisings of his own hands.[2]

268. R. Simeon bar Abba said: Though all [the Sanhedrin's] measures [of justice] have ceased, the [divine] rule of measure for measure has not ceased.[3]

269. We have been taught that R. Meir said: With the same measure a man measures out, it is measured out to him. R. Judah asked: But can we say of a man who metes out a handful [of charity] to a poor man in this world that the Holy One will mete out to him a handful of His bounty in the next?[4] Is it not said of the Holy One, "He meted out all of heaven with His span" (Isa. 40:12)? R. Meir replied: You do not agree with me? Consider then: which measure is greater? That of goodness [i.e., reward] or of punishment? You must admit that the measure of reward is greater than that of punishment. Now, with regard to the measure of punishment, it is written, "Their worm shall not die, neither shall their fire be quenched" (Isa. 66:24). But will not a man in this world who puts his finger into fire be immediately burned? However, just as the Holy One gives the wicked the strength to receive their punishment, so does He give the righteous the capacity to receive their reward.[5]

270. The measure of reward comes quicker than the measure of punishment.[6]

271. "According unto the greatness of Thy loving-kindness" (Num. 14:19). R. Hama bar Hanina said: The verse refers to God's measure of bounty, which is filled to overflowing.[7]

272. Bar Kappara said: The increment given by the Holy One exceeds the principal.[8]

273. R. Isaac said: A man should be judged only according to his deeds at the time of judgment, as is said, "God hath heard the voice of the lad according to what he was then" (Gen. 21:17).[9]

In this connection, R. Simon taught: The ministering angels leaped up to make accusations against Ishmael, saying to God, "Master of the universe, for a person who will one day bring death to Your children by pretending to relieve their thirst,[10] will You now raise up a well?" But the Holy One asked the ministering angels, "At this moment, what sort of person is Ishmael—righteous or wicked?" They answered, "Righteous." God said, "I do not judge a man except for what he is at the time I am judging him."[11]

274. R. Hamnuna said: The Holy One does not requite a man until his measure [of guilt] is full, as is said, "In the fullness of his sufficiency, he shall be in straits" (Job 20:22).[12]

275. Moses said, "He visits the iniquity of the fathers upon the children" (Exod. 34:7). But when Ezekiel came, he revoked it, saying, "The soul that sinneth, it shall die" (Ezek. 18:4).[13]

276. The Holy One does not deal despotically with His creatures.[14]

277. R. Hanina taught: He who says that the Holy One is lawless in the execution of justice will have his life outlawed, for it is said, "The Rock, His work is perfect, for all His ways are just" (Deut. 32:4).[15]

278. R. Hisda said: The verse "O give thanks unto the Lord, for it is the bounty . . ." (Ps. 136:1) means, "Give thanks unto the Lord, who exacts a man's debt from the bounty given to him—an ox from a rich man, a lamb from a poor man, an egg from an orphan, a hen from a widow."[16]

279. Scripture speaks of God as "long in sufferings" (Exod. 34:6), not as "long in suffering," implying that He is willing to suffer the righteous as well as suffer the wicked.[17]

280. R. Hiyya bar Abba said in the name of R. Yohanan: The Holy One does not deprive any creature of the reward due it, even if it is rewarded for no more than a becoming expression.[18]

281. "Therefore any flesh that is torn of beasts in the field, ye shall cast to the dogs" (Exod. 22:30). The verse implies that the Holy One does not deprive any creature of the reward due it. Thus, because Scripture says, "Not a dog shall snarl against any of the Israelites" (Exod. 11:7),

---

1. B. Ket 30a–b; B. Sanh 37b.
2. B. Pes 28a.
3. Gen. R. 9:11.
4. How is a man to cope with such abundance?
5. B. Sanh 100a–b.
6. B. Shab 97a.
7. Yalkut, *Shelah*, §744.
8. Gen. R. 61:4.
9. JV: "God hath heard the voice of the lad where he is."
10. See above, part 1, chap. 3, §15.
11. B. RH 16b; Gen. R. 53:14; Yalkut, *Va-yera*, §94.
12. B. Sot 9a.
13. B. Mak 24a.
14. B. AZ 3a.
15. B. BK 50a.
16. B. Pes 118a.
17. B. BK 50b.
18. B. BK 38b.

the Holy One commanded, "Give the dog his reward." Now, the matter may be argued *a fortiori*: if God did not withhold the reward due an animal, all the less does He withhold the reward due a man.[1]

282. There is the story of a certain butcher in Sepphoris who sold Israelites flesh of animals that died a natural death or were torn by beasts. One Sabbath eve he drank much wine, went up to the roof, fell down, and died. As dogs were licking up his blood, people came and asked R. Hanina: May his body be moved [on the Sabbath] away from the dogs? R. Hanina replied: Let the dogs be, for they are eating what is their due, as is said, "You must not eat flesh torn by beasts; you shall cast it to the dogs" (Exod. 22:30). This one robbed dogs of flesh by feeding it to Israel. Let the dogs be—they are eating what is theirs.[2]

283. "A God of faithfulness, and without iniquity" (Deut. 32:4). "A God of faithfulness": just as the wicked will be requited in the world-to-come even for a slight transgression they had committed, so are the righteous requited in this world even for a slight transgression committed by them. "And without iniquity": just as the righteous will receive a reward in the world-to-come even for an easy precept they had obeyed, so do the wicked receive in this world reward even for an easy precept they had observed.[3]

284. "And with those round about Him it shall be as a hairsbreadth" (Ps. 50:3)[4] implies that the Holy One is exact down to a hairsbreadth with those around Him, an implication that R. Nehunia derived from another verse: "A God greatly dreaded in the council of the holy ones, held in awe by all around Him" (Ps. 89:8).[5]

285. "Thy righteousness is like the mighty mountains; Thy judgments are like the great deep" (Ps. 36:7). R. Akiva said: The Holy One is exact with the righteous as well as with the wicked, searching out the very depths of their being. He is exact with the righteous, holding them to account for the few wrongs they committed in this world, in order to lavish bliss upon them and give them a goodly reward in the world-to-come. On the other hand, He lavishes ease upon the wicked and rewards them in this world for the few good deeds they performed in order to requite them in the world-to-come.[6]

286. R. Eleazar son of R. Zadok said: To what may the righteous be compared in this world? To a tree standing wholly in a place of cleanness, while its foliage overhangs a place of uncleanness; when the foliage is lopped off, the tree stands entirely in a place of cleanness. So, too, does the Holy One bring suffering upon the righteous in this world,[7] in order that they may inherit the world-to-come, as is said, "And though thy beginning is in pain, yet thy latter end shall prosper" (Job 8:7).[8] And to what may the wicked be compared in this world? To a tree standing wholly in a place of uncleanness, while its foliage overhangs a place of cleanness; when the foliage is lopped off, the tree stands entirely in a place of uncleanness. So, too, does the Holy One prosper the wicked in this world, in order to banish them, to consign them to the nethermost rung, for it is said, "There is a way which seemeth right unto a man, but the end thereof are the ways of death" (Prov. 14:12).[9]

287. He whose good deeds are more numerous than his wrongdoings is punished as severely[10] as though he had burned a Torah scroll, leaving not even a single letter. And he whose wrongdoings are more numerous than his good deeds has as much good bestowed upon him as though he had kept the entire Torah, omitting not even a single letter.[11]

288. R. Yohanan said in the name of R. Yose: Moses asked three things of the Holy One, and they were granted to him. He asked that the Presence rest upon Israel, and it was granted to him, for it is said, "Is it not in that Thou goest with us?" (Exod. 33:16). He asked that the Presence not rest upon the idolaters, and it was granted to him, for the verse goes on to say, "So that we are distinguished, I and Thy people" (ibid.). He asked that he be shown the ways of the Holy One, and it was granted to him, for it is said, "Show me now Thy ways" (Exod. 33:13).[12] Moses went on to say before Him: Master of the universe, why is it that some righteous men prosper while others suffer adversity, some wicked men prosper while others suffer adversity? The Holy One replied: Moses, the righteous man who prospers is a righteous man who is the son of a righteous man; the righteous man who suffers adversity is a righteous man who is the son of a wicked man. The wicked man who prospers is a wicked man who is the son of a righteous man; the wicked man who suffers adversity is a wicked man who is the son of a wicked man.

According to some, the Holy One replied to Moses: The righteous man who prospers is completely righteous; the righteous man who suffers adversity is not completely righteous. The wicked man who prospers is not completely wicked; the wicked man who suffers adversity is completely wicked. Now, the [saying of R. Yose] that three

1. Mek, *Mishpatim, Kaspa*, 2.
2. P. Ter 8:4, 5c.
3. B. Ta 11a.
4. JV: "And round about Him it stormeth mightily." But *s'r* ("storm") also means "hairsbreadth."
5. B. BK 50a.
6. Gen. R. 33:1.
7. Thereby purging them of the few sins they do commit—lopping off, so to speak, the branch inclining to an unclean place.
8. JV: "Though thy beginning was small, yet thy end shall greatly increase." But R. Eleazar reads *mitz'ar* ("small") as *mi-tza'ar* ("in pain").
9. B. Kid 40b and En Yaakov, ad loc.
10. Thus purged of his sins in this world, he may enjoy life fully in the world-to-come.
11. So that he may then be entirely condemned to Gehenna. B. Kid 39b.
12. The aforegoing citations show what Moses asked. That God granted his requests is indicated in the reply: "I will also do this thing that thou hast asked" (Exod. 33:17).

things were granted to Moses is in disagreement with the saying of R. Meir. R. Meir said: Two [requests] were granted to Moses, and one was not granted to him. For the Holy One said to Moses, "I will be gracious to whom I will be gracious" (Exod. 33:19), even if he does not deserve it, "and I will show mercy on whom I will show mercy" (ibid.), even if he does not deserve it.[1]

289. R. Levi said: Two men, Abraham and Job, said the same thing. Abraham: "That be far from Thee, to do after this manner, to slay the righteous with the wicked" (Gen. 18:25); Job: "It is all one—therefore I say: He destroyeth the innocent and the wicked" (Job 9:22). Yet Abraham received a reward for what he said, while Job was punished for what he said. The reason: Abraham ate the fig ripe [and spoke after careful consideration of God's ways], while Job swallowed it raw [and spoke rashly]—"It is all one . . . I say."[2]

290. R. Samuel bar Nahmani said in the name of R. Yohanan: Calamity comes upon the world only when there are wicked persons in the world, and it always begins with the righteous,[3] as Scripture says, "If fire break out and catch in thorns" (Exod. 22:5). When does fire break out? When thorns are found nearby. It begins, however, with the righteous, for the verse goes on to say, "And the stack of corn has been consumed [by fire]." Not "And it would consume the stack of corn," but "And the stack of corn has been consumed," implying that the stack of corn had already been consumed.

R. Joseph taught: The verse "And none of you shall go out of the door of his house until the morning" (Exod. 12:22) implies that once permission is granted to the destroyer, he does not distinguish between the righteous and the wicked. Moreover, he even begins with the righteous, as Scripture says, "And I will cut off from thee [first] the righteous and [then] the wicked" (Ezek. 21:8).

R. Joseph wept as he said: So their being righteous counts as nothing! But Abbaye [consoling him] said: Their early death is to their advantage, as Scripture declares, "The righteous is taken away from the evil [to come]" (Isa. 57:1).[4]

291. "But there is that which is swept away without justice" (Prov. 13:23). R. Levi said: Abraham pleaded: Is Your anger like a she-bear ravaging among animals, which, when not finding another animal to destroy, destroys its own young? R. Simon said: [Abraham pleaded: Is Your anger] like a scythe, which cuts down thorns, but when it finds no more, cuts down roses?[5]

292. R. Gorion—some say R. Joseph son of R. Shemaiah—stated: When there are righteous men in a generation, they are held responsible for [the sins of] the generation. When there are no righteous men in a generation, schoolchildren are held responsible.[6]

293. "The Lord testeth the righteous" (Ps. 11:5). R. Jonathan said: Your potter does not test defective vessels, because if he gives them a single rap [to test them], they break. Which vessels does he test? The sound ones, which even if rapped many times will not break. So, too, the Holy One does not test the wicked—only the righteous.

R. Eliezer told the parable of a householder who had two heifers, one whose strength was ample and the other whose strength was limited. Upon which one will he put the yoke? Not on the one whose strength is ample? So, too, the Holy One tests the righteous.[7]

294. R. Yannai said: We did not enter into the tranquility of the wicked, nor did we attain the suffering of the righteous. Hence, neither the tranquility of the wicked nor the suffering of the righteous is within our reach.[8]

295. When R. Joshua ben Levi went to Rome, he entered a palace in which he saw marble pillars covered with wrappings to keep them from [expanding and] cracking during the heat and from [freezing and] contracting during the cold. Then, when he went out into the marketplace, he saw a poor man wrapped in a reed mat [to protect him from the heat and cold]. In regard to the pillars, R. Joshua cited the words "Thy care is like the mighty mountains" (Ps. 36:7); and in regard to the poor man, "Thy judgments are like the great deep" (ibid.).[9]

296. "Sweet is the sleep of a laboring man, whether he eat little or much" (Eccles. 5:11). R. Tanhuma bar Abba said: Solomon was told: Had another person uttered such a thing, we would have laughed at him. How can you, who are described as "wiser than all men" (1 Kings 5:11), have said, "Sweet is the sleep of a laboring man, whether he eat little or much"? It simply is not so. When a man is hungry and eats only a little, sleep will forsake him, but if he eats a lot, his sleep will be sweet. Solomon replied: I spoke only of the righteous and of those who labor in Torah. What do I mean? Well, take a man thirty years old, who since the age of ten has labored at Torah and the doing of precepts and he dies at thirty; another man, eighty years old, who since the age of ten until he died has labored at Torah and the doing of precepts. One might suppose that since the first man labored only twenty years at Torah, while the second labored seventy years, the Holy One will make the reward of the second greater than that of the first. Therefore I say that "whether he eat little or much," the bestowal of reward on the first will be like the bestowal of reward on the second.

R. Levi said: By what parable may the matter be illustrated? By the one of a king who hired laborers to do

1. Since God refuses to divulge the "method" of His mercy and graciousness, R. Meir infers that Moses' request to be shown God's ways was denied. B. Ber 7a; B. BB 15b.
2. Gen. R. 49:9; Tanhuma, *Va-yera*, §5.
3. Cf. 1 Peter 4:17a.
4. B. BK 60a and En Yaakov, ad loc.
5. Gen. R. 49:8 (Gen R. TA, p. 508).
6. B. Shab 33b.
7. Gen. R. 32:2 and 34:2.
8. In short, we are neither perfectly righteous nor perfectly wicked. Avot 4:15; ARNB 33 (trans. Saldarini, p. 197).
9. That is to say, unfathomable. Gen. R. 33:1; Lev. R. 27:1.

his work, and while they were working, the king took one of them to stroll with him. In the evening, when the laborers came to receive their wages, the workman who had been out for a stroll with the king also came to receive his wage. Should the king say to him, "You worked no more than two hours with them. You are therefore to receive a wage in keeping with the time you put in"? The laborer could tell the king, "Had you not idled me by having me stroll with you, my wage would have been equally substantial." So, too, he who exerted himself twenty years at Torah and then died could say to the Holy One, "Had you not removed me from the world in the middle of my years, I would have continued occupying myself with Torah and precepts."[1]

297. When R. Avun son of R. Hiyya died, R. Zera went in and began a eulogy for him with the verse "Sweet is the sleep of a laboring man, whether he eat little or much" (Eccles. 5:11). To whom may R. Avun son of R. Hiyya be compared? To a king who owned a vineyard and hired many laborers to work it. Among them was one laborer far more skillful in his work than the rest. What did the king do? He took him by the hand and walked with him here and there. Toward evening, when the laborers came to receive their wages, this laborer came with them, and the king gave him the full wage. The others, distressed, began to grumble, saying, "We toiled all day, whereas this one toiled for only two hours, and yet the king has given him his full wage." The king replied, "What reason have you for grumbling? This man with his skill achieved in two hours more than you achieved in the entire day." So, too, R. Avun son of R. Hiyya learned more Torah in twenty-eight years than even a distinguished scholar could learn in a hundred years.[2]

298. "Now that I lie still, I am quiet; when I sleep, I am at rest" (Job 3:13). What the righteous are to have bestowed upon them as reward is prepared for them for the time-to-come, but at their departure, while they are still in this world, the Holy One shows them the reward He will bestow upon them. Their souls thus satisfied, they go to sleep.

At the time of R. Abbahu's death, thirteen rivers of balsam passed in front of him. When he asked, "Whose are these?" and was told, "Yours," he said, "All these for Abbahu? 'Yet to me, all my labor seemed useless, my strength worn out in vain. But my case rested with the Lord, and my recompense with my God' " (Isa. 49:14).

The story is told of R. Simeon ben Halafta, who once returned home on a Friday afternoon and found that he had nothing to buy food with [for the Sabbath]. So that afternoon he went outside the city and prayed to the Holy One. At once, a precious stone was given him from heaven. He sold it to a moneychanger and thus was able to provide food for the Sabbath. However, his wife asked him, "Where did all this food come from?" He replied, "From what the Holy One has provided." She said to him, "If you do not tell me truly where all this comes from, I will not touch a morsel." So he began to tell her what happened, concluding, "I prayed thus to God, and He gave me [the precious stone] from heaven." She said in disbelief, "I will still not touch a morsel until you promise me to return the precious stone at the Sabbath's conclusion." He asked her, "Why should I?" She replied, "Do you wish that your table [in heaven] shall be lacking [all good things], while that of your colleague shall be laden with them?"

R. Simeon went and told the story to Rabbi [Judah I, the Patriarch], who said to him, "Go back and tell your wife, 'If anything shall be lacking from your table, I will replenish it from mine.' " When he came back and told this to his wife, she said, "Come with me to him who taught you Torah." [When they got there], she said to Rabbi [Judah], "Master, will a man be able to see his colleague in the world-to-come? Will not each and every righteous man have a world for himself? For Scripture says, 'Man goeth to his own world' " (Eccles. 12:5). After [R. Simeon ben Halafta] heard what his wife had to say, he [quickly] went and returned the precious stone to heaven.

Our masters said: The second miracle was even more difficult [to perform] than the first. For as soon as R. Simeon stretched forth his hand to restore the precious stone to heaven, an angel descended and took it from him.[3]

299. "And I will bestow freely on whom I have no choice but to bestow freely" (Exod. 33:19). At that time the Holy One showed Moses all the treasuries prepared for bestowing reward on the righteous, to each according to his deeds. Moses kept asking, "For whom is this treasury intended?" and God replied, "For masters of Torah." "And this one?" "For givers of charity." And so on with each and every treasury, until he saw a huge treasury and asked, "For whom is this one intended?" God replied, "To him who has [the merit of] good deeds, I give out of the treasury intended for him. But for him who has no such merit, I provide freely and give him out of this [huge treasury], in keeping with 'I will bestow freely on whom I have no choice but to bestow freely.' "[4]

The World-to-Come

300. "Thou dost protect my head on the day of kissing"[5] (Ps. 140:8)—the day when the two worlds kiss each other, the day a man leaves this world and enters the world-to-come.[6]

301. "Make me know the path of life . . . fullness of joy" (Ps. 16:11). David said before the Holy One: Let me know by which gate one is led to life in the world-to-come. The Holy One told David: If you ask for life, you ask for affliction, since "reproofs of affliction are the way to life" (Prov. 10:23).[7]

1. Tanhuma, *Ki Tissa*, §3.
2. Eccles. R. 5:11, §5.
3. P. AZ 3:1, 42c; Exod. R. 52:3; Yalkut, Prov., §890.
4. Tanhuma B, Ki-Tissa, §16; Tanhuma, Ki-Tissa, §28; Exod. R. 45:6.
5. JV: "battle." But *neshek* ("battle") also means "kissing."
6. P. Yev 15:2, 14d.
7. Lev. R. 30:2.

302. Rav had a favorite saying: The world-to-come is not at all like this world. In the world-to-come, there is no eating, no drinking, no procreation, no commerce, no envy, no hatred, no rivalry; the righteous sit with crowns on their heads and enjoy the radiance of the Presence.[1]

303. R. Joshua ben Levi said: In the world-to-come, the Holy One will have each righteous man inherit three hundred and ten worlds, as intimated in the verse "That I may cause those that love Me to inherit *yesh*[2] [whose letters *yod* (ten) and *shin* (three hundred) add up to three hundred and ten]" (Prov. 8:21).[3]

304. Rabbah said in the name of R. Yohanan: In the time-to-come, the Holy One will set up seven canopies for each and every righteous man.

"Smoke, and the shining of fire . . . for each glory shall be a canopy" (Isa. 4:5). The verse implies that the canopy the Holy One makes for each and every righteous man will be in keeping with the glory that is to be accorded him.

Why is smoke required in such a canopy? To teach you, said R. Hanina, that whoever regards disciples of the wise with jaundiced eyes in this world will have his eyes filled with smoke in the world-to-come.

And why is fire required in such a canopy? To teach you, said R. Hanina, that each righteous man will burn [in envy of the superior] canopy of his friend. Alas for such shame! Alas for such a disgrace![4]

305. "When man goeth to his own long habitation" (Eccles. 12:5). R. Isaac said: The verse implies that every righteous man is given a habitation as befits the honor due him. The matter may be understood by the parable of a king who enters a city with his servants. When they enter, all of them enter through the same gate. But when they lodge overnight, each one is given a habitation in keeping with the honor due him.[5]

306. We have been taught that R. Eliezer said: The souls of the righteous are treasured under the throne of glory, as is said, "The soul of my lord shall be treasured in the treasury of life" (1 Sam. 25:29). But the soul of the wicked is tied up and then tossed about. For one angel stands at one end of the world and another angel stands at the other end of the world, and they sling the souls of the wicked to each other, as is said, "The souls of thine enemies, them shall He sling out, as from the hollow of a sling" (ibid.).[6]

307. R. Joseph son of R. Joshua ben Levi became ill, and his spirit flew away. After his spirit returned to him, his father asked him, "What did you see?" He replied, "I saw a world turned upside down—the people high up here were moved down, and the lowly here were moved up." R. Joshua: "My son, you saw a world in which right is made clear. But what of you and me—where were we placed?" "Just as we are esteemed here, so were we esteemed there. I also heard them say, 'Happy is he who comes here with his learning in hand.' I also heard them say, 'They who were martyred by the [Roman] government—no man is allowed to stand within their compartments.' "[7]

308. All Israel have a portion in the world-to-come, as is said, "Thy people are all righteous. They shall inherit the world that is forever: the branch of My planting, the work of My hands, wherein I glory" (Isa. 60:21).

Three kings and four commoners have no portion in the world-to-come. The three kings are Jeroboam, Ahab, and Manasseh. R. Judah, however, said: Manasseh has a portion in the world-to-come, for it is said, "And he prayed unto Him . . . and He hearkened to his supplication and brought him to Jerusalem into his kingdom" (2 Chron. 33:13). The sages retorted to R. Judah: God brought him to his kingdom, but not to life in the world-to-come. The four commoners: Balaam, Doeg, Ahithophel, and Gehazi.

Who enumerated them? The Men of the Great Assembly.

These Men [of the Great Assembly] were about to include one more [Solomon], but the apparition of his father's likeness came and prostrated itself [in supplication] before them. However, they ignored it. Then a fire came down from heaven and licked about their benches, but they ignored it also. At that, a divine voice cried out to them, "Seest thou a man diligent in his business? He shall stand with kings; he shall not stand with mean men" (Prov. 22:29). He who gave precedence to the building of My house over his and built My house in seven years but his own in thirteen, "he shall stand with kings; he shall not stand with mean men." But they ignored that also. Then the divine voice cried out, "Shall his recompense be as thou wilt? . . . Wilt thou choose, and not I?" (Job 34:33).

They who look for the inherent meaning of Scripture maintain: All the aforementioned will enter the world-to-come.[8]

309. The righteous of the nations of the world also have a portion in the world-to-come.[9]

The Garden of Eden and Gehenna

310. R. Joshua ben Levi said: There are two gates of chalcedony in the Garden of Eden, and around them are sixty myriads of ministering angels, the radiance of the countenance of each of whom shines like the splendor of the firmament. When a righteous man comes to them, they remove from him the garments in which he abode in the

---

1. B. Ber 17a.
2. JV: "substance."
3. Uk 3:13.
4. B. BB 75a.
5. B. Shab 152a and En Yaakov, ad loc.
6. B. Shab 152b.
7. B. Pes 50a and En Yaakov, ad loc.
8. B. Sanh 90a and 104b; Yalkut, Prov., §960.
9. Based on Tos Sanh 13:12.

grave and clothe him in eight garments of clouds of glory. They put two crowns on his head, one of precious stones and pearls, and the other of Parvaim gold. They place eight myrtles in his hand and chant praise before him, saying, "Go, eat thy bread with joy" (Eccles. 9:7). Then they bring him to a place of waterbrooks encompassed by eight hundred species of roses and myrtles. Each and every righteous man is given a canopy in keeping with the honor due him. Out of it flow four rivers, one of milk, one of wine, one of balsam, and one of honey. Each and every canopy has above it a vine of gold in which thirty pearls are set, and the brightness of each shines like the brightness of the planet Venus. Each and every canopy has in it a table made of precious stones and pearls. Sixty angels stand at the head of each and every righteous man, and say to him: Come and eat honey in gladness, because you have occupied yourself with Torah, which is likened to honey; and drink the wine kept in its grapes ever since the six days of creation, because you have occupied yourself with Torah, which is likened to wine. The most homely among the angels has a visage like that of Joseph or like that of R. Yohanan.[1] For the righteous, there is no night. During the night's [usual] three watches, life continues to be renewed for the righteous. During the first watch, each righteous man becomes a child and enters the compartment for little children, where he rejoices the way little children rejoice. During the second watch, each righteous man becomes a young man and enters the compartment of young men, where he rejoices the way young men rejoice. During the third watch, each righteous man becomes an old man and enters the compartment for old men, where he rejoices the way old men rejoice.

In the Garden of Eden, in every one of its recesses, there are eighty myriad species of trees, the least of which is more beautiful than all varieties of spice trees. Sixty myriads of ministering angels sing sweetly in each recess of the Garden. The tree of life is in the center, and its foliage spreads over the entire Garden of Eden. The tree has five hundred thousand kinds of fruit, each differing in taste; the appearance of one fruit is not like the appearance of another, and the fragrance of one not like the fragrance of another. Clouds of glory hover above the tree, and from the four points of the compass [breezes] blow at it, so that its fragrance is wafted from world's end to world's end. Under the tree sit disciples of the wise, explaining the Torah. Each of them has two canopies, one studded with stars and the other with the sun and moon. Between each pair of canopies there is a curtain of clouds of glory. Beyond each canopy there is Eden, in which are three hundred and ten worlds. Within Eden are seven companies of the righteous: the first, those slain by the [Roman] government, such as R. Akiva and his companions; the second, those who were made to drown in the sea; the third, Rabban Yohanan ben Zakkai and his disciples; the fourth, those upon whom the cloud descended and covered;[2] the fifth, the penitents, for where penitents stand, not even the wholly righteous may stand; the sixth, bachelors who during their lives did not savor the taste of [sexual] sin; the seventh, the poor who have Scripture, Mishnah, and moral conduct, of whom Scripture says, "So shall those that take refuge in Thee rejoice" (Ps. 5:12). Among them sits the Holy One, explaining the Torah to them, as is said, "Mine eyes are upon the faithful of the land, that they may dwell with Me" (Ps. 101:6). The Holy One did not make known further details of the honor prepared for the righteous, as is said, "No eye except Thine hath seen what will be done for those who trust in Thee, O God" (Isa. 64:3).[3]

311. "God hath set the one close to the other" (Eccles. 7:14). Between the Garden of Eden and Gehenna there is no more than the breadth of a hand.[4]

312. "Who can stand before His indignation? And who can abide in the fierceness of His anger?" (Nah. 1:6). R. Zera began his discourse with the verse "The leech has two daughters: Hav, Hav" (Prov. 30:15), a verse R. Eleazar took to mean that two companies of angels stand at the gates of Gehenna and say, "*Hav, Hav*. 'Bring [(*have*)], bring [(*have*) the wicked to judgment].' "

Why is it called Gehenna?[5] Because the sound of the groaning (*nahamah*)[6] within it goes from world's end to world's end.

There are three gates to Gehenna, one at the sea, another at the wilderness, and the third at inhabited land.

There are five kinds of fire in Gehenna: a fire that eats and drinks, one that drinks but does not eat, one that eats but does not drink, one that neither eats nor drinks, and a fire that eats fire. In Gehenna there are coals as big as mountains, coals as small as hills, coals the size of the Salt Sea, and coals that are no larger than big boulders. Also in Gehenna are rivers of pitch and sulphur flowing in boiling suds, continuously boiling and boiling.

The decree upon a wicked man: angels of destruction push him down on his face, and other such angels receive him from them and shove him farther toward the fire of Gehenna, which opens its mouth and swallows him. But he who possesses Torah and good deeds and has suffered numerous afflictions is delivered from the judgment of Gehenna, as is said, "Even when I walk through the valley of deepest darkness, I will fear no evil. . . . Thy rod and Thy staff, they comfort me" (Ps. 23:4). "Thy rod" refers to afflictions and "Thy staff" to Torah.

R. Joshua ben Levi said: Once, as I was walking on a road, Elijah the Prophet, ever remembered on good occasions, encountered me and said, "Would you like me to set you at the gate of Gehenna?" I replied, "Yes." He [did so and] showed me men suspended by their noses, men suspended by their hands, men suspended by their tongues, men suspended by their feet.[7] He showed me

1. See above, part 2, chap. 1, §404.
2. As the cloud covered Moses at Sinai.
3. Yalkut, *Bereshit*, §2.
4. PRKM 28:3.
5. In Hebrew: Ge-Hinnom ("Valley of Hinnom").
6. Transposing Hinnom [spelled *Hnm*] into *nhm*[*h*].
7. The torments in Gehenna resemble in many ways the kinds of punishment meted out by the Romans at that time. See Saul Lieberman, "Roman Legal Institutions in Early Rabbinics and in the Acta Martyrum," *JQR* 35 (1944): 1–55, in particular pp. 14ff.

women suspended by their teats, men suspended by their eyes, men suspended by their ears. He showed me men made to eat their own flesh, men made to eat [live] coals of broom, men brought back to life and made to sit while worms devoured their flesh. Then he said to me, "These are the ones of whom it is written, 'Their worm shall not die' " (Isa. 66:24). He showed me further men forced to eat sand, which breaks their teeth, while the Holy One says to them, "O wicked ones, when you ate what was stolen, it tasted sweet in your mouths. Now you will have no strength to eat [anything]!"

R. Yohanan said: Each and every angel is appointed to exact punishment for a single transgression. So one angel comes, punishes the sinner, and goes away. Then a second, then a third, and so, too, all the others, until they exact punishment for all the transgressions the man has committed. By what parable may the matter be illustrated? By the one of a man who had many creditors. When they took him to the king, the king said to them, "What am I to do for you? Go and divide him up among yourselves."

Those who go down to Gehenna and are not allowed to come up out of it are, however, taken every Sabbath eve to two mountains of snow and left there. At the Sabbath's end, an angel goes forth and shoves them along until he returns them to their places in Gehenna. [But before leaving], some of them take a handful of snow, which they put in their armpits to keep them cool during the six weekdays. Then the Holy One says to them, "O wicked ones, woe to you, who steal even in Gehenna, as is said, '[Because of] the drought and heat they steal the snow waters—they sin even in Sheol' " (Job 24:19).

Throughout twelve months the wicked are reduced to ash, which the wind scatters under the feet of the righteous. After that, their soul returns to them and they go out of Gehenna, their faces as black as the bottom of a pot. They then declare that they deserved the decree of judgment against them, saying, "Rightly You decreed against us! Properly You punished us," as is said, "With Thee, O Lord, is the right, and the shame of face is on us to this very day" (Dan. 9:7). The nations of the world, however, are punished in seven pyres of fire, twelve months in each and every pyre, where a river of fire which flows forth from under the throne of glory comes down upon them and continues from world's end to world's end.

After all this, the Holy One has mercy on His creatures, as is said, "I will not always contend, I will not be angry forever: I who make spirits flag also create the breath of life" (Isa. 57:16).[1]

313. The Holy One will be seated in the Garden of Eden and expound [Scripture] with all the righteous seated before Him, all the heavenly household standing on their feet, the sun and the planets at the Holy One's right, and the moon and the stars at His left. The Holy One will be seated and expound a new Torah, which He is to give through the Messiah. When He finishes the lesson, Zerubbabel son of Shealtiel will stand up on his feet and say, "May He be magnified and hallowed," and his voice will go from world's end to world's end. All the world's inhabitants from one end of the world to the other will loudly respond, "Amen." Even Israel's wicked and the righteous from among the worshipers of idols still remaining in Gehenna will loudly respond out of Gehenna and say, "Amen." The world will be in such commotion that the sound of their loud response will be heard in the presence of the Holy One, who will ask, "What is this great commotion I hear?" The ministering angels will reply, Master of the universe, these are the wicked of Israel and the righteous of the nations of the world still in Gehenna, who respond with "Amen" and declare their punishment to be just. Then the mercies of the Holy One will surge up mightily for them, and He will say, "What more am I to do about the judgment imposed on them? The impulse to evil is responsible for what has happened to them."

In that instant, in the presence of all the righteous, the Holy One will take the keys to Gehenna, give them to [the angels] Michael and Gabriel, and say to them, "Go, open the gates of [all the] Gehenna[s] and bring them up." Right away, Michael and Gabriel will go with the keys and open the eight thousand gates of Gehenna, each Gehenna being three hundred parasangs in length, three hundred parasangs in width, a thousand parasangs in thickness [of its walls], and a hundred parasangs in depth.[2] Once a wicked man falls into it, he cannot get up out of it. What will Michael and Gabriel do at that time? They will take hold of the hand of each one of them and bring them up, just like a man who brings his fellow up out of a pit by lifting him with a rope. Then the two angels will stand over them, bathe them, anoint them, heal them of the wounds sustained in Gehenna, clothe them in comely vestments, and bring them, thus vested gloriously like priests, before the Holy One and to all the righteous, as is said, "Like Thy priests they will be vested in righteousness, and Thy holy ones [welcoming them] will sing for joy" (Ps. 132:9).

When they are about to arrive at the entrance to the Garden of Eden, Michael and Gabriel will come in first to seek permission from the Holy One, who will respond, saying, "Allow them to come in, that they may behold My glory." When they come in, they will fall on their faces, prostrate themselves before Him, and bless and praise the Name of the Holy One. At once the wholly righteous and upright, who sit in the presence of the Holy One, will voice thanksgivings and exaltation before the Holy One, as is said, "Surely the righteous shall give thanks unto Thy Name, the upright who dwell in Thy presence" (Ps. 140:14); and again, "Let them exalt Him also in the assembly of the people, and praise Him in the seat of the elders" (Ps. 107:32).[3]

314. "This has come to you from My hand. You shall sit down in sorrow" (Isa. 50:11). R. Phinehas said in the

1. *Massekhet Gehinnom*, BhM 1:147–49.

2. The interpretation was provided to the translator by Professor Philip J. Davis of the Mathematics Department of Brown University.

3. Yalkut, Isa., §429.

name of R. Reuben: By what parable may the verse be understood? By the one of a king who arranged a banquet and invited guests to come to him. The king issued an order, saying, "Let each and every man bring something to sit on." Some brought rugs, some brought mats, some brought pillows and bolsters, some brought chairs, some brought logs, and some brought stones. Irritated [at the sight of logs and stones in the palace], the king said, "Every man shall sit on what he brought." Those who were commanded to sit on logs or stones grumbled at the king, saying, "Is such the honor the king is conferring on us, that we have to sit on logs or stones?" When the king heard the complaint, he said brusquely, "It is not enough that you have disfigured with logs and stones the palace erected by me at great cost, but you have the impudence to join in criticism of me. The only honor you will be accorded is the honor you have already accorded yourselves."

So, too, in the time-to-come, when the wicked are condemned to Gehenna, they will grumble at the Holy One, saying, "Behold, we looked for salvation from the Holy One, and this is what happens to us!" The Holy One will reply to them, "In the world in which you spent your lives, were you not men given to bickering, to slander, and to all kinds of evil? Were you not men of strife and violence? 'You are all kindlers of fire, lighters of firebrands' [Isa. 50:11]. Therefore, 'walk by the blaze of your fire, by the brands that you have lit' [ibid.]. And should you say, 'This has come to us from My hand' [ibid.]: not at all! You did it, you did it to yourselves. This has come to you from your own hand. Therefore 'you are to sit down in sorrow' " (ibid.).

R. Simeon ben Lakish used to be greatly absorbed studying Torah in a cave at Tiberias, where every day a potter would place a jar of water for him to drink. Whenever R. Simeon came into the cave feeling very tired, he would take the water jar and drink from it. On one occasion, the potter entered, sat down by R. Simeon, and stayed with him a while to rest. Then he said to R. Simeon, "Master, do you remember when you and I used to go to the same school? But you had the merit [of becoming a student of Torah], while I had no such merit. Pray for me that my portion may be with you in the world-to-come." R. Simeon replied, "How can I pray for you since [it will be your lot to] come in the company of your fellow craftsmen? Because there, in the world-to-come, a man is not allowed to dwell except with the fellows in his craft."[1]

315. R. Abbahu said in the name of R. Eleazar: The fire of Gehenna has no power over disciples of the wise. Infer it *a fortiori* from reflecting upon a salamander. The salamander is no more than an offspring of fire, but the man who anoints himself with its blood is not affected by fire. How much and more is such immunity to fire true of disciples of the wise, whose entire body is fire, as is written, "Is not My word as fire? saith the Lord" (Jer. 23:29).

R. Simeon ben Lakish said: The fire of Gehenna has no power over Israel's transgressors. Infer it *a fortiori* from reflecting upon the golden altar. If the golden altar, whose gold is no more than an overlay of a denar's thickness, was not affected through so many years by fire, how much more and more is this true of Israel's transgressors, all of whose being is as full of good deeds as a pomegranate is of seeds. For in the verse "Thy temples are like a pomegranate split open" (Song 4:3), read not, "Thy temples [*rakkatekh*]," but, "Thy worthless ones [*rekatekh*]": even the worthless ones in your midst are as full of good deeds as a pomegranate is of seeds.[2]

316. R. Akiva used to say: The punishment of the wicked in Gehenna lasts [no more than] twelve months.[3]

317. We have been taught: For a full twelve months, the human body remains in existence while the soul ascends and descends [to join the body]. After twelve months, the body ceases to exist, and the soul ascends [to the treasury of souls] and descends no more.[4]

318. There is the story of R. Akiva, who, while walking along a road, encountered a man blackened by soot, carrying on his shoulders a huge load of fagots and running with them like a horse. R. Akiva ordered him to stop. He said, "I adjure you to tell me whether you belong to the human race or to the demons?" The man replied, "Master, I was a man, and I have already departed from that world. Every day I chop up logs of wood and bring back a load [of fagots] as huge as this one, with which I am incinerated three times every day." R. Akiva asked him, "What did you do during your earthly life?" The man replied, "Nothing prohibited did I overlook. And now guards are appointed over me who give me no rest." R. Akiva asked him, "Did you leave a son?" The man replied, "By your life, do not detain me, for I am afraid of the angels who, while lashing me with thongs of fire, will ask me, 'Why were you delayed?' " R. Akiva: "Answer my question, so that I may be of help to you." The man: "In such-and-such a city, I left a wife, who was pregnant." So R. Akiva went from city to city until he came to that particular city. When he got there, its inhabitants went out to meet him. He asked them, "Where is So-and-so and his house?" They replied, "May the name of the wicked rot" (Prov. 10:7). When R. Akiva asked about the man's wife, they replied, "May her name and her memory be wiped out." When he inquired about the man's son, they replied, "He is uncircumcised—they did not bother even with the precept of circumcision." R. Akiva: "Nevertheless, bring me his son." When they brought him, R. Akiva ordered that he be circumcised; then he had him seated before him to study and taught him the blessings. On the Sabbath, R. Akiva arranged to have the man's son called to read from the Torah scroll. The instant the man's son recited, "Bless ye the Lord who is to be blessed forever and ever," his father was taken out of Gehenna and brought into the Garden of Eden.

1. Eccles. R. 3:9, §1.

2. B. Hag 27a; B. Er 19a.

3. Ed 2:10.

4. B. Shab 152b–153a.

That night the man came to R. Akiva in a dream and said, "Let your mind be at rest, because you have now delivered me from the punishment of Gehenna."[1]

319. R. Joshua ben Levi, associating with sufferers of *raatan*,[2] studied Torah with them. Quoting "A lovely hind and a graceful doe" (Prov. 5:19), he said, "If Torah bestows grace upon those who study it, should it not also protect them from infection?"

When R. Joshua ben Levi was about to die, the angel of death was instructed, "Go and do whatever he wishes." The angel came and revealed himself to R. Joshua, who said to him, "Show me my place in Eden." [The angel: "Very well."] R. Joshua: "But give me your knife, since you might terrify me with it on the way." The angel gave it to him. When they arrived in the Garden of Eden, the angel lifted up R. Joshua and showed him his place. At that, R. Joshua jumped over and landed on the other side [of the wall]. The angel of death seized hold of him by the hem of his cloak, but R. Joshua exclaimed, "I swear, I will not leave!" Then the Holy One said, "If R. Joshua ever had an oath of his annulled, he must return; but if not, he need not return." [Thus, without experiencing death, R. Joshua remained in Eden.] The angel of death said to him, "Give me back my knife," but R. Joshua would not return it to him. A divine voice then went forth, saying to R. Joshua, "Give it back to him, since mortals have need of it."

Elijah the Prophet heralded R. Joshua's arrival, calling out, "Make room for the son of Levi, make room for the son of Levi!" As R. Joshua proceeded on his way, he found R. Simeon ben Yohai seated on thirteen golden mats.[3] R. Simeon: "Are you the son of Levi?" R. Joshua: "Yes." R. Simeon: "Has a rainbow ever appeared in your lifetime?"[4] R. Joshua: "Yes." R. Simeon: "If that is so, you are not the son of Levi."[5]

320. When R. Hanina bar Papa, who had served as escort at R. Joshua ben Levi's wedding,[6] was about to die, the angel of death was instructed, "Go and do whatever he wishes." So he went to R. Hanina's house and revealed himself to him. R. Hanina said, "Allow me thirty days to go over my studies, for the sages have said, 'Happy is he who comes up there in full possession of his learning.' " The angel of death left him and after thirty days appeared to him again. R. Hanina said, "Show me my place [in Eden]." "Very well," the angel replied. R. Hanina: "But give me your knife, since otherwise you might terrify me with it on the way." The angel: "Are you about to play the same trick on me as your friend has done?" R. Hanina: "Bring a Torah scroll and see if there is anything written in it that I have not fulfilled." The angel: "Have you attached yourself to sufferers of *raatan* and engaged in the study of Torah with them, as R. Joshua ben Levi did?"[7]

Nevertheless, when R. Hanina departed, a pillar of fire came between him and the world.[8] And we have a tradition that such a pillar of fire comes to set apart only one person in a generation, or at most two persons in a generation.

Approaching as close as he could to R. Hanina's bier, R. Alexandri said, "Remove the pillar out of deference to the sages." But R. Hanina ignored him. "Remove it out of deference to your father." But again R. Hanina ignored him. "Remove it," R. Alexandri finally pleaded, "out of deference to your own person."[9] And the pillar of fire departed.[10]

321. Rabbah bar Abbahu encountered [the prophet] Elijah standing in a non-Jewish cemetery. Rabbah asked Elijah, "Why are you standing in a cemetery? Are you not a priest [one forbidden to come in contact with the dead]?" Elijah answered, "Did you not study the division Tohorot (Things Clean), where we have been taught, 'The graves of non-Jews do not defile'?" Rabbah: "If I have been unable to learn even four divisions of Mishnah,[11] how can I learn all six?"[12] Elijah: "Why not?" Rabbah: "I am hard pressed to earn a living." So Elijah led him until he brought him into the Garden of Eden, where he said to him, "Take off your cloak, collect some of these leaves, and put them into the cloak." Rabbah gathered them and took them; as he was going out, he heard a voice say, "Who dares consume his [share in the] world-to-come, as [Rabbah bar] Abbahu has just done?"[13] At that, he shook out his cloak and threw away the leaves.

However, he did bring back the cloak that had absorbed the fragrance of the leaves. He sold it for twelve thousand denars, which he divided among his sons-in-law.[14]

322. Even as praise of the Holy One ascends to Him out of the Garden of Eden from the mouths of the righteous,

1. Ka R. 2; Midrash Aseret ha-Dibberot, in Eisenstein, p. 457; Tanhuma, *Noah*, as quoted in *Menorat ha-Maor*.
2. A skin disease causing nervous trembling and extreme weakness (Jastrow). It was so contagious that most people shunned its victims.
3. Persian kings used to sit on no more than seven mats woven with gold thread. Thus Simeon ben Yohai was singled out for much greater distinction (see Daniel Sperber, in Shaul Shaked, ed., *Irano-Judaica* [Jerusalem, 1982], p. 91, and the Hebrew introduction, p. 9). BR mistranslate *taktiki* as "chairs" or "thrones."
4. The rainbow in the sky, the token of God's pledge never again to bring a deluge, does not, according to R. Simeon ben Yohai, appear in the sky during the lifetime of one like himself, wholly righteous, whose presence shields his generation from extinction by floodwaters.
5. That is to say, "You are not wholly righteous." B. Ket 77b.
6. Or, "at whose wedding the angel of death had served as escort." So Rashi, ad loc. The translator follows the Munich ms.
7. "You were not even as pious and staunch in your faith as was R. Joshua ben Levi, who trusted in Torah's power to protect him from all evil. If R. Joshua, despite his extreme piety, did not hesitate to outwit me, the angel of death, how much more likely are you to do so?" (Ket, Soncino, p. 489, n. 2).
8. To show that the rest of mankind are not worthy of being near him.
9. So that you may be eulogized.
10. B. Ket 77b.
11. Festivals, Women, Damages, Things Holy.
12. The remaining two being Seeds and Things Clean.
13. He was about to benefit in this world from what was to be allotted to him in the world-to-come.
14. B. BM 114a–b.

so too it ascends out of Gehenna from the mouths of the wicked, as is said, "Passing through the valley of weeping,[1] they make it a place of fountains" (Ps. 84:7). What is meant by "They make it a place of fountains"? They make their tears flow like fountains until they cool Gehenna with their tears, so that even from there praise goes up, as is said, "Even there, praises clothe the Teacher[2] [ibid.]." What do they say? They say, so taught R. Yohanan, "You spoke well! You judged well! You declared what was clean well! You declared what was unclean well! You taught well! You instructed well! But we would not heed!"[3]

1. JV: "Bakha," a proper noun. But in this comment, *bakha* is taken as a form of *bkh* ("to weep").

2. Usually translated "early rain." But *moreh* can also mean "teacher."

3. Exod. R. 7:4; MTeh 84:3.

PART V

CHAPTER ONE

MAN AND HIS NEEDS

Man at His Birth, in His Old Age, and at His Death

1. Our masters taught: For two and a half years the school of Shammai and the school of Hillel were divided: The first school said: It would have been better for man not to have been created than to have been created. The other said: It is better for man that he was created than it would have been had he not been created. They finally voted and decided: it would have been better for man not to have been created than to have been created. But now that he has been created, let him search his past deeds. Some say: Let him examine what he is about to do.[1]

2. R. Akiva used to say: Beloved is man, for he was created in God's image. Still greater was the love shown him inasmuch as it was made known to him that he was created in God's image, for it is written, "In the image of God made He man" (Gen. 9:6).[2]

3. R. Nehemiah said: What is the proof that one man is equal in worth to all the work of creation? From Scripture: "This is the book of the generations of Adam: In the day that God created man, in the likeness of God made He him" (Gen. 5:1). And earlier: "These are the generations of the heaven and the earth, when they were created, in the day that the Lord God made heaven and earth" (Gen. 2:1). Even as the words "created" and "made" are used in the second verse [which speaks of all the works of creation] so the words "created" and "made" are used in the first verse, which speaks of man.[3]

4. There are four exalted beings in the world: the ox among cattle, the lion among wild beasts, the eagle among birds, and man, who is more greatly exalted than all the others.[4]

5. Our masters taught: six attributes are ascribed to human beings. In regard to three, they are like ministering angels; in regard to three others, like animals. Three like ministering angels: they have understanding like the ministering angels, they walk erect like the ministering angels, they can use the sacred tongue like the ministering angels. Three like animals: they eat and drink like animals, they procreate like animals, and they defecate like animals.[5]

6. R. Hanina bar Papa expounded: The angel in charge of conception, who is called Night, takes the drop of semen, places it before the Holy One, and asks: Master of the universe, what is to happen to this drop? Will it become a strong man or a weak man? A sage or a fool? A rich man or a poor man?[6]

7. Before the formation of the embryo in its mother's womb, the Holy One decrees what it is to be in the end—male or female, weak or strong, poor or rich, short or tall, ungainly or handsome, scrawny or fat, humble or insolent. He also decrees what is to happen to it. But not whether it is to be righteous or wicked, a matter He places solely in the man's power. He beckons the angel in charge of spirits and says to him. "Bring Me such-and-such a spirit, which is in the Garden of Eden, is called So-and-so, and whose appearance is thus-and-so." At once, the angel goes and brings the spirit to the Holy One. When the spirit arrives, it bows and prostrates itself before the King who is King of kings, the Holy One, blessed be He. In that instant the Holy One says to the spirit, "Enter the drop that is in such-and-such an angel's hand." The spirit opens its mouth and says, "Master of the universe, the world in which I have been dwelling since the day You created me is enough for me. Why do You wish to have me, who am holy and pure, hewn from the mass of Your glory, enter this fetid drop?" The Holy One replies, "The world I will have you enter will be more beautiful for you than the one in which you have dwelled. Indeed, when I formed you, I formed you only for this drop." With that, the Holy One makes the spirit enter the drop against its will. Then the angel returns and has the [drop of semen with the] spirit enter the mother's womb. Moreover, two angels are designated for the spirit to guard it, so that it will not leave the embryo or fall out of it. There a lamp is lit over its head, and it is able to look and see from world's end to world's end. The angel takes it from there, leads it to the Garden of Eden, and shows it the righteous seated in glory with crowns upon their heads. The angel asks the spirit, "Do you know who these are?" The spirit: "No, my lord." The angel says, "At the beginning, these that you see were formed like you in their mother's womb; then they went forth into the world and kept the Torah and its commandments. Therefore, they earned the merit of this happiness in which you see them. Know then that in the end you, too, will leave the world. If you succeed in keeping the Holy One's Torah, you will merit like reward and will be seated with these. But if not, know and bear in mind that you will merit another kind of place."

In the evening the angel leads the spirit to Gehenna, where he shows it the wicked, whom angels of destruction

---

1. Past misdeeds cannot be undone; one can only repent and repair any harm caused by them. Future misdeeds can be foreseen and left undone. B. Er 13b.
2. Avot 3:14.
3. ARN 31.
4. Exod. R. 23:13; Yalkut, Exod., §243.
5. B. Hag 16a.

6. B. Nid 16b.

flog with staves of fire. Though the wicked cry out, "Woe, woe!" the angels show them no mercy. The angel asks the spirit, "Do you know who these are?" The spirit: "No, my lord." The angel: "These who are being punished by fire were formed like you, and when they went forth into the world, they did not keep the Holy One's Torah and statutes. Therefore, they came to the disgrace in which you see them. Again I say, know that in the end you are to go forth into the world. Be righteous, be not wicked, and you will merit life in the world-to-come."

Then the angel strolls with the spirit from morning till evening and shows it the place where it is to die and the place where it is to be buried. The angel continues strolling with it throughout the world, showing it the righteous and the wicked, and finally shows it everything. In the evening the angel returns the spirit to its mother's womb, and there the Holy One provides bolted gates for it. The embryo lies in its mother's womb for nine months: the first three months the embryo dwells in the lower compartment of its mother's womb; the next three months in the middle compartment; and the final three months in the upper compartment. And when its time comes to emerge into the air of the world, it rolls down in one instant from the upper compartment to the middle one and then to the lower one. Of all that its mother eats and drinks during this first period, the embryo eats and drinks, but it excretes no feces.

In the end, its time comes to go forth into the world. The same angel appears and says to the spirit, "Your time to go forth into the air of the world has come." The spirit: "Why do you wish to take me out into the air of the world?" The angel: "My son, know that you were formed against your will; know, too, that you will be born against your will, will die against your will, and against your will are to give an account and reckoning before the King who is King of kings, the Holy One, blessed be He." But the spirit refuses to go out of the womb, so that the angel has to beat it and put out the lamp that has been burning over its head, and then he brings it forth into the world against its will. Instantly the infant forgets all that he had seen as he was going forth, and all that he had known. Why does the infant weep as he goes forth? Because he lost a place of repose and comfort—[he weeps] for the world which he was compelled to leave.

When a man's time to die comes, the same angel appears to him and asks, "Do you recognize me?" The man answers, "Yes," and proceeds to inquire, "Why did you come this day and not on any other day?" The angel: "To take you out of the world—your time to depart has arrived." The man begins to weep and makes his voice heard from world's end to world's end. But his fellow creatures are not aware of it, because they cannot hear his voice—except for the cock: he alone can hear it. The man pleads with the angel, "You have already taken me out of two worlds and made me enter this world." The angel: "Have I not told you that you were formed against your will, were born against your will, were alive against your will, and against your will are destined to give an account and reckoning before the Holy One, blessed be He?"[1]

[1] Tanhuma, *Pekudei*, §3.

8. R. Simlai delivered the following discourse: What does an embryo in the womb of its mother resemble? A ledger that stays folded up. The embryo's hands rest on its two temples, its elbows on its two knees, and its heels against its buttocks. Its head lies between its knees, its mouth is closed, and its navel is open. It eats what its mother eats and drinks what its mother drinks, but produces no feces, because otherwise it would kill its mother. (As soon as it goes forth into the air of the world, however, that which has been closed is opened and that which has been open is closed. Otherwise, the embryo could not live one single hour.)

[During the period of gestation] light burns above its head, and it gazes and is able to see from one end of the world to the other. There is no time during which man abides in greater happiness than during those days. At that time he is taught the entire Torah, all of it. But as he comes into the air of the world, an angel appears, strikes him on his mouth, and makes him forget the entire Torah.

The embryo does not leave the womb until it is made to swear an oath. What is the oath it is made to swear? "Be righteous, be not wicked; even if the entire world, all of it, tells you, 'You are righteous,' consider yourself wicked. Always bear in mind that the Holy One is pure, that His ministers are pure, and that the soul I placed in you is pure; if you preserve it in purity, well and good; but if not, I will take it from you."[2]

9. Therefore man was created unique, in order to proclaim the greatness of the Holy One, blessed be He. For if a man strikes many coins from one die, they are all exactly alike. But though the King of kings of kings, the Holy One, blessed be He, has fashioned every man in the stamp of the first man, Adam, not a single one of them is exactly like his fellow. And why are men's faces not like one another? So that no man would see a beautiful dwelling or a beautiful woman and say, "She is mine."[3]

10. Even as men's faces are not alike, so their understanding is not alike. Each man has an understanding that is his very own.[4]

11. We have been taught that R. Meir said: A man differs from his fellow in three ways—in voice, in appearance, and in understanding.[5]

12. The verse "He hath made thee, and placed thee on settings" (Deut. 32:6)[6] implies that the Holy One created in man many organs, each in its own setting, and if any change is made in an organ's setting, the man will die.[7]

13. "For Thou art great, and doest wondrous things" (Ps. 86:10). R. Tanhum said: Should a leather bottle have a

[2] B. Nid 30b.
[3] B. Sanh 37b–38a.
[4] Tanhuma, *Pinhas*, §10.
[5] B. Sanh 38a.
[6] JV: "He hath made thee, and established thee."
[7] B. Hul 56b.

hole in it as small as a needle's eye, all of its air will escape. Yet, though man is formed with many cavities and many orifices, his breath does not escape through them.[1]

14. Our masters taught: The kidneys counsel, the heart discerns, the tongue shapes [words], the mouth articulates them, the windpipe produces the voice, the gullet takes in all kinds of food, the lungs absorb moisture [from the stomach], the liver is the seat of anger, the gall lets a drop fall into the liver and allays the anger, the spleen produces laughter, the large intestine grinds food, the maw produces sleep, and the nose awakens. Should the sleep-inducing organ induce wakefulness, or the wakefulness-inducing organ induce sleep, the man will pine away. The sages taught: Should both induce sleep or both induce wakefulness, the man will die at once.[2]

15. "And He closed up the place with flesh *tahtennah* [instead thereof]" (Gen. 2:21). R. Hanina bar Isaac read *tahtennah* as made up of *noy*, "seemly," and *le-tahtito*, "for the nether part," that is, by a flesh cover the Holy One provided a seemly outlet at man's nether parts, so that [the anus] would not be exposed like that of an animal. Some say: God provided cushions at man's nether part, so that he would feel no pain when sitting down.[3]

16. R. Levi said: Six organs serve a man—three are under his control, and three are not under his control. The ones under his control: the mouth, the hands, and the feet. The ones not under his control: the eyes, the ears, and the nose. And when the Holy One wishes it, even the ones under his control cease to be under it.[4]

17. The face the Holy One created in man is no larger than a *sit* [the distance between the tip of the thumb and the tip of the index finger when held apart]. But though it has many fountains, their fluids do not mingle. The fluid of the eyes is salty, the fluid in the ears is oily, the fluid in the nose is foul, the fluid in the mouth is sweet. Why is the fluid in the eyes salty? Because if a man were to weep over the dead for a long time, his eyes would soon be blinded. But because the fluid is salty,[5] the man stops and weeps no more. Why is the fluid in the ears oily? Because when a man hears bad news, if he should retain it in his ears, it would coagulate in his heart and [cause such pressure] that he might die. However, because the ear fluid is oily, he receives the news in one ear and lets it out at the other. Why is the fluid in the nose foul? Because when a man inhales a bad odor, were it not for the foul fluid in the nose which arrests it, the man would die. Why is the fluid in the mouth sweet? Because sometimes a man eats food that is revolting to him, so that he throws it up, and were the fluid in his mouth not sweet, he would not recover [from his revulsion].[6]

18. R. Tahalifa of Caesarea said in the name of R. Pilla: Pause and consider how many miracles the Holy One performs for man and yet he is not aware of them. If a man swallowed hard bread, it would lacerate his innards as it went down into his bowels. So the Holy One created a fountain [of saliva] in his throat, which conveys the bread down safely.[7]

19. Whatever was created during the six days of creation needs further doing: mustard needs sweetening, lupines need sweetening, wheat needs grinding, even man needs finishing.[8]

20. The tyrant Rufus asked R. Akiva: Whose works are more comely—those of the Holy One or those of flesh and blood? R. Akiva: Those of flesh and blood are more comely. The tyrant Rufus: But think of heaven and earth—can man make anything like them? R. Akiva: Do not speak to me of matters that are above mortals and over which they have no power, but only of matters that are to be found among human beings. The tyrant Rufus: Why do you have yourselves circumcised?[9] R. Akiva: I knew that you were going to ask me this question. That is why I anticipated you by saying, "The works of flesh and blood are more comely than those of the Holy One." [To prove his point] R. Akiva brought Rufus ears of grain and delicate breads, saying, "The ears of grain are the work of the Holy One, the breads the work of flesh and blood—are not the loaves of bread more comely?" Then R. Akiva brought him flax stalks and garments made in Beth-shean, saying, "The first are the work of God; the second, the work of man. Are not the garments more to be admired?" Then the tyrant Rufus asked, "Assuming that He desires circumcision, why does the infant not emerge from his mother's womb circumcised?" R. Akiva replied, "Why does the umbilical cord emerge with the infant? Should not the mother have had the infant's umbilical cord cut off [in the womb]? As to your question of why an infant does not emerge circumcised, it is because the Holy One gave the precepts to Israel to purify them."[10]

21. "The God of Israel said, The Rock of Israel spoke to me" (2 Sam. 23:3). [In thus giving God His full titles], King David meant to intimate: I will thus call attention to the kingship, the greatness, and the might of the Holy One. Every day a man is formed [by Him], every day a man is born; every day a man lives, every day a man dies; every day a man's spirit is taken from him [in sleep] and deposited with the spirit's true Owner; every day he is fed out of the fruit of his deeds, just as the infant is fed out of his mother's breast.[11]

22. R. Samuel bar R. Isaac said in the name of R. Simon ben Eleazar: The seven times Koheleth mentioned "vanity"

---

1. Gen. R. 1:3.
2. B. Ber 61a–b and En Yaakov, ad loc.
3. Gen. R. 17:6; Eccles. R. 3:18, §1.
4. Gen. R. 67:3: Tanhuma B, *Va-yikra*, §18.
5. And causes the eye to smart when shed for a long time.
6. Tanhuma B, *Hukkat*, §1; Num. R. 18:22.
7. Exod. R. 24:1.
8. Circumcision.
9. And thus mutilate a member created by God.
10. Tanhuma B, *Tazria*, §7; Tanhuma, *Tazria*, §5.
11. TdEZ 15 (JPS, p. 463).

correspond to the seven worlds a man beholds. At the age of one, he is like a king lounging in a canopied litter, being hugged and kissed by everyone. At two and three, he is like a pig, sticking his hands into the gutters and putting whatever he finds into his mouth. At ten, he leaps about like a kid. At twenty, he is like a neighing horse, making himself attractive as he goes looking for a wife. Once wed, he has a saddle put upon him, and he works like an ass. After he brings children into the world, he has to brazen his face like a dog in order to provide food for himself and his children. When grown old, he is [bent] like an ape.[1]

23. Judah ben Tema used to say: At the age of five, one is fit for Scripture; at ten, for Mishnah; at thirteen, for [fulfilling the] precepts; at fifteen, for Gemara; at eighteen, for the bridal chamber; at twenty, to pursue [a calling]; at thirty, for the peak of strength; at forty, for understanding; at fifty, for counsel; at sixty, for mature age; at seventy, for a hoary head; at eighty—a sign of exceptional strength; at ninety—bent [beneath the weight of years]; at a hundred—as one that is already dead, who has passed away and ceased to be in this world.[2]

24. We have been taught that R. Simeon ben Eleazar said: If the old say to you, "Demolish," while the young say, "Build," demolish and do not build, because demolition by the old is building, while building by the young is demolition, and the example is Rehoboam son of Solomon.[3]

25. R. Jonathan said, "Solomon first wrote Song of Songs, then Proverbs, and then Ecclesiastes," inferring the order in which these books were written from the way of the world. When a man is young, he utters words of song; when mature, he speaks in proverbs; when old, he talks of [life's] vanities.[4]

26. Old men lack sagacity, and children perspicacity.[5]

27. R. Isaac said: The verse "The vanity of youth leads to blackening" (Eccles. 11:10)[6] implies that the things a man does in his youth blacken his face [with shame] in his old age.[7]

28. R. Joshua bar Nahmani said: Four causes bring old age prematurely to a man: anxiety, provocation by children, a bad wife, and wars.[8]

29. Being steeped in lewdness brings on old age prematurely.[9]

1. Eccles. R. 1:2, §1; Yalkut, Eccles., §966.
2. Avot 5:21.
3. See 1 Kings 12. B. Meg 31b.
4. Song R. 1:1, §10.
5. B. Shab 89b.
6. JV: "For youth and the prime of life are vanity." But *shaharut* ("prime of life") also means "blackness."
7. B. Shab 152a.
8. Tanhuma, *Hayye Sarah*, §2.
9. B. Shab 152a.

30. "Before the days of sorrow come" (Eccles. 12:1), meaning: the days of old age.[10]

31. "Therefore let every pious man pray unto Thee when hard times befall"[11] (Ps. 32:6), "hard times" being old age, according to R. Abba. Concerning his old age, a man should pray that his eyes may [continue] to see, his mouth to eat, and his feet to walk. For when a man grows old, all his functions desert him.[12]

32. Old men's intelligence changes [for the worse], their lips tremble [so that they cannot enjoy their food], and their ears grow hard [of hearing].[13]

33. To an old man, even a tiny mound is like the highest of mountains.[14]

34. Rabbi [Judah I, the Patriarch] asked R. Simeon ben Halafta: Why did we not have the pleasure of receiving you during the [recent] festival, as my forebears had the pleasure of receiving your forebears? R. Simeon replied: [Little] rocks have become tall, near things have become distant, two [legs] have become three, and that which makes peace in the house has ceased to be.[15]

35. A Caesar once asked R. Joshua ben Hananiah: Why did you not attend Be Avidan?[16] He replied: The mountain is covered with snow; it is surrounded by ice; its dogs no longer bark; and its stones no longer grind.[17]

In the school of Rav, it was said [of old age]: What I did not lose, I seek.[18]

We have been taught that R. Yose ben Kisma said: Two are better than three.[19] Alas for the one thing that goes and does not return. What is that? R. Hisda said: One's youth.

When R. Dimi came [from the Land of Israel], he said: Youth is a wreath of roses, old age a wreath of thorns.[20]

36. Happy is our youth if it has not disgraced our old age.[21]

10. B. Shab 151b.
11. JV: "at a time when Thou mayest be found (*metzo*)." But *metzo*, whose meaning is uncertain, has been translated "trouble, anxiety."
12. Tanhuma, *Mi-ketz*, §10.
13. B. Shab 152a and En Yaakov, ad loc.
14. Ibid.
15. I have become old: walking uphill has become harder; my eyes, which once could see far in the distance, barely see at close range; I now walk with the help of a third leg [a walking stick]; my sexual potency is no more. B. Shab 152a.
16. A gathering place for the sages of Rome. For other meanings, see above, part 2, chap. 1, §123.
17. My hair and beard are white, my voice is barely audible, and my teeth are worn to the gums.
18. I walk about bent as though looking for something lost on the ground.
19. Two legs than two legs and a stick.
20. B. Shab 152a.
21. B. Suk 53a.

37. "And Abraham became old" (Gen. 24:1). Until Abraham, there was no old age, so that one who wished to speak with Abraham might mistakenly find himself speaking to Isaac, or one who wished to speak with Isaac might mistakenly find himself speaking to Abraham. But when Abraham came, he pleaded for old age, saying, "Master of the universe, You must make a visible distinction between father and son, between a youth and an old man, so that the old man may be honored by the youth." God replied, "As you live, I shall begin with you." So Abraham went off, passed the night, and arose in the morning. When he arose, he saw that the hair of his head and of his beard had turned white. He said, "Master of the universe, if You have given me white hair as a mark of old age, [I do not find it attractive]." "On the contrary," God replied, "the hoary head is a crown of glory" (Prov. 16:31).[1]

38. "And Abraham was old" (Gen. 24:1). Why does Scripture say it again? Has it not already been said that "Abraham and Sarah were old" (Gen. 18:11)? R. Ammi explained: In the earlier verse, old age combined with virility is meant; while in the latter verse, old age without virility is intended.[2]

39. The glory of a face is its beard.[3]

40. A beard is beauty in a man—in a woman, a blemish.[4]

41. When is a woman old? When she is called "Mother" and doesn't mind.[5]

42. An old man in a house is an obstacle in the house. An old woman in a house is a treasure in the house.[6]

43. "We are strangers before Thee. . . . Our days on the earth are as a shadow" (1 Chron. 29:15). Would that it were as the shadow of a wall or of a tree! But it is as the shadow of a bird in flight, for Scripture also says, "As a shadow that passeth away" (Ps. 144:4). "And without hope" (1 Chron. 29:15)—no one can hope that he will not die, for all know and affirm with their mouth that they will die.[7]

44. "His days are as a passing shadow" (Ps. 144:4). Had Scripture said, "As the shadow of a wall"—that has staying power; "As the shadow of a date palm"—that, too, has staying power. But like what kind of shadow? Like the shadow of a bird, said R. Huna in the name of R. Aha: as it passes, its shadow, too, passes.[8]

45. Mankind are like grasses in the field—while some blossom, others wilt.[9]

46. Flesh and blood: here today tomorrow no more.[10]

47. "Who art thou, that thou art afraid of man?" (Isa. 51:12). R. Judah the son of R. Simeon said: The question may be illustrated by the parable of a man who saw a worm which terrified him—it looked to him like a glowing coal, and we call it night coal [firefly]. He was told: Is this what terrifies you? At night it looks like a fiery burning coal, but when morning comes, you find that it is nothing more than a worm.[11]

48. R. Yohanan said: The word "man" [*adam*] is an acrostic of "dust," "blood," and "gall."[12] The word "flesh" [*basar*] is an acrostic of "shame, "stench," and "worm";[13] according to some, the words are "shame," "Sheol," and "worm."[14]

49. "A time to be born, a time to die" (Eccles. 3:2). At the time one is born, the time he is to die is set. When a man is born, it is decreed for him how many years he is to live. If he merits it, he completes the years given him; if not, their number is diminished. So taught R. Akiva. But the sages said: If he merits it, more years are given him. If not, his years are diminished.

The following story supports the sages.

One of the notables of Sepphoris had occasion to celebrate the circumcision of his son, and the inhabitants of En Te'enah came up to honor him [with their presence], among them R. Simeon ben Halafta. Upon arriving at the gate of the city, they noticed youngsters standing and playing in front of a courtyard. When the youngsters saw R. Simeon ben Halafta, who was both distinguished and handsome, they exclaimed, "We will not let you go until you do a little dance for us." He said to them, "Such is not for me—I am an old man." Though he rebuked them, they were neither frightened nor cowed. He lifted up his face and saw the house in the courtyard about to collapse on the youngsters for their impertinence, so he said to them, "Will you first do what I tell you? Go tell the owner of this courtyard that if he is asleep, he had better wake up, because while the beginning of sin is sweet, its end is bitter."

At the sound of their conversation, the owner of the house woke up. He came out and fell at R. Simeon ben Halafta's feet, saying, "My master, I beg of you, pay no attention to their words—they are but children, and foolish." R. Simeon: "But what can I do, seeing that the decree [that the house collapse] has already been issued? I will, however, postpone it for you until you remove everything

---

1. B. BM 87a; Gen. R. 65:9; Tanhuma, *Hayye Sarah*, §1.
2. Gen. R. 48:16.
3. B. Shab 152a.
4. P. Kid 2:6, 62d.
5. B. Nid 9b.
6. B. Ar 19a.
7. Gen. R. 96:2.
8. Eccles. R. 1:2, §1.
9. B. Er 54a.
10. P. Sanh 6:12, 23d.
11. PR 33:4 (YJS 2:638).
12. The initial letters of these Hebrew words (*efer*, *dam*, *marah*) combine to form *adam*.
13. The initial letters of the three (*bushah*, *seruhah*, *rimmah*) combine to form *basar*.
14. B. Sot 5a.

that you own in this courtyard." As soon as the man had removed all that he owned in the courtyard, the [house] tottered and collapsed.

R. Simeon and his companions then went on to share in the celebration of the circumcision. The child's father served them seven-year-old wine, saying, "Drink some of this superb wine; I trust that at the child's wedding feast, the God of heaven will let me serve you some more of the same vintage, which I intend to age." They responded, "As you have brought this child into the covenant [of Abraham], so may you bring him to Torah and to the nuptial canopy." They went on feasting until midnight.

At midnight R. Simeon ben Halafta, who relied on his [spiritual] strength, set out [with his companions] to walk to his hometown. On the road, the angel of death met him and asked, "Is it because people like you rely on your good deeds that you venture out at a time that is not the time [to be abroad]?" R. Simeon: "And you, who are you?" The angel of death, [smiling]: "I am the emissary of Him who is everywhere." R. Simeon: "Why are you smiling?" The angel: "At the talk of mortals, who say, 'Thus-and-thus shall we do,' though not one of them knows when he may be summoned to die. The same man in whose home you have just feasted, who has said to you, 'I am aging more of this wine to serve at my son's wedding feast'—look, his son's name tag is with me. After thirty days, I am to take him."

R. Simeon ben Halafta then said to the angel of death, "As you live, show me my tag." The angel: "I have no power over you or the likes of you." R. Simeon: "Why not?" The angel: "Because day after day, as you labor in Torah and at precepts, and perform deeds of mercy, the Holy One keeps adding years to your years." R. Simeon: "May it be the Holy One's will that, even as you have no power over our name tags, so shall you have no power to counter our prayers." They besought mercy, and the infant remained alive.

However, R. Akiva said: What relevance does such a story have? The story is of no consequence to me, since there is the explicit verse "The number of thy days I will fulfill" (Exod. 23:26). Consider now: Moses performed so many precepts, so many deeds of charity. Yet in the end he was told, "The time is drawing near for thee to die" (Deut. 31:14). It thus follows: "A time to be born, and a time to die" (Eccles. 3:2).[1]

50. R. Joshua ben Korhah said: When one comes close to his parents' age, let him think of death five years before and five years after.[2]

51. Though a plague may last seven years, no one dies before his time.[3]

52. Our masters taught: One who falls sick and is close to death should be told, "Confess, for all who are sentenced to death should confess." Let one who goes out into the marketplace regard himself as turned over to a Roman officer [for execution]. Let one who has a headache regard himself as restrained with an [iron] collar. Let one who falls down while going up to his couch regard himself as being taken up to the torturer's scaffold for examination. He who is taken up to the scaffold is saved if he has persuasive advocates, but if not, he is not saved. And these are one's advocates: repentance and good deeds. Even if nine hundred and ninety-nine argue for his condemnation and only one argues in his favor, he is saved, for it is said, "If there be for him an angel, an intercessor, one among a thousand, to vouch for the man's uprightness; then He is gracious unto him, and saith: 'Deliver him from going down to the pit, I have found a ransom' " (Job 33:23–24). R. Eliezer son of R. Yose the Galilean said: The verse means that if, in the angel who argues for condemnation, nine hundred and ninety-nine parts tend to condemn but one part argues in the man's favor, he is saved, for the text may be read, "One intercessor who is a thousandth part."[4]

53. The life of any sick person is deemed to be in danger.[5]

54. R. Alexandri said in the name of R. Hiyya bar Abba: The miracle wrought for a sick man is greater than the miracle wrought for Hananiah, Mishael, and Azariah. The miracle for Hananiah, Mishael, and Azariah involved an ordinary fire lit by a human being, but the [fevered] fire of a sick man is from Heaven—who can extinguish that?[6]

55. "God hath heard the voice of the lad because [he prayed] there"[7] (Gen. 21:17), because of his prayer for himself. A sick man's prayer in his own behalf is more effective than those of anyone else.[8]

56. "For this [an easy death] shall everyone that is godly pray unto Thee in the time of finding" (Ps. 32:6). "The time of finding," said R. Nahman bar Isaac, refers to death, as in the verse "Death has many findings (*totzaot*)" (Ps. 68:21).

We have likewise been taught: Nine hundred and three kinds of death have been created in the world, a number intimated in the numerical value of the letters in the world *totzaot*. The most painful of them all is the croup, and the least painful of them all is "the kiss," which is like drawing a bit of hair out of milk.

R. Yohanan said: "The time of finding"—this refers to burial, as is said, "When they can find the grave" (Job 3:22).[9]

57. Our masters taught: If one dies suddenly, that is "death by snatching away." If he is sick one day and then

1. Eccles. R. 3:2, §3; Deut. R. 9:2–3.
2. Gen. R. 65:12.
3. B. Sanh 29a.
4. B. Shab 32a.
5. Eccles. R. 3:2, §2.
6. B. Ned 41a.
7. JV: "the voice of the lad where he is."
8. Gen. R. 53:14.
9. B. Ber 8a.

dies, that is "death by being hustled away." R. Hananiah ben Gamaliel said: That is "death by a stroke." If one dies after two days' illness, that is "delayed death." After three days, it is "death by reproof." After four, it is "death by reprimand." After five, it is "normal death of all men."

If one dies before fifty, that is "premature death."[1] At sixty, it is "death at the hands of Heaven." At seventy, it is "death of a hoary head." At eighty, it is "death at a ripe old age." Rabbah said: From fifty to sixty is "premature death."

When R. Joseph turned sixty, he made a festive day for the sages, saying: I have just passed beyond the age of premature death.

R. Huna died suddenly. When the sages were concerned about the meaning of his death, a pair of sages from Adiabene said to them: What we were taught concerning such a death applies only to one who has not yet reached ripe old age [eighty]. After one has reached it, even sudden death is "death by a kiss."[2]

58. We have been taught: If a man dies smiling, it is a good omen for him; if he dies weeping, it is a bad omen for him. If his face is turned upward, it is a good omen for him; if it is turned downward, it is a bad omen for him. If he faces the people around him, it is a good omen for him; if he faces the wall, it is a bad omen for him. If his face is greenish, it is a bad omen; if bright and ruddy, it is a good omen. If he dies on Sabbath eve, it is a good omen; if at the Sabbath's outgoing, a bad omen. If he dies on the eve of the Day of Atonement, it is a bad omen; if at the outgoing of the Day of Atonement, it is a good omen. If he dies of a disease of the bowels, it is a good omen, because most of the righteous die of such a disease.[3]

59. It is said of the angel of death that he is full of eyes [being, so to speak, everywhere]. Accordingly, when a sick man is about to die, the angel of death stands over the man's pillow, in his hand a drawn sword, a drop of gall hanging from its tip. When the sick man sees him, he trembles and opens his mouth [in terror]. Just then, the angel of death drops the gall into his mouth, and from it he dies—from it, his corpse begins to emit a stench and his face turns green.[4]

60. When the soul leaves the body, its cry [of anguish] goes from one end of the world to the other.

When R. Samuel brother of R. Phinehas son of R. Hama died in Sikhnin,[5] R. Phinehas's associates were sitting with him [in Sepphoris]. Something amusing occurred to them, and they began to laugh. At this, R. Phinehas said to them: The cry of my brother's soul is now breaking cedars and uprooting oaks, and yet you sit here unaware.[6]

61. R. Sheshet, who was blind, sensed the angel of death in the marketplace and said to him: Will you seize me in the marketplace as though I were a beast? Come to my house!

The angel of death appeared to R. Ashi in the marketplace. R. Ashi said to him: Give me thirty days' respite, so that I may go over my studies, inasmuch as it is said [in heaven], "Happy is he who comes here with his learning in hand."

When the angel of death came back on the thirtieth day, R. Ashi asked him: What is the urgency? The angel of death replied: R. Huna [bar Nathan] is close on your heels,[7] and remember, "No sovereignty may encroach upon another even by as little as a hairsbreadth."[8]

62. While seated at the bedside of R. Nahman, Rava saw him lapsing into the sleep of death. Yet R. Nahman managed to say to Rava, "Tell the angel of death not to torment me." Rava replied, "But are you not important enough [to tell him yourself]?" R. Nahman: "Who is sufficiently important, esteemed, or vigorous enough [on his deathbed to make such a request]?" Then Rava implored R. Nahman, "Show yourself to me [in a dream]." When he did show himself [after he died], Rava asked him, "Did you suffer any pain?" and he replied, "As little as taking a hair from milk. Still, if the Holy One were to say to me, 'Go back to that world,' I would not consent, the fear of death being so great."[9]

63. Once, as workers were digging in R. Nahman's ground, R. Ahai bar Josiah [who was buried there] snorted at them. They went and told R. Nahman, "Someone snorted at us." So R. Nahman went to the place and asked him, "Who are you?" "I am Ahai bar Josiah." R. Nahman: "But did not R. Mari say that [even] the righteous will someday become dust?" R. Ahai bar Josiah: "Who is this Mari? I do not know him." R. Nahman: "Yet surely there is the verse 'And the dust shall return to the earth as it was' " (Eccles. 12:7). R. Ahai: "He who taught you Ecclesiastes did not teach you Proverbs, where it is written, 'But envy is rot to the bones' [Prov. 14:30]: he who has envy in his heart—his bones rot away; but he who has no envy in his heart—his bones do not rot away." R. Nahman then felt R. Ahai's person and perceived that it had physical substance. So he said, "Let my master arise and come to my house." R. Ahai: "You now show evidence that you have not studied even the Prophets, for it is written, 'And ye shall know that I am the Lord, when I open your graves, and cause you to come up out of your graves' " (Ezek. 37:13). R. Nahman: "But it is also written, 'For dust art thou, and unto dust thou shalt return' " (Gen. 3:19). R. Ahai: "That will happen only one hour before the resurrection of the dead."[10]

---

1. Literally, "death by excision."
2. B. MK 28a.
3. B. Ket 103b.
4. B. AZ 20b.
5. As in Midrash Sam. 9:30. R. Phinehas lived in Sepphoris, which, like Sikhnin, was in Galilee.
6. B. Yoma 20b; Midrash Sam. 9:3; Gen. R. 6:7.
7. Waiting to succeed you as head of the academy.
8. B. MK 28a.
9. Ibid.
10. It is suggested that the conversation between R. Nahman and R. Ahai bar Josiah took place in a dream (so *Pardes Rimmonim*, cited by Adin Steinsaltz, in his edition of Shab, ad loc.). B. Shab 152b.

64. R. Nathan said: It is a good omen for a dead person if he is punished immediately after death. Thus, if one dies and is not mourned or not buried properly, or a wild beast drags away his body, or rain wets his bier, it is a good omen for him.[1]

65. We have been taught that R. Simeon ben Eleazar said: He who stands by a dying man at the moment of the soul's departure is obligated to rend his garments [even on the Sabbath]. To what may the moment of a soul's departure be likened? To the moment when a Torah scroll is consumed by fire.[2]

66. Our masters taught: There are three partners in man—the Holy One, his father, and his mother. His father inseminates the white substance, out of which are formed the child's bones, sinews, and nails, the brain in his head, and the white of his eye. His mother inseminates the red substance, out of which are formed the child's skin, flesh, and hair, and the black of his eye. The Holy One implants in him spirit, soul, beauty of countenance, eyesight, the capacity to hear, the capacity to speak, and the capacity to walk, as well as knowledge, understanding, and intelligence. When man's time to depart from the world approaches, the Holy One takes away His part and leaves to the father and mother the parts contributed by them.[3]

67. When a man's time comes to die, the Holy One takes His part and leaves the parts contributed by the father and mother before them, and they weep. The Holy One asks them, "Why do you weep? Have I taken anything of yours? I have only taken what belongs to Me!" They reply, "Master of the universe, so long as Your part was mingled with ours, our part was preserved from worms and maggots. But now that You have taken away Your part, behold, our part is exposed and laid open to worms and maggots."

R. Judah [I] the Patriarch used to tell a parable to illustrate what has just been said. A king who owned a vineyard turned it over to a tenant. The king said to his servants, "Go harvest the grapes in my vineyard; take away my share and leave behind the share that belongs to the tenant." They went at once and did what the king ordered, but the tenant began to lament and weep. So the king asked him, "Have I taken anything of yours? Have I not taken only my own?" The tenant replied, "My lord king, so long as your share was with mine, my share was guarded from spoliation and theft. But now that you have removed your share, look, my portion is exposed to spoliation and theft!"[4]

68. R. Judah used to say: Ten strong things have been created in the world. A mountain is strong, but iron cleaves it. Iron is strong, but fire melts it. Fire is strong, but water quenches it. Water is heavy, but clouds carry it. Clouds are heavy, but a wind scatters them. The wind is strong, but the body withstands it. The body is strong, but fear crushes it. Fear is strong, but wine dissipates it. Wine is strong, but sleep works it off. Stronger, however, than all of these is death.[5]

69. In the [margin of] R. Meir's Torah scroll, at the verse "And behold, it was very (*meod*) good" (Gen. 1:31), there was found written: "And behold, death (*mot*) was very good."

R. Samuel bar Nahman said: While perched on my grandfather's shoulder, coming up by way of Beth Shean from my own town to Kefar Hanan, I heard R. Simeon ben Eleazar expounding from a teacher's chair in the name of R. Meir: "And behold, it was very good"—and behold, death was very good.[6]

70. What is the difference between the death of young men and that of old men? R. Judah said: When a lamp goes out of itself, it is good for it and good for the wick; but if it does not go out of itself, it is bad for itself and bad for the wick. R. Nehemiah said: When a fig is gathered at the proper time, it is good for the fig and good for the fig tree; but if it is gathered prematurely, it is bad for itself and bad for the tree.

In this regard, the following story: R. Hiyya the Elder and his disciples—some say R. Akiva and his disciples; others say R. Yose ben Halafta and his disciples—used to rise early and sit and study under a certain fig tree, whose owner rose early to gather its fruit. So they said, "He may well suspect us [of stealing his fruit]." What did they do? They changed their place [of study to someone else's tree]. At that, the owner went to them and said, "My masters, this one merit that you have been conferring upon me by sitting and studying under my fig tree, you have now deprived me of." The sages: "We thought you might suspect us [of stealing your figs]." The owner reassured them, and they returned to their former place. Thereafter, what did the owner do? Upon rising in the morning, he no longer gathered the figs, so when the sun beat down upon them, they became wormy. At that, the sages said, "Even as the owner of the fig tree knows when it is ripe for plucking and plucks it, so the Holy One knows when the time has come for the righteous to be removed from the world and removes them." With regard to such removal, Scripture says, "My Beloved is gone down to His garden . . . to browse in the gardens, and to pick lilies" (Song 6:2).[7]

71. A story of a woman who, grown very old, came before R. Yose ben Halafta and said to him, "Master, I have grown so very old that my life has become hideous. I find no taste in food or drink, and I wish to depart from the world." He asked, "How did you extend your life for so long?" She replied, "Whenever I have something to do, however enjoyable it may be, I am in the habit of putting it aside early every morning and going to the synagogue."

1. B. Sanh 47a.
2. Since a soul released from the dead body and the words in a burned Torah scroll both rise to heaven. B. Shab 105b.
3. B. Nid 31a and En Yaakov, ad loc.
4. Eccles. R. 5:10, §2.
5. B. BB 10a.
6. Gen. R. 9:5.
7. Gen. R. 62:2; Eccles. R. 5:11, §2; P. Ber 2:8, 5b–c.

He said, "For three days, one after another, keep yourself away from the synagogue." She went off and did as he advised, and on the third day she took sick and died.[1]

72. [The city of] Luz[2]—even the angel of death has no authority to enter it. But when the old men in it grow weary of living, they go outside its wall and die.[3]

73. Two Cushites stood in the presence of King Solomon—"Elihoreph and Ahijah sons of Shisha, who were [Solomon's] scribes" (1 Kings 4:3). One day, observing that the angel of death looked distressed, Solomon asked him, "Why are you distressed?" The angel of death replied, "Because the two Cushites seated here are about to be summoned by me." So [to thwart the angel of death] Solomon had spirits take charge of the two and convey them to the city of Luz.[4] But as soon as they reached its wall, they died. The following day, Solomon observed that the angel of death was cheerful. When Solomon asked him, "Why are you so cheerful?" he replied, "You sent them to the very place where they were to be summoned by me."

At that, Solomon spoke up, saying, "A man's feet are responsible for him. They lead him to the place where he is about to be summoned."[5]

74. At the hour of death, a man does not jest, and so the words of a dying man are regarded as signed, sealed, and delivered.[6]

75. The sages taught in the name of R. Meir: When a man comes into the world, his fists are clenched, as though to say, "The whole world is mine, and I shall inherit it." But when he departs from the world, his hands are spread open, as though to say, "I have inherited nothing from this world."[7]

76. "As he came forth of his mother's womb, naked shall he go back as he came" (Eccles. 5:14). Geniva said: The verse is to be understood by the parable of a fox who found a vineyard fenced in on all sides, except for one gap, through which he tried to enter but could not [squeeze himself through it]. What did he do? He fasted for three days, until he became lean and slender, and thus squeezed himself through the gap. But after he had eaten [of the grapes], he became fat again, and when he wished to go out through that gap, he could not. He fasted another three days, until he became lean and slender. Returning to his former size, he was able to go out. After getting out, he turned his face to the vineyard and, gazing at it, said, "O vineyard, O vineyard, how goodly are you, and how goodly is your fruit! All that is within you is beautiful and comely, but what benefit can one derive from you? As one goes into you, so must one come out." Such also is the world.[8]

77. "Though he has not seen the sun . . . the other is better off than the one" (Eccles. 6:5). R. Phinehas said: The verse may be understood by the parable of two men sailing on a ship. When they came to a harbor, one got off the ship, went into the city, and saw much food and much drink there. On returning to the ship, he asked the other, "Why did you not go into the city?" The other: "And you, who did go into the city—what did you see?" "I saw much food and much drink." The other: "Did you enjoy any of it?" "No." The other: "I, who did not go into the city, am much better off than you." Hence, "the other is better off than the one."[9]

78. "A good name is better than precious oil, and the day of death better than the day of one's birth" (Eccles. 7:1). When a person is born, all rejoice; when he dies, all weep. It should not be so. When a person is born, all should not rejoice over him, because it is not known what he will be like when grown and what his deeds will be—whether righteous or wicked, good or evil. When he dies, however, if he departs with a good name and leaves the world in peace, people should rejoice.

R. Levi said: The matter may be illustrated by the parable of two vessels sailing the Great [Mediterranean] Sea, one leaving the harbor and the other entering it. As the one left the harbor, all rejoiced over it, but as the other entered the harbor, all did not rejoice. A clever man who was there said to the people, "As I see it, things should be the other way. When a vessel leaves the harbor, all should not rejoice, because they do not know what its lot will be—what seas it will encounter, what storms it will face. But when a vessel enters the harbor all should rejoice over it, for they then know that it has come back safely from the sea and has safely entered the harbor."

It was of this that Solomon said, "The day of death is better than the day of one's birth."[10]

79. R. Berekhiah said: "The time when one is born is to be like the time when one dies" (Eccles. 3:2). Happy is the man who at the time of his death is [as free of sin] as at the time of his birth.[11]

80. When a man's time to die comes, all have power over him, as Cain said, "It will come to pass, that whosoever findeth me will slay me" (Gen. 4:14).[12]

81. We have been taught that R. Simeon ben Gamaliel said: For a day-old infant, alive, the Sabbath may be desecrated. But for David, king of Israel, dead, the Sabbath may not be desecrated.

R. Simeon ben Eleazar said: A day-old infant, alive,

1. Yelammedenu in Yalkut, Prov., §943.
2. See Judg. 1:26.
3. B. Sot 46b.
4. A city where people live forever.
5. B. Suk 53a.
6. B. BB 175a.
7. Eccles. R. 5:14, §1.

8. Ibid.
9. Eccles. R. 6:5, §1; Yalkut, Eccles., §972.
10. Exod. R. 48:1; Eccles. R. 7:1, §4.
11. P. Meg 1:9, 71c.
12. B. Ned 41a.

requires no protection from a weasel or from rats. But Og, king of Bashan, dead, must be protected from a weasel or from rats, for Noah and his children were told, "The fear of you and the dread of you shall be upon every beast of the earth" (Gen. 9:2)—as long as a man is alive, the fear of him is laid upon creatures; once he is dead, such fear ceases.[1]

82. "The dead cannot praise the Lord" (Ps. 115:17). A man should always occupy himself with Torah and good deeds before he dies. Once he is dead, the obligation of Torah and good deeds ceases, and the Holy One gets no praise from him. With regard to this, R. Yohanan cited the verse "Among the dead I am released"[2] (Ps. 88:6)—when a man dies, he is released from the obligation of Torah and good deeds.[3]

83. At the time of a man's departure from the world, nothing but Torah and good deeds accompany him.[4]

84. In his lifetime, a man has three friends: his sons, his wealth, and good deeds. At the time of his departure from the world, should he gather his sons and say to them, "I beg of you, come and save me from the punishment of death," they will reply, "Have you not heard that there is no prevailing over the day of death? Is it not written, 'No man can by any means redeem his kin' [Ps. 49:8]? Therefore, go in peace and rest on your couch." At this, he gathers his wealth and says, "For you I labored night and day; I beg of you, redeem me from death." But his wealth replies, "Have you not heard that 'wealth is of no avail on the day of passing away' [Prov. 11:4]?" Then he gathers his good deeds, to whom he says, "Come and save me from death—do not let me depart from the world." They reply, "Go in peace. Even before you arrive [in heaven], we shall have come before you, as is said, 'Thy charity shall go before thee' " (Isa. 58:8).[5]

85. "Give ear, all ye weasellike inhabitants"[6] (Ps. 49:2). Why does the psalm liken the inhabitants of the world to a weasel? Because, just as a weasel drags things in and stores them without knowing for whom it is storing them, so the inhabitants of the world drag things in and store them without knowing for whom they store them. "He heapeth up riches, and knoweth not who shall gather them" (Ps. 39:7).[7]

86. "He hath made everything beautiful in its time; also He hath caused to be hidden from their hearts" (Eccles. 3:11). The word *ha-'olam* [*h-'vlm*], "world," spelled here defectively without the letter *vav*, is to be read *he'elim* [*h'lm*], "caused to be hidden." Had not the Holy One hidden the day of death from the heart of man, no man would build a house or plant a vineyard, for he would say, "Tomorrow I may die—why should I get up and weary myself for the sake of others?" Therefore the Holy One hid the day of death from human beings, in order that a man will go on building and planting. If he merits it, it will be his; if he does not merit it, it will be for others.[8]

87. The sons of R. Hiyya went out regularly to cultivate their fields. Consequently, they forgot their studies to such an extent that they had trouble remembering anything. So one asked the other, "Does our [deceased] father know of our trouble?" The other replied, "How could he know? Does not Scripture say, 'Even if his sons are burdened by trouble, he does not know' (Job 14:21)?"[9] The one objected, "But does it not also say, 'He still feels the pain of his flesh, and his spirit mourns in him' [Job. 14:22], regarding which R. Isaac said, 'Worms in a corpse's flesh are as painful as a needle in the flesh of the living'?"

The dead feel their own pain, but they do not feel the pain of others.[10]

88. Zeiri was in the habit of depositing his money with his landlady. [One day] during the time he went to the house of study and came back, she died. So he went seeking her in the cemetery and asked, "Where is my money?" She replied, "Go and take it from under the door socket in such-and-such a place. And tell my mother to send me a comb and a kohl tube with such-and-such a woman, who [will die] tomorrow and come to be with me."[11]

89. Whenever R. Yohanan finished reading the book of Job, he would say: The end of man is to die, and the end of an animal is to be slaughtered. All are doomed to death. Happy is he who was brought up on the Torah, whose labor was in the Torah, and who thus gave pleasure to his Creator; [happy is he] who grew up to earn a good name and who departed from the world with a good name. Of him, Solomon said, "A good name is better than precious oil, and the day of death than the day of one's birth" (Eccles. 7:1).[12]

Man's Soul

90. "Neither root nor branch" (Mal. 3:19). "Root" is the soul, and "branch" is the body.[13]

91. Antoninus [Caesar] asked Rabbi [Judah I, the Patriarch]: When is the soul placed in a man—at the time of the [heavenly] decree [commanding conception] or at

1. B. Shab 151b.
2. JV: "set apart among the dead."
3. B. Shab 30a.
4. Avot 6:9.
5. Cf. the medieval morality play *Everyman*. PRE 34.
6. JV: "inhabitants of the world." But *heled* ("world") also means "weasel."
7. P. Shab 14:1, 14c.
8. Tanhuma, *Kedoshim*, §8; Yalkut, Eccles., §968.
9. JV: "His sons came to honor and he knoweth it not." But the stem *kbd* may mean "burdened by trouble" as well as "honor."
10. B. Ber 18b.
11. Ibid.
12. B. Ber 17a.
13. B. Sanh 110b.

the time of the embryo's creation? Rabbi: At the time of its creation. Antoninus: Can a piece of unsalted meat remain three days without becoming putrid? It must therefore be at the time conception is decreed. Later, Rabbi used to say: Antoninus taught me this matter, and Scripture supports him, for it says, "My spirit preserves me at the time of Thy decree" (Job 10:12).[1]

92. With regard to whom did David say five times, "Bless the Lord, O my soul"? He said these words with regard to the Holy One and with regard to the soul. As the Holy One fills the entire world, so the soul fills the entire body. As the Holy One sees but is not seen, so the soul sees but is not seen. As the Holy One sustains the entire world, all of it, so the soul sustains the entire body. As the Holy One is pure, so the soul is pure. As the Holy One dwells in chambers that are innermost, so the soul dwells in chambers that are innermost. Therefore let him [i.e., man] who has these five characteristics come and praise Him who has these five characteristics.[2]

93. The breath of life is known by five names: life, spirit, soul, the solitary, the one that lives on. "Life" refers to the blood, as is said, "For the blood is the life" (Deut. 12:23). "Spirit" refers to its capacity to go up and down, as is said, "Who knoweth the spirit of man whether it goeth upward" (Eccles. 3:21). "Soul" refers to man's distinctive character. "The solitary": while all other parts of the body are pairs, this one is solitary in the body. "The one that lives on": while all other parts die, it lives on in the body.

The soul fills the entire body, and when a man is asleep, it goes up and draws new life for him from above.[3]

94. The words "Unto Thee, O Lord, do I lift up my soul" (Ps. 25:1) are to be considered in the light of the verse "Into Thy hand I commit my spirit. Thou restorest . . . for Thou, O Lord, art God of truth" (Ps. 31:6). As matters go in the world, a man with whom things are left for safekeeping may confuse one man's things with a second man's things, and the second man's things with the first man's, for some things are not easily told apart. But with the Holy One, there is no such confusion, for "Thou, O Lord, art God of truth" (ibid.). Thus, is it conceivable that a man could rise in the morning and seek his spirit but not find it? Or that he could find his spirit in another's possession, or another's spirit in his possession? Hence it is said, "Thou restorest [what is left with Thee for safekeeping], for Thou, O Lord, art God of truth."

R. Alexandri said: A mortal in whose possession new things are left for safekeeping and with whom the things remain a long time returns them worn and used. Not so the Holy One: With Him, things worn and used are left for safekeeping, and He returns them as good as new. You can see for yourself that this is true: a worker labors the whole day, and his spirit within him grows weary and worn. But when he goes to sleep, he deposits his spirit with the Holy One, and at dawn it returns to his body a new creation, as is said, "[Spirits] are new every morning; great is Thy faithfulness" (Lam. 3:23).[4]

Man's Delight

95. Rav said to R. Hamnuna: My son, if you have the means, treat yourself well. For in Sheol there is no delight, and death is not to be postponed. Should you say, "I will make provisions for my children"—who can tell in what order people will arrive in Sheol?[5] Human beings are like the herbs of the field—some may be blossoming at the time others are wilting.

Samuel said to R. Judah: Keen scholar, snatch and eat, snatch and drink. The world, which we all must leave, lasts no longer than a wedding feast.[6]

96. R. Yose said: A person may not mortify himself by fasting, lest [he fall ill and] become a charge on the community, which will then have to maintain him.

R. Judah said in the name of Rav: What is R. Yose's reason? Because in saying, "And let man become a live soul" (Gen. 2:7), Scripture means: Keep alive the soul I gave you.[7]

97. We have been taught that R. Eleazar ha-Kappar Berabbi said: "And he shall make atonement for him for that he sinned against a soul" (Num. 6:11). But against what soul has the Nazirite sinned?[8] Rather, the verse means that because he afflicted himself through abstention from wine [he sinned against his own soul]. The matter may be argued *a fortiori*: if one who has afflicted himself only by abstaining from wine is called a sinner, how much more by far one who afflicts himself by abstaining from everything. Hence, it follows that one who keeps fasting is called a sinner.[9]

98. We have been taught that Simeon the Righteous said: I have never eaten of the guilt offering brought by a Nazirite who had become defiled,[10] except once. On that occasion a Nazirite [who had become defiled] came up from the south [to bring his guilt offering and shave off the hair of his head].[11] When I saw that he had beautiful eyes, was handsome in appearance, and his curly hair was arranged in symmetrical locks, I asked him, "My son, what was your reason [for becoming a Nazirite, so that now, having become unclean], you must destroy the beautiful hair of

1. God's decree to the spirit to enter a particular drop of semen at the time of conception. See above in this chapter, §6. JV: "Thy providence hath preserved my spirit." B. Sanh 91b.
2. B. Ber 10a.
3. Gen. R. 14:9.
4. MTeh 25:2.
5. Your children may precede you. Cf. Ecclesiasticus 14:11–12.
6. B. Er 54a.
7. B. Ta 22b; Tos Ta 2:12.
8. He did not hurt anyone's soul—he merely denied his body some pleasure.
9. B. Ned 10a.
10. He regarded as a sin the abstention from wine, which Naziriteship required, and therefore would not partake of the guilt offering a Nazirite who had inadvertently become ritually unclean had to bring.
11. See Num. 6:9.

your head?" He replied, "While grazing my father's sheep in my town, I went to draw water from a well and looked at my reflection in the water, whereupon my impulse to evil rushed upon me and endeavored to drive me out of the world [by tempting me to admire my hair]. But I said to it, " 'Wicked one! Why, in a world that is not yours, do you vaunt yourself over one who is destined to turn into worms and maggots? By the Temple service, I swear that I will shave off [the hair on my head] for the sake of Heaven.' "[1] I immediately arose and kissed him on his head, saying, "My son, may there be many Nazirites like you in Israel! Of your [vow to be a Nazirite], Scripture says, 'A Nazirite's vow to set himself apart belongs to the Lord' " (Num. 6:2).[2]

99. Who is a pious fool? He who sees a ripe fig and says, "[Instead of enjoying it myself], I will give it to the first man I meet."[3]

100. Sages said in the name of Rav: A man will have to give reckoning and account for everything that his eye saw and he did not eat.

So concerned was R. Eleazar with carrying out this tradition that he used to collect small change and use it [to purchase bits of new produce]. Thus, throughout the year he was able to taste every kind of food at least once.[4]

101. He who destroys anything from which enjoyment may be derived transgresses "Thou shalt not destroy" (Deut. 20:19).[5]

102. Three things restore a man's spirit: [beautiful] sounds, sights, and scents. Three things increase a man's self-esteem: a beautiful home, a beautiful wife, and beautiful clothes.[6]

103. Spend less on your food and drink, and more on your dwelling.[7]

104. "I forgot what happiness was" (Lam. 3:17) refers, said R. Isaac Nappaha, to a beautiful bed and the beautiful spread on it.[8]

105. At the sight of comely human beings and beautiful trees, one should say, "Blessed be He who has created beautiful creatures."[9]

106. At the sight of beautiful creatures and beautiful trees, one should say, "Blessed be He who has such in His world."[10]

107. "As when new wine is present in the cluster, one saith: 'Destroy it not—a blessing is to be spoken over it' " (Isa. 65:8). There is the story of a pious man who went out to his vineyard on the Sabbath and saw a ripe cluster. [Though he could not pick it because of the Sabbath], he spoke a blessing over it, saying, "This cluster deserves to have a blessing said over it."[11]

108. If a man says no more than "How beautiful is this bread! Blessed be He who is everywhere for having created it," that is sufficient blessing over the bread.[12]

109. There is the story of Rabban Simeon ben Gamaliel, who, while standing on an ascent to the Temple Mount, saw a very beautiful gentile woman. He exclaimed, "How noble are Thy works, O Lord" (Ps. 104:24).

On the other hand, when R. Akiva saw the wife of the wicked tyrant Rufus, he spat, laughed, and wept: spat, because she came from a putrid drop; laughed, because she was eventually to become a proselyte, and he was to wed her; wept, because such beauty would waste in the dust.[13]

110. R. Abbahu taught: What is the proof that the Holy One admires men of high stature? The verse "I destroyed the Amorite . . . whose height was like the height of the cedars" (Amos 2:9).[14]

111. R. Judah said: He who goes outdoors in the days of Nisan and sees trees blooming should say, "Blessed be He who has His world lack nothing and who has created in it goodly creatures and goodly trees for the joy of mankind."

Mar Zutra bar Tobiah said in the name of Rav: What is the proof that one must say a blessing over a fragrant aroma? The verse "Let every breath praise the Lord" (Ps. 150:6). What is the thing that breath enjoys? A fragrant aroma.[15]

112. "No one to converse with (*siah*, 'tree') in the field" (Gen. 2:5). All trees converse (*mesihin*),[16] as it were, with one another. Indeed, one may add, all trees converse with mortals; all trees—created, as trees were, to provide fellowship[17] for mortals.[18]

113. "He that is dead is to be put to death" (Deut. 17:6). While still alive, the wicked is considered the same as dead, because he sees the sun shining but does not say the blessing "He that forms light"; he sees it set but does

1. As required at the end of the period of Naziriteship. Num. 6:13–18.
2. B. Ned 9b.
3. P. Sot 3:4, 19a.
4. P. Kid 4:9, 66d.
5. Midrash Aggadah, *Shofetim* (ed. Buber [Vienna, 1894], p. 199).
6. B. Ber 57b.
7. B. Pes 114a.
8. B. Shab 25b.
9. Tos Ber 6:4.
10. B. Ber 58b.
11. Gen. R. 29:2.
12. Tos Ber 4:4.
13. B. AZ 20a and En Yaakov, ad loc.
14. B. Bekh 45b.
15. B. Ber 43b.
16. The usual word for "tree" is *etz*. Hence *siah* ("conversation"), used instead, is construed in a dual sense: "tree" and "converse, provide fellowship." JV: "Every tree (*siah*) in the field."
17. "Fellowship"—Gen. R. TA; BR: "benefit."
18. Gen. R. 13:2.

not say the blessing "Who bringest on evenings." He eats and drinks but does not say grace. The righteous, however, bless God for each and every thing they eat and drink, see and hear.[1]

Food and Drink

114. R. Avdimi of Haifa said: Before a man eats and drinks, he [being distraught] has two hearts [as it were]. After he eats and drinks, he has but one heart.[2]

115. "He who does good to his own person is a man of mercy" (Prov. 11:17), as may be inferred from what Hillel the Elder once said. After bidding farewell to his disciples, he kept walking along with them. His disciples asked him, "Master, where are you going?" He replied, "To do a good turn to a guest in my house." They said, "Every day you seem to have a guest." He replied, "Is not my poor soul a guest in my body—here today and tomorrow here no longer?"[3]

116. Even if you do no more than go up to the roof [of your own house], take your victuals with you. Even if a hundred pumpkins cost but one *zuz* in town, be sure to have some under your skirts [before you set out to go there].[4]

117. The sages taught in the name of R. Meir: Chew well with your teeth, and you will find [strength] in your legs.[5]

118. A proverb says: The stomach carries the legs.[6]

119. He who prolongs the meal at his table has his days and years prolonged. Why? Because a poor man may come along and the host will give him something to eat. In this connection, it is written, "The altar of wood three cubits high" (Ezek. 41:22), and also, "He said unto me: 'This is the table that is before the Lord' " (ibid.). Why does the verse begin by calling it an altar and end by calling it a table? Because, as R. Yohanan and R. Eleazar both said, as long as the Temple stood, the altar made expiation for Israel, but now a man's table makes expiation for him.[7]

120. Our masters taught: "When the Lord thy God shall enlarge thy border, as He hath promised thee, and thou shalt say, I want to eat meat" (Deut. 12:20). The Torah here teaches the rule of conduct that a person should not eat meat unless he has an urge to eat it. One might suppose that a person may buy meat in the market and eat it; Scripture therefore states, "Thou mayest slaughter of thy cattle and of thy sheep" (Deut. 12:2) [but not those bought in a market]. One might then suppose that he may slaughter all his cattle and eat, all his sheep[8] and eat; the text therefore states, "Of thy cattle," and not all your cattle; "of thy sheep," and not all your sheep. Hence R. Eleazar ben Azariah said, A man whose entire possessions amount to a *maneh* may buy a *litra* of vegetables for his stew; if he has ten *maneh*, he may buy a *litra* of fish for his stew; if he has fifty *maneh*, he may buy a *litra* of meat for his stew; if he has a hundred *maneh*, he may have a full pot of meat put on for him every day. And how often are the others to cook meat? Only on Sabbath eve.

Rav said: We must defer to the opinion of the venerable [R. Eleazar].

R. Yohanan said: Abba[9] comes from a healthy family [and can get along without meat]. But as for us, he who has a penny in his purse should hasten with it to the shopkeeper [to buy meat].

R. Nahman said, As for us, we must even borrow to eat [meat].

"The lambs are for thy clothing" (Prov. 27:26). Your clothing should be of the fleece of your own lambs. "The he-goats, the price of a field" (ibid.). It is better for a person to sell his field and buy he-goats [with the proceeds] than to sell his he-goats and buy a field. "The goats' milk will suffice" (Prov. 27:27). The man will then find the goats' milk and the lambs in his house sufficient to provide for his sundry needs [and he need not slaughter the mothers for meat]. "For thy food, for the food of thy household" (ibid.)—your own sustenance thus has priority over the sustenance of your household. "And life for thy maidens" (ibid.). Mar Zutra son of R. Nahman said: [By disciplining] your maidens, give them life. Here the Torah teaches the rule of conduct that a parent should not accustom his child to meat and wine.[10]

121. A stubborn and rebellious son is condemned because of what he will become in the end.

We have been taught that R. Yose the Galilean said: Is it conceivable that merely because the young man ate a *tartemar*[11] of meat and drank a *log* of Italian wine, the Torah would decree that he be brought before the High Court and put to death by stoning? However, the Torah foresaw the ultimate end of the young man sentenced as a disloyal and defiant son. For in the end, after dissipating his father's possessions, he would continue to seek what he had become accustomed to and, when unable to get it, would go out to a crossroads and commit robbery. Therefore the Torah said, "Let him die while yet innocent, and let him not die guilty." For the death of the wicked benefits themselves and the world, while the death of the righteous injures themselves and the world. Sleep and wine of the

1. Tanhuma, *Berakhah*, §7.
2. B. BB 12b.
3. Lev. R. 34:4.
4. B. Pes 113a.
5. B. Shab 152a.
6. Gen. R. 70:8.
7. B. Ber 54b–55a and En Yaakov, ad loc.
8. If, say, he has only one head of cattle or sheep.
9. Rav's given name. The name Rav, by which he is generally referred to, means "the master."
10. B. Hul 84a.
11. Half a *litra*.

wicked benefit themselves and the world;[1] sleep and wine of the righteous injure themselves and the world.[2]

122. People say: Your belly you fill, all kinds of ill.[3]

123. If a man is not privileged to have words of Torah enter his innards, let him entreat God's mercy that not too much food and drink enter his innards [so that poverty, if not Torah, will purify him], as is said, "I have purged thee through the furnace of poverty" (Isa. 48:10). As you can put into a furnace every kind of wood there is in the world, and the furnace will burn them all up and consume them, so you can put into a man's gullet every kind of food in the world, and the gullet will take it all in.[4]

124. R. Hisda said: He who can eat barley bread but eats wheat bread [is guilty of waste, and therefore] violates "Thou shalt not destroy" (Deut. 20:19).

R. Papa said: He who can drink beer but drinks wine [is guilty of] waste and therefore violates "Thou shalt not destroy."

But neither of the two opinions is right. The injunction [to care for and] not to destroy one's body has priority.[5]

125. In the west [the Land of Israel], there is a proverb: "He who devours the fat-tail (*aliata*) must hide in the loft (*illita*);[6] but he who is content to eat cress (*kikule*) may lie in a place as public as a dunghill (*kikele*)."[7]

126. A certain man turned his slave over to a friend to have him teach the slave how to prepare a thousand kinds of dishes. Since the friend taught the slave only eight hundred, the man summoned him to a lawsuit before Rabbi [Judah I, the Patriarch]. But Rabbi [dismissing the complaint] remarked [to the plaintiff]: Our fathers said, "We have forgotten prosperous living" (Lam. 3:17) [so they conceivably knew such abundance of dishes]. But as for us, we have never even laid eyes on such abundance [so it is remarkable that your friend has taught as many as eight hundred dishes to your slave].[8]

127. The world can live without wine, but the world cannot live without water. The world can live without pepper, but the world cannot live without salt.[9]

128. "From all toil there is some gain," etc. (Prov. 14:23), as may be seen, said R. Simeon bar Abba, from the difference between one who drinks water he took the trouble to boil first and one who drinks water that is cold.[10]

There was a certain man in Sepphoris—some say that it was R. Simeon bar Abba—who used to gather bones [to give them proper burial]. When he saw black bones, he would say, "These are of persons who drank [cold] water." When they were reddish, he would say, "These are of persons who drank wine."[11] When they were white, he would say, "These are of persons who drank hot water."[12]

129. R. Helbo said: It was Phrygian wine and the baths of Emmaus that cut off the ten tribes from Israel.[13] R. Eleazar ben Arakh happened to visit there. He was attracted to its luxuries, and his learning was forgotten. Upon his return, when he arose to read in the Torah scroll, instead of reading, "*Ha-hodesh ha-zeh lakhem*" (Exod. 12:1), he read, "*Ha-horesh hayah libbam.*"[14] The sages besought mercy in his behalf, and his learning was restored to him.[15]

130. We have been taught that R. Meir said: The tree whose fruit Adam ate was a vine, for nothing brings as much woe to man as wine.[16] R. Judah said: It was the wheat plant, for an infant cannot say "Papa" or "Mama" before he has savored the taste of wheat. R. Nehemiah said: It was a fig tree, for, with the very plant with which they disgraced themselves, they were enabled to set themselves right, as is said, "And they sewed fig leaves together" (Gen. 3:7).[17]

131. "Wine (*yayin*) and new wine (*tirosh*) destroy the mind" (Hos. 4:11). Why is wine called *yayin*, and why is it called *tirosh*? It is called *yayin*, said R. Isaac, because it brings (*yelalah*) woe to the world; it is called *tirosh* because he who debauches himself with it becomes poor (*rosh*).[18]

132. "A man who ogles the cup believes himself to be walking on smooth ground" (Prov. 23:31).[19] When a man [lovingly] ogles his cup, the world before him, all of it, appears to be smooth [with neither hollows nor hills].

R. Yohanan said: The *ketiv* [the text as written] is

1. Since they are incapable of inflicting injury while asleep or sodden with wine.
2. B. Sanh 71b–72a.
3. B. Ber 32a.
4. Yalkut, *Va-et'hannan*, §830; TdE, p. 133 (JPS, pp. 328–29).
5. B. Shab 140b.
6. Because he has squandered his money on costly food, he fears his creditors.
7. Not being in debt, he fears no one. B. Pes 114a.
8. B. Ned 50b.
9. P. Hor 3:6, 48c.
10. Heated water aids digestion and, when boiled, is free from pollution.
11. The color was taken to indicate that, because of the wine, the blood had so increased in the body that it had even suffused the bones.
12. Gen. R. 89:1; Yalkut, Prov., §950.
13. Preoccupied with such luxuries, they neglected the study of Torah and lost their faith.
14. The words mean: "This month shall be unto you." What R. Eleazar came up with made no sense: "The plowman was their heart." He could not even distinguish any longer between letters that appear similar.
15. B. Shab 147b.
16. Here there may be a play on words: *yayin* ("wine") and *taniyya veaniyya* ("mourning and moaning").
17. B. Sanh 70a–b.
18. "The first is a play on '*ya, ya*,' exclamation of woe, the second on the second syllable of *tirosh*, which is connected with *rosh*, 'to become poor,' as if *tirosh* meant, 'You will become poor' " (Yoma, Soncino, p. 372, n. 1). B. Yoma 76b.
19. JV: "When it giveth its color in the cup, when it glideth down smoothly." But *ayin* ("color") also means "eye."

kis, "the wallet," while the *keri* [the text as read] is *kos*, "cup," implying that even as the drunkard ogles the cup, the wine seller ogles the drunkard's wallet.[1]

133. As wine enters each and every part of a man's body, it grows lax, and his mind is confused. Once wine enters, reason leaves. Wherever there is wine, reason is no more. When wine comes in, a secret (*sod*) goes out, as intimated by the fact that the numerical value of the letters in *yayin*, "wine," equals seventy,[2] and the numerical value of the letters in *sod* likewise equals seventy.[3]

Man's sources of conscience and reason are distributed in four areas of the body: two portions in the two kidneys,[4] one portion in the heart, and one portion in the mouth. The sources of both conscience and reason are thus located in these four organs. Correspondingly, the sages have given the number four as the measure of drunkenness, that is, four fourths of a *log* of undiluted wine, which is the same as four cups. After a man drinks one cup, which equals one-fourth of a *log*, he loses one-fourth of his intellect. After he drinks two cups, one-half of his intellect leaves him. After he drinks three cups, three-fourths of his intellect leaves him, and his mind is so confused that he begins to speak incoherently. After he drinks the fourth cup, all his intellect leaves him, all his reins are dulled, his mind is confused, and his tongue is tied. He tries to speak but cannot, for his tongue is weighted down.[5]

134. R. Tanhuma said: Wine—its own mother [the vine] cannot stand up under the weight of the juice in the grapes, and you expect to stand up under it? Though the vine is propped up with many reeds and many pronged rods, it cannot stand up [and sags] under the weight of the juice in the grapes. And you expect to stand up under wine?[6]

135. As Noah was about to plant a vineyard, the demon Shamdon met him and suggested: Take me into partnership, but beware, do not trespass into my part. If you do, I will do you harm.[7]

136. When Noah began planting, Satan came by, stationed himself before him, and asked, "What are you planting?" Noah: "A vineyard." Satan: "What is its nature?" Noah: "Its fruit, whether fresh or dried, is sweet, and from it wine is made, which gladdens a man's heart." Satan: "Would you like the two of us, me and you, to plant it together?" Noah: "Very well."

What did Satan do? He brought a ewe lamb and slaughtered it over the vine; then he brought a lion, which he likewise slaughtered over the vine; then a monkey, which he also slaughtered over the vine; and finally a pig, which he again slaughtered over the vine. And with the blood that dripped from them, he watered the vineyard.

The charade was Satan's way of saying that when a man drinks one cup [of wine], he acts like a ewe lamb, humble and meek. When he drinks two, he becomes as mighty as a lion and proceeds to brag extravagantly, saying, "Who is like me?" When he drinks three or four cups, he becomes like a monkey, hopping about, dancing, giggling, and uttering obscenities in public, without realizing what he is doing. Finally, when he becomes blind drunk, he is like a pig, wallowing in mire and coming to rest among refuse.[8]

137. One cup is becoming for a woman; two degrade her. After three, she brazenly solicits sex. After four, she will demand it without a scruple, even of an ass in the marketplace.[9]

138. Wherever you find wine, you will find downfall.[10]

139. Do not get drunk, and you will not sin.[11]

140. R. Isaac said: What is meant by "Look not upon the wine because it reddens" (Prov. 23:31)? Look not upon the wine, because it reddens the faces of the wicked in this world but makes them pale [with shame] in the world-to-come.

Rava read the verse "Look not upon the wine, because it *yitaddam*; in the end it leads to the shedding of blood (*dam*)."[12]

141. There was a man who used to drink twelve jugs of wine every day. One day, after having drunk only eleven, he lay down, but sleep did not come to him. So he got up during the night, went to the keeper of the tavern, and said to him, "Sell me a jug of wine." The keeper of the tavern: "I will not open the inn for you. It is now night, and I am afraid of the town's watchmen." As the man raised his eyes, he saw a hole in the [front] door, so he said to the keeper of the tavern, "Give me some wine through this hole—you pour it out from within, and I shall drink it from without." The keeper did that for the man, who drank and fell asleep in front of the tavern door. The watchmen passed by, took him for a thief, and beat and bruised him. To this man applies the passage "Who hath wounds without cause? Who hath bleary eyes? Those whom the wine keeps till the small hours" (Prov. 23:29–30)—those who are the first to enter a tavern and the last to leave it.[13]

---

1. On *ketiv* and *keri*, see the Glossary. B. Yoma 75a; Tanhuma, *Shemoni*, §5. Midrash Prov. 23:29 (ed. Buber, p. 95).
2. *Yod* (10) + *Yod* (10) + *nun* (50) = 70.
3. *Samekh* (60) + *vav* (6) + *dalet* (4) = 70.
4. The kidneys are conceived in the Bible and in the Talmud as the seat of moral conscience as well as of intellectual deliberation. See H. A. Wolfson, *Philo* (Cambridge, Mass., 1947) 2:185 and n. 124.
5. Num. R. 10:8; Tanhuma, *Shemoni*, §5.
6. Lev. R. 12:4.
7. Gen. R. 36:3 and 31:14.
8. All the above befell Noah. Tanhuma, *Noah*, §13.
9. B. Ket 65a.
10. Tanhuma, *Noah*, §21.
11. B. Ber 29b.
12. B. Sanh 70a.
13. Lev. R. 12:1.

142. A little wine is fine; a lot is not.[1]

143. At the head of all healing [when taken in moderation] am I—wine. At the head of all death [when not taken in moderation] am I—wine. Only where there is no wine are drugs required.[2]

144. R. Kahana explained an inconsistency: the word for "wine" is spelled *tirash* but pronounced *tirosh*. If a man merits it, wine makes him *rosh*, "chief"; if not, it makes him *rash*, "a poor man."

Rava explained another inconsistency: as spelled, the text reads, "Wine that desolates [*yeshammah*]" (Ps. 104:15), but we pronounce the last word "*yesammah* [that maketh glad]." If a man merits it, wine makes him glad; if not, it desolates him. That is what Rava meant when he said: Wine and spices stimulate my mind.[3]

145. R. Samuel bar Nahmani said in the name of R. Jonathan: What is the proof that [the Levites'] song of praise [to God] is sung only over wine?[4] From the verse "And the vine said unto them: Should I leave my wine, which cheereth God and men?" (Judg. 9:13) we understand how wine cheers men, but how does it cheer God? We must therefore conclude that the words "cheereth God" refer to the song of praise [to God], which is to be sung only over wine.[5]

146. No rejoicing [before God] is possible except with wine.[6]

147. Samuel said to R. Judah: Keen scholar, open your feed bag and until you are forty, while food is beneficial, let your food come in; from then on, drink is more beneficial.[7]

148. Aged wine delights the palate of aged men.[8]

149. R. Aha said: There is the story of a man who kept selling his household goods and drinking up the proceeds in wine. So, saying, "[At this rate] our father will leave nothing for us," his sons plied him with drink, made him drunk, took him out of the city, and left him in a cemetery. Just then, some wine merchants happened to pass the gate of the cemetery. When they heard that in the city there was a roundup for compulsory labor service, they left their loads in the cemetery and went to see what was going on in town. In the meantime, the man woke up from his sleep and, seeing a wineskin above his head, untied it and put its opening to his mouth. Three days later, the man's sons said, "Should we not go see what our father is doing?" They got to the cemetery, found him with the wineskin at his mouth, and said, "Even here your Creator has not forsaken you. Since it is He who provides you with wine, we really don't know what to do about you." So they came to an understanding among themselves that each of them in turn was to provide him daily with wine to drink.[9]

150. There was a pious man whose father drank much wine, and every time he collapsed in the marketplace, boys would come, pelt him with stones and pebbles, and mock him: "Look at the drunk!" When his pious son saw this, he was so humiliated that he wanted to die. So every day he would say to his father, "Papa, I will send word and have delivered to your own home all the kinds of wine that are sold in this city, just so you won't have to go to the tavern to drink, for you bring shame upon me and upon yourself." Every day he spoke this way once and twice, until finally the father promised him that he would not go to drink in the tavern. Thereafter, every morning and evening, the pious son would prepare food and drink for his father, put him to sleep in his bed, and then leave him. One time, when it was raining, the pious son went out in the marketplace on his way to the synagogue for prayer and saw a drunkard lying in the marketplace. A stream of rainwater was pouring down upon him, and older and younger boys were pelting him with stones and pebbles, and throwing mud at his face, even into his mouth. When the pious son saw this, he said to himself: I will go get Papa, bring him here, and show him this drunkard and the shame children and teenagers heap upon him—perhaps he will learn to restrain his mouth from drinking in taverns and getting drunk. And so he did: he brought him to the marketplace and showed him the drunkard. But what did his old father do? He went over to the drunkard and asked him in what tavern he had drunk the wine that got him so drunk.[10]

Proper Order and Manners at a Feast

151. What is the proper order at a feast? The guests enter [the waiting room] and sit down on benches or high-backed chairs until all the guests have arrived. After all have arrived, water is brought for washing the hands, each guest washing only his [right] hand.[11] A cup of wine is mixed for them, and each one says the blessing by himself. Then appetizers are brought, and each one says the blessing by himself. After that, they go up to the dining area and recline. Again water is brought to wash the hands. Even though each guest has already washed one hand, he now washes again—both hands. Another cup of wine is mixed for the guests. Even though each guest had already said a blessing over the first cup, another blessing is said over the second cup, but now one guest says it for all the others. More appetizers are brought. Even though each guest had already said a blessing at the first serving, an-

1. DEZ 7.
2. B. BB 58b.
3. B. Yoma 76b.
4. When poured on the altar as a libation at the daily offering.
5. B. Ber 35a.
6. B. Pes 109a.
7. B. Shab 152a.
8. B. Meg 16b.
9. Lev. R. 12:1
10. Tanhuma, *Shemini*, §11.
11. The hand used to pick up the appetizers served before the meal.

other blessing is said over the second serving, but now one guest says it for all the others. After three servings of appetizers, no additional guest may enter.[1]

R. Simeon ben Gamaliel said: In Jerusalem there was the strict custom that, as long as napkins were draped over the door, guests might continue to enter. Once the napkins were removed, no more guests were permitted to enter.

There was another strict custom in Jerusalem. The preparation for the feast was turned over to a caterer. If any item in the feast was spoiled, he was fined, the fine varying with the status of the host and that of the guests.

Pieces of bread [served to the guests] were an important sign for them. As long as the guests saw such pieces of bread, they knew that another course would follow. But when they saw a whole loaf,[2] they knew that no more courses were to follow at this feast.[3]

152. What is the order of reclining? When there are two couches, the senior person reclines first on the first couch and the junior one on the second couch, next to the senior's feet. When there are three couches, the senior reclines first on the middle couch, the junior on the couch next to the senior's head, and the third in seniority on the couch next to the senior's feet. The same order is followed if there are more than three couches.

What is the order for washing one's hands [before the meal]? If there are fewer than five guests, the washing begins with the senior guest. If there are five guests or more, the washing begins with the junior guest, until the fifth guest's turn. Then the customary order is resumed, the washing of hands beginning with the senior. So, too, with the washing of the hands after the meal—the person with whom the customary order of washing the hands resumes is the one who pronounces the appropriate blessing.

What is the order of mixing the cup of wine? During the meal, it begins with the senior. After the meal, it begins with the person who leads in the saying of grace. If he wishes to yield the honor to his teacher or to his senior, he may do so.

When there are two guests, they must wait for each other in taking food from the bowl. If there are three, they need not wait. He who says the blessing [over the bread] may reach first for the food, but if he wishes to yield the honor to his teacher or his senior, he may do so.[4]

153. The scrupulous among the people of Jerusalem would not go to a feast until they learned who was to recline with them.[5]

154. One should break off a piece of bread only from the crusty part [of the loaf] and not from the soft part; nor should one seize with his hand a piece of bread the size of an egg, because one who does so is a glutton and a greedygut. Neither should one drain his cup of wine in one draft; if he does, he is a tippler and a greedygut. How many times should one pause before draining it? Twice, if he has good manners; three times, if he is a show-off.

A man should not start eating a head of garlic or onion before removing its peel. If he starts with the head unpeeled, he is both a glutton and a greedygut. He should not drink two cups [of wine] in reciting grace after meals, because it makes him appear like a tippler.[6]

155. A man should not be given to picking up [and eating] crumbs, emptying his bowl [to the last drop], and tippling.[7]

156. When two sit at a table, the senior guest should reach first for the food, and then the junior; if the junior reaches first, he is a glutton.

The story is told of R. Akiva, who prepared a meal for his disciples. Two dishes were served, one raw and the other cooked. When a raw vegetable was served, the well-mannered disciple took hold of its stalk with one hand and, with the other, tried to pluck it from its stem. When the stalk did not come off, he withdrew his hand and ate only the bread before him. But the ill-mannered disciple took hold of the stalk in one hand and bit it off with his teeth. R. Akiva said to him, "Don't do just that, my son—go ahead and put your foot on the vegetable in the dish!" After that, a cooked dish was served to them, of which they ate their fill. Then R. Akiva said to them, "My sons, I have served [the meal] the way I did only to test whether or not your manners are proper."[8]

157. R. Yose and R. Judah ate porridge [out of the same bowl]. One ate with his finger [as his spoon] and the other with a palm leaf. He who was eating with the palm leaf asked the one who ate with his finger, "How long will you make me eat the filth of your finger?" The one who ate with his finger replied to the one who ate with a palm leaf, "How long will you make me eat your spittle?"[9]

158. A man should not bite into a piece of bread and then give it to his fellow, because people's sense of delicacy varies.[10]

159. R. Abbahu said: Whoever eats bread without scouring his hands is as though he were eating food that is ritually unclean.[11]

160. Foodstuffs are not to be treated with contempt.[12]

161. Our masters taught: Four things have been said concerning bread. Raw meat should not be placed on

1. So that the host will not find himself short of food and be embarrassed.
2. Apparently they kept an unsliced loaf on the table for grace after meals.
3. Tos Ber 4:8–10 and 4:14; P. Ber 6:6, 10d.
4. B. Ber 46b–47a; Tos Ber 5:5–7.
5. B. Sanh 23a.
6. DER 6.
7. DEZ 6.
8. DER 7.
9. B. Ned 49b.
10. DER 9.
11. B. Sot 4b.
12. Sof 3.

bread; a full cup should not be passed along over bread;[1] bread should not be thrown; and a dish should not be propped up on bread.

There is the story of R. Akiva staying with a certain man who took a piece of bread and propped up his bowl with it. R. Akiva snatched up that piece of bread and ate it. The man asked: Master, have you no bread to eat other than the piece I was using to prop up my bowl? R. Akiva: I thought you would be "scalded" with tepid water,[2] but I now see that you are not scalded even with boiling water.[3]

162. It is unbecoming for a host to eat in his guest's presence without asking the guest to join him. It is more unbecoming for a guest to invite another guest. It is even more unbecoming to eat in the presence of a disciple of the wise [without inviting him to join]. More unbecoming than these three is for a guest to cause trouble to his host.[4]

163. R. Yohanan said: One should not talk during a meal, lest the windpipe precede the gullet [in swallowing the food] and thus endanger one's life.[5]

164. R. Huna son of R. Nathan visited the home of R. Nahman bar Isaac. When he was asked, "What is your name?" he replied, "Rav Huna." They said to him, "Will the master sit on the couch?" After he sat down, he was offered a cup, which he accepted at once and drained in two drafts. They then asked him, "Why did you call yourself Rav Huna?" "That is my rightful name." "Why, when you were told, 'Sit on the couch,' did you sit down without hesitation?" "Because whatever your host tells you to do, you must do, except depart." "Why, when you were offered a cup, did you accept at once?" "Because one must appear to be reluctant before a host who is his inferior, but not before a host who is his superior." "Why did you drain the cup in two drafts?" "Because we have been taught: 'He who drains his cup in one draft is a tippler; in two, is well bred; in three, is a show-off.' "[6]

165. The presumption is that no man would drink out of a cup without first examining it thoroughly.[7]

166. A man should not drink from a cup and then pass it to his fellow, because it may endanger his fellow's life. It is told that R. Akiva was staying at the inn of a certain man who offered him a cup of wine after first tasting it. R. Akiva said to him, "Keep it and drink it [all]." The innkeeper then offered R. Akiva another cup of wine, again tasting it first, and again R. Akiva said to him: "Keep it and drink it [all]." Finally Ben Azzai spoke up to the innkeeper: "How long will you keep offering R. Akiva cups of wine that you have tasted first?"[8]

167. A man should not drink from a cup and give that cup to his fellow, because people's sense of delicacy varies.[9]

168. Rav said to his son Hiyya: Wipe [the cup] before drinking, and wipe it again before putting it down. And when you drink water, pour some out,[10] and then you may give it to your disciple.

It once happened that a sage drank some water and, without pouring any out, gave [the cup] to his disciple. But the disciple, being delicate in such matters, would not drink from that cup and died of thirst. Then the sages said: A man should not drink water and give [the cup] to his disciple without first pouring out some of the water [over the rim he drank from].[11]

169. R. Ammi said: At a session of study, precedence is to be given to wisdom; in reclining at a feast, to age.[12]

170. Our masters taught: He who eats in the marketplace is like a dog. Some say, he is unfit to give testimony.[13]

171. "And he shall put off his garments, and put on other garments" (Lev. 6:4). Sages in the school of R. Ishmael taught: The Torah teaches you good manners. The garments in which one cooks a dish for his teacher,[14] he should not wear when he mixes a cup of wine for him.[15]

A Man's Clothing

172. R. Avira expounded: What is meant by the verse "Well is it with the man that dealeth graciously and lendeth freely, but matters concerning his own person he orders fittingly" (Ps. 112:5)? A man should always eat and drink less than his means allow, but clothe himself in keeping with his means.[16]

173. For your belly, count your pence; for your back, spare no expense.[17]

174. R. Yohanan called his garments "my aggrandizers."[18]

1. It might spill.
2. Get the hint that bread should not be treated disrespectfully.
3. B. Ber 50b; DER 9.
4. DEZ 8.
5. B. Ta 5b.
6. B. Pes 86b.
7. B. Ket 75b.
8. DER 9.
9. Tos Ber 5:9.
10. To clean the rim.
11. B. Tam 27b.
12. B. BB 120a.
13. B. Kid 40b.
14. A chore during which one's garments may become soiled.
15. B. Shab 114a.
16. B. Hul 84b.
17. Or: For your stomach, what is adequate; for your back, what is exquisite. B. BM 52a.
18. B. Shab 113a.

175. "Then these men were bound in their cloaks, their tunics, and their robes, and their other garments, and were cast into the midst of the burning fiery furnace" (Dan. 3:21). From this you may infer that even in a time of danger, one should not give up the dignity of one's bearing, for behold, these men were going out to be burned, yet they adorned themselves [with their finery].[1]

176. We have been taught: If a man who is in debt for a thousand *maneh* wears a robe worth a hundred *maneh*, he may be stripped of it. But he must still be provided with a robe that fits his standing, for, as we have been taught in the name of R. Ishmael and of R. Akiva: Everyone in Israel deserves such a robe.[2]

177. "David went and stealthily cut off the corner of Saul's cloak" (1 Sam. 24:5). R. Yose son of R. Hanina said: He who treats garments with contempt ends up by deriving no benefit from them, as is said, "King David was now old, well advanced in years; and though they covered him with bedclothes, he never felt warm" (1 Kings 1:1).[3]

178. The adornment of humans—their garments.[4]

179. In my town, my name's my fame; elsewhere, it's what I wear.[5]

180. He who has only one shirt—his life is no life.[6]

181. "I will provoke them with a vile nation" (Deut. 32:21)—the people of Barbaria[7] and Mauretania, who go about naked in the marketplace. There is none more vile and more abominable than he who goes about naked in the marketplace.[8]

182. R. Judah said in the name of Rav: One should sell even the beams in his house in order to buy shoes for his feet.[9]

Bathing and Anointing

183. The sages said in the name of Rav: It is forbidden to live in a city that has no bathhouse.[10]

184. "I have forgotten that which is good" (Lam. 3:17)—a bathhouse, said R. Jeremiah; washing one's hands and feet in warm water, said R. Yohanan.[11]

185. There are three kinds of sweat that benefit the body: the sweat of sickness, the sweat in a bathhouse, and the sweat of work. The sweat of sickness causes healing, but the sweat in a bathhouse—no [cure] equals it.[12]

186. We have been taught: A man should wash his face, his hands, and his feet every day for the sake of his Maker, as is said, "The Lord hath made everything for His own purpose" (Prov. 16:4).[13]

187. "He who does good to his own person is a man of piety" (Prov. 11:17).[14] Such a one was Hillel the Elder. After taking leave of his disciples, he proceeded to walk along with them. His disciples asked him, "Master, where are you going?" He answered, "To perform a precept." "What precept?" "To bathe in the bathhouse." "But is this a precept?" "It is indeed. Kings' statues set up in theaters and circuses are scoured and washed down by the official specially appointed to look after them, who receives a salary for the work. More—he is esteemed as one of the notables of the empire. How much more and more am I required to scour and wash myself, who have been created in God's image and likeness, as is written, 'In the image of God made He man' [Gen. 9:6]!"[15]

188. Samuel said: A drop of cold water in the morning and washing hands and feet in hot water in the evening are better [for the eyes] than all eye salves in the world.[16]

189. He who bathes in hot water with no cold shower to follow it is like iron heated in the fire but not quenched in cold water to temper it.[17]

190. Samuel said: Neglected and filthy hair causes blindness; neglected and filthy garments cause wit's dulling; a neglected and filthy body causes boils and pimples.[18]

191. "The delights of the children of men" (Eccles. 2:8). These are pools and bathhouses.[19]

192. Proclus son of Philosophus put a question to Rabban Gamaliel, who was bathing in Acco in the bath of Aphrodite.[20] Proclus asked, "It is written in your Torah, 'And there shall cleave nought of the devoted thing to thy hand' [Deut. 13:18]; why then are you bathing in the bath devoted to Aphrodite?" Rabban Gamaliel replied, "Questions [relating to Torah] may not be answered in a bath."[21] When he came out, he said to Proclus, "I did not come

---

1. Tanhuma, *Noah*, §10.
2. B. Shab 128a.
3. B. Ber 62b.
4. DEZ 10.
5. B. Shab 145b.
6. Since he cannot have it washed, he is tormented by lice. So Rashi. B. Betz 32b.
7. Tunis.
8. B. Yev 63b.
9. B. Shab 129a.
10. P. Kid 4:12, 66d.
11. B. Shab 25b.
12. ARN 41.
13. B. Shab 50b.
14. JV: "The merciful man doeth good to his own soul."
15. Lev. R. 34:3.
16. B. Shab 108a.
17. B. Shab 41a.
18. B. Ned 81a.
19. B. Git 68a.
20. Baths were frequently adorned with statues of deities.
21. Where people are naked.

into her domain—she has come into mine.[1] People do not say, 'The bath was made as an adornment for Aphrodite'; they say, 'Aphrodite was made as an adornment for the bath.' "[2]

193. R. Zerika said in the name of R. Eleazar: He who belittles the washing of hands [before a meal] will be rooted out of the world.[3]

194. [Failure to observe the practice of] washing hands before the meal caused one to eat swine's meat. [Failure to observe the practice of] washing hands after the meal slew a person.

The story is told that, during a period of religious persecution, an Israelite shopkeeper used to cook not only ritually clean meat, but pork as well, and sell them, so that it might not be suspected that he was a Jew. Here is how he went about it: when a customer entered his shop [to eat] and did not wash his hands, the shopkeeper, certain that he was a heathen, would place pork before him; but if the customer washed his hands and recited the blessing, the shopkeeper, certain that he was a Jew, fed him kosher meat. One time, a Jew entered the shop to eat and did not wash his hands, so the shopkeeper supposed that he was a heathen and placed pork before him. The man ate and did not say the grace after meals. He then asked to settle the account with the shopkeeper for the bread and meat [he had eaten]. Now pork, it should be said, sold at a higher price. So the shopkeeper said to the man, "You owe me so-and-so much, on account of the meat you ate, each piece of which comes to ten *maneh*." The man said, "Yesterday you served it to me for eight *maneh*, and today you charge me ten?" The shopkeeper replied, "The piece of meat you ate [today] was pork." As soon as the shopkeeper said this to the man, the man's hair stood on end, he fell into a great fright and said under his breath to the shopkeeper, "I am a Jew, and you have fed me pork!" The shopkeeper replied, "May your breath be blasted out! When I saw you eat without washing your hands and without [reciting] a blessing, I thought you were a heathen!"

Another story is told of a man who ate pulse without washing his hands afterward and then went down to the marketplace, his hands still soiled by the pulse. A companion, seeing him, went and said to the man's wife, "Your husband instructs you to send him such-and-such a ring, and in evidence that you may take my word, he told me to say that he had just eaten pulse. She gave him the ring. When after a while her husband returned, he asked her, "Where is the ring?" She replied, "So-and so came with the token you told him to mention to me, and I gave it to him." Filled with rage, he killed her. Hence, when a man does not wash his hands after partaking of food, he may well be like one who kills a human being.[4]

1. The bath existed before the image of Aphrodite was set up in it, and it was constructed for human use.
2. B. AZ 44b.
3. B. Sot 4b.
4. B. Yoma 83b; Tanhuma, *Balak*, §15: Num. R. 20:21.

195. Though anointing [oil] and bath[water] do not enter the body, the body benefits from them.[5]

196. If a man bathes but does not anoint himself, it is like water on top of a [covered] cask.[6]

197. It was told of R. Hanina that, when he was eighty years old, he could take his shoe off or put it on while standing on one foot.

[Speaking of robust old age], R. Hanina said: Warm baths and oil, with which my mother anointed me in my youth, stood me in good stead in my old age.[7]

198. He who wishes to anoint his entire body should first anoint his head, because it is king over all other parts of his body.[8]

Healing the Body

199. "[The Lord will] make strong thy bones" (Isa. 58:11). R. Eleazar said: This is the most perfect of blessings.[9]

200. The sages said in the name of Rav: It is forbidden to live in a city where there is no physician.[10]

201. In a human body, the component parts are dependent on one another. When one ceases to function, so does the other. When they break apart one from the other, the body is stricken and the person dies, like a house that has four sides—if one side breaks away, the house collapses.[11]

202. The sages in the school of R. Ishmael taught: "He shall cause him to be thoroughly healed" (Exod. 21:19). From this verse we infer that permission has been given [by Heaven] to the physician to heal.[12]

203. It is told of R. Ishmael and R. Akiva that, while they were walking through the streets of Jerusalem accompanied by a certain man, a sick person confronted them and said, "Masters, tell me, how shall I be healed?" They replied, "Take such-and-such, and you will be healed." The man accompanying the sages asked them, "Who smote him with sickness?" They replied, "The Holy One." The man: "And you bring yourselves into a matter that does not concern you? God smote, and you would heal?" The sages: "What is your work?" The man: "I am a tiller of

5. B. Ber 57b.
6. Since it is not possible for the water to penetrate the body, the body does not benefit from it. B. Shab 41a.
7. B. Hul 24b.
8. B. Shab 61a.
9. B. Yev 102b.
10. P. Kid 4:12, 66d.
11. Midrash Sam. 4 (ed. Buber [Cracow, 1903], p. 54).
12. B. Ber 60a.

the soil. You see the sickle in my hand." The sages: "Who created the vineyard?" The man: "The Holy One." The sages: "Then why do you bring yourself into a matter that does not concern you? God created it, and you eat the fruit from it!" The man: "Don't you see the sickle in my hand? If I did not go out and plow the vineyard, prune it, compost it, and weed it, it would have yielded nothing." The sages: "You are the biggest fool in the world! Have you not heard the verse 'As for man, his days are as grass' [Ps. 103:15]? A tree, if it is not composted, weeded, and [the area around it] plowed, will not grow; and even if it does grow, if not given water to drink, it will die—will not live. So, too, the human body is a tree, a healing potion is the compost, and a physician is the tiller of the soil."[1]

204. When a man has a pain, he should visit a physician.[2]

205. R. Eleazar said: Honor your physician even before you have need of him.[3]

206. A physician who heals for nothing is worth nothing.[4]

207. A physician not nigh is [as good as] a blind eye.[5]

208. Hapless is the city whose physician has gout.[6]

209. Physician, heal your own lameness![7]

210. The best physician deserves Gehenna.[8]

211. Hezekiah hid away the Book of Cures, and the sages approved.[9]

212. Rav said to his son Hiyya:[10] Don't fall into the habit of taking drugs, don't leap over a sewer,[11] don't have your teeth pulled,[12] don't provoke serpents.[13]

213. "The saving sun with healing in its wings" (Mal. 3:20). Abbaye said: This proves that the shining sun brings healing.[14]

214. People say: When the sun rises, the sick man rises.[15]

Care of the Body

215. Beware of three things. Do not sit too long, for sitting aggravates hemorrhoids. Do not stand too long, for standing too long is harmful to the heart. Do not walk too much, for too much walking is harmful to the eyes. It is best to spend a third of one's time sitting, a third standing, and a third walking.

As for sitting without support at one's back, standing with such support is far more comfortable.[16]

216. "The Lord shall give thee there a trembling heart, and failing of eyes, and languishing of spirit" (Deut. 28:65). Nothing causes greater failing of eyes and languishing of spirit than hemorrhoids.[17]

217. Long steps take away one five-hundredth of a man's sight.[18]

218. Ben Azzai said: Lie on anything, but not on the ground.[19] Sit on anything, except on a beam.[20]

219. Eight things are harmful in large quantities but beneficial in small ones: travel and sexual intercourse, riches and trade, wine and sleep, hot baths and bloodletting.[21]

220. Three things sap a man's strength: anxiety, travel, and sin.[22]

221. R. Tanhum son of R. Hiyya said: Four things sap a man's strength: sin, travel, fasting, and the oppressor's rule. R. Tanhuma said: Trouble also saps a man's strength.[23]

222. Rav said: A sigh breaks half a man's body.[24]

223. "And the Lord will take away from thee all that causes sickness" (Deut. 7:15)—the evil eye. So, in keeping with his opinion, Rav stated that he visited a cemetery and, using certain charms [to determine what caused the death of those buried in it], found that ninety-nine died because of the evil eye and only one from natural causes. But Samuel said, "The verse refers to vapors," and, in keeping with his opinion, Samuel maintained that all sick-

---

1. Midrash Sam. 4.
2. B. BK 46b.
3. P. Ta 3:6, 66d.
4. B. BK 85a.
5. Ibid.
6. And can't get about. Lev. R. 5:6.
7. Gen. R. 23:5.
8. Either because he is haughty or because he occasionally endangers life. B. Kid 82a.
9. For people would no longer trust only in medical treatment. B. Ber 10b.
10. Who was not in good health.
11. So B. Pes 113a; BR: "Don't leap feet-first."
12. Wait for them to get better.
13. B. Pes 113a.
14. B. Ned 8b.
15. B. BB 16b.
16. B. Ket 111b.
17. B. Ned 22a.
18. B. Ber 43b.
19. For fear of serpents.
20. B. Ber 62b.
21. B. Git 70a.
22. Ibid.
23. MTeh 31:9.
24. B. Ber 58b.

ness was caused by miasma. R. Hanina said, "The verse refers to chilly drafts." R. Eleazar said, "The verse refers to diseases of the gall."[1]

224. The sages said in the name of Rav: Better any complaint than a complaint of the bowels, any pain than heart pain, any ache than headache.[2]

225. R. Simeon ben Eleazar said: "And, behold, it was very good" (Gen. 1:31) refers even to sleep. But is there any sleep that is very good? I wonder. After all, have we not been taught: "Only when it is the wicked who indulge in wine and sleep is it comely for them and comely for the world"? What R. Simeon in fact meant was that, because a man sleeps a bit, he is able to get up and labor long at the study of Torah.[3]

226. R. Yohanan said: If one says, "I swear that I will not sleep for three nights," he should be flogged,[4] and afterward he may go right to sleep.[5]

227. R. Judah said: The night was created for no other purpose than sleep.[6]

228. Samuel said: Sleep at the break of dawn is as important for the body as tempering is for iron.[7]

229. Our masters taught: Many things were said of the morning bread. It is an antidote against heat, against cold, against winds, and against demons. It instills wisdom into the simple. It helps a man to be acquitted in a lawsuit. It helps him to study Torah and to teach it; his words are heeded, and he retains what he has learned. His body does not steam [after bathing]. The bread he eats in the morning kills the worms in his intestines. Some say that it also expels jealousy and induces love.

Rabbah asked Rava bar Mari: What is the authority in Scripture for the proverb "Sixty runners speed along but cannot overtake him who breaks bread in the morning" and for the rabbinic dictum "Arise early and eat—in summer, on account of the heat; in winter, on account of the cold"? Rava replied: The verse "When they do not hunger nor thirst, neither cold nor sun shall smite them" (Isa. 49:10).

Rabbah said: You find authority in that verse, but I find it in this one: "When you serve the Lord your God, He shall bless thy bread, and thy water" (Exod. 23:25). "When you serve the Lord your God" refers to the reading of the Shema and the [morning] *Tefillah.* "He shall bless thy bread and thy water" refers to bread seasoned with salt, and a jug of water. Then "I will take sickness away from the midst of thee" (ibid).

We have been taught: By *mahalah*, "the sickness," [illness caused by] the gall is meant. Why is it called "the sickness"? Because it sickens man's entire body.

Another explanation: Because eighty-three[8] sicknesses stem from the gall, and all of them may be eliminated by salted bread and a jug of water taken in the morning.[9]

230. Our masters taught: The first hour of the day[10] is the time for the principal meal for gladiators; the second hour, for brigands; the third, for heirs; the fourth, for the generality; the fifth, for workmen;[11] the sixth, for disciples of the wise.[12] After that, it is like throwing a stone into a bottle.[13]

Abbaye said: What was just asserted is true only if a man has eaten nothing in the morning. But if he has eaten something, there is no objection [to postponing the meal].[14]

231. "Who fed you in the wilderness with manna . . . in order to test you by hardships" (Deut. 8:16). R. Ammi and R. Assi differed [in explaining what hardships were experienced in connection with manna]. One said: The feelings of a man who has bread in his basket are not like the feelings of one who has not.[15] The other said: The feelings of one who sees what he eats are not like the feelings of one who does not see what he eats.[16]

R. Joseph[17] said: In this verse there is the intimation that when the blind eat, they are not satisfied. Therefore, added Abbaye, when a man has a feast, he should have it only in daytime.[18]

232. R. Yose son of R. Bun said: It is forbidden to live in a city that does not have a vegetable garden.[19]

233. R. Hisda said: A young scholar whose provisions are limited should not eat vegetables, because they whet the appetite.

R. Hisda also said: I ate no vegetables, either when poor or when well off. When poor, because they whet the appetite; when well off, because I figured, where vegetables enter, let meat and fish enter instead.[20]

---

1. B. BM 107b.
2. B. Shab 11a.
3. Gen. R. 9:6.
4. Since it is impossible not to sleep for three nights, the man is judged guilty of taking a false oath.
5. He is released from any obligation to try to fulfill his oath. B. Suk 53a.
6. B. Er 65a.
7. B. Ber 62b.
8. The numerical value of the letters that spell the word *mahalah* add up to eighty-three.
9. B. BM 107b; B. BK 92b.
10. Six A.M.
11. Who get through at that time.
12. After they conclude sessions at court.
13. No benefit is derived.
14. B. Shab 10a.
15. They always had to trust that God would send down manna the next day.
16. The variety of foods Israelites tasted when they ate manna was not evident in its outer appearance. See part 1, chap. 5, §8.
17. He was blind.
18. B. Yoma 74b.
19. P. Kid 4:12, 66d.
20. B. Shab 140b.

234. Rav said: Adda the Fisherman told me, "Roast the fish with its brother (salt), plunge it into its father (water), eat it with its son (juice), and after, drink its father (water)."[1]

235. R. Yannai said in the name of Rav: An egg is superior [in food value] to the same quantity of any other kind of food. When Ravin came [from the Land of Israel], he said: A soft-roasted egg is superior to six *log* of fine flour. When R. Dimi came, he said: A soft-roasted egg is superior to six *log* of fine flour; a hard-roasted egg to four *log* of fine flour; and as for a boiled egg, it is superior to any other food of the same quantity except meat.[2]

236. Our masters taught: Milt is good for the teeth but bad for the bowels; bitter vetch is bad for the teeth but good for the bowels. All raw vegetables make the complexion pale, and all things not fully grown retard growth. Living creatures [when eaten] restore vitality, even as the part of a body [such as the neck] that is near the vital organs restores vitality. Cabbage is for sustenance, and beets are for healing. Woe unto the house[3] through which turnips are always passed.[4]

237. We have been taught: Eat salt after every food and drink water after every beverage, and you will come to no harm.

One who has eaten any kind of food without taking salt after it or drunk any kind of beverage without taking water after it is liable to be troubled with bad odor in the mouth during the day and with croup during the night.

Our masters taught: A man who washes down his food with water will not suffer in his bowels. How much should he drink? R. Hisda said: A ladleful to a loaf of bread.

R. Mari said in the name of R. Yohanan: He who is accustomed to eat lentils once in thirty days will keep croup away from his house. He should not, however, eat them every day. Why not? They cause bad odor in the mouth.

R. Mari said further in the name of R. Yohanan: He who customarily uses mustard once in thirty days keeps sickness away from his house. He should not, however, use it every day. Why not? It is bad for the heart.

R. Hiyya bar Ashi said in the name of Rav: He who regularly eats small fish will not suffer in his bowels. Not only that, but small fish stimulate fertility and give nourishment and health to a man's entire body. R. Hama bar R. Hanina said: One who regularly uses black cumin will not suffer from pain in the heart. The sages objected, R. Simeon ben Gamaliel pointing out that black cumin is one of sixty deadly poisons and that even if a man merely sleeps east of a place where black cumin is stored, his blood will be on his own head.[5] There is no contradiction here, however: R. Simeon's statement refers to [inhaling] the odor of black cumin, while R. Hama's statement refers to its taste [when eaten].

R. Jeremiah's mother used to bake bread for him, stick some black cumin on it,[6] and then scrape it off.[7]

238. The sages said in the name of R. Judah bar Ilai: Eat inexpensive onions [*batzel*] and you will afford to live in the shade [*be-tzel*] of your own home. Do not eat geese and fowls, lest your craving for them hound you [out of your house].[8]

239. Radish helps to dissolve food; lettuce, to digest it; cucumbers, to expand the intestines. But did not the sages in the school of R. Ishmael teach that cucumbers are called *kishuim* because they are as injurious [*kashim*] to the body as swords? There is no contradiction: The second statement refers to large cucumbers; the first, to small ones.[9]

240. R. Jeremiah took sick. When the physician who came to heal him saw a pumpkin lying in his house, he left him and went away, saying: This man has the angel of death in his house,[10] yet I am expected to heal him![11]

241. Our masters taught: Five things were said of garlic: it is filling, it keeps the body warm, it brightens the face, it increases semen, and it kills parasites in the bowels. Some say, it brings love and removes jealousy.[12]

242. Our masters taught: Asparagus brew[13] is good for the heart and good for the eyes, and, it goes without saying, also good for the bowels. If one uses it regularly, it is good for the whole body, but if one gets drunk with it, it is bad for the whole body.[14]

243. We have been taught: Three things—coarse bread, new beer, and vegetables—increase feces, bend one's stature, and take away one five-hundredth of a man's vision.[15]

244. Dates are wholesome in the morning and in the evening. They are bad in the afternoon, but at noon there is nothing to match them. Besides, they do away with three things: evil thoughts, sickness of the bowels, and hemorrhoids.[16]

245. The late figs we ate in our childhood were more tasty than the [ripe] peaches we eat in our advanced years.[17]

---

1. During the meal, only wine was drunk. B. MK 11a.
2. B. Ber 44b.
3. That is, the stomach.
4. B. Ber 44b.
5. Because the west wind may carry the odor to him and poison him.
6. So that the bread would absorb the taste of the cumin.
7. To remove the odor. B. Ber 40a.
8. B. Pes 114a.
9. B. AZ 11a and En Yaakov, ad loc.
10. The pumpkin is like poison.
11. B. Ned 49a.
12. B. BK 82a.
13. A beverage made by soaking certain roots in beer or wine.
14. B. Ber 51a.
15. B. Er 55b–56a.
16. B. Ket 10b.
17. P. Pe 7:4, 20a.

246. Our masters taught: One seized by a ravenous hunger should be given honey and all kinds of sweet things to eat,[1] for honey and sweet food light up a man's eyes.

R. Yohanan said: Once, when I was seized by a ravenous hunger, I—mindful of "Wisdom preserveth the life of him who hath it" (Eccles. 7:12)—ran to the eastern [sunny] side[2] of a fig tree and ate its fruit, for R. Joseph taught: He who wishes to savor the fig's full taste should turn to its eastern side.

While R. Judah and R. Yose were walking along a road, ravenous hunger seized R. Judah, who overpowered a shepherd and devoured his bread. R. Yose reproached him: "You overpowered the shepherd!" As they reached the city, ravenous hunger seized R. Yose, and the people of the city plied him with flagons [of honey] and bowls [of sweet food]. At that, R. Judah said, "I overpowered a shepherd, but you overpowered an entire city!"[3]

247. People say: For a tasty bit, there is always room.[4]

248. R. Simeon ben Yohai said: The following acts cause a man to forfeit his life, and his blood is on his own head: eating peeled garlic, peeled onion, or a peeled egg [left to spoil overnight]; drinking liquids that were left [uncovered] overnight;[5] spending the night in a graveyard; and cutting one's fingernails and throwing them into a public thoroughfare.[6]

249. Three kinds of liquids are forbidden when they have been left uncovered: water, wine, and milk.[7]

250. Our masters taught: A man should not drink water from rivers or pools at night. If he drinks, his blood is on his own head—so great is the danger.[8]

251. R. Ammi said: One should be cautious about things that people are cautious about: for example, one should not put small coins into the mouth, a dish of food under a bed, or bread in an armpit; nor should one thrust a knife into a radish or an etrog.[9]

252. R. Yohanan said: It is forbidden to walk four cubits to the east of a leper. R. Simeon [ben Lakish] said: Even a hundred cubits. They did not contradict each other. The one who said four cubits referred to a time when no wind is blowing; the one who said a hundred cubits referred to a time when a wind is blowing.

R. Meir ate no eggs that came from a lepers' alley. R. Ammi and R. Assi would not even enter a lepers' alley. When Resh Lakish saw a leper in the city, he would throw stones in his direction as he said to him, "Go to your own place and do not pollute others!" When R. Eleazar son of R. Simeon saw one of them, he would hide himself from him.[10]

253. R. Yannai said: The verse "All the days of a man poor [in health] are evil" (Prov. 15:15) refers to a man who is finicky about his food. "But he that hath a continual feast is of a merry heart" (ibid.) refers to one whose appetite is robust.[11]

254. Samuel said: Any change in one's regular diet is the beginning of disease of the bowels.

On this subject, if with regard to "All the days of a poor man are evil," one should ask, "But are there not sabbaths and festivals?" the answer lies in Samuel's opinion.[12]

255. We have been taught: If a man eats without drinking, it is as if he ate blood—such eating will bring on stomach trouble. If he eats and does not walk [at least] four cubits, his food will rot within him and bring on a foul odor [from his mouth]. If he feels a need to relieve himself but [suppresses it and] eats, he resembles an oven in which fuel is thrown on top of ashes [from previous heatings] still within it, and this brings on unpleasant [body] odor.[13]

256. Elijah [the Prophet] advised R. Nathan: Fill a third of your stomach with food, a third with drink, and leave a third. Otherwise, should you get angry, the anger will pack your stomach so full [of humors that it will burst].

R. Hiyya taught: One who wishes to avoid stomach trouble should regularly, summer and winter, take bread dipped in wine or in vinegar as a relish. When you are enjoying a meal, withdraw your hand from it just enough for it [not to fill you up]. Do not delay when you feel an urge to relieve yourself.[14]

257. R. Ahai said: He who delays relieving himself violates "Ye shall not make your persons filthy [by retaining waste matter]" (Lev. 20:25).[15]

258. R. Huna asked his son Rabbah, "Why are you not to be found in the presence of R. Hisda, whose traditions are so keen?" Rabbah replied, "Why should I go to him? When I go to him, he treats me to inconsequential matters![16] For instance, he tells me that one who enters a privy

1. Even on the Day of Atonement.
2. Where the fig tree's fruit ripens first.
3. B. Yoma 83b.
4. Or: "There is always room for sweets on a spoon" (Pearl F. Braude). B. Er 82b.
5. A snake might have spit his venom into them.
6. B. Nid 17a.
7. Ter 8:4.
8. B. Pes 112a.
9. The knife might go right through and cause injury. P. Ter 8:3, 45d.
10. Because the man was evil and given to slander, he became a leper, and one should not gaze at the countenance of an evil man. Lev. R. 16:3.
11. B. BB 145b.
12. Rich food on Sabbaths and festivals would effect such a change in the poor man's diet that his health would be harmed. B. Ket 110b.
13. B. Shab 41a.
14. B. Git 70a.
15. B. Mak 16b.
16. I.e., not Torah.

should not sit down abruptly, nor strain overmuch, for the rectum is supported by three toothlike glands, and should these toothlike glands prolapse, his health would be endangered." R. Huna: "R. Hisda discusses matters of health, and you call them inconsequential? All the more reason for you to go to him!"[1]

259. A certain heretic said to R. Judah: Your face is as fat as the faces of those who lend money on interest or raise swine. R. Judah: The two occupations are forbidden to Jews. However, between my home and the house of study there are twenty-four privies, and [as soon as I require it], I enter any one of them.[2]

260. R. Yohanan said in the name of R. Yose ben Ketzartah: There are six kinds of tears, three beneficial and three harmful. Those induced by smoke, by weeping [in grief], and by [pain in] the privy are harmful; those induced by spices, laughter, or plants[3] are beneficial.[4]

261. Excretions from the nose and the ear in excessive quantities show poor health; in small quantities, good health.[5]

262. Regulations concerning danger to life are more stringent than ritual prohibitions.[6]

263. Everything is in the power of Heaven, except the effect on a man of heat and cold, as is said, "Cold and heat are in the path of the contrary person; he who values his life will keep far from them" (Prov. 22:5).[7]

264. One should not depend on a miracle.[8]

265. Miracles are not to be cited as an argument.[9]

266. Miracles do not take place on the hour.[10]

267. Where injury is likely, one should not rely on a miracle.[11]

268. Satan is sure to make accusations in a time of danger.[12]

269. Satan is apt to make accusations in three situations: when a man lives in a dilapidated house, when he walks [alone] on a road, or when he sets out on a sea voyage.[13]

270. R. Isaac said: Three things cause a man's sins to be remembered [in heaven]: passing dangerously near a tottering wall, expecting the fulfillment of prayer,[14] and calling on Heaven to inflict punishment on his fellow.[15]

271. R. Yose ben Halafta entered an alley, his ass drover behind him. When they reached a ditch with water in it, the drover said, "I would like to bathe." R. Yose: "Don't court danger." The drover: "I wish to wash off my uncleanness." R. Yose: "Nevertheless, don't court danger." When the drover still refused to heed him, R. Yose said, "He will go down and is not likely to come up again." Indeed, this is what happened.[16]

272. R. Yannai said: A man should never stand in a place of danger in the expectation that a miracle will be wrought in his behalf. Perhaps it will not be wrought, or if it is wrought, his merits will be diminished as a result. And the proof? R. Hanin's interpretation of "I am become diminished by all the kindness that Thou hast so steadfastly shown Thy servant" (Gen. 32:11)[17] as meaning that Jacob said to the Holy One: I fear that because of the miracle You will perform for me, You will diminish my merits, so that, as a result of all the kindnesses so steadfastly shown me, I will come to be deemed quite unworthy.[18]

273. In Nehardea there was a dilapidated wall beside which Rav and Samuel would not walk, even though it had been standing this way for thirteen years [without collapsing]. Once, when R. Adda bar Ahavah happened to visit there, Samuel said to Rav, "Let us make a detour around it." Rav replied, "No need for it now. Since we have with us R. Adda bar Ahavah, whose merit is so great, I am not afraid.[19]

274. R. Huna had wine stored in a dilapidated building. When he wanted to remove the wine, he took R. Adda bar Ahavah into the building and kept him occupied in a learned discussion until the wine had been removed. Then, the moment they left the building, it collapsed. When R. Adda realized that he had been used for such a purpose, he was annoyed, for he agreed with R. Yannai's view [that one should not stay in a place of danger in the hope that a miracle will be wrought].[20]

275. In all journeys, there is the presumption of mortal danger.[21]

---

1. B. Shab 82a.
2. And thus my body is healthier than that of a usurer or a swineherd. B. Ned 49b and En Yaakov, ad loc.
3. Such as onions or mustard.
4. B. Shab 151b–152a.
5. B. BM 107b.
6. B. Hul 10a.
7. JV: "Thorns and snares are in the way of the froward; he that keepeth his soul holdeth himself far from them." But *tzinnim* ("thorns") also means "cold," and *pahim* ("snares") also means "fiery coals." It is within man's own power to avoid extremes of heat or cold. B. Ket 30a.
8. Based on B. Pes 64b.
9. B. Ber 60a.
10. B. Meg 7b.
11. B. Kid 39b.
12. P. Shab 2:3, 5b; Gen. R. 91:12.
13. Eccles. R. 3:2, §2.
14. In heaven, there will be close scrutiny of the man's deserts.
15. Such a prayer will lead Heaven to compare the two men. B. Ber 55a.
16. P. Ber 3:4, 6c.
17. JV: "I am not worthy of all the mercies and of all the truth which Thou hast shown unto Thy servant."
18. B. Shab 32a; B. Ta 20b and En Yaakov, ad loc.
19. B. Ta 20b.
20. Ibid.
21. P. Ber 4:4, 8b.

276. R. Judah said in the name of Rav: A man should always leave [a place] in [daylight—daylight, which Scripture describes as] "how good" (Gen. 1:4), and enter it in daylight, in keeping with "As soon as the morning was light, the men were sent off" (Gen. 44:3).[1]

277. He who sets out on a journey before cockcrow—his blood is on his own head.[2]

278. Be sure to enter a city in company with [dawning] sunlight.[3]

279. Rav said to R. Assi: Do not live in a city whose mayor is a physician,[4] or in which no horse neighs[5] or no dog barks.[6]

Man's Sustenance—Poverty and Riches

280. "I will make a helpmeet for him" (Gen. 2:18). When the earth heard God's words "I will make a helpmeet for him," it quaked and trembled, saying: Master of the universe, I have not the power to feed the multitudes of mankind [whom the two will generate]. God replied: I and you together will feed them.

Thus they agreed to divide the responsibility equally between them [God sustaining man in the night hours during sleep, while the earth does so in the daytime].[7]

281. R. Joshua ben Levi said: When the Holy One told Adam, "Thorns and thistles shall it bring forth to thee" (Gen. 3:18), Adam's eyes flowed with tears. He spoke up to Him, "Master of the universe, am I and my ass to eat out of the same crib?" But when God replied, "By the sweat of thy brow shalt thou get bread to eat" (Gen. 3:19), his anxiety was set at rest.

Resh Lakish said: Happy are we that we did not remain subject to the first curse.[8]

Abbaye demurred: But we were not saved from it altogether, for we still eat herbs of the field.[9]

282. R. Yohanan said: Man's task of earning his daily bread is twice as difficult as a woman's of giving birth, for while a woman giving birth is told, "In pain (*etzev*) shalt thou bear children" (Gen. 3:16), with regard to one's daily bread, man is told, "In great pain (*itzavon*) shalt thou eat of it" (Gen. 3:17).

R. Yohanan said: To maintain man in his daily bread demands more power than to give redemption, for of his redemption Jacob said, "The *angel* who hath redeemed me from all evil" (Gen. 48:16), but of his daily bread, he said, "The *God* who fed me all my life long unto this day" (Gen. 48:15).

R. Shezbi said in the name of R. Eleazar ben Azariah: The maintenance of man in his daily bread is as awesome as the splitting of the Red Sea, for the verse "Who giveth bread to all flesh" (Ps. 136:25) is aligned as being of equal weight with "Who split apart the Red Sea" (Ps. 136:13).[10]

283. R. Eleazar said: Scripture likens redemption to earning a livelihood, for the verse "He hath redeemed us from our adversaries" (Ps. 136:24) is followed immediately by "He giveth food to all flesh" (Ps. 136:25). As redemption requires [God's working] wonders, so earning a livelihood requires [God's working] wonders.[11]

284. Our masters taught: It happened once that a certain man's wife died and left an infant who had to be suckled. But the man did not have the wherewithal to pay a wetnurse. So a miracle was wrought for him: nipples opened up in his breast, and he gave suck to his child.

R. Joseph said: Pause and consider how great is this man, to have such a miracle performed for him. On the contrary, said Abbaye, how inferior is this man, to have the order of creation changed because of him.[12]

R. Judah said: Pause and consider how difficult earning a livelihood is, since the order of creation was changed for the sake of it.[13]

285. "He hath known thy walking through the great wilderness" (Deut. 2:7) means that God knows of your traveling, your travailing in the grime, your suffering to get a living.[14]

286. A man does not know from what he will earn his living.[15]

287. R. Nathan bar Abba said in the name of Rav: The world is dark for him who must look to the table of others, as is said, "He who has to wander abroad for bread—'Where [is it?]'—becomes aware of the day of darkness as being ready at hand" (Job 15:23). Indeed, said R. Hisda, his life is no life.

Our masters taught: There are three whose life is no life: he who must look to the table of others, he whose wife rules him, and he whose body is racked by suffering. And some say: he who possesses but one shirt.[16]

288. R. Ahai ben Josiah said: He who eats of his own is [as much at ease] as an infant raised at his mother's breast.

1. B. Ta 10b.
2. B. Yoma 21a.
3. B. Ta 10b.
4. Or "a scholar," as both are too busy to attend to the city's needs.
5. The presence of a horse will warn thieves of the likelihood of being pursued.
6. B. Pes 113a.
7. MhG Gen., p. 84; PRE 12.
8. Or we would have had to live on thorns and thistles.
9. B. Pes 118a and En Yaakov, ad loc.
10. Ibid.
11. Gen. R. 20:9.
12. For the child's sake, while no means were provided for the father to dispose of for his own needs.
13. B. Shab 53b.
14. Yalkut, Ps., §690.
15. B. Pes 54b.
16. Since he cannot wash it, he is consumed by vermin. B. Betz 32b and En Yaakov, ad loc.

He also used to say: When a man eats of his own, his mind is at ease. But a man's mind is not at ease when he eats even at his father's table, his mother's table, or his children's table, let alone at a stranger's table.[1]

289. Our masters taught: He who looks to the earnings of his wife or the earnings of his mill[2] will never see a sign of blessing.[3]

290. A man prefers one *kav* of his own food to nine *kav* of his neighbor's.[4]

291. "In her mouth an olive leaf freshly plucked" (Gen. 8:11). Where did the dove bring it? R. Bebai said: The gates of the Garden of Eden were opened for her, and she brought it there. R. Abbahu said to him: Had she brought it from the Garden of Eden, would it not have been something finer, such as a stick of cinnamon or a leaf of balsam? But in truth the dove's olive leaf was a hint to Noah: it is better to have this bitter leaf from the hand of the Holy One than something sweet from your hand.[5]

292. R. Jeremiah ben Eleazar said: What is meant by "And lo, in her mouth an olive leaf freshly plucked" (Gen. 8:11)? That the dove said to the Holy One: Master of the universe, may my sustenance be as bitter as this olive leaf, just so it is proffered by You, rather than be sweet as honey but dependent upon creatures of flesh and blood.[6]

293. Treat your Sabbath like a weekday rather than depend on the [handouts of] others.[7]

294. Sell yourself to work that is alien to you rather than depend on the handouts of others.[8]

295. R. Yohanan and R. Eleazar both said: As soon as a man becomes dependent upon others, his face changes into as many colors as does a *kerum*, as is said, "As a *kerum*, he finds himself disdained among the sons of men" (Ps. 12:9).[9] What is the *kerum*? When R. Dimi came down [from the Land of Israel] he said: There is a bird in cities across the sea, called *kerum*, and when the sun shines on it, it changes into many colors.

Both R. Ammi and R. Assi said: [A man who must depend on others] is as one chastised by two diametrically opposed punishments—fire and water—as is said, "When Thou didst cause men to ride over our heads, it was as though we came through fire and water" (Ps. 66:12).[10]

1. ARN 30.
2. In which others grind their wheat, while the miller does nothing.
3. B. Pes 50b.
4. B. BM 38a.
5. Gen. R. 33:6; Yalkut, *Noah*, §58.
6. B. Er 18b.
7. B. Shab 118a.
8. P. Ber 9:3, 13d.
9. JV: "When vileness is exalted among the sons of men." But *kerum* ("is exalted") is also the name of a bird found in equatorial and western Africa.
10. B. Ber 6b.

296. Poverty in one's house is harder to bear than fifty lashes.[11]

297. No portion in life is harder to bear than poverty, for he who is crushed by poverty is as one beset by all the afflictions in the world, indeed, as one stricken by all the curses listed in Deuteronomy.[12]

Our masters added: Were all afflictions in the world gathered on one side and poverty on the other, poverty would outweigh them all. Come and see: when Satan was pressing charges against Job with the Holy One, he said: You have given Job possessions and children, and You are solicitous about them. At that, the Holy One said to Job: What will you have—poverty or afflictions? Job replied to the Master of the universe: I would rather accept all the afflictions in the world, but not poverty.[13]

298. Immikantron[14] wrote to Hadrian Caesar, "If it is the circumcised you hate, there are also the Ishmaelites. If it is Sabbath observers you hate, there are also the Cutheans.[15] Apparently [it is not their religion but] the people of Israel that you hate. May her God requite a man like you." At that, Hadrian had it proclaimed that the man who had written the missive should make himself known to Caesar, because Caesar wished to give him a gift. Presently a certain man came and represented himself as the writer of the missive. [Though aware that he was not the writer], Caesar ordered, "Let him be beheaded." But [before that was done], he asked the man, "Why did you say such a thing?" The man replied, "Because I knew you would free me from three miserable anxieties." Caesar: "What are they?" The man: "My appetite demands food from me morning and evening, and I have nothing to give it; and my wife and my children make the same demand." Hadrian: "Since he leads such a miserable life, let him go." Then the man applied to himself the verse "So I hated life" (Eccles. 2:17).[16]

299. Poverty is like death. A poor man is like one dead.[17]

300. The torments of poverty deprive a man of his good sense and of the capacity to acknowledge his Creator.[18]

301. We have been taught that R. Eleazar ha-Kappar said: A man should always beseech God's mercy concerning the state of poverty, for if he does not come into it, his son may; and if his son does not come into it, his son's son may, as is said, "Thou shalt surely give thy needy brother . . . because that for (*bi-gelal*) this thing . . ." (Deut. 15:10), the word *bi-gelal* being taken to suggest—so taught sages in the school of R. Ishmael—

11. B. BB 116a.
12. See Deut. 28:15–58.
13. Exod. R. 31:12.
14. A Jew otherwise unknown.
15. Yet you do not persecute the Ishmaelites or the Cutheans.
16. Having been made to live against his will. Eccles. R. 2:17, §1.
17. B. Ned 7b and 64b.
18. B. Er 41b.

that poverty is a wheel (*galgal*) that goes around and around in the world.[1]

302. "For God is a judge; He putteth down one, and lifteth up another" (Ps. 75:8). To what may this world be compared? To a garden's waterwheel: its clay dippers below come up full, and those above go down empty. So, too, not everyone who is rich today will be rich tomorrow, and not everyone who is poor today will be poor tomorrow, for the world is a wheel.[2]

303. A Roman noblewoman asked R. Yose ben Halafta: In how many days did the Holy One create His world? R. Yose replied: In six days, for it is written, "In six days the Lord made heaven and earth" (Exod. 20:11). She asked: And what has He been doing since?[3] R. Yose replied: He has been busy making ladders, having this one ascend and that one descend, making this one rich and that one poor.[4]

304. R. Eleazar ben Pedat was a very poor man. Once, after having himself bled, he had nothing to eat [to regain his strength]. So, coming upon a garlic skin, he put it into his mouth, but he grew faint and fell asleep. The sages, who came in to visit him, found him weeping and smiling [in his sleep], and tongues of fire were issuing from his forehead. When he woke up, they asked him: Why did you smile and weep, and why did tongues of fire issue from your forehead? He replied: [I wept] because I saw the Holy One sitting at my side, and when I asked Him, "How long will I suffer such poverty in this world?" He replied, "Eleazar, My son, would you rather I turn the world back to its very beginnings? Perhaps you might then be born in a more bountiful hour?" I replied, "All this, and then only 'perhaps'?" [I smiled because] when I went on to ask, "Which is the longer part of my life—the one that I have already lived, or the one I am still to live?" He replied, "The one that you have already lived." I said to Him, "If so, I do not want what is left." He replied, "In reward for saying, 'I do not want what is left,' I will give you in the world-to-come thirteen rivers of balsam oil as clear as the Euphrates and the Tigris, which you will be able to enjoy." Finally, tongues of fire issued from my forehead, because when I asked, "Master of the universe—nothing more?" He replied, "And what do you wish Me to give to your fellow men?" I said, "Am I asking a boon from a mere mortal who has nothing to give?" He [playfully] tapped my forehead and exclaimed, "Eleazar, My son, I shall pelt you with My arrows!"[5]

305. "All the days of the poor are evil" (Prov. 15:15). But are there not Sabbaths and festivals?

[However, the verse may be understood in the light of what Samuel had to say, for] he said: A change in diet [which Sabbath and festival fare entails] is the beginning of disease in the bowels.

Ben Sira added: [Not only the days of the poor are evil]—the nights also. For

Lower than all roofs is a poor man's roof.
And his vineyard is on the mountain's highest [and least fertile] summit.
The rain from other roofs pours down on his roof.
Even as the soil of his vineyard washes down to other vineyards.[6]

306. Poverty dogs a poor man's footsteps.[7]

307. The weasel and the cat [make peace to] have a feast on the fat of the luckless.[8]

308. At the gate to emporia, kin and friends are many; at the gate to penury, there are neither kin nor friends.[9]

309. Ben Zoma said: Who is rich? He who delights in his lot.[10]

310. Our masters taught: Who is wealthy? He who is content with his wealth—so said R. Meir. But R. Tarfon said: He who has one hundred vineyards, one hundred fields, and one hundred slaves working in them. R. Akiva said: He who has a wife comely in deeds. R. Yose said: He who has a privy not far from his table.[11]

311. "In want of all things" (Deut. 28:48). R. Ammi said in the name of Rav: This means with neither lamp nor table. R. Hisda said: Without a wife. R. Sheshet[12] said: Without an attendant. R. Nahman said: Without knowledge. Other sages taught: Without salt or fat.[13]

312. Abbaye said: We have a tradition that only he who lacks knowledge is poor.[14]

313. R. Joshua ben Levi said: "All the days of a poor man are evil" (Prov. 15:15) if he is irascible; "but contentment is a feast without end" (ibid.), [even for a poor man] when he is content.[15]

314. Where there is wealth, there should be no penny-pinching.[16]

---

1. B. Shab 151b.
2. Exod. R. 31:3.
3. Apparently an ironical shaft directed at the Jewish idea that creation was a single act of God in the distant past.
4. Tanhuma, *Va-yishlah*, §10.
5. "You win!" B. Ta 25a and En Yaakov, ad loc.
6. The citation from Ecclesiasticus, evidently found among the fragments of the Cairo geniza, is not found in current texts, which are all based on the Greek translation. B. Ket 110b.
7. B. BK 92a.
8. B. Sanh 105a.
9. Avot 4:1.
10. B. Shab 32a.
11. At that time, privies were out in the fields. B. Shab 25b.
12. He was blind (see above, part 2, chap. 1, §632.).
13. B. Ned 41a.
14. Ibid.
15. B. BB 145b.
16. B. Shab 102b.

315. Should you hear that your neighbor is dead, believe it; that your neighbor got rich, do not believe it.[1]

316. All parts of the body depend on the heart. But the heart depends on what's in the purse.[2]

317. Three things are distressing to the body. Disease of the heart is distressing to the body. More distressing than disease of the heart is disease in the bowels. More distressing than either is lack of money in the purse.[3]

318. "And everything in their train that made them stand up" (Deut. 11:6). R. Eleazar said: The verse refers to a man's money, which enables him to stand up on his feet.[4]

319. R. Yohanan said: I remember the time when four *seah* [of wheat] cost as little as one *sela*, yet for lack of a mere *issar* many people in Tiberias were swollen with hunger.[5]

320. A man must not squander his possessions.[6]

321. The Torah wishes to spare Israel unnecessary expense.[7]

322. Scripture says, "And the priest shall command that they empty the house," etc. (Lev. 14:36). What is it that the Torah seeks to spare? Man's earthenware vessels, even his cruse and his ewer.[8] If the Torah is so concerned about property that is of least worth, how much more about property that one prizes most; if about the property of a wicked man,[9] how much more about the property of a righteous man.[10]

323. "And Jacob remained alone" (Gen. 32:25). R. Eleazar said: He remained behind for the sake of some small narrow-necked jugs.[11] From this incident it follows that their property is more precious to the righteous than their body. Why so? Because they do not reach out to seize what is not theirs.[12]

324. Crumbs [scattered] in a house lead to poverty.[13]

325. The angel of poverty was following a certain man but could not get hold of him, because the man was extremely careful about picking up crumbs. One day he ate some bread while he was seated on a grassy spot, and the angel of poverty said: This time he is sure to fall into my hands. But after eating, the man brought a mattock, dug up the blades of grass, and threw them into the river.[14] The man then heard the angel's voice crying: Alas! This man has driven me out of his home!

Abbaye said: At first I used to think that one should pick up crumbs [from the floor] because one should be tidy, but recently my master told me that it was because not doing so leads to poverty.[15]

326. The [heavenly] prince in charge of sustenance is called Nakid, one who picks up crumbs. The prince in charge of poverty is called Naval, one who is wasteful.[16]

327. A man's possessions should not be more precious to him than his person.[17]

328. The presumption is that no man will readily assent to the loss of his money.[18]

329. The reason property is called *nekhasim* is because it conceals itself (*nikhsin*) from one person, and makes itself available to another. Why are certain coins called *zuzim*? Because they remove themselves (*zazim*) from one and give themselves to another. Why is money called *mamon*? Because what you count (*moneh*) so carefully is nothing at all.[19]

330. R. Isaac said: Blessing is possible only in that which is hidden from the eye, as is said, "The Lord will command the blessing for thee only in that which is hidden[20] from thee" (Deut. 28:8).

Sages in the school of R. Ishmael taught: Blessing is possible only in things not under the direct control of the eye, as is said, "The Lord will command the blessing for thee [only] in that which is hidden from thee."

Our masters taught: One who enters his barn to measure the new grain should recite the prayer "May it be Your will, O Lord our God, to send blessing upon the work of our hands." Once he begins to measure, he should say, "Blessed be He who sends blessing into this heap." If, however, he measures and then recites the prayer, it is a prayer in vain—blessing cannot be found in anything already weighed, anything already measured, anything already counted, but only in what is hidden from sight.[21]

---

1. B. Git 30b.
2. P. Ter 8:10, 46b.
3. Eccles. R. 7:26, §2.
4. B. Pes 119a.
5. B. BB 91b.
6. B. Ar 24a.
7. B. RH 27a.
8. Since they cannot be cleansed by immersion, they must be broken if the priest declares the house unclean.
9. Leprosy in a house is considered punishment for the sin of slander.
10. Neg 12:5.
11. Since he had already taken across the ford "that which he had" (Gen. 32:24), he must have come back for some odds and ends left behind.
12. So what they have earned by honest work is more precious to them. B. Hul 91a.
13. Jacob risked his life to save his odds and ends; the righteous earn their property by hard and long labor, not easily by robbery. But cf. below in this chapter, §327. B. Pes 111b.
14. To prevent the crumbs being trod upon and thus wasted, the man threw them into the river for the fish.
15. B. Hul 105b.
16. B. Pes 111b.
17. B. BK 117b.
18. B. Shab 153a.
19. Num. R. 22:8.
20. The word *asamekha* ("thy barns") is here associated with *samuy* ("hidden").
21. B. Ta 8b.

331. He who sees a pot in his dream may anticipate well-being, as is said, "When thou puttest on [a pot], there will be well-being for us" (Isa. 26:12).[1]

332. When the barley is quite gone from the jar, strife comes knocking at the door.[2]

333. We have been taught that R. Simeon ben Eleazar said: Attend to what comes to hand, what you have the means for, and what is still within your power. If you defer today's needs and its obligations to the morrow, the morrow will have [more than] enough to cope with its own needs and obligations—how can it cope with those of yesterday?[3]

334. We have been taught that R. Eliezer the Elder said: He who has a loaf of bread in his basket but says, "What will I eat tomorrow?" is one of those who are lacking in faith.[4]

335. It is written in the book of Ben Sira: "Be not distressed about tomorrow's trouble, for you do not know what the morrow will bring." When the morrow comes, you may be no more, so that you will have worried about a world that is not yours.[5]

336. "Sustenance for each day on its day" (Exod. 16:4). He who created the day creates the sustenance for it. From this verse R. Eleazar of Modiim infers: He who has enough to eat today but wonders, "What will I eat tomorrow?" is lacking in faith.[6]

337. The Holy One sits at the height of the world and apportions sustenance for each creature.[7]

338. The Holy One sits and nourishes the entire world, all of it, from the horns of wild oxen to the eggs of vermin.[8]

339. There is the story of a priest who was reduced to poverty and wanted to go outside the Land. So he called his wife and said to her, "Since people are in the habit of coming to me to have me examine the plague spots on their bodies, come and I will teach you, so that you will know how to examine such spots. When, in examining a man's hair, [you find that] its oil well is dried up, you will know that the man is stricken, because for each and every hair the Holy One created a well of its own from which to drink. When its well is dried up, the hair dries up." His wife responded, "If for each and every hair the Holy One created a well from which to drink, is it not more fitting by far that the Holy One should provide sustenance for you—a man from whom his children derive their sustenance?" So she did not let him go outside the Land.[9]

340. R. Tahalifa the brother of Rabbannai of Hozae taught: Between New Year's Day and the Day of Atonement, all of a man's sustenance [for the coming year] is fixed for him, except his expenses for Sabbaths and festivals, and his expenses for his children's instruction in Torah. If he diminishes any of these, his sustenance is reduced; if he increases these, his sustenance is increased.[10]

341. Rava said: Length of life, children, and sustenance depend not on one's merit, but on one's *mazzal*.[11] Consider Rabbah and R. Hisda. Both were saintly sages—when one prayed for rain, it came; when the other prayed for rain, it also came. Yet R. Hisda lived to the age of ninety-two, but Rabbah only to the age of forty. In R. Hisda's house, sixty wedding feasts were celebrated; in Rabbah's house, sixty bereavements. In R. Hisda's house, there was bread of the finest flour even for dogs, and it went to waste; in Rabbah's house, barley[12] bread was for human beings, and even that was hardly to be had.[13]

342. Sages taught in the name of R. Simeon ben Yohai: The loaf and the rod, wrapped together, were handed down from heaven. Thus the Holy One said to Israel: If you keep the Torah, here is a loaf to eat; if not, here is a rod to be chastised with.[14]

343. Our masters taught: When there is famine in the city, take to your legs, for it is said, "And there was a famine in the Land, and Abram went down to Egypt" (Gen. 12:10).[15]

344. Wealth in abundance—bad; in moderation—good.[16]

345. The more you get, the more you fret.[17]

346. "And Di-zahav"[18] (Deut. 1:1). What is meant by Di-zahav? The sages in the school of R. Yannai taught: Moses protested to the Holy One, saying, "Master of the universe, it is the silver and gold (*zahav*) You showered upon Israel until they said, 'Enough' (*dai*)—it is that which led them to make the [golden] calf." In explaining Moses' protest, sages in the school of R. Yannai quoted the proverb, "A lion roars [in pleasurable delight] not over

1. JV: "Lord, Thou wilt establish peace for us." But the stem *shft* means "establish" as well as "put on [a pot]." B. Ber 56b; Yalkut, Isa., §429.
2. B. BM 59a and En Yaakov, ad loc.
3. B. Shab 151b, as it appears in the Arukh.
4. B. Sot 48b.
5. B. Yev 63b.
6. Mek, *Be-shallah*, *Va-yassa*, 2.
7. B. Pes 118a.
8. B. Shab 107b; B. AZ 3b.
9. Tanhuma B, *Tazria*, §8.
10. B. Betz 15b–16a.
11. Star.
12. Barley was fodder for animals.
13. B. MK 28a.
14. Lev. R. 35:6.
15. B. BK 60b.
16. Based on B. Git 70a.
17. Avot 2:7.
18. An unidentified place.

a heap of straw but over a heap of [freshly killed] flesh."

[In illustrating Moses' protest], R. Oshaia told the parable of a man who had a heifer that was lean but leggy. When he fed her tasty vetches, the heifer kicked him [in sheer delight]. So the man said: What led you to kick me, if not the tasty vetches I myself fed you?

[In explaining Moses' protest], R. Hiyya bar Abba told in the name of R. Yohanan still another parable: A man had a son. He bathed and anointed him, gave him ample food and drink, and hung a purse about his neck. Then he set him down at the door of a brothel. How could the young man do other than sin? R. Sheshet said: This bears out the proverb "A full belly leads to rebellious deeds."

R. Samuel bar Nahmani taught in the name of R. Jonathan: How do we know that in the end the Holy One reversed Himself and admitted to Moses that He was wrong? Because God said, "I multiplied unto her silver and gold, which [I should have known] they would use for Baal" (Hos. 2:10).[1]

The Labor of Man's Hands

347. "That the Lord thy God may bless thee" (Deut. 14:29). Lest it be thought that God's blessing comes to a man who sits in idleness, the verse ends with the injunction "In all the work of thy hand which thou must do" (ibid.). If a man works, he is blessed; if not, he is not blessed.[2]

348. R. Dostai bar Yannai said in the name of R. Meir: In Scripture, Isaac is told, "And I will bless thee" (Gen. 26:24). So, expounding these words,[3] Isaac said: Clearly blessing rests only on the work of one's hands. So he set about sowing, as is said, "And Isaac sowed in that land, and found in the same year a hundredfold" (Gen. 26:12).[4]

349. "God hath seen mine affliction, and the labor of my hands, and gave judgment yesternight" (Gen. 31:42). Because of the labor of Jacob's hands, God warned Laban not to do harm to Jacob. Thus Scripture teaches that a man should not say, "I will eat and drink and enjoy what is good, but will impose no burden on myself, and mercy will be shown [me] from Heaven." Hence Scripture: "Thou hast blessed the work of his hands" (Job 1:10). A man must toil, work with both his hands. Then the Holy One sends His blessing.[5]

350. "Go to the ant, thou sluggard; consider her ways and be wise" (Prov. 6:6). R. Simeon ben Eleazar said: It was sufficient humiliation for man that he had [to be told] to learn from an ant. Had he learned [from her] and done likewise, he would have been sufficiently humbled, but since he was to have learned from her ways and did not, [the humiliation is all the greater].[6]

351. "And the Lord God caused a deep sleep to fall upon the man" (Gen. 2:21). R. Joshua of Sikhnin said in the name of R. Levi: The beginning of man's downfall is sleep. When he sleeps, he does not occupy himself with Torah; when he sleeps, he does no work.[7]

352. R. Simeon ben Eleazar said: Even Adam tasted nothing before he worked, for Scripture says, "And He put him into the Garden of Eden to till it and to tend it" (Gen. 2:15), and only after that, He told him, "Of every tree of the Garden of Eden thou mayest freely eat" (ibid.).

R. Tarfon said: The Holy One did not cause His Presence to dwell among Israel until they did some work, for Scripture says, "And let them make Me the Sanctuary, then shall I dwell among them" (Exod. 25:8).

R. Judah ben Betera said: He who has no work to do—what should he do? If he has a run-down courtyard or a run-down field, let him go and busy himself with it, for Scripture says, "Six days shalt thou labor, and do any kind of thy work" (Exod. 20:9). What is signified by Scripture's saying, "any kind of thy work"? To include him who has run-down courtyards or run-down fields—let him go and busy himself with them.

R. Yose said: Man dies only out of idleness.[8]

353. A parable of a man who had a filly, a she-ass, and a sow. He measured out barley to the she-ass and the filly, but let the sow eat as much as she wanted. The filly complained to the she-ass, "What is the idiot doing? To us, who do the work of the master, he rations food, but to the sow, who does nothing, he gives as much as she wants." The she-ass replied, "The time will come when you will see the sow's downfall, for she is stuffed with fodder not out of deference to her but to her own harm." When the Calends[9] came, they took the sow and stuck her. Later, when barley was placed before the youngling of the she-ass, she sniffed at it without eating it. So her dam said to her: My daughter, not the eating but the idleness leads to being slaughtered.[10]

354. Idleness leads to unchastity. Idleness leads to dull wits.[11]

355. "And when ye come into the Land, ye shall plant" (Lev. 19:23). The Holy One said to Israel: Even though you find it full of all kinds of good, you are not to say, "We will stay put and not plant." But be sure to plant saplings. Even as, when you entered, you found saplings that others planted, so you are to plant for your children.

"He hath made everything beautiful in its time; also

---

1. B. Ber 32a.
2. TdE 14 (JPS, p. 70).
3. The verse reads: "Will bless thee and multiply thy seed." So Isaac inferred that even as multiplication of kind requires sexual intercourse, so growth in possessions requires sowing.
4. Tos Ber 7:8.
5. Tanhuma, *Va-yetze*, §13.
6. Sif Deut., §306.
7. Gen. R. 17:5; Yalkut, *Bereshit*, §26.
8. ARN 11.
9. The first day of the Roman month, usually observed as a feast.
10. Esther R. 7:1; Yalkut, Esther, §1053.
11. B. Ket 59b.

He hath caused to be hidden (*ha-'olam*) for their heart" (Eccles. 3:11). The word *ha-'olam* [*h-'vlm*], spelled here defectively, without the letter *vav*, is to be read *he'elim* "caused to be hidden"—[that is, the Holy One hid the day of death from the heart of man]. Had the Holy One not hidden the day of death from the heart of man, no man would have built or planted, for he would have said, "Tomorrow I may die—why should I get up and weary myself for the sake of others?" Therefore the Holy One hid the day of death from the heart of man, so that a man would build and plant. If he merits it, it will be his; if not, it will be for others.

A story is told of Emperor Hadrian when he was on his way to war, proceeding with his troops to fight a certain province that had rebelled against him. On the road, he encountered an old man who was planting fig saplings. Hadrian asked him, "How old are you now?" The old man: "A hundred years old." Hadrian: "You are a hundred years old, yet you go to all this trouble to plant fig saplings! Do you expect to eat from them?" The old man: "My lord emperor, I am indeed planting. If I am worthy, I shall eat the fruit of my plantings; and if not, then even as my forebears have labored for me, so I labor for my children." After spending three years at war, Hadrian returned and found that old man in the same place. What did the old man do? He took a basket, filled it with beautiful first-ripe figs and presented it to Hadrian, saying, "My lord king, pray accept this from your servant. I am the same old man whom you found busy planting saplings on your march. Behold, He who is everywhere granted me the privilege of eating the fruit of my saplings. The figs in the basket are some of that fruit." Hadrian ordered his servants, "Take the basket from him and fill it with gold coins." His servants did so, and the old man took the basket filled with gold coins and went home. Boasting of it to his wife and children, he told them the entire story. Now, the wife of that old man's neighbor, who was standing there, heard what the old man told and, taunting her husband, said, "All other people get about, and the Holy One provides them with good things, while you stay home in the dark [of poverty]. Look, our neighbor presented the emperor with a basket of figs, and the emperor filled it for him with gold coins. Now you get busy. Take a big basket, fill it with all kinds of good things—apples, figs, and other delicious fruit which he loves very much. Then go and present them to him—perhaps he will fill your basket with gold coins as he did for our old neighbor." Heeding his wife, the man took a big basket, filled it with figs, hoisted it on his shoulder, and approached the emperor on a side road. He stood before him and said, "My lord emperor, I hear that you are fond of fruit, and so I came to present some figs to you." The emperor said to his officers, "Take the figs and pelt his face with them." They promptly stripped him naked and proceeded to pelt his face with the figs until his face swelled up. The officers all but blinded him in their endeavor to make an example of him. Finally, he went home sobbing in despair. When his wife saw him, his face swollen, his body bruised and battered, she asked, "What happened to you?" He replied, "I'll get even with you for all the 'honor' accorded me." She then said to him, "Go and exult before your mother that what was thrown at you was figs and not citrons, and that they were ripe and not green."[1]

356. If a man does not prepare on the eve of the Sabbath, what will he eat on the Sabbath?

If a man does not plow and sow, harvest and vintage during the sunny season, what will he eat during the rainy season?[2]

357. R. Hanina ben Pazzi said: Thorns get neither hoeing nor sowing, yet they grow of themselves and rise up high. Wheat, on the other hand—how much pain and labor is required before it comes up.[3]

358. R. Tarfon used to say: Do not remove yourself from the norm that has no limit and from the task that has no end.[4] By what parable may the matter be understood? By the one of a man who keeps drawing water from the sea and pouring it on dry land—the sea is not diminished, and the dry land is not filled. So, too, if a man grows impatient [about the amount of Torah he acquires], he should be told: Numskull, why are you impatient? [However little you learn], every day you gain the equivalent of a gold denar.[5]

359. R. Sheshet said: Work is excellent for warming up the body [before one sits down to eat].[6]

360. On his way to the house of study, R. Judah used to carry a pitcher on his shoulder, saying, "Great is labor, for it honors the laborer."

R. Simeon used to carry a basket on his shoulder, saying, "Great is labor, for it honors the laborer."[7]

361. R. Meir said: Pause and consider how important is the capacity to work. For an ox [stolen and slaughtered or sold by a thief], the penalty is fivefold, because he took it from its work; but for a lamb [stolen and slaughtered or sold], the penalty is only fourfold, because the thief did not take it away from work.[8]

362. Sages of the school of R. Ishmael taught: "Choose life" (Deut. 30:19) means: choose a craft.[9]

363. Rabban Gamaliel said: To what may he who has a craft be compared? To a vineyard encompassed by a hedge or to a ditch surrounded by a fence. But to what may he who has no craft be compared? To a vineyard not encompassed by a hedge, to a ditch not surrounded by a fence.

R. Eleazar bar Zadok said in the name of Rabban Gamaliel: To what may he who has a craft be likened? To

---

1. Tanhuma, *Kedoshim*, §8; Lev. R. 25:5.
2. Eccles. R. 1:15, §1; Midrash Prov. 6:6.
3. Gen. R. 45:4.
4. Study of Torah.
5. ARN 27.
6. B. Git 67b.
7. B. Ned 49b.
8. B. BK 79b.
9. P. Pe 1:1, 15c.

a hedged vineyard, into which neither cattle nor beast can enter; what is in it, no passersby can eat, and what is in it, no passersby can see. But to what may he who has no craft be compared? To a vineyard whose fence is breached—cattle and beasts can enter it; passersby can eat and see all that is in it.[1]

364. Though the famine lasted seven years, it never so much as passed the craftsman's door.[2]

365. Shemaiah said: Love work, and avoid holding public office.[3]

366. Rabban Gamaliel son of R. Judah [I] the Patriarch said: Study of Torah combined with an occupation is good, for labor at both keeps sin out of one's mind. But study of Torah alone, without an occupation, will in the end come to naught, and even occasion sin.[4]

367. He who is versed in Scripture, Mishnah, and a worldly occupation will not easily sin, for it is said, "A threefold cord is not easily broken" (Eccles. 4:12). But he who is versed in neither Scripture nor Mishnah nor a worldly occupation is not part of the civilized world.[5]

368. R. Ishmael bar R. Nahman said: Worldly occupation preceded the giving of Torah by twenty-six generations. The words "To maintain the way [and then] the tree of life" (Gen. 3:24) refer to this precedence: "the way—that is, the way of an occupation—first, and then "the tree of life," the [giving of] Torah.[6]

369. Our masters taught: "And thou shalt gather in thy corn" (Deut. 11:14). What is the intent of these words? Since Scripture says, "This book of Torah shall not depart out of thy mouth" (Josh. 1:8), we might suppose that the injunction [not to allow Torah's words to depart from one's mouth] is to be taken literally. Therefore Scripture says, "And thou shalt gather in thy corn," a way of saying [that one must combine study of Torah with] a worldly occupation. Such was the view of R. Ishmael. But R. Simeon ben Yohai differed. Is it possible? he asked. If a man plows when plowing is called for, sows when sowing is called for, reaps when reaping is called for, threshes when threshing is called for, and winnows when the wind is blowing, what is to become of the Torah? However, what Scripture means is that when Israel obey the will of Him who is everywhere, their work is performed by others, in keeping with the promise "Strangers shall stand and feed your flocks" (Isa. 61:5). But when Israel do not obey the will of Him who is everywhere, their work must be done by themselves, as Scripture says, "And thou shalt gather in thy corn." Nor is this all: the work of others will also be done by Israel, in keeping with "And thou shalt serve thine enemy" (Deut. 28:48).

Abbaye observed: Many followed R. Ishmael's advice and succeeded [in Torah and in their worldly occupation]; others followed R. Simeon ben Yohai's advice and succeeded in neither.

Rava said to the scholars [who studied with him]: I beg of you not to appear before me during Nisan and Tishri,[7] so that you will not need to worry about your sustenance during the other months of the year.

Rabbah bar Bar Hanah said in the name of R. Yohanan, who quoted R. Judah bar Ilai: Pause and consider the difference between the earlier and later generations. The earlier generations made the study of Torah a primary concern and their daily work a secondary one, and both prospered in their hands. The later generations made their daily work a primary concern and their study of Torah a secondary one, and neither prospered in their hands.[8]

370. R. Joshua said: If a man recites two *Halakhot* in the morning and two *Halakhot* in the evening, and the rest of the day is occupied with his work, it is imputed to him as though he [meditated upon it day and night, and thus] fulfilled the entire Torah, all of it.

"Thou shalt meditate therein day and night" (Josh. 1:8)—[a precept that is impossible to fulfill]. Hence R. Simeon ben Yohai said: Only to men who ate manna[9] was the Torah given to study intensely, since such men had no need to engage in craft or business. Otherwise, could a man sit and study Torah, not knowing where his food and drink would come from or where he would get his clothes or coverings? One must conclude that the Torah was given to be studied intensely only by men who ate manna, and secondly by [priests], who ate heave offerings.[10]

371. R. Hiyya bar Ammi said in the name of Ulla: He who lives from the labor of his hands is greater than he who fears Heaven.[11] For of him who fears Heaven, it is written, "Happy is the man that feareth the Lord" (Ps. 112:1). But of him who lives from the labor of his hands, it is written, "When thou eatest the labor of thy hands, happy shalt thou be; and it shall be well with thee" (Ps. 128:2). "Happy shalt thou be" in this world; "and it shall be well with thee" in the world-to-come.[12]

372. R. Hana the Moneychanger said: Once, Bar Nappaha [came to my banker's table and stood] over me. He asked me for a Gordian denar with which to measure a defect.[13] When I tried to stand up before him, he would

1. Tos Kid 1:11.
2. He could always barter his wares for food. B. Sanh 29a.
3. Avot 1:9.
4. Avot 2:2.
5. B. Kid 40b.
6. Adam was placed in the Garden of Eden to till it and tend it (Gen. 2:15), and twenty-six generations later—ten from Adam to Noah, ten from Noah to Abraham, six from Isaac to Moses—in the generation of Moses, the Torah was given. Lev. R. 9:3.
7. The season of reaping and vintage.
8. B. Ber 35b.
9. Whom God Himself provided with sustenance.
10. Mek, *Be-shallah*, *Va-yassa*, 3; Tanhuma, *Be-shallah*, §20.
11. And depends on others for his livelihood.
12. B. Ber 8a.
13. In an animal's windpipe or skull, to determine whether the animal was kosher.

not allow me, saying: Sit down, my son, sit down—craftsmen engaged in their work are not expected to stand up before disciples of the wise.[1]

373. "It is good for a man that he bear the yoke in his youth" (Lam. 3:27)—the yoke of Torah, the yoke of a wife, the yoke of work.[2]

374. R. Judah said: He who does not teach his son a craft is as though he were teaching him to be a brigand.[3]

375. R. Meir said: A man should teach his son a craft that is honorable[4] and unburdensome; and he should pray to Him to whom riches and possessions belong, for there is no craft in which there are not both poverty and wealth. In truth, poverty does not come from one's craft, nor does wealth; all comes according to one's merit.

R. Simeon ben Eleazar said: Have you ever seen a beast or a fowl practicing a craft? Yet both get their sustenance without toil. Now, were they not created solely to serve me, even as I was created to serve my Maker? Is it not proper then that I also should make my living without toil? The answer is that I have acted evilly and so forfeited my right to sustenance without toil.

We have been taught that R. Simeon ben Eleazar said: I have never seen a lion who was a porter, a gazelle who was a harvester of figs, a fox who was a shopkeeper, a wolf who was a seller of pots—yet they are sustained without toiling. Now, these were created solely to serve me, while I was created to serve my Maker. If these, which were created solely to serve me, are sustained without toil, surely I, who was created to serve my Maker, should make my living without toil. The answer is that I acted evilly and so forfeited my right to sustenance without toil. As Scripture says, "Your iniquities have turned away these things, and your sins have withholden the bounty from you" (Jer. 5:25).[5]

376. Abba Gorion of Zidon said in the name of Abba Guria: A man should not teach his son to be an ass driver, a camel driver, a potter, a mariner, a shepherd, or a shopkeeper, for their craft is the craft of robbers.[6]

R. Judah said in Abba Guria's name: Most ass drivers are crooks. Most camel drivers are honest folk. Most mariners are pious folk. The best of physicians deserves Gehenna.[7] The most law-abiding of butchers is Amalek's partner.[8]

377. Our masters taught: He whose business is with women has a bad character. For example, goldsmiths, carders, hand-mill sharpeners, peddlers, wool dressers, hairdressers, laundrymen, bloodletters, bath attendants, and tanners.[9] From these, neither a king nor a high priest should be appointed. Why? Not because they are [personally] unfit, but because their craft is held in low esteem.

Our masters taught: Ten things are said of a bloodletter. He walks with his arms akimbo, is arrogant, sits [in lordly fashion], is niggardly with his means, begrudges others, and eats much rich food so that he excretes little; he is suspected of unchastity, cheating, and [unwitting] murder.[10]

378. We have been taught that Rabbi [Judah I, the Patriarch] said: Of course, no craft will ever disappear from the world. But happy is he who sees his parents engaged in a superior craft, and alas for him who sees his parents engaged in a mean craft. The world cannot get along without both perfumer or tanner—happy is he whose craft is the perfumer's, and alas for him whose craft is the tanner's.[11]

379. R. Zutra bar Tobiah said in the name of Rav: The verse "He hath made everything beautiful in its time" (Eccles. 3:11) suggests that the Holy One made every trade seem beautiful in the eyes of him who plies it.[12]

380. "And they turned aside thither, and they said unto [the Levite]: 'Who brought thee hither?' " (Judg. 18:3). They asked him, "Are you not a descendant of Moses? And now would you become a priest for the worship of an idol?" He replied, "I have a tradition from my grandfather's house: a man should hire himself out to officiate at idol-worship rather than be dependent on fellow creatures."

The Levite supposed that they were referring to actual *avodah zarah* (idol-worship). But in fact they were not—they meant work that was strange and uncongenial to him.[13] As Rav said to R. Kahana: Flay a carcass in the marketplace to earn a wage and do not say, "I am a priest, I am an important man, and such work is degrading to me."[14]

381. "The Lord is my shepherd" (Ps. 23:1). R. Hama bar Hanina said: You find no occupation more despised than that of the shepherd, who all his days walks about with his staff and his pouch. Yet David called the Holy One a shepherd![15]

382. Should a man say, "I am a descendant of the fathers of the world, of important stock, and it is not proper that I do menial work and be degraded," he should be told, "Fool, He who has formed you has already anticipated

1. B. Hul 54b.
2. Lam. R. 3:27, §9.
3. B. Kid 29a.
4. Literally, "clean," where the temptations to cheat are few.
5. B. Kid 82a; Tos Kid 5:14.
6. Each has an opportunity to steal.
7. Either because of their being haughty before God or because their treatment at times proves fatal.
8. Because he at times sells meat that is not kosher or his temperament is cruel. So Tosefot Yom Tov, ad loc. B. Kid 82a.
9. All these tradesmen make trinkets or garments, repair household tools, or deal in other ways with women.
10. B. Kid 82a.
11. Ibid.
12. B. Ber 43b.
13. *Avodah zarah* may mean either "strange worship" (i.e., idol-worship) or "strange, uncongenial work."
14. B. BB 110a and En Yaakov, ad loc.
15. Yalkut, Ps., §690.

you. For He did work before you came into the world, as is said, 'From all His work that He had done' " (Gen. 2:2).[1]

383. "And all the labor of my hands God saw" (Gen. 31:42). R. Jeremiah said: Labor is more precious than the merit of ancestors, for the merit of ancestors saved wealth, while labor saved lives. Merit of ancestors saved wealth, as Jacob told Laban: "Except the God of my father . . . surely now hadst thou sent me away empty" (ibid.). But labor saved life, as Jacob went on to say, "God hath seen my affliction and the labor of my hands, and gave judgment yesternight" (ibid.).[2]

384. The merit of work stands by a man even where the merit of ancestors cannot.[3]

Work on the Land and the Give-and-Take of Business

385. R. Eleazar stated: There will be a time when all craftsmen will take up work on the land, for it is said, "All the oarsmen, the mariners, and all the pilots of the sea, shall come down from their ships, they shall stand upon the land" (Ezek. 27:29).

R. Eleazar stated further: No occupation is inferior to that of work on the land, for of the aforementioned, it is said, "And they shall come down" (Ezek. 27:29).

Once, when R. Eleazar saw a plot of land that was plowed across its width, he said to it, "Even if you had been plowed across your length as well, turning over merchandise is still preferable."

Once, when Rav entered among growing ears of corn and observed their swaying, he said to them, "Sway, sway, as much as you will; turning over merchandise is still preferable."

Rava said: A hundred *zuz* in merchandise—meat and wine every day; a hundred *zuz* in land—only salt and vegetables. Furthermore, work on the land compels one to sleep on the ground[4] and be embroiled in strife.[5]

386. Better off is the man who has a vegetable patch, manures it, hoes it, and sustains himself from it than he who rents other people's vegetable patches as a sharecropper. As the proverb puts it: "Who rents one patch eats birds; who rents many patches—birds eat him."[6]

387. R. Eleazar said: A man who owns no parcel of land is not a man, for it is said, "The heavens are the heavens of the Lord; but the earth hath He given over to men" (Ps. 115:16).[7]

388. R. Eleazar said: Land is given only to strong men [who can defend it], as is said, "As a strong man, who hath land" (Job 22:8).

Resh Lakish said: The verse "He that labors on his land like a slave shall have food in plenty" (Prov. 12:11) means that if he makes himself a slave to his land, he will have food in plenty; if not, he will not have food in plenty.[8]

389. "A king maketh himself a slave to the fields" (Eccles. 5:8). Even if the king rules from world's end to world's end, he still must make himself a slave to his fields, for he has to keep asking, "Have the fields produced? Have the fields not produced?" Therefore, "he that loveth silver cannot be satisfied with silver, nor he that loveth abundance, unless there be produce [of the fields]" (Eccles. 5:9). He who huffs and puffs after wealth,[9] but owns no land—what joy can be his?[10]

390. There were three who had a passion for land, but no good came to them from it: Cain, tiller of the soil; Noah, the husbandman; and Uzziah, who loved husbandry.[11]

391. "Blessed art thou [if thou hast several crops] in the field" (Deut. 28:3). Your crops should be of three kinds: a third of the field in produce, another third in olives, and still another third in vines.[12]

392. Our masters taught: The verse "And of Asher he said: . . . Let him dip his foot in oil" (Deut. 33:24) speaks of the land of Asher, which, like a spring, flowed with oil.

It is told that when the people of Laodicea were in need of oil, they appointed an agent and instructed him, "Go and purchase for us a hundred myriads' worth of oil." He went first to Jerusalem, where he was told, "Go to Tyre." When he went to Tyre, he was told, "Go to Gush Halav." He went to Gush Halav and was told, "Go to So-and-so, who is out in the field." He went there and found the man breaking up the earth under his olive trees. The agent asked, "Do you have a hundred myriads' worth of oil?" The man replied, "Wait until I finish my work." The agent waited until he finished his work. Then the man slung his tools over his back and proceeded on his way, kicking stones from his path as he went. The agent asked himself: Is it likely that such a man would have a hundred myriads' worth of oil? It seems that the Jews are making sport of me. When the man got to his hometown, his maidservant brought him a kettle of hot water, and he washed his hands and feet in it. Then she brought him a

1. Zohar, Midrash Ne'elam.
2. Gen. R. 74:12.
3. Tanhuma, *Va-yetze*, §13.
4. Since he must remain in his field during the night to guard the crops.
5. With the owners of adjoining fields. B. Yev 63a.
6. Since he cannot possibly watch all the patches, birds devour his crops. Lev. R. 3:1.
7. B. Yev 63a.
8. B. Sanh 58b.
9. In the Hebrew, there is a play on the words *homeh u-mehammeh* ("huffs and puffs") and *mamon* ("wealth").
10. Eccles. R. 5:8, §1.
11. Cain was sentenced to become a wanderer (Gen. 4:12); Noah got drunk and his nakedness was exposed (Gen. 9:20); and Uzziah became a leper (2 Chron. 26:20). Gen. R. 22:3.
12. So that if one crop fails, you will still have the others. B. BM 107a.

golden bowl full of oil, and he dipped his hands and feet in it, in fulfillment of "Let him dip his foot in oil." After they ate and drank, the man measured out to the agent a hundred myriads' worth of oil and then asked, "Do you perhaps need more oil?" The agent: "Yes, but I have no more money with me." The man: "If you wish to buy more, take it, and I will go back with you for the money." The man measured out an additional eighteen hundred myriads' worth of oil. It is said that there was not a horse, a mule, a camel, or an ass in the Land of Israel that the agent did not hire [to transport the oil]. When he got back to his city, the citizens came out to give him a hero's welcome. He said to them, "Do not give such a welcome to me; rather, give it to this man who has come [with me], for he has measured out a hundred myriads' worth of oil, and I still owe him for an additional eighteen myriads' worth."

The story illustrates the verse "There is he that pretendeth himself rich, yet hath nothing; there is he that pretendeth himself poor, yet hath great wealth" (Prov. 13:7).[1]

393. Samuel said: In one matter I am to my father as vinegar is to wine. For my father used to inspect his property twice a day, whereas I do so only once a day. Samuel here followed his own maxim, for Samuel used to say: He who inspects his property [at least once] daily is sure to find at least one *sela*.[2]

Abbaye used to inspect his property daily. One day he met his tenant carrying off a bundle of twigs. Abbaye: "Where is this going to?" The tenant: "To my master's house." Abbaye: "Long have the sages anticipated you."[3]

R. Assi, who used to inspect his property daily, asked, "Where are all those *sela* Master Samuel promised?" One day, when he saw that a water pipe had burst in his field [and inundated it], he took off his cloak, rolled it up, stuffed it into the hole, and began to shout, so that people came and stopped up the break in the pipe. Then he said, "Now I see all those *sela* Master Samuel promised."[4]

394. R. Yohanan said: He who wishes to become rich should occupy himself with [breeding] small cattle. R. Hisda added: The verse "The young (*ashtarot*) of thy flock" (Deut. 7:13) implies that the young of small cattle enrich (*measherot*) their owners.[5]

395. "The lambs will provide you with clothing" (Prov. 27:26). Your clothing should be of the fleece of your own lambs. "The he-goats, the price of a field" (ibid.). It is better for a person to sell his field and buy he-goats [with the proceeds], than to sell his he-goats and buy a field. "The goats' milk will suffice for your food" (Prov. 27:27). The man will then find the goats' milk and the lambs in his house sufficient to provide for his sundry needs [and he need not slaughter the mothers for meat].[6]

396. "The Lord hath delivered me into the hands of those I cannot withstand" (Lam. 1:14). In the west [the Land of Israel], they said: The speaker in the verse is one whose sustenance depends solely on his money.[7]

397. R. Isaac said: A man should always have his money in his hand [so to speak], in keeping with "Bind up the money in thy hand" (Deut. 14:25).

R. Isaac also said: A man should divide his money into three parts: one-third in land, one-third in merchandise, and one-third at hand.[8]

398. "And he divided the people . . . into two camps" (Gen. 32:8). The Torah teaches good sense—a man should not put all his eggs in one basket.[9]

399. R. Judah said: One should always be careful that there is produce in his house, for strife is apt to arise in a man's house largely because of disputes about food, as is said, "He bringeth peace into thy borders, when He satisfieth thee with choice wheat" (Ps. 147:14). R. Papa said: Hence the proverb "When barley is gone from the jar, strife comes knocking at the door."

R. Hinena bar Papa said: A man should always see to it that there is produce in his house, because only when they had no produce left were Israel called "impoverished," as is said, "After Israel had done their sowing, [the foes] would attack them, destroy the produce of the land . . . and Israel was greatly impoverished" (Judg. 6:3–4 and 6:6).[10]

400. R. Hanin said: The words "And thy life shall hang in doubt before thee" (Deut. 28:66) apply to one who purchases produce year after year. "And thou shalt fear night and day" (ibid.) apply to one who purchases produce from Sabbath eve to Sabbath eve. "And shalt have no assurance of thy life" (ibid.) apply to one who depends on a bakeshop [for his bread].[11]

401. R. Ahai ben Josiah said: To whom may he who buys produce in the marketplace be compared? To an infant whose mother has died, and although he is brought around from door to door to different wetnurses, he is never satisfied.[12]

402. Rav said to his son Aibu: I have labored to teach you *Halakhah*, but without success. So come, and I will teach you worldly wisdom: sell your wares while the sand

1. B. Men 85b and En Yaakov, ad loc.
2. The meaning is that he who inspects his property daily will be ahead, for he will make sure that everything is in proper order and that no workman takes advantage of him during his absence.
3. By their advice to inspect one's property daily, whereby pilfering and thievery is stopped.
4. By being on the spot, he was able to halt serious damage to his crop. B. Hul 105a and En Yaakov, ad loc.
5. B. Hul 84b.
6. B. Hul 84a.
7. Since he has no land, he must buy his daily food from others. B. Yev 63b.
8. B. BM 42a.
9. Literally, "all his money in one corner." Gen. R. 76:3.
10. B. BM 59a and En Yaakov, ad loc.
11. B. Men 103b.
12. ARN 30.

is still on your feet.[1] Everything you sell, you may regret,[2] except wine, which you may sell without regret.[3] Drop the money into your purse, then open your sack.[4] Better a *kav* from the ground than a *kor* from the roof.[5] [Once the dates are in your bag, run to the brewery.][6]

403. When you buy, you gain; when you sell, you lose.[7]

404. When merchandise is held in low esteem, its price at rock bottom, go and buy it up, for in the end its price will rise.[8]

405. When merchandise is cheap, hasten to collect [money] and buy some.[9]

406. When a horn is sounded [in the marketplace] in Rome [inquiring about figs], you who are the son of a fig seller, [take advantage of the scarcity and] sell your father's figs [even without his permission].[10]

407. It is the way of the world for people to bring merchandise to a place where there is a demand for it.[11]

408. Bring herbs to Herbtown.[12]

409. R. Papa said: Sow, and you will not need to buy. Sell [even your household effects] to avoid the disgrace of beggary. Stop up [a small hole], and you will not need to repair. Repair, and you will not need to rebuild, for when a man engages in rebuilding, he will be reduced to beggary.[13]

410. R. Yohanan said: He whose father leaves him a great deal of money and wishes to lose it—let him wear linen garments, use glassware, and hire workmen and not be with them [so that they will be idle].[14]

411. "And will do that which is right in His eyes" (Exod. 15:26) while engaged in the give-and-take of business. The verse implies that when a man gives and takes in his business with integrity, and the spirit of his fellow creatures delights in him, it is accounted to him as if he had fulfilled the entire Torah, all of it.[15]

1. After buying, sell quickly.
2. Since the price may go up.
3. Had you waited, it might have turned into vinegar.
4. Be sure to get the money for the merchandise before delivering it to the purchasers.
5. Rather earn a little near home than much far away.
6. To brew beer out of them—otherwise, you may eat them or they may deteriorate. B. Pes 113a.
7. B. BM 51a.
8. Tanhuma, *Mishpatim*, §5.
9. B. Ber 63a.
10. B. Ber 62b.
11. Exod. R. 9:6.
12. Since people come there to buy them. B. Men 85a.
13. B. Yev 63a.
14. B. BM 29b; B. Hul 84b.
15. Such a man will be regarded as "giving ear to His commandments and keeping all His statutes" (Exod. 15:26). So Nahmanides, ad loc. Mek, *Be-shallah*, *Va-yassa*, 1.

412. While R. Giddel was negotiating the purchase of a field, R. Abba came along and bought it. So R. Giddel went and lodged a complaint against R. Abba before R. Zera, who then went and reported the complaint to R. Isaac Nappaha. R. Isaac Nappaha responded, "Wait until R. Abba comes up to us for the next festival." When R. Abba came up, R. Isaac confronted him and asked, "If a poor man is turning a [wheat] cake over the coals, and another person comes along and takes it away from him, what would you call such a person?" R. Abba: "I would call him a scoundrel."

R. Isaac: "Then why, master, did you behave as you did?"

R. Abba: "I did not know that R. Giddel was negotiating the field's purchase."

R. Isaac: "Then let the master turn it over to R. Giddel right now."

R. Abba: "I will not turn it over to him through sale, because it is the first field I have ever bought, and when a man sells his first field, it is a bad omen for him. However, if he is willing to accept it as a gift, he may have it."

Now, R. Giddel refused to take possession of the field, because it is written, "He that hateth gifts shall live" (Prov. 15:27). Nor would R. Abba take possession of the field, because R. Giddel had negotiated its purchase. And so, since neither would take possession, it came to be called the Sages' Field.[16]

413. A seller interprets the terms of a sale liberally.[17]

414. This is the way of traders: they show the inferior wares first, and then display the best.[18]

415. Even he who buys and sells [at the same price] is called a merchant.[19]

416. The profit is mortgaged for the principal.[20]

417. Samuel said: When a man profits, he should profit no more than one-sixth above his cost.[21]

418. Do not pretend to be interested in a purchase if you do not have the money.[22]

419. An article bought has charm in the eyes of its buyer.[23]

420. When a person has made a bad purchase in the marketplace, should one praise it in his presence or disparage it? Surely one should praise it in his presence.[24]

16. B. Kid 59a.
17. Consequently, all parts of the property, unless specifically excluded, are presumed to have been sold or included in the terms of sale. B. BB 37a.
18. Tanhuma, *Shelah*, §6.
19. B. BM 40b.
20. And cannot be collected before it is due for distribution—it may be offset by a loss. B. BM 105a.
21. B. BM 40b.
22. B. Pes 112b.
23. B. Sot 47a.
24. B. Ket 17a.

421. Our masters taught: They who dispose of merchandise at inflated prices[1] with a hullabaloo of false advertising, they who raise small cattle [which destroy crops],[2] they who cut down goodly fruit trees [for kindling], and they who greedily eye the better portion [when sharing with their neighbors] will never see a sign of blessing. Why not? Because people look askance at them.[3]

422. R. Joshua ben Levi said: The Men of the Great Assembly observed twenty-four fasts [to implore Heaven] that they who write Torah scrolls, tefillin, and mezuzot should not get rich, for if they got rich, they would not continue writing.

Our masters taught: They who write Torah scrolls, tefillin, and mezuzot, and those who trade in such articles, and those who trade with those who trade in them—indeed, all who engage in trade with sacred articles, which includes the sellers of blue dye for fringes—will never see a sign of blessing.[4]

423. Our masters taught: Four kinds of small change never bring a sign of blessing: the wages of Torah scribes, the wages of interpreters,[5] the profits of [the money of] orphans [held in trust], and coins that come from a city across the sea.[6]

424. Our masters taught: He who earns his money from trade in reeds and jars will never see a sign of blessing.[7]

425. They who lend money on interest deny the Root of the universe.[8]

426. We have been taught that R. Yose said: Pause and consider the blindness of usurers! When a man calls his neighbor a scoundrel, the neighbor resents it so much that he might even deprive him of his livelihood. But usurers bring witnesses, a scribe, and pen and ink, and they record and seal [a document that in effect declares], "That so-and-so [the usurer] denies the God of Israel."

We have been taught that R. Simeon ben Eleazar said: When a man has money and lends it without interest, Scripture says of him, "He who hath never lent money on interest, or taken a bribe against the innocent—he who acts thus shall never be shaken" (Ps. 15:5). From this verse you may infer that if a man lends money on interest, his possessions shall be shaken.[9]

427. A man should sell his daughter [into servitude] rather than lend money on interest.[10]

428. R. Judah said in the name of Rav: He who has money and lends it without witnesses transgresses "Thou shalt not put a stumbling block before the blind" (Lev. 19:14). And Resh Lakish said: He brings a curse upon himself, for [when he comes to collect without adequate proof, and the borrower denies the loan], people say, "Strike dumb those lying lips, so insolent in pride and scorn against an innocent man" (Ps. 31:19).

The sages said to R. Ashi: Ravina fulfills all that the sages have said. So [to test Ravina], late one Friday afternoon, R. Ashi sent word to Ravina: "Please, master, send me ten *zuz* as a loan, because I have a chance to buy a parcel of land." Ravina replied, "Let the master bring witnesses and draw up a writ of debt." R. Ashi: "Even I?" Ravina: "You, master, immersed as you are in your studies, all the more; for you may forget [that you have borrowed] and cause me to curse you."[11]

429. When R. Dimi came [from the Land of Israel], he said: How do we know that when a man is his neighbor's creditor for a *maneh*, and he knows that his neighbor does not have the money to repay it, he may not even pass in front of him? From the verse "Do not act toward him as a creditor" (Exod. 22:24).[12]

430. We have been taught that R. Simeon ben Yohai said: What is the proof that when a man is his neighbor's creditor, he may not greet him, if such is not his usual practice? The verse "Usury—even a word that may remind one of money owed" (Deut. 23:20).[13] Hence, a word of greeting [by a creditor] is forbidden.[14]

431. R. Simeon said: Usury is indeed grave, if even a greeting is regarded as usury.[15]

432. "Unto thy brother thou shalt not lend upon interest" (Deut. 23:21). What is signified by this verse? Has it not already been stated in the verse just preceding, "Thou shalt not lend upon interest to thy brother" (Deut. 23:20)? However, there is advance interest and there is delayed interest. For example: If a man makes up his mind to borrow money from a neighbor and sends him [a gift], saying, "This is to induce you to lend me"—that is advance interest. If a man borrows from his neighbor, repays

1. See Lieberman, TKF 3:854, n. 71. BR: *Simta* ("narrow streets [that abut public thoroughfares])." But the meaning of *simta* here is obscure.
2. See B. BK 80a.
3. B. Pes 50b.
4. Ibid.
5. The sages spoke in a low voice to these officials, who then repeated the sages' words in a loud voice.
6. The sea voyage being so risky. B. Pes 50b.
7. Because reeds and jars are so bulky, people think the trade is enormous and the profit so high that they begrudge it to traders in such wares.
8. Tos BM 6:17.
9. B. BM 71a.
10. B. Kid 20a.
11. B. BM 75b.
12. Ibid.
13. JV: "interest of anything that is lent upon interest." But R. Simeon construes *davar* ("thing") as though written *dibbur* ("word").
14. B. BM 75b.
15. P. BM 5:10, 10d.

the money, and then sends him [a gift], saying, "This is on account of your money, which lay idle with me"—that is delayed interest.[1]

433. We have been taught that R. Simeon said: They who lend money on interest lose more than they gain [because eventually their wealth will be lost].[2] And more: Presuming to regard Moses our teacher as a fool and his Torah as a lie,[3] they say, "Had Moses our teacher known that in this business [of usury] there is great profit, he would not have set down its prohibition."[4]

434. To what may interest be likened? To a man bitten by a serpent, who is not aware of the bite until a swelling sets in. So, too, with interest—a borrower is not aware of it until it swells up all about him.[5]

1. B. BM 75b; Sif Deut., §263.
2. See above in this chapter, §426.

3. The text reads euphemistically: "to regard Moses our teacher as a sage and his Torah as truth."
4. B. BM 75b.
5. Tanhuma, *Mishpatim*, §9; Exod. R. 31:6.

CHAPTER TWO

A MAN'S HOUSEHOLD

Marriage

1. R. Eleazar said: A man who has no wife is not a [complete] man, for Scripture says, "He created them male and female . . . and He [only then] called their name 'man' [Adam]" (Gen. 5:2).[1]

2. "With the Lord's help I brought a man into being" (Gen 4:1).[2] Prior to Eve's saying this, Adam had been created out of the earth, and Eve had been created out of [the rib of] Adam. Henceforth, [Eve went on], it is to be "in our [joint] image, after our [joint] likeness" (Gen. 1:26)—no man can come into being without a woman, and no woman can come into being without a man, and neither of them can come into being without the Presence.[3]

3. R. Tanhum said in the name of R. Hanilai: When a man is without a wife, he lives without joy, without blessing, without good. In the west [the Land of Israel], they added: Also without Torah, without a [protecting] wall. Rava bar Ulla added: Also without peace.[4]

4. "In want of everything" (Deut. 28:48) means, said R. Hisda, in want of a wife.[5]

5. [In referring to the high priest's] "house" (Lev. 16:6), Scripture means his wife.[6]

6. R. Yose said: I never spoke of my wife as "my wife," or of my ox as "my ox," but always referred to my wife as "my house" and to my ox as "my field."[7]

7. Our masters taught: "A man that hath built a new house . . . a man that hath betrothed a wife" (Deut. 20:5 and 20:7). The Torah teaches proper conduct: a man should first build a house and plant a vineyard, and only after that take a wife. In his wisdom, Solomon also said, "Prepare thy work without, and make it fit for thyself in the field; and afterward build thy house" (Prov. 24:27). "Prepare thy work without"—build a house; "and make it fit for thyself in the field"—plant a vineyard; "and afterward build thy house"—take a wife.[8]

---

1. Hence, an unmarried man is only half a man. B. Yev 63a.
2. JV: "I have gotten a man with the help of the Lord." But *knh* ("get") may also mean "bring into being."
3. Gen. R. 8:9 and 22:2.
4. B. Yev 62b and En Yaakov, ad loc.
5. B. Ned 41a.
6. B. Yoma 2a.
7. B. Shab 118b.
8. B. Sot 44a.

8. We have been taught that R. Simeon reasoned: Why does the Torah say, "If a man sets out to take a wife" (Deut. 22:13), and not simply, "If a wife be taken by a man"? Because it is a man's way to set out in search of a woman, and not a woman's way to set out in search of a man, as may be illustrated by the parable of a man who lost something. Who seeks whom? Clearly the one who lost seeks what he has lost.[9]

9. A Caesar said to Rabban Gamaliel [II], "Your God is a thief, for Scripture says, 'The Lord God caused a deep sleep to fall upon Adam, and he slept, and He took one of his ribs' " (Gen. 2:21). Rabban Gamaliel's daughter said to her father, "Leave him to me, and I will answer him." She said to Caesar, "Give me one [of your] military commanders." Caesar: "Why do you need him?" The daughter: "Robbers came during the night, took a silver ladle from us, and left us one of gold."

Caesar: "Would that such a thief came to *us* every day."

The daughter: "Wasn't it wonderful for Adam that one [of his] ribs was taken from him and he was given instead a wife to serve him?"

Caesar: "I agree with you. But God should have taken the rib from Adam openly."

The daughter: "Bring me a piece of meat." When it was brought to her, she put it under the hot ashes, then took it out and, placing it before Caesar, said to him, "Eat some." Caesar: "I find it repugnant." The daughter: "Even so Adam—had the rib been taken from him openly, Eve would have been repugnant to him.[10]

10. "The Lord God caused a deep sleep to fall upon Adam, and he slept, and He took one of his ribs" (Gen. 2:21). A Roman noblewoman asked R. Yose, "Why by way of thievery?" R. Yose: "Consider a parable. If a man deposits one ounce of silver with you in secrecy, and you in plain sight return to him one *litra* of gold—would that be thievery?" The noblewoman: "But why in secrecy?" R. Yose: "At first God created her in plain sight, but Adam saw her full of various discharges and blood [and found her repulsive]. So God removed her from him. Then He returned and created her a second time in secrecy." The noblewoman: "I can corroborate what you said. I was spoken for to be wed to my mother's brother. But because I grew up with him in the same house, I seemed unattractive to him. So he went and took another wife, even though she is not as comely as I."[11]

---

9. Man lost the rib that God made into a woman. B. Kid 2b and En Yaakov, ad loc.
10. B. Sanh 39a.
11. Gen. R. 17:7.

11. At eighteen, a young man should marry.[1]

12. The sages in the school of R. Ishmael taught: Until a young man reaches the age of twenty, the Holy One sits and waits expectantly: "When will this man take a wife?" But when the young man reaches the age of twenty and has still not wed, He says, "May the bones of this one be blasted."

R. Hisda said: Why am I superior to my colleagues [in learning]? Because I wed at sixteen.[2] Had I wed at fourteen, I would have been able to say to Satan, "An arrow in your eye!"[3]

Rava said to R. Nathan bar Ammi: While you have power over your son,[4] when he is between sixteen and twenty-two (some say, between eighteen and twenty-four), get him married.[5]

13. R. Hisda praised R. Hamnuna before R. Huna as a great man. So R. Huna said, "When he visits you, bring him to me." When R. Hamnuna came, R. Huna noticed that he was not wearing the distinctive turban[6] of scholars. "Why," R. Huna asked, "are you not wearing your turban?" R. Hamnuna: "Because I am not married." R. Huna turned his face away from him and said, "See to it that you do not appear before me again until you are!"[7]

14. R. Huna said: He who at twenty is not married will spend all his days in sinful thought.[8]

15. R. Yohanan said: A bachelor who lives in a large city and does not sin—the Holy One Himself daily proclaims his virtue. Now, R. Safra was just such a bachelor living in a large city. When a Tanna repeated [R. Yohanan's dictum] before Rava and R. Safra, R. Safra's face lit up. But Rava said to him: The dictum does not apply to such as you, sir, but to such as R. Hanina and R. Oshaia, who were cobblers in the Land of Israel and lived in the street of harlots. They made shoes for the harlots, which they would deliver to the brothel. The harlots would gaze [provocatively] at the two sages, but the sages would not so much as lift their eyes to look at them. Henceforth, the oath of those harlots came to be "By the life of the holy sages of the Land of Israel."[9]

16. "The fear of the Lord is clean, enduring forever" (Ps. 19:10). R. Hanina said: The verse applies to him who studies Torah in cleanness. Just what does that mean? That he first marries and then studies Torah.[10]

17. Our masters taught: If there is a question whether to study Torah or take a wife, a man should first study Torah and then take a wife. But if the man cannot live without a woman, he may take a wife and then study Torah. R. Judah said in the name of Samuel: The ruling is: a man must first take a wife and then study Torah. R. Yohanan retorted, With a millstone around his neck, is he expected to study Torah?[11]

18. "Rejoice, O young man, in thy youth. . . . But know thou that for all these things God will bring thee to judgment" (Eccles. 11:9). R. Simeon ben Yohai said: The verse may be understood by the parable of one who, finding fault with women, became a profligate. He used to say, "Where can I find a wife good enough for me?" When he grew old and sought to get married, he was told, "You ill-fated wretch! With your nose dripping, your ears hard of hearing, and your eyes dim, what woman will be willing to have you?"[12]

19. R. Hiyya bar Abba said: The words "Hope deferred maketh the heart sick" (Prov. 13:12) refer to a man who betroths a woman and weds her only after some time. "But desire fulfilled is a tree of life" (ibid.) refers to a man who betroths a woman and weds her right away.[13]

20. Rabbi [Judah I, the Patriarch] was engaged in arranging the marriage of his son into the family of R. Hiyya, and when the time came to write out the *ketubbah*, the bride died. Rabbi was troubled: "Was there, God forbid, anything improper [in the proposed union]?" They carefully examined the lineage of the two families and found that Rabbi was descended from Shephatiah the son of Abital,[14] while R. Hiyya was descended from Shimei, a brother of [King] David.[15]

Later, when Rabbi was engaged in having his son marry into the family of R. Yose ben Zimra, it was agreed that the son was first to spend twelve years in the academy. When the girl was led before Rabbi's son, he said, "Let the period of study be reduced to six years." When the girl was led before him a second time, he said, "Let me marry her now, and then I will go to the academy." But [as he made this request] he was embarrassed by the presence of his father, who [to reassure him] said to him, "My son, the intelligence of your Creator resides in you. For in Scripture it is said first, 'Thou bringest them in, and plantest them in the mountain of Thine inheritance, the place which Thou hast made for Thee to dwell in' [Exod. 15:17],[16] and only subsequently did God request, 'Let them make Me the Sanctuary, that I may dwell among them' " (Exod. 25:8). [After his marriage] Rabbi's son went and sat twelve years in the academy. By the time he returned, his wife had lost the capacity to conceive chil-

1. Literally, "a young man is ready for the *huppah* [wedding canopy]." Avot 5:21.
2. And was thus able to devote myself entirely to study.
3. "You can't incite me to sinful thoughts!"
4. Literally, "your hand is upon his neck."
5. B. Kid 29b–30a.
6. The *sudarium*.
7. B. Kid 29b.
8. Ibid.
9. B. Pes 113a.
10. B. Yoma 72b.

11. B. Kid 29b.
12. Eccles. R. 11:9, §1.
13. PR 15:3.
14. And of King David. See 2 Sam. 3:4.
15. Since the bride was not of direct royal stock, the proposed union was improper.
16. Thus God also hastened the day of His union with Israel.

dren. Rabbi pondered: What are we to do? Shall we have him divorce her? Then people will say, "This poor soul waited in vain." Shall we have him wed another woman? Then people will say, "The other is his [real] wife, and this one is merely his mistress." So Rabbi sought mercy in her behalf, and she was healed.[1]

21. R. Samuel bar Isaac said: When Resh Lakish began to expound on the theme of a wife suspected of infidelity, he would say, "A man is paired with a woman in keeping with the kind of person he is. Thus it is said, 'The rod of wickedness shall not rest upon the lot of the righteous' " (Ps. 125:3). Rabbah bar Bar Hanah said in the name of R. Yohanan: Pairing a man and a woman is as difficult as the splitting of the Red Sea, as is said, "When God bringeth single people to dwell together [in marriage, it is as awesome as when] He brought forth the imprisoned [Israelites] into prosperity" (Ps. 68:7). But is it so? Did not R. Judah say in the name of Rav: Forty days before the formation of a child, a divine voice goes forth and proclaims, "The daughter of So-and-so is to be given to So-and-so, the house of So-and-so to So-and-so, the field of So-and-so to So-and-so"? There is no contradiction, however, for R. Judah's statement refers to a first marriage; the preceding two statements to a second marriage.[2]

22. A [Roman] noblewoman asked R. Yose ben Halafta, "In how many days did the Holy One create His world?" R. Yose replied, "In six days." She asked, "And what has He been doing since?" R. Yose replied, "The Holy One has been busy making matches: the daughter of So-and-so to So-and-so." The noblewoman said, "If that is all He does, I can do the same thing. How many menservants, how many maidservants do I have! In no time at all, I can match them up." R. Yose: "Matchmaking may be a trivial thing in your eyes; but for the Holy One, it is as awesome an act as splitting the Red Sea."

R. Yose ben Halafta left the noblewoman and went away. What did she do? She took a thousand menservants and a thousand maidservants, lined them up in row upon row facing one another, and said, "This man shall marry that woman, and this woman shall be married to that man," and so she matched them all up in a single night. In the morning, the ones thus matched came to the lady, one with his head bloodied, one with his eye knocked out, one with his shoulder dislocated, and another with his leg broken. She asked, "What happened to you?" One replied, "I don't want that woman," and another replied, "I don't want that man."

The noblewoman promptly sent to have R. Yose ben Halafta brought to her. She said to him, "Master, your Torah is completely right, excellent and worthy of praise. All you said is exactly so."[3]

23. Rava overheard a young man seeking [God's] mercy and pleading, "May a certain girl become my wife." Rava said to him, "Do not seek mercy in this way. If she is meant to be yours, she will be yours; and if not, you may [in your frustration be tempted to] deny the Lord." Later [after the young man married the girl], Rava overheard him seeking God's mercy that either he die before her or she die before him. Rava said to the young man, "Did I not tell you that you should not have prayed as you did?"[4]

24. Rav said in the name of R. Reuben the Pinecone Dealer: From the Five Books, from the Prophets, and from the Writings it can be shown that a particular wife is appointed for a man by the Lord. From the Five Books: "Then Laban and Bethuel answered and said: 'The thing proceedeth from the Lord' " (Gen. 24:50). From the Prophets: "But his father and his mother knew not that it was of the Lord" (Judg. 14:4). And from the Writings: "House and riches are the inheritance of fathers; but a prudent wife is from the Lord" (Prov. 19:14).[5]

25. A man's marriage partner is from the Holy One. At times, a man is guided to his spouse's home; at other times, the spouse is guided to the man's home.[6]

26. It is told that King Solomon had a most beautiful daughter, whose like could not be found in the whole Land of Israel. When he gazed at the stars to find out who was her appointed spouse and who was to wed her, he saw that he who was to wed her would be a certain poor man—there was none poorer in Israel than he. What did Solomon do? He built a lofty tower in the open sea and surrounded its four sides with [high] walls. Then he took his daughter and placed her in that lofty tower, in the company of seventy eunuchs selected from the elders of Israel. Solomon provided no doorway into the tower, so that no man would be able to enter. After stocking the tower with ample provisions, he said, "Now I shall see what the acts and doings of His Name will be!"

After a while, the poor man who was to be the maiden's spouse set out by night on a journey. He was naked and barefoot, he was hungry and thirsty [and thoroughly chilled]. When he saw the carcass of an ox cast out in the field, he crept in between its ribs to lessen the chill which overcame him. As soon as he fell asleep, a huge bird came, picked up the carcass, and carried it to the roof of the tower above the maiden's chamber. There the bird ate away the flesh of the carcass, and there, on the roof, the poor man remained.

At daybreak the maiden came out of her chamber, as was her daily custom, to walk on the roof. And there she saw the young man. "Who are you," she asked, "and who brought you here?" The young man: "I am a Jew, of the city of Acco. A bird brought me here." What did she do then? She took him into her chamber, where she had him clothed, bathed, and anointed. And then he appeared so handsome that his like could not be found in all the territories of Israel.

The maiden fell in love with him with all her heart

1. B. Ket 62b.
2. B. Sot 2a.
3. Gen. R. 68:4; Lev. R. 8:1; Num. R. 3:6.
4. B. MK 18b.
5. B. MK 18b.
6. E.g., Jacob to Rachel, and Rebekah to Isaac. Gen. R. 68:3.

and soul. It should be added that the young man was keen, perceptive, and witty, besides being a [skilled] scribe. One day she asked him, "Are you willing to hallow me as your wife?" The young man: "O that such a thing were possible!" What did he do then? He let some blood out of a vein, wrote out the marriage contract for her with his blood, and hallowed her as his wife, saying, "This day the Lord is witness, even as the angels Michael and Gabriel are witnesses." Presently she conceived from him.

When the elders noticed her pregnancy, they said to her, "It seems to us that you are bearing a child." She: "Yes, I am." "And from whom did you conceive?" "Why do you have to know?" At that, the faces of the elders fell, for they feared King Solomon. Then they sent word for him to come. Solomon boarded a ship and came to them [with dispatch]. They said to him, "Our lord king, this is the situation. Let our lord not blame his servants!" Upon hearing the elders' account Solomon summoned his daughter and asked her what had happened. She answered, "The Holy One brought me a handsome and kind youth, who is both scholar and scribe, and he hallowed me as his wife." She summoned the young man, who appeared before the king and showed him the marriage contract he had drawn up for the king's daughter. The king inquired about the young man's father and mother, his family, and the city he came from. From the answers, Solomon understood that this was the one he had seen in the stars. With that, Solomon rejoiced greatly and said, "Blessed be He who is everywhere! It is He who provides a man with the wife meant to be his."[1]

27. R. Papa said: Leap to buy land, lag to place a wedding band. Step down for the woman who'll be your bride; step up for the escort who'll bring you pride.[2]

28. R. Eleazar said: One should always marry into a better family, for take note: from Moses, who wed Jethro's[3] daughter, there issued Jonathan;[4] while from Aaron, who wed Amminadab's daughter, there issued Phinehas.[5]

29. Rava said: He who is about to take a wife should inquire about her brothers, as intimated in Scripture's saying, "Aaron took Elisheba, the daughter of Amminadab, the sister of Nahshon" (Exod. 6:23). Since she is spoken of as the daughter of Amminadab, is it not obvious that she is also the sister of Nahshon? Why, then, is it added that she was also the sister of Nahshon? To intimate that when a man takes a wife, he should inquire about [the character] of her brothers.

The sages taught: Most children take after their maternal uncles.[6]

1. Tanhuma B, introduction, p. 136.
2. A wife of lesser family will look up to her husband; an escort (a best man) of superior lineage will enhance the bridegroom's status. B. Yev 63a.
3. A Midianite priest at an idolatrous shrine.
4. Hired as a priest for Micah's idol. See Judg. 18.
5. Who became a zealous and respected high priest. B. BB 109b.
6. B. BB 110a.

30. Who is rich? R. Akiva said: He who has a wife comely in her deeds.[7]

31. There is a proverb: Ewe follows ewe—as the deeds of the mother, so are the deeds of the daughter.[8]

32. When a man weds a wife who is right for him,[9] [the prophet] Elijah kisses him and the Holy One loves him.[10]

33. Rabbah bar R. Adda said in the name of Rav: He who weds a wife for the sake of money will have unworthy children, as is said, "Since they have dealt treacherously against the Lord, they have begotten children who are estranged" (Hos. 5:7). Should you suppose that their money at least will go unscathed, the verse goes on, "Now shall a moon devour them and their portions." What do these words imply? R. Nahman bar Isaac said: That a moon comes and a moon goes, and their money is lost.

Rabbah bar R. Adda also said (according to some, R. Salla said it in the name of R. Hamnuna): When a man weds a wife who is not fit for him, [the prophet] Elijah binds him and the Holy One flogs him. And the sages taught: Of all such, Elijah writes and the Holy One countersigns: Woe to him who blemishes his seed and dishonors his family.[11]

34. R. Meir used to say: When a man weds a wife who is not right for him, he violates five commandments negative [and positive. Three negative]: "Thou shalt not take vengeance; Thou shalt not bear a grudge" (Lev. 19:18); "Thou shalt not hate thy brother" (Lev. 19:17). [Two positive]: "Thou shalt love thy neighbor as thyself" (Lev. 19:18); "Thy brother shall live with thee" (Lev. 25:36). Moreover, he prevents the birth of children in the world.[12]

35. Our masters taught: Let a man always sell all that he has in order to marry the daughter of a disciple of the wise, for if he should die or be taken into exile, he can be certain that his sons will be disciples of the wise. Let him not marry the daughter of an *am ha-aretz* [an ignorant man], for should he die or be taken into exile, his sons will be ignorant.

Our masters taught also: Let a man always sell all that he has in order to marry the daughter of a disciple of the wise or to have his daughter marry a disciple of the wise, which is like mingling the grapes of one vine with the grapes of another vine, a proper and acceptable procedure. But let him not marry the daughter of an *am ha-aretz*, which is like mingling the grapes of a vine with berries of a thornbush, an improper and unacceptable procedure.

Our masters taught further: Let a man always sell all he has in order to marry the daughter of a disciple of the wise. If he does not find the daughter of a disciple of

7. B. Shab 25b.
8. B. Ket 63a.
9. One whose character and lineage are right.
10. DER 1.
11. B. Kid 70a.
12. Such a misalliance is likely to prove unfruitful. Tos Sot 5:11.

the wise, let him marry the daughter of one of the notables of the generation. If he does not find the daughter of one of the notables of the generation, let him marry the daughter of the head of a synagogue. If he does not find the daughter of the head of a synagogue, let him marry the daughter of a collector of funds for charity. If he does not find the daughter of a collector of funds for charity, let him marry the daughter of a teacher of young children. But let him not marry the daughter of an *am ha-aretz*, because such are detestable, their wives are vermin, and of their daughters it is said, "Cursed be he that lieth with any manner of beast" (Deut. 27:21).[1]

36. "Now Joshua [the High Priest] was clothed with filthy garments" (Zech. 3:3). Was it indeed Joshua's practice to wear filthy garments? No, but the verse indicates that his sons wed women unfit to marry priests, and he did not prevent them from doing so.[2]

37. Our masters taught: A little boy may be trusted if he says, "My daddy told me that this family is fit [to marry into priestly families], while that family is unfit, and we ate at the *Ketzatzah* [the cutting off] when the daughter of So-and-so was married to So-and-so."

What is *Ketzatzah*? If one of several brothers has wed a wife who is not fit for him, the other members of his family come around and bring a jar full of parched corn and nuts, and in the presence of the children break it in the open space [before the house], saying, "Our brethren of the House of Israel, hear! Our brother So-and-so has wed a wife who is not fit for him, and we fear that his issue will commingle with our issue. Come and take some of these as a token for future generations, so that his issue will not commingle with our issue." The children pick up [what has been scattered], saying, "So-and-so has been cut off from his family."

Should the brother divorce such a wife, his family would perform the same ceremony, saying, "So-and-so has returned to his family."[3]

38. We have been taught: "Then the elders of the city shall call him, and impart advice to him" (Deut. 25:8) implies that the brother-in-law who is asked to marry the widow is given suitable advice. If he is young and the widow is old, or if he is old and the widow is young, he should be told, "What will you do with a young girl?" or "What will you do with an old woman? Marry someone your own age, and don't bring disharmony into your household."[4]

39. Resh Lakish said: An unusually tall man should not marry an unusually tall woman, lest their offspring turn out to be as tall as a mast. A dwarf should not marry a dwarf, lest their offspring turn out to be finger-sized. A man whose complexion is abnormally white should not marry a woman whose complexion is abnormally white, lest their offspring turn out to be albino. A man whose complexion is abnormally dark should not marry a woman whose complexion is abnormally dark, lest their offspring turn out to be pitch-black.[5]

40. R. Judah said in the name of Rav: A man may not marry a woman until he has first seen her.[6]

41. "Thine eyes are dovelike" (Song 1:15). As long as a bride's eyes are normal, her body requires no examination [by the prospective husband's kinswomen]; but if her eyes are bleary, her body does require examination.[7]

42. R. Eleazar said: A man may not give his daughter in marriage while she is a minor. He must wait until she grows up and says, "I want So-and-so."[8]

43. When a man sees to it that his sons and daughters are married at the age of their puberty, Scripture says of him, "Thou shalt know that thy tent is in peace" (Job 5:24).[9]

44. Once your daughter has come of age, then [if you cannot find anyone better] free your slave and give him to her [for a husband].[10]

45. R. Judah said in the name of Rav: He who weds his daughter to an old man or takes an adult woman for his immature son, "to the utter ruin of the sated or of the thirsty—him," says Scripture, "the Lord will never forgive" (Deut. 29:18–19).[11]

46. "Profane not thy daughter to make her a harlot" (Lev. 19:29). R. Eliezer said: The verse applies to one who weds his daughter to an old man. R. Akiva said: It also applies to one who lets his grown-up daughter remain unmarried.[12]

47. We have been taught that R. Meir used to say: He who weds his daughter to an *am ha-aretz* [an ignorant person] is as though he bound her and placed her before a lion. As a lion tears and then brazenly devours, so an *am ha-aretz* will beat her and then brazenly copulate with her.[13]

48. There is the story of a woman who, when wed to an associate scholar [haver], would tie the thongs of tefillin to his arm, and subsequently, when wed to a tax collector, would tie to his arm the tax collector's seals.[14]

1. Lacking, as they do, piety, moral sense, and intellectual perception. B. Pes 49a–b.
2. B. Sanh 93a.
3. B. Ket 28b; P. Kid 1:5, 60c.
4. B. Yev 101b.
5. B. Bekh 45b.
6. B. Kid 41a.
7. B. Ta 24a.
8. B. Kid 41a.
9. B. Yev 62b.
10. B. Pes 113a.
11. B. Sanh 76b.
12. B. Sanh 76a.
13. B. Pes 49b.
14. He would remove and distribute these as receipts for taxes paid. B. AZ 39a.

49. There is the story of a maiden whose father was very friendly with a heathen. Once, as they ate and drank and made merry, the heathen said to the maiden's father, "Give your daughter to my son for a wife." The father said, "Very well." Though the maiden heard of the matter, she said nothing until the time of her wedding. When the day of her wedding came, she went up to the roof and jumped to her death.[1]

50. There is the story of a young girl who was walking [one morning] to her father's home. She was very beautiful, and her beauty was further enhanced by gold and silver ornaments. But she lost her way and wandered into uninhabited places. By midday she grew thirsty, for she had brought no water with her. At the sight of a well with a bucket rope hanging at its side, she took hold of the rope and lowered herself [into the well]. After she drank, she wished to go up but could not; so she wept and shouted for help.

A young man passing by heard her voice and stopped at the well. He looked down at her and asked, "Who are you—human or spirit?" "I am human," she cried out. He asked, "What happened to you?" She told him the whole story. The young man: "If I pull you up, will you be my wife?" She replied, "Yes," and he pulled her up.

He wished to mate with her at once. But she asked him, "From what people do you come?" He replied, "I come from the people of Israel, from such-and-such place, and I am a priest." She said to him, "The Holy One chose you, hallowed you out of all Israel, yet now, without *ketubbah*, without marriage rites, you would mate like an animal? Follow me to my father and mother, who are of such-and-such a family, eminent and of noble lineage in Israel, and I shall be betrothed to you." So they pledged faithfulness to each other. When she asked, "But who will act as witness?" a weasel happened to be passing by, so she said, "Let this weasel and this well act as witnesses to our pledge." Then he went his way, and she went hers.

Now, the girl remained true to her pledge, and when anyone came to seek her hand in marriage, she would turn him down. But after her family began pressing her [to accept someone], she proceeded to act like an epileptic, ripping up her own garments and the garments of anyone who touched her. Finally, people left her alone.

As for the young man, as soon as he came back to his city, he violated his pledge, wed another woman, and begot two sons. But one fell into a well and died, and the other died after being bitten by a weasel. The young man's wife asked him, "What is the cause of this, that both our sons have died unnatural deaths?" He told her, "Such-and-such a thing happened." At that, she demanded that he divorce her, saying, "Go to the portion the Holy One has given you."

He went away and, inquiring about the girl in her city, was told, "She is an epileptic, and anyone who wishes to wed her is treated in such-and-such a way." The young man went to her father's house, told him all that had happened, and declared, "I am willing to take her with any blemish she may have." The father called witnesses [to attest the young man's declaration]. When the young man went to see her, she began to act in what had become her customary manner. So he reminded her of the incident with the weasel and the well. Then she said, "Indeed, I have been faithful to my pledge," and immediately became her normal self. She married him, and the two were blessed with many children and possessions. To her apply the words "Mine eyes are on those who are faithful in the Land" (Ps. 101:6).[2]

51. Our masters taught: How does one praise a bride while dancing attendance upon her? The school of Shammai says: Describe the bride as she is. The school of Hillel says: Describe the bride as beautiful and full of grace. The school of Shammai retorted to the school of Hillel: But suppose she is lame or blind. Is one to say, "O bride, beautiful and full of grace," seeing that Scripture declares, "Keep thee far from a false word" (Exod. 23:7)? The school of Hillel replied to the school of Shammai: In your opinion, if a man has made a bad purchase in the marketplace, should a friend praise it to his face or belittle it? Surely he should praise it to his face. Hence, the sages inferred that a man should always endeavor to be pleasant to other people.

It is said of R. Judah bar Ilai that he used to take a myrtle twig and dance before the bride, chanting, "O bride, beautiful and full of grace."

R. Samuel bar R. Isaac used to dance holding three twigs. When R. Zera saw him, [he was so embarrassed that] he tried to keep out of sight, saying, "Look at this old man, how he embarrasses us!" However, when R. Samuel died, there were peals of thunder and lightning for three hours, and finally a divine voice came forth and proclaimed, "R. Samuel bar R. Isaac, the lavish dispenser of kindness, is dead. Let everyone come out to show kindness to him." [When they came out], a pillar of fire stood between him and the rest of the people (and we have a tradition that such a pillar intervenes only for one man, or at most for two, in a generation). R. Zera said: *Shoto*, his twig, benefited the old man. According to some, R. Zera said: *Shetuto*, his folly, benefited the old man. According to others, R. Zera said: *Shitato*, his custom, benefited the old man.

R. Aha used to lift the bride upon his shoulder and dance.

When R. Dimi came [from the Land of Israel], he said: In the west, they sang before a bride, "No kohl, no paint, no waving [of the hair], and still as graceful as a gazelle."[3]

52. Our masters taught: Wine may be drawn through pipes for a groom and a bride.[4] Parched corn and nuts may be thrown before them during the summer, but not during the winter. Fancy cakes are not to be thrown before them either during the summer or during the winter.[5]

---

1. TdE, ed. Friedmann, p. 116 (JPS, p. 293); Yalkut, *Balak*, §766.

2. Rashi on B. Ta 8a; Arukh, s.v. *heled*.

3. B. Ket 16b–17a; P. Pe 1:1, 15d.

4. Either as a prayer for prosperity or to diffuse a pleasant odor. At the pipes' outlet, there is a vessel into which the wine flows.

5. Fancy cakes thrown on the ground would go to waste. B. Ber 50b and En Yaakov, ad loc.

53. It is said of King Agrippa that he made way for a bridal procession and the sages praised him for it. When asked, "Why did you do this?" he replied, "I wear my crown every day, while she will wear hers but a single hour."[1]

54. A groom is [to be treated] like a king.[2]

55. A husband is liable for the maintenance of his wife. For we have been taught that in Scripture's "Her meat [*she'er*] . . . he shall not diminish" (Exod. 21:10), *she'er* refers to a wife's maintenance.[3]

56. If a man maintains his wife through a trustee, [every week] he must give her not less than two *kav* of wheat or four *kav* of barley. R. Yose remarked, "It was R. Ishmael who stipulated the larger amount of barley, because he lived near Edom [where barley is of poor quality]." A man must also give his wife half a *kav* of pulse, half a *log* of oil, and a *kav* of dried figs or a *maneh* of pressed figs. And if he has no [such produce of his own], he must supply her with a corresponding quantity of produce from some other place. He must also provide her with a bed and a mattress, or at least a rush mat. [Once a year] he must also give her a cap for her head and a girdle for her loins; on each major festival, a pair of shoes; and each year, clothing valued at fifty *zuz.* He should not give her new clothes in the summer [because they are too warm] or worn-out clothes in the winter [because they do not provide sufficient protection from the cold]. Rather, he should give her new clothes valued at fifty *zuz* in the winter, so she can wear them the following summer, when they will have been worn thin [and become cool]; these worn-out clothes remain her property. [Every week] he must also give her a silver *maah* for her [other] requirements, and she is to eat with him on every Sabbath eve. If he does not give her a silver *maah* for her other requirements, [the earnings of] her handiwork belong to her.

And what [is the quantity of work that] she must do for him? [She must spin] five *sela* of warp in Judea, which equals ten *sela* in Galilee,[4] or ten *sela* of weft in Judea, which equals twenty *sela* in Galilee. If she is nursing [her child], her handiwork must be reduced and her maintenance increased. All this applies to the poorest in Israel; with more affluent folk, all should be in keeping with the honor due the husband.[5]

57. The following are the kinds of work a wife must perform for her husband: grinding wheat, baking bread, washing clothes, cooking, nursing her child, making her husband's bed, and working in wool. If she brought him one bondwoman [in her dowry], she need not grind, bake, or wash. If she brought two bondwomen, she need not cook or nurse her child. If three, she need not make her husband's bed or work in wool. If four, she may lounge [all day] in an easy chair. R. Eliezer said: Even if she brought him a hundred bondwomen, he may compel her to work in wool, for idleness leads to unchastity. R. Simeon ben Gamaliel said: If a man forbids his wife under a vow to do any work, he must divorce her and pay her the amount stipulated in the *ketubbah*, for idleness leads to stupefaction.[6]

58. In the west [the Land of Israel], when a man married, they used to ask, "*Matza* or *motze*?" By *matza*, they alluded to "Whoso findeth (*matza*) a wife findeth a great good" (Prov. 18:22), and by *motze*, they alluded to "I find (*motze*) more bitter than death the woman" (Eccles. 7:26).[7]

59. It is written in the book of Ben Sira: "A good wife is a precious gift—she is put in the bosom of one who fears God. A bad wife is a plague to her husband. A beautiful wife is a joy to her husband—she doubles the length of his life."[8]

60. R. Akiva expounded: When a husband and wife are worthy, the Presence abides between them; when not worthy, fire consumes them.[9]

61. The sages taught in the name of R. Meir: A husband and a wife: the Presence—the Divine Name YH—is between them: the *yod* in *ish* ("husband") and the *he* in *ishah* ("wife"). If they are worthy, the Presence abides between them, and they are blessed; if they are not worthy, the Presence departs from between them, and the two *ishot* ("fires") in *ish* and *ishah* cling together, so that a fire consumes both husband and wife.[10]

62. R. Yose met [the prophet] Elijah and asked him: It is written, "I will make him a help" (Gen. 2:18). But how does a woman help a man? Elijah: "If a man brings wheat, does he chew the raw wheat? If he brings flax, does he put on the green flax?[11] Does not the woman bring light to his eyes and help him stand on his own two feet?"[12]

63. R. Eleazar said: The verse "I will make him a help over against him" (Gen. 2:18) means: if he is worthy, she is a help to him; if he is not worthy, she is against him.

Others say: R. Eleazar pointed to an apparent inconsistency. The word is written *ke-negdo*, "meet for him," but it can be read *ke-nigdo*, "at him." The answer is that if he is worthy, she is meet for him; if not, she lashes out at him.[13]

---

1. B. Ket 17a; Sem 11:6.
2. Literally, "resembles a king." PRE 16.
3. B. Ket 46b–47b.
4. The Judean *sela* was twice as heavy as the Galilean.
5. B. Ket 64b.
6. B. Ket 59b.
7. B. Ber 8a.
8. Cf. Ecclesiasticus 26:3 and 26:1. B. Yev 63b.
9. "The letters of the word for 'husband' are *alef*, *yod*, and *shin*, and for 'wife' *alef*, *shin*, and *he*. The *yod* and the *he* form the Divine Name; but if they are omitted, only *alef* and *shin* are left, which form the word *esh*, 'fire' " (Sot, Soncino, p. 89, n. 3). B. Sot. 17a.
10. Lekah Tov, *Bereshit*, ed. Buber, p. 23.
11. Clearly not. She grinds and bakes the wheat, and spins and weaves the flax.
12. B. Yev 63a.
13. Ibid.

64. R. Hanina said: "All the days of the poor are evil" (Prov. 15:15). "The poor" applies to a man who has an evil wife. "But he that is of a merry heart hath a continual feast" (ibid.). "A merry heart" applies to him who has a good wife.[1]

65. Rava said: A bad wife is as troublesome as a stormy day.

What is a bad wife? Abbaye said: One who sets out a tray for him,[2] and then belittles him. Rava said: One who sets out a tray for him and then turns her back on him.[3]

66. On account of a bad wife, old age comes to a man quickly.[4]

67. Once, when Rav was taking leave of R. Hiyya, R. Hiyya said to him: May He who is everywhere deliver you from something that is worse than death. "But is there," Rav wondered, "anything worse than death?" He went out to investigate the matter and found the verse "I find more bitter than death the woman" (Eccles. 7:26).[5]

68. R. Judah said: There are fourteen things of which one is stronger than the other, so that each one of these dominates another. The ocean's depth is strong, but earth dominates it. The earth is strong, but mountains dominate it. A mountain is strong, but iron splits it. Iron is strong, but fire penetrates it. Fire is strong, but water quenches it. Water is strong, but clouds carry it. Clouds are strong, but wind disperses them. The wind is strong, but a wall withstands it. A wall is strong, but man demolishes it. Man is strong, but trouble shatters him. Trouble is strong, but wine helps one forget it. Wine is strong, but sleep evaporates it. Sleep is strong, but illness drives it off. Illness is strong, but the angel of death [dominates it and] takes life away.

But a bad wife is stronger than all of these.[6]

69. The sages quoted Rav: Any disease, but not disease of the bowels; any pain, but not pain in the heart; any ache, but not headache; any evil, but not an evil wife.[7]

70. Rav was constantly tormented by his wife. When he said to her, "Prepare some lentils for me," she would prepare beans; if he said, "Beans," she would prepare lentils. After Rav's son Hiyya grew up, he took to reversing his father's requests, until finally Rav said to his son, "Your mother has grown kind [to me]." R. Hiyya said, "It was I who reversed your requests." Rav said, "What you have done bears out the proverb 'Your offspring in season may teach you reason.' Nevertheless, do not continue to do so, lest you become like those of whom Scripture says, 'They have trained their tongues to speak falsely' " (Jer. 9:4).[8]

71. It is unbecoming for a man to walk behind a woman.[9]

72. Rav said: A man who follows his wife's advice will fall into Gehenna, as is said, "But there was none like unto Ahab . . . whom Jezebel his wife stirred up" (1 Kings 21:25).[10]

73. R. Avimi of Hagronia said in the name of Rava: A man whom women have done to death—there is neither judgment nor judge in his behalf.[11]

74. The story of a pious man who was wed to a pious woman, and they did not beget children. Both said, "We are of no use whatever to the Holy One." So he went ahead and divorced her. The husband then married a wicked woman, and she made him wicked, while the divorced wife went and married a wicked man, whom she made righteous. This proves that it all depends on the woman.[12]

75. "Whoso findeth a wife findeth a great good" (Prov. 18:22). Yet in another place it is written, "I find more bitter than death the woman" (Eccles. 7:26). What Scripture means is that if she is a good wife, there is no end to her goodness, but if she is a bad wife, there is no end to her badness.[13]

76. Rava said: Pause and consider how precious is a good wife and how baneful is a bad wife. "How precious is a good wife," for it is written, "Whoso findeth a wife findeth a great good" (Prov. 18:22). Now, if "wife" here means literally a woman, then how precious must a good wife be, since Scripture praises her; if "wife" here means the Torah, then how precious must a good wife be, since Torah is likened to her. "How baneful is a bad wife," for it is written, "I find more bitter than death the woman" (Eccles. 7:26). Now, if "the woman" here means literally a woman, then how baneful must a bad wife be, since Scripture reprehends her; if "the woman" here means Gehenna, then how baneful must a bad wife be, since Gehenna is likened to her.[14]

77. R. Helbo said: A man must always be careful about the deference he shows his wife, for blessing is found in a man's home only on account of his wife, as is said, "And He treated Abram well on account of her" (Gen. 12:16). For this reason, Rava said to the people of Mahoza: Defer to your wives, that you may prosper.[15]

---

1. B. BB 145b.
2. Offers herself.
3. B. Yev 63b.
4. Tanhuma, *Hayye Sarah*, §2.
5. B. Yev 63a.
6. Eccles. R. 7:26, §2.
7. B. Shab 11a.
8. B. Yev 63a and En Yaakov, ad loc.
9. It might stimulate indecent thoughts in him. Gen. R. 60:14.
10. B. BM 59a.
11. Since he had not been man enough to stand up to the women. B. BM 97a.
12. Gen. R. 17:7 and Yalkut, *Bereshit*, §23.
13. MTeh 59:2.
14. B. Yev 63b.
15. B. BM 59a.

78. Our masters taught: He who loves his wife as his own person, who honors her more than his own person, who directs his sons and his daughters onto the right path, and marries them off at puberty—of him, Scripture says, "And thou shalt know that thy tent is in peace" (Job 5:24).[1]

79. People say: If your wife is short, bend down and whisper to her [to solicit her counsel].[2]

80. A man should always be careful about wronging his wife. Since her tears come quickly, punishment for wronging her is quick to come.[3]

81. We have been taught that R. Simeon ben Eleazar said: One's impulse, a child, and a woman—the left hand may thrust them off, but the right hand should bring them near.[4]

82. R. Rehumi used to study Torah in the school of Rava in Mahoza, and he would come home on the eve of the Day of Atonement. Once he became [unusually] involved in his study. His wife, who was expecting him, [kept solacing herself], "He'll be here any minute, he'll be here any minute," but he did not come. She was so disheartened that a tear fell from her eye. R. Rehumi was [at that moment] seated on the roof [of the house of study]—the roof collapsed under him, and he was killed.[5]

83. R. Hiyya was constantly tormented by his wife. Nevertheless, if he came upon something that might please her, he would wrap it in his turban and bring it home. Rav said to him, "But she torments the master." R. Hiyya: "It is enough for us that they rear our children and deliver us from sin."[6]

84. A woman has charm for her husband.[7]

85. Rav said to R. Hiyya, How do women earn merit? By making their sons go to the synagogue to learn Scripture, making their husbands go to the house of study to recite Mishnah, and waiting up for their husbands until they return from the house of study.[8]

86. "It is vain for you that ye rise early, and sit up late, ye that eat the bread of toil! Thus He gives to those that let sleep wander"[9] (Ps. 127:2). R. Isaac said: The verse refers to wives of disciples of the wise who deliberately let sleep wander from their eyes in this world and so merit life in the world-to-come.[10]

87. A story of R. Akiva's son when he got married. How did he conduct himself? After he brought his wife into the nuptial chamber, he stayed awake the whole night reading in the Torah. He said to her, "Fetch a lamp and light it for me." She took a lamp and stood [holding it] over him from evening until morning. In the morning, R. Akiva approached his son and asked him, "My son, [is she] well found or ill found?"[11] His son replied, "[She is] well found."[12]

88. If a man places his wife under a vow that she neither borrow nor lend a winnow, a sieve, a mill, or an oven, he must divorce her and pay her the amount stipulated in her marriage settlement, because [if she were to abide by the vow] he would give her a bad name among the neighbors. So, too, if she herself vows that she will neither borrow nor lend a winnow, a sieve, a mill, or an oven, or that she will not weave beautiful garments for his children, she must be divorced, with forfeiture of the amount due her under her marriage settlement, because [if he allowed her vow to stand], she would give him a bad name among his neighbors.[13]

89. There is the story of a man who vowed to derive no benefit from marriage with his sister's daughter. She was then taken into R. Ishmael's house and adorned to look beautiful. Afterward, when R. Ishmael asked the man, "My son, did you vow not to benefit from this beautiful girl?" the man replied, "Oh, no!" At that, R. Ishmael permitted her to marry him.

At that moment, R. Ishmael wept and said: The daughters of Israel are beautiful, but poverty makes them seem ugly.

The sages taught: She had a false tooth, and R. Ishmael had a gold tooth made for her at his own expense.

When R. Ishmael died, the daughters of Israel raised a lament, saying, "O daughters of Israel, weep for R. Ishmael!"[14]

90. There is the story of a man who said to his wife: "I vow that you are not to benefit from me until you make R. Judah and R. Simeon taste your cooking." R. Judah consented to taste it, reasoning: One may argue the matter *a fortiori*: if, in order to make peace between husband and wife, the Torah quotes God as saying, "Let My Name which is written in sanctity be erased by the water of bitterness, even when the guilt of the woman who is to drink it is in doubt"—how much less should I stand on my dignity [and refuse to taste the food]. R. Simeon, however, did not taste the woman's cooking, exclaiming, "Even if this woman should be widowed and all her children perish, R. Simeon will not budge from his position. Besides, [people should be taught a lesson] not to fall into the habit of making vows."[15]

---

1. B. Yev 62b.
2. B. BM 59a.
3. Ibid.
4. B. Sot 47a.
5. B. Ket 62b.
6. B. Yev 63a.
7. B. Sot 47a.
8. B. Ber 17a.
9. JV: "So He giveth unto His beloved in sleep." But the word *yedido* ("His beloved") is here associated with the stem *ndd* ("wander").
10. B. Yoma 77a.
11. R. Akiva quoted the key words *matza* ("findeth . . . a great good") and *motze* ("find . . . bitter") in Prov. 18:22 and Eccles. 7:26 respectively. See above in this chapter, §58.
12. Yalkut, Prov., §958.
13. B. Ket 72a.
14. B. Ned 66a.
15. B. Ned 66a.

91. There is the story of a Babylonian who went up to the Land of Israel and wed a wife there. When he said to her, "Boil me a couple of lentils," she boiled exactly two lentils for him. He angrily reproved her. The next day, he said to her, "Boil me a bushel of lentils," and she boiled him an entire bushel.[1] Then he said to her, "Bring me two *butzini*,"[2] and she brought him two lamps. He told her, "Smash them against the top of the *bava* [the threshold]." Now, just then Bava ben Buta was seated at the door, engaged in judging a lawsuit. So she broke the lamps over his head. When Bava asked her, "Why are you doing this [to me]?" she replied, "This is what my husband commanded me to do." He said, "You have obeyed the wish of your husband—may He who is everywhere bring forth from you two sons like Bava ben Buta."[3]

92. It once happened that a man said to his wife: I vow that you are to receive no benefit from me until you manage to show R. Ishmael son of R. Yose that at least one of your features is beautiful. So R. Ishmael said to those who reported the incident to him, "Perhaps her head is beautiful?" "It is round," they replied. "Perhaps her hair is beautiful?" "It is like limp stalks of flax." "Perhaps her eyes are beautiful?" "They are bleary." "Perhaps her ears are beautiful?" "They are deformed." "Perhaps her nose is beautiful?" "It is bloated." "Perhaps her lips are beautiful?" "They are thick." "Perhaps her neck is beautiful?" "It is squat." "Perhaps her belly is beautiful?" "It protrudes." "Perhaps her feet are beautiful?" "They are as broad as a duck's." "Perhaps her name is beautiful?" "It is Likhlukhit ['marred']." He said to them, "She is beautifully called *likhlukhit*, marred as she is by her many defects." And he absolved her husband of his vow.[4]

93. The story is told of a woman in Sidon who lived ten years with her husband without bearing a child. Deciding to part from each other, the two came to R. Simeon ben Yohai, who said to them, "By your lives, even as you were paired over food and drink, so must you be parted over food and drink." They followed his advice and, declaring the day a festal day for themselves, prepared a great feast, during which the wife gave her husband too much to drink. In his resulting good humor, he said to her, "My dear, pick any desirable article you want in my home, and take it with you when you return to your father's house." What did she do? After he fell asleep, she beckoned to her menservants and maidservants, and said to them, "Pick him up, couch and all, and carry him to my father's house." At midnight, he woke up from his sleep. The effects of the wine had left him, and he asked her, "My dear, where am I?" She replied, "You are in my father's house." He: "But what am I doing in your father's house?" She: "Did you not say to me last night, 'Pick any desirable article you like from my home and take it with you when you return to your father's house'? There is no desirable article in the world I care for more than for you." So they again went to R. Simeon ben Yohai, and he stood up and prayed for them, and they were remembered [by God and granted children].[5]

94. R. Eleazar said: When a man divorces his first wife, even the altar sheds tears, as is said, "And this further ye do: Ye cover the altar with tears, with weeping, and with sighing, so that He regardeth not the offering any more, neither accepteth what you offer. But you ask, 'Because of what?' Because the Lord hath been witness between thee and the wife of thy youth, against whom thou hast dealt treacherously, though she is thy companion and the wife of thy covenant" (Mal. 2:13–14).[6]

95. "And this ye do a second time: Ye cover the altar with tears, with weeping, and with sighing, so that He regardeth not the offering any more" (Mal. 2:13). R. Haggai said: When Israel came up from the land of exile, the women's faces were blackened by the sun, so that their husbands abandoned them, and went and married heathen wives. The abandoned women would go around the altar weeping. That is why Malachi said of the cause of their weeping, "And this ye do a second time"—a second time, as at Shittim,[7] the Holy One said: Who would accept offerings from husbands who are responsible for the weeping and sighing [of their wives]? Because each of you robbed your wife, did violence to her, and despoiled her of her beauty, and finally you cast her off![8]

96. "For a detested one, divorce" (Mal. 2:16) means, said R. Judah, that when you detest your wife, you may divorce her. [Reading the verse "Detested, the one divorcing"],[9] R. Yohanan said: The man who divorces his wife is to be detested.[10]

97. The school of Shammai says: A man may not divorce his wife unless he has found unchastity in her, for Scripture says, "Because he hath found in her *indecency* in anything" (Deut. 24:1). But the school of Hillel says: [He may divorce her] even if she has merely spoiled his stew, for Scripture says, "Because he hath found in her indecency in *anything*." R. Akiva said: Even if he finds another more beautiful than she, for Scripture also says, "It cometh to pass, if she find no favor in his eyes" (ibid.).[11]

98. A wife who transgresses Jewish practice is liable to divorce with forfeiture of her due under her marriage settlement. And what [conduct is deemed to be transgression of] Jewish practice? If she goes out with her hair loose,

---

1. She boiled a *seah*, the equivalent in volume of 144 eggs.
2. The word means "melons" in the Babylonian dialect and "lamps" in the dialect of the Land of Israel.
3. B. Ned 66b.
4. Ibid.
5. Song R. 1:4, §2.
6. B. Git 90b.
7. See Num. 25.
8. Gen. R. 18:5.
9. Since the two verbs *sane* ("detest") and *shallah* ("divorce") are absolute infinitives, the meaning is ambiguous, making possible two differing interpretations.
10. B. Git 90b.
11. B. Git 90a.

spins in the marketplace [and so exposes her arms], or converses with everybody and anybody. Abba Saul said: Also if she curses his parents in his presence. R. Tarfon said: Also if she is given to shouting. And what kind of woman is deemed a shouter? One whose voice can be heard by her neighbors when she talks in her house.[1]

99. We have been taught that R. Meir used to say: As men differ in their attitude toward food and drink, so they differ in their attitude to women. There is a man who, should a fly fall into his cup, will throw away the cup and not drink from it. This is like the way of Pappus ben Judah, who, upon leaving the house, would lock his wife indoors. There is another man who, should a fly fall into his cup, will toss it away and drink from the cup. This is the way of most men, who do not mind if their wives talk with their brothers and other kinfolk. Then there is the man who, should a fly fall into his soup, will squash it and eat it. This is the way of a bad man who sees his wife go out with her hair loose, spin in the marketplace with her arms and shoulders bare, and bathe in the same place as men. [That husband is unaware that] it is a precept in the Torah to divorce such a wife, as Scripture says, "Because he hath found in her indecency in anything, he is to divorce her" (Deut. 24:1).

"And she goeth and becometh another man's wife" (Deut. 24:2). Scripture calls him "another" to indicate that this one is not a kindred spirit to her first husband. That one put a bad woman out of his house, while this one brought a bad woman into his house. If he is worthy, the second husband too will divorce her, in keeping with "and the latter husband hate her, and write her a bill of divorcement" (Deut. 24:3). If not, she will bury him, in keeping with "If the latter husband die" (ibid.). He deserves to die for having brought a bad woman into his house.[2]

100. A bad wife is a plague to her husband. What remedy does he have? He should divorce her and thus be healed of his plague.[3]

101. "The Lord hath delivered me into the hands of one against whom I am not able to stand" (Lam. 1:14). R. Hisda said in the name of Mar Ukba bar Hiyya: The verse refers to a bad wife whose marriage settlement is substantial.[4]

102. Rava said: A bad wife whose marriage settlement is substantial should be given a rival at her side. As people say: A woman will be chastened quicker by another woman than by a thorn.[5]

103. R. Yohanan said: A man whose first wife has died grieves as much as if the Temple had been destroyed in his lifetime, for Scripture says, "Son of man, behold, I take away from thee the delight of thine eyes with a stroke . . . and at even my wife died" (Ezek. 24:16 and 24:18), and says also, "Behold, I will profane My Sanctuary, the pride of your power, the delight of your eyes" (Ezek. 24:21).

R. Alexandri said: The world grows dark for him whose wife dies during his days [on earth], as is said, "When the light grows dark in his tent [i.e., his wife dies], his lamp over him shall be put out" (Job 18:6). R. Yose bar Hanina added: His steps become unsteady, as the verse goes on to say, "The steps of his strength shall be straitened." And R. Abbahu added: His wits fail him, as the verse concludes, "His own counsel shall cast him down" (ibid.).[6]

104. R. Samuel bar Nahman said: All things can be replaced, except the wife of one's youth, as Scripture says, "A wife of [one's] youth, can she be rejected?" (Isa. 54:6). R. Judah taught his son R. Isaac: Only in his first wife does a man find utter joy, as Scripture says, "Have joy in the wife of thy youth" (Prov. 5:18). R. Isaac asked, "What wife, for example?" R. Judah: "Your mother, for example."[7]

105. We have been taught: A husband's death is felt by none but his wife, and a wife's death is felt by none but her husband. A husband's death is felt by none but his wife, as intimated in "Elimelech, Naomi's husband, died" (Ruth 1:3). A wife's death is felt by none but her husband, as intimated in "And as for me, when I came from Paddan, Rachel died unto me" (Gen. 48:7).[8]

106. He who eyes his wife [in the hope] that she will die, so that he may become her heir, will in the end be buried by her.[9]

107. The sages taught in the name of Rav: The verse "Thy sons and thy daughters shall be given to another people, while thine eyes look on" (Deut. 28:32) refers to a stepmother.[10]

A Woman's Character

108. Women—they are a people unto themselves.[11]

109. "And the Lord God built (*va-yiven*) the rib" (Gen. 2:22). [The text says *va-yiven*, which can also mean], "He considered well (*hitbonen*)[12] out of what part to create her." God said: I will not create her out of Adam's head, lest she be conceited; nor out of the eye, lest she be a coquette; nor out of the ear, lest she be an eavesdropper; nor out of the mouth, lest she be a gossip; nor out of the heart,

1. B. Ket 72a.
2. B. Git 90a–b; Tos Sot 5:9.
3. B. Yev 63b.
4. Ibid.
5. Ibid.
6. B. Sanh 22a.
7. Ibid.
8. Ibid.
9. ARN 3.
10. B. Ber 56a.
11. B. Shab 62a.
12. The commentator regards *va-yiven* as a form of *bin* ("understand").

lest she be prone to jealousy; nor out of the hand, lest she be light-fingered; nor out of the foot, lest she be a gadabout—but rather out of the rib, from a place within Adam's body. And as He was creating each and every part of the woman, He kept saying, "Be a woman [who is capable of 'withinness'], who is retiring." Nevertheless, "ye have set at naught all My counsel" (Prov. 1:25), for all the undesirable qualities mentioned earlier are in her.[1]

110. Our masters taught that women are said to have four traits; they are gluttonous, eavesdropping, slothful, and envious. R. Judah son of R. Nehemiah said: They are also querulous and talkative. R. Levi said: They are also pilferers and gadabouts.[2]

111. R. Dostai son of R. Yannai was asked by his disciples: Why is it that a man goes looking for a woman, but a woman does not go looking for a man? He replied with the parable of a man who lost an article.[3] Who looks for whom? Clearly, he who lost the article goes looking for what he lost.

Why is a man readily pacified, but a woman is not readily pacified? Because he [derives his nature from the yielding earth] out of which he was created, while she [derives her nature from the unyielding bone] out of which she was created.

Why is a woman's voice sweet while a man's voice is not sweet? Because he [derives his voice from the nonresounding earth] out of which he was created, while she [derives hers from the resounding bone] out of which she was created.[4]

112. R. Joshua was asked: Why does a man [at birth] come forth with his face turned downward, while a woman comes forth with her face turned upward? He replied: The man looks down toward the [earth], the place of his creation, while the woman looks up toward [the rib], the place of her creation.

And why must a woman use perfume, while a man does not need to use perfume? He replied: Man was created from the earth, and the earth never becomes putrid, while Eve was created from a bone.[5] Thus, to explain by a parable, if you leave meat unsalted for three days, it will surely become putrid.

And why is a man easily appeased, while a woman is not easily appeased? He replied: Man was created from the earth, and when you pour a drop of water on it, it is absorbed at once; while Eve was created from a bone, which, even if soaked in water many days, will not become saturated.

Why does a man solicit a woman, while a woman does not solicit a man? He replied: The matter may be illustrated by the parable of a man who lost an article—he will be seeking the lost article; the lost article will not be seeking him.

1. Gen. R. 18:2; Tanhuma, *Va-yeshev*, §6.
2. Gen. R. 45:5.
3. The rib that God took.
4. B. Nid 31b.
5. The bone decomposes, however slowly, and is subject to putrefaction.

Why does a man go out with head bare, while a woman goes out with head covered? He replied: One who committed a transgression is ashamed before people. It is for that reason that a woman goes out with her head covered.

Why are women first to pass in front of a corpse? He replied: Because they brought death to the world. Therefore they are the first to pass in front of a corpse.[6]

113. Restrained by feminine delicacy, a woman solicits with her heart, whereas a man solicits with his mouth.[7]

114. Ten *kav* of talk came down to the world; women took nine, and the rest of mankind one.[8]

115. Women seek to know everything.[9]

116. A woman is suspected of uncovering her neighbor's pot to find out what she is cooking.[10]

117. The more wives, the more witchcraft.[11]

118. The most worthy of women is a mistress of witchcraft.[12]

119. There is no wisdom in woman except with the distaff. Thus Scripture says, "And all the women that were wise-hearted did spin with their hands" (Exod. 35:25).[13]

120. Women are lightheaded.[14]

121. Women are incapable of giving legal decisions, and so one is not to rely on what they say.[15]

122. A woman prefers having beautifully decorated rooms and beautifully embroidered clothes to eating fatted calves.[16]

123. "That which I long for" (Hos. 2:7)[17]—the things a woman longs for. And what are they? Adornments.[18]

124. During the week of a festival, a woman may use such adornments of her toilet as our masters taught are permitted, namely, apply kohl to her eyes, braid her hair, and put rouge on her face. [In order to show what may or may not be done], R. Hisda's wife made her toilet in front of her daughter-in-law. R. Huna bar Hinena, who was seated before R. Hisda, said, "The adornments

6. Gen. R. 17:8.
7. B. Er 100b.
8. B. Kid 49b.
9. Yalkut, Esther, §1049.
10. Toh 7:9.
11. Avot 2:7.
12. Sof 15.
13. B. Yoma 66b.
14. B. Shab 33b.
15. Num. R. 10:5.
16. Esther R. 3:10.
17. JV: "My water." But *shikkuyo* ("my water") may also be a form of *shokak* ("to long for").
18. B. Ket 65a.

permitted apply only to a young woman and not to an elderly woman." R. Hisda replied, "By God! Even to your mother, even to your mother's mother, even if she were standing at the brink of the grave. As the proverb has it: At sixty as at six, the sound of the timbrel makes her nimble."[1]

125. "The daughters of Zion are haughty" (Isa. 3:16): that is to say, making themselves erect like spears, they moved about with overweening arrogance. "And walk with stretched-forth necks" (ibid.): when one of them adorned herself, she would bend her neck in one direction and then in another to display her ornaments. "And painted eyes" (ibid.): they painted their eyes with *sikra*—a red dye, according to R. Mani of Caesarea, or, collyrium, according to Resh Lakish—and winked [at men]. "Walking with mincing steps" (ibid): walking heel to toe. A woman who was tall would get two short women to accompany her, one on each side of her, in order to make her appear [by contrast] even taller than she was; on the other hand, a woman who was short would put on shoes with thick soles and get two short women to accompany her, one on each side of her, in order to make herself look tall. "And they beserpent their feet" (Isa. 3:16): as R. Abba bar Kahana explained, each woman used to have the figure of a serpent embossed upon her footwear. According to R. Isaac, the women used to fill their shoes with myrrh and balsam, and thus promenaded in the streets of Jerusalem; when they got close to a group of young men, they would stamp their feet on the ground in order to spray the young men with the fragrance in their shoes, thus injecting them with the evil impulse just as a serpent injects his venom.

The Holy One kept saying to Isaiah, "What are these women doing here? They must be banished hence." And so Isaiah kept telling them, "Vow penitence, so that Israel's foes do not come at you." They replied, "If Israel's foes do come at us, what can they possibly do to us? An officer may see me and take me, a prefect may see me and take me, or even a general may see me and seat me in his carriage."[2]

126. R. Hiyya taught: A wife should be taken mainly for her beauty; a wife should be taken mainly for the sake of bringing children [into the world].

And R. Hiyya taught further: A woman's femininity is brought out by the ornaments she wears.[3]

127. R. Hiyya also taught: He who wishes his wife to look graceful should clothe her in linen garments. He who wishes his daughter to have a light complexion—let him, on the approach of her maturity, feed her with young fowls and give her milk to drink.[4]

128. R. Joshua said: A woman prefers skimpy fare with sexual indulgence to ample fare with continence.[5]

129. Two women in a house, strife in the house.[6]

130. A woman is jealous only of another woman's thighs.[7]

131. "She induced [Othniel] to ask [Caleb] her father for some property—[she did so] by crying out as she pointed to her donkey[8] (Josh. 15:18). Just what did she cry out and say? She said, so taught Rava in the name of R. Isaac: Even as a donkey, when it has no fodder in its trough, will cry out at once, so a woman who knows that she will have no food in her house must cry out at once.[9]

132. [When Abraham asked Sarah to make cakes, he first said], "Of flour" (Gen. 18:6), [then added], "Of choice flour" (ibid.). From Abraham's instructions to his wife, R. Isaac said, one may infer that a woman is more apt than a man to be stingy with guests.[10]

133. "And she said unto her husband: 'Behold now, I perceive that it is a holy man of God' " (2 Kings 4:9). From this verse, said R. Yose son of R. Hanina, one may infer that a woman perceives a guest's character better than a man.

"A holy man." How did she know? Because she never saw a fly pass over his table.[11]

134. "And the Lord God endowed the rib with understanding"[12] (Gen. 2:22). The verse indicates that the Holy One endowed woman with more understanding than man.[13]

135. Daughters of Israel are not wont to be loud-voiced, or given to strutting, or unrestrained in jesting.[14]

136. "Thy wife shall be as a fruitful vine and as the [altar's] sides[15] in your house" (Ps. 128:3). R. Phinehas the Priest bar Hama said: So long as a wife is retiring in

---

1. B. MK 9b.
2. Lev. R. 16:1; Lam. R. 4:18; B. Shab 62b.
3. So apparently two sources cited in Ket, ed. Moshe Hirshler (Jerusalem, 1977) 2:39. BR: "A wife should be taken mainly for the ornaments she wears." B. Ket 59b.
4. Ibid.
5. B. Sot 20a.
6. Tanhuma, *Ki Tetze*, §1.
7. B. Meg 13a.
8. JV: "she alighted from off her ass." But to the commentator, the act seems unnecessary. Hence, he construes *va-titznah* not as "alighted" but as "cried out" and interprets *me-al ha-hamor* not as "from off her donkey" but as "pointed to her donkey" by way of strengthening her plea to be given a dowry, since Othniel, who was to be her husband, was a poor man.
9. B. Tem 16a.
10. B. BM 87a.
11. Even as no fly was ever seen over the altar (Avot 3:2). B. Ber 10b.
12. The commentator takes *va-yiven* ("made") as derived from *bin* ("to understand").
13. B. Nid 45b.
14. Tanhuma, *Naso*, §2.
15. The use of the unusual word *yarkete* ("sides") suggests to the commentator the wife's being compared to the altar, against whose *yerekh*, ("side") the blood of expiation is to be dashed (Lev. 1:11). Tanhuma, *Va-yishlah*, §6.

demeanor in her house, then even as the altar procures forgiveness, so she procures forgiveness for her household.[1]

137. R. Nahman said: Haughtiness does not become women. There were two haughty women, and their names were appropriately odious, one being called Hornet (Deborah), and the other Weasel (Huldah). Of the one called Hornet, Scripture says, "And she sent and called Barak" (Judg. 4:6)—she would not deign to go to him. The one called Weasel, Scripture quotes as saying, "Tell ye the man that sent ye unto me" (2 Kings 22:15)—she would not say, "Tell the king."[2]

138. It is a woman's way to stay in her home. It is a man's way to go out into the marketplace and acquire understanding from other people.[3]

139. It is not a woman's way to sit idle.[4]

140. While a woman talks, she spins.[5]

141. It is not seemly for a woman to keep coming to courts of justice.[6]

142. It is not proper for a woman to go about begging at doorways.[7]

143. Women are merciful.[8]

144. Even more than a man wishes to marry does a woman wish to be married.[9]

145. Better a husband who's not much good than to live alone in widowhood.[10]

146. R. Samuel bar Onia said in the name of Rav: [Before marriage] a woman is an unshaped lump, and she enters into a covenant with him who makes her a [useful] vessel, as is said, "Thy maker is thy husband" (Isa. 54:5).[11]

147. "May ye find ease, each of you in the house of her husband" (Ruth 1:9). From this we infer that a woman has a sense of ease only in her husband's house.[12]

148. "Thy desire shall be to thy husband" (Gen. 3:16). The story is told of a woman of the family of Tabrinus[13] who was married to a brigand, and her husband abused her. When the sages heard of it and came to reprimand her [for remaining with him], she brought forth a golden lampstand with an earthen vessel on top of it.[14]

149. R. Simeon ben Yohai was asked by his disciples: Why does the Torah ordain that after childbirth a woman must bring an offering? He replied: Because when she kneels to give birth, she impetuously swears that she will never again submit to her husband. And since she later violates this oath, the Torah says that she must bring an offering.

"Thy desire shall be to thy husband" (Gen. 3:16). When a woman sits on the birthing stool, she swears, "Never again will I submit to my husband." And the Holy One says to her, "You will return to your desire—you will return to your desire for your husband."[15]

150. A wife longs for her husband when he sets out on a journey.[16]

151. Even if the husband is no larger than an ant, his wife feels she could place her chair among the great.

Though the husband be a mere carder, his wife invites him to the threshold of their home, where she [proudly] sits with him.[17]

152. When a husband moves among pumpkins, the wife will do likewise among melons.[18]

153. One may presume that no wife will dare act insolently in the presence of her husband.[19]

154. A wife is like one's own person.[20]

155. The wife of an associate scholar [*haver*] is like the associate scholar.[21]

156. The wife of a brigand is like the brigand.[22]

157. Whatever a wife acquires belongs to her husband.[23]

158. The sages of the school of R. Eliezer taught: In the verse "These are the ordinances which Thou shalt set before them" (Exod. 21:1), Scripture makes a woman equal to a man in regard to all the ordinances governing relations between one person and another.[24]

The sages of the school of R. Ishmael taught: In the

1. B. Meg 14b.
2. Gen. R. 18:1.
3. P. Ket 5:6, 30a.
4. B. Meg 14b.
5. B. Git 41a.
6. B. Git 41b.
7. B. Ket 67a.
8. B. Meg 14b.
9. B. Yev 113a.
10. B. Yev 118b.
11. B. Sanh 22b.
12. Ruth R. 2:15.
13. Or, Tiberinus. A wealthy family of noble stock.
14. By way of saying that she, a golden article, is willing to submit to "an earthen vessel," her husband. Gen. R. 20:7.
15. B. Nid 31b; Gen. R. 20:7.
16. B. Yev 62b.
17. B. Yev 118b.
18. If one is unfaithful, so will the other be. B. Meg 12b.
19. B. Yev 116a.
20. B. Men 93b.
21. B. AZ 39a.
22. P. Ket 2:9, 26d.
23. B. Git 77b.
24. The inference is not from this verse, but from verse 28 in this chapter, which speaks of "a man or a woman."

verse "When a man or woman commit any sin" (Num. 5:6), Scripture makes a woman equal to a man in regard to all penalties prescribed in the Torah.[1]

Matters between Husband and Wife

159. "Who teacheth us by the beasts of the earth, and maketh us wise by the fowls of heaven" (Job 35:11). R. Yohanan said: Had Torah not been given [to us], we could have learned modesty from the cat, avoiding seizure of others' property from the ant, avoidance of infidelity from the dove, and good manners from the rooster, who first coaxes and only then mates.

How does he go about coaxing? R. Judah said in the name of Rav: [As he lowers his wings, he seems to be saying], "I will buy you a cloak that will reach down to your feet." After the mating, [he lowers his head], as if to say, "May my crest fall off if I have [the money]—I cannot buy you the cloak [I promised]."[2]

160. "And Balaam lifted up his eyes, and he saw Israel dwelling tribe by tribe [in such a way that] he was impelled to exclaim, 'The spirit of God should rest upon Israel' "[3] (Num. 24:2). What did he see? He saw that the entrances to Israel's tents did not face one another [thus ensuring privacy]. So he exclaimed, "These people deserve to have the Presence rest on them."[4]

161. R. Huna said: Israel are holy, and so they do not indulge in sexual intercourse during the day.[5]

162. R. Benjamin bar Japheth said in the name of R. Eleazar: He who sanctifies himself [in his purpose] during sexual intercourse will have male children, as indicated by the fact that the verse "Sanctify yourselves therefore, and be ye holy" (Lev. 11:44) is followed by "If a woman be delivered, and bear a male" (Lev. 12:2).[6]

163. R. Judah said in the name of Rav: Jerusalemites were given to obscenities obscurely worded. One of them would inquire of another: On what did you dine today—on well-kneaded bread or on bread not well-kneaded? On weak-bodied white wine or on full-bodied tawny wine? [Did you recline] on a wide couch or a narrow couch? With a good fellow diner or a poor fellow diner?

All the foregoing expressions, said R. Hisda, allude to the satisfaction of lust.[7]

164. Imma Shalom[8] was asked: Why are your children so handsome? She replied: Because my husband does not cohabit with me at the beginning of the night or at the end of the night, but only at midnight. And when he cohabits with me, he uncovers a handbreadth of my body even as he covers another handbreadth, and he acts as though a demon is driving him. When I ask him, "Why at midnight?" he replies, "So that I give no thought to another woman,"[9] for in that case his children would be [in a manner of speaking] bastards.[10]

165. The sages said: [During intercourse], a man may do with his wife whatever he pleases. An analogy suggests itself with meat that comes from the slaughterhouse: a man may eat it any way he wishes: [raw] with salt, roasted, or stewed. And likewise with fish from the fish market.[11]

166. Do not cook in a pot in which your neighbor has cooked. What does that mean? Do not marry a divorced woman while her husband is still living. For a master said: When a divorced man marries a divorced woman, there are four yearnings in the bed.[12]

167. "That you do not follow your heart . . . in your lustful urge" (Num. 15:39). From this verse it follows, said Rabbi [Judah I, the Patriarch], that one should not drink out of one goblet while thinking of another.[13]

168. Yose ben Yohanan of Jerusalem said: Do not gossip with a woman. The sages said: This applies to one's own wife . . . how much more so to another man's wife. Hence, say the sages, whoever gossips with a woman will bring harm to himself, for he neglects the study of Torah, and in the end will inherit Gehenna.[14]

169. R. Akiva said: Jesting and levity predispose a man to lewdness.[15]

170. R. Yohanan said: It is better to walk behind a lion than behind a woman.

R. Nahman said: Manoah was an unlearned person [*am ha-aretz*], for it is said, "Manoah walked behind his wife" (Judg. 13:11).[16]

171. Samuel said: Even a woman's voice stimulates sexual longing.

R. Sheshet said: Even [the sight of] a woman's hair stimulates sexual longing.[17]

172. Resh Lakish said: Do not suppose that only he who commits the act with his body is called an adulterer. He who commits it merely with his eyes is also called an

1. B. BK 15a.
2. B. Er 100b.
3. So interpreted by Tosafot, ad loc.
4. B. BB 60a.
5. B. Nid 17a.
6. The purpose should be procreation, not mere lust. B. Shevu 18b.
7. B. Shab 62b–63a.
8. The wife of R. Eliezer ben Hyrcanus. See above, part 2, chap. 1, §98.
9. At the beginning of the night and in the early hours of morning, loose women are apt to be abroad.
10. B. Ned 20b.
11. Ibid.
12. B. Pes 112a.
13. B. Ned 20b.
14. Avot 1:5.
15. Avot 3:14.
16. Walking behind a woman arouses a man's lust. B. Ber 61a.
17. B. Ber 24a.

adulterer, for it is said, "The eyes also of the adulterer" (Job 24:15).[1]

173. Our masters taught: If a wife is alone with her husband and is engaged in intercourse with him, while her heart is with another man whom she met on the road, no act of adultery is greater, for it is said, "The wife that committeth adultery, taketh strangers while under her husband" (Ezek. 16:32).[2] But how can a wife who is under her husband commit adultery? Here, however, the verse refers to a woman who has met another man and set her eyes on him, and while she is engaged in intercourse with her husband, her heart is with that man.[3]

174. Our masters taught: He who counts money out of his hand into a woman's hand slowly, so as to gaze at her, even if he possesses as much Torah and as many good deeds as Moses, will not escape the punishment of Gehenna, as is said, "Hand to hand—he shall not be unpunished" (Prov. 11:21): not be unpunished in Gehenna.[4]

175. "And Israel attached itself unto the Baal of Peor" (Num. 25:3). R. Eleazar ben Shammua said: Just as it is impossible for a wooden nail to be wrenched from a door without loss of some wood, so it was impossible for Israel to be wrenched from Peor without loss of some souls.[5]

176. R. Simlai said: Wherever you find lust, you also find pestilence come to the world, slaying the good and the bad. R. Joshua ben Levi added: The Holy One is slow to anger about everything except yielding to lust.[6]

177. The story is told of a certain man who set his eyes on a certain woman and a passion so vehement seized him [that it threatened his life]. People went and consulted physicians, who said: There is no cure for him unless she yields to him. But the sages declared: Let him die rather than have her yield to him. The physicians: Then let her stand before him nude. The sages: Let him die rather than have her stand before him nude. The physicians: Then have her at least converse with him from behind a screen. The sages: Let him die rather than have her converse with him from behind a screen.

But why such rigidity? To prevent, said R. Papa, disgrace to the young woman's family. To prevent, said R. Aha son of R. Ika, dissolute behavior among daughters of Israel.[7]

178. There is no guardian against unchastity.[8]

179. The sages taught: Even the most pious of the pious is not to be appointed guardian where there is the possibility of unchastity.[9]

180. R. Idi said: A woman carries upon herself the weapons of her sex [to protect her from murder].[10]

181. The sages taught: A woman is a leather bag full of excrement, her orifice full of blood, yet all men run after her.[11]

182. The words "Adam knew his wife yet more" (Gen. 4:25) imply that Adam's desire for his wife was increased by much more desire than before: formerly he had felt no desire when he did not see his wife, but now he felt desire for her whether he saw her or not.[12]

183. R. Yohanan said: A man has [on his body] a small member. If he starves it, it is satisfied; if he satisfies it, it is starved.[13]

184. R. Isaac said: Ever since the Temple was destroyed, sexual pleasure has been taken [from those who obey the Torah] and given to those who transgress it, as is said, "Stolen waters are sweet, and bread eaten in secret is pleasant" (Prov. 9:17).[14]

185. The story is told of a certain woman who was propositioned by a certain man. She told him, "Go to such-and-such a place [and I will meet you there]. What did the woman do? She went to the man's wife and told her what had been arranged. So the wife went to the place of assignation, and her husband copulated with her.[15] After that, he regretted what he had done so much that he wished to die. His wife said to him, "You have eaten of your own bread and drunk of your own cup. The trouble with you is that you are presumptuous. You should be satisfied with your own wife, like other men!"[16]

186. "And a spirit of jealousy[17] came upon him, and he accused his wife" (Num. 5:14). The sages in the school of R. Ishmael taught: A man makes such an accusation to his wife only if a spirit enters into him. What kind of spirit? A spirit of impurity, say the sages. On the contrary, says R. Ashi: a spirit of purity.

---

1. Cf. Matthew 5:28. Lev. R. 23:12.
2. JV: "Thou wife that committest adultery, that takest strangers instead of thy husband."
3. Num. R. 9:34; Tanhuma, *Naso*, §7.
4. B. Ber 61a.
5. Abraham, it is said, manages to bring out of Gehenna all kinds of sinners, except such as had intercourse with daughters of idolaters. B. Er 19a. (Reference provided by Johanan Eisenberg in his *Yanhenu* [Warsaw, 1899], ad loc.). Sif Deut., §131.
6. P. Sot 1:5, 17a; Gen. R. 26:5.
7. B. Sanh 75a and En Yaakov, ad loc.
8. B. Ket 13b.
9. P. Ket 1:8, 25d.
10. A man is more likely to rape a woman than murder her. B. Yev 115a.
11. B. Shab 152a.
12. Until the stronger desire was added, Adam—according to rabbinic tradition—was able to live apart from Eve for a hundred and thirty years. Gen. R. 23:5.
13. B. Suk 52b.
14. B. Sanh 75a.
15. Without knowing that it was his own wife.
16. Num. R. 9:3.
17. The commentator's question: Is the husband's jealousy prompted by a spirit of purity that will not put up with immorality or by a wish to make his wife miserable?

It stands to reason that it is a spirit of purity. For we have been taught [in a Baraita]: "And he accused his wife"—it is his option to do so, in the opinion of R. Ishmael; it is his religious duty to do so, in the opinion of R. Akiva. Hence, we must conclude that the husband is moved by a spirit of purity. For should you suppose that he was moved by a spirit of impurity, how can one contend that being moved by such a spirit is an option or a religious duty?[1]

187. How did the husband deal with a wife suspected of infidelity? First, he took her to the local court. Then they brought her to the High Court in Jerusalem, where the judges solemnly admonished her in the way that witnesses in capital cases were admonished. The judges said to her: Daughter, wine does much, levity does much, youth does much, bad neighbors do much. Many preceded you and were swept away. Confess for the sake of the great Name which is written in holiness, so that it will not have to be obliterated by the water of bitterness. They went on to tell her tales of events set down in the early parts of Scripture[2] and uttered blunt warnings, which neither she nor the family of her father's house would otherwise have heard.

Even as she was admonished not to drink the water of bitterness, so was she admonished to drink it.[3] The judges said to her: Daughter, if it is clear to you that you are pure, stand on your innocence and drink, for the waters of bitterness will be no more than a dry salve placed on healthy flesh. If there is a sore in it, the salve will [dissolve and] penetrate deep [into the flesh]; if there is no sore, the salve will have no effect.

If she said, "I am defiled," she forfeited her marriage settlement,[4] [was divorced], and departed. If she insisted, "I am innocent," she was taken to the east gate, in front of the entrance into Nicanor's gate,[5] where women suspected of infidelity were made to drink the waters of bitterness.

A priest roughly gripped her garments—if they tore, they were torn; if the stitches ripped, they were ripped—until he uncovered her bosom and loosened her hair. R. Judah said: If her bosom was comely, he did not uncover it, and if her hair was beautiful, he did not loosen it, to protect young priests [from being stimulated sexually by her]. If she had been clothed in white, the priest clothed her in black; but if black became her, she was stripped and clothed in shabby garments. If she wore golden ornaments and neck chains, earrings and finger rings, they were removed, in order to make her unattractive. R. Yohanan ben Beroka said: Daughters of Israel should not be made unattractive in ways other than those set down in the Torah.

A sheet of byssus linen was then spread between the priest and the people. The priest turned to stand behind her and undid the braids of her hair, to fulfill the precept of undoing them. Afterward, the priest brought an Egyptian[6] rope and tied it above her breasts. Whoever wished to look at her was allowed to come and do so, except her menservants and maidservants, because she felt superior to them [and so would not have been humiliated in front of them]. All women were encouraged to look at her, in keeping with the verse "That all women may be taught not to do after your lewdness" (Ezek. 23:48).

The husband brought her meal offering in an Egyptian basket and made her hold it in order to tire her.[7]

[The priest] next took a new earthenware bowl and poured a *log* of water into it from the laver. Then he entered the Temple Hall and turned right, where there was a place one cubit square, with a marble flagstone to which a ring was attached. Pulling on the ring, he raised the flagstone and from beneath it took some dust, which he put in the bowl—just enough dust to be visible on the surface of the water.

Then the priest entered the Outer Hall leading into the Temple's interior to write out the curses in the scroll. A gold tablet [containing the text of the curses] was affixed on the outside wall of the Temple Hall, which could be seen from the Outer Hall. The priest looked at it as he copied out the text, letter for letter and word for word. He wrote only with ink—writing that can be erased. [After examining carefully what he had written], he went out, stood beside the woman suspected of infidelity, and read [the text of the scroll], expounding it and setting it forth in whatever language she understood, so that she might know exactly why she was being made to drink [the water of bitterness].

If, before [the writing on] the scroll was blotted out [in the water], she said, "I refuse to drink it,"[8] the scroll was hidden [put away] and her meal offering was scattered over the ashes.[9] If, after [the writing on] the scroll was blotted out, she said, "I am defiled," the water was poured out and her meal offering was scattered over the ashes.

If, however, [after the writing on] the scroll was blotted out, she said, "I refuse to drink,"[10] she was compelled and made to drink against her will. R. Judah said: Her mouth was forced open with iron tongs.

She scarcely finished drinking when her face turned yellow, her eyes bulged, and her veins swelled. Everyone cried, "Take her away, so that she may not make the Temple Court unclean."[11]

188. With regard to the woman suspected of infidelity, we find measure for measure—as she measured out, so it was measured out to her. She stood at the doorway of her house to show herself to her lover; therefore the priest

1. B. Sot 3a; Num. R. 9:12.
2. The stories of Reuben and Judah, each of whom confessed his error.
3. Before a wife suspected of infidelity can be made to drink the bitter water, the husband must accuse her in the presence of two witnesses on the evidence of two additional witnesses that she had secreted herself with another man (Sot 1:11).
4. She executed a deed renouncing all claims to it.
5. The place is between the Women's Court and the Court of the Israelites. See above, part 1, chap. 9, §5.
6. Perhaps to show that she followed the Egyptians' proneness to lewd living.
7. And induce her to confess.
8. Conceding her guilt.
9. Of the Temple offerings.
10. Refusing to confess.
11. Sot 1–3; Tos Sot 1–2; Sif Num., §11–12.

stood her at the Nicanor gate to show her disgrace to everyone. She wound beautiful scarves about her head for him; therefore the priest removed the covering from her head and put it under the soles of her feet. She made her face beautiful for him; therefore her face turned yellow. She applied kohl to her eyes; therefore her eyes bulged. She braided her hair for him; therefore the priest undid her hair. She beckoned to him enticingly with her finger; therefore her fingernails fell out. She supported her breasts with a band of fine netting to make herself more alluring to him; therefore the priest fetched Egyptian rope and bound it above her breasts. She thrust her thigh toward her lover; therefore her thigh sagged. She received him on her belly; therefore her belly swelled. She gave him the world's delicacies to eat; therefore her offering consisted of cattle fodder. She gave him rare wine to drink in precious goblets; therefore the priest gave her bitter water to drink in a broken cup of clay. She acted in secret; therefore He who is everywhere exposed her in public.[1]

189. The sages said: A story is told of two sisters who looked exactly alike. One of them was married and settled in one town, and the other married and settled in another town. The husband of one grew so suspicious of her that he wished to have her drink the bitter water in Jerusalem. So she went to the town where her sister had settled. Her sister asked her, "Why did you come here?" She replied, "My husband wishes to make me drink the bitter water, and I am defiled." At this, her sister said, "I will go in your place and drink [the water]." So she said, "Go and do so." What did her sister do? She put on the garments of her adulterous sister, went in her place, drank the bitter water, and was found innocent. When she came back home,[2] the adulterous sister went out to meet her. They embraced and kissed. But as they kissed each other, the adulterous sister got a whiff of the bitter water and died instantly.[3]

190. Once a woman came to Rabbi [Judah I, the Patriarch] and said to him, "I have been raped." R. Judah: "But did you not find the experience pleasing?"[4] The woman: "Suppose someone dipped his finger [in honey] and stuck it in your mouth on the Day of Atonement, would not the experience distress you at first, but after a while please you?"

So R. Judah accepted what she had to say.[5]

191. "A twisted thing cannot be made straight" (Eccles. 1:15). R. Simeon ben Menasya said: He who steals from a man may return what he stole and straighten out matters. He who robs a man may return what he has stolen and straighten out matters. Who, then, is meant by "A twisted thing cannot be made straight"? He who copulates incestuously with a woman and begets a bastard from her.[6]

1. B. Sot 8b–9a.

2. "When she came back home": Num R. 9:9. BR follows Tanhuma, *Naso*, §6: "When she came back to her sister's house."

3. Num. R. 9:9; Tanhuma, *Naso*, §6.

4. If you were a willing partner, you are forbidden to your husband.

5. He declared her permitted to her husband. Num. R. 9:10.

6. B. Hag 9b.

192. "The eye of the adulterer anticipateth the twilight" (Job 24:15). "Saying: 'No eye shall see me' " (ibid.)—neither an eye below nor an eye above—the adulterer keeps asking in anticipation: When will twilight come? When will evening come? "But He who dwells in secret limns a face" (ibid.): the adulterer does not know that He who dwells in the secret place of the world—that is to say, the Holy One—draws the adulterer's features in the newly formed embryo's face, in order to expose him.

R. Levi said: In this connection, consider the parable of a potter's apprentice who stole a lump of his master's clay. When the master detected the theft, what did he do? He proceeded to shape the lump of clay into a vessel, which he hung up before the apprentice. Why all this? To make it known to the apprentice that his master had detected his theft.

R. Judah bar Simon taught in the name of R. Levi ben Perata: "The Artist who begot thee thou dost weaken" (Deut. 32:18). You adulterers weaken the power of the Creator. Consider the parable of an artist who was drawing the features of a sovereign with special care. Even as he was about to complete his work, someone came and said to him: There has been a change of sovereigns. At once the artist's hands grew slack as he said: Whose features am I now to draw? That of the former sovereign or that of the present one? Like the artist, the Holy One occupies Himself with drawing the features of the embryo throughout the first forty days of the woman's pregnancy. But then, at the end of the forty days, she goes off and sins with another man, and thus confuses the paternity of the embryo. At once the hands of the Lord grow slack, if one dare say such a thing, and He says: Whose features am I now to draw? Those of him who possessed her first or of him who possessed her second? Hence, "the Artist who begot thee thou dost weaken."

R. Isaac said: With regard to all other transgressors, we find that the thief gains, while the victim of the theft loses; the robber gains, while his victim loses. In adultery, however, both transgressors benefit. Who loses? The Holy One, for [in order to expose adultery] He destroys the features [He used to indicate the original paternity of the embryo].[7]

193. A king of the Arabs asked R. Akiva, "I am black and my wife is black. Yet she gave birth to a white son. Shall I kill her for having been unfaithful to me?" R. Akiva: "Are the paintings in your house portraits of white or black persons?" The king: "White." R. Akiva: "When you cohabited with her, she fixed her eyes on the portraits of white persons and as a result gave birth to a white child. If you are astonished by what I say, consider our father Jacob's flocks, which were influenced in their conception by rods set up in front of them."[8]

The king of the Arabs agreed that R. Akiva was right.[9]

7. Lev. R. 23:12; Num. R. 9:1.

8. Gen. 30:37–40.

9. Num. R. 9:34.

194. "I further observed all the oppression" (Eccles. 4:1). Daniel the Tailor construed this verse as applying to bastards. "Behold the tears of the oppressed" (ibid.)—if the parents were the transgressors, why should their offspring be subjected to oppression? Let us say the father of one such committed incest with a woman and begot him; in what way did the child sin? "And on the side of their oppressors, there was power" (ibid.)—on the side of Israel's Great Sanhedrin, which, coming at them with the power conferred on them by the Torah, removed them from Israel's fold. "And they have no comforter" (ibid.)—accordingly, the Holy One said: It is for Me to comfort them. For in this world they are deemed dross, but of the time-to-come, Zechariah [speaking of Israel] says, "I have seen, and behold a lampstand all of gold" (Zech. 4:2).[1]

Children and the Rearing of Children

195. We have been taught: He who has no son is as though he were dead, utterly demolished. As though he were dead, for Rachel said, "Give me children, or else I am dead" (Gen. 30:1). As though utterly demolished, for Sarah said, "It may be that I shall be rebuilt through her" (Gen. 16:2), and only that which has been utterly demolished requires rebuilding.[2]

196. "And Isaiah . . . came to him and said unto him: . . . 'Thou shalt die, and not live' " (2 Kings 20:1)—"thou shalt die" in this world "and not live" in the world-to-come. When Hezekiah asked him, "Why punishment so severe?" Isaiah replied, "Because you did not try to have children." Hezekiah: "[I do not] because it was shown to me by the holy spirit that children issuing from me will not be worthy." Isaiah: "What have you to do with the secrets of the Holy One? What you have been commanded, you should have done, and let God do what He pleases."[3]

197. The world was created only for fruition and increase, as is said, "He created it not a waste. He formed it to be inhabited" (Isa. 45:18).[4]

198. We have been taught that R. Eliezer said: He who does not engage in fruition and increase is as though he shed blood, for the verse "Whoso sheddeth man's blood, by man shall his blood be shed" (Gen. 9:6) is followed at once by "Be ye fruitful and multiply" (Gen. 9:7). R. Akiva said: Such a one is as though He diminished God's image, for the verse "In the image of God made He man" (Gen. 9:6) is followed at once by "Be ye fruitful and multiply." Ben Azzai said: He is as one who both sheds blood and diminishes God's image.

R. Eliezer said to Ben Azzai: "Such words sound well when they issue from the mouths of those who practice them. There are some who preach well and practice well; others practice well but do not preach well. You preach well but do not practice well." Ben Azzai replied, "But what shall I do, seeing that my soul yearns for Torah? The world can continue through others."[5]

199. Our masters taught: The verse "And when [the Presence] rested, [Moses] said: 'Return, O Lord, unto the myriads and thousands of Israel' " (Num. 10:36) implies that the Presence rests on no fewer than two thousand and two myriads[6] of Israel. Should the number of Israelites happen to be two thousand and two myriads less one, because this one person has not engaged in fruition and increase, does not that person thereby cause the Presence to stay away from Israel?[7]

200. "To be a God unto thee and to thy seed after thee" (Gen. 17:7). When there exists "seed after thee," the Presence dwells among them; but when there is no "seed after thee," among whom is it to dwell? Among sticks and stones?[8]

201. "They who have no successors, fear not God" (Ps. 55:20) applies to one who has no son.[9]

202. R. Yohanan said in the name of R. Simeon ben Yohai: When a man does not leave a son to inherit from him, the Holy One is filled with wrath at him, for it is said, "You fill Him with wrath[10] when a man's property goes to his daughter [for want of a son]" (Num. 27:8).[11]

203. "The Lord supporteth all that fall" (Ps. 145:14), such as barren women, who fall [in esteem] in their own homes. "And maketh all who are bent stand erect" (ibid.): as soon as the Holy One remembers them with children, they are enabled to stand erect. You can see for yourself that it is so: Leah had been the disdained one in the house, but as soon as the Holy One remembered her with children, she was enabled to stand erect.[12]

204. Our masters taught: If a man takes a wife and lives with her for ten years, and she bears no child, he is to divorce her and return her marriage settlement, for it is possible that it is he who does not merit siring children by her. Even though there is no proof in Scripture for such a requirement, there is an intimation: "And Sarai . . . took Hagar . . . after Abram had dwelt ten years in the land of Canaan, and gave her to Abram" (Gen. 16:3).[13]

205. We have been taught that R. Joshua ben Levi said: If a man married in his youth, he should marry again in

---

1. Lev. R. 32:8; Eccles. R. 4:1, §1.
2. Gen. R. 45:2.
3. B. Ber 10a.
4. Ed 1:13.
5. B. Yev 63b; Tos Yev 8:7.
6. The plurals "thousands" and "myriads" are taken to signify at least two of each.
7. B. Yev 63b–64a.
8. B. Yev 64a.
9. B. BB 116a.
10. The word *ve-haavartem* ("cause to pass") is here derived from the word *evrah* ("wrath").
11. B. BB 116a.
12. Gen. R. 71:2.
13. B. Yev 64a.

his old age; if he had children in his youth, he should also have children in his old age, for it is said, "In the morning sow thy seed, and in the evening withhold not thy hand" (Eccles. 11:6).[1]

206. R. Joshua ben Levi did not go to a house of mourning unless it was the house of one who had left no sons, for it is written, "Weep sore for him that goeth hence" (Jer. 22:10), which, R. Judah said in the name of Rav, means one who goes hence without leaving male children.

R. Phinehas ben Hama expounded: In the verse "When Hadad heard in Egypt that David slept with his fathers, and that Joab the captain of the host was dead" (1 Kings 11:21), why does Scripture use "sleep" with regard to David and "death" with regard to Joab? "Sleep" is used of David because he left a son; "death" is used of Joab because he left no son.[2]

207. "And the Lord had blessed Abraham with everything" (Gen. 24:1). What is meant by "with everything"? That he had no daughter [but only sons], said R. Meir; that he had a daughter [in addition to sons], said R. Judah.[3]

208. It is written in the book of Ben Sira: "A daughter is a deceptive treasure to her father. Because of anxiety on her account, he cannot sleep at night—when she is young, lest she be seduced; when she reaches puberty, lest she play the harlot; after she is grown up, lest she fail to marry; after she is married, lest she have no children; after she has grown old, lest she practice witchcraft" (Ecclesiasticus 42:9–10).[4]

209. R. Hisda said: [The birth of] a female child first is a good sign for the male children [to come].[5]

210. After R. Simeon Berabbi's wife gave birth to a girl, R. Hiyya the Elder happened to see R. Simeon and said to him, "The Holy One has begun to bless you." R. Simeon: "Why do you say that [with regard to the birth of a girl]?" R. Hiyya: "Because Scripture says, 'And it came to pass when man began to multiply . . . daughters were born unto them.' " (Gen. 6:1). Later, when R. Simeon went to see his father [R. Judah], R. Judah asked him, "Did the Babylonian [R. Hiyya] make you feel happy?" R. Simeon: "Yes, and this is what he said to me." "Nevertheless," said R. Judah, "though both wine and vinegar are needed, wine is needed more than vinegar; though wheat and barley are needed, wheat is needed more than barley. Then, too, when a man gives his daughter in marriage and pays the expense for it, he says to her, "May you never need to return here."[6]

211. After a daughter was born to R. Simeon Berabbi, he was disappointed. His father [R. Judah], seeking to comfort him, said, "The possibility for further increase has now come into the world." But Bar Kappara said to R. Simeon, "Your father has offered you vain comfort. The fact is, as we have been taught, the world cannot endure without both males and females. Nevertheless, happy is he whose children are males, and alas for him whose children are females."[7]

212. There are three things a man would rather not have: grass in his standing grain, vinegar in his wine, and a female among his children. Yet all three were created for the world's need.[8]

213. There is a story about a man who made out his will with this provision: my son shall not inherit anything of mine until he acts the fool. R. Yose bar Judah and Rabbi went to R. Joshua ben Korhah to get an opinion about this [strange] provision. When they peeked in from outside [R. Joshua's house], they saw him crawling on his hands and knees, with a reed sticking out of his mouth, and being pulled along by his child. Seeing him thus, they discreetly withdrew, but they came back later and asked him about the provision in the will. He began to laugh and said, "As you live, this business you ask about—acting the fool—happened to me a little while ago." Hence the aphorism "When a man looks on his children, his joy makes him act like a fool."[9]

214. "And to the woman He said: I will greatly multiply thy trouble, and the pain in thy travail" (Gen. 3:16). "Thy trouble" refers to the trouble in rearing children; "the pain in thy travail" to the pain of pregnancy.[10]

215. A woman who eats meat and drinks wine [during her pregnancy] will have healthy children. One who eats eggs will have children with large eyes. One who eats fish will have charming children. One who eats parsley will have exceptionally handsome children. One who eats coriander will have fleshy children. One who eats etrog will have fragrant children.

King Shapur's daughter, whose mother had eaten etrog [while pregnant with her], used to be lifted in front of her father to provide his favorite perfume.[11]

216. A woman should give suck to her child. [Disagreeing with the Mishnah just cited], the school of Shammai says that if a woman has vowed not to give suck to her child, she must pull the nipple out of the infant's mouth.[12] But the school of Hillel maintains that her husband may compel her to nurse the child. If she has been divorced [in the meantime], he may not compel her. If, however, the infant recognizes her [and refuses to be suckled by a wetnurse], the husband is to pay his divorced wife a fee and compel her to give suck, in order to avert harm [to the infant].

1. B. Yev 62b.
2. B. BB 116a.
3. B. BB 16b.
4. B. Sanh 100b.
5. B. BB 141a.
6. Gen. R. 26:4.
7. B. BB 16b.
8. Tanhuma, *Hayye Sarah*, §3.
9. MTeh 92:13; Yalkut, Ps. §846.
10. B. Er 100b.
11. B. Ket 60b–61a.
12. For the woman's vow is valid.

A divorced woman [who refused to give suck to her infant] once appeared before Samuel. He instructed R. Dimi bar Joseph, "Go and determine whether the child recognizes her." R. Dimi arranged to have her sit in a row with other women, then picked up the child and carried it in front of them. When he reached the mother, the child gazed longingly at her face. Wishing to evade him, she covered her eyes, but R. Dimi said to her, "Uncover your eyes, stand up, and take your child."[1]

217. He who brings up a child is called "Father," not he who merely begot him.[2]

218. "Happy are they . . . who do charity at all times" (Ps. 106:3). But is it possible to do charity at all times? Our masters in Yavneh (some say, R. Eliezer) expounded the words as applying to one who sustains his sons and daughters when they are small.[3] R. Samuel bar Nahmani applied these words to him who brings up an orphan boy or an orphan girl in his house and enables them to marry.[4]

219. The sages said in the name of R. Yose bar Hanina: In Usha, an ordinance was enacted that a man is required to maintain his sons and daughters while they are small.[5]

When the question came up before R. Judah, he [concurred with the ordinance of Usha], saying: The sea monster brought forth young and expects the people of the town to maintain them!

When the same question came up before R. Hisda, he would say: Turn a mortar upside down in public, and have the delinquent father stand on it and declare: Even a raven craves to have young, but I do not care for children.

When such a person came to Rava, Rava would ask him: You do not mind having your children maintained by public charity?[6]

220. R. Yose bar Honi said: A man will envy anyone, except his son or his disciple.[7]

221. Is there a father who hates his son?[8]

222. Grandchildren are like one's own children.[9]

223. R. Judah bar Ilai said: Daughters of sons are reckoned as sons, but sons of daughters are not reckoned as sons.[10]

1. B. Ket 59b–60a.
2. Exod. R. 46:5.
3. They have no legal claim upon him for maintenance.
4. B. Ket 50a.
5. Prior to that time, during Hadrian's persecution (135 C.E. and the years that followed), poverty was so widespread that fathers abandoned their children. See *EJ*, s.v. "Usha."
6. B. Ket 49b.
7. B. Sanh 105b.
8. Ibid.
9. B. Yev 62b.
10. In the list of Jacob's descendants (Gen. 46:8–27), the sons of Dinah, Jacob's daughter, are not mentioned. Hence it is concluded that, insofar as the right to inherit is concerned, the sons of a man's daughter(s) are not considered a man's children, belonging as they do to the family of the daughter's husband. Gen. R. 94:6.

224. "That thou wilt not deal falsely with me, nor with my son, nor with my son's son" (Gen. 21:23). A father's compassion for his son reaches only thus far [down the generations].[11]

225. When a man guides his sons and daughters in the right path, Scripture says of him, "And thou shalt know that thy tent is in peace" (Job 5:24).[12]

226. "Train up a child in the way he should go" (Prov. 22:6). R. Eliezer and R. Joshua differed. R. Eliezer said: The verse means that if you train your son with words of Torah until he becomes a young man, he will continue growing in allegiance to them, as the verse concludes, "Even when he is old, he will not depart from it" (ibid.). But R. Joshua said: The child may be compared to a heifer—if she is not taught to plow when young, it will be difficult for her to do so in the end; or to a wine branch—if you do not bend it when it is full of sap, once it hardens, you can do nothing with it.[13]

227. In the main, what children do is bungled.[14]

228. Whatever was created during the six days of creation needs further perfecting. . . . Every man needs finishing.[15]

229. "And when the boys grew up" (Gen. 25:27). R. Levi said: [At first], they were like a myrtle and a wild rose growing side by side. But when they grew up, the former yielded its characteristic fragrance (*reho*), and the latter its thorns (*hoho*). For the first thirteen years, both went together to school and together came home from school. But at the end of the thirteen years,[16] one went to houses of study and the other to shrines of idolatry.

R. Eleazar said: A father must hold himself responsible for his son until the age of thirteen. After that, he should say, "Blessed be He who has freed me of liability for this boy."[17]

230. "Train a lad in the way he should go" (Prov. 22:6). R. Judah and R. Nehemiah differed. One said: "Lad" means from the age of sixteen to twenty-two. The other said: From the age of eighteen to twenty-four.[18]

231. "When you plant any tree . . . ye will find its fruit to be uncircumcised" (Lev. 19:23). These words allude to an infant [whose lips are uncircumcised, not having the capacity to speak]. "For the first three years [of an infant's life], he continues to be for you 'uncircumcised' " (Lev. 19:23), since he cannot converse nor even speak. "But in the fourth year, all its fruit [the infant's speech] shall be

11. Gen. R. 54:2.
12. B. Yev 62b.
13. Midrash Prov. 22:6 (ed. Buber, p. 91).
14. B. Hul 86a.
15. Circumcision. Gen. R. 11:6.
16. Maturity is reached at thirteen years and one day.
17. Gen. R. 63:10.
18. B. Kid 30a.

holy, for giving praise unto the Lord" (Lev. 19:24)—his father should hallow him for study of Torah.[1]

232. "And ye shall teach them to your children by speaking of them" (Deut. 11:19). From this verse, the sages inferred that once an infant begins to speak, the father should speak to him in the holy tongue [Hebrew] and teach him Torah. And if he does not speak to him in the holy tongue and does not teach him Torah, it is as though he were burying him.[2]

233. Our masters taught: A child who knows how to shake the lulav cluster is required to use the lulav cluster. If the child knows how to wrap himself in a prayer shawl, he is required to wrap himself in a prayer shawl. If a child knows how to care for tefillin,[3] his father must acquire tefillin for him. If he knows how to speak, his father must teach him the Shema, Torah, and the holy tongue. If the father does not, it is as though the child had not come into the world.[4]

What is meant here by Torah? R. Hamnuna said: The verse "Moses commanded us Torah, the inheritance of the congregation of Jacob" (Deut. 33:4).

And what is meant here by Shema? Its first verse ["Hear, O Israel: The Lord our God, the Lord is one" (Deut. 6:4)].[5]

234. R. Nahman said: A boy who knows to whom a benediction is addressed may be invited by the partakers to participate in grace after the meal.

[When they were still very young], Abbaye and Rava sat in the presence of Rabbah, who asked them, "Whom do you address when you pronounce a benediction?" The two: "The Holy One, blessed be He."

"And where does the Holy One dwell?"

Rava pointed to the ceiling, while Abbaye went outside and pointed to the sky. At that, Rabbah said to them, "Both of you will grow up to be sages."

Hence the proverb "Each young pumpkin can be told by its stalk."[6]

235. R. Ketina said: When a father has brought a child under the age of six [to school], then later on, even if he runs after the child [to try to restore his failing health], he will not succeed. Others say: If the child's classmates scamper after him [to catch up with his learning], they will not succeed. In fact, both opinions are correct. Such a child's health will be feeble, but he will be learned.[7]

236. R. Joshua ben Levi said: When a man teaches Torah to his grandson, Scripture regards him as though he had received it from [God Himself] at Mount Sinai, for the verse "Make them known to thy children and children's children" (Deut. 4:9) is followed at once by "The day thou stoodest before the Lord thy God at Horeb" (Deut. 4:10).

[Upon learning what R. Joshua ben Levi had said], R. Hiyya bar Abba would not taste meat before going over the Scripture [studied the preceding day] with his child and adding a verse to it. Rabbah bar R. Huna would not taste meat until he brought his child to school.[8]

237. Every Friday afternoon, R. Joshua regularly listened to his grandson's reading of the Scripture lesson [studied during the week]. Once, he forgot to do so, and, when he had already entered the baths of Tiberias, leaning on the shoulder of R. Hiyya bar Abba, he remembered that he had not listened to his grandson's reading of Scripture. So he turned around and left. R. Hiyya bar Abba asked him: Master, did you not teach us that if one has begun [at the bath], one may not interrupt [even for prayer]? R. Joshua answered: Hiyya, my son, is it a small matter to you that he who listens to his grandson's reading of Scripture is as though he were hearing it at Mount Sinai? For it is said, "Make them known unto thy children and thy children's children, as if it were the day that thou stoodest before the Lord thy God in Horeb" (Deut. 4:9–10).[9]

238. Our masters taught: With regard to his son, a father is obligated to circumcise him, to redeem him [if he is the firstborn], to teach him Torah, to teach him a craft, and to get him married. Some say: Also to teach him how to swim. R. Judah said: When a man does not teach his son a craft, it is as though he taught him brigandage.

To teach him a craft—what is the proof? Hezekiah said: The verse "See to a livelihood as eagerly as to the woman whom thou lovest" (Eccles. 9:9). If the term "woman" here refers literally to a wife, then even as a father is required to get a wife for his son, so is he required to teach him a craft [by which to make a livelihood]. If the term "woman" here refers figuratively to Torah, then even as a father is required to teach his son Torah, so is he required to teach him a craft.

Some say: Also to teach him how to swim. The reason? His life may depend on it.

R. Judah said: He who does not teach his son a craft is as though he taught him brigandage. What is the difference between the anonymous teaching [cited at the beginning of this section] that a father should teach his son a craft and R. Judah? They differ in an instance where a father teaches commerce to his son.[10]

Rabbi [Judah I, the Patriarch] said: A father is also required to teach his son civic obligations.

Whatever a father is required to do for his son, should he fail to do it, the son must do it on his own.[11]

---

1. Tanhuma B, *Kedoshim*, §14. The translator is indebted to Professor Jakob J. Petuchowski for the interpretation of this passage.
2. Sif Deut., §46.
3. To stay clean while wearing them.
4. In all these cases, the child is not obligated, but his father should train him to observe the commandments.
5. Tos Hag 1:2; B. Suk 42a.
6. B. Ber 48a.
7. B. Ket 50a.
8. B. Kid 30a.
9. P. Shab 1:1, 3a.
10. The anonymous teaching, without predicting dire consequences, regards a father's teaching the craft of commerce to his son as sufficient; but R. Judah, who predicts dire consequences if a father does not teach his son a craft, does not regard such instruction as sufficient, because commerce is too precarious.
11. B. Kid 29a and 30b; Mek, *Bo, Pis'ha*, 18.

239. When R. Joshua was asked, "May a man teach his son Greek?" he replied, "He may teach it to him at a time that is neither day nor night, for it is said, 'Thou shalt meditate therein [on the Torah] day and night.' " (Josh. 1:8).

If so, a man may not even teach his son a craft. But did not R. Ishmael instruct us that "Choose life" (Deut. 30:19) means teaching a craft?

In the name of R. Yohanan, the sages said: [The prohibition of teaching Greek was imposed only] to lessen the effectiveness of informers.[1]

240. Ben Azzai said: A man is required to teach his daughter Torah.

But R. Eliezer said: Anyone who teaches Torah to his daughter is as though he taught her lechery.[2]

241. R. Abbahu said in the name of R. Yohanan: A man may teach his daughter Greek, because it is an ornament for her. When Simeon bar Abba heard this, he said: Because R. Abbahu wishes to teach his daughter Greek, he hangs the giving of permission on R. Yohanan.

When R. Abbahu heard the charge, he said: May such-and-such befall me if I have not heard it from R. Yohanan![3]

242. R. Akiva used to say: a father transmits to his son good looks, physical strength, wealth, wisdom, and length of years.[4]

243. The son of a sage is [already] half a sage.[5]

244. An heir steps into his father's shoes.[6]

245. Ewe follows ewe—what the mother does, the daughter does.[7]

246. "Like mother, like daughter" (Ezek. 16:44). A heifer gores, her calf kicks.[8]

247. A child's talk in the marketplace is his father's talk or his mother's.[9]

248. As the garden, so the gardener.[10]

249. R. Yohanan said in the name of R. Simeon ben Yohai: A wicked child in a man's household works greater havoc than the wars of Gog and Magog.[11]

250. A rebellious and defiant son (Deut. 21:18–21) is condemned because of what he will become in the end.

We have been taught that R. Yose the Galilean said: Is it conceivable that merely because the young man ate a *tartemar*[12] of meat and drank half a *log* of Italian wine, the Torah would decree that he be brought before the High Court and put to death by stoning? However, the Torah foresaw the ultimate destiny of the young man sentenced as a rebellious and defiant son. For in the end, after dissipating his father's possessions, he will continue to seek what he has become accustomed to and, unable to get it, will go out to a crossroads and rob people. Therefore the Torah said, "Let him die while yet innocent, and not die guilty."

R. Simeon said: Is it conceivable that just because this one ate a *tartemar* of meat and drank half a *log* of Italian wine, his father and mother should take him out to be put to death by stoning? In truth, the rebellious and defiant son never existed and never will exist. Why, then, was the account about him written? So that you will expound the possible reasons for such misconduct and receive a reward doing so.

R. Jonathan, however, said: I saw one such and sat by his grave.[13]

251. R. Huna, in the name of R. Yohanan, told the parable of a certain man who opened a perfume shop for his son in the street of harlots. The street plied its trade, the perfume business plied its trade,[14] and the lad, like any young male, plied his natural inclination—he strayed into depraved ways. When the father came and caught him with a harlot, he began to shout, "I'll kill you!" But the father's friend was there, and he spoke up. "You yourself ruined your son, and now you are yelling at him! You ignored all other occupations and taught him to be a perfumer; you ignored all other streets and deliberately opened a shop for him in the street of harlots!"[15]

252. A story is told of a man who was standing with his son in a synagogue. When all the congregation responded to the reader with "Hallelujah," the man's son responded with some flippant words. "See here," the people said to the father, "your son is responding with flippant words." He replied, "What can I do with him? He is only a child—let him amuse himself." The next day, the same thing happened: as all the congregation responded to the reader with "Hallelujah," the man's son again responded with flippant words. "See here," the people said to the father, "your son is once more responding with flippant words." He replied again, "What can I do? He is only a child—let him amuse himself." All through the eight days of the festival, the son kept on responding with flippant words and the father did not say anything to stop him. Not one year passed by, nor two, nor three, said the sages, but that the father died, his wife died, his son died, his grandson died, and all together fifteen souls departed from his

1. P. Pe 1:1, 15c; P. Sot 9:15, 24c.
2. The laws concerning sexual aberrations may excite her sensuality (so Jastrow). B. Sot 20a.
3. P. Pe 1:1, 15c; P. Sot 9:15, 24c.
4. Ed 2:9.
5. Yalkut, *Va-yera*, §95.
6. Literally, "is his father's leg." B. Er 70b.
7. B. Ket 63a.
8. Gen. R. 80:1; Yalkut, *Va-yishlah*, §133.
9. B. Suk 56b.
10. Gen. R. 80:1.
11. B. Ber 7b.
12. Half a *litra*, whose volume equals an egg and a half.
13. B. Sanh 71a and 72a.
14. Since harlots favor perfume.
15. Exod. R. 43:7; B. Ber 32a.

household. Only two sons were left, one lame and blind, the other half-witted and malicious.[1]

253. R. Hisda said: A man should never terrorize his household. The husband of the concubine of Gibeah terrorized her, and her death precipitated the death of several myriads in Israel.[2]

254. R. Abbahu said: A man should never terrorize his household. A distinguished man—who was he? R. Hanina ben Gamaliel—terrorized his household, and he was served food it is a great sin to eat. What kind of food? A limb cut from a living animal.[3]

255. A man should not threaten a child even with as little a thing as boxing his ears. He should spank him at once or say nothing.

It happened in Lod that when the son of Gorgos ran away from school, the father threatened to box his ears. The son, terrorized by his father, went off and drowned himself in a cistern.

Then, too, it happened in Bene Berak that a child broke a flask on the Sabbath, and his father threatened to box his ears. The child, terrorized by his father, went off and drowned himself in a cistern.[4]

256. R. Simeon ben Eleazar said: Human instinct, a child, and a woman should be thrust off with the left hand only so long as one brings them near with the right hand.[5]

257. R. Isaac stated: In Usha, it was ordained that a man should be patient with his son until the age of twelve. After that, he may even threaten his life.[6]

258. "He that spareth his rod, hateth his son" (Prov. 13:24). The verse is to teach you that when a man refrains from chastising his son, the son will fall into evil ways, so that in the end the father will come to hate his son. Thus it happened with Ishmael, whom his father loved so much that he did not chastise him; then, when Ishmael fell into evil ways, Abraham came to hate him so much that he cast him out empty-handed from his house. What had Ishmael done? When he was fifteen, he began to bring idols from the marketplace, make merry with them, and worship them the way he saw other people worship. "When Sarah saw the son of Hagar the Egyptian making merry . . . she said unto Abraham: 'Cast out this bondwoman and her son' " (Gen. 21:9–10), lest my son learn his ways. There and then, "Abraham rose up early in the morning, and took only bread and a bottle of water" (Gen. 21:14). The meager provisions show that Abraham had come to hate Ishmael so intensely that he decided to send him and his mother away empty-handed when he cast him out of his house. And what was Ishmael's end? After Abraham had driven him out, Ishmael sat at a crossroads and robbed travelers.

The same applies to "Now Isaac loved Esau" (Gen. 25:28); Esau fell into evil ways, because Isaac did not chastise him. It was likewise with David, who did not rebuke his son Absalom or chastise him, so that he fell into evil ways, sought to slay his father, and caused him sorrows without end.[7]

259. "Put not a stumbling block before the blind" (Lev. 19:14). The verse applies to a man who beats his grown-up son.

When a maidservant in the household of Rabbi [Judah I, the Patriarch] saw a man beating his grown-up son, she said: That man should be placed under a ban, for he is violating "Put not a stumbling block before the blind."[8]

260. Rav said: A man should not single out one of his sons for special treatment, for on account of the two *sela* of silk—the one thing Jacob gave to Joseph and not to his other sons—Joseph's brothers grew jealous of him, and the consequences grew until our forebears had to go down into Egypt.[9]

261. If a man bequeaths his estate to others, passing over his own children, what he did is done [valid], but the spirit of the sages finds no pleasure in him. Rabban Simeon ben Gamaliel, however, said: If the man's children did not behave as they should have, it is deemed to the man's credit.

Samuel said to R. Judah: Keen scholar, try to prevent alienation of inheritance, even from a bad son to a good son, because one never knows what issue will come from the bad son; and much more so [when the alienation is] from a son to a daughter.[10]

262. On his deathbed, a certain man bequeathed "the barrel of earth to one son, the barrel of bones to the second, the barrel of hackled wool to the third." They did not know what he meant, so they went to R. Banaah, who asked them, "Do you have land?" They replied, "Yes." "Do you have cattle?" "Yes." "Do you have felt cloaks?" "Yes." "If so," said R. Banaah, "this is what your father had in mind.[11]

263. A certain man overheard his wife say to her daughter, "Why are you not more discreet in your infidelities? I have ten sons, and only one of them is by your father." When the man was dying, he said, "I leave my entire estate to one son." Since they did not know which son he had in mind, they came to R. Banaah, who said to them, "Go and strike your father's grave with sticks until he rises up and tells which one of you he left his estate to." All

1. TdE, ed. Friedmann, pp. 65–66 (JPS, p. 188).
2. See Judg. 19–20. B. Git 6b.
3. When a limb of a slaughtered animal got lost, R. Hanina's servants cut off a limb from a living animal and brought it to him. B. Git 7a.
4. Sem 2:4–5.
5. B. Sot 47a.
6. Literally, "keep at him down to his very life" (by applying the rod, withholding food, etc.). B. Ket 50a.
7. Exod. R. 1:1.
8. The adult son may be moved to strike back, which would make him liable to the death penalty as a rebellious son. B. MK 17a.
9. B. Shab 10b.
10. The daughter's son may take after her husband. See also note to §223 above in this chapter. B. BB 133b; B. Ket 53a.
11. B. BB 58a.

of them went, except the one who was his own son. At that, R. Banaah said, "The entire estate is to go to this one."[1]

264. Happy is the man whose forebears transmit merit to him. Happy is the man who has a noble family tree to hang on to.[2]

Honoring Father and Mother

265. Ulla the Elder expounded at the entrance to the patriarch's house: What is meant by the verse "All the kings of the earth, O Lord, admitted [they were wrong] after they heard the words of Thy mouth" (Ps. 138:4), in which it is said not, "The word of Thy mouth," but, "The words of Thy mouth"? The verse means: when the Holy One said, "I am the Lord thy God" (Exod. 20:2), and "Thou shalt have no other gods before Me" (Exod. 20:3), the nations of the world observed, "He is demanding deference to His own glory." But when He said, "Honor thy father and thy mother" (Exod. 20:12), they recanted and admitted that the first words [were not merely concerned with deference to Him].

Rava said: The same conclusion may be inferred from "The beginning of Thine utterance is true" (Ps. 119:160). Only the beginning of Your utterance, and not the end of Your utterance? No, what Scripture means is that, from the end of Your utterance, its beginning is seen to be true.[3]

266. "Honor thy father and thy mother" (Exod. 20:12) and "Thou shalt not commit murder" (Exod. 20:13). What is signified by having these two commandments next to each other? That if a man has ample provisions in his house, yet refuses to give the benefit of them to his father and mother when they are young, let alone in their old age, it is as if all his days he had been commiting murder in the presence of Him who is everywhere. For this reason the commandment "Honor thy father and thy mother" is followed by "Thou shalt not commit murder."[4]

267. Our masters taught: There are three partners in a man: the Holy One, his father, and his mother. When a man honors his father and his mother, the Holy One says: I account it to them as though I were dwelling among them, and they were honoring Me.

We have been taught that Rabbi [Judah I, the Patriarch] said: It is revealed and known to Him who spoke and the world came into being that a son honors his mother more than his father, because she sways him with her gentle speech. That is why the Holy One put the honor of the father before the honor of the mother. It is known and revealed to Him who spoke and the world came into being that a son fears his father more than his mother, because his father teaches him Torah. That is why the Holy One put the fear of the mother before the fear of the father (Lev. 19:3).

A *tanna*[5] recited before R. Nahman: When a man vexes his father or his mother, the Holy One says: I do well not to live among them, for if I were living among them, they would vex Me, too.[6]

268. When a man curses his father or his mother, or strikes them, leaving bruises on them, the Holy One draws His feet back [in revulsion] under the throne of glory, if one dare say such a thing, as He declares: I made his honoring of his parents equal to his honoring of Me. Had I been dwelling with this man, he would have done the same to Me. I do well not to live in the same house with such a man.[7]

269. R. Simeon ben Yohai said: Great is the duty of honoring one's father and mother, since the Holy One set the honor due them above the honor due to Himself. For concerning the honor due to the Holy One, it is written, "Honor the Lord with thy substance" (Prov. 3:9). How is one to honor God with one's substance? One sets aside gleanings, forgotten sheaves, and the corners of the field; [one gives] heave offerings, the first tithe, the second tithe, the poor man's tithe, and the priest's share of the dough; one makes a lulav, a sukkah, a shofar, tefillin, and ritual fringes; one feeds the hungry, gives drink to the thirsty, and clothes the naked. In short, if you have substance, you are obligated to do all these things; but if you have no substance, you are not obligated to do even one of them. When it comes to honoring father and mother, however, whether you have substance or not, what does Scripture say? "Honor thy father and thy mother," even if you have to go about begging in doorways.[8]

270. Our masters taught: What is "fear," and what is "honor"? "Fear" means that the son is not to stand in his father's place, nor to sit in his place; not to contradict him, nor to tip the scales against him.[9] "Honor" means that the son must supply his father with food and drink, provide him with clothes and footwear, and assist his coming in or going out of the house.[10]

271. We have been taught: When a man's father is [unwittingly] violating a precept of Torah, the man should not say, "Father, you are violating a precept of Torah"; he should rather say, "But, Father, is what you are doing written in the Torah?"

Does it not amount to the same thing?

[Yes]. Hence he should say, "Father, the pertinent verse in Scripture reads thus."[11]

---

1. Ibid.
2. P. Ber 4:1, 7d.
3. B. Kid 31a.
4. TdE, ed. Friedmann, p. 134 (JPS, p. 331).
5. One who memorized Baraitas and recited them before a teacher so that he might expound them.
6. B. Kid 30b–31a.
7. TdE, ed. Friedmann, p. 13 (JPS, p. 331).
8. PR 23/24:2 (YJS 1:499); Mek, *Yitro, Ba-hodesh*, 8; P. Pe 1:1, 15d.
9. When his father is in a dispute concerning *Halakhah* with another sage, the son may not side against him.
10. B. Kid 31b.
11. B. Sanh 81a.

272. When R. Ulla was asked, "How far should honoring one's father and mother extend?" he replied, "Go and see what a certain heathen named Dama ben Netinah did for his father in Ashkelon. Once, the sages sought some merchandise from him involving a profit to him of sixty myriads [of gold denars]. But the key to where the merchandise was kept was under his [sleeping] father's pillow, and he would not disturb him."

R. Judah said in the name of Samuel: When R. Eliezer was asked, "How far should honoring one's father and mother extend?" he replied, "Go and see what a certain heathen named Dama ben Netinah did for his father in Ashkelon. Once, the sages sought some precious stones from him for the ephod at a profit to him of sixty myriads [of gold denars]. But the key to where the stones were kept was under his [sleeping] father's pillow, and he would not disturb him."

The following year, however, the Holy One gave him his reward. A red heifer was born to him in his herd. When the sages of Israel visited him [intending to buy it], he said to them, "I know about you. Even if I were to ask all the money in the world, you would pay me. But all I ask of you is the amount I lost because I honored my father."

R. Hanina said: If one who is not commanded [to honor his parents] and nevertheless does is rewarded thus, how much more by far one who is commanded and does so![1]

273. R. Hezekiah said: There was a heathen in Ashkelon who was the chief of the city fathers. He never presumed to sit on the stone upon which his father sat. And when his father died, he had the stone made into an idol.[2]

274. R. Abbahu said that when R. Eliezer the Elder was asked by his disciples, "How far should one go in honoring one's father and mother?" he replied, "Go and see what Dama ben Netinah of Ashkelon did. When his mother, who was feebleminded, hit him with her sandal in the presence of the entire council over which he presided, he merely said to her, 'Enough, Mother.' Moreover, when her sandal [with which she was hitting him] fell from her hand, [he picked it up and] handed it back to her, so that she would not get upset."[3]

275. When R. Dimi came [from the Land of Israel], he said: Once, while Dama ben Netinah was seated among the notables of Rome, wearing a silk garment embroidered with gold, his mother came, ripped it off him, struck him on the head, and spat in his face. Yet in no way would he put her to shame.[4]

276. When R. Eliezer was asked, "How far is a man to go in honoring his father and mother?" he replied, "So far that, should his father take a purse of denars and toss it into the sea in his presence, he would not put him to shame."[5]

277. It happened that R. Tarfon's mother went forth on the Sabbath for a walk in her courtyard. When her sandal split [and he could not sew it up then and there because it was the Sabbath], R. Tarfon held his hands under the soles of her feet, and she walked on his hands until she reached her couch.

Once, when R. Tarfon took sick and the sages came in to visit him, she said to them, "Pray for my son R. Tarfon, for he treats me with excessive honor." They asked her, "In what way?" So she told them the story. They said, "Even if he had done this a thousand thousand times, he still has not come halfway to showing you the full honor prescribed by the Torah."

R. Ishmael's mother complained to our masters about R. Ishmael. She said to them: Please rebuke my son R. Ishmael, for he does not treat me with honor. At this, the faces of our masters grew pale, and they said: Is it possible that R. Ishmael does not treat his parents with honor? So they asked her: Just what is he doing to you? She replied: When he leaves the house of study [after his daily stint of teaching], I want to wash his feet and drink the water, but he refuses to let me do so. The masters said to him: Since such is her wish, such is the honor due her [from her son].

R. Zera used to grieve, saying: "I wish I had a father and a mother whom I could honor, and thus inherit the Garden of Eden. But after hearing the two tales just told, he said: Blessed be He who is everywhere, that I have neither father nor mother. I could not have acted like R. Tarfon, and [I must confess] I could not have put up with what R. Ishmael had to put up with.

R. Avun said: I was relieved of the obligation to honor father and mother. The sages explained: As soon as his mother conceived him, his father died, and right after he was born, his mother died.[6]

278. R. Yohanan said: Happy is he who has never seen his parents.[7]

R. Yohanan's father died as soon as his mother conceived him, and his mother died right after she gave birth to him.[8]

279. R. Tarfon had an aged mother. Whenever she wished to go up to her couch, he would bend down to let her go up [by stepping on him]; and when she wished to go down, she did so [by stepping on him]. When he went and boasted about it in the house of study, he was told, "You still have not reached half the honor due a mother. Has she ever tossed a purse of gold coins into the sea in your presence, and you did not put her to shame?"[9]

280. When R. Joseph heard the sound of his mother's footsteps, he would say, "I must rise before the Presence, which is approaching."[10]

1. B. Kid 31a.
2. P. Pe 1:1, 15c.
3. Deut R. 1:15; P. Pe 1:1, 15c.
4. B. Kid 31a.
5. B. Kid 32a.
6. P. Pe 1:1, 15c; B Kid 31b.
7. Because it is so difficult to honor them properly.
8. B. Kid 31b.
9. Ibid.
10. Ibid.

281. R. Abbahu said: "He who is like my son Avimi fulfills the precept of honoring one's father." While R. Abbahu was still living, Avimi had five sons who were ordained. Yet, when [his father] R. Abbahu came and called out at the door, Avimi himself would run to open the door for his father, saying, "Coming, coming," until he reached it.

Once R. Abbahu said to Avimi, "Give me a drink of water." By the time Avimi brought it, R. Abbahu had dozed off. Avimi bent down and stood over R. Abbahu until R. Abbahu woke up.[1]

282. A certain widow's son asked R. Eliezer, "If my father says, 'Give me a drink of water,' and my mother says, 'Give me a drink of water,' which request takes precedence?" R. Eliezer replied, "Delay the honor due your mother and accord honor first to your father, since both you and your mother are bound to honor your father."

The widow's son appeared before R. Joshua, who gave him the same answer. He then asked, "Rabbi, what if my mother got divorced?" R. Joshua: "From your eyelids [which seem to have disappeared],[2] it is clear that you are a widow's son. So pour some water into a basin for both your parents and screech to them as to fowls to come and drink."[3]

283. If a man's own lost article and his father's lost article [are to be looked for], his own is to be looked for first. If a man's own lost article and his teacher's lost article [are to be looked for], his own is to be looked for first. And the proof? R. Judah said in the name of Rav: Scripture says, "There shall be no needy in thee" (Deut. 15:4), which implies that you are to look after your own needs before looking after the needs of others.

But R. Judah went on to say in the name of Rav: [Nevertheless], he who does so [all the time] will eventually be brought to poverty.[4]

284. Our masters taught: When a man, his father, and his teacher are in captivity, he has the first right to be ransomed before his teacher, and his teacher before his father. But his mother has the first right to be ransomed before all of them.[5]

285. Avimi the son of R. Abbahu said: There is one who gives his father force-fed birds to eat, yet will inherit Gehenna; and there is another who sets his father grinding at the mill, yet will inherit the Garden of Eden.

How is it possible that one who gives his father fattened birds to eat should inherit Gehenna? There is the story of one who used to provide force-fed chickens for his father. Once, the father said to him, "My son, where did you get these?" The son replied, "Old man, old man, eat and shut up, even as dogs shut up when they eat." Thus, though he gave his father fattened birds, he inherited Gehenna.

How is it possible for one to set his father grinding at the mill and yet inherit the Garden of Eden? There is the story of a young man whose work was grinding wheat. When the king sent word that millers be brought to work for him, the young man said to his father, "Father, you go in to the mill to grind in my stead, and I will go do the king's work. Should there be humiliation in it, I would rather be humiliated, and not you; should there be flogging, let me receive the blows, and not you." Thus, though he made his father grind at the mill, the son inherited the Garden of Eden.[6]

286. "The eye that mocketh at his father, and despiseth [the precept commanding not] to take[7] the mother [bird away from her fledglings], the ravens of the valley shall pick it out, and the young eagles shall eat it." (Prov. 30:17). The ones to pick the eye out, and the others to eat it? Exactly. The Holy One said: Let the raven, who is cruel to its young, come and pick the eye out without benefiting from it; and let the eagle, who is compassionate to its young,[8] come and eat it![9]

287. "Ye shall fear every man his mother and his father" (Lev. 19:3). One might suppose [on the basis of this clause] that if a father [who is a priest] says to his son, "Defile yourself [by coming near the dead]," or "Do not return a lost article," the son must obey his father. Therefore, Scripture says, "Ye shall fear every man his mother and his father," followed immediately by "And ye shall keep My Sabbaths: I am the Lord your God" (ibid.), implying that all of you are bound to honor Me first.[10]

288. Eleazar ben Matia stated: If my father says, "Give me a drink of water," while I have a precept to perform, I must put aside the honor due to my father and perform the precept, since both I and my father are obligated by the precept. But Isi ben Judah added a reservation: If the precept can be performed by others, then let them perform it, while the son attends to his father's honor.[11]

289. The sages said in the name of R. Hisda: If a father renounces the honor due him, it is renounced.[12]

290. Our Masters taught: A man must honor his father in life and honor him in death. How in life? If he is in a

---

1. Ibid.
2. Because his eyes are so swollen from weeping.
3. Since your parents are now both dead, why waste my time with hypothetical questions? The answer is, of course, sarcastic. B. Kid 31a.
4. B. BM 33a.
5. B. Hor 13a.
6. P. Pe 1:1, 15c; B. Kid 31a–b.
7. The word *lykht*, usually rendered "to obey," is here taken as though spelled *lkht* ("to take"). As a matter of fact, the parallel in MhG Exod., p. 423, reads *lkht*, as do some manuscripts of the book of Proverbs.
8. On the eagle's compassion, see Mek, La, 2:202.
9. Tanhuma B, *Ekev*, §3.
10. B. Yev 6a.
11. B. Kid 32a.
12. Ibid.

place where people will heed him out of deference to his father, he should not say, "Allow me to go, because I must attend to my own needs," "Take care of me quickly, because I must attend to my own needs," or, "Dispose of what I require, because I must attend to my own needs." In making such requests, he should say, "Because my father needs me."

How in death? When the son reports something heard from his father, he should not say, "This is what my late father said," but, "This is what my late father, my teacher—may I provide expiation for any punishment that may be his—said." He should speak thus only within the first twelve months following his father's death.[1] After that, he is to say, "May his memory be for a blessing and for life in the world-to-come."[2]

---

1. Punishment in Gehenna ends after twelve months (see above, part 4, chap. 2, §312).
2. B. Kid 31b.

CHAPTER THREE

BETWEEN MAN AND MAN

The Right Course and a Good Name

1. Rabbi [Judah I, the Patriarch] said: Which is the right course for a man to choose? That which is an honor to him and gains him honor from men.[1]

2. R. Hanina ben Dosa used to say: If a man is liked by his fellow men, he is liked by God; if he is not liked by his fellow men, he is not liked by God.[2]

3. R. Akiva used to say: If a man is satisfied with what is his, it is a good sign for him. If he is not satisfied with what is his, it is a bad sign for him.[3]

4. R. Samuel bar Nahman said in the name of R. Jonathan: In the Five Books, in the Prophets, and in the Writings, we find that a man must discharge his obligations before men, even as he must discharge them before God. Where in the Five Books? In the verse "Neither the Lord nor Israel will have any fault to find with you" (Num. 32:22). In the Prophets? In "God, the Lord God, He knoweth, and Israel, too, shall know" (Josh. 22:22). In the Writings? In "So shalt thou find grace and good favor in the eyes of God and men" (Prov. 3:4). Gamaliel Zoga asked R. Yose bar Avun: What is the verse that says it most clearly? R. Yose bar Avun: "Neither the Lord nor Israel will have any fault to find with you."[4]

5. The sages said: Keep far from unseemliness, from what resembles unseemliness, even from what may appear to resemble it.[5]

6. A man should not be awake in the midst of those who are asleep, nor asleep in the midst of those who are awake. He should not weep when in the midst of those who are merry, nor be merry in the midst of those who weep. He should not remain seated in the midst of those who are standing, nor remain standing in the midst of those who are seated. He should not be reading Scripture in the midst of those who recite Mishnah, nor recite Mishnah in the midst of those who read Scripture. The sum of the matter: a man should not depart from the practice of his fellows.[6]

7. Hillel the Elder said: [When others are different in attire or in mood], do not appear naked, do not appear garbed, do not insist on standing, do not insist on sitting, do not be merry, do not be weeping, for it is said, "A time for weeping, and a time for being merry" (Eccles. 3:4).[7]

8. A man's attitude toward his fellow men should always be sympathetic.[8]

9. R. Tanhum bar Hanilai said: One should never depart from custom. Consider! When Moses when up on high, he ate no bread. When angels came down below, they ate bread.[9]

10. When you enter a town, follow its customs.[10]

11. Abbaye had a favorite saying: A man should always be resourceful in the fear of Heaven—"a soft answer turneth away wrath" (Prov. 15:1). A man should speak peaceably with his brothers, his kin, and with every man—indeed, even with a Gentile in the marketplace—so that he may be loved above, sought out below, and deemed agreeable by his fellow creatures.[11]

12. Reflect before a word issues from your mouth. Consider your actions, to have them accord with good manners, and you will be well rewarded for whatever you do. Accept divine judgment against you as right, and keep clear of grumbling.[12]

13. R. Simeon said: There are three crowns: the crown of Torah, the crown of priesthood, and the crown of royalty. But the crown of a good name surpasses them all.[13]

14. You find that a man is given three names—one that his father and his mother call him, one that his fellow men call him, and one that he acquires. The one he acquires for himself is better than all the others.[14]

15. By the name that is rightly yours, you will be called; in the place rightly yours, you will be set; and from that which is rightly yours, you will be given.[15]

16. Your own deeds will bring you near, and your own deeds will remove you far.[16]

---

1. Avot 2:1.
2. Avot 3:13.
3. Tos Ber 3:3.
4. P. Shek 3:2, 47c.
5. B. Hul 44b; Num. R. 10:8.
6. DEZ 5.
7. Tos Ber 2:21.
8. B. Ket 17a.
9. See Exod. 34:28 and Gen. 18:8. B. BM 86b.
10. Gen. R. 48:14.
11. B. Ber 17a and En Yaakov, ad loc.
12. DEZ 3.
13. Without it, the luster of the three aforementioned crowns is tarnished. Avot 4:13.
14. Tanhuma, *Va-yak'hel*, §1.
15. B. Yoma 38a–b.
16. Ed 5:7.

17. "A good name is better than precious oil" (Eccles. 7:1). How far does the oil's fragrance go? From the bedchamber to the dining room. But a good name goes from one end of the world to the other.[1]

The Honor to Be Accorded to One's Fellow Man

18. Ben Zoma said: Who is honored? He who honors his fellow man.[2]

19. R. Eliezer said: Let the honor of your fellow be as dear to you as your own.[3]

20. Be solicitous for the honor of your colleagues.[4]

21. "Thou shalt love thy neighbor as thyself" (Lev. 19:18). R. Akiva said: This is a great principle of the Torah. Ben Azzai said: The verse "This is the book of the descendants of Adam . . . him whom God made in His likeness" (Gen. 5:1) utters a principle even greater: you must not say, "Since I have been humiliated, let my fellow man also be humiliated; since I have been cursed, let my neighbor also be cursed." For, as R. Tanhuma pointed out, if you act thus, realize who it is that you are willing to have humiliated—"him whom God made in His likeness."[5]

22. R. Joshua ben Levi said: When a man walks on the highway, a company[6] of angels goes before him announcing: "Make way for the image of the Holy One, blessed be He."[7]

23. R. Yohanan used to rise before aged heathens and say, "How many troubles must have come to these men!" Rava did not rise, but he showed them respect.

Abbaye used to give his arm to old men [to lean on]. Rava had an emissary of his do so. R. Nahman [bar Abba] had his eunuchs do so, saying, "But for [my learning in] Torah, how many Nahman bar Abbas would there be in the marketplace?"[8]

24. Ben Azzai used to say: Despise no man, and consider nothing as impossible, for there is not a man who has not his hour and not a thing that has not its place.[9]

1. Exod. R. 48:1.
2. Avot 4:1.
3. Avot 2:10.
4. B. Ber 28b.
5. P. Ned 9:4, 41c; Gen. R. 24:7.
6. The Greek *konnion* is a closely packed formation of soldiers (Daniel Sperber, in *Sinai* 87 [Summer 1980]: 151).
7. There is a play here on *ikonia* ("image") and *ikonin* ("company"). MTeh 17:8; Deut. R. 4:4.
8. "R. Nahman means to say: 'I am no better than a dozen men in the marketplace, and by rights I should personally offer my arm to old men to lean on. The reason I dispatch my eunuchs to do it is my learning in Torah—I should not demean the Torah by performing a function that is ordinarily performed by servants.' R. Nahman belonged to the crème de la crème of the aristocracy, and his failure to be helpful to ordinary senior citizens would have been ascribed to sheer arrogance otherwise" (Leon Nemoy). B. Kid 33a.
9. Avot 4:3.

25. "Thou shalt not go up by steps unto Mine altar [rather, on a ramp, slowly, respectfully]" (Exod. 20:23). Now, the matter may be argued *a fortiori:* the stones of the altar have no awareness of what is proper or improper, yet the Holy One said that you should not treat them disrespectfully. How much more by far does it follow that you are not to treat disrespectfully your fellow man, who is made in the image of Him who spoke and the world came into being.[10]

26. "For God will call every creature to account for *all* their conduct" (Eccles. 12:14 [NJV]). Rav said: It includes squashing a louse in the presence of a fellow man, who is disgusted by such an act. Samuel said: It includes spitting in the presence of his fellow man, who is disgusted by such an act.[11]

27. Our masters taught: A man should at all times be pliant as a reed and not hard as a cedar.

A story is told of R. Eleazar son of R. Simeon, who was once returning from his teacher's house in Migdal Eder. He was riding leisurely on his donkey by the lakeshore and felt greatly elated and thoroughly satisfied with himself, because he had studied much Torah. [While in this mood] he chanced upon an exceedingly ugly man, who greeted him, "Peace be upon you, my master." R. Simeon did not return the greeting, but instead said to him, "You worthless creature! How ugly you are! Are all the people of your city as ugly as you?"

The man replied, "What can I do about it? Go tell the Craftsman who made me, 'How ugly is the vessel You have made!' "

No sooner did R. Eleazar son of R. Simeon realize that he had done wrong than he got down from the donkey and, prostrating himself before the man, said to him, "I apologize to you; please forgive me!"

The man replied, "I will not forgive you until you go to the Craftsman who made me and tell Him, 'How ugly is the vessel You have made!' "

R. Eleazar followed him until he reached the man's city. When the people of the city came out to meet R. Eleazar, greeting him with the words "Peace be upon you, my master, my master, my teacher, my teacher," the man asked them, "Whom are you addressing as 'My master, my master'?"

They replied, "The man who is walking behind you." At that, the man said, "If he is the master, may there be no more like him in Israel!" When the people asked him, "Why?" he replied, "This is how the master behaved to me."

They said to him, "Nevertheless, forgive him, for he is a man greatly learned in the Torah."

The man replied, "For your sakes, I forgive him, but only on condition that he not make a habit of such behavior."

R. Eleazar son of R. Simeon immediately entered the house of study and preached on the subject "A man should at all times be pliant as a reed and not hard as a cedar."[12]

10. Mek, *Yitro, Ba-hodesh,* 11.
11. B. Hag 5a.
12. B. Ta 20a; ARN 41.

28. Why is it unusual for disciples of the wise to have disciples of the wise issue from their children? Because, said R. Ashi, they call human beings asses.[1]

29. It once happened that while R. Yannai was on a journey, he saw a man who looked particularly distinguished. So R. Yannai asked him, "Sir, will you deign to visit our home?" The man said, "Yes." R. Yannai brought the man into his house and gave him food and drink. Then R. Yannai tested him in his knowledge of Scripture, and found none; in his knowledge of Mishnah, and found none; in his knowledge of *Aggadah*, and found none; in his knowledge of Talmud, and found none. Finally, when R. Yannai said to him, "Take [the cup of wine] and say grace," the man said evasively, "Yannai should be the one to say grace in his own home." R. Yannai asked the man, "Can you repeat what I am about to say to you?" The man: "Yes." R. Yannai: "Then say, 'A dog has eaten Yannai's bread.' " At that, the guest stood up, took hold of R. Yannai, and said to him, "My inheritance is in your possession, and you hold it back from me." R. Yannai: "What inheritance of yours is in my possession?" The man: "Once, I passed a schoolhouse and heard the voices of young children saying, 'The Torah that Moses commanded the children of Israel is the inheritance of the congregation of Jacob' [Deut. 33:4]—not 'the congregation of Yannai,' but 'the congregation of Jacob.' " R. Yannai: "How have you merited to dine at my table?" The man: "Never in my life, after hearing evil spoken, have I brought it back to the person spoken of, nor have I seen two people quarreling without making peace between them." R. Yannai: "Your conduct is so considerate, and I called you dog!"[2]

30. Sages said in the name of R. Yose of Hutzal: How do we know that when a man is aware that his fellow surpasses him even in one matter, he must show him honor? From Scripture's saying, "Because in [Daniel] there was one surpassing quality, the kind considered setting him over the whole kingdom" (Dan. 6:4).[3]

31. "Boaz . . . said: 'Sit ye down here.' And they sat down" (Ruth 4:2). R. Alexandri commented: From this verse it may be inferred that an inferior person should not sit down [in the presence of a superior] until the superior person says to him, "Sit down."[4]

32. When R. Nehunia ben ha-Kanah was asked by his disciples, "By what merit have you lived such a long life?" he replied, "I never sought to gain honor at the cost of my fellow man's being degraded, the curse of my fellow man never came up [with me] to my couch, and I have always been liberal with my money."

"I never sought to gain honor at the cost of my fellow man's being degraded" may be illustrated by R. Huna, who was once carrying a plowshare on his shoulder. R. Hana bar Hanilai came along and was about to take it away from R. Huna, so R. Huna said, "If you regularly carry such a thing in your own city, carry it. But if not, I do not wish to gain honor at the cost of your being degraded." "The curse of my fellow man never came up [with me] to my couch" may be illustrated by Mar Zutra, who, when he went up to his couch, would say, "Everyone who vexed me is forgiven." "I have always been liberal with my money," for, as a master taught, Job was generous with his money—when [he bought half a *perutah*'s worth of merchandise], he would leave a *perutah* with the storekeeper.[5]

33. R. Yose son of R. Hanina said: He who endeavors to gain honor at the price of his fellow man's being degraded has no portion in the world-to-come.[6]

34. R. Yohanan ben Zakkai said: Pause and consider in what esteem human dignity is held. The penalty for stealing an ox, which walks on its own feet at the thief's side, is fivefold;[7] while for a sheep, which [out of pity] the thief [to his indignity] carries on his shoulder, the penalty is only fourfold.[8]

35. Great is human dignity, since for its sake one may violate a negative precept of the Torah.[9]

36. "If a woman approach unto any beast, and lie down thereto, thou shalt kill the woman and the beast" (Lev. 20:16). In such a case, the human being has committed a sin, but what sin did the animal commit? [None.] However, because the animal was a stumbling block whereby a human being fell into sin, Scripture orders that the animal be stoned to death. Another reason for killing the animal is that, if it were allowed to live, people seeing it pass through the marketplace [would be reminded of the sin and] would be tempted to say, "There's the animal on account of whom So-and-so was stoned to death." The animal is therefore put to death, in order that "bringing an iniquity to remembrance against the House of Israel will not continue to be a source of satisfaction [for malicious people]" (Ezek. 29:16).[10]

37. "Thou mayest ignore them"[11] (Deut. 22:1). There are times when one may ignore such animals. When? When the one who spots them is old, and it does not befit his dignity [to go chasing after them].[12]

38. Our masters taught: On highways, on bridges, or in washing soiled hands [for the saying of grace], one need not give precedence to a superior.

While Ravin and Abbaye were traveling on a [narrow]

1. B. Ned 81a.
2. Lev. R. 9:3.
3. B. Pes 113b.
4. P. Ket 1:1, 25a.
5. B. Meg 28a.
6. P. Hag 2:1, 77c; Gen. R. 1:5.
7. If the ox or sheep stolen was slaughtered or sold (Exod. 21:37).
8. The thief lowers his human dignity by carrying the sheep; hence, his penalty is reduced. B. BK 79b.
9. B. Ber 19b.
10. B. Sanh 54a; Lev. R. 27:3; PRK 9:3.
11. An ox or sheep going astray.
12. JV: "hide thyself from them." B. Ber 19b.

road, Ravin's donkey got in front of Abbaye's donkey, yet Ravin did not stop and say to Abbaye, "Let the master get ahead of me." So Abbaye muttered to himself: Since this student has come up from the west [the Land of Israel], he has grown arrogant. However, when they reached the entrance to the synagogue, Ravin said to Abbaye, "Let the master enter [first]." Abbaye asked, "And have I not been master until now?" Ravin replied, "This is what R. Yohanan taught me: [While on a journey], one gives precedence to one's superior only at an entrance that has doorposts.[1]

39. The people of Galilee were particular about their honor, but not about their money. The people of Judea were particular about their money, but not about their honor.[2]

40. R. Nehorai said: He who humiliates his fellow man will himself be humiliated in the end. More: angels of destruction will thrust at him and expel him from the world as they expose his shame to all mankind.[3]

41. Do not humiliate, and you will not be humiliated.[4]

42. If upward you spit, your own face you'll hit.[5]

43. It is better to submit to being cast into a fiery furnace than to shame a fellow man in public. And the proof? Tamar, who, it is said, "was willing to be brought out [to be burned]" (Gen. 38:25).[6]

44. A *tanna*[7] recited before R. Nahman bar Isaac: He who shames his fellow man in public is as though he shed blood. R. Nahman replied: Well put! Because we see ruddiness depart and paleness take its place [in the face of the man who is humiliated].[8]

45. The fine [for indignity] imposed on one who wounds another is determined according to the status of the one who inflicted the wound and the status of the one upon whom it was inflicted.[9]

46. R. Hanina said: He who strikes a fellow man on the jaw is as though he had struck the jaw of the Presence.

Resh Lakish said: He who merely raises his hand against his fellow man, even if he does not strike him, is called a felon, as is written, "He said unto the felon, 'Why wouldst thou strike thy fellow?' " (Exod. 2:13). Not "Why didst thou strike?" but "Why wouldst thou strike?" indicating that though he had not struck him, he was nevertheless called a felon.[10]

47. If a man cuffs another, he must pay him a *sela*.[11] R. Judah, citing R. Yose the Galilean, said: [He must pay him] a *maneh*.[12] If he slaps him, he must pay him two hundred *zuz;* [if he slaps him] with the back of his hand, he must pay him four hundred *zuz*. If he slits his ear, pulls out his hair, spits so that the spittle reaches him, pulls his cloak off him, disarrays a woman's hair in the marketplace—for any of these, he must pay four hundred *zuz*. However, the general rule is that the amount of the fine must be in keeping with the standing [of the injured person]. But R. Akiva said: Even the poor in Israel, being descendants of Abraham, Isaac, and Jacob, are considered freemen in reduced circumstances.

It once happened that a certain man disarrayed a woman's hair in the marketplace. When the woman came before R. Akiva, he ordered the offender to pay her four hundred *zuz*. The man pleaded, "Rabbi, give me time to pay," and R. Akiva gave him time. After that, the man kept following the woman, until he caught her standing outside the door of her courtyard. Then, in front of her, he broke a pitcher containing an *issar*'s[13] worth of oil. At that, she bared her head [let her hair down], dipped her hands [in the puddle of oil], and worked the oil into her hair. The man [quickly] summoned witnesses to see what she was doing. Then he appeared with them before R. Akiva and said, "Must I give such a woman four hundred *zuz*?" R. Akiva replied, "Your argument has no legal standing. If a person injures himself, though forbidden to do so, he is nevertheless exempt; but if others injure him, they are liable. So, also, he who cuts down his own saplings, though forbidden to do so,[14] is exempt; but if others [cut them down], they are liable."

Even though the offender pays the fine to the victim, the offense is not forgiven until he asks the victim's pardon, as Scripture says, "Now therefore restore the man's wife and [by asking pardon] see to it that he pray in thy behalf" (Gen. 20:7). What is the proof that, should the victim refuse to forgive, he would be [stigmatized as] cruel? The word "So Abraham [not only forgave but even] prayed unto God; and God healed Abimelech," etc. (Gen. 20:17).

Our masters taught: All the aforementioned fines compensate only for the humiliation suffered by the victim. As for the hurt done to his feelings, even if the offender brings all the "rams of Nebaioth" (Isa. 60:7) in the world, the offense is not forgiven until the offender asks for pardon.[15]

1. If such deference were shown on a narrow road, others hurrying to work, etc., would be held back. So Menahem ha-Meiri, quoted by Adin Steinsaltz, Ber, p. 205. B. Ber 46b–47a.
2. P. Ket 4:14, 29b.
3. Ka.
4. B. MK 9b.
5. Eccles. R. 7:9, §1.
6. Though facing death, she did not divulge Judah as the father of her child. B. Ber 43b.
7. One who memorized Baraitas and recited them before a teacher so that he might expound them.
8. B. BM 58b.
9. B. BK 83b.
10. B. Sanh 58b.
11. Half a *zuz*.
12. One hundred *zuz*.
13. An *issar* is one twenty-fourth of a *zuz*.
14. Since he violates the command "Thou shalt not destroy . . . trees" (Deut. 20:19).
15. B. BK 90a–b and 92a.

Love of Fellow Man and Hatred of Fellow Man

48. "Thou shalt love thy fellow man as thyself" (Lev. 19:18). R. Akiva said: This is a great principle in the Torah.

R. Simeon ben Eleazar said: To this utterance a great oath was adjoined, "Thou shalt love thy fellow man as thyself: I the Lord"—I, the Lord, created your fellow man. If you love him, I shall faithfully requite you with ample reward. If not, I shall act as judge to punish you.[1]

49. This is what the Holy One said to Israel: My children, what do I seek from you? I seek no more than that you love one another and honor one another.[2]

50. R. Joshua said: A grudging eye, the evil impulse, and hatred of his fellow men shorten a man's life.

"Hatred of his fellow men"—exactly how is this to be understood? That a man should not set out and say: Love sages but hate disciples, or love disciples but hate the ignorant [the *amme ha-aretz*]. He should say: Love all of them.[3]

51. If others speak ill of you, do not answer them. Should it be a grave calumny, regard it as slight. If, however, you speak ill of others, though the calumny be slight, regard it as so grave that you will feel compelled to go and apologize for having spoken it.

Love your fellow men and honor them.

Set aside your wish in favor of your fellow man's wish, as Rachel did for Leah[4] and David did for Saul.[5]

52. Judah ben Tema used to say: Love Heaven and also be in awe of Heaven, so that you both rejoice [and tremble] in obeying all commandments. If you have done your fellow man a slight wrong, let it seem a serious offense in your eyes. If you have done him a great good, let it seem but a trifle in your eyes. On the other hand, if your fellow man has done you a good that is a mere trifle, let it seem a great thing in your eyes. But if he has done you a great wrong, let it seem a mere trifle in your eyes.[6]

53. Our masters taught: "Thou shalt not hate thy brother in thy heart" (Lev. 19:17). You might suppose that Scripture bids you not to strike him, not to slap him, not to curse him. But in saying, "In thy heart," Scripture also bids you to have no hatred in your heart.[7]

54. Scripture says, "Thou shalt not take vengeance, nor bear a grudge against the children of thy people" (Lev. 19:18). Suppose that, while cutting meat, the knife struck your hand; would you turn around and strike the hand [that held the knife]?[8]

55. We have been taught: What is revenge, and what is bearing a grudge? Suppose A said to B, "Lend me your sickle," and B replied, "No." Then the next day, B said, "Lend me your ax," and A replied, "I will not lend you the ax, just as you did not lend me your sickle." That is taking revenge. And what is bearing a grudge? Suppose A said to B, "Lend me your ax," and B replied, "No." Then the next day, B said, "Lend me your undershirt," and A replied, "Here it is. I am not like you, who would lend nothing to me." That is bearing a grudge.[9]

56. If love depends on something transitory, once the transitory thing passes away, love also passes away; but if love does not depend on something transitory, it will never pass away. What love depends on something transitory? The love of Amnon for Tamar.[10] And what love did not depend on something transitory? The love of David and Jonathan.[11]

57. Love unaccompanied by reproof is not [true] love.[12]

58. We have been taught in the name of R. Simeon ben Eleazar: Love sets aside the conduct expected of men of consequence, as may be seen in the instance of Abraham, who, it is said, "rose early in the morning and saddled his ass" (Gen. 22:3). Did he not have ever so many servants [to do this for him]? Hatred likewise sets aside the conduct expected of men of consequence, as may be seen in the instance of Balaam, who, it is said, "rose up in the morning, and saddled his ass" (Num. 22:21). Did he too not have ever so many servants [to do this for him]?[13]

59. Love upsets usual conduct. Hatred upsets usual conduct.[14]

60. When our love was strong, we could lie on the edge of a sword. Now that our love is not strong, a bed sixty cubits wide is not wide enough for us.[15]

61. It is easy to acquire an enemy, difficult to acquire a friend.[16]

62. Who is the mightiest of the mighty? He who turns his enemy into his friend.[17]

---

1. Sif Lev., ed. Weiss, p. 89b; ARN 16.
2. TdE 26.
3. Avot 2:11; ARN 16.
4. See above, part 1, chap. 3, §71.
5. He refrained from telling Saul that Saul's rule would not be prolonged, since Saul was anointed with a cruse, whereas his, David's, rule would be prolonged, since he was anointed with a horn (see B. Meg 14a). DEZ 1.
6. ARN 41.
7. B Ar 16b.
8. P. Ned 9:4, 41c.
9. B. Yoma 23a and En Yaakov, ad loc.
10. 2 Sam. 13.
11. 2 Sam. 1:26. Avot 5:16.
12. Gen. R. 54:3.
13. B. Sanh 105b; Gen. R. 55:8.
14. Gen. R. 55:8.
15. B. Sanh 7a.
16. Yalkut, *Va-et'hannan*, §845.
17. ARN 23.

63. The proverb says: What is in your heart about your fellow man is likely to be in his heart about you.[1]

64. To the place my heart loves—there my feet lead me.[2]

65. Our masters taught: There are three who love one another: proselytes, slaves, and ravens. There are three who hate one another: dogs, cocks, and Parsee priests. Some say: also disciples of the wise who live in Babylonia.[3]

A Companion

66. "And the Lord said unto Moses: 'Acquire for thyself Joshua the son of Nun' " (Num. 27:18). The word "acquire" here implies acquisition at much cost, for a companion is acquired after difficulties upon difficulties. Hence, say the sages, a man should acquire a companion for [everything]: for reading Scripture with him, reciting Mishnah with him, eating with him, drinking with him, and disclosing all his secrets to him.[4]

67. Either companionship or death.[5]

68. Either [faithful] friends like the friends of Job or death.[6]

69. "Two are better than one" (Eccles. 4:9). When R. Meir saw a man setting out on a journey alone, he would say, "Go in peace, you man of death." When he saw two men, he would say, "May you have peace, you men who are sure to quarrel." When he saw three, he would say, "May you have peace, you men of peace."[7]

70. There is a proverb: If you lift the burden, I will help lift it. If not, I will not.[8]

71. What is the good way a man should cleave to? R. Joshua said: Being a good friend; R. Yose said: Being a good neighbor.

What is the evil way a man should shun? R. Joshua said: Pretending to be a friend; R. Yose said: Being a bad neighbor.[9]

72. Nittai the Arbelite said: Shun a bad neighbor and do not consort with a wicked man.[10]

1. Sif Deut., §24; Tanhuma B, *Shelah*, supplement, §19.
2. Mek, *Yitro, Ba-hodesh*, 11.
3. B. Pes 113b.
4. Sif Deut., §305; ARN 8.
5. B. Ta 23a.
6. B. BB 16b.
7. R. Meir was confident that in the event of a quarrel, the third man would reconcile the two at odds. Eccles. R. 4:9, §1.
8. B. BK 92b.
9. Avot 2:9.
10. Avot 1:7.

73. "He that walketh with wise men shall be wise" (Prov. 13:20). A parable: When a man walks into a spice vendor's shop, even if he sells nothing to the vendor or buys nothing from him, nevertheless, when he leaves, his person and his garments exude a fragrant aroma. And the fragrance will not leave him the entire day.

"But he that walketh with fools shall smart for it" (Prov. 13:20). A parable: When a man walks into a tanner's shop, even if he sells him nothing or buys nothing from him, nevertheless, when the man leaves, his person and his garments reek with stench. And the vile odor from his person and his garments will not leave him the entire day.[11]

74. Rava said to Rabbah bar Mari: Where is the proof in Scripture for the proverb "A bad palm will make its way to [a grove of] barren trees"? Rabbah bar Mari replied: From what is set down in the Five Books, repeated in the Prophets, and mentioned a third time in the Writings; indeed, we have been taught the same in a Mishnah and also in a Baraita. As to what is set down in the Five Books, it is stated, "So Esau went unto Ishmael" (Gen. 28:9). As to the Prophets, it is stated, "And there gathered themselves to Jephthah idle men, and they went out with him" (Judg. 11:3). As to the Writings, it is said, "Every fowl dwells near its kind and man near his equal" (Ecclesiasticus 13:15). As to the Mishnah, "Anything attached to what is itself susceptible to uncleanness is likewise susceptible to uncleanness; anything attached to what is not susceptible to uncleanness is likewise insusceptible to uncleanness" (Kel 12:2). As to the Baraita, "R. Eliezer said, 'Not without cause did the starling follow the raven—it is its own kind.' "[12]

75. In the days of R. Hiyya the Elder, a starling came up to the Land of Israel. Some people brought it to him, inquiring, "May we eat it?" He replied, "Go and place it on a roof, and any bird that comes to rest near it will be of its kind." So they went and placed it on a roof, and an Egyptian raven came and rested near it. At that, R. Hiyya said, "The starling is not kosher, because it belongs to the species of the raven, which Scripture prohibits by saying, 'Every raven after its kind' " (Lev. 11:15). Hence the proverb "The raven went to the starling only because it is of its own kind."[13]

76. One accursed should not unite with one blessed.[14]

77. No man will live with a serpent in the same basket.[15]

78. He who joins himself to those who commit transgressions, though he does not do what they do, will nevertheless receive punishment as one of them.[16]

11. Midrash Prov. 13:20 (ed. Buber, p. 72).
12. B. BK 92b.
13. Gen. R. 65:3.
14. Gen. R. 59:9.
15. B. Yev 112b.
16. ARN 30.

79. Abbaye said: Woe to the wicked and woe to his neighbor. It is well with the righteous and well with his neighbor.[1]

80. When the thornbush is ravaged, so is the cabbage.[2]

81. We have been taught that Rabbi [Judah I, the Patriarch] said: A man should never have a multitude of friends in his house, for it is said, "A man with many friends may be hurt" (Prov. 18:24).[3]

82. A man should always know with whom he is seated, with whom he stands, with whom he reclines at a meal, with whom he converses, and with whom he signs his legal papers.[4]

83. We have been taught that the scrupulous people of Jerusalem would act thus: they never signed a legal document until they knew who would sign it with them; they never sat in judgment until they knew who would sit with them; and they would not go to a banquet until they knew who would recline with them.[5]

84. R. Hiyya bar Abba said in the name of R. Yohanan: When one of several brothers dies, all the other brothers have reason to be concerned. When one member of a fellowship dies, all the others in the fellowship have reason to be concerned.[6]

85. A fellowship and a family are like a pile of stones—when you remove one stone, the pile falls apart.[7]

Rules of Conduct and Good Manners Required between a Man and His Fellow

86. Matia ben Heresh said: Be the first to greet everyone.[8]

87. It is said of R. Yohanan ben Zakkai that no man ever greeted him first, not even a Gentile in the marketplace.[9]

88. R. Helbo said in the name of R. Huna: When a man knows that his friend is in the habit of greeting him [i.e., saying, "Peace be to you"], he should greet him first, for it is said, "Seek peace and pursue it" (Ps. 34:15). If his friend greets him and he does not respond to the greeting, he is called a robber, as is said, "That which you robbed from one who is humiliated [by not being responded to] is in your houses" (Isa. 3:14).[10]

89. A man should never leave the company of his teacher or his friend unless he has previously obtained his permission. Such good manners may be learned from Him who is everywhere: He, if one dare say such a thing, asked Abraham, "May I now leave?" as is stated, "And the Lord went His way, only after having spoken [for permission] to Abraham; and Abraham returned unto his place" (Gen. 18:33).

A man should never enter his friend's home unexpectedly. Such good manners may be learned from Him who is everywhere: He stood at the entrance of the Garden [of Eden] and called to Adam, as is stated, "The Lord God called unto Adam, and said unto him: Where art thou?" (Gen. 3:9).

There is the story of the four sages Rabban Gamaliel, R. Joshua, R. Eleazar ben Azariah, and R. Akiva, who were on their way [to Rome] to attend the [Roman] Privy Council, which had among its members a certain philosopher. R. Joshua asked Rabban Gamaliel, "Master, would you like us to call on our colleague, the philosopher?" He replied, "No." In the morning, he again asked him, "Master, would you like us to call on our colleague, the philosopher?" He replied, "Yes." So they went and arrived at the entrance to the philosopher's house. R. Joshua knocked on the door. The philosopher, speculating on the visitor's identity, said [to himself]: Such manners must be those of a sage.[11] When R. Joshua knocked a second time, the philosopher got up and washed his face, his hands, and his feet. On the third knock, he arose, opened the door, and had the sages of Israel come in, Rabban Gamaliel in the middle, R. Joshua and R. Eleazar ben Azariah on his right, and R. Akiva on his left.

At the sight of them, the philosopher, in a quandary, said [to himself]: How shall I greet these sages of Israel? If I say, "Peace be upon you, Rabban Gamaliel," I will slight the [other] sages. If I say, "Peace be upon you, sages of Israel," I will slight [their chief] Rabban Gamaliel. So, as he approached them, he greeted them with the words "Peace be upon you, sages of Israel, headed by the patriarch Rabban Gamaliel."[12]

90. "And the Lord called unto Moses, and spoke to him" (Lev. 1:1). Why does Scripture put the calling before the speaking? The Torah teaches good manners: a man should say nothing to his fellow man without first calling out to him.[13]

91. R. Simeon ben Yohai said: The man who enters his own house or, needless to say, the house of his fellow man unexpectedly, the Holy One hates, and I too do not exactly love him.

Rav said: Do not enter your city nor even your own home unexpectedly.[14]

When R. Yohanan was about to go in to inquire about the welfare of R. Hanina, he would first clear his throat,

---

1. B. Suk 56b.
2. B. BK 92a.
3. B. Sanh 100b.
4. DEZ 5.
5. B. Sanh 23a.
6. B. Shab 105b–106a.
7. Gen. R. 100:7.
8. Avot 4:15.
9. B. Ber 17a.
10. B. Ber 6b.

11. Apparently most people would walk in without knocking on the door.
12. DER 5; Ka R. 7.
13. B. Yoma 4b.
14. Without informing your kin of your coming.

in keeping with "And his voice shall be heard when he goeth in" (Exod. 28:35).[1]

92. When R. Jeremiah came up to visit R. Assi, R. Assi mixed a cup of wine for him, and he proceeded to examine it. R. Assi's wife said to her husband, "Look what he is doing!" R. Assi replied, "He follows the practice of his teacher, R. Hiyya, who taught that a guest may without hesitation examine what is in the cup [offered him] or in the dish [served him].[2]

93. Shammai said: Receive all men with a cheerful countenance.[3]

94. When a man receives his fellow man with a cheerful countenance, even if he gives him nothing, Scripture credits it to him as though he had given him all the best gifts in the world.[4]

95. He who pays his respects to his fellow man is as though he were paying his respects to the Presence.[5]

96. R. Ishmael said: Receive all men joyfully.[6]

97. Three things make a man beloved by his fellow men: an open hand, a set table, and a sparkling wit.[7]

98. R. Joshua ben Levi said: When a man sees his friend after a lapse of thirty days, he is to say, "Blessed be He who has kept us alive, preserved us, and brought us to this season." After twelve months, he is to say, "Blessed be He who quickens the dead."[8]

99. While R. Papa and R. Huna son of R. Joshua were walking on a road, they met R. Hanina son of R. Ika and said to him: Whenever we see you, we recite two blessings: "Blessed be He who imparted His wisdom to them that fear Him" and "Who has kept us alive." R. Hanina replied: Whenever I see you two, who are deemed by me equal to the sixty myriads of Israel, I recite three blessings: the two you mentioned, and "Blessed be He that discerns secrets."[9]

100. R. Dimi brother of R. Safra taught: Let no man ever talk in praise of his neighbor, for while talking in his praise, he is likely to switch to disparaging him.

When R. Dimi came [from the Land of Israel], he said: What is meant by "He that blesseth his friend with a loud voice, rising early in the morning, it shall be counted as a curse to him" (Prov. 27:14)? The verse refers, for example, to one who stayed at an inn where he was well served. The next day, the guest went out and sat in the marketplace, saying, "May He who is everywhere bless So-and-so [the host], who took such trouble to serve me." Upon hearing such praise, the authorities said: [His business must be thriving], and they clapped a heavier tax on the innkeeper.[10]

101. R. Jeremiah ben Eleazar said: Only a part of man's praise may be said in his presence. But in his absence, all of it may be said. Thus, to Noah, God said, "Thee have I seen righteous before Me in this generation" (Gen. 7:1), but of Noah, it is said, "Noah was in his generations a man righteous and wholehearted" (Gen. 6:9).[11]

102. "And he said unto them: 'Why do ye such things? for I hear evil reports concerning you from all this people' " (1 Sam 2:23). R. Abbahu said: The Torah teaches you right conduct. When you hear a good thing about your fellow man, repeat it in the name of him who said it. When you hear an evil thing about him, say it in behalf of "somebody."[12]

103. R. Simeon ben Eleazar said: Do not try to appease your friend in the hour of his anger; nor comfort him while his dead is lying before him; nor question him in the hour of his vow.[13] And do not endeavor to see him in the hour of his disgrace.[14]

104. R. Yose said: I have never in my life disregarded the words of my colleagues. I know of myself that I am not a priest [who bestows blessing]. Nevertheless, should my colleagues say to me, "Go up on the dais [and pronounce the blessing among the priests]," I would go up.[15]

105. R. Akiva asked R. Nehunia the Elder: How have you managed to live such a long life? [Because Nehunia's attendants regarded his question as impertinent],[16] they began to beat R. Akiva, who clambered up and perched himself at the top of a date palm. R. Nehunia said to his attendants, "Let him be—he is a disciple of the wise." And to R. Akiva, he said, "Never in my life have I accepted gifts; I have been openhanded with my money; I have not insisted on my rights."[17]

106. Our masters taught: Three things are hard to take when excessive, but just right in limited measure: leaven, salt, and declining an invitation.[18]

107. If it is just as easy to be called good, there is no reason to act in such a way as to be dubbed perverse.[19]

---

1. Lev. R. 21:8.
2. P. Shab 1:3, 3b.
3. Avot 1:15.
4. ARN 13.
5. P. Er 5:1, 22a.
6. Avot 3:13.
7. ARNB 31.
8. B. Ber 58b.
9. The blessing prescribed for the sight of sixty myriads of Israel. Ibid.
10. B. Ar 16a.
11. B. Er 18b.
12. Midrash Sam. 7 (ed. Buber, p. 67).
13. He may extend its scope to such an extent that it will be impossible to release him from it.
14. Avot 4:18.
15. B. Shab 118b.
16. They thought R. Akiva begrudged R. Nehunia the length of his life.
17. B. Meg 28a.
18. B. Ber 34a.
19. B. Ber 30a; BK 81b.

108. [The best solution is]: one party derives a benefit, and the other party sustains no loss.[1]

109. One may be compelled not to act in the manner of Sodom.[2]

110. When the Holy One said to Moses, "Come now therefore, and I will send thee unto Pharaoh" (Exod. 3:10), Moses replied, "Master of the universe, I cannot go [without Jethro's permission], because Jethro received me and opened his home to me, so that I am like a son to him. When one man so opens his door to another, the other owes his very life to him."

So, too, you find of Elijah [who did not supplicate that his own parents be brought back to life]. But when he went to the widow in Zarephath whose son died, he began to supplicate and say, "Hast Thou also brought evil upon the widow with whom I sojourn, by slaying her son?" Thus, for the sake of his hostess, he risked his very life [by provoking God]. Clearly, when one man opens his door to another, the other owes greater consideration to him than to his father and mother. Therefore, Moses said to the Holy One, "Jethro has received me and showed me consideration. I cannot go without his permission."[3]

111. "And Moses sent them . . . to the war" (Num. 31:6). The Holy One had spoken to Moses: "Avenge the children of Israel of the Midianites" (Num. 31:2)—you are to do it yourself. Yet he sent others to do it. But because he spent many years in Midian, he said, "It is not right for me to cause distress to one who has been good to me."[4]

112. Rava asked Rabbah bar Mari: What is the source in Scripture for the proverb "Don't throw a stone into the well you drank from"? Rabbah bar Mari replied: The verse "Thou shalt not abhor an Egyptian, because thou wast a stranger in his land" (Deut. 23:8).[5]

113. If a man shares his food with his fellow, be it no more than bread and salt, or a salad leaf to dip [in brine], the fellow who is offered such meager sustenance, though he may have a hundred meals every day like the meals of Solomon in the time of his glory, should express his gratitude right to his benefactor's face.[6]

114. "Whoso rewardeth evil for good, evil shall not depart from his house" (Prov. 17:13). R. Yohanan said: The verse implies that if your neighbor has served you lentils, you should serve him meat. Why? Because he entertained you first.

R. Simeon bar Abba said that this does not exhaust the verse's implication. Not only "whoso rewardeth evil for good," but also he who rewards evil for evil—[in both cases] "evil shall not depart from his house."[7]

115. R. Judah said in the name of Rav: How do we know that a man is not to change his lodging? Because Scripture says of Abraham, "He went . . . unto the place where his tent had been at the beginning" (Gen. 13:3).[8]

116. "Neither will we drink of the water of [our own] well" (Num. 20:17). Should not Scripture have said, "The water of [Edom's] wells"? However, the Torah offers a lesson in proper conduct. When a man goes to a country that is not his, even if he has with him all he needs, he should not eat what is in his hand. Rather, what he has should remain untouched, and he should buy from a shopkeeper, so as to let the shopkeeper make a profit. This is what Moses said: Yes, we do have the well with us, and we do eat manna. But do not suppose that we will be a burden upon you. For you will make a profit from us.[9]

117. "And they said unto him: 'Where is Sarah thy wife?' " (Gen. 18:9). The sages taught in the name of R. Yose: Why are the letters *alef, yod,* and *vav* in the word *elayv* ("unto him") dotted? To indicate that *elayv* may also be read *ayv* [*ayyo*] "where is he?" [Hence, even as the angels asked Abraham, "Where is Sarah?" they also asked Sarah, "Where is Abraham?"] Thus, the Torah offers a lesson in proper conduct, namely, that a guest should make inquiry about both the hostess and the host.[10]

118. R. Simeon ben Gamaliel said: He who gives a piece of bread to a young child should inform the child's mother.[11]

119. R. Hama son of Hanina said: He who gives a gift to his friend need not tell him of it, in keeping with "Moses knew not that the skin of his face sent forth beams, since He had spoken with him" (Exod. 34:29).

However, the sages said in the name of Rav: He who gives a gift to his friend should let him know of it, in keeping with "That ye may know that I the Lord have consecrated you" (Exod. 31:13).[12]

120. When a man asks [God's] mercy for another—even though he himself requires the same thing—his own need will be responded to first.[13]

121. R. Jacob son of Jacob's daughter said: He on whose account his fellow man is punished will not be allowed to enter the precincts of the Holy One.[14]

---

1. B. BK 20b.
2. But to treat one another fairly. B. ER 49a.
3. Exod. R. 4:2.
4. Num. R. 22:4.
5. B. BK 92b; Num. R. 22:4.
6. TdE, ed. Friedmann, p. 89 (JPS, p. 240).
7. He construes the verse as meaning: "evil instead of the good at his disposal." Gen. R. 38:3.
8. B. Ar 16b.
9. Num. R. 19:15.
10. B. BM 87a.
11. B. Shab 10b.
12. Ibid.
13. B. BK 92a.
14. B. Shab 149b.

122. R. Hanan said: He who invokes the judgment of Heaven upon his fellow man will be punished first. Thus, after reporting, "Sarai said unto Abram: 'My wrong be upon thee . . . the Lord judge between thee and me" (Gen. 16:5), Scripture goes on to tell us, "Abraham came to mourn for Sarah, and to weep for her" (Gen. 23:2). When [does he who invokes God's judgment get punished first]? When there is a judge in the Land [to turn to, so that one need have no recourse to the Judge in heaven].

R. Isaac said: Greater is the woe of him who cried [for God's intervention] than the woe of him against whom it is invoked.[1]

123. Rava said: When a man is willing to let his rights pass without insisting on them, all of his transgressions are passed over, as is said, "That pardoneth iniquity, and passeth by transgression" (Mic. 7:18). Whose iniquity does God pardon? That of the man who is willing to let pass the transgression committed against him.

R. Isaac said: Whoever offends his fellow man, even if only with words, should endeavor to reconcile him. R. Hisda added: [If he does not succeed], he should endeavor to pacify him before three groups of people [whom he should successively invite to be present].

R. Yose bar Hanina said: He who seeks pardon of his fellow man need do so no more than three times, for it is said, "Pray (*ana*) forgive, I pray thee (*na*) . . . and now forgive, I pray thee (*na*)" (Gen. 50:17).[2] And if his fellow man is dead, he should bring ten men, have them stand by the grave, and say, "I have sinned against the Lord, the God of Israel, and against So-and-so, whom I have hurt."

Once, when R. Abba had a grievance against R. Jeremiah, R. Jeremiah went and sat down at R. Abba's door [waiting for him to come out so that he might ask to be forgiven]. Just then, a maidservant of R. Abba's came out and emptied dirty water into the dungheap. Some drops of that water fell upon R. Jeremiah's head, at which he remarked, "They have used me as a dungheap," and in his own behalf he prayed, "May He raise up the needy one out of the dungheap" (1 Sam. 2:8). When R. Abba heard what had happened, he came out, but R. Jeremiah turned his face aside and started walking away. R. Abba called to him, "No need for you to beg to be forgiven—now it is up to me to remove [the grievance] from your heart."[3]

124. Matters between you and Him who is everywhere may be forgiven you. Matters between you and your fellow man will not be forgiven until you conciliate him.[4]

125. Valeria the Proselyte put the following question to Rabban Gamaliel: In your Torah, it is written, "Who shows no favor" (Deut. 10:17); yet it is also written, "The Lord will show thee favor" (Num. 6:26). R. Yose the Priest undertook to answer her: I will tell you a parable to explain the apparent contradiction: A man lent *maneh* to his neighbor and fixed a time for it to be repaid in the presence of the king, the borrower swearing by the king's life that he would do so. When the time came and he did not repay the debt, he went to appease the king. The king said, "The wrong done to me is forgiven you. But go and make up with the one who lent you the *maneh*." So it is with regard to the two verses: the first deals with transgressions between a man and his fellow; the second with transgressions between a man and Him who is everywhere.[5]

126. It happened that a certain heathen came before Shammai and said to him, "Take me as a proselyte, but on condition that you teach me the entire Torah, all of it, while I stand on one foot." Shammai instantly drove him away with a builder's measuring rod he happened to have in his hand. When the heathen came before Hillel, Hillel agreed to make him a proselyte, saying "What you don't like, don't do to your neighbor—this is the entire [substance of] Torah, all of it; the rest is commentary. Go and study it."[6]

Theft, Robbery, and Bloodshed

127. R. Yose said: Let the property of your fellow man be as precious to you as your own.[7]

128. There are four types of men: he who says, "Mine is mine, and yours is yours"—the average man; some say, this is the type of Sodom. He who says, "Mine is yours, and yours is mine"—the ignorant man [the *am ha-aretz*]. He who says, "Mine[8] is yours, and yours is yours"—the pious man. And he who says, "Yours is mine, and mine is mine"—the wicked man.[9]

129. He who sets his eyes on what is not his—what he desires is not given him, and what he possesses is taken away from him.[10]

130. R. Yohanan said: When a man robs his fellow even the value of a *perutah*,[11] it is as though he had taken his life away from him, as is said, "So are the ways of everyone that is greedy of gain, which taketh away the life of the owners thereof" (Prov. 1:19).[12]

131. "And God said unto Noah: 'The end of all flesh is come before Me' " (Gen. 6:13). R. Yohanan said: Pause

1. B. BK 93a.
2. The word *na*, repeated three times, is taken to suggest the number of times one is to ask to be forgiven.
3. B. Yoma 87a and En Yaakov, ad loc.; Meg 28a.
4. Sif Lev., ed. Weiss, p. 83a–b.
5. B. RH 17b and En Yaakov, ad loc.
6. B. Shab 31a.
7. Avot 2:12.
8. "Mine" meaning that which was awarded to me in a lawsuit; I prefer that you keep it, since I do not wish to benefit from anything concerning whose ownership there is even a scintilla of doubt. Under similar circumstances, the wicked man reverses matters to suit himself (see Lieberman, TkF 7: 973, n. 16).
9. Avot 5:10.
10. B. Sot 9a.
11. A coin of little value.
12. B. BK 119a.

and consider how powerful is the effect of robbery, for the generation of the flood transgressed all laws, yet the decree of their punishment was sealed only after they reached out for what did not belong to them, as is said, "The earth is filled with robbery through them; and behold, I will destroy them with the earth" (Gen. 6:13). It is also written, "Robbery is risen unto a rod of wickedness," etc. (Ezek. 7:11), which, according to R. Eleazar, means that robbery stood itself upright like a rod, presented itself before the Holy One, and said to Him: Master of the universe, "None of them should remain, nor of their multitude," etc. (ibid.).[1]

132. Samuel said: Even if a man misappropriates a beam and builds it into a palace, he must demolish the entire palace, all of it, and return the beam to its owners.[2]

133. R. Abba said: Grave indeed is the difficulty with food that has been misappropriated and eaten, for even the wholly righteous are unable to return it, as Abraham said, "Save only that which the young men have eaten" (Gen. 14:24).[3]

134. R. Levi said: Misappropriation of things profane is worse than misappropriation of things holy.[4]

135. We have been taught that R. Eliezer ben Jacob said: He who steals a *seah* of wheat, grinds it, kneads it into dough, bakes it, and even sets aside a portion as *hallah*—what blessing could he possibly utter? Surely he may not utter a blessing, for he would be blaspheming, as is said, "The robber who utters a blessing blasphemeth the Lord" (Ps. 10:3).[5]

136. "And you shall take that which is yours . . . fruit of a goodly tree" (Lev. 23:40)—that which belongs to you, not that which was misappropriated.

R. Levi said: A man who uses a lulav cluster got by robbery—to whom may he be likened? To a highwayman who sat at a crossroads, robbing all who came and went. Once, a royal legate passed by on his way to collect the tax of that province, and the highwayman confronted him, overpowered him, and took away all he had. Sometime later, the highwayman was captured and cast into prison. When the king's legate heard this, he went to the highwayman and said to him, "Give me back all that you robbed me of, and I will plead in your behalf before the king." The highwayman answered, "Of all that I seized and took away from you, I have nothing left, except this rug under me, which belongs to you." The legate said to him, "Give it to me, and I shall plead in your behalf before the king." The highwayman said, "Take it."

The next day, the highwayman was taken before the king for judgment. When the king asked him, "Have you anyone to plead for you?" the highwayman replied, "Such-and-such a legate will plead for me." The king sent for the legate and asked him, "Do you know anything in favor of this man?" The legate answered, "I do indeed! When you sent me to collect the tax of that province, this man confronted me and overpowered me, taking away all that I had. This very rug, which belongs to me, is witness against him." Then all the people cried out, "Woe to this one, whose advocate has turned accuser!" Likewise, when, in order to gain merit, a man takes a lulav cluster that was got by robbery, the lulav cluster cries out before the Holy One, "I was got by robbery! I was got by violence!" And the ministering angels say, "Woe to this one, whose advocate has turned accuser."[6]

137. Whenever a man whose hands are soiled by robbery calls to the Holy One, He does not answer.[7]

138. Mar Zutra the Pious once had a silver cup stolen from him at an inn. When he saw one disciple wash his hands and wipe them on another disciple's garments, he said, "That is the one—since he has no consideration for his fellow's property." The disciple was put in fetters, and he confessed.[8]

139. There is the story of a ruler who used to put to death receivers of stolen property but let thieves go. Everyone criticized him for not acting rationally. So what did he do? He had it proclaimed throughout the province, "All people to the arena!" Next, what did he do? He brought weasels and placed before them portions of food. The weasels took the portions and carried them to their holes.

The following day, he again had it proclaimed, "All people to the arena!" Again he brought weasels and placed before them portions of food, but this time he had stopped up the holes, so that when the weasels took their food to the holes and found them stopped up, they returned the portions to where they had been. Thus they demonstrated that, but for receivers, there would be no thievery.[9]

140. A breach in a fence should not be made in front of an honest person, all the less so in front of a thief.[10]

141. A breach invites the thief.[11]

142–43. Not the mouse is the thief, but the hole. Nevertheless, if there were no mouse, how would the hole get filled with stolen goods?[12]

144. Ben Bag Bag said: Do not enter [stealthily] into your neighbor's courtyard to take what belongs to you, lest you appear to him to be a thief. But smash his teeth in as you tell him, "I am taking what belongs to me!"[13]

1. B. Sanh 108a.
2. B. Ta 16a.
3. B. Hul 89a.
4. B. BB 88b.
5. B. BK 94a.
6. Lev. R. 30:6.
7. Exod. R. 22:3.
8. B. BM 24a.
9. Lev. R. 6:2.
10. Tanhuma, *Va-yishlah*, §5.
11. B. Suk 26a.
12. B. Git 45a; B. Ar 30a.
13. B. BK 27b.

145. R. Adda son of R. Ivia asked R. Ashi: What is the difference between a *gazlan* ("robber") and a *hamsan* ("violent man")? R. Ashi answered: A *hamsan* pays for what he takes by violence; a *gazlan* does not pay.[1]

146. We have been taught: "Thou shalt not steal" (Exod. 20:13)—not even [in make-believe] to tease your neighbor. "Thou shalt not steal"—not even with the intention of repaying double.[2]

147. The disciples of Rabban Yohanan ben Zakkai asked him: Why is the Torah more severe with a thief[3] than with a robber?[4] Rabban Yohanan replied: A robber accords equal lack of deference to the slave [his victim] and to the Master, whereas a thief does not accord to the Master the deference he accords to the slave. For the thief acts, if one dare say such a thing, as though the Eye above[5] does not see and the Ear above does not hear, as is said, "Woe unto them that seek deep to hide their counsel from the Lord, and their works are in the dark, and they say: 'Who seeth us? And who knoweth us?' " (Isa. 29:15).

In this regard, R. Meir, citing Rabban Gamaliel, told a parable: How may the conduct of the thief and the robber be illustrated? By the actions of two men who prepared a banquet in the city where they lived. One invited the people of the city but not the royal princes; the other invited neither the people of the city nor the royal princes. Whose punishment is greater? Clearly, the punishment of the one who invited the people of the city but did not invite the royal princes.[6]

148. Once, four hundred jars of wine belonging to R. Huna turned sour. The sages came to visit him and said, "Let the master examine his [past] actions." He asked them, "Am I suspect in your eyes?" They replied, "Is the Holy One suspect of imposing judgment without justice?" He said to them, "If anyone has heard something against me, let him speak up." They replied, "We have heard that the master does not give his tenant his [lawful share of] vine shoots."[7] R. Huna replied, "Does he leave any of them for me? He steals them all!" They said to him, "That is exactly what the proverb says: 'Even if you steal [what is your own] from a thief, you also are a bit of a thief!' " He said to them, "From now on, I pledge myself to give them to him." Some say that then and there the vinegar turned back into wine. Others say that the price of vinegar rose so high that it sold at the same price as wine.[8]

149. A brigand's partner is as bad as the brigand.[9]

150. R. Huna said: How do we know that stealing from a heathen is prohibited? From the verse "Thou mayest consume all the peoples that the Lord thy God shall give unto thee" (Deut. 7:16). Only in time [of war], when they are delivered into your hand [as enemies], is this permitted, but not in time [of peace], when they are not delivered into your hand [as enemies].[10]

151. Torah was given only to hallow God's great Name, as is said, "God said unto me: 'Thou art My servant, Israel, through whom I will be glorified' " (Isa. 49:3). [By your deeds, you will glorify Me among all men.] Hence, the sages said, a man should keep away from dishonesty in dealing, whether with Jew or Gentile; indeed, with anyone in the marketplace. Besides, he who steals from a Gentile will in the end steal from a Jew; he who cheats a Gentile will in the end cheat a Jew; he who swears [falsely] to a Gentile will in the end swear [falsely] to a Jew; he who acts deceitfully toward a Gentile will in the end act deceitfully toward a Jew; he who sheds the blood of a Gentile will in the end shed the blood of a Jew.

That the Torah was given only to hallow God's great Name [in all the world] is shown by the verse "I will work a sign among all the nations and tongues, and send from them survivors . . . to the distant coasts" (Isa. 66:19). And what then? What is declared at the end of the verse: these survivors "shall declare My glory among the nations."[11]

152. When a man cheats a heathen [by swearing a false oath], and the heathen dies before restitution is made, that man's sin cannot be expiated, since [in besmirching Israel's name] he is guilty of profaning God's Name.[12]

153. [He who walks before a dead man's bier, wearing a garment previously rent for another deceased person, cheats the dead]. Cheating the dead is worse than cheating the living, for he who cheats the living can make up with him by making restitution; while he who cheats the dead can never make up with him.[13]

154. In the time-to-come, the mouth and the belly will contend with each other, the mouth saying to the belly, "All that I misappropriated or took by violence, I put into you." But after three days, the belly will burst open and say to the mouth, "Here is all you have misappropriated and taken by violence."[14]

155. Among the inhabitants of large cities, there is likely to be cheating.[15]

---

1. B. BK 62a.
2. Knowing that your neighbor will not accept a gift from you, you resort to a subterfuge, knowing that the law requires you to pay back double the theft. B. BM 61b.
3. He is required to pay double for the animal he stole; and if he has slaughtered or sold it, four- or fivefold.
4. He is merely expected to repay or restore what he has taken.
5. Literally, "below," a euphemism for Heaven.
6. B. BK 79b.
7. The tenant is entitled to as great a share in the shoots cut during the vintage as in the grapes. BM 9:1.
8. B. Ber 5b.
9. P. Sanh 1:2, 19b.
10. B. BK 113b; cf. BK Soncino, ad loc.
11. TdE, ed. Friedmann, p. 140 (JPS, p. 347).
12. Tos BK 10:15 and variant (ed. Zuckermandel).
13. Sem 9:21/22.
14. Gen. R. 100:7.
15. B. Er 21b.

156. A thief about to break in calls on Heaven [for help].[1]

157. When a thief has nothing to steal, he regards his "virtue" as real.[2]

158. If he cannot be trusted in dealing with money, he cannot be trusted in swearing an oath.[3]

159. It once happened to some disciples of R. Akiva that, while journeying to Chezib, they were overtaken by brigands, who asked them, "Where are you going?" They replied, "To Acco."[4] But when they reached Chezib, they said goodbye. The brigands then asked them, "Whose disciples are you?" They replied, "The disciples of R. Akiva." Said the brigands, "Happy are R. Akiva and his disciples, for no evil man will ever get the better of them."

When R. Manasseh was once going to Be Toreta, thieves met him and asked him, "Where are you going?" He said, "To Pumbedita." But when he reached Be Toreta, he said goodbye. They exclaimed, "You must be a disciple of Judah the Teacher of Deceit."[5] He said to them, "Do you indeed know him [as such? For defaming R. Judah], may it be [God's] will that you be put under a ban." For twenty-two years, they went on stealing but met with no success. Finally, realizing the futility of their efforts, they came to ask that the ban be revoked. There was a weaver among them who did not come to have his ban revoked, and he was finally devoured by a lion.

Pause now and consider the difference between thieves of Babylonia and brigands of the Land of Israel.[6]

160. Rava expounded: What is meant by "In the dark they dig into houses, which they had marked for themselves in the daytime" (Job 24:16)? This verse shows that the Sodomites used to cast envious eyes upon men of wealth. In order to mark the exact place where the wealthy men stored their valuables, the Sodomites would deposit their precious scented oil (ostensibly for safekeeping) with the wealthy men, who would store this oil with their own valuables. Later, in the dark of night, these Sodomites would come and like dogs sniff out the oil's whereabouts, dig there, and haul away the wealthy men's valuables.

After R. Yose expounded the verse thus in Sepphoris, that very night there were three hundred burglaries in Sepphoris. The people of the city came and reproached him: "You have taught a method to thieves." He replied, "How was I to know that thieves would come [to hear me]?"[7]

161. R. Eleazar son of R. Simeon once met a detective who was a thief catcher. R. Eleazar asked, "How can you recognize them? Are they not like wild beasts that prowl at night and hide during the day? Perhaps you sometimes arrest the innocent and let the gulity go free?" The detective answered, "What shall I do? It is the king's command." R. Eleazar: "Come, I will teach you what to do. At nine o'clock in the morning,[8] go into a tavern. Should you see a man dozing with a cup of wine in his hand, inquire about him. If he is a disciple of the wise, [you may assume that] he had risen very early in the morning to pursue his studies [and that is why he is dozing]; if he is a laborer, he too must have been up early to do his work. But if he is neither, he is a thief—arrest him." The report [of this conversation] was brought to the king's attention, and the decision was [as the proverb puts it]: "Let the reader of the message become the messenger."[9] R. Eleazar son of R. Simeon was accordingly sent for and was appointed to catch thieves. At that, R. Joshua ben Korhah sent word to him: "O Vinegar son of wine! How long will you deliver up the people of our God for slaughter!" R. Eleazar sent back: "I weed out thorns from the vineyard." R. Joshua replied, "Let the Owner of the vineyard come and Himself weed out its thorns."[10]

162. R. Giddel said in the name of Rav: If a man of Naresh [in Babylonia] kisses you, count your teeth. If a man of Nehar Pekod accompanies you, it is because of the fine garments he sees on you [which he will try to steal]. If a Pumbeditan escorts you, change your lodgings.[11]

163. R. Yohanan said in the name of R. Simeon ben Jehozadak: In the upper chamber of Nitzah's house in Lydda, the sages voted and decided: with regard to all commands in Torah, if a man is told, "Transgress or you will be slain," he may transgress them so as not to be slain, except, however, when told to worship an idol, to commit incest, or to murder.[12]

164. Exile comes to the world because of idolatry, incest, and murder.[13]

165. If a company of people are told by heathens, "Give us one of you, that we may slay him, and if you do not, we will slay all of you," all should let themselves be slain rather than turn over to the heathens even one Jewish person. But if the heathens name the person wanted—as Sheba son of Bichri was named—the company should give him up rather than let all die. Thus Scripture says [of Sheba], "Then the woman came unto all the people in her wisdom," etc. (2 Sam. 20:22). She said to them, "Since Sheba will be slain [in any event, and if you do not sur-

---

1. En Yaakov on B. Ber 63b, missing in Talmud editions.
2. Or: With nothing to steal, the thief regards himself as law-abiding. B. Sanh 22a.
3. B. BM 5b.
4. Acco, located beyond Chezib, made the robbers believe they had ample time to rob R. Akiva's disciples.
5. R. Judah was his master.
6. The brigands of the Land of Israel paid tribute to R. Akiva, while the thieves of Babylonia insulted R. Manasseh. B. AZ 25b–26a.
7. B. Sanh 109a and En Yaakov, ad loc.
8. Literally, the fourth hour of the day.
9. You made the motion, now you can become chairman of the committee.
10. B. BM 83b and En Yaakov, ad loc.
11. He is likely to rob you. B. Hul 127a.
12. B. Sanh 74a.
13. Avot 5:9.

render him], you will be slain, give him up and do not let all of you be slain."[1]

166. Ulla the Conspirator[2] was summoned [on a charge] by the Roman government. He fled and reached the house of R. Joshua ben Levi in Lod. The government sent a detachment of troops after him, who surrounded the city and said to the inhabitants, "If you do not turn him over to us, we will destroy the city." R. Joshua ben Levi undertook to persuade Ulla [to give himself up], saying, "It is better that only you be put to death than that the community be put to death on account of you." Ulla let himself be persuaded, and R. Joshua turned him over to the Romans.

Now, the prophet Elijah, ever remembered on good occasions, used to appear to R. Joshua, but after R. Joshua had done this, Elijah no longer appeared to him. So R. Joshua ben Levi fasted for thirty days, and Elijah again appeared to him. R. Joshua asked, "Master, why did you cease to come?" Elijah answered, "Am I a companion of informers?" R. Joshua: "Did I not act in keeping with the Baraita [that reads: If a company of people are told by heathens, 'Give us one of you, that we may slay him, and if you do not, we will slay all of you,' all should let themselves be slain rather than turn over to the heathens even one Jewish person, but if the heathens name the person wanted, the company should give him up, rather than let all die]?"[3] "But is that a teaching for the pious?" Elijah retorted: "Such an act should have been committed by others, not by you."[4]

167. A man came before Rava and said to him, "The ruler of my city ordered me, 'Go and slay So-and-so. If you do not, I will slay you.' " Rava replied, "Let yourself be slain rather than slay. What makes you think your blood is redder than his? Perhaps that man's blood is redder."[5]

168. R. Yohanan said: What is the meaning of "All faces are turned to paleness" (Jer. 30:6)? The words "all faces" refer to [the angels], God's household in heaven; and to [Israel], God's household on earth, when the Holy One says, "These [the Gentiles] are My handiwork, and those [Israel] are My handiwork—how can I destroy the Gentiles on account of Israel?"[6]

169. There is the story of two brothers, one of whom slew the other. What did their mother do? She took a cup, filled it with the blood of the one slain, and placed it in a turret. Day after day, as she entered the turret, she saw that the blood was seething. One day, when she entered and looked at the cup, she saw that the blood was still. In that instant she knew that her other son was slain, in keeping with the verse "Whoso sheddeth man's blood, by man shall his blood be shed" (Gen. 9:6).[7]

1. Tos Ter 7:20.
2. "Conspirator"—Gen. R. TA, p. 1184; BR: "son of Koshav."
3. Tos Ter 7:20.
4. P. Ter 8:4, 46b; Gen. R. 94:9.
5. B. Pes 25b.
6. B. Sanh 98b.
7. Deut. R. 2:25.

Wronging [Overreaching] and Deception

170. R. Hisda said: All gates may be locked, except the gates through which the prayers of those wronged pass.

R. Eleazar said: [All] evil, except for overreaching, is punished through an emissary.

R. Abbahu said: The curtain [of heaven][8] is never closed before three evils: overreaching, robbery, and idolatry.[9]

171. Our masters taught: "Ye shall do no unrighteousness in judgment, in meteyard, in weight, or in measure" (Lev. 19:35). "Meteyard" means land measurement, [and] it forbids measuring land for one person in summer and for another in winter.[10] "In weight" prohibits the steeping of weights in salt, and "in measure" teaches that one must not cause [a liquid] to foam.[11] Now, the matter may be argued *a fortiori:* if the Torah forbids a [false] *mesurah,* which is but one thirty-sixth of a *log,* how much more and more a *hin,* half a *hin,* a third of a *hin,* and a quarter of a *hin;* a *log,* half a *log,* or a quarter of a *log.*[12]

R. Judah said in the name of Rav: A man is forbidden to keep in his house a measuring vessel smaller or larger [than the standard measure], even if it is to be used as a chamber pot.[13]

172. Our masters taught: What is the proof that a measuring vessel may not be leveled where the practice is to heap it up, and that it may not be heaped up where the practice is to level it? The verse, "A perfect . . . measure" (Deut. 25:15). And what is the proof that if a man says, "I will level where the practice is to heap up, and reduce the price," or, "I will heap up where they level, and raise the price," we may not allow him? The verse, "A perfect and just measure thou shalt have" (ibid.).

Our masters taught: What is the proof that exact weight may not be given where the practice is to allow overweight, and that overweight may not be given where the practice is to give exact weight? The verse "A perfect weight" (Deut. 25:15). And what is the proof that when a man says, "I will give exact weight where the practice is to allow overweight, and reduce the price," or, "I will allow overweight where they give exact weight, and raise the price," we are not to allow him? The verse "A perfect and just weight thou shalt have."

R. Judah of Sura said: "Thou shalt possess nothing in thy house" (Deut. 25:14). Why not? "Because of [thy] diverse measures" (ibid.). "Thou shalt have nothing in thy

8. "Hiding, so to speak, human failings from the divine gaze" (Isidore Epstein, in Bm, Soncino, p. 351, n. 6).
9. B. BM 59a.
10. When brothers divide a landed legacy, one's portion must not be measured off in summer and another's in winter, because the measuring cord expands in winter and shrinks in summer. So Rashi.
11. The incrustation of salt adds to the weight; after the foam subsides, the measure is found to be short.
12. 1 *hin* = 12 *log* = 6.072 liters; 1 *log* = 0.506 liters (about 1 pint). JE 12:484.
13. Even if he does not intend to use it as a measure, others may do so by mistake. B. BM 61b; B. BB 89b.

bag" (Deut. 25:13). Why not? "Because of [thy] diverse weights" (ibid.). But if you keep "a perfect and just weight, thou shalt have [possessions]" (Deut. 25:15), if "a perfect and just measure, thou shalt have [wealth]."[1]

173. Our masters taught: A leveler may not be made wide at one end and narrow at the other.[2] One may not level with a single quick movement, for leveling in this manner causes loss to the seller and gain to the buyer. Nor may one level very slowly, because [this] is disadvantageous to the buyer and advantageous to the seller. Concerning all these [sharp practices of traders], Rabban Yohanan ben Zakkai said: Woe to me if I speak [of them], and woe to me if I do not speak. If I speak of them, knaves might learn [them]; and if I do not speak, the knaves might say, "Disciples of the wise are ignorant of our tricks" [and would deceive us still more].

[The question was raised]: Did Rabban Yohanan finally speak [of these sharp practices] or not? R. Samuel bar R. Isaac said: He did speak [of them]. He based himself on the verse "For the ways of the Lord are right, and the just shall walk in them; but transgressors do stumble therein" (Hos. 14:10).[3]

174. Our masters taught: Abba Saul son of Batnit collected three hundred jugs of wine from the foam in the vessel after it was measured,[4] and his associates collected three hundred jugs of oil from what was left in the vessel after it was measured. They brought the [six hundred] jugs to the treasurers [of the Temple] in Jerusalem[5] and were told, "You are not required to give them up." When Abba Saul and his associates insisted, "We do not wish to retain these jugs," the Temple treasurers replied, "Since you are determined to be stringent with yourselves, sell them and use the money earned for public needs."[6]

175. Our masters taught: As for those who hoard produce, lend money on interest, diminish measures, and raise prices, Scripture quotes such people as "saying: 'When will the new moon be gone, that we may sell grain? And the Sabbath, that we may set forth corn? making the ephah small, and the shekel great, and falsifying the balances of deceit' " (Amos 8:5). And what follows directly? "The Lord hath sworn by the pride of Jacob: Surely I will never forget any of their works" (Amos 8:7).[7]

176. Elijah [the prophet] said: Once a man who had knowledge of Scripture but no knowledge of Mishnah came and sat before me. He said, "Listen, O master, to what happened to me. I sold four *kor* of dates to a heathen, and measured them out half a *kor* by half a *kor* in a dimly lighted room. The heathen said to me, 'You and God in heaven know the measure you are giving me.' Now, [as a matter of fact] I had given him three *seah* of dates less [than he had paid for]. Later, I took the money [he paid me] and with it purchased a jar of oil, which I left on the very spot where I had turned over the dates to the heathen. But the jar split apart, and the oil went to waste." So I said to the man, "My son, blessed be He who is everywhere, in whose presence there is no show of favor! When Scripture says, 'Thou shalt not take advantage of thy neighbor, nor cheat him' [Lev. 19:13], it means that your neighbor [whether Jew or heathen] should be treated like your brother. Hence, you learn that cheating a heathen is still cheating."[8]

177. "Thy silver is become dross, thy wine mixed with water" (Isa. 1:22). When a man went to a silversmith [for currency], he was apt to hear him mutter to his apprentice, "Copper it for him." So, too, when a man went to buy a pint of wine from a wine dealer, he was apt to hear him mutter to his clerk, "Water it for him." Hence it is written, "Thy silver is become dross, thy wine mixed with water."[9]

178. "Thou shalt not put a stumbling block before the blind" (Lev. 19:14)—[not just the physically blind, but] one who is "blind" in a particular matter. Thus, suppose such a one came to you and asked, "Is the daughter of So-and-so fit to marry into a priestly family?" Do not say to him, "She is fit," if in fact she is disqualified. If a man seeks your counsel, do not give him counsel that is not right for him. Do not say to him, "Leave early in the morning," so that brigands will rob him. Do not say to him, "Leave at noon," so that the sun will strike him. Do not say to him, "Sell your field and buy a donkey," so that you may circumvent him and take the field away from him. If you protest, "But it is sensible counsel I am giving him," remember that the matter is turned over to a man's heart, for the verse ends by saying, "Thou shalt fear thy God. I am the Lord." Of any matter that is turned over to a man's heart, Scripture says, "Thou shalt fear thy God."[10]

179. A tale of a city that had no salt. In that city there was a band of muleteers, who said, "Let us go at once to such-and-such a place, fetch salt, and sell it before others have the chance." Now, the muleteers had a chief of the band, and when they said, "Let us go to such-and-such a place," he replied, "I have to plow early tomorrow morning. Wait until I have plowed, and then we will get going." They said, "Very well." But then what did the chief of the band do? He whispered to his wife, "Make sure of this code: if I say, 'Fetch me the yoke,' you are to give me the saddle; if I say, 'Fetch me the plow handle,' you are to give me the sack." [She obeyed him.] Then what did he

---

1. B. BB 89a.
2. When buying grain, the trader will hold the leveler at the wide end, so that its narrow end does not touch the surface of the vessel; as a result, the entire surface is not leveled, thus allowing him a heaping measure. When selling, he holds the leveler at its narrow end, and so diminishes the measure.
3. B. BB 89b.
4. The foam was allowed to run off into a vat.
5. Because they thought that they were required to give them up as property defrauded from their customers.
6. B. Betz 29a; Tos Betz 3:9.
7. B. BB 90b.
8. TdE, ed. Friedmann, pp. 74–75 (JPS, p. 207); Yalkut, *Tzav*, §504.
9. PRKM 15:8 (PRKS, p. 283).
10. Sif Lev., ed. Weiss, p. 88d; B. Kid 32a.

do? He put the sack on the mule and went away [that night], while his fellows slept until morning. When they got up in the morning and called him, the neighbors said, "Whom are you looking for? So-and-so has been gone since last night." The muleteers left the same morning, and on the road they met their chief returning. They asked, "Why have you done this to us?" He replied, "Don't you really know why? If we had all gone, salt would have immediately declined greatly in price. But now I am the only one to bring salt [for sale]. Before you get back, mine will be sold. And when you do get back, you too will sell at a good price." Hence it is said of such men, "They speak falsehood every one with his neighbor; with smooth lip, and with a double heart do they speak" (Ps. 12:3). And so it goes: if you will not call the yoke "saddle" and the plow handle "sack," you cannot make out.[1]

180. A story about R. Jonathan at a time when lentils were scarce [in his town]. He had a kinsman in a certain city, and he went down to him and said, "I am looking for lentils. Are there any to be had in the city?" His kinsman replied, "There are." R. Jonathan asked, "At what price?" His kinsman answered, "At such-and-such a price. Any time that you come here, I shall get them for you." After a while, R. Jonathan went to the city and to his kinsman's house, inquiring after him. His kinsman's wife said, "He is in the field." R. Jonathan waited for him, but since he did not appear, R. Jonathan asked one of the men of the city, "Are there lentils to be had here?" The man answered, "No, but there is wheat." R. Jonathan said, "It's lentils I'm looking for." The man replied, "Would you pay such-and-such a price?" and the man quoted a price higher than the one R. Jonathan's kinsman had given him. Nevertheless, R. Jonathan agreed to the price. When his kinsman came back from the field, R. Jonathan said to him, "Did you not tell me that lentils sold at such-and-such a price? Yet your townsmen charged me a price higher than what you quoted." His kinsman asked, "You didn't mention lentils to them, did you?" R. Jonathan answered, "I did." His kinsman commented, "Had you said to the men of the city, 'It's wheat I'm looking for,' they would have asked you, 'Would lentils do?' But since you told them, 'It's lentils I'm looking for,' they asked you, 'Would you like wheat?' " Hence it is said of such men, "They speak falsehood every one with his neighbor; with smooth lip, and with a double heart do they speak" (Ps. 12:3).

R. Hiyya of Sepphoris went to Sura to buy wheat. R. Jonathan said to him, "When you want wheat, say, 'I am looking for barley,' and when you want barley, say, 'I am looking for wheat,' so that the price will not be increased for you."[2]

181. Abbaye said: One who wishes to present a specimen of his signature at a court of law should not write it at the foot of a [blank] scroll, lest someone find it and write above it that the signer owes him money.

A customs collector once came before Abbaye and said to him, "Will the master let me have his signature, so that when the sages come by and show it to me over your authorization, I will allow them to pass without paying tax."[3] Abbaye wrote it down for him at the head of a blank scroll. As the customs collector kept pulling the scroll up so that a blank space would be left above Abbaye's signature, Abbaye said to him, "The sages have long ago anticipated you."[4]

182. There is the story of a man who came before Rava with a deed bearing the signatures of Rava and R. Aha bar Adda. Rava said to the man, "The signature is mine. But I never signed anything ahead of R. Aha bar Adda." The man was placed under arrest, and he confessed. Then Rava said to him, "I can understand how you forged my signature. But how did you forge the signature of R. Aha bar Adda, whose hand trembles?" The man: "I put my hand on a rope bridge [which vibrates]." According to some, the man stood on a waterskin.[5]

183. There are seven kinds of thieves—the foremost among them is he who steals the good opinion of people.[6]

184. Samuel said: It is forbidden to steal the good opinion of people—even the good opinion of a heathen.[7]

185. Just as there is wronging in business, so there is wronging in speech. A man should not ask, "How much is this article?" if he does not intend to buy it. If a person is a penitent, one is not to say to him, "Remember the way you used to act." If a person is the son of proselytes, one should not taunt him with "Remember the way your fathers acted," as is said, "You shall not wrong a proselyte or oppress him" (Exod. 22:20).[8]

186. Our masters taught: "Ye shall not therefore wrong one another" (Lev. 25:17) means wronging through speech. You say, "Wronging through speech," but does not Scripture here mean wronging in matters of money? No, in saying earlier, "If thou sell aught unto thy neighbor, or acquirest aught of thy neighbor, ye shall not wrong one another" (Lev. 25:14), Scripture has already dealt with wronging in matters of money. Then "Ye shall not therefore wrong each other" must refer to wronging through speech. For example: If a person is a penitent, one should not say to him, "Remember the way you used to act." If he is the son of proselytes, he should not be taunted with "Remember the way your fathers acted." If he is a proselyte and comes to study Torah, one should not say to him, "Shall the mouth that ate unclean and forbidden food, abominable and creeping things, come to study the Torah, which was uttered by the mouth of the Almighty?" If a person is

1. MTeh 12:1; Yalkut, Ps., §656.
2. MTeh 12:1; Yalkut, Ps., § 656.
3. "His possession of Abbaye's signature, he contended, would enable him to verify Abbaye's signature on any authorization that might be presented to him" (BB, Soncino, p. 726, n. 16).
4. B. BB 167a.
5. Ibid.
6. Mek, *Mishpatim, Nezikin,* 13.
7. B. Hul 94a.
8. B. BM 58b.

visited by suffering, afflicted with disease, or has just now had to bury his children, one should not speak to him as Job's companions spoke: "Is not thy fear [of God] thy confidence, and thy hope the integrity of thy ways? Remember, I pray thee, whoever perished, being innocent?" (Job. 4:6ff.). If ass drivers ask to buy grain from him, he should not say to them, "Go to So-and-so, who sells grain," knowing full well that So-and-so has never done any such thing. R. Judah said: One should also not feign interest in a purchase when he has no money, since this is a matter turned over to the heart, and of everything turned over to the heart, it is written, "And thou shalt fear thy God" (Lev. 25:17).

R. Yohanan said on the authority of R. Simeon ben Yohai: Wronging through speech is more heinous than wronging in money matters. For of the first, it is written, "Thou shalt fear thy God," whereas of the second, "Thou shalt fear thy God" is not written. R. Eleazar said: The first affects a victim's very person; the second only his money. R. Samuel bar Nahmani said: For the second, restoration is possible; but not for the first.[1]

187. We have been taught that R. Meir used to say: A man should not urge his friend to dine with him if he knows that his friend will not do so. Nor should he offer him any gifts if he knows that his friend will not accept them. He should not make believe that it is for his guest's sake that he is broaching casks of wine that in fact he intends to turn over to a shopkeeper to be sold—he must inform the guest what his true intentions are. And he should not say to his guest, "Anoint yourself with oil," when he knows that the oil jar is empty. If, however, it is done so that the guest [may appear especially honored in the presence of others], it is permitted.[2]

188. Our masters taught: There are two reasons why a man should not sell his neighbor shoes made of the hide of an animal that died of itself, representing them as made of the hide of an animal that had been slaughtered: first, because he is deceiving him, and secondly, because of the danger.[3] A man should not send his neighbor a cask of wine with oil floating on top. It once happened that a man sent his friend a cask of wine seemingly filled to the brim with oil. [Believing that the cask was full of oil], the friend invited some guests to share it with him. When he dipped into the cask and found that [below the surface] it had only wine, [he was so humiliated that] he hanged himself.[4]

189. Mar Zutra son of R. Nahman was once walking from Sirka to Be Mahoza while Rava and R. Safra were walking to Sirka, and they met on the way. Believing that the two had come to meet him, Mar Zutra asked, "Why did the sages take the trouble to come such a distance [to meet me]?" R. Safra replied, "We did not know that the master was coming; had we known it, we would have come an even greater distance." Later, Rava asked R. Safra, "Why did you tell him what really happened? Now you have embarrassed him." R. Safra: "But if I hadn't told him, we would have been deceiving him." [Rava:] "No, he would have deceived himself."[5]

Returning a Lost Article

190. Our masters taught: In former times, whoever found a lost article used to announce the find during each of the three festivals, and for another seven days following the last festival—three days to allow the owner of the article to go home, another three days to allow him to return to Jerusalem, and another day to announce his loss. After the destruction of the Temple—may it be speedily rebuilt in our own days!—it was enacted that the announcing should be done in synagogues and houses of study. But when oppressors grew in number, it was enacted that only one's neighbors and acquaintances should be informed, and that that sufficed.

Who is meant by "When oppressors grew in number"? People who declared that lost property belonged to the king.

Our masters taught: In Jerusalem, there was a Stone of Losses. He who lost an article went there, and he who found one did likewise. The finder stood up and announced the find, and its owner stood up and called out the identifying marks, and had the article restored to him.[6]

191. A man who finds Torah scrolls must read them at least once every thirty days—if he cannot read, he must roll them open and reroll them.[7] But he must not begin study of new matter in them,[8] nor may another person read them with him.[9] A man who finds a garment must give it a shaking at least once every thirty days, and spread it out [to be aired] to preserve it, but not to enhance his own status.[10] Silver and copper vessels may be used, so that they [do not tarnish but] remain fit—not, however, in such a manner as to wear them out. Gold and glassware may not be touched until Elijah comes.[11] If a man finds a sack, a basket, or any other object it is beneath his dignity to pick up, he need not pick it up.[12]

192. Our masters taught: When a man finds wooden vessels, he may make use of them to keep them from rotting; if copper vessels, he may use them for hot water but may

1. Ibid.
2. B. Hul 94a.
3. "As the animal may have died through the bite of a serpent, and the hide of the animal may have become thereby contaminated" (Hul, Soncino, p. 528, n. 4).
4. B. Hul 94a.

5. B. Hul 94b.
6. B. BM 28b.
7. If left unused, they may become moldy and moth-eaten.
8. The long poring over the scrolls, which would be required, might injure them.
9. Since each is likely to pull the scroll to himself, the scroll may be injured.
10. To show others that he owns fine clothing.
11. The finder may not use them at all, since they do not deteriorate from disuse.
12. B. BM 29b.

not put them directly over the fire, because that wears them out; if silver vessels, he may use them for cold water, but not for hot water, because hot water tarnishes them; trowels and spades may be used with matter that is soft, but not with hard matter, which injures them; gold and glassware he may not touch until Elijah comes. Moreover, what the sages ruled concerning use of lost property, they also ruled concerning personal use of what is deposited in trust.[1]

193. Our masters taught: "And thou mayest hide thyself" (Deut. 22:1).[2] There are times when you may hide yourself and there are times when you may not. When, for example, may you hide yourself? If you are a priest, and the animal has gone astray in a cemetery; or you are an old man, and it is beneath your dignity [to lead an animal home]; or if your own task is more valuable than your neighbor's. Under such circumstances, "thou mayest hide thyself."[3]

194. R. Yohanan said: When a poor man restores a lost article to its owner, the Holy One, blessed be He, daily proclaims his merit.[4]

195. Alexander of Macedon paid a visit to a king at the end of the world[5] who showed him much silver and gold. Alexander said, "I have not come to see your silver and gold—it is your legal customs and practices I have come to observe." As Alexander and the king were engaged in discourse, two men came before the king for judgment. One said, "My lord king, I bought a ruin from this man, and, while clearing it, I found a treasure; and so I said to him, 'Take your treasure. I bought a ruin—I did not buy a treasure.' " The other argued, "Just as you are afraid of the punishment for robbery, so am I afraid of it. The fact is, I sold you the ruin and everything in it—from the depths of the earth to the heights of heaven."

The king addressed one of them and asked him, "Have you a son?" He replied, "Yes." The king asked the other, "Have you a daughter?" He replied, "Yes." "Go, then," said the king, "wed the one to the other, and let the two make use of the treasure." Alexander showed his amazement at this verdict. The king asked, "Have I not judged well?" Alexander: "Yes, well." The king: "If such a case had come up before you in your country, how would you have handled it?" Alexander replied, "I would have chopped off the head of the one and the head of the other, and the treasure would have gone to the king's house." The king: "Does the sun shine for you?" Alexander: "Yes." "Do rains come down upon you?" Alexander: "Yes." The king: "There are small cattle in your country, are there not?" Alexander: "Yes." The king: "May the breath of life in such a man as you be blasted out! It is only for the sake of the small cattle that the sun still shines for you, that the rain still comes down upon you."[6]

196. Simeon ben Shetah was a trader in flax. So his disciples said, "Master, give up this trade. We will buy you a donkey, and you will not have to weary yourself so much." They went and purchased a donkey from an Ishmaelite, which turned out to have a pearl entangled in its neck. They came to their master and said, "From now on, you will not need to weary yourself." When he asked them, "Why not?" they told him, "We bought you a donkey from an Ishmaelite, which has a pearl entangled in its neck." He asked them, "Did its former owner know about the pearl?" They replied, "Of course not." So he said to them, "Go and return it."

They argued with the master: "Even those who say that cheating a Gentile is forbidden nevertheless admit that an article lost by the Gentile may be kept!"

"What do you think?" [replied Simeon]. "That Simeon ben Shetah is a barbarian? Simeon ben Shetah would rather hear 'Blessed be the God of the Jews' than gain any profit in this entire world."[7]

197. R. Samuel bar Sosrati went up to Rome at a time when the empress had lost her ornaments, and he found them. She had it proclaimed throughout the city: "He who returns them within thirty days will receive such-and-such a reward; if after thirty days, he will have his head cut off." R. Samuel did not return them within thirty days; but after the thirty days, he returned them. She asked him, "Were you not in the city?" He said "Yes," [I was here]." "Did you not hear the proclamation?" "Yes, [I heard it]." "Then why did you not return them within thirty days?" "So that you should not say I did it because of fear of you—I did it because of fear of Heaven." At that, she said to him, "Blessed be the God of the Jews."[8]

198. There is the story of a man who passed by the entrance to R. Hanina ben Dosa's house and [inadvertently] left behind some hens, which R. Hanina ben Dosa's wife found. R. Hanina said to her, "Do not eat any of their eggs." The chickens and the eggs kept multiplying, and distressed R. Hanina and his wife so much that he sold them and bought some goats with the proceeds. Then it happened that the man who lost the hens was passing by and said to his companion, "It was here I left my hens." R. Hanina overheard him and asked, "Do you have any mark [to identify them]?" The man said, "Yes." He mentioned the mark and was allowed to take the goats.[9]

199. It is related of R. Phinehas ben Yair that when he was living in a city in the south, two poor men came there to seek a livelihood. They had with them two *seah* of barley, which they deposited with him, but then they forgot about

1. B. BM 30a.
2. "The beginning of the verse reads, 'Thou shalt not see thy brother's ox or his sheep go astray.' In the exegesis that follows, it is assumed that the 'not' may or may not refer to 'and thou shalt hide thyself,' according to circumstances" (BM, Soncino, p. 186, n. 2).
3. B. BM 30a.
4. Paraphrase of B. Pes 113a.
5. Believed to have been Africa, where, according to authors of antiquity, people led ideal lives. The Aramaic *Katzeia* is taken to mean "end of the world." See Saul Lieberman's note in PRKM, p. 274.
6. P. BM 2:5, 8c; Tanhuma, *Emor*, §6.
7. P. BM 2:5, 8c.
8. Ibid.
9. B. Ta 25a.

it and went away. Year after year, R. Phinehas ben Yair sowed the barley, reaped it, and stored it in a granary. After a lapse of seven years, the two men returned and asked for their barley. R. Phinehas ben Yair recognized them and said to them, "First fetch camels and asses, and then come and take your stores [of barley]."[1]

200. A story of a pious man: A Roman noblewoman lost a box full of denars. The pious man found it and took it to her house. When he brought it, people said to her, "He has no idea what is in it—that is why he brought it back to you." She answered, "The box is all gold on the outside, and yet you say that he did not know what is in it!" She said to the pious man, "May your mother be mated to you."[2] They exclaimed, "He returns your lost article, and you curse him!" She replied, "If there were just one more of his kind among his people, we would not last in the world."[3]

Workmen and Slaves

201. We have been taught: "Thou shalt not abuse a hired servant that is poor and needy. . . . In the same day thou shalt give him his hire . . . ; for he . . . setteth his life upon it" (Deut. 24:14–15). Why did the hired man climb a ladder [to build a house] or hang [precariously] from a tree [to gather its fruit] and risk death—was it not for his wage?

In another comment "He . . . setteth his life upon it" is interpreted to mean that he who holds back the wage of a hired person is as though he were taking his life from him.[4]

202. "Thou shalt not abuse a hired servant." But has it not already been said, "Thou shalt not defraud thy neighbor, nor rob him" (Lev. 19:13)? The repetition teaches that he who withholds the wage of a hired servant transgresses five precepts negative and positive. [Three negative]: "Do not defraud." "Do not rob." "The wages of a hired servant shall not abide with thee all night" (Lev. 19:13). [Two positive]: "In the same day thou shalt give him his hire" (Deut. 24:15). "Neither shall the sun go down upon [what is due] him" (ibid.).[5]

203. "In the same day thou shalt give him his hire . . . ; for he . . . setteth his heart upon it" (Deut. 24:15). The verse may be understood by the parable of a man who was walking on a road with his donkey trailing behind him. When a sheaf of corn was sold to the man, he put it on his shoulder. The donkey, plodding on the road behind the sheaf, hoped that he would get to eat it. But what did the owner do to the donkey? When he reached home, he put the donkey in its stall but tied up the sheaf high above it. People said to him, "You cruel man—the donkey kept running all the way because of the sheaf, and in the end you did not put the sheaf within its reach!" So it is with the hired servant who toils and moils all day, hoping for his wages, and you put him out empty-handed![6]

204. There is the story of R. Yohanan ben Matia, who said to his son, "Go out and hire some workmen for us." The son went ahead and contracted to provide them with food. When he came back, his father said to him, "Even if you were to provide them with the kind of banquet that was Solomon's in the time [of his glory], you will not have fulfilled your duty to them [with such an unclear contract], for they are children of Abraham, Isaac, and Jacob. Now, before they begin to work, go out and say to them, 'I engage you on condition that you make no claim upon me [for food] other than for bread and pulse.' "[7]

205. One time R. Yose of Yodkart hired workmen for his field. He was delayed [and] did not bring them their food [when mealtime came]. So they said to his son, "We are hungry." Since they happened to be sitting under a fig tree, the son cried out, "Fig tree, O fig tree, bring forth your fruit, that my father's workmen may eat!" It brought forth its fruit, and they ate. In the meantime, the father came back and said to the workmen, "Bear no grievance against me. I was delayed until now, because I have been occupied with performing a religious duty." They replied, "May He who is everywhere satisfy you, even as your son satisfied us." R. Yose: "In what way?" They told him about the miracle.[8]

206. Some porters [accidentally] broke a cask of wine belonging to Rabbah bar Bar Hanah. So he seized their clothes. When they went and complained to Rav, he said to Rabbah, "Return their clothes." Rabbah: "Is that the law?" Rav: "Yes—'that thou mayest walk in the way of good men' " (Prov. 2:20). So Rabbah returned the clothes to the porters, who then said, "We are poor men. We worked hard all day. We are hungry and have no money [for food]." Rav then said to Rabbah, "Go and pay them their wage." Rabbah: "Is that the law." Rav: "Yes—'keep the path of the saintly' " (ibid.).[9]

207. [A Hebrew may not be sold as a lifelong slave, for God said:] "They are My slaves" (Lev. 25:42). My claim to owning them came first: "whom I brought forth out of the land of Egypt" (ibid.), with the stipulation "that they should not be sold as slaves" (ibid.).[10]

---

1. Deut. R. 3:3; P. Dem 1:3, 22a.
2. So emended by Saul Lieberman. Isaac Katz suggests: "May your people be inferior to you." Ephraim Hurwitz emends *ummatekha* ("your people") to read *ematekha* ("your fear") and translates the passage: "May your fear of God be restricted to you." Literally, "May your people be given over to you." Leon Nemoy suggests: "May your people cast you out from their midst."MTeh, YJS 2:431, n. 3.
3. MTeh 12:1; Yalkut, Ps., §656.
4. B. BM 112a.
5. Sif Deut., §278.
6. Exod. R. 31:7; Tanhuma, *Mishpatim*, §10.
7. B. BM 83a.
8. B. Ta 24a.
9. B. BM 83a.
10. Sif Lev., ed. Weiss, p. 109d.

208. "And his master shall bore his ear through with an awl," etc. (Exod. 21:6). Rabban Yohanan ben Zakkai used to expound this verse in a symbolic way. Why was the ear singled out from all the other parts of the body? Because the Holy One said, "The ear heard My voice on Mount Sinai when I proclaimed, 'For unto Me the children of Israel are servants; they are My servants' [Lev. 25:55], and not servants of servants. Yet this man has gone and acquired a master for himself. Let his ear be bored through!"

"His master . . . shall bring him unto the door, or unto the doorpost" (Exod. 21:6). R. Simeon Berabbi expounded this verse in a symbolic way. Why are the door and the doorpost singled out from all other parts of the house? Because the Holy One said, "The door and the doorpost were witnesses in Egypt when I passed over the lintel and the two doorposts, and proclaimed, 'For unto Me the children of Israel are servants; they are My servants,' and not servants of servants. Then I brought them forth from bondage to freedom, yet this man has gone and acquired a master for himself. Let his ear be bored through in the presence of door and doorpost!"[1]

209. R. Jacob ben Zavdi said: Why is a slave to go free if his master causes him the loss of a tooth or an eye? Because [Canaan, the forebear of slaves, was condemned on account of what] "he saw [with his eye] . . . and told [with his mouth]" (Gen. 9:22).[2]

210. "If thy brother be waxen poor with thee, and sell himself unto thee" (Lev. 25:39). Scripture describes him as "thy brother," implying that you must treat him in a brotherly way. You might suppose that he too should regard himself as your brother. Therefore Scripture goes on to describe him as "slave" (ibid.). How are these seemingly contradictory instructions to be reconciled? You must treat him in a brotherly way, but he must regard himself as being in servitude.

"Do not make him perform the work of a slave" (Lev. 25:39). Do not make him carry [your] personal things before you to the bathhouse, nor put on your shoes for you.[3]

211. "You must not lord it over him harshly" (Lev. 25:43). Do not say to him, "Warm this cup," when you do not need it; "Cool this cup for me," when you do not need it; "Keep hoeing under this vine until I come," if such hoeing is not necessary. Should you protest, "But the fact is, I do need it," the truth of what you say is turned over to the heart. With regard to any matter turned over to the heart, Scripture says, "Thou shalt fear thy God" (Lev. 25:43).[4]

212. Our masters taught: "Since he has fared well with thee" (Deut. 15:16)—"with thee" in food; "with thee" in drink. For you may not eat fine bread while he eats coarse bread. You may not drink aged wine while he drinks new wine. You may not sleep on soft bedding while he sleeps on straw. Hence the saying: When a man buys a Hebrew slave, it is as though he had bought himself a master.[5]

213. "He shall work with thee" (Lev. 25:40). You may not turn over his skill to another person. If, say, he has been a public bath attendant, a public barber, or a public baker he should not continue working in such a capacity. R. Yose differed: If his skill had been thus employed before [he sold himself into servitude], he may continue with the same work; but at the outset, his master may not introduce him to such work.

In any event, the sages say: The slave must cut his master's hair, wash his clothes, and bake his dough.

"Then shall he go out from being with thee" (Lev. 25:41) implies that he should not live in a village while you live in the city or live in the city while you live in a village.[6]

214. R. Yose's wife had a quarrel with her maidservant, and in the maidservant's presence R. Yose declared his wife in the wrong. When she asked him, "Why do you declare me wrong in the presence of my maidservant?" he replied, "Did not Job say, 'If I did despise the cause of my manservant, or of my maidservant, when they contended with me—what then shall I do when God riseth up?' " (Job 31:13).[7]

215. He who is half-slave and half-free must work one day for his master and one day for himself. Such had been the opinion of the school of Hillel. But the school of Shammai said: You have made matters right for the master but not for the slave. He cannot marry a [heathen] bondwoman, for he is already half-free; nor can he marry a freewoman, because he is still half-slave. Shall he remain unmarried? But has not the world been created only for fruition and increase: "He created it not to be a waste, He formed it to be inhabited" (Isa. 45:18)? And so for the sake of the world's well-being, the master is compelled to manumit the slave, who must execute a writ of indebtedness for half his value.

Hearing this argument, the school of Hillel retracted its opinion and ruled in accord with the school of Shammai.[8]

216. There is a story of Rabban Gamaliel, who [accidentally] put out an eye of his slave Tabi. He rejoiced over it greatly [as he had been eager to set Tabi free],[9] and when he met R. Joshua, he said to him, "Do you know that my slave Tabi has gone free?" R. Joshua asked

1. B. Kid 22b, and En Yaakov, ad loc.
2. Since he was condemned through misuse of these organs, he goes free upon the loss of either. Gen. R. 36:5.
3. Sif Lev., ed. Weiss, p. 109b.
4. Ibid.
5. B. Kid 22a.
6. Sif Lev., ed. Weiss, p. 109b.
7. Gen. R. 48:3.
8. B. Pes 88a–b; B. BB 13a.
9. But he could not, because the verse "You are to make them an inheritance for your children after you, to hold for a possession" (Lev. 25:4) is understood as prohibiting the freeing of one's slaves.

him, "What happened?" Rabban Gamaliel replied, "I [accidentally] put out one of his eyes."[1]

217. The instant Rabbi [Judah I, the Patriarch] left the bathhouse, he wrapped himself in his garments and sat down to attend to the needs of the people. His servant mixed a cup of wine for him. Because Rabbi was busy attending to people's needs, he had no opportunity to receive the cup from his servant, who dozed off and fell asleep. When Rabbi turned and looked at him, he said: Well did Solomon say, "Sweet is the sleep of a laboring man . . . but the satiety of the rich will not suffer him to sleep" (Eccles. 5:11)—including the likes of us, who are so busy attending to the needs of people that we are not even allowed to sleep.[2]

218. It is enough for a servant to be like his master.[3]

219. Whatever a slave acquires, his master acquires.[4]

220. Our masters told the story of a man who was engaged in trade and had to put up at inns. [Wherever he went], his slaves went with him. The man had a son in the Land of Israel who labored at the study of Torah. Presently, while the father was staying at an inn, the time of his death approached. So he said, "What shall I do? If I bequeath all my possessions to my son, he will derive no benefit from them, because this slave here will grab everything and take off." Now, what did the man do? He said to the slave, "Go call a scribe for me." Then he said to the scribe, "Write a will giving my son the privilege of choosing any one object he may wish." [Turning to the slave], he went on, "And all the rest is yours." The will was written. The slave rose, folded it up, and brought it to the Land of Israel. When the son heard that his father was dead, he went into mourning for him. After the period of mourning ended, he asked the slave, "Where is my father's money?" The slave: "You have nothing. He bequeathed everything to me. But for you he stipulated that you have the privilege of choosing any one object you may wish—that is the only thing you have." So the son said, "We will go to court tomorrow." In the meantime, the young son went to his teacher and said to him, "I am in great trouble." The teacher: "What happened?" The young son: "My father bequeathed all his money to his slave, and to me he left nothing except for any one object that I may choose. I do not know what to do." The teacher: "Your father conferred a great boon upon you. He was a clever man and knew exactly what he was doing. Tomorrow, when you go to court and the will is read stipulating that everything is the slave's except that you may pick out whatever you want, place your hand on the slave and say, 'This is what I want,' with the result that the slave and all his money will be yours." And the son did just that.[5]

1. Cf above, part 2, chap. 11, §81. B. BK 74b.
2. Eccles. R. 5:11, §1.
3. B. Ber 58b. Cf. Matthew 10:25.
4. B. Pes 88b.
5. Yalkut, Eccles., §968.

221. There is the story of an old slave who [to make himself look younger] went and had his head and beard dyed [black]. He then came to Rava and said, "Buy me." Rava replied by quoting "I prefer to have poor people [not slaves] as servants in my household." The slave then approached R. Papa bar Samuel, who bought him. Once, when R. Papa said to the slave, "Haul up some water for me to drink," the slave [to avoid the hard work] had his head and beard whitened again, and said, "See, I am older than your father."[6] At that, R. Papa bar Samuel quoted against himself the verse "The righteous is delivered out of trouble, and another cometh in his stead" (Prov. 11:8).[7]

222. Ten measures of sleep came down to the world—slaves took nine, and the entire rest of the world took one.[8]

223. R. Nahman said: A slave is not worth the bread it takes to fill his belly. Rava bar R. Joseph commented: What R. Nahman said applies only to such as his slave Daro, who is given to hopping from winehouse to winehouse.[9]

224. Don't put your trust in slaves.[10]

225. The more slaves, the more thievery. The more female slaves, the more lechery.[11]

226. A slave delights in loose living.[12]

227. Wicked slaves first do mischief and then seek advice.[13]

228. Most slaves are arrogant. Most sons of good families are modest.[14]

229. He who calls his fellow man a slave should be placed under a ban.[15]

230. An associate scholar's [*haver*'s] slave is like an associate scholar.[16]

231. Our masters taught: For deceased male or female slaves, no row [of comforters] should be formed, nor should the mourners' grace after meals be spoken, nor condolences offered.

When the bondwoman of R. Eliezer died, his disciples came in to condole with him. At the sight of them, he went up to an upper chamber. They went up after him.

6. It is unseemly for an aged man like me to do menial service for a much younger master.
7. B. BM 60b.
8. B. Kid 49b.
9. B. BK 97a.
10. B. BM 86b.
11. Avot 2:7.
12. B. Git 13a.
13. B. BB 4a.
14. P. Kid 4:11, 66c.
15. B. Kid 28a.
16. B. AZ 39a.

He then went into the bath chamber, and they followed him there. He then went into the great dining hall,[1] and they followed him there. Finally, he said to them: I thought that lukewarm water would be enough to "scald" you, but apparently even boiling water cannot do so. Have I not taught you that no row of comforters is formed at the death of male or female slaves, nor is the mourners' grace after meals spoken, nor condolence offered. What then is said over them? Even as for the loss of an ox or an ass, a man is told, "May He who is everywhere replenish your loss," so, at the death of a male or female slave, he is told, "May He who is everywhere replenish your loss."

We have been taught that no funeral oration is spoken for male and female slaves. R. Yose said: If the slave was a virtuous man, we say, "Alas for a good and faithful man who worked hard for his living." R. Yose was asked, "If so, what have you left to be said about free men who are virtuous?"

When Tabi, Rabban Gamaliel's slave, died, he accepted condolences for him. His disciples asked him, "Master, did you not teach us that condolences are not accepted for slaves?" He replied, "My slave Tabi was not like other slaves—he was a virtuous man."[2]

Compassion for God's Creatures

232. "This is my God, and I will glorify Him (*ve-anvehu*)" (Exod. 15:2). Abba Saul construed the word *ve-anvehu* [as made up of *ani ve-hu*], "I am to be like Him." Hence, as He is gracious and compassionate, so you are to be gracious and compassionate.[3]

233. We have been taught that R. Gamaliel Berabbi quoted, "When He endoweth thee with compassion, He will have compassion upon thee" (Deut. 13:18), and then said: When a man has compassion on God's creatures, compassion is shown him from Heaven. But when a man has no compassion on God's creatures, no compassion is shown him from Heaven.[4]

234. Be filled with compassion for one another, and the Holy One will be filled with compassion for you.[5]

235. Rabban Yohanan ben Zakkai used to say: Because of three sinful things, householders are turned over to the [Roman] government: because they lend money on interest, because they gather paid-up writs of indebtedness,[6] and because they publicly make pledges for charity which they do not pay. Besides, they manage to evade [the Roman government's] yoke and shift it and its taxes onto the helpless poor and needy. Of such householders, Scripture says, "Cursed be he that confirmeth not the words of this Torah by obeying them" (Deut. 27:26), a verse that refers to rapacious householders.[7]

236. R. Nathan bar Abba said in the name of Rav: Babylonia's rich men are sure to go down into Gehenna. Thus, when Shabbetai ben Merinus happened to be in Babylonia and asked its rich men for money to help set him up in business, they did not give it to him. [Then he asked] for mere sustenance, but they did not give him even that. So he said: These rich men must be descendants of the mixed multitude.[8] For Scripture says, "When He endoweth thee with compassion, He will have compassion upon thee and multiply thee as He swore to thy fathers" (Deut. 13:18), proving that he who has compassion on God's creatures is assuredly of our father Abraham's progeny, whereas he who has no compassion on God's creatures is assuredly not of our father Abraham's progeny.[9]

237. "But unto you that fear My Name shall the sun of righteousness shine" (Mal. 3:20). Once, when Abba Tahnah the Pious was entering his city on Sabbath eve at dusk, a bundle slung over his shoulder, he came upon a man afflicted with boils lying [helplessly] at a crossroads. The man said to him, "Master, do an act of kindness for me—carry me into the city." Abba Tahnah replied, "If I abandon my bundle, how shall I and my household support ourselves? But if I abandon a man afflicted with boils, I will forfeit my life!" What did he do? He let his inclination to good overpower his impulse to evil, [set down his bundle on the road], and carried the afflicted man into the city. Then he returned for his bundle and reentered the city with the last rays of the sun. Everybody was astonished[10] and exclaimed, "Is this really Abba Tahnah the Pious?" He too felt uneasy at heart and said to himself: Is it possible that I have desecrated the Sabbath? At that, the Holy One caused the sun to continue to shine [a while longer, delaying the onset of Sabbath].[11]

238. R. Mani taught: When the Holy One said to Saul, "Now go and smite Amalek" (1 Sam. 15:3), Saul said to himself: If at the death of a single person the Torah ordains, "Bring a heifer whose neck is to be broken,"[12] how many more and more such heifers would have to be brought for the death of so many! In any event, if a human being has sinned, what sin has an animal committed? And if grown-ups have sinned, what sin did the little ones commit? At once a divine voice came forth and said, "Be not overly righteous" (Eccles. 7:16). Subsequently, after Saul had said to Doeg, "Turn thou and fall upon the priests" (1

---

1. A mourner usually spent the period of mourning in a room downstairs. R. Eliezer's demonstrative going to the upper chamber, the bathing quarters, and the festive dining area were meant to show that he did not observe mourning for the bondwoman.
2. B. Ber 16b.
3. B. Shab 133b.
4. B. Shab 151b.
5. Gen. R. 33:3.
6. And try to collect on them a second time.
7. ARNB 31.
8. They were not Hebrews. See Exod. 32:38.
9. B. Betz 32b.
10. At seeing the pious man carrying his bundle when the Sabbath was about to begin.
11. Eccles. R. 9:7, §1.
12. See Deut. 21.

Sam. 22:18), another divine voice came forth and said to him, "Be not overly wicked" (Eccles. 7:17).[1]

239. "But Saul and the people had pity on Agag" (1 Sam. 15:9). R. Simeon ben Lakish said: He who shows pity when he should be harsh will in the end be harsh when he should show pity, as is said "And Nob, the city of priests, smote he with the edge of the sword" (1 Sam. 22:19). Nob should not have been treated like Amalek's progeny![2]

240. Scripture prohibits inflicting pain on dumb creatures.[3]

241. The sufferings of Rabbi [Judah I, the Patriarch] came upon him because of an [uncompassionate] act and left him because of a [compassionate] act.

They came to him because of an [uncompassionate] act: once, a calf was being taken to be slaughtered. It broke away, hid its head under the skirts of Rabbi's robe, and lowed pitifully, as though pleading, "Save me." "Go," said Rabbi, "for this you were created."

At that, it was declared [in Heaven], "Since he showed no pity, let sufferings come upon his head."

And left him because of a [compassionate] act: one day, Rabbi's maidservant was sweeping the house. [Seeing] some weasel pups lying there, she was about to sweep them away. "Let them be," he said to her, "for it is written, 'And His compassion is over all His works' " (Ps. 145:9).

At that, it was said [in Heaven], "Since he is compassionate, let us be compassionate to him."[4]

242. R. Judah said in the name of Rav: A man may eat nothing until he has fed his animal, as is said, "And I will give grass in thy fields for thy cattle" (Deut. 11:15), and only after that, "Thou shalt eat and be satisfied" (ibid.).[5]

243. A man may not purchase an animal, tame or wild, or a fowl, unless he has prepared feed for it.[6]

244. A man was walking on a road with his donkey trailing behind him. When a sheaf of corn was sold to the man, he put it on his shoulder. The donkey, plodding on the road behind the sheaf, hoped that he would get to eat it. But what did the owner do to the donkey? When he reached home, he put the donkey in its stall and tied up the sheaf high above it. People said to him, "You cruel man—the donkey kept running all the way because of the sheaf, and in the end you did not put the sheaf within its reach!"[7]

245. R. Jonah lectured at the entrance to Rabbi's house: "The Righteous One is concerned with the cause of the wretched" (Prov. 29:7). The Holy One, concerned about the dog's sustenance, which is scanty,[8] makes the food he eats remain in his stomach for three days.

R. Hamnuna said: It follows from the above that it is the right thing to throw raw meat to a dog. How much? R. Mari said: As much as the size of his ear—and [to discourage his hanging around you] the stick right after.[9]

246. Our masters taught: There are three kinds of men whose life is no life: those who are [overly] compassionate, those who are [too] prone to anger, and those who are [too] fastidious. R. Joseph said: The three qualities are in me.[10]

247. R. Yohanan said: The words "All the days of one prone to be afflicted are evil" (Prov. 29:7) refer to one who is [overly] compassionate. "And he who is pleased with himself hath a continual feast" (ibid.) refer to one who is hardhearted.[11]

Charity

248. R. Hama son of R. Hanina said: "After the Lord your God shall ye walk" (Deut. 13:5). But is it possible for a man to walk right behind the Presence? Has it not already been said, "The Lord thy God is a devouring fire" (Deut. 4:24)? Yes, but what the verse means is that you are to follow the ways of the Holy One. He clothed the naked: "The Lord God made for Adam and for his wife garments of skin, and clothed them" (Gen. 3:21). So should you clothe the naked. The Holy One visited the sick: "The Lord appeared unto him in the terebinths of Mamre" (Gen. 18:1). So should you visit the sick. The Holy One buried the dead: "He buried [Moses] in the valley" (Deut. 34:6). So should you bury the dead. The Holy One comforted mourners: "And it came to pass after the death of Abraham that God bestowed blessing upon Isaac his son" (Gen. 25:11). So should you comfort mourners.[12]

249. R. Assi said: Charity equals in importance all the other precepts combined.[13]

250. R. Eleazar said: Greater is he who does charity than he who offers all the sacrifices, for it is said, "To do charity and justice is more acceptable to the Lord than sacrifice" (Prov. 21:3).[14]

251. R. Eleazar said: When the Temple was standing, a man gave his shekel and thereby procured expiation.

1. B. Yoma 22b and En Yaakov, ad loc.
2. Eccles. R. 7:16, §1.
3. B. Shab 128b.
4. B. BM 85a; Gen. R. 33:3.
5. B. Git 62a.
6. P. Yev 15:3, 14d.
7. Exod. R. 31:7; Tanhuma, *Mishpatim*, §10.
8. Many half-wild dogs roamed the streets of cities in the Middle East.
9. B. Shab 155b.
10. B. Pes 113b.
11. B. BB 145b.
12. B. Sot 14a and En Yaakov, ad loc.
13. B. BB 9a.
14. B. Suk 49b.

But now that the Temple no longer stands, if charity is given, well and good; but if not, the [heathen] nations of the world will come and take it by force.[1]

252. "And you offer your compassion to the hungry" (Isa. 58:10)—to feed the hungry of Jacob, if you merit it; if you do not merit it, to feed the fat ones of Esau.

While asleep on the night of New Year's Day, R. Simeon ben Yohai saw in a dream that his sister's sons were ordered to pay [a tax of] six hundred denars to the [Roman] government. [To protect them], he insisted that they become administrators of charity.[2] When they asked R. Simeon, "Whose money are we to spend?" he replied, "Spend your own money, and keep a record. At the end of the year we will figure out the amount you spent, and pay you." They did so. But at the year's end they were denounced as dealing in silk without paying customs. So a senior official of the [Roman] government came to them and said, "Either you make a purple cloak for the ruler or be fined six hundred denars." [Since they could do neither], the official arrested them and confined them in prison.

When R. Simeon ben Yohai heard what happened, he went to them and asked, "How much did you spend?" They replied, "Here is the record." He proceeded to read it and found that they had spent six hundred denars less six. So he said, "Give me six denars, and I will get you out of prison." They said, "Just look: that senior official demands six hundred denars from us, and this one says, 'Give me six denars, and I will get you out of prison!' " R. Simeon persisted, "Give me six denars, and have no fear." So they took six denars and placed them in R. Simeon's hand, who then went and gave a bribe to the senior official to say nothing to the ruler, and got them out of prison. After they came out, they said to him, "Did you actually know that we would be arrested?" He said to them, "As you live, on the night of New Year's Day I was made aware that you would be fined six hundred denars." They reproached him: "If you had told us, we would have given six more denars to charity." He replied, "If I had told you, you would not have believed me."[3]

253. "The Lord will be thy confidence [*be-kislekha*]" (Prov. 3:26). R. Abba [construing the word *be-kislekha* as portmanteau of *be-kis*, "in the purse," and *lekha*, "to you"] said: The verse means that if you give charity out of your purse, the Holy One will protect you [*lekha*] from tributes, fines, poll taxes, and levies on crops.[4]

254. We have been taught that R. Judah said: Great is charity, for it brings near Israel's deliverance, as is said, "Keep ye justice, and practice charity, then My deliverance will be near to come" (Isa. 56:1).[5]

[1] B. BB 9a.

[2] He hoped that the merit thus gained would relieve them of the tax.

[3] Yalkut, *Be-har*, §665.

[4] P. Pe 1:1, 15b.

[5] B. BB 10a.

255. Our masters taught: It is related of King Monobaz[6] that during years of scarcity he spent all his own treasures and the treasures of his fathers on charity. His brothers and the other members of his family joined together in reproaching him: "Your fathers stored away treasures, adding to the treasures of their fathers, and you squander them!" He replied, "My fathers stored away for the world below, while I am storing away for the world above. My fathers stored away in a place where the hand of others can prevail, while I have stored away in a place where the hand of others cannot prevail. My fathers stored away something that produces no fruit, while I have stored away something that does produce fruit. My fathers stored away treasures of money, while I have stored away treasures of souls. My fathers stored away for others, while I have stored away for myself. My fathers stored away for this world, while I have stored away for the world-to-come."[7]

256. The sages said in the name of R. Eleazar: What is the meaning of "And he put on charity as a coat of mail" (Isa. 59:17)? It tells us that, just as in a coat of mail each and every scale joins the other to form one large piece of armor, so every small coin given to charity combines with the rest to form a large sum. Hence, R. Hanina said: The same lesson may be learned from "All of our acts of charity [together] are as a resplendent[8] garment" (Isa. 64:5). Just as in a garment each and every thread unites with the others to form a whole garment, so every small coin given to charity unites with the rest to form a large sum.[9]

257. R. Dostai son of R. Yannai preached: Pause and consider that the way of the Holy One is not like the way of flesh and blood. How does flesh and blood act? If a man brings a substantial present to the king, it may or may not be accepted; and even if it is accepted, it remains doubtful whether the man will be admitted into the king's presence. Not so with the Holy One. A man who gives but a small coin to a beggar is deemed worthy of being admitted to behold the Presence, as is written, "I shall behold Thy face through charity, and when I awake, shall be satisfied with thy likeness" (Ps. 17:15).

R. Eleazar used to give a small coin to a poor man and then recite the *Tefillah*, because, he said, it is written, "I, through charity, shall behold Thy face."[10]

258. "As for me, I shall behold Thy Presence through charity." Pause and consider how great is the power of charity! Merely because of the one small coin a man gives to the poor, he gets the right to behold the face of the Presence. In the usage of the world, however, a Roman noblewoman wishing to see the emperor and wait upon

[6] King of Adiabene (first century C.E.) who embraced Judaism. See Josephus *Antiquities* 20:2–4.

[7] B. BB 11a.

[8] The word *iddim* ("polluted") may be read *adayim* ("resplendence" or "resplendent"), as here. Moshe Alshekh, ad loc., takes it in this sense.

[9] B. BB 9b.

[10] B. BB 10a.

him must make a wreath befitting her status, and only then, because of the wreath with which she enters to crown the emperor, is she permitted to behold the emperor's face. But on account of the one small coin the man gives to a poor man, he is accorded the right to behold the face of the Presence.

Another comment: What made David single out the power of charity? To prove that even wicked men who had earned no merit other than their having given alms are privileged by this deed alone to have the glory of the Presence revealed to them.[1]

259. R. Akiva gave the following exposition, at times in the name of R. Ammi, and at other times in the name of R. Assi: What is meant by "Thus saith the Lord: Though they be in full strength and likewise many, even so shall they be sheared—that one shall cross" (Nah. 1:12)? When a man sees that his livelihood is barely sufficient, he should nevertheless give charity out of it, and all the more so if it is plentiful. What is meant by the words "Even so shall they be sheared—that one shall cross"? The sages in the school of R. Ishmael taught: Whoever shears off part of his possessions and dispenses it as charity is delivered from the punishment of Gehenna. A parable of two ewes, one shorn and the other unshorn, crossing a body of water: the shorn one gets across; the unshorn one does not.[2]

"And though I have afflicted thee" (Nah. 1:12). Mar Zutra said: Even a poor man who himself subsists on charity should give charity. "I will afflict thee no more" (Nah. 1:12). R. Joseph taught: [If he does that], he will never again experience the trials of poverty.[3]

260. R. Joshua ben Levi said: He who is in the habit of giving charity merits having sons who are masters of wisdom, masters of wealth, and masters of *Aggadah*.[4]

261. R. Joshua taught: More than what a householder does for the poor man, the poor man does for the householder, as is said, "The man's name whom I helped today is Boaz" (Ruth 2:19). Ruth said not, "Who helped me," but, "Whom I helped."[5]

262. We have been taught that R. Meir said: Should a disputant attempt to argue, "If your God loves the poor, why does He not maintain them?" say to him, "So that through the poor we may be saved from the punishment of Gehenna." This very question was actually put by the tyrant Rufus to R. Akiva: "If your God loves the poor, why does He not maintain them?" When R. Akiva replied, "So that we may be saved through them from the punishment of Gehenna," Rufus countered, "On the contrary, it is this which condemns you to Gehenna. I will illuminate the matter by the parable of a king of flesh and blood who became angry with his slave, put him in prison, and ordered that he be given neither food nor drink. A certain man went [to the prison] and gave him food and drink. When the king hears what the man did, would he not be angry with him? And you, after all, are no more than God's slaves, as is written, 'For unto Me the children of Israel are slaves' " (Lev. 25:55). R. Akiva replied, "I will illustrate the matter by another parable, the one of a king of flesh and blood who became angry with his son, put him in prison, and ordered that he be given neither food nor drink. Then a certain man went [to the prison] and gave him food and drink. When the king hears what the man did, would he not send him a present? [Remember that in another verse we are not called slaves]—we are called sons, as is written, 'Sons are ye to the Lord your God' " (Deut. 14:1). Rufus: "You are called both sons and slaves. When you obey the will of Him who is everywhere, you are called sons, but when you do not obey the will of Him who is everywhere, you are called slaves. At the present time, you do not obey the will of Him who is everywhere." R. Akiva replied, "Scripture says, 'Is it not to share thy bread with the hungry, and bring the poor that are cast out to thy house?' [Isa. 58:7]. When is one to bring the poor who are cast out into one's house? At the present time [when we are cast into exile]. Of such a time, we are told 'to share thy bread with the hungry.' "[6]

263. "He will take hold of My strength; he will make peace with Me" (Isa. 27:5). R. Judah son of R. Simeon said: The poor man sits and complains,[7] saying, "How am I different from So-and-so? Yet he sits in his own house, while I sit here; he sleeps in his own house on his own bed, while I sleep on the bare ground." So you come forward and give him something. Then, as you live, I will deem it as though you had made peace between him and Me.[8]

264. We have been taught that R. Eleazar son of R. Yose said: All acts of charity and loving-kindness that Israel performs in this world bring great peace and effective advocates between Israel and their Father in heaven. On the other hand, "for lack of charity and compassion, I have taken away from them, saith the Lord, My [advocates of] peace" (Jer. 16:5).[9]

265. "He who [at once] expects hand for hand is a bad man who will not go unpunished" (Prov. 11:21). R. Phinehas said: The verse spoke of a man who does a charitable act and expects the reward for it at once. Such a man, said R. Simeon, is like one who says [to God], "Here is the sack, the *sela* coin, and the *seah* measure. Get up at once and measure it out."[10]

266. R. Judah used to say: Ten strong things have been created in the world. The [rock of the] mountain is hard,

1. MTeh 17:14.
2. Her unshorn wool absorbs so much water that its weight pulls her under and drowns her.
3. B. Git 7b.
4. B. BB 9b.
5. Lev. R. 34:9.
6. B. BB 10a.
7. The poor man questions Providence.
8. Lev. R. 34:16; Yalkut, Isa., §496.
9. B. BB 10a.
10. Reward for charity is not a buying-and-selling transaction in the marketplace; it is an act of divine justice performed in God's own time. P. Sanh 10:1, 27d.

but iron cleaves it. Iron is hard, but fire softens it. Fire is powerful, but water quenches it. Water is heavy, but clouds bear it. Clouds are thick, but wind scatters them. Wind is strong, but a body resists it. The body is strong, but fear crushes it. Fear is powerful but wine banishes it. Wine is strong, but sleep works it off. Death is stronger than all, yet charity delivers from death, as is written, "Charity delivereth from death" (Prov. 10:2).[1]

267. We have been taught the following incident concerning Benjamin the Righteous, who was supervisor of the charity fund. One day, during a year of scarcity, a woman came to him and said, "Master, provide sustenance for me." He replied, "By the Temple worship, there is no money left in the charity fund." She said, "Master, if you do not provide for me, a woman and her seven children will perish." So he provided for her out of his own pocket. Sometime afterward, he became so ill that he was on the point of death. Then the ministering angels said to the Holy One, "Master of the universe, You have said that he who saves the life of one soul in Israel is considered as if he had saved the entire world. Shall Benjamin the Righteous, who saved the lives of a woman and her seven children, die after so few years of life?" His sentence of death was immediately torn up.

The sages taught that twenty-two years were added to his life.[2]

268. There is a story of a certain pious man who was in the habit of giving charity. Once, while traveling on a ship, a storm arose and the ship sank into the sea. R. Akiva, who saw what happened, came before the court to testify on behalf of the pious man's wife, so that she might be declared free to remarry. Before the time came for R. Akiva to stand up, the pious man entered and stationed himself before him. R. Akiva asked, "Are you not the one who was drowned at sea?" The pious man: "Yes, I am." R. Akiva: "And who brought you up from the sea?" The pious man: "The charity I dispensed—it brought me up from the sea." R. Akiva: "How do you know that?" The pious man: "When I went down to the nethermost depths, I heard a mighty roaring among the waves, one wave calling out to another, 'We must rush to bring this man up from the sea, because he dispensed charity all his days.' " At this, R. Akiva began to say, "Blessed be God, the God of Israel, who has chosen the words of Torah and the sayings of the sages, for the words of Torah and the sayings of the sages endure forever and ever and ever, as it says, 'Cast thy bread upon the waters, for thou shalt find it after many days' [Eccles. 11:1]. And it is also written, 'Charity delivereth from death' " (Prov. 10:2).[3]

269. R. Akiva had a daughter. When astrologers told him, "On the day she is to enter the bridal chamber, a snake will bite her, and she will die," he was extremely distressed about this prediction. On the day [of her marriage], she happened to be holding a long ornamental pin, which she stuck into the opening of a wall. By chance, the pin penetrated the eye of a snake [coiled behind the wall] and remained stuck there. The next morning, when she took out the pin, the dead snake was pulled out with it. Her father asked, "Did you do anything unusual?" She replied, "Last evening a poor man came to the door. Everybody was busy with the banquet, and no one heard him. So I took the gift you had given me and gave it to the poor man." "You have acted in a meritorious manner," he said to her. And then R. Akiva went out and lectured: "Charity delivereth from death" (Prov. 10:2)—not [merely] from an unnatural death, but from death, whatever the cause.[4]

270. R. Hanina had two disciples who went out to chop wood. When an astrologer saw them, he said, "These two will go out and not come back." As they went forth, an old man encountered them and said, "Give me alms—it is three days since I tasted anything." They had only one loaf of bread, but they broke off half of it and gave it to the old man. After he ate, he prayed in their behalf and then said to them, "Even as you have preserved my life this day, so may your life be preserved this day." The two disciples came back as safely as they had gone out. Some men who happened to hear what the astrologer had said asked him, "Did you not say, 'These two will go out and not come back'? We have here," they continued, "a liar, whose astrology is a lie." Nevertheless, they went off, made a search, and found a dead snake, half of it in one bundle of wood and the other half in another bundle.[5] They asked the disciples, "What good deed did you do today?" The disciples told them what had happened. The astrologer said, "What am I to do if the God of the Jews is willing to be seduced by half a loaf?"[6]

271. [One day] Samuel and Avlat, who happened to be sitting together, saw some people going to a meadow. Avlat said to Samuel, "That man is going but will not come back, for a snake will bite him and he will die." Samuel replied, "If he is a Jew, he will go and return." They were still seated there when the man who had gone returned. Avlat arose, removed the man's pack from his back, and found in it a snake cut in two. Samuel asked the man, "What unusual thing did you do?" He replied, "Every day we pool our bread and eat it. But today one of us had no bread, and he was too embarrassed [to ask for some]. So I decided: I shall undertake to [collect the bread and] put it in the basket. When I got to him, I pretended to take bread from him, so that he would not be embarrassed." Samuel said to the man, "You have done a meritorious deed." Then Samuel went out and expounded the words "Charity delivereth from death" (Prov. 10:2)—not merely from unnatural death, but from death, whatever the cause.[7]

---

1. B. BB 10a.
2. B. BB 11a.
3. ARN 3.

---

4. B. Shab 156b.
5. The snake was cut in two.
6. P. Shab 6:9, 8d.
7. B. Shab 156b.

272. "Abraham was old, well advanced in years" (Gen. 24:1). R. Meir happened to go to Mamla, where he saw that all the townspeople had black hair.[1] So he asked, "Are you perhaps of the family of Eli, who were told, 'All the increase of thy house shall die young men' (1 Sam. 2:33)?" They replied, "Master, pray for us." He said, "Go and busy yourselves with charity, and you will attain old age."

What is the proof? "The hoary head is a crown of glory" (Prov. 16:31). Where is a hoary head found? "It is found in the way of charity" (ibid.). From whom may one learn that this is so? From Abraham, of whom Scripture asserts [that he instructed his children] "to keep the way of the Lord, to practice charity, and do justice" (Gen. 18:19). And therefore he attained old age—"Abraham was old, well advanced in years."[2]

273. R. Eleazar of Bartota said: Give Him of that which is really His, for you and what is yours are His. Thus, we find David saying, "Since all things come from Thee, we have given Thee of Thine" (1 Chron. 29:14).[3]

274. It is related that, during a year of scarcity, when a certain pious man gave a denar to a poor man on the eve of New Year's Day, his wife scolded him. So he went and spent the night in the cemetery, where he overheard two spirits conversing with each other. One said to her companion, "My dear, come and let us roam about the world, and learn from behind the [heavenly] curtain what suffering is to come to the world." Her companion replied, "My dear, I cannot roam, buried as I am in a matting of reeds.[4] But you go, and whatever you hear, come back and tell me." So the one went off, roamed about, and returned. When her companion asked, "My dear, what have you heard from behind the [heavenly] curtain?" she replied, "I heard that whoever sows before the first rainfall will have his crop smitten by hail." So the [pious] man went and sowed before the second rainfall, with the result that everyone else's crop was smitten, but his was not.

The next year, he again went and spent the night in the cemetery, where he again overheard the two spirits conversing with each other. One said to her companion, "Come and let us roam about the world, and learn from behind the [heavenly] curtain what suffering is to come to the world." Her companion replied, "My dear, have I not already told you that I cannot roam because I am buried in a matting of reeds? But you go, and whatever you learn, come back and tell me." So the one went off, roamed about the world, and returned. When her companion asked, "My dear, what have you learned from behind the [heavenly] curtain?" she replied, "I learned that whoever sows before the second rainfall will have his crop smitten with blight." So the [pious] man went and sowed before the first rainfall, with the result that everyone else's crop was blighted, but his was not.

The man's wife asked, "How is it that last year everyone else's crop was smitten and yours was not, and this year everyone else's crop is blighted and yours is not?" So he related to her all these happenings.

The story goes that, a few days later, a quarrel broke out between the wife of that pious man and the mother of the young woman [buried in the cemetery]. The wife of the pious man said to the other, "Come, and I will show you that your daughter is buried in a matting of reeds." The next year, the [pious] man again went and spent the night in the cemetery, where he overheard the same two spirits conversing with each other. When the one said, "My dear, come and let us roam about the world, and learn from behind the [heavenly] curtain what suffering is to come to the world," her companion replied, "My dear, leave me alone. Our conversation is already bruited among the living."[5]

275. There is the story of how R. Eliezer, R. Joshua, and R. Akiva went to a suburb of Antioch to make a collection for [the support of] the sages. In that suburb there was one, Abba Yudan by name, who used to give charity with much goodwill, but by that time he had become impoverished. At the sight of our masters, his face turned the color of saffron, and he went home. His wife asked him, "Why is your face sickly?" He replied, "Our masters are here, and I do not know what to do." His wife, who was even more pious than he, said to him, "We have only one field left. Go, sell half of it, and give them [the proceeds]." He went and did so. At that, our masters prayed in his behalf and then said to him, "Abba Yudan, may He who is everywhere make up what you lack." After a while, he went out to plow the half-field that remained his. As he plowed, the ground opened up underneath him, so that his heifer dropped into the hole and its leg was broken. When he went down to bring it up, the Holy One provided light for his eyes, so that he noticed a buried treasure under his heifer. He said, "It was for my sake that my heifer's leg broke."

When our masters came back to the same place, they inquired after him, saying, "How is Abba Yudan doing?" People told them, "Abba Yudan—who can have the privilege of actually seeing his distinguished visage? He is Abba Yudan the possessor of servants, Abba Yudan possessor of goats, Abba Yudan possessor of donkeys, Abba Yudan possessor of camels, Abba Yudan possessor of oxen!" When Abba Yudan heard [of the masters' arrival], he went out to meet them. They asked him, "How is Abba Yudan doing?" He replied, "Your prayer has produced fruit, and fruit from fruit." They said, "As you live, even though others gave more than you did, we wrote you down at the head [of the list]." Then they took him and seated him with themselves, applying to him the verse "A man's gift maketh room for him, and bringeth him before great men" (Prov. 18:16).[6]

276. The story is told of a man who practiced charity so ardently that he sold his house and all he had, and spent

1. None was old enough to have it turn gray.
2. Gen. R. 59:1.
3. Avot 3:7.
4. And ashamed to show myself in such poor garb.
5. B. Ber 18b.
6. P. Hor 5:4, 48a; Lev. R. 5:4; Yalkut, *Re'eh,* §884.

the proceeds on charity. Once, on Hoshana Rabbah[1] his wife gave him ten small coins[2] and said to him, "Go to the market and buy something for your children." No sooner did he leave for the market than the collectors for charity happened to meet him and said, "Here comes the lord of charity! Contribute your share to this charity, for we want to buy a wedding dress for a certain orphan girl." He took the ten coins and gave them to the collectors. Ashamed to go home, he went to the synagogue, where he saw some of the etrogim that the children throw about on Hoshana Rabbah. So he took some, filled his sack with them, and set out on a voyage upon the Great [Mediterranean] Sea, until he reached the king's capital city. It so happened that when he arrived there, the king had a pain in his bowels and was told in a dream, "Eat of the etrogim that the Jews use during their prayers on Hoshana Rabbah, and you will be healed." So they searched all the ships and all the city, but found none. Finally, they came upon that man sitting on his sack and asked him, "Have you anything [for sale] in your sack?" He replied, "I am a poor man and have nothing to sell." But they examined his sack and, finding some etrogim, asked, "Where are these from?" He told them that they were some of those that the Jews use during their prayers on Hoshana Rabbah. So they picked up the sack and brought it to the king, who ate some of the etrogim and was cured. Then they emptied the sack and filled it with denars.[3]

277. There is the story of Bar Mayan, a customs collector, who died on the same day a certain pious man died. All the inhabitants of the city came and formed the funeral procession following the bier of the pious man, while immediately behind, only the customs collector's kinsmen followed his bier. It so happened that foes attacked both processions, and the mourners abandoned both biers and fled, except for one disciple who remained at his master's bier. After a while, when the inhabitants of the city returned to bury the pious man, they mistook the bier of the customs collector for his. Even though the disciple cried out in protest, they paid no attention to him. Thus it came about that only the customs collector's kinsmen buried the pious man.

The disciple kept grieving: "What sin has caused that pious man to be buried in such disgrace, and what merit caused that wicked man to be buried with such great honor?" His pious master appeared to him in a dream and said, "My son, do not grieve. On one occasion I heard disparaging remarks about disciples of the wise and did not protest, and that is why I was punished. As for the customs collector, on one occasion he prepared a banquet for the governor of the city; when the governor of the city did not appear, he distributed the food to the city's poor, and that is why he merited being buried with such honor. But come, and I will show you the honor that is mine in the Garden of Eden, and the punishment that is his in Gehenna." The disciple saw the pious man walking about in gardens and orchards planted by springs of water, and saw Bar Mayan's tongue slavering after the edge of a river in an effort to get to the water, which it could not reach.[4]

278. It is related of R. Tarfon that, although he was very wealthy he did not give many gifts to the poor. Once, R. Akiva met him and said to him, "Master, would you like me to purchase one or two hamlets for you?" He replied, "Yes," and forthwith handed R. Akiva four thousand gold denars. R. Akiva took the money and distributed it among poor disciples of the wise. Later on, R. Tarfon met him and asked, "Where are the hamlets you purchased for me?" R. Akiva took him by the hand and led him to the house of study where he brought over a child holding the book of Psalms in his hand and made him read in it until he came to the verse "He hath scattered abroad; he hath given to the needy; his righteousness endureth forever" (Ps. 112:9). Then R. Akiva said, "This is the hamlet I bought for you." At that, R. Tarfon stood up, kissed him, and said to him, "You are my teacher and my guide—my teacher in wisdom, my guide in proper conduct." And he gave him additional money to distribute.[5]

279. On one occasion, when the sages needed contributions to charity, they sent out R. Akiva and one of the sages with him. As the two were about to enter the house of Bar Buhin,[6] they heard a child's voice asking his father, "What shall we get you for today's meal?" The father replied, "Endives—not today's but yesterday's, because, being wilted, they sell at a low price."

So the sages decided to let Bar Buhin be, and went on. After everyone had contributed, the sages came back to Bar Buhin's house. When he asked them, "Why did you not come to me first, as has been your practice?" they replied, "We did come, and this is what we heard." He said, "What there is between me and the child, you know, but you do not know what there is between me and my Creator. Nevertheless, go and tell my wife that she is to give you a measure of denars." When they went and told her, she asked them, "What did he say to you—a full measure or a skimpy measure?" They replied, "He merely said, 'A measure.' " At this, she responded, "I will give you a full measure. If he said, 'A full measure,' I would have done just what he said. But since he did not say [a full measure], I will deduct the surplus from my marriage settlement." When her husband heard what she had done, he doubled her marriage settlement.[7]

280. When a poor man goes to a householder and says, "Give me something to eat," if the householder gives him something to eat, well and good; if not, "the rich and the poor meet together—but the maker of both is the Lord" (Prov. 22:2). He who made the householder rich will make him poor; He who made the poor man poor will make him rich.[8]

---

1. The seventh day of Tabernacles.
2. Enough to buy a loaf of bread or a *litra* of meat.
3. Lev. R. 37:2.
4. P. Hag 2:2, 77d; Rashi on B. Sanh 44b.
5. Ka 2.
6. So in Esther R. 2:3. In P. Pes: "Ben Mevi Yayin" ("Son of a Wine Buyer").
7. P. Pes 4:9, 31b–c.
8. B. Tem 16a.

281. "The rich and the poor meet together." The rich man may say to the poor man, "Why don't you go out and work at a job? Look at those thighs! Look at those shanks! Look what a belly! Look at that brawn!" The Holy One will then say to the rich man, "Is it not enough for you that you gave him nothing of yours! Must you also cast a grudging eye on what I gave him?"[1]

282. "Rob not the impoverished because he is impoverished" (Prov. 22:22). Our masters said: What is Scripture talking about? If he is impoverished, how can he be robbed? Scripture must be speaking here of gifts to the poor that one is obliged by Torah to give, namely, gleanings, forgotten sheaves, corners of the field, and the poor man's tithe.[2] The Holy One thus admonishes that one is not to rob the poor of the gifts due them. "Because he is impoverished"—sufficient for him is his poverty. It is not enough for the rich man that he lives in comfort while the poor man is in distress; must he also rob the poor of what the Holy One has allotted to him?[3]

283. "He that hath an evil eye hasteneth after riches, and knoweth not that want shall come upon him" (Prov. 28:22). The story is told of a certain man who was scrupulous about paying his tithes. He had a field that yielded a thousand measures, from which he would pay a hundred measures in tithes; from the remainder, he provided for himself and the members of his household. When he was about to die, he called his son and said to him, "My son, give heed to this field, which produces so-and-so many measures, and from which I have been paying so-and-so many measures in tithes. From this field, I sustained myself all my life."

The first year the son sowed the field, it produced a thousand measures, from which he gave a hundred measures in tithes. The second year, however, the evil eye entered into him, and he reduced his tithes by ten. At that, the field in turn produced a hundred measures less. The same thing happened the third, fourth, fifth, [and subsequent] years, until finally the field produced only [one hundred measures], the amount of the original tithe. When his kinsmen observed what had happened, they put on white [festive] undergarments and wrapped themselves in white [festive] outergarments, and went to his house. He asked, "What! Have you come to gloat over me?" They replied, "God's mercy, no! We came only to rejoice with you. In the past, you were the owner and the Holy One was the priest. Now you have become the priest,[4] and the Holy One is the owner."[5]

284. R. Hiyya said to his wife, "When a poor man comes, hurry to offer him bread, so that others may hurry to offer [bread] to your children." She asked, "Are you cursing them by wishing them to be poor?" R. Hiyya replied, "The verse 'For in return (*bi-gelal*) for this thing" (Deut. 15:10)—so it is taught in the school of R. Ishmael—means "a wheel that keeps turning (*galgal*) around and around in the world."[6]

285. R. Joshua ben Korhah said: Anyone who shuts his eye from the obligation of charity is like one who worships idols.[7]

286. "And it came to pass in the days when judges were judged that there was a famine in the Land. And a certain man of Bethlehem . . . went" (Ruth 1:1). Woe to the generation whose judges must be judged. Elimelech was one of the notables of his province and one of the leaders of his generation. But when the years of famine came, he said, "Now all of Israel will come knocking at my door, one with a large basket and another with a small basket [begging for food]." What did he do? He got up and ran away from them.[8]

287. Take care that the doors of your house are not shut when you sit down to eat and drink.[9]

288. It is related that a certain [widow] lived in the vicinity of a landowner, and when her two sons went into his field to glean, he refused them permission. Their mother kept saying, "When my sons return from the field, perhaps I will find something to eat in their hands"; at the same time, the sons were saying, "When shall we return to our mother? Perhaps she has gotten her hands on something to eat." In the end, she got nothing to eat from them, and they got no food with her. So they put their heads between their mother's knees, and all three died the same day. Thereupon the Holy One said to such landowners, "You exact from them nothing less than their lives; as surely as you live, I will exact your lives from you." For it is stated, "Rob not the weak, because he is weak, neither crush the poor in the gate; for the Lord will plead their cause, and despoil of life those that despoil them" (Prov. 22:22).[10]

289. It is related of Nahum of Gamzo[11] that he was blind in both eyes, stumped in both hands, and crippled in both legs; his entire body was covered with boils, and the legs of his bed stood in four basins of water to prevent ants

1. Lev. R. 34:7.
2. Lev. 19:9–10; Deut. 24:19 and 14:28ff.
3. Num. R. 5:2.
4. The point is that the son, who at the end gets only one hundred measures from the field, is getting from it only the amount of the original tithe. And since this amount is what the priest got, the relatives sarcastically designate him a "priest." See Num. 5:10 and Rashi, ad loc.
5. Exod. R. 31:17; Yalkut, Prov., §962.
6. The poor become rich, and the rich become poor.
7. B. Ket 68a.
8. B. Ket 68a. In the source, the idea that not helping a needy person and subversion lead to the worship of idols is described as "belial" [*beli-yaal*], which means "one who casts off [God's] yoke." The man of means should know that what he has came from God, yet he refuses to share what has been entrusted to him.
9. Ruth R. 1:4; Yalkut, Ruth, §598.
10. ARN 38.
11. Gimzo is mentioned in 2 Chron. 28:18 as the name of a place. Here it is a surname or epithet, the combination of *gam* (too) and *zo* ("this")—allegedly derived from Nahum's customary remark when misfortune overtook him: "This, too, is for good."

from crawling all over him. Once, when his bed was in a house about to collapse, his disciples proposed to remove his bed first and then clear the furniture out of the house. But he said to them, "My children, remove the furniture first and then my bed, for you may be sure that, so long as I am in the house, it will not collapse." So they cleared out the furniture first and then removed his bed, and in the next moment the house collapsed. His disciples asked, "Master, since you are so perfectly righteous, why has all this [affliction] come upon you?" He replied, "My children, I invoked it upon myself. Once, I was journeying to my father-in-law's house and had with me three heavily laden asses, one with food, another with drink, and the third with all kinds of delicacies. A poor man appeared on the road and stopped in front of me, saying, 'Master, give me something to sustain me.' I replied, 'Wait until I unload the ass.' I had barely managed to unload the ass when the man's soul departed. I then threw myself over him and cried out, 'Let these eyes of mine, which had no pity upon your eyes, be blinded; let these hands of mine, which had no pity upon your hands, be stumped; let these legs of mine, which had no pity upon your legs, be crippled!' Nor could my conscience rest until I added, 'Let my whole body be covered with boils.' " His pupils exclaimed, "Woe unto us that we see you in such a state!" Nahum replied, "Woe indeed, but unto me if you had not seen me in such a state!"[1]

290. "It is for Saul, and for his bloody house, because he put to death the Gibeonites" (1 Sam. 21:1). But where [in Scripture] do we find that Saul put to death the Gibeonites? [He did not.] However, because he put to the sword Nob, the city of priests, who provided the Gibeonites with water and sustenance, Scripture deems it for him as though he had actually put them to death.[2]

291. We have been taught that Rabban Yohanan ben Zakkai asked his disciples: What is meant by the verse, "Charity exalted the nation, but loving-kindness is a sin for [other] peoples" (Prov. 14:34)? R. Eliezer spoke up and said: "Charity exalteth the nation," that is, Israel, concerning which it is said, "Who is like Thy people, like Israel, a nation one in the earth" (2 Sam. 7:23); "but loving-kindness is a sin for [other] peoples"—even all the acts of charity and loving-kindness that [heathen] peoples of the world perform are deemed a sin for them, because they perform such acts only to enhance their greatness. R. Joshua spoke up and said: "Charity exalteth the nation," that is, Israel; "but loving-kindness is a sin for [other] peoples"—even all the acts of charity and loving-kindness that [heathen] peoples of the world perform are deemed a sin for them, because they perform such acts only to boast of them. Rabban Gamaliel said: We still have to hear the interpretation of the Modiite. R. Eleazar the Modiite said: "Charity exalteth the nation," that is, Israel; "but loving-kindness is a sin for [other] peoples"—even acts of charity and loving-kindness that [heathen] peoples of the world perform are deemed a sin for them, because they perform such acts only to taunt and reproach us [for our failings].[3] R. Nehunia ben ha-Kanah spoke up and read the verse "Charity exalteth the nation, for it is deemed loving-kindness for Israel, but sin for the [heathen] peoples." At that, Rabban Yohanan ben Zakkai said to his disciples: I find the interpretation of R. Nehunia ben ha-Kanah more appealing than mine or yours, because he associates the words "charity" and "loving-kindness" in the verse with Israel, and the word "sin" with the [heathen] peoples of the world.

We have been taught that Rabban Yohanan ben Zakkai interpreted the verse as meaning: Even as a sin offering makes expiation for Israel, so an act of charity [and loving-kindness] makes expiation for [heathen] peoples of the world.[4]

The Ways of Charity

292. Among those asked to give charity are four types: he who wishes to give but does not wish others to give—he is grudging toward others; he who wishes others to give but is himself unwilling to give—he is grudging of his own; he who willingly gives and wishes others to give—the pious man; he who does not give and wishes others not to give—the wicked man.[5]

293. "Happy is he that considereth the poor" (Ps. 41:2): Consider carefully how to benefit him. When R. Jonah saw a man of good family who had lost his money and was ashamed to accept charity, he would go and say to him, "I have heard that an inheritance has come your way in a city across the sea. So here is an article of some value. [Sell it, and use the proceeds.] When you are more affluent, you will repay me." As soon as the man took it, R. Jonah would say, "It's yours as a gift."[6]

294. R. Isaac said: He who gives a small coin to a poor man receives six blessings, and he who speaks to him words of cheer receives eleven blessings.[7]

295. "If thou draw out thy soul to the hungry" (Isa. 58:10). This means, said R. Levi, if you have nothing to give him, comfort him with words. Say to him, "My soul goes out to you, because I have nothing else to give you."[8]

296. When R. Yannai saw a certain man giving a coin to a poor man in front of everyone, he said: It would have been better not to have given it to him than to have given it and put him to shame.[9]

---

1. B. Ta 21a.
2. B. BK 119a.
3. As Nebuzaradan did when he released Jeremiah from his fetters. See Jer. 40:1–4.
4. B. BB 10b.
5. Avot 5:16.
6. Lev. R. 34:1; P. Pe 8:8, 21b.
7. B. BB 9b.
8. Lev. R. 34:15.
9. B. Hag 5b; Eccles. R. 12:14, §1.

297. Which kind of charity saves a man from [an unnatural] death? Charity given without knowing to whom it is given, and received without knowing from whom it is received.[1]

298. R. Eliezer said: A man who gives charity in secret is greater than Moses our teacher. For Moses our teacher, according to Scripture, admitted, "I was afraid of the Anger and the Wrath" (Deut. 9:19); but of one who gives charity in secret, Scripture declares, "A gift in secret subdues Anger" (Prov. 21:14).[2]

299. In Mar Ukba's neighborhood there was a poor man into whose door socket Mar Ukba used to place [secretly] four *zuz* every day. Once the poor man said, "I will go and see who does this kindness for me." It so happened that on that day Mar Ukba stayed late at the house of study, and his wife accompanied him [on his way home]. As soon as the poor man saw the two bending down over the door, he went out after them. They fled from him and entered a furnace from which the fire had just been swept. Mar Ukba's feet were scorched [but not his wife's], and so she said to him, "Place your feet on mine." As he was upset [because a miracle was wrought for her and not for him], she said to him, "I am usually at home and my benefactions to the poor are direct." But why did the two flee into a furnace? Because the sages said: It is better that a man throw himself into a fiery furnace than publicly put his neighbor to shame.[3]

300. Abba the Cupper used to receive daily greetings from the academy on high. What was the special merit of Abba the Cupper? When he let blood, he had a discreet place outside [his office] where the client would put in a few coins. Whoever had money would put it there; but he who had none would sit before Abba the Cupper without feeling embarrassed. Whenever a disciple of the wise came to consult him, he would accept no fee from him, and after the disciple stood up to leave, Abba would give him a few coins and say to him, "Go and get yourself well."

One day, Abbaye sent two disciples of the wise to Abba the Cupper in order to test him. They came to his house, and he had them sit down, gave them food and drink, and in the evening spread woolen mattresses for them [to sleep on]. In the morning, the two disciples of the wise rolled up the mattresses and brought them to the marketplace. When Abba the Cupper came to the marketplace and found the two, they said to him, "Sir, will you estimate how much they are worth?" He replied, "So-and-so much." The two: "Surely they are worth more?" Abba: "This is what I paid for some like them." Then they said to him, "They are yours—we took them away from you."

Then they asked him, "Please tell us what you supposed we were up to?" He replied, "I said to myself: Perhaps you needed money to redeem captives and were too embarrassed to say so to me." The two: "Now, sir, take back what is yours." Abba: "From the moment I missed them, I put them out of my mind by considering them assigned to charity."[4]

301. R. Isaac said: What is the meaning of the verse "He that pursueth charity and compassion, findeth life, charity, and honor" (Prov. 21:21)? That because a man pursues charity, he will find charity? No. Rather, the verse teaches you that when a man pursues every opportunity to give charity, the Holy One will provide him with money to use for it. R. Nahman bar Isaac added: The Holy One will provide for him persons who are fit recipients of charity, so that he may be rewarded for assisting them."[5]

302. Rabbah said: What is the meaning of the verse "[Forgive not their iniquity . . .]. Let them be made to stumble before Thee, in the time of Thine anger deal Thou with them" (Jer. 18:23)? Jeremiah said to the Holy One: Master of the universe, even when the [people of Anathoth] restrain their evil impulse and seek to give charity to impress You, cause them to stumble through men who are not fit recipients, so that they may receive no reward for assisting them.[6]

303. R. Eleazar said: He who gives his bread to one who has no understanding [of Torah] will be assailed by suffering.[7]

304. We have been taught that when a poor man says, "Provide me with clothes," he should be investigated. When he says, "Feed me," he should not be investigated.[8]

305. During years of scarcity, Rabbi [Judah I, the Patriarch] opened storehouses of victuals, proclaiming: Let those who are masters of Scripture, masters of Mishnah, masters of Gemara, masters of *Halakhah*, or masters of *Aggadah* enter. But those who are ignorant may not. Jonathan ben Amram pushed his way up, entered, and said to him, "Master, give me food." [Not recognizing him], Rabbi asked him, "My son, have you studied Scripture?" He replied, "No." "Have you studied Mishnah?" "No." "If not, how can I give you food?" Jonathan: "Then provide me with food as a dog is provided, provide me as a raven is provided."[9] So he gave him some food. After he went away, Rabbi's conscience troubled him, and he said: Woe is me that I have given bread to a man without learning! R. Simeon bar Rabbi ventured to say to him: Perhaps it was your disciple Jonathan ben Amram, who all his life refused to derive any benefit from the honor paid to Torah.

1. B. BB 10a.
2. B. BB 9b.
3. B. Ket 67b.
4. B. Ta 21b–22a and En Yaakov, ad loc.
5. B. BB 9b.
6. Ibid.
7. B. Sanh 92a.
8. But should be fed immediately—he might starve to death during the investigation. B. BB 9a.
9. Jonathan takes the verse "He giveth to the beast his food, to the young ravens which cry" (Ps. 147:9) to mean: "As God feeds these, so you feed me."

Upon inquiry, it was found to be so. At that, Rabbi said, "Let everyone enter."[1]

306. R. Abba used to wrap money in his scholar's turban, sling it on his back [so as not to see who took the money], and, disregarding the possibility of imposters among them, make himself available to the poor.

On every Sabbath eve, R. Hanina used to send regularly four *zuz* to a certain poor man. One day, he sent that sum through his wife. She came back and told him, "He does not need it." R. Hanina asked her, "What did you see?" "I heard that he was asked, 'Will you dine off a cloth of silver or one of gold?' " At this, R. Hanina remarked: Of such, R. Eleazar said, "Come, let us be grateful to imposters. But for them, we would have been sinning every day, for, according to Scripture, 'If [the genuinely poor man] cry unto the Lord against thee, it will be sin in thee' " (Deut. 15:9).[2]

307. R. Yohanan and Resh Lakish went down to bathe in the public baths of Tiberias. When a poor man met them and said to them, "Earn merit by giving me something," they replied, "After we come out, we shall earn merit through you." When they did come out, they found him dead. So they said, "Since we did not earn merit by attending to him in his life, let us attend to him in his death." As they were washing his corpse, they found a bag containing six hundred denars suspended from his neck. So [relieved of the feelings of guilt] they said, "Blessed be He who has chosen the sages and even their [hasty] words. Did not R. Abbahu state in the name of R. Eliezer, 'We ought to be grateful to imposters, since but for imposters among the poor, if anyone begged alms from a person and that person refused, he would immediately be punished.'?"[3]

308. Our masters taught: "Sufficient for his need" (Deut. 15:8) implies that you are enjoined to maintain him, but you are not enjoined to make him rich; "in that which he wanteth" (ibid.) includes even a horse to ride on and a slave to run before him.

It is related about Hillel the Elder that, for a certain poor man who was of a good family, he bought a horse to ride on and a slave to run before him. When on one occasion he could not find a slave to run before the man, he himself ran before him a distance of three *mil*.[4]

309. A poor man came [for sustenance] before R. Nehemiah, who asked, "What do your usual meals consist of?" He answered, "Fat meat and aged wine [from wealthy benefactors]." R. Nehemiah: "Will you join me and make do with a dish of lentils?" The poor man made do with lentils at R. Nehemiah's table, and then died. R. Nehemiah said, "Alas for this man: Nehemiah killed him!"

On the contrary, he should have said, "Alas for Nehemiah: he killed this man!"

On the other hand, [the man himself was to blame]—he should not have coddled himself to such an extent.[5]

310. A poor man once came [for maintenance] before Rava, who asked, "What do your usual meals consist of?" "Fat chicken and aged wine." Rava: "Do you not consider the burden of [such fare on] the community?" The poor man: "Do I eat what's theirs? I eat [the food] of the Holy One. For we are taught: 'The eyes of all wait for Thee, and Thou givest each one food in his season' [Ps. 145:15]—not 'in their season' but 'in his season.' Hence, the Holy One provides food for every person in accordance with his own habits." Just then Rava's sister, who had not seen him for thirteen years, arrived and brought him a fat chicken and aged wine. "What a remarkable coincidence!" Rava exclaimed, and then said to the poor man, "I defer to your request—come and eat."[6]

311. Mar Ukba had in his neighborhood a poor man to whom he regularly sent four hundred *zuz* on the eve of every Day of Atonement. Once he sent them through his son. The son came back and said, "He does not need it." Mar Ukba: "What have you seen [that makes you think so]?" The son: "I saw that [at his dinner] he was served aged wine." Mar Ukba: "So he is that delicate?" And he doubled the amount and sent it back to the poor man.

When Mar Ukba was about to die he requested, "Bring me my charity accounts." Finding there a balance of seven thousand denars, he exclaimed, "The provisions are scanty and the road long," and there and then distributed half of his wealth [to the poor].

But how could he do such a thing? Had not R. Ilai stated, "In Usha, it was ordained that if a man wishes to spend liberally on charity, he may spend no more than one-fifth of his means"? Yes, but this ordinance applies only to a living person, who might have to fall back on his own means if reduced to poverty, but there is no need to fear such a thing after death.[7]

312. Our masters taught: There is a story that every day the people of Upper Galilee bought a pound of meat for a poor member of a good family in the north.[8]

313. This is what R. Tanhum son of R. Hiyya used to do: if he was instructed [by his wife] to buy one pound of meat, he would buy two pounds, one for his household and one for the poor; or two bunches of vegetables, one for his household and one for the poor.[9]

314. On one occasion, Hillel the Elder had a meal prepared for a certain man. In the meantime, a poor man came by, stood at his doorway, and said, "I am to marry today, and I have no provisions whatsoever." At that, Hillel's wife took the entire meal and [without telling her

1. B. BB 8a and En Yaakov, ad loc.
2. B. Ket 67b–68a.
3. Lev. R. 34:10; P. Pe 5:5, 21b.
4. B. Ket 67b.
5. Ibid.
6. Ibid.
7. Ibid.
8. Ibid.
9. Lev. R. 34:5; Eccles. R. 7:14, §2.

husband] gave it to the poor man. Then she kneaded fresh dough, cooked another pot of stew, and came and set it before Hillel and his guest [who were waiting to eat]. Hillel asked, "My dear, why did you not bring it sooner?" She told him what happened. He said, "My dear, the truth is, I did not mean to judge you on the scale of guilt, but rather on the scale of merit, because everything you have done, you have always done for the sake of Heaven."[1]

315. We have been taught that R. Simeon said: For four purposes the Torah ordered *peah* [the corner crop, the poor man's portion of the harvest] to be left at the end of one's field: [as a precaution] against robbing the poor, against wasting [the time of] the poor, against suspicion, and against cheaters. [As a precaution] against robbing the poor: lest the owner, spotting a free moment [when the poor are not present], say to his own poor kinsman, "Right here [in the middle of the field] is *peah* for you." Against wasting [the time of] the poor: so that the poor should not have to sit and be on the lookout for the time when the owner will leave *peah* [in the corner of his field]. Against suspicion: So that passersby should not say, "A curse upon the man who left no *peah* in his field." And as a precaution against cheaters [who might leave no portion at all for the poor].[2]

316. "Thou shalt surely open [thy hand to thy brother, to thy poor]" (Deut. 15:8). From these words it would follow that charity is to be given only to the poor of your city. What is the proof that it is also to be given to the poor of another city? The word "surely," implying: wherever the poor may be.

"Giving[3] thou shalt give"[4] (Deut. 15:10)—the repetition of the verb seems to imply a large sum. What is the proof that the verse also implies a small sum? From the same repetition, implying: giving whatever the gift may be.

"Furnishing thou shalt furnish him liberally" (Deut. 15:14) seems to imply that only if the house has been blessed by a slave's presence[5] is he to be furnished with a gift. What is the proof that he is to be so furnished even if the house has not been blessed because of him? The same repetition implies furnishing under all circumstances.

"Lending thou shalt lend to him" (Deut. 15:8) seems to imply that only if the poor man has nothing and yet does not wish to be maintained at your expense, Scripture says, "Give him by way of a loan." What is the proof that even if the poor has some means, but does not wish to maintain himself [at his own expense], you are to lend to him? From the same repetition, implying: under all circumstances.[6]

317. Our masters taught: If a man has no means and does not wish to be maintained [at public expense], his necessities are first to be given to him as a loan and immediately thereafter presented to him as a gift. Such is the opinion of R. Meir. But R. Simeon asserted: If he has the means but does not wish to maintain himself [at his own expense], there is no need to deal with him. If he has no means but does not wish to be maintained [at public expense], he is to be told, "Bring a pledge, and you will receive a loan on it," so that his spirits will be raised.[7]

318. If a man has fifty *zuz* and trades with them, he may not take of the [gleanings, forgotten sheaves, corners of fields, or poor man's tithe]. He who has no need to take such gifts but nevertheless takes them will not depart this world before he becomes dependent on his fellow men. Whereas he who needs to accept [charity] but does not do so will not die in his old age before becoming able to support others out of what he has. Of such a man, it is written, "Blessed is the man that trusteth in the Lord, and whose trust the Lord is" (Jer. 17:7). And if one is neither lame, nor blind, nor halt, but pretends to be like one of them, he will not die in his old age before he actually becomes one of them, as is said, "He that searcheth for evil, it shall come unto him" (Prov. 11:27).[8]

319. Our masters taught: He who pretends that he is blind or makes believe that his belly is distended [from hunger] or that he is humpbacked will not depart this world until he falls victim to such a condition. He who receives charity even though he does not need it will not depart this world until he comes to real need of it.[9]

320. If a beggar [on his own] goes from door to door, there is no need to respond to him.

A certain poor man who used to go from door to door appeared before R. Papa, who refused him [money]. So R. Samma son of R. Yeva said to R. Papa, "If you, sir, will not respond to him, and no one else will respond to him, is he to die of hunger?"

"But, [R. Papa replied], we have been taught, 'If a poor man goes from door to door, there is no need to respond to him'!"

R. Samma said, "There is no need to respond to him with a large gift, but one should respond to him with a small gift."[10]

321. R. Joseph taught: "If thou lend money to any of My people" (Exod. 22:24) implies that, as between one

1. DER 6.
2. B. Shab 23a–b.
3. The doubling of the verb, translated in JV by "surely," is understood as making the command emphatic. But the rabbinic commentator takes such doubling to require different kinds of giving and, subsequently, to require "furnishing liberally" and "lending" under varying circumstances.
4. The reference is to money lent before the Year of Release (sabbatical year).
5. A contingency that seems to be implied in the verse's conclusion: "As the Lord thy God blessed thee, thou shalt give unto him."
6. B. BM 31b.
7. Being addressed thus, he will be induced to take a loan even though he has nothing of value to pledge. B. Ket 67b.
8. Pe 8:9; P. Pe 8:5, 21b.
9. B. Ket 68a.
10. B. BB 9a.

"of My people" and a heathen, the one "of My people" has precedence. "Even to the poor" (ibid.) implies that, between a poor man and a rich man, the poor man has precedence. "With thee" (ibid.) implies that, between the poor who are your kin and the poor of your city, the poor who are your kin have precedence, and between the poor of your city and the poor of another city, the poor of your city have precedence.[1]

322. For the sake of peace, the poor of the heathens should not be prevented from gathering gleanings, forgotten sheaves, and corners of the field.

Our masters taught: For the sake of peace, the poor of the heathens should be supported as we support the poor of Israel, the sick of the heathens should be visited as we visit the sick of Israel, and the dead of the heathens should be buried as we bury the dead of Israel.[2]

Collectors for Charity

323. The verse "They who provide charity for the many are like the stars forever and ever" (Dan 12:3) refers to collectors for charity.[3]

324. R. Eleazar said: He who causes others to do good is greater than he who himself does good, for it is said, "He who causes the giving of charity confers peace" (Isa. 32:17).[4]

325. R. Nahman said in the name of Rabbah bar Abbahu: Even on Sabbath eve one may insist upon receiving a pledge[5] in lieu of a contribution to charity.

Rava coerced R. Nathan bar Ammi and got him to give four hundred *zuz* to charity.[6]

326. Collectors for charity may accept small contributions from women, but not large ones.

Once, when Ravina happened to be in the city of Mahoza, the women of Mahoza came and brought him gold chains and bracelets, which he accepted from them [as charity]. When Rabbah Tosfaah said to him, "But we have been taught that collectors for charity may accept only small contributions from women, and not large ones," he replied, "Such things are considered small contributions by the people of Mahoza."[7]

327. Our masters taught: A fund for charity must be collected jointly by two persons and distributed by three. It is collected by two, because any office of authority over the community must be held by two persons. The fund must be distributed by three persons, as is the rule with lawsuits involving money [which must be tried by a court of three].[8]

328. Our masters taught: Collectors for charity are not allowed to separate from each other [when collecting] though one may collect at the gate while another collects at a shop [in the same courtyard.].

So, too, if one of them finds money in the street, he may not put it in his purse[9] but only in the charity bag, and then take it out when he comes home.

So, too, if one of the collectors has a debtor repay him a *maneh* in the marketplace, he may not put it in his purse but only in the charity bag, and then take it out when he comes home.

Our masters taught: If collectors have money left but no poor people to distribute it to, they may change the small coins[10] into large ones with other persons, but not with their own money. Stewards of the soup kitchen [who have food left over but] no poor to distribute it to may sell the food to others but not to themselves.[11]

Money collected for charity must be counted not two coins at a time, but one at a time.[12]

329. Abbaye said: At first my master [Rabbah] used to keep two purses, one for the poor of the city and one for the poor from elsewhere. But when he heard what Samuel had said to R. Tahalifa bar Avdimi—namely, "Make one purse only, and stipulate [with the townspeople that it is to be used for both kinds of poor]"—he too kept only one purse and made such a stipulation.

R. Ashi said: I do not need to make such a stipulation, since whoever comes to give charity leaves the matter to my judgment, so that I may give it to whom I wish.[13]

330. Our masters taught: The collectors for charity are not required to provide an account of the moneys given them for charity, nor the treasurers of the Sanctuary for moneys given them for sacred purposes. Even though there is no proof for this rule, there is an intimation in the verse "Moreover they reckoned not with the men, into whose hands they delivered the money . . .; for they dealt faithfully" (2 Kings 12:16).

R. Eleazar said: Even if a man has in his house a steward whom he can trust, he should still keep the money in bags and count [the amount he gives the steward] as is said, "They would put the money into bags and count it. . . . Then they would deliver the money that was weighed out" (2 Kings 12:11–12).[14]

1. B. BM 71a.
2. B. Git 61a.
3. B. BB 8b.
4. B. BB 9a.
5. When the one approached may plead that he is too busy with preparations for the Sabbath.
6. Ordinarily, charity is voluntary. B. BB 8b.
7. They were prosperous. B. BK 119a.
8. B. BB 8b.
9. So that people should not suspect him of appropriating money that belongs to the poor.
10. Small coins are apt to tarnish.
11. So that people will not think they gave small portions to the poor in order to dispose of what is left for their own purposes.
12. Lest people say that the collectors take two coins and count only one. B. BB 8b.
13. B. BB 8b–9a.
14. B. BB 9a.

331. R. Yose said: May my portion be with those who collect charity, and not with those who distribute it.[1]

332. All whose forebears are held to have been eligible to be public officers and collectors for charity are permitted to marry into the priesthood without having their ancestry investigated.[2]

Bringing Up Orphans and Redeeming Captives

333. "He who does charity at all times" (Ps. 106:3) is he, said R. Samuel bar Nahmani, who brings up an orphaned boy or girl in his house and marries him or her off.[3]

334. He who brings up an orphan in his house, Scripture deems it for him as though he had begot him.[4]

335. Our masters taught: If an orphaned boy and an orphaned girl apply for maintenance, the orphaned girl is to be maintained first, and then the orphaned boy, because a man can go begging from door to door, but a woman cannot.

If an orphaned boy and an orphaned girl both apply for marriage grants, the orphaned girl is to be helped to marry first, and then the orphaned boy, because the shame of a woman [without a husband] is greater than the shame of a man [without a wife].[5]

336. Our masters taught: If an orphan applies for assistance to marry, a house must be rented for him and a bed laid out for him, as well as all the household effects he would need, and then he is to be wed to his bride, as is said, "Sufficient for his need whatever he needed" (Deut. 15:8).[6]

337. The sages said in the name of Rav: Better to be under Ishmael than under Edom; under Edom and not under Parsee priests; under Parsee priests and not under a disciple of the wise; under a disciple of the wise and not under an orphan or a widow.[7]

338. Orphans [who are minors] are not subject to the law of atonement.[8]

Orphans who are minors cannot legally renounce [their possessions].[9]

339. Samuel's father was entrusted with some money belonging to orphans. When he died, Samuel was not with his father, and the orphans dubbed Samuel "Son of the Orphans' Money Eater." So he went to the cemetery to locate his father, whom he asked, "Where is the orphans' money?" The father replied, "You will find it in the rack of millstones. The money on the upper and lower millstones is ours; that on the middle one is the orphans'." Samuel: "Why did you put the orphans' money on the middle millstone?" He replied, "So that if thieves got at it [from the top], ours would be stolen; and if the earth eroded it [from below], ours would be eroded."[10]

340. Our masters taught: Four pittances never contain any sign auspicious of blessing: the wage of Torah scribes, the wage of interpreters [in the academy], the profits from orphans' money [kept in trust], and the profits from trade with countries across the sea.[11]

341. R. Anan said in the name of Samuel: Orphans' money may be lent out on interest. R. Nahman differed sharply: Just because they are orphans, am I to stuff their purses with forbidden money? Orphans who live on what is not really theirs might as well follow the parents who left them![12]

342. Whenever collectors for charity caught sight of R. Eleazar of Bartota, they would hide themselves from him, because he was in the habit of giving them all he had. One day, as he was going to the marketplace to buy a wedding outfit for his daughter, the collectors for charity caught sight of him and were about to hide themselves from him. But he ran after them, saying, "I adjure you, tell me for what purpose you are collecting?" They replied, "For the wedding outfit of an orphaned boy and an orphaned girl." R. Eleazar: "By the [Temple] worship, these two have precedence over my own daughter," and he took all he had in his hand and gave it to them. One *zuz*, however, remained with him. With it, he bought some wheat, which he carried up and deposited in the granary. When his wife returned home, she asked her daughter, "What did your father bring you?" She replied, "All that he brought, he carried up into the granary." When the wife went up to open the door of the granary, she found that it was so full of wheat that the grains were forced into the door sockets, and consequently, because of the overflow of wheat, the door could not be opened. The daughter then went to the house of study and said to her father, "Come and see what your Friend has done for you!" At that, he said to her, "By the [Temple] worship, the wheat shall be sacred property, and your share in it shall be the same as that of any other poor person in Israel."[13]

343. Ifra Hormiz, King Shapur's mother, sent a purse of denars to R. Joseph, instructing him that the money be used for a most important precept. R. Joseph tried to figure out what she meant by "a most important precept." Abbaye

1. The temptation to practice favoritism is too great. B. Shab 118b.
2. B. Kid 76a.
3. B. Ket 50a.
4. B. Sanh 19b.
5. B. Ket 67a–b.
6. B. Ket 67b.
7. A disciple of the wise is quick to punish an affront, but God is quick to punish an affront to an orphan or a widow. B. Shab 11a.
8. A sum of money given in lieu of the life of the owner for manslaughter committed by his beast.
9. B. BK 40a; B. BM 22b; B. Pes 50b.
10. B. Ber 18b.
11. Which involve grave risks. B. Pes 50b.
12. B. BM 70a.
13. B. Ta 24a and En Yaakov, ad loc.

said to him: Since R. Samuel bar Judah taught, "Money for charity is not to be levied from orphans, even for the redemption of captives," we may assume that the redemption of captives is "a most important precept."[1]

344. Rava asked Rabbah bar Mari: What is the proof for our masters' statement that redeeming captives is a most important precept? Rabbah answered: From the verse "Such as are for death, for death; and such as are for the sword, for the sword; and such as are for the famine, for the famine; and such as are for captivity, for captivity" (Jer. 15:2). And R. Yohanan added: Each successive punishment in this verse is more severe than the one that precedes it.[2]

Deeds of Loving-kindness

345. R. Simlai expounded: Torah—there is a deed of loving-kindness at its beginning and a deed of loving-kindness at its end. Loving-kindness at its beginning: "the Lord God made for Adam and his wife garments of skins and clothed them" (Gen. 3:21). Loving-kindness at its end: "and he buried [Moses] in the valley" (Deut. 34:6).[3]

346. Once, as R. Yohanan was walking out of Jerusalem, R. Joshua followed him, and, upon seeing the Temple in ruins, he said: Woe unto us that this place is in ruins, the place where atonement was made for Israel's iniquities! R. Yohanan: My son, do not grieve—we have another means of atonement which is as effective. What is it? It is deeds of loving-kindness, concerning which Scripture says, "I desire loving-kindness and not sacrifice" (Hos. 6:6).[4]

347. R. Haggai said in the name of R. Isaac: Everyone is in need of loving-kindness. Even Abraham, for whose sake loving-kindness went around the entire world—even he had need of loving-kindness, as may be inferred by his servant Eliezer's plea, "Show loving-kindness unto thy master Abraham" (Gen. 24:13), meaning: "You have shown him loving-kindness at my journey's beginning, now show it at its end."[5]

348. R. Judah said: When a man denies the obligation to loving-kindness, it is as though he had denied the Root [of Being].[6]

349. A man says to his friend, "Lend me a *kav* of wheat," and the friend replies, "I have none." Or he asks for the loan of a *kav* of barley, and the friend replies, "I have none." Or he asks for a *kav* of dates, and the friend replies, "I have none." Or a woman says to her friend, "Lend me a sieve," and the friend replies, "I have none." Or she says, "Lend me a sifter," and the friend says, "I have none." What does the Holy One do? He causes leprosy to affect the friend's house, and as the household effects are taken out,[7] people seeing them say, "Did not that person say, 'I have none'? See how much wheat is here, how much barley, how many dates are here! The house is rightly cursed with the curses [of want its owner professed]."[8]

350. R. Eleazar said: Loving-kindness is greater than charity, for it is said, "Sow for yourselves according to charity, but reap according to your loving-kindness" (Hos. 10:12). When a man sows, it is in doubt whether he will or will not eat the harvest; but when a man reaps, he will surely eat it.

R. Eleazar said further: The reward for charity depends entirely upon the measure of loving-kindness in the act, as is said, "Sow for yourselves according to your charity, but reap according to your loving-kindness."[9]

351. Our masters taught: Loving-kindness is greater than charity in three ways. Charity is done with one's money, while loving-kindness may be done with one's money or with one's person. Charity is given only to the poor, while loving-kindness may be given both to the poor and to the rich. Charity is given only to the living, while loving-kindness may be shown to both the living and the dead.

R. Eleazar said further: He who executes charity and justice is as though he had filled the entire world, all of it, with loving-kindness, as is said, "When one loveth charity and justice, the earth is full of the loving-kindness of the Lord" (Ps. 33:5). Should you suppose that one may achieve this easily,[10] Scripture says, "How rare is Thy loving-kindness, O God" (Ps. 36:8). Should you suppose that difficulty in executing charity and justice is also true of one who fears Heaven, Scripture says, "But the loving-kindness of the Lord is from everlasting to everlasting with those who fear Him" (Ps. 103:17).[11]

352. "I sleep, but my heart waketh" (Song 5:2). The congregation of Israel said to the Holy One: "I sleep" in neglect of ritual precepts, but "my heart waketh" for the practice of loving-kindness.[12]

353. The sages said in the name of R. Simeon ben Lakish: He who brings up a vicious dog in his house keeps loving-kindness away from his house, as is said, "A dog (*lammos*)—loving-kindness is kept from his fellow man" (Job 6:14).[13] For in Greek, the word *lammos*, usually translated "to him that is ready to faint," means "dog." R. Nahman bar Isaac said: Such a man also casts off the fear of Heaven from himself, for the verse concludes: "And he forsaketh the fear of the Almighty" (ibid.).

---

1. B. BB 8a–b.
2. Ibid.
3. B. Sot 14a.
4. ARN 4; ARNB 8.
5. Gen. R. 60:2.
6. Eccles. R. 7:1, §4.
7. When one suspects "leprosy" in the fabric of a house, "the priest shall command that they empty the house" (Lev. 14:36).
8. Lev. R. 17:2.
9. B. Suk 49b.
10. Literally, "whoever comes to jump can jump."
11. B. Suk 49b.
12. Song R. 5:2, §1.
13. The poor being fearful to approach.

A story is told of a [pregnant] woman who went into a house to do some baking. A dog barked at her, and the embryo within her moved [violently]. The householder sought to reassure her: "Do not be afraid—the dog's teeth have been extracted, and his nails are gone." But she replied, "Keep your favors—throw them to the thorns. The embryo has already been uprooted from its place."[1]

354. R. Abba said in the name of R. Simeon ben Lakish: He who lends money [to a poor man] is greater than he who gives charity; and he who throws money into a common purse [to form a partnership with a poor man] is greater than either.[2]

355. "If thy brother be waxen poor, and his means fail with thee; then thou shalt uphold him" (Lev. 25:35). Don't allow him to fall into utter poverty. The injunction may be explained by analogy with a load on a donkey: as long as he is standing up, one may grab him [to keep from falling] and keep him standing upright. Once he has fallen, five men cannot make him stand up again.[3]

356. What is the proof that if you have already upheld the poor man even four or five times, you should go on upholding him? The statement "Then thou shalt uphold him."[4]

357. The story is told of a pious man whose wife was virtuous. He lost his possessions and became a hired man. One day, as he was plowing in the field, Elijah, ever remembered on good occasions, disguised himself as an Arab, met him, and said to him, "You have six good years [coming to you]—when do you wish them, now or at the end of your days?" The pious man replied, "You must be a sorcerer. I have nothing to give you. Leave me in peace." But Elijah returned three times [with the same question]. Finally, the third time, the pious man said, "I will go and consult my wife." He went to his wife and told her, "Someone came to me and pestered me three times, saying to me, 'You have six good years—when do you wish them, now or at the end of your days?' " Then he asked her, "And what do you say?" She replied, "Go, tell him, 'Bring them now.' " So the pious man went back and said to Elijah, "Go, bring them now." Elijah replied, "Go to your house, and before you reach the gate of your courtyard you will find blessing spread upon your home." It so happened that his children were just then sitting and sifting dirt through their fingers. Suddenly they found enough money to sustain them for six years, so they called to their mother. Even before the pious man reached the gate, his wife came out to meet him and gave him the good tidings. He immediately thanked the Holy One, for he was greatly relieved.

What did his virtuous wife do? She said to him, "As things stand, the Holy One has already twined our lives with the thread of mercy in that He has given us sustenance to last for six years, so let us engage in deeds of loving-kindness during these years—perhaps the Holy One will continue to give us more out of His ample bounty." And this is what she did: each and every day, whatever she gave [to the poor], she told her youngest son, "Record every item we dispense," and he did so.

At the end of six years Elijah, ever remembered on good occasions, came back and said to the pious man, "The time has come to take away what I gave you." The pious man replied, "When I took it, I took it only with my wife's advice. Now that I am to return it, I will return it only with my wife's advice." He went to her and said, "The old man has come back to take away what is his." The wife replied, "Go tell him, 'If you find human beings more reliable than we are, give them what you left in trust with us.' "

When the Holy One considered their words and the acts of charity they had performed, He gave them boon after boon to fulfill what is said: "The work of charity shall convey peace" (Isa. 32:17).[5]

358. Our masters taught: He who loves his neighbors, befriends his kinsmen, marries his sister's daughter,[6] and lends a *sela* to a poor man in his need—of such a one, Scripture says, "When thou seest the naked, that thou cover him, and that thou hide not thyself from thine own flesh. . . . Then thou shalt call, and the Lord will answer; thou shalt cry, and He will say: 'Here I am' " (Isa. 58:7 and 58:9).[7]

359. "That thou hide not thyself from thine own flesh." These words apply to the divorced wife of R. Yose the Galilean [from whom he did not hide].

R. Yose the Galilean had an evil wife, who used to humiliate him in the presence of his disciples and distressed him greatly. When his disciples said to him, "Master, divorce this woman, for she does not treat you with proper respect," he replied, "The marriage settlement I would have to pay her is more than I can afford, so I cannot divorce her." One time, he and R. Eleazar ben Azariah were sitting and studying, and when they finished, R. Yose asked R. Eleazar, "Will the master deign to come with me to my home?" R. Eleazar said, 'Yes." As they entered, R. Yose's wife lowered her face [rudely ignoring the guest]. When R. Yose noticed a pot standing on the stove and asked her, "Is there anything cooking in the pot?" she replied, "There is only hash in it." Upon uncovering the pot, however, he found it full of plump chicks. R. Eleazar ben Azariah was thus made aware that R. Yose's wife was not at peace with her husband. So, as they sat together eating, he observed, "Master, did she not say it was hash? Yet we found chicks in the pot." R. Yose: "The chicks are here because of a miracle." When they finished eating and drinking, R. Eleazar said to R. Yose, "Master, divorce this woman, for she does not treat you with proper respect."

1. B. Shab 63a–b.
2. B. Shab 63b.
3. Sif Lev., ed. Weiss, p. 109b.
4. The statement refers to the future. Ibid.
5. Yalkut, Ruth, §607.
6. The man's affection for his sister is likely to extend to her daughter.
7. B. Yev 62b–63a.

R. Yose replied, "The marriage settlement I would have to pay is more than I can afford, so I cannot divorce her." R. Eleazar: "I will give her the marriage settlement due her." So R. Yose divorced her and was wed to another woman, a much better one.

The divorced wife's sins brought it about that she married the town watchman [a man below her station]. After some time, the watchman was visited with many afflictions: he lost his means and became blind, and his wife had to hold him by the hand and lead him around all the neighborhoods of the town [to beg for alms]. When she reached R. Yose the Galilean's neighborhood, she stopped and turned back. Since her husband was very familiar with all sections of the town, he said to her, "Why don't you lead me to R. Yose the Galilean's neighborhood? He, I heard, gives much to charity." She replied, "I am his divorced wife, and I cannot bring myself to face him." Once, after making the rounds of the entire town and being given nothing, they reached the neighborhood of R. Yose the Galilean, and again she stopped. When her husband [the town watchman] realized why she stopped, he began to beat her, and the noise they made exposed them to shame in the marketplace. Just then, R. Yose happened to look out and, seeing them exposed to public shame in this way, asked the husband, "Why are you beating her?" He replied, "Because every day she causes me the loss of my maintenance from this neighborhood." Upon hearing this, R. Yose took charge of them, settled them in a house he owned, and provided their maintenance for the rest of their lives.

Nevertheless, her voice used to be heard at night as she continued to say, "Was not the pain inflicted on the outside of my body easier to bear than the pain [of humiliation] within my body?"[1]

360. R. Hama bar Hanina said: He who does a favor to someone who does not appreciate it is like one who casts a small stone into a heap of stones [as an offering] to Mercury, as is said, "As a small stone in the heap [of Mercury],[2] so is he that giveth honor to a fool" (Prov. 26:8).[3]

Hospitality to Wayfarers

361. Yose ben Yohanan of Jerusalem said: Let your house be opened wide, and let the poor be members of your household.

Let your house be opened wide—what does this mean? It means that a man's house should be opened wide to the north, to the south, to the east, and to the west, like Job, who provided his houses with four doors. And why did Job provide four doors for his house? In order that the poor should not be put to the distress of having to go around the entire house: he who came from the north could enter directly [through the north door], he who came from the south could enter directly [through the south door], and likewise from the other directions.

And let the poor be members of your household—this does not mean that they should actually become members of your household, but that the poor should be able to talk freely about what they had to eat and drink in your house, just as the poor talked freely about what they had eaten and drunk in Job's house. When one poor man met another, he would ask, "Where are you coming from?" "From Job's house." Or, "Where are you going?" "To Job's house."

When the great calamity befell Job, he pleaded with the Holy One, "Master of the universe, did I not feed the hungry, give drink to the thirsty, and clothe the naked?" The Holy One answered Job, "Job, you have not yet reached half the measure [of hospitality] extended by Abraham. You sat in your house waiting for guests to come to you. To him who was accustomed to eat wheat bread, you gave wheat bread; to him who was accustomed to eat meat, you gave meat; and to him who was accustomed to drink wine, you gave wine. But Abraham did not act thus. He went out, getting about in the world. When he met prospective guests, he brought them to his home. Even to him who was not accustomed to eat wheat bread, he gave wheat bread; to him who was not accustomed to eat meat, he gave meat; and to him who was not accustomed to drink wine, he gave wine. Not only that, but he got busy and built spacious mansions along the highways, and stocked them with food and drink, so that whoever entered ate, drank, and blessed Heaven. Therefore, unusual satisfaction was given to Abraham, and whatever any person requested was to be found in his house.[4]

362. Shammai said: Receive all men with a cheerful countenance. What does this mean? It means that if a man presents the most precious gifts in the world to his fellow, but with a sullen and downcast countenance, Scripture regards that man as though he presented nothing at all to his fellow. On the other hand, he who receives his fellow with a cheerful countenance, even if he gives him nothing—Scripture accounts it to him as though he had presented his fellow with the most precious gifts in the world.[5]

363. R. Judah said in the name of Rav: Receiving wayfarers is greater than welcoming the Presence, for Abraham [wishing to attend to the three wayfarers] pleaded with God, "My Lord, if now I have found favor in Thine eyes, pass not away from thy servant [while I attend to my guests]."[6]

364. R. Yohanan said in the name of R. Yose ben Kisma: The mouthful of food [given to wayfarers] is of great importance, since failure to give it alienated two families from Israel, as is written, "An Ammonite or a Moabite

---

1. P. Ket 11:3, 34b; Gen. R. 17:3; Lev. R. 34:14.
2. JV: "As a small stone in a heap of stones." But *margemah* ("a heap of stones"), found only here, has been variously rendered. The Vulgate follows the rabbinic interpretation, namely, that a shrine of Mercury is referred to.
3. En Yaakov on B. Hul 133b.
4. Avot 1:5; ARN 7.
5. Avot 1:15; ARN 13.
6. B. Shab 127a.

shall not enter into the congregation of the Lord . . . because they met you not with bread and with water" (Deut. 23:4–5). On his own, R. Yohanan said: Not practicing hospitality alienates those who are near, and practicing hospitality brings near those who are alienated, causes [God's] eyes to be averted from the wicked, and makes the Presence rest even on the prophets of Baal. And an unwitting failure to practice it is deemed to be deliberate.[1]

365. R. Nathan said: From Gareb[2] to Shiloh is only a distance of three *mil*, so that the smoke of the woodpile [on the altar] and the smoke of what was offered to Micah's image intermingled. The ministering angels wished to thrust Micah away from there, but the Holy One said, "Let him be—his bread is available to wayfarers."[3]

366. R. Simeon ben Gamaliel used to say: There was a widespread practice in Jerusalem: if a man entrusted [the preparation of] a banquet to another who spoiled it, the other had to compensate the host for the humiliation to himself and to his guests.

There was another widespread practice in Jerusalem: [at the beginning of a meal], a napkin was draped over the entrance to the house. So long as the napkin remained in place, guests entered. When the napkin was removed, no more guests [were permitted to] enter.[4]

367. When R. Huna had a meal, he would open the doors of his house and say, "Let whoever is in need come and eat."[5]

368. It once happened that while R. Yannai was on a journey, he saw a man who looked particularly distinguished. R. Yannai asked him, "Will you, sir, deign to visit our home?" The man said, "Yes." So R. Yannai brought the man into his house and gave him food and drink. Then R. Yannai tested him in his knowledge of Scripture, and found none; in his knowledge of Mishnah, and found none; in his knowledge of *Aggadah*, and found none; in his knowledge of Talmud, and found none. Finally, when R. Yannai said to him, "Take [the cup of wine] and say grace," the guest said evasively, "Yannai should be saying grace in his own house." Then R. Yannai asked him, "Can you repeat what I am about to say to you?" The guest: "Yes." R. Yannai: "Then say, 'A dog has eaten Yannai's bread.' " The guest immediately stood up, took hold of R. Yannai, and said to him, "My inheritance is in your possession, and you keep it from me!" R. Yannai: "What inheritance of yours is in my possession?" The guest: "Once I passed a schoolhouse and heard the voices of young children saying, 'The Torah that Moses commanded the children of Israel is the inheritance of the congregation of Jacob' [Deut. 33:4]—not 'the congregation of Yannai,' but 'the congregation of Jacob.' " R. Yannai: "How have you merited to dine at my table?" The guest: "Never in my life, after hearing evil spoken, have I brought it back to the person spoken of. Nor have I seen two people quarreling without making peace between them." R. Yannai: "You—whose conduct is so extraordinary—I presumed to call 'dog'!"[6]

369. It is unbecoming for a host to eat before his guest. It is unbecoming for a guest to bring another guest. More unbecoming than the two mentioned is the guest who puts his host to great trouble.[7]

370. Guests may not give food set before them to the son or daughter of the host until they receive the host's permission.

R. Eliezer ben Jacob said: Because of disregarding such counsel, three persons perished in Israel. The story is told that, in a time of scarcity, a man invited three guests but had only three eggs to place before them. When the host's child entered and stood before the guests, one of them took his portion and gave it to the child, and so did the second guest, and the third. When the child's father came in and saw one egg stuffed in his mouth and two held in his hands, he lifted the child to his own height and threw him down to the ground so hard that he killed him. When the child's mother saw this, she went up to the roof, threw herself down to her death. Finally, the child's father went up to the roof, and he, too, threw himself down to his death.[8]

371. Do whatever the host says, except "Get out!"[9]

372. A story is told of Simeon ben Antipatros, with whom many guests used to come and stay. When he pressed them to eat and drink, they vowed by the Torah that they would neither eat nor drink, but later they did both eat and drink. When the time came for them to depart, he used to have them flogged. Simeon's actions came to the notice of Rabban Yohanan ben Zakkai and of the sages, who were angered by it and said, "Who will go and tell him how we feel about what he is doing?" R. Joshua replied, "I will go and see what he does."

R. Joshua went, found Simeon at the entrance of his house, and greeted him, "Peace be upon you, master." Simeon replied, "Peace be upon you, master and teacher." R. Joshua: "I need lodging." Simeon replied, "Lodge here in peace." They sat down and occupied themselves until evening with the study of Torah. In the morning, R. Joshua said, "Master, I want to go to the bathhouse." Simeon: "As you wish." After he came back, they ate and drank. Still, R. Joshua was afraid that he would be beaten until he was humpbacked, so he said, "Who will escort me [on my way]?" Simeon: "I will." R. Joshua thought to himself:

1. B. Sanh 103b.
2. See Judg. 17. Both Gareb and Shiloh were in the highlands of Ephraim, in the center of the Land of Israel.
3. B. Sanh 103b.
4. B. BB 93b.
5. B. Ta 20b.
6. Lev. R. 9:3.
7. DEZ 8.
8. B. Hul 94a; DER 9.
9. By getting out, you deprive the host of giving you hospitality and thus cause him to sin. B. Pes 86b; DER 6.

What am I to tell the sages who sent me [since I have not been beaten]? He then turned to look back. Simeon asked him, "Master, why did you turn to look behind you?" R. Joshua: "I have something to ask you. Why did you flog the other guests who stayed with you, and did not flog me?" Simeon: "Master, you are a great sage, and you have good manners. I urged the other guests who stayed with me to eat, but they vowed by the Torah [not to eat] and then broke their vow. And this is what I heard from the mouth of the sages: 'Whoever vows by the Torah and breaks his vow is to be given forty lashes.' " R. Joshua: "May Heaven bless you for what you have done. By your life, and by the life of your head! Whoever behaves in this manner—give him forty lashes on your own account and [another] forty on account of the sages who sent me." R. Joshua then returned and reported to the sages what he had witnessed while he was with Simeon ben Antipatros.[1]

373. Ben Zoma used to say: What does a grateful guest say? "How much trouble the host has gone to for my sake! How much meat he set before me! How much wine he set before me! How many delicate breads he set before me! And all the trouble he went to, he went to only for my sake!" But what does an ungrateful guest say? "What trouble did my host really go to? I ate but one piece of bread, ate but one slice of meat, drank but one cup of wine. All the trouble my host went to, he went to only for the sake of [feeding] his wife and children."[2]

374. In the world's use, when a man receives a guest, the first day he feeds him fatted fowl, the second day ordinary meat, the third day fish, the next day cheese, the following day pulse. Thus, he gives him less and less, until in the end he feeds him greens.[3]

375. R. Ze'era said: Suppose a man has a client [a dependent]. The first time the client comes to visit him, he seats him on a couch; the second time the client comes to visit, he seats him on a chair; the third time, he seats him on a bench; but the fourth time, he says of him, "How this fellow forces himself upon me, and how he burdens me!"[4]

376. [When Abraham asked Sarah to make cakes, he first said], "Of flour" (Gen. 18:6), [then added], "Of fine flour." From Abraham's instructions to his wife, R. Isaac said, one may infer that a woman is more apt to begrudge guests than a man.[5]

377. It is said of R. Phinehas ben Yair: Never in his life did he say grace over a piece of bread not his own.[6]

Once, when Rabbi [Judah I, the Patriarch] heard of the arrival of R. Phinehas, he went out to meet him and asked him, "Will you please dine with me?" "Certainly," R. Phinehas answered. R. Judah's face at once brightened with joy. Seeing that, R. Phinehas said, "Do you suppose that I am forbidden by vow from deriving any benefit from an Israelite? [No, indeed.] The people of Israel are holy. But there are some who desire [to benefit others] and have not the means, while others have the means but not the desire, and it is written, 'Never dine with a niggardly man, never fancy his dainties' " (Prov. 23:6).[7]

378. R. Joshua ben Levi said: The cup of blessing for the grace after meals should be given only to one who is of a generous disposition. "He that hath a bountiful eye shall bless, for he giveth of his bread to the poor" (Prov. 22:9)—read not *yevorakh*, "shall be blessed," but *yevarekh*, "shall recite the blessing."

R. Joshua ben Levi also said: Where is the proof that even birds recognize those of niggardly spirit? The verse "For in vain is the net spread in the eyes of any bird" (Prov. 1:17).

R. Joshua ben Levi also said: Whoever accepts hospitality from men of niggardly spirit transgresses a prohibition: "Never dine with a niggardly man, never fancy his dainties" (Prov. 23:6). R. Nahman ben Isaac said: He thus transgresses two prohibitions: "Never dine" and "Never fancy."

R. Joshua ben Levi also said: [The necessity for] the heifer whose neck is to be broken arises only on account of the niggardly in spirit, as it is said, "The elders shall speak and say, 'Our hands have not shed this blood, neither have our eyes seen it' " (Deut. 21:7). But can it enter our mind that the elders of the High Court might be shedders of blood? No, the meaning of the elders' words is: it is not that the man found dead had come to us for help and we dismissed him without food; we did not see him, and therefore we let him go on without escort.[8]

379. R. Joshua ben Levi also said: Because of the four paces that one Pharaoh had Abraham escorted, as is said, "Pharaoh put men in charge of him and they escorted him"[9] (Gen. 12:20), another Pharaoh [was allowed to] enslave the latter's descendants for four hundred years.

Rav Judah said in the name of Rav: He who accompanies his neighbor for even four cubits in the city will come to no harm [when he himself is on a journey].

Our masters taught: A teacher [should accompany] his pupil as far as the city limit; one associate scholar [should accompany] another as far as the Sabbath limit;[10] a disciple [should accompany] his master an indefinite distance. But exactly how far is that? R. Sheshet said: Up to a parasang, if the master is not a distinguished scholar; if the master is a distinguished scholar, three parasangs.[11]

380. We have been taught that R. Meir used to say: A person may be compelled to escort [a traveler], because

1. DER 6.
2. B. Ber 58a.
3. PRK, ed. Buber, p. 195b; MTeh 23:3.
4. MTeh 4:3.
5. B. BM 87a.
6. That is, he never accepted an invitation.
7. B. Hul 7b.
8. B. Sot 38b.
9. "Escorting" is deemed to cover a minimum of four cubits or four paces.
10. Two thousand cubits.
11. B. Sot 46b and En Yaakov, ad loc.

the reward for such escorting is limitless, as is said, "And the watchers saw a man come forth out of the city, and they said unto him: 'Show us, we pray thee, the entrance into the city, and we will deal kindly with thee' " (Judg. 1:24); and in the next verse, "And he showed them the entrance into the city" (Judg. 1:25). What kindness did they do for him? Although they slew the entire city by the edge of the sword, they let that man and his family go.

"And the man went into the land of the Hittites, and built a city, and called the name thereof Luz" (Judg. 1:26). The sages taught: It is the city of Luz in which the purple dye is made; it is the city of Luz against which Sennacherib marched without disturbing it, against which Nebuchadnezzar marched without destroying it, and through which the angel of death has no permission to pass. And so, when the old men in it become tired of life, they go outside the wall and die [there]. Now, may not the matter be argued *a fortiori*? If this Canaanite, who walked not a step and uttered not a word, caused deliverance for himself and his progeny unto the end of all generations, how much more and more he who provides escort with his own two feet.

How did the Canaanite show them [the way]? He curved his mouth [in that direction] for them, according to Hezekiah. He pointed [the way] for them with his finger, according to R. Yohanan. Because this Canaanite pointed with his finger, as we have been taught in keeping with R. Yohanan's opinion, he caused deliverance for himself and his progeny unto the end of all generations.[1]

381. R. Yohanan said in the name of R. Meir: Whoever does not escort others or allow himself to be escorted is as though he had shed blood, for had the people of Jericho escorted Elisha, he would not have stirred up bears against the children.[2]

382. R. Judah said in the name of Rav: If Jonathan had provided David with two loaves of bread, Nob the city of priests would not have been put to the sword, Doeg the Edomite would not have been expelled [from the world-to-come], and Saul and his three sons would not have been slain.[3]

Saving an Endangered Life

383. "Thou shalt not stand by the blood of thy neighbor" (Lev. 19:16). What is the proof that he who sees his fellow drowning in a river or being dragged by a wild beast or being attacked by brigands must save him? The verse "Thou shalt not stand by the blood of thy neighbor."

Where is the proof that when a man sees his fellow pursued by someone who intends to kill him, he must save him even at the cost of the pursuer's life? The verse "Thou shalt not stand by the blood of thy neighbor."[4]

384. "Why boasteth thou thyself of evil, O mighty man?" (Ps. 52:3). David asked Doeg: Is this really might, for him who sees his fellow at the edge of a pit to push him into it? Or seeing his fellow on top of a roof, to push him off? Is this might? When can a man truly be called a "mighty man"? When his fellow is about to fall into a pit, and he seizes his hand so that he does not fall in. Or when he sees his fellow fallen into a pit, and he lifts him out of it.[5]

385. The reason Adam was created alone in the world is to teach you that whoever destroys a single soul, Scripture imputes it to him as though he had destroyed the entire world; and whoever keeps alive a single soul, Scripture imputes it to him as though he had preserved the entire world.[6]

386. In civil suits, a man may pay money and effect expiation.[7] But in capital cases, he is held responsible for the blood of him [who was wrongfully condemned] and for the blood of the posterity that would have been his until the end of time. Thus we find that Cain, who slew his brother, was told, "The bloods of thy brother cry out unto Me" (Gen. 4:10). Not "the blood of thy brother," but "the bloods of thy brother": his blood and the blood of the posterity [that would have been his].[8]

387. A man sees a child struggling in the river and says, "As soon as I remove my tefillin, I will save him." And even as he is removing them, the child's life gives out. Or he sees a woman drowning in the river and says, "It is improper for me to look at her while I rescue her." Each of these is a foolish pietist.[9]

388. When two are on a journey [far from an inhabited area], and one has a pitcher of water, if both drink, both will die; if only one of them drinks, he will get to a human settlement. Ben Petura preached: It is better that both drink and both die, rather than that one should behold his companion's death. But then R. Akiva came and taught: "That thy brother may live with thee" (Lev. 25:36)—[with *thee*] implies that your life takes precedence over the life of your companion.[10]

389. If a woman is in hard labor, the child in her womb may be cut up and brought out member by member, because the mother's survival has priority over the child's survival. But if the greater part of the child has already emerged, it may not be touched, since one life may not be sacrificed to preserve another.[11]

---

1. B. Sot 46b.
2. The words "[Elisha] went up" (2 Kings 2:23) are taken to mean that he went up unescorted. The escorts would not have allowed the children to abuse Elisha. B. Sot 46b.
3. B. Sanh 104a.
4. B. Sanh 73a.
5. MTeh 52:6.
6. B. Sanh 37a; P. Sanh 4:12, 22b.
7. If he causes financial loss through false testimony.
8. B. Sanh 37a.
9. B. Sot 21b; P. Sot 3:4, 19a.
10. B. BM 62a.
11. In the latter case, the child is regarded as already born; and his life is as sacred as his mother's. Oh 7:6.

390. "And the priest shall command that they empty the house, before the priest go in to see the plague, that all that is in the house be not made unclean" (Lev. 14:36). R. Meir said: But which [of his goods] can become unclean? If you say, "His articles of wood, of cloth, or of metal," these may be immersed, and they become clean. What is it, then, that the Torah seeks to spare? His earthenware vessels—his jar and his pot.[1] If the Torah thus seeks to spare a man's possessions that are of least worth, how much more and more by far possessions that he prizes; if his material possessions, how much more and more by far his sons and daughters; and if what belongs to the wicked, how much more and more by far what belongs to the righteous.[2]

391. Our masters taught: One must remove debris [even] on the Sabbath in order to save a life, and the more eagerly one sets to work at it, the more praiseworthy; and one need not obtain permission first from the court. How so? If a man realizes that a child has fallen into the sea, he may cast a net and bring him up. If a man realizes that a child has fallen into a pit, he may break up a segment [of the wall around the pit] and bring the child up. If a man realizes that a door has [sprung shut and] locked in a child, he may break the door and free the child. One may extinguish and isolate a conflagration on the Sabbath.[3]

392. Water may be heated on the Sabbath for a sick person, even by Israel's notables.[4]

393. We have been taught that R. Simeon ben Gamaliel said: The Sabbath may be desecrated for a one-day-old infant who is alive, because the Torah said: Desecrate for his sake one Sabbath, so that he may keep many Sabbaths. But for David, king of Israel—dead—the Sabbath may not be desecrated: once a man is dead, he is free from the obligation to observe precepts. Thus, R. Yohanan interpreted "Among the dead I am free" (Ps. 88:6) to mean that once a man is dead, he is free from obligation to observe precepts.[5]

394. This question was asked of R. Tanhum of Nevi: What is the law concerning extinguishing a lamp for a sick man on the Sabbath? He replied: A lamp is called a lamp, and man's soul is also called a lamp.[6] It is right that a man's lamp be extinguished for the sake of the Holy One's lamp [a man's soul].[7]

395. R. Ishmael, R. Akiva, and R. Eleazar ben Azariah were once on a journey, with Levi the Net Maker and R. Ishmael son of R. Eleazar ben Azariah walking behind, when this question was asked of them: How do we know that danger to human life supersedes the laws of the Sabbath? R. Ishmael spoke up and quoted: "If a thief be found breaking in, and be smitten so that he dieth, there shall be no bloodguiltiness for the householder" (Exod. 22:1). Now, it is doubtful whether this thief had come to take money or had come to take life, and even though bloodshed pollutes the land and causes the Presence to depart from Israel, yet the householder is allowed to save himself at the cost of the thief's life—how much more and more by far may danger to human life supersede the laws of the Sabbath!

R. Akiva spoke up and said: "If a man come presumptuously upon his neighbor . . . thou shalt take him from My altar, that he may die" (Exod. 21:14). Now if, because of this man—against whom it is unknown whether the charge of murder has substance or not—the service in the Temple, [which is important enough to] supersede the Sabbath, is interrupted, how much more and more by far should the saving of human life supersede the laws of the Sabbath!

R. Eleazar ben Azariah spoke up and said: If circumcision, which involves only one of the two hundred and forty-eight parts of the human body, supersedes the Sabbath,[8] how much more and more by far does the saving of the whole body supersede the Sabbath!

R. Yose the Galilean, quoting "Only ye shall keep My Sabbaths" (Exod. 31:13), said: One might assume that this applies under all circumstances; therefore the test begins with "only," intimating exceptions.

R. Jonathan ben Joseph, quoting "For it is holy unto *you*" (Exod. 31:14), said: The Sabbath is committed into your hands, not you into its hand.[9]

R. Simeon ben Menasya said: "And the children of Israel shall keep the Sabbath" (Exod. 31:16), by which the Torah implied, "Profane for a man's sake *one* Sabbath, so that he may keep many Sabbaths."

R. Judah said in the name of Samuel: If I had been there, I should have quoted—and my verse is more apt than theirs—"He shall live by them" (Lev. 18:5)—he shall not die because of them.[10]

Visiting the Sick

396. We have been taught: There is no measure for visiting the sick. What is meant by "There is no measure for visiting the sick"? R. Joseph thought it meant: "There is no measure for the reward given for it." But is there a definite measure of reward for any precept? Have we not been taught: "Be heedful of a light precept as of a weighty one, for you know not what is given as reward for any precept" (Avot 2:1)? Rather, said Abbaye, it means that a great person should visit a humble one. Rava said: Even a hundred times a day.

1. These cannot be made clean by immersion. See Lev. 15:12.
2. Neg 12:5.
3. B. Yoma 84a.
4. B. Yoma 84b.
5. B. Shab 151b.
6. "The soul of man is the lamp of the Lord" (Prov. 20:27).
7. B. Shab 30a–b.
8. The circumcision must take place on the eighth day, even if that day falls on the Sabbath, thus suspending the laws of the Sabbath, which prohibit any operation, as well as preparations leading to it.
9. Cf. Mark 2:27.
10. B. Yoma 85a; Mek, *Ki Tissa*, *Shabbata*, 1; Yalkut, *Mishpatim*, §367.

R. Aha bar Hanina said: He who visits a sick man takes away one-sixtieth of his illness. So Abbaye said to Rava: If that is the case, let sixty persons come in and thus make the man rise up [well from his sickbed]. Rava replied: The sixtieth part spoken of here is analogous to the tenth part in the school of Rabbi [Judah I, the Patriarch], where the fraction is taken not from the original amount but from the remainder.[1] And besides, each visitor must be of the same age group as the sick man.[2]

397. R. Huna said: When a person visits the sick, the sick man's illness is diminished by one-sixtieth. At this, R. Huna was challenged: If so, let sixty persons visit the sick man, and he immediately will be able to go down with them into the marketplace. R. Huna replied: [It would work] only if each of the sixty loved him as a man loves himself. In any event, they will afford him some relief.[3]

398. R. Helbo fell ill, and even though R. Kahana went out and announced that R. Helbo was ill, no one came to see him. So R. Kahana said to the sages: Did it not once happen that one of R. Akiva's disciples fell ill, and since the sages did not go to visit him, R. Akiva himself went; and because R. Akiva swept and sprinkled the ground before him, the disciple recovered and said, "Master, you have brought me back to life"? Afterward, R. Akiva went out and preached: He who does not visit the sick is as one who sheds blood.

When R. Dimi came [from the Land of Israel], he said: He who visits the sick causes him to live; and he who does not visit the sick causes him to die.[4]

399. R. Anan said in the name of Rav: How do we know that the Presence sustains a sick man? From the verse: "The Lord will sustain him upon his sickbed" (Ps. 41:4).

R. Avin said in the name of Rav: How do we know that the Presence abides over a sick man's bed? From the verse "The Lord over his sickbed will sustain him."

He who visits the sick should sit neither on the bed nor on a chair nor on a bench, but must wrap himself in his robe and sit on the ground, because the Presence abides over a sick man's bed.[5]

400. Our masters taught: He who visits the sick on a Sabbath should say, "It is the Sabbath, when one may not cry out, but recovery will come soon." R. Meir said: One should say, "The Sabbath can have compassion." R. Judah said: "May He who is everywhere have compassion on you and on the sick of Israel." R. Yose said: "May He who is everywhere have compassion on you among [all] the sick of Israel." When Shebna of Jerusalem entered [a sick man's chamber], he would say, "Peace"; and when he left, he would say, "It is the Sabbath, when one may not cry out, but recovery will come soon, for His compassions are abundant. So enjoy the Sabbath in peace."[6]

401. R. Yose bar Parta said in the name of R. Eliezer: One should not visit those ill with sickness of bowels or sickness of eyes, or those who suffer from headaches.[7]

402. Samuel said: A sick person should be visited only after the fever has left him.[8]

403. Whenever Rava fell ill, he would ask on the first day that his sickness not be made known, lest his future be hurt.[9] After that, he would say [to his servants]: Go out to the marketplace and announce, "Rava has fallen ill." [Upon hearing the announcement], my enemies will rejoice, despite being told, "Rejoice not when thine enemy falleth . . . lest the Lord see it and it displeases Him, and He turn away His wrath from him" (Prov. 24:17–18) [so that I will recover]. And they who love me, [hearing of my illness], will entreat mercy on my behalf.[10]

Burying the Dead and Comforting the Mourners

404. "Act in steadfast loyalty to me; . . . carry me out of Egypt, and bury me" (Gen. 47:29–30). Is there such a thing as loyalty that is not steadfast? No, but what Jacob said to Joseph was: If *after* my death you act in loyalty toward me, that will be "steadfast loyalty."

[Why did Jacob speak thus? He spoke in refutation of] the cynical proverb "When your friend's son dies, give your friend sympathy; when your friend himself dies—be on your way!"[11]

405. Our masters taught: He who closes [the eyes of a dying man] at the point of death is a murderer, as may be understood by analogy with a lamp that is flickering out; if one presses one's finger upon it, the lamp goes out at once.

We have been taught that R. Simeon ben Gamaliel said: He who wishes the eyes of a dead man to close should blow wine into his nostrils, apply oil between his eyelids, or take hold of his two big toes, and the eyes will close of themselves.[12]

406. R. Yohanan said in the name of R. Simeon ben Yohai: What is the proof that he who keeps his dead unburied overnight transgresses a negative precept? The verse "His body shall not remain overnight. . . . Thou shalt surely bury him the same day" (Deut. 21:23).

If the relative keeps the body overnight to honor the

1. So there would always be a portion of the man's illness remaining.
2. B. Ned 39b.
3. Lev. R. 34:1.
4. B. Ned 39b–40a.
5. B. Ned 40a and En Yaakov, ad loc.
6. B. Shab 12a.
7. For whom visits are burdensome. B. Ned 41a.
8. Ibid.
9. Through people's idle talk.
10. B. Ned 40a and En Yaakov, ad loc.
11. The friend being dead, there is no one to repay the trouble you may go to for his sake. Gen. R. 96:5.
12. B. Shab 152b.

deceased—to have his death made known in nearby towns, to bring professional women mourners[1] for him, or to procure for him a coffin and shrouds—he violates no precept, for all he does [that brings about delay of burial] is done for the honor of the deceased.[2]

407. R. Yohanan said in the name of R. Simeon ben Yohai: Where in the Torah is burial of the dead alluded to as a precept? In the verse "Bury, thou shalt bury him" (Deut. 21:23).

King Shapur[3] asked R. Hama: From where in the Torah is the obligation to bury the dead derived? R. Hama remained silent, saying nothing in reply. Upon hearing about this incident, R. Aha bar Jacob commented, "The world is given over into the hands of fools! R. Hama should have cited, 'Bury . . . him.' "

[King Shapur might have responded]: Perhaps the words imply that the body must be placed in a coffin?

R. Hama should have quoted the entire verse: "Bury, thou shalt bury him" [where the repetition of the verb indicates burial in the ground].

[Since burying may also refer to a body's being placed in a coffin, King Shapur would have maintained that R. Hama's] inference even from the entire verse was unwarranted.

Should R. Hama have said that the righteous [such as the patriarchs] were buried?

[King Shapur might have retorted]: Merely a matter of general custom.

But the Holy One buried Moses.

He did so merely in order not to depart from the general custom.

R. Hama should have cited "They shall not be buried, neither shall men lament for them" (Jer. 16:6).

[King Shapur would have retorted]: Such a citation indicates that in this instance there was to be a departure from the general custom.[4]

408. When a man finds an unidentified body, he should attend to its needs and bury it in the place where it was found. R. Akiva said: This is how my ministry to the sages began. Once, while walking on a road, I found a slain man. I carried him a distance of four *mil* to a burial place, where I interred him. When I came to R. Eliezer and R. Joshua, I told them what had happened. They said to me, "Every step you took is deemed against you as though you had shed blood." Then I said to myself, reasoning from the minor to the major: If I incurred sin when I thought to do good, how much more sin would I have incurred had I not thought to do good!

Henceforth, I did not budge from ministering to the sages.[5]

409. Our masters taught: One may interrupt the study of Torah to attend a funeral procession.

It is said of R. Judah bar Ilai that he used to interrupt the study of Torah to attend a funeral procession, but only when there were not enough people in the procession. When there are enough, study may not be interrupted. And how many are enough? R. Samuel bar Ini said in the name of Rav: Twelve thousand men and six thousand trumpeters. Ulla said: As many as, say, would form a continuous line from the city gate to the grave. However, R. Sheshet—according to some, R. Yohanan—said: Torah's interruption requires as many to be present as there were when it was given: since the Torah was given in the presence of sixty myriads, so it can be interrupted only if sixty myriads are present.

When may study be interrupted by the presence of sixty myriads? At the funeral of one who read Scripture and recited Mishnah. But at the funeral of one who taught Scripture and Mishnah, there is no limit.[6]

410. Our masters taught: The words "And they did honor him at his death" (2 Chron. 32:33) refer to Hezekiah, king of Judah, before whom thirty-six thousand [warriors] marched with shoulders bare.[7] Such is the opinion of R. Judah. But R. Nehemiah said to him: Was not the same done for Ahab [who was an evildoer]? What did happen was that a Torah scroll was placed on Hezekiah's bier, and the people declared: This one fulfilled all that is written in that scroll.[8]

411. R. Judah said in the name of Rav: A man who sees a corpse [on the way to burial] and does not accompany it shows no concern for the assertion "He that mocketh the poor blasphemeth his Maker" (Prov. 17:5). And if he accompanies it, what is his reward? To him apply the words "He that is gracious unto the poor lendeth unto the Lord" (Prov. 19:7) and "He that is gracious unto the needy honoreth Him" (Prov. 14:31).[9]

412. Our masters taught: A man who transports bones from one place to another should not put them in a saddlebag, place the bag on his donkey's back, and then sit on it, because this is a disrespectful way of treating them. But if he is afraid of heathens or robbers, he may do so. And the rule laid down for bones applies also to a Torah scroll.[10]

---

1. See Jer. 9:16.
2. B. Sanh 46b–47a.
3. Shapur II, king of Persia, 309–380, transferred the royal residence to Ctesiphon, and there came in contact with Jewish sages" (Sanh, Soncino, p. 307, n. 6). Like other magi, he was opposed to burial of corpses in the ground, and he sought to demolish Jewish arguments that burial in the ground should take place. First, he pointed out that burial should include placing the corpse in a casket. When the example of the patriarchs was cited, he dismissed the practice as being no more than a custom—not a prescription. When it was pointed out that God buried Moses, Shapur still insisted that God simply did not wish to depart from the prevailing custom.
4. The ancient Persians regarded burial as a desecration of the earth. Hence King Shapur's question. B. Sanh 46b.
5. P. Naz 7:1, 56a; Sem 4.
6. B. Ket 17a.
7. For an explanation of the number of warriors and the baring of shoulders, see above, part 1, chap. 6, §167.
8. B. BK 16b–17a.
9. B. Ber 18a and En Yaakov, ad loc.
10. Ibid. and En Yaakov, ad loc.

413. R. Aha bar Hanina said: A wicked man should not be buried next to a righteous one; and just as a wicked man should not be buried next to a righteous one, so is a grossly wicked man not to be buried next to one mildly wicked.[1]

414. We have been taught: A man should not walk about in a cemetery with tefillin on his head, nor read from a Torah scroll held on his arm. If he does, he shows no concern for the assertion "He that mocketh the poor[2] blasphemeth his Maker" (Prov. 17:5).[3]

415. Once, while R. Hiyya and R. Jonathan were walking about in a cemetery, the fringes of R. Jonathan's cloak were trailing on the ground. R. Hiyya said to him, "Lift it up, so that the dead should not say, 'Tomorrow they will be coming to join us, yet now they treat us with contempt.' "[4] R. Jonathan replied, "But do they know such things? Is it not written, 'But the dead know not anything' (Eccles. 9:5)?" R. Hiyya: "If you have read the verse once, you have not repeated it; if you have repeated it, you have not gone over it a third time; if you have gone over it a third time, you have not had it explained to you properly. 'For the living know that they shall die' (ibid.)—these are the righteous, who in their death are called living. 'But the dead know not anything'—Such dead are the wicked, who even during their lives are called dead."[5]

416. R. Isaac said: If one makes invidious remarks about the dead, it is like making remarks about a stone. Some say the reason is that they do not know; others say that they know but do not care. But is that so? Has not R. Papa told of a certain man who made derogatory remarks about Samuel while following his bier, and a log fell from the roof and cracked that man's skull? A disciple of the wise [such as Samuel] is different, because the Holy One demands the deference due him.[6]

417. There was a certain magus who used to rummage among graves.[7] When he came to the burial cave of R. Tobi bar Mattenah, R. Tobi grabbed hold of his beard. Abbaye[8] came by and said to Tobi, "Pray, let go of him." A year later, the magus came back, and the dead man again seized hold of his beard. Abbaye came by again [to rescue the magus], but this time the dead man would not let go, so they had to bring scissors and cut off the magus's beard.[9]

418. At one time, providing decent burial was more burdensome for the kin of the deceased than even his death, so they would leave the body and run away, until Rabban Gamaliel [II] came and prescribed a simple style for himself—he was carried out in inexpensive linen shrouds. Thereafter, all the people followed his practice by carrying out their dead in inexpensive linen shrouds.

R. Papa added: And now it is the practice to take out the dead even in a shroud of rough cloth worth no more than a *zuz*.[10]

419. Whoever heaps elaborate shrouds upon the dead transgresses the injunction against wanton destruction. So R. Meir.

R. Eleazar bar Zadok said: "Such a one disgraces the deceased."

Rabban Simeon ben Gamaliel said: "He invites more worms to feed on the deceased."[11]

420. R. Yannai said to his children: My sons, bury me not in white shrouds nor in black shrouds—not in white, lest, lacking merit, I look like a bridegroom among mourners; nor in black, lest, having merit, I look like a mourner among bridegrooms. But bury me in bath attendants' drab-colored cloth that comes from a city across the sea.[12]

421. When R. Yohanan was about to depart from the world, he said to those who were to attend to his burial: Bury me in dun-colored shrouds, neither white nor black, so that if I stand among the righteous, I will not be ashamed, and if I stand among the wicked, I will not be humiliated.

When R. Josiah was about to depart from the world, he asked those who were standing about him, "Call my disciples." When they came, he said to them, "Bury me in [freshly] ironed white shrouds." When they asked him, "Are you better than your master [R. Yohanan]?" he replied, "[It is to show that] I am not ashamed of my deeds when I greet my Creator."[13]

422. Our masters taught: Formerly, the faces of the rich were left uncovered, while the faces of the poor, which during years of drought had turned dark, were covered; understandably, the poor felt humiliated. In deference to their feelings, it was instituted that everybody's face should be covered.

Formerly, the rich were carried out for burial on a state bed, and the poor on a plain bier; understandably, the poor felt humiliated. In deference to their feelings, it was instituted that all should be taken out on a plain bier.

Formerly, a perfuming pan was placed under those

---

1. B. Sanh 47a.
2. The dead are "poor" in that they are incapable of performing precepts.
3. B. Ber 18a.
4. Since the dead are not obligated to observe precepts, dragging the fringes on the ground—tangible evidence of such observance—is both contempt and insult.
5. Unlike the righteous, who prepare for death, the wicked make no such preparations. Hence, says R. Hiyya, the verse R. Jonathan cited did not indicate that the dead were unaware of what was happening around them. B. Ber 18a and En Yaakov, ad loc.
6. B. Ber 19a and En Yaakov, ad loc.
7. Persian fire-worshipers considered it sinful to defile the earth by burying dead bodies in it. They would accordingly exhume bodies and expose them to the birds.
8. He was apparently a friend of the magus.
9. B. BB 58a.
10. B. Ket 8b.
11. Sem 9 (ed. Zlotnick, p. 72).
12. B. Shab 114a.
13. P. Kil 9:4, 32b; Gen. R. 96:5; Tanhuma, *Va-yehi*, §3; Tanhuma B, *Va-yehi*, §6.

who died of disease of the bowels; understandably, the living sufferers from such disease felt humiliated.[1] In deference to their feelings, it was instituted that such a pan should be set under all who died.[2]

423. R. Judah said: Formerly, in Judea, no fewer than seven halts and sit-downs were provided in escorting the dead. It was done thus: [After the escort had rested on the ground], the announcer called out, "Stand up, dear friends, stand up!" And after they had walked for some distance, he again called out, "Sit down, dear friends, sit down!"[3]

424. Our masters taught: Formerly, the mourners used to stand still, while all the people passed in front of them. But there were two families in Jerusalem who contended with each other, each insisting: "We shall pass first." So the masters laid down the rule that the people should remain standing, and the mourners pass in front of them.[4]

425. Our masters taught: Formerly, [victuals] to the house of mourning were conveyed for the rich in silver and gold baskets, and for the poor in baskets of peeled willow shoots, which caused the poor to feel humiliated. In deference to their feelings, it was instituted that victuals for poor and rich alike should be conveyed in baskets of peeled willow shoots.

Formerly, beverages in a rich man's house of mourning were served in white glass vessels, and in a poor man's house of mourning in colored glass, which caused the poor to feel humiliated. In deference to their feelings, it was instituted that beverages for poor and rich alike should be served in colored glass.[5]

426. We have been taught: The sages instituted that ten cups of wine be drunk in the house of a mourner: three before the meal, in order to open the small bowels; three during the meal, in order to dissolve the food in the bowels; and four after the meal—one corresponding to "Who feedeth,"[6] one corresponding to "The blessing for the Land," one corresponding to "Who rebuildeth Jerusalem," and one corresponding to "Who is good and doeth good." Then they added another four cups: one in honor of the town officers, one in honor of the town leaders, one in honor of the Temple, and one in honor of Rabban Gamaliel. But when people began to drink so much that they became intoxicated, the practice of drinking the original number of ten cups was restored.[7]

427. A story is told of one of Kevul's[8] notables who was about to have his son wed. On the fourth day of the week,[9] he invited guests. While they were eating and drinking, he said to his son, "Go up to the upper chamber and get us some good wine out of such-and-such a cask." When the son got there, a serpent bit him, and he died. The father waited for him to come down, but when he did not, the father said: I will go up and see what's happened to my son. He went up and found that a serpent had bitten his son and that he was dead, lying among the wine casks. What did the father do? [Not wishing to dampen the merry mood of his guests], he waited until they had finished their meal. Then, as they were about to say the grace after meals, he spoke out: "Masters, you are not here to say in my son's honor the bridegroom's grace after meals, but rather to say the mourners' grace after meals. You are not here to escort my son to his bridal chamber—come, then, and escort him to his grave." Presently, R. Zakkai of Cabul [lamenting the son's death] concluded his discourse with "If laughter is mingled [with grief], then I say, 'What does mirth accomplish?' " (Eccles. 2:2).[10]

428. "Once, when Jacob was cooking a stew, Esau came in from the open, famished" (Gen. 25:29). On that day Abraham our father died, and our father Jacob made a stew of lentils to comfort Isaac his father. Why lentils? In the west [the Land of Israel], it was said in the name of Rabbah bar Mari: Even as the lentil has, so to speak, no mouth [no cleft], so a mourner has no mouth [he is mute]. According to others: Even as a lentil is round, so mourning comes round in turn to all who enter the world.[11]

429. The sages said in the name of Bar Kappara: When one sheds tears [at the death of] a virtuous man, the Holy One counts them and places them in His treasure house.[12]

430. R. Judah said: Even the poorest man in Israel should provide [for his wife's funeral] not less than two flutes and at least one professional female mourner.[13]

431. During the week of a festival, women may wail but not clap their hands [in a gesture of grief]. However, R. Ishmael said: Those who are next to the bier may clap their hands [in a gesture of grief]. On New Moons, Hanukkah, and Purim, they may both wail and clap their hands. But on none of these days may they chant a dirge.

What is meant by a wail? That all the women wail together. What is meant by a dirge? That one chants [a line] of a dirge, and the others respond [by repeating it].

What did the women say [as they lamented]? According to Rava, the women of Shekanzib[14] used to say:

---

1. To suffer during one's lifetime was bad enough; to be singled out at death was too much.
2. B. MK 27a–b.
3. B. BB 100b.
4. B. Sanh 19a.
5. B. MK 27a.
6. "Who feedeth" is the first blessing in the grace after meals; the blessing "for the Land" is the second; "Who rebuildeth Jerusalem" is the third; and "Who is good and doeth good" is the fourth. See Hertz, *APB*, pp. 966–74.
7. B. Ket 8b; Sem 14.
8. A city in western Galilee near Acco.
9. The day virgins are wed. See Ket 1:1.
10. JV: "I said of laughter: 'It is mad'; and of mirth: 'What doth it accomplish'?" But *meholal* ("mad") can also mean "mingled [with grief]." Lev. R. 20:3; Eccles. R. 2:2, §4.
11. B. BB 16b.
12. B. Shab 105b.
13. B. Ket 46b.
14. Not far from Mahoza, where Rava lived.

Alas for him who is departing,
Alas for the loss [that is ours].
O mountains, enfold yourselves [in clouds]
And cover yourselves [in mourning].
For he is descended from princes, son of great men.
O Sheol, provide a stole of Milesian wool
For this offspring of great men, whose own capacity
to provide has ended.[1]

432. We have been taught: Even as the deceased are requited, so are eulogizers [who do not tell the truth] and they who echo [the falsehoods spoken by] them.[2]

433. In Jerusalem they used to walk in front of the bier reciting the things a deceased person had done, while in Judea they used to recite behind the bier the things he had done. For in Jerusalem they recited in front of the bier only the things he had actually done, while behind the bier they recited the things he had done as well as the things he had not done. However, in Judea they recited in front of the bier the things he had done as well as things he had not done, but those who followed the bier did not respond to all things recited, limiting themselves to only things he had done.[3]

434. Our masters taught: They who are engaged in eulogizing may, as long as the body is still before them, step aside one by one to recite the Shema. When the body is no longer before them, they may sit down to recite it, while the mourner sits in silence. When they stand up to recite the *Tefillah*, the mourner should stand up to resign himself to God's judgment as he says, "Master of the universes, I have sinned greatly before You, and You did not requite me even a thousandth part. May it be Your will, O Lord our God, that in compassion You heal the breaches we have suffered and the breaches suffered by Your entire people Israel."

Abbaye said: A man should not speak thus, for we have been taught in the name of R. Yose that a man should not provide an opening for Satan [to make accusations].[4]

435. R. Simeon ben Eleazar said: Do not try to comfort your friend while the body of his deceased lies before him.[5]

436. It happened that a child of R. Hiyya bar Abba, the teacher of Resh Lakish's son, died. The first day [of R. Hiyya's mourning], Resh Lakish did not go to him. The next day, Resh Lakish took along Judah bar Nahmani, his interpreter,[6] and said to him, "Rise and say something [appropriate] to the death of the child." Judah began his discourse with the verse "When the Lord saw that He was spurned, He [moved] in anger against a man's sons and daughters" (Deut. 32:19).[7] When there is a generation in which fathers spurn the Holy One, He moves in anger against their sons and daughters, so that they die young. Did Judah, invited to comfort R. Hiyya, mean to add to his grief [by speaking] thus? On the contrary—he meant: "You [R. Hiyya] are so important as to be punished [by the loss of your child] for the shortcomings of your generation."

Then Resh Lakish said to Judah, "Rise and say something suitable to the praise of the Holy One." Judah began his discourse by saying, "O God, who is great in the abundance of His greatness, mighty and strong in the multitude of awesome deeds, who with His word revives the dead, who does great things that are unsearchable and wondrous works without number. Blessed are You, O Lord, who revives the dead."

Then Resh Lakish said to Judah, "Rise and say something appropriate to the mourners." Judah began his discourse by saying, "Our brethren, worn out and crushed by this bereavement, set your hearts to consider this: your experience is one that abides forever; it is a path trodden ever since the six days of creation. Many have drunk [this cup of sorrow]; many will drink. Like the drinking of the former, so will be the drinking of the latter. Our brethren, may the Lord of consolations comfort you. Blessed be He who comforts the mourners."

Then Resh Lakish said to Judah, "Rise and say something appropriate to those who comfort mourners." Judah began his discourse by saying, "Our brethren, bestowers of loving-kindnesses, children of bestowers of loving-kindnesses, who hold fast to the covenant of Abraham our father, our brethren, may the Lord of requital give you your reward. Blessed are You, O Lord, who gives the reward due."

Resh Lakish then said to Judah, "Rise and say something capable of consoling all of Israel." Judah began his discourse by saying, "Lord of universes, redeem and save, deliver and rescue Your people Israel from pestilence and from the sword, from plundering and from the blast, from mildew and from all kinds of calamities stirring up to overwhelm the world. Even before we call, may You answer. Blessed are You who stays the plague."[8]

437. When R. Samuel bar Judah's daughter died, the sages said to Ulla: Let us go in and console him. But he answered them: What have I to do with the Babylonian's manner of consolation, which is almost blasphemy? For they say, "What can one do [against God]?" which implies that, were it possible to do anything, they would have done it. He therefore went alone to R. Samuel and said to him: [Scripture says], "And the Lord said unto me: 'Be not at enmity with Moab, neither contend with them in battle' " (Deut. 2:9). Now, there is the question: Would it have entered Moses' mind to wage war against Moab without God's express permission [so that God had to say explicitly, "Do not contend with Moab"]? No, but reasoning *a fortiori*,

1. B. MK 28b.
2. B. Ber 62a.
3. Sem 3 (ed. Zlotnick, p. 38).
4. B. Ber 19a.
5. Avot 4:18.
6. The one who expanded to the public the master's occasionally brief or cryptic utterances spoken in a low voice.
7. JV: "And the Lord saw, and spurned, because of the provoking of His sons and daughters."
8. B. Ket 8b.

Moses said, "Concerning the Midianites, who came only to assist the Moabites, the Torah has commanded 'Vex the Midianites and smite them' [Num. 25:17]). Therefore, all the more should the Moabites themselves be vexed." But the Holy One said to Moses, "The idea that entered your mind is not what entered Mine. There are two good doves I must bring forth from these two nations: Ruth the Moabite and Naamah the Ammonite."[1] Now, may not the matter be argued *a fortiori*? If, for the sake of two good doves [who were to descend from Moab and Ammon], the Holy One showed pity to these two great nations, so that they were not destroyed, does it not follow all the more that if my master [R. Hiyya's] daughter had been fit and worthy to have goodly issue, [she would not have died] but would have remained alive?[2]

438. "Weep not for the dead, neither bemoan him" (Jer. 23:10). "Weep not for the dead" in excess, "neither bemoan him" beyond measure. What does this mean? Three days of weeping, seven for lamenting, and thirty days [for refraining] from wearing pressed clothes and from trimming the hair. "From then on," says the Holy One, "you are not expected to be more compassionate to him than I."[3]

439. When R. Hanina's daughter died and he did not weep for her, his wife asked: Was it a mere hen you carried out of your house? He replied: Do you want me to suffer two evils—not only bereavement but also blindness from incessant weeping?[4]

440. R. Judah said in the name of Rav: When a man indulges in excessive grief for his dead, he will soon find himself weeping for another dead.

In R. Huna's neighborhood, there was a woman who had seven sons. When one of them died, she wept excessively. R. Huna sent word to her: "Don't do this," but she paid no attention to him. He sent word again: "If you listen, well and good; if not, you may find yourself preparing shrouds for your remaining sons." When all of them died, she kept on weeping. Finally, he sent word to her: "Prepare shrouds for yourself," and she, too, died.[5]

441. Rav said: Only after twelve months does one begin to forget the dead.[6]

442. Our masters taught: There are three things God reluctantly thought of, but even if He had not thought of them, they had to be thought of: that a corpse should smell foul,[7] that the dead should be put out of mind, and that produce should rot.[8]

443. R. Meir said: He who finds his fellow mourning after twelve months and speaks words of consolation to him—whom does he resemble? A physician who finds a man whose broken leg had mended and says to him, "Come with me. I will break your leg again and heal it, and you will see how excellent are my medicaments."[9]

---

1. Solomon's wife, through whom the royal house of Judah descended.
2. B. BK 38a–b.
3. B. MK 27b.
4. B. Shab 151b.
5. B. MK 27b.
6. B. Ber 58b.
7. But for that, the kin might keep it and never be consoled.
8. But for that, speculators might hold on to it to raise prices. B. Pes 54b.
9. B. MK 21b.

CHAPTER FOUR

TRAITS AND ATTITUDES

Peace and Strife

1. Rabban Simeon ben Gamaliel said: The world endures on account of three things: on account of justice, truth, and peace.[1]

2. R. Simeon ben Halafta said: The Holy One found no vessel that could contain Israel's blessing except peace, as is said, "In the Lord's wish to give enduring strength to His people, the Lord blessed His people with peace" (Ps. 29:18).[2]

3. "And the Land shall yield her produce" (Lev. 26:4). You might say, "Well, we've got food, we've got drink." Still, if there is no peace, there is nothing at all, for Scripture goes on to say, "And I will give peace in the Land" (Ps. 26:6), which indicates that peace equals all else. Indeed, we say [in the morning *Tefillah*], "When He made peace, He created everything."

R. Levi said: Peace is precious, for the blessings [following the Shema and the blessing at the end of the *Tefillah*] conclude with peace.[3] Then, too, the priests' blessing ends with "The Lord give thee peace" (Num. 6:26), by way of saying that none of the blessings avail at all unless peace is with them.

R. Eleazar ha-Kappar said: Great is peace, for even when Israel worship idols but are together in one band, the measure of justice does not touch them, as is said, "Ephraim is banded to idols, let him alone" (Hos. 4:17). But when they are divided, what is said of them? "Their heart is divided—let them now bear their guilt" (Hos. 10:2).

Hezekiah said: Great is peace, for Scripture says of all the other journeys, "They journeyed" and "They encamped"—that is to say, they set out in strife and encamped in strife. But when they came to Sinai, they encamped as a single encampment: "Israel, there *he* encamped before the mount" (Exod. 19:2). Then the Holy One said: Since they have learned to hate strife and love peace, so that they are now encamped as a single encampment, the time has come for Me to give them My Torah.

R. Eliezer said: Great is peace, for the prophets have implanted in the mouths of people nought but peace.

Bar Kappara said: Great is peace, for even those on high require peace, as is said, "He maketh peace among those of His on high" (Job 25:2). Now, the matter may be argued *a fortiori:* if those on high—among whom there is no hatred, no enmity, no jealousy, no rivalry, no grudging eye—require peace, all the more and more so do human beings, among whom there are such [evil] traits.

R. Joshua said: Great is peace, for the Holy One Himself is called Peace, as is said, "And he called it 'the Lord is peace' " (Judg. 6:24).

R. Joshua ben Levi said: Great is peace; peace is to the world as leaven is to dough.

Great is peace, for even the dead require peace, as when God said to Abram, "Thou shalt go to thy fathers in peace" (Gen. 15:15).

R. Ishmael said: Great is peace, for we find that the Holy One allowed His Name, which is written [in the Torah] in sanctity, to be erased by water in order to bring peace between husband and wife.[4]

Great is peace. For the sake of peace, the Holy One changed words a person uttered, as when the angel quoted Sarah as having said, "Shall I of a surety bear a child, who am old?"[5] (Gen. 18:13).[6]

4. R. Ilai said in the name of R. Eleazar son of R. Simeon: For the sake of peace, one is allowed to change something that has been said, as when the brothers said to Joseph, "Thy father did command. . . . So shall ye say to Joseph: Forgive, I pray thee now" (Gen. 50:16–17).[7]

R. Simeon ben Gamaliel observed: See how much ink was spilled, how many pens broken, how many hides cured, how many children spanked—[all] to learn in the Torah something that had never been said. Consider then how great is the power of peace![8]

5. Hezekiah said: Great is peace, for of all other precepts it is written, "If thou meet thine enemy's ox . . . going astray" (Exod. 23:4), "If thou see the ass of him that hateth thee" (Exod. 23:5), "If a bird's nest chance to be before thee" (Deut. 22:6). These mean: If a precept is at hand, you are required to perform it; but if it is not, you are not required to perform it. Of peace, however, what is said? "Seek peace, and pursue it" (Ps. 34:15), meaning: Seek it where you are and pursue it elsewhere.[9]

6. Hillel said: Be of the disciples of Aaron, loving peace, pursuing peace, loving mankind, and bringing them near to Torah.

---

1. Avot 1:2.
2. Uk 3:12.
3. See Hertz, *APB*, pp. 372 and 154.
4. The passage concerning a woman suspected of infidelity (Num. 5:11–21) is written in ink on a tablet. In the course of the ordeal administered to the woman, it is required that the words of the passage be washed off by water, thus blotting out, so to speak, the Names of God mentioned in it.
5. Actually she said: "my lord being old" (Gen. 18:12).
6. Sif Lev., ed. Weiss, p. 111a; Sif Num., §42; Tanhuma B, *Tzav*, §10; Lev. R. 9:9; Num. R. 11:7; Deut. R. 5:12; Per Sha; Yalkut, *Naso*, §711.
7. Jacob gave no such command.
8. B. Yev 65b; Tanhuma B, *Tzav*, §10.
9. Lev. R. 9:9; P. Pe 1:1, 15d; Per Sha.

Loving peace. What does this mean? It means that a man should love [to foster] peace in Israel between man and man, just as Aaron loved [to foster] peace in Israel between man and man, as is stated, "The law of truth was in his mouth, and unrighteousness was not found in his lips; he walked with Me in peace and uprightness, and did turn away from iniquity" (Mal. 2:6). R. Meir said: What is meant by "and did turn many away from iniquity"? Whenever Aaron walked along the road and met a wicked man, he would greet him warmly. On the following day, when that man was about to commit a transgression, he would say to himself: Woe is me! After doing this, how can I lift my eyes and look Aaron in the face? I would be ashamed before him, since he greeted me so warmly. Consequently, that man will hold himself back from transgression.

Similarly, when two men had quarreled with each other, Aaron would go and sit with one of them and say, "My son, see what your companion is doing! He beats his breast and rends his clothes as he moans, 'Woe is me! How can I lift my eyes and look my companion in the face? I am shamed before him, since it is I who offended him.' " Aaron would sit with him until he had removed all rancor from his heart. Then Aaron would go and sit with the other man and say likewise, "My son, see what your companion is doing! He beats his breast and rends his clothes as he moans, 'Woe is me! How can I lift my eyes and look my companion in the face? I am ashamed before him, since it was I who offended him.' " Aaron would sit with him also until he had removed all rancor from his heart. Later, when the two met, they would embrace and kiss each other. Therefore it is stated, "They wept for Aaron thirty days, even all the House of Israel" (Num. 20:29).[1]

7. Although the school of Shammai and the school of Hillel were in disagreement—what the one forbade, the other permitted—nevertheless, the school of Shammai did not refrain from marrying women [of the families] of the school of Hillel, nor did the school of Hillel refrain from marrying those of the school of Shammai. This should teach you that they showed love and friendship toward one another, thus putting into practice the injunction "Love ye truth, but also peace" (Zech. 8:19).[2]

8. "Do not break up into clusters" (Deut. 14:1).[3] Do not form many [small] clusters, but all of you stay as one cluster.

"Do not break up into clusters." Do not divide in dissent against one another, lest you bring about a "baldness" within your number, as Korah did. He divided Israel, making them into many small clusters, and thus brought about a *korhah*, a "baldness," in Israel.[4]

9. "Ye . . . are alive every one of you this day" (Deut. 4:4). When are you described as "alive"? As [on this day], when "every one of you" is joined together in one cluster.

["When His cluster is one, He will establish it upon the Land" (Amos 9:6).][5] In the way of the world, when a man picks up a cluster of reeds, can he possibly break them all at one time? But if he picks up the reeds one by one, even a child can break them. Thus you find that Israel cannot be redeemed until they are one cluster: "In those days the house of Judah shall walk with the House of Israel, and they shall come together in a cluster out of the land of the north" (Jer. 3:18).[6]

10. Why was "That it was good" not said on the second day of creation? R. Hanina explained: Because on the second day separation [that is to say, disunion] was brought into being, as indicated in "Let [the firmament] separate water from water" (Gen. 1:6). In this regard, R. Tavyomi noted: If there is no mention "that it was good," about an act of separation that is conducive to the world's improvement and well-being, all the less so should these words occur in describing acts of separation that lead to the world's disarray.[7]

11. Any controversy that is carried on for Heaven's sake will in the end be of lasting worth, but any that is not carried on for Heaven's sake will in the end not be of lasting worth. What controversy was for Heaven's sake? The controversy between Hillel and Shammai. What was not for Heaven's sake? The controversy caused by Korah and his entire company.[8]

12. We have been taught that R. Nehemiah said: On account of hatred without rightful cause, strife grows abundant in a man's household.[9]

13. Why was the First Temple destroyed? Because of three evils in it: idolatry, sexual immorality, and bloodshed. But why was the Second Temple destroyed, seeing that, during the time it stood, people occupied themselves with Torah, observance of precepts, and the practice of charity? Because, during the time it stood, hatred without rightful cause prevailed. This should teach you that hatred without rightful cause is deemed as grave as all the three sins of idolatry, sexual immorality, and bloodshed together.[10]

14. "He hangeth the earth on restraint (*belimah*)"[11] (Job 26:7). R. Ilai said: The world endures only on account of him who restrains (*bolem*) himself during strife.[12]

---

1. Avot 1:14; ARN, Soncino, 13.
2. B. Yev 14b.
3. In JV, *titgodedu* is translated "do not cut yourselves." But the verb may also be a form of *aguddah* ("cluster").
4. Sif Deut., §96; Yalkut, *Re'eh*, §891.
5. JV: "And hath founded His vault upon the earth." But *aguddato* ("His vault") also means "His cluster"; and *eretz* ("earth") also means "the Land of Israel."
6. Tanhuma B, *Nitzavim*, §4; Yalkut, *Nitzavim*, §40.
7. Gen. R. 4:6.
8. Avot 5:17.
9. B. Shab 32b.
10. B. Yoma 9b.
11. The word *belimah* means "nothing," as in JV, but it can also mean "restraint."
12. B. Hul 89a.

15. A house in which there is dissension will be destroyed in the end.[1]

16. There were two men who were incited by Satan, so that every Sabbath eve, as the sun was about to set, they fell to quarreling. R. Meir happened to visit them, and for three Sabbaths he stopped them from quarreling, until peace was made between them. Then R. Meir heard Satan wailing: Woe! R. Meir has put me out of my home.[2]

17. Pause and consider how grievous a thing is strife, for the Holy One exterminates the memory of all who help foment it, as is said, "A fire came forth from the Lord, and devoured the two hundred and fifty men" (Num. 16:35).[3]

18. In the time-to-come, when the wicked are condemned to Gehenna, they will complain about the Holy One, saying: Behold, we looked forward to our deliverance by the Holy One. The Holy One will reply: In the world in which you existed, were you not masters of strife, slander, and all kinds of evil? "Behold, all of you kindled a fire, girded yourselves with firebrands" (Isa. 50:11). Therefore, "be gone in the flame of your fire, and among the brands that ye have kindled" (ibid.). And should you ask, "Is it of My hand ye have this?" (ibid.)—no, you did it to yourselves. What you get is of your own doing. Therefore "ye shall lie down in sorrow" (ibid.).[4]

19. Two gladiators cannot sleep on the same board.[5]

20. No good thing can come from a quarrel.[6]

21. Though there be seven pits before the man of peace, [he will not fall into any of them]; but the evildoer will fall even if there is only one pit.[7]

22. R. Huna said: Strife is like an opening made in a dam, which widens as the water presses through it.[8]

Charitable Judgment and Suspicion

23. Hillel said: Judge not your fellow man until you have been in his place.[9]

24. Joshua ben Perahiah said: When you judge anyone, tip the scale in his favor.[10]

25. Our masters taught: He who judges his fellow man on the scale of merit is himself judged favorably.

There is a story of a man who went down from Upper Galilee and hired himself out to a householder in the south for three years. On the eve of the Day of Atonement, the hired man said to the householder, "Give me my wages, so that I may go and maintain my wife and children." The householder: "I have no money." The man: "Give me produce." "I have none." "Give me land." "I have none." "Give me cattle." "I have none." "Give me pillows and bedding." "I have none." So the man tied up his belongings, slung them over his back, and went home in despair. After the holiday, the householder took the wages due the hired man, together with the loads of three asses, a load of food, a load of drink, and a load of delicacies, and went to the hired man's house. After they had eaten and drunk, the householder gave him his wages, and said to him, "When you told me, 'Give me my wages,' and I answered 'I have no money,' what did you suspect me of?"

"I thought perhaps you came upon some merchandise at a low price and purchased it with the money owed me."

"And when you told me, 'Give me cattle,' and I answered, 'I have no cattle,' what did you suspect me of?"

"I thought that they may have been hired out to others."

"And when you said to me, 'Give me land,' and I replied, 'I have no land,' what did you suspect me of?"

"I thought your land was rented out to others."

"And when I told you, 'I have no produce,' what did you suspect me of?"

"I thought perhaps they were not yet tithed."

"And when I told you, 'I have no pillows or bedding,' what did you suspect me of?"

"I thought perhaps you had devoted all your property to Heaven."

The householder exclaimed, "By the Temple service! It was just so. I vowed away all my property because of my son Hyrcanus, who would not occupy himself with Torah, but when I went to my companions in the south, they absolved me of all my vows. And as for you—as you judged me on the scale of merit, so may He who is everywhere judge you on the scale of merit."[11]

26. Our masters taught: There is the story of a certain pious man[12] who ransomed an Israelite maiden from captivity and at the inn had her sleep at his feet. The next day, he went down into a ritual bath, immersed himself, and then taught Mishnah to his disciples, whom he asked, "When I had her sleep at my feet, what did you suspect me of?"

"We thought that perhaps there is a disciple among us whose piety has not been proven to our master."[13]

"When I went down and immersed myself, what did you suspect me of?"

"We thought that, perhaps, because of the fatigue of the journey, the master had had a nocturnal emission."

"By the Temple service," the pious man exclaimed, "it was just so! And as for you—as you judged me on the

---

1. DEZ 9.
2. B. Git 52a.
3. Num. R. 18:4.
4. Eccles. R. 3:9, §1.
5. Since their task is to fight each other. Gen. R. 75:4.
6. Exod. R. 30:17.
7. B. Sanh 7a.
8. Ibid.
9. Avot 2:5.
10. Avot 1:6.
11. According to one tradition, the householder was R. Eliezer ben Hyrcanus and the hired man was Akiva. So *She'eltot*, as quoted by Adin Steinsaltz, Shab, ad loc. B. Shab 127b.
12. R. Judah ben Bava or R. Judah bar Ilai. So Rashi.
13. So the master kept the girl with himself to protect her.

scale of merit, so may He who is everywhere judge you on the scale of merit."[1]

27. Our masters taught: Once the disciples of the wise needed help in a certain matter from a noblewoman of Rome in whose house all the notables of the city used to gather. When the disciples asked, "Who will go to her?" R. Joshua replied, "I will go." So he and his disciples went. As he came within four cubits of the door of her house, he removed his tefillin. Then he went in, shutting the door in their faces. After he came out, he went down to a ritual bath, immersed himself, and then taught Mishnah to his disciples, whom he asked, "When I removed my tefillin, what did you suspect me of?"

"We thought that our master believes 'sacred objects should not be brought into a place of uncleanness.' "

"When I shut the door in your faces, what did you suspect me of?"

"We thought that perhaps he has to discuss with her a matter that concerns the government."

"When I went down to the ritual bath and immersed myself, what did you suspect me of?"

"We thought that perhaps some saliva had sprayed from the woman's mouth upon the master's garments."

"By the Temple service," he exclaimed, "it is just so! And as for you—just as you judged me on the scale of merit, so may He who is everywhere judge you on the scale of merit."[2]

28. "Eli said unto her: 'How long wilt thou be drunken?' . . . And Hannah answered and said: '[Thou art] not my lord' " (1 Sam. 1:14–15). According to Ulla—some say, according to R. Yose son of R. Hanina—Hannah replied: In this matter [of drunkenness], you are not my lord [my superior], nor does the holy spirit rest on you, for you suspect me in this matter.

Some say that this is how Hannah replied: You are not a lord; neither the Presence nor the holy spirit is with you. For you have taken a harsh and not a lenient view of my conduct. Do you not know that "I am a woman of sorrowful spirit" (1 Sam. 1:15)?

"I have drunk neither wine nor strong drink" (1 Sam. 1:15). From these words we may infer, said R. Eleazar, that a man who is wrongfully suspected should make his innocence known.

"Then Eli answered and said: Go in peace" (1 Sam. 1:17). From this we learn, said R. Eleazar, that he who wrongfully suspects his fellow man must placate him. More: he must bestow a blessing upon him, for Eli ended by saying, "The God of Israel grant thy petition" (ibid.)[3]

29. Resh Lakish said: He who is suspicious of innocent people will be smitten in his body. Thus, when Moses said, "But, behold, they will not believe me" (Exod. 4:1), the Holy One, to whom it was known that they would believe this, said to Moses: They are believers, children of believers. It is you who will end up not believing.

And where is the proof that Moses was smitten? The verse "And the Lord said furthermore unto him: 'Put now thy hand into thy bosom.' And he put his hand into his bosom; and when he took it out, behold, his hand was leprous, as white as snow" (Exod. 4:6).[4]

30. R. Reuben ben Itztrobilei said: A person does not incur suspicion unless he has done [what he is suspected of]; or if he did not do all of it, he did part of it; or if he did not do part of it, he yearned in his heart to do it; or if he did not yearn in his heart to do it, he saw others do it and enjoyed [the sight of it].[5]

31. R. Yose said: May my portion be with him who is suspected of something he is innocent of.[6]

Reproof, Flattery, and Hypocrisy

32. We have been taught that Rabbi [Judah I, the Patriarch] said: What is the right way a man should choose for himself? He should love reproofs. As long as there are reproofs in the world, peace of mind comes to the world, good and blessing come to the world, and evil departs from the world, as is said, "But to them that are eager to be reproved, there shall come delight, and the blessing of good shall come upon them" (Prov. 24:25).

R. Samuel bar Nahmani said in the name of R. Jonathan: He who reproves his neighbor for Heaven's sake is deemed worthy of being in the Holy One's own portion, for it is said, "He that reproves a man is to be right behind Me" (Prov. 28:23). More: a thread of favor is to be twined about him, as is said, "He shall find more favor than he that flattereth with his tongue" (ibid.).[7]

33. R. Yose bar Hanina said: Reproof leads to love, as is said, "Reprove a wise man, and he will love thee" (Prov. 9:8). Such is the opinion of R. Yose bar Hanina, who on another occasion said: All love that has no reproof with it is not true love.

Resh Lakish said: Reproof leads to peace. Such is the opinion of the sage, who on another occasion said: All peace that has no reproof with it is not peace.[8]

34. How do we know that when a man observes something unseemly in his neighbor, he should reprove him? From the verse "Thou shalt surely reprove thy neighbor" (Lev. 19:17). How do we know that if he reproved him and his neighbor refused to accept the reproof, he is to reprove him again? From the words "thou shalt *surely* reprove," meaning: under all circumstances. Should you suppose this obligation holds even if the neighbor's face changes color,[9] the verse goes on: "But thou shalt bear no sin because of him" (ibid.).[10]

1. B. Shab 127b.
2. Ibid.
3. B. Ber 31b.
4. B. Shab 97a.
5. B. MK 18b.
6. Ibid.
7. B. Tam 28a.
8. Gen. R. 54:3.
9. Because he is publicly humiliated.
10. B. Ar 16b.

35. Rava said: "Thou shalt surely reprove" (Lev. 19:17)—reprove even a hundred times. I might suppose that only the master must reprove his disciple. But how do I know that a disciple must reprove his master? From Scripture's saying, "Thou shalt surely reprove"—under all circumstances.[1]

36. How far is reproof to go? Rav said: Until the reprover is beaten. Samuel said: Until he is cursed. R. Yohanan said: Until he is reprimanded.[2]

37. R. Zera said to R. Simon: Sir, reprove the people of the exilarch's house. R. Simon replied: They will not be willing to accept any reproof. R. Zera: Even if they are unwilling, you, sir, should nevertheless reprove them.[3]

38. He who can restrain the members of his household [from committing a sin], but does not, will be seized as a pledge [so to speak] for his household. If [he can restrain] the people of his city, he will be seized as a pledge for the people of his city. If [he can restrain] the whole world—all of it—he will be seized as a pledge for the whole world, all of it.[4]

39. R. Hanina said: What is signified by the verse "The Lord will enter into judgment with the elders of His people, and the princes thereof" (Isa. 3:14)? Granted, the princes did sin, but how have the elders sinned? What the verse really means is that "[He will punish] the elders because they did not restrain the princes."[5]

40. R. Eleazar ben Azariah's heifer used to go out [on the Sabbath] with a thong between its horns,[6] contrary to the wishes of the sages.

R. Eleazar ben Azariah's heifer—but did he have only one heifer? Recall what Rav has said: "Year after year, the tithe of R. Eleazar ben Azariah's flock numbered twelve thousand calves." In reply, other sages taught: This particular heifer was not his—it belonged to a woman neighbor. But because he did not protest to his neighbor, the heifer was spoken of as his.[7]

41. R. Aha son of R. Hanina said: Never did a promise of good go forth from the mouth of the Holy One that He later reversed to evil, except in the following instance, where it is written, "And the Lord said unto him: 'Go through the midst of the city, through the midst of Jerusalem, and set a mark upon the foreheads of the men that sigh and that cry for all the abominations that be done in the midst thereof' " (Ezek. 9:4). The Holy One said to Gabriel: Go and set a mark of ink on the foreheads of the righteous, so that the destroying angels may have no power over them; and a mark of blood on the foreheads of the wicked, so that the destroying angels may have power over them. The measure of justice protested before the Holy One: "Lord of the universe, how are these different from those?" God: "Those are completely righteous men, while these are completely wicked." "Master of the universe," the measure of justice continued, "those had the opportunity to protest, but did not." God: "It was clear and manifest to Me that if they had protested, they would not have been heeded." The measure of justice: "Master of the universe, this, to be sure, was clear to You. But was it clear to them?" Then God said to the executioners, "Slay utterly the old man, the young man and the maiden, and little children and women; but come not near any man upon whom is the mark." And—reversing the earlier promise—God said, "Begin at My Sanctuary [*mikdashi*]." "Then they began at the elders that were before the house" (Ezek. 9:6). Read not, taught R. Joseph, *mikdashi* "My Sanctuary," but *mekuddashai*, "my sanctified ones," meaning: those people who fulfilled the Torah, all of it, from *alef* to *tav*[8] [but did not protest against wrongdoing].[9]

42. R. Hanina said: Jerusalem was destroyed only because its inhabitants did not reprove one another, as is said, "Her princes are become like harts that find no pasture" (Lam. 1:6). Like harts, each of whose head is beside the tail of the one before it, so did Israel of that generation keep their faces looking toward the ground and not reprove one another.[10]

43. "Hear, and your soul shall live" (Isa. 55:3). How beloved are Israel, that God draws them to Himself with kind words! He says to them: When a man falls from a roof and his entire body is bruised, the physician comes to him and applies a compress to his head, another to his arms, still another to his legs, and to all [other] parts of his body, so that all of him is covered with compresses. I do not act thus. There are two hundred and forty-eight parts in a human body, and the ear is only one of them; even though the entire body is soiled with transgressions, still, as long as the ear is willing to hear [Me], the entire body is infused with life.[11]

44. Love him who reproves you, and hate him who praises you.[12]

45. We have been taught that R. Tarfon said: I wonder if there is anyone in this generation capable of giving reproof. For if anyone says to another, "Take the chip from between your teeth," the other retorts, "Take the beam from between your eyes."[13] R. Eleazar ben Azariah said: I wonder whether there is anyone in this generation capable of accepting reproof. R. Akiva said: I wonder whether

1. B. BM 31a.
2. B. Ar 16b.
3. B. Shab 55a.
4. B. Shab 54b.
5. B. Shab 54b–55a.
6. The thong, used to restrain an animal, would indicate that this heifer was being made to work, contrary to the command that animals, like humans, were to rest on the Sabbath.
7. B. Shab 54b.
8. The first and last letters of the Hebrew alphabet.
9. B. Shab 55a.
10. B. Shab 119b; Lam. R. 1:6, §33.
11. Exod. R. 27:9.
12. ARN 29.
13. Cf. Matthew 7:4 and Luke 6:41.

there is anyone in this generation who knows how to give reproof [without humiliating the one reproved].

R. Yohanan ben Nuri said: I call heaven and earth to witness that many times R. Akiva was punished on account of me, because I used to bring charges against him before Rabban Gamaliel. Nevertheless, R. Akiva's love for me grew, in keeping with the verse "Reprove a man of sense, and he will love thee" (Prov. 9:8).[1]

46. Abbaye said: When a disciple of the wise is beloved by the people of his city, it is not because he is superior in learning, but because he does not reprove them in matters that concern Heaven.[2]

47. "Remove the chaff from yourselves, then remove it from others" (Zeph. 2:1).[3] Resh Lakish said: Adorn yourself; and after that, adorn others.[4]

48. R. Nathan said: Reproach not your neighbor for a blemish that is yours.[5]

49. R. Ilai said in the name of R. Eleazar son of R. Simeon: Just as it is commendable to say something that will be heeded, so it is commendable not to say something that will not be heeded. R. Abba said: Indeed, it is an obligation not to, in keeping with the verse "Reprove not a scorner, lest he hate thee" (Prov. 9:8).[6]

50. R. Eleazar said: A man given to flattery brings wrath upon the world, for Scripture says, "They whose hearts are given to flattery bring on wrath" (Job 36:13). Moreover, his prayer is not heeded: "They cannot cry for help, for He bindeth them" (ibid.).

R. Eleazar said further: When a man is given to flattery, even embryos in their mother's womb curse him.

R. Eleazar said still further: He who is given to flattery will fall into Gehenna.[7]

51. R. Eleazar said: He who flatters his fellow man will in the end fall into his power. If he does not fall into his power, he will fall into the power of his son, and if not into the power of his son, then into the power of his son's son, as is said, "Then the prophet Jeremiah said unto the prophet Hananiah . . . : 'Amen! The Lord do so! The Lord perform the words which thou hast prophesied' " (Jer. 28:5–6). And it is further written, "And when [Jeremiah] was in the gate of Benjamin, a captain of the ward was there, whose name was Irijah, the son of Shelemiah, the son of Hananiah; and he laid hold of Jeremiah the Prophet . . . and brought him to the princes" (Jer. 37:13–14).[8]

52. R. Eleazar said: A community given to flattery is as loathed as a menstruating woman.[9]

53. R. Eleazar said further: A community given to flattery is banished in the end.[10]

54. A company of flatterers is unable to receive the Presence, for it is said, "The flatterer cannot come into His presence" (Job 13:16).[11]

55. R. Judah bar Maarava—according to some, R. Simeon ben Pazzi—expounded: One may flatter the wicked in this world, for it is said [of the world-to-come], "The vile person shall no more be called liberal, nor the churl said to be noble" (Isa. 32:5). From which it follows that, in this world, such flattery is permitted. R. Simeon ben Lakish drew the same inference from the verse in which Jacob said to Esau, "Forasmuch as I have seen thy face, as one seeth the face of God" (Gen. 33:10). R. Simeon ben Lakish's interpretation of the verse is not like that of R. Levi's. For R. Levi said: What parable explains Jacob's flattery of Esau? The one of a man who invited his friend to dine with him. When the guest perceived that the host planned to murder him, he said, "This dish tastes like the dish I had in the royal palace." So he knows the king, said the host to himself, and, seized with fear, he did not try to go through with his murderous scheme.[12]

56. R. Simeon ben Halafta said: Ever since the day the grip of flattery prevailed, judicial decrees have become so twisted and human conduct so corrupt that no man can say to another, "My conduct is better than yours."[13]

57. King Yannai said to his wife: Do not fear the Pharisees, nor those who are not Pharisees, but fear the hypocrites who make believe they are Pharisees—their deeds are like the deeds of Zimri, but they expect reward like Phinehas.[14]

58. Hypocrites should be exposed to prevent the profanation of the Name.[15]

59. Rabban Gamaliel used to proclaim: No disciple whose inner self does not live up to his [acceptable] exterior[16] may enter the house of study.[17]

---

1. B. Ar 16b and En Yaakov, ad loc.
2. B. Ket 105b.
3. JV: "Gather yourselves together, yea, gather." But *hitkosheshu* ("gather yourselves") is here, as suggested by Rashbam, associated with the noun *kash* ("chaff").
4. Resh Lakish seems to regard *hitkosheshu ve-koshu* (variously interpreted) as a dialectical variation of *hitkeshetu ve-koshetu* (so Leon Nemoy).
5. B. BM 59b.
6. B. Yev 65b.
7. B. Sot 41b.
8. B. Sot 41b–42a and En Yaakov, ad loc.
9. B. Sot 42a.
10. Ibid.
11. Ibid.
12. B. Sot 41b and En Yaakov, ad loc.
13. Ibid.
14. Zimri copulated in public, and Phinehas slew him and his partner. Phinehas's reward was "the covenant of an everlasting priesthood." See Num. 25:6–15. B. Sot 22b.
15. B. Yoma 86b.
16. Literally, whose inside is not as his outside.
17. B. Ber 28a.

60. Ben Azzai used to say: It is easier to rule the entire world, all of it, than to sit and teach in the presence of men who cloak themselves [hypocritically] in sages' robes.[1]

61. When the swine crouches, he displays his cloven hooves as if to say, "Look how kosher I am!"[2]

Slander and Disclosing Another's Secret

62. R. Yohanan said in the name of R. Yose ben Zimra: He who speaks slander is as though he denied the existence of the Lord: "With our tongue will we prevail; our lips are our own; who is Lord over us?" (Ps. 12:5).[3]

63. The company of those who speak slander cannot greet the Presence.[4]

64. R. Hisda said in the name of Mar Ukba: When a man speaks slander, the Holy One says, "I and he cannot live together in the world." So Scripture: "He who slanders his neighbor in secret . . . him I cannot endure" (Ps. 101:5). Read not *oto*, "him," but *itto*, "with him [I cannot live]."[5]

65. R. Mana said: He who speaks slander causes the Presence to depart from the earth below to heaven above: you may see for yourself [that this is so]. Consider what David said: "My soul is among lions; I do lie down among them that are aflame; even the sons of men, whose teeth are spears and arrows, and their tongue a sharp sword" (Ps. 57:5). What follows directly? "Be Thou exalted, O God, above the heavens" (Ps. 57:6). For David said: Master of the universe, what can the Presence do on the earth below? Remove the Presence to the firmament.[6]

66. Behold, how vicious is slander! It is more vicious than murder, unchastity, and idolatry put together. In Scripture, each of these three transgressions is termed "great," but slander is spoken of in the plural as "great things." Thus, Cain said of murder, "My punishment is more great than I can bear" (Gen. 4:13); Joseph exclaimed of unchastity, "How then can I do this great wickedness?" (Gen. 39:9); Moses said of idolatry, "Oh, this people have sinned a great sin" (Exod. 32:31). But of slander it is written, "The Lord shall cut off all flattering lips, the tongue that speaketh great things" (Ps. 12:4), to tell you that slander is more vicious than the other three transgressions.[7]

67. A man is punished for four things in this world, but the principal punishment is meted out in the world-to-come. They are: idolatry, unchastity, bloodshed, [and slander], but the punishment for slander equals the other three put together.[8]

68. Resh Lakish said: He who speaks slander so enlarges his iniquities that they reach up to heaven, as is said, "They have set their mouth against the heavens when their tongue walketh through the earth" (Ps. 73:9).[9]

69. R. Hisda said in the name of Mar Ukba: He who speaks slander deserves death by stoning.[10]

70. R. Sheshet said in the name of R. Eleazar ben Azariah: He who speaks slander, he who accepts slander, and he who gives false testimony against his transgression deserve to be cast to the dogs, for the words "Ye shall cast it to the dogs" (Exod. 22:30) are followed directly by "Thou shalt not take up (*tissa*) a false report" (Exod. 23:1), which may be read, "Thou shalt not spread (*tassi*) [a false report]."[11]

71. He who speaks slander has no portion in the world-to-come.[12]

72. R. Hisda said in the name of Mar Ukba: Of him who speaks slander, the Holy One says to the prince of Gehenna: I, at him from above, and you, at him from below, shall together condemn him.[13]

73. The punishment of him who maligns the young woman he wed as not being a virgin is greater than if he had seduced her or raped her.[14] Thus we find that the decree of death against our forebears in the wilderness was sealed only after the spies had maligned the Land, as is said, "By speaking thus, they tried Me as greatly as the ten other times together [when they did not heed Me]; surely they shall not see the Land which I swore unto their fathers" (Num. 14:22–23).[15]

74. "The men who spread calumnies about the Land died of pestilence [in keeping with the Lord's measure for measure]" (Num. 14:37). They died an unnatural death, said R. Simeon ben Lakish.

[Unnatural in what way?] According to R. Hanina bar Papa, R. Shela of Kefar Temarta expounded the verse as hinting that the tongue of each spy grew so unnaturally long that it reached down to his navel, and worms crawled out of his tongue and entered into his navel, and out of his navel back into his tongue.

According to R. Nahman bar Isaac, the spies choked in a spasm of croup.[16]

---

1. ARN 25.
2. Gen. R. 65:1; Lev. R. 13:5.
3. B. Ar 15b.
4. B. Sot 42a.
5. B. Sot 5a.
6. Deut. R. 5:10.
7. MTeh 52:2; B. Ar 15b.
8. P. Pe 1:1, 15d.
9. B. Ar 15b.
10. Ibid.
11. B. Pes 118a.
12. PRE 53.
13. B. Ar 15b.
14. The penalty for such maligning is one hundred *sela*, while for rape or seduction it is only fifty *sela* (see Deut. 22:29 and Exod. 22:16).
15. B. Ar 15a.
16. B. Sot 35b.

75. R. Eleazar ben Perata said: Pause and consider the spies, and you will understand how pernicious is the effect of calumny. If such befell the spies, who spoke calumny only of trees and stones, how much more and more will befall him who speaks calumny of his neighbor![1]

76. R. Hanina said: Plagues of leprosy come only on account of speaking calumny. For, as the sages said, you can see for yourself that such plagues come on account of calumny. Even the righteous Miriam, who spoke calumny of her brother Moses—plagues clung to her, as a sign [and a warning] to all given to speaking calumny. Hence, "remember what the Lord thy God did unto Miriam" (Deut. 24:9).

Now, the matter may be reasoned *a fortiori:* if Miriam—who made certain not to speak to Moses directly, did so for Moses' own benefit [so he would take back his life and have more children], and spoke for the glory of Him who is everywhere and for the increase of the population of the world—was punished thus, how much more and more will he who speaks publicly in disparagement of his neighbor be punished![2]

77. Resh Lakish said: The verse "This shall be the law concerning the *metzora* [leper]" (Lev. 14:2) means: "This shall be the law concerning *motzi shem ra* [him sho speaks calumny]."[3]

78. "Thinkest thou to kill me, as thou didst kill the Egyptian? And Moses . . . said: 'Surely the thing is known' " (Exod. 2:14). For Moses had been meditating in his heart: How have Israel sinned, that they should be enslaved more than any other nation?" But upon hearing [one of the quarreling men say right out what he, Moses, had done], he said to himself: "Now the thing is known," now I know why the Israelites are enslaved. Talebearing is rife among them. How can they ever be worthy of deliverance?[4]

79. R. Judah said in the name of Rav: When David told Mephibosheth "Thou and Ziba divide the land" (2 Sam. 19:30), a divine voice came forth and said to him: Rehoboam and Jeroboam will divide the kingdom.

R. Judah went on to say in the name of Rav: Had David not heeded the calumny [against Mephibosheth], the kingdom of the house of David would not have been divided, Israel [in the north] would not have served idols, and we would not have been banished from our Land.[5]

80. "A slanderer shall not be established in the earth" (Ps. 140:12). R. Levi said: In the time-to-come, the Holy One will take the [heathen] nations of the world, cast them down into Gehenna, and ask them: Why did you despoil My children with fines? They will reply: Because out of their own ranks came men of evil tongue with tall tales about their neighbors' possessions. Then the Holy One will take both the heathen nations and the slanderers, and cast them down into Gehenna.[6]

81. R. Eleazar son of R. Simeon used to apprehend thieves. So R. Joshua ben Korhah sent word to him: "O Vinegar son of wine! How long will you deliver up the people of our God for slaughter?" R. Eleazar sent word back: "I weed out thorns from the vineyard." R. Joshua replied, "Let the Owner of the vineyard come and Himself weed out the thorns."[7]

82. Mar Ukba[8] sent a message to R. Eleazar, saying, "Certain men are acting against me, but I am able to deliver them into the hands of the government. What shall I do?" R. Eleazar scribbled his answer on the same message: "I said, 'I will take heed to my ways, that I sin not with my tongue; I will keep a curb upon my mouth, while the wicked is before me' " (Ps. 39:2), meaning: Even though the wicked is before me, I will still keep a curb on my mouth. Mar Ukba sent another message to R. Eleazar: They are troubling me very much, and I can put up with them no longer." R. Eleazar replied [with the quotation]: "Resign thyself unto the Lord, and wait patiently [*hit'holel*] for Him" (Ps. 37:7); [that is to say]: Wait for the Lord, and He will utterly prostrate them [*halalim*] before you. In spite of them, go to the house of study morning and evening, and there will soon be an end to them.

R. Eleazar had hardly spoken these words when Geniva[9] was placed in chains for execution.[10]

83. In considering the verse "Death and life are in the hand of the tongue" (Prov. 18:21), R. Hama son of R. Hanina asked: Is it conceivable for the tongue to have a hand? No, but what the verse means is that the tongue can be as murderous as the hand. One might have thought that, just as the hand can kill only what is near it, so the tongue could kill only what is near it; therefore Scripture says, "Their tongue is an arrow shot out" (Jer. 9:7). One might assume that, just as an arrow kills only up to a distance of forty or at most fifty cubits, so the tongue could kill only up to a distance of forty at most fifty cubits; therefore Scripture states, "They have set their mouths against the heavens, while their tongues range over the earth" (Ps. 73:9).[11]

84. "Sharp arrows of the mighty are like coals of broom" (Ps. 120:4). Why does the text liken the evil tongue to an arrow rather than to any other weapon? Because all other weapons strike at close quarters, while the arrow strikes from afar. Likewise the evil tongue—something said in Rome can kill in Syria. Nor is the evil tongue likened to any coals, but only to coals of broom, for all other coals,

1. B. Ar 15b and En Yaakov, ad loc.
2. Deut. R. 6:8; Sif Deut., §275.
3. B. Ar 15b.
4. Exod. R. 1:30.
5. B. Shab 56b.
6. Gen. R. 20:1.
7. B. BM 83b.
8. Mar Ukba II the Exilarch had great influence in the government.
9. He was one of Mar Ukba's chief antagonists.
10. B. Git 7a.
11. B. Ar 15b.

when extinguished without, are also extinguished within; but the coals of broom, even when extinguished without, continue to burn within. So it is with the victim of slander—even though you go and endeavor to appease him, and he acts appeased, yet he continues to burn within.[1]

85. R. Samuel bar Nahman said: Why is the evil tongue called a thrice-slaying tongue? Because it slays three persons: the person speaking, the person spoken to, and the person spoken of. And the proof? Doeg, who spoke evil; Saul, to whom it was spoken; and Nob, the city of priests, of whom it was spoken.[2]

86. The tongue is like an arrow. Why? Because if a man takes his sword in hand to slay his fellow, who then pleads with him and begs for mercy, the would-be slayer can change his mind and return the sword to its sheath. But once the would-be slayer has shot and let fly an arrow, it cannot be brought back even if he wants to do so.[3]

87. R. Yohanan said in the name of R. Yose ben Zimra: What is meant by the verse "What more can be given unto thee, what more can be done [for protection] against thee, thou deceitful tongue?" (Ps. 120:3)? The Holy One said to the tongue: All other parts of a man's body stand erect, but you lie prone. Most other parts of a man's body are outside; you are within. Not only that, but I encompassed you with two walls, one of bone [the teeth] and one of flesh [the cheeks]. "What more can be given unto thee, and what more can be done [for protection] against thee, thou deceitful tongue?"[4]

88. R. Eleazar said in the name of R. Yose ben Zimra: Man has two hundred and forty-eight parts, some prone, some erect. The tongue is placed between the two cheeks, with a water channel [of saliva] passing under it, besides being guarded by several other enfoldings [such as teeth and lips]. Yet pause and consider what searing burns[5] it inflicts! How many more and more such burns would the tongue inflict if it were standing erect![6]

89. How vicious is the evil tongue! A parable of a man smitten on both legs, who greatly disturbed a principality. People said: If he were whole, how much more and more would he disturb! So, too, the tongue. Though cut to small size and placed within the mouth, yet it disturbs the world greatly. To what may the tongue be compared? To a dog: though it is chained and confined, and placed in the innermost of three chambers, yet all people fear it when it barks. If it were outside [unchained], what would it do! So the evil tongue. It is placed within, beyond the opening of the mouth; within, beyond the lips. Yet it smites without cease. If the tongue were outside, how much more and more would it smite!

Hence the Holy One said [to man]: I can save you from all troubles that come upon you. But when it concerns the evil tongue, you must make yourself all but invisible, and you will suffer no injury.[7]

90. Resh Lakish said: [In defense of himself, the serpent could have pleaded]: Does the serpent bite without a whispered command from on high?" (Eccles. 10:11).[8] [Instead of defending himself, he could respond with a question]: "And what advantage does he get who uses his tongue for evil?" (ibid.). Hence, in the time-to-come, when all beasts gather together, go to the serpent, and say, "The lion ramps and devours. The wolf rends and consumes. What enjoyment do you get [from poisoning creatures]?" The serpent will reply, "Well, what advantage does he get who uses his tongue for evil?"[9]

91. R. Samuel son of R. Nahman said: If a serpent is asked, "Why are you found among fences?" it is likely he will answer, "Because I made a breach in the fence of the world." If asked, "Why do you slither along with your tongue darting in the dust?" the serpent is likely to answer, "Because the tongue brought me to this state." If asked, "Why is it that, when other animals bite, their [single] bite does not kill, but when you bite, you kill? What benefit do you derive from that?" the serpent is likely to answer, " 'Does the serpent bite unless there is a whispered command?' [Eccles. 10:11]. If I were not told from heaven, 'Bite!' I would not bite." If asked, "And why, though you bite one limb, do all other limbs feel the poison at once?" the serpent is likely to reply, "Are you asking me? Ask the man of evil tongue who dwells in Rome and slays in Syria, or who dwells in Syria and slays in Rome."[10]

92. "They of my people who live together[11] turn to the sword, smite therefore upon the thigh" (Ezek. 21:17). R. Eleazar said: The verse refers to men who eat and drink with one another, yet stab one another with the swords of their tongues.[12]

93. R. Ishmael taught: "Do not go as a peddler among the people" (Lev. 19:16) refers to peddling by the evil tongue.

R. Nehemiah taught: Do not be like the peddler, who transports the words of one to the other and the words of the other to the one.[13]

94. What constitutes evil speech? Rabbah said: As when one says, There is fire burning in [the oven of] So-and-so's house. Abbaye asked: But what harm does he do? He merely provides information. Nevertheless, [said Rab-

1. Gen. R. 98:19; P. Pe 1:1, 16a.
2. B. Ar 15b; P. Pe 1:1, 16a; Deut. R. 5:10.
3. MTeh 120:4.
4. B. Ar 15b.
5. Cf. James 3:6.
6. Lev. R. 16:4.
7. Yalkut, *Ki Tetze*, §933.
8. JV: "If the serpent bite before it is charmed, then the charmer hath no advantage."
9. B. Ar 15b.
10. P. Pe 1:1, 16a; Tanhuma B, *Hukkat*, §8; Lev. R. 26:2.
11. The word *megurei* ("thrust down") in JV is in this comment taken as a form of *gur* ("live together").
12. B. Yoma 9b.
13. P. Pe 1:1, 16a.

bah], such information may be uttered with the intent to slander, as though he were saying: Where else would such a fire be burning except in the house of So-and-so, who has plenty of meat and fish?[1]

95. When R. Yohanan was asked, "What is evil speech?" he replied, "What is uttered explicitly as well as what is only hinted at."

Thus, when dealers in flax had a gathering to allot to each a portion of a royal levy, one of them, whose name was Ben Hovetz, did not come. So when the question was asked, What shall we eat today? one person answered: *Hovetz*, "soft cheese." At that, the others [reminded of their absent colleague] said: Ben Hovetz should be made to come.

Here, said R. Yohanan, we have an instance of evil speech uttered obliquely.

[Another example]: When the council of Sepphoris held a meeting [for a similar purpose], one of them, whose name was Yohanan, did not come. One of the council asked another: Should we not visit the learned Yohanan today [since he must be ill]? Instantly, all said: Yohanan should be made to come.

Here, said R. Simeon ben Lakish, we have an instance of evil speech disguised as piety.[2]

96. A folded deed was once brought before Rabbi [Judah I, the Patriarch], who remarked, "There is no date on this deed." R. Simeon Berabbi said to Rabbi, "It might be hidden between its folds." On ripping the seams [which held together the deed's folds], Rabbi saw the date. Then he turned around [and] looked at R. Simeon with displeasure.[3] R. Simeon: "I did not write it. R. Judah the Tailor wrote it." Rabbi: "Keep away from such slander!"[4]

Once again, when he was sitting in Rabbi's presence, R. Simeon finished a section of the book of Psalms. Rabbi said, "How accurate this writing is!" R. Simeon: "I did not write it. Judah the Tailor wrote it." Rabbi: "Keep away from such slander!"

In the first instance, one can well understand Rabbi's reproof [since] there was slander; but what slander was there in this instance?

The kind of slander spoken of by R. Dimi. For R. Dimi brother of R. Safra taught: A man should never speak in praise of his friend, because out of praise of him he may [bit by bit] come to dispraise him.[5]

97. "They . . . said: 'We came unto the Land . . . and surely it floweth with milk and honey. . . . Howbeit the people . . . are fierce' " (Num. 13:27–28). This is the way of those who deal in slander—they open with good things and end with evil ones.[6]

98. R. Yohanan said in the name of R. Meir: A slanderous report that does not contain an element of truth in the beginning will not stand up in the end.[7]

99. Even if a word [of slander] is not entirely effective, it will always be partly effective.[8]

100. R. Amram said in the name of Rav: No man escapes—not even for one day—[committing] three transgressions: unchaste thought, insistence on God's immediate response to prayer, and slander. Slander, you say? Yes, at the very least, the fine dust [the overtones] of slander.

R. Judah said in the name of Rav: Most people are guilty of some cheating, a few of unchastity, but all of slander. Slander, you say? Well, at least the fine dust [the overtones] of slander.[9]

101. Rabbah said: Whatever is said in the presence of the person concerned is not considered slander. Abbaye countered: All the more so—it is impudence as well as slander. Rabbah replied: I hold with R. Yose, who asserted, "I never said anything about a person that would make me look back to see if that person were standing behind me."

Rabbah bar R. Huna stated: Repeating what a man said against himself in the presence of three others is not slander. Why not? Because your friend has a friend, and your friend's friend has a friend.[10]

102. R. Menasya grandson of R. Menasya said in the name of R. Menasya the Elder: What is the proof that when a man says something to his friend, the latter may not repeat it unless the man says, "You may go and say it"? The verse "The Lord spoke to him out of the Tent of Meeting, that he was to say (*le'mor*)[11] . . ." (Lev. 1:1).[12]

103. What is the proof that [after a trial is over] and one of the judges leaves [the court], he may not say, "I was for acquittal, but my colleagues were determined to convict. So what could I do, since they were the majority?" Of such a leak, Scripture asserts, "He who revealeth that which is to remain secret is a talebearer" (Prov. 11:13).[13]

104. Our masters taught: The man gathering was Zelophehad. Thus it is said, "And while the children of Israel were *in the wilderness*, they found a man gathering sticks of wood upon the Sabbath day . . . and they stoned him with stones, and he died" (Num. 15:32 and 15:36); while elsewhere the daughters of Zelophehad said, "Our father died *in the wilderness*" (Num. 27:3). Just as in this instance Zelophehad is meant, so, too, Zelophehad [is meant] earlier. Such was R. Akiva's opinion. But R. Judah ben

---

1. B. Ar 15b.
2. P. Pe 1:1, 16a.
3. Because it should not have been so difficult to come upon the date.
4. Why charge R. Judah the Tailor with the error?
5. B. BB 164b.
6. Tanhuma B, *Shelah*, §17.
7. B. Sot 35a.
8. Gen. R. 56:4; Yalkut, *Va-yera*, §101.
9. B. BB 164b–165a.
10. So what was said will inevitably come to be known. B. Ar 15b–16a.
11. Usually translated "saying."
12. B. Yoma 4b.
13. B. Sanh 29a.

Betera said to him, "Akiva, in either case you will have to justify yourself: if you are right, then you have revealed the identity of a man whom the Torah shielded; and if you are wrong, you are casting a stigma upon a righteous man."

Similarly, you read, "And the anger of the Lord was kindled against them; and he departed" (Num. 12:9). The verse teaches that Aaron, too, became leprous. Such was R. Akiva's opinion. But R. Judah ben Betera said to him, "Akiva, in either case you will have to justify yourself for saying such a thing: if you are right, even though the Torah shielded him, you have disclosed what happened to Aaron; and if wrong, you are casting a stigma upon a righteous man."[1]

105. A story is told of a disciple about whom it was reported that, after twenty-two years, he disclosed a matter stated in the house of study [as a secret]. So R. Ammi expelled him from the house of study, saying, "This one discloses secrets."[2]

106. Ignorant men [*amme ha-aretz*] should not be told what is secret.[3]

Truth and Falsehood, Vows and Oaths

107. Rabban Simeon ben Gamaliel said: The world endures because of three things: justice, truth, and peace.[4]

108. R. Hanina said: The Holy One's seal is truth.[5]

109. R. Samuel ben Nahmani said: We find that the Holy One created everything in His world; only the stuff of falsehood He did not create, only the measure of falsehood He did not fashion. Mortals conceived false words out of their own hearts, as is said, "Conceiving and uttering from their own hearts words of falsehood" (Isa. 59:13).[6]

110. A company of liars cannot receive the Presence.[7]

111. R. Eleazar said: He who dissembles in his speech is as one who worships idols, for Jacob [disguised as Esau] said of himself, "I will be in his eyes as one who makes a mockery of him" (Gen. 27:12), and with regard to idols it is said, "They are a delusion, a work of mockery" (Jer. 10:15).[8]

112. Rava said: Jerusalem was destroyed only because men of integrity were no longer found there, as is said, "Roam the streets of Jerusalem, search its squares, look about and take note: You will not find a man—not a one—who acts justly, who seeks integrity, that I may pardon her" (Jer. 5:1).[9]

113. "Ye shall have an honest *ephah* and an honest *hin*" (Lev. 19:36). R. Yose son of R. Judah asked: Why say "honest *hin*"?[10] Is not a *hin* included in the measurement of an *ephah*? Yes, but it suggests that your yea (*hen*) should be as honest as your nay.[11]

114. When a man fulfills his given word, the sages are pleased with him.[12]

115. The sages said: He who has requited the people of the generation of the flood, the people of the generation of the dispersion of men, the people of Sodom and Gomorrah, and the Egyptians at the Red Sea will requite him who does not stand by his word.[13]

116. R. Yose said: I never said something and then retracted it.[14]

117. The letters *alef*, *mem*, and *tav*, which form the word *emet*, "truth," rest on two legs, while the letters *shin*, *kof*, and *resh* [which form the word *sheker*, "falsehood"], rest on one leg, in order to suggest that what is done in truth is fir. .ly based and what is done in falsehood is not. The letters that form the word *emet* are far apart,[15] while the letters that form the word *sheker* closely follow one another, in order to suggest that it is difficult to act in truth, while falsehood is as close as one's ear.[16]

118. Such is the punishment of a liar—even when he speaks the truth, no one listens to him.[17]

119. Rabbah said in the name of R. Yohanan: [In the alphabetical acrostics in Lamentations], why does the letter *pe* precede the letter *ayin*? Because of the spies, who uttered with their mouth [*peh*], what they had not seen with their eye [*ayin*].[18]

120. Hezekiah said: How do we know that he who adds [to the word of God] subtracts from it? From the verse "God hath said: 'Ye shall not eat of it, neither shall ye touch it.' " (Gen. 3:3). But R. Mesharsheya maintained: We derive it from a single word in the verse "*Ammatayim* [two cubits] and a half shall be the length thereof" (Exod. 25:10);[19] while R. Ashi said: We derive it from two words in the verse "*ashte esreh* [eleven] curtains" (Exod. 26:7).[20]

---

1. B. Shab 96b–97a.
2. B. Sanh 31a.
3. B. Pes 49b.
4. Avot 1:18.
5. B. Shab 55a.
6. PR 24:3 (YJS 1:509).
7. B. Sot 42a.
8. B. Sanh 92a.
9. B. Shab 119b.
10. A *hin* equals about six liters; an *ephah*, one bushel.
11. B. BM 49a and En Yaakov, ad loc.
12. Shev 10:9.
13. B. BM 48a.
14. B. Shab 118b.
15. The *alef* at the beginning, the *mem* in the middle, and the *tav* at the end of the alphabet.
16. Yalkut, *Bereshit*, §3, based on B. Shab 104a.
17. B. Sanh 89b.
18. B. Sanh 104b.
19. Had the word read *ma'tayim* ("two hundred") and had the scribe wrongly added an *alef*, making it read *ammatayim* ("two cubits"), God's word would have been diminished.
20. Had the word read *shete esreh* ("twelve") and the scribe wrongly added an *ayin*, making it read *ashte esreh* ("eleven"), God's word would have been diminished. B. Sanh 29a.

121. Weigh carefully what you say before you say it.[1]

122. Teach your tongue to say, "I do not know," lest you be led to lie, and be caught.[2]

123. Love the term "perhaps" and hate the expression "How much [harm will it do me]?" R. Hidka put this in another way: Love the term "perhaps" and hate the expression "[If I sin], what of it?"[3]

124. R. Zera said: A man should not say to a child, "I will give you something," and then not give it to him, because he will thus teach the child to lie, as in the denunciation "They teach their tongue to speak lies" (Jer. 9:4).[4]

125. Rav was constantly tormented by his wife. When he said to her, "Prepare some lentils for me," she would prepare beans; [when he requested] beans, she would prepare lentils. After Rav's son, Hiyya, grew up, he took to reversing his father's requests, until finally Rav said to his son, "Your mother has improved [her behavior toward me]." R. Hiyya confessed, "It was I who reversed your requests when I reported them to her." At that, Rav remarked, "What you have done bears out the saying 'Your offspring in season may teach you reason.' Nevertheless, do not continue to do so, lest you become like those of whom Scripture says, 'They have trained their tongues to speak falsely' " (Jer. 9:4).[5]

126. Rava said: At first, I used to think that there was no truth in the world. But a disciple of the wise, R. Tavut—others say, R. Tavyomi—by name, who would not lie even if he were given all the treasures of the world, told me that he once came to a place called Kushta ("Truth"), where no one ever departed from the truth and where no man ever died before his time. He married one of their women, with whom he had two sons. One day, his wife was sitting and washing her hair when a neighbor, a woman, came and knocked on the door. Thinking to himself that it would not be good manners [to tell her that his wife was washing her hair], he called out, "She is not here." [As a punishment for this], his two sons died. Then people of that town came to him and questioned him, "What is the cause of this?" He related to them what had happened. "We beg of you," they said, "quit this town, and do not incite the angel of death against us."[6]

127. "And when Delilah saw that he had told her all his heart" (Judg. 16:18). How did she know? R. Hanin said in the name of Rav: [Words from the heart], words of truth, are readily recognized.[7]

1. DEZ 3.
2. B. Ber 4a.
3. DEZ 1.
4. B. Suk 46b.
5. B. Yev 63a and En Yaakov, ad loc.
6. B. Sanh 97a.
7. B. Sot 9b.

128. When something is not readily evident, it is made so by citing numerous sources.[8]

129. People say that in Media a camel can dance on a *kav*.[9] Here is a *kav*, here a camel, and here we are in Media—but the camel does not dance![10]

130. People do not lie about what is certain to become known.[11]

131. "And speaketh the truth in his heart" (Ps. 15:2), as, for instance, R. Safra did.

It is told of R. Safra that he had an article to sell, and a certain man came to him while he was reciting the Shema and said, "Let me have the article for such-and-such a price." When R. Safra did not answer, the would-be purchaser, thinking that R. Safra was unwilling to sell for the price offered, kept increasing the amount, saying, "Let me have it for more money." After R. Safra finished the Shema, he said, "Take the article at the price you mentioned first, for I was willing to sell it to you at that price."[12]

132. The Holy One hates him who says one thing in his mouth, and another in his heart.[13]

133. "He who acknowledges the truth" applies to Moses, as is said, "And when Moses heard that, it was well-pleasing in his sight" (Lev. 10:20). So, too, the Holy One acknowledges the truth, as when He said, "The daughters of Zelophehad speak right" (Num. 27:7).[14]

134. The entire world, all of it, was shaken when the Holy One said at Sinai, "Thou shalt not take the Name of the Lord thy God in vain" (Exod. 20:7). With regard to all other transgressions mentioned in the Torah, the hope is held forth that their violator will be held guiltless, but of this one it is said, "The Lord will not hold him guiltless" (ibid.). For all other transgressions mentioned in the Torah, only the transgressor is punished, but for this one, he and his entire family are punished. For all other transgressions mentioned in the Torah, only the transgressor is punished, but for this one, he and the entire world, all of it, are punished. For all other transgressions mentioned in the Torah, if the transgressor has any merit, sentence is suspended for two or three generations,[15] but for this one, he is punished at once.[16]

8. P. Ber 2:3, 4c.
9. A measure equal to four pints. That is, in distant lands, wonderful things happen.
10. B. Yev 45a.
11. B. RH 22b.
12. B. Mak 24a; Rashi, ad loc., based on *She'eltot* of R. Aha, *Va-yehi*, (ed. Vilna, 1861), p. 117.
13. B. Pes 113b.
14. ARN 37.
15. If a son or a grandson of the transgressor repents, the sentence is remitted.
16. B. Shevu 39a.

135. "[The curse] shall enter . . . the house of him that sweareth falsely by My Name . . . and it shall consume it with the timber thereof and the stones thereof" (Zech. 5:4). Hence you learn that a false oath consumes even things that neither fire nor water can consume.[1]

136. "Yes, yes" is an oath. "No, no" is an oath.[2]

137. It is not right for a man to swear an oath even for the truth.[3]

138. R. Judah reported in the name of Rav that, in a year of scarcity, a certain man deposited a gold denar with a widow, who put it in a jar of flour. Subsequently [she forgot it], baked the flour, and gave [the loaf] to a poor man. In the course of time, the owner of the denar came and said to her, "Give me back my denar." She replied, "May death seize upon one of my sons if I have derived any benefit for myself from your denar." Not many days passed—so it is told—before one of her sons died. When the sages heard of the incident, they remarked: If such happens to one who swears truly, what must be the fate of one who swears falsely![4]

139. It happened that a man who had deposited a hundred denars with Bar Telamion came to get them back. Bar Telamion said, "I have already turned over to you what you deposited with me." The man said, "Come [to the synagogue], and I will have you take an oath." What did Bar Telamion do? [On the sly], he took a cane, hollowed it out, put the hundred denars in it, and then leaned on it as if it were a walking stick. When he reached the synagogue, he said to the man, "Hold this cane in your hand, while I swear an oath to you." [Then he said, "I swear by the] master of this house that I have given back to you what you deposited with me." In his rage, the man threw the cane on the ground, and the hundred denars began to roll out. As the man set to gathering them, Bar Telamion said, "Gather them, gather them, it's your own you are gathering!"[5]

140. "Hereby shall ye be proved: as Pharaoh liveth, ye shall not go forth hence," etc. (Gen. 42:15).[6] When Joseph was about to swear falsely, he would say, "As Pharaoh liveth." R. Levi explained the matter by the parable of a kid of the goats that ran away from the pasture and entered the home of a widow. What did she do? She killed it, flayed it, placed it on a bed, and covered it with a sheet. When they came to ask her about the kid, she replied, "May I cut off the flesh of this one lying here and eat it, if I know anything about the kid."[7]

1. Ibid.
2. An emphatic statement has the force of an oath. B. Shevu 36a.
3. Tanhuma, *Va-yikra*, §7.
4. B. Git (Soncino) 35a.
5. Lev. R. 6:3; PR 22:6 (YJS 1: 465–66).
6. Since Joseph did let his brothers go, the commentator explains that the oath was made on the life of Pharaoh, a mortal who was sure to die.
7. The inquirers assumed that the covered form in the bed was her child. Gen. R. 91:7.

141. R. Giddel said in the name of Rav: What is the proof that one may swear to observe a precept? From the verse "I have sworn and have confirmed it, to observe Thy righteous ordinances" (Ps. 119:106).

But why? Has not a Jew been sworn to observe them ever since Sinai? True; but the verse shows that a man may [by an oath] stir his zeal to observe them.[8]

142. R. Akiva said: Vows serve as a hedge for abstinence.[9]

143. R. Giddel said in the name of Rav: He who merely says [without using the standard formula for making a vow], "I will rise early and study this chapter [of Mishnah] or study this tractate [of Talmud]," is deemed to have made a solemn vow to the God of Israel.

R. Giddel said further in the name of Rav: He who merely says to his friend, "Let us rise early and study this chapter," is obliged to rise early.[10]

144. He who makes a vow is as though he put a chain [of iron] about his neck.[11]

145. The sages taught: Do not ever get into the habit of making vows, for you will end up violating even oaths.[12]

146. R. Yannai said: If a man delays fulfilling his vow, his ledger [in heaven] is examined.[13]

147. We have been taught that R. Nathan said: He who vows is as though he built a high place [for an idol] and he who fulfills his vow[14] is as though he brought an offering upon it.[15]

148. R. Dimi the brother of R. Safra said: He who vows, even if he fulfills his vow, is called a sinner. R. Zevid asked: And the proof? "If thou shalt forbear to vow, it shall be no sin in thee" (Deut. 23:23): hence, if you do not forbear, it shall be a sin.[16]

Refined Speech and Lascivious Talk

149. The sages in the school of R. Ishmael taught: A man should always use refined speech: "Thou shalt choose the tongue of the subtle" (Job 15:5); "That which my lips know they shall speak in purity" (Job 33:3).[17]

150. R. Joshua ben Levi said: A man should never let

8. B. Ned 7b–8a.
9. Avot 3:13.
10. B. Ned 8a.
11. B. Ned 9:1, 41b.
12. B. Ned 20a.
13. Gen. R. 81:1.
14. Without seeking to be released from it.
15. B. Ned 22a.
16. B. Ned 77b.
17. B. Pes 3a.

an unseemly word issue from his mouth. Thus, speaking in a roundabout way, Scripture added eight letters in order to avoid uttering an unseemly term, as in the verse "Of clean beasts, and of beasts that are not clean"[1] (Gen. 7:8). R. Papa said: Even nine letters, as in the verse "If there be among you any man that is not clean[2] by reason of that which chanceth him by night" (Deut. 23:11).[3]

151. Two disciples sat before Hillel. One was Rabban Yohanan ben Zakkai–others say it was before Rabbi [Judah I, the Patriarch], and that one was R. Yohanan.[4] The second of the two disciples asked, "Why must we vintage [grapes] in vessels that are clean, yet may gather [olives] in vessels that are unclean?" The first asked [the same question without using the objectionable term "unclean"]: "Why must we vintage [grapes] in vessels that are clean, but need not gather [olives] in vessels that are clean?" Their teacher said, "I am certain that this one [pointing to the first disciple] will be an authorized teacher in Israel." It did not take long before he was indeed an authorized teacher in Israel.

There were three priests. One said, "I received as much as a bean [of the shewbread]"; the second said, "I received as much as an olive"; while the third said, "I received as much as a lizard's tail." The lineage of the third priest was investigated, and a disqualification was found in it.[5]

152. Two disciples sat before Rav. One said, "You made the subject as savory for us as a stuffed pig." The other said, "Your analysis has made me [as tired] as a kid out of breath." Rav would not speak to the first disciple after that.[6]

153. The sages used only genteel language.[7]

154. In punishment for obscene speech, troubles multiply, cruel decrees are proclaimed anew, the young men of Israel—may such things happen to their enemies—die, and the fatherless and widows cry out and receive no answer. For it is said, "Therefore the Lord shall have no joy in their young men, neither shall He have compassion on their fatherless and widows; for everyone is profane and an evildoer, and every mouth speaketh obscenity. For all this His anger is not turned away, but His hand is stretched out still" (Isa. 9:16).[8]

155. R. Hanan bar Rava said: All know why a bride enters the bridal chamber, yet when a man speaks obscenely of it, even if a decree of seventy years' happiness had been sealed for him, it is reversed into [seventy years of] misery.

Rabbah bar Shila said in R. Hisda's name: When a man fouls his mouth with obscenity, Gehenna is made deeper for him, as is said, "A deep pit is for the mouth that speaketh obscenity" (Prov. 22:14). R. Nahman bar Isaac said: Also for him who hears it and remains silent.[9]

156. Our masters taught: A man should not allow his ears to listen to chitchat, because [being delicate] they are, of all parts of the body, the first to "catch fire."[10]

157. Bar Kappara expounded: What is meant by "And thou shalt have a plug among thy weapons" (Deut. 23:14)? Read not *azenekha*,[11] "thy weapons," but *oznekha*, "thine ear," meaning that when a man hears something unseemly, he must place his fingers into his ears. This counsel is in keeping with what R. Eleazar said: Why do a man's fingers resemble plugs? In order to suggest that when a man hears something unseemly, he should plug his ears with his fingers.

The sages taught in the school of R. Ishmael: Why is the entire ear hard and the lobe soft? In order that when a man is about to hear something unseemly, he can plug his ear with the lobe.[12]

158. R. Eliezer ben Jacob said: When a handsome and distinguished man allows an unseemly word to issue from his mouth, what is he like? A large [and well-appointed] dining hall with a tanner's [ill-smelling] drainpipe running through its middle.[13]

159. When R. Kahana fell ill, the sages sent R. Joshua son of R. Idi to find out how he was doing. When he came in and found that R. Kahana had died, he rent his garment but reversed it as he went out weeping, so that the rent part would not be noticed. When he came back to the sages, they asked him, "Is he dead?" R. Joshua: "It was you who said it. I did not say it, for 'he that uttereth evil tidings is a fool' " (Prov. 10:18).[14]

160. Rav was the son of R. Hiyya's brother and the son of R. Hiyya's sister.[15] When Rav came up to the Land of Israel, R. Hiyya asked him, "Is your father still alive?" Rav replied, "You might ask, 'Is Mother still alive?' "[16] "Well, *is* your mother still alive?" R. Hiyya asked. Rav replied, "Is Father still alive?" At that, R. Hiyya said to

1. The word "unclean" would have saved eight letters in the Hebrew text.
2. The word *tamei* ["defiled"] would have saved nine letters in the Hebrew text.
3. B. Pes 3a.
4. R. Yohanan was an Amora in the third century C.E., whereas Rabban Yohanan ben Zakkai was a Tanna in the first century C.E.
5. B. Pes. 3b.
6. Ibid.
7. B. Sanh 68b.
8. B. Shab 33a.
9. Ibid.
10. B. Ket 5b.
11. The usual word for "thy weapons" is *zenekha*. The presence of the letter *alef* at the word's beginning suggests to Bar Kappara the additional meanings.
12. B. Ket 5a–b.
13. DER 3.
14. B. Pes 3b and En Yaakov, ad loc.
15. Aibu, Rav's father, was R. Hiyya's paternal half-brother, while Rav's mother was R. Hiyya's half-sister on his mother's side.
16. Thus implying that his father was dead.

his attendant, "Take off my shoes [but carry my bathing gear after me to the bathhouse]."[1]

161. Yohanan of Hukok[2] went around visiting villages. When he came back, people asked, "Is the wheat crop doing well?" He replied, "The barley crop is doing well." So the people retorted, "Go proclaim the good news to horses and donkeys!"[3]

What should he have said?

"Last year the wheat crop did well," or, "The lentil crop is doing well."[4]

Silence and Speech

162. R. Simeon ben Gamaliel said: I spent all my life among sages and found nothing better for a person than silence. He who talks too much brings on sin.[5]

163. R. Akiva said: Silence is a hedge protecting wisdom.[6]

164. Bar Kappara taught: Silence is seemly for the wise, all the more so for fools. Thus Solomon said, "Even a fool, when he holdeth his peace, is counted wise" (Prov. 17:28). And it goes without saying that it is so when a wise man holds his peace.[7]

165. R. Isaac said: What is meant by "What is politic for men? Silence, yet speak ye the truth" (Ps. 58:2)?[8] It means: What is good policy[9] for a man in this world? To make himself out as mute.[10] Lest it be thought that a man should also remain mute in debate on Torah, the psalm goes on to say, "Yet speak ye the truth."[11]

166. All chitchat is bad, except chitchat about Torah, which is good.[12]

167–68. "A time to keep silence, and a time to speak" (Eccles. 3:7). There are times when a man is silent and receives reward for his silence; and there are other times when a man speaks up and receives reward for speaking up.[13]

169. The story of a peddler who went around the villages of Sepphoris hawking his wares, crying, "Who'd like the elixir of life?" Everybody gathered around and implored him, "Give us the elixir of life." While seated in his reception chamber, busily explaining the literal meaning of Scripture, R. Yannai heard the peddler crying, "Who'd like the elixir of life?" He called out, "Come up here and sell it to me!" The peddler: "Not to you nor to the likes of you." But R. Yannai insisted, so the peddler came up to him, took out a book of Psalms, and showed him the verse "Who is the man that desireth life?'" (Ps. 34:13) and what is written after it: "Keep thy tongue from evil." As he read these words, R. Yannai remarked, "Solomon also proclaimed the same when he said, 'Whoso keepeth his mouth and his tongue keepeth his soul from troubles,' " (Prov. 21:23).

Then R. Yannai added, "All my days I have been reading this verse, but I did not realize its plain meaning until this peddler came by and made me aware of it."[14]

170. R. Simeon ben Gamaliel said to his slave Tabi, "Go to the market and buy me a good piece of meat." So Tabi went out and bought him a tongue. Later, R. Simeon said to Tabi, "Go out and buy me a bad piece of meat at the market." Tabi went out and again bought him a tongue. R. Simeon ben Gamaliel asked him, "Why, when I asked you to buy me a good piece of meat, did you buy a tongue, and when I asked you to buy a bad piece of meat, did you again buy me a tongue?" Tabi replied, "Because from the tongue comes good, and from it comes also evil. When it is good, nothing is better than it; and when it is bad, nothing is more evil than it."[15]

171. "Death and life are in the power of the tongue" (Prov. 18:21). Akila the Translator[16] defined the tongue as a tool having a knife at one end and a spoon at the other[17]—death at one end and life at the other. Even so Ben Sira said, "Blow on a coal to make it glow, or spit on it to put it out; both results come from the same mouth" (Ecclesiasticus 28:12).[18]

172. Rava said: He who wishes to live [can acquire life] through his tongue; he who wishes to die [can find death] through his tongue.[19]

173. A story is told of a king of Persia who became so emaciated that he was about to die. His physicians said, "There is no cure for you until you are brought some milk of a lioness. Drink it, and you will recover." So the king asked the physicians, "Who will fetch some milk of a

1. He meant to show that one may mourn only for an hour if one hears of a death that occurred more than thirty days before. After such a brief period of mourning, R. Hiyya told his attendant to follow him to the bathhouse—he is no longer a mourner, and bathing is now permitted. B. Pes 4a.
2. Hukok is in northern Israel. See Josh. 19:34.
3. Since only animals ate barley.
4. Since wheat and lentils were eaten by humans, Yohanan should have spoken encouragingly of them. B. Pes 3b.
5. Avot 1:17.
6. Avot. 3:13.
7. P. Pes 9:8, 37a; B. Pes 99a.
8. JV: "Do ye indeed speak as a righteous company?"
9. The word *umnam* may be interpreted as "policy," "wisdom," or "indeed."
10. The word *elem* may mean "muteness," "silence," or "company."
11. B. Hul 89a.
12. P. Ber 9:8, 14d.
13. B. Zeb 115b and En Yaakov, ad loc.
14. Lev. R. 16:2; B. AZ 19b.
15. Lev. R. 33:1.
16. The proselyte who prepared a Greek translation of the Bible.
17. Used by soldiers as both tableware and a close-combat weapon.
18. Lev. R. 33:7.
19. By clearing himself or incriminating himself. B. Ar 15b.

lioness?" One of them spoke up and said, "If you wish, I will go, but first you must give me ten goats." They gave him the goats, and he went to a lions' den, where a lioness was sucking her whelps. The first day, he stood at a distance and threw one goat to her, which she devoured. The second day, he came a little closer and threw another goat. And thus he continued day after day. At the end of ten days, he was so close to the lioness that he could play with her and stroke her teats. Thus he drew off some of her milk and went on his way.

Halfway on his journey home, the physician fell asleep and saw in a dream the parts of his body arguing with one another.

The feet were saying, "Among all the parts, there is none like us. Had we not walked, the body would not have been able to fetch any of the milk."

The hands retorted, "There is none like us. Had we not stroked the lioness, the body would not have been able to get any of the milk."

The eyes argued, "We are of greater worth than any of you. Had we not shown him the way, nothing at all would have been accomplished."

Then the heart spoke up: "I am of greater worth than any of you. Had I not given counsel, you would not have succeeded at all in the errand."

Finally, the tongue spoke up and said, "I am better than any of you. Had it not been for speech, what would you have done?"

At that, all the parts of the body joined in responding to the tongue, "How dare you compare yourself with us, you who are lodged in a place of obscurity and darkness—you who, unlike all other parts of the body, have not a single bone?"

But the tongue replied, "This very day you are going to acknowledge that I have power over you!"

After the man woke up from his sleep, he kept the dream in mind and continued on his way. When he came back to the king, he said, "Here is the bitch's milk which I managed to get for you. Drink it."

Immediately the king became angry with the physician and ordered that he be hanged. As he went out to be hanged, all the parts of his body began to tremble. The tongue said to them, "Did I not tell you that there is nothing substantial in you? If I save you now, will you admit that I have power over you?"

They all cried out, "Yes!"

At this, the tongue said to the hangmen, "Take me back to the king." They took the physician back to the king, and he asked him, "Why did you order me hanged?"

The king replied, "Because you brought me the milk of a bitch."

The physician said to the king, "What does that matter to you, as long as it provides healing? Besides, a lioness can be called a bitch."

The milk was taken, tested, and found to be the milk of a lioness.

The king drank it and was healed, and the physician was dismissed in peace.

At that, all the parts of the body said to the tongue, "Now we confess to you that you have power over us all. This is the meaning of the verse "Death and life are in the power of the tongue" (Prov. 18:21).[1]

174. Our masters taught: Two advocates used to stand before Hadrian, one pleading that speech is best, and the other pleading that silence is best. The one said, "Sire, nothing in the world is better than speech. But for speech, how would brides be extolled? How could there be in the world the give-and-take of trade? How could ships sail in the sea?" Then the king asked the one who pleaded that silence was best, "How do you plead in behalf of silence?" As soon as he started to speak, his colleague struck him on the mouth. The king asked, "Why did you strike him?" He replied, "Sire, I pleaded in behalf of what is mine by means that are mine—by speech in behalf of speech. But this one would plead in behalf of what is his by my means. Let him plead in behalf of what is his by means that are his."[2]

175. R. Judah of the village of Gibborayya—according to some, of the village of Gibbor-hayil—interpreted "Silence is praise for Thee" (Ps. 65:2) as meaning that silence is the height of all praises of God.

When R. Dimi came [to Babylonia], he reported: In the West [the Land of Israel], they say: Speech is worth a *sela*, but silence is worth two.[3]

176. Ten measures of speech came down to the world: Women took nine, and the rest of the world, all of it, took one.[4]

177. Even the common talk of Israel is worthy of study.[5]

178. Even the common talk of the people of the Land of Israel is worthy of study.[6]

179. Even the sages' talk concerning profane matters deserves study.[7]

180. From the articulation of your lips, it is evident that you are a disciple of the wise.[8]

181. Silence is tantamount to admission [of guilt].[9]

182. Silence validates [a woman's vow], but silence cannot nullify [it].[10]

---

1. MTeh 39:2; Yalkut, Ps.,§721.
2. Yalkut, *Be-haalotekha*, §738; Yalkut, Prov., §946, citing Yelammedenu.
3. B. Meg 18a.
4. B. Kid 49b.
5. MTeh 104:3.
6. Lev. R. 34:7.
7. B. AZ 19b.
8. B. Me 17b.
9. B. Yev 87b.
10. Tos Ned 7:5.

Anger

183. R. Eliezer said: Be not easily provoked.[1]

184. There are four kinds of dispositions: easy to provoke and easy to reconcile—his loss is compensated by his gain; hard to provoke and hard to reconcile—his gain is offset by his loss; hard to provoke and easy to reconcile—saintly; easy to provoke and hard to reconcile—wicked.[2]

185. Rabbah bar R. Huna said: When a man is angry, even the Presence is deemed by him as of no account, as is said, "At the height of his wrath, the wicked thinks, 'God never punishes,' for all his schemes are based on: 'There is no God' " (Ps. 10:4). R. Jeremiah of Difti said: He also causes his learning to be forgotten and his folly to grow, as is said, "For anger resteth in the bosom of fools" (Eccles. 7:9). Besides, R. Nahman bar Isaac added: It is well known that his transgressions come to be more abundant than his merits, as is said, "A wrathful man aboundeth in transgression" (Prov. 29:22).[3]

186. Resh Lakish said: When a man becomes angry—if he is a sage, his wisdom departs from him; if he is a prophet, his prophecy departs from him. That his wisdom departs from him if he is a sage we learn from Moses, for after saying, "And Moses was wroth with the officers of the host," etc. (Num. 31:14), it is said, "And Eleazar the Priest said unto the men of war . . . that went to the battle: "This is the statute of the law which the Lord hath commanded Moses.' " etc. (Num. 31:21). From the above, it follows that [since Moses was not the one who spoke], the statute had escaped Moses' memory. That his prophecy departs from him if he is a prophet we learn from Elisha, who said in anger, "Were it not that I regard the presence of Jehoshaphat the king of Judah, I would not look toward thee, nor see thee" (2 Kings 3:14). [But overcoming his anger, and joyous because he obeyed God's command], Elisha said: " 'Now bring me a minstrel.' And it came to pass, when the minstrel played, that the hand of the Lord [i.e., the spirit of prophecy] came again upon him" (2 Kings 3:15).

R. Mani bar Pattish said: When a man becomes angry, even if greatness has been decreed for him by Heaven, he is reduced from his greatness. How do we know it? From Eliab, for it is said, "Eliab's anger was kindled against David, and he said: 'I know thy presumptuousness, and the naughtiness of thy heart' " (1 Sam. 17:28). And when Samuel went to anoint David as king, it is written of all his other brothers, "The Lord hath not chosen this one" (1 Sam. 16:8), but it is written of Eliab, "The Lord said unto Samuel, 'Look not on his countenance, or on the height of his stature, because I have rejected him' " (1 Sam. 16:7). Hence it follows that until Eliab became angry, God had favored him greatly.[4]

187. He who succumbs to anger succumbs to bad judgment.[5]

188. R. Huna said: Moses became angry in three instances, and [following each] a law escaped his memory. The instances involved a law about observance of the Sabbath, a law about the purification of unclean metal utensils, and a law about the conduct of a mourner prior to the burial of his dead.

What is the proof that, through anger, Moses forgot to speak of a law about the observance of the Sabbath? [From what happened when the manna was eaten after it first came down.] At that time, we are told, "some of them left it until morning . . . and Moses was angry with them" (Exod. 16:20).[6] Having become angry, a law escaped his memory, and he forgot to speak of a contrary law affecting the Sabbath, for [when the Sabbath came] he said to them, "This is what the Lord hath spoken: . . . 'Eat today [what was left from the prior day], for today is a Sabbath unto the Lord' " (Exod. 16:23 and 16:25). [Moses did not say, "This is what I have spoken," but, "This is what the Lord hath spoken," for he himself had forgotten to speak of it.]

What is the proof that, through anger, Moses forgot to speak of a law regarding the purification of unclean metal utensils? From what happened following the war against Midian. We are told, "Moses was angry with the officers of the host" (Num. 31:14), and in his anger a law escaped his memory, so that he forgot to speak to them of a particular law governing [the purification of unclean] metal utensils. Since Moses did not speak of it to them, Eleazar the Priest had to do so in Moses' stead, as Scripture says, "Eleazar the Priest said unto the men of war: 'This is the statute of the law which the Lord hath commanded Moses' " (Num. 31:21), implying that Eleazar meant: "It was to my master Moses—not to me—that God gave the command."

What is the proof that, through anger, Moses forgot to speak of a law about the conduct of a mourner before the burial of his dead? [From what happened when Nadab and Abihu died, and their brothers Eleazar and Ithamar refused to eat consecrated food.] At that time, we are told, "Moses was angry with Eleazar and with Ithamar" (Lev. 10:16), and, having become angry, he forgot to speak of the law that, prior to the burial of his dead, a mourner may not eat consecrated food. At that, Aaron set forth to Moses an argument *a fortiori:* a man is asked to declare of the tithe, which is of lesser sanctity: "While in mourning, I have not eaten of it prior to the burial of my dead" (Deut. 26:14). How much more by far should a restriction in eating a sin offering, which is of greater sanctity, apply to such a mourner! As soon as "Moses heard that, it was well-pleasing in his sight" (Lev. 10:20), and he issued a proclamation to the entire camp of Israel, saying, "I made an error in the law, and Aaron my brother came and set me straight."[7]

189. R. Samuel bar Nahmani said in the name of R. Yohanan: When a man becomes angry, all sorts of Ge-

1. Avot 2:10.
2. Avot 5:14.
3. B. Ned 22b.
4. B. Pes 66b.
5. Sif Num., §157.
6. For he had previously told them, "Let no man leave of it till the morning" (Exod. 16:19).
7. Lev. R. 13:1; Yalkut, *Mattot*, §785.

henna's evils overpower him, as is said, "If thou removest anger from thy heart, thou puttest away evil from thy flesh" (Eccles. 11:10).[1]

190. A man should always be gentle like Hillel, not irascible like Shammai.[2]

191. Do not seethe with anger, and you will not sin.[3]

192. We have been taught that the sages said in the name of R. Yohanan ben Nuri: You are to regard as an idolater the man who in his anger tears his garments, in his anger smashes his vessels, in his anger scatters his money, because such is the craftiness of the impulse to evil. One day, the impulse says to him, "Do this"; the next day, "Do that"; until finally it says, "Go, worship an idol," and the man goes and worships it. R. Avin said: And the proof? The verse "There shall be no strange god in thee; then thou shalt not worship an alien god" (Ps. 81:10). What strange god is there within a man's body? You must admit, it is the impulse to evil.[4]

193. Once, in the synagogue in Tiberias, it happened that R. Eleazar and R. Yose differed so sharply about a certain ruling that in their rage a Torah scroll got torn. R. Yose ben Kisma, who was there, said, "I shall be surprised if this synagogue does not become a house of idolatry." And so it did.[5]

194. R. Akiva used to say: He who in a rage hurls his bread to the ground or scatters his money will not leave the world before he becomes dependent on [the charity of] mortals.[6]

195. R. Adda bar Ahavah saw a gentile woman in the marketplace who was wearing a garment of linsey-woolsey.[7] Thinking she was Jewish, he stopped and ripped the garment off her. When it turned out that the woman was heathen and the garment was appraised at four hundred *zuz* [which he had to pay], he asked her, "What is your name?" Upon her replying, "Mattun," he said to her, "Mattun, had I been wary (*matun*), it would have been worth [to me] *maatan, maatan* (twice two hundred) *zuz*."[8]

196. R. Yose taught in Sepphoris: "Abba Elijah [the Prophet] is an irascible man." After that, Abba Elijah, who used to visit him regularly, absented himself for three days and did not come. When he finally did come, R. Yose asked him, "Why did my master not come?" Elijah replied [angrily]: "Because you called me irascible." R. Yose: "You, sir, have just proved yourself to be irascible."[9]

197. Bar Kappara taught: A man who is bad tempered achieves nothing but his bad temper.[10]

198. Our masters taught: There are three kinds of men whose life is no life: those who are [too] compassionate, those who are [too] prone to anger, and those who are [too] fastidious.[11]

199. When his disciples asked R. Adda bar Ahavah, "To what do you attribute your long life?" he replied, "I never lost my temper in the midst of my family."[12]

200. Rabbi [Judah I, the Patriarch] made a feast for his disciples, serving them tongues that were tender as well as tongues that were tough. The disciples selected the tender tongues and passed up the tough ones. So he said to them: Take heed of what you are doing—even as you select the tender and pass up the tough, so let your tongues be tender [and not tough] toward one another.[13]

201. A man's character may be discerned by three things: by his tippling, his tipping, and his temper.[14]

202. In the West [the Land of Israel], when two men were quarreling with each other, people watched to see who would be first to stop and would then say, "This one is of better lineage."[15]

203. Happy is the man who, hearing himself abused, remains silent. He thereby wards off a hundred evils from himself.[16]

204. R. Simeon ben Eleazar said: Do not try to pacify your fellow in the hour of his anger.

R. Yohanan said in the name of R. Yose: What is the proof that one should not try to pacify a person in the hour of his anger? The verse "After My countenance goes, I will give thee rest" (Exod. 33:14), in which the Holy One says to Moses, "Wait awhile until My countenance of wrath goes away; then I will give thee rest."[17]

Humility and Pride

205. R. Levitas of Yavneh said: Be very, very humble, for the end of man's hope is the worm.

R. Meir said: Be humble before all men.[18]

---

1. B. Ned 22a.
2. See above, part 2, chap. 1, §15. B. Shab 30b.
3. B. Ber 29b.
4. B. Shab 105b; B. Nid 13b.
5. B. Yev 96b.
6. ARN 3.
7. See Lev. 19:19.
8. A triple play on words: Mattun, the woman's name; *matun* ("wary" or "deliberate"); *maatan* ("two hundred"). B. Ber 20a.
9. B. San 113b.
10. B. Kid 40b–41a.
11. B. Pes 113b.
12. B. Ta 20b.
13. Lev. R. 33:1; Yalkut, Ps., §767.
14. B. Er 65b.
15. B. Kid 71b.
16. B. Sanh 7a.
17. Avot 4:18; B. Ber 7a.
18. Avot 4:4 and 4:12.

206. Our masters taught: Adam was created on the eve of Sabbath, [the last of all created beings]. Why? So that if man's opinion of himself should become overweening, he would be reminded that the gnat preceded him in the order of creation.[1]

207. Whenever Rav saw a crowd [of scholars] follow him [as he was about to enter the court], he would quote, "Though his excellency mount up to the heavens . . . yet he shall perish forever like his own dung" (Job 20:6–7).

As he was carried shoulder high on the Sabbath preceding a festival, Mar Zutra the Pious used to quote, "Riches are not forever; and doth the crown endure unto all generations?" (Prov. 27:24).[2]

208. The following three are of equal importance: wisdom, fear [of God], and humility.[3]

209. The adornment of wisdom is humility; the adornment of humility is fear [of God].[4]

210. R. Isaac ben Eleazar said: That which wisdom has made the crown of her head, humility has made the imprint of her heel. That which wisdom has made the crown of her head, as Scripture says, "The fear of the Lord is the head of wisdom" (Ps. 111:10); humility has made the imprint of her heel, as Scripture says, "The fear of the Lord is humility's heel"[5] (Prov. 22:4).[6]

211. R. Joshua ben Levi said: Humility is greater than all other virtues,[7] for it is said, "The spirit of the Lord God is upon me; because the Lord hath anointed me to bring good tidings unto the humble" (Isa. 61:1)—not "unto the saintly," but "unto the humble." From this you learn that humility is greater than all other virtues.[8]

212. When a house has no lower doorsill, it looks unfinished, left to fall apart. You, too, even if you are endowed with all other virtues but lack humility, are "unfinished."

Rava said: Even as the lower doorsill makes it possible for doors to close and open, so is humility a hedge protecting [the doors of] wisdom.[9]

213. R. Joshua ben Levi said: Pause and consider how great the lowly in spirit are in the presence of the Holy One. For in the days the Temple stood, when a man brought a burnt offering, the reward for a burnt offering was his; a meal offering, the reward for a meal offering was his. But the man whose disposition is lowly—Scripture regards him as though he had brought all the offerings, all of them, as is said, "The sacrifices of God are a broken spirit" (Ps. 51:19).[10]

214. "For My thoughts are not your thoughts, neither are My ways your ways" (Isa. 55:8). When a mortal has a vessel, he rejoices in it as long as it is entire; when it is broken, he has no use for it. Now, what is the Holy One's precious vessel? Man's heart. When the Holy One sees a man proud in heart, He has no use for him, as is said, "Everyone that is proud in heart is an abomination to the Lord" (Prov. 16:5). But when the heart is broken, He says, "This one is Mine," as is said, "The Lord is nigh unto them that are of a broken heart" (Ps. 34:19).[11]

215. "The sacrifices of God are a broken spirit" (Ps. 51:19). R. Abba bar Yudan said: Everything that the Holy One declared unfit in animals, He declared fit in man. In animals, He declared unfit the "blind, broken, or maimed" (Lev. 22:22); but in man, he declared fit the broken and contrite heart.

R. Alexandri said: If an ordinary person uses broken vessels, it is a disgrace to him; but the vessels the Holy One uses are broken ones, as is said, "The Lord is nigh unto them that are of a broken heart" (Ps. 34:19); "Who healeth the broken in heart" (Ps. 147:3); "I dwell in the high and holy place, with him also that is of a contrite and humble spirit" (Ps. 57:15); "The sacrifices of God are a broken spirit" (Ps. 51:19); and "A broken and contrite heart, O God, Thou wilt not despise" (ibid.).[12]

216. R. Joseph said: A man should always learn from the reasoning of his Maker. Behold, the Holy One disregarded all mountains and hills, and caused His Presence to abide on Mount Sinai, even as He disregarded all goodly trees and caused His Presence to abide on a thornbush.[13]

217. Bush, O bush! Not because you are taller than any of the trees in the field did the Holy One cause His Presence to abide on you, but because you are lower than any of the trees in the field did the Holy One cause His Presence to abide on you.[14]

218. R. Abba said in the name of Samuel: For three years there was a dispute between the school of Shammai and the school of Hillel, the one asserting, "The law is according to our views," and the other asserting, "The law is according to our views." Then a divine voice came forth and said, "The utterances of the one and of the other are both the words of the living God, but the law is according to the school of Hillel."

But since both are the words of the living God, by

---

1. B. Sanh 38a.
2. B. Sanh 7b.
3. DEZ 7.
4. "The fear of the Lord is the highest manifestation of wisdom, even as it is the basis of true humility" (Song R., Soncino, p. 12, n. 4). DEZ 5.
5. The word *ekev* may mean "reward" as in JV, or "heel" as here.
6. P. Shab 1:5, 3c; Song R. 1:1, §9; Yalkut, Prov., §960.
7. As enumerated by R. Phinehas ben Yair. See above, part 3, chap. 7, §92.
8. B. AZ 20b.
9. Ka R. 3:6.
10. B. Sot 5b.
11. MhG Gen., p. 641.
12. Lev. R. 7:2.
13. B. Sot 5a.
14. B. Shab 67a.

what merit did the school of Hillel have the law fixed according to their rulings? Because they were kindly and humble, and taught both their own rulings and those of the school of Shammai.[1] Indeed, they taught the rulings of the school of Shammai before their own.

This should prove to you that the man who humbles himself, the Holy One exalts; and the man who exalts himself, the Holy One humbles. From everyone who tries to thrust himself upon eminence, eminence flees. But upon everyone who flees from eminence, eminence thrusts itself. Everyone who tries to force time, time forces back. But everyone who is willing to abase himself before the hour [of success],[2] the hour [of success] remains waiting for him.[3]

219. "Can any hide himself in secret places that I shall not cause him to be seen? saith the Lord" (Jer. 23:24). R. Benjamin bar Levi said: The man who sits in a secret place and occupies himself with Torah, I cause to be seen [and honored] by mortals; by the same token, the man who conceals himself to worship idols, I cause to be seen [and abhorred] by mortals.[4]

220. Ben Azzai said: You will be called by your proper name, you will be seated in your proper place, and you will be given what is properly yours, for no man will be allowed to touch what belongs to another, just as no reign will be allowed to overlap another by a hairsbreadth.[5]

221. R. Akiva used to teach in the name of R. Simeon ben Azzai: Go two or three seats lower than what you believe to be your seat until you are told, "Come up," rather than sit above [your seat] and be told, "Get down."[6] It is better to be told, "Come up, come up," than to be told, "Get down, get down." This, too, is what Hillel used to say: "My abasement of self is my exaltation, my exaltation of self is my abasement." And the proof? "He that exalteth himself is [made to] sit lower, he that abaseth himself is [raised, so that he may be] seen" (Ps. 113:5–8). You find that when the Holy One revealed Himself to Moses from the midst of the thornbush, Moses hid his face from Him. Because of this, the Holy One said to him, "Come now therefore, and I will send thee unto Pharaoh" (Exod. 3:10).[7]

222. When R. Nahman bar R. Hisda said to R. Nahman bar Isaac, "Sir, come up and sit with us," R. Nahman bar Isaac replied, "We have been taught that R. Yose said: A man's place does not honor a man, but a man honors his place. We find this to have been true of Mount Sinai: as long as the Presence abode upon it, the Torah declared, 'Let neither flocks nor herds feed before the mount' [Exod. 34:3]; but once the Presence departed from there, the Torah said, "When the ram's horn soundeth long, they may come up to the mount' [Exod. 19:13]. We also find it to have been true at the Tent of Meeting in the wilderness: as long as the tent remained pitched, the Torah commanded, 'Remove from camp anyone with an eruption or a discharge' [Num. 5:2]; but once its curtains were rolled up [dismantling the tent], both those with a discharge and those with an eruption were allowed to enter." "If so," said R. Nahman bar R. Hisda, "I shall come to sit with you, sir." R. Nahman bar Isaac objected: "It is better for an eminent scholar who is the son of a less eminent scholar to come sit with an eminent scholar who is the son of an eminent scholar, than for an eminent scholar who is the son of an eminent scholar to come sit with an eminent scholar who is the son of a less eminent scholar."[8]

223. A proverb says, "Be head among foxes and not tail among lions."

However, R. Matia ben Heresh said: Be tail among lions and not head among foxes.[9]

224. They sent word from there [the Land of Israel]: Who is destined for the world-to-come? He who is meek and humble, bows on entering and on leaving, continually occupies himself with Torah, and takes no credit to himself. At that, the sages cast their eyes on R. Ulla bar Abba [as endowed with such qualities].[10]

225. R. Yohanan said in the name of R. Yose ben Zimra: To him who invokes his own merit in making a petition, Heaven makes its response depend on the merit of others; whereas to him who invokes the merit of others in making a petition, Heaven makes its response depend on his own merit. Moses invoked the merit of others in his petition, for he said, "Remember Abraham, Isaac, and Israel, Thy servants!" (Exod. 32:13), and Scripture made Heaven's response depend on Moses' own merit: "Therefore He said that He would destroy them, had not Moses His chosen stood before Him in the breach" (Ps. 106:23). On the other hand, Hezekiah invoked his own merit in his petition: "Remember now, O Lord, I beseech Thee, how I have walked before Thee" (Isa. 38:3), and God made His response depend on the merit of others, for God said, "I will

---

1. E.g., in the recital of the Shema, R. Tarfon, a disciple of the school of Hillel, followed a Shammaitic ruling at the risk of his life. B. Ber 10b.
2. Something that Absalom failed to do. See 2 Sam. 15.
3. Brother Caedmon Holmes and Bishop K. Ansgar Nelson helped in translating the preceding paragraph. Leon Nemoy suggests an alternative: "He who persistently pursues eminence, it flees from him; he who flees from it, it persistently pursues him. He who hastens time, time delays him; he who gives way to time, time hastens for him." B. Er 13b and En Yaakov, ad loc.
4. Exod. R. 8:2.
5. B. Yoma 38a–b.
6. Cf. Luke 14:8–11.
7. Lev. R. 1:5.
8. R. Hisda was a more eminent scholar than Isaac, the father of the other R. Nahman, as may be inferred from the fact that the first, being an ordained rabbi, is referred to as R. Hisda, while the second is termed Isaac without the title Rabbi. To show his less-distinguished ancestry, R. Nahman referred to himself as "a *maneh* the son of half a *maneh*," while he referred to R. Nahman as "*maneh* the son of a *maneh*." B. Ta 21b.
9. P. Sanh 4:8, 22b; Avot 4:21.
10. B. Sanh 88b.

defend this city to save it, for Mine own sake and for My servant David's sake" (Isa. 37:35).[1]

226. "Thou didst pluck up a vine out of Egypt" (Ps. 80:9). As in a vine with larger clusters and smaller ones, each large cluster hangs lower than its smaller neighbor, so do Israel: He who is greater than his fellow holds himself to be below him.[2]

227. R. Joshua of Sikhnin said in the name of R. Levi: The other rivers asked the Euphrates, "Why is your sound not very audible?" The Euphrates replied, "I have no need for loud sound: my deeds make me known. When a man plants a sapling at my side, it matures in thirty days; when he sows a vegetable at my side, it is full grown in three days." Then the other rivers asked the Tigris, "Why is your sound so audible?" The Tigris replied, "I wish my sound were heard yet more clearly, so that people would be aware of me." Then they asked the fruit-bearing trees, "Why is your sound not very audible?" They replied, "We do not need to make loud sound, since the fruits we bear testify for us." Then they asked the trees that do not bear fruit, "Why is your sound so audible?" They replied, "We wish our sound were heard yet more clearly, so that people would be aware of us."

R. Huna differed: The preceding explanations do not give the real reason. The fact is that, because fruit-bearing trees are heavy with their fruit, the sound they make is not very audible; while trees that bear no fruit are lightly laden, and so the sounds they make are very audible.[3]

228. "For as the crackling of thorns under a pot" (Eccles. 7:6). When all other kinds of wood are kindled, their sound is not heard; but when thorns are kindled, their sound crackles forth, as though they were saying, "We, too, are wood."[4]

229. A single coin in a bottle goes clink-clink.[5]

230. We have been taught that R. Simeon ben Yohai said: A man should speak of his superiority with a soft voice and of his shortcomings with a loud voice; of his superiority with a soft voice, as may be seen in the confession at tithing;[6] of his shortcomings in a loud voice, as may be seen in the confession at the bringing of firstfruits.[7]

231. Rava said: A man may make himself known in a place where he is not known, as Obadiah did, saying to Elijah, "I, thy servant, fear the Lord from my youth" (1 Kings 18:12).

Then Rava pointed to what appears to be an inconsistency. Here we have "I, thy servant, fear the Lord from my youth," and elsewhere, "Let another man praise thee, and not thine own mouth" (Prov. 27:2). Rava explained: The second verse refers to a place where the man is known, while the first verse refers to a place where the man is not known.

Rava also said: A disciple of the wise may say, "I am a disciple of the wise—put my lawsuit first on the docket."[8]

232. Our masters taught: A man should always be as yielding as a reed and not as unyielding as a cedar.

Now, a reed grows in a well-watered area. Its stock keeps driving up young shoots. And because its roots are many, even if all the winds of the world come and blow at it, they cannot uproot it from its place, for it sways to and fro with them. And once the winds have subsided, the reed resumes its erect stance.

On the other hand, the cedar does not grow in a well-watered area, it does not drive up new shoots, and its roots are few. Still, even if all the winds of the world come and blow at it, they cannot move it from its place. If, however, the [hot] south wind blows at the cedar, it uproots it at once and lays it flat on its face.[9]

233. R. Abba bar Kahana said in the name of R. Levi: He who sets himself head-on against a wave is swept away by it; but he who does not set himself head-on against the wave is not swept away.[10]

234. We have been taught that Rabban Gamaliel said: Once, while traveling on a ship, I saw another ship capsize, and I grieved greatly for a disciple of the wise who was on the ship. (Who was the disciple? R. Akiva.) After I landed, there was R. Akiva, who sat down and held forth before me concerning certain rulings in *Halakhah*. I asked him, "My son, who rescued you?" He replied, "A ship's plank came my way; and as each wave came toward me, I dipped my head under it."[11]

235. R. Eleazar ha-Kappar said: Be not like the upper lintel, which no man's hand can touch; but be like the threshold below, upon which everyone steps—in the end, when the entire structure is demolished, it still remains.[12]

236. R. Yohanan said in the name of R. Simeon ben Yohai: A man who has haughtiness within him is as though he had worshiped an idol, for Scripture says, "Every haughty person is an abomination unto the Lord" (Prov. 16:5), and says elsewhere of an idol, "Thou shalt not bring an abomination into thy house" (Deut. 7:26).

On his own authority, R. Yohanan said: A man who is guilty of such haughtiness is as one who denies the Root

1. B. Ber 10b.
2. Midrash Sam. 16 (ed. Buber, p. 93).
3. Gen. R. 16:3; Eccles. R. 10:11, §1.
4. Eccles. R. 7:6, §1.
5. B. BM 85b.
6. During which one says softly, "I have not transgressed any of Thy commandments, neither have I forgotten them" (Deut. 26:13).
7. During which one is told, "Thou art to speak up and say [loudly], 'A wandering Aramean was my father' " (Deut. 26:5). B. Sot 32b.
8. So that I can get back to my studies. B. Ned 62a.
9. B. Ta 20a; B. Sanh 105b–106a.
10. Gen. R. 44:15.
11. B. Yev 121a.
12. ARN 26; DEZ 3.

of the universe, for of him it is said, "When thy heart wax haughty, thou forgettest the Lord thy God" (Deut. 8:14).[1]

237. R. Hisda (according to some, Mar Ukba), said: Of a man who has haughtiness within him, the Holy One says, "I and he cannot endure together in the world." He declared, "Whoso is haughty of eye and proud of heart, him I cannot endure" (Ps. 101:5). Read not "him" (*oto*), but "together with him" (*itto*).[2]

238. R. Eleazar said: The Presence wails over a man who has haughtiness within him.[3]

239. He who walks even four cubits with a haughty bearing is as though he had pushed aside the feet of the Presence, of which it is written, "The whole earth is full of His glory" (Isa. 6:3).[4]

240. Concerning the despotic, the haughty, the proud, the violent, the insolent, and the aggressive, Scripture says, "The arms of the wicked shall be broken" (Ps. 37:17).

Of those who coo like doves, who make affected gestures with their hands, who kick up their heels and walk mincingly on their toes, Scripture says, "Let not the foot of pride overtake me, and let not the hand of the wicked drive me away" (Ps. 36:12).[5]

241. He who walks into the marketplace with his shoes unlaced is among those who are of haughty spirit. He who walks with his cloak thrown over his shoulder or his cap tilted back, or sits crosslegged, or holds the straps of the tefillin in his hands and throws them behind him while walking in the marketplace—he is among those who are of haughty spirit.[6]

242. R. Alexandri said: The least wind will greatly trouble a man who has haughtiness of spirit,[7] for it is said, "The wicked [haughty ones] are like the troubled sea" (Isa. 57:20). Now, if the sea, which contains so many quarters of *logs* of liquid, is troubled by the least wind, how much more a human being, who has only a quarter of a *log* of blood.[8]

243. R. Judah said in the name of Rav: When a man boasts, if he is a sage, his wisdom departs from him; if he is a prophet, his gift of prophecy departs from him.[9]

244. R. Avira expounded: He in whom there is haughtiness of spirit will presently be reduced in rank, as is said, "They are exalted, then a reduction [in rank]" (Job 24:24). What is meant by "They are cut off as the topmost of ears of corn" (ibid.)? A sage in the school of R. Ishmael taught: It is like a man who, entering his field, plucks the topmost ears.[10]

245. R. Eleazar said: Any man in whom there is haughtiness of spirit deserves being cut down like an *asherah* [a tree sacred to a goddess].[11]

246. R. Levi said: He who is given to boasting is rightly punished by fire, as is said, "This is the law regarding a person given to making himself high—it is that he go up on its burning place" (Lev. 6:2).[12]

247. R. Eleazar said: He in whom there is haughtiness of spirit will not have his dust stirred [at the resurrection], for it is said, "Awake and sing, ye that dwell with the dust" (Isa. 26:19). It is not said, "Ye that dwell in the dust," but, "Ye that dwell with the dust"—each of whom during his life had made himself dwell [in humility] as a neighbor to dust.[13]

248. Bar Kappara expounded: What is meant by the verse "why *teratzedun* [look ye askance] ye mountains of lofty peaks" (Ps. 68:17)? That a divine voice came forth and said to the other mountains, "Why do you seek litigation [*tirtzu din*] with Sinai? Compared to Sinai, all of you are blemished." Said R. Ashi: From this we learn that he who regards himself as being lofty is a blemished person.[14]

249. Nebuchadnezzar said: It is not worth living among the inhabitants of the world. I will provide myself a small cloud and live in it: "I will ascend upon the heights of a cloud" (Isa. 14:14). The Holy One said to him, "Thou saidst in thy heart: I will ascend into heaven," etc. (Isa. 14:13)—I will bring you down to the pit of destruction. You said: It is not worth living among the inhabitants of the world. "Thou shalt be driven from men, and thy dwelling shall be with the beasts of the field, and thou shalt be made to eat grass as oxen . . . and seven times shall pass over thee, till thou know that the Most High ruleth in the kingdom of men, and giveth it to whomsoever He will" (Dan. 4:22).[15]

250. When they who [ostentatiously] draw out their spittle grew more numerous, and the arrogant grew more numerous, disciples became fewer, and Torah had to go around looking for those who would study it.

When the arrogant grew more numerous, the daugh-

1. B. Sot 4b.
2. B. Sot 5a.
3. Ibid.
4. B. Ber 43b.
5. DER 2.
6. DER 11.
7. "The smallest disappointment is liable to discomfit him" (J. N. Epstein in Sot, Soncino, p. 20, n. 2).
8. B. Sot 5a.
9. B. Pes 66b.
10. B. Sot 5a.
11. B. Sot 5a.
12. JV: "This is the law of the burnt offering: it is that which goeth up on its firewood." Lev. R. 7:6.
13. B. Sot 5a.
14. B. Meg 29a.
15. Tos Sot 3:19.

ters of Israel began to wed the arrogant, for our generation looks only at that which is for show.

Is that really true? Behold, he who is arrogant, a master declared, is not acceptable even to members of his own household, as is said, "An arrogant man abideth not at home" (Hab. 2:5), even in his own home.

At first a daughter of Israel jumps at the opportunity to wed such a one, but in the end he becomes repulsive to her.[1]

251. Poverty in Torah is a sign of arrogance.[2]

252. A poor man who is proud—that, the mind cannot comprehend![3]

253. Why are the tallest of the tall and the lowest of the low—the cedar and the hyssop—used in the ritual cleansing of a leper? Because when a man exalted himself like a cedar, he was smitten with leprosy; and when he humbled himself like hyssop, he was healed with hyssop.[4]

Shamefacedness and Brazenness

254. We have been taught: "That the fear of Him may be ever with you" (Exod. 20:20), meaning: shamefacedness; "that ye sin not" (ibid.), implying that shamefacedness brings to fear of sin. Hence, the sages inferred that shyness is a good sign in a man.

Others say: He who has a feeling of shame will not readily sin; whereas he who has no feeling of shame—it is certain that his forebears did not stand at Mount Sinai.[5]

255. There are three signs in this people: they are compassionate, shamefaced, and given to deeds of loving-kindness.[6]

256. Most of those who are of good lineage are shamefaced.[7]

257. Judah ben Tema used to say: The brazen-faced is destined for Gehenna, but the shamefaced for the Garden of Eden.[8]

258. Ulla said: Jerusalem was destroyed only because its inhabitants had no shame of one another: "They shall be put to shame because they have committed abomination; yea, they are not at all ashamed, neither know they how to blush; therefore shall they fall among them that fall" (Jer. 6:15).

R. Isaac said: Jerusalem was destroyed only because the small and the great were made equal, as is said, "Like people, like priest" (Isa. 24:2), which is followed in the next verse by "Therefore shall the earth be utterly emptied.[9]

259. R. Dimi said: Isaiah cursed Israel with eighteen curses, yet he was not content until he said, "The child shall behave insolently against the aged, and the base against the honorable" (Isa. 3:5).[10]

260. Rabbah bar Huna said: Anyone who is brazen-faced may be called "wicked," as is said, "He who makes his face brazen is wicked" (Prov. 21:29). R. Nahman bar Isaac said: One may hate him, as is said, "The brazenness of his face is to be changed" (Eccles. 8:1). Read not *yeshunneh*, "is to be changed," but *yissane*, "is to be hated."[11]

261. Since he is so insolent, he is clearly wicked.[12]

262. R. Nahman said: Impudence avails even against Heaven. Thus, at first God said to Balaam, "Thou shalt not go with them" (Num. 22:12). But finally [giving in to Balaam's insistence] He said, "Rise up, and go with them" (Num. 22:20).

R. Sheshet said: Impudence is kingship without a crown. Thus David admitted, "I am this day weak, though anointed king; and these men, the sons of Zeruiah, are too powerful for me" (2 Sam. 3:39).[13]

263. "And Memucan said" (Esther 1:16). From the fact that he [the least of the king's advisers] was the first to speak, it may be inferred, said R. Kahana, that an ignorant man scrambles to the head of the line.[14]

264. It is better that you be put to shame by yourself than be put to shame by others.[15]

265. R. Abba of Caesarea said: To be put to shame by one's own self is not the same as to be put to shame by others.[16]

266. Ten people get together to steal a beam and feel no shame in the presence of one another.[17]

Joy and Sadness, Frivolity and Levity

267. "Then I commended joy" (Eccles. 8:15)—the joy in obeying a precept. "But of [another kind of] joy, I said, 'What doeth it?' " (Eccles. 2:2)—joy not associated with performing a precept. This should prove to you that the

1. B. Sot 47b.
2. B. Sanh 24a.
3. B. Pes 113b.
4. Num. R. 19:3.
5. B. Ned 20a.
6. B. Yev 79a and En Yaakov, ad loc.
7. P. Kid 4:10, 66c; Sof 15.
8. Avot 5:20.
9. B. Shab 119b.
10. B. Hag 14a.
11. B. Ta 7b.
12. B. BM 83b.
13. B. Sanh 105a.
14. B. Meg 12b.
15. DEZ 2.
16. B. Ta 15b–16a.
17. B. Kid 80b.

Presence rests neither in the midst of sadness, nor in the midst of idleness, nor in the midst of frivolity, nor in the midst of levity, nor in the midst of chitchat, nor in the midst of inane talk, but only in the midst of joy in obeying a precept, as is shown by Elisha. [After Elisha became angry at the king of Israel (2 Kings 3:13–14), his power of prophecy left him. But then, when he overcame his anger, he found such joy] that he said, " 'Now bring me a minstrel. And it came to pass, when the instrument played, that the hand of the Lord [the power of prophecy] came back to him" (2 Kings 3:15).[1]

268. "If there is anxiety in a man's mind, let him quash it (*yash'hennah*)" (Prov. 12:25). R. Ammi and R. Assi differed on how he is to go about it. One said: Let him banish it from his mind (*yasihennah*); the other said: Let him speak about it (*yesihennah*) to others.[2]

269. R. Beroka of Khuzistan used to frequent the marketplace of Be Lapat,[3] where Elijah often appeared to him. Once he asked Elijah, "Is there anyone in this marketplace who is to have a portion in the world-to-come?" Elijah replied, "No."

In the meantime, two men came by, and Elijah said, "These two will have a place in the world-to-come." R. Beroka went over to them and asked them, "What is your occupation?" They replied, "We are jesters. When we see people depressed, we cheer them up; and when we see two people quarreling, we work hard to make peace between them."[4]

270. In the marketplace of Zion, a disciple was following R. Ishmael son of R. Yose, who noticed that he seemed to be fearful and said to him: You must be a sinner, since it is said, "The sinners in Zion are fearful" (Isa. 23:14). The disciple: But is it not also said, "Happy is the man that feareth alway" (Prov. 28:14)? R. Ishmael: That is said about words of Torah.

Judah bar Nathan was following R. Hamnuna, who noticed that he was sighing. So he said to him: You wish to bring affliction upon yourself, since it is said, "The thing which I did fear is come upon me" (Job 3:25). Judah replied: But is it not also said, "Happy is the man that feareth alway?" That, R. Hamnuna replied, is said about words of Torah.[5]

271. Rav said: A sigh breaks half of a man's body, for it is said, "Sigh therefore, thou son of man, with the breaking of thy loins" (Ezek. 21:11). But R. Yohanan said: Man's entire body, for it is said, "And it shall be, when they say unto thee: Wherefore sighest thou? that thou shalt say: Because of the tidings, for when it cometh, every heart shall melt" (Ezek. 21:12).[6]

272. Tears caused by weeping are harmful; tears caused by laughter are beneficial.[7]

273. "And the clouds return after the rain" (Eccles. 12:2). Scripture refers to the light in man's eyes, which is lost after weeping.[8]

274. Rejoicing is designated by ten different terms: joy, gladness, merriment, a ringing cry, leaping, exulting, a shrill cry, jubilation, a resounding cry, shouting.[9]

275. "The heart knoweth its own bitterness, even as with its joy no stranger can intermeddle" (Prov. 14:10). What is meant? Just as the heart first feels the distress which anguishes a man, so, when a man rejoices, the heart is the first to feel the joy.[10]

276. One [occasion for] rejoicing is not to be set at a time when there is another occasion for rejoicing.[11]

277. "Because thou didst not serve the Lord thy God in joyfulness and with gladness of heart" (Deut. 28:47). R. Mattenah said: What service is "in joyfulness and with gladness of heart"? You must conclude that it is [the Levites'] service of song.[12]

278. When the Sanhedrin ceased, song ceased in places of feasting, as is said, "They shall not drink wine with a song" (Isa. 24:9), and it is also said, "When the elders ceased from the gate, the young men ceased from their music" (Lam. 5:15).[13]

279. During the war with Vespasian, the sages decreed against the wearing of crowns by bridegrooms and against sounding the [wedding] drum.

During the war with Quietus,[14] they decreed against the wearing of crowns by brides.

During the last war,[15] they decreed that a bride should not go out in the city [on her way to her groom's house] in a palanquin. But subsequently, other sages permitted it.[16]

280. R. Hisda quoted, "When the miter is removed, the crown is taken off; . . . that which is low shall be exalted,

---

1. "Maharsha observes that the verse is quoted merely to show that the Divine Presence does not rest on a man plunged in gloom, Elisha requiring the minstrel to dissipate the gloom occasioned by Jehoram's visit" (Shab, Soncino, p. 136, n. 6). B. Shab 30b.
2. B. Sanh 100b.
3. The capital of the province of Khuzistan, Persia, during the Sassanid period.
4. B. Ta 22a.
5. Fears lest he forget them. B. Ber 60a.
6. B. Ber 58b.
7. B. Shab 151b–152a.
8. B. Shab 151b.
9. ARN 34; Song R. 1:4, §1.
10. Exod. R. 19:1.
11. Hence, a wedding, an occasion for rejoicing, is not to be set on a Sabbath, which is a day for rejoicing. B. MK 8b.
12. B. Ar 11a.
13. B. Sot 48a.
14. Trajan's general, who fought against the Jews forty-five years after the Temple's destruction; see *Mishnah*, ed. Albeck, 3:260. BR read "Titus."
15. Bar Kokhba's revolt, which began in 132 C.E.
16. B. Sot 49a.

and that which is high abased" (Ezek. 21:31), and then asked: What has the miter to do with the crown? When the miter is on the high priest's head, a crown is on every man's head; when the miter is removed from the high priest's head, the crown is removed from every man's head.[1]

281. An inquiry was addressed to Mar Ukba: Where is the proof that [in our days] singing at secular festivities is forbidden? Mar Ukba scratched his reply on the back of the inquiry: "Rejoice not, O Israel, unto exultation, like the peoples" (Hos. 9:1).

Should he not have replied rather with the verse "They shall not drink wine with music" (Isa. 24:9)?

From the second verse, I might have concluded that the use of musical instruments is prohibited, but not singing. From the first verse, one may infer that singing is also prohibited.[2]

282. R. Yohanan said: He who drinks to the accompaniment of four instruments brings sundry punishments to the world, as is said, "The harp and the lute, the tabret and the pipe, and wine are in their feasts" (Isa. 5:12). And what follows directly? "Therefore my people are gone into captivity, for lack of knowledge" (Isa. 5:13).[3]

283. Rav said: The ear that listens to song shall be torn off.

Rava said: Song in the house brings destruction at its threshold: "When a voice sings in the windows, there shall be desolation in the threshold" (Zeph. 2:14).

R. Huna said: Singing by ship haulers and plowmen is permitted, but not singing by weavers.[4]

284. R. Huna abolished singing [at secular festivities], and though a hundred geese came to be priced at only one *zuz*, and a hundred *seah* of wheat at only one *zuz*, there was no demand for them.[5] R. Hisda came and invalidated R. Huna's decree, and a single goose, sought at even as high a price as one *zuz*, could not be found.[6]

285. R. Joseph said: When men sing and women respond, it is licentiousness. When women sing and men respond, it is fire in tow.[7]

286. Mar the son of Ravina made a marriage feast for his son. When he saw that the sages were getting overly merry, he brought a precious cup worth four hundred *zuz* and smashed it before them, and they grew serious.

R. Ashi made a marriage feast for his son. When he saw that the sages were getting overly merry, he brought a cup of white crystal and smashed it before them, and they sobered up.

At the wedding of Mar the son of Ravina, the sages said to R. Hamnuna the Younger, "Please, sir, sing us something." He sang, " 'Alas' the cry, for we must die! 'Alas' the cry, for we must die!" They asked him, "What refrain are we to sing after you?" He said, "Sing: 'Where is Torah and where mitzvah to ward us, to guard us?' "[8]

287. Let there be rejoicing at the time of rejoicing, and mourning at the time of mourning.[9]

288. "I will spread dung on your faces, even the dung of your feasts" (Mal. 2:3). R. Huna (according to some, R. Hagga) said: The verse is addressed to those who set aside words of Torah and spend their days at feasts.

R. Levi said in the name of R. Papi, who said it in the name of R. Joshua: Three days [after death], the belly of such a man bursts open, and what is in it falls on his face, as though saying to him, "Take back what you put into me."[10]

289. R. Yohanan said in the name of R. Simeon ben Yohai: It is forbidden for a man to fill his mouth with laughter in this world, for Scripture says, "Then will our mouth be filled with laughter, and our tongue with singing" (Ps. 126:2). When? "When it will be said among the nations: 'The Lord hath done great things with these' " (ibid.).

It was told of Resh Lakish that, after he heard these words from his teacher R. Yohanan, he never again filled his mouth with laughter in this world.[11]

290. He who undertakes to be an associate scholar (*haver*) may not be profuse in laughter.[12]

291. Our masters taught: A man should not take leave from his fellow in the midst of ordinary conversation, of levity, of frivolity, or of idle chatter, but should conclude the conversation with a matter of *Halakhah*. For we find that the prophets of old concluded their utterances with words of praise and consolation. So, too, Mari the grandson of R. Huna taught: A man should leave his fellow only with a matter of *Halakhah*, so that he may be remembered thereby.[13]

292. R. Akiva said: Raucous laughter and frivolity predispose a person to unchastity.[14]

293. "Blessed is the man that walketh not in the counsel of the wicked, nor standeth in the way of sinners, nor sitteth in the seat of the scornful" (Ps. 1:1). R. Simeon ben Pazzi commented: If he walks not, how could he be standing on the way?[15] And if he stands not on the way,

---

1. B. Git 7a.
2. B. Git 7a.
3. B. Sot 48a.
4. "Singing helps the former in their work, but with the latter, it is done out of frivolity" (Sot, Soncino, p. 257, n. 7). B. Sot 48a.
5. Because there was no feasting.
6. The demand being great, they were sold out. B. Sot 48a.
7. Ibid.
8. B. Ber 30b–31a.
9. Gen. R. 27:4.
10. B. Shab 151b.
11. B. Ber 31a.
12. Dem 2:3.
13. B. Ber 31a.
14. Avot 3:13.
15. R. Simeon ben Pazzi interprets "Blessed is the man that walketh not in the counsel of the wicked" as meaning "Blessed is the man that walketh not to the theaters and to the circuses of the heathen."

how could he come to sit in the seat of the scornful? And if he sits not [among them], how could he scoff [with them]? The verse means to tell you, however, that when a man walks [among the wicked], he ends up by standing [with them]; when he stands [among them], he ends up sitting [with them]; and when he sits [among them], he ends up by scoffing [with them]. And when he scoffs, it is of him that Scripture says, "If thou scornest, thou alone shalt bear it" (Prov. 9:12).[1]

294. R. Eleazar said: When a man scoffs, suffering will befall him, as is said, "Now therefore do ye not scoff, lest your punishments be made severe" (Isa. 28:22).

Rava said to the sages: I beg of you, do not scoff, so that no suffering will come upon you.

R. Kattina said: When a man scoffs, his victuals will be diminished, as is said, "He withdraweth His hand from scoffers" (Hos. 7:5).

R. Simeon ben Lakish said: He who scoffs will fall into Gehenna, as is said, "A proud and haughty man, whose name is scoffer, worketh for the wrath with which presumptuousness is punished"[2] (Prov. 21:24). And by "wrath" here, Gehenna is meant, as in "That day is a day of wrath" (Zeph. 1:15).

R. Tanhum bar Hanilai said: Anyone who scoffs brings destruction upon the world, as is said, "Now therefore be ye not scoffers, lest your affliction be made severe, for an extermination wholly determined have I heard" (Isa. 28:22).

Said R. Eleazar: Scoffing is indeed a grievous sin, since its beginning is "affliction" and its end "extermination."[3]

295. R. Simeon ben Pazzi expounded: What is meant by "Happy is the man that hath not walked," etc. (Ps. 1:1)? That he has not walked to the theaters and circuses of idolaters. "Nor stood in the way of sinners" (ibid.)? That he did not stand as a spectator at contests of wild beasts. "Nor sat in the seat of the scornful" (ibid.)? That he did not sit at gatherings of intriguers. Lest such a man say, "Since I do not go to theaters or circuses, nor am I a spectator at contests of wild animals, I will go and indulge freely in sleep," Scripture admonishes, "And in His law shall He meditate day and night" (ibid.).[4]

296. Our masters taught: Those who visit stadiums or entertainments at military camps and witness there [the performance] of diviners and charmers, of clowns and buffoons, of comic muleteers and jesters; and who [participate in] bacchanalian and secular festivities—those are spoken of as being in "the seat of the scornful," and concerning them, Scripture says, "Happy is the man that hath not sat in the seat of the scornful," followed at once by "But his delight is in the law of the Lord" (Ps. 1:1–2). From here you may infer that all such activities invariably cause one to neglect the Torah.[5]

297. R. Hisda said in the name of R. Jeremiah bar Abba: The company of scoffers will not receive the Presence, for it is said, "He stretched out His hand against scoffers" (Hos. 7:5).[6]

298. As soon as R. Yassa came up to the Land of Israel, he went and had his hair cut. When he tried to bathe in the springs of Tiberias, a certain wag struck him from behind on the back of his head. R. Yassa said, "The noose intended for this person still hangs loose." An official happened to be seated there, judging a brigand. So the wag went, stationed himself in front of the brigand, and proceeded to mock him. When the official asked the brigand, "Who was with you?" the brigand, lifting his eyes and seeing the wag mocking him, replied, "This one, who is mocking me, was with me." The wag was immediately seized and put to torture, and he confessed that he had killed a certain man. R. Yassa happened to leave the bathhouse and met the two as they were being taken out, carrying their crosses. The wag said to him, "The noose that was hanging loose is now to be made tight." R. Yassa replied, "O ill-starred one, have you not been told, 'Now therefore be ye not scoffers, lest your cords be made tight' (Isa. 28:22)?"[7]

299. R. Nahman said: All scoffing is prohibited, except scoffing at an idol, which is permitted.[8]

Resignation to Suffering

300. A man is required to bless God for evil, even as he is to bless Him for good, as is said, "Thou shalt love the Lord thy God . . . with all thy might (*meodekha*)" (Deut. 6:5). Read rather: "For every measure (*middah*) that may be measured out to you, thank Him (*modeh*)."

R. Meir said: What is the proof that, as one is required to bless for good, so is one required to bless for evil? The verse "Thou shalt bless the Lord [of mercy] as well as thy *Elohim*" (Deut. 8:10)—your Judge,[9] no matter what judgment He decrees for you, whether a measure of prosperity or a measure of suffering.

What is meant by being bound to bless for the evil in the same way as for the good? Shall I say that, just as for good one says the benediction "Who is good and bestows good," so for evil one should say the benediction "Who is good and bestows good"? But we have been taught: For good tidings, one says, "Who is good and bestows good"; for evil tidings, one says, "Blessed be the true Judge." Rava explained: What it really means is that one must accept the evil with gladness. R. Aha said in the name of R. Levi: Where is the proof? From "I will sing of mercy and justice" (Ps. 101:1); be it "mercy," I will sing, or be it "justice," I will sing. R. Samuel bar Nahmani said: We derive it from "In the Lord—I will praise His word:

1. B. AZ 18b.
2. JV: "Even he that dealeth in overbearing pride."
3. B. AZ 18b and En Yaakov, ad loc.; P. Ber 2:8, 5c.
4. B. AZ 18b; P. Ber 2:8, 5c.
5. Ibid.

6. B. Sot 42a.
7. P. Ber 2:8, 5c.
8. B. Meg 25b.
9. Taking *Elohim* ("God") in its alternate meaning of "Judge."

in God—I will praise His word" (Ps. 56:11). "In the Lord—I will praise His word" refers to the measure of good; "In God—I will praise His word" refers to the measure of suffering. R. Tanhum said: We derive it from "I will lift up the cup of salvation, and call upon the Name of the Lord" (Ps. 116:13) and "I found trouble and sorrow, but I still called upon the Name of the Lord" (Ps. 116:3–4). The sages derived it from "The Lord gave, and the Lord hath taken away; blessed be the Name of the Lord" (Job 1:21).[1]

301. The sages said in the name of R. Meir, and other sages taught it in the name of R. Akiva: A man should accustom himself to say, "Whatever the Holy One does is all for good."

Once, while R. Akiva was traveling, he came to a certain town where he looked for lodgings, but none was given him. So, saying, "Whatever the Holy One does is for good," he went to spend the night in the open field. With him, he had an ass, a cock, and a lamp. A lion came and ate the ass, a cat came and ate the cock, and a gust of wind came up and blew out the lamp. Again he said; "Whatever the Holy One does is all for good." The same night, soldiers came and carried off the inhabitants of the town. Then R. Akiva said to his companions, "Did I not tell you that 'whatever the Holy One does is all for good'?"[2]

302. "You shall not behave toward Me," etc. (Exod. 20:20). R. Akiva said: You shall not behave toward Me as others in sundry lands behave. When prosperity comes to them, they honor their deities, as is said, "Therefore they sacrifice unto their trawl" (Hab. 1:16). But when suffering comes to them, they curse their gods, as is said, "They . . . curse their king and their god" (Isa. 8:21). But you [are to act differently]: when I [your God] bring prosperity to you, give thanks, and when I bring suffering upon you, give thanks.[3]

303. R. Huna said: "Behold, it was . . . good" (Gen. 1:31) refers to the measure of prosperity. "Behold, it was very good": (ibid.) [the addition of "very" includes] the measure of suffering. But can suffering be described as "very good"? It seems incredible. But the fact is, it is through suffering that mortals come to life in the world-to-come. Indeed, Solomon said so: "Reproofs of chastisement are the way to life" (Prov. 6:23). Go forth and see what road leads man to life in the world-to-come. You must say it is the measure of suffering.[4]

304. R. Simeon ben Lakish said: The word "covenant" is mentioned with regard to salt (Lev. 2:13), and "covenant" is also mentioned with regard to suffering (Deut. 28:69). What is intended by the covenant of salt? To sweeten the taste of meat, even as suffering is to purge all of man's iniquities.[5]

[1] B. Ber 54a, 48b, and 60b; En Yaakov, ad loc.
[2] B. Ber 60b–61a.
[3] Mek, *Yitro, Ba-hodesh,* 10.
[4] Gen. R. 9:8.
[5] B. Ber 5a.

305. R. Eliezer ben Jacob taught: Scripture says, "Whom the Lord loveth, He chasteneth, even as a father the son in whom he delighteth" (Prov. 3:12). Pause and consider: What was it that made the son become a delight to his father? You must say it was suffering.[6]

306. Our masters taught: When R. Eliezer fell sick, four elders—R. Tarfon, R. Joshua, R. Eleazar ben Azariah, and R. Akiva—came to visit him.

R. Akiva spoke up and said, "Suffering is precious."[7]

At that, R. Eliezer said to his disciples, "Prop me up, that I may hear [better] the words of Akiva, my disciple, who has said, 'Suffering is precious.' What proof have you, Akiva, my son, for saying it?" R. Akiva replied, "Master, I draw such inference from the verse 'Manasseh was twelve years old when he began to reign, and he reigned fifty and five years in Jerusalem . . . and he did that which was evil in the sight of the Lord' [2 Kings 21:1–2]. I consider this verse in the light of another: 'These are also the proverbs of Solomon, which the men of Hezekiah king of Judah copied out [for widespread instruction]' [Prov. 25:1]. Now, is it conceivable that Hezekiah king of Judah taught Torah to the whole world, to all of it, but not to Manasseh, his own son? Of course not! Yet all the pains that Hezekiah took with him and all the labor that he lavished upon him did not bring him onto the right path. Only Manasseh's suffering did so, as is written, 'And the Lord spoke to Manasseh, and to his people; but they gave no heed. Wherefore the Lord brought upon them the captains and the host of the king of Assyria, who took Manasseh captive in manacles. . . . And when [Manasseh] was in distress, he besought the Lord his God, and humbled himself greatly before the God of his fathers, and He answered his entreaty' [2 Chron. 33:10–13)]. You may thus infer how precious is suffering."[8]

307. R. Nathan son of Joseph said: Chastisements are precious. Because of them, the covenant was made with the children of Israel, as is said, "I will bring you into the crucible[9] of the covenant" (Ezek. 20:37).

R. Nehemiah said: Chastisements are precious, for as offerings make atonement, so chastisements make atonement. Of an offering, it is written, "It shall be accepted for him to make atonement for him" (Lev. 1:4); and of suffering under chastisement, it is written, "The land shall lie forsaken without them . . . while they shall make atonement for their iniquity" (Lev. 26:43). Not only this, but even more! Suffering under chastisement is better than offerings for making atonement, for offerings come out of a man's property, but chastisements fall upon a man's very person.[10]

[6] Mek, *Yitro, Ba-hodesh,* 10; Sif Deut., §32.
[7] It makes atonement for the sufferer.
[8] B. Sanh 101a–b; Sif Deut., §32; Yalkut, 2 Kings, §226.
[9] Wordplay on *masoret* ("bond," "tradition") and *masret* (literally "skillet" or "saucepan"), resulting in the figure of "a crucible of suffering."
[10] Mek, *Yitro, Ba-hodesh,* 10: Sif Deut., §32; MTeh 94:2.

308. R. Yudan said: It is written, "If he smite out his bondman's tooth, or his bondwoman's tooth, he shall let him go free for his tooth's sake" (Exod. 21:27). Now, if because of such smitings, which affect not man's entire body but only one of his parts, the Torah says, "He shall go free," how much more and more is a man whose entire body is assailed by suffering certain to be set free [in the world-to-come].[1]

309. R. Simeon ben Yohai said: Chastisements are good; because of them, three precious gifts came to Israel, gifts that the nations of the earth desired for themselves. Yet only because of chastisements were the gifts—Torah, the Land of Israel, and the world-to-come—given to Israel. And the proof that the Torah was so given? "Blessed is the man whom Thou chastenest, O Lord, for thereby Thou teachest him Thy law" (Ps. 94:12). And the proof that the Land of Israel was so given? "As a man chasteneth his son, so the Lord thy God chasteneth thee" (Deut. 8:5). And what follows? "The Lord thy God bringeth thee into a good land" (Deut. 8:7). And the proof that the world-to-come was so given? "Reproofs by chastisement are the way to [future] life" (Prov. 6:23).[2]

310. The sages said in the name of R. Huna: The more pleased the Holy One is with a man, the more He crushes him with suffering, for Scripture says, "The Lord was greatly pleased with [him; hence] he crushed him by disease" (Isa. 53:10). Now, you might think that this is so even if the man did not accept his suffering with love. Therefore the verse goes on to say, "To see if he regarded himself as an offering for guilt" (ibid.).[3]

311. The sages said in the name of R. Huna: When a man sees that sufferings come upon him, he should examine his conduct. If, in examining it, he finds [wrongdoing in himself], let him repent. If, after examining his conduct, he finds no wrongdoing, let him attribute the sufferings to his neglect of the study of the Torah. If, after attempting to attribute them to such neglect, he finds this could not [have been the cause], he may be certain that his sufferings are the chastenings of [God's] love. For "whom the Lord loveth He chasteneth" (Prov. 3:12).[4]

312. "Come, my people, enter thou into thy chambers" (Isa. 26:20). Scrutinize the chambers of your heart [and see] why I brought suffering to you, and you will not then raise a cry against the measure of justice.[5]

313. Happy the man who can withstand the test given him, for there is no mortal whom the Holy One does not test. He tests the rich man to see if his hand will be open to the poor; and He tests the poor man to see whether he will be resigned to suffering and not be filled with resentment.[6]

314. R. Jacob bar Idi and R. Aha bar Hanina [differed with regard to the following]. One said: Chastenings of love are such as do not compel cessation of study of Torah, for Scripture says, "Happy is the man whom Thou chastenest, O Lord, and teachest out of Thy Torah" (Ps. 94:12). The other said: Chastenings of love are such as do not compel the cessation of prayer, for Scripture says, "Blessed be God, who hath not turned away my prayer, nor His mercy from me" (Ps. 66:20). R. Abba son of R. Hiyya said to the two: This is what R. Yohanan taught: Both are chastenings of love, for Scripture says, "Whom the Lord loveth He chasteneth" (Prov. 3:12). Then why does it go on to say, "And teachest him out of Thy Torah"? Read not *telammedennu*, "Thou teachest him," but *telammedeinu*, "Thou teachest us." You teach us such a conclusion out of Your Torah by reasoning *a fortiori* from the law concerning a master's knocking out a slave's tooth or blinding his eye. A tooth or an eye is only one of the parts of a man's body, yet [if it is injured], the slave obtains his freedom because of the injury. How much more and more by far is this true of sufferings that purge a man's entire body![7]

315. "Thy rod and Thy staff they comfort me" (Ps. 23:4). "Thy rod" is affliction, and "Thy staff" is Torah.[8]

316. R. Simeon ben Lakish said: When a man is engaged with Torah, affliction keeps away from him.[9]

317. R. Alexandri said: There is no man without suffering. How happy is he whose suffering comes through [toil in] Torah, as is said, "Happy is the man whom Thou chastenest, O Lord, while Thou teachest him out of Thy Torah" (Ps. 94:12).[10]

318. When R. Hama saw a blind man sitting occupied with Torah, he said to him, "Peace to you, O freedman." The man replied, "Where did you hear that I am the son of a slave?" R. Hama: "I did not, but I meant that you will be a freedman in the world-to-come."[11]

319. R. Bizna said: There is no man in the world without suffering. When he has a pain in his teeth, he does not sleep; in his eyes, he does not sleep. When he toils in the Torah, he does not sleep. In either case, he is awake. "Happy is the man whom Thou chastenest, O Lord, while Thou teachest him out of Thy Torah" (Ps. 94:12).[12]

1. Gen. R. 92:1.
2. Mek, *Yitro, Ba-hodesh,* 10; Sif Deut., §32; MTeh 94:2.
3. B. Ber 5a.
4. Ibid.
5. Yalkut, Isa., §432.
6. Exod. R. 31:3.
7. B. Ber 5a.
8. Song R. 2:1, §3.
9. B. Ber 5a.
10. Rather than being kept up during the night by physical suffering, it is better to be kept awake by the study of Torah. Gen. R. 92:1.
11. Ibid.
12. Tanhuma B, *Mi-ketz,* §16; Yalkut, Ps., §850.

320. "For in much wisdom is much vexation," etc. (Eccles. 1:18). As long as a man increases wisdom, he increases vexation, and as long as he increases knowledge, he increases suffering. Hence Solomon said: Through increasing wisdom I have increased vexation for myself, and through increasing knowledge I have increased suffering for myself.

R. Yohanan said: [Solomon's suffering] may be likened to fine linen garments that come from Beth Shean. If one of them becomes slightly soiled, it is regarded as a serious loss. On the other hand, coarse flaxen garments that come from Arbel—should they become soiled, who cares, for what is their value?[1] So, too, in the way of the world, when two men go into an eating place where one eats coarse bread and pulse, while the other eats delicate bread and choice meat, and drinks aged wine, the man who ate fine food is apt to suffer intestinal discomfort, while he who had coarse food is not apt to suffer. Likewise, have you ever seen an ass suffering from chills or a camel suffering from nervous stomach? By whom are such sufferings experienced? Only by human beings.[2]

321. R. Huna said: Suffering is divided into three portions: the patriarchs and all the generations of men took one portion; the generation that lived in the time [of Hadrian's] persecution took the second portion; and the generation of the king Messiah will take the third.[3]

322. R. Eleazar son of R. Simeon invoked painful afflictions upon himself, so that even though sixty felt pads were spread under him in the evening [when he went to bed], sixty basins of blood and pus were removed from under him the next morning. Every morning his wife prepared for him a mixture of sixty kinds of fig pap, and after he ate of it, he felt better. However, that evening R. Eleazar would invoke his afflictions back again, saying, "Come back, my brethren and familiars!" And in the morning he would say to them, "Depart, lest you disturb my studies!"[4]

323. Rabbi [Judah I, the Patriarch] invoked painful afflictions upon himself for thirteen years, six through stones in the kidneys and seven through scurvy.

Rabbi's steward was wealthier than King Shapur. [So numerous were his cattle that] when he set out fodder for them, their lowing could be heard for three *mil;* and he deliberately set out their fodder just when Rabbi was entering the privy [so that Rabbi's cries of pain would not be heard]. Yet even so, Rabbi's voice [lifted in pain] was louder than the lowing of the cattle and could be heard even by seafarers [far away].[5]

324. When R. Yohanan fell ill, R. Hanina, went to visit him and asked, "Are your sufferings welcome to you?" R. Yohanan replied, "Neither they nor their reward." R. Hanina: "Give me your hand." R. Yohanan gave him his hand, and R. Hanina raised him up from his sickbed [fully cured].[6]

325. R. Akiva used to say: A king had four sons. One was silent when thrashed; another protested when thrashed; the third begged for mercy when thrashed; and the fourth, when thrashed, said to his father, "Go on thrashing me." The one who remained silent when thrashed—Abraham; the one who protested when thrashed—Job; the one who begged for mercy when thrashed—Hezekiah; the one who, when thrashed, said to his Father, "Go on thrashing me"—David.[7]

326. The man who stubbornly refuses to learn from his suffering must suffer doubly for his stubbornness.[8]

327. Our masters taught: They who are insulted but do not insult, they who hear themselves reviled without replying, they who act out of love and rejoice in suffering—Scripture says of such, "They who love Him will [ultimately] be as the sun when He goeth forth in His might" (Judg. 5:31).[9]

328. R. Abbahu said: A man should always strive to be of the persecuted and not of the persecutors, for among birds none are more persecuted than doves and pigeons, yet only these were declared by Scripture fit for the altar.[10]

329. "When a bullock, or a sheep, or a goat is born" (Lev. 22:27). The Holy One said: A bullock is pursued by a lion, a goat by a leopard, a sheep by a wolf—do not offer to Me any of the pursuers, only of the pursued.[11]

330. "God seeketh that which is pursued" (Eccles. 3:15). R. Huna said in the name of R. Yose: God always seeks [with His love] the pursued. You find that when a righteous man pursues a righteous man, "God seeks him who is pursued." When a wicked man pursues a righteous man, "God seeks him who is pursued." When a wicked man pursues a wicked man, "God seeks him who is pursued." Under all circumstances, He seeks [with love] him who is pursued.[12]

331. R. Meir said: When a man suffers, what expression does the Presence use? "My head is too heavy for Me, My arm is too heavy for Me."[13]

---

1. "Their cost is small, and not much loss is incurred. Similarly, nobody takes much notice if an ordinary person does wrong; but the matter is serious if it happens to be a scholar" (Eccles. R., Soncino, p. 49, n. 5).
2. Gen. R. 19:1; Eccles. R. 1:18, §1.
3. MTeh 2:9.
4. B. BM 84b.
5. B. BM 85a.
6. B. Ber 5b.
7. Sem 8.
8. TdE, ed. Friedmann, p. 12 (JPS, p. 65).
9. B. Shab 88b.
10. B. BK 93a.
11. Lev. R. 27:5.
12. Eccles. R. 3:15, §1.
13. Because of this man's suffering, God's sympathy impels Him to say, "I too am weighed down by his suffering." B. Sanh 46a.

332. "The Lord said unto Satan: 'Behold, he is in thy hand; only spare his life' " (Job 2:6). R. Isaac said: Satan's distress was greater than Job's—he was like a servant told by his master: Break the cask, but spare its wine.[1]

333. "The sorrows of death compassed me (*afafuni*)" (Ps. 18:5). What is the literal meaning of *afafuni*? It means "waves of sorrow have come up to the nose."[2]

Another interpretation: Do not read *afafuni* but *'afafuni*—sorrows, swift flying, swoop down like birds (*'of*) of prey upon me.

Another interpretation: Sorrows come rolling over me like wheels (*ofan*)—solid and spoked wheels.[3]

334. When afflictions are dispatched to a man, they are adjured: Be sure to arrive only on such-and-such a day, and be sure to depart only on such-and-such a day, at such-and-such an hour, through [the healing effected by] So-and-so, by means of such-and-such a potion.[4]

335. Our masters taught: There are three whose life is no life: he who depends on his neighbor's table, he whose wife dominates him, and he whose body is overwhelmed by afflictions. Some say: Also he who has only one shirt.[5]

336. At what point may [divine] visitations be said to commence?[6] R. Eleazar said: If a man had a garment woven for him to wear, and it does not fit him. Rava the Younger (or, according to others, R. Samuel bar Nahmani) disagreed: Something more unpleasant: If hot wine was ordered, but it was served cold; or if cold wine was ordered, but it was served hot [this is a divine visitation]. Mar son of Ravina said: Even if he finds his shirt turned inside out. Some say: Even if one puts his hand inside his purse expecting to find three coins, but finds only two.[7]

337. When Rabbi Judah I, the Patriarch, stubbed his small toe, he applied to himself the words "Many are the sufferings of the wicked" (Ps. 32:10).[8]

338. Nittai the Arbelite said: Do not delude yourself into thinking that [divine] punishment will not come.[9]

339. The sages in the school of R. Ishmael taught: He who has passed forty days without any kind of suffering is [in a manner of speaking] deemed to have received his reward in this world. In the west [the Land of Israel], they say: [He who has passed forty days without any kind of suffering is to know that] suffering [which will effect atonement] still awaits him.[10]

340. Rava said: A man is not held responsible for what he says in the hour of his distress.[11]

341. Sufficient unto the hour is the trouble thereof.[12]

342. Troubles dim the eyes.[13]

343. The later troubles cause one to forget the earlier ones.[14]

344. A proverb says: When your sieve is clogged, strike it.[15]

345. R. Levi said: No trouble comes to a man that does not bring profit to others.[16]

Analysis of Human Traits

346. Whoever possesses these three qualities is of the disciples of Abraham our father; and [whoever possesses] three other qualities is of the disciples of Balaam the Wicked. The disciples of Abraham our father [possess] a generous eye, a humble spirit, and a lowly soul. The disciples of Balaam the Wicked [possess] an evil eye, a haughty spirit, and an overambitious soul.

What is [the difference] in the treatment given to the disciples of Abraham our father and that given to the disciples of Balaam the Wicked? The disciples of Abraham our father enjoy [their share in] this world and inherit the world-to-come, as is said, "That I may cause those that love Me to inherit substance, and that I may fill their treasuries" (Prov. 8:21). But the disciples of Balaam the Wicked inherit Gehenna and descend into the nethermost pit, as is said, "But Thou, O God, wilt bring them down to the nethermost pit; men of blood and deceit shall not live out half their days" (Ps. 55:24).[17]

347. Rabban Yohanan ben Zakkai had five [distinguished] disciples, to whom he said: Go forth and discover what characteristic should be cultivated as a way of life. [When they came back], R. Eliezer declared: A generous eye. R. Joshua declared: Being a good friend. R. Yose: Being a good neighbor. R. Simeon: The capacity to consider the consequences of one's action. R. Eleazar [ben Arakh]: A joyous heart. Rabban Yohanan said to them: I prefer what Eleazar ben Arakh has said to what you have said, because his definition includes all of yours.

---

1. B. BB 16a.
2. *Afafuni* is taken here as a derivative of *af* ("nose").
3. MTeh 18:10.
4. B. AZ 55a.
5. Betz 32b.
6. These are considered "chastisements" that would have been his in the world-to-come. Hence, he will come to enjoy sooner the reward for his good deeds.
7. B. Ar 16b–17a.
8. Lev. R. 15.4.
9. Avot 1:6.
10. B. Ar 16b–17a.
11. B. BB 16b.
12. No need to keep harping on it. B. Ber 9b.
13. Lekah Tov, Gen. 48:10.
14. B. Ber 13a.
15. So, too, when one forgets his obligations, he is jolted by suffering. Gen. R. 81:2; Tanhuma, *Va-yishlah*, §8.
16. Gen. R. 38:10.
17. Avot 5:19.

Then he said: Go forth and discover what characteristic should be shunned. [When they came back], R. Eliezer declared: A grudging eye. R. Joshua declared: Pretending to be a friend. R. Yose: Being a bad neighbor. R. Simeon: Borrowing and not repaying—in borrowing thus from man, it is as if he borrowed thus from God, for "when the wicked man borroweth and payeth not, the Righteous One, who dealeth graciously, giveth to the one thus wronged" (Ps. 37:21). R. Eleazar ben Arakh: A despondent heart. R. Yohanan said to them: I prefer what R. Eleazar ben Arakh has said to what you have said, because his definition includes all of yours.[1]

348. R. Joshua said: The evil eye, the impulse to evil, and hatred of [God's] creatures put a man out of the world.[2]

349. R. Eleazar ha-Kappar said: Envy, lust, and ambition put a man out of the world.[3]

350. R. Dosa ben Horkinas said: Sleep into the morning, wine at midday, childish chatter, and sitting in at gatherings of the ignorant [*amme ha-aretz*] put a man out of the world.[4]

351. R. Yudan said in the name of R. Aibu: No man departs from the world with even half his desire gratified. If he has one hundred, he wants to turn it into two hundred, and if he has two hundred, he wants to turn it into four hundred.[5]

352. The Holy One said, "In sundry actions, endeavor to rival Me." But for such rivalry, the world could not endure, for no man would build a house, no man would plant a vineyard, and no man would wed a wife.[6]

353. "Envy is rottenness in the bones" (Prov. 14:30). When a man has envy in his heart, his bones rot; but when he has no envy in his heart, his bones do not rot.[7]

354. Better to die a hundred deaths than to experience envy once.[8]

355. R. Levi said: Six organs serve man—three are under his control, and three are not under his control. The eyes, the ears, and the nose are not under his control: he sees what he does not wish to see, he hears what he does not wish to hear, and he smells what he does not wish to smell. The mouth, the hands, and the feet are under his control: the mouth, if he wishes, will occupy itself with Torah or, if he prefers, slander, revile, and blaspheme. The hands, if he wishes, will distribute charity or, if he prefers, steal and slay. The feet, if he wishes, will walk to synagogues and houses of study or, if he prefers, walk to theaters and circuses.

But when a man has merit, the Holy One has even those organs that are under his control cease to be under it.[9]

356. R. Ilai said: A man's character may be known through three things: his tippling, his tipping, and his temper. Some say: Also through what makes him titter.[10]

357. By three things is a man tested: by his give-and-take in business, by the amount of wine he imbibes, and by the length of his talk.[11]

358. Three the Holy One loves: him who does not show temper, him who does not get drunk, and him who does not insist on his full rights.

Three the Holy One hates: him who says one thing with his mouth and another in his heart, him who knows of evidence in favor of his neighbor and does not testify for him, and him who sees something unseemly in his neighbor and is the only one to testify against him.[12]

359. Four are called wicked: he who raises a hand against his neighbor to strike him, he who borrows and does not repay, he who is brazen-faced, and he who is given to quarreling.[13]

360. R. Jeremiah bar Abba said: Four companies will not receive the Presence: the company of scoffers, the company of hypocrites, the company of liars, and the company of slanderers.[14]

361. Four are hard to put up with: a poor man who is proud, a rich man who falsely denies [a claim against him], an old man who is lecherous, and a leader who without justification would lord it over the community. Some say: Also he who divorces his wife, [remarries her], divorces her again, and remarries her again.[15]

362. [There are] seven things [characteristic] in a man whose mind is imperfectly developed, and seven in a wise man. A wise man does not speak before one who is greater than he in wisdom, does not break in on the words of his fellow, is not hasty to answer, asks what is relevant and answers what is appropriate, speaks on the first [point] first and on the last [point] last, says of that which he has not heard: "I have not heard it," and acknowledges the

1. Avot 2:9.
2. Avot 2:11.
3. Avot 4:21.
4. Avot. 3:10.
5. Eccles. R. 1:13.
6. MTeh 37:1.
7. B. Shab 152b.
8. Deut. R. 9:9.
9. Thus Isaac was made to say of Jacob, "He must remain blessed" (Gen. 27:33). See also 1 Kings 3:15 and Prov. 1:15. Gen. R. 67:3; Yalkut, 1 Kings, §202.
10. B. Er 65b.
11. ARNB 31.
12. Since the evidence of only one witness is not sufficient in court, he is in effect a slanderer. B. Pes 113b.
13. Tanhuma, *Korah*, §8.
14. B. Sot 42a.
15. B. Pes 113b.

truth. The reverse of these [is characteristic] of a man whose mind is imperfectly developed.[1]

363. R. Akiva said: A hedge around wisdom—silence; a hedge around honor—avoidance of frivolity; a hedge around things holy—purity; a hedge around vows—abstinence; a hedge around Torah—tradition.[2]

364. Hillel used to say: The more flesh, the more worms; the more property, the more anxiety; the more wives, the more witchcraft; the more bondwomen, the more lewdness; the more slaves, the more thievery. On the other hand, the [more] study of Torah, the more life; the more sitting down [to study and contemplate], the more wisdom; the more counsel, the more understanding; the more charity, the more peace. He who has acquired a good name has acquired something that [unlike property] remains his own; he who has acquired words of Torah has acquired for himself life in the world-to-come.[3]

365. "Who teacheth us through the beasts of the earth, and maketh us wise through the fowls of heaven" (Job 35:11). R. Yohanan said: Had the Torah not been given to Israel, we might have learned modesty from the cat,[4] respecting others' property from the ant, chastity from the dove, and proper courtship from the rooster.[5]

366. The adornment of God—men; the adornment of men—Torah; the adornment of Torah—wisdom; the adornment of wisdom—humility; the adornment of humility—fear [of God]; the adornment of fear [of God]—the performance of precepts. The adornment of performance of precepts is modesty.[6]

367. R. Phinehas ben Yair said: Zeal [in the study and practice of Torah] leads to fastidiousness, fastidiousness leads to cleanness, cleanness leads to abstinence, abstinence leads to purity, purity leads to holiness, holiness leads to humility, humility leads to fear of sin, fear of sin leads to pious conduct, pious conduct leads to the holy spirit, the holy spirit leads to the resurrection of the dead.[7]

1. Avot 5:7.
2. ARNB 33.
3. Avot 2:7.
4. A cat is discreet about its feces.
5. B. Er 100b and En Yaakov, ad loc.
6. DEZ 5.
7. Song R. 1:1, §9; B. Sot 49b; AZ 20b; P. Shab 1:3, 3c; P. Shek 3:4, 47c.

CHAPTER FIVE

THE COMMUNITY, THE STATE, AND THEIR REQUIREMENTS

The Individual and the Community

1. Our masters taught: He who sees hosts of Israelites should say, "Blessed be He who discerns secrets," for the mind of each of them is not like the mind of any other, nor is the countenance of each of them like the countenance of any other.[1]

2. Ben Zoma once saw such a host on one of the steps of the Temple Mount. He said, "Blessed be He who discerneth secrets, and blessed be He who has created all these people to serve me." For he used to say: How many labors did Adam have to engage in before he obtained bread to eat! He plowed, he sowed, he reaped; he stacked the sheaves, threshed the grain, winnowed the chaff, selected the good ears, ground [them], sifted [flour], kneaded the dough, and baked. And only then did he eat. Whereas I get up and find all these things done for me. How many labors did Adam have to engage in before he obtained a garment to wear! He sheared the sheep, washed [the wool], combed it, spun it, wove it, dyed the cloth, and sewed it. And only then did he have a garment to wear. Whereas I get up and find all these things done for me. All kinds of craftsmen come early to the door of my house, and when I rise in the morning, I find all these things ready for me.

He also used to say: What does a good guest say? "How much trouble my host has taken [for me]! How much meat he set before me! How much wine he set before me! How many cakes he set before me! And all the trouble he has taken was only for my sake!" But what does a bad guest say: "How much, after all, has my host put himself out? I have eaten one piece of bread, I have eaten one slice of meat, I have drunk one cup of wine! All the trouble my host has taken was only for the sake of his wife and his children."[2]

3. Our masters taught: The verse "And when it halted, he would say, 'Rest O Lord, upon the myriads and thousands of Israel' " (Num. 10:36) teaches that the Presence does not rest on fewer than two thousand and two myriads of Israel.[3]

4. R. Isaac said: Let respect for the community always be with you, for you will note that [when blessing the worshipers], the priests' faces were turned toward the people and their backs were toward the Presence. R. Nahman derived this rule from "Then David the king stood up upon his feet and said: "Hear me, my brethren, and my people.' " (1 Chron. 28:2).[4]

5. Hillel said: Do not separate yourself from the community.[5]

6. Samuel said: A man should never extrude himself from the community.[6]

They Who Labor for the Community and Endeavor to Benefit Its People

7. Rabban Gamaliel son of R. Judah [I] the Patriarch said: All who labor for the community should labor with them for Heaven's sake, for then the merit of the community's forebears will sustain them, and their beneficence will endure forever. And as for you [who labor thus], I regard you as deserving great reward, as though you had accomplished it all [on your own].[7]

8. "A man of heave offerings destroys it" (Prov. 29:4).[8] A man who regards himself as though he were a [holy] heave offering set apart in a corner of the house and says, "What concern have I with the community's burden? What concern have I with their lawsuits? What concern have I with listening to their pleas? My own well-being is my one and only concern"[9]—such a man destroys the world, as is said, "A man of heave offerings destroys it."

A story is told of R. Ammi that, as he was about to depart from the world, his sister's son came to visit him and found him weeping. So he asked him: Master, why are you weeping? Is there Torah that you neither learned nor taught? Look, the disciples you taught are seated in front of you. Is there any act of kindness you failed to do? And beyond all your other qualities, you have removed yourself from adjudging lawsuits; nor have you allowed yourself to be charged with handling the community's needs. R. Ammi answered: My son, for this very reason I weep. I will very likely have to give an account and reckoning because I could have dealt with Israel's lawsuits [and chose not to].[10]

---

1. B. Ber 58a.
2. B. Ber 58a and En Yaakov, ad loc.
3. The plurals "myriads" and "thousands" are taken to denote at least two myriads and two thousand—hence, twenty-two thousand. B. Yev 63b–64a.
4. B. Sot 40a.
5. Avot 2:4.
6. B. Ber 49b.
7. Avot 2:2.
8. JV: "But he that exacteth gifts overthroweth it." The word *terumot* ("gifts") also means "heave offerings."
9. Literally, "Peace be upon thee, O my soul!"
10. Tanhuma, *Mishpatim*, §2.

9. When there is a disciple of the wise in a city, all the needs of the community are cast upon him.[1]

10. R. Huna said: If a man stumbles into a transgression for which he incurs the penalty of death at the hands of Heaven, what should he do to stay alive? If he has been in the habit of reading one page of Scripture, let him read two. If he has been in the habit of reciting one chapter of Mishnah, let him recite two. But if he has not been in the habit of reading Scripture or reciting Mishnah, what is he to do to stay alive? Let him go and become either an official of the community or a collector for charity, and he will stay alive. For had Scripture said, "Cursed be he that studieth not," he—may such a thing happen to Israel's foes—would not have been able to stay alive; but it says, "Cursed be he who does not enable the words of this Torah to stand" (Deut. 27:26). Had Scripture said, "[Torah] is a tree of life for those who toil in it," he—may such a thing happen to Israel's foes—would not have been able to stay alive; but it says, "[Torah] is a tree of life to those who uphold it" (Prov. 3:18). Thus, "the shelter of wisdom is assured by the shelter of gifts of money" (Eccles. 7:12).[2]

11. He who leads the many to virtue—no sin shall come about through him; but he who leads the many to sin shall not be given the means to repent.[3] Moses was virtuous and led the many to virtue; therefore, the merit of the many was ascribed to him, as is said, "Because he executed the Lord's design, the merit for Israel's obedience to His ordinances [was ascribed to Moses]" (Deut. 33:21). Jeroboam sinned and caused the many to sin;[4] therefore, the sin of the many was ascribed to him: "All the sins of Jeroboam which he sinned by causing Israel to sin" (1 Kings 15:30).[5]

12. Those in Israel who transgress by defiling their bodies and those among the Gentiles who transgress by defiling their bodies will go down to Gehenna and be punished there for twelve months. After twelve months, their bodies will be consumed and their souls burned, and the wind will scatter their ashes under the soles of the feet of the righteous. But as for the heretics, the informers, and the scoffers, who denied the Torah, denied the resurrection of the dead, abandoned the ways of the community, struck terror in the land of the living, and, like Jeroboam the son of Nebat and his companions, sinned and caused the many to sin—these will go down to Gehenna and be punished there for generations upon generations. Gehenna will be consumed, but they will not be consumed.[6]

1. B. MK 6a.
2. Lev. R. 25:1.
3. It would not be right for him to repent and go free while those he caused to sin undergo punishment.
4. See above, part 2, chap. 6, §127–30.
5. Avot 5:18.
6. Presumably, Gehenna will come to an end but their punishment will be unending. B. RH 17a.

The Leader of a Community

13. R. Isaac said: A leader is not to be appointed for a community without its being consulted, for Scripture says, "Consider, the Lord hath called by name Bezalel" (Exod. 35:30). When the Holy One asked Moses, "Moses, do you consider Bezalel suitable?" he replied, "Master of the universe, if he is deemed suitable by You, surely he is for Me." But God said, "Nevertheless, go and consult them." So Moses went and asked Israel, "Do you consider Bezalel suitable for you?" They replied, "Moses our teacher, if he is deemed suitable by the Holy One and by you, surely we must consider him so."[7]

14. Our masters taught: "And seventy of the elders of Israel" (Exod. 24:1). Why were the names of the elders not mentioned? So that a man should not query, "Is So-and-so the equal of Moses and Aaron? Is So-and-so the equal of Nadab and Abihu? Is So-and-so the equal of Eldad and Medad?" Scripture also says, "And Samuel said to the people, 'It is the Lord that appointed Moses and Aaron' " (1 Sam. 12:6), and [in the same passage], "And the Lord sent Jerubaal, and Bedan,[8] and Jephthan, and Samuel" (1 Sam. 12:11). Thus Scripture places three less-worthy chiefs on the same level as three of Israel's most estimable leaders, to teach you that in his generation Jerubaal is to be considered as Moses was in his generation; Bedan in his generation is to be considered as Aaron was in his generation; Jephthah in his generation is to be considered as Samuel was in his generation. To teach you also that the least worthy, once appointed leader of a community, is to be esteemed as the most eminent among the eminent. In regard to such deference, Scripture says, "Thou shalt come unto the priests the Levites, and unto the judge that shall be in those days" (Deut. 17:9). Can you imagine a man's going to a judge who is not in his days? But what Scripture means is that you are to be content to go to the judge who is in your days. Scripture says also, "Say not, 'How was it that the former days were better than these?' " (Eccles. 7:10).[9]

15. "And I will make them (*va-asimem*) heads over you" (Deut. 1:13). Since the word is spelled without the letter *yod*, it may be read *va-ashamam*, "their guilt be on your heads." According to R. Joshua ben Levi, Moses said to Israel, "If you will not obey those who are appointed leaders, the sin will be on your heads." The matter may be illustrated by a parable: The serpent's tail said to its head, "How much longer will you move first? I want to go first." The head: "Go!" So the tail went ahead, and when it got to a water hole, it flung the serpent's head into the water; when it encountered fire, it flung the serpent's head into the fire; and when it came to thorns, it flung the serpent's head into their midst. What caused such mishaps to the serpent? Allowing its head to follow its tail. So, too, when

7. B. Ber 55a.
8. Samson.
9. B. RH 25a–b.

the rank and file follow the guidance of their notables, the notables decree in the presence of Him who is everywhere, and He does what they decree; but when the notables allow themselves to follow the rank and file, they inevitably share in the mishaps that follow.

Another explanation: R. Hoshaia said: The matter may be illustrated by the parable of a bride who, while standing under the bridal canopy, discovers that her hands are soiled. If she wipes them on the wall, the wall will become dirty, yet her hands will not become clean; if on the pavement, the pavement will be blackened, yet her hands will still not be clean. If, however, she wipes them on her hair, her hair [will become more black, and thus] improve in appearance, and her hands will become clean. So, too, when Israel follow their notables but their notables do not attend to Israel's wants, the guilt is on the heads of their notables; but when Israel do not follow their notables, the guilt is on Israel's own heads.[1]

16. R. Akiva said: Israel may be likened to a bird: as the bird cannot fly without wings, so Israel can do nothing without their elders.

R. Yose ben Halafta said: Great is eldership. When elders are aged, they are beloved; when they are young, their youthfulness is regarded as an incidental matter, for we have been taught that R. Simeon ben Yohai said: Not in one instance, nor in two instances, but in many instances do we find the Holy One according honor to elders.[2]

17. R. Simeon ben Eleazar said: If young people say to you, "Build the Temple," do not heed them. But if elders say to you, "Destroy the Temple," heed them. For building done by young people may be equivalent to destruction, while the destruction done by old people is equivalent to building. And the proof for this assertion is Rehoboam, the son of Solomon.[3]

18. A prophet and an elder—by what parable may their authority be illustrated? By the one of a king who sends two of his emissaries to a province. Concerning one, he writes, "If he does not show you my seal and my signet, do not believe him"; and of the other, he writes, "Even if he does not show you my seal and my signet, believe him without seal or signet." So, too, of a prophet it is written, "He must give thee a sign or a wonder" (Deut. 13:2), while of elders it is written, "According to the Torah which they shall teach thee" (Deut. 17:11).[4]

19. One verse says to Joshua, "Thou must go with this people [as their equal]" (Deut. 31:7), while another verse says to him, "Thou [as leader] shalt bring the children of Israel" (Deut. 31:23). R. Yohanan explained the apparent inconsistency: In the first verse, Moses told Joshua, "You, on a par with the elders of the generation, are to go in with the people"; while in the second verse, the Holy One said to Joshua, "Take a stick and, if necessary, strike them on their pates. A generation can have but one leader, not two."

Likewise, concerning David, Scripture says, "Then David the king stood up upon his feet and said, 'Hear me, my brethren and my people' " (1 Chron. 28:2). If he called them "my brethren," why "my people"? And if "my people," why "my brethren"? R. Eleazar explained that David said to Israel: If you heed me, you are my brethren; but if not, you are my people, and I shall rule you with a rod.[5]

20. When a good leader is available, the Holy One Himself proclaims his identity, as is said, "The Lord spoke to Moses, saying: "See, I have called by name Bezalel' " (Exod. 31:2).[6]

21. "Through Thee comes kingship, O Lord, and through Thee he who has charge of anything is raised up" (1 Chron. 29:11).[7] Rav said: Even the man in charge of water pits is raised to his office by Heaven.[8]

22. R. Eleazar said: When the Holy One assigns high rank to a man, He assigns it to his children and his children's children unto the end of all generations. But if that man becomes arrogant, the Holy One brings him low.[9]

23. "Whom thou knowest to be the people's elders" (Num. 11:16)—you must know whether they have in fact been approved by the people. The words "the people's elders" suggest that a man should not be considered for office until people sing his praise, saying, "So-and-so is virtuous, pious, and fit to be declared a sage."[10]

24. "Thou shalt not take the Name of the Lord thy God in vain" (Exod. 20:7)—do not rush to accept authority when you are not fit for such authority. R. Jacob, citing R. Mani, supported this interpretation by citing the verse "Go not forth hastily to strive" (Prov. 25:8), where the word for "to strive," *le-riv*, is written defectively, so that it can also be read *le-rav*, "for authority."

According to R. Abbahu, God said: I am called holy, and [when you take on authority], you, too, will be called holy. Unless you have all attributes of Mine [which I revealed to Moses (Exod. 34:6–7)], you may not take on such authority.[11]

25. In expounding the verse "Then it shall be, if it is done in error by the eyes of [the leaders of] the congregation" (Num. 15:24), Oshaia, the youngest of the asso-

---

1. Deut R. 1:10; Yalkut, Deut., §802.
2. Lev. R. 11:8; Sif Num., §92.
3. See 1 Kings 12:1–17. Tos AZ 1:19; B. Ned 40a.
4. P. Ber 1:7, 3b.
5. B. Sanh 8a; B. Sot 40a and En Yaakov, ad loc.
6. B. Ber 55a.
7. JV: "Thine, O Lord, is the kingship, and Thou art exalted as head over all."
8. B. BB 91b.
9. B. Meg 13b.
10. Sif Num., §92.
11. PR 22:4 (YJS, 1: 457–58).

ciate scholars [*haverim*], told the parable of a bride who lives in her father's house. So long as her eyes are beautiful, her body needs no examination; however, should her eyes be bleary, her entire body needs examination.[1]

26. "This is the generation and those who seek its welfare" (Ps. 24:6).[2] R. Judah [II] the Patriarch and the sages differed about this matter. According to one opinion, the character of a generation is determined by its leader. According to the other opinion, the character of its leader is determined by the generation.[3]

27. In the synagogue in Maon,[4] while interpreting in Aramaic the verse, "Hear this, O ye priests" (Hos. 5:1), Yose of Maon said: The Holy One will fetch the priests, have them stand for judgment, and ask them, "Why did you not labor in study of Torah? Did you not enjoy twenty-four gifts[5] as your prerogative?" The priests will reply, "But Israel give us nothing now."[6]

Then Yose went on, " 'Attend, ye House of Israel' [Hos. 5:1]—why, O Israel, did you not give to the priests the twenty-four gifts I commanded you at Sinai to give?" Israel will reply, "But the servants of the patriarch's household take everything."

Then Yose went on, " 'Give ear, O royal house of the patriarch,[7] for unto you will come judgment' [Hos. 5:1]. Is it not to you that I said, 'This then shall be what is adjudged to belong to the priests' [Deut. 18:3]? Therefore at you and against you will judgment be turned when I sit in judgment over the royal patriarch's house to bring their rule to an end and have them perish from the world."

When R. Judah the Patriarch heard what Yose had said, [he was enraged], and Yose, frightened, fled. In the evening, Resh Lakish went in to pay his respects to R. Judah and to pacify him concerning Yose of Maon, saying, "Master, we should be grateful to the nations of the world, who bring mimes into their theaters and circuses to entertain them, and thus induce them to converse amicably among themselves without lapsing into foolish quarrels. [It was in order to wean people from vain pursuits that] Yose of Maon expounded words of Torah, yet you are enraged at him." R. Judah: "But does he know anything at all of Torah?" Resh Lakish: "Yes, he is an eminent scholar." R. Judah: "Will he be able to answer any question I may put to him?" Resh Lakish: "Yes." R. Judah: "If so, let him come to see me." When Yose came in, R. Judah asked him, "What is meant by 'Behold, everyone that useth proverbs shall use this proverb against thee, saying: Like mother, like daughter' (Ezek. 16:44)?" Yose: "Like mother, like daughter—like the generation is its patriarch; like the altar are its priests. As people say in the proverb, 'Like the garden is the gardener.' "

At that, Resh Lakish said to Yose, "Even before I finish pacifying R. Judah for one insult, you hurl another insult at him for us to cope with."[8]

28. Resh Lakish went up to pay his respects to our Rabbi [Judah I, the Patriarch]. "Pray for me," R. Judah begged him, "for this Roman government is exceedingly evil."[9] "Take nothing from anyone," Resh Lakish told him, "and then you will not have to give anything [to anyone]." While Resh Lakish was sitting with R. Judah, a woman came in, bringing R. Judah a dish with a knife in it. He took the knife and returned the dish to the woman. At that moment an imperial courier came in and saw the knife, took a fancy to it, and carried it off. Toward evening, Resh Lakish went again to pay his respects to our Rabbi and saw him laughing. "Why are you laughing?" asked Resh Lakish. R. Judah: "That knife you saw—an imperial courier came in, saw it, coveted it, and took it away." Resh Lakish: "Did I not tell you that if you take nothing from anyone, you will not have to give anything to anyone?"[10]

29. R. Hanina said: Why is it written, "The Lord will indict the elders of His people and the princes thereof" (Isa. 3:14)? Granted, the princes sinned, but in what way did the elders sin? You must therefore conclude: God will indict the elders because they did not protest against the princes' doings.[11]

30. R. Mana used to ridicule those who were appointed to office through money. R. Ammi applied to them the verse "Gods of silver, or gods of gold, ye shall not make unto you" (Exod. 20:20).

Rav said: One need not stand in the presence of a judge appointed through money, nor need one call him "Master." As for the judicial stole placed upon him, it is worth no more than the packsaddle of a donkey.

While R. Ze'era and one of the sages were sitting together, one of those who were appointed to office through money passed by. The sage said to R. Ze'era: Let us make believe that we are reciting Mishnah, so that we will not have to stand up for him.

Jacob of Kefar Gibborayya interpreted the verse "Woe unto him that saith to the wood: 'Awake,' to the dumb stone: 'Arise!' Can this teach?" (Hab. 2:19)—can such a one teach? "Behold, he is overlaid with gold and silver" (ibid.)—was he not appointed through money? "Within him there is no spirit at all" (ibid.)—he never learned anything at all. If you wish to appoint [one that is fit], "the Lord is in His holy Temple" (Heb. 2:20)—look, R. Isaac son of R. Eleazar is in the synagogue at the gate of Caesarea.[12]

---

1. By the groom's family. Bleary eyes suggest an unhealthy body. B. Ta 24a.
2. JV: "Such is the generation of them that seek after Him." But the object of the verb "seek" may refer to God or to the generation.
3. B. Ar 17a.
4. A town near Tiberias, which was the seat of the patriarch.
5. Most of them are listed in Num. 18. Receipt of them, it was anticipated, would have given priests time to study Torah.
6. Now that the Temple is no longer in existence, and the priests are not serving there.
7. JV: "Give ear, O house of the king."
8. P. Sanh 2:6, 20d; Gen. R. 80:1.
9. Its demands are exorbitant.
10. Gen. R. 78:12.
11. B. Shab 54b–55a.
12. P. Bik 3:3, 65d.

31. The body follows the head.[1]

32. Once the head is removed, what good is the body? Once the body is taken away, what good is the head?[2]

33. When a shepherd is angry at his flock, he appoints for it a bellwether that is blind.[3]

34. When the shepherd is lost, so are the sheep.[4]

35. Alas for a principality whose physician is lame and whose guide has but one eye.[5]

36. "And they spoke unto him, saying: 'If thou wilt be a servant unto this people.' " etc. (1 Kings 12:7). The verse teaches you that he who is appointed over a community becomes the servant of the community.

Rabban Gamaliel made up his mind to place R. Eleazar Hisma and R. Yohanan ben Gudgada in posts of authority. He sent for them, but they did not come. He sent for them again, and they came. He then said to them: You apparently suppose that I am about to bestow rulership upon you. What I am bestowing upon you is servitude, as is said, "And they spoke unto him, saying: 'If thou wilt be this day a servant unto this people.' "[6]

37. A story is told of R. Yohanan ben Nuri and R. Eleazar ben Hisma, whom Rabban Gamaliel placed in authority at the academy. However, the disciples took no cognizance of them, and in the evening the two quietly sat down among the disciples. When Rabban Gamaliel came in and found the two seated among the disciples, he said: R. Yohanan ben Nuri and R. Eleazar ben Hisma, you dealt ill[7] with the academy's community in not exercising authority over it. In the past, you were subject to your own governance. But henceforth [like it or not] you are in servitude to the community.[8]

38. Rabbi [Judah I, the Patriarch] came out of the bathhouse, wrapped himself in his garments, and sat down to attend to the needs of the people. Rabbi's servant mixed a cup of water and wine for him, but since Rabbi was so busy attending to people's needs, he could not spare a moment to take it from his servant, who [kept holding it] until he dozed off and fell asleep. When Rabbi finally turned and looked at him, he said, Solomon put it well: "Sweet is the sleep of the laboring man, whether he eat little or much; but the satiety of the rich will not suffer him to sleep" (Eccles. 5:11). Those [rich in Torah] like ourselves are so busy attending to the needs of the people that we are not even allowed to sleep.[9]

39. "And Moses went down from the mount unto the people" (Exod. 19:14). This shows that Moses did not turn to his own affairs, did not even go down to his house, but went directly "from the mount unto the people."[10]

40. Before God confers high office on a man, He first tests him in a little thing, and only then promotes him to high office. Here you have two of the world's great, whom God first tested in a little thing, found trustworthy, and then promoted to high office. He tested David by sheep, which he led far into the wilderness in order to keep them from despoiling [the fields of others]. Eliab referred to this practice when he said to David, "And with whom hast thou left those few sheep [far] in the wilderness?" (1 Sam. 17:28). Then God said to David, "You have been found trustworthy in tending sheep; come now and tend My sheep," as is said, "From following the ewes that give suck, He brought him to be shepherd over Jacob His People" (Ps. 78:71). So, too, Scripture says of Moses, "And he led the flock to the farthest end of the wilderness" (Exod. 3:1), in order to keep them from despoiling [the fields of others]. Therefore God took him to tend Israel, as is said, "Thou didst lead Thy people like a flock, by the hand of Moses and of Aaron" (Ps. 77:21).[11]

41. "The Lord testeth the righteous" (Ps. 11:5). How does He test him? By having him pasture sheep. He tested David by means of a flock and found him a good shepherd, as is said, "God took him because of [his] separations[12] of the sheep" (Ps. 78:70). What is meant by the phrase "his separations"? It means that David kept some sheep separate from others. He would lead out the lambs and let them feed on the upper part of the herbage. He would then lead out the old ewes and let them feed on the middle part of the herbage; and finally he would lead out the rams and let them feed on the stubble of the herbage. Accordingly, the Holy One said: Seeing that David knows how to feed the sheep, each according to its capacity, let him come and feed My sheep, the people of Israel, as is said, "From following the ewes that give suck, He brought him to be shepherd over Jacob His people" (Ps. 78:71).

Moses was also tested by the Holy One by means of the flock, as our masters explained: When Moses our teacher was tending Jethro's flock in the wilderness, a lamb scampered off, and Moses ran after it, until it approached a shelter under a rock. As the lamb reached the shelter, it came upon a pool of water and stopped to drink. When Moses caught up with it, he said, "I did not know that you ran away because you were thirsty. Now you must be tired." So he hoisted the lamb on his shoulders and

1. B. Er 41a.
2. PRK 16:5 (PRKS, p. 293); Gen. R. 100:9.
3. B. BK 52a.
4. PRE 42; B. BK 52a.
5. So Musaf he-Arukh. BR take *aktuta*, ("guide") to mean "eye doctor." Lev. R. 5:6.
6. B. Hor 10a–b; Yalkut, 1 Kings, §197.
7. Reading *hare'otem* ("you dealt ill"), as in Sif Deut., ed. Finkelstein, p. 26, instead of BR's *hoda'tem* ("announced, told").
8. Sif Deut., §16.
9. Eccles. R. 5:11, §1.
10. Mek, *Yitro, Ba-hodesh*, 6 (La 2:215).
11. Exod. R. 2:3.
12. Usually translated "from the sheepfolds."

started walking back with it. The Holy One then said: Because you showed such compassion in tending the flock of a mortal, as you live, you shall become shepherd of Israel, the flock that is Mine.[1]

42. If there were no flock, what need for a shepherd?[2]

43. "Take [the elders of Israel] unto the Tent of Meeting" (Num. 11:16). God said to Moses: Take them by persuasive words. First speak to them words of praise: "Happy are you that you were appointed." Then speak to them words to Israel's discredit: "You are to know that they are litigious and contrary. So you are taking this responsibility upon yourselves with the understanding that they may curse you, may throw stones at you." [To drive the point home, God finished by saying]: What I set forth clearly to you [Moses], you are to set forth clearly to the elders.[3]

44. When R. Yose came to Kufrah, he wanted to appoint leaders over the people, but they refused to accept office. So, quoting to them "Ben Bebai was in charge of the wicks [for the Temple lampstand],"[4] he said: If he who was appointed to have charge of wicks merited being mentioned with the notables of his generation, how much greater by far will be your merit, for you are to have charge of the vital needs of human beings.

When R. Haggai appointed community leaders, he would have them carry a Torah scroll, by way of saying that every sort of authority bestowed is bestowed with Torah's authorization, as Torah said, "By me kings reign, by me rulers rule" (Prov. 8:15–16).

When people wanted to appoint R. Akiva a community leader, he said, "Let me consult my family." The people followed him and [in response to the family's advice that he accept] heard him say, "Even if it means being abused, even if it means being regarded as reprehensible."[5]

45. "Take thee Joshua, the son of Nun, a man in whom is spirit" (Num. 27:18), a man who will have the capacity to stand up to the spirit of each and every one.[6]

46. "And Moses called unto Joshua, and said unto him in the sight of all Israel: 'Be strong and of good courage' " (Deut. 31:7). The people I am turning over to you are still kids of the goats, being very young. Do not be provoked by what they do, even as their Lord was not provoked by what they did, as He said, "Because Israel was young, I loved him" (Hos. 11:1).[7]

47. "My son, if thou art become surety for thy neighbor" (Prov. 6:1). R. Nehemiah said: This verse is addressed to scholars. As long as one is but a scholar [engaged in his studies], he is not responsible for the community and will not be punished [for its lapses], but as soon as he is appointed a leader and dons the stole [of authority], he may no longer say, "I will engage only in what is of benefit to me. I am not responsible for the community." On the contrary, the community's entire burden is henceforth on his shoulders. If he sees a man resorting to violence against another or engaging in a forbidden sexual act and does not endeavor to prevent him, he will be punished because of what that man did, while the holy spirit laments, "My son, if thou art become surety for thy neighbor," you are responsible for him. [Once you assume office], you put yourself in the arena, and he who puts himself in the arena is either conquered or conquers.[8]

48. R. Eleazar said: Any leader who guides a community gently will merit guiding it in the world-to-come.[9]

49. When a leader lords it over a community, the Holy One weeps every day because of him.[10]

50. "Who struck terror in the land of the living" (Ezek. 32:24) refers, said R. Hisda, to a leader who strikes terror in a community not for the sake of Heaven.

R. Judah said in the name of Rav: A leader who strikes terror in a community not for the sake of Heaven will never have a disciple of the wise for a son.[11]

51. "And Samson called unto the Lord, and said: 'O Lord God, remember me, I pray Thee, and strengthen me, I pray Thee, only this once' " (Judg. 16:28). Samson pleaded with the Holy One: Master of the universe, remember on my behalf the twenty-two years I judged Israel and never presumed to say to anyone, "Carry my staff from here to there."[12]

52. R. Yohanan said in the name of R. Simeon ben Jehozadak: One should not appoint a leader over a community unless he has a basket of reptiles hanging behind him,[13] so that if he becomes arrogant, people may say to him, "Look behind you."[14]

53. "The heads of your tribes, your elders, and your officers" (Deut. 29:9). Even though I appointed over you heads, elders, and officers, all of you are equal before Me, for the verse concludes, "All are men of Israel" (ibid.).[15]

54. "I went down into the garden of nuts" (Song 6:11). Resh Lakish said: The nut tree is smooth. Anyone who would climb to its top without considering how to do it is sure to fall to his death, thus taking his punishment from the tree. So, too, he who would exercise authority over a

1. Exod. R. 2:2; MTeh 78:21; Yalkut, Ps., §883.
2. Yalkut, *Bo*, §187.
3. Sif Num., §92.
4. Shek 5:1.
5. P. Pe 8:6, 21a.
6. Sif Zuta, *Pinhas*, §16.
7. Sif Deut., §305; Yalkut, *Va-yelekh*, §941.
8. Exod. R. 27:9.
9. B. Sanh 92a.
10. B. Hag 5b.
11. B. RH 17a.
12. B. Sot 10a.
13. Something shameful in his past.
14. B. Yoma 22b.
15. Tanhuma, *Nitzavim*, §2.

community in Israel without considering how to do it is sure to fall and take his punishment from the hands of the community.[1]

55. "When [a son of] Ephraim spoke, making [Solomon] tremble" (Hos. 13:1). When Jeroboam son of Nebat came and spoke reprimands to Solomon, the Holy One said to Jeroboam: Why do you reprimand him? "He is a prince of Israel" (Hos. 13:1). As you live, I will have you taste his authority, and you will be unable to cope with it. We are told that as soon as Jeroboam attained kingship, he "became guilty through Baal and died" (ibid.).[2]

56. R. Judah said: Three things shorten a man's days and years: being given a Torah scroll to read and refusing to read it; being given a cup of blessing to say grace and refusing to say it; and taking on airs of authority.

R. Hama bar Hanina said: Why did Joseph die before his brothers?[3] Because he took on an air of authority.[4]

57. Power buries those who possess it. A man enters the world naked and leaves it naked. Would that on leaving it he were [as free of sin] as on entering it.[5]

58. R. Yohanan said: Woe to authority, for it buries its possessor. There was not a prophet that did not outlive four kings who were his contemporaries.[6]

59. R. Eleazar ben Azariah said, "I am some seventy years old." Though he had attained authority, he nevertheless lived long. Thus you learn that authority generally shortens life.[7]

60. Woe unto authority, for it buries those who possess it. Woe unto [the kind of] authority that does not do good to the world.[8]

61. "Gather unto Me seventy men of the elders of Israel" (Num. 11:16). R. Abba bar Kahana said: After the elders were appointed, all Israel kindled lamps in their honor as they rejoiced over them. When Miriam saw the lamps lit, she asked Zipporah, "What is the meaning of these lamps alight?" After Zipporah explained the matter to Miriam, Miriam said, "[How] happy these men's wives must be at what they see—how their husbands have risen to authority." Zipporah replied, "Alas for these wives."[9]

62. "Joshua . . . said: 'My lord Moses, make them cease' " (Num. 11:28). How? Joshua meant: Throw on them the cares of the community, and they will as a matter of course cease prophesying.[10]

63. He who pursues office, office flees from him; he who flees from it, it pursues him.[11]

64. Shemaiah said: Shun authority.

Just what does this mean? That a man should not on his own place a crown upon his head. But others may do so.[12]

65. We have been taught that R. Joshua ben Perahiah said: Formerly, had a man said to me, "Accept this office," I would have been ready to bind him and place him before a lion. Now, however, were a man to say to me, "Give up this office," I would feel like pouring a kettle of boiling water over him. Note that at first Saul fled from high office, but after he reached it, he sought to slay David.[13]

66. R. Joshua ben Kevusai said: All my days, I fled from office. But now that I have achieved it, were anyone to attempt to oust me, I would go at him with this kettle. Even as a kettle scalds, maims, or blackens, so would I go at him.[14]

67. It is easy to go up to a dais, tough to come down.[15]

68. Our Rabbi [Judah I, the Patriarch] was very modest and used to say, "I am prepared to do anything a person tells me, except what the elders of Betera did for my ancestor [Hillel]—they actually relinquished their high office and promoted him to it. Still, if R. Huna the Exilarch were to come up to the Land, I would rise up out of respect for him [relinquish my office, and] seat him above me, for he is descended from Judah on the male side, while I am descended from Judah only on the female side." But when R. Hiyya the Elder said to him, "Look, R. Huna is outside!" Rabbi's face went pale. When R. Hiyya saw that Rabbi's face had gone pale, he said, "It is R. Huna's coffin that has come."[16]

69. "When a ruler sinneth . . . through error . . . he shall bring his offering" (Lev. 4:22). R. Yohanan ben Zakkai said: Happy is the generation whose ruler brings an offering in expiation of his error. If the ruler must bring an offering, is there any need to add that a commoner must also bring an offering? And if the ruler must bring an offering for an error, is there any need to add that he must do so if he committed a sin wittingly?[17]

---

1. Song R. 6:11, §1.
2. Lev. R. 12:5.
3. As intimated in "And Joseph died, and then all his brothers" (Exod. 1:6).
4. B. Ber 55a.
5. B. Yoma 86b.
6. Thus, for example, Isaiah and Hosea outlived Uzziah, Jotham, Ahaz, and Hezekiah. B. Pes 87b.
7. R. Eleazar, being an exception to the general rule, confirms it. P. Ber 1:9, 3d.
8. TdE 11 (ed. Friedmann, p. 55).
9. Yalkut, *Be-haalotekha*, §738, citing Yelammedenu.
10. B. Sanh 17a.
11. Tanhuma B, *Va-yikra*, §4; Tanhuma, *Va-yikra*, §3.
12. Avot 1:9; ARN 11.
13. B. Men 109b.
14. P. Pes 6:1, 35a.
15. Yalkut, *Va-et'hannan*, §845, citing Midrash Esfah.
16. P. Kil 9:3, 32b; Gen. R. 33:3.
17. B. Hor 10b.

70. Happy is the generation in which the greater defer to the lesser and, it goes without saying, the lesser to the greater.[1]

71. "When our rulers are willing to bear burdens, there will be no breach, no sortie, and no outcry in our broad places" (Ps. 144:14). R. Yohanan said: The psalm does not say, "Rulers are burdened," but says, "*Our* rulers are burdened," meaning that when the great are willing to shoulder the burdens of the lesser, "there will be no breach, no sortie, and no outcry in our broad places." R. Simeon ben Lakish finds in the verse the opposite meaning: The psalm does not say, "Our rulers bear burdens," but says, "Our rulers are borne as burdens," meaning that when the lesser bear the greater as burdens, "there will be no breach, no sortie, and no outcry in our broad places."[2]

72. R. Yohanan said: In saying, "And it came to pass when the generation judged its judges" (Ruth 1:1),[3] Scripture means that the generation had to judge its judges. When a judge would say, "Remove the toothpick from between your teeth," the accused would reply, "Remove the beam from between your eyes." When a judge would say, "Thy silver is become dross" (Isa. 1:22), the accused would reply, "Thy wine is mixed with water" (ibid.).[4]

73. "And it came to pass in the days when the judges were judged" (Ruth 1:1). Woe unto the generation that judges its judges, and woe unto the generation whose judges are in need of being judged.[5]

74. Samuel said: As soon as a man is appointed leader of a community, he becomes rich. First it is written of Saul, "He counted them by means of pebbles" (1 Sam. 11:8), but subsequently it is said, "He counted them by means of sheep" (1 Sam. 15:4).[6]

75. If a prophet wishes to benefit from the hospitality of others, let him do it in the manner of Elisha [who accepted the hospitality of the Shunammite woman]. But if he does not wish to benefit, he may refuse to do so, as did Samuel the Ramathite, of whom it is said, "His return was to Ramah, even though wherever [he judged Israel] . . . was his home" (1 Sam. 7:17), which R. Yohanan took to mean that he provided himself a home of his own at all the places he went in circuit.[7]

1. B. RH 25b.
2. "The general idea is that rule is a two-way street: the ruled must obey the ruler, but the ruler must also defer to the rights and needs of the ruled" (Leon Nemoy). P. RH 2:8, 58b; Yalkut, Ps., §888.
3. JV: "And it came to pass in the days when the judges judged." But R. Yohanan's reading of the verse is also admissible.
4. B. BB 15b and En Yaakov, ad loc.
5. Ruth R. 1:1.
6. B. Yoma 22b.
7. R. Yohanan regards the words "for there was his home" as superfluous. Hence he construes 1 Sam. 7:17 as saying: "Wherever he judged Israel—at Bethel, Gilgal, Mizpah—there was his home." B. Ber 10b.

76. As Rabbi [Judah I, the Patriarch] lay dying, he said: I require the presence of my eldest son. When R. Gamaliel entered, he entrusted to him the regulations of the patriarchate. "My son," he said, "surround your patriarchate with the best people and discipline the students with severity."[8]

77. R. Huna bar Idi said in the name of Samuel: [In order to maintain the dignity of his position], a man appointed to high office in a community may not do any manual work in the presence of three persons.[9]

78. R. Hanina once visited R. Yudan the Patriarch, who came out to him wearing his linen undershirt. R. Hanina said, "Go back and put on your toga, for it is said, 'Thine eyes shall see the king in his beauty' " (Isa. 33:17).

R. Yohanan once visited R. Yudan the Patriarch, who came out to him wearing a plain flaxen garment. R. Yohanan said, "Go back and put on your woolen garment, in keeping with what we are told: 'Thine eyes shall see the king in his beauty.' "

As R. Yohanan left, he saw [R. Yudan's coadjutor] R. Hanina bar Sisi splitting wood. So he said, "This does not befit your dignity." R. Hanina: "But what am I to do? I have no one to help me." R. Yohanan: "If you could not afford to engage help, you should not have accepted high office."[10]

79. "And the people spoke against God, and against Moses" (Num. 21:5). If they dared speak against God, is it not implied *a fortiori* that they also spoke against Moses? Yes, but adding "against Moses" is meant to teach that speaking against [Israel's] faithful shepherd is like speaking against Him who commanded and the world came into being.[11]

80. An elder to whom something unseemly has happened should not be reduced in rank, but should be told, "Stay home and enjoy thy glory" (2 Kings 14:10).[12]

The King

81. We have been taught that R. Yose said: Three commandments were given to Israel when they entered the Land: to appoint for themselves a king; to cut off the seed of Amalek; and to build themselves the house chosen [by God]. I would not have known which of them had priority but for Scripture's saying, "The hand upon the throne of the Lord, the Lord will have war with Amalek" (Exod. 17:16), from which you are bound to infer that first they were to appoint a king, for the term "throne" implies the existence of a king, as in the verse "Then Solomon sat on the throne of the Lord as king" (1 Chron. 29:23). Yet I still would not have known which was to come next: the

8. B. Ket 103b.
9. B. Kid 70a.
10. P. Sanh 2:6, 20c–d.
11. Mek, *Be-shallah, Va-yehi*, 7 (La 1:252).
12. P. MK 3:1, 81d.

building of the house chosen by God or cutting off the seed of Amalek. However, from Scripture's saying, "When He giveth you rest from all your enemies . . . then it shall come to pass that the place which the Lord your God shall choose," etc. (Deut. 12:10), you are bound to infer that the cutting off of the seed of Amalek was to come before the building of the Temple. Indeed, the verse "And it came to pass when [David] the king dwelt in his house, and the Lord had given him rest from his enemies round about" (2 Sam. 7:1) is followed at once by "The king said unto Nathan the Prophet: "Here I am dwelling in a house of cedars while the Ark of God abides in a tent" (2 Sam. 7:2).[1]

82. We have been taught that R. Eliezer said: The elders of the generation made a proper request when they said, "Give us a king to judge us" (1 Sam. 8:6). But the ignorant [the *amme ha-aretz*] in Israel spoiled it by adding, "That we also may be like all the nations; and that our king may judge us, and go out before us, and fight our battles" (1 Sam. 8:20).[2]

83. R. Yose said: A king is allowed to do all that is set forth in chapter 8 [of the book of Samuel] concerning the actions of a king. But R. Judah said: The king's possible actions were set forth in that chapter only to inspire the people with fear, in keeping with "Thou shalt [be free to] set a king upon thee" (Deut. 17:15), that the fear of him shall be upon you. R. Nehorai said: The actions of a king were set forth in that chapter only in anticipation of the people's future complaints, for in declaring, "And shalt say [on thine own]: I will set a king upon me," etc. (Deut. 17:14), [Scripture implies that kingship is a choice, not an obligation].[3]

84. "Thou shalt in any wise set him king upon thee" (Deut. 17:15), that the awe of him shall be upon you. Hence, the sages said: One is not to mount the steed of a king of Israel, nor sit on his throne, nor make use of his crown or his scepter or any of his utensils. When he dies, all these are burned in front of his corpse. Nor is one to gaze upon him when he is naked, when his hair is being sheared, or when he is in the bathhouse, in deference to "Thine eyes shall see the king in his beauty" (Isa. 33:17).[4]

85. R. Yannai said: The awe of kingship should always be upon you. Thus Moses said, "And all these thy servants shall come down unto me, and bow down unto me" (Exod. 11:8). Even though he knew that Pharaoh also would come down, he did not, in deference to the king's person, say that Pharaoh would bow down to him. R. Yohanan drew the same inference from "The hand of the Lord was on Elijah, and he girded up his loins, and ran before Ahab" (1 Kings 18:46).[5]

1. Proving that the building of the Temple came last. B. Sanh 20b.
2. Ibid.
3. Ibid.
4. Sif Deut., §157; P. Sanh 2:6, 20c.
5. Even though Elijah disapproved strongly of Ahab, he showed him respect. B. Zev 102a; Exod. R. 7:3.

86. It is not proper for a king to do anything himself. He should issue an order and have others do it for him.[6]

87. The king's highway has no limits, for he may breach a wall to make a way for himself and no one may prevent his doing so.[7]

88. Our masters taught: A funeral procession must make way for a bridal procession, and both must make way for a king of Israel.

It was said of King Agrippa that he made way for a bride, and the sages commended him.

You say, "Commended him," implying that he acted properly. But did not R. Ashi say: Even he who maintains that if a patriarch forgoes the honor due him, it is forgone, [admits] that if a king forgoes the honor due him, it is not forgone, because, as a master taught, "Thou shalt in any wise set him king upon thee," implies that the awe of him shall be upon you [always].

It [the incident with the bride] took place at a crossroads.[8]

89. When a king and a bride meet, the bride must make way in deference to the king. Nevertheless, King Agrippa made way for a bride, and the sages commended him. When they asked him, "What made you do so?" he replied, "I wear a crown every day; let her wear her crown for a brief hour."[9]

90. R. Yudan said: He who is insolent toward a king is as though he were insolent toward the Presence.[10]

91. R. Simeon ben Lakish said: The words "Behold, it was . . . good" (Gen. 1:31) apply to the kingdom of Heaven. The full statement "Behold, it was very good" applies to the Roman Empire. But how can the Roman Empire be described as "very good"? What a baffling statement! Well, the empire merits such designation because it exacts justice for human beings.[11]

92. "And Thou makest man as the fishes of the sea" (Hab. 1:14). As among the fishes of the sea, the greater swallow the smaller, so it is with humankind: were it not for fear of government, the stronger would swallow the weaker. This is indeed what we have been taught: R. Hanina, deputy high priest, used to say: Pray for the well-being of the [Roman] government—but for the fear of it, men would swallow one another alive.[12]

93. The sages said in the name of Rav: If all the seas were ink, all reeds were pens, all skies parchment, and

6. Exod. R. 40:20.
7. B. BB 100b.
8. Hence, seeing Agrippa giving way to the bride, people would have supposed he was heading in another direction and not yielding way to her. B. Ket 17a.
9. Sem 11.
10. Gen. R. 94:9.
11. Gen. R. 9:13.
12. B. AZ 4a.

all men scribes, they would be unable to set down the full scope of the [Roman] government's concerns. And the proof? The verse, said R. Mesharsheya, "Like the heaven for height, and the earth for depth, so is the heart of kings unfathomable" (Prov. 25:3).[1]

94. "Pharaoh dreamed" (Gen. 41:1). I wonder, do not all human beings dream? Yes, but in saying that the dream was Pharaoh's [a king's], Scripture asserts that the dream was inspired by the King of the entire universe.[2]

95. "They shall suck the abundance of the seas" (Deut. 33:19). Two take in abundance and give in abundance: the sea and the government. As the sea takes in abundance and gives in abundance, so the government takes in abundance and gives in abundance.[3]

96. Our masters taught: On seeing kings of Israel, one is to say, "Blessed be He who gave a portion of His glory to those who fear Him"; on seeing kings of the nations of the world, one is to say, "Blessed be He who has given of His glory to His creatures."

R. Yohanan said: A man should always endeavor to go out to greet kings of Israel, and this applies not only to kings of Israel but to kings of the nations of the world as well, so that if he merits [seeing the Messiah], he will see how much more distinguished kings of Israel will be than kings of the nations of the world.[4]

97. R. Sheshet was blind. Still, on one occasion when all the people went out to welcome the king, R. Sheshet arose and went with them. A certain heretic came across him and said to him, "Whole pitchers go to the river, but cracked ones—whither?" R. Sheshet replied, "Come along, and you will see that I know more than you."

As the first detachment was passing by and a shout arose, the heretic said, "Here comes the king." But R. Sheshet retorted, "Not yet." As the second detachment was passing by and again a shout arose, the heretic said again, "Here comes the king." But R. Sheshet once more retorted, "The king has not yet come." Then the third detachment passed by in perfect silence, R. Sheshet said to the heretic, "Now, for certain, the king is coming." The heretic asked, "How do you know this?" R. Sheshet replied, "Royalty on earth is like royalty in heaven, concerning which it is written, 'Behold, the Lord passed by, and a great and a strong wind rent the mountains and broke in pieces the rocks before the Lord, but the Lord was not in the wind; and after the wind an earthquake, but the Lord was not in the earthquake; and after the earthquake a fire, but the Lord was not in the fire; and after the fire a still small voice' " (1 Kings 19:11–12).

When the king came by, R. Sheshet pronounced the appropriate blessing over him. At that, the heretic asked, "How can you pronounce a blessing over one you cannot see?" R. Sheshet fixed his eyes upon him, and the heretic collapsed into a heap of bones.[5]

98. At one time, Diocletian[6] was a swineherd near Tiberias. Whenever he approached the house of study of R. Yudan the Patriarch, the children used to go out and rough him up. By and by, when he became emperor, he took up residence near Panias[7] and sent a letter to Tiberias: I command the notables of the Jews to come and appear before me immediately after the outgoing of the Sabbath. He also commanded his emissary: Be sure to give the letter to the Jews only on Sabbath eve as it begins getting dark.

When R. Samuel bar Nahman went down to bathe, he saw R. Yudan the Patriarch standing in front of the great house of study, his face quite pale. R. Samuel bar Nahman asked him, "Why is your face so pale?" R. Yudan replied, "Such-and-such an order was sent to me by the [Roman] government." R. Samuel bar Nahman: "Come [with me] and bathe, for your Creator will perform miracles for us." When the two entered the bathhouse, a bath sprite came jesting and dancing toward them. R. Yudan the Patriarch wished to scold him, but R. Samuel bar Nahman said, "Master, leave him alone, for sometimes he shows himself just before miracles." Then, to the sprite: "Your master is in distress, yet you stand here jesting and dancing?" The sprite: "Eat and drink and keep the Sabbath with good cheer, for your God will perform miracles for you, and I will set you down before the emperor immediately after the conclusion of the Sabbath."

At the outgoing of the Sabbath, immediately after the service, the sprite took both of them and set them down in front of the gate of Panias. When the emperor was informed, "Lo, they are standing before the gate," he ordered, "Shut the gate." But the sprite took them and set them down upon the walls of the town. When the emperor was informed of it, he exclaimed, "I command that the bathhouse be heated for three days, then have them enter and bathe, and, after that, appear before me." The bathhouse was heated for three days, but the sprite entered it [first] and tempered the heat for them, so that when they entered it, they could bathe. Then they appeared before the emperor, who said to them, "Because [you know that] your God performs miracles for you, you contemn the emperor?" They replied, "Diocletian the Swineherd we do contemn, but to Diocletian the Emperor we willingly submit." "Even so," the emperor replied, "you should not contemn the humblest Roman citizen or the lowest-ranking [Roman] soldier."[8]

99. Our masters taught: Three must not be provoked: an insignificant Gentile, a young snake, and a humble disciple. Why not? Because, though they are still wet behind the ears, their rise to power is likely [if not certain].[9]

---

1. B. Shab 11a.
2. Gen. R. 89:4.
3. Sif Deut., §354; Yalkut, *Berakhah*, §961.
4. B. Ber 58a.
5. B. Ber 58a.
6. Emperor of Rome from 285 to 305 C.E.; his father had been a slave.
7. Caesarea Philippi, a city in the north of Palestine.
8. P. Ter 8:8, 46b–c; Gen. R. 63:8.
9. When they mature, they might take revenge; B. Pes 113a.

100. R. Joseph taught that the verse "Behold, I made thee [Edom] small among the nations" (Obad. 1:2) applies [to Rome], where no dynastic continuity exists, because they do not put the king's son on the throne.[1]

101. "And these are the kings that reigned in the land of Edom" (Gen. 36:31). R. Isaac began his discourse with the verse [in which Tyre is told], "From the oak trees of Bashan they made thine oars" (Ezek. 27:6). The nations of the world are likened to a ship: as a ship is provided with a mast from one place and an anchor from another place, so are the nations of the world provided with [their oarsmen, their kings]: "Samlah from Masrekah . . . Shaul from Rehoboth by the River" (Gen. 36:36–37).[2]

102. "Out of them shall come forth the cornerstone, out of them the stake, out of them the battle bow" (Zech. 10:4). Pause and consider! The nations of the world, when about to set up a king for themselves, used to bring him from all sorts of places and set him over themselves: "And in Edom there reigned . . . one of Dinhabah . . . later one of Bozrah" (Gen. 36:32–33), and likewise all their successors [from a variety of places]. But with Israel, it was not so. Out of their own midst came their notables, out of their own midst their kings, out of their own midst their priests, out of their own midst their prophets, out of their own midst their princes.[3]

103. "One from among thy brethren shalt thou appoint king over thee" (Deut. 17:15); indeed, the appointments you make to every kind of office are to be from among your own brethren.[4]

104. "Saul clad David with his garment" (1 Sam. 17:38), even though it is written of Saul, "From his shoulders and upward he was higher than any of the people" (1 Sam. 9:2). After Saul clad David with his garment and saw that it fit him, he immediately cast an evil eye on him. Observing [Saul so disturbed that] his face turned white, "David said: 'I cannot walk in your garment, for I am not used to it.' So David took it off" (1 Sam. 17:39). From [this incident] you learn that even a man who is short, once appointed king, grows tall. How does such a thing come about? The instant he is anointed with the anointing oil, he becomes superior to all his brethren.[5]

105. "And he took the crown of Malcam from off his head; and the weight thereof was a talent of gold; . . . and it was put on David's head" (2 Sam. 12:30). But how could David have put it on? R. Judah said in the name of Rav: What the verse means is that the dimensions of the crown fit the dimensions of David's head. R. Yose son of R. Hanina said: There was a lodestone in the crown, which kept it suspended above David's head.[6]

106. "Then they brought out the king's son, and put upon him the *nezer* and the evidence" (2 Chron. 23:11). *Nezer* means "crown." "Evidence," said R. Judah in the name of Rav, means that the crown provided evidence that young Joash was of the house of David, for the crown fit him who could claim kingship by virtue of his descent, but it did not fit him who could make no such claim.[7]

107. We have been taught: "And he shall write him the repetition of this law" (Deut. 17:18). The king should write out two copies—one that goes out and comes in with him, and the other that is kept in his archives. The one that goes out and comes in with him [should be written out in small letters so that it is] as small as an amulet, which he should suspend from his arm, in keeping with "I have set the Lord always before me; surely He is at my right hand, I shall not be moved" (Ps. 16:8).[8]

108. At the conclusion of the first day of the Festival of Tabernacles, in the eighth year, at the outgoing of the sabbatical year in a septennate, a wooden dais is erected for the king in the Temple Court, and he sits on it. The sexton of the synagogue takes the Torah scroll and gives it to the head of the synagogue, the head of the synagogue gives it to the deputy high priest, the deputy high priest gives it to the high priest, and the high priest gives it to the king. The king stands up to receive it, but sits down when he is to read it. King Agrippa,[9] however, stood up to receive it and read it standing, for which the sages commended him. When he reached the words "Thou shalt not put a foreigner over thee" (Deut. 17:15), tears flowed from his eyes. So the sages said to him, "Fear not, Agrippa, you are our brother, you are our brother."

It was taught in the name of R. Nathan: Because the sages flattered Agrippa, Israel at that moment incurred the penalty of extermination.[10]

109. One of King Yannai's slaves killed a man. Simeon ben Shetah said to the sages, "Set your eyes [boldly] upon him and let us judge him." So they sent word to King Yannai, "Your slave killed a man." The king sent him to them [to be tried]. But they again sent word to him, "You, too, must come here, for the Torah says, 'If warning has been given to his owner' [Exod. 21:29], meaning that the owner must come and stand by his ox."[11] The king came, was given a seat next to Simeon ben Shetah, and sat down.

Then Simeon ben Shetah said, "Stand up on your feet, King Yannai, and let the witnesses testify against you—you are standing not before us but before Him who spoke and the world came into being, for it is said, 'The two men who have a dispute shall stand before the Lord' " (Deut. 19:17). The king replied, "[I shall do not] what you say, but what [all] your colleagues say." Simeon turned

1. B. AZ 10a. See also below, part 6, chap. 4, §4n.
2. The allusion may be to the time in Roman history when the emperors were not Romans. Gen. R. 83:1.
3. Exod. R. 37:1.
4. B. Kid 76b.
5. Lev. R. 26:9.
6. B. AZ 44a.
7. Ibid.
8. B. Sanh 21b.
9. Agrippa I (10 B.C.E.–44 C.E.). Only his mother was of Jewish descent.
10. The assertion is hyperbolic. Its purpose is pedagogical, to emphasize the heinous character of flattery. B. Sot 41b.
11. The owner is responsible for his slave, whose legal status is that of chattel.

to the right, but they looked down to the ground; he turned to the left, but they too looked down to the ground. Then Simeon ben Shetah said to his colleagues, "You appear to be given to deep thought. Let the Master of men's thought come and requite you." At once Gabriel came down and smote them to the ground, so that their souls left them.

At that time, the sages declared: A king is not to sit in judgment, nor is he to be judged; he is not to testify nor to be testified against.[1]

110. "The king's heart is in the hand of the Lord as the watercourses; He turneth it whithersoever He will" (Prov. 21:1). When you place water in a vessel, you may turn it in any direction you wish. So, too, when a mortal rises to kingship, his heart is placed in the hand of the Holy One. If the world merits it, the Holy One turns his heart to beneficent decrees; if the world is guilty, He turns his heart to maleficent decrees. But every decree that issues from a king's mouth issues first from the Holy One's Presence.[2]

111. Samuel said: The law of the land is law.[3]

112. Do not seek to evade customs.[4]

113. A king's emissary is like the king himself.[5]

114. The chiefs [mentioned in Genesis 36] are uncrowned kings.[6]

115. There is no need to anoint a king who is the son of a king.[7]

116. One reign may not overlap another even by a hairsbreadth.[8]

117. Is it possible for two kings to wear the same crown?[9]

118. Is a king appointed unless he knows the tactics of government?[10]

119. A government that has no counselors is not a proper government.[11]

120. A fox in its hour—bow down to it.[12]

121. "As far as the great river, the river Euphrates" (Deut. 1:7). Simeon ben Tarfon said: Mentioning the Euphrates in connection with the Holy Land accounts for its being called "great," just as when you touch a person anointed with oil, you too will become anointed with oil. The sages in the school of R. Ishmael taught: A king's servant is like the king himself.[13]

A proverb says: Attach yourself to the captain, and people will bow down to you.[14]

122. A high dignitary took us by the hand, and his [sweet] scent entered our hand.[15]

123. Lying does not become a king.[16]

124. Because oil cannot be adulterated, kings are anointed with it.[17]

125. "Come not nigh to the door of her house" (Prov. 5:8)—to the door of the ruling power.[18]

126. Shemaiah said: Do not become intimate with the ruling power.[19]

127. Rabban Gamaliel son of R. Judah the Patriarch said: Be circumspect in your dealings with the ruling power. They bring no man near them save for their own need: they appear to be friends when it is to their gain, but they do not stand with a man in the hour of his distress.[20]

Judgment and Judges

128. Rabban Simeon ben Gamaliel said: The world stands on three things: on truth, on justice, and on peace, as is said, "Execute truth, justice, and peace within your gates" (Zech. 8:16).

These three are interlinked: when justice is done, truth is achieved, and peace is established.[21]

129. Rabban Simeon ben Gamaliel said: Make no mockery of justice, for it is one of the world's three pillars. How so? Because the sages have taught: The world stands on three things: on justice, on truth, and on peace. Take care not to subvert justice, for if you subvert justice, you shake the world, one of whose pillars is justice.[22]

130. "Now these are the judgments which thou art to set before them" (Exod. 21:1). One would have expected

1. B. Sanh 19a–b; Tanhuma B, *Shofetim*, §6.
2. Midrash Prov. 21 (ed. Buber, p. 89).
3. B. BK 113a.
4. B. Pes 112b.
5. B. BK 113b.
6. B. Sanh 99b.
7. B. Hor 11b.
8. B. Ber 48b.
9. B. Hul 60b.
10. B. Shab 31a.
11. PRE 3.
12. B. Meg 16b.
13. Of the rivers mentioned in Gen. 2:11–14 , the Euphrates is regarded as the smallest. But since it is spoken of in connection with the Holy Land, it is described as "the great river."
14. B. Shevu 47b; Sif Deut., §6.
15. B. Zev 96b.
16. B. Tam 32a.
17. Mek, *Mishpatim, Nezikin*, 13.
18. B. AZ 17a.
19. Avot 1:9.
20. Avot 2:3.
21. Avot 1:18; P. Ta 4:2, 68a.
22. Deut. R. 5:1; Yalkut, *Shofetim*, §907.

Scripture to say, "Which thou art to teach them." However, as R. Jeremiah (according to some, R. Hiyya bar Abba) explained, Scripture means that the judges' implements are to be set before them.

Before leaving for the court, R. Huna used to say: Bring forth the implements of my trade: my rod, my sandal, my horn, and my lash.[1]

131. R. Hisda and Rabbah bar R. Huna sat in court the entire day and grew faint. So R. Hiyya bar Rav of Difti recited to them, "When the people stood about Moses from the morning till the evening" (Exod. 18:13). Can you possibly suppose that Moses sat in court the entire day? When would his study of Torah have been done? However, even when only on one occasion a judge issues a true verdict in keeping with the facts as he ascertained them, Scripture deems it for him as though he had become the partner of the Holy One in the [six days'] work of creation. This is intimated in "And when the people stood about Moses, [the time they spent in his court was equivalent to] 'the morning till the evening' [of each day of creation]," as suggested by the similarly worded "There was evening and there was morning, the first day" (Gen. 1:5).[2]

132. R. Samuel bar Nahmani said in the name of R. Jonathan: When a judge issues a true verdict in keeping with the facts as he has ascertained them, he causes the Presence to abide in Israel, as is said, "God standeth in the congregation of God, when judgment is determined in awareness of God" (Ps. 82:1).[3] But when a judge does not issue a true verdict in keeping with the facts as he should have ascertained them, he causes the Presence to depart from Israel, as is said, " 'Because of the oppression of the poor, because of the sighing of the needy, now will I arise,' saith the Lord" (Ps. 12:6).[4]

133. What is the proof that when three judges sit in court, the Presence is among them? The verse "He [God] judgeth among the judges" (Ps. 82:1).[5]

134. When a judge issues a true verdict in keeping with the facts, the Holy One, if one dare say such a thing, leaves the heaven of heavens and causes His Presence to be at the judge's side, for Scripture says, "And when the Lord raised them up judges, then the Lord was with the judge" (Judg. 2:18). But when He sees that a judge shows partiality, He, if one dare say such a thing, removes His Presence and goes back to heaven. When the angels ask Him, "Master of the universe, what happened?" He replies, "I saw that the judge was partial, and I have removed Myself from there," as Scripture says, " 'For the oppression of the poor, for the sighing of the needy, now will I arise,' saith the Lord" (Ps. 12:6). What does the Holy One do? He draws His sword in front of Him to make it known that there is a Judge above, as it says, "Be ye afraid of the sword; for wrath bringeth the punishments of the sword, that ye may know there is *shaddun*" (Job 19:29); the last word, though read *shaddun*, is written *she-din*, "there is judgment" in the world.[6]

135. "Judges and officers shalt thou appoint" (Deut. 16:18). R. Levi said: By what parable may the command [to appoint officers concerned with justice] be illustrated? By the one of a king who had many sons but loved the youngest more than the others. He also had an orchard which he loved more than anything else he had. So the king said: I will give this orchard, which I love more than anything else I have, to my youngest son, whom I love more than any of my other sons. So, too, the Holy One said: Of all the nations I created, I love only Israel. Of all else I created, I love only justice. So I will give what I love to the nation I love.

The Holy One said to Israel: My children, as you live, I am exalted because of your intense concern for justice: "The Lord of hosts is exalted through justice" (Isa. 5:16).[7]

136. We have been taught that R. Yose ben Elisha said: If you see a generation overcome by many troubles, go forth and investigate the conduct of Israel's judges, for all punishment that comes to the world comes only on account of the conduct of Israel's judges, as is said, "Hear this, I pray you, ye heads of the house of Jacob, and rulers of the House of Israel, that abhor justice. . . . The heads thereof judge for bribes, and the priests thereof teach for hire, and the prophets thereof divine for money" (Mic. 3:9 and 3:11). Therefore the Holy One will bring three punishments upon them, corresponding to the three sins they commit, as is said, "Assuredly, because of you shall Zion be plowed as a field, and Jerusalem shall become heaps of ruins, and the Temple Mount a shrine in the woods" (Mic. 3:12). And the Holy One will not cause His Presence to rest again upon Israel until the wicked leaders and officers cease out of Israel, for it is said, "And I will turn My hand upon thee, and purge away thy dross as with lye. . . . And I will restore thy judges as at the first, and thy counselors as at the beginning" (Isa. 1:25–26).[8]

137. R. Melai said in the name of R. Eleazar son of R. Simeon: What is meant by "The Lord hath broken the staff of the wicked, the scepter of the rulers" (Isa. 14:5)? "The Lord hath broken the staff of the wicked" refers to judges who make themselves, as it were, into a staff for their sheriffs.[9] "The scepter of the rulers" refers to the disciples of the wise in families of judges [who cover up the unfitness of their kinsmen]. Mar Zutra said: They are the disciples of the wise who teach ignorant judges [the minimal amount of Torah and proper conduct that the public expects, but the judges remain unfit].[10]

---

1. The rod to beat disturbers; the sandal to be used in the *halitzah* ceremony (see Deut. 25:5–9); the horn to be used in the ritual of excommunication; and the lash to flag offenders. B. Sanh 7b.
2. B. Shab 10a.
3. JV: "in the midst of the judges He judgeth."
4. B. Sanh 7a.
5. The word *Elohim* ("God") also means "judges." B. Ber 6a.
6. Exod. R. 30:24.
7. Deut. R. 5:7.
8. B. Shab 139a.
9. So Adin Steinsaltz, Shab, ad loc.
10. B. Shab 139a.

138. R. Eleazar said: What is the proof that a judge on his way to court should not press through, so that he all but steps on the holy people [seated on the ground in the house of study]? The verse "Do not ascend my altar by stepping [on others]" (Exod. 20:23), which is followed directly by "This applies also to those concerned with decisions about justice" (Exod. 21:1).[1]

139. "So that the judgment is left to God" (Deut. 1:17). According to R. Hama son of R. Hanina, the Holy One said: It is not enough for the wicked that they take money from one and unjustly give it to another, but they put upon Me the task of recompensing the true owner.[2]

140. R. Samuel bar Nahmani said in the name of R. Jonathan: When a judge unjustly takes from one and gives to another, the Holy One will take the judge's life, for it is said, "Rob not the poor because they are poor . . . for the Lord will plead their cause, and will despoil of life those that despoil them" (Prov. 22:22–23).[3]

141. R. Samuel bar Nahmani said in the name of R. Jonathan: A judge should always regard himself as though a sword were hanging over his head[4] and Gehenna gaping beneath him.[5]

142. Whenever Rava was leaving for the court, he would say: Of his own will [a judge] goes to meet death. He makes no provisions for the needs of his household, since he comes home empty-handed. O if only he might return [from court as free of sin] as when he went.[6]

143. It is written, "And I charged your judges at that time" (Deut. 1:16); it is also written, "And I charged you at that time" (Deut. 1:18). R. Eleazar said in the name of R. Simlai: The second verse is an admonition to the community that awe for a judge be upon them; and the first verse is an admonition to a judge that he be patient with the community. To what extent? R. Hanin (according to some, R. Shabbetai) said, "As a nurse carries an infant" (Num. 11:12).[7]

144. "Go to the ant; . . . consider her ways and be wise" (Prov. 6:6). R. Simeon ben Halafta said: Once it happened that an ant dropped a grain of wheat, and though all the other ants came by and sniffed at that grain, not one of them touched it, until the one to whom it belonged came back and took it. Ponder the wisdom an ant has! Ponder the rectitude an ant has! She learned her ways from no other creature. She has no ruler or officer over her, as is said, "Without leaders, officers, or rulers" (Prov. 6:7). Hence, you, for whom I have appointed magistrates and clerks—how much more by far should you be willing to heed them, as enjoined in the verse "Ye shall appoint magistrates and clerks in all your settlements" (Deut. 16:18).[8]

145. "Thou shalt not revile a judge" (Exod. 22:27). Our masters taught: It once happened that a man with a lawsuit came before a judge, who gave the verdict in his favor. When he left the judge's presence, he said, "Judge So-and-so—there is no sage in the world like him! He is an angel!" In the course of time, the man had another lawsuit and came again before the same judge, who this time gave a verdict against him. When he left the judge's presence, he said, "In the entire world, there is no fool like him!" People asked him, "Yesterday an angel, and today a fool?" Hence Scripture admonishes you, "Thou shalt not revile a judge."[9]

146. R. Ishmael son of R. Yose said: He who shuns the office of judge rids himself of enmity, robbery, and false swearing. On the other hand, he who is overly confident in giving a verdict is foolish, wicked, and arrogant.[10]

147. Rav said: To whom does the verse "Many are wounded by the immature, but because of those who hold back, all may be slain" (Prov. 7:26)[11] apply? The words "Many are wounded by the immature" apply to a disciple of the wise who is not mature enough to give decisions, yet gives them; and the words "because of those who hold back, all may be slain" apply to a disciple of the wise who is mature enough to give decisions, but holds back from giving them.[12]

148. "Ye shall not be partial [in appointing men who are to sit] in judgment" (Deut. 1:7) applies to the man charged with appointing judges. He should not say, "So-and-so once lent me money; I will appoint him judge," or "So-and-so commands many languages; I will appoint him judge," with the result that the one appointed will be acquitting the guilty and sentencing the innocent, not because he is wicked, but because he does not know better. Scripture accounts it to him who has appointed such a judge as though he himself had been partial in judgment.[13]

149. Resh Lakish said: He who appoints a judge that is unfit is as though he had planted in Israel a pole sacred to an idol, for it is said, "Judges and officers shalt thou appoint unto thee" (Deut. 16:18), and soon after that, "Thou shalt not plant thee a pole sacred to an idol" (Deut. 16:21). R. Ashi added: And if such an appointment is made where a disciple of the wise is available, it is as

---

1. JV: "These are the ordinances." But the paraphrase appears to be required by the comment. B. Sanh 7b.
2. B. Sanh 8a.
3. B. Sanh 7a.
4. Literally, "placed between his flanks."
5. B. Sanh 7a.
6. B. Sanh 7b; B. Yoma 86b–87a.
7. B. Sanh 8a.
8. Deut. R. 5:2.
9. Exod. R. 31:8; Tanhuma, *Mishpatim*, §10.
10. Avot 4:7.
11. JV: "For she hath cast down many wounded; yea, a mighty host are all her slain." But Rav associates the word *hippilah* ("cast down") with "cast down prematurely"—hence, "immature"; and *atzumim* ("mighty") with the verb "*otzem*" ("shut, refrain, hold back").
12. B. AZ 19b.
13. Sif Deut., §17; Yalkut, *Devarim*, §802.

though he had planted that pole near [God's] altar, for the verse goes on to say, "Beside the altar of the Lord thy God" (ibid.).[1]

150. He who is wise, humble, clear-headed, and fearful of sin; whose youth was of unblemished repute; and the spirit of his fellows takes delight in him—he may be made a judge in his city.[2]

151. R. Yohanan said: Those appointed to the Sanhedrin are to be men of stature, men of wisdom, men of good appearance, men of mature years, men who know witchcraft, and who are conversant with the world's seventy languages, lest the Sanhedrin have need to listen to an interpreter.

R. Judah said in the name of Rav: Only he who is so subtle that he can prove from Scripture that a reptile is clean may be appointed to the Sanhedrin.[3]

152. We have been taught: A man who is old, castrated, or has no children may not be appointed to the Sanhedrin. R. Judah added: Nor one who is cruel.[4]

153. R. Judah said in the name of Samuel: He who has drunk a fourth of a *log* of wine may not issue a decision.[5]

154. The scrupulous men of Jerusalem would not sit in at a trial unless they knew who was to sit with them.[6]

155. When the sages ordained R. Zera, they began the ordination with a wedding song: "No kohl, no rouge, no hair dye—yet a graceful gazelle!"

When the sages ordained R. Ammi and R. Assi, they sang to them: "Such as these, such as these, ordain for us. Do not ordain for us those whose speech is confusing and whose reasoning is flawed"—or, as some say—"those who jump to conclusions and whose utterances are not thought through."[7]

156. The patriarch's household once appointed a judge who was no scholar. So the sages said to Judah bar Nahmani, Resh Lakish's interpreter: Stand at his side as interpreter. Judah stood at his side and bent down to hear him, but he said nothing. Then Judah bar Nahmani discoursed on the verse "Woe unto him that saith to the wood: 'Awake,' to the dumb stone: 'Arise!' Can this one teach? Behold, he is overlaid with gold and silver, and there is no spirit at all in the midst of him" (Hab. 2:19). The Holy One will call to account those responsible for appointing him, as is said, "The Lord is in His holy Temple; let all the earth keep silence before Him" (Hab. 2:20).[8]

157. R. Ishmael son of R. Yose used to say: Judge not alone, for none may judge alone save One. Do not peremptorily say, "Go by my opinion." When your colleagues in the court are in a majority, they have the right to decide—not you.[9]

158. R. Judah ben Pazzi said: Even the Holy One does not judge alone, for it is said, "All the host of heaven standing by Him on His right hand and on His left" (1 Kings 22:19), some inclining toward the scale of merit, others inclining toward the scale of guilt; and the Holy One engages in give-and-take with them. After the verdict is decided upon, the Holy One enters a place where the host of heaven may not enter and by Himself seals the verdict.[10]

159. R. Joshua ben Levi said: When ten men sit in judgment, the collar of responsibility is on all of them.

When a case was brought before R. Huna, he summoned ten disciples of the wise from the house of study, saying, "So that each of us may carry a chip of the beam."[11]

160. "Hear out your fellow men, and decide justly" (Deut. 1:16). Should the same case come before you once, twice, and a third time, do not say, "This case has already come before me once, twice, and a third time," but be patient. Indeed, this is what the Men of the Great Assembly used to say: "Be patient in judgment."[12]

161. R. Josiah (according to others, R. Nahman bar Isaac) discoursed as follows: What is meant by "O house of David, thus saith the Lord: Execute justice in the morning, and deliver the spoiled out of the hand of the oppressor" (Jer. 21:12)? Is it only in the morning that one acts as a judge, and the rest of the day there is no judging? Of course not. It means that if a judgment [you are about to give] is as clear to you as the morning light, pronounce it; but if not, do not pronounce it. R. Hiyya bar Abba, citing R. Yohanan, derived it from "Say unto wisdom, 'Thou art my sister' " (Prov. 7:4): if the judgment [you are about to give] is as clear to you as the law that you may not marry your sister, pronounce it; but if not, do not pronounce it.[13]

162. "Bless him who leavens" (Isa. 1:17).[14] Rava said: Blessed be the judge who allows the "leavening" of his judgments.[15]

163. What is the proof that a disciple who sees his master erring in a judgment should not say, "I will wait until he carries it out, then demolish his judgment and set up mine,

1. B. Sanh 7b.
2. Tos Sanh 7:1.
3. B. Sanh 17a.
4. B. Sanh 36b.
5. B. Er 64a.
6. B. Sanh 23a.
7. So interpreted by Geonim (see B. Sanh 14a in the edition of Adin Steinsaltz, p. 59). B. Ket 17a.
8. B. Sanh 7b.
9. Avot 4:8.
10. P. Sanh 1:1, 18a; Tanhuma, *Shemot*, §18.
11. Carry a share of the blame for a decision that may be wrong. B. Sanh 7b.
12. Sif Deut., §16.
13. B. Sanh 7b.
14. JV: "Relieve the oppressed." But *asheru* ("relieve") can also mean "bless," and *hamotz* ("oppressed") can also mean "leaven."
15. He does not rush to issue a verdict. B. Sanh 35a.

which will thereafter be called by my name"? The verse "Keep thou far from a false matter" (Exod. 23:7).[1]

164. "Remove the chaff from yourselves, then remove it from others" (Zeph. 2:1).[2] Resh Lakish said: Adorn yourself, and after that, adorn others.

A story. In R. Yannai's field, there was a tree that overhung a public thoroughfare, and another man also had a tree overhanging the same thoroughfare. People passing along the thoroughfare objected to the other man's tree. The man came before R. Yannai, who said to him, "You may leave now, but come back tomorrow." During the night, R. Yannai sent out his workmen and had his own tree cut down. The next day, the man came back, and R. Yannai told him, "Go and cut down your tree." The man objected: "But you also have such a tree." R. Yannai: "Go out and see. If I have cut down mine, you should cut down yours; if not, you need not."

What was R. Yannai's idea at first [when he had his tree], and what was it afterward?

At first, he thought that passersby in the public thoroughfare would be pleased with it, because they could sit in its shade. But when he saw that they objected to it, he sent to have it cut down.[3]

165. "Their mother hath played the harlot, she that conceived them hath acted shamefully" (Hos. 2:7). According to R. Simlai, the Holy One said: Israel's leaders put My own words to shame before the common people. How? A sage in the teacher's chair expounds in public "Thou shalt not lend money on interest," yet he himself lends his money on interest; "Thou shalt not rob," yet he himself robs; "Thou shalt not steal," yet he himself steals.

R. Berekhiah said: There is the story of a man whose cloak was stolen. He went to complain about the matter to a judge, and found the cloak spread over the judge's bed. There is also the story of a woman whose kettle was stolen. When she went to complain about the matter to a judge, she found the kettle set upon the judge's stove.

Such is the import of "Their mother hath played the harlot, she that conceived them hath acted shamefully."[4]

166. A judge who is sued is not worthy of the name "judge."

But if that is so, anyone can come in from the street, file suit, and disqualify him.

No, what the statement means is that a judge who is sued [found guilty], and sentenced to pay money is not worthy of the name "judge."[5]

167. R. Yohanan said: In times past, when a man would go up to Jerusalem to plead a lawsuit, the judge would say, "Split a couple of logs for me," "Fill a couple of casks of water for me," [and so on. While the man was doing such chores], his money ran out, and he would have to leave Jerusalem with a broken spirit. When a widow happened to meet him on the way and asked him, "How did your lawsuit come out?" he would reply, "My money ran out, and I got nowhere at all." The widow would then say, "If this person, who is a man, got nowhere at all with his case, all the more certain will I, who am a widow, get nowhere with mine."

Thus were fulfilled literally the words "The cause of a widow doth not come unto them" (Isa. 1:23).[6]

168. While R. Judah was sitting before Samuel, a woman came before Samuel crying [about a wrong done to her], but he ignored her. When R. Judah asked Samuel, "Does not the master realize that 'whoso stoppeth his ears at the cry of the poor, he also shall cry himself, but shall not be answered' (Prov. 21:13)?" Samuel replied, "Sharp-tongued one, [I], your superior, will be punished only with cold water, but your superior's superior will be punished with hot water, for he, Mar Ukba, the president of the court, is sitting [here], and [he, being a descendant of David], is told, "O house of David . . . execute justice in the morning, and deliver the spoiled from the hand of the oppressor, lest My fury go forth like fire' " (Jer. 21:12).[7]

169. The sword comes to the world on account of delay in justice, on account of subversion of justice, and on account of those who interpret the Torah not in keeping with accepted traditions.[8]

170. When R. Simeon ben Gamaliel and R. Ishmael were brought [before the Roman officials], and it was decreed that they be executed, R. Ishmael wept. R. Simeon said to him, "Avrekh,[9] you are but two steps away from being put in the bosom of the righteous, yet you weep!" R. Ishmael replied, "I weep because we are about to be executed in the same way as murderers and desecrators of the Sabbath." So R. Simeon asked him, "Did someone perhaps come to you for judgment or with a question, and you kept him waiting while you sipped your cup, tied your sandal, or put on your cloak, even though the Torah says, 'If thou afflict in any wise . . . I will kill you with the sword' [Exod. 22:23]—whether the affliction be severe or the affliction be light?"[10]

Taking Bribes and Showing Favor

171. R. Nahman bar Kohen expounded the verse "The king by justice establisheth the land, but he that loveth gifts overthroweth it" (Prov. 29:4). If the judge is like a king, who feels that he has no need for material help, he preserves the land; but if he is like a priest, who goes

1. B. Shevu 31a.
2. JV: "Gather yourselves together, yea, gather together." But the stem *kshsh* ("gather") is here associated with *kash* ("stubble").
3. B. BB 60a–b; Tanhuma, *Shofetim*, §3.
4. Deut. R. 2:19; Yalkut, Isa., §391; Yalkut, Hos., §517.
5. B. BB 58b.
6. PRKM 15:9 (PRKS, p. 284); Yalkut, Isa., §391.
7. B. Shab 55a.
8. Avot 5:8.
9. The word is taken to be portmanteau for *av* ("father [in wisdom]") though *rakh* ("tender [in years]").
10. Mek, *Mishpatim, Nezikin,* 18; Sem 8.

around threshing floors to collect the gifts due him, he will destroy it.[1]

172. We have been taught: "Thou shalt take no bribe" (Exod. 23:8). What is the purpose of such a statement? If to teach not to acquit the guilty and not to condemn the innocent, it has already been said: "Do not subvert the rights of the needy in their disputes" (Exod. 23:6). The Torah's intention, however, is to say that a bribe is not to be taken even if it be to acquit the innocent and condemn the guilty.

If one takes a fee for acting as judge, his decisions are null and void. What is the proof? R. Judah said in the name of Rav: The verse "Behold, I have taught you statutes and ordinances, even as the Lord your God commanded me" (Deut. 4:5), intimating that just as I [your God] give statutes and ordinances at no fee, so you must give judgments at no fee.

We have been taught: The judge who takes a fee for pronouncing judgment is contemptible, but his decision is valid.

But we have been taught: If one takes a fee for acting as judge, his decisions are null and void. Yes, but one may take a fee as compensation for time taken from engaging in other work. Karna used to take an *istira*[2] from the party he was going to declare innocent and an *istira* from the party he was going to declare guilty, and then give his decision.

How could he do so? Have we not been taught: The judge who takes a fee is contemptible?

This applies only to a fee for loss of time from performing nonessential work. But Karna used to take a fee for loss of time from performing essential work, for he was regularly occupied in a wineshop, where he sampled the aroma of wines to determine [whether they could be stored], and for that he would receive a *zuz*.

When a lawsuit was brought to R. Huna, he used to say to the litigants: Provide me a man who will draw irrigation water in my stead, and I will give you my decision.

Jerusalem's judges of civil law used to receive a fee of ninety-nine *maneh* from the Temple funds.[3] If the amount proved insufficient, an increase was given them, even if they were unwilling to accept it.[4]

173. Rava said: Why is accepting a bribe prohibited? Because when one accepts a bribe from another, one becomes so well disposed to the other that the other becomes like one's own person, and no man sees his own person in the wrong.[5]

174. What is intimated in *shohad*, "bribe"? *She-hu*, "that he [the recipient] becomes" *had*, "one [with the giver]."[6]

1. B. Sanh 7b; B. Ket 105b.
2. A silver coin worth a third of a denar.
3. Literally, "from the heave offering of the chamber [where the shekels were kept]."
4. B. Ket 105a; B Bekh 29a.
5. B. Ket 105b.
6. Ibid.

175. R. Abbahu said: Come and see how blind are the eyes of those who accept a bribe. When a man has a pain in his eyes and pays money to a physician, he may be cured or may not be cured. Yet these take the equivalent of a small coin and surely blind their own eyes, as is said, "For a bribe doth blind them that have sight" (Exod. 23:8).[7]

176. "For a bribe doth blind the sages" (Deut. 16:19). Even a great sage who accepts a bribe will not depart from this world without his mind being dulled. "And pervert the words of the righteous" (ibid.). Even a wholly righteous man who accepts a bribe will not depart from this world without his mind being addled.[8]

177. "For a bribe doth blind," etc. (Deut. 16:19). In this connection, the sages said: He who takes money to subvert judgment will not leave this world before the light of his eyes is diminished. R. Nathan said: [He will not leave this world] before one of the following three things happens: his mind becomes so addled in his grasp of Torah that he declares the unclean clean and the clean unclean; he becomes dependent on charity; or his eyesight is diminished.[9]

178. A man once brought to R. Ishmael son of R. Elisha[10] th first of the fleece. R. Ishmael asked him, "Where are you from?" The man: "From such-and-such a place." "But," R. Ishmael asked, "between there and here, was there no priest to whom you might have given the first of the fleece?" The man: "I have a lawsuit, and I thought that while I was at it, I might as well bring the first of the fleece to the master." R. Ishmael refused to accept the first of the fleece from him, saying, "I am now disqualified from trying your lawsuit," and had two disciples of the wise seated to try the man's suit. Even as he was going about arranging the matter, he found himself thinking: If the man wished, he might plead thus; or if he preferred, he might plead otherwise. Then he exclaimed, "May the breath of those who accept bribes be blasted! If I, who did not accept the first of the fleece—and if I had accepted it, would only have taken what was rightfully due me—find myself so concerned about his suit, how much more by far would this be true of those who accept a bribe!"[11]

179. The tenant of R. Ishmael son of R. Yose, who was in the habit of bringing him a basket of fruit every Friday, once brought it to him on a Thursday. R. Ishmael asked him, "Why was the day changed?" The tenant: "I have a lawsuit, and I thought that while I was at it, I might as well bring [the basket of fruit] to the master." Refusing to accept the basket from the tenant, R. Ishmael said, "I am now disqualified as judge in your case," and had two disciples of the wise seated to try the man's suit. Even as

7. B. Ket 105a.
8. B. Ket 105a–b.
9. Mek, *Mishpatim*, *Kaspa*, 3 (La 3: 172–73).
10. Who was a priest and entitled to the priestly dues.
11. B. Ket 105b.

he was going about arranging the matter, he found himself thinking: If the tenant wished, he might plead thus; or if he preferred, he might plead otherwise. Then he exclaimed, "May the breath of those who accept bribes be blasted! If I, who have not accepted [the basket of fruit]—and if I had taken it, would only have taken what is rightfully due me—am in such a dither, how much more by far would this be true of those who accept bribes!"[1]

180. R. Eliezer's wife, Imma Shalom, was Rabban Gamaliel's sister. Now, in Rabban Gamaliel's neighborhood there lived a certain [Christian] philosopher who gave it out that, when [acting as judge] he took no bribes. In an attempt to expose his true character, Imma Shalom brought him a golden lamp and then appeared before him in court, saying, "I wish to have a share given me of my [deceased] father's estate." He ordered, "Let them divide it [equally]." Then Rabban Gamaliel spoke up: "In our Scripture it is written, 'Where there is a son, a daughter does not inherit.' " The philosopher: "Ever since the day you were exiled from your Land, the Torah of Moses has been abrogated and another Torah[2] given, in which it is written, 'A son and a daughter inherit equally.' " The next day, Rabban Gamaliel came back and brought him a Lybian ass, whereupon the philosopher said to them, "I read on to the end of the book, where it is written, 'I came not to detract from the Torah of Moses but to add to the Torah of Moses,'[3] and [as you said] in that Torah is written, 'A daughter does not inherit where there is a son.' " At this, Imma Shalom said to the philosopher, "May your light shine forth like a lamp." And Rabban Gamaliel said to him, "But an ass came and knocked over the lamp!"[4]

181. Resh Lakish went to pay his respects to our rabbi [Judah I, the Patriarch]. "Pray for me," R. Judah begged him, "for this Roman government is very evil."[5] "Take nothing from anyone," Resh Lakish told him, "and then you will not have to give anything." While Resh Lakish was sitting with R. Judah, a woman came in, bringing R. Judah a dish with a knife in it. He took the knife and returned the dish to the woman. Later, an imperial courier came in and saw the knife, took a fancy to it, and carried it off. Toward evening, Resh Lakish again went to pay his respects to our rabbi and saw him chuckling. "Why are you chuckling?" asked Resh Lakish. R. Judah: "That knife you saw—an imperial courier came in, eyed it, coveted it, and took it away." Resh Lakish: "Did I not tell you that if you take nothing from anyone, you will not have to give anything to anyone?"[6]

182. Our masters taught: "Thou shalt take no bribe" (Exod. 23:8). It goes without saying that a bribe of money is prohibited, but even a bribe of beguiling words is prohibited, for Scripture does not say, "Thou shalt take no gain."[7]

183. What is meant by a bribe of pleasant words? Such a bribe as the one offered to Samuel. He was once crossing a river on a rope bridge when a man came along and offered him his hand [to assist him]. Samuel asked him, "How do you happen to be here?" The man replied, "I have a lawsuit." Samuel: "I am disqualified from acting as judge in your suit."

Amemar was once presiding at a lawsuit. When a bird flew down onto his head and a certain man came up and removed it, Amemar asked him, "How do you happen to be here?" The man replied, "I have a lawsuit." Amemar: "I am now disqualified as judge in your suit."[8]

184. A man once brought a bale of small marsh fish to R. Anan. "What is your business here?" R. Anan asked him. "I have a lawsuit," the man replied. R. Anan did not accept the fish, saying, "I am now disqualified as judge in your suit." "I do not request," the man said to him, "the master's decision [in my lawsuit]; will the master, however, at least accept [the present], so that I may not be prevented from offering my firstfruits. For we have been taught: "And there came a man from Baal-shalishah, and brought the man of God bread of the firstfruits, twenty loaves of barley, and fresh ears of corn in his sack' " (2 Kings 4:42). But was Elisha entitled to eat firstfruits? This, however, was intended to inform you that he who brings a gift to a scholar [is doing as good a deed] as if he had offered firstfruits. ["It was not my intention to accept your gift"], said R. Anan, "but now that you have given me a valid reason, I will accept it from you." He then sent him to R. Nahman with the message "Let the master try [the suit of] this man, for I, Anan, am disqualified as judge for him." Since he has sent me such a message, R. Nahman thought, he must be his relative. An orphans' lawsuit was then in progress before him, and he reflected: An orphans' suit is subject to a positive precept [and should not be postponed]; on the other hand, to show respect to Torah scholars is also a positive precept. But the positive precept of showing respect for Torah must take precedence. So he postponed the orphans' case and brought up that man's suit. When the opponent of the man sent by R. Anan noticed the honor R. Nahman was showing his adversary, he found himself unable to present his evidence.

[Until that happened], Elijah [the prophet] was a frequent visitor to R. Anan, whom he was teaching the tractate Order of Elijah, but as soon as R. Anan acted in the manner described [Elijah] stayed away. R. Anan spent his time fasting and praying for [God's] mercy [until Elijah] came to him again.[9]

185. R. Papa said: A man should not act as judge when one he loves or one he hates is involved—he is not likely

1. Ibid.
2. Or, as in the Oxford Codex: "and the law of the Evangelium has been given."
3. See Matthew 5:17 et seq.
4. B. Shab 116a–b.
5. Its demands are exorbitant.
6. Gen. R. 78:12.
7. That would have meant only a monetary gain. B. Ket 105b.
8. Ibid.
9. B. Ket 105b–106a.

to find fault in the one he loves nor to find merit in the one he hates.[1]

186. Mar bar R. Ashi said: I am disqualified as judge when a disciple of the wise is involved, for he is as precious to me as my own person, and no man can find fault with his own person.[2]

187. "Ye shall not be afraid of the face of any man" (Deut. 1:17). Resh Lakish said: When two men, one weak [i.e., of little influence], the other strong [i.e., of great influence], come to you in a lawsuit, before you have heard their case or even after you have heard their case, you may—so long as you are still undecided in whose favor judgment is tending—tell them, "I choose not to act as judge in your case," lest the party of great influence be found guilty and use his influence to harass the judge. But after you have heard their case and know in whose favor judgment is tending, you may not withdraw and say, "I choose not to act as judge in your case," because it is written, "Ye shall not be afraid of the face of any man."

R. Joshua ben Korhah said: How do we know that a disciple who is present when his master judges a case and sees a point in favor of the poor party or against the rich party should not remain silent? From the verse "Ye shall not be afraid [*lo taguru*] of the face of any man," which R. Hanin took to mean, "You shall not hold back [*lo teageru*] your words because of anyone." Further, witnesses should know against whom [God] they are giving evidence, before whom they are giving evidence, and who will call them to account [in the event of false evidence]. For Scripture says, "Then both the men, between whom the controversy is, shall stand before the Lord" (Deut. 19:17). Judges should also know whom it is they are judging, before whom they are judging, and who will call them to account [if they subvert justice], as is written, "God standeth in the congregation of God, in the midst of judges doth He judge" (Ps. 82:1). And thus it is said of Jehoshaphat, "He said to the judges, Consider what ye do; for ye judge not for man but for the Lord" (2 Chron. 19:6). And lest a judge say, "Why should I go to such trouble?" Scripture reassures him, "He is with you in giving judgment" (ibid.)—a judge is held responsible only for what he can make out with his own eyes.[3]

188. What is the proof that a judge who knows that a plea is false should not say, "Since witnesses testify in support of it, I will give a decision and let the collar of blame hang around the witnesses' necks"? The verse "Keep thee far from a false matter" (Exod. 23:7).[4]

189. Judah ben Tabbai said: Do not [as a judge] play the part of an advocate. While the litigants stand before you, let them be regarded by you as guilty; and when, after submitting to the judgment, they leave your presence, let both be regarded as guiltless.[5]

190. "Ye shall hear the small and the great alike" (Deut. 1:17). Resh Lakish said: Let a lawsuit involving a mere *perutah* be as important to you as one involving a hundred *maneh*.[6]

191. "Hear [the pleas] between your brethren, and judge righteously" (Deut. 1:16). R. Hanina said: This verse serves warning on the judge that he should not listen to the pleading of one of the litigants in the absence of the other; and to the litigant that he should not set forth his plea to the judge before his opponent has arrived.[7]

192. Who is a cunning rogue? He, said R. Yohanan, who sets forth his plea to the judge before his opponent has arrived.[8]

193. Our masters taught: "In righteousness shalt thou judge thy neighbor" (Lev. 19:15). One litigant should not sit while the other stands; one should not be allowed to say all he needs while the other is told, "Be brief."

Another interpretation: "In righteousness shalt thou judge thy neighbor" (Lev. 19:15)—judge your neighbor on the scale of merit.[9]

194. R. Huna's widow had a lawsuit before R. Nahman, who said to himself: What shall I do? If I rise for her, her opponent will feel hindered in his plea. If I do not rise for her, I will be doing wrong, for a scholar's wife should be treated like a scholar. So he said to his attendant, "Go and make a duck fly at me, and [to ward it off] I will have to rise."[10]

195. Rabbah bar R. Huna said: When a disciple of the wise and an ignorant person (*am ha-aretz*) have a dispute [and come to court], the disciple of the wise should be invited to sit down, and the ignorant person should also be told, "Sit down." But if he remains standing, it does not matter.[11]

196. How do we know that if two litigants come to court, one dressed in rags and the second in a stole worth a hundred *maneh*, the second should be told, "Dress like your opponent, or see to it that he is dressed like you"? Because Scripture says, "Keep far from a false matter" (Exod. 23:7).[12]

197. If a wicked man and a virtuous one stand before you in a lawsuit, do not say, "Since this man is wicked,

1. B. Ket 105b.
2. B. Shab 119a.
3. B. Sanh 6b.
4. B. Shevu 30b–31a.
5. Avot 1:9.
6. B. Sanh 8a.
7. B. Sanh 7b and En Yaakov, ad loc.
8. B. Sot 21b.
9. B. Shevu 30a.
10. I will rise for R. Huna's widow, but her opponent will think I do so to ward off the duck. B. Shevu 30b.
11. Ibid.
12. Since the poorly dressed litigant may feel hindered in his plea, his side of the dispute will not be presented properly, and the judges may come to a false decision. B. Shevu 31a.

I will turn the judgment against him." For Scripture says, "Thou shalt not pervert the justice due to the needy in his lawsuit" (Exod. 23:6), even if he is needy [not in worldly goods but] in good deeds.[1]

198. Such was the practice of R. Ishmael: When two men, one a heathen and the other an Israelite, appeared before him in a lawsuit, if the heathen wished to be judged according to the law of Israel, R. Ishmael tried the case according to the law of Israel; if he wished to be judged according to the law of the nations of the world, R. Ishmael tried the case according to the law of the nations.[2]

Compromise [Arbitration] and Going Beyond the Letter of the Law

199. We have been taught: "Justice, justice shalt thou follow" (Deut. 16:20) One mention of justice refers to decisions based on strict law [which should be just]; the other, to compromises [which should be just]. How are compromises worked out? Say, two boats sailing in the same direction meet at [a narrow channel of] a river. If both attempt to pass side by side, both will sink; but if one is willing to proceed behind the other, both can sail safely. Likewise, two camels meet as they go up the ascent to Beth-horon. If both attempt to go up at the same time, both will fall [into the valley below]; but if one follows the other, both will go up [safely]. How should a compromise be worked out? If one is laden and the other not laden, the unladen should give way to the laden. If one is near [its destination] and the other not near, the one near its destination should give way to the one not near. If both are [equally] near or equally far [from their destination], a compromise should be made between them, the one [who is to go first] compensating the other [who is asked to give way].[3]

200. R. Eliezer son of R. Yose the Galilean said: It is forbidden to arbitrate [in a dispute before the court], and he who arbitrates commits a sin. The law must prevail, even if it involves cutting through a mountain, for it is said, "Judgment is God's" (Deut. 1:17).[4] Thus, Moses used to say, "Let the law cut through the mountain." Aaron, however, who loved peace and pursued peace, made peace between a man and his fellow [before they came to court], for of Aaron it is said, "The law of truth was in his mouth . . . ; he walked with Me in peace and uprightness" (Mal. 2:6).

R. Joshua ben Korhah said: Settlement by arbitration is a meritorious act, for it is written, "Execute the judgment of truth and of peace in your gates" (Zech. 8:16). But is it not true that where there is [strict] justice, there is no peace, and where there is peace, there is no [strict] justice? However, what is the kind of justice with which peace can abide? You must admit, it is justice through arbitration. Thus, of David we are told, "David executed justice and charity" (2 Sam. 8:15). Is it not true that where there is [strict] justice, there is no charity, and where there is charity, there is no [strict] justice? However, what is the kind of justice with which charity can abide? You must admit, it is justice through arbitration.[5]

201. R. Simeon ben Menasya said: There are times when one should arbitrate and times when one should not arbitrate.

For example, when two men come before you in a lawsuit, and before you have heard their case or even after you have heard their case, if you have not made up your mind which way the judgment is tending, you may suggest to them, "Go out and settle the matter between the two of you." But once you have heard their case and have made up your mind which way the judgment is tending, you are not at liberty to say to them, "Go out and settle the matter between the two of you." For it is written, "If you wish to dispose of a dispute that may rush on like water, do so at the trial's beginning—before the arguments are made patent, you may ask that it cease" (Prov. 17:14).[6] Before the arguments are made patent, you may suggest closing the dispute [through arbitration]. But after the arguments are made patent, you may not suggest that the dispute close thus.[7]

202. R. Joseph taught: In the verse "Thou shalt show them . . . the practice that they are to follow" (Exod. 18:20), "the practice" refers to practice in keeping with the letter of the law, and "that they are to follow" refers to decisions that go beyond the letter of the law.[8]

203. R. Yohanan said: Jerusalem was destroyed only because judges based decisions on the letter of the law and refused to go beyond the letter of the law.[9]

204. Some porters [through carelessness] broke a cask of wine belonging to Rabbah bar Bar Hanah, so he seized their garments. When they went and complained to Rav, he said to Rabbah, "Return their garments." Rabbah: "Is that the law?" Rav: "Yes—'that thou mayest walk in the way of good men' " (Prov. 2:20). So Rabbah returned the garments to the porters, who said to him, "We are poor men, and we worked hard all day. We are hungry and do not have a penny." Rav then said to Rabbah, "Go and pay them their wage." Rabbah: "Is that the law?" Rav: "Yes, 'keep the path of the righteous' " (ibid.).[10]

---

1. Mek, *Mishpatim, Kaspa*, 3.
2. Sif Deut., §16.
3. B. Sanh 32b.
4. And no court has a right to hinder the law's course.
5. B. Sanh 6b.
6. Thus, according to Rashi (ad loc.), is the verse to be understood. JV: "The beginning of strife is as when one letteth out water; therefore leave off contention, before the quarrel break out."
7. B. Sanh 6b; Tos Sanh 1:6.
8. B. BM 30b.
9. Ibid.
10. B. BM 83a and En Yaakov, ad loc.

205. The brother of Mari bar Isaac came to see him from Be Hozae, saying, "Divide our father's estate with me." Mari: "I do not know you." When they came to have the dispute adjudicated by R. Hisda, he said to Mari's brother, "Mari spoke properly to you, for it is written, 'Joseph knew his brethren, but they knew him not' [Gen. 42:8], which implies that he left them when he had no beard and met them again when he had one. Go and bring witnesses that you are his brother." The brother: "I have witnesses, but they are afraid of him, because he is a powerful man." So R. Hisda said to Mari, "You go and bring witnesses that he is not your brother." Mari: "Is this the law? The burden of proof lies rather on the claimant." R. Hisda: "This is the way you and all powerful men like you are to be judged."[1]

206. After considering a dispute, the judge acquits the innocent and condemns the guilty. But on seeing that the guilty one is poor, the judge pays the penalty out of his own purse. "Such a judge practiceth justice and charity" (2 Sam. 8:15)—justice to the one and charity to the other: justice to the innocent by repaying him the money owed him, and charity to the guilty one by paying for him out of his own means.[2]

Courts and Judicial Procedure

207. We have been taught that R. Yose said: Formerly there were not many differences of opinion in Israel in matters of law. There were the Sanhedrin of seventy-one judges sitting in the Chamber of Hewn Stone; two courts of twenty-three judges, one sitting at the entrance to the Temple Mount and the other at the entrance to the [Temple] Court; and other courts of twenty-three sitting in various cities in the Land of Israel. When a man needed to inquire about a particular matter, he made inquiry of the court in his city. If there was no court in his city, he went to the court nearest his city. If its members had a tradition concerning this matter, they stated it to him; if not, the inquirer, together with the most expert judge of that court, went to the court situated at the entrance to the Temple Mount. If its members had a relevant tradition, they stated it to these two; if not, the two, together with the most expert judge of that higher court, went to the court situated at the entrance to the Temple Court, and the sage [who differed from his colleagues] declared, "I have expounded the law thus, and my colleagues have expounded it otherwise; I have taught thus, and my colleagues have taught otherwise." If the members of that highest court had a relevant tradition, they stated it to the three inquirers; if not, the members of the three aforementioned courts proceeded to the great court in the Chamber of Hewn Stone. There the Great Sanhedrin sat from the time the morning offering was brought until the time of the evening offering; on Sabbaths and festivals, the Great Sanhedrin sat in the promenade encompassing the Temple Court. The inquiry was then put before them. If they had a relevant tradition, they stated it; if not, they decided the matter by vote. If they who voted "unclean" were in the majority, the matter was declared unclean; if they who voted "clean" were in the majority, the matter was declared clean. The ruling went forth from there and spread throughout Israel. But when Shammai's and Hillel's disciples, who had not waited sufficiently on their masters, increased in number, there were so many differences of opinion in Israel that the Torah became as two Torahs.

Emissaries were sent from the Chamber of Hewn Stone to all Israel to investigate [candidates for judges]. If a candidate was wise, humble, and sin-fearing, and his conduct as a young man was exemplary, so that he was esteemed by his fellow men, the emissaries appointed him judge in his own city. After being appointed judge in his own city, he might in due course be promoted and might [eventually] be seated in the Chamber of Hewn Stone.[3]

208. Civil actions should be tried by three judges, each litigant choosing one judge and both litigants jointly choosing the third. Such is the opinion of R. Meir. But the sages say: The two judges choose the third.

What procedure is followed in judging? The judges are seated, and the litigants stand before them. The plaintiff is the first to speak. If there are witnesses, they are brought into a chamber and earnestly admonished [to tell the truth]. Then they are taken outside, leaving behind the oldest witness, who is asked, "Tell us, how do you know that the defendant owes money to the plaintiff?" If he answers, "He himself told me that he owes the money," or "So-and-so told me that the defendant owes the money," his testimony is invalid unless he declares, "The defendant admitted to the plaintiff in our presence that he owes him two hundred *zuz*." Then the second witness is brought in and similarly examined. If their statements tally, the judges debate the case.

R. Nehemiah observed: Such was the practice of the morally fastidious men in Jerusalem: the judges bring in the litigants and hear what they have to say; then they bring in the witnesses and hear what they have to say. After that, the judges order the litigants and witnesses to leave the court while they debate the case. If two judges find the defendant not liable and one judge finds him liable, he is declared not liable; if two find him liable and one not liable, he is declared liable; if one finds him liable and one not liable, while the third judge says, "I do not know," more judges are added.

Once the verdict is arrived at, the litigants are brought back, and the senior judge says, "So-and so, you are not liable," or "So-and-so, you are liable."

And how do we know that a judge may not say on leaving, "I was for acquittal, but my colleagues were for conviction. What could I do, seeing that they were in the majority"? Of such a judge, it is written, "A base fellow giveth away secrets" (Prov. 11:13).[4]

1. B. BM 39b.
2. B. Sanh 6b.
3. B. Sanh 88b; Tos Sanh 7:1; Tos Hag 2:2.
4. B. Sanh 23a, 29a, and 30b; Tos Sanh 6:3.

209. Capital cases were tried by twenty-three judges.

The Sanhedrin's seating was in a semicircle, the way people sit halfway around a threshing floor, so that the judges could conveniently see one another. The patriarch [who was the chief judge] sat in the center, and the coadjutors at his right and at his left. Before them stood the two court scribes, one to the right and one to the left, and they wrote down the arguments of those who were for acquittal and the arguments of those who were for conviction. R. Judah said: There were three scribes: one wrote down the arguments of those who were for acquittal; another wrote down the arguments of those who were for conviction; and the third wrote down the substance of the arguments of those who were for acquittal as well as the substance of the arguments of those who were for conviction.

In front of them sat three rows of disciples of the wise, each of whom knew the place where he was to sit [in keeping with his rank].

How were witnesses in capital cases earnestly admonished? In capital cases, they were brought in and admonished this way: Perhaps what you say is but conjecture, or hearsay (and thus secondhand testimony), or something heard from a man you consider trustworthy. Perhaps you do not know that we shall test you by a thoroughgoing inquiry? You should know that capital cases are not like civil cases: in civil cases, the guilty makes restitution and is absolved; but in capital cases, the witness is held responsible for the blood of him [who is wrongfully condemned] and for the blood of his posterity [that should have been born to him] to the world's end of time. Thus we find that after Cain slew his brother, he was told, "The bloods of thy brother cry" (Gen. 4:10). Not "the blood of thy brother" but "the bloods of thy brother"—his blood and the blood of his posterity. That is why man was created alone: to show you that if a man causes a single soul to perish, Scripture imputes it to him as though he had destroyed the entire world; conversely, if a man preserves a single soul, Scripture imputes it to him as though he had preserved the entire world. You might be tempted to say, "Why should we get involved in such a miserable business?" Is it not written of such as you, "He being a witness, whether he hath seen or known, if he do not utter it, then shall he bear his iniquity" (Lev. 5:1)? And should you say, "Why should we be responsible for the blood of this man?"—is it not written of such as you, "When the wicked perish, there is joy" (Prov. 11:10).

The judges used to examine each of the witnesses with seven searching queries: In what septennate of the Jubilee? In what year? In what month? On what day of the month? On what day [in the week]? In what hour? In what place? [They also asked]: Do you know him? Did you warn him?

The judge who crossexamines most thoroughly is most praiseworthy. Ben Zakkai once examined witnesses with regard to stalks of figs. He asked the witnesses, "Were the stalks of the fig tree thin or thick? Were the figs black or white?"

If the testimony of the witnesses tallies, the judges begin to examine the evidence in favor of the accused.

Should one of the disciples say, "I wish to plead for conviction," he is silenced. But if he says, "I wish to plead for acquittal," he is greeted with friendly countenance, brought up to the dais, and seated among the judges, and he does not come down from there the entire day. If there is any substance in what he says, he is listened to. Even if the accused himself says, "I wish to plead for my acquittal," he is listened to, provided there is some substance in what he says.

If at this stage the judges find the accused innocent, he is set free; if not, the continuation of his trail is postponed to the following day, while the judges go about in pairs [discussing the charge], eating little, drinking no wine at all the entire day, and debating the matter through the entire night. Early the next day, the judges come to the court. The judge who favors acquittal says, "I held him innocent [yesterday], and I still hold him innocent"; and the judge who favors conviction says, "I held him guilty [yesterday], and I still hold him guilty." The judge who [the day before] argued for conviction may now argue for acquittal, but the judge who [the day before] argued for acquittal may not retract his previous opinion and argue for conviction. If on that day the judges find the accused innocent, he is set free: if not, the judges proceed to vote. If twelve favor acquittal and eleven favor conviction, he is set free; if twelve favor conviction and eleven favor acquittal, or even if eleven favor acquittal and eleven favor conviction, and one says, "I do not know," or even if twenty-two favor acquittal or favor conviction, and one says, "I do not know," more judges are to be added. Up to what number of judges may be added? They may be added by twos up to seventy-one. If thirty-six then favor acquittal and thirty-five favor conviction, the accused is held innocent; if thirty-six favor conviction and thirty-five favor acquittal, the judges are to debate with one another until one of those who favored conviction comes to agree with the opinion of those who favored acquittal.

If at the end of the trial the sentence [of stoning] has been passed, the condemned is taken out to be stoned. (The place of stoning was outside of the court [far away].) A man is stationed at the entrance to the court with kerchiefs in his hand, and another man is mounted on a horse, some distance away [but near enough] to see him. If one [of the judges] says, "I have something to argue in favor of acquittal," that man waves his kerchiefs, and the man on the horse trots up to stop the one condemned [from continuing on his way to be stoned]. Even if the condemned himself says, "I have something more to argue in favor of my acquittal," he must be brought back, as many as four or five times, provided that there is some substance in what he says. If the judges then find a reason for acquittal, he is set free. If not, he goes forth to be stoned. A herald goes out before him [crying], "So-and-so the son of So-and-so is going forth to be stoned for having committed such-and-such offense, and witnesses against him are So-and-so and So-and-so. If any man knows an argument in favor of acquittal, let him come and state it."

When the condemned is about ten cubits from the place of stoning, he is told, "Make your confession," for the way of all who are to be executed is to make confession, since everyone who makes such confession has a share in the world-to-come. If he does not know how to make confession, he is told, "Say, 'May my death be atonement for all my sins.' "

The condemned is not buried in the burial place of his fathers. Two burial places were prepared by the court, one for those who were stoned or burned, and one for those who were beheaded or strangled.

Once the flesh has decayed, the bones are gathered and buried in their proper place.[1] [After the condemned has been put to death], his kinsmen come and greet the judges and the witnesses, as if to say, "We have nothing in our hearts against you, for you have pronounced a true judgment."[2]

210. Our masters taught: It happened once that a man who was taken to be executed said, "If I am guilty of this sin, may my death not atone for any of my sins; but if I am innocent of this sin, may my death expiate all my sins. [I declare that] the court and all Israel are guiltless, but the witnesses—may they never be forgiven." When the sages heard of the matter, they said: It is impossible to recall him, since the sentence has already been pronounced. Let him be executed, and may the collar [of responsibility] hang on the necks of the witnesses.[3]

211. Our masters taught: What is meant by evidence based on conjecture? When the judge suggests to the witnesses: Perhaps you saw the accused running after another man into a ruin, and you ran after him and found him, sword in hand, with blood dripping from it, while the murdered man was writhing [in agony]. If this is all you saw, you saw nothing [that constitutes evidence].

We have been taught that R. Simeon ben Shetah said: May I never behold consolation if I did not see a man running after another man into a ruin. I ran after him and saw him, sword in hand, with blood dripping from it, and the murdered man writhing. I called to him: You criminal! Who slew this man? It must be either you or I! But what can I do, since your blood [i.e., life] does not rest in my hand, for the Torah says, "At the mouth of two witnesses . . . shall he that is to die be put to death" (Deut. 17:6)? May He who knows men's thoughts exact vengeance from him who slew his fellow man!

It is related that before they moved from the place, a serpent came and bit the murderer, and he died.[4]

212. R. Hiyya bar R. Ashi said in the name of R. Hisda: The man who is led out to be executed is given a grain of frankincense in a goblet of wine, in order to make him numb, in keeping with "Give strong drink unto him that is about to perish, and wine unto the bitter in soul" (Prov. 31:6).

We have been taught that the noblewomen of Jerusalem volunteered to provide the wine.[5]

1. The family's burial place.
2. Sanh 4:1–6:6; P. Sanh 4:9–12, 22b; Tos Sanh 8:2–5.
3. B. Sanh 44b.
4. B. Sanh 37b.
5. B. Sanh 43b.

213. R. Nahman said in the name of Rabbah bar Abbahu: "Thou shalt love thy neighbor as thyself" (Lev. 19:18) implies also: Choose an easy death for him.[6]

214. "His body shall not remain all night upon the tree . . . for he that is hanged is a reproach unto God" (Deut. 21:23). We have been taught that R. Meir said: By what parable may the meaning of the verse be made clear? By the one of twin brothers who lived in a certain city. One was appointed king, and the other took to brigandage. The king commanded that his brother be hanged, and whoever saw the corpse said, "The king is hanged."[7] When that happened, the king commanded that the corpse be taken down.[8]

215. R. Meir said: When a man is in distress, what does the Presence say? "My head weighs Me down, My arm weighs Me down"—if one dare attribute such words to God.[9] Now if He who is everywhere grieves over the blood of the wicked that is shed, how much more and more by far over the blood of the righteous.[10]

216. R. Akiva said: Where is the proof that a Sanhedrin that condemns a person to death is to taste nothing at all that day? The verse "Ye shall eat nothing at [the shedding of] blood" (Lev. 19:26).[11]

217. A Sanhedrin that issues a sentence of execution once in seven years is a murderous tribunal. R. Eleazar ben Azariah said: Once in seventy years. R. Tarfon and R. Akiva said: If we were members of the Sanhedrin, no man would ever be executed. To this, Rabban Simeon ben Gamaliel replied: Yes; and they would thus increase shedders of blood in Israel.[12]

218. A sentence postponed overnight is a sentence nullified.[13]

219. No punishment may be imposed unless a warning preceded it.[14]

220. No mercy may be shown in a matter of law.[15]

221. Whoever judges a fool will himself be judged.[16]

222. When the court declares a thing ownerless (*hefker*), ownerless it is. R. Isaac said: What is the proof for the

6. B. Sanh 45a.
7. Man, having been created in God's image, resembles God.
8. B. Sanh 46b.
9. Because of this man's suffering, God's sympathy impels Him to say, "I, too, am weighed down by suffering."
10. B. Sanh 46a.
11. B. Sanh 63a.
12. B. Mak 7a.
13. B. Sanh 95a.
14. B. Yoma 81a; Sif Deut., §173.
15. B. Ket 84a.
16. Lam. R., proem 14.

dictum "When the court declares a thing ownerless, ownerless it is"? The verse "Whosoever came not within three days, according to the counsel of the princes and the elders, all his substance should be forfeited, and himself separated from the congregation of the captivity" (Ezra 10:8). However, R. Eleazar stated that [the deduction is made] from "These are the inheritances, which Eleazar the Priest and Joshua the son of Nun, and the heads of the fathers' houses of the tribes of the children of Israel, distributed for inheritance" (Josh. 19:51). [Since "heads of the tribes" would have been sufficient], what analogy between "heads" and "fathers" is suggested [by what appears to be a gratuitous introduction of the phrase "fathers' houses"]? The suggestion is that even as fathers may distribute whatever they wish as an inheritance to their children, so may the heads [of courts] distribute whatever they wish as an inheritance to the people.[1]

223. No court can annul the ordinances of another court, unless it is superior to it in wisdom and in number.[2]

224. R. Hiyya bar Abba said: He who [without witnesses] pleads against an act of the court[3] [contending that he had already paid] says nothing [that is taken notice of].[4]

225. When a man leaves court deprived of the cloak he stole, he should sing a song of relief as he goes on his way.[5]

226. Simeon ben Shetah said: Interrogate witnesses diligently, but be careful in what you say, lest from your words they learn how to speak falsely.[6]

227. The oath taken by witnesses and the oath imposed by judges may be uttered in any language. How is the witnesses' oath administered? Witnesses are made to swear five times in any language they understand, and if [swearing falsely], they answer [each time], "Amen," they are liable. How is the oath imposed by judges administered? When a man is bound to swear an oath to his fellow man, the court says to the man: Know that the entire world, all of it, was shaken when the Holy One said at Sinai, "Thou shalt not take the Name of the Lord thy God in vain" (Exod. 20:7). For with regard to all transgressions mentioned in Torah, there is the possibility, according to Scripture, of being held "guiltless" (ibid.); but with regard to one who swears a false oath, Scripture states, "He will not be held guiltless" (ibid.).[7]

228. Three the Holy One hates: him who says one thing with his mouth and another in his heart; him who possesses evidence in favor of his neighbor but fails to testify in his behalf; and him who, seeing something improper in his neighbor, acts as the sole witness against him.[8] Such a thing happened when Tobiah sinned, and Zigud came and testified against him before R. Papa, whereupon R. Papa had Zigud flogged. When Zigud protested, "Tobiah sinned, and Zigud gets flogged!" R. Papa replied, "Yes, because it is said, 'One witness shall not rise up against a man' [Deut. 19:15], yet you were the only one testifying against him—all you do is bring ill repute upon him."[9]

229. R. Sheshet said in the name of R. Eleazar ben Azariah: He who speaks slander, who accepts slander, or who gives false testimony against his neighbor deserves to be cast to the dogs.[10]

230. A witness who has testified [in favor of someone] cannot [retract and] testify again [against him].[11]

231. R. Hisda said: Evidence may be remembered for sixty years—longer than that, it may not be remembered.[12]

232. A litigant's admission is worth one hundred witnesses.[13]

233. It is told that, in the days of King Solomon, three men were journeying on the eve of Sabbath, just as the Sabbath day's sanctity set in. So, saying to one another, "Come, let us hide our money in one place," they went and hid their money in a place agreed upon. At midnight, one of the three arose, took the money, and hid it in another place. At the Sabbath's outgoing, when they were ready to continue their journey, they went to the place [where they had hid their money], and, not finding it, one said to the other, "You stole it." The other said to the one, "You stole it. "So they went to try the matter before King Solomon. Now, when they had set forth to him all that happened, he said, "In the morning, there will be judgment" (Jer. 21:12). Then what did he do? He sat down and, with his wisdom and understanding, sought to figure out a response whereby he might catch them through their own words.

When they came back to him, he said to them, "I hear of you that you are masters of Torah and masters of wisdom and law. So I beg permission to consult with you about a suit in law: a certain king sent me a request for advice on something that happened in his realm. A young boy and a young girl who lived in the same courtyard came to long for each other. So the young boy said to the young girl, 'Come, let us make a sworn stipulation between us that whenever anyone wishes to betroth you, you will not respond to him except with my permission.' She so swore to him.

1. B. Yev 89b.
2. B. Meg 2a.
3. Such as one requiring him to pay a marriage settlement or provide sustenance for a wife and daughter.
4. B. BM 17a.
5. Happy that he was relieved of something he had no right to. B. Sanh 7a.
6. Avot 1:9.
7. B. Shevu 38b–39a; Tos Sot 7:12.
8. Since the testimony of a sole witness is not accepted in court, he is in effect a slanderer.
9. B. Pes 113b.
10. B. Pes 118a.
11. B. Ket 18b.
12. B. Ket 20b.
13. B. Kid 65b.

"After a while, the young girl was betrothed, but when the groom came to her, she said to him, 'I will not respond to you until I go to So-and so and ask his permission, since this is what I swore to him.'

"What did she do then? She went to her childhood sweetheart and said to him, 'Take much silver and gold, and release me to him who is to be my husband.' He replied, 'Since you have been faithful to your oath, I release you to him who is to be your husband, and I will take nothing from you.' And to the young man who came with her, he said, 'Rejoice in your lot in peace.'

"So off they went. On their way back, they were attacked by brigands. Among them was an elderly man who seized for himself the young woman, all the silver and gold that she and her betrothed had, and all the ornaments worn by them; further, he wanted to rape her. She said to the elderly brigand, 'I beseech you to wait awhile, until I tell you something that has happened to me.' And she told him the whole story. She added, 'If my betrothed, though in the vigor of youth, overcame his impulse and would not touch me, how much more and more should you who are already on in years [restrain yourself]! Take all the silver and gold that I have, and let me depart in peace, to go with him who is to be my husband.' When the elderly man heard her, he lifted his eyes to heaven and began to reason with himself: I, who am on in years, and day by day drawing nearer to the edge of my grave—shall I now do such a [sinful] thing?

"What did he do? He released her, and she went off with her betrothed. He even returned to her all the ornaments, all the silver and gold that he had taken from them, refusing to touch anything that they had or to benefit at all from anything that was theirs.

"Now, the king has sent a request to me to explicate which of these people is the most praiseworthy. Tell me your judgment."

The first of the three men spoke up and said, "I praise the young woman who stood by her oath." The second spoke up and said, "I praise her betrothed, who conquered his impulse and did not touch her." The third spoke up and said: "I praise the brigand who despoiled them of their possessions and then returned all the possessions he had taken, denying himself the use of them."

Solomon immediately spoke up and said, "If, merely from hearing the story, the third of you, who was not there, thought about the material possessions he had not seen, how much more would he think of them in the present instance!" King Solomon ordered that he be put in fetters and flogged until he confessed in the king's presence and revealed the place where he had hidden the money.

"Then they saw that the wisdom of God was within him to do justice" (1 Kings 3:28).[1]

234. There is the story of Alexander of Macedon coming to pay a visit to a king at the end of the world,[2] who showed him much silver and gold. Alexander said, "I have not come to see your silver and gold—it is your customs and legal practices I have come to observe."

As Alexander and the king were engaged in discourse, two men came before the king for judgment. One said, "My lord king, I bought a ruin from this man, and, while clearing it, I found a treasure; so I said to him, 'Take your treasure. I bought a ruin,—I did not buy a treasure.' " The other replied, "Just as you are afraid of the punishment for robbery, so am I afraid of it. The fact is, I sold you the ruin with everything in it—from the depths of the earth to the heights of heaven."

The king addressed one of them and asked him, "Have you a son?" He replied, "Yes." The king asked the other, "Have you a daughter?" He replied, "Yes." "Go, then," said the king, "wed the one to the other, and let the two make use of the treasure." Alexander showed his amazement at this verdict. The king asked, "Have I not judged well?" Alexander: "Yes, well." The king: "If such a case had come up before you in your country, how would you have handled it?" Alexander replied, "I would have chopped off the head of the one and the head of the other, and the treasure would have gone to the king's house." The king: "Does the sun shine where you dwell?" Alexander: "Yes." "Does rain come down upon you?" Alexander: "Yes." The king: "There are small cattle in your country, are there not?" Alexander: "Yes." The king: "May the breath of life in such a man as you be blasted out! It is only for the sake of the small cattle that the sun still shines for you, that the rain still comes down upon you."[3]

235. When Levi visited a certain place, a man came before him and said: So-and-so *kava*'ed me. Since Levi did not know what the man meant, he went and inquired at the house of study, where he was told that the man meant, "So-and-so robbed me," as in the verse 'Will a man rob [*yikba*] God?' " (Mal. 3:8).

Rava of Barnash said to R. Ashi: Had I been there, I would have asked the man, "How did he *kava* you? Of what did he *kava* you? Why did he *kava* you?" And I would have found out the meaning of the word.[4]

236. Hanan the Scoundrel boxed a man on the ear and was brought before R. Huna, who said to Hanan, "Pay the man half a *zuz*." Hanan had a *zuz*—a defectively minted one—and he wanted the man to give him back half a *zuz* in change. Since the man refused to do so, Hanan boxed him on the ear a second time, and let him keep the whole *zuz*.[5]

Cities of Refuge

237. "Ye shall appoint you cities to be cities of refuge for you, that the manslayer that killeth . . . may flee thither" (Num. 35:11). R. Hama bar Hanina began his

1. Midrash Aseret ha-Dibberot (BhM 1:86–87).
2. Believed to have been Africa, where, according to authors of antiquity, men lived ideal lives. The Aramaic *Katzia* is taken to mean "end of the world." See Saul Lieberman's note in PRKM, p. 274.
3. Tanhuma, *Emor*, §6.
4. B. RH 26b.
5. B. BK 37a.

discourse on this theme with "Good and upright is the Lord, therefore doth He instruct sinners in the way" (Ps. 25:8). If He instructs sinners, how much more so the righteous!

R. Simeon ben Lakish opened his discourse [on this theme] with these [two verses]: "And if a man lie not in wait, but God cause it to come to hand; then I will appoint thee a place whither he may flee" (Exod. 21:13) and "As saith the proverb of the ancients: Out of the wicked cometh forth wickedness; but my hand shall not be upon thee" (1 Sam. 24:14). Of whom does Scripture speak? Of two men, each of whom had slain a person. One had slain unwittingly, and the other with intent, and there were no witnesses against either of the two. So the Holy One has the two men come to the same inn, where the one who has slain with intent sits under a ladder, and the one who has slain unwittingly comes down the ladder, falls on top of the one who has slain with intent, and kills him. Thus, he who has slain with intent is slain, while he who has slain unwittingly goes into banishment [to a city of refuge].[1]

238. "Ye shall appoint you cities to be cities of refuge" (Num. 35:11). Moses asked, "Master of the universe! If a man in the north or in the south unwittingly slays another, how is he to know where the cities of refuge are, so that he may flee there?" God replied, "Thou shalt prepare (*takhin*) thee the way" (Deut. 19:3), implying: You are to prepare direct (*tekhavven*) roads, so that a manslayer shall not miss the way and, upon being found by the blood avenger, be killed. Still Moses asked, "But how?" God replied, "Set up posts pointing toward the cities of refuge, and on each post let there be an inscription "Manslayer—to the cities of refuge."[2]

239. We have been taught that R. Eliezer ben Jacob said: The words *miklat*, *miklat* [refuge, refuge] were inscribed at crossroads, so that the manslayer might see them and turn in the right direction. "What is the proof?" R. Kahana asked. The verse "Thou shalt prepare thee the way"—prepare suitable directions to the roads.[3]

240. "He showeth sinners the way" (Ps. 25:8). R. Avin said: At every *mil* along the way there was a station, and at each station there was a figure whose hand pointed toward the cities of refuge.[4]

241. Our masters taught: A private road should be four cubits wide, a public road sixteen cubits, and a road to the cities of refuge thirty-two cubits.[5]

242. "Thou shalt prepare thee the way" (Deut. 19:3). You are to prepare side roads leading into the main roads [to the cities of refuge].[6]

1. B. Mak 10b.
2. Num. R. 3:13; Tanhuma B, *Mas'e*, §8.
3. B. Mak 10b; Tos Mak 3:5.
4. MTeh 25:10; Yalkut, *Shofetim*, §519.
5. B. BB 100a–b.
6. Sif Deut., §180.

243. We have been taught: Neither small fortified villages nor large cities are to be picked as cities of refuge, but only midsized towns located in the vicinity of water. Where there is no water at hand, it should be brought there [by pipes]. Cities of refuge are to be located only near markets [where sufficient food is available] and only in well-populated areas. If the population diminishes, it is to be increased: if the number of residents in the town has fallen off, priests, Levites, and Israelites should be brought in. No weapons—not even hunters' gear—should be sold there. Such is the opinion of R. Nehemiah, but the sages permit such sales. However, both agree that no traps are to be set, nor are nooses to be knotted in these towns, so that a blood avenger may not be tempted to acquire those weapons while visiting a city of refuge.

R. Isaac asked: What is the proof [for all the foregoing provisions to protect the manslayer]? The verse "That fleeing unto one of these cities he might live" (Deut. 4:42), which means: Provide him with whatever he needs, so that he may remain alive.[7]

244. "He must remain in his city of refuge until the death of the high priest" (Num. 35:28). For that reason, mothers of high priests used to provide food and clothing for manslayers, so that they should not pray for their sons' death.[8]

245. "Ye shall appoint you cities to be cities of refuge for you, that the manslayer that killeth . . . may flee thither" (Num. 35:11). R. Eliezer ben Jacob said: What does Scripture imply by repeating the word "thither" three times?[9] That there is to be the manslayer's dwelling, there is to be his dying, and there is to be his burial.[10]

For the Public Weal

246. Our masters taught: A man should not clear stones out of his own domain and throw them into the public domain.

There is the story of a man who was clearing stones out of his own domain and throwing them into the public domain. A pious man, seeing him, said to him, "Wretch, why do you remove stones from a domain that is not yours to a domain that is yours?" The man just laughed at him. After a time, that man had to sell his field, and, walking on that very public domain, he stumbled over the stones [he had thrown]. He said, "How well that pious man put it: 'Why do you remove stones from a domain that is not yours to a domain that is yours?' "[11]

247. If a man digs a pit in his private domain and opens it onto a public domain, he is liable [even if someone falls into the part of the opening that is in his private domain].[12]

7. B. Mak 10a.
8. B. Mak 11a.
9. In verses 11, 15, and 25.
10. Tos Mak 3:5.
11. His domain may not remain his own, whereas his right to use the public domain will always remain his. B. Bk 50b.
12. If the pit had its opening only in the private domain, there would have been no liability.

Our masters taught: If a man digs a pit and leaves it open, but then turns its ownership over to the public, he is exempt from liability. Such was the custom of Nehunia, a digger of pits, ditches, and caves. He used to dig them and leave them open, but he turned their ownership over to the public. When the sages heard of his procedure, they said, "This man is fulfilling the *Halakhah* just mentioned."[1]

248. [Even during the rainy season], if a man pours out water into the public domain and another is injured thereby, he is liable for the other's injury. If a man hides [but not thoroughly] thorns or glass fragments in the public domain, or covers his fence with thorns [which jut out into the public domain], or allows his fence to collapse into the public domain [and does not clear it at once], and others are injured thereby, he is liable for their injury.

Our masters taught: The pious men of old used to bury their thorns and their broken pieces of glass in the middle of their fields at a depth of three handbreadths, so that the plow could not bring them up again.[2] R. Sheshet used to throw them in the fire. Rava threw them into the Tigris.[3]

249. We have been taught that R. Nathan said: Where is the proof that a man should not raise a vicious dog in his house, nor set up a rickety ladder in his house? The verse "Thou bring not blood upon thy house" (Deut. 22:8).[4]

250. Our masters taught: A man should not rear a dog unless he keeps it chained. But he may rear one in a city near the border, chaining it during the day and letting it loose at night.

R. Dostai of Birei expounded: The verse "And when it rested, Moses said: 'Return, O Lord, unto the myriads and thousands of Israel' " (Num. 10:36) implies that the Presence will rest on no fewer than two thousand and two myriads[5] of Israel. Should the number of Israelites happen to be two thousand and two myriads less one, and among them is a pregnant woman capable of completing the minimum number, but a dog barks at her and she miscarries, the dog's owner would turn out to be the one who forces the Presence to remove itself from Israel.[6]

251. A story is told of a [pregnant] woman who went into a house to do some baking, and a dog barked at her. When its master reassured her, "Don't fear the dog—its teeth are gone," she replied, "Keep your favors—throw them to the thorns! The fetus has already been uprooted."[7]

1. B. BK 50a.
2. "So that the plow could not bring them up again"—Rome ms. of Maimonides, Code; BR: "so that the plow would not be hindered."
3. B. BK 30a.
4. B. BK 15b.
5. The plurals "thousands" and "myriads" are taken to signify at least two of each.
6. B. BK 83a; B. Yev 64a.
7. B. BK 83a.

252. R. Judah said in the name of Rav: When a city has [steep] grades up and down, men and cattle in it are old by the time they reach half their life span.[8]

253. On the fifteenth of the month of Adar, officials must go forth to clear the roads of thorns, to mend plazas and streets, to measure the dimensions of ritual baths, and to attend to other public needs.

And what is the proof that if the officials fail to go forth and attend to all these things, any blood [shed as a result of their neglect] is regarded by Scripture as though the officials themselves had shed it? The verse "And so blood be upon thee" (Deut. 19:10).[9]

254. "To him that setteth right the way will I show the salvation of God" (Ps. 50:23) applies to people who light lamps in order to provide light for the public. For R. Simeon ben Lakish said: Saul merited kingship only because his grandfather had lit lamps for the public.[10] It is said there were dark alleys between his own house and the house of study, and he used to light lamps in them to give light to the public.[11]

255. On one occasion, when R. Judah, R. Yose, and R. Simeon ben Yohai were seated in teachers' chairs, R. Judah commenced the discussion by observing, "How noble are the works of this Roman nation! They laid out streets, they built bridges, they erected baths." R. Yose remained silent, but R. Simeon ben Yohai spoke up and said, "All that they have done, they did for themselves: they laid out streets to settle harlots in them; baths, to pamper themselves; bridges, to levy tolls."[12]

256. Fruits and items such as wines, oils, and various kinds of flour, which are necessary to sustain life, may not be hoarded; but one may hoard spices, cumin, and pepper. These restrictions apply only to what one buys in the markets; one may hoard what is grown in one's own field or vineyard. In the Land of Israel, one may store fruits for the following three years: the year preceding the sabbatical year, the sabbatical year, and the year following the sabbatical year.[13] In years of scarcity, one may not hoard even one *kav* of carobs,[14] because such hoarding will result in privation for Israel.[15]

In the Land of Israel, one may not profit from things that are life's necessities, such as wines, oils, and various kinds of flour.[16]

8. B. Er 56a.
9. B. MK 5a and 6a.
10. The comment is no doubt inspired by 1 Chron. 8:33, where Saul's grandfather is called Ner, "the lamplighter."
11. Lev. R. 9:2.
12. B. Shab 33b.
13. During the year preceding the sabbatical year, produce must be stored for the following year; and during the year following it, there will be no produce until its conclusion.
14. The cheapest fruit.
15. "Will result in privation for Israel"—Rome ms. of Maimonides, Code; BR: "will bring a curse on prices."
16. B. BB 90b–91a; Tos AZ 4:1.

257. Our masters taught: One is not permitted to export from the Land of Israel items such as wines, oils, and various kinds of flour, which are life's necessities. R. Judah ben Betera allows the export of wine, since lack of it reduces frivolity.[1]

258. One should not raise small cattle in the Land of Israel. They may, however, be raised in Syria or in the desert regions of the Land of Israel. One should not breed poultry in Jerusalem on account of the holy offerings,[2] nor may priests do so throughout the entire Land of Israel, on account of their food, which has to be ritually clean. One may not raise pigs in any place whatsoever. No man should raise a dog unless he keeps it chained. One may not spread nets to snare doves unless these are a distance of thirty *ris*[3] from inhabited areas.[4]

Even though the sage said, "One may not raise small cattle," one may nevertheless rear large cattle, for no restriction is imposed on a community unless a majority of the community can abide it: small cattle can be imported from outside the Land; large cattle cannot be imported from outside the Land.[5]

259. Just as the sages said, "One may not raise small cattle," so they also said, "One may not raise small wild beasts." However, R. Ishmael said: One may raise village dogs,[6] cats, monkeys, and porcupines, as these help rid the house [of rodents].[7]

260. Our masters taught: There was once a certain pious man who coughed [blood] from his heart, and the physicians who were consulted said that there was no remedy for him unless he sucked warm milk every morning. So a she-goat was brought to him and fastened to the legs of his bed, and every morning he sucked milk directly from its udder. After some days, his colleagues came to visit him, but when they saw the goat fastened to the legs of his bed, they drew back, saying, "An armed robber[8] is in the house of this man—how can we come visit him?" Nevertheless, they sat down and, after inquiring into his conduct, found no fault in him except the sin of keeping the she-goat. At the time of his death, he too proclaimed, "I know that no sin can be imputed to me except that of the she-goat, when I contravened the opinion of my colleagues."[9]

261. We have been taught that a disciple of the wise may not live in a city that does not have the following ten institutions and officials: a court that imposes floggings and fines, a charity fund collected by two officials and distributed by three, a synagogue, a [public] bathhouse, a [public] privy, a physician, a cupper, a scribe, [a ritual slaughterer], and a teacher of young children. The sages said in the name of R. Akiva: Also several kinds of fruit trees, because their fruit gives light to the eyes.[10]

262. R. Huna said: A disciple of the wise may not live in a city that has no vegetable garden.[11]

263. "Come, my Beloved, and let us go out into the field" (Song 7:12). The congregation of Israel pleaded with the Holy One: Do not judge me as You judge dwellers in big cities, among whom there exist robbery, unchastity, meaningless oaths, and false oaths.[12]

264. R. Yose son of R. Hanina said: Where is the proof that dwelling in big cities is hard? The verse "The people blessed all the men that willingly offered themselves to dwell in Jerusalem" (Neh. 11:2).[13]

265. The sages said in the name of Rav: A man should always see to it that he dwells in a city whose settlement is recent, for inasmuch as its settlement is recent, its iniquities are few, as Lot said, "Behold now, this city is recent, so one should flee there: [its iniquities are] few" (Gen. 19:20).[14] Because its settlement is recent, its iniquities are few.[15]

Widespread Trouble and the Community's Fast

266. Our masters taught: When Israel are in distress, and one of their number separates himself from them, the two ministering angels who accompany every individual come and place their hands on his head and say, "So-and-so here, who separated himself from the community, will not behold the comforting of the community."

We have also been taught: When the community is in distress, let no man say, "I will go to my house, eat and drink, and live it up." But if a man does so nevertheless, Scripture says of him, "And behold joy and gladness, slaying oxen and killing sheep, eating flesh and drinking wine—'Let us eat and drink, for tomorrow we shall die' " (Isa. 22:13). What follows this verse? "And the Lord of hosts revealed Himself in mine ears: Surely this iniquity shall not be expiated by you till ye die" (Isa. 22:14). This is the conduct of the ordinary man [who is afraid of death]. But what does Scripture say of the conduct of a wicked man? "Come ye [says he], I will fetch wine, and we will fill ourselves with strong drink; and tomorrow shall be as this day" (Isa. 56:12). What follows this verse? "The righteous perisheth, and no man layeth it to heart . . . that the righteous is taken away because of the

1. B. BB 90b.
2. These might become unclean through contact with the unclean insects that infest fowl.
3. Four miles.
4. To make certain that no privately owned doves would be snared.
5. B. BK 79b.
6. They are small and harmless.
7. B. BK 80a.
8. For it grazes in the fields of other people, and thus "robs" the public.
9. They ruled that a goat may not be raised even when bound to a bedstead. B. BK 80a.
10. B. Sanh 17b.
11. B. Er 55b.
12. B. Er 21b.
13. B. Ket 110b.
14. JV: "Behold now, this city is near to flee unto, and it is a little one."
15. B. Shab 10b.

wickedness of such as he" (Isa. 57:1). Therefore, a man should share in the distress of the community. Thus we find that Moses our teacher shared in the distress of the community, as is said, "But Moses' hands were heavy; and they took a stone, and put it under him, and he sat thereon" (Exod. 17:12). But did not Moses have at least one bolster or cushion to sit on? However, Moses said to himself: Since Israel are in distress, I, too, will share their distress with them. For he who shares in the distress of the community will deserve to behold the community's comforting. Should a man say, "Who is going to testify against me?"—the very stones of his house and the beams on his roof will testify against him, as is written, "For the stone shall cry out of the wall, and the beam out of the timber shall answer it" (Hab. 2:11).[1]

267. "Miriam died there. . . . And there was no water for the congregation, and they assembled themselves together against Moses and against Aaron" (Num. 20:1–2). When Miriam died, and Moses and Aaron were occupied with her [funeral], Israel were seeking water, which they could not find. So they gathered together against Moses and Aaron. When the two saw them coming, Moses said to Aaron, "Can you tell me what this assembly means?" Aaron replied, "Are they not children of Abraham, Isaac, and Jacob, themselves bestowers of loving-kindness, and children of bestowers of loving-kindness?" Moses said, "You do not know how to distinguish between one assembly and another. This is not an assembly bent on doing what is right, but one bent on destruction. Had it been an assembly bent on doing what is right, officers of thousands and officers of hundreds would have been at its head. Yet you say they are come to bestow loving-kindness!"

At once the assembly spoke contentiously against Moses, as is said, "The people strove with Moses" (Num. 20:3). When Moses and Aaron saw their angry faces, they fled to the Tent of Meeting. By what parable may their flight be illustrated? By the one of a notable who fled to the royal palace when the people of his province were stirred up. "And the glory of the Lord appeared unto them" (Num. 20:6).[2] The Holy One said to the servants of the community, "Leave this place quickly. My children are near death with thirst, and you sit here mourning for that old woman [Miriam]."[3]

268. R. Yohanan said: There are three things the Holy One Himself proclaims, namely, famine, plenty, and a good leader. Famine, for it is said, "The Lord hath called for a famine" (2 Kings 8:1); plenty, for it is said, "I will call for the corn, and will increase it" (Ezek. 36:29); and a good leader, for it is said, "See, I have called by name Bezalel, the son of Uri" (Exod. 31:2).[4]

269. The alarm should be sounded on account of any visitation that may come upon a community.

If rain has not come down upon a city, or if there is an epidemic in it, or if its houses are collapsing, that city should fast and sound the alarm, while the people in surrounding towns should fast but not sound the alarm. R. Akiva said: They should only sound the alarm; they need not fast.

On the following occasions, the alarm should be sounded everywhere: on account of a plague of blight, mildew, locust, hoppers, wild beasts, and the enemy's sword, because each is a moving plague. Regarding any other visitations that may suddenly come upon a community, such as epidemic eruptions in the skin, grasshoppers, flies, hornets, mosquitoes, and bands of serpents and scorpions, no alarm is sounded [in public services], but a cry is raised [by private recitation of prayers]. R. Akiva said: For blight and mildew, the alarm must be sounded in whatever measure they appear. For locusts and hoppers, the alarm must be sounded at once, even if only one of these winged creatures appears anywhere in the Land of Israel.

The story is told of certain elders who traveled from Jerusalem to their own cities and decreed a fast, because in Ashkelon there was seen a blight which injured just enough grain to bake one ovenful [of bread]. They also decreed a fast because wolves had devoured two children on the other side of the Jordan. R. Yose said: The fast was decreed not because the wolves had devoured children, but merely because wolves had been seen.

For the following, the alarm should be sounded even on the Sabbath: for a city surrounded by heathens or threatened by a flooding river, or for a ship about to founder in the sea. R. Yose said: It is to be sounded to secure people's help, but not by way of crying [to God]. Simeon the Temanite said: The alarm may also be sounded for an epidemic. But the other sages did not agree with him.[5]

270. What is the order [of service during the last seven] days of fasting?[6] The Ark is taken out to the broad place of the town, and wood ashes are placed on it, on the head of the patriarch, and on the head of the president of the Sanhedrin. Everyone else present takes some ashes and puts them on his own head. The eldest among them admonishes them with these words: Our brethren, Scripture does not say of the people of Nineveh, "God saw their sackcloth and their fasting," but "God saw their works, in that they turned from their evil way" (Jon. 3:10); and elsewhere in an utterance received from God, it is said, "Rend your heart and not your garments" (Joel 2:13). Let no man feel too ashamed to confess before his fellow, too ashamed to make amends for his wrongdoing. It is better to feel shame before his fellow and for his wrongdoing than to have himself and his children distressed by famine. If a man is holding an [unclean] reptile [wrongdoing] in his hand, even if he immerses himself in the water of Siloam—indeed, in all the water of creation—he will never become clean. But once he flings the reptile from his hand, an immersion in a mere forty *seah* of water will be effective in cleansing him.

---

1. B. Ta 11a.
2. The next verse is a command to act, which the commentator paraphrases.
3. Yalkut, *Hukkat*, §763, which quotes Yelammedenu.
4. B. Ber 55a.
5. B. Ta 18b, 19a, and 22b; B. BK 80b.
6. See Ta 1:6.

Our masters, as mentioned earlier, taught: The eldest among them addresses them with words of admonition. If an elder is present, he is the one who addresses them; if not, a sage addresses them; and if not, a man of imposing presence addresses them, as follows: "Our brethren, neither sackcloth nor fasting is of any effect, but only penitence and good deeds, for we find that Scripture does not say of the men of Nineveh, 'And God saw their sackcloth and their fasting,' but, 'God saw their works, in that they turned from their evil way' " (Jon. 3:10).

"But let them be covered with sackcloth, both man and beast" (Jon. 3:8). What did they do with the beasts? They penned the dams separately, and their sucklings separately, and said, "Master of the universe, if You show no mercy to us, we will show no mercy to these."

"And let them cry unto God by speaking of His might" (Jon. 3:8). What did they say? They said, "Master of the universe, if one can be humbled, and the other cannot [i.e., One is mighty, and the other is not], if One is [invariably] righteous and the other is [not infrequently] wicked, which of the two should yield?"

"Let them turn, everyone, from his evil way and from the violence that is in their hands" (Jon. 3:8). What is the meaning of "from the violence that is in their hands"? Samuel said: If one had stolen a joist, even though he had used it in building a fort, he should raze the entire fort and restore the joist to its owner.

When they stand up to pray, they send to the Ark [as reader] an old and experienced man, who has children and whose home is empty [of possessions], so that his heart may be wholly given to prayer.

Our masters taught: When they stand up to pray, even if there is present among them an elder or a sage, they should place before the Ark [as reader] only a man conversant with the prayers. R. Judah said: They should place before the Ark a man who has a large family and no means of support; who draws his subsistence from [the produce of] his field,[1] but whose house is empty; whose youth was unblemished; who is modest and well liked by the people; who is skilled in chanting, has a sweet voice, and is well versed in the Five Books, the Prophets, and the Writings, in Midrash of *Halakhot* and *Haggadot*, and in all the blessings.[2]

271. R. Eliezer said: Fasting is greater than charity. The reason? It is done with one's body, while the other is done with one's money.[3]

272. When R. Sheshet was fasting, he would, after finishing his *Tefillah*, add: Master of universes, it is manifest to You that while the Temple was standing, if a man sinned, he presented an offering, and though all that was offered was its fat and its blood, atonement for him was brought about. Now that I have been fasting, my own fat and my own blood have been diminished. May it be Your will that my diminished fat and blood be deemed as though I had presented them on the altar as an offering before You, entreating that You favor me.[4]

273. Rava would not decree a fast on a cloudy day, because of the verse "Thou didst cover Thyself with a cloud so that no prayer can pass through" (Lam. 3:44).[5]

274. Our masters taught: Once it happened that most of [the month of] Adar passed by, and rain did not come down. So the people sent word to Honi the Circle Maker: "Pray for rain to fall." He replied, "Go out and bring in the ovens [in which you roast] the paschal lambs, so that they do not disintegrate."[6] He then prayed, but no rain came down. What did he do? He drew a circle and stationed himself within it, as the prophet Habakkuk had done—Habakkuk, who is quoted as having said, "I will stand upon my watch, and station me within a circle" (Hab. 2:1). Then Honi exclaimed before the Holy One, "Master of the universe, Your children have turned to me because they regard me as a member of Your household. By Your great Name I swear that I will not move from here until You have mercy on Your children." At once rain began to fall drop by drop. His disciples said, "Master, only because of your merit have we been allowed to see you [cause such a miracle] without being struck dead. But it seems to us that the rain is coming down merely to release you from your vow." In reply, he exclaimed, "Not for this [gentle] rain did I pray, but for pouring rain that would fill cisterns, ditches, and caves." The rain immediately began to come down so furiously that each drop was the size of the mouth of a cask, and the sages estimated that no drop was less than a *log*[7] in bulk. Again the disciples said, "Master, only because of your merit have we been allowed to see you without being struck dead. But it seems to us that the pouring rain is coming down to destroy the world."

Again Honi exclaimed before God, It is not for this that I prayed, but for rains of benevolence, benediction, and grace." At once the rain moderated to a normal pace but continued so steadily that all the people had to go up to the Temple Mount [to escape the rising water]. Then they said to Honi, "Master, just as you have prayed for rain to come down, pray now for it to cease." He replied, "I have it by tradition that one may not pray for the cessation of superabundant good. Nevertheless, bring me a bullock for a thank offering." They brought him the bullock. He laid both his hands upon it and said to the Holy One, "Master of the universe, Your people Israel, whom You have brought out of Egypt, cannot endure either superabundant good or superabundant punishment. When You are angry with them, they cannot endure it; and when You shower superabundant good upon them, they cannot endure it. May it be Your will that the rains cease and there be relief in the world." Immediately a wind blew, the clouds dispersed, and the sun shone. The people went

1. And is fully aware of the critical need for rain.
2. B. Ta 15a and 16a; Tos Ta 2:8.
3. B. Ber 32b.
4. B. Ber 17a.
5. B. Ber 32b.
6. These portable ovens were usually made of clay.
7. The equivalent of six eggs.

out into the fields and began to gather mushrooms and truffles.

Simeon ben Shetah sent word to Honi: "Were you not Honi, I would place you under a ban.[1] But what can I do to you, seeing that you ingratiate yourself with Him who is everywhere, who then grants you your wish, just like a son ingratiating himself with his father, who then grants him his wish? Thus the son may say, 'Father, take me to where I may bathe in warm water,' and he takes him there; 'to where I may shower in cold water,' and he takes him there; 'Give me walnuts, almonds, peaches, and pomegranates,' and he gives them to him. Of you [Honi], Scripture says, 'Thy-Father-and-thy-Mother [God] is glad, so she [the congregation of Israel] that bore thee must rejoice' " (Prov. 23:25).

Our masters taught: They who sat in the Chamber of Hewn Stone [the Sanhedrin] sent the following missive to Honi the Circle Maker: "Thou decreest a thing, and because of thee it is established" (Job 22:28ff.)—[on the earth] below you decree, and [in heaven] above the Holy One fulfills your word. "And light shines upon thy ways" (ibid.)—with your prayer you give light to a generation in darkness. "When they were cast down, thou saidst: 'There is lifting up' " (ibid.)—with your prayer you lifted the spirit of a generation that was cast down. "The lowly person thou savest" (ibid.)—with your prayer you saved a generation whom [sin] brought low. "Thou didst deliver him that is not innocent" (ibid.)—with your prayer you delivered a generation that is not innocent. "Yea, it was delivered through the cleanness of thy hands" (ibid.)—you, through the deeds of your clean hands, have delivered it.[2]

275. Hanan ha-Nehba ["the timid soul"] was a son of the daughter of Honi the Circle Maker. When the world was in need of rain, the sages would send schoolchildren to him. They would take hold of the hem of his garment and say to him, "Papa, papa, give us rain." Then he would plead with the Holy One, "Master of the universe, do it for the sake of these [little ones] who do not know the difference between the Father who can give rain and a papa who cannot."[3]

276. Our masters taught: It once happened that when all Israel came up to Jerusalem for a festival, there was no water to drink. So Nakdimon ben Gorion went to the [Roman] commander and said to him, "Lend me the water of twelve wells for those who have come up for the pilgrimage, and I will repay you with the water of twelve wells; if I cannot do so, I will pay you instead twelve talents of silver." And he fixed the day [for repayment]. When the time [for repayment] arrived and no rain had yet come down, the commander sent word in the morning to Nakdimon: "Deliver to me either the water or the money you owe me." Nakdimon replied, "I have still time; the entire day is as yet before me." At noon, the commander again sent word: "Deliver either the water or the money you owe me." Nakdimon replied, "Some hours are still left in the day." In the afternoon, the commander [again sent] word: "Deliver either the water or the money you owe me." Nakdimon replied, "A little while is still left in the day." Scorning Nakdimon's reply, the commander said to himself: No rain came down the entire year; is rain going to come down now? [With great glee, the commander set off for the bathhouse. At the same time] Nakdimon, greatly depressed, entered the Temple, wrapped himself in his prayer shawl, and stood in prayer to the Holy One, saying, "Master of the universe, to You it is clear and manifest that I made this commitment not for my own glory or for the glory of my father's house—I made it for Your glory, so that water might be made available for the pilgrims." Immediately the sky became covered with clouds, and so much rain came down that the commander's twelve wells were filled with water and even overflowed. As the commander was coming out of the baths, Nakdimon ben Gorion came out of the Temple, and the two met. Nakdimon said to the commander, "Pay me the money for the additional water you have received." The commander replied, "I know that it is only for your sake that the Holy One has shaken His world, but I still have a legitimate argument against you, for the sun had already set. Consequently, when the rains came down, they came down as my property." At this, Nakdimon ben Gorion again entered the Temple, wrapped himself in his prayer shawl, stood in prayer, and said to the Holy One, "Master of the universe, make it known that You have beloved ones in Your world." Immediately a wind began to blow, the clouds were dispersed, and the sun shone out again [showing that the day had not yet ended]. Then the commander said to Nakdimon, "Had not the sun broken through[4] [again], I would still have had a legitimate argument to exact from you the money that was due me."[5]

277. Once Samuel the Little ordained a fast [for the following day], but rain fell before sunrise [before the people had begun to fast and pray]. The people thought that it was due to the merit of the congregation,[6] but Samuel said to them: To make you understand what happened, let me tell you the parable. A servant asked his master for an extra ration of bread, and the master said to his other servants, "Give it to him, just so I don't have to listen to his whining."

Another time, Samuel the Little ordained a fast [for the following day], and the rain fell the next day after sunset [after the people had fasted and entreated God]. The people thought that it was due to the merit of the congregation. But Samuel said to them: No; rain came not because of the congregation's merit. To make you understand what happened, let me tell you the parable. A servant asked his master for an extra ration of bread, and the

1. God must have imposed the drought in punishment for Israel's transgressions, and pressing Him to cancel His judgment would have been sinful.
2. B. Ta 19a and 23a; En Yaakov, ad loc.
3. B. Ta 23a–b.
4. The word for "broken through," *nakedah*, suggests Nakdimon—"the man for whom the sun broke through."
5. B. Ta 19b–20a and En Yaakov, ad loc.
6. Inasmuch as rain came even before their prayers of entreaty.

master said to his other servants, "Keep him waiting until he is weakened by hunger and wracked by pain. Then give it to him."

So how, according to Samuel the Little, is one ever to determine whether a congregation's own merit is responsible for the coming down of rain? Only when a congregation recites [the prayer], "He who causeth the wind to blow," and the wind begins to blow at once; and when it recites, "He who causeth the rain to fall," and rain begins to fall at once.[1]

278. We have been taught: No more than thirteen [consecutive] fasts may be decreed for a community, since it is not right to put too great a burden on a community.

Our masters taught: Once it happened that R. Eliezer decreed thirteen fasts for a community, and no rain came. Finally, when people began to leave [the synagogue], he said, "Have you got graves ready for yourselves?" At this, the people broke into sobbing, and rain began to fall.[2]

279. In the days of R. Tanhuma, Israel had need of rain, so they came to him and said, "Master, decree a fast." He proclaimed a fast for one day, for a second day, and for a third day, yet no rain came down. Then he entered [the synagogue] and preached to them, saying, "My children, be filled with compassion for one another, and the Holy One will be filled with compassion for you." Consequently, as they were distributing charity to the poor, they saw a man conversing with his divorced wife and even giving her money. At that, they went to R. Tanhuma and cried out, "While we sit here, something reprehensible is taking place out there!" R. Tanhuma: "What have you seen?" "We saw So-and-so conversing with his divorced wife, and he even gave her money." He sent for the couple, who were brought before the community, and he asked the man, "What is this woman to you?" The man: "She is my divorced wife." R. Tanhuma: "Why did you give her money?" The man: "Master, I saw her in great distress and was filled with compassion for her." At this, R. Tanhuma turned his face to Him above and exclaimed, "Master of all universes! When this man—upon whom this woman has no claim for maintenance—saw her in distress, he was filled with compassion for her. Now, since it is written of You that You are gracious and compassionate, and since we are children of Your beloved ones, children of Abraham, Isaac, and Jacob, and so have a claim upon You for our maintenance, surely, surely You should be filled with compassion for us!" Immediately rain began to come down, and the world enjoyed relief.[3]

280. R. Hama ben Hanina decreed a fast, but no rain came. He was asked, "Why is it that when R. Joshua ben Levi decrees a fast, rain does come?" He replied, "I am merely I, while he is the son of Levi."[4] So the people said to R. Hama ben Hanina, "Come, let us prepare our hearts for prayer. Perhaps the community will turn contrite in their hearts, and rain will come down." All besought God's mercy, and still no rain came. R. Hama ben Hanina then asked the people, "Are you united in praying that rain come down for us?" The people: "Yes." So he said, "Sky, O sky, cover your visage [with clouds]." But the sky did not cover itself. Then he said, "How impudent is the sky's visage!" At that, it covered itself with clouds, and rain began to fall.[5]

281. Levi decreed a fast and implored God's mercy, but no rain came down. So he said to the Holy One, "Master of the universe, You have gone up and taken Your seat in heaven, and have no compassion for Your children." Rain did fall, but Levi became lame.

R. Eliezer said: A man must never speak to Him above in reproach, for, lo, a great man spoke to Him above in reproach, and he became lame. Who was it? Levi.[6]

282. R. Judah [II] the Patriarch decreed a fast, during which he prayed for God's compassion, but no rain came. So he said, "What a difference between Samuel the Ramathite and Judah ben Gamaliel! [Samuel the Ramathite decreed no fast, yet rain fell,[7] while Judah decrees a fast, and no rain falls.] Alas for the generation that is in such a plight. Alas for him to whom such a thing happens!" He felt humiliated, and then rain came.[8]

283. Once R. Judah, seeing two men playfully tossing bread at each other, exclaimed, "It seems that there is a superfluity of food in the world!" He cast an angry look at the wasters, and a famine ensued. So the sages said to R. Kahana son of R. Nehunia, a disciple ministering as R. Judah's attendant, "You, sir, who are constantly with him, should persuade him to go out by the door next to the marketplace."[9] He prevailed upon him, and R. Judah went out into the marketplace. Seeing a large crowd there, he asked, "What is the matter?" He was told, "They stand around the offal of ground dates, which is for sale." He exclaimed, "There is evidently famine in the world," and said to his attendant, "Take off my shoes." As soon as the attendant had taken off one shoe, rain began to fall. As the attendant was about to take off the other shoe [the prophet] Elijah appeared and said to him, "The Holy One said: If you take off the other shoe, I will lay waste to the world [with a flood]."[10]

284. Once Rabbah decreed a fast and besought God's mercy, but rain did not fall. He was asked, "Why was it that whenever R. Judah decreed a fast, rain did fall?" Rabbah replied, "What can I do? If it is because of learning, we are superior to them, for in R. Judah's days all

1. B. Ta 25b.
2. B. Ta 14b and 25b.
3. Gen. R. 33:3; Lev. R. 34:14.
4. And thus a Levite, more important than I, a commoner.
5. B. Ta 25a.
6. Ibid.
7. See 1 Sam. 7:5–6.
8. B. Ta 24a. and En Yaakov, ad loc.
9. That he might see for himself how people were suffering because of the famine he had brought about.
10. R. Judah should not importune God with too much self-humiliation, as rain was about to come. B. Ta 24b and En Yaakov, ad loc.

of them studied only the division Nezikin, whereas we study all six divisions of the Mishnah. And yet when R. Judah had just one of his shoes taken off, rain fell, while we cry out for rain all day long, and no one heeds us. If it is because of good deeds—if anyone has seen something wrong in me, let him come and say so. Well, what can a generation's leaders do when the generation does not appear good enough [in the eyes of God]?"[1]

285. Once R. Nahman decreed a fast and besought God's mercy, but rain did not fall. When he went home, he said, "Take Nahman and throw him from the roof to the ground," he felt so humiliated. And then the rain came down.[2]

286. R. Papa decreed a fast.[3] Feeling weak, he gulped down a plateful of grits, then resumed his prayer for God's mercy, but no rain came. R. Nahman bar Ish Prati ("Man of the Euphrates")[4] said tauntingly, "If the master would only gulp down another plateful of grits, rain will surely come." R. Papa felt ashamed and humiliated. And then the rain came.[5]

287. R. Hiyya bar Luliani said: I heard the clouds say, "Let us go and bring down rain on Ammon and Moab." So I said to them, "When the Holy One was about to give the Torah, He went around with it to every nation and tongue, but none accepted it, until Israel came forward and accepted it. Yet you would now leave Israel and bring down rain upon Ammon and Moab! Pour down the rain on the spot where you are." And they did so.[6]

288. "Ask ye of the Lord rain . . . the Lord maketh *hazizim*" (Zech. 10:1). What is meant by "the Lord maketh [many] *hazizim*"? R. Yose son of R. Hanina said: The verse implies that the Holy One makes a *haziz* [a rain cloud] for each and every righteous man for his own need.

"And He will give them showers of rain—to everyone [a bed of] grass in the field" (Zech. 10:1). R. Daniel bar Ketina had a garden patch, which he used to examine every day and say, "This bed needs water and that one does not." At that, rain would come down and water every spot that needed water.[7]

289. R. Simeon ben Yohai said: When Israel merit it, rains come down on all that grows—trees and sown produce—and the world is blessed. But when they sin, the rains come down only into seas and rivers.[8]

290. Resh Lakish said: What is implied in "And He will shut up the heavens" (Deut. 11:17)? That when the heavens are "shut up," unable to bring down dew and rain, they are like a woman who is in labor but cannot bring forth.[9]

291. R. Yohanan said: *Porehot* are a sign that rain is coming. But what are *porehot*? R. Papa said: Thin clouds under thick ones.

When Ulla visited Babylonia and saw *porehot*, he said to the people, "Bring your [perishable] things indoors, for rain will come soon." But in the end, no rain came. Ulla said, "As the Babylonians are deceivers, so their rains are deceivers."[10]

292. R. Hama bar Hanina said: A day when rain comes is as great as the day heaven and earth were created.

R. Oshaia said: Great is the day when the rain comes, for on it even deliverance is increased and multiplied, as is said, "Let the earth open, that the rains bring forth deliverance and loving-kindness" (Isa. 45:8).[11]

293. "The Lord will open unto thee His good treasure" (Deut. 28:12). See how great is the coming down of rain. R. Judah son of R. Ezekiel said: Whenever my late father saw rain coming down, he recited the prayer: May the Name of Him who spoke and the world came into being be magnified, hallowed, blessed, and exalted, for He appoints thousands of thousands and myriads of myriads of angels for each and every drop that comes down. Why? Because from here to the sky is a distance that takes five hundred years to traverse, yet when rain comes down, not one drop intermingles with another.[12]

294. R. Abbahu said: The day when rain comes is greater than the day of resurrection, since the day of resurrection is only for the righteous, whereas the day when rain comes is for both the righteous and the wicked.

R. Judah said: The day when rain comes is as great as the day on which the Torah was given, for it is said, "My doctrine shall drop as the rain" (Deut 32:2), and "doctrine" here means Torah, as in "I give you good doctrine; forsake ye not My teaching" (Prov. 4:2). Rava said: Even greater than the day the Torah was given, for it is said, "My doctrine shall drop as the rain." Now, which is usually compared to which? You must admit that [God's doctrine] the less important is compared to the more important [rain].[13]

295. R. Simeon ben Yohai said: Three things—earth, man, and rain—are equal in importance. And each of the three, R. Levi bar Hiyya pointed out, is made up of three letters.[14] This should teach you that if there were no earth, there would be no rain; if there were no rain, there would

1. B. Ta 24b.
2. B. Ta 24a and En Yaakov, ad loc.
3. The words "but rain did not come" are omitted, as in B. Ta.
4. Or, as suggested by Leon Nemoy, "Man of Sparta."
5. B. Ta 24b.
6. B. Ta 25a and En Yaakov, ad loc.
7. B. Ta 9b.
8. Tanhuma, *Mi-ketz*, §1.
9. B. Ta 8a.
10. B. Ta 9b.
11. B. Ta 7b.
12. Deut. R. 7:7; P. Ber 9:3, 14a.
13. B. Ta 7a.
14. *'rtz* ("earth") *'dm* ("man"), and *gshm* ("rain").

be no earth; and if there were neither, man could not exist.[1]

296. R. Tanhum bar Hiyya said: The sending of rain is greater than the giving of Torah, for while the giving of Torah was a joy to Israel, the sending of rain gives joy to all the world—to cattle, to wild beasts, and to fowl.[2]

297. R. Hiyya bar Abba said: The power of rain is greater than the resurrection of the dead, since resurrection is for man alone, while rain is for both man and beast; resurrection is for Israel alone, while rain is not only for Israel but also for the nations of the world.[3]

298. A certain heathen inquired of R. Joshua ben Korhah, saying to him: You have your festivals, and we have ours. When you are rejoicing, we are not, and when we are rejoicing, you are not. When do both we and you rejoice? When rain comes down. And the proof? The verse "The meadows are clothed with flocks; the valleys also are covered with corn; they shout for joy, yea, they sing" (Ps. 65:14). And what follows directly? "Shout unto the Lord, all the earth" (Ps. 66:1)—not just priests, Levites, or lay Israelites, but all the earth.[4]

299. R. Hisda said: Ever since the day the Temple was destroyed, rain does not come down from the good treasury, for it is said, "[In the Land which the Lord swore unto thy fathers to give thee], the Lord will open unto thee His good treasury" (Deut. 28:11–12). When Israel obey the will of Him who is everywhere and so dwell in their own Land, rains come down from the good treasury; but when Israel do not dwell in their own Land, rains do not come down from the good treasury.[5]

300. We have been taught that R. Eleazar ben Perata said: Ever since the day the Temple was destroyed, the rains have become irregular and arbitrary for the world. One year the rains are abundant, another year they are meager; one year rain comes down in season, another year it does not.

What parable shows what happens in a year when rain comes down in season? The one of a servant to whom his master gives the weekly food allowance [in advance] on the first day of the week, with the result that the dough is well baked and the bread palatable. What parable shows what happens in a year when the rains do not come down in season? The one of a servant to whom his master gives the weekly food allowance late on Friday, with the result that the dough is not well baked[6] and the bread is not palatable.

What parable shows what happens in a year when the rains are abundant? The one of a master who gives his servant the [yearly] food allowance all at once: the waste in the mill when grinding a *kor* [of grain] is no more than [the waste] in grinding a *kav*;[7] and likewise the waste in the trough when kneading a *kor* [of flour] is no more than when kneading a *kav*. What parable shows what happens in a year when the rains are meager? The one of a master who gives his servant the [yearly] food allowance little by little: the waste in the mill when grinding a *kav* [of grain] is no less than in grinding a *kor*; and likewise the waste in the trough when kneading a *kav* [of flour] is no less than when kneading a *kor*. Another illustration: What parable shows what happens when the rains are abundant? The one of a man molding clay: if he has abundant water, it will not give out and the clay will be molded well; but if the available water is meager, it will soon give out, and the clay will not be well molded.[8]

301. Our masters taught: "I will give you rains in their season" (Lev. 26:4), with the result that the soil will be neither soaked nor parched, but moderately watered. Whenever rains are excessive, they wash away the soil, so that it yields no fruit. Another interpretation: "In their season," so that rains come down only on the eves of Wednesday and Friday. Thus we find that in the days of Simeon ben Shetah, rains came down for them on the eves of Wednesdays and Fridays, so that grains of wheat grew as large as kidney beans, and grains of barley as large as olive pits, and lentils as large as gold denars. Specimens of them were kept for future generations, to show what loss sin causes, as is said, "Your iniquities have turned away these things, and your sins have withheld bounty from you" (Jer. 5:25). We also find that in the days of Herod, when the people were occupied with the rebuilding of the Temple, rain would come down during the night, but in the morning the wind blew, the clouds dispersed, and the sun shone, so that all the people were able to go out to their work—thus they knew that they were engaged in work for the sake of Heaven.[9]

302. Our masters taught: The alarm may be sounded on account of any calamity that comes upon a community except excessive rain. Why not? R. Yohanan said: Because we should not pray for the cessation of superabundant blessing, for it is said, "I will surely open for you the windows of heaven, and pour out a blessing for you that there shall be more than enough" (Mal. 3:10). What is meant by "more than enough"? Rami bar R. Hiyya said: That your lips will grow weary[10] saying, "It is enough." However, in the Diaspora,[11] said Rama bar R. Judah in the name of Rav, the alarm may be sounded on account of such superabundance.

In a year of abundant rain, the lay posts in the provinces would send word to their delegates on the watch [in Jerusalem]: "[When praying], direct your thoughts to your

1. Gen. R. 13:3.
2. MTeh 117:1.
3. Gen. R. 13:6.
4. Ibid.
5. B. BB 25b.
6. Since once Sabbath eve sets in, baking is forbidden.

7. A *kor* contains thirty *seah*, and a *seah* contains six *kav*.
8. B. Ta 19b.
9. B. Ta 22b–23a.
10. The word *beli* in the phrase *ad beli* ("more than") is construed as a form of *billah* ("wear out" or "worn out").
11. That is in Babylonia. Since it is a low-lying country, abundant rain would swamp it.

brethren in the Diaspora, so that their houses may not become their graves."

When R. Eliezer was asked, "How long must rain keep coming down before we are allowed to pray for it to cease?" he replied, "When a man standing on the wall of Ophel is able to splash his feet in the water" [of the brook of Kidron, which is considerably below the wall of Ophel. For as] Rabbah bar Bar Hana related, "Once, while standing on the wall of Ophel,[1] I saw [below] an Arab riding on a camel and holding a spear in his hand—to me, the Arab looked as small as a flax worm.[2]

303. "I will pour out a blessing for you that there shall be more than enough" (Mal. 3:10), which means—so said the sages in the name of Rav—until your lips will grow weary saying, "It is enough." For in this world [excessive] rains inconvenience human beings: they who set out on a journey are distressed by them, they who sail the sea are distressed by them, they who tread wine vats and who plaster roofs are distressed by them. But in the time-to-come, the Holy One will make them [always] a blessing.[3]

304. Our masters taught: ["The alarm may be sounded if houses are collapsing"]. The collapsing of houses spoken of here refers to sound houses, not to rickety ones; to such as are not liable to collapse, not to such as are liable to collapse.[4]

305. Our masters taught: The alarm for wild beasts, of which the sages have spoken, is to be sounded when the beasts constitute a visitation, but not otherwise. When are wild beasts considered a visitation, and when not? When they appear in the city, it is a visitation: when only in the fields, it is not. If by day, it is a visitation; if only by night, it is not. If a beast, seeing two persons together, pursues them, it is a visitation; but if it hides itself on seeing them, it is not. If it has torn two persons and devoured only one of them,[5] that is a visitation; but if it has devoured both of them, it is not. If it has climbed to a roof and seized an infant out of his cradle, it is a visitation.[6]

306. Rami bar Hama said: No wild beast prevails over a human being until he seems to it to be like a beast, as is said, "When he is like the beasts, he perisheth" (Ps. 49:13).[7]

307. In the days of R. Hiyya bar Abba, a [*re'em*'s] whelp invaded the Land of Israel and left no tree that it did not uproot. A fast was proclaimed, and R. Hiyya prayed. As a result, the whelp's dam roared out of the wilderness, and at the sound of her voice, it went down [to the wilderness to meet her].[8]

308. What is an epidemic? When, in a city capable of furnishing five hundred foot soldiers, three men [in normal health] die, one each day, on three successive days, that is an epidemic. When fewer than three men [in normal health] die, it is not an epidemic.[9]

309. Our masters taught: When there is an epidemic in the city, keep your feet [within your house], as is said, "Come, my people, enter thou into thy chambers . . . until the rage passes" (Isa. 26:20).

During an epidemic, Rava used to keep [his] windows shut in fear of "Death is come up into our windows" (Jer. 9:20).

Our masters taught: When there is famine in a city, take to your heels, as is said, "And there was a famine in the Land, and Abram went down into Egypt" (Gen. 12:10).

When there is an epidemic in a city, one should not walk in the middle of the road, because [at such a time] the angel of death walks in the middle of the road. When there is peace in a city, one should not walk at the sides of the road.[10]

When there is an epidemic in a city, a man should not enter the synagogue alone, because the angel of death deposits his implements there. This, however, is true only of a synagogue in which children do not read Scripture and ten adults do not pray together.

When dogs howl, the angel of death has come to the city. When dogs frolic, the prophet Elijah has come.[11]

310. R. Joseph taught: What is implied by "None of you shall go out of the house until the morning" (Exod. 12:22)? That once permission is granted to the angel of destruction, he does not distinguish between the righteous and the wicked.[12]

311. The sages taught: Michael arrives [at his destination] with but one flap of his wings; Gabriel, with two flaps; Elijah, with four; the angel of death, with eight—but during an epidemic, he arrives with but one flap of his wings.[13]

312. The croup—if people die of it, the alarm should be sounded; if not, the alarm need not be sounded.[14]

313. In the days of R. Samuel ben Nahmani, there was famine accompanied by pestilence. The sages said: What are we to do? Shall we beseech mercy for the cessation of both? One may not pray [at the same time for the cessation

1. See 2 Chron. 27:3. When the brook Kidron rose, one could sit on the wall of Ophel and dangle his feet in the water. See Tos Ta 3:1.
2. B. Ta 22b and En Yaakov, ad loc.
3. Lev. R. 35:12.
4. B. Ta 20b.
5. "That is to say, it tore one person and devoured him, and tore another without devouring him. That is considered a visitation, because the animal tore the second person after it had stilled its hunger" (Ta, trans. Henry Malter, p. 160, n. 311).
6. B. Ta 22a.
7. B. Sanh 38b.
8. Gen. R. 31:13.
9. B. Ta 19a.
10. Where, at such a time, the angel of death stalks his prey.
11. B. BK 60b.
12. B. BK 60a; Yalkut, *Bo*, §206.
13. B. Ber 4b.
14. Tos Ta 2:9.

of two afflictions]. So we shall beseech mercy for the cessation of the epidemic, and [resign ourselves to] suffer hunger. But R. Samuel ben Nahmani said to them: Let us rather pray for the cessation of the famine, for when the Holy One gives plenty, He gives it only to the living, as is said, "Thou openest Thy hand, and satisfiest every living thing with favor" (Ps. 145:16).[1]

314. Our masters taught: The sword concerning which sages said [the alarm should be sounded] is the sword [of soldiers] moving from place to place, even if it be the sword of peace, let alone the sword intended as punishment.[2]

Warfare

315. People may not be sent to fight in an optional war without consent of the court of seventy-one.[3]

316. "And it shall be, when ye draw nigh unto the battle, that the priest shall approach" (Deut. 20:2)—the priest anointed for battle. "And speak unto the people" (ibid.)—speak in the holy tongue. "And shall say unto them: 'Hear, O Israel, ye draw nigh this day unto battle against your enemies' " (Deut. 20:3)—not against your brethren, not Judah against Simeon nor Simeon against Benjamin, so that if you fall into their hands, they are likely to have mercy upon you, as it is said, "And the men that have been mentioned by name rose up, and took the captives, and with the spoil clothed all that were naked among them, and arrayed them, and shod them, and gave them to eat and to drink, and anointed them, and carried all the feeble of them upon asses, and brought them to Jericho, the city of palm trees, unto their brethren; then they returned to Samaria" (2 Chron. 28:15). [Remember that] you march against your enemies, who will have no mercy upon you if you should fall into their hands. "Let not your heart faint" (Deut. 20:3) at the neighing of horses and the flashing of swords. "Fear not" (ibid.) because of the crash of shields and the noise of soldiers' nail-studded boots. "Nor be alarmed" (ibid.) at the sound of trumpets. "Neither be ye affrighted" (ibid.) at the sound of war cries. "For the Lord your God is He that goeth with you" (Deut. 20:4). They come [relying] on the strength of flesh and blood, but you come [relying] on the strength of Him who is everywhere. The Philistines came [relying on] the strength of Goliath. But what was his end? In the end he fell by the sword, and they fell with him. The Ammonites came [relying] on the strength of Shobach. But what was his end? In the end he fell by the sword, and they fell with him. But with you it is otherwise: "The Lord your God is He that goeth with you to fight for you against your enemies" (Deut. 20:4). [This alludes to] the Ark bivouacked [with Israel's army].[4]

317. "Let not your heart faint; fear not, nor be alarmed, neither be ye affrighted at them" (Deut. 20:3). [These four expressions] correspond to the four means adopted by the nations of the world [to terrorize the enemy]: they crash [their shields], blast [trumpets], shout [battle cries], and stamp [with their horses].[5]

318. "And the officers shall speak unto the people, saying: 'What man is there that hath built a new house, and hath not dedicated it? let him go and return to his house,' " etc. (Deut. 20:5). All such—after hearing the words of the priest appointed to go with the Ark to war concerning the regulations governing those who are required to go to war—return to their homes, where they send supplies of water and food, and where they keep the roads in repair.[6]

319. "And the officers shall speak further to the people, and they shall say: 'What man is there that is fearful and faint-hearted?' " (Deut. 20:8). R. Akiva said: "Fearful and faint-hearted" is to be understood literally, that he is unable to stand in the line of battle and look at a drawn sword. R. Yose the Galilean said: "Fearful and faint-hearted" means that he is fearful because of the transgressions he committed. That is why the Torah gave him the opportunity to return for the other reasons [such as that he has built a house or planted a vineyard].[7]

320. R. Yohanan ben Zakkai said: Come and see how considerate the Holy One is of human dignity. When someone returns because he is fearful and faint-hearted, people who see him [avoiding military service] will merely say, "Perhaps he has just built a house," "Perhaps he has recently planted a vineyard," "Perhaps he has recently betrothed a wife."

Yet in all these cases, the people claiming exemption from military service [on the ground that they have just built a new house or recently planted a vineyard, or that they are newly wed] have to bring witnesses to attest that this is really so. The exception is the man who is fearful and faint-hearted—he is his own witness: when he hears the sound of crashing shields, he is frightened; the sound of neighing horses, he trembles; the sound of blasting trumpets, he panics. When he sees the unsheathing of swords, urine streams down between his knees [and he doesn't have to prove to others that he is faint-hearted].[8]

321. "And it shall be, when the officers have made an end of speaking unto the people, that army guards shall be posted in front of [and behind] the people" (Deut. 20:9): in front of and behind the rearmost contingent of the people are set guards against desertion, with iron axes in their hands. Should anyone wish to flee, they have the authority to strike his thighs, because flight is the beginning of defeat.

To what do such precautions apply? To optional wars.

1. B. Ta 8b.
2. B. Ta 22b; Tos Ta 2:10.
3. B. Sanh 2a.
4. B. Sot 42a.
5. B. Sot 42a–b.
6. B. Sot 43b.
7. So that he would not be called upon to publicly confess his sins. B. Sot 44a.
8. Sif Deut., §192. Professor Jakob J. Petuchowski provided the interpretation.

But in obligatory wars, all must go forth, even a bridegroom from his nuptial chamber and a bride from her bridal bower.[1]

322. In session, none is as good as a man on in years; and in war, none as good as a young man.[2]

323. Common soldiers advance and start the battle, but it is the seasoned veterans who go down into the fray and win victory.[3]

324. "And he shall stand before Eleazar the Priest, who shall inquire for him by the judgment of the Urim before the Lord" (Num. 27:21). The verse shows that when Israel go out to war, the court above sits to decide whether they are to be victorious or defeated.[4]

325. "And it came to pass, when Moses held up his hand, that Israel prevailed" (Exod. 17:11). But did the hands of Moses actually wage war or win victories? Not actually; what the text means is that as long as Israel turned their thoughts upward and submitted their hearts to their Father in heaven, they prevailed. Otherwise, they fell.[5]

326. We have been taught: When heathens lay siege to towns in Israel, one may not go forth with weapons [on the Sabbath] on account of them, nor on account of them profane the Sabbath in any way. When does this rule apply? When the heathens come to seize money. But when they come to destroy lives, one may go forth with weapons on account of them and profane the Sabbath on account of them. When the town is near the border, even if the heathens come not to destroy lives, but only to get hold of straw and stubble, one may go forth with weapons on account of them and profane the Sabbath on their account.[6]

327. We have been taught: Formerly [Jews returning from war on a Sabbath] would leave their weapons in a house near the town wall.[7] One time, the heathens became aware of what the Jews had been doing. So they kept pursuing them. When the Jews rushed back into that house to get their weapons, with the heathens right behind them, the Jews pushed against one another so hard that they accidentally slew more than the heathens had slain. Then it was ordained that Jews may return to their own homes with their weapons.[8]

328. A man should not go out on the Sabbath carrying a sword, a bow, a shield, a lance, or a spear. R. Eliezer objected: They are his ornaments. But the sages said: They are in fact a reproach to him, for Scripture says, "They shall beat their swords into plowshares, and their spears into pruning hooks; . . . neither shall they learn war any more" (Isa. 2:4).[9]

329. R. Eliezer ben Jacob said: What is the proof that a woman may not go forth with weapons to war? From "A warrior's[10] gear may not be put on a woman" (Deut. 22:5).[11]

1. See Joel 2:16. B. Sot 44a–b.
2. B. Hag 14a.
3. B. Ber 53b.
4. P. Shab 2:3, 5b.
5. B. RH 29a.
6. B. Er 45a.
7. To avoid carrying them inside the town on the Sabbath.
8. B. Er 45a.
9. B. Shab 63b.
10. The word *gever* ("man") may also be read *gibbor* ("mighty man," "warrior").
11. B. Naz 59a.

PART VI

CHAPTER ONE

THE WORLD AND ALL THAT IT HOLDS

The World

1. "Lo, these are but the outskirts of His ways; and how small a whisper is heard of Him! But the thunder of His mighty deeds who can understand?" (Job 26:14). R. Huna said: All you see is but the outskirts of the Holy One's ways. If a man say to you, "I can comprehend the order of the world," reply, "Since you cannot comprehend [the ways of] a mortal king, how do you suppose you can comprehend [the ways of] the King who is King of kings, the Holy One, blessed be He?"[1]

2. Three things were created before the creation of the world—water, wind, and fire. The water conceived and gave birth to thick darkness; the fire conceived and gave birth to light; the wind conceived and gave birth to wisdom. For this reason did David say, "Bless the Lord, O my soul! O Lord my God, Thou art very great . . . who layest the beams of Thine upper chambers in the waters . . . who walkest upon the wings of the wind . . . the flaming fires Thy messengers" (Ps. 104:1–4). For when man sees a beautiful pillar, he exclaims, "Blessed be He who has created the source from which this was hewn." When he sees how beautiful the world is, he says, "Blessed be the Omnipresent who has hewed it out and created it with the word; happy are you, O world, because the Holy One rules you."[2]

3. R. Judah said in the name of Rav: At the time the Holy One created the world, it went on extending farther [in both directions], like two unwound clews of thread, until the Holy One rebuked it and brought it to a standstill: "The pillars of heaven swayed [hither and yon], until they were appalled at the thunder of His rebuke" (Job 26:11). That, too, is what Resh Lakish said: What is meant by "I am God Shaddai" (Gen. 17:2 and 35:11)? I am He who said to My world: "*Dai*, Enough!"

Resh Lakish also said: When the Holy One created the sea, it went on extending, until the Holy One rebuked it and caused it to dry up, as is said: "He rebuked the sea and made it dry" (Nah. 1:4).[3]

4. The world is formed like an orb, and the sea like a bowl.

R. Jonah said: Alexander of Macedon wished to ascend on high, and he ascended [on a couch][4] higher and higher until he saw the world like an orb and the sea like a bowl. On account of this, they depict him [Alexander] with an orb in his hand.[5]

5. We have been taught that R. Yose said: Alas for human beings who see but know not what they see, stand but know not on what they stand. On what does the earth rest? On pillars, for it is said, "Who shaketh the earth out of her place, and the pillars thereof tremble" (Job 9:6). The pillars [rest] upon the waters: "To Him that spread forth the earth above the waters" (Ps. 136:6). The waters, upon the mountains: "The waters stood upon the mountains" (Ps. 104:6). The mountains, on the wind: "For lo, He that formeth the mountains and createth the wind" (Amos 4:13). The wind [rests] upon the storm: "The wind—the storm executeth its command" (Ps. 148:8). Storm is suspended above the arm of the Holy One: "And underneath are the everlasting arms" (Deut. 33:27). But the sages said: [The world] rests on twelve pillars: "He set the [number of] borders for the peoples to be the same number as the tribes] of Israel" (Deut. 32:8); some say on seven pillars: "Wisdom . . . hath hewn out her seven pillars" (Prov. 9:1). R. Eleazar ben Shammua said: [It rests] on one pillar, whose name is Righteous: "Righteous is the foundation of the world" (Prov. 10:25).[6]

6. There are seven levels to the universe; the upper level [of the heavens], the lower level, the world's atmosphere, and the four upper spheres.[7]

7. R. Judah said: There are two firmaments, for it is said, "Behold, unto the Lord thy God belongeth heaven, and the heaven above heaven" (Deut. 10:14). Resh Lakish said: Seven, namely, Curtain, Expanse, Grinders, Habitation, Dwelling, Treasury, Heavy Clouds. The Curtain serves no function other than to be placed in its sheath in the morning and taken out of its sheath in the evening, thus renewing daily the work of creation. The Expanse is that wherein sun, moon, stars, and planets are fixed. The Grinders is that in which millstones stand and grind manna for the righteous. Habitation is that in which Jerusalem, the Temple, and the altar are built—the altar where Michael, the great prince, stands and daily brings an offering. The Dwelling is that in which there are innumerable companies of ministering angels, who utter song at night and are hushed during the day in deference to Israel [who intone song during the day]. The Treasury is that in which there are stores of snow, stores of hail, the loft of noxious

1. Gen. R. 12:1.
2. Exod. R. 15:22.
3. B. Hag 12a and En Yaakov, ad loc.
4. The couch was tied to two eagles, above whom meat was suspended. The sight of the meat spurred the eagles to fly higher and higher (Eisenstein, p. 463).
5. P. AZ 3:1, 42c; Num. R. 13:14. The translator follows the reading in Num. R: not *lah* ("her,") but *leyh* ("him,"), that is, Alexander; and not *be-yadah* ("in her hand") but *bi-yedeh* ("in his hand").
6. B. Hag 12b and En Yaakov, ad loc.
7. ARN 37 (YJS, p. 154).

dews, the loft of raindrops, the chamber of the storm and of the whirlwind, and the cave of vapor—the doors of all these are of fire. Heavy Cloud is that in which are stored righteousness, judgment, and mercy; the treasures of life, the treasures of peace, and the treasures of blessing; the souls of the righteous and the spirits and souls of those yet to be created; and the dew with which the Holy One will revive the dead. There also are the *ofannim*,[1] the seraphim, the celestial creatures, the ministering angels, and the throne of glory; the King, the living and enduring God, high and exalted, dwells above them, surrounded by darkness, cloud masses, and thick clouds.

R. Aha bar Jacob said: There is still another firmament above the heads of the celestial creatures.

So far you have permission to speak—beyond this, you have no permission to speak, for thus it is written in the book of Ben Sira:

Do not pry into things too hard for you.
Or examine what is beyond your reach.
Meditate on the commandments you have been given;
What the Lord keeps secret is no concern of yours.[2]

8. We have been taught: Rabban Yohanan ben Zakkai asked: What answer did the divine voice give that wicked [Nebuchadnezzar] when he said, "I will ascend above the heights of the clouds; I will be like the Most High" (Isa. 14:14)? [Rabban Yohanan declared]: The divine voice went forth and said: O wicked man, son of a wicked man, grandson of the wicked Nimrod who during his reign stirred the entire world, all of it, to rebel—how many are man's years? "Three score years and ten, or even by reason of strength fourscore years" (Ps. 90:10). But it is a five hundred years' journey from earth to heaven, and a five hundred years' journey across the thickness of heaven, and a similar distance from each heaven to the one above it. Above the heavens are the celestial creatures. The journey across each of the feet of the celestial creatures takes as much time as all the previous journeys together; the journey across the ankles of each of the celestial creatures takes as much time as all the previous journeys together; the journey across each of the legs of the celestial creatures takes as much time as all the previous journeys together; the journey across each of the knees of the celestial creatures takes as much time as all the previous journeys together; the journey across each of the thighs of the celestial creatures takes as much time as all the previous journeys together; the journey across the body of each of the celestial creatures takes as much time as all the previous journeys together; the journey across the neck of each of the celestial creatures takes as much time as all the previous journeys together; the journey across the head of each of the celestial creatures takes as much time as all the previous journeys together; the journey across each of the horns of the celestial creatures takes as much time as all the previous journeys together. Above them is the throne of glory, and the journey across each of the legs of the throne of glory takes as much time as all the previous journeys together. And above them dwells God, living and enduring, lofty and exalted. And yet you [Nebuchadnezzar] say, "I will ascend above the heights of the clouds; I will be like the Most High."[3]

9. Four quarters have been created in the world: a quarter facing the east, one facing the west, one facing the south, and one facing the north. From the quarter facing the east, light goes forth to the world. From the quarter facing south, dews of blessing go forth to the world. From the quarter facing west, where are the treasuries of snow and the treasuries of hail, come forth into the world cold, heat, and rains. The quarter facing north, God created but did not complete, for He said: Anyone who dares declare, "I am a God," let him come and complete this quarter which I left [incomplete].

There [in the north] is the abode of agents of destruction—[evil] spirits and demons; from there, evil goes forth into the world, as is said, "Out of the north, evil shall break forth" (Jer. 1:14).[4]

10. Seven qualities minister before the throne of glory: faithfulness, righteousness, justice, loving-kindness, compassion, truth, and peace, as is said, "[I will betroth thee unto Me in righteousness and in justice, in loving-kindness and in compassion], and I will betroth thee unto Me in faithfulness, and thou shalt know the Lord" (Hos. 2:21); [and "Mercy and truth are met together; righteousness and peace have kissed each other" (Ps. 85:11)].[5]

11. "God also created the one over against the other" (Eccles. 7:14). For everything God created, He created its counterpart: He created mountains, and He created hills; He created seas, and He created rivers.[6]

12. "God also created the one over against the other" (Eccles. 7:14). The Holy One created the world in pairs, one an opposite to the other, and the other an opposite of the one, so that it might be known that each and every thing has a mate and has an opposite, and but for the one, the other would not be. But for death, there would be no life, and but for life, there would be no death. But for peace, there would be no evil, and but for evil, there would be no peace. If all human beings were fools, they would not be regarded as fools, and if all human beings were sages, they would not be recognized as sages. But for poor people, the rich would not be recognized, and but for rich people, the poor would not be recognized. He created grace and created ugliness, males and females, fire and water, iron and wood, light and darkness, heat and cold, eating and hunger, drinking and thirst, sea and dry land, work and idleness, anxiety and ease of mind, laughter and weeping, healing and sickness. If there is no cleanness, there is no uncleanness, and if there is no

1. Wheel-angels.
2. B. Hag 12b–13a and En Yaakov, ad loc.
3. B. Hag 12b–13a.
4. PRE 3.
5. So suggested by Elijah of Vilna (Avot d-R. Nathan, Soncino, p. 185, n. 19). ARN 37.
6. B. Hag 15a.

uncleanness, there is no cleanness. If there is no righteous man, there is no wicked man; and if no wicked man, no righteous man. [All the aforegoing] to make known the might of the Holy One, who created everything in pairs and to be mated. For all things there is an opposite, except for the Holy One, who is One and has no second.[1]

13. Pause and consider that all the Holy One's creatures borrow one from the other. The day borrows from the night and the night from the day, yet they do not strive with each other as human beings do. The moon borrows from the stars and the stars from the moon; the light borrows from the sun and the sun from the light; the heavens borrow from the earth and the earth from the heavens; wisdom borrows from understanding and understanding from wisdom; loving-kindness borrows from righteousness and righteousness from loving-kindness; Torah borrows from precepts and precepts from Torah.[2] The Holy One's creatures borrow from each other and repay each other. It is only mortal man who borrows from his fellow, and his fellow seeks to swallow him with usurious interest and cheating.

Moreover, he who exacts interest says to the Holy One, "Why do You not take payment from Your world in which Your creatures are—payment from the earth, to which You give drink; payment from the flowers, which You make grow; payment from the lights, which You cause to shine; payment from the soul, which You breathe into them; payment from the body, which You preserve?" The Holy One replies, "See how much I lend, yet take no interest, and how much the earth lends and takes no interest. I take only the capital I lent, even as the earth takes her capital, for Scripture declares, 'The dust returneth to the earth as it was, and the spirit returneth unto God who gave it' " (Eccl. 12:7).[3]

Heaven and the Luminaries

14. *Shamayim*, "heaven," said R. Yose bar Hanina, is a composite of *sham*, "there," and *mayim*, "water." The sages taught in a Baraita that the word is a composite of *esh*, "fire," and *mayim*, "water." This proves that the Holy One worked them into each other until He made the firmament out of them.

Another explanation: *Shamayim* is so called because men wonder (*mishtomemim*) at it, saying: Of what (*shel mah*) is it composed? Of fire? Of water? It is an enigma.[4]

15. The Holy One created twelve constellations in the firmament. For each and every constellation, He created thirty hosts; and for each and every host, He created thirty legions; and for each and every legion, He created thirty cohorts; and for each and every cohort, thirty camps; and to each and every camp He appended three hundred and sixty-five thousands of myriads of stars, corresponding to the days of the solar year.[5]

16. There is a constellation that completes its circuit in twelve months—the sun; and there is a constellation that completes its circuit in thirty days—the moon; there is a constellation that completes its circuit in twelve years—Jupiter; and there is a constellation that completes its circuit in thirty years—Saturn. Aside from the aforementioned, Mercury, Venus, and Mars complete their circuits in four hundred and eighty years.[6]

17. The Pleiades gives taste to fruit, and Orion draws together each nodule [of the fruit] to the one adjoining it.[7]

18. At night, though it be night, one has the light of the moon, the stars, and the planets. Then when is it really dark? Just before dawn! After the moon sets and the stars set and the planets vanish, there is no darkness deeper than the hour before dawn. And in that hour the Holy One answers the world and all that are in it: out of the darkness He brings forth the dawn and gives light to the world.

The hind of the dawn [the morning star]—its light rays out as it rises. At the beginning, light comes little by little; then it spreads wider and wider, grows and increases; and at last it bursts into shining glory.[8]

19. We have been taught that Rabbi [Judah I, the Patriarch] said: The moon's column of light is not like the sun's column of light: the moon's column rises straight like a rod; while the sun's column rays out in all directions.[9]

20. Rav said: When the orb of the sun and the orb of the moon enter to get permission from the Holy One, their eyes are dimmed by the radiance of the Presence, so that when they wish to go out to give light to the world, they can see nothing at all. What then does the Holy One do to them? He shoots ahead of them arrows by whose light they go: "When the sun and the moon have come to a standstill in their habitations, they go by the light of Thine arrows, by the shining of Thy glittering spear" (Hab. 3:11).

R. Levi said: Each and every day the Holy One has to sit in judgment over the sun and the moon, because the sun and the moon do not wish to go forth to give light to the world. What reason do they give? They say, "Mortals offer incense to us, mortals bow down to us." What does the Holy One do about them? R. Yusta bar Shunem said:

---

1. Midrash Tem 2 (BhM, 1:107–8).
2. "On certain occasions, a command—such as the reading of the Megillah—is regarded as more pressing than the study of the Torah; and he who makes the Torah his life study need not perform so many commandments" (Exod. R., Soncino, p. 396, n. 7).
3. Tanhuma, *Mishpatim*, §12; Exod. R. 31:15.
4. B. Hag 12a; Gen. R. 4:7.
5. "The picture is primarily astronomical: the belt of the heavens (360°) divided into the twelve constellations, in turn divided into 30 *hayil* (or *hel*, in the sense of degrees), a *hayil* into 30 *rihaton* [in reality 60 minutes]" (Ber, trans. A. Ehrman [Ramat-Gan-Givatayim, 1973], p. 66a). Paraphrase of B. Ber 32b.
6. Gen. R. 10:4.
7. Gen. R. 10:6.
8. MTeh 22:4 and 22:13; Aggadat Esther 7:10 (ed. Buber, p. 68); B. Yoma 29a.
9. B. Yoma 28b.

He sits in judgment over them, until reluctantly they go forth to give light to the world, as is said, "Every morning doth He send down His judgment to the light, that it faileth not" (Zeph. 3:5).[1]

21. When the sun and the moon are about to go back in, they cannot tell where to go because of the radiance from above, and so they stand in the firmament and dawdle before entering, but the Holy One hurls torches, arrows, and spears of light before them. And toward the place where He hurls them, there they go.[2]

22. "The chariot of it is purple" (Song 3:10). The sun, which is set on high, rises in a chariot[3] and gives light to the world as it rides forth garlanded like a bridegroom, in keeping with "The sun, which is as a bridegroom coming out of his chamber," etc. (Ps. 19:6).[4]

23. The orb of the sun is kept within a sheath, in front of which there is a pool of water. When the sun comes out, the Holy One tempers its strength in the water, so that as it goes forth it will not incinerate the world.[5]

24. R. Levi said: Why is a man's voice not as audible by day as it is by night? Because of the sun's orb, which saws [its way] through the firmament as a carpenter saws through cedars. Even though the "sawdust" of the sun is called *la*, "nothing," [the sound made by the sawing of the sun's orb is deafening].[6]

25. Our masters taught: Were it not for the sound made by the sun's orb, the sound of Rome's tumult would be heard; and were it not for the sound of Rome's tumult, the sound of the sun's orb would be heard.

Our masters taught: There are three sounds that go from one end of the world to the other, yet the creatures within the world are not even aware of them: the sound of the sun's orb, the sound of Rome's tumult, and the sound of the soul as it leaves the body.[7]

26. Our masters taught: As to twilight, it is doubtful whether it is part day and part night, or whether all of it is day or all of it is night. How long does twilight last? After sunset, as long as the east still has a reddish glow: when the lower [sky] is pale but not the upper, it is twilight; [but] when the upper [sky] is as pale as the lower, it is night. Such is the opinion of R. Judah. R. Nehemiah said: [Twilight lasts after sunset] as long as it takes a man to walk half a *mil*. R. Yose said: Twilight is like the twinkling of an eye as night enters and the day departs, and it is impossible to determine its length.[8]

1. Lev. R. 31:9.
2. MTeh 19:11.
3. Cf. "the chariots of the sun" (2 Kings 23:11).
4. Num. R. 12:4; PRE 6.
5. Gen. R. 6:6.
6. B. Yoma 20b.
7. B. Yoma 20b; Gen. R. 6:7.
8. B. Shab 34b.

27. To what may twilight be compared? R. Tanhuma said: To a drop of blood placed on the tip of a sword—the instant it takes the drop to divide into two parts, that is twilight.[9]

28. R. Hanina said: He who wishes to know the length of twilight as defined by R. Nehemiah should leave Carmel's summit while the sun is still shining, go down and take a dip in the sea, and come up again—such is R. Nehemiah's estimate of the duration of twilight.[10]

29. At evening prayer, a man should say, "May it be Your will, O Lord my God, that You bring me forth from darkness into light." At morning prayer, a man should say, "I thank You, O Lord my God, that You have brought me out of darkness into light." At afternoon prayer, a man should say, "May it be Your will, O Lord my God, that as You have privileged me to see the sun's rising, You will privilege me to see its setting."[11]

30. Our masters taught: He who sees the sun at its cycle's beginning,[12] the moon in its power,[13] the stars in their orbits [as at the beginning of time], and the signs of the zodiac in their original order should say, "Blessed be He who wrought the work of creation."[14]

31. We have been taught that R. Eliezer said: The world is like an exedra,[15] with its north side not enclosed, and so when the sun reaches the northwest corner, it makes a detour as it returns above the firmament [to the east]. However, R. Joshua said that the world is like a tent,[16] with its north side also enclosed, and so when the sun reaches the northwest corner, it goes around the tent's rear [until it reaches the east],[17] as Scripture says, "It goeth toward the south and turneth again toward the north" (Eccles. 1:6)—"it goeth toward the south" by day and "turneth again toward the north" by night. "It turneth about continually in its course, and the wind returneth again to its circuits" (Eccles 1:6): this refers to the eastern and western sides of heaven, which at times the sun traverses and at other times runs parallel to.[18]

9. P. Ber 1:1, 2b.
10. B. Shab 35a.
11. Gen. R. 68:9.
12. At the beginning of a twenty-eight-year period, when the sun appears as it did at the time of creation.
13. That is, "its fullness."
14. B. Ber 59b; Lev. R. 23:8.
15. That is, closed on three sides and open on the fourth.
16. That is, completely enclosed by the firmament. "The opinions of R. Eliezer and R. Joshua appear to reflect the difference between two cosmologies. The exedra is a flat, semicircular shape, and so R. Eliezer advocates a two-dimensional model of the sun–earth. The tent is a solid object, and R. Joshua therefore proposes a three-dimensional model" (Professors Philip J. Davis and David Pingree of Brown University).
17. R. Eliezer and R. Joshua endeavor to set forth just where the sun disappears during the night.
18. B. BB 25b and En Yaakov, ad loc.

32. The Holy One created three hundred and sixty-five windows for the world to use: one hundred and eighty-two in the east, one hundred and eighty-two in the west, and one in the firmament's middle, out of which the sun issued at the beginning of the work of creation.[1]

33. R. Simeon ben Yohai said: We do not know whether the sun and the moon fly through the air, glide across the firmament, or have a regular route assigned to them. It is an exceedingly difficult matter, and no person can fathom it.[2]

34. Antoninus asked Rabbi [Judah I, the Patriarch], "Why does the sun rise in the east and set in the west?" Rabbi: "Were it the other way around, you would have asked the same question." Antoninus: "My question still stands—why should the sun set in the west? [Why does it not return to the east, where it rose, or to any other point in the sky?"] Rabbi: "The sun sets in the west to make obeisance to its Maker, as is said, 'The host of the heavens make obeisance to Thee' " (Neh. 9:6). Antoninus: "Then let the sun go midway in heaven, make obeisance, and set at once." Rabbi: "[The sun sinks gradually] for the sake of workers and wayfarers."[3]

35. Our masters taught: The sages of Israel maintain that the sphere is stationary, but the constellations revolve; while the sages of the nations of the world maintain that the sphere revolves and the constellations in it are stationary. Rabbi [Judah I, the Patriarch] observed: The fact that we never find the Wain in the south or Scorpio in the north is a refutation of what the sages of the nations maintain.

The sages of Israel maintain that the sun travels beneath the sky by day, [and thus is seen] and above the sky at night; while the sages of the nations of the world maintain that it travels beneath the sky by day and below the earth at night. Said Rabbi: Their view is preferable to ours, for springs are cold during the day but hot during the night.[4]

We have been taught that R. Nathan said: In summer, the sun travels in the high part of heaven; therefore the whole world is hot, while the springs are cold. In winter, the sun travels in the lower part of heaven; therefore the whole world, all of it, is cold, while the springs are hot.

Our masters taught: The sun travels over four courses: during Nisan, Iyyar, and Sivan, it travels over the mountains, in order to melt the snows; during Tammuz, Av, and Elul, over the inhabited world, to ripen the fruits; during Tishri, Marheshvan, and Kislev, over seas, to dry up the rivers; during Tevet, Shevat, and Adar, through the wilderness, so as not to dry up the seeds [planted in the ground].[5]

1. P. RH 2:5, 58a.
2. Gen. R. 6:8.
3. If the sun sank suddenly, they would have no way of planning when to stop work or to halt in their journey. B. Sanh 91a.
4. They are warmed by the sun, which, as the sages of the nations maintain, is beneath the earth.
5. B. Pes 94b (Soncino).

36. R. Judah bar Ilai said: The sun is kept within its sheath, as is said, "As for the sun, He set into a tent" (Ps. 19:5). But during the Tammuz solstice, it emerges from its sheath to ripen fruits.[6]

37. We have been taught that R. Eliezer the Elder said: By the time the fifteenth day in the month of Av comes, the power of the sun is depleted.[7]

38. "Day unto day . . . poureth out [time] by a mere word," etc. (Ps. 19:3). The "pouring out" of time refers to the four seasons of the year. On the first day of the vernal equinox and on the first day of the autumnal equinox, day and night are equal. From the beginning of the vernal equinox up until the summer solstice, the day borrows time from the night; from the summer solstice until the autumnal equinox, the day yields time to the night; from the autumnal equinox until the winter solstice, the night borrows from the day; and from the winter solstice until the vernal equinox, the night yields time to the day, so that by the time of the vernal equinox and of the autumnal equinox, neither owes any time to the other. They borrow one from the other, in trust, and yield one to the other, in trust, and no creature hears a word exchanged between them: "There is no speech, there are no words, neither are their voices heard" (Ps. 19:4).[8]

39. R. Yohanan said: What is implied in the verse "Dominion and fear are with Him; He maketh peace in His high places" (Job 25:2)? That the sun has never seen the [dark], unshining face of the moon; nor has it seen the [dark], unshining face of the rainbow.

R. Levi said: Not one of the planets that travels through the sky ever sees the planet in front of it, only the one behind it, much like a man who goes down a ladder with his face turned backward. This is done in order that each and every planet might say, "I am the first." In such ways "He maketh peace in His high places."

R. Simeon ben Yohai taught: The firmament is water, and the stars are fire, yet they dwell with each other and do no harm one to the other, as is written, "He maketh peace in His high places."[9]

40. The tail of Scorpio is placed in the river of fire.[10]

41. "The Bear will be comforted for her children" (Job 38:32). Why does the Bear follow the Pleiades? Because the Bear says to the Pleiades, "Give me back my children." For at the time the Holy One wanted to bring a flood to the world, He took two stars from the Pleiades and brought the flood to the world. Then, when He wanted to stop it, He took two stars from the Bear and stopped it.[11]

6. Tanhuma B, *Tetzavveh*, §6; Tanhuma, *Tetzavveh*, §8.
7. B. BB 121b.
8. MTeh 19:10; MhG Gen. pp. 43–44.
9. B. RH 23b; P. RH 2:4, 58a; Deut. R. 5:12.
10. B. Ber 58b.
11. B. Ber 59b.

42. What are *zikin?*[1] Samuel said: A comet.

Samuel said further: The lanes of heaven are as familiar to me as the lanes of Nehardea, except the comet—I do not know what it is. We have a tradition that it never passes through Orion. If it did pass through Orion, the world would be destroyed.

But we saw it pass through.

Only its radiance passed through, which made it seem as though it had passed through. R. Huna son of R. Joshua said: The heaven called Curtain was pulled aside and rolled up, so that the light of the firmament was seen.[2]

43. Our masters taught: When the sun is in eclipse, it is a bad omen for the entire world, for all of it. By what parable may the matter be illustrated? By the one of a king of flesh and blood who made a banquet for his servants and put up a lamp for them. But when he became angry at them, he said to his attendant, "Take away the lamp from them, and let them sit in the dark."

We have been taught that R. Meir said: Whenever the luminaries are in eclipse, it is a bad omen for Israel, since they are the ones most likely to receive blows, as may be illustrated by a parable: A schoolteacher comes to school with a strap in his hand. Who is the one apprehensive? The pupil who is accustomed to being punished daily.

Our masters taught: When the sun is in eclipse, it is a bad omen for the nations of the world; when the moon is in eclipse, it is a bad omen for Israel, since Israel reckon time by the moon, while the nations of the world count it by the sun. If the sun is in eclipse in the east, it is a bad omen for those who dwell in the east; if in the west, it is a bad omen for those who dwell in the west; if in the center of heaven, it is a bad omen for the entire world, for all of it. If its visage is as red as blood, [it is a sign that] the sword is coming to the world; if it is the color of sackcloth, the arrows of famine are coming to the world; if it resembles both,[3] then both the sword and the arrows of famine are coming to the world. If the eclipse is at sunset, punishment will tarry in coming; if at dawn, punishment hastens to come to the world. Some say the meaning of the signs is to be reversed. No nation is smitten but that its gods are smitten together with it, as is said, "And against all the gods of Egypt I will execute judgments" (Exod. 12:12). But when Israel carry out the will of Him who is everywhere, they need have no fear of any of these [omens]: "Thus saith the Lord: Learn not the way of the nations, and be not dismayed at the signs of heaven, for the nations are dismayed at them" (Jer. 10:2). The Gentiles will be dismayed, but Israel will not be dismayed.[4]

44. R. Simeon ben Pazzi said in the name of R. Joshua ben Levi, who cited Bar Kappara: When a man knows how to calculate the seasons and planetary courses, but does not, Scripture says of him, "They regard not the work of the Lord, neither have they considered the operation of His hands" (Isa. 5:12).

R. Samuel ben Nahmani said in the name of R. Jonathan: What is the proof that it is a man's obligation to calculate the seasons and the planetary courses? The verse "This is your wisdom and understanding in the sight of the peoples" (Deut. 4:6). What is wisdom and understanding in the sight of the peoples? The capacity to calculate seasons and courses of the planets.[5]

The Earth

45. Rabban Simeon ben Gamaliel said: The earth has four names: *eretz*, *tevel*, *adamah*, and *arka*, to correspond to the four seasons. *Eretz*, corresponds to the vernal equinox, when the earth forces up (*meritzah*) its produce; *tevel* corresponds to the summer solstice, when the earth seasons (*metabbelet*) its produce; *adamah* corresponds to the autumn equinox, when the ground is broken up by the rains into many clods of earth (*adamah*); and *arka* corresponds to the winter solstice, which causes crops to wither (*moreket*).[6]

46. The entire world, all of it, is made up of one-third of seas, one-third of deserts, and one-third of arable land.[7]

47. Egypt was four hundred parasangs by four hundred parasangs. Now Egypt is one-sixtieth of Ethiopia, Ethiopia one-sixtieth of the world, the world one-sixtieth of the Garden [of Eden], the Garden one-sixtieth of Eden, and Eden one-sixtieth of Gehenna. Thus the entire world, all of it, is something like the lid of a pot for Gehenna.[8]

48. R. Nathan said: The entire inhabited world is situated under a single star. You can see this for yourself. If a man fixes his eye on a star and goes east, he finds himself still under it; in fact, if he goes in any of the four directions of the world, he will find himself under it.[9]

49. R. Yose bar Hanina said: What is meant by "In a land that no man passed through, where Adam had not intended for anyone to dwell" (Jer. 2:6)? Since no man has ever passed through it, how could anyone be said to dwell there? However, the verse asserts that a land Adam decreed should be inhabited became inhabited, and a land concerning which Adam did not so decree did not become inhabited.[10]

50. Alexander of Macedon put a question to the elders of the Negev, [the south country]. He asked: Which is farther—from heaven to earth, or from east to west? They

1. Shooting stars.
2. B. Ber 58b.
3. If it is pale red.
4. B. Suk 29a, and En Yaakov, ad loc.
5. B. Shab 75b; Yalkut, Isa., §402.
6. Gen. R. 13:12.
7. Tosafot on Pes 94a, citing a Midrash.
8. B. Pes 94a.
9. Ibid.
10. B. Sot 46b and En Yaakov, ad loc.

replied: From east to west. The proof is that when the sun is in the east, [it is so far away that] all men can look at it. When the sun is in the west, [it is also so far away that] all men can look at it. But when the sun is in the center of the sky, [it is so close that] no one look at it.

However, the sages said: The distance from earth to heaven and from east to west is the same. But what is the reason that, when the sun is in the center of the sky, no one look at it? Because it is completely visible, nothing obstructing the view of it.[1]

51. We have been taught: R. [Simeon ben] Gamaliel had a tube through which he looked and could see as far as two thousand cubits on dry land, and, correspondingly, two thousand cubits on the sea. If one wished to know the depth of a valley, R. Simeon would bring the tube, look through it, and ascertain the valley's depth. Incidentally, when one wished to know the height of a palm tree, he would measure his own height and his own shadow, then the shadow of the palm tree, and thus know [more or less] the height of the palm tree.[2]

Lightnings and Thunders, Clouds and Rains, Rainbows and Earthquakes

52. On seeing shooting stars, earthquakes, thunderclaps, and lightnings, one should say, "Blessed be He whose strength and might fill the world." On seeing mountains, hills, seas, rivers, and deserts, one should say, "Blessed be He who wrought the work of creation." R. Judah said: He who sees the Great [Mediterranean] Sea should say, "Blessed be He who made the Great Sea," but only if he sees it at considerable intervals.[3]

53. R. Berekhiah the Priest said: Lightning is something generated by the fire from on high. Hence, when it goes forth, its light illuminates the world from end to end.[4]

54. Rava said: A single flash, white lightning, green lightning, clouds that rise in the west and move from the south, and two clouds that rise facing each other are all [signs of] trouble. When? At night. But in the morning there is no significance to any of these phenomena.

What causes thunder? Samuel said: Clouds that rub against each other while whirling about, as Scripture says, "The voice of Thy thunder was in the whirlwind; the lightning lighted up the world, the earth trembled and shook" (Ps. 77:19). The sages, however, said: Clouds that pour water into each other. R. Aha bar Jacob said: A powerful lightning that strikes clouds and breaks off chunks of ice. R. Ashi said: There are hollows in the clouds, and when a blast of wind comes and blows through these hollows, it makes a sound like wind blowing across the opening of a cask. R. Aha bar Jacob's explanation is the most likely, for when lightning flashes, the clouds rumble, and then rain begins to fall.[5]

55. "A path for thunderclaps" (Job 38:25). I have created many thunderclaps in the clouds, and for each clap a separate path, so that two claps should not travel by the same path. For if two claps did travel by the same path, they would devastate the entire world.[6]

56. "Lo, these are but parts of His ways; . . . but the thunder of His mighty deeds who can understand?" (Job 26:14). R. Huna said: When thunder goes forth in the fullness of its force, no creature can understand it. Nevertheless, the clearheaded surmise His hints and His thoughts.[7]

57. R. Joshua ben Levi said: Thunders were created only to straighten out the crookedness of the heart: "God hath so devised it, that men should fear before Him" (Eccles. 3:14).[8]

58. R. Yohanan and R. Simeon ben Lakish differed: Cloud vapors, said R. Yohanan, come only from above, for they are described as "clouds of heaven" (Dan. 7:13). But R. Simeon ben Lakish said that cloud vapors come only from below, for "He causeth the vapors to ascend from the ends of the earth" (Ps. 135:7). R. Yohanan's view is that God's giving of the vapors is like a man's giving a cask of wine to his friend, container and all. R. Simeon's view is that even as a man says to his friend, "Lend me a measure of wheat," and his friend declares, "Bring your basket and measure it out for yourself," so the Holy One declares to the earth, "Bring Me your cloud vapor, and you will receive rain."[9]

59. R. Hanan of Sepphoris said in the name of R. Samuel bar Nahman: The Holy One changed the original order of things and caused the earth to be watered from above[10] for four reasons: (1) to restrain strong-arm men;[11] (2) to wash away noxious dews; (3) to water the high places as well as the low; and (4) to make all living things lift their eyes to heaven.[12]

60. We have been taught that R. Eliezer said: The earth drinks only from the waters of the Ocean, as is said, "There rose up a mist from the earth and watered the whole face of the ground" (Gen. 2:6). R. Joshua asked him: But are not the waters of the Ocean salty? R. Eliezer replied: They are made sweet in the clouds.

Nevertheless, R. Joshua maintained: The entire

---

1. B. Tam 31b–32a.
2. B. Er 43b.
3. B. Ber 54a.
4. Tanhuma B. *Be-haalotekha*, §7; Lev. R. 31:8

5. B. Ber 59a.
6. B. BB 16a.
7. That God asks them to repent (*Yefeh Toar*, ad loc.). Gen. R. 12:1.
8. B. Ber 59a.
9. Gen. R. 13:11.
10. See Gen. 2:5–6. Verse 6 reads: "There went up a mist from the earth, and watered the whole face of the ground."
11. If it gathered on the ground, they would steal the water belonging to others.
12. Gen. R. 13:9; P. Ta 3:3, 66c.

earth, all of it, drinks from the upper waters, for "the earth . . . drinketh water of the rain of heaven" (Deut. 11:11). If so, what is signified by "There went up a mist from the earth"? The verse shows that, by a great effort, the clouds rise up to the firmament, where they open their mouths like a leather bottle and receive the rainwater: "As with a gourd, they gather water out of His vapor" (Job 36:27).[1] Since the clouds are perforated like a sieve, they distill water to the ground, as is said, "Distilling waters from the thick clouds" (2 Sam. 22:12).[2] And between one drop and the next, there is only a hairsbreadth.[3]

61. "[The Lord answered]: . . . Who hath cleft a channel for the waterflood?" (Job 38:25). I have created many drops in the clouds, and for each and every drop I created a mold of its own, so that two drops should not issue from the same mold. For if two drops were to issue from the same mold, they would make the soil so muddy that it would yield no fruit.[4]

62. The firmament is like a lake. Above the lake is a vault, and [because of the heat of the lake] the vault exudes heavy drops of water, which, though descending into salt water, do not mingle with it.

R. Yohanan observed: Do not wonder at this, for even though the Jordan passes through the lake of Tiberias, its water does not mingle with the lake's water.

In this matter, there is the working of a miracle. For when a man sifts stalks of stubble or grains of wheat in a sieve, they intermingle while dropping a distance of two or three fingerbreadths. Yet, though the raindrops have been traveling ever so many years, they do not intermingle.[5]

63. R. Simeon ben Eleazar said: Not one handbreadth [of rain] descends from above without the earth bringing up two handbreadths [of moisture] to meet it.

R. Levi said: The upper waters are male while the lower are female, and the upper waters say to the lower waters, "Receive us. You are the Holy One's creatures, while we are His messengers." At once the lower waters receive the upper waters, as is written, "Let the earth open [to receive], that it may bear the fruit of salvation with righteousness in blossom at its side. I the Lord have created it" (Isa. 45:8). I created rain for the specific purpose of benefiting the world and making it habitable.[6]

64. "When my doctrine shall break down their stubbornness, there will be rain" (Deut. 32:2).[7] R. Berekhiah said: After human beings break their stubbornness, rain will come down at once.

"And water the whole ground" (Gen. 2:6). R. Eleazar said in the name of R. Yose bar Zimra: [Through rain], everything is blessed—the give-and-take of commerce is blessed, and merchants make a profit. R. Hiyya bar Abba said: The sick too are relieved; their limbs become more supple.

Avimi of Havraya used to visit the sick. When autumn rain fell and he was asked, "How are the sick faring?" he would answer, "They feel relieved."

R. Abba said: Even a precious stone feels the rain. The sages said: Even fish feel it.

R. Phinehas related: It once happened that a fish caught off the coast of Acco was estimated to weigh three hundred *litra*, yet, when weighed, it came to only two hundred *litra*. An old fisherman who was there said, "That is because autumn rain has not yet fallen." After rain fell, they caught another fish that was estimated to weigh two hundred *litra* but, when weighed, was found to be three hundred *litra*.[8]

65. R. Joshua ben Levi said: When rain comes down, cattle long to rut.[9]

66. R. Hana of Baghdad said: Rainwater soaks, saturates, and fertilizes [the earth], and thus gives size and plumpness to fruit.[10]

67. [A cloud is called] *haziz* because it produces [magnificent] visions (*hezyonot*) in the sky and causes the holy spirit to rest on human beings.[11]

68. R. Joshua ben Levi said: When rain comes down, it [makes plants grow and thereby] gives contour to the face of the earth.[12]

69. "I will give the rain of your Land in its season, the former rain (*yoreh*), and the latter rain (*malkosh*)" (Deut. 11:14). Our masters taught: The former rain is called *yoreh* because it instructs (*yoreh*) people to plaster their roofs, to gather in their produce, and to attend to all their [other] needs [for the winter]. Another explanation: It is called *yoreh* because it saturates the soil and waters it to its nethermost depths: "Saturating (*ravveh*) her furrows, leveling her ridges, Thou makest her soft with showers; Thou blessest the growth thereof" (Ps. 65:11). Another explanation: It is called *yoreh* because it comes down gently (*yored*), not vehemently. But is it not possible that it is called *yoreh*, "that which shoots down," because it makes fruit fall from trees—even [young] trees—and washes away seeds? No. Scripture has here also *malkosh*, "latter rain," implying that as the latter rain is a blessing, so also is the former rain. But may not the latter rain be called *malkosh* because it knocks down houses, shatters trees,

1. The word *yazokku* ("they gather") is connected with *zika* ("a water gourd"). Literally, "They pour down rain according to the vapor thereof."
2. Literally, "Binding (*heshrat*) of waters, thick clouds." But here *heshrat* is derived from *hashar* ("to sift," "to distill drops as from a sieve.").
3. B. Ta 9b.
4. B. BB 16a.
5. Gen. R. 4:5; Yalkut, *Bereshit*, §5.
6. Gen R. 13:13.
7. JV: "My doctrine shall drop as the rain." But R. Berekhiah derives *yaarof* ("shall drop") from *araf* ("break the neck").
8. Gen. R. 13:14 and 13:16; Yalkut, *Bereshit*, §2.
9. Gen. R. 13:6.
10. B. Ket 10b.
11. Gen R. 13:12.
12. Gen. R. 13:17.

and brings up the locusts (*lekesh*)? No. Scripture has here *yoreh*, implying that as the former rain is a blessing, so also is the latter rain. How do we know that the former rain is a blessing? From the verse "Be glad then, ye children of Zion, and rejoice in the Lord your God; for He giveth you the former rain (*moreh*) in [His] kindness. Now He causeth the rain to come down for you as before, the former rain and the latter rain" (Joel 2:23).[1]

70. If a man extracts rainwater from the air of Sodom and irrigates a garden bed with it, the bed will not sprout.[2]

71. R. Judah said: Wind after rain is as beneficial as rain, clouds after rain as beneficial as rain, sunshine after rain as beneficial as two rainfalls.

Rava said: One snowfall is as beneficial to mountains as five rainfalls are to level ground.

Rava said further: Snow is beneficial to mountains, vehement rain to trees, gentle rain to the produce of fields, drizzling rain even to kernels under hard clods.[3]

72. R. Yohanan said: *Porehot* are a sign that rain is coming. But what are *porehot*? R. Papa said: Thin clouds under thick clouds. R. Judah said: A mist before rain is a sign that rain is coming; in order to remember this, think of a sieve.[4] A mist after rain indicates the cessation of rain; in order to remember this, think of the excrements of goats.[5]

73. When Ulla visited Babylonia and saw *porehot*, he said, "Bring your [perishable] things indoors, for rain will come soon." But in the end, no rain came. So he said, "As the Babylonians are deceivers, so their rains are deceivers."

In the west [the Land of Israel], they say: When clouds are dark, they contain much water; but when they are light, they contain little water.[6]

74. R. Alexandri said in the name of R. Joshua ben Levi: He who sees the rainbow in the cloud should fall on his face [and pray]. In the west [the Land of Israel], they cursed anyone who did so, because it looked as though he were bowing down [in worship] to the rainbow.[7]

75. R. Judah bar Nahmani, Resh Lakish's interpreter, expounded: When a man looks at a rainbow, his eyes grow dim, for it is said, "As the appearance of the bow that is in the cloud in the day of rain . . . so was the appearance of the likeness of the glory of the Lord" (Ezek. 1:28).[8]

76. What are *zevaot*? R. Ketina said: A rumbling.

Once, while R. Ketina was walking along a road, a rumbling was heard the instant he reached the entrance to the house of a certain necromancer. So he said, "Perhaps the necromancer knows the meaning of this rumbling." Raising his voice, the necromancer said, "Ketina, Ketina, why should I not know? When the Holy One calls to mind His children who abide in anguish in the midst of the nations of the world, He lets fall two tears into the Great [Mediterranean] Sea, and the sound is heard from one end of the world to the other—that is the cause of the rumbling [you heard]." R. Ketina's own explanation of the rumbling was that the Holy One claps His hands; R. Nathan's explanation, that the Holy One emits a sigh; and the Sages said that He stamps upon the firmament. R. Aha bar Jacob said that He presses his feet together beneath the throne of glory.[9]

Fire and Wind

77. We have been taught that R. Yose said: It had been God's intention to create fire on the eve of the Sabbath, but it was not created until Sabbath's outgoing. At the Sabbath's outgoing, the Holy One gave Adam the kind of knowledge that is analogous to the knowledge above, so that he fetched two stones, rubbed one against the other, and from between them fire came forth.[10]

78. The sages taught: Fire and hybrids were not created during the six days of creation, although it had been God's intention that they be created.[11]

79. Our masters taught that there are six kinds of fire: fire that devours but does not lap up; fire that laps up but does not devour; fire that both devours and laps up; fire that devours moist matter as well as dry matter; fire that pushes another fire away; and fire that devours fire. Fire that devours but does not lap up—that is our fire [which is quenched by water]; laps up but does not devour—a sick man's fever; devours and laps up—that of Elijah, of which it is written, "It lapped up the water that was in the trench" (1 Kings 18:38); devours both moist and dry matter—the fire of the woodpile [on the altar]; fire that pushes another fire away—that of Gabriel;[12] and fire that devours fire—that of the Presence, concerning which a master said: He put forth His finger among the angels and incinerated them.[13]

80. "And behold, the bush burned with fire, but the bush was not consumed" (Exod. 3:2). From this verse, the sages inferred that the fire above leaps up like a palm branch

1. B. Ta 6a.
2. Gen. R. 51:5.
3. B. Ta 3b–4a.
4. "From which the finest flour resembling a mist comes first, and then the heavier, thicker parts, resembling drops of rain" (Ta, trans. Henry Malter, p.64, n. 157).
5. "First the animal discharges with force, and then relaxes" (Ta trans. Henry Malter, p.64, n. 158). B. Ta 9b.
6. B. Ta 9b–10a.
7. B. Ber 59a.
8. Hence, the human eye cannot bear it. B. Hag 16a.
9. B. Ber 59a.
10. B. Pes 54a.
11. Gen. R. 82:15.
12. He went down into the furnace into which Hananiah, Mishael, and Azariah had been cast, and pushed away the fire.
13. B. Yoma 21b.

in tongues of flame,[1] burns but does not consume,[2] and is black. Whereas the fire below does not leap up like a palm branch, is red in color, and both burns and consumes.[3]

81. There are many kinds of light in fire.[4]

82. Fire is one-sixtieth of Gehenna.[5]

83. "He appointeth a weight for the wind" (Job 28:25). R. Joshua bar Hananiah said: When the wind goes forth from the Holy One, it endeavors to destroy the world. But the Holy One slows it down with mountains and breaks it up with hills as He commands it, "Take care not to harm My creatures."

R. Huna said: On three occasions when winds went forth, the pressure of their weight unrestrained, the world might have been destroyed by them: one in the days of Jonah, another in the days of Job, and the third in the days of Elijah.[6]

84. Once R. Huna and R. Hisda were sitting together when Geniva happened to pass by. Said one to the other, "Let us stand up for him—he is a man of Torah learning." The other replied: "Shall we stand up for a quarrelsome man?" In the meantime, Geniva came up to them and asked, "What are you occupied with?" They replied, "With winds." He said, "R. Hanan bar Rava, citing Rav, asserted the following: Every day four winds blow, and the north wind blows with each of them. Were it not so, the world could not continue to exist for a single hour. The south wind is the most violent, and if the angel who resembles the hawk did not hold it back, it would have destroyed the entire world, all of it."[7]

85. Once Rava and R. Nahman bar Isaac were sitting together when R. Nahman bar Jacob went by in a gilded litter, a cloak of shaggy green cloth spread over him. Rava went out to meet him, but R. Nahman bar Isaac did not stir, saying, "He is probably a member of the exilarch's court, whom Rava needs, while I do not need them." However, when R. Nahman bar Isaac saw that it was R. Nahman bar Jacob, he also went out to meet him. Presently, R. Nahman bar Jacob bared his arm, saying, "The east wind is blowing." Rava observed: "This is what Rav said: 'Because of it, a woman will miscarry'; while Samuel said, 'Because of it, even a pearl of the sea will rot.' "

"Though he be fruitful among his brothers, when an east wind cometh," etc. (Hos. 13:15). Rava said, "Because of it, even the pin in a plowshare becomes loose." R. Jospeh said, "Because of it, even a peg in a wall becomes loose." R. Aha bar Jacob said, "Because of it, even cane in a wicker basket becomes slack."[8]

86. The east wind is always good; the west wind always bad. The north wind is good for wheat grown to one-third [of its size] and bad for olives when they are budding. The south wind is bad for wheat grown to one-third [of its size] and good for olives when they are budding.[9]

87. R. Judah said: What is meant by the word *yaarof* in "My doctrine shall drop [*yaarof*] as the rain," etc. (Deut. 32:2)? The word *yaarof* [suggests] the west wind, which comes from the world's back [*oref*].[10] In "My speech which is like dew is deemed worthless [*tizzal*]" (ibid.),[11] the word *tizzal* [suggests] the coming of the north wind, which [withers crops and leads to such scarcity that] even gold becomes worthless [*mazzelet*]. In "As the he-goats [*seirim*] upon the tender grass" (ibid.), the word *seirim* suggests the east wind, which rages through the world like a he-goat [*seir*]. And in "As showers [*revivim*] upon the herb" (ibid.), the word *revivim* [suggests] the south wind, which brings up showers and causes the growth of herbage.[12]

88. "And it came to pass, when the sun arose, that God prepared a *harishit* east wind" (Jon. 4:8). What is the root meaning of *harishit*? That when it blows, said R. Judah, it plows [*horeshet*] the sea into many furrows. That when it blows, said Rabbah, its presence stills[13] all other winds.

89. We have been taught that Abba Saul said: Fine weather at Pentecost is a good sign for the year.

R. Zevid said: If the first day of New Year is warm, the year will be warm; if cold, the year will be cold.[14]

90. R. Isaac bar Avdimi said: On the night following the seventh day of Tabernacles, all watched for the smoke rising from the pile of wood [on the altar]. If the smoke inclined toward the north, poor people rejoiced and the [prosperous] householders were dejected, because the rains of the coming year were going to be excessive, and their produce would have to be left to rot.[15] If the smoke inclined toward the south, poor people were dejected and the [prosperous] householders rejoiced, because the rains of the coming year were going to be scanty, and the produce would be preserved. If the smoke turned toward the east, everyone rejoiced;[16] if toward the west, all were dejected.[17]

1. *Labbat* ("flame") is associated with lulav, ("palm branch").
2. The bush remained unconsumed.
3. "Both burns and consumes"—Mah; "burns but does not consume"—BR. Exod. R. 2:5.
4. B. Ber 52b.
5. B. Ber 57b.
6. Jon. 1:4; Job 1:19; 1 Kings 19:11; Gen. R. 24:4; Lev. R. 15:1.
7. B. Git 31b; B. BB 25a.
8. B. Git 31b–32a.
9. B. Yoma 21b.
10. The east wind being called *kedem* ("front").
11. JV: "My speech shall distill as the dew."
12. B. BB 25a.
13. Rabbah associates the word *harishit* with *heresh*, ("be still"). B. Git 31b.
14. B. BB 147a.
15. So the poor would be able to buy them cheaply.
16. Since it indicated normal rainfall and normal prices.
17. Because the east wind dries up the seeds and causes famine. B. BB 147a; B. Yoma 21b.

91. R. Nahman said: The heat emitted by the cloud-covered sun is more intense than the direct heat of the sun; in order to remember this, think of a cask of vinegar.[1] The dazzling sunlight [coming through breaks in the clouds] is worse than direct sunlight; in order to remember this, think of drippings from the roof.[2] The end of the summer is more trying than the summer itself; in order to remember this, think of a reheated oven.[3]

92. R. Levi said: Behold, you have labored—you have plowed, sown, weeded, and cropped, hoed and reaped, bound the sheaves, threshed and stacked the sheaves; still, if the Holy One did not bring forth a little wind to winnow for you, how would you stay alive?[4]

93. R. Simeon ben Halafta was a corpulent man. One day, the heat all but overpowered him. So he climbed to the top of a boulder, where he sat down and said to his daughter, "Daughter, fan me with your fan, and I will give you two talents' worth of spikenard." Just then a breeze began to blow. So he said; "How many talents' worth of spikenard do we owe the Master of this breeze?"[5]

94. There is the story of Rabban Gamaliel and R. Akiva, who [during Tabernacles] were traveling on a ship. R. Akiva put himself to the trouble of erecting a sukkah on the ship's bow. The next day, a wind blew and ripped it away. Rabban Gamaliel said to him, "Akiva, now where is your sukkah?"[6]

Seas and Rivers

95. R. Judah said in the name of Rav: At the time the Holy One was about to create the world, He said to the prince of the sea, "Open your mouth and swallow all the water in the world."[7] The prince of the sea replied, "Master of the universe, I have all I can do to put up with the water that already belongs to me." At once, God kicked and slew him: "He struck the sea with His power, and through His understanding smote Rahab" (Job 26:12). From this verse, said R. Isaac, it follows that the name of the prince of the sea was Rahab. Incidentally, had the waters not covered him, no creature could have endured the foul odor that his carcass emitted.[8]

96. When the word went forth from the mouth of the Almighty, "Let the waters . . . be gathered together" (Gen. 1:9), the mountains and the hills rose up from the uttermost parts of the earth and were scattered over the whole earth, so that many valleys were formed in the earth's surface, and the waters rolled down and were gathered into the valleys. The waters immediately lifted themselves up and rose to cover the earth as in the beginning. But the Holy One rebuked them, subdued them beneath the soles of His feet, and measured out their extent with His span, so that they should neither enlarge nor diminish. As a man makes a hedge for his vineyard, so He made the sand into a hedge for the sea. Thus, when the waters rise and see the sand before them, they turn back.[9]

97. "Like the raging sea" (Isa. 57:20). One wave says, "When I rise up, I will overwhelm the entire world, all of it." But when that wave reaches the sand, it submits to it. Still, the next wave learns nothing from the first.[10]

98. "The fountain of God is full of water" (Ps. 65:10). A certain heretic asked R. Meir, "Is it possible that 'the fountain of God remained full of water' [ibid.] and has not diminished at all since the six days of Creation? Such a thing is incredible!"[11] R. Meir replied, "Go in and bathe, and weigh yourself before you enter and after." The heretic went and weighed himself, and his weight had not diminished at all. R. Meir asked him, "All that perspiration—did it not ooze out of you?" The heretic: "Yes." R. Meir: "If your fountain—though you are but flesh and blood—has in no way diminished [by losing sweat], how much less by far should this be true of the fountain of the Holy One!"[12]

99. It happened that Hadrian Caesar sought to fathom the depth of the Adriatic Sea. He took ropes and kept lowering them for three and a half years, until he heard a heavenly voice say, "Cease and desist, Hadrian!"

Again, Hadrian Caesar sought to know how the waters praise the Holy One, so he made chests of glass, into which he put men, and then lowered the chests into the Great [Mediterranean] Sea. When the men came up, they said: We have heard the waters of the Great Sea praise the Holy One thus: "The Lord on high is mighty" (Ps. 93:4).[13]

100. "All the rivers run into the sea, yet the sea is not full" (Eccles. 1:7). There is the story of R. Eliezer and R. Joshua, who were sailing in the Great Sea, and their ship entered an area where the water was becalmed. R. Eliezer said to R. Joshua, "We have been brought here for no purpose other than [to prove that what Ecclesiastes says about the waters of the sea is true]." So they filled a cask to the brim with that water. When they arrived in Rome, Hadrian asked them, "What is distinctive about the water of the Great Sea?" They replied, "Its water

---

1. It emits a stronger smell through a tiny crack than when open.
2. Immersion in water is more agreeable than being under such drippings.
3. An oven, once heated, is quickly reheated, even as more heat affects a person more quickly at the end of a hot summer. B. Yoma 28b–29a.
4. PR 18:1 (YJS 1:381); Yalkut, *Emor*, §653.
5. B. BM 86a.
6. A sukkah on a ship's bow was not a proper sukkah to begin with. B. Suk 23a.
7. So that the dry land may be seen.
8. B. BB 74b and En Yaakov, ad loc.
9. MTeh 93:5; PRE 5.
10. Yalkut, Isa., §490, citing Yelammedenu.
11. Then where does the rain come from?
12. Gen. R. 4:4.
13. MTeh 93:6.

absorbs other water." He said, "Let me have some of this water." They gave him a flaskful, and though more water was poured into it, the flask kept absorbing it.[1]

101. "The rivers have lifted up *dokhyam*"[2] (Ps. 93:3). R. Levi said: The waters were whispering to one another, asking, "Where shall we go?" and answering, "To the sea [*derekh yam*]! To the sea!" However, according to the sages, the waters said, "We are being crushed [*dakkim*], receive us! We are being reduced to submission [*meduk-kakim*], receive us!"[3]

102. All rivers are useful when flowing over land—blessed by sweetness, so that the world derives benefit from them. But once they flow into the sea, they become useless—cursed by bitterness, so that the world has no benefit from them.[4]

103. R. Judah said in the name of Rav: All rivers are lower in altitude than the three [Pishon, Gihon, and Hiddekel (Tigris)], and these three are lower in altitude than the Euphrates.[5]

What is the etymology of Hiddekel? R. Ashi said: Its waters are pungent [*had*] and swift [*kal*]. What is the etymology of Euphrates [Perat]? Its waters are fruitful [*porim*] and ever more abundant.[6]

104. R. Hiyya said: When a man goes up to the summit of Carmel and espies a kind of sieve in the Sea of Tiberias, that is Miriam's well.[7]

105. The Jordan issues from the cavern of Panias, flows through the lake of Sibkay,[8] the lake of Tiberias, and the lake of Sodom, and goes on until it falls into the Great [Mediterranean] Sea. Then it rolls on and on downward until it reaches Leviathan's mouth.[9]

106. The Jordan traverses the Sea of Tiberias but does not mingle with it.[10]

107. "The gathering together of the waters called He seas" (Gen. 1:10). R. Yose bar Halafta said: Since there is only one [Mediterranean] Sea, why does Scripture speak of seas? Well, the taste of fish caught in Acco is not like the taste of fish caught in Tyre; nor is the fish caught in Tyre like the fish caught in Apamea.[11]

108. There is a spring that nurtures strong men and a spring that nurtures weak men; a spring that nurtures handsome men and a spring that nurtures homely men; a spring that nurtures chaste men and a spring that nurtures men steeped in lewdness. Now, the spring of Shittim was one of harlotry, for it was the one that watered the land of Sodom. Therefore, Israel became depraved at that spring, as Scripture says, "When Israel abode in Shittim, the people began to commit harlotry with the daughters of Moab" (Num. 25:1). The Holy One will dry up that spring, as is said, "A spring shall come forth out of the house of the Lord, and shall water the riverbed of Shittim" (Joel 4:18).[12]

109. Samuel said: A river is replenished by the water coming down its [banks from the river's source],[13] thus disagreeing with Rav, for R. Ammi said in the name of Rav: When there is rain in the west [the Land of Israel], the Euphrates is a convincing witness of it.[14]

110. "He giveth a way in the sea" (Isa. 43:16). R. Isaac bar Maryon said: But that "He giveth a way in the sea," a man would perish at once whenever he ventured down into it.

The sages said: "He giveth a way in the sea" between Pentecost and the Feast of Tabernacles, "and a path in the mighty waters" (ibid.) between the Feast of Tabernacles and Hanukkah.

R. Nathan Kohen the brother of R. Hiyya bar Abba, about to set out on a sea voyage that was to last from the Feast of Tabernacles to Hanukkah, said to his brother, "Pray for me." The brother replied, "How can I pray for you? Rather, after tying up your lulav cluster [on Tabernacles], you should tie up your feet and not travel.[15] [Besides], when you enter a synagogue and hear [the congregation] praying for rain, do not rely upon my prayer in your behalf."[16]

R. Joshua son of R. Tanhum son of R. Hiyya of Kefar Hanun was in Esya[17] and wished to embark on a sea journey that would last from the Feast of Tabernacles to Hanukkah, but a [Roman] noblewoman cautioned him: "Should one set out on a sea voyage at this time of the year?" Moreover, his father appeared to him in a dream [and warned him]: "My son, [you will die] without burial: 'not to be accorded a burial' " (Eccles. 6:3). But R. Joshua paid no heed either to the words of his father or to the words of the noblewoman, and the warning was fulfilled [he was drowned].[18]

111. Rabban Gamaliel and R. Joshua once traveled on a ship. R. Gamaliel had only bread, while R. Joshua had both bread and fine flour. When R. Gamaliel's bread was used up, he had to depend on R. Joshua's flour. So R. Gamaliel asked R. Joshua, "Was it because you knew that

1. Gen. R. 13:9.
2. JV: "their roaring."
3. Gen. R. 5:3; MTeh 93:5; Yalkut, Ps., §848.
4. PRE 9.
5. All rivers draw their supply from it.
6. B. Ber 59b.
7. P. Kil 9:4, 32c; B. Shab 35a.
8. The Sea of Samachonitis, north of Tiberias.
9. B. BB 74b; B. Bekh 55a.
10. Gen. R. 4:5.
11. Sif Deut., §39; Gen. R. 5:8.
12. Tanhuma, *Balak*, §17; Yalkut, Joel, §538.
13. Not directly by rain.
14. It receives much of the rainwater. B. Bekh 55b.
15. Since the sea is dangerous after Tabernacles.
16. My prayer will be overwhelmed by those of the congregation, and abundant rain naturally increases the danger of a sea voyage.
17. Perhaps Ezion, a port in the Gulf of Aqaba on the Red Sea.
18. P. Shab 2:3, 5b; Gen. R. 6:5.

we would be so greatly delayed that you brought flour with you?" R. Joshua answered, "Once every seventy years, a certain star rises and leads sailors astray, so I thought perhaps it will rise and lead us astray."[1]

112. A large ship was once sailing on the Great [Mediterranean] Sea when a gale seized it and drove it to a place where the water was becalmed. When the passengers saw that they were in real trouble, they said, "Come, let us share our provisions, so that if we die, we all die, and if we survive, we will all survive." [As a reward], He who is everywhere gave light to their eyes [enabling them to devise a plan]. They took a kid, roasted it, and hung it up on the ship's western side. A large sea beast, attracted by the odor, came up and began to pull the ship until it drew it to where the water was flowing, and they were able to resume their voyage. When they reached their destination and entered Rome, they recounted the incident to R. Eliezer and R. Joshua, who applied to them the text "Cast thy bread upon the waters, for thou shalt find it after many days" (Eccles. 11:1).[2]

113. A valiant captain had a ship in which he prevailed over both waters and winds. When pirates came against him, he rose up and slew them all. After a while, just as he reached the entrance to a port, a violent wind came, and his ship broke apart. He began beseeching mercy of the people [on shore]: "I beg of you, save me." They replied, "Yesterday you prevailed over winds and slew pirates, and now you ask others to save you?" He said, "As long as my ship was in existence, I was valiant and did not need to have people help me. But now that my ship has broken apart, my strength, too, is broken."[3]

Gold and Precious Stones

114. There were three special ports, two belonging to the Romans and one belonging to the Persians. At the Roman ports they brought up coral; at the Persian port they brought up pearls. How did they go about it? They would bring six thousand men to a large Liburnian ship for twelve months, and the men loaded it with sand until it rested on the sea bottom. Than a diver would go down and tie flaxen ropes from the coral to the ship. The sand was then taken and thrown overboard, and, as the boat rose, it pulled up the coral with it.[4]

115. There are seven kinds of gold: good gold, pure gold, locked gold, brilliant gold, refined gold, spun gold, and Parvaim gold. Good gold is literally—as R. Isaac put it—"good for him who has it in his house and good for him whose escort it is." Pure gold is so pure that, when put into [furnace] fire, its weight is not diminished,[5] even as we have been taught: It is related that the golden lampstand Moses made in the wilderness was overweight by one gold denar, and though it was put into a furnace eighty times, its weight was not diminished. Locked gold is so called because when it becomes available, all other shops are locked [since no one will buy their inferior gold]. Brilliant gold is as brilliant as fire kindled by sulfur. Refined gold is cut up into pieces the size of olives, covered with dough, and fed to ostriches, which filter it; some say it is buried in manure for seven years. Spun gold is drawn out like wax and spun like thread. Hadrian had an egg's weight of it, Diocletian had a Gordian denar's weight of it. Parvaim gold is as red as the blood of bullocks [*parim*].[6]

116. "And the gold of that land is good [everywhere]" (Gen. 2:12). R. Abbahu said: The Holy One bestowed a great boon upon His world, for a man may change just one gold denar and make use of it for ever so many purposes.[7]

117. There is the story of a man who went to Rome to sell a sapphire. A would-be purchaser said to him, "I will buy it provided that I may first test it." He laid the sapphire on an anvil and began to strike it with a hammer—the anvil split and the hammer was smashed, but the sapphire remained intact.[8]

Grasses and Trees

118. R. Simon said: There is not one herb without its own constellation (*mazzal*) in heaven, which slaps it and says, "Grow!"[9]

119. R. Hanina ben Pazzi said: Thorns need not be hoed nor sown—they sprout on their own, rise straight up, and grow. But wheat—how much pain, how much labor is needed before it can be made to grow![10]

120. There is a story of an old man who was a guest in a certain place at the home of a pious man, and great deference was shown him. At noon, the householder's wife asked her husband, "My lord, what shall we eat tonight in our guest's honor?" He replied, "Our own *adam*." When the old man heard this, he was greatly disturbed, as he said to himself: It appears that in this place the people eat one another; and even as they are about to eat a man in my honor, it may be that when another guest comes after me, they will eat me in his honor. What did the old man do? He left that house and went off to another. At mealtime, the first householder went around and asked all his neighbors, "Have you seen the old man who came to my house today?" One replied, "I saw him enter the house of So-and-so." The householder went there and found the old man seated at the table. So he asked him, "Sir, what

---

1. B. Hor 10a.
2. Eccles R. 11:1, §1.
3. Aggadat Bereshit 34 (ed. Buber, pp. 66–67).
4. B. RH 23a.
5. It contains no dross.
6. B. Yoma 44b–45a; P. Yoma 4:4, 41d.
7. Gen R. 16:2.
8. Lam. R. 4:7, §10.
9. Gen. R. 10:6.
10. Gen. R. 45:4.

made you leave my house? Please leave this house and come back to me." The old man: "I will not go." Though the householder besought him again and a third time, he would not go, so the householder went away. Then the second householder asked the old man: "Why did you act that way, shaming that pious man?" The old man replied, "I heard such-and-such, and out of fear fled and came here." The householder burst into laughter and said to the old man, "In our area, *adam* is a kind of vegetable, so called because it resembles a human being."[1]

121. There is the story of two men walking on a road, one sighted and the other blind. When they sat down to eat, they reached out for the [edible] grasses in the field, and ate them. As a result, he who was sighted became blind, and he who was blind regained his sight. By the time they moved from that place, the first had to lean on the second, who until then had been leaning on him.[2]

122. There is the story of a certain man who was on his way from Babylonia to the Land of Israel and sat down at the side of the road to eat. He noticed two birds fighting with each other, until one killed the other. The victor then went and fetched an herb; it placed it in the mouth of the dead bird and brought it back to life. So the man took the herb, which had fallen from the bird, and set out to bring the dead of the Land of Israel back to life. When he arrived at the Ladder of Tyre, he saw a dead lion cast on the road. So, saying to himself: It would be a good idea to try the herb on this lion, he placed the herb in the lion's mouth and brought it back to life. Immediately, the lion leaped up and devoured the man. This bears out the popular saying: "Don't be kind to the bad, and you won't be had."[3]

123. R. Samuel bar Nahmani said in the name of R. Yohanan: What is meant by "These are the sons of Seir the Horite, the inhabitants of the earth" (Gen. 36:20)? Could the verse possibly suggest that other human beings are inhabitants of the firmament? On the contrary, what the verse intimates is that they were expert in that which makes the earth habitable. They used to say, "This square rod of land is fit for olives, that square rod for vines, and the other for figs." The word Horite means that they smelled (*merihin*) the soil, and the word Hivite (Gen. 36:2), R. Papa said, means that they tasted the soil in the manner of a snake (*hivya*).[4]

124. We have been taught that Rabban Simeon ben Gamaliel said: Gallnut oak trees mark hilly terrain; palm trees mark valleys; reeds mark riverbeds; sycamores mark lowlands.[5]

1. Tanhuma B, introduction.
2. Tanhuma B, *Hukkat*, §1.
3. Lev. R. 22:4; Num. R. 18:22; Tanhuma B, *Hukkat*, §1; Eccles. R. 5:8, §5.
4. B. Shab 85a and En Yaakov, ad loc.
5. B. Pes 53a.

125. R. Judah said: When a man goes out to the country in the month of Nisan [springtime] and sees trees bring forth blossoms, he is to say, "Blessed be He who has His world lack nothing, having created in it comely creatures and beautiful trees, so that human beings may enjoy them."[6]

126. R. Yannai said: The way it is with mankind, when a man buys a pound of meat in the marketplace, how much he wearies himself, how much trouble he goes to in order to cook it! Yet, while mortals are asleep in their beds, the Holy One causes winds to blow, clouds to rise, rains to come down, dews to bespangle plants, plants to spring up, fruits to grow plump.[7]

127. There is a tree whose roots go down twenty cubits, another whose roots go down thirty, and still another, fifty, while there are some trees whose roots go down no more than three handbreadths. If the rain coming down from above were to water only the trees whose roots go down three handbreadths, those whose roots go down fifty cubits would wither; on the other hand, if the rain watered the trees whose roots go down fifty cubits, then those that go down three handbreadths would be flooded. Hence, the deep above calls unto the deep below, saying, "Rise up, and I will come down," and the deep below replies, "Come down, and I will rise up." Thus, the deep above comes down and waters the trees whose roots go down three handbreadths, while the deep below rises up and waters the trees whose roots go down fifty cubits.

Pause and consider how vast is the distance between the deep above and the deep below, yet they call across it one to the other. And human beings in between the two do not hear their call. Is this not a proof that "God thundereth marvelously with His voice" (Job 37:5)?[8]

128. Roots of wheat penetrate fifty cubits into the soil. Roots of the fig tree are frail, yet they penetrate a flinty rock.[9]

129. R. Eleazar son of R. Simeon said: The earth drinks no deeper than its upper layer. If so, how do roots of the carob and the roots of the sycamore tree manage? Well, each tree gets rain to the depth it requires. R. Levi said to R. Eleazar: It is as you say—no deeper than the earth's upper layer. As for the carob tree and sycamore tree, once every thirty days the deep rises and irrigates them.[10]

130. R. Samuel bar Nahman said in the name of R. Jonathan: There are twenty-four kinds of sturdy trees, and the best are seven—those mentioned in the verse "I will plant cedars in the wilderness, acacias and myrtles and oleasters; I will set cypresses in the desert, box trees and elms as well" (Isa. 41:19).[11]

6. B. Ber 43b.
7. PRKM 8:1; Yalkut, *Emor*, §643.
8. Exod. R. 5:9.
9. P. Ber 9:3, 14a; Gen. R. 13:17.
10. Gen. R. 13:17.
11. Gen R. 15:1.

131. R. Huna said: All creatures seek their mate. R. Ammi said: Even cedars seek their mate. You can see this for yourself. For in Babylon there had been no cedars,[1] and when Nebuchadnezzar came here [to the Land of Israel], he uprooted cedars from here and planted them in Babylon. When he died, the cedars here rejoiced[2] at his downfall. It was of their rejoicing that Scripture said to Nebuchadnezzar, "Even pines rejoice at thy downfall, and [it goes without saying] the cedars of Lebanon" (Isa. 14:8).[3]

132. R. Tanhuma said: It happened that a female palm that stood in Hammetan yielded no fruit. A scion of a male palm was grafted onto it, but it still yielded no fruit. A palm grower who passed by saw it and said, "She gazes upon a palm at Jericho and has a desire for it." When they went and got a scion of that palm and grafted it onto the female, she yielded fruit right away.[4]

133. The male palm has neither hollows nor knots, and it casts a long shadow.

In the female palm, nothing goes to waste—its dates are eaten, its fronds are used during the *Hallel*, and its twigs are used to cover the sukkah: its bast is for ropes, its leaves for sieves, and its planed trunks for ceiling a house.[5]

134. R. Yohanan said: Once [on the Day of Atonement] I was seized by a ravenous hunger, so I ran to the eastern side of a fig tree, thus making true for myself "Wisdom revives the life of him who hath it" (Eccles. 7:12). For R. Joseph taught: One who would savor a fig's full taste should turn to the tree's eastern side, as is said, "The most precious things are the fruits of the sun" (Deut 33:14).[6]

135. When a broom shrub is set on fire, it makes coals that cannot be extinguished.

Once it happened that two men who were going through the wilderness sat down under a broom shrub, gathered some fallen twigs of the broom, cooked themselves a meal, and ate it. A year later, they came back to the same place, found the ashes of the fire they had kindled, and said, "It is now twelve months since we came through here and ate in this place." As they scrabbled the ashes and walked over them, their feet were burned by the live coals [still glowing] under the ashes.[7]

136. "Coals of broom" (Ps. 120:4). All other coals, when extinguished on the outside, are also extinguished inside. But coals of broom, even when extinguished on the outside, continue to burn within.

It once happened that a man left such coals burning on the Festival of Tabernacles, and when he came back on Passover, he found that they were still burning.

It once happened that a broom tree was set on fire, and it kept burning for eighteen months[8]—winter, summer, and another winter.[9]

137. "A tree that may be eaten" (Lev. 19:23)—that is, a tree whose wood and whose fruit taste the same. What is it? The pepper plant.[10]

138. When a tree that bears fruit is cut down, its moan goes from one end of the world to the other, yet no sound is heard.[11]

Various Kinds of Creatures

139. R. Akiva used to quote, "What variety thou hast created, O Lord!" (Ps. 104:24). You have creatures that grow in the sea, and You have creatures that grow on dry land. If those of the sea were to come up on the dry land, they would immediately die; and if those of the dry land were to go down into the sea, they too would immediately die. You have creatures that grow in fire,[12] and You have creatures that grow in the air. If those of the fire were to come up into the air, they would immediately die. If those of the air were to come down into the fire, they too would immediately die. "What variety Thou hast created, O Lord!"[13]

140. Our masters taught: Everything that exists on dry land exists also in the sea, except the weasel.[14]

141. Resh Lakish said: What is meant by the verse "I will sing unto the Lord, for He is highly exalted" (Exod. 15:1)? It means a song to Him who is exalted above the exalted ones. For a master taught: The king of wild beasts is the lion; the king of cattle is the ox; the king of birds is the eagle—but man is exalted over them. However, the Holy One is exalted over all these and over the entire world, all of it.[15]

142. R. Simeon ben Lakish said: There are three insolent ones: Israel among the nations, the dog among beasts, and the cock among fowls. Some say, also the goat among small cattle. And some say, also the caper shrub among trees.[16]

143. Our masters taught: There are three who gather strength as they get older: a fish, a snake, and a pig.[17]

---

1. Because the land is swampy.
2. Because he had deprived them of their mates.
3. Lam. R. 1:4, §30.
4. Gen. R. 41:1; Num. R. 3:1.
5. Gen. R. 41:1.
6. B. Yoma 83b.
7. MTeh 120:4.
8. BR has "twelve months."
9. P. Pe 1:1, 16a; Gen. R. 98:19.
10. B. Ber 36b.
11. PRE 34.
12. Salamanders were believed to live in fire.
13. B. Hul 127a.
14. Ibid.
15. B. Hag 13b.
16. The caper is the first to sprout. B. Betz 25b.
17. B. Shab 77b.

144. R. Yohanan said: The best of cattle is the ox; the best of fowls is the chicken.[1]

145. R. Joshua ben Levi said: An unclean animal can never be impregnated by a clean one, nor can a clean animal be impregnated by an unclean one. Large cattle can never be impregnated by small cattle, nor small cattle by large cattle. Domestic animals can never be impregnated by wild beasts, nor can wild beasts be impregnated by domestic animals. The one exception [is the *koi*],[2] discussed by R. Eliezer and his disputants, who agree that this wild beast can be impregnated by a domestic animal.[3]

146. Our masters taught: An unclean fish gives birth to live young, while a clean fish lays eggs. Whatever gives birth to live young gives suck [that is, has breasts]. Whatever lays eggs supports its young by gathering food for them. The one exception is the bat, for though it lays eggs, it gives suck to its young. Dolphins multiply and increase by coupling like human beings. What are dolphins? R. Judah said: Humans of the sea.

Whatever animal has its male genital outside gives birth; and whatever has its male genital inside lays eggs. Whatever copulates during the day gives birth in the day; and whatever copulates during the night gives birth in the night. Whatever copulates during the day as well as the night gives birth in the day as well as the night. Whatever copulates during the day gives birth in the day—the hen. Whatever copulates during the night gives birth in the night—the bat. Whatever copulates during the day as well as the night gives birth in the day as well as the night—man and all creatures resembling him.

All animals whose [manner of] copulating and [length of] pregnancy are alike can give birth from one another and nurse each other's young.

All male animals copulate with their faces to the female's back, except three, which copulate face to face—fish, man, and serpents. The sages taught: Camels copulate back to back.

Our masters taught: The hen lays its eggs twenty-one days after impregnation, and its counterpart among trees is the almond.[4] The dog carries its young fifty days [after impregnation], and its counterpart among trees is the fig. The cat carries its young fifty-two days [after impregnation], and its counterpart among trees is the mulberry. The pig carries its young sixty days [after impregnation], and its counterpart among trees is the apple. The fox and all kinds of varmint carry their young six months, and their counterpart among trees is field produce [wheat].[5] Small animals that are clean carry their young five months, and their counterpart among trees is the vine. Large animals that are unclean carry their young twelve months, and their counterpart among trees is the date palm. Large animals that are clean carry their young nine months, and their counterpart among trees is the olive. The wolf, the lion, the bear, the leopard, the *bardeles* [panther?], the elephant, the tailless ape, and the long-tailed ape carry their young three years, and their counterpart among trees is the fig tree that grows white figs. The viper carries its young seventy years, and its counterpart among trees is the carob, for it takes seventy years from the time the carob is planted to the time its fruit ripens; the time of its "pregnancy,"[6] which lasts three years, [is included in the seventy years of the carob's growth]. The serpent carries its young seven years, and for that creature we can find no counterpart tree. Some say its counterpart is a species of fig tree bearing inferior figs.[7]

147. A certain philosopher wanted to know how long after impregnation a serpent gives birth. So when he saw a pair of serpents copulating, he took them, placed them in a cask, and fed them until they bore young. When the sages visited Rome, the philosopher asked Rabban Gamaliel how long after impregnation it takes a serpent to bear. Since Rabban Gamaliel did not know what to answer, he turned pale [with shame]. R. Joshua met him and, seeing that his face was pale, asked him, "Why is your face so pale?" Rabban Gamaliel: "I was asked a question and could not answer it." R. Joshua: "What was the question?" Rabban Gamaliel: "How long after impregnation does a serpent bear?" R. Joshua: "After seven years." Rabban Gamaliel: "How do you know that?" R. Joshua: "Because the dog, which is an unclean beast, bears after fifty days, and cattle, also unclean, bear after twelve months. Now, the serpent was told, 'Cursed art thou above all cattle, and [they] above all beasts of the field' [Gen. 3:14]: hence, just as cattle are seven times more accursed than a beast of the field, so is the serpent seven times more accursed than cattle." Toward evening, Rabban [Gamaliel] went and told this to the philosopher, who proceeded to beat his head against the wall [in grief] as he cried out, "All that took me seven years to achieve, this man handed to me on the tip of a reed!"[8]

148. We have been taught: After seven years, the male *tzavua* [hyena] turns into a bat; after seven years, the bat turns into an *arpad* [another small bat]; after seven years, the *arpad* turns into a *kimosh* [a thorny weed]; after seven years, the *kimosh* turns into a thorn; after seven years, the thorn turns into a demon [*shed*]. After seven years, a man's spine [*sheder*] turns into a serpent.[9]

149. We have been taught that R. Simeon ben Eleazar said: In all my days I have never seen a lion work as a porter, a deer as a gatherer of fruit, a fox as a shopkeeper,

1. B. BM 86b.
2. An antelope or a bearded deer, believed to be the offspring of a he-goat and a hind.
3. B. Bekh 7a.
4. From the time it sends forth blossoms to the ripening of its fruit.
5. Wheat is here described as a tree, in accordance with the belief that the tree from which Adam ate was a wheat tree. See above, part 1, chap. 2, §91.
6. From the time it sends forth blossoms until its fruit ripens.
7. B. Bekh 7b–8a.
8. Gen. R. 20:4.
9. B. BK 16a.

or a wolf as a seller of pots; yet they are provided food without toil.[1]

150. Cattle have a language—each species its own.[2]

Fowl

151. When the hen's chicks are tiny, she gathers them under her wings, warms them, and grubs for them. But when they grow up and one of them wants to get near her, she pecks at its head and says, "Go grub in your own dungheap."[3]

152. R. Simeon ben Halafta had a hen that lost her femur. So they provided her with a tube of reed for support, and she recovered.

It is said of R. Simeon ben Halafta, who was an observer of nature, that he did something to disprove R. Judah's view, for R. Judah maintained, "If a bird's down is gone, it is unfit to be eaten." Now, R. Simeon ben Halafta had a hen whose down was entirely gone. So, after first wrapping the hen in a bronze workers' [warm] leather apron, he kept her in an oven, and the new down she grew was more abundant than before.[4]

153. "On eagles' wings" (Exod. 19:4). All other birds carry their young between their legs for fear of other birds flying above them. But the eagle is afraid only of man, who might shoot an arrow at him. So the eagle says, "It is better that the arrow lodge in me than in my young."[5]

154. An eagle does not enter its nest at once, but first claps its wings between one tree and the next, between one thicket and the next, so that its eaglets wake up and have the strength to receive it.[6]

155. R. Simeon ben Halafta was an observer of nature. Now, in his orchard he had a tree trunk, and he saw a hoopoe building its nest in it. So, saying to himself: What business does this unclean bird have in my orchard? R. Simeon ben Halafta proceeded to demolish the nest. The hoopoe went and repaired it. What did R. Simeon ben Halfta do then? He brought a board, placed it at the opening of the nest, and made it stay put by driving a nail into it. What did the hoopoe do? It brought a certain herb, placed it on the nail, and pulled it out. R. Simeon ben Halafta decided: It would be a good idea if I were to hide this herb, so that thieves may not learn to do likewise and bring mankind to ruin.[7]

156. "Oh that I had wings like a dove!" (Ps. 55:7). R. Azariah said in the name of R. Yudan: All other birds, when tired, rest on a rock or a tree, but the dove, when she gets tired while flying, draws in one of her wings[8] and keeps flying with the other.[9]

157. A dove fleeing from a hawk was about to enter a cleft in a rock when she found a serpent nesting there. If she entered, there was the serpent hissing at her; if she turned back, there was the hawk standing outside. What did the dove do? She began to cry and clap her wings, so that the devecote's owner would hear her and come to save her.[10]

158. The sages said: The raven is cruel—when he begets fledglings and sees that they are white while he is black, he abandons them and goes away. Then the Holy One provides sustenance for them.

R. Assi was an observer of nature. When he once saw a raven building its nest, laying eggs, and hatching fledglings, he took the fledglings and put them in a new pot, whose top he sealed with plaster. After three days, he opened the top to find out what the fledglings were doing and found that their droppings had produced gnats, which the fledglings ate as they flew up. R. Assi applied to them the verse "Who provideth for the raven his prey" (Job 38:41).[11]

159. In the days of R. Hiyya the Elder, a starling migrated to the Land of Israel. The people came and brought it to him, inquiring, "May we eat it?" He replied, "Go and place it on a rooftop, and any bird that comes to rest next to it is of its kind." So they went and placed it on a rooftop, and an Egyptian raven came by and rested next to it. Accordingly, R. Hiyya said, "The starling is unclean, because it belongs to the species of the raven, which Scripture prohibits by saying, 'Every raven after its kind' " (Lev. 11:16). Hence the proverb: "Not for nothing did the starling go to the raven—it is, after all, its kind."[12]

160. The partridge brings eggs of other birds and sits on them, until they emerge from their shells as chicks. They then climb on his back, pluck his feathers, and eat them. When the partridge wishes to flee from them, he cannot, because his feathers have been plucked. Then, when a reptile or a beast come upon him, it eats him. What brought such a fate upon him? The fact that he brooded on eggs that were not his.[13]

161. R. Ilish was taken captive, together with a man who understood the language of birds. When a raven came by and crowed, R. Ilish asked the man, "What does it

1. Cf. Matthew 6:26. B. Kid 82b; Tos Kid 5:15.
2. Lekah Tov, Gen. 3:1 (ed. Buber, p. 24).
3. Lev. R. 25:5
4. B. Hul 57b.
5. Mek, *Yitro*, *Ba-hodesh*, 2.
6. Sif Deut., §314; Lekah Tov, Deut. 32:11 (ed. Buber, p. 112); Yalkut, *Haazinu*, §944.
7. Lev. R. 22:4; Eccles. R. 5:8, §5.
8. To rest her body on it.
9. Gen. R. 39:8.
10. Mek, *Be-shallah*, *Va-yehi*, 3 (La 1:211); Song R. 2:14, §2.
11. Lev. R. 19:1
12. Gen. R. 65:3; B BK 92b.
13. Tanhuma; Yalkut, Jer., §297.

say?" The man replied, "It says, 'Ilish, flee! Ilish, flee.' " So R. Ilish said, "The raven is a liar, and one should not rely on it." Then a dove came along and called. R. Ilish again asked the man, "What does it say?" The man replied, "Ilish, flee! Ilish, flee!' " [Said R. Ilish], "Since the congregation of Israel is likened to a dove, I am being told that a miracle will be wrought for me." So both men made a break for it. A miracle was performed for R. Ilish and he got safely across the bridge [on the river], but the man with R. Ilish was caught and put to death.[1]

162. R. Judah said, The *hasidah* (Lev. 11:19) is a white stork. Why is it called *hasidah*? Because it does kindness (*hasidut*) to its mates.[2]

163. R. Judah also said: The *kaat* (Lev. 19:18) is a pelican. The *raham* (ibid.) [is a pelican that] cries, *Sherakrak*."[3] Why is it called *raham*? Because when it appears, *rahamim*, "compassion," appears in the world; provided, said R. Bebai bar Abbaye, it is perched on something when it cries, *Sherakrak*." We have a tradition that if a pelican perches on the ground and cries, "*Sherakrak*," the Messiah will come presently, in keeping with "I will *sherakrak*[4] to them, and I will gather them" (Zech. 10:8).

But did not a *raham* once settle on a furrow, and when it cried "*Sherakrak*," a piece of marble fell on it and split its head? That bird was an imposter [not a real *raham*].[5]

164. In cities far across the sea there is a bird called *kerum*,[6] and when the sun shines on it, it changes into ever so many colors.[7]

165. The *tzavua*, the colored animal,[8] has three hundred and sixty-five colors, corresponding to the days of the solar year.[9]

166. "I shall multiply my days as the *hol*, the phoenix" (Job 29:18). The school of R. Yannai maintained: The *hol* lives a thousand years, at the end of which a fire issues from its nest and burns it up, leaving only as much as an egg's bulk, and from that it grows new limbs and lives again. R. Yudan bar R. Simeon said: [It lives a thousand years], at the end of which its body is consumed and its wings drop off, yet, from the egg-sized bulk left, it grows new limbs and lives again.[10]

Reptiles and Creeping Things

167. R. Judah said in the name of Rav: Of all that the Holy One created in His world, He did not create a single thing that is useless. Even those creatures you may look upon as superfluous in the world, such as serpents and scorpions, flies, fleas, or gnats—they too are part of the entirety of creation.[11]

168. "A serpent in the way" (Gen. 49:17). All other beasts go in pairs, whereas the serpent goes its way alone.[12]

169. "Dust shall be the serpent's food" (Isa. 65:25). R. Ammi and R. Assi differed. One said: Even when the serpent eats any of the world's delicacies, he tastes in them only the taste of dust. And the other said: Even if he eats any of the world's delicacies, he is not content until he eats dust.[13]

170. R. Safra said in the name of R. Joshua of the South: A serpent's venom is of three kinds: When the serpent is young, it sinks to the bottom [of what the snake is drinking]. When in the middle years, it permeates [the liquid]. When old, it floats [on top].[14]

171. Our masters taught: The wilderness of Shur was eight hundred parasangs by eight hundred parasangs, and full of serpents, scorpions, and wild beasts. R. Yose said: In it were serpents as thick as the beams of an olive press, and scorpions the length of a span. Thus, as Scripture speaks of it: "Who led thee through the great and dreadful wilderness, wherein were serpents, fiery serpents, and scorpions" (Deut. 8:15). It is reported that when King Shapur wished to go through that wilderness, his first caravan, endeavoring to go through, was swallowed by a serpent; the next caravan was swallowed by the same serpent; and so was the third. As the king sat in great distress, the sages who were with him said, "Why are you putting up with this? Summon ten strong men," and he summoned them. Then they said, "Fill ten hides with straw."[15] They kept filling the hides with straw and rolling them before the serpent, while he continued swallowing the straw until his belly was so swollen that he could not move. Then they attacked and slew him.[16]

172. It is reported that when the viper merely glances at a flying bird's shadow, the bird, at once spellbound [by the viper's glance] at its shadow, falls to pieces limb by limb.[17]

173. R. Aha said: R. Hiyya the Elder told me the following: There was a man in the Land of Israel who was

1. B. Git 54a.
2. B. Hul 63a.
3. An onomatopoeic attempt to imitate its sound.
4. English: "whistle" or "hiss."
5. And should not have cried. B. Hul 63a.
6. "[Yehudi Leib] Lewysohn . . . identifies the bird with 'the bird of paradise' " (Ber, Soncino, p. 28, n. 8).
7. B. Ber 6b.
8. "The leopard, or perhaps the striped hyena" (Gen R., Soncino, p. 51, n. 9).
9. Gen. R. 7:4.
10. Gen. R. 19:5; Midrash Sam. 12 (ed. Buber, p. 81).
11. B. Shab 77b; Gen. R. 10:7; Exod. R. 10:1.
12. Gen. R. 99:11.
13. B. Yoma 75a.
14. B. AZ 30b.
15. To make the serpent believe they were animals.
16. Mek, *Be-shallah*, *Va-yassa*, 1; Tanhuma B, *Be-shallah*, §17.
17. Ibid.

called Baldhead. Why was he called Baldhead? Because, so it is said, he once went up to the top of a mountain to gather wood. There he saw a serpent the size of a beam in an olive press, sound asleep. And even though the serpent did not see him, the man's hair fell out, and no hair grew on him again to the day of his death. So he was called Baldhead.[1]

174. R. Phinehas told in the name of R. Hanan of Sepphoris the story of a certain man who was reaping and binding sheaves in the valley of Beth-tofet. When the heat [of the day] came on, he took some herbs and made them into a wreath, which he tied to his head. Later, a big snake came to attack him, and he rose up and killed it. A snake charmer passed by, saw the dead snake, fixed his eyes on the man, and said, "I am amazed! Who slew this snake?" The man: "I slew it." When the snake charmer noticed the herbs made into a wreath on the man's head, he asked him, "Did you really kill this snake?" The man: "Yes." The snake charmer: "Would you mind removing the herbal [wreath] from your head?" The man: "Not at all." The charmer: "Would you mind picking up the snake with my staff?" The man: "Not at all." But as soon as the man drew near to the snake, even before he touched it, he fell to pieces limb by limb.[2]

175. Once, a man was walking in a field, holding a jug of milk in his hand. A snake moaning with thirst met him. "Why are you moaning?" asked the man. "Because I am thirsty," replied the snake; "what is that you have in your hand?" The man: "Milk." The snake: "Give me the milk to drink, and I will show you so much money that you will be rich." The man gave the milk to the snake, and it drank.

After the snake had drunk, the man said, "Show me the money you spoke of." The snake: "Follow me." He followed it until they came to a big stone. The snake said, "The money is hidden under this stone." The man lifted the stone, dug down, and found the money, which he took and was about to carry to his house.

But what did the snake do? It sprang up and coiled itself around the man's neck. "Why are you doing this?" the man asked. The snake: "I am going to kill you because you took all my money." The man: "Come with me to Solomon before his court."

They went and appeared before Solomon, the snake still coiled around the man's neck. The man made his plea to the king.

"What are you after?" the king asked the snake. It answered, "I want to kill him." "Get off his neck," said the king; "Since both of you are in court, it is not right that you should have a hold on him while he has no hold on you." So the snake slithered off the man's neck to the ground. The king: "Now you can have your say." The snake began his plea: "I wish to slay the man, in keeping with what the Holy One said to me: 'Thou shalt strike him in the heel' " (Gen. 3:15). Then the king said to the man, "And the Holy One commanded you, 'He is to strike you in the head' (ibid.)." The man immediately sprang forward and smashed its head.

Hence the proverb "Smash the head of even the best of snakes."[3]

176. "When a man's ways please the Lord, He maketh even his enemies eager to give up life for him" (Prov. 16:7). By "enemy" here, according to R. Joshua ben Levi, is meant a snake [as is proven by the following story].

A man ground up some garlic in his house [for his meal]. A desert snake came and ate of it, and a pet snake saw him. When the people of the house sat down to eat, the pet snake began to scatter dust at them, but they did not understand what it meant. So it threw itself into the [venom-soaked] garlic [and died].[4]

177. "Even the jackals draw out their breast, they give suck to their young ones" (Lam. 4:3). The wild ass spreads a kind of veil over its face when it suckles its young, in order not to see their red coloring and devour them.[5]

178. R. Muna bar Torta said: Once I went to a place where crossbreeding was practiced, and I saw a snake wrapped around a lizard. After some days, an *arod* emerged from between them. When I came [with this story] before R. Simeon the Pious, he said to me: The Holy One declares: These people have been bringing into being creatures that I did not create in My world; I too will bring upon them a [vastly more dangerous] creature that I did not create in My world.[6]

179. Our masters taught: In a certain place there was once an *arod*[7] who used to injure people. People came and told R. Hanina ben Dosa about this. He said, "Show me its hole." They did so, and he put his heel over the hole. The *arod* came out, bit him, and immediately died. He hoisted it on his shoulder, brought it to the house of study, and said, "See, my children, it is not the venomous lizard [*arod*] that kills, it is sin that kills!"

On that occasion, they said: Woe unto the man who meets up with a venomous lizard, and woe unto the venomous lizard who meets up with R. Hanina ben Dosa.[8]

180. When a *havarbar* lizard stings a man, if the man is the first to get to water, the lizard will die; but if the lizard is the first to get to water, the man will die.

It is told that while R. Hanina ben Dosa was standing for the *Tefillah*, a *havarbar* lizard came and stung him, but he did not interrupt his *Tefillah*. Then they went and found that lizard dead at the entrance to his hole. When R. Hanina's disciples asked him, "Master, did you not feel the sting?" he replied, "May such-and-such come

1. Ibid.; Exod. R. 24:4.
2. Gen. R. 10:7; Num. R. 18:22
3. Tanhuma B, introduction, p. 157.
4. P. Ter 8:3, 45c.
5. Lam. R. 4:3, §6.
6. B. Hul 127a.
7. Perhaps a crossbreed of a snake and a lizard.
8. B. Ber 33a and En Yaakov, ad loc.

upon me if I felt anything, my heart being concentrated utterly on the *Tefillah.*"

R. Isaac bar Eleazar said: [To save R. Hanina's life], the Holy One created a kind of fountain under his feet, in keeping with "He will fulfill the desire of them that fear Him; He also will hear their cry, and will save them" (Ps. 145:19).[1]

181. The Holy One carries out a mission of His through everything, even through a snake, even through a scorpion, even through a frog, even through a gnat.

R. Hanan of Sepphoris said: There is the story of a scorpion proceeding to the other side of the Jordan to carry out a mission given him. The Holy One provided him with a frog, upon whose back he crossed the river; then, moving on, he stung a man to death. His mission thus completed, the scorpion was brought back to his place by the frog.[2]

182. As R. Yannai was sitting and lecturing at the gate of his town, he saw a snake slithering rapidly toward the town. When it was chased away from one side [of the road], it resumed its journey on the other side; when chased away from that side, it kept going forward on the side where it had been first. So R. Yannai said, "This creature is on its way to carry out a mission." Soon after, a report spread in the town: "So-and-so was bitten by a snake and is dead."[3]

183. Samuel saw a scorpion mount a frog, cross a river, and bite a man, who then died. Accordingly, he applied to the frog and the scorpion the verse "They stand this day [to carry out] Thy judgments, for all are Thy servants" (Ps. 119:91).[4]

184. It is reported of King David that when he finished the book of Psalms, he became so arrogant that he said to the Holy One, "Master of the universe, is there anyone in the world who has uttered as many songs as I?" In that instant, a frog confronted him and said, "Do not be so arrogant—I utter more songs than you."[5]

185. Three creatures—the *ishut* (mole), the snake, and the frog—differ from all other creatures. The mole: if it could see light, no creature could stand up against it. The snake: if it had feet, it could overtake a horse in full stride and kill him. The frog: if it had teeth, no creature would enter the water for fear of it.[6]

186. What is an *ishut*? R. Judah said: It is a creature that has no eyes. Accordingly, the *ishut* must be a mole rat. Though there is no proof for this identification, there is an intimation of it in the verse "Let them be as a snail which melteth and passeth away, like an untimely birth or like an *eshet*,[7] that hath not seen the sun" (Ps. 58:9).[8]

187. Moles do not see the sun, but burrow into the earth and remain there.[9]

188. There are creatures that grow in fire but cannot grow in the air. What is one? The salamander. How does it come into being? When makers of glass heat their furnace seven successive days and seven successive nights, there emerges from the fierceness of the fire a creature resembling a mouse, which people call "salamander." If a man applies its blood to his hand or to any of his limbs, fire has no power over that spot. Why not? Because the salamander's origin is from fire.[10]

189. R. Eleazar was asked by his disciples: Why do all people persecute mice? Because of their malicious nature. In what way does it show itself? Rava said: They chew up even clothing.[11] R. Papa said: They will chew up even the handle of a mattock.[12]

190. Mice are feral [and want to devour everything before their eyes]. So when they see a great deal of produce, they call their comrades to help them eat.[13]

191. There is the story of a king of Saracenia who happened to drop a pearl. A mouse [scampered by and] swallowed it. So the king came to R. Phinehas ben Yair, who asked him, "Am I a magician?" The king: "I came because of your good name." So R. Phinehas commanded all mice to gather around him. When he saw one of them come waddling in, he said, "Here, the pearl is in this one." Then he commanded the mouse to disgorge, and it spewed out the pearl.[14]

192. Go out into a valley, and you will see a mouse that today is half-flesh and half-earth, and tomorrow it will have become a reptile, so that all of it will be flesh.

Go up a mountain, and you will see that today there is only one snail, but tomorrow, after rain comes down, the whole mountain will be filled with snails.[15]

193. R. Yose said: Once, while I was on a journey from Chezib to Tyre, I encountered an old man whom I greeted and asked, "How do you make your living?" The old man replied, "From purple snail."[16] I asked: "But can it be found?" He replied, "By Heaven, there is an area in the sea where the creature lies between mountains. Spiders sting it, and when it dies, it dissolves in its place." I said,

1. P. Ber 5:1, 9a.
2. Gen. R. 10:7; Num. R. 18:22.
3. Gen. R. 10:7; Tanhuma B, *Hukkat*, §1.
4. B. Ned 41a.
5. Perek Shirah.
6. MTeh 58:4
7. JV: "like the untimely births of a woman."
8. B. MK 6b; P. MK 1:4, 80c.
9. MTeh 58:4
10. Tanhuma, *Va-yeshev*, §3; B. Hag 27a.
11. Even though it is not food.
12. B. Hor 13a.
13. P. BM 3:5, 9b.
14. P. Dem 1:3, 22a.
15. B. Sanh 91a.
16. A snail yielding *tekhelet*, a special kind of blue dye.

"By Heaven, they do say that it is kept for the righteous in the time-to-come."[1]

194. Our masters taught: The purple snail resembles the sea in its essence: its shape resembles a fish; it comes up from the sea once in seventy years; and the blue thread is dyed with its blood. It is for this reason that it is so expensive.[2]

195. The snail—all the time it is growing, its shell grows with it.[3]

196. It is said of R. Simeon ben Halafta that he was an experimenter with natural phenomena.

In what way did he experiment? R. Mesharsheya gave an example: Scripture admonishes:

> Look to the ant, thou sluggard;
> Consider her ways, and be wise,
> Which having no chief, overseer, or ruler,
> Provideth her bread in the summer
> (Prov. 6:6–8).

R. Simeon said: I will go and see whether it is true that ants have no king. So, during the summer solstice,[4] he went and spread his cloak over an anthill. When one came out, he put a mark on it. It went in and reported to the others, "A shadow has fallen."[5] The instant the other ants came out, he lifted his cloak, and the sun beat down upon them. So they set on that ant and killed it. R. Simeon concluded: From this incident, one may infer that ants have no king. If they had a king, he reasoned, would they not have had to obtain royal sanction [to kill the ant]?

R. Aha son of Rava said to R. Ashi: But the king may have been with them, or the king's permission may have been given them [to act in an instance of deception]. Or perhaps it was an interregnum [when there was no authority], a time such as Scripture mentions: "In those days there was no king in Israel, every man did that which was right in his own eyes" (Judg. 28:25). But no; Solomon's testimony in Proverbs [quoted above] is good enough for us.[6]

197. The ant has three stories in her hill, but she brings no food into the top story because of the roof's drippings, nor into the bottom story because of the soil's moisture; only into the middle story. She lives only six months. Why so short a time? Because a creature that has neither sinews nor bones can live only six months. Though the entire amount of her food is only a grain and a half of wheat, yet throughout the summer she goes about gathering all the wheat, the barley, and the lentils she can find. R. Tanhuma said, "But why does she do so? Because she says, 'Perhaps the Holy One will decree a longer life for me, and then I will have what I need to eat.' "

R. Simeon ben Yohai said: It is told that three hundred *kor* of wheat were found in one ant hole, which a single ant had gathered that summer for the winter. Therefore Solomon said, "Go to the ant, thou sluggard; consider her ways, and be wise" (Prov. 6:8).

What else is intimated in "Consider her ways, and be wise"? Consider her good conduct, how she avoids taking what belongs to others. Thus, according to R. Simeon ben Halafta's account, an ant once dropped a grain of wheat, and though all the other ants came and sniffed at it, not one of them touched it, until the ant to whom it belonged came and took it. Consider therefore the wisdom an ant has.[7]

198. How are ants' holes destroyed? R. Simeon ben Gamaliel said: Earth is brought from one hole and placed in another hole, and the ants strangle one another.[8]

R. Yemar bar Shelemia said in the name of Abbaye: Such a measure is effective only if a river separates the two ant holes, with no bridge between them or no plank [on the river] between them or no rope to cross by. How far apart should the two holes be? At least a parasang.[9]

199. Once, while seated in his garden, David, king of Israel, saw a wasp eating a spider. David spoke up to the Holy One: Master of the universe, what benefit is there from these two You created in Your world? The wasp merely despoils the nectar of flowers—no benefit from it. The spider spins all year but makes no garments. The Holy One replied: David, you belittle My creatures! The time will come when you shall have need of both of them.

Later, while fleeing from King Saul, David took refuge in a cave, and the Holy One sent a spider, which spun a web across the cave's entrance, sealing it. When Saul came and saw the cave's entrance with the web across it, he said, "Surely no man has come in here, for had he done so, he would have torn the web." So Saul went away without going into the cave.

As David left the cave and saw the spider, he blew it a kiss, saying: Blessed be your Creator, and blessed be you.

Subsequently, David found Saul asleep within a barricade [in the royal tent], with Abner lying prone across the tent's entrances, his head in one entrance and his feet in the opposite entrance. Abner's knees were raised up, and so David was able to come in under them and pick up the cruse of water.[10] As he was about to leave the way he came, Abner stretched out his legs, which were like two gigantic columns in size, pinning David down. David, beseeching the Holy One's compassion, prayed, "My God, My God, why hast Thou forsaken me?" (Ps. 22:2). At that, the Holy One performed a miracle for him—He sent him a big wasp, which stung Abner's legs so that he again raised his knees, and thus David was free to leave.

In that instant, David said in praise of the Holy One:

---

1. Sif Deut., §354; Yalkut, *Berakhah*, §961.
2. B. Men 44a.
3. PRKM 11:12 (PRKS, p. 219).
4. Literally, "the cycle of Tammuz."
5. Ants shun the sun's heat.
6. B. Hul 57b.
7. Deut. R. 5:2; Yalkut, Prov., §968.
8. Since the ants in one heap do not know the ants in the other, and take them for invaders.
9. A parasang is four Roman miles. B. MK 6b–7a.
10. See 1 Sam. 26:12.

Master of the universe, "who can imitate Your works, Your mighty acts?" (Deut. 3:24)—all Your works are beautiful![1]

Domesticated and Wild Animals

200. "His firstling bullock, majesty is his; and his horns are the horns of the *re'em*" (Deut. 33:17).

The bull: his strength is awesome, but his horns are not beautiful; on the other hand, the *re'em*: his horns are beautiful, but his strength is not awesome.[2]

201. Do not stand in front of a bull when he comes up from the meadow, because Satan dances between his horns.[3] Samuel said: This applies only to a black bull, and only in the month of Nisan.

R. Oshaia taught: One should keep fifty cubits away from a bull that has never gored; and completely out of sight of a bull known to be a gorer.

The sages taught in the name of R. Meir: [Even] when the bull's head is in a feed basket, climb to the upper chamber and push away the ladder from under you.[4]

202. Our masters taught: Rams used to be brought [as temple offerings] from Moab, lambs from Hebron, calves from the Sharon, and pigeons from King's Mountain. R. Judah said: They used to bring lambs that were as wide as they were tall.[5]

203. The sages in the school of R. Ishmael taught: "The camel, because it cheweth the cud" (Lev. 11:4). The Ruler of His world knows that there are no creatures other than the camel [and the rock badger (Lev. 11:5)] that chew the cud and yet are unclean. Therefore, Scripture made a point of singling out the camel [as well as the rock badger] with the pronoun "it."

"And the swine because it parteth the hoof" (Lev. 11:7). The Ruler of His world knows that there is no creature other than the swine that has a parted hoof and yet is unclean. Therefore, Scripture made a point of singling out the swine with the pronoun "it."

R. Hisda said: If a man walks in the desert and finds an animal with its hooves cut off, he should examine its mouth: if it has no upper teeth, he may be certain that it is clean; if it has upper teeth, he may be certain that it is unclean—provided, however, he knows a young camel when he sees one.[6]

R. Hisda also said: If a man walks along a road and finds an animal whose mouth is toothless, he should examine its hooves: if its hooves are cloven, he may be certain that it is clean; if not, he may be certain that it is unclean—provided, however, he recognizes the swine.

R. Hisda also said: If a man walks in the desert and finds an animal whose mouth is toothless and whose hooves are cut off, he should examine its flesh: if it runs crosswise,[7] he may be certain that it is clean; if not, he may be certain that it is unclean—provided, however, he can recognize the wild ass.[8]

204. R. Hanan bar Rava said: The *shesuah*[9] (Deut. 14:7) is a specific creature that has two backs and two spines. But was Moses our teacher a hunter or an archer?[10] From here, one may draw a refutation of him who says, "Torah is not from Heaven."[11]

205. Six things are said of a horse: it loves promiscuity, it loves battle, its spirit is haughty, it despises sleep, it eats much but excretes little, and it walks at the sides of the road. Some say, it also wishes to slay [its master] in battle.[12]

206. How long is a horse's nap? Sixty breaths.[13]

207. A donkey is cold even during the summer solstice.[14]

208. Abbaye said: The mule: if its voice is harsh, it is the offspring of a she-ass; if shrill, the offspring of a mare. R. Papa said: If its ears are big and its tail short, it is the offspring of a she-ass; if its ears are small and its tail long, it is the offspring of a mare.[15]

209. "[On the Sabbath], ewes may not go out protected [*hanunot*] in a certain way" (Shab. 5:4). "Protected" here means, said R. Aha bar Ulla while seated before R. Hisda, that after a ewe is shorn, a compress saturated with oil is placed on her forehead, so that she will not catch cold. R. Hisda replied, "If so, you would treat a ewe as though she were Mar Ukba!"[16] But R. Papa bar Samuel, while seated before R. Nahman, said: "Protected" means that when a ewe is about to kneel for lambing, two compresses saturated with oil are made for her, one placed on her forehead, and the other over her womb, so that she may keep warm. R. Nahman replied, "If so, you would treat a ewe as though she were Yalta!"[17] Finally, to explain "protected," R. Huna said: There is a certain wood in

1. Alphabet of Ben Sira, in Eisenstein.
2. Sif Deut., §393.
3. The bull is then mad.
4. B. Pes 112b; B. Ber 33a.
5. B. Men 87a.
6. It has no teeth.
7. "The muscles of the rump under the tail run in a crisscross fashion, one series of muscles running downward and another transversely" (Hul, Soncino, p. 326, n. 2).
8. B. Hul 59a.
9. In JV, "cloven." But in rabbinic interpretation, the word "cloven" signifies a particular animal whose back and spine are "cloven."
10. On his own, Moses could not have known the characteristics of various animals, particularly one so rare. Hence, God must have informed him.
11. B. Hul 60a.
12. Since the horse is so eager to enter the fray. B. Pes 113b and En Yaakov, ad loc.
13. B. Suk 26b.
14. B. Shab 53a.
15. B. Hul 79a.
16. He was an exilarch.
17. She was the wife of R. Nahman, who was the exilarch's son-in-law.

cities far across the sea called *hanun,* a chip of which is brought and placed in the ewe's nostril to make her sneeze and thus expel the worms inside her head.[1]

210. R. Yose ben Nehorai said: There was a ewe in our neighborhood in whose windpipe there was a hole, and when a tube of reed was fitted into it, the ewe recovered.[2]

211. While alive, a sheep has but one voice. After it dies, its voice is multiplied sevenfold. How is its voice multiplied sevenfold? Its two horns are made into two trumpets; its two leg bones into two flutes; its hide into a drum; its entrails are used for lyres, and its chitterlings for harps.[3]

212. A *koi* is a wild ram. Some say: It is the offspring of a he-goat and a hind. R. Yose said: [It is not a hybrid but] a distinct creature. However, the sages have not decided whether it is a species of wild animal or a species of cattle. R. Simeon ben Gamaliel said: It is a species of cattle, and the family of Doshai used to breed many herds of them.[4]

213. R. Zera found R. Judah standing by the door of his father-in-law's house and noticed that he was in such a cheerful mood that if he asked him about all the secret processes of the universe, he would tell them to him. So he asked him: Why do the dark-colored goats walk at the head of the flock, while the [light-colored] sheep follow after? R. Judah: It is in keeping with the order of creation—darkness first and light afterward.

Why is the rear end of sheep covered with a fat-tail, while goats are uncovered? Those whose wool we cover ourselves with are themselves covered, while those whose fur we do not cover ourselves with are uncovered.

Why is a camel's tail short? Because it feeds on thorns.[5]

Why is an ox's tail long? Because it dwells in meadows and needs a long tail to beat off the gnats.

Why is the proboscis of a locust flexible? Because it dwells among swaying young shoots. If the proboscis were hard, it would be dislocated, and the locust would go blind. For, as Samuel said, if one wishes to blind a locust, let him extract its proboscis.

Why is a fowl's [lower] eyelid raised upward?[6] Because it dwells among the rafters, and if smoke entered its eyes, it would go blind.[7]

214. R. Hanina ben Dosa had some goats and was told, "Your goats are causing damage." He replied, "If they really cause damage, may bears devour them; if not, may each of them bring a bear impaled on its horns this evening." That evening, each of them brought home a bear on its horns.[8]

215. A story: The donkey of R. Hanina ben Dosa was stolen by brigands, who tied it up in a yard and put straw, barley, and water before it. But it would neither eat nor drink. So, saying, "Why should we let it die and stink up our yard?" they opened the gate and chased it out.

It walked along braying until it reached the house of R. Hanina ben Dosa. As soon as it reached the house, his son heard its voice. "Father," he said, "this sounds like our beast." R. Hanina said to him, "Son, open the gate, for it must be almost dead of hunger." The son rose up, opened the gate, and put straw, barley, and water before the donkey, which it ate and drank.

Therefore it is said: Even as the righteous of old were saintly, so their beasts, like their masters, were saintly.[9]

216. While on a journey, R. Phinehas ben Yair came to a certain inn, where some barley was placed before his she-ass, which she would not eat. It was mashed, but the she-ass would not eat it. It was carefully picked; still the she-ass would not eat it. "Perhaps," suggested R. Phinehas, "the barley had not been tithed?" So the barley was tithed, and only then did the she-ass eat it. R. Phinehas said, "This poor creature is on a journey to do the will of her Creator, and you would feed her untithed produce!"[10]

217. R. Yose of Yodkart had a donkey. When hired out for the day, the pay would be sent attached to the donkey's back, and he would bring it to his master [R. Yose]. If the amount was too much or too little, the donkey would not move from his place. Once, a pair of sandals were forgotten on the donkey['s back], and he refused to budge until they were removed.[11]

218. There is the story of a certain pious man who owned a plowing heifer. In the course of time, his wealth slipped out of his hand, and he had to sell her to a heathen. The new master plowed with her during the six [working] days of the week. On the Sabbath, he brought her out again to plow for him, but she lay down under the yoke and would not work. Though he kept beating her, she would not budge from her place. Seeing this, the heathen went to the pious man and said to him, "Come, take back your heifer. Six days I worked her, but when I took her out on the Sabbath, she lay down under the yoke and would do no work whatever. And though I beat her again and again, she would not budge from her place."

After the heathen spoke, the pious man understood why the heifer would do no work—it was because she had become accustomed to rest on the Sabbath. So he said to the heathen, "Come along, and I will get her up and make

1. B. Shab 54b.
2. B. Hul 57b.
3. Kin 3:6.
4. B. Hul 80a.
5. In which a long tail would be entangled.
6. When its eyes are closed, the lower eyelid turns upward and lies on the upper. So Rashi. The reference is to a thin membrane beneath the lower lid of the eye which is capable of extending across the eyeball.
7. B. Shab 77b.
8. B. Ta 25a.
9. ARN 8.
10. B. Hul 7a–b.
11. B. Ta 24a.

her plow." When he came to the heifer, he whispered into her ear "O heifer, heifer, you know that when you were in my domain, you were allowed to rest on the Sabbath. But since my sins brought it about that I had to sell you to this heathen, I beg of you, stand up and do the will of your [new] master."

At once the heifer stood up and was ready to work.

The heathen then said to the pious man, "I won't let you go until you tell me what you did to her and what you whispered in her ear. Perhaps you bewitched her."

The pious man replied, "I put it to her thus and so."

On hearing these words the heathen, shaken and amazed, reasoned with himself: If a heifer, which has neither speech nor knowledge nor understanding, could acknowledge her Creator, shall not I, whose Maker made me in His own image and likeness, and put knowledge and understanding into me—shall not I acknowledge my Creator?

At once he went off, became a proselyte, and was privileged to acquire so much Torah that he came to be called R. Yohanan ben Torta ("son of a heifer")[1]

219. R. Eleazar's pupils asked him, "Why does a cat not recognize its master the way a dog does?" He replied, "If a man who eats what a mouse has bitten into is forgetful,[2] all the more so by far the creature that eats the mouse itself."[3]

220. After herdsmen had milked a cow, a snake came and drank of the milk, and a dog saw it drinking. When the herdsmen sat down to partake of the milk, the dog began to bark [warningly] at them, but they did not understand what his barking meant. Finally, the dog sprang forward, drank of the [venom-spattered] milk, and died. When the herdsmen buried him, they set a monument over him, which to this day is called the Dog's Monument.[4]

221. A certain man invited a sage to his home and seated a dog next to him. When the sage asked his host, "Do I deserve such humiliation from you?" the host replied, "Master, I owe the dog much gratitude: slavers came into the city, and when one of them sought to rape my wife, the dog [saved her by springing on him and] biting off his testicles."[5]

222. R. Tanhum bar Maryon said: In Rome, there are dogs who know how to outwit people. Thus, a dog slumps down in a baker's shop and pretends he has dozed off. When the owner of the bakeshop also dozes off, the dog dislodges a few loaves to the ground. While the loaves are being gathered up, the dog makes off with a loaf and gets away.[6]

223. R. Jonah lectured at the entrance to the patriarch's academy: What is meant by "The Righteous One knoweth the cause of the poor" (Prov. 29:7)? The Holy One knows that a dog's food is scanty,[7] so He enables it to keep food in its stomach for three days.

R. Hamnuna said: This proves that it is proper to throw a hunk of raw meat to a dog. And how large? R. Mari said: The size of its ear, and a stick right after [to drive it away].[8]

224. Dogs: when one of them barks, the rest gather and bark for no reason.[9]

225. A dog: when a man throws him a piece of bread, he shuts the dog's mouth.[10]

226. Our masters taught: When dogs howl, the angel of death has come to the city. When dogs frolic, the prophet Elijah has come to the city. This is so, however, only when there is no bitch among them.[11]

227. Dogs and cocks hate each other.[12]

228. Our masters taught: Five things are said of a mad dog: its mouth is open, its saliva drips, its ears flap, its tail hangs between its legs, and it walks on the edge of roads. Some say: It also barks, but is not heard.[13]

229. R. Papa said: No one is poorer than a dog or richer than a pig.[14]

230. Hang the heart of a palm on a pig, and he will do his usual thing with it.[15]

231. R. Gamda paid four *zuz* to sailors to bring him a certain thing, but since they could not find it, they brought him a monkey, which slipped away and scurried into a hole. The sailors dug their way into the hole and found the monkey squatting on precious stones, which they took and brought to R. Gamda.[16]

232. R. Hami bar Ukba said in the name of R. Yose bar R. Hanina: The sages surmised that a mountain animal will not grow in a valley and a valley animal will not grow on a mountain.

Diocletian used to oppress the inhabitants of Panias, who said to him, "We will go elsewhere." His counselor advised him, "They will not go away, and if they do go, they will come back. Should you wish to test the matter, get hold of some gazelles and send them to a distant land—

1. PR 14:2; Midrash Aseret ha-Dibberot (BhM 1:74–75).
2. See below, part 6, chap. 2, §79.
3. B. Hor 13a.
4. PRKM 10:1 (PRKS, p. 201).
5. P. Ter 8:7, 46a.
6. Gen. R. 22:6; Yalkut, Ps., §840.
7. In the ancient East, semiwild dogs roamed the streets.
8. B. Shab 155b.
9. Exod. R. 31:9.
10. Yelammedenu, *Devarim*, ed. L. Grünhut (Jerusalem, 1904), p. 90b. Yalkut, Isa., §485.
11. B. BK 60b.
12. B. Pes 113b.
13. B. Yoma 83b; P. Yoma 8:5, 45b.
14. Unlike a dog, a pig is provided with ample food. B. Shab 155b.
15. The pig will take even this delicacy to a dungheap to eat it there. B. Ber 43b.
16. B. Ned 50b.

in the end, they will return to their native place." He did so. He got hold of some gazelles, covered their horns with silver, and sent them off to Africa. At the end of three years, they [all] returned to their native place.[1]

233. A gazelle sleeps with one eye open and the other closed.[2]

234. "Knowest thou the time when the wild goats of the rocks bring forth?" (Job 39:1). The wild goat is cruel toward her young, and when about to crouch to give birth, she goes up to the top of a mountain, so that the young will fall out of her and be killed. Hence, the Holy One readies a vulture for her, to catch the young on its wings and set it down before its dam. Not even by an instant does the vulture come too soon or too late, for if the vulture were an instant too soon or too late, the youngling would be killed.

"Canst thou mark when the hinds calve?" (Job 39:1). The hind has a narrow womb. When she crouches to be delivered, the Holy One provides her with a drago,[3] which bites her in the abdomen, so that the fawn is loosened from its place [and falls out]. Were the drago there an instant too soon or too late, the fawn would die. And after the hind gives birth, what does the Holy One do? He provides an herb for her, which she eats and is healed by.[4]

235. "The high mountains are for wild goats" (Ps. 104:18). R. Yudan said: For whose sake were high mountains created? For the wild goats' sake. There, a wild she-goat, weak and afraid of predatory beasts, [may find shelter]. Then, too, when she wishes to drink, the Holy One throws her into a state of frenzy, so that she strikes the ground with her horns. When the predatory beast hears the noise she makes, it flees.[5]

236. When a hind is thirsty, she digs a hole, fixes her horns in it, and in her distress pants before the Holy One. The Holy One brings up the deep for her, and the deep brings up water for her.[6]

237. R. Ila said in the name of R. Simeon ben Lakish that R. Meir used to say: The *tahash*[7] of Moses' day was a distinct species, and the sages are undecided whether it belonged to the genus of wild beasts or to the genus of domestic animals. On its forehead it had one horn. During the construction of the Tabernacle, the animal was provided for Moses. After he made [the coverings for the] Tabernacle out of its skins, the *tahash* disappeared.[8]

238. The *keresh*[9] is of the genus of wild beasts and has only one horn.[10]

239. R. Judah said: The *keresh* is the stag of [the forest] on high; the *tigres* is the lion of [the forest] on high.

R. Joseph said: The hide of the stag of the [forest] on high is sixteen cubits long.

R. Kahana said: The distance from one ear of the lion of the [forest] on high to the other is nine cubits.[11]

240. A Caesar once said to R. Joshua ben Hananiah, "Your God is likened to a lion, for it is written, 'The lion hath roared, who will not fear? The Lord God hath spoken, who can but prophesy?' [Amos 3:8]. Wherein lies His greatness? Surely a horseman can [easily] kill a lion!" R. Joshua: "He has been likened not to an ordinary lion but to the lion of [the forest] on high!" "I desire," said Caesar, "that you show it to me." R. Joshua: "You will be unable to look at it." Caesar: "Nevertheless, I insist." So R. Joshua entreated God's mercy, and the lion [of the forest on high] was forced to move from its place. When it was four hundred parasangs distant, it roared once; all the pregnant women miscarried, and the walls of Rome collapsed. When it was three hundred parasangs distant, it roared again; the teeth of men fell out, and Caesar himself fell from his throne to the ground. "I beg of you," he implored, "entreat God's mercy that this lion may return to its place." R. Joshua did entreat God's mercy, and it was returned.[12]

241. Once, R. Hanina ben Dosa saw a lion and said to him: O you weakling of a king, have I not adjured you not to be seen in the Land of Israel? The lion fled at once, but R. Hanina ran after him and said: Forgive my having called you "weakling," for He who created you called you "mighty"—"the lion which is mightiest among the beasts" (Prov. 30:30).[13]

242. While R. Simeon ben Halafta was walking on the road, he was met by lions, who roared at him. So he quoted, "The young lions roar after their prey" (Ps. 104:21). At that, two joints of meat came down [from heaven], and the lions ate one and left the other. R. Simeon ben Halafta took the joint they left to the house of study and inquired about it: Is it unclean or is it clean [and fit to be eaten]? The sages replied: Nothing unclean comes down from heaven.[14]

243. R. Papa said: We have a tradition that a lion will not attack two persons.

But we see that it does. However, so Rami bar Abba explained, no wild beast will endeavor to overpower a human being unless he appears to it to be an animal, as

1. P. Shev 9:2, 38d.
2. Song R. 8:14, §1.
3. A flying lizard.
4. B. BB 16b; Yalkut, Ps., §862.
5. Gen. R. 12:9.
6. Aggadat Esther 7:10 (ed. Buber, p. 68); MTeh 22:14.
7. Dugong.
8. B. Shab 28b.
9. A kind of antelope; a unicorn. So Jastrow.
10. B. Shab 28b.
11. B. Hul 59b.
12. Ibid.
13. Tanhuma, *Va-yiggash*, §3.
14. B. Sanh 59b.

is said, "Man will not abide in honor when he appears to be an animal—he will perish" (Ps. 49:13).[1]

244. While David was tending sheep, he came upon the *re'em* asleep in the wilderness. Thinking it was a mountain, he climbed upon it and continued to tend his sheep. The *re'em* woke up and arose, and David, astride its horns, was lifted as high as the heavens. At that moment David prayed to the Holy One to bring him down from the *re'em.* What did the Holy One do? He caused a lion to come [toward the *re'em*], and when the *re'em* saw the lion, he was afraid of it and cringed before it, for the lion is king of all beasts and cattle. When David saw the lion, he also was afraid of it. But then the Holy One caused a stag to come along, and as the lion sprang away in pursuit of it, David descended and went his way. Hence he said, "Save me from the lion's mouth; for Thou hast answered me from the horns of the *re'mim* (Ps. 22:22).[2]

245. It happened that a lion, a dog, and an Ethiopian gnat[3] were together. The lion was about to mangle the dog, but when he saw the Ethiopian gnat, he drew back in fear, for the Ethiopian gnat is the scourge of the lion, even as the dog is the scourge of the Ethiopian gnat. Thus, the three creatures did no harm to one another. When R. Akiva saw this, he quoted, "How manifold are Thy works, O Lord! In wisdom hast Thou made them all" (Ps. 104:24).[4]

246. Our masters taught: There are five instances in which the weak cast fear on the strong: the fear of a certain reptile on a lion, the fear of a gnat on an elephant,[5] the fear of a spider on a scorpion,[6] the fear of a swallow on an eagle,[7] and the fear of a stickleback on Leviathan. R. Judah said in the name of Rav: And the proof? "He strengtheneth the despoiled over the strong" (Amos 5:9).[8]

247. R. Judah said in the name of Rav: All that the Holy One created in His world, He created male and female. So, too, Leviathan the bolt-straight serpent and Leviathan the coiled serpent, He created male and female, and if they had mated with each other, [their numerous progeny] would have destroyed the entire world, all of it. What did the Holy One do? He castrated the male and killed the female, preserving her in brine for the righteous in the world-to-come. Also the Behemoth,[9] which [daily] eats up the grass of a thousand hills, He created male and female. And if they had mated with each other, [their numerous progeny] would have destroyed the entire world, all of it. What did the Holy One do? He castrated the male and froze the female, preserving her for the righteous in the time-to-come.[10]

248. R. Yohanan said: When Leviathan is hungry, it emits a fiery breath from its mouth and brings all the waters of the deep to a boil, and but for Leviathan's sticking its head into the Garden of Eden, no creature could endure the stench of its breath. When Leviathan is thirsty, it makes many furrows in the sea.[11]

249. "Mine . . . is the Behemoth upon a thousand hills" (Ps. 50:10). I, says God, have a unique creature whom I made for your sustenance in the time-to-come. It is the Behemoth, couched on a thousand mountains, and these thousand mountains provide it with all kinds of herbs and all kinds of other victuals to eat.

How does it drink? Some say: Its head is opposite the mouth of the Jordan, with its mouth directly against the river, so that the Jordan pours into its mouth, and thus it drinks its waters. And some say that it swallows in a single draft all the water that the Jordan gathers up in six months.[12]

Travelers' Tales

250. Rabbah bar Bar Hanah reported: Seafarers told me:[13] The wave capable of sinking a ship looks as though a white fringe of fire is at its crest, and if we strike it with clubs on which is engraved "I am that I am, Yah, the Lord of Hosts, Amen, Amen, Selah," it wanes.

More. Seafarers also told me: Between one wave and the next there is a distance of three hundred parasangs, and the height of each wave is three hundred parasangs. Once, while we were on a sea voyage, a wave lifted us up so high that we saw the resting place of the smallest star—it was the size of a field in which forty *seah* of mustard seed could be sown. Had the wave lifted us a bit higher, we would have been incinerated by the star's heat. Then we heard one wave calling to the other, "Mate, if there is anything in the world that you did not sweep away, I will go and destroy it." The other replied, "Go forth and behold the power of your Creator, who gave us no permission to go beyond the sand [on the shore], be it even as little as the breadth of a thread."[14]

251. Rabbah bar Bar Hanah said further: I saw Ormuzd the son of Lilith running so fast on the parapet of Mahoza's wall that a rider galloping below on horseback could not keep up with him. Once, the people of Mahoza saddled for Ormuzd two she-mules which stood on the two bridges of the Robnag; and he jumped from one she-mule to the other, and back again from the other to the one, while

1. JV: "But man abideth not in honor; he is like the beasts that perish." B. Shab 151b; B. Sanh 38b.
2. MTeh 22:28.
3. Or "lizard."
4. MTeh 104:19.
5. In whose trunk it enters.
6. In whose ear it enters.
7. It goes under the eagle's wings and prevents their being spread.
8. JV: "That causeth destruction to flash upon the strong." B. Shab 77b.
9. See Ps. 50:10.
10. B. BB 74b.
11. B. BB 75a.
12. PR, supplement A (YJS 2:823–24); Lev. R. 22:10.
13. The following apparent hyperboles may be allegories on the political and social conditions of the time.
14. B. BB 73a.

holding in his hands two cups of wine, pouring from one to the other, and back again from the other to the one, and not a drop fell to the ground. He was able to do so even though it was the sort of day when "waves mounted up to heaven and plunged down to the depths" (Ps. 107:26).[1]

252. Rabbah bar Bar Hanah said: I saw a *re'em* only a day old that was as big as Mount Tabor. The length of its neck was three parasangs, and the place where its head rested was a parasang and a half. When it dropped its turds, they stopped the Jordan's flow.[2]

253. Rabbah bar Bar Hanah further stated: I saw a frog the size of the Fort of Hagronia. A serpent came and swallowed the frog; then came a raven, and, after swallowing the serpent, it flew up and perched high on a tree. Pause and consider how strong that tree must have been [to support such a giant raven]. R. Papa bar Samuel said: Had I not been there myself, I would not have believed it.[3]

254. Rabbah bar Bar Hanah said further: Once, while traveling on a ship, we saw a fish in whose nostrils a stickleback had entered, so that the fish died. When the water cast the dead fish onto the shore, sixty towns were destroyed thereby, sixty towns ate of it, and sixty towns salted [what was left of it], and three hundred kegs of oil were filled from one of its eyeballs. On returning after twelve months, we saw that building joists were being sawn from its skeleton, and with these the towns were rebuilt.[4]

255. Rabbah bar Bar Hanah said further: Once, while traveling on a ship, we saw a fish whose back was covered by a sandbank upon which reeds grew. Thinking that we had come upon dry land, we went up and baked and cooked on the fish's back. However, when its back became hot, the fish turned over, and had not the ship been close by, we would have drowned.[5]

256. Rabbah bar Bar Hanah said further: Once, while we were traveling on a ship, it sailed for three days and three nights between one fin of a fish and the other. The fish was swimming against the wind, while we were sailing with the wind. Lest you suppose that the ship did not sail very fast, R. Dimi, when he came [from the Land of Israel], stated that the ship covered sixty parasangs in the time it takes to heat a kettle of water. When a horseman shot an arrow, the ship kept ahead of the arrow.[6]

257. Rabbah bar Bar Hanah said further: Once, while traveling on a ship, we saw a bird standing up to its ankles in water, while its head reached the sky. Supposing that the water was not deep, we were about to go down into it to cool ourselves, but a divine voice called out, "Do not go down here, for seven years ago a carpenter's adze was dropped [into this water], and it has not yet reached the bottom." And not only because the water is so deep, but because it is so rapid.

That bird, R. Ashi said, was *ziz* of the fields [which darkens the sun with its wings].[7]

258. Rabbah bar Bar Hanah said further: Once, while traveling in a desert, we saw geese that were so fat their feathers were forced out, and streams of fat flowed from under them. When I asked them, "May I have a share of your flesh in the world-to-come?" one lifted up its wing for me and the other lifted up its leg for me.[8]

When I came before R. Eleazar, he said to me: Israel will be called to account for [the sufferings[9] of] these [geese].[10]

259. Rabbah bar Bar Hanah related: Once, while traveling in a desert, we were joined by an Arab merchant who would pick up some sand, smell it, and say, "This road leads to such-and-such a place, and that road leads to such-and-such a place." We asked him, "How far are we from water?" He replied, "Give me some sand." We gave it to him, and he said, "Eight parasangs." After traveling several parasangs, we gave him more sand, and he smelled it and told us that we were three parasangs away. When I substituted sand from one place with sand from another place, he was not fooled.

That Arab also said to me, "Come, and I will show you the Israelites who died [during the forty years' wandering] in the wilderness." I went [with him] and saw them. They appeared to be in a state of exhilaration, lying on their backs. The knee of one of them was raised up, and the Arab merchant passed under that knee, riding his camel and holding his spear erect, without touching the knee's hamstring. I snipped off a corner of the purple cloak of one of them; and suddenly we found ourselves unable to budge from the place where we were. The Arab said to me, "You've taken something from them, haven't you? Return it, for we have a tradition that he who takes anything from them cannot move from his place." After I returned the corner of the cloak, we were able to move on.

That Arab also said to me, "Come, and I will show you Mount Sinai." I went and saw that it was surrounded by scorpions, which stood there as [large as] white asses. Then I heard a divine voice: "Woe is Me that I uttered an oath [to send Israel into exile]. Who will nullify it for Me?"

When later I came before the sages, they said to me, "Every Rabbah is an ass, and every bar Bar Hanah is a fool. You should have said; 'Your oath is nullified, Your oath is nullified.' "

---

1. B. BB 73a–b and En Yaakov, ad loc.
2. Ibid. and En Yaakov, ad loc.
3. Ibid.
4. Ibid.
5. Ibid.
6. Ibid.

---

7. B. BB 73b.
8. As though to intimate, "These portions are yours."
9. "The protracted suffering of the geese caused by their growing fatness is due to Israel's sins, which delay the coming of the Messiah, or the era denoted by the expression 'the world-to-come' " (BB, Soncino, p. 292, n. 5).
10. B. BB 73b.

That Arab also said to me, "Come, and I will show you the men of Korah who were swallowed by the earth." I went and saw two cracks in the ground, out of which smoke was rising. I then took fleeces of wool, dipped them in water, stuck them on the tip of a spear, and lowered it into one of the cracks. When I pulled the spear out, the fleeces were singed. The Arab then said to me, "Listen closely. What do you hear?" I heard the men of Korah crying out, "Moses and his Torah are truth, and we are liars." The Arab said to me, "Every thirty days, Gehenna, turning them around like meat in a stew pot, returns them here, and they cry out, 'Moses and his Torah are truth, and we are liars.' "

The Arab also said to me, "Come, and I will show you the spot where heaven and earth kiss each other." I went and saw that heaven was provided with ever so many windows. So I took my basket [which contained my food] and put it into a window in heaven. When I finished my *Tefillah*, I looked for the basket but did not find it, so I asked, "Are there thieves here?" The Arab replied, "Heaven is a revolving wheel—wait until tomorrow, and you will find the basket coming back."[1]

260. R. Yohanan related: Once we were traveling on a ship and saw a fish raise its head out of the sea. Its eyes seemed like two moons, and as much water gushed from its two nostrils as from both rivers of Sura.[2]

261. R. Safra related: Once, while traveling on a ship, we saw a fish that raised its head out of the sea. It had horns on which was engraved: "I, one of the lesser creatures of the sea, am three hundred parasangs long, and yet I can fit into Leviathan's mouth."

R. Ashi said: This fish was a sea-goat [which has to dig for its food, and that is why it has horns].[3]

262. R. Yohanan related: Once, while traveling on a ship, we saw a chest set with precious stones and pearls, and encompassed by a species of fish called *karsha*. When a diver went down to bring up the chest, a fish attacked him and was about to bite off his thigh. But the diver threw a bottle full of vinegar at it and was able to continue his dive. Just then, a divine voice came forth, saying, "What have you people to do with the chest that belongs to R. Hanina ben Dosa's wife, who is to store in it purple dye for the righteous in the world-to-come!"[4]

263. Rav Judah the Indian related: Once, while we were traveling on a ship, we saw in the sea a precious stone that was encompassed by a serpent. When a diver descended to bring it up, the serpent came and was about to swallow the ship. But along came a raven and bit off the serpent's head, and the water turned into blood. Immediately, a second serpent came, took the precious stone, hung it over the dead serpent, and brought it back to life. So again it was about to swallow the ship. But along came a bird, bit off its head, took hold of the precious stone, and threw it into the ship. We had a supply of salted birds in the ship, and when we touched them with the stone, [they revived] and flew off, taking the stone with them.[5]

264. R. Ashi said: R. Huna bar Nathan told me [the following]: Once, while walking in the desert, we happened to have with us a leg of meat, which we cut up, porged,[6] and put on the grass. Even before we could bring kindling wood, the leg [which had been cut up into pieces] became whole. We roasted it, and when we returned to that place after twelve months, we found the coals of the fire we had made still glowing. When I came before Amemar, he said to me, "That grass was dragon's blood [a resin]; those coals were broom."[7]

265. R. Ishmael ben Satriel of Arkat-livnah testified before Rabbi: Lettuces in our place have sixty myriads of peelings [around their core], and a gnat in our place has sixty myriads of membranes in its stomach.

Once a cedar fell in our place, and sixteen wagons side by side passed across the most slender part of its trunk. Once the egg of a *bar-yokani*[8] fell, and it drowned sixty large cities and shattered three hundred cedars.[9]

Human Beings

266. There are seven created things, each higher in importance than the other.

Higher in importance than the earth, the Holy One created a firmament.

Higher in importance than the firmament, He created stars to give light to the world.

Higher in importance than the stars, He created trees, which yield fruit, while the stars yield no fruit.

Higher in importance than the trees, He created winds, which are able to go hither and yon, while trees cannot stir from their place.

Higher in importance than the winds, He created animals, which are able to eat and drink, while winds neither eat nor drink.

Higher in importance than the animals, He created man, in whom there is understanding, while in animals there is no understanding.

Higher in importance than man, He created ministering angels, who are able to go from one end of the world to the other, whereas man cannot.[10]

267. Our masters taught: Six things are said concerning human beings. In regard to three, they are like ministering

1. B. BB 73b–74a and En Yaakov, ad loc.
2. B. BB. 74a.
3. Ibid.
4. B. BB 74a–b.
5. B. BB 74b.
6. Removed the forbidden fat and the sciatic muscle.
7. B. BB 74b.
8. "A fabulous bird of the ostrich family" (Bekh, Soncino, p. 391, n. 6).
9. B. Bekh 57b and En Yaakov, ad loc.
10. ARN 37; ARNB 29.

angels; in regard to three others, like animals. Three like ministering angels: they have understanding like the ministering angels, they walk erect like the ministering angels, they can use the sacred tongue like the ministering angels. Three like animals: they eat and drink like animals, they procreate like animals, and they excrete like animals.[1]

268. We have been taught that R. Meir used to say: One man differs from another in three ways: in voice, in appearance, and in understanding.[2]

269. We have been taught: With what part of the body does the formation of an embryo begin? With the head. Abba Saul said: With the navel, which sends its roots in every direction.[3]

270. Abba Saul said: In its primary stage, the fetus resembles a locust, its two eyes being like the two eyes of a fly. The two, according to R. Hiyya, are far removed from each other. Its two nostrils are also like the two eyes of a fly, being near each other, according to R. Hiyya. Its two ears are also like the two eyes of a fly. Its two arms are like scarlet ribbons. Its mouth is as narrow as a hair stretched out. Its body is as round as a lentil, with its limbs pressed together as a shapeless lump. If the fetus is a female, its body is the size of a barley grain with a slit across its length. [It goes without saying that] the fetus has no outlines of either hands or feet.[4]

271. R Eleazar stated: What does a fetus resemble when it is in its mother's womb? A nut floating in a bowl of water. Should a man put his finger on it, the finger would sink whatever it touched.[5]

272. Our masters taught: During the first three months [of pregnancy], the fetus occupies the lowest chamber [in the womb]; during the middle months, it occupies the middle chamber; and during the last three months, it occupies the uppermost chamber. When the time arrives for the fetus to emerge, it turns over and emerges—the turning over is the cause of the woman's pains.

The pain in giving birth to a female child is more intense than in giving birth to a male, for a female turns its face upward while a male does not.[6]

273. R. Hinena bar Papa expounded as follows: What is implied in "Who doeth great things past finding out; yea, marvelous things without number" (Job 9:10)? That you are to pause and consider the contrast between the Holy One's capacity and man's capacity. Man's capacity: if he put a valuable article in a well-tied skin bottle with its orifice turned upward, it may or may not stay safe. Whereas the Holy One fashions the embryo in a woman's inner part, which is open and whose orifice is turned downward, yet the embryo stays safe.

[Another difference]: When man places articles in the pan of a scale, the pan sinks lower and lower as the weight increases. [When] the Holy One [places a fetus in the womb], it rises higher and higher [from the lowest chamber in the womb to the uppermost] as the fetus's weight increases.

R. Yose the Galilean expounded: What is implied in the verse "I will give thanks unto Thee, for I am fearfully and wonderfully made; wonderful are Thy works; and that my soul knoweth right well" (Ps. 139:14)? That you are to pause and consider the contrast between the Holy One's capacity and man's capacity. Man's capacity: if he plants various seeds in a bed, each will grow only into its own species; whereas the Holy One fashions the embryo in a woman's innards in such a way that the seed of the male and the seed of the female grow into a single species.

According to some, R. Yose expounded the psalm verse in another way: If a dyer puts different ingredients into a caldron, they all unite into one color, whereas the Holy One fashions the embryo in a woman's innards in such a way that each element develops into a distinct entity.[7]

274. R. Simlai delivered the following discourse: What does an embryo in the womb of its mother resemble? A writing tablet that stays folded up. The embryo's hands rest on its two temples, both its elbows on its two knees, and its heels against its buttocks. Its head lies between its knees, its mouth is closed, and its navel is open. It eats what its mother eats and drinks what its mother drinks, but it produces no feces, because otherwise it would kill its mother. However, as soon as it goes forth into the air of the world, that which had been closed is opened, and that which had been open is closed. Otherwise, the newborn could not live even one hour.[8]

275. There are two hundred and forty-eight parts in a man: thirty in the foot,—there being six in each toe—ten in the ankle, two in the shank, five in the knee, one in the thigh, three in the hip, eleven ribs, thirty parts in the hand—there being six in each finger—two in the forearm, two in the elbow, one in the upper arm, and four in the shoulder. Thus, there are one hundred and one parts on one side of the body and one hundred and one parts on the other side of the body. There are also eighteen vertebrae in the spine, nine parts in the head, eight in the neck, six in the breast, and five in the orifices [of generation and excretion].[9]

276. R. Judah related in the name of Samuel: R. Ishmael's disciples once dissected the body of a prostitute who had been condemned by the king to be burned. Upon examination, they found in it two hundred and fifty-two

---

1. B. Hag 16a.
2. B. Sanh 38a.
3. B. Yoma 85a.
4. B. Nid 25a and En Yaakov, ad loc.; Lev. R. 14:8.
5. B. Nid 31a.
6. Ibid.

7. The male seed develops into bones, sinews, nails, etc., while the female seed develops into skin, flesh, etc. Ibid.
8. B. Nid 30b.
9. Oh 1:8.

parts. So the disciples came to R. Ismael and asked, "How many parts in a human being?" He replied, "Two hundred and forty-eight." The disciples: "But we examined a body and found two hundred and fifty-two parts." R. Ishmael: "Perhaps you examined a woman, in whom, according to Scripture, two hinges [in her sexual organ] and two doors [of the womb] are added."[1]

277. Our masters taught: The kidneys counsel, the heart discerns, the tongue shapes [words], the mouth articulates, the windpipe produces the voice, the gullet takes in all kinds of food, the lungs absorb all kinds of moisture [from the stomach], the liver is the seat of anger, the gall lets a drop fall into the liver and allays anger, the spleen produces laughter, the large intestine grinds food, the maw produces sleep, and the nose awakens. Should the organ that induces sleep awaken, or the wakener fall asleep, the man would pine away. The sages taught: Should both organs cause sleep or both keep awake, the man would die at once.[2]

278. R. Tahalifa of Caesarea said in the name of R. Fila: Pause and consider how many miracles the Holy One performs for man and he knows it not. If a man swallowed dry bread, it would go down into his bowels and lacerate his innards. So the Holy One created a fountain of saliva in his throat, which conveys the bread down safely.[3]

279. [The food proceeds] from the mouth to the gullet, from the gullet to the stomach, from the stomach to the digestive organ, from the digestive organ to the duodenum, from the duodenum to the second stomach, from the second stomach to the small winding intestine, from the small winding intestine to the large winding intestine, from the large winding intestine to the mucal sieve, from the mucal sieve to the rectum, from the rectum to the anus, and from the anus to outside the body.[4]

280. R. Levi said: Six organs serve a man—three are under his control, and three are not under his control. The ones under his control: the mouth, the hands, and the feet; the ones not under his control: the eyes, the ears, and the nose. And when the Holy One wishes it, even the ones under his control are no longer under his control.[5]

281. The face that the Holy One created in man is no more than the distance between the tip of the thumb and the tip of the index finger when held apart; and though it has many fountains, the fluids do not mingle. The fluid of the eyes is salty, the fluid in the ears greasy, the fluid in the nose foul, the fluid in the mouth sweet. Why is the fluid in the eyes salty? Because if a man were able to weep for the dead all the time, his eyes would soon be blinded. But because the fluid is salty,[6] the man stops and weeps no more. Why is the fluid in the ears greasy? Because when a man hears bad news, if it were retained in his ears, it would penetrate his heart, and he would die. However, because the ear fluid is greasy, he takes the news in at one ear and lets it out at the other. Why is the fluid in the nose foul? Because when a man inhales a bad odor, if it were not for the foul liquid in the nose, which arrests it, the man would immediately die. Why is the fluid in the mouth sweet? Because sometimes a man eats food that disagrees with him, so that he throws it up, and if the fluid in the mouth were not sweet, he would not recover [from his revulsion].[7]

282. The verse "He that made thee, and placed thee on settings" (Deut. 32:6) implies that the Holy One created in man many organs, each in its own setting, and if any change is made in an organ's setting, the man will be unable to go on living.[8]

283. "For Thou art great, and doest wondrous things" (Ps. 86:10). R. Tanhum said: Should a leather bottle have a hole in it as small as a needle's eye, all of its air will escape. Yet though man is formed with many hollows and many orifices, his breath does not escape through them.[9]

284. We have been taught that Abba Saul said: When I was a gravedigger, I made a practice of carefully observing the bones of the dead. The bones of one who drank undiluted wine are burned, those of one who drank wine excessively diluted are translucent, and those of one who drank wine properly mixed are full of marrow. The bones of a person whose drinking exceeded his eating are burned, those of one whose eating exceeded his drinking are translucent, and those of one who ate and drank in a proper balance are full of marrow.[10]

285. We have been taught that Abba Saul (according to some, R. Yohanan) said: When I was a gravedigger, on one occasion, while pursuing a stag, I entered the thighbone of a corpse, and though I pursued the stag for three parasangs, I reached neither the stag nor the end of the thighbone. When I came back out, I was told that the thighbone was Og's, king of Bashan.[11]

286. We have been taught that Abba Saul said: When I was a gravedigger, on one occasion a cave opened under me, and I found myself standing up to my nose in the eyeball of a corpse. When I came back out, I was told that it was Absalom's eye.[12]

1. B. Bekh 45a.
2. B. Ber 61a–b and En Yaakov, ad loc.
3. Exod. R. 24:1.
4. Lev. R. 3:4; Eccles. R. 7:19, §3.
5. Gen. R. 67:3; Tanhuma B, *Va-yikra*, §10.
6. And smarts when shed for a long time.
7. Tanhuma B, *Hukkat*, §1; Num. R. 18:22.
8. B. Hul 56b.
9. Gen. R. 1:3.
10. B. Nid 24b.
11. Ibid.
12. Ibid.

CHAPTER TWO

MATTERS PERTAINING TO DIVINATION AND HEALING

The Influence of Constellations

1. In the notebook of R. Joshua ben Levi, it was recorded: He who is born on the first day of the week [Sunday] will be either completely virtuous or completely wicked. What is the reason? Because on that day light and darkness were created. He who is born on the second day of the week [Monday] will be bad tempered. What is the reason? Because on that day the waters were divided. He who is born on the third day of the week [Tuesday] will be wealthy and carnal. What is the reason? Because on that day herbs were created.[1] He who is born on the fourth day of the week [Wednesday] will be endowed with wisdom and understanding. What is the reason? Because on that day the luminaries were suspended in the sky. He who is born on the fifth day of the week [Thursday] will practice benevolence. What is the reason? Because on that day fishes and birds were created.[2] He who is born on the eve of the Sabbath [Friday] will be a seeker, which means, as R. Nahman bar Isaac indicated, a seeker after good deeds.[3] He who is born on the Sabbath will die on the Sabbath, because, in order to assist in his delivery, the great day of the Sabbath had to be desecrated.[4]

R. Hanina said to his disciples: Go out and tell the son of Levi: not the constellation of the day but the planet regnant in the hour of a man's birth is the determining influence. He who is born under the sun will be radiant in his appearance; he will eat and drink what is his, and his secret deeds will be quickly uncovered, so that if he should try to take what is not his, he will not succeed. He who is born under Venus [Nogah] will be wealthy and carnal. What is the reason? Because the fire [of lust] hangs from it. He who is born under Mercury [Kokhav] will be perceptive and wise. What is the reason? Because Mercury is the sun's scribe. He who is born under the moon will be a man to suffer illness; he will build and demolish, demolish and build,[5] eat and drink that which is not his;[6] and his secrets will stay hidden,[7] so that if he takes what is not his, he will succeed. He who is born under Saturn [Shabbetai] will be a man whose plans will be frustrated.[8] Others say: [All] malicious designs against him will be frustrated. He who is born under Jupiter [Tzedek] will be a right-doing man [*tzadkan*]. He who is born under Mars [Maadim] will be a shedder of blood,[9] which, as R. Ashi observed, means either a surgeon, a brigand, a slaughterer, or a circumciser. Rabbah said: I was born under Mars [and I am none of these]. Abbaye retorted: You too, sir, [as judge], inflict punishment and put to death.[10]

2. R Hanina said: The planetary influence gives wisdom, the planetary influence gives wealth; and Israel also stands under planetary influence. But R. Yohanan maintained: Israel is free from planetary influence. Now, R. Yohanan is consistent with his view set forth elsewhere, for R. Yohanan said: How do we know that Israel is free from planetary influence? Because it is said, "Thus saith the Lord: Learn not the way of the nations, and be not dismayed at the signs of heaven, for only the nations need be dismayed by them" (Jer. 10:2): they are to be dismayed—not Israel. Rav, too, holds that Israel is free from planetary influence, for R. Judah said in the name of Rav: How do we know that Israel is free from planetary influence? Because "He brought him forth beyond [heaven's planets]" (Gen. 15:5). When Abraham stated before the Holy One, "Master of the universe, one born in my house is to be mine heir" (Gen. 15:3), the Holy One replied, "Not so, thine heir will be he that shall come forth out of thine own bowels" (Gen. 15:4). Abraham spoke up: "Master of the universe, I gazed into what my planet bodes and found that I am not fated to beget a child." The Holy One replied, "Give up gazing at planets; [Israel is free from planetary influence]. How have you reached your conclusion? Is it because Jupiter [Tzedek, your planet], stands in the [chilly] west?[11] I will turn it back and place it in the [warm] east."[12]

3. R. Nahman bar Isaac's mother was told by astrologers, "Your son will be a thief." So she did not let him be bareheaded, saying to him, "Cover your head, so that the fear of Heaven may be upon you, and pray for God's mercy." Now, he did not know why she spoke to him thus. One day, while he sat and studied under a date palm, the cover fell off his head. Just then he looked up and saw the dates on the palm, and his evil inclination took hold of him. So he climbed up and bit off a cluster of dates with his teeth.[13]

4. Rava said: [Length of] life, children, and sustenance depend not on merit but on *mazzal* [planetary influence]. Take Rabbah and R. Hisda, both of whom were sages,

---

1. All kinds of them grow together—"promiscuously," so to speak.
2. Their sustenance derives from God's benevolence.
3. In the manner of the Sabbath keeper, who seeks to acquire all kinds of provisions for the Sabbath.
4. Thus, measure for measure.
5. Like the moon, which grows and diminishes each month.
6. Like the moon, which takes its light from the sun.
7. Like the moon, which comes out when it is dark.
8. *Shabbetai* means "made to cease," "frustrated."
9. *Maadim* means "the reddener."
10. B. Shab 156a.
11. It is thus not suitable for begetting children.
12. B. Shab 156a–b.
13. The tree did not belong to him. B. Shab 156b.

both saintly. When one prayed, rain came, even as when the other prayed, rain came. Yet R. Hisda lived to the age of ninety-two,[1] while Rabbah lived only to the age of forty.[2] In R. Hisda's house, there were sixty[3] wedding feasts; in Rabbah's house, sixty bereavements. In R. Hisda's house, dogs were fed bread of fine flour, which was not missed; in Rabbah's house, barley bread was for human beings, and even that was hardly to be had.[4]

5. The sages said in the name of R. Yose of Hutzal: What is the proof that one should not consult astrologers [about the influence of the planets]? "You shall be wholehearted with the Lord your God" (Deut. 18:13).[5]

Dreams

6. R. Samuel bar Nahmani said in the name of R. Jonathan: A man is shown in a dream only matters that are already in his own thoughts, as is said, "As for thee, O king, thine own thoughts come [into thy mind] upon thy bed" (Dan. 2:29); or, if you prefer, from here, "That thou mayest know the thoughts of thy heart" (Dan. 2:30). Rava said: You can see it for yourself: a man is never shown in a dream a date palm of gold or an elephant going through the eye of a needle.[6]

7. A Caesar asked R. Joshua ben Hananiah: You say that you are great sages. Tell me, then—what will I see in my dream? R. Joshua: You will see the Persians come upon you, enslave you, despoil you, and make you graze unclean animals with a gold crook [in your hand]. Caesar thought of R. Joshua's prediction all day and saw it [in his dream] that night.[7]

8. King Shapur [I] said to Samuel, "You say that you are great sages. Tell me then—what will I see in my dream?" Samuel: "You will see the Romans come, take you into captivity, and make you grind date pits in a golden mill. The king thought of that prediction all day and saw it [in his dream] that night.[8]

9. A man sleeping here in Babylonia might see a dream taking place in Spain.[9]

10. "The prophet that hath a dream, let him tell a dream. What hath the straw to do with the wheat?" (Jer. 23:28). What connection is there between straw and wheat, and a dream? Well, R. Yohanan said in the name of R. Simeon ben Yohai, just as there can be no wheat without straw, so there can be no dream without some stuff of nonsense.[10]

11. R. Berekhiah said: Even if part of a dream is fulfilled, all of it is never fulfilled. And the proof? From Joseph, who in his dream saw "the sun and the moon bow down. . . . And his father . . . said unto him: . . . 'Shall I and thy mother indeed come?' " (Gen. 37:9–10). [How could his mother come?] At that time, she was no longer in the world.[11]

12. When Samuel had a bad dream, he used to say, "The dreams speak falsely" (Zech. 10:2). When he had a good dream, he would say, "I wonder if dreams ever speak falsely—is it not said, 'I [God] speak with him in a dream' (Num. 12:6)?"[12]

13. Dreams have no significance, one way or another.[13]

14. A dream is one-sixtieth of prophecy.[14]

15. R. Yohanan said: If at the moment of rising, a scriptural text comes to a man's mouth, that is a minor prophecy.[15]

16. R. Yohanan said: Three kinds of dreams are fulfilled: a morning dream, a dream that a friend has about one, and a dream that is interpreted in the midst of a dream. Some say: Also a dream that is repeated.[16]

17. R. Huna said: A good man is shown a bad dream, and a bad man is shown a good dream: in all of David's years, he never had a good dream; in all of Ahithophel's years, he never had a bad dream.[17]

18. R. Ze'era said: A man who goes seven days without a dream is called evil, for Scripture says, "He that hath it shall abide satisfied; he shall not be visited with evil" (Prov. 19:23). Read not *savea*, "satisfied," but *sheva*, "seven."[18]

19. "There shall no evil befall thee" (Ps. 91:10). This means, said R. Hisda, citing R. Jeremiah bar Abba, that no bad dreams or evil thoughts will disturb you.[19]

20. The sages said in the name of Rav: Fasting is as effective against a dream as fire against woodchips. Pro-

1. He died in 390 C.E.
2. He died in 330 C.E.
3. A proverbial round number.
4. B. MK 28a.
5. B. Pes 113b.
6. B. Ber 55b.
7. B. Ber 56a.
8. Ibid.
9. B. Nid 30b.
10. B. Ber 55a.
11. B. Ber 55a.
12. Ibid. and En Yaakov, ad loc.
13. B. Git 52a.
14. B. Ber 57b.
15. B. Ber 55b.
16. Ibid.
17. Ibid.
18. R. Ze'era reads the verse: "He who abides seven days without being visited [by a dream is known to be one associated] with evil." B. Ber 14a and 55b.
19. B. Ber 55b.

vided, said R. Hisda, the fast was on the same day as the dream. Even, added R. Joseph, on the Sabbath.[1]

21. R. Hisda said: There is reality in every dream except one that occurs during a fast. As long as a dream is not interpreted, it is like a letter that has not been read.[2] Neither a good dream nor a bad dream is ever entirely fulfilled. A bad dream is better[3] than a good dream. The sadness caused by a bad dream is in itself enough, and the joy caused by a good dream is in itself enough. A bad dream is worse than being flogged.

R. Joseph said: In a good dream, the joy is such that, [blind though I am], it all but gives me sight.[4]

22. The sages said in the name of R. Yohanan: He who has a dream and is worried about it should have it given a good meaning in the presence of three. He should bring three [friends] and say to them, "I saw a good dream," and they should say to him, "It is good, and may it be good. May He who is everywhere turn it to good. Seven times may it be decreed for you from heaven that it should be good," and it will be good.[5]

23. He who had a dream but does not remember what he saw should stand before the priests at the time when they lift their hands in blessing and pray thus: "Master of the universe, I am Yours and my dreams are Yours. I dreamed a dream, but I do not know what it is. Whether I have dreamed about myself, or my colleagues dreamed about me, or I dreamed about others—if the dreams are good dreams, strengthen them and confirm them like the dreams of Joseph; and if they require healing, heal them, as the waters of Marah were healed by Moses our teacher, as Miriam was healed of her leprosy, as Hezekiah was healed of his sickness, and as the waters of Jericho were healed by Elisha. As You turned the curse of the wicked Balaam into a blessing, so may You turn all my dreams into something good for me." He should endeavor to conclude his *Tefillah* when the priests conclude their blessing, so that the congregation may answer, "Amen!" If he cannot manage this, he should say, "You who are majestic on high, who abide in might, You are peace, and Your Name is peace. May it be Your will to bestow peace upon us."[6]

24. R. Birayim, citing a certain elder—who was the elder? R. Banaah—said: In Jerusalem, there were twenty-four interpreters of dreams. Once I dreamed a dream and went to all of them, and not one agreed with the other in the interpretation of my dream, yet all the interpretations were fulfilled, confirming the saying, "All dreams follow the utterances of the mouth." R. Eleazar asked: What is the proof that all dreams follow the [utterances of the] mouth? "It came to pass, as he interpreted to us, so it was" (Gen. 41:13). Rava said: This is so, provided the interpretation corresponds to the substance of the dream, for "to each man according to his dream he did interpret" (Gen. 41:12).[7]

25. Bar Hadaya was an interpreter of dreams. He would give a favorable interpretation to one who paid him [a fee] and an unfavorable interpretation to one who did not. Abbaye and Rava each had [the same] dream. Abbaye gave him a *zuz*, and Rava gave him nothing. The two said to him: In our dream, we had read to us the verse, "Thine ox shall be slain before thine eyes, and thou shalt not eat of it" (Deut. 28:31). To Rava, Bar Hadaya said: Your merchandise will depreciate, and because of the distress in your heart, you will be unable to eat. To Abbaye, he said, Your merchandise will appreciate so much that you will be unable to eat because of the joy in your heart.

The two reported: We had read to us the verse "Thou shalt carry much seed out into the field, and shalt gather little in" (Deut. 28:38). To Abbaye, [Bar Hadaya] interpreted only the first half of the verse; to Rava, only the second half.

The two reported: We had read to us the verse "And all the peoples of the earth shall see that the Name of the Lord is called upon thee; and they shall be afraid of thee" (Deut. 28:10). To Abbaye, Bar Hadaya said: Your fame will go forth, you will become head of the academy, and all people will fear you. To Rava, he said: You will be arrested in the company of thieves, and because of what will be done to you, all will be the more afraid for themselves. The next day, the royal treasury was broken into by thieves, and the authorities arrested Rava. So people were afraid and said: If Rava was arrested, how much more and more are we likely to be.

The two told Bar Hadaya: We saw a head of lettuce lying over the mouth of a cask. To Abbaye, Bar Hadaya said: Your business will double as speedily as the growth of a lettuce. To Rava, he said: Your business will prove as bitter as a lettuce.

Later, Rava went to Bar Hadaya by himself and reported: I saw two doves flying away. Bar Hadaya: You will divorce two wives. Rava said to him, I saw two turnip tops.[8] He replied: You will receive two blows with a cudgel. Rava went and sat all that day in the house of study, where he came upon two blind men quarreling with each other and went to separate them, and they gave him two blows with their cudgels. They raised their cudgels to give Rava a third blow, but he said, "Enough! [In my dream] I saw only two."

Finally, Rava went over, paid Bar Hadaya a fee, and reported: I saw a wall fall down. To which Bar Hadaya replied: You will acquire wealth without limit.

Rava reported: I saw my own house collapse, and everyone came and took it away brick by brick. Bar Hadaya replied, Your teachings will spread throughout the world.

Rava reported: I dreamed that my head was split open

1. B. Shab 11a.
2. A dream follows its interpretation.
3. Since it stirs one to repent.
4. Instead of BR's *mefakahto* ("nullifies it"), the text is read *mefakahti* ("gives me sight"). B. Ber 55a.
5. B. Ber 55b.
6. Ibid.
7. Ibid.
8. Which look like cudgels.

and my brains spilled out. Bar Hadaya replied: The feathers stuffed in your pillow will burst out bit by bit. He reported: In my dream I had the *Hallel* of Egypt[1] read to me. Bar Hadaya replied: Miracles will happen to you.

Once, when Bar Hadaya was traveling with Rava by ship, he said to himself: Why would I accompany a man to whom a miracle will happen?[2] As Bar Hadaya was disembarking, he accidentally dropped a book, which Rava found. He saw written in it: All dreams follow the [interpreter's] mouth. At that, Rava exclaimed, "Wretch! It all depended on you, and you caused me such great distress![3]

26. Ben Dama, the son of R. Ishmael's sister, asked R. Ishmael: I saw that my two jaws fell in. [What does this mean]? R. Ishmael: Two Roman legionaries "jawed" evil against you, and they died.

Bar Kappara said to Rabbi [Judah I, the Patriarch]: I dreamed that my nose fell off. Rabbi: Fierce anger[4] has been removed from you. Bar Kappara: I dreamed that both my hands were cut off. Rabbi: You will not be in need of the labor of your hands. Bar Kappara: I dreamed that both my legs were cut off. Rabbi: You [will do so well that you] will be able to afford to ride horseback.[5]

27. R. Joshua ben Levi said: He who sees a river in his dream should rise early and say, "Behold, I will extend peace to her like a river" (Isa. 66:12), before another sort of verse, such as "Distress will come in like a river" (Isa. 59:19), occurs to him. He who sees a bird in his dream should rise early and say, "As birds hovering, so will the Lord of hosts protect" (Isa. 31:5), before another sort of verse, such as "Like a sparrow wandering from its nest, so is a man that wandereth from his place" (Prov. 27:8), occurs to him. He who sees grapes in his dream should rise early and say, "I found Israel like grapes in the wilderness" (Hos. 9:10), before another sort of verse, such as "Their grapes are grapes of gall" (Deut. 32:32), occurs to him.[6]

28. R. Hanina said: He who sees a well in a dream will experience peace. R. Hanan said: There are three images in dreams that signify peace: a river, a bird, and a pot.[7]

29. He who sees olive oil in his dream may hope for the light of the Torah.

He who sees an etrog [the *hadar* tree's fruit] in his dream will be honored [*hadur*] in the sight of his Maker.

He who sees a cock in his dream may expect a male child; if a hen, a fine garden and joy.[8]

He who sees [whole] eggs[9] in his dream—his petition will be held in abeyance; if broken eggs—his petition will be granted. This holds true also of nuts, cucumbers, all vessels of glass, and all other breakable things like them.

He who dreams that he goes up to a roof will attain high position; that he goes down, will be demoted. He who in a dream enters a big city will have his desires fulfilled; who enters a marsh will be made head of an academy;[10] who enters a forest will become head of students who are mature.[11]

30. R. Levi said: One should await fulfilment of a good dream for as long as twenty-two years. And the proof? Joseph, of whom Scripture says, "Joseph being seventeen years old . . . dreamed a dream (Gen. 37:25), and says later. "Joseph was thirty years old when he stood before Pharaoh" (Gen. 41:46). From seventeen to thirty is how many years? Thirteen, which—together with the seven years of plenty and two years of famine—add up to twenty-two.[12]

Destructive Forces That Afflict Mankind

31. Demons were created at twilight on the eve of the first Sabbath.[13]

32. "Let the earth bring forth living creatures" (Gen. 1:25). These, according to Rabbi [Judah I, the Patriarch] were the demons. The Holy One created their souls, but when He was about to create their bodies, the Sabbath's sanctity began, and He would not create them.[14]

33. R. Jeremiah ben Eleazar said: In all the years that Adam was under the ban,[15] he begot evil spirits—male demons and female demons. For it is said, "Adam lived a hundred and thirty years, and begot a son in his own likeness, after his own image" (Gen. 5:3), from which it follows that until that time [the end of the one hundred thirty years mentioned in the verse] he did not beget after his own image.[16]

34. Our masters taught: Six things are said concerning demons. In regard to three, they are like ministering angels, and in regard to three, they are like human beings. In regard to three, they are like ministering angels: they have wings like ministering angels, they fly from world's end to world's end like ministering angels, and, like min-

1. Ps. 113–18, recited on Passover Eve to celebrate the going forth from Egypt.
2. As much as to say, "He will be saved, but I will not."
3. B. Ber 56a–b and En Yaakov, ad loc.
4. *Af*, the Hebrew word for "nose," also means "God's anger."
5. B. Ber 56b.
6. Ibid.
7. B. Ber 57b.
8. The word *tarnegolet* ("hen") is taken to be portmanteau for *tar* [*bitza*] ("garden"), *naeh* ("fine"), and *gilah* ("joy").
9. The Aramaic for "egg," *beya*, also means "petition."
10. "The short and long reeds in a marsh are figurative of the different ages and standards of those attending the academy" (Ber, Soncino, p. 354, n. 5).
11. "The full-grown trees in a forest represent students who are mature" (Ber, Soncino, p. 354, n. 6). B. Ber 57a.
12. B. Ber 55b.
13. Based on Avot 5:6.
14. Gen. R. 7:5.
15. Because he ate the fruit of the tree of knowledge.
16. Semen discharged not for procreation is said to be utilized by evil spirits to procreate their own kind. B. Er 18b.

istering angels, they can hear what goes on behind the curtain [of heaven]. In regard to three, they are like human beings: they eat and drink like human beings, they increase and multiply like human beings, and they die like human beings.[1]

35. We have been taught that Abba Benjamin said: If the eye had permission to see [what is invisible], not a creature could withstand demons. Abbaye said: They are more numerous than we are, and they surround us like the ridge encompassing a water ring [dug around a tree]. R. Huna said: Each and every one among us has a thousand [demons] at his left and ten thousand at his right. Rava said: The crush at the *Kallah*[2] lectures is due to them, fatigue in the knees is due to them, the wearing out of sages' garments is due to demons rubbing against them, the bruising of feet is due to them.

He who wishes to become aware of demons' existence should take well-sifted ashes and sprinkle them around his bed. In the morning, he will see something like the tracks of a cock. He who wishes to see them should take the afterbirth of a black cat that is the offspring of a black cat and firstborn of a firstborn; he should parch the afterbirth in fire, grind it into powder, and put a generous pinch of the mix into his eyes—then he will see the demons. He should pour the rest of the mix into an iron tube and seal it with an iron signet, lest they steal it from him; he should also cover his mouth, so that he will come to no harm.

Though R. Bebai bar Abba did all this, nevertheless, when he saw the demons, he came to harm. But the sages entreated God's mercy in his behalf, and he recovered.[3]

36. Abbaye said: At first I used to say that people should not sit under a drainpipe in order to avoid being drenched with wastewater. But then my master told me: It is because demons are present there.

There is a story of porters who were carrying a cask of wine. Wishing to rest, they put it under a drainpipe, and the cask burst. So they came to Mar bar R. Ashi, who brought rams' horns and exorcised the destructive creature, which then appeared in his presence. When Mar bar R. Ashi asked the demon, "Why did you do this?" the demon replied, "What else could I have done, since they put the cask at my ear." Mar bar R. Ashi: "What business do you have in a place where there are many people? Since you have departed from what is prescribed for you, go and reimburse the porters." The demon: "If the master will fix the time right now when I am to pay them, I will do so." So Mar bar R. Ashi fixed a time, but when the time came, the demon was not there. When he did come, Mar bar R. Ashi asked him, "Why did you not come at the time agreed upon?" The demon replied, "We have no right to take anything that is tied up, sealed, measured, or counted. So I had to wait until I found money that was ownerless [and that money I bring now]."[4]

37. There is the story of what happened to a spirit who abode at a certain well, and another spirit came and wished to expel him from there. Now, a certain pious man whose name was Yose of Tzaytor used to sit and study near that well. So the spirit who had been abiding at the well appeared to him and said, "My master, I have been here in this place many years, and though you and your wives pass here at noon and at night, I have not injured anyone. But of late, a certain spirit has been contending with me each day and seeks to banish me from this place—he is very wicked and cruel, and will not suffer any creature to remain alive." Abba Yose asked, "What are we to do?" The spirit replied, "Go and tell the people of the city: At high noon, take your clubs and sickles, and go at that spirit, shouting, 'Our spirit prevails, our spirit prevails!' and the intruding spirit will flee."

They did as he asked and succeeded in having the intruder take flight. It is said that they did not budge from the place until they saw a kind of blood spot floating in the water [of the well].[5]

38. We have been taught: One should not go out alone on certain nights. Not on the nights of Wednesday or the nights of Sabbath, because Igrat the daughter of Mahalath—she and eighteen myriads of angels of destruction—go forth, and each angel has permission to wreak destruction on his own. Formerly, they were about every day in the week. On one occasion, Igrat met R. Hanina ben Dosa and said to him, "Had they not proclaimed in heaven concerning you, 'Beware of Hanina and his Torah learning,' I would have put you in danger." R. Hanina: "If, [as you say], I am of account in heaven, I decree that you are nevermore to pass through inhabited areas." Igrat: "I beg of you, leave me just a bit of space." So he left her Sabbath nights and Wednesday nights.

On another occasion, Igrat met Abbaye and said to him, "Had they not proclaimed in heaven concerning you, 'Beware of Nahmani[6] and his Torah learning,' I would have put you in danger." Abbaye: "If [as you say], I am of account in heaven, I decree that you nevermore pass through inhabited areas."

But we see that she does pass through them.

Those are the narrow paths in vineyards, which Igrat's host frequents: when their horses bolt [into inhabited areas], Igrat's host follows them to retrieve them.[7]

39. R. Jacob son of R. Aha bar Jacob was once sent by his father to study under Abbaye. When R. Jacob returned, and his father saw that his learning was not overly acute, he said, "Since I appear to be more apt than you, you remain here while I go [and study under Abbaye]." Pres-

1. B. Hag 16a and En Yaakov, ad loc.
2. The semiannual gatherings of Babylonian sages during the months of Adar and Elul.
3. B. Ber 6a.
4. B. Hul 105a.
5. Tanhuma, *Kedoshim*, §9; Lev. R. 24:3; MTeh 20:7.
6. Abbaye was so called because he was brought up in the house of Rabbah bar Nahmani.
7. B. Pes 112b–113a.

ently, Abbaye heard that R. Aha was coming. Now, it so happened that at that time a certain demon haunted Abbaye's house of study, so that even during the day, though people entered in pairs, they were harmed. Accordingly, Abbaye ordered his disciples: "Let no one offer lodging to R. Aha [so that he will have to spend the night in the house of study]. Perhaps through his merit a miracle will occur. So R. Aha went into the house of study, where he spent the night. [During the night] the demon appeared to him in the guise of a seven-headed dragon. But each time R. Aha fell on his knees in prayer, one of the demon's heads fell off. The next day, R. Aha chided them: "Had a miracle not occurred, you would have endangered my life."[1]

40. R. Huna said in the name of R. Yose: The demon Bitter Destruction is covered all over with scales and hair, [and he glares] with his one eye, and that eye is in the middle of his chest. He has no power when it is cool in the shade and hot in the sun, but only when it is hot in both shade and sun. He rolls like a ball, and from the seventeenth day of Tammuz to the ninth day of Av, he has power after ten o'clock in the morning and up to three o'clock in the afternoon.[2] And anyone who sees this demon falls upon his face and dies.[3]

41. A demon changes into many colors.[4]

42. R. Joshua ben Levi said: It is forbidden to greet one another by night, for we fear that the other might be a demon.[5]

43. R. Hanina said: It is forbidden to sleep in a house alone, for he who sleeps in a house alone is seized by Lilith [the night demon].[6]

44. To a single person, a destructive spirit may show itself and harm him. To two, it may show itself but not harm them. To three, it will not show itself at all.

R. Zutra bar Tobiah said in the name of Rav: A torch is as protective as two persons, and moonlight as protective as three.[7]

45. R. Hanina said: The demon Jonathan told me: Demons have a shadow, but not the shadow of a shadow.[8]

Sorceries and Optical Illusion

46. Ten measures of witchcraft came down to the world. The Egyptians took nine, and the rest of the world, all of it, took one.[9]

47. R. Yohanan said: Why are sorcerers called *mekhashefim?* Because they diminish (*makh'hishim*) the power of the household (*familia*) above.

"There is no one beside Him" (Deut. 4:35). Even by means of sorcery, said R. Hanina, no one can stand up against Him.

When a woman sought to take earth from under R. Hanina's feet [in order to bewitch him], he said to her, "If you can do it, go and practice [your sorcery], but remember Scripture's admonition: 'There is no one beside Him.' "

But is that really so? Did not R. Yohanan say, "Why are sorcerers called *mekhashefim?* Because they diminish the power of the household above"? However, R. Hanina is different, because his merit is so abundant.[10]

48. A *baal ov* (Lev. 19:31) is a ventriloquist who speaks out of his armpit. The *yiddeoni*, "wizard" (ibid.), is one who puts a bone of the *yiddoa*[11] in his mouth and speaks out of this bone.[12]

49. Three things have been said about him who brings up a dead person: he who brings him up sees him but does not hear his voice; he who needs him hears his voice but does not see him; and he who does not need him neither sees him nor hears his voice.[13]

50. Our masters taught: A *meonen*[14] is, according to R. Simeon, one who applies the semen of seven species to his eyes [in order to perform witchcraft]. According to the sages, he is one who causes an optical illusion.[15] According to R. Akiva, he is one who calculates seasons and hours, and declares, "Today is propitious for setting out, tomorrow is propitious for making purchases; wheat ripening on the eve of a sabbatical year is generally sound; [instead of waiting for the usual harvest time], the beans should be pulled up to save them from becoming wormy."[16]

51. Our Masters taught: A *menahesh* is a diviner who announces, "So-and-so's bread has fallen out of his mouth," "His staff has fallen from his hand," "So-and-so has called him from behind," "A raven has screamed at him," "A dog has barked at him," "A deer has crossed his path," "A snake has passed at his right and a fox at his left." Or who says, "Do not start anything with me now—it is morning, it is the New Moon, it is the Sabbath's outgoing."

Our masters taught: "Ye shall not use divinations" (Lev. 19:26)—the kind of those who resort to divination by means of weasels, birds, fish, and stars.[17]

---

1. B. Kid 29b.
2. Literally "between the fourth hour and the ninth hour," the count beginning at dawn, which is set at 6 A.M.
3. MTeh 91:3; Num. R. 12:3.
4. B. Yoma 75a.
5. B. Meg 3a.
6. B. Shab 151b.
7. B. Ber 43b.
8. B. Yev 122a.
9. B. Kid 49b.
10. B. Sanh 67b.
11. An unidentified beast or bird.
12. B. Sanh 65a–b.
13. Lev. R. 26:7.
14. JV: "Observer of times" (Deut. 18:10).
15. Possibly taking *meonen* as a form of *anan* ("cloud"); hence, "one who beclouds the eyes." Also a play on the root *'yn* ("eye").
16. Sif Deut., §171; Tos Shab 8:13–14; B. Sanh 65b.
17. B. Sanh 65b–66a.

52. We have been taught: In the words "Or that consulteth the dead" (Deut. 18:11), Scripture refers to him who starves himself and then spends the night in a cemetery, so that an unclean spirit may rest upon him [to enable him to hear what the dead say]. Whenever R. Akiva reached this verse, he would burst into tears [and say]: If an unclean spirit does come to rest upon a person who fasts in order that it should do so, how much more and more should the desire be fulfilled of him who fasts in order that the pure spirit [the Divine Presence] rest upon him! But alas! Our sins have driven it away from us, as is written, "Your iniquities have been a barrier between you and your God" (Isa. 59:2).[1]

53. Rava said: If the righteous desired it, they could create a world.

Indeed, Rava created a man and sent him to R. Zera. When R. Zera spoke to him and received no answer, he said to him, "You are a creature of one of the sages. Return to your dust."

R. Hanina and R. Oshaia spent every Sabbath eve studying the Book of Creation, by means of which they created—and ate—a calf developed to one-third of its growth.[2]

54. "Then the magicians said unto Pharaoh, 'This is the finger of God' " (Exod. 8:15).[3] R. Eleazar said: This proves that a demon cannot create a creature smaller than a barleycorn. R. Papa said: By God! Even a creature as large as a camel he cannot create![4]

55. When two women sit at a crossroads, one on one side and one on the other, facing each other, it is clear that they are engaged in witchcraft. What is the remedy? If there is another road, let the traveler take it; if there is no other road, then, if another man is with him, let the two hold each other's hands and pass; if there is no other man, let the traveler say, "Agrat, Ozlat, Usia, Belusia have been slain with a dark[?] arrow."[5]

56. Yohani daughter of Retivi was a widowed witch. Whenever a woman's time to give birth had come, Yohani would shut the woman's womb by witchcraft. After the woman had suffered greatly, the witch would say, "I will go and implore [God's] mercy—perhaps my prayer will be heard." Then she went and undid her witchcraft, and the child emerged. Once, when she went to the house of a woman about to give birth, [leaving behind] in her own house a man hired by the day, the hired man heard the sound of witchery knocking about in a vessel, as an embryo is knocked about in its mother's womb. When he removed the vessel's stopper, the witcheries went out, and the child was born. Then all knew that the widow was a mistress of witchcraft.[6]

57. There is the story of R. Eliezer, R. Joshua, and Rabban Gamaliel, who went up to Rome and entered a certain place where they found children piling up small mounds and saying, "This is what the people of the Land of Israel do as they say, 'This is the heave offering, and this is the tithe.' " So the sages said: It is evident that there are Jews here. Then they went to another place where they stayed as guests of a certain man. When they sat down to eat, every course that was put before them was first taken into a small chamber. Afraid that they were about to eat sacrifices offered to deities that are no deities, they asked their host, "Why do you not bring us any course without first taking it into the small chamber?" Their host replied, "I have an old father who has imposed upon himself the resolution that he would not leave his small chamber until he saw the sages of Israel." So they said, "Go and tell him, 'Come out to them, they are here.' " When the father came out to them, they asked him, "What reason did you have for such a resolution?" He replied, "[I imposed this resolution upon myself out of grief for my son, who was waiting for the sages to come to pray in his behalf. Now that you are here], pray in behalf of my son, who is still childless." So R. Eliezer said to R. Joshua, "Now then, Joshua ben Hananiah, see what you can do." R. Joshua: "Bring me some flaxseed." Flaxseed was brought to him. He made as though he were sowing it on the tabletop, then as though he watered it, then as though the seed had sprouted, then as though the stalks had come up, and then as though he plucked the stalks, until finally [he made as though] he raised up a woman by the braids of her hair. He said to her, "Undo the spell you wove." She replied, "I will not undo it." R. Joshua: "If you do not undo it, I will make known what you are." The woman: "I can do nothing, since I threw my cords of witchery into the sea." R. Joshua then imposed a decree upon the prince of the sea, and he disgorged them. The three sages prayed in behalf of their host, and he was given the privilege of begetting R. Judah ben Betera. So the three sages said, "If we had come up to Rome only to help in begetting such a righteous man, it would have been enough for us."[7]

58. The more women, the more witchcraft.[8]

59. After R. Simeon ben Shetah was designated head of the Sanhedrin, some people came and told him, "There are eighty witches in a cave in Ashkelon, bent on destroying the world. On that day there was a heavy rainstorm. Still, R. Simeon ben Shetah arose at once, gathered eighty young men, and took them with him. He gave each one a new jug with a clean cloak folded up in it, and they placed the jugs upside down on their heads. Then R. Simeon said to them, "When I chirp the first time,[9] put on your cloaks. When I chirp a second time, all of you enter the cave together. After you enter, each one of you is to take one of the witches into his arms and lift her off the ground,

1. B. Sanh 65b.
2. Ibid.
3. The verse refers to the plague of gnats.
4. B. Sanh 67b.
5. B. Pes 111a and En Yaakov, ad loc.
6. Rashi on B. Sot 22b.
7. P. Sanh 7:14, 52d.
8. Avot 2:7.
9. From the cave, which he was to enter alone.

for such is the way of a witch—once you lift her off the ground, she can do nothing at all."

Then R. Simeon went and stationed himself at the entrance to the cave, and called to the witches, "*Oyim, oyim,*[1] open for me, for I am one of you." They asked, "How did you manage to come here bone-dry at such a rainy hour?" He replied, "I walked between the raindrops." They: "What did you come to do here?" He: "To study and to teach, and to have each of you do what she knows." So one intoned whatever [incantation] she intoned and produced a loaf of bread; another intoned something else and produced a cut of meat; a third produced a cooked dish; and a fourth produced wine. Then they asked him, "And you, what can you do?" He said, "I can chirp twice and produce for you eighty young men wearing dry cloaks. They will find joy in you and will give joy to you." He chirped once, and the young men put on their cloaks. He chirped a second time, and all of them entered the cave together. R. Simeon said, "Let each select his mate." They picked them up, went out, and hanged them.[2]

60. Zeiri happened to go to Alexandria in Egypt, where he bought an ass. When he was about to give it water, it was released from its spell and turned back into a landing bridge. The vendors then said to him, "If you were not Zeiri, we would not return your money to you: [in this place of witchcraft], does anyone buy anything without first testing it by water?"[3]

Yannai came to an inn and said, "Give me a drink of water"; a woman offered him a drink of barley flour and honey. When he noticed that her lips were moving, he [covertly] spilled a little of it, and it turned into scorpions. He said, "As I have drunk of yours, now you drink of mine." So he gave her to drink, and she turned into a she-ass. He mounted her and rode to the marketplace. There her friend came and undid the spell [changing her back into human form], and Yannai was thus seen riding upon a woman in public.[4]

61. R. Ashi said: I saw Karna's father [a magician] blow his nose violently and eject streamers of silk from his nostrils.[5]

62. Rav said to R. Hiyya, "I saw an Arab take a sword and cut up his camel. Then he struck a tabor, and the camel stood up whole." R. Hiyya asked Rav, "Was there any blood or dung?" Rav: "No." R. Hiyya: "Since there was not, it must have been an optical illusion."[6]

63. R. Yannai said: I was once walking in the marketplace of Sepphoris, where I saw a heretic take a pebble and toss it upward, and when it came down, it had turned into a calf. But did not R. Eleazar say in the name of R. Yose bar Zimra, "If all the world's inhabitants assembled, they could not create a single gnat and cast the breath of life into it"? What really happened was that the heretic called to a trickster, who stole a calf from the flock and [covertly] brought it to him.

R. Hinena son of R. Hananiah said: I was walking in Nufta, near Sepphoris, and saw a heretic take a round stone and toss it upward; when it came down, it had become a calf. When I came back and told my father about it, he said: If you were able to eat it, it was real; if not, it was no more than an optical illusion.[7]

Whispered Charms and Sundry Kinds of Healing

64. Amemar related: The queen of witches said to me: He who meets witches should say, "May boiling excrement in a perforated basket [be forced] into your mouths, O witches! May your heads become bald, wind carry off the crumbs you [use in sorcery], your spices be scattered, and wind carry off the new saffron in your hands, O witches!"[8]

65. Our masters taught: The following three are not to pass between two [men], nor is one to pass between any two of them: a dog, a date palm, and a woman. Some say, also a pig. And some say, also a snake. If one did go between them, what is the remedy? R. Papa said: He should recite the two verses that begin with El ("God") and end with El,[9] or he should begin with a verse that starts with *lo* ("not") and end [with a verse that also starts with] *lo*.[10]

66. Resh Lakish said: If a man does one of the following four things, his bloodguilt is upon himself when he loses his life: if he relieves himself between a date palm and a wall, if he passes between two date palms, if he drinks borrowed water, or if he walks over spilt water, even if his own wife spilled it in his presence.[11]

67. R. Isaac said: To whom does the verse "Yea, though I walk through the valley of the shadow of death, I will fear no evil, for Thou art with me" (Ps. 23:4) refer? To him who sleeps in the shadow of a single date palm or in a shadow [produced] by the moon.

Four kinds of shade [are haunted by demons]: the shade of a single date palm, the shade of a *kinnara*,[12] the shade of a caper, and the shade of thorny bushes whose fronds are made edible.[13] Some say, also the shade of a ship, and the shade of a willow. This is the general rule: Whatever has many branches, its shade is dangerous; and whatever has hard thorns, its shade is dangerous. The

1. A cry used by sorcerers to summon their creations.
2. P. Hag 2:2, 77d; Rashi on B. Sanh 44b.
3. Water is effective in dissolving spells.
4. B. Sanh 67b.
5. Ibid.
6. Ibid.
7. P. Sanh 7:13, 25d.
8. B. Pes 110a.
9. Num. 23:22 and 23:23.
10. Num. 23:19 and 23:21. B. Pes 111a.
11. B. Pes 111a.
12. Christ's-thorn or jujube.
13. After they are sweetened (private communication to the translator from Professor Yehuda Feliks of Bar Ilan University).

exception is the thorny bush whose fronds are made edible; its shade is not dangerous, even though its thorns are hard, for Shida [the female demon] said to her son, "Stay away from the thorny bush whose fronds are made edible, because that is the one that killed your father."

In a place of capers, there are spirits. In a place of thorny bushes with edible fronds, there are demons. On rooftops, there are fiery-bolt demons. What are the practical consequences? In the writing of an amulet [it is important to know the identity of the agent who caused the injury].

A thorny bush with edible fronds near a town is haunted by no fewer than sixty demons. What is the practical consequence? In the writing of an amulet [it is necessary to know the number of demons who caused the injury].

When the prefect of a certain city went and stood by a thorny bush with edible fronds near the city, he was set upon by sixty demons, and his life was in danger. So he went to a certain sage who did not know that it was a thorny bush with edible fronds haunted by sixty demons, and so he wrote a one-demon amulet for it. Then he heard the demons dancing in the tree and singing, "Though this sage's head scarf is like a sage's, we have examined him [and find] that he does not know how to make the blessing before putting on such a scarf." Then another sage came who knew that the cause was the thorny bush with edible fronds that is haunted by sixty demons, and he wrote a sixty-demon amulet for the prefect's injury. Then he heard the demons say, "Clear your vessels away from here."[1]

68. R. Ishmael ben Elisha said: Suriel, the prince of the [Divine] Presence, told me three things: when dressing in the morning, do not take your shirt from the hand of your attendant, do not let water be poured over your hands by one who has not already washed his own hands, and do not return a cup of wine brewed with asparagus to anyone save to the one who has handed it to you, because a company of demons—according to some, a band of destroying angels—lie in ambush for a man and say, "When will somebody come to do one of these things, so that we can trap him?"[2]

69. R. Joshua ben Levi said: The angel of death told me three things: when dressing in the morning, do not take your shirt from your attendant, do not let water be poured over your hands by one who has not already washed his own hands, and do not stand in front of women when they are returning from the presence of a deceased person, because, sword in hand, I go leaping in front of them, and have permission to do harm. If one should happen to meet such women, what is his remedy? He should remove himself a distance of four cubits; if there is a river nearby, let him cross it; if there is another road, let him take it; if there is a wall, let him stand behind it. If he cannot do any of these things, let him turn his face away and say, "The Lord said unto Satan, 'The Lord rebuke thee, O Satan,' " etc. (Zech. 3:2), until they have passed by.[3]

70. R. Assi said: No blessing is to be said over an unlucky cup. What is an unlucky cup? "The second [of two cups]," said R. Nahaman bar Isaac.[4]

71. He who drinks an even number of cups should not say grace.[5]

72. Our masters taught: He who drinks an even number of cups—his blood is upon his own head. R. Judah said: When is this so? Only when he does not step outside [between drinks]. But if he does step outside, he may drink an even number. R. Ashi said: I saw Hananiah bar Bebai step outside after each cup. However, what the sages meant is that drinking an even number of cups is harmful only when one is about to set out on a journey; when one intends to remain home, it is not harmful. R. Zera observed: And going to sleep is like setting out on a journey.

Ulla said: Ten cups are not subject to the danger in even numbers.

R. Joseph said: Joseph, the expert in ways of demons, told me: Ashmedai, king of demons, has charge of all matters concerned with even numbers, and it does not befit the dignity of a king to be called harmful. But some say: On the contrary, since a king has the power, he does whatever he wishes.

R. Papa stated: Joseph, the expert in ways of demons, told me [that demons say]: For two cups, we kill; for four, we do not kill—we only injure the drinker. For two cups, we kill, whether [drunk] unwittingly or deliberately; for four cups, only if drunk deliberately, but not if drunk unwittingly.

And if a man forgetfully drinks [an even number of cups] and goes out, what is his remedy? Let him take the thumb of his right hand with his left hand, and the thumb of his left hand with his right hand, and say, "You [two thumbs] and I surely are three!" But if he hears a voice say, "You [three] and I are surely four!" let him retort, "[Not so]—you and I are surely five!" And if he hears a voice say, "You and I are six!" let him retort, "[Not so]—you and I are seven." Once it happened that the drinker kept on counting until he reached one hundred and one, whereupon the demon disintegrated.[6]

73. In the west [the Land of Israel], they were not particular about even numbers. R. Dimi of Nehardea was particular even about an even number of marks on a [wine] cask. He became particular after a cask [with such a number] burst. This is the general rule: when a man is particular about such numbers, the demons are particular with him, and when a man is not particular about such

1. B. Pes 111a–b.
2. B. Ber 51a and En Yaakov, ad loc.
3. Ibid. and En Yaakov, ad loc.
4. Ibid.
5. Ibid.
6. B. Pes 110a and En Yaakov, ad loc.

numbers, the demons are not particular with him. Nevertheless, one should be cautious.[1]

74. R. Joseph said: The following three things take away a man's sight: combing one's head while the hair is dry, drinking the drippings [of wine], and putting on shoes while one's feet are still wet.[2]

75. Food suspended [from the ceiling] in a house brings on poverty, as people say, "He who suspends a basket [of food] puts his sustenance in suspense." Bran in a house brings on poverty. Crumbs in a house bring on poverty. A bowl covering the spout of a jug brings on poverty. He who drinks water out of a bowl is liable to get a cataract in his eye. He who eats cress without first washing his hands will live in fear for thirty days. He who undergoes bloodletting without first washing his hands will live in fear for seven days. He who trims his hair without first washing his hands will live in fear for three days. He who pares his nails without first washing his hands will live in fear for one day without knowing the cause of his fear. Putting a hand on one's nostrils is a step to fear. Putting a hand on one's forehead is a step to sleep.[3]

76. The sages taught: Even if covered by iron vessels, food and drink kept under a bed will have a baneful spirit rest on them.[4]

77. Our masters taught: A man must not drink water either on the night ushering in Wednesday or the night ushering in the Sabbath, and if he does drink, his blood is on his own head because of the danger. What danger? An evil spirit. But if he is thirsty, what is he to do? He should recite the verses in which "the voice of the Lord" occurs seven times,[5] verses that David uttered over the water, and then he may drink. But if [he does] not [say these verses], let him say, "*Lul shafan anigeron anirdafon*, I dwell among the stars, I walk among lean and fat people." If he does not say this, then, if there is another man with him, he should wake him up and say to him, "So-and-so son of So-and-so, I am thirsty for water," and then he may drink. But if there is no other man with him, he should knock the lid against the pitcher and then drink. But if [there is neither lid nor pitcher], he should throw something into the water and then drink.

Our masters taught: A man should not drink water from rivers or pools at night, and if he drinks, his blood is on his own head because of the danger. What danger? The danger of temporary blindness. But if he is thirsty, what should he do? If another man is with him, he should wake him up and say to him, "So-and-so son of So-and-so, I am thirsty for water." But if there is no other man with him, he should knock the lid against the pitcher and say to himself, "O So-and-so son of So-and-so, your mother told me, 'Beware of Shabriri'[6]—Shabiri, beriri, riri, iri, ri. I am thirsty for water in white cups."[7]

78. Ravina said: He who is frightened, even though he sees nothing—it is because his planet sees it. What is the remedy? He should recite the Shema, and if he stands in a place soiled with excreta [where the Shema may not be recited], he should remove himself a distance of four cubits from that place and say, "The he-goat at the butcher's is fatter than I."[8]

79. Our masters taught: Five things make man forget his learning: eating something of which a mouse or a cat has eaten, eating the heart of a beast, frequent consumption of olives, drinking waste bathwater, and washing one's feet one foot above the other. Some say: Also he who puts his clothes under his pillow [forgets his learning].

Five things improve one's learning: eating wheat bread—and much more so, wheat itself[9]—eating a roasted egg without salt, frequent consumption of olive oil, frequent indulgence in wine and spices, and drinking the water that is left from kneading [dough]. Some say, also dipping one's finger into salt and licking it.[10]

80. R. Yohanan said: While olives cause one to forget seventy years of study, olive oil restores seventy years of study.[11]

81. Ten things adversely affect one's capacity to learn: passing under a camel's bit—and all the more so, under the camel itself—passing between two camels, passing between two women, a woman passing beneath two men, passing within smelling distance of a [decaying] carcass, passing under a bridge beneath which no water has flowed for forty days, eating bread insufficiently baked, eating meat out of a soup ladle, drinking from a water channel that runs through a graveyard, and looking into the face of a dead body. Others say: He who reads the inscription on a grave is also [subject to the same disability].[12]

82. Abba Saul said in the name of R. Akiva: He who whispers an incantation over a wound, saying, "I will put none of the diseases upon thee which I have put upon the Egyptians; for I am the Lord that healeth thee" (Exod. 15:26), and then spits will have no portion in the world-to-come.[13]

83. [On the Sabbath], one may go out carrying a cricket's egg, a fox's tooth, or a nail from [the gallows of] an impaled

---

1. B. Pes 110b.
2. B. Pes 111b.
3. B. Pes 111b–112a.
4. B. Pes 112a.
5. Ps. 29:3–5 and 29:7–9.
6. A demon and the affliction it caused (see below in this chapter, §101 and note). It was exorcised by repeating its name while dropping the initial syllables.
7. B. Pes 112a; B. AZ 12b.
8. B. Meg 3a.
9. "Wheat bread—and much more so, wheat itself": Munich ms; BR: "bread baked on coals—and much more so, coal itself."
10. B. Hor 13b.
11. Ibid.
12. Ibid. and En Yaakov, ad loc.
13. B. Sanh 90a; Tos Sanh 12:10.

convict as a means of healing. So said R. Meir. But the sages forbid such practices even on weekdays, as following "the ways of the Amorite."[1]

[On the Sabbath], one may go out carrying a cricket's egg to cure an ear discharge; a fox's tooth to cure sleep disorders—a live fox's tooth for excessive sleepiness, a dead fox's tooth for sleeplessness; and a nail from [the gallows of] an impaled convict to heal an inflammation.

Both Abbaye and Rava maintained: Whatever is effective as a remedy is not [forbidden] on account of "the ways of the Amorite."[2]

84. When R. Joshua ben Levi's grandson had an obstruction in his throat, a certain man came and whispered into his ear a spell in the name of [Jesus], the well-known heretic, and he began to breathe again. As the man was leaving, R. Joshua asked him, "What did you whisper in his ear?" The man: "Such-and-such a spell." R. Joshua: "It would have been better if my grandson died rather than recover by such means." And, "like an error which proceedeth from the mouth of a ruler [a ruler in matters of Torah]" (Eccles. 10:5), his thoughtless imprecation caused the death of his grandson.

It once happened to R. Eleazar ben Dama, the son of R. Ishmael's sister, that he was bitten by a snake, and Jacob of Kefar Sekhania[3] came to treat him in the name of Jesus son of Pandera,[4] But R. Ishmael did not allow him to. R. Eleazar ben Dama pleaded, "R. Ishmael, my brother, allow him to treat me—I can bring proof from the Torah that this is permitted." No sooner did he finish than his soul departed and he died. R. Ishmael exclaimed, "Happy are you, Ben Dama, that your body is pure, that your soul left you while you were in a state of purity, and that you have not breached the fence [the injunctions] of the sages who used to quote, 'He who breaketh through a fence, a serpent shall sting him' " (Eccles. 10:8).

But a snake did sting him [before he violated the words of the sages].

The verse refers to the "snake" [sting] of sages' words, for which there is no remedy.

What is the verse that R. Eleazar ben Dama should have quoted? It is "Keep My statutes . . . which if a man do, he shall live by them" (Lev. 18:5) and not die by them.[5]

85. Our masters taught: Demons may not be consulted on the Sabbath. R. Yose: This is forbidden even on weekdays.

It is permitted to consult by incantation the guardian spirits of oil and of eggs, but [sometimes] they give false answers.[6]

86. [On the Sabbath], boys may go out with *kesharim*. What are *kesharim?* The sages said in R. Judah's name: They are garlands of dyer's madder [used as a remedy].

Abbaye said: My [foster] mother told me that three such garlands halt an illness, five cure it, and seven are efficacious even against witchcraft. R. Aha bar Jacob observed: [That is so], provided the sick man does not look at the sun or the moon or at rain; does not hear the sound of iron, the cry of a fowl, or the sound of footsteps.[7]

R. Nathan bar Isaac said: [For all practical purposes], madder's dye—you may as well chuck it into a pit![8]

87. Avin bar Huna said in the name of Hama bar Guria: When a child yearns greatly for his father, the father should take a strap from his right shoe and tie it to the child's left arm.[9] It is dangerous to reverse the tying as prescribed.[10]

88. Abbaye said: My [foster] mother told me that all incantations which are repeated several times should mention the mother [of the one for whom the incantation is whispered]; and all straps must be tied on the left arm. All incantations should be repeated the prescribed number of times; and if the number has not been specified, the incantation shall be repeated forty-one times.[11]

89. Abbaye also said: My [foster] mother told me that for a daily fever one should take a new *zuz* coin, go to a salt deposit, take the *zuz*'s weight in salt, and tie the salt inside the collar of his shirt with a band of twined strands of wool. If this remedy does not help, the patient should sit at a crossroads, and when he sees a large ant carrying something, he should take it, put it into a brass tube, close the tube's openings with lead, and seal it with sixty seals. He should shake it, lift it on his back, and say to it, "Your burden be upon me, and my burden be upon you." If this remedy does not help, he should take a new jar, small in size, go to the river, and say to it, "River, O river, lend me a jarful of water for a guest who happens to be visiting me." He should circle the jar seven times about his head, then pour its water behind his back and say to it, "River, O river, take back the water you gave me, for the guest who visited me came for a day and left the same day."[12]

90. R. Huna said: [As a remedy] for tertian fever, one should procure seven prickles from seven date palms, seven chips from seven beams, seven pegs from seven bridges, seven handfuls of ash from seven ovens, seven pinches of earth from seven graves, seven bits of pitch from seven ships, seven seeds of cumin, and seven hairs from the beard of an old dog, and tie them inside the collar of his shirt with a band of twined strands of wool.[13]

---

1. In Jewish lore, Amorites were regarded as masters of witchcraft and magic spells.
2. B. Shab 67a.
3. Possibly James son of Alphaeus (Mark 3:18), or James the Younger (Mark 15:40). So Isidore Epstein in Soncino, p. 85, n. 3.
4. A pejorative implying that a soldier named Pandera seduced Jesus' mother.
5. B. AZ 27b; P. Shab 14:4, 14d; Tos Hul 2:22–23.
6. B. Sanh 101a.
7. "It is useless as a remedy, since no one can take such precautions."
8. B. Shab 66b.
9. These, according to him, are the *kesharim* mentioned in §86 above in this chapter.
10. B. Shab 66b.
11. Ibid.
12. Ibid.
13. B. Shab 67a.

91. R. Yohanan said: For fever accompanied by shivering, one should take a knife made entirely of iron, go to a place where there is a thornbush, and tie to it bands of twined strands of wool. On the first day, he should make a slight notch in the bush and say, "The angel of the Lord appeared unto him. . . . And Moses said: . . . I will turn aside now . . . and see why the bush is not burnt" (Exod. 3:2–3). On the following day, he should make another small notch and say, "When the Lord saw that he turned aside to see" (Exod. 3:4). The next day, he should make a third small notch and say, "Draw not nigh hither" (Exod. 3:5). And when the fever has ceased, he should bend the bush and then cut it down as he says, "Thornbush, O thornbush, not because you are higher than all other trees in the field did the Holy One have His Presence abide upon you, but He had His Presence abide upon you because you are lower than all other trees in the field. And even as the fire fled Hananiah, Mishael, and Azariah when it saw them, so may the "fire" that sees So-and-so son of So-and-so flee from him."[1]

92. For a rash, one should say, "Bazbaziah, Masmasiah, Kaskasiah, Sharlai, and Amarlai"—these are the angels who were sent out from the land of Sodom to heal those smitten with a rash—"Bazakh, Bazikh, Bazbazikh, Masmassikh, Kammon, Kamikh, your color is to remain what it is now, your color is to remain what it is now. Your place is to be confined to where it is now. Like one whose seed is locked up, or like a mule that is not fruitful and cannot increase, so may your seed not be fruitful nor increase in the body of So-and-so son of So-and-so.[2]

93. Against epilepsy, one should say, "A sword drawn, a sling stretched, its name is not to be Yukhav—'sickness and pain.' "[3]

94. Against a demon, one should say, "Even as you have been shut in, stay shut in. Cursed, shattered, and banished shall be Bar Tit, Bar Tamei, Bar Tina, Kashmaggaz, Merigaz, and Istamai."[4]

95. For the demon of the privy, one should say, "On the head of a lion and on the snout of a lioness did we find the demon Bar Shirikai Pandai; with a bed of leeks I felled him, and with the jawbone of an ass I smote him"[5]

96. If a man is seized by depression, what is the means of healing him? Red meat broiled over coals, and diluted wine.[6]

97. Abbaye said: My [foster] mother told me that the remedy for a fever on the first day is to drink a small pitcher of water; if the fever lasts two days, to let blood; if three days, to eat red meat broiled over coals and drink diluted wine. For continuing fever, a man should get a black hen, tear it lengthwise and crosswise, shave the middle of his head, put the hen on his head, and leave it there till it sticks fast; then he should go down [to the river] and stand in the water up to his neck until he is quite faint, and then he should take a dip and come up.

For fever [as already said], one should eat red meat broiled over coals and drink diluted wine. For a chill, one should eat fat meat broiled over coals and drink undiluted wine.[7]

98. For blood rushing to the head, a man should take bark of a box tree, a willow, a myrtle, an olive tree, a sea willow, and a cynodon, and boil them all together. Then he should pour three hundred cups [of the brew] on one side of his head and three hundred cups on the other side. If this remedy does not help, he should take white roses all of whose leaves are on one side of the stem, boil them, and pour sixty cups of the boiled roses on one side of his head and sixty cups on the other side of his head.[8]

99. For migraine, a man should take a woodcock and cut its throat with a white silver coin over the side of the head where the pain is concentrated, taking care that the blood does not blind his eyes. Then he should hang the bird on his doorpost, so that he can rub against it when he comes in and when he goes out.[9]

100. For a cataract, a man should take a seven-hued scorpion, dry it out in the shade, and mix two parts of ground kohl to one part of ground scorpion; then, with a paintbrush, apply three drops to each eye—no more, lest the eye burst.[10]

101. For night blindness,[11] a man should take a rope made of wool and with it tie one of his own legs to the leg of a dog, and children should rattle potsherds behind him, saying, "Old dog, stupid cock." He should collect seven pieces of raw meat from seven houses, place them [for a while] in a door socket, and then have [the dog] eat them over the ash pit of the town. After that, he should untie the rope, and people should say to him, "Blindness of So-and-so son of So-and-so, let go of So-and-so son of So-and-so, and instead seize the pupils of the dog's eyes."

For day blindness, a man should take seven milts from the insides of animals and roast them over a bloodletter's shard. And while the blind man sits inside the house, another man should sit outside, and the blind man should say to him, "Give me something to eat." The sighted

1. Ibid.
2. Ibid.
3. Ibid.
4. Ibid.
5. Ibid.
6. B. Git 67b.
7. Ibid.
8. B. Git 68b.
9. Ibid.
10. B. Git 69a.
11. "*Shabrire*, a *shafel* form of *brr* ('clear'), a euphemism for blindness. In this affliction, ascribed to the demons, a distinction was made between day *shabrire* and night *shabrire*, which are said to correspond with hemeralopia and nyctalopia. J. Preuss and AZ, Soncino (Isidore Epstein in Git, Soncino, p. 327, n. 4).

man should reply, "Take and eat." After the blind man has eaten, he should break the shard; otherwise, the blindness will come back.[1]

102. To stop a nosebleed, a man should call a priest whose name is Levi and write "Levi" backward, or else call any other man and write backward, "I am Papi Shila bar Sumki," or else write, "The taste of the bucket in water of silver, the taste of the bucket in water of blemish." If this remedy does not help, he should take roots of clover, rope of an old bed, papyrus, saffron, and the red part of a palm branch, and burn them all together; then he should take a fleece of wool, twine it into two wicks, steep these in vinegar, roll them in the ashes, and put them into his nostrils. If this remedy does not help, he should look for a water channel running from east to west, stand astride it, pick up some clay with his right hand from under his left foot and with his left hand from under his right foot, twine two more fleeces of wool into wicks, rub these in the clay, and put them into his nostrils. If this remedy does not help either, he should sit under a drainpipe and have people bring water, and sprinkle it over him as they say, "Even as these waters will stop, so shall the blood of So-and-so son of So-and-so stop."[2]

103. To stop bleeding from the mouth, the blood should be tested by means of a wheaten straw. If the straw is softened, the blood comes from the lung and there is a remedy for that; if the straw is not softened, the blood comes from the liver, and there is no remedy for that.

If the blood comes from the lung, what is the remedy? He should take seven fistfuls of hashed beets, seven fistfuls of mashed leeks, five fistfuls of jujube berry, three fistfuls of lentils, a fistful of cumin, a fistful of string, and a quantity equal to all these of the ileum of a firstborn animal; then he should cook the mixture and eat it, washing it down with strong beer made during [the month of] Tevet.[3]

104. For a toothache, Rabbah bar R. Huna said: A man should take a whole head of garlic, grind it with oil and salt, and apply it on his thumbnail to the side where the tooth aches; but he must put a rim of dough around it, thus taking care that it does not touch his flesh, as it may cause leprosy.[4]

105. For catarrh in the head, a man should take gum ammoniac equal to the size of a pistachio nut, galbanum equal to the size of a walnut, honey cake, a spoonful of white honey, and a Mahozan *natla*[5] of clear wine, and boil them together; when the gum ammoniac comes to a boil, all the others have boiled enough. If this remedy does not help, he should take a quarter of a *log*[6] of milk of white goats, let it drip on three stalks of cabbage, and stir it with a stem of marjoram; when that stem comes to a boil, all the others have boiled enough. If even this remedy does not help, he should take the excrement of a white dog and knead it with balsam; but if he can possibly avoid it, he should not resort to eating the dog's excrement, as it disintegrates the limbs.[7]

106. For swelling of the spleen, a man should take seven water leeches and dry them in the shade, and every day drink two or three in wine. If this remedy does not help, he should take the spleen of a she-goat that has not yet had young, stick it inside an oven, stand by it, and say, "As this spleen has dried up, so may the spleen of So-and-so son of So-and-so dry up." If this remedy does not help, he should look for the corpse of a person who died on the Sabbath, take the corpse's hand, put it against his own spleen, and say, "As the hand of this one has dried up, so may the spleen of So-and-so son of So-and-so dry up."[8]

107. Abbaye said: He who is unsure of his virility should bring three small measures of thorny saffron, pound it, boil it in wine, and drink it. R. Yohanan said, "This is just what restored me to the vigor of my youth."[9]

108. Abbaye said: My [foster] mother told me: He who suffers from weakness of the heart should get meat from the right leg of a ram and dried cattle turd dropped during the month of Nisan—if he has no dried cattle droppings, he should get chips of willow—roast the meat over them, and eat it, and then drink diluted wine.[10]

109. Abbaye said: My [foster] mother told me: A six-year-old child stung on his birthday by a scorpion is not likely to live. What is a [possible] remedy? The gall of a white stork in beer. This is to be rubbed into the wound, and the rest should be given to the child to drink. A one-year-old stung on his birthday by a wasp is also not likely to live. What is a [possible] remedy? The bast of a date palm in water. This is to be rubbed into the wound, and the rest should be given to the child to drink.[11]

110. Samuel said: A [sword] wound is to be regarded as so dangerous that the Sabbath may be profaned for it. What is the remedy? To stop the bleeding, pepperwort in vinegar; to induce new growth of flesh, peelings of cynodon and the paring of a thornbush, or worms from a dunghill.[12]

111. R. Safra said: A berry-sized growth on the eye is an emissary of the angel of death. What is the remedy for it? Rue in honey or parsley in an inferior wine. In the meantime, a berry resembling it in size should be brought and rolled over it: a white berry for a white growth, and a black berry for a black growth.[13]

---

1. B. Git 69a.
2. Ibid.
3. Ibid.
4. In the winter, when the paste is made strong. Ibid.
5. A small vessel holding a quarter of a *log*.
6. Equal to the bulk of an egg and a half.
7. B. Git 69a–b.
8. B. Git 69b.
9. B. Git 70a.
10. B. Er 29b.
11. B. Ket 50a.
12. B. AZ 28a.
13. Ibid.

112. Rava said: A carbuncle is a forerunner of fever. What is the remedy for it? It should be snapped sixty times with the middle finger and then cut open crosswise and lengthwise. This should be done only if its head is not white; if its head is white, it is not dangerous.[1]

113. When R. Jacob was suffering from a fissure in the rectum, R. Ammi—some say, R. Assi—directed him to take seven grains from the purple alkali plant, wrap them up in the collar [of a shirt], tie around it a white wool thread, dip the poultice in white naphtha, burn it, and powder the fissure with the ashes. While preparing the poultice, he was to take kernels of the nut of a thornbush and apply their split side to the fissure. This should be done if the fissure is external. What should be done if it is internal? One should take some fat of a she-goat that has borne no young, melt it, and apply it within the anus. If this remedy does not help, one should take three melon leaves that have been dried in the shade, burn them, and powder the fissure with the ashes. If this remedy does not help, one should apply olive oil mixed with wax and cover the fissure with strips of linen in summer and cotton wool in winter.[2]

114. R. Abbahu had an earache. So R. Yohanan—some say, the sages in the house of study—instructed him: he should take the kidney of a hairless goat, cut it crosswise and lengthwise, put it over glowing coals, and pour the water that comes out of it—neither hot nor cold, but tepid—into the ear. If this remedy does not work, he should take the fat of a large scarab beetle, melt it, and let it drip [into the ear]. If this remedy does not work either, the ear should be filled with oil; then seven wicks should be made out of clover stalks, with a garlic stem and a woolen tassel attached to one end of each wick, and the wick set alight. The other end is placed inside the ear. The ear should be exposed to the fire, but care must be taken that there be no wind: each wick should be replaced by another when it is used up. If this remedy does not work, he should take tow of the *danda* plant [*ceterach officinalis*] that has not been combed and place it within the ear, and place the ear near the fire; but care should be taken that there be no wind. If this remedy does not work, he should take the tube of an old cane [that has been detached from the soil] for about a hundred years, fill it with rock salt, then burn it and apply the ashes to the sore part [of the ear].[3]

115. When R. Yohanan suffered from scurvy, he went to a Roman noblewoman, who prepared something for him on Thursday and Friday. What did she prepare for him? R. Aha son of R. Ammi said: The water of leaven, olive oil, and salt. R. Yemar said: Leaven itself, olive oil, and salt. R. Ashi said: The fat of a goose together with its wing. Abbaye said: I tried all of these without effecting a cure for myself, until an Arab recommended: "Take the pits of olives that have not grown to one-third of their size, burn them in fire on a new rake, and stick them to the inside of the gums." I did so and was cured.[4]

116. One attacked by jaundice should be fed the flesh of a donkey. One bitten by a mad dog should be fed the lobe of its liver. So said R. Matia ben Heresh. But the sages said: There is no healing whatever in such remedies.[5]

117. What causes a dog to go mad? Because women given to witchery have sported with it. So said Rav. Because an evil spirit rested on it. So said Samuel. What is the practical difference between the two opinions? [If the dog's madness is because an evil spirit rested on it], the dog must be killed by something thrown at him.[6]

We have been taught that Samuel's opinion is right: when the dog is killed, he should be killed only [at a distance], with something thrown at him. One against whom a mad dog rubs itself is in danger. One whom it bites will die.

"One against whom a mad dog rubs itself is in danger." What is the remedy? He should remove his garments and run. Once, in the marketplace, a mad dog rubbed itself against R. Huna son of R. Joshua. R. Huna removed his garments and ran, saying [later]: I applied to myself "Wisdom preserveth the life of him who hath it" (Eccles. 7:12).

"One whom such a dog bites will die." What is the remedy? Abbaye said: He should take the skin of a male hyena and write on it: I, So-and-so, the son of So-and-so, have written against you on the skin of a male hyena: "*Kanti, kanti, kleros* (some say, *Kandi, kandi, kloros*), God, God, Lord of hosts, Amen, Amen, Selah." Then he should remove his garments and bury them in a cemetery for twelve months. After that, he should take them out, burn them in an oven, and scatter their ashes at a crossroads. During those twelve months, when he drinks water, he should drink it only through a copper tube, lest he sees the demon's shadow and be endangered. The mother of Abba bar Martha, who is Abba bar Minyomi, made a gold [drinking] tube for her son.[7]

118. [As a remedy] for worms in the bowels, pennyroyal should be eaten. With what should it be eaten? With seven black dates. What causes worms in the bowels? Raw meat and water on an empty stomach, fat meat on an empty stomach, ox meat on an empty stomach, nuts on an empty stomach, or shoots of fenugreek eaten on an empty stomach and washed down with water. If there are no black dates, one should swallow white cress. If that does not help, he should fast, then fetch some fat meat, put it over glowing coals, suck out the marrow from a bone, and gulp down vinegar. Not vinegar, others say, because it affects the liver. If that does not help, he should procure the scrapings

---

1. Ibid.
2. B. AZ 28a–b.
3. B. AZ 28b.
4. B. Yoma 84a; B. AZ 28a.
5. B. Yoma 84a.
6. To avoid contact with the evil spirit.
7. B. Yoma 83b–84a.

of a thornbush that were scraped from top to bottom—not from the bottom to the top, lest the worms issue through his mouth—and boil the scrapings in beer at twilight. The next day, he should hold his nose and make himself drink it. When he relieves himself, he should do so on the stripped parts of a date palm.[1]

119. As an antidote for drinking uncovered water,[2] [juice of the] shepherd's flute plant should be drunk. If that does not help, one should get five roses and five cups of beer, boil them together until the brew reduces to an *anpak*,[3] and drink it. The mother of R. Ahadboi bar Amni prepared [a potion of] one rose and one cup of beer for a certain man. She brought the mix to a boil and made him drink it. Then she lit the oven, swept it out [to cool it], placed a brick in it, and had him sit on it [to perspire], and the poison [of the snake's venom] oozed out of him [in a liquid the color of] a green palm leaf. R. Ivia suggested [as an antidote for uncovered water]: a fourth of a *log*[4] of milk from a white goat. R. Huna bar Judah said: He should obtain a sweet etrog, scoop it out, fill it with honey, set it over burning embers [to boil], and then eat it. R. Hanina said: [He should drink] some urine forty days old [as a remedy]: a *barzina*[5] of it for a wasp sting; a fourth of a *log* for a scorpion's sting; and half a *log* for uncovered water. A *log* [of urine] is effective even against witchcraft.[6]

120. He who swallows a [baby] snake should eat cuscuta with salt and run three *mil*. R. Shimi bar Ashi saw a man swallow a [baby] snake; he appeared to the man in the guise of a horseman and made him eat cuscuta with salt and run three *mil* before him, and the snake issued from the man rib by rib. Some say that R. Shimi bar Ashi himself swallowed a [baby] snake. Elijah [the Prophet] appeared to him in the guise of a horseman, made him eat cuscuta with salt and run three *mil* before him, and the snake issued from R. Shimi rib by rib.

He who is bitten by a snake should procure the embryo of a white she-ass, tear it open, and put it over him; provided, however, that the ass was not found to be suffering from a serious organic disease. A certain officer of Pumbedita was bitten by a snake. Now, there were thirteen white she-asses in Pumbedita; all were torn open, and each was found to be suffering from a serious organic disease. There was another she-ass on the outskirts of the city, but before they could go and bring it, a lion devoured it. Then Abbaye suggested, "Perhaps he was bitten by 'the snake of the sages,'[7] for which there is no cure." The people replied, "This is so, our master, for when Rav died, R. Isaac bar Bisna decreed that [in token of mourning], myrtles and palm branches should not be brought to a wedding feast to the sound of bells, yet this officer did go and bring myrtles and palm branches to a wedding feast [to the sound of bells]." So a snake bit him, and he died.

If a snake winds itself around a man, he should wade into water, put a basket over his head, and dislodge the snake—when the snake climbs up to the basket, he should shove the basket onto the water, go up out of the water, and get away [as fast as he can].

When a man is scented by a snake, if he has a companion with him, he should ride upon the companion's shoulders a distance of four cubits. If he has no companion, he should jump over a ditch full of water. If there is no ditch, he should ford a river. And at night he should place his bed on four casks and sleep [outdoors] under the vault of heaven. He should also bring four she-cats and tie them to the four legs of the bed, then scatter chips of wood all around, so that when the cats hear the sound of the snake coming [over the chips], they will devour it.

He who is chased by a snake should run toward sandy places.[8]

121. He who has a meatbone stuck in his throat should bring more of that kind of meat, place it on his head, and say, "One by one, go down, swallow; swallow, go down, one by one." If it is a fishbone, he should say, "You are stuck like a pin, locked up as in a cuirass. Go down, go down."[9]

122. A tree that loses its fruit should be painted red and loaded with stones. It is loaded with stones to lessen its strength;[10] and covered with red paint so that people who see it may implore [God's] mercy in the tree's behalf.[11]

The Ways of the Amorites and Omens

123. The following practices are [forbidden as] ways of the Amorites:[12] cutting the hair from ear to ear in the forepart of the head, and leaving the hair at the back [which is to be offered at puberty to an idol]; reviving a [dead] child by dragging it around in the cemetery; attaching a precious stone to the girdle above the thigh or a red thread to one's finger; counting pebbles while throwing them into the sea or into a river [and observing their manner of sinking for omens]. The aforementioned are ways of the Amorites.

Striking hips, clapping hands, and dancing before a fire [in order to extinguish it] are also ways of the Amorites.

If bread falls from a man's mouth and he says to another, "Give it back to me, lest the benefit from what I

1. B. Shab 109b.
2. There was fear that water left uncovered overnight might be lapped up by a snake, who would leave his venom in it.
3. A fourth of a *log*.
4. The bulk of an egg and a half.
5. One thirty-second of a *log*.
6. B. Shab 109b.
7. That is, he disobeyed an edict of theirs.
8. B. Shab 109b–110a.
9. B. Shab 67a.
10. In order that the tree will produce fewer blossoms and less fruit, and so not lose them.
11. B. Shab 67a.
12. In Jewish lore, the Amorites were regarded as masters of witchcraft and magic spells.

have eaten be lost to me"; if a man says, "Place a lamp on the ground [near the deceased], so that the deceased will be distressed," or, "Do not place a lamp on the ground, so that they will not be distressed"; if sparks fall from the lamp and a person says, "We will have guests today"—the aforementioned are ways of the Amorites.

If a person, as he begins a task, says, "Let So-and-so, whose hands are lucky, come and begin it," or, "Let So-and-so, whose feet are lucky, come and pass before us"—these, too, are ways of the Amorites.

Or when a person beginning work on a cask or a lump of dough says, "Let So-and-so, whose hands are blessed, come and begin it"—this is one of the ways of the Amorites. When one is in the room of a woman about to give birth and plugs [a hole in] the window with a thorn or ties iron around the legs of the bed or sets a table before her [for luck][1]—these, too, are ways of the Amorites. However, one may plug the window with a jar or a sheaf of grain, or place a bowl of water before the woman, or tie a hen in front of her for companionship—these are not [necessarily] Amorite ways.

A person who says, "Slaughter this cock who chants in the evening,"[2] or, "Slaughter this hen who clucks like a cock," or, "Make her eat a cock's comb, since she crows as though she were a male"—these are ways of the Amorites. If a person calls to a raven, "Scream," or to a she-raven, "Screech, and for my sake turn your tail as a sign for good"—these are ways of the Amorites. If one says, "Eat this date or this leaf of lettuce, so that you may remember me," or, "Do not eat it because it may cause cataracts"; or, "Sleep in the coffin intended for a dead person, so that you may see him in the night," or, "Do not sleep in the coffin intended for a dead person, lest you see him in the night"; or "Turn your undershirt inside out, so that you will have good dreams," or, "Do not turn your undershirt inside out, so as not to have dreams"; or, "Sit on the broom, so that you will dream good dreams," or, "Do not sit on the broom, so as not to have dreams"—all these are ways of the Amorites.

If one says, "Do not sit on the plow, so that the work will not become too hard for us," or "Do not sit on the plow, so that it will not break"—these are ways of the Amorites. But if he says it out of certain knowledge that the plow will break under the man's weight, it is permitted.

If one says, "Do not twist your hands behind your back, lest we be prevented from doing our work"—that is a way of the Amorites. If one drives a firebrand into a wall [to extinguish it] and says, "This!"—that is a way of the Amorites. But if he does it [to warn people] of the sparks, it is permitted. If one spills water in a public thoroughfare and says, "This!"—that is a way of the Amorites. But if he cautions passersby [so that they will not be drenched], it is permitted. If one throws iron into a cemmetery and says, "This!"—that is a way of the Amorites. But if he does it to alert passersby, it is permitted. If one places a partly burned firebrand and [a rod of] iron under his head—that is a way of the Amorites. But if he puts the two there only to protect them [from thieves], it is permitted.

If a woman shouts at an oven that the bread being baked in it should not fall in, or puts chips of wood into the handles of a pot lest it should boil over, or spills some of the contents of the pot behind her back—these are ways of the Amorites. But chips of mulberry wood and slivers of glass may be put into a pot so that it will come to a boil quicker. The sages forbid slivers of glass because of the danger involved.

If a woman does a jig so that a sour-milk pudding may rise, or bids people to be still so that lentils may cook properly, or whistles so that rice may get cooked, or claps her hands for grits to cook—these are ways of the Amorites.

If a snake falls upon a bed and one says that the owner of the bed, who is poor, will become rich, or that the pregnant woman will bear a male child, or that the maiden will wed a distinguished man—such auguries are Amorites' ways.

If a woman about to set down [a chicken] for hatching says, "I must have a virgin do it," or, "I must strip naked to do it," or, "I must see to it that the chicken is set down with the left hand" or "with both hands"; or if one who, as he pays the [symbolic] coin to his bride, does so with both hands, or hands over the bill of divorcement with both hands; or if one says at the end of a meal, "Bring more food to the table [in sign of blessing]"—all these are ways of the Amorites.

If a woman uses eggs to attach herbs to a wall, covers them with plaster, and counts to seventy-one—that is a way of the Amorites.

If a woman puts chicks in a sieve or places pieces of iron between them—that is a way of the Amorites. If she does so to protect them from thunder or lightning, it is permitted.

If a man inquires of his walking stick, "Shall I go or not go?"—that is a way of the Amorites. Even though there is no proof for this interdict, there is an intimation of it in Scripture: "My people ask counsel at their stock, and their staff declareth unto them" (Hos. 4:12).

He who says [to one who sneezes], "May it be for healing"—that is a way of the Amorites. He who says [while gathering his crop], "All I have of this is really left over from last year's, for this year's crop yielded nothing"[3]—that is a way of the Amorites. He who says, "I will drink and leave some [for luck]"—that is a way of the Amorites. He who says, "No, no! [May such a thing not befall me!]"—that is a way of the Amorites. He who says, "Do not pass between the two of us, lest our affection for each other cease"—that is a way of the Amorites. But if such a request is made out of deference, it is permitted.[4]

124. The following practices are permitted: When a man begins a task, he may utter praise and thanks to Him who is everywhere. When he begins work on a cask or a lump

1. See Isa. 65:11.
2. BR: "who crows like a raven."

3. Or, as Leon Nemoy suggests: "may the harvest be overflowing."
4. Tos Shab 7 and 8:4–12 (ed. Saul Lieberman, pp. 22–27 and notes); B. Shab 67b.

of dough, he may pray that a blessing come into these and that a curse not come.

Wine and oil may be drawn through pipes in honor of grooms and brides with no concern that the Amorites observe this practice. There is the story that when Judah and Hillel, sons of Rabban Gamaliel, came to Cabul, the inhabitants of the city had wine and oil drawn for them through pipes.[1]

125. Our masters taught: A lump of salt may be placed in a lamp in order to make it burn brightly, and mud and potter's clay may be placed under [the oil in] a lamp to make the oil burn slowly.[2]

126. R. Levi said: He who resorts to augury will find that what he fears will come upon his own person. And the proof? "There is no (*lo'*) augury in Jacob" (Num. 23:23), where the word *lo'*, "no," is to be read *lo*, "on his own person."[3]

127. Ahavah son of R. Zera taught: He who does not resort to augury will be brought into a precinct that even ministering angels are not allowed to enter, as is said, "When there is no augury in Jacob . . . then inquiry will be directed [by the ministering angels] to Jacob . . . : 'What hath God done?' " (Num. 23:23).[4]

128. Rav said: All augury that is not like the augury of Eliezer, Abraham's servant,[5] or like the augury of Jonathan son of Saul[6] [each of whom relied on augury] is not [the kind of] augury [that is prohibited].[7]

129. We have been taught that R. Simeon ben Eleazar said: Although the building of a house, the birth of a child, and the taking of a wife are not to be construed as auguries, they may be regarded as auspicious events.[8]

130. An omen is to be taken seriously.[9]

131. R. Ammi said: He who wishes to ascertain whether he will live through the year or not should, during the ten days between New Year's Day and the Day of Atonement, kindle a lamp in a house where there is no draft. If the light continues to burn, he may be certain that he will live through the year.

He who wishes to engage in business and wants to ascertain whether he will succeed or not should rear a cock; if it grows plump and handsome, he will succeed.

He who wishes to set out on a journey and wants to ascertain whether he will return to his home safely or not should stand in a dark house. If he sees the reflection of his shadow, he may be certain that he will return to his home safely. However, such a procedure is not desirable, for his courage may fail him, and in consequence he may meet with misfortune.

Abbaye commented: Now that it has been stated that omens are to be taken seriously, a man should regularly eat pumpkins, fenugreek, leeks, beets, and dates on New Year's Day.[10]

132. The sages taught in the name of R. Yose: A man should never give Satan the opportunity to open his mouth.[11]

133. Our masters taught: When dogs howl, the angel of death has come to the city. When dogs frolic, the prophet Elijah has come to the city. This is so, however, only when there is no bitch among the dogs.[12]

134. He who does badly in one town and does not go to another [to improve his situation] is among those who are not heeded when they cry out.[13]

135. One who takes sick should not speak of it the first day, lest his luck turn worse. After the first day, he may speak freely of his sickness.[14]

136. R. Isaac said: He who wishes to become wise should turn southward when praying; and he who wishes to become rich should turn northward when praying. Why think so? [In the Tabernacle], the table [symbol of plenty] is in the north[15] and the lampstand [symbol of wisdom] is in the south.[16] But R. Joshua ben Levi said: One should always turn in prayer to the south, for when one becomes wise, he is also likely to become rich, as is said, "Length of days is in [wisdom's] right hand; in her left hand are riches and honor" (Prov. 3:16).[17]

The Evil Eye

137. "And the Lord shall take away from thee all sickness" (Deut. 7:15). That is, said Rav, [take away] the evil eye.[18]

Rav's reason [for this interpretation] was the follow-

1. Tos Shab 8:22 and 16.
2. Tos Shab 2:7; B. Shaba 67b.
3. P. Shab 6:9, 8d.
4. B. Ned 32a.
5. Gen. 24:14.
6. 1 Sam. 14:9–10.
7. B. Hul 95b.
8. Consequently, following such events, one may enter into other ventures with good hope of success. Ibid.
9. B. Ker 6a.
10. Symbols of fertility and prosperity. B. Hor 12a.
11. B. Ber 60a.
12. B. BK 60b.
13. Either to a court below or to God above. B. BM 75b.
14. B. Ber 55b.
15. "Thou shalt put the table on the north side" (Exod. 26:35).
16. "Thou shalt set . . . the lampstand over against the table . . . toward the south" (ibid.).
17. B. BB 25b.
18. Rav takes the verse to mean that God will take away the cause of all sickness, namely, the evil eye.

ing: Rav went to a cemetery, did what he did[1] [to find out what caused the death of the people buried in it], and concluded: ninety-nine of them died because of the evil eye, and only one died in a natural way [the end of his days having come].[2]

138. R. Yohanan was in the habit of sitting at the gate of places where women went to immerse themselves, saying: When the daughters of Israel come up from their immersion, let them look at me and have children as handsome as I.[3]

The sages asked him, "Are you not afraid that you might be affected by the evil eye?" But he replied, "I am the progeny of Joseph, over whom the evil eye has no power, as is said, 'Joseph is a fruitful vine, a fruitful vine above the eye'"[4] (Gen. 49:22)." Hence, R. Yose son of R. Hanina said: [The proof of the immunity of Joseph's progeny is in] "Let them multiply like fish in the midst of the earth" (Gen. 48:16). Just as the fish in the sea are covered by water and the evil eye has no power over them, so the evil eye has no power over Joseph's progeny.[5]

139. The sages said in the name of Rav: One should not stand in his neighbor's field when the crop is fully grown.[6]

140. He who enters a city and is afraid of the evil eye should take hold of the thumb of his right hand with his left hand and the thumb of his left hand with his right hand, and say, "I, So-and-so son of So-and-so, come from the seed of Joseph, over whom the evil eye has no power." If he is afraid of his own evil eye, he should point [his thumb] toward the wall of his left nostril.[7]

1. Through inquiry in a dream. So R. Hananel, as cited by N. Zobel and C. Z. Dimitrovsky in their translation of BM into Hebrew (Jerusalem, 1960), p. 207.
2. B. BM 107b.
3. See above, part 2, chap. 1, §402.
4. JV: "a fruitful vine by a fountain." But *ayin* ("fountain") also means "eye."
5. B. Ber 20a.
6. If it fails, he will be charged with having given it the evil eye. B. BM 107a.
7. B. Ber 55b.

CHAPTER THREE

PARABLES, PROVERBS, AND SAYINGS

Parables

1. A certain man owned a well-kept orchard which produced some luscious newly ripened figs. He appointed two watchmen to take care of it, one lame and the other blind. One day, the lame man said to the blind one, "I see some luscious early figs in the orchard. Come, put me upon your shoulder, and we will pick and eat them." So the lame watchman mounted the blind one's back and picked the figs, and the two ate them. Some time later, the owner of the orchard came and inquired, "Where are those beautiful early figs?" The lame watchman replied, "Have I feet to walk with?" The blind one replied, "Have I eyes to see with?" What did the owner of the orchard do? He mounted the lame watchman on the blind one's back and passed judgment against the two as though they were one.[1]

2. On a pitch-black night, a blind man was walking on a road with a torch in his hand. When he was asked, "What use is a torch to you?" he replied, "As long as the torch is in my hand, people see me and save me from pits, thorns, and briers."[2]

3. A man had two wives, one very young and the other of advanced years. The young one used to pluck out his white hair, while the old one used to pluck out his black hair—in the end he became quite bald.[3]

4. There were two men: one had a mound in the middle of his field, while the other had a ditch in the middle of his field. The owner of the mound said, "Who will sell me that ditch?" The owner of the ditch said, "Who will sell me that mound?" One day, the two met, and the owner of the ditch said to the owner of the mound, "Sell me your mound." The other replied, "Would that such a request had been made long ago! Take it for nothing."[4]

5. A king became angry at his son and, noticing a large stone before him, swore that he would hurl it at his son. But then the king changed his mind, saying, "If I hurl it at my son, his life will end. Still, it is impossible to nullify my oath." What did the king do? He ordered that the stone be broken up into small pebbles and that these be thrown at his son one by one. Thus, the king spared his son and yet kept his royal oath.[5]

6. A man walked into a garden, gathered some mulberries, and ate them. The owner of the garden ran after him and asked, "What do you have in your hand?" The man: "I have nothing in my hand." The owner: "But aren't your hands stained?"[6]

7. A stag grew up in the wilderness and on his own joined a shepherd's flock. The shepherd not only gave him food and drink but loved him more than the other animals in his flock. He was asked, "How is it that you love the stag more than any in the flock?" He replied, "I had to perform many kinds of labor for my flock. I took them out in the morning and brought them back in the evening, until they grew up. But this one [I did not have to labor over]—he grew up in the wilderness and forests, and came on his own into my flock. Should I not love him more?"[7]

8. As a lion was devouring his prey, a bone stuck in his throat. So he said, "I shall give a reward to anyone who comes and removes it." An Egyptian heron, which has a long beak, came along, stuck his beak into the lion's mouth, pulled out the bone, and demanded, "Give me my reward." The lion roared, "Off with you! Go boast, 'I entered a lion's mouth in peace and came out in peace.' There can be no greater reward for you than that."[8]

9. A fox was walking on a river bank and, seeing schools of fish swimming here and there, asked them, "From whom are you fleeing?" They replied, "From the nets and traps set for us by men." So the fox said to them, "How would you like to come up on dry land, so that you and I could live together, the way my ancestors lived with yours?" They replied, "You—the one they call the cleverest of animals—are in fact a fool. If we are fearful in the place where we can stay alive, how much more fearful would we be in a place where we are sure to die!"[9]

10. A lion became angry at all beasts, wild and tame. So they said, "Who will go and pacify him?" The fox spoke up: "Come with me to him. I know three hundred parables with which to pacify him." They replied, "Let's go." After walking a short distance, he stopped. So they asked him, "What is the matter?" The fox: "I forgot a hundred parables." They: "There is ample power for good in two hundred." He walked a little farther and stopped again. They again asked, "What is the matter?" The fox: "I forgot another hundred." They: "There is ample power for good even in a hundred parables." When they were nearing

1. B. Sanh 91a–b.
2. B. Meg 24b.
3. B. BK 60b.
4. B. Meg 13b–14a.
5. MTeh 6:3; Yalkut, Ps., §635.
6. Gen. R. 22:9.
7. Num. R. 8:2; MTeh 146:8.
8. Gen. R. 64:10.
9. B. Ber 61b; Yalkut, *Va-et'hannan*, §837.

their destination, he said, "I forgot them all. Each one of you—go and pacify the lion in your own behalf."[1]

11. A lion, some other beasts, and a fox, were about to sail on a ship. The ass was collecting the fare for the journey, saying to each animal, "Pay me the fare." The fox said to the ass, "How dare you! You know that the king of beasts is with us, and yet you demand the fare." The ass replied, "I collect the fare, even from the king, and I deposit the proceeds in the king's treasuries." [Upon hearing these words], the lion ordered, "Bring the ship to." He then got off, ripped the ass apart, and told the fox, "Lay out the parts of this fool's carcass for me [to dine on]." The fox laid them out. But when he saw the ass's heart, he ate it up. When the lion came back and saw all the parts cut up, he asked, "Where is the fool's heart?" The fox replied, "My lord king, he had no heart.[2] If he had had one, he would not have presumed to collect the fare from the king."[3]

12. The lion gave a feast to all animals, wild and tame, and provided a pavilion for them out of lions' skins. After they had eaten and drunk, they said, "Who will compose an appropriate verse for our entertainment?" and looked to the fox. He asked, "Will you respond ['Amen'] to what I am about to say?" They: "Yes." The fox lifted his eyes toward the skins above and said, "May He who has shown us what happened to those above show us what is to happen to the one below."[4]

13. A story: The fox said to the wolf, "Go into a Jewish courtyard on a Sabbath eve and help them prepare whatever is needed for the meal, and you will eat with them on the Sabbath." But when the wolf was about to enter, the courtyard's residents banded together against him with clubs.

Then the wolf was set on killing the fox, but the fox said, "They beat you only because of your father, who on one occasion helped them prepare a meal and then devoured every luscious morsel." The wolf: "Should I be beaten up because of my father?" The fox: "Yes—'fathers eat sour grapes, and their children's teeth are blunted' [Ezek. 18:2]. But come with me, and I will show you a place where you can eat your fill." The fox led the wolf to a well. Across the well's mouth was a beam with a rope wound over it. At each end of the rope was tied an empty bucket. The fox climbed into the upper bucket, and his weight caused it to plunge downward, while the lower bucket flew upward. The wolf called down to him, "Why did you go down there?" The fox: "Because here there is meat and cheese enough to eat one's fill," and he pointed to the moon's reflection in the water. It looked like a round cheese. The wolf: "How am I to go down?" The fox: "Climb into the upper bucket." The wolf did so, and his weight caused it to plunge down, while the bucket with the fox flew up. The wolf: "How am I to get up again?" The fox: " 'The righteous is delivered out of his trouble, and the wicked cometh in his stead' [Prov. 11:1]. Is it not written, 'Just balances, just weights' (Lev. 19:36)?"[5]

14. A fox found a vineyard that was fenced in on all sides, except for one narrow gap through which he tried to enter but could not. What did he do? He fasted for three days, until he became lean and slender, and thus got through the gap. But then, after he ate [his fill of the grapes], he became fat again, so that when he tried to leave through the same gap, he could not. He again fasted three days, until he once more became lean and slender; thus having returned to his former size, he was able to leave. He turned his face back to the vineyard, and gazed at it, said, "O vineyard, vineyard, how good are you, and how good is the fruit within you! All that is within you is beautiful and comely. But what benefit can one derive from you? As one goes into you, so must one come out."[6]

15. A certain man had a filly, a she-ass, and a sow. He measured out fodder to the she-ass and the filly, but let the sow eat as much as she wanted. The filly complained to the she-ass, "What is the idiot doing? To us, who do the work of the master, he rations food, but to the sow, who does nothing, he gives as much as she wants." The she-ass replied, "The time will come when you will see that she is stuffed with fodder not out of deference to her but to her own harm." When the Roman Calends[7] came, they took the sow and stuck her.[8]

16. A she-bear adorned with precious stones and pearls was standing in the marketplace. People said, "Whoever jumps her will get what she has on." A knowing man who was there said, "All you can see is what she is adorned with, but I see her fangs."[9]

17. A man walking on a road saw a pack of dogs and felt afraid of them, so he sat down in their midst.[10]

18. Two dogs watching a flock were jealous of each other. But when a wolf came and attacked one of them, the other said to himself: If I do not help, the wolf will kill him today, and tomorrow he will have a go at me! So both dogs went at the wolf and killed him.[11]

19. When a pig crouches, it displays its cloven hoof, as if to say, "See how kosher I am!"[12]

---

1. Gen. R. 78:7.
2. The heart was presumed to be the seat of understanding.
3. Yalkut, *Va-era*, §182.
4. Esther R. 7:3; Yalkut, Esther, §1054.
5. Rashi on B. Sanh 39a.
6. Eccles. R. 5:14, §1.
7. The first day of the Roman month, usually observed as a feast.
8. Esther R. 7:1; Midrash Abba Gorion on Esther 3:1 (ed. Buber, p. 20).
9. Gen. R. 86:4.
10. To disguise his fear. Had he run, they would have chased him. Gen. R. 84:5.
11. B. Sanh 105a.
12. A cloven hoof is the mark of a kosher animal, which the pig is not, because it does not chew the cud (see Lev. 11:7). Gen. R. 65:1; Lev. R. 13:5.

20. The pig said to a kosher animal, "You should be grateful to us. But for me and my mates, you would not be known as kosher."[1]

21. A wolf comes to snatch a lamb. The shepherd runs after the lamb to snatch it from the wolf's mouth, but between the shepherd and the wolf, the lamb is torn apart.[2]

22. When the hen's chicks are tiny, she gathers them under her wings, keeps them warm, and grubs for them. But once they grow up, when one of them tries to get near her, she pecks at its head and says, "Go grub in your own dungheap."[3]

23. A bird made its nest at the edge of the sea, only to have it swept away when the tide rose. What did the bird do? It proceeded to take into its beak water from the sea and pour it out on the dry land, then take sand from the dry land and drop it into the sea. His companion stopped to watch, then asked, "What are you doing, wearing yourself out like this?" The bird answered, "I will not budge from here until I turn the sea into dry land and the dry land into sea." His companion said, "You are the biggest fool in the world! After all this effort, what do you think you can accomplish?"[4]

24. A bird was confined in a cage. Another bird flew up, perched above the caged one, and said, "How happy you must be that your food is provided for you." The bird in the cage responded, "Bad luck to you! All you see is the food; you don't see the bars on the cage."[5]

25. A dove pursued by vultures and ravens managed to flee from them and reach her nest, where she settled in. Some people were saying, "Those eggs must have been sired by a vulture"; others said, "Those eggs must have been sired by a raven." One person spoke up: "As long as they are eggs, it cannot be known whether they are the raven's or the vulture's. Wait until the dam hatches them and they become chicks; then you will know whose they are."[6]

26. A heron used to sing in the house of his master. While he sat and dined, the heron would sing. Presently the master brought a young hawk into the house. When the heron saw it, he fled under the bed, hid himself, and would no longer open his mouth. The master came in to dine and asked a member of his household, "Why doesn't the heron sing?" He was told, "Because you brought a young hawk in on him, he has ceased to sing out of fear. Remove the young hawk, and the heron will sing again."[7]

27. Why does the raven move about by hopping? Because one time the raven saw a dove moving about in a manner more beautiful than that of any other bird. The dove's movement was so appealing to the raven that he said to himself: I will move about like the dove. He all but broke his bones in his endeavor to do so, and the other birds made fun of him. Put to shame, the raven decided: I will return to my previous manner of moving about. When he tried to return to it, he could not, because he had forgotten his previous manner of moving. So he became a creature that hops—he could manage neither his previous nor his latter way of moving about.[8]

28. A bird hunter caught a bird and was about to catch a second when that bird perched itself on a king's statue. At this, the hunter stood still, perplexed, and said to himself: If I throw stones at her, I will forfeit my life, and if I try poking at her with my stick, I am afraid I might strike the king's image. I don't know what to say to you, [birdie], except that you fled to a perfect place and made good your escape.[9]

29. A cock and a bat were both waiting for the dawn. The cock said to the bat, "I am waiting for dawn, because dawn is mine [to announce]. But of what use is the dawn to you?"[10]

30. The serpent's tail said to his head, "How much longer will you go first? Let me go first." The head: "Go!" The tail went ahead, but when it got to a water hole, it flung the serpent's head into the water. When it got to fire, it flung the serpent's head into the fire. When it came to thorns, it flung the serpent's head into their midst. What caused the serpent such mishaps? Allowing his head to follow his tail.[11]

31. A man saw an insect that looked like a live coal—what we call a firefly—and it terrified him. He was asked, "Is this what terrifies you? At night it is a fiery, blazing thing, but when morning comes, you can see it is nothing more than a worm."[12]

32. Straw, stubble, and chaff were disputing with one another, one saying, "The field was sown for my sake," and another saying, "The field was sown for my sake." [Overhearing them], the ear of wheat retorted, "Wait till harvest time comes and we will know for whose sake the field was sown." When harvest time came, the owner proceeded to winnow the crop. The chaff was scattered before the wind; the owner threw the straw on the ground; he burned the stubble. But he took the wheat and piled it up in a heap—and everyone who passed by kissed it.[13]

---

1. Midrash Tem 2 (BhM 1:108).
2. Exod. R. 5:21.
3. Lev. R. 25:55.
4. Esther R. 7:10; Yalkut, Esther, §1054.
5. Eccles R. 11:9, §1: Yalkut, Eccles., §979; PRKM 24:14.
6. Aggadat Bereshit 37 (ed. Buber, p. 75).
7. Aggadat Bereshit 58 (ed. Buber, p. 116).
8. Alphabet of Ben Sira, in Eisenstein, p. 48.
9. Exod. R. 27:6.
10. B. Sanh 98b.
11. Deut. R. 1:10.
12. PR 33:4 (YJS 2:638).
13. Gen. R. 83:5.

33. The tares said to the wheat, "We are more comely than you, even though the rain comes down on you and on us, and the sun shines for both of us." The wheat replied, "It is not what you say, nor what we say. The fact is that when the winnower comes, he will set us aside for the storehouse, and you [will be thrown] as food for birds."[1]

34. A myrtle and a wild rose grew side by side. But when they grew up, the myrtle yielded its characteristic fragrance [*reho*] and the rose its thorns (*hoho*).[2]

35. A king had an orchard planted with a row of fig trees, a row of grapevines, a row of pomegranate trees, and a row of apple trees. He turned it over to a keeper and went away. After a while, the king came back, looked into the orchard to see how it was doing, and found it overgrown with thorns and briers. He was about to bring woodcutters to cut down the orchard, but when he looked closely at the thorns, he saw among them a rose-colored lily. He picked it up and breathed in its fragrance, and his spirit was calmed. The king said: Because of this lily, let the entire orchard be spared.[3]

36. A reed grows in a well-watered area. Its stock keeps driving up young shoots, and, because its roots are many, even if all the winds of the world come and blow at it, they cannot uproot it from its place, swaying as it does in harmony with them. When the winds subside, the reed resumes its erect stance.

The cedar does not grow in a well-watered area. It does not drive up new shoots, and its roots are few. Still, even if all the winds of the world come and blow at it, they cannot move it from its place. However, when the [hot] south wind blows at the cedar, it immediately uproots it and throws it flat on its face.[4]

37. The other rivers asked the Euphrates, "Why do you not make your voice more audible?" The Euphrates: "I don't need to—my deeds make me known. When a man plants a sapling at my side, it matures in thirty days; when he sows a vegetable at my side, it is full grown in three days." Then the rivers asked the Tigris, "Why is your voice so audible?" The Tigris: "I wish my voice could be heard even more, so that I might be noticed."

When the trees that bear fruit were asked, "Why is your voice not very audible?" they replied, "We have no need—our fruits bear witness for us." When the trees that do not bear fruit were asked, "Why is your voice so audible?" they replied, "We wish our voices could be heard even more, so that we might be noticed."[5]

38. "As the crackling of thorns under a pot" (Eccles. 7:6). When all other kinds of wood are kindled, their sound is not heard. But when thorns are kindled, their sound crackles forth, as if to say, "We, too, are wood."[6]

39. When iron was created, the trees began to tremble. The iron said to them, "Why are you trembling? Let no piece of your wood become part of me, and not one of you will be harmed."[7]

1. Aggadat Bereshit 23 (ed. Buber, p. 48).
2. Gen. R. 63:10.
3. Lev. R. 23:3.
4. B. Ta 20a; B. Sanh 105b–106a.
5. Gen. R. 16:3; Eccles. R. 10:11, §1.
6. Eccles. R. 7:6, §1.
7. The iron ax head can be used only with a wooden handle. Gen. R. 5:9.

CHAPTER FOUR

A MISCELLANY

Series of Matters Set Forth by Number

1. Three love one another: proselytes, slaves, and ravens.[1]

2. A man has three friends: his children, his possessions, and his good deeds.[2]

3. There are three wrongs before which the curtain [of heaven] is never closed: cheating, robbery, and idolatry.[3]

4. Three should not be provoked: a young Gentile, a young snake, and a humble pupil. Why not? Because, though they are still wet behind the ears, their rise to power is likely [if not certain].[4]

5. Three will not see Gehenna's face: they who undergo the torments of poverty, they who are sick in their bowels, and they who are hounded by the authorities. Some say, also he who has a bad wife.[5]

6. Three come unawares: the Messiah, something found, and a scorpion.[6]

7. The road does three things: it wears out one's clothing, grinds down one's body, and diminishes one's money.[7]

8. Three organs are under man's control: the mouth, the hands, and the feet. Three are not under his control: the eyes, the ears, and the nose.[8]

9. The prolonging of three acts prolongs a man's days and years: prolonging the *Tefillah*, prolonging his stay at the table, and prolonging his stay in the privy.[9]

10. Three things nullify an evil decree: prayer, charity, and repentance.[10]

11. Three things deplete a man's strength: fear, travel, and sin.[11]

12. Three things the Holy One Himself proclaims: famine, plenty, and a good leader.[12]

13. Three things take away man's reason and belief in his Creator: idolatry, an evil spirit, and the torments of poverty.[13]

14. Three things are said about finger- and toenails: he who burns them is a pious man, he who buries them is a righteous man, and he who throws them away is a wicked man.[14]

15. Three things were given as a gift to the world: Torah, rain, and the luminaries.[15]

16. Three things were given conditionally: The Land of Israel, the Temple, and the royal house of David.[16]

17. There are three things God reluctantly thought of, but even if He had not thought of them, they had to be thought of: that a corpse give off a stench, that a dead person be put out of mind, and that produce rot.[17] Some say, also that coins be accepted everywhere.[18]

18. There are three things whose sound goes from one end of the world to the other, and though mortals are in between, they are not aware of it: the sound of the day['s sun revolving on its course], the [sound of] rain[clouds moving across the firmament], and the sound of the soul when it leaves the body.[19]

19. Three things are grave threats to the body: heart disease, disease of the bowels, and an empty purse—which is a graver threat to the body than the preceding two.[20]

20. There are three things of which a large quantity and a small quantity are bad, while a moderate quantity is good: leaven, salt, and refusal of an invitation. At first one should decline, then one should hesitate, but finally one should eagerly accept.[21]

---

1. B. Pes 113b.
2. PRE 34.
3. Heaven is always open to hear the cries of the victims. B. BM 59a.
4. When they grow up, they may take revenge. Leon Nemoy writes, "This is too free for my taste," and suggests: "Because their rise to power stands [as close to them as] the back of their ears." B. Pes 113a.
5. B. Er 41b.
6. B. Sanh 97a.
7. MTeh 23:3. Cf. Gen. R. 39:14.
8. Tanhuma, *Toledot*, §12.
9. B. Ber 54b.
10. P. Ta 5:1, 65b.
11. B. Git 70a.
12. B. Ber 55a.
13. B. Er 41b.
14. There was great aversion, possibly for hygienic reasons, to exposing clipped nails. B. Nid 7a.
15. Gen. R. 6:7.
16. Mek, *Yitro, Amalek*, 4 (La 2:188).
17. Otherwise, the corpse would be kept at home for a long time; the memory of the loss would be kept fresh; and speculators would hold on to produce indefinitely and inflate prices.
18. But for that, commerce would cease. B. Pes 54b.
19. Gen. R. 6:7.
20. Eccles R. 7:26, §2.
21. P. Ber 5:3, 9c.

21. Three things are equal in importance: the earth, rain, and man. And [in the Hebrew] each of these words is made up of three letters.[1] This should teach you that if there were no earth, there would be no rain; if there were no rain, the earth would not endure; and if there were neither, man could not exist.[2]

22. Three the Holy One loves: him who does not succumb to anger, him who does not get drunk, and him who does not insist on his full rights.[3]

23. For three the Holy One weeps every day: for him who could occupy himself with Torah but does not; for him who cannot occupy himself with Torah, yet does; and for a leader who lords it over the community.[4]

24. Three the Holy One hates: him who says one thing with his mouth while another is in his heart, him who possesses evidence in his neighbor's favor but does not testify for him, and him who sees something indecent in his neighbor and appears as the only witness against him.[5]

25. Three have returned to the place where they first came into being: Israel,[6] Egypt's money,[7] and the script of the Tablets.[8]

26. There are three whose life is no life: he who has to rely on his neighbor's table, he whose wife rules him, and he whose body is racked by suffering. And some say, also he who owns only one shirt.[9]

27. There are three whose life is no life: those who are [too] compassionate, those who are too prone to anger, and those who are [too] fastidious.[10]

28. Suffering is divided into three portions: the patriarchs and all the generations of men took one, the generation that lived in the time of [Hadrian's] persecution took one, and the lord Messiah will take one.[11]

29. There are three kinds of magnetism in the world: the magnetism of a place for its inhabitants, the magnetism of a wife for her husband, and the magnetism of an article in the estimate of its purchaser.[12]

30. There are three who gather strength as they get older: a fish, a snake, and a pig.[13]

31. There are three crowns: the crown of Torah, the crown of priesthood, and the crown of royalty. But the crown of a good name surpasses them all.[14]

32. There are three whose sins are forgiven: the proselyte, the one who rises to an important office, and the one who weds a wife.[15]

33. There are three concerning whom the Holy One makes proclamation every day: the bachelor who lives in a large city but does not succumb to sin, the poor man who returns a lost article to its rightful owner, and the rich man who tithes his produce in privacy.[16]

34. There are three who will inherit the world-to-come: he who lives in the Land of Israel, he who brings up his sons to the study of Torah, and he who recites the *Havdalah* blessing over wine at the Sabbath's outgoing.[17]

35. Three bear witness in behalf of one another: the Holy One, Israel, and the Sabbath.[18]

36. Three things have something of the world-to-come: the Sabbath, the sun, and sexual intercourse.[19]

37. In the hand of the Holy One, there are three keys that no creature—neither an angel nor a seraph—can take possession of: the key to rain, the key to the womb, and the key [to the grave] at the resurrection of the dead.[20]

38. Three things increase a man's self-esteem: a beautiful dwelling, a beautiful wife, and beautiful appointments.[21]

39. Three things restore a man's spirit: [beautiful] sounds, [beautiful] sights, and [beautiful] fragrances.[22]

40. Three take in abundance and give in abundance: the earth, the sea, and the [Roman] government.[23]

41. There are three insolent ones: Israel among the nations, a dog among beasts, and the cock among fowls.[24]

1. *'dm* ("man"), *'rtz* ("earth"), and *gshm* ("rain").
2. Gen. R. 13:3.
3. B. Pes 113b.
4. B. Hag 5b.
5. Since the testimony of one witness is insufficient in court, he is in effect a slanderer. B. Pes 113b.
6. They were exiled to Babylon, whence their forebear Abraham had come.
7. In the days of Rehoboam, Shishak king of Egypt took away all the treasures of Jerusalem (2 Chron. 12:9).
8. The Tablets are described as written "with the finger of God" (Exod. 31:18), and when they were broken, the letters, according to legend, flew to heaven. B. Pes 87b.
9. B. Betz 32b.
10. B. Pes 113b.
11. MTeh 16:3.
12. B. Sot 47a; P. Yoma 4:1, 41b.
13. B. Shab 77b.
14. Avot 4:13.
15. P. Bik 3:3, 65d.
16. B. Pes 113a.
17. Ibid.
18. Quoted from Tosafot on B. Hag 3b.
19. B. Ber 57a.
20. B. Ta 2a; Deut. R. 7:6.
21. B. Ber 57b.
22. Ibid.
23. Lev. R. 4:2.
24. B. Betz 25b.

42. Three cry and receive no response [from a court on earth or in heaven]: he who has money and lends it without witnesses, he who acquires a master for himself, and he whose wife rules him.[1]

43. There are three things for which one entreats [God's] mercy: a good king, a good year, and a good dream.[2]

44. Three require watching: a sick person, a groom, and a bride. Some say, also a disciple of the wise at night.[3]

45. Three sounds go from one end of the world to the other: the sound of the sun's orb, the sound of Rome's tumult, and the sound of the soul when it leaves the body. Some say, also the sound of childbirth. The sages entreated mercy for the soul when it leaves the body and had the sound [of its anguish] stopped.[4]

46. Three things are hard to take when excessive, but just right in limited measure: leaven, salt, and declining an invitation.[5]

47. Three men made requests in careless language: two were answered favorably and one unfavorably. The three: Abraham's servant Eliezer, Saul son of Kish, and Jephthah the Gileadite. As to Abraham's servant Eliezer, he requested, "So let it come to pass, that the damsel to whom I shall say: Let down thy pitcher, I pray thee, that I may drink . . . Thou hast appointed for Thy servant, even for Isaac" (Gen. 24:14), a request that could have included a lame or blind damsel. However, he was answered favorably in that Rebekah came out to meet him. As to Saul son of Kish, it was requested in his behalf, "And it shall be, that the man who killeth Goliath, the king will enrich him with great riches, and will give him his daughter, and make his father's house free in Israel" (1 Sam. 17:25), a request that might have included a slave or a bastard. However, he was answered favorably in that David came forth. As to Jephthah the Gileadite, he requested, "Then it shall be, that whatsoever cometh forth of the doors of my house to meet me when I return in peace from the children of Ammon, it shall be the Lord's, and I will offer it up for a burnt offering" (Judg. 11:31), a request that might have included an unclean creature [unfit for an offering]. And, indeed, he was answered unfavorably in that his own daughter came out of his house.[6]

48. Three hate one another: dogs, cocks, and Parsee priests. Some say, also harlots. And others say, also disciples of the wise in Babylonia.[7]

---

1. B. BM 75b.
2. B. Ber 55a.
3. B. Ber 54b.
4. B. Yoma 20b–21a.
5. B. Ber 34a.
6. B. Ta 4a.
7. B. Pes 113b.

49. A man is called by three names: one given him by his father and mother, one that others call him, and one that [through his deeds] he causes himself to be called by.[8]

50. There are three partners in man's making: the Holy One, his father, and his mother.[9]

51. One man differs from his fellow in three ways: in voice, in appearance, and in understanding.[10]

52. A man's true character may be recognized by three things: his tippling, his tipping, and his temper. Some say, also by what makes him titter.[11]

53. In three instances [a man is apt to die because] Satan is ready to bring charges against him: when he lives in a house on the verge of collapsing, when he walks on a road alone, or when he sets out on the Great [Mediterranean] Sea.[12]

54. For three reasons one should not enter a dilapidated house: because of suspicion [of lewdness], because of its possible collapse, and because of demons.[13]

55. The world stands on three things: on Torah, worship, and loving-kindness.[14]

56. The world endures because of three things: justice, truth, and peace.[15]

57. Three may be called virgin: a human virgin, virgin soil, and a virgin sycamore tree.[16]

58. Three good gifts—Torah, the Land of Israel, and the world-to-come—the Holy One bestowed on Israel, and they were bestowed only through suffering.[17]

59. Three endowments [wisdom, strength, and wealth] were created in the world. He who acquires any one of them may be said to have acquired [the most precious] thing in the world. If he acquires wisdom, he has attained everything. If he acquires strength, he has attained everything. If he acquires wealth, he has attained everything. When is this so? When they are endowments from Heaven and come to one through the power of Torah. But strength and wealth originating in mortals are worth nothing.[18]

---

8. Eccles. R. 7:1, §3; Tanhuma, *Va-yak'hel*, §1.
9. B. Kid 30b.
10. B. Sanh 38a.
11. B. Er 65b.
12. Eccles R. 3:2, §2; P. Shab 2:3, 5b.
13. B. Ber 3a.
14. Avot 1:2.
15. Avot 1:17.
16. B. Nid 8b.
17. B. Ber 5a.
18. Num. R. 22:7.

60. Not a day does a man escape three transgressions: unchaste thoughts, inattention during prayer, and slander.[1]

61. There are three kinds of torpor: the torpor of sleep, the torpor of prophecy, and the torpor of unconsciousness.[2]

62. Four are hard to put up with: a poor man who is proud, a rich man who falsely denies a claim against him, an old man who is lecherous, and a leader who [without justification] lords it over his community. Some say, also he who divorces his wife, [remarries her], divorces her again, and then marries her again.[3]

63. The Holy One showed Abraham four things—Gehenna, [the yoke of] the [heathen] kingdoms, the giving of Torah, and the Temple—and said to him: If your children are deeply occupied with the latter two, they will be saved from the former two.[4]

64. Four things tear up a [divine] decree issued against a man: charity, supplication, a change of name, and a change of conduct. Some say, also a change of residence.[5]

65. Four things drain a man's strength: iniquity, wayfaring, fasting, and the [Roman] Empire.[6]

66. Four are regarded as if dead: a poor man, a leper, a blind man, and a man who has no children.[7]

67. Four the Holy One regrets having created: exile, Chaldeans, Ishmaelites, and the impulse to evil.[8]

68. Four are called scoundrel: he who raises his hand against a neighbor to strike him, even though he does not strike him; he who borrows and does not repay; he who is brazen-faced; and he who is given to quarreling.[9]

69. Four things need to be done with vigor: study of Torah, good deeds, prayer, and one's daily task.[10]

70. Four are required to give thanks: they who have gone down to the sea, they who have journeyed through the desert, he who had been ill and has recovered, and he who had been confined in prison and has been released.[11]

71. Five things are a sixtieth of something else: fire, honey, Sabbath, sleep, and a dream. Fire is one-sixtieth of Gehenna; honey, one-sixtieth of manna; Sabbath, one-sixtieth of the world-to-come; sleep, one-sixtieth of death; a dream, one-sixtieth of prophecy.[12]

72. Five possessions the Holy One declared as His very own in His world: Torah is one such possession; heaven and earth are one such possession; Abraham is one such possession; Israel is one such possession; the Temple is one such possession.[13]

73. A man enjoys the fruits of six things in this world, while the principal reward abides for him in the world-to-come: hospitality to wayfarers, visiting the sick, concentration during prayer, early attendance at the house of study, rearing one's sons in the study of Torah, judging a neighbor on the scale of merit.[14]

74. Seven things are hidden from man: no man knows the day of [his] death, the day of [Israel's] comforting, the ultimate truth in divine judgments, what is in his neighbor's heart, what he will earn, when the sovereignty of the house of David will return, or when the kingdom of Edom will collapse.[15]

75. Seven things were created before the world was created: they are Torah, repentance, the Garden of Eden, Gehenna, the throne of glory, the Temple, and the name of the Messiah.[16]

76. Seven are as if under Heaven's ban: a man who has no wife, who has a wife but no children, who has children but does not rear them in the study of Torah; who has no tefillin on head and arm, no fringes on his garment, no mezuzah at the entrance to his house; and who denies shoes to his feet. Some say, also he who never participates in a company gathered for a religious purpose.[17]

77. Eight things are harmful in large quantities, but in small quantities are beneficial: travel, sexual intercourse, wealth, gainful trade, wine, sleep, hot baths, and cupping.[18]

78. Ten things serve the soul: the gullet for food, the windpipe for voice, the liver for temper, the lungs to absorb liquids, the first stomach to grind food, the spleen for laughter, the maw for sleep, the gall bladder for jealousy, the kidneys for thought, and the heart for decision-making. And above all these is the soul.[19]

---

1. B. BB 164b.
2. Gen. R. 17:6 (Soncino, p. 136).
3. B. Pes 113b.
4. Gen. R. 44:21.
5. B. RH 16b.
6. Lam. R. 1:14, §43; MTeh 31:9.
7. B. Ned 64b.
8. B. Suk 52b.
9. Tanhuma, *Korah*, §8.
10. B. Ber 32b.
11. Cf. Ps. 107; B. Ber 54b.
12. B. Ber 57b.
13. Avot 6:10.
14. B. Shab 127a.
15. B. Pes 54b.
16. B. Pes 54a.
17. B. Pes 113b.
18. B. Git 70a.
19. Lev. R. 4:4.

Sundry Matters

79. Hillel used to say: An empty-headed person does not dread sin, an ignorant one [*am ha-aretz*] cannot be pious, one who is too bashful [to ask questions] cannot learn, an irritable man cannot teach, and he that is engrossed in trade cannot become a sage; and where there are no men, strive to be a man.[1]

80. He used to say: The more flesh, the more worms; the more property, the more worry; the more wives, the more witchcraft; the more female slaves, the more lewdness; the more male slaves, the more thievery; the more Torah [study], the more life; the more schooling, the more wisdom; the more counsel, the more understanding; the more charity, the more peace. He who has acquired a good name has acquired something truly his own; he who has acquired for himself words of Torah has acquired for himself life in the world-to-come.[2]

81. R. Hanina ben Hakinai said: He who, while awake at night or while walking alone on a road, turns his heart to that which is idle forfeits his life.[3]

82. R. Dosa ben Korkinas said: Morning sleep, wine at noon, children's chatter, and attending the meeting places of the ignorant [*amme ha-aretz*] put a man out of the world.[4]

83. R. Eleazar of Modim said: He who profanes things sacred, who scorns the festivals, who causes his fellow man to go pale with shame in public, who nullifies the covenant [circumcision] of Abraham our father, who misinterprets the Torah—even if he possesses Torah learning and good deeds—has no share in the world-to-come.[5]

84. R. Akiva said: The traditionally fixed text of Scripture is a [protective] fence for Torah, tithes are a fence for wealth, vows a fence for abstinence. For wisdom, silence is a fence.[6]

85. R. Eleazar ben Azariah said: When there is no study of Torah, there is no proper conduct; when there is no proper conduct, there is no study of Torah. When there is no wisdom, there is no fear [of God]; when there is no fear [of God], there is no wisdom. When there is no understanding, there is no knowledge; when there is no knowledge, there is no understanding. When there is no flour [for bread], there is no study of Torah; when there is no study of Torah, there is no bread.[7]

1. Avot 2:5.
2. Avot 2:7.
3. Avot 3:4.
4. Avot 3:11.
5. Ibid.
6. Avot 3:13.
7. Avot 3:17.

86. Ben Zoma said: Who is wise? He who is willing to learn from all men, as is written, "Because of all, who taught me, I gained insight" (Ps. 119:99). Who is mighty? He who subdues his impulse to evil, as is written, "He that is slow to anger is better than the mighty; and he that ruleth his spirit than he that taketh a city" (Prov. 16:32). Who is rich? He who is happy with his portion, as is written, "When thou art content to eat the labor of thy hands, happy shalt thou be, and it shall be well with thee" (Ps. 128:2): "happy shalt thou be" in this world, "and it shall be well with thee" in the world-to-come. Who is honored? He who honors others, as is written, "For them that honor Me [by honoring mankind created in My image] I will honor, and they who despise Me shall be lightly esteemed" (1 Sam. 2:30).[8]

87. Ever since pleasure seekers have multiplied, justice has come to be subverted,[9] human conduct has deteriorated, and God has no satisfaction in the world.

Ever since they who display partiality in judgment have multiplied, the command "Ye shall not be afraid of the face of any man" (Deut. 1:17) has become void; the command "Ye shall not respect persons in judgment" (ibid.) has ceased to be obeyed; people have thrown off the yoke of Heaven and have placed upon themselves the yoke of mortals.

Ever since they who convey whispered hints to judges have multiplied, [God's] fierce anger has so greatly increased against Israel that the Presence has departed [from them] because, as Scripture says, "God standeth in the congregation of God only when He judgeth among the judges" (Ps. 82:1).

Ever since [men of whom it is said], "Their heart goeth after their gain" (Ezek. 33:31), have multiplied, they "who call evil good and good evil" (Isa. 5:20) have also multiplied.

Ever since men "who call evil good and good evil" have multiplied, cries of "woe!"[10] have increased in the world.

Ever since men who ostentatiously draw in their spittle have multiplied, the arrogant have increased, disciples have become few, and Torah has had to go about looking for people to study it.

Ever since men who make much of their outer appearance have multiplied, the daughters of Israel have begun to marry such men, because our generation looks only to the outward appearance.

Ever since judges who force their goods upon householders and make them trade in their behalf have multiplied, bribery, as well as miscarriage of justice, has increased and fairness [in justice] has ceased.

Ever since judges who say, "I accept your favor," and, "I shall appreciate your favor," have multiplied, there has been an increase of "every man doing that which is right in his own eyes" (Judg. 17:6); low persons have been raised to eminence; the eminent have been brought low; and the kingdom [of Israel] has continued to deteriorate.

Ever since the niggardly have multiplied, despoilers

8. Avot 4:1.
9. Since people do not take the trouble to study what the law says.
10. The word "woe" occurs five times in Isa. 5.

of the poor have also multiplied, and so have those who harden their hearts and close their hands from lending to the needy, thus transgressing what is written in the Torah: "Beware that there be not a base thought in thy heart" (Deut. 15:9).

Ever since people eager to accept gifts have multiplied, the days [of human life] have become fewer, even as the years have been shortened: "It is he that spurneth gifts who shall live" (Prov. 15:27).

Ever since the haughty of heart have multiplied, controversies have increased in Israel. Ever since disciples of Shammai and of Hillel who had not ministered sufficiently to their teachers have multiplied, controversies have increased in Israel and the Torah has become like two [contradictory] Torahs.

Ever since those willing to accept charity from Gentiles have multiplied, Israel has sunk to the bottom, while Gentiles have risen to the top; Israel has gone backward, while Gentiles have come forward.[1]

88. "And they dwelt there" (Gen. 11:2). R. Isaac said: Whenever people seek to dwell [in tranquility], Satan leaps in [to disrupt]. R. Helbo said: Whenever you find contentment, Satan levels charges. R. Levi said: Whenever you find [too much] eating and drinking, Satan levels charges.[2]

89. "All the days of the poor are evil" (Prov. 15:15) refers, according to R. Hanina, to one who has an evil wife. "But he that is of a merry heart hath a continual feast" (ibid.) refers to a man who has a good wife.

R. Yannai said: "All the days of the poor are evil" refers to one who is overly fastidious. "But he that is of a merry heart hath a continual feast" refers to one who is of a more balanced disposition.

R. Yohanan said: "One who so grieves[3] [for the suffering of others] that [he deems] all his days blemished," is truly compassionate. "But he whose heart is so merry that he is continually feasting" is [uncaring, indeed,] cruel.

However, R. Joshua ben Levi said: "All the days of the poor [in spirit] are evil" refers to one who is ungenerous. "But he that is of a merry heart hath a continual feast" refers to one who is generous.[4]

90. "When a man's ways please the Lord, He maketh even his enemies to be at peace with him" (Prov. 16:7). "Enemy," said R. Yohanan, refers to a man's wife. "To a snake," said Samuel. "To the impulse to evil," said R. Joshua ben Levi. R. Berekhiah said: In saying "even his enemies," Scripture includes pests in a man's house, such as gnats, fleas, and flies.[5]

91. Happy is the man whose wife is from his own city, whose source of Torah learning is from his own city, and whose livelihood is from his own city.[6]

92. The sages taught in the name of R. Meir: He who is a permanent resident in the Land of Israel, eats his [daily]—[nonsacral]—food in ritual purity, speaks Hebrew, and recites the Shema morning and evening may be certain that life in the world-to-come will be his.[7]

93. The merit in attending a [Torah] lecture is in the running [to hear it]. The merit in attending a *Kallah*[8] session is in [the willingness to endure] the crush. The merit in listening to a halakhic tradition is in the reasoning it stimulates. The merit in attending a house of mourning is in the silence imposed. The merit in a fast is the [required] giving of charity. The merit of a eulogy is in the [listeners'] loud lament in response. The merit in attending a wedding is in the good wishes expressed to the bride and groom.[9]

94. Rava asked Rabbah bar Mari: Where does the proverb "When the thorn is ravaged, so is the cabbage" come from?

Rabbah bar Mari: From the verse "Wherefore will ye contend with Me? Ye all have transgressed against Me, saith the Lord" (Jer. 2:29).[10]

"Wherever the poor goes, poverty tags along"?

Rabbah bar Mari: We have been taught: "The rich bring their firstfruits in baskets overlaid with silver and gold; while the poor bring them in wicker baskets made of peeled willow branches, and give both baskets and fruits to the priests" (Bik 3:8).

"Sixty men may run but not catch up with him who has a meal early in the morning"?

Rabbah bar Mari: From the verse "They do not hunger or thirst, neither the sun nor the moon shall smite them" (Isa. 49:10).

"When your friend calls you an ass, put a saddle on your back"?

Rabbah bar Mari: From the verse "And he said: 'Hagar, *slave* of Sarai, whence camest thou? and whither goest thou?' And she said: 'I flee from the face of my *mistress* Sarai' " (Gen. 16:8).

"If there is anything unfavorable in you, be the first to admit it"?

Rabbah bar Mari: From "[Eliezer] said: I am Abraham's slave" (Gen. 24:34).

"Though a duck keeps its head down while walking, its eyes range far and wide"?

Rabbah bar Mari: From "[Aware of what was to happen to David], Abigail said to him: 'When the Lord shall have dealt well with my lord, then remember thy handmaid' " (1 Sam. 25:31).

"Sixty pains afflict the tooth that sees another tooth chomping while it does not"?

Rabbah bar Mari: [Nathan, who saw Adonijah's men eat and drink, said ruefully], "But me, even me thy servant . . . hath he not called" (1 Kings 1:26).

1. B. Sot 47b.
2. Gen. R. 38:7.
3. The word *ani* ("poor") may also mean "one who grieves."
4. B. BB 145b.
5. P. Ter 8:7, 46a; Gen. R. 54:1.
6. Midrash Prov. 5:18 (ed. Buber, p. 52).
7. P. Shab 1:5, 3c.
8. The semiannual gatherings of Babylonian sages during the months of Adar and Elul.
9. B. Ber 6b.
10. Surely not *all*—not, for example, Jeremiah—have transgressed.

"The wine belongs to the owner, but the butler gets the thanks"?

Rabbah bar Mari: From "Joshua the son of Nun was full of the spirit of wisdom; for Moses had laid his hands upon him" (Deut. 34:9).[1]

"A hungry dog will swallow his own excrement"?

Rabbah bar Mari: From "The full soul loatheth a honeycomb; but to the hungry soul every bitter thing is sweet" (Prov. 27:7).

"A bad date palm will make its way to a grove of barren trees"?

Rabbah bar Mari: This matter is dealt with in the Five Books, repeated in the Prophets, said again in the Writings, taught in the Mishnah, and repeated in a Baraita. In the Five Books: "Esau went to Ishmael" (Gen. 28:9). In the Prophets: "Men of low character gathered about Jephthah and went out raiding with him" (Judg. 11:3). In the Writings: "Every bird dwells with its own kind, even as men with his like" (Ecclesiasticus 13:19). In the Mishnah: "Anything joined to what is susceptible to uncleanness is itself susceptible to uncleanness, and what is joined to what is not susceptible to uncleanness is itself not susceptible to uncleanness" (Kel 12:2). In a Baraita: "R. Eliezer said: Not for naught did the starling to go the raven—it is, after all, its kind."

"If you summon your neighbor [to have a dispute arbitrated] and he will not respond, you may use any means[2] to get from him what belongs to you"?

Rabbah bar Mari: From "Because I have purged thee and thou wast not purged of thine uncleanness, thou shalt not be purged from thy filthiness any more, till I have satisfied My fury upon thee" (Ezek. 24:13).

"Do not throw a stone into the well from which you once drank"?

Rabbah bar Mari: From "Thou shalt not abhor an Edomite, for he is thy brother; thou shalt not abhor an Egyptian, because thou wast a stranger in his land" (Deut. 23:8).

"If you join me in lifting the burden, I too will lift it; if not, I will not lift it"?

Rabbah bar Mari: From "Barak said unto her: 'If thou wilt go with me, then I will go; but if thou wilt not go with me, I will not go' " (Judg. 4:8).

"When we were young, we were treated as men, but now that we have grown old, we are treated as children"?

Rabbah bar Mari: In the beginning it is said, "The Lord went before them . . . to lead them the way" (Exod. 13:21). But in the end God said to Israel, "Behold, I send an angel before thee, to guard thee on the way" (Exod. 23:20).

"Be ready to pull even chips of wood behind a man of wealth"?

Rabbah bar Mari: From "Lot also, who went with Abram, had flocks, and herds, and tents" (Gen. 13:5).[3]

95. The following is a tradition from our forebears, the Men of the Great Assembly: whenever Scripture says, "And it came to pass (*va-yehi*)," it means that there was trouble.[4]

96. The sages said to R. Perida: "R. Ezra, the grandson of R. Avtolas, who was the tenth generation from R. Eleazar ben Azariah, who in his turn was the tenth generation of Ezra, is standing at the door." R. Perida: "Why such a recital of forebears? If he is a man of Torah, it is well. If he is both a man of Torah and a scion of distinguished ancestors, it is doubly well. However, if he is merely a scion of distinguished forebears but not a man of Torah, may fire consume him." The sages: "He is a man of Torah." R. Perida: "Then let him come in." When he entered, R. Perida saw that R. Ezra was troubled. So R. Perida began to discourse on the verse "I have said unto the Lord: 'Thou art my Lord!' But My gratitude, [God answered], is not to thee" (Ps. 16:2). Then R. Perida went on: The congregation of Israel said to the Holy One, "Master of the universe, show gratitude to me having made You known in the world." God replied, "My gratitude is not to you, but to Abraham, Isaac, and Jacob, who first made Me known to the world." As the next verse says, "The holy that are in the earth, they are the mighty in whom is all My delight" (Ps. 16:3). As soon as R. Ezra heard the word "mighty," he began an allocution, saying:

> Let the Mighty come and for the sake of the mighty
> requite the mighty by means of the mighty.[5]
> Let the beloved, scion of the beloved, come and build
> A beloved house for the Beloved in the beloved's
> portion,
> Where the beloved may procure atonement.[6]
> Let the good come and receive the good from the
> Good for the sake of the good.[7]
> Let this one come and receive this Torah from
> This Unique One for the sake of this people.[8]

97. [When a meal was over, and it was time for the young disciples to leave], the maidservant of the household of Rabbi [Judah I, the Patriarch] would speak in enigmatic language and say:

> The dipper is already knocking at the sides of the
> empty jug.
> Let the young eagles fly to their eyries.

When she wished them to sit down for a meal, she would say:

> If need be, let the stopper be pulled out even from
> a second jug,

---

1. As though wisdom emanated not from God but from Moses.
2. Literally, "you may lift a big wall and throw it at him."
3. B. BK 92a–93a.
4. B. Meg 10b.
5. Requite the Egyptians with the mighty waters.
6. The beloved (*Yedidiah*) Solomon (see 2 Sam. 12:25), scion of the beloved Abraham, is to build the Temple in Benjamin's portion for the beloved people of Israel.
7. The good Moses is to receive the Torah for the good people of Israel.
8. The refrain of "this" is based on Exod. 32:1, Deut. 4:44, Exod. 15:2, and Isa. 43:21, where Moses, Torah, God, and Israel are singled out by the demonstrative "this." B. Men 53a–b.

so that the dipper float in it,
like a ship sailing the sea.

When R. Yose bar Asyan spoke in enigmatic language, he would say, "Prepare for me *tordin*, "beets," with *hardal*, "mustard that the poor use."[1]

When he would ask an innkeeper what the menu for the day was, he would say:

For a man whose mouth—
The one here—is raw[2] with hunger,
What tasty morsels are there?

When R. Abbahu spoke in enigmatic language, he would say:

Make the coal [glow] like etrogim,
Then make the golden glow sky-blue,
And prepare for me two cocks who during thick darkness announce [the dawn]."[3]

98. A certain disciple sitting before R. Samuel bar Nahmani said in the course of an exposition: Job never was, never came into being—he is merely a parable. R. Samuel: To such as you, Scripture retorts, "There was a man in the land of Uz, whose name was Job" (Job 1:1).

The disciple: But then, what of "The poor man had nothing, save one little ewe lamb," etc. (2 Sam. 12:3)? Was there such a poor man? No; the story of the poor man is a parable, even as the story of Job is a parable.[4]

99. We have been taught: "In the middle of the altar there was a mound of ash, whose bulk at times was as much as three hundred *kor*."[5] "This," said Rava, "is hyperbole."

"They gave a lamb about to be the daily offering a drink from a cup of gold." "This," said Rava, "is hyperbole."

R. Ammi said: The Five Books used hyperbole. The Prophets used hyperbole. The sages used hyperbole, as we have just mentioned. The Five Books used hyperbole, as in the verse "The cities are great and fortified up to heaven" (Deut. 1:28). The Prophets used hyperbole, as in the verse "The earth was split open by the uproar" (1 Kings 1:40).

R. Isaac bar Nahmani said in the name of Samuel: Of three matters, the sages used hyperbole—of the mound on the altar, the vine, and the Temple curtain. The mound, as we have mentioned above. The vine, as we have been taught: At the entrance to the Temple Hall, there stood a vine, trellised over columns and laden with gold; for whoever presented a berry or a cluster of golden grapes would bring it and hang it there. [So abundant was the gold on the vine], said R. Eleazar son of R. Zadok, that on one occasion three hundred priests were assigned to clear it.

The curtain, as we have been taught: R. Simeon ben Gamaliel said in the name of R. Simeon, deputy [high priest]: The curtain[6] was a handbreadth thick and was woven on seventy-two strands, each strand consisting of twenty-four threads. Its length was forty cubits and its breadth twenty cubits, made up in its entirety of eighty-two myriads [of threads]. They used to make two curtains every year, and three hundred priests were needed to immerse them.[7]

100. Samuel said: In the Sanctuary, there was a [musical instrument called] a *magrefah*. It had ten holes, each of which produced ten different kinds of pitches. Thus, it produced one hundred different kinds of pitches altogether.

[In a differing tradition], the sages taught in a Baraita: The instrument was one cubit long and one cubit high. A handle projected from it which had ten holes, each producing one hundred different kinds of pitches. Thus, it produced one thousand different kinds of pitches.

R. Nahman bar Isaac said: You are to remember who is prone to such hyperbole: [Not the Mishnah, but] the Baraita exaggerates.[8]

101. The sages said to R. Hamnuna: R. Ammi wrote out four hundred Torah scrolls. R. Hamnuna: Are you sure he didn't copy just the words "Moses commanded us the Torah" (Deut. 33:4) four hundred times?

Rava said to R. Zera: R. Yannai planted four hundred vineyards. R. Zera: Are you sure these "vineyards" weren't of [the minimal definition], namely, two pairs of vines facing each other, with one vine jutting out as a kind of tail?[9]

102. Ulla said: Italy of the idolaters is the great city of Rome, which covers an area of three hundred parasangs by three hundred parasangs. In it are three hundred and sixty-five marketplaces, corresponding to the days of the solar year. The smallest of them—that of the poultry sellers—is sixteen *mil* by sixteen *mil*. Every day the emperor dines in one of them. Whoever lives in the city, even if not born there, receives a daily portion of food from the emperor's palace. So, too, does he who was born there receive such a daily portion from the emperor's palace, even if he no longer lives there. In the city are three thousand bathhouses whose five hundred [tall] flues convey their smoke beyond the city wall. One side of the city is bounded by the sea, another side by mountains and hills, a third side by a barrier of iron, and a fourth side by sand dunes and swamps.[10]

1. It sounded as though he asked for *tor* ("an ox") and *din* ("judgment"), and for *har* ("mount") and *dal* ("poor").
2. He asked for the menu by taking *ushpizkana* ("innkeeper") as a portmanteau for *ish* ("man"), *peh* ("mouth"), *zeh* ("the one here"), *na* ("raw [with hunger]").
3. B. Er 53b.
4. B. BB 15b.
5. A *kor* is eleven bushels.
6. Between the Holy of Holies and the Temple Hall, where the golden altar stood.
7. If they became unclean. B. Hul 90b; B. Tam 29b.
8. B. Ar 10b–11a.
9. B. BB 14a.
10. Or, as in En Yaakov, *metzudah* ("traps"). B. Meg 6b and En Yaakov, ad loc.

GLOSSARY

Adar see Months

Afternoon prayer (*Minhah*) recited from half an hour after midday until sunset, corresponding to the time set for the daily burnt offering in the afternoon

Aggadah (pl. *Aggadot*) that part of talmudic (and of later rabbinic) literature that does not deal with legal matters

Altar unless otherwise specified, refers to the Outer Altar, also known as the Altar of Burnt Offering (Exod. 25:6), situated in the courtyard of the Tabernacle or the Temple Court; upon it were burned all sacrifices except the incense and were offered all sprinklings of blood except those of certain sin offerings

Am ha-aretz a person who knows neither Scripture nor Mishnah and, in his limited understanding of Jewish conduct, acts like a heathen

Amalek in the Bible (Exod. 17:8–16 and 1 Sam. 15), a people totally evil—hence, *the* symbol of evil to the rabbis

Amidah literally, "standing"; see *Tefillah*

Amoraim literally, "expounders, expositors"; talmudic authorities who flourished about 200–500 C.E. and whose discussions are embodied in the Gemara

Analogy the use of a similar expression occurring elsewhere in Scripture in order to apply to one subject a rule, characteristic, or concept already known to apply to another

Av see Months

Baraita an extraneous Mishnah containing a tannaitic tradition not incorporated in the Mishnah as collected by Rabbi Judah I, the Patriarch (ca. 200 C.E.), but cited in the Gemara, the Midrash, or the Tosefta

Bible the Hebrew Bible consists of three main groups: (1) the Torah, i.e., the five books of the Pentateuch; (2) the Prophets, subdivided into Prior Prophets (Joshua through Kings) and Latter Prophets (Isaiah through Malachi); and the Writings (Psalms through Chronicles); see also *Oral Law*

Burnt offering offered for sinful desire, for evil thoughts that come into one's mind; cf. Lev. R. 7:3

Clean and unclean animals see Lev. 11

Cubit unit of length measured from the elbow to the tip of the middle finger; about 18 inches

Daily burnt offerings two he-lambs were offered daily in the Temple, one in the morning and one in the afternoon at dusk; see Num. 28:1–8

Day and night in the Jewish system of reckoning time, the twenty-four-hour day begins with the preceding night; the night is counted from dusk to dawn, and the day from dawn to dusk or sunrise to sunset; a daylight hour means a twelfth part of the day as thus defined

Denar a silver coin worth a quarter of a *sela* or $^1/_{24}$ of the gold denar; the approximate equivalent of 25 cents in modern American currency

Diverse kinds of seeds or plants, which may not be sown together; of garment stuffs, which may not be worn together; of cattle, which may not be bred to each other; see Lev. 19:19 and Deut. 22:9–11

Dough offering (*Hallah*) the portion of dough that belongs to a priest (see Num. 15:20ff.); in the Diaspora, this was not given to the priest but burned

Edom a rabbinic designation for Rome

Eighteen Benedictions (*Shemoneh Esreh*) see *Tefillah*

Elul see *Months*

Ephah standard biblical dry measure, equal to ten *omer* (Exod. 16:36) or 3 *seah;* approximately the bulk of 432 eggs—a little more than 1 bushel

Eruv literally, "intermingling, blending"; specifically, a symbolic act of "blending" several domains or limits together for the purpose of making it lawful to walk or transport things from one to the other on the Sabbath

Esau a rabbinic designation for Rome

Etrog a species of citron (*Citrus medica L.*) used with the festive cluster on the Feast of Sukkot; see also *Lulav*

Excision literally, "cutting off"; shortening one's life or depriving one of progeny; divine punishment for sins for which no penalty by an earthly court is specified

Firstfruits a portion of the first ripe fruits, brought by the owner of the field to the Temple in thanksgiving and then consumed by the priests; see Num. 18:17–18

Firstling the firstborn male of cattle and sheep, brought by the owner to the Temple as a hallowed offering consumed by the priests; see Num. 18:17–18

Four Kingdoms Babylonia, Media and Persia, Greece, and Rome, which kept Israel in subjection; see Dan. 7

Gemara the major part of the Talmud, containing the comments of the Amoraim on the Mishnah

Geonim heads of the Babylonian academies of Sura and Pumbedita and major legal authorities in the post-talmudic period (7th to 11th centuries)

Geullah benediction a section recalling the redemption from Egypt and ending with a blessing over future redemption, that occurs between the Shema and the Amidah in morning and evening prayers

Haggadah (pl. *Haggadot*) a variant spelling of *Aggadah*

Halakhah (pl. *Halakhot*) that part of talmudic (and of later rabbinic) literature dealing with legal matters; also, a section of a chapter in the Mishnah

Hallah see *Dough offering*

Hallel Ps. 113–18, as used for liturgical recitation

Hanukkah minor Jewish festival of eight days, beginning on the 25th day of Kislev, commemorating the rededication of the Temple by the Maccabees in 165 B.C.E.

Havdalah the benediction of "separation," recited at the close of the Sabbath or holy day

Heave offering a portion of the produce (about two percent on average) given to the priests, who alone were permitted to eat it; see Num. 18:8, Lev. 22:10, and Deut. 18:4

Heave offering of the tithe out of the tithe offering he received, the Levite was obliged to give a tenth part to the priest; in other words, one one-hundredth of the original produce harvested by the Israelite; see Num. 18:25–32

Heshvan see *Months*

Holy spirit the quickening of man's natural faculties by divine inspiration—a level of inspiration below that of prophecy, whereby a prophet received divine communications in a supranatural manner; see Maimonides, *Guide of the Perplexed,* trans. Shlomo Pines (Chicago, 1963), 2:45

Hours, daylight see *Day and Night*

Immersion pool for ritual purification, primarily by women; it must contain 40 *seah* (approximately 60 gallons or 270 liters) of water, which may not be drawn, but must be taken directly from a river or spring, or must consist of rainwater led straight into the bath

Issar a coin worth $^1/_{24}$ of a denar or eight *perutot*

Iyar see *Months*

Jubilee year the year concluding a series of seven sabbatical cycles comprising 49 years; see Lev. 25:8–16

Kav the equivalent of the bulk of 15 eggs; 4 pints

Keri the Masoretic instruction for reading, as opposed to *ketiv,* the traditional spelling of biblical words

Ketiv the traditional spelling of biblical words, as opposed to the *keri,* the Masoretic instruction for reading

Kiddush the ceremony of drinking wine after a blessing in the synagogue or home, by which the advent of the Sabbath or festivals is sanctified

Kislev see *Months*

Kor 11 bushels

Law, the see *Bible*

Levite (a) a descendant of the tribe of Levi (see Num. 3:5ff.); (b) as contrasted to "priest" and "[lay] Israelite"

Log a liquid measure said to be equal to the displacement of 6 eggs (see B. Er 83a)—1 pint

Lulav the palm branch carried with the festival cluster during the Festival of Sukkot—see Lev. 23:40; or, more generally, the cluster of palm branch, myrtle, and willow used with the *etrog* on that festival

Maneh money worth 100 *zuz*

Mezuzah literally, "doorpost" (Deut. 6:9); a piece of parchment bearing the verses Deut. 6:4–9 and 11:13–21 enclosed in a cylinder and fastened to the right-hand doorpost

Midrash exposition or exegesis of Scripture

Mil (= mille), a Roman mile; about 1,620 yards

Mishnah (pl. *Mishnayyot*) literally, "teaching"; the collection of legal decisions of the sages of the first two centuries C.E. (the Tannaim), edited and arranged into six orders by Rabbi Judah I, the Patriarch (ca. 200 C.E.); the Mishnah provides the text to which the Gemara is the commentary, the two together constituting the Talmud

Mitzvah (pl. *Mitzvot*) a divine "commandment" from the Torah as interpreted by the rabbis

Months the Hebrew names of the months are: Nisan, Iyar, Sivan, Tammuz, Av, Elul, Tishri, Heshvan (Marheshvan), Kislev, Tevet, Shevat, and Adar; in an intercalated year, a thirteenth month, called 2d Adar, is added

Musaf (*Additional Offering*) special offering for Sabbaths, New Moons, and festivals brought in addition to the regular daily offerings—see Num. 28:9–31; after the destruction of the Temple, replaced by the Additional (*Musaf*) Prayer

Nazirite one who vows to dedicate himself to the service of God; his vow implies abstention from all products of the grapevine, letting his hair grow, and avoidance of contact with a dead body (see Num. 6:2–8)

Nisan see *Months*

Noachide Commandments in rabbinic thought, seven universal precepts held to be incumbent not only upon Israelites but upon all the "sons of Noah," i.e., upon the whole human race

Notarikon script a rabbinic system of interpretation in which words are shortened or one letter of each word is written (as in an acrostic)

Ofanim see *Wheel-angels*

Omer the sheaf of barley, also called the "sheaf of waving," brought as an offering on the 16th day of Nisan (see Lev. 23:9–14); also a standard dry measure (see *ephah*)

Oral Law the authoritative exposition of the written Torah received by Moses at Sinai was never meant to be committed to writing; eventually, it was, in the Mishnah and Talmud

Parasang a distance of 8,000 cubits or 4,000 yards

Peace offering sacrifice betokening the nearness and communion between God and man

Perutah (pl. *perutot*) see *Issar*

Priestly watch the priests and Levites were divided into 24 guards or watches, each one of which was on duty for one week every six months; see 1 Chron. 24:4

Prophets see *Bible*

Purim the Feast of Lots, observed on the 14th day of Adar in commemoration of the salvation of the Jews in Persia; its full story is recorded in the book of Esther

Rabbi literally, "my master"; a term of respect used in direct address by a disciple to his teacher and generally by the public to a scholar known for his learning. It was only much later that the term assumed its present meaning of the spiritual leader of a Jewish community

Ram's horn see *Shofar*

Red Heifer in Num. 19, a cow whose ashes purify people and objects that have been defiled by contact with a corpse

Re'em a wild ox

Ritual bath see *Immersion pool*

Sabbath limit one may not walk on the Sabbath beyond the distance of 2,000 cubits from the city or place where one resides

Sages the postbiblical scholars dating back to Ezra the Scribe (ca. 440 B.C.E.); the term is loosely used to apply to the rabbis of the subsequent period who preserved and transmitted the Oral Law

Sanhedrin council, high court; the Great Sanhedrin was the supreme court consisting of 71 members; a Small Sanhedrin was a high court consisting of 23 members

Scripture see *Bible*

Seah a third of an *ephah;* the equivalent of the bulk of 144 eggs, or about 12 quarts

Sheaf of barley see *Omer*

Shekhinah "the Presence" of God, as a circumlocution when Scripture speaks of God's dwelling in a place or removing from one, and the like

Shema the name and the first word ("Hear, [O Israel]!") of a group of passages from Scripture (Deut. 6:4–9 and 11:13–21; Num. 15:37–41) that must be recited daily in the morning and evening

Shevat see *Months*

Shofar ram's horn sounded on New Year's Day and other occasions (see Num. 29:1 and Lev. 25:9); the notes produced by it were: sustained note (*tekiah*), tremolo (*teruah*), and broken note (*shevarim*)

Sifra a Midrash commenting on the book of Leviticus in sequence

Sifre a Midrash commenting on the books of Numbers and Deuteronomy in sequence

Sivan see *Months*

Sukkah the booth used in observance of the Festival of Sukkot

Tallit a prayer shawl with 4 fringes (see *Tallit*) to remind the Jew of the divine commandments; see Num. 15:38

Talmud the two collections of rabbinic law and lore comprising Mishnah and Gemara; the Palestinian (also known as the Jerusalemite) Talmud was redacted by the disciples of R. Yohanan, ca. 300 C.E.; the Babylonian Talmud was redacted by R. Ashi and Ravina, ca. 450 C.E.

Tammuz see *Months*

Tannaim authorities cited in the Mishnah and the Baraita, who flourished up to ca. 200 C.E.

Tefillah the name of one of the principal prayers in the daily services, consisting on weekdays of 19 (originally 18) benedictions. Hence, also called Eighteen Benedictions (*Shemoneh Esreh*) and, since it is usually recited while standing, *Amidah* (*Standing* [*Prayer*])

Tefillin phylacteries; small leather cases, one worn on the arm and the other on the head during the recital of weekday prayers. Each case contains parchment strips upon which are written four passages from Scripture: Exod. 13:1–10, Exod. 13:11–16, Deut. 6:4–9, and Deut. 11:13–21

Tekiah see *Shofar*

Teruah see *Shofar*

Tevet see *Months*

Tishri see *Months*

Tithe (*maaser*) an offering of the tenth part of the produce or cattle. Tithes were of three kinds: the first tithe was given to the Levites in each of the first six years of the sabbatical cycle; the second tithe was separated in the first, second, fourth, and fifth years of the cycle and was consumed by the owner in Jerusalem; the poor man's tithe was given to the poor in the third and sixth years of the cycle

Torah see *Bible*

Tosefta (pl. *Toseftot*) a collection of those legal decisions of the Tannaim that were not included in the Mishnah; redacted by R. Hiyya, a disciple of Rabbi Judah I, the Patriarch

Tzitzit 4 fringes attached to the *tallit*

Urim and Tummim the 12 precious stones in the "breastplate of judgment," upon which were engraved the names of the 12 tribes of Israel (Exod. 28:15–30); the letters served as an oracle

Wheel-angels (*ofannim*) in the strange "chariot" vision of Ezekiel 1:15, they (along with the *hayyot* angels) bear the throne of God

Writings see *Bible*

Zuz (pl. *zuz* or *zuzim*) another name for a denar during the Roman period in Palestine; a Sassanid drachm in third-century Babylonia

REFERENCES

B. prefixed to the name of a tractate indicates a reference to the Babylonian Talmud; P. indicates a reference to the Palestinian (Jerusalem) Talmud; Tos refers to the Tosefta in the Zuckermandel edition given in Other Sources, below. Otherwise, the reference is to tractates of the Mishnah.

Unless another edition is specified, the Midrash Rabbah used—on the Pentateuch as well as on the five scrolls—is the Vilna, 1878, edition.

Abbreviations of Tractates

Ar	Arakhin	Hal	Hallah	Mik	Mikvaot	Shevu	Shevuot
ARN	Avot de-Rabbi Natan	Hor	Horayot	MK	Moed Katan	Sof	Soferim
Avot	Avot	Hul	Hullin	MSh	Maaser Sheni	Sot	Sotah
AZ	Avodah Zarah	Ka	Kallah	Naz	Nazir	ST	Sefer Torah
BB	Bava Batra	Kel	Kelim	Ned	Nedarim	Suk	Sukkah
Bekh	Bekhorot	Ker	Keritot	Neg	Negaim	Ta	Taanit
Ber	Berakhot	Ket	Ketubbot	Nid	Niddah	Tam	Tamid
Betz	Betzah	Kid	Kiddushin	Oh	Ohalot	Tef	Tefillin
Bik	Bikkurim	Kil	Kilayim	Or	Orlah	Tem	Temurah
BK	Bava Kamma	Kin	Kinnim	Par	Parah	Ter	Terumot
BM	Bava Metzia	Kut	Kutim	Pe	Peah	Toh	Toharot
De	Demai	Maas	Maaserot	Per Sha	Perek ha-Shalom	TY	Tevul Yom
DER	Derekh Eretz Rabbah	Mak	Makkot	Pes	Pesahim	Tz	Tzitzit
DEZ	Derekh Eretz Zuta	Makh	Makhshirin	RH	Rosh ha-Shanah	Uk	Uktzin
Ed	Eduyyot	Me	Meilah	Sanh	Sanhedrin	Yad	Yadayim
Er	Eruvin	Meg	Megillah	Sem	Semahot	Yev	Yevamot
Ger	Gerim	Men	Menahot	Shab	Shabbat	Yoma	Yoma
Git	Gittin	Mez	Mezuzah	Shek	Shekalim	Zav	Zavin
Hag	Hagigah	Mid	Middot	Shev	Sheviit	Zev	Zevahim

Other Sources

Alfasi — Isaac ben Jacob Alfasi [North Africa, 1013–1103], commentary on the Talmud (in standard editions)

APB — *The Authorized Daily Prayer Book of the United Hebrew Congregations of the British Empire*, with a translation by Simeon Singer [1848–1906], 13th ed., London, 1925

ARN — Avot de-R. Nathan, published in two columns, A and B, ed. Solomon Schechter [1847–1915], Vienna, 1887; *The Fathers according to Rabbi Nathan*, trans. Judah Goldin [1914–], New Haven, Conn., 1955 (YJS 10)

ARNA — Column A of ARN

ARNB — *The Fathers according to Rabbi Nathan* (version B of ARN), trans. Anthony Saldarini, [1941–] Leiden, 1975

Arukh — Nathan ben Yehiel of Rome [11th century], *Aruch Completum*, ed. Alexander Kohut [1842–94], facsimile reprint, 8 vols., Vienna, 1926

AV — The Authorized version of the English Bible, also known as the King James Version, first published in 1611

B — Appended to a title: ed. Solomon Buber [1827–1906]

B. — Babylonian Talmud

Bah — Joel Sirkes [1561–1640], *Haggahot ha-Bah*, marginal notes on the Babylonian Talmud

Bertinoro — Obadiah ben Abraham of Bertinoro [d. ca. 1500], commentary on the Mishnah

BhM — Bet ha-Midrash, ed. A. Jellinek [1820–93], vols. 1–4: Leipzig, 1853–57; vols. 5–6: Vienna, 1873–77

BR — The Hebrew edition of this volume,

	Sefer ha-Aggadah, published in Odessa in 1908–11, and the revised and expanded 2d edition, Tel Aviv, 1936
Darkhe Moshe	by Moses ben Israel Isserles [16th century], commentary on Tur Yoreh Deah, printed in most editions of the Tur
Samuel Edels	Samuel Eliezer ben Judah Edels [1555–1631], novellae on the Babylonian Talmud (in the Vilna, 1880, ed.)
Eisenstein	Judah David Eisenstein [1854–1956], *Otzar Midrashim*, an anthology of midrashic texts, New York, 1928
EJ	*Encyclopaedia Judaica*, 16 vols., Jerusalem, 1973
Elegant Compositions	*Hibbur Yafeh me-ha-Yeshu'ah*, by Nissim ben Jacob ben Nissim ibn Shahin [11th century]; *Elegant Compositions Concerning Relief after Adversity*, trans. William M. Brinner [1924–], New Haven, Conn., 1977 (YJS 20)
En Yaakov	by Jacob ben Solomon ibn Habib [ca. 1460–1516], compilation of the aggadic passages in the Babylonian Talmud and in the orders Zeraim and Moed of the Palestinian Talmud, 4 vols., New York, 1955
ET	*Entzyklopediah Talmudit*, 18 vols., Jerusalem, 1955–84
Etz Yosef	by Chanoch Zundel ben Joseph [d. 1867], commentaries on Tanhuma, ed. Warsaw, after World War I; and on Midrash Rabbah on the Pentateuch, Vilna, 1897
EV	English versions of Scripture (as distinguished from special interpretations made by a rabbinic commentator)
Gen. R. TA	Genesis Rabbah: Julius Theodor, [1849–1924], *Midrasch Bereschit Rabbah*, Berlin, 1907–17; completed by Chanoch Albeck [1890–1972], *Minhat Yehudah*, Berlin, 1928–36
Gesenius, *Lexicon*	Wilhelm Gesenius, *A Hebrew and English Lexicon of the Old Testament*, trans. Edward Robinson; ed. Francis Brown, S. R. Driver, and Charles A. Briggs, Oxford, 1907
Ginzberg, *Legends*	Louis Ginzberg [1873–1953], *Legends of the Jews*, 7 vols., Philadelphia, 1908–38
Goldschmidt	Lazarus Goldschmidt [1871–1950], *Der babylonische Talmud*, Berlin, 1930–36
Hai Gaon	Hai ben Sherira (Babylonia, 939–1038), head of the Pumbedita academy and a major post-talmudic legal authority
R. Hananel	Hananel ben Hushiel [Kairouan, d. 1055], legal authority and Talmud commentator
Hertz, *APB*	Joseph Herman Hertz [1872–1946], *The Authorized Daily Prayer Book*, rev. ed., New York, 1954
David Hoffmann	[1843–1921], *Midrasch Tannaim zum Deuteronomium*, 2 vols., Berlin, 1908–9
HUCA	*Hebrew Union College Annual*
Iyyun Yaakov	Jacob ben Joseph Reischer [1670–1733] Vilna, 1884
Jastrow	Marcus Jastrow [1829–1903], *A Dictionary of the Targumim, the Talmud Babli and Yerushalmi, and the Midrashic Literature*, 2 vols., London and New York, 1903
JE	*The Jewish Encyclopedia*, 12 vols., New York, 1901–6
JPS	Jewish Publication Society of America
JQR	*The Jewish Quarterly Review*
JV (Jewish Version)	*The Holy Scriptures according to the Masoretic Text*, Philadelphia, 1917
Kimhi	David Kimhi [ca. 1160–1235], commentary on the Bible
Lekah Tov	by Tobiah ben Eliezer [11th century]; Midrash Lekah Tov, ed. Solomon Buber [1827–1906], Vilna, 1880
Levy, *Wörterbuch*	Jacob Levy [1819–92], *Neuhebräisches und chaldäisches Wörterbuch über die Talmudim und Midraschim*, 4 vols., Leipzig, 1867–89
Lieberman, TKF	Saul Lieberman [1898–1983], Tosefta Ki-feshutah, 12 vols., New York, 1955–73
David Luria	[1798–1855], comments on the Midrash Rabbah (in the Vilna, 1878, ed. of that Midrash)
Mah	by Ze'ev Wolf Einhorn [d. 1862], commentary on Midrash Rabbah, Vilna, 1878
Maimonides, Code	The Code of Maimonides (in progress), New Haven, Conn., 1949– (YJS)
Malbim	Meir Lev ben Yehiel Michael [1809–80], *Ha-Torah ve-ha-Mitzvah*, commentary on Torah and Sifra, Warsaw, 1874–80
Mattenot Kehunnah	by Issachar Berman Ben Naphtali ha-Kohen (Berman Ashkenazi) [16th century], comments on the Midrash Rabbah (in the Vilna, 1878, ed. of that Midrash)
Megillat Ta	Megillat Taanit, earliest printing, Mantua, 1513; critical ed. by H. Lichtenstein, *Hebrew Union College Annual* 8–9 (1931–32): 257–351
Mek; Mek, La	*Mekilta de-Rabbi Ishmael*, ed. Jacob Zallel Lauterbach [1873–1942], 3 vols., Philadelphia, 1933
Mek RSbY	Mekhilta de-Rabbi Simeon bar Yohai, ed. D. Hoffmann [1843–1921], Frankfurt am Main, 1905
MhG Exod.	Midrash ha-Gadol on Exodus, ed. Mordecai Margulies [1910–68], Jerusalem, 1956

MhG Gen. Midrash ha-Gadol on Genesis, ed. Mordecai Margulies [1910–68], Jerusalem, 1947

MhG Num. Midrash ha-Gadol on Numbers, ed. Solomon Fisch [1898–], 2 vols., London, 1957–63

Midrash Avkir A midrash no longer extant; excerpts quoted in Yalkut Shimoni

Mishnah (ed. Albeck) *The Mishnah*, ed. Chanoch Albeck [1890–1972], 6 vols., Jerusalem, 1952–58; and introductory vol., Jerusalem, 1959

Montefiore, *RA* Claude Goldsmid Montefiore [1859–1939] and Herbert Loewe [1882–1940], *Rabbinic Anthology*, London, 1938

Moore, *Judaism* George Foot Moore [1851–1931], *Judaism in the First Centuries of the Christian Era: The Age of the Tannaim*, 3 vols., Cambridge, Mass., 1927–30

MTeh Midrash Tehillim, ed. Solomon Buber [1827–1906], Vilna, 1891; *Midrash on Psalms*, trans. William G. Braude [1907–88], New Haven, Conn., 1959 (YJS 13)

Nahmanides Moses ben Nahman [1194–ca. 1270], commentary on the Pentateuch (printed in rabbinic Bibles)

R. Nissim Nissim ben Reuben Gerondi [Spain, 14th century], commentary and novellae to the Talmud

NJV *A New Translation of the Holy Scriptures*, Philadelphia, 1962–85

Obermeyer Jacob Obermeyer [1845–1935], *Die Landschaft Babylonien*, Frankfurt am Main, 1929

Onkelos *see* Targum

Ot Emet Meir ben Samuel Benveniste [16th century], Jerusalem, 1969

P. Palestinian Talmud

Pene Moseh by Moses Margalit [18th century], commentary on the orders Nashim, Zeraim, and Moed of the Palestinian Talmud, ed. Vilna, after World War I

PR Pesikta Rabbati, an early medieval Midrash on Jewish festivals; *Pesikta Rabbati: Discourses for Feasts, Fasts, and Special Sabbaths*, trans. William G. Braude [1907–88], New Haven, Conn., 1968 (YJS 18)

PRE Pirke de-Rabbi Eliezer, an eighth-century midrashic narrative, Warsaw, 1852; trans. Gerald Friedländer [1871–1923], London, 1916; reprint, New York, 1965

PRF Pesikta Rabbati, ed. Meir Friedmann [1831–1908], Vienna, 1880

PRK Pesikta de-Rav Kahana, an early homiletic Midrash, ed. Solomon Buber [1827–1906], Lyck, 1868

PRKM Pesikta de-Rav Kahana, ed. Bernard Mandelbaum [1922–], 2 vols., New York, 1962

PRKS Pesikta de-Rav Kahana, trans. William G. Braude [1907–88] and Israel J. Kapstein [1904–82], Philadelphia, 1975

R. Preceding a name: Rabbi; after a text: Rabbah

Rashba Solomon ben Abraham Adret [Spain, 13th century], a major legal authority who published responsa to legal questions and novellae on the Talmud

Rashbam Samuel ben Meir [1080–1158], grandson of Rashi; an important scholar whose commentaries on the Torah and the Talmud are published in rabbinic Bibles and Talmud editions

Rashi R. Solomon ben Isaac of Troyes [1040–1105], author of commentaries on the Hebrew Bible and the Babylonian Talmud

RV Revised Standard Version of the King James Bible, Testament (first published in 1885)

Shibbolei ha-Leket a collection dealing with laws and holidays, ed. Solomon Buber [1827–1906], Vilna, 1886

Sif Sifra, a Midrash commenting on the book of Leviticus in sequence, and Sifre, a Midrash commenting on the books of Numbers and Deuteronomy in sequence

Soncino The English translations of the Babylonian Talmud (1935–52), the Midrash Rabbah (1939), and the Zohar (1931–34) issued by the Soncino Press in London

SOR Seder Olam Rabbah, ed. Ber Ratner [1852–1916], Vilna, 1894

Strashun Samuel Strashun [1794–1872], novellae on Midrash Rabbah (in the Vilna, 1878, edition of that Midrash)

Tanhuma an early medieval homiletic Midrash, sometimes called Tanhuma Yelammedenu, ed. Warsaw, after World War I

Tanhuma B ed. Solomon Buber [1827–1906], Vilna, 1885

Targum Ancient translations or paraphrases of the Bible into Aramaic. The most important of these is the translation of the Pentateuch ascribed to Onkelos the Proselyte, a mishnaic teacher of the first century C.E. The Targum Jonathan is a freer paraphrase of the Bible, ascribed to Jonathan ben Uzziel, a pupil of Hillel

TdE, TdEZ Seder Eliyyahu Rabbah and Seder Eliyyahu Zuta (also known as Tanna de-Bei Eliyyahu), ed. Meir Friedmann

[1831–1908], Vienna, 1902, 1904; *Tanna de-Bei Eliyyahu: The Lore of the School of Elijah*, trans. William G. Braude [1907–88] and Israel J. Kapstein [1904–82], Philadelphia, 1980 (JPS)

Tos — Tosefta, a collection of material supplementary to the Mishnah, from the mishnaic period, ed. Moshe Shemuel Zuckermandel, Pasewalk, 1880; reprint, Jerusalem, 1969

Tosafot — Critical and explanatory glosses on the Talmud by the successors of Rashi

Tur — Arbaah Turim, by Jacob ben Asher [1270?–1340], a four-part code of Jewish law, first published in Italy in 1475

Tur Yoreh Deah — Part 2 of the Tur

Yalkut — The compilation or catena on Scripture known as Yalkut Shimoni; the word Yalkut followed by other names are other collections of midrashic texts

Yede Moshe — by Jacob Moses Helin [17th century], comments on Midrash Rabbah, Frankfurt-on-Oder, 1705 (in the Vilna, 1878, ed. of that Midrash)

Yefeh Toar — by Samuel ben Isaac Jaffe [16th century], comments on Midrash Rabbah (in the Vilna, 1878, ed. of that Midrash)

YJS — Yale Judaica Series

Zayit Raanan — Abraham Abele Gumbiner [ca. 1635–83], comments on the Yalkut (in the Warsaw, 1876, edition of that compilation)

INDEX OF NAMES AND SUBJECTS

Note: In personal names, the terms "bar" and "ben" both denote "son of." Names in this index are listed under all three terms as they appear in the text of this translation.

INDEX OF BIBLICAL REFERENCES

Biblical verses are in **bold face,** *followed by book page and paragraph number.*

EXODUS

NUMBERS

DEUTERONOMY

II KINGS

ISAIAH

PROVERBS

JOB

SONG OF SONGS

RUTH

LAMENTATIONS

ECCLESIASTES

ESTHER

Hayim Nahman Bialik (1873–1934) was the poet of the Jewish national renaissance. Born in the Hasidic environment of northern Ukraine, he moved to Odessa in 1891, where he was drawn to Ahad Ha'am and the circle of intellectuals involved in creating a modern Jewish culture. In 1921, he left Soviet Russia for Berlin and emigrated to Palestine in 1924.

Yehoshua Hana Ravnitzky (1859–1944) was an early Zionist publicist and pioneer of modern Hebrew journalism and publishing. A native of Odessa, he became Bialik's first patron and later his closest collaborator. Together they founded the publishing house of Moriah, which brought forth the first edition of *Sefer Ha-Aggadah* in 1908–11. Ravnitzky settled in Tel Aviv in 1921, where he and Bialik subsequently founded the Dvir Publishing House.

William G. (Gershon Zev) Braude (1907–1988) was born in Telz, a center of Lithuanian Jewish learning, and emigrated to America in 1920. After being ordained at Hebrew Union College in Cincinnati and earning his Ph.D. at Brown University, he served as Rabbi of Congregation Sons of Israel and David, Temple Beth El, in Providence, Rhode Island. Through a series of major translations, including *Midrash on Psalms*, *Pesikta Rabbati*, *Pesikta De-Rab Kahana*, and *Tanna Debe Eliyyahu*, he established a reputation as a leading interpreter of classical rabbinic literature.